W9-COI-353

The Dictionary of Classical Hebrew

Volume I

The Dictionary of Classical Hebrew

David J.A. Clines
Editor

Philip R. Davies   John W. Rogerson
Consulting Editors

Volume I

א

John Elwolde
Executive Editor

Kate Dove Davis, Richard S. Hess, David Stec, David Talshir,
Zipora Talshir, Wilfred G.E. Watson
Research Associates

Published under the auspices of
The Society for Old Testament Study

and with the support of
The University of Sheffield

The Dictionary of Classical Hebrew

David J.A. Clines
Editor

Volume I

John Elwolde
Executive Editor

Sheffield
Sheffield Academic Press

1993

Published by Sheffield Academic Press Ltd
343 Fulwood Road
Sheffield S10 3BP
England

Typeset by Sheffield Academic Press
and
Printed on acid-free paper in Great Britain
by Bookcraft
Midsomer Norton, Somerset

British Library Cataloguing in Publication Data

Dictionary of Classical Hebrew. – Vol. 1: Aleph
I. Clines, David J. A.
492.43

ISBN 1-85075-244-3

CONTENTS

PREFACE

It is with some hesitancy but also with a certain pride that we launch this Dictionary, the first dictionary of the Classical Hebrew language ever to be published. Unlike all previous dictionaries of ancient Hebrew, this work does not restrict itself to, or privilege in any way, those ancient Hebrew texts found in the Hebrew Bible. Rather, it views Hebrew simply as a language like any other ancient language, for which it is necessary to examine the evidence of all the extant texts. We feel convinced that such a Dictionary, which will give the user a greater control over the material than previous dictionaries have allowed, is much needed, both by professional scholars of the Hebrew language and literatures and by students. This Dictionary marks an important departure from the tradition of Hebrew lexicography, and it is our hope that it will be judged according to its own stated designs and not according to the norms with which scholars have long been familiar.

The realities of preparing a Hebrew dictionary are no doubt unfamiliar to most scholars and to most users of this Dictionary, so it is perhaps not out of place to report on the contexts and practicalities of the research that the Dictionary project has entailed.

Most scholars can easily imagine what writing an article for a learned journal on the meaning of a Hebrew word would be like, and feel like—even if they have never done it—and they could be forgiven for thinking that writing a Hebrew dictionary is very much like that, repeated thousands of times. In fact, however, while the preparation of a Hebrew dictionary involves research activity of that kind, there are many other aspects of the research it requires as well: for it collapses the distinction between pure and applied research, demands that a variety of contexts for research that are usually invisible be constantly foregrounded and, above all, sets research in a social and economic context.

When researchers write scholarly papers for a learned journal they do not have to consider the market. However hard they will try to make their work intelligible and attractive, they do not have to ask themselves how many people will want to read their article, or whether readers will take out or cancel subscriptions to the journal because of their article. They have only to concern themselves with whether the editor will accept it or not. If the editor does, they have nothing more to do except read the proofs. The business of the production and publication of their scholarly work is not their affair.

Everything is different with a dictionary on this scale. In three important respects it brings into the foreground contexts for research, each of them creating a constraint upon the scholarly ambitions and targets of the work. These contexts, however, do not only form constraints, for it is precisely the contexts that constitute the scholarly opportunity. No one would set about writing a Hebrew dictionary if the scholarly community already had a perfectly serviceable Hebrew dictionary; it is the market niche, and the dictionary-makers' perception of the users' needs, that create the possibility for the scholarly activity. To be sure, people would go on writing journal articles on particular words even if we had a thoroughly satisfactory dictionary for most practical purposes. But the kind of scholarly activity that results in the composition of a unified work such as a dictionary is in fact market-led—not by the market in some narrow sense of cash and profit but by the market as a negotiation between providers and consumers.

1. *Economics*. Let us begin with the kind of money involved. It has not been customary for scholars in the humanities to talk about money, but we need to recognize that it is an inescapable dimension of all research, and especially of large-scale research projects. The cost of producing this Dictionary is upwards of a million pounds, at 1993 values, and it can be reckoned like this. To produce Aleph, the first of our projected eight volumes, has cost us about ten person-years. At an average cost of £20,000 for a postdoctoral research associate, that is £200,000 per volume. If we multiply by the eight volumes, we have a total of about £1,600,000. It will be nearer a million pounds if our rate of progress improves, as we intend it shall. Perhaps this is a lot of money to pay for a Hebrew dictionary, perhaps it is not. It is roughly equivalent to the income of a university professor over 35 years. We could think it cheap to get

a Hebrew dictionary for the cost of one scholarly career. In science research terms it would be cheap; a million pounds is not infrequently the price of one piece of equipment that must be bought before the research project itself begins. In this case, however, it is the cost of the research itself.

However, needless to say, no one has a million pounds to spare, at least no one we know. Public and private research funding bodies are on the whole not sympathetic to projects of this size in the humanities. Most publishers are not interested in investing in such a project, because they are mostly owned by mega-companies that are responsible to their shareholders and banks to produce profits in three to five years. So who will pay £1,000,000 for a Hebrew dictionary? The only answer can be: 2500 scholars and libraries at, let us say, £400 for the set of eight volumes (or, alternatively, 1000 libraries at £400 and 3000 scholars and students at £200 for the set). That is to say, if 3000 or 4000 people will buy volume 1, there will be enough money for us to write volume 2, and so on. Old-fashioned patronage is still very welcome for long-term meritorious undertakings like the present one, but the realities of our market economies will no doubt dictate that it will be the end-users who carry the cost. And that is perhaps not such a bad thing: it means that the scholarly community can, if it chooses, actually take the ownership of the project—not only of the volumes that libraries and individuals possess when they have bought them, but of the project itself.

What constraints do the economics of the project make on the scholarship that goes into it? They are principally the constraints of cost-effectiveness and time. There are many desirable things to do in scholarship that we would have done if there had been time—which is to say, if there had been the funds to employ people to do them. For example, we should like to have read all the secondary scholarly literature on Hebrew words, to have satisfied ourselves about the location of geographical places mentioned in the texts and about the identification of birds, animals and plants, to have organized the Hebrew word-stock by semantic field and have identified the contexts in which one term and not a near synonym is used, to have weighed the emendations of the texts that have been suggested and make a judgment of our own about each proposal. All these things need to be done, and most of them should be done afresh in each generation. But such tasks cannot be ours. On matters like these we can hope to do no more than report the position of the best scholarship we can find. Critics can easily think of many things we might have done, and blame us for these omissions. They have already started to make such criticisms, and most of their criticisms are valid. In the end, though, we have to say that we prefer our way of writing a Hebrew dictionary to their way of not writing a Hebrew dictionary.

2. *The reader*. The dictionary is a product, produced by a manufacturing industry and sold in the market, and readers are the customers who will spend, or refuse to spend, their money on the product. The makers of dictionaries cannot therefore simply serve disinterested scholarship; they must be aware of what readers will count as value for money. But readers are of course not only people with money in their pockets; they are potential users of the book. So as dictionary-makers we have to be sure we are addressing not only the pockets but the needs of the customers.

If we were starting again, we would do a systematic market research that asked many individual Hebrew dictionary users what they want and what is wrong with the dictionaries they are currently using. Before 1988, when we began the composition of the Dictionary, we had conversations with very many people about what they thought the Dictionary should look like; but perhaps the uses that professional scholars make of the dictionaries already available—and it was in the main other scholars whom we consulted—would not be a good guide to the needs of the whole range of potential readers of this Dictionary.

But despite our only partial acquaintance with the needs and interests of future readers of the Dictionary, we have tried to put ourselves in the shoes of such readers as we have written and revised the proofs of the Dictionary. The readers, we feel sure, want an alphabetical dictionary; the readers want all the Hebrew to be accompanied by an English gloss; the readers want comprehensiveness, so as to be sure of locating a particular text under one or another semantic heading; the readers want help with difficult verb forms; the readers want an English–Hebrew index. We have tried to serve the needs of such readers.

3. *The staff*. Most research in the humanities differs fundamentally from the Hebrew Dictionary project: most of the time scholars are lone workers in

the library or at their keyboards. The result is that scholars have little experience of collaborative work, perhaps even less of research management. Most of them do not know what are the effects of managing a research project upon the kind of scholarship that can be produced in it. It is not worse scholarship than that of the lone researcher; it is just different. The two main elements that are different, in our experience, are the need for inflexibility and the significance of responsibility.

First, when scholars have sole charge of their own research, they can make up the rules as they go along. They control the data and the methods themselves, they can reshape their paper or book at any point, right up to the latest phase of its redaction, they can make their own decisions on what to include, expand, omit. A group, on the other hand, cannot have this degree of flexibility; and a unified work like a dictionary must not show too evidently that it is the product of several minds. So a vast array of rules and procedures has to be drawn up and followed strictly, and before very long the point is reached where it becomes difficult, and then impossible, to change them even when it becomes clear that they were not the best rules that could have been formulated. Fortunately, many technical and editorial rules for the redaction of the Dictionary are rather arbitrary, so not a lot hangs upon which option has been chosen. But once it has been chosen, it has to be followed rigidly. If an individual scholar were writing the dictionary personally, it would undoubtedly look rather different.

Secondly, the composition of such a dictionary is far too big a task for one scholar, and so the manager of the project has to delegate most of the work. And yet there is very little training in the field of the humanities in how to delegate scholarship. It goes against the grain of most scholarly instincts to rely on someone else's work and especially to envisage a work going out under one's name which one cannot personally guarantee in its detail. It is not at all easy to entrust the responsibility for research to younger scholars, who are not indeed less clever than the manager of the project but certainly less experienced. And yet it has to be recognized that this is a corporate project, and that no one person can take credit, or accept blame, for the line by line contents of the work. If a Hebrew dictionary is to be done, there can be little doubt that this is the way it has to be done, these days. We will not find a Brown, a Driver and a Briggs who will devote so much of their scholarly careers and their personal life to composing a dictionary. None of us has servants any longer, and most of us do not expect our wives or our husbands to service our scholarship. In any case, there may, in fact, be long-term rewards in training younger scholars to do Hebrew lexicography: some of them may be managing the next dictionary project before their career is finished, whereas the skills of Brown, Driver and Briggs, we must suppose, more or less died with them.

Publication of the first volume of the Dictionary gives a welcome opportunity to acknowledge the support it has received from many quarters. The project has been funded in the five years since its inception by substantial grants from the Laing Trust, from Sheffield Academic Press, and from the Research Stimulation Fund of the University of Sheffield. Smaller grants have been received from the British Academy, from the Bethune-Baker Fund in the University of Cambridge, and from The Society for Old Testament Study, as well as from several private donors.

The roll-call of workers on the Dictionary is already quite lengthy. Throughout the period, the project has been excellently carried forward by John Elwolde, research associate from September 1988 to December 1992, and thereafter executive editor. Beside him there was in the first year Richard S. Hess, David Talshir and Zipora Talshir as talented research associates. In the last two years the work has also benefited from the appointment of David M. Stec. Susan Halpern served capably as secretary to the project through most of the period. In addition, there have been several very competent students from the Department: Noel Bailey, Kate Dove Davis, Becca Doyle, Jonathon Dyck, Mark Love, Paulson Pulikottil, and Jonathan Williams. A special acknowledgment must be made of the generous contribution of time made to the later stages of the work of the Dictionary by Wilfred Watson despite his own scholarly commitments. John Jarick carried out a meticulous last-minute proofreading of the Hebrew of the entire text. The editorial board of reference, drawn from the membership of the Society for Old Testament Study, has been an important source of support for the principles of the Dictionary. Robert Gordon, a member of the Board of Reference, should be specially mentioned for his continuing concern for the wellbeing of the project and for his highly successful contacts with funding bodies on the Dictionary's behalf. Graham Davies most helpfully provided us from time to time with the successive drafts of his corpus of ancient Hebrew inscriptions (now published). Heather McKay has given ideas (both lateral and linear), encouragement and criticism unstintingly throughout the project. George Brooke provided essential materials and advice on Qumran texts. Hilary Feldman of Oxford University Press kindly made available the manuscript of D. Winton Thomas's revision of Brown–Driver–Briggs, which he was engaged upon at the time of his death. And my two colleagues, Philip Davies and John Rogerson, who have acted as consulting editors, have been, from the very inception of the project, a ready resource; their support, extending even to carrying the editor's undergraduate teaching load for two years in the early phases of the project, has been indispensable, and it has been deeply appreciated.

This volume is dedicated to the memory of my father, Alfred William Clines, a master cartographer and Bible scholar, whose exactitude, love of learning and independence of mind have been a cardinal influence on the editor of this Dictionary. And this is the place also to record my indebtedness to my former teachers of Hebrew, E.C.B. MacLaurin of Sydney, and D. Winton Thomas, Sebastian Bullough, OP, and Erwin I.J. Rosenthal of Cambridge, who, each in his own way, left an indelible stamp upon his pupil.

DJAC
November 21, 1993

Introduction

1. *Main Characteristics of the Dictionary*

There are two main characteristics of this dictionary that distinguish it from other Hebrew dictionaries:

1. The range of texts it includes. This dictionary differs from traditional Hebrew lexica in that it designates and defines a phase of the language as Classical Hebrew. By that we mean all kinds of Hebrew from the period prior to about 200 CE, that is, earlier than the Hebrew of the Mishnah. Unlike other dictionaries of the ancient Hebrew language, which cover only the texts of the Hebrew Bible, whether exclusively or principally, this dictionary systematically records the language of all texts written in Hebrew from the earliest times down to the second century of the common era. For this purpose, we have divided all the texts into four corpora: (1) The Hebrew Bible (excluding the Aramaic portions); (2) Ben Sira; (3) the Qumran manuscripts (Dead Sea Scrolls) and related texts; (4) inscriptions and other occasional texts. The non-biblical texts are in extent about 15% of the size of the Hebrew Bible; so while references to biblical material predominate in this dictionary, an important place is given, for the first time, to the other evidence for the classical Hebrew language. For further details of the texts used for this dictionary, see below, The Sources.

2. The linguistic principles on which it is based. Unlike previous dictionaries, the Dictionary of Classical Hebrew has a theoretical base in modern linguistics. This theoretical base comes to expression primarily in the overriding concern in this dictionary for the *uses* of words in the language, especially the regular and normal uses in the written texts; we subscribe to the dictum that the meaning of a word is its use in the language. The focus here, then, is not so much on the meanings, or the translation equivalents, of individual words

as on the patterns and combinations in which words are used; and attention is paid primarily not to the unusual and difficult words but to the common words. Our especial concern has been to display the full evidence for the way Classical Hebrew words were used in our extant texts; so we report, for example, in exhaustive detail, all the subjects and objects that are attested for every verb, and, for nouns, all the verbs and all the other nouns with which they are connected. Many other features of the dictionary, such as the priority given to the most commonly attested sense, the avoidance of historical reconstructions, of the evidence of cognate languages, and of marking certain usages as 'figurative' or 'metaphorical', likewise depend upon the commonly accepted principles of modern linguistic theory.

2. *Other Features of the Dictionary*

Among features of this dictionary that users will notice as distinctive, the following may be mentioned:

1. We have striven to make this dictionary as user-friendly as possible. By design, it is very technical and detailed, but we have borne in mind the needs of a wide range of potential users, and would claim that it is both intelligible to the beginner in Hebrew (or even to the non-Hebraist) and instructive to the professional scholar. It is for this reason that the Dictionary is arranged on a strictly alphabetical principle, and that the 'root' forms of verbs are used as headwords, no matter how suspect such forms may be methodologically speaking. Indeed, the Dictionary should for the most part be quite intelligible to persons who have only the most rudimentary acquaintance with the language: once the reader has located the page on which the word in question is dealt with (there will be an English–Hebrew index in each volume), the semantic structure of the word, our differentiation of senses and the meaning of the citations should all be easily accessible.

2. The principle has also been followed, for the sake of potential users, that all Hebrew words and phrases, whether as the headword or in the body of an article, should be accompanied by an English translation (except when the same Hebrew word has been translated a line or two above). This practice of offering translations for the Hebrew is indeed a little imprudent, for it has

necessitated our offering renderings of very many words that we have not yet studied; and we can of course easily envisage that by the time we have finished the work there will be many renderings embedded in it that we would no longer wish to stand by. But the alternatives are worse; and we did not see this work as directed only to professional scholars and researchers but also to any readers of Hebrew texts who have progressed beyond the most elementary stages.

3. The Dictionary is professedly a dictionary of the extant texts rather than of the classical Hebrew language as spoken and written in its own time. Thus, for example, we list all the forms of a verb that are actually attested in the texts, and not those we could postulate as having existed.

4. The Dictionary studies the classical Hebrew language as if it were a synchronic system. It is not a historical dictionary, and it does not aim at tracing the development of the meaning of words. For most purposes we regard the classical language as constituting a single phase in the history of the Hebrew language. There were of course changes in the meanings of words throughout the millennium or more in which 'Classical Hebrew' was used, and in some cases developments can be inferred from the data in the Dictionary. For example, it is only in the Qumran texts, from the latest period of Classical Hebrew, that אַהֲרֹן *Aaron* is used in the sense of 'the priesthood, the priests collectively' (in biblical Hebrew it is the phrase בְּנֵי אַהֲרֹן *the sons of Aaron* that is used in this sense). So for some words it would have been possible to organize an article historically; but in general it proves impossible to prepare a dictionary of the classical phase of the Hebrew language on historical principles, since so few of the texts we have can be dated with any certainty.

5. The Dictionary attempts to use consistently gender-inclusive language: אָדָם is usually translated *humankind*, for example, though אִישׁ is *man*. Further, in the brief encyclopaedic information given about persons, the traditional suppression of data about women in many previous dictionaries is avoided; thus, for example, אַהֲרֹן *Aaron* is said to be 'son of Amram and Jochebed', not just 'son of Amram', and he is also 'brother of Miriam', just as Miriam will be said to be 'sister of Aaron'. We must, however, acknowledge that we cannot justify our practice of generally putting the father's name first.

6. The policy for the Dictionary concerning emendations has been this. We

do not attempt to evaluate emendations, or recommend readers to accept particular emendations of the texts. We do not regard this as lexicographers' business; it is only for us to report on the work of text-critics. In practice, we have tried as a rule to include all emendations that are adopted in the dictionaries of Brown–Driver–Briggs and Koehler–Baumgartner as well as those mentioned in the critical apparatus to *Biblia hebraica stuttgartensia*, since that edition is the standard scholarly text of the Hebrew Bible. We think it will be helpful to users of the Hebrew Bible to find the emendations of this edition reported on in the relevant places in the Dictionary; and those consulting the Dictionary on a particular word might benefit from being made aware that its use has been postulated for some other places in the Bible apart from those where it clearly occurs. But we never say whether we agree with an emendation or not; when we say 'or em.' we mean that what follows is an emendation that has been proposed, and when we say 'if em.' we mean that such and such is the result of accepting an emendation. There are of course cases in our printed texts of the Hebrew Bible where emendation is unquestionably required; for example, there are several cases where אֱדוֹם *Edom* is undoubtedly a scribal error for אֲרָם *Aram*, and vice versa. But there are very many more cases where emendation is questionable, and our policy has been to avoid making judgments on such issues. We always register a word in the places where it appears in the Masoretic text of the Hebrew Bible as it is printed in the edition of the *Biblia hebraica stuttgartensia*, even if we ourselves think the word needs to be emended. In the case of fragmentary non-biblical texts, the rule is that all words that are wholly or largely supplied by the editor of the primary published text in order to fill a lacuna are entered in the Dictionary, but such words are not counted in the tally of occurrences, even if their restoration is certain.

7. Cognates in other Semitic languages have not been listed in this Dictionary. Such information has become traditional in Hebrew lexica of the last two centuries, but its presence in a Hebrew dictionary is highly problematic, and it is difficult to see what purpose it serves. Theoretically speaking, that is, data about the meaning of cognate words in Akkadian and Arabic, for example, are strictly irrelevant to the Hebrew language; and, practically speaking, there is evidence that the significance of the cognates has been

systematically misunderstood by many users of the traditional dictionaries. It is often said, for example, that the function of noting the cognates is to indicate how it is that we know the meaning of the Hebrew word to be such and such; but this is incorrect, since there is usually a quite complex set of evidences for such matters, ranging from internal consistency within the Hebrew texts to the testimony of ancient versions and to Jewish lexicographical and exegetical tradition; and there is no reason to privilege the particular type of evidence, problematic as it is, that is provided by the cognate languages. We have not, in fact, seen it as our task to justify the meanings we propose for the Hebrew words; that is too complex a task to be accomplished within the confines of a dictionary.

3. *The Structure of Typical Articles*

The main elements of an article in this Dictionary are as follows:

1. *Headword (or, Lemma).* In the case of a verb, the headword (or, lemma) is given in the 'root' or unvocalized form; in the case of a noun, it is given in the form of the singular absolute, vocalized where possible. If the noun does not actually occur in the extant texts in the singular absolute, the lemma is placed within square brackets to indicate that the form has been reconstructed.

2. *Number of occurrences.* The number of occurrences of the word is divided among the four groups of texts that constitute our corpus: 1. the Hebrew Bible; 2. Ben Sira; 3. the Dead Sea Scrolls and related texts; 4. inscriptions and other such texts. In the case of אָדָם *human being,* for example, the notation indicates that the noun occurs 548 times in the Hebrew Bible, 31 times in Ben Sira, 101 times in the Dead Sea Scrolls, and twice in other Hebrew texts.

3. *Part of speech.* The designation of a word as verb, noun, adjective, and so on, is traditional and generally uncontroversial.

4. *Gloss.* A simple translation of the Hebrew headword follows, in order to identify the word. The gloss may consist of more than one word if the range of meanings for the Hebrew word is a wide one.

5. *Morphology.* Here are listed all forms of the headword that exist in the texts. Within round brackets are variants of a given form, whether orthographic, pausal, or suffixal. When a form occurs only as an unvocalized word,

the corpus to which it belongs is indicated by Q for Qumran texts, S for Ben Sira and Inscr for inscriptions. Verb forms prefixed with Waw are not termed 'consecutive' or 'preterite', but are simply prefaced with the rubric '+ waw'. Accents are marked when the stress is not on the last syllable (pausal forms show the Masoretic mark of accentuation).

6. *Semantic analysis.* This element forms the body of the article. Here the 'meanings' or 'senses' that may be attributed to the word are analysed. Thus, for example, the word אֹהֶל *tent* is said to have three senses: 1. tent for human habitation; 2. tent of soldiers; 3. tent, tabernacle as divine habitation. It needs to be stressed that all such analyses have a large subjective element in them, and that our perception of senses is often dependent on the semantic structure of the English language. That is how it must be, and should be, of course, in an interlingual dictionary. No rigid schematization is followed for the semantic analysis; rather, the structure of each article is developed from the nature and range of the attestations of the word. The only basic principle that is commonly employed is that the senses of a word are generally arranged in order of frequency of attestation. In this respect, the Dictionary of Classical Hebrew differs from many other dictionaries, in which so-called concrete senses normally precede metaphorical ones.

7. *Syntagmatic analysis.* This is a second level of arrangement, designed to display the contexts within which the word in question is used, that is, the syntagmatic relationships of the word. If the semantic or 'sense' divisions are close to one another, the syntagmatic analysis follows the semantic analysis as a whole; but if the senses are more distinct, the syntagmatic analysis is carried out for each sense separately. So, for example, in the case of the noun אַהֲבָה *love*, the senses are 1. love among humans; 2. love between deity and humans; here the senses are judged to be close, and the syntagmatic analysis follows the two semantic analyses. In the case of אכל *eat*, however, the two main senses that have been isolated—1. eat food, 2. devour—are regarded as more distinct, and so separate syntagmatic analyses follow each of the two senses.

The nature of the syntagmatic analysis differs according to the part of speech of the word in question. In the case of a verb, syntagmatic analysis means that the subjects and objects attested for the word are registered. So, for example, in the case of אכל, *eat*, under the heading 'eat food' everyone and everything that is said to eat food is listed, individuals, kings, shepherds, fools and so on; then everything that is said to be eaten as food is listed, bread, flesh, fruit, animals and so on. Following that, under the heading 'devour', everything that devours, fire, famine, enemies, and so on, is noted, and everything they devour, trees, nations, tents and so on. Further syntagmatic analysis of verbs is carried out by identifying the prepositions with which the verb is used, and by noting other typical collocations in which it is attested.

In the case of a noun, the syntagmatic analysis includes the following elements: the verbs of which it is the subject or object ; the nouns that are related to it; the adjectives used to modify the noun; and the prepositions and verb-prepositional phrases used with the noun. Thus in the case of אֹזֶן *ear*, we find that ears hear, attend, receive, tingle, rejoice and so on, and that people or things uncover ears, and bend, waken, or plant them and so on. We also find references to the ears of Pharaoh, Jerusalem, elders, dust, dogs and so on, and to the tip, hearing, heaviness of ears and so on (the two kinds of 'construct' relationship, one taking the headword as the *nomen regens*, the other taking it as the *nomen rectum*, are here analysed). The analysis of adjectives shows that ears are said to be right, attentive and uncircumcised. The analysis of the use of prepositions lists the examples of 'in', 'with' and 'to' ears.

Other parts of speech have their own system of syntagmatic analysis.

The syntagmatic analysis sometimes requires a certain amount of transformation of the surface structure of the text. So, for example, participles and infinitives are analysed for subjects and objects as if they were finite verbs. Thus, in the phrase בְּאַהֲבַת יהוה אֶת־יִשְׂרָאֵל *because Yahweh loved Israel* (1 Kings 10.9), 'Yahweh' is analysed as the subject of the verb אהב, and 'Israel' as its object. Even though grammatically speaking it is incorrect to regard 'Yahweh' here as the subject, the justification for treating infinitives and finite verbs alike is that semantically their function is the same; that is to say, the clause cited is evidence that 'Yahweh' can function as the subject of אהב *love*, and 'Israel' can be its object. Another example of transformation is the identification of the subject of verbs where none is specifically expressed. For example, in Genesis 3.6, וַתֵּרֶא הָאִשָּׁה ... וַתִּקַּח מִפִּרְיוֹ וַתֹּאכַל וַתִּתֵּן *and the woman saw ... and she took from its fruit and she ate and she gave*, the word אִשָּׁה *woman* is to be understood as the subject of the four verbs ראה *see,* לקח *take,* אכל *eat,* and נתן *give*—even though it is explicitly only the subject of the first. Consequently, in the article אִשָּׁה *woman,* the word is registered as the subject of all four verbs.

8. *Paradigmatic analysis.* Especially within the syntagmatic analysis a note has been made of any synonym or antonym of the word in question that is attested at that point in the text. This feature addresses to some extent another concern of modern linguistics: the place of a word within the semantic field of words provided by the language. That is, the meaning of a word in a given text is not only determined by its position in that text and its grammatical relationship to other words in the same sentence, but also by its relationship to all similar words in the language. It is impossible to combine a thorough paradigmatic analysis of the language with a dictionary of the present kind; a systematic notation of the attested synonyms and antonyms can however be a partial and preliminary attempt at paradigmatic analysis. The data of synonyms and antonyms displayed in the body of the article are summarized in the section headed <SYN>, which constitutes an index to the synonyms and antonyms that have already been mentioned. It needs to be noted, however, that it is not always the case that words and phrases marked in the body of the article (with the signs || or :: or +) as 'parallels' or as 'opposites' or as being in a more loose association qualify as true synonyms and antonyms (and it is in any case very debatable what true synonyms and antonyms actually are, and even whether they exist). Only words belonging to the same part of speech as the headword are listed in the Synonym section, whereas in the body of the article there are often other words or phrases that are noted by the signs || or ::. And no word is noted among Synonyms unless it occurs at least twice as a synonym in the body of the article. Words occurring in antithetical or antonymous relationship more than once are listed in the section labelled <ANT>.

9. *Index.* In the case of verbs, the paragraph that begins with an arrow (⇨) lists all the words, including proper names, that may clearly be 'derived', morphologically speaking, from the verbal 'root'. In the case of nouns, the verbal 'root' from which the noun is 'derived' is noted, if it is attested; in some cases, another noun appears as the indexial word in this paragraph. It should be noted that no historical implications about the derivations of words

are intended by this section; it is not concerned with the etymology of words.

4. *The Recent History of Hebrew Lexicography*

This Dictionary of Classical Hebrew has been conceived as the successor of the most famous of all Hebrew dictionaries, at least in the English-speaking world: *A Hebrew and English Lexicon of the Old Testament, with an Appendix containing the Biblical Aramaic, based on the Lexicon of William Gesenius as translated by Edward Robinson ... Edited with constant reference to the Thesaurus of Gesenius as completed by E. Rödiger, and with authorized use of the latest German editions of Gesenius's Handwörterbuch über das Alte Testament*, by Francis Brown, with the co-operation of S.R. Driver and Charles A. Briggs. Known familiarly as BDB, from the initials of its editors' surnames, or as The Oxford Lexicon, it began to appear with the issue of its First Part in 1891; the complete dictionary was published in 1907. Since that time a corrected edition has been issued, in 1955, containing 'many hundreds' of small corrections by G.R. Driver, either incorporated in the sheets of the text without resetting, or contained at the end of the volume in the eight pages of 'addenda et corrigenda', to which asterisks in the body of the text refer.

In brief, it is a hundred years since there has been a major dictionary of the ancient Hebrew language in English. A hundred years is a long time in lexicography, even in the lexicography of ancient languages. It would have seemed so, we can be sure, to the editors of BDB itself. For, although they remarked in 1906 that 'the need of a new Hebrew and English Lexicon of the Old Testament has been so long felt that no elaborate explanation of the appearance of the present work seems called for', the previous lexicon was no more than 32 years old when the first fascicle of BDB appeared. It was an edition of Gesenius prepared by S.P. Tregelles. The editors of BDB showed how ancient a work they thought it when they referred to it as a work that 'dates back as far as 1859'! There had in fact been in the intervening period yet another English dictionary of Hebrew, published in 1867, namely the translation by Samuel Davidson of *A Hebrew and Chaldee Lexicon to the Old Testament*, translated as a 'third edition' from the second edition of Julius Fuerst's Dictionary of 1863.

Beyond the English-speaking world, there have been of course very considerable achievements in Hebrew dictionary-making in the present century. In the front rank must be set the *Lexicon in Veteris Testamenti Libros* of Ludwig Koehler, to which a dictionary of the Aramaic parts of the Old Testament was supplied by Walter Baumgartner. This volume was published by E.J. Brill of Leiden in 1953, and was notable, if not unique, among dictionaries of ancient languages for its provision of both German and English renderings of the words. This practice was continued into the second edition (1958), which consisted of the first edition reprinted, plus a second volume, *Supplementum ad Lexicon Veteris Testamenti Libros*, put into its final form by Baumgartner. This *Supplementum* contained 84 pages of 'additions and corrections' (pp. 125-208), a further collection of 'most recent additions' ('Additamenta Novissima', pp. 209-25), and yet further 'corrections most recently discovered' ('Correctiones nuperrime repertae', pp. 226-27). It is no reflection on the scholarly quality of this dictionary to observe that any user laboured under the disadvantage of needing to look in four different places in order to discover the definitive statement of this edition of the dictionary on any matter.

The third edition of Koehler–Baumgartner, of which the fourth and final volume of the Hebrew part of the lexicon has recently appeared, more than compensates for the inconveniences of the second edition, for it is a thoroughgoing revision with several new features. However, from the standpoint of the English-speaking scholar or student, it is a step backwards, in that it entirely omits English renderings. This fact is implicitly announced by the change of title from a Latin one to a German one, *Hebräisches und aramäisches Lexikon zum Alten Testament*.

Two new lexicographical projects are in course of publication at the present time. There is the eighteenth edition of the standard German dictionary of Wilhelm Gesenius, edited by Rudolf Meyer and Herbert Donner: *Wilhelm Gesenius. Hebräisches und aramäisches Handwörterbuch über das Alte Testament*, of which the first part (Alpeh to Gimel) appeared in 1987. And there is the new Spanish dictionary project edited by Luis Alonso Schökel, *Diccionario bíblico hebreo–español*, of which the first fascicle, containing most of the letter Aleph, appeared in 1990.

We should not of course overlook the smaller dictionary of Biblical Hebrew prepared by Georg Fohrer (and translated into English by William

Johnstone), and that by William L. Holladay, an abbreviation of the second edition of Koehler–Baumgartner. But however useful these dictionaries may be for pedagogical purposes, nothing has yet been produced—it seems safe to say—that can in any way rival the dominance of BDB in the English-speaking world. The announced English translation of Koehler–Baumgartner, of which the first volume is expected in late 1993, will undoubtedly be a competitor; and so also, we hope, will the Dictionary of Classical Hebrew!

Nevertheless, the need for a new Hebrew dictionary arises not simply from the lapse of time since the last work of this kind. The era since the publication of BDB has seen the discovery of the Ugaritic texts and the Qumran scrolls, to name only the most notable discoveries, and to say nothing of the creation of the science of modern linguistics, the name for which did not even exist in the days of Brown, Driver and Briggs. The Old Testament no longer stands, as it did in their days, in linguistic isolation; the classical Hebrew language is no longer more or less co-terminous with the language of the Hebrew Bible, for it now embraces a very much larger corpus of texts.

For these reasons, any dictionary of the ancient Hebrew language prepared at the end of the century should be a dictionary of the classical language as a whole, in which the language of the Bible is not privileged over that of the non-biblical texts: the book of Ben Sira, the Qumran manuscripts and the Hebrew inscriptions from many periods.

5. *A Hebrew Dictionary at the End of the Twentieth Century*

One of the strengths of the great lexica of the past is that they have stood in a lexicographical tradition, and have, more often than not, been revisions and adaptations of previous lexica. Thus, for example, the Brown–Driver–Briggs Lexicon announced itself on its title page as 'based on' the lexicon of Gesenius, while the new German dictionary currently in progress, under the editorship of Donner and Meyer, presents itself unambiguously as essentially a revision of Gesenius, bearing as it does an engraved portrait of Wilhelm Gesenius himself as its frontispiece.

The Dictionary of Classical Hebrew is, by contrast, an entirely new work. The editors and researchers of the Dictionary of Classical Hebrew have, needless to say, systematically read the entries in the standard lexica of the past; but the dictionary as a whole is designed on independent lines, as will be evident to any user on opening the first volume. The focus in modern linguistics has rightly been upon sentences as wholes, rather than upon individual words, and although a dictionary must remain a word book and be organized alphabetically by the words it discusses, it must pay a great deal of attention to the contexts in which words occur, and the place they hold within the total system of the language. A modern dictionary, therefore, will concern itself not only with meanings, but with syntagmatic and paradigmatic relationships.

That is to say, the fundamental questions about every word for which an entry is written in the dictionary must be: 1. How is it used and in what kind of sentences and connections? 2. How is it related in meaning and use to other similar or opposite words? To a remarkable extent the great dictionaries of Hebraists of the past have answered these questions, though never explicitly. BDB, for example, is rich in citations of usages, phrases and idioms—all of which provide important syntagmatic information. What is lacking, however, is any systematic exploitation of the data, or presentation of them in a form that trains the mind of the user to recognize that these two questions must always be at the forefront of any inquiry about a word.

The Dictionary of Classical Hebrew is one of the first Hebrew dictionaries to be informed by linguistics rather than philology (the Spanish dictionary being edited by L. Alonso Schökel is the other noteworthy example of the impact of modern linguistics on Hebrew lexicography). The great philological enterprise, a legacy of nineteenth-century historical scholarship, was essentially an historical enquiry after original meanings and historical developments. In Hebrew studies, it was stimulated by the discovery of two important members of the Semitic language family, Akkadian and Ugaritic, both of them older than any attestations of the Hebrew language, and therefore meat and drink to historically inclined philologians. The era of philology, even at the present time, shows no signs of drawing to a close, and there can be no doubt that it remains an important and productive area of research. However, a search for origins is not an appropriate way of inquiring after meaning, and the success of BDB, for example, lay not in its comparative Semitic philology but in its sensitivity to the regularities and irregularities of Hebrew usage within the Bible. Nevertheless, in traditional philology, of which BDB is one of the finest examples, the concentration has been on the word, the individual word, the meaning of the word; the orientation of modern linguistics, by contrast, is toward the sentence or the unit of discourse. By design, then, this new Dictionary systematically deflects attention from the word to the larger units of meaning.

This Dictionary is therefore not simply a word-book. Its function is not primarily to tell the user the meaning of words. It has not been written in order to help readers of Hebrew texts to discover how to translate those texts. It would indeed be a very inconvenient way of studying a Hebrew text to look up the meanings of all the words in this large and exhaustive work. Rather, the primary function of this Dictionary is to organize and rationalize the available data about Hebrew words, enabling readers to make their own decisions about the meaning of words in the light of all the evidence, which has been arranged in such a way as to make that task feasible.

At the end of the twentieth century, it is only right that a Hebrew dictionary should reflect something of the spirit of the age. And if our age can in any sense be characterized as post-modern—that is to say, as resisting concepts of authority, determinate meanings and the like, and as emphasizing instead the perpetual deferral of meaning as well as the plurality and historical conditionedness of scholarly values (as of all values)—then a dictionary for the age should be short on authority and prescription and long on reader-involvement, open-endedness and uncertainty. Faced on many occasions, for example, with decisions about what data we should select and what we should compress, we have found ourselves concluding that there is no way of predicting which pieces of information will prove interesting and important to which users. So we have consistently regarded our task as providing and organizing the data that others will use as they think best, rather than imposing our own views as to what is significant.

Because it is not a conventional Hebrew dictionary, many readers will miss elements they have been familiar with, and may find several of its novelties of little use to themselves. We will all have to learn how to use this Dictionary, and invent new questions to which it will provide the answers. Developers of computer software cannot envisage the range of uses to which their customers will put their product; no more can we.

6. *The Dictionary of Classical Hebrew Project*

This Dictionary of Classical Hebrew had its inception in 1983, when proposals concerning its principles and methods were first discussed in Sheffield. The actual composition of the Dictionary began in September, 1988, when the first research associates were appointed.

The Dictionary is a research project of the Department of Biblical Studies in the University of Sheffield under the editorship of David J.A. Clines. He is assisted by an committee of Philip R. Davies and John W. Rogerson, as consulting editors. The drafting of the articles for this volume has been carried out by the research associates appointed as members of the Department's staff. Since January 1993 the work of the research associates has been under the direction of the executive editor for Volume 1, John Elwolde. The project is being undertaken under the auspices of the Society for Old Testament Study, which has appointed a Board of Reference from among the members of that Society. The Dictionary of Classical Hebrew is recognized by the University of Sheffield as part of its research activity, and it has its office within the Humanities Research Institute of the University.

Future volumes of the Dictionary are expected to follow this plan:

vol. no.	Hebrew letters	% of total work	estimated no. of pages
1	א	9.7	372
2	ב ג ד ה ו	13.9	533
3	ז ח ט	10.6	407
4	י כ ל	12.6	483
5	מ נ	15.1	579
6	ס ע פ	13.8	529
7	צ ק ר	11.8	453
8	שׂ שׁ ת	12.5	479
Totals		100.0	3835

As will be seen from the foregoing table, the contents of the present volume form a little under ten per cent of the Dictionary as a whole. The number of pages devoted to Dictionary articles proper is somewhat smaller than it will be in subsequent volumes; but the Introduction to this first volume makes the total length of this volume about average for the set as a whole. The whole work is planned to be completed in eight volumes.

The following statistics show the comparative extent of the various corpora of texts surveyed for the Dictionary. The material from Qumran will of course be enlarged in coming years by the further publication of manuscripts.

	estimated length of text (in words)	text length as % of Classical Hebrew texts	text length as % of Hebrew Bible (BHS)	number of occurrences of Aleph words in Dictionary
Biblical				
BHS	305500	86.4	100.0	61883
Non-biblical				
Ben Sira	7020	2.0	2.3	1422
Qumran	38349	10.9	12.6	7768
Inscr	2528	0.7	0.8	512
Total	353396			71585
Non-biblical texts as % of all Classical Hebrew texts		13.6		
Non-biblical texts as % of the Hebrew Bible (BHS)			15.7	

The foregoing statistics of the size of the various corpora of Hebrew texts have ben derived in the following way. From the totals in the table, Words Beginning with Aleph in Order of Frequency, it can be seen that we have identified 61,883 occurrences of words in the Hebrew Bible (*Biblia hebraica stuttgartensia*) beginning with Aleph. Knowing that there are some 305,500 words in the Hebrew Bible (the figure comes from Francis I. Andersen and A. Dean Forbes, *The Vocabulary of the Old Testament* [Rome: Pontifical Biblical Institute, 1989], p. 23), we can assume that, roughly speaking, the 1,422 occurrences of Aleph words in ben Sira imply a text of c. 7,020 words (i.e. 1422 divided by 61833 and multiplied by 305500). Similarly, the total of 7,768 occurrences in the Qumran and related materials implies a corpus of c. 38,300 words (in the non-biblical texts already published, that is).

THE SOURCES

The purview of this Dictionary, as has already been noted, differs from all previous dictionaries of the ancient Hebrew language in that it comprehends not only the biblical texts but all Hebrew texts of whatever description from the earliest times down to c. 200 CE. Locating the varied materials for a Hebrew dictionary remains a formidable task, since, except for the Bible, there exist no standard and comprehensive editions. In the case of the Qumran texts especially, recourse must be had to a multitude of periodical and other publications, not always easy to obtain. In many cases, no standard nomenclature for the texts exists. For the work of the Dictionary it has been necessary to draw up check lists of the materials known to us and to determine forms of citation in cases where they do not already exist. What follows is, we think, the most comprehensive list of classical Hebrew texts that readers will have easy access to.

a. *Hebrew Bible*

The edition of the Hebrew Bible used in this Dictionary is *Biblia hebraica stuttgartensia* (ed. K. Elliger and W. Rudolph; Stuttgart: Deutsche Bibelstiftung, 1967). Both the text of the Bible itself and the text of the critical apparatus have been used as source texts for this Dictionary.

b. *Ben Sira*

The edition used as the primary text for this Dictionary is that of the Academy of the Hebrew Language: *Materials for the Dictionary. Series I. 200 B.C.E.—300 C.E.* (Jerusalem: The Academy of the Hebrew Language—The Historical Dictionary of the Hebrew Language, 1988). This text was previously published in *The Book of Ben Sira: Text, Concordance and an Analysis of the Vocabulary* (Jerusalem: The Academy of the Hebrew Language and the Shrine of the Book, 1973).

c. *Qumran and Related Non-Biblical Texts*
The base text used for the Qumran and related materials has been the edition from the Academy of the Hebrew Language, published in microfiche as its *Materials for the Dictionary. Series I. 200 B.C.E.—300 C.E.* (Jerusalem: The Academy of the Hebrew Language—The Historical Dictionary of the Hebrew Language, 1988). This text (here referred to as AHL) was chosen at the inception of the present project for the following reasons: 1. It provided in a handy format a complete set of the texts that had been already published, including, for example, the Temple Scroll. 2. It was accompanied by a concordance, on microfiche, which facilitated the locations of occurrences of words. 3. It incorporated various previous editions of the texts, together with improvements of its own, and so represented something of a scholarly norm. 4. It displayed lacunae and uncertainties in the text clearly, and was conservative in filling lacunae.

This base text (AHL) has been compared with the editions of texts in the 'official' publications in the series Discoveries in the Judaean Desert (DJD) and with other scholarly editions. Where the editor of another major edition offers a reading different from AHL, the alternative reading is also given in the articles of the Dictionary, with the editor's name in brackets. Many texts in AHL have at the present time not appeared in DJD.

The corpus of Qumran texts has of course been greatly increased in extent by the publication in 1991 and 1992 of photographs and editions of many of the known Dead Sea Scrolls, years before their anticipated publication by the official group of scholars to whom they were entrusted. First came the volume by B.Z. Wacholder and M.G. Abegg, *A Preliminary Edition of the Unpublished Dead Sea Scrolls: The Hebrew and Aramaic Texts from Cave Four* (1991), a reconstruction of the text of the Cave Four manuscripts of the Damascus Document and of 4QMishmarot (4Q320–330) from the excerpts of these manuscripts in the handwritten *Preliminary Concordance* compiled by R.E. Brown, J.A. Fitzmyer, W.G. Oxtoby and J. Teixidor. Though the materials in the concordance are simply excerpts written on filing cards, they represent the readings of the original group of Qumran specialists, and the reconstruction of the text they presume is quite serviceable. Following the first volume by Wacholder and Abegg, Robert H. Eisenman and James M. Robinson published a *Facsimile Edition of the Dead Sea Scrolls* (1991), containing about 1800 photographs of the unpublished manuscripts, and in 1992 Eisenman and Michael Wise produced *The Dead Sea Scrolls Uncovered: The First Complete Translation and Interpretation of 50 Key Documents Withheld for Over 35 Years*, with a transcription and translation of about 33 Hebrew manuscripts from Cave Four. In 1992 Wacholder and Abegg published the second volume of their reconstructed texts, which they had now been able to check against the photographs.

Officially or not, these texts are now in the public domain, and we felt obliged to incorporate them as best we could in the Dictionary, even at a very late stage in its redaction, and even in the knowledge that the editions available in 1993 leave much to be desired in several respects. It is estimated that these new publications have added between 300 and 400 non-biblical texts to the corpus of Qumran literature, the extent of which may now be reckoned to be as large as 30% to 40% of the length of the Hebrew Bible (much more, of course, if the biblical manuscripts are included). We did not have time to incorporate the manuscripts published in the second volume by Wacholder and Abegg, but we intend to include in future volumes of this Dictionary both those and other manuscripts promised for later publication.

The policy of the editors of the Dictionary has been that the edition of Eisenman and Wise (EW) has been taken as a norm for the 33 texts they have published. When their text disagrees verbally with that of manuscripts in the first volume by Wacholder and Abegg, the readings of the latter are also given, with their name (WA); graphic variations are ignored. Other texts are cited according to the readings of Wacholder and Abegg (WA). Any subsequent detailed scholarly edition of a particular manuscript is given preference to the editions of EW and of WA, and the graphic readings of those two editions are in those cases ignored. But if either of these editions differs verbally from a later edition, the verbal reading of EW or WA is reported. Our normal practice has been that the proposals of the primary editor(s) for reconstructing lacunae are registered in the Dictionary, but such reconstructions are not counted as occurrences of the word in question. This practice has also been followed with respect to the newly published manuscripts.

In brief, the edition that has been followed as the primary text for each of the Qumran and related manuscripts is shown in the lists of sources, below, in the column headed Edition.

A distinction needs to be made between *texts* and *manuscripts.* A text is a literary work, of which there may be more than one copy, or, manuscript, in existence. At Qumran, what have been discovered are of course manuscripts (or rather, fragments of manuscripts) rather than texts or literary works; and it is not always easy to say whether two manuscripts containing different wording are copies of the one text or not. We have not attempted to make any decisions of our own, but have simply tried to follow what seems to be the consensus among Qumran specialists on this matter. In the currently fluid state of Qumran scholarship, that is easier said than done, however; for example, the Temple Scroll is the name given to the *work* that exists in the *manuscript* 11QT, but most people do not observe the distinction and speak interchangeably of the Temple Scroll and 11QT.

The principle that has been followed for the Dictionary is that *manuscripts* are not registered, but all *texts* are (though texts can only be referred to as they are attested in manuscripts!). In practice, this means that all biblical manuscripts from Qumran are excluded from the Dictionary (except where they have a text different from the Masoretic text), but that the Qumran commentaries (*pesharim*) are included. Thus, for example, of the Isaiah Scroll (1QIsa^{a}) only differences from the Masoretic text of the Hebrew Bible are mentioned, whereas from the Commentary on Isaiah (1QpIsa) all the material is included, except for the citations of the biblical text. The Temple Scroll (11QT) has been considered an independent work, and so citations and rephrasings of the biblical text in 11QT are indicated by an equals sign between the biblical reference and the Qumran citation (e.g. Nm 30_{5}=11QT 53_{17}), and the word that occurs in Numbers 30 and Column 53 of the Temple Scroll is counted as occurring twice, even though the wording of the Temple Scroll has been taken from Numbers.

When there are multiple copies of the same text or work (as in the case of the Damascus Document or the Book of Jubilees, of which 14 or 15 copies are known), for the purposes of the Dictionary we have regard only to the one *text*. Thus a given word may occur in 14 different manuscripts of Jubilees, but it will be noted and counted only once in the Dictionary.

There follow lists of all known non-biblical Qumran and related texts; those that have been published have been incorporated in the Dictionary. There is, first, a list arranged by order of cave number (e.g. 1QS, 4QM, 11QT), and, within each cave, alphabetically if the texts are known only by a name or siglum (e.g. 1QS), and then numerically if they are known by a number (e.g. 4Q153). And there is, secondly, for the texts known also by a siglum (e.g. 1QDM, 4QFlor, 4QVisSam), an alphabetical list of the sigla; these are the names by which we refer to these texts in the Dictionary. Only the texts in Hebrew are included in these lists, and only the non-biblical texts.

The following lists combine data from publications by Eisenman and Wise, Fitzmyer, García Martínez, Tov, and Wacholder and Abegg (see the Bibliography below for details). Abbreviations used in these lists are explained in the Bibliography.

Qumran and Related Non-Biblical Texts in Cave and Number Order

In this list there appears, in the five columns, the following:

(1) The number by which the texts are known (in the case of four major Qumran texts from Cave 1, no number is assigned, and the text is known simply by its siglum; such cases are listed first).

(2) The generally agreed siglum or abbreviation of name by which the text is usually referred to; in the few cases where the siglum used in the Dictionary differs from that in current use, this Dictionary's siglum is given first.

(3) The name of the text that prevails in current scholarship (occasionally two names are in current use, in which case they are separated by an oblique line); if no name seems to have been agreed, some indication of the nature of the work is given in lower-case letters (e.g. 'sapiential', 'liturgical').

(4) A reference to the edition of the text that has been the standard for this Dictionary (where page numbers alone are given, the reference is to the Academy of the Hebrew Language edition [AHL]).

(5) Other principal editions that are also cited in the Dictionary from time to time, and other sources of information about the texts (for example, in cases where a text has not been published, 'cf.' directs the reader to some description of the text).

This list attempts to be a complete list of known non-biblical Hebrew texts, published and unpublished, from Qumran (from related sites, on the other hand, only those texts that have been published are included). With a very few exceptions, all published texts—that is, texts that have been printed in transcription, with or without translation and technical notes—have been read for the Dictionary and incorporated in it. For all the texts used in the Dictionary there is an entry in the fourth column, which notes the primary edition we have followed. When further texts are published, their data will be included in future volumes of the Dictionary.

No.	Siglum	Name / Description	Edition	Reference
Cave 1				
	1QH	Hymns / Hodayot	228-52	Licht
	1QM	War Scroll	157-76	Yadin
	1QpHab	Habakkuk Pesher	258-63	Burrows, I
	1QS	Community Rule / Manual of Discipline	110-24	Burrows, II
1Q14	1QpMic	Micah Pesher	264-65	DJD, I, 77-80
1Q15	1QpZeph	Zephaniah Pesher	266	DJD, I, 80
1Q16	1QpPs	Psalms Pesher	267-70	DJD, I, 81-82
1Q17	1QJub[a]	Jubilees	97-99	DJD, I, 82-83
1Q18	1QJub[b]	Jubilees	97-99	DJD, I, 83-84
1Q19	1QNoah	Noah	207	DJD, I, 84-86
1Q19b	1QNoah	Noah	207	DJD, I, 152
1Q22	1QDM	Dibre Mosheh / Words of Moses	205-206	DJD, I, 91-97
1Q25		prophecy	208-209	DJD, I, 100-101
1Q26		sapiential	289	DJD, I, 101-102
1Q27	1QMyst	prophecy	253-54	DJD, I, 102-107
1Q28a	1QSa	Community Rule	110-24	DJD, I, 108-11
1Q28b	1QSb	Community Rule	110-24	DJD, I, 118-30
1Q29		Three Tongues of Fire	225	DJD, I, 130-32
1Q30		liturgical	299	DJD, I, 132-33
1Q31		liturgical	300	DJD, I, 133-34
1Q33	1QM	War Scroll	171	DJD, I, 135-36
1Q34	1QLitPr[a]	Festival Prayers	301	DJD, I, 136
1Q34a	1QLitPr[b]	Festival Prayers	301	DJD, I, 152-55
1Q35	1QH/1QH[b]	Hymns / Hodayoth	228-52	DJD, I, 136-38
1Q36		hymns	302-303	DJD, I, 138-41
1Q37–40		hymns	305-307	DJD, I, 141-43
1Q41–62		unidentified	330-42	DJD, I, 144-47
1Q69		unidentified	DJD, I, 148	

Cave 2

2Q19	2QJub^{a}	Jubilees	97-99	DJD, III, 77-78
2Q20	2QJub^{b}	Jubilees	97-99	DJD, III, 78-79
2Q21	2QapMoses	Apocryphon of Moses	290	DJD, III, 79-81
2Q22	2QapDavid	Apocryphon of David	291	DJD, III, 81-82
2Q23	2QapProph	prophecy	292	DJD, III, 82-84
2Q25		halakah	329	DJD, III, 90
2Q27–33		unidentified	343-46	DJD, III, 91-93

Cave 3

3Q4	3QpIsa	Isaiah Pesher	199-204	DJD, III, 95-96
3Q5	3QJub	Jubilees	197-99	DJD, III, 96-98
3Q6	3QHymn	hymnic	308	DJD, III, 98
3Q7	3QTJud	Testament of Judah	347	DJD, III, 99
3Q8		Angel of Peace	348	DJD, III, 100
3Q9		sectarian	349	DJD, III, 100-101
3Q10-11		unidentified	DJD, III, 101-102	
3Q15	3QTr	Copper Scroll	387-91	DJD, III, 211-302

Cave 4

4Q158	4QBibPar	Biblical Paraphrase	DJD, V, 1-6	
4Q159	4QOrd^{a}	Ordinances	153-55	DJD, V, 6-9
4Q160	4QVisSam	Visions of Samuel	188	DJD, V, 9-11
4Q161	4QpIsa^{a}	Isaiah Pesher	199-204	DJD, V, 11-15
4Q162	4QpIsa^{b}	Isaiah Pesher	199-204	DJD, V, 15-17
4Q163	4QpIsa^{c}	Isaiah Pesher	199-204	DJD, V, 17-27
4Q164	4QpIsa^{d}	Isaiah Pesher	199-204	DJD, V, 27-28
4Q165	4QpIsa^{e}	Isaiah Pesher	199-204	DJD, V, 28-30
4Q166	4QpHos^{a}	Hosea Pesher	271-73	DJD, V, 31-32
4Q167	4QpHos^{b}	Hosea Pesher	271-73	DJD, V, 32-36
4Q168	4QpMic	Micah Pesher	DJD, V, 36	
4Q169	4QpNah	Nahum Pesher	274-75	DJD, V, 90-93
4Q170	4QpZeph	Zephaniah Pesher	DJD, V, 42	
4Q171	4QpPs^{a}	Psalms Pesher	267-70	DJD, V, 42-51
4Q172	4QpUnid	unidentified pesher	277	DJD, V, 50-51
4Q173	4QpPs^{b}	Psalms Pesher	267-70, 369	DJD, V, 51-53
4Q174	4QFlor	Florilegium	278-79	DJD, V, 53-57
4Q175	4QTestim	Testimonia	177	DJD, V, 57-60
4Q176	4QTanḥ	Consolations	309-10	DJD, V, 60-67
4Q176.19-21	4QJub^{f}	Jubilees	310	Kister, *RQ* 12 (1987)
4Q177	4QCat^{a}	Catena	281-83	DJD, V, 67-74
4Q178		unidentified	326	DJD, V, 74-75
4Q179	4QapLam	Lamentation on Jerusalem	218-19	DJD, V, 75-77

4Q180	4QAges	Pesher on the Periods	285	DJD, V, 77-79
4Q181		Ages of Creation	286	DJD, V, 79-80
4Q182	4QCat^{b}	Catena	284	DJD, V, 80-81
4Q183		historical	257	DJD, V, 81-82
4Q184	4QWiles	Wiles of the Wicked Woman	323-24	DJD, V, 82-85
4Q185		Eulogy on Wisdom	220-21	DJD, V, 85-87
4Q186	4QCrypt	horoscopes	325	DJD, V, 88-91
4Q200	4QTob	Tobit		cf. Milik, *RB* 73 (1966) 522
4Q215	4QTNaph	Testament of Naphtali	EW, 159	
4Q216	4QJub^{a}	Jubilees^{a}	VanderKam–Milik, *JBL* 110 (1991)	
4Q217	4QJub^{b}	Jubilees^{b}		
4Q218	4QJub^{c}	Jubilees^{c}		
4Q219	4QJub^{d}	Jubilees^{d}	VanderKam–Milik, *Bib* 73 (1992)	
4Q220	4QJub^{e}	Jubilees^{e}		
4Q221	4QJub^{f}	Jubilees^{f}		cf. VanderKam, *Madrid*
4Q222	4QJub^{g}	Jubilees^{g}		
4Q223–224	4QJub^{h}	Jubilees^{h}		
4Q225	4QpsJub^{a}			
4Q226	4QpsJub^{b}			
4Q227	4QpsJub^{c}	Pseudo-Jubilees	EW, 96-97	
4Q228		work citing Jubilees		
4Q229		pseudepigraphon (Mishnaic)		
4Q230		Catalogue of Spirits^{a}		
4Q231		Catalogue of Spirits^{b}		
4Q232		New Jerusalem (?)		
4Q233		place names		
4Q234		exercise on Genesis 27		
4Q237		psalter		
4Q239		pesher on the true Israel		
4Q240		commentary on Canticles (?)		
4Q241		fragments citing Lamentations		
4Q247		pesher on Apocalypse of Weeks		cf. Milik, *Enoch*, 256
4Q248		Acts of a Greek King		
4Q249	4QMSM	Midrash Sepher Mosheh		Milik, *JJS* 23 (1972)
4Q250		text on verso of MSM		
4Q251		Halakah / A Pleasing Fragrance	EW, 202-203	Baumgarten, *JJS* 27 (1976)
4Q252	4QpGen^{a}	Patriarchal Blessings / Genesis Florilegium	EW, 86-87	AHL, 280
4Q253	4QpGen^{b}	Patriarchal Blessings		
4Q254	4QpGen^{c}	Patriarchal Blessings		
4Q255	4QS^{a}	Community Rule		cf. Milik, *RB* 67 (1960)
4Q256	4QS^{b}	Community Rule (previously 4QS^{d})		Vermes, *JJS* 42 (1991)
4Q257	4QS^{c}	Community Rule		

4Q258	4QS^{d}	Community Rule (previously 4QS^{b})		Vermes, *JJS* 42 (1991)
4Q259	4QS^{e}	Community Rule		WA, I, 96-101; cf. Milik, SVT 4 (1957)
4Q260	4QS^{f}	Community Rule		cf. Milik, *RB* 67 (1960)
4Q261	4QS^{g}	Community Rule		cf. Milik, *RB* 67 (1960)
4Q262	4QS^{h}	Community Rule		cf. Milik, *RB* 67 (1960)
4Q263	4QS^{i}	Community Rule		cf. Milik, *RB* 67 (1960)
4Q264	4QS^{j}	Community Rule		cf. Milik, *RB* 67 (1960)
4Q265	4QSD	Community Rule + Damascus Document		cf. Milik, *Ten Years*, 96
4Q266	4QD^{a}	Damascus Document (prev. 4QD^{b}) 198		WA, I, 1, 21-22; Baumgarten, *Madrid*, 506
4Q267	4QD^{b}	Damascus Document^{b} (prev. 4QD^{d}) EW, 218		WA, I, 3-22
4Q268	4QD^{c}	Damascus Document^{c} (prev. 4QD^{a})		WA, I, 23-27
4Q269	4QD^{d}	Damascus Document^{d} (prev. 4QD^{f})		WA, I, 28-35; Baumgarten, *JJS* 41 (1990)
4Q270	4QD^{e}	Damascus Document^{e}		WA, I, 36-47
4Q271	4QD^{f}	Damascus Document^{f} (prev. 4QD^{g})		WA, I, 48-53
4Q272	4QD^{g}	Damascus Document^{g}		WA, I, 54-56; Baumgarten, *JJS* 41 (1990)
4Q273	4QD^{h}	Damascus Document^{h}		WA, I, 57-59; Baumgarten, *JJS* 41 (1990)
4Q274	4QToh A	Purities	EW, 207-208	
4Q275	4QToh B	Purities		cf. Milik, *JJS* 23 (1972)
4Q276	4QToh B^{a}	Laws of the Red Heifer	EW, 226	
4Q277	4QToh B^{b}	Laws of the Red Heifer	EW, 210	
4Q278	4QToh C?			
4Q279	4QToh D$^{a?}$	Laws		
4Q280	4QToh D	Curses against Melkiresha	214	Milik, *JJS* 23 (1972)
4Q281–282		4QToh E^{a}?		
4Q283	4QToh F?			
4Q284	4QNid	Rule of the Menstruants		
4Q284a		Leqet		
4Q285		Destruction of the Kittim / Messianic Leader	EW, 24	Vermes, *JJS* 43 (1992) Milik, *JJS* 23 (1972)
4Q286	4QBer^{a}	The Chariots of Glory	EW, 226-28	AHL, 287
4Q287	4QBer^{b}	The Chariots of Glory	EW, 228	
4Q288	4QBer^{c}			
4Q289	4QBer^{d}			
4Q290	4QBer^{e}			
4Q291–293		prayers		
4Q294–297		rules and prayers		
4Q298		Admonitions to the Sons of Dawn EW, 164-65		

4Q299	4QMyst[a]	= 1Q27		
4Q300–301	4QMyst[b]	= 1Q27		
4Q301	4QMyst[c]	= 1Q27		
4Q302		Praise of God		
4Q302a		Parable of the Tree		
4Q303		Meditation on Creation A[a]		
4Q304		Meditation on Creation A[b]		
4Q305		Meditation on Creation B		
4Q306		Men of People who Err		
4Q307		sapiential		
4Q308		sapiential		
4Q311		unidentified		
4Q312		Hebrew text in cursive Phoenician?		
4Q313		unidentified cryptic script		
4Q316		unidentified		
4Q317		Phases of Moon (cryptic script)		Milik, *Enoch*, 68-69
4Q319	4QOtot	Heavenly Concordances	EW, 130-31	
4Q320	4QMish A	Priestly Courses II	EW, 116-18	WA, I, 60-67
4Q321	4QMish B[a]	Priestly Courses I	EW, 109-11	WA, I, 68-73
4Q321a	4QMish B[b]	Priestly Courses I		WA, I, 74-76
4Q322	4QMish C[a]	Priestly Courses III	EW, 122-23	WA, I, 77-78
4Q323	4QMish C[b]	Priestly Courses III	EW, 123-24	WA, I, 79-81
4Q324	4QMish C[c]	Priestly Courses III	EW, 124	WA, I, 81-82
4Q324a	4QMish C[d]	Priestly Courses III	EW, 124	WA, I, 82-84
4Q324b	4QMish C[e]	Priestly Courses III	EW, 124-25	WA, I, 84-85
4Q324c	4QMish C[f]			
4Q325	4QMish D	Priestly Courses IV	EW, 127*	WA, I, 86-87
4Q326	4QMish E[a]			WA, I, 88
4Q327	4QMish E[b]			WA, I, 89-91
4Q328	4QMish F[a]			WA, I, 92
4Q329	4QMish F[b]			WA, I, 93-95
4Q329a	4QMish G			WA, I, 94
4Q330	4QMish H			WA, I, 95
4Q331		Historical Work[a]		
4Q332		Historical Work[b]		
4Q333		Historical Work[c]		
4Q334	4QOrdo	Ordo		
4Q335–336		astronomical		
4Q337		calendar		
4Q338		genealogical		
4Q339		list of false prophets		
4Q340		list of Nethinim		
4Q341		list of proper names	Naveh, *IEJ* 36 (1986) 52-55	

4Q344		debt acknowledgment		
4Q348		act regarding ownership		
4Q349		sale of property		
4Q356		account of money		
4Q360		exercise / Therapeia		
4Q362		cryptic script		
4Q363		cryptic script		
4Q363a		cryptic script		
4Q364	4QPentPar[a]	Pentateuchal Paraphrase	White, *Madrid*, 217-28	
4Q365	4QPentPar[b]	Pentateuchal Paraphrase	White, *Madrid*, 217-28	
4Q365a		Temple Scroll?		
4Q366	4QPentPar[c]	Pentateuchal Paraphrase		
4Q367	4QPentPar[d]	Pentateuchal Paraphrase		
4Q368		Pentateuch Apocryphon		
4Q369		Prayer of Enosh?		
4Q370		Flood Apocryphon	Newsom, *RQ* 13 (1988)	
4Q371	4QApocJos[a]	Joseph Apocryphon	Schuller, *Madrid*, 529-30*	
4Q372	4QApocJos[b]	Joseph Apocryphon	Schuller, *RQ* 14 (1990) Schuller, *Madrid*, 528-29	
4Q373	4QApocJos[c]	Joseph Apocryphon	Schuller, *Madrid*, 515-27	
4Q374	4QApocMos A	Moses Apocryphon A	Newsom, *Forty Years*, 40-52	
4Q375	4QApocMos B	Moses Apocryphon B	Strugnell, JSPS, VIII, 221-34	
4Q376		Three Tongues of Fire	Strugnell, JSPS, VIII, 234-45	
4Q377	4QApocMos C	Moses Apocryphon C		
4Q378	4QPsJos[a]	Psalms of Joshua	Newsom, *JJS* 39 (1988) 56-65	
4Q379	4QPsJos[b]	Psalms of Joshua	Newsom, *JJS* 39 (1988) 65-73	
4Q380	4QapPs[a]	Non-Canonical Psalms A	Schuller, *Non-Canonical*, 241-65	
4Q381	4QapPs[b]	Non-Canonical Psalms B	Schuller, *Non-Canonical*, 61-240	
4Q382		Kings paraphrase		
4Q383	4QApocJer A	Jeremiah Apocryphon A		
4Q384	4QApocJer B	Jeremiah Apocryphon B		
4Q385	4QpsEzek[a]	Pseudo-Ezekiel	EW, 57-58, 60	Strugnell–Dimant, *RQ* 13 (1988), *RQ* 14 (1990)
4Q385a	4QpsMos[a]	Pseudo-Moses		
4Q385b	4QApocJer C	Jeremiah Apocryphon C		
4Q386–389	4QpsEzek[b]	Second Ezekiel, etc.	EW, 60-62	
4Q390	4QpsMos[e]	Pseudo-Moses Apocalypse / Angels of Mastemoth	Dimant, *Madrid*, 405-47; EW, 55-56	
4Q391	4QpsEzek[g]	Pseudo-Ezekiel		
4Q392–393		liturgical		
4Q394-399	4QMMT A	Halakah / 1st Letter on Works	EW, 188-92	Qimron–Strugnell, *BAT*, 400-407
	4QMMT B /	Halakah / 2nd Letter on Works	EW, 198-99	

4Q400	4QShirShab[a]	Songs of the Sabbath Sacrifice	Newsom, *Songs*, 85-123	AHL, 293-98
4Q401	4QShirShab[b]	Songs of the Sabbath Sacrifice	Newsom, *Songs*, 125-46	
4Q402	4QShirShab[c]	Songs of the Sabbath Sacrifice	Newsom, *Songs*, 147-66	
4Q403	4QShirShab[d]	Songs of the Sabbath Sacrifice	Newsom, *Songs*, 185-247	AHL, 293-98
4Q404	4QShirShab[e]	Songs of the Sabbath Sacrifice	Newsom, *Songs*, 249-55	
4Q405	4QShirShab[f]	Songs of the Sabbath Sacrifice	Newsom, *Songs*, 257-354	AHL, 293-98
4Q406	4QShirShab[g]	Songs of the Sabbath Sacrifice	Newsom, *Songs*, 255-57	
4Q407	4QShirShab[h]	Songs of the Sabbath Sacrifice	Newsom, *Songs*, 259-60	
4Q408		sapiential		
4Q409		liturgical	Qimron, *JQR* 80 (1990)	
4Q410–413		sapiential		
4Q414		Baptismal Hymn	EW, 231-32	
4Q415		Sapiential Work A[d]		
4Q416		Sapiential Work A[b]/ The Children of Salvation	EW, 244-49	
4Q417		Sapiential Work A[c]		
4Q418		Sapiential Work A[a]/ The Children of Salvation	EW, 244-49	
4Q419		Sapiential Work B		
4Q420		Ways of Righteousness[a]		
4Q421		Ways of Righteousness[b]		
4Q422		Treatise on Genesis and Exodus		
4Q423		Sapiential Work A[e]		
4Q423a		Sapiential Work E		
4Q424		sapiential / The Sons of Righteousness	EW, 166-67	
4Q425		Sapiential Work C		
4Q426		sapiential		
4Q427	4QHod[a]	Hymns		
4Q428	4QHod[b]	Hymns		
4Q429	4QHod[c]	Hymns		
4Q430	4QHod[d]	Hymns		
4Q431	4QHod[e]	Hymns		
4Q432	4QHod[f]	Hymns		
4Q433		hymnic		
4Q434	4QBark[a]	Barki Naphshi[a]	EW, 238-39	
4Q434a		Grace after Meals	EW, 238-39	Weinfeld, *JBL* 111 (1992)
4Q435	4QBark[b]	Barki Naphshi[b]		
4Q436	4QBark[c]	Barki Naphshi[c]		
4Q437	4QBark[d]	Barki Naphshi[d]		
4Q438	4QBark[e]	Barki Naphshi[e]		
4Q439		similar to Barki Naphshi		
4Q440		hymnic		

4Q441–444		prayers		
4Q445–447		poetic		
4Q448		Paean for King Jonathan		
		Apocryphal Psalms	EW, 280	
4Q449–457		prayers		
4Q458		The Tree of Evil	EW, 46	
4Q459–460		pseudepigraphic		
4Q461		narrative		
4Q462		Second Exodus /		
		The Era of Light is Coming	EW, 268-69	Smith, *RQ* 15 (1991)
4Q463		sapiential		Steudel, *Eschatologie*
4Q464		Exposition on the Patriarchs		Stone–Eshel, *Muséon* 105
4Q464a–b		unidentified		
4Q464–465		unidentified		
4Q466–469		apocryphon		
4Q470		Zedekiah fragment		
4Q471	4QM[g]	The Servants of Darkness	EW, 31-32	Eshel, *Madrid,* 611-20
4Q471a		polemical	Eshel–Kister, *JJS* 43 (1992)	
4Q472		sapiential		
4Q473		The Two Ways		
4Q474–476		sapiential		
4Q477		Decrees of Sect / He Loved		
		His Bodily Emissions	EW, 272-73	
4Q479–481a-f		unidentified		
4Q482		Jubilees?	100	DJD, VII, 1-2
4Q483		Jubilees?	DJD, VII, 2	
4Q484	4QTJud	Testament of Judah	DJD, VII, 3	
4Q485	4QProph	prophetic or sapiential	103	DJD, VII, 4
4Q486	4QSap[a]	sapiential	104	DJD, VII, 4-5
4Q487	4QSap[b]	sapiential	105-107	DJD, VII, 5-10
4Q491	4QM[a]	War Scroll	157-76	DJD, VII, 12-44
4Q492	4QM[b]	War Scroll	157-76	DJD, VII, 45-49
4Q493	4QM[c]	War Scroll	157-76	DJD, VII, 49-53
4Q494	4QM[d]	War Scroll	157-76	DJD, VII, 53-54
4Q495	4QM[e]	War Scroll	157-76	DJD, VII, 54-56
4Q496	4QM[f]	War Scroll	157-76	DJD, VII, 57-68
4Q497	4QM[g(?)]	War Scroll	DJD, VII, 69-72	
4Q498	4QHymSap	hymnic or sapiential	256	DJD, VII, 73-74
4Q499	4QHymPr	hymnic or prayers	108	DJD, VII, 74-79
4Q500	4QBen	Song of the Vineyard	109	DJD, VII, 78-79
4Q501	4QapLam[b]	Lamentation	276	DJD, VII, 79-80
4Q502	4QRitMar	Ritual of Marriage	125-30	DJD, VII, 81-105
4Q503	4QPrQuot	Daily Prayers	131-39	DJD, VII, 105-36

4Q504	4QDibHam[a]	Words of the Luminaries	178-86	DJD, VII, 137-68
4Q505	4QDibHam[b]	Words of the Luminaries	178-86	DJD, VII, 168-70
4Q506	4QDibHam[c]	Words of the Luminaries	178-86	DJD, VII, 170-75
4Q507	4QPrFêtes[a]	Festival Prayers	140-47	DJD, VII, 175-77
4Q508	4QPrFêtes[b]	Festival Prayers	140-47	DJD, VII, 177-84
4Q509	4QPrFêtes[c]	Festival Prayers	140-47	DJD, VII, 184-215
4Q510	4QShir[a]	Songs of the Sage	311-20	DJD, VII, 215-19
4Q511	4QShir[b]	Songs of the Sage	311-20	DJD, VII, 219-62
4Q512	4QRitPur	Ritual of Purification	148-52	DJD, VII, 262-86
4Q513	4QOrd[b]	Ordinances	153-55	DJD, VII, 287-95
4Q514	4QOrd[c]	Ordinances	224	DJD, VII, 295-98
4Q515–520		unidentified fragments	225-27	DJD, VII, 299-312
4Q521		Messiah of Heaven and Earth	EW, 21-23	Puech, *RQ* 15 (1992)
4Q522		Joshua Apocryphon	EW, 90-91	
4Q523		Hebrew fragment B		
4Q524		halakic		
4Q525		Beatitudes / The Demons of Death	EW, 172-75	Puech, *RB* 98 (1991)
4Q526		Hebrew fragment C		
4Q527		Hebrew fragment D		
4Q528		Hebrew fragment E		
4QAcademyFr		Academy Fragments	368	

Cave 5

5Q9		toponyms	359	DJD, III, 179-80
5Q10	5QapMal	Malachi Pesher?	288	DJD, III, 180
5Q11	5QS	Community Rule	110-24	DJD, III, 180-81
5Q12	5QD	Damascus Document	189-98	DJD, III, 181
5Q13	5QRègle	Damascus Document + Rule	210-11	DJD, III, 181-83
5Q14		curses	322	DJD, III, 183-84
5Q16–24		unclassified	323, 360-65	DJD, III, 193-96
5Q25		unclassified	366	DJD, III, 196-97

Cave 6

6Q9	4QapSam/Kings	Samuel–Kings apocryphon	212-13	DJD, III, 119-23
6Q10	6QProph	prophetic	217	DJD, III, 123-25
6Q11	6QAllegory	Song of the Vine	352	DJD, III, 125-26
6Q12	6QapProph	prophetic	353	DJD, III, 126
6Q13	6QPriestProph	priestly prophecy	354	DJD, III, 126-27
6Q15	6QD	Damascus Document	189-98	DJD, III, 128-31
6Q16	6QBen	blessings	355	DJD, III, 131-32

6Q17	6QCal	calendar	356	DJD, III, 132-33
6Q18	6QHym	hymnic	327-28	DJD, III, 133-36
6Q20	6QDeut(?)	Deuteronomy-related?	357	DJD, III, 136-37
6Q21	6QfrProph	unidentified	358	DJD, III, 137
6Q22		unidentified	358	DJD, III, 137
6Q24–25		unidentified	DJD, III, 138	
6Q26		account or contract		
6Q27–31		unclassified		
6QX1–2		unclassified		
Cave 8				
8Q3	8QPhyl	phylactery	DJD, III, 149-57	
8Q5	8QHymn	hymnic	321	DJD, III, 161-63
Cave 9				
9Q		unclassified	DJD, III	
Cave 10				
10Q		ostracon?	DJD, III	
Cave 11				
11Q11	11QapPs[a]	Apocryphal Psalms	Puech, *RQ* 14 (1990)	
11Q12	11QJub	Jubilees	97-98	van der Woude, *Fs Kuhn*
11Q13	11QMelch	Melchizedek	215	van der Woude, *OTS* 14; Puech, *RQ* 12 (1987)
11Q14	11QBer	Benedictions (= 4Q285)	370	van der Woude, *Bibel und Qumran*
11Q15	11QHod[a]	Hymns		cf. van der Ploeg, *RQ* 12 (1985) 11
11Q16	11QHod[b]	Hymns		cf. van der Ploeg, *RQ* 12 (1985) 11
11Q17	11QShirShabb	Songs of the Sabbath Sacrifice	Newsom, *Songs*, 361-87	
11Q19–20	11QT	Temple Scroll	61-93	Yadin, *Temple Scroll*
11Q21–23		unidentified		
Masada				
	MasShirShabb	Songs of the Sabbath Sacrifice	Newsom, *Songs*, 167-84	
Murabba'at				
Mur 6		hymnic	222	DJD, II, 86
Mur 7		contract	398	DJD, II, 86
Mur 22		deed of sale of land	399	DJD, II, 86
Mur 24		farming contracts	402	DJD, II, 122-34

Mur 29		deed of sale	405	DJD, II, 140-44
Mur 30		deed of sale	411	DJD, II, 144-48
Mur 42	MurEpBeth-Mashiko	letter of administrators	413	DJD, II, 155-59
Mur 43	MurEpBarC[a]	letter of Shimon b. Kosibah	414	DJD, II, 155-61
Mur 44	MurEpBarC[b]	letter of Shimon b. Kosibah	415	DJD, II, 161-63
Mur 45		letter	416	DJD, II, 163-64
Mur 46	MurEpJonathan	letter of Jonathan	417	DJD, II, 164-66
Mur 47		letter	418	DJD, II, 166-67
Mur 48		letter	419	DJD, II, 167-68

Naḥal Ḥever

5/6 ḤevBA 44	contract	406
5/6 ḤevBA fr. 1–2	contract	406
5/6 ḤevBA 45	contract	407
5/6 ḤevBA 45 fr. 1–2	contract	407
5/6 ḤevBA 46	contract	410
5/6 ḤevEp 1	letter	420
5/6 ḤevEp 5	letter	421
5/6 ḤevEp 12	letter	422
5/6 ḤevEp 12 fr.	letter	422

QUMRAN AND RELATED NON-BIBLICAL TEXTS IN ALPHABETICAL ORDER OF SIGLA

1QDM	1Q22	Dibre Mosheh / Words of Moses	205-206	DJD, I, 91-97
1QH		Hymns / Hodayot	228-52	Licht
1QH/1QH[b]	1Q35	Hymns / Hodayoth	228-52	DJD, I, 136-38
1QJub[a]	1Q17	Jubilees	97-99	DJD, I, 82-83
1QJub[b]	1Q18	Jubilees	97-99	DJD, I, 83-84
1QLitPr[a]	1Q34	Festival Prayers	301	DJD, I, 136
1QLitPr[b]	1Q34a	Festival Prayers	301	DJD, I, 152-55
1QM	1Q33	War Scroll	171	DJD, I, 135-36
1QM		War Scroll	157-76	Yadin
1QMyst	1Q27	prophecy	253-54	DJD, I, 102-107
1QNoah	1Q19	Noah	207	DJD, I, 84-86
1QNoah	1Q19b	Noah	207	DJD, I, 152
1QpHab		Habakkuk Pesher	258-63	Burrows, I
1QpMic	1Q14	Micah Pesher	264-65	DJD, I, 77-80
1QpPs	1Q16	Psalms Pesher	267-70	DJD, I, 81-82

1QpZeph	1Q15	Zephaniah Pesher	266	DJD, I, 80
1QS		Community Rule / Manual of Discipline	110-24	Burrows, II
1QSa	1Q28a	Community Rule	110-24	DJD, I, 108-11
1QSb	1Q28b	Community Rule	110-24	DJD, I, 118-30
2QapDavid	2Q22	Apocryphon of David	291	DJD, III, 81-82
2QapMoses	2Q21	Apocryphon of Moses	290	DJD, III, 79-81
2QapProph	2Q23	prophecy	292	DJD, III, 82-84
2QJub[a]	2Q19	Jubilees	97-99	DJD, III, 77-78
2QJub[b]	2Q20	Jubilees	97-99	DJD, III, 78-79
3QHymn	3Q5	hymnic	308	DJD, III, 98
3QJub	3Q4	Jubilees	197-99	DJD, III, 96-98
3QpIsa		Isaiah Pesher	199-204	DJD, III, 95-96
3QTJud	3Q7	Testament of Judah	347	DJD, III, 99
3QTr	3Q15	Copper Scroll	387-91	DJD, III, 211-302
4QAcademyFr		Academy Fragments	368	
4QAges	4Q180	Pesher on the Periods	285	DJD, V, 77-79
4QapLam	4Q179	Lamentation on Jerusalem	218-19	DJD, V, 75-77
4QapLam[b]	4Q501	Lamentation	276	DJD, VII, 79-80
4QApocJer A	4Q383	Jeremiah Apocryphon A		
4QApocJer B	4Q384	Jeremiah Apocryphon B		
4QApocJer C	4Q385b	Jeremiah Apocryphon C		
4QApocJos[a]	4Q371	Joseph Apocryphon	Schuller, *Madrid*, 529-30*	
4QApocJos[b]	4Q372	Joseph Apocryphon	Schuller, *RQ* 14 (1990) Schulker, *Madrid*, 528-29	
4QApocJos[c]	4Q373	Joseph Apocryphon	Schuller, *Madrid*, 515-27	
4QApocMos A	4Q374	Moses Apocryphon A	Newsom, *Forty Years*, 40-52	
4QApocMos B	4Q375	Moses Apocryphon B	Strugnell, JSPS, VIII, 221-34	
4QApocMos C	4Q377	Moses Apocryphon C		
4QapPs[a]	4Q380	Non-Canonical Psalms A	Schuller, *Non-Canonical*, 241-65	
4QapPs[b]	4Q381	Non-Canonical Psalms B	Schuller, *Non-Canonical*, 61-240	
4QBark[a]	4Q434	Barki Naphshi[a]	EW, 238-39	
4QBark[b]	4Q435	Barki Naphshi[b]		
4QBark[c]	4Q436	Barki Naphshi[c]	EW, 238-39	
4QBark[d]	4Q437	Barki Naphshi[d]		
4QBark[e]	4Q438	Barki Naphshi[e]		
4QBen	4Q500	Song of the Vineyard	109	DJD, VII, 78-79
4QBer[a]	4Q286	The Chariots of Glory	EW, 226-28	AHL, 287
4QBer[b]	4Q287	The Chariots of Glory	EW, 228	
4QBer[c]	4Q288			
4QBer[d]	4Q289			
4QBer[e]	4Q290			
4QBibPar	4Q158	Biblical Paraphrase	DJD, V, 1-6	

4QCat^{a}	4Q177	Catena	281-83	DJD, V, 67-74
4QCat^{b}	4Q182	Catena	284	DJD, V, 80-81
4QCrypt	4Q186	horoscopes	325	DJD, V, 88-91
4QD^{a}	4Q266	Damascus Document (prev. 4QD^{b})	98	WA, I, 1, 21-22; Baumgarten, *Madrid*, 506
4QD^{b}	4Q267	Damascus Document^{b} (prev. 4QD^{d})	EW, 218	WA, I, 3-22
4QD^{c}	4Q268	Damascus Document^{c} (prev. 4QD^{a})		WA, I, 23-27
4QD^{d}	4Q269	Damascus Document^{d} (prev. 4QD^{f})		WA, I, 28-35; Baumgarten, *JJS* 41 (1990)
4QD^{e}	4Q270	Damascus Document^{e}		WA, I, 36-47
4QD^{f}	4Q271	Damascus Document^{f} (prev. 4QD^{c})		WA, I, 48-53
4QD^{g}	4Q272	Damascus Document^{g}		WA, I, 54-56; Baumgarten, *JJS* 41 (1990)
4QD^{h}	4Q273	Damascus Document^{h}		WA, I, 57-59; Baumgarten, *JJS* 41 (1990)
4QDibHam^{a}	4Q504	Words of the Luminaries	178-86	DJD, VII, 137-68
4QDibHam^{b}	4Q505	Words of the Luminaries	178-86	DJD, VII, 168-70
4QDibHam^{c}	4Q506	Words of the Luminaries	178-86	DJD, VII, 170-75
4QFlor	4Q174	Florilegium	278-79	DJD, V, 53-57
4QHod^{a}	4Q427	Hymns		
4QHod^{b}	4Q428	Hymns		
4QHod^{c}	4Q429	Hymns		
4QHod^{d}	4Q430	Hymns		
4QHod^{e}	4Q431	Hymns		
4QHod^{f}	4Q432	Hymns		
4QHymPr	4Q499	hymnic or prayers	108	DJD, VII, 74-79
4QHymSap	4Q498	hymnic or sapiential	256	DJD, VII, 73-74
4QJub^{a}	4Q216	Jubilees^{a}	VanderKam–Milik, *JBL* 110 (1991)	
4QJub^{b}	4Q217	Jubilees^{b}		
4QJub^{c}	4Q218	Jubilees^{c}		
4QJub^{d}	4Q219	Jubilees^{d}	VanderKam–Milik, *Bib* 73 (1992)	
4QJub^{e}	4Q220	Jubilees^{e}		
4QJub^{f}	4Q221	Jubilees^{f}		cf. VanderKam, *Madrid*, 635-48
4QJub^{g}	4Q222	Jubilees^{g}		
4QJub^{h}	4Q223–224	Jubilees^{h}		
4QM^{a}	4Q491	War Scroll	157-76	DJD, VII, 12-44
4QM^{b}	4Q492	War Scroll	157-76	DJD, VII, 45-49
4QM^{c}	4Q493	War Scroll	157-76	DJD, VII, 49-53
4QM^{d}	4Q494	War Scroll	157-76	DJD, VII, 53-54
4QM^{e}	4Q495	War Scroll	157-76	DJD, VII, 54-56
4QM^{f}	4Q496	War Scroll	157-76	DJD, VII, 57-68

4QM^{g}	4Q471	The Servants of Darkness	EW, 31-32	Eshel, *Madrid*, 611-20
4QM$^{g(?)}$	4Q497	War Scroll	DJD, VII, 69-72	
4QMish A	4Q320	Priestly Courses II	EW, 116-18	WA, I, 60-67
4QMish B^{a}	4Q321	Priestly Courses I	EW, 109-11	WA, I, 68-73
4QMish B^{b}	4Q321a	Priestly Courses I		WA, I, 74-76
4QMish C^{a}	4Q322	Priestly Courses III	EW, 122-23	WA, I, 77-78
4QMish C^{b}	4Q323	Priestly Courses III	EW, 123-24	WA, I, 79-81
4QMish C^{c}	4Q324	Priestly Courses III	EW, 124	WA, I, 81-82
4QMish C^{d}	4Q324a	Priestly Courses III	EW, 124	WA, I, 82-84
4QMish C^{e}	4Q324b	Priestly Courses III	EW, 124-25	WA, I, 84-85
4QMish C^{f}	4Q324c			
4QMish D	4Q325	Priestly Courses IV	EW, 127*	WA, I, 86-87
4QMish E^{a}	4Q326			WA, I, 88
4QMish E^{b}	4Q327			WA, I, 89-91
4QMish F^{a}	4Q328			WA, I, 92
4QMish F^{b}	4Q329			WA, I, 93-95
4QMish G	4Q329a			WA, I, 94
4QMish H	4Q330			WA, I, 95
4QMMT A	4Q394–396	Halakah / 1st Letter on Works	EW, 188-92	Qimron–Strugnell, *BA*
4QMMT B	4Q397–399	Halakah / 2nd Letter on Works	EW, 188-92, 198-99	
4QMSM	4Q249	Midrash Sepher Mosheh		Milik, *JJS* 23 (1972)
4QMyst^{a}	4Q299	= 1Q27		
4QMyst^{b}	4Q300–301	= 1Q27		
4QMyst^{c}	4Q301	= 1Q27		
4QNid	4Q284	Rule of the Menstruants		
4QOrd^{a}	4Q159	Ordinances	153-55	DJD, V, 6-9
4QOrd^{b}	4Q513	Ordinances	153-55	DJD, VII, 287-95
4QOrd^{c}	4Q514	Ordinances	224	DJD, VII, 295-98
4QOrdo	4Q334	Ordo		
4QOtot	4Q319	Heavenly Concordances	EW, 130-31	
4QPentPar^{a}	4Q364	Pentateuchal Paraphrase	White, *Madrid*, 217-28	
4QPentPar^{b}	4Q365	Pentateuchal Paraphrase	White, *Madrid*, 217-28	
4QPentPar^{c}	4Q366	Pentateuchal Paraphrase		
4QPentPar^{d}	4Q367	Pentateuchal Paraphrase		
4QpGen^{a}	4Q252	Patriarchal Blessings /		
4QpGen^{b}	4Q253	Patriarchal Blessings		
4QpGen^{c}	4Q254	Patriarchal Blessings		
4QpHos^{a}	4Q166	Hosea Pesher	271-73	DJD, V, 31-32
4QpHos^{b}	4Q167	Hosea Pesher	271-73	DJD, V, 32-36
4QpIsa^{a}	4Q161	Isaiah Pesher	199-204	DJD, V, 11-15
4QpIsa^{b}	4Q162	Isaiah Pesher	199-204	DJD, V, 15-17
4QpIsa^{c}	4Q163	Isaiah Pesher	199-204	DJD, V, 17-27
4QpIsa^{d}	4Q164	Isaiah Pesher	199-204	DJD, V, 27-28

4QpIsa^{e}	4Q165	Isaiah Pesher	199-204	DJD, V, 28-30
4QpMic	4Q168	Micah Pesher	DJD, V, 36	
4QpNah	4Q169	Nahum Pesher	274-75	DJD, V, 90-93
4QpPs^{a}	4Q171	Psalms Pesher	267-70	DJD, V, 42-51
4QpPs^{b}	4Q173	Psalms Pesher	267-70, 369	DJD, V, 51-53
4QPrFêtes^{a}	4Q507	Festival Prayers	140-47	DJD, VII, 175-77
4QPrFêtes^{b}	4Q508	Festival Prayers	140-47	DJD, VII, 177-84
4QPrFêtes^{c}	4Q509	Festival Prayers	140-47	DJD, VII, 184-215
4QProph	4Q485	prophetic or sapiential	103	DJD, VII, 4
4QPrQuot	4Q503	Daily Prayers	131-39	DJD, VII, 105-36
4QpsEzek^{a}	4Q385	Pseudo-Ezekiel	EW, 57-58,	Strugnell–Dimant, *RQ* 13 (1988)
			60	Dimant–Strugnell, *RQ* 14 (1990)
4QpsEzek^{b}	4Q386–389	Second Ezekiel, etc.	EW, 60-62	
4QpsEzek^{g}	4Q391	Pseudo-Ezekiel		
4QPsJos^{a}	4Q378	Psalms of Joshua	Newsom, *JJS* 39 (1988) 56-65	
4QPsJos^{b}	4Q379	Psalms of Joshua	Newsom, *JJS* 39 (1988) 65-73	
4QpsJub^{a}	4Q225	Pseudo-Jubilees		
4QpsJub^{b}	4Q226	Pseudo-Jubilees		
4QpsJub^{c}	4Q227	Pseudo-Jubilees	EW, 96-97	
4QpsMos^{a}	4Q385a	Pseudo-Moses		
4QpsMos^{e}	4Q390	Pseudo-Moses Apocalypse / Angels of Mastemoth	Dimant, *Madrid*, 405-47; EW, 55-56	
4QpUnid	4Q172	unidentified pesher	277	DJD, V, 50-51
4QpZeph	4Q170	Zephaniah Pesher	DJD, V, 42	
4QRitMar	4Q502	Ritual of Marriage	125-30	DJD, VII, 81-105
4QRitPur	4Q512	Ritual of Purification	148-52	DJD, VII, 262-86
4QS^{a}	4Q255	Community Rule		cf. Milik, *RB* 67 (1960)
4QSap^{a}	4Q486	sapiential	104	DJD, VII, 4-5
4QSap^{b}	4Q487	sapiential	105-107	DJD, VII, 5-10
4QS^{b}	4Q256	Community Rule (previously 4QS^{d})		Vermes, *JJS* 42 (1991)
4QS^{c}	4Q257	Community Rule		
4QSD	4Q265	Community Rule + Damascus Document		cf. Milik, *Ten Years*, 96
4QS^{d}	4Q258	Community Rule (previously 4QS^{b})		Vermes, *JJS* 42 (1991)
4QS^{e}	4Q259	Community Rule		WA, I, 96-101; cf. Milik, SVT 4 (1957) 25
4QS^{f}	4Q260	Community Rule		cf. Milik, *RB* 67 (1960)
4QS^{g}	4Q261	Community Rule		cf. Milik, *RB* 67 (1960)
4QS^{h}	4Q262	Community Rule		cf. Milik, *RB* 67 (1960)
4QShir^{a}	4Q510	Songs of the Sage	311-20	DJD, VII, 215-19
4QShir^{b}	4Q511	Songs of the Sage	311-20	DJD, VII, 219-62
4QShirShab^{a}	4Q400	Songs of the Sabbath Sacrifice	Newsom, *Songs*, 85-123	AHL, 293-98

4QShirShab[b]	4Q401	Songs of the Sabbath Sacrifice	Newsom, *Songs*, 125-46	
4QShirShab[c]	4Q402	Songs of the Sabbath Sacrifice	Newsom, *Songs*, 147-66	
4QShirShab[d]	4Q403	Songs of the Sabbath Sacrifice	Newsom, *Songs*, 185-247	AHL, 293-98
4QShirShab[e]	4Q404	Songs of the Sabbath Sacrifice	Newsom, *Songs*, 249-55	
4QShirShab[f]	4Q405	Songs of the Sabbath Sacrifice	Newsom, *Songs*, 257-354	AHL, 293-98
4QShirShab[g]	4Q406	Songs of the Sabbath Sacrifice	Newsom, *Songs*, 255-57	
4QShirShab[h]	4Q407	Songs of the Sabbath Sacrifice	Newsom, *Songs*, 259-60	
4QS[i]	4Q263	Community Rule		cf. Milik, *RB* 67 (1960)
4QS[j]	4Q264	Community Rule		cf. Milik, *RB* 67 (1960)
4QTanḥ	4Q176	Consolations	309-10	DJD, V, 60-67
4QTestim	4Q175	Testimonia	177	DJD, V, 57-60
4QTJud	4Q484	Testament of Judah	DJD, VII, 3	
4QTNaph	4Q215	Testament of Naphtali	EW, 159	
4QTob	4Q200	Tobit		cf. Milik, *RB* 73 (1966) 522
4QToh A	4Q274	Purities	EW, 207-208	
4QToh B	4Q275	Purities		cf. Milik, *JJS* 23 (1972)
4QToh B[a]	4Q276	Laws of the Red Heifer	EW, 226	
4QToh B[b]	4Q277	Laws of the Red Heifer	EW, 210	
4QToh C?	4Q278			
4QToh D	4Q280	Curses against Melkiresha	214	cf. Milik, *JJS* 23 (1972)
4QToh D[a]?	4Q279	Laws		
4QToh E[a]?	4Q281–282			
4QToh F?	4Q283			
4QVisSam	4Q160	Visions of Samuel	188	DJD, V, 9-11
4QWiles	4Q184	Wiles of the Wicked Woman	323-24	DJD, V, 82-85
5QapMal	5Q10	Malachi Pesher?	288	DJD, III, 180
5QD	5Q12	Damascus Document	189-98	DJD, III, 181
5QRègle	5Q13	Damascus Document + Rule	210-11	DJD, III, 181-83
5QS	5Q11	Community Rule	110-24	DJD, III, 180-81
5/6 ḤevBA 44		contract	406	
5/6 ḤevBA fr. 1–2		contract	406	
5/6 ḤevBA 45		contract	407	
5/6 ḤevBA 45 fr. 1–2		contract	407	
5/6 ḤevBA 46		contract	410	
5/6 ḤevEp 1		letter	420	
5/6 ḤevEp 5		letter	421	
5/6 ḤevEp 12		letter	422	
5/6 ḤevEp 12 fr.		letter	422	
6QAllegory	6Q11	Song of the Vine	352	DJD, III, 125-26
6QapProph	6Q12	prophetic	353	DJD, III, 126
6QBen	6Q16	blessings	355	DJD, III, 131-32
6QCal	6Q17	calendar	356	DJD, III, 132-33
6QD	6Q15	Damascus Document	189-98	DJD, III, 128-31

6QDeut(?)	6Q20	Deuteronomy-related?	357	DJD, III, 136-37
6QfrProph	6Q21	unidentified	358	DJD, III, 137
6QHym	6Q18	hymnic	327-28	DJD, III, 133-36
6QPriestProph	6Q13	priestly prophecy	354	DJD, III, 126-27
6QProph	6Q10	prophetic	217	DJD, III, 123-25
8QHymn	8Q5	hymnic	321	DJD, III, 161-63
11QapPs[a]	11Q11	Apocryphal Psalms	Puech, *RQ* 14 (1990) 377-408	
11QBer	11Q14	Benedictions (= 4Q285)	370	van der Woude, *Bibel*
11QHod[a]	11Q15	Hymns		van der Ploeg, *RQ* 12 (1985) 11
11QHod[b]	11Q16	Hymns		van der Ploeg, *RQ* 12 (1985) 11
11QJub	11Q12	Jubilees	97-98	van der Woude, *Fs Kuhn*
11QMelch	11Q13	Melchizedek	215	van der Woude, *OTS* 14 (1965); Puech, *RQ* 12 (1987)
11QShirShabb	11Q17	Songs of the Sabbath Sacrifice	Newsom, *Songs*, 361-87	
11QT	11Q19–20	Temple Scroll	61-93	Yadin, *Temple Scroll*
MasShirShabb		Songs of the Sabbath Sacrifice	Newsom, *Songs*, 167-84	
MurEpBarC[a]	Mur 43	letter of Shimon b. Kosibah	414	DJD, II, 155-61
MurEpBarC[b]	Mur 44	letter of Shimon b. Kosibah	415	DJD, II, 161-63
MurEpBeth-Mashiko	Mur 42	letter of administrators	413	DJD, II, 155-59
MurEpJonathan	Mur 46	letter of Jonathan	417	DJD, II, 164-66

Bibliography

AHL, *see Materials for the Dictionary*

Allegro, John M. , *Qumrân Cave 4. I (4Q158–4Q186)* (Discoveries in the Judaean Desert of Jordan, 5; Oxford: Clarendon Press, 1968)

Baillet, M., *Qumrân Grotte 4 (4Q482–4Q520)* (Discoveries in the Judaean Desert, 7; Oxford: Clarendon Press, 1982)

—, J.T. Milik and R. de Vaux, *Les 'petites grottes' de Qumrân* (Discoveries in the Judaean Desert of Jordan, 3; Oxford: Clarendon Press, 1962)

Barthélemy, D. and J.T. Milik, *Qumran Cave I* (Discoveries in the Judaean Desert, 1; Oxford: Clarendon Press, 1955)

Baumgarten, Joseph, 'The Disqualifications of Priests in 4Q Fragments of the "Damascus Document", a Specimen of the Recovery of pre-Rabbinic Halakha', in *The Madrid Congress: Proceedings of the International Congress on the Dead Sea Scrolls, Madrid, 18–21 March 1991* (ed. J. Trebolle Barrera and L. Vegas Montaner; Studies on the Texts of the Desert of Judah, 11; Madrid: Universidad Complutense and Leiden: E.J. Brill, 1992), pp. 503-13

—'The 4Q Zadokite Fragments on Skin Disease', *Journal of Jewish Studies* 41 (1990), pp. 153-65

Benoit, P., J.T. Milik and R. de Vaux, *Les grottes de Murabba'ât* (Discoveries in the Judaean

Desert, 2; Oxford: Clarendon Press, 1961)
Burrows, M. (ed.), *The Dead Sea Scrolls of St. Mark's Monastery*, 2 vols. (New Haven: American Schools of Oriental Research, 1951)
Dimant, Devorah, 'New Light from Qumran on the Jewish Pseudepigrapha—*4Q390*', in *The Madrid Congress: Proceedings of the International Congress on the Dead Sea Scrolls, Madrid, 18–21 March 1991* (ed. J. Trebolle Barrera and L. Vegas Montaner; Studies on the Texts of the Desert of Judah, 11; Madrid: Universidad Complutense and Leiden: E.J. Brill, 1992), pp. 405-48
—and John Strugnell, 'The Merkabah Vision in *Second Ezekiel* (*4Q385* 4)', *Revue de Qumran* 14 (1990) 331-48
DJD, I, *see* Barthélemy, D. and J.T. Milik
DJD, II, *see* Benoit, P., J.T. Milik and R. de Vaux
DJD, III, *see* Baillet, M., J.T. Milik and R. de Vaux
DJD, IV, *see* Sanders, J.A.
DJD, V, *see* Allegro, J.M.
DJD, VI, *see* Vaux, R. de and J.T. Milik
DJD, VII, *see* Baillet, M.
Eisenman, Robert H. and Michael Wise, *The Dead Sea Scrolls Uncovered* (Shaftesbury, Dorset: Element, 1992)
Eshel, Esther and Hanan, '4Q471 Fragment 1 and *Ma'amadot* in the War Scroll', in *The Madrid Congress: Proceedings of the International Congress on the Dead Sea Scrolls, Madrid, 18–21 March 1991* (ed. J. Trebolle Barrera and L. Vegas Montaner; Studies on the Texts of the Desert of Judah, 11; Madrid: Universidad Complutense and Leiden: E.J. Brill, 1992), pp. 612-20
Eshel, Esther and Menahem Kister, 'A Polemical Qumran Fragment', *Journal of Jewish Studies* 43 (1992), pp. 277-81
EW, *see* Eisenman and Wise
Fitzmyer, Joseph A., SJ, *The Dead Sea Scrolls. Major Publications and Tools for Study* (revised edition; SBL Resources for Biblical Study, 20; Atlanta: Scholars Press, 1990)
García Martínez, Florentino, 'Lista de mss procedentes de Qumran', *Henoch* 11 (1989), pp. 149-232
—*Textos de Qumrán. Introducción y edición* (Madrid: Editorial Trotta, 1992), pp. 483-518
Kister, M., 'Newly Identified Fragments of the Book of Jubilees: Jub. 23:21-23, 30-31', *Revue de Qumran* 12 (1985–87), pp. 529-36
Licht, J., *The Thanksgiving Scroll* (Jerusalem, 1965) [Hebrew]
Materials for the Dictionary. Series I. 200 B.C.E. —300 C.E. (The Academy of the Hebrew Language—The Historical Dictionary of the Hebrew Language; Jerusalem, 1988)
Milik, J.T., *Ten Years of Discovery in the Wilderness of Judaea* (trans. J. Strugnell; London: SCM Press, 1959)
—'Le travail d'édition des manuscrits du désert de Juda', *SVT* 4 (1957), pp. 17-26
—'Notes d'épigraphie et de topographie palestiniennes', *RB* 67 (1960), pp. 354-67, 550-91
—'Fragment d'une source du Psautier (4Q Ps 89) et fragments des Jubilés, du Document de Damas, d'un phylactère dans la grotte 4 de Qumrân', *RB* 73 (1966), pp. 94-106

—*The Books of Enoch: Aramaic Fragments of Qumran Cave 4* (Oxford: Clarendon Press, 1976)

—'*Milkî-ṣedeq* et *Milkî-reša*' dans les anciens écrits juifs et chrétiens', *Journal of Jewish Studies* 23 (1972), pp. 95-144

—'Numérotation des feuilles des rouleaux dans le scriptorium de Qumrân', *Semitica* 27 (1977), pp. 75-81

Naveh, Joseph, 'A Medical Document or a Writing Exercise? The So-called 4Q Therapeia', *IEJ* 36 (1986), pp. 52-55

Newsom, Carol, *Songs of the Sabbath Sacrifice: A Critical Edition* (Harvard Semitic Studies, 27; Atlanta: Scholars Press, 1985)

—'The "Psalms of Joshua" from Qumran Cave 4', *Journal of Jewish Studies* 39 (1988), pp. 56-73

—'*4Q370*: An Admonition Based on the Flood', *Revue de Qumran* 13 (1988), pp. 23-41

—'4Q374: A Discourse on the Exodus/Conquest Tradition', in *The Dead Sea Scrolls: Forty Years of Research* (ed. Devorah Dimant and Uriel Rappaport; Leiden: E.J. Brill; Jerusalem: Magnes Press and Yad Izhak Ben-Zvi, 1992), pp. 40-52

Ploeg, J. van der, 'Les manuscrits de la grotte XI de Qumran', *Revue de Qumran* 12 (1985), pp. 3-15

Puech, Emile, '*11QPsAp^a*: Un rituel d'exorcismes. Essai de reconstruction', *Revue de Qumran* 14 (1990), pp. 377-408

—'4Q Apocalypse Messianique (4Q521)', *Revue de Qumran* 15 (1992)

Qimron, Elisha, 'Times for Praising God: A Fragment of a Scroll from Qumran (4Q409)', *Jewish Quarterly Review* 80 (1990), pp. 341-47

—and John Strugnell, 'An Unpublished Halakhic Letter from Qumran', in *Biblical Archaeology Today: Proceedings of the International Congress on Biblical Archaeology, Jerusalem, April 1984* (Jerusalem: Israel Exploration Society, 1985), pp. 400-407

Sanders, J.A., *The Psalms Scroll of Qumrân Cave 11* (Discoveries in the Judaean Desert of Jordan, 4; Oxford: Clarendon Press, 1965)

Schuller, Eileen, *Non-Canonical Psalms from Qumran: A Pseudepigraphic Collection* (Harvard Semitic Studies, 28; Atlanta: Scholars Press, 1986)

—'*4Q372* 1: A Text about Joseph', *Revue de Qumran* 14 (1990), pp. 349-76

—'A Preliminary Study of *4Q373* and Some Related (?) Fragments', in *The Madrid Congress: Proceedings of the International Congress on the Dead Sea Scrolls, Madrid, 18–21 March 1991* (ed. J. Trebolle Barrera and L. Vegas Montaner; Studies on the Texts of the Desert of Judah, 11; Madrid: Universidad Complutense and Leiden: E.J. Brill, 1992), pp. 515-30

Smith, M., '*4Q462* (Narrative) Fragment 1: A Preliminary Edition', *Revue de Qumran* 15 (1991), pp. 55-77

Steudel, A. *Der Midrash zur Eschatologie aus der Qumrangemeinde (4QMidrEschat^b)* (PhD, University of Göttingen, 1991)

Stone, M.E. and E. Eshel, 'An Exposition on the Patriarchs (4Q464) and Two Other Documents (4Q464^a and4Q464^b)', *Le Muséon* 105 (1992), pp. 243-64

Strugnell, John, 'Moses-Pseudepigrapha at Qumran: 4Q375, 4Q376, and Similar Works', in *Archaeology and History in the Dead Sea Scrolls: The New York University Conference in Memory of Yigael Yadin* (ed. Lawrence H. Schiffman; Journal for the Study of the Pseudepigrapha Supplement Series, 8; JSOT/ASOR Monographs, 2; Sheffield: JSOT Press,

1990), pp. 221-56
— and Devorah Dimant, '4Q Second Ezekiel', *Revue de Qumran* 13 (1988), pp. 45-58
Sukenik, E.L., *The Dead Sea Scrolls of the Hebrew University* (Jerusalem: The Magnes Press, 1955)
Tov, Emanuel, 'The Unpublished Qumran Texts from Caves 4 and 11', *Biblical Archaeologist* 55 (1992), pp. 94-104
—(ed.), *The Dead Sea Scrolls on Microfiche: A Comprehensive Facsimile Edition of the Texts from the Judean Desert. Companion Volume* (Leiden: E.J. Brill and IDC, 1993)
VanderKam, J.C., 'The Jubilees Fragments from Qumran Cave 4', in *The Madrid Congress: Proceedings of the International Congress on the Dead Sea Scrolls, Madrid, 18–21 March 1991* (ed. J. Trebolle Barrera and L. Vegas Montaner; Studies on the Texts of the Desert of Judah, 11; Madrid: Universidad Complutense and Leiden: E.J. Brill, 1992), pp. 635-48
—and J.T. Milik, 'The First *Jubilees* Manuscript from Qumran Cave 4: A Preliminary Publication', *Journal of Biblical Literature* 110 (1991), pp. 243-70
—and J.T. Milik, 'A Preliminary Publication of a Jubilees Manscript from Qumran Cave 4: 4QJub^{d} (4Q219)', *Biblica* 73 (1992), pp. 62-83
Vaux, R. de and J.T. Milik, *Qumrân Grotte 4:* I. *Archéologie.* II. *Tefillin, Mezuzot et Targums (4Q128–4Q157)* (Discoveries in the Judaean Desert, 6; Oxford: Clarendon Press, 1977)
Vermes, G., 'Preliminary Remarks on Unpublished Fragments of the Community Rule from Qumran Cave 4', *Journal of Jewish Studies* 42 (1991), pp. 250-55
—'The Oxford Forum for Qumran Research—Seminar on the Rule of War from Cave 4', *Journal of Jewish Studies* 43 (1992), pp. 85-90
WA, *see* Wacholder and Abegg
Wacholder, Ben Zion and Martin G. Abegg, *A Preliminary Edition of the Unpublished Dead Sea Scrolls: The Hebrew and Aramaic Texts from Cave Four,* Fascicle 1 (Washington, DC: Biblical Archaeology Society, 1991)
Weinfeld, Moshe, 'Grace after Meals in Qumran', *Journal of Biblical Literature* 111 (1992), pp. 427-40
Woude, Adam van der, 'Melchisedek als himmlisch Erlösergestalt in den neugefundenen eschatologischen Midraschim aus Qumran Höhle XI', *Oudtestamentische Studiën* 14 (1965), pp. 354-73
—'Ein neuer Segensspruch aus Qumran (11QBer)', in *Bibel und Qumran: Beiträge zur Erforschung der Beziehungen zwischen Bibel- und Qumranwissenschaft: Hans Bardtke zum 22.8.1966* (ed. S. Wagner; Berlin: Evangelische Haupt-Bibelgesellschaft, 1968)
—'Fragmente des Buches Jubiläen aus Qumran Höhle XI (11QJub)', in *Tradition und Glaube: Das frühe Christentum in seiner Umwelt: Festgabe für Karl Georg Kuhn zum 65. Geburtstag* (ed. J. Jeremias *et al.*; Göttingen: Vandenhoeck & Ruprecht, 1971), pp. 140-46
Yadin, Yigael, *The Scroll of the War of the Sons of Light against the Sons of Darkness* (Oxford: Oxford University Press, 1962)
—(ed.) *The Temple Scroll* (3 vols.; Jerusalem: Israel Exploration Society, 1983)
* publication in part

d. *Inscriptions*

The primary source text for the Hebrew inscriptions from the period prior to 200 BCE has been that of Graham I. Davies, *Ancient Hebrew Inscriptions: Corpus and Concordance* (Cambridge: Cambridge University Press, 1991). This collection has been supplemented by that of William Horbury and David Noy, *Jewish Inscriptions from Graeco-Roman Egypt* (Cambridge: Cambridge University Press, 1992).

The following list is arranged alphabetically by the abbreviation used in this Dictionary for each inscription, seal, and the like. The reference numbers in the first column are those assigned by Davies, or in the case of texts included in the Academy of the Hebrew Language corpus (AHL), the page reference in that corpus.

AHL, 94 Alexander Jannaeus Coin 5, 12, 13, 14, 17
AHL, 95 Alexander Jannaeus Seal
AHL, 427 Alma 3
AHL, 102 Antigonus Coin 30, 31, 34

2.089 Arad inscr. 89
2.091 Arad inscr. 91
2.092 Arad inscr. 92
2.093 Arad inscr. 93
2.095 Arad inscr. 95
2.097 Arad inscr. 97
2.098 Arad inscr. 98
2.099 Arad inscr. 99
2.101 Arad inscr. 101
2.102 Arad inscr. 102
2.103 Arad inscr. 103
2.104 Arad inscr. 104
2.001-018 Arad ost. 1-18
2.019 Arad ost. 19
2.020-031 Arad ost. 20-31
2.032 Arad ost. 32
2.033 Arad ost. 33
2.035-042 Arad ost. 35-42
2.044 Arad ost. 44
2.047-049 Arad ost. 47-49
2.050 Arad ost. 50
2.051 Arad ost. 51
2.052 Arad ost. 52
2.053 Arad ost. 53
2.054 Arad ost. 54
2.055-062 Arad ost. 55-62
2.064 Arad ost. 64
2.067-069 Arad ost. 67-69
2.071-072 Arad ost. 71-72
2.074 Arad ost. 74
2.076 Arad ost. 76
2.080 Arad ost. 80
2.088 Arad ost. 88
2.110-112 Arad ost. 110-112

AHL, 60 Aristobulus Coin 28, 29
4.211 Armenian garden inscr.
6.001 Aroer ost. 1
6.002 Aroer ost. 2

AHL, 408 Bar-Kochba Deed of Sale
AHL, 400 Bar-Kochba Revolt Year 1 Coins 165–167, 169, 171, 173, 176
AHL, 401 Bar-Kochba Revolt Year 2 Coins 176, 178, 181, 183, 186, 187, 190A, 193, 194

AHL, 409	Bar-Kochba Revolt Year 3 Coins 199, 213, 214
5.005	Beersheba graf. 1
5.006	Beersheba graf. 2
5.007	Beersheba graf. 3
5.008	Beersheba graf. 4
5.010	Beersheba graf. 6
5.013	Beersheba jug inscr.
5.001-002	Beersheba ost. 1-2
5.003	Beersheba ost. 3
16.001	Beth-Shean Valley spindle whorl
AHL, 428	Beth Shearim Inscr. 17
AHL, 429	Beth Shearim Inscr. 22
17.001	Beth-Shemesh inscr.
4.121	City of David ashlar inscr.
4.119	City of David jar inscr.
4.122	City of David jug inscr.
4.120	City of David monumental inscr.
4.123	City of David ost.
20.001	En-Gedi amphora inscr.
20.002	En-Gedi cave inscr.
21.001	Eshtemoa jug inscr.
AHL, 375	Frey 1247
AHL, 384	Frey 1285/6
AHL, 372	Frey 1294
AHL, 373	Frey 1295
AHL, 374	Frey 1308
AHL, 376	Frey 1317
AHL, 377	Frey 1372
AHL, 378	Frey 1373
AHL, 379	Frey 1374
AHL, 380	Frey 1410
AHL, 381	Frey 1411
AHL, 423	Frey 1413
AHL, 423	Frey 1534
AHL, 425	Frey 1536
AHL, 96	Gezer Boundary Inscr. (Frey 1183)
10.001	Gezer calendar
22.001-012	Gibeon jar handle inscr. 1-12
22.014-019	Gibeon jar handle inscr. 14-19
22.021-052	Gibeon jar handle inscr. 21-52
22.054-062	Gibeon jar handle inscr. 54-62
AHL, 54	GnzPs (Geniza Psalm)
24.005	Hazor inscr. 5
24.006	Hazor inscr. 6
24.007	Hazor inscr. 7
24.008	Hazor inscr. 8
24.011	Hazor ost. 1
24.012	Hazor bowl inscr. 2
24.014	Hazor bowl inscr. 4-6
24.018	Hazor ost. 10
24.020	Hazor ost. 12
26.003	Hebron bowl inscr.
26.001	Hebron jar inscr. 1
26.002	Hebron jar inscr. 2
26.004	Hebron jar inscr. 3
26.006	Hebron jug inscr.
37.001	Ḥorvat 'Uza ost. 1
37.002	Ḥorvat 'Uza ost. 2
37.003	Ḥorvat 'Uza ost. 3
AHL, 223	Hosea Seal
AHL, 59	Hyrcanus I Coins 26, 27
AHL, 101	Hyrcanus II Coins 18, 18A, 19, 20, 22, 23
99.001	Ivory pomegranate inscr.
35.001	Izbet Ṣarṭah ost.
4.206	Jerusalem decanter inscr.
44.001	Jerusalem jar handle inscr.
4.204	Jerusalem Jar inscr.
4.201-202	Jerusalem ost. 1-2
4.207	Jerusalem pithos inscr.
AHL, 382	JerusInscr 31
AHL, 392	Jewish War Year 1 Coins 148, 149, 150
AHL, 393	Jewish War Year 2 Coins 151–53, 514
AHL, 394	Jewish War Year 3 Coins 154–56, 524
AHL, 396	Jewish War Year 4 Coins 158–63
AHL, 396	Jewish War Year 5 Coin

3.041	Samaria ost. 41
3.042-059	Samaria ost. 42-59
3.060	Samaria ost. 60
3.061	Samaria ost. 61
3.062	Samaria ost. 62
3.063-064	Samaria ost. 63-64
3.066	Samaria ost. 66
3.067	Samaria ost. 67
3.072-073	Samaria ost. 72-73
3.078	Samaria ost. 78
3.080	Samaria ost. 80
3.081	Samaria ost. 81
3.082	Samaria ost. 82
3.083	Samaria ost. 83
3.084	Samaria ost. 84
3.089	Samaria ost. 89
3.090	Samaria ost. 90
3.099	Samaria ost. 99
3.100	Samaria ost. 100
3.101	Samaria ost. 101
3.102	Samaria ost. 102
3.301	Samaria-Sebaste ost. 1101
3.302	Samaria-Sebaste ost. 1265
3.303	Samaria-Sebaste ost. 1142
3.304	Samaria-Sebaste ost. 1012
3.305	Samaria-Sebaste ost. 689
3.306	Samaria-Sebaste ost. 857
3.307	Samaria-Sebaste ost. 1220
3.308	Samaria-Sebaste ost. 1307
3.309	Samaria-Sebaste ost. 1266
3.310	Samaria-Sebaste ost. 4236
3.312	Samaria stele inscr.
100.001	Seal 1 (7th cent.)
100.002	Seal 2
100.003	Seal 3 (Megiddo, 8th cent.)
100.004	Seal 4 (Nablus, 8th cent.)
100.005	Seal 5 (8th cent.)
100.007	Seal 7 (Megiddo, 8th cent.)
100.008	Seal 8 (T. el-Far'ah, 8th cent.)
100.009	Seal 9 (Carthage)
100.011	Seal 11
100.012	Seal 12
100.013	Seal 13 (Jerusalem?, 8th cent.)
100.014	Seal 14 (Ashkelon?, 7th cent.)
100.015	Seal 15 (Gezer, 7th cent.)
100.016	Seal 16 (7th cent.)
100.018	Seal 18 (Cyprus)
100.019	Seal 19 (Jerusalem, 7th cent.)
100.020	Seal 20 (Jerusalem, c. 700)
100.021	Seal 21
100.022	Seal 22 (8th cent.)
100.023	Seal 23 (Babylonia?, 8th/7th cent.)
100.024	Seal 24 (Jerusalem, 7th cent.)
100.025	Seal 25 (Jerusalem, 7th cent.)
100.026	Seal 26 (6th cent.)
100.027	Seal (Palestine, 7th cent.)
100.030	Seal 30 (Es-Soda, 8th cent.)
100.031	Seal 31 (7th cent.)
100.032	Seal 32 (Es-Soda, 8th cent.)
100.033	Seal 33 (Syria?, 8th/7th cent.)
100.034	Seal 34 (Cyrene, 7th cent.)
100.035	Seal 35 (7th cent.)
100.036	Seal 36 (Syria?, 7th cent.)
100.037	Seal 37 (Palestine)
100.038	Seal 38 (8th cent.)
100.039	Seal 39 (Palestine, 7th cent.)
100.040	Seal 40 (Aleppo?, 7th cent.)
100.042	Seal 42 (Palestine)
100.043	Seal 43 (Palestine)
100.044	Seal 44 (Jericho, 8th cent.)
100.045	Seal 45 (Jerusalem)
100.046	Seal 46 (Palestine, 8th cent.)
100.047	Seal 47 (7th cent.)
100.048	Seal 48 (Beth-Shemesh, 7th cent.)
100.049	Seal 49 (Jerusalem, 8th/7th cent.)
100.050	Seal 50 (Jerusalem, 7th cent.)
100.051	Seal 51 (Palestine, 7th cent.)
100.052	Seal 52 (Palestine)
100.053	Seal 53 (Jerusalem)
100.054	Seal 54 (Egypt, 7th cent.)
100.055	Seal 55 (T. el-Judeideh)
100.056	Seal 56
100.057	Seal 57 (Lachish, 7th cent.)

100.058 Seal 58 (Egypt)
100.059 Seal 59 (Palestine?, 7th cent.)
100.060 Seal 60 (Palestine, 7th cent.)
100.061 Seal 61 (7th cent.)
100.062 Seal 62 (Ashkelon)
100.063 Seal 63
100.065 Seal 65 (8th cent.)
100.067 Seal 67 (Palestine, 8th cent.)
100.068 Seal 68 (Megiddo, 8th cent.)
100.069 Seal 69 (T. en-Naṣbeh, 8th/7th cent.)
100.070 Seal 70
100.071 Seal 71 (Jerusalem)
100.072 Seal 72 (Palestine, 7th cent.)
100.074 Seal 74 (7th cent.)
100.075 Seal 75
100.080 Seal 80 (8th cent)
100.081 Seal 81 (8th/7th cent)
100.082 Seal 82
100.083 Seal 83 (Nablus, 8th cent.)
100.087 Seal 87 (7th cent.)
100.088 Seal 88 (8th cent.)
100.089 Seal 89 (Beirut, 7th cent.)
100.090 Seal 90 (Phoenicia, 7th/6th cent.)
100.092 Seal 92 (Babylonia, 7th cent.)
100.094 Seal 94 (5th cent.)
100.095 Seal 95 (Cadiz, 8th/7th cent.)
100.096 Seal 96
100.099 Seal 99 (Samaria, 8th cent.)

100.100 Seal 100 (Jerusalem?, 7th cent.)
100.101 Seal 101 (Beirut, 8th cent.)
100.105 Seal 105 (Samaria, 8th cent.)
100.106 Seal 106 (T. el-Judeideh, 7th cent.)
100.107 Seal 107 (Beth-Shemesh, 8th cent.)
100.108 Seal 108 (Beth-Shemesh, 8th cent.)
100.109 Seal 109 (Lachish, 8th/7th cent.)
100.110 Seal 110 (Beth-Zur, 7th/6th cent.)
100.120 Seal 120 (T el-Judeideh, 8th cent.)
100.121 Seal 121 (T. el-Judeideh, 8th cent.)
100.122 Seal 122 (8th cent.)
100.123 Seal 123 (Palestine, 8th cent.)
100.124 Seal 124 (7th cent.)
100.125 Seal 125 (T. Qasile, 5th/4th cent.)
100.126 Seal 126 (8th/7th cent.)
100.127 Seal 127 (Palestine?, 8th cent.)
100.128 Seal 128 (Syria, 8th/7th cent.)
100.129 Seal 129 (Transjordan, 7th cent.)
100.130 Seal 130 (Persian period)
100.132 Seal 132 (Judaea?)
100.136 Seal 136 (Megiddo, 7th cent.)
100.138 Seal 138 (8th/7th cent.)
100.139 Seal 139 (Lachish, 8th/7th cent.)
100.140 Seal 140 (8th cent.)
100.141 Seal 141 (8th cent.)
100.142 Seal 142 (Judaea?, 7th cent.)
100.143 Seal 143 (Jerusalem?, Persian period)
100.144 Seal 144 (Jerusalem, 8th/7th cent.)
100.145 Seal 145 (Judaea?, 8th cent.)
100.146 Seal 146 (Judaea?, c. 600)
100.147 Seal 147 (Jerusalem, 7th cent.)
100.148 Seal 148 (Jerusalem, early Persian period)
100.149 Seal 149 (Lachish, 7th cent.)

100.150 Seal 150 (Lachish, 8th/7th cent.)
100.151 Seal 151 (Judaea?, 7th cent.)
100.152 Seal 152 (Judaea?, 7th cent.)
100.153 Seal 153 (Judaea?, 6th cent.)
100.154 Seal 154 (Beth-Shemesh, 8th/7th cent.)
100.155 Seal 155 (7th/6th cent.)
100.156 Seal 156 (T. eṣ-Ṣafi, 7th cent.)
100.157 Seal 157 (Amman, c. 600)
100.158 Seal 158 (Gaza, 5th cent.)
100.160 Seal 160 (Jerusalem, 5th cent.)
100.161 Seal 161 (Jerusalem, 7th cent.)
100.162 Seal 162 (Palestine, 7th cent.)
100.163 Seal 163 (Gezer, 6th-4th cent.)
100.167 Seal 167 (c. 700)
100.168 Seal 168 (7th cent.)
100.169 Seal 169 (Judaea, 7th cent.)
100.170 Seal 170 (c. 600)
100.171 Seal 171 (7th cent.)
100.172 Seal 172 (7th cent.)
100.174 Seal 174 (Cairo, 6th cent.)
100.175 Seal 175 (6th cent.)

100.176 Seal 176 (Judaea, 7th cent.)
100.177 Seal 177 (Samaria, 8th cent.)
100.178 Seal 178 (8th cent.)
100.179 Seal 179 (7th cent.)
100.180 Seal 180 (6th cent.)
100.181 Seal 181 (8th/7th cent.)
100.182 Seal 182 (Aleppo, 8th/7th cent.)
100.185 Seal 185 (Samaria)
100.186 Seal 186 (Gibeon, 8th cent.)
100.187 Seal 187 (Gibeon, 8th cent.)
100.188 Seal 188 (Gibeon, 8th cent.)
100.189 Seal 189 (Gibeon, 8th cent.)
100.190 Seal 190 (Gibeon, 8th cent.)
100.191 Seal 191 (Gibeon)
100.192 Seal 192 (Gibeon, 8th cent.)
100.193 Seal 193 (Nebi Rubin, 7th cent.)
100.196 Seal 196 (Ramat Raḥel, 8th cent.)
100.197 Seal 197 (Ramat Raḥel, 8th cent.)
100.198 Seal 198 (Ramat Raḥel, 8th cent.)
100.199 Seal 199 (Ramat Raḥel, 8th cent.)

100.202 Seal 202 (7th cent.)
100.203 Seal 203 (Tel Aviv, 7th cent.)
100.204 Seal 204 (Revadim, 7th cent.)
100.205 Seal 205 (Dan, 9th/8th cent.)
100.206 Seal 206 (Shechem, 7th cent.)
100.207 Seal 207 (En-Gedi, 7th cent.)
100.208 Seal 208 (En-Gedi, 6th cent.)
100.209 Seal 209 (c. 700)
100.210 Seal 210 (8th cent.)
100.211 Seal 211 (Kiriath-jearim, 7th/6th cent.)
100.212 Seal 212 (Arad, 8th cent.)
100.213 Seal 213 (Jerusalem, 7th cent.)
100.214 Seal 214 (Nablus?, 8th cent.)
100.215 Seal 215 (8th/7th cent.)
100.218 Seal 218 (6th cent.)
100.220 Seal 220 (c. 700)
100.222 Seal 222 (Ramat Raḥel)
100.223 Seal 223 (Ramat Raḥel, 8th cent.)
100.224 Seal 224 (Ramat Raḥel)
100.226 Seal 226 (7th cent.)
100.228 Seal 228 (8th cent.)
100.230 Seal 230 (Arad, 7th cent.)
100.231 Seal 231 (Arad, 7th cent.)
100.232 Seal 232 (Arad, 7th cent.)
100.233 Seal 233 (Palestine, 7th cent.)
100.235 Seal 235 (7th cent.)
100.236 Seal 236 (8th cent.)
100.238 Seal 238 (8th cent.)
100.239 Seal 239 (8th/7th cent.)
100.240 Seal 240 (8th/7th cent.)
100.241 Seal 241 (7th/6th cent.)
100.242 Seal 242 (6th cent.)
100.243 Seal 243 (7th cent.)
100.244 Seal 244 (7th/6th cent.)
100.245 Seal 245 (7th/6th cent.)
100.246 Seal 246 (7th cent.)
100.247 Seal 247 (8th/7th cent.)
100.248 Seal 248 (8th cent.)
100.249 Seal 249 (8th cent.)

100.250 Seal 250 (7th cent.)
100.251 Seal 251 (8th/7th cent.)
100.252 Seal 252 (7th/6th cent.)
100.253 Seal 253 (Lachish, 7th cent.)
100.254 Seal 254 (Lachish, 7th cent.)
100.255 Seal 255 (Lachish, 7th cent.)
100.256 Seal 256 (Lachish 7th cent.)
100.257 Seal 257 (Lachish, 7th cent.)
100.258 Seal 258 (Lachish, 7th cent.)
100.268 Seal 268 (Jerusalem, 7th cent.)
100.270 Seal 270 (T. el-Judeideh, 8th cent.)
100.272 Seal 272 (8th cent.)
100.273 Seal 273 (Gibeon)
100.274 Seal 274 (Jerusalem, 8th cent.)
100.276 Seal 276
100.277 Seal 277 (Ramat Raḥel, 8th cent.)
100.278 Seal 278 (7th/6th cent.)
100.279 Seal 279 (4th/3rd cent.)
100.280 Seal 280 (Lachish, 7th cent.)
100.281 Seal 281 (Beer-Sheba, 8th cent.)
100.282 Seal 282 (Arad, 7th cent.)
100.288 Seal 288 (T. en-Naṣbeh, 8th cent.)
100.289 Seal 289 (Lachish, 8th cent.)
100.291 Seal 291 (T. el-Judeideh, 8th cent.)

100.293 Seal 293 (Beirut)
100.294 Seal 294 (Hebron, 8th cent.)
100.295 Seal 295 (Kh. Rabud, 8th cent.)
100.296 Seal 296 (Kh. Rabud, 8th cent.)
100.299 Seal 299 (8th cent.)

100.300 Seal 300 (8th cent.)
100.301 Seal 301 (9th cent.?)
100.307 Seal 307 (6th/5th cent.)
100.308 Seal 308 (6th/5th cent.)
100.309 Seal 309 (6th/5th cent.)
100.310 Seal 310 (6th/5th cent.)
100.311 Seal 311 (6th/5th cent.)
100.312 Seal 312 (6th/5th cent.)
100.313 Seal 313 (6th/5th cent.)
100.316 Seal 316 (Hebron?, 8th/7th cent.)
100.317 Seal 317 (6th cent.)
100.318 Seal 318 (7th cent.)
100.321 Seal 321 (Hebron, 8th/7th cent.)
100.322 Seal 322 (8th cent.)
100.323 Seal 323
100.324 Seal 324 (7th cent.)
100.325 Seal 325 (7th cent.)
100.326 Seal 326 (8th/7th cent.)
100.327 Seal 327 (8th-6th cent.)
100.328 Seal 328 (7th–6th cent.)
100.329 Seal 329 (7th–6th cent.)
100.330 Seal 330 (8th–6th cent.)
100.331 Seal 331 (8th–6th cent.)
100.332 Seal 332 (8th–6th cent.)
100.333 Seal 333 (8th–6th cent.)
100.334 Seal 334 (8th–6th cent.)
100.335 Seal 335 (8th–6th cent.)
100.336 Seal 336 (6th cent.)
100.337 Seal 337 (8th–6th cent.)
100.338 Seal 338 (8th–6th cent.)
100.339 Seal 339 (8th–6th cent.)
100.340 Seal 340 (8th–6th cent.)
100.341 Seal 341 (7th cent.)
100.342 Seal 342 (8th–6th cent.)
100.343 Seal 343 (7th cent.)
100.344 Seal 344 (7th cent.)
100.345 Seal 345 (7th cent.)
100.346 Seal 346 (7th/6th cent.)
100.347 Seal 347 (8th–6th cent.)

100.351 Seal 351 (8th cent.)
100.354 Seal 354 (7th/6th cent.)
100.355 Seal 355 (T. Zakariya/Gezer, 8th cent.)
100.358 Seal 358 (Lachish, 8th cent.)
100.359 Seal 359 (8th/7th cent.)
100.360 Seal 360 (7th cent.)
100.361 Seal 361 (7th cent.)
100.362 Seal 362 (7th cent.)
100.363 Seal 363 (8th/7th cent.)
100.364 Seal 364 (8th/7th cent.)
100.365 Seal 365 (8th/7th cent.)
100.366 Seal 366 (7th cent.)
100.367 Seal 367 (8th/7th cent.)
100.368 Seal 368 (8th/7th cent.)
100.369 Seal 369 (8th/7th cent.)
100.370 Seal 370 (8th/7th cent.)
100.371 Seal 371 (8th cent.)
100.372 Seal 372 (8th/7th cent.)
100.373 Seal 373 (8th/7th cent.)
100.374 Seal 374 (7th cent.)
100.375 Seal 375 (8th/7th cent.)
100.376 Seal 376 (8th cent.)
100.377 Seal 377 (8th/7th cent.)
100.378 Seal 378
100.379 Seal 379 (8th/7th cent.)
100.380 Seal 380
100.381 Seal 381 (7th cent.)
100.392 Seal 392 (Lachish, c. 700)
100.393 Seal 393 (Buqei'ah Valley, 7th cent.)
100.396 Seal 396 (Lachish, 8th cent.)
100.397 Seal 397 (7th cent.)

100.402 Seal 402 (7th/6th cent.)
100.404 Seal 404 (Lachish, 8th cent.)
100.406 Seal 406 (7th cent.)
100.407 Seal 407 (7th cent.)
100.408 Seal 408 (Wadi ed-Daliyeh, Seal 4th cent.)
100.409 Seal 409 (Beth-Shemesh, 8th cent.)

100.410	Seal 410 (T. ed-Judeideh, 8th cent.)
100.411	Seal 411 (Beth-Shemesh, 7th/6th cent.)
100.412	Seal 412 (Jerusalem, 7th cent.)
100.413	Seal 413 (8th/7th cent.)
100.414	Seal 414 (8th/7th cent.)
100.415	Seal 415 (7th/6th cent.)
100.416	Seal 416 (8th/7th cent.)
100.418	Seal 418 (8th/7th cent.)
100.419	Seal 419 (7th cent.)
100.420	Seal 420 (8th/7th cent.)
100.421	Seal 421 (7th cent.)
100.422	Seal 422 (7th cent.)
100.423	Seal 423 (7th/6th cent.)
100.424	Seal 424 (7th/6th cent.)
100.425	Seal 425 (7th/6th cent.)
100.426	Seal 426 (7th cent.)
100.427	Seal 427 (7th cent.)
100.428	Seal 428 (7th/6th cent.)
100.429	Seal 429 (8th/7th cent.)
100.430	Seal 430 (6th cent.)
100.431	Seal 431 (7th cent.)
100.432	Seal 432 (7th cent.)
100.435	Seal 435 (7th/6th cent.)
100.436	Seal 436 (7th cent.)
100.437	Seal 437 (7th/6th cent.)
100.438	Seal 438 (7th/6th cent.)
100.452	Seal 452 (T. Sandahannah, 8th cent.)
100.453	Seal 453 (T. eṣ-Ṣafi, 8th cent.)
100.454	Seal 454 (T. Zakariya, 8th cent.)
100.455	Seal 455 (T. Sandahannah?, 8th cent.)
100.456	Seal 456 (T. el-Judeideh)
100.457	Seal 457 (T. el-Judeideh, 8th cent.)
100.459	Seal 459 (Gezer)
100.460	Seal 460 (Jerusalem)
100.461	Seal 461 (T. el-Judeideh)
100.463	Seal 463 (Gezer)
100.464	Seal 464 (T. el-Judeideh)
100.465	Seal 465 (T. en-Naṣbeh)
100.466	Seal 466 (Gezer)
100.467	Seal 467 (T. el-Judeideh)
100.469	Seal 469 (Lachish, 8th cent.)
100.470	Seal 470 (Lachish, 8th cent.)
100.471	Seal 471 (Lachish, 7th cent.)
100.472	Seal 472 (Lachish, 8th cent.)
100.473	Seal 473 (Lachish, 8th/7th cent.)
100.474	Seal 474 (Lachish, 8th cent.)
100.475	Seal 475 (Lachish, 8th/7th cent.)
100.476	Seal 476 (Lachish, 8th cent.)
100.477	Seal 477 (Lachish, 8th/7th cent.)
100.478	Seal 478 (Lachish, 8th/7th cent.)
100.479	Seal 479 (Lachish, 8th/7th cent.)
100.480	Seal 480 (Lachish, 8th/7th cent.)
100.481	Seal 481 (Lachish, 8th/7th cent.)
100.482	Seal 482 (Lachish, 8th/7th cent.)
100.483	Seal 483 (Lachish, 8th/7th cent.)
100.485	Seal 485 (Beirut, 8th cent.)
100.486	Seal 486 (T. Beit Mirsim, 8th cent.)
100.488	Seal 488 (Ramat Raḥel, 8th cent.)
100.489	Seal 489 (Lachish)
100.491	Seal 491 (Ramat Raḥel)
100.493	Seal 493 (Ramat Raḥel, 8th cent.)
100.494	Seal 494 (7th cent.)
100.495	Seal 495 (8th cent.)
100.496	Seal 496 (7th cent.)
100.497	Seal 497 (7th/6th cent.)
100.498	Seal 498 (7th cent.)
100.499	Seal 499 (Kh. Shovev, 8th cent.)
100.501-509	Seal 501-509 (T. Beit Mirsim?, 7th/6th cent.)
100.510	Seal 510 (T. Beit Mirsim?, 7th/6th cent.)
100.511-535	Seal 511-535 (T. Beit Mirsim?, 7th/6th cent.)
100.536	Seal 536 (T. Beit Mirsim?, 7th/6th cent.)
100.537-550	Seal 537-550 (T. Beit Mirsim?, 7th/6th cent.)
100.551	Seal 551 (T. Beit Mirsim?, 7th/6th cent.)
100.552-557	Seal 552-557 (T. Beit Mirsim?, 7th/6th cent.)
100.558	Seal 558 (T. Beit Mirsim?, 7th/6th cent.)

100.559-575 Seal 559-575 (T. Beit Mirsim?, 7th/6th cent.)
100.576 Seal 576 (T. Beit Mirsim?, 7th/6th cent.)
100.577-580 Seal 577-580 (T. Beit Mirsim?, 7th/6th cent.)
100.581 Seal 581 (T. Beit Mirsim?, 7th/6th cent.)
100.582 Seal 582 (T. Beit Mirsim?, 7th/6th cent.)
100.583-608 Seal 583-608 (T. Beit Mirsim?, 7th/6th cent.)

100.609 Seal 609 (T. Beit Mirsim?, 7th/6th cent.)
100.610-628 Seal 610-628 (T. Beit Mirsim?, 7th/6th cent.)
100.629 Seal 629 (T. Beit Mirsim?, 7th/6th cent.)
100.630-639 Seal 630-639 (T. Beit Mirsim?, 7th/6th cent.)
100.640 Seal 640 (T. Beit Mirsim?, 7th/6th cent.)
100.641-662 Seal 641-662 (T. Beit Mirsim?, 7th/6th cent.)
100.663 Seal 663 (T. Beit Mirsim?, 7th/6th cent.)
100.664-669 Seal 664-669 (T. Beit Mirsim?, 7th/6th cent.)
100.670 Seal 670 (T. Beit Mirsim?, 7th/6th cent.)
100.671 Seal 671 (T. Beit Mirsim?, 7th/6th cent.)
100.672 Seal 672 (T. Beit Mirsim?, 7th/6th cent.)
100.673 Seal 673 (T. Beit Mirsim?, 7th/6th cent.)
100.674 Seal 674 (T. Beit Mirsim?, 7th/6th cent.)
100.675 Seal 675 (T. Beit Mirsim?, 7th/6th cent.)
100.676 Seal 676 (T. Beit Mirsim?, 7th/6th cent.)
100.677 Seal 677 (T. Beit Mirsim?, 7th/6th cent.)
100.678 Seal 678 (T. Beit Mirsim?, 7th/6th cent.)
100.679 Seal 679 (T. Beit Mirsim?, 7th/6th cent.)
100.680 Seal 680 (T. Beit Mirsim?, 7th/6th cent.)
100.683 Seal 683 (T. Beit Mirsim?, 7th/6th cent.)
100.684 Seal 684 (T. Beit Mirsim?, 7th/6th cent.)
100.689 Seal 689 (T. Beit Mirsim?, 7th/6th cent.)
100.690 Seal 690 (T. Beit Mirsim?, 7th/6th cent.)
100.694 Seal 694 (T. Beit Mirsim?, 7th/6th cent.)
100.695 Seal 695 (T. Beit Mirsim?, 7th/6th cent.)
100.696 Seal 696 (T. Beit Mirsim?, 7th/6th cent.)

100.702 Seal 702 (T. Beit Mirsim?, 7th/6th cent.)
100.712 Seal 712 (8th cent.)
100.713 Seal 713 (8th cent.)
100.714 Seal 714 (7th cent.)
100.715 Seal 715 (7th/6th cent.)
100.716 Seal 716 (6th cent.)
100.718 Seal 718 (7th/6th cent.)
100.719 Seal 719 (Judaea, 7th cent.)
100.720 Seal 720
100.721 Seal 721 (7th cent.)
100.722 Seal 722 (7th cent.)
100.723 Seal 723 (7th cent.)
100.724 Seal 724 (7th cent.)
100.725 Seal 725 (7th/6th cent.)
100.726 Seal 726 (7th/6th cent.)
100.727 Seal 727 (7th cent.)
100.728 Seal 728 (8th/7th cent.)
100.729 Seal 729 (7th cent.)
100.730 Seal 730 (8th/7th cent.)

100.731 Seal 731 (En-Gedi, 7th/6th cent.)
100.733 Seal 733 (Jerusalem, 7th cent.)
100.734 Seal 734 (8th/7th cent.)
100.735 Seal 735 (9th/8th cent.)
100.736 Seal 736 (7th cent.)
100.737 Seal 737 (8th/7th cent.)
100.738 Seal 738 (7th cent.)
100.739 Seal 739 (7th cent.)
100.740 Seal 740 (8th/7th cent.)
100.743 Seal 743 (Naḥal 'Arugot, 8th cent.)
100.744 Seal 744 (c. 700)
100.745 Seal 745 (c. 700)
100.746 Seal 746 (c. 700)
100.747 Seal 747 (c. 700)
100.748 Seal 748 (c. 700)
100.749 Seal 749 (c. 700)

100.750 Seal 750 (7th cent.)
100.751 Seal 751 (8th/7th cent.)
100.752 Seal 752 (7th cent.)
100.753 Seal 753 (c. 700)
100.754 Seal 754 (c. 700)
100.755 Seal 755 (c. 700)
100.756 Seal 756 (c. 700)
100.757 Seal 757 (8th-6th cent.)
100.758 Seal 758 (c. 700)
100.759 Seal 759 (Umm el-Qanafid, 7th cent.)
100.760 Seal 760 (8th cent.)
100.761 Seal 761 (8th/7th cent.)
100.762 Seal 762 (7th cent.)
100.763 Seal 763 (c. 700)
100.764 Seal 764 (8th/7th cent.)
100.765 Seal 765 (7th cent.)
100.766 Seal 766 (7th cent.)
100.767 Seal 767 (8th/7th cent.)
100.768 Seal 768 (5th cent.)
100.769 Seal 769 (T. en-Naṣbeh, 7th cent.)
100.770 Seal 770 (Ophel, 7th cent.)
100.771 Seal 771 (Beth-Shemesh, 8th cent.)
100.772 Seal 772 (Beth-Shemesh, 8th cent.)
100.773 Seal 773 (Beth-Shemesh, 8th cent.)
100.774 Seal 774 (Jerusalem, 7th cent.)
100.776 Seal 776 (Beth-Shemesh, 8th cent.)
100.777 Seal 777 (Sebaste, 8th cent.)
100.778 Seal 778 (T. el-Ḥesi, 7th/6th cent.)
100.779 Seal 779 (Lachish)
100.780 Seal 780 (7th cent.)
100.781 Seal 781 (7th cent.)
100.782 Seal 782 (7th cent.)
100.783 Seal 783 (7th cent.)
100.784 Seal 784 (6th cent.)
100.785 Seal 785 (8th/7th cent.)
100.786 Seal 786 (Jerusalem)
100.787 Seal 787 (Jerusalem, 8th cent.)
100.788 Seal 788 (Jerusalem, 8th cent.)
100.789 Seal 789 (Jerusalem, 8th cent.)
100.790 Seal 790 (T. Batash, 8th cent.)
100.791 Seal 791 (Lachish, 8th cent.)
100.792 Seal 792 (Lachish, 8th cent.)

100.801-805 Seal 801-805 (City of David, 7th/6th cent.)
100.807-810 Seal 807-810 (City of David, 7th/6th cent.)
100.812-814 Seal 812-814 (City of David, 7th/6th cent.)
100.817 Seal 817 (City of David, 7th/6th cent.)
100.819-820 Seal 819-820 (City of David, 7th/6th cent.)
100.823 Seal 823 (City of David, 7th/6th cent.)
100.828-829 Seal 828-829 (City of David, 7th/6th cent.)
100.831-836 Seal 831-836 (City of David, 7th/6th cent.)
100.839 Seal 839 (City of David, 7th/6th cent.)
100.845 Seal 845 (City of David, 7th/6th cent.)
100.848 Seal 848 (City of David, 7th/6th cent.)

100.850-851 Seal 850-851 (City of David, 7th/6th cent.)
100.852 Seal 852 (7th cent.)
100.853 Seal 853 (7th cent.)
100.854 Seal 854
100.855 Seal 855 (7th cent.)
100.856 Seal 856
100.857 Seal 857

100.858 Seal 858
100.859 Seal 859
100.860 Seal 860 (7th cent.)
100.861 Seal 861 (8th)
100.862 Seal 862 (7th cent.)
100.863 Seal 863
100.864 Seal 864
100.865 Seal 865
100.866 Seal 866 (8th/7th cent.)
100.867 Seal 867 (8th/7th cent.)
100.868 Seal 868 (8th cent.)
100.869 Seal 869 (8th cent.)
100.870 Seal 870 (7th cent.)
100.871 Seal 871 (8th/7th cent.)
100.872 Seal 872 (7th/6th)
100.873 Seal 873 (7th cent.)
100.874 Seal 874 (7th cent.)
100.875 Seal 875 (8th/7th cent.)
100.876 Seal 876
100.877 Seal 877 (8th cent.)
100.878 Seal 878 (7th cent.)
100.879 Seal 879 (7th/6th cent.)
100.880 Seal 880 (7th cent.)
100.881 Seal 881 (8th cent.)
100.882 Seal 882 (T. Dan, 8th cent.)
100.883 Seal 883 (7th cent.)
100.884 Seal 884 (8th cent.)
100.885 Seal 885 (7th cent.)
100.886 Seal 886 (7th cent.)
100.887 Seal 887 (7th cent.)
100.888 Seal 888 (7th/6th cent.)
100.889-895 Seal 889-895 (7th cent.)
100.896 Seal 896 (7th cent.)
100.897 Seal 897 (7th cent.)
100.898 Seal 898 (8th/7th cent.)
100.899 Seal 899 (Babylon?, 8th/7th cent.)
100.900 Seal 900 (Jerusalem, 8th cent.)

4.116 Siloam tunnel inscr.
4.401 Silwan royal steward tomb inscr. 1
4.402 Silwan royal steward tomb inscr. 2
4.404 Silwan tomb inscr.
106.001 Stamp/Coin 1 (5th/4th cent.)
106.002 Stamp/Coin 2 (5th/4th cent.)
106.003 Stamp/Coin 3 (Ramat Raḥel, 5th/4th cent.)
106.004 Stamp/Coin 4 (3rd/2nd cent.)
106.005 Stamp/Coin 5 (4th cent.)
106.006 Stamp/Coin 6 (5th/4th cent.)
106.008 Stamp/Coin 8 (5th/4th cent.)
106.009 Stamp/Coin 9 (5th/4th cent.)
106.010 Stamp/Coin 10 (5th/4th cent.)
106.011 Stamp/Coin 11 (5th cent.)
106.012 Stamp/Coin 12 (6th cent.)
106.013 Stamp/Coin 13 (5th/4th cent.)
106.014 Stamp/Coin 14 (5th/4th cent.)
106.015 Stamp/Coin 15 (5th/4th cent.)
106.016-018 Stamp/Coin 16-18 (5th/4th cent.)
106.019 Stamp/Coin 19 (5th/4th cent.)
106.021 Stamp/Coin 21 (3rd cent.)
106.031 Stamp/Coin 31 (6th/5th cent.)
106.032 Stamp/Coin 32 (6th/5th cent.)
106.041-044 Stamp/Coin 41-44 (4th cent.)
106.045 Stamp/Coin 45 (3rd cent.)
106.046 Stamp/Coin 46 (3rd cent.)
106.047 Stamp/Coin 47 (Samaria?, 4th cent.)
106.048 Stamp/Coin 48 (Nablus, 4th cent.)
106.049 Stamp/Coin 49 (4th cent.)
106.050 Stamp/Coin 50 (4th cent.)
106.051 Stamp/Coin 51 (3rd cent.)
106.052 Stamp/Coin 52 (3rd cent.)
107.001 Stamp/Coin 53
109.001 Susa inscribed measure 1
109.002 Susa inscribed measure 2

39.001 T. 'Amal jar handle inscr.
40.001 T. Batash bowl rim inscr.
40.002 T. Batash jar inscr.
18.001 T. Beit Mirsim inscr. 1
18.002 T. Beit Mirsim inscr. 2
18.003 T. Beit Mirsim inscr. 3
18.004 T. Beit Mirsim inscr. 4
18.005 T. Beit Mirsim inscr. 5
19.001 T. Dan graf.
29.001 T. el-Hamme jar handle inscr.
23.001 T. el-Hesi ost. 1

23.002	T. el-Hesi ost. 2
38.001	T. el-'Oreme jug graf.
38.002	T. el-'Oreme ost.
30.001	T. en-Naṣbeh inscr. 1
30.002	T. en-Naṣbeh inscr. 2
30.003	T. en-Naṣbeh inscr. 3
30.004	T. en-Naṣbeh inscr. 4
30.005	T. en-Naṣbeh inscr. 5
30.006	T. en-Naṣbeh inscr. 6
30.007	T. en-Naṣbeh inscr. 7
12.001	T. esh-Shari'a ost.
12.002	T. esh-Shari'a jug inscr.
14.001	T. Gat jar inscr.
13.003	T. 'Ira jar inscr. 1
13.004	T. 'Ira jar inscr. 2
13.001-002	T. 'Ira ost. 1-2
11.001-002	T. Qasile ost. 1-2
AHL, 386	Temple Mt Inscr.
AHL, 385	Temple Seal
108.011	Weight 11
108.012	Weight 12
108.021	Weight 21
108.031	Weight 31
108.033	Weight 33
108.043	Weight 43
108.051	Weight 51 (6th/5th cent.)
108.052	Weight 52
108.053	Weight 53 (Samaria, 8th cent.)
108.054	Weight 54 (7th cent.)
108.055	Weight 55 (Lachish, 7th/6th)

WORDS BEGINNING WITH ALEPH IN ORDER OF FREQUENCY

In this table are listed all the words beginning with Aleph (850 words, including proper names), in descending order of their frequency of occurrence in the corpus of classical Hebrew. Words that are conjectured, and for which therefore no occurrence statistics are noted in the Dictionary, are of course absent from this list. Words for which the lemma form is reconstructed (for example, when only plural forms are attested and the presumed singular form is therefore shown within square brackets) are included, without their square brackets.

Following the Hebrew word itself, and (in the case of homonyms) a Roman numeral to distinguish one word from another spelled alike, five columns of figures follow. They record the number of occurrences of the word in the four corpora of texts that comprise classical Hebrew—the Masoretic text of the Hebrew Bible (MT), Ben Sira (Si), the Dead Sea Scrolls (Qumran and related texts) (Q) and the Hebrew inscriptions (Inscr)—and the total number of occurrences. This total determines a word's position in the table. In the next column the part of speech is noted, and a simple gloss follows, to identify the word in question.

The significance of the comparative frequency of occurrence in the four corpora can be best appreciated by reference to the table of word-lengths of the corpora, to be found at the end of the Introduction. By way of example, readers are invited to consider the statistics for the words אֵל *god*, אַל *not*, אֱמֶת *truth*, אוֹת *sign*, אמן *be trustworthy*, אָמֵן *amen*, אַחֲרִית *end*, and אַשְׁמָה *guilt*, as well as for the personal names אֶלְעָזָר *Eleazar*, אֶלְיָשִׁיב *Eliashib*, and אֲמַרְיָהוּ *Amariah*.

This table may also be used in order to discover, for example, which words in classical Hebrew beginning with Aleph are not attested in the

Hebrew Bible, which are used only in the Bible, and, by inference, what the size of the Qumran vocabulary is. There are, according to this table, little more than 200 words in the Qumran texts beginning with Aleph, and, since Aleph is about 10% of the total Hebrew vocabulary, the Qumran word-stock is likely to be about 2000 words.

		MT	Si	Q	Inscr	Total	Part of Speech	Gloss
אֵת	I	10898	55	866	33	11826	part.	object-marker
אֲשֶׁר		5495	57	944	29	6499	part.	*which*
אֶל		5464	79	229	33	5805	prep.	*to*
אמר		5299	28	187	9	5523	vb.	*say*
אֱלֹהִים		2603	29	213	3	2848	n.m.pl.	*God*
אֶרֶץ		2504	24	224	3	2755	n.f.m.	*land*
אִישׁ	I	2179	80	466	9	2734	n.m.	*man*
אָב		1215	20	84		1319	n.m.	*father*
אִם		1071	68	125	6	1270	conj.	*if*
אַל	I	725	245	206	2	1178	adv.	*no[t]*
אֶחָד		970	13	150		1133	adj.	*one*
אַיִן	I	790	55	228	3	1076	part.	*not*
אֵת	II	931	7	41	9	988	prep.	*with*
אֲנִי		871	4	103	1	979	pron.	*I*
אכל		809	11	100		920	vb.	*eat*
אַתָּה		744	7	163	1	915	pron.	*you*
אֵלֶּה		755	17	139	1	912	pron.	*these*
אִשָּׁה		782	42	57	7	888	n.f.	*woman*
אֵל	I	240	64	501	2	807	n.m.	*god*
אָח	I	628	10	51	5	694	n.m.	*brother*
אָדָם	I	548	31	101	2	682	n.m.	*human being*
אַחֲרֵי		619	13	44		676	prep.	*after*
אַרְבַּע	I	454	1	117	2	574	n.m.f.	*four*
אֶלֶף	I	496	6	45	4	551	n.m.	*thousand*
אֲדֹנָי		425	6	52		483	pr.n.m.	*Adonai*
אֵשׁ	I	379	17	49		445	n.f.m.	*fire*
אוֹ		320	2	84		406	conj.	*or*
אָנֹכִי		359		32		391	pron.	*I*
אַהֲרֹן		347	5	38		390	pr.n.m.	*Aaron*
אָדוֹן		334	5	13	32	384	n.m.	*lord*
אַמָּה	I	246		124	3	373	n.f.	*cubit*
אַף	II	277	12	71		360	n.m.	*nose, anger*

Words Beginning with Aleph

אֹהֶל	I	345	2	12		359	n.m.	*tent*
איב		283	5	50		338	vb.	*be an enemy*
אֱמֶת		127	7	204		338	n.f.	*truth*
אֶבֶן		277	7	34		318	n.f.	*stone*
אַתֶּם		279		12		291	pron.	*you*
אהב		208	40	38		286	vb.	*love*
אֵם		220	9	23		252	n.f.	*mother*
אוֹר		115	7	116		238	n.m.f.	*light*
אֲדָמָה	I	225	1	11		237	n.f.	*earth*
אסף		200	7	23		230	vb.	*gather*
אבד		185	11	30		226	vb.	*die*
אֹזֶן		187	10	27		224	n.f.	*ear*
אַיִל	I	182		38		220	n.m.	*ram*
אֲרוֹן		201		3	2	206	n.m.f.	*ark*
אַחֵר	I	166	5	24		195	adj.	*another*
אַחַר		96	9	87	1	193	prep.	*after*
אֶפְרַיִם	I	180	2	11		193	pr.n.m.	*Ephraim*
אַבְרָהָם		175	3	12		190	pr.n.m.	*Abraham*
אָז		144	3	36	2	185	adv.	*then*
אַךְ		164	10	1		175	adv.	*surely*
אוֹת		79	6	84	1	170	n.m.f.	*sign*
אַף	I	134	4	24		162	conj.	*also*
אַשּׁוּר		150	1	5		156	pl.n.	*Assyria*
אֲרָם		143		3		146	pr.n.m.	*Aram*
אמן	I	90	18	27		135	vb.	*be trustworthy*
אָחוֹת		114		10		124	n.f.	*sister*
אֹרֶךְ		95	1	20		116	n.[m.]	*length*
אֲנַחְנוּ		104		11		115	pron.	*we*
אַבְשָׁלוֹם		111		2		113	pr.n.m.	*Absalom*
אַחֲרִית		61	14	34		109	n.f.	*end*
אֶלְעָזָר		72	3	27	2	104	pr.n.m.	*Eleazar*
אֱדוֹם		100		1	2	103	pr.n.m.	*Edom*
אַחְאָב		93			8	101	pr.n.m.	*Ahab*
אוֹצָר		80	8	12		100	n.m.	*treasure*
אַשְׁמָה		19		78		97	n.f.	*guilt*
אֶבְיוֹן		61	3	27		91	adj.	*poor*
ארר		63		22	6	91	vb.	*curse*
אֱמֹרִי		86		3		89	gent.	*Amorite*
אָוֶן	I	80	2	6		88	n.m.	*iniquity, misfortune*
אסר		72		15		87	vb.	*bind*
אֵצֶל		61	2	24		87	prep.	*beside*
אחז		76	3	7		86	vb.	*hold*
אֱנוֹשׁ	I	42	19	25		86	n.m.	*person*

אֶ֫רֶז		73	1	11		85	n.m.	*cedar*
אור		50	3	26	2	81	vb.	*be light*
אֵלִיָּ֫הוּ		71	1		6	78	pr.n.m.	*Elijah*
אִשֶּׁה		65	3	8		76	n.m.	*fire offering*
אַחֲרוֹן		51	2	18		71	adj.	*last*
אֹ֫מֶר		55	5	11		71	n.m.	*word*
אֲחֻזָּה		66		4		70	n.f.	*possession*
אֲבִימֶ֫לֶךְ		67				67	pr.n.m.	*Abimelech*
אֹ֫רַח		59	4	4		67	n.m.	*way*
אָמָה		56		8	2	66	n.f.	*maidservant*
אָמֵן		30		35	1	66	adv.	*amen*
אֱמוּנָה		49	5	11		65	n.f.	*faithfulness*
אַבְנֵר		63			1	64	pr.n.m.	*Abner*
אֵיךְ		61		3		64	adv.	*how*
אֱלִישָׁע		58		1	5	64	pr.n.m.	*Elisha*
אַשְׁרֵי		45	8	11		64	interj.	*happy*
אַבְרָם		61		2		63	pr.n.m.	*Abram*
אַתְּ		60		2		62	pron.	*you*
אָחוֹר		51	3	7		61	n.[m.]	*rear part*
אֱלוֹהַּ		57	1	3		61	n.m.	*God*
אַלּוּף	I	60				60	n.m.	*chief*
אַלְמָנָה		56	2	2		60	n.f.	*widow*
אִיּוֹב		58	1			59	pr.n.m.	*Job*
אַהֲבָה		40	1	17		58	n.f.	*love*
אָסָא		58				58	pr.n.m.	*Asa*
אבה		54	3			57	vb.	*be willing*
אֶ֫דֶן		57				57	n.m.	*base*
אֶ֫פֶס		43	4	10		57	n.m.	*end*
אֶסְתֵּר		55				55	pr.n.f.	*Esther*
אֵפֹד	I	52	1	2		55	n.m.	*ephod*
אוּלָם	II	49		4		53	n.m.	*porch*
אֹכֶל		43	2	7		52	n.m.	*food*
אוּרִיָּה		39		1	11	51	pr.n.m.	*Uriah*
אמץ		41	3	6	1	51	vb.	*be strong*
אָשָׁם		46		5		51	n.m.	*guilt*
אזן	I	41	3	6		50	vb.	*hear*
אָשֵׁר		43		5		48	pr.n.m.	*Asher*
אָסָף		46			1	47	pr.n.m.	*Asaph*
אֲשֵׁרָה		40		1	6	47	n.f.	*Asherah*
אַיֵּה		46				46	adv.	*where?*
אָלָה		37	1	8		46	n.f.	*curse*
אַרְיֵה	I	45	1			46	n.m.	*lion*
אשׁם		36	1	9		46	vb.	*be guilty*

אוּלַי	I	45				45	adv.	*perhaps*
אָחָז		41			4	45	pr.n.m.	*Ahaz*
אֵיפָה		41	1	3		45	n.f.	*ephah*
אַרְגָּמָן		39	1	5		45	n.m.	*purple*
אבל	I	39	1	4		44	vb.	*mourn*
אוֹפַן		35	1	8		44	n.m.	*wheel*
אֵי		41	1			42	adv.	*where?*
אָן		42				42	adv.	*where?*
אִמְרָה		37	1	4		42	n.f.	*word*
אֶצְבַּע		31		10		41	n.f.	*finger*
אֲמַצְיָהוּ		40				40	pr.n.m.	*Amaziah*
ארך		34	2	4		40	vb.	*be long*
אֲחַזְיָהוּ		37			2	39	pr.n.m.	*Ahaziah*
אִי		36	1	2		39	n.m.f.	*island*
אֶלְיָשִׁיב		17		1	21	39	pr.n.m.	*Eliashib*
אֲרִי		35	1	3		39	n.m.	*lion*
אַדִּיר		28	3	7		38	adj.	*majestic*
אֲבִיָּה		26		4	7	37	pr.n.m.f.	*Abijah*
ארב	I	26	4	6		36	vb.	*wait in ambush*
אוה	I	26	3	7		36	vb.	*desire*
אֵבֶל		24	1	10		35	n.m.	*mourning*
אִוֶּלֶת		25	5	5		35	n.f.	*folly*
אֲחִימֶלֶךְ		17			18	35	pr.n.m.	*Ahimelech*
אֱוִיל	I	26	4	4		34	adj.	*foolish*
אָתוֹן		34				34	n.f.	*she-ass*
אֲדֹנִיָּהוּ		26			7	33	pr.n.m.	*Adonijah*
אַרְמוֹן		32		1		33	n.m.	*fortress*
אֶתְמוֹל		31	2			33	n.[m.]	*previous time*
אֲחַשְׁוֵרוֹשׁ		31				31	pr.n.m.	*Ahasuerus*
אחר		17	6	7	1	31	vb.	*delay*
אֵפֶר		22	3	6		31	n.[m.]	*dust*
אֱלִישָׁמָע		17			13	30	pr.n.m.	*Elishama*
אֶבְיָתָר		30				30	pr.n.m.	*Abiathar*
אֲחִיָּה		24			6	30	pr.n.m.	*Ahijah*
אָרֹךְ		18	1	11		30	adj.	*long*
אֲחִיקָם		20			8	28	pr.n.m.	*Ahikam*
אַמְנוֹן		28				28	pr.n.m.	*Amnon*
אֲבִישַׁי		25		2		27	pr.n.m.	*Abishai*
אֵיכָה		18		9		27	adv.	*how*
אוֹי		24		2		26	interj.	*woe*
אַרְבֶּה		24	1	1		26	n.m.	*locust*
אֲמַרְיָה		16			9	25	pr.n.m.	*Amariah*
אפה		25				25	vb.	*bake*

אַרְנוֹן		25				25	pl.n.	*Arnon*
אֵיד		24				24	n.m.	*disaster*
אֱלִיל		20	1	3		24	n.m.	*worthlessness*
אֳנִיָּה		20		4		24	n.f.	*ship*
אִיתָמָר		21		2		23	pr.n.m.	*Ithamar*
אֲנָחָה		11	4	8		23	n.f.	*sigh(ing)*
אִיזֶ֫בֶל		22				22	pr.n.f.	*Jezebel*
אַ֫יִל	II	22				22	n.[m.]	*pillar*
אֵימָה		16	2	4		22	n.f.	*terror*
אתה		21	1			22	vb.	*come*
אזר		16	1	4		21	vb.	*gird*
אָכִישׁ		21				21	pr.n.m.	*Achish*
אֱלִיאָב		21				21	pr.n.m.	*Eliab*
אֲרַוְנָה		21				21	pr.n.m.	*Araunah*
אָפִיק	I	18	1	2		21	n.m.	*channel*
אוּלָם	I	19	1			20	conj.	*however*
אֶזְרָח		18		2		20	n.m.	*native*
אֲחִיתֹ֫פֶל		20				20	pr.n.m.	*Ahithophel*
אֲבִיגַיִל		17			2	19	pr.n.f.	*Abigail*
אַבִּיר		17	2			19	adj.	*mighty*
אַיִן	II	18	1			19	adv.	*where?*
אָכְלָה		18		1		19	n.f.	*food*
אָכֵן		19				19	part.	*indeed*
אֱלִיעֶ֫זֶר		14		5		19	pr.n.m.	*Eliezer*
אֶלְקָנָה		19				19	pr.n.m.	*Elkanah*
אִסָּר		11		8		19	n.m.	*vow*
אָדָם	V	9	1	8		18	pr.n.m.	*Adam*
אוֹב	I	16	2			18	n.m.	*ghost*
אֵזוֹר		14	2	2		18	n.m.	*girdle*
אֲנוּ		1		17		18	pron.	*we*
אֵלָה	I	17				17	n.f.	*terebinth*
אָמוֹן	III	17				17	pr.n.m.	*Amon*
אָמוֹץ		13		2	2	17	pr.n.m.	*Amoz*
אנח		12	3	2		17	vb.	*sigh*
אַשְׁדּוֹד		17				17	pl.n.	*Ashdod*
ארג		14	1	2		17	vb.	*weave*
אוֹפִיר	I	12	1	2	1	16	pl.n.	*Ophir*
אֵיתָן	I	14	1	1		16	adj.	*continuous*
אֶלְנָתָן		7			9	16	pr.n.m.	*Elnatan*
אמן	II	9	1	6		16	vb.	*foster*
אנף		14	1	1		16	vb.	*be angry*
אוֹן	I	13	1	2		16	n.m.	*strength*
אוץ		10	3	2	1	16	vb.	*urge*

אמל		16				16	vb.	*be feeble*
אֲהָהּ		15				15	interj.	*alas*
אֲחִיטוּב		15				15	pr.n.m.	*Ahitub*
אֲחִימַעַץ		15				15	pr.n.m.	*Ahimaaz*
אֱלִיפַז		15				15	pr.n.m.	*Eliphaz*
אַמְתַּחַת		15				15	n.f.	*sack*
אָנָּא		13		2		15	interj.	*oh!*
אֵפוֹא		15				15	part.	*then*
אֲפֵלָה		10		5		15	n.f.	*darkness*
אֶלֶף	III	13		2		15	n.m.	*clan*
אֲבַדּוֹן		6		8		14	n.f.	*destruction*
אָבֵל	I	8	2	4		14	adj.	*mourning*
אַכְזָרִי		8	4	2		14	adj.	*cruel*
אלם	I	8		6		14	vb.	*be dumb*
אָסִיר		13		1		14	n.m.	*prisoner*
אשר	II	9	5			14	vb.	*be happy*
אֲבִינָדָב		13				13	pr.n.m.	*Abinadab*
אָבֵל	II	13				13	pl.n.	*Abel*
אֲדֹמִי		12			1	13	gent.	*Edomite*
אַיָּל		11		2		13	n.m.	*deer*
אֵלָה	II	13				13	pr.n.m.	*Elah*
אנשׁ		9		4		13	vb.	*be weak*
אֲרַמִּי		13				13	gent.	*Aramaean*
ארשׂ		11		2		13	vb.	*betroth*
אֲבִיהוּא		12				12	pr.n.m.	*Abihu*
אֲבִירָם		11	1			12	pr.n.m.	*Abiram*
אֲבָל		11	1			12	adv.	*indeed*
אַדֶּרֶת		12				12	n.f.	*majesty, cloak* "
אֵזוֹב		10		2		12	n.m.	*hyssop*
אַשְׁקְלוֹן		12				12	pl.n.	*Ashkelon*
אֶתְנַן	I	12				12	n.m.	*fee*
אִמֵּר	II	8		4		12	pr.n.m.	*Immer*
אָבִיב		9		2		11	n.m.	*ear (of cereal)*
אַבְנֵט		9		2		11	n.[m.]	*girdle*
אוֹדָה		11				11	n.f.	*cause*
אַיָּלָה		11				11	n.f.	*hind*
אֵיפֹה		10		1		11	adv.	*where?*
אִישׁ־בֹּשֶׁת		11				11	pr.n.m.	*Ish-bosheth*
אֵלוֹן		10		1		11	n.m.	*terebinth*
אֱלִיהוּא		11				11	pr.n.m.	*Elihu*
אפק		7	1	3		11	vb.	*be strong*
אֲרֻבָּה		9		2		11	n.f.	*window*
ארח		6	2	2		10	vb.	*journey*

אֲגַם	I	9		1		10	n.[m.]	*pool*
אִגֶּרֶת		10				10	n.f.	*letter*
אדם		10				10	vb.	*be red*
אָדֹם		9		1		10	adj.	*red*
אֵהוּד		9			1	10	pr.n.m.	*Ehud*
אוֹרָה	I	3		7		10	n.f.	*light*
אוּרִים		7		3		10	n.m.pl.	*Urim*
אטם		9		1		10	vb.	*block*
אַיָּלוֹן		10				10	pl.n.	*Aijalon*
אֱלִיאֵל		10				10	pr.n.m.	*Eliel*
אֱלִיפֶלֶט		9			1	10	pr.n.m.	*Eliphelet*
אֹפֶל		9		1		10	n.m.	*darkness*
אַרְפַּכְשַׁד		9		1		10	pr.n.m.	*Arpachshad*
אשׁ				10		10	n.m.	*foundation*
אָשֻׁר		10				10	n.f.	*step*
אַזְכָּרָה		7	2			9	n.f.	*token offering*
אליקם					9	9	pr.n.m.	*Elikam*
אַלּוֹן	I	9				9	n.m.	*oak*
אָמְנָם		9				9	adv.	*truly*
אֲפֵק		9				9	pl.n.	*Aphek*
אַרְתַּחְשַׁסְתְּ		9				9	pr.n.m.	*Artaxerxes*
אשיהו					9	9	pr.n.m.	*Ashiah*
אֶשְׁכּוֹל	I	9				9	n.m.	*cluster*
אַשְׁמוּרָה		7	1	1		9	n.f.	*watch*
אִתַּי		9				9	pr.n.m.	*Ittai*
אשא					8	8	pr.n.m.	*Isha*
אֶפְרָתָה	II	8				8	pl.n.	*Ephrathah*
אֲגַג		8				8	pr.n.m.	*Agag*
אֲגַף	I	7		1		8	n.[m.]	*troop*
אדר		4	3	1		8	vb.	*be majestic*
אֲדָר		8				8	pr.n.[m.]	*Adar*
אֶדְרֶעִי		8				8	pl.n.	*Edrei*
אָהֳלִיבָמָה		8				8	prnfm	*Oholibamah*
אַוָּה		7		1		8	n.f.	*desire*
אוּט				8		8	n.[m.]	*storehouse*
אוֹנָן		8				8	pr.n.m.	*Onan*
אוּרִי		8				8	pr.n.m.	*Uri*
אחא					8	8	pr.n.m.	*Aha*
אֲחִינֹעַם		7			1	8	pr.n.f.	*Ahinoam*
אֵילַת		8				8	pl.n.	*Elath*
אֵיתָן	II	8				8	pr.n.m.	*Ethan*
אִכָּר		7		1		8	n.m.	*farmer*
אֵל	II	5	2	1		8	n.m.	*power*

אַלּוּף	II	8				8	adj.	*tame*
אלעז					8	8	pr.n.m.	*Eliaz*
אֶלֶף	II	8				8	n.m.	*cattle*
אֱנוֹשׁ	II	7	1			8	pr.n.m.	*Enosh*
אָסוֹן		5	3			8	n.m.	*harm*
אֶפְרֹחַ	II				8	8	pr.n.m.	*Ephroah*
אצל		5	3			8	vb.	*withhold*
אַשְׁפֹּת		6		2		8	n.[m.]	*refuse heap*
אשר	I	7	1			8	vb.	*go forward*
אֹמֶץ		1	1	6		8	n.[m.]	*might*
אֲבִיעֶזֶר		7				7	pr.n.m.	*Abiezer*
אָבִיר		6	1			7	adj.	*mighty*
אַחְיוֹ		6			1	7	pr.n.m.	*Ahio*
אֲחֹרַנִּית		7				7	adv.	*backwards*
אֵיבָה		5		2		7	n.f.	*enmity*
אֵילוֹן	I	6			1	7	pr.n.m.	*Elon*
אֶלְיוֹעֵינַי		7				7	pr.n.m.	*Elioenai*
אִלֵּם		6		1		7	adj.	*dumb*
אַמִּיץ		6	1			7	adj.	*mighty*
אֳנִי		7				7	n.m.	*fleet*
אפף		5		2		7	vb.	*surround*
אָשֵׁד		7				7	n.f.	*slope*
אַשְׁפָּה		6			1	7	n.f.	*quiver*
אֶשְׁתָּאֹל		7				7	pl.n.	*Eshtaol*
אֵיכָכָה		4	2	1		7	adv.	*how?*
אֵמֻן	I	5		2		7	n.[m.]	*faithfulness*
אַלְיָה		5		1		6	n.f.	*fat tail*
אָשִׁישׁ		1		5		6	n.m.	*adult*
אָבָק		6				6	n.m.	*dust*
אֲדַמְדָּם		6				6	adj.	*reddish*
אָהֳלִיבָה		6				6	pr.n.f.	*Oholibah*
אוּר	I	6				6	n.m.	*fire*
אות		4		2		6	vb.	*agree*
אֲחִיעֶזֶר		6				6	pr.n.m.	*Ahiezer*
אַיָּה	II	6				6	pr.n.m.	*Aiah*
אֵילִם		6				6	pl.n.	*Elim*
אִישׁוֹן		4	1	1		6	n.[m.]	*pupil*
אלה	I	6				6	vb.	*curse*
אֶלְחָנָן		4			2	6	pr.n.m.	*Elhanan*
אֱלִימֶלֶךְ		6				6	pr.n.m.	*Elimelech*
אֶלְיָסָף		6				6	pr.n.m.	*Eliasaph*
אֱלִיצָפָן		6				6	pr.n.m.	*Elizaphan*
אַלְמֻג		6				6	n.[m.]	*algum*

אֶלְעָשָׂה		6				6	pr.n.m.	*Eleasah*
אֵמֻן	II	3	1	2		6	adj.	*faithful*
אֶמֶשׁ		5			1	6	n.[m.]	*evening*
אפס		5	1			6	vb.	*cease*
אֶפְרֹחַ	I	4		2		6	n.m.	*nestling*
אָצֵל		6				6	pr.n.m.	*Azel*
אֲרוּכָה		6				6	n.f.	*restoration*
אֲרֻחָה		6				6	n.f.	*ration*
אַרְכִּי		6				6	gent.	*Archite*
אַרְפַּד		6				6	pl.n.	*Arpad*
אַשְׁדּוֹדִי		6				6	gent.	*Ashdodite*
אֲבֵדָה		4		1		5	n.f.	*lost object*
אֲבִידָן		5				5	pr.n.m.	*Abidan*
אֲבִיָּם		5				5	pr.n.m.	*Abijam*
אֲבִישַׁג		5				5	pr.n.f.	*Abishag*
אֲבִישׁוּעַ		5				5	pr.n.m.	*Abishua*
אֲגָגִי		5				5	gent.	*Agagite*
אַגְמוֹן		5				5	n.[m.]	*rush*
אַדְמָה		5				5	pl.n.	*Admah*
אָהֳלָה		5				5	pr.n.f.	*Oholah*
אָהֳלִיאָב		5				5	pr.n.m.	*Oholiab*
אוֹנוֹ		5				5	pl.n.	*Ono*
אוּר	II	4		1		5	pl.n.	*Ur*
אזל	I	5				5	vb.	*go*
אֶזְרוֹעַ		2		3		5	n.f.	*arm*
אֲחִילוּד		5				5	pr.n.m.	*Ahilud*
אֲחִימַן		4			1	5	pr.n.m.	*Ahiman*
אֲחִירַע		5				5	pr.n.m.	*Ahira*
אחמא					5	5	pr.n.m.	*Ahima*
אַט		5				5	n.m.	*gent.leness*
אָטֵר		5				5	pr.n.m.	*Ater*
אֱלִיצוּר		5				5	pr.n.m.	*Elizur*
אֲלֻמָּה		5				5	n.f.	*sheaf*
אֶלְעָלֵה		5				5	pl.n.	*Elealeh*
אַמָּה	III			5		5	n.f.	*conduit*
אָמְנָם		5				5	adv.	*truly*
אנה	II	4	1			5	vb.	*happen*
אֹנֶה		3		2		5	n.m.	*distress*
אֲנָקָה	I	4	1			5	n.f.	*groaning*
אֶפְעֶה	II	1		4		5	n.[m.]	*nothing*
אֶפְרָתִי		5				5	gent.	*Ephrathite*
אצר		5				5	vb.	*store up*
אֶצֶר		5				5	pr.n.m.	*Ezer*

אֲרִיאֵל	II	5				5	pl.n.	*Ariel*
אֲרָמִית		5				5	adv.	*in Aramaic*
אָשִׁיחַ			1	4		5	n.m.	*reservoir*
אֵת	III	5				5	n.[m.]	*blade*
אַתִּיק		5				5	n.m.	*ledge*
אַתֵּ֫נָה		5				5	pron.	*you*
אֶבְיָסָף		4				4	pr.n.m.	*Ebiasaph*
אֲבִיחַ֫יִל		4				4	pr.n.m.	*Abihail*
אֲבִינֹ֫עַם		4				4	pr.n.m.	*Abinoam*
אֵ֫בֶר		3		1		4	n.[m.]	*wing*
אֶבְרָה		4				4	n.f.	*wing*
אֹבֹת	I	4				4	pl.n.	*Oboth*
אֲגֻדָּה		4				4	n.f.	*bond*
אַגָּן		3			1	4	n.[m.]	*bowl*
אֹ֫דֶם		3	1			4	n.[f.]	*ruby*
אהל	I	3		1		4	vb.	*pitch tent*
אָהָל		4				4	n.[m.]	*aloe*
אוּלָם	III	4				4	pr.n.m.	*Ulam*
אוֹנָם		4				4	pr.n.m.	*Onam*
אוּרִיאֵל		4				4	pr.n.m.	*Uriel*
אֲחֹחִי	II	4				4	gent.	*Ahohite*
אֲחַשְׁדַּרְפַּן		4				4	n.m.	*satrap*
אָטָד		4				4	n.m.	*bramble*
אַכְזִיב		4				4	pl.n.	*Achzib*
אַכְזָר		4				4	adj.	*cruel*
אֶלְיָדָע		4				4	pr.n.m.	*Eliada*
אַלְמָנוּת		4				4	n.f.	*widowhood*
אלף	I	4				4	vb.	*learn*
אֲמָנָה	I	2		2		4	n.f.	*agreement*
אֲנָךְ		4				4	n.[m.]	*lead*
אנק		4				4	vb.	*groan*
אַסִּיר	I	4				4	n.m.	*prisoner*
אַסִּיר	II	4				4	pr.n.m.	*Assir*
אָסֹף		3		1		4	n.[m.]	*storehouse*
אַצִּיל		3	1			4	n.[f.]	*joint*
אֲצַלְיָ֫הוּ		2			2	4	pr.n.m.	*Azaliah*
אַרְגֹּב	II	4				4	pl.n.	*Argob*
אֻרְוָה		4				4	n.f.	*stall*
אָרַח		4				4	pr.n.m.	*Arah*
אֲרָרַט		4				4	pl.n.	*Ararat*
אַשְׁחוּר		2			2	4	pr.n.m.	*Ashhur*
אֲשִׁישָׁה		4				4	n.f.	*raisin cake*
אֶשְׁכּוֹל	III	4				4	pl.n.	*Eshcol*

אָשֵׁם		3		1		4	adj.	*guilty*
אֶשְׁתְּמֹעַ	I	4				4	pl.n.	*Eshtemoa*
אֵתָם		4				4	pl.n.	*Etham*
אֶלְגָּבִישׁ		3		1		4	n.[m.]	*hail*
אֻמָּה		3		1		4	n.f.	*people*
אֶפְרָ֫תָה	I	3				3	pr.n.f.	*Ephrathah*
אוּד		3				3	n.m.	*firebrand*
אִי	II	3				3	n.m.	*jackal*
אַכְשָׁף		3				3	pl.n.	*Achshaph*
אֵב		2		1		3	n.m.	*greenness*
אבא					3	3	pr.n.m.	*Abba*
אֵבוּס		3				3	n.m.	*trough*
אֲבִיאֵל		3				3	pr.n.m.	*Abiel*
אֲבִיעֶזְרִי		3				3	gent.	*Abiezrite*
אֶ֫בֶן		2		1		3	n.[m.]	*stone*
אגר		3				3	vb.	*gather*
אֶגְרֹף		2		1		3	n.[m.]	*fist*
אַדְמוֹנִי		3				3	adj.	*ruddy*
אֲדֹנִי בֶ֫זֶק		3				3	pr.n.m.	*Adoni-bezek*
אֲדֹנִיקָם		3				3	pr.n.m.	*Adonikam*
אַדְרַמֶּ֫לֶךְ		3				3	pr.n.m.	*Adrammelech*
אַ֫הַב		2	1			3	n.[m.]	*lover*
אַהֲוָא		3				3	pl.n.	*Ahava*
אוּבָל		3				3	n.[m.]	*river*
אוֹמָר		3				3	pr.n.m.	*Omar*
אוֹן	II	3				3	pl.n.	*On*
אֶזְרָחִי		3				3	gent.	*Ezrahite*
אָח	II	3				3	interj.	*alas*
אָח	II	3				3	n.f.	*brazier*
אָ֫חוּ		3				3	n.m.	*reed*
אֲחִי		2			1	3	pr.n.m.	*Ahi*
אֲחִיסָמָךְ		3				3	pr.n.m.	*Ahisamach*
אַיָּה	I	3				3	n.f.	*falcon*
אָיֹם		3				3	adj.	*terrible*
אִיתִיאֵל		3				3	pr.n.m.	*Ithiel*
אֵלָא		1			2	3	pr.n.m.	*Ela*
אֶלְדָּד		3				3	pr.n.m.	*Eldad*
אֱלָהוּת				3		3	n.[f.]	*divinity*
אֱלוּל	I	1		2		3	pr.n.[m.]	*Elul*
אלזכר					3	3	pr.n.m.	*Elzachar*
אלח		3				3	vb.	*be corrupt*
אליאר					3	3	pr.n.m.	*Eljair*
אֱלִיעָם		2			1	3	pr.n.m.	*Eliam*

אֱלִישָׁה		3				3	pr.n.m.	*Elishah*
אלמא				3		3	pr.n.m.	*Alma*
אַלְמֹנִי		3				3	n.m.	*such-and-such*
אלסמך					3	3	pr.n.m.	*Elisamach*
אֶלְפַּעַל		3				3	pr.n.m.	*Elpaal*
אלרם					3	3	pr.n.m.	*Eliram*
אֹם				3		3	n.m.	*nation*
אֵמִים		3				3	gent.	*Emim*
אניהו					3	3	pr.n.m.	*Oniah*
אנס		1	1	1		3	vb.	*force*
אֵסוּר		3				3	n.m.	*bond*
אָסִיף		2			1	3	n.[m.]	*harvest*
אָסָם		2		1		3	n.m.	*storehouse*
אָסְנַת		3				3	pr.n.f.	*Asenath*
אֹסֶף		3				3	n.m.	*harvest, group*
אֵסַר־חַדֹּן		3				3	pr.n.m.	*Esarhaddon*
אֶפְעֶה	I	3				3	n.[m.]	*viper*
אַרְבַּע	II	3				3	pr.n.m.	*Arba*
אַרְגַּז		3				3	n.m.	*box*
אֲרִיאֵל	I	3				3	pr.n.m.	*Ariel*
אֲרִיאֵל	II	3				3	n.[m.]	*altar hearth*
אַשְׂרִיאֵל		3				3	pr.n.m.	*Asriel*
אִשׁ		3				3	part.	*there is*
אַשְׁבֵּל		3				3	pr.n.m.	*Ashbel*
אַשְׁכְּנַז		3				3	pr.n.m.	*Ashkenaz*
אֶשְׁכָּר		2			1	3	n.[m.]	*payment*
אֶשֶׁל		3				3	n.[m.]	*tamarisk*
אֶשְׁנָב		2	1			3	n.m.	*window*
אֶדֶר		2		1		3	n.[m.]	*majesty*
אנן		2	1			3	vb.	*sigh*
אִי	V	2				2	interj.	*alas*
אֲסַפְסֻף		1		1		2	n.[m.]	*rabble*
אֹבֵד		2				2	n.[m.]	*destruction*
אַבְדָן		2				2	n.[m.]	*destruction*
אֲבִידָע		2				2	pr.n.m.	*Abida*
אֲבִיהַיִל		2				2	pr.n.f.	*Abihail*
אֲבִיטַל		2				2	pr.n.f.	*Abital*
אֲבִימָאֵל		2				2	pr.n.m.	*Abimael*
אֲבִישׁוּר		2				2	pr.n.m.	*Abishur*
אבמעץ					2	2	pr.n.m.	*Abmaaz*
אבס		2				2	vb.	*fatten*
אֲבַעְבֻּעָה		2				2	n.f.	*blister*
אֲבִעֶזֶר					2	2	pl.n.	*Abiezer*

אִבְצָן		2				2	pr.n.m.	*Ibzan*
אבק		2				2	vb.	*wrestle*
אֲגַרְטָל		2				2	n.m.	*basket*
אֵד		2				2	n.m.	*stream*
אַדְבְּאֵל		2				2	pr.n.m.	*Adbeel*
אִדּוֹ		2				2	pr.n.m.	*Iddo*
אֲדֻמִּים		2				2	pl.n.	*Adummim*
אַדָּן		2				2	pl.n.	*Addan*
אֲדֹנִי־צֶדֶק		2				2	pr.n.m.	*Adoni-zedek*
אֲדֹנִירָם		2				2	pr.n.m.	*Adoniram*
אַדָּר	II	2				2	pl.n.	*Addar*
אֲדֹרָם		2				2	pr.n.m.	*Adoram*
אֹהַב		2				2	n.[m.]	*display of love*
אֹהַד		2				2	pr.n.m.	*Ohad*
אֹהֶל	II	1			1	2	pr.n.m.	*Ohel*
אוּזָל	I	2				2	pr.n.m.	*Uzal*
אֱוִי		2				2	pr.n.m.	*Evi*
אֱוִיל מְרֹדַךְ		2				2	pr.n.m.	*Evil-merodach*
אוּלַי	II	2				2	pl.n.	*Ulai*
אוּפָז		2				2	pl.n.	*Uphaz*
אוֹפִיר	II	2				2	pr.n.m.	*Ophir*
אזה					2	2	pl.n.	*Azzah*
אָזֵק		2				2	n.[m.]	*manacle*
אֹחַ		1		1		2	n.[m.]	*owl*
אחאמה					2	2	pr.n.m.	*Ahamah*
אַחֲוָה	II	1		1		2	n.f.	*declaration*
אַחְזַי		1			1	2	pr.n.m.	*Ahzai*
אֲחִיאָם		2				2	pr.n.m.	*Ahiam*
אַחְלַי		2				2	interj.	*if only!*
אַחְלַי		2				2	pr.n.m.f.	*Ahlai*
אַחְלָמָה		2				2	n.[f.]	*amethyst*
אֲחַשְׁתְּרָן		2				2	adj.	*royal*
אִטֵּר		2				2	adj.	*shut*
אִיכָבוֹד		2				2	pr.n.m.	*Ichabod*
אֱיָל		1		1		2	n.[m.]	*help*
אֵילוֹן	II	2				2	pl.n.	*Elon*
אִישׁ־טוֹב		2				2	pr.n.m.	*Ishtob*
אַכְזָב		2				2	adj.	*deceptive*
אֶלְדָּעָה		2				2	pr.n.m.	*Eldaah*
אֶלָּה				2		2	adv.	*except*
אִלּוּ		2				2	conj.	*(even) if*
אַלּוּף	II	1	1			2	n.m.	*cow*
אָלוּשׁ		2				2	pl.n.	*Alush*

אֶלְזָבָד		2				2	pr.n.m.	*Elzabad*
אֱלִיאָתָה		2				2	pr.n.m.	*Eliathah*
אֶלְיַחְבָּא		2				2	pr.n.m.	*Eliahba*
אֱלִיפְלֵהוּ׳		2				2	pr.n.m.	*Elipheleh*
אֱלִישׁוּעַ		2				2	pr.n.m.	*Elishua*
אַלְלַי		2				2	interj.	*alas*
אֵלֶם		2				2	n.[m.]	*silence*
אַלְמוֹדָד		2				2	pr.n.m.	*Almodad*
אֶלָּסָר		2				2	pl.n.	*Ellasar*
אֶלְעָדָה		1			1	2	pr.n.m.	*Eleadah*
אָלֶף				2		2	n.[m.]	*aleph*
אֶלְתּוֹלַד		2				2	pl.n.	*Eltolad*
אֶלְתְּקֵא		2				2	pl.n.	*Eltekeh*
אָמוֹן	V	2				2	pr.n.m.	*Amon*
אָמִיר		2				2	n.m.	*branch*
אמליוס				2		2	pr.n.m.	*Aemilius*
אֲמָנָה	II	2				2	pl.n.	*Amana*
אָמְנָה	I	2				2	adv.	*indeed*
אָמֹץ	I	2				2	adj.	*dappled*
אַמְצִי		2				2	pr.n.m.	*Amzi*
אֶמְצַע				2		2	n.m.	*middle*
אַמְרָפֶל		2				2	pr.n.m.	*Amraphel*
אִמְרִי		2				2	pr.n.m.	*Imri*
אִמֵּר	I	2				2	pl.n.	*Immer*
אֲמִתַּי		2				2	pr.n.m.	*Amittai*
אנה	I	2				2	vb.	*mourn*
אֲנִיָּה		2				2	n.f.	*mourning*
אֲנָפָה		2				2	n.f.	*heron*
אסם					2	2	vb.	*store*
אפד		2				2	vb.	*dress in ephod*
אַפַּיִם	II	2				2	pr.n.m.	*Appaim*
אֶפְלָל		2				2	pr.n.m.	*Ephlal*
אֹפֶן		1	1			2	n.[m.]	*occasion*
אפצח					2	2	pr.n.	*Epezach*
אֲפֵר		2				2	n.[m.]	*covering*
אֶצְבּוֹן		2				2	pr.n.m.	*Ezbon*
אֹצֶם		2				2	pr.n.m.	*Ozem*
אֶצְעָדָה		2				2	n.f.	*bracelet*
אֲרָא		1			1	2	pr.n.m.	*Ara*
אַרְאֵלִי	I	2				2	pr.n.m.	*Areli*
אֶרֶב		2				2	n.[m.]	*lying in wait*
אֹרֶב		2				2	n.[m.]	*ambush*
אֶרֶג		2				2	n.[m.]	*shuttle*

אַ֫רְדְּ		2				2	pr.n.m.	*Ard*
ארה		2				2	vb.	*pluck*
אַרְוַד		2				2	pl.n.	*Arvad*
אַרְוָדִי		2				2	gent.	*Arvadite*
אֹרְחָה		2				2	n.f.	*caravan*
אַרְיוֹךְ		2				2	pr.n.m.	*Arioch*
אֲרָן		2				2	pr.n.m.	*Aran*
אַרְנֶ֫בֶת		2				2	n.f.	*hare*
אֶשְׁבָּן		2				2	pr.n.m.	*Eshban*
אֶשְׁבַּ֫עַל		2				2	pr.n.m.	*Eshbaal*
אֶשְׁכּוֹל	II	2				2	pr.n.m.	*Eshcol*
אשנא					2	2	pr.n.m.	*Ashna*
אַשְׁנָה		2				2	pl.n.	*Ashnah*
אַשָּׁף		2				2	n.m.	*conjuror*
אֶשְׁפָּר		2				2	n.[m.]	*date cake*
אֹ֫שֶׁר		1	1			2	n.[m.]	*happiness*
אֶשְׁתְּמֹעַ	II	2				2	pr.n.m.	*Eshtemoa*
אֶשְׁתּוֹן		2				2	pr.n.m.	*Eshton*
אֲמָם		1			1	2	pl.n.	*Amam*
אֲלַ֫כְסָא				1		1	pr.n.[m.]	*Alexander*
אֹ֫פֶס		1				1	n.m.	*extremity*
אָצַל		1				1	pl.n.	*Azal*
אַרְגֹּב	I	1				1	pr.n.m.	*Argob*
אָשֵׁרִי		1				1	gent.	*Asherite*
אבבעל					1	1	pr.n.m.	*Abibaal*
אֲבַגְתָא		1				1	pr.n.m.	*Abagtha*
אֵ֫בֶה		1				1	n.[m.]	*reed*
אֲבוֹי		1				1	interj.	*alas*
אִבְחָה		1				1	n.f.	*slaughter*
אֲבַטִּיחַ		1				1	n.[m.]	*melon*
אָבִי	I	1				1	interj.	*if only*
אֲבִיהוּד		1				1	pr.n.m.	*Abihud*
אֲבִיּוֹנָה		1				1	n.f.	*caper-berry*
אביחי					1	1	pr.n.m.	*Abihai*
אֲבִיטוּב		1				1	pr.n.m.	*Abitub*
אֲבִי־עַלְבוֹן		1				1	pr.n.m.	*Abi-albon*
אבך		1				1	vb.	*turn*
אֶ֫בֶץ		1				1	pl.n.	*Ebez*
אֲבָקָה		1				1	n.f.	*powder*
אבר		1				1	vb.	*fly*
אבריהו					1	1	pr.n.m.	*Abraiah*
אַבְרֵךְ		1				1	n.m.	*hail*
אבשעל					1	1	pr.n.m.	*Abshaal*

Words Beginning with Aleph

אָגֵא		1				1	pr.n.m.	*Agee*
אגד				1		1	vb.	*bind*
אֱגוֹז		1				1	n.[m.]	*nut*
אָגוּר		1				1	pr.n.m.	*Agur*
אֲגוֹרָה		1				1	n.f.	*payment*
אֵגֶל		1				1	n.[m.]	*drop*
אֶגְלַיִם		1				1	pl.n.	*Eglaim*
אָגֵם		1				1	adj.	*distressed*
אדב		1				1	vb.	*be sick*
אֲדַד		1				1	pr.n.m.	*Adad*
אֲדוֹרַיִם		1				1	pl.n.	*Adoraim*
אֲדַלְיָא		1				1	pr.n.m.	*Adalia*
אָדָם	V	1				1	pl.n.	*Adam*
אֲדָמָה	II	1				1	pl.n.	*Adamah*
אֲדָמִי הַנֶּקֶב		1				1	pl.n.	*Adami-nekeb*
אַדְמָתָא		1				1	pr.n.m.	*Admatha*
אַדָּר	I	1				1	pr.n.m.	*Addar*
אדשׁ		1				1	vb.	*thresh*
אַדְשָׁךְ				1		1	n.[m.]	*rafter*
אדתא					1	1	pr.n.f.	*Adatha*
אהל	II	1				1	vb.	*be bright*
אוּאֵל		1				1	pr.n.m.	*Uel*
אוֹב	II	1				1	n.m.	*wineskin*
אוֹבִיל		1				1	pr.n.m.	*Obil*
אוה	II	1				1	vb.	*mark out*
אוּזַי		1				1	pr.n.m.	*Uzai*
אוטרפלוס				1		1	pr.n.m.	*Eutrapelos*
אוֹיָה		1				1	interj.	*woe*
אוּל	I	1				1	n.[m.]	*body*
אֱוִלִי		1				1	adj.	*foolish*
אוֹן	II	1				1	pr.n.m.	*On*
אֹנֶס			1			1	n.[m.]	*force*
אוֹצָרָה				1		1	n.f.	*treasure*
אוּר	II	1				1	pr.n.m.	*Ur*
אֶזְבַּי		1				1	pr.n.m.	*Ezbai*
אזל	II	1				1	vb.	*weave*
אזן	II	1				1	vb.	*weigh*
אָזֵן		1				1	n.[m.]	*tool*
אַזְנוֹת תָּבוֹר		1				1	pl.n.	*Aznoth-tabor*
אָזְנִי	I	1				1	pr.n.m.	*Ozni*
אָזְנִי	II	1				1	gent.	*Oznite*
אֲזַנְיָה		1				1	pr.n.m.	*Azaniah*
אֻזֵּן שֶׁאֱרָה		1				1	pl.n.	*Uzzen-sheerah*

אַחְבָּן		1			1	pr.n.m.	*Ahban*
אחד		1			1	vb.	*be united*
אֵחוּד		1			1	pr.n.	*Ehud*
אַחֲוָה	I	1			1	n.f.	*brotherhood*
אֲחוֹחַ		1			1	pr.n.m.	*Ahoah*
אֲחוּמַי		1			1	pr.n.m.	*Ahumai*
אֲחֻזָּם		1			1	pr.n.m.	*Ahuzzam*
אחזר			1		1	pl.n.	*Hazor*
אֲחֻזַּת		1			1	pr.n.m.	*Ahuzzath*
אֲחֹחִי	I	1			1	pr.n.m.	*Ahohi*
אֵחִי		1			1	pr.n.m.	*Ehi*
אחיאל				1	1	pr.n.m.	*Ahiel*
אֲחִיהוּד		1			1	pr.n.m.	*Ahihud*
אֲחִיחֻד		1			1	pr.n.m.	*Ahihud*
אֲחִימוֹת		1			1	pr.n.m.	*Ahimoth*
אַחְיָן		1			1	pr.n.m.	*Ahian*
אֲחִינָדָב		1			1	pr.n.m.	*Ahinadab*
אֲחִירָם		1			1	pr.n.m.	*Ahiram*
אֲחִירָמִי		1			1	gent.	*Ahiramite*
אֲחִישַׁחַר		1			1	pr.n.m.	*Ahishahar*
אֲחִישָׁר		1			1	pr.n.m.	*Ahishar*
אחך				1	1	pr.n.m.	*Ahicha*
אַחְלָב		1			1	pl.n.	*Ahlab*
אֲחַסְבַּי		1			1	pr.n.m.	*Ahasbai*
אַחֵר	II	1			1	pr.n.m.	*Aher*
אַחֲרָאִי			1		1	n.m.	*guarantor*
אַחְרַח		1			1	pr.n.m.	*Aharah*
אֲחַרְחֵל		1			1	pr.n.m.	*Aharhel*
אַחֲרַי		1			1	adv.	*afterwards*
אֲחַשְׁתָּרִי		1			1	pr.n.m.	*Ahashtari*
אחתמלך				1	1	pr.n.f.	*Ahathmelech*
אֵטוּן		1			1	n.[m.]	*linen*
אִטִּי		1			1	n.m.	*ghost*
אטר		1			1	vb.	*shut*
אִי	III	1			1	adv.	*not*
אֱיָלוּת		1			1	n.f.	*help*
אִילָן			1		1	n.[m.]	*tree*
אֵיל פָּארָן		1			1	pl.n.	*El-paran*
איעדה				1	1	pr.n.	*Iadah*
אִיעֶזֶר		1			1	pr.n.m.	*Iezer*
אִיעֶזְרִי		1			1	gent.	*Iezrite*
אִישְׁהוֹד		1			1	pr.n.m.	*Ishhod*
אִיתוֹן		1			1	n.m.	*entrance*

אַכַּד		1				1	pl.n.	*Accad*
אַכְזְרִיּוּת		1				1	n.[m.]	*cruelty*
אֲכִילָה		1				1	n.f.	*meal*
אֻכָל		1				1	pr.n.m.	*Ucal*
אַכְסַדְרָן				1		1	n.m.	*vestibule*
אכף		1				1	vb.	*press*
אֶכֶף		1				1	n.m.	*pressure*
אַכְפָּה			1			1	n.[f.]	*pressure*
אלאמר					1	1	pr.n.m.	*Eleamar*
אלבא					1	1	pr.n.m.	*Elba*
אלה	II	1				1	vb.	*mourn*
אַלָּה		1				1	n.[f.]	*terebinth*
אִלּוּלֵי				1		1	conj.	*if not*
אַלּוֹן	II	1				1	pr.n.m.	*Allon*
אליבר					1	1	pr.n.m.	*Elibar*
אֱלִיחֹרֶף		1				1	pr.n.m.	*Elihoreph*
אֱלִיעֵנַי		1				1	pr.n.m.	*Elienai*
אֱלִיפַל		1				1	pr.n.m.	*Eliphal*
אֱלִיקָא		1				1	pr.n.m.	*Elika*
אלירב					1	1	pr.n.	*Elirab*
אֱלִישֶׁבַע		1				1	pr.n.f.	*Elisheba*
אֱלִישָׁפָט		1				1	pr.n.m.	*Elishaphat*
אלם	II	1				1	vb.	*bind*
אַלַּמֶּלֶךְ		1				1	pl.n.	*Allammelech*
אַלְמָן		1				1	adj.	*widowed*
אַלְמֹן		1				1	n.[m.]	*widowhood*
אלמתן	I				1	1	pl.n.	*Elmattan*
אֵלֹנִי		1				1	gent.	*Elonite*
אֶלְנַעַם		1				1	pr.n.m.	*Elnaam*
אלסמכי					1	1	pr.n.m.	*Elsamchi*
אֶלְעָד		1				1	pr.n.m.	*Elead*
אֶלְעוּזַי		1				1	pr.n.m.	*Eluzai*
אלעש					1	1	pr.n.m.	*Eleash*
אלף	II	1				1	vb.	*be a thousand*
אלץ		1				1	vb.	*press*
אַלְקוּם		1				1	n.[m.]	*God*
אֶלְקֹשִׁי		1				1	gent.	*Elkoshite*
אלשגב					1	1	pr.n.f.	*Elsagab*
אֶלְתְּקֹן		1				1	pl.n.	*Eltekon*
אַמָּה	II	1				1	n.f.	*doorpost*
אַמָּה	IV	1				1	pl.n.	*Ammah*
אָמוֹן	I	1				1	n.m.	*confidant*
אָמוֹן	II	1				1	n.m.	*multitude*

אָמִי		1			1	pr.n.m.	*Ami*
אמיה				1	1	pr.n.f.	*Ammia*
אֻמְלַל		1			1	adj.	*languishing*
אֲמֵלָל		1			1	adj.	*feeble*
אָמָּן		1			1	n.m.	*artisan*
אֹמֶן		1			1	n.m.	*faithfulness*
אָמְנָה	II	1			1	n.f.	*fosterage*
אֹמְנָה		1			1	n.f.	*doorpost*
אַמְצָה		1			1	n.f.	*might*
אֲנָחֲרַת		1			1	pl.n.	*Anaharath*
אני				1	1	pr.n.m.	*Ani*
אָנִין			1		1	n.[m.]	*sighing*
אֲנִיעָם		1			1	pr.n.m.	*Aniam*
אֲנָקָה	II	1			1	n.f.	*gecko*
אנתיכוס			1		1	pr.n.m.	*Antiochus*
אָסוּךְ		1			1	n.m.	*jar*
אסטאן			1		1	n.[m.]	*portico*
אַסְנָה		1			1	pr.n.m.	*Asnah*
אֲסֵפָה		1			1	n.f.	*gathering*
אֲסֻפָּה		1			1	n.f.	*collection*
אספי				1	1	pr.n.m.	*Aspi*
אַסְפָּתָא		1			1	pr.n.m.	*Aspatha*
אִסְתִּרָא			1		1	n.[f.]	*stater*
אֵפֹד	II	1			1	pr.n.m.	*Ephod*
אַפֶּדֶן		1			1	n.[m.]	*palace*
אֲפִיחַ		1			1	pr.n.m.	*Aphiah*
אָפִיל		1			1	adj.	*late*
אָפִיק	II	1			1	adj.	*mighty*
אָפֵל		1			1	adj.	*dark*
אפלי				1	1	pr.n.m.	*Aphulai*
אֹפֶס		1			1	n.m.	*ankle*
אֶפֶס דַּמִּים		1			1	pl.n.	*Ephes-dammim*
אֲפֵקָה		1			1	pl.n.	*Aphekah*
אַפִּרְיוֹן		1			1	n.[m.]	*palanquin*
אֶפְרַיִם	II	1			1	pl.n.	*Ephraim*
אָצִיל	I	1			1	n.[m.]	*side*
אָצִיל	II	1			1	n.[m.]	*leader*
אָצֵל		1			1	pl.n.	*Azel*
אֶקְדָּח		1			1	n.[m.]	*beryl*
אַקּוֹ		1			1	n.[m.]	*wild goat*
אַרְאֵלִי	II	1			1	gent.	*Arelite*
אֲרַב		1			1	pl.n.	*Arab*
אָרְבָּה		1			1	n.f.	*skill*

אֲרֻבּוֹת		1			1	pl.n.	*Arubboth*
אַרְבִּי		1			1	gent.	*Arbite*
אַרְדּוֹן		1			1	pr.n.m.	*Ardon*
אַרְדִּי		1			1	gent.	*Ardite*
אֲרִדַי		1			1	pr.n.m.	*Aridai*
אֹרָה		1			1	n.[f.]	*mallow*
אֲרוֹד		1			1	pr.n.m.	*Arod*
אֲרוֹדִי	I	1			1	pr.n.m.	*Arodi*
אֲרוֹדִי	II	1			1	gent.	*Arodite*
אָרוּז		1			1	adj.	*secure*
אֲרוּמָה		1			1	pl.n.	*Arumah*
אַרְזָה		1			1	n.f.	*cedar work*
אֲרִידָתָא		1			1	pr.n.m.	*Aridatha*
אַרְיֵה	II	1			1	pr.n.m.	*Arieh*
אֲרִיסַי		1			1	pr.n.m.	*Arisai*
אֶרֶךְ		1			1	pl.n.	*Erech*
אַרְמֹנִי		1			1	pr.n.m.	*Armoni*
אֹרֶן	I	1			1	n.[m.]	*laurel*
אֹרֶן	II	1			1	pr.n.m.	*Oren*
אַרְנָן		1			1	pr.n.	*Arnan*
אַרְצָא		1			1	pr.n.m.	*Arza*
ארצטון			1		1	pr.n.m.	*Ariston*
אֲרֵרָה			1		1	n.[f.]	*curse*
אֲרֶשֶׁת		1			1	n.f.	*desire*
אֲשַׂרְאֵל		1			1	pr.n.m.	*Asarel*
אֲשַׂרְאֵלָה		1			1	pr.n.m.	*Asarelah*
אַשְׂרִאֵלִי		1			1	gent.	*Asrielite*
אַשְׁבֵּלִי		1			1	gent.	*Ashbelite*
אֱשׁוּן		1			1	n.[m.]	*beginning*
אַשּׁוּרִם		1			1	pr.n.m.	*Asshurim*
אֲשׁוּרִי		1			1	gent.	*Ashurite*
אָשְׁיָה		1			1	n.f.	*tower*
אֲשִׁימָא		1			1	pr.n.f.	*Ashima*
אֶשֶׁךְ		1			1	n.[m.]	*testicle*
אַשְׁמָן		1			1	adj.	*healthy*
אֶשְׁעָן		1			1	pl.n.	*Eshan*
אַשְׁפְּנַז		1			1	pr.n.m.	*Ashpenaz*
אֶשְׁקְלוֹנִי		1			1	gent.	*Ashkelonite*
אשרחי				1	1	pr.n.m.	*Asherahi*
אשש		1			1	vb.	*be firm*
אֶשְׁתָּאֻלִי		1			1	gent.	*Eshtaolite*
אֶתְבַּעַל		1			1	pr.n.m.	*Ethbaal*
אֶתְנִי		1			1	pr.n.m.	*Ethni*

אֶתְנַן	II	1				1	pr.n.m.	*Ethnan*
אֲתָרִים		1				1	pl.n.	*Atharim*
Totals		61883	1422	7768	512	71585		

Abbreviations and Signs

Texts

Gn Ex Lv Nm Dt Jos Jg 1 S 2 S 1 K 2 K Is Jr Ezk Ho Jl Am Ob Jon Mc Na Hb Zp Hg Zc Ml Ps Jb Pr Ru Ca Ec Lm Est Dn Ezr Ne 1 C 2 C

Si Si_M (Sirach from Masada)

1QpHb 1QS 1QM 1QH 11QT (etc.)

GnzPs (Cairo Geniza psalms)

Other abbreviations will be found in the section entitled, The Sources

Signs

+ = the following is used in association with the preceding

:: = the following is used in contrast or opposition to the preceding

|| = the following is used in parallel to the preceding

§ = section

† = not all these occurrences are listed in this article

Abbreviations

abs. = absolute

add. = additional (inscription)

adj. = adjective

adv. = adverb

AHL = Academy of the Hebrew Language

alw. = always

anat. = anatomical

app. = apposition

architect. = architectural

assoc. = associated, association

BHS = *Biblia hebraica stuttgartensia*

cent. = century

coll. = miscellaneous collocations

conj. = conjunction

corrupt. = corruption

cstr. = construct

del. = delete

der. = derivands, derivatives, i.e. morphologically related forms

descr. = describing, description

design. = designation, designating

du. = dual

em., *see* if em., or em.

emph. = emphatic

encl. = enclitic

esp. = especially

f., fem. = feminine

fr. = fragment

freq. = frequently

gent. = gentilic

Gnz = Genizah fragment, manuscript

graf. = graffito

hi. = hiphil

ho. = hophal

htp. = hithpael

htpal = hithpalel

htpalp. = hithpalpel

htpo. = hithpoel

htpol. = hithpolal, hithpolel

I = inscription

ident. = to be identified

if em. = the foregoing results from an

emendation
impf. = imperfect
impv. = imperative
inf. = infinitive
ins. = insert
inscr. = inscription
intens. = intensive
interj. = interjection
intrans. = intransitive
interrog. = interrogative
Kh. = Khirbet
Kt = ketiv
L = Codex Leningradensis B19 A
lit. = literally
m., masc. = masculine
mg = marginal, sublinear, supralinear reading
mod. = modern
ms = manuscript
n. = noun
ni. = niphal
nom. cl. = noun clause
obj. = object
oft. = often
or em. = the foregoing will not be the case if the following emendation is accepted
orig. = originally
ost. = ostracon
part. = particle
pass. = passive
perh. = perhaps
pf. = perfect
pi. = piel
pilp. = pilpel
pl., plur. = plural
pl.n. = place name
po. = poel, po'al,
pol. = polal, polel
prep. = preposition
pr.n. = personal name
prob. = probably
pron. = pronoun
pronom. = pronominal
ptc. = participle
pu. = pual
Q = Qumran
Qr = qere
ref. = reference
Seb = Sebir (supposed reading)
sf. = suffix
sg. = singular
Si = Ben Sira
sim. = similar, similarly
sing. = singular
specif. = specifially
subj. = subject
Sup = supplementary text(s)
syn. = synonym
T. = Tel, Tell
t = times
trans. = transitive
usu. = usually
var. = variant
vb. = verb
W. = Wadi
Y. = Yhwh

א

אָב 1215.20.84 n.m. **father**—cstr. אֲבִי ,אֲב; sf. אָבִי, אָבִ֫יךָ, אָבִ֫ינוּ, אָבִ֫יהָ, (אביה Q, אָבִ֫יהוּ) אָבִיו, אָבִיךְ, (אביכה Q), אֲבִיכֶם ,אֲבִיכֶן ,אֲבִיהֶם ,אֲבִהֶן; pl. abs. אָבוֹת (אָבֹת); cstr. אֲבוֹת; sf. אֲבוֹתַי (אֲבֹתַי ,אֲבוֹתָי), אֲבוֹתֶ֫יךָ (אֲבֹתֶ֫יךָ), אֲבֹתֵ֫ינוּ) אֲבוֹתֵינוּ, (אֲבֹתָיו) אֲבוֹתָיו, (אבותיכה Q), (אבותיכמה Q ,אֲבֹתֵיכֶם ,אֲבוֹתֵכֶם) אֲבוֹתֵיכֶם, (אבויתינו Q), אֲבוֹתָם (אֲבֹתָם ,אֲבוֹתֵיהֶם ,אֲבֹתֵיהֶם, אבותיהמה Q).

1. usu. **father,** sometimes, esp. in pl., **parent** (e.g. Ex 205 347 Dt 83.16 2416 Jr 621 3129 Ezk 510 182 Ml 324 Pr 176; in sg., e.g. Is 3819 Ezk 184 Pr 1721 Si 38), father of rain Jb 3828, tree as father Jr 227, pit as father Jb 1714.

2a. ancestor, rare in sg. (e.g. Dt 265 Jos 243 Is 4327), grandfather (e.g. Gn 4815.16 4929 2 S 163), remote ancestors of various generations (e.g. Ex 135 Nm 2015 Dt 437 1022 265 305 Jos 242.3.14.15 1 S 126.8 1 K 853 99 2 K 2115 Is 4327 Jr 318 725 114 1722 Ezk 2027 Ho 910 Ps 442 959 1067 Pr 2228 Ne 916 Si 441).

2b. founding father, of city, nation, group, Gn 420.21 918.22 1021 174.5 1937.38 2221 369.43 1 C 829 935 Si 4419.

3. father figure, as protector, counsellor, etc., e.g. Gn 458 Jg 1710 1819 Is 95 Jb 2916 Si 410 1QM 21.3 1QH 720, God as father, Dt 326 Is 6316.16 647 Jr 34.19 Ml 210 Ps 686 8927 1 C 2210 (in both, as father to Solomon) 2910 1QH 935; אָבִי *my father* in address, as term of respect, 1 S 2412 (David to Saul, unless אָבִי *if only*; or em. :וְאָבִי he is the anointed of Y. *and my father as well*) 2 K 212.12 (Elisha to Elijah) 513 (servants to Naaman, unless אָבִי *if only*) 621 1314.14 (king to Elisha).

4. בֵּית(־)אָב **father's household, phratry,** as kinship and perh. military unit (but distinction from less technical usage oft. unclear), in pl. (בֵּיתן־]אָבוֹת) except Gn 4631.31 4712 508.22 Nm 324.30.35 1717 181 2514.15 Jos 212.18 625 2214 Jg 615.27 91.5.18 112.7 1631 1 S 227.28.30.31 920 1725 221.11.15.16.22 2 S 329 1929 149 2417||1 C 2117 1 K 231 1818 Is 717 2223.24 Jr 126 Ps 4511 Est 414 1 C 919 1229 2311 246 266 284.4 2 C 2113 11QT 2516 5716.19 11QPsa 1917; מַטֵּה אָב *father's tribe* Nm 366.8, מַטֵּה אָבוֹת *fathers' tribe* 147 132 364.7, מַטּוֹת אָבוֹת *fathers' tribes* 2655 3354, שֵׁבֶט אָבִיךָ *your father's tribe* 182.

5. רָאשֵׁי אָבוֹת **heads of fathers' households,** Ex 625 Nu 3126 3228 361 Jos 141 1951 211.1 Ezr 15 268||Ne 770 Ezr 312 42.3 81 1016 Ne 769 813 1212.22.23 1 C 711 86.10.13.28 99.33.34 1512 239.24 246.31 2621.26.32 271 2 C 12 198 232 2612 1QSa 124.25 216 1QM 27 34, רָאשִׁים לְאָבוֹת in same sense Ne 1113, נְשִׂיאֵי הָאָבוֹת *the princes of fathers' households* 1 K 81||2 C 52, שָׂרֵי(־)הָאָבוֹת in sim. sense Ezr 829 1 C 296 1QSa 116(erased).

<SUBJ> היה *be* Gn 420.21 Dt 265, ראה *see* Gn 4235 Ex 106.6 Jg 193.5.6.8.9 2 S 135, גלה *reveal* 1 S 202, סתר hi. *conceal* 202, שׁמע *hear* Nm 305.6=11QT 5317.20 2 K 2213 Jr 3414 Ne 916, קשׁב hi. *pay attention* 934, חרשׁ hi. *be silent* Nm 305=11QT 5318, משׁשׁ *feel* Gn 2712.22, ידע *know* Dt 83.16 137 2836.64 Jg 144 1 S 203 2317 1 K 232 Jr 915 1613 194 443 Dn 1138 1QH 935, hi. *make known* Is 3819 (+ לְבָנִים *to children*), שׂכל hi. *perceive* Ps 1067, פקד *notice* 1 S 206, שׁכח *forget* Jr 2327.

אמר *say* Gn 276.18.22.26.32 3710 4236 432.11 4425.27 4819 505 Dt 2119=11QT 643 Dt 2216=11QT 6510 Jg 143 152 195.6.8 1 S 203 Zc 133, דבר pi. *speak* Gn 276 4928 1 K 1312, נגד hi. *tell* Dt 327, ספר *count* 2 C 216, pi. *relate* Jg 613 Ps 442 783, למד pi. *teach* Jr 913 4Q525 411 (+ אֵל *God*), ענה *answer* Gn 2739 1 S 2010, קרא *call, name* Gn 2618 3518.

ברך pass. *be blessed* 1 C 2910, pi. *bless* Gn 2734.38.41 4928.28, כבד ni. *be honoured* 4Q521 1.32, הלל pi. *praise* Is 6410, שׁבע hi. *adjure* Gn 505 1 S 1427.28, צוה pi. *command* Gn 5016 Jr 356.8.10, גער *rebuke* Gn 3710.

עכר *cause trouble* 1 S 1429, קצף hi. *anger* Zc 814, כלם hi. *humiliate* 1 S 2034, יסר pi. *punish* Dt 2118=11QT 642 1 K 1211.14||2 C 1011.14, עצב *hurt* 1 K 16, גדף *revile* Ezk 2027, קשׁה hi. *harden* 1 K 124||2 C 104 Ne 916, כבד *make heavy* 1 K 1210||2 C 1010 1 K 1214, עמס hi. *burden* 1211||2 C 1011.

לחם ni. *fight* Jg 917, תפשׂ *seize* Dt 2119=11QT 643, לכד *capture* 2 C 172, ירשׁ *take possession* Dt 305, עשׁק *extort* Ezk 1818, גזל *rob* 1818 (obj. אָח *brother*), בער pi. *set on fire* Jr 718 (|| בֵּן *child*, אִשָּׁה *woman*), דקר *stab* Zc 133,

אבד pi. *destroy* 2 K 213, שׁחת pi. *destroy* 1912||Is 3712 (hi.), חרם hi. *destroy* 2 C 3214, נתץ pi. *demolish* 333.

בוא *come* Gn 471.5 Jg 2122 2 S 135 4QTNaph 27, הלך *go* Jg 217 1 K 314 94||2 C 717 2 K 2121 Jr 25 1611 Am 24.7, htp. *keep going* Gn 4815, יצא *go out* 1 S 223 2 K 2115 Jr 725, hi. *take out* Dt 2119=11QT 643 Dt 2215=11QT 659, ירד *go down* Nm 2015 Dt 1022 265 Jg 145.10, כשׁל *stumble* Jr 621, נפל *fall* 2 C 299, hi. *cast* lots 1 C 2431, קום *arise* Gn 2731.

עשׂה *do* Nm 328 1 S 202 2 S 102||1 C 192 1 K 1422 153 2254 2 K 32 143 153||2 C 264 2 K 159.34||2 C 272 2 K 1741 183||2 C 292 2 K 2120||2 C 3322 2 K 2332.37 249 Jr 4417 Ezk 1818 Dn 1124.24 Ne 934 1318 2 C 2422 296 3213 3322, *make* Jos 2228 1 K 1512 Pr 2228, חדל *cease* 1 S 95.

נתן *give, allow* Ex 2216 Jg 151 2 C 213 Jb 4215, *place* 1 K 129||2 C 109 2 C 296, לקח *take* Dt 2215=11QT 659 1 K 2034, חזק *urge* Jg 194, נוא hi. *restrain* Nm 306.6=11QT 5320.21, מאן pi. *refuse* Gn 4819 Ex 2216, בקשׁ pi. *seek* 1 S 192, מצא *find* Jr 25, שׁמר *keep* Gn 3711 Jg 222 Jr 1611 1 C 919 2 C 3421.

שׁית *place* Gn 4817, שׂים *place* 1 K 2034 1 C 2610, כון hi. *establish* 2 C 26, נטה hi. *turn* trans. Jr 3414 2 C 296, סבב hi. *turn* trans. 296, חלף hi. *change* trans. Gn 317, נשׂא *carry* Ezk 1820, נטשׁ *leave* 1 S 102, עזב *desert* Jr 1611.11 Ps 2710 2 C 296 4Q372 116 (|| אֱלֹהִים *God*), רחק *be far* Jr 25, פנה hi. *turn* intrans. 473 (+ אֶל־בָּנִים *to children*).

גור *sojourn* Dt 265, נחל *inherit* Jr 1619, ישׁב *dwell* Jos 242 Ezk 3725 1 C 829 935, לון *spend the night* 2 S 178, אצר *store up* 2 K 2017||Is 396, אכל *eat* Gn 2710.31 Jr 2215 3129 Ezk 510 (obj. בֵּן *son*) 182, שׁתה *drink* Jr 2215, ירק *spit* Nm 1214.

ילד *beget* Zc 133 Is 4510 (hi.) Pr 2322, קנה *create* Dt 326, מות *die* Gn 4422 5015 Nm 273 Ezk 1818 2 C 254, hi. *kill* 1 S 192, ho. *be put to death* Dt 2416 2 K 146 (both + עַל־בָּנִים *on account of children*), חלה *be ill* Gn 481, ענה htp. *be afflicted* 1 K 226, בכה *bewail* Gn 3735, אבל htp. *mourn* 1 C 722, זעק *cry out* 1 S 128.

עבד *serve* Jos 2414.15 2 K 2121 Jr 1611, שׁחה htpal. *bow down* 1611, קטר pi. *offer incense* 4421, קדשׁ hi. *consecrate* 2 K 1219, כנע ni. *humble oneself* 2 C 3323.

ירא *fear* Gn 4235, שׂער perh. *fear* Dt 3217, דאג *be anxious* 1 S 95 102, בטח *trust* Ps 225, נסה pi. *test* 959, רצה *like* Pr 312, אהב *love* Gn 279.14 374 4420, רחם pi. *pity* Ps 10313 CD 139, שׂמח *be happy* Jg 193 Pr 1721 2325 (both || ילד ptc. *parent*), גיל *rejoice* 2324(Qr).

חטא *sin* Is 4327 Jr 325 Lm 57 Dn 98 1QS 125 ([חט]אנו ... [א]בותינו), פשׁע *sin* Ezk 23 1QS 125, רשׁע *be wicked* 1QS 125 (hi.) CD 2029, מעל *transgress* Ezk 2027 2 C 296, זוד hi. *be insolent* Ne 916, תלל hi. *deceive* Gn 317, הבל *become deluded* Jr 25.

<NOM CL> מִי אֲבִיהֶם *who is their father?* 1 S 1012, אִם־אָב אָנִי *if I am a father* Ml 16 (|| אָדוֹן *master*), אָב אָנֹכִי לָאֶבְיוֹנִים *I was a father to the poor* Jb 2916, [אנכי ... אב] *I am the father* of the sons of Jacob 4QJuba 49 (|| אֱלֹהִים *God*), אָבִי אַתָּה *you are my father* Jr 227 Ps 8927 (|| אֵל *God*) Jb 1714 (+ אֵם *mother*, אָחוֹת *sister*) Si 5110, אָבִינוּ ... אַתָּה *you ... are our father* Is 6316.16 (|| גאל ptc. *redeemer*), var. 647, אתה אב לכול [בנ]י אמתכה *you are a father to all who are faithful to you* 1QH 935, הֲלוֹא־הוּא אָבִיךָ *is he not your father?* Dt 326, הוּא ... אָבִי *he is ... my father* 2 S 2412 (if em. וְאָבִי : הוּא to : הוּא וְאָבִי), יֶשׁ־לָנוּ אָב *we have a father* Gn 4420, sim. 4419, הֲיֵשׁ־לַמָּטָר אָב *does the rain have a father?* Jb 3828, הֲלוֹא אָב אֶחָד לְכֻלָּנוּ *is there not one father for us all?* Ml 210, אֵין לָהּ אָב *she had no father* Est 27, אֲבוֹתֵיכֶם אַיֵּה־הֵם *as for your ancestors, where are they?* Zc 15.

אֲרַמִּי ... אָבִי *my ancestor was ... an Aramaean* Dt 265, אָבִיךְ הָאֱמֹרִי *your father was the Amorite* Ezk 163, sim. 1645, אָבִיו אִישׁ־צֹרִי *his father was a Tyrian* 1 K 714||2 C 213, אָבִיךָ אִישׁ מִלְחָמָה *your father is a man of war* 2 S 178, גִּבּוֹר אָבִיךָ *your father is a warrior* 1710, תִּפְאֶרֶת בָּנִים אֲבוֹתָם *children's crowning glory is their parents* Pr 176 (|| זָקֵן *old*), אָבִינוּ זָקֵן *our father is old* Gn 1931, הַעוֹד אָבִי חָי *is my father still alive?* 453, sim. 437.

הוּא אֲבִי(־) *he was the father of* + pr.n.m. Ru 417 1 C 242 411 731, מָעוֹן אֲבִי בֵית־צוּר *Maon was the father of Beth-zur* 1 C 245, sim. 44.4, אֲבִי עֲמָשָׂא יֶתֶר *the father of Amasa was Jether* 217, אֵלֶּה אֲבִי עֵיטָם *these were (the sons of) the father of Etam* 43.

וּבְנֵי אֵשֶׁת הוֹדִיָּה ... אֲבִי קְעִילָה ... וְאֶשְׁתְּמֹעַ *and the sons of Hodiah's wife ... were the fathers of Keilah ... and Eshtemoa* 1 C 419, בְּנֵי שֵׁלָה ... עֵר אֲבִי לֵכָה וְלַעְדָּה אֲבִי מָרֵשָׁה *the sons of Shelah ... were Er the father of Lecah and Laadah the father of Mareshah* 421.

<OBJ> עזב *leave* Gn 2$_{24}$ (|| אֵם *mother*) 44$_{22.22}$ Ru 2$_{11}$ Si 3$_{16(C)}$ 4QpsMos^{e} 1$_{7}$, קרא *meet* Gn 46$_{29}$, מצא *find* 44$_{34}$ Ne 9$_{32}$ (לְ for אֶת־), לקח *take* Gn 45$_{18}$ Jos 24$_{3}$, אסף *gather* 2$_{18}$ (|| אֵם, אָח *brother*), בוא hi. *bring* Gn 47$_{7}$, יצא hi. *bring out* Jos 6$_{23}$ (|| אֵם, אָח) 24$_{6}$ 1 S 12$_{8}$ 1 K 8$_{53}$ 9$_{9}$ Jr 7$_{22}$ 11$_{4}$ 11QT fr. 1$_{2}$, ירד hi. *take down* Gn 45$_{13}$, עלה hi. *take up* Jos 24$_{17}$ 1 S 12$_{6}$, נשׂא *raise* Gn 45$_{19}$ 46$_{5}$, נשׂג hi. *overtake* Zc 1$_{6}$, שׂים *place*, i.e. appoint as 1QH 7$_{20}$ (+ לבני חסד *to loyal children*; || אמן ptc. *guardian*).

שׁקה hi. *give to drink* Gn 19$_{32.33.35}$, ילד *bear* (of mother) 1 C 2$_{24.49.49}$ 4$_{18.18.18}$ 7$_{14}$, hi. *beget* 2$_{44}$ 4$_{12.14}$, הרה *conceive* 4$_{17}$, חיה hi. *allow to live* Jos 2$_{13}$ (|| אֵם, אָח, אָחוֹת *sister*), נחל hi. *give inheritance (to)* Jr 3$_{18}$, ישׁב hi. *settle* Gn 47$_{6.11}$ (both || אָח) 11QT fr. 1$_{2}$, כול pilp. *provide for* 47$_{12}$ (|| אָח), עבד *serve* 31$_{6}$, פלט pi. *rescue* Ps 22$_{5}$.

שׁאל *ask* Dt 32$_{7}$ (|| זָקֵן *elder*) Jos 4$_{21}$, חקר *search*, i.e. discover father's feelings 1 S 20$_{12}$, ראה *see* Ho 9$_{10}$, שׁמע *hear* Gn 27$_{6}$, ענה *answer* 34$_{13}$ 1 S 20$_{32}$, בשׂר pi. *bring good news (to)* Jr 20$_{15}$, צוה pi. *command* Jg 2$_{20}$ 3$_{4}$ 1 K 8$_{58}$ 2 K 17$_{13}$ Jr 7$_{22}$ 11$_{4}$ 17$_{22}$ Ps 78$_{5}$.

שׂמח pi. *gladden* Pr 10$_{1}$ 15$_{20}$ (both || אֵם) 29$_{3}$, ידע *know* 2 S 17$_{8}$ 1 K 5$_{17}$, אהב *love* Dt 4$_{37}$ (|| זֶרַע *offspring*), כבד pi. *honour* Ex 20$_{12}$ Dt 5$_{16}$ (both || אֵם) 2 S 10$_{3}$||1 C 19$_{3}$ Ml 1$_{6}$ (|| אָדוֹן *lord*) Si 3$_{8}$ 4Q416 10.2$_{16}$, ירא *fear* Lv 19$_{3}$ (|| אֵם), הלל pi. *praise* Si 44$_{1}$ (|| אִישׁ loyal *man*), בזה *despise* 3$_{16(A)}$, מאס *despise* Jb 30$_{1}$, קלל pi. *insult* Ex 21$_{17}$ Lv 20$_{9.9}$ Ezk 22$_{7}$ (hi.; || אֵם), Pr 20$_{20}$ 30$_{11}$ (all || אֵם), קלה hi. *dishonour* Dt 27$_{16}$ (|| אֵם), נבל pi. *dishonour* Mc 7$_{6}$ (|| אֵם), כלם hi. *humiliate* Pr 28$_{7}$, קבב *curse* Si 41$_{7(B)}$ ([יקו]ב).

חלל pi. *profane* Lv 21$_{9}$, שׁדד pi. *ruin* Pr 19$_{26}$ (|| אֵם), גזל *rob* 28$_{24}$ (|| אֵם), שׂרף *burn* Jg 15$_{6}$ (or em. אֶת־אָבִיהָ *her father* to אֶת־בֵּית אָבִיהָ *her father's house*), נכה hi. *strike* Ex 21$_{15}$ 2 K 14$_{5}$||2 C 25$_{3}$, נפץ pi. *shatter* Jr 13$_{14}$, אכל *eat* Ezk 5$_{10}$ (subj. בֵּן *child*), משׁח *anoint* Ex 40$_{15}$, חנט *embalm* Gn 50$_{2}$, קבר *bury* 50$_{5.6.7.14.14}$, בכה *bewail* Dt 21$_{13}$=11QT 63$_{13}$ (|| אֵם).

<CSTR> אֲבִי *father of* + pr.n.m. Abraham Jos 24$_{2}$, Nahor 24$_{2}$, Shechem Gn 33$_{19}$ 34$_{6}$ Jos 24$_{32}$ Jg 9$_{28}$, Anak Jos 15$_{13}$ 21$_{11}$, Gilead 17$_{1}$ 1 C 2$_{21.23}$ 7$_{14}$, Amasa 2$_{17}$, Tekoa 2$_{24}$ 4$_{5}$, Ziph 2$_{42}$, Hebron 2$_{42}$, Jorkeam 2$_{44}$, Bethzur 2$_{45}$, Madmannah 2$_{49}$, Machbenah 2$_{49}$, Gibea 2$_{49}$, Kireath-jearim 2$_{50.52}$, Bethlehem 2$_{51}$ 4$_{4}$, Beth-gader 2$_{51}$, Etam 4$_{3}$, Gedor 4$_{4.18}$, Hushah 4$_{4}$, Eshton 4$_{11}$, Irnahash 4$_{12}$, Ge-harashim 4$_{14}$, Estemoa 4$_{17.19}$, Soco 4$_{18}$, Zanoah 4$_{18}$, Keilah 4$_{19}$, Lecah 4$_{21}$, Mareshah 4$_{21}$, Birzaith 7$_{31(Qr)}$, Jesse Ru 4$_{17}$, Saul 1 S 9$_{3}$ 14$_{51}$, Abner 14$_{51}$, David Ru 4$_{17}$; + pr.n.f. Milcah Gn 11$_{29}$, Iscah 11$_{29}$, Bilhah 4QTNaph 2$_{8}$; אֲבִי בֵית־רֵכָב *the ancestor of the family of Rechab* 1 C 2$_{55}$.

אֲבִי *ancestor of* + gent. or pr.n.m. of a country or people, Aram Gn 22$_{21}$, Ammonites 19$_{38}$, Canaan 9$_{18.22}$, Edom 36$_{9.43}$, Moab 19$_{37}$, Gibeon 1 C 8$_{29}$ 9$_{35}$, אֲבִי כָּל־בְּנֵי־עֵבֶר *ancestor of all the descendants of Eber* Gn 10$_{21}$, אַב(־)הֲמוֹן גּוֹיִם *ancestor of a multitude of nations* 17$_{4.5}$ Si 44$_{19}$, אֲבִי יֹשֵׁב אֹהֶל *ancestor of whoever dwells in a tent* Gn 4$_{20}$, אֲבִי כָּל־תֹּפֵשׂ כִּנּוֹר *ancestor of everyone who plays the lyre* 4$_{21}$.

אֲבִי־עַד *father*, i.e. counsellor, *of eternity* Is 9$_{5}$, אֲבִי צַדִּיק *father of a righteous one* Pr 23$_{24}$ (|| ילד ptc. *parent*), נָבָל *of a fool* 17$_{21}$, אִמֵּךְ *of your mother* Gn 28$_{2}$, אִמּוֹ *of his mother* Jg 9$_{1}$, אמי *of my mother* 4QTNaph 2$_{8}$, הַנַּעֲרָה *of the girl* Dt 22$_{15(Qr).16(Qr).19}$=11QT 65$_{9.10.15}$ Dt 22$_{29(Qr)}$=11QT 66$_{10}$ Jg 19$_{3.4.5.6.8.9}$ 4QRitMar 108$_{3}$ ([אב]י), יְתוֹמִים *of orphans* Ps 68$_{6}$ (|| דַּיָּן *judge*), אָבוֹת הָרֹאשׁ perh. *most important fathers* (lit. *fathers of the head*) 1 C 24$_{31}$, אבות העדה *fathers of the community* 1QM 2$_{1.3}$ (|| ראשׁ *head*), אבות עולם *ancestors of eternity*, i.e. *ancient ancestors* Si 44$_{1}$.

אָב, אָבוֹת, etc. *of father(s), ancestor(s)*, with these nouns in construct sg. or pl., מוֹלֶדֶת *offspring* Lv 18$_{11}$, בַּת *daughter* Gn 20$_{12}$ Lv 18$_{9}$ 20$_{17}$ Dt 27$_{22}$ Ezk 22$_{11}$ 1 C 2$_{21}$ 11QT 66$_{14}$ 4Q251 7$_{2}$ ([בת אביו]), בֵּן *son* Gn 42$_{32}$ 49$_{8}$ 1 C 2$_{23.42}$ 28$_{4}$ 11QT 54$_{19}$ 66$_{13}$ 11QPs^{a} 28$_{3}$, אָח *brother* Gn 29$_{12}$ Lv 18$_{14}$ Nm 27$_{4.7.10}$ Jos 17$_{4}$ CD 5$_{11}$ 4Q251 7$_{4}$ ([אח]י), אָחוֹת *sister* Lv 18$_{12}$ 20$_{19}$ 11QT 66$_{15}$ 4QTNaph 2$_{1}$ 4Q251 7$_{4}$ ([אב]יו), אִשָּׁה *wife* Gn 37$_{2}$ Lv 18$_{8.11}$ 20$_{11}$ Dt 23$_{1}$=11QT 66$_{12}$ Dt 27$_{20}$ 1 C 2$_{24}$ (if em.; see App.), פִּלֶגֶשׁ *concubine* Gn 35$_{22}$ 2 S 3$_{7}$ 16$_{21.22}$, רֵעַ *friend* Pr 27$_{10(Qr)}$, עֶבֶד *servant* Gn 26$_{15}$ 2 S 15$_{34}$ 1 K 11$_{17}$, נָבִיא *prophet* 2 K 3$_{13}$.

בֵּית *house(hold)* of father, in technical sense (§4), Gn 46$_{31.31}$ 47$_{12}$ (+ כָּל־ *all*; + אָב) 50$_{8}$ (all four + אָח *brother*)

50$_{22}$ Ex 6$_{14}$ (+ רֹאשׁ לְ *head of*) 12$_3$ Nm 1$_2$ (+ לְ *[arranged] according to*; + מִשְׁפָּחָה *family*) 1$_4$ (+ רֹאשׁ לְ; + מַטֶּה *tribe*) 1$_{18+12t}$ (all thirteen + מִשְׁפָּחָה) 1$_{44.45}$ 2$_{2.32}$ (all seventeen + לְ) 2$_{34}$ (+ עַל *according to*; + מִשְׁפָּחָה) 3$_{15}$ (+ מִשְׁפָּחָה) 3$_{20}$ (both + לְ) 3$_{24.30.35}$ (all three נְשִׂיא בֵית־אָב לְ *chief of the father's household of*) 4$_{2+7t}$ (all eight + לְ; + מִשְׁפָּחָה) 7$_2$ (+ רֹאשׁ *head* of; + מַטֶּה) 17$_{17.17}$ (both + לְ) 17$_{18}$ (+ רֹאשׁ) 17$_{21}$ (+ לְ) 18$_1$ 25$_{14}$ (נְשִׂיא בֵית־אָב לְ) 25$_{15}$ (רֹאשׁ אֻמּוֹת בֵּית־אָב בְּמִדְיָן *head of peoples of a father's household in Midian*) 26$_2$ 34$_{14.14}$ (all three + לְ) Jos 2$_{12.18}$ (+ כָּל־) 6$_{25}$ 22$_{14}$ (+ לְ) 22$_{14}$ (+ רֹאשׁ) Jg 6$_{15.27}$ 9$_1$ (כָּל־מִשְׁפַּחַת בֵּית־אֲבִי אִמּוֹ *all the family of his mother's father's household*) 9$_{5.18.20}$ (+ כֹּל *all*) 11$_{2.7}$ 16$_{31}$ (+ כָּל־; + אָח) 1 S 2$_{27.28.30}$ (+ בַּיִת *household*) 2$_{31}$ 17$_{25}$ 22$_1$ (+ כָּל־; + אָח) 22$_{11}$ (כָּל־בֵּית אָבִיו הַכֹּהֲנִים *all his father's household, the priests*) 22$_{15.16}$ (both + כָּל־) 22$_{22}$ 24$_{22}$ 2 S 3$_{29}$ (+ כָּל־) 14$_9$ 19$_{29}$ (+ כָּל־) 24$_{17}$||1 C 21$_{17}$ 1 K 2$_{31}$ 18$_{18}$ Is 7$_{17}$ 22$_{23.24}$ (+ כָּבוֹד *glory* of) Jr 12$_6$ (+ אָח) Ps 45$_{11}$ Est 4$_{14}$ Ezr 2$_{59}$||Ne 7$_{61}$ (+ זֶרַע *offspring*) Ezr 10$_{16}$ (+ לְ) Ne 1$_6$ 10$_{35}$ (+ לְ) 1 C 4$_{38}$ 5$_{13}$ (+ לְ) 5$_{15.24}$ (both + רֹאשׁ לְ) 5$_{15}$ (+ רֹאשׁ לְ) 5$_{24}$ (+ רֹאשׁ) 5$_{24}$ 7$_2$ (both + רֹאשׁ לְ) 7$_4$ (+ לְ; + תּוֹלְדָה *generation*) 7$_{7.9.40}$ (all three + רֹאשׁ) 9$_9$ (+ לְ) 9$_{13}$ (+ רֹאשׁ לְ) 9$_{19}$ (+ לְ *belonging to*) 12$_{29.31}$ (+ לְ) 23$_{11.24}$ (+ לְ *[arranged] according to*) 24$_4$ (+ רֹאשׁ לְ) 24$_{6.30}$ 26$_{6.13}$ (all three + לְ) 28$_4$ (+ כֹּל) 28$_4$ 2 C 17$_{14}$ (+ לְ) 21$_{13}$ (+ אָח) 25$_5$ 31$_{17}$ 35$_4$ (all three + לְ) 35$_5$ (+ פְּלֻגָּה *division* of) 35$_5$ (+ חֲלֻקָּה *division* of) 35$_{12}$ (+ לְמִפְלַגּוֹת לְ *according to the divisions of*) 11QT 25$_{16}$ 42$_{14}$ (ראשי בתי האבות ל *heads of the fathers' houses of* Israel) 57$_{16.19}$ (both + מִשְׁפָּחָה) 11QPs^a 19$_{17}$ (+ אָח).

מַטֶּה *tribe* of father Nm 1$_{47}$ 13$_2$ (both + לְ) 26$_{55}$ (+ שֵׁם *name* of) 33$_{54}$ (+ לְ) 36$_4$ (+ נַחֲלָה *inheritance* of) 36$_6$ (+ מִשְׁפָּחָה *family* of) 36$_7$ (+ נַחֲלָה) 36$_8$ (+ מִשְׁפָּחָה), שֵׁבֶט *tribe* 18$_2$ (+ מַטֶּה *tribe*).

בַּיִת *house(hold)* of father, in less technical sense, Gn 12$_1$ 20$_{13}$ 24$_{7.23.38.40}$ 28$_{21}$ 31$_{14.30}$ 34$_{19}$ 38$_{11.11}$ 41$_{51}$ Lv 22$_{13}$ Nm 30$_4$=11QT 53$_{17}$ Nm 30$_{17}$ Dt 22$_{21}$ Jg 14$_{15.19}$ 15$_6$ (if em. אָבִיהָ; see Obj.) 19$_{2.3}$ 1 S 18$_2$ 2 S 3$_8$ Is 3$_6$ Si 42$_{10}$.

מִשְׁפָּחָה *family* of father Nm 36$_{12}$ 1 S 18$_{18}$ 11QT 57$_{17}$, אֶרֶץ *land* Gn 31$_3$ 48$_{21}$ 11QT 59$_{12}$, מַמְלְכוּת *kingdom* 2 S 16$_3$, מַמְלָכָה *kingdom* 2 C 21$_4$, אֲחֻזָּה *inheritance* Lv 25$_{41}$, נַחֲלָה *inheritance* Nm 27$_7$ 36$_{3.8}$ 1 K 21$_{3.4}$ Is 58$_{14}$ Pr 19$_{14}$.

מִקְנֶה *livestock* of father Gn 31$_9$, צֹאן *flock* 37$_{12}$ Ex 2$_{16}$ 1 S 17$_{15}$, לֶחֶם *food* Lv 22$_{13}$, כָּנָף *hem* Dt 23$_1$=11QT 66$_{12}$ Dt 27$_{20}$, שְׂרֵפָה *fire*, i.e. fire in honour of 2 C 21$_{19}$, מַשְׂרֵפָה *fire* Jr 34$_5$, קֹדֶשׁ *holiness*, i.e. holy object 1 K 7$_{51}$||2 C 5$_1$ 1 K 15$_{15}$||2 C 15$_{18}$, כִּסֵּא *throne* 1 K 2$_{12.24}$ 2 K 10$_3$ 11QT 59$_{15}$, מִשְׁכָּב *bed* Gn 49$_4$=4QpGen^a 4$_5$, יָצוּעַ *bed* 1 C 5$_1$, קֶבֶר *grave* Jg 8$_{32}$ 16$_{31}$ 2 S 2$_{32}$ 17$_{23}$ 19$_{38}$ 21$_{14}$ 1 K 13$_{22}$ Ne 2$_{3.5}$ 2 C 35$_{24}$.

דָּבָר *word* of father Gn 27$_{34}$, מִצְוָה *commandment* Jr 35$_{14.16}$ Pr 6$_{20}$, חֹק *statute* 1 K 3$_6$ Ezk 20$_{18}$, בְּרִית *covenant* Dt 4$_{31}$ Ml 2$_{10}$ 1QSb 2$_{1(Milik)}$ ([ברית א]בותיכה) CD 8$_{18(A)}$=19$_{31(B)}$, מוּסָר *discipline* Pr 1$_8$ 4$_1$ 13$_1$ 15$_5$, בְּרָכָה *blessing* Gn 49$_{26}$ Si 3$_9$ 4QpGen^a 3$_{13}$, כָּבוֹד *honour* Si 3$_{11.12}$, צְדָקָה *charity*, i.e. charity done to 3$_{14}$, שֶׁבַח *praise*, i.e. in praise of 44$_1$, עֲבוֹדָה *service*, i.e. work for 1 K 12$_4$||2 C 10$_4$.

דֶּרֶךְ *way* of father 1 K 15$_{26}$ 22$_{43}$||2 C 20$_{32}$ 1 K 22$_{53}$ 2 K 22$_2$||2 C 34$_2$ Ezk 20$_{30}$ 2 C 17$_3$ 21$_{12}$, חֵקֶר *investigation* Jb 8$_8$, מָגוֹר *sojourning* Gn 37$_1$, יְגִיעַ *toil* Jr 3$_{24}$, עֳנִי *affliction* Ne 9$_9$, שֵׁם *name* Gn 48$_{16}$ Nm 27$_4$ Jos 19$_{47}$ Jg 18$_{29}$, דּוֹר *generation* Ps 49$_{20}$, יוֹם pl. *days*, i.e. lifetime Jl 1$_2$ Ml 3$_7$ Ezr 9$_7$, חַיִּים *life* Gn 47$_9$, מָוֶת *death* Est 2$_7$ 2 C 22$_4$, אֵבֶל *mourning*, i.e. mourning for Gn 27$_{41}$.

עָוֹן *evil* of father Ex 20$_5$ 34$_7$ (both + פקד ... עַל־בָּנִים *visit* evil *upon [the] children*) Lv 26$_{39.40}$ Nm 14$_{18}$ Dt 5$_9$ (both + פקד ... עַל־בָּנִים) Is 14$_{21}$ 65$_7$ Jr 11$_{10}$ 14$_{20}$ 32$_{18}$ (+ שׁלם ... אֶל־חֵיק בְּנֵיהֶם pi. *recompense* evil *against their children*) Ezk 18$_{17.19.20}$ Ps 109$_{14}$ Dn 9$_{16}$ Ne 9$_2$ 4QDibHam^a 1.6$_6$ 4QDibHam^c 31$_{12(Baillet)}$ ([עוונות]) 4QBark^a 2.2$_3$, רָעָה *evil* Jr 44$_9$, חַטָּאת *sin* 1 K 15$_3$ Ezk 18$_{14}$, תּוֹעֵבָה *abomination* 20$_4$, גִּלּוּל *idol* 20$_{24}$, מַעַל *treachery* 1QH 4$_{34}$, קָלוֹן *shame* Si 3$_{10}$.

פָּנִים *face* of father Gn 31$_5$ 50$_1$, יָד *hand* 48$_{17}$ 1 S 23$_{17}$ 2 K 13$_{25}$ 2 C 32$_{15}$ (both + מִן *from*), מָתְנַיִם *loins* 1 K 12$_{10}$||2 C 10$_{10}$, עֹרֶף *neck* 2 K 17$_{14}$, קוֹל *voice* Dt 21$_{18}$=11QT 64$_2$ (אביה[ון]) 1 S 2$_{25}$ Jr 35$_8$, נֶפֶשׁ *life* Ezk 18$_4$ (|| בֵּן *child*), לֵב *heart* Ml 3$_{24}$=Si 48$_{10}$ (+ עַל־בָּנִים *toward children*), עֶרְוָה *nakedness* Gn 9$_{22.23.23}$ Lv 18$_{7.8}$ 20$_{11}$ Ezk 22$_{10}$, שְׁאֵר *flesh* Lv 18$_{12}$.

רֹאשׁ *head* of fathers' households (§5) Ex 6$_{25}$ (+ אֵלֶּה *these are*, הַלְוִיִּם *of the Levites*) Nu 31$_{26}$ (+ הָעֵדָה *of the community*) 32$_{28}$ (+ הַמַּטּוֹת *of the tribes*) 36$_1$ (+ נָשִׂיא

chief) Jos 14$_{1}$ (+ הַמַּטּוֹת) 19$_{51}$ (+ לְ heads of fathers' households *of*) 21$_{1}$ (+ הַלְוִיִּם) 21$_{1}$ (+ הַמַּטּוֹת) Ezr 1$_{5}$ (+ לְ *of* Judah & Benjamin; + כֹּהֵן *priest*, לֵוִי *Levite*) 2$_{68}$||Ne 7$_{70}$ (+ מִן *some of*) Ezr 3$_{12}$ (+ הַזְּקֵנִים *the old* heads of fathers' households; + לֵוִי ,כֹּהֵן) 4$_{2.3}$ (+ לְ; + שְׁאָר *rest of*) 8$_{1}$ (+ אֵלֶּה) 10$_{16}$ (+ אִישׁ *man*) Ne 7$_{69}$ (+ מִקְצָת *some of*) 8$_{13}$ (+ לְ *of* Israel; + לֵוִי ,כֹּהֵן) 12$_{12}$ (+ לְ) 12$_{22}$ (both + כֹּהֵן) 12$_{23}$ (+ לֵוִי) 1 C 7$_{11}$ (+ לְ *[arranged] according to*) 8$_{6}$ (+ לְיוֹשְׁבֵי *of the inhabitants of*; + אֵלֶּה הֵם *these are the ones who were*) 8$_{10}$ (+ בֵּן *son*) 8$_{13}$ (+ לְיוֹשְׁבֵי; + הֵמָּה *these are*) 8$_{28}$ (+ אֵלֶּה; + רֹאשׁ *chief*) 9$_{9}$ (+ אִישׁ) 9$_{33}$ (+ שִׁיר pol. ptc. *singer*) 9$_{34}$ (+ רֹאשׁ *chief*; both + אֵלֶּה) 15$_{12}$ (+ אַתֶּם *you are*; all three + לַלְוִיִּם *of the Levites*) 23$_{9}$ (+ לְ) 23$_{24}$ (+ בְּנֵי־לֵוִי *Levites*; both + אֵלֶּה) 24$_{6}$ (+ שַׂר *officer*) 24$_{31}$ (both + לַכֹּהֲנִים וְלַלְוִיִּם *of the priests and of the Levites*; both + מֶלֶךְ *king*) 26$_{21}$ (+ לְ; + בֵּן *son*) 26$_{26}$ (+ לְשָׂרֵי *to the officers of* [or em. וְשָׂרֵי *and the officers of*]; + מֶלֶךְ, שַׂר) 26$_{32}$ (+ בֶּן־חַיִל *capable man*) 27$_{1}$ (+ שַׂר ,שֹׁטֵר *official*) 2 C 1$_{2}$ (+ נָשִׂיא) 19$_{8}$ (+ מִן *some of*; + כֹּהֵן) 23$_{2}$ (both + לְ *of* Israel; both + לֵוִי) 26$_{12}$ (+ לְ; + מִסְפַּר *number of*) 1QSa 1$_{24}$ (על יד ראשי [א]בות העדה *under the control of the heads of fathers' households of the community*) 1$_{25}$ (כול ראשי אבות העדה) 2$_{16}$ ([ר]אשי א[בות הע]דה) 1QM 2$_{7}$ (כול ראשי אבות העדה) 3$_{4}$ (ראשי אבות העדה; + אנשי השם *persons of renown*) 4QApocMos B 1.2$_{8}$.

שַׂר *prince* of fathers' households (§5) Ezr 8$_{29}$ (+ לְיִשְׂרָאֵל *of Israel*; + שָׂרֵי הַכֹּהֲנִים וְהַלְוִיִּם *princes of the priests and Levites*) 1 C 29$_{6}$ (+ וְשָׂרֵי שִׁבְטֵי יִשְׂרָאֵל *and the princes of the tribes of Israel*) 1QSa 1$_{16(erased)}$ (+ כֹּהֵן *priest*), נָשִׂיא *prince* 1 K 8$_{1}$||2 C 5$_{2}$ (+ רָאשֵׁי הַמַּטּוֹת *the heads of tribes*).

אֱלֹהֵי אָבִי *God of my father* Gn 31$_{5.42}$ 32$_{10.10}$ Ex 15$_{2}$ 18$_{4}$ Si 51$_{1}$, אֱלֹהֵי אֲבֹתֵינוּ *God of our ancestors* Dt 26$_{7}$ Ezr 7$_{27}$ 1 C 12$_{18}$ 29$_{18}$ 2 C 20$_{6}$ 1QM 13$_{7}$ (אֵל).

אֱלֹהֵי אָבִיךָ *God of your* (sg.) *father/ancestor* 46$_{3}$ 49$_{25}$ (אֵל) 50$_{17}$ Ex 3$_{6}$ 2 K 20$_{5}$||Is 38$_{5}$ 1 C 28$_{9}$ 2 C 21$_{12}$, אֱלֹהֵי אֲבֹתֶיךָ *God of your* (sg.) *ancestors* Dt 1$_{21}$ 6$_{3}$ 12$_{1}$ 27$_{3}$ (אֱלֹהֵי־), אֱלֹהֵי אֲבִיכֶם *God of your* (pl.) *father* Gn 31$_{29}$ 43$_{23}$, אֱלֹהֵי אֲבֹתֵיכֶם *God of your* (pl.) *ancestors* Ex 3$_{13.15.16}$ Dt 1$_{11}$ 4$_{1}$ Jos 18$_{3}$ Ezr 8$_{28}$ 10$_{11}$ 1 C 13$_{12}$ 2 C 28$_{9}$ (אֱלֹהֵי־) 29$_{5}$ 11QT 54$_{13}$.

אֱלֹהֵי אָבִיו *God of his father* Gn 46$_{1}$ 2 C 17$_{4}$, אֱלֹהֵי אֲבִיהֶם *God of their*, i.e. each one's, *father* Gn 31$_{53}$, אֱלֹהֵי אֲבֹתָיו *God of his ancestors* 2 K 21$_{22}$ Dn 11$_{37}$ (אֱלֹהֵי = *gods of*) 2 C 21$_{10}$ 28$_{25}$ 30$_{19}$ 33$_{12}$, אֱלֹהֵי אֲבוֹתֵיהֶם *God of their ancestors* Ex 4$_{5}$ Dt 29$_{24}$ Jg 2$_{12}$ (all three אֲבֹתָם) 1 C 5$_{25}$ 29$_{20}$ 2 C 7$_{22}$ 11$_{16}$ 13$_{18}$ 14$_{3}$ 15$_{12}$ 19$_{4}$ 20$_{33}$ 24$_{18.24}$ 28$_{6}$ (אֲבֹתָם) 30$_{7.22}$ 34$_{32.33}$ 36$_{15}$ 4Q385 1$_{8}$.

פַּחַד אָבִיו *fear of his father* Gn 31$_{53}$, מִקְוֵה אֲבוֹתֵיהֶם *hope of their ancestors* Jr 50$_{7}$, כָּל־אֲבוֹתָי *all my ancestors* Ps 39$_{13}$, כָּל־אֲבֹתֵינוּ *all our ancestors* 1 C 29$_{15}$.

<APP> אָב *father, ancestor (of)* preceded by pr.n.m., Ham Gn 9$_{22}$, Shem 10$_{21}$, Kemuel 22$_{21}$, Esau 36$_{9.43}$, Terah 11$_{28}$ Jos 24$_{2}$, Abraham Gn 22$_{7}$ 26$_{3.15.18.24}$ 28$_{13}$ Is 51$_{2}$ 1 C 29$_{18}$ Si 44$_{19.22}$, Isaac Gn 27$_{22.26.30.32.39}$ 28$_{8}$ 31$_{18}$ 35$_{27}$ 1 C 29$_{18}$, Bethuel Gn 28$_{2}$, Hamor 33$_{19}$ 34$_{4.6.13}$ Jos 24$_{32}$ Jg 9$_{28}$, Arba Jos 15$_{13}$ 21$_{11}$ (both + קִרְיַת *city of*), Zibeon Gn 36$_{24}$, Jacob (Israel) 42$_{29.36}$ 43$_{8.11}$ 45$_{25.27}$ (+ רוּחַ *spirit* of) 46$_{5.29}$ 47$_{7}$ 49$_{2}$ Is 58$_{14}$ 1 C 29$_{18}$ 4QTNaph 2$_{7.10}$ (יעקו[ב]), Dan Jos 19$_{47}$ Jg 18$_{29}$, Ephraim 1 C 7$_{22}$, Reuel Ex 2$_{18}$, Aaron Nm 3$_{4}$ 1 C 24$_{19}$, Jonadab Jr 35$_{6.8.10}$ Machir Jos 17$_{1}$ 1 C 2$_{21.23}$ 7$_{14}$, Ashhur 2$_{24}$ 4$_{5}$, Hezron 2$_{24}$ (if em. אֲבִיָּה *Abijah* to אָבִיהוּ/אָבִיהָ *his* [Caleb's] *father*), Mareshah 2$_{42}$, Raham 2$_{44}$, Shaaph 2$_{49}$, Sheva 2$_{49}$, Shobal 2$_{50.52}$, Salma 2$_{51}$, Hareph 2$_{51}$, Hammath 2$_{55}$, Ephrathah 4$_{4}$ (+ בְּכוֹר *first-born* of), Tehinnah 4$_{12}$, Joab 4$_{14}$, Ishbah 4$_{17}$, Jered 4$_{18}$, Heber 4$_{18}$, Jekuthiel 4$_{18}$, Er 4$_{21}$, Laadah 4$_{21}$, Rotheos 4QTNaph 2$_{8}$ (רתיו[ס]), Joash Jg 8$_{32}$, Manoah 16$_{31}$, Kish 1 S 9$_{3}$ 14$_{51}$ (unless קִישׁ אֲבִי־שָׁאוּל = *Kish was the father of Saul*) 2 S 21$_{14}$, Jesse Ru 4$_{17}$, Ner 1 S 14$_{51}$, Saul 19$_{4}$ 20$_{32}$ 23$_{17.17}$ 2 S 3$_{8}$ 9$_{7}$, Jonathan 9$_{7}$, David 1 K 2$_{12.24}$ 2$_{26.44}$ 3$_{3.6}$||2 C 1$_{8}$ 1 K 3$_{7.14}$ 5$_{17.19}$ 6$_{12}$ 7$_{51}$||2 C 5$_{1}$ 1 K 8$_{15.17}$||2 C 6$_{4.7}$ (+ לֵבָב *heart* of) 1 K 8$_{18.20.24.25}$||2 C 6$_{8.10.15.16}$ 1 K 8$_{26}$ 9$_{4.5}$||2 C 7$_{17.18}$ 1 K 11$_{4}$ (+ לֵבָב) 11$_{6.12.27}$ (+ עִיר *city* of) 11$_{33.43}$||2 C 9$_{31}$ (+ עִיר) 1 K 15$_{3}$ (+ לֵבָב) 15$_{11.24}$ 22$_{51}$ (both + עִיר) 2 K 14$_{3}$ 15$_{38}$ (+ עִיר) 16$_{2}$||2 C 28$_{1}$ 2 K 18$_{3}$||2 C 29$_{2}$ 2 K 20$_{5}$||Is 38$_{5}$ 2 K 22$_{2}$||2 C 34$_{2}$ 1 C 29$_{23}$ 2 C 1$_{9}$ 2$_{2.6.13}$ (+ חָכָם pl. *wise ones*, i.e. craftsmen, of) 2$_{16}$ 3$_{1}$ 8$_{14}$ (+ מִשְׁפָּט *judgment* of) 17$_{3}$ 21$_{12}$ 34$_{3}$, Solomon 1 K 12$_{6}$||2 C 10$_{6}$, Asa 1 K 22$_{43.47}$ 2 C 17$_{2}$, Jehoshaphat 21$_{12}$, Ahab 2 K 9$_{25}$, Jehoiada 2 C 24$_{22}$, Joash 2 K 14$_{3}$, Jehoahaz 13$_{25}$, Amaziah 15$_{3}$||2 C 26$_{4}$, Uzziah 2 K 15$_{34}$||2 C 27$_{2}$, Hezekiah 2 K 21$_{3}$||2 C 33$_{3}$, Manasseh

2 K 21$_{20}$||2 C 33$_{22.23}$, Josiah 2 K 23$_{34}$ Jr 22$_{11}$.

With name following, Jeiel 1 C 9$_{35(Qr)}$, Abraham Gn 32$_{10}$ Jos 24$_{3}$, Isaac Gn 31$_{53}$ 32$_{10}$ 46$_{1}$, David 1 K 2$_{32}$, Asa 2 C 20$_{32}$, Amaziah 2 K 14$_{21}$||2 C 26$_{1}$, Jeduthun 1 C 25$_{3}$; Jehoshaphat and Jehoram and Ahaziah, his ancestors, kings of Judah 2 K 12$_{19}$.

יי ... אָבִינוּ *Y. ... our father* 1 C 29$_{10}$, חֹתְנוֹ אֲבִי הַנַּעֲרָה *his father-in-law, the father of the girl* Jg 19$_{4.9}$, עַבְדְּךָ אָבִי *your servant, my father* Gn 44$_{24.27.30}$, sim. 43$_{28}$ 44$_{31}$, הַמֶּלֶךְ אָבִיו *the king, his father* 2 K 14$_{5}$||2 C 25$_{3}$.

<ADJ> אָב אֶחָד *one father* Ml 2$_{10}$, אָב זָקֵן *old father* Gn 43$_{27}$ 44$_{20}$, אב רשע *wicked father* Si 41$_{7}$, אָבִיךָ הָרִאשׁוֹן *your first ancestor* Is 43$_{27}$, אבותינו הרישנים *our first ancestors* 1QM 10$_{18}$ + Sup 4QDibHam^{c} 31$_{12}$.

<PREP> לְ of direction, *to*, + בוא hi. *bring* Gn 27$_{10.31}$, שׁלח *send* 45$_{23}$, נתן *give* Dt 1$_{35}$ 19$_{8}$ 22$_{19}$=11QT 65$_{15}$ Dt 22$_{29}$=11QT 66$_{10}$ Jos 21$_{43}$ 1 K 8$_{34.40.48}$||2 C 6$_{25.31.38}$ 1 K 14$_{15}$ 2 K 21$_{8}$ Jr 7$_{7.14}$ 16$_{15}$ 23$_{39}$ 24$_{10}$ 25$_{5}$ 30$_{3}$ 32$_{22}$ 35$_{15}$ Ezk 20$_{42}$ 36$_{28}$ 47$_{14}$ Ne 9$_{36}$ 4Q185 1.2$_{14}$, אמר *say* to Gn 27$_{31.34}$ Dt 33$_{9}$ (לְ = *concerning*), Is 45$_{10}$ Ne 9$_{23}$, דבר pi. *speak* 1 K 8$_{26}$ Dn 9$_{6}$ 11QT 55$_{12}$, ספר pi. *relate* 1 K 13$_{11}$, נגד hi. *tell* Gn 29$_{12}$ 45$_{13}$ Jg 14$_{2.6.16}$ 1 S 14$_{1}$, שׁבע ni. *swear* Ex 13$_{5.11}$ Nm 11$_{12}$ 14$_{23}$ Dt 1$_{8}$ 6$_{10.18.23}$ 7$_{8.12.13}$ 8$_{1.18}$ 9$_{5}$ 10$_{11}$ 11$_{9.21}$ 13$_{18}$ 19$_{8}$ 26$_{3.15}$ 28$_{11}$ 29$_{12}$ 30$_{20}$ 31$_{7.20}$ Jos 1$_{6}$ 5$_{6}$ 21$_{44}$ Jg 2$_{1}$ Jr 11$_{5}$ 32$_{22}$ Mc 7$_{20}$ 4QJub^{a} 2$_{2}$ (נשבעתי] [לאבותיהם]), שׁמע *listen* Pr 23$_{22}$, ראה לְ ni. *appear to* 2 C 3$_{1}$.

לְ of benefit, *to, for* Gn 27$_{9}$ 45$_{23}$, + עשׂה *do* 50$_{10}$ Jg 9$_{56}$ 1 K 2$_{44}$, טמא htp. *defile oneself* Lv 21$_{2.11}$ Nm 6$_{7}$ Ezk 44$_{25}$, עמד hi. *establish* 2 C 33$_{8}$, שׁמר *keep* promise 1 K 8$_{24.25}$||2 C 6$_{15.16}$, רעה *tend* asses Gn 36$_{24}$, כַּעַס לְ *vexation for* Pr 17$_{25}$, הַוֹּת לְ *disaster for* 19$_{13}$, מִשְׁפָּט לְ *judgment for* CD 16$_{12}$, of possession, *belonging to, of* Gn 29$_{9}$ 31$_{1.1.19}$ 43$_{28}$ Jg 6$_{25.25}$ 1 S 17$_{34}$ Dn 9$_{8}$ Si 42$_{9}$, + היה *be* Nm 27$_{11}$ Pr 4$_{3}$ 1 C 25$_{2}$ 4$_{5}$.

כרת לְ *make (covenant) with* 2 C 7$_{18}$ 1QM 13$_{7}$ ([כ]רתה), שׁמר לְ *keep* covenant *with* 14$_{8}$, חטא לְ *sin against* Gn 44$_{32}$, היה לְ *be as* 17$_{4}$ Jg 17$_{10}$ 18$_{19}$ (both || כֹּהֵן *priest*) 2 S 7$_{14}$||1 C 17$_{13}$ (|| בֵּן *son*) Is 22$_{21}$ Jr 31$_{9}$ 1 C 22$_{10}$ 28$_{6}$ (both || בֵּן), שׂים לְ *place, appoint as* Gn 45$_{8}$ (+ לְפַרְעֹה *to Pharaoh*; || אָדוֹן *lord*), נשׁק לְ *kiss* 1 K 19$_{20}$, לעג לְ *mock* Pr 30$_{17}$, רעע לְ hi. *hurt* Nm 20$_{15}$, נשׂא לְ *forgive* 4QDibHam^{a} 1.2$_{8}$ ([נ]שא[תה]), לְאָבוֹת *(arranged) according to (their) fathers* (cf. §4) 1 C 6$_{4}$ (לַאֲבוֹתֵיהֶם) 26$_{31}$ (|| תּוֹלְדָה *generation*).

היה בְּ *be against* 1 S 12$_{15}$, קדשׁ בְּ htp. *sanctify oneself because of* 2 C 31$_{18}$ (if em. בֶּאֱמוּנָתָם *in their office of trust*), משפטו בנו ובאבותי[נו] *his judgment on us and on our fathers* 1QS 1$_{26}$, חשׁק בְּ *desire* Dt 10$_{15}$, בחר בְּ *choose* 4QD^{b} 1$_{1}$ (בח[ר]תה), עוד בְּ hi. *warn* Jr 11$_{7}$.

כְּ *as* Ps 39$_{13}$ 78$_{8}$ 1 C 29$_{15}$, + היה *be* Zc 1$_{4}$ 2 C 30$_{7}$ Si 4$_{10}$ (+ ליתומים *to orphans*; || בַּעַל *husband*), עשׂה *do* 1 K 11$_{33}$ 15$_{11}$ (in both obj. יָשָׁר *right*) 2 K 3$_{2}$ (obj. רַע *evil*) 14$_{3}$ 16$_{2}$||2 C 28$_{1}$ (in both obj. יָשָׁר), גדל *grow up* Jb 31$_{18}$ (or em. גְּדֵלַנִי *he grew up to me* to גִּדְּלַנִי *he* (Y.) *reared me* or אֲגַדְּלֶנּוּ *I shall rear him*), pi. *raise* child 31$_{18}$ (if em.), רצה *like* Pr 3$_{12}$, רחם pi. *have pity* CD 13$_{9}$ (+ לבניו *to his children*), מלא pi. *wholly follow* Y. 1 K 11$_{6}$, בגד *be treacherous* Ps 78$_{57}$, סוג ni. *depart* 78$_{57}$, קשׁה hi. *harden* neck 2 C 30$_{8}$, כאב לאיש כן אבריהו *as a father is to a person, thus are his limbs* 4Q416 10.2$_{17}$.

מִן of direction, *from*, + נצל hi. *seize* Gn 31$_{16}$, כחד pi. *hide* Jb 15$_{18}$, בוא *come* 1 C 2$_{55}$, שׁמע *hear* Si 5$_{9}$, of instrument, *by means of*, + חיה pi. *preserve alive* Gn 19$_{32.34}$, הרה hi. *become pregnant* 19$_{36}$, of comparison, *(more) than* 1 K 19$_{4}$ Jb 15$_{10}$, + שׁחת hi. *act corruptly* Jg 2$_{19}$, רעע *do evil* Jr 7$_{26}$ 16$_{12}$, בחר *choose* David 2 S 6$_{21}$, יטב hi. *do good (to)* offspring Dt 30$_{5}$, רבה *multiply* offspring 30$_{5}$, בושׁ מִן *be ashamed because of* Si 41$_{17}$, מאבי ידעתני perh. *from my father*, i.e. from his begetting me, *you have known me* 1QH 9$_{29}$.

אֶל of direction, *to*, + בוא *come* Gn 15$_{15}$ 27$_{10}$ 31$_{18}$ 35$_{27}$ 42$_{29}$ 44$_{30}$ 45$_{25}$ Ex 2$_{18}$, hi. *bring* Gn 27$_{18}$ 37$_{2.32}$, הלך *go* Jg 14$_{9}$, נגשׁ *approach* Gn 27$_{22}$, יצא *go out* 2 K 4$_{18}$, עלה *go up* Gn 44$_{17.24.34}$ 45$_{9}$, שׁוב *go back* Jg 11$_{39}$, hi. *take back* Gn 37$_{22}$, אסף *gather* to ancestors 2 C 34$_{28}$ (||2 K 22$_{20}$ עַל; || קֶבֶר *grave*), ni. *be gathered* Jg 2$_{10}$, אמר *say* Gn 27$_{19.38}$ 31$_{35}$ 34$_{4.11}$ 42$_{37}$ 43$_{8}$ 48$_{9.18}$ Jg 11$_{37}$ 14$_{3}$ 1 K 8$_{18}$||2 C 6$_{8}$ 2 K 4$_{19}$, דבר pi. *speak* 1 S 19$_{3.4}$ 1 K 5$_{19}$ 6$_{12}$ Dn 9$_{6}$, ספר pi. *tell* Gn 37$_{10}$, שׁמע *listen* 28$_{7}$ 49$_{2}$ Dt 21$_{18}$=11QT 64$_{2}$, נבט hi. *look* at Is 51$_{2}$, קבר אֶל *bury with* Gn 49$_{29}$, יטב אֶל hi. *be pleasing to* 1 S 20$_{13}$, נחם אֶל pi. *console regarding* 2 S 10$_{2}$ (||1 C 19$_{2}$ עַל).

עַל *on account of* Jr 16$_{7}$, + מות *die* 2 C 25$_{4}$, ho. *be put to death* Dt 24$_{16}$ 2 K 14$_{6}$, לְבַד מִמְכָּרָיו עַל־הָאָבוֹת perh. *apart from his sales on account of the ancestors*, i.e. *apart from inherited wealth* Dt 18$_{8}$=11QT 60$_{15}$ (ממכר), דבר עַל pi. *say to*, i.e. promise 1 K 9$_{5}$, אמר עַל *say concerning* Jr 16$_{3}$, שׂושׂ עַל *rejoice in* Dt 30$_{9}$, נחם עַל pi. *console regarding* 1 C 19$_{2}$ (||2 S 10$_{2}$ אֶל), קצף עַל *be angry with* Zc 1$_{2}$, שׁוב עַל hi. *turn* heart *toward* Ml 3$_{24}$, אסף עַל *gather to* ancestors 2 K 22$_{20}$ (||2 C 34$_{28}$ אֶל).

תַּחַת *instead of*, + היה *be* Ps 45$_{17}$, מלך *reign* Jr 22$_{11}$, hi. *make king* 1 K 3$_{7}$ 2 K 14$_{21}$||2 C 26$_{1}$ 2 K 23$_{30}$||2 C 36$_{1}$ 2 K 23$_{34}$, משׁח *anoint* as king 1 K 5$_{15}$, ישׁב *sit*, i.e. be enthroned 1 C 29$_{23}$, קום *arise*, i.e. succeed to throne 1 K 8$_{20}$||2 C 6$_{10}$, כהן pi. *serve as priest* Lv 16$_{32}$, לבשׁ *be clothed* in priestly garments 11QT 15$_{16}$ (ללובן]שׁ ... [אבי]הו).

אֶת *with* Gn 42$_{13.32}$, + שׁכב *lie down* for sex Gn 19$_{33.34}$, in grave 2 S 7$_{12}$, דבר pi. *speak* 1 K 8$_{15}$||2 C 6$_{4}$ Jr 7$_{22}$, עשׂה *do* 1 S 12$_{7}$, שׁפט ni. *enter dispute* Ezk 20$_{36}$, כרת *make (covenant)* Dt 5$_{3}$ 2 K 17$_{15}$ Jr 11$_{10}$ 31$_{32}$ 34$_{13}$, באשׁ אֶת ni. *be loathsome to* 2 S 16$_{21}$.

עִם *with* 2 C 1$_{9}$, + היה *be* 1 S 20$_{13}$ 1 K 8$_{57}$, חטא *sin* Ps 106$_{6}$, כרת *make (covenant)* 1 K 8$_{21}$, שׁכב *lie down* in grave (alw. with אָבוֹת *ancestors*) Gn 47$_{30}$ Dt 31$_{16}$ 1 K 1$_{21}$ 2$_{10}$ 11$_{21.43}$||2 C 9$_{31}$ 1 K 14$_{20.31}$||2 C 12$_{16}$ 1 K 15$_{8}$||2 C 13$_{23}$ 1 K 15$_{24}$||2 C 16$_{13}$ 1 K 16$_{6.28}$ 22$_{40.51}$||2 C 21$_{1}$ 2 K 8$_{24}$ 10$_{35}$ 13$_{9.13}$ 14$_{16.22}$||2 C 26$_{2}$ 2 K 14$_{29}$ 15$_{7}$||2 C 26$_{23}$ 2 K 15$_{22.38}$||2 C 27$_{9}$ 2 K 16$_{20}$||2 C 28$_{27}$ 2 K 20$_{21}$||2 C 32$_{33}$ 2 K 21$_{18}$||2 C 33$_{20}$ 2 K 24$_{6}$ 4Q464 3.2$_{5}$ ([אבותיו]), קבר *bury* 2 K 9$_{28}$ 12$_{22}$ 15$_{7}$||2 C 26$_{23}$ 2 C 25$_{28}$, ni. *be buried* 1 K 14$_{31}$ 15$_{24}$ 22$_{51}$||2 C 21$_{1}$ 2 K 8$_{24}$ 14$_{20}$ 15$_{38}$ 16$_{20}$, הלך *walk* 1 C 17$_{11}$, עשׂה עִם *do for* 2 C 2$_{2}$, עשׂה חֶסֶד עִם *show loyalty to* 1 K 3$_{6}$||2 C 1$_{8}$.

בוא עַד hi. *bring to* 1 S 20$_{8}$; ערב מֵעִם *take on pledge from* Gn 44$_{32}$, כלה מֵעִם *be determined by* 1 S 20$_{9.33}$; מֵאֵת *from*, + לקח *take* 1 K 20$_{34}$, שׁאל *ask* Jg 1$_{14}$; לִפְנֵי *before*, of space, + עבד *serve* 2 S 16$_{19}$, נשׂא *bear* ark 1 K 2$_{26}$, עמד *stand* 2 C 10$_{6}$ (||1 K 12$_{6}$ אֶת־פְּנֵי), נתן *place* Jr 44$_{10}$, of time, + מות *die* 1 C 24$_{2}$, *against*, חַטָּאתִי לִפְנֵי *my sin against* 1 S 20$_{1}$; עמד אֶת־פְּנֵי *stand before* 1 K 12$_{6}$ (||2 C 10$_{6}$ לִפְנֵי); עמד לְיַד *stand next to* 1 S 19$_{3}$; עשׂה נֶגֶד *do in the presence of* Ps 78$_{12}$; בְּיַד *by (order of)* 1 C 24$_{19}$; עַל יְדֵי *under the charge of* 1 C 25$_{3.6}$.

בֵּין אָבִי וּבֵין אָבִיךָ *between my father and your father* 1 K 15$_{19}$||2 C 16$_{3}$, בֵּין־אָב לְבִתּוֹ *between a father and his daughter* Nm 30$_{17}$ (+ בֵּין אִישׁ לְאִשְׁתּוֹ *between a man and his wife*); א[צל] אביך *with your father* Mur 45$_{5(\text{Milik})}$; אַחֲרֵי *after*, + רדף *pursue* Jos 24$_{6}$, רכב *ride* 2 K 9$_{25}$; לְמַעַן *because of* 1 K 11$_{12}$; בַּעֲבוּר *on account of* Si 44$_{22}$.

<COLL> אָבִי in exclamations, *oh, my father* Gn 22$_{7}$ 27$_{18.38}$ 48$_{18}$ 2 K 2$_{12.12}$ 5$_{13}$ 6$_{21}$ 13$_{14.14}$ Is 8$_{4}$ Jr 3$_{4.19}$, as vocative, *O my father* Gn 27$_{34.38}$ Jg 11$_{36}$ 1 S 24$_{12}$ 4Q473 1$_{16}$.

הֵמָּה וַאֲבִיהֶם *they and their father* Gn 42$_{35}$, הֵמָּה וַאֲבוֹתָם *they and their ancestors* Jr 9$_{15}$ Ezk 2$_{3}$, var. Jr 19$_{4}$ 4QpsMos[e] 1$_{7}$, אֲנִי וַאֲבוֹתַי *I and my ancestors* 2 C 32$_{13}$, אֲנַחְנוּ וַאֲבוֹתֵינוּ *we and our ancestors* Jr 3$_{25}$ 44$_{17}$, var. 1QS 1$_{25}$ ([וא]בותינו), sim. Gn 47$_{3}$ 1QS 1$_{26}$ (ואבותי[נו]) CD 20$_{29}$, אַתָּה וַאֲבֹתֶיךָ *you* (sg.) *and your ancestors* Dt 13$_{7}$ 28$_{36.64}$, אַתֶּם וַאֲבוֹתֵיכֶם *you* (pl.) *and your ancestors* Jr 16$_{13}$ 44$_{3.21}$.

אִישׁ וְאָבִיו *a man and his father* Am 2$_{7}$, אֲבֹתֶיךָ וַאֲבוֹת אֲבֹתֶיךָ *your fathers and your fathers' fathers* Ex 10$_{6}$, sim. Dn 11$_{24}$, וְהָאָבוֹת וְהַבָּנִים יַחְדָּו *the parents and the children together* Jr 13$_{14}$, אֵין אָב *without a father* Lm 5$_{3}$.

אָב ... אֵם *father ... mother* Gn 2$_{24}$ 20$_{12}$ 28$_{7}$ Ex 20$_{12}$ 21$_{15.17}$ Lv 18$_{7.9}$ 20$_{9.17}$ 21$_{11}$ Nm 6$_{7}$ (+ אָח *brother*, אָחוֹת *sister*) Dt 5$_{16}$ 21$_{13}$=11QT 63$_{13}$ Dt 21$_{18.19}$=11QT 64$_{2(\text{Yadin}).3}$ Dt 22$_{15}$=11QT 65$_{9}$ Dt 27$_{16.22}$ 33$_{9}$ (+ בֵּן *child*) Jos 2$_{13}$ (+ אָחוֹת) 2$_{18}$ 6$_{23}$ (all four + אָח) Jg 14$_{2+6t}$ 1 S 22$_{3}$ 2 S 19$_{38}$ 1 K 19$_{20}$ 22$_{53}$ 2 K 3$_{2.13}$ Is 8$_{4}$ Jr 16$_{7}$ Ezk 16$_{3}$ 22$_{7}$ (+ גֵּר *foreigner*, יָתוֹם *orphan*, אַלְמָנָה *widow*) 44$_{25}$ (+ בֵּן *son*, בַּת *daughter*, אָח, אָחוֹת) Mc 7$_{6}$ (+ חָמוֹת *husband's mother*) Zc 13$_{3.3}$ Ps 27$_{10}$ Jb 17$_{14}$ (+ אָחוֹת) Pr 1$_{8}$ 4$_{3}$ 6$_{20}$ 10$_{1}$ 15$_{20}$ 19$_{26}$ 20$_{20}$ 23$_{22.25}$ 28$_{24}$ 30$_{11.17}$ Ru 2$_{11}$ Est 2$_{7}$ Si 3$_{9.16}$ 41$_{17}$ 11QT 54$_{19}$ 66$_{13.14.15}$ 1QH 9$_{29.35}$ 4Q251 7$_{2}$ ([אביו ... אמו]) 7$_{4}$ (א[ביו ... אמו]) 7$_{4}$ 4Q416 10.2$_{16.17}$, var. Lv 19$_{3}$ 20$_{19}$ 21$_{2}$ (+ אָח) Jr 16$_{3}$ (אִמּוֹת ... אָבוֹת; both + בֵּן, בַּת) Ezk 16$_{45}$, non-parallelistic Gn 27$_{14}$ 37$_{10}$ (+ אָח) 44$_{20}$ 2 K 4$_{19}$ Si 3$_{11}$.

אָב ... אָח/אַחִים *father ... brother(s)* Gn 28$_{2}$ 34$_{11}$ 37$_{10}$ 43$_{7}$ 44$_{19.20}$ 47$_{1.5.6.11.12}$ (+ בֵּית אָב *father's household*) Lv 21$_{2}$ (+ אֵם, בֵּן, בַּת) Nm 6$_{7}$ (+ אֵם, אָחוֹת) Dt 33$_{9}$ (+ בֵּן) Jos 2$_{13}$ (+ אָחוֹת) 2$_{18}$ (+ בֵּית אָב) 6$_{23}$ (all four + אֵם) Jg 21$_{22}$

Ezk 44$_{25}$ (+ אָחוֹת, בַּת, בֵּן, אֵם), var. Gn 37$_{11}$, non-parallelistic Gn 9$_{22}$ 27$_{6.30.41}$ 37$_{4.12}$ 42$_{13.32}$ 45$_{3}$ 50$_{14.15}$ Jg 9$_{5.56}$ 16$_{31}$ 2 S 3$_{8}$ (+ מֵרֵעַ *friend*) Isa 3$_{6}$ Ezk 18$_{18}$ Jb 42$_{15}$ 1 C 7$_{22}$ 2 C 21$_{4}$. Very freq. is בֵּן ... אָב *father/parent ... son/child*.

Also 4QRitMar 15$_{1}$ 39$_{3}$ (אב[ינו]) 1QNoah 3$_{4}$ 5QRègle 22$_{7}$ 4QCat^{a} 1$_{11}$ 4QShir^{b} 127$_{1}$ Samaria-Sebaste ost. 9$_{2}$ 4Q521 3.2$_{9}$ 4QapPs^{b} 93$_{1}$.

→ אבא *Abba*, אבאחי *Abahai*, אבגר *Abgar*, אֲבִיאֵל *Abiel*, אֲבִיגַיִל *Abigail*, אֲבִידָן *Abidan*, אֲבִידָע *Abida*, אֲבִיָּה *Abijah*, אֲבִיהוּא *Abihu*, אֲבִיהוּד *Abihud*, אֲבִיהַיִל *Abihail*, אביחי *Abihai*, אֲבִיטוּב *Abitub*, אֲבִיטַל *Abital*, אֲבִיָם *Abijam*, אֲבִימָאֵל *Abimael*, אֲבִימֶלֶךְ *Abimelek*, אֲבִינָדָב *Abinadab*, אֲבִינֹעַם *Abinoam*, אֶבְיָסָף *Ebiasaph*, אֲבִיעֶזֶר *Abiezer*, אֲבִי־עַלְבוֹן *Abi-albon*, אֲבִירָם *Abiram*, אֲבִישַׁג *Abishag*, אֲבִישׁוּעַ *Abishua*, אֲבִישׁוּר *Abishur*, אֲבִישַׁי *Abishai*, אֶבְיָתָר *Abiathar*, אבמעץ *Abmaaz*, אַבְנֵר *Abner*, אבבעל *Abibaal*, אַבְרָהָם *Abraham*, אבריהו *Abraiah*, אַבְרָם *Abram*, אַבְשָׁלוֹם *Absalom*, אבשעל *Abshaal*, אָהֳלִיאָב *Oholiab*, אֱלִיאָב *Eliab*.

[אֵב] 2.0.1 n.m. **greenness**—sf. אִבּוֹ; pl. cstr. אִבֵּי—in ref. to flowering, blossoming of plants, עֹדֶנּוּ בְאִבּוֹ לֹא יִקָּטֵף ... יִיבָשׁ *... while it* (papyrus) *is still in its flower (and) it is not cut down ... it withers* Jb 8$_{12}$, לִרְאוֹת בְּאִבֵּי הַנָּחַל *to look at the blossoms of the valley* Ca 6$_{11}$ (+ פָּרְחָה *sprouting*, הֵנֵצוּ *blossoming*), כול האב אשר בתוכו קודש *all the greenness that is in its middle*, i.e. in the garden of Eden, *is holiness* 4Q251 3$_{14}$.

→ אָבִיב *ear (of cereal)*.

אֹב, see אוֹב I–II.

אבא 0.0.0.3 pr.n.m. **Abba, 1.** Seal 160$_{1}$ (Jerusalem, 5th cent.). **2.** Seal 204 (Revadim, 7th cent.). **3.** Seal 485 (Beirut, 8th cent.).

→ אָב *father*.

[אבאחי] pr.n.m. **Abahai,** Seal 105 (אב[אח]י; Samaria, 8th cent.).

→ אָב *father*.

אבבעל 0.0.0.1 pr.n.m. **Abibaal, 1.** Samaria ost. 2$_{4}$. **2.** one of David's warriors, appar. ident. with Abi-albon (אֲבִי־עַלְבוֹן) at 2 S 23$_{31}$, 1 C 11$_{32}$ (if em. אֲבִיאֵל *Abiel* to אֲבִיבַעַל *Abibaal*).

→ אָב *father* + בַּעַל *Baal*.

[אבגד], see אַבְגָּר.

[אֲבִגַיִל], see אֲבִיגַיִל.

[אַבְגָּר] pr.n. **Abgar** Lachish ost. 24 (others אבגד *Avigad* or alphabetic sequence).

אֲבַגְתָא 1 pr.n.m. **Abagtha,** eunuch at court of Ahasuerus Est 1$_{10}$.

אבד 185.11.30 vb. **die, be destroyed, disappear, be lost—Qal** Pf. אָבַד (אָבֶד), אָבְדָה (אָבֵדָה), אָבַדְתָּ, אָבַדְתְּ, אָבַדְתִּי (אָבֵדְתִּי), אָבְדוּ (אָבֵדוּ), אָבַדְנוּ (אָבֵדְנוּ); impf. יֹאבַד (יֹאבֵד), תֹּאבַד (תֹּאבֵד, Q תובד), יֹאבְדוּ (יֹאבֵדוּ, Q יבדו, יובדו), תֹּאבְדוּ (תֹּאבֵדוּ), תֹּאבַדְנָה, תֹּאבֵדוּן, נֹאבֵד (נֹאבְדָה); + waw וְאָבַד, וְאָבְדָה, וְאָבְדוּ (וְאָבֵדוּ), וַאֲבַדְתֶּם; וַיֹּאבְדוּ, וַתֹּאבַדְנָה, Si ויאבד; ptc. אֹבֵד (אוֹבֵד), cstr. אֹבַד, אוֹבֶדֶת (Q אובדה), אוֹבְדִים, אוֹבְדוֹת; pass. Si אבוד; inf. אָבֹד, אֲבֹד, אַבֶּדְךָ (אָבְדְךָ), אֲבָדְכֶם, אָבְדָם (Q [א]ובדם).

1a. die, be destroyed, disappear, of persons, oft. as divine judgment, **<SUBJ>** Israel Lv 26$_{38}$ Dt 4$_{26.26}$ (אָבֹד תֹּאבֵדוּן *you will be utterly destroyed*; :: תַּאֲרִיכֻן יָמִים *you will live long*) 8$_{19.19}$ (אָבֹד תֹּאבֵדוּן) 8$_{20}$ 11$_{17}$ 28$_{20}$ (‖ שׁמד ni. *be exterminated*) 28$_{22}$ 30$_{18.18}$ (אָבֹד תֹּאבֵדוּן; :: תַּאֲרִיכֻן יָמִים) Jos 23$_{13.16}$ Jer 27$_{10.15}$ Ob$_{12.13}$ (if em. אֵידוֹ *his disaster* to אָבְדוֹ *his perishing*) CD 3$_{9.10}$ Mur 45$_{7}$, remnant of Judah Jr 40$_{15}$; other nations Dt 7$_{20}$ Is 60$_{12}$ (‖ חָרֹב יֶחֱרָבוּ *will be utterly laid waste*) Ps 10$_{16}$, remnant of Philistines Am 1$_{8}$, Moab Nm 21$_{29.30}$, Cain Nm 24$_{24}$ (if em. אֹבֵד unto *destruction* to אָבַד יֹאבֵד *he will perish* unto *eternity*), Egypt Ex 10$_{7}$, Egyptians 4QPentPar^{b} 6.2$_{5}$, Tyre Ezk 26$_{17}$, Ninevites Jon 3$_{9}$; humans in general Jb 4$_{20}$, בָּשָׂר *flesh* 4QapPs^{b} 29$_{3}$ (כל בש[ר]), רבים *many* 4QpIsa^{a} 2$_{4}$ ([יוב]דו) 4QJub^{a} 2$_{7}$ (אבדו [רבי]ם); family of Korah Nm 16$_{33}$, of Ahab 2 K 9$_{8}$, of Esther Est 4$_{14}$; the foolish Ps 49$_{11}$, those far from God

73$_{27}$ (|| צמת hi. *put an end to*), those incensed against Israel Is 41$_{11}$ (|| היה כְּאַיִן *become as nothing*), cities and families 4QpNah 3.2$_{9}$, Yahweh's enemies Jg 5$_{31}$ Ps 80$_{17}$ 83$_{18}$ (|| בהל ni. *be dismayed*) 92$_{10}$ (|| פרד htp. *be scattered*), psalmist's enemies 9$_{4}$, wicked Jb 4$_{9}$ Ps 37$_{20}$ (|| בֶּעָשָׁן כָּלוּ [mss כֶּעָשָׁן] *as smoke they vanish*) 68$_{3}$ (|| כְּהִמֵּס דּוֹנַג מִפְּנֵי־אֵשׁ *as wax melts before fire*) Pr 11$_{10}$ 28$_{28}$ (:: קום *arise*) 4QpPs^{a} 1.2$_{1}$ 1.3$_{4.8}$, cursed ones 1QDM 1$_{10}$ ([א]ובדם), sailors Jon 1$_{6.14}$; individuals Mc 4$_{9}$ Zc 9$_{5}$ Ps 2$_{12}$ 119$_{92}$ Est 4$_{16.16}$ 11QapPs^{a} 3$_{4}$, צַדִּיק *righteous* Is 57$_{1}$ (|| אסף ni. *be taken away*) Ec 7$_{15}$, חָסִיד *pious* Mc 7$_{2}$, נָקִי *innocent* Jb 4$_{7}$ (|| כחד ni. *be destroyed*), slave Si 30$_{40}$, עָנָו *poor person* 4Q372 1$_{17}$, רוּשׁ ptc. *poor person* 1$_{17}$, opponent of a rich man Si 8$_{2}$ (ישקל מחירך ואבדת *he may pay out your price and you will perish*), false witness Pr 19$_{9}$ 21$_{28}$; אֹבְדֵי לֵב *those perishing in respect of heart* Is 46$_{12}$ (if em. אַבִּירֵי *mighty of heart*); non-human subjs. לַיִשׁ *lion* Jb 4$_{11}$ (+ מִבְּלִי טָרֶף *for lack of prey*).

1b. be about to die, be in danger of death, always ptc. except Nm 17$_{27}$ (אָבַדְנוּ *we are about to die*), **<SUBJ>** Israelites in wilderness Nm 17$_{27.27}$ (|| גוע *expire*), in Assyria Is 27$_{13}$, destitute person Jb 29$_{13}$ 31$_{19}$ (+ מִבְּלִי לְבוּשׁ *for lack of clothing*); תְּנוּ שֵׁכָר לְאוֹבֵד *give strong drink to one in danger of dying* Pr 31$_{6}$, אֲרַמִּי אֹבֵד *an Aramaean on the point of death* Dt 26$_{5}$, גּוֹי אֹבַד עֵצוֹת *a nation about to perish in respect of counsel* Dt 32$_{28}$ = CD 5$_{17}$, רשש ואבד מהלך *poor and about to die*, lit. *about to perish in respect of his (life-)journey* Si 11$_{12}$, אבד תקוה *about to perish in respect of hope* 41$_{2(B)}$ (M אבוד).

2. be destroyed, perish, of inanimate objects, **<SUBJ>** קִיקָיוֹן *gourd* Jon 4$_{10}$ (|| יבשׁ *dry up*; :: היה *come into being*), מָקוֹם *place* 4QMMT B$_{5}$ (אבד[ו מקצת] מקומות), אֶרֶץ *countryside* Jr 9$_{11}$ (|| נִצְּתָה כַמִּדְבָּר *laid waste as a desert*), עֵמֶק *valley* 48$_{8}$ (|| שׁדד *destroy*, שׁמד ni. *be destroyed*), earth and heavens Ps 102$_{27}$ (|| כַּבֶּגֶד יִבְלוּ *they will wear out as a garment*; :: עמד *stand, endure*), קָצִיר *harvest* Jl 1$_{11}$ (|| אמל pulal *wither*, appar. יבשׁ hi. *be withered*), בָּתֵּי הַשֵּׁן *houses of* (decorated with) *ivory* Am 3$_{15}$ (|| סוף *come to an end*), אָרְחוֹת *caravans* Jb 6$_{18}$, waters 11QT 32$_{14}$, כְּלֵי מִלְחָמָה *weapons of war* 2 S 1$_{27}$ (|| נפל *fall*), idols Jr 10$_{15}$=51$_{18}$, מחמדיהם *their precious things* GnzPs 2$_{21}$, [עריצי הברית] *ruthless ones of the covenant* 4QpPs^{a} 1.4$_{18(Horgan)}$; כְּלִי אֹבֵד *a destroyed vessel* Ps 31$_{13}$ (|| כְּמֵת *as a dead person*) 1QH 4$_{9}$ (אובד).

3. cease, vanish, fade away, of abstracts, **<SUBJ>** תִּקְוָה *hope* Ezk 19$_{5}$ 37$_{11}$ (|| יָבְשׁוּ עַצְמוֹתֵינוּ *our bones have dried up*) Ps 9$_{19}$ 11QPs^{a} 22$_{8}$ (both || שׁכח ni. *be forgotten*) Jb 8$_{13}$ Pr 10$_{28}$ 11$_{7.23(ms)}$ (L עֶבְרָה *wrath*; or em. עָבָרָה *has passed away*) 4QPentPar^{b} 6.2$_{4}$, תּוֹחֶלֶת *hope* 11$_{7}$ Lm 3$_{18}$, זֵכֶר *remembrance* Ps 9$_{7}$ Jb 18$_{17}$ (|| לֹא־שֵׁם לוֹ *he has no name*) 4QJub^{d} 1.2$_{27}$, שֵׁם *name* Ps 41$_{6}$ (|| מות *die*) 4QJub^{f} 21$_{22}$ 4QJub^{d} 1.2$_{27}$, מָנוֹס *(place of) escape* Jr 25$_{35}$ Am 2$_{14}$ Ps 142$_{5}$ Jb 11$_{20}$, פְּלֵיטָה *deliverance* Jr 25$_{35}$, נֵצַח *(power of) endurance* Lm 3$_{18}$, תַּאֲוָה *longing* Ps 112$_{10}$, אֱמוּנָה *truth* Jr 7$_{28}$ (|| כרת ni. *be cut off*), עֵצָה *advice* Jr 49$_{7}$ 4QpNah 3.3$_{7}$, תּוֹרָה, עֵצָה, דָּבָר *torah, advice, word* (of prophecy) Jr 18$_{18}$ Ezk 7$_{26}$ (lacking דָּבָר), חָכְמָה *wisdom* Is 29$_{14}$ (|| סתר htp. *be hidden*), חָזוֹן *vision* Ezk 12$_{22}$, זכרך *your memory* Jub 21$_{22}$, עֶשְׁתֹּנוֹת *thoughts* Ps 146$_{4}$, לֵב *courage* Jr 4$_{9}$, אַהֲבָה, שִׂנְאָה, קִנְאָה *love, hate, ambition* Ec 9$_{6}$, ממש[ל]ה *dominion* Si 41$_{6(M)}$, דֶּרֶךְ *way* Ps 1$_{6}$, כֶּלַח *vigour* Jb 30$_{2}$, יִתְרָה *wealth* Jr 48$_{36}$, עֹשֶׁר *wealth* Ec 5$_{13}$, יוֹם *day* Jb 3$_{3}$.

4. be lost, stray, **<SUBJ>** שֶׂה *sheep* Ps 119$_{176}$ (+ תעה *go astray*), צֹאן *sheep* Jr 50$_{6}$ (+ תעה hi. *lead astray*), sheep Ezk 34$_{4.16}$ (both || נדח ni. *be expelled*), אֲתֹנוֹת *she-asses* 1 S 9$_{3.20}$, אֲבֵדָה *something lost* Dt 22$_{3}$; כל האובד *any missing thing* CD 9$_{10}$, האובד בשדה *what has gone astray in the field* (of fallen fruit, etc.) 10$_{22}$.

<PREP> מִן of place, *from* Mc 7$_{2}$ Zc 9$_{5}$ Ps 10$_{16}$ Jb 18$_{17}$ (also מֵעַל *from upon* Jos 23$_{13.16}$, מִתּוֹךְ *from among* Nm 16$_{33}$), esp. of person(s), *from* Jr 25$_{35}$ 49$_{7}$ Ezk 7$_{26}$ Am 2$_{14}$ Ps 142$_{5}$ Jb 11$_{20}$ Lm 3$_{18}$ (+ 'י Y.) (all with abstract subj.) Dt 22$_{3}$ (with concrete subj.) (also מִפְּנֵי *from before* Ps 9$_{4}$ 68$_{3}$); לְ (stray) *from* a person 1 S 9$_{3.20}$ (or לְ = she-asses *belonging to*); בְּ of place, *in* 4QPentPar^{b} 6.2$_{5}$, of instrument, *because of, by* Jon 1$_{14}$ Ps 119$_{92}$ Jb 4$_{11}$ 31$_{19}$ Ec 5$_{13}$ 7$_{15}$ perh. 4QpPs^{a} 2$_{1}$ 3$_{4}$ CD 3$_{9.10}$ Mur 45$_{7}$; מִפְּנֵי *because of* Dt 28$_{20}$; בְּתוֹךְ *in the middle of* 11QT 32$_{14}$.

<COLL> מ[כה גדול]ה אשר לאבדך *a great blow that will be for your perishing* 11QapPs^{a} 3$_{4}$.

<SYN> שׁמד ni. *be destroyed*, יבשׁ *dry up*, נדח ni. *be expelled*.

Pi. Pf. אִבַּד (אִבְּדָם), אִבַּ֫דְתָּ, אִבַּדְתִּי; impf. יְאַבֵּד (יְאַבֶּד־, Si יאבדנה), 2ms תְּאַבֵּד (תְּאַבְּדֵם), Q יאבדו, תְּאַבְּדוּ (תְּאַבְּדוּן); + waw וְאִבַּד, וְאִבַּדְתִּי, וְאִבַּדְתֶּם; Q ויאבד (וַיְאַבְּדֵם), וַתְּאַבֵּד, וָאַבֶּדְךָ, וַיְאַבְּדוּם; ptc. Si מאבד, מְאַבְּדִים; inf. אַבֵּד, (אַבְּדֵנִי, Q אבדו, אַבְּדָם).

1. kill, destroy, **<SUBJ>** Y. Dt 11_{4} Is 26_{14} (|| שׁמד hi. *destroy*) Jr 12_{17} (|| נתשׁ *pluck up*) 15_{7} (|| שׁכל pi. *bereave*) 51_{55} Ezk 6_{3} Zp 2_{13} Ps 5_{7} 9_{6} (|| שְׁמָם מָחִיתָ *you have blotted out their name*) Jb 12_{23} Lm 2_{9} (|| שׁבר pi. *break*) Si 46_{18} ([ויא]בד), cherub Ezk 28_{16} (if em. וְאִבַּדְךָ to וָאַבֶּדְךָ or וַיְאַבֶּדְךָ), kings 2 K 13_{7} (+ וַיְשִׂמֵם כֶּעָפָר לָדֻשׁ *and made them as the dust at threshing*) 2 K 19_{18}=Is 37_{19} (by burning) 2 K 21_{3} (:: בנה *build*) Ps 21_{11}, queen 2 K 11_{1}, princes Ezk 22_{27}, executors of Haman's decree Est $3_{9.13}$ (|| שׁמד hi. *destroy*, הרג *kill*) 4_{7} 7_{4} (|| שׁמד hi., הרג) 8_{5} $9_{24.24}$ (|| המם *crush*), Israel (and Jews) Nm $33_{52.52}$ (|| שׁמד hi.) Dt $12_{2.3}$ Est 8_{11} (|| שׁמד hi., הרג) $9_{6.12}$, wicked Ps 119_{95} Ec 9_{18}; שַׁלְוָה *complacency* Pr 1_{32}, מַתָּנָה *bribe* Ec 7_{7}.

<OBJ> nation(s) Dt 11_{4} Jr 12_{17} Zp 2_{13}, Israel Jr 15_{7} Est $3_{9.13}$ 4_{7} 7_{4} 8_{5} $9_{24.24}$, enemies of Jews Est $9_{6.12}$, זֶרַע הַמַּמְלָכָה *royal family* 2 K 11_{1}, פְּרִי *fruit* + זֶרַע *offspring* of enemies Ps 21_{11}, army 2 K 13_{7} Est 8_{11} (or del. חֵיל *army of* the people), gods 2 K 19_{18}=Is 37_{19}, רבים *many* 1QpHab 2_{13} 6_{10}, fools Pr 1_{32}; individuals, king of Tyre Ezk 28_{16}, wicked Ps 9_{6}, liars 5_{7}, psalmist Ps 119_{95}, נְפָשׁוֹת *lives* Ezk 22_{27}, נפשו *his soul*, i.e. himself Si $20_{22.22(\text{Segal})}$ (יאבדנה; AHL יורישנה *he dispossesses it*), כל סרני פלישתים *all the princes of the Philistines* Si 46_{18}, מַשְׂכִּית, מַסֵּכֹת, צַלְמֵי *figured stones, molten images* Nm $33_{52.52}$, cult places Dt $12_{2.2}$ 2 K 21_{3} Ezk 6_{3}, bars of city gates Lm 2_{9}; קוֹל גָּדוֹל *mighty voice* of Babylon Jr 51_{55}, memory Is 26_{14}, name (of idols) Dt 12_{3}, טוֹבָה *good* Ec 9_{18}, לֵב *mind* 7_{7} (|| הלל pol. *make a fool of*), חלק *portion* Si 14_{9}.

2. lose, waste, **<OBJ>** wealth Pr 29_{3} 1QS 7_{6}, צֹאן *flock* Jr 23_{1} (|| פוץ hi. *scatter*); obj. not specified Ec 3_{6} (:: בקשׁ pi. *seek*) Si 8_{12}. **<PREP>** בְּ of instrument, *by* 1QpHab 6_{10}; מִן of place, *from* Ps 21_{11} Jr 51_{55}; מִתּוֹךְ *from among* Ezk 28_{16}. **<COLL>** עַד הַיּוֹם הַזֶּה *to this day* Dt 11_{4}.

<SYN> §1 שׁמד hi. *destroy*, הרג *kill*.

Hi. Pf. הֶאֱבַ֫דְתָּ; impf. אֹבִידָה; + waw וְהֶאֱבִיד, וְהַאֲבַדְתִּיךָ, וְהַאֲבַדְתִּיךָ (וְהַאֲבַדְתִּי, וְהַאֲבַדְתָּם) וְהַאֲבַדְתָּ; ptc. מַאֲבִיד; inf. הַאֲבִיד, הַאֲבִידוֹ, הַאֲבִידֵ֫נוּ, Q האבידמה.

destroy, kill, **<SUBJ>** Y. Lv 23_{30} Dt 7_{10} 8_{20} 28_{63} (|| שׁמד hi. *destroy*) Jos 7_{7} 1 S 12_{15} (if em. וּבַאֲבֹתֵיכֶם *and against your fathers* to וּבְמַלְכְּכֶם לְהַאֲבִידְכֶם *and against your king to destroy you*) Jr 18_{7} (|| נתשׁ *pluck up*, נתץ *break down*) 25_{10} 31_{28} (|| הרס *overthrow*, רעע hi. *hurt*, נתשׁ, נתץ) 49_{38} Ezk 25_{7} (|| כרת hi. *cut off*, שׁמד hi. *destroy*) 25_{16} (|| כרת hi. *cut off*) 30_{13} (|| שׁבת hi. *put an end to*) 32_{13} Ob_{8} Mc 5_{9} (|| כרת hi. *cut off*) Zp 2_{5} Ps 143_{12} (|| צמת hi. *exterminate*) Jb 14_{19} 11QapPs[a] 5_{2} ([יהו]ה יאביד), Israel Nm 24_{19} Dt 8_{20} 9_{3} (|| ירשׁ hi. *dispossess*), foreign nations Dt 28_{51} 2 K 24_{2}, Egypt like a flooding river Jr 46_{8}, Jehu 2 K 10_{19}, Jeremiah Jr 1_{10}=Si 49_{7} (|| נתשׁ, נתץ, הרס).

<OBJ> Israel Dt $28_{51.63}$ Jos 7_{7} 1 S 12_{15} (if em.; see Subj.) 2 K 24_{2} Jr 31_{28}, nation(s) Dt 8_{20} Jr 18_{7} Ezk $25_{7.16}$ Zp 2_{5}, Elam's king and princes Jr 49_{38}, worshippers of Baal 2 K 10_{19}, [בני בל]יעל *sons of Belial* 11QapPs[a] 5_{2}, those who hate Y. Dt 7_{10}, wise men Ob_{8}, נֶפֶשׁ *person* Lv 23_{30}, שָׂרִיד *survivor* Nm 24_{19}, city and its inhabitants Jr 46_{8}; animals Ezk 32_{13}, קֶרֶן *horn* 4QFlor 6_{1}, chariots Mc 5_{9}, images Ezk 30_{13}, קוֹל שָׂשׂוֹן *sound of mirth* Jr 25_{10}, name Dt 7_{24}, תְּבוּנָה *understanding* Ob_{8}, תִּקְוָה *hope* Jb 14_{19}.

<PREP> מִן of place, *from* Nm 24_{19} Dt 7_{24} Jr 49_{38} Ezk 25_{7} Ob_{8}, of person, *from* Jr 25_{10}; מֵעַל of place, *from beside* Ezk 32_{13}; מִקֶּרֶב *from among* Lv 23_{30}, מִפְּנֵיכֶם *from before you* Dt 8_{20}. **<COLL>** מַהֵר *quickly* Dt 9_{3}.

<SYN> כרת hi. *cut off*, שׁמד hi. *destroy*, נתשׁ *pluck up*, נתץ *break down*, הרס *overthrow*.

Also 4QpNah 1_{8} 4QTanḥ $14_{7(\text{Allegro})}$ 4Q515 22_{1}.

→ אֹבֵד *destruction*, אֲבֵדָה *lost object*, אֲבַדּוֹן *Abaddon*, אַבְדָן, אָבְדָן *destruction*.

[אָבָד], see אֹבֵד.

אֹבֵד 2 n.[m.] **destruction,** אַחֲרִיתוֹ עֲדֵי אֹבֵד *his* (Amalek's) *end is unto destruction* Nm 24_{20} (Sam עד יאבד *until he perishes*; or em. אָבָד *eternity*), גַּם־הוּא עֲדֵי אֹבֵד *he* (appar. Kain) *too is unto destruction* 24_{24} (Sam עד יאבד; or em. אָבָד יֹאבֵד *he will perish* unto *eternity*,

i.e. eternally).
→ אבד *die*.

אֲבֵדָה 4.0.1 n.f. **lost object**—cstr. אֲבֵדַת—<SUBJ> היה *be* CD 9_{14} (+ לכהנים *for the priests*), אבד *be lost* Dt 22_3 (+ שִׂמְלָה *garment*, חֲמוֹר *ass*), מצא ni. *be found* CD 9_{14}.

<OBJ> מצא *find* Lv $5_{22.23}$ Dt 22_3, שׁוב hi. *return*, i.e. make restitution for Lv 5_{23} (|| גְּזֵלָה *theft*, עֹשֶׁק *[gain by] extortion*, פִּקָּדוֹן *deposit*).

<CSTR> אֲבֵדַת אָחִיךָ *lost thing of*, i.e. thing lost by, *your brother* Dt 22_3; כָּל־אֲבֵדָה *any lost thing* Ex 22_8 Dt 22_3 (אֲבֵדַת) CD 9_{14}.

<PREP> עשׂה לְ *do with respect to* Dt 22_3; כחשׁ בְּ pi. *lie about* Lv 5_{22}; בוא עַל *come* to court *concerning* Ex 22_8 (+ שׁוֹר *ox*, חֲמוֹר *ass*, שֶׂה *sheep*, שַׂלְמָה [Sam שִׂמְלָה] *garment*).

<COLL> כָּל־אֲבֵדָה אֲשֶׁר יֹאמַר כִּי־הוּא זֶה *anything lost (of) which one says, This is it* Ex 22_8.
→ אבד *die*.

[אֲבַדֹּה] see אֲבַדּוֹן.

אֲבַדֹּו, see אֲבַדּוֹן.

אֲבַדּוֹן 6.0.8 n.f. **destruction**—אֲבַדֹּו (Kt אבדה); sf. Q אבדונו; pl. Q אבדונים; cstr. אבדוני—**destruction**, but oft. almost as pr.n. or pl.n. in ref. to death or abode of the dead, **Abaddon**, <SUBJ> אמר *say* Jb 28_{22} (|| מָוֶת *death*), שׂבע *be satisfied* Pr 27_{20} (Kt אבדה; Qr אֲבַדֹּו; Qrmss אֲבַדּוֹן; || שְׁאוֹל *Sheol*).

<NOM CL> אֲבַדּוֹן נֶגֶד י׳ *Abaddon is (exposed) before Y.* Pr 15_{11} (|| שְׁאוֹל *Sheol*).

<CSTR> אבדוני שאול *Abaddon(s) of Sheol* 1QM $14_{18(mg)}$ + Sup (main text אבדו, as Pr 27_{20}); רו[ח האב]דון *the spirit of destruction* (|| שַׁחַת *pit*) 4QBer[a] 3.2_7, שאול אבדון *Sheol of Abaddon* 1QH 3_{19} (+ שַׁחַת), מחשכי אבדונים *dark places of Abaddon(s)* 1QM $14_{18(mg)}$ + Sup (main text אבנים *of stones*), כול אבדו[ן] *all Abaddon* 4QApocJos[b] 2_2 (+ תְּהוֹם *abyss*), קללת האב[דון] *curse of Abbadon* 11QapPs[a] 3_{10}.

<PREP> אֵין כְּסוּת לָאֲבַדּוֹן *there is no covering for Abaddon* Jb $26_{6(L)}$ (mss לַאֲבַדּוֹן; + שְׁאוֹל *Sheol*), יבקעו לאבדון נחלי בליעל *the rivers of Belial break through to Abaddon* 1QH 3_{32}.

ספר בְּ pu. *be recounted in* (of Y.'s reliability) Ps 88_{12} (|| קֶבֶר *grave*, + חֹשֶׁךְ *darkness*, אֶרֶץ נְשִׁיָּה *land of oblivion*), בכול אבדו[ן] *in all Abaddon* 4QApocJos[b] 2_2, באבדונו *in his destruction* 1QM 18_{17}, [אש בו]ערת במחשכי אבדונים באבדוני שאול תוק[ד] *a burning fire will be kindled in the dark places of Abaddon(s), in Abaddon(s) of Sheol* 1QM $14_{18(mg, Baillet)}$ + Sup.

משאול אבדון העליתני לרום עולם *from Sheol of Abaddon you raised me to an eternal height* 1QH 3_{19}; אכל עַד *burn unto* (of adultery as fire) Jb 31_{12}.

<COLL> [תהום] רבה ואבדון *a great abyss and Abaddon* 4QDibHam[a] $1.7_{8(Baillet)}$.

<SYN> שְׁאוֹל *Sheol*.
→ אבד *die*.

אָבְדָן 2 n.[m.] **destruction**—אָבְדָן; cstr. אָבְדַן (as if from אָבְדָן)—<NOM CL> הוא אבדן *that is destruction* 4QpIsa[a] $14_{3(Allegro)}$. <OBJ> נכה hi. *strike* enemies *(with)* Est 9_5 (+ מַכָּה *striking*, הֶרֶג *slaughter*). <CSTR> אָבְדַן מוֹלַדְתִּי *destruction of my kin* Est 8_6. <PREP> ראה בְּ *look at* Est 8_6.
→ אבד *die*.

[אָבְדָן], see אַבְדָן.

אבה 54.3 vb. **be willing**—**Qal** Pf. אָבָה, אָבִיתִי, אָבוּ (אָבוּא), אֲבִיתֶם; impf. יֹאבֶה, תֹּאבֶה (תֹּבֵא, תֹּאבֶה, Si תובא), יֹאבוּ, תֹּאבוּ; ptc. אֹבִים.

1. be willing (with negative particle except Is 1_{19} Jb 39_9 Si 6_{33}). **a.** followed by לְ + inf. cstr. of שׁלח *stretch out* hand 1 S 22_{17} 26_{23}, pi. *release* Ex 10_{27} (+ חזק pi. *harden* heart), עלה *go up* Dt 1_{26} (+ מרה hi. *rebel*), שׁחת hi. *destroy* 2 K 8_{19}||2 C 21_7, לין *pass the night* Jg 19_{10}, סור *turn* intrans. 2 S 2_{21}, hi. *bring back* 6_{10}, הלך *go* Gn $24_{5.8}$ 2 S 13_{25}, בוא *come* $14_{29.29}$, שׁתה *drink* $23_{16.17}$||1 C $11_{18.19}$, ישׁע hi. *save* 1 C 19_{19} (|| 2 S 10_{19} וַיִּרְאוּ *and they feared* for לֹא אָבָה *was not willing*), שׁמע *heed* Lv 26_{21} (+ הלך קְרִי *go contrary*) Dt 23_6 Jos 24_{10} Jg 19_{25} 20_{13} 2 S $13_{14.16}$ Ezk $3_{7.7}$ 20_8 (+ מרה) Si 6_{33} (+ חפץ *desire*, שׂום *apply* mind, נטה hi. *incline* ear), סלח *pardon* 2 K 24_4.

b. followed by inf. cstr. (without לְ) of עבר hi. *let pass* Dt 2_{30} (+ קשׁה hi. *harden* spirit, אמץ pi. *harden* heart), שׁחת hi. *destroy* Dt 10_{10} 2 K 13_{23}, חרם hi. *exterminate* 1 S 15_{9}, שׁמע *hear*, i.e. heed Is 28_{12} 30_{9} (+ עַם מְרִי *a rebellious people*, בָּנִים כֶּחָשִׁים *deceitful children*), עבד *serve* Jb 39_{9}, סלח *pardon* Dt 29_{19}, יבם pi. *fulfil duty as husband's brother* 25_{7} (:: מאן pi. *refuse*; + חפץ *desire*).

c. followed by inf. abs. of הלך *go* Is 42_{24} (+ שׁמע *hear*).

d. used absolutely (with ellipsis of verb), Jg 11_{17} (|| שׁמע *hear*) 1 S 31_{4}||1 C 10_{4} 2 S 12_{17} 1 K 20_{8} (|| שׁמע) 22_{50} Is 30_{15} Pr 1_{10} 6_{35} (+ נשׂא פָּנִים *be favourable*, חמל *pity*) Si 34_{10} (but perh. connect with להרע *to do evil*, as §1a).

e. followed by *waw*-consecutive, אִם־תֹּאבוּ וּשְׁמַעְתֶּם ... תֹּאכֵלוּ *if you are willing and obey ... you will eat* Is 1_{19} (:: מאן pi. *refuse*, + מרה *rebel*).

2. consent to, accept, a. followed by לְ, לֹא תֹאבֶה לוֹ *you shall not accede to him* Dt 13_{9} (|| שׁמע *hear*, i.e. heed), יִשְׂרָאֵל לֹא־אָבָה לִי *Israel would not accede to me* Ps 81_{12} (|| שׁמע), לֹא־אָבוּ לַעֲצָתִי *they would not accept my advice* Pr 1_{30} (:: נאץ *spurn*).

b. with direct obj., תּוֹכַחְתִּי לֹא אֲבִיתֶם *you would not accept my reproof* Pr 1_{25} (:: פרע *neglect*), perh. Si 14_{1} לא אבה עליו דין לבו *his heart does not consent to judgment against him* (or em. לא הביא עלוי דין לבו *his heart does not bring remorse against him*).

<SUBJ> Israel Lv 26_{21} Dt 1_{26} 13_{9} Is 1_{19} 28_{12} (אָבוּא) $30_{9.15}$ 42_{24} Ezk $3_{7.7}$ 20_{8} Ps 81_{12}, Aram 1 C 19_{19}, Benjaminites Jg 20_{13}, עַם *people* 1 S 15_{9}, Y. Dt 10_{10} 23_{6} 29_{19} Jos 24_{10} 2 K 8_{19}||2 C 21_{7} 2 K 13_{23}, Rebekah Gn $24_{5.8}$, Saul 1 S 15_{9}, David 26_{23} 2 S 6_{10} 12_{17} 13_{25} $23_{16.17}$||1 C $11_{18.19}$, Jehoshaphat 1 K 22_{50}, Asahel 2 S 2_{21}, Joab $14_{29.29}$, Amnon $13_{14.16}$, Pharaoh Ex 10_{27}, Sihon Dt 2_{30} Jg 11_{17}.

מֶלֶךְ *king* Jg 11_{17} 1 K 20_{8}, עֶבֶד *servant* 1 S 22_{17}, נשׂא ptc. *one who carries* armour or weapons 31_{4}||1 C 10_{4}, אִישׁ *man* Jg $19_{10.25}$ Si 34_{10}, גֶּבֶר *man* Pr 6_{35}, יָבָם *husband's brother* Dt 25_{7}, בֵּן *son* Pr 1_{10} Si 6_{33}, פֶּתִי *simple one* Pr 1_{25}, רְאֵם *wild ox* Jb 39_{9}, לֵב *heart* Si 14_{1}.

<OBJ> see §2b.

<PREP> see §2.

<SYN> שׁמע *hear*.

<ANT> מאן pi. *refuse*.

[אֵבֶה] 1 n.[m.] **reed**—אֵבֶה—יָמַי ... חָלְפוּ עִם־אֳנִיּוֹת אֵבֶה *my days ... have been changed*, or *have passed, with*, i.e. as, *ships (made) of reed* Jb 9_{26}.

[אבוגיל], see אֲבִיגַיִל.

אֲבוֹי 1 interj. **alas**—Gnz אֲבוֹי—**alas** (or perh. noun, **discomfort**), לְמִי אֲבוֹי *to whom is there*, i.e. to whom does one say, *Alas!?* Pr 23_{29} (+ אוֹי *woe*, מִדְיָן *contention*, שִׂיחַ *complaint*, פֶּצַע *bruise*, חַכְלִלוּת *dullness* of eyes), אֲבוֹי יִבָּחֵן אִיּוֹב *alas, Job will be tested* Jb 34_{36} (if em. אָבִי *if only*).

אֵבוּס 3 n.m. **trough**—cstr. אֵבוּס; sf. אֲבוּסֶךָ—**trough** for feeding, or perh. **stall** for sleeping, <NOM CL> אֵבוּס בָּר *a trough is clean*, i.e. empty Pr 14_{4} (or perh. *[there is] a trough [full] of corn*, or em. אֶפֶס *there is no* corn; + בְּאֵין אֲלָפִים *without oxen*). <OBJ> ידע *know* (of ass) Is 1_{3}. <CSTR> אֵבוּס בְּעָלָיו *trough of his master* Is 1_{3}. <PREP> לין על *pass the night at* (of wild ox) Jb 39_{9}.
→ אבס *fatten*.

אָבוֹת, see אוֹב I–II.

[אִבְחָה] 1 n.f. **slaughter**—cstr. אִבְחַת—נָתַתִּי אִבְחַת־חָרֶב against all their gates *I have placed destruction of*, i.e. by, *sword* Ezk 21_{20} (or em. טֶבַח הַחֶרֶב or טִבְחַת־חֶרֶב in same sense).

[אֲבַטִּיחַ] 1 n.[m.] **melon**—pl. אֲבַטִּחִים—perh. watermelon (*citrullus vulgaris*), among foods eaten in Egypt, זָכַרְנוּ ... אֶת הָאֲבַטִּחִים *they remembered ... the melons* Nm 11_{5} (|| קִשֻּׁאָה *cucumber*, בָּצָל *onion*, שׁוּם *garlic*, + דָּגָה *fish*, חָצִיר *leeks*).

אָבִי I 1 interj. **if only**, perh. var. of בִּי *pray*, or 1cs impf. ביה *entreat*, אָבִי יִבָּחֵן אִיּוֹב *if only Job were tested* Jb 34_{36} (or em. אֲבָל *alas* or אֲבוֹי *alas*), אָבִי דָּבָר גָּדוֹל הַנָּבִיא דִּבֶּר אֵלֶיךָ perh. *if only the prophet had spoken to you*, i.e. ordered you to do, *a great thing* 2 K 5_{13} (or אָבִי = *my* *father*, as term of respect; perh. ins. אִם *if* he had said), וְאָבִי רְאֵה גַּם רְאֵה perh. *and if only you would see* (lit. *see!, again, see!*) 1 S 24_{12} (or אָבִי = *my father*, or em. וְאָבִי : he is the anointed of Y. *and my father as well*).

אָבִי II, see חוּרָם אָבִי.

אֲבִי, see אֲבִיָּה.

אֲבִיאֵל 3 pr.n.m. **Abiel, 1.** father of Kish and Ner, 1 S 9_1 14_{51}. **2.** one of David's warriors, appar. ident. with Abi-albon at 2 S 23_{31}, 1 C 11_{32} (or em. אֲבִיבַעַל *Abibaal*).
→ אָב *father* + אֵל *God*.

אֲבִיאָסָף, see אֶבְיָסָף.

אָבִיב 9.0.2 n.m. **ear (of cereal)**—pl. Q אביבות—**1. ear** of cereal, usu. collective, in ref. to uncut or freshly cut, unprocessed, cereal, specif. barley (Ex 9_{31}), **<SUBJ>** קלה pass. *be roasted* Lv 2_{14}. **<NOM CL>** הַשְּׂעֹרָה אָבִיב *the barley was (in the) ear* Ex 9_{31} (|| גִּבְעֹל *bud* of flax). **<OBJ>** קרב hi. *present* in sacrifice Lv 2_{14}. **<APP>** אָבִיב ... גֶּרֶשׂ כַּרְמֶל *ears ..., groats, fresh fruit* Lv 2_{14}, לחם חדש אביבות ומלילות *new bread (made of) ears of various cereals* (lit. *ears and ears*) 11QT 19_7 + Sup.

2. Abib, as month of first ears (אָבִיב), month of exodus and feast of unleavened bread and passover festivals, ident. with later Nisan, **<CSTR>** חֹדֶשׁ הָאָבִיב *the month of Abib* Ex 13_4 23_{15} 34_{18} (both + מוֹעֵד *appointed time of*) 34_{18} (Sam בוֹ *in it* for בְּחֹדֶשׁ הָאָבִיב *in the month of Abib*) Dt $16_{1.1}$.

<PREP> עם האביב יעק[וב ירד] *with Abib Jacob went down* to Egypt 4Q462_{10}.

Also Gezer calendar$_8$ (אבי[ב]; others אבי[ה] *Abijah*).
→ אֵב *greenness*, perh. תֵּל אָבִיב *Telabib*.

[אֲבִיבַעַל], see אבבעל.

אֲבִיגַיִל 17.0.0.2 pr.n.f. **Abigail**—אֲבִיגַיִל (אֲבִגַיִל), אֲבִיגַל, Kt אבוגיל—**1.** wife of Nabal and then of David, 1 S 25_3 (אֲבִגַיִל) $25_{14.18}$ (Kt אבוגיל) $25_{23.32}$ (אֲבִיגַל) $25_{36.39.40.42}$ 27_3 30_5 2 S 2_2 3_2||1 C 3_1 (2 S Kt אביגל). **2.** sister of David, wife of Ithra/Jether, and mother of Amasa, 2 S 17_{25}||1 C 2_{17} (2 S אֲבִיגַל *Abigal*) 1 C 2_{16} (אֲבִיגַיִל). **3.** wife of Asaiah (עשיהו), Seal 62_1 (Ashkelon). **4.** daughter of Elhanan (אלחנן), Seal 867_1 (8th/7th cent.).
→ אָב *father* + גיל *rejoice*.

אֲבִיגַל, see אֲבִיגַיִל.

אֲבִידָן 5 pr.n.m. **Abidan,** son of Gideoni and leader of tribe of Benjamin, Nm 1_{11} 2_{22} $7_{60.65}$ 10_{24}.
→ אָב *father* + דין *judge*.

אֲבִידָע 2 pr.n.m. **Abida,** son of Midian, Gn 25_4||1 C 1_{33}.
→ אָב *father* + ידע *know*.

אֲבִיָּה 26.0.4.7 pr.n.m. & f. **Abijah**—אֲבִיָּהוּ, אֲבִי, I אביו—as pr.n.m. **1.** king of Judah (ident. with Abijam at 1 K 14_{31} [mss אֲבִיָּה] $15_{1.7.7.8}$), son of Rehoboam, 1 C 3_{10} 2 C $11_{20.22}$ 12_{16} 13_{1+10t} ($13_{20.21}$ אֲבִיָּהוּ). **2.** second son of Samuel, 1 S 8_2 1 C 6_{13}. **3.** son of Jeroboam I, 1 K 14_1. **4.** Benjaminite, son of Becher, 1 C 7_8. **5.** head of priestly family at time of David, 1 C 24_{10}. **6.** head of priestly family at time of Nehemiah, Ne 10_8 $12_{4.17}$. **7.** perh. scribe, Gezer calendar$_8$ (אבי[ה]; others אבי[ב] *Abib*). **8.** perh. son of Zibiah (צבי), papMurPalimp$^b{}_2$ (אבי). **9.** Arad ost. 27_6 (אביהו). **10.** Seal 513_2 ([א]ביהו; T. Beit Mirsim?, 7th/6th cent.). **11.** Samaria ost. 50_2 (אביו; others אריו *Uriah*) 52_2 (אביו). **12.** Seal 65_1 (אביו; 8th cent.). **13.** Seal 123_1 (אביו; Palestine, 8th cent.). **14.** Seal 9_1 (אביו; others יואב *Joab*; Carthage).

As pr.n.f. **15.** wife of Hezron, 1 C 2_{24} (unless em. וְאֵשֶׁת חֶצְרוֹן אֲבִיָּה *and the wife of Hezron was Abijah* to אֵשֶׁת חֶצְרוֹן אָבִיהוּ/אֲבִיָּה Ephrathah, *wife of Hezron his* [Caleb's] *father*). **16.** daughter of Zechariah and mother of Hezekiah, 2 K 18_2||2 C 29_1 (2 K אֲבִי).

As name of priestly course (derived from §5) and period during which this course holds office, alw. באביה *in Abijah*, 4QMish A 1.1_{13} ([ב-2 באביה] *on the second of Abijah*) 4QMish B^a 1.1_1 (בשנים באב[יה] *on the second of Abijah)* 1.24 2.14 (both שבת באביה *[on the] sabbath of Abijah)* 1.37 (בארבעה באביה *on the fourth of Abijah)* 2.24 ([באביה] בוא הפסח *in Abijah comes the passover)* 2.27 ([השמיני באביה] *the [beginning of the] eighth [month] is in Abijah)* 2.28 (באביה בוא הפסח) 2.31 ([השביעי באביה] *the [beginning of the] seventh [month] is in Abijah)* 2.35 ([באביה השביע׳] *in Abijah is the [beginning of the] seventh [month]*).

→ אָב *father* + ׳י Y.

אֲבִיָּהוּ, see אֲבִיָּה.

אֲבִיהוּא 12 pr.n.m. **Abihu**, son of Aaron and Elisheba, Ex 623 241.9 281 Lv 101 Nm 32.4 2660.61 1 C 529 241.2 1QM 172 2QapMoses 11 (both אבי[הוא]).

→ אָב *father* + הוּא *he.*

אֲבִיהוּד 1 pr.n.m. **Abihud**, son of Bela, Benjaminite, 1 C 83 (or em. אֲבִי אֵהוּד *father of Ehud*).

→ אָב *father* + הוֹד *splendour.*

אֲבִיהַ֫יִל 2 pr.n.f. **Abihail**—אֲבִיהָ֫יִל—**1.** wife of Abishur and mother of Ahban and Molid, 1 C 229 (mss אֲבִיחַ֫יִל *Abihail*). **2.** daughter of Eliab son of Jesse, and either wife of Rehoboam or mother of Mahalath and mother-in-law of Rehoboam (if em. וַאֲבִיהַ֫יִל *and [of] Abihail*), 2 C 1118.

→ אָב *father.*

אֲבִיו, see אֲבִיָּה.

אֶבְיוֹן 61.3.27 adj. **poor**—Q איביון; sf. אֶבְיֹנְךָ; pl. abs. אֶבְיוֹנִים (אֶבְיֹנִים); cstr. אֶבְיוֹנֵי (אֶבְיֹנֵי); sf. אֶבְיֹנֶיהָ, Q אביונינו—esp. assoc. with dependence on divine help. **1.** used as adj., **poor, needy,** + אִישׁ *man* Ps 10916 (|| עָנִי *poor,* כאה ni. ptc. *disheartened*), שָׂכִיר *hired worker* Dt 2414 (|| עָנִי), אָח *brother* 157.9.

2. used as noun, **poor one, needy person** (described in Jb 244–11), also in ref. to soul (Ec 125 [if em.; see Subj.]).

<SUBJ> היה *be* Dt 154.7 (both + בְּ *among*), אכל *eat* Ex 2311, חדל *cease* Dt 1511 (+ מִן *from* the land), רבץ *lie down* Is 1430 (|| דַּל *poor*), גיל *rejoice* 2919 (|| עָנָו *poor*), בקשׁ pi. *seek* 4117 (|| עָנִי *poor*), שׁכח ni. *be forgotten* Ps 919 (+ עָנִי [Kt עָנָו]), אזן hi. *hear* 493 (:: עָשִׁיר *rich*), דבר pi. *speak* Is 327 (+ עָנִי [Kt עָנָו]), הלל pi. *praise* Ps 7421 (|| עָנִי), פרר hi. *frustrate* Ec 125 (if em. אֲבִיּוֹנָה *caper-berry* to אֶבְיוֹנָה *poor one,* i.e. soul).

<NOM CL> תועבת עשיר אביון *the poor is the abomination of the rich* Si 1320 (|| עֲנָוָה *humility*), אֲנִי עָנִי וְאֶבְיוֹן *I am a poor and needy man* Ps 4018 706, sim. 861 10922, עביון אתה *you are poor* 4Q416 10.29.13 (+ רושׁ ptc. *poor*).

<OBJ> ינה hi. *oppress* Ezk 1812 2229 (+ גֵּר *sojourner;* both || עָנִי *poor*), מכר *sell* Am 26 (|| צַדִּיק *righteous*), קנה *acquire* 86 (|| דַּל *poor*), עזב *forsake* Is 4117 (|| עָנִי), רצץ *crush* Am 41 (|| דַּל), שׁאף *crush* 84 (+ עָנִי [Kt עָנָו]), נטה hi. *turn aside* 512 (+ צַדִּיק) Jb 244 (+ עָנִי), נפל hi. *cause to fall* Ps 3714 (|| עָנִי; + יָשָׁר *upright*), קטל *kill* Jb 2414 (|| עָנִי), אכל *consume* Pr 3014 (+ מִן *from* human beings; || עָנִי), כלה pi. *destroy* 1QpHab 126, נצל hi. *deliver* Ps 3510 (+ מִגֹּזְלוֹ *from his despoiler*) 7212 (+ אֵין־עֹזֵר לוֹ *one who has no helper;* both || עָנִי) 824 (+ מִן *from* the wicked; || דַּל), פלט pi. *deliver* 824, ישׁע hi. *deliver* Jb 515 (+ מִן *from* the strong), דין *judge* Pr 319 (|| עָנִי), רום hi. *raise* 1 S 28=Ps 1137 (+ מִן *from* refuse heap; || דַּל), שׂגב pi. *raise* Ps 10741 (+ מִן *from* affliction), חנן *be gracious (to)* Pr 1431 (+ דַּל), ענה *answer* Is 4117 (|| עָנִי), שׂבע hi. *satisfy* Ps 13215 (+ לֶחֶם *[with] bread*).

<CSTR> אֶבְיוֹנֵי אָדָם *poor ones of humanity* Is 2919 GnzPs 321, פדותכה *of your redemption,* i.e. redeemed by you 1QM 119, חסד *of loyalty* 1QH 522, אֶבְיֹנֵי עַמֶּךָ *poor ones of your people* Ex 2311; נֶפֶשׁ אֶבְיוֹן *life of a poor one* Jr 2013 1QH 232 ([נפ]ש) 325 518 4QBarka 2.11 (+ עָנִי *poor,* דַּל *poor*), יְמִין at *right hand of* Ps 10931, יַד־עָנִי וְאֶבְיוֹן *hand of a poor and needy man* Ezk 1649 CD 621 (+ גֵּר *sojourner*) 1414(Yadin) (+ יָתוֹם *orphan* [(יתו)מים]), זָקֵן *old,* אִישׁ *man* who is homeless, בְּתוּלָה *virgin,* עַלְמָה *young woman* [(ולע(למה], אשר ישבה *one held captive*), דִּין־עָנִי וְאֶבְיוֹן *judgment of a poor and needy man* Jr 2216, צעקת איביון *cry of a poor one* GnzPs 48, מִשְׁפַּט אֶבְיֹנְךָ *judgment of your poor one* Ex 236, בְּנֵי אֶבְיוֹן *children of a poor man* Ps 724 (+ עָנִי *poor,* עשׁק ptc. *oppressor*), מִשְׁפַּט אֶבְיֹנִים *judgment of poor ones* Jr 528 (+ יָתוֹם) Ps 14013 (|| עָנִי), אֶנְקַת *groaning of* Ps 126(L) (|| עָנִי), יד *hand* of 1QM 11₉ (אביוני) 11₁₃, עצת *counsel of* 4QMa fr. 11.1₁₁, הון *wealth of* 1QpHab 12₁₀, נַפְשׁוֹת אֶבְיוֹנִים *souls of poor ones* Jr 2₃₄ Ps 72₁₃, עדת האביונים *congregation of the poor ones* 4QpPsa 1.2₉ 1.3₁₀, כול אביוני *all the poor ones of* 1QH 5₂₂.

<ADJ> אֶבְיוֹנִים נְקִיִּים *innocent poor ones* Jr 2₃₄.

<PREP> לְ of direction, *to* (but in some perh. לְ of benefit), + פתח *open* hand Dt 15₁₁ (|| עָנִי *poor*, אָח *brother*), שׁלח pi. *extend* hand Pr 31₂₀ (|| עָנִי), ישׁט hi. *extend* hand Si 7₃₂ (לאביון הו[שיט), נתן *give* Ps 112₉ Si 32₁₃(mg), ירשׁ *give as inheritance* GnzPs 3₂₁.

לְ of benefit, *to, for* Jb 29₁₆ (+ אָב *father*) Est 9₂₂ (+ מַתָּן *gift*), + היה *be* stronghold Is 25₄ (|| דַּל *poor*), אֵין כְּסוּת לָאֶבְיוֹן *there is no covering for the poor man* Jb 31₁₉, עגם לְ *grieve concerning* 30₂₅.

פלה בְּ hi. *act wonderfully for* 1QH 5₁₆; שׁמע אֶל *listen to* Ps 69₃₄ (+ אָסִיר *prisoner*); עִם *with* 1QM 13₁₄ (+ יָד *hand*); עַל *against, with*, + גמל *give retribution* to 1QpHab 12₃, גבר htp. *act haughtily* 4QapLamb₉ (|| עָנִי), חוס עַל *have pity on* Ps 72₁₃ (|| דַּל), [ר]חמיו על אביונ[*his compassion for the poor (of)* 1QH fr. 16₃.

Also 4QMg(?) 14₂ ([אב]יונים) 4QPrFêtesb 21₂ (|| ארח ptc. *traveller*) 4QPrFêtesc 8₇ 4QShirb 17₂ (דל א[ב]יוני) 4Q416 9.1₁₇.

<SYN> עָנִי *poor*, דַּל *poor*.

אֲבִיּוֹנָה 1 n.f. **caper-berry,** perh. *capparis spinosa*, appar. used for whetting appetite, תָּפֵר הָאֲבִיּוֹנָה *the caper-berry frustrates (desire)* Ec 12₅ (or em. אֶבְיוֹנָה *poor one*, i.e. soul, and/or תֻּפַּר *is made ineffectual* or תִּפְרֶה *bears fruit* or תִּפְרַח *sprouts*).

אביחי 0.0.0.1 pr.n.m. **Abihai,** Arad ost. 39₁₁.
→ אָב *father* + חיה *live*.

אֲבִיחַ֫יִל 4 pr.n.m. & f. **Abihail**—אֲבִיחָיִל; Sam אביחל—**1.** father of Esther and uncle of Mordecai, descendant of Benjamin, Est 2₁₅ 9₂₉. **2.** father of Zuriel, head of father's house of Merari, Nm 3₃₅ (Sam mss אֲבִיחֵל *Abihel*). **3.** son of Huri, descendant of Gad, 1 C 5₁₄. **4.** as pr.n.f., wife of Abishur and mother of Ahban and Molid, 1 C 2₂₉(mss) (L אֲבִיהָיִל *Abihail*).

→ אָב *father* + חַיִל *strength*.

אֲבִיחֵל, see אֲבִיחַיִל.

אֲבִיטוּב 1 pr.n.m. **Abitub,** son of Hushim (unless em. מֵחֻשִׁים *from Hushim* to מִמַּחְשָׁם *from Mahsham*) and Shaharaim, Benjaminite, 1 C 8₁₁ (mss אֲחִיטוּב *Ahitub*).
→ אָב *father* + טוב *be good*.

[אֲבִיטַל] 2 pr.n.f. **Abital**—אֲבִיטָל—wife of David and mother of Shephatiah, 2 S 3₄||1 C 3₃.
→ אָב *father* + טַל *dew*.

אֲבִיָּם 5 pr.n.m. **Abijam, 1.** king of Judah (ident. with Abijah at ||2 C 12₁₆ 13₁.₂₂.₂₃), son of Rehoboam, 1 K 14₃₁ (mss אֲבִיָּה *Abijah*) 15₁.₇.₇.₈.
→ אָב *father*.

אֲבִימָאֵל 2 pr.n.m. **Abimael,** son of Joktan, Gn 10₂₈||1 C 1₂₂.
→ אָב *father*.

אֲבִימֶ֫לֶךְ 67 pr.n.m. **Abimelech**—L אֲבִימֶ֫לֶךְ—**1.** Philistine king of Gerar, Gn 20₂₊₉ₜ 21₂₂₊₆ₜ 26₁ (L אֲבִימֶלֶךְ) 26₈₊₅ₜ. **2.** son of Gideon, called Jerubbaal at Jg 6₃₂ etc. and Jerubbesheth at 2 S 11₂₁, and king of Israel, Jg 8₃₁ 9₁₊₃₇ₜ 10₁. **3.** king of Gath, ident. with Achish at 1 S 21₁₁, Ps 34₁. **4.** priest, son of Abiathar, 1 C 18₁₆ (mss, ||2 S 8₁₇ אֲחִימֶלֶךְ *Ahimelech*).
→ אָב *father* + מלך *reign*.

אֲבִינָדָב 13 pr.n.m. **Abinadab, 1.** inhabitant of Kiriath-jearim, keeper of ark after return from Philistines, father of Eleazar (1 S 7₁) and of Uzzah and Ahio (2 S 6₃), 1 S 7₁ 2 S 6₃ (both + בֵּית *house of*) 6₃||1 C 13₇ 2 S 6₄ (both + בֵּית). **2.** second son of Jesse and brother of David, 1 S 16₈ 17₁₃ 1 C 2₁₃. **3.** son of Saul killed by Philistines, appar. ident. with Ishvi (יִשְׁוִי) at 1 S 14₄₉, 1 S 31₂||1 C 10₂ 1 C 8₃₃ 9₃₉. **4.** father (or perh. more remote ancestor) of one of Solomon's administrators, 1 K 4₁₁ (בֶּן־אֲבִינָדָב *son of Abinadab* or *Ben-abinadab*).
→ אָב *father* + נדב *impel*.

אֲבִינֹעַם 4 pr.n.m. **Abinoam, 1.** father of Barak Jg 46.12 51.12. **2.** Samaria ost. 92 102 (both אבנעם; others אחנעם *Ahinoam* or אדנעם *Adonoam*).
→ אָב *father* + נעם *be pleasant.*

אֲבִינֵר, see אַבְנֵר.

אֶבְיָסָף 4 pr.n.m. **Ebiasaph, Abiasaph**—אֲבִיאָסָף—son (or, at 1 C 68, descendant) of Korah, Ex 624 (אֲבִיאָסָף; Sam אֶבְיָסָף) 1 C 68.22 (mss in both אֲבִיאָסָף) 919.
→ אָב *father* + אסף *gather.*

אֲבִיעֶזֶר 7 pr.n.m. **Abiezer, 1.** nephew of Gilead, descendant of Manasseh, appar. ident. with Iezer (אִיעֶזֶר [Sam אֲחִיעֶזֶר *Ahiezer*]) at Nm 2630, Jos 172 1 C 718. **2.** family descended from preceding, Jg 634 82 (:: אֶפְרַיִם *Ephraim*). **3.** Abiezer the Anathothite (הָעֲנְתוֹתִי/הָעַנְּתֹתִי), one of David's warriors, descendant of Benjamin, 2 S 2327ǁ1 C 1128 1 C 2712.
→ אָב *father* + עזר *help.*

[אֲבִיעֶזְרִי] 3 gent. **Abiezrite**—אֲבִי הָעֶזְרִי—appar. ident. with Iezrite (אִיעֶזְרִי) at Nm 2630. **1.** as adj., **Abiezrite,** of family of Abiezer, descendant of Manasseh, Jg 611 (+ יוֹאָשׁ *Joash*) 832 (+ עָפְרָה *Ophrah*; mss עָפְרַת *Ophrah of,* as §2). **2.** as coll. noun, **Abiezrites,** Jg 624 (+ עָפְרָת [mss עָפְרַת] *Ophrah of*) 832(mss).
→ אָב *father* + עזר *help.*

אֲבִי־עַלְבוֹן 1 pr.n.m. **Abi-albon,** Arbathite (עַרְבָתִי), i.e. from Beth-arabah, one of David's warriors, appar. ident. with Abiel (or em. אֲבִיבַעַל *Abibaal*) at 1 C 1132, 2 S 2331.
→ אָב *father.*

[אָבִיר] 6.1 adj. **mighty**—cstr. אֲבִיר—alw. as noun, **mighty one,** with ref. to Y., **<SUBJ>** גאל *redeem* Is 4926 6016 (both + ׳י *Y.*). **<CSTR>** אֲבִיר יַעֲקֹב *mighty one of Jacob* Gn 4924 Is 4926 6016 Ps 1322.5 Si 5112, יִשְׂרָאֵל *of Israel* Is 124; אֲבִיר ... נְאֻם *utterance of ... the mighty one of* Is 124, מִידֵי *from the hands of* Gn 4924 (+ אֵל *God,* שַׁדַּי *Shaddai,* רעה ptc. *Shepherd,* אֶבֶן *Rock*). **<APP>** הָאָדוֹן י׳ צְבָאוֹת אֲבִיר יִשְׂרָאֵל *the Lord, Y. of hosts, mighty one of Israel* Is 124. **<PREP>** נדר לְ *vow to* Ps 1322 (+ ׳י *Y.*), ידה לְ hi. *give praise to* Si 5112, מִשְׁכָּנוֹת לְ find *dwelling place for* 1325 (+ ׳י); ירד כְּ hi. *bring down* kings *as* Is 1013 (if em. כַּאבִּיר *as a bull*).
→ אַבִּיר *mighty.*

אַבִּיר 17.2 adj. **mighty**—כַּאבִּיר; cstr. אַבִּיר; pl. abs. אַבִּירִים (Si אברים; L כְּאַבְּרִים); cstr. אַבִּירֵי; sf. אַבִּירַי, אַבִּירָיו, אַבִּירֶיךָ (mss אַבִּירְךָ).

Alw. as noun. **1. mighty one, hero,** with ref. to humans, 1 S 218 Is 4612 Jr 4615 Ps 766 (unless em. in all three) Jb 2422 3420 Lm 115, appar. angels, Ps 7825 Si 435.

2. mighty animal. **a. bull,** Is 1013 (unless em.) 347 Jr 4615 (if em.; see Subj.) Ps 2213 5013 6831 Si 731. **b. stallion,** Jg 522 Jr 816 473 5011.

<SUBJ> עמד *stand* Jr 4615, נוס *flee* 4615 (if em. נִסְחַף *is swept away* to נָס חַף *Apis,* your bull, *has fled*), סור *depart* Jb 3420 (if em. יָסִירוּ אַבִּיר *they remove a mighty one* to יָסוּרוּ אַבִּירִים *mighty ones depart*), סחף ni. *be swept away* Jr 4615, כתר pi. *surround* Ps 2213 (ǁ פַּר *bull*), שׁלל htpo. *be plundered* 766 (or em.; see Cstr.; + אַנְשֵׁי־חַיִל *men of valour*), שׁמע *hear* Is 4612 (or em.; see Cstr.; + רָחוֹק *far* from deliverance).

<OBJ> הדף *thrust* Jr 4615, משׁך *drag* Jb 2422, סור hi. *remove* 3420, סלה pi. *reject* Lm 115 (+ בָּחוּר *youth*), נצח pi. *cause to shine* Si 435.

<CSTR> אַבִּיר הָרֹעִים *mighty one,* i.e. chief, *of the herdsmen* 1 S 218, אַבִּירֵי לֵב *mighty ones of heart* Is 4612 (or em. אֹבְדֵי *ones perishing of* heart) Ps 766 (or em. כָּל־בַּעֲרֵי *all the brutish of* heart) 4QapPsb 489 ([אבירי]), בָּשָׁן *of Bashan* 2213; לֶחֶם אַבִּירִים *food of mighty ones* Ps 7825 Si 731 (לחם אברים appar. *flesh of bulls,* unless אברים = *limbs [of sacrifices]*; or em. אשׁמים *of guilt offerings*), בְּשַׂר *flesh of* Ps 5013 (ǁ עַתּוּד *goat*), עֲדַת *congregation,* i.e. herd, *of* 6831 (+ חַיָּה *beast,* עֵגֶל *calf*), דַּהֲרוֹת אַבִּירָיו *gallopings of his stallions* Jg 522 (+ סוּס *horse*), קוֹל מִצְהֲלוֹת *sound of the neighings of* Jr 816 (ǁ סוּס), קוֹל שַׁעֲטַת פַּרְסוֹת *sound of the stamping of the hooves of* 473 (+ רֶכֶב *chariot*), כָּל־אַבִּירַי *all my mightyones* Lm 115.

<APP> חַף אַבִּירֶ֫ךָ Apis, *your bull* Jr 46$_{15(mss)}$ (if em. נִסְחַף).

<PREP> כְּ *as*, + צהל *neigh* Jr 50$_{11}$ (L כָּאֲבִרִים), ירד hi. *bring down* kings Is 10$_{13}$ (כַּאבִּיר; or em. כְּאָבִיר *as the mighty one*, i.e. God, or בֶּעָפָר *into the dust* or בָּאֵפֶר *into the dust*); ירד עִם *go down with* Is 34$_{7}$ (subj. פַּר *bull*; + רְאֵם *wild ox*).

<SYN> §2b סוּס *horse*.

→ אָבִיר *mighty*.

אֲבִירָם 11.1 pr.n.m. **Abiram, 1.** Reubenite, son of Eliab and brother of Dathan, Nm 16$_{1+5t}$ 26$_{9.9}$ Dt 11$_{6}$ (=8QPhyl אבהו *Abihu*) Ps 106$_{17}$ Si 45$_{18}$. **2.** son of Hiel the Bethelite, 1 K 16$_{34}$.

→ אָב *father* + רום *be high*.

אֲבִישַׁג 5 pr.n.f. **Abishag,** Shunammite, female servant of David, 1 K 1$_{3.15}$ 2$_{17.21.22}$.

→ אָב *father*.

אֲבִישׁוּעַ 5 pr.n.m. **Abishua, 1.** son of Phinehas and father of Bukki, Ezr 7$_{5}$ 1 C 5$_{30.31}$ 6$_{35}$. **2.** Benjaminite, son of Bela (or, if em., of Ehud), 1 C 8$_{4}$. **3.** Seal 1 (אבשוע; others אבשדי *Abshaddai*; 7th cent.).

→ אָב *father* + perh. שׁוע *cry out*.

אֲבִישׁוּר 2 pr.n.m. **Abishur,** son of Shammai and father of Ahban and Molid, descendant of Judah, 1 C 2$_{28.29}$.

→ אָב *father* + perh. שׁוּר *wall*.

אֲבִישַׁי 25.0.2 pr.n.m. **Abishai**—אַבְשַׁי—grandson of Jesse, son of Zeruiah (sister of David) and brother of Joab, 1 S 26$_{6.6.7.8.9}$ 2 S 2$_{18.24}$ 3$_{30}$ 10$_{10}$||1 C 19$_{11}$ (אַבְשַׁי; 2 S mss אֲבִישַׁי) 2 S 10$_{14}$||1 C 19$_{15}$ (2 S mss, 1 C אַבְשַׁי) 16$_{9.11}$ 18$_{2.5.12}$ 19$_{22}$ 20$_{6.10}$ 21$_{17}$ 23$_{18}$||1 C 11$_{20}$ (1 C אַבְשַׁי) 1 C 2$_{16}$ 18$_{12}$ (or em. וְאַבְשַׁי בֶּן־צְרוּיָה *and Abishai the son of Zeruiah* to וּבְשׁוּבוֹ מִצּוֹבָה *and when he returned from Zobah*). **2.** party to land conveyance, Mur 22$_{3}$ (אב[ש]י) 22$_{11.12(Milik)}$ (אב[ש]י).

→ אָב *father*.

אֲבִישָׁלוֹם, see אַבְשָׁלוֹם.

אֲבִית, see בַּיִת.

אֶבְיָתָר 30 pr.n.m. **Abiathar,** son of Ahimelech and priest at time of David and Solomon, 1 S 22$_{20.21.22}$ 23$_{6.9}$ 30$_{7.7}$ 2 S 8$_{17}$||1 C 18$_{16}$ 2 S 15$_{24+5t}$ 17$_{15}$ 19$_{12}$ 20$_{25}$ 1 K 1$_{7.19.25.42}$ 2$_{22.26.27.35}$ 4$_{4}$ 1 C 15$_{11}$ 24$_{6}$ 27$_{34}$.

→ אָב *father* + יתר *remain*.

אבך 1 vb. **turn—Htp.** Impf. + waw וַיִּתְאַבְּכוּ—**swirl, billow,** וַתִּצַּת בְּסִבְכֵי הַיַּעַר וַיִּתְאַבְּכוּ גֵּאוּת עָשָׁן *and it* (wickedness) *has kindled in the thickets of the forest and they have billowed (as) a plume of smoke* Is 9$_{17}$.

אבל I 39.1.4 vb. **mourn—Qal** Pf. אָבַל, אָבְלָה, אָבְלוּ; impf. תֶּאֱבַל (תֶּאֱבָל), Q יאבלו; + waw וְאָבַל, וְאָבְלוּ—**mourn, grieve,** because of calamity, drought, etc.

<SUBJ> שׁלך hi. ptc. *one who casts* hook, i.e. fisherman Is 19$_{8}$ (|| אנה *mourn*, אמל pulal *languish*), כֹּהֵן *priest* Jl 1$_{9}$, ישׁב ptc. *one who dwells* in land Am 8$_{8}$ 9$_{5}$, עַם *people* of Samaria Ho 10$_{5}$, יְהוּדָה *Judah* Jr 14$_{2}$ (or em. עַל־הַבַּצֹּרֶת *because of the drought*; || אמל pulal, קדר *be dark*), נֶפֶשׁ *soul* Jb 14$_{22}$ (|| כאב *suffer pain*).

אֶרֶץ *earth* Is 24$_{4}$ (|| נבל *wither*, אמל pulal *languish*) Jr 4$_{28}$ (|| קדר *be dark*) Ho 4$_{3}$ (|| אמל pulal, אסף ni. *be gathered* in death), *land* Is 33$_{9}$ (or em. אֲבָל *alas*; || אמל pulal, חפר hi. *be ashamed*, קמל *wither*) Jr 12$_{4}$ (|| יבשׁ *be dry*, ספה *be destroyed*) 12$_{11}$ (|| שׁמם ni. *be desolated*) 23$_{10}$ (|| יבשׁ).

אֲדָמָה *ground* Jl 1$_{10}$ (|| שׁדד pu. *be ravaged*, יבשׁ hi. *be dry*, אמל pulal *languish*), פֶּתַח *entrance* to city Is 3$_{26}$ (|| אנה *mourn*, + נקה ni. *be cleaned*), נָוֶה *meadow* Am 1$_{2}$ (|| יבשׁ *be dry*), תִּירוֹשׁ *new wine* Is 24$_{7}$ (|| אמל pulal, אנח ni. *groan*); subj. not specified, 4Q525 4$_{16}$ (+ יַחַד *together*; || זכר *remember*)

<PREP> עַל *for, over* Beth-aven Ho 10$_{5}$, soul Jb 14$_{22}$, *before* Y. Jr 12$_{11}$.

<SYN> אנה *mourn*, אמל pulal *languish*, יבשׁ *be dry*, קדר *be dark*.

Hi. Pf. הֶאֱבַלְתִּי; + waw וַיְאַבֶּל־—**1. cause mourning,** of Y., for Assyria (or em. תְּאַשּׁוּר *box tree*) Ezk 31$_{15}$

(unless אבל III *shut* abyss; || כסה pi. *cover*). **2. cause to mourn,** of Y., causing חֵיל *rampart* and חוֹמָה *wall* of Jerusalem to mourn Lm 2$_{8}$ (+ אמל pulal *languish*).

Htp. Pf. הִתְאַבֵּל; impf. יִתְאַבָּל, תִּתְאַבְּלוּ; +waw וַיִּתְאַבֵּל, וָאֶתְאַבְּלָה, וַיִּתְאַבְּלוּ (וַיִּתְאַבָּלוּ); impv. Si התאבל, הִתְאַבְּלִי; ptc. מִתְאַבֵּל, מִתְאַבֶּלֶת, מִתְאַבְּלִים.

1. be in mourning for death or disappearance, usu. for son (except 2 S 14$_{2}$ 2 C 35$_{24}$), <SUBJ> Jacob Gn 37$_{34}$ (+ יָמִים רַבִּים *many days;* + קרע *tear* mantle, שׂים *place* sackcloth on loins), David 2 S 13$_{37}$ (+ כָּל־הַיָּמִים *all the days* [mss יָמִים רַבִּים]) 19$_{2}$ (+ בכה *weep*), Ephraim 1 C 7$_{22}$ (+ יָמִים רַבִּים), אִשָּׁה wise *woman* 2 S 14$_{2}$, Judah and Jerusalem 2 C 35$_{24}$.

<PREP> עַל *for* Joseph Gn 37$_{34}$, Absalom 2 S 13$_{37}$ 19$_{2}$, Saul 1 S 16$_{1}$(mss), Josiah 2 C 35$_{24}$, מֵת *dead person* 2 S 14$_{2}$.

2. lament, in distress, penitence, etc., <SUBJ> Samuel 1 S 15$_{35}$ 16$_{1}$ (+ עַד־מָתַי *how long?*), Ezra Ezr 10$_{6}$ (+ אכל not *eat*, שׁתה not *drink*), Nehemiah Ne 1$_{4}$ (+ יָמִים *days;* + ישׁב *sit*, בכה *weep*, צום *fast*, פלל htp. *intercede*), Daniel Dn 10$_{2}$ (+ שְׁלֹשָׁה שָׁבֻעִים יָמִים *three weeks [of] days;* + אכל not *eat* [or drink], סוך not *anoint oneself*), תָּם *pure (one)* 11QPs^{a} 22$_{8}$, גּוֹרָל *lot* of light 4QCat^{a} 1$_{8.8}$, מכר ptc. *one who sells* Ezk 7$_{12}$ (:: שׂמח *rejoice*), מֶלֶךְ *king* 7$_{27}$ (+ לבשׁ שְׁמָמָה *be clothed [in] desolation*, בהל ni. *be confused*), עַם *people* of Israel Ex 33$_{4}$ (+ שׁית *place* ornaments on oneself) Nm 14$_{39}$ (+ מְאֹד *greatly*) 1 S 6$_{19}$ Ne 8$_{9}$ (+ כְּשָׁמְעָם *when they heard;* || בכה *weep*); subj. unspecified, Is 66$_{10}$.

<PREP> בממשלת בל[יעל] *during,* or *because of, the dominion of Belial* 4QCat^{a} 1$_{8}$; אֶל *for* Saul 1 S 15$_{35}$ 16$_{1}$; עַל *over* Jerusalem Is 66$_{10}$ 11QPs^{a} 22$_{8}$, *because of* transgression Ezr 10$_{6}$.

3. behave as a mourner, <SUBJ> אִשָּׁה wise *woman* 2 S 14$_{2}$ (+ לבשׁ *be clothed [in]* mourning clothes, סוך not *anoint oneself*); subj. unspecified, Si 7$_{34}$. <PREP> עם אבלים התאבל *with mourners behave as a mourner* Si 7$_{34}$.

→ אָבֵל *mourning*, אֵבֶל *mourning*.

[אבל] II, see אבל I, Qal.

[אבל] III, see אבל I, Hi.

אָבֵל I 8.2.4 adj. **mourning**—cstr. אֲבֶל־; pl. אֲבֵלִים (אבילים), אֲבֵלוֹת; cstr. אֲבֵלֵי (Q אבילי); sf. אֲבֵלָיו—as noun, **mourner,** because of death (Gn 37$_{35}$ Ps 35$_{14}$ 4QapLam^{a} 2$_{8}$) or other calamity, perh. sg. as collective, **mourners** (4QCat^{a} 1$_{9}$).

<NOM CL> דַּרְכֵי צִיּוֹן אֲבֵלוֹת *Zion's paths are mourning* Lm 1$_{4}$ (|| שׁמם *be desolate*, אנח ni. *groan*).

<OBJ> נחם pi. *console* Is 61$_{3}$ Jb 29$_{25}$ Si 48$_{24}$ 1QH fr. 21$_{3}$.

<CSTR> אֲבֶל־אֵם *one mourning a mother* Ps 35$_{14}$ (see Prep.), אֲבֵלֵי צִיּוֹן *mourners of Zion* Is 61$_{3}$ Si 48$_{24}$; ראשי אבל *heads of mourners* 4QCat^{a} 1$_{9}$ (unless אֵבֶל *mourning*, i.e. those in charge of mourning), כָּל־אֲבֵלִים *all mourners* Is 61$_{2}$.

<PREP> לְ of direction, *to,* + שׂים *place,* i.e. give Is 61$_{3}$, נתן *give* oil of joy instead of mourning 61$_{3}$, שׁלם pi. *repay* consolations 57$_{18}$.

בנותיה כאבלות *her daughters are as women mourning* 4QapLam^{a} 2$_{8}$ (+ עַל *for* husbands; || שׁכל pi. ptc. *bereaved one*), כַּאֲבֶל־אֵם קֹדֵר שַׁחוֹתִי *as one mourning a mother, I have bowed down, darkened* Ps 35$_{13}$ (+ ענה pi. *humble* soul by fasting, לְבוּשִׁי שָׂק *my clothing was sackcloth*).

אבל עם htp. *behave as mourner with* Si 7$_{34}$.

לֹא יִפְרְסוּ לָהֶם עַל־אָבֵל *they will not tear at themselves for a mourner* Jr 16$_{7}$ (if em. אֵבֶל *mourning*).

<COLL> אֵרֵד ... אָבֵל שְׁאֹלָה *I (Jacob) will go down ..., a mourner, to Sheol* Gn 37$_{35}$ (+ בכה *weep*, נחם htp. not *be consoled*), וְהָמָן נִדְחַף אֶל־בֵּיתוֹ אָבֵל וַחֲפוּי רֹאשׁ *and Haman hurried to his house, (as) a mourner and with his head covered* Est 6$_{12}$.

Also 1QH 18$_{15}$ (+ [נכ]אי רוח *ones stricken of spirit*).

→ אבל *mourn*.

אָבֵל II 13 pl.n. **Abel**—+ ה- of direction אָבֵלָה—**1.** אָבֵל בֵּית־מַעֲכָה **Abel-beth-maachah,** perh. ident. with T. Abil, 7 km WNW of T. Dan, 2 S 20$_{14}$ (וּבֵית מַעֲכָה *and Beth-maachah*) 20$_{15}$ (mss וּבֵית) 1 K 15$_{20}$ 2 K 15$_{29}$. **2. Abel,** ident. with preceding, 2 S 20$_{18}$ 2 C 16$_{4}$ (if em. מַיִם Abel-*maim* to מִיָּם they struck Abel *from the sea;*

||1 K 15$_{20}$ בֵּית מַעֲכָה Abel-*beth-maachah*). **3.** אָבֵל מַיִם **Abel-maim**, see preceding. **4.** אָבֵל הַגְּדוֹלָה **Abel-hagedolah, Great Abel**, on Philistine border, 1 S 6$_{18}$ (mss אֶבֶן large *stone*).

5. אָבֵל מְחוֹלָה **Abel-meholah**, in Gilead Jg 7$_{22}$ 1 K 4$_{12}$ 19$_{16}$. **6.** אָבֵל הַשִּׁטִּים **Abel-shittim**, also called Shittim (Nm 25$_{1}$), in Moab, perh. ident. with T. Kefrēn, 9 km E of Jordan, Nm 33$_{49}$ (הַשִּׁטִּים [Sam שִׁטִּים]) 4QPsJos[a] 14$_{2}$ ([אבל השטים]). **7.** אָבֵל כְּרָמִים **Abel-keramim**, in Ammon, Jg 11$_{33}$. **8.** אָבֵל מִצְרַיִם **Abel-mizraim**, near R. Jordan, Gn 50$_{11}$ (+ אֵבֶל־ לְמִצְרָיִם כָּבֵד זֶה *for Egypt, this was a deep mourning*, as origin of name).

אֵבֶל 24.1.10 n.m. **mourning**—cstr. אֵבֶל; sf. אֶבְלֵךְ (Q אבלכה), Si אבלו, Q אבלה, אֶבְלָם; pl. Q אבליהמה—**mourning, mourning ritual, period of mourning**, for the dead or for calamity, **<SUBJ>** עבר *pass* 2 S 11$_{27}$. **<NOM CL>** אֵבֶל ... זֶה *this was ... a mourning* Gn 50$_{11}$ (+ לְמִצְרָיִם *on the part of Egypt*), בְּכָל־מְדִינָה ... אֵבֶל *in every city ... there was mourning* Est 4$_{3}$ (+ לַיְּהוּדִים *on the part of the Jews*; || צוֹם *fasting*, בְּכִי *weeping*, מִסְפֵּד *mourning*).

<OBJ> עשׂה *do*, i.e. perform Gn 50$_{10}$ (+ לְאָבִיו *for his father*, שִׁבְעַת יָמִים *seven days*; + מִסְפֵּד *mourning*) Jr 6$_{26}$ (+ לָךְ *on your part*; || מִסְפֵּד) Ezk 24$_{17}$ (+ מֵתִים *[for the] dead*) Mc 1$_{8}$ (+ כַּבְּנוֹת יַעֲנָה *as ostriches*; || מִסְפֵּד), שׂית *place*, i.e. perform Si 38$_{17}$ (+ מִסְפֵּד), הפך *change* into joy Jr 31$_{13}$ (+ יָגוֹן *sorrow*), ראה *see* Gn 50$_{11}$.

<CSTR> אֵבֶל יָחִיד *mourning of*, i.e. for, *only child* Jr 6$_{26}$ Am 8$_{10}$ (+ יוֹם מָר *bitter day*), אֵבֶל אָבִי *mourning of*, i.e. for, *my father* Gn 27$_{41}$, אֵבֶל מֹשֶׁה *mourning of*, i.e. for, *Moses* Dt 34$_{8}$, אבל יגון *mourning of sorrow* 1QS 4$_{13}$ (|| רָעָה *evil*) 1QH 2$_{5}$ (mg לאבול) 11$_{22(mg)}$ ([יג]ון; || מִסְפֵּד *mourning*), אבל מרורים *mourning of bitterness(es)* 11$_{19}$.

בִּגְדֵי־אֵבֶל *clothes of mourning* 2 S 14$_{2}$, בֵּית אֵבֶל *house of mourning* Ec 7$_{2}$ (בֵּית־; :: מִשְׁתֶּה *feast*) 7$_{4}$ (:: שִׂמְחָה *joy*), יְמֵי אֵבֶל *days of mourning* Gn 27$_{41}$ Is 60$_{20}$ (אֶבְלֵךְ), יְמֵי בְכִי אֵבֶל *days of weeping (because) of mourning* Dt 34$_{8}$ 4QPsJos[a] 14$_{2}$ ([ימי בכי]), perh. ראשי אבל *heads*, i.e. those in charge, *of mourning* 4QCat[a] 1$_{9}$ (but prob. אָבֵל *of mourners*), כול אבל *all mourning of* 1QH 11$_{22(mg)}$.

<ADJ> אֵבֶל גָּדוֹל *great mourning* Est 4$_{3}$, אֵבֶל־כָּבֵד *heavy*, i.e. deep, *mourning* Gn 50$_{11}$.

<PREP> לְ of direction, *to*, + שׁמע hi. *proclaim* joy 1QH 2$_{5}$ (mg לאבול), היה לְ *be (turned into)* 2 S 19$_{3}$ (+ לְכָל־הָעָם *on the part of all the people*; subj. תְּשׁוּעָה *victory*) Jb 30$_{31}$ (subj. כִּנּוֹר *harp*; + קוֹל בֹּכִים *sound of weepers*), הפך לְ *change* feasts *into* Am 8$_{10}$ (|| קִינָה *lament*), ni. *be changed into* Lm 5$_{15}$ (subj. מָחוֹל *dancing*) 4QpHos[a] 2$_{17}$, שׁדד לְ ho. *be ravaged by, because of* (subj. evil spirits) 1QH fr. 5$_{6}$, ואנחה בכנור קינה ל *and I shall groan with the harp a lamentation for* 11$_{22(mg)}$, מקור ל *fountain for* 11$_{19}$, לאבליהמה שמחת עולם *instead of their mourning(s), eternal joy* 4Q416 9.1$_{12}$.

שׂמח בְּ *rejoice during* 4Q416 9.1$_{10(mg)}$, כול קציהם באבל יגון ... *all their times ... are (spent) in mourning of sorrow* 1QS 4$_{13}$.

שׂים כְּ *place*, i.e. make, *as* Am 8$_{10}$.

הפך מִן ni. *be changed from* to holiday Est 9$_{22}$ (|| יָגוֹן *sorrow*).

קרא אֶל *call to (attendance at)* Am 5$_{16}$ (+ מִסְפֵּד *mourning*).

נחם עַל ni. *be consoled because of* 4QBark[c] 1, וְלֹא יִפְרְסוּ לָהֶם עַל־אֵבֶל *and they will not tear at themselves because of mourning* Jr 16$_{7}$ (or em. אָבֵל *mourner*; mss לֶחֶם tear *bread*).

נתן תַּחַת *give* to mourners oil of joy *instead of* Is 61$_{3}$ (|| אֵפֶר *ashes*, + רוּחַ כֵּהָה *crushed spirit*).

<SYN> מִסְפֵּד *mourning*, יָגוֹן *sorrow*.

→ אבל *mourn*.

אֲבָל 11.1 adv. **indeed, however, alas, 1.** adversative, **however, on the contrary** (but distinction from emphatic usage not alw. clear), **a.** with verb, מצא ni. *be found* 2 C 19$_{3}$, מלך hi. *make king* 1 K 1$_{43}$, זבח *sacrifice* 2 C 33$_{17}$, עלה hi. *bring up* 1$_{4}$, נפל *fall* Dn 10$_{7}$, נגד hi. *tell* 10$_{21}$, שׁפט ni. *be judged* Si 36$_{8(F)}$. **b.** with nom. cl., אֲבָל הָעָם רָב וְהָעֵת גְּשָׁמִים *but the people are numerous and the time is (of) rains* Ezr 10$_{13}$.

2. emphatic, **indeed, a.** with verb, ילד *give birth* Gn 17$_{19}$. **b.** with nom. cl., אֲבָל אֲשֵׁמִים אֲנַחְנוּ *indeed we are guilty* Gn 42$_{21}$.

3. interjection, **alas** (but perh. emphatic), אֲבָל אִשָּׁה־אַלְמָנָה אָנִי *alas, I am a widow* 2 S 14$_{5}$, אֲבָל בֵּן אֵין־לָהּ וְאִישָׁהּ זָקֵן *alas, she has no son and her husband is old* 2 K 4$_{14}$, אֲבָל אֻמְלְלָה אָרֶץ *alas, the land has languished* Is 33$_{9}$ (if em. אָבַל *has mourned*), אֲבָל יִבָּחֵן אִיּוֹב *alas, Job will be tested* Jb 34$_{36}$ (if em. אָבִי *if only*).

אֵבָל, see אוּבָל.

אבמעץ 0.0.0.2 pr.n.m. **Abmaaz,** Seal 274 (Jerusalem, 8th cent.) 454 (א[ב]מעץ; T. Zakariya, 8th cent.) 790 (T. Batash, 8th cent.) (all three + לצפן *to Zaphan*).

→ אָב *father.*

אֶ֫בֶן 277.7.34 n. f. **stone**—אָ֫בֶן; cstr. אֶ֫בֶן; sf. אַבְנוֹ; pl. abs. אֲבָנִים; cstr. אַבְנֵי; sf. אֲבָנֶ֫יךָ, אֲבָנָיו, אֲבָנֶ֫יהָ, אַבְנֵיהֶם—stone, either viewed as a substance, or as an individual piece of rock, large or small; the sg. can be used collectively, and in many contexts sg. and pl. are equally possible (e.g. gods of עֵץ וָאֶבֶן *wood and stone,* or עֵצִים וַאֲבָנִים *wood* [pl.] *and stones*).

1a. as material for building, crafting, Gn 11$_{3}$ Lv 14$_{40.42.43.45}$ 2 S 5$_{11}$ 1 K 6$_{18}$ 7$_{10.10.10.10}$ 15$_{22}$||2 C 16$_{6}$ Is 60$_{17}$ Ezk 26$_{12}$ Mc 1$_{6}$ Hb 2$_{11}$ Hg 2$_{15.15}$ Zc 5$_{4}$ Ps 102$_{15}$ Pr 24$_{31}$ Lm 4$_{1}$ Ne 3$_{34.35}$ 1 C 22$_{14.15}$ 29$_{2}$ 4QBen 1$_{3}$ 1QpHab 10$_{1}$ perh. Mur 30$_{15}$ (unless stone as hewn, quarried, as §1b); foundation stone Is 28$_{16.16}$ 54$_{11}$ Jr 51$_{26}$ 1QH 6$_{26}$; corner-stone Jr 51$_{26}$ Zc 4$_{7}$ Ps 118$_{22}$ Jb 38$_{6}$ 2QapProph 1$_{6}$; for altar, unhewn stones Ex 20$_{25}$ Dt 27$_{5.6}$ Jos 8$_{31}$ 1 K 18$_{31.32.38}$, hewn stone Ezk 40$_{42}$, unspecified Is 27$_{9}$; material for vessels Ex 7$_{19}$; material for images of gods Dt 4$_{28}$ 28$_{36.64}$ 29$_{16}$ 2 K 19$_{18}$||Is 37$_{19}$ Jr 2$_{27}$ 3$_{9}$ Ezk 20$_{32}$ Hb 2$_{19}$ 11QT 59$_{3}$ 1QpHab 13$_{2}$.

b. large stones (see also §5, named standing stones), as memorial Gn 28$_{18.22}$ 31$_{45}$ 35$_{14}$ Dt 27$_{2.4.8}$ (also engraved, as §1e) Jos 4$_{3+7t}$ 24$_{26.27}$ 1 S 6$_{14.15.18}$ (if em.; see Prep.) 7$_{12}$ 14$_{33}$ 2 S 20$_{8}$ Jr 43$_{9.10}$; as hewn, quarried Dt 10$_{1.3}$ 1 K 5$_{31.31.32}$ 6$_{7}$ 7$_{9.11}$ 2 K 12$_{13.13}$ 22$_{6}$||2 C 34$_{11}$ Ec 10$_{9}$ 1 C 22$_{2}$; covering entrance to well or cave Gn 29$_{2.3.3.8.10}$ Jos 10$_{18.27}$; in instructions for locating treasure 3QTr 8$_{5}$ 10$_{9}$ 12$_{2}$; place of slaughter Jg 9$_{5.18}$; burden Si 6$_{21}$.

c. small stones, in heap Jb 8$_{17}$ Ec 3$_{5.5}$ Lm 3$_{53}$; as memorial cairn Gn 31$_{46.46}$ Jos 7$_{26}$ 8$_{29}$ 2 S 18$_{17}$.

d. stone as weapon, 4QApocJos^{b} 2$_{13}$, in the hand Ex 21$_{18}$ Nm 35$_{17}$, thrown 35$_{23}$ Jg 20$_{16}$ 2 S 16$_{6.13}$, sling-stone 1 S 17$_{40.49.50}$ Zc 9$_{15}$ (or em.; see Cstr.) Jb 41$_{20}$ Pr 26$_{8}$ 1 C 12$_{2}$ 2 C 26$_{14}$, catapulted 26$_{15}$; as instrument of capital punishment Lv 20$_{2.27}$ 24$_{23}$ Nm 14$_{10}$ 15$_{35.36}$ Dt 13$_{11}$ 17$_{5}$=11QT 55$_{21}$ Dt 21$_{21}$=11QT 64$_{5}$ Dt 22$_{21.24}$ =11QT 66$_{2}$ Jos 7$_{25.25}$ 1 K 12$_{18}$||2 C 10$_{18}$ 1 K 21$_{13}$ Ezk 16$_{40}$ 23$_{47}$ 2 C 24$_{21}$.

e. stone as engraved object, for tables of the law Ex 24$_{12}$ 31$_{18}$ 34$_{1.4}$ Dt 4$_{13}$ 5$_{22}$ 9$_{9.10.11}$ Jos 8$_{32}$ 1 K 8$_{9}$; as divine image Lv 26$_{1}$=11QT 52$_{2}$ 11QT 51$_{21}$; generally 2 C 2$_{13}$; engraved precious stones Ex 28$_{11}$ Zc 3$_{9}$ (both in §2).

f. stone as naturally occurring, as interfering with agriculture 2 K 3$_{19.25.25}$ Jb 5$_{23}$; as substance of the earth 28$_{6}$; as ore producing iron and copper Dt 8$_{9}$ Jb 28$_{2.3}$; gleaming like fire Ezk 28$_{14.16}$; in underworld Is 14$_{19}$; conveying defilement after contact with human corpse CD 12$_{15}$.

g. stone as support, for head (pillow) Gn 28$_{11}$; to sit upon Ex 17$_{12}$; for 'sea' in temple 2 K 16$_{17}$.

h. stone as symbol, of heaviness Ex 15$_{5}$ Zc 12$_{3}$ Pr 27$_{3}$ Ne 9$_{11}$, dumbness Hb 2$_{19}$ (also material for building, as §1a), stillness, lifelessness Ex 15$_{16}$ 1 S 25$_{37}$ Ezk 11$_{19}$ 36$_{26}$ 1QH 18$_{26}$, commonness 1 K 10$_{27}$||2 C 1$_{15}$=9$_{27}$, strength Jb 6$_{12}$, endurance 14$_{19}$, hardness 38$_{30}$ 41$_{16}$ perh. 4QCrypt 1.2$_{2}$, cause of stumbling Is 8$_{14}$ 62$_{10}$ Ps 91$_{12}$ 1Q38 1.1$_{2}$, recompense Pr 26$_{27}$, Y. Gn 49$_{24}$ (or em.; see App).

<SUBJ> היה *be* Gn 28$_{22}$ (+ בֵּית *house* of God) Jos 4$_{7}$ (+ לְזִכָּרוֹן *as a memorial*) 4$_{9}$ (+ שָׁם *there*) 24$_{27}$ (+ לְעֵדָה *as a witness*) Ps 118$_{22}$ (+ לְרֹאשׁ פִּנָּה *head of the corner*) 1QpHab 10$_{1}$ (+ בעשק *with oppression*), הפך ni. *be turned into* stubble Jb 41$_{20}$, שׁוב *come back* Pr 26$_{27}$, שׂים pass. *be placed* Hg 2$_{15}$, זעק *cry out* Hb 2$_{11}$, עור *awake* 2$_{19}$, טבע *sink* 1 S 17$_{49}$, נפץ pu. *be shattered* Is 27$_{9}$, ראה ni. *be seen* 1 K 6$_{18}$, שׁמע *hear* Jos 24$_{27}$, שׁפך htp. *be scattered* Lm 4$_{1}$, גרר po. *be sawn* 1 K 7$_{9}$, יצק pass. *be smelted* Jb 28$_{2}$ (or em. יוּצַק, ho. be smelted; + עָפָר *dust*), גאל pu. *be defiled* CD 5$_{12}$, ילד *give birth to* Jr 2$_{27}$.

<NOM CL> הָאֶבֶן גְּדֹלָה עַל־פִּי הַבְּאֵר *the stone was large over the mouth of the well* Gn 29$_{2}$ (or em. אֶבֶן *there was a* large *stone*), Ex 39$_{14}$, אֲבָנֶיהָ בַרְזֶל *its* (land's) *stones are iron* Dt 8$_{9}$, מְקוֹם־סַפִּיר אֲבָנֶיהָ *its* (earth's) *stones are a place of sapphires* Jb 28$_{6}$, בצדו המערבי אבן *on its western side is a* black *stone* 3QTr 10$_{9}$, מְיֻסָּד אֲבָנִים *the foundation was stones* 1 K 7$_{10}$, מִלְמַעְלָה אֲבָנִים *above were stones* 7$_{11}$, הֵמָּה ... אֶבֶן *they are ... stone* 2 K 19$_{18}$||Is 37$_{19}$, מָה הָאֲבָנִים הָאֵלֶּה *what are these stones?* Jos 4$_{6.21}$, שָׁם אֶבֶן *there was a stone there* 1 S 6$_{14}$, עֵד הָאֶבֶן *the stone is a witness* 6$_{18}$ (if em. עַד אֶבֶן *unto (the) meadow* [mss; L עַד אָבֵל *unto* Great *Abel*]), [ל]לו[קח] וא[בנים וכ]לאת שעליו *to the purchaser are both the stones and the enclosures which are upon it* (land) Mur 30$_{15}$.

<OBJ> חצב *hew* 2 C 2$_{2}$, נסע hi. *quarry* 1 K 5$_{31.31}$ Ec 10$_{9}$ (|| עֵץ *wood*), לקט *gather* Gn 31$_{46}$, כנס *gather* Ec 3$_{5}$, חקר *search* Jb 28$_{3}$, לקח *take* Gn 28$_{18}$ 31$_{45.46}$ Ex 17$_{12}$ Lv 14$_{42}$ Jos 4$_{20}$ 24$_{26}$ 1 S 7$_{12}$ 17$_{49}$ 1 K 18$_{31}$ Jr 43$_{9}$ 51$_{26}$ (+ לְפִנָּה *for a corner*) 51$_{26}$ (+ לְמוֹסָדוֹת *for foundations*), כון hi. *prepare* Jos 4$_{3}$ 1 K 5$_{32}$ 1 C 22$_{14}$ 2 C 26$_{14}$ (if em.; see Prep.), נשׂא *lift up* Jos 4$_{8}$ 1 K 15$_{22}$||2 C 16$_{6}$ (|| עֵץ), רום hi. *raise up* Gn 31$_{45}$ (+ מַצֵּבָה *as a pillar*) Jos 4$_{5.20}$, שׂים *place* Gn 28$_{11.18.22}$ (both + מַצֵּבָה) Jos 10$_{27}$ Is 27$_{9}$ Ezk 26$_{5}$, *reckon* CD 12$_{15}$ (+ כְּ as human beings), *make into* Zc 12$_{3}$, נוח hi. *place* Jos 4$_{3.8}$, נתן *place* Lv 26$_{1}$ (|| אֱלִיל *idol*, מַצֵּבָה *pillar*) 11QT 51$_{21}$, יסד pi. *lay as foundation* Is 28$_{16}$, נטה *lay* 1QH 6$_{26}$ (לְ[נ]טות), ירה *set* cornerstone Jb 38$_{6}$, קום hi. *set up* Dt 27$_{2.4}$ Jos 4$_{9}$ 24$_{26}$, רבץ hi. *lay* Is 54$_{11}$ (+ בַּפּוּךְ *in antimony*), שׁאר hi. *leave* 2 K 3$_{25}$, טמן *hide* trans. Jr 43$_{9}$ (+ בַּמֶּלֶט *in the mortar*) 43$_{10}$, חלץ pi. *pull out* Lv 14$_{40.43}$, נתץ *pull down* 14$_{45}$, כלה pi. *destroy* Zc 5$_{4}$, יצא hi. *bring out* 4$_{7}$, גלל *roll* Gn 29$_{3.8}$ Jos 10$_{18}$ 1 S 14$_{33}$ Pr 26$_{27}$ (+ שַׁחַת *pit*), hi. Gn 29$_{10}$, שׁוב hi. *put back* 29$_{3}$, עבר hi. *remove* Jos 4$_{3.8}$, אכל *consume* 1 K 18$_{38}$ (|| עֵץ, עָפָר *dust*, עֹלָה *burnt offering*), רגם *pelt with* Lv 24$_{23}$ Jos 7$_{25}$ 1 K 12$_{18}$||2 C 10$_{18}$ Ezk 23$_{47}$ 24$_{21}$, שׁלך hi. *cast* 2 K 3$_{25}$ Ec 3$_{5}$, ידה pi. *cast* Lm 3$_{53}$, נפל hi. *cast* Nm 35$_{23}$ (if em.; see Prep), נגר hi. *pour down* Mc 1$_{6}$, שׁחק *wear away* Jb 14$_{19}$ (|| עָפָר), צרר *bind* Pr 26$_{8}$, קשׁר *bind* Jr 51$_{63}$, כבשׁ *subdue* Zc 9$_{15}$ (or em.; see Cstr.), שׂיד *plaster* Dt 27$_{2.4}$, עשׂה *make* 11QT 52$_{2}$, קנה *buy* 2 K 22$_{6}$||2 C 34$_{11}$, חיה pi. *revive* Ne 3$_{34}$, מאס *reject* Ps 118$_{22}$, רצה *take delight in* 102$_{15}$ (|| עָפָר), ראה *see* Dt 29$_{16}$, שׁרת pi. *worship* Ezk 20$_{32}$, עבד *serve* Dt 4$_{28}$ 28$_{36.64}$ 11QT 59$_{3}$ 1QpHab 13$_{2}$.

<CSTR> אֶבֶן קִיר *stone of wall* 2 S 5$_{11}$ (|| עֵץ *wood*), צונם *of granite* 4QCrypt 1.2$_{2}$, מַשְׂכִּית *of figure*, i.e. carved stone Lv 26$_{1}$ 11QT 51$_{21}$ 52$_{2}$ ([א]ב[ן] [מ]שכית), פנת *of the corner of* 2QapProph 1$_{6}$, פִּנָּתָהּ *of its corner* Jb 38$_{6}$, הָרֹאשָׁה *of*, i.e. at, *the top* Zc 4$_{7}$ (if em.; see App.), יָד *of*, i.e. in the, *hand* Nm 35$_{17}$, דּוּמָם *of stillness*, i.e. inert stone Hb 2$_{19}$, מַעֲמָסָה *of heaviness* Zc 12$_{3}$, מַשָּׂא *of burden* Si 6$_{21}$, בֹּחַן *of testing*, i.e. pyramidion Is 28$_{16}$ 1QH 6$_{26}$, נֶגֶף *of striking* Is 8$_{14}$ (|| צוּר *rock*) 1Q38 1.1$_{2}$, אֹפֶל וְצַלְמָוֶת *of darkness and deep darkness* Jb 28$_{3}$, יִשְׂרָאֵל *of Israel*, i.e. Y. Gn 49$_{24}$ (or em.; see App.), אבן המז[ור] *the stone of wound(ing)* 4QApocJos[b] 2$_{13}$.

אַבְנֵי־גִר *stones of chalk* Is 27$_{9}$, שַׁיִשׁ *of marble* 1 C 29$_{2}$, אֵשׁ *of fire* Ezk 28$_{14.16}$, בּוֹר *of Pit* Is 14$_{19}$, קֶלַע *of*, i.e. for, *sling* Zc 9$_{15}$ (or em. בְּנֵי קֶלַע / קֹבַע *sons of Kela/Koba*) Jb 41$_{20}$ (קֶלַע), קְלָעִים *of slings* 2 C 26$_{14}$, קֹדֶשׁ *of holiness* Lm 4$_{1}$, מַחְצֵב *of*, i.e. from, *quarry* 2 K 12$_{13}$ 22$_{6}$||2 C 34$_{11}$, גָּזִית *of hewing*, i.e. hewn stones 1 K 5$_{31}$ Ezk 40$_{42}$ 1 C 22$_{2}$ 11QT 3$_{7}$, הַשָּׂדֶה *of the field* Jb 5$_{23}$, מִזְבֵּחַ *of altar* Is 27$_{9}$, הַמָּקוֹם *of the place* Gn 28$_{11}$ 1QJub[a] 27$_{20}$, עֶשֶׂר אַמּוֹת *of ten cubits* 1 K 7$_{10}$, שְׁמֹנֶה אַמּוֹת *of eight cubits* 7$_{10}$, אַבְנֵי הָרָמָה *stones of Ramah* 1 K 15$_{22}$||2 C 16$_{6}$.

מַצֶּבֶת אֶבֶן *pillar of stone* Gn 35$_{14}$ (אָבֶן), כֹּבֶד־אֶבֶן *heaviness of stone* Pr 27$_{3}$ (|| חול *sand*), חָרָשֵׁי *workers of* 2 S 5$_{11}$ 1 C 22$_{15}$, לֵב הָאֶבֶן *heart of stone* Ezk 11$_{19}$ 36$_{26}$ 1QH 18$_{26}$, חוֹצְבֵי *cutters of* 2 K 12$_{13}$, לֻחֹת *tablets of* Ex 24$_{12}$ 31$_{18}$ (אֶבֶן) 4QJub[a] 1$_{3}$ ([לוחות האבן]) 1$_{6}$ ([לוחות]).

גַּל־אֲבָנִים *mound of stones* Jos 7$_{26}$ 8$_{29}$ 2 S 18$_{17}$, לֻחֹת *tablets of* Ex 34$_{1.4.4}$ Dt 4$_{13}$ (לֻחוֹת) 5$_{22}$ 10$_{1}$ (לוּחֹת) 10$_{3}$, לוּחֹת הָאֲבָנִים 9$_{9.10.11}$ (לֻחֹת) 1 K 8$_{9}$ (לֻחֹת), מִזְבַּח אֲבָנִים *altar of stones* Ex 20$_{25}$ Dt 27$_{5}$ Jos 8$_{31}$, מַרְצֶפֶת *pavement of* 2 K 16$_{17}$, בֵּית *house*, i.e. place, *of* Jb 8$_{17}$ (or em. בֵּין *among* stones), גֶּדֶר אֲבָנָיו *wall of its stones* Pr 24$_{31}$, חוֹמַת אַבְנֵיהֶם *wall of their stones* Ne 3$_{35}$, כֹּחַ אֲבָנִים *strength of stones* Jb 6$_{12}$, מחשכי *darkness of* 1QM 14$_{18}$ + Sup (mg אבדונים *of Abaddon[s]*), חַלֻּקֵי־ *smooth ones of*, i.e. smooth stones 1 S 17$_{40}$, כָּל־אֶבֶן *any stone* Nm 35$_{23}$, כָּל־אַבְנֵי *all stones of* altar Is 27$_{9}$.

<APP> אֱלֹהִים מַעֲשֵׂה יְדֵי אָדָם עֵץ וָאֶבֶן *gods, the work of* *human hands, wood and stone* Dt 4_{28}, sim. 2 K 19_{18}||Is 37_{19} 11QT 59_3, אֱלֹהִים ... עֵץ וָאֶבֶן *gods, ... wood and stone* Dt $28_{36.64}$, שִׁקּוּצֵיהֶם גִּלֻּלֵיהֶם עֵץ וָאֶבֶן כֶּסֶף וְזָהָב *their detestable things, their idols, wood and stone, silver and gold* 29_{16}, רֹעֶה אֶבֶן *the Shepherd, the Rock of* Israel Gn 49_{24} (or em. מִשָּׁם רֹעֶה אֶבֶן *from there the Shepherd, the Rock of* to מִשֵּׁם עֹזֵר *by the name of the helper of*), הָאֶבֶן הָרֹאשָׁה *the stone, the top,* i.e. the topmost (or, corner) stone Zc 4_7 (or em. אֶבֶן *stone of* the top).

<ADJ> אַחֵר *other* Lv 14_{42}, אֶחָד *one* Jos 4_5 Jg $9_{5.18}$ 1 S 7_{12}, גָּדוֹל *great* Gn 29_2 (if em.; see Nom Cl.) Dt 27_2 Jos $10_{18.27}$ 24_{26} 1 S $6_{14.15.18(mss)}$ (אֶבֶן הַגְּדוֹלָה; or em. הָאֶבֶן; L אָבֵל Great *Abel*) 14_{33} 2 S 20_8 1 K 5_{31} 7_{10} Jr 43_9 2 C 26_{15}, יְמָנִי *right* 1Q29 $2_{2(Milik)}$ ([הא]בן), יָקָר *costly* (of building stones) 1 K 5_{31} $7_{9.10.11}$, שָׁחֹר *black* 3QTr 10_9 12_2, שָׁלֵם *whole*, i.e. unhewn Dt 27_6 Jos 8_{31}, *finished*, i.e. hewn 1 K 6_7.

<PREP> אמר לְ *say to* Jr 2_{27} Hb 2_{19} (both || עֵץ *wood*), היה לְ *be as* Gn 11_3 (+ לְבֵנָה *brick*) Is 8_{14}, *become*, i.e. be paralysed 1 S 25_{37}, שׂים לְ *make as* Is $54_{12.12}$, שׂים מִמַּעַל לְ *place above* Jr 43_{10}, כון לְ hi. *prepare* stones 2 C 26_{14} (or em. לְאַבְנֵי to אַבְנֵי).

בְּ of instrument, *with* perh. 4QApocJos^b 2_{13}, + נכה hi. *strike* Ex 21_{18} (|| אֶגְרֹף *fist*) Nm 35_{17}, נגף *strike* Ps 91_{12}, סקל *pelt* Dt 13_{11} 17_5=11QT 55_{21} Dt $22_{21.24}$=11QT 66_2 ([אבנים]) Jos 7_{25} 1 K 21_{13}, pi. 2 S $16_{6.13}$, רגם *pelt* Lv $20_{2.27}$ Nm 14_{10} $15_{35.36}$ Dt 21_{21}=11QT 64_5 (א[בנ]ם) Ezk 16_{40}, קלע *sling* Jg 20_{16}, נפל hi. *cast* Nm 35_{23} (or del. בְּ, and understand as obj.), ימן hi. *use the right hand* 1 C 12_2, שׂמאל hi. *use the left hand* 12_2, ירה *shoot* 2 C 26_{15} (|| חֵץ *arrow*), חזק *prevail* 1 S 17_{50} (|| קֶלַע *sling*), כאב hi. *damage* land 2 K 3_{19}, עשׂה *work* 2 C 2_{13} (|| זָהָב *gold*, כֶּסֶף *silver*, נְחֹשֶׁת *bronze*, בַּרְזֶל *iron*, עֵץ *wood*, אַרְגָּמָן *purple material*, תְּכֵלֶת *blue material*, כַּרְמִיל *crimson material*, בּוּץ *fine linen*), בנה pass. *be built* 4QBen 1_3 ([בנ]וי), of place, *in*, + היה *be* Ex 7_{19} (+ דָּם *blood*).

כְּ *as* 1 K 10_{27}||2 C 1_{15}=9_{27} Ne 9_{11}, + היה *be* Si 6_{21} (+ חָכְמָה *wisdom*), שׂים *make* Is 27_9, דמם *be still* Ex 15_{16}, חבא htp. *congeal* Jb 38_{30}, יצק pass. *be cast* Jb 41_{16}, ירד *go down* Ex 15_5.

מִן *from* 2QapProph 1_6, סקל מֵאֶבֶן pi. *clear of stones* Is 62_{10}, לקח מִן *take (one) of* Gn 28_{11} 1QJub^a 27_{20} (ויק[ח]).

עַל *upon, over* 3QTr 8_5, + הרג *kill* Jg $9_{5.18}$, כתב *write* Dt 27_8 Jos 8_{32}, ישׁב *sit* Ex 17_{12}, נוח hi. *place* 1 S $6_{15(mss)}$ (L אֶל) $6_{18(mss)}$ (L אָבֵל at the side of Great *Abel*), נוף hi. *wave* Dt 27_5 Jos 8_{31}; אֶל *to*, + ירד *go down* Is 14_{19}, *upon*, + שׂים *place* 1 S 6_{15}, pass. *be placed* Hg 2_{15}; נאף אֶת *commit adultery with* Jr 3_9; עִם *with* 2 S 20_8 Jb 5_{23}; תַּחַת *under* 3QTr 12_2, *instead of*, + בוא *bring* Is 60_{17} (|| עֵץ *wood*, נְחֹשֶׁת *bronze*, בַּרְזֶל *iron*); הלך בְּתוֹךְ htp. *walk among* Ezk 28_{14}, אבד מִתּוֹךְ pi. *destroy from among* 28_{16}, עַד אֶבֶן *unto (the) stone* 1 S $6_{18(mss)}$ (L אָבֵל Great *Abel*; or em. עֵד הָאֶבֶן *the stone is a witness*).

<COLL> עֵץ וָאֶבֶן (וָאֶבֶן) divine images of *wood and stone* Dt 4_{28} $28_{36.64}$ (both + אֱלֹהִים אֲחֵרִים *other gods*) 29_{16} 2 K 19_{18}||Is 37_{19} Ezk 20_{32} 11QT 59_3, עֵצִים וַאֲבָנִים *wood* (pl.) *and stones* (and vars.) Ex 7_{19} 1 K 5_{32} 2 K 12_{13} 22_6 Zc 5_4 1 C 22_{14} CD 12_{15}, אֶבֶן וָעֵץ *stone and wood* (and vars.) Jr 3_9 1 C 22_{15} 1QpHab 13_2, אֲבָנִים וְעֵצִים *stones and wood* (and vars.) Lv 14_{45} Ezk 26_{12} 2 C 2_{13} 34_{11}, אֶבֶן שְׁלֵמָה מַסָּע נִבְנָה *it was built with stone finished at the quarry* 1 K 6_7, בנה אֲבָנִים *build with stones* Ex 20_{25} Dt 27_6 1 K 18_{32}, שְׁתֵּים עֶשְׂרֵה אֲבָנִים *twelve stones* (and vars.) Jos $4_{3.8.9.20}$ 1 K 18_{31}.

2. precious stone (of many kinds), with or without adj. יָקָר *precious*, **<SUBJ>** היה *be* Ex 28_{21} (+ עַל *according to* names), מצא ni. *be found* 1 C 29_8, סבב ho. *be surrounded* Ex 28_{11}, גלה ni. *be revealed* 4Q376 1.2_1. **<NOM CL>** שָׁם ... אֶבֶן *there ... was stone* Gn 2_{12} (|| בְּדֹלַח *bdellium*), זֹאת הַתְּרוּמָה ... אַבְנֵי *this is the offering ... stones of* Ex 25_7, הָאֲבָנִים עַל־שְׁמֹת בְּנֵי־יִשְׂרָאֵל הֵנָּה שְׁתֵּים עֶשְׂרֵה *the stones were according to the names of the sons of Israel, twelve* 39_{14}, אֶבֶן ... הַשֹּׁחַד *a stone is ... a bribe* Pr 17_8, וּבָהּ אֶבֶן *and in it* (crown) *was* precious *stone* 1 C 20_2 (|| 2 S 12_{30} וְאֶבֶן *and*, i.e. with, precious *stone*), אֶבֶן יְקָרָה מְסֻכָתֶךָ *precious stone was your cover* Ezk 28_{13}.

<OBJ> בוא hi. *bring* Ex $35_{9.27}$ (|| בֹּשֶׂם *spice*, שֶׁמֶן *oil*) 1 K 10_{11}||2 C 9_{10} (|| עֵץ *wood*) 4QDibHam^a 4_{10}, כון hi. *prepare* 1 C 29_2 (|| זָהָב *gold*, כֶּסֶף *silver*, נְחֹשֶׁת *bronze*, בַּרְזֶל *iron*, עֵץ), עשׂה *make* Ex 28_{11}||39_6, נשׂא *carry* 1 K 10_2||2 C 9_1 (|| זָהָב, בֹּשֶׂם), שׂים *place* Ex 28_{12}||39_7, נתן *give* 1 K 10_{10}||2 C 9_9 (|| זָהָב, בֹּשֶׂם) Zc 3_9, לקח *take* Ex 25_7||35_9

(|| זָהָב ,כֶּסֶף ,נְחֹשֶׁת ,תְּכֵלֶת *blue material,* אַרְגָּמָן *purple material,* שֵׁשׁ *fine linen,* עֵז *goat hair,* עוֹר *skin,* עֵץ, שֶׁמֶן, בֹּשֶׂם; + תּוֹלַעַת שָׁנִי *scarlet material)* 28$_{9}$, פתח pi. *engrave* 28$_{11}$, צפה pi. *overlay* 2 C 3$_{6}$, מלא pi. *fill,* i.e. set Ex 28$_{17}$, פאר pi. *adorn* Si 45$_{11.11}$.

<CSTR> אֶבֶן־חֵן *stone of grace,* i.e. precious stone Pr 17$_{8}$, חֵפֶץ *of pleasure,* i.e. gems Is 54$_{12}$ Si 45$_{11}$ 50$_{9}$ 1QM 5$_{6.9.14}$ 12$_{12}$ 4Q525 3$_{3}$ (אבני), אֶבֶן תַּרְשִׁישׁ *stone of beryl* Ezk 10$_{9}$, הַשֹּׁהַם *of onyx* Gn 2$_{12}$, סַפִּיר *of sapphire* 1$_{26}$ (אֶבֶן) 10$_{1}$, הספיר 4QpIsa^{d} 1$_{3}$, פּוּךְ וְרִקְמָה *of antimony and variegated colours* 1 C 29$_{2}$, שֹׁהַם *of onyx* Ex 25$_{7}$ ||35$_{9.27}$ (אַבְנֵי הַשֹּׁהַם) 28$_{9}$ 39$_{6}$ (אַבְנֵי הַשֹּׁהַם) 1 C 29$_{2}$, אַבְנֵי אֶקְדָּח *stones of beryl* Is 54$_{12}$, זִכָּרֹן *of remembrance* Ex 28$_{12}$||39$_{7}$ (זִכָּרוֹן), מִלֻּאִים *of settings,* i.e. for inlay 25$_{7}$||35$_{9.27}$ (הַמִּלֻּאִים) 1 C 29$_{2}$ (אַבְנֵי־ ... מִלּוּאִים), אַבְנֵי־נֵזֶר *stones of crown* Zc 9$_{16}$; חָרַשׁ אֶבֶן *engraver of stone* Ex 28$_{11}$, חֲרֹשֶׁת *cutting of* 31$_{5}$||35$_{33}$ (|| עֵץ *wood;* + זָהָב *gold,* כֶּסֶף *silver,* נְחֹשֶׁת *bronze),* עֵין *gleam of* Ezk 10$_{9}$, מַרְאֵה *appearance of* 1$_{26}$, מִלֵּאת *setting of* Ex 28$_{17}$, טוּרֵי *rows of* 39$_{10}$ (אָבֶן), כָּל־אֶבֶן *every stone* Ezk 27$_{22}$ 28$_{13}$ 1 C 29$_{2}$ (כֹּל) Si 45$_{11}$ GnzPs 2$_{29}$ (כל אבנ[ים]) 4Q525 3$_{3}$ (כול אבני).

<APP> אַרְבָּעָה טוּרִים אָבֶן *four rows, stones,* i.e. four rows of stones Ex 28$_{17}$, מנחתם ... אבן *their offering ... stone* 4QDibHam^{a} 4$_{10}$.

<ADJ> יָקָר *precious* stone(s) (perh. collective) 2 S 12$_{30}$||1 C 20$_{2}$ 1 K 10$_{2.10.11}$||2 C 9$_{1.9.10}$ Ezk 27$_{22}$ 28$_{13}$ Dn 11$_{38}$ 1 C 29$_{2}$ 2 C 3$_{6}$ 32$_{27}$ Si 45$_{11}$ 4QDibHam^{a} 4$_{10}$, טוֹב *good* GnzPs 2$_{29}$, אֶחָד *one* Ex 28$_{10}$ Zc 3$_{9}$, שֵׁנִי *second* Ex 28$_{10}$, שְׂמָאלִי *left* 4Q376 1.2$_{1}$.

<PREP> עשׂה לְ *make* treasuries *for* 2 C 32$_{27}$ (|| כֶּסֶף *silver,* זָהָב *gold,* בֹּשֶׂם *spice,* מָגֵן *shield,* כְּלִי *vessel),* שׂים לְ *make of* Is 54$_{12}$; כבד בְּ pi. *honour with* Dn 11$_{38}$ (|| זָהָב, כֶּסֶף, חֲמוּדָה *precious thing),* נתן עִזָּבוֹן בְּ *trade wares in exchange for* Ezk 27$_{22}$ (|| בֹּשֶׂם ,זָהָב); כְּ *as* Ezk 10$_{1}$ 4QpIsa^{d} 1$_{3}$, + נסס htpo. *be prominent* Zc 9$_{16}$ (if em. כִּי אַבְנֵי־ *for stones of* to כְּאַבְנֵי־); טוֹב מִן *better than* GnzPs 2$_{29}$ (|| מַרְגָּלִית *jewel);* עַל *upon,* + פתח pi. *engrave* Ex 28$_{9.10.10}$ Zc 3$_{9}$, אחז ni. *be caught up* Si 50$_{9}$; appar. לקח עם ni. *be taken,* i.e. bought, *with* 4Q525 3$_{3}$; בְּתוֹךְ *among* 4QpIsa^{d} 1$_{3}$.

<COLL> שְׁתֵּי הָאֲבָנִים *the two stones* Ex 28$_{11.12}$, var. 28$_{9}$, שְׁתֵּים עֶשְׂרֵה ... הָאֲבָנִים *the stones ... twelve* 39$_{14}$.

3a. weight, **<SUBJ>** היה *be* Lv 19$_{36}$ Dt 25$_{13.15}$ (all three + לְ *to* Israel). **<NOM CL>** אֶבֶן שְׁלֵמָה רְצוֹנוֹ *a full weight is his delight* Pr 11$_{1}$, מַעֲשֵׂהוּ ... אַבְנֵי־כִיס *the weights of the bag ... are his work* 16$_{11}$, תּוֹעֲבַת י׳ אֶבֶן וָאָבֶן *diverse weights are an abomination to Y.* 20$_{23}$, var. 20$_{10}$. **<OBJ>** שׁלך hi. *cast* Zc 5$_{8}$.

<CSTR> אֶבֶן הַמֶּלֶךְ *weight of the king,* i.e. the royal standard weight 2 S 14$_{26}$, עֹפֶרֶת *of lead,* as a cover Zc 5$_{8}$, אַבְנֵי־כִיס *weights of the bag,* i.e. portable weights Pr 16$_{11}$, צֶדֶק *of righteousness,* i.e. true weights Lv 19$_{36}$, מִרְמָה *of deceit,* i.e. fraudulent weights Mc 6$_{11}$ (אַבְנֵי); אבן ... תמחי *cleansing of ... weight* Si 42$_{4(M)}$ (B תמהות appar. err. for תמחות *cleansing of;* Bmg תמרות *exchanging of;* || אֵיפָה *measure),* כִּיס אַבְנֵי *bag of weights of* Mc 6$_{11}$, כָּל־אַבְנֵי *all the weights of* Pr 16$_{11}$. **<ADJ>** שָׁלֵם *full* Dt 25$_{15}$ Pr 11$_{1}$. **<PREP>** שׁקל בְּ *weigh by* 2 S 14$_{26}$.

<COLL> אֶבֶן וָאָבֶן *weight and weight,* i.e. diverse (fraudulent) weights Dt 25$_{13}$ Pr 20$_{10}$ (וְאָבֶן; || אֵיפָה *measure)* 20$_{23}$, איפה ואבן *measures and weights* Si 42$_{4}$.

3b. plummet, **<OBJ>** נטה *stretch* Is 34$_{11}$, ראה *see* Zc 4$_{10}$. **<CSTR>** אַבְנֵי־בֹהוּ *plummets of emptiness* Is 34$_{11}$ (|| קַו *line).* **<APP>** הָאֶבֶן הַבְּדִיל *the plummet, the tin* Zc 4$_{10}$.

3c. weight, to sink book Jr 51$_{63}$.

4. hailstone, **<SUBJ>** נפל *fall* Ezk 13$_{11}$, היה *be* 13$_{13}$ (+ לְכָלָה *for destruction).* **<OBJ>** מטר hi. *rain down* Ezk 38$_{22}$ (|| גֶּשֶׁם *rain,* אֵשׁ *fire,* גָּפְרִית *brimstone),* שׁלך hi. *cast* Jos 10$_{11}$, גדע pi. *break down* Si 43$_{15}$. **<CSTR>** אֶבֶן בָּרָד *hailstone* Is 30$_{30}$, אַבְנֵי הַבָּרָד *hailstones* Jos 10$_{11}$ Si 43$_{15}$ (א[ב]ני ברד) 46$_{5(Segal)}$ ([ברד]), אַבְנֵי אֶלְגָּבִישׁ *hailstones* Ezk 13$_{11.13}$ 38$_{22}$ Si 46$_{5(Segal)}$ (אבני ... [א]לגביש). **<ADJ>** גָּדוֹל *great* Jos 10$_{11}$. **<PREP>** בְּ of instrument, *with,* + ענה *answer* Si 46$_{5}$, ראה hi. *show* sweep of arm Is 30$_{30}$ (|| זֶרֶם *downpour,* נֶפֶץ *cloudburst,* לַהַב *flame,* זַעַף *anger),* מוּת בְּ *die because of* Jos 10$_{11}$.

5. named stones, a. אֶבֶן בֹּהַן בֶּן־רְאוּבֵן *the stone of Bohan, son of Reuben,* on the boundary between Judah and Benjamin W. of Jericho, mod. Ḥağar el-Aṣbāḥ, Jos 15$_{6}$ 18$_{17}$. **b.** אֶבֶן הַזֹּחֶלֶת *the stone of Zoheleth* (or perh. *the serpent's stone*), in the Kidron valley 1 K 1$_{9}$. **c.** (הָ)אֶבֶן הָעֵזֶר *Ebenezer,* i.e. the stone (called) Help, between Mizpah and Jerusalem 1 S 4$_{1}$ 5$_{1}$ 7$_{12}$.

d. הָאֶבֶן הָאָזֶל *the stone of Ezel* 1 S 20$_{19}$ (or em. הָאַרְגָּב הַלָּאז *this stone heap*).

Also 11QT 11$_{17}$ 4QpIsa^{c} 2$_{5}$ 1Q29 1$_{2}$ 1Q46 1$_{2}$ 4Q376 1.1$_{4}$.

<SYN> §1 עָפָר *dust*, בַּרְזֶל *iron*; §§1, 2 עֵץ *wood*, זָהָב *gold*, כֶּסֶף *silver*, נְחֹשֶׁת *bronze*; §2 בֹּשֶׂם *spice*, שֶׁמֶן *oil*; §3 אֵיפָה *measure*.

→ אֶבֶן *stone*.

[אֹבֶן] 2.0.1 n.[m.] **stone**—du. אָבְנַיִם (Q הבנים = אָבְנַיִם or הָאָבְנָיִם)—alw. du., **pair of stones,** appar. circular, like millstone, and used in pottery (Jr 18$_{3}$ appar. 1QH fr. 2.1$_{8}$) and, perh., childbirth (as seat for mother) (Ex 1$_{16}$). <PREP> עֹשֶׂה מְלָאכָה עַל־הָאָבְנָיִם *doing work on the (potter's) stones* Jr 18$_{3}$, על הבנים תבחנני appar. *over the (potter's) wheels you will test me* 1QH fr. 2.1$_{8}$, וּרְאִיתֶן עַל־הָאָבְנָיִם *and you have seen (the mothers) upon the stones* Ex 1$_{16}$.

→ אֶבֶן *stone*.

[אַבְנָה], see אֲמָנָה II.

אַבְנֵט 9.0.2 n.[m.] **girdle**—cstr. אַבְנֵט; sf. אַבְנֵטְךָ; pl. אַבְנֵטִים—of priest, also of royal officer (Is 22$_{21}$), <OBJ> עשׂה *make* Ex 28$_{4}$ (‖ אֵפֹד *ephod*, מְעִיל *robe*, כְּתֹנֶת *tunic*, מִצְנֶפֶת *turban*) 28$_{39}$ (+ מִצְנֶפֶת, כְּתֹנֶת) 28$_{40}$ (+ כְּתֹנֶת, מִכְנָסַיִם, מִגְבָּעָה, מִצְנֶפֶת, כְּתֹנֶת + מִגְבָּעָה *bonnet*) 39$_{29}$ (+ *breeches*), חגר *gird* priests *(with)* Ex 29$_{9}$‖Lv 8$_{13}$ (+ כְּתֹנֶת, מִגְבָּעָה), חזק pi. *fasten (onto)* Eliakim Is 22$_{21}$ (‖ כְּתֹנֶת, + מֶמְשָׁלָה *government*). <CSTR> אַבְנֵט בַּד *girdle of linen* Lv 16$_{4}$ 1QM 7$_{10}$ 4QM^{a} fr. 1$_{18}$ ([ב]ד). <APP> (הָ)אַבְנֵט ... מַעֲשֵׂה רֹקֵם *(the) girdle ..., work of an embroiderer* Ex 28$_{39}$ 39$_{29}$, הָאַבְנֵט שֵׁשׁ מָשְׁזָר וּתְכֵלֶת וְאַרְגָּמָן וְתוֹלַעַת שָׁנִי *the girdle, fine twined linen and of blue and purple and scarlet material* 39$_{29}$ 1QM 7$_{10}$ (משוזר תכלת), בְּגָדִים ... אַבְנֵט *garments ... a girdle* Ex 28$_{4}$. <PREP> חגר בְּ *gird (oneself) with* Lv 8$_{7}$ (+ כְּתֹנֶת, מְעִיל, אֵפֹד) 16$_{4}$ (+ כְּתֹנֶת, מִצְנֶפֶת, מִכְנְסֵי) 1QM 7$_{10}$ (+ מִכְנָסַיִם, כְּתֹנֶת).

<SYN> כְּתֹנֶת *tunic*, אֵפֹד *ephod*, מְעִיל *robe*, מִצְנֶפֶת *turban*.

[אבנעם], see אֲבִינֹעַם.

אַבְנֵר 63.0.0.1 pr.n.m. **Abner**—אֲבִינֵר—**1.** son of Ner and commander of Saul's army, father of Jaasiel (1 C 27$_{21}$), 1 S 14$_{50}$ (אֲבִינֵר; mss אבנר) 14$_{51}$ 17$_{55.55.55.57}$ 20$_{25}$ 26$_{5+5t}$ 2 S 2$_{8+15t}$ 3$_{6+27t}$ 4$_{1.12}$ 1 K 2$_{5.32}$ 1 C 8$_{33}$‖9$_{39}$ (if em. קִישׁ *Kish*) 26$_{28}$ 27$_{21}$. **2.** Seal 163$_{1}$ (Gezer, 6th–4th cent.).

→ אָב *father* + נֵר *lamp*.

אבס 2 vb. **fatten**—ptc. pass. אָבוּס, אֲבוּסִים—**fatten** for eating, or perh. **keep in stall** for rest or restraint, בַּרְבֻּרִים אֲבוּסִים *fatted fowl* 1 K 5$_{3}$, שׁוֹר אָבוּס *fatted ox* Pr 15$_{17}$.

→ אֵבוּס *trough*, מַאֲבוּס *granary*.

[אֲבַעְבֻּעָה] 2 n.f. **blister**—pl. אֲבַעְבֻּעֹת—שְׁחִין פֹּרֵחַ אֲבַעְבֻּעֹת *inflammation erupting (in) blisters* Ex 9$_{9}$, sim. 9$_{10}$.

[אֲבִעֶזֶר] 0.0.0.2 pl.n. **Abiezer,** appar. W of Shechem (unless perh. name of family, אֲבִיעֶזֶר *Abiezer*, §2), Samaria ost. 13$_{1}$ 28$_{1}$.

→ אָב *father* + עזר *help*.

[אֶבֶץ] 1 pl.n. **Ebez**—אֶבֶץ—town in Issachar, Jos 19$_{20}$.

אִבְצָן 2 pr.n.m. **Ibzan,** judge after Jephthah, Jg 12$_{8.10}$.

אבק 2 vb. **wrestle—Ni.** + waw וַיֵּאָבֵק; inf. הֵאָבְקוֹ—<SUBJ> אִישׁ *man* Gn 32$_{25.26}$. <PREP> עִם *with* Jacob Gn 32$_{25.26}$.

אָבָק 6 n.m. **dust**—cstr. אֲבַק; sf. אֲבָקָם—**dust, fine dust.** <SUBJ> כסה pi. *cover* Tyre Ezk 26$_{10}$.

<NOM CL> עָנָן אֲבַק רַגְלָיו *a cloud is the dust of his feet* Na 1$_{3}$. <OBJ> נתן *give*, i.e. cause (rain) to be Dt 28$_{24}$ (‖ עָפָר *dust*).

<ADJ> דַּק *fine* Is 29$_{5}$.

<PREP> לְ *as*, + היה *be* (of ashes) Ex 9$_{9}$; כְּ *as*, + היה *be* (of multitude) Is 29$_{5}$ (+ מֹץ *chaff*), עלה *go up*, i.e. disappear (of blossom) 5$_{24}$ (+ מַק *rottenness*).

<COLL> אָבָק וְעָפָר *powder and dust* Dt 28$_{24}$.

→ אֲבָקָה *powder*.

[אֲבָקָה] 1 n.f. **powder**—cstr. מְקֻטֶּרֶת ... מִכֹּל—אַבְקַת אַבְקַת רוֹכֵל *perfumed ... with every powder of a merchant* Ca 3_{6} (+ מוֹר וּלְבוֹנָה *myrrh and frankincense*).
→ אָבָק *dust*.

אבר 1 vb. **fly**—**Hi.** Impf. ־יַאֲבֶר—**fly**, perh. **grow wings**, הֲמִבִּינָתְךָ יַאֲבֶר־נֵץ *is it by your wisdom that the hawk flies?* Jb 39_{26} (|| פרשׂ *spread* wings, גבה hi. *soar*).
→ אֵבֶר *wing*, אֶבְרָה *wing*.

אֵבֶר 3.0.1 n.[m.] **wing**, **1.** in sg., as collective, **wings, wingfeathers**, <OBJ> עלה hi. *raise*, i.e. grow Is 40_{31} (+ כֹּחַ *strength*, כַּנְּשָׁרִים *as the eagles*), נתן *give* Ps 55_{7} (+ כַּיּוֹנָה *as the dove*). <CSTR> אֶרֶךְ הָאֵבֶר *long of the wings* Ezk 17_{3} (+ כָּנָף *wing*, נוֹצָה *plumage*, הַנֶּשֶׁר הַגָּדוֹל *the great eagle*).

2. in pl., **limb, member**, esp. of sacrificial animal, לחם אברים perh. *flesh of limbs* Si 7_{31} (but prob. אברים = *bulls*; see אַבִּיר *mighty*), וארביה לבד יהיו[ן] *and its limbs will be (kept) apart* 11QT 24_{8} (corr. for אבריה).

3. quarter of city, ישב ... באברו אליו *he is to dwell ... in his quarter (that is to him)* 4QToh A 1.1_{2}.

4. meaning uncertain, ושניו רומות לאבר appar. *and his teeth are uneven* 4QCrypt 1.3_{3}.
→ אבר *fly*.

אֶבְרָה 4 n.f. **wing**—sf. אֶבְרָתוֹ, אֶבְרוֹתֶיהָ—**wing**, perh. also collective, **wings**, of dove, stork, eagle, Y. as bird, <SUBJ> חפה ni. *be covered* with gold Ps 68_{14} (|| כָּנָף *wing*).

<NOM CL> אִם־אֶבְרָה appar. *is it (the) wing?*, i.e. is it like the wing? Jb 39_{13}.

<APP> אֶבְרָה חֲסִידָה וְנֹצָה appar. *the wing (of) the stork and (her) plumage* Jb 39_{13}. <PREP> סכך בְּ hi. *cover with* Ps 91_{4} (+ כָּנָף *wing*); נשׂא עַל *carry upon* Dt 32_{11} (+ כָּנָף). <SYN> כָּנָף *wing*.
→ אבר *fly*.

אַבְרָהָם 175.3.15 pr.n.m. **Abraham**, patriarch, formerly called Abram (Gn 17_{5} 1 C 1_{27}; see also אַבְרָם *Abram*), sometimes representative of Israel (Gn 18_{19} Mc 7_{20}), Gn 17_{5} (+ אַב־הֲמוֹן גּוֹיִם *father of a multitude of nations*) 17_{9+8t} 18_{6+12t} $19_{27.29}$ 20_{1+7t} 21_{2+17t} 22_{1+19t} 23_{2+11t} $24_{1.1.2.6.9.12}$ (+ אֱלֹהֵי *God of*) $24_{12.15.27}$ (+ אֱלֹהֵי) $24_{34.42.48}$ (both + אֱלֹהֵי) $24_{52.59}$ 25_{1+12t} $26_{1.3.5.15.18.18.24}$ (+ אֱלֹהֵי) 26_{24} (+ עֶבֶד *servant* of Y.) $28_{4.4.9.13}$ (+ אָב *ancestor* of Jacob) $31_{42.53}$ 32_{10} (all four + אֱלֹהֵי) $35_{12.27}$ $48_{15.16}$ $49_{30.31}$ $50_{13.24}$ Ex 2_{24} (+ בְּרִיתוֹ אֶת־ *his covenant with*) $3_{6.15}$ (both + אֱלֹהֵי) 3_{16} 4_{5} (+ אֱלֹהֵי) $6_{3.8}$ 32_{13} (+ עֶבֶד) 33_{1} Lv 26_{42} (+ בְּרִיתִי *my covenant [with]*) Nm 32_{11} Dt 1_{8} 6_{10} $9_{5.27}$ 29_{12} 30_{20} 34_{4} Jos $24_{2.3}$ 1 K 18_{36} (+ אֱלֹהֵי) 2 K 13_{23} (+ בְּרִיתוֹ אֶת־) Is 29_{22} 41_{8} (+ זֶרַע *seed of*, אהב ptc. *friend* of Y.) 51_{2} (+ אָב *ancestor* of Israelites) 63_{16} Jr 33_{26} (+ זֶרַע) Ezk 33_{24} Mc 7_{20} Ps 47_{10} (+ אֱלֹהֵי) 105_{6} (||1 C 16_{13} יִשְׂרָאֵל *Israel*; + עֶבֶד, זֶרַע) $105_{9.42}$ (+ עֶבֶד) Ne 9_{7} 1 C $1_{27.28.32.34}$ 16_{16} 29_{18} (+ אָב *ancestor* of Israelites) 2 C 20_{7} (+ זֶרַע, אהב ptc.) 30_{6} (+ אֱלֹהֵי) Si 44_{19} (+ אב המון גוים) 44_{22} 51_{12} (+ מגן *shield of*) 3QJub $23_{6.6}$ (in both [א]ברהם) 4QJub[a] 2_{2} (+ אָב) CD 3_{2} 12_{11} (+ ברית *covenant of*) 16_{6} 5QRègle 2_{5} 5Q22 1_{5} (אברה[ם]) 4QJub[d] 1.1_{11} ([אברהם]) 1.2_{36} 4QPsJos[a] 22.1_{4} 4QPsJos[b] 11_{3} 17_{4} 4Q386–9 4_{8} ([הברית אשר כרתי] עם אב[רהם ועם י]צחק *the covenant that I made with Abraham and with Isaac*) 4QpGen[a] 2_{8} (אהב ptc.) $3_{7.13}$ (+ ברכת אביכה [אברהם] *blessing of your father/ancestor, Abraham*) 4Q464 1_{1} (+ בן [תרח] *son of Terah*) 3.2_{3} (אברה[ם]) 3.1_{6}.
→ אָב *father*.

אבריהו 0.0.0.1 pr.n.m. **Abraiah**, Seal 330 (8th-6th cent.).
→ perh. אבר *fly* + יו Y.

אַבְרֵךְ 1 appar. interj., perh. **bow down** or **hail, minister**, etc., וַיִּקְרְאוּ לוֹ אַבְרֵךְ *and they called (to) him, Abrek* Gn 41_{43}.

אַבְרָם 61.0.2 pr.n.m. **Abram**, patriarch, son of Terah, father of Isaac and Ishmael (see also אַבְרָהָם *Abraham*), Gn 11_{26+5t} 12_{1+11t} 13_{1+8t} $14_{12.13}$ (+ בְּרִית *covenant of*) 14_{14+5t} 15_{1+7t} 16_{1+11t} $17_{1.1.3.5}$ Ne 9_{7} Ezk 33_{24} 4QpGen[a] 2_{9} (אב[רם]) $2_{10.11.13}$ (אב[רם]).
→ אָב *father* + רום *be high*.

[אבשדי], see אֲבִישׁוּעַ.

[אבשוע], see אֲבִישׁוּעַ.

אַבְשַׁי, see אֲבִישַׁי.

אַבְשָׁלוֹם 111.0.2 pr.n.m. **Absalom**—אֲבִישָׁלוֹם, אַבְשָׁלֹם —**1. Absalom,** son of David and Maacah, 2 S 3_{3} 13_{1+20t} 14_{1+12t} 15_{1+17t} 16_{8+10t} 17_{1+14t} 18_{5+8t} $18_{18.18}$ (+ יַד *hand,* i.e. pillar, *of*) $18_{29.32}$ 19_{1+8t} 20_{6} 1 K 1_{6} $2_{7.28}$ Ps 3_{1} 1 C 3_{2} 3QTr 10_{12} (+ יד). **2. Abishalom,** maternal grandfather of Abijam (Abijah) and Asa, 1 K 15_{2} (||2 C 13_{2} אוּרִיאֵל *Uriel*) 15_{10} (both אֲבִישָׁלוֹם) 2 C $11_{20.21}$. **3.** perh. pejorative term for leader of a religious party, בית אבשלום *house of Absalom* 1QpHab 5_{9}.
→ אָב *father* + שָׁלוֹם *peace.*

אבשעל 0.0.0.1 **Abshaal,** Seal 712 (8th cent.).
→ אָב *father.*

אֹבֹת I 4 pl.n. **O b o t h,** station of exodus, perh. Qaṣr ʿĒn Ḥarūf (Meṣad Rāḥēl) in W. Arabah, Nm $21_{10.11}$ $33_{43.44}$.

אֹבֹת II, see אוֹב I.

אָגֵא 1 pr.n.m. **Agee,** father of Shammah (L שַׁמָּא; mss שַׁמָּה), one of David's warriors, 2 S 23_{11}.

אֲגַג 8 pr.n.m. **Agag**—אֲגָג—**1.** king of Amalek, 1 S $15_{8.9}$ (אֲגָג) $15_{20.32.32.32.33}$ (both אֲגָג). **2.** person mentioned in oracle of Balaam, perh. ident. with preceding, וְיָרֹם מֵאֲגַג מַלְכּוֹ *and his king will be more exalted than Agag* Nm 24_{7} (Sam וירם מגוג מלכו *and Magog, his king, will arise*).
→ אֲגָגִי *Agagite.*

אֲגָגִי 5 gent. **Agagite,** of family of, or perh. of same nature as, Agag the Amalekite, הָמָן בֶּן־הַמְּדָתָא הָאֲגָגִי *Haman son of Hammedatha, the Agagite* Est $3_{1.10}$ 8_{3} (הָמָן הָאֲגָגִי) 8_{5} 9_{24}.
→ אֲגַג *Agag.*

אגד 0.0.1 vb. **bind**—inf. Q אגוד—ותתן לו לאגוד *and you gave to,* i.e. enabled, *him* (Levi) *to (un)bind* 5QRègle 2_{7}.
→ אֲגֻדָּה *bond.*

אֲגֻדָּה 4 n.f. **bond**—cstr. אֲגֻדַּת; sf. אֲגֻדָּתוֹ; pl. cstr. אֲגֻדּוֹת—in ref. to restraining **bond** (Is 58_{6} perh. Am 9_{6}), of plants or persons bound together, **bunch** (Ex 12_{22}), **band, troop** (2 S 2_{25}), perh. of heavens as joined together, **vault** (Am 9_{6}).
<OBJ> לקח *take* Ex 12_{22}, appar. טבל *dip* in blood 12_{22}, נתר hi. *release* Is 58_{6} (|| חַרְצֻבָּה *bond*), יסד *establish* Am 9_{6} (+ עַל־אֶרֶץ *upon/over [the] earth*). <CSTR> אֲגֻדַּת אֵזוֹב *bunch of hyssop* Ex 12_{22}, אֲגֻדּוֹת מוֹטָה *bonds of,* i.e. tying one to, *bar (of yoke)* Is 58_{6}. <ADJ> אֲגֻדָּה אֶחָת *a single troop* 2 S 2_{25}. <PREP> היה לְ *be as* 2 S 2_{25}.
→ אגד *bind.*

אֱגוֹז 1 n.[m.] **nut,** perh. specif. **walnut, walnut tree** (*juglans regia*), used collectively, אֶל־גִּנַּת אֱגוֹז יָרַדְתִּי *I went down into (the) garden of nuts* Ca 6_{11} (Gnz אֱגוֹז).

אָגוּר 1 pr.n.m. **Agur,** author of proverbs, son of Jakeh, Pr 30_{1}.

[אֲגוֹרָה] 1 n.f. **payment**—cstr. אֲגוֹרַת—**payment** or perh. **piece, coin** of silver, לְהִשְׁתַּחֲוֹת לוֹ לַאֲגוֹרַת כֶּסֶף וְכִכַּר־לָחֶם *to bow down to him for payment (consisting) of,* or *for a piece of, silver and a morsel of bread* 1 S 2_{36}.

[אַגְזָרִי], see אַכְזָרִי.

[אֵגֶל] 1 n.[m] **drop**—pl. cstr. אֶגְלֵי—מִי־הוֹלִיד אֶגְלֵי־טָל *who begat (the) drops of dew?* Jb 38_{28} (+ מָטָר *rain*).

אֶגְלַיִם 1 pl.n. **Eglaim,** town in Moab, perh. Kh. eṭ-Ṭelīse, just S of Kerak, Is 15_{8}.

[אגם], see אַגְמוֹן.

אֲגַם I 9.0.1 n.m. **pool**—cstr. אֲגַם; pl. אֲגַמִּים; cstr. אַגְמֵי; sf. אַגְמֵיהֶם—perh. specif. **swamp** (e.g. Jr 51_{32}, unless אֲגַם II *bulwark*), assoc. with renewal of dry or waste land (Is 35$_{7}$ 41$_{18}$ Ps 107$_{35}$ 114$_{8}$), with devastation after destruction of city (Is 14$_{23}$).

<SUBJ> היה *be* turned into blood Ex 7$_{19}$. <OBJ> יבשׁ hi. *make dry* Is 42$_{15}$ (+ נָהָר *river,* הַר *mountain,* גִּבְעָה *hill,* עֵשֶׂב *grass*), הפך *turn* rock *into* Ps 114$_{8}$, שׂרף *burn* Jr 51$_{32}$ (+ מַעְבָּרָה *ford,* אִישׁ *man* of war), שׂוך *close* 4QapPs^{b} 14 (‖ יְאֹר *stream*).

<CSTR> אֲגַם־מַיִם *pool of water* Is 41$_{18}$ (or em. אֲגַמִּים *pools;* + מוֹצָאֵי מַיִם *springs of water*) Ps 107$_{35}$ (+ מֹצָאֵי מָיִם) 114$_{8}$ (+ מַעְיְנוֹ־מָיִם *fountain of water*), אַגְמֵי־מַיִם *pools of water* Is 14$_{23}$ (+ מוֹרָשׁ קִפֹּד *possession of hedgehog[s]*). <APP> מֵימֵי מִצְרַיִם ... אַגְמֵיהֶם *waters of Egypt ... their pools* Ex 7$_{19}$ (or ins. וְ *and* before two preceding nouns).

<PREP> היה לְ *be as,* i.e. turn into (of parched land) Is 35$_{7}$ (+ מַבּוּעַ *spring,* קָנֶה *reed,* גֹּמֶא *reed*), שׂים לְ *place as,* i.e. turn (Babylon, desert) into Is 14$_{23}$ 41$_{18}$ Ps 107$_{35}$; נטה עַל *extend* hand *over* Ex 7$_{19}$ (+ כָּל־מִקְוֵה מֵימֵיהֶם *all their deposits of water*) 8$_{1}$ (both ‖ נָהָר *river,* יְאֹר *stream*).

Also 4QJub^{a} 6$_{2}$ (האג[מים]).

→ אַגְמוֹן *rush.*

[אֲגַם] II, see אֲגַם I.

[אָגֵם] 1 adj. **distressed**—pl. cstr. אַגְמֵי—וְהָיוּ ... כָּל־עֹשֵׂי שֶׂכֶר אַגְמֵי־נָפֶשׁ *and all who work (for) hire will be distressed of soul* Is 19$_{10}$ (or em. שֵׂכָר *hire* or שֵׁכָר who make *strong drink;* + דכא pu. ptc. *crushed*).

אַגְמוֹן 5 n.[m.] **rush**—אַגְמֹן (Q אוגמן)—as lowly, weak (Is 9$_{13}$ 19$_{15}$ 58$_{5}$), used as barb (Jb 40$_{26}$), <SUBJ> עשׂה *do* work Is 19$_{15}$ (:: כִּפָּה *branch,* ‖ זָנָב *tail*). <OBJ> כרת hi. *cut* Is 9$_{13}$ (:: כִּפָּה *branch,* ‖ זָנָב *tail*), שׂים *place* in snout Jb 40$_{26}$ (+ חוֹחַ *hook* or perh. *thorn,* חַכָּה *hook,* חֶבֶל *cord*). <PREP> כפף כְּ *bow* head *as* Is 58$_{5}$ (1QIsa^{a} כאוגמן), מִנְּחִירָיו יֵצֵא עָשָׁן כְּדוּד נָפוּחַ וְאַגְמֹן appar. *from his nostrils there goes out smoke as (from) a boiling pot or (burning) rush(es)* Jb 41$_{12}$ (or em. וְאֹגֵם a boiling *and seething* pot).

→ אֲגַם *pool.*

אַגְמֹן, see אַגְמוֹן.

[אַגָּן] 3.0.0.1 n.[m.] **bowl**—cstr. אַגַּן; pl. אַגָּנוֹת (אַגָּנֹת), Q אגונות, I אגנת—**bowl** or perh. **goblet,** small vessel (Is 22$_{24}$) for blood, wine, etc., <SUBJ> חסר *lack* drink Ca 7$_{3}$. <NOM CL> שָׁרְרֵךְ אַגַּן הַסַּהַר *your navel is a round bowl* Ca 7$_{3}$. <CSTR> אַגַּן הַסַּהַר *bowl of (the) roundness,* i.e. round bowl Ca 7$_{3}$; יין האגנת *wine of the bowls* Arad ost. 1$_{10}$, כְּלֵי הָאַגָּנוֹת *vessels (consisting) of (the) bowls* Is 22$_{24}$ (+ נֵבֶל *jug*). <PREP> שׂים בְּ *place* blood *in* Ex 24$_{6}$.

[אֲגַף] I 7.0.1 n.[m.] **troop**—pl. cstr. Q אגפי; sf. אֲגַפֶּיךָ, אֲגַפֶּיהָ, אֲגַפָּיו—**troop, division** of army, belonging to Gog and his allies Ezk 38$_{6.6.9.22}$ 39$_{4}$, king of Judah 12$_{14}$ 17$_{21}$.

<SUBJ> היה *be* Ezk 38$_{9}$ (+ כְּ *as* devastation, cloud; + עַמִּים רַבִּים *many peoples*), בוא *come* 38$_{9}$, עלה *go up* 38$_{9}$, נפל *fall* 17$_{21}$ (if em. בְּכָל־אֲגַפָּיו *among all his troops*) 39$_{4}$.

<OBJ> יצא hi. *take out* Ezk 38$_{6.6}$ (+ עַמִּים רַבִּים *many peoples*), זרה pi. *scatter* 12$_{14}$ (+ עֶזְרֹה *his help* [or em. עֹזְרָיו *his helpers*]).

<CSTR> כול אגפי רום *all troops of height,* i.e. mighty troops 1QH 3$_{29}$ (but prob. אֲגַף II *[river] bank*), כָּל־אֲגַפָּיו *all his troops* (and vars.) Ezk 12$_{14}$ 17$_{21}$ 38$_{6.6.9}$ 39$_{4}$ (mss + עַמִּים רַבִּים *many peoples* [L lacks רַבִּים]).

<PREP> כָּל־מִבְרָחָיו בְּכָל־אֲגַפָּיו בַּחֶרֶב יִפֹּלוּ *all his fugitives among all his troops will fall by the sword* Ezk 17$_{21}$(Qr) (mss מִבְחָרָיו *his choicest warriors;* or em. וְכָל־אֲגַפָּיו *and all his troops* will fall); מטר עַל hi. *cause* pouring rain, hailstones, fire, brimstone *to rain upon* Ezk 38$_{22}$ (+ עַמִּים רַבִּים *many peoples*), הלך עַל *go over* (of torrents of Belial) 1QH 3$_{29}$(mg) (but prob. אֲגַף II *[river] bank*); ריק אַחֲרֵי hi. *empty,* i.e. draw (sword) *after,* i.e. in pursuit of Ezk 12$_{14}$.

<COLL> אַתָּה וְכָל־אֲגַפֶּיךָ *you* (Gog) *and all your troops* Ezk 38$_{9}$ 39$_{4}$, עָלָיו וְעַל־אֲגַפָּיו *upon him* (Gog) *and upon all his troops* 38$_{22}$, גֹּמֶר וְכָל־אֲגַפֶּיהָ *Gomer and all its troops* 38$_{6}$, בֵּית תּוֹגַרְמָה ... וְכָל־אֲגַפָּיו *Beth-togarmah ... and all its troops* 38$_{6}$ (if em. וְאֶת־כָּל־ in same sense).

[אֲגַף] II, see אֲגַף I.

אגר 3 vb. **gather**—**Qal** Pf. אָגְרָה; impf. תֶּאֱגֹר; ptc. אֹגֵר—<SUBJ> נְמָלָה *ant* Pr 6$_{8}$ (+ בַקָּצִיר *in the harvest;* ‖ כון hi.

prepare), בֵּן intelligent *child* Pr 10$_{5}$ (+ בַּקַּיִץ *in the summer;* :: רדם ni. *sleep deeply*), Israel Dt 28$_{39}$ (|| שׁתה *drink* wine, + נטע *plant* vineyard, עבד *serve*, i.e. work). **<OBJ>** מַאֲכָל *food* Pr 6$_{8}$; obj. not specified, Dt 28$_{39}$ Pr 10$_{5}$.

[אֶגְרוֹף], see אֶגְרֹף.

[אֲגַרְטָל] 2 n.m. **basket**—pl. cstr. אֲגַרְטְלֵי—cultic vessel, perh. in shape of basket, ... אֲגַרְטְלֵי זָהָב אֲגַרְטְלֵי־כֶסֶף *baskets of gold*, thirty, *baskets of silver*, a thousand Ezr 1$_{9}$ (+ מַחֲלָפִים *knives*, or em. מָחֳלָפִים *replaced;* + כְּפוֹר *bowl*, כְּלִי *vessel*).

אֶגְרֹף 2.0.1 n.[m.] **fist**—Q אגרוף; cstr. אֶגְרֹף (Q גורף)—prob. **fist** (esp. CD 11$_{6}$), perh. **club** or other instrument, used to strike beast (CD 11$_{6}$), neighbour (Ex 21$_{18}$), **<CSTR>** אֶגְרֹף רֶשַׁע *fist of wickedness* Is 58$_{4}$ (1QIsa[a] גורף). **<PREP>** נכה בְּ hi. *strike with* Ex 21$_{18}$ (|| אֶבֶן *stone*) Is 58$_{4}$ CD 11$_{6}$.

→ perh. גרף *sweep*.

אִגֶּרֶת 10 n.f. **letter**—cstr. אִגֶּרֶת; pl. אִגְּרוֹת; cstr. אִגְּרוֹת; sf. אִגְּרֹתֵיהֶם—alw. of an official nature, **<SUBJ>** הלך *go* from nobles Ne 6$_{17}$ (+ עַל *to* Tobiah), בוא *come* from Tobiah 6$_{17}$ (+ אֶל *to* nobles), פתח pass. *be opened* 6$_{5}$ (+ בְּיָדוֹ *in his hand*). **<OBJ>** נתן *give* Ne 2$_{7}$ (+ עַל *to/for* governors) 2$_{8}$ (+ אֶל *to/for* Asaph) 2$_{9}$, כתב *write* 2 C 30$_{1}$ (+ שׁלח עַל *send [command] to*), שׁלח *send* Ne 6$_{19}$, קום pi. *confirm* Est 9$_{29}$ (or em. לְקַיֵּם תֹּקֶף אִגֶּרֶת *to confirm the force of the letter of*), רבה hi. *multiply* Ne 6$_{17}$.

<CSTR> אִגֶּרֶת הַפּוּרִים *the letter of*, i.e. concerning, *Purim* Est 9$_{29}$, אִגְּרוֹת הַמֶּלֶךְ *letters of*, i.e. from, *the king* Ne 2$_{9}$; דִּבְרֵי הָאִגֶּרֶת *words of the letter* Est 9$_{26}$. **<ADJ>** הַזֹּאת *this letter* Est 9$_{26}$ (+ סֵפֶר *letter* 9$_{20.25}$) 9$_{29}$, שֵׁנִית *second* 9$_{29}$ (unless del. הַשֵּׁנִית). **<PREP>** הלך בְּ *go with* (of couriers) 2 C 30$_{6}$ (+ מִיַּד *from the hand of*), כתב בְּ pass. *be written in* Ne 6$_{5}$.

אֵד 2 n.m. **stream**—sf. אֵדוֹ—**stream** or perh. **mist**, וְאֵד יַעֲלֶה מִן־הָאָרֶץ וְהִשְׁקָה אֶת־כָּל־פְּנֵי־הָאֲדָמָה *and a stream, or mist, would come up from the ground and it watered all the surface of the land* Gn 2$_{6}$, יָזֹקּוּ מָטָר לְאֵדוֹ *they* (drops of water) *refine rain to his* (God's) *stream*, or *into its mist* Jb 36$_{27}$ (or em. יָזֹק *he* [God] *refines*), פָּרַשׂ עָלָיו אֵדוֹ *he has spread over it* (appar. cloud) *his stream*, or *mist* 36$_{30}$ (if em. אוֹרוֹ *his light*).

אדב 1 vb. **be sick—Qal, be sick,** ptc. as noun, אל תשא לב מאודב *do not raise (your) heart from*, i.e. forget about, *one that is sick* Si 7$_{35}$ (if em. אוהב *friend*).

Hi. Inf. לַאֲדִיב—**sicken,** אִישׁ לֹא־אַכְרִית ... לְכַלּוֹת אֶת־עֵינֶיךָ וְלַאֲדִיב אֶת־נַפְשֶׁךָ *one man I shall not cut off ... in order to wear out your eyes and to sicken your soul* 1 S 2$_{33}$ (or em. לְהָדִיב [from דוב] in same sense; 4QSam[a] עיניו ... נפשו *his eyes ... his heart*).

אַדְבְּאֵל 2 pr.n.m. **Adbeel,** son of Ishmael, Gn 25$_{13}$||1 C 1$_{29}$.

→ אֵל *God*.

אֲדַד 1 pr.n.m. **Adad,** prob. ident. with or em. to הֲדַד *Hadad*, 1 K 11$_{17}$.

אִדּוֹ 2 pr.n.m. **Iddo,** leader of Jews of Casiphia at time of Ezra, Ezr 8$_{17.17}$.

אֱדוֹם 100.0.1.2 pr.n.m. (sometimes f.), **Edom**—I אדם—**1a. Edom,** territory and state in mountainous region east and south of Judah. **b.** as collective noun, **Edomites** (distinction not alw. clear), e.g. Gn 36$_{9.43.43}$ Ex 15$_{15}$ Nm 20$_{20.21}$ 2 S 8$_{14}$||1 C 18$_{13}$ 2 K 8$_{20.21.22}$||2 C 21$_{8.9.10}$ 2 K 14$_{7.10}$ Ezk 16$_{57(mss)}$ 25$_{12}$ Am 1$_{11}$ 9$_{12}$ Ml 1$_{4}$ Ps 60$_{2}$ 137$_{7}$ Lm 4$_{21.22}$ 1 C 1$_{51.54}$ 18$_{12}$ 2 C 25$_{19}$ Arad ost. 24$_{20}$ 40$_{10.15}$ ([אד]ם).

<SUBJ> היה *be* 2 S 8$_{14}$||1 C 18$_{13}$ (+ עֲבָדִים *servants*) Jr 49$_{17}$ (+ שַׁמָּה *horror*) Ezk 35$_{15}$ (+ שְׁמָמָה *waste;* + הַר־שֵׂעִיר *Mt Seir*) Jl 4$_{19}$ (+ מִדְבַּר שְׁמָמָה *desert waste;* || מִצְרַיִם *Egypt*) Nm 24$_{18}$ (+ יְרֵשָׁה *possession*), בוא *come* Arad ost. 24$_{20}$, יצא *go out* Nm 20$_{20}$, מלט ni. *escape* Dn 11$_{41}$ (|| מוֹאָב *Moab*, + בְּנֵי עַמּוֹן *Ammonites*), נתן *give* Nm 20$_{21}$ Ezk 27$_{16(mss)}$ (L אֲרָם *Aram*) 36$_{5}$, עשׂה *do* 25$_{12}$ Arad ost. 40$_{15}$ ([אד]ם עשתה), אמר *say* Nm 20$_{18.20}$ Ml 1$_{4}$, ידע *know* Ezk 35$_{15}$, פשׁע *rebel* 2 K 8$_{20.22}$=2 C 21$_{8.10}$, מאן pi.

refuse Nm 20$_{21}$.

<NOM CL> אֱדוֹם ... מִשְׁלוֹח יָדָם *Edom ... is (the object of) the outstretching of their hand* Is 11$_{14(L)}$ (mss מִשְׁלֹחַ; ‖ מוֹאָב *Moab*, בְּנֵי עַמּוֹן *Ammonites*).

<OBJ> נכה hi. *defeat* 2 S 8$_{13(mss)}$ (L אֲרָם) 2 K 8$_{21}$‖2 C 21$_{9}$ 2 K 14$_{7.10}$ Ps 60$_{2}$ 1 C 18$_{12}$ 2 C 25$_{19}$, כרת hi. *cut off* 1 K 11$_{15}$ (if em. בִּהְיוֹת *when he was*), נתן *give*, i.e. make (desolate) Jr 25$_{21}$ (‖ מוֹאָב *Moab*, בְּנֵי עַמּוֹן *Ammonites*, etc.), שׁקה hi. *give to drink* 25$_{21}$.

<CSTR> אֶרֶץ אֱדוֹם *land of Edom* Gn 36$_{16.17.21.31}$‖1 C 1$_{43}$ Nm 20$_{23}$ (אֶרֶץ־) 21$_{4}$ 33$_{37}$ Jg 11$_{18}$ 1 K 9$_{26}$‖2 C 8$_{17}$ Is 34$_{6}$, גְּבוּל *border of* Jos 15$_{1.21}$, דֶּרֶךְ *way of* 2 K 3$_{20}$, מִדְבַּר *desert of* 3$_{8}$, שְׂדֵה *field of* Gn 32$_{4}$ (‖ שֵׂעִיר *Seir*) Jg 5$_{4}$, מֶלֶךְ *king of* Nm 20$_{14}$ (or del. מֶלֶךְ; see Prep.) Jg 11$_{17.17}$ 2 K 3$_{9}$ (‖ יִשְׂרָאֵל *Israel*, יְהוּדָה *Judah*) 3$_{12.26}$ 16$_{6}$ (if em. מֶלֶךְ־אֲרָם *king of Aram*) Jr 27$_{3}$ (‖ מוֹאָב *Moab*, צֹר *Tyre*, צִידוֹן *Sidon*, בְּנֵי עַמּוֹן *Ammonites*) Am 2$_{1}$ (מֶלֶךְ־), אֲבִי *ancestor of*, i.e. Esau Gn 36$_{9.43}$, שְׁאֵרִית *remnant of* Am 9$_{12}$, בַּת־ *daughter of* Lm 4$_{21}$ (+ עוּץ *Uz*) 4$_{22}$ (+ צִיּוֹן *Zion*).

בְּנֵי *sons of* Ps 137$_{7}$, אַלּוּפֵי *chiefs of* Gn 36$_{43}$ Ex 15$_{15}$ (‖ מוֹאָב *Moab*) 1 C 1$_{51.54}$, גִּבּוֹרֵי *warriors of* Jr 49$_{22}$, גְּדוּדֵי *troops of* 2 K 24$_{2}$ (if em. אֲרָם *Aram*; ‖ מוֹאָב, בְּנֵי־עַמּוֹן *Ammonites*) 1QM 1$_{1}$ (גדוד; + מואב, בני עמון), בְּנוֹת *daughters of* Ezk 16$_{57(mss)}$ (L אֲרָם), אָהֳלֵי *tents of* Ps 83$_{7}$ (+ מוֹאָב, יִשְׁמְעֵאלִים *Ishmaelites*, הַגְרִים *Hagrites*), אֱלֹהֵי *gods of* 2 C 25$_{20}$, פִּשְׁעֵי *sins of* Am 1$_{11}$, כָּל־אֱדוֹם *all Edom* 2 S 8$_{14.14}$‖1 C 18$_{13}$ Ezk 35$_{15}$.

<APP> אֱדוֹם כֻּלָּא *Edom, all (of it)* Ezk 36$_{5}$ (mss כֻּלָּהּ), אֱדוֹם כֻּלָּהּ *Edom, all of it* 35$_{15}$ 36$_{5(mss)}$, מֵעֵבֶר לַיָּם מֵאֱדוֹם *from across the sea, from Edom* 2 C 20$_{2(ms)}$ (L אֲרָם *Aram*), כָּל־הַגּוֹיִם ... אֱדוֹם *all the nations ... Edom* Jr 25$_{21}$ 1 C 19$_{11}$‖2 S 8$_{12(mss)}$ (L אֲרָם), בְּכָל־אֹיְבָיו ... בֶּאֱדוֹם *against all his enemies ... against Edom* 1 S 14$_{47}$, כָּל־מוּל בְּעָרְלָה ... אֱדוֹם *all uncircumcised of foreskin ... Edom* Jr 9$_{25}$.

<PREP> לְ of direction, *to*, + שׁוב hi. *give back* 2 K 16$_{6}$ (if em. אֲרָם *Aram*), סגר hi. *deliver* Am 1$_{6.9}$, אמר לְ *say concerning* Jr 49$_{7}$ Ob$_{1}$.

בְּ of place, *in* + היה *be* 1 K 11$_{15(mss)}$ (L אֶת־ *with*), עשׂה *do* Ezk 25$_{14}$ (perh. בְּ = *against*), שׂים *place* garrisons 2 S 8$_{14}$‖1 C 18$_{13}$ 2 S 8$_{14}$, מלך *rule* Gn 36$_{32}$ (perh. בְּ = *over*), מִזֶּרַע הַמֶּלֶךְ ... בֶּאֱדוֹם *one of the king's descendants ... in Edom* 1 K 11$_{14}$, כָּל־זָכָר בֶּאֱדוֹם *every male in Edom* 11$_{15.16}$, מֶלֶךְ אֵין בֶּאֱדוֹם *there was no king in Edom* 22$_{48}$, הַיְּהוּדִים אֲשֶׁר ... בֶּאֱדוֹם *the Judaeans who were ... in Edom* Jr 40$_{11}$ (‖ מוֹאָב *Moab*, בְּנֵי־עַמּוֹן *Ammonites*), *against*, + לחם ni. *fight* 1 S 14$_{47}$ (‖ מוֹאָב, בְּנֵי־עַמּוֹן, etc.), נתן *give* vengeance Ezk 25$_{14}$.

מִן of place, *from*, + בוא *come* Is 63$_{1}$ (or em. מְאָדָּם *reddened*; ‖ בָּצְרָה *Bozrah*), 2 C 20$_{2(ms)}$ (L אֲרָם *Aram*), אבד hi. *cause* wise *to perish* Ob$_{8}$ (‖ הַר עֵשָׂו *Mt Esau*), כרת hi. *cut off* life Ezk 25$_{13}$, נחא *lead* Nm 23$_{7}$ (if em. אֲרָם), נשׂא *carry* treasure 1 C 18$_{11}$ (‖ מוֹאָב *Moab*, עֲמָלֵק *Amalek*, בְּנֵי עַמּוֹן *Ammonites*, פְּלִשְׁתִּים *Philistines*), קדשׁ pi. *consecrate* 2 S 8$_{12(mss)}$ (L אֲרָם), [המכתבים מ]אדם *the letters from the Edomites* Arad ost. 40$_{10}$, הַכֶּסֶף וְהַזָּהָב ... מֵאֱדוֹם *the silver and the gold ... from Edom* 2 S 8$_{12(mss)}$ (L אֲרָם *Aram*).

היה אֵת *be with* 1 K 11$_{15}$ (mss בְּ *in*); שׁלח אֶל *send to* Nm 20$_{14}$ (if del. מֶלֶךְ *king of*), יעץ אֶל *advise* Jr 49$_{20}$; נחה עַד *lead to* Ps 60$_{11}$‖108$_{11}$.

עַל of place, *upon, over*, + ירד *go down* Is 34$_{5}$, שׁלך hi. *throw* Ps 60$_{10}$‖108$_{10}$, מלך *reign* 1 K 11$_{25(mss)}$ (L אֲרָם *Aram*), *across*, + עבר *pass* Jr 49$_{17}$, *against*, + נטה *extend* hand Ezk 25$_{13}$, דבר pi. *speak* 36$_{5}$, + פקד עַל *punish* Jr 9$_{25}$ (‖ מוֹאָב *Moab*, בְּנֵי עַמּוֹן *Ammonites*, יְהוּדָה *Judah*, מִצְרַיִם *Egypt*), היה עַל־יְדֵי *be alongside* Nm 34$_{3}$.

2. Esau, son of Isaac and Rebekah, twin brother of Jacob Gn 25$_{30}$, עֵשָׂו הוּא אֱדוֹם *Esau, who is Edom* Gn 36$_{1.8}$, sim. 36$_{19}$.

3. in pr.n.m. **Obed-edom** (usu. אֱדֹם).

Also perh. Arad ost. 21$_{5}$.

→ אֲדֹמִי *Edomite*; עֹבֵד אֱדֹם *Obed-edom*.

[אֲדוֹמִי], see אֲדֹמִי.

אָדוֹן 334$_{.5.13.32}$ n.m. **lord**—אָדוֹן (אָדֹן); cstr. אֲדוֹן; sf. אֲדֹנִי (Q אדוני, לַאדֹנִי/בַּ/וַ), אֲדֹנֵנוּ; pl. אֲדֹנִים (Q אדונים); cstr. אֲדֹנֵי; sf. אֲדֹנַי (אֲדֹנָי) אֲדֹנֶיךָ (לַאדֹנֶיךָ), אֲדֹנַיִךְ, אֲדֹנָיו (Kt אֲדֹנֵיו, לַ/כַּאדֹנָיו) אֲדֹנֶיהָ (אֲדוֹנֶיהָ), אֲדֹנֵינוּ (אֲדוֹנֵינוּ), אֲדֹנֵיהֶם (Q אדוניכמה) אֲדֹנֵיכֶם.

1a. usu. **lord, master** (human), superior of other persons, freq. in contrast to words for servant (עֶבֶד *slave, servant*, נַעַר *lad*, נַעֲרָה *lass*, שִׁפְחָה *maid*); except for אֲדֹנִי *my master*, suffixed forms usu. pl., even when in ref. to single individual (e.g. אֲדֹנֶיךָ *your master*). **b. husband,** Gn 18_{12} Am 4_1 Mur 30_{27} perh. Ps 45_{12}. **c.** perh. **employer,** Si 42_3. **d. owner** of hill, 1 K 16_{24}.

<SUBJ> היה *be* 2 S 15_{21}, זקן *be old* Gn 18_{12}, ברך pass. *be blessed* En-Gedi cave inscr.$_7$ (others אדני[הו] *Adonijah*), חיה *live* 1 K 1_{31}, מות *die* Jg 3_{25} 2 S 2_7, בוא *come* Gn 39_{16} 2 S 19_{31} 24_{21} 2 K 5_{18}, יצא *go out* 2 S 19_{20}, סור *turn* Gn 19_2 Jg 4_{18}, hi. *remove* Is 3_1, עבר *pass* Gn 33_{14}, עזב *leave* 1 S 30_{13}, שוב hi. *take back* Ho 12_{15}, רדף *pursue* 1 S 26_{18}, ארץ *hasten* Lachish ost. 8_7 ([י]אץ).

קום *arise* Jg 19_{27}, נפל *fall* Jg 3_{25}, שכב *lie* 1 K 1_{21}, חנה *camp* 2 S 11_{11}, שלח *send* 1 K 18_{10} 2 K 5_{22} 18_{27}||Is 36_{12} 2 K 19_4||Is 37_4 Lachish ost. 3_6 $4_{2.4}$ ([אדני]) 4_5 6_3 18_3, pi. *dispatch* Is 10_{16}, נגש hi. *bring* Ex 21_6, לקח *take* Gn 39_{20} 2 S 24_{22}, נתן *give* Gn 39_{20} Ex 21_4 Lachish ost. 4_{12}, עלה hi. *offer up* 2 S 24_{22}.

אמר *say* Jg 19_{12} 1 S 16_{16} 2 S 13_{32} 2 C 2_{14} Lachish ost. 3_8, דבר *speak* Nm 32_{27}, pi. Gn 44_7 Jos 5_{14} 2 S $14_{18.19}$ 1 K 2_{38} Dn 10_{19}, שאל *ask* Gn 44_{19}, צוה pi. *command* Nm 32_{25} 2 S 9_{11}, pu. Nm 36_2, שבע ni. *promise* 1 K $1_{13.17}$, hi. Gn 24_{37}, ידע *know* 33_{13} 39_8 1 K $1_{11.18}$, חשב *reckon* 2 S 19_{20}, חפץ *desire* 2 S 24_3, זכר *remember* Lachish ost. 2_4.

שׂים *place*, i.e. pay attention 1 S 25_{25} 2 S 13_{33}, appoint (as) Ps 105_{21} (|| משל ptc. *ruler*), בחר *choose* 2 S 15_{15}, טמן hi. *conceal* Si $41_{15(Bmg)}$ (B, M איש מצפן *a person that conceals*), בקשׁ pi. *seek* 1 C 21_3, ראה *see* Gn 39_3 2 K 2_{19}, שמע *hear* Gn $23_{6.11.15}$ 39_{19} 1 S 26_{19} Jr 37_{20} Meṣad Ḥashavyahu ost. 1_1, בשׂר htp. *hear good news* 2 S 18_{31}, perh. כתב *write* Lachish ost. 6_8 ([א]דני), בכה *weep* 2 K 8_{12}.

עשׂה *do* 1 C 21_{23} Arad ost. 21_3, לחם ni. *fight* 1 S 25_{28}, ישׁע hi. *be victorious, save* 1 S 25_{31} 2 K 6_{26}, בעל *be master (of)* Is 26_{13}, חשׂך *spare* 2 K 5_{20}, כלא *restrain* Nm 11_{28}, מלך hi. *make king* 1 K 1_{43}, רצע *pierce* Ex 21_6, שׁתה *drink* Gn 24_{18} 44_5.

<NOM CL> הוא *he* Gn 24_{65} Ps 45_{12}, חָכָם *wise* 2 S 14_{20}, כְּמַלְאַךְ הָאֱלֹהִים *as a holy angel* 2 S 14_{17} 19_{28}, לְאֵלֶּה *for these sheep* 1 K 22_{17}||2 C 18_{16}, לִפְנֵי הַנָּבִיא *before the prophet* 2 K 5_3, שָׁם *there* Jg 19_{26}.

<OBJ> אהב *love* Ex 21_5, כבד pi. *honour* Ml 1_6, ירא *fear* Dn 1_{10}, ברך pi. *bless* Gn 24_{35} 1 S 25_{14} 1 K 1_{47}, קלל *curse* 2 S 16_9, הרג *murder* 2 K 9_{31}, לקח *take* 2 K $2_{3.5}$, צוה pi. *command* Nm 36_2, שמע hi. *cause to hear* Lachish ost. 2_2 3_3 4_1 5_1 ([אד]ני) 8_1 ([אדני]) 9_1, בקשׁ pi. *seek* 2 K 2_{16}, ראה hi. *show* Lachish ost. 6_2, קרא *meet* 2 S 19_{21}, שׁמר *protect* Pr 27_{18}, בכר perh. *cause to be early (for)* Lachish ost. 2_5 (א[דנ]י; others אי *no matter* and/or יעכר *may he discomfit* for יבכר).

<CSTR> אֲדֹנֵי הָאָרֶץ *lord of the land* Gn $42_{30.33}$, אֲדֹנֵי יוֹסֵף *Joseph's master* 39_{20}, אֲדֹנֵי הַשָּׂדֶה *lords of the field*, i.e. demons Jb 5_{23} (if em. אַבְנֵי *stones of*), אֲדֹנֵי הָהָר *owner of the hill* 1 K 16_{24}.

אֵשֶׁת אֲדֹנִי *wife of my lord* Gn 24_{36}, אֵשֶׁת אֲדֹנָיו *wife of his lord* 39_7 (אֵשֶׁת־) 39_8, נְשֵׁי אֲדֹנֶיךָ *wives of your lord* 2 S 12_8.

בֶּן־אֲדֹנִי *son of my lord* Gn 24_{44}, בֶּן־אֲדֹנֶיךָ *son of your lord* 24_{51} 2 S $9_{9.10.10}$ 16_3, בְּנֵי אֲדֹנֵיכֶם *sons of your lord* 2 K $10_{2.3.6}$ (בְּנֵי־; mss בֵּית *house of*), אֲחִי אֲדֹנִי *brother of my lord* Gn 24_{27} (if em. אֲחֵי *brothers of*) 24_{48}.

עֶבֶד אֲדֹנִי *servant of my lord* Dn 10_{17}, עַבְדֵי אֲדֹנִי *servants of my lord* 1 S 25_{41} 2 S 11_{11} 2 K 18_{24}||Is 36_9, עַבְדֵי אֲדֹנֶיךָ *servants of your* (sg.) *lord* 1 S 29_{10} 2 S 20_6, עַבְדֵי אֲדֹנֵיכֶם *servants of your* (pl.) *lord* 1 K 1_{33}, עַבְדֵי אֲדֹנָיו *servants of his lord* 2 S $11_{9.13}$ 2 K 9_{11}.

אֱלֹהֵי אֲדֹנִי *God of my lord* Gn $24_{12.27.42.48}$ 1 K 1_{36}, אֹיְבֵי *enemies of* 1 S 29_8 2 S 18_{32}, נַעֲרֵי *lads of* 1 S 25_{25}, חַכְמֵי *skilled ones of* 2 C 2_{13}, אָזְנֵי *ears of* Gn 44_{18}, עֵינֵי *eyes of* 31_{35} $33_{8.15}$ 47_{25} 2 S 24_3, עֵינֵי אֲדֹנֶיהָ *eyes of her lord* Ex 21_8.

יַד אֲדֹנִי *hand of my lord* 1 S 30_{15} (יַד־), יַד אֲדֹנִים *hand of a lord* Is 19_4, יַד אֲדוֹנֵיהֶם *hand of their lords* Ps 123_2 (|| גְּבֶרֶת *mistress*, עֶבֶד *servant*).

נֶפֶשׁ אֲדֹנִי *soul of my lord* 1 S 25_{29}, נֶפֶשׁ אֲדֹנָיו *soul of his lord* Pr 25_{13}, perh. כלב אדני *according to the heart of my lord* Lachish ost. 12_1 (unless כֶּלֶב *dog*).

רַגְלֵי אֲדֹנִי *feet of my lord* 1 S 25_{27}, רַגְלֵי אֲדֹנָיו *feet of his lord* 2 K 6_{32}, בֵּית אֲדֹנֶיךָ *house of your* (sg.) *lord* Gn 44_8 2 S 12_8 Is 22_{18}, בֵּית אֲדֹנֵיכֶם *house of your* (pl.) *lord* 2 K 10_3, בֵּית אֲדֹנָיו *house of his lord* Gn 39_2 40_7, בֵּית אֲדֹנֵיהֶם *house of their lord* Zp 1_9, גְּמַלֵּי אֲדֹנָיו *camels of his lord* Gn 24_{10}, עֲבֹדַת אֲדֹנֵיהֶם *work of their lord* Ne 3_5 (perh. אָדוֹן = *Lord*, as §2).

כִּסֵּא אֲדֹנִי *throne of my lord* 1 K $1_{20.27.37}$, אַף *anger of*

Ex 32$_{22}$, דְּבַר־ *word of* 2 S 14$_{17}$, דִּבְרֵי *words of* Gn 44$_{24}$, טוּב אֲדֹנָיו *goodness of his lord* 24$_{10}$, חשבון חובר ואדון *reckoning of a partner and an employer* Si 42$_{3(B)}$ (erased חשבון ב *reckoning with;* Bmg שותף וארח *partner and [fellow] traveller;* M שותף ודרך in same sense).

<APP> with title, אֲדֹנִי(־)הַמֶּלֶךְ *my lord, the king* 1 S 24$_9$ 26$_{17.19}$ 29$_8$ 2 S 3$_{21}$ 4$_8$ 9$_{11}$ 13$_{33}$ 14$_{9+6t}$ 15$_{15.21}$ 16$_{4.9}$ 18$_{28.31.32}$ 19$_{20+8t}$ 24$_{21.22}$ 1 K 1$_{2+11t}$ 2$_{38}$ 20$_{4.9}$ 2 K 6$_{12.26}$ 8$_5$ Jr 37$_{20}$ 38$_9$ Dn 1$_{10}$ 1 C 21$_{3.23}$, הַמֶּלֶךְ אֲדֹנִי *the king, my lord* 2 S 14$_{15}$, אֲדֹנֶיךָ הַמֶּלֶךְ *your lord, the king* 1 S 26$_{15}$, אֲדֹנֵינוּ הַמֶּלֶךְ־דָּוִד *our lord, the king, David* 1 K 1$_{43}$, לַאֲדֹנֵיהֶם לְמֶלֶךְ מִצְרָיִם *against their lord, the king of Egypt* Gn 40$_1$, אֶת־אֲדֹנִי אֶת־מֶלֶךְ אַשּׁוּר *with my lord, the king of Assyria* 2 K 18$_{23}$ (|| Is 36$_8$ אֶת־אֲדֹנִי הַמֶּלֶךְ אַשּׁוּר), אֲדֹנִי אִישׁ הָאֱלֹהִים *my lord, the man of God* 2 K 4$_{16}$, אדני השר *my lord, the official* Meṣad Ḥashavyahu ost. 1$_1$.

Followed by pr.n.m., Abraham Gn 24$_{12.27.42.48}$, David 2 C 2$_{13}$, Eliashib Arad ost. 18$_1$, Elijah 1 K 18$_7$, Gediah Arad ost. 71$_3$ (אדן גדי[הו] perh. pr.n. *Adon*), Hanun 2 S 10$_3$, Jaush Lachish ost. 2$_1$ 3$_2$ (ל[אד]ני [יאו]ש) 6$_1$, Joab 2 S 11$_{11}$, Saul 2 S 2$_7$ 1 C 12$_{20}$, Moses Nm 11$_{28}$, אֲדֹנָיו הַמִּצְרִי *his master, the Egyptian* Gn 39$_2$, לַאדֹנִי לְעֵשָׂו *to my lord, to Esau* Gn 32$_{5.19}$; preceded by pr.n.m., Abraham Gn 24$_9$, Ahab 2 K 9$_7$, David 1 K 1$_{11}$, Hadadezer 1 K 11$_{23}$, מֶלֶךְ־אַשּׁוּר אֲדֹנָיו *the king of Assyria, his lord* 2 K 19$_4$||Is 37$_4$.

<ADJ> אֲדֹנִים קָשֶׁה *hard,* i.e. harsh, *lord* Is 19$_4$.

<PREP> לְ of possession, *of, (belonging) to* Gn 24$_{36}$ (+ בֵּן *son*) 44$_{16.33}$ (both + עֶבֶד *servant*) 1 S 25$_{31}$ 1 C 21$_3$ Kadesh Barnea oil lamp inscr. (others אדנ[הו] *Adonijah*), + היה *be* Gn 44$_9$ Ex 21$_4$.

לְ of benefit, *for,* + בקשׁ pi. *seek* virgin 1 K 1$_2$, חמם *be warm* 1$_2$, טוב hi. *be good* 1 S 25$_{31}$, עשׂה *do* 24$_7$ 25$_{30}$, *make* house 25$_{28}$.

לְ of direction, *to* Gn 24$_{54.56}$ 32$_{19}$ 1 S 25$_{27}$, + אמר *say* Gn 32$_5$ 44$_{16}$ 1 K 18$_{8.11.14}$ 20$_9$ Am 4$_1$ Kuntillet ʿAjrud inscr. E2.2$_1$, נגד hi. *tell* Gn 32$_6$ 2 K 5$_4$ Lachish ost. 3$_2$ (הג[ד] ל[אד]ני), ho. *be told* 1 K 18$_{13}$, נתן *give* Ex 21$_{32}$ 2 S 4$_8$ Arad ost. 40$_{10}$, שׁלם pi. *repay* 21$_4$ ([אדנ]י).

שִׂים לְ *place,* i.e. appoint, *as* Gn 45$_{8.9}$ (both || אָב *father,* i.e. counsellor), חטא לְ *sin against* 40$_1$, נְאֻם י׳ לַאדֹנִי *utterance of Y. to my lord* Ps 110$_1$, אַנְשֵׁי־מָוֶת לַאדֹנִי *(as) men of,* i.e. destined for, *death before my lord* 2 S 19$_{29}$.

בְּ *against,* + שׁלח *send* hand, i.e. harm 1 S 24$_{11}$, נשׂא *raise* hand 2 S 18$_{28}$.

וְהָיָה ... כַּעֶבֶד כַּאדֹנָיו *and the servant will be as his master* Is 24$_2$.

מִן of direction, *from* perh. Arad ost. 26$_2$, + נצל ni. *be saved* Dt 23$_{16}$, כחד pi. *conceal* Gn 47$_{18}$, עֶבֶד חָפְשִׁי מֵאֲדֹנָיו *a servant is free of his master* Jb 3$_{19}$, טוֹב מִן *better than* Si 41$_{15(Bmg)}$ (B, M אִישׁ *man;* :: אִישׁ *[common] man*), בּוֹשׁ מִן *be ashamed before* 41$_{18}$ (|| גְּבֶרֶת *mistress*).

אֶל of benefit, respect, *for, concerning,* + היה *be* burden 2 S 19$_{36}$ (ms לְ), כלה *be determined* (of evil) 1 S 25$_{17}$ (mss עַל *against*), בקשׁ *seek* evil 25$_{26}$, צוה pi. *command* Jr 27$_4$, of possession, *(belonging) to* Gn 47$_{18}$.

אֶל of direction, *to,* + בוא *come* Gn 33$_{14}$ 1 S 20$_{38}$ 2 K 8$_{14}$, hi. *bring* 2 S 1$_{10}$, הלך *go* 2 K 6$_{22.23}$, שׁוב *go back* 1 K 12$_{27}$, hi. *return* letters Lachish ost. 5$_7$, נפל *fall,* i.e. desert 1 C 12$_{20}$, שׁלח *send* Is 36$_{12}$ (||2 K 18$_{27}$ עַל) Lachish ost. 3$_{21}$, קבץ *gather* Israel 2 S 3$_{21}$, סגר hi. *hand back* servant Dt 23$_{16}$, רגל pi. *slander* servant 2 S 19$_{28}$, לשׁן hi. *denounce* servant Pr 30$_{10(Qr)}$, אמר *say* Gn 24$_{39}$ 44$_{20.22}$ Jg 19$_{11}$ 2 S 10$_3$ 2 K 19$_6$||Is 37$_6$ Jr 27$_4$, דבר pi. *speak* 2 S 14$_{12.15}$, כתב *write* Arad ost. 40$_6$ (וכתבת[י]).

אֶל *to, for the attention of* addressee Lachish ost. 2$_1$ 6$_1$ Arad ost. 18$_1$, רצה אֶל htp. *make oneself pleasing to* 1 S 29$_4$, עמד אֶל *stand before* 2 K 5$_{25}$, שׁמר אֶל *guard* 26$_{15}$ (mss אֶת־ object-marker).

עַל *against,* + קשׁר *plot* 2 K 10$_9$, מרד *rebel* 2 C 13$_6$, שׁמר עַל *keep watch over* 1 S 26$_{16}$.

אֵת *with,* + עשׂה *do,* i.e. show loyalty to Gn 24$_{49}$, ערב htp. *exchange pledges* 2 K 18$_{23}$||Is 36$_8$; היה מֵאֵת ni. *be caused by* 1 K 12$_7$, שׁאל מֵאֵת *ask (for)* child *from* 2 K 4$_{28}$.

עִם *with,* + היה *be* (of Y.) 1 K 1$_{37}$ Kuntillet ʿAjrud inscr. E2.2$_2$ (אד[נ]י), עבר *cross* Jordan 2 S 19$_{38}$, + עשׂה *do,* Gn 24$_{12.14}$ 2 S 2$_5$ (4QSam^a עַל), דבר pi. *speak* Dn 10$_{17}$; עזב מֵעִם *leave from* (of loyalty and truth) Gn 24$_{27}$.

לִפְנֵי *before* 2 K 5$_1$, + שׁאר ni. *remain* Gn 47$_{18}$; פרץ מִפְּנֵי htp. *break away from* 1 S 25$_{10}$.

<COLL> אֲדֹנִי *sir,* as term of address to superior 1 S

22$_{12}$ 25$_{24.26}$, to heavenly being Zc 1$_{9}$ 4$_{4}$ 6$_{4}$ Dn 10$_{16}$ 12$_{8}$, בִּי אֲדֹנִי *please, sir* Gn 43$_{20}$ 44$_{18}$ Nm 12$_{11}$ Jg 6$_{13}$ 1 S 1$_{26}$ 1 K 3$_{17.26}$, לֹא אֲדֹנִי *no, sir* Gn 42$_{10}$ 1 S 1$_{15}$ 2 K 6$_{12}$ Zc 4$_{5.13}$ 6$_{12}$, אַל אֲדֹנִי *do not, sir* Gn 19$_{18}$ 2 K 4$_{16}$, אֲהָהּ אֲדֹנִי *alas, my lord* 2 K 6$_{5.15}$, הוֹי אָדוֹן *alas, lord* Jr 22$_{18}$ 34$_{5}$, אֶמְצָא־חֵן בְּעֵינֶיךָ אֲדֹנִי *may I find grace in your eyes, O my lord* 2 S 16$_{4}$, sim. 14$_{22}$ Ru 2$_{13}$, בבית[ך] אדוני *in your house, O my lord* Mur 30$_{27}$, אָדוֹן לְבֵיתוֹ *lord to*, i.e. over, *his house* Ps 105$_{21}$, מִי אָדוֹן לָנוּ *who is our master?* Ps 12$_{5}$.

2. Lord (divine), **<SUBJ>** אמר *say* Is 51$_{22}$, בוא *come* Ml 3$_{1}$, שׁלח pi. *send* Is 10$_{16}$, מהה htp. *delay* Si 32$_{22(mg)}$, סאף pi. *prune* Is 10$_{33}$, ברך htp. *be blessed* GnzPs 4$_{11}$ 4QShirShab^{d} 1.1$_{28}$ ([ה]אד[ו]ן), רום htp. *be exalted* GnzPs 4$_{11}$.

<NOM CL> אֲנִי *I* Ml 1$_{6}$, אתה *you* 1QH 10$_{8}$, הואה *he* 11QPsa^{a} 18$_{6}$, גָּדוֹל *great* Ps 135$_{5}$ 147$_{5}$.

<OBJ> ברך pi. *bless* 4Q409 1$_{6}$ ([ברך ... אדו]ן]) 1$_{8}$ ([בר]ך).

<CSTR> [אדון] אדונים *Lord of lords* 1QNoah 2$_{5}$, אֲדֹנֵי הָאֲדֹנִים *Lord of lords* Dt 10$_{17}$ Ps 136$_{3}$=11QPs^{a} 15$_{7}$ (אדון האדונים) (both || אֱלֹהֵי הָאֱלֹהִים *God of gods*) 4QapPs^{b} 76$_{14}$ (האדונים), אדון יעקוב *Lord of Jacob* 11QPs^{a} 18$_{6}$, אֲדוֹן כָּל־הָאָרֶץ *Lord of all the earth* Jos 3$_{11.13}$ Mc 4$_{13}$ (|| ׳י Y.) Zc 4$_{14}$ 6$_{5}$ Ps 97$_{5}$ (|| ׳י) 114$_{7}$ (if em.; see Prep.; || אֱלוֹהַּ *God*), אדון כול איל[י] *Lord of all gods of* 4QShirShab^{d} 1.2$_{33}$, אדון כל הדורות *Lord of all the generations* GnzPs 4$_{11}$, אדון הכול *the Lord of all* 4Q409 1$_{6}$ ([אדו]ן) 1$_{8}$; נְאֻם הָאָדוֹן *utterance of the Lord* Is 1$_{24}$ 19$_{4}$ (or del. הָאָדוֹן), מעשי אדון *works of (the) Lord* 11QPsa^{a} 28$_{7}$.

<APP> הָאָדוֹן ׳י *the Lord, Y.* Ex 23$_{17}$ 34$_{23}$ (Sam אֲרוֹן *ark of* Y. in both) Is 1$_{24}$ 3$_{1}$ 10$_{16.33}$ 19$_{4}$, ׳י אֲדֹנֶיךָ *your Lord, Y.* Is 51$_{22}$, ׳י אֲדֹנֵינוּ *Y., our Lord* Ps 8$_{2.10}$ Ne 10$_{30}$, [ה]אד[ו]ן מל[ך ה]כול] *the Lord, the king of all* 4QShirShab^{d} 1.1$_{28}$.

<PREP> חרם לְ hi. *devote* wealth *to* Mc 4$_{13}$, שׂנא לְ pass. *be hated by* Si 10$_{7}$ (+ אִישׁ *man*), ידה לְ hi. *praise* Ps 136$_{3}$, הלל לְ pi. *praise* 4QShirShab^{d} 1.2$_{33}$, קָדוֹשׁ הַיּוֹם לַאֲדֹנֵינוּ *today is holy to our Lord* Ne 8$_{10}$.

עמד עַל *stand by* Zc 4$_{14}$, יצב עַל htp. *take one's stand*, i.e. present oneself, *to* 6$_{5}$.

ראה אֶל־פְּנֵי ni. *appear in the presence of* Ex 23$_{17}$ (Sam אֶת־פְּנֵי אֲרוֹן *in the presence of the ark of*); ראה אֶת־פְּנֵי ni. *appear in the presence of* Ex 34$_{23}$ (Sam אֲרוֹן).

מִלִּפְנֵי *(from) before*, + מסס ni. *be melted* Ps 97$_{5}$, חול *dance* Ps 114$_{7}$ (or רקד *dance*, if em. חוּלִי אָרֶץ *dance, O earth* to כָּל־הָאָרֶץ Lord of *all the earth*).

<COLL> אדון לכול רוח *Lord of every spirit* 1QH 10$_{8}$, אדון לכול קדושים *Lord of all the saints* 4QShir^{a} 1$_{2}$, לאדון ואנשים *by the Lord and (by) people* Si 10$_{7}$.

Also 1QpMic 14$_{1}$ 1QSb 5$_{8}$ Lachish ost. 12$_{6}$ 17$_{2.3}$ ([א]דני) Arad ost. 26$_{4}$.

→ אֲדֹנָי *my Lord*, אֲדֹנִיָּהוּ *Adonijah*, אדניחי *Adonihai*, אֲדֹנִיקָם *Adonikam*, אֲדֹנִירָם *Adoniram*, אֲדֹנִי בֶזֶק *Adoni-bezek*, אֲדֹנִי־צֶדֶק *Adoni-zedek*, טוֹב אֲדוֹנִיָּה *Tob-adonijah*.

אֲדוֹן, see אָדֹן.

אֲדוֹנִירָם, see אֲדֹנִירָם.

אֲדוֹרַיִם 1 pl.n. **Adoraim,** town in Judah fortified by Rehoboam, mod. Dūra, 8 km WSW of Hebron, 2 C 11$_{9}$.

אדות, see אוֹדָה.

[אדי] pr.n.m. **Addai,** father of Joseph, perh. purchaser of land, Mur 22$_{4}$ ([אד]י).

אַדִּיר 28.3.7 adj. **majestic**—sf. אדירנו, אַדִּירוֹ; f. אַדֶּרֶת; pl. אַדִּירִים (אדרים, אַדִּרִים); cstr. אַדִּירֵי; sf. אַדִּירֶיךָ, אַדִּירָיו, אַדִּירֵיהֶם (אַדִּרֵיהֶם)—**1.** as attributive adj., **majestic, mighty, noble,** of מַיִם *water*, i.e. waves Ex 15$_{10}$=1QH 8$_{19}$ (אדיר[ם]) 4QPentPar^{b} 6.2$_{5}$, מִשְׁבָּר *breaker, wave* Ps 93$_{4}$ (unless מַיִם רַבִּים אַדִּירִים מִשְׁבְּרֵי־יָם = *many waters, majestic ones, breakers of the sea*, i.e. as §2, or em. אַדִּיר מִמִּשְׁבְּרֵי *more majestic than the breakers of*).

אָפִיק *channel* Si 40$_{13(B)}$ (+ אֵיתָן *continuous*), צִי *ship* Is 33$_{21}$, אֶרֶז *cedar* Ezk 17$_{23}$, גֶּפֶן *vine* 17$_{8}$, קוֹל *sound* of trumpet Si 50$_{16}$, פֶּקַע *blast* of thunder 46$_{17}$, מֶלֶךְ *king* Ps 136$_{18}$ (|| גָּדוֹל *great*), גּוֹי *nation* Ezk 32$_{18}$ (or em. אַדִּרִם to אֹרִדֵם *I shall bring them down*), אֱלֹהִים *gods* 1 S 4$_{8}$.

2. as predicative adj. or noun, **majestic (one),**

mighty (one), noble (one), of Y., name of Y. (Is 33$_{21}$ Ps 8$_{2.10}$ 42$_{5}$ [if em.] 76$_{5}$ 93$_{4}$ 1QM 19$_{1}$), of noble man, esp. assoc. with rulers and shepherds as rulers, of majestic tree (Is 10$_{34}$ Zc 11$_{2}$).

<SUBJ> היה *be* Jr 30$_{21}$ (or em. אַדִּירוֹ מִמֶּנּוּ *his noble one* will be *one of his own* to אַדִּיר מֵהֶם he will be *mightier than them;* || משׁל ptc. *ruler*), זכר ni. *be remembered* Na 2$_{6}$ (if em. יִזְכֹּר *he will remember*), שׁלח *send* Jr 14$_{3(Qr)}$ (obj. צְעִירֵיהֶם *their little ones,* i.e. servants), פלשׁ htp. *roll about* in mourning 25$_{34}$ (|| רעה ptc. *shepherd*), שׁכן *dwell* Na 3$_{18}$ (or em. יָשְׁנוּ *they sleep;* || רעה ptc.), כשׁל ni. *stumble* 2$_{6}$ (or em. לֹא יִכָּשְׁלוּ *they will not stumble*), בוא hi. *bring* neck, perh. exercise oneself Ne 3$_{5}$, שׁדד pu. *be devastated* Zc 11$_{2}$.

<NOM CL> + ׳׳ *Y.* Is 33$_{21}$ (+ לָנוּ *for us*) Ps 93$_{4}$ (+ בַּמָּרוֹם *on high*), אַתָּה *you* (Y.) Ps 76$_{5}$ (+ אור ni. *be illuminated [in glory]*), שֵׁם *name* of Y. Ps 8$_{2.10}$ (both + בְּכָל־הָאָרֶץ *in all the world*); קדוש אדירנו *our noble one* (Y.) *is holy* 1QM 19$_{1}$ (+ מלך הכבוד *the king of glory*).

<OBJ> זכר *remember* Na 2$_{6}$ (or em. יִזָּכְרוּ *are remembered*), לקח *take* 2 C 23$_{20}$ (|| שַׂר *captain* of a hundred, משׁל ptc. *ruler*), appar. קפד *gather up* 4Q521 3.2$_{7}$ ([אדירן[ים).

<CSTR> אַדִּירֵי הַצֹּאן *nobles of the flock,* i.e. national leaders Jr 25$_{34.35.36}$ (all three + רעה ptc. *shepherd*), וְאַדִּירֵי כָּל־חֶפְצִי־בָם *and noble ones of all in whom is my delight* Ps 16$_{3}$ (or em. כָּל־חֶפְצֵי־בָם *all who delight in them* and וַאֲרוּרִים *and cursed are* or יַאְדִּיר *he will glorify,* or הָאַדִּיר כָּל־חֶפְצוֹ בָם *[as for] the noble one, all of his delight is in them*).

סֹךְ אַדִּר *shelter of (the) noble one* (Y.) Ps 42$_{5}$ (if em. בַּסָּךְ אֲדַדֵּם *in the throng I led them in procession;* or em. בְּסוֹד אַדִּירִים *in the company of noble ones*), סָךְ אַדִּרִם *throng of nobles* 42$_{5(mss)}$, סֵפֶל אַדִּירִים *bowl of,* i.e. fit for, *nobles* Jg 5$_{25}$, יד אדירים *hand of mighty ones* 1QH 2$_{35}$ (+ יד חזק ממנו *hand of one stronger than him*), עצם אדירים *bone(s) of noble ones* 5$_{7}$ (|| גִּבּוֹר *warrior*), וִילְלַת אַדִּירֵי *and wailing of nobles of* the flock Jr 25$_{36}$ (mss וְיִלְלַת).

<APP> אֲחֵיהֶם אַדִּירֵיהֶם *their brothers, their nobles,* i.e. heads of family Ne 10$_{30}$, אַדִּיר ... מְקוֹם־נְהָרִים יְאֹרִים *a noble one ... a place of two rivers, of* broad *streams* Is 33$_{21}$ (or del. נְהָרִים).

<PREP> שָׂרִיד לְאַדִּירִים *remnant of noble ones,* i.e. Israelite tribes Jg 5$_{13}$ (+ גִּבּוֹר *warrior*), ... טוֹבָתִי לִקְדוֹשִׁים ... וְאַדִּירֵי *my goodness is for holy ones ... and (for) nobles of* all in whom is my delight Ps 16$_{3}$ (or em.; see Cstr.); [ו]יתננו לאלוהים על אדירים *and he made him as God to the mighty ones* 4QApocMos A 2.2$_{6}$.

הַלְּבָנוֹן בְּאַדִּיר יִפּוֹל *Lebanon with its majestic one(s),* i.e. trees, *will fall* Is 10$_{34}$=4Q285 7$_{2}$ (לבנון באדיר [י]פול).

אבד מִן *disappear from* (of escape) Jr 25$_{35}$.

חזק על hi. *join with, support* Ne 10$_{30}$.

<COLL> אַדִּיר מִן *more majestic than* Jr 30$_{21}$ (if em.; see Subj.) Ps 76$_{5}$ (+ הַר *mountain*) 93$_{4}$ (if em.; see §1), מָה־אַדִּיר *how majestic* Ps 8$_{2.10}$.

<SYN> §2 משׁל ptc. *ruler,* רעה ptc. *shepherd,* גִּבּוֹר *warrior.*

→ אדר *be majestic.*

אֲדַלְיָא 1 pr.n.m. **Adalia,** son of Haman, Est 9$_{8}$.

אדם 10 vb. **be red—Qal** Pf. אָדְמוּ—**be red,** אָדְמוּ עֶצֶם מִפְּנִינִים *(their) bone(s) were redder than corals* Lm 4$_{7}$ (or em. אָדַם עוֹרָם *their skin was redder* or אָדְמָה שְׂפָתָם *their lip[s] were redder;* + צחח *glisten,* זכך *be pure,* חשׁך *be dark*).

Pu. Ptc. מְאָדָּמִים, מְאָדָּם—**be made red,** **<SUBJ>** מָגֵן *shield* Na 2$_{4}$ (+ תלע pu. *be scarlet*), עוֹר *skin* of ram Ex 25$_{5}$||35$_{7}$ 26$_{14}$||36$_{19}$ 35$_{23}$ 39$_{34}$. **<COLL>** מִי־זֶה בָּא מְאָדָּם *who is this, coming reddened?* Is 63$_{1}$ (if em. מֵאֱדוֹם *from Edom,* + חמץ *be red*).

Hi. Impf. יַאְדִּימוּ—**be red,** **<SUBJ>** חֵטְא *sin* Is 1$_{18}$ (1QIsa^{a} ידומו perh. *are like;* + כַּתּוֹלָע red *as scarlet*).

Htp. Impf. יִתְאַדָּם—**be red,** **<SUBJ>** יַיִן *wine* Pr 23$_{31}$ (+ נתן *give* eye, i.e. sparkle, הלך *go about* smoothly).

→ אָדוֹם *red,* אֲדַמְדָּם *reddish,* אַדְמֹנִי *ruddy,* אֹדֶם *ruby,* אָדָם *human being,* אֱדוֹם *Edom,* אֲדָמָה I *earth,* II *Adamah,* אַדְמָה *Admah,* אֲדֻמִּים *Adummim,* אֲדָמִי הַנֶּקֶב *Adami-nekeb.*

אָדָם I 548.31.101.2 n.m. **human being**—cstr. Q אדם—**1.** collective, **humanity, people** (as distinct from God or animals), persons in general (usu. without regard to sex, e.g. Gn 52), human race as a whole, also with ref. to smaller groups, e.g. inhabitants of a city; of persons in general. Distinction between אָדָם as collective and as individual not alw. clear, perh. also at times אָדָם *Adam* (pr.n.m.) is intended; rarely, אָדָם takes pl. verb (e.g. Jr 472 Zp 117).

<SUBJ> חיה *live* Ex 3320 Lv 185 Dt 524 83.3 Ezk 2011.13.21 Ne 929 4QDibHama 617 CD 316 4QDb12, לין *pass the night*, i.e. endure Ps 4913 (or em. בין *understand*), משל ni. *be comparable (to)* Ps 4913=21 (+ בְּהֵמָה *beast*), דמה *be like* 1444, יצר ni. *be fashioned* Si 3610, רבב *become many* Gn 61, רבה *be numerous* Ezk 3611, פרה *be fruitful* 3611, ישׁב *dwell* Jr 26 (|| אִישׁ *man*), אמר *say* 5812, נגד hi. *tell* 6410, קרא *call* Jon 38, זעק *cry out* Jr 472 (+ כֹּל יוֹשֵׁב הָאָרֶץ *every inhabitant of the country*), בטא *utter* Lv 54.

הלך *go* Jr 503 Zp 117, יצא *go out* Ps 10423 (+ לְפָעֳלוֹ *to his work*), שׁוב *return* Jb 3415 (+ עַל־עָפָר *to dust*; + כָּל־בָּשָׂר *all flesh*), נוד *wander* Jr 503, משׁך *follow* Jb 2133, ירשׁ *possess* Ezk 3612, עשׂה *do* Lv 185 Ezk 2011.13.21 Ps 5612 1186 Ne 929 CD 316 4QDb12 4QDibHama 617(Baillet) ([יעשה]) 4QShirb 306(Baillet) (|| אִישׁ *man*), *make* idols, gods Is 220 Jr 1620, חלל hi. *begin* Gn 61, שׁלך hi. *throw away* idols Is 220, שׁתה *drink* Jon 37, טעם *taste* 37, רעה *feed* 37.

ראה *see* Ex 3320 (obj. God) 1 S 167.7 (:: Y.) Ps 6410(mss), שׁעה *look* Is 177, חזה *look* Jb 3625 (|| אֱנוֹשׁ *person*), ידע *know* Jon 411 Pr 282 (or em. יֹדֵעַ כֵּן יַאֲרִיךְ by *knowledgeable* people, *thus will it endure* to יִדְעָכוּן *they will be extinguished*) Ec 91.12, בין *understand* Ps 4913 (if em. לין *pass the night*) 4921, hi. Pr 282, שׂכל hi. *understand* Ps 6410, זכר *remember* Ec 915, כזב *lie* Ps 11611, pi. CD 1925, קבע *rob* God Ml 38 (or em. עקב *trick*), מעל *be disloyal* CD 108, חטא *sin* Zp 117, ירא *fear* Ps 6410 (mss ראה *see*), רעשׁ *quake* Ezk 3820, ענה pi. *afflict* Is 585 (obj. נַפְשׁוֹ *oneself*), שׁחח ni. *be humbled* 29=515 (both || אִישׁ *man*), כסה htp. *cover oneself* Jon 38, חפשׂ pu. *be sought*, i.e. be hidden Pr 2812 (or em. htp. *disguise oneself*), סתר ni. *be hidden* 2828.

<NOM CL> אֵין הָאָדָם *there was no one* Jr 425 (+ עוֹף הַשָּׁמַיִם *birds of the sky*), אָדָם אַתֶּם *you are people* Ezk 3431 (or del.; + אֲנִי אֱלֹהֵיכֶם *I am your God*), הָאָדָם עֵץ הַשָּׂדֶה *the trees of the field are human* Dt 2019 (or em. *are they human?*), מִצְרַיִם אָדָם *Egypt is human* Is 313 (+ וְלֹא־אֵל *and not God*), מָה־אָדָם *what is humanity?* Ps 1443.

<OBJ> subject God עשׂה *make* Gn 126 66 Is 177 Jr 275 (|| אֶרֶץ *world*) Hb 114=1QpHab 512 Ec 729 (+ יָשָׁר *upright*) Si 5022 4QJuba 72 4QapPsa 1.21, ברא *create* Gn 127 51 67 Dt 432 Is 4512 (|| אֶרֶץ) Si 1514, יצר *fashion* 1QH 115 (+ בתבל *in the world*), גדל pi. *make grow* Si 5022, רבה hi. *make numerous* Ezk 3610.11, שׂים *place* Jb 204 (+ עֲלֵי־אָרֶץ *on the earth*), שׁית *place* Si 1514(Segal) (+ ביד חותפו *into the hand of his adversary*), נתן *place* Is 434 (or em. אֲדָמֹת *lands*; + לְאֻמִּים *nations*) Si 1514 (+ ביד יצרו *into the hand of his own desire*), מצא hi. *cause to be found* Zc 116, סור hi. *remove* Jb 3317, רחק pi. *remove* Is 612 4Q386–9 412 (+ אֶרֶץ *land*), הלך hi. *cause to walk* Ezk 3612, שׁלח pi. *send* Zc 810, ידע *know* Ps 1443 (|| בֶּן־אֱנוֹשׁ *person*), נצר *watch* Jb 720, יקר hi. *make precious, rare* Is 1312 (|| אֱנוֹשׁ *person*), למד pi. *teach* Ps 9410 (+ גּוֹיִם *nations*), ישׁע hi. *save* Ps 367, מחה *wipe out* Gn 67, שׁבת hi. *destroy* Jr 3629, כרת hi. *cut off* Ezk 1413.17.19.21 2513 298 Zp 13, סוף hi. *put an end (to)* 13, נכה hi. *strike* Jr 216 335.

Other subjects, נבט hi. *look (at)* Is 3811, נסף hi. *incite* CD 1925, שׁמד hi. *destroy* (of Israelites) Jos 1114, נכה hi. *strike* fatally (of Israelites) 1114 (+ שָׁלָל *booty*, בְּהֵמָה *cattle*), זבח *sacrifice* Ho 132, אכל *eat* Ezk 193.6 (both with subj. lion) 3613.14 (both with subj. land; + גּוֹיֵךְ *your people*), בלע *swallow* (of earth) Nm 1632 (|| רְכוּשׁ *property*).

<CSTR> אדם רשעה *people of wickedness, wicked humanity* 1QS 119 (+ סוד בשר עול *company of flesh of iniquity*).

לֵב אָדָם *heart of a human being* Gn 821, בְּשַׂר *flesh of* Ex 3032, עַצְמוֹת *bones of* 1 K 132 2 K 2314.20, רוּחַ *spirit of* Zc 121 1QH 115, חיי *life of* Si 3926(Segal), נֶפֶשׁ *life of*, i.e. human being Lv 2417 Nm 3135 (+ מִן־הַנָּשִׁים *consisting of the women*) 3140.46 Ezk 2713 1 C 521 4Q251 26 4QMMT A 281 ([נפש] האדם), בכור *first-born of* 4Q251 64 ([ב]כור האד[ם]) 65 ([ב]כור), נִבְלַת *corpse(s) of* Jr 921, פִּגְרֵי *corpses of* 335, יַד־ *hand*, i.e. power, *of* Gn 95 (+ כָּל־חַיָּה *every living being*) 2 S 2414||1 C 2113 (:: Y., as merciful) Jb 37$_{7}$ (בְּיַד־כָּל־; or em. בְּעַד *around;* + אֲנָשִׁים *men)* 4QBark^{a} 2.1$_{8}$ ([מיד]), יְדֵי *hands of* Dt 4$_{28}$ 2 K 19$_{18}$=Is 37$_{19}$ (both + מַעֲשֵׂה *work of)* Ezk 1$_{8(Kt)}$ 10$_{21}$ Ps 115$_{4}$ 135$_{15}$ 2 C 32$_{19}$ 11QT 59$_{3}$ (all four + מַעֲשֵׂה), רֶגֶל *foot of* Ezk 29$_{11}$ 32$_{13}$, זֶרַע *seed of* Jr 31$_{27}$ 1QLitPr^{b} 1.2$_{3}$ ([אד]ם) 4QPrFêtes^{c} 97.1$_{1(Baillet)}$ (ז]רע [האדם)), עַיִן *eye of* Zc 9$_{1}$ (but perh. אָדָם III surface of the *earth;* or em. עֵין אֲרָם *eye of Aram* or עָרֵי אֲרָם *cities of Aram* or עָוּו אֲרָם *Aram has acted wickedly),* עֵינֵי *eyes of* Pr 3$_{4}$ (|| אֱלֹהִים *God)* 27$_{20}$, דְּמֵי *blood,* i.e. murders, *of* Hb 2$_{8.17}$=1QpHab 9$_{8}$ 12$_{1}$ (both + חֲמַס־אֶרֶץ *violence against the earth),* חַבְלֵי *cords of* Ho 11$_{4}$ (perh. אָדָם II *leather;* || אַהֲבָה I/II *love/leather),* דִּבְרֵי *words of* 1 S 24$_{10}$.

ברית *covenant of* human beings 1QH 17$_{27}$, עידי *witnesses of* GnzPs 1$_{1}$, מַחְשְׁבוֹת *thoughts of* Ps 94$_{11}$, בִּינַת *intelligence of* Pr 30$_{2}$ (|| אִישׁ *man),* עֲבֹדַת *labour of* Ps 104$_{14}$, עֲמַל *labour of* Ec 6$_{7}$, פְּעֻלּוֹת *deeds of* Ps 17$_{4}$ 4QBark^{a} 1$_{8}$ (פעולות), שְׂכַר *hire of* Zc 8$_{10}$, חֵלֶק־ *portion of* a person from God Jb 20$_{29}$ 27$_{13}$, מקדש *sanctuary of* 4QFlor 1.1$_{6}$, מוֹתַר *superiority of* Ec 3$_{19}$, חַטֹּאת *sins of* Nm 5$_{6}$, רָעַת *evil of* Gn 6$_{5}$, גַּבְהוּת *pride of* Is 2$_{11.17}$ (both + אֲנָשִׁים *men),* חֲמַת *anger of* Ps 76$_{11}$, עֹשֶׁק *oppression of* 119$_{134}$, טֻמְאַת *uncleanness of* Lv 5$_{3}$ 7$_{21}$ CD 12$_{16}$, טמאו[ת] *uncleannesses of* 1QSa 2$_{4}$, צֵאַת *excrement of* Ezk 4$_{12}$, גֶּלְלֵי *faeces of* 4$_{15}$, בְּכוֹר *firstborn of* Ex 13$_{13}$ (+ בְּבָנֶיךָ *among your sons)* 13$_{15}$, תּוֹרַת *law of,* i.e. applicable to 2 S 7$_{19}$ (||1 C 17$_{17}$ תּוֹר *plait of),* דְּמוּת *appearance of* Ezk 1$_{5}$, רֶכֶב *chariotry (consisting) of* Is 22$_{6}$ (or em. אֲרָם *Aram),* תְּשׁוּעַת *victory of* Ps 60$_{13}$||108$_{13}$, נְסִיכֵי *princes of* Mc 5$_{4}$, מושלי *rulers of* GnzPs 2$_{12}$ (|| תֵּבֵל *world),* בחירי *elect of* 1QS 11$_{16}$, גדולי *great (ones) of* GnzPs 3$_{19}$ (:: קטני אינוש *least ones of humanity),* הולכי *those who go of,* i.e. among 4Q416 1$_{16}$, אֶבְיוֹנֵי *poor (ones) of* Is 29$_{19}$ GnzPs 3$_{21}$, צֹאן *flock of* Ezk 36$_{37.38}$, רֹב (רָב־) *crowd of* Ezk 23$_{42}$ Zc 2$_{8}$ Pr 20$_{6}$ (|| אִישׁ *man),* מעוט *diminution of* 4QpIsa^{c} 4.2$_{8}$, חֶרְפַּת *reproach of* Ps 22$_{7}$, כָּל־אָדָם (and vars.) *all people* Gn 7$_{21}$ Ex 9$_{19}$ Nm 12$_{3}$ 16$_{29.29}$ (+ מוֹת *death of,* פְּקֻדַּת *fate of)* 16$_{32}$ Jos 11$_{14}$ Jg 16$_{17}$ Ezk 38$_{20}$ Zc 8$_{10}$ (or del. אֶת־כָּל־) Ps 64$_{10}$ 116$_{11}$ Jb 21$_{33}$ 36$_{25}$ (+ אֱנוֹשׁ *person)* 37$_{7}$ (+ אִישׁ *man).*

<APP> אָדָם פָּרָשִׁים *people, (namely) horseriders* Is 22$_{6}$ (or em. אֲרָם פֹּרְשִׁים in the chariots *of Aram are riders).*

<ADJ> רַע *evil* Ps 140$_{2}$ (|| אִישׁ *man),* רַב *numerous* Jb 36$_{28}$ (but perh. אָדָם III great *earth).*

<PREP> לְ *to, for* Pr 24$_{9}$ (+ לֵץ *scoffer)* 27$_{19}$ 1 C 29$_{1}$ 2 C 19$_{6}$ (both :: Y.), *against* Jb 21$_{4}$, + אמר *say* Jb 28$_{28}$, נגד hi. *tell* Am 4$_{13}$, ידע ni. *be known* 11QPs^{a} 18$_{4}$, צרר hi. *cause distress* (subj. Y.) Zp 1$_{17}$, שׁרת pi. *minister* 4QapPs^{b} 1$_{1}$.

בְּ *among* Ex 8$_{13.14}$ 9$_{10}$ 13$_{2}$ Nm 8$_{17}$ 18$_{15}$ 31$_{11}$ Jr 49$_{15}$ (+ גּוֹיִם *nations)* Mc 7$_{2}$ (|| אֶרֶץ *land)* Ps 78$_{60}$ Pr 23$_{28}$ 4Q521 1.3$_{2}$, *with* Pr 28$_{2}$, *consisting of* Nm 31$_{26}$ Ps 68$_{19}$, + משׁל בְּ *rule over* 2 S 23$_{3}$, בטח בְּ *trust in* Ps 118$_{8}$ (:: Y.), וּבְיִשְׂרָאֵל וּבָאָדָם *both in Israel and in humanity at large* Jr 32$_{20}$ (but perh. אָדָם III *earth;* or em. וּבָאֲדָמוֹת *and in the [other] lands).*

כְּאָדָם *as humans are wont to do* (or perh. *as Adam)* Ho 6$_{7}$ (or em. בְּאָדָם *at Adam)* Jb 31$_{33}$ Ps 82$_{7}$ (+ שָׂרִים *princes),* כְּאַחַד הָאָדָם *as one of the ordinary people* Jg 16$_{7.11}$.

מִן *from (among)* Gn 6$_{7}$ 7$_{23}$ Lv 27$_{28.29}$ Nm 3$_{13}$ 31$_{28.30.47}$ Is 2$_{22}$=1QS 5$_{17}$ Jr 51$_{62}$ (לְמֵאָדָם) Ho 9$_{12}$ Ps 135$_{8}$ 140$_{2}$ (|| אִישׁ *man)* Pr 30$_{14}$ (but perh. אָדָם III *earth;* or em. מֵאֲדָמָה *from the earth;* + אֶבְיוֹן *poor person;* || אֶרֶץ *earth)* CD 9$_{1}$ 11QapPs^{a} 4$_{6}$ ([מ]אדם), הֵמָּה מֵאָדָם *they are but humans* Is 44$_{11}$, *because of* Mc 2$_{12}$, הִרְחִיק מִן *at a distance (away) from* or *(higher) than* Jos 3$_{16(Qr)}$ (Kt באדם *at Adam,* as pl.n.).

מֵאֵין *without* (in ref. to depopulation by war, etc.) Is 6$_{11}$ Jr 32$_{43}$ 33$_{10.10.12}$, + עלם ni. *be hidden* Si 11$_{4(A)}$ ([מ]אדם; B מאנוש).

אֶל *to* Jb 32$_{21}$ (|| אִישׁ *man);* עַל *upon* Ex 9$_{9.22}$ Jr 7$_{20}$ Hg 1$_{11}$ Jb 36$_{28}$ (יִרְעֲפוּ עֲלֵי *they* [clouds] *drip upon;* but perh. אָדָם III *earth)* Ec 6$_{1}$.

עִם *with* Ps 73$_{5}$ (|| אֱנוֹשׁ *people);* אֵת *with,* + דבר pi. *speak* (of God) Dt 5$_{24}$, ישׁב *dwell* (of God) 2 C 6$_{18}$; בַּעֲבוּר *on account of* Gn 8$_{21}$; חתם בְּעַד *place seal around* Jb 37$_{7}$ (if em. בְּיַד *into the hand of).*

<COLL> אָדָם ... בְּהֵמָה *humanity ... beasts,* i.e. all living creatures Gn 6$_{7}$ 7$_{23}$ Ex 8$_{13.14}$ 9$_{9.10.19.22.25}$ 12$_{12}$ 13$_{2.15}$ Lv 27$_{28}$ Nm 3$_{13}$ 8$_{17}$ 18$_{15}$ 31$_{11.26.47}$ Jr 7$_{20}$ 21$_{6}$ 27$_{5}$ 31$_{27}$ 32$_{43}$ 33$_{10.10.12}$ 36$_{29}$ 50$_{3}$ 51$_{62}$ Ezk 14$_{13.17.19.21}$ 25$_{13}$ 29$_{8.11}$ 32$_{13}$ 36$_{11}$ Jon 3$_{7.8}$ 4$_{11}$ Zp 1$_{3}$ Hg 1$_{11}$ Zc 2$_{8}$ 8$_{10}$ Ps 36$_{7}$ 135$_{8}$ Ec 3$_{19}$, נֶפֶשׁ ... אָדָם *an individual person ... humans* (in general) Lv 5$_{4}$ 7$_{21}$, with number Jon 4$_{11}$ (120,000),

אֲשֶׁר יַעֲשֶׂה אֹתָם הָאָדָם וָחַי בָּהֶם (and vars.) commandments, etc. *that people should do and live by them* Lv 18$_{5}$ Ezk 20$_{11.13.21}$ Ne 9$_{29}$ CD 3$_{16}$, אָדָם כַּיֶּלֶק מִלֵּאתִיךְ *I have filled you (with) people (numerous) as locusts* Jr 51$_{14}$, הָאָדָם אֲשֶׁר נְשָׁמָה בְּאַפּוֹ *humankind, in whose nostril is breath* Is 2$_{22}$=1QS 5$_{17}$.

2a. individual, whether a particular person or a typical human, **<SUBJ>** היה *be* Lv 16$_{17}$ Ec 2$_{18}$ 11QT 32$_{15}$ (+ נוגעים *those who touch*) 49$_{16}$, יכל ho. *be able* Ec 6$_{10}$ 8$_{17}$, כון ni. *be established* Pr 12$_{3}$ (+ בְּרֶשַׁע *in wickedness*), חיה *live* Ec 11$_{8}$, ילד pass. *be born* Jb 14$_{1}$, ni. *be born* 4QDibHam^{c} 31$_{6}$ ([א]דם), pu. *be born* Jb 5$_{7}$ (+ לְעָמָל *for trouble*), מות *die* Nm 19$_{14}$ 11QT 49$_{5}$, גוע *die* Jb 14$_{10}$ (|| גֶּבֶר *man*).

הלך *go* Pr 6$_{12}$ Ec 12$_{5}$ (+ אֶל־בֵּית עֹלָמוֹ *to the house of his eternity, to his grave*), בוא *come* 2$_{12}$ Ne 2$_{10}$, ho. Lv 13$_{2.9}$, יצא *go out* perh. Si 16$_{14}$ (or em. ימצא *will find*), קום *arise* 1 S 25$_{29}$ (+ לִרְדָפְךָ *to pursue you*) Ps 124$_{2}$, נוס *flee* Pr 28$_{17}$, נוח *rest* 21$_{16}$, קרב hi. *bring near* a sacrifice Lv 1$_{2}$, נשׂא *bear, accept* Ec 5$_{18}$ (obj. חֶלְקוֹ *his portion*), חזק hi. *grasp* 4Q185 1.2$_{13}$, פתח *open* tomb Silwan royal steward tomb inscr. 1$_{2}$, מצא *find* Pr 3$_{13}$ (obj. wisdom) Ec 3$_{11}$ 7$_{14}$ 8$_{17.17}$ Si 16$_{14}$ (if em. יצא *will go out*), פוק hi. *obtain* wisdom Pr 3$_{13}$, לקח *take* Is 44$_{15}$, גמל *repay* Pr 3$_{30}$, ירשׁ *possess* 4Q185 1.2$_{13}$, נחל *inherit* Si 10$_{11}$ (+ רמה *corruption*), קנה hi. *cause to acquire* Zc 13$_{5}$ (but perh. אָדָם III *earth*, as obj., or em. אָדָם הִקְנַנִי *man has caused me to possess* to אֲדָמָה קִנְיָנִי *land was my acquisition*).

בקשׁ pi. *seek* Ec 8$_{17}$ Ne 2$_{10}$ 4Q185 1.2$_{13}$, בקר pi. *ask* Pr 20$_{25}$, דבר pi. *speak* CD 14$_{11.11}$, ענה *answer* Si 46$_{19}$, אנן htp. *complain* Lm 3$_{39}$ (|| גֶּבֶר *man*), לוע *utter* Pr 20$_{25}$, שׁמע *hear* 8$_{34}$, ראה *see* Ec 3$_{13.22}$, hi. 2$_{24}$, שׁקד *watch* Pr 8$_{34}$, שׁמר *guard* 8$_{34}$, ידע *know* Ec 10$_{14}$, נכר hi. *recognize* 4QRitMar 1$_{1}$ ([א]דם), חבר pu. *associate (with)* Si 13$_{16}$, בין *understand* Pr 20$_{24}$, זכר *remember* Ec 11$_{8}$, יאל *be willing* 4Q185 1.2$_{13}$, ערב *guarantee* Pr 17$_{18}$, בטח *trust* Ps 84$_{13}$, שׂמח *rejoice* Ec 3$_{22}$ 5$_{18}$ 8$_{15}$ 11$_{8}$, אשׁר pu. *be considered happy* Si 11$_{27}$.

אהב *love* (obj. הדומה לו *what is like him*) Si 13$_{15}$, חפץ pi. *desire* 15$_{17}$, פאר pi. *glorify* 11QPs^{a} 18$_{7}$, בער ni. *be stupid* Jr 10$_{14}$=51$_{17}$ (|| צֹרֵף *smith*), פחד pi. *fear* Pr 28$_{14}$, עזז pu. *be enraged* Si 10$_{12}$, עשׂה *do* 4Q185 1.2$_{13}$, *make* idol Is 44$_{15}$, פעל *make* idol 44$_{15}$, עמל *labour* Ec 1$_{3}$ 2$_{21}$ 8$_{17}$, מלך *rule* Jb 34$_{30}$, שׁלט *dominate* Ec 8$_{9}$, עשׁק *oppress* Ps 105$_{14}$, דין *judge* Ec 6$_{10}$, בחן ni. *be tested* 11QPs^{a} 22$_{10}$ (+ כדרכו *according to his behaviour*, || אִישׁ *man*), שׁחה htpal. *bow down* Is 44$_{15}$, סגד *bow* 44$_{15}$, עבר עַל *pass over, ignore* Pr 19$_{11}$ (+ פֶּשַׁע *fault*), פסד ni. *be mistreated* MurEpBarC$^{a}_{5}$ (יפס[ד]), כסה *cover* knowledge Pr 12$_{23}$, חרם hi. *put to the ban* CD 9$_{1}$, תקע *strike* hand in agreement Pr 17$_{18}$, נגע *touch* 11QT 50$_{8}$.

חמם *be warm* Is 44$_{15}$, בער pi. *burn* 44$_{15}$, שׂלק hi. *light a fire* 44$_{15}$, אפה *bake* 44$_{15}$, אכל *eat* Ec 2$_{24}$ 3$_{13}$ 5$_{18}$ 8$_{15}$, שׁתה *drink* Ec 2$_{24}$ 3$_{13}$ 8$_{15}$, בלע pi. *swallow up* Pr 21$_{20}$, כבס pi. *wash* clothes 11QT 49$_{16}$ 50$_{8}$, רחץ *wash oneself* 49$_{16}$ 50$_{8}$, טהר *be clean* 50$_{8}$, עשׁק pass. *be oppressed* Pr 28$_{17}$ (+ בְּדַם־נָפֶשׁ *by the blood of a person*), חטא *sin* 1 K 8$_{46}$||2 C 6$_{36}$, טמא ho. *be made unclean* 11QT 49$_{21}$, תעה *err* Pr 21$_{16}$, בזה *despise* 15$_{20}$.

<NOM CL> + יֵשׁ *there is* Ec 2$_{21}$, אַיִן *there is not* Gn 2$_{5}$ (אַיִן) 1 K 8$_{46}$||2 C 6$_{36}$ Ec 7$_{20}$ 8$_{8}$ Lachish ost. 4$_{5}$ (אין שם אדם *no one is there*), הוּא אָדָם *he is a person* Ec 6$_{10}$, לֹא אָדָם הוּא *he* (God) *is not a human being* 1 S 15$_{29}$, אַתָּה אָדָם וְלֹא־אֵל *you are a human being, not God* Ezk 28$_{2.9}$. + הֶבֶל *breath* Ps 39$_{6.12}$ Si 41$_{11}$ (הבל אדם בגויתו *a mere breath is a person in one's body*), עָמֵל *labouring* Ec 2$_{22}$, אַשְׁרֵי *happy* Ps 32$_{2}$ 84$_{6.13}$ Pr 3$_{13}$ 8$_{34}$ 28$_{14}$ 4Q185 1.2$_{8.13}$, ארור *cursed* Silwan royal steward tomb inscr.$_{2}$.

<OBJ> (1) subj. God עשׂה *make* Gn 9$_{6}$ Si 10$_{12}$, פגע *meet* with kindness Is 47$_{3}$, נוח hi, *allow* Ps 105$_{14}$ (+ מְלָכִים *kings*), שׁלט hi. *empower* Ec 5$_{18}$, רצה *be pleased (with)* 11QPs^{a} 18$_{7}$.

(2) subj. humans מצא *find* Ec 7$_{28}$, בוא hi. *bring* 3$_{22}$, אשׁר pi. *consider happy* Si 11$_{27}$ (תאשׁ[רה]ו), הלל pi. *praise* 11$_{2}$ (|| אָדָם), מות hi. *kill* CD 9$_{1}$, נכה hi. *strike fatally* Lv 24$_{21}$ (:: בְּהֵמָה *animal*), תעב pi. *despise* Si 11$_{2}$ (|| אָדָם), חטא hi. *regard as sinful* Is 29$_{21}$, יכח hi. *reprove* Pr 28$_{23}$, חקר *examine* Si 11$_{27}$, עות pi. *subvert* Lm 3$_{36}$ (|| גֶּבֶר *man*), אסר *bind* 11QapPs^{a} 2$_{9}$ (ל[אסור האדם]).

<CSTR> נֶפֶשׁ *life of* Gn 9$_{5}$, *body of* Nm 9$_{6.7}$ 19$_{11.13}$ CD 11$_{16}$, לֵב *heart of* Pr 16$_{9}$ (:: Y.) 27$_{19}$, *courage of* 1 S 17$_{32}$ (or em. אֲדֹנִי *of my lord*), דַּם *blood of* Gn 9$_{6}$ 11QT 50$_{6}$ 4QJub^{d} 1.2$_{18}$ ([דם]) 1.2$_{19.20}$ (both [דם האדם]), עֶצֶם

bone of Nm 19$_{16}$ Ezk 39$_{15}$ 11QT 50$_{5}$, יַד *hand of* Ezk 10$_{8}$ 4QpsEzek^{a} 4$_{10}$ (אדם [יד]), יְדֵי *hands of* Pr 12$_{14}$ (|| אִישׁ *man*), פְּנֵי *face of* Ezk 1$_{10}$ 10$_{14}$ 41$_{19}$, פֶּה *mouth of* Ex 4$_{11}$, לשון *tongue of* Si 5$_{13}$, קוֹל־ *voice of* 2 K 7$_{10}$ (|| אִישׁ *man*) Dn 8$_{16}$, נִשְׁמַת *breath of* Pr 20$_{27}$, פֹּעַל *deed of* Jb 34$_{11}$ (|| אִישׁ *man*), תַּאֲוַת *desire*, i.e. what is desired, *of* Pr 19$_{22}$, גיל *happiness of* Si 30$_{22}$.

אחרית *end of* Si 11$_{25}$ (א[ד]ם), סוף *end of* 11$_{27}$, מוֹת *death of* Pr 11$_{7}$ Si 10$_{11}$ (מ[ו]ת), מֵת *dead of*, i.e. dead person Ezk 44$_{25}$, רָעַת *misfortune of* Ec 8$_{6}$ (mss דַּעַת *knowledge of*), מוֹקֵשׁ *trap of*, i.e. for Pr 20$_{25}$, הוֹן *wealth of* 12$_{27}$, מַתָּן *gift of* 18$_{16}$, גמול *reward of* Si 32$_{24}$ (|| אֱנוֹשׁ *person*), כֶּרֶם *vineyard of* Pr 24$_{30}$ (|| אִישׁ *man*), מַרְאֵה *appearance of* Ezk 1$_{26}$ Dn 10$_{18}$, תִּפְאֶרֶת *splendour of* Is 44$_{13}$ (|| אִישׁ), דַּעַת *knowledge of* Ec 8$_{6(mss)}$, חָכְמַת *wisdom of* Ec 8$_{1}$, שֶׂכֶל *intelligence of* Pr 19$_{11}$, אִוֶּלֶת *stupidity of* 19$_{3}$, גַּאֲוַת *pride of* 29$_{23}$, חֶרְדַּת *terror of* 29$_{25}$ (:: Y.), כְּסִיל *fool of* 15$_{20}$ 21$_{20}$, כָּל־אָדָם (and vars.) *every, each person* Lv 16$_{17}$ 1 K 5$_{11}$ 8$_{38}$||2 C 6$_{29}$ Jr 31$_{30}$ 51$_{17}$ Ps 39$_{6.12}$ Ec 3$_{13}$ 5$_{18}$ 7$_{2}$ (+ סוֹף *end of*) 12$_{13}$ Si 13$_{15}$ (+ כל בשר *all flesh*) 16$_{14}$ 30$_{38}$ 34$_{31(F)}$ 46$_{19}$ 11QT 32$_{15}$ 49$_{9}$ (+ מישראל *from Israel*) 50$_{8}$ MurEp BarC$_{a5}$ CD 9$_{1}$ 14$_{11}$ 11QapPs^{a} 2$_{8}$ ([א]דם).

<APP> אָדָם בְּלִיַּעַל *person (who is) worthless(ness)* Pr 6$_{12}$ (or em. אֲדַם *person of*; + אִישׁ אָוֶן *man of iniquity*), אַרְבַּע הָאָדָם הַגָּדוֹל *Arba, the great(est) man of the* Anakim Jos 14$_{15}$.

<ADJ> הֲרִאישׁוֹן אָדָם תִּוָּלֵד *are you the first person to be born?* Jb 15$_{7}$, חַי *living* Lm 3$_{39}$, מֵת *dead* 11QT 50$_{5.6}$, עָרוּם *crafty* Pr 12$_{23}$, שַׁלִּיט *having mastery* Ec 8$_{8}$ (+ בָּרוּחַ *over the spirit*), גָּדוֹל *great* Jos 14$_{15}$, חֲסַר־לֵב *lacking mind, unintelligent* Pr 17$_{18}$ 24$_{30}$, רָשָׁע *wicked* 11$_{7}$, חָנֵף *irreverent* Jb 34$_{30}$, אֶחָד *one* Ec 7$_{28}$ (+ מֵאֶלֶף *out of a thousand*).

<PREP> לְ *to, for* 1 K 8$_{38}$||2 C 6$_{29}$ Is 44$_{15}$ Jr 10$_{23}$ (|| אִישׁ *man*) Ec 1$_{3}$ (+ יִתְרוֹן *advantage*) 2$_{21.22}$ 6$_{11}$ (+ יֹתֵר *advantage*) 6$_{12}$ 8$_{15}$ 11QT 49$_{9}$ 1QS 11$_{10}$ (+ דרכו *his way*; || אֱנוֹשׁ *person*), לְאָדָם מַעַרְכֵי־לֵב וּמֵי' מַעֲנֵה לָשׁוֹן *to a person belong the plans of the mind, but from Y. is the tongue's response* Pr 16$_{1}$, + נגד hi. *tell* Jb 33$_{23}$ Ec 6$_{12}$ Ne 2$_{12}$, נתן *give* Ec 2$_{26}$ GnzPs 4$_{21}$ (+ כדרכיו *according to his behaviour*), נוח hi. *leave* Ec 2$_{18}$, שׁוב hi. *give back* Pr 24$_{12}$, אחד של אדם *(there was) one (face) that was of a human being* 4QpsEzek^{a} 4$_{9}$.

בְּ *in* Lv 13$_{9}$ 24$_{20}$ (+ מוּם *disfigurement*), *as for* 11QT 49$_{21}$, *on account of* Gn 9$_{6}$, *for* Ec 2$_{24}$, דין בְּ appar. *strive against* Gn 6$_{3}$ (=4QpGen^{a} דור ב *dwell in*), בטח בְּ *rely on* Jr 17$_{5}$ (|| בָּשָׂר *flesh*, :: Y.), נגע בְּ *touch* Lv 22$_{5}$ 4QToh A 1.1$_{8}$ (ה[נ]וגע[ )), שָׁלַט הָאָדָם בְּאָדָם *one man dominates another* Ec 8$_{9}$.

שכבת זרע מאדם *lying of seed*, i.e. semen, *from a human being* 4QToh A 2.1$_{4}$, לִפְנֵי *in front of* Si 15$_{17}$ (+ חיים ומוות *life and death*); לְעֵינֵי *in the sight of* Si 34$_{31(F)}$; עִם *with* Jg 18$_{7.28}$ (or em. אֲרָם *Aram* in both), + ריב *contend* Pr 3$_{30(Qr)}$.

עַל *upon*, וְעַל־גּוֹי וְעַל־אָדָם יַחַד *whether upon a nation or an individual* Jb 34$_{29}$, + יתר hi. *be overbearing* Si 30$_{38}$, ישׁ[ל]ח[ו] על [כול האר]ץ חטא ועל כול א[דם רשע] *they sent sin over all the earth and wickedness over every human being* 11QapPs^{a} 2$_{8}$.

<COLL> as vocative (*O human!*) Mc 6$_{8}$, [האדם] ואשתו *the man and his wife* 4QRitMar 1$_{3(Baillet)}$, לֹא לְאָדָם דַּרְכּוֹ *not to a person is one's way*, i.e. one does not control one's own destiny Jr 10$_{23}$, פֶּרֶא אָדָם *a wild ass of a human* Gn 16$_{12}$ (but perh. אָדָם III *earth*), עַיִר פֶּרֶא אָדָם יִוָּלֵד *a colt of a wild ass is born a human* Jb 11$_{12}$ (|| אִישׁ *man*).

מִדְבָּר לֹא־אָדָם בּוֹ *desert where there is no human being* 38$_{26}$ (|| אִישׁ *man*), (בְּ)חֶרֶב לֹא־אָדָם *(by) a sword not of*, i.e. wielded by, *a person* Is 31$_{8}$=1QM 11$_{12}$ (|| אִישׁ *man*), אדם לבד[ו] *a human alone* 4QShir^{b} 96$_{3}$, כְּסִיל אָדָם *a fool of a person* Pr 21$_{20}$.

2b. with article, **the man,** i.e. Adam, in Gn 2–3, **<SUBJ>** היה *be* Gn 2$_{7}$ (+ נֶפֶשׁ חַיָּה *living being*) 2$_{18}$ (+ לְבַדּוֹ *on his own*) 2$_{25}$ (+ עָרוּם *naked*) 3$_{22}$ (+ כְּאַחַד מִמֶּנּוּ *as one of us*), חיה *be alive* 3$_{22}$, לקח *take* 3$_{22}$, שׁלח *send, stretch out* hand 3$_{22}$, עבד *work* 2$_{15}$, שׁמר *keep* 2$_{15}$, ידע *know* 3$_{22}$ 4$_{1}$, אמר *say* 2$_{23}$ 3$_{12}$, קרא *call* 2$_{19.19.20}$ 3$_{20}$, אכל *eat* 2$_{16}$ 3$_{22}$, ישׁן *sleep* 2$_{21}$, חבא htp. *hide oneself* 3$_{8}$.

<OBJ> subj. God יצר *fashion* Gn 2$_{7.8}$, שׂים *place* 2$_{8}$, נוח hi. *set down* 2$_{15}$, לקח *take* 2$_{15}$, גרשׁ pi. *drive out* 3$_{24}$.

<PREP> לְ *to* Gn 2$_{20}$ 3$_{17.21}$ (if em. לְאָדָם to לָאָדָם); לקח מִן *take from* Gn 2$_{22}$; אֶל *to*, + בוא hi. *bring* Gn 2$_{19.22}$, קרא *call* 3$_{9}$; עַל *upon*, + צוה pi. *lay commandment* Gn 2$_{16}$, נפל hi. *make* sleep *fall* upon 2$_{21}$.

3. בֶּן־אָדָם **son of a person, individual, a.** in Ezk (also 4Q385 3$_4$ [(בן אדם)] 4QpsEzek^a 2$_4$ [(בן אדם)] 4Q386–9 3.2$_2$), alw. as vocative, **you**, in address to prophet, <SUBJ> היה *be* 2$_8$ (+ מְרִי *rebellious*), עשׂה *make* 12$_3$, שׁוב *do again* 8$_{6.15}$, ישׁב *dwell* 12$_2$, הלך *go* 3$_{1.4}$, יצא *go out* 3$_{25}$, גלה *go into exile* 12$_{3.3}$, בוא *come* 3$_4$, עבר hi. *make to pass* 5$_1$, ירד hi. *send down* 32$_{18}$, עמד *stand* 2$_1$, לקח *take* 3$_{10}$ 4$_1$ 5$_{1.1.1}$ 37$_{16.16}$, נתן *place* 4$_1$, שׂים *place* 6$_2$ 13$_{17}$ 21$_{2.7}$ 25$_2$ 28$_{21}$ 29$_2$ 35$_2$ 38$_2$ (all nine with obj. face, i.e. look) 40$_4$ 44$_{5.5}$ (all three with obj. heart, i.e. pay attention) 21$_{24}$, נשׂא *raise* 8$_5$ (obj. eyes) 27$_2$ 28$_{12}$ 32$_2$ (all with obj. קִינָה *lament*), פצה *open* mouth 2$_8$, נכה hi. *strike*, i.e. clap hand 21$_{19}$, אכל *eat* 2$_8$ 3$_{1.1}$ 12$_{18}$, שׁתה *drink* 12$_{18}$, ראה *see* 8$_{6.6.12.15.15.17}$ 40$_{4.4}$ 44$_5$ 47$_6$.

אמר *say* 13$_2$ 20$_{3.27}$ 21$_{14.33.33}$ 22$_{24}$ 28$_{2.12}$ 30$_2$ 31$_2$ 32$_2$ 33$_{2.10.12}$ 34$_2$ 36$_1$ 37$_9$ 38$_{14}$ 39$_{1.17}$, דבר pi. *speak* 3$_{1.4}$ 20$_{3.27}$ 33$_2$, נבא ni. *prophesy* 6$_2$ 11$_{4.4}$ 13$_{2.17}$ 21$_{2.7.14.19.33}$ 25$_2$ 28$_{21}$ 29$_2$ 30$_2$ 34$_{2.2}$ 35$_2$ 36$_1$ 37$_{9.9}$ 38$_{2.14}$ 39$_1$ 4QpsEzek^a 2$_4$ ([בן אדם הנ[בא]), ידע hi. *make known* Ezk 16$_2$ 20$_4$ 22$_2$, נגד hi. *tell* 23$_{36}$ 40$_4$ 43$_{10}$, נטף hi. *proclaim* 21$_{2.7}$, חוד *set a riddle* 17$_2$, משׁל *say a proverb* 17$_2$.

אנח ni. *groan* 21$_{11.11}$, זעק *cry out* 21$_{17}$, ילל hi. *wail* 21$_{17}$, ספד *mourn* 24$_{16}$, נהה *mourn* 32$_{18}$, בכה *weep* 24$_{16}$, זהר hi. *warn* 3$_{17}$ 33$_7$, בין htpol. *consider* 4Q386–9 3.2$_2$, שׁפט *judge* Ezk 20$_{4.4}$ 22$_{2.2}$ 23$_{36}$, כתב *write* 24$_{2(Qr)}$ 37$_{16.16}$, חקק *inscribe* 4$_1$, חלק *split* 5$_1$, שׁמע *hear* 2$_8$ 3$_{10.17}$ 33$_7$ 40$_4$ 44$_5$, ירא *fear* 2$_6$, חתר *dig* 8$_8$.

<APP> without verb 2$_3$ 3$_3$ 4$_{16}$ 11$_{2.15}$ 12$_{9.22.27}$ 14$_{3.13}$ 15$_2$ 22$_{18}$ 23$_2$ 24$_{2(Kt).25}$ 26$_2$ 29$_{18}$ 30$_{21}$ 33$_{24.30}$ 36$_{17}$ 37$_{3.11}$ 43$_{7.18}$, וְאַתָּה בֶן־אָדָם *and you, son of man* 2$_{6.8}$ 3$_{25}$ 4$_1$ 5$_1$ 7$_2$ 12$_3$ 13$_{17}$ 21$_{11.19.24.33}$ 22$_2$ 24$_{25}$ 27$_2$ 33$_{7.10.12.30}$ 36$_1$ 37$_{16}$ 39$_{1.17}$ 43$_{10}$ (lacks וְ).

b. outside Ezk, <SUBJ> חזק hi. *hold fast* Is 56$_2$ (|| אֱנוֹשׁ *person*), יכח hi. *argue* Jb 16$_{21}$, בין hi. *understand* Dn 8$_{17}$, נתן ni. *be given* as grass, i.e. be mortal Is 51$_{12}$ (|| אֱנוֹשׁ), גור *dwell* Jr 49$_{18.33}$ 50$_{40}$, עבר *pass* Jr 51$_{43}$, appar. דמה *be similar* 4Q416 7$_{11}$ (|| אֱנוֹשׁ).

<NOM CL> מָה ... בֶן־אָדָם *what is ... a human being?* Ps 8$_5$, לֹא אִישׁ אֵל ... וּבֶן־אָדָם *God is not a man ... nor a human being* Nm 23$_{19}$, מה אף הואה בן אדם (and var.) *what, indeed, is a* (mere) *human?* 1QS 11$_{20}$ (+ ילוד אשה *one born of a woman*) 1QH 10$_3$, תּוֹלֵעָה *worm* Jb 25$_6$ (|| אֱנוֹשׁ *person*).

<OBJ> פקד *notice* (of God) Ps 8$_5$ (|| אֱנוֹשׁ *person*), אמץ pi. *strengthen* (of God) 80$_{18}$ (|| אִישׁ *man*).

<CSTR> דְּמוּת *likeness of* Dn 10$_{16}$ (בְּנֵי; ms בֶּן).

<PREP> לְ *to* Jb 35$_8$ (|| אִישׁ *man*) 1QH 4$_{30}$ (+ תום דרך *purity of behaviour*, || אֱנוֹשׁ *person*) 10$_{28}$ (לבן א[דם]; others לבן א[מתכה] *to the son of your handmaid*); בטח בְּ *trust in* Ps 146$_3$ (+ נָדִיב *noble*); ירא מִן *fear (from)* Is 51$_{12}$; עַל *upon* Ps 80$_{18}$.

<COLL> לֹא ... אִישׁ ... וְלֹא ... בֶּן־אָדָם *no ... man ... and no ... human* Jr 49$_{18.33}$ 50$_{40}$ 51$_{43}$ (var. 2$_6$).

c. בְּנֵי(־)אָדָם **persons**, sometimes appar. *persons of high standing* Ps 49$_3$ (+ בְּנֵי־אִישׁ *persons of low degree*, עָשִׁיר וְאֶבְיוֹן *rich and poor*) 62$_{10}$, <SUBJ> עשׂה *do* Ec 2$_3$, ענה *be occupied* 1$_{13}$ 3$_{10}$, בנה *build* Gn 11$_5$, חסה *take refuge* Ps 36$_8$, שׁוב *turn back* Ps 90$_3$ (|| אֱנוֹשׁ *person*), ידע *know* 1QH 4$_{32}$, אמר *say* 4QpsEzek^a 3$_1$ ([בני]), סות hi. *incite* 1 S 26$_{19}$ (:: Y.), יקשׁ pu. *be trapped* Ec 9$_{12}$.

<NOM CL> אַתֶּם *you* 4Q185 1.1$_9$ (or perh. app., *you, mortals*), הֶבֶל *breath* Ps 62$_{10}$, אֲרוּרִים *cursed* 1 S 26$_{19}$.

<OBJ> (1) subj. God ברא *create* Ps 89$_{48}$, פרד hi. *disperse* Dt 32$_8$, בחן *test* Ps 11$_4$, ברר *test* Ec 3$_{18}$, שׁפט *judge* Ps 58$_2$, ראה *see* 33$_{13}$, חזה *see* 11$_4$. (2) subj. lions להט *burn up* Ps 57$_5$.

<CSTR> דִּבְרַת *matter of*, i.e. concerning Ec 3$_{18}$, נִגְעֵי *blows of*, i.e. from 2 S 7$_{14}$ (+ אֲנָשִׁים *people*), דַּרְכֵי *ways of* Jr 32$_{19}$ (|| אִישׁ *[each] man*), מִקְרֶה *fate of* Ec 3$_{19}$ (|| בְּהֵמָה *beast*), לֵב *heart of* Ec 8$_{11}$ 9$_3$ 4Q416 7$_4$ ([אדם]), לְבַב *heart of* 1 K 8$_{39}$||2 C 6$_{30}$, לִבּוֹת *hearts of* Pr 15$_{11}$, רוּחַ *spirit of* Ec 3$_{21}$ (:: בְּהֵמָה *beast*), עשתוני *thoughts of* Si 3$_{24}$, חטאת *sin of* 1QS 11$_{15}$ (|| אֱנוֹשׁ *person*) 4Q181 1$_1$, תַּעֲנוּגֹת *delights of* Ec 2$_8$, דְּמוּת *appearance of* Dn 10$_{16}$ (ms בֶּן *son of*), מע[שי בני ה]אדם *the deeds of humanity* 4QJub^d 1.2$_{23}$, כָּל־בְּנֵי הָאָדָם (and var.) *all humans* 1 K 8$_{39}$ Ps 33$_{13}$ Si 16$_{17}$ 4QpsEzek^a 3$_1$ ([כל בני] האדם).

<PREP> לְ *to, for* Mc 5$_6$ (|| אִישׁ *man*) Ps 107$_{8.15.21.31}$ (all + נִפְלְאוֹתָיו *his* [Y.'s] *miracles*) 12$_9$ Ec 2$_3$ 1QH 12$_7$ (:: God) 4$_{32}$ perh. 4Q521 5$_4$ ([אד]ם) 4QapPs^b 76$_2$, + נתן *give* Ps 115$_{16}$ (:: Y.) Ec 1$_{13}$ 3$_{10}$ (obj. עִנְיָן *matter*), חלק *apportion* Si 16$_{16}$, ידע hi. *make known* Ps 145$_{12}$.

מִן *from* Jl 1$_{12}$ Ps 12$_2$ 21$_{11}$ (|| אֶרֶץ *world*) Si 38$_8$ 4QShir^b 26$_{3(\text{Baillet})}$ (+ ומסוד[בשר] *and of the company of flesh*), + סתר ni. *be hidden* 1QS 11$_6$ (|| אֱנוֹשׁ *person*), אין אשה מבני אדם *she is not a woman from among humans*, i.e. she is exceptional Si 36$_{28}$, comparative, *than* Is 52$_{14}$ (|| אִישׁ *man*), + יפה pe'al'al *be fair* Ps 45$_3$.

אֶל *to* Pr 8$_4$ (+ אִישִׁים *people*); עַל *against* Ps 66$_5$, *upon* Si 40$_1$ (+ עול כבד *heavy yoke*) CD 12$_4$ (+ משמורו [duty of] *guarding him*), + שׁקף hi. *look down* Ps 14$_2$ 53$_3$ (subj. God).

אֵת *with* Pr 8$_{31}$ (+ אֶרֶץ *world*); בְּתוֹךְ *among* Ezk 31$_{14}$ (+ יוֹרְדֵי בוֹר *those who go down to the pit*, i.e. mortals) 1QH 6$_{11}$ 11$_6$ 4Q416 1$_3$; נֶגֶד *in the presence of* Ps 31$_{20}$ 1QH 2$_{25}$ 5$_{15}$ 4QBark^a 2.2$_2$ ([ב]נ׳), + סתר pi. *hide someone* 1QH 5$_{11}$; לְעֵינֵי *in the sight of* Si 34$_{31(Bmg)}$ ([אד]ם); אֶל־תּוֹךְ *(in)to the middle of* 4QpsJub^c 2$_3$.

<COLL> ובני אדם מה יוסיף אומ[צם] *as for humans, what can their power add?* 11QPs^a 24$_{15}$.

d. בְּנוֹת אָדָם **women,** <SUBJ> ילד *give birth* Gn 6$_4$. <OBJ> ראה *see* Gn 6$_2$ (subj. בְּנֵי־הָאֱלֹהִים *the sons of God, deities*).

<PREP> בוא אֶל *come to* for sex Gn 6$_4$ (subj. בְּנֵי הָאֱלֹהִים).

Also Si 39$_{26}$ 11QJub 5$_2$ ([כו]ל [אדם]) 1QH 13$_4$ ([ב]נ׳) 4$_{38}$ (ולא לאדם) 10$_{26}$ 15$_{12}$ (|| אֱנוֹשׁ) 19$_4$ fr. 34$_2$ 4QDibHam^a 8$_{13}$ 4QShir^b 44$_5$ 111$_1$ 4QpIsa^c 31$_{2(Allegro)}$ 4QTanḥ 40$_{2(Allegro)}$ 4QWiles 4$_4$ (+ ורוחו *and his spirit*) 4Q178 4$_2$ (לאדם) 4Q181 2$_2$ 1Q36 20$_{1(Milik)}$ ([בני] אדם) 4Q521 4$_6$.

[אָדָם] II, see אָדָם I, §1, Cstr.

[אָדָם] III, see אָדָם I, §1, Cstr., Prep.; §2a, Subj., Coll.

אָדָם IV 9.1.8 pr.n.m. **Adam, 1.** first human being (distinction אָדָם *human being* oft. uncertain), as first name in genealogy 1 C 1$_1$.

<SUBJ> היה *be* 130 years old Gn 5$_3$, חיה *be alive* 5$_5$, ידע *know* (sexually) 4$_{25}$ (or em. הָאָדָם *the human*), ילד hi. *beget* 5$_{3.4}$, שׁמע *hear* 3$_{17}$ (or em. לְאָדָם *to the human*), קרא *call*, i.e. name child Gn 4$_{25(Sam)}$ (MT וַתִּקְרָא *and she called*) 5$_3$, אכל *eat* 3$_{17}$ (or em. לְאָדָם), מות *die* 5$_5$. <CSTR> תבנית אדם *design of Adam* 1QM 10$_{14}$ (Yadin + ותול[דות צל]ע *and the generations of*, i.e. issuing from, *his rib*), תפארת *splendour of* Si 49$_{16}$ (+ Shem, Seth, Enosh), כול כבוד *all the glory of* 1QS 4$_{23}$ CD 3$_{20}$ (כל) 1QH 17$_{15}$, כול נחלת *all the inheritance of* 4QpPs^a 3.1$_2$, תּוֹלְדֹת אָדָם *generations of Adam* Gn 5$_1$, יְמֵי *days of* 5$_4$ (יְמֵי־) 5$_5$.

<PREP> אמר לְ *say to* Gn 3$_{17}$ (or em. לְאָדָם *to the man*), עשׂה לְ *make* tunic *for* 3$_{21}$ (or em. לְאָדָם; + לְאִשְׁתּוֹ *for his wife*), לְאָדָם לֹא־מָצָא עֵזֶר *as for Adam, he did not find help* 2$_{20}$ (or em. לְאָדָם), לאדם ולבנ[יו] *to Adam and to his children* 4QShir^b 52$_2$; כְּאָדָם perh. *as Adam* (or *as a human being [is wont to do]*), + עבר *transgress* covenant Ho 6$_7$ (or em. בְּאָדָם *at Adam* = אָדָם V), מות *die* Ps 82$_7$, כסה pi. *cover* sin Jb 31$_{33}$; מִן *from* 4QJub^a 17$_{14}$.

2. son of Jekamiah, Arad ost. 39$_1$ ([א]דם).

Also 11QJub 4$_{10}$ (ואד[ם]).

→ אדם *be red.*

[אָדָם] V 1 pl.n. **Adam, 1.** town in Jordan Valley, appar. ident. with Adamah, T. ed-Dāmye, S of confluence of Jabbok and Jordan, קָמוּ נֵד־אֶחָד הַרְחֵק מְאֹד באדם הָעִיר אֲשֶׁר מִצַּד צָרְתָן *the waters arose, a single pile, at a considerable distance, at Adam, the town beside Zarethan* Jos 3$_{16(Kt)}$ (Qr מֵאָדָם *away from*, or *[higher] than, a human being*, [at] the town), בְּאָדָם עָבְרוּ בְרִית *at Adam they transgressed the covenant* Ho 6$_7$ (if em. כְּאָדָם *as a human being*).

→ אדם *be red.*

אָדֹם 9.0.1 adj. **red**—אָדוֹם, f. אֲדֻמָּה; pl. אֲדֻמִּים—**red, brown, 1.** used as adj., of סוּס *horse* Zc 1$_{8.8}$ (|| שָׂרֹק *sorrel*, לָבָן *white*) 6$_2$ (|| שָׁחֹר *black*, בָּרֹד, לָבָן *dappled*), פָּרָה *cow* Nm 19$_2$, דּוֹד (complexion of) *lover* Ca 5$_{10}$ (|| צַח *shining*), מַיִם *water* 2 K 3$_{22}$ (+ כַּדָּם *as blood*), לְבוּשׁ *clothing* Is 63$_2$ (+ כְּדֹרֵךְ בְּגַת *as one who treads in a winepress*), perh. שִׁית *pit* 3QTr 4$_{9(Milik)}$ (others בשית האדמא *in the pit of clay*, i.e. אֲדָמָה *land*).

2. used as noun, **red, brown one, red, brown stuff,** with ref. to סוּס *horse*, נָזִיד *stew*, אַרְגָּמָן *purple*, <SUBJ> יצא *go out* Zc 6$_6$ (if em. אֲשֶׁר־בָּהּ הַסּוּסִים *in which were the black horses* to ⌈הָאֲדֻמִּים יֹצְאִים אֶל־אֶרֶץ הַקֶּדֶם⌉ *the brown ones are going out to the land of the east, and*; || שָׁחֹר *black*, לָבָן *white*, בָּרֹד *dappled*).

<PREP> הַלְעִיטֵנִי נָא מִן־הָאָדֹם הָאָדֹם הַזֶּה *please let me eat some of the brown stuff, this brown stuff* Gn 25₃₀ (unless em. אֱדֹם II both times, as name of food requested by Esau). <APP> perh. ארגמן אדום *purple, red stuff* (with ref. to temple furnishings) 11QT 10₁₂.

<SYN> שָׁחֹר *black,* לָבָן *white,* בָּרֹד *dappled.*

→ אדם *be red.*

אֹדֶם 3.1 n.[f.] **ruby**—Si אודם—**ruby, sardius,** or similar (semi-)precious stone, in Aaron's breastplate, <NOM CL> כָּל־אֶבֶן יְקָרָה מְסֻכָתֶךָ אֹדֶם פִּטְדָה וְיָהֲלֹם *every precious stone was your covering—ruby, topaz and diamond* Ezk 28₁₃. <CSTR> טוּר אֹדֶם פִּטְדָה וּבָרֶקֶת *a row of ruby, topaz and emerald* Ex 28₁₇‖39₁₀, כומז אדם *ornament of ruby* Si 35₅(C) (B אודם; + בָּרֶקֶת *emerald*). <APP> אֶבֶן יְקָרָה ... אֹדֶם *precious stone ... ruby* Ezk 28₁₃.

→ אדם *be red.*

אֱדֹם I, see אֱדוֹם, עֹבֵד אֱדֹם.

אֱדֹם II, see אָדֹם, §2.

[אֲדַמְדָּם] 6 adj. **reddish**—אֲדַמְדָּם; f. אדמדמת (אֲדַמְדֶּמֶת); pl. f. אֲדַמְדַּמֹּת—**reddish, light red,** used attributively (Lv 13₁₉.₂₄.₄₂ 14₃₇) and predicatively (Lv 13₄₃.₄₉) of נֶגַע *stroke,* i.e. diseased, rotten area of flesh, Lv 13₄₂, cloth 13₄₉, שְׂאֵת *swelling* of lesion 13₄₃, בַּהֶרֶת *brightness,* i.e. lesion 13₁₉.₂₄, שְׁקַעֲרוּרָה infected *depression* in wall 14₃₇. <COLL> לְבָנָה אֲדַמְדֶּמֶת (and vars.) *reddish-white* Lv 13₁₉.₂₄.₄₂.₄₃, יְרַקְרַק אוֹ אֲדַמְדָּם (and var.) *greenish or reddish* 13₄₉ 14₃₇.

→ אדם *be red.*

אֲדָמָה I 225.1.11 n.f. **earth**—Q אדמא; cstr. אַדְמַת; sf. אַדְמָתִי, אַדְמָתְךָ (אַדְמָתֶךָ) אַדְמָתוֹ, אַדְמָתָהּ, אַדְמָתֵנוּ, אַדְמָתָם, אַדְמַתְכֶם; pl. אֲדָמוֹת.

1. land, ground, in contrast to water, etc., especially as productive, **clay, soil,** <SUBJ> רמשׂ *creep* with Gn 9₂ Lv 20₂₅, מלא *be full of* Ex 8₁₇ (‖ בַּיִת *house*), בקע ni. *be split* Nm 16₃₁, פצה *open* mouth Gn 4₁₁ Nm 16₃₀, בלע *swallow* 16₃₀, יצא hi. *bring forth* Hg 1₁₁, ירא *fear* Jl 2₂₁ (‖ בְּהֵמָה *beast*), חתת *be dismayed* Jr 14₄ (+ אֶרֶץ *soil*), אבל *mourn* Jl 1₁₀ (‖ שָׂדֶה *field*), ארר *be cursed* Gn 3₁₇, שׁאה ni. *be laid waste* Is 6₁₁ (+ שְׁמָמָה as a *desolation*), נתן *give* Gn 4₁₂ Dt 11₁₇, יסף hi. *do,* i.e. give strength, *again* Gn 4₁₂.

<NOM CL> הַמָּקוֹם ... אַדְמַת־קֹדֶשׁ הוּא *the place ... is holy ground* Ex 3₅, אֲדָמָה עַל־רֹאשׁוֹ *soil was upon his head* in mourning 1 S 4₁₂ 2 S 1₂ 15₃₂, sim. Ne 9₁, מה אפהו אדם ואדמה הוא *what, therefore, is a person? It is dust* 1QH 10₃.

<OBJ> עבד *cultivate* Gn 2₅ 3₂₃ 4₂.₁₂ 2 S 9₁₀ Is 30₂₄ Zc 13₅ Pr 12₁₁=28₁₉ (אֲדָמָה = *plot,* as §2b), שׂדד pi. *harrow* Is 28₂₄, פתח pi. *open* 28₂₄, זרע *sow* Gn 47₂₃ Is 30₂₃, אכל *eat* Gn 3₁₇ Is 1₇, לכד *capture* Ne 9₂₅ (‖ עִיר *city*), קלל pi. *curse* Gn 8₂₁, ארר *curse* 5₂₉, אהב *love* 2 C 26₁₀.

<CSTR> אַדְמַת־עָפָר *ground of dust,* i.e. dusty ground, or, dust of the earth Dn 12₂, אַדְמַת־קֹדֶשׁ *ground of holiness,* i.e. holy ground Ex 3₅, אַדְמַת עַמִּי *soil of my people* Is 32₁₃ (for parallels, see Prep.); צֶמַח הָאֲדָמָה *vegetation of the ground* Gn 19₂₅ (+ יֹשְׁבֵי הֶעָרִים *inhabitants of the cities*), רֶמֶשׂ *creeping creature of* 1₂₅ 6₂₀ Ho 2₂₀, עֲבֹדַת *cultivation of* 1 C 27₂₆, תְּבוּאַת *produce of* Is 30₂₃, אִישׁ *man of,* i.e. farmer Gn 9₂₀, מִזְבַּח *altar of* earth Ex 20₂₄, עֲבִי *thickness of* soil 2 C 4₁₇ (mss עֳבִי; ‖1 K 7₄₆ מַעֲבֵה *thickness,* or *mould, of* soil; but perh. אֲדָמָה II *Adamah*), שִׁית *pit of* clay 3QTr 4₉ (or red *pit;* see אֹדֶם *red*), פְּרִי *fruit of* Gn 4₃ Dt 26₂.₁₀ Jr 7₂₀ (‖ שָׂדֶה *field*) Ml 3₁₁.

פְּרִי אַדְמָתְךָ *fruit of your ground* Dt 28₄.₁₁ (אַדְמָתֶךָ; ‖ בְּהֵמָה *beast*) 28₁₈ (אַדְמָתֶךָ; all three ‖ בֶּטֶן *womb*) 28₃₃.₄₂.₅₁ (פְּרִי־אַדְמָתֶךָ), (בְּהֵמָה ‖ both ,בֶּטֶן ‖) 30₉ (פְּרִי־) *fruit of your ground* 7₁₃ (‖ בֶּטֶן), פְּרִי אַדְמָתָם *fruit of their land* Ps 105₃₅ (‖ אֶרֶץ *land*), מַעְשַׂר אַדְמָתֵנוּ *tithe of our ground* Ne 10₃₈, טוב אדמתו *goodness of his soil* CD 1₈.

פְּנֵי הָאֲדָמָה *surface of the ground* Gn 8₈ (+ מֵעַל *from upon*) 8₁₃ 1 K 17₁₄ 18₁ (both + נתן עַל־ *give* rain *upon*) Jr 8₂ 16₄ 25₃₃ (all three היה לְדֹמֶן עַל־ *be as dung upon*) Ps 104₃₀ (פְּנֵי אֲדָמָה), חַרְשֵׂי *potsherds of* clay Is 45₉ 4QpGen[a] 1₂₂ ([מעל פני האדמה]), בִּכּוּרֵי אַדְמָתְךָ *first fruits of your land* Ex 23₁₉ 34₂₆, בִּכּוּרֵי אַדְמָתֵנוּ *first fruits of our land* Ne 10₃₆ (+ עֵץ *tree*).

<APP> מַשָּׂא צֶמֶד־פְּרָדִים אֲדָמָה *a burden of a pair of mules, soil* 2 K 5₁₇.

<ADJ> אֲדָמָה שְׁמֵנָה *fat land* Ne 9_{25}.

<PREP> שׁוב לְ *go back to* Ps 146_4, הָיוּ דֹמֶן לְ *they were as dung for* Ps 83_{11} (but perh. אֲדָמָה II *Adamah*); רמשׂ בְּ *creep upon* Dt 4_{18}; שׁוב אֶל *go back to* Gn 3_{19}; מִן of direction, *from*, + עלה *go up* Am 3_5 (subj. פַּח *trap*), צמח *sprout* Jb 5_6 (‖ עָפָר *dust*), hi. *make sprout* Gn 2_9, צעק *cry* 4_{10}, ארר pass. *be cursed* 4_{11} (or מִן of comparison, *more than*), יצר מִן *form* animals *from* 2_{19}, עָפָר מִן־הָאֲדָמָה *dust from the ground* 2_7 (+ יצר *form* human being), עִצְּבוֹן יָדֵינוּ מִן־הָאֲדָמָה *the pain of our hands from (working) the land* 5_{29}; עַל of place, *upon* Ex 8_{17}, + נפל *fall* 2 S 17_{12}, רמשׂ *creep* Gn 7_8 Ezk 38_{20}, ספד עַל *beat* breast *for* Is 32_{13} (‖ שָׂדֶה *field*, גֶּפֶן *vine*, בַּיִת *house*, קִרְיָה *city*; but perh. תַּעֲלֶה ... עַל = *goes up ... upon*); בַּעֲבוּר *on account of* Jr 14_4.

<COLL> הָאֲדָמָה אֲשֶׁר לֻקַּח מִשָּׁם *the ground from which he was taken* Gn 3_{23}.

2a. area of **land, territory,** plur. only in Ps 49_{12}, <SUBJ> היה *be* Is 19_{17} (+ לְמִצְרַיִם לְחָגָּא *to Egypt for a terror*), עזב ni. *be abandoned* Is 7_{16}, שׁמם ni. *be desolated* Ezk 25_3 (‖ מִקְדָּשׁ *sanctuary*), זוב *flow* with (see also App.) Dt 31_{20}.

<OBJ> נתן *give* Dt 21_{23}=11QT 64_{12} (+ נַחֲלָה *[as a] possession*) Dt 26_{15} 28_{11} 30_{20} Jos $23_{13.15}$ 1 K $8_{34.40}$‖2 C $6_{25.31}$ 1 K 9_7 14_{15} 2 K 21_8 Jr 16_{15} 24_{10} 25_5 35_{15} Ezk 11_{17} 28_{25} Am 9_{15}, עמד hi. *assign* 2 C 33_8, ירשׁ *possess* Lv 20_{24} Dt 30_{18} 31_{13} 32_{47}, חלק pi. *divide* Dn 11_{39}, ראה *see* Nm 32_{11}, ברך pi. *bless* Dt 26_{15} (‖ עַם *people*), כפר pi. *atone for* 32_{43} (but see App.), טמא pi. *defile* 21_{23}‖11QT 64_{12} Ezk 36_{17}.

<CSTR> אַדְמַת הַקֹּדֶשׁ *the land of holiness*, i.e. holy land Zc 2_{16}, ״ *of Y.* Is 14_2, יְהוּדָה *of Judah* 19_{17}, יִשְׂרָאֵל *of Israel* Ezk 7_2 11_{17} $12_{19.22}$ 13_9 18_2 $20_{38.42}$ $21_{7.8}$ 25_3 (+ בֵּית יְהוּדָה *the house of Judah*) 25_6 33_{24} 36_6 37_{12} $38_{18.19}$ 4Q386–9 3.2_2, עַמּוֹ *of his people* Dt $32_{43(Sam)}$, שְׁאֵרִית אֲדָמָה *remnant of (the) land* Is 15_9.

<APP> הָאֲדָמָה ... אֶרֶץ זָבַת חָלָב וּדְבָשׁ *the land ... a land flowing with milk and honey* Dt 11_9 26_{15}, var. Lv 20_{24}, אַדְמָתוֹ עַמּוֹ appar. *his land, his people* (unless *land of his people*) Dt 32_{43} (but perh. אֲדָמָה III *blood* of his people; + דַּם־עֲבָדָיו *blood of his servants* [4QDeut[b] בניו *of his sons*]).

<ADJ> הָאֲדָמָה הַזֹּאת *this land* Gn 28_{15}, הָאֲדָמָה הַטּוֹבָה הַזֹּאת *this good land* Jos $23_{13.15}$ 1 K 14_{15}, אֲדָמָה טְמֵאָה *unclean land* Am 7_{17}.

<PREP> אמר לְ *say to* Ezk 7_2 21_8; בְּ מצא ni. *be found in* Dt 21_1 (subj. חָלָל *one slain*), בין בְּ htpol. *consider* 4Q386–9 3.2_2, יושבי בה אדמה perh. *those that live in it, a land* 4QBer[a] 2_1; אֶל of direction, *to*, + בוא *come* Ezk 13_9 20_{38} (+ אֶרֶץ *land*), hi. *bring* Dt 31_{20} Ezk 20_{42} (‖ אֶרֶץ) 34_{13} 36_{24} $37_{12.21}$, שׁוב *go back* Dn 11_9, hi. *bring back* Gn 28_{15} 1 K 8_{34}‖2 C 6_{25} Jr 16_{15} 42_{12}, of place, *in*, Ezk 12_{19}, + ישׁב *dwell* Jr 35_{15}, *against*, + נבא ni. *prophesy* Ezk 21_7, שׂמח *rejoice* 25_6, אמר *say* 25_3 (+ הֶאָח *aha!*; ‖ מִקְדָּשׁ *sanctuary*).

עַל of place, *in, upon* Dt 7_{13} 12_{19} 28_{11} 31_{13} (+ חַי *alive*) Ezk 12_{22} (perh. עַל = *concerning*) 33_2 Zc 2_{16}, + היה *be* Ezk 34_{27} 38_{19} Jon 4_2, מות *die* Am 7_{17}, נוח hi. *place* Is 14_1 Ezk 37_{14}, *leave* Jr 27_{11}, נטע *plant* returning exiles Am 9_{15}, נטשׁ ni. *be abandoned* 5_2, ישׁב *dwell* Dt 30_{20} Jr 23_8 25_5 Ezk 28_{25} 36_{17} 39_{26}, נסס htpol. *be prominent* Zc 9_{16}, ברך pi. *bless* Dt 7_{13}, שׁיר *sing* Ps 137_4, יתר hi. *make abundant* Dt 28_{11}, ארך hi. *extend* days Ex 20_{12}‖Dt 5_{16} Dt 4_{40} 11_9 25_{15} 30_{18} 32_{47}, רבה *be many* 11_{21}, נחל htp. *possess* Is 14_2.

עַל *against*, + בוא *come* Ezk 38_{18}, נבא ni. *prophesy* 36_6, כנס עַל pi. *gather into* 39_{28}, נשׂא עַל *carry to* Nm 11_{12}, משׁל עַל *speak proverb concerning* Ezk 18_2, קָרְאוּ בִשְׁמוֹתָם עֲלֵי אֲדָמוֹת *they named lands their own* (lit. *they called with their names upon lands*) Ps 49_{12}; עַל־פְּנֵי *upon (the face of)* 1 K 8_{40}‖2 C 6_{31} (+ חַי *alive*), + חיה *live* Jr 35_7.

מֵעַל *from (upon)*, + גלה *go into exile* 2 K 17_{23} 25_{21}‖Jr 52_{27} Am $7_{11.17}$, אבד *perish* Jos 23_{13}, תמם *be consumed* Jr 24_{10}, כלה pi. *destroy* Dt 28_{21}, שׁמד hi. *destroy* Jos 23_{15}, כרת hi. *cut off* 1 K 9_7 (מֵעַל פְּנֵי *from upon the face of*), נתשׁ *pluck up* Dt 29_{27} 1 K 14_{15} Jr 12_{14} 2 C 7_{20}, ni. *be plucked up* Am 9_{15}, נסח ni. *be torn* Dt 28_{63}, רחק hi. *remove* Jr 27_{10}, סור hi. *remove* 2 C 33_8.

מִן *from*, + נדח hi. *expel* Si 47_{24} (מ[א]דמתם), נוד hi. *cause to wander* 2 K 21_8.

<COLL> אדמתנו וכול יבולה *our land and all its produce* 4QRitMar 9_6, הָאֲדָמָה אֲשֶׁר נִשְׁבַּעְתָּ לַאֲבֹתָיו *the land which you swore (to give) to his fathers* Nm 11_{12}, sim. 32_{11} Dt 31_{20}, הָאֲדָמָה אֲשֶׁר אַתֶּם גָּרִים שָׁם *the land where*

you are sojourners Jr 35$_7$.

2b. used of a smaller (owned) area, **plot, farmland,** <SUBJ> היה *be* Gn 47$_{19}$ (+ עֶבֶד *servant*) 47$_{26}$ (+ לְפַרְעֹה *to Pharaoh*), שׁאר ni. *remain* 47$_{18}$ (|| גְּוִיָּה *body*), מות *die* 47$_{19}$, שׁמם *be desolate* 47$_{19}$, זעק *cry out* Jb 31$_{38}$, חלק pu. *be divided* Am 7$_{17}$.

<OBJ> קנה *buy* Gn 47$_{19.20.22.23}$, מכר *sell* 47$_{22}$. <CSTR> אַדְמַת מִצְרַיִם *farmland of Egypt* Gn 47$_{20.26}$, הַכֹּהֲנִים *of the priests* 47$_{22.26}$. <PREP> חֹק עַל *a statute concerning* Gn 47$_{26}$. <COLL> אֲנַחְנוּ ... אַדְמָתֵנוּ *we ... our land* Gn 47$_{19.19}$.

3. earth, world, <CSTR> פְּנֵי־הָאֲדָמָה *the face of the earth* Gn 2$_6$ (see also עַל־פְּנֵי under Prep.), מִשְׁפְּחֹת *families of* 12$_3$ 28$_{14}$ Am 3$_2$, מַלְכֵי *kings of* Is 24$_{21}$ (:: מָרוֹם *high place, heaven*), יושבי *inhabitants of* 1QH fr. 5$_{12}$.

<PREP> למשל בכל אלה באדמה *to rule over all these on earth* 4QapPs^b 1$_7$; עַל *upon* Dt 4$_{10}$ 12$_1$ 1 S 20$_{31}$ (all three + חַי *alive*) Is 24$_{21}$ 1QH fr. 5$_{12}$, היה *be* Ex 10$_6$, עַל־פְּנֵי *upon (the face of)* Gn 7$_{23}$ Ex 33$_{16}$ Nm 12$_3$ Dt 7$_6$ 14$_2$ Is 23$_{17}$ Jr 25$_{26}$ Ezk 38$_{20}$ 4QapPs^b 46$_8$ (עלפני), + רבב *be many* Gn 6$_1$, שִׂים *place* 2 S 14$_7$, מֵעַל פְּנֵי, + כלה pi. *destroy* Ex 32$_{12}$, שׁמד hi. *destroy* Dt 6$_{15}$ 1 K 13$_{34}$ Am 9$_8$, כחד hi. *destroy* 1 K 13$_{34}$, כרת hi. *cut off* 1 S 20$_{15}$ Zp 1$_3$, מחה *blot out* Gn 6$_7$ 7$_4$, אסף *gather* trans. Zp 1$_2$, שׁלח pi. *send away* Jr 28$_{16}$, גרשׁ pi. *drive out* Gn 4$_{14}$.

<COLL> כָּל־מַמְלְכוֹת הָאָרֶץ עַל־פְּנֵי הָאֲדָמָה *all the kingdoms of the world upon the face of the earth* Is 23$_{17}$, sim. Jr 25$_{16}$.

Also 1QDM 1$_6$ (האד[מה]).

<SYN> §1 בְּהֵמָה *beast*, בֶּטֶן *womb*, בַּיִת *house*, שָׂדֶה *field*; §§1–2a אֶרֶץ *land*.

→ אדם *be red*.

אֲדָמָה II 4 pl.n. **Adamah, 1.** town in Naphtali, near Sea of Galilee, perh. Ḥağar ed-Damm (Even Peleṭ), Jos 19$_{36}$. **2.** town in Jordan Valley, appar. ident. with Adam (Jos 3$_{16[Kt]}$ Ho 6$_7$ [if em.]), T. ed-Dāmye, S of confluence of Jabbok and Jordan, הָאֲדָמָה בֵּין סֻכּוֹת וּבֵין צָרְתָן *Adamah, between Succoth and Zarethan* 1 K 7$_{46}$||2 C 4$_{17}$ (unless אֲדָמָה I *earth*), הָיוּ דֹמֶן לָאֲדָמָה *they became dung at Adamah* Ps 83$_{11}$ (unless אֲדָמָה I *earth*; + עֵין־דֹּאר *En-dor* [or em. עֵין־חֲרֹד *En-harod*]).

→ אדם *be red*.

[אֲדָמָה] III, see אֲדָמָה I, §2a, App.

אַדְמָה 5 pl.n. **Admah,** Canaanite town near Dead Sea, alw. followed by Zeboim and, except at Ho 11$_8$, preceded by Sodom and Gomorrah, Gn 10$_{19}$ 14$_{2.8}$ Dt 29$_{22}$ Ho 11$_8$.

→ אדם *be red*.

אַדְמוֹנִי 3 adj. **ruddy**—אַדְמֹנִי—as predicative adj. or noun, **(one that is) ruddy,** הוּא אַדְמוֹנִי *he* (David) *was ruddy* 1 S 16$_{12}$ (+ יְפֵה *fair* of eyes, טוֹב *good* in appearance), הָיָה נַעַר וְאַדְמֹנִי *he* (David) *was a youth and ruddy* 17$_{42}$ (+ יְפֵה *fair* of appearance [mss of eyes]), וַיֵּצֵא הָרִאשׁוֹן אַדְמוֹנִי כֻּלּוֹ כְּאַדֶּרֶת שֵׂעָר *and the first one* (Esau) *came out ruddy—all of him was as a cloak of hair* Gn 25$_{25}$.

→ אדם *be red*.

אֲדֹמִי 12.0.0.1 gent. **Edomite**—pl. אֲדוֹמִים (אֲדֹמִים, I אדמם), אֲדֹמִיֹּת, אֲדֹמִית—**1.** as plur. (1 K 11$_1$ 2 K 16$_{6[Qr]}$ 2 C 25$_{14}$ 28$_{17}$) or collective sing. (Jg 1$_{36}$ Ezr 9$_1$ [if em. in both]) noun, **Edomites,** <SUBJ> בוא *come* 2 K 16$_{6(Qr)}$ (Kt, mss אֲרָמִים *Aramaeans*) 2 C 28$_{17}$, ישׁב *dwell* 2 K 16$_{6(Qr)}$, נכה hi. *strike* 2 C 28$_{17}$, שׁבה *take captive* 28$_{17}$. <OBJ> נכה hi. *strike* 2 C 25$_{14}$, אהב *love* 1 K 11$_1$. <CSTR> גְּבוּל הָאֲדֹמִי *border of the Edomites* Jg 1$_{36}$ (if em. הָאֱמֹרִי *of the Amorites*). <APP> נָשִׁים נָכְרִיּוֹת ... אֲדֹמִיֹּת *foreign women ... Edomites* 1 K 11$_1$. <PREP> כְּתוֹעֲבֹתֵיהֶם לַכְּנַעֲנִי ... וְהָאֲדֹמִי *according to (their) abominations of the Canaanite(s) ... and the Edomite(s)* Ezr 9$_1$ (if em. אֱמֹרִי *Amorites*).

2. as sing. noun, a particular **Edomite,** לֹא־תְתַעֵב אֲדֹמִי כִּי אָחִיךָ הוּא *you are not to abominate an Edomite, for he is your brother* Dt 23$_8$, דֹּאֵג הָאֲדֹמִי *Doeg the Edomite* 1 S 21$_8$ 22$_{9.18(Qr).22(Qr)}$ Ps 52$_2$ (all three דּוֹאֵג), הֲדַד הָאֲדֹמִי *Hadad the Edomite* 1 K 11$_{14}$ (mss הֲדַר *Hadar*).

3. as attributive adj., **Edomite,** אֲנָשִׁים אֲדֹמִיִּים *Edomite men* 1 K 11$_{17}$.

Also Arad ost. 3$_{12}$.

→ אֱדוֹם *Edom*.

אֲדָמִי הַנֶּקֶב 1 pl.n. **Adami-nekeb**, town in Naphtali, perh. Kh. ed-Dāmiye (Ḥorbat Dāmīm), NE of Mt Tabor, Jos 19_{33} (or em. אֲדָמִים *Adamim*).
→ אדם *red.*

[אֲדָמִים], see אֲדָמִי הַנֶּקֶב.

אֲדֻמִּים 2 pl.n. **Adummim,** on border of Judah and Benjamin, Ṭal'at ed-Damm, between Jerusalem and Jericho, Jos 15_{7} 18_{17} (both + מַעֲלֵה *ascent* of).
→ אדם *red.*

אַדְמֹנִי, see אַדְמוֹנִי.

אַדְמָתָא 1 pr.n.m. **Admatha,** Persian prince, one of Ahasuerus's counsellors, Est 1_{14}.

[אֶדֶן] 57 n.m. **base**—אֶדֶן; pl. abs. אֲדָנִים; cstr. אַדְנֵי; sf. אֲדָנָיו, אֲדָנֶיהָ, אַדְנֵיהֶם—usu. metal base supporting pillars, <SUBJ> היה *be* Ex $26_{25.25.25}$||$36_{30.30.30}$ 38_{27}, טבע ho. *be sunk* (of the earth's foundation) Jb 38_{6}.

<NOM CL> אַדְנֵיהֶם שְׁלֹשָׁה *their bases are three* Ex $27_{14.15}$||$38_{14.15}$ (both || עַמּוּד *pillar*), אַרְבָּעָה *are four* 27_{16}||38_{19} (|| עַמּוּד), עֲשָׂרָה *are ten* 27_{12}||38_{12} (|| עַמּוּד), עֶשְׂרִים נְחֹשֶׁת *are twenty, bronze* $27_{10.11}$||$38_{10.11}$ (both || עַמּוּד), חֲמִשָּׁה נְחֹשֶׁת *are five, bronze* 36_{38}, אַדְנֵיהֶם נְחֹשֶׁת *their bases are bronze* 27_{17} (|| וָו *hook*) 27_{18}, var. 38_{17}, פְּקֻדַּת מִשְׁמֶרֶת ... אֲדָנָיו ... אַדְנֵיהֶם *the office of the charge* of the sons of Merari was *its* (the tabernacle's) *bases* ... and the pillars of the court ... and *their bases* Nm 3_{36-37}, (+ קֶרֶשׁ *frame*, בְּרִיחַ *bar*, עַמּוּד *pillar*, כְּלִי *vessel*, עֲבֹדָה *service*, יָתֵד *peg*, מֵיתָר *cord*), זֹאת מִשְׁמֶרֶת מַשָּׂאָם ... אֲדָנָיו ... אַדְנֵיהֶם ... *this is the charge of their burden ... its* (the tabernacle's) *bases* ... and the pillars of the court and *their bases* 4_{31-32} (+ קֶרֶשׁ, בְּרִיחַ, עַמּוּד, כְּלִי, עֲבֹדָה, יָתֵד, מֵיתָר), וְאַדְנוֹ/וַאֲדָנָיו וְקִירֹתָיו עֵץ *and its base(s) and its walls were wood* Ezk 41_{22} (if em. וְאָרְכּוֹ *and its length*).

<OBJ> עשׂה *make* Ex $26_{19.19.19.21.21.21}$||$36_{24.24.24.26.26.26}$ 35_{11} (|| קֶרֶס *hook*, קֶרֶשׁ *frame*, בְּרִיחַ *bar*, עַמּוּד *pillar*, etc.) 35_{17} (|| עַמּוּד, etc.) 38_{30} (|| מִזְבַּח *altar*, מִכְבָּר *grating*, כְּלִי *vessel*) $38_{31.31}$ (|| יָתֵד *peg*), יצק *cast* 26_{37} 36_{36} $38_{27.27}$, בוא hi. *bring* 39_{33} (|| קֶרֶס, קֶרֶשׁ, בְּרִיחַ, עַמּוּד, etc.) 39_{40} (|| עַמּוּד, etc.), נתן *set* 40_{18} (|| קֶרֶשׁ, בְּרִיחַ, עַמּוּד).

<CSTR> אַדְנֵי־כֶסֶף *bases of silver* Ex 26_{19}||36_{24} 26_{32}||36_{36} (כֶּסֶף), פָּז *of gold* Ca 5_{15}, אַדְנֵי נְחֹשֶׁת *bases of bronze* Ex 26_{37}, הַקֹּדֶשׁ *of the sanctuary* 38_{27}, הַפָּרֹכֶת *of* (the pillars supporting) *the curtain* 38_{27}, פֶּתַח *of the door of* tent 38_{30}, הֶחָצֵר *of the courtyard* 38_{31}, שַׁעַר *of the gate of* courtyard 38_{31}.

<PREP> כִּכָּר לָאָדֶן *a talent per base* Ex 38_{27}; עַל *upon* Ex 26_{32}, + יסד pu. *be set* Ca 5_{15} (+ עַמּוּד *pillar*).

<COLL> שְׁמֹנָה קְרָשִׁים וְאַדְנֵיהֶם כֶּסֶף *eight frames and their bases of silver* Ex 26_{25}||36_{30}, מְאַת אֲדָנִים *one hundred bases* 38_{27} (Sam הָאֲדָנִים), אַרְבָּעִים אַדְנֵי *forty bases of* silver 26_{19}||36_{24}, אַרְבָּעִים אַדְנֵיהֶם כֶּסֶף *their forty bases of silver* 26_{21}||36_{26}, שִׁשָּׁה עָשָׂר אֲדָנִים *sixteen bases* 26_{25}||36_{30}, חֲמִשָּׁה אַדְנֵי *five bases of* bronze 26_{37}, אַרְבָּעָה אַדְנֵי *four bases of* silver 26_{32}||36_{36}, שְׁנֵי אֲדָנִים *two bases* $26_{19.19}$||$36_{24.24}$ (both + תַּחַת הַקֶּרֶשׁ הָאֶחָד לִשְׁתֵּי יְדֹתָיו *under one frame for its two tenons*) $26_{21.21}$||$36_{26.26}$ (both + תַּחַת הַקֶּרֶשׁ הָאֶחָד *under one frame*) $26_{25.25}$||$36_{30.30}$ (+ תַּחַת הַקֶּרֶשׁ הָאֶחָד); see also Nom. Cl. for other uses with numerals.

<SYN> עַמּוּד *pillar*, קֶרֶשׁ *frame*, קֶרֶס *hook*, בְּרִיחַ *bar*, כְּלִי *vessel*, יָתֵד *peg*.

אַדָּן 2 pl.n. **Addan**—אַדּוֹן—**Addan** or **Addon,** a place in Babylonia from where returning exiles departed, Ezr 2_{59}||Ne 7_{61} (אַדּוֹן; perh. join with preceding word as composite name, Cherub-addan/addon).

אדני, see אֲדֹנִיָּהוּ.

אֲדֹנָי $425.6.52$ pr.n.m. **(my) Lord**—אֲדֹנָי (Q אדוני, וַ/בַּ/לַאדֹנָי)—**1. my Lord, Adonai,** as name of Y., and term of address to Y. (see Coll.), <SUBJ> היה *be* Mc 1_{2} (+ לְעֵד *as a witness*, מֵהֵיכַל קָדְשׁוֹ *from his holy temple*) Ps 90_{1} (+ מָעוֹן *dwelling place*) Lm 2_{5} (mss ״ Y.; + כְּאוֹיֵב *as an enemy*), עשׂה *act* Ps 109_{21} Dn 9_{19} 4QDibHam[a] 1.27 ([אדו]ני), יסף hi. *do again* Is 11_{11} Ps 77_{8}, ישׁב *sit* Is 6_{1}, נצב ni. *stand* Am 7_{7} 9_{1}, בוא *come* Ps 68_{18} (if em.; see Nom. Cl.), הלך *walk* Ex 34_{9}, דרך *tread* Lm 1_{15}, hi. *cause to tread* Hb 3_{19}, חושׁ *hasten* Ps 38_{23}, עור *rouse one* *self* 44_{24}, hi. 35_{23} perh. 73_{20}, קיץ hi. *wake up* 35_{23} 44_{24} 73_{20} (or em. אֵינֶנּוּ *it is not*), יקץ *wake up* 78_{65}, נתן *give* 1 K 22_6 Lm 1_{14} (mss ׳י Y.) Dn 1_2 (all three + בִּידֵי/בְּיַד *into the hand[s] of*) Is 7_{14} 30_{20} Ps 68_{12} (obj. אֹמֶר *word*).

סור hi. *remove* Is 3_{18}, סכך *cover* Ps 140_8, עלה hi. *raise* Is 8_7, נשׂא *raise* 1QSb $5_{23(Milik)}$ ([י]ש[אכ]ה), ni. *be raised up* Is 6_1, רום *be high* 6_1 1QM 12_{18} (ר[ום]) 4QpIsa^c 23.2$_8$, שׁלח *send* Ex $4_{13.13}$ 5_{22}, Is 9_7 (obj. word), שׁלך hi. *cast* Lm 2_1, נגע hi. *bring to* 2_2, יצא hi. *bring out* Dn 9_{15} (from Egypt), קנה *buy (back)* Is 11_{11}, גאל *rescue* Lm 3_{58}, שׁלם pi. *repay* Ps 62_{13}, ערב *go surety* Is 38_{14}, ריב *argue* Lm 3_{58} (mss ׳י), אמץ pi. *strengthen* Si $42_{17(M)}$, חלם hi. *heal* Is 38_{16}, חיה hi. *revive* 38_{16}, שׂים *place* Hb 3_{19}.

פתח *open* lips Ps 51_{17}, רחץ *wash* Is 4_4, ראה *see* Ps 35_{17} Lm 3_{36}, שׁמע *hear* Ps 66_{18} 130_2 Dn 9_{19} (mss ׳י), hi. *make to hear* 2 K 7_6, קשׁב hi. *listen* Dn 9_{19}, אמר *say* Is $21_{6.16}$ (both + כֹּה *thus*) 29_{13} Ezk 21_{14} (+ כֹּה) Am 7_8 9_1 Ps 68_{23}, דבר pi. *speak* 4Q521 4_{10}, צוה pi. *order* Lm 3_{37}, ענה *answer* Ps 38_{16}, שׁבע ni. *swear* 89_{50}, בצע pi. *finish* Is 10_{12}, קרא *call* Lm 1_{15}, יטב hi. *do good* 11QPs^a 9_{10}, ברך pass. *be blessed* Ps 68_{20} 1QLitPr^b 1.1$_7$ 4QPrFêtes^a 2_2 3_1 (אד[וני]; both [ב]רוך) 4QPrFêtes^c 3_9 ([ברו]ך) $4_{4(Baillet)}$ $18_{3(Baillet)}$ ([א]דוני; both [ברוך]) 206_1 4QDibHam^a $4_{14(Baillet)}$ ([ברוך]) 6_{20}, pi. *bless* 1QSb $1_{3(Milik)}$ ([א]דוני) 3_{25}, ירא ni. *be feared* Ne 4_8, למד pi. *teach* 11QPs^a 9_{10}, ידע hi. teach 4QDibHam^a 4_{14} (הודי[ענו]), בין hi. *give understanding* 4QPrFêtes^c 4_4 ([א]דוני), חשׁב *consider* Ps 40_{18}.

נשׂא *raise* face, i.e. show favour to 1QSb 3_1, זכר *remember* Ps 89_{48} (if em. אֲנִי *I*) 89_{51} 1QLitPr^b 1.1$_9$ (זכ[ור אד]וני) 4QPrFêtes^b 2_2 4QDibHam^a 3.2$_5$ 5.2$_3$ ([ז]כ[ור]), pass. *be remembered* 4QDibHam^a 8_1 ([זכו]ר אד[וני]), שׁכח *forget* Is 49_{14} (|| ׳י), חנן *be gracious to* Ps 86_3 (mss ׳י) 1QSb 2_{22} 4QpIsa^c 23.2$_8$ ([ח]ננכמה), בקר pi. *visit* loyal ones 4Q521 1.2$_5$, רחם pi. *have mercy* 4QpIsa^c 23.2$_8$, חמל *spare* 1QIsa^a 9_{16} (MT שׂמח *rejoice*) Lm 2_2, סלח *forgive* Dn 9_{19}, רצה *be favourable* Ps 77_8, שׂמח *rejoice* Is 9_{16} (or em. יִשְׂמַח *will rejoice* to יְשַׁמַּח *will be merciful*; 1QIsa^a חמל), pi. *gladden* 1QLitPr^b 1.1$_7$ 4QPrFêtes^c 3_9, ישׁן *sleep* Ps 44_{24}, חכה pi. *wait* 4QpIsa^c 23.2$_8$, אחר pi. *delay* Dn 9_{19}, רחק *be distant* Ps 35_{22}, מנע *hold back* 59_{12} (if em.; see App.).

רעע hi. *cause misfortune* Ex 5_{22}, עוב hi. *becloud* Lm 2_1 (mss ׳י), זנח *reject* Ps 44_{24} 77_8 Lm 2_7 3_{31} (mss ׳י in both), סלה pi. *reject* 1_{15} (mss ׳י), בזה *despise* Ps 73_{20}, נאר pi. *despise* Lm 2_7, לעג *mock* Ps 2_4, שׂחק *laugh* 37_{13}, מחץ *crush* 110_5, הרג *kill* Gn 20_4, נכה hi. *strike*, i.e. hurl Zc 9_4, ערה pi. *uncover* soul Ps 141_8, בלע pi. *consume* 55_{10} (obj. tongue) Lm $2_{2.5}$ (in both mss ׳י), פלג pi. *divide* tongue Ps 55_{10}, הרס *pull down* Lm 2_2, שׁחת pi. *destroy* 2_5, סגר hi. *hand over* 2_7, ירשׁ hi. *disinherit* Zc 9_4 (mss ׳י), חלל pi. *profane* Lm 2_2, שׂפח pi. *uncover* forehead Is 3_{17} (|| ׳י), גלח pi. *shave* Is 7_{20}, רבה hi. *increase* trans. Lm 2_5.

<NOM CL> אֲדֹנָי אָתָּה *you are my Lord* Ps 16_2, אֲדֹנָי בָם *my Lord is among them* 68_{18} (or em. בָּם to בָּא *came* from Sinai), קדוש אדוני *my Lord is holy* 1QM 12_8, גדול אדני *my Lord is great* Si $43_{5(M)}$ (B ׳י Y.), אֲדֹנָי חֵילִי *my Lord is my strength* Hb 3_{19}, אֲדֹנָי עֹז יְשׁוּעָתִי *my Lord is the strength of my salvation* Ps 140_8, אֲדֹנָי בְּסֹמְכֵי נַפְשִׁי *my Lord is among my supporters* 54_6 (mss ׳י), אֲדֹנָי עַל־יְמִינְךָ *the Lord is at your right hand* 110_5 (mss ׳י), אַתָּה אֲדֹנָי אֵל־רַחוּם וְחַנּוּן *you, my Lord are a compassionate and merciful God* 86_{15} (mss ׳י).

<OBJ> ראה *see* Is 6_1 Am 9_1, זכר *remember* Ne 4_8, ברך pi. *bless* Ps $68_{27(mss)}$ (L ׳י Y.) 4QBark^a 2.1$_1$, זמר pi. *laud* Ps 57_{10} 68_{33}, ידה hi. *praise* 57_{10} 86_{12} 1QH $2_{20.31}$ $3_{19.37}$ 4_5 $5_{5.20}$ $7_{6.34}$ 14_{23} ([אוד]ך), דרשׁ *seek* Ps 77_3, בקשׁ pi. *seek* 4Q521 1.2$_3$, מצא *find* 1.2$_4$, חרף pi. *reproach* Ps 79_{12} 2 K 19_{23}||Is 37_{24}.

<CSTR> מִקְדַּשׁ אֲדֹנָי *sanctuary of my Lord* Lm 2_{20} (mss ׳י *of Y.*), אֲרוֹן בְּרִית־ *ark of the covenant of* 1 K 3_{15} (mss ׳י), שֻׁלְחַן *table of* Ml 1_{12}, כֹּחַ *strength of* Nm 14_{17} (mss ׳י), קוֹל *voice of* Is 6_8, דבר *word of* Si $43_{10(M)}$ (B אל *of God*), אמר *word of* $42_{15(M)}$ (B אלהים *of God*), פְּנֵי *presence of* Lm 2_{19} (mss ׳י), מעשה *deed of* 4Q521 1.2$_{11}$, ברכת *blessing of* 1.3$_3$, [כ]בוד *glory of* Si $42_{16(M)}$ (B ׳י), נֹעַם *pleasantness of* Ps 90_{17}, דֶּרֶךְ *way of* Ezk $18_{25.29}$ $33_{17.20}$ (in all four mss ׳י; all four + תכן ni. *be correct*), עֲצַת *counsel of* Ezr 10_3 (mss ׳י), יִרְאַת *reverence of*, i.e. for Jb 28_{28}.

<APP> with אֲדֹנָי preceding, אֲדֹנָי תְּשׁוּעָתִי *my Lord, my salvation* Ps 38_{23}, אדני עושהו *my Lord its maker* Si $43_{5(M)}$ (B ׳י Y.), אדוני יוצר *my Lord the creator* 1QH $16_{8(Holm-Nielsen)}$ (AHL [אדני גדול הע]צה *my Lord, great* *of counsel*), אֲדֹנָי הָאֱלֹהִים *my Lord God* Dn 9$_{3}$, אֲדֹנָי אֱלֹהַי *my Lord, my God* Ps 38$_{16}$ 86$_{12}$, אֲדֹנָי אֱלֹהֵינוּ *the Lord our God* Ps 90$_{17}$ Dn 9$_{9.15}$, אֲדֹנָי הָאֵל הַגָּדוֹל וְהַנּוֹרָא *my Lord the great and terrible God* 9$_{4}$, אדוני אל הרחמ[ים] *my Lord God of mercy* 1QH 10$_{14}$; with אֲדֹנָי following, י׳ אֲדֹנָי *Y. my Lord* 1QpMic 1$_{1(Milik)}$ ([י]הוה [אדוני]; MT אֲדֹנָי י׳ *the Lord Y.*) Hb 3$_{19}$ Ps 68$_{21}$ 109$_{21}$ 140$_{8}$ 141$_{8}$ (mss אֱלֹהִים אֲדֹנָי *God, my Lord*; in all five Kt י׳, Qr אֱלֹהִים), י׳ אֱלֹהֵי צְבָאוֹת אֲדֹנָי *Y. God of hosts, my Lord* Am 5$_{16}$, אֱלֹהַי וַאדֹנָי *my God and my Lord* Ps 35$_{23}$, מָגִנֵּנוּ אֲדֹנָי *Lord our shield* 59$_{12}$ (or em. מָגִנֵּנוּ to מְנָעֵמוֹ *hold them back*), אַתָּה אֲדֹנָי *you, my Lord* 86$_{15}$.

<ADJ> גָּדוֹל *great* Ne 4$_{8}$, סַלָּח *forgiving* Ps 86$_{5}$ (mss י׳ *Y.*), טוֹב *good* 86$_{5}$ 11QPs^{a} 9$_{10}$.

<PREP> לְ *(belonging) to* Is 28$_{2}$ Dn 9$_{7}$ (+ צְדָקָה *righteousness*) 9$_{9}$, *to, for,* Ps 130$_{6}$, + ספר pu. *be recounted* 22$_{31}$, זבח *sacrifice* Ml 1$_{14}$, חרה לְ *become angry* Gn 18$_{30.32}$; יטב בְּעֵינֵי *be pleasing in the eyes of* 1 K 3$_{10}$.

אֶל of direction, *to*, + נשׂא *lift* soul Ps 86$_{4}$, נתן *give*, i.e. turn, face Dn 9$_{3}$, דבר pi. *speak* Gn 18$_{27.31}$, צעק *cry* Lm 2$_{18}$, קרא *cry* Ps 86$_{3}$, חנן htp. *beseech* Ps 30$_{9}$ (|| י׳).

לְמַעַן *for the sake of* Dn 9$_{17}$; שׁחה לִפְנֵי htpal. *bow down before* Ps 86$_{9}$ (mss י׳); נֶגֶד *before* 38$_{10}$.

<COLL> as vocative, *O my Lord* Is 21$_{8}$ Ps 39$_{8}$ 57$_{10}$ 79$_{1}$ 86$_{8.12}$ 130$_{3}$ (|| יָהּ *Y.*) Dn 9$_{16}$ Si 51$_{15(B)}$ 1QH 2$_{20.31}$ 3$_{19.37}$ 4$_{5}$ 5$_{5.20}$ 7$_{6.28.34}$ 14$_{23}$ 4QDibHam^{a} 1.6$_{3(mg)}$ 4$_{16}$ 4QPrFêtes^{b} 13$_{1}$, אִם־נָא מָצָאתִי חֵן בְּעֵינֶיךָ אֲדֹנָי *if, pray, I find grace in your eyes, my Lord* (and var.) Gn 18$_{3}$ Ex 34$_{9}$, בִּי אֲדֹנָי *please, my Lord* Ex 4$_{10.13}$ Jos 7$_{8}$ Jg 6$_{15}$ 13$_{8}$, אָנָּא אֲדֹנָי *pray, my Lord* Dn 9$_{4}$ 4QDibHam^{a} 1.2$_{7}$ ([אדו]ני) 1.6$_{10}$ Ne 1$_{11}$ (אָנָּה), אַל־נָא אֲדֹנָי *pray, let not my Lord* Gn 18$_{30.32}$ 19$_{18}$, עַד־מָתַי אֲדֹנָי *how long, my Lord?* Is 6$_{11}$, אֲדֹנָי כַּמָּה *my Lord, how long?* Ps 35$_{17}$, ברוך אתה אדוני *blessed are you, my Lord* 1QH 5$_{20(mg)}$ 10$_{14}$ 11$_{33}$ ([את]ה) 14$_{8(Holm-Nielsen)}$ ([ברוך אתה]) 16$_{8}$ fr. 15.1$_{6(Holm-Nielsen)}$ ([ברוך]), אֲדֹנָי מֵהֵיכַל קָדְשׁוֹ *my Lord from his holy temple* Mc 1$_{2}$.

2. followed by י׳ (Qr אֱלֹהִים *God*), **my Lord Y.**, **<SUBJ>** היה *be* Mc 1$_{2}$ (1QpMic [Milik] [י]הוה [אדוני] *Y. my lord*; || אֲדֹנָי), גדל *be great* 2 S 7$_{22}$, עשׂה *make* Is 10$_{23}$ (obj. כָּלָה *destruction*) Jr 32$_{17}$ (obj. the world) Ezk 11$_{13}$ (obj. כָּלָה) Am 3$_{7}$, חלל hi. *begin* Dt 3$_{24}$, חדל *desist* Am 7$_{5}$, בוא *come* Is 40$_{10}$, hi. *bring* 2 S 7$_{18}$, יצא hi. *bring out* from Egypt 1 K 8$_{53}$, עבר hi. *bring across* Jordan Jos 7$_{7}$, שׁלח *send* Is 48$_{16}$, נתן *give* Gn 15$_{2}$ Jos 7$_{7}$ Is 50$_{4}$, פתח *open* ear 50$_{5}$, עזר *help* 50$_{7.9}$, צמח hi. *make flourish* 61$_{11}$, אמר *say* (with כֹּה *thus*, except Is 22$_{14}$ Jr 32$_{25}$ Am 1$_{8}$ 7$_{6}$) Is 7$_{7}$ 10$_{24}$ 22$_{14.15}$ 28$_{16}$ 30$_{15}$ 49$_{22}$ 52$_{4}$ 65$_{13}$ Jr 7$_{20}$ 32$_{35}$ Ezk 2$_{4}$ 3$_{11.27}$ 5$_{5.7.8}$ 6$_{3.11}$ + 114 times Am 1$_{8}$ 7$_{6}$ 3$_{11}$ 5$_{3}$ Ob$_{1}$, דבר pi. *speak* 2 S 7$_{19.28.29}$ 1 K 8$_{53}$ Am 3$_{8}$.

שׁבע ni. *swear* Am 4$_{2}$ 6$_{8}$, קרא *call* 7$_{4}$ Is 22$_{12}$, תקע *sound the alarm* Zc 9$_{14}$, ידע *know* 2 S 7$_{20}$ Ezk 37$_{3}$, זכר *remember* Jg 16$_{28}$, סלח *forgive* Am 7$_{2}$, מחה *wipe* tear Is 25$_{8}$, ראה hi. *show* Dt 3$_{24}$ Am 7$_{1.4}$ 8$_{1}$, נשׁא hi. *deceive* Jr 4$_{10}$, מות hi. *kill* Is 65$_{15}$, אבד hi. *destroy* Jos 7$_{7}$, שׁחת hi. *destroy* Dt 9$_{26}$ Ezk 9$_{8}$.

<NOM CL> אֲנִי אֲדֹנָי י׳ *I am the Lord Y.* Ezk 13$_{9}$ 23$_{49}$ 24$_{24}$ 28$_{24}$ 29$_{16}$, אֲדֹנָי י׳ אַתָּה־הוּא הָאֱלֹהִים *You, Lord Y., are God* 2 S 7$_{28}$, אַתָּה תִקְוָתִי אֲדֹנָי י׳ מִבְטַחִי *you, my Lord Y., are my hope, my trust* Ps 71$_{5}$.

<CSTR> אֲרוֹן אֲדֹנָי י׳ *ark of my Lord Y.* 1 K 2$_{26}$, נְאֻם(־) *oracle of* Is 3$_{15}$ 56$_{8}$ Jr 2$_{19.22}$ 49$_{5}$ 50$_{31}$ Ezk 5$_{11}$ 11$_{8.21}$ 12$_{25.28}$ + 76 times in Ezk Am 3$_{13}$ 4$_{5}$ 8$_{3.9.11}$, דְּבַר־ *word of* Ezk 6$_{3}$ 25$_{3}$ 36$_{4}$ גְּבֻרוֹת *mighty deeds of* Ps 71$_{16}$, רוּחַ *spirit of* Is 61$_{1}$, יַד־ *hand of* Ezk 8$_{1}$, עֵינֵי *eyes of* Am 9$_{8}$ (or em. עֵינֵי אֲדֹנָי י׳ to עֵינַי *my eyes*).

<APP> אֲדֹנָי י׳ צְבָאוֹת *my Lord Y. of hosts* Is 3$_{15}$ 10$_{23.24}$ 22$_{5.12.14.15}$ 28$_{22}$ Jr 2$_{19}$ 46$_{10.10}$ 49$_{5}$ 50$_{25.31}$ Am 9$_{5}$ (הַצְּבָאוֹת) Ps 69$_{7}$, אֲדֹנָי י׳ אֱלֹהֵי הַצְּבָאוֹת *my Lord Y., the God of hosts* Am 3$_{13}$, אֲדֹנָי י׳ קְדוֹשׁ יִשְׂרָאֵל *my Lord Y., the Holy One of Israel* Is 30$_{15}$.

<PREP> לְ *(belonging) to* Is 22$_{5}$ Jr 46$_{10}$ (both + יוֹם *day*) 46$_{10}$ (+ זֶבַח *sacrifice*) 50$_{25}$ (+ מְלָאכָה *mission*); בְּ *in* Ps 73$_{28}$ (+ מַחְסֶה *refuge*); מֵאֵת *from* Is 28$_{22}$; מִפְּנֵי of place, *from before* Zp 1$_{7}$.

<COLL> *my Lord Y.*, as vocative Gn 15$_{8}$, אֲהָהּ אֲדֹנָי י׳ *alas, my Lord Y.* Jos 7$_{7}$ Jg 6$_{22}$ Jr 1$_{6}$ 4$_{10}$ 14$_{13}$ 32$_{17}$ Ezk 4$_{14}$ 9$_{8}$ 11$_{13}$ 21$_{5}$ (or del. אֲדֹנָי in all four), חַי־אֲדֹנָי י׳ *as my Lord Y. lives* Jr 44$_{26}$, וִידַעְתֶּם כִּי אֲנִי אֲדֹנָי י׳ *so that you may know that I am the Lord Y.* Ezk 13$_{9}$ 23$_{49}$ 24$_{24}$, vars. 28$_{24}$ 29$_{16}$.

Also 4QPrFêtes^{c} 11$_{7}$ 4QVisSam 7$_{4}$ 4Q521 5$_{7}$.

→ אָדוֹן *lord*.

אֲדֹנִי בֶזֶק 3 pr.n.m. **Adoni-bezek**—אֲדֹנִי־בֶזֶק—appar. Canaanite king of Bezek, perh. ident. with Adoni-zedek (אֲדֹנִי־צֶדֶק) at Jos $10_{1.3}$ (or em. in both אֲדֹנִי בֶזֶק), Jg $1_{5.6.7}$ (אֲדֹנִי־בֶזֶק; or em. in all three אֲדֹנִי־צֶדֶק).
→ אָדוֹן *lord* + בֶּזֶק *Bezek.*

אֲדֹנִיָּה, see אֲדֹנִיָּהוּ.

אֲדֹנִיָּהוּ 26.0.0.7 pr.n.m. **Adonijah**—אֲדֹנִיָּה, L אֲדֹנִיָּהוּ, I אדני—**1.** son of David and Haggith, 2 S 3_4||1 C 3_2 1 K $1_{5.7}$ (all four אֲדֹנִיָּה) $1_{8.9.11.13}$ (L אֲדֹנִיָּהוּ; mss אֲדֹנִיָּהוּ) 1_{18} (אֲדֹנִיָּה) $1_{24.25.41.42.43.49.50.51}$ $2_{13.19.21.22.23.24}$ 2_{28} (אֲדֹנִיָּה). **2.** Levite at time of Jehoshaphat, 2 C 17_8. **3.** leader of people at time of Nehemiah, perh. ident. with Adonikam at Ezr 2_{13} 8_{13} Ne 7_{18}, Ne 10_{17} (אֲדֹנִיָּה). **4.** father of Shallum (שלם), Seal 75_2 (אדניה). **5.** son of Jekamiah (יקמיהו), Seal 511_1 (T. Beit Mirsim?, 7th/6th cent.). **6.** perh. ident. with preceding, Seal 501_1 502_1 625_2 (אדני[הו]) 665_2 (all four T. Beit Mirsim?, 7th/6th cent.). **7.** Seal 96_2 (אדני). **8.** Kadesh Barnea oil lamp inscr. (אדני[הו]; others אדני *my lord*). **9.** En-Gedi cave inscr.$_7$ (אדני[הו]; others אדני *my lord*). **10.** Seal 891_1 (7th cent.). **11.** Samaria ost. 42_3 (אדניו; others מרניו *Maraniah*).
→ אָדוֹן *lord* + י׳ *Y.*

[אדניו], see אֲדֹנִיָּהוּ.

[אדניחי] 0.0.0.1 pr.n.m. **Adonihai,** son of Shahar (בן ש[חר]) and father of Mattan (מתן), Seal 613_2 ([א]דניחי; T. Beit Mirsim?, 7th/6th cent.).
→ אָדוֹן *lord* + חיה *live.*

אֲדֹנִי־צֶדֶק 2 pr.n.m. **Adoni-zedek,** Canaanite king of Jerusalem, perh. ident. with Adoni-bezek (אֲדֹנִי בֶזֶק) at Jg $1_{5.6.7}$ (or em. in all three אֲדֹנִי־צֶדֶק), Jos $10_{1.3}$ (or em. in both אֲדֹנִי בֶזֶק).
→ אָדוֹן *lord* + צדק *be righteous.*

אֲדֹנִיקָם 3 pr.n.m. **Adonikam,** head of family of returning exiles, appar. ident. with Adonijah (אֲדֹנִיָּה) at Ne 10_{17}, Ezr 2_{13} 8_{13} Ne 7_{18}.
→ אָדוֹן *lord* + קום *arise.*

אֲדֹנִירָם 2 pr.n.m. **Adoniram**—ms אֲדוֹנִירָם—son of Abda (עַבְדָּא) and in charge of forced labour under Solomon, appar. ident. with Adoram (אֲדֹרָם) at 2 S 20_{24} 1 K 12_{18} and Hadoram at 2 C 10_{18}, 1 K 4_6 5_{28} $12_{18(ms)}$ (אֲדוֹנִירָם; L אֲדֹרָם).
→ אָדוֹן *lord* + רום *be high.*

[אדנעם], see אֲבִינֹעַם.

אדר 4.3.1 vb. **be majestic**—**Ni.** Impf. Si יאדר, Sam תאדר; ptc. נֶאְדָּר (cstr. נֶאְדָּרִי), Si נאדרה—**be exalted, <SUBJ>** Y. Ex 15_{11} (Sam נאדרי; + ירא ni. *be feared*), יָמִין *right hand* of Y. 15_6, Esau Gn $27_{40(Sam)}$ (MT תָּרִיד *you will be restless*), קֶשֶׁת *bow* Si $43_{11(B)}$ (Bmg, M נהדר[ה] *is made glorious*), זֵכֶר *memory* of Nehemiah 49_{13}. **<PREP>** בְּ of accompaniment, *with, in* Ex 15_6 (+ כֹּחַ *strength*) 15_{11} (+ קֹדֶשׁ *holiness*) Si 43_{11} (+ [בכ]בוד *in glory*).

Hi. Pf. Q האדיר; impf. יַאְדִּיר (Q יאדרהה); impv. Si האדר—**make glorious, <SUBJ>** Y. Is 42_{21} Ps 16_2 (if em. וְאַדִּירֵי כָּל־חֶפְצִי־בָם *and noble ones of all [whom] my delight is in them* to יַאְדִּיר כָּל־חֶפְצֵי־בָם *he will make glorious all who delight in them*) 1QM 17_6.

<OBJ> תּוֹרָה *law* Is 42_{21} (1QIsa[a] ויאדירה; || גדל hi. *magnify*), יָד *hand* of Y. Si $33_{7(B)}$ (Bmg האריך *stretch out*; || אמץ pi. *strengthen*), those who delight in saints Ps 16_2 (if em.; see Subj.).

<PREP> האדיר למשרת perh. *he has made glorious for the authority of* 1QM 17_6.
→ אַדִּיר *majestic,* אֶדֶר *majesty,* אַדֶּרֶת *majesty,* אֲדָר I–II *Addar,* אֲדוֹרַיִם *Adoraim,* אַדְרַמֶּלֶךְ *Adrammelech.*

אֶדֶר 2.0.1 n.[m.] **majesty**—cstr. אֶדֶר—הַשְׁלִיכֵהוּ אֶל־הַיּוֹצֵר אֶדֶר הַיְקָר אֲשֶׁר יָקַרְתִּי *throw it* (money) *to the potter—the majesty of preciousness,* i.e. wonderful price, *(at) which I was valued* Zc 11_{13} (or em. הָאוֹצָר *to the treasury* and יָקַרְתָּ *you were valued*), מִמּוּל שַׂלְמָה אֶדֶר תַּפְשִׁטוּן appar. *from the front of a garment you strip off (its) majesty* Mc 2_8 (or em. מֵעַל שְׁלֹמֹה/שְׁלֵמִים אַדֶּרֶת *from one that is at peace with him/peaceable ones* you

strip off *a cloak*), אדר נציב כבודם *the majesty of a pillar is their glory* 4QapPs^b 31$_7$.
→ אדר *be majestic.*

אֲדָר 8 pr.n.[m.] **Adar,** final month of Babylonian-based calendar, corresponding to February/March, alw. <CSTR> חֹדֶשׁ אֲדָר *month of Adar* Est 3$_{7.13}$ 8$_{12}$ (all three + חֹדֶשׁ שְׁנֵים־עָשָׂר *month twelve*) 9$_1$ (+ שְׁנֵים עָשָׂר חֹדֶשׁ *twelve,* i.e. twelfth, *month*) 9$_{15.17.19.21}$.

אַדָּר I 1 pr.n.m. **Addar,** son of Bela, descendant of Benjamin, appar. ident. with Ard (אַרְדְּ) at Gn 46$_{21}$ ||Nm 26$_{40}$, 1 C 8$_3$ (mss אַרְדְּ).
→ אדר *be majestic.*

אַדָּר II 2 pl.n. **Addar**—+ ה of direction אַדָּרָה—on southern border of Judah, also חֲצַר־אַדָּר *Hazar-addar* (Nm 34$_4$), perh. ʿĒn el-Qudērāt, Nm 34$_4$ Jos 15$_3$.
→ אדר *be majestic.*

[אֲדַרְכּוֹן], see דַּרְכְּמוֹן.

אֲדֹרָם 2 pr.n.m. **Adoram,** official in charge of forced labour under David and Rehoboam, appar. ident. with Adoniram (אֲדֹנִירָם) at 1 K 4$_6$ 5$_{28}$ and Hadoram (הֲדֹרָם) at 2 C 10$_{18}$, 2 S 20$_{24}$ (ms אֲדוֹנִירָם) 1 K 12$_{18}$ (||2 C 10$_{18}$ הֲדֹרָם).

אַדְרַמֶּלֶךְ 3 pr.n.m. **Adrammelech, 1.** god of Sepharvaim, 2 K 17$_{31}$. **2.** son and assassin of Sennacherib, 2 K 19$_{37}$||Is 37$_{38}$.

אֶדְרֶעִי 8 pl.n. **Edrei**—אֶדְרֶעִי (mss אֶדְרֶעִי)—**1.** city in Manasseh, captured from Og, king of Bashan, mod. Derʿā, on border with Syria, Nm 21$_{33}$||Dt 3$_3$ Dt 1$_4$ (בְּעַשְׁתָּרֹת בְּאֶדְרֶעִי *at Ashtaroth in Edrei*; ms וּבְאֶדְרֶעִי *and at Edrei*; mss אֶדְרֶעִי) 3$_{10}$ Jos 12$_4$ 13$_{12.31}$ (all three + עַשְׁתָּרוֹת *Ashtaroth*). **2.** town in Naphtali, Jos 19$_{37}$.

אַדֶּרֶת 12 n.f. **majesty, cloak**—(perh. fem. of אַדִּיר *majestic [one]*) אַדֶּרֶת; cstr. אַדֶּרֶת; sf. אַדַּרְתּוֹ, אַדַּרְתָּם—**1. majesty** of tree, vine, etc., <SUBJ> שׁדד pu. *be devastated* Zc 11$_3$ (+ אַדִּיר *majestic [tree]*, גָּאוֹן *pride*). <CSTR> גֶּפֶן אַדֶּרֶת *vine of majesty* Ezk 17$_8$.

2. cloak, coat, as costly or royal (Jos 7$_{21}$ Jon 3$_6$), or worn by prophet (Zc 13$_4$ 1 K 19$_{13.19}$ 2 K 2$_{8.13.14}$).

<SUBJ> נפל *fall* 2 K 2$_{13.14}$, טמן pass. *be concealed* Jos 7$_{21}$ (+ כֶּסֶף *silver*, זָהָב *gold*). <OBJ> לבשׁ *be dressed (in)* Zc 13$_4$, פשׁט hi. *strip off* Mc 2$_8$ (if em. אֶדֶר *majesty*), עבר hi. *cause to pass,* i.e. take off Jon 3$_6$ (:: שַׂק *sackcloth*), לקח *take* Jos 7$_{21.24}$ (+ כֶּסֶף, זָהָב) 2 K 2$_{8.14}$, רום hi. *raise* 2$_{13}$, עלה *take up* Jos 7$_{21}$, שׁלך hi. *throw* 1 K 19$_{19}$, ראה *see* Jos 7$_{21}$, חמד *desire* 7$_{21}$, appar. גלם *wrap* 2 K 2$_8$, appar. שׂרף *burn* Jos 7$_{25}$, appar. סקל *stone* 7$_{25}$.

<CSTR> אַדֶּרֶת שִׁנְעָר *cloak of,* i.e. from, *Shinar* Jos 7$_{21}$, אַדֶּרֶת שֵׂעָר *cloak (made) of hair* Gn 25$_{25}$ Zc 13$_4$, אַדֶּרֶת אֵלִיָּהוּ *cloak of Elijah* 2 K 2$_{13.14}$. <ADJ> אַדֶּרֶת שִׁנְעָר אַחַת טוֹבָה *one good cloak of Shinar* Jos 7$_{21}$. <PREP> בְּ לוט hi. *wrap* face *in* 1 K 19$_{13}$; כֻּלּוֹ כְּאַדֶּרֶת שֵׂעָר *all of him was as a cloak of hair* Gn 25$_{25}$.
→ אדר *be majestic.*

אדשׁ 1 vb **thresh—Qal** Inf. אָדוֹשׁ—לֹא לָנֶצַח אָדוֹשׁ יְדוּשֶׁנּוּ *not for ever does one continue to thresh* (lit. *[to] thresh, he threshes*) bread, i.e. bread grain Is 28$_{28}$ (appar. byform of, or em. to דּוֹשׁ *[to] thresh*; 1QIsa^a הדש appar. *does the thresher?*).

[אַדְשָׁךְ] 0.0.1 n.[m.] **rafter**—pl. Q אדשכים—**rafter** or perh. **doorway,** מקורים באדשכים עץ ארז ומצופים זהב *(the) beams will be in rafters,* or *the beams at the doorways will be, (made of) wood of cedar and covered with gold* 11QT 41$_{16}$, גובהמה שמונה ועשרים באמה עד [האד]שכים *their height will be twenty-eight cubits up to the rafters,* or *doorways* 41$_{16(erased)}$ + Sup.

אדתא 0.0.0.1 pr.n.f. **Adatha,** wife of Pashhur (פשחר), Seal 152$_1$ (Judaea?, 7th cent.).

אהב 208.40.38 vb. **love—Qal** Pf. 3ms אָהֵב (אָהַב, אֲהֵב, sf. אֲהֵבוֹ, אֲהֵבָהּ, אֲהֵבְךָ), 3fs אָהֲבָה (sf. אֲהֵבַתְהוּ, אֲהֵבַתֶךְ), 2ms אָהַבְתָּ (Q אהבתה, sf. אֲהַבְתָּנוּ, אֲהַבְתָּנִי), 2fs אָהַבְתְּ, 1s אָהַבְתִּי (אָהָבְתִּי, sf. אֲהַבְתִּיךָ, אֲהַבְתִּיךְ), 3mp אָהֲבוּ (sf. אֲהֵבוּם, אֲהֵבוּךָ), 2mp אֲהַבְתֶּם; impf. 3ms יֶאֱהַב (יֶאֱהָב,

sf. יֶאֱהָבְךָ, יֶאֱהָבֵנִי), 2ms תֶּאֱהַב (תֶּאֱהָב), 1cs אֹהַב (sf. אֹהֲבֵם, Q אהבנו), 2mpl תֶּאֱהֲבוּ (תֶּאֱהָבוּן, תֶּאֱהָבוּ).

+ waw וַאֲהֵבְךָ, וְאָהַבְתָּ, וַאֲהַבְתֶּם; וַיֶּאֱהַב (וַיֶּאֱהָבֵהוּ [Kt ויאהבו], וַיֶּאֱהָבֶהָ), 2ms וַתֶּאֱהַב, וָאֹהַב (Q ואהבכה, וָאֹהֲבֵהוּ, וָאֹהֲבֵם); impv. אֱהַב (Q אהוב, אֱהָבֶהָ), אֶהֱבוּ (אֱהָבוּ); ptc. אֹהֵב (אוֹהֵב, sf. אֹהֲבִי, אוֹהַבְךָ, אֹהַבְךָ, אוֹהֲבוֹ), אֹהֶבֶת (אוֹהֶבֶת, sf. אוֹהַבְתִּי, אֹהַבְתִּי), אֹהֲבִים (אוֹהֲבִים, אוֹהֲבַי, אֹהֲבַי, אֹהֲבֶיהָ, אוֹהֲבֶיהָ, אֹהֲבֶיךָ, אוֹהֲבֶיךָ, Q אהביך, אוֹהֲבַיִךְ, אוֹהֲבָיו, אֹהֲבֶיהָ, אוֹהֲבֶיהָ, Q אוהביהא), אוֹהֲבֵי־; ptc. pass. אָהוּב, אֲהוּבָה, אֲהֻבַת־, Q אהובים; inf. אֱהוֹב, אַהֲבָה, אַהֲבַת (Q אהבתו, אֲהָבָם).

1. love another human, a. in family, father for son, Gn 22$_{2}$ 25$_{28}$ 37$_{3.4}$ 44$_{20}$ Pr 13$_{24}$; mother for son, Gn 25$_{28}$; daughter-in-law for mother-in-law, Ru 4$_{15}$.

b. as friend, patron, etc., Lv 19$_{18}$ 2 S 19$_{7}$ 1 K 5$_{15}$ Jr 20$_{4.6}$ Mc 6$_{8}$ Pr 9$_{8}$ 12$_{1}$ 15$_{12}$ 16$_{13}$ 17$_{19.19}$ 21$_{17.17}$ 29$_{3}$ Ec 3$_{8}$ 5$_{9.9}$ Est 5$_{10.14}$ 6$_{13}$ 2 C 19$_{2}$ Si 34$_{2}$ 46$_{13}$ 1QS 1$_{3.9}$ CD 6$_{20}$ 1QH 14$_{19}$ GnzPs 1$_{9}$ 4Q525 4$_{14}$; of slave for master, Ex 21$_{5}$ Dt 15$_{16}$; of master for servant, Si 7$_{21(C)}$; of Israelite for sojourner, Lv 19$_{34}$ Dt 10$_{19}$; of friends, 1 S 18$_{1.3}$ 20$_{17.17}$ Jb 19$_{19}$ Si 47$_{22}$; of colleagues, companions, Pr 17$_{17}$ Si 6$_{13}$ 37$_{1(Bmg, D)}$ 2 S 19$_{7}$; of superior and inferior, 1 S 16$_{21}$ 1 S 18$_{22}$ 1 S 18$_{16}$; oneself, Pr 19$_{8}$.

c. sexually, Gn 24$_{67}$ 29$_{18.20.30.32}$ 34$_{3}$ Dt 21$_{15.15.16}$ Jg 14$_{16}$ 16$_{4.15}$ 1 S 1$_{5}$ 18$_{20.28}$ 2 S 13$_{1.4.15}$ 1 K 11$_{1.2}$ Ezk 16$_{37}$ Ho 3$_{1.1}$ Ca 1$_{3.4.7}$ 3$_{1.2.3.4}$ Ec 9$_{9}$ Lm 1$_{2}$ Est 2$_{17}$ 2 C 11$_{21}$ Si 9$_{8}$ (but prob. אָהֵב *loved one*).

2. love humans, of Y., Dt 4$_{37}$ 7$_{8.13}$ 10$_{15.18.19}$ 23$_{6}$ 2 S 12$_{24}$ 1 K 10$_{9}$ Is 43$_{4}$ 48$_{14}$ 61$_{8}$ Jr 31$_{3}$ Ho 3$_{1}$ 9$_{15}$ 11$_{1}$ 14$_{5}$ Ml 1$_{2.2.2}$ 2$_{11}$ Ps 11$_{7}$ 33$_{5}$ 37$_{28}$ 47$_{5}$ 78$_{68}$ 87$_{2}$ 97$_{10}$ (if em.; see Subj.) 99$_{4}$ 146$_{8}$ Pr 3$_{12}$ 15$_{9}$ 22$_{11}$ (if em.; see Subj) Ne 13$_{26}$ 2 C 2$_{10}$ 9$_{8}$ Si 4$_{14}$ 1QS 3$_{26}$ CD 2$_{3}$ 8$_{15.17(A)}$=19$_{28.30(B)}$ 1QH 14$_{10}$ 17$_{24}$ 4QDibHam[a] 4$_{4}$.

3. love a deity, a. Y., Ex 20$_{6}$||Dt 5$_{10}$ 6$_{5}$ 10$_{12}$ 11$_{1.13.22}$ 13$_{4}$=11QT 54$_{12}$ Dt 7$_{9}$=CD 19$_{2}$ 19$_{9}$ 30$_{6.16.20}$ Jos 22$_{5}$ 23$_{11}$ Jg 5$_{31}$ 1 K 3$_{3}$ Is 56$_{6}$ Ps 31$_{24}$ 97$_{10}$ (or em.; see Subj.) 116$_{1}$ 145$_{20}$ Dn 9$_{4}$=Ne 1$_{5}$ Si 7$_{30}$ 47$_{8}$ GnzPs 3$_{25}$ CD 20$_{21}$ 1QH 14$_{26}$ 15$_{9.10}$ 16$_{13}$ 4QTanḥ 16$_{5}$ 11QPs[a] 19$_{12}$ 4Q525 2.4$_{8}$ 4Q416 4$_{9}$, for name of Y., Ps 5$_{12}$ 69$_{37}$ 119$_{132}$ 11QPs[a] 19$_{6}$ 4QpsEzek[a] 2$_{1}$.

b. other gods, Jr 2$_{25}$ 8$_{2}$ Ezk 16$_{37}$ Ps 116$_{1}$.

4. like, love objects or actions, Gn 27$_{4.9.14}$ Is 1$_{23}$ 56$_{10}$ 57$_{8}$ 66$_{10}$ Jr 5$_{31}$ 14$_{10}$ Ho 3$_{1}$ 4$_{18}$ 9$_{1}$ 10$_{11}$ 12$_{8}$ Am 4$_{5}$ 5$_{15}$ Mc 3$_{2}$ 6$_{8}$ Zc 8$_{17.19}$ Ps 4$_{3}$ 11$_{5}$ 26$_{8}$ 34$_{13}$ 40$_{17}$=70$_{5}$ 45$_{8}$ 52$_{5.6}$ 109$_{17}$ 116$_{1}$ 119$_{47.48.97.113.119.127.140.159.163.165.167}$ 122$_{6}$ Pr 1$_{22}$ 4$_{6}$ 8$_{17.17.21.36}$ 12$_{1.1}$ 15$_{12}$ 16$_{13}$ 17$_{19.19}$ 18$_{21}$ 20$_{13}$ 21$_{17.17}$ 22$_{11}$ 29$_{3}$ Ec 5$_{9.9}$ 2 C 26$_{10}$ Si 3$_{26}$ 4$_{12.12}$ 13$_{15}$ 34$_{5}$ 1QH 2$_{14}$ 16$_{7}$ 1QDM 1$_{5}$ GnzPs 2$_{26}$ 4QpPs[a] 1.1$_{15}$ 4Q181 2$_{4}$ 11QPs[a] 22$_{2}$ 4Q298 3$_{7}$ 4Q477 2$_{8}$ Ketef Hinnom inscr. 1$_{3}$.

<SUBJ> Rebekah Gn 25$_{28}$, Michal 1 S 18$_{20.28}$, Abraham Gn 22$_{2}$, Isaac 24$_{67}$ 25$_{28}$, Jacob 29$_{18.20.30}$ 37$_{3}$, Shechem 34$_{3}$ (+ וַתִּדְבַּק נַפְשׁוֹ *and his soul cleaved*, דבר עַל־לֵב pi. *speak to the heart*, i.e. persuade), Samson Jg 14$_{16}$ (:: שׂנא *hate*) 16$_{4.15}$ (+ לִבְּךָ אֵין אִתִּי *your heart is not with me*), Elkanah 1 S 1$_{5}$, Samuel Si 46$_{13}$, Saul 1 S 16$_{21}$, Jonathan 18$_{1.3}$ 20$_{17.17}$, David 2 S 19$_{7}$ (:: שׂנא) Si 47$_{8}$, Amnon 2 S 13$_{1.4.15}$ (:: שׂנא), Solomon 1 K 3$_{3}$ 11$_{1.2}$ Ne 13$_{26}$, Hiram 1 K 5$_{15}$, Rehoboam 2 C 11$_{21}$, Hosea Ho 3$_{1}$ (:: שׂנא), Job Jb 19$_{19}$, Jehoshaphat 2 C 19$_{2}$.

כַּלָּה *daughter-in-law* Ru 4$_{15}$, עַלְמָה *young woman* Ca 1$_{3.4}$, אָדָם *human being* Mc 6$_{8}$, אִישׁ *man* Ps 4$_{3}$ (בְּנֵי אִישׁ *humans*) 34$_{13}$ (|| חפץ *desire*) Pr 29$_{3}$ CD 6$_{20}$ 4Q298 3$_{7}$ (|| רדף *pursue*), *husband* Gn 29$_{32}$, father 27$_{9.14}$ 37$_{4}$ 44$_{20}$ Pr 13$_{24}$ (:: שׂנא *hate*), slave Ex 21$_{5}$ Dt 15$_{16}$ 1 S 18$_{22}$, master Si 7$_{21(C)}$, מֶלֶךְ *king* 1 K 11$_{1}$ Ps 45$_{8}$ Pr 16$_{13}$ Est 2$_{17}$, שַׂר *prince* Is 1$_{23}$, גִּבּוֹר *warrior* Ps 52$_{5.6}$, רֵעַ *neighbour* Pr 17$_{17}$, חָכָם *wise person* 9$_{8}$ (:: שׂנא), אהב ptc. *friend* Si 37$_{1(Bmg, D)}$, אמר ptc. *one who says* 37$_{1(B)}$, קנה ptc. *one who acquires* wisdom Pr 19$_{8}$, פעל ptc. *doer* of good GnzPs 1$_{9}$, נֶפֶשׁ *soul* Ca 1$_{7}$ 3$_{1.2.3.4}$.

Israelites Lv 19$_{18.34}$ Dt 6$_{5}$ 10$_{12.19}$ 11$_{1.13.22}$ 13$_{4}$=11QT 54$_{12}$ 19$_{9}$ 30$_{6.16.20}$ Jos 22$_{5}$ 23$_{11}$ 1 S 18$_{16}$ Is 57$_{8}$ Jr 2$_{25}$ 8$_{2}$ (|| עבד *serve*, הלך אַחֲרֵי *walk after*, דרשׁ *seek*, שׁחה לְ htpal. *bow down to*) 5$_{31}$ 14$_{10}$ Ho 3$_{1}$ 4$_{18}$ 9$_{1}$ Am 4$_{5}$ 5$_{15}$ Mc 3$_{2}$ (both :: שׂנא *hate*) Zc 8$_{17.19}$ 1QDM 1$_{5}$ 4QpsEzek[a] 2$_{1}$, foreigners Is 56$_{6}$, psalmist Ps 26$_{8}$ perh. 109$_{17}$ 116$_{1}$ 119$_{47.48.97}$ (:: שׂנא) $_{113.119.127.140.159}$ (:: שׂנא) $_{163.167}$ GnzPs 2$_{26}$ 1QH 14$_{19.26}$ 15$_{10}$ (both + נְדָבָה *freely*) 11QPs[a] 19$_{12}$ 22$_{2}$, חָסִיד *pious one* Ps 31$_{24}$.

Y. Dt 4$_{37}$ 7$_{8.13}$ 10$_{15.18}$ 23$_{6}$ 2 S 12$_{24}$ 1 K 10$_{9}$ Is 43$_{4}$ 48$_{14}$ (|| יקר *be valuable*, כבד ni. *be honoured*) 48$_{14}$ (or em. אֲהֵבוֹ *has loved him* to הֱבִיאוֹ *has brought him*) 61$_{8}$ Jr 31$_{3}$ Ho 3$_{1}$ 9$_{15}$ 11$_{1}$ 14$_{5}$ (+ נְדָבָה *freely*) Ml 1$_{2.2.2}$ 2$_{11}$ Ps 11$_{7}$ 33$_{5}$ 37$_{28}$ 47$_{5}$ 78$_{68}$ 87$_{2}$ 97$_{10}$ (if em. אֹהֲבֵי י׳ שִׂנְאוּ רָע *those who love Y., hate evil* to אֹהֵב י' שֹׂנְאֵי רָע *Y. loves those who hate evil*) 146$_{8}$ Pr 3$_{12}$ 15$_{9}$ Pr 22$_{11}$ (if em. אֹהֵב י' *Y. loves*) Ne 13$_{26}$ 2 C 2$_{10}$ 9$_{8}$ Si 4$_{14}$ (if em אלהי במא ויהא to אוהביה אוהב י' *Y. loves those who love her*) 4QDibHam^{a} 4$_{4}$ 1QS 3$_{26}$ CD 2$_{3}$ 8$_{15.17(A)}$=19$_{28.30(B)}$ 1QH 14$_{10}$ 17$_{24}$.

צפה ptc. *one keeping watch* Is 56$_{10}$, כְּנַעַן *merchant* Ho 12$_{8}$, פֶּתִי *simple one* Pr 1$_{22}$, חָכְמָה *wisdom* 8$_{17}$, שׂנא pi. ptc. *one who hates* wisdom 8$_{36}$, אהב ptc. *one who loves* wisdom Si 4$_{12}$, סתר hi. ptc. *one who hides* counsel 34$_{2}$, ליץ ptc. *scoffer* Pr 15$_{12}$, זנה ptc. *prostitute* Ezk 16$_{37}$, בָּשָׂר *flesh*, i.e. human being Si 13$_{15}$, עֹז *strength* of king Ps 99$_{4}$, עֶגְלָה *heifer* Ho 10$_{11}$.

Subj. not specified, Ex 20$_{6}$||Dt 5$_{10}$ Dt 7$_{9}$=CD 19$_{2}$ 2 S 19$_{7}$ Jg 5$_{31}$ Is 66$_{10}$ Jr 20$_{4.6}$ Ps 5$_{12}$ 11$_{5}$ 40$_{17}$=70$_{5}$ 69$_{37}$ 97$_{10}$ (or em.; see above) 119$_{132.165}$ 122$_{6}$ 145$_{20}$ Pr 4$_{6}$ 8$_{17.21}$ 12$_{1}$ 17$_{19.19}$ 18$_{21}$ 20$_{13}$ 21$_{17.17}$ 22$_{11}$ (unless em.; see above) Ec 3$_{8}$ 5$_{9.9}$ 9$_{9}$ Lm 1$_{2}$ Est 5$_{10.14}$ 6$_{13}$ Dn 9$_{4}$=Ne 1$_{5}$ Si 3$_{26}$ 6$_{13}$ (|| שׂנא *hate*) 9$_{8}$ 47$_{22}$ GnzPs 3$_{25}$ (+ חָסִיד *pious one*) CD 20$_{21}$ (|| שׁמר *keep*) 1QH 2$_{14}$ 15$_{9}$ (יא[הבו]) 16$_{13}$ 4QTanḥ 16$_{5}$ 4QpPs^{a} 1.1$_{15}$ 4Q181 2$_{4}$ 11QPs^{a} 19$_{6}$ 4Q525 2.4$_{8}$ 4$_{14}$ ([אוהביכה]) 4Q416 1$_{8}$ 4Q477 2$_{8}$ Ketef Hinnom inscr. 1$_{3}$ ([א]הב) 1$_{5}$ אה[ביו]/אה[בי]; others אה[רן] *Aaron*)

Subj. of passive verb (*be loved*), אִשָּׁה *wife* Dt 21$_{15.15.16}$ (all three :: שׂנא *hate*) Ho 3$_{1}$.

<OBJ> Isaac Gn 22$_{2}$, Rebekah 24$_{67}$, Esau 25$_{28}$, Jacob 25$_{28}$ Ml 1$_{2}$ (:: שׂנא *hate*), Rachel 29$_{18.20.30}$, Leah 29$_{32}$, Joseph 37$_{3.4}$ 44$_{20}$, Delilah Jg 16$_{4.15}$, Hannah 1 S 1$_{5}$, David 16$_{21}$ 18$_{1.3.16.20.22.28}$ 20$_{17.17}$ 2 S 19$_{7}$, Tamar 13$_{1.4.15}$, Solomon 12$_{24}$ Ne 13$_{26}$, Pashhur Jr 20$_{4.6}$, Maacah 2 C 11$_{21}$, Naomi Ru 4$_{15}$, Esther Est 2$_{17}$, Haman 5$_{10.14}$ 6$_{13}$.

אָדוֹן *master* Ex 21$_{5}$, רֵעַ *neighbour* Lv 19$_{18}$ Ho 3$_{1}$ (if em. אֲהֻבַת רֵעַ a woman *beloved of a neighbour* to אֹהֶבֶת רֵעַ a woman *who loves a neighbour*), אָח *brother* CD 6$_{20}$, גֵּר *sojourner* Lv 19$_{34}$ Dt 10$_{18.19}$, זור ptc. *stranger* Jr 2$_{25}$, master Dt 15$_{16}$, עֶבֶד *slave* Si 7$_{21(C)}$, מַת *man* Jb 19$_{19}$, one who reproves Pr 9$_{8}$ 15$_{12}$, דבר ptc. *one who speaks* uprightness 16$_{13}$, נֶפֶשׁ *self* 19$_{8}$, שׂנא ptc. *one who hates* Ps 97$_{10}$ (if em.; see Subj.) 2 C 19$_{2}$, בֵּן *son* Pr 13$_{24}$ 1QS 1$_{9}$, נַעֲרָה *young woman* Gn 34$_{3}$, Samson's wife Jg 14$_{16}$, אהב ptc. *one who loves* Pr 8$_{17}$, pagan nations as lovers Ezk 16$_{37}$, אִשָּׁה *woman, wife* 1 K 11$_{1}$ Ho 3$_{1.1}$ Ec 9$_{9}$ Si 9$_{8}$ (but prob. אֲהַב *loved one*), male lover Ca 1$_{3.4.7}$ 3$_{1.2.3.4}$, אָב *father* Dt 4$_{37}$ 10$_{15}$, רִאשׁוֹן *first one* CD 8$_{16(A)}$=19$_{29(B)}$, Israel Dt 7$_{13}$ 23$_{6}$ 1 K 10$_{9}$ Is 43$_{4}$ Jr 31$_{3}$ Ho 9$_{15}$ 11$_{1}$ 14$_{5}$ Ml 1$_{2.2}$ 2 C 2$_{10}$ 9$_{8}$ 4QDibHam^{a} 4$_{4}$, עַם *people* Si 46$_{13}$ (|| רצה pass. *be favoured*), צַדִּיק *righteous one* Ps 146$_{8}$, רדף pi. ptc. *one who pursues* righteousness Pr 15$_{9}$, טָהוֹר *one pure* of heart 22$_{11}$, בוא ptc. *one coming* after CD 8$_{17(A)}$=19$_{30(B)}$, wisdom's devotees Si 4$_{14}$, אֶחָד *one* (spirit of light) 1QS 3$_{26}$.

Y. Ex 20$_{6}$||Dt 5$_{10}$ 6$_{5}$ Dt 7$_{9}$=CD 19$_{2}$ (|| שׁמר *keep* commandments) Dt 10$_{12}$ 11$_{1.13.22}$ 13$_{4}$=11QT 54$_{12}$ Dt 19$_{9}$ 30$_{6.16.20}$ Jos 22$_{5}$ 23$_{11}$ Jg 5$_{31}$ 1 K 3$_{3}$ Ps 31$_{24}$ 97$_{10}$ (or em.; see Subj.) 116$_{1}$ (if em. אָהַבְתִּי י' *I love Y.*) 145$_{20}$ Dn 9$_{4}$=Ne 1$_{5}$ (|| שׁמר *keep* commandments) Si 47$_{22}$ (אוה[ביו]; + נֶכֶד *posterity*) GnzPs 3$_{25}$ CD 20$_{21}$ 1QH 14$_{26}$ 15$_{9.10}$ 16$_{13}$ 4QTanḥ 16$_{5}$ (both + שׁמר *keep* commandments) 4Q525 2.4$_{8}$ 4Q416 1$_{8}$ Ketef Hinnom inscr. 1$_{5}$ (אה[ביו]/אה[בי]), עשׂה ptc. *maker* Si 7$_{30}$ 47$_{8}$, שֵׁם *name* of Y. Ps 5$_{12}$ 69$_{37}$ 119$_{132}$ Is 56$_{6}$ 1QH 16$_{7}$ ([שמך]) 11QPs^{a} 19$_{6.12}$ 4QpsEzek^{a} 2$_{1}$ (אה[בו]), קֹדֶשׁ *sanctuary* of Y. Ml 2$_{11}$, מָעוֹן *habitation* of house Ps 26$_{8}$ GnzPs 2$_{26}$, מָקוֹם *place* of dwelling of glory Ps 26$_{8}$, שַׁעַר *gate* of Zion 87$_{2}$, הַר *mountain* of Zion 78$_{68}$, גָּאוֹן *pride* of Jacob 47$_{5}$, עִיר *city* Lm 1$_{2}$, יְרוּשָׁלַםִ *Jerusalem* Is 66$_{10}$ (|| אבל htp. *mourn*) Ps 122$_{6}$, ציון Zion 11QPs^{a} 22$_{2}$.

שֶׁמֶשׁ *sun*, Jr 8$_{2}$, יָרֵחַ *moon* 8$_{2}$, צָבָא *host* of heaven 8$_{2}$, מַטְעַם *tasty food* Gn 27$_{4.9.14}$, שֹׁחַד *bribe* Is 1$_{23}$, מִשְׁכָּב *bed* 57$_{8}$, אֲשִׁישָׁה *(raisin) cake* Ho 3$_{1}$, קָלוֹן *shame* 4$_{18}$ (or em. אָהֲבוּ הֵבוּ *they have loved* to אָהֹב אָהֲבוּ *they have indeed loved*; || זנה *act as prostitute*), אֶתְנָן *fee* for prostitution 9$_{1}$, מְחִיר *price* Si 34$_{5(B)}$ (|| רדף *pursue* gold), יוֹם *day* Ps 34$_{13}$, שֶׁמֶן *oil* Pr 21$_{17}$, יַיִן *wine* 21$_{17}$, כֶּסֶף *silver* Ec 5$_{9}$, הָמוֹן *wealth* 5$_{9}$ (if em.; see Prep.), אֲדָמָה *the soil* 2 C 26$_{10}$, מִין *kind* Si 13$_{15}$, פרע *(long) locks* 4QpPs^{a} 1.1$_{15(Allegro)}$.

טוֹב *good* Am 5$_{15}$, טוֹבָה *good thing* Si 3$_{26}$, רָע *evil* Ps 52$_{5}$ Mc 3$_{2}$, חֶסֶד *loyalty* 6$_{8}$ 4Q298 3$_{7}$, בְּרִית *covenant* Ketef Hinnom inscr. 1$_{3}$ ([א]הב הבר[ית]), שְׁבוּעָה false *oath* Zc 8$_{17}$, שָׁלוֹם *peace* 8$_{19}$, אֱמֶת *truth* 8$_{19}$, מִשְׁפָּט *justice* Is 61$_{8}$ Ps 33$_{5}$ 37$_{28}$ 99$_{4}$, צְדָקָה *righteousness* Ps 11$_{7}$ 33$_{5}$, עַוְלָה *iniquity* 4Q181 2$_{4}$, חָמָס *violence* Ps 11$_{5}$, תְּשׁוּעָה *deliverance* 40$_{17}$=70$_{5}$, רִיק *vanity* 4$_{3}$, צֶדֶק *righteousness* 45$_{8}$, דָּבָר devouring *word* 52$_{6}$, אִמְרָה *word* 119$_{140}$, לָשׁוֹן

tongue Pr 18$_{21}$ (or em. אֹהֲבֶיהָ *those who love it*, i.e. tongue, to אֹחֲזֶיהָ *those who hold it*), קְלָלָה *cursing* Ps 109$_{17}$.

חָכְמָה *wisdom* Pr 4$_{6}$ (:: עזב *abandon*) 8$_{17.21}$ 29$_{3}$ Si 4$_{12}$ (|| בקשׁ pi. *seek*) 4$_{14}$ (if em.; see Subj.) CD 2$_{3}$, תּוּשִׁיָּה *wisdom* 2$_{3}$, בִּינָה *discernment* Pr 4$_{6}$, מוּסָר *discipline* 12$_{1}$ 1QH 2$_{14}$, דַּעַת *knowledge* Pr 12$_{1}$ CD 2$_{3}$, מִצְוָה *command* Ps 119$_{47.48.127}$, תּוֹרָה *law* 119$_{97.113.163.165}$, עֵדָה *testimony* 119$_{119.167}$, פִּקּוּד *precept* 119$_{159}$, פֶּשַׁע *transgression* Pr 17$_{19}$, מַצָּה *quarrelling* 17$_{19}$, שֵׁנָה *sleep* 20$_{13}$, מָוֶת *death* 8$_{36}$, חַיִּים *life* Si 4$_{12}$, שִׂמְחָה *joy* Pr 21$_{17}$, פֶּתִי *simplicity* Pr 1$_{22}$, שֶׁפֶךְ *emission* of flesh 4Q477 2$_{8}$, כֹּל *all* that Y. has chosen 1QS 1$_{3}$.

Obj. not specified, Ps 116$_{1}$ (unless em. אָהַבְתִּי *I have loved* to אָהַבְתִּי י׳ *I have loved Y.*) Pr 3$_{12}$ 17$_{17}$ Ec 3$_{8}$ Si 6$_{13}$ 34$_{2}$ 1QH 14$_{10.19}$ 17$_{24}$ 4Q525 4$_{14}$ ([אוהביכה]).

<PREP> לְ have love *for* Lv 19$_{18}$ (+ רֵעַ *neighbour*) 19$_{24}$ (+ גֵּר *sojourner*) 1 K 5$_{15}$ (+ דָּוִד *David*) 2 C 19$_{2}$ (+ שׂנא ptc. *one who hates*); בְּ appar. of price, *for* Ec 5$_{9}$ (or em. בֶּהָמוֹן *for wealth* to הָמוֹן *wealth*) Si 34$_{5(Bmg)}$, of place *in* GnzPs 1$_{9}$ (+ לֵבָב *heart*); אָהַבְתָּ רָע מִטּוֹב *you love evil more than good* Ps 52$_{5}$; כְּ *as* oneself Lv 19$_{18.34}$ 1 S 18$_{1}$ Si 7$_{21}$ 34$_{2}$ CD 6$_{20}$.

<COLL> אַהֲבַת נַפְשׁוֹ אֲהֵבוֹ *he loved him as he loved himself* 1 S 20$_{17}$, דבק בְּ לְאַהֲבָה *cling to* wives *in love* 1 K 11$_{2}$, עֵת לֶאֱהֹב *a time to love* Ec 3$_{8}$ (:: שׂנא *hate*), אהב כֵּן *love* (it to be) *thus* Jr 5$_{31}$ Am 4$_{5}$, אהב + inf. נום *sleep* Is 56$_{10}$, נוע *wander* Jr 14$_{10}$, דושׁ *thresh* Ho 10$_{11}$, עשׁק *defraud* 12$_{8}$, ראה *see* good Ps 34$_{13}$.

<SYN> שׁמר *keep* commandments.

<ANT> שׂנא *hate*.

5. ptc. as noun (some ptcs. in §§ 1–3 perhaps belong here), **friend, lover a.** of other human, Ps 38$_{12}$ 88$_{19}$ Pr 14$_{20}$ 18$_{24}$ 27$_{6}$ Si 6$_{1.5.7.8.9.10.14.14.15.16}$ 7$_{18.35}$ 9$_{10.10}$ 12$_{8}$ 14$_{13}$ 30$_{28}$ 36$_{6}$ 37$_{1(Bmg, D).1(Bmg, D).1(Bmg, D).4.5}$ 41$_{22}$.

b. of Y., Is 41$_{8}$ 2 C 20$_{7}$ CD 3$_{2.3}$ 4QpGen^{a} 2$_{8}$ 4Q372 1$_{21}$.

<SUBJ> אמר *say* Si 37$_{1(D)}$, עמד *stand* Ps 38$_{12}$ (|| רֵעַ *friend*, קָרוֹב *relative*) Si 6$_{8}$ 37$_{4}$, חשׂף *strip*, i.e. reveal Si 6$_{9}$, ידע ni. *be known* Si 12$_{8}$ (:: שׂנא ptc. *one who hates*), מצא ni. *be found* 6$_{10}$, נבט hi. *look* 37$_{4}$, לחם ni. *fight* 37$_{5(B)}$, נחל *inherit* Si 37$_{5(Bmg)}$, חזק hi. *hold* 37$_{5}$, הפך ni. *be turned* 6$_{9}$ (+ לשׂנא *into an enemy*), דבק *cleave* Pr 18$_{24}$ (+ מֵאָח *more than a brother*), שׂנא *hate* Si 36$_{6}$.

<NOM CL> אֹהֲבֵי עָשִׁיר רַבִּים *the friends of the rich are many* Pr 14$_{20}$ (+ רֵעַ *friend*), יֵשׁ אֹהֵב *there is a friend* 18$_{24}$ (+ רֵעַ) Si 6$_{8.9.10}$ 37$_{1(Bmg, D)}$ (+ שם אהב appar. *[who is] a name of a friend*, i.e. a friend in name only), אוהב אמונה אוהב תקוף *a faithful friend is a strong friend* 6$_{14}$, צרור חיים אוהב אמונה *a faithful friend is a bundle of life* 6$_{16}$, יי[ן] חדש אוהב *a new friend is new wine* 9$_{10}$, כסוס מוכן אוהב *a friend* who hates *is as a horse prepared* (for battle) Si 36$_{6(F)}$ (E אוהב [כסוס מיזן] [Segal]).

<OBJ> רחק hi. *remove* Ps 88$_{19}$ (|| רֵעַ *friend*; + ידע pu. ptc. *acquaintance*), רבה hi. *multiply* Si 6$_{5}$, קנה *acquire* 6$_{7}$, מור hi. *exchange* Si 7$_{18}$ (+ במחיר *for a price*; || אָח *brother*), משׁל hi. *let rule over* 30$_{28}$ (|| בֵּן *son*, אִשָּׁה *wife*, רֵעַ *friend*), מצא *find* 6$_{14}$.

<CSTR> אוהב אמונה *friend of faithfulness* Si 6$_{14.15.16}$, תקוף *of strength* 6$_{14}$, אֹהֲבֵי עָשִׁיר *friends of the rich* Pr 14$_{20}$, שם אוהב *name of friend* Si 37$_{1(Bmg)}$ (D אהב), זֶרַע ... אֹהֲבִי *seed*, i.e. offspring, *of ... my friend* Is 41$_{7}$ 2 C 20$_{7}$ (אֹהַבְךָ *your friend*), בני אהביך *sons of your friend* 4Q 372 1$_{21}$, פִּצְעֵי אוֹהֵב *wounds of a friend* Pr 27$_{6}$.

<APP> אוהב חבר שלחן *a friend, a table companion* (lit. *companion of a table*) Si 6$_{10}$, מרע אוהב *one who does evil, a friend* 37$_{4}$, אַבְרָהָם אֹהֲבִי *Abraham, my friend* Is 41$_{8}$ 2 C 20$_{7}$ (אֹהַבְךָ *your friend*) 4QpGen^{a} 2$_{8}$ (אהבו *his friend*), אהביך יעקב *your friend, Jacob* 4Q372 1$_{21}$.

<ADJ> יָשָׁן *old* Si 9$_{10}$, חָדָשׁ *new* 9$_{10}$ ([חדש]) 9$_{10}$ (ח[ד]ש), טוֹב *good* 37$_{5}$, דָּבֵק *clinging* Pr 18$_{24}$.

<PREP> לְ *to* Si 6$_{15}$, + טוב hi. *do good* Si 14$_{13}$, נתן *give* 4QpGen^{a} 2$_{8}$, *make into* Si 14$_{13}$; נשׂא מִן *raise* heart *from*, i.e. forget about Si 7$_{35}$ (or em. אודב *one that is sick*), בושׁ מִן *be ashamed of* 41$_{22}$; תַּחַת *instead of* Si 6$_{1}$, *beneath* 36$_{6(F)}$ (E [Segal] [רוכב] *rider* for אוהב); בטח עַל *trust in* Si 6$_{7}$.

<COLL> ויעל אוהב *he* (Abraham) *was reckoned a friend* CD 3$_{2}$, ויכתבו אוהבים *they* (Isaac and Jacob) *were written down as friends* 3$_{3}$.

<SYN> רֵעַ *friend*.

Ni. Impf., Si תאהב; ptc. הַנֶּאֱהָבִים—**be loved,** <SUBJ> Saul and Jonathan 2 S 1$_{23}$ (|| נְעִימִם *pleasant one*), בֵּן *son* Si 3$_{17}$, subject not specified 7$_{35}$.

<PREP> מִן of comparison, *than*, Si 3_{17} (A + נתן ptc. *giver* of gifts, C + אִישׁ *man* of a gift), of cause, *because of* 7_{35}.

Pi. Ptc. מְאַהֲבַי (מְאַהֲבָי, מְאַהֲבַיִךְ, מְאַהֲבָיִךְ, מְאַהֲבֶיהָ)—**love** (or lover, if ptcs. are used as nouns), **a. as a friend,** Zc 13_6.

b. sexually, Jr $22_{20.22}$ 30_{14} Ezk $16_{33.36.37}$ $23_{5.9.22}$ Ho $2_{7.9.12.14.15}$ Lm 1_{19}.

<SUBJ> Subj. not specified, Jr $22_{20.22}$ 30_{14} Ezk $16_{33.36.37}$ $23_{5.9.22}$ Ho $2_{7.9.12.14.15}$ Zc 13_6 Lm 1_{19}.

<OBJ> Oholah Ezk $23_{5.9}$, Oholibah 23_{22}, יְרוּשָׁלַםִ *Jerusalem* Ezk 16_{33} Lm 1_{19}, appar. Jr $22_{20.22}$ 30_{14}, זוֹנָה *harlot*, i.e. Jerusalem Ezk $16_{36.37}$, נָבִיא *prophet* Zc 13_6, אֵם *mother* Ho $2_{7.9.12.14.15}$.

Hi. Imv. Si האהב—**cause to be loved, endear,** האהב לנפשך לעדה *endear yourself to the assembly* Si 4_7.

Also 4Q487 7_2 4QPrFêtes[c] 146_2 1QH 17_{28} 4Q416 4_9 4Q477 4_{10}.

→ אַהֲבָה *love*, אֹהַב *display of love*, אַהַב *loved one*.

[אֹהַב] 2 n.[m.] **display of love**—sf. אֳהָבִם; pl. אֳהָבִים—נִתְעַלְּסָה בָּאֳהָבִים *let us delight ourselves with displays of love* Pr 7_{18} (+ דֹּדִים *acts of love*), וַיִּהְיוּ שִׁקּוּצִים כְּאָהֳבָם *and they became abominations (just) as their display of love* Ho 9_{10} (or em. אֹהֲבָם *the one who loved them*).

→ אהב *love*.

[אַהַב] 2.1 n.[m.] **lover, loved one, love-token**—pl. אֲהָבִים; sf. Si אהביה—הִתְנוּ אֲהָבִים *they* (Ephraim) *have hired loved ones*, i.e. lovers Ho 8_9 (or em. נָתְנוּ *they have given* love-tokens), אהביה באש תלהט appar. *she* (woman) *sets her loved ones*, i.e. lovers, *aflame with fire* Si 9_8 (or *those who love her burn with fire*), אַיֶּלֶת אֲהָבִים *hind of loved ones*, i.e. cherished hind Pr 5_{19} (+ יַעֲלַת חֵן *doe of grace*).

→ אהב *love*.

אַהֲבָה I 40.1.17 n.f. **love**—cstr. אַהֲבַת; sf. אַהֲבָתִי, אַהֲבָתְךָ (Q אהבתכה), אַהֲבָתוֹ, אַהֲבָתָהּ, אַהֲבָתָם—**1. love among humans. a.** friendship, loyalty, affection, 1 S 20_{17} 2 S 1_{26} Ps $109_{4.5}$ Pr 10_{12} 15_{17} 17_9 27_5 Ca 3_{10} Ec $9_{1.6}$ Si 40_{20} 1QS 2_{24} $5_{4.25}$ 8_2 $9_{16.21}$ 10_{26} CD 13_{17} 4QRitMar 14_5. **b.** sexual love, Gn 29_{20} 2 S 1_{26} 13_{15} Jr 2_{33} Pr 5_{19} Ca $2_{4.5}$ 2_7=3_5=8_4 5_4 $8_{6.7.7}$; as term of address for beloved woman, Ca 7_7 (or em.; see Subj.).

2. love between deity and humans, a. of Y. for his people, Is 63_9 Jr 31_3 Ho 11_4 Zp 3_{17} 4QPrFêtes[b] 13_1 GnzPs $1_{13.26}$ 2_9 perh. 2_{25} (אהבתם appar. *their love*, i.e. Y.'s love for them). **b.** of people for Y., Jr 2_2.

<SUBJ> פלא ni. *be wonderful* 2 S 1_{26}, יפה *be beautiful* Ca 7_7 (or em. אֲהֻבָה *O beloved*), נעם *be pleasant* 7_7, חפץ *desire* 2_7=3_5=8_4 (or em. הָאֲהֻבָה *the beloved one*), כסה pi. *cover* Pr 10_{12} (+ עַל כָּל־פְּשָׁעִים *over all transgressions*; :: שִׂנְאָה *hatred*), סתר pu. *be hidden* 27_5 (or em. אֵיבָה *enmity*; + תּוֹכַחַת *reproof*), אבד *perish* Ec 9_6 (|| שִׂנְאָה, קִנְאָה *jealousy*).

<NOM CL> דִּגְלוֹ ... אַהֲבָה *his banner ... is love* Ca 2_4 (or em. דִּגְלוּ *they raised* love *as a banner*), עַזָּה כַמָּוֶת אַהֲבָה *love is as strong as death* 8_6 (|| קִנְאָה *jealousy*), אַהֲבָה־שָׁם *love is there* Pr 15_{17} (:: שִׂנְאָה *hatred*), כן אהבתו עם שנאתו *thus is his love with*, i.e. and, *his hatred* 1QS 9_{16}, משניהם אהבת דודים *better than both of them* (wine and strong drink) *is the love of friends* Si 40_{20}.

<OBJ> בקשׁ pi. *seek* Jr 2_{33} Pr 17_9, עשׂה *practise* 1QS 5_4 8_2, עור hi. *arouse* Ca 2_7=3_5=8_4 (or em.; see Subj.), pol. *arouse* 2_7=3_5=8_4 (or em.; see Subj.), חדשׁ pi. *renew* Zp 3_{17} (if em.; see Prep.), ידע *know* Ec 9_1 (|| שִׂנְאָה *hatred*), זכר *remember* Jr 2_2 (|| חֶסֶד *loyalty*), דגל *set up as a banner* Ca 2_4 (if em.; see Nom. Cl.), כבה pi. *extinguish* 8_7, שׁטף *wash away* 8_7, אהב *love* (cognate acc.) 1 S 20_{17} 2 S 13_{15} (:: שִׂנְאָה) Jr 31_3.

<CSTR> אַהֲבַת נַפְשׁוֹ *love of himself* 1 S 20_{17}, נָשִׁים *of women* 2 S 1_{26}, דודים *of friends* Si 40_{20}, עוֹלָם *of eternity*, i.e. eternal Jr 31_3, חסד *of loyalty* 1QS 2_{24} (|| מַחֲשָׁבָה *purpose*) 5_4 (|| יַחַד *unity*, צְדָקָה *righteousness*, מִשְׁפָּט *judgment*, + הצנע לכת *modesty of going*) 5_{25} (all three || עֲנָוָה *humility*) 8_2 (|| מִשְׁפָּט, צְדָקָה, + הצנע לכת; all four || אֱמֶת *truth*) 10_{26} (+ לנוכנעים *for the oppressed*; || חֹזֶק *strength* of hands, i.e. encouragement) CD 13_{17} (+ עֲנָוָה) 4QRitMar 14_5, כְּלוּלֹתָיִךְ *of your betrothal* Jr 2_2; יחד ... אהבת *community ... of love of* 1QS 2_{24}, עֲבֹתוֹת אַהֲבָה *bands of love* (unless אַהֲבָה II *leather*) Ho 11_4 (|| אָדָם I *human being*, or II *leather*).

<PREP> אלה תכוני הדרך ... לאהבתו *these are the rules of conduct ... with respect to his love* 1QS 9₂₁ (+ עם שנאתו *with his hatred*).

בְּ of accompaniment, *with, in* CD 13₁₇ perh. 4Q462₅, + יכח hi. *rebuke* 1QS 5₂₅ ([להו]כיח), חרש hi. *be silent* Zp 3₁₇ (or em. יְחַדֵּשׁךָ *he will renew you*), עזר *help* GnzPs 1₂₆, of cause, *because of* Gn 29₂₀ 4QPrFêtes[b] 13₁, + גאל *redeem* Is 63₉, שׁגה *err*, i.e. be infatuated Pr 5₁₉, אמר htp. *boast* 4Q448 2₁, of instrument, *by, with*, + כפר *make atonement* GnzPs 1₁₃ (+ על כל פשעינו *for all our transgressions*), רפא *heal* fracture 2₉, נתן בְּ *give in exchange for* Ca 8₇.

מִן of comparison, *than* 2 S 1₂₆ (+ פלא ni. *be wonderful*) 13₁₅ (+ גָּדוֹל *great*) Pr 27₅ (or em.; see Subj.; + טוֹב *good*); בַּעֲבוּר *on account of* GnzPs 2₂₅.

תַּחַת־אַהֲבָתִי יִשְׂטְנוּנִי *in return for my love they accuse me* Ps 109₄ (or del. תַּחַת־אַהֲבָתִי), וַיָּשִׂימוּ עָלַי ... שִׂנְאָה תַּחַת אַהֲבָתִי *and they have set against me ... hatred in return for my love* 109₅ (‖ טוֹבָה *good*; or em. אַהֲבָה *love*).

<COLL> רָצוּף אַהֲבָה מִבְּנוֹת יְרוּשָׁלָם (interior of palanquin) *inlaid with love from the daughters of Jerusalem* Ca 3₁₀ (or em. אַהֲבָה מִבְּנוֹת to הָבְנִים׃ בְּנוֹת *ebony. Daughters of*), חוֹלַת אַהֲבָה אָנִי *I am sick from* (lit. *of*) *love* 2₅ 5₈.

Also 4QRitPur 226₂ (אהב[תכה]).

<SYN> קִנְאָה *jealousy*, שִׂנְאָה *hatred*, צְדָקָה *righteousness*, מִשְׁפָּט *judgment*, עֲנָוָה *humility*, אֱמֶת *truth*.

<ANT> שִׂנְאָה *hatred*.

→ אהב *love*.

[אַהֲבָה] II, see אַהֲבָה I, Cstr., Coll.

[אֲהַבְהָב], see הַבְהָב.

אֹהַד 2 pr.n.m. **Ohad,** son of Simeon, Gn 46₁₀‖Ex 6₁₅.

אֲהָהּ 15 interj. **alas,** usu. with addressee immediately following, אֲהָהּ אֲדֹנָי י׳ *alas, my Lord Y.* Jos 7₇ Jg 6₂₂ Jr 1₆ 4₁₀ 14₁₃ 32₁₇ Ezk 4₁₄ 9₈ 11₁₃ 21₅ (or del. אֲדֹנָי in all four), אֲהָהּ אֲדֹנִי *alas, my lord* 2 K 6₅.₁₅, אֲהָהּ בִּתִּי *alas, my daughter* Jg 11₃₅, without addressee following 2 K 3₁₀; אֲהָהּ לַיּוֹם *alas for the day* (of Y.) Jl 1₁₅; matter lamented by speaker introduced by אֵיכָה *how?* 2 K 6₁₅, אָכֵן *indeed* Jr 4₁₀, הֲ־ interrog. Ezk 9₈ 11₁₃ (if em. כָּלָה you are making *an end* of the remnant of Israel to הֲכָלָה *are* you making *an end?*), הַכְרֵעַ הִכְרַעְתַּנִי *how you have made me bow down* Jg 11₃₅ (or em. עָכוֹר עֲכַרְתַּנִי *you have troubled me*), הִנֵּה *behold* Jr 1₆ 14₁₃ 32₁₇ Ezk 4₁₄ 21₅(Gnz) (L הֵמָּה *they* are saying), וְהוּא שָׁאוּל *and it was borrowed!* 2 K 6₅, כִּי *for* Jg 6₂₂ 2 K 3₁₀ Jl 1₁₅, לָמָּה *why?* Jos 7₇.

אַהֲוָא 3 pl.n. **Ahava,** river (or canal) in Babylonia and/or place through which it flows, נְהַר אַהֲוָא *river (of) Ahava* Ezr 8₃₁, הַנָּהָר אַהֲוָא *the river, Ahava* 8₂₁, הַנָּהָר הַבָּא אֶל־אַהֲוָא *the river that comes into Ahava* 8₁₅.

אֵהוּד 9.0.0.1 pr.n.m. **Ehud**—I אחד—**1.** judge who assassinated Eglon of Moab, son of Gera and descendant of Benjamin, Jg 3₁₅₊₆ₜ 4₁. **2.** perh. ident. with preceding, ancestor of heads of fathers' houses, son of Gera and descendant of Benjamin, 1 C 8₃ (if em. וַאֲבִיהוּד *and Abihud* to אֲבִי אֵהוּד *father of Ehud*) 8₆ (if em. אֵחוּד *Ehud*). **3.** son of Bilhan, descendant of Benjamin, 1 C 7₁₀. **4.** T. ʿIra jar inscr. 2 (אהד; perh. אֹהַד *Ohad*).

[אֱהִי], see אַיֵּה §§a, e.

אהל I 3.0.1 vb. **pitch tent—Qal** Impf. mss יָהֵל [= יֶאֱהַל]; + waw וַיֶּאֱהַל—**move tent,** <SUBJ> Abram Gn 13₁₈ (+ בוא *come*, ישׁב *dwell*), Lot 13₁₂, עֲרָבִי *Arab* Is 13₂₀(mss) (L pi. *pitch tent*). <PREP> עַד סְדֹם *toward, in the direction of Sodom* Gn 13₁₂. **Pi.** Impf. יַהֵל [= יְאַהֵל], Q תאהל (perh. Qal)—**pitch tent, establish dwelling place,** <SUBJ> עֲרָבִי *Arab* Is 13₂₀ (mss Qal; + שָׁם *there*; + רבץ hi. *cause* beasts *to lie*), prostitute 4QWiles 1₇ (+ תו[ש]כון באהלי דומה *she dwells in tents of silence*).

→ אֹהֶל I *tent*, II *Ohel*, אָהֳלָה *Oholah*, אָהֳלִיאָב *Oholiab*, אָהֳלִיבָה *Oholibah*, אָהֳלִיבָמָה *Oholibamah*.

אהל II 1 vb **be light—Hi.** Impf. יַאֲהִיל—**shine,** הֵן עַד־יָרֵחַ וְלֹא יַאֲהִיל *behold, even (the) moon, (and) it does not shine* Jb 25₅ (ms יָהֵל [from הלל] in same sense]; ‖ זכך *be pure*).

[אהל] III, see אֹהֶל I, App., and אֵלֶה, §2 (1).

אֹהֶל I $_{345.2.12}$ n.m. **tent**—אֹהֶל (+ ה of direction הָאֹהֱלָה); cstr. אֹהֶל; sf. אָהֳלִי, אָהָלְךָ אֹהָלְךָ (אָהֳלֶךָ), אָהֳלֵךְ, אָהֳלוֹ (Q אוהלו[ן], אָהֳלֹה); pl. אֹהָלִים (בָּאֳהָלִים); cstr. אָהֳלֵי (L אָהֳלֵי); sf. אֹהָלַי, אֹהָלֶיךָ (אֹהָלֶךָ), אֹהָלָיו, אָהֳלֵיהֶם, אָהֳלֵיכֶם.

1. tent of human beings (distinction of categories not always clear). **a.** as abode of individuals, Gn 9$_{21}$ 12$_{8}$ 13$_{3.5}$ 18$_{2.6.9.10}$ 24$_{67}$ 26$_{25}$ 31$_{25.33.33.33.33.33.34}$ 33$_{19}$ 35$_{21}$ Ex 16$_{16}$ 18$_{7}$ 33$_{8.10}$ Lv 14$_{8}$ Nm 11$_{10}$ 16$_{26.27}$ 19$_{14.14.14.18}$ Dt 11$_{6}$ Jos 7$_{21.22.22.23.24}$ Jg 4$_{11.17.18.20.21}$ 20$_{8}$ 2 S 16$_{22}$ Is 16$_{5}$ Dn 11$_{45}$ 1 C 4$_{41}$ 4Q251 2$_{4}$.

b. as abode of group, Gn 4$_{20}$ (or em.; see below) 25$_{27}$ Jg 5$_{24}$ 8$_{11}$, Rechabites Jr 35$_{7.10}$, pilgrims at festival Ho 9$_{6}$ 12$_{10}$, perh. Dt 16$_{7}$ 11QT 17$_{9}$, shepherds, herdsmen Gn 4$_{20}$ (if em. יֹשֵׁב אֹהֶל וּמִקְנֶה *one dwelling [in] a tent, and cattle* to יֹשֵׁב אָהֳלֵי מִקְנֶה *one dwelling in tents of cattle*) Is 38$_{12}$ 2 C 14$_{14}$, shepherds as warriors Jr 6$_{3}$, warriors Jg 6$_{5}$ 7$_{8.13.13}$ 1 S 17$_{54}$ 2 K 7$_{7.8.8.10}$ Jr 37$_{10}$.

c. tents of foreign tribes, nations, Gn 9$_{27}$ Jr 49$_{29}$ Hb 3$_{7}$ Ps 78$_{51}$ 83$_{7}$ 120$_{5}$ Ca 1$_{5}$ 4QpGen^{a} 2$_{7}$.

d. tents of specif. Israelite tribes, Dt 33$_{18}$ Jos 22$_{4.6.7.8}$ Zc 12$_{7}$ 1 C 5$_{10}$.

e. tents of Israel at the exodus (see also Jr 30$_{18}$ Ml 2$_{12}$ at §1e, g), Nm 24$_{5}$ Dt 1$_{27}$ 5$_{30}$ Jos 3$_{14}$ Ps 78$_{55}$ 106$_{25}$ CD 3$_{8}$.

f. with ref. to home, dwelling place in general, Jg 19$_{9}$ 1 S 4$_{10}$ 13$_{2}$ 2 S 18$_{17}$ 19$_{9}$ 20$_{1.22}$ 1 K 8$_{66}$||2 C 7$_{10}$ 1 K 12$_{16.16}$||2 C 10$_{16.16}$ 2 K 8$_{21}$ 13$_{5}$ 14$_{12}$||2 C 25$_{22}$ Jr 4$_{20}$ 10$_{20.20}$ 30$_{18}$ Ps 52$_{7}$ 69$_{26}$ 91$_{10}$ 122$_{6(ms)}$ 132$_{3}$ Jb 5$_{24}$ 11$_{14}$ 18$_{6.14.15}$ 19$_{12}$ 20$_{26}$ 22$_{23}$ 29$_{4}$ 31$_{31}$ Si 14$_{25}$ 4QapPs^{b} 31$_{2}$.

g. dwelling place of robbers Jb 12$_{6}$, righteous Ps 118$_{15}$, upright Pr 14$_{11}$, wicked, wickedness Ps 84$_{11}$ Jb 8$_{22}$ 21$_{28}$, bribery 15$_{34}$, silence 4QWiles 1$_{7}$, security perh. 1QH 12$_{3}$.

h. with ref. to Jerusalem, Is 33$_{20}$, to territory or population, Is 54$_{2}$ Lm 2$_{4}$ Ml 2$_{12}$ Ps 78$_{67}$, to heavens, as dwelling place for sun, Ps 19$_{5}$, as expanse above earth, Is 40$_{22}$.

2. tent of sanctuary of Y., tabernacle, oft. with ref. to outer covering of מִשְׁכָּן *tabernacle* (e.g. Ex 26$_{7}$||36$_{14}$ 26$_{12.13}$ 40$_{19}$ Nm 3$_{25}$; in list of furnishings, Ex 35$_{11}$||39$_{33}$ Nm 4$_{25}$) or to מִשְׁכָּן itself (e.g. Nm 9$_{15}$ 2 S 7$_{6}$||1 C 17$_{5}$ Ps 78$_{60}$), but distinction oft. unclear.

a. tent in wilderness, Ex 26$_{7}$||36$_{14}$ 26$_{9.11}$||36$_{18}$ 26$_{12.13.14}$||36$_{19}$ 26$_{36}$||36$_{37}$ 27$_{21}$ 28$_{43}$ 29$_{4+6t}$ 30$_{16.18.20.26.36}$ 31$_{7}$ 33$_{7+8t}$ 35$_{11}$||39$_{33}$ 35$_{21}$ 38$_{8.30}$ 39$_{32.38.40}$ 40$_{2+13t}$ Lv 1$_{1.3.5}$ 3$_{2.8.13}$ 4$_{4+7t}$ 6$_{9.19.23}$ 8$_{3.4.31.33.35}$ 9$_{5.23}$ 10$_{7.9}$ 12$_{6}$ 14$_{11.23}$ 15$_{14.29}$ 16$_{7+5t}$ 17$_{4.5.6.9}$ 19$_{21}$ 24$_{3}$ Nm 1$_{1}$ 2$_{2.17}$ 3$_{7.8.25.25.25.38}$ 4$_{3+15t}$ 6$_{10.13.18}$ 7$_{5.89}$ 8$_{9+5t}$ 9$_{15.17}$ 10$_{3}$ 11$_{16.24.26}$ 12$_{4.5.10}$ 14$_{10}$ 16$_{18.19}$ 17$_{7+5t}$ 18$_{2+8t}$ 19$_{4}$ 20$_{6}$ 25$_{6}$ 27$_{2}$ 31$_{54}$ Dt 31$_{14.14.15.15}$ 4QToh B^{a} $_{5}$.

b. tent elsewhere, 2 S 7$_{6}$||1 C 17$_{5.5}$, specif. Jerusalem 2 S 6$_{17}$||1 C 16$_{1}$ 1 K 1$_{39}$ 2$_{28.29.30}$ perh. 7$_{45(Kt)}$ 8$_{4.4}$||2 C 5$_{5.5}$ Ezk 41$_{1}$ Ps 15$_{1}$ 27$_{5.6}$ 61$_{5}$ 1 C 6$_{17}$ 9$_{19.21.23}$ 15$_{1}$ 23$_{32}$ 2 C 1$_{4}$ 24$_{6}$ Si 50$_{5}$ CD 7$_{15}$ perh. 1QH 12$_{3}$ 4Q372 1$_{13}$, Shiloh Jos 18$_{1}$ 19$_{51}$ 1 S 2$_{22}$ Ps 78$_{60}$, Gibeon 2 C 1$_{3.6.13}$.

<SUBJ> היה *be* Gn 13$_{3}$ (+ שָׁם *there*) 13$_{5}$ (+ לְלוֹט *to Lot*; || צֹאן *flock*, בָּקָר *herd*), פרח hi. *flourish* Pr 14$_{11}$ (or em. יַפְרִיחַ *it will flourish* to יַעֲמֹד *it will stand*; || בַּיִת *house*), עמד *stand* 14$_{11}$ (if em.; see above), נסע *set out* Nm 2$_{17}$, צען *travel*, i.e. be moved Is 33$_{20}$ (+ יָתֵד *peg*, חֶבֶל *cord*), עלה *come up* Jg 6$_{5}$ (|| מִקְנֶה *cattle*), נפל *fall* 7$_{13.13}$, שׁדד pu. *be destroyed* Jr 4$_{20}$ (|| יְרִיעָה *curtain*) 10$_{20}$ (+ מֵיתָר *cord*), שׁלה *be at peace* Ps 122$_{6}$ (ms; L אֹהֲבָיִךְ *those who love you*) Jb 12$_{6}$, טוב *be pleasing* Nm 24$_{5}$ (|| מִשְׁכָּן *dwelling place*).

<NOM CL> שָׁלוֹם אָהֳלֶךָ *your tent is peace*, i.e. at peace Jb 5$_{24}$ (+ נָוֶה *abode*), אֹהֶל רְשָׁעִים אֵינֶנּוּ *as for the tent of the wicked, it is not*, i.e. does not exist 8$_{22}$, אֹהָלִים כַּאֲשֶׁר־הֵמָּה *tents were as they had been* 2 K 7$_{10}$ (or em. הָאֹהָלִים *the tents*), מִשְׁמֶרֶת בְּנֵי־גֵרְשׁוֹן ... הָאֹהֶל *the charge of the sons of Gershon was ... the tent* Nm 3$_{25}$ (|| מִשְׁכָּן *tabernacle*; + מִכְסֶה *covering*, מָסָךְ *screen*, קֶלַע *hanging*, מֵיתָר *cord*).

<OBJ> עשׂה *make* Ex 31$_{7}$ 35$_{11}$ perh. 1 K 7$_{45(Kt)}$ (see App.), שׂים *place* Ps 19$_{5}$ (+ לַשֶּׁמֶשׁ *for the sun*), פרשׂ *spread* Ex 40$_{19}$, חבר pi. *fasten* 26$_{11}$||36$_{18}$, נטה *pitch* Gn 12$_{8}$ 26$_{25}$ 33$_{19}$ 35$_{21}$ Jg 4$_{11}$ Jr 10$_{20}$ (|| יְרִיעָה *curtain*) Dn 11$_{45}$ (if em.; see below) 1 C 15$_{1}$ 2 C 1$_{4}$ Si 14$_{25}$ (|| שֶׁכֶן *dwelling place*), hi. 2 S 16$_{22}$ (+ לְאַבְשָׁלוֹם *for Absalom*), תקע *pitch* Gn 31$_{25}$ Jr 6$_{3}$, נטע *plant* Dn 11$_{45}$ (or em. וְיִטַּע *and he will plant* to וְיֵטֶה *and he will pitch*), לקח *take* Ex

337 Jos 724 Jr 4929 (|| יְרִיעָה, כְּלִי *vessel*, צֹאן *flock*; + גָּמָל *camel*), נשׂא *carry* Nm 425, בוא hi. *bring* Ex 3933, עלה hi. *bring up* 1 K 84||2 C 55 (|| אֲרוֹן *ark*, כְּלִי), שׁכן hi. *cause to dwell* Jos 181, pi. Ps 7860 (unless em. שִׁכֵּן *he caused to dwell* to שָׁכַן *he dwelt*; || מִשְׁכָּן *tabernacle*).

קדשׁ pi. *consecrate* Ex 2944 (+ מִזְבֵּחַ *altar*, אַהֲרֹן *Aaron*, בֵּן *son*), משׁח *anoint* 3026, כפר pi. *atone for* Lv 1620 (|| קֹדֶשׁ *sanctuary*) 1633 (+ מִקְדַּשׁ הַקֹּדֶשׁ *holy sanctuary*; both || מִזְבֵּחַ), עבד *serve* Nm 815, משׁשׁ pi. *search* Gn 3134, ראה *see* Is 3320 Hb 37 (+ יְרִיעָה *curtain*), כסה pi. *cover* Ex 4034 (of cloud), אכל *consume* Jb 1534, נכה hi. *smite* 1 C 441, בלע *swallow* Dt 116 (|| בַּיִת *house*, יְקוּם *living being*), נכה hi. *strike* Jg 713 2 C 1414, הפך *overturn* trans. Jg 713 (+ לְמַעְלָה *upwards*), עזב *abandon* 2 K 77 (|| סוּס *horse*, חֲמוֹר *donkey*), נטשׁ *abandon* Ps 7860, ישׁע hi. *deliver* Zc 127.

<CSTR> אֹהֶל מוֹעֵד *tent of meeting* Ex 2721 2843 294+6t 3016.18.20.26.36 317 337.7 3521 388.30 3932 3940 402+8t Lv 11.3.5 32.8.13 44+7t 619.23 83.4.31.33.35 95 107.9 1514.29 167+5t 174.5.6.9 1921 243 Nm 11 37.8.25.25 43+15t 610.13.18 75.89 89+5t 103 1116 124 1410 1618.19 177.8.15.19 184+5t 206 256 3154 Dt 3114.14 Jos 181 1951 1 S 222 1 K 84||2 C 55 1 C 921 2 C 13.6.13 4QMMT A 234 ([אהל מועד]), אֹהֶל־מוֹעֵד Ex 406.29 Lv 69 126 1423 Nm 22.17 338 194 272 1 C 2332.

אֹהֶל הָעֵדֻת *tent of the testimony* Nm 915 (+ מִשְׁכָּן *tabernacle*) 1722.23 (הָעֵדוּת) 182 2 C 246 (הָעֵדוּת), בֵּיתִי *of my house* Ps 1323, ״ *of Y.* 1 K 228.29.30, בַּת־צִיּוֹן *of the daughter of Zion* Lm 24, צִיּוֹן *of Zion* 4Q372 113, לֵאָה *of Leah* Gn 3133.33, רָחֵל *of Rachel* 3133, יַעֲקֹב *of Jacob* 3133 (אֹהֶל־), יָעֵל *of Jael* Jg 417, דָּוִד *of David* Is 165.

אֹהֶל רֹעִים *tent of shepherds* Is 3812 (if em., see Adj.), מִשְׁכְּנוֹת *of the dwelling places of* the wicked Jb 2128, רְשָׁעִים *of wicked persons* 822, יְשָׁרִים *of upright persons* Pr 1411, אֹהֶל שְׁתֵּי הָאֲמָהֹת *tent of the two maidservants* Gn 3133, אָהֳלֵי הָאֲנָשִׁים הָרְשָׁעִים *tents of the wicked people* Nm 1626, צַדִּיקִים *of righteous persons* Ps 11815.

אָהֳלֵי מִקְנֶה *tents of cattle* Gn 420 (if em.; see above, §1b) 2 C 1414, רֶשַׁע *of wickedness* Ps 8411 (אָהֳלֵי־ || בֵּית *house*), שֹׁחַד *of bribery* Jb 1534 (אָהֳלֵי־), בטח *of safety* 1QH 123 ([ב]אהלי בט[ח]; or perh. [ב]אהלו בט[ח] dwell *in his* [Y.'s] *tent securely*), מות *of death* 4QapPsb 312, דומה *of silence* 4QWiles 17, אָהֳלֵי אַפַּדְנוֹ *tents of his palace* Dn 1145(L).

אָהֳלֵי שֵׁם *tents of Shem* Gn 927 (אָהֳלֵי־) 4QpGena 27, קֵדָר *of Kedar* Ps 1205 Ca 15 (|| יְרִיעָה *curtain*), חָם *of Ham* Ps 7851 (אָהֳלֵי־), כּוּשָׁן *of Cushan* Hb 37, יַעֲקֹב *of Jacob* Jr 3018 (יַעֲקוֹב; + מִשְׁכָּן *dwelling place*) Ml 212, יְהוּדָה *of Judah* Zc 127, אֱדוֹם *of Edom* Ps 837, אַבְרָהָם *Abraham* 4710 (if em. עַם אֱלֹהֵי *people of the God of* to עִם אָהֳלֵי *with the tents of*).

פֶּתַח הָאֹהֶל *entrance of the tent* Gn 181 (פֶּתַח־) 182.10 Ex 2636 339.10 3637 3938 Nm 125 Dt 3115 Jg 420, פֶּתַח אֹהֶל *entrance of (the) tent of* Ex 294.11.32.42 388.30 4012 Lv 13.5 32 44.7.18 83.4.31.33.35 107 126 1411.23 1514.29 167 174.5.6.9 1921 Nm 325 425 610.13.18 103 1618.19 1715 206 256 272 Jos 1951 1 S 222, פֶּתַח אָהֳלוֹ *entrance of his tent* Ex 338.10 Nm 1110.

יְתַד הָאֹהֶל *peg of the tent* Jg 421, מִכְסֶה *covering of* Ex 4019, חֲצַר אֹהֶל *court of (the) tent of* Lv 69.19, מְקוֹם אָהֳלֵךְ *place of your tent* Is 542 (+ מִשְׁכָּן *dwelling place*; מֵיתָר *cord*, יָתֵד *peg*), בֵּית־הָאֹהֶל *house of the tent* 1 C 923 (+ בֵּית־״ *house of Y.*), מִשְׁכַּן אֹהֶל *tabernacle of the tent of* Ex 3932 402.6 1 C 617 4QMMT A 234 ([משכן אהל]), רֹחַב הָאֹהֶל *width of the tent* Ezk 411 (or em. הָאַיִל *of the pillar*).

עֲבֹדַת הָאֹהֶל *service of the tent* Nm 184, עֲבֹדַת אֹהֶל *service of the tent of* Ex 3016 Nm 430 75 824 186.21.23, מִשְׁמֶרֶת *service of* 184 1 C 2332, מִשְׁמֶרֶת כָּל־הָאֹהֶל *service of all the tent* Nm 183, מְלֶאכֶת אֹהֶל *work of the tent of* Ex 3521, סֵתֶר אָהֳלוֹ *secret place of his tent* Ps 275 (+ סֻכָּה *shelter*, צוּר *rock*).

יֹשֵׁב אֹהֶל *one who dwells of*, i.e. in, *a tent* Gn 420 (or em.; see above, §1b), יְרִיעֹת הָאֹהֶל *curtains of the tent* Ex 2612.13, מְתֵי אָהֳלִי *men of my tent* Jb 3131, כְּלֵי אֹהֶל *vessels of the tent of* Nm 38, יֹשֵׁב אֹהָלִים *one who dwells of*, i.e. in, *tents* Gn 2527, פֶּתַח אָהֳלֵיהֶם *door of their tents* Nm 1627, יֹשֵׁב אָהֳלֵי *one who dwells of*, i.e. in, *tents of* Gn 420 (if em.; see above, §1b), שְׁבוּת אָהֳלֵי *restoration of the tents of* Jacob Jr 3018, שׁוֹכְנֵי אֹהָלִים *ones who dwell of*, i.e. in, *tents* Jg 811 (if em.; see below, Coll.), כָּל־הָאֹהֶל *all the tent* Gn 3134 Nm 183.

<APP> אָהֳלוֹ מִבְטַחוֹ *his tent, his security* Jb 1814, יְרוּשָׁלַםִ ... נָוֶה ... אֹהֶל *Jerusalem ... an abode ... a tent* Is 3320, perh. כָּל־הַכֵּלִים הָאֹהֶל *all the vessels (of* or *and) the* tent 1 K $7_{45(Kt)}$ (Qr הָאֵלֶּה *these* vessels).

<ADJ> רֹעִי *shepherd* (or em. רֹעִים tent of *shepherds*) Is 38_{12}, אֶחָד *one* 2 K 7_{8}, אַחֵר *another* 7_{8}.

<PREP> לְ of direction, *to*, + הלך *go* Dt 16_{7} Jos 22_{4} Jg 19_{9} 20_{8} 1 K 8_{66} 12_{16} 2 C 10_{16} 11QT 17_{9} ([לאוהלו]), שׁוב *go back* Dt 5_{30}, נוס *flee* 1 S 4_{10} 2 S 18_{17} 19_{9} (both + אִישׁ *each man*) 2 K 8_{21} 14_{12}||2 C 25_{22} (+ אִישׁ), פוץ *be scattered* 2 S 20_{22} (+ אִישׁ), without verb, אִישׁ לְאֹהָלֶיךָ יִשְׂרָאֵל *each one to your tents, Israel* 2 C 10_{16} (||1 K 12_{16} lacks אִישׁ), var. 2 S 20_{1}, חנה סָבִיב לְ *encamp around* Nm 2_{2} Jb 19_{12}, ישׁב מִחוּץ לְ *remain outside* Lv 14_{8} 4QMMT A 27_{5} ([י]שב מחוץ [לאוהלו]).

לְ of possession, *of, to* 1 C 9_{19} (+ סַף *threshold*) 9_{21} (+ פֶּתַח *entrance*) 2 C 1_{6}, of benefit, *for* Ex 39_{40}, + בוא hi. *bring* 2 C 24_{6}, כסה pi. *cover* Nm 9_{15}, עשׂה *do* Lv 16_{16}, *make* Ex 26_{7}||36_{14} (obj. יְרִיעָה *curtain*; + עַל־הַמִּשְׁכָּן *over the tabernacle*) 26_{14}||36_{19} (obj. מִכְסֶה *cover*), נטה לְ *pitch* 33_{7}, כסה לְ pi. *cover* Nm 9_{15}, קרא לְ *call*, i.e. name Ex 33_{7}.

בְּ of place, *in, at* Gn 18_{9} Ex 16_{16} Lv $4_{7.18}$ 16_{17} 24_{3} Nm 3_{25} 4_{4+6t} 18_{31} 19_{14} Jg 5_{24} 1 K 8_{4}||2 C 5_{5} Ho 9_{6} Ps 118_{15} Jb 20_{26} perh. 4QapLam[a] 2_{3} perh. 4Q458 1_{3}, + היה *be* Lv 16_{17} (+ כָּל־אָדָם *any person*), עשׂה *do* Nm 4_{3} (obj. מְלָאכָה *work*), עבד *serve* 4_{23} (obj. עֲבֹדָה *service*) $4_{37.41.43.47}$ $8_{19.22}$ (all three, obj. עֲבֹדָה), שׁרת pi. *serve* 8_{26}.

נתן *place* Ex 30_{36} 40_{22}, שׂים *place* $40_{24.26}$ 1 S 17_{54}, נוח hi. *place* Nm $17_{19.22}$, טמן pass. *be hidden* Jos $7_{21.22}$, מות *die* Nm 19_{14}, קרב *approach* Ps 91_{10}, בוא *come* Gn $31_{33.33.33.33}$ Ps 132_{3}, הלך htp. *go about* 2 S 7_{6}, יצב htp. *take one's stand* Dt $31_{14.14}$.

ישׁב *sit* Is 16_{5}, *dwell* 2 K 13_{5} Ps 69_{26} (+ היה *be*, טִירָה *encampment*) Jr $35_{7.10}$ 1 C 5_{10}, hi. *cause to dwell* Ho 12_{10}, שׁכן *dwell* (see also Coll.) Gn 9_{27} Jb 18_{15} (+ נָוֶה *abode*) 4QWiles 1_{7} (ות[ש]כון) 4QpGen[a] 2_{7}, hi. *cause to dwell* Jb 11_{14} Ps 78_{55}, דור *dwell* 84_{11}, נוח *rest* 1QH $12_{3(Licht)}$ ([אנוחה לי ב]אלהי), גור *sojourn* Ps 15_{1} (+ הַר *mountain*) 61_{5} (+ סֵתֶר *secret place*).

שׁאר ni. *remain* Jr 37_{10} (+ אִישׁ *each person*), חשׁך *be dark* Jb 18_{6}, רעה *feed* intrans. 20_{26}, נכה hi. *strike* Ps 78_{51}, שׂמח *rejoice* Dt 33_{18} (unless em. וְיִשָּׂשכָר *and Issachar* to וְשִׂישׂ יִשָּׂשכָר *and rejoice, Issachar*), שׂישׂ *rejoice* 33_{18} (if em.; see above), ערך *arrange* Ex 27_{21} Lv 24_{3}, זבח *sacrifice* Ps 27_{6}, דבר pi. *speak* Nm 1_{1}, ראה ni. *appear* 14_{10} Dt 31_{15}, שׁפך *pour out (upon)* La 2_{4}, רגן ni. *murmur* Dt 1_{27} Ps 106_{25} CD 3_{8}, מאס בְּ *reject* Ps 78_{67} (|| שֵׁבֶט *tribe*).

כְּ *as* Is 38_{12} (+ דּוֹר *dwelling place*) 40_{22} (+ לָשָׁבֶת *for dwelling*; || דֹּק *curtain*), שְׁחוֹרָה אֲנִי וְנָאוָה ... כְּאָהֳלֵי קֵדָר *I am dark and lovely ... as the tents of Kedar* Ca 1_{5}.

מִן of place, *from*, + יצא *go out* Gn 31_{33}, hi. *bring out* 4Q251 2_{4} ([יוציא]), נסע *set out* Jos 3_{14}, עלה hi. *bring up* 4QapPs[b] 31_{2}, לקח *take* 1 K 13_{9}, רחק hi. *remove* Jb 22_{23}, גלה hi. *send into exile* CD 7_{15} (מאהלי דמשק *from my tent [to] Damascus*; = Am 5_{27} מֵהָלְאָה לְדַמָּשֶׂק *beyond Damascus*), כרת hi. *cut off* Ml 2_{12}, נסח *tear out* Ps 52_{7}, נתק ni. *be torn* Jb 18_{14}, שׁגח hi. *gaze* Si 50_{5} (+ בית הפרכת *house of the veil*, i.e. tabernacle), דבר pi. *speak* Lv 1_{1}, וָאֶהְיֶה מֵאֹהֶל אֶל־אֹהֶל *and I have been from tent to tent* 1 C 17_{5} (or em. וָאֶהְיֶה מִתְהַלֵּךְ *I have been moving about* from tent to tent; || מִשְׁכָּן *tabernacle*).

אֶל of direction, *to, into*, + לקח *take* Nm 11_{16}, קרב *approach* 18_{22}, הלך *go* Jos 22_{6}, בוא *come* Ex 28_{43} 29_{30} 30_{20}=40_{32} 40_{35} Lv 9_{23} 10_{9} 16_{23} Nm 7_{89} 17_{23} 19_{14} 1 K 2_{30} 2 K $7_{8.8}$, hi. *bring* Lv $4_{5.16}$ Nm 31_{54}, ho. *be brought* Lv 6_{23}, יצא *go out* Ex $33_{7.8}$ Nm 12_{4}, שׁוב *go back* Jos 22_{8}, נוס *flee* Jg 4_{17} 1 K $2_{28.29}$, שׁלח pi. *send* Jos 22_{7} Jg 7_{8} 2 C 7_{10}, פנה *turn* intrans. Nm 17_{7}.

לקח אֶל־פְּנֵי *take before* Lv 9_{5}, בוא אֶל־פְּנֵי *come before* Nm 17_{8}, כפל אֶל־מוּל פְּנֵי *fold* curtain *at the front of* Ex 26_{9}, הזה אֶל־נֹכַח פְּנֵי *sprinkle* blood *before the front of* Nm 19_{4} 4QToh B[a] $_{5}$ ([א]ל נכח א[ו]הל).

עַל *upon* Jb 29_{4} (עָלֵי), + נזה hi. *sprinkle upon* Nm 19_{18}; מֵעַל *from upon*, + עלה ni. *be taken up* Nm 9_{17}, סור *depart* 12_{10} 16_{26}, גדף עַל pi. *revile agsinst* 4Q372 1_{13}; מִתּוֹךְ *from inside*, + לקח *take* Jos 7_{23}, מושׁ hi. *depart* Ex 33_{11}; בְּתוֹךְ *inside*, + גלה htp. *lie uncovered* Gn 9_{21}, טמן pass. *be hidden* Jos 7_{21}, יצג hi. *place* ark 2 S 6_{17}||1 C 16_{1}.

שׁכן עִם *dwell with* Ps 120_{5}, אסף עִם ni. *be gathered with* 47_{10} (if em. עַם אֱלֹהֵי *people of the God of* to עִם אָהֳלֵי *with the tents of*); בוא עַד *come to* Jg 7_{13}; לִפְנֵי *before* Nm 18_{2}, + שׁמר *keep* charge 3_{7}, קרב hi. *bring near* Ex 29_{10} Nm 8_{9}, בוא hi. *bring* Lv 4_{14}, שׁרת pi. *serve* Nm 18_{2}, שׁחט *slaughter* Lv $3_{8.13}$, חנה *encamp* Nm 3_{38} (+

מִשְׁכָּן *tabernacle*); בוא מִלִּפְנֵי *come from before* 2 C 1_{13}.

וְנָתַתָּ ... בֵּין־אֹהֶל מוֹעֵד וּבֵין הַמִּזְבֵּחַ *and you will place ... between the tent of meeting and the altar* Ex 30_{18} $40_{7.30}$ (וַיָּשֶׂם *and he placed*); עמד סְבִיבֹת hi. *position* elders *around* Nm 11_{24}.

ה of direction, הָאֹהֱלָה *to the tent*, + מהר pi. *hurry* Gn 18_{6}, בוא *come* Ex 18_{7} $33_{8.9}$, hi. *bring* Gn 24_{67}, יצא *go out* Nm 11_{26}, רוץ *run* Jos 7_{22}, סור *turn* intrans. Jg 4_{18}.

<COLL> הַשְּׁכוּנֵי בָאֳהָלִים appar. *those who dwell in tents* Jg 8_{11} (or em. שֹׁכְנֵי אֹהָלִים *dwellers of*, i.e. in, *tents*), אֹהֶל שָׁכַן בָּאָדָם *a tent [in which] he dwelt among people* Ps 78_{60} (if em.; see Obj.), הָאֹהֱלָה שָׂרָה אִמּוֹ appar. *to the tent (of) Sarah, his mother* Gn 24_{67} (or del. שָׂרָה אִמּוֹ).

Also Arad ost. 15_{5} ([א]הל).

<SYN> §1 בַּיִת *house*, נָוֶה *abode*, מִשְׁכָּן *dwelling place*, יְרִיעָה *curtain*, צֹאן *flock*; §2 מִשְׁכָּן *tabernacle*, מִזְבֵּחַ *altar*, §§1–2 כְּלִי *vessel*.

→ אהל *pitch tent*.

אֹהֶל II 1.0.0.1 pr.n.m. **Ohel**—I אוהל—**1.** son of Zerubbabel, 1 C 3_{20}. **2.** father of Elikam (אליקם), Seal 829_{2} (אוהל; City of David, 7th/6th cent.).

→ אהל *pitch tent*.

[אָהָל] 4 n.[m]. **aloe**—pl. אֲהָלִים, אֲהָלוֹת—**aloe, aloe wood,** used to perfume clothes, bed, etc., perh. *aloexylon agallochum* or *aquilaria agallocha*, <NOM CL> אֲהָלוֹת ... כָּל־בִּגְדֹתֶיךָ *all your garments are ... aloes* Ps 45_{9} (|| קְצִיעָה *cassia*, מֹר *myrrh*).

<OBJ> נטע *plant* Nm 24_{6} (or em. אֵילִים *terebinths* or אַלּוֹנִים *oaks*; || אֶרֶז *cedar*), נוף *sprinkle* Pr 7_{17} (as second obj.; + מִשְׁכָּב *bed*; || מֹר *myrrh*, קִנָּמוֹן *cinnamon*).

<CSTR> אֲהָלוֹת קְצִיעוֹת perh. *aloes of cassia* Ps 45_{9} (but prob. *aloes [and] cassia*, as nom. cl.; mss וּקְצִיעוֹת); מֹר אֲהָלִים perh. *myrrh of aloes* Pr 7_{17} (but prob. *myrrh [and] aloes*, as obj.; or em. וַאֲהָלִים).

<APP> פְּרִי מְגָדִים ... אֲהָלוֹת *choicest fruit ... aloes* Ca 4_{14} (|| מֹר *myrrh*, + קִנָּמוֹן *cinnamon*, נֵרְדְּ *nard*, כֹּפֶר *henna*, כַּרְכֹּם *saffron*, קָנֶה fragrant *reed*, לְבוֹנָה *frankincense*).

<PREP> כְּ + נטה *plant* Israel's tents *as* Nm 24_{6}; פַּרְדֵּס עִם *orchard with, containing* Ca 4_{14}.

<SYN> מֹר *myrrh*.

אָהֳלָה 5 pr.n.f. **Oholah,** Samaria as adulterous wife of Y., elder sister of Oholibah, i.e. Jerusalem, Ezk $23_{4.4.5.36.44}$.

→ אהל *pitch tent*.

אֳהָלוֹת, see אָהָל.

אָהֳלִיאָב 5 pr.n.m. **Oholiab,** chief assistant of Bezalel in construction of tabernacle, etc., son of Ahisamach, descendant of Dan, Ex 31_{6} 35_{34} $36_{1.2}$ 38_{23}.

→ אהל *pitch tent* + אָב *father*.

אָהֳלִיבָה 6 pr.n.f. **Oholibah,** Jerusalem as adulterous wife of Y., younger sister of Oholah, i.e. Samaria, Ezk $23_{4.4.11.22.36.44}$.

→ אהל *pitch tent*.

אָהֳלִיבָמָה 8 pr.n.f. and m. **Oholibamah, 1.** wife of Esau, Gn $36_{2.5.14.18.18.25}$. **2.** Edomite tribal chief, Gn 36_{41}||1 C 1_{52}.

→ אהל *pitch tent*.

אֲהָלִים, see אָהָל.

אַהֲרֹן 347.5.38 pr.n.m. **Aaron**—Q אהרון—**1.** priest, spokesman for Moses, son of Amram and Jochebed, brother of Moses and Miriam, husband of Elisheba, father of Nadab, Abihu, Eleazar and Ithamar, Ex $4_{27.28.30}$ 6_{23} $7_{7.9.19}$ $8_{1.2.12.13}$ $16_{9.10.33.34}$ 18_{12} 28_{1+8t} $29_{5.26.29}$ $30_{7.8.10}$ 32_{1+8t} $34_{30.31}$ 39_{1} 40_{13} Lv $8_{12.23}$ $9_{7.8.21.22}$ $10_{3.4.8.19}$ 16_{3+6t} 21_{17} 24_{3} Nm $8_{2.3.11.21.21}$ $12_{10.11}$ 16_{11} $17_{11.12.15.18}$ $18_{1.8.20}$ 20_{24+6t} 26_{60} 33_{39} Dt $9_{20.20}$ 10_{6} Ps 133_{2} 1 C 12_{28} 23_{13} 27_{17} Si $45_{6.20}$ 4QApocMos B 1.2_{6} (אה[ר]ון).

<CSTR> בֶּן־אַהֲרֹן *son of Aaron* Ex 6_{25} 38_{21} Nm 3_{32} $4_{16.28.33}$ 7_{8} 17_{2} $25_{7.11}$ 26_{1} Jos 24_{33} Jg 20_{28} Ezr 7_{5} 1QapMoses 1_{3} (ב[ן] אהר[ו]ן), *descendant of Aaron* Ne 10_{39}, בְּנֵי(־)אַהֲרֹן *sons of Aaron* Ex $28_{1.40}$ $8_{13.24}$ $9_{9.12.18}$ $10_{1.16}$ 16_{1} Nm $3_{2.3}$ 10_{8} 1 C 5_{29} 6_{35} 24_{1} 1QM 17_{2}, *descendants of Aaron* Lv $1_{5.7.8.11}$ 2_{2} $3_{2.5.8.13}$ $6_{7.11}$ (+ כָּל־זָכָר בְּ

every male among) 7$_{10.33}$ 21$_1$ (in all fourteen perh. בְּנֵי = *sons of)* Jos 21$_{4.10.13.19}$ Ne 12$_{47}$ 1 C 6$_{39.42}$ 15$_4$ 23$_{28.32}$ 24$_{1.31}$ 2 C 13$_{9.10}$ 26$_{18}$ 29$_{21}$ 31$_{19}$ 35$_{14.14}$ Si 50$_{13.16}$ 11QT 22$_5$ + Sup 34$_{13}$ 44$_5$ 1QS 5$_{21}$ 9$_7$ 1QSa 1$_{16}$ ([אהר]ון) 1$_{23}$ 2$_{13(Barthélemy)}$ ([בני]) 4QOrd^b 10.2$_8$ ([אהרו]ן) 1QM 7$_{10}$ 4QM fr. 3$_1$ ([אהרו]ן) 4QD^a$_{13}$ 5Q20 1$_2$ 4QpsMos^e 1$_2$ ([אהר]ון) 1$_3$ 4QMMT A 2$_{12}$ ([בני אהרו]ן) 2$_{17.86}$ 4QD^a 6.2$_{5.8.10}$ ([מבני]) 6.2$_{12}$ (+ עֲצַת *counsel of).*

אֲחוֹת אַהֲרֹן *sister of Aaron* Ex 15$_{20}$, דֹּד אַהֲרֹן *uncle of Aaron* Lv 10$_4$, זֶרַע אַהֲרֹן *offspring of Aaron* Lv 21$_{21}$ 22$_4$ Nm 17$_5$ 4Q251 3$_3$, בֵּית(־)אַהֲרֹן *house of Aaron* Ps 115$_{10.12}$ 118$_3$ 135$_{19}$, נחלת אהרן *inheritance of Aaron* Si 45$_{25}$, מַטֵּה(־)אַהֲרֹן *Aaron's rod* Ex 17$_{12}$ Nm 17$_{21.23.25}$, מטה לוי ואהרן *tribe of Levi and Aaron* CD 10$_5$.

<APP> אַהֲרֹן הַכֹּהֵן *Aaron the priest* Ex 31$_{10}$ 35$_{19}$ 38$_{21}$ 39$_{41}$ Lv 1$_7$ 7$_{34}$ 13$_2$ 21$_{21}$ Nm 3$_{6.32}$ 4$_{16.28.33}$ 7$_8$ 17$_2$ 18$_{28}$ 25$_{7.11}$26$_{1.64}$ 33$_{38}$ Jos 21$_{4.13}$ Ezr 7$_5$, אַהֲרֹן אָחִיךָ *Aaron your brother* Ex 4$_{14}$ 7$_{1.2}$ 28$_{1.2.4.41}$ Lv 16$_2$ Nm 20$_8$ 27$_{13}$ Dt 32$_{50}$ 11QT 44$_5$ (אחיכה), אַהֲרֹן אֲבִיהֶם *Aaron their father* Nm 3$_4$ 1 C 24$_{19}$.

<COLL> מֹשֶׁה וְאַהֲרֹן *Moses and Aaron* (and vars.) Ex 4$_{29}$ 5$_{1.4.20}$ 6$_{13.27}$ 7$_{6.8.10.20}$ 8$_{4.8.21}$ 9$_{8.27}$ 10$_{3.8.16}$ 11$_{10}$ 12$_{1.28.31.43.50}$ 16$_{2.6}$ 17$_{10}$ 24$_9$ 40$_{31}$ Lv 9$_{23}$ 11$_1$ 13$_1$ 14$_{33}$ 15$_1$ Nm 1$_{17.44}$ 2$_1$ 3$_{38.39}$ 4$_{1+6t}$ 8$_{20}$ 9$_6$ 12$_4$ 13$_{26}$ 14$_{2.5.26}$ 15$_{33}$ 16$_{3.18.20}$ 17$_{6.7.8}$ 19$_1$ 20$_{2.6.10.12.23}$ 26$_{9.64}$ 33$_1$ Jos 24$_5$ 1 S 12$_{6.8}$ Mc 6$_4$ Ps 77$_{21}$ 99$_6$ 105$_{26}$ 106$_{16}$ 6QD 3$_{1(Baillet)}$ ([משה ו]אהרון) CD 5$_{18}$, אַהֲרֹן וּמֹשֶׁה *Aaron and Moses* (and vars.) Ex 6$_{20.26}$ Nm 3$_1$ 26$_{59}$ 1 C 5$_{29}$ 23$_{13}$.

אַתָּה וְאַהֲרֹן *you and Aaron* Ex 19$_{24}$ 24$_1$ Nm 1$_3$ 16$_{17}$ 20$_8$, sim. 16$_{16}$, אַהֲרֹן וְחוּר *Aaron and Hur* Ex 17$_{10.12}$ 24$_{14}$, אַהֲרֹן וּמִרְיָם *Aaron and Miriam* (and vars.) Nm 12$_{4.5}$ Mc 6$_4$ 1 C 5$_{29}$, מִרְיָם וְאַהֲרֹן *Miriam and Aaron* Nm 12$_1$.

אַהֲרֹן וּבָנָיו *Aaron and his sons, descendants* (and vars.) Ex 27$_{21}$ 28$_{1.41.43}$ 29$_{4+13t}$ 30$_{19.30}$ 31$_{10}$ 39$_{27}$ 40$_{12.31}$ Lv 2$_{3.10}$ 6$_{2.9.13.18}$ 7$_{31.34.35}$ 8$_{2+10t}$ 9$_1$ 10$_{12}$ 17$_2$ 21$_{24}$ 22$_{2.18}$ 24$_9$ Nm 3$_{9.10.38.48.51}$ 4$_{5.15.19.27}$ 6$_{23}$ 8$_{13.19.22}$ 1 C 6$_{34}$.

2. as priestly community, descended from Aaron, CD 1$_7$ 6$_2$ (both ‖ יִשְׂרָאֵל *Israel*) perh. 4QM^g 1$_2$ ([אהרון]) Ketef Hinnom inscr. 1$_5$ ([לאה]רן; others [לאה]ביו/ [לאהב]י *to those who love him/me*), המתנדבים לקודש באהרון *those in Aaron who freely devote themselves to holiness* 1QS 5$_6$ (‖ יִשְׂרָאֵל), סוד קודש קודשים לאהרון *council of complete holiness for, or, consisting of, Aaron* 8$_6$, sim. 8$_9$ 9$_6$ (‖ יִשְׂרָאֵל), משיח אהרן *messiah of Aaron* CD 19$_{11(B)}$ 14$_{19}$ ([מש]יח), sim. 20$_{1(B)}$ 12$_{23}$ (משוח; all four ‖ יִשְׂרָאֵל), משיחי אהרון *messiahs of Aaron* 1QS 9$_{11}$ (‖ יִשְׂרָאֵל), שם ישראל ואהרון *the name of Israel and Aaron* 1QM 3$_{14}$, sim. 5$_1$ (+ לֵוִי *Levi*), [יש]ראל ואהרון *Israel and Aaron* 4QFlor 5$_2$.

Also 4QRitMar 2$_8$ ([א]הרון).

אוֹ 320.2.84 conj. **or, 1.** expressing alternatives, without clear preference for either, e.g. עַל־יָמִין אוֹ עַל־שְׂמֹאל *to the right or to the left* Gn 24$_{49}$, 24$_{50}$ 31$_{43}$ 44$_{8.19}$ Ex 4$_{11.11.11.11}$ 5$_3$ 19$_{13}$ 21$_{4+14t}$ 22$_{4+8t}$ 23$_4$ 28$_{43}$ 30$_{20}$ Lv 1$_{10.14}$ 3$_6$ 5$_{4+10t}$ 7$_{16.21.21}$ 11$_{32.32.32}$ 12$_{6.6}$ 12$_{7.8}$ 13$_{2+45t}$ 14$_{22.30.37}$ 15$_{3.14.25.29}$ 17$_{3.3.3.8.13}$ 18$_{9.9.10}$ 19$_{20}$ 20$_{17.27.27}$ 21$_{18+10t}$ 22$_{4.5.5}$ 22$_{21.21}$ 22$_{22+7t}$ 25$_{14.47.49.49.49}$ 26$_{41}$ (if em. אוֹ־אָז *or then* to וְאָז *and then)* 27$_{10}$ Nm 5$_{6.30}$ 6$_{2.10}$ 9$_{10+5t}$ 11$_8$ 14$_2$ 15$_{3+9t}$ 18$_{17}$ 19$_{16+5t}$ 22$_{18}$ 24$_{13}$ 30$_3$=11QT 53$_{16}$ Nm 30$_{7.11.15}$ 35$_{20.21.22.23}$ Dt 4$_{16.32.34}$ 13$_{2.2.4.6.7.7.7.7}$=11QT 54$_{8.8.11.15.19.19.20.20}$ Dt 13$_8$ 14$_{21}$ 15$_{12.21}$ 17$_{2.3.3.5}$=11QT 55$_{16.18.18.21}$ Dt 17$_{5.6.12}$=11QT 56$_9$ Dt 19$_{15}$=11QT 61$_7$ Dt 22$_1$=11QT 64$_{13}$ Dt 22$_{4.6.6.6}$=11QT 65$_{2.3.3}$ Dt 24$_3$ 24$_{14}$ 27$_{22}$ 29$_{17.17.17}$ Jos 7$_3$ Jg 11$_{34}$ 19$_{13}$ 21$_{22}$ 1 S 2$_{14.14.14}$ 13$_{19}$ 14$_6$ 20$_2$ 21$_{4.9}$ 22$_{15}$ 26$_{10.10}$ 2 S 2$_{21}$ 3$_{35}$ 17$_9$ 1 K 8$_{46}$‖2 C 6$_{36}$ 1 K 20$_{39}$ 2 K 2$_{16}$ 4$_{13}$ 13$_{19}$ Is 7$_{11}$ 27$_5$ Is 41$_{22}$ 50$_1$ Jr 23$_{33.33}$ 40$_5$ Ezk 21$_{15}$ (if em. אוֹ נָשִׂישׂ שֵׁבֶט בְּנִי מֹאֶסֶת *or shall we rejoice, rejecting [the] rod, my son* to אֵיךְ אֲשִׁיבֶנּוּ שֵׁבֶט מָאַסְתְּ *how shall I return it, [the] rod you have rejected,* or אֵין יְשִׁיבֶנּוּ *no one will return it)* 46$_{12}$ Am 3$_{12}$ Ml 2$_{17}$ Jb 3$_{15.16}$ 12$_8$ 13$_{22}$ 16$_3$ 22$_{11}$ (if em. אוֹ־חֹשֶׁךְ *or darkness* to אוֹר חָשַׁךְ *light has become darkness)* 35$_7$ 38$_5$ 38$_{6.28.31.36}$ Pr 30$_{31}$ 31$_{4(Kt)}$ (Qr אֵי *where?*; or em. אַוֵּה/אַוּוֹ *to desire* or רָוֹו/רְאוֹ *to drink heavily)* Ca 2$_7$=3$_5$ 2$_{9.17}$ 8$_{14}$ Si 13$_2$ 16$_{21}$ 11QT 20$_{10}$ 27$_7$ 48$_{17}$ 50$_{6.6.6}$ 52$_{10.10}$ 52$_{15}$ 53$_{10.17}$ 54$_{2.9(mg).19}$ 55$_{18}$ 64$_{13}$ 66$_{13.14.15.17}$ 1QS 5$_{25.26}$ 6$_{4.5}$ 6$_{16}$ 7$_{1.1(erased).1.5.25}$ 8$_{22}$ 1QSa 1$_{25.26}$ 2$_{5.6.6.6.6.7}$ 4QRitPur 40$_{2(mg)}$ 4QOrd^a 2$_1$ 1QM 7$_{4.4.4.4}$ CD 9$_{4.10}$ 11$_{3.4.23}$ 12$_{14.17}$ 4QD^a$_{6(mg).15}$ Mur 22 2$_{11}$ ([א]ו) Mur 30 1$_3$ ([א]ו) 2$_{14}$ 11QPs^a 22$_9$ 4Q525 3$_2$ ([או]) 6.10$_7$ (אוספיח *or what grows of itself)* 4QMMT A 2$_{82}$ 4Q251 2$_3$ 4$_3$ 7$_2$ ([או]) 4QToh A 1.1$_{4(mg)}$ 1.17$_8$ ([או]) 4QD^b$_3$ ([או]) 4Q376 1.3$_{2.2}$.

2. rather, or rather, expressing preference,

יָמִים אוֹ עָשׂוֹר *(a few) days or ten* Gn 24$_{55}$, 1 S 29$_{3}$.

3. אוֹ ... אוֹ **either ... or,** אוֹ רָאָה אוֹ יָדָע *whether he has seen or heard (it)* Lv 5$_{1}$, 5$_{2}$, perh. also, from §1, Lv 13$_{48.49.51.52.53.56.57.58.59}$.

4. אִם ... אוֹ **whether ... or,** אִם עַל־הַמִּשְׁכָּב הוּא אוֹ עַל־הַכְּלִי *whether it is upon the bed or upon the vessel* Lv 15$_{23}$.

5. הֲ ... אוֹ **is ... or?,** in disjunctive questions, הֲטוֹב ... אוֹ *is it better ... or?* Jg 18$_{19}$, 2 K 6$_{27}$ Ml 1$_{8}$ Ec 2$_{19}$ 11$_{6}$.

6. or if, introducing a sentence, esp. stating a particular case under a general principle, אוֹ־בֵן יִגָּח *or if he gore a son* Ex 21$_{31}$, 21$_{36}$ Lv 4$_{23.28}$ (if in both em. אוֹ[־]הוֹדַע *or if one makes known* to אִם הוֹדַע *if one makes known* or וְהוֹדַע *and one makes known*) 5$_{2.3.4.21.22}$ 13$_{16.24}$ 25$_{49}$ Nm 5$_{14}$ 15$_{6}$ 35$_{18}$ (MSS וְאִם *and if*) 2 S 18$_{13}$ 1 K 21$_{6}$ (אוֹ אִם *or if*) Ezk 14$_{17.19}$.

7. if (by chance), מִי יַגִּיד לִי אוֹ מַה־יַּעַנְךָ אָבִיךָ קָשָׁה *who will tell me if what your father answers you is harsh* 1 S 20$_{10}$ (or em. אוֹ מַה־ to אִם־ *if*).

8. unless, אֲצִיתֶנָּה יָּחַד׃ אוֹ יַחֲזֵק בְּמָעוּזִּי *I should burn her unless he take hold of my refuge* Is 27$_{5}$.

Also 4QToh A 3.1$_{3}$.

אוּאֵל 1 pr.n.m. **Uel,** one who divorced non-Israelite wife at time of Ezra, Ezr 10$_{34}$.

→ אוה *desire* + אֵל *God.*

אוֹב I $_{16.2}$ n.[m.] **ghost**—pl. אֹבוֹת (אֹבֹת)—**ghost,** in contexts of divination, but perh. sometimes (e.g. 1 S 28$_{3.9}$ 2 K 21$_{6}$||2 C 33$_{6}$) **medium, necromancer,** i.e. one who consults a ghost.

<SUBJ> היה *be* Lv 20$_{27}$ (|| יִדְּעֹנִי *wizard*), צפף pilp. *chirp* Is 8$_{19}$ (|| יִדְּעֹנִי), הגה hi. *mutter* 8$_{19}$.

<OBJ> שׁאל *ask* Dt 18$_{11}$||11QT 60$_{18}$ (|| יִדְּעֹנִי *familiar spirit*; + עבר hi. *make* child *pass* into fire, קסם *practice divination,* ענן po. *practice soothsaying,* נחשׁ pi. *practice divination,* כשׁף pi. *practice sorcery,* חבר *cast spell,* דרשׁ *inquire* of dead), עשׂה perh. *appoint* 2 K 21$_{6}$||2 C 33$_{6}$ (|| יִדְּעֹנִי; + עבר hi., ענן po., נחשׁ pi., כשׁף pi. [2 C only]), סור hi. *expel* 1 S 28$_{3}$ (|| יִדְּעֹנִי), כרת hi. *cut off* 28$_{9}$ (|| יִדְּעֹנִי), בער pi. *put away* 2 K 23$_{24}$ (|| יִדְּעֹנִי, תְּרָפִים *teraphim,* גִּלּוּל *idol,* שִׁקּוּץ *abomination*).

<CSTR> אֵשֶׁת בַּעֲלַת־אוֹב *a woman of a possessor,* i.e. that has control, *of a ghost* 1 S 28$_{7.7}$, כמשפט האוב *as the case of the ghost* CD 12$_{3}$ (|| יִדְּעֹנִי *familiar spirit*).

<PREP> קסם בְּ *practise divination by means of* 1 S 28$_{8}$, שׁאל בְּ *inquire of* 1 C 10$_{13}$ (+ לִדְרוֹשׁ *in order to seek [guidance]*); היה כְּ *be as* Is 29$_{4}$ (subj. קוֹל *voice*); פנה אֶל *turn to* Lv 19$_{31}$ 20$_{6}$ (both || יִדְּעֹנִי *familiar spirit*), דרשׁ אֶל *inquire of* Is 8$_{19}$ (|| יִדְּעֹנִי) 19$_{3}$ (|| אֱלִיל, יִדְּעֹנִי *idol,* אִטִּי *ghost*).

<SYN> יִדְּעֹנִי *familiar spirit.*

[אוֹב] II 1 n.m. **wineskin**—pl. אֹבוֹת—כְּאֹבוֹת ... בִּטְנִי חֲדָשִׁים יִבָּקֵעַ *my stomach ... would break out as (wine from) new wineskins* Jb 32$_{19}$ (+ יַיִן *wine*).

אוֹבִיל 1 pr.n.m. **Obil,** Ishmaelite keeper of David's camels, 1 C 27$_{30}$.

[אוּבָל] 3 n.[m.] **river**—אֻבָל; cstr. אוּבַל—**river, stream, canal,** or perh. **tower,** הָיִיתִי עַל־אוּבַל אוּלָי *I was by the River (of) Ulai* Dn 8$_{2}$, אַיִל ... עֹמֵד לִפְנֵי הָאֻבָל *ram ... standing before the river* 8$_{3.6}$.

אוגמן, see אַגְמוֹן.

אוּד 3 n.m. **firebrand**—pl. אוּדִים—<SUBJ> נצל ho. *be rescued* or *be snatched* from fire Am 4$_{11}$ Zc 3$_{2}$. <NOM CL> הֲלוֹא זֶה אוּד *is this not a firebrand?* Zc 3$_{2}$. <CSTR> עשן האוד *the smoke of a firebrand* 4QpPs^{a} 3$_{8(Allegro)}$, מִשְּׁנֵי זַנְבוֹת הָאוּדִים *from the two tails,* i.e. stumps, *of firebrands* Is 7$_{4}$. <ADJ> הָאוּדִים הָעֲשֵׁנִים הָאֵלֶּה *these smoking firebrands* Is 7$_{4}$. <PREP> היה כְּ *be as* Am 4$_{11}$.

[אוֹדָה] 11 n.f. **cause, matter**—pl. אֹדוֹת; cstr. אֹדוֹת (אוֹדֹת); sf. אֹדוֹתַי, אֹדוֹתֶיךָ—alw. עַל אוֹדֹת (and vars.). **1.** as prep., **a. about, concerning, with regard to,** וַיַּגִּדוּ לוֹ עַל־אֹדוֹת הַבְּאֵר *and they told him about the well* Gn 26$_{32}$, sim. 21$_{25}$ (+ יכח hi. *reprove* concerning), הַדָּבָר אֲשֶׁר־דִּבֶּר י׳ ... עַל אֹדוֹתַי וְעַל אֹדוֹתֶיךָ *the matter (about) which Y. spoke ... concerning me and concerning you* Jos 14$_{6}$, sim. Nm 12$_{1}$, וַתֹּאמֶר לוֹ עַל־אוֹדֹת הָרָעָה

הַגְּדוֹלָה הַזֹּאת *and she said to him, With regard to this greater evil* 2 S 13₁₆(mss) (L אַל־אוֹדֹת perh. *there is no cause*; or em. אַל־אָחִי *no, my brother*).

b. on account of, because of, כָּל־אֲשֶׁר עָשָׂה י׳ לְפַרְעֹה ... עַל אוֹדֹת יִשְׂרָאֵל *everything that Y. had done to Pharaoh ... on account of Israel* Ex 18₈, עַל אוֹדוֹת הָאֶשְׁכּוֹל אֲשֶׁר־כָּרְתוּ *because of the cluster (of grapes) that they had cut* Nm 13₂₄, הִנְּךָ מֵת עַל־אוֹדוֹת הָאִשָּׁה *behold, you will be dead because of the woman* Gn 20₃(Sam) (MT lacks אוֹדוֹת), וַיֵּרַע הַדָּבָר מְאֹד בְּעֵינֵי אַבְרָהָם עַל אוֹדֹת בְּנוֹ *and the matter was very bad in the eyes of Abraham, because of his son* 21₁₁ (unless, as §1a, *[that is, the matter] concerning his son*), זָעֲקוּ ... עַל אוֹדֹת מִדְיָן *they cried out ... because of Midian* Jg 6₇ (unless, as §1a, *concerning Midian*).

2. as conj., עַל־כָּל־אוֹדוֹת אֲשֶׁר **because,** נִאֲפָה ... שִׁלַּחְתִּיהָ *because she had fornicated so often ... I sent her away* Jr 3₈.

[אוֹדוֹת], see אוֹדָה.

[אוֹדֶם], see אֹדֶם.

אוֹדֹת, see אוֹדָה.

אוה I 26.3.7 vb. **desire—Pi.** Pf. אִוָּה, אִוְּתָה, 2ms Si איותה, Si אויתי (אִוִּתִיךָ, אִוִּתִיהָ); impf. 3fs תְּאַוֶּה; ptc. Si מאויה—**desire, yearn for.**

<SUBJ> Y. Ps 132₁₃ (|| בחר *choose*) 132₁₄, psalmist Is 26₉ (|| שׁחר pi. *seek*) Ps 119₃₀ (if em. שִׁוִּיתִי *I have set* to אִוִּיתִי *I have desired*) 1QH 15₂₃ ([אוי[תי]), בֵּן *son* Si 63₇, Ben Sira 30₁₅, נֶפֶשׁ *soul*, with ref. to Y. Jb 23₁₃, prophet Mc 7₁, Israelite Dt 12₂₀=11QT 53₂ ([א]ותה) Dt 14₂₆ 1 S 2₁₆ 4Q416 6₂, 'teacher' 1QS 10₁₉, רֹזֵן *governor* Pr 31₄ (if em. Kt או *or* to אַוֵּה), wicked person Pr 21₁₀, David 1 S 20₄ (if em. תֹּאמַר *says* to תְּאַוֶּה *desires*) 2 S 3₂₁, Jeroboam 1 K 11₃₇, subj. not specified Si 4₁₄ (if em. אלהו במא ויהא to אל אוהב מאויה *God loves those who desire her*).

<OBJ> Y. Is 26₉, Zion Ps 132₁₃.₁₄, בִּכּוּרָה *early fig* Mc 7₁, רַע *evil* Pr 21₁₀, חַיִּים *life*, i.e. health of body Si 30₁₅, הוֹן *wealth* 1QS 10₁₉, חָכְמָה *wisdom* Si 4₁₄ (if em.; see Subj.), מִשְׁפָּט *justice* Ps 119₃₀ (if em.; see Subj.), שֵׁכָר *beer* Pr 31₄ (if em.; see Subj.); obj. not specified Dt 14₂₆ 1 S 2₁₆ (both with ref. to food or drink) 2 S 3₂₁ 1 K 11₃₇ (both with ref. to rule of king) Jb 23₁₃ Si 63₇.

<PREP> בְּ of time, *at* Is 26₉ (+ לַיְלָה *night*); מִן of comparison, *(more) than* Si 30₁₅ (+ פָּז *gold*).

<COLL> נַפְשִׁי אִוִּיתִיךָ *I yearn for you with my soul* Is 26₉, נַפְשׁוֹ אִוְּתָה וַיָּעַשׂ *he* (Y.) *does what he desires* Jb 23₁₃, ואותה נפשכה כי תבוא *and your soul will desire that it should come* 4Q416 6₂; with infin. of אכל *eat* Dt 12₂₀ =11QT 53₂, בוא *enter* 1QH 15₂₃(Licht).

Htp. Pf. הִתְאַוָּה, הִתְאַוִּיתִי, הִתְאַוּוּ; impf. יִתְאַוֶּה, (יִתְאָו), 2ms תִּתְאַוֶּה, Q, Kt תתאו (Qr תִּתְאָיו); + waw וְהִתְאַוִּיתֶם; וַיִּתְאַוֶּה, וַיִּתְאָו, וַיִּתְאַוּוּ; ptc. מִתְאַוָּה, מִתְאַוִּים—**desire, crave.**

<SUBJ> אֲסַפְסֻף *rabble* Nm 11₄, עָם *people* 11₃₄, Israel Dt 5₂₁ (Sam חמד *desire*; || חמד), David 2 S 23₁₅||1 C 11₁₇, Jeremiah Jr 17₁₆, מֶלֶךְ *king* Ps 45₁₂, נֶפֶשׁ *soul* (perh. *appetite*) Pr 13₄ (or del. נַפְשׁוֹ *his soul* and em. מִתְאַוָּה *desiring* [fem.] to מִתְאַוֶּה [masc.] with עָצֵל *idle[r]* as subj.), עָצֵל *idle(r)* 13₄ (if em.) 21₂₆ (or em. הִתְאַוָּה תַאֲוָה lit. *he has desired* desire to הִתְאַוָּה עַוָּל/ רָשָׁע/אֱוִיל *[the] wicked one/evil one/fool has desired*), one who dines with a ruler 23₃, one who dines with a miser 23₆, wealthy person Ec 6₂, שׂכל hi. ptc. *teacher* 1QS 9₂₅; subj. not specified, Am 5₁₈ Pr 24₁ Si 16₁ 11QPsª 22₄ 4Q416 10.2₉.

<OBJ> תַּאֲוָה *desire* Nm 11₄ Ps 106₁₄ Pr 21₂₆ (unless em.; see Subj.), בַּיִת *house* Dt 5₂₁, שָׂדֶה *field* 5₂₁, עֶבֶד *male slave* 5₂₁, אָמָה *female slave* 5₂₁, שׁוֹר *ox* 5₂₁, חֲמוֹר *ass* 5₂₁, כֹּל *anything* belonging to neighbour 5₂₁, יוֹם *day* Jr 17₁₆ Am 5₁₈, יֳפִי *beauty* Ps 45₁₂, תֹּאַר *form* of worthless children Si 16₁, obj. not specified Nm 11₃₄ 2 S 23₁₅||1 C 11₁₇ Pr 13₄ Ec 6₂.

<PREP> לְ to express object Pr 23₃.₆ (both + מַטְעַם *delicacy*), 11QPsª 22₄ (+ יוֹם *day* of salvation); בְּ of place, *in* Ps 106₁₄ (+ מִדְבָּר *desert*), to express object 1QS 9₂₅ (+ כֹּל *anything* that Y. has not commanded).

<COLL> + infin. of היה *be* Pr 24₁; אל תתאו זולת נחלתכה *do not desire anything except your own inheritance* 4Q416 10.2₉.

→ אַוָּה *desire*, תַּאֲוָה *desire*, מַאֲוַי *desire*, אוּאֵל *Uel*.

אוה II 1 **mark out**—Htp. Pf. + waw וְהִתְאַוִּיתֶם—וְהִתְאַוִּיתֶם לָכֶם לִגְבוּל קֵדְמָה מֵחֲצַר עֵינָן שְׁפָמָה *and you shall mark out your eastern border from Hazar-enan to Shepham* Nm 34_{10} (or em. וְהִתְאִיתֶם or וְתֵאִיתֶם *and you shall mark out,* i.e. תאה *mark out*).

→ perh. אוֹת *sign.*

[אַוָּה] 7.0.1 n.f. **desire**—cstr. אַוַּת; sf. אַוָּתִי—usu. אַוַּת נֶפֶשׁ *desire of the soul,* i.e. one's own desire.

<NOM CL> אִם יֵשׁ אַוַּת־נַפְשְׁכֶם *if it is the desire of your soul* Gn 23_8 (if em. אֶת־נַפְשְׁכֶם), יֵלְכוּ ... אַוָּתָם *their inclination was ... that they should go* Ezk 10_{22} (if em. אוֹתָם), אֵין־אַוַּתְכֶם אֵלַי *your desire was not towards me* Hg 2_{17} (if em. אֶתְכֶם *you were*).

<OBJ> אַוָּתָם זָכָר *he* (avenger of blood) *remembers their desire* Ps 9_{13} (if em. אוֹתָם he remembers *them*). <CSTR> אַוַּת נַפְשְׁךָ *desire of your soul* Dt $12_{15.20.21}$ (נַפְשֶׁךָ) 1 S 23_{20}, נַפְשׁוֹ *of his soul* Dt 18_6=11QT 60_{13} Jr $2_{24(Kt)}$, נַפְשָׁהּ *of her soul* Jr $2_{24(Qr)}$; כָּל־אַוַּת *all the desire of* Dt $12_{15.20.21}$ (כֹּל) 18_6=11QT 60_{13} (כול) 1 S 23_{20}.

<PREP> לְכָל־אַוַּת נַפְשְׁךָ לָרֶדֶת רֵד *according to all your desire to come down, come down* 1 S 23_{20}; בְּכָל־אַוַּת נַפְשְׁךָ and vars., *as much as you desire, whenever you desire,* + זבח *sacrifice* Dt 12_{15}, אכל *eat* $12_{15.20.21}$, בוא *come* 18_6=11QT 60_{13}, בְּאַוַּת נַפְשָׁהּ שָׁאֲפָה רוּחַ (Kt נפשו) *in her* (wild ass's) *desire she sniffs the wind* Jr 2_{24} (+ תַּאֲנָה *time of heat*), בְּאַוָּתִי וְאֶסֳּרֵם *when I desire I will discipline them* Ho 10_{10} (or em. וּבָאתִי *I will come*).

→ אוה *desire.*

אוהל, see אֹהֶל II.

אוּזַי 1 pr.n.m. **Uzai,** father of Palal, who helped repair walls of Jerusalem, Ne 3_{25} (mss אוּרִי *Uri,* mss אוּזָל *Uzal*).

אוּזָל I 2 pr.n.m **Uzal,** son of Joktan, Gn 10_{27}‖1 C 1_{21} (Gn Sam איזל *Izal*). **2.** father of Palal, who helped repair walls of Jerusalem, Ne $3_{25(mss)}$ (L אוּזַי *Uzai*).

[אוּזָל] II pl.n. **Uzal,** perh. ident. with Izāl or Azāl (ancient Ṣan'a) in the Yemen, trading partner of Tyre, Ezk 27_{19} (if em. מְאוּזָּל *woven material*).

[אוט] 0.0.8 n.[m.] perh. **storehouse**—אוט; cstr. אוט; sf. אוטו (אוטהו), אוטכה—<NOM CL> בידכה אוטהו *in your hand is his storehouse* (+ טֶנֶא *basket*) 4Q416 5_{12}. <OBJ> מיד כול מֹשל *rule* 4Q416 9.2_7 ([מו]של אוטכה). <CSTR> מיד כול אוט אנשים *from (the hand of) every storehouse of human beings* 4Q416 5_2, מחסור אוטו *need of his storehouse* 5_{13} 9.2_1 (מחסורי), חכמת אוטו *wisdom of his storehouse* 9.2_{12}, חפצי אוט *delights of (the) storehouse* 6_5. <COLL> אוט לכול הולכי אדם perh. *a storehouse for all who go of,* i.e. among, *human beings* 4Q416 1_{16}.

אוטרפלוס 0.0.1 pr.n.m. **Eutrapelos,** father of Kleopos, signatory as vendor to deed of sale, Mur 29_2.

אוֹי 24.0.2 interj. **woe, 1.** as general expression of dismay, אוֹי מִי יִחְיֶה מִשֻּׂמוֹ אֵל *woe!, who will live when,* or *unless, God places,* i.e. allows, *it?* Nm 24_{23} (Sam יהיה *will be;* or em. מִשְּׁמְאֵל *from Shameal* or מִשְּׂמֹאל *from the north* or מִיִּשְׁמְעֵאל *from Ishmael*).

2. in lamenting one's own situation, אוֹי לִי *woe to me* (and vars.), i.e. Isaiah Is 6_5 (אוֹי־; 1QIsa[a] אילי in same sense; + כִּי *for*) 24_{16} (or em. אוֹי לַבֹּגְדִים *woe to the traitors*), Jeremiah Jr 10_{19} 15_{10} (אוֹי־), Baruch 45_3 (אוֹי־נָא לִי), Jerusalem 4_{13} (אוֹי לָנוּ) 4_{31} (אוֹי־נָא לִי) Lm 5_{16} (אוֹי־נָא לָנוּ; all five + כִּי) 4QapLam[a] 14 2_1, Philistines 1 S 4_7 (both + כִּי) 4_8 (all four אוֹי לָנוּ).

3. in announcing disaster for others, אוֹי עִיר הַדָּמִים *woe (to you), city of blood,* i.e. Jerusalem Ezk $24_{6.9}$; אוֹי־לָךְ *woe to you* (and vars.), i.e. Jerusalem Jr 13_{27} (אוֹי לָךְ; perh. ins. כִּי *for*) Ezk 16_{23} (אוֹי אוֹי לָךְ), Moab Nm 21_{29} Jr 48_{46} (+ כִּי), אוֹי לָהֶם *woe to them* (Ephraimites) Ho 7_{13} (+ כִּי) 9_{12}.

אוֹי לְנַפְשָׁם *woe to their* (Judah's and Jerusalem's) *soul* Is 3_9, אוֹי לְרָשָׁע *woe to a wicked one* 3_{11} (both + כִּי), אוֹי לַבֹּגְדִים *woe to the traitors* 24_{16} (if em.; see §2), לְמִי אוֹי *to whom is there,* i.e. to whom does one say, *Woe!?* Pr 23_{29} (+ אֲבוֹי *alas,* מִדְיָן *contention,* שִׂיחַ *complaint,* פֶּצַע *bruise,* חַכְלִלוּת *dullness* of eyes).

→ אוֹיָה *woe.*

אֱוִי 2 pr.n.m. **Evi,** ruler of Midian, Nm 31$_{8}$=Jos 13$_{21}$.

אוֹיֵב, see אֹיֵב.

אוֹיָה 1 interj. **woe,** אוֹיָה־לִי כִּי־גַרְתִּי מֶשֶׁךְ *woe to me, for I have sojourned (in) Meshech* Ps 120$_{5}$.

→ אוֹי *woe.*

אֱוִיל I 26.4.4 adj. **foolish**—cstr. אֱוִיל; pl. (אֱוִלִים) אֱוִילִים; cstr. Q אוילי—specif. in matters of speech (Pr 10$_{8.10}$ [unless em. in both; see Subj.] 10$_{14}$ 12$_{16}$ 14$_{3}$ 17$_{28}$ 20$_{3}$ 27$_{3}$ 29$_{9}$ Si 8$_{4}$), religion (Jr 4$_{22}$ Ho 9$_{7}$ Pr 14$_{9}$ 4QCat^{a} 9$_{7}$), morality and discipline (Is 35$_{8}$ Ps 107$_{17}$ [unless em.; see Subj.] Jb 5$_{2}$ Pr 1$_{7}$ 7$_{22}$ [unless em.; see Cstr.] 10$_{21}$ 15$_{5}$ Si 6$_{20}$ 34$_{7}$ 41$_{5}$).

1. as attributive adj., **foolish,** of אִישׁ *man* Pr 29$_{9}$ (unless del. אִישׁ) Si 8$_{4}$, נֶכֶד *descendants* 41$_{5}$.

2. usu. as predicative adj. or noun, **foolish (one), fool.**

<SUBJ> היה *be* CD 15$_{15}$ (|| שׁגע pu. ptc. *madman*), שׁרשׁ hi. *take root* Jb 5$_{3}$, חרשׁ *be silent* Pr 17$_{28}$, חשׁב ni. *be reckoned* wise 17$_{28}$, מות *die* 10$_{21}$ (+ צַדִּיק *righteous person*), ענה htp. *be oppressed* because of wickedness Ps 107$_{17}$ (or em. אֱוִלִים to אֻמְלָלִים *languishing* or חוֹלִים *sick*), שׁמד ni. *be destroyed* 4Q416 4$_{8}$, לבט ni. *be ruined* Pr 10$_{8}$ (or em. שְׂפָתַיִם יִלָּבֵט a fool of *lips will be ruined* to שְׁבָטִים יֵדַע *will know rods,* i.e. blows) 10$_{10}$ (or em. וּמוֹכִיחַ יַעֲשֶׂה שָׁלוֹם to אֱוִיל שְׂפָתַיִם יִלָּבֵט *and one who reproves will make peace*), גלע htp. *break out* in contention 20$_{3}$.

ידע *know* blows Pr 10$_{8}$ (if em.), hi. *make* anger *known* 12$_{16}$ (if em. יִוָּדַע *is known;* see Coll.), בזה *despise* wisdom and discipline 1$_{7}$, נאץ *despise* discipline 15$_{5}$ (Gnz pi.; + שֹׁמֵר תּוֹכַחַת *one who observes reproof*), ליץ *scorn* guilt offering 14$_{9}$ (or em. אֱוִלִים יָלִיץ to בְּבָתֵּי אֱוִילִים יָלִין *in the houses of fools* wickedness *passes the night;* + יָשָׁר *upright person*), תעה *err* Is 35$_{8}$ (+ טָמֵא *unclean one*).

<NOM CL> אֱוִיל הַנָּבִיא *the prophet is a fool* Ho 9$_{7}$ (|| שׁגע pu. ptc. *madman*), אֱוִיל עַמִּי *my people are fool(s)* Jr 4$_{22}$, עֶבֶד אֱוִיל לַחֲכַם־לֵב *a fool is a servant to the wise of heart* Pr 11$_{29}$, אֱוִלִים שָׂרֵי צֹעַן *the princes of Zoan are fools* Is 19$_{11}$.

<OBJ> ראה *see* Jb 5$_{3}$, כתשׁ *grind* in mortar Pr 27$_{22}$.

<CSTR> אֱוִיל שְׂפָתַיִם *one foolish of lips* Pr 10$_{8.10}$ (or em. in both; see Subj.), אוילי לב 4Q416 4$_{4.8}$ (+ בני עולה *children of iniquity*); דֶּרֶךְ אֱוִיל *way of a fool* Pr 12$_{15}$ (+ חָכָם *wise one*), פִּי־ *mouth of* 10$_{14}$ (+ חָכָם) 14$_{3}$ (:: חָכָם), כַּעַס *anger of* 27$_{3}$, מוּסַר *correction of* 7$_{22}$ (or em. מוֹסֵר אֱיָל *a deer* enters *a trap*) 16$_{22}$ (אֱוִלִים), זִמַּת *devising of* 24$_{9}$ (if em. אִוֶּלֶת *folly*), בָּתֵּי אֱוִילִים *houses of fools* 14$_{9}$ (if em.; see Subj.), כָּל־אֱוִיל *every fool* 20$_{3}$.

<PREP> הרג לְ *kill* Jb 5$_{2}$ (|| פתה ptc. *simple person*), עקובה היא לאויל *it is difficult for the fool* Si 6$_{20}$ (+ חסר לב *one lacking intelligence*), תקלה הוא לאויל *it is an obstacle for the fool* 34$_{7}$ (+ פתה), רָאמוֹת לֶאֱוִיל חָכְמוֹת *wisdom is (as) corals,* i.e. unattainable treasure, *to a fool* Pr 24$_{7}$ (unless רָאמוֹת = רָמוֹת too *high* for; or em. דּוּמַת *[if] you are silent* before).

שׁפט אֶת ni. *contend with* Pr 29$_{9}$ (del. אִישׁ *man*).

<COLL> אֱוִיל בַּיּוֹם יִוָּדַע כַּעְסוֹ *as for a fool, his anger is known on the (same) day* Pr 12$_{16}$ (or em. יוֹדַע *he makes known;* + עָרוּם *crafty one*), צדיק ורשע אויל ופת[י] *(the) righteous and (the) wicked, (the) fool and (the) simple* 4QCat^{a} 7$_{16}$.

<SYN> שׁגע pu. ptc. *madman,* פתה ptc. *simple person.*

<ANT> חָכָם *wise (one).*

→ אֱוִלִי *foolish,* אִוֶּלֶת *folly.*

[אֱוִיל] II, see אַיִל I, §2, Obj.

אֱוִיל מְרֹדַךְ 2 pr.n.m. **Evil-merodach,** king of Babylon who released Jehoiachin from prison, 2 K 25$_{27}$||Jr 52$_{31}$.

[אוּל] I 1 n.[m.] **body**—sf. אוּלָם—**body** or perh. **belly,** וּבָרִיא אוּלָם *and fat is their body* Ps 73$_{4}$ (or em. לְמוֹתָם *for their death* to לָמוֹ תָּם *for them; sound* and fat).

Also perh. 4QTanḥ 14$_{4(mg)}$ (אולנו).

[אוּל] II, see אַיִל I, §2, Obj.

אֱוִלִי 1 adj. **foolish,** כְּלִי רֹעֶה אֱוִלִי *implement of a foolish shepherd* Zc 11$_{15}$, רֹעִי הָאֱוִלִי עֹזְבִי הַצֹּאן *my foolish* *shepherd, who abandons the flock* 11_{17} (if em. רֹעִי הָאֱלִיל *the shepherd of worthlessness*).

→ אֱוִיל *foolish*.

אוּלַי I $_{45}$ adv. **perhaps**—אֻלַי—**1. perhaps, it may be that,** also, in question or statement understood as question (e.g. Gn $18_{24.28.29.30.31.32}$ $24_{5.39}$), **supposing that, what if?, a.** with impf., חיה pi. *let live* 1 K 20_{31}, חנן *be merciful (to)* Am 5_{15}, כפר pi. *atone* Ex 32_{30}, ישׁר *be right* in God's eyes Nm 23_{27}, יכל *be able* 22_{11} Is 47_{12}, *prevail* Nm 22_{6}, עשׂה *do*, i.e. work, perform 1 S 14_{6} 2 S 14_{15}, קרה ni. *do by chance* Nm 23_{3}, הלך *go* Gn 24_{39} (אֻלַי), שׁוב *go back* Jr 26_{3}, נפל *fall*, i.e. be presented 36_{7}, נשׂא *raise* face Gn 32_{21}, קלל hi. *lighten* hand 1 S 6_{5}, ערץ *terrify* Is 47_{12}, חטא *sin* Jb 1_{5}.

אבה *desire* Gn 24_{5}, עשׁת htp. *think* Jon 1_{6}, ראה *see* 2 S 16_{12} Ezk 12_{3}, שׁמע *hear* 2 K 19_{4}||Is 37_{4} (but perh. אוּלַי = *if* Y. hears, then he will reprove, as §2) Jr 26_{3} 36_{3}, משׁשׁ *feel* Jacob Gn 27_{12}, נגד hi. *tell* direction 1 S 9_{6}, חסר *lack* Gn 18_{28}, מצא *find* 1 K 18_{5}, ni. *be found* Gn $18_{29.30.31.32}$, בנה ni. *be built* 16_{2}, פתה pu. *be enticed* Jr 20_{10}, רפא ni. *be healed* 51_{8}, סתר ni. *be hidden* Zp 2_{3}.

b. with pf., ישׁן *sleep* 1 K 18_{27}.

c. with ptc., ישׁב *dwell* Jos 9_{7} (but perh. אוּלַי = *if* you dwell among us, how can we make a covenant with you?, as §2).

d. in nom. cl., אוּלַי מִשְׁגֶּה הוּא *perhaps it was a mistake* Gn 43_{12}, אוּלַי יֵשׁ חֲמִשִּׁים צַדִּיקִם *supposing there are fifty righteous individuals* 18_{24}, אוּלַי יֵשׁ תִּקְוָה *perhaps there is hope* Lm 3_{29}.

2. if (but at Jr 21_{2} Ho 8_{7} perh. אוּלַי = *supposing that,* as §1), אוּלַי י׳ אוֹתִי וְהוֹרַשְׁתִּים *if Y. is with me I shall dispossess them* Jos 14_{12}, אוּלַי יַעֲשֶׂה י׳ אוֹתָנוּ ... וְיַעֲלֶה מֵעָלֵינוּ *if Y. deals* miraculously *with us ... he* (Nebuchadrezzar) *will go up (away) from us* Jr 21_{2}, אוּלַי יַעֲשֶׂה זָרִים יִבְלָעֻהוּ *if it yields, strangers will swallow it* Ho 8_{7} (or em. תַּעֲשֶׂהוּ *it yields it*).

3. unless, אוּלַי נָטְתָה ... אַתְּכָה הָרַגְתִּי *unless she had turned aside ... I would have killed you* Nm 22_{33} (or em. וְלוּלֵי *and unless*).

[אוּלַי] II $_{2}$ pl.n. **Ulai**—אוּלָי—river in Elam, mod. R. Kārūn, Dn $8_{2.16}$.

אוּלָם I $_{19.1}$ conj. **however, although,** perh. also **(but) indeed** (e.g. Ex 9_{16} Jb 5_{8} 13_{3} 14_{18} 33_{1}), usu. וְאוּלָם (except Jb 2_{5} 5_{8} 13_{3} Si $44_{10[M]}$).

a. with nom. cl., וְאוּלָם לוּז שֵׁם־הָעִיר לָרִאשֹׁנָה *but Luz was the name of the city at first* Gn 28_{19}, sim. Jg 18_{29}, וְאוּלָם אַתֶּם טֹפְלֵי־שָׁקֶר *but you are smearers of deceit* Jb 13_{4}, ואולם אלה אנשי חסד *but these were loyal people* Si $44_{10(B)}$ (M אולם).

b. with verb, גדל *be great* Gn 48_{19}, מלא *be full* Mc 3_{8}, נבל *be worn out* Jb 14_{18} (or em. הַר־נוֹפֵל יִבּוֹל *a falling mountain will be worn out* to הַר־נָפוֹל יִפּוֹל *a mountain will gradually fall*), לחם ni. *fight* 1 K 20_{23}, שׁוב *go back* Jb 17_{10}, נפל *fall* 14_{18} (if em.), עמד hi. *raise* Ex 9_{16}, שׁלח *send*, i.e. extend hand Jb 1_{11} 2_{5}, דרשׁ *seek* 5_{8}, שׁאל *ask* 12_{7}, דבר pi. *speak* 13_{3}, שׁמע *hear* 33_{1}.

c. before oath, wish, חַי־אָנִי *as I live* Nm 14_{21}, חַי־י׳ *as Y. lives* 1 S 20_{3} 25_{34}, מִי־יִתֵּן *if only* Jb 11_{5}.

אוּלָם II $_{49.0.4}$ n.m. **porch**—אֻלָם; cstr. אוּלָם (אֻלָם); sf. Kt אלמו (אֵילַמּו); pl. אֻלַמּוֹת; cstr. אֻלַמֵּי (Q אוּלמי); sf. Qr אֵלַמָּיו (אֵילַמָּיו) (forms in Ezk 40_{16-36} as if from אֵילָם)—**porch, hall, portico, 1.** of temple of Solomon, <NOM CL> הָאוּלָם (אֲשֶׁר) עַל־פְּנֵי הֵיכַל הַבַּיִת *the porch (which was) in front of the hall of the house* 1 K 6_{3}||2 C 3_{4} (if em. עַל־פְּנֵי הָאֹרֶךְ *in front of the length* to עַל־פְּנֵי הֵיכַל הַבַּיִת ... הָאֹרֶךְ *in front of the hall of the house ... the length*).

<CSTR> אֻלָם הַהֵיכָל *porch of the temple* 1 K 7_{21}, הַבָּיִת *of the house* 7_{12}, י׳ *of Y.* 2 C 15_{8} 29_{17} (both אוּלָם); תַּבְנִית הָאוּלָם *plan of the porch* 1 C 28_{11}, דַּלְתוֹת *doors of* 2 C 29_{7}.

<PREP> לְ *(belonging) to* 1 K 7_{12}, קום לְ hi. *raise up* pillars *at* 7_{21}, בוא לְ *come to* 2 C 29_{17}; בְּ of place, *in* 1 K 7_{19} (ms כְּ *as*; or em. כֻּלָּם *all of them*), בֵּין *between* porch and altar Ezk 8_{16}, + בכה *weep* Jl 2_{17}, לִפְנֵי (of altar) *in front of* 2 C 15_{8}, + בנה *build* altar 8_{12}.

<COLL> וְהָאוּלָם ... עֶשְׂרִים אַמָּה אָרְכּוֹ ... עֶשֶׂר בָּאַמָּה רָחְבּוֹ *as for the porch ... its length was 20 cubits ... its width was ten cubits* 1 K 6_{3}, וְהָאוּלָם ... הָאֹרֶךְ ... אַמּוֹת עֶשְׂרִים וְהַגֹּבַהּ מֵאָה וְעֶשְׂרִים *as for the porch ... the length*

... was twenty cubits and the height was a hundred and twenty 2 C 3$_4$ (or ins. הָרֹחַב אַמּוֹת עֶשֶׂר the width was ten cubits after וְהָאוּלָם).

2. of temple in Ezekiel's vision, **<SUBJ>** היה *be* Ezk 40$_{21}$ (+ כְּ *as*; || אַיִל *pillar*), ספן pass. *be panelled* 41$_{16}$ (if em. הַסִּפִּים *the thresholds* to סְפֻנִים *were panelled*).

<NOM CL> אֻלָם שַׁעַר מֵהַבָּיִת *the porch of the gate was on the inside* Ezk 40$_9$, אֵלַמָּיו ... כְּמִדַּת הַשַּׁעַר *its porches ... were as the dimension of the gate* 40$_{22(Qr)}$ (|| חַלּוֹן *window*, תִּמֹרָה *palm-tree*), sim. 40$_{29.33}$ (both || אַיִל *pillar*, תָּא *chamber*), אֵ(י)לַמָּיו לִפְנֵיהֶם *its porches were in front of them* 40$_{22(Qr).26(Qr)}$, אֵלַמּוֹת סָבִיב סָבִיב *porches were all round* 40$_{30}$, אֵלַמָּיו אֶל־חָצֵר הַחִיצוֹנָה *its porches were towards*, i.e. faced, *the outer court* 40$_{31(Qr)}$, sim. 40$_{34.37}$ (if em. אֵילָיו *its pillars*).

<OBJ> מדד *measure* Ezk 40$_{8.9.9.24.36}$ (|| תָּא *chamber*, חַלּוֹן *window*; all three || אַיִל *pillar*) 41$_{15}$ (unless em.; see Subj.), בוא *enter* 11QT 4$_8$ (or em. ובתאה *and you shall enter* to ובניתה *and you shall build*).

<CSTR> אֻלָם הַבַּיִת *porch of the temple* Ezk 40$_{48}$, הַשַּׁעַר *of the gate* 40$_7$ (אולם) 40$_{8.9.9.14}$ (if em.; see Prep.) 40$_{15.38}$ (אולם; if em.; see Prep.) 40$_{39.40}$ 44$_3$ 46$_{2.8}$ (both אולם), אֵלַמֵּי הֶחָצֵר *porches of the court* 41$_{15}$ (or em. אֵלַמּוֹ הַחִצוֹן *its outer porch* or הָאֻלָם הַחִיצוֹן *the outer porch*); אֵל אֻלָם *pillar of (the) porch* 40$_{48}$ (or em. אֵיל־הָאֻלָם), אֹרֶךְ הָאֻלָם *length of the porch* 40$_{49}$, כִּתְפוֹת *sides of* 41$_{26}$ (הָאוּלָם), דֶּרֶךְ אוּלָם *way of porch of* gate 44$_3$ (אֻלָם) 46$_{2.8}$.

<ADJ> הָאֻלָם הַחִצוֹן *the outer porch* Ezk 41$_{15}$ (if em.; see Cstr.).

<PREP> חַלּוֹנוֹת לוֹ וּלְאֵ(י)לַמָּיו *there were windows for it and its porches* Ezk 40$_{25(Qr).29(Qr).33(Qr)}$, כֵּן לְאֵלַמּוֹ חַלּוֹנוֹת *likewise for its porch there were windows* 40$_{16}$ (if em. כֵּן אֵלַמּוֹת וְחַלּוֹנוֹת *likewise for the porches, and [there were] windows*), מִחוּצָה לְאוּלָם *on the outside of the porch* Ezk 40$_{40}$ (if em. עֹלֶה *one who goes up*).

בְּ of place, *in* Ezk 40$_{38}$ (if em. בְּאֵילִים הַשְּׁעָרִים *at the pillars, the gates* to בְּאוּלָם הַשַּׁעַר *in the porch of the gate*) 40$_{39}$; בוא אֶל hi. *bring to* Ezk 40$_{48}$; אֶל־פְּנֵי *in front of* Ezk 41$_{25}$; עַל־פְּנֵי *in front of* Ezk 40$_{14}$ (if em. וַיַּעַשׂ אֶת־אֵילִים *and he made [the] pillars* to עַל־פְּנֵי אֻלָם הַשַּׁעַר *and in front of the porch of the gate [were]*); עַל־לִפְנֵי *to the front of* Ezk 40$_{15}$ (mss עַד־לִפְנֵי *to the front of*); מֵאֵצֶל *beside* Ezk 40$_7$.

3. of heavenly temple, **<CSTR>** אולמי מבואיהם *porches of their entrances* 4QShirShab^{f} 14$_4$, sim. 14$_5$ 11QShirShab c$_2$ ([מ]בואי); [מו]צא אול[מי] *exit of the porches of* 11QShirShab k$_2$. **<PREP>** פתח בְּ pu. *be engraved on* 4QShirShab^{f} 14$_5$.

4. of palace of Solomon, **<NOM CL>** אוּלָם עַל־פְּנֵיהֶם וְעַמֻּדִים *there was a porch in front of them with pillars* 1 K 7$_6$.

<OBJ> עשׂה *make* 1 K 7$_{6.7.7}$.

<CSTR> אוּלָם הַכִּסֵּא *hall of the throne* 1 K 7$_7$, הַמִּשְׁפָּט *of judgment* 7$_7$ (אֻלָם), הָעַמּוּדִים *of the pillars* 7$_6$.

<PREP> מִבֵּית לְ *within* 1 K 7$_8$; כְּ *as* 7$_8$ (+ בַּיִת *house*).

אוּלָם III 4 pr.n.m. **Ulam, 1.** son of Peresh (or perh. of Sheresh) and father of Bedan, descendant of Manasseh, 1 C 7$_{16.17}$ **2.** son of Eshek and ancestor of famous archers, descendant of Benjamin, 1 C 8$_{39.40}$.

אִוֶּלֶת 25.5.5 n.f. **folly**—cstr. אִוֶּלֶת; sf. אִוַּלְתִּי, אִוַּלְתּוֹ—particularly associated with indiscipline (Pr 5$_{23}$ 22$_{15}$), shortness of temper (14$_{17.29}$ 1QS 4$_{10}$), and rashness of speech (Pr 12$_{23}$ 15$_2$ 18$_{13}$); contrasted with knowledge (Pr 14$_{18}$ 15$_{14}$), wisdom (14$_{1.8}$), and understanding (14$_{29}$ 15$_{21}$ 16$_{22}$); included among attributes of רוח עולה *spirit of iniquity* (1QS 4$_{10}$).

<SUBJ> הרס *tear down* Pr 14$_1$ (+ חַכְמוֹת נָשִׁים *wisest of women*), סלף pi. *ruin* 19$_3$, סור *depart* 27$_{22}$, קשׁר pass. *be bound* 22$_{15}$ (+ בְּלֶב־נַעַר *in the heart of a lad*).

<NOM CL> אִוֶּלֶת שִׂמְחָה *folly is a joy* Pr 15$_{21}$ (+ לַחֲסַר־לֵב *to one lacking in understanding*), אִוֶּלֶת כְּסִילִים מִרְמָה *the folly of fools is deception* 14$_8$, אִוֶּלֶת כְּסִילִים אִוֶּלֶת *the folly of fools is folly* 14$_{24}$ (:: עֹשֶׁר *wealth*), מוּסַר אֱוִלִים אִוֶּלֶת *the discipline of fools is folly* 16$_{22}$ (+ שֵׂכֶל *intelligence*), אִוֶּלֶת הִיא *it is folly* 18$_{13}$, אין שם לעו[ד] אולת *folly is never there* 1QMyst 1.1$_7$ (+ דֵּעָה *knowledge*).

<OBJ> רחק hi. *remove* Pr 22$_{15}$, פרשׂ *spread* 13$_{16}$ (+ כְּסִיל *fool*, עָרוּם *shrewd person*, דַּעַת *knowledge*), רום hi. *raise* 14$_{29}$ (+ תְּבוּנָה *understanding*, קְצַר־רוּחַ *short-tempered person*, אֶרֶךְ־אַפַּיִם *patient person*), נבע hi. *pour out* 15$_2$ (:: דַּעַת; + כְּסִיל, חָכָם *wise person*), צפן hi. *conceal* Si

41$_{15(B)}$ (:: חָכְמָה wisdom), טמן hi. *conceal* 41$_{15(M)}$ ([מטמ]ן :: חָכְמָה).

עשׂה *do* Pr 14$_{17}$ (+ קְצַר־אַפַּיִם *short-tempered person,* מְזִמָּה *intrigue*), קרא *proclaim* 12$_{23}$ (+ דַּעַת, עָרוּם, כְּסִיל), נחל *inherit* 14$_{18}$ (:: דַּעַת; + פֶּתִי *simple person,* עָרוּם), רעה *graze on* 15$_{14}$ (:: דַּעַת; + כְּסִיל, בין ni. ptc. *intelligent person*).

<CSTR> אִוֶּלֶת אָדָם *the folly of a human being* Pr 19$_3$, כְּסִילִים *of fools* 14$_8$ (:: חָכְמָה *wisdom;* + עָרוּם *shrewd person*), פנים *of face,* i.e. foolish appearance Si 20$_{22}$ (+ בֹּשֶׁת *shame*); זִמַּת אִוֶּלֶת *intrigue of folly* Pr 24$_9$, רֹב *greatness of* 5$_{23}$ (אִוַּלְתּוֹ; + אֵין מוּסָר *lack of discipline*) 1QS 4$_{10}$ (רוב), רחב *(one) broad of* Si 47$_{23}$ (:: בִּינָה *understanding*), דרכי *ways of* 4Q525 2$_2$.

<PREP> יָדַעְתָּ לְאִוַּלְתִּי *you know (of) my folly* Ps 69$_6$ (+ אַשְׁמָה *guilt*); בְּ of accompaniment, *in, with,* + הלך htp. *walk* 1QS 4$_{24}$ (:: חָכְמָה *wisdom*), עלה htp. *raise oneself up* Si 30$_{13(mg)}$, כְּסִיל בְּאִוַּלְתּוֹ *a fool in his folly* Pr 17$_{12}$, of instrument, *by, with,* + ספה ni. *be swept away* Si 8$_{15}$, ירשׁ hi. *dispossess* 20$_{22}$, לעב htp. *mock* 30$_{13}$ (יתלעבך; Segal, יתלע בך), כְּסִיל שׁוֹנֶה בְאִוַּלְתּוֹ *a fool repeats his folly* Pr 26$_{11}$ (|| קֵא *vomit*); ענה כְּ *answer* fool *according to* Pr 26$_{4.5}$; מִפְּנֵי *because of* Ps 38$_6$.

Also 1QH 13$_{6.7}$ (ואול[ת]).

<ANT> דַּעַת *knowledge,* חָכְמָה *wisdom.*

→ אֱוִיל *foolish,* אֱוִלִי *foolish.*

[אוֹם], see אם.

[אוֹמֶץ], see אֹמֶץ.

אוֹמָר 3 pr.n.m. **Omar,** Edomite tribal chief, son of Eliphaz, Gn 36$_{11}$||1 C 1$_{36}$ Gn 36$_{15}$.

אוֹמֶר, see אֹמֶר.

אָוֶן I 80.2.6 n.m. **iniquity, misfortune,**—sf. אוֹנְךָ, אוֹנִי, אוֹנוֹ, Q אונה, אוֹנָם; pl. Si אונים—(for Jb 18$_{7.12}$ Pr 11$_7$, see און *strength*) **1. misfortune, trouble.**

<SUBJ> יצא *go forth* Jb 5$_6$ (|| עָמָל *trouble*), אנה pu. *be sent* Pr 12$_{21}$ (|| רַע *harm*).

<NOM CL> וְאָוֶן וְעָמָל בְּקִרְבָּהּ *both misfortune and trouble are within it* Ps 55$_{11}$, רָהְבָּם עָמָל וָאָוֶן *their pride is toil and trouble* 90$_{10}$. <OBJ> נבט hi. *observe* Nm 23$_{21}$ (Sam עָוֹן *iniquity;* || עָמָל *trouble*), ראה hi. *show* Hb 1$_3$ (|| עָמָל), שׁמע hi. *proclaim* Jr 4$_{15}$, קצר *reap* Pr 22$_8$ (+ עַוְלָה *iniquity*), צפן *store* Jb 21$_{19}$, מוט hi. *drop* Ps 55$_4$.

<PREP> תַּחַת *under,* i.e. suffering Hb 3$_7$ (or em. תַּחַת אָוֶן *under misfortune* to תֵּחָתְאָנָה *shall be snatched away* or תְּחִתֶּין *shall be dismayed*).

2. iniquity, evil, sin, <NOM CL> תַּחַת לְשׁוֹנוֹ עָמָל וָאָוֶן *under his tongue are wrongdoing and sin* Ps 10$_7$, דִּבְרֵי־פִיו אָוֶן וּמִרְמָה *the words of his mouth are iniquity and deceit* 36$_4$, הֵן כֻּלָּם אָוֶן *behold, all of them are iniquity* Is 41$_{29}$ (or em. אַיִן *nothing*), אִם־גִּלְעָד אָוֶן *if (in) Gilead is iniquity* Ho 12$_{12}$ (+ שָׁוְא *falsehood*), אָוֶן וּתְרָפִים הַפְצַר *arrogance is (as) iniquity and teraphim* 1 S 15$_{23}$ (or em. עֲוֹן תְּרָפִים *the iniquity of* consulting *teraphim*).

<OBJ> ילד hi. *give birth* Is 59$_4$ Jb 15$_{35}$ (|| מִרְמָה *deceit;* both || עָמָל *trouble*), חבל pi. *conceive* Ps 7$_{15}$ (|| עָמָל, שֶׁקֶר *deceit*), חשׁב *plot* 1QIsa^a 32$_6$ (MT עשׂה *do*) Ezk 11$_2$ Mc 2$_1$ (both || רַע *evil*) Ps 36$_5$, בגד *treacherously plot* 59$_6$, חרשׁ *plough* Jb 4$_8$(|| עָמָל), קבץ *gather* Ps 41$_7$ (|| שָׁוְא *falsehood*), ראה *see* 66$_{18}$ Jb 11$_{11}$ (+ שָׁוְא), שׁקד *watch for* Is 29$_{20}$, יכל *endure* 1$_{13}$ (|| עֲצָרָה *assembly*), רחק hi. *put far away* Jb 11$_{14}$ (|| עַוְלָה *evil*), בלע pi. *swallow up* Pr 19$_{28}$, עשׂה *do* Is 32$_6$ (1QIsa^a חשׁב), פעל *do* Pr 30$_{20}$, דבר pi. *speak* Is 58$_9$ Zc 10$_2$ (|| שֶׁקֶר *deceit*) 1QS 11$_2$, ברך pi. *bless* Is 66$_3$ (perh. in concr. sense *idol*), שׁוב hi. *repay* Ps 94$_{23}$ Pr 20$_{26}$ (if em. אוֹפַן *wheel*), שׁלט hi. *give dominion* Ps 119$_{133}$.

<CSTR> אִישׁ אָוֶן *man of iniquity* Is 55$_7$ (+ רָשָׁע *wicked person*) Pr 6$_{12}$ (+ אָדָם בְּלִיַּעַל *worthless person*), שְׂפַת־ *lip of* 17$_4$ (|| הַוָּה *destruction*), [מ]קור *source of* 1QH fr. 12$_2$, משגת *error of* 4QFlor 1$_{9(Brooke)}$ (א[ו]נ[מה]), מְתֵי־ *men of* Jb 22$_{15}$, אַנְשֵׁי־ *men of* 34$_{36}$, בַּחוּרֵי *youths of* Ezk 30$_{17}$ (or em. און *On*), בעלי *lords of* 4Q416 5$_6$, חללי *slain ones of,* i.e. the wicked slain 1QM 6$_3$, מַעֲשֵׂי־ *deeds of* Is 59$_6$ (|| חָמָס *violence*), מַחְשְׁבוֹת *thoughts of* 59$_7$ (+ שֹׁד *devastation,* שֶׁבֶר *destruction*) Jr 4$_{14}$ (אוֹנֵךְ) Pr 6$_{18}$ (+ רָעָה *evil*) 4QFlor 1$_9$, חִקְקֵי־ *decrees of* Is 10$_1$ (|| עָמָל *trouble*).

<PREP> פלט עַל pi. *expel because of* Ps 56$_8$; שׁוב מִן *return from* Jb 36$_{10}$; כל מאונ(י)ם אל און(י)ם ישוב *everything* that comes *from sin will return to sin* Si 41$_{10(Bmg)}$

(B, M אפס אל אפס *nothing to nothing*); פנה אֶל *turn to* Jb 36$_{21}$ (:: עֳנִי *affliction*).

3. בֵּית אָוֶן **house of iniquity,** appar. as dysphemism for בֵּית אֵל *Bethel* (lit. *house of God*), and in contrast to pl.n. Beth-aven (Jos 7$_2$ 18$_{12}$ 1 S 13$_5$ 14$_{23}$), בֵּית־אֵל יִהְיֶה לְאָוֶן *the house of God will become (the house of) iniquity* Am 5$_5$ (+ גִּלְגָּל *Gilgal*), אַל־תַּעֲלוּ בֵּית אָוֶן *do not go up to the house of iniquity* Ho 4$_{15}$ (+ גִּלְגָּל), הָרִיעוּ בֵּית אָוֶן *shout out (at) the house of iniquity* 5$_8$ (+ גִּבְעָה *Gibeah*, רָמָה *Ramah*), עֶגְלוֹת בֵּית אָוֶן *calves of the house of iniquity* 10$_5$ (or em. עֵגֶל *calf of*), בָּמוֹת בֵּית־אָוֶן *high places of the house of iniquity* Ho 10$_{8(ms)}$ (L lacks בֵּית־), perh. בִּקְעַת־אָוֶן *valley of (the house of) iniquity* Am 1$_5$ (+ דַּמֶּשֶׂק *Damascus*, בֵּית עֶדֶן *Beth-eden*).

4. פֹּעֲלֵי אָוֶן **evildoers,** אָוֶן = *harm, iniquity,* <SUBJ> ידע *know* Ps 14$_4$||53$_5$, יכל *be able* 36$_{13}$, דבר pi. *speak* 94$_4$, נבע hi. *pour out* words 94$_4$, אמר htp. *boast* 94$_4$, אכל *eat* 14$_4$||53$_5$, קרא *call upon* 14$_4$||53$_5$, סור *turn away* 6$_9$, נפל *fall* 36$_{13}$, דחה pu. *be pushed down* 36$_{13}$, קום *rise* 36$_{13}$, ציץ hi. *bloom* 92$_8$ (|| רָשָׁע *wicked person*), שמד ni. *be destroyed* 92$_8$, פרד htp. *be scattered* 92$_{10}$ (|| איב ptc. *enemy*), סתר ni. *be hidden* Jb 34$_{22}$.

<OBJ> שׂנא *hate* Ps 5$_6$ (+ הלל ptc. *boaster*), כרת hi. *cut off* 101$_8$ (|| רָשָׁע *wicked person*).

<CSTR> עֶזְרַת פֹּעֲלֵי אָוֶן *helper of evildoers* Is 31$_2$, קִרְיַת *city of* Ho 6$_8$, רִגְשַׁת *tumult of* Ps 64$_3$ (|| רעע hi. ptc. *evil one*), מֹקְשׁוֹת *traps of* 141$_9$.

<APP> אִישִׁים פֹּעֲלֵי־אָוֶן *men* who are *evildoers* Ps 141$_4$.

<PREP> נֵכֶר לְ *disaster is for* Jb 31$_3$ (|| עַוָּל *evildoer*), מְחִתָּה לְ *destruction for* Pr 10$_{29}$ (|| תֹּם *innocence*, i.e. *innocent one*) 21$_{15}$.

עִם *with*, + משך *drag off* Ps 28$_3$ (|| רָשָׁע *wicked person*), ארח לְחֶבְרָה *go in company* Jb 34$_8$ (+ אַנְשֵׁי רֶשַׁע *wicked persons*), יצב עִם htp. *take a stand against* Ps 94$_{16}$ (|| רעע hi. ptc. *wicked one*).

אֵת *with*, + עלל htpo. *busy oneself* Ps 141$_4$, הלך hi. *cause to walk* 125$_5$.

נצל מִן hi. *deliver from* Ps 59$_3$ (+ אַנְשֵׁי דָמִים *bloodthirsty men*).

Also 1QSb 1$_7$.

<SYN> עָמָל *trouble*, רַע *evil*, עַוְלָה *evil*, שֶׁקֶר *deceit*, שָׁוְא *falsehood*.

אָוֶן II, see בֵּית אָוֶן.

אוֹן I $_{13.1.2}$ n.m. **strength, wealth**—sf. אוֹנִי, אוֹנוֹ (אֹנוֹ), אוֹנָם; pl. אוֹנִים (Si אוינים)—**1. strength, virility,** <SUBJ> היה *be* Jb 18$_{12}$ (+ רָעֵב *hungry*; perh. אֹנוֹ = *his offspring*, i.e. fruit of his virility, or *his misfortune*, from אָוֶן *iniquity*).

<NOM CL> אוֹנוֹ בִּשְׁרִירֵי בִטְנוֹ *his strength is in the muscles of his belly* Jb 40$_{16}$ (|| כֹּחַ *strength*).

<CSTR> רֵאשִׁית אוֹנִי *first of my strength*, i.e. my first-born Gn 49$_3$=4QpGen^a 4$_4$ (רישית; + כֹּחַ *strength*, עֹז *strength*, בְּכוֹר *first born*, שְׂאֵת *dignity*), רֵאשִׁית אֹנוֹ *first of his strength*, i.e. his first-born Dt 21$_{17}$ (+ בְּכֹרָה *birthright*), צַעֲדֵי אוֹנוֹ *steps of his strength*, i.e. his strong steps (unless אוֹנוֹ = *his iniquity*, from אָוֶן *iniquity*) Jb 18$_7$, רֵאשִׁית אוֹנִים *first of strength(s)*, i.e. first-born Ps 78$_{51}$ (+ בְּכוֹר *first-born*).

איש אונים *man of strength(s)* (unless אונים = *of sorrows*, from אֲנָה *distress*) Si 41$_{2(B)}$ (Smend אננים *of mourners*, from אנן *sigh*; || עָצְמָה *power*), רֹב אוֹנִים *greatness of strength(s)* Is 40$_{26}$ (+ אַמִּיץ כֹּחַ *mighty of strength*) 4QShir^b 17$_4$ (רוב אונ[י]ם), כָּל־אוֹנָם *all their strength* Ps 105$_{36}$ (+ רֵאשִׁית לְ *first of*, בְּכוֹר *first-born*).

<PREP> בְּאוֹנוֹ שָׂרָה אֶת־אֱלֹהִים *in his strength he struggled with God* Ho 12$_4$ (+ בַּבֶּטֶן *in the womb*). <COLL> אֵין אוֹנִים *(person) without strength* Is 40$_{29}$ (+ יָעֵף *weary one*, כֹּחַ *strength*) Si 41$_{2(M)}$ (אוינים; both || עָצְמָה *power*).

2. wealth, <OBJ> מצא *find* Ho 12$_9$ (+ עשׁר *be rich*, יְגִיעַ *gain*), שׁוב hi. *give back* Jb 20$_{10}$, לקח *take* 5$_5$ (if em. וְאֶל־מִצִּנִּים appar. *and from out of thorns* to וְאֹנָם צִנִּים *and as for their wealth, thorns*, i.e. sharp weapons, take it). <CSTR> תּוֹחֶלֶת אוֹנִים *hope of wealth* (unless אוֹנִים = *strength[s]*, as §1, or, *iniquity*, from אָוֶן *iniquity*) Pr 11$_7$ (+ אָדָם רָשָׁע *wicked person*).

<SYN> §1 כֹּחַ *strength*, עָצְמָה *power*.

→ אוֹן II *On*, אוֹנָם *Onam*, אוֹנָן *Onan*.

אוֹן II $_1$ pr.n.m. **On,** son of Peleth, descendant of Reuben, leading participant in rebellion of Korah,

Nm 16$_{1}$ (or em. הוּא *he* [Eliab] was the son of Peleth).
→ אוֹן *strength.*

אוֹן III 3 pl.n. **On**—אֹן—Egyptian city, also known as בֵּית שֶׁמֶשׁ *Beth-shemesh,* i.e. Heliopolis (Jr 43$_{13}$), ident. with Maṭariyē N of Cairo, פּוֹטִי פֶרַע כֹּהֵן אֹן *Potiphera, priest of On* Gn 41$_{45.50}$ (און) 46$_{20}$, בַּחוּרֵי אוֹן וּפִי־בֶסֶת *youths of On and Pibeseth* Ezk 30$_{17}$ (if em. אָוֶן *of iniquity*).

[אוֹן] IV, see אָנָה.

אוֹנוֹ 5 pl.n. **Ono,** town in Benjamin, established (בנה) by Shemed (1 C 8$_{12}$; mss שֶׁמֶר *Shemer*), ident. with Kafr ʿĀna (Newē Efrayīm), 9 km NW of Lod, Ezr 2$_{33}$||Ne 7$_{37}$ (+ בְּנֵי *sons of* [or em. אַנְשֵׁי *men of*]) Ne 6$_{2}$ (+ בִּקְעַת *valley of*) 11$_{35}$ 1 C 8$_{12}$.

אוֹנִי, see אָנָה.

[אוֹנִיָּה], see אֳנִיָּה.

אוֹנִים, see אָוֶן I, אוֹן I, אָנָה.

אוֹנָם 4 pr.n.m. **Onam, 1.** son of Shobal and grandson of Seir the Horite, Gn 36$_{23}$||1 C 1$_{40}$ (1 C ms אוֹנָן *Onan*). **2.** son of Jerahmeel and Atarah and father of Shammai and Jada, descendant of Judah, 1 C 2$_{26.28}$.
→ אוֹן *strength.*

אוֹנָן 8 pr.n.m. **Onan, 1.** son of Judah and of the daughter of Shua, Gn 38$_{4.8.9}$ 46$_{12.12}$ Nm 26$_{19.19}$ 1 C 2$_{3}$. **2.** son of Shobal and grandson of Seir the Horite, 1 C 1$_{40(ms)}$ (L, ||Gn 36$_{23}$ אוֹנָם *Onam*).
→ אוֹן *strength.*

[אוֹנֶס] 0.1 n.[m.] **force,** כן עושה באונס משפט *thus is one who does judgment,* i.e. imposes justice, *by force* Si 20$_{4(B)}$ (Bmg בגזל *by robbery*).
→ אנס *force.*

אוּפָז 2 pl.n. **Uphaz,** appar. foreign source of gold, כֶּסֶף מְרֻקָּע מִתַּרְשִׁישׁ יוּבָא וְזָהָב מֵאוּפָז *beaten silver is brought from Tarshish and gold from Uphaz* Jr 10$_{9}$ (or em. אוֹפִיר *Ophir*), מָתְנָיו חֲגֻרִים בְּכֶתֶם אוּפָז *their loins were girded with gold of Uphaz* Dn 10$_{5}$ (or em. אוֹפִיר or וּפָז *and pure gold*).

אוֹפִיר I 12.1.2.1 pl.n. **Ophir**—אֹפִיר, I אפר; Q אופירים; + ־ה of direction אוֹפִירָה—source of gold and other valuable items, in Arabia, India or eastern or southern Africa.

<CSTR> כֶּתֶם אוֹפִיר *pure gold of Ophir* Is 13$_{12}$ Ps 45$_{10}$ Jb 28$_{16}$ Dn 10$_{5}$ (if em. אוּפָז *Uphaz*) 4QM^{a} fr. 11.1$_{18}$ (אופירים), זְהַב אוֹפִיר *gold of Ophir* 1 C 29$_{4}$ Si 7$_{18}$ T. Qasile ost. 2$_{1}$ (אפר; + לבית חרן *for Beth-horon*), מעשי אופירים *works of,* perh. *from, Ophir(s)* 4QShirShab^{f} 23.2$_{9}$.

<PREP> אֲשֶׁר־נָשָׂא זָהָב מֵאוֹפִיר הֵבִיא מֵאֹפִיר the fleet *that carried gold from Ophir (also) brought from Ophir* almug trees and precious stones 1 K 10$_{11}$, sim. ||2 C 9$_{10}$, יוּבָא ... זָהָב מֵאוֹפִיר *from Ophir gold ... is brought* Jr 10$_{9}$ (if em. אוּפָז *Uphaz*; || תַּרְשִׁישׁ *Tarshish*), וַיָּבֹאוּ אוֹפִירָה וַיִּקְחוּ מִשָּׁם זָהָב *and they came to Ophir and took from there gold* 1 K 9$_{28}$, sim. ||2 C 8$_{18}$, לָלֶכֶת אוֹפִירָה לַזָּהָב *to go to Ophir for gold* 1 K 22$_{49}$.

<COLL> וְשִׁית־עַל־עָפָר בָּצֶר וּבְצוּר נְחָלִים אוֹפִיר *or place ore on (the) dust and (gold of) Ophir in the rock of streams* Jb 22$_{24}$ (or em. וְשַׁתָּ *or you placed*).

Also perh. 4QApocMos A 4$_{2}$.

אוֹפִיר II 2 pr.n.m. **Ophir**—אוֹפִר—son of Joktan, descendant of Noah, Gn 10$_{29}$||1 C 1$_{23}$ (Gn אוֹפִר).

אוֹפַן 35.1.8 n.m. **wheel**—אוֹפָן; cstr. אוֹפַן (אֹפַן); pl. אוֹפַנִּים; cstr. אוֹפַנֵּי (Q אופני); sf. אוֹפַנֵּיהֶם (Q אופניהמה)—wheel of chariot, etc. (Ex 14$_{25}$ 1 K 7$_{33}$ Is 28$_{27}$ Na 3$_{2}$ 4QBer^{a} 1$_{2}$), in Ezekiel's vision (e.g. Ezk 1$_{15.16.19}$ 4QpsEzek^{a} 4$_{11.13}$), of base of laver (1 K 7$_{30.32.33}$), used in threshing (Is 28$_{27}$ Pr 20$_{26}$).

<SUBJ> היה *be* Ezk 1$_{16}$ 10$_{10}$ (both + בְּתוֹךְ *within*), הלך *go* 1$_{19}$ 10$_{16}$ 4QShirShab^{f} 20.2$_{9}$, חזר *turn* intrans. Si 36$_{5}$ (|| גַּלְגַּל *wheel*), נשׂא ni. *rise* Ezk 1$_{19.20.21}$, מלא *be full* of eyes 10$_{12}$, סבב *turn* intrans. 10$_{16}$, ho. *roll over* Is

28$_{27}$, חבר pass. *be joined* 4QpsEzek^a 4$_{11}$, ברך pi. *bless* 4QShirShab^d 1.2$_{15}$ (+ כְּרוּב *cherub*).

<NOM CL> מחשבותיו ... אופן *his thoughts are ... a wheel* Si 36$_5$, אוֹפַנֵּי נְחֹשֶׁת לַמְּכוֹנָה *there were wheels of bronze to the stand* 1 K 7$_{30}$, לְאַרְבַּעְתָּם אוֹפַנֵּיהֶם *there were their wheels to the four of them* Ezk 10$_{12}$, הָאוֹפַנִּים לְמִתַּחַת *the wheels were under* the panels 1 K 7$_{32}$, הָאוֹפַנִּים לְעֻמָּתָם *the wheels were beside them* Ezk 10$_{19}$ 11$_{22}$, אוֹפַן ... אֵצֶל הַכְּרוּב *a wheel ... was beside the cherub* 10$_{9.9}$, sim. 10$_9$, אוֹפַן ... בָּאָרֶץ *a wheel was ... upon the earth* Ezk 1$_{15}$.

<OBJ> שׁוב hi. *turn* trans. Pr 20$_{26}$ (or em. אוֹנָם *their iniquity*), סור hi. *remove* Ex 14$_{25}$.

<CSTR> אֹפַן מַרְכְּבֹתָיו *the wheel of his chariots* Ex 14$_{25}$, אוֹפַן הַמֶּרְכָּבָה *the wheel of the chariot* 1 K 7$_{33}$, אוֹפַן עֲגָלָה *wheel of a cart* Is 28$_{27}$, אוֹפַנֵּי נְחֹשֶׁת *wheels of bronze* 1 K 7$_{30}$, אופני אור *wheels of light* 4QShirShab^f 20.2$_3$ (‖ כְּרוּב *cherub*); רַעַשׁ אוֹפָן *the noise of a wheel* Na 3$_2$, קוֹמַת הָאוֹפָן *the height of the wheel* 1 K 7$_{32}$, יְדוֹת הָאוֹפַנִּים *the axles of the wheels* 7$_{32}$, מַעֲשֵׂה אוֹפָן *the work,* i.e. structure, *of the wheel* 7$_{33}$, מַעֲשֵׂה הָאוֹפַנִּים *the work of the wheels* 7$_{33}$, מַרְאֵה *appearance of* Ezk 1$_{16}$ 10$_9$, שני עברי הא[ופנים] *the two sides of the wheels* 4QpsEzek^a 4$_{11}$, קוֹל *sound of* Ezk 3$_{13}$.

<ADJ> אֶחָד *one* Ezk 1$_{15}$ 10$_{9.9}$, sim. 1 K 7$_{32}$.

<PREP> בְּ *in* Ezk 1$_{20.21}$; היה בְּתוֹךְ *be within* Ezk 1$_{16}$ 10$_{10}$; לָאוֹפַנִּים לָהֶם קוֹרָא הַגַּלְגַּל *as for the wheels, it was called to them,* i.e. they were called, *the whirling (wheels)* Ezk 10$_{13}$; אופן חבור אל אופן *a wheel was joined to a wheel* 4QpsEzek^a 4$_{11}$; עמד אֵצֶל *stand beside* Ezk 10$_6$; [בינת] האופנים והחיות והאופנים *between the wheels and the living creatures and the wheels* 4QpsEzek^a 4$_{13}$.

<COLL> אַרְבָּעָה אוֹפַנִּים (and vars.) *four wheels* 1 K 7$_{30.32}$ Ezk 10$_{9.12}$, מרכבות כבודכה בן[ר]וביהמה ואופניהמה *the chariots of your glory with their multitudes and their wheels* 4QBer^a 1$_2$.

<SYN> כְּרוּב *cherub*.

Also 4QpsEzek^a 4$_{10}$ ([הא]ופנים).

[אוֹפֶן], see אֹפֶן.

[אוֹפָנָה], see פון.

אוֹפִר, see אוֹפִיר II.

אוץ 10.3.2.1 vb. **urge**—**Qal** Pf. אָץ, אַצְתִּי (Q אצותי [as if from אצץ]); ptc. אָץ, אָצִים; inf. Q (Yadin) אוץ—**1.** usu. **urge** oneself **on, hasten, be impatient** (at Ex 5$_{13}$ perh. אי״ץ = *urge on, hasten* another, with ellipsis of object). **2.** of space, **be narrow,** Jos 17$_{15}$, of time, **be short,** 1QM 18$_{12}$.

<SUBJ> Jeremiah Jr 17$_{16}$, אִישׁ *man* Gn 19$_{15}$ (if em.) Pr 29$_{20}$, נגשׂ ptc. *taskmaster* Ex 5$_{13}$, שֶׁמֶשׁ *sun* Jos 10$_{13}$ 1QM 18$_5$, הַר *mountain,* i.e. Mt Ephraim Jos 17$_{15}$, יוֹם *day* 1QM 18$_{12}$; subj. unspecified, Pr 19$_2$ (אָץ ... חוֹטֵא *one that hastens ... misses*) 21$_5$ (כָּל־אָץ אַךְ לְמַחְסוֹר *everyone that hastens is [destined] only for need* [or em. כָּל־מַחְשְׁבוֹת אָץ *all the thoughts of one that hastens;* + חָרוּץ *diligent*) 28$_{20}$ (אָץ ... לֹא יִנָּקֶה *one that hurries ... will not be held innocent*) Si 11$_{10}$ (אץ ... לא ינקה).

<PREP> לְךָ be (too) narrow *for you* Jos 17$_{15}$; בְּרַגְלַיִם *with (one's) legs* Pr 19$_2$, בִּדְבָרָיו *in his words* 29$_{20}$; מֵרֹעֶה *from (being) a shepherd* Jr 17$_{16}$ (or em. מֵרָעָה *from wickedness* or רָעָה *to wickedness*).

Hi. Impf. Si תאיץ, תָּאִיצוּ; + waw וַיָּאִיצוּ—as Qal, **be impatient, hasten**—<SUBJ> מַלְאָךְ *angel* Gn 19$_{15}$ (or em. אִישׁ *man*), בַּלָּהָה *terror* Jb 18$_{11}$ (if em. וֶהֱפִיצֻהוּ *and they will scatter him* וֶהֱאִיצֻהוּ *and they will hasten him* to his feet); subj. unspecified, Is 22$_4$ (אַל־תָּאִיצוּ *do not hasten*) Si 7$_{15}$ (or em. אל תאיץ *do not hasten* to אל תקוץ *do not feel nauseated* by) 7$_{17}$ (אל תאיץ *do not hasten*).

<PREP> לְרַגְלָיו *to his feet* Jb 18$_{11}$ (if em.); בְּלוֹט be impatient *with Lot* Gn 19$_{15}$.

<COLL> (Qal and Hi.) followed by infinitive (except at Si 7$_{15}$, with לְ) of אמר *say* Si 7$_{17}$, בוא *come* Jos 10$_{13}$ 1QM 18$_5$(Yadin) (באוץ השמש לבוא), נחם pi. *console* Is 22$_4$, עשׁר hi. *enrich (oneself)* Pr 28$_{20}$, צבא *serve* Si 7$_{15}$ (or em. בצבא), רבה hi. *multiply (activities)* 11$_{10}$, רדף *pursue* 1QM 18$_{12}$.

Also Lachish ost. 8$_7$ (א[י]ץ).

אוֹצָר 80.8.12 n.m. **treasure, treasury**—Q (Allegro) אצר; cstr. אוֹצַר; sf. אוֹצָרוֹ (Q [Milik] אוצרה); pl. אוֹצָרוֹת (אוֹצָרֹת, אֹצָרוֹת); cstr. אוֹצְרוֹת (אֹצְרוֹת); sf. אוֹצְרֹתַי (אוֹצְרֹתָיו), אוֹצְרוֹתָיו, אוֹצְרוֹתַיִךְ, אוֹצְרוֹתֶיךָ (אֹצְרֹתָי),

(אֹצְרֹתֵיהֶם) אוֹצְרֹתָם, (אֹצְרֹתֶיהָ) אוֹצְרֹתֶיהָ, (אֹצְרֹתָיו).

1. treasure (oft. pl.), distinction from §2 oft. uncertain. **a.** valuables in temple, palace, etc., 1 K 14$_{26.26}$‖2 C 12$_{9.9}$ 1 K 15$_{18}$ (unless em.; see Obj.) 2 K 24$_{13.13}$ 1 C 26$_{22.24}$ 2 C 8$_{15}$ 25$_{24}$ (‖2 K 14$_{14}$ אוֹצָר = *treasury*, as §2a) 36$_{18.18}$ Jr 20$_{5}$ GnzPs 3$_{15}$. **b.** wealth of nations, cities, etc., Is 27 30$_{6}$ 33$_{6}$ Jr 15$_{13}$ 17$_{3}$ 48$_{7}$ 49$_{4}$ 50$_{37}$ 51$_{13}$ Ho 13$_{15}$ Lm 2$_{7}$ (if em.; see Cstr.). **c.** wealth of individuals, Is 45$_{3}$ Pr 10$_{2}$ 15$_{16}$ 21$_{6.20}$ Si 40$_{18}$ 41$_{12.14}$. **d.** supplies, stores of food, drink, etc., Mc 6$_{10}$ (if em.; see App.) Ne 12$_{44}$ 1 C 27$_{25.25.27.28}$ 2 C 11$_{11}$ 3QTr 1$_{10(\text{Allegro})}$ perh. 4Q416 9.1$_{19}$.

2. treasury, storehouse (oft. sg.), **a.** of temple, palace, etc., Jos 6$_{19.24}$ 1 K 7$_{51}$‖2 C 5$_{1}$ 1 K 15$_{18}$‖2 C 16$_{2}$ 1 K 15$_{18}$ (if em.; see Obj.) 2 K 12$_{19}$ 14$_{14}$ 16$_{8}$ 18$_{15}$ 20$_{13.15}$‖Is 39$_{2.4}$ Jr 38$_{11}$ Ezk 28$_{4}$ Zc 11$_{13.13}$ (if em.; see Prep.) Dn 1$_{2}$ Ezr 2$_{69}$‖Ne 7$_{70}$ Ne 7$_{69}$ 10$_{39}$ 1 C 9$_{26}$ 26$_{20.20.26}$ 28$_{12.12}$ 29$_{8}$ 2 C 32$_{27}$ 3QTr 8$_{1(\text{Allegro})}$. **b.** for private wealth, Pr 8$_{21}$. **c.** for food, Jl 1$_{17}$ Mc 6$_{10}$ (unless em.; see App.) Ml 3$_{10}$ Ne 13$_{12.13}$ Mur 24 2$_{19}$ 3$_{17}$. **d.** for wisdom, understanding, 4QBer[a] 1$_{7}$ 4Q289 2$_{9}$ perh. 4Q416 1$_{9}$. **e.** heaven as storehouse of wind, rain, etc., Dt 28$_{12}$ Jr 10$_{13}$‖51$_{16}$‖Ps 135$_{7}$ Ps 33$_{7}$ Jb 38$_{22.22}$ Si 39$_{17}$ 43$_{23(\text{Bmg})}$ 1QS 10$_{2}$ 1QH 1$_{12}$ 1QM 10$_{12}$ 11QBer 2$_{7}$; of divine punishments, Dt 32$_{34}$ Jr 50$_{25}$ Si 39$_{30}$ 43$_{14}$.

<SUBJ> בזז pu. *be plundered* Jr 50$_{37}$, שׁמם ni. *be desolate* Jl 1$_{17}$ (‖ מְגוּרָה *storehouse*, if em. מַמְּגֻרוֹת appar. *granaries* to מְגֻרוֹת *storehouses*), סתר ho. *be concealed* Si 41$_{14(\text{B})}$ (Bmg סימה *treasure*, M שימה *treasure*; ‖ חָכְמָה *wisdom*), חסר *be lacking* 4Q416 9.1$_{19}$, חמד ni. *be desirable* Pr 21$_{20}$ (‖ שֶׁמֶן *oil*), יעל hi. *profit* 10$_{2}$, שׁכן *dwell* 21$_{20}$ (if em.; see Nom. Cl.).

<NOM CL> יִרְאַת י׳ הִיא אוֹצָרוֹ *the fear of Y. is his treasure* (or em. אוֹצָרָהּ *her* [Zion's] *treasure*) Is 33$_{6}$, הַאִשׁ ... אֹצְרוֹת רֶשַׁע *are there ... treasuries of wickedness?* Mc 6$_{10}$ (or em. הַאִשׁ to הַאֶשֶּׁה *shall I forget?* [from נשׁה *forget*], or הַאֶשָּׂא *shall I bear?* [from נשׂא *carry*]; ‖ אֵיפָה *ephah*), אוֹצָר ... וָשֶׁמֶן בִּנְוֵה חָכָם *treasure ... and oil is in the dwelling of a wise person* Pr 21$_{20}$ (or em. וָשֶׁמֶן בִּנְוֵה to יִשְׁכֹּן בְּפִי *shall dwell in the mouth of*), ומוצא פיו אוצרו appar. *and the utterance of his mouth is his storehouse* Si 39$_{17}$ (unless יעריך ... אוצרו = *he arranges ... his storehouse*, or em. יעמיד *he establishes*; perh. also em. ומוצא to ובמוצא *and with the utterance of*).

<OBJ> נתן *give, place* 1 K 15$_{18}$ (or em. וְאֶת־אוֹצְרוֹת *and the treasures of* to וּבְאוֹצְרוֹת *and in the treasuries of*) Is 45$_{3}$ (‖ מַטְמוֹן *treasure*) Jr 15$_{13}$ 17$_{3}$ (both + לָבַז *as a spoil*; ‖ חַיִל *wealth*) 20$_{5}$ (‖ חֹסֶן *wealth*, יְגִיעַ *gain*, יְקָר *precious object*) 2 C 11$_{11}$ (‖ נָגִיד *leader*) GnzPs 3$_{15}$ (‖ חַיִל, חֶמְדָּה *desire*), בוא hi. *bring* Jr 20$_{5}$ 2 C 36$_{18.18}$ (‖ כְּלִי *vessel*), מלא pi. *fill* Pr 8$_{21}$, אצר *store up* Mc 6$_{10}$ (if em.; see App.), עשׂה *make* 2 C 32$_{27}$ (+ לְ *for* valuables; ‖ מִסְכְּנוֹת *storehouses*, אֻרְוָה *stall*), פעל *make* Pr 21$_{6}$ (if em.; see Cstr.), ברא *create* Si 43$_{14(\text{B})}$ ([אוצ]ר), ערך hi. *arrange* 39$_{17}$ (see Nom. Cl.), עמד hi. *establish* 39$_{17}$ (if em.; see Nom Cl.).

פתח *open* Dt 28$_{12}$ Jr 50$_{25}$ 1QS 10$_{2}$ 11QBer 2$_{7}$, פרע *loose* Si 43$_{14(\text{M})}$, לקח *take* 1 K 14$_{26.26}$‖2 C 12$_{9.9}$ 1 K 15$_{18}$ (or em.; see above) Jr 20$_{5}$, יצא hi. *take out* 2 K 24$_{13.13}$, נשׂא *carry* Is 30$_{6}$ (‖ חַיִל) Mc 6$_{10}$ (if em.; see Nom Cl.), שׁלח *send* 1 K 15$_{18}$ (or em.; see above), שׁוב hi. *take back* 2 C 25$_{24}$ (if em.; see Prep.), נטה *extend*, i.e. place Si 43$_{23(\text{Bmg})}$ (B איים *islands*; or em. ויט *and he extended* to ויטע *and he planted*), נטע *plant* 43$_{23(\text{Bmg})}$ (if em.; see above).

בזז *plunder* Jr 20$_{5}$, שׁסה *plunder* Ho 13$_{15}$ (or em. יְשַׁסֶּה אוֹצַר *he will plunder the treasury of* to יַשְׁאֶה אַרְצוֹ *he will destroy his land* [from שׁאה *crash*]), בלע pi. *swallow* Pr 21$_{20}$, מצא *find* Si 40$_{18(\text{B})}$ (mg סימה *treasure*; ‖ חָכְמָה *wisdom*), ראה *see* Jb 38$_{22}$, נשׁה hi. *forget* Mc 6$_{10}$ (if em.; see Nom. Cl.).

<CSTR> אוֹצַר י׳ *treasury of Y.* Jos 6$_{19}$, בֵּית י׳ *of the temple of Y.* 6$_{24}$ 1 C 29$_{8}$, אֱלֹהָיו *of his god* Dn 1$_{2}$, הַמְּלָאכָה *of the work* Ezr 2$_{69}$‖Ne 7$_{70}$, כָּל־כְּלִי חֶמְדָּה *of every desirable object* Ho 13$_{15}$ (or em.; see Obj.), שׂכל *of wisdom* 4QBer 1$_{7}$, בינות *of understanding* 4Q298 2$_{9}$, אֹצְרוֹת בֵּית י׳ *treasuries of the house of Y.* 1 K 7$_{51}$ 14$_{26}$‖2 C 12$_{9}$ 1 K 15$_{18}$‖2 C 16$_{2}$ (1 K אוֹצְרוֹת) 2 K 12$_{19}$ 24$_{13}$ (אוֹצְרוֹת) 1 C 26$_{22}$ 2 C 36$_{18}$, בֵּית הָאֱלֹהִים *of the house of God* appar. 1 C 9$_{26}$ (הָאֹצָרוֹת; or em.; see App.) 26$_{20}$ (אוֹצְרוֹת) 28$_{12}$ 2 C 5$_{1}$, הַקֳּדָשִׁים *of holy objects* 1 C 26$_{20.26}$ 28$_{12}$, בֵּית הַמֶּלֶךְ *of the house of the king* 14$_{26}$‖2 C 12$_{9}$ (1 K אוֹצְרוֹת) 1 K 15$_{18(\text{Qr})}$‖2 C 16$_{2}$ (1 K Kt אוֹצְרוֹת בֵּית מלך) 2 K 12$_{19}$ 14$_{14}$‖2 C 25$_{24}$ 2 K 16$_{8}$ 18$_{15}$ 24$_{13}$ (אוֹצְרוֹת), הַמֶּלֶךְ

of the king 1 C 27_{25} 2 C 36_{18} (+ וְשָׂרָיו *and [of] his officials*), אוצרות מלכים *treasures of kings* GnzPs 3_{15}, אוֹצְרוֹת מַלְכֵי יְהוּדָה *treasures of the kings of Judah* Jr 20_{5}, חֹשֶׁךְ *of darkness* Is 45_{3}, חכמה *of wisdom* Si $41_{12(B)}$ (mg סומות חמדה *treasures of desire*, i.e. precious treasures), אֹצְרוֹת רֶשַׁע *treasuries of wickedness* Mc 6_{10} Pr 10_{2}, הַיַּיִן *of the wine* 1 C 27_{27}, הַשֶּׁמֶן *of the oil* 27_{28}, מַאֲכָל וְשֶׁמֶן וָיָיִן *of food and oil and wine* 2 C 11_{11}, שֶׁלֶג *of snow* Jb 38_{22}, בָּרָד *of hail* 38_{22}, אוצרות כבו[וד] *treasures of glory* 1QM $10_{12(Yadin)}$, אוצרות מחשבת perh. *hidden treasuries* (lit. *treasuries of thought*) 1QH 1_{12}.

ב׳[ת] אוצר *house of treasury*, i.e. treasury 3QTr $8_{1(Allegro)}$ (others ב׳[ת] אחצר *Beth-hazor*), בֵּית אוֹצַר *house of the treasury of* Dn 1_{2}, בֵּית הָאוֹצָר *house of the treasury* Ml 3_{10} Ne 10_{39}, גג אוצר *roof of the storehouse* Mur 24 $2_{19(Milik)}$ ([גג]) $3_{17(Milik)}$ (אוצרה *his storehouse*), מֶלְתַּחַת הָאוֹצָר *wardrobe of the treasury* Jr 38_{11} (if em.; see Prep.), פֹּעַל אוֹצָרוֹת *making of treasures* Pr 21_{6} (or em. פֹּעֵל *one who makes*), רַבַּת אוֹצָרֹת *one great of*, i.e. with many, *treasures* Jr 51_{13}, חֶמְדַּת אֹצְרוֹתֶיהָ *delight of her treasures* Lm 2_{7} (if em. חוֹמֹת אַרְמְנוֹתֶיהָ *walls of her fortresses*), אלפי אוצרות *thousands of treasures* Si 41_{12}, כָּל־אֹצְרוֹת *all the treasuries of* 1 C 26_{26}.

<APP> אוֹצָרוֹ ... הַשָּׁמַיִם *his treasury ..., the heavens* Dt 28_{12}, בֵּית רָשָׁע אֹצְרוֹת רֶשַׁע *house of the wicked, treasures of wickedness* Mc 6_{10} (unless אֹצְרוֹת is obj. and בֵּית רָשָׁע is vocative, *O house of the wicked*), הַלְּשָׁכוֹת ... הָאֹצְרוֹת בֵּית הָאֱלֹהִים *the chambers ... (and) the treasuries (of) the house of God* 1 C 9_{26} (or em. הָאֹצָרוֹת), האצר השבוע *the store, the seventh-year (produce)* 3QTr $1_{10(Allegro)}$ (others האצרה שבע *the treasure—seven [talents]*; see אוֹצָרָה *treasure*).

<ADJ> אוֹצָרוֹ הַטּוֹב *his good storehouse* Dt 28_{12}=11QBer 2_{7}, אוֹצָר רָב *great treasure* Pr 15_{16}.

<PREP> לְ of possession, *of, to* Is 2_{7} (|| מֶרְכָּבָה *chariot*, + זָהָב *gold*, כֶּסֶף *silver*, סוּס *horse*), of direction, *to*, + בוא hi. *bring* Ne 13_{12}, נתן *give* Ezr 2_{69}||Ne 7_{70} Ne 7_{69} 1 C 29_{8}, of benefit, *to, for* Ne 12_{44} (|| תְּרוּמָה *contribution*, רֵאשִׁית *firstfruits*, מַעֲשֵׂר *tithe*) 1 C 26_{20} 27_{27} $28_{12.12}$, מִצְוַת הַמֶּלֶךְ ... לָאֹצָרוֹת *commandment of the king ... concerning the treasuries* 2 C 8_{15} (|| דָּבָר *matter*).

בְּ of place, *in* Si $39_{30(B)}$, + היה *be* 2 K 20_{15}||Is 39_{4}, יתר ni. *be left* 1 K $15_{18.18}$ (if em.; see Obj.), פקד ni. *be deposited* Si $39_{30(Bmg)}$, מצא ni. *be found* 2 K 12_{19} 14_{14} 16_{8} 18_{15} 20_{13}||Is 39_{2}, חתם pass. *be sealed* Dt 32_{34}, נתן *place* 1 K 7_{51}||2 C 5_{1} Ps 33_{7} (without בְּ, Jos 6_{24}), עשׂה *make*, i.e. gather (silver) Ezk 28_{4}, בטח בְּ *trust in* Jr 48_{7} (|| מַעֲשֶׂה *work*; or em. בְּמַעֲשַׂיִךְ וּבְאוֹצְרוֹתַיִךְ *in your works and in your treasures* to בְּמָעֻזַּיִךְ בִּמְצָדוֹתַיִךְ *in your strongholds, in your refuges*) 49_{4}, משׁל בְּ hi. *give authority over* 4Q416 1_{9}, מה תועלה ב *what value is in?* Si $41_{14(B)}$.

יצא מִן hi. *bring out from* Jr 10_{13}||51_{16}||Ps 135_{7} 2 C 16_{2}, טוֹב מִן *better than* Pr 15_{16}, אֶל *(in)to*, + בוא *come* Jb 38_{22} (without אֶל, Jos 6_{19}), שׁלך hi. *cast*, i.e. deposit (silver) Zc $11_{13.13}$ (if em. הַיּוֹצֵר *the potter* to הָאוֹצָר *the treasury* in both), חֶרֶב אֶל־אוֹצְרֹתֶיהָ *a sword to her treasures* Jr 50_{37} (|| סוּס *horse*, עֶרֶב *foreign population*, רֶכֶב *chariot*); וַיָּבֹא ... אֶל־תַּחַת הָאוֹצָר *and he came ... to below the treasury* 38_{11} (or em. [אֶל־]מֶלְתַּחַת הָאוֹצָר *[to] the wardrobe of the treasury*).

שׁוב אֶת *go back with* 2 C 25_{24} (or em. וַיָּשָׁב *and he went back* to הֵשִׁיב *he took back*, + זָהָב *gold*, כֶּסֶף *silver*, כְּלִי *vessel*, בְּנֵי הַתַּעֲרֻבוֹת *hostages*).

עַל *over, in charge of* 1 C $26_{20.22.24.26}$ $27_{25.25.28}$, + היה *be* 9_{26} (|| לִשְׁכָּה *chamber*), אצר hi. *appoint as treasurer* Ne 13_{13} (or em.; see אצר *store up*), צוה pi. *give charge* 13_{13} (if em.; see אצר).

הכל של הדמע והאצר *all of the contribution and the store* 3QTr $1_{10(Allegro)}$.

Also 5QRègle 1_{4}.

<SYN> §1 חַיִל *wealth*, חָכְמָה *wisdom*.

→ אצר *store up*.

[אוֹצָרָה] 0.0.1 n.f. **treasure**—Q אצרה—הכל של הדמע והאצרה שבע *all the contribution and the treasure—seven (talents)* 3QTr 1_{10} (Allegro והאצר השבוע *and the store, the seventh-year [produce]*; see אוֹצָר *treasure*, §1d).

→ אצר *store up*.

אוֹר 50.3.26.2 vb. **be light**—**Qal** Pf. אוֹר, אֹרוּ; + waw וְאוֹר; וַתָּאֹרְנָה; impv. אוֹרִי; ptc. אוֹר, Q אורה, Si אורים—**1. be light, bright, shine,** Gn 44_{3} 1 S $14_{27.29}$ 29_{10} Is 60_{1} Jb 33_{30} (if em.; see Ni., Prep.) Pr 4_{18} Si 13_{26} 1QM 1_{8}.

2. ptc. as adj., **enlightened,** ויהי דויד ... חכם ואור *and David was ... wise and enlightened* 11QPs^{a} 27$_{2}$, רוח נבונה ואורה *an understanding and enlightened spirit* 27$_{4}$.

<SUBJ> בֹּקֶר *morning* Gn 44$_{3}$, עַיִן *eye*, i.e. strength is regained, 1 S 14$_{27(Qr)}$ (Kt ותראנה) 14$_{29}$, פָּנִים *face* Si 13$_{26}$, אֹרַח *path* of the righteous Pr 4$_{18}$, צֶדֶק *righteousness* 1QM 1$_{8(Yadin)}$ (צ[דק]), דַּעַת *knowledge* 1QM 1$_{8(Yadin)}$ ([ד]עת), Zion Is 60$_{1}$ (|| קום *rise*; + זרח *shine*); subj. not specified, 1 S 29$_{10}$.

<PREP> וְאוֹר לָכֶם *and (when) it is light*, i.e when day breaks, *for you* 1 S 29$_{10}$.

<COLL> הוֹלֵךְ וָאוֹר *shining more and more* Pr 4$_{18}$, sim. 1QM 1$_{8}$ (הלוך).

Ni. Impf. + waw וַיֵּאֹר; ptc. נָאוֹר; inf. לֵאוֹר (= לְהֵאוֹר)—as Qal, **be light, bright, shine,** <SUBJ> גֶּבֶר *man* Jb 33$_{30}$ (or em.; see Prep), Y. Ps 76$_{5}$ (or em. נוֹרָא *terrible*; + אַדִּיר *majestic*); subj. not specified, 2 S 23$_{2}$.

<PREP> וַיֵּאֹר לָהֶם *and (when) it was light*, i.e. day broke, *for them* 2 S 23$_{2}$; לֵאוֹר בְּאוֹר הַחַיִּים *to shine*, i.e. so that he shines, *with the light of life* Jb 33$_{30}$ (or em. לָאוֹר *to shine*, i.e. Qal, or לִרְאוֹת *to see*).

Hi. Pf. הֵאִירָה, Q האירותה ,הֵאִירוּ; impf. יָאִיר (juss. יָאֵר), תָּאִיר (Si תאר), יְאִירוּ (Q יאירוכה), תָּאִירוּ; + waw וַיָּאֶר; וְהֵאִיר; impv. הָאֵר (הָאִירָה); ptc. מְאִירַת ,מֵאִיר, Q מאירים ,מְאִירוֹת; inf. הָאִיר (Q לאיר)—**1. give light, shine,** Gn 1$_{15.17}$ Ex 13$_{21}$ 25$_{37}$ Nm 8$_{2}$ Is 60$_{19}$ Ezk 43$_{2}$ Ps 118$_{27}$ (unless em.; see Obj.) 139$_{12}$ Jb 41$_{24}$ (if subj.) 11QT 9$_{12}$ 1QM 1$_{8.8}$ 5$_{10}$ 14$_{17(Yadin)}$ 4QPrQuot 1$_{12}$ 10$_{1}$ 48$_{7}$ 4QShirShab^{f} 23.2$_{9}$ 4QJub^{a} 6$_{6}$ 11QapPs^{a} 4$_{10}$.

2. cause to shine, Jb 41$_{24}$ (if obj.) 1QIsa^{a} 13$_{10}$ Ezk 32$_{7}$ 1QH 9$_{27}$ 4QShir^{b} 2.1$_{4}$.

3. trans. **light up, illuminate,** Ex 14$_{20}$ (unless em.; see Subj.) Ps 77$_{19}$ 97$_{4}$ 105$_{39}$ 118$_{27}$ (if em.; see Obj.) Ne 9$_{12.19}$.

4. kindle fire, lamp, etc., Is 27$_{11}$ 50$_{11}$ (if em.; see Subj.) Ml 1$_{10}$ Ps 18$_{29}$ CD 6$_{12}$.

5a. enlighten someone, **make shine** mentally and morally, 1QM 17$_{7}$ 1QS 2$_{3}$ 4QShir^{b} 2.1$_{4}$ 18.2$_{8}$ 4QShirShab^{d} 1.2$_{35}$ 4QWiles 1$_{8}$. **b. give enlightenment,** Ps 119$_{130}$ 1QS 4$_{2}$ 4QpIsa^{d} 1$_{5}$ 4QShirShab^{f} 19$_{5}$.

6. with obj. פָּנִים **make one's face shine, a. show favour,** Nm 6$_{25}$ Ps 31$_{17}$ 67$_{2}$ 80$_{4.8.20}$ 119$_{135}$ Dn 9$_{17}$ Si 7$_{24}$ 11QBer 1.2$_{6}$ 4QApocMos A 2.2$_{8}$ 11QapPs^{a} 4$_{11}$ Ketef Hinnom inscr. 1$_{16}$ 2$_{8}$. **b. be cheerful,** Si 32$_{11}$. **c. make cheerful,** Ec 8$_{1}$. **d. cause to shine, enlighten,** i.e. teach 1QH 3$_{3}$ 4$_{5.27}$ 1QSb 4$_{27}$.

7. with obj. עֵינַיִם, **enlighten the eyes,** i.e. revive, Ps 13$_{4}$ 19$_{9}$ Pr 29$_{13}$ Ezr 9$_{8}$.

perh. **Pol.** Ptc. מְאוֹרֲרִים—**make clear, evident,** of water, Nm 5$_{18.19.22.24.27}$ (if em. in all הַמְאָרֲרִים waters *that bring a curse*).

<SUBJ> מָאוֹר *luminary* Gn 1$_{15.17}$ 1QSb 4$_{27}$, יָרֵחַ *moon* Is 60$_{19}$ Ezk 32$_{7}$ (+ כסה pi. *cover* sun, קדר hi. *darken* luminaries), שֶׁמֶשׁ *sun* 4QPrQuot 10$_{1}$, כּוֹכָב *star* 1QIsa^{a} 13$_{10}$ (MT יָהֵלּוּ *they shine*), כְּסִיל *constellation* 13$_{10}$, נֵר *lamp* Ex 25$_{37}$ Nm 8$_{2}$ 11QT 9$_{12}$ ([יא]ירו), לַהַב *blade* 1QM 5$_{10}$, לַיְלָה *night* Ps 139$_{12}$ (:: חשך hi. *be dark*), אֶרֶץ *earth* Ezk 43$_{2}$, פֵּתַח *opening* of words Ps 119$_{130}$, אוֹר *light* 1QM 14$_{17(Yadin)}$ ([יא]יר) 11QapPs^{a} 4$_{10}$ ([יאיר אור]), אֵשׁ *fire* Ps 105$_{39}$, עַמּוּד *pillar* of fire Ex 13$_{21}$ Ne 9$_{12.19}$, בָּרָק *lightning* Ps 77$_{19}$ 97$_{4}$, מַעֲשֶׂה *work* 4QShirShab^{f} 23.2$_{9}$.

Y. Nm 6$_{25}$ (|| חנן *be gracious*, נשׂא *lift up* countenace, שׂים *place* = give peace) Ps 13$_{4}$ (:: ישׁן *sleep* in death) 18$_{29}$ (||2 S 22$_{29}$ omits) 31$_{17}$ (|| ישׁע hi. *save*) 67$_{2}$ (|| חנן, ברך pi. *bless*) 80$_{4.8}$ (both || שׁוב hi. *restore*, + ישׁע ni. *be saved*) 80$_{20}$ (+ ישׁע ni.) 118$_{27}$ 119$_{135}$ Pr 29$_{13}$ Dn 9$_{17}$ Ezr 9$_{8}$ (+ נתן *give* revival) 1QS 2$_{3}$ 1QH 3$_{3}$ 4$_{5}$ (+ לבריתכה *for your covenant*) 4$_{27}$ 9$_{27}$ 4QShir^{b} 2.1$_{4}$ 18.2$_{8}$ (ה[א]יר) 11QBer 1.2$_{6}$ (+ ברך pi.) 4QApocMos A2.2$_{8}$ Ketef Hinnom inscr. 1$_{16}$ 2$_{8}$, רוּחַ *spirit* 4QShirShab^{f} 19$_{5}$.

אִשָּׁה *woman* Is 27$_{11}$, father Si 7$_{24}$, כֹּהֵן *priest* Ml 1$_{10}$, perh. מַלְאָךְ *angel* of Y. Ex 14$_{20}$ (or em. וַיַּעַבְרוּ *and they passed*, or וַיָּאֶר *and he cast a spell* upon the night, from ארר *curse*), Michael 1QM 17$_{7}$, perh. twelve leaders 4QpIsa^{d} 1$_{5}$, מִצְוָה *commandment* Ps 19$_{9}$ (|| שׂמח pi. *make happy*), חָכְמָה *wisdom* Ec 8$_{1}$, צֶדֶק *righteousness* 1QM 1$_{8(Yadin)}$ (צ[דק]), דַּעַת *knowledge* 1$_{8(Yadin)}$ ([ד]עת), רום *height* of majesty 1$_{8}$, perh. נָתִיב *path* Jb 41$_{24}$ (or understand as obj.), one brought into covenant CD 6$_{12}$; subj. not specified, Is 50$_{11}$ (if em. מְאַזְּרֵי *ones who gird* to מְאִירֵי *ones who kindle*; || קדח *kindle* fire) Si 32$_{1}$ (ה[א]ר) 4QWiles 1$_{8}$ 4QShirShab^{d} 1.2$_{35}$.

<OBJ> אוֹר *light* 1QIsa^{a} 13$_{10}$ Ezk 32$_{7}$ 4QShir^{b} 2.1$_{4}$ 4QShirShab^{f} 23.2$_{9}$ ([א]ור), נֹגַהּ *light* 4QWiles 1$_{8}$

(Allegro מאזרי *ones who gird*), מָאוֹר *luminary* 1QH 9$_{27}$, נֵר *lamp* Ps 18$_{29}$ (lacking in ||2 S 22$_{29}$), זִק *spark* Is 50$_{11}$ (if em.; see Subj.), perh. נָתִיב *path* Jb 41$_{24}$ (or understand as subj.), דֶּרֶךְ *way* Ne 9$_{12.19}$, לַיְלָה *night* Ex 14$_{20}$ (or em.; see Subj.) Ps 105$_{39}$, תֵּבֵל *world* 77$_{19}$ 97$_4$, קָצִיר *branch* Is 27$_{11}$, פָּנִים *face* Nm 6$_{25}$ Ps 31$_{17}$ 67$_2$ 80$_{4.8.20}$ 119$_{135}$ Ec 8$_1$ Dn 9$_{17}$ Si 7$_{24}$ 32$_{11}$ 1QH 3$_3$ ([פני]) 4$_{5.27}$ 1QSb 4$_{27}$ 11QBer 1.2$_6$ Ketef Hinnom inscr. 1$_{16}$ ([פ]נ[יו]) 2$_8$ 4QApocMos A 2.2$_8$ 11QapPs^a 4$_{11}$ ([לה]איר ... פניו]), עַיִן *eye* Ps 13$_4$ 19$_9$ Pr 29$_{13}$ Ezr 9$_8$, לֵב *heart* 1QS 2$_3$, דַּעַת *knowledge* 4QShir^b 18.2$_8$ 4QShirShab^d 1.2$_{35}$, בְּרִית *covenant* with Israel 1QM 17$_7$ (Yadin ב]ית י]שראל *house of Israel*), perh. אסר ptc. pass. *bound one*, i.e. sacrificial victim Ps 118$_{27}$ (if em. אִסְרוּ *bind!*); obj. of place מִזְבֵּחַ *altar* Ml 1$_{10}$ CD 6$_{12}$ (both + חִנָּם *in vain*).

<PREP> לְ of benefit, *to, for* Ex 13$_{21}$ Is 60$_{19}$ Ps 118$_{27}$ Ne 9$_{12.19}$ (both + אָב *father*) Si 7$_{24(C)}$ (+ בֵּן *son*), of direction, *to* 1QM 1$_8$ (+ קָצָה *end* of world), of time, *to, until* 1$_8$ (+ קֵץ *appointed time*).

בְּ of accompaniment, *with, in* Si 32$_{11}$ (+ מ[ע]שיך *your deeds*) 1QM 17$_7$ (+ שִׂמְחָה *joy*), of instrument, *by, through* 1QS 2$_3$ (+ שֵׂכֶל *wisdom* of life) 1QH 4$_{27}$, of place, *in, among* 4$_2$ 4QShir^b 18.2$_8$ (both + לֵבָב *heart*) 4QShirShab^d 1.2$_{35}$, of direction, *upon* Ps 119$_{135}$ (+ עֶבֶד *servant*), of method, *in* 4QpIsa^d 1$_5$ (+ מִשְׁפָּט *manner* of Urim and Thummim); כְּ *as* Ps 139$_{12}$ (+ יוֹם *day*).

אֶל *upon* Nm 6$_{25}$ Si 7$_{24(A)}$ (+ בַּת *daughter*) 11QBer 1.2$_6$ 4QApocMos A 2.2$_8$ Ketef Hinnom inscr. 2$_8$ ([א]ל[יך]); עַל *upon* Gn 1$_{15.17}$ (both + אֶרֶץ *earth*) Ex 25$_{37}$ (+ עֵבֶר *side*) Ps 31$_{17}$ (+ עֶבֶד *servant*) Dn 9$_{17}$ (+ מִקְדָּשׁ *sanctuary*) 4QPrQuot 1$_{12}$ (+ אֶרֶץ) 10$_1$ (+ [אר]ץ) 48$_7$ ([להא]יר; + [א]רץ]) 4QJub^a 6$_6$ ([להאיר על]); מִן of place, *from* 1QH 9$_{27}$ (+ חֹשֶׁךְ *darkness*), of cause, *because of* Ezk 43$_2$ (+ כָּבוֹד *glory*); אֵת *with* Ps 67$_2$; אַחֲרֵי Jb 41$_{24}$ (+ לִוְיָתָן *Leviathan*).

Also 4Q376 1.2$_1$

<SYN> חנן *be gracious*, ברך pi. *bless*.

→ אוֹר *light*, אוֹרָה *light*, אוּר I *fire*, מָאוֹר *luminary*, מְאוּרָה *light-hole*, אוּר II *Ur*, אוּרִיאֵל *Uriel*, אוּרִיָּה *Uriah*, יָאִיר *Jair*, יָאִירִי *Jairite*, אוּרִים *Urim*.

אוֹר 115.7.116 n.m. (sometimes f.) **light**—cstr. אוֹר, sf. אוֹרִי, אוֹרְךָ (אוֹרֶךָ, Q אורכה), אוֹרֵךְ, אוֹרוֹ, אוֹרֵהוּ (אוֹרֵהוּ), אוֹרָם; pl. אוֹרִים.

1. daylight, by contrast with darkness, Gn 1$_{3.3.4.4.5.18}$ Ex 10$_{23}$ Is 5$_{30}$ 18$_4$ 45$_7$ 1QIsa^a 53$_{11}$ Am 8$_9$ Zc 14$_6$ (unless em.; see Subj.) 14$_7$ Ps 37$_6$ 49$_{20}$ 104$_2$ 139$_{11}$ (unless em.; see Nom. Cl.) Jb 3$_{9.16.20}$ 12$_{22.25}$ 17$_{12}$ 18$_{18}$ 24$_{16}$ 25$_3$ (unless em.; see Subj.) 26$_{10}$ 28$_{11}$ 33$_{28}$ 38$_{19}$ Ec 2$_{13}$ 11$_7$ 12$_2$ Si 3$_{25}$ 36$_{14}$ 39$_{17}$ (if em.; see Obj.) 42$_1$ 1QS 10$_{1.2}$ 1QH 12$_{4.6.7}$ 4QPrQuot 1$_{9.10}$ 7$_2$ 15$_6$ 19$_2$ 29$_{10}$ 33$_1$ 35$_2$ 51$_{5(mg)}$ GnzPs 1$_4$ 11QPs^a 139$_{12}$ 4QBer^a 1$_{13}$ 4QBark^a 2.1$_9$ 4QJub^a 5$_{10}$ 6$_{7.9}$ 7$_5$ 11QapPs^a 1$_{13}$ 3$_8$ 4$_{10.10}$ 11QShirShab 1$_4$.

2. luminaries, sun, moon, stars, Is 60$_{19}$ Ps 136$_7$ Jb 31$_{26}$ 37$_{21}$ 1QS 3$_{20}$ CD 5$_{18}$ 4QPrQuot 13$_1$ 29$_9$.

3. light given by luminaries, Is 13$_{10.10}$ 30$_{26.26.26}$ Jr 4$_{23}$ 31$_{35.35}$ Ezk 32$_{7.8}$ Ps 148$_3$ Si 36$_7$ 43$_9$ 50$_6$ 4QpIs^d 1$_6$ 4QShirShab^f 20.2$_9$ 11QShirShab 4$_2$ 5$_{2.2}$ 11QPs^a 27$_2$.

4. dawn, Jg 16$_2$ 19$_{26}$ 1 S 14$_{36}$ 25$_{34.36}$ 2 S 17$_{22}$ 23$_4$ 2 K 7$_9$ Am 8$_8$ (unless em.; see Prep.) Mc 2$_1$ Zp 3$_5$ Jb 24$_{14}$ Pr 4$_{18}$ Ne 8$_3$.

5. lightning, Jb 36$_{30}$ (unless em.; see Obj.) 36$_{32}$ 37$_{3.11}$ (unless em.; see Cstr.) 37$_{15}$, perh. 38$_{24}$ (unless em.; see Subj.).

6. light from other sources, Is 50$_{11}$ (fire; if em.; see Cstr.), Jr 25$_{10}$ (lamp), Hb 3$_{11}$ (arrows), Ps 78$_{14}$ (fire), Jb 41$_{10}$ (sneezing of crocodile) 4QBer^a 1$_3$ (fire) 4QShirShab^f 23.2$_{10}$ (gold).

7. light as representing goodness, hope, salvation, justice, etc. (distinction from §1 oft. uncertain), Is 2$_5$ 5$_{20.20}$ 9$_{1.1}$ 10$_{17}$ 26$_9$ (if em.; see Prep.) 42$_{6.16}$ 49$_6$ 51$_4$ 58$_{8.10}$ 59$_9$ 60$_{1.3.19.20}$ Jr 13$_{16}$ Ho 6$_5$ Am 5$_{18.20}$ Mc 7$_{8.9}$ Ps 27$_1$ 36$_{10.10}$ 38$_{11}$ 43$_3$ 44$_4$ 56$_{14}$ 89$_{16}$ 97$_{11}$ 112$_4$ 119$_{105}$ Jb 18$_{5.6}$ 22$_{28}$ 29$_{24}$ 24$_{13}$ 29$_3$ 30$_{26}$ 33$_{30}$ (unless em.; see Cstr.) 38$_{15}$ Pr 6$_{23}$ 13$_9$ 16$_{15}$ Si 11$_{21}$ 16$_{16}$ Lm 3$_2$ GnzPs 2$_{10}$, esp. at Qumran, 1QM 1$_{1.3.9.11.13}$ 13$_{5.9.15}$ 14$_{17}$ 17$_6$ 1QH 6$_{17}$ 7$_{24}$ 9$_{26}$ 12$_{15}$ 18$_{3.29}$ 1QS 1$_9$ 2$_{16}$ 3$_{3.7.13.19.20.24.25.25}$ 4$_8$ 11$_{3.5}$ CD 13$_{12}$ 4QToh D$_1$ 4QPrQuot 10$_2$ 15$_6$ 21$_1$ 51$_{14}$ 4QShir^a 1$_7$ 4QShir^b 2.1$_4$ 4QCat^a 1$_8$ 7$_8$ 12.1$_7$ 4QCrypt 1.2$_7$ 1.3$_6$ 1QMyst 1.1$_6$ 4Q416 4$_{14}$ 4Q462$_{8.9}$ 4QShirShab^d 1.1$_{45}$ 1.2$_{35}$ 4QShirShab^e 5$_4$ 4QShirShab^f 46$_2$ 11QapPs^a 4$_7$.

<SUBJ> היה *be* Gn 13.3 Ex 1023 (+ לְכָל־בְּנֵי יִשְׂרָאֵל *to all the people of Israel*) Is 1017 (+ לְאֵשׁ *for a fire*) 3026.26 Zc 146 (or em. קוֹר *cold* or אוֹר *heat*) 147 (+ לְעֶת־עֶרֶב *at evening time*) 4Q4628 (+ עִם *with* Y.), בוא *come* Is 601 (|| כָּבוֹד *glory* of Y.), hi. *bring* Ps 433, יצא *go*, i.e. shine, *out* Ho 65 (or em.; see Prep.), בקע ni. *break* Is 588 (+ כַּשַּׁחַר *as the dawn*), עבר *pass* 11QapPsa 410 ([יבעור]), אור hi. *give light* 1QM 1417(Yadin) ([יא]יר) 4QShirb 2.14 11QapPsa 410 ([יאיר אור]), זרח *shine* Is 5810 Ps 9711 (if em. זָרֻעַ *is sown*) 1124 Pr 139 (if em. יִשְׂמָח *will rejoice*), הלל hi. *shine* Jb 3126, זהר hi. *shine* Si 439 (+ במרומי אל *in the high places of God*), נגה *shine* Is 91 Jb 2228, יפע hi. *shine* 1QH 926.

שׂמח *rejoice* Pr 139 (ms צמח *spring up*; || נֵר *lamp*), זרע pass. *be sown* Ps 9711 (+ לַצַּדִּיק *for the righteous one*, שִׂמְחָה *joy*; or em. זָרַח *has arisen*), צמח *spring up* Pr 139(ms) (L שׂמח *rejoice*), קום *rise* Jb 253 (or em. אוֹרְבוֹ *his ambush* or אִמְרָהוּ *his word*), חסר *be lacking* Si 325 (|| חָכְמָה *wisdom*), חשׁך *be darkened* Is 530 (if em. חֹשֶׁךְ צַר וָאוֹר *darkness [and] distress and light* to חֹשֶׁךְ צָר וְאוֹר *darkness [and] distress. And light* is darkened) Jb 186 (+ בְּאָהֳלוֹ *in his tent*; || נֵר *lamp*) Ec 122 (|| שֶׁמֶשׁ *sun*, יָרֵחַ *moon*, כּוֹכָב *star*), דעך *be extinguished* Jb 185 (|| שָׁבִיב *flame*), מנע ni. *be withheld* 3815 (+ מֵרְשָׁעִים *from the wicked*).

נסע *depart* Ps 47 (if em. נָסָה *raise*), חלק ni. *be divided* Jb 3824 (or em. רוּחַ *wind*, or אוּר *fire*), שׁכן *dwell* 3819, שׁנה *be different* Si 367 (+ [מ]על שמש *than [the] sun*), נחה hi. *lead* Ps 433, נחם pi. *comfort* 433(mss) (L נחה), ישׁע hi. *save* 444 (|| זְרוֹעַ *arm*, יָמִין *right hand*).

<NOM CL> וַיַּרְא אֱלֹהִים אֶת־הָאוֹר כִּי־טוֹב *and saw the light, that it was good* Gn 14, דְּבָרֶךָ ... אוֹר לִנְתִיבָתִי *your word is ... a lamp to my path* Ps 119105 (|| נֵר *lamp*), לַיְלָה אוֹר *night is light* 13911 (or em. יְסֻגַּר *closes* around me; 11QPsa אזר *girdles*), אוֹר קָרוֹב מִפְּנֵי־חֹשֶׁךְ *light is near darkness* Jb 1712 (+ יוֹם *day*), מָתוֹק הָאוֹר *the light is sweet* Ec 117, אֵין אוֹרָם *there was not their* (heavens') *light* Jr 423, אוֹרוֹ עַל־כַּנְפוֹת הָאָרֶץ *his lightning is to the ends of the earth* Jb 373 (unless obj. of יִשְׁרֵהוּ *he releases*), מִשְׁפָּטֶיךָ אוֹר *your judgments are light* Ho 65 (unless em.; see Prep.), חֹשֶׁךְ יוֹם י׳ וְלֹא־אוֹר *the day of Y. is darkness and not light* Am 520, var. 518, י׳ אוֹרִי *Y. is my light* Ps 271 (|| יֵשַׁע *salvation*, מָעוֹז *stronghold*), var. Mc 78, חשך אתה ולוא אור *you* (Belial) *are darkness and not light* 11QapPsa 47, תּוֹרָה אוֹר *teaching is light* Pr 623 (|| נֵר), אוֹר־עֵינַי גַּם הֵם אֵין אִתִּי *the light of my eyes is* (lit. *are*) *also not with me* Ps 3811, אתכה אור *with you is light* 1QH 183, perh. אור בלבבי *light is in my heart* 1QS 115 (Wernberg-Møller) (for AHL, see Cstr.).

<OBJ> אור hi. *give (light)* 1QIsaa 1310 Ezk 327 4QShirShabf 23.210 ([א]ור), הלל hi. *cause to shine* Is 1310 Jb 4110, נגה hi. *cause to shine* Is 1310, גבר hi. *magnify* 1QM 1315 (:: חֹשֶׁךְ *darkness*), עשׂה *make* Ps 1367, ברא *create* 4QJuba 510 ([אור]), יצר *create* Is 457 (|| שָׁלוֹם *peace* [1QIsaa טוֹב *good*]; :: חֹשֶׁךְ *darkness*), פתח *open* 1QS 113, ידע *know* Jb 2416, ראה *see* Gn 14 Is 91 1QIsaa 5311 (perh. יִרְאֶה = *is sated with*, from רוה) Ps 3610 4920 Jb 316 3126 (|| יָרֵחַ *moon*) 3721, נתן *give* 320 (|| חַיִּים *life*), שׂים *place* Is 520 (+ לְחֹשֶׁךְ *for darkness*), פרשׂ *spread* Jb 3630 (or em. אֵדוֹ *his mist*), חלק *apportion* Si 1616 (+ לבני אדם *to human beings*; || שֶׁבַח *praise*), שׁלח *send forth* Ps 433 (|| אֱמֶת *truth*), נסה *raise* 47 (or em. נטה *extend*; ms נשׂא *raise*), נטה *extend* 47 (if em.), נפל hi. *cause to fall* Jb 2924, צוה pi. *command* Si 3917 (if em. אוצרו *his storehouse* to אור צוה *he commanded light*).

<CSTR> אוֹר הַבֹּקֶר *light of the morning* Jg 162 1 S 1436 2534.36 2 S 1722 2 S 234 (בֹּקֶר) 2 K 79 Mc 21, אור [היו]ם *light of the day* 4QPrQuot 19, היומם *of the day* 110 הַלְּבָנָה *of the moon* Is 3026, ([א]ור) 515(mg) ([א]וֹר) 156 331 ([א]ור) 71 ([י]ומם) הַשֶּׁמֶשׁ *of the sun* 11QPsa 272, הַחַמָּה *of the sun* Is 3026, נֹגַהּ *of brightness* Pr 418, עוֹלָם *of eternity* Is 6019.20 1QH 127 ([עו]לם) 4Q416 414, עֲנָנוֹ *of his cloud* Jb 3715, אֵשׁ *of fire* Is 5011 (if em. אוּר אֶשְׁכֶם *flame of your fire*) Ps 7814, נֵר *of a lamp* Jr 2510, גודלכה *of your majesty* 1QM 1417, [כ]בודו *of his glory* 4QPrQuot 211, י׳ *of Y.* Is 25 Si 1121 1616, יִשְׂרָאֵל *of Israel* Is 1017 (אוֹר־; || קָדוֹשׁ *holy one*).

אור עולמים *light of eternity* 1QS 48 1QM 135 ([עולמ]ים) 176, אור אורתים *light of (two) lights*, i.e. perfect light 1QH 1829, sim. 4QShirShabd 1.145 (אורתם perh. *of their light*) 4QShirShabe 54 (אורותם perh. *of their lights*), צַדִּיקִים *of righteous ones* Pr 139 (אוֹר־), רְשָׁעִים *of wicked ones* Jb 185, שִׁבְעַת הַיָּמִים *of the seven days* of creation Is 3026, אורים *of lights* 11QShirShab 42

5$_{2}$ (אור[י]ם), חִצֶּיךָ of your arrows Hb 3$_{11}$ (|| נֹגַהּ brightness), עֵינַי of my eyes Ps 38$_{11}$, פְּנֵי of the countenance of king Pr 16$_{15}$ (אוֹר־), פָּנֶיךָ of your countenance Ps 4$_{7}$ 44$_{4}$ 89$_{16}$ (אוֹר־), פָּנַי of my countenance Jb 29$_{24}$, הַחַיִּים of life Ps 56$_{14}$ Jb 33$_{30}$ (or em. אֶרֶץ land of) 1QS 3$_{7}$, שבעתים of sevenfold, i.e. sevenfold light 1QH 7$_{24}$ ([א]ור), גּוֹיִם of the nations Is 42$_{6}$ (|| בְּרִית covenant) 49$_{6}$ GnzPs 2$_{10}$ (הגוים), עַמִּים of peoples Is 51$_{4}$.

יום אור day of light, i.e. daylight Am 8$_{9}$, מבוא coming of, i.e. sunrise 1QH 12$_{4}$, מוצא outgoing of, i.e. sunset 12$_{6}$, פנו[ת] turn of 12$_{7}$ (Licht מפני from before), כוכב אור star of light Si 50$_{6}$, רקיע האור firmament of the light 4QShirShab^{f} 20.2$_{9}$, עֲנַן אוֹרוֹ cloud of his lightning Jb 37$_{11}$ (or em. אֵדוֹ his mist), תַּכְלִית אוֹר the end, i.e. boundary, of light 26$_{10}$, בית house of 4QCrypt 1.2$_{7}$ 1.3$_{6}$ (both האור).

מעון אור abode of light 1QS 3$_{19}$ (:: חֹשֶׁךְ darkness) 11QapPs^{a} 3$_{8}$ ([מ]עון אור]), מעין fountain of 1QH 6$_{17}$, ממשלת dominion of 1QS 10$_{1}$ (+ עם תקופתו at its coming round), ממשל dominion of 4QPrQuot 15$_{6}$, יִתְרוֹן superiority of Ec 2$_{13}$ (הָאוֹר; + מִן־הַחֹשֶׁךְ over the darkness), קֵץ age of 4Q462$_{9}$ (האור; :: חֹשֶׁךְ), גורל lot of 1QM 13$_{9}$ 4QCat^{a} 1$_{8}$ ([ג]ו[רל]) CD 13$_{12}$ (הא[ור]).

מְאוֹרֵי אור luminaries of light Ezk 32$_{8}$, כּוֹכְבֵי stars of Ps 148$_{3}$ (|| שֶׁמֶשׁ sun, יָרֵחַ moon), שערי gates of 4QPr Quot 7$_{2}$ ([או]ר) 19$_{2}$ 29$_{10}$, כלי vessels of 1$_{9}$, מֹרְדֵי rebels of, i.e. against Jb 24$_{13}$ (אוֹר־), משפטי judgments of 1QS 11$_{5}$.

בני sons of 1QS 1$_{9}$ 2$_{16}$ 3$_{13.24.25}$ 1QM 1$_{1.3.9.11}$ (:: הַחֹשֶׁךְ darkness) 1$_{13}$ 4QToh D$_{1}$ ([הא]ור) 4QCat^{a} 7$_{8}$ (האור) 12.1$_{7}$ 4QShir^{a} 1$_{7}$ ([או]ר), גורלות lots of 4QPrQuot 51$_{14}$, דגלי standards, i.e. troops, of 10$_{2}$, דרכי ways of 1QS 3$_{3.20}$, רוחות spirits of 3$_{25}$ (:: הַחֹשֶׁךְ), נהרי rivers of 4QShir Shab^{f} 15.2$_{2}$, אופני wheels of 20.2$_{3}$ (|| קֹדֶשׁ holiness), אלי gods of 4QShirShab^{d} 1.2$_{35}$, צבעי colours of 4QShirShab^{f} 23.2$_{8}$.

שר אורים prince of lights 1QS 3$_{20}$ CD 5$_{18}$ (האורים), אל God of 4QPrQuot 29$_{9}$ (או[ר]ים), רוח spirit 4QShir Shab^{f} 14$_{5}$, אלוהי God of 46$_{2}$ 4QPrQuot 13$_{1}$, נה[ו]רי fires of 4QBer^{a} 1$_{3}$, כול אורו all its (the sun's) light 4QpIs^{d} 1$_{6}$.

<ADJ> אוֹר גָּדוֹל a great light Is 9$_{1}$, אוֹרִים גְּדֹלִים great lights Ps 136$_{7}$.

<PREP> גורל אל לאור the lot of God is for eternal light 1QM 13$_{5}$, כובדכה לאור your glory is for an eternal light 1QH 12$_{15}$, היה לְ be a light Is 60$_{19}$ (+ שֶׁמֶשׁ sun) 60$_{19}$ (+ י׳ Y.), יצב לְ htp. stand as 1QH 18$_{29(Licht)}$ ([ולהתיצב]), נתן לְ give as Is 42$_{6}$ (obj. עַבְדִּי my servant; || בְּרִית covenant) 49$_{6}$ (obj. עַבְדִּי) Jr 31$_{35.35}$ (obj. luminaries) GnzPs 2$_{10}$ (obj. עבדו his servant, i.e. psalmist), make dark places light 4QBark^{a} 2.1$_{9}$, שִׂים לְ place darkness as Is 5$_{20}$ (:: חֹשֶׁךְ darkness) 42$_{16}$ (|| מִישׁוֹר level place), יצא לְ go, i.e. shine, out as 51$_{4}$ (subj. מִשְׁפָּט judgment, if em. verse division), יחל לְ pi. wait for Jb 30$_{26}$ (|| טוֹב good), קוה לְ pi. wait for Is 59$_{9}$ (|| נְגֹהָה brightness) Jr 13$_{16}$ (:: צַלְמָוֶת gloom) Jb 3$_{9}$ Si 11$_{21}$ (א[ו]רה), לְ of time, at, + קום rise Jb 24$_{14}$ (or em. לְאוֹר at the light to לֹא אוֹר [when there is] not light), עדר ni. be lacking Zp 3$_{5}$, לְ of place, direction, to, + הלך go Is 60$_{3}$ (|| נֹגַהּ brightness), walk in Jb 29$_{3}$ (+ חֹשֶׁךְ darkness), יצא hi. bring out Mc 7$_{9}$ Jb 12$_{22}$, רגע לְ hi. perh. cause judgment to rest, i.e. to be, as Is 51$_{4}$, קרא לְ call, i.e. name Gn 1$_{5}$ (:: חֹשֶׁךְ), הבדלתה עולם בין חושך לאור you have divided the world between darkness and light GnzPs 1$_{4}$ (|| טָהוֹר clean thing; + צֶדֶק righteousness).

בְּ of place, in Pr 16$_{15}$ 1QS 4$_{8}$ 4QPrQuot 21$_{1}$ 4QJub^{a} 7$_{5}$ ([באור]) 11QShirShab 4$_{2}$, + ראה see Ps 36$_{10}$ (+ מְקוֹר חַיִּים fountain of life), הלך walk Is 2$_{5}$ 50$_{11}$ (if em.; see Cstr.) Ps 89$_{16}$, htp. 56$_{14}$ 4Q416 4$_{14}$ (יתה[לכו]), [כ]בוד באור glory in light 4QShirShab^{d} 1.1$_{45}$ 4QShirShab^{e} 5$_{4}$, of time, at, + עשה do Mc 2$_{1}$, of instrument, through, by, with, perh. 11QShirShab 5$_{2}$, + אור ni. be enlightened Jb 33$_{30}$ (if em.; see Cstr.), חדש pi. renew joy 4QPrQuot 35$_{2}$ (או[ר]), האדיר למשרת מיכאל באור עולמים he has magnified the authority of Michael through eternal light 1QM 17$_{6}$, יפע בְּ hi. shine with 1QH 7$_{24}$ ([א]ור), ראה בְּ see Jb 33$_{28}$, נבט בְּ hi. look at 1QS 3$_{7}$.

כְּ as 2 S 23$_{4}$ Is 26$_{9}$ (if em. כַּאֲשֶׁר when to כָּאוֹר as the light) 30$_{26.26}$ Zp 3$_{5}$ (if em. לָאוֹר at the light) Ps 37$_{6}$ (|| צָהֳרָיִם midday) 11QPs^{a} 139$_{12}$ (MT כָּאוֹרָה) 27$_{2}$, + יצא go, i.e. shine, out Ho 6$_{5}$ (if em. מִשְׁפָּטֶיךָ אוֹר יֵצֵא your judgments are light (that) goes forth to מִשְׁפָּטִי כָאוֹר יֵצֵא my judgment goes forth as the light).

וַיִּקְרָא־בוֹ ... מִן־הָאוֹר and he read it from light, i.e. dawn, until midday Ne 8$_{3}$, יֶהְדְּפֻהוּ מֵאוֹר אֶל־חֹשֶׁךְ they *thrust him from light to darkness* Jb 18$_{18}$; מִפְּנֵי *from before*, + אסף ni. *be gathered* (of darkness) 1QS 10$_{2}$ 1QH 12$_{7(\text{Licht})}$ (AHL [מפנו]ת *from the turn of*), גלה *be exiled* (of darkness) 1QMyst 1.1$_{6(\text{Milik})}$; בדל בֵּין hi. *separate between* light and darkness Gn 1$_{4.18}$ 4QJub[a] 6$_{7}$ (להב[דיל בין אור]) 6$_{9}$ (ו[יבדיל בין האור]) 11QapPs[a] ([בין האור]).

כְּחֹם צַח עֲלֵי אוֹר *as glowing heat in the (day)light* Is 18$_{4}$, חסף עַל *lay bare to*, i.e openly reveal secret Si 42$_{1(\text{Bmg})}$ (B lacks על אור), צוה עַל pi. *command* Jb 36$_{32}$.

עַד *until, when*, + הרג *kill* Jg 16$_{2}$, בזז *spoil* 1 S 14$_{36}$, יתר ni. *remain* 25$_{34}$, נגד hi. *tell* 25$_{36}$, עדר ni. *be lacking* 2 S 17$_{22}$, חכה pi. *wait* 2 K 7$_{9}$, נפל *fall*, i.e. lie Jg 19$_{26}$, נוכח האור ח[ושך] *opposite to the light is darkness* Si 36$_{14}$.

<COLL> עטה אוֹר *wrap oneself (in) light* Ps 104$_{2}$, עַל־כַּפַּיִם כִּסָּה־אוֹר *he covers his hands with lightning* Jb 36$_{32}$, יצא אוֹר hi. *bring out to light* 28$_{11}$, חֹשֶׁךְ וְלֹא־אוֹר *(into) darkness without light* 12$_{25}$ Lm 3$_{2}$.

אורתים *lights* 1QH 4$_{6.23}$ 18$_{29}$ may be אור תום *light of perfection*; see אוֹרָה *light*.

Also 4QMg(?) 9$_{2}$ 4QPrQuot 7$_{5}$ 13$_{2}$ 15$_{6}$ (ל[א]ור) 29$_{8\ 9}$ 56.2$_{2}$ 65$_{3}$ ([א]ור) 215$_{7}$ 1QH 18$_{1.2}$ 4QShirShab[c] 3.2$_{7}$ (+ בינ[ה] *understanding*) 7$_{2}$ 12$_{1}$ 4QShirShab[d] 6$_{3}$ (+ דַּעַת *knowledge*) 6$_{6}$ (+ כָּבוֹד *glory*) 11QShirShab 1$_{4}$ o$_{1}$ 8QHymn 1$_{3}$ 4QBer[a] 1$_{13}$ ([א]ור) 4QOtot 1$_{10}$ 4Q477 2$_{2}$ 4QapPs[a] 7.2$_{3}$ 11QShirShab 1$_{3.4}$ o$_{1}$.

<SYN> §7 נֵר *lamp*.

<ANT> §§1, 7 חֹשֶׁךְ *darkness*.

→ אור *be light*.

אוּר I 6 n.m. **fire**—cstr. אוּר; pl. אֻרִים—**1. fire,** Is 31$_{9}$ 44$_{16}$ 47$_{14}$ Ezk 5$_{2}$ (unless em.; see Prep.) Jb 38$_{24}$ (if em.; see Subj.).

2a. light, Is 50$_{11}$. **2b.** in pl., appar. **region of light, east,** Is 24$_{15}$ (unless em.; see Prep.).

3. heat, Zc 14$_{6}$ (if em.; see Subj.).

<SUBJ> היה *be* Zc 14$_{6}$ (if em. אוֹר *light*), חלק ni. *be divided* Jb 38$_{24}$ (if em. אוֹר). **<NOM CL>** י׳ אֲשֶׁר־אוּר לוֹ בְּצִיּוֹן *Y. who has a fire in Zion* Is 31$_{9}$ (‖ תַּנּוּר *furnace*). **<OBJ>** ראה *see* 44$_{16}$ (+ חמם *be warm*). **<CSTR>** אוּר אֶשְׁכֶם *light of your fire* Is 50$_{11}$ (+ זִק *spark*).

<PREP> בְּ בער hi. *burn* hair *in* Ezk 5$_{2}$ (or em. בָּעוֹר *burning* or בָּאֵשׁ *in the fire*), הלך בְּ *walk by means of* Is 50$_{11}$, בָּאֻרִים *in the east* 24$_{15}$ (or em. בְּאִיֵּי הַיָּם *in the islands of the sea*; + אִיֵּי הַיָּם), נֶגֶד *in front of*, + ישׁב *sit* Is 47$_{14}$ (‖ גַּחֶלֶת *coal*), חמם *be warm* 1QIsa[a] 44$_{16}$.

→ אור *be light*.

אוּר II 1 pr.n.m. **Ur,** father of Eliphal, one of David's warriors, 1 C 11$_{35}$.

→ אור *be light*.

אוּר III pl.n. 4.0.1 **Ur,** alw. אוּר כַּשְׂדִּים *Ur of the Chaldaeans*, in southern Babylon, on right bank of Euphrates, mod. T. el-Muqayyar, Gn 11$_{28.31}$ 15$_{7}$ Ne 9$_{7}$ 4QpGen[a] 2$_{9}$ (אור כשדיים).

אוֹרָה I 3.0.7 n.f. **light**—cstr. Q אורת; appar. du. Q אורתים; pl. אוֹרֹת—**1. light, a.** as opposed to darkness, Ps 139$_{12}$. **b.** as representing revival, success, Is 26$_{19}$ Est 8$_{16}$. **2.** mental, spiritual **illumination,** 1QS 11$_{3}$ 1QH 4$_{6.23}$ 18$_{29}$.

<SUBJ> היה *be* Est 8$_{16}$ (+ לַיְּהוּדִים *to the Jews*; + יְקָר *honour*, שָׂשׂוֹן *joy*, שִׂמְחָה *joy*), נבט hi. *look* 1QS 11$_{3}$ (+ ברז *at the secret of*; + עַיִן *eye*; but perh. אורת לבבי ברז = *the light of my heart is in the secret of*).

<CSTR> אורת לבבי *light of my heart* 1QS 11$_{3}$; אור אורתים *light of (two) lights*, i.e. perfect light 1QH 18$_{29}$, sim. 4QShirShab[d] 1.1$_{45}$ (אורתם perh. *of their light*) 4QShirShab[e] 5$_{4}$ (אורותם perh. *of their lights*), טַל אוֹרֹת *dew of*, i.e. that is, *light(s)* Is 26$_{19}$.

<PREP> לאור[תי]ם הופעתה לי *you have shone for me as (two) lights* 1QH 4$_{6}$, sim. 4$_{23}$; כַּחֲשֵׁיכָה כָּאוֹרָה *as darkness, as light*, i.e. darkness is as light Ps 139$_{12}$ (11QPs[a] כחושך כאור).

Also 4QShirShab[d] 1.2$_{1}$ (אורתום).

→ אור *be light*.

[אוֹרָה] II, see אֻרָה.

[אֻוָרָה], see אֻרְוָה.

אוּרִי 8 pr.n.m. **Uri**—אֻרִי—**1.** son of Hur and father of Bezalel, Ex 31$_{2}$‖35$_{30}$ (31$_{2}$ Sam mss חוּרִי *Huri*) 38$_{22}$ 1 C

2_{20}. **2.** father of Geber, one of Solomon's officers, 1 K 4_{19} (אֻרִי). **3.** gatekeeper at time of Ezra, Ezr 10_{24}. **4.** father of Palal, who helped repair walls of Jerusalem, Ne $3_{25(mss)}$ (L אוּזַי *Uzai*).

→ אור *be light*.

אוּרִיאֵל 4 pr.n.m. **Uriel, 1.** son of Tahath and father of Uzziah, descendant of Kohath, 1 C 6_9. **2.** Kohathite leader at time of David, perh. ident. with preceding, 1 C $15_{5.11}$. **3.** maternal grandfather of Abijah, king of Judah, 2 C 13_2 (‖1 K 15_2 אֲבִישָׁלוֹם *Abishalom* for אוּרִיאֵל מִן־גִּבְעָה *Uriel from Gibeah*).

→ אור *be light* + אֵל *God*.

אוּרִיָּה 39.0.1.11 pr.n.m. **Uriah**—אוּרִיָּהוּ (I אריהו), I אוריו, אריו—**1.** Hittite warrior, husband of Bathsheba, 2 S 11_{3+19t} $12_{9.10.15}$ 23_{39}‖1 C 11_{41} 1 K 15_5 CD 5_5. **2.** priest at time of Ahaz, 2 K $16_{10.11.11.15}$ (or del. and em. Qr וַיְצַוֶּה to וַיְצַוֵּהוּ *and he commanded him*) 16_{16} Is 8_2 (all + הַכֹּהֵן *the priest*). **3.** prophet at time of Jehoiakim, Jr $26_{20.21.23}$ (all אוּרִיָּהוּ). **4.** father of priest at time of Ezra and Nehemiah, Ezr 8_{33} Ne $3_{4.21}$. **5.** companion of Ezra, perh. ident. with preceding, Ne 8_4. **6.** owner of tomb, Kh. el-Qom tomb inscr. $3_{1.2}$. **7.** son of Raga, Arad ost. 31_2 (אוריהו). **8.** father of Jehoaddan, Seal 855_2 (אריהו; 7th cent.). **9.** Samaria ost. 50_2 (אריו; others אביו *Abijah*).

10. perh. ident. with preceding, Samaria ost. 304_4 (ארי[ו]). **11.** Ophel ost.$_8$ (אוריהו; others הודיהו *Hodiah*). **12.** Seal 495 (אריהו; 8th cent.). **13.** Seal 23_2 (אריה; others תריה *Tiria*, תדיה *Todiah*; Babylonia?, 8th/7th cent.). **14.** Seal 429_1 (אריהו; 8th/7th cent.). **15.** Seal 770_2 (אריהו; Ophel, 7th cent.). **16.** Seal 208_1 (אריהו; En-Gedi, 7th cent.). **17.** Seal 430_1 (אריהו; 6th cent.). **18.** Stamp/coin 8 (אוריו; 5th/4th cent.). **19.** Arad ost. 26_1 (אריהו; others [ע]זריהו *Azariah*).

→ אור *be light* + י״ *Y*.

אוּרִיָּהוּ, see אוּרִיָּה.

אוּרִיו, see אוּרִיָּה.

אוּרִים 7.0.3 n.m.pl. **Urim**—Sam ארים; sf. אוּרֶיךָ (Q אורך, אוריכה)—sacred oracle in high priest's breastplate, usu. + תֻּמִּים *Thummim* (אורתום is perh. contraction of אורים ותומים at 1QH $4_{6[Licht].23[Licht]}$ $18_{29[Licht]}$ [AHL אורתים *[two] lights* in all three] 4QShirShab[d] 1.1_{45} [אורתם] 1.2_1 [אורתום] 4QShirShab[e] 5_4 [אורותם]).

<SUBJ> היה *be* Ex 28_{30} (Sam; see Obj.; + עַל *upon* Aaron's heart).

<NOM CL> אוּרֶיךָ לְאִישׁ חֲסִידֶךָ *your Urim are,* i.e. belong, *to your loyal one* Dt 33_8 (4QTestim; see Obj.).

<OBJ> נתן *place* Ex 28_{30} Lv 8_8 (both + אֶל *into* [Sam עַל *upon*] breastplate), יהב *give* 4QTestim Dt 33_8, עשׂה *make* Ex $28_{30(Sam)}$.

<CSTR> מִשְׁפַּט הָאוּרִים *judgment of the Urim* Nm 27_{21} 11QT $58_{18.20}$ 4QpIsa[d] 1_5.

<PREP> כֹּהֵן לְ *priest (qualified) for,* i.e. able to give a decision Ezr 2_{63}‖Ne 7_{65}; ענה בְּ *answer by means of* 1 S 28_6 (‖ חֲלוֹם *dream,* נָבִיא *prophet*).

Also 4QFlor 6_7 ([או]רים) perh. 4Q376 1.1_3.

→ perh. אור *be light* or ארר *curse*.

אורנה, see אֲרַוְנָה.

[אוּשׁ], see אשׁ.

אות 4.0.2 vb. **agree—Ni.** Impf. נֵאוֹת, יֵאֹתוּ, Q יאות (נְאוֹתָה); + waw וַיֵּאֹתוּ—**agree, consent,** <SUBJ> sons of Jacob Gn $34_{15.22}$, Hamor, Shechem and people of city 34_{23}, כֹּהֵן *priest* 2 K 12_9, אִישׁ *man* CD 20_7. <PREP> לְ agree *with*, consent *to* someone Gn $34_{15.22.23}$; עִם in same sense CD 20_7 4QD[b] 1_5 ([י]אות); בְּ *about, in respect of* wealth CD 20_7. <COLL> with infin., Gn 34_{22} (לָשֶׁבֶת *to dwell*) 2 K 12_9 (לְבִלְתִּי קְחַת־ *not to take*).

אוֹת 79.6.84.1 n.m. (sometimes f.) **sign**—אֹת; cstr. אוֹת; pl. אֹתֹת, אוֹתֹת (Q אותות); cstr. אֹתוֹת (Q אותות); sf. אֹתֹתַי, אוֹתֹתֶיךָ (Q אתותך), אֹתוֹתָיו (אֹתֹתָיו), אֹתוֹתֵינוּ, אוֹתֹתָם (אֹתֹתָם, Q אותותם).

1. sign, a. as reminder, memorial, of rainbow, Gn $9_{12.13.17}$ Si 44_{18}; circumcision, Gn 17_{11}; festival of unleavened bread, Ex 13_9 (‖ זִכָּרוֹן *reminder*); redemption of firstborn, 13_{16} (‖ טוֹטָפוֹת *frontlets*); sabbath, 31_{13} (+

לָדַעַת in order *to know*) 31$_{17}$ (+ לְעֹלָם *for ever*) Ezk 20$_{12.20}$ 4QJub^{a} 5$_{3}$ 7$_{5}$; altar, pillar, Is 19$_{20}$ (|| עֵד *witness*); altar covering made from censers of Korah and other rebels, Nm 17$_{3}$; Aaron's rod, 17$_{25}$; tassel on garment, 15$_{39}$ (if em.; see Prep.); words, Dt 6$_{8}$ 11$_{18}$ (both + טוֹטָפוֹת); stones, Jos 4$_{6}$; trees, Is 55$_{13}$ (|| שֵׁם *name*, i.e. testimony); iron plate, Ezk 4$_{3}$; idolater, 14$_{8}$ (|| מָשָׁל *byword*); judgment on the wicked, 1QH 15$_{20}$ (|| מ]ופת] *wonder*).

b. as token, proof, Ex 3$_{12}$ Dt 13$_{2.3}$=11QT 54$_{8.9}$ (both || מוֹפֵת *wonder*) Dt 28$_{46}$ (|| מוֹפֵת) Jos 2$_{12}$ Jg 6$_{17}$ 1 S 2$_{34}$ 10$_{7.9}$ 14$_{10}$ Is 7$_{11.14}$ 8$_{18}$ (|| מוֹפֵת) Jr 44$_{29}$ Ps 86$_{17}$ (+ לְטוֹבָה *of favour*) Si 44$_{16}$ 1QMyst 1.2$_{10}$, 4Q386–9 4$_{5.14}$.

c. as portent of the future, 2 K 19$_{29}$||Is 37$_{30}$ 2 K 20$_{8}$||Is 38$_{22}$ 2 K 20$_{9}$||Is 38$_{7}$ Is 20$_{3}$ (|| מוֹפֵת *wonder*) 44$_{25}$ Jr 10$_{2}$ Jl 2$_{23}$ (if em.; see Obj.) Ps 65$_{9}$.

d. as miraculous event, indicating divine action, Ex 4$_{8.8.9.17.28}$ (|| דָּבָר *word*) 4$_{30}$ 7$_{3}$ (|| מוֹפֵת *wonder*) 8$_{19}$ 10$_{1.2}$ (+ אֲשֶׁר הִתְעַלַּלְתִּי *how I made sport of Egypt*) Nm 14$_{11.22}$ (|| כָּבוֹד *glory*) Dt 4$_{34}$ (|| מַסָּה *testing*, מִלְחָמָה *war*, מוֹרָא *terror*, זְרוֹעַ outstretched *arm*, יָד mighty *hand*) 6$_{22}$ 7$_{19}$ (|| מַסָּה; all three || מוֹפֵת) 11$_{3}$ (|| מַעֲשֶׂה *deed*, מוּסָר *discipline*, גֹּדֶל *greatness*) 26$_{8}$ (|| מוֹרָא; all three || זְרוֹעַ, יָד) 29$_{2}$ (|| מַסָּה *testing*) 34$_{11}$ (all three || מוֹפֵת) Jos 24$_{17}$ Jr 32$_{20.21}$ (|| מוֹרָא, יָד, אֶזְרוֹעַ *arm*) Ps 78$_{43}$ (all three || מוֹפֵת) 105$_{27}$ (|| מוֹפֵת if em.; see Obj.) 135$_{9}$ Ne 9$_{10}$ Si 33$_{6}$ (all three || מוֹפֵת) 45$_{19}$ 48$_{12}$ (|| מוֹפֵת) 11QapPs^{a} 2$_{3}$ (|| מוֹפֵת).

e. as marker of seasons, Gn 1$_{14}$ (|| מוֹעֵד *season*, יוֹם *day*, שָׁנָה *year*) Si 43$_{6}$ 1QS 10$_{4}$ (|| יום [AHL]) 4QPrQuot 51$_{14}$ 64$_{4}$ 1QH 12$_{8}$ 4QJub^{a} 6$_{7}$; in 4QOtot with ref. to year in which vernal equinox coincides with new moon (e.g. 1$_{11.12}$ 2$_{5}$ 3$_{8}$).

f. as mark of identification, on Cain, Gn 4$_{15}$; of blood on doorposts and lintel, Ex 12$_{13}$; of nations, Is 66$_{19}$.

g. as evidence, character, Jb 21$_{29}$ 1QS 3$_{14}$.

h. as code, previous instructions, Lachish ost. 4$_{11}$.

2. standard, ensign of a military unit, Nm 2$_{2}$ Ps 74$_{4.9}$ (or em.; see Obj.) 1QpHab 6$_{4}$ 1QM 3$_{13.13.14.15.17}$ 4$_{1.1.2.3.4.6.7.8.9.9.11.13.15.15.15.16.17}$ perh. 4QM^{a} fr. 1$_{2}$.

<SUBJ> היה *be* Ex 8$_{19}$ (+ לְמָחָר *tomorrow*), בוא *come* Dt 13$_{3}$=11QT 54$_{9}$ Jos 4$_{6}$ (+ זֹאת *this*) 1 S 2$_{34}$ 10$_{7.9}$, ירה hi. *teach*, i.e. point (to) Jl 2$_{23}$ (if em.; see Obj.).

<NOM CL> זֹאת אוֹת *this is the sign of* the covenant Gn 9$_{12.17}$, זֶה־לְּךָ הָאוֹת *this is the sign for you* Ex 3$_{12}$ 1 S 2$_{34}$ 2 K 19$_{29}$||Is 37$_{30}$ 2 K 20$_{9}$||Is 38$_{7}$, vars. 1 S 14$_{10}$ Jr 44$_{29}$ 1QMyst 1.2$_{10 (Milik)}$ 4Q386–9 4$_{5.14}$, אוֹת הִיא *it is a sign* Ex 31$_{13 (Qr).17 (Qr)}$ (both + בֵּין *between* Y. and Israel) Ezk 4$_{3}$ (+ לְ *to* Israel), מָה אוֹת *what is (the) sign?* 2 K 20$_{8}$||Is 38$_{22}$ (or em. 2 K הָאוֹת *the sign*), בהתחדשם ... אות *when they are renewed ... it is a sign* 1QS 10$_{4}$ (+ למפתח חסדיו *of the release of his mercy*).

<OBJ> שׂים *place* Gn 4$_{15}$ Ex 10$_{2}$ Is 66$_{19}$ Jr 32$_{20}$ Ps 74$_{4}$ (+ אֹתוֹת *as ensigns*) 78$_{43}$ 105$_{27}$ (if em. שָׂמוּ בָם דִּבְרֵי אֹתוֹתָיו *they placed among them the words of his signs* to שָׂם בְּמִצְרַיִם אֹתוֹתָיו *he placed his signs in Egypt*), שׁית *place* Ex 10$_{1}$, עשׂה *do* 4$_{17.30}$ Nm 14$_{11.22}$ Dt 11$_{3}$ 34$_{11}$ Jos 24$_{17}$ Jg 6$_{17}$ Ps 86$_{17}$ 4QapPs^{b} 15$_{3}$ ([אות]) 11QapPs^{a} 2$_{3}$ ([ע]שה ... האותות]), נתן *give* Dt 6$_{22}$ 13$_{2}$=11QT 54$_{8}$ Jos 2$_{12}$ Is 7$_{14}$ Jl 2$_{23}$ (if em. אֶת־הַמּוֹרֶה *the early rain* to אֹת־הַמּוֹרֶה *a sign which points* to prosperity) Ne 9$_{10}$ Lachish ost. 4$_{11}$ 4QJub^{a} 7$_{5}$ ([ויתן ... אות]), בוא hi. *bring* Si 45$_{19}$, קום hi. *establish* Gn 9$_{17}$, שׁלח *send* Ps 135$_{9}$, צוה pi. *command* Ex 4$_{28}$, חדשׁ pi. *renew* Si 33$_{6}$, רבה hi. *multiply* Ex 7$_{3}$ Si 48$_{12}$, ראה *see* Nm 14$_{22}$ 15$_{39}$ (if em.; see Prep.) Dt 11$_{3}$ 29$_{2}$ Ps 74$_{9}$ (or em. אֹתִיּוֹתֵינוּ *our future things*, i.e. ptc. אתה *come*), ידע *know* Dt 11$_{3}$, נכר pi. *recognize* Jb 21$_{29}$ (or נכר = *treat as strange*, i.e. deny), פרר hi. *annul* Is 44$_{25}$, שׁאל *ask* 7$_{11}$ (+ מֵעִם י׳ *from Y.*), נגד hi. *tell* Ex 4$_{28}$, ספר pi. *tell* 10$_{2}$, זכר *remember* Dt 7$_{19}$.

<APP> מִשְׁמֶרֶת *keeping*, i.e. something kept Nm 17$_{25}$, [אות ... יום] השבת *a sign, ... the sabbath day*4QJub^{a} 7$_{5}$.

<ADJ> גָּדוֹל *great* Jos 24$_{17}$ 1QM 3$_{13}$ 4QJub^{a} 6$_{7}$ ([אות גד]ול), רִאשׁוֹן *first* Ex 4$_{8}$ 1QM 4$_{9}$, שֵׁנִי *second* 4$_{9}$, אַחֲרוֹן *latter* Ex 4$_{8}$.

<CSTR> אוֹת אֱמֶת *sign of truth*, i.e. true sign Jos 2$_{12}$, דעת *of knowledge* Si 44$_{16}$, עוֹלָם *of eternity* Is 55$_{13}$ Si 43$_{6}$44$_{18}$, בְּרִית *of (the) covenant* Gn 9$_{13}$ 17$_{11}$, אוֹת־הַבְּרִית *sign of the covenant* 9$_{12.17}$, אות של[ושת] *banner of three* 1QM 4$_{15}$, העשרה *of the ten* 4$_{4.17}$, החמשים *of the fifty* 4$_{3}$, המאה *of the hundred* 3$_{17 (Yadin)}$ ([המאה]) 4$_{2}$, הא[לף] *of the thousand* 4$_{1}$, רבוא *of ten thousand* 4$_{16}$, מררי *of Merari* 4$_{1}$, השבט *of the tribe* 3$_{15}$ ([א]ות), כול העדה *of all the* congregation 4$_{15}$.

אות שכניה *sign of Shecaniah* 4QOtot 1$_{11.11}$ ([או]ת [שכניה]) 1$_{12}$ ([אות שכ[נ]י]ה) 1$_{13}$ ([או]ת]) 1$_{13}$ ([שכניה]) 1$_{14}$ ([או]ת ש]כנ[י]ה]) 1$_{15}$ ([שכניה]) 1$_{15}$ ([או]ת ש]כניה]) 1$_{18}$ ([אות) 1$_{18}$ ([א]ות]) 1$_{19}$ 2$_{1.1}$ (both [אות שכניה]) 2$_{2}$ ([א]ות שכניה]) 2$_{3.3}$ ([אות שכניה]) 2$_{4}$ ([אות] שכני[ה]) 2$_{6.7}$ ([או]ת]) 2$_{8}$ ([אות]) 2$_{8.9.10}$ ([שכניה]) 2$_{11}$ ([שכ]ניה]) 2$_{11.13.14}$ ([אות]) 2$_{15.15.16}$ (both [אות שכניה]) 2$_{17}$ ([א]ות ש]כניה]) 2$_{17.18}$ 3$_{1}$ (all three [אות שכניה]) 3$_{2.3}$ ([או[ת]) 3$_{3}$ ([שכניה]) 3$_{4.5.6.7}$ ([אות שכניה]) 3$_{10.11.12}$ (all three [אות שכניה]) 3$_{12}$ ([או]ת שכניה]) 3$_{13.14.15.16}$ ([אות שכניה]), גמול *of Gamul* 1$_{11}$ ([אות גמול]) 1$_{12}$ ([ג]מול]) 1$_{12}$ ([אות גמ]ול]) 1$_{13}$ ([או]ת]) 1$_{14}$ ([גמו]ל]) 1$_{14}$ ([או]ת) 1$_{15}$ ([אות ג]מול]) 1$_{16}$ ([אות גמול]) 1$_{18}$ ([גמו[ל]) 1$_{19.19}$ (both [גמו]ל]) ([או]ת [גמו]ל) 2$_{1.2.2.3.4}$ (all five [אות ג]מול) 2$_{6}$ ([אות גמול]) 2$_{7}$ ([או]ת גמול) 2$_{7.8}$ ([אות ג]מול) 2$_{9}$ ([גמול]) 2$_{10.10.11}$ ([אות]) 2$_{14.14.15}$ (both [אות גמול]) 2$_{16}$ ([ג]מול]) 2$_{16.17}$ (both [אות גמול]) 2$_{18}$ ([ג]מול]) 3$_{1.2}$ (both [אות גמול]) 3$_{3}$ ([גמו]ל]) 3$_{4.4}$ ([אות]) 3$_{5.6.10}$ (both [אות גמול]) 3$_{11}$ ([גמו]ל]) 3$_{12}$ ([אות]) 3$_{13}$ ([אות גמול]) 3$_{14}$ ([אות ג]מול]) 3$_{14}$ ([אות]) 3$_{15}$ ([גמול]), סוף *of end* of Jubilee 1$_{16}$ ([ס]וף]) 2$_{4}$ ([אות סוף]) 2$_{12}$ ([או]ת סוף]) 2$_{18}$ ([אות סוף]) 3$_{7(mg).16}$, היו]בלים *of the jubilees* 3$_{8}$.

אותות (כול) העדה *banners of (all) the congregation* 1QM 3$_{13}$ 4$_{9}$, ראשי המחנות *of the chiefs of the camps* 3$_{14}$, אֹתוֹת הַשָּׁמַיִם *signs of*, i.e. in, *the heavens* Jr 10$_{2}$, בַּדִּים *of idle talkers* Is 44$_{25}$ (or em. בַּדִּים to בָּרִים *diviners*), היובל *of the jubilee* 4QOtot 1$_{16}$ ([אתות הי]ובל]) 2$_{5}$ 1$_{12}$ ([אתות היובל]) 2$_{19}$ ([אתות היובל]) 3$_{7}$ ([אתות]); קֹל הָאֹת *voice*, i.e. testimony, *of the sign* Ex 4$_{8.8}$, [אורך האו]תות] *length of the banners* 1QM 4$_{15(Yadin)}$, סרך אותות *order of the banners of* 3$_{13}$ 4$_{9}$, דִּבְרֵי אֹתוֹתָיו *words of his signs* Ps 105$_{27}$ (or em.; see Obj.), כָּל־הָאֹתוֹת *all the signs* 1 S 10$_{7(mss)}$ (L lacks ־כָּל) 10$_{9}$ Nm 14$_{11}$ (כל) Lachish ost 4$_{11}$ (האתת).

<PREP> לְ *as* sign Nm 17$_{25}$ (+ לִבְנֵי מֶרִי *for the rebels*) Is 8$_{18}$ 4QM^{a} fr. 1$_{2}$, היה לְ *be as* Gn 1$_{14}$ 9$_{13}$ 17$_{11}$ Ex 12$_{13}$ (+ הַדָּם *the blood*) 13$_{9}$ 13$_{16}$ (both + עַל *upon* your hand) Nm 15$_{39}$ (if em. לְצִיצִת *as a tassel*) 17$_{3}$ (+ לִבְנֵי יִשְׂרָאֵל *to the people of Israel*) Dt 28$_{46}$ Is 19$_{20}$ 55$_{13}$ Ezk 20$_{12.20}$ (both + שַׁבָּת *sabbath*) 1QH 15$_{20}$, נתן *give as* 4QJub^{a} 5$_{3}$ 6$_{7}$ (both [ויתן ... לאות]), קשׁר *tie as* Dt 6$_{8}$ (+ עַל־יָדֶךָ) 11$_{18}$ (+ עַל־יֶדְכֶם *upon your hand*), שׂים לְ hi. *make into* Ezk 14$_{8}$ (or em. to qal וְשַׂמְתִּיהוּ *and I will make him*), זבח לְ *sacrifice to* standard 1QpHab 6$_{4}$, אמן לְ hi. *believe* sign Ex 4$_{9}$.

בְּ *despite* Nm 14$_{11}$, of accompaniment, *with* 2$_{2}$ 1QS 3$_{14}$, + כרת ni. (of covenant) *be made* Si 44$_{18}$, of instrument, *by, with*, + יצא hi. *bring out* Dt 26$_{8}$ Jr 32$_{21}$, לקח *take* Dt 4$_{34}$, ידע בְּ *know* sign 4QPrQuot 51$_{14}$ ([אותו]ת]), בתכונם באותותם *in their order, in their signs* 1QH 12$_{8}$.

כְּ *according to* Lachish ost 4$_{11}$.

חתת מִן *be dismayed at* Jr 10$_{2}$, ירא מִן *be afraid of* Ps 65$_{9}$.

כתב על *write on* standard 1QM 3$_{13.14.15}$ ([ע]ל [א]ות]) 3$_{17(Yadin)}$ ([יכתובו]) 4$_{1.1.2..3.4.6.7.8.9.9.11.13}$.

<COLL> הָלַךְ ... עָרוֹם וְיָחֵף ... אוֹת *he has walked ... naked and barefoot ... as a sign* Is 20$_{3}$, אות לנו ללילה [במועד] *a sign for us of the night at the festival* 4QPrQuot 64$_{4}$.

אוֹת + number 2, 4QOtot 2$_{6.13(mg)}$ 3$_{8.18}$ ([אתות]); 3, 1$_{17}$ 3$_{1}$ ([אתות]); 16, 2$_{5}$ 3$_{8}$ ([אתות]) 3$_{17}$; 17, 2$_{12}$.

Also 1QH 13$_{1}$ 4Q487 12$_{4}$ 11QShirShab h$_{1.4}$ perh. 4Q522 2$_{6}$.

<SYN> §1 מוֹפֵת *wonder*, טוֹטָפֹת *frontlets*, מוֹרָא *fear*, מַסָּה *testing*, זְרוֹעַ *arm*, יָד *hand*.

→ perh. אוה II *mark out*.

אָז 144.3.36.2 adv. **then, at that time**—אָז (אֱזַי)—whether temporally or logically (but not in the sense of 'subsequently, next'), **1.** temporal, **then, at that time**, **a.** in ref. to **past time**, (1) with perf., e.g. אָז הוּחַל לִקְרֹא בְּשֵׁם י׳ *then they began to call on the name of Y.* Gn 4$_{26}$, Ex 4$_{26}$ 15$_{15}$ Jos 10$_{33}$ Jg 5$_{11.13.19.22}$ 8$_{3}$ 13$_{21}$ 2 S 21$_{17.18}$‖1 C 20$_{4}$ 1 K 8$_{12}$‖2 C 6$_{1}$ 1 K 9$_{24}$ 22$_{50}$ 2 K 14$_{8}$ Jr 11$_{18}$ Ml 3$_{16}$ Ps 40$_{8}$ 89$_{20}$ Jb 28$_{27}$ 1 C 15$_{2}$ 16$_{7}$ (+ בַּיּוֹם הַהוּא *on that day*) 2 C 8$_{12.17}$ 24$_{17}$ Si 51$_{11}$ 11QPs^{a} 26$_{12}$ 28$_{13}$ 4QpGen^{a} 4$_{5}$ 4QJub^{a} 5$_{10}$ perh. 4Q370 1$_{2}$.

(2) with impf., e.g. אָז יָשִׁיר־מֹשֶׁה *then Moses sang* Ex 15$_{1}$, אֹזֵל לוֹ אָז יִתְהַלָּל *when he goes off, at that time he boasts* Pr 20$_{14}$, Nm 21$_{17}$ Dt 4$_{41}$ Jos 8$_{30}$ 10$_{12}$ (אָז ... בְּיוֹם *then ... on the day of*) 22$_{1}$ 1 K 3$_{16}$ 8$_{1}$‖2 C 5$_{2}$ 1 K 9$_{11}$ 11$_{7}$ 16$_{21}$ 2 K 8$_{22}$‖2 C 21$_{10}$ (+ בָּעֵת הַהִיא *at the same time*) 2 K 12$_{18}$ 15$_{16}$ 16$_{5}$ Jb 38$_{21}$ Pr 1$_{28}$ Si 50$_{16.20}$ 4QapPs^{b} 69$_{6}$.

(3) with ptc., e.g. וְהַכְּנַעֲנִי ... אָז יֹשֵׁב בָּאָרֶץ *and at that time the Canaanites ... were living in the land* Gn 13$_{7}$, Jr 32$_{2}$.

(4) without a finite verb, e.g. וְהַכְּנַעֲנִי אָז בָּאָרֶץ *and at that time the Canaanites were in the land* Gn 12$_{6}$, Jos 14$_{11}$ (:: עַתָּה *now*) Jg 5$_{8}$ (or em. אָז לָחֶם שְׁעָרִים *then war was [in] the gates* to מֵאָז לֹא לָהֶם שְׁעָרִים *(which) had not been known to them in the past*) 2 S 23$_{14.14}$||1 C 11$_{16.16}$ Ho 2$_{9}$ (:: עַתָּה *now*).

b. in ref. to **future time,** (1) with impf., e.g. אָז תִּרְצֶה הָאָרֶץ אֶת־שַׁבְּתֹתֶיהָ *then the land will enjoy its sabbaths* Lv 26$_{34}$, 26$_{34.41.41}$ Dt 29$_{19}$ Jos 20$_{6}$ 1 S 20$_{12}$ 2 S 5$_{24}$||1 C 14$_{15}$ 2 S 5$_{24}$ Is 35$_{5.6}$ 41$_{1}$ 58$_{8.9}$ 60$_{5}$ Jr 22$_{22}$ 31$_{13}$ Ezk 32$_{14}$ Mc 3$_{4}$ (+ בָּעֵת הַהִיא *at the same time*) Zp 3$_{9.11}$ Ps 51$_{21.21}$ 56$_{10}$ (+ בְּיוֹם אֶקְרָא *on a day I call*) 96$_{12}$||1 C 16$_{33}$ Ps 119$_{6}$ 126$_{2.2}$ Jb 33$_{16}$ 1QS 4$_{19.20}$ 1QH 6$_{29}$ 11$_{22}$ 4Q521 1.2$_{12}$ 4Q416 9.1$_{15}$.

(2) with perf., e.g. אָז חֻלַּק עַד־שָׁלָל *then prey of spoil will be divided* Is 33$_{23}$, Hb 1$_{11}$.

2. logical, **a. if so, in that case, e.g.** אָז תִּנָּקֶה מֵאָלָתִי *in that case you will be freed from my adjuration* Gn 24$_{41}$, Ex 12$_{44.48}$ Jos 1$_{8.8}$ 1 S 6$_{3}$ 2 K 13$_{19}$ Jr 11$_{15}$ Ps 19$_{14}$ 69$_{5}$ Jb 3$_{13}$ 11$_{15}$ 13$_{20}$ 22$_{26}$ Pr 3$_{23}$ Ec 2$_{15}$ (or em. אֵין *not*) 1QS 3$_{11}$ 4Q416 1$_{18}$ 9.2$_{8.15}$ 10.2$_{8.10.16}$.

b. therefore, e.g. עָשָׂה מִשְׁפָּט וּצְדָקָה אָז טוֹב לוֹ *he dispensed justice and righteousness, therefore it was well with him* Jr 22$_{15}$ (or em. וְטוֹב *and it was well*), Jos 22$_{31}$ Jr 22$_{16}$ Ps 2$_{5}$ Ca 8$_{10}$.

c. then, introducing apodosis after conditional clause, אִם ... אָז *if ... then* Is 58$_{14}$ Jb 9$_{31}$ Pr 2$_{5.9}$, אָז ... אִם *then ... if* 1 C 22$_{13}$, כִּי ... אָז *when ... then* Gn 49$_{4}$, לוּלֵא ... כִּי אָז *if not ... then* 2 S 2$_{27}$, לוּלֵי ... אָז *if not ... then* 119$_{92}$, לוּלֵי י׳ ... אֲזַי ... בְּלָעוּנוּ ... אֲזַי הַמַּיִם שְׁטָפוּנוּ ... אֲזַי עָבַר *were it not (for) Y. ... then they would have swallowed us, ... then the waters would have drowned us, ... then it would have passed* over our necks Ps 124$_{2\text{-}5}$, כִּי לוּ ... כִּי־אָז *if not ... then* 2 S 19$_{7(Qr)}$, אִילוּלֵי ... אָז *if not ... then* MurEpBeth-Mashiko$_{5}$ (אללי שהגיים קרבים אלנו אזי עלתי *had the Gentiles not closed in on us, then I should have gone up*), אַחֲלֵי ... אָז *would that ... then* 2 K 5$_{3}$.

4. מֵאָז, **a.** as adv., **from of old,** usu. of distant past, Is 44$_{8}$ 45$_{21}$ (+ מִקֶּדֶם *from of old*) 48$_{3.5.7}$ (:: עַתָּה *now*) 48$_{8}$ Ps 93$_{2}$ (+ מֵעוֹלָם *from eternity*) Pr 8$_{22}$ 1QM 1$_{10}$ 10$_{2}$ 11$_{6.11}$ 13$_{10.14}$ 16$_{15}$ 18$_{7.10}$ 4QM^{a} fr. 11.1$_{10}$ 1QH fr. 47$_{3}$; of the nearer past, e.g. עֶבֶד אָבִיךָ וַאֲנִי מֵאָז *I was your father's servant in the past* 2 S 15$_{34}$ (:: עַתָּה *now*), Jg 5$_{8}$ (if em.; see §1a) Is 16$_{13}$ (:: עַתָּה).

b. as conj., **since,** (1) with perf., e.g. מֵאָז הִפְקִיד אֹתוֹ ... וַיְבָרֶךְ י׳ אֶת־בֵּית הַמִּצְרִי *from the time he put him in charge ... Y. blessed the house of the Egyptian* Gn 39$_{5}$, Ex 5$_{23}$ 9$_{24}$ Jos 14$_{10}$ Is 14$_{8}$ Jr 44$_{18}$ (מִן־אָז) Lachish ost. 6$_{12}$ ([מ]אז).

(2) with inf., מֵאָז דַּבֶּרְךָ *since you have spoken* Ex 4$_{10}$, מאז שלחך *since you sent* Lachish ost. 3$_{7}$.

c. as prep. **since, from,** מֵאָז הַבֹּקֶר *from early morning* Ru 2$_{7}$ (+ עַד־עַתָּה *until now*), מִי־יַעֲמֹד לְפָנֶיךָ מֵאָז אַפֶּךָ *who can stand before you once your anger is roused?* Ps 76$_{8}$ (or em. מֵעֹז אַפֶּךָ *from the strength of your anger,* as in 90$_{11}$).

Also 1QM 1$_{16}$ 4QRitPur 42.2$_{6}$ ([א]זי) 5Q25 2$_{2}$ 4Qap Ps^{b} 36$_{2}$.

אֶזְבָּי 1 pr.n.m. **Ezbai**—אֶזְבָּי—father of Naarai and warrior of David, 1 C 11$_{37}$ (נַעֲרַי בֶּן־אֶזְבָּי *Naarai the son of Ezbai*; ||2 S 23$_{35}$ פַּעֲרַי הָאַרְבִּי *Paarai the Arbite*).

אזה 0.0.0.2 pl.n. **Azzah, 1.** perh. ident. with Zawāta, 5 km SE of Samaria, Samaria ost. 2$_{3}$ 17$_{1}$. **2. Azzath-paran,** Samaria ost. 14$_{2}$ (מא[ז]ת פראן; others גת *Gath-paran*).

אזוב 10.0.2 n.m. **hyssop**—אֵזוֹב—aromatic plant used in purification, perh. *origanum maru* or *majorana syriaca*, <SUBJ> יצא *go out* 1 K 5$_{13}$ (+ בַּקִּיר *from the wall*; :: אֶרֶז *cedar*). <OBJ> לקח *take* Lv 14$_{4.6.49.51}$ Nm 19$_{6}$ (all five + צִפּוֹר *bird*, עֵץ אֶרֶז *cedar wood*, שְׁנִי תוֹלַעַת *scarlet material*) 19$_{18}$, טבל *dip* Lv 14$_{6.51}$ Nm 19$_{18}$, שׁלך hi. *cast* 4QToh B^{a}$_{5}$ (ארז [...] אזוב ... שני[ן] תולע *cedar ... hyssop ... scarlet material*). <CSTR> אֲגֻדַּת אֵזוֹב *bunch of hyssop* Ex 12$_{22}$. <PREP> בְּ of instrument, *with* 11QT 49$_{3}$ (+ עֵץ אֶרֶז *cedar wood*), + חטא pi. *purify* Lv 14$_{52}$ Ps 51$_{9}$; מִן־הָאֶרֶז ... וְעַד הָאֵזוֹב *from the cedar ... to the hyssop* 1 K 5$_{13}$. Also 4QToh B^{b}$_{1}$.

אֵזוֹר $_{14.2.2}$ n.m. **girdle,** short waist-cloth of linen or leather.

<SUBJ> היה *be* Is 11$_{5}$ (or em. אֵסוּר *girdle;* + צֶדֶק *righteousness*) 11$_{5}$ (+ אֱמוּנָה *faithfulness*) 1QSb (+ צֶדֶק), אזר pass. *be girded* around loins 2 K 1$_{8}$, דבק *be attached* to loins Jr 13$_{11}$, פתח ni. *be opened* Is 5$_{27}$, שׁחת ni. *be marred* Jr 13$_{7}$, צלח *be useful* 13$_{7.10}$.

<NOM CL> הָאֵזוֹר ... אֲשֶׁר עַל־מָתְנֶיךָ *the girdle ... which is around your loins* Jr 13$_{4}$.

<OBJ> אסר *bind* around loins of kings Jb 12$_{18}$, עטה *wrap oneself (in),* i.e. wear Si 11$_{4(B)}$ (Amg אֵפֶר *ashes*), נקף hi. *place around* Aaron 45$_{10}$ (|| אֵפֹד *ephod,* חֹשֶׁן *breastplate*), קנה *buy* Jr 13$_{1.2.4}$, שׂים *place* around loins 13$_{1.2.4}$, בוא hi. *bring* into water 13$_{1}$, לקח *take* 13$_{4.6.7}$, טמן *conceal* in rock 13$_{4.5.6.7}$.

<CSTR> אֵזוֹר חֲלָצָיו *girdle of his loins* Is 5$_{27}$ 11$_{5}$, חלציכה *of your loins* 1QSb 5$_{26}$, מָתְנָיו *of his loins* Is 11$_{5}$, עוֹר *of leather* 2 K 1$_{8}$, פִּשְׁתִּים *of linen* Jr 13$_{1}$; חֲגוֹרֵי אֵזוֹר *girded of,* i.e. by, *a girdle* around their loins Ezk 23$_{15}$ (+ טְבוּל *turban*).

<ADJ> זֶה *this* Jr 13$_{10}$.

<PREP> כְּ היה *be as* Jr 13$_{10}$; עַל *upon* Dt 23$_{14}$ (if em. אֲזֵנֶךָ *your tool*).

→ אזר *gird.*

[אֲזוּרָה] pr.n.f. **Azurah,** daughter of Cain, 11QJub 4$_{8}$ ([אזור]ה).

אֲזַי, see אָז.

אַזְכָּרָה $_{7.2}$ n.f. **token offering**—sf. אַזְכָּרָתָהּ (L אַזְכָּרָתָהּ)—a handful of fine flour, oil, and incense, taken from grain offering (מִנְחָה) or sin offering (חַטָּאת, Lv 5$_{12}$).

<OBJ> קטר hi. *burn* Lv 2$_{2.9.16}$ (+ מִגִּרְשָׂהּ וּמִשַּׁמְנָהּ *from its* [cereal offering's] *crushed grain and from its oil*) 5$_{12}$ (+ עַל אִשֵּׁי י׳ *upon the fire offerings of Y.*) 6$_{8}$ Nm 5$_{26}$ Si 45$_{16}$ (+ ריח ניחח *pleasing odour*), קמץ *take handful (of)* Lv 5$_{12}$ Nm 5$_{26}$, רום hi. *raise,* i.e. offer Lv 2$_{9}$, נגשׁ hi. *present* Si 38$_{11(Segal)}$ ([הגש]), נתן *give* 38$_{11(Smend)}$ (|| מִנְחָה *grain offering* [מ(נח)ה], דֶּשֶׁן *fatness,* i.e. fat of offering).

<APP> אַזְכָּרָתָהּ ... אִשֶּׁה *a token offering of it ... a fire offering* Lv 2$_{2.9}$ (both אִשֵּׁה *fire offering of* pleasing odour) 2$_{16}$ 24$_{7}$ (אַזְכָּרָה אִשֶּׁה *a token offering, a fire offering*), רֵיחַ נִיחֹחַ אַזְכָּרָתָהּ *a pleasing odour, its token offering* 6$_{8}$, מְלֹא קֻמְצוֹ ... אַזְכָּרָתָהּ *a handful of it ..., its token offering* 5$_{12}$, [ניחוח] אזכרה *a soothing (odour), a token offering* Si 38$_{11(Segal)}$.

<PREP> וְהָיְתָה לַלֶּחֶם לְאַזְכָּרָה *and it will be as a token offering for the bread* Lv 24$_{7}$=11QT 8$_{10(Yadin)}$ ([והית]ה).

<SYN> אִשֶּׁה *fire offering.*

→ זכר *remember.*

אזל I $_{5}$ vb **go—Qal** Pf. אָזַל, אָזְלַת, אָזְלוּ; impf. 2fs תֵּזְלִי; ptc. אֹזֵל—**go (away), be gone,** <SUBJ> קנה ptc. *buyer* Pr 20$_{14}$, יָד *hand,* i.e. strength Dt 32$_{36}$, לֶחֶם *food* 1 S 9$_{7}$, מַיִם *water* Jb 14$_{11}$, Israel Jr 2$_{36}$ (unless em.; see Coll.). <PREP> וְאֹזֵל לוֹ *when he goes off* Pr 20$_{14}$; מִכֵּלֵינוּ *from our vessels* 1 S 9$_{7}$, מִנִּי־יָם *from (the) sea* Jb 14$_{11}$. <COLL> מַה־תֵּזְלִי מְאֹד *how you have gone (astray) so very much* Jr 2$_{36}$ (or em. תֵּזֵלִּי, from זלל hi., how very *easy it is*).

Ni. Impf. Sam ותאזל—**go out,** <SUBJ> אִמְרָה *word* Dt 32$_{2(Sam mss)}$ (MT נזל *flow;* || ערף *drip*).

אזל II $_{1}$ vb **weave—Pu.** Ptc. מְאוּזָל—**be woven,** מְאוּזָּל בְּעִזְבוֹנַיִךְ נָתָנוּ *they give woven material in exchange for your wares* Ezk 27$_{19}$ (unless em. מֵאוּזָל *from Uzal,* i.e. אוּזָל II).

[אֶזֶל], see אֶבֶן, §6.

אזן I $_{41.3.6}$ vb. **hear—Hi.** Pf. הֶאֱזִין, הֶאֱזִינוּ; impf. יַאֲזִין, יַאֲזִינוּ, אָזִין; + waw וְהַאֲזַנְתָּ, וְהַאֲזִין, Si ויאזין; impv. הַאֲזִינָה, הַאֲזִינוּ (Q אזינו), הַאֲזִינִי, הַאֲזִנָה; ptc. מֵזִין (Si מאזין); inf. Si האזין—**hear, listen,** oft. **obey.**

<SUBJ> אִישׁ *man* Jb 32$_{11}$ (|| יחל hi. *wait,* בין htpo. *consider*) 4Q298 1$_{1}$ ([האזינו]), אִשָּׁה *wife* Gn 4$_{23}$ (|| שׁמע *hear*), בֵּן *son* Ps 49$_{2.2}$ Si 5$_{11}$ (+ היה ממהר ל *be quick to;* + שׁוב hi. *return* answer), בַּת *daughter* Is 32$_{9}$ (|| שׁמע), Balak Nm 23$_{18}$ (|| שׁמע), Job Jb 33$_{1}$ (|| שׁמע) 37$_{14}$ (|| בין htpo.), אֶבְיוֹן *poor person* Ps 49$_{2}$, עָשִׁיר *rich person* 49$_{2}$, רזן ptc. *ruler* Jg 5$_{3}$ (|| שׁמע), ישׁב ptc. *inhabitant* Jl 1$_{2}$ Ps 49$_{2}$ (both || שׁמע), ידע ptc. *one who knows* Jb 34$_{2}$ (|| שׁמע), שֶׁקֶר *deceiver* Pr 17$_{4}$ (if em.; see below), שׁקר pi.

ptc. *deceiver* 17$_{4}$ (if em.; see below).

Y. Ps 5$_{2}$ (‖ בין *consider*) 17$_{1}$ (both ‖ קשׁב hi. *pay attention*) 39$_{13}$ 54$_{4}$ (all three ‖ שׁמע) 55$_{2}$ (:: עלם htp. *hide oneself*; ‖ קשׁב hi.) 77$_{2}$ 84$_{9}$ (‖ שׁמע) 86$_{6}$ (‖ קשׁב hi.) 140$_{7}$ 141$_{1}$ (‖ חושׁ *hurry*) 143$_{1}$ (‖ שׁמע) Jb 9$_{16}$ Si 51$_{11}$ 11QPs[a] 28$_{8}$ (both ‖ שׁמע), רעה ptc. *shepherd* of Israel, i.e. Y. Ps 80$_{2}$, idols Ps 135$_{17}$.

Israelites Ex 15$_{26}$ Dt 1$_{45}$ (both ‖ שׁמע) Ne 9$_{30}$ 2 C 24$_{19}$, בַּיִת *house(hold)* of king Ho 5$_{1}$ (‖ שׁמע, קשׁב hi.), עַם *people* Is 1$_{10}$ (‖ שׁמע) Ps 78$_{1}$ (‖ נטה hi. *extend* ear, i.e. hear), לְאֹם *nation* Is 51$_{4}$ (‖ קשׁב hi.).

שֶׁקֶר *falsehood* Pr 17$_{4}$ (‖ קשׁב hi.; or em. שַׁקָּר or מְשַׁקֵּר *deceiver*), מֶרְחָק *distant place* Is 8$_{9}$, שָׁמַיִם *heavens* Dt 32$_{1}$ Is 1$_{2}$ (both ‖ שׁמע); subj. not specified, Is 28$_{23}$ 42$_{23}$ (both ‖ קשׁב hi.) 64$_{3}$ Jr 13$_{15}$ Jb 34$_{16}$ Si 4$_{15}$ (all six ‖ שׁמע) 1QH 4$_{17}$ fr. 12$_{5}$ (ל[ה]אזין) CD 20$_{32}$ 4Q525 6.10$_{2}$.

<OBJ> אִמְרָה *word* Gn 4$_{23}$ Is 32$_{9}$, אֹמֶר *word* Ps 5$_{2}$, דָּבָר *word* Jb 33$_{1}$, תּוֹרָה *law* Is 1$_{10}$ Ps 78$_{1}$, תְּפִלָּה *prayer* 17$_{1}$ 55$_{2}$ 86$_{6}$ perh. 84$_{9}$, שַׁוְעָה *cry* 39$_{13}$, קוֹל *voice* 140$_{7}$ 141$_{1}$ Jb 9$_{16}$ 1QH fr. 12$_{5}$, זֹאת *this* Is 42$_{23}$ Jb 37$_{14}$, perh. Ho 5$_{1}$ Jl 1$_{2}$ Ps 49$_{2}$; without object (or preposition), Dt 32$_{1}$ Jg 5$_{3}$ Is 1$_{2}$ 8$_{9}$ 28$_{23}$ 64$_{3}$ Jr 13$_{15}$ Ps 80$_{2}$ 135$_{17}$ Ne 9$_{30}$ 2 C 24$_{19}$ Si 5$_{11}$ 11QPs[a] 28$_{8}$, perh. Ho 5$_{1}$ Jl 1$_{2}$ Ps 49$_{2}$ 84$_{9}$.

<PREP> לְ *to* person Jb 34$_{2}$ Si 4$_{15}$ 4Q298 1$_{1}$ (האזי[נו]) 4Q525 6.10$_{2}$, message, etc. Ex 15$_{26}$ (+ מִצְוָה *command*) Ps 54$_{4}$ (+ אֹמֶר *word*) 143$_{1}$ (+ תַּחֲנוּן *supplication*) Jb 34$_{16}$ (+ קוֹל *voice*) 1QH 4$_{17}$ (+ דָּבָר *word*) CD 20$_{32}$ (+ קוֹל).

אֶל *to* person Dt 1$_{45}$ Is 51$_{4}$ Ps 77$_{2}$, message, etc. 143$_{1}$ Si 51$_{11}$ (both + תַּחֲנוּן *supplication*); עַד *to* person Nm 23$_{18}$, עַד־תְּבוּנֹתֵיכֶם *to your insights* Jb 32$_{11}$; עַל־לְשׁוֹן הַוֺּת *to a destructive tongue* Pr 17$_{4}$.

Also 4Q298 3$_{4}$.

<SYN> שׁמע *hear*, קשׁב hi. *pay attention*.

→ אֹזֶן *ear*, אֲזַנְיָה *Azaniah*, יַאֲזַנְיָהוּ *Jaazaniah*, אָזְנִי I *Ozni*, II *Oznite*, אַזְנוֹת תָּבוֹר *Aznoth-tabor*, אֻזֵּן שֶׁאֱרָה *Uzzen-sheerah*.

אזן II 1 vb. **weigh—Pi.** Pf. אִזֵּן—וְאִזֵּן וְחִקֵּר תִּקֵּן מְשָׁלִים הַרְבֵּה *and he* (Qoheleth) *weighed and researched (and) corrected many proverbs* Ec 12$_{9}$ (or אזן I, *hear* i.e. listen intently).

→ מֹאזְנַיִם *scales*.

אֹזֶן 187.10.27 n.f. **ear**—Q אוזן; cstr. אֹזֶן (Q אוזן); sf. אָזְנִי (Si, Q אוזני), אָזְנְךָ (אָזְנֶךָ) אָזְנֵךְ, Q אוזנכה, אָזְנוֹ, Si אזננו (Q אוזננו), אָזְנְכֶם, אָזְנָם; du. אָזְנַיִם (אָזְנָיִם); cstr. אָזְנֵי; sf. אָזְנַי (אָזְנָי), אָזְנֶיךָ, אָזְנַיִךְ (אָזְנָיִךְ), אָזְנָיו (Q אוזניו), אָזְנֵינוּ, אָזְנֵיכֶם, אָזְנֵיהֶם (Q אוזניהם).

<SUBJ> שׁמע *hear* 2 S 22$_{45}$ Is 30$_{21}$ Ps 92$_{12}$ Jb 13$_{1}$ 29$_{11}$ (both ‖ עַיִן *eye*) Pr 15$_{31}$ 20$_{12}$ (‖ עַיִן) 25$_{12}$ Si 16$_{5}$ 1QH 7$_{3}$ (both ‖ עַיִן) 4Q424 2$_{5}$, קשׁב *attend* Is 32$_{3}$ (‖ עַיִן), hi. Ps 10$_{17}$ Pr 2$_{2}$ Si 3$_{29}$ (+ לֵב *heart*), פתח ni. *be opened* Is 35$_{5}$ (‖ עַיִן) 48$_{8}$ (if em.; see pi.), pi. *open* 48$_{8}$ (or em. פִּתְּחָה your ear *opened* to פִּתַּחְתָּ *you opened* your ear, or פֻּתְּחָה or נִפְתְּחָה your ear *was opened*), pu. *be opened* 48$_{8}$ (if em.; see pi.), לקח *receive* Jr 9$_{19}$ (obj. דָּבָר *word*) Jb 4$_{12}$, צלל *tingle* 1 S 3$_{11}$ 2 K 21$_{12}$ Jr 19$_{3}$, מוט htpol. *be tossed about* Si 36$_{2(E)}$ (or em. אזנו *his ear* to אוני *ship*), בקשׁ pi. *seek* Pr 18$_{15}$ (‖ לֵב), בחן *test* Jb 12$_{11}$ 34$_{3}$ (both + חֵךְ *palate*), כבד *be heavy*, i.e. deaf Is 59$_{1}$ (‖ יָד *hand*), חרשׁ *become deaf* Mc 7$_{16}$, מלא ni. *be full* Ec 1$_{8}$ (+ עַיִן), שׂמח *rejoice* Si 3$_{29}$, היה *be* Ps 130$_{2}$ 2 C 6$_{40}$ 7$_{15}$ (all three + קַשֻּׁב *attentive*) Ne 1$_{6}$ (all four ‖ עַיִן) 1$_{11}$ (both + קַשָּׁב *attentive*).

<NOM CL> אָזְנַיִם לָהֶם *ears are to them*, i.e. they have ears Jr 5$_{21}$ Ezk 12$_{2}$ Ps 115$_{6}$ (‖ אַף *nose*, רֶגֶל *foot*, יָד *hand*) 135$_{17}$ (both ‖ פֶּה *mouth*; all four ‖ עַיִן *eye*), sim. Is 43$_{8}$ (+ עַיִן), אָזְנָיו אֶל־שַׁוְעָתָם *his ears are (directed) towards their cry* Ps 34$_{16}$ (+ עַיִן), אָזְנֵי כָל־הָעָם אֶל־סֵפֶר הַתּוֹרָה *the ears of all the people were (directed) towards the book ofthe law* Ne 8$_{3}$, עֲרֵלָה אָזְנָם *their ear is uncircumcised* Jr 6$_{10}$.

<OBJ> נטה hi. *bend, incline* (oft. with שׁמע *hear*) 2 K 19$_{16}$=Is 37$_{17}$ Is 55$_{3}$ Jr 7$_{24.26}$ 11$_{8}$ 17$_{23}$ 25$_{4}$ 34$_{14}$ 35$_{15}$ 44$_{5}$ Ps 17$_{6}$ 31$_{3}$ 45$_{11}$ 49$_{5}$ (+ פֶּה *mouth*, לֵב *heart*) 71$_{2}$ 78$_{1}$ (+ פֶּה) 86$_{1}$ 88$_{3}$ 102$_{3}$ 116$_{2}$ Pr 4$_{20}$ 5$_{1.13}$ 22$_{17}$ (+ לֵב) Dn 9$_{18}$ (‖ עַיִן *eye*) Si 4$_{8}$ 6$_{33}$ 51$_{16}$ 11QPs[a] 24$_{4}$ 4QBark[a] 2.1$_{2}$ (‖ עַיִן), פקח *open* Is 42$_{20}$ 4QBark[a] 2.1$_{3}$ (‖ עַיִן; א[וזניה]ם), perh. hi. Lachish ost. 3$_{5}$ (perh. הִפָּקַח *be opened*; others עין *eye*, רזם *he has alluded*), פתח *open* Is 48$_{8}$ (if em.; see Subj.) 50$_{5}$, כבד hi. *make heavy*, i.e. deaf 6$_{10}$ (‖ עַיִן; + לֵב) Zc 7$_{11}$ (‖ כָּתֵף *shoulder*), אטם *close* Is 33$_{15}$ Pr 21$_{13}$, hi. Ps 58$_{5}$, עלם hi. *shut* Lm 3$_{56}$, גלה *uncover*, i.e. reveal to (אֹזֶן alw. in sg.) 1 S 9$_{15}$ 20$_{2.12.13}$ 22$_{8.17}$ 2 S 7$_{27}$ Jb 33$_{16}$ 36$_{10.15}$ Ru 4$_{4}$ 1 C 17$_{25}$ CD 2$_{2}$ 1QH 1$_{21}$ 2$_{37(Licht)}$ ([גליתה]) 6$_{4}$ 18$_{4}$ fr. 4$_{7.12}$ (או[זן]) 5$_{10}$ 1Q26 1$_{4}$ 4Q416 10.2$_{19}$, נתן *cause* Dt

29$_3$ (+ לִשְׁמֹעַ *to hear*) 4QDibHam^a 18$_{3(Baillet)}$ ([אוזנ[ים]; + [לשמוע]), עור hi. *waken* Is 50$_4$ (+ לִשְׁמֹעַ), בוא hi. *bring* Pr 23$_{12}$ (|| לֵב), סור hi. *turn away* 28$_9$ (+ מִשְּׁמֹעַ), *remove* Ezk 23$_{25}$ (|| אַף *nose*), רצע *pierce* in manumission ritual Ex 21$_6$, כרה *dig* Ps 40$_7$, נטע *plant*, i.e. provide 94$_9$ (|| עַיִן).

<CSTR> אֹזֶן עַבְדְּךָ *ear of your servant* 2 S 7$_{27}$ Lachish ost. 3$_5$ (others עַיִן *eye of*, רזם your servant *has alluded*), הַמִּטַּהֵר *of the one to be cleansed* Lv 14$_{14.17.25}$ (אֹזֶן) 14$_{28}$, of Aaron Ex 29$_{20}$||Lv 8$_{23}$ (אֹזֶן), of Samuel 1 S 9$_{15}$, אוזן עפר *ear of dust*, i.e. mortal's ear 1QH 18$_{27}$ (|| לֵב *heart*), בשר *of flesh*, i.e. mortal's ear 1QH fr. 5$_{10}$, אֹזֶן חֲכָמִים *ear of wise people* Pr 18$_{15}$, בָּנָיו *of his sons* Ex 29$_{20}$.

אָזְנֵי הַמֶּלֶךְ *ears of the king* Jr 36$_{20.21}$, אֲדֹנִי *of my lord* Gn 44$_{18}$, בִּנְךָ וּבֶן־בִּנְךָ *of your son and your son's son* Ex 10$_2$, הָעָם *of the people* Ex 11$_2$ 24$_7$ Dt 32$_{44}$ Jg 7$_3$ 1 S 11$_4$ 2 K 18$_{26}$||Is 36$_{11}$ Jr 28$_7$ (כָּל־הָעָם *of all the people*) 36$_{6.10}$ (כָּל־הָעָם) 36$_{13.14}$ Ne 8$_3$ (כָּל־הָעָם) 13$_1$, עַם־הָאָרֶץ *people of the land* Gn 23$_{13}$, כָּל־קְהַל יִשְׂרָאֵל *of the whole assembly of Israel* Dt 31$_{30}$, כָּל־יְהוּדָה *of all Judah*, of Y. Nm 11$_{1.18}$ 1 S 8$_{21}$, of Pharaoh Gn 50$_4$, of Joshua Ex 17$_{14}$, of David 1 S 18$_{23}$ 2 S 3$_{19}$, of Jeremiah Jr 29$_{29}$, of Jerusalem 2$_2$, of (tribe of) Benjamin 2 S 3$_{19}$, אָזְנֵי־כֶלֶב *ears of a dog* Pr 26$_{17}$.

אָזְנֵי חֵרְשִׁים *ears of the deaf* Is 35$_5$, שֹׁמְעִים *of those who hear* 32$_3$, זִקְנֵי הָעִיר *of the elders of the city* Jos 20$_4$, כָּל־בַּעֲלֵי שְׁכֶם *of all the lords of Shechem* Jg 9$_{2.3}$, בְּנֵי־חֵת *of the Hittites* Gn 23$_{10.16}$, נְשֵׁיכֶם בְּנֵיכֶם וּבְנֹתֵיכֶם *of your wives, your sons, and your daughters* Ex 32$_2$.

תְּנוּךְ אֹזֶן *lobe of the ear of* Ex 29$_{20}$ (אֹזֶן) Lv 8$_{23}$ (|| Ex 29$_{20}$ אֹזֶן) 8$_{24}$ (אָזְנָם) 14$_{14.17}$ (both אֹזֶן) 14$_{25.28}$ (אֹזֶן), בְּדַל־אֹזֶן *tip of ear* of savaged animal Am 3$_{12}$, שֵׁמַע־ *hearing of* Ps 18$_{45}$ (שֵׁמַע) Jb 42$_5$ Si 43$_{24(B)}$ (אוזנו; M אזנינו), כבוד אוזן *heaviness*, i.e. deafness, *of ear* 1QS 4$_{11}$ (|| עַיִן *eye*, עֹרֶף *neck*, לֵב *heart*), כבד *one who is heavy of* ear, i.e. deaf 4Q424 2$_4$ (אוזן), ערל *one who is uncircumcised of* ear 1QH 18$_{20}$, מגולי *ones who are open of* ear 1QM 10$_{11}$, מִשְׁמַע אָזְנַיִם *hearing of ears* Is 11$_3$, הַשְׁמָעוּת אָזְנַיִם *informing of ears* Ezk 24$_{26}$.

<ADJ> יָמִין *right* Lv 8$_{23.24}$ 14$_{14.17.25.28}$ (all six || יָד *hand*, רֶגֶל *foot*), עָרֵל *uncircumcised* Jr 6$_{10}$.

<PREP> תעודות ננתנו לאוזנים *testimonies were given to ears* 1QH 23$_7$, דובר לאוזן *one who speaks to an ear* 4Q424 2$_5$; בְּ (with noun in pl. except Dt 15$_{17}$ 1QH 18$_{27}$) of place, direction, *in(to)* the ears (or, hearing) of, Gn 35$_4$ Ex 32$_3$ 1 S 15$_{14}$ 2 S 22$_7$ Is 5$_9$ Jb 13$_{17}$ 15$_{21}$, + דבר *speak* Dt 5$_1$ Jr 28$_{7.7}$, pi. Gn 20$_8$ 23$_{13.16}$ 44$_{18}$ 50$_4$ Ex 11$_2$ Nm 14$_{28}$ Dt 31$_{28.30}$ 32$_{44}$ Jos 20$_4$ Jg 9$_{2.3}$ 1 S 8$_{21}$ 11$_4$ 18$_{23}$ 25$_{24}$ (+ שמע *hear*), 2 S 3$_{19.19}$ 2 K 18$_{26}$=Is 36$_{11}$ Jr 26$_{15}$ Pr 23$_9$.

אמר *say* Jg 17$_2$ Is 49$_{20}$ Ezk 9$_5$ Jb 33$_8$ (+ שמע *hear*), נגד hi. *tell* Jr 36$_{20}$, צוה pi. *command* 2 S 18$_{12}$, ספר pi. *relate* Ex 10$_2$, גלה ni. *be revealed* Is 22$_{14}$, ענה *reply* Gn 23$_{10}$, קרא *read* (aloud) Ex 24$_7$ Dt 31$_{11}$ Jg 7$_3$ 2 K 23$_2$ Jr 29$_{29}$ 36$_{6+7t}$ 2 C 34$_{30}$ 1QSa 1$_4$ (בא[וזניהם]) 1QM 15$_4$, *call, proclaim* Jr 2$_2$ Ezk 8$_{18}$ 9$_1$ (both + קוֹל גָּדוֹל *[with] a loud voice*), ni. *be read* Ne 13$_1$, pu. *be called*, i.e. named Ezk 10$_{13}$, אנן htpol. *complain* Nm 11$_1$ (+ שמע).

בכה *wail* Nm 11$_{18}$, שמע *hear* 1 C 28$_8$ (if ins. שִׁמְעוּ אֶת־דְּבָרַי *hear my word* after בְּאָזְנֵי אֱלֹהֵינוּ *in the hearing of our God*; || עַיִן *eye*), בוא *come* Ps 18$_7$, בוא *come* 4QapPs^b 24$_9$, עלה *go up* 2 K 19$_{28}$||Is 37$_{29}$, נתן *place* Dt 15$_{17}$ 1QH 18$_{27}$, שׂים *place* Ex 17$_{14}$.

בְּ of instrument, *by, with*, + שמע *hear* 2 S 7$_{22}$ Jr 26$_{11}$ Ezk 3$_{10}$ (|| לֵבָב *heart*) 40$_4$ 44$_5$ (both || עַיִן *eye*, + לֵב *heart*) Ps 44$_2$ Jb 28$_{22}$ 1 C 17$_{20}$, חזק בְּ hi. *seize by* Pr 26$_{17}$; מוֹכִיחַ חָכָם עַל־אֹזֶן שֹׁמָעַת *a wise reprover for a hearing ear* Pr 25$_{12}$, נתן עַל *place* jewellery *upon* Ezk 16$_{12}$ (|| אַף *nose*, ראשׁ *head*).

<COLL> שְׁתֵּי אָזְנָיו *his two ears* 1 S 3$_{11}$ 2 K 21$_{12}$.

Also 4Q487 36$_2$ 1QH fr. 18$_2$ 4QShir^b 70$_2$.

<SYN> עַיִן *eye*, לֵב *heart*, יָד *hand*, רֶגֶל *foot*, אַף *nose*, פֶּה *mouth*.

→ אזן *hear*.

[אָזֵן] 1 n.[m.] **tool**—sf. אֲזֵנֶךָ; pl. sf. Gnz, mss אֲזֵנֶיךָ—perh. collective, **tool(s)** or **weapon(s)**, וְיָתֵד תִּהְיֶה לְךָ עַל־אֲזֵנֶךָ *and a peg* (for digging) *you are to have upon your tool* Dt 23$_{14}$ (Gnz, mss אֲזֵנֶיךָ *your tools*; or em. אֵזֹרֶךָ *your girdle*).

אֻזֵּן שֶׁאֱרָה 1 pl.n. **Uzzen-sheerah**—mss אָזֵן, אֹזֶן, אזן—in Ephraim, established (בנה) by Sheerah daughter of Ephraim, perh. Bēt Ṣīra 5 km N of Beth-horon, 1 C

7$_{24}$. → אזן *hear.*

אַזְנוֹת תָּבוֹר 1 pl.n. **Aznoth-tabor,** in Naphtali, perh. Kh. Umm Ǧubbēl (T. Aznōt Tāvōr), 5 km N of Mt Tabor, Jos 19$_{34}$.
→ אזן *hear.*

אָזְנִי I 1 pr.n.m. **Ozni,** son of Gad, appar. ident. with Ezbon at Gn 46$_{16}$, Nm 26$_{16}$.
→ אזן *hear.*

אָזְנִי II 1 gent. **Oznite,** מִשְׁפַּחַת הָאָזְנִי *the family of the Oznites* Nm 26$_{16}$.
→ אזן *hear.*

אֲזַנְיָה 1 pr.n.m. **Azaniah,** father of Jeshua, Levite at the time of Nehemiah, Ne 10$_{10}$.
→ אזן *hear.*

[אָזֵק] 2 n.[m.] **manacle**—pl. הָ/בָּאזִקִּים—**<PREP>** הוּא־אָסוּר בָּאזִקִּים *he* (Jeremiah) *was bound with manacles* Jr 40$_{1}$, פִּתַּחְתִּיךָ הַיּוֹם מִן־הָאזִקִּים אֲשֶׁר עַל־יָדֶךָ *I have today released you from the manacles that were around your hand(s)* 40$_{4}$ (mss יָדֶיךָ *your hands*).
→ זֵק *fetter.*

אזר 16.1.4 vb. **gird**—**Qal** Pf. אָזְרוּ; impf. 2ms תֶּאְזֹר, sf. יַאַזְרֵנִי; impv. אֱזָר־; ptc. pass. אָזוּר—**1a. gird oneself,** for battle, dispute, etc., 1 S 2$_{4}$ Jr 1$_{17}$ Jb 38$_{3}$ 40$_{7}$. **1b.** pass. **be girded,** for support, of belt, 2 K 1$_{8}$. **2. bind, be tight** around, 11QPs^{a} 139$_{11}$ Jb 30$_{18}$.

<SUBJ> Jeremiah Jr 1$_{17}$ (‖ קום *stand up*), Job Jb 38$_{3}$ 40$_{7}$, כשל ni. ptc. *one who stumbles* 1 S 2$_{4}$ (+ חַיִל *[with] strength*), לְבוּשׁ *clothing* Jb 30$_{18}$ (+ חפשׂ htp. perh. *be sought*), לַיְלָה *night* 11QPs^{a} 139$_{11}$ (MT אוֹר *light*); pass., אֵזוֹר *belt* 2 K 1$_{8}$.

<OBJ> חֲלָצַיִם *waist* Jb 38$_{3}$ 40$_{7}$, מָתְנַיִם *waist* Jr 1$_{17}$, Job Jb 30$_{18}$, worshipper 11QPs^{a} 139$_{11}$.

<PREP> בְּמָתְנָיו *around his waist* 2 K 1$_{8}$; כְּ *as* Jb 30$_{18}$ (+ פֶּה *mouth,* i.e. collar) 38$_{3}$ (+ גֶּבֶר *man* [ms גִּיבּוֹר *warrior*]) 40$_{7}$ (+ גֶּבֶר); בעדי *around me* 11QPs^{a} 139$_{11}$.

Ni. Ptc. נֶאְזָר—**be girded,** for battle, of Y., נֶאְזָר בִּגְבוּרָה *girded with strength* Ps 65$_{7}$.

Pi. Impf. אֲאַזֶּרְךָ; + waw Si ויאזרהו, 2ms וַתְּאַזְּרֵנִי (וַתְּזְרֵנִי); ptc. מְאַזְּרֵנִי, מְאַזְּרֵי—**1.** as Qal, **gird oneself,** with sparks, light, Is 50$_{11}$ (unless em.; see Subj.) 4QWiles 1$_{8}$(Allegro).

2a. gird someone, for battle, 4QSam^{a} 2 S 22$_{33}$‖Ps 18$_{33}$ 2 S 22$_{40}$‖18$_{40}$, with joy, Ps 30$_{12}$. **2b. envelop** someone, Is 45$_{5}$ Si 45$_{7}$.

<SUBJ> Y. 4QSam^{a} 2 S 22$_{33}$‖Ps 18$_{33}$ (2 S MT מָעוּזִּי *my refuge*) 2 S 22$_{40}$‖Ps 18$_{40}$ (2 S וַתַּזְרֵנִי) Ps 30$_{12}$ Is 45$_{5}$ Si 45$_{7}$ (‖ לבשׁ hi. *clothe*), Israelites Is 50$_{11}$ (or em. מְאִירֵי *who light* sparks); subj. not specified, 4QWiles 1$_{8}$ (Allegro) (AHL מאירי).

<OBJ> David 4QSam^{a} 2 S 22$_{33}$‖Ps 18$_{33}$ (MT; see Subj.) 2 S 22$_{40}$‖Ps 18$_{40}$ (all + חַיִל *[with] strength*), worshipper Ps 30$_{12}$ (+ שִׂמְחָה *[with] joy*), Aaron Si 45$_{7}$, Israel Is 45$_{5}$, זֵק *spark* 50$_{11}$, נֹגַהּ *light* 4QWiles 1$_{8}$(Allegro) (AHL; see Subj.).

<PREP> בתועפות ראם *with the eminence of a wild ox* Si 45$_{7}$(B) (Bmg תואר with eminence *of form*).

Htp. Pf. הִתְאַזָּר; impf. Q יתאזר, Q יתאזרו; impv. הִתְאַזָּרוּ; ptc. Q מתאזרים; inf. cstr. התאזר—as Qal, **gird oneself,** for battle, etc., **<SUBJ>** Y. Ps 93$_{1}$ (+ עֹז *[with] strength;* ‖ לבשׁ *be clothed*), מֶרְחָק *distant place* Is 8$_{9.9}$ (both + חתת *be shattered*), חַיִל *army* of Belial 1QM 1$_{13}$, Belial 16$_{9}$, גִּבּוֹר *warrior* 15$_{14}$ ([ג]בורי).

<PREP> למלחמ[ה] *for battle* 1QM 15$_{4}$, לע[ז]רת בני חושך *for the help of the sons of darkness* 16$_{9}$.
→ אֵזוֹר *belt.*

אֶזְרוֹעַ 2.0.3 n.f. **arm**—sf. אֶזְרֹעִי—**1. arm,** perh. specif. **forearm** of human being or Y., **<SUBJ>** שבר ni. *be broken* Jb 31$_{22}$ (+ מִקָּנָה *from [its humeral] bone;* ‖ כָּתֵף *shoulder*) 4QpPs^{a} 1.2$_{23}$(Allegro) (אזרועות ... תשברנה]), נטה pass. *be extended* Jr 32$_{21}$ (‖ יָד *hand*). **<CSTR>** אזרוע[ות רשעים] *arms of wicked ones* 4QpPs^{a} 1.2$_{23}$ (Allegro). **<PREP>** יצא בְּ hi. *take out* from Egypt *with,* or *by means of* Jr 32$_{21}$.

2. in 11QT, **leg, foreleg** of sacrificial animal, **<OBJ>** רום hi. *raise,* i.e. sacrifice 11QT 20$_{16}$ 22$_{9}$(Yadin) ([האזרוע]), נוף hi. *wave,* i.e. make wave-offering 20$_{16}$. **<PREP>** השכם הנשאר מן האזרוע *(any of) the shoulder left*

עד עצם השכם *the foreleg up to the shoulder bone* 11QT *over from the foreleg* 11QT 20$_{16}$ + Sup. <COLL> האזרוע 20$_{16}$, [האזרוע]ת והלחיים *the forelegs and the cheeks* 20$_{16(Yadin)}$ + Sup, var. 22$_{9(Yadin)}$ ([האזרוע]).

→ זְרוֹעַ *arm*.

אֶזְרָח 18.0.2 n.m. **native**—cstr. אֶזְרַח—**1. native inhabitant, citizen,** of Israel, as opposed to sojourner (גֵּר).

<SUBJ> היה *be* Nm 15$_{29}$ (or em. לָאֶזְרָח; + תּוֹרָה *law*), עשׂה *do* Lv 16$_{29}$ 18$_{26}$ Nm 15$_{13}$, ישׁב *dwell* in booths Lv 23$_{42}$ 11QT fr. 1$_{1}$, קרב hi. *bring* sacrifice Nm 15$_{13}$.

<CSTR> אֶזְרַח הָאָרֶץ *native inhabitant of the country* Ex 12$_{19.48}$ Nm 9$_{14}$; כָּל־הָאֶזְרָח *every native inhabitant* Lv 23$_{42}$ (+ בְּיִשְׂרָאֵל *in Israel*) Nm 15$_{13}$ 11QT fr. 1$_{1}$ 1QSa 1$_{6}$ (both כול; both + בְּיִשְׂרָאֵל).

<PREP> לְ *for* 1QSa 1$_{6}$ (+ סֶרֶךְ *rule*), + היה *be* (of law, statute) Ex 12$_{49}$ Nm 9$_{14}$ 15$_{29}$ (if em.; see Subj.; + בִּבְנֵי יִשְׂרָאֵל *among the Israelites*); בְּ *among*, + אכל *eat* Lv 17$_{15}$, כרת ni. *be cut off* Ex 12$_{19}$; כְּ *as*, + היה *be* Ex 12$_{48}$ Lv 19$_{34}$ (+ מִכֶּם *from you*, i.e. of your own kin) 24$_{22}$ Ezk 47$_{22}$ (+ בִּבְנֵי יִשְׂרָאֵל *among the Israelites*), מות ho. *be put to death* Lv 24$_{16}$, עמד *stand* Jos 8$_{33}$; מִן *from (among)*, + עשׂה *do* Nm 15$_{30}$.

<COLL> אֶזְרָח ... גֵּר *native inhabitant ... sojourner* Ex 12$_{49}$ Lv 16$_{29}$ 17$_{15}$ 18$_{26}$ Nm 15$_{29.30}$, גֵּר ... אֶזְרָח Ex 12$_{19.48}$ Lv 19$_{34}$ 24$_{16.22}$ Nm 9$_{14}$ Jos 8$_{33}$ Ezk 47$_{22}$, one law for both Ex 12$_{49}$ Lv 24$_{22}$ Nm 9$_{14}$ 15$_{29}$.

2. something that grows up in its native place, **plant, tree,** מִתְעָרֶה כְּאֶזְרָח רַעֲנָן *spreading himself as a leafy tree* Ps 37$_{35}$ (or em. מִתְעַלֶּה כְּאַרְזֵי הַלְּבָנוֹן *exalting himself as the cedars of Lebanon*).

<ANT> §1 גֵּר *sojourner*.

אֶזְרָחִי 3 gent. **Ezrahite,** of the family or guild of Zerah (see 1 C 2$_{6}$), 1 K 5$_{11}$ (+ אֵיתָן *Ethan*) Ps 88$_{1}$ (+ הֵימָן *Heman*) 89$_{1}$ (+ אֵיתָן).

→ זֶרַח *Zerah*.

[אזת פראן], see אזה.

אָח I 628.10.51.5 n.m. **brother**—אָח; cstr. אֲחִי; sf. אָחִי, אָחִיךָ, אָחִינוּ, אָחִיהָ, (אָחִיהוּ) אָחִיו, אָחִיךְ, (אחך I, אחיכה Q), אֲחִיכֶם, אֲחִיהֶם; pl. אַחִים; cstr. אֲחֵי; sf. אַחַי (אֶחָי), אַחֶיךָ (אחיכה Q), אֶחָיו, אַחֶיהָ, אַחֵינוּ, אֲחֵיכֶם (אחיכן Q), אֲחֵיהֶם (אחיהמה Q).

1a. usu. **brother,** including half-brother (e.g. Jg 11$_{3}$ 2 S 13$_{20}$ 2 C 11$_{22}$), e.g. Gn 20$_{5.13}$ (both || אָחוֹת *sister*) 24$_{55}$ (|| אֵם *mother*) 27$_{29}$ (+ בֶּן אֵם *mother's son*) 34$_{11}$ (|| אָב *father*) 37$_{10}$ (|| אֵם, אָב) 37$_{19}$ 42$_{21.28.28}$ Gn 50$_{8}$ (+ בֵּית אָב *father's household*) Jr 9$_{3.3}$ (both || רֵעַ *friend*) 22$_{18}$ (|| אָחוֹת *sister*) Ps 50$_{20}$ 69$_{9}$ (both + בֶּן אֵם *mother's son*) Pr 17$_{2.17}$ (|| רֵעַ) 18$_{24}$ (:: אהב ptc. *friend*) Jb 42$_{15}$ CD 5$_{8}$ 11QT 66$_{17}$ (both || אָחוֹת) 11QPs^{a} 28$_{3}$ (+ בֶּן אָב *father's son*).

1b. used collectively, **brother tribe, nation,** of Judah/Israel in relation to Edom Nm 20$_{14}$ Am 1$_{11}$ Ob$_{10.12}$ Ml 1$_{2}$, Judah and Simeon Jg 1$_{3.17}$, בִּנְיָמִן אָחִי/ו the tribe of *Benjamin, my/his brother* 20$_{23.28}$ 21$_{6}$.

2a. nephew, Gn 14$_{14.16}$ 24$_{27}$ 29$_{12.15}$ Jg 9$_{3.18}$. **2b. cousin,** 1 C 23$_{22}$. **2c.** other close relative, **kinsman,** Gn 13$_{11}$ Lv 10$_{4}$ 25$_{25}$ (protected by גֹּאֵל *redeemer*) 25$_{35.36.39.47}$ Nm 27$_{4}$ Jos 15$_{17}$ 17$_{4.4}$ Jg 1$_{13}$ 3$_{9}$ 9$_{26.31.41}$ 2 S 3$_{8}$ (|| מֵרֵעַ *friend*) 2 K 10$_{13.13}$ Jr 12$_{6}$ Pr 19$_{7}$ (|| מֵרֵעַ) 27$_{10}$ (|| רֵעַ *friend*, אָב *father*) 27$_{10}$ (:: שָׁכֵן *neighbour*) Jb 42$_{11}$ (|| אָחוֹת *kinswoman*) Ru 4$_{3.10}$ Ezr 3$_{2}$ 10$_{18}$ Ne 1$_{2}$ 7$_{2}$ Si 14$_{16}$ CD 8$_{6}$ 19$_{18}$ (both || רֵעַ), אָח ... רֵעַ ... קָרוֹב *kinsman ... friend ... neighbour* Ex 32$_{27}$, אָח תָּלוּי *a dependent relative* Si 7$_{18}$ (|| אוהב *friend*) 40$_{24(Segal)}$ (|| [אוהב]).

3. fellow member of group, esp. a tribe or nation, **a.** of Israelites (includes non-Israelite kinsmen of Israelites), Gn 31$_{23+6t}$ Ex 2$_{11.11}$ 4$_{18}$ Lv 19$_{17}$ (|| עָמִית *kinsman*) 25$_{46}$ Nm 20$_{3}$ 25$_{6}$ 32$_{6}$ Dt 1$_{16.16}$ (:: גֵּר *alien*) 1$_{28}$ 3$_{20}$||Jos 1$_{15}$ Dt 10$_{9}$ 15$_{2}$ (|| רֵעַ *friend*) 15$_{3}$ (+ נָכְרִי *foreigner*) 15$_{7.7.11}$ 17$_{15}$=11QT 56$_{14}$ Dt 17$_{20}$ (both king's fellow-countrymen) 18$_{2.15.18}$ 23$_{20.21}$ (:: נָכְרִי) 24$_{7.14}$ (|| גֵּר *alien*) 25$_{3}$ Jos 22$_{3.4.7.8}$ Jg 14$_{3}$ 18$_{8.8.14}$ (all three Danites) 2 S 2$_{26.27}$ 1 K 20$_{32.33}$ (both of Ben-hadad and Ahab) Is 9$_{18}$ 66$_{5}$ Jr 29$_{16}$ 34$_{14.17}$ (|| רֵעַ *friend*) Ho 2$_{3}$ (|| אָחוֹת *sister*) Mc 5$_{2}$ Ml 2$_{10}$ Ps 122$_{8}$ (|| רֵעַ) Est 10$_{3}$ Ne 5$_{5.7.8}$ 1 C 8$_{32.32}$||9$_{38.38}$ 9$_{6.9.13}$ 12$_{2.30.33.40}$ 13$_{2}$ 2 C 11$_{4}$ 28$_{11.15}$ 30$_{7}$ (|| אָב *forefather*) 30$_{9}$ (|| בֵּן *descendant*) 35$_{6}$ Si 50$_{1}$ (|| עַם *people*) 11QPs^{a} 19$_{17}$ (+ בֵּית אָב *father's household*) 5/6ḤevEp 12$_{4}$, including females, אָחִיךָ הָעִבְרִי אוֹ הָעִבְרִיָּה *your kinsman the Hebrew man* *or the Hebrew woman* Dt 15$_{12}$, אֲחֵיהֶם ... נָשִׁים בָּנִים וּבָנוֹת *their kinsmen ... women, sons, and daughters* 2 C 28$_{8}$, יְהוּדִי אָחִיהוּ *a Jew, his kinsman* Jr 34$_{9}$, sim. Ne 5$_{1.8}$, אַחֶיךָ אַחֶיךָ אַנְשֵׁי גְאֻלָּתֶךָ *your kinsmen, your kinsmen, the people of your kin* Ezk 11$_{15}$ (or em. גָּלוּתֶךָ *of your exile,* i.e. exiled with you), אִישׁ נָכְרִי אֲשֶׁר לֹא־אָחִיךָ הוּא *a foreign man, who is not your kinsman* Dt 17$_{15}$=11QT 56$_{15}$, אַחַי אַתֶּם עַצְמִי וּבְשָׂרִי *you are my kinsmen, my own bone and flesh* 2 S 19$_{13}$, אָח ... רֵעַ ... חָבֵר *kinsman ... friend ... colleague* Si 7$_{12}$, אֲחֵיכֶם כָּל־בֵּית יִשְׂרָאֵל *your kinsmen, all the house of Israel* Lv 10$_{6}$, אֲחֵיכֶם בְּנֵי־יִשְׂרָאֵל *your kinsmen, the sons of Israel* Dt 3$_{18}$ Jos 1$_{14}$ 1 K 12$_{24}$, sim. Jg 20$_{13}$, אַחֵינוּ אִישׁ יְהוּדָה *our kinsmen, the men of Judah* 2 S 19$_{42}$, אֲחֵיכֶם ... זֶרַע אֶפְרָיִם *your kinsmen ... the seed of Ephraim* Jr 7$_{15}$, אֲחֵיכֶם בְּנֵי־עֵשָׂו *your kinsmen, the sons of Esau* Dt 2$_{4}$, sim. 2$_{8}$, לֹא־תְתַעֵב אֲדֹמִי כִּי אָחִיךָ הוּא *do not despise an Edomite, for he is your kinsman* 23$_{8}$, אָח הוּא לְבַעַל מַשְׁחִית *he* (idler) *is a kinsman to,* i.e. akin to, *a destructive person* Pr 18$_{9}$, אֲחֵיהֶם אַדִּירֵיהֶם *their kinsmen, their nobles,* the family heads Ne 10$_{30}$, אֲחֵיכֶם בְּנֵי הָעָם *your kinsmen, the laity* 2 C 35$_{5}$, אֶחָיו לְמִשְׁפְּחֹתָיו *his kinsmen, according to their clans* 1 C 5$_{7}$, sim. 5$_{13}$ 7$_{5}$.

b. of non-Israelites, 2 S 15$_{20}$ (Gittites) Is 19$_{2}$ (Egyptians; ‖ רֵעַ *friend*) Jr 49$_{10}$ (Edomites, זַרְעוֹ וְאֶחָיו וּשְׁכֵנָיו *his offspring and his kinsmen and his neighbours*) Am 1$_{9}$ (Edomites, Tyre) Jb 6$_{15}$ 19$_{13}$ (‖ ידע ptc. *acquaintance*) 22$_{6}$ (all three, Job's kinsmen) Ne 3$_{34}$ (Samarians), עַל־פְּנֵי כָל־אֶחָיו *alongside all his* (Ishmael's) *kinsmen* Gn 16$_{12}$ 25$_{18}$, וַיֹּאמַר אַל־נָא אַחַי תָּרֵעוּ *and he* (Lot) *said, Please, my kinsmen* (Sodomites), *do not behave wickedly* 19$_{7}$, sim. Jg 19$_{23}$ (Benjaminites), אָח הָיִיתִי לְתַנִּים *I* (Job) *have become a kinsman to jackals* Jb 30$_{29}$ (‖ רֵעַ *friend*).

4. without emphasis on consanguinity, **fellow** (see esp. Coll.), **a.** of Israelites, Ex 16$_{15}$ Lv 25$_{14}$ (+ עָמִית *kinsman*) Nm 14$_{4}$ Dt 19$_{18.19}$=11QT 61$_{10.10}$ Dt 22$_{1.1.2}$ =11QT 64$_{13.14.14}$ Dt 22$_{2.3.4}$ 25$_{11}$ Is 66$_{20}$ Jr 13$_{14}$ 23$_{35}$ (‖ רֵעַ *friend*) 31$_{34}$ (‖ רֵעַ) 41$_{8}$ Ezk 4$_{17}$ 24$_{23}$ 33$_{30}$ 47$_{14}$ Mc 7$_{2}$ Zc 7$_{9.10}$ Ps 49$_{8}$ (but see אָח *alas*) 22$_{23}$ (‖ קָהָל *congregation*) 133$_{1}$ Pr 6$_{19}$ Ne 4$_{13}$ CD 14$_{5}$.

b. of non-Israelites, Ex 10$_{23}$ (Egyptians) Ezk 38$_{21}$ (Gog), מִיַּד הָאָדָם מִיַּד אִישׁ אָחִיו אֶדְרֹשׁ אֶת־נֶפֶשׁ הָאָדָם *I will seek* recompense *for the life of a human being, from human being, from each man* the life of *his brother* Gn 9$_{5}$.

5. colleague, fellow member of institution, organization, etc., בין אחים ראשם נכבד *among colleagues, their leader is honoured* Si 10$_{20}$, אֲנִי אַחַי וּנְעָרַי *I* (Nehemiah), *my colleagues, and my servants* Ne 4$_{17}$ 5$_{10.14}$ (lacks וּנְעָרַי), used of **a.** priests, Levites, etc. (but oft. perh. §3a because of hereditary nature of priesthood; see, e.g., 1 C 24$_{31}$), Lv 21$_{10}$ Nm 8$_{26}$ 16$_{10}$ 18$_{2.6}$ Dt 18$_{7}$ 2 K 23$_{9}$ Ezr 8$_{24}$ Ne 3$_{18}$ 10$_{11}$ 11$_{12.13.14.17.19}$ 12$_{8.9.24.36}$ 13$_{13}$ 1 C 6$_{24}$ 9$_{17.19.25.32}$ 15$_{5.+7t}$ 16$_{7.37.38}$ 24$_{31}$ 25$_{7}$ 26$_{12+6t}$ 2 C 19$_{10.10}$ 29$_{15}$ 31$_{12.13.15}$ 35$_{9}$ Si 50$_{12}$ 1QSa 1$_{18}$ 1QM 15$_{7}$.

אֶחָיו הַכֹּהֲנִים *his colleagues, the priests* Ezr 3$_{2.8}$ (+ וְהַלְוִיִּם *and the Levites*) Ne 3$_{1}$ 1 C 16$_{39}$ 1QM 13$_{1}$ (הכ[וה]נים) 15$_{4}$ ([הכ[והנים]); both + והלויים *and the Levites*) 4QDa 6.2$_{4}$, sim. Ezr 6$_{20}$, הַכֹּהֲנִים וַאֲחֵיהֶם *the priests and their colleagues* Ne 12$_{7}$, אֲחֵיכֶם הַלְוִיִּם *your colleagues, the Levites* Nm 18$_{6}$, sim. 18$_{2}$ Dt 18$_{7}$ Ezr 3$_{9}$ 1 C 6$_{33}$ 2 C 29$_{34}$ 35$_{15}$ 11QT 60$_{14}$, בְּנֵי אַהֲרֹן אֲחֵיהֶם *the sons of Aaron, their colleagues* 1 C 23$_{32}$, sim. 24$_{31}$ 11QT 44$_{5}$, בְּנֵי מְרָרִי אֲחֵיהֶם *the sons of Merari, their colleagues* 1 C 6$_{24}$ 15$_{17}$, אֲחֵיהֶם הַמְשֹׁרְרִים *their colleagues, the singers* 15$_{16}$, אִדּוֹ אָחִיו הַנְּתִינִים *Iddo* and *his colleagues, the temple-servants* Ezr 8$_{17}$(Qr), בָּנִים וְאַחִים *juniors and peers* Ezr 3$_{9}$ 8$_{18.19}$ 1 C 25$_{10+21t}$ 26$_{8.9.11}$ 2 C 5$_{12}$, sim. 1 C 25$_{9}$, אֲחֵיהֶם הַמִּשְׁנִים *their brothers, the seconds,* i.e. their subordinates 15$_{18}$.

b. members of a religious group, Jr 35$_{3}$ 1QS 6$_{10.22}$ CD 6$_{20}$ 7$_{1.2}$ 20$_{18}$ (‖ רֵעַ *friend*) 4QCata 12.1$_{6}$, perh. 1 K 13$_{30}$.

c. soldiers, Lv 26$_{37}$ Dt 20$_{8}$=11QT 62$_{4}$ Jos 14$_{8}$ 2 K 7$_{6}$ 9$_{2}$ Jl 2$_{8}$ Hg 2$_{22}$ 11QT 58$_{14}$ Mur 45$_{8}$ Arad ost. 15$_{1.5}$ 16$_{1}$.

d. others, specif. craftsmen, Is 41$_{6}$ (‖ רֵעַ *friend*), reapers, Meṣad Ḥashavyahu ost. 1$_{10.11}$, kings, Jr 25$_{26}$.

6. in vocative, **my brother,** oft. as polite or official form of address, Gn 29$_{4}$ (Jacob to shepherds) 33$_{9}$ (Esau to Jacob) 1 S 30$_{23}$ (David to troops) 2 S 20$_{9}$ (Joab to Amasa) 1 K 9$_{13}$ (Hiram to Solomon) 1 C 28$_{2}$ (David to chiefs of Israel; ‖ עַם *people*); also in laments, 2 S 1$_{26}$, הוֹי אָחִי *alas, my brother* 1 K 13$_{30}$ Jr 22$_{18}$ 4QPsJosa 6.1$_{7}$.

7. partner, of inanimate objects, faces of cherubim Ex 25$_{20}$‖37$_{9}$ (אִישׁ אֶל־אָחִיו *the one facing the other*), scales of Behemoth cleaving אִישׁ־בְּאָחִיהוּ *one to the other* Jb 41$_{9}$.

<SUBJ> היה *be* Ex 7$_{1}$ (+ נָבִיא *prophet*), יכל *be able* Gn 45$_{3}$, עשׂה *do, make* 31$_{46}$ 45$_{17}$ 1 S 30$_{23}$ Ne 11$_{12}$, יסף *do again* Gn 37$_{5.8}$, כלה pi. *complete* 1QS 6$_{10}$, כון hi. *provide* 1 C 12$_{40}$ 2 C 35$_{15}$, פרה *be fruitful* 4Q525 2$_{10}$, ילד ni. *be born* Pr 17$_{17}$, גדל *grow great* Gn 48$_{19}$, יצא *go out* Jr 29$_{16}$ 11QPs^{a} 28$_{9}$, from mother's womb Gn 25$_{26}$ 38$_{29.30}$, עזב *leave* Gn 50$_{8}$, בוא *come* 27$_{35}$ 37$_{10}$ 42$_{6.15}$ 44$_{14}$ 45$_{16.17}$ 46$_{31}$ 47$_{1.5}$ Nm 32$_{6}$ Jg 9$_{26.31}$ 21$_{22}$ Jb 42$_{11}$ Ne 1$_{2}$ 1 C 7$_{22}$ 9$_{25}$, הלך *go* Gn 37$_{12}$ 45$_{17}$ 50$_{18}$, עבר *pass* Jg 9$_{26}$ Jb 6$_{15}$, שׁוב *go back* Gn 50$_{14}$ 2 C 30$_{9}$, נגשׁ *approach* Gn 45$_{4.4}$, קרא *meet* 11QPs^{a} 28$_{9}$, שׁלח *send* Arad ost. 15$_{1}$ ([אח]ך שלח) 16$_{1}$, עלה *go up* Jos 14$_{8}$ Jg 16$_{31}$, hi. *take up* 1 C 15$_{12}$.

עמד *stand* Ezr 3$_{9}$, קום *stand up* 3$_{2.2}$ Ne 3$_{1}$, ירד *go down* Gn 42$_{3}$ 44$_{23}$ Jg 16$_{31}$ 1 S 22$_{1}$ 2 K 10$_{13}$ 4QPsJos^{a} 6.1$_{5}$, שׁחה htpal. *prostrate oneself* Gn 37$_{10}$ 42$_{6}$, נפל *fall down* Gn 44$_{14}$ 50$_{18}$, מוך *sink* into debt Lv 25$_{25.35.39.47}$, עבד *serve* Nm 18$_{6}$, שׁרת pi. *serve* in cult 18$_{2}$ 1 C 26$_{12}$, קדשׁ htp. *sanctify oneself* 1 C 15$_{12}$, נתן pass. *be assigned* 1 C 6$_{33}$, לקח *take* Gn 27$_{35}$ 31$_{46}$, לקט *gather* 31$_{46}$, נשׁה *lend* Ne 5$_{10}$, קנה *buy* 5$_{8}$, שׁבר *buy* grain Gn 42$_{3}$, מכר *sell* Lv 25$_{25}$, ni. *be sold, sell oneself* Lv 25$_{39.47.48}$ Dt 15$_{12}$ Ne 5$_{8.8}$ (or em. וְנִכְרוּ *that we might buy*).

אכל *eat* Gn 31$_{46.54.54}$ Ne 5$_{14}$, הרג *kill* Gn 37$_{26}$ 2 S 3$_{30}$, קבר *bury* Gn 50$_{14.14}$ (obj. אָב *father*) Jg 16$_{31}$, רעה *tend animals* Gn 37$_{12.13}$, טען *load* beasts 45$_{17}$, שׁבה ni. *be captured* 14$_{14}$, אסר ni. *be imprisoned* 42$_{19}$, שׁדד pu. *be devastated* Jr 49$_{10}$, מקק ni. *fade away* Ezk 4$_{17}$, גוע *die* Nm 20$_{3}$, מות *be dead* Gn 42$_{38}$ 44$_{20}$ Ex 1$_{6}$.

דרשׁ *look for* Dt 22$_{2}$, בקשׁ pi. *seek* Nm 16$_{10}$, צור *besiege* Jg 9$_{31}$, נדה pi. *drive away* Is 66$_{5}$, ירשׁ *take possession of* Dt 3$_{20}$, בנה *build* Ezr 3$_{2.2}$ Ne 3$_{1}$, חזק hi. *repair* walls 3$_{18}$, ישׁב *dwell* Gn 47$_{6}$ Dt 24$_{8}$ 25$_{5}$ Ps 133$_{1}$ 2 C 19$_{10}$, חיה *live* with redeemer Lv 25$_{35}$, לוה ni. *associate (with)* Nm 18$_{2}$, שׁאר ni. *remain* 1 C 13$_{2}$, לין *spend the night* Gn 31$_{54}$, פשׁט *strip* clothes Ne 4$_{17}$, ענה pi. *rape* 2 S 13$_{12}$, נשׂא *take (as wife)* 1 C 23$_{22}$, *carry* Jg 16$_{31}$.

ראה *see* Gn 37$_{4}$ 50$_{15}$, נכר hi. *recognize* 42$_{8}$, ידה hi. *praise* 49$_{8}$, שׂמח *rejoice* 11QPs^{a} 19$_{17}$, שׂנא *hate* Gn 37$_{5.8}$ Is 66$_{5}$, קנא *be jealous of* Gn 37$_{11}$, עקב *cheat* Jr 9$_{3}$, גנב *steal* 2 S 19$_{42}$, סות hi. *seduce* Dt 13$_{7}$=11QT 54$_{19}$ (שׂות), בגד *betray* Jr 12$_{6}$ Jb 6$_{15}$, מעל *be unfaithful* 2 C 30$_{7}$, כסה pi. *conceal* murder Gn 37$_{26}$.

מסס hi. *cause* heart *to melt* Dt 1$_{28}$ Jos 14$_{8}$, בהל ni. *be terrified* Gn 45$_{3}$, שׁמם ni. *be appalled* Ezk 4$_{17}$, קלה ni. *feel humiliated* Dt 25$_{3}$, פשׁע ni. *be offended* Pr 18$_{19}$ (or em. מוֹשִׁיעַ *is one who delivers* or שׁוֹעַ *free*), רגז *quarrel* Gn 45$_{24}$, נצה ni. *struggle* Dt 25$_{11}$, בכה *bewail* Lv 10$_{6}$, נחם pi. *console* 1 C 7$_{22}$.

אמר *say* Gn 24$_{55}$ 37$_{8}$ 47$_{3}$ 50$_{15.18}$ Nm 20$_{14}$ Dt 1$_{28}$ 13$_{7}$ Jg 18$_{8}$, דבר pi. *speak* Gn 45$_{15}$ Ex 7$_{2}$ Jg 9$_{3}$ 1QS 6$_{10}$, צוה pi. *command* 1 S 20$_{29}$, למד pu. *be taught* 1 C 25$_{7}$, ענה *answer* Gn 45$_{3}$, *testify* Meṣad Ḥashavyahu ost. 1$_{10.11}$, שׁמע *hear* Gn 37$_{27}$ 1 S 22$_{1}$.

<NOM CL> הוּא אָחִי *he is my brother* 1 K 2$_{22}$, אָחִי הוּא *he is my brother* Gn 20$_{5.13}$ 1 K 20$_{32}$, אַחַי בְּנֵי־אִמִּי הֵם *they were my brothers, the sons of my own mother* Jg 8$_{19}$, אָחִיךְ הוּא *he is your* (fem.) *brother* 2 S 13$_{20}$, אָחִינוּ ... הוּא *he is ... our brother* Gn 37$_{27}$ Jg 9$_{3}$, אֲחִי אָבִיהָ הוּא *he was her father's kinsman* Gn 29$_{12}$, אָחִי אַתָּה *you are my kinsman* 29$_{15}$, הֲלוֹא־אָח עֵשָׂו לְיַעֲקֹב *is not Esau a brother of Jacob?* Ml 1$_{2}$, אֲנִי ... אֲחִיכֶם *I am ... your brother* Gn 45$_{4}$, אֲחִיכֶם הוּא *he is your* (pl.) *brother* Jg 9$_{18}$, אֲחִיכֶם אִתְּכֶם *your* (pl.) *brother is with you* Gn 43$_{3.5}$, sim. 44$_{26.26}$, הֲזֶה אֲחִיכֶם *is this your* (pl.) *brother?* 43$_{29}$, אֲחִי מִיכָה יִשִּׁיָּה *the brother of Micah was Isshiah* 1 C 24$_{25}$, לָכֶם אָח *you* (pl.) *have a brother* Gn 43$_{6.7}$ 44$_{19}$, וּלְרִבְקָה אָח *and Rebekah had a brother* 24$_{29}$, וְאָחִיו מַחַת *and his brother was Mahath* 1 C 6$_{10}$ (if em. וַאֲחִימוֹת *and Ahimoth*).

אַחִים אֲנַחְנוּ *we are brothers* Gn 13$_{8}$ 42$_{13}$, var. 42$_{32}$, אֲחֵי אֲחַזְיָהוּ אֲנַחְנוּ *we are Ahaziah's relatives* 2 K 10$_{13}$, וְלוֹ־אַחִים *and he* (Jehoram) *had brothers* 2 C 21$_{2}$, אחים לי *I have brothers* 4QRitMar 9$_{11}$, וְאֶחָיו לֶאֱלִיעֶזֶר appar. *and his brothers were to,* i.e. under the charge of, *Eliezer* 1 C 26$_{25}$, שִׁמְעוֹן וְלֵוִי אַחִים *Simeon and Levi are brothers* Gn 49$_{5}$, אֲחֵיהֶם ... אֱלִיהוּ וּסְמַכְיָהוּ *their brothers ... were Elihu and Semachiah* 1 C 26$_{7}$, אִם־אֵין ... אַחִים *if there are no ... brothers* Nm 27$_{10.11}$.

<OBJ> ילד *give birth to* Gn 4$_{2}$ 4QTNaph 2$_{10}$, חיה hi. *preserve life of* Jos 2$_{13}$, גאל *redeem* Lv 25$_{48}$, שׁמר *guard* Gn 4$_{9}$, חזק hi. *support* Lv 25$_{35}$, pi. *assist* 2 C 29$_{34}$, כול pilp. *provide for* Gn 47$_{12}$, שׁאל *ask* 1 S 17$_{22}$, צוה pi.

command Ne 7$_{2}$, בקשׁ pi. *seek* Gn 37$_{16}$, מצא *find* 37$_{17}$ 2 K 10$_{13}$, ישׁב hi. *resettle* Gn 47$_{6.11}$, עבד *serve* 27$_{40}$, שׁרת pi. *serve* in cult Nm 8$_{26}$, מלך hi. *make king* 2 C 36$_{4.10}$.

נתן *give* Gn 42$_{34}$, מור hi. *exchange* Si 7$_{18}$, לקח *take* Gn 31$_{23}$ 42$_{16}$ 43$_{13}$ Nm 18$_{6}$ Jr 35$_{3}$ 2 C 36$_{4}$, אסף *gather* Jos 2$_{18}$ 2 C 29$_{15}$, תפשׂ *seize* Is 3$_{6}$, נוח hi. *lead* Jos 6$_{23}$, *leave behind* Gn 42$_{33}$ 11QT 58$_{14}$, עזב *leave* Jos 22$_{3}$ 1 C 16$_{37.38.39}$, בוא hi. *bring* Gn 42$_{20.34}$ Is 66$_{20}$ 2 C 36$_{4}$, יצא hi. *bring out* Jos 6$_{23}$, ירד hi. *send down* Gn 43$_{7}$, עלה hi. *send up* Gn 50$_{24}$, קום hi. *raise* CD 5$_{19}$, עמד hi. *position* 1 C 15$_{16}$, שׁוב hi. *bring back* Gn 14$_{16}$ 2 S 15$_{20}$, קרב hi. *advance* Nm 16$_{10}$ 18$_{2}$, דחק *impede* Jl 2$_{8}$, נשׂא *carry* Lv 10$_{4}$, רחק hi. *make distant* Jb 19$_{13}$, שׁלח pi. *send* Gn 43$_{4.14}$ 45$_{24}$, שׁלך hi. *cast out* Jr 7$_{15}$, pi. *release* from slavery 34$_{14}$, מכר *sell* Gn 45$_{4}$ Ne 5$_{8}$, כרה *buy* 5$_{8}$ (if em. וְנִמְכְּרוּ *that they might be sold*), פדה *redeem* Ps 49$_{8}$ (but perh. אָח II *alas;* mss אַךְ *indeed*), רדף *pursue* Am 1$_{11}$, צוד *hunt* Mc 7$_{2}$, גרשׁ pi. *drive out* Jg 9$_{41}$.

שׂנא *hate* Lv 19$_{17}$, אהב *love* CD 6$_{20}$, ינה hi. *oppress* Lv 25$_{14}$, צדק hi. *make righteous* CD 20$_{18}$, עקב *cheat* Ho 12$_{4}$, נגשׂ *exact (from)* Dt 15$_{2}$, חבל *pledge* Jb 22$_{6}$, נכה hi. *strike* 2 S 14$_{7}$ 1 C 20$_{5}$, הרג *kill* Gn 37$_{26}$ Ex 32$_{27}$ Jg 9$_{5.24.56}$ 2 S 14$_{7}$ 2 C 21$_{4.13}$, פשׁט hi. *strip* clothes Gn 37$_{23}$, ראה *see* 42$_{7}$ 43$_{29}$ 1 S 20$_{29}$, פקד *notice* Gn 50$_{24}$, *ask* 1 S 17$_{18}$, נכר hi. *recognize* Gn 42$_{7.8}$ Dt 33$_{9}$, htp. *feign ignorance (of)* Gn 42$_{7}$, קרא *invite* 1 K 1$_{9.10}$, למד pi. *teach* Jr 31$_{34}$, יכח hi. *reprove* CD 7$_{2}$.

<CSTR> אֲחִי *brother, kinsman of* followed by pr.n.m. Abra(ha)m Gn 14$_{12}$ 22$_{23}$ 24$_{15}$, Ahaziah 2 C 22$_{8}$, Caleb Jos 15$_{17}$ Jg 1$_{13}$ 3$_{9}$, David 2 S 13$_{3.32}$ 21$_{21}$||1 C 20$_{7}$, Goliath 1 C 20$_{5}$, Ichabod 1 S 14$_{3}$, Japheth Gn 10$_{21}$, Jerahmeel 1 C 2$_{42}$, Joab 1 S 26$_{6}$ 2 S 18$_{2}$ 23$_{18.24}$||1 C 11$_{20.26}$ 1 C 27$_{7}$, Joseph Gn 42$_{4}$, Micah 1 C 24$_{25}$, Nathan 11$_{38}$, Shammai 2$_{32}$, Shuhah 4$_{11}$; pr.n.f. Rebekah Gn 28$_{5}$, (־)אֲחֵי *brothers of* followed by pr.n.m. Ahaziah 2 K 10$_{13.13}$, David 1 C 27$_{18}$, Joseph Gn 42$_{3.6}$ 50$_{15}$, Saul 1 C 12$_{2.30}$; pr.n.f. Dinah Gn 34$_{25}$.

אֲחֵי־רָשׁ *poor man's kinsmen* Pr 19$_{7}$, אֲחִי אָב *father's brother, uncle* Lv 18$_{14}$ CD 5$_{10}$ 4Q251 7$_{4}$, אֲחֵי אָב *father's brothers, kinsmen* Nm 27$_{4.7.10}$ Jos 17$_{4}$, אֲחִי אֵם *mother's brother, uncle* Gn 28$_{2}$ 29$_{10.10.10}$ (all + Laban) 4Q251 7$_{4}$, אֲחֵי אֵם *mother's brothers, uncles* Jg 9$_{1.3}$.

בֵּית אֲחֵי אֲדֹנִי *the house of my master's kinsmen* Gn 24$_{27}$, בֵּית אָח *brother's house* Dt 25$_{9}$ Pr 27$_{10}$ Jb 1$_{13.18}$, אֵשֶׁת אָח *brother's wife, sister-in-law* Gn 38$_{8.9}$ Lv 18$_{16}$ 20$_{21}$ 11QT 66$_{13}$, בֶּן־אָח *brother's son, nephew* Gn 12$_{5}$ 2 K 11$_{2}$ (if em. אֲחַזְיָה *Ahaziah* to אָחִיהָ *her brother*), בֶּן אַחִים *a son of kinsmen* Ho 13$_{15}$ (or em. כְּאָחוּ *as reeds*), בְּנֵי אַחִים *brothers' sons, nephews* 2 C 22$_{8}$, בַּת־אָח *brother's (grand-)daughter, (great-)niece* Gn 24$_{48}$ CD 5$_{8.10}$ 11QT 66$_{17}$ 4Q251 7$_{3}$, בְּנוֹת אַחִים *kinsmen's daughters* Jg 14$_{3}$, חֵי אָחִיךָ *your kinsman's life* Lv 25$_{36}$, שֵׁם אָחִיו *his brother's name* Gn 4$_{21}$ 10$_{25}$||1 C 1$_{19}$ Dt 25$_{6}$ 1 C 7$_{16}$, שֵׁם אֲחֵיהֶם *their brothers' name* Gn 48$_{6}$, בְּרִית אַחִים *covenant of kinsmen*, perh. blood-ties Am 1$_{9}$, חֲמוֹר אָחִיךָ *your kinsman's ass* Dt 22$_{4}$, שׁוֹר אָחִיךָ *your kinsman's ox* 22$_{1}$=11QT 64$_{13}$, כָּל־אֲבֵדַת אָחִיךָ *anything lost of* (by) *your kinsman* Dt 22$_{3}$, גֵּזֶל אָח *something stolen from a brother* Ezk 18$_{18}$.

מִמְכַּר אָחִיו *(proceeds of) sale of* (by) *kinsman* Lv 25$_{25}$, נְזִיר אֶחָיו *elect of his brothers* Gn 49$_{26}$ Dt 33$_{16}$, גדול אחיו *greatest of his kinsmen* Si 50$_{1}$, רְצוּי אֶחָיו *favourite of his brothers* Dt 33$_{24}$, שלום אחיהו seek *his brother's peace*, i.e. see how he fares CD 7$_{1}$, שְׁלוֹם אַחֶיךָ see *your brothers' peace* Gn 37$_{14}$, קוֹל אֲחֵיהֶם *the voice of their kinsmen* Jg 20$_{13}$, נֶפֶשׁ אָחִיו *his brother's life* 2 S 14$_{7}$, בְּשַׂר אַחֵינוּ *our brothers' flesh* Ne 5$_{5}$, יד אחיו *his colleagues' hand(s)* Si 50$_{12}$ (+ מִן *from*), פִּי אַחִים *colleagues' mouth(s)*, i.e their consent 1QM 15$_{7}$, דְּמֵי אָחִיךָ *your brother's blood* Gn 4$_{10.11}$, עֶרְוַת אָח *brother's nakedness* Lv 18$_{14.16.21}$ CD 5$_{10}$, כנף אחיהו *his brother's skirt* 11QT 66$_{13}$, לְבַב אֶחָיו *his kinsmen's courage* Dt 20$_{8}$=11QT 62$_{4}$, חֲמַת אָחִיךָ *your brother's fury* Gn 27$_{44}$, אַף־אָחִיךָ *your brother's fury* 27$_{45}$, פֶּשַׁע אַחֶיךָ *your brothers' sin* 50$_{17}$, חֲמַס אָחִיךָ *violence of* (to) *your brother* Ob$_{10}$, יוֹם אָחִיךָ *your brother's day* of distress Ob$_{12}$.

יַד אָח *brother's hand, control* Gn 32$_{12}$ (+ מִן *from*), חֶרֶב אָחִיו *his fellow's sword* Hg 2$_{22}$, גְּבוּל אֲחֵיכֶם *your brothers' boundary* Dt 2$_{4}$, אַחַד אַחֶיךָ *one of your kinsmen* Dt 15$_{7}$, רֹב אֶחָיו *majority of his kinsmen* Est 10$_{3}$, יֶתֶר אֶחָיו *rest of his kinsmen* Mc 5$_{2}$, שְׁאָר אֲחֵיהֶם *rest of their kinsmen* Ezr 3$_{8}$, קְצֵה אֶחָיו *the extremity of*, i.e. all, *his brothers* Gn 47$_{2}$.

כָּל־אָח *every brother* Jr 9$_{3.3}$, כָּל אֲחֵי *all brothers of* Pr

19$_{7}$, כל אחי *all my brothers* 4Q372 1$_{19}$ Meṣad Ḥashavyahu ost. 1$_{10}$, כָּל־אָחִיךָ *all your* (sg.) *colleagues* Nm 16$_{10}$, כָּל־אֶחָיו *all his brothers, kinsmen, colleagues* Gn 16$_{12}$ 25$_{18}$ 27$_{37}$ 37$_{4}$ 45$_{15}$ Dt 18$_{7}$ Jb 42$_{11}$ 2 C 21$_{4}$ 1QM 15$_{7}$ 11QT 60$_{14}$, כָּל־אֲחֵיכֶם *all your* (pl.) *kinsmen* Jr 7$_{15}$, כָּל־אֲחֵיהֶם *all their kinsmen* 1 C 12$_{33}$.

<APP> + pr.n. Aaron Ex 4$_{14}$ 7$_{1.2}$ 28$_{1.2.4.41}$ Lv 16$_{2}$ Nm 20$_{8}$ 27$_{13}$ Dt 32$_{50}$, Abel Gn 4$_{2.8.8.9}$, Abimelech Jg 9$_{21.24}$, Abishai 1 S 26$_{6}$ 2 S 3$_{30}$ 10$_{10}$||2 C 19$_{11.15}$ 2 S 18$_{2}$ 20$_{10}$ 23$_{18}$||1 C 11$_{20}$, Absalom 2 S 13$_{4.20.20}$ 1 K 2$_{7}$, Adonijah 1 K 2$_{21}$, Ahitub 1 S 14$_{3}$, Amnon 2 S 13$_{7.8.10.20.26}$, Asahel 3$_{27.30}$ 23$_{24}$||1 C 11$_{26}$ 1 C 27$_{7}$, Asaph 6$_{24}$, Baanah 2 S 4$_{6.9}$, Ben-Hadad 1 K 20$_{33}$, Benjamin Gn 42$_{4}$ 43$_{29}$ 45$_{12.14}$, Buz 22$_{21}$, Caleb 1 C 24$_{2}$, Chelub 4$_{11}$, Dan 4QTNaph 2$_{10}$, Eliab 1 S 17$_{28}$, Eliakim 2 C 36$_{4}$, Elimelech Ru 4$_{3}$, Esau Gn 27$_{6.11.23.30.42}$ 32$_{4.7.12.14.18}$ 35$_{1}$ 4QTNaph 2$_{7}$, Eshek 1 C 8$_{39}$, Hanani Ne 7$_{2}$, Hananiah Arad ost. 16$_{1}$, Helem 1 C 7$_{35}$, Jacob Gn 27$_{41}$ 36$_{6}$ Ob$_{10}$, Jada 1 C 2$_{32}$, Jehoahaz 2 C 36$_{4}$, Joab 2 S 2$_{22}$, Joel 1 C 11$_{38}$ 26$_{22}$, Joha 11$_{45}$, Jonathan 2 S 1$_{26}$, Joseph Gn 45$_{4}$, Laban 27$_{43}$ 28$_{5}$ 29$_{10.10.10}$, Lahmi 1 C 20$_{5}$, Lot Gn 14$_{16}$, Nahor 22$_{20.23}$ 24$_{15}$, Othniel Jos 15$_{17}$ Jg 1$_{13}$ 3$_{9}$, Shallum 1 C 9$_{19}$, Shemer 7$_{34}$ (or em. אֲחִי *Ahi*), Shimeah 2 S 13$_{3.32}$ 21$_{21}$||1 C 20$_{7}$, Shimei 2 C 31$_{12.13}$, Simeon Jg 1$_{3.17}$, Solomon 1 K 1$_{10}$, Zedekiah 2 C 36$_{10}$, Zelophehad Nm 36$_{2}$; with אָח in pl. Gn 34$_{25}$ Ne 10$_{11}$ 12$_{9.36}$ 1 C 23$_{22}$ 2 C 35$_{9}$.

אֲנָשִׁים אַחִים *men* (who are) *relatives* Gn 13$_{8}$, אָחִינוּ בְשָׂרֵנוּ *our brother, our flesh* 37$_{27}$, אֶחָיו בְּנֵי־יְרֻבַּעַל *his brothers, the sons of Jerubbaal* Jg 9$_{5}$, אַחִים ... בְּנֵי אִישׁ־אֶחָד *brothers ... sons of just one man* Gn 42$_{13}$, sim. 42$_{32}$, אָח בֶּן־אֵם *a brother, the son of one's own mother* 43$_{29}$ Dt 13$_{7}$=11QT 54$_{19}$ (+ בן אביכה *son of one's own father*), מַמְרֵא הָאֱמֹרִי אֲחִי אֶשְׁכֹּל וַאֲחִי עָנֵר *Mamre the Amorite, relative of Eshcol and relative of Aner* Gn 14$_{13}$, אחו הכהנים *his brothers, the priests* 4QD^{a} 6.2$_{4}$ (WA אחי).

<ADJ> אָח גָּדוֹל *older brother* Gn 10$_{21}$ 1 S 17$_{28}$ 1 K 2$_{22}$, אָח בְּכוֹר *eldest brother* Jb 1$_{13.18}$, אָח קָטֹן *younger brother* Gn 42$_{15.20.34}$ 43$_{29}$ 44$_{23.26.26}$ 48$_{19}$ Jg 1$_{13}$ 3$_{9}$ 1 C 24$_{31}$, אֲחִיכֶם הָאֶחָד *your one brother,* i.e. one of your brothers Gn 42$_{19(Sam)}$ (MT אֶחָד) 42$_{33}$, אָחִיךָ הָאֶבְיוֹן *your poor kinsman* Dt 15$_{7.9}$, אִם־לֹא קָרוֹב אָחִיךָ אֵלֶיךָ *if your kinsman is not near to you* Dt 22$_{2}$=11QT 64$_{14}$, אָח רָחוֹק *a far-off brother* Pr 27$_{10}$, אָחִיו הָעִבְרִי *his Hebrew kinsman* Jr 34$_{14}$, אָחִיו הַמֵּת *his dead brother* Dt 25$_{6}$, אָח שׁוֹעַ *a free brother* Pr 18$_{19}$ (if em. נִפְשָׁע *[who] is offended*).

<PREP> לְ of possession, *of, (belonging) to* Gn 9$_{25}$ (+ עֶבֶד *servant*) 1 K 2$_{15}$ Ru 4$_{3}$ 1 C 4$_{27}$ 4QpGen^{a} 2$_{6}$ (+ עֶבֶד), of direction, *to* + לקח *take* 1 S 17$_{17}$ (perh. לְ of benefit) 17$_{17}$, נתן *give* Gn 20$_{16}$ 24$_{53}$ (+ אֵם *mother*) 47$_{11}$ (|| אָב *father*) Nm 27$_{9.10}$ Dt 3$_{20}$ 2 C 31$_{15}$ Si 14$_{16}$, ni. *be given* 4Q251 7$_{4}$ ([תנתן]), שׁוב hi. *bring back* Dt 22$_{1}$=11QT 64$_{14}$ Dt 22$_{2}$, עשׂה *do* Dt 19$_{19}$=11QT 61$_{10}$, נוח hi. *give rest* Dt 3$_{20}$||Jos 1$_{15}$ Jos 22$_{4}$, פתח *open* hand in generosity Dt 15$_{11}$, חלק *distribute* Ne 13$_{13}$, נשׁך hi. *charge interest* Dt 23$_{20.21}$, אמר *say* Gn 31$_{46}$ Is 41$_{6}$ Ho 2$_{3}$, נגד hi. *tell* Gn 37$_{5}$, ספר pi. *relate* 37$_{9}$ Ps 22$_{23}$, קרא *call* Gn 31$_{54}$ Jr 34$_{17}$, עזר *give assistance* Is 41$_{6}$.

לְ of benefit, *for*, + קום hi. *establish* descendants/name (for dead brother) Gn 38$_{8}$ Dt 25$_{7}$, נתן *establish* name Gn 38$_{9}$, טמא htp. *become unclean* Lv 21$_{2}$ Nm 6$_{7}$ Ezk 44$_{25}$, שׁחט *slaughter* Ezr 6$_{20}$, כון hi. *prepare* 2 C 35$_{6}$.

לְ *according to* 2 C 35$_{5}$, היה מוּזָר לְ *become stranger to* Ps 69$_{9}$, דמה לְ *be like* 4QPsJos^{a} 6.1$_{5}$, היה גְּבִיר לְ *be master over* Gn 27$_{29}$, נקם ונטר ל *taking revenge and bearing a grudge against* CD 8$_{6}$ 19$_{18}$, דאג ל *care about* 5/6ḤevEp 12$_{4}$, נשׁק לְ pi. *kiss* Gn 45$_{15}$.

בְּ *among* 1 C 5$_{2}$ 2 C 11$_{22}$, *against* Ex 32$_{29}$ Dt 15$_{9}$ 19$_{18}$=11QT 61$_{10}$ Dt 28$_{54}$ Ezk 38$_{21}$ Ml 2$_{10}$ Ps 50$_{20}$, + לחם ni. *fight* Is 19$_{2}$.

כְּ *as*, + היה *be* 2 C 30$_{7}$, מות *die* Gn 38$_{11}$, כֹּרֵעַ כְּאָח לִי *bowing down, as (though it were for) a brother of mine* Ps 35$_{14}$ (if em. כְּרֵעַ כְּאָח *as a friend, as a brother*), מִי יִתֶּנְךָ כְּאָח לִי *would that you were as a brother of mine* Ca 8$_{1}$, כאח חשבו[הו] *regard him as a brother* Si 30$_{39}$.

מִן of direction, *from* Dt 15$_{7}$ 17$_{20}$ 2 C 19$_{10}$ perh. 4QM^{g} 1$_{2}$, partitive, *some, any (of)* Ex 2$_{11}$ Lv 25$_{48}$ Dt 18$_{15}$ 24$_{7.14}$ Ezr 8$_{24}$ Ne 1$_{2}$ 11$_{17}$ 1 C 9$_{32}$ 12$_{2}$ 15$_{17}$ 27$_{18}$ 2 C 28$_{8.11}$, ואל ישמש מאח appar. *and let him not depart from a brother* Si 38$_{12(Bmg)}$ (or em. ולא ימוש מאתך *so that he does not depart from you*), of comparison, *than* Lv 21$_{10}$ Pr 18$_{24}$ 27$_{10}$ Ne 4$_{13}$ 1 C 4$_{9}$ 11QPs^{a} 28$_{3}$ 4Q372 1$_{9}$.

עַל *against* 2 C 19$_{10}$ Si 7$_{12}$, *because of* Gn 42$_{21}$ Ne 4$_{8}$, +

בכה *weep* Gn 45$_{15}$, *more than* 48$_{22}$, בטח עַל *trust in* Jr 9$_{3}$, חזק עַל hi. *help* Ne 10$_{30}$, שׁלח עַל *send to* 1 C 13$_{2}$, הוי אחי עליכמה *woe, my brothers to you* 4QPsJos^{a} 6.1$_{7}$.

אֶל of direction, *to* Gn 32$_{4.7}$ 37$_{23.30}$ Ex 2$_{11}$ 4$_{18}$ Nm 25$_{6}$ Jg 9$_{1}$ 18$_{8}$, + אמר *say* Gn 34$_{11}$ 37$_{26}$ 42$_{21.28}$ 45$_{3.4.17.24}$ 46$_{31}$ 47$_{3}$ 50$_{24}$ Jg 18$_{14}$ 2 K 7$_{6}$ Jr 23$_{35}$, ספר pi. *relate* Gn 37$_{10}$, נהם *moan* Ezk 24$_{23}$, ידע htp. *make oneself known* Gn 45$_{1}$, קָרוֹב אֶל *near to* Jr 25$_{26}$, עשׂה אֶל *show* loyalty *to* 2 S 3$_{8}$, חמל אֶל *show compassion towards* Is 9$_{18}$, כמר אֶל ni. *be warm*, i.e. tender, *towards* Gn 43$_{30}$, נפץ אֶל pi. *smash* person *against* fellow Jr 13$_{14}$, צְעָקָה אֶל *outcry against* Ne 5$_{1}$.

נגשׁ עַד *approach* Gn 33$_{3}$; לִפְנֵי *in front of* Dt 31$_{8}$||Jos 1$_{14}$ Ne 3$_{34}$, מֵאַחֲרֵי *from after*, + שׁוב *turn* 2 S 2$_{26}$, עלה ni. *give up* 2$_{27}$; הלך אַחַר *follow after* Gn 37$_{17}$; נֶגֶד *in the presence of* Gn 31$_{32.37.37}$ 1 C 8$_{32}$||9$_{38}$; מִפְּנֵי *from the presence of* Gn 35$_{1.7}$ 36$_{6}$ Jg 11$_{3}$; מִלִּפְנֵי *from the presence of* 4QTNaph 2$_{7}$.

מֵעִם *away from* Ru 4$_{10}$; מֵעַל *away from* Gn 13$_{11}$; מִקֶּרֶב *from among* Dt 17$_{15}$=11QT 56$_{14}$ 18$_{18}$; מִתּוֹךְ *from among* 2 K 9$_{2}$.

בְּקֶרֶב *among* Dt 18$_{2}$ 1 S 16$_{13}$; בְּתוֹךְ *among* Nm 27$_{4.7}$ Jos 17$_{4.4}$ 2 K 23$_{9}$ Jb 42$_{15}$ Pr 17$_{2}$ 1QS 6$_{22}$ 1QSa 1$_{18}$, *with* Jr 41$_{8}$.

מֵאֵת *from* Gn 38$_{1}$; עִם *with* Gn 44$_{33}$ Dt 10$_{9}$ 22$_{4}$ Jos 22$_{7.8}$ 1 C 8$_{32}$||9$_{38}$ 25$_{7}$, + היה *be* 4Q372 1$_{10}$, לחם ni. *fight* 1 K 12$_{24}$||2 C 11$_{4}$; אֵת *with* Gn 31$_{25}$ 37$_{2}$ 42$_{4}$ Dt 15$_{3}$ Ezk 33$_{30}$, + עשׂה חֶסֶד *behave with integrity* Zc 7$_{9}$.

בֵּין *between* Dt 1$_{16.16}$ Pr 6$_{19}$; אֵצֶל *alongside* 2 C 28$_{15}$; לְמַעַן *for the sake of* Ps 122$_{8}$; לְעֻמַּת *corresponding to* 1 C 24$_{31.31}$ 26$_{12}$.

<COLL> שְׁנֵי־אֶחָיו *his two brothers* Gn 9$_{22}$ 4Q372 1$_{10}$, אִישׁ ... אָחִיו *one man ... another man* 13$_{11}$ Ex 10$_{23}$ 32$_{27}$ Lv 25$_{14}$ Dt 1$_{16}$ 25$_{11}$ 2 S 2$_{27}$ Jr 34$_{14}$ Ezk 4$_{17}$ 33$_{30}$ Jl 2$_{8}$ Mc 7$_{2}$ Hg 2$_{22}$ Zc 7$_{9}$ Ps 49$_{8}$ (if not II אָח *alas*) Ne 4$_{13}$ CD 6$_{20}$ 7$_{1.2}$ 20$_{18}$.

אִישׁ אֶל־אָחִיו *the one to the other* Gn 42$_{28}$ Is 9$_{18}$ Jr 13$_{14}$ 25$_{26}$ Ezk 24$_{23}$, + אמר *say* Gn 37$_{19}$ 42$_{21}$ Ex 16$_{15}$ Nm 14$_{4}$ 2 K 7$_{6}$ Jr 23$_{35}$, אִישׁ לְאָחִיו *a man to his fellow* Is 41$_{6}$ Jr 34$_{17}$ CD 8$_{6}$ 19$_{18}$, אִישׁ בְּאָחִיו *a man against his fellow* Lv 25$_{46}$ 26$_{37}$ Is 3$_{6}$ 19$_{2}$ Ezk 38$_{21}$ Ml 2$_{10}$ Ne 5$_{7}$, אִישׁ כְּאָחִיו *a man like his fellow*, i.e. equally Lv 7$_{10}$ Ezk 47$_{14}$, איש אחר אחיו *one after the other* CD 14$_{5}$, רַעַת אִישׁ אָחִיו *evil against one another* (lit. *evil of a man, his kinsman*) Zc 7$_{10}$.

וְאֶחָיו *and his brothers, kinsmen, colleagues* + pr.n.m. Adaiah Ne 11$_{13}$, Amminadab 1 C 15$_{10}$, Asaiah 15$_{6}$, Asaph 16$_{7.37}$, Eliashib Ne 3$_{1}$, Eliel 1 C 15$_{9}$, Gaal Jg 9$_{26.31.41}$, Hashabiah 1 C 26$_{30}$, perh. Jerijah 26$_{32}$, Jaazaniah Jr 35$_{3}$, Jeshua Ezr 3$_{2.9}$ 10$_{18}$, Joel 1 C 15$_{7}$, Judah Gn 44$_{14}$, Shallum 1 C 9$_{19}$, Shelomith 26$_{28}$, Shelomoth 26$_{26}$, Shemaiah 15$_{8}$, Uriel 15$_{5}$, Zadok 16$_{39}$, Zechariah Ne 12$_{36}$, Zerubbabel Ezr 3$_{2}$, וַאֲחֵיהֶם *and their kinsmen, colleagues* + pr.n.m. Ne 11$_{14.19}$ 12$_{24}$ 1 C 9$_{6.9.13}$ 16$_{38}$.

יחנה ואחיהו *Jannes and his brother* CD 5$_{19}$, כְּאָח לִי *as my brother* Ps 35$_{14}$ (|| רֵעַ *friend*, + אֵם *mother*), מִי יִתֶּנְךָ כְּאָח לִי יוֹנֵק שְׁדֵי אִמִּי *would that you were as a brother of mine, sucking my mother's breasts* Ca 8$_{1}$, אַל־אָחִי *my brother, don't* 2 S 13$_{12}$, אָב אוֹ־אָח *a father or a brother* Gn 44$_{19}$, sim. Jg 21$_{22}$, אָב וְאַחִים *father and brothers* Gn 47$_{1.5.6.11.12}$, אַחִים וּבֵית אָב *brothers and father's household* 46$_{31.31}$ Jr 12$_{6}$, sim. 1 S 22$_{1}$ 2 C 21$_{13}$, בֵּן וְאָח *son and brother* Ex 32$_{29}$ Ec 4$_{8}$, אֵם ... אָב ... בֵּן ... בַּת ... אָח *mother ... father ... son ... daughter ... brother* Lv 21$_{2}$, sim. Nm 6$_{7}$ Dt 33$_{9}$ Jos 2$_{13.18}$ 6$_{23}$ Ezk 44$_{25}$, ... אָח בֵּן ... בַּת ... אִשָּׁה ... בַּיִת *brother ... son ... daughter ... wife ... house* Ne 4$_{8}$, שִׁבְעִים אֶחָיו *his seventy brothers* Jg 9$_{56}$; הלקח אח perh. *what is taken by a brother*, i.e. a brother's share of an inheritance Si 14$_{14}$.

<SYN> רֵעַ *friend*, אָחוֹת *sister*, אֵם *mother*, אָב *father*.

<ANT> נָכְרִי *foreigner*.

→ אַחֲוָה *brotherhood*, אָחוֹת *sister*, אחא *Aha*, אַחְאָב *Ahab*, אֵחִי *Ahi*, אַחְיוֹ *Ahio*, אחיאל *Ahiel*, אֲחִיאָם *Ahiam*, אֲחִיָּה *Ahijah*, אֲחִיהוּד *Ahihud*, אֲחַזְיָהוּ *Ahaziah*, אֲחִיחֻד *Ahihud*, אֲחִיטוּב *Ahitub*, אֲחִילוּד *Ahilud*, אחימות *Ahimoth*, אֲחִימֶלֶךְ *Ahimelech*, אֲחִימַעַץ *Ahimaaz*, אֲחִימַן *Ahiman*, אַחְיָן *Ahian*, אֲחִינָדָב *Ahinadab*, אֲחִינֹעַם *Ahinoam*, אֲחִיסָמָךְ *Ahisamach*, אֲחִיעֶזֶר *Ahiezer*, אחיקם *Ahikam*, אֲחִירָם *Ahiram*, אֲחִירָמִי *Ahiramite*, אֲחִירַע *Ahira*, אֲחִישַׁחַר *Ahishahar*, אֲחִישָׁר *Ahishar*, אֲחִיתֹפֶל *Ahithophel*, אַחְלַי *Ahlai*, אחמא *Ahima*, אֲחַרְחֵל *Aharhel*, perh. אחך *Achicha*.

אָח II 3 interj. **alas**, אֱמָר־אָח אֶל כָּל־תּוֹעֲבוֹת *say, Alas,* *about all the abominations of* Ezk 6$_{11}$ (or em. הֶאָח *aha*, expressing satisfaction), וְעָשָׂה אָח מֵאַחַד מֵאֵלֶּה appar. *if he does, alas, any one of these* 18$_{10}$ (or del. אָח; mss מֵאַחַת *any one of*), אִבְחַת־חָרֶב אָח עֲשׂוּיָה לְבָרָק *slaughter of*, i.e. by, *a sword, alas, made like lightning* 21$_{20}$ (or em. אַךְ *indeed* it is made), אָח לֹא־פָדֹה יִפְדֶּה אִישׁ *alas, one cannot save oneself* Ps 49$_8$ (but prob. אָח I *brother*; mss אַךְ *indeed*).

אָח III 3 n.f. **brazier**, אֶת־הָאָח לְפָנָיו מְבֹעָרֶת *the brazier was in front of him, burning* Jr 36$_{22}$ (or em. ־אֵשׁ *fire of* the brazier), הָאֵשׁ אֲשֶׁר עַל/אֶל־הָאָח *the fire that was in the brazier* Jr 36$_{23.23}$.

[אֹחַ] 1.0.1 n.[m.] **owl**—pl. אֹחִים—וּמָלְאוּ בָתֵּיהֶם אֹחִים *and their houses will be full of owls* Is 13$_{21}$ (+ צִיִּי *wild beast*, בַּת־יַעֲנָה *ostrich*, שָׂעִיר *satyr*, אִי *jackal*, תַּן *jackal*), ל בן[הל] כול רוחי מלאכי חבל ורוחות ממזרים ... אחים *to terrify all spirits of the angels of destruction and the spirits of incestuous issue: ... owls* 4QShir^a 1$_5$ (+ שד אים לילית *demons, jackals, Lilith*), [לפלט מכול נגע הר]וחות והשדים [והלילית והאחים והציים] *to deliver (him) from every assault of the spirits and the demons and the liliths and the owls and the howling creatures* 11QapPs^a 2$_{12}$.

אחא 0.0.0.8 pr.n.m. **Aha**, **1.** father of Hananiah (חנניה[ו]), Seal 834$_2$ (City of David, 7th/6th cent.). **2.** אחא [ה]יהד[י] *Aha the Judaean* Samaria ost. 51$_3$. **3.** Seal 120$_2$ ([אחא]) 121$_2$ (both T. el-Judeideh, 8th cent.) 295$_2$ 296$_2$ (both Kh. Rabud, 8th cent.; all four + שלם *Shallum*). **4.** Arad ost. 49$_5$ 67$_4$ (אח[א]) 74$_2$. **5.** Kh. el-Meshash ost. 1543.1$_4$.
→ אָח *brother*.

אַחְאָב 93.0.0.8 pr.n.m. **Ahab**—אֶחָב—son of Omri and his successor as king of Israel, husband of Jezebel, 1 K 16$_{28+5t}$ 17$_1$ 18$_{1+16t}$ 19$_1$ 20$_{2.13.14}$ 21$_{1+14t}$ 22$_{20}$||2 C 18$_{19}$ 1 K 22$_{39.40.41.50.52}$ 2 K 1$_1$ 3$_{1.5}$ 8$_{16.18.18}$||2 C 21$_{6.6}$ 2 K 8$_{25.27.27}$ ||2 C 22$_{3.4}$ 2 K 8$_{27.28.29}$||2 C 22$_{5.6}$ 2 K 9$_{7+5t}$ 10$_{1+6t}$ 21$_{3.13}$ 2 C 18$_{1.2.2.3}$ 21$_{13}$ 22$_{7.8}$ Mc 6$_{16}$. **<APP>** אַחְאָב בֶּן־עָמְרִי *Ahab, son of Omri* 1 K 16$_{29.30}$, אַחְאָב מֶלֶךְ־יִשְׂרָאֵל *Ahab, king of Israel* 1 K 20$_2$ 21$_{18}$ 22$_{41}$ 2 K 21$_3$ (both מֶלֶךְ) 2 C 18$_{3.19}$, אַחְאָב מֶלֶךְ שֹׁמְרוֹן *Ahab, king of Samaria* 1 K 21$_1$, אַחְאָב אֲדֹנֶיךָ *Ahab, your lord* 2 K 9$_7$.

2. son of Kolaiah and prophet at time of Jeremiah, Jr 29$_{21.22}$ (אֶחָב; Qr^{Or} אַחְאָב). **3.** father of Eliaz (אלעז), Seal 517$_2$ 518$_2$ (both T. Beit Mirsim?, 7th/6th cent.). **4.** father of Helez (חלץ [בן]), perh. ident. with preceding, Seal 560$_2$ (T. Beit Mirsim?, 7th/6th cent.). **5.** son of Ephroah (אפרח), perh. ident. with one or both of the preceding, Seal 519$_1$ (T. Beit Mirsim?, 7th/6th cent.). **6.** perh. ident. with one or more preceding, Seal 516$_2$ (T. Beit Mirsim?, 7th/6th cent.). **7.** T. el-Hamme jar handle inscr. **8.** Seal 57$_2$ (Lachish, 7th cent.). **9.** Seal 156$_2$ (אחאב; others אהאב; T. eṣ-Ṣafi, 7th cent.). **10.** Seal 876$_2$.
→ אָח *brother* + אָב *father*.

אחאמה 0.0.0.2 pr.n.m. **Ahamah**, **1.** son of Jekamiah, Seal 366$_1$ (7th cent.). **2.** father of Pashhur, Seal 651$_2$ (T. Beit Mirsim?, 7th/6th cent.).
→ אָח *brother*.

[אחאמר], see אֲחִיסָמָךְ.

אֶחָב, see אַחְאָב.

אַחְבָּן 1 pr.n.m. **Ahban**, son of Abihail and Abishur, descendant of Judah, 1 C 2$_{29}$.
→ אָח *brother* + בין *understand*.

אחד 1 vb. **be united—Htp.** Impv. הִתְאַחֲדִי—הִתְאַחֲדִי הֵימִנִי הָשִׂימִי הַשְׂמִילִי *do it at all at once* (O sword of Y.), *(turn) to the right, place yourself, (turn) to the left* Ezk 21$_{21}$ (mss הִתְאַחֲרִי *turn to the rear*; or em. הִתְחַדִּי *sharpen yourself*).
→ אֶחָד *one*.

אֶחָד †970.13.151 adj. **one**—masc. אֶחָד (חַד, אַחַד, Kt אחת); cstr. אַחַד (Kt אחת); pl. אֲחָדִים; fem. אַחַת (אֶחָת, אֶחָד, Kt אחד); cstr. אַחַת (Kt אחד)—**1a.** as adj. of quantity, **one (whole), single, same,** of אֵל *God* Ml 2$_{10}$, רוּחַ *spirit* Ec 3$_{19}$, עַם *people* Gn 11$_6$ 34$_{16.22}$ 2QapMoses 1$_6$, גּוֹי *nation* Ezk 37$_{22}$, שֵׁבֶט *tribe* Jg 21$_{3.6}$, מַטֶּה *tribe* Nm 1$_{44}$

(if ins. לְמַטֶּה אֶחָד אִישׁ רֹאשׁ *per one tribe, each being a head*), אֲגֻדָּה military *unit* 2 S 2$_{25}$, perh. צָבָא *army* Nm 31$_{28}$ (לַצָּבָא אֶחָד; or em.; see §2a), בַּיִת *house(hold)* 1 K 3$_{17}$ 1 C 24$_{6.6.6}$ (if em. אָחֻז *taken* in both).

אָב *father* Ml 2$_{10}$, בַּת *daughter* 4QTNaph 2$_{8}$ ([בת] [אחת]), נָשִׂיא *chief* Nm 7$_{11.11}$ 34$_{18.18}$ Jos 22$_{14.14}$, נֶפֶשׁ *person* Nm 31$_{28(Sam)}$ (MT אֶחָד נֶפֶשׁ), אָדָם *man* Ec 7$_{28}$, עֵד *witness* Nm 35$_{30}$ Dt 17$_{6}$ 19$_{15}$=11QT 61$_{6}$, חטא ptc. *sinner* Ec 9$_{18}$ (or em. חֵטְא *sin*), שְׁגָגָה *sin of inadvertence* 1QS 9$_{1}$.

אַיִל *ram* Gn 22$_{13}$ (if em. אַחַר *behind*) Lv 16$_{5}$ Nm 6$_{14}$ 7$_{15+11t}$ 28$_{11.19.27}$ 29$_{2.8.9.14.36}$ Dn 8$_{3}$ 11QT 14$_{1(Yadin)}$ ([איל אחד]) 14$_{4(Yadin)}$ ([לאיל האחד]) 14$_{12.16}$ ([ה]אחד]) 15$_{4(Yadin)}$ ([לאיל ה]אחד]) 18$_{9}$ 21$_{2(Yadin)}$ + Sup ([איל] [אחד]) 21$_{2}$ + Sup ([איל אח]ד]) 21$_{3(Yadin)}$ + Sup ([איל] אח]ד) 22$_{12.12.13}$ 23$_{6}$ 25$_{7}$ + Sup 25$_{13}$, שָׂעִיר *goat* Lv 23$_{19}$ Nm 7$_{16+11t}$ 28$_{15.22.30}$ 29$_{5+9t}$ 11QT 17$_{14}$ 25$_{14}$ 28$_{4.8.11}$ 4QApocMos B 1.2$_{5}$ ([האחד]), פַּר *bull* Lv 23$_{18}$ Nm 7$_{15+11t}$ 29$_{2.8.14.36}$ 11QT 23$_{6(mg)}$ 25$_{13}$, כֶּבֶשׂ *lamb* Nm 6$_{14}$ 7$_{15+11t}$ 29$_{4.10}$ 11QT 21$_{2(Yadin)}$ + Sup ([כבש אחד]) 21$_{2}$ + Sup 21$_{3(Yadin)}$ + Sup 22$_{12.12.13}$ 23$_{6(Yadin)}$ ([כב]ש אחד]), כַּבְשָׂה *ewe-lamb* Lv 14$_{10}$ Nm 6$_{14}$, אַרְבֶּה *locust* Ex 10$_{19}$.

מָקוֹם *place* Gn 1$_{9}$ Ec 3$_{20}$ 6$_{6}$ 4QM^{a} fr. 1$_{15(Baillet)}$ ([במקום]), חֶבֶל *cord*, i.e. territory Jos 17$_{14.17}$, מִדָּה *measurement* Ex 26$_{2.8}$||36$_{9.15}$ 1 K 6$_{25}$ 7$_{37}$, תִּיכוֹן *capacity* 4QOrd^{b} 1.1$_{3}$ ([תכ]ון]), עִשָּׂרוֹן *tenth* Nm 29$_{4}$, לֹג *log* Lv 14$_{10}$, קֶצֶב *design* 1 K 6$_{25}$ 7$_{37}$, דְּמוּת *likeness* Ezk 1$_{16}$ 10$_{10}$ (אֶחָד; or em. אַחַת), גּוֹרָל *lot* Lv 16$_{8}$=11QT 26$_{4}$ ([גו]רל א]חד]) Lv 16$_{8}$=11QT 26$_{4(Yadin)}$ ([גורל אחד]) Jos 17$_{14}$, אחז ptc. pass. *selection* Nm 31$_{30}$ (or del. אָחֻז; see §2a), אֶבֶן *stone* Jos 4$_{5}$ Zc 3$_{9}$, נֵד *pile* Jos 3$_{13.16}$, שְׁכֶם *shoulder*, i.e. slope Gn 48$_{22}$, שַׁעַר *gate* 1QM 7$_{16}$, שָׂפָה *lip*, i.e. language Gn 11$_{1.6}$, דָּבָר *word* Jos 23$_{14.14}$ 1 K 8$_{56}$ CD 9$_{21}$ (if em. אחר *another*), שְׁאֵלָה *request* 1 K 2$_{20}$, תּוֹרָה *law* Ex 12$_{49}$ Lv 7$_{7}$ Nm 15$_{16.29}$, חֻקָּה *statute* 9$_{14}$, מִשְׁפָּט *judgment* Lv 24$_{22}$ (if em.; see §2d) Nm 15$_{16}$, סֵפֶר *book* 3QTr 6$_{5}$, בְּרָכָה *blessing* Gn 27$_{38}$, מִקְרֶה *fate* Ec 2$_{14}$ 3$_{19}$ 9$_{2.3}$, דֶּרֶךְ *way* Dt 28$_{7.25}$ (both + שֶׁבַע *seven*) Jr 32$_{39}$, בָּשָׂר *flesh* Gn 2$_{24}$, עֶצֶם *bone* 4QMMT A 24$_{9}$.

תַּנּוּר *oven* Lv 26$_{26}$, טַבַּעַת *ring* Ex 26$_{24}$||36$_{29}$ (perh. אֶחָד = *first*, as §5a), לָשׁוֹן *tongue*, i.e. bar (of gold) Jos 7$_{21}$, עֲנָק *pendant* of necklace Ca 4$_{9}$, מִקְשָׁה *hammered work* Ex 25$_{36}$||37$_{22}$, שְׂבָכָה *network* 1 K 7$_{18.42}$||2 C 4$_{13}$, קְעָרָה *bowl* Nm 7$_{13+11t}$, מִזְרָק *basin* 7$_{13+11t}$, כַּף *spoon* 7$_{14+11t}$, שִׁדָּא *chest* 3QTr 12$_{5}$, כִּיס *purse* Pr 1$_{14}$, צִנְצֶנֶת *jar* Ex 16$_{33}$, לַפִּיד *torch* Jg 15$_{4}$, קָנֶה *stalk* Gn 41$_{5.22}$, עֵץ *stick* Ezk 37$_{19}$, לֶחֶם *loaf* Ex 29$_{23}$, חַלָּה *loaf* 29$_{23}$ Lv 8$_{26.26}$ Nm 6$_{19}$ 11QT 15$_{10}$ + Sup, מַצָּה *unleavened loaf* Nm 6$_{19}$, רָקִיק *wafer* Lv 8$_{26}$ 11QT 15$_{10(Yadin)}$ + Sup ([אחד]).

שָׁנָה *year* Ex 23$_{29}$ Dt 24$_{5}$ 1QS 6$_{25.27}$ ([אח]ת]) 7$_{3.4.8(mg).16}$, רֶגַע *instant* Ex 33$_{5}$, פַּעַם *occasion*, i.e. once Jos 6$_{3.11.14}$ 10$_{42}$ 1 S 26$_{8}$ 2 S 23$_{8}$||1 C 11$_{11}$ Is 66$_{8}$ 11QT 22$_{16}$ 27$_{5}$ 4QOrd^{a} 1.2$_{7(Allegro)}$ ([פ]עם]) 11QT 18$_{9(Yadin)}$ ([אחת]; AHL [בשנה]).

יוֹם *day* Gn 33$_{13}$ Lv 22$_{28}$ 1 S 2$_{34}$ 1 K 20$_{29}$ Is 10$_{17}$ 47$_{9}$ 66$_{8}$ (all six + בְּ *on*) Jon 3$_{4}$ Zc 3$_{9}$ Est 3$_{13}$ 8$_{12}$ (all three + בְּ) Ne 5$_{15}$ (if em. אַחַר *after* to לְיוֹם אֶחָד *per one day*) 5$_{18}$ (+ לְ) 2 C 28$_{6}$ (+ בְּ) Si 46$_{4}$ 11QT 52$_{6}$ (+ בְּ) 4Q185 1.2$_{5}$, specif. *on the same day* Gn 27$_{45}$ Is 9$_{13}$ 4QMMT A 24$_{4}$ (+ בְּ), *continuous daytime* Zc 14$_{7}$.

אִישׁ *man* Nm 14$_{4}$ 13$_{2.2}$ 16$_{22}$ Dt 1$_{23}$ Jos 3$_{12.12}$ 4$_{2.2.4.4}$ 22$_{20}$ 23$_{10}$ (:: אֶלֶף *thousand*) Jg 9$_{2}$ (:: שִׁבְעִים *seventy*) 18$_{19}$ 1 K 22$_{8}$||2 C 18$_{7}$ Is 4$_{1}$ (:: שֶׁבַע *seven*) Ezk 9$_{2}$, כְּאִישׁ אֶחָד *as one man*, i.e. with one accord, of Israel Jg 20$_{1.8.11}$ 1 S 11$_{7}$ 2 S 19$_{15}$ Ezr 3$_{1}$ Ne 8$_{1}$, of the destruction of a nation *as though it were just a single man* Nm 14$_{15}$ Jg 6$_{16}$, לֵב אֶחָד *(with) a single heart, singlemindedly* Jr 32$_{39}$ Ezk 11$_{19}$ Ps 83$_{6}$ (if em. יַחְדָּו *together*) 1 C 12$_{39}$ 2 C 30$_{12}$ 4Q183 1.2$_{4}$, פֶּה אֶחָד *(with) a single mouth, unanimously* Jos 9$_{2}$ 1 K 22$_{13}$||2 C 18$_{12}$, שְׁכֶם אֶחָד *(with) a single shoulder, jointly* Zp 3$_{9}$, קוֹל אֶחָד *(with) a single voice, (in) unison* Ex 24$_{3}$ 2 C 5$_{13}$ 1QM 8$_{10}$ 4QM^{a} fr. 13$_{8}$ ([קו]ל [אח]ד]) 18$_{2}$ ([ק]ול אח]ד]), דְּבָרִים אֲחָדִים *(with the) same words* Gn 11$_{1}$.

אַחַת דָּתוֹ *his law*, i.e. the law applying to him, *is the same* Est 4$_{11}$, כָּמוֹךָ כְמוֹהֶם אֶחָד *as you (or) as them is the same*, i.e. they are the same as you Jg 8$_{18}$, אַחַת הִיא *it is one*, i.e. it is all the same Jb 9$_{22}$, אחד הוא מעולם *he* (Y.) *is the same for ever* Si 42$_{21}$, אחד עבדך *(if) your servant is one*, i.e. if you have just one servant 30$_{39.39}$, אחד יהי דברך *may your word be one*, i.e. straightforward 5$_{10}$.

1b. as adj. of quality, **unique, singular,** of גּוֹי *nation* 2 S 7$_{23}$||1 C 17$_{21}$, רֹעֶה *shepherd* Ec 12$_{11}$, רָעָה *disaster* Ezk 7$_{5}$, יי אֶחָד *Y. is unique* Dt 6$_{4}$ Zc 14$_{9}$ (+ וּשְׁמוֹ אֶחָד *and* *his name will be unique*), אַחַת הִיא *she* (beloved) *is the only one* Ca 6$_{9.9}$.

1c. as particularizing adj., **a certain, a(n),** of אִישׁ *man* Gn 42$_{11.13}$ Jg 13$_2$ 1 S 1$_1$ 2 S 18$_{10}$ 1 K 20$_{35}$ Ezk 33$_2$ Dn 10$_5$ 4QTestim 1$_{23(mg)}$, נֶפֶשׁ *person* Lv 4$_{27}$ Nm 15$_{27}$, ארר pass. ptc. *cursed one* 4QTestim 1$_{23}$, קָדוֹשׁ *holy one* Dn 8$_{13}$, אִשָּׁה *woman* Jg 9$_{53}$, עַם *people* Est 3$_8$, אַיִל *ram* Dn 8$_3$, עִיר *city* 2 S 12$_1$, מוֹשָׁב *assembly* 1QS 7$_{11}$, גִּבְעָה *hill* 2 S 2$_{25}$, יוֹם־אֶחָד *one day*, i.e. some day (in the future) 1 S 27$_1$, יָמִים אֲחָדִים *some days, a few days* Gn 27$_{44}$ 29$_{20}$ Dn 11$_{20}$.

2. as noun. **a.** almost as indefinite article, אַחַד (מִן), אֶחָד מִן **(any)one of, a(n),** with pl. or collective noun, מָקוֹם *place* Jg 19$_{13}$ 2 S 17$_{9.12}$, חֵלֶק *portion* Ezk 45$_7$ 48$_8$, אַף *side* 1 S 1$_5$, הַר *hill* Gn 22$_2$ 2 K 2$_{16}$, גַּיְא *valley* 2$_{16}$, שִׂיחַ *bush* Gn 21$_{15}$, בּוֹר *well* 37$_{20}$, פַּחַת *pit* 2 S 17$_9$, עִיר *city* Dt 4$_{42}$ 13$_{13}$ 19$_{5.11}$ Jos 10$_2$ 1 S 27$_5$ 2 S 2$_1$, שַׁעַר *gate* Dt 15$_7$ 16$_5$ 17$_2$ 18$_6$ 23$_{17}$ 11QT 55$_{15}$ 60$_{12}$, לִשְׁכָּה *chamber* Jr 35$_2$, כְּלִי *instrument* CD 12$_{18}$, צֶלַע *rib* Gn 2$_{21}$.

דָּבָר *word* 1QS 1$_{13}$ 3$_{11}$, מִצְוָה *commandment* Lv 4$_{13.22.27}$ 5$_{17}$, טֻמְאָה *uncleanness* 1QSa 2$_3$ (טמאו[ת]) CD 11$_{19}$, שָׂרָף *seraph* Is 6$_6$, צְבִי *gazelle* 2 S 2$_{18}$, גּוּר *lion cub* Ezk 19$_{3.5}$, אָתוֹן *she-ass* 2 K 4$_{22}$, עַם *people* Gn 26$_{10}$ 1 S 26$_{15}$, שֵׁבֶט *tribe* Gn 49$_{16}$ Dt 12$_{14}$ Jg 21$_8$ 2 S 7$_7$ 15$_2$ 4QApoc Mos B 1.1$_8$.

שַׂר *prince* Ps 82$_7$ Dn 10$_{13}$, שׁפט ptc. *judge* 1 C 17$_6$, כֹּהֵן *priest* 2 K 17$_{27.28}$ 1QS 7$_2$ 4QpIsa^a 8$_{24}$, כְּהֻנָּה *priesthood*, i.e. priestly duty 1 S 2$_{36}$, בֶּן־נָבִיא *prophet's son* 2 K 9$_1$, בֵּן *son* Lv 13$_2$ Nm 36$_3$ Jg 17$_{5.11}$ 2 S 9$_{11}$, אָח *brother* Lv 25$_{48}$ Dt 15$_7$ Ne 1$_2$, אָדָם ordinary *human beings* Jg 16$_{7.11}$, רֵיק *worthless person* 2 S 6$_{20}$, נָבָל *fool* 13$_{13}$ Jb 2$_{10}$ (נְבָלוֹת), עֶבֶד *servant* 2 K 3$_{11}$ 6$_{12}$ 18$_{24}$‖Is 36$_9$ Ezk 46$_{17}$, שִׁפְחָה *maidservant* Ru 2$_{13}$, אָמָה *maidservant* 4QTNaph 2$_2$, סָרִיס *eunuch* Est 7$_9$, נַעַר *lad*, i.e. soldier 1 S 9$_3$ 16$_{18}$ 25$_{14}$ 26$_{22}$ 2 S 1$_{15}$ 2$_{21}$ 2 K 4$_{22}$.

אַחַת מִשְּׁתֵי עֵינַי *one of my two eyes* Jg 16$_{28}$, בְּאַחַת מֵעֵינַיִךְ *with one* glance *of your eyes* Ca 4$_{9(Qr)}$, אֶחָד מֵחֲמֵשׁ הַמֵּאוֹת *one of the five hundreds*, i.e. one in every five hundred Nm 31$_{28}$ (if del. נֶפֶשׁ *soul*), אֶחָד מִן־הַחֲמִשִּׁים *one of the fifties*, i.e. one in every fifty 31$_{30}$ (if del. אָחֻז *selection*), בְּאַחַת יָדוֹ *with one hand* Ne 4$_{11}$, אֶחָד מִמִּשְׁפַּחַת *someone from the family of* Nm 36$_8$.

אֶחָד מִמֶּנּוּ *one of us* Gn 3$_{22}$, [א]חד מכם *one of you* 11QapPs^a 1$_5$, אַחַד מֵהֶם, אַחַת מֵהֵנָּה *one of them* Lv 4$_2$ Nm 16$_{15.15}$ Dt 25$_5$ 28$_{55}$ 1 S 17$_{36}$ 2 S 24$_{12}$‖1 C 21$_{10}$ 1 K 19$_2$ 22$_{13}$‖2 C 18$_{12}$ Is 34$_{16}$ Ob$_{11}$ Ps 34$_{21}$ 106$_{11}$ (אֶחָד) Si 35$_1$, אַחַת מֵאֵלֶּה *one of these* Lv 5$_{4.5.13}$ Ezk 18$_{10(mss)}$ (L אַחַד), אֶחָד מִן *one out of* + number Nm 31$_{28.30}$ 31$_{47}$ Jb 9$_3$ 33$_{23}$ Ec 7$_{28}$ Ne 11$_1$ Si 6$_6$ 11QT 58$_{13.13}$ 60$_{4.8.9}$ 4Q416 5$_1$.

2b. one of us, you, them, with ref. to one of a known group, oft. of two, Gn 44$_{28}$ Ex 8$_{27}$ 9$_6$ 36$_{10+9t}$ Lv 5$_{7.7}$ perh. 7$_{14}$ 12$_{8.8}$ 14$_{22.22}$ 15$_{15.15}$ Nm 6$_{11.11}$ 10$_4$ Dt 21$_{15.15}$ Jg 16$_{29.29}$ 20$_{31.31}$ 1 S 10$_{3.3.3}$ 14$_5$ (וְהָאֶחָד = *and the other one*) 1 K 3$_{25.25}$ Is 19$_{18}$ Jr 3$_{14}$ Zc 8$_{21.21}$ 11$_{7.7}$ Ne 4$_{11}$ 11QT 13$_{5.5}$ 15$_{17}$ 21$_{15}$ 25$_{16}$ 1QM 2$_2$ 9$_{14.14}$ ([א]ח ד) 4QCrypt 1.3$_6$ (+ [ש]מנה *eight*) 4QTNaph 2$_9$.

כי באחת לא תנקה *even in respect of one of them* (sins) *you will not be held innocent* Si 7$_8$, אחת אהב ... אחת תעב *one of them he loved … one of them he loathed* 1QS 3$_{26}$, שֵׁם הָאֶחָד בּוֹצֵץ וְשֵׁם הָאֶחָד סֶנֶּה *the name of one of them was Bozez and the name of one of them was Seneh* 1 S 14$_4$ (mss הַשֵּׁנִי[ת] *of the second*, i.e. שֵׁם הָאֶחָד = *the name of the first one*, as §5b).

אחד גוע ואחד גומל *one perishes, one matures* Si 14$_{18(mg)}$, אחד משפיל ואח[ד] מירים *one he debases, one he exalts* GnzPs 3$_{21}$, שְׁנֵי אֲנָשִׁים ... אֶחָד עָשִׁיר וְאֶחָד רָאשׁ *two men, … one was rich and one was poor* 2 S 12$_1$, [דמות] הפ[נ]ים אחד ארי אח[ד] נשר ואחד עגל ואחד של אדם *as for the shape of their faces, one was a lion, one was an eagle, and one was a calf, and one was of a human being* 4QpsEzek^a 4$_9$.

וַיַּכּוֹ הָאֶחָד אֶת־הָאֶחָד *and one of them struck the other* 2 S 14$_6$, אֶחָד אֶל־אֶחָד *one of them to the other* Ezk 37$_{17}$, אֶחָד בְּאֶחָד יִגַּשׁוּ *one of them approaches another* Jb 41$_8$, הָאֶחָד יָקִים אֶת־חֲבֵרוֹ *the one supports the other* (lit. *his partner*) Ec 4$_{10}$, וְהָאֶחָד אֵינֶנּוּ *and one of us* (Jacob's sons) *is no more* Gn 42$_{13}$, הָאֶחָד בָּא־לָגוּר *this one came to sojourn* 19$_9$.

2c. a person alone, a single individual, אֵיכָה יִרְדֹּף אֶחָד אֶלֶף *how does one person pursue a thousand?* Dt 32$_{30}$, טוב אחד עושה רצון מאלף *one person who does what is pleasing is better than a thousand (others)* Si 16$_3$, אֶחָד קְרָאתִיו *I called him* (Abraham) when he was just *one person* Is 51_{2}, אֶחָד הָיָה אַבְרָהָם *Abraham was but a single person* Ezk 33_{24}.

יֵשׁ אֶחָד וְאֵין שֵׁנִי *there is a person alone with no partner* (lit. *no second*) Ec 4_{8}, לְאֶחָד אֵיךְ יֵחָם *as for a person on his own, how can he be warm?* 4_{11}, מאחד ערירי *through one, childless, person* Si 16_{4}, והוא אחד *and he is one*, i.e. if he is alone CD 9_{17}, לפני אחד *in front of one person* $9_{19.20}$, אֶחָד לְמֵאָה *one man for*, i.e. over, *a hundred* 1 C 12_{15} כבודו אשר מאחד ימלא *his glory which is from the one, fills* the seas and the earth 4Q462$_{7}$.

לֹא אֶחָד *no one* Jb 14_{4}, עַד־אֶחָד not *unto one*, not *a single one* Ex 9_{7} 14_{28} Jg 4_{16} 2 S 17_{22}, גַּם־אֶחָד not *even one* 17_{12} Ps 14_{3}=53_{4}, וְלֹא־נוֹתַר ... אֶחָד *and not one person (survived)* 2 S 13_{30} 17_{12}, sim. Ps 106_{11}, אף כי אחד *had there been but one person* Si 16_{11} (if em. אחר *another*).

2d. a single thing, just one thing, אַחַת שָׁאַלְתִּי *I have asked one thing* Ps 27_{4}, אַחַת דִּבֶּר אֱלֹהִים *one thing God has spoken* 62_{12}, [אין] צריך לו אחת אלה שלו *there need be to him not one thing other than that which is (already) his* MurEpJonathan$_{6(Milik)}$, sim. Mur 48_{5} ([כ]ל אחת), יָמִים יֻצָּרוּ וְלֹא אֶחָד בָּהֶם *the days were created* (for unborn child), *though* he had *not* yet had *even one of them* Ps 139_{16}, מִשְׁפַּט אֶחָד appar. *judgment (consisting) of one (judgment)* Lv 24_{22} (or em. מִשְׁפָּט one *judgment*).

2e. one time, once, אַחַת בַּשָּׁנָה *once a year* Ex $30_{10.10}$, אַחַת לְשָׁלֹשׁ שָׁנִים *once every three years* 2 K 10_{22}||2 C 9_{21}, וַיֵּלֶךְ בַּבַּיִת אַחַת הֵנָּה וְאַחַת הֵנָּה *and he walked through the house, once here and once there* 2 K 4_{35}, אַחַת דִּבַּרְתִּי ... וּשְׁתַּיִם *I have spoken once ... indeed twice* Jb 40_{5}, כִּי־בְאַחַת יְדַבֶּר־אֵל וּבִשְׁתַּיִם *for God speaks on one occasion, and on two*, i.e. at various times 33_{14}, לֹא־אַחַת וְלֹא שְׁתָּיִם *not once and not twice* (but often) 2 K 6_{10}, אַחַת נִשְׁבַּעְתִּי *I have sworn once* Ps 89_{36}, בְּאַחַת *at one time, all at once* Jr 10_{8} Pr 28_{18}, עוֹד אַחַת *once again* Hg 2_{6}.

3a. as adj., **each,** of קְעָרָה *bowl* Nm 7_{85}, מִזְרָק *basin* Nm 7_{85}, כִּיּוֹר *laver* 1 K $7_{38.38}$, מְכוֹנָה *stand* $7_{27.30.34.38}$, צִנָּה *shield* 10_{16}||2 C 9_{15}, מָגֵן *shield* 1 K 10_{17}||2 C 9_{16}, כֹּתֶרֶת *capital* Jr 52_{22}, יְרִיעָה *curtain* Ex $26_{2.2.8.8}$ ||$36_{9.9.15.15}$, חַלָּה *loaf* Lv 24_{5} 11QT 18_{15}, אַיִל *ram* Nm 15_{11} $28_{12.28}$ 29_{14}, פַּר *bull* $28_{12.28}$ 29_{14}, שׁוֹר *ox* 15_{11}, שֶׂה *sheep* 15_{11}, כֶּבֶשׂ *lamb* $29_{4.10.15}$ 11QT $14_{6.18(Yadin)}$ ([לכבש]), חַיָּה *creature* 4QpsEzek[a] 4_{7}, מַחֲלֹקֶת *division* 1 C 27_{1}, אִישׁ *man* 2 K 15_{20}.

3b. as noun, **each one,** לְאֶחָד and vars. *for each one*, with reference to persons Ex 16_{22} Nm 7_{3} 15_{12}, to heavenly beings Is 6_{2} Ezk $1_{6.6}$ $10_{14.21.21}$, אחד א[ח]ד *each one*, i.e. angel 4QShirShab[f] 20.2_{12}, אַחַת לְאַחַת *one by one* Ec 7_{27}, לְאַחַד אֶחָד Is 27_{12}, כל אחד ואח[ד] *each and every one, one by one*, (lit. every one and one) 3QTr 12_{13}, כל אחד מן *any one of* 1QS 1_{13}.

בפי אחד *by the mouth of anyone* CD 6_{7}, על אחד *it is the responsibility of each person* 9_{23}, יצר אחד *the mind of each person* Si 27_{6}, שבעה סדרי פנים למערכה האחת *seven frontal arrays to each battle line* 1QM 5_{4}, sim. 6_{11} ([הא]חת), שקיו עבות ומלאות [ש]ער לאחת *his thighs are thick and full of hair—each one* 4QCrypt 1.3_{4}.

4. (as) one, united, a single unit, וְהָיָה הַמִּשְׁכָּן אֶחָד *and the tabernacle shall be a single unit* Ex 26_{6}||36_{13}, sim. 26_{11}||36_{18} Ezk 37_{19}, [יהיה לב]בם אח[ד] *their heart shall be one* 4QTNaph 4_{7}, מוּצָק אֶחָד *cast as one*, i.e. alike 1 K 7_{37}, לחת מוצקות והמקבל מהמה כהם לחה אחת *the moisture of poured (liquids) and of the (vessel) receiving them is like them, one (and the same) moisture* 4QMMT A 2_{66}, כְּאֶחָד *as one, united* Is 65_{25} Ec 11_{6} Ezr 2_{64}||Ne 7_{66} Ezr 3_{9} 6_{20} 2 C 5_{13}, לַאֲחָדִים *as one, united* Ezk 37_{17}, הוּא בְאֶחָד וּמִי יְשִׁיבֶנּוּ *he* (Y.) *is as a unity, so who can turn him back?* Jb 23_{13}.

5. as ordinal number, **a.** as adj., **first,** with nouns (oft. + שֵׁנִי *second*) מַחֲנֶה *camp* Gn 32_{9}, אֶבֶן *stone* Ex 28_{10}, שֵׁן *rock* 1 S 14_{5}, עֵבֶר *side* 1QM 6_{9}, צֶלַע *side* Ex 25_{12}||37_{3} 26_{26}||36_{31}, יְרִיעָה *curtain* $26_{4.5}$||$36_{11.12}$ 26_{10}, פֵּאָה *side* 27_{9}, כֹּתֶרֶת *capital* 1 K $7_{16.17}$, דֶּלֶת *door* 6_{34}, כֶּבֶשׂ *lamb* Nm 28_{4}, צִפּוֹר *bird* Lv $14_{5.50}$, כְּרוּב *cherub* 1 K 6_{24} 2 C 3_{12} (or em. אַחֵר *other*), כֹּהֵן *priest* 1QM 7_{12}, אִשָּׁה *woman* 1 K 3_{17}.

יוֹם אֶחָד *the first day*, or perh., *day one* (as §6), of creation Gn 1_{5} (+ שֵׁנִי *second* 1_{8}), בְּאֶחָד לַחֹדֶשׁ *(on) the first (day) of the month* Gn $8_{5.13}$ Ex $40_{2.17}$ Lv 23_{24} Nm $1_{1.18}$ 29_{1} 33_{38} Dt 1_{3} Ezk 26_{1} 29_{17} 31_{1} 32_{1} 45_{18} Hg 1_{1} (בְּיוֹם אֶחָד) Ezr 3_{6} (מִיּוֹם אֶחָד) $7_{9.9}$ 10_{16} (בְּיוֹם אֶחָד) 10_{17} (עַד יוֹם אֶחָד) Ne 8_{2} (בְּיוֹם אֶחָד) 2 C 29_{17} 1QJub $27_{19(Milik)}$ ([באחד לחודש]) 11QT 14_{9} (לחודש) 1QDM 1_{2}

([באחד לחוד]ש) 4QpGen^{a} 1$_{19}$ ([א]חד), sim. Ex 12$_{18}$ Hg 2$_{1}$, [באחד בחדש הראשו]ן *on the first (day) of the first month* 4QpGen^{a} 1$_{22}$, באחד *on the first (day)* of the month 4QpGen^{a} 1$_{11}$ 4QMMT A 1$_{95}$ ([באחד]), זה אחד *this is the first (day)* of the month 4QMish C^{c}$_{2}$ ([זה אח]ד) 4QMish C^{c}$_{5}$ ([זה א]חד) 4QMish C^{d} 1.2$_{7}$ 2$_{5}$ ([זה אחד]) 3$_{2}$ ([זה אחד]), באחד ביויריב *on the first of* (the priestly course) *Joirarib* 4QMish B^{a} 1.1$_{5}$, sim. 1.1$_{1}$ ([באחד]) 1.2$_{1.1.5.5}$ ([באחד]) 1.3$_{3.4.6.7}$ (all three [באחד]) 1.3$_{8.8}$ ([באחד]) 2.1$_{1.2.5}$, אחר האחד השני *after the first and second (days)* 4QMMT A 1$_{45.92}$ (both [אחר האחד השני]) 1$_{139}$ ([אחר ה]אחד] השנ]י) 1$_{171}$ ([אחר [האחד השני]), באחד בשבת *on the first (day) after the sabbath* 4QpGen^{a} 1$_{4.13.17.19}$ ([אחד]) 2$_{2.3}$, באחד עשר *on the eleventh (day)* of the month 4QMish C^{c}$_{7}$ 4QMish C^{d} 1.2$_{8}$ 2$_{6}$ ([באחד עשר]), באחד [ע]שר בה *on the eleventh day of it* (the tenth month) 4QMish C^{b} 2$_{2}$, באחד ועשרים *on the twenty-first (day)* of the month 4QMish B^{a} 1.3$_{5}$ ([באחד ועשרים]) 2.1$_{4}$ ([ועשרים]), בעשרים ואחד *on the twenty-first (day)* of the month 4QMMT A 1$_{39}$ ([בעשרים ואחד]) 1$_{79.133}$ ([בע[שר]ים]) 1$_{170}$ ([בעשרים ואחד]) 4QMish C^{c}$_{3}$ ([בע]שרים ואחד]) 4QMish C^{d} 1.2$_{5}$ ([בעשרים ואחד]) 2$_{2}$ ([ב]עשרים [ואחד]) 4QMish D 2$_{6}$ ([בעשרים ואחד]), [בשלושים] באחד *on the thirty-first (day)* of the month 4QMish B^{a} 1.2$_{6}$.

בְּאַחַת [שנה השבועה השנית] באחד 1QJub 27$_{19(Milik)}$, וְשֵׁשׁ־מֵאוֹת שָׁנָה *in the six hundred and first year* Gn 8$_{13}$ 4QpGen^{a} 2$_{1}$ ([מאו]ת), בִּשְׁנַת אַחַת לְ *in the first year of (the reign of)* Dn 9$_{1.2}$ 11$_{1}$ Ezr 1$_{1}$ 2 C 36$_{22}$, שנת אחת לגאלת ישראל *the first year of the redemption of Israel* Mur 22 1$_{1}$ (לגאולת י[שר]אל) Bar-Kochba Revolt Year 1 Coin 165 166 (ישר) 169 171 173 176, בַּשָּׁנָה הָאַחַת עֶשְׂרֵה *in the eleventh year* 1 K 6$_{38}$.

5b. as noun, **first one, former,** שֵׁם הָאֶחָד/הָאַחַת *the name of the first one* Gn 2$_{11}$ 4$_{19}$ 10$_{25}$ Ex 1$_{15}$ 1 S 14$_{4(mss)}$ Jb 42$_{14}$ Ru 1$_{4}$, כְּנַף הָאֶחָד *the wing of the first one* 2 C 3$_{11}$, וְהָאַחַת גְּבֹהָה מִן־הַשֵּׁנִית הָאַחַת מֵהֶם *the first of them* Dn 8$_{9}$, *and the first was higher than the second* 8$_{3}$.

6. in lists, etc., as cardinal number, **one,** מֶלֶךְ ... אֶחָד *the king of* Jericho, etc. ..., *one* Jos 12$_{9+30t}$, כָּל־מְלָכִים שְׁלֹשִׁים וְאֶחָד *all (the) kings, thirty-one* 12$_{24}$, ו[גוב]הו אחת [ועשרים באמה] *and its height (is) twenty-one in cubits* 11QT 6$_{7(Yadin)}$.

7. in **other numbers,** 11 = אַחַד עָשָׂר Gn 32$_{23}$ 37$_{9}$ Dt 1$_{2}$ 4QPrQuot 1$_{13}$ ([א]חד ע[ש ר]), אַחַת עֶשְׂרֵה 2 K 9$_{29}$ 23$_{36}$||2 C 36$_{5}$ 2 K 24$_{18}$||Jr 52$_{1}$||2 C 36$_{11}$ 1 K 6$_{38}$ Ezk 30$_{20}$ 31$_{1}$ (all + שָׁנָה *year*) Jos 15$_{51}$ 6QapSam/Kings 1$_{1}$ ([א]חת עשרא) 3QTr 8$_{15}$ (עסרה), 21 = אֶחָד/אַחַת וְעֶשְׂרִים Ex 12$_{18}$ 1 C 25$_{28}$ 11QT 4$_{12}$ 6$_{7(Yadin)}$ ([ועשרים]) 31$_{10}$, עֶשְׂרִים וְאֶחָד/אַחַת 2 K 24$_{18}$||Jr 52$_{1}$||2 C 36$_{11}$ Hg 2$_{1}$ Ezr 2$_{26}$, 31 = שְׁלֹשִׁים וְאֶחָד/אַחַת Jos 12$_{24}$ 2 K 22$_{1}$||2 C 34$_{1}$ 1 K 16$_{23}$ 4QpGen^{a} 1$_{20}$ ([שלוש]ים [ואחד]), 41 = אֶחָד וְאַרְבָּעִים Nm 1$_{41}$ 2$_{28}$, אַרְבָּעִים וְאַחַת 1 K 15$_{10}$ 14$_{21}$||2 C 12$_{13}$ 2 K 14$_{23}$ 2 C 16$_{13}$, 51 = אֶחָד וַחֲמִשִּׁים Nm 2$_{16}$, 61 = אֶחָד וְשִׁשִּׁים 31$_{34.39}$, 601 = אַחַת וְשֵׁשׁ־מֵאוֹת Gn 8$_{13}$.

Also 4Q487 19$_{2}$ (כאחד) 4QPrQuot 7$_{3}$ (באחד) 11QT 14$_{12(AHL)}$ 25$_{7}$ + Sup ([א]ח[ד]) 4QpGen^{a} 2$_{4}$ 4Q464 3.1$_{4}$.

→ אחד *be united.*

[אחה], see נוח.

אָחוּ 3 n.m. **reed,** used collectively, <SUBJ> שׂגה *grow* Jb 8$_{11}$ (+ בְּלִי־מָיִם *without water;* || גֹּמֶא *reed*). <PREP> רעה בְּ *graze among* (of cows, along Nile) Gn 41$_{2.18}$; בֵּין אָחוּ/אַחִים יַפְרִיא *among reeds he will bear fruit* Ho 13$_{15}$ (if em. בֵּן אַחִים *son of brothers;* perh. also em. יַפְרִיד *he will separate*).

אֵחוּד 1 pr.n. **Ehud,** descendant of Benjamin, 1 C 8$_{6}$ (or em. אֵהוּד *Ehud*).

אַחֲוָה I 1 n.f. **brotherhood,** <OBJ> פרר hi. *annul* Zc 11$_{14}$ (+ בֵּין *between* Judah and Israel). <COLL> הוֹי אַחְוָתוֹ *alas, his brotherhood* Jr 22$_{18}$ (if em. אָחוֹת *sister;* || אָח *brother*).

→ אָח *brother.*

[אַחֲוָה] II 1.0.1 n.f. **declaration**—sf. אַחֲוָתִי—<NOM CL> וְאַחֲוָתִי בְּאָזְנֵיכֶם *and my declaration is in your ears* Jb 13$_{17}$ (or em. וַאֲחַוֶּה *and I shall declare;* + מִלָּה *word*), מָה אַחֲוַיַת אֵלֶּה *what is the declaration of these things?*, i.e. what are they saying? Dn 12$_{8}$ (if em. אַחֲרִית *end of*).

Also 4QPrQuot 51$_{3}$ (אחות).

→ חוה *speak.*

אָחוּז, see אחז, Qal, §2.

אֲחוֹחַ 1 pr.n.m. **Ahoah**, grandson of Benjamin and son of Bela, 1 C 8_4 (or em. אֲחִיָּה *Ahijah*).
→ אֲחֹחִי *Ahohi(te)*.

אֲחוֹחִי, see אֲחֹחִי II.

אֲחוּמַי 1 pr.n.m. **Ahumai**, son of Jahath, descendant of Judah, 1 C 4_2.

אָחוֹר 51.3.7 n.[m.] **rear part**—pl. cstr. אֲחֹרֵי; sf. אֲחֹרָי, אֲחֹרֵיהֶם—**1.** as adv. indicating direction, **backwards,** with verb, סוג ni. *turn* intrans. 2 S 1_{22} Is 42_{17} 50_5 Jr 38_{22} 46_5 Ps 35_4 40_{15} 44_{19} 70_3 129_5, ho. Is 59_{14}, שׁוב *turn* Ps 9_4 56_{10} Lm 1_8 1QM 15_9 4QM^{a} fr. 14_6 (תשו[בו]) 1QH $13_{21.22}$ 1QMyst 1.1_8 4QMMT B_{25} ([אחו]ר), hi. trans. Is 44_{25} Ps 44_{11} Lm 1_{13} 2_3, סבב *turn* intrans. Ps $114_{3.5}$ 4QpsEzek^{a} 4_7 ([יסבו]), הלך *go* Jr 15_6 Jb 23_8 (:: קֶדֶם *forwards*), נפל *fall* Gn 49_{17}, כשׁל *stumble* Is 28_{13}, נכה hi. *strike* (so as to make fall backwards) Ps 78_{66}, זור *be estranged* (so as to turn back from someone) Is 1_4.

<PREP> וַיִּהְיוּ לְאָחוֹר וְלֹא לְפָנִים *and they went* (lit. *were*) *backwards and not forwards* Jr 7_{24}.

2. as adv. indicating position, **to the rear, a.** without prefixed prep., with verb כתב pass. *be written* Ezk 2_{10} (פָּנִים וְאָחוֹר *at the front and back*, subj. מְגִלָּה *scroll*), היה *be* 1 C 19_{10} (פָּנִים וְאָחוֹר, subj. פָּנִים *face* of battle), צור *besiege* Ps 139_5 (אָחוֹר וָקֶדֶם *behind and in front*); in nom. cl. הַמִּלְחָמָה פָּנִים וְאָחוֹר *the battle was*, i.e. engulfed them, *in front and behind* 2 C 13_{14}.

2b. with prefixed preposition מֵאָחוֹר **from the rear,** with verb היה *be* 2 S 10_9 (+ מִפָּנִים *from the front*; ||1 C 19_{10} is without prep.); in nom. cl. אֲרָם מִקֶּדֶם וּפְלִשְׁתִּים מֵאָחוֹר *Aram was in front and (the) Philistines were behind* Is 9_{11} (perh. אָחוֹר = *west*, קֶדֶם = *east*); בְּאָחוֹר **at the back,** with verb שׁבח pi. *hold back* passions Pr 29_{11}, מימין ומשמאול ובא[חור ובפנים] *from right and from left, at the back and in the front* 4QM^{a} fr. $1_{14(Baillet)}$.

3. as pl. noun, **rear parts, back,** of Y. Ex 33_{23}, worshippers Ezk 8_{16}, oxen 1 K 7_{25}||2 C 4_4, tabernacle Ex 26_{12}. <OBJ> ראה *see* Ex 33_{23} (:: פָּנִים *face*).

<NOM CL> אֲחֹרֵיהֶם אֶל־הֵיכַל י׳ *their backs were towards the temple of Y.* Ezk 8_{16} (:: פָּנִים *face*), וְכָל־אֲחֹרֵיהֶם בָּיְתָה *and all their backs were towards the inside* 1 K 7_{25}||2 C 4_4.

<CSTR> אֲחֹרֵי הַמִּשְׁכָּן *back of the Tabernacle* Ex 26_{12}.

<PREP> בַּאֲחֹרֵי הַחֲנִית he struck him *with (the) back of the spear* 2 S 2_{23} (if em. בְּאַחֲרֵי *with the back*); סרח עַל *hang over* Ex 26_{12}, הַגִּזְרָה ... עַל־אֲחֹרֶיהָ *the space ... at its*, i.e. temple's, *back* Ezk 41_{15} (if em. אַחֲרֶיהָ *its back*).

4. as sg. noun, **future,** <PREP> לְאָחוֹר *in the future, from now on,* + אתה *come* Is 41_{23}, שׁמע *listen* 42_{23}, מצא *find* Si 6_{28}, נשׂג hi. *appreciate* words 12_{12}.

5. as adj. used as noun, **another** (or em. אַחֵר *other*), ויתן קרנם לאחור *and he gave their horn to another* Si 49_5 (|| גּוֹי *nation*).

Also 1QH fr. 1_{10}.

<ANT> פָּנִים to the *front*, i.e. forwards (§1), at the *front* (§2), *face* (§3), קֶדֶם to the *front*, i.e. forwards (§1), at the *front* (§2).
→ אחר *delay*.

אָחוֹת 114.0.10 n.f. **sister**—cstr. אֲחוֹת; sf. אֲחֹתִי (אֲחוֹתִי), אֲחוֹתֵנוּ (אֲחֹתֵנוּ), אֲחֹתָהּ (אֲחוֹתָהּ), אֲחֹתוֹ, אֲחוֹתֵךְ, אֲחוֹתְךָ, אֲחוֹתָם (אֲחֹתָם); pl. Q אחיות; cstr. Q אחיות; sf. אַחְיֹתַי, אֲחוֹתַיִךְ (אֲחוֹתֵךְ, אַחְיוֹתֵךְ), אַחְיוֹתָיו (Kt אחיתיו), אַחְיֹתֵיהֶם, אַחְיוֹתֵיכֶם—**1. sister,** also half-sister (e.g. 2 S 13) or kinswoman (e.g. Nm 25_{18}); esp. in Jr and Ezk, country or city depicted as woman; term of endearment to lover (Ca 4-5).

<SUBJ> היה *be* Gn 24_{60} (+ לְ *as*) Lv 21_3 (+ לְאִישׁ *[married] to a man*) Ezk 16_{56} (+ לִשְׁמוּעָה *as a byword*) 23_4 (+ לִי *to me*) 44_{25} (+ לְאִישׁ) 2 C 22_{11} (+ הִיא *she* [Jehoshabeath]), עשׂה *do* Ezk 16_{48}, *prepare* food 2 S 13_5, ישׁב *dwell* Ezk $16_{46.46}$ (both + בַּת *daughter*), הלך *go* Jr 3_8, בוא *come* 2 S $13_{5.6.11}$ Jb 42_{11} (|| אָח *brother*, ידע ptc. *acquaintance*), שׁוב *go back* Jr 3_{10} Ezk 16_{55}, יצב htp. *position oneself* Ex 2_4, שׁכב *lie* with 2 S 13_{11}, זנה *prostitute oneself* Jr 3_8, ילד *give birth (to)* 1 K 11_{20} Ezk 23_4 1 C 7_{18}, לקח *take* Ex 15_{20} 2 K 11_2, נתן *give*, i.e. place child 11_2 (if ins. וַתִּתֵּן), חזק hi. *hold* hand Ezk 16_{49}, פתח *open* Ca 5_2.

ברה hi. *feed* brother 2 S 13_{5}, לבב pi. *make cakes* 13_{6}, אכל *eat* Jb 1_{4} 42_{11}, שׁתה *drink* 1_{4}, גנב *steal* child 2 K 11_{2}, סתר hi. *conceal* child 11_{2}, ראה *see* Jr $3_{7(Qr)}$ Ezk 23_{11}, ירא *fear* Jr 3_{8}, געל *despise* husband and sons Ezk 16_{45}, שׁחת hi. *corrupt* 23_{11}, צדק *be righteous* 16_{52}, אמר *say* Ex 2_{7}, חרשׁ hi. *be silent* 2 S 13_{20}, לבב pi. *steal heart* Ca $4_{9.9}$, נוד *show sympathy* Jb 42_{11}, נחם pi. *console* 42_{11}, נכה ho. *be struck* Nm 25_{18}, perh. מלך *rule* 1 C 7_{18} (unless הַמֹּלֶכֶת = *Hammolecheth*).

<NOM CL> + אַתְּ *you* Gn 12_{13} Ezk 16_{45} Pr 7_{4} (+ מֹדַע *acquaintance*), הִיא *she* Gn 12_{19} $20_{2.5.12}$ $26_{7.9}$ Lv 18_{11} (all seven Qr), Naamah Gn 4_{22}, Timna 36_{22}||1 C 1_{39}, Zeruiah 1 C 2_{16}, Abigail 2_{16}, Tamar 3_{9}, Shelomith 3_{19}, Samaria Ezk 16_{46}, Sodom 16_{46}, אֲחֹתָהּ ... טוֹבָה מִמֶּנָּה *her sister ... is better than her* Jg 15_{2}, לְאַבְשָׁלוֹם ... אָחוֹת *to Absalom ... there was a sister* 2 S 13_{1}, אָחוֹת לָנוּ *we have a sister* Ca 8_{8}, גַּן נָעוּל אֲחֹתִי *my sister is a locked garden* 4_{12}.

<OBJ> עשׂה *make* Gn 34_{31} (כְּזוֹנָה *as a prostitute*), ילד *give birth (to)* Nm 26_{59}, hi. *beget* 1 C 7_{32}, חיה hi. *keep alive* Jos 2_{13}, נתן *give* Ezk 16_{61}, in marriage Gn 34_{14} 1 K $11_{19.19}$, לקח *take* Ezk 16_{61}, in marriage Gn 36_{3} Ex 6_{23} Lv 20_{17} 11QT $66_{14.15.15}$ 4Q251 7_{2} ([א]חותו) 11QJub 4_{9} (אחו[תו]), שׁלח pi. *send away* Gn 24_{59}, טמא pi. *defile* $34_{13.27}$, ענה pi. *rape* 2 S $13_{22.32}$ Ezk 22_{11}, גלה *uncover* Lv $20_{19(mss).19(mss)}$ (L עֶרְוַת אֲחוֹת *nakedness of sister of*), אהב *love* 2 S 13_{4}, צדק pi. *justify* Ezk $16_{51.52}$.

<CSTR> אֲחוֹת *sister of* + pr.n.m. Tubal-Cain Gn 4_{22}, Laban 25_{20}, Nebaioth 28_{9} 36_{3}, Lotan 36_{22}||1 C 1_{39}, Nahshon Ex 6_{23}, Aaron 15_{20}, Absalom 2 S 13_{4}, Ahaziah 2 K 11_{2} 2 C 22_{11}, Naham 1 C 4_{19}; + pr.n.f. Zeruiah 2 S 17_{25}, Tahpenes 1 K $11_{19.20}$.

אֲחוֹת אָבִיךָ *your* (masc.) *father's sister* Lv 18_{12} (אֲחוֹת־) 20_{19}, אחות אביהו *his father's sister* 11QT 66_{15} 4Q251 7_{4} ([א]ביו), אֲחוֹת אִמְּךָ *your* (masc.) *mother's sister* Lv 18_{13} (אֲחוֹת־) 20_{19}, אחות אמו *his mother's sister* 11QT 66_{15} 4Q251 7_{4} ([אחות אמו]), אֲחוֹת אֲחוֹתֵךְ appar. *your* (fem.) *sisters' sister* Ezk 16_{45} (mss אֲחוֹתַיִךְ), אֲחוֹת אִשְׁתּוֹ *his wife's sister* 1 K 11_{19}, אחיות אבי *my father's sisters* 4QTNaph 2_{1}.

עֶרְוַת אֲחוֹת *nakedness of the sister of* Lv 18_{9} (אֲחוֹתְךָ) $18_{12.13}$ both אֲחוֹת־) $20_{19.19}$ (mss lack עֶרְוַת) 4Q251 $7_{4.4}$ (ערות אחות), דֶּרֶךְ אֲחוֹתֵךְ *way of your sister* Ezk 23_{31}, כּוֹס *cup of* $23_{32.33}$, בת אחותו *his sister's daughter* 11QT 66_{17} CD 5_{8} (both || אָח *brother*) 4Q251 7_{3} ([א]חותו), בֶּן־אֲחֹתוֹ *his sister's son* Gn 29_{13}, שֵׁם אֲחֹתוֹ *the name of* 1 C 7_{15} (ms אִשְׁתּוֹ *his wife*; or em. אֲחֹתָם *their sister*), שֵׁם אֲחוֹתָם *their sister* 4_{3} (or em. אֲחוֹתָהּ *her sister*) 7_{15} (if em.).

עֲוֹן ... אֲחוֹתֵךְ *iniquity of ... your sister* Ezk 16_{49}, דְּבַר ... אֲחֹתָם *matter of*, i.e. concerning ..., *their kinswoman* Nm 25_{18}, יְדֵי אֲחֹתוֹ *his sister's hands* Gn 24_{30}, זְנוּנֵי אֲחוֹתָהּ *her sister's licentiousness* Ezk 23_{11}, כָּל־אַחְיֹתָיו *all his sisters* Jb 42_{11}.

<APP> with pr.n. or pl.n. preceding, Rebekah Gn $24_{30.59}$ 25_{20}, Mahalath 28_{9} $36_{3(Sam)}$, Basemath 36_{3}, Dinah 34_{13}, Serah 46_{17}||1 C 7_{30}, Elisheba Ex 6_{23}, Miriam 15_{20} Nm 26_{59}, Cozbi 25_{18}, Tamar 2 S $13_{2.4.5.6.22.32}$, Abigal 17_{25}, Jehosheba 2 K 11_{2}, Shua 1 C 7_{32}, Oholibah Ezk 23_{4}, Judah Jr 3_{8}, Sodom Ezk $16_{48.49.56}$; with pr.n.f. or pl.n. following, Oholibah Ezk 23_{11}, Hammolecheth 1 C 7_{18} (unless הַמֹּלֶכֶת = *who ruled* in place of her brother), Judah Jr $3_{7.10}$, Samaria Ezk 16_{55} 23_{33}, Sodom 16_{55}.

+ נְבִיאָה *prophetess* Ex 15_{20}, אִשָּׁה *wife* 1 C 4_{19}, אֵם *mother* 4QTNaph 2_{1} ([א]מי), בַּת *daughter* Gn 20_{12} 25_{20} 28_{9} 36_{3} Ex 6_{23} Nm 25_{18} 2 S 17_{25} 2 K 11_{2}, אֲחֹתוֹ בַת־אָבִיו אוֹ בַת־אִמּוֹ *his sister, the daughter of his father or the daughter of his mother* Lv 20_{17} Dt 27_{22} 11QT 66_{14} (אביהו) 4Q251 7_{2} ([א]חותו בת אביו או בת אמו), sim. Lv 18_{9} Ezk 22_{11}.

אֲחוֹת אִשְׁתּוֹ אֲחוֹת תַּחְפְּנֵיס *the sister of his wife, the sister of Tahpenes* 1 K 11_{19}, אֲחֹתוֹ הַבְּתוּלָה הַקְּרוֹבָה אֵלָיו *his virgin sister, who is closest to him* Lv 21_{3}, אֲחֹתִי כַלָּה *my sister, the bride* Ca $4_{9.10.12}$ 5_{1}, גַּנִּי אֲחֹתִי *my garden, my sister* 5_{1}, אֲחֹתִי רַעְיָתִי יוֹנָתִי תַמָּתִי *my sister, my companion, my dove, my perfection* 5_{2}.

<ADJ> קָטָן *young(er)* Jg 15_{2} Ezk $16_{46.61}$ Ca 8_{8}, גָּדוֹל *elder* Ezk $16_{46.61}$, יָפֶה *fair* 2 S 13_{1}, בָּגוֹד *treacherous* Jr $3_{7.10}$.

<PREP> לְ of direction, *to* perh. 4QTNaph 2_{11} (ל[ש]תי אחיות) perh. 4QRitMar 96_{1}, + אמר *say* Ho 2_{3} (|| אָח), of possession, *(belonging) to*, + היה *be* Ezk 16_{49} (|| בַּת *daughter*), of benefit, *to, for*, + טמא htp. *defile oneself* Lv $21_{3.3}$ Nm $6_{7.7}$ Ezk 44_{25}, פלל pi. *intercede* Ezk 16_{52},

עשׂה *do* Ca 88.

קנא בְּ pi. *be jealous of* Gn 301, דבר בְּ pu. *be spoken about* Ca 88.

קרב אל *approach* sexually CD 59, לקח אֶל *take* wife *as well as* her sister Lv 1818; עִם *with* 4QTNaph 21.1 (ואחו[תה]), + פתל ni. *wrestle* Gn 308, שׁכב *lie* Dt 2722; נקע מֵעַל *be estranged from* Ezk 2318; יצא אַחֲרֵי *go out after* Ex 1520; חלה בַּעֲבוּר htp. *pretend to be sick on account of* 2 S 132.

<COLL> אָב ... אֵם ... אָח ... אָחוֹת *father ... mother ... brother ... sister* Nm 67 Jos 213 Ezk 4425 (+ בֵּן ... בַּת *son ... daughter*), sim. Lv 213 (+ בֵּן ... בַּת), אִמִּי וַאֲחֹתִי *my mother and my sister* Jb 1714 (+ אָב *father*), הוֹי אָחוֹת *alas, sister* Jr 2218 (or em. אַחֲוָתוֹ *his brotherhood*; ‖ אָח *brother*), שְׁלֹשֶׁת אַחְיֹתֵיהֶם *their three sisters* Jb 14 (ms שְׁלֹשׁ), ל[ש]תי אחיות *to the two sisters (of)* 4QTNaph 211, אֲחֹתֵנוּ אַתְּ הֲיִי *O our sister, may you be* Gn 2460.

2. partner, with ref. to inanimate objects, אִשָּׁה אֶל־אֲחֹתָהּ *each one to its partner* (lit. *sister*) Ex 263.3.5.6.17 (Sam and ‖3610.10.12.13.22 אַחַת אֶל־אַחַת lit. *one to one*) Ezk 19.23 313, with ref. to יְרִיעָה *curtain* (Ex 263.3.6), לוּלָי *loop* (Ex 265), יָד *handle* (Ex 2617), כָּנָף *wing* (Ezk 19.23 313).

<SYN> §1 אָח *brother*, בַּת *daughter*.

→ אָח *brother*, אחתמלך *Ahathmelech*.

אחז 76.3.7 vb. **hold—Qal** Pf. אָחַז (אֲחָזַנִי) אָחֲזָה, אֲחָזָתְנִי, אֲחָזֻנִי) אָחֲזוּ, אֲחָזְתִּיו, אֲחַזְתִּיו, אָחָזְתְּ, (אֲחָזָתַם, אֲחָזָתְהָה; impf. יֹאחֵז, יֹאחֲזוּן, 3fs (יֹאחֲזֻמוֹ), וְתֹאחֵז (וְתֹאחֲזֵנִי), 2ms תֶּאֱחֹז, אֹחֲזָה, (יֹאחֲזוּךְ, יֹאחֲזוּנִי).

+ waw וַיֹּאחֶז (וַיֶּאֱחֹז, Q [ו]יאחזהו), 3fs וַתֹּאחֶז (וַתֹּחֶז), וָאֹחֵז (וְאֹחֲזָה), (וַיֹּאחֲזוּהוּ) וַיֹּאחֲזוּ, וְאֹחֲזִי־, וֶאֱחֹז; impv. אֱחֹז, אֶחֱזוּ־ (וֶאֱחֹזוּ); ptc. אֹחֵז, אֹחֶזֶת (Q אוחזת), Q אוחזי, אֹחֲזוּ, (אָחֻז), אֲחֻזִים, אֲחֻזוֹת (mss אֲחֻזוֹת), אֲחֻזֵי; inf. אֱחֹז (Si אחוז), בֶּ/לֶאֱחֹז.

1. hold, seize, grasp, <SUBJ> Moses Ex 44 (‖ חזק hi. *seize*), Jacob 4QBibParaph 1-24 ([ו]יאחזהו; ‖ אבק ni. *wrestle*), David 2 S 410 (+ הרג *kill*), Samson Jg 163, Adonijah 1 K 151, Asahel 2 S 221, Uzzah 2 S 66‖1 C 139, Job Jb 3813, Ruth Ru 315, Qoheleth Ec 23, Levite Jg 206.

אָצִיל *leader* Ex 2411(Sam), צַדִּיק *righteous man* Jb 179, lover Ca 34 (:: רפה hi. *release*) 79, warrior 2 C 255, יצר ptc. *creator* Si 3613, guards Ne 73, Philistines Jg 1621 Ps 561, tribesmen of Judah Jg 16 (+ רדף *chase*), tribesmen of Gilead Jg 126, קַדְמֹנִי *person from the east* Jb 1820, enemy of Babylon Ps 1379, כְּפִיר *(young) lion* Is 529, God Ps 7323 (+ נחה hi. *lead*) 775 Jb 1612.

יָד *hand* Gn 2526 Dt 3241, יַד־יְמִין *right hand of* 2 S 209 (ותאחז=וַתֹּחֶז; 1QSam), יָמִין *right hand* Ps 13910 (‖ נחה hi. *lead*), רֶגֶל *foot* Jb 2311, פַּח *trap* Jb 189, יָצִיעַ *structure* 1 K 610 (Kt יצוע).

חִיל *writhing* Ex 1514, רַעַד *trembling* Ex 1515 1QH 433, רְעָדָה *trembling* Is 3314 Ps 487, רֶתֶת *shivering* 1QH 433, שָׁבָץ *agony* 2 S 19, צָרָה *distress* Jr 4924 (‖ חזק hi. *seize*), צִירִים *writhings* Is 138 213, חֲבָלִים *pains* Is 138 Jr 1321 4924, בָּשָׂר *flesh* Jb 216, יְמֵי־עֹנִי *days of affliction* Jb 3016, זַלְעָפָה *burning* anger Ps 11953, pl. 4QapLamb6; subj. not specified, 1 K 66 Pr 1821 (if em.; see Obj.) Ca 215 Ec 718.

<OBJ> Y. Ex 2411(Sam) (MT וַיֶּחֱזוּ *and they saw*, from חזה), Samson Jg 1621, Saul 2 S 19, David Ps 561, Job Jb 3016, Adoni-bezek Jg 16, prophet Is 213, angel 4QBibParaph 1–24, worshipper Ps 11953 13910 1QH 433 4QapLamb6, lover Ca 34, חנף ptc. *irreligious person* Is 3314, heathen kings Ps 487, עוֹלֵל *child* 1379, אָב *father* 1QS 29 4QToh D4 (אב[ות]), אֶחָד *individual* 2 S 221.

ישׁב ptc. *inhabitant* of Philistia Ex 1514, אַיִל *chief* of Moab Ex 1514, Ephraimite Jg 126, people of Judah Jr 1321, Damascus Jr 4924, טֶרֶף *prey* Is 529, שַׂעַר *horror* Jb 1820, שׁוּעָל *fox* Ca 215, פַּלָּצוּת *shuddering* Jb 216, שְׁמֻרָה *eyelid* Ps 775, לָשׁוֹן *tongue*, i.e. be able to speak well Pr 1821 (if em. אֹהֲבֶיהָ *those who love her*).

דֶּלֶת *gate* of city Ne 73 (אחז = *fasten securely*, ‖ גוף hi. *lock*), בַּיִת *Temple* 1 K 610, רֹמַח *spear* 2 C 255, צִנָּה *shield* 255 (with both objects, אחז = *be able to hold, handle,* or *comprehend*), דֶּרֶךְ *way* of behaving Jb 179 (אחז = *hold to, persist in*); without obj. (or prep.), Is 138.

<PREP> בְּ introducing object, sometimes perh. intensifying action of verb or as instrumental (e.g. hold *by* the hand), Gn 2526 (+ עָקֵב *heel*) Ex 44 (+ זָנָב *tail*) Dt 3241 (+ מִשְׁפָּט *justice*) Jg 163 (+ דֶּלֶת *door*) 206 (+ פִּלֶגֶשׁ *concubine*) 2 S 410 (+ נגד hi. ptc. *messenger*) 66 (+ אֲרוֹן *ark*) 209 (+ זָקָן *beard*) 1 K 151 (+ קֶרֶן *horn* of altar) Ps 7323 (+ יָד *hand*) Jb 1612 (+ עֹרֶף *neck*) 189 (+ עָקֵב)

38$_{13}$ (+ כָּנָף *end* of the earth) Ru 3$_{15.15}$ (both + מִטְפַּחַת *mantle*) Ca 7$_{9}$ (+ סַנְסִן *palm branch*) Ec 2$_{3}$ (+ סִכְלוּת *folly*) 7$_{18}$ (+ זֶה *this* quality; + אַל־תַּנַּח אֶת־יָדֶךָ *do not release your hand*) 4QDa$_{3(AHL)}$ (האוחזו[ת]; + עוֹר *skin*) 4QDa$_{6}$ (AHL).

בְּגַת *in Gath* Ps 56$_{1}$, לְבִלְתִּי אֲחֹז בְּקִירוֹת־הַבָּיִת *so as not to hold (anything) within the walls of the Temple* 1 K 6$_{6}$, בַּאֲשֻׁרוֹ אָחֲזָה רַגְלִי *in his trail my foot holds*, i.e. persists Jb 23$_{11}$.

<COLL> לאחוז רצון *to handle according to (his) will* Si 36$_{13}$, אָחַז בְּשָׂרִי פַּלָּצוּת *my flesh has seized*, i.e. has been seized by, *shuddering* Jb 21$_{6}$, קַדְמֹנִים אָחֲזוּ שָׂעַר *those who live in the east have grasped*, i.e. are gripped by, *horror* 18$_{20}$.

2. in passive אָחֻז (Ezk 41$_{6.6}$ Est 1$_{6}$ אָחוּז), **a. be held, be taken, held, <SUBJ>** צִפּוֹר *bird* Ec 9$_{12}$ (אֲחֻזוֹת; mss אֲחוּזוֹת; ‖ אחז ni. *be held*, יקשׁ pu. *be trapped*) Si 11$_{30}$, fabric Est 1$_{6}$, גִּבּוֹר *warrior* Ca 3$_{8}$ (אֲחֻזֵי חֶרֶב *held of*, appar. holding, or comprehending, *a sword*; or em. אֹחֲזֵי i.e. active ptc. in same sense; + למד pu. *be trained* in warfare), אֶחָד *one* father's household 1 C 24$_{6}$ (mss אֶחָד *one [of them]*) 24$_{6(mss)}$ (L אָחֻז *selection*, as §2b).

<PREP> לְ of benefit, *for*, or instrument, *by* 1 C 24$_{6.6}$; בְּ of place, *in*, or instrument, *by* Ec 9$_{12}$ (+ פַּח *trap*) Est 1$_{6}$ (+ חֶבֶל *cord*) Si 11$_{30}$ (+ כְּלוּב *cage*).

2b. as noun (1) in sg., **selection,** אָחֻז אָחֻז לְאִיתָמָר *a selection selected for Ithamar* 1 C 24$_{6}$ (mss אֶחָד *one* was selected), תִּקַּח אֶחָד אָחֻז מִן־הַחֲמִשִּׁים *you* (Moses) *are to take one selection of the fifty* Nm 31$_{30}$ (or del. אָחֻז), וַיִּקַּח מֹשֶׁה ... אֶת־הָאָחֻז אֶחָד מִן־הַחֲמִשִּׁים *and Moses took the selection, one from the fifty* 31$_{47}$ (or del. אֶת־הָאָחֻז); (2) in pl., **support** for side-chambers of temple, **<SUBJ>** היה *be*, i.e. function as Ezk 41$_{6.6}$.

<SYN> חזק hi. *seize*.

Ni. Pf. נֶאֱחַז, נֹאחֲזוּ; + waw וְנֹאחֲזוּ, וַיֵּאָחֲזוּ; impv. וְהֵאָחֲזוּ; ptc. Si נאחז, שֶׁנֶּאֱחָזִים—**1a. be held, trapped, <SUBJ>** נאחזו אשר לא שמרו מצות אל *those who did not observe the laws of God were trapped* CD 2$_{18}$, אַיִל *ram*, trapped in thicket by its horns Gn 22$_{13}$, דָּג *fish*, caught in net Ec 9$_{12}$ (‖ אחז qal pass.). **<PREP>** בְּ of place, *in*, Gn 22$_{13}$ (+ סְבַךְ *thicket*) Ec 9$_{12}$ (מְצוֹדָה *net*; perh. בְּ of instrument), of instrument, *by*, Gn 22$_{13}$ (+ קֶרֶן *horn*).

1b. be set, held in place, of jewels, ... ככלי זהב הנאחז על אבני חפץ *as a vessel of gold ... set about with precious stones* Si 50$_{9}$.

2. hold property (perh. denom. from אֲחֻזָּה *possession*), **<SUBJ>** sons of Jacob Gn 34$_{10}$ (‖ סחר *trade*), Israel 47$_{27}$, tribesmen of Gad and Reuben (and Manasseh) Nm 32$_{30}$ Jos 22$_{9.19}$.

<PREP> בְּ of place, *in*, + אֶרֶץ *land*, Gn 34$_{10}$ 47$_{27}$ Nm 32$_{30}$ Jos 22$_{9}$; בְּתוֹךְ *among* Nm 32$_{30}$ Jos 22$_{19}$.

Pi. Ptc. מְאַחֵז—**cover, <SUBJ>** God Jb 26$_{9}$ (‖ פרשׁז pilel *spread*). **<OBJ>** פְּנֵי *surface* of throne Jb 26$_{9}$.

Ho. Ptc. מָאֳחָזִים—**be held,** fastened, ... מַעֲלוֹת לַכִּסֵּא מָאֳחָזִים *steps ... attached to the throne* 2 C 9$_{18}$.

→ אֲחֻזָּה *possession*, אָחָז *Ahaz*, אַחְזַי *Ahzai*, אֲחַזְיָהוּ *Ahaziah*, אֲחֻזָּם *Ahuzzam*, אֲחֻזַּת *Ahuzzath*, יְהוֹאָחָז *Jehoahaz*, יוֹאָחָז *Joahaz*.

אָחָז 41.0.0.4 pr.n.m. **Ahaz, 1.** king of Judah, son of Jotham and father of Hezekiah, 2 K 15$_{38}$‖2 C 27$_{9}$ 2 K 16$_{1.2}$‖2 C 28$_{1}$ 2 K 16$_{5}$=Is 7$_{1}$ 2 K 16$_{7}$‖2 C 28$_{16}$ 2 K 16$_{8.10.10.11.11.15.16.17.19.20}$‖2 C 28$_{27}$ 2 K 17$_{1}$ 18$_{1}$ 20$_{11}$ 23$_{12}$ 1 C 3$_{13}$ 2 C 28$_{19.21.22.24}$ 29$_{19}$ Is 1$_{1}$ 7$_{3.10.12}$ 14$_{28}$ (or em. אָחָז הָיָה *Ahaz there was* to וָאֶחֱזֶה *and I saw*) 38$_{8}$ Ho 1$_{1}$ Mc 1$_{1}$.

2. son of Micah and father of Jehoaddah (יְהוֹעַדָּה 1 C 8$_{36}$) or Jarah (יַעְרָה 1 C 9$_{42}$; mss יַעְדָּה *Jadah*), descendant of Jeiel and Saul, 1 C 8$_{35.36}$‖1 C 9$_{42}$. **3.** master of Ashna (לאשנא עבד אחז), Seal 141$_{2}$ (8th cent.). **4.** Samaria ost. 2$_{5}$. **5.** Samaria-Sebaste ost. 1220. **6.** Seal 44 (Jericho, 8th cent.).

→ אחז *hold*.

אֲחֻזָּה 66.0.4 n.f. **possession**—cstr. אֲחֻזַּת (Q אוחזת); sf. אֲחֻזָּתְךָ, אֲחֻזָּתוֹ, אֲחֻזַּתְכֶם, אֲחֻזָּתָם (Q אחוזתם)—**possession, inheritance, property,** usu. **(a)** in ref. to small areas or plots of land (Gn 23$_{4.9}$ 23$_{20}$ 47$_{11}$ 49$_{30}$ 50$_{13}$ Lv 25$_{10.13.25.27.28.41}$ 27$_{16.21.22.24.28}$ Nm 27$_{4.7}$ 35$_{28}$ Jos 21$_{12}$ Ezk 44$_{28.28}$ 45$_{5.6.7.7.8}$ 46$_{16.18.18.18}$ 48$_{20.21.22.22}$ Ne 11$_{3}$ 1 C 7$_{28}$ 9$_{2}$ 2 C 31$_{1}$), specif. of Levitical cities (Lv 25$_{32.33.33.34}$ Nm 35$_{2}$ 2 C 11$_{14}$); also **(b)** in ref. to whole countries, esp. Canaan as promised land (Gn 17$_{8}$ 48$_{4}$ Lv 14$_{34.34}$ 25$_{24}$ Nm 32$_{5.22.29.32}$ Jos 22$_{4.9.19.19}$ Ps 2$_{8}$), as well as **(c)**

to non-Israelite purchased as slave (Lv $25_{45.46}$) and **(d)** possession of knowledge, etc. (1QS 11_7 4Q416 7_{12}).

<SUBJ> היה *be* Lv 27_{21} (+ לַכֹּהֵן *for the priest*) Ezk $48_{22.22}$ (if, in both, em. מֵאֲחֻזַּת *some of the possession of*; + לַנָּשִׂיא *for the prince*).

<NOM CL> אֲנִי אֲחֻזָּתָם *I* (Y.) *am their inheritance* Ezk 44_{28} (‖ נַחֲלָה *inheritance*), אֲחֻזָּתָם הִיא בְּנַחֲלָה *it is their land as an inheritance* 46_{16} (‖ נַחֲלָה), וַאֲחֻזָּתָם וּמֹשְׁבוֹתָם בֵּית־אֵל וּבְנֹתֶיהָ *and their properties and dwelling places were Bethel and its daughters*, i.e. nearby villages 1 C 7_{28}, אֲשֶׁר־לוֹ אֲחֻזַּת הָאָרֶץ *one for whom it is an inheritance of the land*, i.e. rightful property Lv 27_{24}, בָּתֵּי עָרֵי הַלְוִיִּם הִוא אֲחֻזָּתָם *the houses of the cities of the Levites are their property* 25_{33}, אֲחֻזַּת עוֹלָם הוּא לָהֶם *a possession of eternity it* (field) *is to them* 25_{34} (Sam הִיא; mss לָכֶם *to you*), אֲחֻזָּתְךָ עַד־אַפְסֵי־אָרֶץ *your inheritance will be unto the ends of the earth* Ps $2_{8(ms)}$, אִתָּנוּ אֲחֻזַּת נַחֲלָתֵנוּ *the possession of our inheritance*, i.e. the territory to be inherited by us, *is with us* Nm 32_{32} (or em. אַתָּ[ה] תְּנָה *you, give!* or אָתָנוּ *has come to us*).

<OBJ> נתן *give* Gn 23_4 47_{11} 48_4 Nm $27_{4.7}$ 32_{32} (if em.) Ezk 44_{28} 45_6 Ps 2_8 (second object; + אַפְסֵי־אָרֶץ *ends of the earth*; ‖ נַחֲלָה *inheritance*), עזב *leave* 2 C 11_{14} (‖ מִגְרָשׁ *open land*), ירשׁ *inherit* Lv 25_{46}, נחל *inherit* 4Q416 7_{12}.

<CSTR> אֲחֻזַּת עוֹלָם *possession of eternity* Gn 17_8 48_4 Lv 25_{34} 1QS 11_7 (אוחזת עולם) 4Q416 7_{12}, נַחֲלָה *of inheritance*, i.e. able to be inherited Nm $27_{4(Sam).7}$ 32_{32} (נַחֲלָתֵנוּ *of our inheritance*), קֶבֶר *of a grave*, i.e. land for it Gn $23_{4.9}$ (קָבֶר) 23_{20} (קָבֶר) 49_{30} (קָבֶר) 50_{13} (all five אֲחֻזַּת־), אֲבֹתָיו *of his ancestors*, i.e. his family property Lv 25_{41}, בְּנֵי־יִשְׂרָאֵל *of the children of Israel* (as distinct from Levites) Nm 35_8 Jos 21_{41}, הַלְוִיִּם *of the Levites* Ezk 48_{22}, הָעִיר *of the city* $45_{6.7.7}$ $48_{20.21.22}$, הָאָרֶץ *of the land* Lv 27_{24}.

שְׂדֵה אֲחֻזָּתוֹ *field of his (inherited) possession*, i.e. owned by him Lv $27_{16.22}$ (+ שְׂדֵה מִקְנָתוֹ *field of his purchase*, i.e. land bought by him) 27_{28}, עִיר *city of*, i.e. to which he belongs 25_{33}, עָרֵי אֲחֻזָּתָם *cities of their inheritance* Lv 25_{32}, נַחֲלַת אֲחֻזָּתָם *inheritance of their possession*, i.e. property they have inherited Nm 35_2, אֶרֶץ אֲחֻזַּתְכֶם *land of your inheritance* Gn 36_{43} (אֲחֻזָּתָם *of their inheritance*) Lv 14_{34} 25_{24} Nm 35_{28} (אֲחֻזָּתוֹ *of his possession*) Jos $22_{4.9}$ (אֲחֻזָּתָם) $22_{19.19}$ (אֲחֻזַּת י׳ *of the inheritance of Y.*).

<APP> אֶרֶץ ... אֲחֻזָּה *land ... possession* Gn 48_4, לַאֲחֻזָּתוֹ לְעָרֵיהֶם *to their inheritance, to their towns* 2 C 31_1, sim. Ne 11_3 1 C 9_2.

<PREP> לְ of direction, *to*, + שׁוּב *go back* Lv $25_{27.28}$ 2 C 31_1, of possession, *of, (belonging) to* Ezk 45_7 48_{21}, *for, as* possession/inheritance, + היה *be* Lv 25_{45} Nm 32_{22} Ezk $45_{5(Qr).8}$, נתן *give* Gn 17_8 23_9 Lv 14_{34} Nm 32_{29} Dt 32_{49} 1QS 11_7, ho. *be given* Nm 32_5, קָנָה *buy* Gn 49_{30} 50_{13}, קוּם *arise*, i.e be transferred 23_{20}.

נתן בְּ *give as* Jos 21_{12}, of place, *in* 1 C 9_2, + ישׁב *dwell* Ne 11_3.

מִן partitive, *(some) of*, + היה *be* Ezk $48_{22.22}$ (or em. both to וַאֲחֻזַּת *and the possession of*), מכר *sell* Lv 25_{25}, נתן *give* Nm 35_8, נחל hi. *cause to inherit* Ezk 46_{18}, of direction, *from*, + ינה hi. *oppress* so as to drive out from inheritance Ezk 46_{18} (or del. מֵאֲחֻזָּתָם), פוץ *be scattered* 46_{18}.

אֶל of direction, + שׁוּב *go back* Lv 25_{10} (‖ מִשְׁפָּחָה *family*) $25_{13.41}$ (‖ מִשְׁפָּחָה), *as well as* Ezk 48_{20}; אֶל־פְּנֵי *in front of* Ezk 45_7; בְּתוֹךְ *among* Jos 21_{41}.

<SYN> נַחֲלָה *inheritance*, מִשְׁפָּחָה *family*.

Also CD 16_{16} 4QpsMos^e 2.2_{10}.

→ אחז *hold*.

אַחְזַי 1.0.0.1 pr.n.m. **Ahzai, 1.** son of Meshillemoth (or em. מְשַׁלֵּמוֹת *Meshallemoth*) and father of Azarel (mss עֲזַרְיאֵל *Azriel*), ancestor of priest at time of Nehemiah, appar. ident. with Jahzerah (יַחְזֵרָה) at 1 C 9_{12}, Ne 11_{13} (mss אַחֲזַי). **2.** Samaria ost. 25_3. **3.** Stamp/Coin 16_1 (others אחיו *Ahijah*).

→ אחז *hold*.

אֲחַזְיָה, see אֲחַזְיָהוּ.

אֲחַזְיָהוּ 37.0.0.2 pr.n.m. **Ahaziah**—אֲחַזְיָה—**1.** king of Israel, 1 K $22_{40.50.52}$ 2 K 1_2 (אֲחַזְיָה) 1_{18} 2 C 20_{35} (אֲחַזְיָה) 20_{37}. **2.** king of Judah, 2 K 8_{24}‖2 C 22_1 2 K $8_{25.26}$‖2 C 22_2 2 K 8_{29}‖9_{16} (אֲחַזְיָה; ‖2 C 22_6 עֲזַרְיָהוּ *Azariah*) $9_{21.23.23}$ (אֲחַזְיָה) 9_{27}‖2 C 22_8 (2 K אֲחַזְיָה) 2 K 9_{29} (אֲחַזְיָה) $10_{13.13}$ 11_1‖2 C 22_{10} 2 K $11_{2.2}$‖2 C 22_{11} (2 K אֲחַזְיָה; or

em. אָחִיהָ *her brother*) 12₁₉ 13₁ 14₁₃ (||2 C 25₂₃ יְהוֹאָחָז *Jehoahaz*) 1 C 3₁₁ 2 C 20₃₇ 22₁₊₁₀t **3.** Seal 342₂ (8th-6th cent.). **4.** Seal 769₁ (T. en-Naṣbeh, 7th cent.).
→ אחז *hold* + יִ *Y*.

אֲחֻזָּם 1 pr.n.m. **Ahuzzam,** son of Naarah and Ashhur, descendant of Judah, 1 C 4₆.
→ אחז *hold*.

אחזר 0.0.1 pl.n. **Hazor,** W of Beth-hazor (בית אחצר), perh. ident. with Hazor (חָצוֹר) at Ne 11₃₃, 3QTr 8₂ (שמזרח אחזר *which is east of Hazor*; Allegro שמיד אתון *which is beside [the] entrance* [i.e. אִיתוֹן]).

אֲחֻזַּת 1 pr.n.m. **Ahuzzath,** adviser to Abimelech, king of Gerar, Gn 26₂₆.
→ אחז *hold*.

אֲחֹחִי I 1 pr.n.m. **Ahohi,** father of Dodo (Qr דּוֹדוֹ; Kt דדי *Dodai*) and grandfather of Eleazar, one of David's warriors, 2 S 23₉ (or em. אִישׁ חַיִל *man of valour*; ||1 C 11₁₂ דּוֹדוֹ הָאֲחוֹחִי *Dodo the Ahohite*).

אֲחֹחִי II 4 gent. **Ahohite**—אֲחוֹחִי—with ref. to warriors of David, Dodo (דּוֹדוֹ) 1 C 11₁₂ (אֲחוֹחִי; ||2 S 23₉[Qr] אֲחֹחִי Dodo, son of *Ahohi*), Dodai (דּוֹדַי) 1 C 27₄ (אֲחוֹחִי), Zalmon, 2 S 23₂₈ (||1 C 11₂₉ עִילַי הָאֲחוֹחִי *Ilai the Ahohite*).

אֵחִי 1 pr.n.m. **Ehi,** son of Benjamin, Gn 46₂₁ (or em. אֵחִי וְרֹאשׁ *Ehi and Rosh* to וַאֲחִירָם *and Ahiram*).
→ אָח *brother*.

אֲחִי 2.0.0.1 pr.n.m. **Ahi, 1.** son of Abdiel and head of father's house, descendant of Gad, 1 C 5₁₅. **2.** son of Shemer (ms שׁוֹמֵר *Shomer*), descendant of Asher, 1 C 7₃₄(Qr) (or em. בְּנֵי שָׁמֶר אֲחִי *the sons of Shemer were Ahi* ... to בְּנֵי שֶׁמֶר אָחִיו *the sons of Shemer his brother were* ... **3.** Arad ost. 39₆.
→ אָח *brother*.

אחיאיל, see אֲחִיאָם.

אחיאל 0.0.0.1 pr.n.m. **Ahiel,** City of David jug inscr. City of David ost.₁ (אחיא[ל]).
→ אָח *brother* + אֵל *God*.

אֲחִיאָם 2 pr.n.m. **Ahiam, 1.** one of David's warriors, 2 S 23₃₃||1 C 11₃₅. **2.** father of Shallum, Arad ost. 35₃ (others אחיאיל *Ahiayil*).
→ אָח *brother*.

אֲחִיָּה 24.0.0.6 pr.n.m. **Ahijah**—אֲחִיָּהוּ—**1.** son of Ahitub and priest at time of Saul, 1 S 14₃.₁₈. **2.** prophet at time of Solomon and Jeroboam, 1 K 11₂₉.₃₀ 12₁₅||2 C 10₁₅ (אֲחִיָּהוּ) 1 K 14₂.₄.₄.₅.₆.₁₈ (all four אֲחִיָּהוּ) 2 C 9₂₉. **3.** father of Baasha, 1 K 15₂₇.₃₃ 21₂₂ 2 K 9₉. **4.** scribe at time of Solomon, son of Shisha (שִׁישָׁא; or em. שַׁוְשָׁא *Shavsha*), 1 K 4₃.

5. son of Jerahmeel, descendant of Judah, 1 C 2₂₅ (or em. מֵאֲחִיָּה *from Ahijah*, as n.f., wife of Jerahmeel). **6.** Pelonite (הַפְּלֹנִי), one of David's warriors, appar. ident. with Eliam the Gilonite at ||2 S 23₃₄, 1 C 11₃₆. **7.** son of Ehud, descendant of Benjamin, appar. ident. with Ahoah at 1 C 8₄ (or em. אֲחִיָּה), 1 C 8₇. **8.** Levite at time of David and overseer of treasuries, 1 C 26₂₀ (or em. אֲחֵיהֶם *their brothers*). **9.** leader at time of Nehemiah, Ne 10₂₇ (or em. אָחִיו *his brother*).

10. father of Hodaviah, Lachish ost. 3₁₇ (אחיהו). **11.** son of Hashoreq or member of sorrel horse clan (בן השרק), Ophel ost.₂ (אחיהו). **12.** father of Shaphat (שפט בנ[ן]), Seal 666₂ (אחיהו; T. Beit Mirsim?, 7th/6th cent.). **13.** T. Qasile ost. 1₃ ([א]חיהו; others חיהו *Haiah*). **14.** Ramat Raḥel ost.₁ (אחיהו). **15.** Seal 246₁ (אחיהו; 7th cent.). **16.** Seal 513₁ ([א]חיהו; T. Beit Mirsim?, 7th/6th cent.). **17.** Seal 809₂ (אחיהו; City of David, 7th/6th cent.).
→ אָח *brother* + יִ *Y*.

אֲחִיָּהוּ, see אֲחִיָּה.

אֲחִיהוּד 1 pr.n.m. **Ahihud, 1.** son of Shelomi, descendant of Asher, involved in allotment of land, Nm 34₂₇. **2.** son of Gera, descendant of Benjamin, 1 C 8₇(mss) (L אֲחִיחֻד).

→ אָח *brother* + הוֹד *splendour.*

אַחְיוֹ 6.0.0.1 pr.n.m. **Ahio, 1.** son of Abinadab and brother of Uzzah (עֻזָּה/עֻזָּא), 2 S 6_{3}||1 C 13_{7} 2 S 6_{4}. **2.** son of Elpaal, descendant of Benjamin, 1 C 8_{14} (or em. וְאָחִיו or וַאֲחֵיהֶם *and his brother/s was/were*). **3.** son of Jeiel, descendant of Benjamin, 1 C 8_{31}=9_{37}. **4.** son of Sheal (שאל), Seal 339_{1} (8th–6th cent.). **5.** Stamp/Coin 16_{1} (others אחזי *Ahzai*; 5th/4th cent.).
→ אָח *brother* + י״ *Y.*

אֲחִיהֻד 1 pr.n.m. **Ahihud,** son of Gera, descendant of Benjamin, 1 C 8_{7} (mss אֲחִיהוּד).
→ אָח *brother* + הוֹד *splendour.*

אֲחִיטוּב 15 pr.n.m. **Ahitub, 1.** father of Ahijah, 1 S 14_{3} $22_{9.11.12.20}$. **2.** priest, father of Zadok, 2 S 8_{17}||1 C 18_{16} 5_{33}||6_{37} $5_{34.37.38}$ Ezr 7_{2}. **3.** father of Meraioth and grandfather of Zadok, Ne 11_{11}||1 C 9_{11}. **4.** son of Hushim and Shaharaim, descendant of Benjamin, 1 C $8_{11(mss)}$ (L אֲבִיטוּב *Abitub*).
→ אָח *brother* + טוב *be good.*

אֲחִילוּד 5 pr.n.m. **Ahilud, 1.** father of Jehoshaphat, recorder at time of David, 2 S 8_{16}||20_{24}||1 C 18_{15} 1 K 4_{3}. **2.** father of Baana, one of Solomon's administrators, 1 K 4_{12}.
→ אָח *brother.*

אחימה, see אחמא.

אֲחִימוֹת 1 pr.n.m. **Ahimoth,** Levite, son of Elkanah, 1 C 6_{10} (or em. אָחִיו מַחַת *his brother, Mahath*).
→ אָח *brother* + מות *die.*

אֲחִימֶלֶךְ 17.0.0.18 pr.n.m. **Ahimelech**—I אחמלך—**1.** priest at time of Saul and David, son of Ahitub and father of Abiathar, 1 S $21_{2.2.3.9}$ $22_{9.11.14.16.20}$ 23_{6} 30_{7} Ps 52_{2} (mss אֲבִימֶלֶךְ *Abimelech*). **2.** son of Abiathar and priest at time of David, 2 S 8_{17}||1 C $18_{16(mss)}$ (L אֲבִימֶלֶךְ) 1 C $24_{3.6.31}$. **3.** Hittite, one of David's warriors, 1 S 26_{6}. **4.** father of Hamiadan (חמיעדן), Seal 324_{2} (אחמלך; 7th cent.).
5. Samaria ost. 22_{2} 23_{2} (both אחמלך) 24_{1} (אחמל[ך]) 25_{2} ([א]חמלך) 26_{1} ([אחמלך]) 27_{2} 28_{2} 29_{2} 48_{2} (all four אחמלך). **6.** Arad ost. 72_{2}. **7.** Seal 124 ([א]חמלך; 7th cent.). **8.** Seal 139_{2} (אחמלך; Lachish, 8th/7th cent.). **9.** Seal 154_{2} (אחמלך; Beth-Shemesh, 8th/7th cent.). **10.** Seal 358_{2} (אחמלך; Lachish, 8th cent.). **11.** Seal 424_{2} (אחמלך; 7th/6th cent.). **12.** Seal 629 (אחמלך; T. Beit Mirsim?, 7th/6th cent.). **13.** Seal 739_{2} (אחמלך; 7th cent.). **14.** Seal 762_{2} (אחמלך; 7th cent.). **15.** Seal 792_{2} (Lachish, 8th cent.). **16.** Seal 878_{2} (7th cent.). **17.** Seal 890_{1} (אחמלך; 7th cent.).
→ אָח *brother* + מֶלֶךְ *king.*

אֲחִימַן 4.0.0.1 pr.n.m. **Ahiman**—אֲחִימָן—**1.** descendant of Anak, Nm 13_{22} Jos 15_{14} Jg 1_{10}. **2.** gatekeeper, 1 C 9_{17}. **3.** Seal 130 (Persian period).
→ אָח *brother.*

אֲחִימַעַץ 15 pr.n.m. **Ahimaaz**—אֲחִימָעַץ—**1.** father-in-law of Saul, 1 S 14_{50}. **2.** son of Zadok, 2 S $15_{27.36}$ $17_{17.20}$ 18_{19+5t} 1 C $5_{34.35}$ 6_{38}. **3.** administrator at time of Solomon and husband of Basemath, daughter of Solomon, perh. ident. with preceding, 1 K 4_{15}.
→ אָח *brother.*

אַחְיָן 1 pr.n.m. **Ahian,** son of Shemida (שְׁמִידָע), descendant of Manasseh, 1 C 7_{19}.
→ אָח *brother.*

אֲחִינָדָב 1 pr.n.m. **Ahinadab,** son of Iddo and one of Solomon's administrators, 1 K 4_{14}.
→ אָח *brother* + נדב *impel.*

אֲחִינֹעַם 7.0.0.1 pr.n.f. **Ahinoam**—I אחנעם—**1.** daughter of Ahimaaz and wife of Saul, 1 S 14_{50}. **2.** wife of David, 1 S 25_{43} 27_{3} 30_{5} 2 S 2_{2} 3_{2}||1 C 3_{1}. **3.** Samaria ost. 19_{3}.
→ אָח *brother* + נעם *be pleasant.*

אֲחִיסָמָךְ 3 pr.n.m. **Ahisamach, 1.** father of Oholiab, Ex 31_{6} 35_{34} 38_{23}. **2.** Seal 280_{2} (אחסמך; others אחאמר

Ahiamar; Lachish, 7th cent.).
→ אָח *brother* + סמך *lean*.

אֲחִיעֶ֫זֶר 6 pr.n.m. **Ahiezer, 1.** son of Ammishaddai and leader of Dan, Nm 1_{12} 2_{25} $7_{66.71}$ 10_{25}. **2.** one of David's warriors, brother of Joash and son of Shemaah (or em. יְהוֹשָׁמַע *Jehoshama*; but perh. also em. יוֹאָשׁ בֶּן־ *Joash, son of* Shemaah/Jehoshama), 1 C 12_3. **3.** descendant of Gilead, appar. ident. with Abiezer (אֲבִיעֶזֶר) at Jos 17_2 1 C 7_{18}, Nm $26_{30(Sam)}$ (MT אִיעֶזֶר *Iezer*).
→ אָח *brother* + עזר *help*.

אֲחִיקָם 20.0.0.8 pr.n.m. **Ahikam**—I אחקם—**1.** official at time of Josiah, son of Shaphan and father of Gedaliah, 2 K 22_{12}||2 C 34_{20} 2 K 22_{14} 25_{22} Jr 26_{24}, 39_{14} $40_{5.6.7.9.11.14.16}$ $41_{1.2.6.10.16.18}$ 43_6. **2.** son of Shemaiah (שמעיהו), Arad ost. 31_5. **3.** son of Menahem (מ[נ]חם), Ḥorvat ʿUza ost. 1_1 (אחקם). **4.** son of Tobiah (ב[ן] טביהו), Seal 514_1 (אחק[ם]; T. Beit Mirsim?, 7th/6th cent.). **5.** City of David ost.$_2$. **6.** Seal 865_1. **7.** Seal 210_2 (אחקם; 8th cent.). **8.** Seal 515_1 (אחקם; T. Beit Mirsim?, 7th/6th cent.). **9.** Seal 516_1 (אחקם; T. Beit Mirsim?, 7th/6th cent.). **10.** Seal 764_1 (אחקם; 8th/7th cent.).
→ אָח *brother* + קום *arise*.

אֲחִירָם 1 pr.n.m. **Ahiram,** head of Benjaminite family, Gn 46_{21} (if em.; see אֵחִי *Ehi*) Nm 26_{38} 1 C 8_1 (if em.; see אַחְרַח *Aharah*). → אָח *brother* + רום *be high*.

אֲחִירָמִי 1 gent. **Ahiramite,** of the family of Ahiram, Nm 26_{38}.
→ אָח *brother* + רום *be high*.

אֲחִירַע 5 pr.n.m. **Ahira,** son of Enan and leader of tribe of Naphtali, Nm 1_{15} 2_{29} $7_{78.83}$ 10_{27}.
→ אָח *brother* + perh. רעה *associate with*.

[אֲחִישַׁ֫חַר] 1 pr.n.m. **Ahishahar**—אֲחִישָׁחַר—Benjaminite, son of Bilhan, 1 C 7_{10}.
→ אָח *brother* + שַׁחַר *dawn*.

אֲחִישָׁר 1 pr.n.m. **Ahishar,** overseer (עַל־הַבָּיִת *over the house*) of Solomon's palace, 1 K 4_6 (ms אֲחִי שָׂר).
→ אָח *brother*.

אֲחִיתֹ֫פֶל 20 pr.n.m. **Ahithophel,** adviser to David, 2 S $15_{12.31.31.34}$ $16_{15.20.21.23.23}$ 17_{1+7t} 23_{34} 1 C $27_{33.34}$.
→ אָח *brother*.

אחך 0.0.0.1 pr.n.m. **Ahicha,** Beth-Shemesh inscr.
→ perh. אָח *brother*.

אַחְלָב 1 pl.n. **Ahlab,** town assigned to, but not occupied by, Asher, appar. ident. with Mehebel (unless מֵחֶבֶל = *from the territory of* Achzib; or em. מְחַלֵּב *Mehalleb* or מַחֲלֵב *Mahaleb*), perh. Kh. el-Maḥālib NNE of Tyre, Jg 1_{31}.

אַחֲלַי 2 interj. **if only**—אַחֲלֵי—**1.** with verb אַחֲלַי יִכֹּנוּ דְרָכָי לִשְׁמֹר חֻקֶּיךָ *if only my ways were set to keep your decrees* Ps 119_5. **2.** with nom. cl., as protasis, אַחֲלֵי אֲדֹנִי לִפְנֵי הַנָּבִיא ... אָז יֶאֱסֹף *if only my lord were before the prophet ... then he would gather* 2 K 5_3.

[אַחְלַי] 2 pr.n.m. & f. **Ahlai**—אַחְלָ֑י—**1.** son of Sheshan, descendant of Judah, 1 C 2_{31}. **2.** father of Zabad, one of David's warriors, 1 C 11_{41}.

אַחְלָמָה 2 n.[f.] **amethyst**—**amethyst, jasper,** or similar (semi-)precious stone, in Aaron's breastplate, הַטּוּר הַשְּׁלִישִׁי לֶשֶׁם שְׁבוֹ וְאַחְלָמָה *the third row is,* i.e. comprises, *an opal, an agate, and an amethyst* Ex 28_{19}||39_{12}.

אחמא 0.0.0.5 pr.n.m. **Ahima**—אחימה—**1.** Samaria ost. 32_3 37_2 38_2 39_2. **2.** Seal 845_1 (אחימה; City of David, 7th/6th cent.).
→ אָח *brother*.

אחמלך, see אֲחִימֶ֫לֶךְ.

אחנעם, see אֲחִינֹ֫עַם.

אֲחַסְבַּי 1 pr.n.m. **Ahasbai,** father of Eliphelet, one of David's warriors, 2 S 23$_{34}$.

[אחסמך], see אֲחִיסָמָךְ.

אחצר, see בית אחצר.

אחקם, see אֲחִיקָם.

אחר 17.6.7.1 vb. **delay** (intrans.)—**Qal** + waw וָאֵחַר—**stay behind, delay** (intrans.), <SUBJ> Jacob Gn 32$_5$ (+ גור *sojourn*). <PREP> עַד־עָתָּה *until now* Gn 32$_5$.

Pi. Pf. אֵחַר, אֵחֲרוּ; impf. יְאַחֵר (Si ויאחר), תְּאַחֵר (תְּאַחֲרוּ), תְּאַחֵר תְּאַחַר; ptc. pl. מְאַחֲרִים; cstr. מְאַחֲרֵי—**1. stay behind, delay** (intrans.), as Qal, <SUBJ> Eliashib Arad ost. 2$_6$, פַּעַם *sound* of chariots Jg 5$_{28}$, תְּשׁוּעָה *salvation* Is 46$_{13}$, חָזוֹן *vision* Hb 2$_3$, Y. Dt 7$_{10}$ Ps 40$_{18}$ ‖ 70$_6$ Dn 9$_{19}$ GnzPs 1$_{14}$; subject not expressed, Is 5$_{11}$ Pr 23$_{30}$.

<PREP> לְמַעַנְךָ *for your sake* Dn 9$_{19}$; מְאַחֲרִים עַל־הַיָּיִן *those who linger over wine* Pr 23$_{30}$; מְאַחֲרֵי בַנֶּשֶׁף *those who stay behind into the twilight* to drink wine Is 5$_{11}$; לֹא יְאַחֵר לְשֹׂנְאוֹ *he will not delay with one who hates him* Dt 7$_{10}$.

2. detain, delay (trans.), <SUBJ> brother and mother of Rebekah Gn 24$_{56}$, Israel Ex 22$_{28}$, sinner Si 35$_{17(E, Bmg)}$ (B ואחר *and after*), community member 1QS 5$_{24}$, אִישׁ *man* 4Q251 5$_2$. <OBJ> servant of Abraham Gn 24$_{56}$, מְלֵאָה *full produce* Ex 22$_{28}$ 4Q251 5$_2$, דֶּמַע *juice* Ex 22$_{28}$, צֹרֶךְ *need* Si 35$_{17(E, Bmg)}$. <PREP> כְּ *in accordance with* perverseness 1QS 5$_{24}$.

3. be slow, late to, **hold back** from, with inf. + לְ, עשׂה *do* Gn 34$_{19}$, שׁלם pi. *repay* Dt 23$_{22}$=11QT 53$_{11}$ Ec 5$_3$, שׁלך hi. *throw* Si 6$_{21}$, שׁוב *turn* intrans. 5$_7$, ישׁב *sit* Ps 127$_2$ (lacks לְ; :: שׁכם hi. *be early*), בקר pi. *seek* Pr 20$_{25}$ (if em. אַחַר *after*; or em. לַבֹּקֶר *until the morning*). <SUBJ> נַעַר *youth* Gn 34$_{19}$, Y. Dt 7$_{10}$, Israel Dt 23$_{22}$=11QT 53$_{11}$, אֱוִיל *fool* Si 6$_{21}$, אָדָם *person* Pr 20$_{25}$ (if em.); subject not specified, Ps 127$_2$ Ec 5$_3$ Si 5$_7$.

Hi. + waw Qr וַיּוֹחֶר (Kt וייחר, perh. Qal, Pi., or Hi.)—**stay behind, delay** (intrans.), as Qal, <SUBJ> Amasa 2 S 20$_5$. <PREP> מִן־הַמּוֹעֵד *beyond the appointed time* 2 S 20$_5$.

Htp. Impf. Q יתאחר, Si תתאחר; ptc. Si מתאחר; inf. Q התאחר—**1. delay** (intrans.), **be late, hold back** (intrans.), **be held back,** <SUBJ> עמל ptc. *labourer* Si 11$_{11}$, community member 1QS 1$_{14}$ (:: קדם pi. *cause to be early*) CD 11$_{23}$ (:: קדם htp. *be early*); subj. not specified, Si 7$_{34}$ 35$_{11}$. <PREP> מִן of place/time, *from* Si 7$_{34}$ (+ בכה ptc. *one who weeps*) 1QS 1$_{14}$ (+ מוֹעֵד *appointed time*).

2. turn to the rear, in address to sword, הִתְאַחֲרִי הֵימִנִי הָשִׂימִי הַשְׂמִלִי *turn to the rear, (turn) to the right, place yourself, (turn) to the left* Ezk 21$_{21}$ (L הִתְאַחֲדִי *do it all at once*; or em. הִתְחַדִּי *sharpen yourself*).

Also 4Q521 1.2$_{10}$.

→ אָחוֹר *behind*, אַחֵר *other*, אַחֲרָאי *guarantor*, אַחֲרוֹן *latter*, אַחֲרֵי *after*, אַחֲרִית *end*, אֲחֹרַנִּית *backwards*; אַחֵר *Aher*, perh. אַחְרַח *Aharah*, אֲחַרְחֵל *Aharhel*.

אַחֵר I 166.5.24 adj. **another**—fs אַחֶרֶת, mpl אֲחֵרִים (אֲחֵרִין), fpl אֲחֵרוֹת.

1. of contrast, **another, other, different,** of אִישׁ *man* Gn 29$_{19}$ Lv 27$_{20}$ Dt 20$_{5.6.7}$ 24$_2$ 28$_{30}$ 1 S 10$_6$ 1 K 20$_{37}$ Jr 3$_1$, אִשָּׁה *woman* Jg 11$_2$, עַם *people* Dt 28$_{32}$ Ps 105$_{13}$‖1 C 16$_{20}$, מַטֶּה *tribe* Nm 36$_9$, דּוֹר *generation* Jg 2$_{10}$, זֶרַע *offspring* Gn 4$_{25}$ (‖11QJub 4$_7$; see §3), מַלְאָךְ *angel* Zc 2$_7$, לֵב *heart* 1 S 10$_9$, רוּחַ *spirit* Nm 14$_{24}$, לָשׁוֹן *tongue* Is 28$_{11}$ 1QH 2$_{19}$ 4$_{16}$, שֵׁם *name* Is 65$_{15}$.

אֵל *god* Ex 34$_{14}$=11QT 2$_{11(Yadin)}$ ([אחר]ל), אֱלֹהִים *god* Ex 20$_3$=Dt 5$_7$ Ex 22$_{19}$ (if em. לָאֱלֹהִים to לֵאלֹהִים אֲחֵרִים) 23$_{13}$ Dt 6$_{14}$ 7$_4$ 8$_{19}$ 11$_{16.28}$ 13$_{3.7}$=11QT 54$_{10.21}$ Dt 13$_{14}$ 17$_3$=11QT 55$_{17}$ Dt 18$_{20}$=11QT 61$_1$ (אלו]הים אחר[ים) Dt 28$_{14.36.64}$ 29$_{25}$ 30$_{17}$ 31$_{18.20}$ Jos 23$_{16}$ 24$_{2.16}$ Jg 2$_{12.17.19}$ 10$_{13}$ 1 S 8$_8$ 26$_{19}$ 1 K 9$_{6.9}$‖2 C 7$_{19.22}$ 1 K 11$_{4.10}$ 14$_9$ 2 K 5$_{17}$ 17$_{7.35.37.38}$ 22$_{17}$ Jr 1$_{16}$ 7$_{6.9.18}$ 11$_{10}$ 13$_{10}$ 16$_{11.13}$ 19$_{4.13}$ 22$_9$ 25$_6$ 32$_{29}$ 35$_{15}$ 44$_{3.5.8.15}$ Ho 3$_1$ 2 C 28$_{25}$ 34$_{25}$ 4Q386–9 4$_{15}$ 4QJub^a 2$_4$ ([אחרנ]ים).

מָקוֹם *place* Nm 23$_{13.27}$ Ezk 12$_3$ Est 4$_{14}$ 4QD^{b}4.5a (ר[אח]), שָׂדֶה *field* Ru 2$_{8.22}$, אֶרֶץ *land* Dt 29$_{27}$ Jr 22$_{26}$ (if em. הָאָרֶץ to אֶרֶץ), דֶּרֶךְ *way* 1 K 13$_{10}$, בֶּגֶד *garment* Lv 6$_4$ 1 S 28$_8$ Ezk 42$_{14}$ 44$_{19}$ 4QToh B$_4$ ([בגדים אחרים]), כְּלִי *vessel* Jr 18$_4$ Ezr 1$_{10}$, אֶבֶן *stone* Lv 14$_{42}$, עָפָר *clay* 14$_{42}$, דָּבָר *matter* CD 9$_{21}$ (or em. אֶחָד *one*), פָּרָה *cow* Gn

41$_{3.19}$, יוֹם *day* 2 S 18$_{20}$, עֵילָם *Elam* Ezr 2$_{31}$ Ne 7$_{34}$, נְבוֹ *Nebo* Ne 7$_{33}$.

2. of similarity, **a. another, other, additional,** of אִישׁ *man* 2 S 18$_{26}$, אִשָּׁה *wife* 1 C 2$_{26}$ 11QT 57$_{17}$, בֵּן *son* Gn 30$_{24}$ 1 C 23$_{17}$, שַׂר *captain* 2 K 1$_{11}$, מַלְאָךְ *messenger* 1 S 19$_{21}$, חֲלוֹם *dream* Gn 37$_{9}$ (+ עוֹד *again*), כֶּסֶף *silver* 43$_{22}$, מְגִלָּה *scroll* Jr 36$_{28.32}$, מַעֲרָכָה *battle line* 1QM 16$_{12}$, בְּאֵר *well* Gn 26$_{21.22}$, חוֹמָה *wall* 2 C 32$_{5}$ (if em. הַחוֹמָה to חוֹמָה), אֹהֶל *tent* 2 K 7$_{8}$, דּוֹר *generation* Jl 1$_{3}$ Ps 109$_{13}$, יוֹם *day* Gn 8$_{10.12}$ 2 C 30$_{23}$ 4QpGen[a] 1$_{15}$ ([א]חרים]) 1$_{18}$ ([אחרןים]), שָׁנָה *year* Gn 29$_{27.30}$ 11QT 43$_{5}$.

2b. with article (except Gn 43$_{14}$), **the next, the second, the other,** of יוֹם *day* 2 K 6$_{29}$, שָׁנָה *year* Gn 17$_{21}$, אִשָּׁה *woman* 1 K 3$_{22}$, אָח *brother* Gn 43$_{14}$ (Sam הָאֶחָד *one*), כְּרוּב *cherub* 2 C 3$_{11.12}$, כָּנָף *wing* 3$_{11.12}$, כָּתֵף *side* Ezk 40$_{40}$, חָצֵר *court* 1 K 7$_{8}$, פִּנָּה *corner* 3QTr 3$_{5}$.

3. as noun, **another one,** <SUBJ> לקח *take* Ps 109$_{8}$, צמח *sprout* Jb 8$_{19}$ Si 14$_{18}$ (גמל *ripen* erased), עלה *go up* Dn 8$_{8}$ (if em. חָזוּת *conspicuousness* to אֲחֵרוֹת *others*), ישׁב *dwell* Is 65$_{22}$, אכל *eat* 65$_{22}$ Jb 31$_{8}$, כרע *crouch* Jb 31$_{10}$, עמד *stand* Dn 12$_{5}$.

<NOM CL> אֵין אַחֶרֶת זוּלָתָהּ בָּזֶה (of sword) *there is no other except it here* 1 S 21$_{10}$, אין אחר זולתכה (of Y.) *there is no other except you* 1QS 11$_{18}$, ואין אחר עמו (of Y.) *no one else is with him* 1QH 12$_{11}$.

<OBJ> מהר *acquire* Ps 16$_{4}$ (or em. אַחֵר מָהָרוּ to אֲחֵרִים יִירָאוּ *they fear others* or אָרְחָם הֵרֵעוּ *they make evil their way* or אָרְחָם הֵמִירוּ *they change their way*), לקח *take (in marriage)* Ex 21$_{10}$, נשׂא *take (in marriage)* 11QT 57$_{19}$, עמד hi. *cause to stand* Jb 34$_{24}$, קלל pi. *curse* Ec 7$_{22}$.

<CSTR> סוֹד אַחֵר *secret of another* Pr 25$_{9}$, שְׂדֵה *field of* Ex 22$_{4}$.

<PREP> לְ of possession, *to* Ezk 41$_{24}$ (‖ אֶחָד *one*) Ne 5$_{5}$ (or em. לַחֹרִים *to the nobles*), of direction/benefit, *to, for* Dn 11$_{4}$ (+ מִלְּבַד־אֵלֶּה *besides these*), + נתן *give* Is 42$_{8}$ 48$_{11}$ Jr 8$_{10}$ Pr 5$_{9}$ Si 30$_{28}$, עזב *leave* Ps 49$_{11}$ Si 11$_{19}$ (ע[ז]בו) 14$_{15}$, טחן *grind* Jb 31$_{10}$, סבב ni. *be turned over* Jr 6$_{12}$, קבץ *gather* Si 14$_{4}$; מִן of comparison, *(greater) than* 2 S 13$_{16}$; וַיִּסֹּב מֵאֶצְלוֹ אֶל־מוּל אַחֵר *and he turned away from him toward another* 1 S 17$_{30}$.

<COLL> שְׁנַיִם אֲחֵרִים *two others* Dn 12$_{5}$, חנין בר חנינא ואחרים *Hanin bar Hananiah and others* Mur 22$_{3.12}$ ([ח]נין), חוני ו[א]חרים *Huni and others* Mur 22$_{11}$, אחר תחת הבל *another one instead of Abel* 11QJub 4$_{7}$ (‖Gn 4$_{25}$; see §1), זה ... ואחר *the one ... and the other* Si 18$_{14}$.

Also 4Q485 1$_{5}$ 6QapSam/Kings 64$_{1}$ 4QToh B[b]$_{9}$ ([א]חרת).

⇒ אחר *delay.*

אַחֵר II $_{1}$ pr.n.m. **Aher,** a Benjaminite 1 C 7$_{12}$.

⇒ אַחֵר *other.*

אַחַר $_{96.9.87.1}$ prep. **after,** of time or place—sf. Q, Kt אחרו (Qr אַחֲרָיו), אַחַר כֵּן, אַחַר זֶה—**1.** of time, **after, following, a.** preceding noun, דָּבָר *event* Gn 15$_{1}$ 22$_{1}$ 39$_{7}$ 40$_{1}$ 1 K 13$_{33}$ 17$_{17}$ 21$_{1}$ Est 2$_{1}$ 3$_{1}$ Ezr 7$_{1}$ 1QM 17$_{10}$ 4QRitPur 24$_{4}$ (הדב[רי]ם), מַבּוּל *flood* Gn 9$_{28}$ 10$_{1}$ 10$_{32}$ 11$_{10}$, נֶדֶר *vow* Pr 20$_{25}$ (or em. אֵחַר *he delayed*), יוֹבֵל *jubilee* Lv 25$_{15}$ 27$_{18}$ 6QapProph 1$_{3}$, שְׁמִטָּה *(year of) release* 4QOtot 1$_{13.15}$ ([אחר השמט]ה) 1$_{19}$ (השׁ[מטה]) 2$_{3}$ ([אחר השמט]ה) 2$_{7.9}$ ([אחר]) 2$_{12.15}$ ([אחר השמטה]) 2$_{18}$ ([אחר ה]שמטה) 3$_{5}$ ([השמטה]) 3$_{10.13}$ (both [אחר השמט]ה), רוּחַ *wind* 1 K 19$_{11}$, רַעַשׁ *earthquake* 19$_{12}$, אֵשׁ *fire* 19$_{12}$, גֵּז *mowing* Am 7$_{1}$, כָּבוֹד *honour* Zc 2$_{12}$ (or em. אֹרַח *path of*), גֶּשֶׁם *rain* Ec 12$_{2}$, שַׁבָּת *sabbath* Ne 13$_{19}$ MurEpBarC[b]$_{9}$ 4QMish C[c]$_{2}$ ([אחר שבת]) 4QMish D 1$_{3.7}$ 2$_{2.5}$ (both [אחר שבת]), מָוֶת *death* 1 C 2$_{24}$, מַעֲשֶׂה *deed* Si 35$_{19}$, מִלְחָמָה *battle* 1QM 1$_{3}$, מְנַשֶּׁה *Manasseh* 4QpNah 3.4$_{6}$, עֹלָה *burnt offering* 11QT 23$_{8}$ 24$_{10}$, שְׁחִיטָה *slaughtering* 4QMMT A 2$_{46}$ ([לאחר שחיטתו]), שִׁלּוּחִים *sending away* Ex 18$_{2}$, ברך pi. ptc. *blessing* 1QS 2$_{10}$, קלל pi. ptc. *cursing* 2$_{10}$, האחד והשני *the first and second (days)* 4QMMT A 1$_{44.91}$ (both [אחר האחד והשני]) 1$_{138}$ ([אחר ה]אחד] והשנ[י]).

1b. preceding infinitive, שׁלח pi. *send away* Jr 40$_{1}$, דבר pi. *speak* Jb 21$_{3}$, גלח htp. *shave* Nm 6$_{19}$, עלה ni. *be raised* 1QM 14$_{2}$, נזה ho. *be sprinkled* 4QRitPur 1$_{7}$ (וא[חר ה]וזותו).

1c. as conjunction, introducing finite verb, חלץ pi. *withdraw* Lv 14$_{43}$ (‖ אַחֲרֵי *after* + infin. cstr.), נכה hi. *strike* Jr 41$_{16}$, נקף pi. *strike off* Jb 19$_{26}$, דבר pi. *speak* Jb 42$_{7}$, עלה ni. *be taken up* 4Q376 1.1$_{2}$; אַחַר אֲשֶׁר + נכה ho.

be conquered Ezk 40_{1}, למד pi. *teach* 4QpsJub^{c} 2_{1}.

2. of place, **a. behind, to the rear of, after,** following verb, עלל *glean* Si 30_{25} ([אח]ר), לקט pi. *glean* Ru 2_{2}, כתב ni. *be written* CD 14_{5}, הלך *go* Gn 37_{17} CD 11_{5}, בוא *come* Nm 25_{8} Jg 3_{22} 1QpHab 4_{12}, עבר *pass* 1QS $2_{20.21}$, נהג *drive* Ex 3_{1}, עמד *stand* Ca 2_{9}, רדף *pursue* 2 K 25_{5}, שׁמם pol. *appal* Si 9_{7} (or em. לשומם to לשוטט *to wander*), ישׁב *sit* 1QS 7_{20}, שׂים *place* Is 57_{8}, סרך *arrange* 1QM 2_{1}, סדר pi. *arrange* 5_{16}, לחם ni. *fight* 4QM^{a} fr. $13_{7(\text{Baillet})}$ (נלח[מים]), מות *die* Ex 11_{5}; in nom. cl., הַשְּׁלִשִׁית ... אַחַר *a third were ... behind* 2 K 11_{6} (or em. אַחֵר *another*). Preceding noun, אָח *brother* Gn 37_{17} CD 14_{5}, אִישׁ *man* Nm 25_{8} 1QS 7_{20}, כֹּהֵן *priest* 1QM 2_{1}, מִשְׁנֶה *deputy* 2_{1}, רוץ ptc. *guard* 2 K 11_{6} (or em. אַחַר הָרָצִים *behind the guards* to אַחֵר *another* gate), מֶלֶךְ *king* 25_{5}, בְּהֵמָה *beast* CD 11_{5}, מִדְבָּר *desert* Ex 3_{1}, רֵחֶה *hand mill* 11_{5}, דֶּלֶת *door* Is 57_{8}, מְזוּזָה *doorpost* 57_{8}, כֹּתֶל *wall* Ca 2_{9}, בַּיִת *house* Si 9_{7}, לַהַב *blade* Jg 3_{22}; in distributive phrases, זה אחר זה *one after the other* 1QS $2_{20.21}$ 1QpHab 4_{12} (ה[ז]), sim. 4QM^{a} fr. $13_{7(\text{Baillet})}$, איש אחר איש *(one) man after another* 1QM 5_{4}, מערכה אחר מערכה *one battle-line after the other* 5_{16}; preceding verbal clause, אֲשֶׁר אֶמְצָא־חֵן בְּעֵינָיו *him in whose sight I find favour* Ru 2_{2}.

2b. מֵאַחַר **from behind,** after verb, לקח *take* 2 S 7_{8} (mss מֵאַחֲרֵי) 11QPs^{a} 28_{11}, סוג ni. *turn back* intrans. Is 59_{13}, בוא hi. *bring* Ps 78_{71}.

Preceding noun, צֹאן *flock* 2 S 7_{8} (+ נָוֶה *pasture*) 11QPs^{a} 28_{11}, עול ptc. *ewe giving suck* Ps 78_{71}, אֱלֹהִים *God* Is 59_{13}.

3. of personal relationship, **a. after, in support of,** with verb, היה *be* 1 S 12_{14}, הלך *go* 2 K 13_{2} 23_{3} Is 65_{2} Ezk 13_{3} Jb 31_{7} 4QJub^{a} $2_{5\text{-}6}$ (וילך]כו אחר ... ואחר ...) [ואחר), יצא *come out* 1 S 11_{7}, טהר htp. *purify oneself* Is 66_{17}, קדשׁ htp. *sanctify oneself* 66_{17}, דרשׁ *seek* Jb 39_{8}, רדף *pursue* 1QpHab 11_{5} 4Q416 7_{9}, פנה *turn* 4QJub^{a} 2_{4} ([פנו]), רצה *desire* 4Q424 1_{9}, לוז ni. *err* Si 34_{8}, תעה *stray* 1QS 5_{4}, זנה *fornicate* 1QpHab 5_{7}.

Preceding noun, י׳ *Y.* 1 S 12_{14} 2 K 23_{3}, אֱלֹהִים *God* 4QJub^{a} 2_{4}, חַטָּאת *sin* of Jeroboam 2 K 13_{2}, כְּלִמָּה *shame* 4QJub^{a} 2_{6} ([אחר כ]ל[מתם]), חֶרְפָּה *shame* 2_{6} (אחר] [חרפת]ם), מַחֲשָׁבָה *imagination* Is 65_{2} 1QS 5_{4}, אֱמֶת *truth* 4Q424 1_{9}, שֹׁרֶשׁ *root* of understanding 4Q416 7_{9}, עַיִן *eye* Jb 31_{7} 1QS 5_{4} 1QpHab 5_{7}, לֵבָב *heart* 1QS 5_{4}, רוּחַ *spirit* Ezk 13_{3}, אֶחָד *one* Is $66_{17(\text{Kt})}$ (Qr אַחַת *one*), יָרוֹק *green thing* Jb 39_{8}, מָמוֹן *wealth* Si 34_{8}, מורה hi. ptc. *teacher* of righteousness 1QpHab 11_{5}, Samuel 1 S 11_{7}, גּוֹי *nation* 4QJub^{a} 2_{5} ([אחר הגו]ים).

3b. מֵאַחַר **from after,** after verb, שׁוב *turn aside* 1QS 1_{17}, hi. *cause to turn* CD 6_{1}, סוג ni. *turn aside* Is 59_{13}; preceding noun, אֵל *God* CD 6_{1}, אֱלֹהִים *God* Is 59_{13}; מאחרו *from after him* (Y.) 1QS 1_{17}.

4. besides, וַיִּקְחוּ מֵהֶם בְּלֶחֶם וָיַיִן אַחַר כֶּסֶף *they took from them bread and wine besides silver* Ne 5_{15} (or em. לְיוֹם אֶחָד *for one day*).

5. according to, אחר צרכו ימשוך תורה *according to his need he pulls*, i.e. distorts, *the law* Si $35_{17(\text{B})}$ (Bmg, E, F ויאחר *and he delays*).

6a. as adv. of time, **afterwards, then,** with verb, הלך *go* Gn 24_{55} Jos 2_{16} Jg 19_{5}, נסע *journey* Nm 12_{16}, בוא *come* Ex 5_{1} Lv 14_{8} Nm 19_{7} 31_{24} 1 C 2_{21} CD 12_{5} 1QS 6_{15} 11QT 39_{10} $45_{9.16}$ 63_{14} 4QRitPur 42.2_{2} $48_{5(\text{Baillet})}$ ([בוא]) 4Q414 1.2_{5}, נגשׁ *approach* Gn 33_{7}, יצא *go out* 38_{30} 4QpGen^{a} 2_{10}, hi. *lead out* Jos 24_{5} 11QT 22_{11}, ירד *descend* Jg 1_{9}, עבר *pass by* Gn 18_{5}, שׁחט *slaughter* Lv 14_{19}, טהר *be clean* 15_{28} 11QT 51_{5}, אכל *eat* Lv 22_{7} 11QT 22_{14} 63_{15} 4QOrd^{c} 1.1_{6} (יא[כ]לו) 1.1_{9} 4QToh A $1.1_{3.5}$, שׁקה hi. *cause to drink* Nm 5_{26}, שׁתה *drink* 6_{20} Si 9_{10} (ת[ש]תינו), אסף ni. *be gathered* Nm 12_{14} 31_{2} 1QM 19_{11} + Sup, פוץ ni. *be scattered* Gn 10_{18}, חזק *become strong* Jg 7_{11}, חדל *cease* 15_{7}, שׁמע *listen* Ezk 20_{39}, ילד *bear* Gn 30_{21}, שׁוב *return* Nm 32_{22} Ho 3_{5} 1QM^{a} 1_{17} 11QT 59_{9} 4Q414 4_{6}, pol. *respond* 4Q525 4_{24}, סבב *recline* Si 35_{1}, רבץ *recline* 35_{2}, לקח *take* Ps 73_{24} (or em. אֹרַח *[in] the path of* glory), דבר pi. *talk* Jb 18_{2} 4QRitMar 19_{5} ([אח]ר), מלא ni. *be full* Pr 20_{17}, בנה *build* 24_{27}, תקע *sound* trumpet 1QM $8_{2.13}$ 16_{3} 4QM^{a} fr. 18_{2} ([א]חר [יתק]עו), כון hi. *prepare* 2 C 35_{14}, תנן *repeat* Lachish ost. 3_{12} (אחר אתננהו; others ולא אתן בה), היה *be* Si $5_{10(\text{C})}$ (A אחר *one*) 11QT 34_{7} (+ טֶבַח *slaughter*), זוף hi. *reprove* Si 11_{7}, זעם *curse* 4QBer^{a} 3.2_{1} ([א]חר; EW [א[ז *then*), עשׂה *do* Si 36_{4} 11QT 24_{11} $25_{7(\text{Yadin})}$ ([תעשו]) 27_{3}, נגה hi. *cause to shine* Si 36_{4}, גלה ni. *be revealed* 1QpHab 11_{1}, שׁאל *ask* 1QS 7_{21}, כתב *write* 1QS 9_{2} (יכתוב perh. ni.), ni. *be* *written* 8_{19} (יכת[ב]), ישב *sit* 1QSa 2_{14}(Barthélemy) ([י]שב), שלח *stretch* hand 2_{20} (אח]ר יש[לח), עלה *rise* 1Q29 2_4, hi. *offer* sacrifice 11QT 18_9, קום *rise* 4QM^a fr. 1_{13}, סור *depart* 4QpIsa^a 5_2 (יס[ו]ר), רמס ni. *be trampled* 4QpNah 3.1_3, ענג htp. *delight* 4QpPs^a 1.2_{10}, סוך *anoint oneself* 11QT 22_{14}; with nom. cl., [אחר ... הנף העמר] *afterwards ... it is the waving of the omer* 4QMMT A 1_{13}, [אחר ... חג השבועות] *afterwards ... it is the festival of weeks* 13_5, [אחר ... מועד התירוש] *afterwards ... it is the festival of the new wine* 16_1, [אח[ר] ... קרבן] העצים] *afterwards ... it is the offering of the wood* 18_5.

6b. אַחַר כֵּן **afterwards,** with verb בוא *come* Lv 14_{36} Dt 21_{13} 1 S 10_5.

6c. אַחַר זֶה **after this,** with verb שׁלח *send forth* 2 C 32_9.

7. as adv. of space, **behind,** in nom. cl., וְהִנֵּה־אַיִל אַחַר *and behold, behind him was a ram* (mss אֶחָד *one* ram) Gn 22_{13}, אַחַר נֹגְנִים *behind are musicians* Ps 68_{26}.

Also Mur 48_4 ([א]חר) Mur 30 2_{27} 5QRègle 2_{10} 11QT 19_6 4QShir^b 3_2 ([א]חר) 4QRitPur 16_{13} 15.2_4 4QToh A 1.1_9 (אח[ר]).

→ אחר *delay*.

[אַחֲרָאי] 0.0.1 n.m. **guarantor,** כל שיש לי ושאקנה אח[ר]אים וערבים *all that I have and that I shall acquire are guarantors and sureties* Mur 30 2_{24}.

→ אחר *delay*.

אַחֲרוֹן 51.2.18 adj. **last**—אַחֲרֹן, f. אַחֲרוֹנָה (אַחֲרֹנָה); pl. אַחֲרוֹנִים (אַחֲרֹנִים), f. Q אחרונות—**1a. last, latter,** with noun, דָּבָר *word* 2 S 23_1 1 C 23_{27}, *deed* of king 29_{29} 2 C 9_{29} 12_{15} 16_{11} 20_{34} 25_{26} 26_{22} 28_{26} 35_{27} (all nine :: רִאשׁוֹן *first*), מִדְרָשׁ *midrash* of the law 4QD^b 2_1 (... [מ]דר[ש] [האחרון]), חֶסֶד *loyalty* Ru 3_{10} (:: רִאשׁוֹן), אוֹת *sign* Ex 4_8; יוֹם *day* Is 30_8 Pr 31_{25} Ne 8_{18} (:: רִאשׁוֹן), עֵת *time* Is 8_{23} (:: רִאשׁוֹן), קֵץ *end time* 1QpHab $7_{7.12}$ 4QpNah 3.4_3 1QS 4_{17}, דּוֹר *generation* Dt 29_{21} Ps 48_{14} $78_{4.6}$ 102_{19} 1QpHab 2_7 7_2 1QpMic 17_5 CD $1_{12.12}$, יוֹבֵל *jubilee* 11QMelch 1_7 (האח[ר]ון), אִישׁ *husband* Dt $24_{3.3}$, כֹּהֵן *priest* 4QpHos^b 2_3 1QpHab 9_5, בַּיִת *temple* Hg 2_9 (:: רִאשׁוֹן *first*).

1b. as noun, **last one, latter one,** <SUBJ> היה *be* 2 S $19_{12.13}$ Ec 1_{11} (:: רִאשׁוֹן *first one*), קום *rise* Jb 19_{25}, שׂמח *rejoice* Ec 4_{16}, שׁקד *watch* Si 36_{16} (or perh. אחריו *after him*). <NOM CL> אֲנִי רִאשׁוֹן וַאֲנִי אַחֲרוֹן *I am the first and the last* Is 44_6, sim. 48_{12}, ראשנים ואחרנים עמך *first and last are with you* Si 41_3(B).

<OBJ> עשׂה *make* MasShirShab 1_4 (:: רִאשׁוֹן *first one*), שׂים *place* Gn $33_{2.2}$ (:: רִאשׁוֹן), זכר *remember* Si 41_3(M) (:: קַדְמוֹן *former one*), ידע hi. *make known* 4QJub^a 1_{11} ([ויודיעהו ... האחרונים]), מאס *reject* CD 20_9 (:: רִאשׁוֹן), עצם pi. *break bones* Jr 50_{17}.

<APP> גם אני אחרון *I too, (the) last* Si 36_{16}, בְּנֵי אֲדֹנִיקָם אַחֲרֹנִים *the descendants of Adonikam, (the) last ones* Ezr 8_{13}. <PREP> אֶת־אַחֲרֹנִים *with (the) last ones* Is 41_4 (+ רִאשׁוֹן *first one*).

2a. western, הַיָּם הָאַחֲרוֹן *the western sea,* i.e. Mediterranean Dt 11_{24} 34_2 Jl 2_{20} Zc 14_8 (both :: קַדְמֹנִי *eastern* sea, i.e. Dead Sea).

2b. as noun, **one from the west,** <SUBJ> שׁמם ni. *be horrified* Jb 18_{20} (:: קַדְמֹנִי *one from the east*).

3. אַחֲרֹנָה used as adv., **afterwards, at the last,** alw. preceded by prep. (1) בָּאַחֲרֹנָה + verb, היה *be* Dt 13_{10} 17_7 (both :: רִאשֹׁנָה *first* [adv.]) 2 S 2_{26} (בָּאַחֲרוֹנָה), עשׂה *make* 1 K 17_{13} (:: רִאשֹׁנָה), עבר *pass* 1 S 29_2, עלה *go up* Dn 8_3. (2) לָאַחֲרֹנָה + verb, נסע *set out* Nm 2_{31}, היה *be* Ec 1_{11}. (3) כָּאַחֲרֹנָה + verb, היה *be* Dn 11_{29}.

Also 4QDibHam^a 18_4 ([א]חרון) 4QShir^b 11_9 (אחר[ו]ן) 11_{10} 4QD^a 6.2_1(WA) 4QJub^a 4_3 ([ה]אחרני[ם]).

<ANT> §1 רִאשׁוֹן *first (one);* §2 קַדְמֹנִי *eastern* §3 רִאשֹׁנָה *first.*

→ אחר *delay*.

אֲחַרַח 1 pr.n.m. **Aharah,** son of Benjamin, 1 C 8_1 (or em. אֲחִירָם *Ahiram*).

→ perh. אחר *delay*.

אֲחַרְחֵל 1 pr.n.m. **Aharhel,** son of Harum, 1 C 4_8.

→ perh. אחר *delay*.

אַחֲרֵי 619.13.44 prep. **after**—in form, אַחֲרֵי is pl. cstr. of אַחַר; sf. אַחֲרַי (אַחֲרָי), אַחֲרֶיךָ (Q אחריכה), אַחֲרַיִךְ (אַחֲרָיִךְ), אַחֲרָיו, אַחֲרֶיהָ, אַחֲרֵינוּ, אַחֲרֵיכֶם, אַחֲרֵיהֶם (Q אחריהמה), אַחֲרֵיהֶן.

אַחֲרֵי

1a. prep. of time, **after.** (1) Preceding **infinitive cstr.** of בוא *come* 2 S 5$_{13}$ 2 C 25$_{14}$, הלך *go* 2 S 17$_{21}$, יצא *go out* Jr 29$_{2}$ Ezk 46$_{12}$, שׁוב *go back* Gn 14$_{17}$ Jr 31$_{19}$, נפל *fall* 2 S 1$_{10}$, שׁכב *lie down* 2 K 14$_{22}$||2 C 26$_{2}$, עשׂה *do* Jr 3$_{7}$, נתן *give* 32$_{16}$, כרת *cut*, i.e. make, covenant 34$_{8}$, ילד hi. *beget* Gn 5$_{4+8t}$ 11$_{11+7t}$ (all except 5$_{4.22}$ + חיה *live*), קבר *bury* 50$_{14}$ 1 K 13$_{31}$, גלה hi. *exile* Jr 24$_{1}$, נכה hi. *strike* Ex 7$_{25}$ Dt 1$_{4}$, שׁבר *break* Jr 28$_{12}$, קצה hi. *cut* Lv 14$_{43}$ (|| אַחַר *after* + finite verb), נתשׁ *pluck* Jr 12$_{15}$, שׂרף *burn* 36$_{27}$, אכל *eat* 1 S 1$_{9}$ 1 K 13$_{23}$, שׁתה *drink* 1 S 1$_{9}$ (inf. abs.) 1 K 13$_{23}$, ראה *see* Gn 46$_{30}$, ni. *show oneself* Lv 13$_{7}$, שׁמע *hear* Nm 30$_{16}$, ידע ni. *be informed* Jr 31$_{19}$, פרד ni. *be separate* Gn 13$_{14}$, בלה *be worn out* 18$_{12}$, כבס hothp. *be washed* Lv 13$_{55.56}$, טוח ni. *be smeared* 14$_{43}$ (|| אַחַר + finite verb) 14$_{48}$, משׁח ni. *be anointed* Nm 7$_{88}$, שׁמד ni. *be destroyed* Dt 12$_{30}$.

(2) Preceding **noun**, דָּבָר *event* Gn 22$_{20}$ 48$_{1}$ Jos 24$_{29}$ 2 C 32$_{1}$, *speech* Jb 29$_{22}$, סְפָר *count* 2 C 2$_{16}$, רֳאִי *vision* Gn 16$_{13}$, זִקְנָה *old age* 24$_{36}$ (+ ילד *give birth*), מַגֵּפָה *plague* Nm 25$_{19}$, מָוֶת *death* (alw. cstr. מוֹת) Gn 25$_{11}$ 26$_{18}$ Lv 16$_{1}$ Nm 35$_{28}$ Dt 31$_{27.29}$ Jos 1$_{1}$ Jg 1$_{1}$ 2 S 1$_{1}$ 2 K 1$_{1}$ 14$_{17}$||2 C 25$_{25}$ Ru 2$_{11}$ 2 C 22$_{4}$ 24$_{17}$ Si 46$_{20}$, יוֹם *day* Jr 31$_{33}$, שָׁבוּעַ *week* Dn 9$_{26}$, מֶלֶךְ *king* Ec 2$_{12}$, אֵם *mother*, i.e. mother's death Gn 24$_{67}$, טָהֳרָה *cleansing* Lv 13$_{35}$ Ezk 44$_{26}$, רָעָה *evil* 16$_{23}$, מַתַּת *gift*, i.e. after giving a present Si 41$_{22(B)}$ (M אַחַר); אַחֲרֵי הַנִּרְאָה אֵלַי בַּתְּחִלָּה *after the one that appeared to me first* Dn 8$_{1}$, אַחֲרֵי כָּל־הַבָּא עָלֵינוּ *after all that has come upon us* Ezr 9$_{13}$, אַחֲרֵי מָתַי עֹד *after how much longer?* Jr 13$_{27}$, ומטהרים את הנשכות זואת אחרי זאות *purifying the chambers, one after the other* 11QT 45$_{6}$, [אחרי כל אלה] *after all these (amimals)* 4QJub[a] 7$_{1}$, [ש]ל[חז]ק[יא] אח[רי ב]פ[ר]ע[ן] *which will belong to Hezekiah after payment* Mur 22 1$_{2}$.

(3) As conjunction, preceding **finite verb, a.** אַחֲרֵי, with verb, סבב hi. *bring round* 1 S 5$_{9}$, מכר ni. *be sold* Lv 25$_{48}$. **b.** אַחֲרֵי אֲשֶׁר, with verb, יצא *go out* Jos 2$_{7}$ (כַּאֲשֶׁר), הפך *turn* tail 7$_{8}$, נוח hi. *give rest* 23$_{1}$, יטב hi. *do good* 24$_{20}$, כרת *cut*, i.e. make, covenant 9$_{16}$, טמא hothp. *be defiled* Dt 24$_{4}$. **c.** אַחֲרֵי־כֵן, with verb, ספר *count* 2 S 24$_{10}$.

1b. (1) With pronom. suff. referring to an object, period, or person that has ceased to be, **after the death, reign, end, etc.,** followed by verb, מלך *reign* after (David) 1 K 1$_{13.17.24.30}$, שׁפט *judge* after (judge) Jg 12$_{8.11.13}$, ישׁב *sit* (on throne) after (David) 1 K 1$_{20.27}$, עמד *arise* (of one prophet, king after another) Si 47$_{1.12}$, קום *arise* Gn 41$_{30}$ (of years of famine after years of plenty) Jg 2$_{10}$ (of new generation after old) 10$_{3}$ (of Jair as judge after Tola) 1 K 3$_{12}$ 2 K 23$_{25}$ (both of successor to outstanding king; || לְפָנַי *before*, + כְּ *as* you, him), בוא *come* Jr 51$_{46}$ (of second rumour coming after first year) CD 4$_{7}$ 8$_{17(A)}$=19$_{30(B)}$ (both of descendants), לקח *take (in marriage)* (Maacah after Abihail) 2 C 11$_{20}$, מצא *find* (what happens after death) Ec 7$_{14}$, עזב *leave* successor Si 47$_{23}$ ([אח]ריו), ילד hi. *beget* (further children after first-born) Gn 48$_{6}$, יתר ni. *be left* (of descendants of destroyed nation) 1 K 9$_{21}$||2 C 8$_{8}$, שׁמם ni. *be* left *devastated* (of land after departure of exiles) Zc 7$_{14}$, קטר hi. *offer* burnt offering (after completion of previous one) 11QT 23$_{10}$, עשׂה *offer* burnt offering (after completion of previous one) 24$_{12}$, יסף hi. *recur* (of day) Jl 2$_{2}$, היה *be* Ex 10$_{14}$ (of plague after plague of locusts) Jg 3$_{31}$ 2 K 18$_{5}$ (both of successor to judge, king) Is 43$_{10}$ (of successor to Y.; || לְפָנַי) Ec 2$_{18}$ (of one's heir) 3$_{22}$ 6$_{12}$ (both of events after one's death) 2 C 1$_{12}$ (of successor to outstanding king; || לְפָנַי *before*, + כֵּן *such*), לֹא הָיָה כַּיּוֹם הַהוּא לְפָנָיו וְאַחֲרָיו *there has not been as that day before it or after it* Jos 10$_{14}$; without verb, אַחֲרָיו אֶל־הַמֵּתִים perh. *after it* (destiny) *to the dead* Ec 9$_{3}$ (or em. אַחֲרִיתָם *their destiny* is [to go] to the dead).

(2) מֵאַחֲרָיו in same sense, אֲשֶׁר יָקוּמוּ מֵאַחֲרֵיכֶם your children *who will appear after you* Dt 29$_{21}$, אֲשֶׁר יִהְיֶה מֵאַחֲרָיו *what will be after him*, i.e. after his death Ec 10$_{14}$.

(3) With **personal name** instead of suffix, Jos 24$_{31}$||Jg 2$_{7}$ (of elders who outlive Joshua) Jg 10$_{1}$ (of Tola as successor to Abimelech) 1 K 1$_{6}$ (of Adonijah born after Absalom).

1c. (which comes) after, etc., in prepositional phrases, etc., where one object or state follows another, but without close ref. to verbal action, בעשר השנים אשר אחריהם *in the ten years that come after them* 1QM 2$_{13}$, שָׁנָה אַחֲרֵי שָׁנָה *year after year* 2 S 21$_{1}$,

דֹּרוֹתֵינוּ אַחֲרֵינוּ *the generations after us* Jos 22_{27}, בֵּיתוֹ אַחֲרָיו *his household after him* Gn 18_{19} Jb 21_{21}, זַרְעֲךָ אַחֲרֶיךָ *your seed after you* Gn $17_{7.7.8.9.10}$ 35_{12} 48_{4} 2 S 7_{12}||1 C 17_{11}, sim. Gn 9_{9} 17_{19} Ex 28_{43} Nm 25_{13} Dt 1_{8} 4_{37} 10_{15} 1 S 24_{22} 4QDibHam[a] 5.2_{1} 4QDibHam[c] $24_{2(\text{Baillet})}$ ([בזורעם אח]ריהם), בָּנֶיךָ אַחֲרֶיךָ *your children after you* Dt 4_{40} $12_{25.28}$ 11QT 53_{7}, sim. Ex 29_{29} Lv 25_{46} 1 K 15_{4} Jr $32_{18.39}$ Pr 20_{7} 1 C 28_{8} Si $44_{9(B)}$ (מאחריהם) 11QT 59_{21} 4Q185 1.2_{2}.

1d. after he had done, etc., where suffix has ref. more to the action performed than to its agent, followed by verb (the preceding verb is given in brackets), חלל hi. *begin* 11QT 21_{6} + Sup, אמר *say* 1QS 1_{20} (ברך pi. *bless*) 2_{18} (אמר), ידה hi. *praise* 1_{24} (ספר pi. *recount*), עבר *enter (covenant)* 2_{20} (|| ברשונה *first*, בשלישית *thirdly*), יצא *go out* 1QM $6_{1.4}$ (in both שׁוב *go back*), שׁתה *drink* Jr 25_{26} (שׁקה hi. *give to drink*), חזק hi. *repair* Ne 3_{16+14t} (Kt $3_{30.31}$ appar. אַחֲרַי *afterwards*); with elision of verb, Ne 3_{25} (mss include verb חזק hi.) 11QT 15_{18} + Sup (סמך *rest* hands); suffix refers only to action, not agent (cf. אַחֲרֵי־כֵן, §1e), ... יְשָׁרֵהוּ אַחֲרָיו יִשְׁאַג *he lets loose ... After it he roars* Jb 37_{4}.

1e. אַחֲרֵי־כֵן **afterward,** with verb, בוא *come* Lv $16_{26.28}$ Nm 4_{15} $8_{15.22}$, נסע *set out* 9_{17}, שׁוב *go back* Jr 34_{11} 4QJub[a] 2_{17} ([ואחרי כן ישובו]), hi. *bring back* 49_{6}, יצא *go out* Gn 15_{14} 25_{26} Ex 11_{8}, נגשׁ *approach* 34_{32}, קום *arise* 1 S 24_{9}, עמד *arise* 4QCat[a] 5_{3} ([וא]חרי כן יעמו[ד]), עשׂה *offer* sacrifice Ezr 3_{5} (אַחֲרֵיכֵן), שׁלח *send* Jr 16_{16}, pi. *dispatch* Israelites Ex 3_{20} 11_{1}; נתן *give* Jr 21_{7}, ni. *be given* 4QpPs[a] 1.2_{19} (ואחר[י] כן), פתח *open* Jb 3_{1} 4QM[c]$_{2}$ (ואח[ר]י כן יפת[חו]), נכה hi. *strike* Jos 10_{26}, קבר *bury* Gn 23_{19}, עתר ni. *be appeased* 2 S 21_{14}, ראה *see* Gn 32_{21}, דבר pi. *speak* 45_{15} (אַחֲרֵי כֵן), שׁמע *hear* 2 S 3_{28} (מֵאַחֲרֵי כֵן), קרא *read* Jos 8_{34}, pass. *be called* Is 1_{26}, חבר htp. *make alliance* 2 C 20_{35} (אַחֲרֵיכֵן), בנה *build* 33_{14}, שׁכן *dwell* Jr 46_{26}, אכל *eat* 1 S 9_{13}.

וַיְהִי אַחֲרֵי־כֵן *and it came to pass afterwards* Jg 16_{4} 1 S 24_{6} 2 S 2_{1} 8_{1}||1 C 18_{1} 2 S 10_{1}||1 C 19_{1} 2 S 13_{1} 15_{1} (מֵאַחֲרֵי כֵן) 21_{18}||1 C 20_{4} (אַחֲרֵיכֵן) 2 K 6_{24} Jl 3_{1} (וְהָיָה) 2 C 20_{1} 24_{4} (both אַחֲרֵיכֵן), הָרָעָב הַהוּא אַחֲרֵי־כֵן *that famine thereafter* Gn 41_{31}, בַּיָּמִים הָהֵם וְגַם אַחֲרֵי־כֵן *in those days, and afterwards too* 6_{4}, וַיִּנָּשֵׂא ... מֵאַחֲרֵי־כֵן *and he was exalted ... from then on* 2 C 32_{23}; אַחֲרֵי־זֹאת *after this* Jb 42_{16} Ezr 9_{10}, אַחֲרֵי כָל־זֹאת *after all this* 2 C 21_{18} 35_{20} (כָּל־).

2a. prep. of place, **after, (approaching) towards the rear of,** with verbs of motion (distinction from §2b not alw. clear), oft. of following or pursuing hostilely; sometimes merely expressing accompaniment (e.g. Gn 24_{5} 1 S 25_{42}) or direction or motion towards (e.g. 1 S $12_{20.21}$ 20_{37} 22_{20} 2 K 19_{21}||Is 37_{22}).

With verb, הלך *go* Gn $24_{5.8.39.61}$ 32_{20} Nm 16_{25} Jos 3_{3} $6_{8.9.13}$ (all three + לִפְנֵי *in front of*) Jg 9_{49} 13_{11} 19_{3} 1 S 6_{12} $17_{13.14}$ 25_{42} 30_{21} 2 S 3_{16} (+ אֵת *with*) 3_{31} 13_{34} (or em. חֹרֹנַיִם the road to *Horonaim*) 1 K 13_{14} $19_{20.21}$ 2 K 4_{30} 6_{19} 7_{15} Is 45_{14} Jr $2_{2.25}$ 48_{2} Ezk 10_{11} 33_{31} Ho $2_{7.15}$ 5_{11}=CD 4_{19} Am 2_{4} Pr 7_{22} (or em. אַחֲרֶיהָ פִּתְאֹם go *after her suddenly* to אֹרַח פְּתָאִים go *the way of the naive*) Ru 2_{9} 3_{10} Ne 12_{32} Si 5_{1}, of showing allegiance to a god Dt 4_{3} 6_{14} 8_{19} 11_{28} $13_{3.5}$=11QT 54_{13} Dt 28_{14} Jg $2_{12.19}$ 1 K $11_{5.10}$ 14_{8} $18_{18.21.21}$ 21_{26} 2 K 17_{15} Jr $2_{5.8.23}$ $7_{6.9}$ 8_{2} 9_{13} 11_{10} 13_{10} 16_{11} 25_{6} 35_{15} Ezk 20_{16} Ho 11_{10} 2 C 34_{31} (|| 2 K 23_{3} אַחַר), or a person Jg 9_{4} 2 K 17_{15} CD 19_{32}.

בוא *come* Ex $14_{17.23.28}$ 1 S 11_{5} 25_{19} (|| לִפְנֵי *in front of*) 26_{3} 2 S 20_{14} 1 K 1_{14} 2 K 11_{15}||2 C 23_{14} 2 C 26_{17}, יצא *go out* Ex 15_{20} Jos $8_{6.17}$ 1 S 11_{7} (|| אַחַר *after*) 17_{35} 24_{15} 2 S 11_{8} 20_{7} Si 14_{22}, נסע *set out* Ex 14_{10}, עבר *cross over* 2 S 20_{13} Ezk 9_{5}, ירד *go down* Jg 3_{28} 1 S $14_{36.37}$ Ps 49_{18}, עלה *go up* Gn $41_{3.19.27}$ (אַחֲרֵי perh. temporal in all three) 1 S 14_{12} 25_{13} 2 S 20_{2} 1 K $13_{5.40}$ 1 C 14_{14}, צמח *sprout up* Gn $41_{6.23}$ (אַחֲרֵי perh. temporal in both), משׁך *pull* Ca 1_{4}, *go* Jb 21_{33} (|| לִפְנֵי) Si 14_{19} (אַחֲרֵי perh. temporal in both), רכב *ride* 2 K 9_{25} (or em. צְמָדִים אַחֲרֵי *teams after* to צֶמֶד מֵאַחֲרֵי *a team away from*).

שׁוב *go back* to 1 S 15_{31} 2 S 23_{10} Ru 1_{15} (|| אֶל *towards*), פנה *turn* intrans., i.e. look behind oneself Jos 8_{20} Jg 20_{40} 2 S 1_{7} 2_{20} 2 K 2_{24}, *turn* to (another, for help) Ezk 29_{16}, נטה *turn* (intrans.) to the pursuit of (gain) 1 S 8_{3}, hi. *turn* someone's heart, to follow (idols) 1 K $11_{2.4}$, סור *turn* intrans., to follow (idols) 1 S 12_{21}, רדף *pursue* (of hostile pursuit except Jg 3_{28} 2 K 5_{21} 4QBark[a] 1_{6}) Gn 31_{23} 35_{5} 44_{4} Ex $14_{4.8.9}$ Dt 11_{4} 19_{6} Jos $2_{5.7.7}$ $8_{16.16.17}$ 10_{19} 20_{5} 24_{6} Jg 1_{6} 3_{28} $4_{16.16}$ 7_{23} $8_{5.12}$ 1 S $23_{25.28}$ 24_{15} 26_{18} 30_{8} 2 S $2_{19.24.28}$ 17_{1} 18_{16} $20_{6.7.10.13}$ 2 K 5_{21} 9_{27} Jr 29_{18}

395||528 (|| 2 K 255 אַחַר) 2 C 1319 4QBarka 16.

דבק *stay close* to, i.e. pursue Jr 4216 Ps 639, hi. Jg 2045 1 S 1422 1 C 102.2 (|| 1 S 312.2 object-marker אֶת), דלק *hotly pursue* Gn 3136 1 S 1753, רוץ *run* after 2 S 1822 1 K 1920 2 K 520.21, ברח *flee* to 1 S 2220, תעה *stray* after (idols) Ezk 4410 (+ מֵעַל *away from Y.*), שלח *send* (messenger, etc.) after, to 2 S 326 2 K 714 1419||2 C 2527, pi. *dispatch* (sword) after, against Jr 915 4937, שׁלך hi. *throw away* behind (oneself) 1 K 149 Is 3817 Ezk 2335 Ps 5017 Ne 926 4QpHosa 1.24.

ריק hi. *unsheathe* (sword) after, against Lv 2633 Ezk 52.12 1214, בער pi. *blaze up* after, against 1 K 1410 2121, hi. 163.3, חרם hi. *destroy*, i.e. pursue destructively Jr 5021, פקד *visit*, i.e. send (destruction) against 1QS 26, זעק ni. *be called*, i.e. rallied behind Jg 634.35, צעק ni. *be called*, i.e. rallied behind 1 S 134, קבץ htp. *be gathered*, i.e. rallied behind 2 S 225, נקשׁ ni. *be lured* after, i.e. be deceived into following Dt 1230, נבט hi. *look* behind (oneself) Gn 1917 1 S 249, *look* at (another) Ex 338, קרא *call* after, to 1 S 2037.38 249 Jr 126, זנה *prostitute oneself* with, i.e. disloyally follow another god Ex 3415.16 Lv 177 205.5.6 (+ פנה אֶל *turn to*) Nm 1539 Dt 3116 Jg 217 827.33 Ezk 69 (+ מֵעַל) 2030 2330 1 C 525 11QT 213(Yadin) ([וזנו]), pu. *be followed for prostitution* with Ezk 1634, נהה ni. *lament*, i.e. follow repentantly 1 S 72, חרד *tremble*, i.e. follow trembling 137, חשׁל ni. *be shattered*, i.e. follow wearily Dt 2518, שׂדד pi. *harrow* behind (farmer) Jb 3910; אַחֲרֵי גִּלּוּלֵי אֲבוֹתָם הָיוּ עֵינֵיהֶם *their eyes were (attracted) towards their fathers' idols* Ezk 2024, נפשי נתתי אחריה *I have given my life to (go) after her* Si 5120(B).

מֵאַחֲרֵי in same sense, preceded by verb, הלך *go* Ex 1419 (|| לִפְנֵי *in front of*), נבט hi. *look* Gn 1926.

Without verb, אַחֲרֶיךָ בִנְיָמִין (they are) *behind you, Benjamin* Jg 514 Ho 58 (or em. הַחֲרִדוּ *terrify* Benjamin), אַחֲרֵי יוֹאָב *follow Joab* 2 S 2011.

2b. without implied motion towards, **at the back of, behind, after,** with verb, שׁמע *hear* (sound) at (one's) back Ezk 312, שׁאר hi. *leave* (blessing) behind Jl 214, אור *illuminate* (path) in the wake of Jb 4124, סגר *close* door Gn 196, נעל *lock* door 2 S 1317.18, להט pi. *blaze* Jl 23 (|| לִפְנֵי *in front of*), מות pol. *kill* 1 S 1413, חנה *encamp* behind (tabernacle) Nm 323, פקד *muster* 1 K 2015, שׁקד *keep watch* behind (someone) Si 3616 (אחריו; or perh. אחרון *last*).

פאר pi. *strip (branches)* behind (harvester) Dt 2420, עלל po. *glean* behind (harvester) 2421, לקט pi. *gather* (trans.) behind (harvester) Ru 23, אסף *gather* (trans.) behind (harvester) 27, נוע hi. *shake* (head) at 2 K 1921||Is 3722, רצה *be pleased* behind (someone), i.e. express pleasure when someone has passed by Ps 4914 (or em. אַחֲרִיתָם *their end*, or אָרְחוֹתָם *their way*), חלק hi. *make* tongue smooth behind, i.e. flatter someone Pr 2823 (if em. לָשׁוֹן אַחֲרָיו *tongue behind him*), מצא *find* favour with person or by action 2823(ms) (without movement to end of verse), ... יכתובו על אותותם ... ואחריהם כול ... שמותם *they are to write on their banners* 'God's truth', etc. ... *and after them* (the texts) *all ... their names* 1QM 46.7.

מֵאַחֲרֵי in same sense, with verb, עמד *stand* Ex 1419 (+ מִפְּנֵי *from before*), שׁמע *hear* Is 3021, נפל *fall* Jr 921.

In Nom. Cl., *after* (with or without motion) with subject, pronoun Gn 1810 3219 1 S 2110 Ne 1238, Jacob Gn 3221, אִישׁ *man* Jg 414 Ne 417 (plur. in both), נֹשֵׂא כֵלִים *armour-bearer* 1 S 1413, שַׂר *officer* Ne 410, בְּתוּלָה *virgin* in the train of (princess) Ps 4515, סוּס *horse* Zc 18, חַיִל *army* 1 K 2019, מִדְבָּר *desert* Jl 23 (|| לִפְנֵי *in front of*), הָמוֹן *roar* of water 11QPsa 2610 (|| לִפְנֵי), קוֹל רַגְלֵי אֲדֹנָיו אַחֲרָיו *the sound of his master's feet is behind him* 2 K 632, אַחֲרֵיהֶם ... הַנֹּתְנִים אֶת־לְבָבָם *behind them ... were all who placed their mind on* Y. 2 C 1116.

מֵאַחֲרֵי in nom. cl. with subject, מַאֲרָב *ambush* (|| לִפְנֵי *in front of*) 2 C 1313; רֹאשׁ־עָגֹל לְכִסֵּה מֵאַחֲרָיו *behind the throne there was a round head* 1 K 1019, וָאַעֲמִיד ... מֵאַחֲרֵי לַחוֹמָה *and I stationed ... behind the wall* Ne 47.

Followed by noun (§2a–b), מִי *whom?* 1 S 2415.15, אֱלֹהִים *God/god* Ex 3415.16 Dt 614 819 1128 133 2814 3116 Jg 212.17.19 1 K 112.4.10 Jr 76.9 1110 1310 1611 256 3515 1 C 525 11QT 213 ([אל[והיהמה), גִּלּוּל *idol* 1 K 2126 Ezk 69 2016.24 4410, שִׁקּוּץ *abomination* Ezk 2030, תֹּהוּ *formlessness* 1 S 1221, הֶבֶל *vanity* 2 K 1715 Jr 25, צַו *command* Ho 511(or em. שָׁוְא *vanity*) CD 419, דֶּרֶךְ *way* 4QBarka 16, אַחֲרֵי לֹא־יוֹעִלוּ they went *after what did not help* Jr 28.

אִישׁ *man* Gn 444 1 K 1314, אִשָּׁה *wife* Jg 1311, יְבָמָה *sister-in-law* Ru 115, אהב pi. ptc. *lover* Ho 27.15, אָב *father* Jos 246, בֵּן *son* Gn 355 Ex 148 1 C 102, נַעַר *lad* 1 S 2037.38, בָּחוּר *youth* Ru 310, מֶלֶךְ *king* Jr 528, מַלְאָךְ *messenger* 1 S 2542, עֶבֶד *servant* 2618, קצר ptc. *reaper* Jr 921 Ru 23.7, איב ptc. *enemy* Jos 1019, רצח ptc. *killer* Dt 196, בַּיִת *household* 1 K 1410 163 Ne 410.

עֵדֶר *herd* Gn 3220, בָּקָר *cattle* 1 S 115, כֶּלֶב *dog* 2415, פַּרְעֹשׁ *flea* 2415, מִשְׁכָּן *tabernacle* Nm 323, אֲרוֹן *ark* Jos 69.13, אֵפוֹד *ephod* 1 S 2110, מִטָּה *bier* 2 S 331, רֶכֶב *chariotry* Jg 416, מַחֲנֶה *camp* 416 2 K 714, גְּדוּד *troop* 1 S 308, גַּו *back* 1 K 149 Is 3817 (גֵּו) Ezk 2335 Ne 926 4QpHosa 1.24, בֶּצַע *bribery* 1 S 83 Ezk 3331.

Moses Ex 338, Joshua Jos 816, Zebah Jg 85, Abimelech Jg 949, Saul 1 S 117 134 1531 1713.14 249 1 C 102, David 1 S 2220 2325.28 2513 3021 2 S 171, Abner 219.24.25 326, Joab 2013, Sheba 202.7.10.13, Jeroboam 2 C 1319, Baasha 1 K 163, Ahab 2 K 925, Elijah 1 K 1920.21, Naaman 2 K 521, Cushite 2 S 1822, Molech Lv 205, בַּעַל *Baal(im)* Dt 43 Jg 833 1 K 1818 Jr 223 913, Ashtoreth 1 K 115, אֵל *God* CD 1930, Y. Dt 135=11QT 5413 Ho 1110 2 C 3431, Israel Jos 817.17 2 S 228 1816, Midian Jg 723, Philistines 1 S 1436.37 1753, גּוֹיִם *nations* 2 K 1715 Ezk 2330.

2c. of greater distance, **beyond,** הֵמָּה ... אַחֲרֵי דֶּרֶךְ *they are ... beyond the* west *road* Dt 1130 (+ מוּל *opposite,* אֵצֶל *alongside*), הִנֵּה אַחֲרֵי קִרְיַת יְעָרִים *behold, it is beyond Kiriath-jearim* Jg 1812.

3. perh. **junior to,** i.e. below in status (but spatial and temporal senses might also be valid), אַחֲרָיו שַׁמָּא *after him was Shammah* 2 S 2311, sim. 239(Qr)||1 C 1112 Ne 118 1 C 277.34, אָנֹכִי אַחֲרֶיךָ *I am behind you*, in terms of kinship proximity Ru 44, אחריהם ראשי הלויים *after them are the heads of the Levites* 1QM 22, sim. 23 4QMd6 ([ואחר]יהם רא[שי]).

4. behind, in support of, with verb, היה *be* Ex 232 2 S 210 1513 (subj. לֵב *heart*) 1 K 1220 1621.21, נטה *turn* intrans. Ex 232 Jg 93 1 K 228.28, מלא pi. *be wholehearted* in support of Y. Nm 1424 3211.12 Dt 136 Jos 148.9.14 1 K 116 Si 466.10, עזר *give help* to1 K 17, רעה *be a shepherd* in the service of, who follows (a master) Jr 1716, עור hi. *be active* in the service of, in following (Y.) CD 817(A), עוד hi. *testify* (against people) in following (Y.) 1930(B).

In nom. cl., עַם אֲשֶׁר אַחֲרֵי *people who were in support of* 2 S 179 1 K 1622.22, אַחֲרָיו כָּל־יִשְׁרֵי־לֵב *in support of it* (judgment) *are all the upright* Ps 9415 (or em. אַחֲרִית there is a *future*).

Followed by noun, Abimelech Jg 93, (House of) David 2 S 210 1 K 1220, Absalom 2 S 1513 179 1 K 228, Adonijah 17 228, Tibni 1621.22, Omri 1621.22, רַבִּים *(the) many* Ex 232.2.

5. in accordance with, with verb, תור *go, behave* Nm 1539.39 CD 311, הלך *go, behave* Jr 317 913 1612 1812 Si 52; preceding noun, לֵב *heart* Nm 1539 (לֵבָב) Si 52, עַיִן *eye* Nm 1539 Si 52, שְׁרִירוּת *stubbornness* Jr 317 913 1612 CD 311, מַחֲשָׁבָה *thought* Jr 1812.

6. because, seeing that, as conj. introducing verb in causal clause, ידע hi. *inform* Gn 4139; אַחֲרֵי אֲשֶׁר in same sense, עשׂה *do* Jg 1136, בוא *come* 1923 2 S 1931, נתן *give* 1 S 3023 (if em. אֵת object-marker appar. introducing subject of transitive verb).

7. מֵאַחֲרֵי from behind, (away) from (following), with verb, בוא *come* 2 C 1313, עלה *go up* 1 S 1446 2 S 202, ni. *depart* 227, תעה *stray* Ezk 1411, שׁוב *turn* intrans. Nm 1443 3215 Dt 2315 Jos 2216.18.23.29 1 S 1511 242 2 S 226.30 1115 1 K 96 1921 2233||2 C 1832 Jr 319 3240 (|| מֵעַל *away from*) Ru 116, hi. trans. 1 S 67 4QApocMos B 1.15 (להש[יבכה]), סור *turn* intrans. 1220 2 S 221.22 2 K 1029 186 Jb 3427 2 C 3433 Si 419 CD 165, hi. trans. Dt 74 11QT 5619, נטה *turn* intrans. 2 S 219, סוג ni. *turn* intrans. Zp 16 Si 4611 1QS 217, נזר ni. *be separated* Ezk 147, לקח *take* Am 715 1 C 177 (מִן־אַחֲרֵי; || 2 S 78 מֵאַחַר), זנה *prostitute oneself* Ho 12, ארב *lay ambush* Jos 82.4.14, נדח hi. *push* 2 K 1721(Qr).

Preceding noun, עִיר *city* Jos 84.14, צֹאן *sheep* Am 715 1 C 177, אָח *brother* 2 S 226.27, אֵל *God* Si 4611 1QS 217, Y. Nm 1443 Jos 2216.18.23.29 1 S 1220 2 K 1721 Ho 12 Zp 16 2 C 3433, David 2 S 202, Abner 219.30, Philistines 1 S 1446 242.

8. אַחֲרֵי as noun, **back parts, rear,** בְּאַחֲרֵי הַחֲנִית he struck him *with (the) back of the spear* 2 S 223 (or em. בְּאַחֲרֵי *with the back part*), מֵאַחֲרָיו the spear protruded *from his back* 2 S 223, אֶל־אַחֲרֵי go *to rear of* troops 523, charioteer 2 K 918.19, horses Zc 66 (or em.

אֶל־אֶרֶץ הַיָּם *to the west*), הַגִּזְרָה ... עַל־אַחֲרֶיהָ *the space ... at its* (the temple's) *back* Ezk 41$_{15}$ (or em. אַחֲרֶיהָ *its rear*).

Also 5QS5 4QMa fr. 1$_{5}$ (ואחר[י]) 17$_{2}$ (ואח[רי]) 6Q10 1.2$_{2}$ 4QFlor 2$_{4}$ 4QPentPara 3.2$_{6}$ Nimrud ivory inscr. 1$_{2}$ ([מא]חרי).

→ אחר *delay*.

אַחֲרַי 1 adv. **afterwards,** מוֹכִיחַ אָדָם אַחֲרַי חֵן יִמְצָא *one that reproves a person will afterwards find favour* Pr 28$_{23}$ (unless אַחֲרַי adj., person *that turns backward* or, perh. *responsible* person; ms אַחֲרָיו *with him* or *by it* [reproof]; or em. אַחֲרָיו and move to end of verse), אחרי הֶחֱזִיק *afterwards, he* (Hananiah, Malchijah) *strengthened* wall Ne 3$_{30(Kt).31(Kt)}$ (Qr אַחֲרָיו *after him*).

→ אחר *delay*.

אַחֲרִית 61.14.34 n.f. **end**—cstr. אַחֲרִית; sf. אַחֲרִיתִי, אַחֲרִיתוֹ, אַחֲרִיתֵךְ (אחריתכה Q), אַחֲרִיתְךָ (אַחֲרִיתֶךָ), אַחֲרִיתָהּ, אַחֲרִיתֵנוּ, אַחֲרִיתְכֶן, אַחֲרִיתָם, אַחֲרִיתָן.

1. in ref. to place, **end, edge,** אַחֲרִיתָהּ דַּרְכֵי־מָוֶת *its end is the ways of death* Pr 14$_{12}$=16$_{25}$ (or em. דַּרְכֵי to יַרְכְּתֵי *depths of*), אֶשְׁכְּנָה בְּאַחֲרִית יָם *I dwell at the end of the sea* Ps 139$_{9}$.

2. in ref. to time, consequence, **end, result, future,** <SUBJ> היה *be* Nm 23$_{10}$ (+ כְּ *as*) Pr 24$_{20}$ (+ לָרָע *to the evil one*) 29$_{21}$ (+ מָנוֹן perh. *rebellious*) Si 11$_{25}$ (+ עַל *upon*) 16$_{3}$ (+ לְ of possession, *to*), שׂגה *be great* Jb 8$_{7}$ (:: רֵאשִׁית *beginning*), ברך pu. *be blessed* Pr 20$_{21}$, באשׁ *be odious* Si 3$_{26}$.

<NOM CL> מָה אַחֲרִיתָם *what is their end?* Dt 32$_{20}$, sim. Dn 12$_{8}$ (or em. אַחֲוָיַת *declaration of*), זֶה ... אַחֲרִיתָם *this is ... their end* Ps 49$_{14}$ (if em. אַחֲרֵיהֶם *after them*), זה הוא אחרית הימים *this is the end of the days* 4QMMT B$_{24}$, כֵּן אַחֲרִית *such is the end of* Jb 8$_{13}$ Pr 1$_{19}$ (if in both em. אָרְחוֹת *paths of*), אַחֲרִיתָהּ מָרָה כַלַּעֲנָה *her end is bitter as wormwood* Pr 5$_{4}$, וְאַחֲרִיתָהּ שִׂמְחָה תוּגָה *and as for its end, joy is grief* Pr 14$_{13}$ (or em. וְאַחֲרִית הַשִּׂמְחָה *the end of joy* is grief), יֵשׁ אַחֲרִית *there is a future* 23$_{18}$ 24$_{14}$ (both || תִּקְוָה *hope*), אַחֲרִית לְכָל־יִשְׁרֵי־לֵב *there is a future to all the upright of heart* Ps 94$_{15}$ (if em. אַחֲרָיו כָּל־ *all* are *in support of it*), טוֹב אַחֲרִית דָּבָר מֵרֵאשִׁיתוֹ *better is the end of a matter than its beginning* Ec 7$_{8}$, אַחֲרִית פִּיהוּ הוֹלֵלוּת *the end of his speech is madness* 10$_{13}$, אַחֲרִיתוֹ עֲדֵי אֹבֵד *his end is to destruction* Nm 24$_{20}$, אַחֲרִיתָם אֶל־הַמֵּתִים *their end is (to go) to the dead* Ec 9$_{3}$ (if em. אַחֲרָיו *after it*).

<OBJ> ידע *know* Is 41$_{22}$ Si 12$_{11}$, זכר *remember* Is 47$_{7}$ Lm 1$_{9}$ Si 7$_{36}$ 38$_{20(B)}$ (Bmg נכר hi. *regard*), נגד hi. *tell* Is 46$_{10}$ (+ מֵרֵאשִׁית *from the beginning*, אֲשֶׁר לֹא־נַעֲשׂוּ *what is not yet done*), ראה *see* Jr 12$_{4}$ (or em. אָרְחוֹתֵנוּ *our path*), חזה *see* Si 48$_{24}$, נתן *give* Jr 29$_{11}$ (|| תִּקְוָה *hope*), שׂים *set* Am 8$_{10}$, ברך pi. *bless* Jb 42$_{12}$ (+ מֵרֵאשִׁתוֹ *more than his beginning*).

<CSTR> אַחֲרִית דָּבָר *end of a matter* Ec 7$_{8}$, פִּיהוּ *of his speech* 10$_{13}$, שָׁנָה *of a year* Dt 11$_{12}$ (mss, Sam הַשָּׁנָה; :: רֵשִׁית *beginning*), הקץ *of endtime* 4QpNah 3.3$_{3}$ 4QpPsb 1$_{5}$ (הק[ץ]), העת *of time*, i.e. the end time 4QMMT B$_{15}$ (אחר[י]ת [העת]) 4QMMT B$_{33}$, אִיּוֹב *of Job* Jb 42$_{12}$, הַזָּעַם *of the indignation* Dn 8$_{19}$, מַלְכוּתָם *of their reign* 8$_{23}$, קנאה *of jealousy* Si 12$_{11}$, אדם *of a person* Si 11$_{25}$, כָּל־שֹׁכְחֵי אֵל *of all who forget God* Jb 8$_{13}$ (if em.; see Nom. Cl.; :: תִּקְוָה *hope*), כָּל־בֹּצֵעַ בָּצַע *of everyone who makes gain by violence* Pr 1$_{19}$ (if em.; see Nom. Cl.).

אַחֲרִית הַיָּמִים *the end of the days*, i.e. the latter days, the future Gn 49$_{1}$ Nm 24$_{14}$ Dt 4$_{30}$ 31$_{29}$ Is 2$_{2}$||Mc 4$_{1}$ Jr 23$_{20}$ 30$_{24}$ 48$_{47}$ 49$_{39}$ Ezk 38$_{16}$ Ho 3$_{5}$ Dn 10$_{14}$ 1QSa 1$_{1}$ 4QDibHama 1.3$_{13}$ 4QPrFêtesc 7$_{5}$ CD 4$_{4}$ 6$_{11}$ 4QpIsaa 5$_{9}$ 8$_{17(Horgan)}$ (אח[רית הימים]) 4QpIsab 1.2$_{1}$ 4QpIsac 4.2$_{14}$ (Allegro) ([ה]ימים]) 13$_{3(Allegro)}$ (אחר[י]ת) 23.2$_{10}$ 4QpIsad 1$_{7(Allegro)}$ ([א]חרית הימים]) 11QMelch 1$_{4}$ 1QpHab 2$_{5}$ 9$_{6}$ 4QpNah 3.2$_{2}$ 4QFlor 1$_{2.12}$ (both [א]חרית) 1$_{15}$ ([ה]ימים) 1$_{19}$ 4QCata 1$_{5}$ ([ה]ימ[י]ם) 1$_{7(Allegro)}$ ([ה]ימים) 7$_{11}$ ([א]חרית) 9$_{2(Allegro)}$ (באחרי[ת הימים]) 12.1$_{2}$ ([ה]ימים) 4QCatb 1$_{1}$ ([א]חרית הימים) 2$_{1}$ ([ה]ימים) 4Q178 3$_{4}$ (אח[רית הימ]ם) 4QpGena 4$_{2}$ 4QMMT B$_{13.24}$.

אַחֲרִית הַשָּׁנִים *the end of the years*, i.e. the latter years Ezk 38$_{8}$.

<ADJ> אחרית טובה *a good future* Si 16$_{3}$.

<PREP> לְ *concerning* 4QpIsad 1$_{7(Allegro)}$ ([לא]חרית), + כתב pass. *be written* 4QFlor 1$_{15}$, פשר הדבר לאחרית הימים *the interpretation of the matter concerning the latter days* 4QpIsab 1.2$_{1}$ 4QpIsac 4.2$_{14(Allegro)}$ 23.2$_{10}$, sim. 4QpIsaa 5$_{9(Horgan)}$ (פשר ה[פתגם]), *in, at* 4QpIsac

13$_3$ (Allegro) ([לאחר]ית) 4QpPs^b 1$_5$ 4QCat^a 12.1$_2$ 4QCat^b 2$_1$, + בגד *be treacherous* 1QpHab 2$_5$, נתן ni. *be given* 1QpHab 9$_6$, דרשׁ *seek* smooth things 4QpNah 3.2$_2$, עשׂה *do* Jr 5$_{31}$, בין לְ *discern* Dt 32$_{29}$ Ps 73$_{17}$.

בְּ *in, at* 4QFlor 1$_{2.12}$ (both [בא]חרית) 4QCat^a 1$_{5.7}$ 7$_{11}$ ([בא]חרית) 9$_2$ (Allegro) (באחרי[ת]) 4QFlor 1$_{19}$ 4QPrFêtes^c 7$_5$ 4QMMT B$_{15}$ ([באחרי]ת), הסרך לכל עדת ישראל באחרית הימים *the rule for all the congregation of Israel in the latter days* 1QSa 1$_1$, + היה *be* Is 2$_2$‖Mc 4$_1$ Jr 17$_{11}$ 49$_{39}$ Ezk 38$_{16}$ Dn 8$_{19}$, קרא *befall* Gn 49$_1$ Dt 31$_{29}$, קרה *occur* Dn 10$_{14}$, קרא ni. *be proclaimed* 11QMelch 1$_4$ (Milik) ([ותקרא ב]אחרית הימים), גלה ni. *be uncovered* 4QpNah 3.3$_3$, בוא *come* Ezk 38$_8$ 4QMMT B$_{13}$ ([יבו]א), עשׂה *do* Nm 24$_{14}$ Pr 25$_8$, שׁלח *send* evil 4QDibHam^a 1.3$_{13}$ ([ש]לחתה), מחה *wipe out* 4QpGen^a 4$_2$, יטב hi. *do good* Dt 8$_{16}$, שׁוב *restore* fortunes Jr 48$_{47}$, שׂמח *rejoice* 4QMMT B$_{33}$, נהם *groan* Pr 5$_{11}$, חכם *be wise* 19$_{20}$ (or em. בְּאָרְחֹתֶיךָ *in your paths*), בין htpol. *understand* Jr 23$_{20}$ 30$_{24}$, עמד *arise* Dn 8$_{23}$ CD 4$_4$ 6$_{11}$ 4QpIsa^a 8$_{17}$ (Allegro) ([באח]רית), נשׂג hi. *attain to* Si 34$_{22}$, נכר ni. *be recognized* 11$_{28}$, מצא *find* Dt 4$_{30}$ Si 34$_{22}$, אשׁר pu. *be called blessed* 11$_{27}$, פחד *fear* Ho 3$_5$, שׁמר בְּ ni. *be watchful concerning* Si 35$_{22}$ (B), זהר בְּ ni. *take heed concerning* Si 35$_{22}$ (Bmg, E, F).

עַד *until* Dt 11$_{12}$.

<COLL> אַחֲרִיתוֹ כְּנָחָשׁ יִשָּׁךְ *its end (is that) it* (wine) *bites as a snake* Pr 23$_{32}$, אחריתכה תנחל שמחה *as your end you will inherit joy* 4Q416 10.2$_8$.

3. in ref. to position, status, **last,** הִנֵּה אַחֲרִית גּוֹיִם מִדְבָּר צִיָּה וַעֲרָבָה *behold the last of nations, a desert, dry land and steppe* Jr 50$_{12}$ (or ins. הִיא *she [shall be]* after הִנֵּה).

4. in ref. to persons, **a. descendants, posterity, <SUBJ>** היה *be* Ps 109$_{13}$ (+ לְהַכְרִית *to cut off*), כרת ni. *be cut off* 37$_{38}$. **<NOM CL>** אַחֲרִית לְאִישׁ שָׁלוֹם *there is posterity for a peaceful person* Ps 37$_{37}$. **<OBJ>** כרת hi. *cut off* Ps 109$_{13}$. **<CSTR>** אחרית זדון *posterity of insolence* Si 16$_{3.3}$, רְשָׁעִים *of the wicked* Ps 37$_{38}$. **<PREP>** יֵשׁ־תִּקְוָה לְאַחֲרִיתֵךְ *there is hope for your posterity* Jr 31$_{17}$, לֹא לְאַחֲרִיתוֹ *not for his posterity* Dn 11$_4$; [טו]ב ... מן *better ... than* Si 16$_{3.3}$.

4b. remnant, <SUBJ> נפל *fall* Ezk 23$_{25}$, אכל ni. *be consumed* 23$_{15}$. **<OBJ>** הרג *kill* Am 9$_1$, נשׂא pi. *take* 4$_2$.

Also 1QpMic 6$_2$ 4QpHos^a 1$_{11}$ (Horgan) ([אח]רית) 4QpIsa^c 13$_4$ 4QFlor 14$_2$ (לאחרית) 4QCat^a 12.2$_3$ (ל[א]חרית) 5Q16 3$_5$.

<SYN> תִּקְוָה *hope.*

<ANT> רֵאשִׁית *beginning.*

→ אחר *delay.*

אַחֹרַנִּית 7 adv. **backwards,** with verb, הלך *go* Gn 9$_{23}$, נפל *fall* 1 S 4$_{18}$, סבב hi. *turn* trans. 1 K 18$_{37}$, שׁוב *turn* intrans. 2 K 20$_{10}$, hi. *turn* trans. 20$_{11}$ Is 38$_8$; in nom. cl., פְּנֵיהֶם אֲחֹרַנִּית *their faces were backwards,* i.e. turned the other way Gn 9$_{23}$.

→ אחר *remain behind, delay.*

[אֲחַשְׁדַּרְפָּן] 4 n.m. **satrap**—pl. אֲחַשְׁדַּרְפְּנִים; cstr. אֲחַשְׁדַּרְפְּנֵי—**<SUBJ>** נשׂא pi. *help* Est 9$_3$ (‖ שַׂר *prince,* פֶּחָה *governor,* עשׂה ptc. *one who does* work for king) Ezr 8$_{36}$ (‖ פֶּחָה). **<CSTR>** אֲחַשְׁדַּרְפְּנֵי הַמֶּלֶךְ *satraps of the king* Est 3$_{12}$ (אֲחַשְׁדַּרְפְּנֵי־ ‖ פֶּחָה, שַׂר) Ezr 8$_{36}$. **<PREP>** נתן לְ *give to* Ezr 8$_{36}$; כתב אֶל pass. *be written to* Est 3$_{12}$ 8$_9$ (‖ יְהוּדִי *Jew,* שַׂר, פֶּחָה); נפל עַל *fall upon* (of fear) Est 9$_3$.

<SYN> שַׂר *prince,* פֶּחָה *governor.*

אֲחַשְׁוֵרוֹשׁ 31 pr.n.m. **Ahasuerus**—אֲחַשְׁוֵרֹשׁ, L אֲחַשְׁוֵרוֹשׁ, Kt אחשרש—Persian king Xerxes, Est 1$_{1.1}$ (mss omit) 1$_{2+6t}$ 2$_{1.12.16.21}$ 3$_{1.6.7.8.12}$ 6$_2$ 7$_5$ 8$_{1.7.10.12}$ 9$_2$ (L אֲחַשְׁרֹשׁ; mss אֲחַשְׁוֵרוֹשׁ) 9$_{20.30}$ 10$_1$(Qr) (Kt אחשרש) Dn 9$_1$ Ezr 4$_6$.

אֲחַשְׁוֵרֹשׁ, see אֲחַשְׁוֵרוֹשׁ.

אֲחַשְׁתָּרִי 1 pr.n.m. **Ahashtari,** son of Naarah and Ashhur, descendant of Judah, 1 C 4$_6$ (הָאֲחַשְׁתָּרִי perh. *Haahashtari* or *the Ahashtarite,* as gent.).

→ אֲחַשְׁתְּרָן *royal.*

[אֲחַשְׁתְּרָן] 2 adj. **royal**—pl. רֹכְבֵי הָרֶכֶשׁ—אֲחַשְׁתְּרָנִים הָאֲחַשְׁתְּרָנִים appar. *riders of the royal steeds* Est 8$_{10.14}$.

→ אֲחַשְׁתָּרִי *Ahashtari.*

אחתמלך 0.0.0.1 pr.n.f. **Ahathmelech,** wife of Joshua, Seal 63_{1}.
→ אָחוֹת *sister* + מֶלֶךְ *king*.

אַט 5 n.[m.] **gentleness**—Q אוט; sf. אִטִּי—**a.** with prep., לְאַט *according to,* or *with, gentleness,* i.e. gently, + הלך *go* (of waters of Shiloah) Is 8_{6}, נהל htp. *travel by stages* (of Jacob) Gn 33_{14} (לְאִטִּי lit. *according to my gentleness;* + לְרֶגֶל *at the leg,* i.e. pace, *of*); without verb, לְאַט־לִי לַנַּעַר (*deal*) *gently, for my sake, with the lad* 2 S 18_{5}, דָּבָר לְאַט עִמָּךְ *a word (spoken) gently with you* Jb 15_{11} (לָאַט; + מְעַט *little*).

b. without prep. (but in same sense), + הלך pi. *wander* (of Ahab) 1 K 21_{27} (mss htp. in same sense), perh. אכל hi. *feed* (of Y.) Ho 11_{4} (but prob. וָאֵט = *and I turned,* from נטה).

Also perh. 4Q424 1_{6}.

אָטָד 4 n.m. **bramble,** perh. *lycæum europæum,* singular or collective (Ps 58_{10}), **<SUBJ>** אמר *say* Jg 9_{15}, הלך *go* 9_{14}, מלך *rule* 9_{14}. **<OBJ>** משׁח *anoint* Jg 9_{15}, בין *understand,* i.e. be aware of (of boiling pot) Ps 58_{10}. **<PREP>** אמר אֶל *say to* Jg 9_{14}; יצא מִן *go out,* i.e. spread (of fire), *from* 9_{15}.
→ גֹּרֶן הָאָטָד *Goren-haatad.*

[אֵטוּן] 1 n.[m.] **linen**—cstr. חֲטֻבוֹת אֵטוּן מִצְרָיִם—אֵטוּן *quilts (made of) thread of,* i.e. from, *Egypt* Pr 7_{16} (or em. הִטִּיתִי *I have stretched out* linen).

[אִטִּי] 1 n.m. **ghost**—pl. אִטִּים (sg. perh. אַט or אֵט)—וְדָרְשׁוּ ... אֶל־הָאִטִּים *and they will inquire of ... the ghosts* Is 19_{3} (‖ אֱלִיל *idol,* אוֹב *ghost,* יִדְּעֹנִי *familiar spirit*).

אטם 9.0.1 vb. **block**—**Qal** Ptc. אֹטֵם, אֹטְמִים (Q אטומים), אֹטְמוֹת—**a. block, shut, <SUBJ>** בְּאֵר *pit* Ps 69_{16} (if em. אטר *shut*); subj. not specified, Is 33_{15} Pr 17_{28} 21_{13}. **<OBJ>** שָׂפָה *lip* Pr 17_{28}, פֶּה *mouth* of pit Ps 69_{16} (if em.), אֹזֶן *ear* Is 33_{15} (‖ נער *shake* hands, עצם *shut* eyes) Pr 21_{13}. **<PREP>** מִזַּעֲקַת־דָּל *from (the) cry of the poor* Pr 21_{13}, מִשְּׁמֹעַ דָּמִים *from hearing (about) bloodshed* Is 33_{15}; עָלַי *over* me Ps 69_{16} (if em.).

b. pass. ptc., perh. **be recessed, <SUBJ>** חַלּוֹן *window* 1 K 6_{4} Ezk 40_{16} $41_{16.26}$ 11QT 33_{11}. **<PREP>** אֶל־הַתָּאִים וְאֶל אֵלֵיהֵמָה *towards the chambers and their pillars* Ezk 40_{16}.

Hi. Impf. יַאְטֵם—**block, <SUBJ>** פֶּתֶן deaf *adder* Ps 58_{5} (or em. יֶאְטַם, Qal). **<OBJ>** אֹזֶן *ear* Ps 58_{5} (or em.).

אטר 1 vb. **shut**—**Qal** Impf. תֶּאְטַר—**shut,** אַל־תֶּאְטַר־עָלַי בְּאֵר פִּיהָ *may not (the) pit shut its mouth over me* Ps 69_{16} (or em. תֶּאְטַם/תַּאְטֵם in same sense).
→ אִטֵּר *shut,* אָטֵר *Ater.*

אָטֵר 5 pr.n.m. **Ater, 1.** returning exile and signatory to Nehemiah's pledge, Ezr 2_{16}‖Ne 7_{21} Ne 10_{18}. **2.** ancestor of gatekeepers returning from exile, Ezr 2_{42}‖Ne 7_{45}.
→ אטר *shut.*

אִטֵּר 2 adj. **shut,** אִישׁ ... אִטֵּר יַד־יְמִינוֹ *man ... shut in respect of his right hand* Jg 3_{15} 20_{16}, i.e. left-handed or perh. ambidextrous, of Benjaminites (lit. *sons of the right hand;* see 1 C 12_{2} ... נֹשְׁקֵי קֶשֶׁת מַיְמִינִים וּמַשְׂמִאלִים מִבִּנְיָמִן *ones equipped with a bow, capable with right hand and left hand, ... from Benjamin*).
→ אטר *shut.*

אֵי 41.1 interrog. adv. **where?**—sf. אַיֵּכָה, אַיּוֹ, אַיָּם—**1.** with verb, **where?,** אֵי לָזֹאת אֶסְלַח־לָךְ *where,* i.e. how, *might I forgive you for this?* Jr $5_{7(\text{Qr})}$.

2. in nom. cl., **where is?, a.** with noun, אֱלֹהִים *gods* Dt 32_{37} (Sam אַיֵּה *where?*), הֶבֶל *Abel* Gn 4_{9}, אָח *brother* 4_{9}, חֲנִית *spear* 1 S 26_{16} (+ ראה *see* where), צַפַּחַת *jar* 26_{16} (if em. אֶת־ appar. introducing subject/predicate of nom. cl.), שֵׁכָר *beer* Pr $31_{4(\text{Qr})}$ (Kt אוֹ *or;* or em. אַוֵּה/אַוּוֹ *to desire* or רָאוֹ/רָווֹ *to drink heavily*).

b. with pronom. sf., אַיּוֹ *where is he?* Ex 2_{20} (+ לָמָּה *why?*) 2 K 19_{13} (ms and ‖Is 37_{13} אַיֵּה *where is?;* + מֶלֶךְ *king*) Jr $37_{19(\text{Kt})}$ (Qr אַיֵּה *where are?;* + נְבִיאֵיכֶם *your prophets*) Mc 7_{10} (or em. אַיֵּה *where is?;* + יי *Y.*) Jb 14_{10} (ms וְאֵין *and there is not,* i.e. he no longer exists) 20_{7}; אַיָּם *where are they?* Is 19_{12} (+ חָכָם *wise one*) Na 3_{17} (or em. אֵיכָה *how?* or אוֹי מָה *woe!, why* have they slept?);

אַיֶּכָּה *where are you?* Gn 3$_9$.

3. אֵי־זֶה **whither?, in which direction?, a.** with verb, אֵי־זֶה עָבַר רוּחַ־י׳ מֵאִתִּי *in which direction did the spirit of Y. pass from me?* 1 K 22$_{24}$ (ms and ||2 C 18$_{23}$ אֵי זֶה הַדֶּרֶךְ *where is the way?*).

b. in nom. cl., **where is?**, with (pro)noun, בַּיִת *house* 1 S 9$_{18}$ (+ נגד hi. *tell* me) Is 66$_1$, מָקוֹם *place* 66$_1$ Jb 28$_{12.20}$ (both אֵי זֶה; + מֵאַיִן *whence?*) 38$_{19}$, דֶּרֶךְ *way* 1 K 13$_{12}$ 2 C 18$_{23}$||1 K 22$_{24(ms)}$ (2 C אֵי זֶה) 2 K 3$_8$ Jr 6$_{16}$ Jb 38$_{19.24}$, סֵפֶר *document* Is 50$_1$ (אֵי זֶה), הוּא *he* Est 7$_5$ (+ מִי *who?*).

4. אֵי־זֶה **what?, which?, a.** with verb, אֵינְךָ יוֹדֵעַ אֵי זֶה יִכְשַׁר הֲזֶה אוֹ־זֶה *you do not know which will prosper—this one or this one* Ec 11$_{6(L)}$. **b.** in nom. cl., עַד אֲשֶׁר־אֶרְאֶה אֵי־זֶה טוֹב *until I might see what is good* Ec 2$_3$. **c.** בְּאֵיזֶה **by which?**, באיזה ד[רך תבקשנו] *by which way will you seek him?* Si 30$_{40(Segal)}$.

5. אֵי־מִזֶּה **whence?, a.** with verb, בוא *come* Gn 16$_8$ (+ אָנָה *whither*) 2 S 1$_3$ Jb 2$_2$ (both אֵי מִזֶּה). **b.** in nom. cl., with pronoun, אַתָּה *you* 1 S 30$_{13}$ (+ לְמִי *to whom?*) 2 S 1$_{13}$ (both אֵי מִזֶּה), הוּא *he* Jg 13$_6$ (+ שׁאל *ask* him), הֵמָּה *they* 1 S 25$_{11}$ (אֵי מִזֶּה; + ידע *know*).

6. אֵי־מִזֶּה **from which?**, אֵי־מִזֶּה עִיר אַתָּה *from which town are you?* 2 S 15$_2$, אֵי־מִזֶּה עַם אָתָּה *from which people are you?* Jon 1$_8$.

→ אֵיפֹה *where?*

אִי I $_{36.1.2}$ n.m. (sometimes f.) **island**—cstr. אִי; pl. אִיִּים (אִיִּן, Q אים); cstr. אִיֵּי—**1. island. 2. coast, coastland,** e.g. Is 20$_6$ 23$_{2.6}$ Jr 25$_{22}$ Ezk 27$_{35}$ 39$_6$ Ps 72$_{10}$, distinction from §1 not alw. clear (perh. אִי = *dry land*, i.e. island or coast).

<SUBJ> שׂמח *rejoice* Ps 97$_1$ (+ אֶרֶץ *land*), שׁיר *sing* Is 42$_{10}$ (+ יוֹרְדֵי הַיָּם וּמְלֹאוֹ *those who go down [to] the sea and its fulness*), ראה *see* 41$_5$ 66$_{19}$ (1QIsa^a אים), שׁמע *hear* Is 49$_1$ (|| לְאֹם *people*) 66$_{19}$, חרשׁ hi. *listen* 41$_1$ (+ לְאֻמִּים), יחל pi. *wait* 42$_4$ 51$_5$, קוה pi. *wait* 51$_5$ 60$_9$ (or em. כְּלֵי אִיִּים יִקָּווּ *the vessels of the islands are gathered;* + אֳנִיּוֹת תַּרְשִׁישׁ *ships of Tarshish*), ירא *fear* 41$_5$ (+ קְצוֹת הָאָרֶץ *ends of the earth*), חרד *fear* Ezk 26$_{18}$, בהל ni. *be dismayed* 26$_{18}$ (הָאִיִּן; mss הָאִיִּים), רעשׁ *shake* 26$_{15}$, שׁחה htpal. *bow down* Zp 2$_{11}$, פרד ni. *be spread out* Gn 10$_5$, נטל ni. *be lifted up*, i.e. be weighed Is 40$_{15}$ (if em. יִטּוֹל *he has raised* to יִטְּלוּ), ישׁב *dwell (in)* 42$_{10}$ (see also Cstr.).

<NOM CL> אִיִּים רַבִּים סְחֹרַת יָדֵךְ *many islands are the merchandise of your hand*, i.e. trade under your control Ezk 27$_{15}$ (+ בְּנֵי דְדָן *children of Dedan*), הָאִיִּים אֲשֶׁר־בַּיָּם *the islands that are in the sea* 26$_{18}$, הָאִי אֲשֶׁר בְּעֵבֶר הַיָּם *the coast that is across the sea* Jr 25$_{22}$ (+ צֹר *Tyre*, etc.).

<OBJ> נטה hi. *spread out* Si 43$_{23(B)}$ (+ בתהום *in the ocean*), נטל *lift* Is 40$_{15}$ (or em. יִטְּלוּ *are weighed;* + כַּדַּק *as the dust;* + גּוֹי *nation*), לכד *seize* Dn 11$_{18}$, עבר *cross (to)* Jr 2$_{10}$.

<CSTR> אִי כַפְתּוֹר *island of Caphtor* Jr 47$_4$ (2QJer איי *islands of;* + פְּלִשְׁתִּים *Philistines*), אִיֵּי אֱלִישָׁה *islands of Elishah* Ezk 27$_7$, כִּתִּיִּים *of (the) Kittim* Jr 2$_{10}$ Ezk 27$_{6(Qr)}$ (Kt כתים), הַיָּם *of the sea* Is 11$_{11}$ (+ אַשּׁוּר *Assyria*, etc.) 24$_{15}$ (if em. בָּאֻרִים *in the east*) 24$_{15}$ Est 10$_1$ (+ אֶרֶץ *land*) 1QpHab 3$_{11}$, הַגּוֹיִם *of the nations* Gn 10$_5$ Zp 2$_{11}$.

שְׁאֵרִית אִי *remnant of the island of* Jr 47$_4$ (2QJer איי *of the islands of*), יֹשֵׁב הָאִי *dweller(s) of*, i.e. in, *the coastland* Is 20$_6$, יֹשְׁבֵי אִי *dwellers of*, i.e. in, *(the) coastland* 23$_{2.6}$ (both + צֹר *Tyre*, צִידוֹן *Sidon*, etc.), יֹשְׁבֵי הָאִיִּים *dwellers of*, i.e. in, *the islands* Ezk 27$_{35}$ 39$_6$.

מַלְכֵי הָאִי *kings of the island* Jr 25$_{22}$, מַלְכֵי תַרְשִׁישׁ וְאִיִּים *kings of Tarshish and (the) islands* Ps 72$_{10}$, כְּלֵי אִיִּים *vessels of (the) islands* Is 60$_9$ (if em. כִּי־לִי *for* islands wait *for me*), כֹּל אִיֵּי *all the islands of* Zp 2$_{11}$.

<APP> אִיֵּי הַגּוֹיִם ... אִישׁ *islands of the nations ..., each one* Gn 10$_5$ (unless ins. אֵלֶּה בְּנֵי יֶפֶת *these arethe sons of Japheth* after הַגּוֹיִם), sim. Zp 2$_{11}$, ממרחק ... מאיי הים *from afar ..., from the islands of the sea* 1QpHab 3$_{11}$.

<ADJ> הָאִי הַזֶּה *this coast* Is 20$_6$, הָאִיִּים הָרְחֹקִים *the distant islands* 66$_{19}$, אִיִּים רַבִּים *many islands* Ps 97$_1$ Ezk 27$_{3.15}$ Dn 11$_{18}$ (elliptical).

<PREP> לְ of direction, *to*, + שׁוב hi. *turn* face Dn 11$_{18}$, שׁלם pi. *repay* recompense Is 59$_{18}$ (+ איב ptc. *enemy*, צַר *adversary*), וְשַׂמְתִּי נְהָרוֹת לָאִיִּים *and I shall turn rivers into (the) islands* Is 42$_{15}$ (or em. לְצִיּוֹת *into dry places* or תַּלְאֻבִים *[into areas of] drought*).

בְּ of place, *in, among*, + כבד pi. *honour* name of Y. Is 24$_{15}$, Y. 24$_{15}$ (if em. בָּאֻרִים *in the east*; perh. also em. עַל־כֵּן *therefore* to עָלְזוּ *rejoice* among the islands), + נגד

hi. *tell* 42$_{12}$ Jr 31$_{10}$ (+ מִמֶּרְחָק *from afar*; + גּוֹי *nation*).

מִן of direction, *from* Ezk 27$_{6.7}$, + בוא *come* 1QpHab 3$_{11}$, קנה *acquire* Is 11$_{11}$; רכל אֶל *trade with* Ezk 27$_{3}$; שׂים עַל *place*, i.e. impose, tribute *upon* Est 10$_{1}$.

Also 4QBer^a 2$_4$.

[אִי] II $_3$ n.m. **jackal**—pl. אִיִּים—jackal or similar animal, <SUBJ> ענו *dwell* Is 13$_{22}$ (+ בְּאַלְמְנוֹתָיו [L] *among his widows* [or em. בְּאַרְמְנוֹתֶיהָ *in her fortifications*]; + אֹחַ *owl*, צִי *wild beast*, בַּת־יַעֲנָה *ostrich*, שָׂעִיר *satyr*, תַּן *jackal*). <OBJ> פגשׁ *meet* Is 34$_{14}$ (1QIsa^a אייאמים [perh. conflation of אִי and אֵימָה *terror*]; + צִי, שָׂעִיר), בהל pi. *terrify* 4QShir^a 1$_5$ (ל[בהל]). <APP> כול רוחי מלאכי חבל ורוחות ממזרים שד אים *all spirits of the angels of destruction and the spirits of incestuous issue: demons, jackals* 4QShir^a 1$_5$ (or שדאים = שֵׁדִים *demons*; + לילית אחים *Lilith, owls*). <PREP> ישׁב אֶת *dwell with* Jr 50$_{39}$ (+ צִי, בַּת־יַעֲנָה).

אִי III $_1$ adv. **not**, יְמַלֵּט אִי־נָקִי *he will deliver (one that is) not innocent* Jb 22$_{30}$ (or em. אֶת־ object-marker or אִישׁ־ innocent *man* or אֱלֹהִים *God* delivers an innocent one), יבכר י׳ אי דבר אשר לא ידעתה perh. *may Y. cause to be early no matter that you do not know* Lachish ost. 2$_6$ (others א[דנ]י *[for] my lord* and/or יעכר *may he discomfit* for יבכר).

אִי IV $_2$ interj. **alas**—אִילוֹ, Q אילי—אִילוֹ הָאֶחָד שֶׁיִּפּוֹל וְאֵין שֵׁנִי לַהֲקִימוֹ *but alas for him, the (solitary) one, who falls and with no partner to help him up* Ec 4$_{10}$ (mss אִי לוֹ in same sense; or em. אִילוּ *if*), אִי־לָךְ אֶרֶץ שֶׁמַּלְכֵּךְ נָעַר *alas for you, O land whose king is a lad* 10$_{16}$ (:: אַשְׁרֵי *happy*), אילי כי נדמיתי *alas for me, for I am destroyed* 1QIsa^a 6$_5$ (MT אוֹי־לִי in same sense).

איב 28$_{3.5.50}$ vb. **be an enemy—Qal** + waw וְאָיַבְתִּי; ptc. masc. אוֹיֵב (אֹיֵב); sf. אֹיְבִי, אוֹיִבְךָ (אֹיִבְךָ, אֹיִבְךָ), אֹיִבֵךְ, אוֹיְבֵנוּ, אֹיְבוֹ; pl. אוֹיְבִים (אֹיְבִים); cstr. אוֹיְבֵי (אֹיְבֵי); sf. אוֹיְבַי (אוֹיְבַי, אֹיְבַי), אוֹיְבֶיךָ (אֹיְבֶיךָ, Q איביכה), אֹיְבַיִךְ, אֹיְבֵיכֶם, אוֹיְבֵינוּ (אֹיְבֵינוּ), אוֹיְבָיו (אֹיְבָיו), אֹיְבֶיהָ, (אֹיְבֶיהָ) אוֹיְבֵיהֶם (אֹיְבֵיהֶם, Q אויביהמה); ptc. fem. sf. אֹיַבְתִּי—**1. be an enemy to, be at enmity with,** וְאָיַבְתִּי אֶת־אֹיְבֶיךָ וְצַרְתִּי אֶת־צֹרְרֶיךָ *and I* (Y.) *shall be an enemy to your enemies and an adversary to your adversaries* Ex 23$_{22}$, וַיְהִי שָׁאוּל אֹיֵב אֶת־דָּוִד כָּל־הַיָּמִים *and Saul was an enemy to David all the time* 1 S 18$_{29}$.

2. ptc. אוֹיֵב as a noun, **enemy, a.** usu. collective **enemy of Israel** (including Jerusalem, etc.), foreign nation or army, or groups in foreign nations (e.g. Est 8$_{13}$ 9$_{1.5.16.22}$ Ne 4$_9$ 6$_1$; for individual enemies, see §2g); e.g. Jg 2$_{18}$ (|| לחץ ptc. *oppressor*, דחק ptc. *oppressor*) Is 62$_8$ (+ בְּנֵי־נֵכָר *foreigners*) Zp 3$_{15}$ (|| מִשְׁפָּט *judgment*; or שׁפט po. ptc. *one who condemns*, if em. מְשֹׁפְטַיִךְ to מִשְׁפָּטַיִךְ) Ps 74$_{18}$ (+ עַם נָבָל *an ignoble people*) 80$_7$ (|| שָׁכֵן *neighbour*) Lm 1$_2$ (:: רֵעַ *friend*) Ne 6$_{16}$ (|| גּוֹי foreign *nation*) Si 46$_1$ (:: יִשְׂרָאֵל *Israel*) 1QM 12$_{11}$ (|| חָלָל *slain one*), אוֹיְבֵי יִשְׂרָאֵל *enemies of Israel* 2 C 20$_{29}$, אֹיְבֵי הַיְּהוּדִים *enemies of the Jews* Est 9$_1$, הַגּוֹיִם אוֹיְבֵינוּ *the nations, our enemies* Ne 5$_9$; עַמִּי לְאוֹיֵב יְקוֹמֵם *my people arises as an enemy* Mc 2$_8$, אֶת־אוֹיְבֵיהֶם כִּסָּה הַיָּם *the sea covered their enemies* Ps 78$_{53}$.

2b. enemy of the king, or other leader, Jg 11$_{36}$ (enemies of Jephthah) 1 S 14$_{47}$ 2 S 5$_{20}$||1 C 14$_{11}$ 2 S 7$_{1.9.11}$ 22$_{1.4.18.38.41.49}$||Ps 18$_{1.4.18.38.41.49}$ (|| קום ptc. *opponent*; + אִישׁ חֲמָסִים *violent man*) 1 K 3$_{11}$ Ps 61$_4$ 72$_9$ (|| צִי *wild beast*; or צַר *adversary*, if em. צִיִּים to צָרִים or צָרָיו) 89$_{23}$ (+ בֶּן־עַוְלָה *wicked man*) 89$_{43}$ 110$_2$ 1 C 17$_{10}$ 21$_{12}$ (:: י׳ Y.) 22$_9$ 4Q385 2$_3$, אוֹיְבֵי הַמֶּלֶךְ *enemies of the king* 1 S 18$_{25}$ Ps 45$_6$, אוֹיְבֵי דָוִד *David's enemies* 1 S 20$_{15.16}$ 25$_{22}$, sim. 19$_{17}$ 25$_{29}$ 26$_8$ 2 S 4$_8$ 18$_{19}$, שָׁאוּל אֹיִבְךָ *Saul, your enemy* 4$_8$, תִּמְצָא יָדְךָ לְכָל־אֹיְבֶיךָ *your hand will reach all your enemies* Ps 21$_9$, עַד־אָשִׁית אֹיְבֶיךָ הֲדֹם לְרַגְלֶיךָ *until I place your enemies as a footstool to your feet* 110$_1$, אוֹיְבָיו אַלְבִּישׁ בֹּשֶׁת *his enemies I shall clothe with shame* 132$_{18}$; יִהְיוּ כְנָבָל אֹיְבֶיךָ *may your enemies be as Nabal* 1 S 25$_{26}$ (+ מְבַקֵּשׁ רָעָה *one who seeks harm*), יִהְיוּ כַנַּעַר אֹיְבֵי אֲדֹנִי הַמֶּלֶךְ *may the enemies of my lord the king be as the lad* (Absalom) 2 S 18$_{32}$, הַמְצָאתַנִי אֹיְבִי (Ahab to Elijah) *have you found me, my enemy?* 1 K 21$_{20}$; enemies of הַכּוֹהֵן הָרָשָׁע *the wicked priest* who will afflict (ענה pi.) and exhaust (בלה pi.) him 1QpHab 9$_{10}$.

2c. enemy of Y., Ex 15$_6$ Nm 10$_{35}$ 32$_{21}$ Dt 32$_{42}$ Jg 5$_{31}$ (:: אהב ptc. *friend*) Is 1$_{24}$ 42$_{13}$ 59$_{18}$ 66$_{6.14}$ (:: עֶבֶד *servant*)

Na 1$_{8}$ Ps 8$_{3}$ 66$_{3}$ 68$_{2.22.24}$ 83$_{3}$ 89$_{11}$ (|| רַהַב *Rahab*) 89$_{52}$ 92$_{10.10}$ (+ פֹּעֲלֵי אָוֶן *workers of iniquity*) Jb 13$_{24}$ 33$_{10}$ 1QpMic 11$_{4}$, אוֹיְבֵי י׳ *enemies of Y.* 1 S 30$_{26}$ Ps 37$_{20}$, כִּי־נִאֵץ נִאַצְתָּ אֶת־אֹיְבֵי י׳ *because you have utterly despised the enemies of Y.* (or del. אֹיְבֵי *enemies of*) 2 S 12$_{14}$, יַד־י׳ אֶת־עֲבָדָיו וְזָעַם אֶת־אֹיְבָיו *the hand of Y. is with his servants, but he is angry with his enemies* Is 66$_{14}$, חֵמָה ... נוֹטֵר הוּא לְאֹיְבָיו *wrath ... he keeps for his enemies* Na 1$_{2}$.

2d. enemy of worshipper, 1 S 2$_{1}$ Ps 6$_{11}$ 9$_{4.7}$ 13$_{3.5}$ 25$_{2.19}$ 27$_{2}$ (|| רעע hi. ptc. *evildoer*) 27$_{6}$ 30$_{2}$ 31$_{9.16}$ (|| רדף ptc. *pursuer*) 35$_{19}$ 41$_{3.6.12}$ 42$_{10}$ 43$_{2}$ 54$_{9}$ 55$_{4.13}$ 56$_{10}$ 59$_{2}$ 64$_{2}$ 69$_{5.19}$ 71$_{10}$ (+ שֹׁמְרֵי נַפְשִׁי *those who watch for my life,* i.e. who seek to kill me) 102$_{9}$ (|| הלל po. ptc. *one who raves against*) 119$_{98}$ 138$_{7}$ 139$_{22}$ 143$_{9.12}$, יִרְמֹס לָאָרֶץ חַיַּי *let him* (enemy) *trample my life into the ground* 7$_{6}$, דִּכָּא לָאָרֶץ חַיָּתִי *he* (enemy) *crushes my life into the ground* 143$_{3}$, הִכִּיתָ אֶת־כָּל־אֹיְבַי לֶחִי *you* (Y.) *have struck all my enemies on the face* 3$_{8}$, אֹיְבַי בְּנֶפֶשׁ *my enemies in respect of* my *soul,* i.e. deadly enemies 17$_{9}$, אֹיְבַי חַיִּים *my enemies* (in respect of) *life,* i.e. deadly enemies 38$_{20}$, אֹיְבַי סְבִיבוֹתַי *my enemies around me* Ps 27$_{6}$.

2e. enemy of foreign people or ruler, Jr 49$_{37}$ Na 3$_{11.13}$, מֶלֶךְ־בָּבֶל אֹיְבוֹ *the king of Babylon, his enemy* Jr 44$_{30}$; for Balaam to curse Nm 23$_{11}$ 24$_{10}$, אוֹיְבֵי אֲדֹנִי הַמֶּלֶךְ *enemies of my lord the king* (Achish) 1 S 29$_{8}$.

2f. a person as enemy of a nation, אִישׁ צַר וְאוֹיֵב הָמָן הָרָע הַזֶּה *the man* who is *an adversary and an enemy is this evil Haman* Est 7$_{6}$, וַיֵּהָפֵךְ לָהֶם לְאוֹיֵב *and he* (Y.) *turned into their* (Israel's) *enemy* Is 63$_{10}$, שִׁמְשׁוֹן אוֹיְבֵנוּ *Samson, our enemy* Jg 16$_{23}$ (+ מַחֲרִיב אַרְצֵנוּ וַאֲשֶׁר הִרְבָּה אֶת־חֲלָלֵינוּ *one who has ravaged our land and who has multiplied our casualties*), אוֹיֵב בַּדָּרֶךְ *an assailant along the route* Ezr 8$_{22}$, אוֹיֵב וְאוֹרֵב *assailant or robber* 8$_{31}$.

2g. personal enemy of individual, Pr 24$_{17}$, אם בעיניו ידמיע אויב אם מצא עת לא ישבע דם *even though an enemy weeps with his eyes, if he finds an opportunity, he will not be satisfied with any amount of blood* Si 12$_{16}$, יְהִי כְרָשָׁע אֹיְבִי *may my enemy be* treated *as a wicked person* Jb 27$_{7}$, אֹיְבֵי אִישׁ אַנְשֵׁי בֵיתוֹ *a man's enemies are men of his own household* Mc 7$_{6}$, וְהוּא לֹא־אוֹיֵב לוֹ וְלֹא מְבַקֵּשׁ רָעָתוֹ *though he was not his enemy, and was not seeking to harm him* Nm 35$_{23}$, וְכִי־יִמְצָא אִישׁ אֶת־אֹיְבוֹ וְשִׁלְּחוֹ בְּדֶרֶךְ טוֹבָה *and if a man encounters his enemy, does he let him go away unharmed* (lit. *on a level path*)? 1 S 24$_{20}$, גַּם־אוֹיְבָיו יַשְׁלִם אִתּוֹ *even his enemies he reconciles to himself* Pr 16$_{7}$, כִּי־יְדַבְּרוּ אֶת־אוֹיְבִים בַּשָּׁעַר *when they speak with* their *enemies at the gate* Ps 127$_{5}$, שׁוֹר אֹיִבְךָ *your enemy's ox* Ex 23$_{4}$, ידי הא[יבם] *hands of the enemies* (of Jaosh) Lachish ost. 6$_{7 (Lemaire)}$ (others הא[נשים] *of the people* or הא[רץ ו]ה[עיר] *of the land and the city*).

<SUBJ> היה *be* Nm 24$_{18}$ (+ יְרֵשָׁה *a possession*) Jb 27$_{7}$ (+ כְרָשָׁע *as a wicked one*), אמר *say* Ex 15$_{9}$ Ezk 36$_{2}$ Ps 13$_{5}$ 41$_{6}$ 71$_{10}$ Lm 2$_{16}$ Si 33$_{12 (mg)}$ 4QCat^{a} 7$_{12}$, נשא hi. *deceive* Ps 89$_{23}$, ראה *see* Mc 7$_{10}$ Lm 2$_{16}$, שׁמע *hear* 1$_{21}$ Ne 4$_{9}$ 6$_{16}$, ידע *know* 6$_{16}$, קוה pi. *hope* Lm 2$_{16}$, שׂבר pi. *hope* Est 9$_{1}$, אכל *eat* Lv 26$_{16}$, לחך pi. *lick* dust Ps 72$_{9}$, לעג *mock* 80$_{7}$, המה *roar* 83$_{3}$, פצה *open* mouth Lm 2$_{16}$ 3$_{46}$, חרק *gnash* teeth 2$_{16}$, שׂישׂ *rejoice* 1$_{21}$, רום *be exalted* over Ps 13$_{3}$, עלץ *exult* over 25$_{2}$, שׂמח *rejoice* Mc 7$_{8}$ Ps 35$_{19}$, רוע hi. *shout in triumph* 41$_{12}$, שׁמם *be appalled* Lv 26$_{32}$ 11QT 59$_{5}$, בהל ni. *be dismayed* Ps 6$_{11}$, חרף pi. *despise* Ps 55$_{13}$ 74$_{18}$ 89$_{52}$ 102$_{9}$, נאץ pi. *despise* 74$_{10}$, שׂנא *hate* 25$_{19}$, קום *rise up* Dt 28$_{7}$, בוא *come* Jos 10$_{19}$ Lm 4$_{12}$, יצא *go out* to battle Dt 28$_{7}$, רבב *be many* Ps 25$_{19}$, עצם *be powerful* 38$_{20}$ 69$_{5}$, גדל hi. *triumph* Lm 1$_{9}$, גבר *be strong* 1$_{16}$, שׁלט *rule* over Est 9$_{1}$, שׁלה *prosper* Lm 1$_{5}$, בקשׁ pi. *seek* life 2 S 4$_{8}$, צוד *hunt* Lm 3$_{52}$, מצא *find* 1 K 21$_{20}$ Lm 2$_{16}$, רדף *pursue* Ex 15$_{9}$ Ho 8$_{3}$ Ps 7$_{6}$ 143$_{3}$, נשׂג hi. *overtake* Ex 15$_{9}$ Ps 7$_{6}$, נקף hi. *surround* Ps 17$_{9}$, צרר *press upon* 1 K 8$_{37}$||2 C 6$_{28}$, יכל *prevail* against Ps 13$_{5}$, צוק hi. *oppress* Jr 19$_{9}$, צמת hi. *destroy* Ps 69$_{5}$, רעע hi. *do damage* 74$_{3}$, ריק hi. *draw* sword Ex 15$_{9}$, חלק pi. *divide* booty 15$_{9}$, שׁכן hi. *place* Ps 7$_{6}$, ישׁב *resettle* land Lv 26$_{32}$ 4Q372 1$_{20}$, hi. *resettle* person Ps 143$_{3}$, דכא pi. *crush* 143$_{3}$, צוק hi. *oppress* Dt 28$_{53.55.57}$, לחץ *oppress* Ps 106$_{42}$, אבד *perish* Jg 5$_{31}$ Ps 9$_{4}$ 92$_{10.10}$, כלה *vanish* Ps 37$_{20.20}$, pi. *destroy* Lm 2$_{22}$, תמם *be destroyed* Ps 9$_{7}$, כרת ni. *be cut off* Mc 5$_{8}$, נפל *fall* Lv 26$_{7.8}$ (both + לֶחָרֶב *by* the *sword*) Ps 27$_{2}$ Pr 24$_{17}$ Ne 6$_{16}$ (+ בְּעֵינֵיהֶם *in their own eyes*), כשׁל ni. *stumble* Ps 9$_{4}$ 27$_{2}$ Pr 24$_{17}$, שׁוב *turn back* Ps 6$_{11}$ 9$_{4}$ 56$_{10}$, נוס *flee* Dt 28$_{7}$, פוץ *be scattered* Nm 10$_{35}$ Ps 68$_{2}$, מלט ni. *escape* 1 S 19$_{17}$, כחשׁ ni. perh. *cringe* Dt

33$_{29}$, pi. *cringe* Ps 66$_3$, בּוֹשׁ *be put to shame* 6$_{11.11}$, נגף ni. *be defeated* Dt 28$_7$ 1QM 3$_2$ 9$_2$.

<NOM CL> אֹיְבֵינוּ פְּלִילִים perh. *our enemies are judges* Dt 32$_{31}$, חֶרֶב לְאֹיֵב מָגוֹר מִסָּבִיב *the enemy has a sword, terror is all around* Jer 6$_{25}$, אֹיְבֵי י׳ כִּיקַר כָּרִים *the enemies of Y. are as the glory of the pastures* Ps 37$_{20}$.

<OBJ> ראה *see* Ps 25$_{19}$, עבד *serve* Dt 28$_{48}$, hi. *make someone serve* Jr 17$_4$, שׂמח pi. *gladden* Ps 30$_2$ Lm 2$_{17}$, hi. *gladden* Ps 89$_{43}$, לחם ni. *fight against* Jos 10$_{25}$, נתן *give, hand over* Ex 23$_{27}$ Dt 21$_{10}$ 23$_{15}$ Jos 10$_{19}$ 21$_{44}$ Jg 3$_{28}$ Jg 16$_{23.24}$ 1 S 24$_5$ 2 S 22$_{41}$||Ps 18$_{41}$ (+ עֹרֶף with their *backs* to me, i.e. fleeing) 11QT 59$_{19}$, *cause* someone to do something Dt 28$_7$, *allow* Jos 10$_{19}$, שׁלח pi. *dispatch* Dt 28$_{48}$ 4QDibHam^a 1.6$_{8(mg)}$, *send away*, so as to escape 1 S 19$_{17}$, עבר hi. *bring across* Jr 15$_{14}$, איב *be an enemy to* Ex 23$_{22}$, דין *judge* 1QpMic 11$_4$, קבב *curse* Nm 23$_{11}$ 24$_{10}$, סוך pilp. *antagonize* Is 9$_{10}$, סגר pi. *hand over* 1 S 26$_8$, hi. *hand over* 1QM 11$_{13}$, רדף *pursue* Lv 26$_7$ 2 S 22$_{38}$||Ps 18$_{38}$ 1QM 9$_6$, pi. *pursue* Na 1$_8$, זנב pi. *attack in the rear* Jos 10$_{19}$, פרץ *break out against* 2 S 5$_{20}$||1 C 14$_{11}$, הדף *push away* Dt 6$_{19}$ Si 33$_9$, פנה pi. *clear away* Zp 3$_{15}$, פוץ hi. *scatter* 1QM 3$_5$, פזר pi. *scatter* Ps 89$_{11}$, פזר pi. *scatter* 4QapPs^b 15$_5$ ([פוזרת איביך]), רמס trample 1QM 9$_{12}$ (ר[מוס]; Yadin ה[מים], from מסס hi. *intimidate*), שׁלל *plunder* 1QM 10$_2$, נכה hi. *strike* 1 S 26$_8$ Ps 3$_8$, נצח *prevail* over 11QT 58$_{12}$, כנע hi. *subjugate* Ps 81$_{15}$ 1 C 17$_{10}$, שׁבת hi. *silence* Ps 8$_3$, כרת hi. *cut off* 1 S 20$_{15}$ 2 S 7$_9$||1 C 17$_8$, שׁמד hi. *destroy* 2 S 22$_{38}$ (||Ps 18$_{38}$ נשׂג hi. *overtake*) 1QM 9$_5$, כלה pi. *destroy* 2 S 22$_{38}$||Ps 18$_{38}$, צמת hi. *destroy* Ps 143$_{12}$, רעץ *shatter* Ex 15$_6$, שׁבר *shatter* 11QT 58$_{12}$, נקם *be avenged on* Jos 10$_{13}$, שׁבה *capture* Dt 21$_{10}$, ירשׁ hi. *dispossess* Nm 32$_{21}$, פגע hi. *cause to entreat* Jr 15$_{11}$ (or em. אֶת־הָאֹיֵב to אֶל־הָאֹיֵב *make entreaty to the enemy*).

<CSTR> [או]יבי כול הארצות *enemies of*, i.e. from, *all lands* 1QM 11$_{13}$; מַכַּת אוֹיֵב *blow of*, i.e. from, *an enemy* Jr 30$_{14}$, לַחַץ *oppression of*, i.e. from, Ps 42$_{10}$ 43$_2$, כַּעַס *provocation of*, i.e. by, Dt 32$_{27}$, אַף *anger of* Ps 138$_7$, ממ[ש]ל[ת] *government of* 1QM 18$_{11}$, נִקְמֵי *vengeances of* Si 46$_1$, פַּחַד *fear of*, i.e. about, Ps 64$_2$ 4QpNah 3.2$_5$, אֶרֶץ *land of* 1 K 8$_{46}$ Jr 31$_{16}$, רֹאשׁ פַּרְעוֹת *heads of hair*, i.e. hairy heads, *of* Dt 32$_{42}$, ראשׁ פאתי *head of temples of* Si 33$_{12(Bmg)}$ (B מואב *of Moab*), לב *heart of* 1QM 8$_{10}$, חללי *slain ones of*, i.e. among, 1QM 14$_3$, קוֹל *sound of* Ps 55$_4$, מערכת האויב *battle line of the enemy* 1QM 3$_7$ 6$_{2.6(mg)}$ (אויב) 8$_{8.13}$, מערכות *battle lines of* fr. 1$_5$ ([הא]ויב]), מלחמת *battle of* (against) *the enemy* 1QM 3$_{11}$, כול האויב *all the enemy* 9$_6$.

יַד־אוֹיֵב *hand, control, of enemy*, + נפל בְּ *fall into* 4QJub^a 2$_7$ ([ביד האויב]), סגר בְּ hi. *hand over to* Ps 31$_9$ Lm 2$_7$, גאל מִן *redeem from* Ps 106$_{10}$, יַד אוֹיְבִים *hand, control, of enemies*, + ישׁע מִן hi. *deliver from* Jg 2$_{18}$ 2 S 3$_{18}$ 11QT 59$_{11}$, נצל מִן hi. *deliver from* Jg 8$_{34}$ 1 S 12$_{10.11}$ 2 K 17$_{39}$ Ps 31$_{16}$ (יַד־), בקשׁ pi. *seek* revenge on 1 S 20$_{16}$, שׁפט מִן *give judgment* so that one escapes *from* 2 S 18$_{19}$, נתן בְּ *hand over to* 2 K 21$_{14}$ Jr 20$_5$ 21$_7$ 34$_{20.21}$ 44$_{30}$ 1QpHab 9$_{10}$ 4QpsMos^e 1$_9$, עזב *leave* Ne 9$_{28}$, מכר בְּ *sell into* Jg 2$_{14}$; כַּף אוֹיֵב *hand, control, of enemy*, + נצל מִן hi. *deliver from* Ezr 8$_{31}$, כַּף אוֹיְבִים *hand, control, of enemies*, + ישׁע מִן hi. *deliver from* 1 S 4$_3$, נצל מִן hi. *deliver from* 2 S 19$_{10}$ 22$_1$||Ps 18$_1$, גאל מִן *redeem from* Mc 4$_{10}$, נתן בְּ *hand over to* Jr 12$_7$.

חֶרֶב אוֹיְבִים *sword of enemies* Jr 20$_4$ 1 C 21$_{12}$, שַׁעַר *gate of* Gn 22$_{17}$, אֶרֶץ *land of* Lv 26$_{34.38.41.44}$ 1 K 8$_{48}$ 4QBark^a 2.1$_3$ ([ארץ]), אַרְצוֹת *lands of* Lv 26$_{36.39}$ Ezk 39$_{27}$ 11QT 59$_5$, שְׁלַל *booty of*, i.e. from, Dt 20$_{14}$ Jos 22$_8$ 1 S 14$_{30}$ 20$_{36}$ 11QT 62$_{11}$, עֹרֶף *neck of* Gn 49$_8$ 1QM 12$_{11}$19$_3$, רֹאשׁ *head of* Ps 68$_{22}$, לֵב *heart of* Ps 45$_6$, נֶפֶשׁ *life of* 1 S 25$_{29}$ 1 K 3$_{11}$ Ps 41$_3$ 4Q385 2$_3$, במו[תי אויב]יכה *backs of your enemies* 4Q525 4$_{11}$.

יֶתֶר אֹיְבֵינוּ *the rest of our enemies* Ne 6$_1$, כָּל־אוֹיְבִים *all enemies* Dt 12$_{10}$ 25$_{19}$ Jos 10$_{25}$ 21$_{44.44}$ 23$_1$ Jg 5$_{31}$ 8$_{34}$ 1 S 14$_{47}$ 2 S 3$_{18}$ 7$_{1.9.11}$ 22$_1$||Ps 18$_1$ 2 K 17$_{39}$ Mc 5$_8$ Ps 3$_8$ 6$_{11}$ 21$_9$ 89$_{43}$ Lm 1$_{21}$ 2$_{16}$ Est 9$_5$ Ne 6$_{16}$ 1 C 17$_{8.10}$ 22$_9$ 11QT 59$_{19}$ 1QM 10$_2$.

<APP> אוֹיְבִים *enemies*, named 1 S 14$_{47}$, עם אויב *a people, an enemy* 4Q372 1$_{20}$, אֹיְבֶיךָ ... בְּנֵי עַמּוֹן *your enemies ... the Ammonites* Jg 11$_{36}$, שֵׂעִיר אֹיְבָיו *Seir, his enemies* Nm 24$_{18}$, אֹיְבֵיכֶם ... מוֹאָב *your enemies ... Moab* Jg 3$_{28}$.

<PREP> לְ *to, for,* 4QapPs^b 28$_3$, + עשׂה *do* 1 S 25$_{22}$, נתן *give* Dt 28$_{31}$ 2 K 21$_{14}$ (+ לְבַז וְלִמְשִׁסָּה *as plunder and spoil*) Is 62$_8$, מכר htp. *be sold* Dt 28$_{68}$, שׁלם pi. *repay* Is 59$_{18}$ 66$_6$, לְאֹיְבַיִךְ פָּתוֹחַ נִפְתְּחוּ your gates *are open wide* *to your enemies* Na 3_{13}, הָיָה לְ *become* Ps 139_{22} Lm 1_{2}, חשב לְ *consider* someone to be Jb 13_{24} 33_{10}.

בְּ, + ראה *look* at Ps 54_{9}, לחם ni. *fight* against 1 S 14_{47} 29_{8} 1QM 11_{8}, נקם ni. *be avenged* on 1 S 18_{25}, נכה hi. *strike* at Est 9_{5}, רדה *rule* over Ne 9_{28}; בְּקֶרֶב *in the middle of* Ps 110_{2}; כְּ *as* Lm $2_{4.5}$.

מִן partitive, *(one) of* Jos 21_{44} Ps 68_{24}, of comparison, *than* Ps 119_{98}, *from* (see also כַּף, יַד *hand of*, in Cstr.) Na 3_{11} (+ מָעוֹז *refuge*), + נצל hi. *rescue* 2 S 22_{18} ||Ps 18_{18} Ps 59_{2} 143_{9}, ישׁע ni. *be delivered* Nm 10_{9} 2 S 22_{4}||Ps 18_{4}, נוח *get respite* Est $9_{16.22}$, hi. *give respite* Dt 12_{10} 25_{19} Jos 23_{1} 2 S $7_{1.11}$ 1 C 22_{9}, יצא hi. *deliver* 2 S 22_{49}||Ps 18_{49}, שׂמח מִן pi. *make someone rejoice over* 2 C 20_{27}, עזר מִן *help against* Ezr 8_{22}, נקם מִן ni. *take vengeance on* Isa 1_{24} 1 S 14_{24} Est 8_{13}, עשׂה נְקָמוֹת מִן *take vengeance on* Jg 11_{36}.

פגע אֶל hi. *make entreaty to* Jr 15_{11} (if em.; see Obj.); עַל *because of* 4QDibHam[a] 1.5_{4}, *against* Dt 20_{3} 30_{7} 1 S 2_{1} 2 C 26_{13} 1QM 9_{6} 18_{12} (ל[ע]), + יצא *go out* Dt 20_{1}=11QT 61_{13} Dt 21_{10}=11QT 63_{10} Dt 23_{10} 1 K 8_{44}||2 C 6_{34} 11QT $58_{6.16}$, גבר htp. *display might* Is 42_{13}; לחם עִם ni. *fight against* Dt 20_{4} 2 C 20_{29}.

לִפְנֵי *in the presence of* Lv 26_{37}, + הפך *turn* neck Jos 7_{8}, פנה *turn* neck 7_{12}, קום *rise* $7_{12.13}$, עמד *stand* Jg 2_{14}, פוץ hi. *scatter* Jr 18_{17}, נפל hi. *cause to fall* 19_{7}, כשׁל hi. *cause to fall* 2 C 25_{8}, חתת hi. *terrify* Jr 49_{37}, הלך *go* into captivity Am 9_{4}, נגף ni. *be defeated* by Lv 26_{17} Nm 14_{42} Dt 1_{42} 28_{25} 1 K 8_{33}||2 C 6_{24}, נתן *give* to 1 K 8_{46}||2C 6_{36}, *give* to sword before Jr 15_{9}; מִפְּנֵי *because of* Ps 44_{17}, *in the presence of* 61_{4} Lm 2_{3}.

רדף אַחֲרֵי *pursue after* Jos 10_{19}; לִקְרַאת *opposite* 1QM 7_{9}; לְמַעַן *because of* Ps 69_{19}.

<COLL> אוֹיְבִים מִסָּבִיב *enemies all around* Dt 12_{10} 25_{19} Jos 23_{1} Jg 2_{14} 8_{34} 1 S 12_{11} 1 C 22_{9} Si 46_{16} (ו[א]יביו); אוֹיֵב parallel with צַר *adversary* Dt 32_{27} Is 1_{24} 9_{10} 59_{18} Mc 5_{8} Na 1_{2} Ps 13_{5} 27_{2} 81_{15} 89_{43} Lm 1_{5} $2_{4.17}$ 4_{12} Si 33_{9}, צרר ptc. *oppressor* Ex 23_{22} Ps 143_{12}, שׂנא ptc. *one who hates* Lv 26_{17} Dt 30_{7} 2 S 22_{18}||Ps 18_{18} Ps 21_{9} 35_{19} 38_{20} 68_{24} 74_{10} 106_{10} Est $9_{1.5.16}$ 11QT 59_{11}, pi. ptc. Nm 10_{35} 2 S 22_{41}||Ps 18_{41} 55_{13} 68_{2} 83_{3} 1QM 3_{5}, בקשׁ pi. ptc. *one who seeks* another's life (נֶפֶשׁ) Jr $19_{7.9}$ 21_{7} $34_{20.21}$ $44_{30.30}$ 49_{37}, נקם htp. ptc. *avenger* Ps 8_{3} 44_{17}, רָשָׁע *wicked person* Ps 3_{8} 17_{9} 37_{20} 55_{4}, קום htpol. ptc. *opponent* Ps 59_{2} Jb 27_{7}.

Also 11QT 3_{3} 1QM fr. 4_{4} 4Q183 1.2_{1} 1QpMic 11_{2} 4QpNah 3.4_{8} 4Q376 1.3_{2}.

→ אֵיבָה *hostility*.

אֵיבָה 5.0.2 **enmity**—cstr. אֵיבַת—of Philistines towards Israel Ezk 25_{15}, of Esau for Jacob 1QJub[b] 35_{9}, of Edom for Israel 35_{5}, of nations for returning exiles Ezr 3_{3} (if em.), between killer and victim Nm $35_{21.22}$, between (descendants of) Eve and (descendants of) serpent Gn 3_{15}, between truth and iniquity 1QS 4_{17}.

<SUBJ> היה *be* Ezk 35_{5}. **<OBJ>** נתן *give*, i.e. place (of God) 1QS 4_{17}, שׁית *place* (of God) Gn 3_{15}. **<CSTR>** אֵיבַת עוֹלָם *enmity of eternity*, i.e. eternal enmity Ezk 25_{15} (+ בִּשְׁאָט בְּנֶפֶשׁ *with contempt in [their] soul*) 35_{5} 1QS 4_{17}. **<PREP>** בְּ of accompaniment, *with, in*, + נכה hi. *strike* Nm 35_{21}, הדף *push* 35_{22} (Sam hi.; בְּלֹא־אֵיבָה *without enmity*; + בְּפֶתַע *suddenly*), רדף *pursue* 1QJub[b] $35_{9(Milik)}$ ([ירדפנו] באיבה), שׁחת hi. *destroy* Ezk 25_{15} (if em. לְמַשְׁחִית אֵיבַת עוֹלָם *to destroy [with] eternal enmity*; or em. אַהֲבַת *love of*, i.e. destroy love for ever), בְּאֵיבָה עֲלֵיהֶם מֵעַמֵּי הָאֲרָצוֹת perh. *some of the peoples of the lands were against them in enmity*Ezr 3_{3} (if em. בְּאֵימָה *with terror*).

→ איב *be an enemy*.

אֵיד 24 n.m. **disaster**—cstr. אֵיד; sf. אֵידִי, אֵידְךָ, אֵידוֹ, אֵידָם, אֵידְכֶם—**disaster, calamity,** for nations (oft. caused by God), for ignorant, wicked, poor, **<SUBJ>** בוא *come* Jr 48_{16} (|| רָעָה *misfortune*) Jb 21_{17} Pr 6_{15} (+ פִּתְאֹם *suddenly*), אתה *come* 1_{27} (+ כְּסוּפָה *as a whirlwind*; || פַּחַד *fear*), קום *arise* 24_{22} (+ פִּתְאֹם *suddenly*), כון ni. *be ready* Jb 18_{12} (+ לְצַלְעוֹ *at his side*).

<NOM CL> + פַּחַד *fear* Jb 31_{23} (perh. also app., פַּחַד אֵלַי אֵיד אֵל *fear was upon me, disaster from God*), קָרוֹב *near* Jr 48_{16}, לְ *(destined) for* (+ עַוָּל *unjust one*) Jb 31_{3}, וְדֶרֶךְ בֹּגְדִים אֵידָם *and the way of traitors is*, i.e. leads to, *their disaster* Pr 13_{15} (if em. אֵיתָן *continuous*).

<OBJ> בוא hi. *bring* Jr 49_{8} (+ עֵת פְּקַדְתִּיו *the time I have punished him*) 49_{32}.

<CSTR> אֵיד אֵל *disaster of*, i.e. from, *God* Jb 31_{23}, עֵשָׂו *of Esau* Jr 49_{8}, מוֹאָב *of Moab* 48_{16} (־אֵיד).

יוֹם אֵיד *day of disaster* for enemies of Israel Dt 32$_{35}$ (אֵידָם; + עָתִיד *future*), for David 2 S 22$_{19}$||Ps 18$_{19}$ (אֵידִי), for Israel Jr 18$_{17}$ (אֵידָם), for Judah Ob$_{13}$ (אֵידָם; or em. אוֹנוֹ *his misfortune*) Ob$_{13}$ (אֵידָם) Ob$_{13}$ (אֵידוֹ; or em. אָבְדוֹ *his perishing*), for Egypt's mercenaries Jr 46$_{21}$ (אֵידָם; || פְּקֻדָּה *punishment*), for wicked person Jb 21$_{30}$ (|| עֶבְרָה *wrath*), for individual Pr 27$_{10}$ (אֵידֶךָ) 4QapPs^b 24$_7$ ([א]ידי).

עֵת אֵידָם *time of their* (Edom's) *disaster* Ezk 35$_5$ (+ עָוֹן *iniquity*), אָרְחוֹת אֵידָם *paths of their disaster* Jb 30$_{12}$.

<PREP> שָׂמֵחַ לְ *(one who is) happy at,* i.e. laughs at, because of, *disaster* Pr 17$_5$ (|| רָשׁ *poor [person]*).

שׂחק בְּ *laugh at, because of* Pr 1$_{26}$ (+ פַּחַד *fear*).

אַיָּה I $_3$ n.f. **falcon** or other bird of prey (e.g. kite), prohibited for consumption, <SUBJ> אכל ni. *be eaten* Lv 11$_{14}$. <OBJ> שׁקץ pi. *despise* Lv 11$_{14}$ (+ דָּאָה *kite*), אכל *eat* Lv 11$_{14(Sam)}$||Dt 14$_{13}$ (+ דַּיָּה *kite* [unless del. and em. רָאָה to דָּאָה]). <CSTR> עֵין אַיָּה *eye of falcon* Jb 28$_7$ (+ עַיִט perh. *hawk*), לֶחֶם אַיָּה *food of,* i.e. for, *falcon* Jb 15$_{23}$ (if em. אַיֵּה *where is it?*). <COLL> הָאַיָּה ... לְמִינָהּ *the falcon ... of any kind* Lv 11$_{14}$||Dt 14$_{13}$.

→ אַיָּה *Aiah.*

אַיָּה II $_6$ pr.n.m. **Aiah**—BHS אַיָּה—**1.** father of Rizpah, concubine of Saul, 2 S 3$_7$ 21$_{8.10.11}$. **2.** Horite, son of Zibeon (צִבְעוֹן) and descendant of Seir, Gn 36$_{24}$||1 C 1$_{40}$ (Gn BHS אַיָּה).

→ אַיָּה *falcon.*

אַיֵּה $_{46}$ interrog. adv. **where?,** alw. (except Jb 15$_{23}$) preceding noun with article, oft. with restrictive clause (relative or appositional) following. In nom. cl., **where is?, a.** with name, Sarah Gn 18$_9$, Ahimaaz and Jonathan 2 S 17$_{20}$, Y. 2 K 2$_{14}$ Jr 2$_{6.8}$ Mc 7$_{10}$ (if em. אַיּוֹ *where is he?*).

b. with animate noun, אִישׁ *man* Gn 19$_5$ Is 40$_{13}$ (if em. וְאִישׁ to וְאַיֵּה אִישׁ), נָבִיא *prophet* Jr 37$_{19(Qr)}$ (Kt אַיּוֹ *where is he?*), בֵּן *son* 2 S 16$_3$, מֶלֶךְ *king* Is 37$_{13}$ (||2 K 19$_{13}$ אַיּוֹ *where is he?*) Ho 13$_{10}$ (if em. אֱהִי *shall I be?*), קְדֵשָׁה *prostitute* Gn 38$_{21}$, אֱלֹהִים *God, gods* Dt 32$_{37(Sam)}$ (MT אֵי *where?*) 2 K 18$_{34.34}$||Is 36$_{19.19}$ Jr 2$_{28}$ Jl 2$_{17}$ Ml 2$_{17}$ Ps 42$_{4.11}$ 79$_{10}$ 115$_2$, אֱלוֹהַּ *God* Jb 35$_{10}$, שֶׂה *sheep* Gn 22$_7$, עֵדֶר *flock* Jr 13$_{20}$; אֲבוֹתֵיכֶם אַיֵּה־הֵם *your fathers, where are they?* Zc 1$_5$.

c. with participle of ספר *count* Is 33$_{18.18}$, שׁקל *weigh* 33$_{18}$, עלה hi. *raise* 63$_{11}$, שׂים *place* 63$_{11}$, טוח *paint* Ezk 13$_{15}$ (if em. אֵין *there are none*).

d. with inanimate noun, פֶּה *mouth* Jg 9$_{38}$, טִיחַ *mud* Ezk 13$_{12}$, דָּגָן *corn* Lm 2$_{12}$, יַיִן *wine* 2$_{12}$, מָעוֹן *dwelling place* Na 2$_{12}$, בַּיִת *house* Jb 21$_{28}$, אֹהֶל *tent* 21$_{28}$, קִיר *wall* Ezk 13$_{15}$ (if em. אֵין *there are none*).

e. with abstract noun, פלא ni. ptc. *wonder* Jg 6$_{13}$, דֶּבֶר *plague* Ho 13$_{14}$ (if em. אֱהִי *shall I be?*), קֶטֶב *destruction* Ho 13$_{14}$ (if em. אֱהִי), חֵמָה *anger* Is 51$_{13}$, כָּבוֹד *honour* Ml 1$_6$, מוֹרָא *fear* 1$_6$, קִנְאָה *jealousy* Is 63$_{15}$, דָּבָר *word* of Y. Jr 17$_{15}$, חֶסֶד *loyalty* Ps 89$_{50}$, תִּקְוָה *hope* Jb 17$_{15}$.

<COLL> אַיֵּה אֵפוֹ(א) *where, then?* Jg 9$_{38}$ Jb 17$_{15}$ Ho 13$_{10}$ (if em. אֱהִי *shall I be?*), אַיֵּה־נָא *where, pray?* Ps 115$_2$ (4QPs^b איה), נֹדֵד הוּא לַלֶּחֶם אַיֵּה *he wanders for bread—where (is it)?* Jb 15$_{23}$ (unless אַיֵּה = *any* bread; or em. אַיָּה for the food of a *falcon*).

Also Si 11$_{24}$ (א[י]ה).

→ אֵי *where?*

אִיּוֹב $_{58.1}$ pr.n.m. **Job**, non-Israelite worshipper of Y., model of righteous person (Ezk 14$_{14.20}$ Si 49$_9$), Ezk 14$_{14.20}$ Jb 1$_{1.5.5.5.8}$ (+ עַבְדִּי *my servant*) 1$_{9.14.20.22}$ 2$_3$ (+ עַבְדִּי) 2$_{7.10.11}$ 3$_{1.2}$ 6$_1$ 9$_1$ 12$_1$ 16$_1$ 19$_1$ 21$_1$ 23$_1$ 26$_1$ 27$_1$ 29$_1$ 31$_{40}$ 32$_{1.2.3.4.12}$ 33$_{1.31}$ 34$_{5.7.35.36}$ 35$_{16}$ 37$_{14}$ 38$_1$ 40$_{1.3.6}$ 42$_{1.7.8.8.8}$ (all three + עַבְדִּי) 42$_{9+6t}$ Si 49$_9$ (+ נ[ב]יא *a prophet*).

אִיזֶבֶל $_{22}$ pr.n.f. **Jezebel**—אִיזָבֶל—daughter of Ethbaal, king of Sidon, and wife of Ahab, 1 K 16$_{31}$ 18$_{4.13.19}$ 19$_{1.2}$ 21$_{5+8t}$ 2 K 9$_{7+6t}$.

→ perh. אֵי *where?* + זבל *honour.*

אֵיךְ $_{61.0.3}$ interrog. adv. **how?, 1.** introducing rhetorical question, **how is it possible that?, surely it is not possible that?,** but distinction from §2 oft. uncertain, with verb, יכל *be able* Deut 7$_{17(Sam, 5QDeut)}$ (MT אֵיכָה *how?*) 1QH 15$_{21}$, חיה *live* Ezk 33$_{10}$, עשׂה *do* Gn 39$_9$ Jr 9$_6$

125, הלך *go* 1 S 162, בוא *come* 2 S 69, עלה *go up* Gn 4434, חרה htp. *contend*, i.e. race Jr 125, רדף *pursue* Dt 3230(Sam) (MT אֵיכָה), נשׂא *raise* face 2 S 222 2QapMoses 15 ([א]אשׁ; || מָה *what?*), שׁוב hi. *turn* face *aside* 2 K 1824||Is 369, עמד *stand* 2 K 104, מלט ni. *escape* Is 206, שׁית *place* Jr 319, שׂים *place* Ho 118, נתן *give* 118.8, מגן pi. *hand over* 118, גנב *steal* Gn 448, חלל ni. *be profaned* Is 4811, כרת *cut*, i.e. make covenant Jos 97, אמר *say* Gn 269 (:: כִּי *because*) Jg 1615 2 S 1218 Is 1911 Jr 223 4814 Ps 111, שׁיר *sing* 1374, שׁקט *be silent* Jr 477, שׁמע *hear* Ex 612.30, ידע *know* 2 S 15 11QT 612 (א[י]ך), ירא *fear* 2 S 114, נחם pi. *console* Jb 2134.

2. introducing simple question, **how?, by what method?**, with verb, שׁאר ni. *remain* Jg 2117 (if em. יְרֻשַּׁת *inheritance of* to אֵיךְ תִּשָּׁאֵר), הפך ni. *be turned around* Jr 221, נפל *fall* Ru 318 (+ ידע *know*), כתב *write* Jr 3617 (+ נגד hi. *tell*), יעץ ni. *advise* 1 K 126||2 C 106, חמם *be warm* Ec 411, ידע *know* Dt 1821(Sam) (MT אֵיכָה *how?*), ירא *fear* 2 K 1728 (+ ירה hi. *teach*), עבד *worship* Dt 1230(Sam) (MT אֵיכָה).

3. as interj. expressing enormity of catastrophe, typically within lament (קִינָה), **how terribly!**, with verb, היה *be* Jr 5023 5141 Zp 215 Ps 7319 (all + לְשַׁמָּה *as a desolation*), שׁבת *cease* Is 144, ni. *be silenced* Ezk 2617 (if em.; see below), דמה ni. *be silenced* Ob5, סוף *be ended* Ps 7319, אבד *disappear* 2 S 127 Ezk 2617 (or em. אֵיךְ אָבַדְתְּ נוֹשֶׁבֶת *how terribly have you disappeared, you who were inhabited* to נִשְׁבַּתְּ *have you been silenced*), מות *die* Ec 216, שׁדד pu. *be devastated* Jr 918, חתת *be shattered* 4839, שׁבר ni. *be broken* 5023, גדע ni. *be hewn down* 5023.

נפל *fall* 2 S 119.25.27 (all three with subj. גִּבּוֹר *warrior*) Is 1412, פנה hi. *turn* neck Jr 4839, מושׁ hi. *remove* Mc 24 (or em. אֵיךְ יָמִישׁ לִי *how terribly he removes from me* to אֵין מֵשִׁיב *there is none that gives back*), עזב pu. *be abandoned* Jr 4925, שׂנא *hate* Pr 512, נאץ *depise* 512, לכד ni. *be captured* Jr 5141, תפשׂ ni. *be seized* 5141, חפשׂ ni. *be searched* Ob6, בעה ni. *be requested* Ob6.

→ אֵיכָה *how?*, אֵיכָכָה *how?*

אִיכָבוֹד 2 pr.n.m. **Ichabod**—אִי־כָבוֹד—son of Phinehas son of Eli, 1 S 421 (אִי־כָבוֹד) 143.

→ אִי *not* + כָּבוֹד *glory*.

אֵיכָה 18.0.9 interrog. adv. **how?, where?**—אֵיכֹה—**1.** introducing rhetorical question, **how is it possible that?, surely it is not possible that?**, but distinction from §2 oft. uncertain, with verb, יכל *be able* Dt 717 (Sam, 5QDeut אֵיךְ *how?*) 1QH 1514, עמד *stand* 1QH fr. 36, נשׂא *carry* Dt 112 1QDM 27(Baillet) ([אשא] א[י]כה), רדף *pursue* Dt 3230 (Sam אֵיךְ), אמר *say* Jr 88, ידע *know* Ps 7311, נום *sleep* Na 317 (if em. אַיָּם *where are they?*).

2. introducing simple question, **how?, by what method?**, with verb, היה ni. *occur* Jg 203, עשׂה *do* 2 K 615, עבד *worship* Dt 1230 (Sam אֵיךְ *how?*), ישׁר pi. *make straight* 1QH 1234 (+ מָה *what?*), שׂכל hi. *instruct* 106 (|| מָה), קמם htpol. *be exalted* 1235, ידע *know* Dt 1821 (Sam אֵיךְ), בין hi. *understand* 1QH 1233 (|| מָה), שׁוב hi. *bring back*, i.e. reply 107 (|| מָה), אמר *say*4Q416 411.

3. as interj. expressing enormity of catastrophe, **how terribly!**, note אֵיכָה as title of Lamentations, with verb, היה *become* Is 121 (לְזוֹנָה *as a prostitute*), ישׁב *sit* Lm 11, שׁבר ni. *be broken* Jr 4817 (KtOr אֵיךְ), עמם ho. *be dimmed* Lm 41, שׁנה *change* 41, חשׁב ni. *be considered* 42, עוב hi. *becloud* 21.

4. where?, a. with verb, רעה *tend (beasts)* Ca 17, רבץ hi. *cause (beast) to crouch* 17.

b. in nom. cl., **where is?**, with pronoun, וּרְאוּ הוּא *and see where he is* 2 K 613 (אֵיכֹה; + ראה *see*).

<SYN> §2 מָה *what?*

Also 4Q485 12(Baillet) 4QPrFêtesb 402 (איכ[ה]).

→ אֵיךְ *how?*

אֵיכֹה, see אֵיכָה.

אֵיכָכָה 4.2.1 interrog. adv. **how?**—אֵיכָכָה—**1.** introducing rhetorical question, **how is it possible that?, surely it is not possible that?**, with verb, יכל *be able* Est 86.6, לבשׁ *be clothed* Ca 53, טנף pi. *make* feet *dirty* 53.

2. as conj., **how much more**, הנכבד בעיניו בעשרו איככה ונקלה בעשרו בעיניו איככה *the one who is great in his own eyes, how much more*, i.e. how much greater, *with wealth, and one who is despised because of wealth, how much more (despised he will be) in his own eyes!* Si 1031(B).

Also 4QapPsb 316. → אֵיךְ *how?*

אַיִל I $_{182.0.38}$ n.m. **ram**—אַ֫יִל; cstr. אֵיל (אֵל); pl. אֵילִים (אֵילִם, אֵלִים); cstr. אֵילֵי (אֵלֵי, Kt אולי)—**1. ram,** usu. as sacrifice, oft. in lists of sacrificial animals, symbol of arrogance (Dn), <SUBJ> היה *be* Lv 23$_{18}$ (+ עֹלָה *sacrifice*) Ezk 46$_{6}$ (+ תָּמִים *complete,* i.e. unblemished) 2 C 29$_{32}$ (+ מִסְפַּר הָעֹלָה *number of [beasts for] the sacrifice*), עשׂה *do* Dn 8$_{4}$, גדל hi. *be great* 8$_{4}$, שׁרת pi. *minister* Is 60$_{7}$, עמד *stand* Dn 8$_{3.6}$, עלה *go up* Is 60$_{7}$ (+ עַל ... מִזְבְּחִי *onto ... my altar*), אחז ni. *be held* Gn 22$_{13}$ (+ בַּסְּבַךְ בְּקַרְנָיו *in a thicket, by its horns*), נגח pi. *thrust* Dn 8$_{4}$.

<NOM CL> הָאַיִל ... מַלְכֵי מָדַי וּפָרָס *the ram ... is the kings of Media and Persia* Dn 8$_{20}$, כִּי אֵיל מִלֻּאִים הוּא *for it is a ram of ordination* Ex 29$_{22}$, וְקָרְבָּנוֹ ... אַיִל *and his sacrifice shall be ... a ram* Nm 7$_{15.27.33.39.45.51.57.63.69.75.81}$, וְהָעֹלָה ... אַיִל *and the sacrifice will be ... a ram* Ezk 46$_{4}$, וַאֲשָׁמָם אֵיל־צֹאן *and their guilt offering was a ram of the flock* Ezr 10$_{19}$ (if em. וַאֲשֵׁמִים *and as for the guilty ones*).

<OBJ> לקח *take* Gn 15$_{9}$ 22$_{13}$ Ex 29$_{1.15.19.31}$ Lv 8$_{2}$ 9$_{2}$ 16$_{5}$ (both + לְעֹלָה *as a burnt offering*) Jb 42$_{8}$ 4QApoc Mos B 1.2$_{3}$ ([איל]), נתן *give* 11QT 22$_{12.12.13}$, בוא hi. *bring* Lv 5$_{15.18.25}$ 19$_{21}$ 2 C 17$_{11}$ 29$_{21}$, שׁוב hi. *bring back,* i.e. give 2 K 3$_{4}$, שׁחט *slaughter* Ex 29$_{16.20}$ Lv 9$_{18}$ 2 C 29$_{22}$, נתח pi. *cut up* Ex 29$_{17}$||Lv 8$_{22}$, זבח *sacrifice* Lv 9$_{4}$ 1 C 15$_{26}$, קרב hi. *present in sacrifice* Ex 29$_{3}$ Lv 8$_{18}$ (Sam נגשׁ hi. *bring forward*) 8$_{22}$ 23$_{18}$ Nm 6$_{14}$ 7$_{21}$ 28$_{11.19.27}$ 29$_{8.13.36}$ Ezk 43$_{23}$ (+ מִן־הַצֹּאן *from the flock*) Ezr 8$_{35}$ 11QT 14$_{1(Yadin)}$ ([תקריבו ... איל]) 17$_{13}$ 19$_{16(Yadin)}$ + Sup ([והקריבו את האי]לים) 25$_{5(Yadin)}$ + Sup ([וחק]רבתמה) 25$_{13.16}$, עלה hi. *offer in sacrifice* Gn 22$_{13}$ Nm 23$_{2.4.14.30}$ 1 C 29$_{21}$ 11QT 18$_{9}$, קטר hi. *burn in sacrifice* Ex 29$_{18}$||Lv 8$_{21}$, נוף hi. *offer as wave offering* 11QT 15$_{12}$ + Sup, אכל *eat* Gn 31$_{38}$ Dt 32$_{14}$ (both non-sacrificial), כון hi. *prepare* Nm 23$_{1.29}$, עשׂה *make,* i.e. present as sacrifice 6$_{17}$ 29$_{2}$ Ezk 43$_{25}$ (+ מִן־הַצֹּאן *from the flock*) 45$_{23}$ 11QT 14$_{12(Yadin)}$ ([ועשיתמה]) 27$_{3}$ (ה[אי]ל), חצץ *divide* 11QT 15$_{4}$, ראה *see* Dn 8$_{4.6.20}$, נכה hi. *strike* Dn 8$_{7}$.

<CSTR> אֵיל הָעֹלָה *ram of the sacrifice* Lv 8$_{18}$, אֵיל הָאָשָׁם *ram of the guilt-offering* Lv 5$_{16}$ 19$_{21.22}$ CD 9$_{14}$, כול אלי אשמות *all the rams of the guilt offerings* 11QT 35$_{14}$ (or em. אלו אשמות *these guilt offerings*), אֵיל מִלֻּאִים *ram of ordination* Ex 29$_{22.26.27.31}$ Lv 8$_{22.29}$, כול אי[לי המלואים] *all the rams of ordination* 11QT 15$_{4(mg, Yadin)}$, אֵיל הַכִּפֻּרִים *ram of expiation* Nm 5$_{8}$, אֵילֵי נְבָיוֹת *rams of Nebaioth* Is 60$_{7}$, אֵיל־צֹאן *ram of (the) flock* Ezr 10$_{19}$, אֵילֵי צֹאנְךָ *the rams of your flock* Gn 31$_{38}$, אֵילֵי חֶמְדָּה *rams of desire,* i.e. choice rams Jr 25$_{34}$ (if em. כְּלִי *vessel of*), רֹאשׁ הָאָיִל *head of the ram* Ex 29$_{15.19}$||Lv 8$_{18.22}$, עֹרֹת אֵילִם מְאָדָּמִים (and var.) *reddened skins of rams* Ex 25$_{5}$ 26$_{14}$ 35$_{7.23}$ 36$_{19}$ 39$_{34}$, בְּשַׂר הָאַיִל *flesh of the ram* Ex 29$_{32}$ 4QApocMos B1.2$_{5}$ (האי[ל]), כָּל־הָאַיִל *all the ram* Ex 29$_{18}$||Lv 8$_{21}$, חֵלֶב אֵילִים *fat of rams* 1 S 15$_{22}$, חֵלֶב כָּרִים וְאֵילִים *fat of lambs and rams* Dt 32$_{14}$ (Sam חמת *cream of*), חֵלֶב כִּלְיוֹת אֵילִים *fat of the kidneys of rams* Is 34$_{6}$, עֹלוֹת אֵילִים *sacrifices of rams* Is 1$_{11}$, קְטֹרֶת אֵילִים *smoke of rams* Ps 66$_{15}$, אַלְפֵי אֵילִים *thousands of rams* Mc 6$_{7}$, כול האילים *all the rams* 11QT 15$_{4}$ + Sup.

<APP> הָאַיִל ... בַּעַל הַקְּרָנַיִם *the ram, the possessor of two horns* Dn 8$_{6.20}$ (הַקְּרָנַיִם), וְאֵילִים בְּנֵי־בָשָׁן *and rams, (children) of Bashan* Dt 32$_{14}$, אֲשָׁמוֹ ... אַיִל *his guilt-offering ..., a ram* Lv 5$_{15.25}$, אֵילִים צָמֶר *rams, (namely, their) wool* 2 K 3$_{4}$, צֹאן אֵילִים *herd-animals, (namely) rams* 2 C 17$_{11}$.

<ADJ> אֶחָד *one, a (single), each,* etc. Gn 22$_{13}$ (if em. אַחַר *behind*) Ex 29$_{15}$ Lv 16$_{5}$ Nm 6$_{14}$ 7$_{15.21.27.33.39.45.51.57.63.69.75.81}$ 15$_{11}$ 28$_{11.12.14(Sam).19.27.28}$ 29$_{2.8.9.14.36}$ Dn 8$_{3}$ 11QT 14$_{1(Yadin).4(Yadin)}$ (both [איל אחד]) 14$_{12.16}$ (ה[א]חד) 15$_{4(mg, Yadin)}$ ([לאיל ה[א חד]) 18$_{9}$ 21$_{1(Yadin)}$ ([איל אח]ד) 21$_{1}$ + Sup (אי[ל]) 21$_{2(Yadin)}$ ([איל אחד]) 22$_{12.12.13}$ 23$_{6}$ 25$_{5}$ + Sup 25$_{13}$ 4QApocMos B 1.2$_{5}$ ([איל אחד]), תָּמִים *complete,* i.e. unblemished Ex 29$_{1}$ Lv 5$_{15.18.25}$ 9$_{2}$ Nm 6$_{14}$ Ezk 43$_{23.25}$ 45$_{23}$ 46$_{4.6}$ 11QT 14$_{12(Yadin)}$ ([תמימים]), הָאַיִל הַשֵּׁנִי *the second ram* Ex 29$_{19}$||Lv 8$_{22}$, אַיִל מְשֻׁלָּשׁ *three-year-old ram* Gn 15$_{9}$, לאיל הזה *for this ram* 11QT 18$_{2}$.

<PREP> לְ of benefit, *for* Nm 28$_{12.28}$ 29$_{3.9.14.14.18.21.24.27.30.33.37}$ Ezk 46$_{7}$ 11QT 14$_{4(Yadin)}$ ([לאיל]) 15$_{4(mg)}$ ([לכול אי[ל]) 15$_{4(mg, Yadin)}$ ([לאיל]) 17$_{15}$ 18$_{2}$ 19$_{16}$ + Sup 19$_{16}$ + Sup 25$_{15}$ 28$_{5}$ ([לאל]ים) 28$_{9}$ 29$_{1(Yadin)}$ ([לאיל]), + היה *be* Nm 28$_{14}$ (Sam יַיִן *of wine* for יִהְיֶה *will be*) Ezk 46$_{11}$ Dn 8$_{7}$, עשׂה *do, make* Nm 15$_{6.11}$ (ni. *be done*) 28$_{20}$ Ezk 45$_{24}$ 46$_{5}$ 11QT 24$_{7(Yadin)}$ ([יעשו]), קרב hi. *present as sacrifice* 11QT 14$_{16(Yadin)}$ (תקריבו) 22$_{4(Yadin)}$ + Sup,

בֵּין־שֶׂה לָשֶׂה לָאֵילִים וְלָעַתּוּדִים *between sheep and sheep, rams and goats* Ezk 34$_{17}$.

בְּ of instrument, *by means of*, + כפר pi. *atone with* Lv 5$_{16}$ 19$_{22}$, מלא pi. *fill* hand, i.e. consecrate 2 C 13$_{9}$ (with ellipsis of בְּ), בוא בְּ *come with* Lv 16$_{3}$ (with ellipsis of בְּ; + לְעֹלָה *as a burnt offering*), בְּכָרִים וְאֵילִים ... בָּם סֹחֲרָיִךְ *in lambs and goats ..., in these they traded with you* Ezk 27$_{21}$, רצה בְּ *take pleasure in* Mc 6$_{7}$ (בְּאַלְפֵי אֵילִים *in thousands of rams*), לֹא־הָיָה כֹחַ בָּאַיִל *there was no strength in the ram* Dn 8$_{7}$.

כְּ *as*, + נפל *fall* Jr 25$_{34}$ (if em. כִּכְלִי *as a vessel of*), ירד hi. *take down* Jr 51$_{40}$, רקד *dance* Ps 114$_{4.6}$.

מִן *(as sacrificial gift) from, out of* Lv 9$_{19}$ 11QT 15$_{6}$ 20$_{15(Yadin)}$ + Sup ([מן האי]לים) 21$_{1(Yadin)}$ + Sup ([מ]ן), + רום ho. *be raised*, i.e. be taken Ex 29$_{27}$, + לקח *take* Ex 29$_{20.26}$||Lv 8$_{29}$ Nm 6$_{19}$, לְבַד מִן *apart from* CD 9$_{14}$.

מִלְּבַד *apart from* Nm 5$_{8}$; בוא עַד *come to* Dn 8$_{6}$; נגע אֵצֶל hi. *reach* Dn 8$_{7}$.

<COLL> וְהִנֵּה(־)אַיִל *and behold, a ram* Gn 22$_{13}$ Dn 8$_{3}$, אֵילִים ... עַתּוּדִים *rams ... (male) goats* Jr 51$_{40}$ Ezk 27$_{21}$ 34$_{17}$ 39$_{18}$, איל איל לכול [יום ויום] *a ram for every day* 11QT 15$_{3(Yadin)}$ + Sup, איל ואיל *each ram* 11QT 24$_{7}$.

With number, 2. Ex 29$_{1.3}$||Lv 8$_{2}$ Lv 23$_{18}$ Nm 29$_{13.14.17.20.23.26.29.32}$ 11QT 25$_{16}$ 28$_{3(Yadin)}$ ([אלים שנים]) 28$_{7.10}$; 5. Nm 7$_{17.23.29.35.41.47.53.59.65.71.77.83}$; 7. Nm 23$_{1.29}$ Jb 42$_{8}$ 2 C 13$_{9}$ 29$_{21}$; 12. Nm 7$_{87}$ Ezk 45$_{23}$ 1 C 15$_{26}$ 11QT 19$_{16}$; 20. Gn 32$_{15}$; 60. Nm 7$_{88}$; 96. Ezr 8$_{35}$; 100. 2 C 29$_{32}$; 1000. 1 C 29$_{21}$; 7,700. 2 C 17$_{11}$; 100,000. 2 K 3$_{4}$.

2. leader of a nation, <SUBJ> דבר pi. *speak* Ezk 32$_{21}$, עמד *stand* Ezk 31$_{14}$ (but prob. אֲלֵיהֶם = *their trees*, i.e. אֵלָה *terebinth* or em. אֲלֵיהֶם *to/over them*). <OBJ> אחז *seize* Ex 15$_{15}$ (subj. רַעַד *shaking*), לקח *take* Ezk 17$_{13}$, הלך hi. *lead away* 2 K 24$_{15(Qr)}$ (Kt אולי appar. אול II *leader* or אֱוִיל II *leader*; + גּוֹלָה *[into] exile*), שׁבת hi. *eliminate* Ezk 30$_{13}$ (if em. אֱלִילִים *idols*, || נָשִׂיא *prince*).

<CSTR> אֵילֵי הָאָרֶץ *leaders of the country* 2 K 24$_{15(Qr)}$ Ezk 17$_{13}$, אֵלֵי גִבּוֹרִים *leaders of warriors* Ezk 32$_{21}$, אֵילֵי מוֹאָב *leaders of Moab* Ex 15$_{15}$ (|| אַלּוּף *leader*), בְּיַד אֵיל הַגּוֹיִם *into the hand of a leader of the nations* Ezk 31$_{11}$.

Also 6QHymn 4$_{1}$ Arad ost. 12$_{6}$ 4QpGen^{a} 2$_{11}$ 4Q376 1.1$_{2}$.

אַיִל II $_{22}$ n.[m.] **pillar**—cstr. אֵיל (אֶל); sf. Kt אילו (אלו), pl. אֵילִים (אֵלִם); sf. Qr אֵילָיו (אֱלָיו), אֵלֵיהֶמָה—usu. rounded or angled edge of section of wall used to support frame or post of door (1 K 6$_{31}$), window (Ezk 40$_{16}$), gateway (e.g. Ezk 40$_{24}$), <SUBJ> היה *be* Ezk 40$_{21}$(+ כְּמִדַּת *as the dimension of*; || אוּלָם *porch*).

<NOM CL> הָאַיִל מְזוּזוֹת חֲמִשִׁית *the pillar (and) door posts were*, i.e. occupied, *a fifth* 1 K 6$_{31}$, ... אֵילָיו כַּמִּדּוֹת הָאֵלֶּה *its pillars ... were as these dimensions* Ezk 40$_{29(Qr).33(Qr)}$ (אֵלָיו; both || תָּא *chamber*, אוּלָם *porch*), וְאֵילָיו לֶחָצֵר *and its pillars were by the court* 40$_{37(Qr)}$ (or em. אֵלַמּוֹ *its porch*), לוֹ ... אֵילָיו *it had ... pillars* 40$_{36(Qr)}$ (unless obj. of מדד *measure*).

<OBJ> עשׂה *make* Ezk 40$_{14}$ (or em. וַיַּעַשׂ אֶת־אֵילִים *and he made [the] pillars to* וְעַל־פְּנֵי אֻלָם הַשַּׁעַר *and in front of the porch of the gate [were]*; + שִׁשִּׁים אַמָּה *sixty cubits* [or em. חֲמִשִּׁים *fifty*]), מדד *measure* 40$_{9}$ (+ שְׁתַּיִם אַמּוֹת *two cubits*; || אוּלָם *porch*) 40$_{24.36}$ (unless nom. cl.; || תָּא *chamber*, חַלּוֹן *window*; all three || אוּלָם *porch*) 40$_{48}$ 41$_{1}$ (+ שֵׁשׁ אַמּוֹת *six cubits*) 41$_{3}$ (+ שְׁתַּיִם אַמּוֹת).

<CSTR> אֵיל הֶחָצֵר *pillar of*, i.e. in, *the court* Ezk 40$_{14}$, אֵיל־הַפֶּתַח *pillar of the entrance* 41$_{3}$, אֵל אֻלָם *pillar of (the) porch* 40$_{48}$ (or em. אֵיל־הָאֻלָם), רֹחַב הָאַיִל *width of the pillar* Ezk 41$_{1}$ (if em. הָאֹהֶל *of the tent*).

<APP> אֵילִים הַשְּׁעָרִים *pillars, the gates*, perh. pillars of the gates Ezk 40$_{38}$ (or em. אוּלָם הַשַּׁעַר *porch of the gate*), הָאַיִל מְזוּזוֹת *the pillar (and) door posts* 1 K 6$_{31}$.

<PREP> מִדָּה אַחַת לָאֵילִם *there was a single measure for the pillars* Ezk 40$_{10}$.

לִשְׁכָּה וּפִתְחָהּ בְּאֵילִים *and a chamber and its entrance were next to pillars* Ezk 40$_{38}$ (or em.; see App.).

אֲטֻמוֹת אֶל perh. *recessed towards* Ezk 40$_{16}$ (|| תָּא *chamber*; or em. וְאֶל אֵלֵיהֶמָה *and towards their pillars to* לְאֵלַמּוֹ חַלּוֹנוֹת *[belonging] to its porch. Windows*), וְאֶל־אֵיל הֶחָצֵר הַשַּׁעַר סָבִיב סָבִיב appar. *and next to the pillar of the porch was the gate all around* 40$_{14}$, וְעַמֻּדִים אֶל־הָאֵילִים *and there were columns by the pillars* 40$_{49}$ (or em. עַל *by*) וְתִמֹרִים אֶל־אֵילָיו (and var.) *and (decorative) palm trees were on its pillars* 40$_{26.31(Qr).34(Qr)}$ (אֵלָיו) 40$_{37(Qr)}$, sim. 40$_{16.26}$ (or em. עַל in all five).

[אַיִל] III, see אֵלָה I.

אֱיָל 1.0.1 n.[m.] **help**—sf. Q אילך—**help** or perh. **strength, arbitration,** כְּגֶבֶר אֵין־אֱיָל *as a man (for whom) there is no help* Ps 88_{5}, באילך מאסור *by your arbitration from a prisoner* 4Q416 2_{9}
→ אֱיָלוּת *help.*

אַיָּל 11.0.2 n.m. (sometimes f.) **deer**—Q איאל; pl. אַיָּלִים—permitted for food (Dt 12_{15}=11QT 53_{5} Dt 12_{22} 14_{5} 15_{22}=11QT 52_{11}), consumed by Solomon (1 K 5_{3}), <SUBJ> מצא *find* pasture Lm 1_{6}, ערג *crave* Ps 42_{2} (or em. אַיֶּלֶת *hind*), אכל ni. *be eaten* Dt 12_{22} (|| צְבִי *gazelle*). <OBJ> אכל *eat* Dt 14_{5} (|| צְבִי). <CSTR> עֹפֶר הָאַיָּלִים *young deer (of deer)* Ca $2_{9.17}$ (Gnz עֲפַר) 8_{14} (all three + צְבִי), עכס (pi.) *catch by leg* Pr 7_{22} (if em. וּכְעֶכֶס אֶל־מוּסַר אֱוִיל *and as (one wearing) anklets to the disciplining of a fool*). <PREP> כְּ *as*, + היה *be* (of princes) Lm 1_{6}, ערג *crave* (of soul) Ps 42_{2}, דלג pi. *leap* Is 35_{6} 4QapPs[b] 48_{6} ([כאי]ל]), רדף *chase* Jb 19_{22} (if em. כְּמוֹ־אֵל *as God*), אכל כְּ *eat (something) as though it were* a deer Dt 12_{15}=11QT 53_{5} Dt 15_{22}=11QT 52_{11}; לְבַד מִן *apart from* 1 K 5_{3} (+ צְבִי).
<SYN> צְבִי *gazelle.*
→ אַיָּלָה *hind,* אַיָּלוֹן *Aijalon.*

אַיָּלָה 11 n.f. **hind**—abs. אַיֶּלֶת; cstr. אַיֶּלֶת; pl. abs. אַיָּלוֹת; cstr. אַיְלוֹת—proverbial for agility (2 S 22_{34}||Ps 18_{34} Hb 3_{19}) and tenderness (Jr 14_{5} Pr 5_{19}), <SUBJ> חול pol. *writhe* Jb 39_{1} (+ יָעֵל *mountain goat*), ילד *give birth* Jr 14_{5} (+ בַּשָּׂדֶה *in the field*), עזב *leave* fawns 14_{5}, שׁלח pass. *be released* Gn 49_{21} (or em. אֵילָה slender *terebinth*) 4QpGen[a] 6_{1} ([אילה]), נתן *give* 49_{21} (obj. אִמְרֵי־שָׁפֶר *lovely sayings*), ערג *be thirsty* Ps 42_{2} (if em. אַיָּל *hart*; + עַל־אֲפִיקֵי־מָיִם *for channels of water*).
<NOM CL> נַפְתָּלִי אַיָּלָה *Naphtali is a hind* Gn 49_{21} (or em. אֵילָה *terebinth*). <OBJ> חול pol. *make calve* Ps 29_{9} (or em. אֵילוֹת *terebinths*).
<CSTR> אַיֶּלֶת אֲהָבִים *hind of loves,* i.e. hind whom one loves Pr 5_{19}, אַיֶּלֶת הַשַּׁחַר *hind of the dawn* (title of melody) Ps 22_{1}, אַיְלוֹת הַשָּׂדֶה *hinds of the field* Ca 2_{7} 3_{5} (both + צְבִי *gazelle*). <APP> אֵשֶׁת נְעוּרֶךָ אַיֶּלֶת אֲהָבִים *the wife of your youth, a hind whom one loves* Pr 5_{19} (|| יַעֲלָה *doe*).
<PREP> שׁבע בְּ hi. *adjure* daughters of Jerusalem *by* Ca 2_{7}=3_{5}; כְּ *as* Ps 42_{2} (if em.; see Subj.), וַיָּשֶׂם רַגְלַי כָּאַיָּלוֹת *and he has placed my feet as (those of) the hinds* Hb 3_{19} (+ עַל בָּמוֹת *on high places*), sim. 2 S $22_{34(Qr)}$||Ps 18_{34} (+ עַל בָּמוֹת); עַל *according to* melody Ps 22_{1}.
→ אַיָּל *deer.*

אִילוּ, see אִי IV.

[אִילוּ], see אִלּוּ.

[אִילוּלֵי], see אִלּוּלֵי.

אַיָּלוֹן 10 pl.n. **Aijalon**— + ־ה of direction אַיָּלֹנָה—**1.** Canaanite town that passed, as Levitical city, to Dan (also attributed to Ephraim, 1 C 6_{54}, and Benjamin, 1 C 8_{13} 2 C 11_{10}), ident. with Yālō 20 km NW of Jerusalem, Jos 10_{12} (+ עֵמֶק *valley of*) 19_{42} 21_{24} (ms Kt אלון *Elon*) Jg 1_{35} 1 S 14_{31} 1 K 4_{9} (if em. אֵילוֹן בֵּית חָנָן *Elon-beth-hanan* to אַיָּלוֹן וּבֵית חָנָן *Aijalon and Beth-hanan*) 1 C 6_{54} 8_{13} 2 C 11_{10} 28_{18}. **2.** in Zebulun, burial place of Elon, Jg 12_{12}.
→ אַיָּל *deer.*

אֵילוֹן I 6.0.0.1 pr.n.m. **Elon**—אֵלוֹן, אֵילֹן, אלן I—**1.** Hittite (Sam חִוִּי *Hivite*), father of Basemath wife of Esau, Gn 26_{34} (אֵילֹן). **2.** Hittite, father of Adah wife of Esau, perh. ident. with preceding, Gn 36_{2}. **3.** son of Zebulun, Gn 46_{14} Nm 26_{26} (both אֵלוֹן). **4.** judge after Ibzan and descendant of Zebulun, Jg $12_{11.12}$ (אֵלוֹן; mss אֵילוֹן). **5.** son of Elibar (אליבר), Seal 397_{1} (אלן; 7th cent.).
Also Arad ost. 69_{6} (אלן).
→ אֵלוֹן *terebinth.*

אֵילוֹן II 2 pl. n. **Elon,** town in Dan, Jos 19_{43} perh. 1 K 4_{9} (Or em. אֵילוֹן בֵּית חָנָן *Elon-beth-hanan* to אַיָּלוֹן וּבֵית חָנָן *Aijalon and Beth-hanan*).

אֵילוֹת, see אֵילַת.

[אֱיָלוּת] 1 n.f. **help**—sf. אֱיָלוּתִי—**help,** or perh. **strength,** אֱיָלוּתִי לְעֶזְרָתִי חוּשָׁה *my help, to my assistance hasten* (in address to Y.) Ps 22$_{20}$.
Also 4QM(g?) 5$_{2}$.
→ אֱיָל *help.*

[אֵילָם], see אוּלָם II.

אֵילִם 6 pl.n. **Elim**—+ ־ה of direction אֵילִמָה—second station of exodus, Ex 15$_{27}$ 16$_{1.1}$ Nm 33$_{9.9.10}$.
→ אֵלוֹן *terebinth.*

אֵילֹן, see אֵילוֹן I.

[אִילָן] 0.0.1 n.[m.] **tree**—used collectively, של הירק ושל האילן *of the vegetable(s) and of the tree(s)* 5/6ḤevBA 46$_{9}$.

אֵיל פָּארָן 1 pl.n. **El-paran,** on edge of desert, perh. ident. with Elath (אֵילַת), Gn 14$_{6}$.

אֵילַת 8 pl.n. **Elath**—אֵלוֹת, אֵילוֹת, mss אֵלַת—Red Sea port, used by Solomon for trade with Ophir (1 K 9$_{26}$‖2 C 8$_{17}$), rebuilt by Azariah/Uzziah (2 K 14$_{22}$‖2 C 26$_{2}$), captured by Edomites (2 K 16$_{6}$ [if em. אֲרָם *Aram*]), perh. ident. with El-paran at Gn 14$_{6}$, Dt 2$_{8}$ 1 K 9$_{26}$‖2 C 8$_{17}$ (1 K אֵלוֹת; mss אֵלַת; 2 C אֵילוֹת) 2 K 14$_{22}$‖2 C 26$_{2}$ (2 C אֵילוֹת) 2 K 16$_{6.6}$ (אֵילוֹת; mss אֵלַת) 16$_{6}$.

אַיֶּלֶת, see אַיָּלָה.

אָיֹם 3 adj. **terrible**—Q איום; f. אֲיֻמָּה—אָיֹם וְנוֹרָא הוּא *terrible and fearful it* (nation) *is* Hb 1$_{7}$ (1QpHab איום), אֲיֻמָּה כַּנִּדְגָּלוֹת woman lover is *terrible as those that carry banners* Ca 6$_{4.10}$.
→ אֵימָה *terror,* אֵמִים *Emim.*

אֵימָה 16.2.4 n.f. **terror**—אֵימָתָה, Q אמה; cstr. אֵימַת; sf. אֵימָתִי (אֵמָתִי), אֵימָתְךָ (אֵמָתְךָ) אֵימָתוֹ (אֵמָתוֹ), אֵימַתְכֶם, Q אימתם; pl.abs. אֵימִים (אֵמִים); cstr. אֵימוֹת, אֵמֶיךָ—**1.** feeling of terror, **dread,** <SUBJ> נפל *fall* Gn 15$_{12}$ Ex15$_{16}$ (‖ פַּחַד *fear*) Jos 2$_{9}$ Ps 55$_{5}$, חרף pi. *reproach* Si 43$_{16(B)}$ (M אִמְרָתוֹ *his word*). <NOM CL> אימתם על כול הגואים *the nations* 1QpHab 3$_{4}$ (‖ פַּחַד *fear*). <OBJ> שׁלח pi. *send* Ex 23$_{27}$.

<CSTR> אימת מות *dread of death* Si 40$_{5}$ (+ פַּחַד *fear,* דְּאָגָה *worry,* קִנְאָה *envy,* תַּחֲרָה *strife*), אֵימוֹת מָוֶת *dread(s) of death* Ps 55$_{5}$; רשית ... אימה *the beginning of ... dread* 1QS 10$_{15}$ (‖ פַּחַד *fear*), כול ... אימה *all ... dread* 1$_{17}$ (‖ פַּחַד). <APP> אֵימָה חֲשֵׁכָה גְדֹלָה *a dread, great darkness* Gn 15$_{12}$. <PREP> בְּ נתן ni. *be given* to enemy *with* 1QpHab 4$_{7}$ (‖ פַּחַד *fear*), שׁוב מִן *go back because of* 1QS 1$_{17}$ (‖ פַּחַד, מַצְרֵף *testing*).

2. source of terror (but distinction from §1 not alw. clear). **a. terror,** <SUBJ> שׁכל pi. *bereave* Dt 32$_{25}$ (or understand וּמֵחֲדָרִים אֵימָה as nom. cl., *and from inside is terror*), בעת pi. *terrify* Jb 9$_{34}$ 13$_{21}$ 33$_{7}$, הלך *go* 20$_{25}$. <NOM CL> הוֹד נַחְרוֹ אֵימָה *the majesty of his snorting is a terror* Jb 39$_{20}$, סְבִיבוֹת שִׁנָּיו אֵימָה *terror is around his teeth* 41$_{6}$, נַהַם כַּכְּפִיר אֵימַת מֶלֶךְ *the terror of,* i.e. inspired by, *a king is a growl as (that of) a lion* Pr 20$_{2}$. <OBJ> נשׂא *bear* Ps 88$_{16}$, הגה *meditate on* Is 33$_{18}$.

<CSTR> אֵימַת מֶלֶךְ *terror of a king* Pr 20$_{2}$. <PREP> בְּאֵימָה עֲלֵיהֶם מֵעַמֵּי הָאֲרָצוֹת perh. *some of the peoples of the lands were against them with terror* Ezr 3$_{3}$ (or em. בְּאֵיבָה *with enmity*).

2b. idol, perh. as source of terror, אֶרֶץ פְּסִלִים הִיא וּבָאֵימִים יִתְהֹלָלוּ *it is a land of images, and they act like madmen with their idols* Jr 50$_{38}$.
Also 1QIsa[a] 34$_{14}$ (אייאמים; see אִי *jackal,* Obj.).
<SYN> §1 פַּחַד *fear.*
→ אָיֹם *terrible.*

אֵימָה, see אָיֹם.

[אֵימִי], see אֵמִים.

אֵימִים, see אֵמִים.

אַיִן I 790.55.228.3 negative part. **not**—abs. אַיִן; cstr. אֵין (L אין); sf. אֵינֶנִּי (Q איני), אֵינְךָ, אֵינֵךְ, 3ms אֵינֶנּוּ (Q אננו), אֵינֶנָּה, 1cp אֵינֶנּוּ, אֵינְכֶם, אֵינָם, אֵינָמוֹ (אֵינָמוֹ), Q אינמה)—in its syntax, when compounded with suffixes, אַיִן

resembles יֵשׁ.

1a. there is not (present) (oft. preceded by כִּי *that, because*), as predicate of **noun without article** (usu. sg.), Gn 41$_{49}$ 45$_{6}$ Ex 2$_{12}$ 12$_{30}$ 21$_{11}$ 32$_{18.18}$ Nm 11$_{6}$ 20$_{19}$ (+ רַק *only*) 21$_{5.5}$ Dt 8$_{15}$ 32$_{4}$ Jg 18$_{7}$ (if em.; see §2a) 19$_{19}$ 1 S 20$_{21}$ 1 K 5$_{18.18}$ 18$_{26.29.29.43}$ 2 K 4$_{2}$ Is 33$_{19}$ 40$_{16.16}$ 41$_{28}$ 59$_{15.16}$ Jr 2$_{32}$ 5$_{21}$ 6$_{14}$=8$_{11}$ 8$_{15}$=14$_{19}$ 14$_{6}$ Ezk 13$_{10.16}$ Ho 3$_{4.4.4.4.4}$ Jl 1$_{6}$ Mc 3$_{7}$ Na 3$_{9}$ Zc 10$_{2}$ Ps 19$_{4.4}$ 37$_{10}$ 69$_{3}$ 88$_{5}$ 104$_{25}$ 105$_{34}$ 144$_{14.14}$ Jb 5$_{9}$ 19$_{7}$ 21$_{33}$ Pr 6$_{15}$ 10$_{25}$ 25$_{3}$ 28$_{3.24}$ 29$_{1.9.19}$ Ec 4$_{8}$ Lm 2$_{9}$ 5$_{3}$ 1 C 29$_{15}$ 2C 20$_{24}$ Si 13$_{24}$ 3QJub 23$_{12.23}$ 1QS 4$_{23}$ 4QPrFêtes[c] 13$_{4}$ 1QM 14$_{5}$ 4QDibHam[a] 1.4$_{12}$ CD 9$_{13}$ 20$_{16}$ 4Q185 1.1$_{12}$ 1.2$_{6}$ 1QH 5$_{34}$ 6$_{32(Licht)}$ 9$_{3}$ 10$_{18}$ 11$_{26}$ 12$_{10}$ 15$_{16}$ fr. 2.1$_{11}$ 1QpHab 3$_{12}$, אֵין אָדָם אֲשֶׁר לֹא־יֶחֱטָא *there is not a person who does not sin* 1 K 8$_{46}$||2 C 6$_{36}$; and all refs. in §5, except §5a [3] and Is 57$_{1}$ Jr 19$_{11}$ 48$_{9}$ Ezk 33$_{28}$ Ml 2$_{13}$ 2 C 14$_{12}$ Si 8$_{16}$ 1QM 18$_{11}$ 1QM 19$_{11(Baillet)}$ + Sup, and, in §4e, Jg 18$_{10}$ 2 S 7$_{22}$ 1 K 22$_{7}$||2 C 18$_{6}$ 2 K 3$_{11}$ 4$_{6}$ 7$_{5.10}$ Is 23$_{10}$ 34$_{12}$ 43$_{11}$ 44$_{6}$ 45$_{5.21}$ 46$_{9}$ Jr 8$_{22}$ 48$_{2}$ Ho 13$_{4}$ Ps 14$_{3}$||53$_{4}$ 74$_{9}$ 1 C 17$_{20}$ Si 33$_{5}$ 1QH 12$_{18}$ Lachish ost. 4$_{5}$ 1QMyst 1.1$_{7}$ Silwan royal steward tomb inscr. 1$_{1}$.

אַיִן oft. introduces a circumstantial clause, e.g. שְׁבִי־לָאָרֶץ אֵין־כִּסֵּא *sit on the ground, there being no*, i.e. without, *throne* Is 47$_{1}$, יוֹנָה פוֹתָה אֵין לֵב *a foolish dove, without a mind* Ho 7$_{11}$, ואין עולה יבדלו *there being no wickedness, they divide* 1QS 8$_{10(mg)}$, sometimes without verbal force, **without,** פַּחַד וְאֵין שָׁלוֹם *fear and not peace* Jr 30$_{5}$, Ca 6$_{8}$ 1 C 22$_{3}$ Si 37$_{25(D)}$ 1QH 6$_{31}$ 4QapPs[b] 76$_{12}$.

1b. with **noun with article**, thus **cease to be, vanish, die,** אֵין הַנַּעַר וָמֵת *the lad there was not*, i.e. was no more, *and was dead* Gn 44$_{31}$, הִנֵּה אֵין יוֹנָתָן *behold, Jonathan there was not*, i.e. he had vanished, 1 S 14$_{17}$, sim. Jr 4$_{23.25}$ 22$_{17}$ 48$_{2}$ (+ עוֹד *any more*) Ezk 13$_{15}$ (or em. אַיֵּה *where is?*), perh. אֵין אֱלֹהִים *God is not present* Ps 10$_{4}$ 14$_{1}$||53$_{2}$, אֵין זֹאת *this there is not*, i.e. this is not so, 1 S 20$_{2}$ Am 2$_{11}$, אֵין זֶה כִּי(־)אִם *there is not*, i.e. nothing, *except this* place, etc. Gn 28$_{17}$ Ne 2$_{2}$, sim. Jg 7$_{14}$.

Oft. when subj. has article אַיִן has a resumptive pronoun suffix, e.g. וְהוּא אֵינֶנּוּ *and he, he was not*, i.e. he disappeared 1 K 20$_{40}$, sim. Gn 37$_{30}$ 42$_{13.32.36.36}$ Zc 8$_{10}$, אֹהֶל רְשָׁעִים אֵינֶנּוּ *(the) tent of (the) wicked is no more* Jb 8$_{22}$.

1c. אַיִן forms complete clause with pronoun suffix, **I am no more,** etc., e.g. בְּטֶרֶם אֵלֵךְ וְאֵינֶנִּי *before I go and am no more* Ps 39$_{14}$, הַמְחַכִּים לַמָּוֶת וְאֵינֶנּוּ *who wait for death, but there is none* Jb 3$_{21}$, א[יננו] עוד *he is no more* 1QMyst 1.1$_{6}$, var. 1.1$_{7}$, sim. Gn 5$_{24}$ Is 17$_{14}$ 19$_{7}$ Jr 10$_{20}$ 31$_{15}$ 49$_{10}$ (or em.; see §2a) 50$_{20}$ Ezk 26$_{21}$ 27$_{36}$ 28$_{19}$ (both + עַד־עוֹלָם *forever*) Ps 37$_{10.36}$ 59$_{14}$ 73$_{20}$ (if em. אֲדֹנָי *Adonai*) 103$_{16}$ Jb 7$_{8.21}$ 23$_{8}$ 24$_{24}$ 27$_{19}$ Pr 12$_{7}$ 23$_{5}$ Lm 5$_{7}$.

1d. there is none, with ellipsis of previously stated subj., esp. in context of search or expectation, מְבַקְשִׁים מַיִם וָאַיִן *seeking water but there is none* Is 41$_{17}$, נְקַוֶּה לַמִּשְׁפָּט וָאַיִן *we look for justice but there is none* 59$_{11}$, וַנִּרְאֶה כִּי־אַיִן *and we saw that there were none* (she-asses) 1 S 10$_{14}$, sim. 1 S 9$_{4}$ 1 K 18$_{10}$ Ezk 7$_{25}$ Ps 69$_{21}$ Jb 3$_{9}$ Pr 14$_{6}$ 20$_{4}$ Si 51$_{7}$.

With subj. not stated, מִתְאַוָּה וָאַיִן נַפְשׁוֹ *his soul craves, but there is nothing* Pr 13$_{4}$, כִּי־אַיִן פָּקַד אַפּוֹ appar. *because there is not* (perh. *because nothing has been decided*) *his anger has punished* Jb 35$_{15}$ (or em. אֵין פֹּקֵד his anger *does not punish*).

הֲיֵשׁ ... אִם־אַיִן *is there ... or isn't there?*, הֲיֵשׁ־בָּהּ עֵץ אִם־אַיִן *are there trees there or aren't there?* Nm 13$_{20}$, Ex 17$_{7}$ Jb 33$_{33}$ Si 5$_{12}$ (both אִם יֵשׁ).

1e. אַיִן as whole clause, **no, there isn't,** Jg 4$_{20}$ 4QM[a] fr. 11.1$_{16}$ 4QShir[b] 18.2$_{5}$.

2a. there is no one who, nothing that, followed by **participle** e.g. אֵין רֹאֶה *there is no one who sees* Ex 22$_{9}$, of ראה *see* Ex 22$_{9}$ 1 S 26$_{12}$ Is 47$_{10}$, גלה *uncover* 1 S 22$_{8}$, אמר *say* Is 42$_{22}$ Jr 49$_{10}$ (if em. אֵינֶנּוּ *he is no more* to וְאֵין אֹמֵר *and there is none who says*), דבר *speak* Jb 2$_{13}$, ענה *reply* Jg 19$_{28}$ 1 S 14$_{39}$ 1 K 18$_{26.29}$ Is 50$_{2}$ 66$_{4}$, קרא *call* 59$_{4}$ 64$_{6}$ Ho 7$_{7}$, פתר *explain* Gn 40$_{8}$ 41$_{8.15}$, נגד hi. *tell, explain* 41$_{24}$ Is 41$_{26}$, יעץ *advise* 41$_{28}$, יכח hi. *reprove* Jb 32$_{12}$ CD 20$_{16}$, שמע *hear* 2 S 15$_{3}$ Is 41$_{26}$, hi. *tell* 41$_{26}$, קשב hi. *listen* Pr 1$_{24}$, ידע *know* 1 S 26$_{12}$, נכר hi. *know* Ps 142$_{5}$, בין ni. *be intelligent* Gn 41$_{39}$, hi. *understand* Is 57$_{1}$ Dn 8$_{27}$ 4QapPs[b] 44$_{4}$, דרש *seek* Jr 30$_{17}$ Ezk 34$_{6}$ Ps 142$_{5}$ CD 14$_{16}$ 4QTanḥ 14$_{6}$, בקש pi. *request* Ezk 34$_{6}$, כתב pass. *be written* CD 9$_{5}$.

אנס *compel* Est 1$_{8}$, כלם hi. *humiliate* Jg 18$_{7}$ (or em.

אֵין־מַכְלִים דָּבָר appar. *there was no one who humiliated [them] in any way* to אֵין־מַחְסוֹר כָּל־דָּבָר *there was no lack of anything* or אֵין־מֶלֶךְ מַדְבֵּר *there was no oppressive king*) Jb 11$_3$, שׁחת hi. *destroy* 4QShir^b 1$_6$ ([אי]ן), שׁפט ni. *contest legally* Is 59$_4$, הנה ni. *enjoy* Si 30$_{19(Bmg)}$, חרד hi. *terrify* Lv 26$_6$ Dt 28$_{26}$ Is 17$_2$ Jr 7$_{33}$ 30$_{10}$=46$_{27}$ Ezk 34$_{28}$ 39$_{26}$ Mc 4$_4$ Na 2$_{12}$ Zp 3$_{13}$ Jb 11$_{19}$, חלה *be sick* 1 S 22$_8$, הלל *be mad* 1QH 4$_{20}$, גרע ni. *be diminished* Ex 5$_{11}$, פתל ni. *be twisted* Pr 8$_8$, שׁוה *be equitable* Est 3$_8$, סתר ni. *be hidden* Ps 19$_7$ Si 39$_{19}$ (mg pu.), כון ni. *be stable, prepared* Ps 5$_{10}$ Ne 8$_{10}$, קִיץ hi. *awake* 1 S 26$_{12}$, פלא ni. *be wonderful* Si 39$_{20}$.

ישׁב *dwell* Jr 44$_2$ 48$_9$, עמד *stand* Dn 11$_{16}$, בוא *come* Jos 6$_1$, הלך *go* Ezk 7$_{14}$, יצא *go out* Jos 6$_1$ Ps 144$_{14}$, עבר *pass* intrans. Ezk 33$_{28}$ Is 34$_{10}$ 60$_{15}$, רדף *pursue* Lv 26$_{17.36.37}$ (אַיִן) Pr 28$_1$, כשׁל *stumble* Is 5$_{27}$ Ps 105$_{37}$, נשׂג hi. *place* 1 S 14$_{26}$, שׂים *place* Jr 12$_{11}$, סגר *close* Is 22$_{22}$, פתח *open* 22$_{22}$ Jr 13$_{19}$ 4QShir^b 30$_3$, שׁוב hi. *return* trans. 1QSb 5$_{29(Milik)}$ ([מש]ב) 4QapLam$^b_3$, פנה hi. *turn* trans. Na 2$_9$, נטה *extend* trans. Jr 10$_{20}$, פרשׂ *extend* intrans. Lm 4$_4$, פגע hi. *intervene* Is 59$_{16}$, חזק hi. *grasp* 51$_{18}$, קום hi. *raise* 10$_{20}$ Jr 50$_{32}$ Am 5$_2$, דלג *leap*, i.e. transgress statute 4QShirShab^f 23.1$_{10}$.

ישׁע hi. *deliver* Dt 22$_{27}$=11QT 66$_8$ Dt 28$_{29.31}$ 1 S 11$_3$ 2 S 22$_{42}$||Ps 18$_{42}$ Is 47$_{15}$ 11QT 59$_8$, נצל hi. *deliver* Dt 32$_{39}$ Jg 18$_{28}$ 2 S 14$_6$ Is 5$_{29}$ 42$_{22}$ 43$_{13}$ Ho 5$_{14}$ Mc 5$_7$ Ps 7$_3$ 50$_{22}$ 71$_{11}$ Jb 5$_4$ 10$_7$ Dn 8$_4$ Si 8$_{16}$ 1QM 14$_{11}$ 18$_{13(Yadin)}$ ([מציל]), פרק *deliver* Lm 5$_8$, עזר *help* 2 K 14$_{26}$ Is 63$_5$ Ps 22$_{12}$ 72$_{12}$ 107$_{12}$ Lm 1$_7$ Dn 11$_{45}$ Si 51$_7$ 1QM 1$_6$, נחם pi. *comfort* Ec 4$_{1.1}$ Lm 1$_{2.9.17.21}$, דין *judge* Jr 30$_{13}$, סמך *support* Is 63$_5$, חבשׁ *bind* 4QapLam$^b_3$.

עשׂה *do* Ps 14$_{1.3}$||53$_{2.4}$, קנה *buy* Dt 28$_{68}$, כבה pi. *extinguish* Is 1$_{31}$ Jr 4$_4$ 21$_{12}$ Am 5$_6$ 4QapPs^b 24$_2$, קבץ pi. *gather* Is 13$_{14}$ Jr 49$_5$ Na 3$_{18}$, אסף *gather* Jr 9$_{21}$, שׂנא *hate* 4Q416 9.1$_7$, מות *die* Ex 12$_{30}$, שׁכל pi. *be bereaved* 11QBer 1.2$_{10}$, קבר *bury* 2 K 9$_{10}$ Ps 79$_3$ 1QM 11$_1$ 4QTanḥ 1.1$_4$, pi. *bury* Jr 14$_{16}$ 1QM 19$_{11(Baillet)}$ + Sup (מ[קב]ר), וְאֵין הַטָּחִים אֹתוֹ *and there are none who paint it* Ezk 13$_{15}$ (or em. אַיֵּה *where are?*), מגר *throw*, i.e. pour 4QapLam^a 1.2$_{8(Allegro)}$.

2b. there is no one who is, nothing that is, followed by **adjective,** טוֹב *good* 1 S 27$_1$ Ec 2$_{24}$ 3$_{12.22}$ 8$_{15}$, קָדוֹשׁ *holy* 1 S 2$_2$, צַדִּיק *righteous* 1QH 12$_{19}$, יָשָׁר *righteous* Mc 7$_2$ (יָשָׁר ... אָיִן), קָטָן *small* Si 39$_{20}$, גָּדוֹל *great* 10$_{24(A)}$ ([אי]ן), חָזָק *strong* 39$_{20}$, נָקִי *exempt* 1 K 15$_{22}$, עָיֵף *tired* Is 5$_{27}$, שַׁכּוּל *bereaved* Ca 4$_2$=6$_6$, רַע *wicked* Ml 1$_{8.8}$ Si 14$_6$, טָמֵא *impure* 4QShirShab^a 1.1$_{14}$ ([אי]ן), עִקֵּשׁ *twisted* Pr 8$_8$, אֵין אַחֶרֶת *there is no other* 1 S 21$_{10}$, var. 1QS 11$_{18}$ 1QH 12$_{11}$.

3. there is no one, nothing, (1) followed by **preposition,** כְּ *like* Ex 8$_6$ 9$_{14}$ Dt 33$_{26}$ 1 S 10$_{24}$ 2 S 7$_{22}$ 1 K 8$_{23}$||2 C 6$_{14}$ Ps 86$_{8.8}$ Jb 1$_8$ 2$_3$ 1 C 17$_{20}$ 4QpIsa^a 5$_{11}$ perh. 1QH fr. 35$_2$, מֵאֵין כָּמוֹךְ perh. *there is no one like you* Jr 10$_{6.7}$ (or em. אֵין or מֵאַיִן *whence is* [one] like you?) 4QapPs^b 44$_4$ 76$_{14}$; בְּ of place, accompaniment, *in, with,* etc., 1 K 8$_9$||2 C 5$_{10}$ 1QH 9$_{16}$ MasShirShab 1$_4$ 4QMMT A 2$_{63}$; עִם *(compared) with* 2 C 14$_{10}$ 1QH 10$_{10}$, אֵין עִמָּדִי *it is not with me* Jb 28$_{14}$; אֵין־אֶתְכֶם אֵלַי *you were not*, i.e. did not return, *to me* Hg 2$_{17}$; אֶת־מִי־אֵין כְּמוֹ־אֵלֶּה *with whom are there not (things) as these?* Jb 12$_3$; אין לנגד כבודכה *there is no one in the presence of your glory* 1QH 10$_{10}$, sim. 12$_{31}$.

(2) with **adverb,** עוֹד *besides, more* Dt 4$_{35.39}$ 1 K 8$_{60}$ Is 45$_{5.6.14.18.22}$ 46$_9$ Jl 2$_{27}$ 1QM 18$_{11}$, בִּלְתִּי *besides* 1 S 2$_2$, זוּלַת *besides* Is 45$_{21}$ (אַיִן) Si 33$_{12}$ 4QDibHam^a 1.5$_9$ 1QH 7$_{32}$ 10$_9$.

4. is not, in a negative **nom. cl., a.** predicate is continued by **prepositional phrase,** (1) אֵין לְ **there is not,** i.e. there does not belong, **to,** with pronoun following, e.g. שָׁדַיִם אֵין לָהּ *she does not have breasts* Ca 8$_8$, sim. Lv 22$_{13}$ Nm 27$_8$ Dt 25$_5$ Jg 18$_{7.28}$ 2 K 4$_{14}$ Is 1$_{30}$ 27$_4$ Jr 30$_{13}$ 46$_{11}$ 49$_{1.1}$ Ezk 38$_{11}$ Am 3$_{4.5}$ Pr 30$_{27}$ Ec 4$_8$ 9$_6$ 1QH 7$_{17}$ Mur 30 1$_6$ 2$_{28}$ 4Q371 1.2$_2$ 4QApocMos A 2.2$_4$.

With noun following, e.g. כֹּל אֲשֶׁר אֵין־לוֹ סְנַפִּיר *anything which does not have a fin* Lv 11$_{10}$||Dt 14$_{10}$ Lv 11$_{12}$, sim. Gn 11$_{30}$ Ex 22$_1$ Lv 25$_{31}$ Nm 5$_8$ 27$_{4.9.10.17}$ 35$_{27}$ Dt 12$_{12}$ 14$_{27.29}$ 22$_{26}$=11QT 66$_6$ Jos 22$_{25.27}$ 1 S 14$_6$ 2 S 18$_{18}$ 19$_7$ 20$_1$ 21$_{4.4}$ 1 K 22$_{17}$||2 C 18$_{16}$ 2 K 4$_2$ Is 8$_{20}$ 55$_1$ Jr 8$_{17}$ 14$_{19}$ 39$_{10}$ 46$_{23}$ Ezk 42$_6$ Ho 8$_7$ Ml 1$_{10}$ Ps 119$_{165}$ 146$_3$ Pr 6$_7$ Est 2$_7$ 2 C 14$_{12}$ 35$_3$ Si 3$_{22(A).28}$ 7$_6$ 13$_{22}$ 15$_{12(B)}$ 36$_{31}$ 38$_{21}$ 44$_9$ GnzPs 2$_{24}$ CD 9$_{14}$ 14$_{16}$ ([אי]ן) 20$_{10}$ 4QShir^b 3$_5$ ([ל]כם) 2Q28 2$_2$ 5/6Ḥev BA 45$_4$ (ל[ה]ם).

אֵין לְאֵל יָדֵנוּ *there is not according to the power of our hand*, i.e. *we are powerless* Ne 5$_{5}$ (mss יָדֵינוּ *our hands*) 4QapLam^{a} 1.1$_{2}$, vars. Dt 28$_{32}$ Jg 11$_{34}$ Ec 12$_{1}$ Ex 22$_{2}$ Pr 22$_{27}$ Dn 9$_{26}$ (or ins. after אֵין לוֹ *there is nothing he has* דִּין *judgment* or אָוֶן *iniquity*, i.e. although *he has no judgment/iniquity*) 2 C 22$_{9}$ 4QOrd^{a} 1.2$_{4}$.

אֵין separated from or following לְ, e.g. אֵין אַחִים לְאָבִיו *his father does not have brothers* Nm 27$_{11}$, לוֹ אֵין מִשְׁפַּט־מָוֶת *for him there is no capital penalty* Dt 19$_{6}$, sim. Gn 47$_{4}$ Jos 18$_{7}$ Jg 6$_{5}$ 7$_{12}$ 1 S 1$_{2}$ 18$_{25}$ 2 S 12$_{3}$ Is 27$_{7}$ 9$_{6}$ 40$_{28}$ 45$_{9}$ 48$_{22}$=57$_{21}$ 50$_{10}$ 51$_{18}$ Jr 12$_{12}$ Ho 10$_{3}$ Jl 1$_{18}$ Na 2$_{10}$ 3$_{3.19}$ Zc 8$_{10}$ Ps 3$_{3}$ 34$_{10}$ 55$_{20}$ 73$_{4}$ 145$_{3}$ 147$_{5}$ Jb 22$_{5}$ 26$_{6}$ 31$_{19}$ Pr 25$_{28}$ Ec 1$_{11}$ 2$_{16}$ 4$_{8.16}$ 8$_{15}$ 9$_{5}$ 10$_{11}$ Ne 2$_{20}$ 1 C 4$_{27}$ 22$_{14.16}$ 2 C 12$_{3}$ 15$_{5}$ Si 6$_{15.15}$ 12$_{3}$ 26$_{15(C)}$ 39$_{18}$ 1QS 4$_{14}$ 1QM 14$_{8.11}$ CD 2$_{6}$ 4QpNah 3.2$_{6}$ 4Q181 2$_{6}$ 1QH 1$_{5(Licht)}$ ([לרחמכה]) 6$_{33}$ 7$_{11.17(Licht)}$ ([ליצר]) 8$_{27}$ 9$_{17.17.17}$ (Licht) ([אין]) 10$_{10}$ 5QCurses 1$_{5}$ (לְ elided) 11QPs^{a} 19$_{9}$ 4Q416 9.2$_{16}$ 4QapPs^{b} 33$_{3}$ ([לחכמתך]) 76$_{11}$.

(2) אֵין בְּ *there is not in*, e.g. אֵין־בִּי כֹחַ *there is not in me strength*, i.e. I have none Is 50$_{2}$, var. 2 C 20$_{12}$, sim. Gn 19$_{31}$ 37$_{24}$ 47$_{13}$ Lv 13$_{21.26.31}$ Nm 5$_{13}$ (בְּ = *against*) 19$_{2}$ Dt 32$_{28}$ Jg 14$_{3.6}$ 19$_{1}$ 1 S 17$_{50}$ 24$_{12}$ 30$_{4}$ 1 K 5$_{20}$ 22$_{48}$ Is 1$_{6}$ 43$_{12}$ Jr 5$_{13}$ 8$_{19.22}$ 16$_{19}$ Ezk 37$_{8}$ Mc 4$_{9}$ Hb 2$_{19}$ Ps 6$_{6}$ 32$_{2}$ 38$_{15}$ Ca 4$_{7}$ Ec 5$_{13}$ Dn 1$_{4}$ Si 40$_{26}$ CD 5$_{17}$ 10$_{12}$ 4QShirShab^{f} 23.1$_{10}$ 4QapLam^{a} 1.1$_{6.11}$ 1.2$_{10}$ 4Q372 1$_{18}$.

אֵין and בְּ separated, Gn 20$_{11}$ 37$_{29}$ 39$_{11}$ Ex 14$_{11}$ Nm 14$_{42}$ Dt 31$_{17}$ Jg 17$_{6}$ 18$_{1}$ 21$_{25}$ 1 S 18$_{25}$ 2 K 1$_{3.6.16}$ 5$_{15}$ Is 3$_{7}$ 14$_{31}$ 59$_{8}$ Jr 8$_{13.13}$ 22$_{28}$ 38$_{6.9}$ 48$_{38}$ 49$_{7}$ Ho 4$_{1}$ 8$_{8}$ Ob 7 Hb 3$_{17.17}$ Zc 9$_{11}$ Ps 38$_{4.4.8}$ 135$_{17}$ 139$_{4}$ 144$_{14}$ Jb 6$_{13}$ 18$_{19}$ 24$_{7}$ Pr 7$_{19}$ Ec 5$_{3}$ 8$_{8.8}$ 9$_{10}$ Si 15$_{12(A)}$ 18$_{33(C)}$ 30$_{23}$ 41$_{4(mg)}$ GnzPs 4$_{22}$ ([אין ב[כל) 4$_{22}$ CD 20$_{5(erased)}$ 1QH 12$_{16(Licht)}$ ([בכול]) 12$_{17(Licht)}$ ([בממשלתכה]) 4QWiles 1$_{7}$, with pronom. sf., אֵינֶנִּי בְּקִרְבְּכֶם *I am not in your middle* Dt 1$_{42}$, בַּעֲמַל אֱנוֹשׁ אֵינֵמוֹ *they are not in the trouble of men* Ps 73$_{5}$.

(3) עִם *with* Gn 31$_{50}$ Ex 22$_{13}$ Dt 29$_{14}$ 32$_{12.39}$ Jg 13$_{9}$ Ne 2$_{12}$ 2 C 14$_{5}$ 19$_{7}$ 25$_{7}$ Si 32$_{15}$ 1QH 12$_{11}$, with pronom. sf., Gn 31$_{2}$ 2 S 3$_{22}$; אֵת *with* Jg 16$_{15}$ 1 S 21$_{2}$ 1 K 3$_{18}$ Is 63$_{3}$ Jr 10$_{5}$ (אוֹתָם) Si 16$_{2}$ 4QJub^{d} 1.2$_{4}$, with pronom. sf., Gn 44$_{26.30.34}$, הֵם אֵין אִתִּי *they are not with me* Ps 38$_{11}$; כְּ *as* 1 S 2$_{2}$; עַל *over, upon* Nm 19$_{15}$ Jb 41$_{25}$ Si 30$_{16}$.

אֶל *towards* Jr 15$_{1}$ Ml 2$_{13}$, אֵינֶנּוּ אֵלַי כִּתְמוֹל שִׁלְשֹׁם *he is not*, i.e. does not behave, *toward me as previously* Gn 31$_{5}$; אֶל־תַּחַת *below* 1 S 21$_{5}$; תַּחַת *below* Ec 1$_{9}$ 2$_{11}$; מִן partitive, *some of* Si 36$_{28}$; בֵּין *between* 1 K 22$_{1}$ 4QM^{a} fr. 13$_{7}$ 1QH 6$_{13}$; לְנֶגֶד *in front of* Ps 36$_{2}$, *against* Pr 21$_{30}$.

4b. predicate is continued by **adjective** (אַיִן with pronom. sf., Gn 7$_{8}$ 30$_{33}$ 39$_{9}$ Lv 13$_{21.26.34}$ Ec 1$_{7}$), טוֹב *good* 1 S 9$_{2}$, גָּדוֹל *great* Gn 39$_{9}$, שַׁלִּיט *dominant* Ec 8$_{8}$, טָהוֹר *pure* Gn 7$_{8}$, צַדִּיק *righteous* Ec 7$_{20}$, נָקֹד *speckled* Gn 30$_{33}$, שָׁפָל *low* Lv 13$_{21.26}$, עָמֹק *deep* 13$_{4.31.32.34}$, מָלֵא *full* Ec 1$_{7}$, חַי *alive* 1 K 21$_{15}$, אין אתה צריך *you do not need* 4Q372 1$_{17}$.

4c. (1) predicate is continued by **participle**, Gn 39$_{23}$ Ex 5$_{16}$ 33$_{15}$ Lv 14$_{21}$ Jg 19$_{15.18}$ 1 S 3$_{1}$ 1 K 6$_{18}$ Is 57$_{1}$ Jr 4$_{29}$ 8$_{6}$ Ezk 8$_{12}$ 9$_{9}$ Ps 33$_{16}$ Ec 8$_{11}$ 9$_{1}$ Est 2$_{20}$ 3$_{5}$ 7$_{4}$ 10$_{21}$ Ezr 3$_{13}$ Ne 4$_{17}$ 7$_{4}$ 4QToh B^{b}$_{11}$, with double negative, אֵין כֶּסֶף לֹא נֶחְשָׁב *money was not considered* 1 K 10$_{21}$ (||2 C 9$_{20}$ lacks לֹא), with pronom. sf., לַזֹּבֵחַ וְלַאֲשֶׁר אֵינֶנּוּ זֹבֵחַ *to one who sacrifices and to one who does not sacrifice*) Ec 9$_{2}$, Ex 3$_{2}$ Lv 11$_{4.26.26}$ 1 S 11$_{7}$ Jr 38$_{4}$ Ec 5$_{11}$ Est 5$_{13}$, אין הם מבדיל *they do not divide* CD 5$_{6}$, אין הוא בחון *he is not expert* 13$_{3}$.

(2) אַיִן with suffixed **subject pronoun** and **participle** of יצא *go out* 2 S 19$_{8}$, עבר *cross* river Dt 4$_{22}$, נפל *fall* Jr 37$_{14}$, שׂים *place* Ml 2$_{2}$, שׁלח pi. *send* Gn 43$_{5}$ Ex 8$_{17}$ Lachish ost. 4$_{7}$ ([אינ[נ]י)), שׁוב hi. *return* trans. Gn 20$_{7}$, נתן *give* Ex 5$_{10}$, ראה *see* Dt 4$_{12}$ Jr 7$_{17}$ Ec 8$_{16}$ 4QMMT A 25$_{8.59}$, שׁמע *hear* Dt 21$_{18}$=11QT 64$_{2}$ ([א]ננו [שומע]) Dt 21$_{20}$=11QT 64$_{5}$ Is 1$_{15}$ Jr 7$_{16}$ 11$_{14}$ 14$_{12}$ 32$_{33}$ 44$_{16}$ Ezk 20$_{39}$, ni. *be heard* Ec 9$_{16}$, ידע *know* 2 K 17$_{26}$ Ec 4$_{17}$ 8$_{7}$ 11$_{5.6}$, נכר hi. *know* Ne 13$_{24}$, אמן hi. *believe* Dt 13$_{2}$, נבא htp. *prophesy* 2 C 18$_{7}$, אבה *consent* Ezk 3$_{7}$, רצה *desire* Jr 14$_{12}$, ירא *fear* 2 K 17$_{34}$ Ec 8$_{13}$, עשׂה *do* 2 K 17$_{34}$ Ezk 33$_{32}$ (אַיִן follows ptc.) Est 3$_{8}$ 11QapPs^{a} 2$_{9}$ ([עושים]), יכל *be able* Arad ost. 40$_{13}$ ([אי]ננו), חזק pi. *strengthen* 2 K 12$_{8}$, שׁמר *keep* Ml 2$_{9}$, חסר *lack* Ec 6$_{2}$, חלה *be ill* Ne 2$_{2}$, קשׁר ni. *be tied* CD 13$_{18}$, שׁחט *slaughter* 4QMMT A 24$_{3}$ ([אי]נם), אכל *eat* 1 K 21$_{5}$, פתח *open* Jg 3$_{25}$, ישׁע hi. *deliver* 12$_{3}$, מלט pi. *rescue* 1 S 19$_{11}$, נגע *touch* Dn 8$_{5}$ (if em. אֵינֶנּוּ), בדל hi. *divide* 4QMMT A 26$_{4}$.

4d. predicate followed by לְ (except Ec 12$_{12}$) +

infinitive, (1) with subject, **there is no ... to,** אֵין כֹּחַ לַעֲמוֹד *there is not strength to stand* Ezr 10$_{13}$ 4Q185 1.1$_{7}$, Gn 2$_{5}$ (אַיִן) Ex 17$_{1}$ Nm 20$_{5}$ (אַיִן) 22$_{26}$ 1 S 9$_{7}$ 14$_{6}$ 2 S 21$_{4}$ 2 K 19$_{3}$||Is 37$_{3}$ (אַיִן) Is 47$_{14}$ Jr 19$_{11}$ 49$_{12}$ Mc 7$_{1}$ Jb 20$_{21}$ 34$_{22}$ Ec 4$_{10}$ 12$_{12}$ Dn 11$_{15}$ Ne 2$_{14}$ Si 7$_{6}$ 40$_{29}$ 1QS 11$_{18}$ 4Q185 1.1$_{7}$ (ו[אין]) 1QH 6$_{23}$ 7$_{17}$ 11$_{22}$ MasShirShab 14$_{(Newsom)}$ Mur 30 1$_{6}$ 2$_{28}$.

(2) without subj. **there is no one, nothing to,** אין להשיב *there is none to return* 1QH 7$_{28}$, Pr 22$_{27}$ Ru 4$_{4}$ (+ זוּלַת *besides*) 4QWiles 1$_{12(Allegro)}$ (להרג[ן יעה]).

4e. אַיִן modified by **adverb,** שָׁם *there* Gn 39$_{11}$ Jg 18$_{10}$ 21$_{9}$ 2 K 7$_{5.10}$ Is 34$_{12}$ Jr 8$_{22}$ Lachish ost. 4$_{5}$ 1QMyst 1.1$_{7}$; פֹּה *here* 1 S 21$_{9}$ (אַיִן) 2 K 3$_{11}$ Silwan royal steward tomb inscr. 1$_{1}$ ([פ]ה), with pronom. sf. Dt 29$_{14}$ (|| יֵשׁ *there is*); עוֹד *again, besides* 1 K 22$_{7}$||2 C 18$_{6}$ 2 K 4$_{6}$ Is 23$_{10}$ 45$_{21}$ 46$_{9}$ Jr 38$_{9}$ 48$_{2}$ 49$_{7}$ Ml 2$_{13}$ Ps 74$_{9}$ Ec 9$_{5}$ 1QH 12$_{18}$ ([א]ין) perh. 4QTanḥ 8$_{14}$, with pronom. sf. Ps 104$_{35}$ (עוֹד אֵינָם); זוּלַת *apart from* 1 S 21$_{10}$ 2 S 7$_{22}$ Is 45$_{5}$ 1 C 17$_{20}$ Si 33$_{5}$ 1QS 11$_{18}$, בִּלְתִּי *apart from* Ho 13$_{4}$ (אַיִן); מִבַּלְעָדַי *apart from* Is 43$_{11}$ 44$_{6}$ 45$_{21}$; אֵין גַּם־אֶחָד *there is not even one* Ps 14$_{3}$||53$_{4}$.

4f. אַיִן introducing circumstantial clause, **while not,** וְאֵין נֹגֵעַ בָּאָרֶץ *and without touching the ground* Dn 8$_{5}$ (or em. וְאֵינֶנּוּ *and he was not* touching, as §4c [2]).

5. אַיִן with **prefixed preposition, a.** introducing **final** clause, **so that there is not, (so that it is) without, beyond,** (1) מֵאַיִן, וְהַאֲבַדְתִּיךְ מֵאֵין יוֹשֵׁב *and I shall destroy you so that there is not one inhabitant* Zp 2$_{5}$, sim. Is 5$_{9}$ 6$_{11.11}$ Jr 4$_{7}$ 26$_{9}$ 32$_{43}$ 33$_{10.10.10.10.10.12}$ 34$_{22}$ 44$_{22}$ 46$_{19}$ 48$_{9}$ 51$_{29.37}$ Ezk 33$_{28}$ Zp 3$_{6}$ Lm 3$_{49}$.

(2) לְאַיִן, וַיִּפֹּל מִכּוּשִׁים לְאֵין לָהֶם מִחְיָה *and the Cushites fell so that there was not to them survival,* i.e. they had no survivors 2 C 14$_{12}$, sim. Ezr 9$_{14}$ 1 C 22$_{4}$ 2 C 20$_{25}$ 21$_{18}$ 1QS 2$_{7.14}$ 4$_{14}$ 5$_{13}$ 1QM 1$_{6}$ 4$_{2}$ 18$_{2(Yadin).11.13}$ 19$_{11(Baillet)}$ + Sup CD 2$_{6}$ 4QToh D$_{5.5}$ 4Q185 1.2$_{15}$ 1QH 2$_{26}$ 3$_{20.27}$ 5$_{21.28.29.38(Licht)}$ 6$_{3.3.7.27}$ 8$_{17.30}$ 18$_{30}$, perh. 1QM 16$_{17}$ + Sup 4QShir^{b} 2.1$_{3}$ 4QBer^{a} 3.2$_{10}$ (ל[אין]).

(3) לְאַיִן followed by inf. absol. (cf. §6b), ונפלו ... לאין קום *and they will fall ... so that there is not rise,* i.e. so that is impossible to rise 1QM 18$_{2}$, sim. 1QH 3$_{27.28}$ 5$_{37.39(Licht)}$ (ל[אין פלט]) 6$_{12.18}$ 7$_{15(Licht)}$ (ה[סר]) 8$_{28}$ 11$_{23}$ 18$_{2}$ (השב[ת]) fr. 10$_{5(Licht)}$ (השׁ[בת]) perh. 9$_{39}$ ([א]ין).

(4) עַד־אַיִן *until there is no* Ps 40$_{13}$ Jb 5$_{9}$ 9$_{10.10}$ 2 C 36$_{16}$ 1QH 4$_{27}$ (both עַד לְאֵין) 9$_{37}$.

5b. introducing **causal** clause, **because there is not, through lack of,** (1) מֵאַיִן, תִּבְאַשׁ דְּגָתָם מֵאֵין מַיִם *their fish stinks because there is not water* Is 50$_{2}$, sim. Jr 7$_{32}$ 19$_{11}$ Ezk 34$_{8}$ Ml 2$_{13}$ Si 20$_{6(C)}$.

(2) בְּאַיִן (some perh. circumstantial), הוּא יָמוּת בְּאֵין מוּסָר *he dies through lack of discipline* Pr 5$_{23}$, sim. 11$_{14}$ 15$_{22}$ 26$_{20}$ (|| בְּאֶפֶס *for lack of*) 29$_{18}$ Si 3$_{25.25}$ 36$_{30.30}$.

5c. introducing **circumstantial** clause, **while there is not, without there being,** (1) בְּאַיִן, אַנְשֵׁי־חֶסֶד נֶאֱסָפִים בְּאֵין מֵבִין *faithful people are taken away without anyone understanding (why)* Is 57$_{1}$, sim. Ezk 38$_{11}$ Pr 8$_{24.24}$ 14$_{4}$ Si 8$_{16}$ 11$_{9}$ 1QH 10$_{6}$.

(2) לְאַיִן, Si 51$_{4}$ 1QM 11$_{1}$ 1QH 6$_{7}$ 4Q 416 9.2$_{19.19}$.

<COLL> (1) אַיִן *one for whom there is not,* + כֹּחַ *strength* 2 C 14$_{10}$, אוֹנִים *strength(s)* Is 40$_{29}$ Si 41$_{2(M)}$, עֵינַיִם *eyes* Is 59$_{10}$; אֵין נָכוֹן לוֹ *one for whom nothing is prepared* Ne 8$_{10}$, לאין משכלה *to those without sense* 4Q385 3$_{4}$, לאין לב *as for those without understanding* 4QapPs^{b} 1$_{2}$.

(2) אַיִן with pronoun, והוא אין הוא לבוש *and he, he is not dressed* 11QT 35$_{6}$, הוא אין הוא כוהן *he, he is not a priest* 35$_{4}$, אַבְנֵר אֵינֶנּוּ עִם־דָּוִד *Abner was not with David* 2 S 3$_{22}$, הַמֵּתִים אֵינָם יוֹדְעִים *the dead do not know* Ec 9$_{5}$, השלישית איננו עם *the third is not a nation* Si 50$_{25}$, איני צריך *I am not in need (of)* 5/6ḤevBA 46$_{2}$.

(3) אַיִן(־)יֵשׁ־ *there is not* Ps 135$_{17}$, אֵין יֶשׁ־פֹּה ... חֲנִית *here there is not ... a spear* 1 S 21$_{9}$ (mss אַיִן; or em. אַיֵּן *where is?* or אִם *is?* or הֵן *behold*).

(4) Subjects of clauses with אַיִן (אַיִן abs. alw. after noun, Gn 2$_{5}$ Nm 20$_{5}$ 2 K 19$_{3}$||Is 37$_{3}$ Ho 13$_{4}$ Pr 25$_{14}$). Nouns usu. sg., but also pl. (e.g. Nm 27$_{10.11}$ Jr 22$_{17}$ 49$_{1}$ Ezk 38$_{11}$ Ps 19$_{4}$ Ne 7$_{4}$ CD 9$_{13.14}$ Mur 30 1$_{6}$) or multiple (e.g. Gn 45$_{6}$ 1 S 14$_{17}$ Jr 22$_{17}$ Ho 3$_{4}$ Pr 6$_{7}$ Ec 4$_{8}$ 9$_{10}$ Ne 4$_{17.17}$ 4QDibHam^{a} 1.4$_{12}$ 1QH 11$_{26}$).

אֱלֹהִים *God* Dt 31$_{17}$ 32$_{29}$ 2 S 7$_{22}$ 2 K 1$_{3.6.16}$ 5$_{15}$ Is 44$_{6}$ 45$_{5.21}$ Ps 10$_{4}$ 14$_{1}$||53$_{2}$ 1 C 17$_{20}$ Si 33$_{5}$, אֵל *god* Dt 32$_{12}$, אָדָם *human being* Gn 2$_{5}$ 1 K 8$_{46}$||2 C 6$_{36}$ Is 6$_{11}$ Jr 4$_{25}$

32$_{43}$ 33$_{10.10.12}$ Ec 7$_{20}$ 8$_8$ 9$_1$ Lachish ost. 4$_5$, אִישׁ *man* Gn 19$_{31}$ 31$_{50}$ 39$_{11}$ Ex 2$_{12}$ Jg 13$_9$ 19$_{15.18}$ 21$_9$ 1 S 9$_2$ 21$_2$ 2 S 21$_4$ 1 K 5$_{20}$ 2 K 7$_{5.10}$ Is 41$_{28}$ 50$_2$ 57$_1$ 59$_{16}$ 63$_3$ Jr 4$_{29}$ 8$_6$ 12$_{11}$ 38$_4$ Pr 7$_{19}$ Ne 4$_{17}$ Si 36$_{28}$, ישׁב ptc. *inhabitant* Is 5$_9$ 6$_{11}$ Jr 4$_7$ 26$_9$ 33$_{10}$ 34$_{22}$ 44$_{22}$ 46$_{19}$ 48$_9$ 51$_{29.37}$ Zp 2$_5$ 3$_6$, אִשָּׁה *woman* Jg 14$_3$ Si 36$_{30}$, אֶחָד *one* person Gn 42$_{13.32}$ Ps 14$_3$‖52$_4$ Dn 10$_{21}$, שֵׁנִי *second* person Ec 4$_{8.10}$, שלישית *third* nation Si 50$_{25}$, עַם *people* Ezr 3$_{13}$.

מֶלֶךְ *king* Jg 17$_6$ 18$_1$ 19$_1$ 21$_{25}$ 1 K 22$_{48}$ Jr 8$_{19}$ Ho 3$_4$ 10$_3$ Mc 4$_9$ Ps 33$_{16}$ Pr 30$_{27}$, שַׂר *prince* Gn 39$_{23}$ 2 S 19$_7$ Ho 3$_4$, שׁפט ptc. *judge* CD 20$_{16}$, קָצִין *ruler* Pr 6$_7$, perh. פֶּחָה *governor* Si 51$_4$, נָבִיא *prophet* 1 K 22$_7$‖2 C 18$_6$ 2 K 3$_{11}$ Ps 74$_9$, כֹּהֵן *priest* 11QT 35$_4$, בַּעַל *master* Ex 22$_{13}$ CD 9$_{13.14}$, עֵד *witness* Nm 5$_{13}$, רעה ptc. *shepherd* 27$_{17}$ 1 K 22$_{17}$‖2 C 18$_{16}$ Ezk 34$_8$ Zc 10$_2$, נהל pi. ptc. *guide* Is 51$_{18}$, ליץ hi. ptc. *mediator* 1QH 6$_{13}$, רפא ptc. *physician* Jr 8$_{22}$ 4QPrFêtes[c] 13$_4$.

זור ptc. *stranger* 1 K 3$_{18}$ Is 43$_{12}$, בוא ptc. *visitor* to festival 4QapLam[a] 1.1$_{11}$, ישׁע hi. ptc. *saviour* Is 43$_{11}$ Ho 13$_4$ 4Q386–9 4$_3$, גאל ptc. *redeemer* Nm 5$_8$ CD 14$_{16}$ (גו[וא]ל), רָשָׁע *evildoer* Ps 37$_{10}$ 104$_{35}$ Pr 10$_{25}$, צרר ptc. *enemy* Est 7$_4$, שָׂטָן *adversary* 1 K 5$_{18}$ 4QDibHam[a] 1.4$_{12}$, רגן ni. ptc. *slanderer* Pr 26$_{20}$, בדד ptc. *straggler* Is 14$_{31}$, שָׂרִיד *survivor* Jb 18$_{19}$ 20$_{21}$.

יֶלֶד *child* Gn 37$_{30}$ 1 S 1$_2$, וָלָד *child* Gn 11$_{30}$, זֶרַע *seed, child* Lv 22$_{13}$, ירשׁ ptc. *heir* Jr 49$_1$, נַעַר *youth* Gn 44$_{30.31.34}$ Ne 4$_{17}$, בֵּן *son* Nm 27$_{4.8}$ Dt 25$_5$ Jg 11$_{34}$ 2 S 18$_{18}$ 2 K 4$_{14}$ Jr 49$_1$ Ec 4$_8$ 1 C 4$_{27}$, בַּת *daughter* Nm 27$_9$ Jg 11$_{34}$, אָח *brother* Gn 44$_{26}$ Nm 27$_{10.11}$ Ec 4$_8$ Ne 4$_{17}$, אָב *father* Lm 5$_3$ Est 2$_7$, אֵם *mother* Est 2$_7$.

מַיִם *water* Gn 37$_{24}$ Ex 17$_1$ Nm 20$_5$ 21$_5$ Dt 8$_{15}$ Is 1$_{30}$ 50$_2$ Jr 38$_6$ Zc 9$_{11}$, מַעְיָן *spring* Pr 8$_{24}$, יָם *sea* Ec 1$_7$, תְּהוֹם *abyss* Pr 8$_{24}$, גֶּשֶׁם *rain* 25$_{14}$, צוּר *rock* 1 S 2$_2$ Is 44$_8$, אֶבֶן *stone* 1 K 6$_{18}$, מַצֵּבָה *cultic stone* Ho 3$_4$, גַּחֶלֶת *coal* Is 47$_{14}$, סְנֶה *bush* Ex 3$_2$, חָרִישׁ *ploughing* Gn 45$_6$, מִרְעֶה *pasture* Gn 47$_4$ Jl 1$_{18}$, תֶּבֶן *straw* Ex 5$_{16}$, עֵשֶׂב *grass* Jr 14$_6$, צֶמַח *growth* Ho 8$_7$, יְבוּל *produce* Hb 3$_{17}$, לֶחֶם *bread* Gn 47$_{13}$ Nm 21$_5$ 1 S 21$_5$ Is 3$_7$ Jr 38$_9$ Pr 28$_3$, אֶשְׁכּוֹל *cluster* Mc 7$_1$, עֵנָב *grape* Jr 8$_{13}$, תְּאֵנָה *fig* 8$_{13}$.

מָקוֹם *place* Jr 7$_{32}$ 19$_{11}$ Ne 2$_{14}$ Si 13$_{22}$, תְּקוּמָה *position* 5/6ḤevBA 45$_4$ (ת[קומה]), דֶּרֶךְ *way* Nm 22$_{26}$, נְתִיבָה *path* 1QH 6$_{23}$, מָבוֹא *entrance* 6$_{27}$, חֵלֶק *portion* Dt 12$_{12}$ 14$_{27.29}$ Jos 18$_7$ 22$_{25.27}$ 2 S 20$_1$ Ec 9$_6$ Ne 2$_{20}$ CD 20$_{10}$, נַחֲלָה *inheritance* Dt 12$_{12}$ 14$_{27.29}$ 4QWiles 1$_7$, גּוֹרָל *lot* CD 20$_5$, מָעֳמָד *foothold, resistance* Ps 69$_3$ 1QM 14$_8$ 16$_{17}$ + Sup 18$_{13}$.

בַּיִת *house* Ex 12$_{30}$ Ne 7$_4$, אֹהֶל *tent* Jb 8$_{22}$, קֵן *nest* Si 36$_{31}$, חֹמָה *wall* Lv 25$_{31}$ Ezk 38$_{11}$, קִיר *wall* 13$_{15}$, גָּדֵר *wall* Si 36$_{30}$, עַמּוּד *pillar* Ezk 42$_6$, קֶבֶר *grave* Ex 14$_{11}$, דֶּלֶת *door* Ezk 38$_{11}$, צָמִיד *lid* Nm 19$_{15}$, מוֹקֵשׁ *trap* Am 3$_5$, כְּסוּת *covering* Jb 24$_7$ 26$_6$ 31$_{19}$, שִׂמְלָה *coat* Is 3$_7$, חֶרֶב *sword* 1 S 17$_{50}$, חֲנִית *spear* 21$_9$, אֵפוֹד *ephod* Ho 3$_4$, כִּסֵּא *throne* Is 47$_1$, תְּשׁוּרָה perh. *gift* 1 S 9$_7$, זֶבַח *sacrifice* Ho 3$_4$.

מִחְיָה *survival* 2 C 14$_{12}$, שְׁאֵרִית *remnant* Ezr 9$_{14}$ 1QS 4$_{14}$ 5$_{13}$ 1QM 1$_6$ 4$_2$ 14$_5$ 18$_{2(\text{Yadin})}$ ([שארית]) CD 2$_6$ 4QToh D$_5$ 1QH 6$_{32(\text{Licht})}$ (ש א[רית]) fr. 7.2$_2$ 4QApocMos A 2.2$_4$ (שרית), פְּלֵיטָה *escape* Ezr 9$_{14}$ 2 C 20$_{24}$ 1QS 4$_{14}$ CD 2$_6$ 4QToh D$_5$ 3Q11 2$_{3(\text{Baillet})}$ (פלי[טה]) 4QApocMos A 2.2$_4$, מָנוֹס *escape* 1QM 14$_{11}$ 1QH 5$_{29.38(\text{Licht})}$ ([מנוס]) 6$_{33}$, מַחְסֶה *refuge* 7$_{17}$, מָעוֹז *refuge* 8$_{27}$.

רְפֻאָה *healing* Jr 30$_{13}$ Si 3$_{28}$, מַרְפֵּא *healing* Jr 14$_{19}$ Pr 6$_{15}$ 29$_1$ 2 C 21$_{18}$ 36$_{16}$ 1QH 2$_{26}$, תְּעָלָה *healing* Jr 46$_{11}$, צֳרִי *healing* 8$_{22}$, לַחַשׁ *spell* 8$_{17}$, חֶבֶר *spell* 1QH 5$_{28}$, כֵּהָה *alleviation* Na 3$_{19}$, הֲפוּגָה *cessation* Lm 3$_{49}$, קֵץ *end* Is 9$_6$ Jb 22$_5$ Ec 4$_{8.16}$ 12$_{12}$ 4QpNah 3.2$_6$ 1QH 6$_{31}$, קָצֶה *end* Is 2$_{7.7}$ Na 2$_{10}$ 3$_{3.9}$, כָּלָה *end* 1QH 5$_{34}$, אֶפֶס *end* 6$_{17}$ 12$_{10}$.

קֶשֶׁב *attentiveness* 1 K 18$_{29}$ 2 K 4$_{31}$, בִּינָה *understanding* Is 33$_{19}$ CD 5$_{17}$, תְּבוּנָה *understanding* Dt 32$_{28}$ Ob7 Pr 21$_{30}$, חָכְמָה *wisdom* Jr 49$_7$ Pr 21$_{30}$ Ec 9$_{10}$, דַּעַת *knowledge* Ho 4$_1$ Ec 9$_{10}$ Si 3$_{25}$, תִּקְוָה *hope* 38$_{21}$ 1QH 3$_{27}$, מִקְוֶה *hope* 1 C 29$_{15}$ 4Q185 1.1$_{7.12}$, שִׂמְחָה *joy* GnzPs 2$_{24}$, חֶסֶד *loyalty* Ho 4$_1$, אֱמֶת *faithfulness* 4$_1$ 4QJub[d] 1.2$_{24}$, צְדָקָה *righteousness* 1QH 7$_{17}$, טוֹב *goodness* Jr 8$_{15}$ 14$_{19}$ Ec 8$_{15}$, טוֹבָה *goodness* Si 12$_3$ 30$_{16}$, הֵיטִיב *goodness* Jr 10$_5$, רַחֲמִים *mercy* 1QS 2$_7$ 1QH 9$_3$, חֲנִינָה *mercy* 3QJub 23$_{23}$, סְלִיחָה *forgiveness* 1QS 2$_{14}$.

חֵפֶץ *delight* 1 S 18$_{25}$ Jr 22$_{28}$ 48$_{38}$ Ho 8$_8$ Ml 1$_{10}$ Ec 5$_3$ 12$_1$ Si 15$_{12(\text{B})}$ 4QapLam[a] 1.2$_{10}$, רָצוֹן *pleasure* 1QH 10$_6$, תְּהִלָּה *praise* Jr 48$_2$, מְתֹם *soundness* Is 1$_6$ Ps 38$_{4.8}$, שָׁלוֹם *wellbeing, peace* Is 48$_{22}$=57$_{21}$ Jr 6$_{14}$=8$_{11}$ 12$_{12}$ 30$_5$ Ezk 13$_{10.16}$ Zc 8$_{10}$ Ps 38$_4$ 2 C 15$_5$ 3QJub 23$_{12}$ 4QShir[b] 3$_5$

אַיִן

([שׁל]ום), תְּשׁוּעָה *salvation* Ps 146$_3$, יְשׁוּעָה *salvation* 3$_3$, עֶזְרָה *help* Jb 6$_{13}$, אֱיָל *help* Ps 88$_5$, כֹּחַ *strength* 1 S 30$_4$ 2 K 19$_3$||Is 37$_3$ Is 44$_{12}$ 50$_2$ Dn 11$_{15}$ Ezr 10$_{13}$ 2 C 14$_{10}$ 20$_{12}$ 4Q185 1.1$_7$ 4QapPs^b 53$_4$ ([א]ין), אוֹן *strength* Is 40$_{29}$ Si 41$_{2(M)}$, חַיִל *strength* 7$_6$, שִׁלְטוֹן *dominion* Ec 8$_8$, חָמָס *violence* 4Q372 1$_{18}$.

קוֹל *voice* Ex 32$_{18.18}$ 1 K 18$_{26.29}$ 2 K 4$_{31}$ 7$_{10}$, לֵב *heart* Jg 16$_{15}$ Jr 5$_{21}$ 22$_{17}$ Ho 7$_{11}$ 4QapPs^b 1$_2$, אֹזֶן *ear* 4Q424 2$_5$, פָּנִים *face* Ex 33$_{15}$, עַיִן *eye* Is 59$_{10}$ Jr 22$_{17}$, אִישׁוֹן *pupil of eye* Si 3$_{25}$, פֶּה *mouth* 1QH 7$_{11}$, יָד *hand* Lv 14$_{21}$ Dt 28$_{32}$ Ne 5$_5$ 4QapLam^a 1.1$_2$, *handle* Is 45$_9$, שַׁד *breast* Ca 8$_8$, שֵׂעָר *hair* Lv 13$_{21.26.31}$, דָּם *blood* Ex 22$_1$ Nm 35$_{27}$, רוּחַ *breath* Ezk 37$_8$ Hb 2$_{19}$ (כָּל־רוּחַ אַיִן *there is no breath at all*) Ps 135$_{17}$ Pr 25$_{14}$ 4QM^a fr. 13$_7$, נֶפֶשׁ *soul* Jr 15$_1$, חַיִּים *life* Si 40$_{29}$, מַרְאֶה *appearance* Lv 13$_{4.31.32.34}$.

סְנַפִּיר *fin* Lv 11$_{10}$||Dt 14$_{10}$ Lv 11$_{12}$, פַּרְסָה *hoof* 11$_4$, שֶׁסַע *cleft* 11$_{26}$, גֵּרָה *cud* 11$_{26}$, בָּקָר *cattle* Hb 3$_{17}$, בְּהֵמָה *beast* Gn 7$_8$ Jr 32$_{43}$ 33$_{10.10}$ Ne 2$_{12}$, אֶלֶף *ox* Pr 14$_4$, צָפִיר *goat* Dn 8$_5$ (or em. אֵינֶנּוּ), טֶרֶף *prey* Am 3$_4$.

מוּם *flaw* Nm 19$_2$ Ca 4$_7$, מְאוּם *flaw* Dn 1$_4$, חֵטְא *sin* Dt 22$_{26}$=11QT 66$_6$, פֶּשַׁע *sin* 1 S 24$_{12}$ Pr 28$_{24}$, עָוֶל *wickedness* Dt 32$_4$ 1QH 6$_7$, עַוְלָה *wickedness* 2 C 19$_7$ 1QH 12$_{17(Licht)}$ (ע[ולה]) 1QS 4$_{23}$ 8$_{10}$ 4QapPs^b 76$_{12}$, עָוֹן *wickedness* Si 13$_{24}$, רָעָה *wickedness* 1 S 24$_{12}$, רְמִיָּה *deceit* Ps 32$_2$ 1QH 12$_{16}$, כָּזָב *falsehood* GnzPs 4$_{22}$, כַּחַשׁ *deceit* 4$_{22}$ (אי[ן כחש]), אִוֶּלֶת *folly* 1QMyst 1.1$_7$, חֵמָה *anger* Is 27$_4$, חַרְצֻבָּה *pain* Ps 73$_4$, עַצָּבָה *pain* Si 11$_{9(A)}$, נֶגַע *affliction* 1QH 11$_{22}$, יָגוֹן *sorrow* 11$_{26}$, יִרְאָה *fear* Gn 20$_{11}$ Si 16$_2$, פַּחַד *fear* Ps 36$_2$, צְוָחָה *cry* Ps 144$_{14}$, מַדְהֵבָה *tribulation* 1QH 12$_{18}$, מִלְחָמָה *war* 1 K 22$_1$ 2 C 14$_5$.

מִשְׁפָּט *judgment* Dt 19$_6$ Is 59$_{8.15}$ Jr 26$_{16}$ 49$_{12}$ Jb 19$_7$, תּוֹכָחָה *rebuke* Ps 38$_{15}$ Si 41$_{4(mg)}$, עֵצָה *advice* Pr 21$_{30}$ Si 11$_{9(B)}$ (א[ין]), סוֹד *advice* Pr 15$_{22}$, תַּחְבֻּלָה *advice* 11$_{14}$, חֵקֶר *investigation* Is 40$_{28}$ Ps 145$_3$ Jb 5$_9$ 9$_{10}$ Pr 25$_3$ 4Q185 1.2$_{15}$ 1QH 3$_{20}$ 6$_3$ 8$_{17}$ 18$_{30}$ (both ח[קר]) 4Q181 2$_6$ (חק[ר]) 11QPs^a 19$_9$ 4QapPs^b 33$_3$, מוּסָר *discipline* Pr 5$_{23}$, תּוֹרָה *law* Lm 2$_9$, חֹק *statute* 2Q28 2$_2$ (אין לו חוק; Baillet דין לרתוק *judgment for one who is joined*), חָזוֹן *vision* 1 S 3$_1$ Pr 29$_{18}$, בְּשֹׂרָה *good news* 2 S 18$_{22}$.

מִכְשׁוֹל *obstacle* Ps 119$_{165}$ 1QH 10$_{18}$, מַעְצוֹר *restraint* 1 S 14$_6$ Si 39$_{18}$, מַעְצָר *restraint* Pr 25$_{28}$, מֵזַח perh. *restraint* Is 23$_{10}$, מַחְסוֹר *lack* Jg 18$_{10}$ 19$_{19}$ Ps 34$_{10}$ Pr 28$_{27}$ Si 40$_{26}$ 1QH 15$_{16}$, צֹרֶךְ *need* Si 15$_{12(A, Bmg)}$ (צ[ורך]), דַּי *enough* Is 40$_{16.16}$ CD 10$_{12}$ 5QCurses 1$_5$ (דיו), שָׂבָע *abundance* Ec 5$_{11}$, שָׂבְעָה *satisfaction* 1QpHab 3$_{12}$, יעל hi. ptc. *profit* Jr 16$_{19}$, יִתְרוֹן *profit* Ec 2$_{11}$ 10$_{11}$, עֹשֶׁר *wealth* Si 30$_{16}$, כֶּסֶף *silver* Ex 21$_{11}$ 2 S 21$_4$ 1 K 10$_{21}$||2 C 9$_{20}$ Is 55$_1$ Silwan royal steward tomb inscr. 1$_1$, מִשְׁקָל *weight, value* 1 C 22$_3$ Si 6$_{15}$ 26$_{15(C)}$, מְחִיר *price* 6$_{15}$ 1QH 9$_{17(Licht)}$ 10$_{10}$ 4Q416 9.2$_7$, שָׂכָר *reward* Zc 8$_{10}$ Ec 9$_5$, תּוֹעֶלָה *profit* Si 30$_{23}$.

מֹשֶׁל *similarity* Jb 41$_{25}$, חֲלִיפָה *change* Ps 55$_{20}$, זֵכֶר *remembrance* 6$_6$ Si 44$_9$, זִכְרוֹן *remembrance* Ec 1$_{11}$ 2$_{16}$, נַחַת *quiet* Pr 29$_9$, מָנוֹחַ *rest* 1QH 8$_{30}$, נִיחֹחַ *pacification* 4QapLam^a 1.1$_6$, נֹגַהּ *brightness* Is 50$_{10}$, שַׁחַר *dawn* Is 8$_{20}$, חֹשֶׁךְ *darkness* Jb 34$_{22}$ 4Q185 1.2$_6$, צַלְמָוֶת *gloom* Jb 34$_{22}$.

מַשָּׂא *burden, raising* 2C 19$_7$ 20$_{25}$ 35$_3$ Si 32$_{15}$ 4QShir^b 17$_3$, פֶּרֶץ *breach* of womb Ps 144$_{14}$, מַעֲשֶׂה *action* Ec 9$_{10}$, פֶּגַע *occurrence* 1 K 5$_{18}$ 4QDibHam^a 1.4$_{12}$, עֵסֶק *business* Si 3$_{22(A)}$, מִשְׁלַחַת *discharge* Ec 8$_8$, פנה inf. cstr. *turning* Ml 2$_{13}$, תְּשׁוּבָה *return* 1QH fr. 2.1$_{11}$.

מִסְפָּר *number* Gn 41$_{49}$ Jg 6$_5$ 7$_{12}$ Jr 2$_{32}$ 46$_{23}$ Jl 1$_6$ Ps 40$_{13}$ 104$_{25}$ 105$_{34}$ 147$_5$ Jb 5$_9$ 9$_{10}$ 21$_{33}$ Ca 6$_8$ 1 C 22$_{4.16}$ 2 C 12$_3$ Si 37$_{25}$ 1QH 1$_5$ 4$_{27}$ 6$_{3(Licht)}$ ([מספר]) 9$_{37}$ (מס[פר]) 4QapPs^b 76$_{11}$, מִדָּה *measure* 5$_{21}$ 9$_{17}$, דָּבָר *word, matter, anything* Nm 20$_{19}$ Jg 18$_{7.28}$ 1 S 20$_{21}$ Ps 19$_4$ Mur 30 1$_6$ 2$_{28}$ (דב[רי]ם) 4Q285 3$_6$ (דב[ר]), דִּבֵּר *speaking* Jr 5$_{13}$, אֹמֶר *utterance* Ps 19$_4$, מִלָּה *word* 139$_4$, פִּתְגָם *decree* Ec 8$_{11}$, מַעֲנֶה *answer* Mc 3$_7$ Jb 32$_5$ Pr 29$_{19}$ Si 20$_{6(C)}$.

כֹּל *(anything at) all* Gn 30$_{33}$ Nm 11$_6$ 2 S 12$_3$ 2 K 4$_2$ Pr 13$_7$, מְאוּמָה *anything* Jg 14$_6$ 1 K 18$_{43}$ Jr 39$_{10}$ Ec 5$_{13}$ Si 18$_{33(C)}$ (מאומ[ה]), כָּל־זֶה *all this* Est 5$_{13}$, כָּל־חָדָשׁ *anything new* Ec 1$_9$.

With personal name, Gn 37$_{29}$ 42$_{36.36}$ Ex 14$_{11}$ Nm 14$_{42}$ Dt 31$_{17}$ Jg 13$_9$ 1 S 14$_{17}$ 2 S 3$_{22}$ 1 K 21$_{15}$ Jr 8$_{19}$ Ezk 8$_{12}$ 9$_9$ Est 2$_{20}$ 3$_5$ 2 C 25$_7$; noun with article (or determined construct chain), Gn 37$_{30}$ 42$_{13.32}$ 44$_{26.30.34}$ Ex 22$_{13}$ Jr 5$_{13}$ 8$_{19}$ 38$_9$ 49$_{12}$ Zc 8$_{10}$ Ps 33$_{16}$ 38$_{11}$ Jb 6$_{13}$ Pr 7$_{19}$ Ec 5$_{11}$ 9$_1$ Est 7$_4$ Ezr 3$_{13}$ Si 36$_{28}$ 40$_{29}$ CD 20$_{5(erased)}$ 1QH 10$_6$ 4QWiles 1$_7$; independent subject pronoun, 1 K 20$_{40}$ Ps 38$_{11}$ Ne 4$_{17.17}$ 11QT 35$_4$ CD 5$_6$ 13$_3$; demonstr. pronoun, Gn 28$_{17}$ Jg 7$_{14}$ 1S 20$_2$ Am 2$_{11}$ Ne 2$_2$.

6a. appar. negating **indicative** verb, ... יִהְיוּ־לְךָ וְאֵין לְזָרִים *they will be for you ... and not for strangers* Pr 5$_{17}$, אֵין הַמֶּלֶךְ יוּכַל *the king cannot* Jr 38$_5$, נטמאו אין עוד perh. *no longer were they unclean* 11QT 50$_3$ + Sup.

6b. אֵין לְ + inf. cstr. **it is not possible, permitted to, one cannot, may not, need not,** מִמֶּנּוּ אֵין לִגְרֹעַ *it is not possible to diminish it* Ec 3$_{14}$, אָכוֹל וְאֵין לְשָׂבְעָה *eating without it being possible to be satisfied* Hg 1$_6$, הִתְקַדְּשׁוּ אֵין לִשְׁמוֹר מַחְלְקוֹת *they sanctified themselves, there being no need to keep rank* 2 C 5$_{11}$, sim. Hg 1$_{6.6}$ Ec 3$_{14.14}$ Est 4$_2$ 8$_8$ Ezr 9$_{15}$ 1 C 23$_{26}$ 2 C 20$_6$ 22$_9$ 35$_{15}$ Si 10$_{23.23}$ 14$_{16}$ 39$_{21.34(mg)}$ 40$_{26}$ 1QS 3$_{10.16}$ 4QOrd^b 10.2$_3$ CD 4$_{11}$ (+ עוֹד *any more*) 1QH 8$_{33}$ (ו[אי]ן) 8$_{34.35}$ 12$_{30}$ 1QLitPr^b 1.2$_2$ perh. 4QOrd^b 12$_3$ 4QMMT A4 ([אי]ן) 2$_{5.22.44.51.51}$(all three [אי]ן) 2$_{52}$ (אי[ן]) 2$_{53}$ ([אי]ן) 2$_{66.79}$ 4QapPs^b 14$_3$, אֵין עֲרֹךְ אֵלֶיךָ *it is impossible to draw comparisons with you* Ps 40$_6$, כְּפֶרֶד אֵין הָבִין *as a mule—it cannot understand* 32$_9$.

7. (וְ)אִם־אַיִן **(and) if not, otherwise,** הָבָה־לִּי בָנִים וְאִם־אַיִן מֵתָה אָנֹכִי *give me children, otherwise I am dead* Gn 30$_1$, הֲנַעֲשֶׂה אֶת־דְּבָרוֹ אִם־אַיִן אַתָּה דַבֵּר *shall we follow his advice—if not, you must say something* 2 S 17$_6$, אִם בֶּאֱמֶת אַתֶּם מֹשְׁחִים אֹתִי ... חֲסוּ בְצִלִּי וְאִם־אַיִן תֵּצֵא אֵשׁ *if you are genuinely anointing me ... take shelter in my shade, and if not, let fire spread* Jg 9$_{15}$, sim. Ex 32$_{32}$ Jg 9$_{20}$ 2 K 2$_{10}$.

8. אָיִן abs. perh. as abstract noun, **nothing(ness), vanity,** <NOM CL> מוֹתַר הָאָדָם מִן־הַבְּהֵמָה אָיִן *the superiority of human beings over the animals is nothing* Ec 3$_{19}$ (but perh. as §1a, *there is no superiority*). <CSTR> לֶב־אָיִן *heart of nothingness, empty mind* Pr 17$_{16}$ (but perh. as §1a, *there is no mind*).

<PREP> כְּאַיִן *as nothing,* i.e. worthless, oft. in comparison with Y., Is 40$_{17}$ (+ נֶגֶד *before Y.*; + אֶפֶס *nothing*) 41$_{11.12}$ (|| אֶפֶס, both + היה *become*) 1QM 14$_{12}$ 4QDibHam^a 1.3$_3$ (both כא[י]ן; + נֶגֶד, || אֶפֶס, תֹּהוּ *void*); of temple Hg 2$_3$ (+ בְּעֵינֵיכֶם *in your eyes*), חֶלֶד *lifetime* Ps 39$_6$ (+ נֶגֶד), כְּאַיִן שֻׁפְּכוּ אֲשֻׁרָי appar. *my feet were almost made to slip* Ps 73$_{2(Qr)}$ (+ כִּמְעַט *almost*), נאלמו כאין *they will become silent as nothing* 1QH 8$_{39}$. הַנּוֹתֵן רוֹזְנִים לְאָיִן *who turns rulers into nothing* Is 40$_{23}$, [תהיה] לאין wickedness *will be as nothing* 1QH fr. 3$_{10(Licht)}$ (|| אֶפֶס); אַתֶּם מֵאַיִן *you are (made) of nothing* Is 41$_{24}$ (|| אֶפַע *nothing*), גָּדוֹל הַיּוֹם הַהוּא מֵאַיִן כָּמֹהוּ *that day is greater than any* (lit. *none*) *like it* Jr 30$_7$.

Also Si fr. (ms C) 4QM^a fr. 11.1$_{13.21}$ 1QH 10$_1$ (both [אי]ן) fr. 51$_5$ 4QapLam^a 1.1$_9$ 4QCat^a 7$_6$ 12.1$_5$ 4QShir Shab^f 40$_4$ 1Q31 2$_1$ (לאין) 4Q416 9.1$_{12}$ ([אי]ן) 9.2$_2$ 4Q477 2$_7$ 4QapPs^b 14$_4$ 18$_5$ 31$_8$ 69$_8$ 4QAocMos A 10$_3$ 4QApocJos^a 3$_2$.

אַיִן II $_{18.1}$ interrog. adv. **where?—1.** without מִן, **where?,** אֵין יֶשׁ־פֹּה ... חֲנִית *where is there here ... a spear?* 1 S 21$_9$ (if em. אֵין [mss אַיִן] *there is not*).

2. מֵאַיִן **whence? a.** with verb, בוא *come* Gn 42$_7$ Jos 9$_8$ (|| מִי *who?*) Jg 17$_9$ 19$_{17}$ (|| אָן *where?*) 2 K 20$_{14}$||Is 39$_3$ (|| מָה *what?*) Jon 1$_8$ (|| מָה, אֵי *where?*) Ps 121$_1$ (הֶהָרִים מֵאַיִן *the hills whence*) Jb 1$_7$ 28$_{20}$ (|| אֵי), מצא ni. *be found* 28$_{12}$ (|| אֵי), ישׁע hi. *deliver* 2 K 6$_{27}$, בקשׁ pi. *seek* Na 3$_7$ (|| מִי).

b. in nom. cl., **whence is?,** with (pro)noun, בָּשָׂר *flesh* Nm 11$_{13}$, שָׁלוֹם *peace* Si 13$_{18}$ (if em. מאישׁ *from a man*) 13$_{18}$, גֵּחֲזִי *Gehazi* 2 K 5$_{25(Qr, mss)}$ (Kt מֵאָן *whence?*), אַתֶּם *you* Gn 29$_4$, הֵמָּה *they* Jos 2$_4$ (+ ידע *know*); מֵאֵין כָּמוֹךָ *whence is (one) as you?* Jr 10$_{6.7}$ (if em. מֵאַיִן perh. *there is no one*).

<SYN> אֵי *where?,* מָה *where?,* מִי *who?*

אִין, see אַיִן I, Coll.

איעדה $_{0.0.0.1}$ pr.n. **Iadah,** Seal 151 (Judaea?, 7th cent.).

אִיעֶזֶר $_1$ pr.n.m. **Iezer,** descendant of Gilead, appar. ident. with Abiezer (אֲבִיעֶזֶר) at Jos 17$_2$ 1 C 7$_{18}$, Nm 26$_{30}$ (Sam אחיעזר *Ahiezer*).

→ עזר *help.*

אִיעֶזְרִי $_1$ gent. **Iezrite,** as noun, **Iezrites,** descendants of Iezer, appar. ident. with Abiezrite (אֲבִיעֶזְרִי) at Jg 6$_{11.24}$ 8$_{32}$, Nm 26$_{30}$.

→ עזר *help.*

אֵיפָה 41.1.3 n.f. **ephah**—אֵפָה; cstr. אֵיפַת—**1. ephah,** unit of dry measure, about 40 litres, ten omers (Ex 16$_{36}$) and one tenth of a homer (Ezk 45$_{11}$), and equal to liquid measure bath (Ezk 45$_{11}$), esp. in cult (e.g. Lv 5$_{11}$ 6$_{13}$ Nm 28$_5$ Ezk 45$_{24}$).

<SUBJ> היה *be* Lv 19$_{36}$ (|| מֹאזְנַיִם *scales,* אֶבֶן *stone,* i.e. weight, הִין *hin*) Dt 25$_{14.15}$ (|| אֶבֶן) Ezk Ezk 45$_{10}$ (all four + לְ *to* Israelite; || מֹאזְנַיִם, בַּת *bath*) 45$_{11}$ (+ תֹּכֶן אֶחָד *one measure*) 46$_{11.11}$ (both + מִנְחָה *grain offering*), נשׂא *bear,* i.e. contain 45$_{11}$, זעם pass. *be cursed* Mc 6$_{10}$.

<NOM CL> מִנְחָה אֵיפָה *the grain offering is an ephah* Ezk 46$_5$, הָעֹמֶר עֲשִׂרִית הָאֵיפָה הוּא *the omer is one tenth of an ephah* Ex 16$_{36}$ הַאִשׁ ... אֵיפַת *is there ... the ephah of* smallness Mc 6$_{10}$ (or em. הַאִשׁ to הַאֶשֶּׁה *shall I forget?*or הַאֶשָּׂא *shall I endure?*).

<OBJ> עשׂה *make,* i.e. yield Is 5$_{10}$ (|| בַּת *bath*), *prepare* Jg 6$_{19}$ Ezk 45$_{24.24}$ 46$_{7.7}$ (all four + מִנְחָה *as a grain offering*), לקח *take* 1 S 17$_{17}$, קטן hi. *diminish* Am 8$_5$ (:: שֶׁקֶל *shekel*), נשׁה *forget* Mc 6$_{10}$ (if em.; see Nom. Cl.), נשׂא *bear,* i.e. endure 6$_{10}$ (if em.; see Nom. Cl.), שׁשׁה pi. *give a sixth part of* Ezk 45$_{13}$ (unless em.; see Cstr.).

<CSTR> אֵיפַת צֶדֶק *ephah of righteousness,* i.e. just ephah Lv 19$_{36}$ Ezk 45$_{10}$ (אֵיפַת־), אמת *of truth* 4Q416 1$_9$, רָזוֹן *of smallness* Mc 6$_{10}$, הַקָּלִיא הַזֶּה *of this roasted grain* 1 S 17$_{17}$ (mss הַקָּלִי), קֶמַח *of flour* Jg 6$_{19}$ (אֵיפַת־); תמחי איפה *cleansing of ephah* Si 42$_{4(M)}$ (B תמהות appar. error for תמחות *cleansing of;* Bmg תמורת אפה *exchanging of ephah;* || אֶבֶן *stone,* i.e. weight), שִׁשִּׁית הָאֵיפָה *sixth part of the ephah* Ezk 45$_{13.13}$ (if em. וְשִׁשִּׁיתֶם *and you shall give a sixth part of* the ephah) 46$_{14}$, עֲשִׂירִת *tenth part of* Lv 5$_{11}$ 6$_{13}$ (both הָאֵפָה) Nm 5$_{15}$ 28$_5$ (עֲשִׂירִית), מעשׂר *tithe of* 4QOrd^{b} 1.1$_4$.

<ADJ> קָטָן *small* Dt 25$_{14}$, גָּדוֹל *large* 25$_{14}$, שָׁלֵם *whole* 25$_{15}$ (שְׁלֵמָה וָצֶדֶק *whole and righteous[ness]*), אֵיפָה אַחַת *one ephah* 1 S 1$_{24}$.

<PREP> עלה בְּ hi. *bring up with* 1 S 1$_{24}$ (|| פַּר *bull,* נֵבֶל *skin* of wine); כְּ *about* Ru 2$_{17}$; שֶׁמֶן הִין לְאֵיפָה *wine, a hin for (each) ephah* Ezk 45$_{24}$ 46$_{5.7.11}$.

<COLL> אֵיפָה וְאֵיפָה *ephah and ephah,* i.e. two kinds of ephah Dt 25$_{14}$ Pr 20$_{10}$ (|| אֶבֶן *stone*) Si 42$_{4(Bmg)}$ (אפה ואפה), אֵיפָה לַפָּר וְאֵיפָה לָאַיִל *an ephah for the bull and an ephah for the ram* Ezk 45$_{24}$ 46$_{7.11}$, אֵיפָה לָאַיִל *an ephah for the ram* 46$_5$.

2. ephah container, measure, <SUBJ> יצא *go out* Zc 5$_5$ (if em. מָה *what* to הָאֵיפָה *the ephah*) 5$_6$. <NOM CL> זֹאת הָאֵיפָה *this is the ephah container* Zc 5$_6$. <OBJ> נשׂא *lift up* Zc 5$_9$, הלך hi. *take* 5$_{10}$. <PREP> ישׁב בְּתוֹךְ *sit inside* Zc 5$_7$, שׁלך אֶל־תּוֹךְ hi. *thrust into* 5$_8$.

Also 4QOrd^{a} 1.2$_{13}$ (א[י]פה).

<SYN> אֶבֶן *stone,* i.e. weight, בַּת *bath,* מֹאזְנַיִם *scales.*

אֵיפֹה 10.0.1 interrog. adv. **where?, 1. where?,** with verb, היה *be* Jb 38$_4$ (+ מִי *who?*), שׁגל pu. *be violated* Jr 3$_2$, כחד ni. *be effaced* Jb 4$_7$ (+ מִי), לקט pi. *glean* Ru 2$_{19}$ (+ אָן *where?*).

2. in nom. cl., **where?,** with (pro)noun, עַם *people* 1QMyst 1$_{11}$ (+ מִי), אִישׁ *man* Jg 8$_{18}$ (but perh. אֵיפֹה = *how?,* i.e. of what character?), אַתֶּם *you* Jr 36$_{19}$ (+ ידע *know*), הוּא *he* 2 S 9$_4$, הֵם *they* Is 49$_{21}$ (+ מִי), אֵיפֹה הֵם רֹעִים *where are they shepherding?* Gn 37$_{16}$ (+ נגד hi. *tell*), אֵיפֹה שְׁמוּאֵל וְדָוִד *where are Samuel and David?* 1 S 19$_{22}$.

→ אֵי *where?* + פֹּה *here.*

[אִיץ], see ארץ.

אִישׁ I +2179.80.466.9 n.m. **man**—I אשׁ; cstr. אִישׁ; sf. אִישִׁי, אִישֵׁךְ, אִישׁוֹ, אִישָׁהּ; pl. אֲנָשִׁים (Q הנשים [= האנשים], I אנשם), אִישִׁים; cstr. אַנְשֵׁי (Q אנישי, Q הנשי, Q אנש); sf. אֲנָשַׁי, אֲנָשֶׁיךָ, אֲנָשֶׁיהָ, אֲנָשָׁיו (Kt, I אנשו), אֲנָשֵׁינוּ, אַנְשֵׁיהֶם (Q אנשיהמה), אַנְשֵׁיהֶן—**1a.** usu. **man, person,** oft. without contextual emphasis on gender, e.g. Ex 1$_1$ Nm 14$_{15}$ 16$_{22}$ Dt 3$_{11}$ Jg 1$_{25}$ 6$_{16}$ 8$_{21}$ 9$_{36}$ 18$_{19}$ 20$_{1.8.11}$ 1 S 1$_{21}$ 9$_{17}$ 10$_6$ 11$_7$ 27$_3$ 2 S 2$_3$ 19$_{15}$ 2 K 14$_{6(Qr)}$||2 C 25$_4$ (אִישׁ בְּחֶטְאוֹ יוּמָת *a man,* or *person shall be put to death for his own sin*) Is 53$_3$ Jr 23$_{34}$ 31$_{30}$ Mc 2$_2$ Ps 1$_1$ 49$_3$ 112$_{1.5}$ Jb 38$_{26}$ Ezr 3$_1$ Ne 6$_{11}$ 8$_1$ Si 13$_{17}$ 14$_2$ 34$_8$ 37$_{25(B)}$ 50$_{28}$ Nimrud ivory inscr. 1$_2$.

1b. distributively, **each,** of individuals, e.g. Gn 9$_5$ 10$_{5.5}$ 11$_{3.7}$ 13$_{11}$ 15$_{10}$ 26$_{31}$ 31$_{49}$ 37$_{19}$ 40$_5$ 41$_{11.12}$ 42$_{21}$ 43$_{33}$ Ex 12$_4$ 16$_{16.16.18.21}$ 18$_{16}$ 36$_4$ Lv 7$_{10}$ 15$_2$ 17$_{3.8.10}$ 19$_{3.11}$ 24$_{19}$ 25$_{17}$ Nm 1$_4$ 2$_{34}$ 7$_5$ 17$_{17}$ Dt 1$_{16}$ 16$_{17}$ Jg 17$_6$ 21$_{25}$ 2 S 20$_1$

1 K $5_{7.8}$ $18_{4.13}$ 22_{36} 2 K 15_{20} 23_{35} Jr 7_{5} 22_{7} 23_{36} 25_{26} Ezk 18_{8} 46_{16} Ps 87_{5} Pr 20_{6} Est 1_{8} Ne 4_{13} 2 C 31_{2} Si 16_{12} 46_{11} 11QPs^{a} 22_{10} 1QS $1_{9.10}$ 2_{25} $5_{21.23.24}$ $6_{4.7.8.9}$ $9_{12.15.15.18}$ 1QSa 1_{23} 2_{16} 1QM 5_{4} 8_{6} CD 3_{6} $8_{7(A)}$=$19_{20(B)}$ $14_{5.11}$ $20_{24(mg)}$ 1QH fr. 11_{4} 4Q181 1_{5} 4QCat^{a} 1_{11} 1QpHab 4_{11} 4QpsMos^{e} $2.1_{9.9}$ 4Q416 1_{3} Siloam tunnel inscr.$_{2.2.4}$.

1c. distributively, **each,** of groups, objects, tribes, Nm 26_{54} 35_{8}; gods, 2 K 18_{33}||Is 36_{18}; cherubim, Ezk $1_{9.11.11.12.23.23}$ 10_{22}; faces of cherubim, Ex 25_{20}||37_{9} =11QT $7_{12(Yadin)}$ ([א]יש]); scales of behemoth, Jb 41_{9}; engravings on stones of breastpiece, Ex 28_{21}||39_{14}; islands, Zp 2_{11}; supports, surfaces of stands, 1 K $7_{30.36}$.

2. one, someone, sim. to indefinite pronoun, esp. in negative clauses, e.g. Gn 13_{16} 19_{31} (but perh. אִישׁ = *man*, as §3) 23_{6} Ex 34_{24} Nm 31_{49} Dt 34_{6} Jos 21_{44} 23_{9} Jg 4_{20} $19_{15.18}$ $21_{1.8}$ 1 S $2_{25.25}$ 9_{9} 10_{12} 11_{13} 12_{4} $14_{28.36}$ $21_{2.3}$ 24_{20} $30_{2.17}$ 2 S $16_{23(Qr)}$ 2 K 10_{14} 12_{10} 23_{8} 1 C 16_{21} Lachish ost. 3_{9}.

3. man, husband, as distinct from woman, e.g. Gn $2_{23.24}$ $3_{6.16}$ 16_{3} $19_{5.8}$ 20_{7} 24_{16} 26_{11} $29_{19.32.34}$ $30_{15.18.20}$ 34_{14} 38_{25} Ex 2_{1} 11_{2} 21_{28} 22_{15}=11QT 66_{8} Ex $35_{22.29}$ 36_{6} Lv $13_{29.38}$ $15_{18.24.33}$ $19_{20.20}$ 20_{10+9t} $21_{3.7}$ 22_{12} 24_{10} Nm 5_{6+12t} 6_{2} $25_{8.14}$ 30_{3}=11QT 53_{14} Nm 30_{7+10t} Dt $17_{2.5}$=11QT $55_{16.21}$ Dt $20_{7.7}$ 21_{15} $22_{13.16.18}$=11QT $65_{7.11(mg).14}$ Dt $22_{22.22.23.23.24.25}$=11QT $66_{3.4}$ Dt $22_{25.25}$=11QT 66_{5} Dt $22_{28.29}$=11QT $66_{8.10}$ Dt 23_{1}=11QT 66_{12} Dt 23_{11} $24_{1.3.3.5}$ $25_{5.7.9.11}$ $28_{30.54.56}$ 31_{12} Jos 6_{21} 8_{25} Jg $9_{49.51}$ 11_{39} $13_{2.6.9.10}$ 14_{15} $16_{27.27}$ $19_{3.22.25}$ 20_{4} 21_{21} 1 S $1_{8.11.23}$ 2_{19} $4_{19.21}$ 15_{3} 22_{19} 25_{3} 27_{9} 30_{22} 2 S $3_{15.16}$ 6_{19}||1 C 16_{3} 2 S 11_{26} $14_{5.7}$ 25_{19} 2 K $4_{1.9.14.22.26}$ Is 4_{1} Jr 3_{1} 6_{11} 18_{21} 29_{6} 40_{7} $44_{7.15.19}$ Ezk $16_{32.45.45}$ $22_{11.11.11}$ $23_{14.40}$ Ho $2_{4.9.18}$ Am 2_{7} Pr 6_{26} 7_{19} Ru $1_{1.2.3.5.9}$ $2_{1.11}$ Ezr $10_{1.17}$ Ne 4_{17} 8_{3} Si $25_{17.20}$ 36_{28} $42_{10.14}$ 11QT 45_{11} 54_{3} $66_{12.14.15.16}$ CD 5_{8} 12_{1} $16_{10.11}$.

4. armed man, warrior, e.g. Ex 15_{3} Nm $31_{23.28.49.53}$ Dt $2_{14.16}$ Jos 5_{4} 17_{1} Jg 3_{29} $20_{2.44.46}$ 1 S 14_{12} 16_{18} $17_{4.23.33}$ 31_{12}||1 C 10_{12} 2 S $8_{4.10}$||1 C $18_{4.10}$ 2 S 11_{16} 23_{20}||1 C 11_{22} 2 S 24_{9} Is 5_{22} Jr 6_{23}||50_{42} Pr 6_{11}=24_{34} Ec 12_{3} 1 C 12_{9} 19_{18} 26_{8} Si 44_{6} 11QT 57_{6} $58_{7.8.10.16}$ 1QM $2_{7.8}$ $3_{1.7}$ $5_{17(Yadin)}$ $6_{9.10(mg).11.12.13}$ $7_{1.5.12.16}$ $8_{1.4}$ $9_{3.5}$ 15_{4} 16_{4} 17_{13} 1QM 14_{18} + Sup 4QM^{c}$_{2}$ CD 20_{14} 1QH 7_{22} 9_{22} 1Q36 16_{2} 4QpIsa^{a} 1_{3} 4QpNah 3.3_{11}.

5. oft. **servant, member of retinue,** alw. pl., e.g. Gn $24_{32.54.59}$ Jg 9_{28} 1 S 18_{27} $23_{3.5.12.24.25}$ $24_{3.5.7}$ 27_{3} $28_{1.8}$ 2 S $2_{29.31.32}$ 5_{6} $13_{9.9}$ 15_{22} 17_{8} 19_{42} 20_{7} 21_{17} 1 K 10_{8}||2 C 9_{7} 2 K $25_{23.23}$||Jr $40_{7.8}$ Zc 7_{2} Pr 25_{1} Ne 2_{12} Si 45_{18} Lachish ost. 3_{18} Arad ost. 24_{19}.

6a. mortal, as distinct from God, Gn 32_{29} Nm 23_{19} Dt 1_{17} Jos 10_{14} Jg $9_{9.13}$ 1 S $2_{25.26}$ 26_{15} Is 7_{13} 31_{8} 40_{13} Ho 11_{9} Ps 4_{3} 62_{10} Jb 9_{32} 32_{13} Lm 3_{33} Si $10_{4.7}$ 45_{1} 11QPs^{a} 27_{3} 11QT 64_{12} 1QS 3_{13} $4_{15.20.26}$ 1QM 1_{11} 11_{14} 1QM $14_{17(Baillet)}$ + Sup 2_{15} 1QH 3_{22} fr. 10_{8} $11_{4(Licht)}$ 1Q36 25.2_{5} 4QWiles 1_{17} 4QShir^{b} 1_{11} 4QShirShab^{a} $2_{2.3}$ 4QShirShab^{b} 14.1_{8} Kuntillet ʻAjrud add. inscr. 2.

6b. human being, as distinct from other animal, Ex 11_{7} 19_{13} 34_{3} Is 66_{3} Ps 22_{7} 147_{10} Si 13_{18} (or em.; see Prep.).

7. male animal, מִן־הַבְּהֵמָה ... אִישׁ וְאִשְׁתּוֹ *from the beasts ... a male and his mate* Gn $7_{2.2}$.

<SUBJ> היה *be* Gn 6_{9} (+ נֹחַ *Noah*) 46_{32} (+ אִישׁ) 46_{34} (+ עֶבֶד *servant*) Lv 20_{21} (+ עֲרִירִי *childless*) Nm 1_{4} (+ אֵת *with*) 1_{4} (+ רֹאשׁ *chief*, if em. הוּא *he* to יִהְיוּ *they will be*) 31_{3} (+ עַל *against*) Dt 23_{11} (+ טָהוֹר *clean*) 24_{5} (+ נָקִי *innocent*) Jos 17_{1} (+ הוּא *he*) Jg 12_{2} (+ אֲנִי *I*) 1 S 11_{8} (+ number) 22_{2} (+ עִם *with*) 2 S 19_{29} (+ בַּיִת *household*) 1 K 5_{27} (+ מַס *levy*) 2 K 5_{1} (+ גִּבּוֹר *warrior*) Jr 41_{2} (+ אֵת) Ezk 18_{5} (+ צַדִּיק *righteous*) Jb 1_{1} (+ תָּם וְיָשָׁר *pure and upright*) 1_{3} (+ גָּדוֹל *great*) Dn 10_{7} (+ עִם) Ne 4_{16} (+ מִשְׁמָר *guard*) 1 C 8_{40} (+ בֵּן *child*) 21_{5} (+ number; perh. nom. cl.) 22_{9} (+ הוּא) 25_{1} (+ מִסְפָּר *number*) Si 6_{6} (+ רַב *many*) 42_{8} 1QS 6_{3} (+ שָׁם *there*) 1QM 7_{1} (+ מִן *from* the age of) 7_{5} (+ כולם *all of them*) 7_{6} (+ טָהוֹר) 8_{6} (+ פשט ni. ptc. *arrayed*) 1QM fr. $1_{10(Baillet)}$ (+ [טהור]) 1QH 2_{14} 4QCrypt 1.1_{4} 4QToh A 2.1_{6} (+ במחנה *in the camp*).

+ לְ of possession, etc. Gn 44_{17} Ex 22_{30} Nm 1_{44} Jg 10_{18} 1 S 29_{4} etc., + בְּ of place, etc. Nm $9_{10.13}$ 26_{64} 2 S 12_{1} 1QS 7_{22}, + כְּ *as* Nm 17_{5} 2 S 14_{25} 1 K 3_{13} Is $32_{2.2}$ etc., + pr.n.m. Gn 25_{27} 39_{2} 2 S 8_{10}||1 C 18_{10} 2 S 24_{9}||1 C 21_{5} 2 K 5_{1}, + ptc. 2 S 10_{5} 2 K 7_{3} Jr 18_{21} 26_{20} Ezk 43_{6} Mc 2_{11} etc. 11QT 57_{8} 1QM 2_{6}, וַיְהִי(־)אִישׁ *and there was a man* Jg 13_{2} 17_{1} 19_{1} 1 S 1_{1} 9_{1} etc., sim. 2 S 4_{2} 2 K 7_{3} 11QT 64_{7} 1QS 9_{23} 1QM $14_{10(Baillet)}$ + Sup (א[נ]שי]).

יתר ni. *remain* Nm 26_{65} 1 K 20_{30} Am 6_{9}, hi. *leave over*

Ex $16_{19.20}$, שׁאר ni. *remain* Nm 11_{26} Jos 8_{17} 2 K 10_{21} Jr 37_{10} 38_4, עדר ni. *be missing* Is 40_{26}, אחר pi. *delay* 4Q251 5_2, פקד pass. *be appointed* 1QS 6_{14}, ni. *be appointed* Ne 12_{44}, *be unaccounted for* Nm 31_{49} 2 S 2_{30} 1 K 20_{39} 2 K 10_{19}, htp. *rally* intrans. Jg $20_{15.15.17}$, חדל *cease* Nm 9_{13}, שׁבת *cease* Jb 32_1, חרשׁ hi. *be silent* Nm $30_{8.12.15.15}$ Pr 11_{12}, שׁקט *be silent* Ru 3_{18} Si 41_1, דמם ni. *be silenced* Jr 49_{26}||50_{30} 1QpHab 5_{10}.

בוא *come* Gn $19_{5.8}$ 24_{32} Ex 1_1 35_{21} etc. 11QT $45_{11.12}$ 1QSa 1_{19} $2_{3.10}$ 4QM^a fr. 1_{10} (יבו[א]) CD $8_{21(A)}$=$19_{33(B)}$ Nimrud ivory inscr. 1_2 ([איש ... יב]א), *come* for sex Dt 22_{13}, hi. *bring* Gn 19_{10} $43_{17.24}$ Ex $35_{23.29}$ etc. 1QS 6_1 CD $9_{2.2}$, הלך *go* Gn 14_{24} 18_{22} 24_{65} 26_{13} Ex 2_1 etc. 11QT 17_9 Dt 20_8=11QT 62_3 1QS 2_2 $5_{4.10}$ $7_{15.16}$ $8_{2.20.20}$ $9_{8.19}$ 1QM $7_{4.4}$ CD 11_5, pi. *walk* Pr 6_{28}, hi. *lead* 16_{29} 4Q251 3_5 ([איש]), htp. *go about* Jos 18_4 Jg 21_{24} 1 S $23_{13.13}$ 30_{31} etc. 1QS 6_2 CD $10_{20.20}$ 20_7, נדד *wander* Pr 27_8, נוע *wander* CD 14_{15}, סחר *roam* Gn 34_{21}, נסע *set out* Nm $2_{17.34}$ Jg 18_{11}, ארח *travel* 19_{17}, נגשׁ *approach* Lv 21_{21} Dt 25_1 1 K 20_{28} Jl 4_9, hi. *bring forward* 1 S $14_{34.34.34}$, קרב *approach* Lv 18_6 $21_{17.18.21}$ 22_3 etc., hi. *bring forward* $22_{18.21}$ Nm 9_{13} 25_6.

יצא *go out* Ex 12_{22} 16_{29} Nm 11_{26} 31_{28} Dt 13_{14}=11QT 55_3 (אנש[י]ם) etc. 11QT 58_{16} 1QM 3_1 7_{16} 9_3 16_4, hi. *take out* Gn 19_{16} Nm 14_{37} Dt $22_{13.18}$=11QT $65_{7.14}$ Dt 24_{11} 4QOrd^a 2_8 (Allegro יוצו, with אִישׁ as obj.) CD 11_7 4Q251 2_4 ([יוציא אי]ש), ירד *go down* Gn 43_{15} Jos 2_{23} Jg 15_{11} 1 S 17_8 25_{20} etc. 1QM 7_6, hi. *take down* Gn 44_{11}, עלה *go up* Ex 34_3 Nm 13_{31} 32_{11} Jos $6_{5.20}$ etc., ni. *be removed* 2 S 2_{27}, hi. *take up* Gn 37_{28} Ex $32_{1.23}$ 1 S 7_1 Ezk 14_3 etc. CD 11_{17} 4Q251 2_5, *offer (sacrifice)* 1 S 6_{15} Jr 33_{18} CD 11_{17}, עבר *cross over* Jos 2_{23} 18_9 Jg 12_1 1 S 27_2 29_2 etc., *transgress* Jr 34_{18} 1QS 8_{21}, hi. *take across* 2 S 19_{42} 2 K 23_{10} Ezk 47_3.

שׁוב *go back* Lv $25_{10.10.13}$ Nm 14_{36} Dt 3_{20} $20_{5.6.7.8}$=11QT 62_3 etc. Si 8_5 1QS 5_1 $7_{16.17.18}$ CD 19_{33} 20_{14} 1QH fr. $1_{7(Licht)}$ ([שב]), hi. *take back* Jr $34_{16.16}$ Ezk $18_{7.8}$ Jon 1_{13} Si 36_{25}, *answer* Dt 1_{22} Ezk 9_{11} 1QS 6_9, סור *turn* intrans. 1 K 20_{39} Ps 139_{19} Jb 2_3 1QS 8_{16} 1QSa 1_2 (ס[רו]) CD 19_{33}, hi. *remove* 1 S 17_{26} Jr 4_4, פנה *turn* intrans. Gn 18_{22} Jos 8_{20} Jg $20_{41.47}$ Is 13_{14} etc., סוג ni. *turn* intrans. Jr 38_{22}, נטה hi. *turn aside* trans. Si 35_{17} 11QT 51_{16}, נוע hi. *remove* 2 K 23_{18}, סבב *go round* Jos 6_3, ni. *surround* Gn 19_4 Jg 19_{22}, hi. *remove* 2 S 20_{12}, עטר *close in* 1 S 23_{26}, הפך *turn* intrans. Jg $20_{39.41}$ 2 K 5_{26}, לפת ni. *turn over* intrans. Ru 3_8.

שׁגה *stray* Ezk 45_{20}, תעה *stray* Is 47_{15}, hi. *lead astray* CD 1_{14} 4QpPs^a 1.1_{18}, בדל ni. *separate oneself* Ezr 10_{16} 1 C 12_9 1QS 9_5, ho. *be separated* CD 9_{21}, נזר ni. *separate oneself* Ezk 14_7, פרד ni. *separate oneself* Gn 10_5 13_{11}, htp. *be separated* Jb 41_9, לוה ni. *be joined* Gn 29_{34}, צמד ni. *be joined* Nm 25_5, ערב htp. *associate oneself* 1QS 7_{24} 8_{23} perh. CD 11_4, פוץ *be dispersed* 2 S 20_{22} Ezk 46_{18}, מושׁ *depart* 1QS $6_{3.6}$ CD 13_2, פטר ni. *depart* 1QS 7_{10}, עזב *abandon* Gn 2_{24} 1 S 31_7||1 C 10_7 Is 55_7 Ezk 20_8 11QT 57_6, ni. *be abandoned* 1QH 8_{27}.

רוץ *run* 1 S 4_{12} 2 S 15_1 $18_{24.26.26}$ etc., רדף *pursue* Jos 2_7 23_{10} Jg 7_{23} 1 S 7_{11} 17_{52} etc. 1QM 9_5 4Q298 3_6, דבק *cleave* Gn 2_{24} Nm $36_{7.9}$ 2 S 20_2, hi. *overtake* Jg 18_{22}, *pursue* 1 S 14_{22}, pu. *be joined* Jb 41_9, ברח *flee* 1 K 11_{17} Jr 39_4||52_7 Dn 10_7 Ne 6_{11} (+ כָּמוֹנִי a person *like me*) 13_{10} 11QT 64_9, נוס *flee* Dt 19_{11} Jos 7_4 Jg 9_{51} 20_{47} 1 S 4_{10} etc., מלט ni. *escape* Jg 3_{29} 1 S 30_{17} 1 K 18_{40} 2 K 10_{24}, pi. *rescue* Jr $51_{6.45}$, חבא htp. *hide oneself* 1 S 14_{22}, עלם htp. *hide oneself* CD $8_{6(A)}$=$19_{18(B)}$, סתר ni. *be hidden* Gn 31_{49} Jr 23_{24}, נצל ni. *be saved* Ezk $14_{16.18}$, hi. *save* Ex 2_{19} 2 K 18_{33}||Is 36_{18} Ezk 14_{16} Ho 2_{12}, pi. *save* Ezk 14_{14}, ישׁע hi. *save* 1 S 9_{16}, פדה *redeem* Ps 49_8 CD 16_7, גאל *redeem* Lv 27_{31}.

קום *arise* Gn 18_{16} 24_{54} 43_{15} Ex 10_{23} perh. Nm 16_2 Dt 19_{11} 22_{26}=11QT 66_7 etc. 1QM 12_{10} CD $16_{1.4.7.9}$ (יקו[ם]), hi. *establish* Nm 30_{14}=11QT 54_3 (יקי[מנו]) Nm $30_{15.15}$ Jr 34_{18} Ne 5_{13} CD $16_{4.9}$, עמד *stand* Gn 24_{30} 43_{15} 45_1 Nm 1_5 16_{18} etc. Si 10_4 Dt 19_{17}=11QT 61_8 1QS 6_{13} 1QSa 1_{22} 1QM 5_{17} (אנש[י]) 15_4 16_4 4QTestim $1_{23(mg)}$ CD 1_{14} 4_{11} 4QCat^a 1_6 4QpsEzek^a 2_9, יצב htp. *position oneself* Nm 11_{16} Dt 7_{24} 11_{25} Jos 1_5 Jg 20_2 etc. 1QM 16_5 17_{11} (התיצבם אי[ש]), נצב ni. *stand* Gn 18_2 Ex 33_8 Jg 18_{16}, hi. *erect* Jos 6_{26}, נפל *fall* Ex 32_{28} Jg $20_{44.46}$ 1 S 31_1||1 C 10_1 2 S 1_2 etc., hi. *cause to fall* 4QD^a 6.2_{10} ([איש]), שׁכב *lie down* Jos 2_1 Is 14_{18} Jb 14_{12}, שׁכב *lie (with)* sexually Dt $28_{30(Qr)}$, שׁכב אֶת *lie with* sexually Lv $15_{18.24}$ 19_{20} $20_{11.12}$ etc., שׁכב עִם *lie with* sexually Ex 22_{15} Lv 15_{33} Dt $22_{22.22.23.25.25}$=11QT $66_{4.5}$ Dt $22_{28.29}$=11QT $66_{8.10}$ etc.

11QT 45$_{11}$ CD 12$_{1}$, מוך *be low* Si 25$_{20}$, שׁפל *be low* Is 2$_{9}$ 5$_{15}$ (both || אָדָם *human being*) 1QS 2$_{23}$, שׁחה htpal. *bow down* Gn 24$_{26}$ Ex 33$_{10}$ 2 S 1$_{2}$ Zp 2$_{11}$, קדד *bow down* Gn 24$_{26}$.

שׁלח *send* Jos 10$_{6}$ 2 K 6$_{9}$ 22$_{15}$||2 C 34$_{23}$ CD 11$_{19}$, *extend* hand Gn 19$_{10}$ 1QSa 2$_{18(\text{Barthélemy})}$ ([ישלח]) 1QM 17$_{13}$, pi. *send away* Gn 12$_{20}$ Ex 21$_{26}$ 22$_{4}$ Dt 24$_{1.3}$ etc., pu. *be sent away* Gn 44$_{3}$, פרשׂ *spread out* hands 1 K 8$_{38}$||2 C 6$_{29}$, שׁלך hi. *throw* Ex 7$_{12}$ Jg 8$_{25}$ 2 S 20$_{12}$ 2 K 3$_{25}$ 6$_{6}$ etc., זרק *toss* Jb 2$_{12}$, נזה hi. *sprinkle* Nm 19$_{18}$ 4Q251 3$_{3}$ 4QToh B$^{b}{}_{6}$ ([יזה]) 4QToh B$^{b}{}_{6}$ ([והזה]), נדף *push*, i.e. defeat Jb 32$_{13}$, דחק *push aside* Jl 2$_{8}$, נדח ni. *be pushed aside* Jr 49$_{5}$, hi. *push aside* Dt 13$_{14}$=11QT 55$_{3}$, נדה ni. *be banisdhed* 4QD^{a} 6.2$_{10}$, משׁך *pull* Gn 37$_{28}$ 1 K 22$_{34}$||2 C 18$_{33}$, נהל pi. *lead* 2 C 28$_{15}$, נהג *lead* 1 S 30$_{22}$ (+ בֵּן *child*).

רום *be high* 1QS 2$_{23}$, hi. *raise* Gn 41$_{44}$ Jos 4$_{5}$ Dn 12$_{7}$ 1QM 16$_{6}$ 17$_{12}$, נטל *raise* CD 11$_{9}$, עמס *load* Gn 44$_{13}$, סמך *support* Si 12$_{17}$, *lean* trans. Am 5$_{19}$, ni. intrans. 2 K 18$_{21}$||Is 36$_{6}$, שׁען ni. *lean* intrans. 1QS 5$_{18}$, נשׂא *carry* Lv 20$_{17.20}$ 24$_{15}$ Nm 9$_{13}$ (|| נֶפֶשׁ *person*) Dt 1$_{31}$ etc. CD 11$_{9}$, *take* 13$_{14}$, pi. *help* Ezr 1$_{4}$, נגע *touch* Lv 15$_{5}$ 22$_{5}$ 2 S 23$_{7}$ 2 K 13$_{21}$ Hg 2$_{12}$ Dn 9$_{21}$ 11QT 50$_{5.21}$ 1QS 8$_{16}$, hi. *reach* 1QM 17$_{12}$, pu. *be struck* 1QSa 2$_{3.4}$ 1QM 7$_{4}$ 4QM^{a} fr. 1$_{6}$ ([מנו]גע]), נשׁק *kiss* 1 S 20$_{41}$, אמץ pi. *strengthen* Pr 24$_{5}$, htp. *defy* 2 C 13$_{7}$, קשׁה hi. *harden* Pr 29$_{1}$, עזז hi. *strengthen* 21$_{29}$, חדה hi. *sharpen* 27$_{17}$, לטשׁ *sharpen* 1 S 13$_{20}$, ישׁר pi. *straighten* Pr 15$_{21}$, קפא *become thick* Zp 1$_{12}$, רעשׁ hi. *shake* trans. Is 14$_{16}$, רגז hi. *shake* trans. 14$_{16}$, רקק *spit* 1QS 7$_{13}$.

רפה pi. *cause to drop* Jr 38$_{4}$, פתח *open* Gn 44$_{11}$ Ex 21$_{33}$, ni. *be released* Jb 12$_{14}$, סגר *close* Gn 19$_{10}$ Jg 9$_{51}$, כסה pi. *cover* Ex 21$_{33}$ Lv 17$_{13}$ Ezk 18$_{7.16}$ Si 35$_{18}$, חפה *cover* 2 S 15$_{30}$, שׁית *place* Ex 33$_{4}$, שׂים *place* Nm 4$_{19}$ Dt 22$_{13}$=11QT 65$_{7}$ Dt 27$_{15}$ Jg 9$_{49}$ 20$_{36}$ etc., נוח hi. *place* Gn 19$_{16}$ Nm 19$_{9}$.

אהב *love* Gn 29$_{32}$ Ps 34$_{13}$ Pr 21$_{17}$ 29$_{3}$ CD 6$_{20}$, אבה *be willing* Jg 19$_{10.25}$, אוה htp. *desire* Ec 6$_{2}$, חמד *desire* Ex 34$_{24}$, חפץ *desire* Dt 25$_{7}$ Ps 112$_{1}$, רצה *desire* 4Q424 2$_{8}$ Arad ost. 40$_{7}$, htp. *ingratiate oneself* 1 S 29$_{4}$, ארשׂ pi. *become engaged (to)* Dt 20$_{7}$, בעל *marry* 24$_{1}$ 11QT 65$_{7}$, שׂנא *hate* Ex 18$_{21}$ Dt 19$_{11}$ 22$_{13.16}$=11QT 65$_{7.11}$ Dt 24$_{3}$ Pr 29$_{10}$ CD 8$_{6(A)}$=19$_{18(B)}$, ni. *be hated* Pr 14$_{17}$, נאץ pi. *despise* 1 S 2$_{17}$, שׁקץ pi. *make detestable* CD 7$_{4}$ 12$_{11}$, בוז *scorn* Si 8$_{4}$, צחה perh. *mock* 1QS 7$_{4}$, זבל *honour* Gn 30$_{20}$, ירא *fear* 20$_{8}$ 43$_{18}$ Ex 18$_{21}$ Lv 19$_{3}$ Dt 20$_{8}$=11QT 62$_{3}$ etc., פחד *fear* Jr 36$_{16}$, pi. *fear* Si 37$_{12(\text{Bmg, D})}$, חרד *tremble* Gn 42$_{28}$ Ezk 32$_{10}$ Ru 3$_{8}$, רגז *tremble* Pr 29$_{9}$, חלה pi. *entreat* 1 K 13$_{6}$, כפר pi. *appease* Pr 16$_{14}$, חמל *spare* 2 S 12$_{4}$ Is 9$_{18}$ Ml 3$_{17}$, חנן *be merciful* Ps 112$_{5}$.

חשׁב *think* Ezk 11$_{2}$ Zc 8$_{17}$ Ps 140$_{5}$, ni. *be reckoned* CD 19$_{33}$, חלם *dream* Gn 40$_{5}$ 41$_{11}$, הגה *ponder* Si 50$_{28}$, ידע *know* Gn 25$_{27}$ Dt 34$_{6}$ 1 S 16$_{16}$ 21$_{3}$ 2 S 15$_{11}$ etc. Si 40$_{29}$ 47$_{5}$ 1QS 2$_{22.22}$ 8$_{16}$ CD 16$_{11}$ ([י]דענה]) 4Q424 2$_{7}$, *know* sexually Gn 24$_{16}$ Jg 19$_{25}$, pass. *be knowledgeable* Dt 1$_{13.15}$, ni. *be known* 1 S 22$_{6}$, hi. *inform* Is 40$_{13}$ CD 9$_{22}$ 15$_{10}$, זכר *remember* Si 15$_{8}$, שׁמר *keep* commandment Lv 19$_{3}$ Dt 31$_{12}$ 1QSa 1$_{3}$, ni. *guard oneself* Jr 9$_{3}$, למד *learn* Dt 31$_{12}$, pass. *be trained* 1 C 5$_{18}$, pi. *teach* Jr 31$_{34.34}$, pu. *be taught* 1QM 6$_{13}$, בין *understand* Jr 9$_{11}$ Pr 28$_{5}$, hi. *understand* 1 C 27$_{32}$ Si 36$_{3}$, ni. *be intelligent* Gn 41$_{33}$ Dt 1$_{13}$ 1 S 16$_{18}$ Si 36$_{3}$, pol. *be expert* CD 13$_{2}$, לבב ni. *become intelligent* Jb 11$_{12}$, בחן pass. *be expert* CD 13$_{3}$, צנע pass. *be discreet* Si 42$_{8}$, בער *be bestial* Ezk 21$_{36}$.

נסה pi. *test* Nm 14$_{22}$ Lachish ost. 3$_{9}$, בחר *choose* 2 S 16$_{18}$ CD 8$_{8(A)}$=19$_{20(B)}$, pass. *be chosen* Jg 20$_{15.16.34}$ 1 S 24$_{3}$ 26$_{2}$ etc., ni. *be chosen* Si 34$_{16}$, מאן pi. *refuse* 1 K 20$_{35}$, מאס *reject* Is 31$_{7}$ 1QpHab 5$_{11}$, נאץ pi. *reject* Nm 16$_{30}$, בטח *trust* Jg 20$_{36}$ Jr 9$_{3}$, אמן ni. *be trustworthy* CD 10$_{2}$, hi. *believe* Jon 3$_{5}$.

ראה *see* Ex 10$_{23}$ Lv 20$_{17}$ Nm 14$_{22}$ 17$_{24}$ 32$_{11}$ etc. Si 15$_{7}$ (|| מַת *man*) CD 9$_{22}$, ni. *be seen* Ex 34$_{3}$ Jg 13$_{10}$, hi. *show* Jg 1$_{24}$, גלה pi. *reveal* nakedness Lv 20$_{11.17.18.20.21}$ etc. Dt 23$_{1}$=11QT 66$_{12.12}$ 4Q251 7$_{3}$ ([יגל]) 7$_{6}$, ערה hi. *expose* vulva Lv 20$_{18}$, נבט hi. *look* Nm 21$_{9}$, שׁקף hi. *look down* Gn 18$_{16}$, נכר hi. *recognize* Ru 3$_{14}$, ni. *be recognized* Si 11$_{28}$, שׁאה htp. *gaze* Gn 24$_{21}$, שׁגח hi. *gaze* Si 40$_{29}$, תור *spy* Nm 13$_{2}$, רגל pi. *spy* Jos 2$_{1}$ 6$_{22}$ 7$_{2.2}$, שׁמע *hear* Gn 11$_{7}$ Nm 11$_{10}$ 14$_{22}$ 30$_{8.9.12.13}$=11QT 54$_{3}$ etc. 11QT 56$_{8}$, ni. *obey* 1QS 5$_{23}$, אזן hi. *hear* 4Q298 1$_{1}$ ([האזי]נו]).

אמר *say* Gn 11$_{3}$ 19$_{12}$ 37$_{17.19}$ 38$_{21}$ etc. Dt 22$_{13}$=11QT 65$_{7}$ 1QS 6$_{13}$, דבר pi. *speak* Gn 24$_{30}$ 42$_{30}$ Ex 33$_{11}$ Jg 13$_{11}$ 1 S 9$_{6}$ etc. 1QS 6$_{10.11.11}$ 4QRitMar 19$_{5}$ CD 10$_{17}$ 12$_{2(\text{mg})}$ 4Q251 1$_{6}$, ni. *converse* Ml 3$_{16}$, נגד hi. *tell* Jg 13$_{6}$ 14$_{15}$ 1 S

4$_{14}$ 9$_{6.8}$ etc., ספר *count* 11QT 45$_{15}$, pi. *tell* Jos 2$_{23}$ Jg 7$_{13}$ Jr 23$_{27}$ CD 9$_{2}$, מנה *count* Gn 13$_{16}$, בשׂר pi. *bring news* Jr 20$_{15}$, שׁאל *ask* Gn 26$_{7}$ 37$_{15}$ 43$_{7}$ Ex 11$_{2}$ 18$_{7}$ etc. 1QS 6$_{12}$, ni. *be asked* 6$_{4.11}$, ענה *answer* Jg 8$_{8.8}$ 18$_{14}$ 20$_{4}$ 1 S 10$_{12}$ etc., יעץ *advise* Ezk 11$_{2}$, מרא hi. *urge* CD 11$_{12}$, ירה hi. *teach* Jg 13$_{8}$, נטף hi. *preach*. lit. *drop* CD 1$_{14}$, שׁבע ni. *swear* Gn 26$_{31}$ Nm 30$_{3}$=11QT 53$_{14}$ Jg 21$_{1}$ 2 S 21$_{17}$ Dn 12$_{7}$, hi. *cause to swear* CD 9$_{9}$, נדר *vow* Nm 30$_{3}$=11QT 53$_{14}$ Jon 1$_{16}$ CD 16$_{13}$ ([א]יש), עוד hi. *testify* Gn 43$_{3}$ 1 K 21$_{10.13}$, ברך pi. *bless* Dt 33$_{1}$ 2 K 4$_{29}$, קלל pi. *curse* Lv 20$_{9.9}$ 24$_{15}$ 2 S 16$_{5}$ 11QT 64$_{9}$, שׁקר pi. *lie* 1QS 6$_{24}$.

קרא *call* Jg 1$_{26}$ 1 K 13$_{4}$ 2 K 23$_{16.16.17}$ etc., pass. *be called* 2 S 15$_{11}$ 1QM 2$_{6}$, ni. *be called* 2 S 20$_{1}$ Est 4$_{11}$ 1QSa 1$_{27}$, זעק *call* Jon 1$_{5}$, ni. *be summoned* Jg 18$_{22}$, צעק ni. *be summoned* 7$_{23.24}$ 12$_{1}$, רוע hi. *shout* 1 S 17$_{52}$ 2 C 13$_{15.15}$, שׁיר pol. *sing* Jb 36$_{24}$.

לחם ni. *fight* 1 S 17$_{19}$ 2 S 11$_{17}$ Is 19$_{2.2}$ (|| עִיר *city*, מַמְלָכָה *kingdom*), צבא *wage war* Nm 31$_{42}$, פשׁט *raid* 1 S 27$_{8}$, עלל po. *pick off* stragglers Jg 20$_{45}$, נצה ni. *struggle* Ex 2$_{13}$ 21$_{22}$ Lv 24$_{10}$ Dt 25$_{11}$, ריב *struggle* Ex 21$_{18}$ Jg 8$_{1}$ Ho 4$_{4}$, איב *be an enemy* Mc 7$_{6}$ Est 7$_{6}$, פגע *attack* Jg 18$_{25}$, ארב *ambush* Dt 19$_{11}$ Si 11$_{32}$, מרה *rebel* 1 K 13$_{26}$, hi. *rebel* Jos 1$_{18}$, מרד *rebel* 1QpHab 8$_{11}$, סרר *rebel* 1QH 5$_{24}$.

ערך *form battle-line* Jg 20$_{20.22.33}$ 1 S 17$_{2}$, *prepare* 1 C 12$_{9}$ 4QOrd^{c} 1.1$_{10}$ ([א]יש), חלץ ni. *arm oneself* Nm 31$_{3}$, אבק ni. *wrestle* Gn 32$_{25}$, שׁלף *draw* sword Jg 8$_{10}$ 20$_{2.46}$ 2 S 24$_{9}$||1 C 21$_{5}$ 2 K 3$_{26}$ etc., *remove* shoe Ru 4$_{7}$, דרך *bend* bow 1 C 5$_{18}$ 8$_{40}$, גבר *prevail* 1 S 2$_{9}$ 2 S 11$_{23}$.

נכה hi. *strike* Ex 2$_{11}$ 21$_{18.20.26}$ Lv 24$_{17}$ etc. 4Q251 4$_{1}$ ([יכה איש]), ho. *be struck* Nm 25$_{14.14}$ 1 S 5$_{12}$, נגף *strike* Ex 21$_{22}$, ni. *be struck* 2 S 2$_{17}$, דפק htp. *knock* Jg 19$_{22}$, נקשׁ ni. *be struck down* Si 41$_{2(B)}$, הרג *kill* Gn 26$_{7}$ Ex 32$_{27.27.27}$ Nm 25$_{5}$ etc., רצח *murder* Dt 22$_{26}$=11QT 66$_{7}$, טבח *slaughter* Ex 21$_{37}$, שׁחט *slaughter* Lv 17$_{3.3}$ Jr 41$_{7}$, שׁחת pi. *destroy* Ex 21$_{26}$, hi. Pr 28$_{24}$, שׂרף *burn* 1 S 31$_{12}$, הרס *tear down* Pr 29$_{4}$, בזז *plunder* Nm 31$_{53.53}$, רגם *stone* Dt 21$_{21}$=11QT 64$_{5}$, סקל *stone* Dt 22$_{21}$.

ינה *oppress* Ezk 18$_{7}$, hi. *oppress* Lv 25$_{14.17}$ Ezk 18$_{16}$, נגשׂ ni. *oppress* Is 3$_{5.5}$, *be oppressed* 1 S 14$_{24}$, עשׁק *oppress* 4QpsMos^{e} 2.1$_{9}$, עמר htp. *enslave* Dt 24$_{7}$, חטף *seize* Jg 21$_{21}$, ענה pi. *violate* Dt 22$_{24.29}$=11QT 66$_{3.10}$ Ezk 22$_{11}$, htp. *humble oneself* 11QT 27$_{6}$, שׁגל *violate* Dt 28$_{30(Kt)}$, עלל htp. *torment* Jg 19$_{25}$.

לון ni. *complain* Nm 14$_{36(Kt)}$ 1QS 7$_{17}$, hi. *complain* 1QH 5$_{24}$, *cause to complain* Nm 14$_{36(Qr)}$, כאה ni. *be cowered* Ps 109$_{16}$, כנע ni. *humble oneself* 2 C 30$_{11}$, פגר pi. *be exhausted* 1 S 30$_{10.21}$, לאה *be weary* Gn 19$_{11}$, יעף ho. *be wearied* Dn 9$_{21}$, כשׁל *stumble* Lv 26$_{37}$ Si 41$_{2}$ 1QSa 2$_{7}$, שׁבר ni. *be broken* Pr 29$_{1}$, פרר htpo. *be split* 1QH 7$_{22(Licht)}$ (ויתפ[וררו]), בלע pu. *be swallowed* Jb 37$_{20}$, עצב htp. *feel hurt* Gn 34$_{7}$, המה *murmur* Ezk 7$_{16}$ 1QH 2$_{16}$, נהם *groan* Ezk 24$_{23}$, אנח ni. *groan* 9$_{4}$, אנק ni. *groan* 9$_{4}$.

שׁמם ni. *be appalled* Ezk 4$_{17}$, בהל ni. *be dismayed* Jg 20$_{41}$ Jr 51$_{32}$, *do quickly* Pr 28$_{22}$, דהם ni. *be astonished* Jr 14$_{9}$, פלא hi. *do something extraordinary* Lv 27$_{2}$ Nm 6$_{2}$, תמה *be amazed* Gn 43$_{33}$ Is 13$_{8}$, בושׁ *be ashamed* Zc 13$_{4}$, בכה *weep* Nm 11$_{10}$ 1 S 20$_{41}$ 2 S 3$_{16}$ 15$_{30}$ 2 K 8$_{11}$.

ילד ni. *be born* 1 C 7$_{21}$, hi. *beget* Ec 6$_{3}$, pi. *help give birth* CD 11$_{13}$, pu. *be born* Ps 87$_{5}$, חיה *live* Ex 19$_{13}$ Nm 21$_{9}$ 2 K 13$_{21}$ Ec 6$_{3}$, pi. *keep alive* Is 7$_{21}$, נקב ni. *be named* Nm 1$_{17}$ 2 C 28$_{15}$ 31$_{19}$, מול ni. *be circumcised* Jr 4$_{4}$, גדד htpo. *cut oneself* 41$_{5}$, דקר pu. *be stabbed* 37$_{10}$, שׂרע pass. *be long-limbed* Lv 21$_{18}$, חרם pass. *be short-limbed* 21$_{18}$, צרע pass. *be leprous* 13$_{44}$, עות htp. *be bent* Ec 12$_{3}$, נבב pass. *be hollow* Jb 11$_{12}$, גלח pu. *be shaven* Jr 41$_{5}$, שׁגע pu. *be mad* 29$_{26}$ Ho 9$_{7}$, htp. *be mad* 1 S 21$_{15}$.

כון ni. *be established* Ps 140$_{12}$, hi. *establish* Jr 10$_{23}$, צמח *grow* intrans. Zc 6$_{12}$, גדל *become great* Gn 26$_{13.13.13}$, hi. *increase* Ps 41$_{10}$, רבה hi. *increase* trans. 1 C 8$_{40}$, פרץ *increase* intrans. Gn 30$_{43}$, htp. *break away* 1 S 25$_{10}$, עשׁר hi. *become rich* Ps 49$_{17}$, צלח hi. *be successful* Gn 39$_{2}$ Si 41$_{1}$, שׂבע *be satisfied* Pr 12$_{14}$ 14$_{14}$, הלל pu. *be praised* 12$_{8}$, htp. *boast* 25$_{14}$, כבד ni. *be honoured* Si 10$_{30(B)}$ 1QSa 1$_{18}$ 4Q416 7$_{10}$, שׂחק *laugh* Pr 29$_{9}$, שׂמח *rejoice* 1 S 11$_{9.15}$, pi. *gladden* Dt 24$_{5}$ Pr 29$_{3}$, קלה ni. *be insignificant* 1 S 18$_{23}$, רושׁ *be poor* 18$_{23}$ 2 S 12$_{4}$.

תמם *be finished* Dt 2$_{14.16}$ Jr 44$_{27}$ CD 20$_{14}$, מות *die* Ex 4$_{19}$ 21$_{12.28}$ Lv 20$_{20}$ Nm 14$_{37}$ etc. 11QT 64$_{9}$, ho. *be put to death* Lv 20$_{2.9.11.12.13}$ etc. 11QT 51$_{16}$ 56$_{10}$ 66$_{5}$, גוע *die* Jos 22$_{20}$, אבד *perish* Is 41$_{11}$, ישׁב *dwell, remain* Gn 34$_{21}$ Ex 16$_{29}$ Jg 19$_{7}$ 20$_{47}$ 1 S 24$_{4}$ etc., *sit* 1 K 8$_{25}$||2 C 6$_{16}$ 1 K 13$_{14}$ 21$_{13}$ 22$_{10}$||2 C 18$_{9}$ 2 K 18$_{27}$||Is 36$_{12}$ etc. 11QT 59$_{14.17}$ 1QS

$6_{4.9}$, hi. *marry* Ezr 10_{17}, חנה *encamp* Nm 1_{52} 2_2 1 S 17_2, זור *be foreign* Lv 22_{12} Nm 17_5 Dt 25_5.

אכל *eat* Gn 3_6 24_{54} 43_{16} Ex 2_{20} Lv 17_{10} etc. CD $10_{22.22}$ 4QOrd[c] 1.$1_{10(\text{Baillet})}$ ([יאכ]אל) 4Q251 5_5 (א[י]ש) 4QToh A 3.1_7 4QD[b]$_{15}$, hi. *give food (to)* 2 C 28_{15}, שׁתה *drink* Gn 24_{54} 2 K 18_{31}||Is 36_{16} Jb 15_{16} CD 10_{22} 4QOrd[c] 1.1_{10} (יש[תה]), לקק pi. *lap* Jg 7_7, שׁקה hi. *give drink to* Ex 2_{19} 2 C 28_{15} 4QToh A 3.1_9 ([ישק[ה]), צום *fast* 1 C 10_{12}, רעה *graze* intrans. Jr 6_3, trans. Gn 46_{32}, רחץ *wash* 43_{24} Lv $15_{5.16.18}$ 11QT 45_{15} CD 10_{11} 4QToh A 1.1_3 4QToh B[b]$_5$ ([רחץ ... איש]), כבס pi. *wash* clothes 1.1_3 2.1_9 4QToh B[b]$_3$ ([ויכבסו ... האנשים]), זכך hi. *purify* 1QS 9_8, לבשׁ *wear (clothes)* Jon 3_5 4QToh B[b]$_3$ ([ל[בשו ... [האנשים]), pass. *be clothed* Ezk $9_{2.3.11}$ $10_{2.6}$ etc., hi. *clothe* 2 C $28_{15.15}$, תלע pu. *be dressed in scarlet* Na 2_4, נעל hi. *give shoes (to)* 2 C 28_{15}, חגר *gird* weapon Dt 1_{41} 1 S $25_{13.13}$, pass. *be girded* with weapons Jg $18_{11.16.17}$, אזר pass. *be girded* 2 K 1_8, אסר *bind* 1 S 6_{10}, *be girded* Ne 4_{12}.

חצב *hew* 2 C 2_1, קצב *chop* 2 K 6_6, כרת *cut* Jg 9_{49}, *make (covenant)* Jr 34_{18}, ni. *be cut off* Ex $30_{33.38}$ Lv $17_{4.9}$ 20_{17} etc. 11QT 27_6 (ו[נ]כרתו) 59_{17}, זמר *prune* 1QDM 3_2 ([א[י]ש), קצר *reap* $3_{3(\text{Milik})}$ ([יקצור איש]), קשׁשׁ po. *gather* wood Nm 15_{32}, חתה *seize* coals Pr 6_{27}, יצת hi. *kindle* Jg 9_{49}, כרה *dig* Ex 21_{33} Pr 16_{27}, חתר *row* boat Jon 1_{13}, טבל *dip* Nm 19_{18}, צוף hi. *cause to float* 2 K 6_6, רקח *compound* oil Ex 30_{33}, דלה *draw* water 2_{19} Pr 20_5, כבס pi. *wash* clothes Lv 15_5, קרע *tear* clothes 2 S 1_{11} Jb 2_{12}, ni. *be torn* Jr 41_5, קבר *bury* 2 S 2_4 1 C 10_{12}, pass. *be buried* 1 K 13_{31}, pi. *bury* Ezk 39_{14}, מדד *measure* 47_3.

נטע *plant* Dt 20_6, בנה *build* 20_5 25_9 Jos 6_{26} Jg 1_{26} Zc 6_{12} etc., יסד pi. *lay foundation* Jos 6_{26}, גדר *repair (wall)* Ezk 22_{30}, חנך *dedicate* Dt $20_{5.5}$, פרר hi. *annul* Nm $30_{9.13.13.14}$=11QT 54_3 ([יפר]נו), נוא hi. *forbid* Nm $30_{9.12}$ CD $16_{10.11}$, קדשׁ hi. *consecrate* Lv $27_{14.16.26}$, pi. *sanctify* CD $16_{14.16}$ ([יקד]ש איש), זבח *sacrifice* 1 S $2_{13.15}$ 6_{15} Jon 1_{16}, קטר hi. *offer (sacrifice)* Jr 33_{18}, נוף hi. *make wave offering* Ex 35_{22}, יצק *pour* Nm 5_{15}, שׁפך *pour* Lv 17_{13}, נתך ni. *be poured* CD 20_3, משׁח *anoint* 2 S 2_4, סוך *anoint* 2 C 28_{15}, מלך hi. *make king* 1 K 11_{24}, נגן pi. *play (instrument)* 1 S 16_{16}, חרשׁ *engrave* 1 K 7_{14}, כתב *write* Dt 24_1 Jos $18_{4.9}$ Jb 31_{35}, ni. *be recorded* CD 19_{33}, עתק hi. *copy* Pr 25_1, רכב *ride* 1 S 30_{17} 2 S 13_{29} Zc 1_8 1QM 6_{13}, צוד *hunt* Lv 17_{13} Mc 7_2.

לכד *capture* Jg 7_{24}, ni. *be captured* Jr 6_{11}, htp. *grip* Jb 41_9, תפשׂ *seize* Dt 22_{28} Is 3_6 4QpHos 16_2, שׁבה *take captive* 1QM 12_{10}, יקשׁ ni. *be trapped* Si 41_2, גזל *steal* Ezk $18_{7.16}$ 4QpsMose[e] 2.1_9 ([א[י]ש]), גנב *steal* Ex 21_{37} Dt 24_7 2 S 19_{42}, pi. *steal* Jr 23_{30}, כלא *withhold* Gn 23_6 1 S 6_{10}, חזק hi. *seize* Gn 19_{16} Dt 22_{25}=11QT 66_4 Jg 19_{25} 2 S 2_{16} Zc 8_{23} etc., *hold (position)* 1QSa 2_4, *repair* Ne $3_{7.22.28}$, htp. *rally onerself* Jg 20_{22}, *retain* Ezk 7_{13}, perh. *stand still* 1QSa 2_7.

אסף *gather* trans. Nm 19_9 1QDM $3_{3(\text{Milik})}$ ([איש ...]אסוף[י]), ni. *be gathered* Jg 20_{11} 1 S 17_2 Is 57_1, pi. *gather* trans. Jg $19_{15.18}$, לקט *gather* trans. Ex $16_{16.18.21}$, htp. intrans. Jg 11_3, קבץ ni. *gather* intrans. 2 C 13_7, htp. 1 S $22_{2.2.2}$, קהל ni. *be assembled* 1 K 8_2||2 C 5_3 4QD[b]$_{17}$ ([אנשי]; EW [יושבי]), לקח *take* Gn 24_{22} 34_{25} $43_{15.15}$ Ex 2_1 etc. Si 35_{18} 11QT 51_{16} CD 11_3 4Q251 2_2 ([יקח איש]), *take (in marriage)* Ex 2_1 Lv $20_{14.17.21}$ Dt $20_{7.7}$ 22_{13}=11QT 65_7 Dt 23_1=11QT 66_{12} etc. 11QT $66_{12.14.15.16}$ CD 5_8 4Q251 $7_{2.2}$ ([יקח ... איש]) 7_7, קבל pi. *accept* 4Q424 2_7, פוק hi. *obtain* 2_7, צבר *amass* Ps 39_7, ירשׁ *inherit* Nm 36_8, נחל *inherit* 35_8, *cause to inherit* 34_{17} Ezk 47_{14}, htp. *take possession* Nm 32_{18}.

צפן hi. *conceal* Si $41_{15(B).15}$, טמן hi. *conceal* 41_{15} (Bmg, M) ([מטמ[ן]), נטר *keep* CD $8_{6(A)}$=$19_{18(B)}$, בקשׁ pi. *seek* Ex 4_{19} Jg 6_{29} 2 K $2_{16.17}$ Jr 11_{21} etc., דרשׁ *seek* Jg 6_{29} Jr 38_4 1QS $6_{6.14}$ 8_{11} CD 6_{21}=6QD 4_3 4QD[b]$_{15}$, חפר *search* Dt 1_{22}, נחשׁ pi. *divine* Gn 44_{15} 1 K 20_{33}, מצא *find* Gn 37_{15} Lv 25_{26} Nm 31_{50} Dt $22_{23.25}$=11QT 66_4 Dt 22_{28} etc. Si 44_{23}, ni. *be found* Dt 17_2=11QT 55_{16} Dt 22_{22} 24_7 2 K $25_{19.19}$||Jr $52_{25.25}$ Jr 41_8 Si 34_8 11QT 59_{14} 1QS 6_{24} 4QpPs[a] 1.2_7, פגשׁ *meet* intrans. Pr 29_{13}.

נתן *give* Gn $43_{24.24}$ Ex $22_{6.9}$ 30_{12} etc. Dt 22_{29}=11QT 66_{10} 4QOrd[a] 1.2_6 CD 13_{14} Arad ost. 40_8 ([נת[ן]), *place* Gn 15_{10} Ex 30_{33} Lv 24_{19} Nm $5_{15.20}$ etc., *treat* Gn 42_{30}, ho. *be given* 2 S $21_{6(\text{Qr})}$, מכר *sell* Gn 37_{28} 47_{20} Ex $21_{7.37}$ Lv 25_{29} etc. CD 12_8, לוה hi. *lend* Ps 112_5 Pr 22_7, נשׁא *lend* Ne 5_7, נשׁה hi. *lend* CD 10_{17}, חבל *take in pledge* Ezk 18_{16}, שׁלם pi. *pay* Ex 21_{37} $22_{4.13}$, htp. *be paid* 11QPs[a] 22_{10} (|| אָדָם *human being*), שׁקל *weigh* for payment Si 8_2, מהר *pay bride-price* Ex 22_{15}, גמל *repay* Pr 11_{17}.

יעד ni. *be appointed* 1QSa 2$_{22}$ ([יו]עדו), ברר pass. *be selected* CD 10$_{4}$, משל *rule* Gn 3$_{16}$ Jg 9$_{2}$ Is 28$_{14}$ 2 C 7$_{18}$ Si 41$_{2(Bmg)}$ CD 13$_{12}$, בקר pi. *oversee* 1QS 6$_{11.19}$, נבא ni. *prophesy* Zc 13$_{3}$, htp. *prophesy* Nm 11$_{25.26}$ 1 K 22$_{8}$||2 C 18$_{7}$ Jr 29$_{26}$, שפט *judge* Is 5$_{3}$ Ezk 23$_{45}$ 4Q424 2$_{1}$, ni. *contend* Pr 29$_{9}$, *be judged* CD 12$_{2(mg)}$ 20$_{24(mg).32}$, יסר pi. *punish* Dt 8$_{5}$ 4QDibHam 1.3$_{6}$ 6$_{15}$, יכח hi. *reprove* Ezk 3$_{26}$ Ho 4$_{4}$ CD 7$_{2}$ 20$_{4}$, נקם *take vengeance* 8$_{6(A)}$=19$_{18(B)}$, נחם ni. *repent* Jr 8$_{6}$, ענש ni. *be fined* 1QS 7$_{13.18}$, צדק *be justified* Jb 11$_{2}$ 1QH 13$_{20}$ 16$_{11}$, hi. *justify* CD 20$_{18}$ (ל[הצדי]ק), נקה ni. *be exonerated* Nm 5$_{31}$, טהר *be clean* Lv 22$_{4}$ 11QT 45$_{15}$ 50$_{5}$, pi. *clean* CD 10$_{11}$, htp. *be cleansed* Lv 14$_{11}$, טמא *be unclean* Lv 15$_{5.16.18.24}$ 22$_{5}$ etc., pi. *defile* Lv 20$_{3}$ Ezk 22$_{11}$ 33$_{26}$ 11QT 45$_{12}$, htp. *defile oneself* Ezk 20$_{7}$, חלל pi. *profane* Dt 20$_{6.6}$ Ezk 20$_{39}$ CD 11$_{15}$, hi. *breach (vow)* Nm 30$_{3}$=11QT 53$_{14}$, *begin* Jg 10$_{18}$ 1QS 9$_{10}$ 1QM 14$_{18}$ + Sup 4QM^{a} fr. 1$_{13(Baillet)}$ ([יחלו]).

חטא *sin* Nm 16$_{22}$ 1 S 2$_{25.25}$ 1 K 8$_{31}$||2 C 6$_{22}$ Dt 19$_{15}$=11QT 61$_{6}$, htp. *cleanse oneself* Nm 19$_{20}$, פשע *sin* Is 66$_{24}$, רעע hi. *do evil* Jr 38$_{9}$, רשע htp. *be wicked* 1QM 14$_{10}$ + Sup, מעל *transgress* CD 7$_{1}$ 9$_{17}$, אשם *be guilty* 1$_{9}$, נאף *commit adultery* Lv 20$_{10}$.

ארר *curse* 4QD$^{b}_{17}$ ([אנשי]; EW [יושבי]), pass. *be cursed* Dt 27$_{15}$ Jos 6$_{26}$ 1 S 14$_{24.28}$ Jr 11$_{3}$ etc. 4QTestim 1$_{23(mg)}$ 4QPsJos^{b} 22.2$_{9}$ ([אר]ור [איש]), קנא pi. *be jealous* Nm 5$_{30}$ Si 45$_{18}$ 1QS 9$_{23}$ 4Q424 2$_{8}$, קצף *be angry* 2 K 13$_{19}$, זיד *be insolent* Ex 21$_{14}$ Jr 43$_{2}$, גרה pi. *antagonize* Pr 15$_{18}$ 29$_{22}$, פוח hi. *inflame* 29$_{8}$, דמה pi. *plot* 2 S 21$_{5}$, פתה *be simple* 1QSa 1$_{19}$, pi. *entice* Ex 22$_{15}$=11QT 66$_{8}$ Pr 16$_{29}$, pu. *be enticed* 1QH fr. 4$_{8(AHL)}$, סות hi. *entice* Jr 38$_{22}$, רמה pi. *deceive* Pr 26$_{19}$, נשא hi. *deceive* Ob$_{7}$, תלל hi. *deceive* Jr 9$_{4}$, כזב pi. *lie* Mc 2$_{11}$, כחש *lie* 4Q251 1$_{7}$, בגד *betray* Ml 2$_{10}$ CD 19$_{33}$.

עשה *do* Gn 43$_{17}$ Ex 36$_{1.6}$ Lv 18$_{27}$ 20$_{12}$ etc. 11QT 27$_{6}$ Dt 17$_{2.5}$=11QT 55$_{16.21}$ 11QT 56$_{8}$ 64$_{7}$ CD 3$_{6.12}$ 8$_{7(A)}$=19$_{20(B)}$ 10$_{14}$ 1QpHab 7$_{10}$, *make* Ex 30$_{38}$ Dt 27$_{15}$ Jg 17$_{5}$ 2 K 17$_{30.30.30}$ etc. 4QOrd^{a} 1.2$_{3(Allegro)}$ ([ו]עשה) CD 13$_{15}$, *perform* sacrifice Nm 9$_{10}$ Jr 33$_{18}$, כול pilp. *conduct* affairs Ps 112$_{5}$, יטב hi. *do well* 1 S 16$_{17}$, יסף *add, do again* Lv 22$_{14}$ Nm 11$_{25}$, hi. Lv 27$_{31}$ Jg 20$_{22}$, יכל *be able* Gn 13$_{16}$ Nm 9$_{6}$ Dt 22$_{29}$=11QT 66$_{10}$ 2 K 3$_{26}$ Jon 1$_{13}$ etc. 4QShir^{b} 30$_{6}$, *prevail* Jr 38$_{22}$ Ob$_{7}$, אות ni. *agree* Gn 34$_{22}$ CD 20$_{7}$ 4QD$^{b}_{15}$, חרם hi. *proscribe* Lv 27$_{28}$, בער hi. *allow to graze* Ex 22$_{4}$.

כלה pi. *finish* Ru 3$_{3.18}$ 1QM 8$_{1}$, *destroy* 2 S 21$_{5}$, חצה *divide* Ps 55$_{24}$ Jg 7$_{16}$, עור ni. *be roused* Zc 4$_{1}$ Jb 14$_{12}$, קיץ hi. *wake up* intrans. 14$_{12}$, מהר pi. *do quickly* Jos 8$_{14}$ 1 S 4$_{14}$ 1 K 20$_{33}$, אוץ *do quickly* Pr 29$_{20}$, פחז *be reckless* Jg 9$_{4}$, שכם hi. *rise early* Jos 8$_{14}$ Jg 6$_{28}$ 1 S 29$_{11}$, עצר ni. *be detained* 21$_{8}$, לון *pass the night* Gn 24$_{54}$ Jg 19$_{7}$ 2 S 19$_{8}$ Ne 4$_{16}$, שבת hi. *pass Sabbath* CD 11$_{14}$, נדב htp. *volunteer* Ne 11$_{2}$ 1QS 5$_{1}$ 1Q31 1$_{1}$ ([המתנד]בי[ם]), מלא pi. *do wholeheartedly* Nm 32$_{11}$, ni. *be filled*, i.e. armed 2 S 23$_{7}$, pi. *fill* Jg 17$_{5}$, עזר *help* Is 41$_{6}$ 2 C 20$_{23}$ 1QpHab 5$_{10}$, עדר *help* 1 C 12$_{39}$, עבד *serve* Ex 10$_{7}$ Ezk 20$_{39}$ 4QCat^{a} 7$_{16}$, *enslave* Jr 34$_{9}$, *work* land Zc 13$_{5}$, שרת pi. *minister* 1QM 2$_{3}$.

<NOM CL> + pr.n.m., Gn 25$_{27}$ 27$_{11}$ Ex 15$_{3}$ Jg 3$_{17}$ etc., 4QMMT B$_{28}$. + pronoun אָנֹכִי *I* Gn 27$_{11}$ Ex 4$_{10}$ 1 S 18$_{23}$ Is 6$_{5}$ Ho 2$_{4}$ etc., אֲנִי *I* 2 K 1$_{10.12}$ 1QH fr. 1$_{4}$, אֲנַחְנוּ *we* Gn 13$_{8}$ Jr 48$_{14}$, אַתָּה *you* Jg 13$_{11}$ 1 S 26$_{15}$ 2 S 12$_{7}$ 16$_{8}$ 18$_{20}$ etc., הוּא *he* Lv 13$_{44}$ Dt 24$_{12}$ 1 S 17$_{33}$ 2 S 19$_{33}$ 1 K 13$_{26}$ etc. CD 20$_{3}$, הֵם *they* 1 K 9$_{22}$ CD 1$_{9}$ 4QpIsa^{b} 1.2$_{6}$ 4QpNah 3.3$_{11}$, הֵמָּה *they* 1 S 9$_{22}$ Zc 3$_{8}$ 2 C 8$_{9}$ 1QSa 1$_{3}$, זֶה *this* 2 S 18$_{27}$ Is 14$_{16}$, אֵלֶּה *these* Ezk 11$_{2}$ 1 C 4$_{12}$ 9$_{9}$ Si 44$_{10}$ 1QSa 1$_{27}$ (הנשים) 2$_{2}$ 4QM^{a} fr. 1$_{12}$, מִי *who?* Nm 22$_{9}$ Dt 20$_{5.6.7.8}$=11QT 62$_{3}$ etc.

+ noun אִישׁ *man* 2 S 24$_{9}$, רֹאשׁ *chief* Nm 1$_{4}$ Jos 22$_{14}$, עָנָו *humble person* Nm 12$_{3}$, עַם *people* 13$_{32}$, אָב *father* 2 S 17$_{8}$ 1 K 7$_{14}$||2 C 2$_{13}$, בֵּן *son* Jg 19$_{16}$ 2 S 12$_{5}$ Ne 11$_{6}$, אָח *brother* Dt 17$_{15}$=11QT 56$_{15}$, גִּבּוֹר *warrior* Jos 10$_{2}$ 1 K 11$_{28}$, נָבִיא *prophet* 1 K 18$_{22}$ Zp 3$_{4}$, בַּעַל *possessor* Si 9$_{16}$, עֵדוּת *testimony* Ps 119$_{24}$, תּוֹעֵבָה *abomination* Pr 29$_{27}$, נֶטַע *planting* Is 5$_{7}$, עֶצֶב *pot* Jr 22$_{28}$, עִיר *city* Pr 25$_{28}$, נָשִׂיא *cloud* 25$_{14}$, מֵפִיץ *scatterer* 25$_{18}$, מִסְפָּר *number* 1 C 7$_{40}$, מְעַט *a few* Ec 9$_{14}$.

הָאֲנָשִׁים אֲשֶׁר־פֶּתַח הַבַּיִת *the people who were (at) the entrance of the house* Gn 19$_{11}$, sim. Ezk 8$_{16}$, הַקֶּבֶר אִישׁ־הָאֱלֹהִים *the grave is (that of) the man of God* 2 K 23$_{17}$, לֹא אִישׁ אֵל ... וּבֶן־אָדָם *God is not a man ... or a human being* Nm 23$_{19}$, אֵל אָנֹכִי וְלֹא־אִישׁ *I am God and not a man* Ho 11$_{9}$, הֲלוֹא־אִישׁ אַתָּה *are you not a man?* 1 S 26$_{15}$, לֹא־אִישׁ כָּמֹנִי *he is not a man like me* Jb 9$_{32}$, אָנֹכִי תוֹלַעַת וְלֹא־אִישׁ *I am a worm and not a man* Ps 22$_{7}$.

+ adj. גָּדוֹל *great* Ex 11$_{3}$ 1 S 25$_{2}$ Est 9$_{4}$ (הוֹלֵךְ וְגָדוֹל *continually increasing*), רַב *great* Pr 28$_{20}$, טוֹב *good* 1 S 9$_{2}$ 25$_{15}$ Ps 112$_{5}$, חָכָם *wise* Pr 28$_{11}$, זָקֵן *old* 1 S 4$_{18}$ 17$_{12}$ 2 K 4$_{14}$, כָּבֵד *heavy* 1 S 4$_{18}$, קָשֶׁה *hard* 25$_{3}$ 2 S 3$_{29}$, רַע *wicked* Gn 13$_{13}$ 1 S 25$_{3}$, חַטָּא *sinful* Gn 13$_{13}$, טָהוֹר *clean* Nm 9$_{13}$ 4QToh B^{b}2 ([איש]), שָׁלֵם *peaceful* Gn 34$_{21}$, יָקָר *precious* Pr 17$_{27(Qr)}$, קָרוֹב *near* Ru 2$_{20}$.

+ prep. בְּ of place Gn 19$_{31}$ Dt 31$_{12}$ Jg 18$_{22}$ 20$_{13}$ 1 S 9$_{6}$ etc. Si 41$_{4(B)}$ (Bmg אין *there are no* reproofs) 1QS 6$_{12}$ 8$_{1}$ 4QpIsa^{b} 1.2$_{6.10}$, *against* Ex 32$_{29}$, בְּיַד *under the control of* Nm 31$_{49}$, אֵת *with* Gn 24$_{32}$ Jg 7$_{19}$ 8$_{4}$ 1 S 22$_{6}$ 26$_{2}$ etc., עִם *with* Gn 24$_{54}$ 31$_{50}$ 32$_{7}$ 33$_{1}$ 1 S 27$_{2}$ etc., מִן of direction Jg 19$_{16}$, מִמַּעַל *above* Dn 12$_{6.7}$, עַל *in charge of* Gn 43$_{19}$, *at* table Ne 5$_{17}$, כְּ *as* Gn 44$_{15}$ Si 27$_{5}$, אַחֲרֵי *after* Jg 4$_{14}$ Ne 4$_{17}$, לִפְנֵי *in front of* Ezk 9$_{6}$, לְפִי judged *according to* Pr 27$_{21}$, לְיַד *alongside* 1QM 8$_{4}$, לְעוּמָּה *opposite* 4QM^{a} fr. 1$_{12}$ ([אנש]ין).

+ adverb שָׁם *there* Gn 39$_{11}$ 1 S 9$_{10}$ 21$_{8}$ 2 S 11$_{16}$, כֵּן *thus* Pr 27$_{8}$ Si 6$_{1}$ 36$_{31}$, אַיֵּה *where?* Gn 19$_{5}$, אֵיפֹה *where?* Jg 8$_{18}$.

+ יֵשׁ *there is* Gn 47$_{6}$ Dt 29$_{17}$ Jg 4$_{20}$ 2 K 2$_{16}$ Si 10$_{30(B)}$, עוֹד *there still is* 1 K 22$_{8}$||2 C 18$_{7}$, אַיִן *there is not* Ex 2$_{12}$ Jg 13$_{9}$ 21$_{9}$ 1 S 21$_{2}$ 2 S 21$_{4}$ etc. Si 36$_{28}$, אֶפֶס *there is not* 2 S 9$_{3}$.

<OBJ> איב *be an enemy to* Mc 7$_{6}$, שׂנא *hate* 1 K 22$_{8}$||2 C 18$_{7}$ 1QS 1$_{10}$, תעב pi. *despise* Ps 5$_{7}$, געל *loathe* Ezk 16$_{45.45}$ (both || בֵּן pl. *children*), קלל pi. *curse* 1QS 2$_{4}$, ריב *struggle (with)* Dt 33$_{8}$, פגע *attack* Am 5$_{19}$, דקר *stab* Nm 25$_{8}$, יקע hi. *impale* 2 S 21$_{6}$, נגח *gore* Ex 21$_{28}$ 4Q251 4$_{3}$ ([איש ...]יגח), שׂסע pi. *tear (at)* 1 S 24$_{8}$, נשׁך *bite* Nm 21$_{9}$ Am 5$_{19}$, מות hi. *kill* Ex 21$_{29}$ Lv 20$_{4}$ Jg 20$_{13}$ 1 S 11$_{12}$ 2 S 21$_{4}$ etc., הרג *kill* Gn 4$_{23}$ (|| יֶלֶד *youth*) 49$_{6}$ (|| שׁוֹר *ox*) Nm 25$_{5}$ Jg 8$_{17.18}$ etc., אבד pi. *destroy* Est 9$_{6.12}$, שׁחט *slaughter* 2 K 10$_{7}$, שׁחת hi. *destroy* Jg 20$_{21.25.35}$, שׁמד hi. *destroy* Dt 4$_{3}$, כרת hi. *cut off*, i.e. kill Lv 20$_{3.5}$ 1 S 2$_{33}$ 20$_{15}$ Jr 44$_{7}$ 1QH 4$_{20}$, סקל *stone* Dt 17$_{5}$=11QT 55$_{21}$ Dt 22$_{24}$=11QT 66$_{3}$.

אכל *consume* Nm 16$_{35}$ 26$_{10}$, נכה hi. *strike* Gn 19$_{11}$ Ex 21$_{12}$ Dt 25$_{11}$ Jos 7$_{5}$ 8$_{21}$ etc., שׁבר *break* 1 K 13$_{26}$, נפץ pi. *shatter* Jr 13$_{14}$ 51$_{22}$, נער pi. *shake out* Ne 5$_{13}$, שׁלך hi. *throw* 2 K 13$_{21}$, רגם *stone* Lv 20$_{27}$ Nm 15$_{35}$, תלה *hang* Dt 21$_{22}$=11QT 64$_{9}$ 11QT 64$_{7}$ 4QpNah 3.1$_{7}$, שׂרף *burn* Lv 20$_{14}$, צוד *hunt* Ps 140$_{12}$, רדף *pursue* Jos 7$_{5}$ Ps 109$_{16}$, כשׁל hi. *trip* 4QWiles 1$_{14}$, בקשׁ pi. *seek* Jg 4$_{22}$ 1 S 13$_{14}$ 16$_{16}$ 24$_{3}$ 2 S 17$_{3}$ etc., חכה pi. *await* Ho 6$_{9}$.

לכד *capture* 2 S 8$_{4}$||1 C 18$_{4}$ Jr 5$_{26}$, תפשׂ *capture* 1 S 23$_{26}$, שׁמר *keep* 1 K 20$_{39}$, לקח *take* Gn 7$_{2.2}$ 30$_{15}$ (|| דּוּדַי *mandrake*) 47$_{2}$ Nm 1$_{17}$ 11$_{16}$ Dt 1$_{23.23}$ etc. Dt 22$_{18}$ =11QT 65$_{14}$ Lachish ost. 3$_{18}$, גנב *steal* Ex 21$_{16}$, מכר *sell* 21$_{16}$, יהב *provide* Dt 1$_{13}$ Jos 18$_{4}$, נתן *give* Jg 20$_{13}$ 1 S 11$_{12}$ 14$_{12}$ 17$_{10}$ 1 K 13$_{26}$, *place* Ex 18$_{25}$ Dt 1$_{15}$ 17$_{15}$=11QT 56$_{15}$ Jr 29$_{26}$, *allow* Jg 3$_{28}$ 1 S 24$_{8}$, *cause to be* Jr 34$_{18}$ Ezk 33$_{2}$, סגר hi. *hand over* 1 S 23$_{12}$, pi. *hand over* 2 S 18$_{28}$, סור hi. *remove* 1 K 20$_{24}$ Is 3$_{2}$, ירשׁ hi. *dispossess* Jg 2$_{21}$, *cause to inherit* 4Q416 1$_{3}$, חסר pi. *deprive* Si 14$_{2}$, עזב *abandon* Ex 2$_{20}$, קבר *bury* 2 K 13$_{21}$.

בוא *come (upon)* Pr 28$_{22}$, hi. *bring* Gn 43$_{16.17.24}$ 1 S 21$_{15}$ 1 K 20$_{39}$ etc. Si 11$_{29}$ CD 13$_{13}$, פגשׁ *meet* 1 S 25$_{20}$, קרא *meet* Jg 19$_{3}$ 2 K 8$_{8}$ 1 C 19$_{5}$, מצא *find* Gn 41$_{38}$ Nm 15$_{32}$ Jos 2$_{23}$ 1 S 10$_{2}$ 30$_{11}$ 1 K 13$_{14}$ etc., hi. *hand over* Zc 11$_{6}$ Jb 34$_{11}$, בחר *choose* Ex 17$_{9}$ 18$_{25}$ Nm 16$_{7}$ 17$_{20}$ Jos 8$_{3}$ etc. 1QM 2$_{7}$ 4QM^{g} 4$_{7}$ ([יבחרו ... אנשי]), ברר *choose* 11QT 57$_{6}$, שׁלח *send* Nm 13$_{2.2.3.16}$ 14$_{36}$ etc. 11QT 58$_{10}$ 4Q424 2$_{3.3}$ ([איש]) 2$_{6}$, Arad ost. 24$_{19}$, pi. *send away* Gn 24$_{59}$ Ex 10$_{7}$ Jos 24$_{28}$ Jg 1$_{25}$ 7$_{8}$ etc. 1QS 7$_{16.17}$.

אסף *gather* Gn 29$_{22}$ Nm 11$_{16.24}$ 1 S 14$_{52}$ 2 K 5$_{7}$, קבץ *gather* Jg 12$_{4}$ 1 K 11$_{24}$ 22$_{6}$||2 C 18$_{5}$, עבר hi. *take across* 2 S 19$_{42}$, עלה hi. *take up* 2 S 2$_{3}$ 1QS 5$_{24}$, הדף *push* Si 47$_{5}$, בדל hi. *separate* Ezk 39$_{14}$ 1QS 6$_{24}$ 7$_{15}$, יצא hi. *take out* Gn 45$_{1}$ Dt 17$_{5}$=11QT 55$_{21}$ Dt 22$_{24}$=11QT 66$_{3(Yadin)}$ ([והוציאו]) Jos 2$_{3}$ Jg 19$_{22}$ etc. Si 44$_{23}$ (א[י]צ[ויו]), שׁוב hi. *take back* 1 S 29$_{4}$ Jr 12$_{15.15}$, הלך hi. *lead* 2 K 24$_{16}$, נשׂג hi. *overtake* Gn 44$_{4}$ Jos 2$_{5}$, יצג hi. *present* Gn 47$_{2}$, ישׁב hi. *seat* 1 K 21$_{10}$, שׂים *place* Gn 47$_{6}$ Dt 1$_{13}$ Jos 8$_{12}$ 2 K 10$_{24}$, hi. *cause to be* Ezk 14$_{8}$, עמד hi. *position* Lv 14$_{11}$ Nm 11$_{24}$, חבא hi. *conceal* 1 K 18$_{13}$, צפן *conceal* Jos 2$_{4}$, סתר pi. *conceal* 1QH 6$_{11(Licht)}$ ([לסתר את]).

נסה pi. *test* Dt 33$_{8}$, שׁפט *judge* 25$_{1}$ Ezk 18$_{30}$ 33$_{20}$ Si 16$_{12}$ 1QS 8$_{25}$, רשׁע hi. *condemn* Pr 12$_{2}$, צדק hi. *vindicate* 2 S 15$_{4}$, פתה pi. *entice* Jg 14$_{15}$, אלה hi. *cause to swear* 1 K 8$_{31}$||2 C 6$_{22}$, יסר pi. *punish* Dt 22$_{18}$=11QT 65$_{14}$ Ps 39$_{12}$, ענשׁ *fine* Dt 22$_{18}$=11QT 65$_{14}$, יכח hi. *reprove* 1QS 5$_{25}$, כלם hi. *humiliate* Si 8$_{5}$, לאה hi. *weary* Is 7$_{13}$, עשׁק *oppress* Mc 2$_{2}$ (|| גֶּבֶר *man*).

יתר hi. *leave over* Ezk 12_{16}, שׁאר hi. *leave over* 1 S 14_{36} 2 K 10_{14}, נצל hi. *save* Dt 25_{11}, ישׁע hi. *save* 1QH $13_{20(Licht)}$ ([תושיענו]), חיה pi. *let live* 1 S $27_{9.11}$, חלם hi. *strengthen* Si $15_{20(A)}$, נחם pi. *console* Is 66_{13} 4QBark$^{c}_{6}$, אהב *love* 1QS 1_9, ברך pi. *bless* Gn 49_{28} 2 K 4_{29} 1QS 2_2, שׂמח pi. *gladden* Jg 9_{13} 2 C 20_{27}, לבשׁ hi. *clothe* Est 6_9, שׁקה hi. *give water to* 1 S 30_{11}, לוה hi. *lend to* Si 8_{12}.

ראה *see* Gn 41_{33} Ex 2_{11} Jg 1_{24} $19_{3.17}$ etc. 4QWiles 1_{14} ([לראו]ת]), hi. *show* Jos 5_6 Jg 4_{22} 2 K 6_6, חזה *see* Pr 22_{29} 29_{20}, *provide* Ex $18_{21.21}$, שׁמע *hear* Dn 12_7, קרא *call* Is 46_{11}, *name* Ho 2_{18} (+ בַּעַל *husband/Baal*), קהל hi. *assemble* Dt 31_{12}, זעק hi. *summon* 2 S 20_4, שׁאל *ask* Gn 38_{21} Jg 13_6, ענה *answer* 2 K 4_{29} $7_{2.19}$, ירה hi. *teach* Ps 25_{12}.

ידע *know* 2 S 17_8 2 K 9_{11} (|| שִׂיחַ *talk*) 4Q416 10.2_6, sexually Gn $19_{5.8}$ Nm 31_{17} Jg 11_{39} 19_{22} etc., hi. *teach* 8_{16}, זכר *remember* Ec 9_{15}, אמן hi. *trust* 4Q424 1_7 ([תא]מין]) 1_8 ([תאמ]ין]), כסס *compute* Ex 12_4, כתב *register* Jr 22_{30}, ספר *count* 2 C $2_{1.16.16}$, פקד *number* 1 S 13_{15}, *appoint* Nm 4_{49} 27_{16}, hi. *appoint* Jos 10_{18}, *entrust* Jr 40_7, משׁל hi. *put in charge* 4Q424 1_{10}, חלץ *equip* 1QM 2_8, חשׁב *consider* 4Q416 9.1_7.

קנה *acquire* Gn 4_1, נצח pi. *direct* 1QM 8_1, מלך hi. *make king* 2 K 10_5, משׁח *anoint* 1 S 9_{16}, כון hi. *appoint* Jos 4_4, מלא pi. *appoint* 4Q181 $1_{5(Allegro)}$ ([מ]לאו]), כבד pi. *honour* Jg 9_9 Si 10_{23} 1QH 10_{28}, פאר pi. *glorify* 13_{20}, הלל pi. *praise* Si $44_{1.3.6}$, שׁלט hi. *empower* Ec 6_2, שׁרת pi. *minister to* 2 K 6_{15}, עבד *serve* Jg 9_{28} Ml 3_{17}, עשׁר hi. *enrich* 1 S 17_{25}, צוה pi. *appoint* Gn 12_{20} 1 S 13_{14}, *command* Jg 21_{10} Ezk 10_6, שׂכר *hire* Jg 9_4 2 S 10_6.

<CSTR> אִישׁ הָאֲדָמָה *man of,* i.e. working, *the land* Gn 9_{20}, שָׂדֶה *of,* i.e. working in, *a field* Gn 25_{27}, מַתָּן *of a gift,* i.e. generous Pr 19_6 Si $3_{17(C)}$, זְרוֹעַ *of an arm,* i.e. strong Jb 22_8, מָגֵן *of,* i.e. carrying, *a shield* Pr 6_{11}=24_{34}, רִיב *of strife* Jg 12_2 Jr 15_{10} Jb 31_{35} (רִיבִי) 1QH 2_{14}, מָדוֹן *of contention* 2 S $21_{20(Qr)}$ Jr 15_{10} Pr $26_{21(Kt)}$ (מדונים), מִלְחָמָה *of war* Ex 15_3 Jos 17_1 Jg 20_{17} 1 S 16_{18} 17_{33} 2 S 8_{10}||1 C 18_{10} (מִלְחֲמוֹת) 2 S 17_8 Is 3_2 42_{13} (מִלְחָמוֹת) Ezk 39_{20} 1 C 28_3 (מִלְחָמוֹת) 11QT 57_6, חַיִל *of valour* Jg 3_{29} (חָיִל) 1 S 31_{12}||1 C 10_{12} 2 S $23_{20(Qr)}$||1 C 11_{22} 2 S 24_9 1 C 26_8 (all three אִישׁ־) 4Q424 2_8, *of ability* 1 K 1_{42}.

בְּשֹׂרָה *of,* i.e. bearing, *news* 2 S 18_{20}, כבוד *of glory* 1QM 12_{10}, אֱמֶת *of truth* Ne 7_2, חֶסֶד *of mercy* Pr 11_{17}, תְּבוּנָה *of understanding* 10_{23} 11_{12} (תְּבוּנוֹת) 15_{21} 17_{27} 20_5, שֵׂכֶל *of intelligence* Ezr 8_{18} 4Q424 2_7, שָׁלוֹם *of peace* Ps 37_{37} 41_{10} (שְׁלוֹמִי), מְנוּחָה *of rest* 1 C 22_9, תֹּאַר *of (fair) form* 1 S 16_{18}, מִדָּה *of (large) dimension* 1 C 11_{23} 20_6, מַרְאֶה *of (striking) appearance* 2 S $23_{21(Qr)}$, מָצוֹק *of distress* 1 S 22_2, מַחְסוֹר *of poverty* Pr 21_{17}, חֵמָה *of anger* 15_{18} 22_{24} (חֵמוֹת).

דַּעַת *of,* i.e. posssessing, *knowledge* Pr 24_5 (אִישׁ־), בַּעַר *of brutishness* Ps 92_7 (אִישׁ־), אַף *of anger* Pr 29_{22} (אִישׁ־), חָמָס *of violence* Ps 18_{49} (||2 S 22_{49} חֲמָסִים) $140_{2.5}$ (both חֲמָסִים) 140_{12} (אִישׁ־) Pr 3_{31} etc. Si $10_{23(B)}$ $35_{17(Bmg, F).18(Bmg, F)}$, תלונה *murmuring* 4Q424 1_7, לָשׁוֹן *of a (slanderous) tongue* Ps 140_{12} Si 8_3 9_{18}, רָכִיל *of slander* 11QT 64_7, כָּזָב *of a lie* Pr 19_{22} CD 20_{15} 1QpHab 2_1 5_{11} 4QpPs^{a} 1.1_{18} (all four הכזב), מִרְמָה *of deceit* Ps 5_7 (אִישׁ־דָּמִים וּמִרְמָה) 43_1 (אִישׁ־), תהו *of emptiness* 1QH $7_{27(Licht)}$ ([תהו]) 7_{32}, בְּלִיַּעַל *of worthlessness* 1 S 25_{25} (הַבְּלִיַּעַל) 30_{22} (כָּל־אִישׁ־רָע וּבְלִיַּעַל) 2 S 16_7 (הַבְּלִיַּעַל) 20_1 Pr 16_{27} Si 11_{32} 4QPsJos^{b} 22.2_9 ([איש בליעל]).

רָע *of evil* Pr 29_6, רע עין *of evil eye,* i.e. covetous 4Q424 1_{10}, אָוֶן *of evil* Is 55_7 Pr 6_{12}, פֶּשַׁע *of sin* 1QH fr. 1_4, עָוֶל *of injustice* Pr 29_{27} 4Q416 9.1_7, עַוְלָה *of injustice* Ps 43_1 (אִישׁ־מִרְמָה וְעַוְלָה), מָוֶת *of,* i.e. destined for, *death* 1 K 2_{26}, הקודש *of holiness* 1QS 5_{18}, הָרוּחַ *of the spirit,* i.e. prophet Ho 9_7, הלצון *of mockery* CD 1_{14}, הַבֵּנַיִם *of the spaces between (armies),* i.e. champion 1 S 17_4 (אִישׁ־) 17_{23}.

עֲצָתִי *of my counsel* Is $46_{11(Qr)}$, חֶרְמִי *of my ban,* i.e. whom I condemned 1 K 20_{42} (אִישׁ־), חֲסִידֶךָ *of,* i.e. loyal to, *your devotee,* i.e. Levi Dt 33_8.

אִישׁ הָאִשָּׁה *husband of the woman* Jg 20_4, נָעֳמִי *of Naomi* Ru 1_3, חֵיקָהּ *of her bosom* Dt 28_{56} (|| בֵּן *son*, בַּת *daughter*).

אִישׁ יִשְׂרָאֵל *Israelite(s)* Nm $25_{8.14}$ Dt 27_{14} 29_9 Jos 9_6 etc. 1QS 2_{22} 5QRègle 1_{13}, אִישׁ־יִשְׂרָאֵל Nm 25_8 Jos 9_7 Jg 7_{23} 8_{22} 20_{36} etc., אִישׁ יְהוּדָה *Judahite(s)* Jg 15_{10} 1 S 11_8 (+ בְּנֵי־יִשְׂרָאֵל *Israelites*) 15_4 2 S $19_{17.42}$ etc., אִישׁ־יְהוּדָה 19_{15} 20_4 Jr 18_{11}, אִישׁ אֶפְרַיִם *Ephraimite(s)* Jg 7_{24} 8_1 12_1, אִישׁ בִּנְיָמִן *Benjaminite(s)* Jg 20_{41} 1 S 4_{12} (אִישׁ־), אִישׁ אֱלֹהִים *man of God* 2_{27} 9_6 (both אִישׁ־) 1 K 13_1 17_{24} 2 K 1_{10} 4_9, אִישׁ הָאֱלֹהִים Dt 33_1 Jg $13_{6.8}$ 1 S $9_{7.8}$ etc.

אִישׁ־הָאֱלֹהִים Jos 14_{6} 1 K 12_{22}‖2 C 11_{2} 1 K $13_{4.6.8}$ 4QapPs^{b} 24_{4} (האל[הי]ם) etc.

אִישׁ דְּבָרִים *man of words*, i.e. good speaker Ex 4_{10}, שְׂפָתַיִם *of lips*, i.e. garrulous Jb 11_{2}, תְּרוּמוֹת *of contributions*, i.e. one who exacts Pr 29_{4}, אונים *of riches* Si $41_{2(B)}$, מְזִמּוֹת *of intrigues* Pr 12_{2} 14_{17}, תַּהְפֻּכוֹת *of perversity* 16_{28}, אֱמוּנִים *of faithfulness* 20_{6}, חֲמֻדוֹת *of preciousness* Dn $10_{11.19}$ (both ־אִישׁ), דָּמִים *of blood(s)*, i.e. murderer 2 S 16_{7} (הַדָּמִים) 16_{8} Ps 5_{7} (־אִישׁ), תְּכָכִים *of oppressions*, i.e. oppressor Pr 29_{13}, מַכְאֹבוֹת *of pains* Is 53_{3}, תּוֹכָחוֹת *of*, i.e. subject to, *reproofs* Pr 29_{1} (or em. שׂוֹנֵא *one who hates*) Si $41_{4(B)}$ (Bmg אין *there are no*), ההודות *of the*, i.e. worthy of, *praises* 4QRitMar $24_{2(mg)}$, רֵעִים *of*, i.e. with, *friends* Pr 18_{24} (but prob. אִישׁ II *there are*).

אַנְשֵׁי הָעִיר *men of the city* Gn 19_{4} 24_{13} 34_{20} (עִירָם) Dt 21_{21}=11QT 64_{5} (עִירוֹ) Dt 22_{21} (עִירָהּ) Jos 8_{14} (־עִיר) Jg $6_{27.28.30}$ 8_{17} 14_{18} 19_{22} 1 S 5_{9} 2 S 11_{17} 1 K 21_{11} (עִירוֹ) 2 K 2_{19} 23_{17}, הכרך *of the fortress* MurEpBarCa$_{2(AHL)}$ (Milik הברך *of Habbaruch*), המחנה *of the camp* 4QD^{b}$_{17}$ ([אנש]; EW [יושבי]), הַמָּקוֹם *of the place* Gn $26_{7.7}$ 29_{22} 38_{21} (מְקֹמָהּ) 38_{22} Jg 19_{16} Ezr 1_{4} (מְקֹמוֹ), הָאָרֶץ *of the land* Lv 18_{27} (־אַנְשֵׁ), הַבַּיִת *of the house(hold)* Gn 17_{23} (בֵּית) 17_{27} (בֵּיתוֹ) $39_{11.14}$ (בֵּיתָהּ) Mc 7_{6} (בֵּיתוֹ) 2QJub $23_{7(Baillet)}$ ([אנש]י ביתו]) 3QJub 23_{6} ([אנש]י) 1QH $5_{24(Licht)}$ ([בי]ת), היחד *of the assembly* 1QS $5_{1.2.15}$ 6_{21} $7_{20.24}$ ([יח]ד) $8_{11.16}$ $9_{5.7.10.19}$ CD 20_{32} (היחיד perh. = *of the unique one*) 4QPBless 1.1_{5} 4QCat^{a} $5_{1(Allegro)}$ ([הי]חד) 1Q31 1_{1}, השחת *of*, i.e destined for, *the pit* 1QS $9_{16.22}$ (שחת) $10_{19(mg)}$ (אנש) 4QpGen^{a} 5_{5}.

הַמִּלְחָמָה *of (the) war* Nm $31_{28.49}$ Dt $2_{14.16}$ Jos 5_{4} (‖ זָכָר *male*) etc. 11QT $58_{7.8.16}$ (all eight הַמִּלְחָמָה) 1QM 2_{7} 9_{5} (both lack ה) CD 20_{14} 1QH 7_{22} (מלחמתי) 9_{22} ([מלחמ]תי), הַצָּבָא *of the army* Nm $31_{21.53}$ 1 C 12_{9} (lacks הַ) 11QT 58_{10}, הַמִּשְׁמָר *of the guard* Ne 4_{17}, המשמרת *of the guard* 1Q36 16_{2} ([א]נשי), הַמַּצָּבָה *of the outpost* 1 S 14_{12}, הרכב *of the chariotry* 1QM 8_{4} 4QM^{a} fr. $1_{12(Baillet)}$ ([אנש]י הרכב), הקלע *of the sling*, i.e. sling-men 1QM 8_{1}, הסרך *of the order (of battle)* $6_{10(mg)}$ (סרך המערכות) 6_{11} 7_{1} 15_{4}, המערכה *of the battle-line* 7_{12}.

החרש *of the craftsman*, i.e. craftsmen 4QM^{a} fr. 1_{7}, הַשֵּׁם *of name*, i.e. of renown Gn 6_{4} Nm 16_{2} (אַנְשֵׁי־שֵׁם) 1 C 5_{24} 12_{31} (both שְׁמוֹת) Si 44_{3} (שם) 1QSa 2_{2} (אנישי) 2_{8} (א[נ]ישי) $2_{11.13}$ (אנישי) 1QM 2_{6} 3_{3}, העול *of evil* 1QS $5_{2.10}$ 8_{13} (הנשי) 9_{17}, הַבְּלִיַּעַל *of worthlessness* 1 K 21_{13} 4QCat^{a} 7_{5} (בליעל), תמים הקדש *of the perfection of holiness* 1QS 8_{20} (התמים קודש) CD $20_{2.5}$ (קדש) 20_{7}, נדבת מלחמה *of voluntariness of*, i.e. who have volunteered for, *war* 1QM 7_{5}.

חזונכה *of your vision* 1QH 14_{7}, עֲצָתִי *of my counsel* Ps 119_{24} 1QSa 1_{3} (אנישי עצתו) 1QSb 4_{24} (עצת) 1QH $6_{11.13}$ (both עצתכה) 1QpHab 5_{10} (עצתם) 9_{10} 4QpPs^{a} 1.2_{18} 4QpNah 3.1_{5} 4QCat^{a} 1_{14} ([א]נשי) 1_{16} (all five עצתו), סודי *of my counsel* 1QH 14_{18}, גְּאֻלָּתֶךָ *of your kin* Ezk 11_{15}, גָּלוּתֶךָ *of your exile* 11_{15} (if em. גְּאֻלָּתֶךָ).

שְׁלֹמֶךָ *of your peace* Jr 38_{22} Ob$_{7}$ (שְׁלֹמֶךָ) Si 6_{6} (שלומך), בְּרִיתֶךָ *of your covenant* Ob$_{7}$ 1QS 5_{9} 6_{19} (both בריתם) 1QH fr. 4_{8} (אנישי ברית; others אנוש וברית *humankind and the covenant of*) 1Q36 7_{2} 4QShir^{b} 63.3_{5} (both ברית), גורלו *of his lot* 1QS $2_{2.4}$ (both גורל) 1QM 1_{5} $1_{15(Yadin)}$ ([גורלו]) 4_{2} 11QMelch 1.1_{8} (אנש]י ג[ורל) 4QCat^{a} 12.1_{11}, תעודתו appar. *of his enrolment*, i.e. under his charge 1QM 4_{5}, ממשלתו *of his government* 14_{10} ([אנ]שי), רִיבֶךָ *of your contention*, i.e. your opponents Is 41_{11}, מַצֻּתֶךָ *of your struggle*, i.e. your opponents 41_{12}, מַעֲשֵׂהוּ *of his action* Jb 37_{7} (or em. אֲנָשִׁים so that *men* might know his action).

מִקְנֶה *of cattle*, i.e. herdsmen Gn $46_{32.34}$, מְלָאכָה *of work*, i.e. craftsmen 1 C 25_{1}, חַיִל *of valour* Jg $20_{44.46}$ (both חָיִל) 2 S 11_{16} (all three ־אַנְשֵׁי) Is 5_{22} Jr 48_{14} Na 2_{4} Ps 76_{6} (all four ־אַנְשֵׁי) Ec 12_{3} (הֶחָיִל) Si 44_{6} 1QM 2_{8} 6_{13} 4QpIsa^{a} 1_{3} (חילו) 4QpNah 3.3_{11} ([חי]לה) 4QM^{g} 4_{7} ([אנשי חיל]) perh. 4QapPs^{b} 48_{9} ([אנשי חיל]), *of ability* Gn 47_{6} Ex $18_{21.25}$ (all three ־אַנְשֵׁי) 2 K 24_{16} (הַחַיִל) Ne 11_{6} (אַנְשֵׁי־חָיִל) 1QSa 1_{28} (החיל), לֵבָב *of heart*, i.e. wise Jb $34_{10.34}$ (‖ גֶּבֶר *man*) 4Q298 1_{1}, בִּינָה *understanding* 3_{4}, דעות *of knowledge* CD 20_{4}, חֶסֶד *of loyalty* Is 57_{1} (־אַנְשֵׁי) Si $44_{1.10}$, אֱמֶת *of truth* Ex 18_{21} 11QT 57_{8} 1QH 14_{2} 1QpHab 7_{10} (האמת) 4Q298 3_{6}, קֹדֶשׁ *of holiness* Ex 22_{30} (־אַנְשֵׁי) 1QS 5_{13} $8_{17.23}$ 9_{8} (all four הקודש), צֶדֶק *of righteousness* Si 9_{16}, שֵׂיבָה *of old age* Dt 32_{25}, מטה *of a yoke* 1QS 11_{1}, מִדָּה *of (large) dimension* Nm 13_{32} (מִדּוֹת) Is 45_{14}, מִסְפָּר *of number*, i.e. few Ezk 12_{16}.

אַשְׁמָה *of guilt* 1QH 6_{18}, רָעָה *of evil* Pr 24_{1}, רָע *of evil*

28$_{5}$ (־אַנְשֵׁי; or em. רֹעַ *of evil*), רֶשַׁע *of evil* Jb 34$_{8}$ (־אַנְשֵׁי), אָוֶן *of evil* 34$_{36}$ (־אַנְשֵׁי), עולה *of evil* Si 41$_{8(M, Yadin)}$ ([עו]לה) 1QS 10$_{20}$, לָצוֹן *of scoffing* Is 28$_{14}$ Pr 29$_{8}$ CD 20$_{11}$ 4QpIsa^{b} 1.2$_{6.10}$ (all three הלצון), זדון *of insolence* Si 15$_{7(A)}$, רָכִיל *of slander* Ezk 22$_{9}$, מָוֶת *of*, i.e. condemned to, *death* 2 S 19$_{29}$ (־אַנְשֵׁי), חמס *of violence* Si 13$_{13}$ 15$_{12}$ 1QpHab 8$_{11}$, מִרְמָה *of deceit* Ps 55$_{24}$ (דָּמִים וּמִרְמָה *of murder and deceit*) 1QH 4$_{20}$, רמיה *of deceit* 1QS 9$_{8}$ (הרמיה) 1QH 2$_{16}$ 14$_{14}$, כזב *of a lie* Si 15$_{8(A).20}$, מוֹפֵת *of*, i.e. who are, *a sign* Zc 3$_{8}$ 1QH 7$_{21}$.

אַנְשֵׁי *men of* + place name, Sodom Gn 13$_{13}$ 19$_{4}$, Ai Jos 7$_{4.5}$ 8$_{20.21.25}$, Gibeon 10$_{6}$, Succoth Jg 8$_{5.8.14.15.16}$, Penuel 8$_{8.9}$, Shechem 9$_{57}$, Gilead 12$_{4.4.5}$, Ashdod 1 S 5$_{7}$, Gath 1 C 7$_{21}$, Beth-shemesh 1 S 6$_{15.19.20}$, Kireath-jearim 7$_{1}$ Ne 7$_{29}$, Jabesh(-gilead) 1 S 11$_{1.5.9}$ (אִישׁ) 11$_{9.10}$ etc., Babylon 2 K 17$_{30}$, Cuth 17$_{30}$, Hamath 17$_{30}$, Anathoth Jr 11$_{21.23}$ Ezr 2$_{23}$||Ne 7$_{27}$, Kir-heres Jr 48$_{31.36}$, Nineveh Jon 3$_{5}$, Netophah Ezr 2$_{22}$||Ne7$_{26}$, Michmas Ezr 2$_{27}$||Ne 7$_{31}$, Bethel Ezr 2$_{28}$||Ne 7$_{32}$, Bethlehem Ne 7$_{26}$, Beth-azmaweth 7$_{28}$, Ramah 7$_{30}$, Nebo 7$_{33}$, Jericho 3$_{2}$, Gibeon 3$_{7}$, Recah 1 C 4$_{12}$, Cozeba 4$_{22}$, Habbaruch MurEpBarC^{a}$_{2(Milik)}$ (AHL הכרך *the fortress*), En-gedi 5/6ḤevEp 12$_{1}$.

אַנְשֵׁי *men of* + pr.n.m. Hamor Jg 9$_{28}$, Dathan and Abiram Si 45$_{18}$, David 1 S 23$_{3}$ 24$_{5}$ 2 S 19$_{42}$ 21$_{17}$, Abner 2$_{31}$, Joab 20$_{7}$, Hezekiah Pr 25$_{1}$, אַנְשֵׁי יִשְׂרָאֵל *Israelites* 1 S 7$_{11}$ 8$_{22}$ 11$_{15}$ 17$_{52}$ 31$_{1}$ etc., אַנְשֵׁי־יִשְׂרָאֵל 31$_{7}$, אַנְשֵׁי עַם יִשְׂרָאֵל *men of the people of Israel* Ezr 2$_{2}$||Ne 7$_{7}$, אַנְשֵׁי יְהוּדָה *men of Judah* 2 S 2$_{4}$ 1 K 1$_{9}$ Ezr 10$_{9}$ (־אַנְשֵׁי), אַנְשֵׁי הַכִּכָּר *men of the plain* Ne 3$_{22}$.

אַנְשֵׁי הַתָּרִים *men of the spies*, i.e. merchants 1 K 10$_{15}$||2 C 9$_{14}$, הפנים *of the front (of battle)* 1QM 5$_{17(Yadin)}$, הב(י)נים *of the spaces between (armies)*, i.e. skirmishers 3$_{1.7}$ 5$_{17(Yadin)}$ (אנש]י הבינים]) 6$_{9.12}$ (אנש[י]) 7$_{16}$ (lacks ה) 9$_{3}$ 16$_{4}$ 17$_{12(Yadin)}$ ([הבינים]) 17$_{13}$ 4QM^{a} fr. 1$_{12(Baillet)}$ (ה]בינ[ים]) 1$_{13(Baillet)}$ ([הבינים]) 2$_{9}$ (הבי[נ]י[ם]) 4QM^{c}$_{2}$ (לא]נשי]), דָּמִים *of blood(s)*, i.e. murderers Ps 26$_{9}$ 55$_{24}$ 59$_{3}$ 139$_{19}$ Pr 29$_{10}$, בֹּגְדוֹת *of treachery* Zp 3$_{4}$, אֳנִיּוֹת *of ships*, i.e. sailors 1 K 9$_{27}$.

אֲנָשִׁים/אִישׁ *of man (men)*, after construct (sg. or pl.) of nouns, יָד *hand* Gn 9$_{5}$ (|| אָדָם *humankind*) 1 S 12$_{4}$ (both + מִן *from*) Ezk 40$_{5}$ 1QS 6$_{19}$ (+ אֶל *[in]to*), כַּף *hand* 2 S 14$_{16}$ (+ מִן) 1 K 18$_{44}$, שֹׁעַל *palm* 4QShir^{b} 30$_{4}$, אֹזֶן *ear* Jb 33$_{16}$, רֶגֶל *foot* Gn 24$_{32}$, שׁוֹק *leg* Ps 147$_{10}$, מָתְנַיִם *hips* Jr 13$_{11}$, ראשׁ *head* Nm 31$_{49}$ 1 S 29$_{4}$, עַיִן *eye* Nm 5$_{13}$ 16$_{14}$ Jr 19$_{10}$ 43$_{9}$ (both לְעֵינֵי *in the presence of*) Pr 21$_{2}$ 26$_{12}$ (both בְּעֵינֵי *in the presence of*), פֶּה *mouth* Jr 44$_{26}$ Jb 32$_{5}$ Pr 12$_{14}$ 13$_{2}$ 18$_{4}$ etc., פָּנִים *face* Gn 44$_{26}$ Jb 32$_{21}$, מֵצַח *forehead* Ezk 9$_{4}$, קוֹל *voice* Jos 10$_{14}$ Siloam tunnel inscr.$_{2}$, לֵב *heart* 2 S 15$_{6.13}$ Pr 12$_{25}$ 18$_{12}$ 19$_{21}$ etc. 4QCat^{a} 7$_{10}$, לֵבָב *heart* 2 S 19$_{15}$ 1QS 4$_{2}$, קֶרֶב *innards* Ps 64$_{7}$, דָּם *blood* 2 S 23$_{17}$||1 C 11$_{19}$, בָּשָׂר *flesh* Jb 12$_{10}$, נֶפֶשׁ *soul* Jon 1$_{14}$ Pr 13$_{8}$, רוּחַ *spirit* 18$_{14}$, חַיִּים *life* Si 30$_{22}$ (|| אָדָם *human being*) 37$_{25(B)}$ (D אֱנוֹשׁ *human being*; || עַם *people*), שָׁנָה *year* 1QSa 1$_{19}$.

מַרְאֶה *appearance* Si 25$_{17}$, תַּבְנִית *pattern* Is 44$_{13}$ (|| אָדָם *human being*), שֵׁם *name* Nm 1$_{5}$ 13$_{16}$ 25$_{14}$ 34$_{17.19}$ etc. 1QM 4$_{5}$, כָּבוֹד *glory* Si 3$_{11}$, רָצוֹן *pleasure* Est 1$_{8}$, מִקְרָא *proclamation* 1QM 3$_{7}$, תְּרוּעָה *shout* 1$_{11}$, נְבֵלָה *corpse* 1 K 13$_{29}$, פֶּגֶר *corpse* Is 66$_{24}$ Jr 41$_{9}$, אִשָּׁה *woman* Gn 20$_{7}$ Pr 6$_{26}$, בַּת *daughter* Gn 24$_{13}$ 38$_{2}$ Lv 21$_{9}$, בֵּן *son* Gn 42$_{11.13}$ Lv 24$_{10}$ 1 S 9$_{1}$ 17$_{12}$ etc., specif. בְּנֵי אִישׁ *sons of a man* Ps 4$_{3}$ 62$_{10}$ (+ בְּנֵי־אָדָם *human beings*) Lm 3$_{33}$ (־בְּנֵי) 1QS 3$_{13}$ 4$_{15.20.26}$ 1QM 11$_{14}$ 1QH fr. 10$_{8}$ 11$_{4(Licht)}$ 1Q36 25.2$_{5}$ 4QWiles 1$_{17}$, appar. *sons of an (ordinary) man* Ps 49$_{3}$ (+ בְּנֵי אָדָם appar. *nobles*).

נַעַר *lad* 2 K 8$_{4}$, קָצִין *leader* Jos 10$_{24}$, עֶבֶד *servant* Ex 12$_{44}$, שׁוֹר *ox* 21$_{35}$, כִּבְשָׂה *ewe-lamb* 2 S 12$_{4}$, נַחֲלָה *inheritance* 1QS 4$_{16.24}$, חֵלֶק *portion* Gn 14$_{24}$, [ש]ארית *remnant* 1QH 7$_{22}$ (Licht כפו]ארות] shake warriors *as branches*), זֶרַע *seed*, i.e. male offspring 1 S 1$_{11}$, אֹהֶל *tent* Nm 16$_{26}$, בַּיִת *house(hold)* Ex 22$_{6}$ Nm 30$_{11}$ Jg 18$_{19}$ (+ שֵׁבֶט *tribe*, מִשְׁפָּחָה *family*) 19$_{26}$ 2 S 17$_{18}$ Jb 1$_{4}$ etc. Si 42$_{10(B)}$ (א]יש[ה]), שָׂדֶה *field* Pr 24$_{30}$, אוט *storehouse* 4Q416 5$_{2}$, שֻׁלְחָן *table* Si 34$_{12(mg)}$, מִטָּה *bed* 2 K 4$_{21}$, חֲצֹצְרָה *trumpet* 1QM 3$_{3}$, כֶּסֶף *silver* Gn 43$_{21}$ 44$_{1}$, הוֹן *wealth* 1QS 9$_{8.8}$ 1QpHab 8$_{11}$ 4Q416 9.1$_{21}$ (אנש[ים]), כָּנָף *hem* Zc 8$_{23}$, לֶחֶם *bread* Ezk 24$_{17.22}$, עֹלָה *sacrifice* Lv 7$_{8}$.

עֵדָה *assembly* 1QS 5$_{2}$ 1QSa 2$_{8}$ CD 20$_{2}$ 4QpIsa^{b} 1.2$_{10}$, יַחַד *assembly* 4QpIsa^{e} 9$_{3}$ (היח[ד]) 1QH 14$_{18}$, כְּנֶסֶת *assembly* 4QPBless 1.1$_{6}$, מוֹשָׁב *assembly* 1QS 8$_{13}$ (הנשי) 1QSa 2$_{11}$ ([מו]שב), קְהִלָּה *assembly* 1QM 1$_{11}$, מַעֲמָד *station* CD 20$_{5}$, סוֹד *council* 4QRitPur 36$_{3}$ (אנש[ים]) CD 14$_{10}$ 4QShir^{b} 1$_{11}$, עֵצָה *council* 1QS 8$_{11}$, מוֹסָד *foundation*, i.e. company 4QSirShab^a 2$_2$ 4QShir Shab^b 14.1$_8$ ([מו]סדי).

עֶרֶךְ *value* 2 K 12$_5$ (or em. עֹבֵר *current* money), מַעַר *space* 1 K 7$_{36}$, מִסְפָּר *number* Ezr 2$_2$||Ne 7$_7$, מִצְעָר *few* 2 C 24$_{24}$, רֹב *multitude* 1QS 5$_{2.9}$ 6$_{19}$, שְׁלִישִׁית *a third* 11QT 58$_8$, חֲמִישִׁית *a fifth* 58$_7$, מִשְׁקָל *weight* 1QS 9$_{12}$, אַמָּה *cubit*, i.e. common cubit Dt 3$_{11}$, טוֹבָה *success* Si 12$_9$, דָּבָר *word* 2 S 19$_{44.44}$ 1 K 13$_4$ 2 K 5$_{14}$ 8$_2$, *matter* concerning 1 S 11$_5$, מִלָּה *word* 4QTanḥ 16$_{4(Allegro)}$ (AHL פעולת *deed of*), תּוֹרָה *law* 2 C 30$_{16}$, תֹּכֶן *rule* 1QS 9$_7$, מִשְׁפָּט *judgment* Pr 29$_{26}$ 1QSa 1$_2$, *appearance* 2 K 1$_7$, מִצְוָה *commandment* Is 29$_{13}$ Ne 12$_{24}$ 2 C 8$_{14}$, שִׁיר *song* Ne 12$_{36}$, מַעֲשֶׂה *deed* 4QShir^b 63.3$_2$, מִפְעָל *deed* Si 15$_{19}$, פְּעֻלָּה *deed* 4QTanḥ 16$_4$, דֶּרֶךְ *way* Jb 34$_{21}$ Pr 5$_{21}$ 16$_{2.7}$ 21$_2$ etc. 1QS 3$_6$, אֹרַח *way* Jb 34$_{11}$, טָהֳרָה *purification* 1QS 5$_{13}$ 8$_{17}$.

מִלְחָמָה *war* 4Q183 1.2$_{2(Allegro)}$, רִיב *strife* 1QS 10$_{19}$ 4Q424 2$_4$, רֶכֶב *chariotry* Is 21$_9$ 1QM 6$_{11}$, חֶרֶב *sword* Jg 7$_{22}$ 1 S 14$_{20}$ Is 31$_8$ (חֶרֶב לֹא־אִישׁ *a sword not of mortals;* || אָדָם *human beings*) Ezk 38$_{21}$, שֵׁבֶט *rod* 2 S 7$_{14}$ (|| בֶּן־אָדָם *human being*), מַעֲרָכָה *battle-line* 1QS 10$_{14}$ 1QM 6$_9$, רֹכֶס *conspiracy* Ps 31$_{21}$, רַע *evil* Si 42$_{14(Bmg, M)}$ (+ טוב אשה *a woman's goodness*), רָעָה *evil* Jg 9$_{57}$ Zc 7$_{10}$, פֶּשַׁע *sin* Pr 29$_6$, רוּם *haughtiness* Is 2$_{11}$=2$_{17}$ (|| אָדָם *human being*), מַעַל *unfaithfulness* 1QS 10$_{23}$, קִנְאָה *jealousy* Ec 4$_4$, מָוֶת *death* Ru 2$_{11}$.

תַּרְבּוּת אֲנָשִׁים *breed of men* Nm 32$_{14}$, עַל־שְׂמֹאול אִישׁ *to a man's left* 2 K 23$_8$, מֵעֵבֶר אִישׁ *from the side of each* 1 K 7$_{30}$, אַשְׁרֵי־אִישׁ *happy is (the) man* 1 K 10$_8$||2 C 9$_7$ (אֲנָשֶׁיךָ; or em. נָשֶׁיךָ *your women;* || עֶבֶד *servant*) Ps 1$_1$ (הָאִישׁ) 112$_1$ Si 14$_2$ 34$_8$ 50$_{28}$, [אהוב] ... אנשים *beloved of ... men* Si 45$_{1(Segal)}$, מקוללי ... אנשים *cursed of ... men* 11QT 64$_{12}$.

כֹּל אִישׁ *each man* Ex 36$_1$ Dt 29$_9$ Jg 20$_{33}$ 1 S 14$_{22}$, כָּל־אִישׁ Gn 45$_1$ Ex 25$_2$ 35$_{21.22.23}$ etc., כ(ו)ל איש Si 10$_{23}$ 11$_{29}$ 11QT 35$_{2.3.5}$ (א[יש]) 45$_{12.15}$ 49$_8$ 50$_{5.21}$ 1QS 2$_{22}$ 6$_{12}$ 7$_{22}$ 8$_{16.21}$ 9$_{20}$ 1QSa 1$_{19}$ 2$_{3.4}$ 1QM 7$_6$ 4QM^a fr. 16$_{10}$ CD 9$_2$ 12$_{2(mg)}$ 4QD$_{14}$ 5QRègle 1$_{13}$ 4QpPs^a 1.2$_7$ 4QM^g 4$_2$ 4QToh B$^b_5$ ([כל איש]) 4Q416 10.2$_6$, כָּל־הָאִישׁ Dt 4$_3$ 2 S 15$_2$ Ne 5$_{13}$, כול האיש 11QT 27$_6$, כֹּל אַנְשֵׁי *all the men of* Jos 5$_4$ 8$_{25}$ Jl 4$_9$ Ob$_7$, כָּל־אַנְשֵׁי Gn 17$_{27}$ 29$_{22}$ Dt 21$_{21}$=11QT 64$_5$ 1 S 11$_{1.15}$ etc., כֹּל־אַנְשֵׁי Jos 6$_3$, כול אנשי 2QJub 23$_7$ (אנש[י]) 1QS 2$_{2.4}$ 5$_{10}$ 7$_{20}$ 1QM 1$_{5.15}$ 4$_2$ 7$_{12}$ 9$_3$ 15$_4$ CD 20$_{14}$ (כל) 1QH 2$_{16(Licht)}$ ([וכול]) 4$_{20}$ 6$_{13.18}$ 9$_{22(Licht)}$ ([לכול]) 14$_{18}$ 4QCat^a 12.1$_{11}$ 1Q31 1$_{1(Milik)}$ ([כ]ול) 1Q36 7$_2$ 4QShir^b 63.3$_5$ 6QBen 1$_2$ 4Q298 1$_1$ ([כ]ול), כֹּל הָאֲנָשִׁים *all the men* Ne 11$_2$ CD 8$_{21(A)}$=19$_{33(B)}$ 4QToh B$^b_3$ (כול [האנשים]), כָּל־הָאֲנָשִׁים Nm 14$_{22}$ Jg 9$_{51}$ 2 S 17$_{12}$ Jr 44$_{15}$ 2 C 2$_{16}$, כָּל־אֲנָשֶׁיהָ *all her* (city's) *men* Jos 10$_2$, כָּל־אֲנָשָׁיו *all his men* 1 S 31$_6$ 2 S 15$_{22}$.

<APP> + הוּא *he* Nm 16$_7$ Jos 22$_{20}$ z1QH 7$_{32}$, אֵלֶּה *these* 1 C 12$_{39}$, אֶחָד *one* 4QTestim 1$_{23(mg)}$, כֹּל *all* 1QM 9$_5$, אִישׁ *man* 2 S 23$_{21(Qr)}$||1 C 11$_{23}$ Ps 140$_{12}$ 1 C 5$_{24}$ Si 41$_{1.2(B)}$, אָדָם *human being* Pr 6$_{12}$ 20$_6$.

אָח *brother* Gn 13$_8$ 2 S 19$_{42}$ Ezk 11$_{15}$ 1 C 26$_8$, מוֹדַע *relative* Ru 2$_{1(Qr)}$, אָב *father* Si 44$_1$, נַעַר *lad* 1 S 30$_{17}$, בֵּן *son* Jg 9$_{2.5.18}$ 2 S 3$_{39}$ 2 K 10$_6$ etc., צַר *enemy* Est 7$_6$, אָדוֹן *lord* Gn 42$_{30.33}$ 2 K 4$_{16}$, שַׂר *prince* Ex 2$_{14}$ 2 S 4$_2$, נָשִׂיא *prince* Nm 16$_2$, סָגָן *ruler* Ne 5$_{17}$.

רֹאשׁ *chief* Nm 13$_3$ Dt 1$_{15}$ Ezr 10$_{16}$ 1 C 5$_{24}$ 9$_9$, *column* 1QM 8$_6$, זָקֵן *elder* 1 K 21$_{11}$, חֹר *noble* 21$_{11}$, כֹּהֵן *priest* Lv 21$_9$ Ne 3$_{22}$ 1QS 6$_3$ CD 13$_2$ 4QToh B$^b_6$, נָבִיא *prophet* Jg 6$_8$, עֶבֶד *servant* 1 K 1$_9$ 9$_{27}$ 2 K 4$_1$, סָרִיס *eunuch* Jr 38$_7$, סַבָּל *porter* 2 C 2$_1$, כְּסִיל *fool* Pr 14$_7$ Si 34$_{20}$, בַּעַל *possessor* Jg 19$_{22.23}$ 2 K 1$_8$ Si 6$_1$, חָרָשׁ *craftsman* Ezk 21$_{36}$, גֵּר *sojourner* 2 S 1$_{13}$ 2 C 2$_{16}$, עַיִט *bird of prey* Is 46$_{11}$, גִּבּוֹר *warrior* Gn 6$_4$ Jos 8$_3$ 1 S 9$_1$ Ru 2$_1$ 1 C 5$_{24}$ 12$_9$ etc. 11QT 58$_{16}$ 1QM 11$_1$ 12$_{10}$ 4QpNah 3.3$_{11}$ (גבור[י]), בֶּן־חַיִל *warrior* Jg 18$_2$ 2 K 2$_{16}$, ירה hi. ptc. *archer* 1 S 31$_3$, שַׁעֲשֻׁעִים *delight* Ps 119$_{24}$.

דּוֹר *generation* Dt 2$_{14}$, גּוֹי *nation* Jos 5$_6$, קָהָל *assembly* Ezr 10$_1$, עַם *people* Nm 11$_{10}$ Dt 31$_{12}$ Jg 20$_{22}$ 2 S 16$_{15}$ 4QpsEzek^a 2$_9$ (ע[ם]), מחצית העם *half of the people* 11QT 58$_{10}$, חמישית העם *a fifth of the people* 58$_{16}$.

איש עוז נפש *a man (who has) strength of soul* Si 40$_{30}$, אֲנָשִׁים בְּנֵי־בְלִיַּעַל *men (who are) sons of worthlessness* Dt 13$_{14}$=11QT 55$_3$ (אנש[י]ם [בנ]י [בלי]ע ל) Jg 19$_{22}$ (אַנְשֵׁי) 20$_{13}$ 1 K 21$_{13}$ 2 C 13$_7$, כָּל־מַרְבִּית בֵּיתְךָ ... אֲנָשִׁים *all the increase of your household ... (namely) men* 2 S 2$_{33}$.

+ pr.n.m. Gabriel Dn 9$_{21}$, Noah Gn 9$_{20}$ Ezk 14$_{14}$, Daniel 14$_{14}$ Dn 10$_{11}$, Job Ezk 14$_{14}$ Jb 1$_8$ 2$_3$, Lot Gn 19$_9$, Joseph Ps 105$_{17}$, Potiphar Gn 39$_1$, Moses Ex 11$_3$ 32$_{1.23}$ Nm 12$_3$ Dt 33$_1$ etc., Joshua Nm 27$_{18}$, Ehud Jg 3$_{15}$, Gideon 7$_{14}$, Tola 10$_1$, Micah 17$_5$, Elkanah 1 S 1$_{21}$,

David Ne 12$_{24.36}$ 2 C 8$_{14}$, Goliath 1QM 11$_1$, Nabal 1 S 25$_{25}$, Paltiel 2 S 3$_{15}$, Sheba 20$_1$, Jeroboam 1 K 11$_{28}$, Shemaiah 12$_{22}$||2 C 11$_2$, Elisha 2 K 5$_{20}$, Coniah Jr 22$_{28}$, Uriah 26$_{20}$, Elnathan 26$_{22}$, Hanan 35$_4$, Ebed-melech 38$_7$, Mordecai Est 2$_5$ 9$_4$, Sabaeans Is 45$_{14}$.

אִישָׁהּ *her husband*, preceded by pr.n.m. Abram Gn 16$_3$, Manoah Jg 13$_9$, Elkanah 1 S 1$_{8.23}$, Uriah 2 S 11$_{26}$ (|| בַּעַל *husband*), אִישָׁהּ נָבָל *her husband, Nabal* 1 S 25$_{19}$, אִישׁ ... פַּלְטִיאֵל *a husband ..., Paltiel* 2 S 3$_{15}$.

<ADJ> חַי *alive* 4QpNah 3.1$_7$, טוֹב *good* 2 S 18$_{27}$ 1 K 2$_{32}$ Pr 14$_{14}$ Si 36$_{14}$, קָדוֹשׁ *holy* 2 K 4$_9$, יָשָׁר *upright* 4Q424 2$_8$ 4QPsJos^a 3.2$_6$, צַדִּיק *righteous* Gn 6$_9$ 1 K 2$_{32}$ Ezk 23$_{45}$, תָּם *innocent* Gn 25$_{27}$ Jb 1$_8$ 2$_3$ (both + יָשָׁר), חָכָם *wise* Gn 41$_{33}$ Dt 1$_{13.15}$ 2 S 13$_3$ 1 K 2$_9$ etc. Si 10$_{23(A)}$ ([ח]כם) 35$_{17(B).18(B).18(B)}$, חֲכַם־לֵב *wise of heart* Ex 36$_{1.2}$, וָתִיק *experienced* Si 36$_{25}$, עָשִׁיר *rich* 2 S 12$_4$ Pr 28$_{11}$ Si 10$_{30(B)}$, שָׁלֵו *at ease* 41$_1$, יָפֶה *beautiful* 2 S 14$_{25}$, טָהוֹר *clean* Nm 19$_{9.18}$ 11QT 49$_8$ 4QToh B^b$_6$ ([טה]ור).

עָנִי *poor* Dt 24$_{12}$ Ps 109$_{16}$, אֶבְיוֹן *poor* 109$_{16}$, מִסְכֵּן *poor* Ec 9$_{15.15}$, חָסֵר *lacking* Si 41$_{2(B)}$, רֵיק *empty-headed* Jg 9$_4$ 11$_3$ 2 C 13$_7$, אֱוִיל *foolish* Pr 29$_9$ Si 8$_4$, טָמֵא *unclean* CD 11$_{19}$, טְמֵא־שְׂפָתַיִם *unclean of lips* Is 6$_5$ (+ עַם *people*), כבד אזן *heavy*, i.e. poor, *of hearing* 4Q424 2$_3$ ([איש]), שמן לב *stout*, i.e. hard *of heart* 2$_6$, רָשָׁע *wicked* Nm 16$_{26}$ 2 S 4$_{11}$ Pr 21$_{29}$ 1QH 7$_{27(Mansoor)}$ ([רשע]; Licht [תהו] *emptiness*) 4QpPs^a 1.2$_7$ (ר[שע]), רַע *evil* 1 S 30$_{22}$ Si 6$_1$ 37$_{11}$, רַע עַיִן *evil of eye* Pr 28$_{22}$ Si 14$_3$, שוע עינים *poor of eyesight* 4Q424 2$_3$, חַטָּא *sinful* Nm 32$_{14}$, מַר־נֶפֶשׁ *bitter of soul* Jg 18$_{25}$ (מָרֵי) 1 S 22$_2$, זידן *insolent* 1QH fr. 45$_5$ (others זודן).

גָּדוֹל *great* 2 S 19$_{33}$ 2 K 5$_1$ Si 8$_1$ 34$_{12(mg)}$ 4QPsJos^a 3.2$_6$, גִּבּוֹר *strong* 1 S 14$_{52}$ (+ בֶּן־חַיִל *warrior*), חָזָק *strong* Si 8$_{12}$, עָצוּם *powerful* 4QWiles 1$_{14(Allegro)}$ ([ע]צום), מָהִיר *quick* Pr 22$_{29}$, עִתִּי *prepared* Lv 16$_{21}$=11QT 26$_{13}$, קָרִיא *invited* 1QSa 2$_{2.11(Barthélemy)}$ ([קריא]), חָפֵץ *desiring* Ps 34$_{13}$, יָעֵף *weary* Jg 8$_{15}$, עָצֵל *lazy* Pr 24$_{30}$, רַךְ *gentle* Dt 28$_{54}$, רַךְ לֵבָב *fainthearted* 20$_8$=11QT 62$_3$, עָנֹג *delicate* Dt 28$_{54}$.

שָׂעִר *hairy* Gn 27$_{11}$, חָלָק *smooth* 27$_{11}$, בָּרִיא *fat* Jg 3$_{17}$, זָקֵן *old* 19$_{16.17.20.22}$ 1 S 28$_{14}$ etc. 1QSa 2$_7$, יָשִׁישׁ *old* Si 25$_{20}$, עִוֵּר *blind* Lv 21$_{18}$ 11QT 45$_{12}$, פִּסֵּחַ *lame* Lv 21$_{18}$, אִטֵּר יַד־יְמִינוֹ *constricted in his right hand* Jg 3$_{15}$ 20$_{16}$, שִׁכּוֹר *drunk* Jr 23$_9$ (|| גֶּבֶר *man*), אַחֵר *another* Gn 29$_{19}$ Lv 27$_{20}$ Dt 20$_{5.6.7}$ etc., אֶחָד *one, a certain* Gn 42$_{11.13}$ Nm 1$_{44}$ 13$_{2.2}$ etc. 4QM^g 4$_4$ ([אחד]; see also Prep, כְּ), נָכְרִי *foreign* Dt 17$_{15}$=11QT 56$_{15}$ Ec 6$_2$, רִאשׁוֹן *first* husband Ho 2$_9$, אַחֲרוֹן *latter* husband Dt 24$_{3.3}$, אִישׁ רַגְלִי *man on foot, foot-soldier* Jg 20$_2$ 2 S 8$_4$||1 C 18$_4$ (+ פָּרָשׁ *horseman*) 1 C 19$_{18}$.

+ gentilic, Hebrew Ex 2$_{11.13}$, Israelite Lv 24$_{10}$ (אִישׁ הַיִּשְׂרְאֵלִי), Judaean Jr 43$_9$ Zc 8$_{23}$ Est 2$_5$ 4Q324A 4$_1$, Levite Jg 19$_1$ 20$_4$, Benjaminite 1 S 9$_1$ 2 S 20$_1$ Est 2$_5$, Canaanite Gn 38$_2$, Egyptian 39$_1$ Ex 2$_{11.19}$ Lv 24$_{10}$ 1 S 30$_{11}$ etc., Amalekite 30$_{13}$, Midianite Gn 37$_{28}$, Edomite 1 K 11$_{17}$, Adullamite Gn 38$_1$, Ephrathite 1 S 17$_{12}$, Tyrian 1 K 7$_{14}$||2 C 2$_{13}$.

הָאִישׁ הַזֶּה *this man* Gn 24$_{58}$ 26$_{11}$ Dt 22$_{16}$=11QT 65$_{11}$ Jg 19$_{23.24}$ etc. 8QHymn 1$_2$, הָאִישׁ הַלָּזֶה *that man* Gn 24$_{65}$, הָאִישׁ הַהוּא *that man* Lv 17$_{4.4.9}$ 20$_{3.4}$ etc. Dt 17$_5$=11QT 55$_{21}$ Dt 17$_{12}$=11QT 56$_{10}$ Dt 22$_{18(Sam)}$=11QT 65$_{14}$, הָאֲנָשִׁים הָאֵלֶּה *these men* Gn 19$_8$ (הָאֵל) 34$_{21}$ Nm 1$_{17}$ 16$_{26.30}$ 22$_9$ etc., הָאֲנָשִׁים הָהֵם *those men* 9$_7$ (הָהֵמָּה) 14$_{38}$ 16$_{14}$ 1 S 29$_4$.

<PREP> לְ of direction, *to* MurEpBarC^a$_2$ 5/6ḤevEp 12$_1$, + בוא hi. *bring* 1 S 9$_{7.7}$ 2 K 4$_{42}$ 1QH 6$_{13}$, שׁוב hi. *take back* Lv 25$_{27}$ 1 S 26$_{23}$ Pr 24$_{29}$ 1QS 10$_{17}$, ירד hi. *take down* Gn 43$_{11}$, שׁלח *send* Ezk 23$_{40}$, נפל hi. *cause* lot *to fall* 1QH 3$_{22}$, נתן *give* Gn 3$_6$ 16$_3$ 45$_{22}$ 1 S 9$_8$ 1 K 8$_{39}$ etc. CD 14$_{15}$ (perh. לְ of benefit, *for*), specif. *give (in marriage)* Gn 29$_{19}$ 30$_{18}$ 34$_{14}$ Dt 22$_{16}$=11QT 65$_{11(mg)}$ Jr 29$_6$, מכר *sell* Lv 25$_{27}$ 27$_{20}$, שׁלם pi. *pay* Ps 62$_{13}$ 1QS 10$_{18}$, חלק pi. *apportion* 2 S 6$_{19}$||1 C 16$_{3.3}$.

אמר *say* Jos 5$_{13}$ 6$_{22}$ Jg 1$_{24}$ 8$_{5.9}$ etc., דבר pi. *speak* 1 K 13$_{26}$, נגד hi. *tell* Gn 43$_6$ Jg 13$_{10}$ 1 S 11$_9$ 25$_{19}$ 2 K 4$_7$, קרא *call* Gn 39$_{14}$ Ex 2$_{20}$ Jg 16$_{19}$ 2 S 15$_2$ 1 K 1$_9$, שׁבע ni. *swear* Jos 5$_6$ 2 K 25$_{24}$||Jr 40$_9$, ענה ni. *answer* Ezk 14$_{4.7}$, למד pi. *teach* Si 15$_{20(B)}$, ידע ni. *make oneself known* Ru 3$_3$, pu. *be known* 2$_{1(Kt)}$, hi. *make known* 1QH 7$_{27}$, שׁמע hi. *make heard* 4QShir^b 63.3$_5$, נוח hi. *give rest* 1 C 22$_9$, *permit* 16$_{21}$ (||Ps 105$_{14}$ אָדָם *person*), אַהֲבָה לְ *love towards* 1QS 5$_{25}$.

לְ of possession, *of, (belonging) to* Nm 5$_8$ Dt 19$_{17}$=11QT 61$_8$ 1 S 30$_{13}$ Jr 26$_{11}$ Ps 37$_{37}$ etc. Si 36$_{31}$ 11QT 46$_{18}$ 1QS 11$_1$ 1QM 15.1$_5$ 6$_{10}$ CD 12$_6$ 4QCat^a 1$_{11}$ 4QapPs^b 24$_4$, + היה *be* Nm 5$_{10.10}$ Dt 21$_{18}$=11QT 64$_2$ Jos

17$_1$ Jg 20$_{38}$ 1 S 9$_1$ Ec 6$_3$, specif. *be married* to Lv 21$_3$ 22$_{12}$ Nm 30$_7$ Dt 21$_{15}$ 22$_{29}$=11QT 66$_{10}$ (לוא) etc., חשׁב לְ ni. *be reckoned to* Lv 17$_4$, ארשׂ לְ pu. *be engaged to* 19$_{20}$, חָבֵר לְ *companion of* Pr 28$_{24}$, לֹא־לְאִישׁ *it is not in the power of a man* Jr 10$_{23}$ (|| אָדָם *human being*), סֶרֶךְ לְ *order of* 1QS 5$_1$, כֵּן לְ *this applies to* 7$_{10}$, [לאי]שה *it depends on her husband* CD 16$_{10}$, הֲשָׁלוֹם לְאִישֵׁךְ *is there peace to your husband?* 2 K 4$_{26}$ (|| יֶלֶד *child*), מוֹדַע לְאִישָׁהּ *a kinsman of her husband* Ru 2$_{1(Qr)}$, איש לו שפתים *the man who has (cunning) lips* 4Q424 1$_8$.

לְ of benefit, *to, for* Pr 10$_{23}$ 15$_{23}$ Si 25$_{20.20}$ 40$_{29}$ 1QH fr. 1$_7$, + שׂים *establish* heir 2 S 14$_7$, ילד *bear (children)* Dt 21$_{15}$, אמן *be foster-parent* 1QH 7$_{21}$, פלל htp. *intercede* 1 S 2$_{25}$, יצק *pour* 2 K 4$_{40}$, פתח *open* gates 4QM^{c}2$_{(Baillet)}$, אור ni. *be light, dawn* 2 S 23$_2$, טמא *be unclean* 11QT 49$_8$, חרף ni. *be designated* Lv 19$_{20}$, עשׂה *do* to, for Gn 19$_8$ Jg 19$_{24}$ 2 S 3$_{20}$ 12$_4$, ni. *be done* to, for Lv 24$_{19}$ Dt 25$_9$ 1 S 17$_{26.27}$ Est 6$_{9.11}$, כרת hi. *cut off* Ml 2$_{12}$, בוז לְ *scorn* Ca 8$_7$, נשׂא לְ *forgive* Is 2$_9$, ברך לְ pi. *bless* Ne 11$_2$, מתק לְ hi. *be sweet to* Si 40$_{30}$, עָרֵב לְ *sweet to* Pr 20$_{17}$, [מ]ר ל *bitter to* Si 41$_1$ 4Q416 10.2$_{16}$ (|| גֶּבֶר *man*), טוב ל *good for* Si 41$_{2(B)}$, נאוה ל *suitable for* 14$_3$, [ל...] מכשול *stumbling-block to* 1QH 9$_{22(Licht)}$, הַמַּשָּׂא יִהְיֶה לְאִישׁ דְּבָרוֹ *the burden will be for each man his own word* Jr 23$_{36}$.

לְ of agent, *by*, + דרשׁ ni. *be sought* Ezk 14$_3$, שׂנא pass. *be hated* Si 10$_7$, מצא ni. *be found* 1QS 8$_{11}$, הרה *conceive* Gn 38$_{25}$, *against*, + חרץ *sharpen* tongue, i.e. slander Jos 10$_{21}$, חטא *sin* 1 S 2$_{25}$, שׁחר ni. *break out* (of illness) 5$_9$.

הפך לְ ni. *be changed into* 1 S 10$_6$, שׂים לְ *appoint as* Ex 2$_{14}$, היה לְ *be(have) as* 1 S 4$_{9.9}$ 1 K 2$_2$ Ezk 32$_6$, קוה לְ pi. *wait for* Mc 5$_6$ (|| בֶּן אָדָם *human being*), חזק לְ hi. *grasp* 2 S 15$_5$, נשׁק לְ *kiss* 15$_5$; מִנֶּגֶד לְ *from the presence of* Pr 14$_7$.

בְּ of place, *in, among, with* Gn 17$_{23}$ Dt 13$_5$ Jg 20$_{39}$, + בוא *come* 1 S 17$_{12}$, יתר ni. *remain* 2 S 17$_{12}$, מצא ni. *be found* Jr 11$_9$, מלט ni. *escape* 41$_{15}$, חלל hi. *begin* Ezk 9$_6$, כלה pi. *finish* Ezr 10$_{17}$, קום *arise*, i.e. endure Jos 2$_{11}$, רבץ בְּ *settle on* Dt 29$_{19}$, of agent, *by*, + ישׁע hi. *save* Jg 7$_7$, נכה hi. *strike* 4QpNah 3.1$_5$, חרה htp. *be angered* Ps 37$_7$, שַׁכּוּל בְּ *bereaved by* Pr 17$_{12}$, partitive, *some (of)*, + נכה hi. 1 S 6$_{19}$, אכל *consume* 1QM 15$_3$ + Sup, of essence, *as* Jb 34$_{36}$, ערך בְּ *form battle-line comprising* 2 C 13$_3$.

בְּ *against* Dt 29$_{19}$ 1QM 4$_2$, + היה *be* Dt 21$_{22}$=11QT 64$_9$ CD 13$_5$, פגע *attack* 1 K 2$_{32}$, נגשׂ ni. *oppress* Is 3$_5$, פצר *press* Gn 19$_9$ Jg 19$_7$, קום *stand* Dt 19$_{15.16}$=11QT 61$_{6.7}$, נתן *set* face Lv 20$_3$ Ezk 14$_8$, שׂים *set* face Lv 20$_5$, שׁלח *extend* hand 4QpPs^a 1.2$_{18}$, מעל *transgress* Nm 5$_{12.27}$, רעע *be evil* Dt 28$_{56}$, חרה *be hot* (of anger) 2 S 12$_5$, ענה *answer* Dt 19$_{16}$=11QT 61$_7$, נשׂא *impose* oath on 1 K 8$_{31(mss)}$||2 C 6$_{22(mss)}$ (L נשׁא appar. *exact* oath from).

קנא בְּ pi. *be jealous of* Pr 3$_{31}$ 24$_1$ Si 9$_{11}$, עשׂה בְּ *do for* Est 6$_6$, ב[איש ...]ישה *he lends ... to a man* 1QDM 3$_{5(Milik)}$, בטח בְּ *trust* Ps 41$_{10}$, בחר בְּ *choose* 2 C 6$_5$, נגע בְּ *touch* Gn 26$_{11}$, חזק בְּ hi. *seize* Is 4$_1$, *keep* Jg 7$_8$, רציתה ב[איש] *you took pleasure in a man* 1QH fr. 1$_{12(Licht)}$, חפץ ב *delight in* Si 15$_{12(B)}$, רצ]ונכה ב] *your goodwill towards* 1QH 16$_4$, צורך ב *need of* Si 15$_{12(A, Bmg)}$ (Bmg [צ]ורך).

בְּיַד *by means of* Lv 16$_{21}$=11QT 26$_{13}$ CD 11$_{19}$, *into the control of*, + נתן *give* Jr 38$_{16}$ Ezk 21$_{36}$, ni. *be given* Jr 39$_{17}$; בְּתוֹךְ *in the middle of* 1QS 6$_{21}$ 9$_{17.19}$.

מִן partitive, *some (of), any (of)*, + חיה *live* Nm 14$_{38}$, לכד *capture* Jg 8$_{14}$, מלט ni. *escape* 2 K 10$_{24}$, אִישׁ מֵאַנְשֵׁי (not) *one of the men of* Gn 39$_{11}$ 1QS 5$_{15}$ 7$_{24}$ 8$_{16.23}$, sim. 1 S 30$_{22}$, (לְ)מֵאִישׁ וְעַד־אִשָּׁה *both man and woman* Jos 6$_{21}$ 8$_{25}$ 1 S 15$_3$ (lacks וְ) 22$_{19}$ 2 S 6$_{19}$||1 C 16$_3$ etc., לְמֵאִישׁ וְעַד־בְּהֵמָה *both man and beast* Ex 11$_7$.

מִן of direction, *from*, + רחק *be far* Si 9$_{13}$, שׁוב hi. *take back* 1QS 10$_{20}$ 4Q416 1$_{10}$, בדל ni. *separate oneself* 1QS 5$_{10}$ 9$_{20}$, גרשׁ pass. *be divorced from* Lv 21$_7$, לקח *take* Ex 25$_2$ (מֵאֵת) 2 S 3$_{15}$ (מֵעִם) 4Q416 10.2$_6$, pu. *be taken* Gn 2$_{23}$, חצה *separate* Nm 31$_{42}$, נצל hi. *save* 2 S 22$_{49}$||Ps 18$_{49}$ Pr 2$_{12}$, ישׁע hi. *save* Ps 59$_3$, פלט pi. *save* 43$_1$, נצר *guard* 140$_2$ (|| אָדָם *human being*) 140$_5$, עלם hi. *hide* eyes Lv 20$_4$, שׁאל *ask* Kuntillet ʿAjrud add. inscr. 2, מאיש שלום צבוע אל כלב *from a man, is there peace of jackal with dog?* Si 13$_{18}$ (or em. מֵאַיִן *whence is there* peace?).

מִן of comparison, *(more) than* Pr 19$_{22}$ 26$_{12}$ 29$_{20}$ 30$_2$ Ec 7$_5$ Si 3$_{17}$ 41$_{15}$ 1QH 10$_{28}$, מִשְׁחַת מֵאִישׁ *disfigurement unlike that of a man* Is 52$_{14}$ (+ בְּנֵי אָדָם *human beings*), *on account of* Ezk 45$_{20}$, שׁאר מִן ni. *be left without* Ru 1$_5$ (|| יֶלֶד *child*), פ[לא] מאלוהים ואנשים *a wonder among gods and men* 4QShirShab^{a} 2.2$_{3}$; לְבַד מִן *apart from* 1 K 10$_{15}$||2 C 9$_{14}$; דרשׁ מֵאֵת *inquire by means of* 2 K 8$_{8}$; דרשׁ מֵעִם *require from* Dt 18$_{19}$; מִבְּלִי *without* Jr 9$_{9}$ Zp 3$_{6}$; מִבַּלְעֲדֵי *apart from* Nm 5$_{20}$ Jr 44$_{19}$.

אֶל of direction, *to*, + בוא *come* Gn 24$_{30}$ Jg 8$_{15}$ 13$_{11}$ 1 S 30$_{21}$ 2 K 4$_{25}$ etc., הלך *go* Jos 5$_{13}$, hi. *lead* 2 K 6$_{19}$, שׁוב *go back* Gn 43$_{13}$ 2 K 5$_{15}$ Ho 2$_{9}$, נגשׁ *approach* Gn 43$_{19}$, אצל ni. *draw near* Si 13$_{17}$ (:: עָשִׁיר *wealthy man*) ירד *go down* 2 K 7$_{17}$, עבר *cross over* 1 S 14$_{8}$, רוץ *run* Gn 24$_{29}$, שׁלח *send* 2 S 2$_{5}$ 1 K 21$_{11.11}$, גלה ni. *reveal oneself* 1 S 14$_{8}$, נתן *give* Nm 7$_{5}$, אמר *say* Gn 44$_{4}$ Dt 27$_{14}$ Jos 2$_{9}$ 7$_{2}$ 9$_{6}$ etc., דבר pi. *speak* Gn 34$_{20}$ 43$_{19}$ Jos 14$_{6}$ 1 S 17$_{28}$ 1 K 13$_{7}$ etc., קרא *call* Ex 36$_{2}$ Jos 4$_{4}$ 10$_{24}$ 1 K 13$_{21}$ 2 K 4$_{22}$ etc., צהל *neigh* Jr 5$_{8}$, היה *be (directed)* 1 K 12$_{22}$||2 C 11$_{2}$, אֶל־אִישֵׁךְ תְּשׁוּקָתֵךְ *your desire will be towards your husband* Gn 3$_{16}$.

אֶל *against*, + צור *besiege* 1 S 23$_{8}$, עטר *close in* on 23$_{26}$, בוא hi. *bring* evil Jr 11$_{23}$ 36$_{31}$, שׂים לֵב אֶל *pay attention to* 1 S 25$_{25}$, הגה אֶל *moan for* Jr 48$_{31}$, המה אֶל *moan for* 48$_{36}$, בוא אֶל ho. *be brought in addition to* Ezk 23$_{42}$.

כְּ *as* Is 66$_{13}$ Zc 4$_{1}$ Si 12$_{17}$ 1QSb 4$_{24}$ (Milik באישׁ) 4QBarkc$_{6}$ 4Q416 10.2$_{17}$ (|| גֶּבֶר *man*), + היה *be* Jr 14$_{9}$ (|| גִּבּוֹר *warrior*) 1QH 8$_{27}$, עור hi. *rouse* jealousy Is 42$_{13}$, עלה *go up* Jl 2$_{7}$ (|| גִּבּוֹר), חמל *love* 4Q416 9.2$_{13}$, אכל *eat* Si 34$_{16}$, ערך pass. *be arranged*, i.e. equipped for battle Jr 6$_{23}$||50$_{42}$, סבב hi. *sit at table* Si 34$_{16}$, כְּאִישׁ אֶחָד *as one man* Nm 14$_{15}$ Jg 6$_{16}$ 20$_{1.8.11}$ 1 S 11$_{7}$ 2 S 19$_{15}$ Ezr 3$_{1}$ Ne 8$_{1}$, כָּאִישׁ גְּבוּרָתוֹ *as the man is his strength* Jg 8$_{21}$, צֵל ... כָּאֲנָשִׁים *a shadow ... as men* 9$_{36}$.

עַל *upon* Ezk 9$_{6}$, + היה *be* Ps 80$_{18}$, נפל *fall* 1 K 20$_{30}$ Jb 4$_{13}$ 33$_{15}$ Dn 10$_{7}$, כבד *make* burden *heavy* Ex 5$_{9}$, נתן *place* Nm 11$_{25}$, נוח *rest* (of spirit) 11$_{25}$, עבר *pass*, i.e. become incumbent Dt 24$_{5}$, *against* perh. 4QCat^{a} 5$_{1}$, + היה *be* 2 S 11$_{23}$, סגר *close in* on Jb 12$_{14}$, ענה *answer* 2 S 19$_{43}$, חרשׁ perh. *be angry* Si 8$_{2}$ ((עַ[ל])), קנא pi. *be zealous* 1QH 14$_{14}$, עזר *help* 1QpHab 5$_{11}$.

עַל *concerning*, + אמר *say* Jr 11$_{21}$, נגד hi. *tell* 1 C 19$_{5}$, פשׁרו על *its interpretation concerns* 1QpHab 7$_{10}$ 4QpPs^{a} 1.1$_{18}$ ((פשׁר]ו)), פקד עַל ho. *be placed in charge of* 2 C 34$_{12}$, פָּקִיד עַל *overseer in charge of* 2 K 25$_{19}$||Jr 52$_{25}$, שׂים עַל *place in charge of* 1 S 18$_{5}$, *appoint* time *for* Jb 34$_{23}$, נצח עַל pi. *oversee* 2 C 2$_{1}$, שׁלח עַל *send to* 2 K 18$_{27}$||Is 36$_{12}$, שׁור עַל appar. *look at* Jb 33$_{27}$ (unless em. יָשִׁיר *sings* or יָשֵׁר *proclaims* to), אסר עַל ni. *be composed of* 1QM 5$_{3}$, שׂטה על *stray from* in adultery Si 42$_{10(M)}$, פקד עַל *punish* Jr 23$_{34}$ Zp 1$_{12}$, הות על pol. perh. *attack* Ps 62$_{4}$, נגשׁ על *approach* Ezk 9$_{6}$; נתן עַל־יַד *hand over to* Est 6$_{9}$; הלך עַל פְּנֵי pi. *walk in front of* 1QM 7$_{12}$.

עִם *with* Dt 32$_{25}$ 1 S 2$_{26}$ Si 34$_{20}$ 1QpHab 2$_{1}$ 4QPBless 1.1$_{5}$ 4QpGen^{a} 5$_{5}$, + הלך *go* Gn 24$_{58}$ Nm 22$_{35}$ (|| שַׂר *prince*) Jb 34$_{8}$, pi. *go* Si 13$_{13}$, יצא *go out* 1QM 6$_{12}$, ירד *go down* 2 S 19$_{17}$, שׁוב *go back* CD 20$_{11.15}$ ((ע]ם)), רגל hi. *be familiar* Si 8$_{4}$, שׁתה *drink* 4QOrd^{c} 1.1$_{10}$ ((יש]תה ... א]ישׁ)), אסף *gather* life Ps 26$_{9}$, עשׂה *work* Ru 2$_{19}$, יעץ ni. *consult* Si 37$_{11}$, *against* 1QS 9$_{22}$, + שׂרה *struggle* Gn 32$_{29}$, ריב *contend* Si 8$_{1}$, htpol. *dispute* 1QS 9$_{16}$, נצה ni. *struggle* Si 8$_{3}$, עשׂה חֶסֶד עִם *behave loyally to* 2 S 9$_{3}$.

אֵת *with* 1QS 6$_{12}$, + היה *be* Pr 24$_{1}$, ישׁב *dwell* Ex 2$_{21}$ Jg 17$_{11}$, בוא *come* Pr 22$_{24}$, הלך *go* Nm 22$_{20}$, htp. *go about* 1 S 25$_{15}$, עלה *go up* 2$_{19}$, שׁלם hi. *cause to be at peace* Pr 16$_{7}$, *against*, + שׁפט ni. *contend* Pr 29$_{9}$, חשׁב אֵת pi. *keep a check on* 2 K 12$_{16}$.

עַד *towards*, + רוץ *run* 2 K 4$_{22}$, נטה *turn* intrans. Gn 38$_{1}$, *up to, at least* 1QSa 2$_{22}$ CD 13$_{1}$, ממלך גדל [ו]עד אישׁ *from a great king to a (common) man* Nimrud ivory inscr. 1$_{2}$; אַחֲרֵי *behind*, + הלך *go* Gn 24$_{61}$, רדף *pursue* 44$_{4}$ Jos 2$_{5.7}$, דבק hi. *cleave to*, i.e. pursue Jg 20$_{45}$, זנה *prostitute oneself* Lv 20$_{5}$; ישׁב אַחַר *sit behind* 1QS 7$_{20}$, אישׁ אחר אישׁ *one behind the other* 1QM 5$_{4}$, sim. CD 14$_{5}$; סור מֵאַחַר *turn* (intrans.) *from* CD 16$_{4}$; נֶגֶד *in the presence of* Ne 8$_{3}$; לִפְנֵי *before* Pr 14$_{12}$=16$_{25}$ 11QPs^{a} 27$_{3}$, + נוס *flee* Jos 7$_{4}$, פנה *turn* intrans. Jg 20$_{42}$, נתן *give* Gn 43$_{14}$, *place* 2 K 4$_{43}$ Ne 1$_{11}$, עמד *stand* 2 K 5$_{15}$, חזק htp. *resist* 2 C 13$_{7}$; יגר מִפְּנֵי *be afraid of* Dt 1$_{17}$ (+ אֱלֹהִים *God*) Jr 39$_{17}$ (יָגוֹר *fearful*); תַּחַת *from (under)*, + שׂטה *stray* in adultery Nm 5$_{19.20.29}$, נאף pi. *commit adultery* Ezk 16$_{32}$; בֵּין אִישׁ בֵּין אֲנָשִׁים struggle *between men* Dt 25$_{1}$, וּבֵין רֵעֵהוּ *between one man and another* Ex 18$_{16}$ Jr 7$_{5}$, sim. Dt 1$_{16}$ Ezk 18$_{8}$ 1QS 5$_{21}$, בֵּין אִישׁ לְאִשְׁתּוֹ בֵּין־אָב לְבִתּוֹ *between a man and his wife, between a father and his daughter* Nm 30$_{17}$; בְּעַד *concerning* Si 9$_{18}$ (but text prob. corrupt); נֹכַח *opposite* Si 36$_{14}$.

<COLL> הִנֵּה הָאִישׁ *behold, the man* 1 S 9_{17}, אֶרֶץ לֹא־אִישׁ *a land without a man* Jb 38_{26}, חֲדַל אִישִׁים *lacking men* Is 53_{3}, אִישׁ וּבֵיתוֹ *a man and his household* Ex 1_{1} 1 S 27_{3} 2 S 2_{3}, sim. 1 S 1_{21} Jr 23_{34}, אִישׁ וְנַחֲלָתוֹ *a man and his inheritance* Mc 2_{2} (|| גֶּבֶר *man*), אֶת־הָאִישׁ וְאֶת־כָּל־מִשְׁפַּחְתּוֹ *the man and all his family* Jg 1_{25}.

אִישׁ ... רֵעֵהוּ *a man ... his fellow* Gn $11_{3.7}$ 15_{10} 31_{49} 43_{33} etc. 1QS 2_{25} 6_{7} 4Q251 4_{1} ([איש ... רעהו]) 4Q416 7_{10} 4QpsMos^{e} 2.1_{9} ([אי]ש ... לר[ע]הו) 2.1_{9} Siloam tunnel inscr.$_{2.2.4}$ etc., אִישׁ ... אָחִיו *a man ... his brother* Gn 9_{5} 13_{11} 26_{31} 37_{19} 42_{21} etc., אִישׁ ... עֲמִיתוֹ *a man ... his fellow* Lv 19_{11} 24_{19} 25_{17}, איש לפני רעהו *one in front of the other* 1QS 5_{23}, sim. 1QpHab 4_{11}, רְחֹקִים אִישׁ אֶל־אָחִיו *far from each other* Jr 25_{26}, sim. Ne 4_{13}.

איש בשמו *each by his name* Si 46_{11}, איש בסרכו *each in his rank* 1QSa 1_{23}, איש בתכונו *each in his rank* 1QS $6_{8.9}$, אי[ש] על [מצבו] *each at his post* 4QM^{a} fr. $13_{4(Baillet)}$, איש בתרו *each in turn* CD 14_{11}, אִישׁ חָדְשׁוֹ *each (during) his month* 1 K 5_{7}, אִישׁ וְכֵלָיו *each with his weapons* Jr 22_{7}, מֵאָה נְבִאִים ... חֲמִשִּׁים אִישׁ בַּמְּעָרָה *a hundred prophets ..., fifty to each cave* 1 K 18_{4}, sim. 18_{13}, אִישׁ אֶל־עִירוֹ וְאִישׁ אֶל־אַרְצוֹ *each to his city, each to his land* 22_{36}, אִישׁ לְאֹהָלָיו *each to his tents* 2 S 20_{1}.

אִישׁ אִישׁ *each one, anyone* Ex 36_{4} (אִישׁ־אִישׁ) Lv 15_{2} $17_{3.8.10}$, אִישׁ וָאִישׁ *everyone* Ps 87_{5} Est 1_{8} (אִישׁ־וָאִישׁ) 1QS 9_{12} 4QCat^{a} 1_{11}, אִישׁ כְּאָחִיו *each one as the other* Lv 7_{10}.

אִישׁ לְפִי *each according to* Ex 12_{4} $16_{16.18}$ Nm 26_{54} 1QS 5_{24} 1QSa 2_{15} ([אי]ש) $2_{16.21(Barthélemy)}$ (א[יש לפי]) CD $20_{24(mg)}$ 1QH fr. $11_{4(AHL)}$ 4Q181 1_{5}, אִישׁ כְּפִי in same sense Ex 16_{21} Nm 7_{5} 35_{8} 2 C 31_{2}, אִישׁ כְּ in same sense Gn 40_{5} $41_{11.12}$ Dt 16_{17} 1 K 5_{8} 2 K 23_{35} etc. Si 16_{12} 1QS $1_{9.10}$ 6_{4} $9_{15.15.18}$ 11QPs^{a} 22_{10}, אִישׁ לְ in samesense Gn $10_{5.5}$ Ex 16_{16} Nm 1_{4} 2_{34} etc., אִישׁ מִמֶּנּוּ *one of us* Gn 23_{6} Jg 21_{1}, sim. Nm 31_{49} 1 S 30_{17} 2 K 10_{14}.

הָאֲנָשִׁים עַל־הַנָּשִׁים *the men as well as the women* Ex 35_{22}, הָאֲנָשִׁים וְהַנָּשִׁים *the men and the women* Jg 9_{51} 16_{27} Ne 8_{3}, אֲנָשִׁים וְנָשִׁים וָטַף *men, women, and children* Jr 40_{7}, sim. Dt 31_{12} Ezr 10_{1}, אִישׁ עִם־אִשָּׁה *man with woman* Jr 6_{11}, אִישׁ וְאִשָּׁה *man and woman* Ex 35_{29} 36_{6} Jg 9_{49} 16_{27} 1 S 27_{9} etc., אִישׁ־וְאִשָּׁה Jr 44_{7}, אִישׁ אוֹ אִשָּׁה *man or woman* Lv 13_{29}, אִישׁ אוֹ־אִשָּׁה 13_{38} 20_{27} Nm 5_{6} 6_{2} Dt 17_{2}=11QT 55_{16} etc., sim. Dt 17_{5}=11QT 55_{21}, חֲמִיהָ וְאִישָׁהּ *her father-in-law and her husband* 1 S $4_{19.21}$, אִישׁ ... אִשְׁתּוֹ *a man ... his wife* Gn 26_{11} 1 S 25_{3} Ru $1_{1.2}$, אַנְשֵׁי מְחֻקֶּה עַל־הַקִּיר *(images of) men carved on the wall* Ezk 23_{14} (or em. אֲנָשִׁים חֲקֻקִים *men carved*).

וַאֲנָשָׁיו *and his men* following pr.n.m., Saul 1 S $23_{25.26}$, David $23_{5(Qr).24.26.26}$ 24_{3} etc., Abner 2 S 2_{29}, Joab 2_{32}, Ittai 15_{22} (וְכָל־; + טַף *children*), Regem-melech Zc 7_{2}, Hodaviah Lachish ost. 3_{18}, הַמֶּלֶךְ וַאֲנָשָׁיו *the king and his men* 2 S 5_{6}, אֲנִי וַאֲנָשִׁים מְעַט עִמִּי *I and a few men with me* Ne 2_{12}, האנשם את אלישע perh. *the men with Elisha* Arad ost. 24_{19}.

אֱלֹהִים וַאֲנָשִׁים *gods and men* Jg $9_{9.13}$ Si 45_{1} ([א]להים) 11QT 64_{12} 4QShirShab^{a} 2_{3}, sim. Gn 32_{29}, אלים ואנשים *gods and men* 1QM 1_{11} 1QM $14_{17(Baillet)}$ + Sup ([אל]ים) 4QShir^{b} 1_{11}, sim. 1QM 15_{3} + Sup, אל ואנשים *God and men* 11QPs^{a} 27_{3}, לאדון ואנשים *to the Lord and men* Si 10_{7}, אֲנָשִׁים ... יי *Y. ... men* 1 S 2_{26}, אִם־בְּהֵמָה אִם־אִישׁ *whether beast or man* Ex 19_{13}.

אֲנָשִׁים *men* + number., 2. שְׁנֵי(־) Ex 2_{13} Nm 11_{26} Dt 19_{17}=11QT 61_{8} 1 S 10_{2} 28_{8} etc., שְׁנַיִם(־) Jos 2_{1} 6_{22} 1 K 21_{10}; 3. Gn 18_{2} Jos 18_{4} 1 S 10_{3} Ezk $14_{14.16}$ etc. 4QAges 2.2_{2} ([האנשי]ם); 4. 2 K 7_{3}; 5. Gn 47_{2} Jg $18_{2.7.14.17}$; 6. Ezk 9_{2}; 7. 2 S 21_{6}; 8. Jr 41_{15}; 9. 1QM 4_{5}; 10. Jg 6_{27} 20_{10} 2 K 25_{25}||Jr $41_{1.2.8}$ etc. 1QS 6_{3} 1QSa 2_{22} ([אנש]ים) 4QOrd^{a} $2_{3(Allegro)}$ ([עשר]ה) CD 10_{4} 13_{1}; 12. Dt 1_{23} Jos 4_{2} 4QpGen^{a} 3_{2} ([אנש]ים); 20. 2 S 3_{20}; 30. Jr 38_{10}; 50. 2 K 2_{16} 1QM 7_{16}; 200. 1 S 30_{21}; 468. Ne 11_{6}; 500. 1 C 4_{42}; 26,000. 1 C 7_{40}.

אִישׁ collective *men* + number. 12. Nm 1_{44} Jos 3_{12} 4_{4} 1QS 8_{1}; 19. 2 S 2_{30}; 15. 4Q251 3_{7} ([חמשה ע]שר איש); 20. 1 S 14_{14}; 25. Ezk 8_{16} 11_{1}; 30. Jg 14_{19} $20_{31.39}$ 1 S 9_{22}; 36. Jos 7_{5}; 42. 2 K 10_{14}; 50. 2 S 15_{1} 1 K $18_{4.13}$ 2 K $2_{7.17}$ etc.; 70. Nm $11_{16.24.25}$ Jg $9_{2.5}$ etc.; 77. Jg 8_{14}; 80. 2 K 10_{24}; 85. 1 S 22_{18}; 100. Jg 7_{19} 1 K 18_{13} 2 K 4_{43}; 150. Ne 5_{17}; 200. 1 S 18_{27} 30_{10} 2 S 15_{11}; 250. Nm 16_{35} 26_{10}; 300. Jg $7_{6.7.8.16.22}$ etc.; 360. 2 S 2_{31}; 400. Gn 32_{7} 33_{1} 1 S 22_{2} 25_{13} 30_{10}; 450. 1 K 18_{22}; 500. Est $9_{6.12}$; 600. Jg 3_{31} $18_{11.16.17}$ 20_{47} etc.; 700. Jg $20_{15.16}$ 2 K 3_{26}.

1000. Jg 9_{49} $15_{15.16}$ 2 S 10_{6} 19_{18}; 2000. Jos 7_{3} Jg 20_{45}; 3000. Ex 32_{28} Jos $7_{3.4}$ Jg 15_{11} 16_{27} etc; 4000. 1 S 4_{2}; 5000. Jos 8_{12} Jg 20_{45}; 10,000. Jg 1_{4} 3_{29} $4_{6.10.14}$ etc; 12,000. Jg 21_{10} 2 S 10_{6} 17_{1} 11QT 57_{6}; 18,000. Jg $20_{25.44}$; 20,000. 2 S

8$_{4}$||1 C 18$_{4}$; 22,000. Jg 20$_{21}$ 2 S 8$_{5}$||1 C 18$_{5}$; 25,000. Jg 20$_{46}$; 25,100. 20$_{35}$; 26,000. Jg 20$_{15}$; 27,000. 1 K 20$_{30}$; 28,000. 1QM 9$_{5}$; 30,000. Jos 8$_{3}$ 1 K 5$_{27}$; 40,000. 1 C 19$_{18}$; 50,000. 1 S 6$_{19}$; 70,000. 2 S 24$_{15}$||1 C 21$_{14}$ 2 C 2$_{1}$; 80,000; 2 C 2$_{1}$; 120,000. Jg 8$_{10}$; 400,000. Jg 20$_{2.17}$ 2 C 13$_{3}$; 470,000 1 C 21$_{5}$; 500,000. 2 C 13$_{17}$; 800,000. 2 S 24$_{9}$ 2 C 13$_{3}$; 1,100,000. 1 C 21$_{5}$.

Also 11QT 58$_{2}$ 4Q487 1.2$_{6}$ 7$_{3}$ 20$_{3}$ 23$_{2}$ 4QM^{a} fr. 19$_{4}$ (אנ[שי]) 4QRitMar 30$_{2}$ (אנש[י]) 1QH fr. 28$_{3}$ (לאנשי) 1QDM 13$_{2}$ 4QpHos^{b} 5$_{1}$ 4QFlor 6$_{7}$ (לאיש) 4QCat^{a} 5$_{10}$ 7$_{7}$ 12.2$_{8}$ 1Q36 15$_{3}$ (ל[א]יש) 4QCrypt 1.2$_{3}$ 5Q16 3$_{1}$ 4Q251 1$_{6}$ 2$_{3}$ 4Q424 1$_{13}$ 2$_{8}$ 4QToh A 3.2$_{6}$ 4QToh B^{b}$_{1}$ (א[יש]) 4Q298 1$_{3}$ (א[נשי]) 4Q414 1.2$_{8}$ 4Q477$_{1}$ 4QMish C^{b} 3$_{5}$ ([אנש]ים) 4QD^{a} 6.24 ([איש]) 4Q522 2$_{6}$ 4Q416 2$_{4.5}$ 4QapPs^{a} 2$_{6}$ 4QapPs^{b} 75$_{2}$.

אִישׁ־בֹּשֶׁת 11 pr.n.m. **Ish-bosheth**—אִישׁ בֹּשֶׁת, mss אִישְׁבֹּשֶׁת—son of Saul, ident. with Eshbaal (אֶשְׁבַּעַל) at 1 C 8$_{33}$ 9$_{39}$, 2 S 2$_{8}$ (אִישׁ בֹּשֶׁת; mss אִישׁ־בֹּשֶׁת) 2$_{10.12}$ (mss in all three אִישְׁבֹּשֶׁת) 2$_{15}$ (אִישׁ בֹּשֶׁת; mss אִישְׁבֹּשֶׁת/אִישׁ־בֹּשֶׁת) 3$_{8.14.15}$ 4$_{5}$ (both אִישׁ בֹּשֶׁת) 4$_{8.8.12}$ (BHS אִישׁ־בֹּשֶׁת; 4QSam^{a} מפיבשת *Mephibosheth*).

→ אִישׁ *man* + בּוֹשׁ *be ashamed.*

אִישְׁהוֹד 1 pr.n.m. **Ishhod,** son of Hammolecheth, descendant of Manasseh, 1 C 7$_{18}$.

→ אִישׁ *man* + הוֹד *splendour.*

[אִישׁוֹן] 4.1.1 n.[m.] **pupil**—Si אישון; cstr. אִישׁוֹן—<NOM CL> באין אישון יחסר אור *without a pupil, light is lacking* Si 3$_{25}$ (|| דַּעַת *knowledge*). <CSTR> אִישׁוֹן עֵינוֹ *pupil of his* (Y.'s) *eye* Dt 32$_{10}$ 4QToh A 3.1$_{1}$, אִישׁוֹן עֵינֶיךָ *pupil of your* (child's) *eyes* Pr 7$_{2}$, אִישׁוֹן בַּת־עָיִן *pupil of (the daughter of) the eye* Ps 17$_{8}$ (or del. בַּת), אִישׁוֹן לַיְלָה *pupil*, i.e. very middle, *of night* Pr 7$_{9}$ (or em. אֱשׁוּן *beginning of*), אִישׁוֹן חֹשֶׁךְ *pupil*, i.e. middle, *of darkness* 20$_{20(Kt)}$ (Qr אֱשׁוּן). <PREP> בְּ of place/time, *in, at,* + הלך *go* (of lad) Pr 7$_{9}$ (or em. בֶּאֱשׁוּן *at the beginning of*), דעך *be extinguished* (of lamp) 20$_{20(Kt)}$ (Qr בֶּאֱשׁוּן); כְּ *as,* + נצר *keep* Israel (of Y.) Dt 32$_{10}$, שׁמר *keep* worshipper, instruction Ps 17$_{8}$ Pr 7$_{2}$. <COLL> גולת אל את אישון עינו appar. *God's revelation of,* or *exiling of, the apple of his eye* 4QToh A 3.1$_{1}$.

→ אִישׁ *man.*

[אֱישׁוֹן], see אֱשׁוּן.

אִישׁ־טוֹב 2 pr.n.m. **Ishtob**—אִישׁ טוֹב—ally of Ammonites against David (unless אִישׁ(־)טוֹב = *man,* i.e. warriors, *of Tob*), 2 S 10$_{6}$ (אִישׁ טוֹב; 4QSam^{a} [א]ישטוב) 10$_{8}$.

אִישַׁי, see יִשַׁי.

אִיתוֹן 1 n.m. **entrance**—Kt יאתון, Q (Allegro) אתון—וְעַל פְּנֵי הַשַּׁעַר הָאִיתוֹן *and at the front of the gate, the entrance,* i.e. the entrance gate, Ezk 40$_{15(Qr)}$ (or em. וּמִלִּפְנֵי הַשַּׁעַר הַחִיצוֹן *and from before the outer gate,* or אִתְיוֹן הַשַּׁעַר *entrance of the gate;* + הַשַּׁעַר הַפְּנִימִי *the inner gate*), מיד אתון *beside (the) entrance* of temple court 3QTr 8$_{2(Allegro)}$ (others מזרח אחזור *east of Hazor;* see אחזור).

אִיתַי, see אִתַּי.

אִיתִיאֵל 3 pr.n.m. **Ithiel, 1.** appar. recipient of words of Agur, Pr 30$_{1.1}$ (or em. לָאִיתִי אֵל *I am weary, O God,* or לְאֵה אֶת־[הָ]אֵל *one who has wearied himself with God* or לֹא אָנֹכִי/אֲנִי אֵל *I am not God* or לֹא אִתִּי אֵל *God is not with me* or לוּ אִתִּי אֵל *if only God were with me*). **2.** son of Jeshaiah and father of Maaseiah, descendant of Benjamin, Ne 11$_{7}$.

→ אֵל *God.*

אִיתָמָר 21.0.2 pr.n.m. **Ithamar,** son of Aaron and Elisheba, Ex 6$_{23}$ 28$_{1}$ 38$_{21}$ Lv 10$_{6.12.16}$ Nm 3$_{2.4}$ 4$_{28.33}$ 7$_{8}$ 26$_{60}$ 1 C 5$_{29}$ 24$_{1+6t}$ Ezr 8$_{2}$ 1QM 17$_{3}$ 4QPsJos^{b} 17$_{5}$.

אֵיתָן I 14.1.1 adj. **continuous**—אֵתָן; sf. אֵיתָנוֹ; pl. אֵיתָנִים (אֵתָנִים)—**a.** as predicative adj. or noun, **continuous (one), continuity, perennial (one), eternal (one), eternity, reliable (one), reliability.**

<SUBJ> שׁמע *hear* Mc 6$_{2}$ (or em.; see App.). <NOM CL> + דֶּרֶךְ *way* of traitors Pr 13$_{15}$ (or em. אֵידָם

their disaster), רִיב *strife* of bones of afflicted Jb 33$_{19(Kt)}$ (Qr רוֹב *multitude* of bones), מוֹשָׁב *dwelling place* of Kenites Nm 24$_{21}$. **<OBJ>** סלף pi. *overthrow* Jb 12$_{19}$ (|| כֹּהֵן *priest,* שֹׁפֵט *judge,* יֹעֵץ *counsellor,* + מֶלֶךְ *king,* נֶאֱמָן *reliable one).*

<CSTR> נְוֵה אֵיתָן *pasture of continuity* or *dwelling place of an eternal one* Jr 49$_{19}$ 50$_{44}$ (both + גְּאוֹן הַיַּרְדֵּן *swelling of the Jordan),* נַהֲרוֹת אֵיתָן *rivers of continuity* Ps 74$_{15}$. **<APP>** הָאֵתָנִים מֹסְדֵי אָרֶץ *the reliable ones, foundations of (the) earth* Mc 6$_{2}$ (or em. וְהַאֲזִינוּ *and hear!;* || הָר *mountain).*

<PREP> שׁוּב לְאֵיתָנוֹ *go back to its continuity,* i.e. to its normal state (of sea) Ex 14$_{27}$; וַתֵּשֶׁב בְּאֵיתָן קַשְׁתּוֹ *and his* (Joseph's) *bow dwelt as a continuous one* Gn 49$_{24}$ (or em. וַתִּשָּׁבֵר *and* his *bow was broken* by an eternal one, i.e. Y.), חָכְמוֹת תָּשִׂים בְּאֵיתָן בֵּיתָהּ *wisdom places her house with reliability,* i.e. securely Pr 14$_{1}$ (if em. חַכְמוֹת נָשִׁים בָּנְתָה בֵּיתָהּ *the wisest one of women has built her house).*

b. perh. as attributive adj. (unless cstr.), of נַחַל *stream* Dt 21$_{4}$=11QT 63$_{2}$ Am 5$_{24}$ Si 40$_{13(B)}$ (|| אַדִּיר *majestic),* גּוֹי *nation* Jr 5$_{15}$ (+ מֵעוֹלָם *from of old).*

c. as pr.n.m. of month, **Ethanim,** ... יֶרַח הָאֵתָנִים הַחֹדֶשׁ הַשְּׁבִיעִי *the month of Ethanim ... the seventh month* 1 K 8$_{2}$.

→ אֵיתָן *Ethan.*

אֵיתָן II 8 pr.n.m. **Ethan, 1.** Ethan the Ezrahite (הָאֶזְרָחִי), perh. ident. with following, 1 K 5$_{11}$ Ps 89$_{1}$. **2.** Levitical singer, son of Kishi (1 C 6$_{29}$ [mss קוּשִׁי *Kushi*]) or Kushaiah (1 C 15$_{17}$), 1 C 6$_{29}$ 15$_{17.19}$. **3.** Levite, ancestor of Asaph, colleague of preceding, 1 C 6$_{27}$. **4.** son of Zerah and father of Azariah, descendant of Judah, 1 C 2$_{6.8}$.

→ אֵיתָן *reliable.*

[אֵיתָנִים], see אֵיתָן I.

אַךְ 164.10.1 adv. **surely, only, however, 1.** asseverative **surely, certainly, indeed,** (1) in nom. cl., אַךְ הִנֵּה אִשְׁתְּךָ *surely she is your wife* Gn 26$_{9}$, אַךְ עַצְמִי וּבְשָׂרִי אָתָּה *surely you are my bone and my flesh* 29$_{14}$, אַךְ ... יוֹם הַכִּפֻּרִים הוּא *surely ... it is the day of atonement* Lv 23$_{27}$, אַךְ נֶגֶד י׳ מְשִׁיחוֹ *surely before Y. is his anointed* 1 S 16$_{6}$, אַךְ מֶלֶךְ־יִשְׂרָאֵל הוּא *surely it is the king of Israel* 1 K 22$_{32}$, אַךְ־אֱוִלִים שָׂרֵי צֹעַן *surely the princes of Zoan are fools* Is 19$_{11}$, אַךְ בָּךְ אֵל *surely God is with you* Is 45$_{14}$, אַךְ־עַמִּי הֵמָּה *surely they are my people* 63$_{8}$, אַךְ זֶה חֳלִי *surely this is my sickness* Jr 10$_{19}$, אַךְ־פְּרִי לַצַּדִּיק *surely there is a reward for the righteous* Ps 58$_{12}$, אַךְ יֵשׁ־אֱלֹהִים *surely there is a God* who judges 58$_{12}$, אַךְ טוֹב לְיִשְׂרָאֵל אֱלֹהִים *surely God is good to Israel* 73$_{1}$, אַךְ קָרוֹב לִירֵאָיו יִשְׁעוֹ *surely his salvation is near to those who fear him* 85$_{10}$, אַךְ־אֵלֶּה מִשְׁכְּנוֹת עַוָּל *surely these are dwellings of an evil person* Jb 18$_{21}$, מַחְשְׁבוֹת חָרוּץ אַךְ־לְמוֹתָר *the plans of the diligent are,* i.e. lead, *surely to abundance* Pr 21$_{5}$, אך קנאה דאגה ופחד *surely there is envy, trouble and fear* Si 40$_{5}$.

(2) with perfect verb, שׁמר *guard* 1 S 25$_{21}$, היה *be* 2 K 24$_{3}$ Ho 12$_{12}$, רגע hi. *repose* Is 34$_{14}$, קבץ ni. *be gathered* 34$_{15}$, שׁוב *turn* Jr 2$_{35}$, עשׁר *be rich* Ho 12$_{9}$, עצה *plan* Ps 62$_{5}$, זכה pi. *keep clean* 73$_{13}$, לאה hi. *make weary* Jb 16$_{7}$, זור *be estranged* 19$_{13}$, אמר *say* 33$_{8}$, קוה pi. *wait for* Lm 2$_{16}$.

(3) with imperfect verb, דרשׁ *require* Gn 9$_{5}$, אות ni. *consent* 34$_{23}$, שׁבת hi. *remove* Ex 12$_{15}$, אכל *eat* Dt 12$_{22}$, שׁמר *observe* Ex 31$_{13}$, חגג *celebrate* Lv 23$_{39}$, ירא *fear* Zp 3$_{7}$, רדף *follow* Ps 23$_{6}$ (or §2), מחץ *shatter* 68$_{22}$, שׁית *set* 73$_{18}$, מצה *drain* by drinking 75$_{9}$, שׁוף *crush* 139$_{11}$, ידה hi. *praise* 140$_{14}$, שׂים *set* Jb 23$_{6}$, שׁלח *stretch out* hand 30$_{24}$, שׁמע *hear* 35$_{13}$, שׁוב *do again* Lm 3$_{3}$ (+ הפך *turn).*

(4) with imperative, ידע *know* 2 K 5$_{7}$, ראה *see* 5$_{7}$, ירא *fear* 1 S 12$_{24}$.

(5) with participle, בהל ni. *be sudden* Zp 1$_{18}$.

(6) with infinitive absolute + perfect verb, טרף pu. *be torn* Gn 44$_{28}$; + participle, נגף ni. *be struck down* Jg 20$_{39}$.

(7) with adjective, תֶּהְגּוּ אַךְ־נְכָאִים *you shall mourn, utterly stricken* Is 16$_{7}$.

2a. restrictive **only, except,** (1) in nom. cl., וְעוֹד לוֹ אַךְ הַמְּלוּכָה *what else is there for him except the kingdom?* 1 S 18$_{8}$, אַךְ־דְּבַר־שְׂפָתַיִם עֵצָה *apart from words, is there a plan?* 2 K 18$_{20}$||Is 36$_{5}$, אַךְ בַּי׳ .... צְדָקוֹת וָעֹז *only in Y. ... are righteousness and strength* Is 45$_{24}$, אַךְ־דַּלִּים הֵם *these are only the poor* Jr 5$_{4}$,

אַךְ אֶל־אֱלֹהִים דּוּמִיָּה נַפְשִׁי *only in God is there quiet for my soul* 62$_{2}$, sim. 62$_{6}$, אַךְ־הוּא צוּרִי וִישׁוּעָתִי מִשְׂגַּבִּי *he alone is my rock and my salvation; he is my fortress* 62$_{3.7}$, אַךְ הֶבֶל בְּנֵי־אָדָם *human beings are only a breath* 62$_{10}$, sim. 39$_{12}$, תַּאֲוַת צַדִּיקִים אַךְ־טוֹב *the desire of the righteous is*, i.e. brings, *only good* Pr 11$_{23}$, אַךְ־לְמַחְסוֹר *it is*, i.e. leads, *only to lack* 11$_{24}$ 14$_{23}$ 21$_{5}$ 22$_{16}$.

(2) with perfect verb, דבר pi. *speak* Nm 12$_{2}$, ידע *know* 1 S 20$_{39}$, שׁמר ni. *keep oneself* 1 S 21$_{5}$, היה *be* 2 S 2$_{10}$, נחל *inherit* Jr 16$_{19}$, נצב ni. *stand* Ps 39$_{6}$, עמד *stand* Ezr 10$_{15}$; with perfect + waw, Dt 16$_{15}$ 28$_{29}$.

(3) with imperfect verb, אות ni. *consent* Gn 34$_{15.22}$, אכל ni. *be eaten* Ex 12$_{16}$, דבר pi. *speak* Nm 22$_{20}$, היה *be* Ezk 46$_{17}$, הלך htp. *walk back and forth* Ps 39$_{7}$, המה *be in commotion* 39$_{7}$, כאב *be in pain* Jb 14$_{22}$, בקשׁ pi. *seek* Pr 17$_{11}$, עשׂה *do* Jb 13$_{20}$; with imperfect verb + waw, שׁאר ni. *remain* Gn 7$_{23}$.

(4) with imperative, ידע *know* Jr 3$_{13}$.

(5) with participle, סכך hi. *cover* feet, i.e. relieve oneself Jg 3$_{24}$ (or §1), עשׂה *do* Jr 32$_{30}$ (+ היה *be*), כעס hi. *provoke* 32$_{30}$.

(6) with infinitive construct, פשׁט pi. *strip* 2 S 23$_{10}$, רעע hi. *do evil* Ps 37$_{8}$.

2b. אַךְ הַפַּעַם **only this time,** i.e. **once more,** (1) with imperfect verb, דבר pi. *speak* Gn 18$_{32}$ Jg 6$_{39}$ (+ רַק הַפַּעַם *once more*). (2) with imperative, נשׂא *forgive* Ex 10$_{17}$, חזק pi. *strengthen* Jg 16$_{28}$.

3a. adversative **however, but, yet,** (1) in nom. cl., אַךְ לֹא בַת־אִמִּי *but* she is *not my mother's daughter* Gn 20$_{12}$, אך יש אוכל *but there is food* Si 36$_{23(B)}$ (Bmg מאכל *food*), אך יש אשה *yet there is a* beautiful *woman* 36$_{26(Bmg)}$, אך יש אהב *but there is a friend* 37$_{1}$, אך יש יועץ דרך *but there is one who counsels a way* 37$_{7}$.

(2) with perfect verb, אמר *say* 1 S 29$_{9}$, שׁוב *turn* intrans. 2 K 23$_{26}$, ערך hi. *tax* 23$_{35}$, עבד hi. *burden* Is 43$_{24}$, יגע hi. *make weary* 43$_{24}$, שׁבר *break* Jr 5$_{5}$, נתק pi. *tear* 5$_{5}$, היה *be* Jr 26$_{24}$, נשׂג hi. *overtake* Zc 1$_{6}$, שׁכן *dwell* Ps 68$_{7}$, סור *turn aside* intrans. 1 S 12$_{20}$ 2 K 13$_{6}$, *be removed* 1 K 22$_{44}$‖2 C 20$_{33}$, כנע ni. *be humbled* 2 C 30$_{11}$.

(3) with imperfect verb, דבר pi. *speak* Jr 12$_{1}$, אכל *eat* Gn 9$_{4}$ Lv 11$_{4.21}$ Dt 14$_{7}$, היה *be* Lv 11$_{36}$ Nm 36$_{6}$ Jos 3$_{4}$, בוא *enter* Lv 21$_{23}$, נגשׁ *touch* 21$_{23}$, קדשׁ hi. *dedicate* 27$_{26}$, מכר ni. *be sold* 27$_{28}$, גאל ni. *be redeemed* 27$_{28}$, פדה *redeem* Nm 18$_{17}$ Ps 49$_{16}$, מרד *rebel* Nm 14$_{9}$, נתן *give* 1 C 22$_{12}$, פקד *number* Nm 1$_{49}$, חלק ni. *be apportioned* 26$_{55}$, בחן ni. *be tested* 1QS 9$_{1}$, חטא htp. *be purified* Nm 31$_{23}$, מות *die* Dt 18$_{20}$, קום hi. *establish* 1 S 1$_{23}$, עשׂה *do, make* 1 K 11$_{12}$ Jr 30$_{11}$, ni. *be made* 2 K 12$_{14}$, ענה pi. *afflict* 1 K 11$_{39}$, יסף hi. *do again* Jon 2$_{5}$ (+ נבט hi. *look*), חשׁב ni. *be accounted* 2 K 22$_{7}$, עלה *go up* 23$_{9}$, ירד ho. *be brought down* Is 14$_{15}$, עבר hi. *make pass through* Nm 31$_{22}$, קרב *draw near* 18$_{3}$, יכח hi. *defend* Jb 13$_{15}$ (or §2), ריב *dispute* Ho 4$_{4}$, יעץ ni. *consult* Si 37$_{12}$, כרת ni. *be cut off* 41$_{11}$, בושׁ *be ashamed* 42$_{1}$, נחל *obtain property* 45$_{22}$.

(4) with imperative, שׁמע *hear* Gn 27$_{13}$ Jr 28$_{7}$ 34$_{4}$, היה *be* 1 S 18$_{17}$, לחם ni. *fight* 18$_{17}$, נצל hi. *deliver* Jg 10$_{15}$, שׁמר *keep*, i.e. spare, life Jb 2$_{6}$, עשׂה *make* 1 K 17$_{13}$, יסר pi. *train* Jr 10$_{24}$.

(5) with participle, שׁאל *request* 2 S 3$_{13}$.

(6) with infinitive absolute + imperfect verb, פדה *redeem* Nm 18$_{15}$, עוד hi. *warn* 1 S 8$_{9}$ (אַךְ כִּי *except that*), ידע *know* Jr 26$_{15}$.

3b. אַךְ אִם **but if,** introducing conditional sentence, אַךְ אִם־אַתָּה לוּ שְׁמָעֵנִי *but if you will, hear me* Gn 23$_{13}$, אַךְ אִם־טְמֵאָה אֶרֶץ אֲחֻזַּתְכֶם עִבְרוּ לָכֶם אֶל־אֶרֶץ *but if the land of your possession is unclean, pass over into the land of* Jos 22$_{19}$, אַךְ אִם־יוֹם אוֹ יוֹמַיִם יַעֲמֹד לֹא יֻקַּם *but if he* (slave) *survives a day or two, he* (the master) *shall not be punished* Ex 21$_{21}$.

4. restrictive in temporal sequence **hardly, just when,** (1) with perfect verb, עלה *go up* 1 K 9$_{24}$. (2) with infinitive absolute + perfect verb, יצא *leave* Gn 27$_{30}$, קום hi. *set* Jg 7$_{19}$.

אַכַּד 1 pl.n. **Accad,** Mesopotamian city, perh. near Sippar (T. Abū Ḥabba), Gn 10$_{10}$.

אַכְזָב 2 adj. **deceptive,** alw. as noun, **deceptive one,** בָּתֵּי אַכְזִיב לְאַכְזָב לְמַלְכֵי יִשְׂרָאֵל *the houses of Achzib are as one that is deceptive for the kings of Israel* Mc 1$_{14}$ (or em. יוֹשֶׁבֶת *the one that dwells of*, i.e. in, Achzib, or בַּת *daughter of* Achzib and/or לְמֶלֶךְ *for the king of*), תִּהְיֶה לִי כְּמוֹ אַכְזָב מַיִם לֹא נֶאֱמָנוּ *you are to me as one that is deceptive, (as) waters that are not reliable*

Jr 15$_{18}$. → כָּזַר *lie.*

[אַכְזִב], see אַכְזִיב.

אַכְזִיב 4 pl.n. **Achzib**—+ ־ה of direction אַכְזִ֫יבָה—**1.** town in lowland of Judah, appar. ident. with Chezib (כְּזִיב) at Gn 38$_{5}$, perh. T. el-Bēḍā (Ḥorbat Lavnīn) N of Lachish, Jos 15$_{44}$ Mc 1$_{14}$ perh. Lachish ost. 8$_{6}$ (but perh. אֲכַזֵּב *I shall lie;* others אֶכְתֹּב *I shall write*) 22$_{10}$ (בית אכזי[ב] *house of Achzib* unless *Beth-achzib,* as separate pl.n.). **2.** coastal town in Asher, perh. Ez-Zīb (T. Akzīv) 15 km N of Akko, Jos 19$_{29}$ Jg 1$_{31}$.

אַכְזָר 4 adj. **cruel, fierce, 1.** used attributively of ראשׁ *poison* Dt 32$_{33}$. **2.** used predicatively or as noun, **cruel (one), fierce (one),** לֹא־אַכְזָר כִּי יְעוּרֶ֫נּוּ *he is not (so) fierce,* or *there is none (so) fierce, that he will rouse himself* Jb 41$_{2}$ (mss יְעִירֶ֫נּוּ *he will rouse him*), תֵּהָפֵךְ לְאַכְזָר לִי *you turn into one that is cruel to me* 30$_{21}$, בַּת־עַמִּי לְאַכְזָר *the daughter of my people has become cruel* Lm 4$_{3}$ (or em. בְּנוֹת *daughters of*).

→ אַכְזָרִי *cruel,* אַכְזְרִיּוּת *cruelty.*

אַכְזָרִי 8.4.2 adj. **cruel**—Q אגזרי; fem. Q אכזריה—**1a.** used attributively of מַלְאָךְ *messenger* Pr 17$_{11}$, מוּסָר Jr 30$_{14}$ (if em., see §2a Cstr.); יוֹם־י׳ בָּא אַכְזָרִי *the day of Y. is coming, a cruel (day)* Is 13$_{9}$ (1QIsa[a] אגזרי; perh. אַכְזָרִי = *cruelty,* as §2b). **b.** used predicatively of nation Jr 6$_{23}$=50$_{42}$ (+ לֹא יְרַחֵמוּ *they have no compassion*), רַחֲמִים *compassion* of the wicked Pr 12$_{10}$, בַּת *daughter* 4QapLam[a] 1.2$_{4}$.

2. used as noun, **a. cruel one,** <SUBJ> עכר *trouble* Pr 11$_{17}$ (+ אִישׁ חֶסֶד *kind man*). <CSTR> מוּסַר אַכְזָרִי *chastisement of a cruel one* Jr 30$_{14}$ (|| איב ptc. *enemy;* or em. מוּסָר אַכְזָרִי *cruel chastisement*), מתני *loins of* Si 32$_{22}$. <PREP> לְ נתן *give* years *to* Pr 5$_{9}$ (|| אַחֵר *another person*); עִם *with,* + הלך *go* Si 8$_{15}$, יעץ ni. *consult* 37$_{11}$ (+ על טוב בשר *about physical fitness,* איש רע *evil man*).

2b. cruelty, <NOM CL> רוח עולה ... אכזרי ורוב חנף *the spirit of falsehood is ... cruelty and much hypocrisy* 1QS 4$_{9}$. <OBJ> נתן *give,* i.e. practise Si 13$_{12}$ (+ לא יחמל *does not spare*).

→ אַכְזָר *cruel.*

[אַכְזְרִיּוּת] 1 n.[m.] **cruelty**—appar. cstr. אַכְזְרִיּוּת—אַכְזְרִיּוּת חֵמָה *(there is) cruelty of anger,* or, *cruelty is anger* Pr 27$_{4}$ (|| שֶׁטֶף *overflow* of wrath, + קִנְאָה *jealousy*).

→ אַכְזָר *cruel.*

אֲכִילָה 1 n.f. **meal,** וַיֹּאכַל וַיִּשְׁתֶּה וַיֵּלֶךְ בְּכֹחַ הָאֲכִילָה הַהִיא *and he* (Elijah) *ate and drank, and he went in the strength of,* i.e. given him by, *that meal* 1 K 19$_{8}$.

→ אכל *eat.*

אָכִישׁ 21 pr.n.m. **Achish,** Philistine king of Gath, 1 S 21$_{11.12.13.15}$ 27$_{2+6t}$ 28$_{1.2.2}$ 29$_{2.3.6.8.9}$ 1 K 2$_{39.40}$.

אכל 809.11.100 vb. **eat**—**Qal** Pf. 3ms אָכַל (אָכָ֑ל, אֲכָלַ֫נִי, אֲכָלַ֫תְהוּ ,אֲכָלַתְךָ), 3fs אָכְלָה (אָכָ֑לָה ,אֲכָלַ֫תְנִי ,אֲכָלַ֫תְךְ ,אֲכָלוֹ), 2ms אָכַ֫לְתָּ (אָכָ֑לְתָּ ,אֲכַלְתֶּ֫הוּ), 2fs Qr אָכַלְתְּ (Kt אכלתי), 1cs אָכַ֫לְתִּי (אָכָ֑לְתִּי), 3mpl אָכְלוּ (אָכָ֫לוּ ,אֲכָלוּם), 2mpl אֲכַלְתֶּם (Q אכלתמה), אָכַ֫לְנוּ.

Impf. יֹאכַל (יֹאכֵ֑ל, Q יוכל ,יֹאכְלֶ֫נּוּ ,יֹאכְלֶ֫נָּה ,יֹאכְלֵ֫מוֹ, Q יוכלם ,יֹאכְלֵם ,יואכלנה Q), 3fs תֹּאכַל (תֹּאכֵ֑ל, תֹּאכְלֵ֫הוּ ,תֹּאכְלֶ֫נּוּ ,תֹּאכְלֵךְ ,תואכל Q ,תוכל Q), 2ms תֹּאכַל (תֹּאכֵ֑ל ,תֹּאכְלֶ֫נּוּ ,תֹּאכְלֵם ,תֹּאכְלֵם), תֹּאכְלֶ֫נָּה ,תואכלנו Q ,תֹּאכְלֶ֫נּוּ ,תֹּאכֲלֶנּוּ ,תואכל Q), 2fs תֹּאכְלִי, 1cs אֹכַל (אֹכֵ֑ל ,אֹכְלָה ,(תואכלנה Q)), 3mpl יֹאכְלוּ (יֹאכֵ֫לוּ ,יוֹכְלוּ ,יֹאכְלוּן ,יֹאכֵלוּן ,Q יואכלו ,יֹאכְלֻהוּ ,יֹאכְלוּהָ ,יֹאכְלוּם ,Q יא[וכ]לום), 3fpl תֹּאכַ֫לְנָה, 2mpl תֹּאכְלוּ (תֹּאכְלוּן ,תֹּאכֵ֫לוּ ,Q תוכלו ,Q תואכלו ,תֹּאכְלֻ֫הוּ ,תֹּאכְלוּם), 1cpl נֹאכַל (נֹאכֵ֑ל).

+ waw 3ms וַאֲכָלָ֫הּ, 3fs וַאֲכָלָ֫תַם, 2fs וְאָכַלְתְּ (Si, Q ואכלתה), 3mpl וַאֲכָלֻ֫הוּ (Q ואכלוהו), 1cpl וַאֲכַלְנֻהוּ; 3ms וַיֹּאכַל (וַיֹּאכֵ֑ל, Si ויאכלם), 3fs וַתֹּאכַל (וַתֹּאכֵ֑ל), 2ms וַתֹּאכַל, 1cs וָאֹכַל (וָאֹכֵ֑ל ,וָאֹכְלָה ,וָאֹכֵלָה) וָאֹכְלֵם, 3mpl וַיֹּאכְלוּ (וַיֹּאכֵ֫לוּ ,וַיֹּאכְלוּ), 2fpl וַתֹּאכַ֫לְנָה, 1cpl וַנֹּאכְלָה (וַנֹּאכֵלָה ,וַנֹּאכְלֶ֫נּוּ ,וַנֹּאכְלֵהוּ).

Impv. אֱכוֹל (אֱכֹל ,אֱכָל־ ,אֱכֹל ,וְאֶכְלָה), אִכְלוּ (וֶאֱכֹ֫לוּ); ptc. אֹכֵל (אוֹכֵל ,אֹכֵל ,אֹכְלָה ,(אֹכֵלָה) ,אֹכְלֵהוּ ,אֹכְלֹהוּ) ,וְאֹכְלוּהָ) אֹכֶ֫לֶת, אֹכְלִים (Q אוכלים ,אכלין ,Q אוכלת ,אֹכֶ֫לֶת), sf. אֹכְלַיִךְ ,אֹכְלֵי (Q או[כלי], אֹכְלֶ֫יהָ ,אֹכְלָיו); inf. אָכֹל (אֱכוֹל ,אֱכֹל), אֱכֹל־ ,אֲכָלְךָ ,אֲכָלוֹ ,אָכְלָה ,אָכְלֵנוּ ,אֲכָלְכֶם (אֱכֹל ,אֱכוֹל ,אֱכָל־ ,אֶכְלְךָ), אָכְלָם, Q אוכלמה).

אכל

1. eat food or ingredients of food, oft. sacrificial food, e.g. Gn 31$_{46}$ Ex 12$_{7+15t}$ 29$_{33.33}$ Lv 6$_{22}$ 7$_{6}$ Nm 18$_{11}$ 25$_{2}$ 1 S 9$_{13.13.13.19.24.24}$ Ps 106$_{28}$.

<SUBJ> named man, Gn 9$_{4}$ 25$_{34}$ (|| קום *arise*, הלך *go*) 26$_{30}$ (both || שתה *drink*) 27$_{4.7.10.19}$ (|| ישב *sit*) 27$_{25.25}$ (|| שתה) 27$_{31.33}$ 31$_{38.46}$ (+ שָׁם *there*) Ex 29$_{32.33}$ 34$_{28}$ (|| שתה) Lv 6$_{9.9}$ 8$_{31}$ (|| בשל pi. *boil*; + שָׁם) 8$_{31}$ 10$_{12}$ (|| לקח *take*) 10$_{13.14.17.18.19}$ 24$_{9}$ Dt 9$_{9.18}$ (both || שתה) Jg 14$_{9}$ (|| הלך) 1 S 9$_{19.24.24}$ 20$_{5}$ (+ ישב) 20$_{34}$ 28$_{20.22.23.25}$ 2 S 9$_{7.10.11.13}$ (+ ישב) 11$_{11}$ (|| שתה, שכב *lie* with wife) 11$_{13}$ (|| שתה) 12$_{20}$ (+ שים *set* table) 12$_{21}$ (|| קום, :: צום *fast*; + בכה *weep*) 13$_{5}$ (|| ראה *see*) 13$_{9.11}$ 17$_{29}$ 19$_{36}$ (|| שתה) 1 K 1$_{25}$ (|| שתה; + אמר *say*) 14$_{1}$ 18$_{41.42}$ (|| עלה *go up*, שתה) 19$_{5}$ (|| קום) 19$_{6}$ (|| שתה, קום, שוב *go back*, שכב) 19$_{7}$ (|| קום) 19$_{8}$ (|| שתה, קום) 21$_{4.5.7}$ (|| קום, טוב *be good*) 2 K 4$_{8.8}$ 9$_{34}$ (|| שתה; + בוא *come*) 19$_{29.29}$||Is 37$_{30.30}$ (+ זרע *sow*, קצר *harvest*, נטע *plant*) 2 K 25$_{29}$ Is 7$_{15}$ Jr 16$_{8}$ (|| שתה) 41$_{1}$ (+ שָׁם) 51$_{34}$ (|| המם *discomfit*, בלע *swallow*, מלא pi. *fill* stomach) 52$_{33}$ Hg 1$_{6}$ (+ אֵין־לְשָׂבְעָה *without satisfaction*; || שתה, לבש *be clothed*) Jb 31$_{17}$ 42$_{11}$ Ru 3$_{7}$ (|| שתה, יטב *be good*) Est 4$_{16}$ Dn 1$_{12}$ (|| שתה) 10$_{3}$ (|| סוך *anoint oneself*) Ezr 10$_{6}$ Ne 5$_{14}$.

Adam and Eve Gn 3$_{1.2.3}$ (|| נגע *touch*) 3$_{5}$ (see also below, אָדָם *human being*), Hannah 1 S 1$_{7.8}$ (both :: בכה *weep*) 1$_{9}$ (|| שתה *drink*), Ruth Ru 2$_{14}$ (|| נגש *approach*, טבל *dip*) 2$_{14}$ (|| ישב, שבע, יתר hi. *leave*).

Israel, Israelite(s) Ex 34$_{15.18}$ Dt 2$_{28}$ (|| שתה *drink*) 6$_{11}$ (|| שבע *be satisfied*) 8$_{9.10.12}$ (both || שבע) 11$_{15}$ (|| שבע) 12$_{7}$ (|| שמח *be merry*; + שָׁם *there*) 12$_{15}$ (|| זבח *sacrifice*) 12$_{16}$.(:: שפך *pour*) 12$_{17.18}$ (|| שמח) 12$_{20.21}$ (|| זבח) 12$_{22.23.23.24}$ (:: שפך) 12$_{25.27}$ (:: שפך ni. *be poured*) 14$_{3.4.6.7.8}$ (|| נגע *touch*) 14$_{9.9.10.11.12.20.21.23.26}$ (|| שמח) 15$_{22.23}$ 16$_{3.8}$ 20$_{14}$=11QT 62$_{11}$, 20$_{19}$ 26$_{14}$ 28$_{31.53.55}$ 29$_{5}$ (|| שתה) 32$_{13}$ 1 K 4$_{20}$ (|| שתה, שמח) Is 1$_{19}$ Jr 2$_{7}$ 7$_{21}$ Ezk 4$_{16}$ (|| שתה) Ho 8$_{13}$ Jl 2$_{26}$ (|| שבע, הלל pi. *praise*) Am 6$_{4}$ 9$_{14}$ (|| ישב *sit*, שתה) Mc 6$_{14}$ (:: שבע; || סוג hi. *remove*) Ps 78$_{24.29}$ (|| שבע) 106$_{28}$ (|| צמד ni. *join*) Pr 23$_{7}$ (|| שתה) 23$_{8}$ 25$_{16}$ 2 C 31$_{10}$ (|| יתר hi. *have food left over*; both || שבע) Ezr 9$_{12}$ (|| חזק *be strong*) 4QOrd^{a} 1.2$_{4}$ (|| כנס *gather*) CD 3$_{6}$ 4Q416 9.1$_{20}$ 4QJub^{a} 2$_{3}$, Jerusalem Ezk 16$_{13}$, Ephraim Ho 9$_{3}$ (|| שוב *go back*).

בְּנֵי־יִשְׂרָאֵל *people of Israel* Gn 32$_{33}$ Ex 16$_{3}$ (+ לָשֹׂבַע *to satisfaction*) 16$_{12}$ (|| שבע *be satisfied*) 16$_{25.35.35}$ 22$_{30}$ 23$_{15}$ Lv 3$_{17}$ 7$_{23\ 24.25.26}$ 11$_{2.3.4.8}$ (|| נגע *touch*) 11$_{9.9.11}$ (|| שקץ pi. *make detestable*) 11$_{21.22.40}$ (|| נשא *carry*) 11$_{42}$ 17$_{14.14}$ 22$_{16}$ 23$_{6\ 14}$ 25$_{12.19}$ (+ לָשֹׂבַע *to satisfaction*; || ישב *sit*) 25$_{20.22.22}$ 26$_{5}$ (+ לָשֹׂבַע; || ישב) 26$_{10.26}$ (:: שבע), 26$_{29.29}$ Nm 11$_{5}$ 15$_{19}$ Dt 31$_{20}$ (|| דשן *grow fat*, שבע) Jos 5$_{11.12.12}$ Ezk 4$_{13}$ Ezr 6$_{21}$, בֵּית יִשְׂרָאֵל *house of Israel* Ezk 24$_{22}$ (|| עטה *cover* lip).

עַם *people* Ex 13$_{6}$, Nm 11$_{13.18.18.19.21}$ 23$_{24}$ (|| שתה *drink*) 25$_{2}$ Dt 2$_{6}$ (|| שתה) 27$_{7}$ (+ שָׁם *there*; || זבח *slaughter*, שמח *be merry*) 28$_{33}$ Jos 24$_{13}$ 1 S 9$_{13}$ 14$_{30.32.33}$ 1 K 19$_{21}$ 2 K 4$_{41.42.43.43.44}$ Is 65$_{4}$ Is 65$_{21}$ Ho 4$_{10}$ (:: שבע, || זנה hi. *fornicate*) Ne 5$_{2}$ (|| לקח *take*, חיה *live*), 8$_{10}$ (|| הלך *go*, שתה, שלח *send*) 8$_{12}$ (|| שתה, שלח pi. *send*) 2 C 30$_{18}$, עֵדָה *congregation* of Israel Ex 12$_{7.8.8.9}$ (+ יתר hi.) 12$_{11+5t}$ Lv 19$_{8.25.26}$ (:: שבע), קָהָל *assembly* 1 C 29$_{22}$ (|| שתה).

נֶפֶשׁ *person* Ex 12$_{15.19}$ Lv 7$_{18.20.21}$ (|| נגע *touch*) 7$_{25.27}$ 17$_{10.12.15}$ 22$_{6.7.8.11}$, *desire* Dt 12$_{20}$.

אִישׁ *man, husband* Gn 3$_{6}$ 18$_{8}$ 24$_{33.33.54}$ (|| שתה) 43$_{16.25}$ (+ שָׁם) Ex 2$_{20}$ Lv 9$_{11}$ 17$_{10}$ 22$_{14}$ Nm 6$_{3}$ (|| שתה) 6$_{4}$ Jg 19$_{4}$ (|| לין *spend night*, ישב + שתה) 19$_{8.21.21}$ (both || רחץ *wash*, שתה *drink*) 1 S 14$_{24.28.34.34}$ (|| שחט *slaughter*; + לֹא־תֶחֶטְאוּ *you shall not sin*) 30$_{11}$ (+ נתן *give* food, שקה hi. *give water*) 30$_{12}$ (+ שוב *go back*) 30$_{12}$ (|| שתה) 2 S 19$_{43}$ 1 K 13$_{8}$ (+ בוא *come*) 13$_{9}$ (|| שוב; both || שתה) 13$_{15}$ (+ הלך) 13$_{16.17}$ (+ שָׁם *there*, שוב) 13$_{18.19.22}$ (both + שוב) 13$_{22}$ (all six || שתה) 2 K 4$_{40.40.40}$ 18$_{27}$||Is 36$_{12}$ 18$_{31}$ (both || שתה) Is 7$_{22}$ 9$_{19}$ (|| גזר *cut off*, :: שבע *be satisfied*) 9$_{19}$ 36$_{16}$ (|| שתה) Jr 19$_{9}$ Ezk 18$_{6}$ 22$_{9}$ Ps 41$_{10}$ 78$_{25}$ Ru 3$_{3}$ (|| שתה) 1 C 12$_{40}$ (|| שתה) CD 10$_{22.23}$ (|| שתה) 1QS 6$_{2}$ (+ יַחַד *together*, || ברך pi. *bless*, יעץ ni. *take counsel*) 6$_{4}$, 5/6ḤevEp 12$_{3}$ (|| ישב, שתה) 4QToh A 1.1$_{3}$ 3.1$_{7}$ 4Q251 5$_{5}$ (א[י]ש).

אָדָם *human being* Gn 2$_{16.17.17}$ 3$_{11.12.17.17.17.18.19.22}$ (|| לקח *take*) Is 44$_{16}$ (|| שבע *be satisfied*) 44$_{19}$ (both || צלה *roast*) Jr 30$_{30}$ 8$_{15}$ (|| שתה *drink*, שמח *be merry*) Ec 2$_{24}$ (|| שתה, ראה hi. *cause to see*) 3$_{13}$ (|| שתה, ראה), בֶּן־אָדָם *human being* Ezk 2$_{8}$ (|| פצה *open* mouth) 3$_{1.1.3}$ 4$_{9.10.10.12.14}$ 12$_{18}$ (|| שתה) 24$_{17}$ (|| עטה *cover* lip).

אִשָּׁה *woman, wife* Gn 3$_{6}$ (|| לקח *take*) 3$_{13}$ Nm 6$_{3}$ (|| שתה *drink*) 6$_{4}$ Jg 13$_{4.7.14}$ (all three || שתה) 13$_{14}$ 1 S 1$_{18}$ 1 K 17$_{12}$ (|| מות *die*) 17$_{15}$ 2 K 6$_{28.28.29.29}$ (|| בשל pi. *boil*) Is 4$_{1}$ (|| לבש *wear* clothes) Pr 30$_{20}$ (|| מחה *wipe*, אמר *say*)

31_{27} (or em.; see Hi. Obj.) Lm 2_{20} (|| עלל po. *act arbitrarily*) 11QT $63_{15.15}$, *(each) one* (of sheep) Zc 11_{9}.

אָב *father* Jg 14_{9} $19_{4.6}$ (|| ישב *sit*; both || שתה *drink*) Jr 22_{15} (|| שתה) 31_{29}=Ezk 18_{2} (+ קהה *be blunted*, of teeth) Ezk 5_{10}, אֵם *mother* Jg 14_{9}, חֹתֵן *father-in-law* Jg 19_{8}, בֵּן *son* 2 S 9_{10} 1 K 1_{25} (|| שתה; + אמר) 17_{12} Ezk 5_{10} $18_{11.15}$ Jb $1_{13.18}$ (both || שתה) Pr 24_{13}, *descendant* Ne 9_{25} (|| שבע, שמן hi. *grow fat*), בַּת *daughter* Lv $22_{12.13}$ Jb $1_{13.18}$ (both || שתה), חָתָן *son-in-law* Jg 19_{6} (|| ישב, שתה), יֶלֶד *youth* Dn $1_{13.15}$, נַעַר *lad* Gn 14_{24} 2 S 16_{2} (|| רכב *ride*, שתה), אָח *brother, relative* Gn $31_{54.54}$ (|| לין *spend night*) 37_{25} (+ ישב) 43_{2}, אָחוֹת *sister* Jb 1_{4} (|| שתה).

מֶלֶךְ *king* 1 S 20_{24} (|| ישב) Jr 50_{17} (+ עצם pi. *crush* bones) 51_{34}, אָצִיל *leader* Ex 24_{11} (|| שתה), קָצִין *ruler* Mc 3_{3}, רֹאשׁ *chief* 3_{3} (both + פשט hi. *strip* flesh, פצח pi. *crush* bones), שַׂר *prince* Ec $10_{16.17}$ 1 K 1_{25} (|| שתה, + אמר), נָשִׂיא *prince* Ezk 44_{3}, אַלּוּף *chief* Zc 12_{6}, שָׁלִישׁ *officer* 2 K $7_{2.19}$ (both || ראה *see*; + שָׁם *there*), בַּעַל שְׁכֶם *citizen of Shechem* Jg 9_{27} (|| שתה, קלל pi. *revile*).

priest Gn 47_{22} Lv 6_{19} Lv 21_{22} 22_{4} Nm 18_{10} Dt 18_{1} 2 K 23_{9} Ezk 42_{13} (+ שָׁם) 44_{29} 31 Ho 4_{8} Zc $7_{6.6}$ (both || שתה) Ezr 2_{63}||Ne 7_{65} 11QT $19_{5(\text{Yadin})}$ + Sup 20_{12} (יא]וכ[לום; + מ[צות] with *unleavened bread*), Levite Nm 18_{31} Dt 14_{29} (|| שבע *be satisfied*) 18_{8} 26_{12} (|| שבע) 2 C 30_{22}, נָבִיא *prophet* 1 K 13_{23} (|| שתה) 18_{19}, רֹאֶה *seer* 1 S $9_{13.13}$, חֹזֶה *seer* Am 7_{12} (|| נבא ni. *prophesy*; + שָׁם *there*), psalmist 1QH 5_{33}.

רעה ptc. *shepherd* Ezk 34_{3} (|| לבשׁ *wear* clothes, זבח *slaughter*, :: רעה *tend*) Zc 11_{16} (|| פרק *tear off* hoof), עֶבֶד *servant* Gn 24_{54} (|| שתה) Ex 12_{44} Is 65_{13} (|| שתה, שמח *be merry*, :: רעב *be hungry*, צמא *thirst*, בושׁ *be shamed*), עבד ptc. *labourer* Ec 5_{11}, שָׂכִיר *hired labourer* Ex 12_{45} Lv 22_{10}.

אֶבְיוֹן *poor person* Ex 23_{11}, עָנָו *poor person* Ps 22_{27} (|| שבע), עָנִי *poor person* Ps $102_{5.10}$ (|| מסך *mix*), רעב ptc. *hungry person* Is 29_{8} (|| שתה), Jb 5_{5}, צַדִּיק *righteous person* Pr 13_{25}, כְּסִיל *fool* Ec 4_{5} (|| חבק *clasp* hands), צָמֵא *thirsty person* Is 55_{1} (|| הלך *go*, שבר *buy*) 55_{2} (|| ענג htp. *enjoy*), דָּשֵׁן *fat*, i.e. vigorous, *person* Ps 22_{30} (|| שחה htpal. *bow down*), קדשׁ htp. ptc. *sanctified person* Is 66_{17}, טהר htp. ptc. *ritually clean person* 66_{17}, טָהוֹר *clean person* Lv 7_{19} Nm $18_{11.13}$ Dt $12_{15.22}$, טָמֵא *unclean person* $12_{15.22}$, זוב ptc. fem. sg. *woman with issue* 4QToh A 1.1_{5}, צרע pu. pass. ptc. *leper* 2 K 7_{8} (|| שתה, נשׂא *carry*).

גּוֹי *nation* Dt 28_{51}, ישב ptc. *inhabitant* Is 23_{18} (+ לְשָׂבְעָה *to satisfaction*) Ezk 12_{19} (|| שתה) 33_{25} (|| נשׂא *raise*, שפך *shed* blood), גֵּר *sojourner* Lv 17_{12} Dt $14_{21.29}$ 26_{12} (both || שׂבע *be satisfied*), גור ptc. *sojourner* Is 5_{17} (or em. גָּרִים to גְּדָיִים *kids* or כָּרִים *lambs*), תּוֹשָׁב *sojourner* Ex 12_{45} Lv 22_{10}, בֶּן־נֵכָר *alien* Ex 12_{43}, גּוֹלָה *exiles* Jr 29_{5} || 29_{28} (|| נטע *plant*; + בנה *build*, ישב *dwell*), ערל ptc. *uncircumcised person* Ex 12_{48}, אַלְמָנָה *widow* Dt 14_{29} 26_{12} (both || שׂבע) 1 K 17_{12}, יָתוֹם *orphan* Dt 14_{29} 26_{12} (both || שׂבע) Jb 31_{17}, מִצְרִי *Egyptian* Gn 39_{6} $43_{32.32}$, בֶּן־קֶדֶם *Kedemite* Ezk 25_{4} (|| שתה), גְּדוּד *troop* 1 S 30_{16} (|| שתה, חגג *celebrate*), זָכָר *male* Lv $6_{11.22}$ 7_{6} Nm 18_{10}.

אהב ptc. *lover* Pr 18_{21}, דּוֹד *beloved one* Ca 4_{16} 5_{1} (|| שתה), אכל ptc. *eater* Dn 11_{26} 2 S 19_{29} 1 K 2_{7} 1QH 5_{23}, רֵעַ *friend* Ca 5_{1}, קרא pass. ptc. *guest* 1 S 9_{13}.

אֵלֶּה *these* (prisoners) 2 K $6_{22.23}$ (both || שתה, הלך *go*), appar. הַר *mountain* of Israel Ezk $36_{13.14}$ (both || שכל pi. *bereave*), אַחֵר *another person* Is 65_{22} Jb 31_{8}, יתר ni. ptc. *remainder* 1 S 2_{36} Is 7_{22}, אסף pi. ptc. *gatherer* 62_{9} (|| הלל pi. *praise*, שתה), מִי *whoever* (|| חושׁ *enjoy*), delicate woman Dt 28_{57}, חֵךְ *palate* Jb 34_{3}, גַּרְגֶּרֶת *throat* Si 36_{23} (mg [כ]רש *stomach*).

אֱלֹהִים *God* Ps 50_{13} (|| שתה), *gods* Dt 4_{28} (|| ראה *see*, שמע *hear*, ריח hi. *smell* trans.) 32_{38} (|| שתה), אֱלִיל *idol* Si $30_{19(\text{Segal})}$ (אל[י]לי), מַלְאָךְ *angel* Gn 19_{3} Jg 13_{16}, Y. Ho 13_{8} (+ שָׁם *there*; perh. אכל = *destroy*) Ps 50_{13}.

חַיָּה *wild animal* Gn $37_{20.33}$ Ex 23_{11} Is 56_{9} Ezk 33_{27} 34_{28} $39_{17.18.19}$ (all three || שתה) Ho 2_{14} perh. Si 36_{23}, בְּהֵמָה *animal* Jr 15_{3} (|| שחת hi. *destroy*), פָּרָה *cow* Gn $41_{4.20}$, בָּקָר *ox* Is 11_{7} 65_{25} Jb 40_{15}, אֶלֶף *ox* Is 30_{24}, שׁוֹר *ox* Ps 106_{20}, עַיִר *ass* Is 30_{24}, כִּבְשָׂה *ewe-lamb* 2 S 12_{3} (|| שתה, + שכב *lie* (on breast), כֶּלֶב *dog* 1 K 14_{11} 16_{4} $21_{23.24}$ 2 K $9_{10.36}$ Ps 59_{16} 4QMMT A 2_{66}, אַרְיֵה *lion* 1 K 13_{28} (|| שבר *maul*) Is 11_{7} 65_{25}, כְּפִיר *lion cub* (perh. אכל = *destroy*) Ezk $19_{3.6}$ (both + טרף *tear*), זְאֵב *wolf* Gn 49_{27}, locust (perh. אכל = *destroy*) Ex $10_{5.5.12.15}$ Jl $1_{4.4.4}$ 2_{25} Am 4_{9} 7_{2} Ps $105_{35.35}$ 2 C 7_{13}, עָרֹב *swarm* Ps 78_{45} (|| שחת hi.), נָחָשׁ *snake* Gn 3_{14}, תּוֹלַעַת *worm* Dt 28_{39}, עָשׁ *moth* (perh. אכל = *destroy*) Is 50_{9} 51_{8} Jb 13_{28}, סָס *moth* (perh. אכל = *destroy*) Is 51_{8}, עוֹף *bird* Gn $40_{17.19}$ 1 K 14_{11} 16_{4}

21$_{24}$ Jr 15$_{3}$, נֶשֶׁר *eagle* Hb 1$_{8}$ Pr 30$_{17}$ (בְּנֵי־נֶשֶׁר).

Subj. not specified, Gn 3$_{11}$ Lv 14$_{47}$ (|| שׁכב *lie*) Dt 31$_{17}$ Is 21$_{5}$ 22$_{13.13}$ (all three || שׁתה *drink*) 55$_{10}$ 59$_{5}$ Jr 2$_{3}$ 30$_{16}$ Ho 9$_{4}$ Mc 7$_{1}$ Ps 127$_{2}$ Jb 20$_{21}$ Pr 25$_{27}$ Ec 5$_{16.17}$ (|| שׁתה, ראה *see*) 9$_{7}$ (|| שׁתה) Lm 4$_{5}$ Si 6$_{19}$ 1QS 5$_{16}$ (|| שׁתה, לקח *take*) 4QMMT A 2$_{4}$ ([לאכול]) 2$_{45}$ ([האוכל]) 2$_{45}$ 4QJub^{d} 1.1$_{38}$ ([אכול]) 1.2$_{17}$ ([תאכלו]) 1.2$_{17}$ ([תאכל]).

<OBJ> לֶחֶם *bread, food* (oft. pleonastic for אכל alone) Gn 3$_{19}$ 28$_{20}$ (|| לבשׁ *wear* clothes) 31$_{54.54}$ 37$_{25}$ 39$_{6}$ 43$_{25.32}$ Ex 2$_{20}$ 16$_{3}$ 18$_{12}$ 34$_{28}$ Lv 21$_{22}$ 23$_{14}$ 26$_{5.26}$ (|| שׂבע *be satisfied*) Dt 8$_{9}$ 9$_{9.18}$ 29$_{5}$ 1 S 14$_{24.28}$ 20$_{34}$ 28$_{20}$ 30$_{12}$ 2 S 9$_{7.10.10}$ 12$_{21}$ 16$_{2(Qr)}$ 1 K 13$_{8+9t}$ 21$_{4.5.7}$ (|| קום *arise*) 2 K 4$_{8.8}$ 25$_{29}$||Jr 52$_{33}$ Is 4$_{1}$ Jr 41$_{1}$ Ezk 4$_{9.13.16}$ 12$_{18.19}$ 24$_{17.22}$ 44$_{3}$ Ho 9$_{4}$ Am 7$_{12}$ Ps 14$_{4}$ 41$_{10}$ 53$_{5}$ 78$_{25}$ 102$_{5}$ 127$_{2}$ Jb 42$_{11}$ Pr 31$_{27}$ (or em.; see Hi. Obj.) Ec 9$_{7}$ Dn 10$_{3}$ Ezr 10$_{6}$ Ne 5$_{14}$ 4QOrd^{c} 1.1$_{6.9}$ 1QH 5$_{23}$ (see Coll.).

בָּשָׂר *flesh* (sometimes human), *food* (sometimes pleonastic for אכל alone) Gn 9$_{4}$ 40$_{19}$ Ex 12$_{8.8.11.11}$ 16$_{8.12}$ (|| שׂבע) 29$_{32}$ Lv 7$_{19.20}$ 26$_{29.29}$ Nm 11$_{13.18.18.19.21}$ Dt 12$_{15}$ (|| זבח *slaughter*) 12$_{15.20.20}$=11QT 53$_{2.3}$ (both ב[שר]) Dt 12$_{22.27}$ 28$_{53}$ Jg 6$_{21}$ 2 K 9$_{36}$ Is 9$_{19}$ (|| שׂבע) 22$_{13}$ 44$_{16.19}$ 65$_{4}$ 66$_{17}$ Jr 7$_{21}$ 19$_{9}$ Ezk 39$_{17.18}$ Ho 8$_{13}$ (|| זבח) Zc 11$_{9.16}$ Ps 27$_{2}$ 50$_{13}$ Ec 4$_{5}$ 2QapProph 1$_{3}$ (ב[שר]) 11QT 52$_{19}$ 53$_{3}$ (ב[שר]) 4QJub^{d} 1.1$_{38}$ ([בשרו אכול]), שְׁאֵר human *flesh* Mc 3$_{3}$, 4Q251 4$_{4}$ ([יאכל ... בשר]ן).

פְּרִי *fruit, produce, food* (see also §4) Lv 19$_{25}$ Dt 28$_{33.51.51.53}$ 2 K 19$_{29}$||Is 37$_{30(Qr)}$ Is 65$_{21.22}$ (all three || נטע *plant*) Jr 2$_{7}$ 29$_{5}$ (|| נטע) 29$_{28}$ Ezk 25$_{4}$ Am 9$_{14}$ Ps 105$_{35}$ (perh. אכל = *destroy*) Pr 18$_{21}$ Ca 4$_{16}$ Lm 2$_{20}$ Ne 9$_{36}$ Si 6$_{19}$ 4QBark^{c} $_{4}$ 4QapPs^{b} 1$_{8}$, אֹכֶל *food* Dt 2$_{6}$ (|| שׁבר *purchase* food) 2$_{28}$ (|| שׁבר hi. *sell* food), מַאֲכָל *food* Ezk 4$_{10.10}$, תְּבוּאָה *produce* Lv 25$_{7.12}$ Jr 2$_{3}$ 11QT 38$_{10(Yadin)}$ + Sup, יְגִיעַ *produce* Dt 28$_{33}$ Jr 3$_{24}$ Ps 128$_{2}$, תְּנוּבָה *produce* Dt 32$_{13}$, טוּב *produce* Is 1$_{19}$ Jr 2$_{7}$ Ezr 9$_{12}$ 4QBark^{c} $_{4}$, טוֹב *good (things)* (see also §4) Is 55$_{2}$ (perh. = *eat well*), חֹק *statutory ration* Gn 47$_{22}$, בִּכּוּרִים *firstfruits* Nm 18$_{13}$.

בְּהֵמָה *animal* Dt 14$_{4}$ 11QT 52$_{17}$, חַיָּה *wild animal* Lv 11$_{2}$, אַיִל *ram* Gn 31$_{38}$, כַּר *lamb* Am 6$_{4}$, פָּרָה *cow* Gn 41$_{4.20}$, עֵגֶל *calf* Am 6$_{4}$, צֹאן *flock* Jr 5$_{17}$, בָּקָר *herd* 5$_{17}$, דָּגָה *fish* Nm 11$_{5}$, עוֹף *bird* Dt 14$_{20}$, (un)clean animal Lv 11$_{3.4.9.9}$||Dt 14$_{6.7.9.9}$ Lv 11$_{21.22.42}$ Dt 14$_{10.11.12}$, טֶרֶף *prey* Nm 23$_{24}$, טְרֵפָה *savaged animal* Ex 22$_{30}$ Lv 17$_{15}$ 22$_{8}$ Ezk 4$_{14}$ 44$_{31}$, נְבֵלָה *carcase* Lv 17$_{15}$ 22$_{8}$ Dt 14$_{21.21}$ 1 K 13$_{28}$ Ezk 4$_{14}$ 44$_{31}$ 11QT 48$_{6}$, מות ptc. *corpse* 1K 14$_{11.11}$ 16$_{4.4}$ 21$_{24.24}$, אָדָם *human being* (perh. אכל = *destroy*) Ezk 19$_{3.6}$ 36$_{13.14}$, אָב *father* 5$_{10}$, בֵּן *son* Dt 28$_{55.57}$ 2 K 6$_{28.28.29.29}$ (|| בשׁל pi. *boil*) Jr 5$_{17}$ Ezk 5$_{10}$ 16$_{20}$, וָלָד *foetus* 4QMMT A 2$_{45}$ ([האוכל את הולד]) 2$_{45}$.

גִּיד *sinew* Gn 32$_{33}$, חֵלֶב *fat* 45$_{18}$ (+ הָאָרֶץ *of the land*) Lv 3$_{17}$ 7$_{23.24.25.25}$ Dt 32$_{38}$ Ezk 34$_{3}$ (|| לבשׁ *wear* clothes) 39$_{19}$ 4QapPs^{b} 1$_{8}$, דָּם *blood* Lv 3$_{17}$ 7$_{26.27}$ 17$_{10.10.12.12.14.14}$ Dt 12$_{16.23}$=11QT 53$_{5}$ Dt 12$_{24.25}$ 15$_{23}$=11QT 52$_{11}$ CD 3$_{6}$ 4QJub^{d} 1.2$_{17}$ ([תאכלו ... דם]), נֶפֶשׁ *life-source* Dt 12$_{23}$ =11QT 53$_{6}$, חָזֶה *breast* of sacrificial animal Lv 10$_{14}$, שׁוֹק *thigh* of sacrificial animal 10$_{14}$, עַיִן *eye* of mocker Pr 30$_{17}$.

מַצָּה *unleavened bread* Ex 12$_{15.18.20}$ 13$_{6}$ 23$_{15}$ 34$_{18}$ Lv 23$_{6}$ Dt 16$_{8}$ 2 K 23$_{9}$, פַּת *morsel* of bread 1 S 2$_{36}$ 28$_{22}$ Jb 31$_{17}$ Pr 23$_{8}$, חָמֵץ *leaven* Ex 12$_{15}$, מַחְמֶצֶת *leaven* 12$_{19.20}$, מָן *manna* 16$_{25.35.35}$ Ps 78$_{24}$, עֻגָה *cake* Ezk 4$_{12}$, דְּבַשׁ *honey* Jg 14$_{9}$ Is 7$_{15.22}$ Ezk 16$_{13}$ Pr 24$_{13}$ 25$_{27}$ Ca 5$_{1}$, יַעַר *honeycomb* 5$_{1}$, חֶמְאָה *curd* Is 7$_{15.22.22}$, פַּתְבַּג *delicacies* Dn 1$_{13.15}$ 11$_{26}$, מַשְׁמָן *delicacy* Ne 8$_{10}$, מְעַט *a little* Ec 5$_{11}$, הַרְבֵּה *a lot* 5$_{11}$, דַּי *sufficiency* of honey Pr 25$_{16}$.

עֵשֶׂב *grass* Gn 3$_{18}$ Ex 10$_{12.15}$ Am 7$_{2}$ Ps 105$_{35}$ (in all four perh. אכל = *destroy*) 106$_{20}$ 4QDibHam^{a} 16$_{2}$ ([א]כל), חָצִיר *grass* Jb 40$_{15}$, תֶּבֶן *straw* Is 11$_{7}$ 65$_{25}$, בְּלִיל *fodder* 30$_{24}$, קָצִיר *harvest* Jr 5$_{17}$ Jb 5$_{5}$, יָשָׁן *old crop* Lv 25$_{22}$ 26$_{10}$, שֶׁבֶר *grain* Gn 43$_{2}$, דָּגָן *grain* Is 62$_{9}$ Ne 5$_{2}$ 11QT 43$_{6}$, חִטָּה *wheat* 4Q251 5$_{5}$, קָלִי *parched grain* Lv 23$_{14}$ Ru 2$_{14}$ (|| שׂבע *be satisfied*, יתר hi. *leave over*), כַּרְמֶל *fresh grain* Lv 23$_{14}$, סָפִיחַ *wild cereal* 2 K 19$_{29}$||Is 37$_{30}$, סָחִישׁ *wild cereal* 2 K 19$_{29}$ (||Is 37$_{30}$ שָׁחִיס *wild cereal*), זֶרַע *seed* Lv 26$_{16}$ (|| זרע *sow*), אֲדָמָה *land* Gn 3$_{17}$.

קֶמַח *flour* 1 K 17$_{12}$, סֹלֶת *flour* Ezk 16$_{13}$, שֶׁמֶן *oil* 1 K 17$_{12}$ Ezk 16$_{13}$, גַּנָּה *garden* Am 4$_{9}$ (unless em. הַרְבּוֹת perh. *in quantity* to הֶחֱרַבְתִּי *I dried up*), כֶּרֶם *vineyard* Dt 28$_{39}$ Jos 24$_{13}$ (both || נטע *plant*) Am 4$_{9}$ (unless em.; see above), גֶּפֶן *vine* 2 K 18$_{31}$||Is 36$_{16}$ Jr 5$_{17}$ Ho 2$_{14}$, עֵנָב *grape* Nm 6$_{3}$ Dt 23$_{25}$, בֹּסֶר *sour grapes* Jr 31$_{29.30}$ Ezk 18$_{2}$, אֶשְׁכּוֹל *cluster* Mc 7$_{1}$, זַיִת *olive-tree* Jos 24$_{13}$ (|| נטע) Am 4$_{9}$, תְּאֵנָה *fig* 2 K 18$_{31}$||Is 36$_{16}$ Jr 5$_{17}$ Ho 2$_{14}$ Am 4$_{9}$, קַיִץ *summer fruit* 2 S 16$_{2}$.

מִנְחָה *meal offering* Lv 6$_{11}$ 10$_{12.13}$ Ezk 44$_{29}$, חַטָּאת *sin offering* Lv 10$_{17.18.19}$ Ezk 44$_{29}$ Ho 4$_{8}$ 11QT 38$_{10}$ + Sup, אָשָׁם *guilt offering* Ezk 44$_{29}$, אִשֶּׁה *offering by fire* Dt 18$_{1}$ Si 45$_{21}$, שֶׁלֶם *peace offering* Dt 27$_{7}$ (|| זבח *sacrifice*), זֶבַח *sacrifice* Lv 19$_{8}$ 11QT 63$_{15.15}$ (all three + שֶׁלֶם) Ps 106$_{28}$, פֶּסַח *passover meal* 2 C 30$_{18}$ 11QT 17$_{8(Yadin)}$ ([פסח]), מוֹעֵד *(food at) festival* 2 C 30$_{22}$, קֹדֶשׁ *holy thing* Lv 22$_{10.10.14.16}$ Ezk 42$_{13}$ 4QD[a] 6.2$_{7}$, מַעֲשֵׂר *tithe* Dt 12$_{17.18}$ 14$_{23}$, יתר ni. ptc. *remnants* of sacrifice 11QT 20$_{11}$, חֵלֶק *portion* Dt 18$_{8}$=11QT 60$_{15}$.

עַד *booty* Gn 49$_{27}$, שָׁלָל *booty* Dt 20$_{14}$=11QT 62$_{11}$, בֶּגֶד *garment* Jb 13$_{28}$ (perh. אכל = *destroy*), מְגִלָּה *scroll* Ezk 2$_{8}$ 3$_{1.1.3}$, דָּבָר *word* of Y. Jr 15$_{16}$, שָׁנָה *year* Jl 2$_{25}$ (perh. אכל = *destroy*), טָמֵא *unclean food* Ho 9$_{3}$, תּוֹעֵבָה *abomination* Dt 14$_{3}$ 11QT 48$_{7}$, יֶתֶר *remainder* Ex 10$_{5}$ Jl 1$_{4.4.4}$, אֵפֶר *ash* Ps 102$_{10}$, עָפָר *dust* Gn 3$_{14}$, צוֹאָה *excrement* 2 K 18$_{27(Qr)}$||Is 36$_{12(Qr)}$, חֶרֶא *excrement* 18$_{27(Kt)}$||Is 36$_{12(Kt)}$.

<PREP> בְּ of place, *in, at*, + מָקוֹם *(holy) place* Lv 10$_{13.14.17}$ 24$_{9}$ Nm 18$_{31}$ Dt 14$_{23}$ 15$_{20}$=11QT 52$_{9}$ Dt 16$_{7}$ (|| בשׁל pi. *boil*) 1 K 13$_{8.22}$ 11QT 52$_{15}$, אֶרֶץ *land* Dt 8$_{9}$, Shiloh 1 S 1$_{9}$, Assyria Ho 9$_{3}$, שַׁעַר *gate* Dt 12$_{17.21}$ (|| זבח *slaughter*) 15$_{22}$=11QT 52$_{11}$ Dt 26$_{12}$ (|| שׂבע *be satisfied*) 11QT 52$_{17}$ 53$_{4}$, בַּיִת *house* Ex 12$_{7}$ Lv 14$_{47}$ (|| שׁכב *lie down*) 1 K 13$_{19}$ Jb 1$_{13.18}$ 42$_{11}$, חָצֵר *enclosure* Lv 6$_{9}$ 11QT 19$_{5}$ + Sup ([בחצ]ר) 20$_{11}$ 22$_{13}$, קֹדֶשׁ *sanctuary* Nm 18$_{10}$, רֹאשׁ *summit* Ex 24$_{17}$.

Of time, *in, on, at*, + יוֹם *day* 1 S 20$_{34}$ 1 C 29$_{2}$ 11QT 21$_{3(Yadin)}$ + Sup ([ביום]) 22$_{13}$ 43$_{15.16}$ CD 10$_{22}$ 4QJub[d] 1.13$_{8}$ ([אכול ביום]), לַיְלָה *night* 11QT 17$_{8}$ ([בל]ילה]), בֹּקֶר *morning* Gn 49$_{27}$ Ec 10$_{16}$, צָהֳרַיִם *noon* Gn 43$_{16}$, שָׁנָה *year* Lv 25$_{20}$, עֵת *appointed time* Ec 10$_{17}$.

Of accompaniment, *with*, + חִפָּזוֹן *urgency* Ex 12$_{11}$, סֵתֶר *secrecy* Dt 28$_{57}$ (+ בְּחֹסֶר־כֹּל *due to utter want*), מִסְתָּר *secrecy* Hb 3$_{14}$, חֹשֶׁךְ *darkness* Ec 5$_{16}$, שְׁגָגָה *inadvertence* Lv 22$_{14}$, טֻמְאָה *impurity* 4QOrd[c] 1.1$_{7.8(mg)}$, מִסְכֵּנוּת *poverty* Dt 8$_{9}$, אָוֶן *sorrow* 26$_{14}$, דְּאָגָה *anxiety* Ezk 4$_{16}$ 12$_{19}$, רַעַשׁ *trembling* 12$_{18}$, שִׂמְחָה *joy* Ec 9$_{7}$ 1 C 29$_{22}$, שָׂבָע *satisfaction* 11QPs[a] 18$_{11}$, בְּמִשְׁקָל *by weight*, i.e. in small amounts Ezk 4$_{16}$, of instrument, *with*, + עִצָּבוֹן *toil* Gn 3$_{17}$, זֵעָה *sweat* 3$_{19}$.

Partitive, *(some) of*, + פֶּסַח *passover sacrifice* Ex 12$_{43.44.45.48}$, קֹדֶשׁ *holy thing* Lv 22$_{4.11}$, sim. 22$_{12}$, לֶחֶם *bread, food* 22$_{11.13}$ Jg 13$_{16}$ 1QH 5$_{33}$, יאכל בפיהו *he is to eat with his mouth* (i.e. perh. only he, not his family) 4QOrd[a] 1.2$_{5}$.

לְשֹׂבַע *to satisfaction* Ex 16$_{3}$ Lv 25$_{19}$ 26$_{5}$ Pr 13$_{25}$ (לְ), לְשָׂבְעָה *to satisfaction* Is 23$_{18}$ Ezk 39$_{19}$ Hg 1$_{6}$, הָאֹכְלִים לְמַעֲדַנִּים *those who feed on dainties* Lm 4$_{5}$.

כְּ *as*, + לָבִיא *lion* Ho 13$_{8}$, אִישׁ *man* Si 34$_{16(mg).16}$.

מִן of place, *from*, + עֵץ *tree* Gn 2$_{16.17}$ 3$_{1}$ $_{+6t}$ Dt 20$_{19}$, סַל *basket* Gn 40$_{17}$, יָד *hand* 2 S 13$_{5}$, partitive, *(some) of* Nm 6$_{4}$ Jg 13$_{14}$ 2 K 7$_{2.19}$ 11QT 43$_{16}$ 4QOrd[b] 1$_{11}$ (י[אוכ]לו) CD 10$_{22}$, + פְּרִי *fruit, produce* (see also §4) Gn 3$_{2.3}$, תְּבוּאָה *produce* Lv 25$_{22}$ Jos 5$_{12}$, עָבוּר *produce* 5$_{11.12}$, דָּגָן *grain* of Gentiles 4QMMT A 2$_{4}$ ([לאכול]), לֶחֶם *bread* Lv 22$_{13}$ Nm 15$_{19}$ Ru 2$_{14}$, בָּשָׂר *flesh* Ex 12$_{9}$ Lv 7$_{18.21}$ 11$_{8}$||Dt 14$_{8}$ Lv 11$_{11}$, שָׁלָל *booty* 1 S 14$_{30}$, נְכָס *wealth* 5/6ḤevEp 12$_{3}$, קֹדֶשׁ *holy thing* Lv 22$_{6.7}$ Dt 26$_{14}$ Ezr 2$_{63}$=Ne 7$_{65}$ 4QD[a] 6.2$_{11}$, זֶבַח *sacrifice* Ex 34$_{15}$, פַּת *morsel* 2 S 12$_{3}$ Jb 31$_{17}$, לֵחָה *moisture* of dew 4QToh A 3.2$_{5}$, חַיָּה *animal* CD 12$_{12}$, שׁוֹר *ox* Dt 28$_{31}$ (|| טבח pass. *be slaughtered*), צַיִד *game* Gn 27$_{19.25}$, שֶׁרֶץ *swarming animal* 11QT 48$_{3(Yadin)}$ ([משר]ץ) 48$_{4}$, רֶמֶשׂ *creeping animal* CD 12$_{12}$, נָזִיד *stew* 2 K 4$_{40}$, בֵּיצָה *egg* Is 59$_{5}$, זַיִת *olive* 11QT 22$_{15}$ (|| סוך *anoint oneself*), נְבֵלָה *carcase* Lv 11$_{40}$ (|| נשׂא *carry*), הוֹן *property* 1QS 5$_{16}$, מקצת עצמות *some of the bones* 4QMMT A 2$_{66}$, מִן־הַמֶּלֶךְ *at the king's expense* 2 S 19$_{43}$.

עַל *on, with*, + דָּם *blood* Lv 19$_{26}$ 1 S 14$_{32.33.34}$ (אֶל־) Ezk 33$_{25}$, מַצָּה *unleavened bread* Nm 9$_{11}$ Dt 16$_{3}$, חָמֵץ *leaven* Dt 16$_{3}$, שְׂמֹאל *the left* Is 9$_{19}$ (L שְׂמֹאול), עַל שֻׁלְחָן *at table* 2 S 9$_{7.10.11.13}$.

אֶל־הֶהָרִים *on the mountains* Ezk 18$_{6.11.15}$ (עַל־) 22$_{9}$.

אֵת *with* someone Gn 43$_{16.32.32}$; עִם *with* someone Ex 18$_{12}$ 1 S 9$_{19.24}$ Jb 1$_{4}$ 42$_{11}$, אָכַלְתִּי יַעְרִי עִם־דִּבְשִׁי *I have eaten my honeycomb with my honey (in it)* Ca 5$_{1}$ (|| ארה *pluck*); בְּתוֹךְ *among* others 2 K 23$_{9}$, *in* city 11QT 52$_{19}$; אֵצֶל *next to*, + מִזְבֵּחַ *altar*, שַׁעַר *gate* Lv 10$_{12}$ 11QT 38$_{6}$ ([אוכ]לים]); לִפְנֵי *in the presence of* someone Dt 12$_{7}$=11QT 52$_{15}$ (|| שׂמח *be merry*) Dt 12$_{18}$ 14$_{23.26}$ 15$_{20}$ ||11QT 52$_{9}$ (all seven + Y.) 2 S 11$_{13}$ 1 K 1$_{25}$ 2 K 25$_{29}$||Jr 52$_{33}$ Ezk 44$_{3}$ 1 C 29$_{22}$ (both + Y.); עַד *until* evening 1 S 14$_{24}$; אכל בְּלִי־כֶסֶף *eat without money*, i.e. for free Jb 31$_{39}$.

<COLL> אכל || שׁתה *drink*, e.g. Gn 26$_{30}$ Ex 24$_{11}$ 32$_{6}$ Jg 9$_{27}$ 19$_{4}$ 1 S 30$_{16}$ 2 S 11$_{11}$ (|| שׁכב *sleep* with wife) 19$_{36}$ (+ טעם *taste*) 1 K 4$_{20}$ (|| שׂמח *be merry*) 18$_{41.42}$ 19$_{6}$ 2 K 6$_{22.23}$ 7$_{8}$ 9$_{34}$ Is 21$_{5}$ (+ ערך שֻׁלְחָן *set table*) 22$_{13}$ 29$_{8}$ 65$_{13}$ Jr 16$_{8}$ Pr 23$_{7}$ Ru 3$_{7}$ (|| יטב *be glad*) Ec 2$_{24}$ (|| ראה נֶפֶשׁ טוֹב hi. *cause one's soul to see good, enjoy oneself*) 3$_{13}$ 5$_{17}$ (both || ראה *see* good, i.e. enjoy oneself) 8$_{15}$ (|| שׂמח) Est 4$_{16}$ Dn 1$_{12}$ Ne 8$_{12}$ 1 C 12$_{40}$ 11QT 38$_{3}$ (ושו[תים]) 1QS 5$_{16}$ (|| לקח *take*) 6$_{4}$ 4QRitPur 7$_{3}$ (ולש[תות]) CD 10$_{23}$ 5/6ḤevEp 12$_{3}$ (|| ישׁב *sit*).

אכל *eat food/a meal*, i.e. with no explicit object, e.g. 1 S 28$_{23.25}$ 30$_{11.12}$ 2 S 12$_{20}$ 1 K 17$_{15}$ 19$_{5}$ (|| קום *arise*) 19$_{6.7.8}$ (both || קום) 19$_{21}$ 2 K 4$_{40.40.41.42.43.43.44}$ (both || יתר hi. *have* food *left over*) Ps 22$_{30}$ (or em. אָכְלוּ וַיִּשְׁתַּחֲווּ *they ate and they bowed down* to אַךְ לוֹ יִשְׁתַּחֲווּ *surely to him they bowed down*, or אֵיךְ לוֹ יִשְׁתַּחֲווּ *how they bowed down to him!*) Pr 30$_{20}$ 1QDM 2$_{4}$ (ואכל[ת ה]) 4QDibHam^{a} 1.4$_{14}$ (ויואכ[לו]; both || שׂבע *be satisfied*) 11QBer 1.2$_{10}$ (both || דשׁן hthp. *grow fat*) 1QS 6$_{2}$.

אכל (finite) preceded by inf. absol. Gn 2$_{16}$ Lv 7$_{24}$ 10$_{18}$ 1 S 14$_{30}$ (perh. אכל = *use*) 2 S 19$_{43}$, followed by inf. absol. Gn 31$_{15}$ (§3) Jl 2$_{26}$ (|| שׂבע *be satisfied*), אֵין־שָׂרִיד לְאָכְלוֹ *there was nothing left after he had eaten* Jb 20$_{21}$, לֶאֱכֹל לְטַפְּכֶם *to eat for your children*, i.e. for your children to eat Gn 47$_{24}$.

אכל preceded by לֹא *you shall not* Gn 2$_{17}$ 3$_{1.3.17}$ 9$_{4}$ Ex 12$_{20}$ 22$_{30}$ Lv 3$_{17}$ 7$_{23.24.26}$ 11$_{4.8}$||Dt 14$_{7.8}$ Lv 11$_{11.42}$ 17$_{12.14}$ 19$_{26}$ 23$_{14}$ Dt 12$_{23}$=11QT 53$_{6}$ Dt 12$_{24.25}$ 14$_{3.10.12.21}$ 15$_{23}$=11QT 52$_{11}$ Dt 16$_{3}$ 1 K 13$_{9.17}$ Ezk 24$_{17.22}$ 11QT 48$_{6.7}$ 52$_{19}$, preceded by אַל *do not* Ex 12$_{9}$ Jg 13$_{4.7.14}$ (3fs) 1 K 13$_{22}$ Est 4$_{16}$ 11QT 50$_{4}$ + Sup.

כָּכָה יֹאכְלוּ *you are to eat it thus* Dt 12$_{22}$, כֵּן תֹּאכְלֶנּוּ *they will eat thus* Ezk 4$_{13}$, ככה יהיו אוכלים אותו *they will eat it thus* 11QT 43$_{5}$, הָלוֹךְ וְאָכֹל *eating as he went* Jg 14$_{9}$, אֶזְרְעָה וְאַחֵר יֹאכֵל *may I sow and another eat* Jb 31$_{8}$, שִׁבְרוּ וֶאֱכֹלוּ *buy food and eat!* Is 55$_{1}$, מִי יֹאכַל וּמִי יָחוּשׁ חוּץ מִמֶּנִּי *who eats and who feels pleasure apart from me?* Ec 2$_{25}$.

לֶאֱכֹל *to eat, eating*, + e.g. מאן pi. *refuse* 2 S 13$_{9}$, כלה pi. *finish* 1 K 14$_{1}$ Ru 3$_{3}$, נגשׁ hi. *bring* food for someone 2 S 13$_{11}$ 17$_{29}$, אתה *come* Is 56$_{9}$, טעם *taste* food Jb 34$_{3}$, ערך *prepare* table 1QS 6$_{4}$, ישׁב *sit down* 1 S 20$_{5.24}$.

אֹכְלֵי שֻׁלְחָן *those who eat at table* 2 S 19$_{29}$ 1 K 2$_{7}$ 18$_{19}$, [או]כלי לחמי *those who eat my bread*, i.e. my close companions 1QH 5$_{23}$, וְנָתַן ... לֶחֶם לָאֹכֵל *and it gives ... bread to the eater* Is 55$_{10}$ (|| זרע *sow*).

2. destroy, devour, oft. by burning; distinction from §1 not always clear, e.g., lion as הָאֹכֵל *the eater/destroyer* Jg 14$_{14}$, פִּי אוֹכֵל *destroyer's mouth* Na 3$_{12}$, וְאָכְלָה חֶרֶב *and a sword will devour* (|| שׂבע *be satisfied*, רוה *be drunk*) Jr 46$_{10}$.

<SUBJ> אֵשׁ *fire* Ex 24$_{17}$ Lv 6$_{3}$ 9$_{24}$ 10$_{2}$ Nm 11$_{1}$ (+ בער *burn*) 16$_{35}$ 21$_{28}$ 26$_{10}$ Dt 4$_{24}$ 5$_{25}$ 9$_{3}$ 32$_{22}$ Jg 6$_{21}$ 9$_{15\ 20\ 20}$ (all three || יצא *go out*) 2 S 22$_{9}$||Ps 18$_{9}$ (|| עלה *go up* , בער *burn*) 1 K 18$_{38}$ (+ נפל *fall*) 2 K 1$_{10.10.12.12.14}$ (all five || ירד *descend*) Is 5$_{24}$ (לְשׁוֹן אֵשׁ *tongue of fire*) 9$_{17}$ 10$_{17}$ (|| בער) 26$_{11}$ 29$_{6}$ (לַהַב אֵשׁ *flame of fire*) 30$_{27.30}$ (לַהַב אֵשׁ) 33$_{11.14}$ Jr 5$_{14}$ 17$_{27}$ (:: כבה *douse*) 21$_{14}$ 48$_{45}$ 49$_{27}$ 50$_{32}$ Ezk 15$_{4.5.7}$ 19$_{12.14}$ 21$_{3}$ 28$_{18}$ Ho 8$_{14}$ Jl 1$_{19}$ (|| להט pi. *consume*) 1$_{20}$ 2$_{3}$ (|| להט pi.) 2$_{5}$ (לַהַב אֵשׁ) Am 1$_{4.7.10.12.14}$ 2$_{2.5}$ 5$_{6}$ (:: כבה pi.) 7$_{4.4}$ Ob$_{18}$ (|| דלק *ignite* intrans.) Na 3$_{13.15}$ Zc 11$_{1}$ Ps 21$_{10}$ 50$_{3}$ 78$_{63}$ Jb 1$_{16}$ (אֵשׁ אֱלֹהִים *fire of God*, || בער *burn*) 15$_{34}$ 20$_{26}$ 22$_{20}$ 31$_{12}$ (|| שׁרשׁ *consume to the roots*) Lm 2$_{3}$ (+ בער) 4$_{11}$ 2 C 7$_{1}$ 1QM 11$_{10}$ (לפיד אש *torch of fire*) 4QShir^{b} 16$_{3(\text{Baillet})}$ ([אש]) 1QH 2$_{26}$ 3$_{29}$ (|| תמם hi. *destroy*) 3$_{30.31}$ 4QapPs^{b} 17$_{3}$ (תא[כלם אש]).

שַׁלְהֶבֶת *flame* 1QH 8$_{30}$ (שלבתה), לַהַב *flame* (|| בער *burn*), חֶרֶב *sword* Dt 32$_{42}$ 2 S 2$_{26}$ (+ לָנֶצַח *for ever*) 11$_{25}$ 18$_{8}$ Is 31$_{8}$ Jr 2$_{30}$ 12$_{12}$ 46$_{10.14}$ Ho 11$_{6}$ (|| כלה pi. *destroy*) Na 2$_{14}$ 3$_{15}$ 1QM 6$_{3}$ 12$_{12}$ 19$_{4}$, אֶבֶן *stone* Zc 9$_{15}$ (or em. וְיָכְלוּ *and they shall prevail*), יַעַר *forest* 2 S 18$_{8}$, אֶרֶץ *land* Lv 26$_{38}$ Nm 13$_{32}$, בֹּשֶׁת *shame* Jr 3$_{24}$, מצא ptc. *one who finds* Jr 50$_{7}$, חֹרֶב *heat* Gn 31$_{40}$, קֶרַח *frost* 31$_{40}$, רָעָב *famine* Ezk 7$_{15}$, דֶּבֶר *plague* 7$_{15}$, חָרוֹן *wrath* Ex 15$_{7}$ (+ כַּקַּשׁ *as stubble*), קִנְאָה *zeal* Ps 69$_{10}$, perh. נָקָם *vengeance* 1QM 15$_{3}$ + Sup, נֶפֶשׁ *soul*, i.e. passion Si 6$_{3}$, אֵיד *disaster* Jb 18$_{13}$ (or em.; see Ni. Prep.), בְּכוֹר *first-born of* death Jb 18$_{13}$, אָלָה *curse* Is 24$_{6}$, חֹדֶשׁ *new moon* Ho 5$_{7}$.

איב ptc. *enemy* Lv 26$_{16}$ (perh. אכל = *eat*) Jr 8$_{16}$, גּוֹי *(enemy) nation* 5$_{17.17.17.17}$ 10$_{25.25}$ (|| כלה pi. *destroy*) Ps 79$_{7}$ (|| שׁמם hi. *devastate*), Aram and Philistines Is 9$_{11}$ (+ בְּכָל־פֶּה *with all mouth*, i.e. greedily), Kittim 1QpHab 3$_{11}$ (:: שׂבע *be satisfied*), זור ptc. *stranger* Lv 22$_{10.13}$ Is 1$_{7}$, foreigner 4Q372 1$_{15}$, נָבִיא *prophet* Ezk 22$_{25}$, Y. Si 45$_{19}$ (||

כלה pi. *consume*) דּוֹר *specific class of people* Pr 30$_{14}$, Jeremiah Jr 15$_{16}$, פעל ptc. *doer (of iniquity)* Ps 14$_{4.4}$||Ps 53$_{5.5}$, to foreign gods as lovers Ezk 16$_{20}$, Israel, Israelite Dt 7$_{16}$, Nm 24$_{8}$ Ho 7$_{7}$, perh. פָּרָז *warrior* Hb 3$_{14}$, רעע hi. ptc. *evildoer* Ps 27$_{2}$, ירא ptc. *one who fears Y.* 128$_{2}$, יָלִיד *one born* Lv 22$_{11}$.

<OBJ> עֵץ *tree, wood* Ex 10$_{5}$ (perh. אכל = *eat*) 1 K 18$_{38}$ Jr 5$_{14}$ Ezk 21$_{3}$ (+ בְּךָ *in you*) 1QH 2$_{26}$, אֶרֶז *cedar* Jg 9$_{15}$, עָלֶה *leaf* Si 6$_{3}$, קַשׁ *stubble* Is 5$_{24}$ Jl 2$_{5}$, שָׁמִיר *thorn* Is 9$_{17}$ 10$_{17}$, שַׁיִת *thorn-bush* 9$_{17}$ 10$_{17}$ (both || בער pi. *burn*), תְּהוֹם *abyss* Am 7$_{4}$, אֶרֶץ *land* Dt 32$_{22}$ Is 24$_{6}$ Jr 8$_{16}$ 2 C 7$_{13}$ (perh. אכל = *eat*), אֲדָמָה *land* Is 1$_{7}$, חֵלֶק *portion* Ho 5$_{7}$ Am 7$_{4}$, נָוֶה *pasture* Jl 1$_{19.20}$, יְבוּל *produce* Dt 32$_{22}$, פְּרִי *fruit* Ezk 19$_{14}$.

נֶפֶשׁ *life* Ezk 22$_{25}$, בָּחוּר *youth* Ps 78$_{63}$, שפט ptc. *judge* Ho 7$_{7}$, עַם *people* Dt 7$_{16}$ Zc 12$_{6}$ Ps 14$_{4}$=53$_{5}$ 1QpHab 3$_{11}$, גּוֹי *nation* Nm 24$_{8}$, צַר *enemy* 24$_{8}$, עָנִי *poor person* Hb 3$_{14}$ Pr 30$_{14}$, אֶבְיוֹן *poor person* 30$_{14}$, חָלָל *battle-victim* 1QM 6$_{3}$, individuals Gn 31$_{40}$ Jg 9$_{20.20}$ 2 K 1$_{10.10.12.12.14}$ Si 45$_{19}$ etc., כְּפִיר *lion cub* Na 2$_{14}$, אֹהֶל *tent* Jb 15$_{34}$, אַרְמוֹן *citadel* Jr 17$_{27}$ 49$_{27}$ Ho 8$_{14}$ Am 1$_{4.7.10.12.14}$ 2$_{2.5}$, יְסוֹד *foundation* Lm 4$_{11}$, אֶבֶן *stone* 1 K 18$_{38}$, עָפָר *dust* 18$_{38}$, בְּרִיחַ *bar* Na 3$_{13}$, מַטֶּה *rod* Ezk 19$_{12}$, עֹלָה *sacrifice* Lv 6$_{3}$ (+ דֶּשֶׁן consume to *ashes*) 9$_{24}$ 1 K 18$_{38}$ 2 C 7$_{1}$, חֵלֶב *fat* Lv 9$_{24}$, בָּשָׂר *flesh* Dt 32$_{42}$ Zc 9$_{15}$ (if em. וְכָבְשׁוּ *and they will subjugate* to בָּשָׂר) 1QM 12$_{12}$ 19$_{4}$ 1QH 17$_{3}$ ([בש]ר), פֵּאָה *forehead* Jr 48$_{45}$, בַּד *limb* Jb 18$_{13}$ (or em.; see Ni. Prep.) 18$_{13}$, כֹּחַ *strength* 4Q372 1$_{15}$, רִשְׁעָה *wickedness* 1QM 11$_{10}$, יֶתֶר *remainder* Jb 22$_{20}$.

<PREP> בְּ partitive, *(some) of*, + עַם *people* 2 S 18$_{8}$, אִישׁ *man* 1QM 15$_{3}$ + Sup, אֵל *god* 15$_{3}$ + Sup, אֶרֶז *cedar* Zc 11$_{1}$, מוּסָד *foundation* 4QShir^{b} 16$_{3}$ ([א]וכלת), אֹשׁ *foundation* 1QH 3$_{30}$, רָקִיעַ *surface* 3$_{30}$, שֶׁנְהָב perh. *ivory* 3$_{29}$, of place/instrument, *in, with*, + שָׁבִיב *flame* Si 45$_{19}$, of time, *in*, + יוֹם *day* Gn 31$_{40}$, לַיְלָה *night* 31$_{40}$.

לִפְנֵי *in front of* Y. Jl 2$_{3}$ Ps 50$_{3}$; לְנֶגֶד *in the presence of* Is 1$_{7}$; וְאָכְלוּ עַל־יָמִין וְעַל־שְׂמֹאול *and they shall destroy to the right and to the left* Zc 12$_{6}$, sim. Is 9$_{19}$ (§1); אכל מֵאֶרֶץ *destroy* (so as to remove) *from the world* Pr 30$_{14}$; עַד־אֲבַדּוֹן תֹּאכֵל *it devours even to Abaddon* Jb 31$_{12}$, ותאכל עד תהום רבה *it devours even to the great deep* 1QH 3$_{31}$, עד ימימה תואכל *it devours for days* 8$_{30}$.

<COLL> גער בְּאֹכֵל *rebuke the destroyer* Ml 3$_{11}$, וְהָיָה לֶאֱכֹל *and he will be (ready) for destroying*, i.e. to be destroyed Dt 31$_{17}$, אֹכְלַיִךְ יֵאָכֵלוּ *those who destroy you will be destroyed* Jr 30$_{16}$, מוֹצְאֵיהֶם אֲכָלוּם *those who found them destroyed them* 50$_{7}$.

3. use, use up, enjoy, **<SUBJ>** זור ptc. *stranger* Ho 7$_{9}$, Laban Gn 31$_{15}$, Job Jb 31$_{39}$, אִישׁ *man* Ec 6$_{2.2}$, אָדָם *human being* 5$_{18}$, זֶה *this person* Jb 21$_{25}$, אַתִּיק *ledge* Ezk 42$_{5}$, אָב *father*, i.e. ancestor Ne 9$_{36}$.

Subj. not specified, Is 61$_{6}$, Ec 5$_{10}$.

<OBJ> כֶּסֶף *money* Gn 31$_{15}$, טוֹבָה *goods* Ec 5$_{10}$, עֹשֶׁר *wealth* 6$_{2}$, נֶכֶס *wealth* 6$_{2}$, חַיִל *wealth* Is 61$_{6}$, כָּבוֹד *honour* Ec 6$_{2}$, כֹּחַ *strength* Ho 7$_{9}$ Jb 31$_{39}$.

<PREP> מִן partitive, *(some) of*, + עֹשֶׁר *wealth* Ec 5$_{18}$ 6$_{2}$, נֶכֶס *wealth* 5$_{18}$ 6$_{2}$, כָּבוֹד *honour* Ec 6$_{2}$, טוֹבָה *good* Jb 21$_{25}$ Si 11$_{19}$ ([מ]טוב[ת]), יוֹכְלוּ אַתִּיקִים מֵהֵנָּה *ledges used up from them*, i.e. used up their space Ezk 42$_{5}$ (mss יֹאכְלוּ).

4. experience consequences of actions, **<SUBJ>** צַדִּיק *righteous person* Is 3$_{10}$, Israelite Ho 10$_{13}$, נצר ptc. *keeper* (of fig-tree) Pr 27$_{18}$ (|| כבד pu. *be honoured*), אִישׁ *man* Pr 13$_{2}$, פֶּתִי *simple person* Pr 1$_{31}$.

<OBJ> פְּרִי *fruit, result* Is 3$_{10}$ Ho 10$_{13}$ Pr 27$_{18}$, טוֹב *good (results)* 13$_{2}$. **<PREP>** יֹאכְלוּ מִפְּרִי דַרְכָּם *they shall experience (some) of the fruit*, i.e. result, *of their behaviour* Pr 1$_{31}$.

Also 11QT 37$_{13}$ + Sup ([ואכ]ל) 38$_{1.4}$ ([וי]אכל) 38$_{10}$ 45$_{18}$ + Sup ([אכ]ל) 52$_{1}$ 4QOrd^{b} 24$_{4(mg)}$ 4QOrd^{c} 1.1$_{2.4}$ 1QDM 3$_{1}$ (perh. לְאָכְלָה *for food*) 4QToh A 1.2$_{1}$ (יא[וכל]) 4QD^{a} 6.2$_{13}$.

<SYN> §1 שׁתה *drink*, שׂבע *be satisfied*, יתר hi. *have food left over*, דשן (htp.) *grow fat*, נטע *plant*, זרע *sow*, זבח *slaughter*, לקח *take*, יצג hi. *place*, בשל pi. *boil*, צלה *roast*, שׂמח *be merry*, הלל pi. *praise*, ישב *sit*, שכב *lie down*, קום *arise*, הלך *go*, שוב *go back*, לין *spend night*, נשא *carry*, לבש *wear* clothes, עטה *cover*, סוך *anoint oneself*, ראה *see*, נגע *touch*, שבר *buy*, שחת hi. *destroy*; §2 כלה pi. *destroy*, להט pi. *consume*, בער *burn*, יצא *go out*, ירד *descend*.

<ANT> §1 שׁפך *pour*, שׂבע *be satisfied*; §2 כבה pi. *douse*.

Ni. Impf. יֵאָכֵל, 3fs תֵּאָכֵל, יֵאָכְלוּ (יֵאָכֵלוּ), 3fpl

תֵּאָכַלְנָה; + waw וַיֵּאָכֵל ,וְנֶאֱכַל; ptc. נֶאֱכֶלֶת; inf. הֵאָכֹל—**1. be eaten,** <SUBJ> אֹכֶל *food* Lv 11$_{34}$, מַאֲכָל *food* Gn 6$_{21}$, פֶּסַח *passover meal* Ex 12$_{46}$, חָמֵץ *leaven* 13$_{3}$, מַצָּה *unleavened bread* 13$_{7}$ Nm 28$_{17}$ Ezk 45$_{21}$, פְּרִי *fruit* Lv 19$_{23}$, תְּאֵנָה *fig* Jr 24$_{2.3.8}$ 29$_{17}$ (all + מֵרֹעַ *because they are bad*), בָּשָׂר *flesh* Ex 21$_{28}$ Lv 7$_{15.19}$ Nm 12$_{12}$ (perh. אכל = *be destroyed*), יתר ni. ptc. *remnants* of sacrifice Ex 29$_{34}$ Lv 6$_{9}$ (+ מַצּוֹת *as unleavened loaves*) 7$_{16}$ 11QT 43$_{11}$, תָּפֵל *bland food* Jb 6$_{6}$, sacrifices (various) Lv 6$_{16.19.23}$ 7$_{6.16}$ 19$_{6.7}$ 22$_{30}$ 11QT 20$_{12}$ (+ חמץ with *leaven*) 20$_{12}$ 4QMMT A 2$_{11}$ (נא[כלת]); + על החלבים *with the fat*), חַיָּה *animal* Lv 11$_{47.47}$, צַיִד *game* 17$_{13}$, עוֹף *bird* 17$_{13}$, צְבִי *gazelle* Dt 12$_{22}$, אַיָּל *deer* 12$_{22}$, שֶׁרֶץ *swarming creature* Lv 11$_{41}$, דָּג *fish* CD 12$_{13}$.

<PREP> בְּ of place, *in*, + מָקוֹם *place* Lv 6$_{19}$ 7$_{6}$ 19$_{6.7}$ 22$_{30}$, בַּיִת *house* Ex 12$_{46}$, of time, *in*, + יוֹם *day* Lv 7$_{15.18}$ 19$_{6.7}$ 22$_{30}$ 11QT 20$_{12}$ 43$_{4.17.17}$; לְ of agent, *by* Ex 12$_{16}$; מִן partitive, *(some) of* + בָּשָׂר *flesh* Lv 7$_{18}$.

<COLL> (for Jr 30$_{16}$, see Qal, Coll.) אִם הֵאָכֹל יֵאָכֵל *if any of it is eaten* Lv 7$_{18}$ 19$_{7}$, אל יאכלו *let them not be eaten* CD 12$_{13}$.

2. be destroyed, devoured, <SUBJ> עוֹר *skin* Jb 18$_{13}$ (if em.; see Prep.), גָּדִישׁ *stack of grain* Ex 22$_{5}$, קָמָה *standing grain* 22$_{5}$, שָׂדֶה *field* 22$_{5}$, אֶרֶץ *earth* Zp 1$_{18}$ 3$_{8}$, Tyre Zc 9$_{4}$, אַחֲרִית *survivors* Ezk 23$_{25}$.

<PREP> בְּ of agent/place, *by*, *in*, + אֵשׁ *fire* Ezk 23$_{25}$ Zp 1$_{18}$ 3$_{8}$ Zc 9$_{4}$, דְּוַי *illness* Jb 18$_{13}$ (if. em. יֹאכַל בַּדֵּי disaster *will consume the limbs of* to יֵאָכֵל בִּדְוַי *it will be consumed by illness*).

Pu. Pf. אֻכְּלוּ; impf. תְּאֻכְּלוּ; ptc. אֻכָּל—**be destroyed,** <SUBJ> סְנֶה *bush* Ex 3$_{2}$, Israelites Is 1$_{20}$ (+ חֶרֶב = בחרב 1QIsa[a] *by the sword*), איב ptc. *enemy* Na 1$_{10}$, שַׁעַר *gate* Ne 2$_{3.13}$.

<PREP> בָּאֵשׁ *in/by means of the fire* Ne 2$_{3.13}$; כְּקַשׁ יָבֵשׁ *as dry stubble* Na 1$_{10}$.

Hi. Pf. הֶאֱכַלְתָּם ,הֶאֱכַלְתִּי (הֶאֱכַלְתִּיךָ); impf. יַאֲכִלֵנוּ, (Sam יאכלהו), תַּאֲכִל ,אוֹכִיל; + waw 3ms Q והאכילכה, 3fs Si והאכילתהו, 1cs וְהֶאֱכַלְתִּי (וְהַאֲכַלְתִּיךָ ,וְהַאֲכִלְתִּים); 3ms וַיַּאֲכִלֵנִי ,וַיַּאֲכִלְךָ ,וַיַּאֲכִילֵהוּ, 3mpl וַיַּאֲכִלוּם; impv. הַאֲכִלֵהוּ ,וְהַאֲכִ(י)לֻהוּ; ptc. מַאֲכִיל (מַאֲכִלְךָ ,מַאֲכִילָם); inf. הָכִיל, Q לְ[ה]אכילם—**1. feed, force to eat** (Is 49$_{26}$); subj. Y. except 1 K 22$_{27}$‖2 C 18$_{26}$ Ezk 3$_{3}$ Pr 25$_{21}$ 31$_{27}$ (if em.; see Obj.) 2 C 28$_{15}$ (persons) Si 15$_{3}$ (Wisdom); subj. not specified, 4QMMT A 2$_{79}$.

<OBJ> recipient of food, Israelites Ex 16$_{32}$ Nm 11$_{4.18}$ Dt 8$_{3.16}$ 32$_{13(Sam)}$ Jr 9$_{14}$ 19$_{9}$ Ezk 16$_{19}$ Ho 11$_{4}$ Ps 80$_{6}$ 81$_{17}$ 2 C 28$_{15}$, ינה hi. ptc. *oppressor* Is 49$_{26}$, שׂנא ptc. *enemy* Pr 25$_{21}$, religious person Si 15$_{3}$, נָבִיא false *prophet* Jr 23$_{15}$, Micaiah 1 K 22$_{27}$‖2 C 18$_{26}$, Ezekiel Ezk 3$_{2}$, בֶּטֶן *stomach* 3$_{3}$, one impure with skin disease 4QMMT A 2$_{79}$.

Food given, לֶחֶם *bread* Ex 16$_{32}$ 1 K 22$_{27}$‖2 C 18$_{26}$ Ps 80$_{6}$ Pr 25$_{21}$ (‖ שׁקה hi. *give to drink*) 31$_{27}$ (if em. תֹּאכַל *she eats* to תַּאֲכִל *she feeds*) Si 15$_{3}$ (‖ שׁקה hi.), בָּשָׂר *flesh* Nm 11$_{4.18}$ Is 49$_{26}$ Jr 19$_{9}$, מָן *manna* Dt 8$_{3.16}$, תְּנוּבָה *produce* Dt 32$_{13}$ (Sam), סֹלֶת *fine flour* Ezk 16$_{19}$ (+ נתן *give* food), שֶׁמֶן *oil* 16$_{19}$, דְּבַשׁ *honey* 16$_{19}$, מַיִם *water* 1 K 22$_{27}$‖2 C 18$_{26}$, לַעֲנָה *wormwood* Jr 9$_{14}$ 23$_{15}$ (both ‖ שׁקה hi.), מְגִלָּה *scroll* Ezk 3$_{2.3}$ (‖ מלא pi. *fill*); without second obj. Ho 11$_{4}$ 2 C 28$_{15}$ (‖ לבשׁ hi. *clothe*, נעל hi. *provide with shoes*, שׁקה hi.).

<PREP> בְּ of place, *in*, + מִדְבָּר *desert* Ex 16$_{32}$ Dt 8$_{16}$; מִן feed someone *from/with*, + חֵלֶב *fat* of wheat Ps 81$_{17}$ (‖ שׂבע hi. *satisfy*), תְּרוּמָה *contribution* 4QOrd[b] 2.2$_{3}$ (לְ[ה]אכילם), holy things 4QMMT A 2$_{79}$; אוֹכִיל לוֹ *I would feed him* Ho 11$_{4}$ (if em. אוֹכִיל : לֹא *I would feed (him). He will not* return).

2. destroy, חֶרֶב ... מְרוּטָה לְהָכִיל *a sword ... polished to destroy* Ezk 21$_{33}$ (but perh. כול hi. *contain*; or em. לְכָלָה *for destruction*).

3. cause to enjoy, וְהַאֲכַלְתִּיךָ נַחֲלַת יַעֲקֹב *and I shall cause you to enjoy the inheritance of Jacob* Is 58$_{14}$.

<SYN> §1 שׁקה hi. *give* liquid *to drink*.

→ אֹכֶל *food*, אָכְלָה *food*, מַאֲכָל *food*, מַכֹּלֶת *food*, אֲכִילָה *meal*, מַאֲכֹלֶת *fuel*, מַאֲכֶלֶת *knife*.

אֹכֶל 43.2.7 n.m. **food**—abs. Si, Q אוכל; cstr. אֹכֶל; sf. אָכְלְךָ ,אָכְלוֹ ,אָכְלְכֶם ,אָכְלָם (Q אוכלמה)—**food** sometimes as **prey** (Ps 104$_{21}$ Jb 9$_{26}$ 39$_{29}$) or **produce, harvest**;(Gn 41$_{35.35.36.48}$ Hb 3$_{17}$ Pr 13$_{23}$), <SUBJ> אכל ni. *be eaten* Lv 11$_{34}$, בזה ni. *be despised* Ml 1$_{12}$, היה *be* Gn 41$_{36}$ (+ לְפִקָּדוֹן *as a reserve*) 11QT 47$_{6}$ (+ טָהוֹר *clean*; ‖ שׁקה ho. ptc. *moistened food*; שֶׁמֶן *oil*, יַיִן *wine*), טמא *be unclean* 49$_{7}$ (‖ שׁקה ho. ptc., כְּלִי *vessel*), כרת ni. *be cut off* Jl 1$_{16}$. <NOM CL> אָכְלָם בְּפִיהֶם *their food was in their* *mouth* Ps 78$_{30}$, יש אוכל *there is food* Si 36$_{23(B)}$ (Bmg מאכל *food*).

<OBJ> עשה *produce* Hb 3$_{17}$, קבץ *gather* Gn 41$_{35.48}$, צבר *store* 41$_{35}$, נתן *give* 41$_{48.48}$ Lv 25$_{37}$ (‖ כֶּסֶף *silver*) Ps 104$_{27}$ Jb 36$_{31}$, בוא hi. *bring* 11QT 47$_{13}$ (‖ שֶׁמֶן *oil*, יַיִן *wine*), לקח *take* Gn 14$_{11}$ (‖ רְכוּשׁ *property*), שבר *buy* 42$_{7.10}$ 43$_{4.20.22}$ 44$_{25}$ Dt 2$_{6}$, hi. *sell* 2$_{28}$, שפך *pour* 4Q370 1$_{1}$, בקשׁ pi. *seek* Lm 1$_{19}$ Ps 104$_{21}$ (+ טֶרֶף *prey*), חפר *seek* Jb 39$_{29}$, שׁאל *request* Ps 78$_{18}$, טעם *taste* Jb 12$_{11}$, תעב pi. *loathe* Ps 107$_{18}$; מלא pi. *fill* Gn 44$_{1}$ (as second obj.; + אַמְתַּחַת *sack*), עטר pi. *crown* 11QPs^{a} 26$_{13}$ (as second obj.; + הַר *mountain*; + לכול חי *for every living being*).

<CSTR> אֹכֶל שְׂדֵה־הָעִיר *food of*, i.e. from, *the field of the city* Gn 41$_{48}$, אֹכֶל הַשָּׁנִים *food of*, i.e. harvested during, *years* 41$_{35}$, sim. 41$_{48}$, אוכל בית *food of a house* Si 11$_{30(Segal)}$ (AHL; see Prep.); נֶשֶׁךְ אֹכֶל *interest of*, i.e. on, *food* Dt 23$_{20}$ (‖ כֶּסֶף *silver*), מְעַט־ *little of* Gn 43$_{2}$ 44$_{25}$, רָב־ *abundance of* Pr 13$_{23}$ Si 37$_{30(Bmg, D)}$, עֵת הָאֹכֶל at *the time of*, i.e. for, *food* Ru 2$_{14}$, כָּל־אֹכֶל *all of (the) food* Gn 14$_{11}$ (אָכְלָם) 41$_{35.48}$ Lv 11$_{34}$ (הָאֹכֶל) Ps 107$_{18}$ 11QT 49$_{7}$ 4QRitPur 67$_{3}$ (מכול א[וכ]ל).

<APP> following בַּר *grain* Gn 41$_{35}$, נִיב *fruit* Ml 1$_{12}$; אֹכֶל ... שִׂמְחָה וָגִיל *food ..., joy and gladness* Jl 1$_{16}$. **<ADJ>** טוב *good* 11QPs^{a} 26$_{13}$.

<PREP> יִהְיֶה ... לְאָכְלְכֶם *it will be ... as your food* Gn 47$_{24}$ (+ זֶרַע *seed*; if em. לֶאֱכֹל לָכֶם *for eating by you*), בעדן [לתענוג לאכל] *in Eden for pleasure and for food* 4QJub^{a} 6$_{4}$; ככלב הוא באוכל בית *as a dog he is at the food of a house* Si 11$_{30(Segal)}$ (AHL הוא בא וכל בית *he comes, and every house*), נתן בְּ *give in exchange for* Lm 1$_{11}$; יש אוכל [מאוכל נעים] *there is food more pleasant than (other) food* Si 36$_{23(Segal)}$; תחסרון מאוכלה *you will be in lack of her food* 51$_{24}$ (if em.; see אֵלּוּ *these*); טוש עַל *swoop upon* Jb 9$_{26}$; לְפִי *according to*, + כסס *determine* Ex 12$_{4}$, לקט *gather* 16$_{16.18.21}$ (כְּפִי); תעה לִבְלִי *wander without* Jb 38$_{41}$.

<COLL> [ל[ש]בי ולמ]שמות [ולאכל] *for captivity, devastation and devouring* 4QJub^{a} 2$_{15}$.

Also 4Q285 5$_{3}$.

<SYN> שקה ho. ptc. *moistened food*, שֶׁמֶן *oil*, יַיִן *wine*, כֶּסֶף *silver*.

⇒ אכל *eat*.

אֻכָל 1 pr.n.m. **Ucal**—אֻכָל (mss אֻכָל)—appar. addressed by Agur, Pr 30$_{1}$ (or em. וָאֵכֶל *and I am exhausted* or וְאֻכָל *and I have endured* or וְאֻכָל *that I should prevail* or וַיּוּכָל *and he has prevailed*).

אָכְלָה 18.0.1 n.f. **food, fuel**—Q אוכלה—**1.** usu. **food. 2. fuel**for fire, Ezk 15$_{4.6}$ 21$_{37}$ 23$_{37}$.

<PREP> alw. לְאָכְלָה *for*, or *as*, *food* (usu. + לְ as food *for*), + היה *be* Gn 1$_{29}$ (subj. עֵשֶׂב *grass*, עֵץ *tree*) 6$_{21}$ (subj. מַאֲכָל *food*) 9$_{3}$ (subj. רֶמֶשׂ *moving being*) Lv 25$_{6}$ (subj. שַׁבָּת *sabbath*) Ezk 21$_{37}$ (subj. Ammonites) 34$_{5.8.10}$ (in all three, subj. צֹאן *flock*) 11QT 59$_{7}$ (subj. Israelites).

נתן *give* Ex 16$_{15}$ (obj. לֶחֶם *bread*) Ezk 15$_{6}$ (obj. עֵץ *tree*) 29$_{5}$ (obj. פַּרְעֹה *Pharaoh*) 39$_{4}$ (obj. גּוֹג *Gog*), ni. *be given* 15$_{4}$ (subj. (עֵץ) 35$_{12}$ (subj. הַר *mountain*), עבר hi. *cause* children *to pass* through fire 23$_{37}$, אתה hi. *bring* animals Jr 12$_{9}$ (or em. אֵתָיו לְאָכְלָה *come to food*, i.e. to eat it, of animals).

אֶת־כָּל־יֶרֶק עֵשֶׂב לְאָכְלָה appar. *every green grass is for food* Gn 1$_{30}$ (mss וְאֶת; or em. נָתַתִּי *I have given*). מִן־הַבְּהֵמָה אֲשֶׁר־הִיא ... לְאָכְלָה *any animal that is ... for food* Lv 11$_{39}$.

⇒ אכל *eat*.

אָכֵן 19 emph. part. **indeed, however, 1.** emphatic, **indeed, surely** (distinction from §2 not alw. clear), **a.** with verb, סור *turn* intrans. 1 S 15$_{32}$, נטה hi. *turn* trans. 1 K 11$_{2}$, עשׂה *do* Jr 8$_{8}$, נשׁא hi. *deceive* 4$_{10}$, בגד *betray* 3$_{20}$ (or em. אַךְ כִּבְגֹד *but as* a woman *betrays*), ידע ni. *be known* Ex 2$_{14}$.

b. with nom. cl., אָכֵן יֵשׁ י׳ בַּמָּקוֹם הַזֶּה *surely Y. is in this place* Gn 28$_{16}$, אָכֵן חָצִיר הָעָם *surely the people is grass* Is 40$_{7}$, אָכֵן לַשֶּׁקֶר מִגְּבָעוֹת *surely it is in vain (to expect salvation) from (the) hills* Jr 3$_{23}$ (or em. הַגְּבָעוֹת surely *the mountains* are useless), אָכֵן בַּי׳ ... תְּשׁוּעַת יִשְׂרָאֵל *surely in Y. ... is the salvation of Israel* 3$_{23}$, אָכֵן אַתָּה אֵל מִסְתַּתֵּר *indeed you are a hidden God* (unless, as §1a, *surely, God, you hide yourself*) Is 45$_{15}$ (or em. אִתָּךְ surely *with you* there is).

2. adversative, **however, nonetheless, a.** with verb, נשׂא *carry* Is 53$_{4}$, סבל *carry* 53$_{4}$, נפל *fall* Ps 82$_{7}$, שׁכם hi. *rise early* Zp 3$_{7}$, שׁחת hi. *make corrupt* 3$_{7}$, שׁמע *hear* Ps

31$_{23}$ 66$_{19}$, קשׁב *pay attention* 66$_{19}$, מות *die* 82$_{7}$.

b. with nom. cl., אָכֵן מִשְׁפָּטִי אֶת־י׳ וּפְעֻלָּתִי אֶת־אֱלֹהָי *nonetheless, my judgment is with Y. and my reward is with my God* Is 49$_{4}$, אָכֵן רוּחַ־הִיא בֶאֱנוֹשׁ *nonetheless, there is a spirit in a person* Jb 32$_{8}$.

[אַכְסַדְרָן] 0.0.1 n.[m.] **vestibule,** בקבר צדוק תחת עמוד האכסדרן *in the grave of Zadok, below the column of the vestibule* 3QTr 11$_{3}$.

אכף 1 vb. **press—Qal** Pf. אָכַף—אָכַף עָלָיו פִּיהוּ *his mouth,* perh. his hunger, *has pressed him (to continue labouring)* Pr 16$_{26}$, כאכפו/כאכפם ל[ו איבים מסביב] *when enemies around pressed against him* Si 46$_{5(Segal)}$ (if em. כאכפה *when pressure* was), sim. 46$_{16}$.

→ אֶכֶף *pressure,* אַכְפָּה *pressure.*

[אֶכֶף] 1 n.m. **pressure**—sf. אַכְפִּי—**pressure,** or perh., **hand,** אַכְפִּי עָלֶיךָ לֹא־יִכְבָּד *my pressure against you will not be heavy* Jb 33$_{7}$ (|| אֵימָה *terror* [or em. אַמָּה *cubit*] i.e. arm; sim. 13$_{21}$ כַּף *hand*).

→ אכף *press.*

[אַכְפָּה] 0.1 n.[f.] **pressure,** כאכפה ל[ו איבים מסביב] appar. *when enemies around were pressure to him* Si 46$_{5(Segal).16}$ (כאכפה לו איב[י]ו מסביב]; or em. in both כְּאָכְפָם or כְּאָכְפוֹ *when they pressed*).

⊞ אכף *press.*

אִכָּר 7.0.1 n.m. **farmer**—pl. אִכָּרִים, sf. אִכָּרֵיכֶם—<SUBJ> היה *be* 2 C 26$_{10}$ (+ לוֹ *to him,* but perh. אִכָּרִים... בֶּהָרִים is nom. cl., *farmers were in the hills;* || כרם ptc. *vinedresser*), בושׁ *be ashamed* Jr 14$_{4}$, hi. Jl 1$_{11}$ (|| כרם ptc.), חפה *cover* Jr 14$_{4}$, ישׁב *dwell* 31$_{24}$.

<NOM CL> בְּנֵי נֵכָר אִכָּרֵיכֶם *foreigners are your farmers* Is 61$_{5}$ (|| כרם ptc. *vinedresser*). <OBJ> נפץ pi. *shatter* Jr 51$_{23}$ (|| רעה ptc. *shepherd;* + פֶּחָה *governor*), קרא *call* Am 5$_{16}$ (+ אֶל־אֵבֶל *to mourning;* || מִסְפֵּד *lamentation,* or, || ידע ptc. *one who knows* mourning, if em. וּמִסְפֵּד אֶל־ *and* call *lamentation to* to וְאֶל־מִסְפֵּד *and to lamentation*).

<COLL> אִכָּרִים וְנָסְעוּ בַּעֵדֶר *farmers and those who move with flocks* Jr 31$_{24}$, רֹעֶה וְעֶדְרוֹ ... אִכָּר וְצִמְדּוֹ *a shepherd and his flock ... a farmer and his team* 51$_{23}$.

Also 4Q416 2$_{1}$.

<SYN> כרם ptc. *vinedresser.*

אַכְשָׁף 3 pl.n. **Achshaph,** originally Canaanite town on border of Asher, perh. T. Kēsān (T. Kīsōn) 9 km SE of Akko and/or Kh. Iksāf 27 km E of Tyre, Jos 11$_{1}$ 12$_{20}$ (or em. in both אַכְשִׁף *Achshiph;* both + מֶלֶךְ *king of*) 19$_{25}$.

אַל I 725.245.206.2 adv. **no(t). 1.** as adverb, expressing desire that an action will not occur, **may it** (etc.) **not,** or prohibiting an action, **do not, you** (etc.) **are not to.** Often || to לֹא *not,* e.g. אַל־תֵּלְכִי ... וְגַם לֹא תַעֲבוּרִי *do not go ... and do not leave either* Ru 2$_{8}$, Ex 23$_{1}$ 34$_{3}$ Lv 10$_{6}$ 11$_{43}$ 19$_{4}$ Jg 13$_{14}$ 1 K 20$_{8}$ Jr 7$_{6}$ Mc 2$_{6}$ Pr 22$_{24}$ 27$_{2}$ Ezr 9$_{12}$. Often אַל with a verb follows a positive impv., e.g. אֱמֶת קְנֵה וְאַל־תִּמְכֹּר *buy truth, do not sell it* Pr 23$_{23}$; rarely, the verb with אַל comes after the positive impv., e.g. אל תועץ עם חמיך וממקנא העלים סוד *do not take advice from your father-in-law, and hide your counsel from one who is envious* Si 37$_{10}$.

1a. with impf., juss., or cohort. verb (e.g. 1cs 11QPs[a] 19$_{14}$, 1cpl Jon 1$_{14}$, 2fs 2 S 13$_{20}$, 2fpl Ru 1$_{20}$, 3fs Gn 49$_{6}$, 3fpl Jr 14$_{17}$), with verb usu. immediately following (except לָעַד *for ever* Is 64$_{8}$, בְּאַפְּךָ *in your wrath* Jr 10$_{24}$ Ps 6$_{2}$ 38$_{2}$, בַּחֲמָתְךָ *in your wrath* 6$_{2}$, בְּקֶצְפְּךָ *in your wrath* 38$_{2}$, לְאֶרֶךְ אַפְּךָ *in your patience* Jr 15$_{15}$; אל שיח תשפך *do not pour out your thoughts* Si 35$_{4[F]}$; אַל־נָא *do not, please,* e.g. Gn 13$_{8}$ 18$_{3.30.32}$ 19$_{7}$ 47$_{29}$ Nm 10$_{31}$ 12$_{11.12}$ 22$_{16}$ Jg 6$_{18}$ 1 S 3$_{17}$ 25$_{25}$ 2 S 13$_{25}$ 14$_{18}$ Jr 44$_{4}$ Jon 1$_{14}$ Jb 32$_{21}$), with היה *be* Gn 13$_{8}$ 37$_{27}$ Nm 12$_{12}$ 1 S 18$_{17}$ Jr 17$_{17}$ 20$_{14}$ 50$_{26.29}$ Ezk 2$_{8}$ Zc 1$_{4}$ Ps 32$_{9}$ 69$_{26}$ 109$_{12.12}$ Jb 6$_{29}$ 16$_{18}$ Pr 3$_{7}$ 22$_{26}$ 23$_{20}$ 24$_{28}$ Ec 7$_{16.17}$ 2 C 30$_{7}$ Si 3$_{22}$ 4$_{29.30.31}$ 5$_{9}$ 6$_{1}$ 18$_{33}$ 42$_{11}$ 47$_{23}$ 4QOrd[a] 2$_{6}$ (||Dt 22$_{5}$ לֹא) 1QH 16$_{15(Licht)}$ ([י]היה]) 4QapLam[b] $_{7}$).

חיה *live* Si 40$_{28}$, נצץ hi. *blossom* 11QPs[a] 24$_{13}$, אבד *perish* Jon 1$_{14}$, מות *die* Dt 33$_{6}$ 1 S 12$_{19}$, hi. *kill* 1 K 3$_{26}$ Jr 41$_{8}$ GnzPs 2$_{25}$, ho. *be killed* 2 K 11$_{15}$, כרת ni. *be destroyed* 2 S 3$_{29}$, hi. *destroy* Nm 4$_{18}$, סתר *tear down* Si 35$_{1(F)}$.

אבל htp. *mourn* Ezk 7_{12} Ne 8_{9}, עצב ni. *be distressed* Gn 45_{5} Ne $8_{10.11}$, נוד *show grief* Jr 16_{5} 22_{10}, hi. *cause to wander* Ps 36_{12}, בכה *weep* Jr 22_{10} Mc 1_{10} Ne 8_{9}, אהב *love* Zc 8_{17} Pr 20_{13}, חמד *desire* 6_{25} Si 14_{14}, אוה htp. *desire* Pr $23_{3.6}$ 24_{1} Si 16_{1} 4Q416 10.2_{9}, חפץ *desire* 7_{13}, אבה *be willing* Pr 1_{10}, אות ni. *agree* CD 20_{7}, הבל *be deluded* Ps 62_{11}, בקשׁ pi. *seek* Lv 19_{31} Jr 45_{5} Si $7_{4.6}$, דרשׁ *seek* Am $5_{5.14}$ Jb 3_{4} Si 3_{21} 4Q416 9.2_{19}, חקר *investigate* 3_{21}, תור *seek out* $11_{9(B)}$, ענג htp. *indulge oneself* $37_{29(Bmg, D)}$, שׂמח *rejoice* Is 14_{29} Ezk 7_{12} Ho 9_{1} Ob$_{12}$ Mc 7_{8} Ps $35_{19.24}$ Pr 24_{17} Si 16_{1} 18_{32} 4Q416 9.1_{10}, בוע *rejoice* 16_{2}, גיל *rejoice* Pr 24_{17}, חדה *rejoice* Jb 3_{6}, עלץ *rejoice* Ps 25_{2}.

חרה *become hot, angry* Gn $18_{30.32}$ 31_{35} 44_{18} 45_{5} Ex 32_{22} Jg 6_{39}, ni. *become angry* Si $11_{9(A)}$ (תאחר), htp. *become heated* Ps $37_{1.7.8}$ Pr 24_{19} Si $35_{21(F)}$ $38_{16(mg)}$, קצף *be angry* Is 64_{8}, htp. *be enraged* Si $35_{19(B)}$.

חטא *sin* Gn 42_{22} 1 S 19_{4} Ps 4_{5}, רעע *be evil* Gn 19_{7} 21_{12} Jg 19_{23} 2 S 11_{25}, hi. *harm* Ps 105_{15}||1 C 16_{22} Si $7_{20(C)}$, רשׁע *be wicked* Ec 7_{17}, hi. *condemn* Jb 10_{2} Si 7_{7}, חמס *oppress* Jr 22_{3}, חלל pi. *defile* Lv 19_{29} CD 11_{15}, טמא htp. *defile oneself* Lv 18_{24} Ezk $20_{7.18}$, חבל *corrupt* 4Q416 10.2_{7}, אשׁם *be culpable* Ho 4_{15}, נקה pi. *exonerate* 1 K 2_{9}, מחה ni. *be wiped out* (of sins) Ps 109_{14} Ne 3_{37}, hi. *wipe out* Jr 18_{23} Ne 13_{14}, פדה *redeem* CD 16_{8}, כפר pi. *atone for* Jr 18_{23}, חוס *show pity* Gn 45_{20} Ezk 9_{5}, חמל *spare* Jr 50_{14} 51_{3} Ezk 9_{5}, חנן *spare* Ps 59_{6}, קדשׁ hi. *sanctify* CD 16_{14} ([אל]) 16_{15} (יקד[שׁ]), צדק htp. *justify oneself* Si 7_{5}, טהר pi. *clean* CD 10_{12}, נזה hi. *sprinkle* 4Q251 3_{3} (ל[א]) 4QToh A 2.1_{2} 4QToh B$^{b}_{7}$.

קשׁר *conspire* Si 7_{8}, סות hi. *incite* 2 C 32_{15}, כזב pi. *deceive* 2 K 4_{16} 4Q416 9.1_{22}, כחשׁ pi. *deceive* Si $37_{6(Bmg)}$, נשׁא hi. *deceive* 2 K 18_{29}||Is 36_{14}||2 C 32_{15} 2 K 19_{10}||Is 37_{10} Jr 29_{8} 37_{9}, גבה *be haughty* 13_{15}, כבד *be honoured* 4Q416 9.1_{4}, htp. *honour oneself* Si 3_{10} 10_{26} (תתכבו[ד]) 4Q416 9.2_{20}, הדר htp. *honour oneself* Pr 25_{6}, זוד hi. *act arrogantly* Si $37_{29(D)}$, רהב *act arrogantly* 13_{8}, פרר hi. *break* covenant Jr 14_{21}, מרד *rebel* Nm 14_{9} Jos $22_{19.19}$ (L אֶל), מרה hi. *rebel* Ex 23_{21} 4Q185 1.2_{3} (ו[א]ל; Allegro יצל *let him deliver*) perh. Si 3_{23}, סרב pi. *rebel* 4_{25}.

ירא *fear* Gn 15_{1} 21_{17} 26_{24} 35_{17} 43_{23} (+ 69t in MT, all 2 masc. or fem.) 1QM 15_{8} 17_{4}, פחד *dread* Is 44_{8} Si 9_{13} 41_{3}, ירה *fear* Is 44_{8}, ערץ *tremble* Dt 20_{3} 31_{6} Jos 1_{9} 1QM 15_{8}, חפז *be alarmed* Dt 20_{3} 1QM 15_{8}, חתת *be dismayed* Dt 1_{21} Jos 8_{1} 10_{25} Is 51_{7} Jr 1_{17} 10_{2} 17_{18} 30_{10}=46_{27} Ezk 2_{6} 1 C 22_{13} 28_{20} 2 C $20_{15.17}$ 32_{7} 1QM 15_{8} (תח[תו]) 4QPsJos^{a} 3.2_{10}, תמה *be astounded* Ec 5_{7} Si 11_{21} ([א]ל ת[ת]מה).

חפר *feel shame* Ps 34_{6}, בושׁ *feel shame* Jr 17_{18} Ps $25_{2.20}$ $31_{2.18}$ 69_{7} 71_{1} Si $4_{20.22(C).26}$ 42_{1}, hi. *shame* Ps $119_{31.116}$, pi. *shame* Si 8_{6}, כלם ni. *be humiliated* Is 54_{4} Ps 69_{7}, hi. *humiliate* Si 3_{13} 8_{5}, ענה pi. *humiliate* 2 S 13_{12}, pu. *be humiliated* 1Q25 4_{3}.

שׂנא *hate* 1QS $5_{26(mg)}$, צור *show hostility to* Dt $2_{9.19}$, תעב pi. *loathe, cause to be odious* Si 7_{26} 11_{2}, קוץ *loathe* Pr 3_{11} Si 4_{9} 6_{25}, שׁקץ pi. *make detestable* Lv 11_{43} CD 12_{11}, בוז *despise* Pr 23_{22} Si 34_{22}, בזה *despise* 7_{11}, מאס *despise* Pr 3_{11} Jb 5_{17} Si 7_{19} 8_{9} 38_{4} 1QH 13_{7}, נאץ *despise* Jr 14_{21} Si 41_{22}, נטר *harbour grudge* CD 13_{17}, קלל pi. *curse* Ec $10_{20.20}$, hi. *lighten* 4Q416 9.2_{21}, נבל pi. *treat as foolish* Jr 14_{21}, התל pi. *mock* Si $11_{4(A)}$, ליץ htpo. *mock* Is 28_{22}, לעג *mock* Si 4_{1} $34_{22(mg)}$, hi. *mock* 34_{22}, קלס pi. *mock* $11_{4.4(B)}$, זנח *reject* Ps 44_{24}, קנא pi. *be jealous* 37_{1} Pr 3_{31} 23_{17} $24_{1.19}$ Si $9_{1.2.11}$ ([אל]) 30_{39} (ל[א]).

כחד pi. *conceal* Jos 7_{19} 1 S 3_{17} 2 S 14_{18} Jr $38_{14.25}$ 50_{2}, עלם hi. *conceal* Lm 3_{56}, htp. *hide oneself* Ps 55_{2} Si 4_{4} 38_{16}, צפן hi. *conceal* $4_{23(A)}$, סתר hi. *conceal* Ps 27_{9} 69_{18} 102_{3} 119_{19} 143_{7} GnzPs 2_{25} 1QS 8_{12}, htp. *hide oneself* 4Q487 2_{4} (יסתת[ר]).

מור hi. *exchange* Si 7_{18} 4Q416 9.2_{6}, מכר *sell* CD $12_{8.10.10}$ 4Q416$9.2_{18}$, ערב *guarantee* Si 8_{13}, *give in pledge* 4Q416 9.2_{18}, htp. *mingle* Pr 24_{21} 4QToh A 1.1_{5} (ל[א]), שׁחד *bribe* Si 32_{14}, שׁלם pi. *repay* 10_{6}, גמל *repay* $37_{11(B)}$ (Bmg עַל).

ידע *know* 1 S 20_{3} 21_{3} Is 6_{9} Jr 36_{19} 38_{24} Si $7_{3.20(A)}$ 1QS 8_{18}, ni. *be known* Ru $3_{3.14}$, hi. *make known* CD 15_{10}, חשׁב *think* 2 S 19_{20} Zc 7_{10} 8_{17} 4Q416 9.1_{7}, hi. *reckon* Si 7_{16}, חרשׁ *devise* Pr 3_{29} Si 7_{12} 8_{2}, בין *discern* Is 6_{9}, hi. *consider* Si $42_{12(M)}$, htpol. *be attentive* Is 43_{18} Si 7_{5} 9_{5}, יעץ ni. *be advised* 37_{10}, למד *learn* Jr 10_{2}, בחר *choose* Pr 3_{31}, זכר *remember* 2 S 19_{20} Is 43_{18} 64_{8} Ps 25_{7} 79_{8} Si 38_{21} CD 15_{2}, ni. *be remembered* 11QPs^{a} 24_{11}, שׁכח *forget* Dt 9_{7} Ps 10_{12} $74_{19.23}$ 103_{2} Pr 3_{1} 4_{5} Si 3_{14} 37_{6} 11QPs^{a} 24_{10}, חכם htp. *appear wise* Ec 7_{16} Si 10_{26}, אמן ni. *be trusted* CD 10_{2}, hi. *trust* Jr 12_{6} Mc 7_{5} Jb 15_{31} Pr 26_{25} 2 C 32_{15} Si 7_{26} 12_{10}

13$_{11}$ 4Q424 1$_{7}$ ([תא]מין]) 1$_{8}$ ([תאמ]ין]), בטח *trust* Jr 7$_{4}$ 9$_{3}$ Mc 7$_{5}$ Ps 62$_{11}$ 146$_{3}$ Si 5$_{5.8}$ 13$_{11}$ 16$_{3}$ 32$_{15}$ 35$_{21.21(B)}$ 4Q416 9.2$_{14}$, hi. *cause to trust* 2 K 18$_{30}$||Is 36$_{15}$, רעה htp. *make friends* Pr 22$_{24}$, דמה *be like* 4QPsJos^{a} 6.1$_{5}$.

אמר *say, think* Dt 9$_{4}$ 2 S 13$_{32}$ 1 K 22$_{8}$||2 C 18$_{7}$ Is 56$_{3.3}$ Jr 1$_{7}$ Ps 35$_{25.25}$ Pr 3$_{28}$ 20$_{22}$ 24$_{49}$ Ec 5$_{5}$ 7$_{10}$ Si 5$_{1.3.4.6}$ 11$_{23.24}$ 15$_{11}$ 16$_{17}$ 34$_{12.31}$, דבר pi. *speak* Ex 20$_{19}$ 2 K 18$_{26}$||Is 36$_{11}$ Pr 23$_{9}$ Si 11$_{8}$ 1QS 5$_{25}$ 6$_{10.10.11}$ CD 10$_{17.19}$, נטף hi. *speak* Mc 2$_{6}$, נדר *vow* CD 16$_{13}$, שׁבע ni. *swear* Ho 4$_{15}$ 4Q416 9.2$_{18}$, נגד hi. *tell* 2 S 1$_{20}$ Mc 1$_{10}$, בשׂר pi. *proclaim* 2 S 1$_{20}$, ענה *answer* Pr 26$_{4}$, קרא *call* Ru 1$_{20}$, ni. *be called* Si 5$_{14.14}$, סלף pi. *declare corrupt* 11$_{7}$, אשׁר pi. *call happy* 11$_{27}$ (תאשׁ]רהו]) 11$_{28}$, גלה pi. *reveal* Is 16$_{3}$ Pr 25$_{9}$ Si 8$_{19}$ 4Q251 7$_{3}$ ([אל יגל]) 7$_{6}$, כתב ni. *be written* Ps 69$_{29}$, גדל hi. *magnify* Ob$_{12}$, פגע *entreat* Jr 7$_{16}$ Ru 1$_{16}$, פלל htp. *pray* Jr 7$_{16}$=11$_{14}$=14$_{11}$, יכח hi. *reprove* Ho 4$_{4}$ Ps 6$_{2}$ 38$_{2}$ Pr 9$_{8}$ Si 34$_{31}$, יסר pi. *chastise* Ps 6$_{2}$.

סוד perh. *boast* Si 7$_{14}$, htp. *take secret counsel* 8$_{17}$ 9$_{3}$ 42$_{12}$, הלל *boast* Ps 75$_{5}$, pi. *praise* Pr 27$_{2}$ Si 11$_{2}$, htp. *boast* 1 K 20$_{11}$ Jr 9$_{22.22.22}$ Pr 27$_{1}$ Si 8$_{7}$ 4Q185 1.2$_{9}$, פאר htp. *gloat* Si 11$_{4(B)}$, לשׁן hi. *slander* Pr 30$_{10}$, רגז *quarrel* Gn 45$_{24}$, רגל pi. *slander* Si 5$_{14.14}$, hi. *be familiar with* 8$_{4}$ ([אל]).

עשׂה *do* Gn 19$_{8}$ 22$_{12}$ Jg 19$_{23}$ 2 S 13$_{12}$ Jr 5$_{10}$ 39$_{12}$ 40$_{16}$ 44$_{4}$ Jb 13$_{20}$ Si 7$_{1}$ 8$_{18}$ CD 10$_{14}$ 13$_{15}$ 4Q464 6$_{3}$ ([אל תעש]), פעל *do* Si 35$_{19}$, יסף hi. *repeat* Ex 8$_{25}$ 10$_{28}$ (L אֶל) Dt 3$_{26}$ Jb 40$_{32}$ Pr 30$_{6}$ 11QPs^{a} 24$_{12}$ 4Q416 9.1$_{18.20}$ 9.2$_{10}$ ([א]ל), שׁנה *repeat* Si 7$_{14}$, דמה *cease* Jr 14$_{17}$ 4Q416 2$_{3}$, פתח *open* Si 34$_{12}$ 4Q487 16$_{2}$ CD 11$_{9(Schechter, AHL)}$ (י]פתח]), אטר *close* Ps 69$_{16}$, קפץ *close* Si 4$_{23(C)}$, htp. perh. *be impatient* 35$_{19(E, F)}$, גרע *withhold* Jr 26$_{2}$, חשׂך *withhold* Is 54$_{2}$ 58$_{1}$, כלא *withhold* 43$_{6}$, מנע *withhold* Pr 3$_{27}$ 23$_{13}$ 30$_{7}$ Si 4$_{3.23}$ 7$_{21.33}$ 14$_{14}$ (אל ת]מנע]) 35$_{3}$ GnzPs 3$_{4}$ 11QPs^{a} 24$_{5}$, ni. *be withheld* Nm 22$_{16}$, עצר *restrain* 2 K 4$_{24}$ 2 C 14$_{10}$, מאן pi. *refuse* Si 4$_{27}$.

נתן *give, allow* Dt 21$_{8}$=11QT 63$_{7}$ Jos 10$_{19}$ 1 S 1$_{16}$ Is 62$_{7}$ Jl 2$_{17}$ Jon 1$_{14}$ Ps 27$_{12}$ 41$_{3}$ 74$_{19}$ 121$_{3}$ 140$_{9}$ Pr 6$_{4}$ 30$_{8}$ 31$_{3}$ Lm 2$_{18}$ Ec 5$_{5}$ 7$_{21}$ Ezr 9$_{12}$ Si 8$_{3}$ 9$_{6}$ 12$_{5.5}$ 30$_{21.28.31}$ 37$_{27}$ 42$_{12(B)}$ CD 13$_{14}$ 4QapLam$^{b}_{1}$ 4QapPs^{b} 45$_{4}$, ni. *be given (in marriage)* 4Q251 7$_{4}$ ([אל תנתן]), קבל pu. *be accepted* CD 9$_{23}$, שׁמר *keep* Ezk 20$_{18}$, סגר hi. *hand over* Ob$_{14}$, נשׁה *lend* CD 10$_{18}$, לוה hi. *lend* Si 8$_{12}$, אסף *gather* Ps 26$_{9}$, לקח *take* Lv 25$_{36}$ 2 K 12$_{8}$ Jr 15$_{15}$ Ps 51$_{13}$ Pr 6$_{25}$ 8$_{10}$ CD 11$_{3}$ 16$_{14}$ 4Q424 1$_{4}$ 4Q251 2$_{2}$ ([י]קח]) 7$_{2.2}$ ([אל יקח]) 7$_{7}$ 4Q416 10.2$_{6}$, נצל hi. *seize* Ps 119$_{43}$, גזל *rob* Pr 22$_{22}$, סוג hi. *remove* Pr 22$_{28}$ 23$_{10}$.

שׂים *place* 1 S 9$_{20}$ (+ לֵב *heart*, i.e. pay attention) 22$_{15}$ 25$_{25}$ 2 S 13$_{33}$ (both + לֵב) Ps 39$_{9}$, שׁית *place* Ex 23$_{1}$ Nm 12$_{11}$ 2 S 13$_{20}$ Ps 62$_{11}$ (both + לֵב) Si 34$_{14(mg)}$ 38$_{20(mg)}$ (+ לֵב), נשׂא *raise* Is 2$_{9}$ Jr 7$_{16}$=11$_{14}$ 17$_{21}$ Pr 19$_{18}$ Jb 32$_{21}$ Si 4$_{22}$ 7$_{35}$ 30$_{11}$ 42$_{1}$ CD 11$_{9.11}$ 12$_{7}$ 13$_{14}$, *take (as wife)* Ezr 9$_{12}$, נטל *carry* CD 11$_{10}$, פוק hi. *bring out* Ps 140$_{9}$, קום hi. *establish* CD 11$_{14}$ 16$_{9.12}$, po. *raise oneself* Si 11$_{9}$ 35$_{9}$, מגר pi. *cast down* 11QPs^{a} 24$_{5}$, שׁלך hi. *throw* Ps 51$_{13}$ 71$_{9}$, שׁלח *send* Gn 22$_{12}$ 37$_{22}$ 1 S 6$_{3}$ Ob$_{13}$ Jb 1$_{12}$ CD 11$_{2.18}$ 12$_{6}$ 4Q424 1$_{6}$ 2$_{3.4.6}$ 4Q416 10.2$_{5}$, יצע hi. *spread* trans. Si 4$_{27}$.

נדח hi. *banish* Si 8$_{19}$, עזב *abandon* Nm 10$_{31}$ 1 K 8$_{57}$ Ps 27$_{9}$ 38$_{22}$ 71$_{9.18}$ 119$_{8}$ Pr 3$_{3}$ 4$_{2.6}$ 27$_{10}$ Si 3$_{12}$ 37$_{6}$ 1QH fr. 4$_{18}$ 4Q525 2.4$_{3}$ ([אל]) 4QapPs^{b} 79$_{6}$ 4Q372 1$_{16}$, נטשׁ *abandon* Ps 27$_{9}$ Pr 1$_{8}$ 6$_{20}$ Si 8$_{8}$ 9$_{10}$ 4QDibHam^{a} 7$_{10}$, שׁגה hi. *mislead* Ps 119$_{10}$, נוח hi. *give rest, leave* Jr 14$_{9}$ Ec 7$_{18}$ 10$_{4}$ 11$_{6}$, נוע hi. *disturb* 2 K 23$_{18}$, קצר htp. *be cut short* Si 7$_{10}$, רבה hi. *increase* 1 S 2$_{3}$ Si 35$_{9.12}$, קשׁה hi. *harden* Ps 95$_{8}$ 2 C 30$_{8}$.

שׁכן hi. *accommodate* Jb 11$_{14}$, שׁען ni. *lean* Pr 3$_{5}$ Si 5$_{1.1}$, תמך *grasp* Pr 28$_{17}$, משׁך *drag* Ps 28$_{3}$, רכב *ride* Si 8$_{16}$, נוא hi. *restrain* Ps 141$_{5}$ CD 16$_{10}$, פרע *loosen* Lv 10$_{6}$ Pr 8$_{33}$ 11QPs^{a} 24$_{5}$, מרא pi. *urge on* CD 11$_{12}$, שׁאב *draw water* 11$_{1}$, שׁפך *pour* trans. Gn 37$_{22}$ Jr 7$_{6}$ 22$_{3}$ Si 35$_{4.4(F)}$ 37$_{29(B)}$ CD 10$_{18(Rabin)}$ 4Q525 4$_{22}$ ([אל]), רעה *pasture* Ex 34$_{3}$ Jon 3$_{7}$, קבר *bury* Gn 47$_{29}$, ערה pi. *lay bare* Ps 141$_{8}$, זרה *scatter* Si 37$_{29(Bmg)}$, זרע *sow* seed Jr 4$_{3}$ Si 7$_{3(AHL)}$ (if em. תדע) 37$_{29(B)}$, כסה pi. *cover* Jb 16$_{18}$ Ne 3$_{37}$, חמר hi. *cause to ferment* Si 4$_{2}$, אור hi. *give light* 7$_{24}$, יפע hi. *shine* Jb 3$_{4}$.

משׁל *rule* Ps 19$_{14}$ CD 13$_{12}$, hi. *cause to rule* Si 30$_{11.28}$ 4Q424 1$_{10}$ 2$_{2}$, שׁלט hi. *rule* Ps 119$_{133}$ Si 30$_{29}$ 11QPs^{a} 19$_{15}$, שׁפט *judge* Ps 69$_{16}$ CD 10$_{18(AHL)}$ 11QPs^{a} 24$_{7}$, ni. *contend* Si 8$_{14}$, שׁמשׁ pi. *minister* 38$_{12(mg)}$ (or from מושׁ *depart*), ירשׁ *inherit* 11QPs^{a} 19$_{16}$, סוך *anoint* 2 S 14$_{2}$, ישׁע hi. *save* Jos 22$_{22}$ 2 K 6$_{27}$ (but see Coll.), ילד pi. *assist at birth* CD 11$_{13}$.

עמד *stand* Gn 19$_{17}$ 45$_{9}$ Jos 10$_{19}$ 1 S 20$_{38}$ Jr 4$_{6}$ 51$_{50}$ Ob$_{14}$ Pr 25$_{6}$ Ec 8$_{3}$ Si 4$_{26}$ 6$_{8}$, hi. *position* 12$_{12}$, יצב htp. *position oneself* CD 10$_{7}$, ישׁב *sit* Si 8$_{14}$, hi. *seat* 12$_{12}$, בוא

come Gn 49$_6$ Lv 16$_2$ Jr 16$_5$ 42$_{19}$ Ho 4$_{15}$ Ob$_{13}$ Ps 36$_{12}$ 69$_{28}$ 143$_2$ Jb 36$_7$ Pr 4$_{14}$ 23$_{10}$ 27$_{10}$ Ru 3$_{17}$ 2 C 23$_6$ 25$_7$ 1QS 5$_{13}$ 6$_1$ 1QSa 1$_{20}$ 2$_{4.8}$ ([יב]ואו) CD 11$_{9.22}$ 15$_{16}$ 4QWiles 6$_2$ 4Q424 1$_4$ 4QD^a 6.2$_{5(WA)}$ ([אל]), hi. *bring* 1QS 6$_1$ 11QPs^a 24$_{10}$, הלך *go* 2 S 13$_{25}$ 2 K 2$_{18}$ Jr 6$_{25}$ 16$_5$ 25$_6$ 35$_{15}$ Ezk 20$_{18}$ Pr 1$_{15}$ Ru 2$_8$ Si 5$_{2.9(C)}$ 8$_{15}$ 35$_{20}$ 4Q251 3$_5$ ([אל ילך]), pi. *walk about* 10$_6$ 13$_{13}$, htp. *walk about* CD 10$_{20.21}$ 11$_5$, יצא *go out* Ex 16$_{29}$ 2 K 9$_{15}$ 10$_{25}$ Jr 6$_{25}$ Pr 25$_8$ Si 6$_{35}$, hi. *take out* CD 11$_{7.7.8}$ 4Q251 2$_4$ ([יוציא]), עלה *go up* Nm 14$_{42}$ Jos 7$_3$ Ho 4$_{15}$, hi. *raise* Ex 33$_{15}$ Ps 102$_{25}$ CD 11$_{17.17}$ 4Q251 2$_5$, htp. *raise oneself* Jr 51$_3$ (if em. אֶל־), רום *be exalted* Ps 66$_{7(Qr)}$, hi. *raise* 66$_{7(Kt)}$ 75$_{5.6}$ CD 11$_6$, ירד *go down* Gn 26$_2$, רחק *be far* Ps 22$_{12.20}$ 35$_{22}$ 38$_{22}$ 71$_{12}$, hi. in same sense Jos 8$_4$, htp. *keep oneself distant* Si 13$_{10}$, קרב *approach* Ex 3$_5$ Jos 3$_4$ Pr 5$_8$ Si 9$_3$, htp. 13$_{10}$, נגשׁ *approach* Ex 19$_{15}$ Is 65$_5$ Ezk 9$_6$ 4QD^a 6.2$_6$, זוח perh. *move* intrans. Si 8$_{11}$.

אחר pi. *delay* intrans. Ps 40$_{18}$||70$_6$ Ec 5$_3$ Dn 9$_{19}$ Si 5$_7$ 4Q251 5$_2$ Arad ost. 2$_6$, trans. Gn 24$_{56}$, htp. *be delayed* Si 7$_{34}$ 35$_{11}$, רוץ *run* 3$_{28}$, בהל ni. *hurry* Ec 8$_3$, pi. 5$_1$ 7$_9$, מהר pi. *hurry* 5$_1$ Si 6$_7$ 25$_{21}$ ([א]ל), אוץ *hurry* Is 22$_4$ Si 7$_{15.17}$, אשׁר pi. *advance* Pr 4$_{14}$, צעד *step* 4Q185 1.2$_4$, נשׂג hi. *overtake* Si 7$_1$, ערב htp. *be mixed* 1QS 6$_{17}$ 9$_8$ CD 11$_4$.

פנה *turn* intrans. Lv 19$_{4.31}$ Nm 16$_{15}$ Dt 9$_{27}$ Jb 36$_{21}$, נטה *turn* intrans. Pr 4$_{5.27}$, hi. trans. Ps 27$_9$ 119$_{36}$ 141$_4$ Jb 36$_{18}$, סור *turn* intrans. Jos 1$_7$ 1 S 12$_{20}$ Pr 5$_7$ 4Q525 2$_{12}$ ([א]ל), שׁוב *turn* intrans. Ps 74$_{21}$ 85$_9$ 1QM 15$_8$, hi. trans. 1 K 2$_{16.20}$ Jr 37$_{20}$ Ps 132$_{10}$ 2 C 6$_{42}$ Si 11$_8$ 38$_{20}$ 1QH 16$_{18}$ 18$_9$, pol. *reply* 4Q525 4$_{20}$ ([אל]) 4$_{23}$ ([אל]), שׂטה *turn* intrans. Pr 7$_{25}$.

עבר *cross* Gn 18$_3$ Pr 4$_{15}$ Si 14$_{14}$ 4Q416 9.1$_{14}$, hi. *take across* Nm 32$_5$, htp. *postpone* Si 5$_7$ 7$_{10}$ 38$_9$, תעה *stray* Pr 7$_{25}$, רחב *be far* 4Q416 9.1$_8$, מושׁ *depart* Jg 6$_{18}$ 1QS 6$_{3.6}$ CD 13$_2$, *remove* 4Q416 9.1$_9$, לוז *depart* Pr 3$_{21}$, hi. *send away* 4$_{21}$, נוס *flee* Jr 46$_6$ 1QM 15$_{9(Yadin)}$ ([תנוסו]), מלט ni. *escape* 1 K 18$_{40}$ Jr 46$_6$ Si 16$_{13}$ (לא erased).

תקל ni. *stumble* Si 35$_{20}$, כשׁל ni. *stumble* 4$_{22(A)}$ 30$_{21}$, hi. *cause to stumble* 30$_{21(mg)}$, נפל *fall* 1 S 17$_{32}$ 26$_{20}$ 2 S 24$_{14}$||1 C 21$_{13}$ Si 6$_2$ 25$_{21}$, hi. *let fall* Est 6$_{10}$ Si 7$_7$, שׁפל *be low* 4Q416 9.2$_{15}$, רפה *droop* Zp 3$_{16}$ 2 C 15$_7$, hi. *let go* Jos 10$_6$ Ps 138$_8$ Pr 4$_{13}$ Si 6$_{27}$ 51$_{10}$ 4Q416 9.2$_8$, טבע *sink* intrans. Ps 69$_{15}$.

יגע *toil* Pr 23$_4$, pi. *burden* Jos 7$_3$, לבשׁ *be dressed* 4QOrd^a 2$_7$ (||Dt 22$_5$ לא), רחץ *wash* CD 10$_{10}$, אכל *eat* Ex 12$_9$ Jg 13$_{4.7.14}$ 1 K 13$_{22}$ Est 4$_{16}$ 11QT 50$_4$ + Sup CD 10$_{22.23}$ 12$_{13}$ 4QOrd^c 1.1$_{2.7.8}$ 4Q251 5$_5$ 4QToh A 3.1$_6$ ([אל]) 3.1$_7$ 4QD^a 6.2$_7$, לחם *eat* Pr 23$_6$, בלע *swallow* Ps 69$_{16}$, htp. *be swallowed up* 4Q416 10.2$_9$, עיט *be greedy* Si 34$_{16}$, לעע *gulp down* 34$_{17}$, טעם *taste* Jon 3$_7$ Si 9$_9$, שׁתה *drink* Lv 10$_9$ Jg 13$_{4.7.14}$ 1 K 13$_{22}$ Jon 3$_7$ Est 4$_{16}$ CD 10$_{23}$ 4QOrd^c 1.1$_{10}$ ([יש]תה) 4Q416 9.2$_{19}$, סבב *dine* Si 9$_9$ ([אל ת]סב).

ישׁט hi. *extend* hand Si 34$_{14.18}$, פוח *blow* 4$_2$, שׁאף *gasp* Jb 36$_{20}$, לאה *be weary* Si 43$_{30(mg)}$, שׁכב *lie down* CD 12$_1$, דמך *sleep* Si 9$_4$, נום *sleep* Ps 121$_3$, לין *spend night* Jg 19$_{20}$ 2 S 17$_{16}$, שׁבת hi. *observe sabbath* CD 11$_{14}$.

נבט hi. *look* Gn 19$_{17}$ 1 S 16$_7$ Si 9$_8$, ראה *see* Gn 21$_{16}$ Nm 11$_{15}$ Ob$_{12.13}$ Jb 3$_9$ 20$_{17}$ Pr 23$_{31}$ Ca 1$_6$, ni. *be seen* Ex 34$_3$, שׁעה *gaze* 5$_9$, htp. *look around* Is 41$_{10}$, שׁמע *hear, obey* 1 K 20$_8$ 2 K 18$_{31}$||Is 36$_{16}$ 2 K 18$_{32}$ Jr 23$_{16}$ 27$_{9.14.16.17}$ 29$_8$ papMurPalimp^b 2, hi. *cause to hear* Jg 18$_{25}$, קשׁב hi. *listen* Jr 18$_{18}$, שׁקד *be wakeful* 4Q416 9.2$_{14}$, נגע *touch* Nm 16$_{26}$ Is 52$_{11}$ Ps 105$_{15}$||1 C 16$_{22}$ Lm 4$_{15}$ 1QS 6$_{20}$ 8$_{17}$ 4QToh A 1.1$_{4.6.7}$ ([יגע]) 2.1$_{3.7}$ 4Q416 9.2$_{16}$.

ארב *lie in wait* Pr 24$_{15}$, בגד *betray* Ml 2$_{15}$, בעת pi. *overwhelm* Jb 9$_{34}$ 13$_{21}$, הרס *break through* Ex 19$_{24}$, גבר htp. *prove one's strength* Si 34$_{25}$, לחם ni. *fight* 2 C 13$_{12}$, נצה ni. *struggle* Si 8$_3$, ריב *contend* Ho 4$_4$ Pr 3$_{30(Qr)}$ Si 8$_{1.1}$ 34$_{31}$, גרה htp. *make war* Dt 2$_{5.9.19}$ Si 37$_{11}$ (or תגר htp. *bargain with*), דרך *draw* bow Jr 51$_3$ (if em. אֶל־), שׁדד pi. *attack* Pr 24$_{15}$.

שׁחת hi. *ruin* Dt 9$_{26}$ 1 S 26$_9$ Is 65$_8$ Ps 57$_1$ 58$_1$ 59$_1$ 75$_1$ (all four as title of melody, etc.) 2 C 35$_{21}$ Si 5$_{15}$, בזז *plunder* 4Q416 9.2$_{21}$ ([אל]), דאב hi. *make weary* 4$_1$, יגה hi. *cause suffering* 34$_{31}$, ינה hi. *oppress* Lv 25$_{14}$ Jr 22$_3$, עשׁק *oppress* Zc 7$_{10}$ Ps 119$_{122}$, כאב hi. *cause pain* Si 4$_3$, קמע hi. perh. *cause pain* 34$_{31}$, דכא pi. *crush* Pr 22$_{22}$, הרג *slay* Ex 23$_7$ Ps 59$_{12}$.

צלח *succeed* Si 8$_{10}$, קלה htp. *be dishonoured* 11QPs^a 19$_{14}$, עזז *be strong* Ps 9$_{20}$, hi. *strengthen* Si 8$_{16}$, רכך *be tender* Dt 20$_3$ Is 7$_4$, עצל ni. *be slow* Jg 18$_9$, htp. *be idle* 11QPs^a 18$_2$, דמה *be like* Si 13$_8$, pi. *imagine* Est 4$_{13}$, יחד *be united* Gn 49$_6$ Si 34$_{14(mg)}$, יתר hi. *excel* Gn 49$_4$ Si 30$_{38}$ 35$_1$ 4QpGen^a 4$_4$, *leave over* Ex 16$_{19}$, *be abundant* 4Q416

9.2_{10}, דמם *be silent* Lm 2_{18}, ni. *be silenced* Jr 51_6, חרשׁ *be silent* Ps 28_1 35_{22} 39_{13} 50_3 83_2 109_1, hi. *be deaf* 1 S 7_8, שׁקט *be silent* Ps 83_2, שׁלה ni. *be slack* 2 C 29_{11}, מעט *be small* Jr 29_6 Ne 9_{32}, hi. *stint* 2 K 4_3 4Q416 9.2_6, חסר *be lacking* Ca 7_3 Ec 9_8, פקד ni. *be lacking* 2 K 10_{19}, hi. *appoint* 4Q424 1_6.

1b. with other forms of the verb, (1) perfect, אַל־פְּשַׁטְתֶּם appar. *did you (not) raid?* 1 S 27_{10}; (2) infinitive, אל לאמר *not to say,* i.e. do not say Si 39_{34} (or em. אין, as mg and 39_{21}); (3) imperative, אל פתח *do not open* CD $11_{9(\text{Rabin})}$.

1c. without a verb following, *no!, not,* Gn 19_{18} 33_{10} Nm 12_{13} (if em. אֵל נָא *God, please*), אַל *no!* 2 K 3_{13}, אַל־יוֹשִׁעֵךְ י׳ מֵאַיִן אוֹשִׁיעֵךְ *No! May Y. save you! From where can I save you?* 2 K 6_{27}; קִרְעוּ לְבַבְכֶם וְאַל־בִּגְדֵיכֶם *tear your hearts, not your garments* Jl 2_{13} 4QD^b$_{5a}$, דִּרְשׁוּ־טוֹב וְאַל־רָע *seek good, not evil* Am 5_{14}, הַט־לִבִּי אֶל־עֵדְוֹתֶיךָ וְאַל אֶל־בָּצַע *incline my heart to your commandments, not to corruption* Ps 119_{36}, קְחוּ־מוּסָרִי וְאַל־כָּסֶף *take my instruction, not money* Pr 8_{10}, פָּגוֹשׁ דֹּב שַׁכּוּל בְּאִישׁ וְאַל־כְּסִיל בְּאִוַּלְתּוֹ better for *a man to meet a bereaved bear—not a fool in his stupidity* 17_{12}, יְהַלֶּלְךָ זָר וְלֹא־פִיךָ נָכְרִי וְאַל־שְׂפָתֶיךָ *let another praise you, not your own mouth—a stranger, not your own lips* 27_2, הֵאָסְפִי אַל־תַּעְרֵךְ appar. *be gathered—not,* i.e. without, *your scabbard* Jr $47_{6(L)}$ (mss אֶל־ be gathered *to*).

<COLL> אַל before person addressed, בָּנָי *my sons* 1 S 2_{24}, בְּנֹתַי *my daughters* Ru 1_{13}, and before following verb, בְּנִי *my son* 2 S 13_{25}, אָחִי *my brother* 13_{12}, אֲדֹנִי *sir* 2 K 4_{16}; אַל־אוֹדֹת appar. corrupt for עַל־אוֹדֹת *concerning* 2 S 13_{16}; for אַל prob. corrupt for אֶל, see אֶל *to,* §19.

2. as negative particle, **let there not be,** אַל־טַל וְאַל־מָטָר עֲלֵיכֶם *let there not be dew and let there not be rain upon you* 2 S 1_{21}, אַל־דֳּמִי לָכֶם/־לָךְ *let there not be silence for you* Is 62_6 Ps 83_2, אַל־מָוֶת *let there be no death* Pr 12_{28} (mss אֶל), אַל לַמְלָכִים *let it not be for kings* $31_{4.4}$ (+ ־שְׁתוֹ *to drink*).

3. as noun, **nothing,** וְיָשֵׂם לְאַל מִלָּתִי *and he will make my word as nought* Jb 24_{25}.

Also Si 9_{12} 4Q487 6_4 $8_{3.5}$ 9_2 16_3 4QRitMar 21_2 1QM 16_{16} + Sup 4QVisSam 1_5 4QapLamb_6 4QWiles 5_3 3QTr 8_3 4Q251 2_3 3_6 5_6 6_2 4Q416 9.$1_{13.21}$ 9.2_3 10.2_{11} 4QD^a 6.$2_{1(\text{WA})}$ ([א]ל).

[אַל] II, see אַל I, §1b.

אֵל I $_{240.64.501.2}$ n.m. **God**—sf. אֵלִי; pl. אֵלִים (Q אילים); cstr. Q אלי.

1a. god, freq. in pl., oft. as constituting divine/angelic assembly (Ex 15_{11} Ps 29_1 89_7 Jb 41_{17} Dn 11_{36} 4QPrQuot 65_2 1QM $1_{10.11}$ 1QM $14_{15.16}$ 17_7 1QM 15_3 +Sup 4QM^a fr. 11 $1_{12.14.18}$ $24_{3.4}$ 1QDM 4_1 11QMelch 1.1_{14} 1QH 7_{28} 10_8 19_3 fr. 2 $1_{3.10}$ 4QpHos^a 1.2_6 4QShir^a 1_2 4QShir^b 1_{11} 16_4 4QShirShab^a 1.$1_{4.20}$ 1.2_{17} $2_{1.7}$ 4QShirShab^b 14.$1_{5.5}$ 4QShirShab^c 4_8 4QShirShab^d 1.$1_{21.26.31.33.38.38}$ 1.$2_{26.33.35}$ 4QShirShab^e 2_2 4_6 4QShirShab^f 14_3 19_3 23.1_8 MasShirShab $1_{9.11}$ 11QShirShab 5_6 c_1 m_5 o_2 11QapPs^a 1_{11}).

<SUBJ> היה *be* Ps 81_{10} (+ בְּךָ *among you*), בוא *come* 4QShirShab^f 23.1_8, עשׂה *do* Dt 3_{24}, יצר ni. *be formed* Is 43_{10}, גור *be frightened* Jb 41_{17}, חפץ *delight* Ps 5_5 (mss lack אֵל), ידה hi. *praise* 4QShirShab^d 1.$1_{38.38}$ 4QShirShab^e 4_6.

<NOM CL> אֵל אָנִי *I am a god* Ezk 28_2 (+ אֱלֹהִים *god*), אַתָּה אָדָם וְלֹא־אֵל *you are human and not a god* $28_{2.9}$ (both + אֱלֹהִים), מִצְרַיִם אָדָם וְלֹא־אֵל *Egypt is human and not a god* Is 31_3 (|| רוּחַ *spirit*), אֵין עִמּוֹ אֵל *there was no god with him* Dt 32_{12}, אַתָּה ... לֹא אֵל *you are ... not a god* who delights in wickedness Ps 5_5, מִי־אֵל *who is a* great *god* in heaven or on earth? Dt 3_{24} Ps 77_{14} (+ כֵּאלֹהִים *as God*), מי כמוכה באלים *who is as you among the gods?* 1QH 7_{28}.

<OBJ> עבד *serve* 4QDibHam^a 1.5_3.

<CSTR> אלי [הצדק] *gods of righteousness* 11QMelch 1.$1_{14(\text{Milik})}$, ההוד *of majesty* 4QShirShab^d 1.1_{38}, טוהר *of purity* 4QBer^a 3.1_6, דעת *of knowledge* 4QShirShab^a 2_1 4QShirShab^d 1.$1_{31.38}$ (אילי) 4QShir Shab^e 4_7 (א[י]לי) 4QShirShab^f 23.1_8, רום *of height* 4QShirShab^d 1.1_{33}, אור *of light* 1.2_{35}, עולמים *of ages* 4QShirShab^f 19_3 MasShirShab 1_{11}, אלים *of gods* 4QShirShab^b 14.1_5; בַּת־אֵל *daughter of a god* Ml 2_{11}, עֲדַת *council of* Ps 82_1 (|| אֱלֹהִים *God*), עדת אלים *council of gods* 1QM 1_{10} fr. 11 1_{12} 1QDM 4_1, סוד *council of* 4QShir^b 1_{11} (אילים)

4QShirShab^a 1.2$_9$ (אל[ים]) 4Q416 4$_{15}$, תרועת battle cry of 1QM 1$_{11}$ (|| אִישׁ man), שַׂר prince of 1QH 10$_8$, אֵל God of Dn 11$_{36}$ 1QM 18$_6$ 4QShir^a 1$_2$ (|| קָדוֹשׁ holy one) 4QShirShab^d 1.2$_{26}$ 4QShirShab^f 14$_3$, דעת knowledge of 4QShirShab^a 2$_7$ (אל[ים]) MasShirShab 1$_{11}$ ([ד]עת אלי[ ]), ממשלת ... [ה]א[ל]ים dominion of ... the gods 4QM^a fr. 24$_3$, בְּנֵי אֵלִים sons of gods Ps 29$_1$ 89$_7$ 4QM^a fr. 24$_4$ 1QH fr. 2 1$_{3.10 (Holm-Nielsen)}$ ([בני]) 11QShirShab o$_2$ (אל[ים]), צבאות hosts of 4QPrQuot 65$_2$, גבורי mighty ones of 1QM 15$_{14}$, גבורות strengths of 4QShirShab^e 2$_2$ (גבורו[ת אל]ים), אלוהי God of 4QShir^b 16$_4$ (אל[ים]) 4QShirShab^a 1.1$_{20}$ ([א]ל[והי]) 4QShirShab^c 4$_8$ 9$_2$ ([א]לוהי אל[ים]) 4QShirShab^d 1.1$_{26}$ ([א]ל[ו]הי) Mas Shir Shab 1$_9$ ([א]ל[והי]) 11QShirShab 5$_6$ c$_1$ (אל[והי] [אל]ים) m$_5$ (אל[ים]) 11QapPs^a 1$_{11}$ ([אלוהי אלים]), אלי gods of 4QShirShab^b 14.1$_5$, רוחי spirits of 4QShirShab^f 19$_3$ (אלי), כול אל every god Dn 11$_{36}$ (כָּל־) MasShirShab 2$_5$, כול [ה]א[ל]ים all the gods 4QM^a fr. 24$_3$, כול אלי all the gods of 11QMelch 1.1$_{14}$ 4QShirShab^a 1.1$_4$ 4QShir Shab^d 1.1$_{18}$ (אי[לי]) 1.1$_{31.38.38}$ (כל אילי) 1.2$_{33}$ (אדון כול אילי[ ] lord of all gods of) 1.2$_{35}$ 4QShirShab^e 4$_6$ 4QShir Shab^f 13$_2$ (אי[לי]).

<ADJ> אַחֵר another Ex 34$_{14}$ 11QT 2$_{11 (Yadin)}$ ([אחר]), נֵכָר foreign Dt 32$_{12}$ Ml 2$_{11}$ Ps 81$_{10}$ 4QDibHam^a 1.5$_3$, זָר strange Ps 44$_{21}$ 81$_{10}$, גָּדוֹל great 77$_{14}$.

<PREP> לְ of possession, of 4QShirShab^a 1.1$_4$ (+ עֵדָה congregation), of direction, to + שׁחה htpal. bow down Ex 34$_{14}$ Ps 81$_{10}$ 11QT 2$_{11 (Yadin)}$ ([א]ל), פרשׂ extend hands Ps 44$_{21}$, ברך לְ pi. bless 4QShirShab^d 1.1$_{18}$ (אי[לי]); בְּ in, among Ex 15$_{11}$ 1QH 7$_{28}$, + אכל eat 1QM 15$_3$ + Sup, רום hi. raise kingdom 1QM 17$_7$, הלל pi. praise 4QShirShab^a 2$_1$ 4QShirShab^d 1.1$_{31}$, אור hi. give light 1.2$_{35}$, קנא בְּ pi. provoke to jealousy with Dt 32$_{21}$ (|| הֶבֶל idol; :: עַם people); כְּ as 4QpHos^a 1.2$_6$; מִן partitive, (some) of, + שׁפל hi. make low 1QM 14$_{15}$ (:: עָפָר dust), אלוהים מאלי רום gods from among the gods of height, i.e. most exalted gods 4QShirShab^d 1.1$_{33}$; פלל אֶל htp. pray to Is 45$_{20}$ (+ פֶּסֶל idol); גדל עַל htp. exalt oneself against Dn 11$_{36}$; עִם with 4QM^a fr. 11 1$_{18}$ (|| בֵּן son of king), + חשׁב htp. be reckoned fr. 11 1$_{14}$, רוד wander Ho 12$_1$ (or em. אֵל to אֵלִים gods or בַּעַל Baal; || קָדוֹשׁ holy one).

<COLL> לֹא־אֵל a non-god Dt 32$_{21}$, אֵל לֹא יוֹשִׁיעַ a god that cannot save Is 45$_{20}$.

1b. image of a god, <SUBJ> נצל hi. deliver Is 44$_{17}$. <NOM CL> אֵלִי אָתָּה you are my god Is 44$_{17}$. <OBJ> עשׂה make Is 46$_6$, יצר form 44$_{10}$ (|| פֶּסֶל idol), פעל make 44$_{15}$ (|| פֶּסֶל). <APP> פֶּסֶל idol Is 44$_{17}$. <PREP> עשׂה לְ make into Is 44$_{17}$.

1c. as pr.n., **El,** in אֵל בְּרִית El-Berith Jg 9$_{46}$.

2. God, a. of patriarchs, usu. with other divine name or adj., עֶלְיוֹן Most High Gn 14$_{18.19.20.22}$, רֳאִי seeing 16$_{13}$, שַׁדַּי Shaddai 17$_1$ 28$_3$ (=4QpGen^a 3$_{12}$) 35$_{11}$ 43$_{14}$ 48$_3$ 49$_{25}$ (if em.; see Subj.) Ex 6$_3$, עוֹלָם eternal Gn 21$_{33}$, בֵּית־אֵל Bethel 31$_{13}$ 35$_7$.

<SUBJ> ברך pass. be blessed Gn 14$_{20}$, pi. bless 28$_3$ (=4QpGen^a 3$_{12}$) 48$_3$ 49$_{25}$ (if em. אֵת to אֵל), פרה hi. make fruitful 28$_3$ 48$_3$, רבה hi. multiply 28$_3$ 48$_3$, נתן give 43$_{14}$ 48$_3$, לקח take Jb 5$_5$ (if em. וְאֶל־מִצִּנִּים appar. and from out of thorns to וְאֵל מִשִּׁנָּיו and God takes it from his teeth), שׁלח pi. send Gn 43$_{14}$, ראה ni. appear 35$_1$ 46$_3$ (if em.; see Nom. Cl.) 48$_3$, אמר say 48$_3$, ענה answer 35$_3$, מגן pi. deliver 14$_{20}$, עזר help 49$_{25}$.

<NOM CL> אַתָּה אֵל רֳאִי you are the God of seeing Gn 16$_{13}$, אֲנִי־אֵל שַׁדַּי I am the God Shaddai 17$_1$ 35$_{11}$, אָנֹכִי הָאֵל בֵּית־אֵל I am the God Bethel 31$_{13}$ (or ins. הַנִּרְאָה אֵלֶיךָ בְּ who appeared to you at after הָאֵל), אָנֹכִי הָאֵל I am God 46$_3$.

<CSTR> אֵל אָבִיךָ God of your father Gn 49$_{25}$.

<APP> אֵל עֶלְיוֹן קֹנֵה שָׁמַיִם וָאָרֶץ God Most High, possessor, i.e. creator, of heaven and earth Gn 14$_{19}$, י׳ אֵל עֶלְיוֹן קֹנֵה שָׁמַיִם וָאָרֶץ Y., God Most High, possessor of heaven and earth 14$_{22}$ (or del. י׳ Y.), [אל] קן ארץ God, possessor of the earth Jerusalem ost. 1$_3$, י׳ אֵל עוֹלָם Y., God eternal Gn 21$_{33}$, הָאֵל אֱלֹהֵי אָבִיךָ God, the God of your father 46$_3$.

<PREP> לְ to, for 4QpGen^a 2$_{11}$, + עשׂה make altar Gn 35$_{1.3}$, ברך לְ pass. be blessed by 14$_{19}$, כֹּהֵן לְ priest of 14$_{18}$; ראה בְּ ni. appear as Ex 6$_3$; רום יָד אֶל hi. raise hand, i.e. swear oath, to Gn 14$_{22}$; פזז מִן be supple by means of Gn 49$_{25}$; הלך לִפְנֵי htp. walk before Gn 17$_1$.

<COLL> וַיִּקְרָא לַמָּקוֹם אֵל בֵּית־אֵל he called the place God of Bethel Gn 35$_7$.

2b. of Israel, oft. || אֱלֹהִים God, י׳ Y., שַׁדַּי Shaddai, or used with divine name or adj., שַׁדַּי *Shaddai* Ezk 10$_{5}$, עֶלְיוֹן *Most High* Ps 78$_{35}$ Si 46$_{5.5}$ 47$_{5.8}$ 48$_{20}$ 1QM 19$_{13}$ + Sup ([א]ל) 1QH 4$_{31}$ 6$_{33}$ 11QBer 1.2$_{3.6}$ 4QJub^{d} 1.2$_{21}$ 1.2$_{25.28}$ (both [אל עליון]) 1.2$_{32}$ (אל ע[ליון]), י׳ *Y.* Is 42$_{5}$ Ps 85$_{9}$ (or em.; see Subj.) GnzPs 2$_{2}$ 4$_{13}$ 4QJub^{d} 1.2$_{21}$ (יהו[ה]), אֱלֹהִים י׳ *God Y.* Jos 22$_{22.22}$ Ps 50$_{1}$; see also App. and Adj.

<SUBJ> היה *be* Ps 99$_{8}$ (+ י׳ *Y.*), רפא *heal* Nm 12$_{13}$ (or em. אַל *do not*) Si 38$_{9}$, זכר *remember* GnzPs 4$_{13}$ CD 6$_{2}$, שכח *forget* Ps 10$_{11.12}$ 77$_{10}$ (+ חנן *be gracious*), אסף *gather* 1QM 3$_{10}$, בחר *choose* 1QS 4$_{22}$ 11$_{7}$ 1QSb 3$_{23}$ CD 2$_{7}$ 4QpPs^{a} 1.3$_{16(Horgan)}$ ([ב]חר), ספר *number* 1QpHab 2$_{9}$, קפץ *shut up* compassion Ps 77$_{10}$, מאס *reject* Jb 8$_{20}$ 36$_{5}$, נאץ *despise* 1QH 4$_{12}$, כנע hi. *humble* 1QM 16$_{17}$ + Sup, ענה pi. *humble* Ps 55$_{20}$.

שמע *hear* Ps 17$_{6}$ 55$_{20}$ (or em. יִשְׁמָעֵאל *Ishmael*) Jb 27$_{9}$ 35$_{13}$ (‖ שַׁדַּי *Shaddai*), נטה hi. *incline* ear Ps 17$_{6}$, ראה *see* Ps 10$_{11}$ 4Q416 9.1$_{15}$, שׁור *regard* Jb 33$_{14}$, אמר *say* Nm 23$_{19}$ Is 42$_{5}$ CD 6$_{13}$ 8$_{9(A)}$=19$_{22(B)}$, דבר pi. *speak* Nm 23$_{19}$Ps 50$_{1}$ 85$_{9}$ (or em. הָאֵל י׳ *God, Y.* to הֲלֹא י׳ *Y., will he not*) Jb 33$_{14}$ CD 4$_{13}$ 1QpHab 7$_{1}$, קרא *call* Ps 50$_{1}$ Si 4$_{10}$ 1QM 16$_{1}$ CD 6$_{6}$, כזב pi. *lie* Nm 23$_{19}$, חרשׁ *be silent* Ps 83$_{2}$, שׁקט *be silent* 83$_{2}$, ענה *answer* 17$_{6}$ 55$_{20}$ (unless em. יַעֲנֵם *he will answer them* to יַעְלָם *Jalam*) Si 46$_{5}$ GnzPs 2$_{2}$ 1QH 4$_{18}$, צוה pi. *command* 1QS 1$_{16}$ 4QRitMar 14$_{4}$ 1QH 6$_{20}$, ידע *know* Jos 22$_{22}$ Ps 73$_{11}$ (+ עֶלְיוֹן *Most High*) 139$_{23}$ Jb 22$_{13}$, hi. *make known* Ps 77$_{15}$ 1QH 10$_{14}$ 11$_{15}$ 1QpHab 7$_{4}$, גלה *reveal* or *exile* appar. 4QToh A 3.1$_{1}$, pi. *reveal* CD 3$_{13}$, למד pi. *teach* 4Q525 4$_{11}$, בין *understand* CD 1$_{10}$.

חקר *search* Ps 139$_{23}$, בחן *test* 139$_{23}$, בדל hi. *set apart* 1QS 2$_{16}$ CD 7$_{4}$ 4QRitPur 40$_{3}$ (ותב[דל]), קום *rise* Ps 10$_{12}$ Jb 31$_{14}$, hi. *raise, establish* Nm 23$_{19}$ 1QS 11$_{15}$ 1QSb 5$_{27}$ CD 3$_{13.21}$ 4$_{9}$, רום *rise* 1QM 14$_{16}$, hi. *raise* 1QH 7$_{23}$ 1QM 15$_{13}$, pol. *be exalted* 4$_{8}$, כון hi. *establish* 1QS 11$_{15}$ 1QSb 3$_{20}$ 1QH 12$_{10}$ fr. 4$_{15}$ (הכינו[תה]) 4QpPs^{a} 1.3$_{16}$, pol. 1QNoah 15$_{1}$, ערך *arrange* Ps 78$_{19}$.

שׁפט *judge* Jb 21$_{22}$ 22$_{13}$, po. 1QpHab 12$_{5}$, פקד *visit* Jb 31$_{14}$ Si 32$_{21}$ 1QS 2$_{6}$ CD 5$_{16}$ 7$_{9(A)}$=19$_{6(B)}$ 8$_{3(A)}$=19$_{15(B)}$, ריב *plead* cause 1QH 9$_{23}$, מהה htpalp. *delay* Si 32$_{22(B)}$ (Bmg אדון *the Lord*), אהב *love* 1QS 3$_{26}$ CD 2$_{3}$, רצה *accept* 1QS 3$_{26}$ 11$_{15}$, נחם htp. *repent* Nm 23$_{19}$, שׂנא *hate* Si 12$_{6}$ 34$_{13}$ CD 19$_{31(B)}$ 4QM^{g} 4$_{8}$, תעב pi. *abhor* 1QS 3$_{26}$ CD 19$_{31}$, קצף *be angry* Nm 16$_{22}$, זעם *be angry* Ps 7$_{12}$ (+ אֱלֹהִים *God*), נקם *avenge* Na 1$_{2}$, רעם hi. *thunder* Ps 29$_{3}$ Jb 37$_{5}$ 1QH 3$_{34}$, קבב *curse* Nm 23$_{8}$ (‖ י׳ *Y.*), רשׁע hi. *act wickedly* Jb 34$_{12}$ (‖ שַׁדַּי *Shaddai*), *condemn* 4QPs^{a} 1.4$_{9(Allegro)}$ ([ירשיענו]), כלה pi. *destroy* 1QpHab 5$_{3}$ 13$_{3}$, נתץ *pull down* Ps 52$_{7}$, חתה *snatch away* 52$_{7}$, נסח *tear away* 52$_{7}$, נגף *strike* 1QM 3$_{9}$, נדף *blow away* Jb 32$_{13(L)}$ (ms הדף *thrust*; ms רדף *pursue*; :: אִישׁ *man*), עלה hi. *remove* Ps 102$_{25}$, סור hi. *remove* Jb 27$_{2}$ (‖ שַׁדַּי) 34$_{5}$.

כפר pi. *atone for* CD 3$_{18}$ 4$_{7.10}$ 20$_{34}$, נשׂא *lift up* Ps 10$_{12}$ (or del.) CD 3$_{18}$, *forgive* Mc 7$_{18}$ Ps 99$_{8}$ CD 3$_{18}$, ni. *be exalted* 1QM 14$_{16}$, עבר *pass over*, i.e. forgive Mc 7$_{18}$, שׂים *place* Nm 24$_{23}$ (or em. מִשֻּׂמוֹ אֵל *when God places* to מִשַּׁמְאָל *from Sham'al* or מִשְּׂמֹאל *from the north* or מִיִּשְׁמָעֵאל *from Ishmael*) Si 34$_{13}$ 1QS 4$_{16.25}$ 1QH 6$_{25}$ 8$_{16}$ perh. 4Q416 5$_{14}$ (unless אַל *not*), נצב hi. *set* wisdom CD 2$_{3}$, עמד hi. *make stand* 4QPrQuot 34$_{4}$, חתם *seal* 4QShir^{b} 30$_{3}$ (חתמ[תה]), נוח hi. *give rest* Si 47$_{13}$, חנן *be merciful* Ml 1$_{9}$ 1QS 2$_{8}$=4QToh D$_{3}$ perh. Kh. Beit Lei graf. 6 (others אתה *you*), ברך pi. *bless* 11QBer 1.2$_{6}$ 4QpGen^{a} 2$_{7}$, ברך pass. *be blessed* 4QRitMar 24$_{2}$ 96$_{2}$ (ב[רוך]) 4QPrQuot 1$_{2.6}$ 7$_{6}$ 34$_{4}$ (ברו[ך]) 35$_{11}$ (בר[וך]) 36$_{3}$ 48$_{7}$ 51$_{6.12}$ 65$_{4}$ 69$_{2}$ 74$_{3}$ (ברו[ך]) 139$_{1}$ 4QRitPur 40$_{3}$ (בר[וך]) 1QM 13$_{2}$ 14$_{4}$ 4QDibHam^{a} 3.2$_{2}$ ([א]ל) 1QH 10$_{14}$ 11$_{29}$ fr. 4$_{15}$ 4QShir^{b} 52$_{4(Baillet)}$ ([ברוך]), כבד ni. *be honoured* 4QShirShab^{d} 1.1$_{5}$.

שׁמר *keep* Dt 7$_{9}$ Ps 16$_{1}$ Dn 9$_{4}$ (+ אֲדֹנָי *Lord*) Ne 1$_{5}$ 9$_{32}$ 1QM 14$_{4.8}$, סמך *sustain* 4QpIsa^{a} 8$_{18}$, חזק pi. *strengthen* 4QJub^{d} 1.2$_{32}$ ([יחזק ... אל]), hi. *grasp* hand Jb 8$_{20}$, פתח *open* 1QS 11$_{15}$ 1QH 5$_{32}$ 11QBer 1.2$_{6}$, סגר *close* 1QH 5$_{14}$ (סג[רתה]), hi. *hand over* Jb 16$_{11}$, ירט pi. *thrust* 16$_{11}$, יצא *go forth* 1QpMic 12$_{3}$, hi. *bring forth* Nm 23$_{22}$ 24$_{8}$ Si 38$_{4}$, ירד hi. *bring down* 2 S 22$_{48}$ (4QSam^{a} רדד pi. *subdue*), יכל *be able* Ps 78$_{19}$, עשׂה *do, make* Nm 23$_{19}$ Ps 77$_{15}$ 106$_{21}$ Jb 37$_{5}$ GnzPs 3$_{6}$ 1QM 18$_{8}$ 1QH 18$_{21}$ 4QAges 1$_{1}$ 4Q416 6$_{5}$, פעל *do* Nm 23$_{23}$ Jb 33$_{29}$, ברא *create* Ml 2$_{10}$ Si 16$_{26}$, יצר *form* 1QH 4$_{31}$, גמר *accomplish* Ps 57$_{3}$, חדשׁ pi. *renew* Si 33$_{6(Bmg)}$ 4QPrQuot 29$_{9}$, פלא ni. *be wonderful* 4Q372 1$_{29}$, hi. *make wonderful* 4QPrQuot 15$_{8}$ (המפ[ליא]) 1QM^{a} 1$_{6}$ (המ[פ]ליא) 1QH 11$_{3}$, גדל *be great* 1QM 4$_{8}$, hi. *act greatly* 18$_{6}$, גבר hi. *act mightily* 1QH 11$_{3}$, ברר pi.

purify 1QS 4_{20}, זקק pi. *purify* 4_{20}, תמם hi. *make perfect* 1QH 4_{31}, חול pol. *give birth* Dt 32_{18} (|| צור *rock*).

חלק pi. *apportion* Si 34_{13} 38_{1} 40_{1}, פלג pi. *apportion* 4Q416 1_{20}, נתן *give* 2 S 22_{48}||Ps 18_{48} Ps 18_{33} 68_{36} (+ אֱלֹהִים *God*) 1QS 2_{6}=4QToh D_{3} 1QS 4_{18} 1QH 7_{10} 12_{11} 1QpHab 2_{8} 5_{4} 9_{10} 10_{3} 4Q298 2_{4} 4Q416 7_{6} ([יתן]), שׁלם pi. *repay* 1QS 10_{18} 4QPs^a 1.4_{9}(Allegro) ([אל]), אור hi. *give light to* Ps 118_{27} 11QBer 1.2_{6}, יפע hi. *shine forth* Ps 94_{1}, אזר pi. *gird* 18_{33}, עזר *help* 1QS 3_{24} 1QH 2_{34} 7_{23} ([א]לי), ישׁע hi. *save* Is 45_{21} (+ י׳ *Y.*, אֱלֹהִים) Ps 106_{21} 4Q183 1.2_{3} 4QpPs^a 1.4_{21}, נצל hi. *deliver* 1QpHab 8_{2} 4QpPs^a 1.4_{21}, מלט pi. *deliver* 4Q183 1.2_{3}, פלט pi. *deliver* 1QH 5_{18}, פדה *redeem* Ps 31_{6} 1QH 2_{34} 4QpPs^a 1.2_{18}, נתר hi. *set free* 2 S 22_{33}, אמן ni. *be faithful* Dt 7_{9}, ירא ni. *be feared* Dt 7_{21} 10_{17} Ps 89_{8} Dn 9_{4} Ne 1_{5} 9_{32} 1QM 10_{1} 12_{7} ([נ]ורא) 4Q372 1_{29}, ערץ ni. *be feared* Ps 89_{8}, שׂוך *hedge* 1QH 8_{11} ([א]ל), רכך hi. *make weak* Jb 23_{16} (|| שַׁדַּי *Shaddai*), ירשׁ hi. *drive out* Jos 3_{10} Jb 20_{15}, קדשׁ ni. *show oneself holy* Is 5_{16} (|| י׳), htp. 1QM 17_{2}, שׂגב hi. *act exaltedly* Jb 36_{22}, חבא pi. *hide* 1QH 5_{11}, סתר pi. *hide* 5_{11}, hi. *hide* face Ps 10_{11} 4QpHos^b 2_{6} ([יסתי]ר), htp. *keep oneself hidden* Is 45_{15} (+ אֱלֹהִים), נטשׁ *abandon* Si 47_{22} ([א]ל), עזב *leave* Ps $22_{2.2}$ CD 5_{6} 4QpPs^a 1.2_{14} 1.4_{9}(Allegro) ([יעזבנו]), עות pi. *pervert* Jb 8_{3} (|| שַׁדַּי).

<NOM CL> אֲנִי־אֵל *I am God* Is 43_{12} (+ י׳ Y.) 45_{22}, אָנֹכִי אֵל *I am God* 46_{9} (|| אֱלֹהִים *God*), אֵל אָנֹכִי *I am God* Ho 11_{9} (|| קָדוֹשׁ *holy one*; :: אִישׁ *man*), זֶה אֵלִי *this is my God* Ex 15_{2} (|| אֱלֹהִים), אַתָּה אֵל *you are God* Ps 90_{2} Si 36_{22} 4QPrQuot 35_{7} (א[תה א]ל) 4QDibHam^a 1.5_{9}, אתה אלי *you are my God* 1QH 5_{32} (את) 4QShir^b 52_{1}, var. Ps 89_{27}, אֵלִי אַתָּה *you are my God* 22_{11} 63_{2} (+ אֱלֹהִים) 118_{28} 140_{7} (+ י׳), י׳ ... אֵלִי *Y. is ... my God* Ps 18_{3} (mss אֱלֹהֵי *the God of* my rock), אֵל י׳ *Y. is God* Ps 118_{27}.

אָנֹכִי י׳ אֱלֹהֶיךָ אֵל *I, Y. your God, am ... a God* Ex 20_{5} Dt 5_{9} (jealous), י׳ אֱלֹהֶיךָ ... אֵל *Y. your God is ... a God* 4_{24} (jealous), הוּא ... אֵל *he is ... a God* Ex 34_{14} (jealous; + י׳) Jos 24_{19} (jealous + י׳, אֱלֹהִים) 4Q416 3_{5} (הוא[ה]; of truth), י׳ אֱלֹהֶיךָ ... אֵל *Y. your God is ... a God* Dt 4_{31} (compassionate) 6_{15} (jealous), אַתָּה אֵל *you are a God* Jon 4_{2} (merciful and compassionate) 1QM 13_{7} (of our fathers) 4QDibHam^a 4_{4} (of knowledge), אַתָּה ... אֵל *you are ... a God* Ne 9_{31} (merciful and compassionate) 1QH 7_{31} (eternal) 15_{25} (of truth), אַתָּה ... אֵל *you are ... a God* Ps 86_{15} (compassionate and merciful; + אֲדֹנָי *Lord* [L], י׳ [mss]), י׳ ... אֵל *Y. is ... a God* 1 S 2_{3} (of knowledge) Jr 51_{56} (of retribution) Na 1_{2} (jealous and avenging) Ps 94_{1} (of vengeance) 95_{3} (great; + י׳, אֱלֹהִים), י׳ אֱלֹהֶיךָ ... אֵל *Y. your God is ... a God* Dt 7_{21} (great and terrible), י׳ אֱלֹהֵיכֶם הוּא ... הָאֵל *Y., your God is ... the God* 10_{17} (great, mighty, terrible).

אֵל כַּבִּיר *God is mighty* Jb 36_{5}, אֵל שַׂגִּיא *God is great* Jb 36_{26}, אל גדול קדוש גבור ואדיר *God is great, holy, mighty and majestic* 4Q372 1_{29}, אל ארך אפים הוא *as for God, he is slow to anger* Si 5_{4}, לֹא אִישׁ אֵל *God is not a man* Nm 23_{19}, מִי־אֵל *who is God?* 2 S 22_{32} (+ י׳ Y.) Mc 7_{18}, חַי־אֵל *as God lives* Jb 27_{2}, אֵל ... בְּקִרְבְּכֶם *God is ... among you* Jos 3_{10}, בָּךְ אֵל *God is among you* Is 45_{14} (+ אֱלֹהִים *God*), אל עמכם *God is with you* 11QBer 2_{13}, עִמָּנוּ אֵל *God is with us* Is $8_{8.10}$ (cf. 7_{14}, §2c), הָאֵל מָעוּזִּי חָיִל *God is my strong refuge* 2 S 22_{33}, אֵל יְשׁוּעָתִי *God is my salvation* Is 12_{2} (+ י׳), הָאֵל יְשׁוּעָתֵנוּ *God is our salvation* Ps 68_{20} (+ אֲדֹנָי *Lord*), הָאֵל לָנוּ אֵל *God is for us a God* of salvation 68_{21} (+ י׳ אֲדֹנָי *Y., the Lord*), אֵל ... גֹּאֲלָם *God is ... their redeemer* 78_{35} (|| אֱלֹהִים), אֵל יַעֲקֹב בְּעֶזְרוֹ *the God of Jacob is his help* 146_{5} (or del. בְּ; + י׳ אֱלֹהָיו *Y. his God*).

<OBJ> נסה pi. *test* Ps $78_{18.41}$ (|| קָדוֹשׁ *holy one*) 106_{14}, זעם *provoke* Si 31_{6}, רגז hi. *provoke* Jb 12_{6} (+ אֱלוֹהַּ *God*), יגע hi. *weary* 4QDibHam^a 1.5_{19}(mg) (|| צור *rock*), גדף pi. *blaspheme* Si 48_{18}, appar. מרה hi. *rebel against* 4Q370 1_{2} (ויאמרו), שׂנא pi. *hate* 1QM 3_{6}, שׁכח *forget* Dt 32_{18} Ps 106_{21} Jb 8_{13} 4QpHos^a 2_{3}, דמה pi. *liken* Is 40_{18}, שׁחר pi. *seek* Ps 78_{34}, דרשׁ *seek* Si $35_{14(Bmg).14(B)}$ 1QS 1_{2}, קרא *call* Ps 17_{6}, שׁוב hi. *return* trans. 1QH 5_{18}, *answer* Jb 31_{14}, ידע *know* 18_{21} 1QH 12_{11}, הלל pi. *praise* Ps 150_{1} 1QM 19_{13} 6QHymn 6_{5}, ידה hi. *give thanks to* Ps 118_{28} 1QH $11_{3.15}$ (|| צור), ברך pi. *bless* 1QS 1_{19} 4QRitMar 105_{1} (יבר[כו]) 1QM 13_{1} 14_{4} 18_{6} 4QBer^a 3.1_{8}, כבד pi. *honour* Si 7_{31} (|| כֹּהֵן *priest*), נוה hi. *adorn* Ex 15_{2}, ירא *fear* Si 6_{16} CD 10_{2} 20_{20} 4QCat^a 12.1_{10} (יר[א]י), pi. 4QShir^b 35_{6}, פחד *fear* Si 7_{29} (+ כֹּהֵן), עזב *leave* 1QpHab 8_{10} 4QpHos^b 7_{2} ([ע]זבו).

<CSTR> אֵל אֱמֶת *God of truth* Ps 31_{6} 1QH 15_{25} 4Q416 3_{5}, אֱמוּנָה *of faithfulness* Dt 32_{4}, ה[צ]דק *of righteousness*

1QM 18$_{8}$, הצדק והשכל *of righteousness and insight* 1QH fr. 7.2$_{8}$, התשבחות *of praises* Si 51$_{12}$, הַכָּבוֹד *of glory* Ps 29$_{3}$ (אֵל־) MasShirShab 2$_{13}$, שלום *of peace* 1QM 16$_{17}$ + Sup, עולם *of eternity* Si 36$_{22}$ ([עו]ל[ם]) 1QH 7$_{31}$, כל חי *of all living* 40$_{1(Bmg)}$ (B אם *mother of*), יִשְׂרָאֵל *of Israel* Ps 68$_{36}$ 1QS 3$_{24}$ 4QRitMar 8$_{5}$ 9$_{2}$ ([א]ל) 9$_{14}$ 14$_{4}$ 24$_{2}$ 105$_{1}$ (י[שראל]) 4QPrQuot 7$_{6}$ (י[שראל])14$_{2}$ 15$_{8}$ (ישר[אל]) 15$_{12}$ (ישרא[ל]) 34$_{4}$ (א[ל י]שראל) 40.2$_{3(Baillet)}$ (ישרא[ל]) 48$_{3.7}$ (יש[ראל]) 51$_{6}$ ([י]שראל) 51$_{12}$ 62$_{1}$ (ישר[אל]) 66$_{2}$ (ישרא[ל]) 68$_{2}$ (יש[ראל]) 69$_{2}$ (ישר[אל]) 90$_{2}$ (יש[ראל]) 4QRitPur 1$_{2(Baillet)}$ 11$_{5}$ (ישר[א]ל) 29$_{21}$ (יש[ראל]) 40$_{3}$ (ישר[אל]) 64$_{5}$ (י[שראל]) 1QM 1$_{9}$ 6$_{6}$ 10$_{8}$ 13$_{1.2.13}$ 14$_{4.4}$ 15$_{13}$ 16$_{1}$ 18$_{3.6}$ 19$_{13}$ + Sup 4QFlor 4$_{7(Allegro)}$ (י[שר]אל; but perh. אל = *to*) 4QCat^{a} 1$_{9}$ (ישרא[ל]) 6QHymn 8$_{1}$ (ישר[אל]), יַעֲקֹב *of Jacob* Ps 146$_{5}$, יְשֻׁרוּן *of Jeshurun* Dt 33$_{26}$ (if em. כָּאֵל *as God* to כְּאֵל *as the God of*), דֵּעוֹת *of knowledge* 1 S 2$_{3}$, הדעות 1QS 3$_{15}$ 4QDibHam^{a} 4$_{4}$ 1QH 1$_{26}$ 12$_{10}$ (ה[ד]ע[ו]ת) fr. 3$_{12}$ fr. 4$_{15}$, גְּמֻלוֹת *of retribution* Jr 51$_{56}$, נְקָמוֹת *of vengeance* Ps 94$_{1}$ (אֵל־) 1QS 4$_{12}$ (נקמ[ות]), החסדים *of mercy* 1QM 14$_{8.10}$ + Sup (ה[חס]דים), הרחמ[ים] *of mercy* 1QH 10$_{14}$, הרחמים וה[ח]נינה *of compassion and mercy* 11$_{29}$, או[ר]ים *of lights* 4QPr Quot 29$_{9}$, הַשָּׁמָיִם *of the heavens* Ps 136$_{26}$, אבותינו *of our fathers* 1QM 13$_{7}$, חַיָּי *of my life* Ps 42$_{9(L)}$ (mss חָי *living* God), אֵלִים *of gods* Dn 11$_{36}$ 1QM 14$_{16}$ 18$_{6}$ (א[ל]ים) 4QShir^{a} 1$_{2}$ (+ אדון *Lord*) 4QShirShab^{d} 1.2$_{26}$ 4QShirShab^{f} 14$_{3}$.

כְּבוֹד־אֵל *glory of God* Ps 19$_{2}$ 1QS 10$_{9}$ 1QSb 4$_{25}$ 1QM 4$_{6.8}$ CD 20$_{26}$ 1QNoah 13$_{1}$ Mur 6 1$_{6}$, נצח *success of* 1QM 4$_{13}$, שם *name of* 4QRitMar 8$_{5}$ 4QPrQuot 40.2$_{3}$ 11QBer 1.2$_{3}$ Kuntillet ʿAjrud plaster inscr.$_{3}$, מאת *hundred of* 1QM 4$_{3}$, סרך *military order of* 3$_{3}$, מלחמת *battle of* 4$_{12}$ 9$_{5}$ 15$_{12}$, נס *banner of* 3$_{15}$, חרב *sword of* 15$_{3}$ 19$_{11}$ 1QH 6$_{29}$, קהל *congregation of* 1QM 4$_{10}$ perh. 1QSa 2$_{4}$ (see אֵלֶּה *these*, §1, Coll.), עצת *council of* 1QS 1$_{8.10}$ 1QSb 4$_{24}$ 4QShir^{b} 48$_{1}$, עדת *assembly of* 1QM 4$_{9}$, עדת שערי *assembly of gates of*, i.e. city court Si 7$_{7}$, יחד *community of* 1QS 1$_{12}$ 2$_{22}$, עם *people of* 1QM 1$_{5}$ 3$_{13}$, גורל *lot of* 1QS 2$_{2}$ 1QM 13$_{5}$ 15$_{1}$ 17$_{7}$, תרומת *offering of* 4$_{1}$, אֵיד *disaster of* Jb 31$_{23}$, חֶסֶד *love of* Ps 52$_{3}$ (or em. אֶל־חָסִיד *to*, i.e. against, *the pious one*), אמת *truth of* 1QS 3$_{6}$ 11$_{4}$ 1QM 4$_{6}$, אהבת *love of* CD 8$_{16(A)}$=19$_{29(B)}$, יראת *fear of* Si 35$_{12}$ 1QSb 5$_{25}$, דבר *word of* Si 43$_{10}$ 46$_{13(Segal)}$ ([דבר]) 48$_{3}$, דרך *way of* CD 20$_{18}$, ברית *covenant of* 1QS 5$_{8}$ 10$_{10}$ 1QM 16$_{17}$ + Sup CD 3$_{11}$ 5$_{12}$ 7$_{5}$ 13$_{14}$ 14$_{2}$ 20$_{17}$ 5QRègle 28$_{3}$ 1QpHab 2$_{4}$ 4QBer^{a} 3.2$_{12}$ ([א]ל), שיר *song of* Si 35$_{5(B)}$ (Bmg, F שירת *singing of*), תהלת *praise of* 1QM 4$_{14}$ 4QTNaph 4$_{4}$, תשבוחת *praise of* 1QM 4$_{8}$, [ש]מחת *joy of* 4$_{14}$, קוֹל *voice of* Ezk 10$_{5}$, נִשְׁמַת־ *breath of* Jb 37$_{10}$, רוּחַ־ *spirit of* 33$_{4}$ (|| שַׁדַּי *Shaddai*), פי *mouth of* 1QH 12$_{9}$ 1QpHab 2$_{3}$ (פיא), אף *anger of* 1QS 2$_{15}$ 1QM 4$_{1}$ 6$_{3}$ CD 2$_{1}$ 3$_{8}$ 8$_{13(A)}$=19$_{26(B)}$ 10$_{9}$ 20$_{16}$ 4QapLam^{a} 1.2$_{1}$, עברת *anger of* 1QS 4$_{12}$ 4QBer^{a} 3.2$_{10}$ ([א]ל), חמת *wrath of*1QpHab 11$_{15}$ ([א]ל), נקמת *vengeance of* 1QS 1$_{11}$ 1QM 4$_{12}$, גמול *reward of* 4$_{12}$, מהומת *commotion of* 4$_{7}$, כלת *annihilation of* 4$_{12}$, ריב *contention of* 4$_{12}$, מצרף *crucible of* 17$_{9}$, כוח *strength of* 1QM 4$_{12}$ 13$_{13}$ 4Q416 5$_{9}$, יַד־ *hand of* Jb 27$_{11}$ (+ שַׁדַּי) Si 43$_{12}$ 1QM 1$_{14}$ 18$_{1.3}$ 4QM^{a} fr. 1$_{4}$ fr. 14$_{6(Baillet)}$ ([יד]) 4QCat^{a} 12.1$_{9}$, ימין *right hand of* 1QM 4$_{7}$, גבורת *might of* 1$_{11.14}$ 3$_{8}$ 4$_{4.12}$ 6$_{2.6}$ 10$_{5}$ 14$_{6}$ + Sup (גב[ו]רת), רצון *will of* Si 15$_{15}$ 16$_{3}$ 1QS 9$_{13.24}$ 1QM 2$_{5}$, מעשה *deed of* Si 36$_{15}$ 39$_{33}$, תורת *law of* 1QpHab 1$_{11}$ 4Q525 2$_{6}$ 4QMMT A 2$_{1}$ ([תורת א]ל) 4QMMT B$_{25}$ (ת[ורת אל]), חוק *statute of* 4QRitMar 1$_{2}$, מצות *commandment of* CD 9$_{7}$, משפט *judgment of* 1QS 9$_{25}$ 1QM 4$_{6}$ 6$_{3.5}$, צדק *righteousness of* 4$_{6}$, צדקת *righteousness of* 1QS 10$_{25}$ 11$_{12}$, קודש *holiness of* 4Q416 7$_{8}$ ([א]ל), מקדש *sanctuary of* 1QpHab 12$_{9}$, מועד *appointed time of* 1QM 1$_{8}$ 3$_{8}$ 4$_{7}$, עזר *help of* 4$_{13}$, משענת *support of* 4$_{13}$, ברכת *blessing of* Si 11$_{22}$ 30$_{25(Segal)}$ (ב[רכ]ת) 4QRit Mar 45$_{1}$, שלום *peace of* 4QPrQuot 29$_{11}$ 1QM 3$_{5}$ 4$_{14}$, פדות *redemption of* 1$_{12}$.

עיני אל *eyes of God* Si 15$_{19}$, פְּנֵי־ *face of* Ml 1$_{9}$ 4Q482 3$_{1}$, חסדי *mercy of* 1QS 11$_{12}$, רחמי *compassion of* 4Q181 1$_{3}$ 4QShir^{b} 1$_{9}$, תעודות *summoned ones of* 1QM 3$_{4}$, בחירי *chosen ones of* 1QpHab 10$_{13}$ 4QPs^{a} 1.4$_{14(Allegro)}$ (ב[חיר]י), קדושי *holy ones of* Si 42$_{17(B)}$ (F קדשי) 11QMelch 1$_{9}$, למודי *disciples of* CD 20$_{4}$, קריאי *those called of*, i.e. by, *God* 1QM 4$_{11}$ (קרואי) 3$_{2}$, דגלי *divisions of* 3$_{6}$ 4$_{10}$, צבאות *hosts of* 4$_{11}$, כּוֹכְבֵי־ *stars of* Is 14$_{13}$, אִמְרֵי־ *words of* Nm 24$_{4.16}$ (both || שַׁדַּי *Shaddai*) Ps 107$_{11}$ (both || עֶלְיוֹן *Most High*), דברי *words of* 1QS 1$_{14}$, חוקי *statutes of* 1$_{7.12}$ 3$_{8}$ 11QMelch 1.1$_{12(Milik)}$ 4QShir^{b} 48$_{5}$, מצות *commands of* CD 2$_{18}$ 3$_{2.6.12}$ 5$_{21}$ 8$_{19(A)}$=19$_{32(B)}$,

[משמ]רות אל] *obligations of God* 4QJub^{d} 1.2$_{28}$, משפטי *judgments of* 1QS 3$_{6}$ 4$_{3}$ 11QMelch 1.1$_{13}$ ([מש]פט[י א]ל]) 1.1$_{24}$ ([משפט]י]), צדקות *righteous deeds of* 1QS 1$_{21}$ 10$_{23}$, חפצי *desires of* Si 35$_{14}$, שלומי *retributions of* 1QM 4$_{12}$, ישועות *salvation of* 4$_{13}$, רוֹמְמוֹת *high praises of* Ps 149$_{6}$, הודות *thanksgivings of* 1QM 4$_{14}$, גילות *joys of* 3$_{11}$, רנות *joys of* 4$_{5}$, תַּנְחֻמוֹת *consolations of* Jb 15$_{11}$, גבורות *mighty deeds of* 1QM 3$_{5}$ 4Q181 1$_{2}$, נִפְלְאוֹת *wonders of* Jb 37$_{14}$, מַעַלְלֵי־ *deeds of* Ps 78$_{7}$ (+ אֱלֹהִים *God*), מעשי *deeds of* Si 39$_{16(Segal)}$ ([מעשׂי]) 42$_{15}$ 1QS 4$_{4}$ CD 1$_{2}$ 2$_{15}$ 13$_{8}$ 1QH 5$_{36}$ fr. 15 1$_{1}$, בְּנֵי־ *sons of* Ho 2$_{1}$, חללי *slain ones of* 1QM 4$_{7}$, דַּרְכֵי־ *ways of* Jb 40$_{19}$ 1QS 3$_{10}$ 4QTNaph 4$_{6}$, רזי *mysteries of* 1QS 3$_{23}$ 1QM 3$_{9}$ 16$_{11.16}$ 17$_{17(Yadin)}$ ([ר]זי]) 1QpHab 7$_{8}$, מִקְדְּשֵׁי־ *sanctuaries of* Ps 73$_{17}$, מוֹעֲדֵי־ *meeting places of* 74$_{8}$, ק[י]צי *end times of* 1QpHab 7$_{13}$, מחני *camps of* 1QM 4$_{9}$, שבטי *tribes of* 4$_{10}$, משפחות *families of* 4$_{10}$, מרומי *high places of* Si 43$_{9}$, נשיאי *princes of* 1QM 3$_{3}$, הַרְרֵי־ *mountains of* Ps 36$_{7}$ 50$_{10}$ (if em. אֶלֶף *cattle*), אַרְזֵי־ *cedars of* 80$_{11}$, הֲלִיכוֹת אֵלִי *processions of my God* 68$_{25}$ (|| אֱלֹהִים).

<APP> אלי מלך הכ[בו]ד *my God, the king of glory* 4QShir^{b} 52$_{4}$, אֵלִי מַלְכִּי *my God, my king* Ps 68$_{25}$, אל ... מלך *God ... king* 4QShirShab^{d} 1.2$_{26}$, אָבִי ... אֵלִי וְצוּר יְשׁוּעָתִי *my father, my God, and the rock of my salvation* 89$_{27}$, הַצּוּר ... אֵל *the rock ... a God of* faithfulness Dt 32$_{4}$, אֵל סַלְעִי *God, my rock* Ps 42$_{10}$, סַלְעִי וּמְצוּדָתִי וּמְפַלְטִי אֵלִי צוּרִי ... מָגִנִּי וְקֶרֶן־יִשְׁעִי מִשְׂגַּבִּי *my rock, and my fortress, and my deliverer, my God, my rock ... my shield, and the horn of my salvation, my refuge* 18$_{3}$, אֵל שִׂמְחַת גִּילִי *God, the joy of my rejoicing* 43$_{4}$, י׳ אֵל *Y., a* compassionate and merciful *God* Ex 34$_{6}$, *Y., the God of* truth Ps 31$_{6}$, אֱלֹהֵי הָאֱלֹהִים וַאֲדוֹנֵי הָאֲדֹנִים הָאֵל *God of gods and Lord of lords, the* great, mighty and terribble *God* Dt 10$_{17}$, אדוני אל *Lord, God of* mercy 1QH 10$_{14}$, אֱלֹהֵינוּ הָאֵל *our God, the* great, mighty and terrible *God* Ne 9$_{32}$, אֵל אֱלֹהֵי הָרוּחֹת *God, the God of the spirits* Nm 16$_{22}$, [אל] ... אלוהי אלוהיכה *God, ... my God and your God* 4QJub^{d} 1.32.

<ADJ> אֶחָד *one* Ml 2$_{10}$, חַי *living* Jos 3$_{10}$ Ho 2$_{1}$ Ps 42$_{3.9(mss)}$ (L חַיָּי God of *my life*) 84$_{3}$ 4QDibHam^{a} 1.5$_{9}$ 8$_{12}$ 5QapMal 1$_{4}$, קָדוֹשׁ *holy* Is 5$_{16}$, צַדִּיק *righteous* Is 45$_{21}$, קַנָּא *jealous* Ex 20$_{5}$ 34$_{14}$ Dt 4$_{24}$ 5$_{9}$ 6$_{15}$ 11QT 2$_{12}$, קַנּוֹא *jealous* Jos 24$_{19}$ Na 1$_{2}$, רַחוּם וְחַנּוּן *compassionate and merciful* Ex 34$_{6}$ Ps 86$_{15}$, חַנּוּן וְרַחוּם *merciful and compassionate* Jon 4$_{2}$ Ne 9$_{31}$, רַחוּם *compassionate* Dt 4$_{31}$, גָּדוֹל *great* 7$_{21}$ 10$_{17}$ Jr 32$_{18}$ Ps 95$_{3}$ Dn 9$_{4}$ Ne 1$_{5}$ 9$_{32}$ 1QM 10$_{1}$, גִּבּוֹר *mighty* Dt 10$_{17}$ Is 9$_{5}$ 10$_{21}$ Jr 32$_{18}$ Ne 9$_{32}$, טוֹב *good* 4QShirShab^{d} 1.1$_{5}$ ([ה]טוב]).

<PREP> לְ of direction, *to, towards* Ps 42$_{9}$ Jb 33$_{6}$ perh. 4QShirShab^{d} 1.1$_{5}$ 1.2$_{26}$, + אמר *say* Ps 42$_{10}$ Jb 21$_{14}$ 22$_{17}$ (+ שַׁדַּי *Shaddai*) 1QS 10$_{11}$ (|| עֶלְיוֹן *Most High*), דבר pi. *speak* Jb 13$_{7}$, קרא *cry* Ps 57$_{3}$ (|| אֱלֹהִים *God*; + עֶלְיוֹן), למד pi. *teach* Jb 21$_{22}$, רבה hi. *multiply* words 34$_{37}$, רנן hi. *shout for joy* 4QDibHam^{a} 1.7$_{11}$, ידה *give thanks* 4QShirShab^{d} 1.1$_{4}$, hi. Ps 136$_{26}$ Si 51$_{12}$ 1QS 11$_{15}$ (|| עֶלְיוֹן) 4QRitMar 9$_{10}$ 4QShirShab^{f} 14$_{3}$ MasShirShab 2$_{13}$, נתן *give* Si 32$_{12(Bmg)}$ (B לו *to him*) 47$_{8}$, כחש pi. *act deceptively* Jb 31$_{28}$ (+ מִמָּעַל *from above*), of possession, *to, of* 1QS 11$_{2}$ 11$_{10}$ 1QM 6$_{6}$ 1QM 15$_{13}$ ([ל]אל]) perh. 19$_{13}$ + Sup (ל[א]ל) CD 3$_{4}$ 1QH 4$_{31}$ perh. 6$_{33}$, of benefit, *to, for* + ריב *plead* Jb 13$_{8}$, סכן *be of use* 22$_{2}$, צמא לְ *thirst for* Ps 42$_{3}$ (|| אֱלֹהִים), ערך לְ *compare with* Is 40$_{18}$, חָלִלָה לָאֵל מֵרֶשַׁע *far be wickedness from God* Jb 34$_{10}$ (|| שַׁדַּי).

אֶל of direction, *to*, + שׁוב *return* intrans. Is 10$_{21}$ Si 40$_{1(Bmg)}$ (B אם *mother*) 4QD^{b}5, hi. *return* trans. Jb 15$_{13}$, בוא *enter* Ps 43$_{4}$ (+ אֱלֹהִים *God*), אמר *say* Jb 34$_{31}$, רנן pi. *sing joyfully* Ps 84$_{3}$ (+ י׳ Y.), עתר hi. *pray* Si 37$_{15}$ 38$_{14}$, פלל htp. *pray* 38$_{9(B)}$ (Bmg pi.), הלך *go* Jb 34$_{23}$ (+ בַּמִּשְׁפָּט *in judgment*), שׁוע pi. *cry* 38$_{41}$, קרא *call* Si 46$_{5.16(Segal)}$ ([קרא א]ל [א]ל) 47$_{5}$ 48$_{20}$ (וי[קר]או) 4Q372 1$_{16}$, נשׂא *raise* heart Lm 3$_{41}$ (+ בַּשָּׁמָיִם *in heaven*), גלל *roll*, i.e. rely on Si 7$_{17}$, תמם hi. *make perfect* heart49$_{3}$, נטה אֶל *stretch* hand *against* Jb 15$_{25}$ (|| שַׁדַּי *Shaddai*), דרשׁ אֶל *seek* 5$_{8}$ (|| אֱלֹהִים), שׁחר אֶל pi. *seek* 8$_{5}$ (|| שַׁדַּי).

בְּ *at, against* 6QHymn 8$_{1}$, + מרד *rebel* 1QpHab 8$_{11}$, חסה בְּ *take refuge in* Ps 16$_{1}$; כְּ *as* Dt 33$_{26}$ Jb 40$_{9}$ Si 7$_{15}$ (or em. מאל *from God*); עִם *with* 2 S 23$_{5}$ Jb 27$_{13}$ (|| שַׁדַּי *Shaddai*), + צדק *be righteous* 9$_{2}$, יכח hi. *argue* 13$_{3}$ (|| שַׁדַּי), צדק *be justified* 25$_{4}$, סרב עִם *rebel against* Si 4$_{25}$; אֵת *with* 1QS 10$_{18}$, + אמן ni. *be faithful* Ps 78$_{8}$; שׁוב עַד *return unto* CD 20$_{24(Rabin)}$ (AHL עוד אל *again to*); מִן *from* Jb 20$_{29}$ (|| אֱלֹהִים *God*) 35$_{2}$ Si 7$_{15}$ (if em.; see above) 15$_{11}$ 41$_{4}$ 1QS 3$_{15}$ 4QM^{a} fr. 25$_{1}$, + בקשׁ pi. *seek* Ps 104$_{21}$

Si 7_{4}, סתר ni. *be hidden* 16_{17}, חלק ni. *be allotted* 15_{9} (Amg), פשע מִן hi. *make rebel against* 4QWiles 1_{16}; חכם מֵאֵת *have skill from* Si 38_{2}; מֵאַחֲרֵי *from (after)*, + סוג ni. *backslide* Si 46_{11} 1QS 2_{17}, שׁוב hi. *cause to turn away* CD 6_{2}; שׁען על ni. *lean upon* CD 20_{23}, דבר עַל pi. *speak against* Dn 11_{36}, ענג על htp. *delight in* 4Q525 4_{10} (א[ל]).

לִפְנֵי *before* 11QPs^{a} 27_{3} (|| אִישׁ *man*) 1QM 1_{9} 1QNoah 1_{4}, + גרע *diminish* meditation Jb 15_{4}, מעט *be little* Ne 9_{32}, ידה htp. *confess* CD 20_{28}, אשׁם *be guilty* 4QJub^{d} 1.2_{25} ([לפני אל]), מצא *find* Si 3_{18}, עבר *enter* covenant 1QS 1_{16}, רצה ni. *be accepted* 1QS 3_{11} 4QJub^{d} 1.2_{21} ([וירצה לפני]), שׁרת pi. *serve* 1QM 2_{2}; אַחֲרֵי *after*, + מלא pi. *fill*, i.e. wholly follow Si 46_{6}, עוד hi. *testify* in favour of CD 19_{30}.

<COLL> אל ישראל ומלאך אמתו *the God of Israel and his true angel* 1QS 3_{24}, וַיִּקְרָא שְׁמוֹ ... אֵל גִּבּוֹר *his name shall be called ... mighty God* Is 9_{5}, הָאֵל ... י׳ צְבָאוֹת שְׁמוֹ *God ... Y. of hosts is his name* Jr 32_{18}, מַה־יָּקְרוּ רֵעֶיךָ אֵל *how precious are your thoughts, O God* Ps 139_{17}, הָאֵל תָּמִים דַּרְכּוֹ *as for God, his way is perfect* 2 S 22_{31}||Ps 18_{31} (+ י׳ *Y.*), אב ואלכה *your father and God* 4Q525 4_{11}.

2c. as element in names, usu. personal, including עִמָּנוּ אֵל *Immanuel*, i.e. *God is with us* Is 7_{14}, אֵל אֱלֹהֵי יִשְׂרָאֵל *El-Elohe-Israel* Gn 33_{20} (as name of altar).

<SYN> §1a אֱלֹהִים *god*, קָדוֹשׁ *holy one*; §1b פֶּסֶל *idol*; §2b אֱלֹהִים *God*, י׳ *Y.*, שַׁדַּי *Shaddai*, עֶלְיוֹן *the Most High*, צוּר *rock*, קָדוֹשׁ *holy one*, כֹּהֵן *priest*.

<ANT> אִישׁ *man*.

Also Kuntillet ʻAjrud plaster inscr.$_{1}$ Kh. el-Qom bowl inscr. Si 50_{21} (ל[א]) 4Q487 $8_{3.5}$ 9_{2} 23_{3} 1QS 2_{26} (ל[א]) 4QRitMar 21_{1} (א[ל]) 104_{6} 4QPrQuot 48_{8} 72_{2} 73_{5} 4QOrd^{a} 5_{1} 1QM 14_{18} + Sup 6QD 5_{5} 1QH fr. 18_{6} 21_{5} 4QPs^{a} 4_{27} 4QCat^{a} 12.2_{6} 19_{2} 4QTanḥ 21_{4} 4QShir^{b} 8_{10} 48_{6} 130_{2} 4QShirShab^{a} 1.2_{17} 4QShirShab^{b} 16_{1} (ם[אלי]) 30_{1} 4QShirShab^{c} 6_{3} 4QShirShab^{d} 1.1_{21} 4QShirShab^{f} 6_{8} 4Q416 5_{14} 4Q285 $4_{2.8}$ (both perh. אֶל *to*) 4Q372 1_{9} 4QPsJos^{b} 22.2_{6}.

→ אֲבִיאֵל *Abiel*, אלאמר *Eleamar*, אלבא *Elba*, אלדגן *Eldagan*, אֶלְדָּד *Eldad*, אלדלה *Eldalah*, אֶלְדָּעָה *Eldaah* , אֶלְעוּזַי *Eluzai*, אֶלְזָבָד *Elzabad*, אלזכר *Elzachar*, אֶלְחָנָן *Elhanan*, אֱלִיאָב *Eliab*, אֱלִיאֵל *Eliel*, אליאר *Eljair*, אֱלִיאָתָה *Eliathah*, אליבר *Elibar*, אֶלְיָדָע *Eliada*, אֵלִיָּהוּ *Elijah*, אֱלִיהוּא *Elihu*, אֶלְיוֹעֵינַי *Elioenai*, אֶלְיַחְבָּא *Eliahba*, אֱלִיחֹרֶף *Elihoreph*, אֱלִימֶלֶךְ *Elimelech*, אֶלְיָסָף *Eliasaph*, אֱלִיעֶזֶר *Eliezer*, אֱלִיעָם *Eliam*, אֱלִיעֵנַי *Elienai*, אֱלִיפַל *Eliphal*, אֱלִיפַז *Eliphaz*, אֱלִיפְלֵהוּ *Elipheleh*, אֱלִיפֶלֶט *Eliphelet*, אֱלִיצוּר *Elizur*, אֱלִיצָפָן *Elizaphan*, אֱלִיקָא *Elika*, אליקם *Elikam*, אֶלְיָקִים *Eliakim*, אלירב *Elirab*, אֱלִישֶׁבַע *Elisheba*, אֱלִישׁוּעַ *Elishua*, אֶלְיָשִׁיב *Eliashib*, אֱלִישָׁמָע *Elishama*, אֱלִישָׁע *Elisha*, אֱלִישָׁפָט *Elishaphat*, אֶלְנַעַם *Elnaam*, אֶלְנָתָן *Elnathan*, אלסמך *Elsamach*, אלסמכי *Elisamchi*, אֶלְעָד *Elead*, אֶלְעָדָה *Eleadah*, אלעז *Eliaz*, אֶלְעָזָר *Eleazar*, אֶלְעָלֵה *Elealeh*, אלעש *Eleash*, אֶלְעָשָׂה *Eleasah*, אֶלְפַּעַל *Elpaal*, אלצדק *Elzedek*, אֶלְקָנָה *Elkanah*, אלרלה *Elralah*, אלרם *Eliram*, אלשגב *Elsagab*, אל *suffixed*, אַדְבְּאֵל *Adbeel*, אוּאֵל *Uel*, אוּרִיאֵל *Uriel*, אִיתִיאֵל *Ithiel*, אֲרִיאֵל *Ariel*, אֲשַׂרְאֵל *Asarel*, אֲשַׂרְאֵלָה *Asarelah*, אַשְׂרִיאֵל *Asriel*, בדאל *Badiel*, בידאל *Bejadiel*, בעדאל *Beadel*, בְּצַלְאֵל *Bezalel*, בָּרַכְאֵל *Barachel*, גְּאוּאֵל *Geuel*, גַּבְרִיאֵל *Gabriel*, גַּדִּיאֵל *Gaddiel*, גַּמְלִיאֵל *Gamliel*, דָּנִאֵל *Daniel*, דְּעוּאֵל *Deuel*, זַבְדִּיאֵל *Zabdiel*, חִיאֵל *Hiel*, חַמּוּאֵל *Hammuel*, חַנִּיאֵל *Hanniel*, חֲנַמְאֵל *Hanamel*, טָבְאֵל *Tabeel*, יְדִיעֲאֵל *Jediael*, יְזִיאֵל *Jeziel*, יזנאל *Jezanel*, יַחְדִּיאֵל *Jahdiel*, יַחֲזִיאֵל *Jahaziel*, יְחֶזְקֵאל *Ezekiel*, יְחִיאֵל *Jehiel*, יַהְלֶלְאֵל *Jahleel*, יַחְצְאֵל *Jahzeel*, יְמוּאֵל *Jemuel*, יְעוּאֵל *Jeuel*, יַעֲזִיאֵל *Jaaziel*, יְקוּתִיאֵל *Jekuthiel*, יְרַחְמְאֵל *Jerahmeel*, יְרִיאֵל *Jeriel*, יְשִׂימִאֵל *Jesimiel*, יִשְׂרָאֵל *Israel*, יִשְׁמָעֵאל *Ishmael*, יַתְנִיאֵל *Jathniel*, לְמוּאֵל *Lemuel*, מַגְדִּיאֵל *Magdiel*, מְהֵיטַבְאֵל *Mehetabel*, מַהֲלַלְאֵל *Mahalalel*, מְחוּיָאֵל *Mehujael*, מִיכָאֵל *Michael*, מִישָׁאֵל *Mishael*, מַלְכִּיאֵל *Malchiel*, מְשֵׁיזַבְאֵל *Meshezabel*, נְמוּאֵל *Nemuel*, נְתַנְאֵל *Nethanel*, עַבְדְּאֵל *Abdeel*, עדאל *Adael*, עֲדִיאֵל *Adiel*, עַדְרִיאֵל *Adriel*, עזאל *Azael*, עֻזִּיאֵל *Uzziel*, עֲזַרְאֵל *Azarel*, עַזְרִיאֵל *Azriel*, עַמִּיאֵל *Ammiel*, עִמָּנוּאֵל *Immanuel*, עֲשָׂהאֵל *Asahel*, עֲשִׂיאֵל *Asiel*, עשנאל *Ashnel*, עָתְנִיאֵל *Othniel*, פַּגְעִיאֵל *Pagiel*, פְּדָהְאֵל *Pedahel*, פּוּטִיאֵל *Putiel*, פַּלְטִיאֵל *Paltiel*, פְּנוּאֵל *Penuel*, פְּתוּאֵל *Pethuel*, צוּרִיאֵל *Zuriel*, קַדְמִיאֵל *Kadmiel*, קְמוּאֵל *Kemuel*, רְעוּאֵל *Reuel*, רְפָאֵל *Rephael*, שְׁאַלְתִּיאֵל *Shealtiel*, שְׁבוּאֵל *Shebuel*, שְׁלֻמִיאֵל *Shelumiel*, שלמאל *Shalmael*, שַׁלְתִּיאֵל *Shaltiel*, שְׁמוּאֵל *Samuel*.

אֵל II 5.2.1 n.m. **power**—cstr. יֶשׁ־לְאֵל יָדִי—אֵל *there is according to the power of my hand*, i.e. *I have the power*

Gn 31_{29} (+ לַעֲשׂוֹת *to do*) Si 5_{1}, var. Mc 2_{1} (יָדָם *their hand*), אֵין לְאֵל יָדֵנוּ *there is not according to the power of our hand,* i.e. *we are powerless* Ne 5_{5} (mss יָדֵינוּ *our hands*) 4QapLam^{a} 1.1_{2}, var. Dt 28_{32} (יָדֶךָ *your hand* [mss יָדֶיךָ *your hands*]), בִּהְיוֹת לְאֵל יָדְךָ *when it is according to the power of your hand,* i.e. *when you have the power* Pr $3_{27(Qr)}$ (Kt ידיך *your hands;* + לַעֲשׂוֹת *to do*), לאל ידך הדשן *according to the power of your hand,* i.e. as you are able, *make yourself fat* Si 14_{11}.

אֵל III, see אַיִל I–II, אֵלָה I, אֵלֶּה.

אֶל †5464.79.229.33 prep. **to**—usu. אֶל־ (אֱלֵי); sf. אֵלַי (אֱלָי), אֵלֶיךָ אֵלַיִךְ (אֵלָיִךְ, Q אליכה, אלך I), אֵלָיו (Kt, אלו I, Q אלוהיהי), אֵלֶיהָ, אֵלֵינוּ (Q אלנו), אֲלֵיכֶם (אֲלֵכֶם), אֲלֵיהֶם (אֲלֵהֶם, אֵלֵימוֹ, Q אליהמה), אֲלֵיהֶן (אֲלֵהֶן)—exact meaning oft. uncertain, oft. ‖ לְ (e.g. Gn 30_{25} Dt 13_{9} Jos 17_{17} 2 S 1_{8} 2 K 2_{20}) or variation (or corruption) of עַל (e.g. 2 K 18_{27} Jr 11_{2} 18_{11} 19_{15}).

1a. to, of movement, usu. horizontal, where goal of movement is reached, **into,** esp. where goal is place or structure, + בוא *come* (1) to Gn 6_{20} $7_{9.15}$ 8_{11} 14_{7} etc. 11QT 26_{10} 53_{9} Dt 17_{14}=11QT 56_{12} Dt $18_{6.9}$=11QT $60_{13.16}$ fr. 14 3QJub 23_{6} 1QM 3_{11} 4QOrd^{a} $1.2_{5(Allegro)}$ 4QTNaph 2_{7} 4QpGen^{a} $1_{15.15}$ (אל ה[תבה]) 4QpGen^{a} 1_{16} 4Q251 3_{17} ([אל תבוא]) 4QPentPar^{b} 23.2_{4} perh. 4QapPs^{b} 31_{3} Lachish ost. $3_{11.20}$ 11QapPs^{a} 4_{5} 4QApocMos B 1.1_{8} ([א]ל), specif. for sex Gn 6_{4} $16_{2.4}$ $29_{21.23}$ etc. Dt 21_{13}=11QT 63_{14}, (2) right up to (so as to be in contact with) 2 K 9_{20} (עַד־אֲלֵיהֶם) Ezk 44_{25} Jb 4_{5} (‖ עַד *up to*), (3) into Gn 6_{18} $7_{1.7.9.13}$ etc. 11QT $45_{7.10.10.11.16}$ 45_{18} + Sup 46_{8} $49_{6.17}$ 50_{11} CD 6_{12} 11_{21} 12_{6} 15_{17} ([א]ל), (4) before (princes, of lawsuits) Is 1_{23}, *pass* (of food) into (stomach) Gn $41_{21.21}$, *arrive* at, *attain* to (membership of group) 2 S 23_{23}‖1 C 11_{25}, *flow* (of river) into Ezk 47_{8} (if em. אֶל־הַיָּמָּה הַמּוּצָאִים appar. *which are taken out into the sea* to אֶל־הַמַּיִם הַחֲמוּצִים *into the bitter waters*) 47_{9} Ezr 8_{15}, hi. *bring* Gn $2_{19.22}$ 6_{19} 8_{9} 19_{10} etc. Si 11_{29} 46_{8} 11QT $33_{6(Yadin)}$ ([והבאי]ם) 47_{9} 4QOrd^{a} 1.2_{5} 1QM 7_{11} 12_{14}=19_{6} + Sup ([אל]יך) 4QDibHam^{a} 6_{7} CD 11_{9} (+ מִן *from*) 13_{13} 4QMMT B_{6} ([א]ל) appar. 4Q386–9 3.3_{1} Lachish ost. 5_{9} ([ב]א; others לעבדך for אל עבדך), ho. *be brought* (1) to Lv $13_{2.2.9}$ 14_{2}, (2) into 6_{23} 10_{18} 4Q251 3_{18}.

הלך *go* (1) to Gn 12_{1} 13_{4} $22_{2.3.19}$ etc. 1QJub $35_{10(Milik)}$ (ל[כת]) 4QD^{b}$_{4}$, for sex Am 2_{7}, (2) before (God, for judgment) Jb 34_{23}, *run* (of water) into Ec $1_{7.7}$ 11QT 32_{14} ([א]ליה) Siloam tunnel inscr.$_{5}$ (+ מִן *from*), hi. *lead, bring* Dt 28_{36} 2 K 6_{19} Jr 31_{9} 52_{26} Ezk 43_{1}, htp. *wander* Ps $105_{13.13}$‖1 C $16_{20.20}$ (both + מִן *from*) 4Q525 5_{2} (ות[ת]הלך).

יצא *go out* Gn 14_{17} $19_{6.14}$ 34_{6} Ex 2_{11} etc. 4QM^{a} fr. 1_{9} ([י]אצאו) 1_{9} ([יצ]או) 4QpGen^{a} $2_{10.13}$ (both [אל]), specif. progress (from one evil) to (another) Jr 9_{2}, hi. *take out* Gn $19_{5.8}$ 43_{23} Ex 16_{3} Lv 4_{12} etc. 11QT 22_{11} $33_{6(Yadin)}$ Dt $21_{19.19}$=11QT $64_{3.4}$ Dt 22_{15}=11QT 65_{10} CD 11_{8} (+ מִן *from*), ho. *be taken out* Jr 38_{22} Ezk 47_{8} (or em. אֶל־הַמַּיִם הַחֲמוּצִים *into the bitter waters*), עלה *go up* (on)to (see also §2b) Gn $44_{17.24.34}$ 45_{9} Ex 2_{23} etc. 11QT 46_{7} 4QJub^{a} 1_{4} ([עלה]) 1_{7} ([עלה אלי]) 1_{7} ([ויעל ... אל]), *lead up* (of steps) Ezk 40_{49}, hi. *take up* Gn 50_{24} Ex 3_{8} (both + מִן) $3_{8.8.17.17}$ etc., ירד *go down* Gn 37_{35} Ex 11_{8} 19_{14} (+ מִן *from*) 19_{20} (+ עַל *onto*) 19_{25} etc. 3QTr 1_{13} (or read בירדא ל), *lead down* (of paths) Pr 7_{27}, hi. *take down* Gn 44_{21} Dt 1_{25} 21_{4}=11QT 63_{2} ([ו]הור[ידו]) Jg $7_{4.5}$ etc., ho. *be taken down* Is $14_{15.15}$ Ezk 31_{18}.

נגש *approach, come near* Gn 43_{19} 44_{18} 45_{4} Ex 24_{14} etc., for sex 19_{15}, ni. 19_{22} 20_{21} 24_{2} 2 S $11_{20.21}$ etc., hi. *bring near* to Gn $48_{10.13}$ Ex $21_{6.6.6}$ etc., קרב *come near* to Gn 37_{18} Ex 14_{20} 32_{19} 36_{2} etc. Si 6_{19}, for sex Gn 20_{4} Dt 22_{14}=11QT 65_{9} Is 8_{3} Ezk 18_{6} Si 9_{3} 1QSa $1_{10(Barthélemy)}$ ([קרב]י), ni. Ex 22_{7} 4QpsEzek^{a} 2_{5} (הקרבו עצם אל] [עצם), htp. 4QM^{a} fr. 14_{8} ([אלי]כם), hi. *bring near* Ex 28_{1} 29_{4} 40_{12} Lv $1_{3.15}$ etc. perh. 1QS$6_{19(erased)}$, pi. Ezk 37_{17} 1QS 6_{19}, סור hi. *bring* ark 2 S 6_{10}‖1 C $13_{13.13}$ (‖2 S 6_{10} עַל).

שׁוב *go back* Gn $8_{9.12}$ 16_{9} $18_{10.14}$ etc. Si $40_{1.11.11}$ $41_{10.10}$ 11QT 62_{3} (=Dt 20_{8} לְ) 1QS 7_{24} 1QM $14_{3.18}$ + Sup 4Q285 6_{9} 4QJub^{a} 2_{17} ([ישובו]), in penitence, etc. 1 K 8_{48} $12_{27.27.27}$ Is 10_{21} 44_{22} etc Si 5_{7} GnzPs 2_{16} 11QT 59_{10} 1QS 5_{8} CD 15_{9} (א[ל]) $15_{10.12}$ $16_{1.5}$ 20_{24} (שבו עוד אל *they returned again to;* Rabin שבו עד אל *they returned unto God*) 1QH 16_{17} 4QD^{b}$_{5}$ 4QMMT B_{14}, *be returned,* i.e. transformed into (dust) Gn $3_{19.19}$ Ps 104_{29} Ec 3_{20} 1QH

12$_{31}$ 1QH fr. 1$_{4}$ (שׁ]ב]) 4$_{11}$, *be restored* (of healed hand) to (person) 1 K 13$_{6.6}$, hi. *bring back* Gn 24$_{5}$ 28$_{15}$ 37$_{22}$ 42$_{25}$ 44$_{8}$ etc. 11QMelch 1.1$_{6}$ Lachish ost. 5$_{7}$, specif. return sword to sheath 1 C 21$_{27}$, of reply to questioner Est 4$_{13.15}$ Lachish ost. 9$_{5}$ ([אל]), of converting faithless to Y. Ne 9$_{26.29}$ 2 C 24$_{19}$, *place* (hand) on (mouth) 1 S 14$_{27}$, *repay* (reproach) to (bosom, head of offender) Ps 79$_{12}$ Ne 3$_{36}$, *return* (someone), i.e. transform into (dust) Jb 10$_{9}$, שׁוב אֶל־לֵב hi. *bring to (the) heart*, i.e. pay attention to Dt 4$_{39}$ 30$_{1}$ (Sam mss לְבָב ;עַל) 1 K 8$_{47}$‖2 C 6$_{37}$ (לְבָב) Is 44$_{19}$ Lm 3$_{21}$ 4QDibHam[a] 1.5$_{13}$ (לְבָב) 4QMMT B$_{14}$ (והשיבות]ה אל] ל]בב[ך), ho. *be returned* Ex 10$_{8}$, pol. *restore* someone Is 49$_{5}$ Jr 50$_{19}$.

הפך *restore* (speech) to (people) Zp 3$_{9}$ 4Q464 3.1$_{9}$ ([הפך]), סבב *go (round)* Nm 36$_{7}$ (+ מִן *from*) 2 S 14$_{24.24}$ Ezk 42$_{19}$ Ec 1$_{6}$ Si 10$_{8}$ (+ מִן), *surround, come near* to 2 K 8$_{21}$‖2 C 21$_{9}$, hi. *bring* 1 S 5$_{10}$ 1 C 13$_{3}$ Ezk 47$_{2}$, specif. cause allegiance, kingdom to be transferred 2 S 3$_{12}$ 1 C 12$_{24}$, עבר *cross over* (in)to (land) Gn 31$_{52.52}$ Nm 32$_{7}$ 33$_{51}$ Dt 2$_{29}$ etc., hi. *bring over* Jos 4$_{8}$ Ezk 46$_{21}$, נפל *go over, desert* 2 K 7$_{4}$ Jr 37$_{13}$ (‖ עַל 37$_{14}$) 38$_{19}$ 52$_{15}$ 1 C 12$_{20}$ (‖ עַל), נהר *flow* (of nations) Is 2$_{2}$ (=Mc 4$_{1}$ עַל) Jr 31$_{12}$ 51$_{44}$, עוף *fly* Is 6$_{6}$ 60$_{8}$, שׁאף *gasp*, i.e. come gasping Ec 1$_{5}$ (or em. שָׁב אַף *and [then] returning*).

רוץ *run* Gn 18$_{7}$ 24$_{29.29}$ 1 S 3$_{5}$ Is 55$_{5}$, מהר pi. *hurry* Gn 18$_{6}$ Pr 7$_{23}$, דחף ni. *hurry* Est 6$_{12}$, שׁחר *hurry* Jb 8$_{5}$, שׁכם *wake early* (to go) Gn 19$_{27}$, קום *rise* (and go) Est 7$_{7}$, ברח *flee* Gn 27$_{43}$ Nm 24$_{11}$ 1 S 23$_{6}$ 1 K 2$_{39}$ 11$_{40}$ etc., *pass through* (of bar) to (other side) Ex 36$_{33}$, hi. 26$_{28}$, נוס *flee* Nm 35$_{32}$ Dt 4$_{42}$ 19$_{5.11}$ Jos 20$_{4}$ etc. 6QapSam/Kings 33$_{3}$ (+ מִן *from*), hi. *cause to flee* Ex 9$_{20}$, מלט ni. *escape* 1 S 22$_{1}$ 27$_{1}$, נצל ni. *escape* Dt 23$_{16}$ (+ מֵעִם *from*), פוץ hi. *scatter* Ezk 34$_{21}$.

נשׂא *carry* Lv 16$_{22}$ 2 K 4$_{19}$ Ml 2$_{3}$ (or perh. אֶל = *with it*, i.e. as well as it, as §13, or em. וְנָשָׂאתִי אֶתְכֶם מֵעָלָי *and I shall carry you away from me*), hi. 2 S 17$_{13}$, שׁבה *take as captive* 1 K 8$_{46}$‖2 C 6$_{36}$, ni. *be taken as captive* 4QTNaph 2$_{3}$ ([אל]יה), גלה *go into exile* Ezk 12$_{3}$, hi. *send into exile* (1) to (place) 1 C 8$_{6}$ 2 C 36$_{20}$, (2) among (nations) Ezk 39$_{28}$, נוע *wander* Am 4$_{8}$, גלל *roll* (stone) to (person) 1 S 14$_{33}$, *roll* deeds, lawsuit, i.e. entrust to Ps 22$_{9}$ Pr 16$_{3}$ Si 7$_{17(A)}$ (object omitted).

שׁלח *send* Gn 32$_{4}$ 38$_{25}$ 46$_{28}$ Ex 3$_{10.13}$ etc. 4QpPs[a] 1.4$_{9}$ 4QpHos[a] 1.2$_{4}$ 4QpsMos[e] 1$_{6}$ 4QJub[a] 2$_{11}$, Lachish ost. 3$_{6.7.21}$ 4$_{4}$ (א]לי]) 5$_{4}$ (של]חת]) Arad ost. 6$_{2}$ (+ מֵאֵת *from*), *extend* (channels) to (trees) Ezk 31$_{4}$, *put* (hand) into (bag) 1 S 17$_{49}$, ni. *be sent* (of letters) Est 3$_{13}$, pi. *send* Gn 25$_{6}$ (+ מֵעַל *from*) Jos 22$_{7}$ Is 66$_{19}$ (+ מִן *from*) Jr 27$_{3.3.3.3.3}$ etc., *extend* (shoots, roots) to (river) Ps 80$_{12}$ (‖ עַד *up to*) 1QH 8$_{10}$, pu. *be sent* Dn 10$_{11}$, נחה *lead* Ex 32$_{34}$ Ps 107$_{30}$, נהל pi. *lead* Ex 15$_{13}$, נתק *draw* Jg 20$_{32}$ (+ מִן), משׁך *draw* Jg 4$_{7.7}$ 4QMMT A 2$_{9}$, יבל ho. *be brought* (of tribute) to (place) Is 18$_{7}$ (‖ לְ *to* Y.), גנב pu. *be brought by stealth* to (person) Jb 4$_{12}$, נטה hi. *move* trans. 1 C 13$_{13}$ (‖2 S 6$_{10}$ lacks אֶל) Si 41$_{19(B)}$ (41$_{19(M)}$ עַל).

לקח *take, bring* Gn 48$_{9}$ Ex 27$_{20}$‖Lv 24$_{2}$ Nm 11$_{16}$ 19$_{2}$ 23$_{14}$ etc., ni. *be taken* Est 2$_{8.16.16}$, נתן *give* Gn 18$_{7}$ 21$_{14}$ 35$_{4}$ Ex 22$_{6.9}$ etc. Dt 13$_{2}$=11QT 54$_{8}$ Meṣad Ḥashavyahu ost. 1$_{13}$ (ו[תת]ן), *give* blood, i.e. assign guilt to Jr 26$_{15.15}$ (‖ עַל), *place* (sword) over (neck) Ezk 21$_{34}$, *place* (bracelets) on, around (hands) 23$_{42}$, *place* (blood) on (altar, etc.) 43$_{20.20}$ (‖ עַל) 45$_{19.19}$ (‖ עַל), נתן אֶל־לֵב *place on*, i.e. lay to, *heart* Ec 7$_{2}$ 9$_{1}$, ni. *be given* Ezk 31$_{14}$ (‖ לְ) 31$_{14}$ (unless אֶל = *together with*, as §13), עשׂה pass. *be executed* (of carving, etc.) on (house, door) 41$_{19.25.25}$ (‖ לְ), מכר *sell* Gn 37$_{36}$ Jl 4$_{8}$ (‖ לְ), סגר hi. *hand over* Dt 23$_{16}$ Jb 16$_{11}$, שׁלם pi. *repay* wickedness Jr 32$_{18}$ Jb 21$_{19}$, מצא hi. *give* Lv 9$_{12.13.18}$, כנה pi. *give (flattering) title* Jb 32$_{21}$, שׁוב hi. *make restitution* Nm 5$_{8}$, נטה *turn* trans., i.e. give Gn 39$_{21}$ Is 66$_{12}$, אפק htp. *restrain oneself* from Is 63$_{15}$ (or em.; see אפק).

שׁלך hi. *throw (away)* (1) to (person) 2 S 20$_{22}$ 1 K 19$_{19}$, (2) to, into (place, vessel) Gn 37$_{22}$ Ex 15$_{25}$ Lv 1$_{16}$ 14$_{40}$ Dt 9$_{21}$ etc. 1QM 6$_{1}$, ho. *be thrown* to (Joab) 2 S 20$_{21}$, שׁפך *pour* (in)to (place) Lv 14$_{41}$, מגר pass. *be thrown* to (sword) Ezk 21$_{17}$, דחה ni. *be pushed* to (friend) Si 13$_{21}$ (+ מִן *from*), הדף *push* (wicked) into (darkness) Jb 18$_{18}$ (+ מִן *from* light), נדח hi. *push* (northerner) into (desert) Jl 2$_{20}$, גיח *burst out* (of water) into (mouth) Jb 40$_{23}$.

מדד *measure* (from one place) to (another) Ezk 40$_{23.27}$, בקע hi. *force a way through* to (person) 2 K 3$_{26}$, הרס *break through* (cordon) to (Y.) Ex 19$_{21}$, ברך hi.

cause to kneel at, i.e. lead camels to (water) Gn 24$_{11}$ (+ מִחוּץ לְ *from out of* city), חבר *join forces* at (valley) 14$_{3}$, קרא *summon* (to come) to 31$_{4}$ Ex 19$_{20}$ 2 S 9$_{2}$ 1 K 12$_{20}$ 2 K 10$_{19}$ etc., צעק hi. *summon* (to come) to (person) 1 S 10$_{17}$, זעק hi. *summon* (to come) to (place) Jg 4$_{13}$ (+ מִן *from*).

אסף *gather* trans. (1) around (person) Gn 6$_{21}$ Jos 2$_{18}$ 20$_{4}$ Jg 3$_{13}$ 1 S 5$_{8}$ etc., gather to ancestors in death 2 C 34$_{28}$ (||2 K 22$_{20}$ עַל), (2) at, into (place) Gn 42$_{17}$ Ezk 24$_{4}$ Zc 14$_{2}$, return sword to scabbard 1QH 5$_{15}$, ni. *be assembled* (1) around (person) Ex 32$_{26}$ Ezr 9$_{4}$ Ne 8$_{13}$ 1QM 18$_{4}$, be gathered to ancestors in death Gn 25$_{8.17}$ 35$_{29}$ 49$_{29.33}$ etc., (2) at (place) Lv 26$_{25}$ Nm 11$_{30}$ Ezr 3$_{1}$ Ne 8$_{1}$ 2 C 12$_{5}$, be gathered to grave in death 2 K 22$_{20}$||2 C 34$_{28}$, *withdraw* into (place) 2 S 17$_{13}$ 1QH 12$_{7(mg)}$, *be gathered* into scabbard Jr 47$_{6(mss)}$ (L אַל־ *not*), יעד ni. *be assembled* (1) around (person) Nm 10$_{3.4}$, (2) at (place) 10$_{3}$ Ne 6$_{10}$, po. *assemble* people at (place) 1 S 21$_{3}$ (if em. יוֹדַעְתִּי *I have made known* concerning, as §7; 4QSam[b] יעדתי *I have made an appointment* at).

קבץ *assemble* people (1) around (person) 1 K 18$_{19}$ Hb 2$_{5}$ 2 C 32$_{6}$, (2) at (place) 1 K 18$_{19.20}$ Est 2$_{3.3}$ Ezr 8$_{15}$ 2 C 32$_{6}$, ni. *be assembled* (1) around (person) Jr 40$_{15}$ 4QapPs[b] 76$_{1}$, (2) at (place) Est 2$_{8}$ Ezr 10$_{1}$ Ne 4$_{14}$ 1 C 11$_{1}$ 13$_{2}$, htp. *be assembled* around (person) 1 S 22$_{2}$, קהל ni. *be assembled* around (person) Jg 20$_{1}$ 1 K 8$_{2}$||2 C 5$_{3}$ Jr 26$_{9}$, hi. *assemble* people (1) around (person) Dt 31$_{28}$ 1 K 8$_{1}$, (2) at (place) Lv 8$_{3.4}$ Nm 16$_{19}$ (|| עַל *around* person) 1 C 15$_{3}$ 28$_{1}$ (note distance from verb) 2 C 5$_{2}$, לקט htp. *be assembled* around person Jg 11$_{3}$, קוה ni. *be gathered* at (place) Gn 1$_{9}$ Jr 3$_{17}$.

סמך *lean* against, i.e. lay siege to (Jerusalem) Ezk 24$_{2}$, לחץ *squeeze* (foot) against (wall) Nm 22$_{25}$, ni. *squeeze oneself* against (wall) 22$_{25}$, נזה *spurt* (of blood) against (wall, horses) 2 K 9$_{33.33}$, hi. *sprinkle* (blood) on (house) Lv 14$_{51}$, נפץ pi. *smash* (someone) against Jr 13$_{14}$ Ps 137$_{9}$, נכה hi. *clap* (one hand) against (the other) Ezk 21$_{19.22}$, *strike* (Goliath) on (forehead) 1 S 17$_{49}$, *strike* (person) through (ribs) 2 S 2$_{23}$ 4$_{6}$ 20$_{10}$, דקר *stab* (woman) through (stomach) Nm 25$_{8}$, נטה hi. *stretch* (sackcloth) over (rock) 2 S 21$_{10}$, נשק hi. *brush* against Ezk 3$_{13}$, דבק *stick* (intrans.) to (body) 2 S 23$_{10}$ Jr 13$_{11}$ Lm 4$_{4}$, hi. (trans.) Jr 13$_{11}$ Ezk 3$_{26}$.

נגע *reach, come right up* to (person) Jon 3$_{6}$ Dn 9$_{21}$, *touch, make contact* with Nm 4$_{15}$ 1 K 6$_{27}$ Jr 51$_{9}$ (|| עַד *up to*) Hg 2$_{12.12.12.12}$ (|| בְּ) Jb 2$_{5.5}$, hi. *reach, come right up* to, *lead* to 1 S 14$_{9}$ Zc 14$_{5}$ Si 37$_{2(B)}$ (Bmg עַל; D עַד *up to*) 37$_{12(B).30(B)}$ (D עַל), *cause to touch, bring* to Ex 12$_{22.22}$ Ezk 13$_{14}$ Si 12$_{5}$ 50$_{19}$, כלה pi. *complete* (work) up to, to within (a cubit) Gn 6$_{16}$, מדד *measure* (recompense, so as to reach) to (bosom) Is 65$_{7(Qr)}$ (Kt עַל), תנן *repeat* (words) down to (last detail) Lachish ost. 3$_{12}$ (others כל *all*), עצב אֶל־לֵב htp. *be grieved to the heart*, i.e. greatly Gn 6$_{6}$, גלל *roll* (stone) against (cave entrance) Jos 10$_{18}$ (10$_{27}$ עַל).

לוה ni. *be joined* to (person) Gn 29$_{34}$ Is 56$_{3}$ Jr 50$_{5}$ Zc 2$_{15}$ 11QPs[a] 22$_{7}$, חבר *be joined* to Ex 26$_{3.3}$ Ezk 1$_{9}$ Si 12$_{14}$ 13$_{1}$, pi. *join* to Ex 26$_{6}$||36$_{13}$ 36$_{10.10}$ Si 7$_{25}$, pu. *be joined* to Ex 28$_{7(Sam)}$ (MT אֶל־שְׁנֵי קְצוֹתָיו וְחֻבָּר there will be to it *at its two edges, and [thus] it will be joined*; Gnz, ||39$_{4}$ עַל) Ec 9$_{4(Qr)}$ Si 13$_{16.17}$, htp. *make alliance* with Dn 11$_{23}$ Si 13$_{2.2.2}$, שׁלב pu. *be joined* to (one another) Ex 26$_{17}$||36$_{22}$, בדל ni. *separate oneself* (so as to become attached) to (group, Torah) Ezr 6$_{21}$ Ne 10$_{29}$ 1 C 12$_{9}$ (all + מִן separate oneself *from*), ספח *attach* (someone) to, i.e. employ in (priestly work) 1 S 2$_{36}$, רכס *tie* to (ring) Ex 28$_{28}$||39$_{21}$ (+ מִן *from* another ring), אסר *tie* to ring 11QT 34$_{6}$.

היה *be* of Y. moving from tent to tent 1 C 17$_{5.5}$ (if ins. אֶל־מִשְׁכָּן from tabernacle *to tabernacle*), of word of Y., vision, coming to Gn 15$_{1}$ 1 S 15$_{10}$ 2 S 7$_{4}$||1 C 17$_{3}$ 2 S 24$_{11}$ 1 K 6$_{11}$ etc., of rumour, turning into fresh rumour Ezk 7$_{26}$ (|| עַל).

In nom. cl., דְּבַר־י׳ *message from Y.* to Abram Gn 15$_{4}$, prophet 1 K 13$_{17}$ (דָּבָר אֵלַי בִּדְבַר י׳ *a message was to me by a word of Y.*; ms כֵּן צִוָּה אוֹתִי בִּדְבַר י׳ *thus did Y. command me with the [following] message*; ms דִּבֶּר י׳ אֵלַי בִּדְבַר י׳ *Y. spoke to me by a word of Y.*), Elijah 19$_{9}$.

With adj., קָרוֹב אֶל־ *near(est) to* Gn 45$_{10}$ Ex 12$_{4}$ Lv 21$_{2.3}$ 25$_{25}$ Nm 27$_{11}$ Dt 4$_{7}$ 13$_{8}$ (+ רָחוֹק מִן *far from*) 21$_{3.6}$=11QT 63$_{4}$ Dt 22$_{2}$=11QT 64$_{15}$ Dt 30$_{14}$ Jos 9$_{16}$ 2 S 19$_{43}$ 1 K 8$_{59}$ perh. Jr 25$_{26}$ Ezk 43$_{19}$ Est 1$_{14}$ 1 C 12$_{41}$ CD 5$_{14}$, קָרֵב אֶל־ *(one) coming near to* Nm 17$_{28}$ 1 S 17$_{41}$ 1 K

5$_7$ Ezk 40$_{46}$ (+ מִן nearer *than*) Si 12$_{13}$ 6QD 2$_2$ MurEp Beth-Mashiko$_5$.

<COLL> noun affixed by אֶל of direction and ה *locale* Ezk 34$_{21}$ (פוץ אֶל־הַחוּצָה hi. *scatter* flocks *to outside*) 47$_8$ (or em. אֶל־הַיָּמָּה הַמּוּצָאִים appar. *which are taken out into the sea* to אֶל־הַמַּיִם הַחֲמוּצִים *into the bitter waters*) בוא אֶל־הַיָּמָּה *come to the sea*), ישר אל *straight to* 1QM 5$_{12}$, מַהֲלָךְ ... אֶל־הַפְּנִימִית *a way ... (leading) to the inside* Ezk 42$_4$, מִי לַי׳ אֵלָי *whoever is for Y., (come) to me* Ex 32$_{26}$, אִישׁ אֶל־עִירוֹ וְאִישׁ אֶל־אַרְצוֹ *each (return) to his city, and each (return) to his land* 1 K 22$_{36}$, מִיּוֹם אֶל־יוֹם *from day to day* Nm 30$_{15}$ 1 C 16$_{23}$ (‖Ps 96$_2$ לְ) Si 5$_{7(A)}$ (C לְ), מֵעֵת אֶל־עֵת *from time to time* 1 C 9$_{25}$, מאדם עד אליו *from Adam until him* (Jacob?) 4QJub^a 7$_{14}$, משאה אל משואה *from ruin to desolation* 1QH 9$_6$ (א erased to read למשואה), מִשְּׂפָתוֹ אֶל־שְׂפָתוֹ *from (its) edge to (its) edge* 2 C 4$_2$ (‖1 K 7$_{23}$ עַד), מִגְּבוּל ... אֶל־גְּבוּל *from border of ... to border of* Ezk 45$_7$, נַחֲלָה אֶל־הַיָּם הַגָּדוֹל *(from the) Wadi to the Great Sea* 47$_{19}$, מִפֶּה אֶל־פֶּה be filled *from end to end* Ezr 9$_{11}$ (or em. פֹּה from *here* to *here*), מפנה אל פנה *from corner to corner* 11QT 30$_6$, sim. 30$_8$ ([אל]) 36$_7$, מעמוד אל עמוד *from column to column* 42$_{11}$, מִזַּן אֶל־זַן bring forth *from (one) kind to (another) kind*, i.e. all kinds of (produce) Ps 144$_{13}$, מחול אל חול *(what comes) from sand (returns) to sand* Si 40$_{13(B)}$, כַּדּוּר אֶל־אֶרֶץ *(as a) ball (thrown) to a land* Is 22$_{18}$ (or em. כְּצֶנֶף הַכַּדּוּר *as the winding of a ball* to the earth), אֲחוֹתַיִךְ הַגְּדֹלוֹת מִמֵּךְ אֶל־הַקְּטַנּוֹת מִמֵּךְ *your sisters—(from) those who are older than you to those who are younger than you* Ezk 16$_{61}$.

1b. towards, in the direction of, where contact is not made, + קלע *sling* stone at Jg 20$_{16}$, נוף hi. *wield* pick in the direction of (mate) Siloam tunnel inscr.$_2$, גדל *grow* towards south, etc. Dn 8$_{9.9.9}$, ירא hi. *shoot* at 2 S 11$_{24}$, רדף *pursue, chase* after Jg 7$_{25}$, הלך אל־עֵבֶר *go in the direction of* Ezk 1$_{9.12}$ 10$_{22}$, נשׂג hi. *stretch* hand towards mouth 1 S 14$_{26}$, שׁלח *stretch* hand, branch Ezk 2$_9$ (pass.) 8$_{17}$ 10$_7$ (+ מִן *from*), פרשׂ *stretch* hands, in entreaty Ex 9$_{29.33}$ 1 K 8$_{38}$‖2 C 6$_{29}$ Jb 11$_{13}$ Ezr 9$_5$ Si 48$_{20}$ 4QWiles 2$_4$ ([פ]רושׂ), pi. Is 65$_2$ Ps 143$_6$, שׁטח pi. *stretch out* hands, in entreaty 88$_{10}$, אטם pass. *be blocked*, i.e. recessed towards Ezk 40$_{16.16}$ (or em. וְאֶל אֵלֵיהֶמָּה *and towards their pillars* to לְאֵלָמּוֹ חַלּוֹנוֹת *[belonging] to its porch. Windows*), שׁפד pass. *be tapered* 1QM 5$_{10(Yadin)}$.

נשׂא *raise* hand(s), in blessing Lv 9$_{22}$, in command Is 49$_{22}$, in oath Dt 32$_{40}$, in desire Ps 119$_{48}$, in entreaty Lm 2$_{19}$, eyes, face, i.e. look (up) at 2 K 9$_{32}$ Ps 121$_1$, in blessing, greeting Nm 6$_{26}$ 2 S 2$_{22}$ 1QSb 3$_{1.3(Milik)}$ ([ישׂא]), in desire Gn 39$_7$ Ezk 23$_{27}$, in entreaty Ezk 18$_{12.15}$ 33$_{25}$ Jb 22$_{26}$, soul, in desire Ho 4$_8$ Pr 19$_{18}$, in trust Ps 25$_1$ 86$_4$ 143$_8$, heart, in need, entreaty Dt 24$_{15}$ Lm 3$_{41}$, רום hi. *raise* hand, in oath Gn 14$_{22}$ Dn 12$_7$, standard, in command Is 49$_{22}$, face, i.e. look (up) at (person) Ezr 9$_6$.

פתח pass. *be open* (of roots) to (water) Jb 29$_{19}$, of eyes, i.e. have regard for 1 K 8$_{29.29}$‖2 C 6$_{20.20}$ 1 K 8$_{52.52}$, פצה *open* mouth, i.e. swear to Jg 11$_{35.36}$, סבב ni. *swing open* (of door) Ezk 26$_2$, *turn* (intrans.) Jos 15$_{10}$ (+ מִן *from*), hi. *turn* face 2 K 20$_2$‖Is 38$_2$, נתן *turn* face Gn 30$_{40}$, in entreaty Dn 9$_3$.

פנה *turn* (intrans.) Ex 16$_{10}$ Nm 17$_7$ Jos 15$_7$ 1 S 13$_{17.17}$ etc., turn mentally, have regard for Lv 19$_{4.31.31}$ 20$_6$ etc. Si 51$_{23}$ 4QapPs^b 15$_2$, turn in expectation Hg 1$_9$, hi. *turn* (tail) towards (tail) Jg 15$_4$, נטה *turn* (intrans.) Gn 38$_{16.16}$ Ps 40$_2$ Si 9$_9$ ([א]ליה), hi. Ho 11$_4$, *direct* heart, ear Jos 24$_{23}$ 1 K 8$_{58}$ Ps 31$_3$ 71$_2$ 119$_{36.36}$ Si 9$_9$ 1QM 10$_{17(Yadin)}$ ([הטה ... אוזני]כה) 4QBark^a 2.1$_2$ Arad ost. 40$_5$, שׁוב hi. *direct* heart Si 38$_{20(B)}$, סור *turn* intrans. Gn 19$_{2.3}$ Jg 4$_{18.18}$ 19$_{11.12}$ etc., turn in obedience 1 S 22$_{14}$, הפך *turn* intrans. Ezk 4$_8$ (+ מִן *from*), ni. *turn tail* toward (or perh. *turn* into [another kind of person], as §3a) Jos 8$_{20}$, שׂטה *turn* (intrans.) to (evil ways) Pr 7$_{25}$, תאר *turn* intrans. Jos 15$_9$ (+ מִן *from*).

שׂים *place* face Ezk 6$_2$ 13$_{17}$ 21$_7$ 25$_2$ 28$_{21}$ etc., heart, i.e. pay attention to Ex 9$_{21}$ 1 S 25$_{25}$ (‖ עַל) 2 S 18$_{3.3}$ Jb 34$_{14}$, שׁית *turn* face Nm 24$_1$, heart, i.e. pay attention to Jb 7$_{17}$, כון hi. *turn* face Ezk 4$_{3.7}$, heart, in faith 1 S 7$_3$ 1 C 29$_{18}$, פחד *fear*, i.e. turn fearfully towards Jr 2$_{19}$ (if em. פַּחְדָּתִי אֵלַיִךְ *fear of me was to you*) 36$_{16}$ Ho 3$_{5.5}$ Mc 7$_{17}$, חרד *tremble*, i.e. with trembling turn towards Gn 42$_{28}$, נסע *set out* on journey towards Nm 10$_{29}$, הלך *go* in the direction of (corner) Ezk 10$_{11}$.

שׁחה htpal. *bow down* in direction of (place) Ps 5$_8$ 138$_2$, פלל htp. *pray* towards (place) 1 K 8$_{29.30.42}$‖2 C

$6_{20.21.32}$, נוע hi. *shake* head, in mockery Si 13_7, היה *be*, of face, turned toward Ex 25_{20}||37_9, of territory, roots, extended toward Jos 15_1 Ezk 31_7.

In nom. cl., of face turned toward face Ex 25_{20}||37_9, palm-motif Ezk $41_{19.19}$, of eye(s) turned toward manna Nm 11_6, Y. Ps 25_{15}, worshippers 33_{18}, righteous 34_{16}, superiors $123_{2.2}$, Y. 123_2 141_8, of ear turned toward cry 34_{16}, Torah Ne 8_3, of voice directed to Elijah 1 K 19_{13}, Y. Ps $77_{2.2}$, humans Pr 8_4, of soul inclined toward people Jr 15_1, of backs turned to temple Ezk 8_{16}, of gate positioned to north 8_{14}, of vestibule positioned toward court 40_{31}, of edge of sword tapering toward tip 1QM $5_{10(AHL)}$, פָּנָיו אֶל־הַיָּם ... וְסֹפוֹ אֶל־הַיָּם *(so that) his front is towards the* eastern *sea … and his rear is towards the* western *sea* Jl 2_{20}.

<COLL> יְשָׁרוֹת אִשָּׁה אֶל־אֲחוֹתָהּ *the one (stretched out) straight towards the other* Ezk 1_{23}, פָּנִים אֶל־פָּנִים *face to face* (with God) Gn 32_{31} Ex 33_{11} Dt 34_{10} Jg 6_{22} Ezk 20_{35} 4QDibHam[a] 3.2_{17} 4QDibHam[c] 25_1 ([פנ]ים אל פ[נים]), also פֶּה אֶל־פֶּה *mouth to mouth* Nm 12_8, בְּיָדָם אֶל־פִּיהֶם drinking *with their hand to their mouth* Jg 7_6, אֶל־חִכְּךָ שֹׁפָר *to your palate—a trumpet* Ho 8_1, מִקְצֵה לְמַטֵּה ... אֶל־גְּבוּל אֱדוֹם *the extreme south … toward the border of Edom* Jos 15_{21}, sim. 18_{19}, אֶל־הַיָּמִין *to the right* Ezk 1_{10} (|| מִן *on* the left), sim. 1 S 23_{24}, הַבִּנְיָן אֶל־הַצָּפוֹן *the building to the north* Ezk 42_1, רֹחַב הַקִּיר ... אֶל־הַחוּץ *the width of the wall … towards the outside*, i.e. the width of the outer wall 41_9.

2. on(to), into, expressing vertical motion. **a.** downward motion, + נפל *fall* (1) in obeisance, onto (face) Jos 5_{14} 2 S 14_{22} Ezk 43_3 44_4, (2) into (water, pit) 2 K 6_5 Is 24_{18} Jr 48_{44} CD $11_{16.16}$ 4Q251 2_5 ([א]ל המי[ם]) 2_6 ([המי]ם), over (one another) Jr 46_{16}, hi. *drop* (newborn) into (cistern, pit) CD $11_{13.14}$, שׁוח *sink* Pr $2_{18.18}$, עיט *swoop down* on (booty) 1 S $14_{32(Qr)}$ 15_{19}, צלח *rush* (of spirit) onto (person) 16_{13} 18_{10}, דלג pi. *leap* (from one city) to (another) Si 36_{31}, פגע *touch, light* upon Jos 19_{11}, שׁקף hi. *look down* on Ex 14_{24} 2 K 9_{32}, טול hi. *cast* into (sea) Jon $1_{4.5.12.15}$, מחה *wipe off* into (water) Nm 5_{23}, רדה *scrape off* into (hand) Jg 14_9.

נוח hi. *place* (up)on (rock, ass, mountain, table) Jg 6_{20} 1 K 13_{29} Ezk $40_{2.42}$, *cause* blessing, wrath *to rest* on 44_{30} Si $5_{6(A)}$ (C עַל), שׂים *place* in, on (cart, bed, stone, step) 1 S $6_{11.15}$ 19_{13} 2 K 9_{13} (+ תַּחַת *under*) Hg 2_{15}, שׂים אֶל־לֵב *place on (the) heart*, i.e. pay attention 2 S 13_{33} 19_{20}, שׁית אֶל־לֵב in same sense $13_{20(mss)}$ (L אֶת־), נתן *place* into Gn 39_{20} 40_3 Ex $25_{16.21}$ (+ נתן אֶל *give to*) 28_{30} etc., נתן אֶל־לֵב *place into (the) heart*, i.e. suggest Ne 2_{12} 7_5, שׂכר htp. *earn* (money to place) into (bag) Hg 1_6.

אור hi. *cause* face *to shine* on Nm 6_{25} Si $7_{24(A)}$ (C לְ) 11QBer 1.2_6 4QApocMos A 2.2_8, Ketef Hinnom inscr. 2_{10} ([אל]יך), שׁרק hi. *shine* on Si 50_7, נתך ni. *be poured out* (of wrath) Jr 7_{20} (|| עַל), קיא hi. *vomit* onto Jon 2_{11}, שׁפך *pour out* wrath Ps 79_6 (or em. עַל ; || עַל) 4QDibHam[a] 1.3_{10}, יצק *pour* (oil) onto (head) 2 K 9_6 (9_3 עַל), *pour* (of blood) into (chariot) 1 K 22_{35}, ריק ho. *be emptied* (from one vessel) into (another) Jr 48_{11}, ערה pi. *empty* (water) into Gn 24_{20}, שׂחט *squeeze* (juice) into (cup) 40_{11}, זרע *sow* among (thorns) Jr 4_3.

חול *whirl around (back)* (of bloodguilt) onto (wicked's head) 2 S 3_{29} (|| עַל), כרת pass. *be cut off* (so as to fall) onto (ground) 1 S 5_4 (mss עַל), שׁחט perh. *slaughter* (bird) so as to let blood fall into (vessel) Lv $14_{5.50}$, פלח pi. *chop* (food, so as to fall) into (pot) 2 K 4_{39}, עכס pi. *catch by the foot* in (trap) Pr 7_{22} (if em. וּכְעֶכֶס אֶל־מוּסַר אֱוִיל *and as [one wearing] an anklet [comes] to the punishment of a fool* to וּכְעַכֵּס אֶל־מוֹסֵר אַיָּל *and as one catches a deer in a trap*), כתב *write* in, on (book, scroll) Jr 30_2 36_2 ($36_{4.18}$ עַל) 51_{60} Ezk 2_{10} (pass.).

כבד *be heavy* (of hand) upon 1 S 5_6, שׁקה hi. *drench* (earth) right down (perh. up) to (mountains) Ezk 32_6 (or move מִדָּמְךָ *with your blood* and del. אֶל־הֶהָרִים *to the mountains*), היה *be*, of Y.'s spirit, hand, upon 1 S 16_{23} (+ מֵעַל depart *from*) 19_9 1 K 18_{46} 2 K 2_9 Ezk 33_{22}, of burden, to 2 S 19_{36} (ms לְ).

In nom. cl., דָּמִי אֶל־ *let* (the guilt for shedding) *my blood fall upon* Jr 51_{35} (|| עַל).

2b. onto, of upward motion, + עלה ni. *raise oneself* (from one place) to (another) Ezk 9_3, hi. *lift* onto, into (bed, chariot) 1 K 17_{19} (+ עַל when no motion towards implied) 2 K $10_{15.15}$, עלה אֶל־לֵב hi. *lift up to the heart*, i.e. have regard for Ezk 14$_{4.7}$, נשׂא *raise* (heart) onto (hands) Lm 3$_{41}$ (or em. עַל), (Job) onto (wind) Jb 30$_{22}$ (or em. עַל), רכב hi. *mount* on (cart) 2 S 6$_3$ (mss, 4QSam[a], ||1 C 13$_7$ עַל), נתק ni. *be pulled up* (from water) onto (dry land) Jos 4$_{18}$, שׁאב *draw* (water) into (vessel) CD 11$_1$, אסף *gather*, i.e. lift up (feet) onto (bed) Gn 49$_{33}$.

3a. of perceptual and verbal acts and dispositions of one person **to(wards)** another person, place, etc., + אמר *say* Gn 3$_{1.2.4.14.16}$ etc. Dt 20$_3$=11QT 61$_{15}$ Dt 21$_{20}$=11QT 64$_4$ Dt 22$_{16}$=11QT 65$_{11}$ 4QM[a] fr. 14$_5$ 4Q385 3$_4$ 4QpsEzek[a] 2$_3$ 3$_4$ 4Q386–9 3.2$_1$ 4QJub[a] 1$_{12}$ ([ויאמר אליו]) 4$_6$ (both [ויאמר אל]) 5$_1$ ([ויאמר ... אל]) 4QApocMos A 9$_3$, ni. *be said* Ezk 13$_{12}$, אמר אֶל־לֵב *say to (the) heart*, i.e. think Gn 8$_{21}$ 1 S 27$_1$ 11QT 61$_{2(mg)}$, דבר *speak* to Gn 16$_{13}$ Jr 38$_{20}$ Jon 3$_2$ Jb 2$_{13}$ Dn 10$_{11}$, pi. Gn 8$_{15}$ 12$_4$ 18$_{27.29.31}$ etc. 11QT 31$_9$ Dt 13$_3$=11QT 54$_9$ Dt 20$_2$=11QT 61$_{15}$ Dt 20$_{8.9}$=11QT 62$_{3.5}$ 11QT fr. 1$_{3.4}$ 4QPrFêtes[c] 2$_4$ (אל[ין]) 1QS 5$_{25}$ 1QSa 2$_9$ 1QDM 2$_{11(Milik)}$ (לדב[ר]) 1Q29 1$_{5(Milik)}$ (חמד[בר]) 1QpHab 7$_1$ papMurPalimp[b] 1$_2$ 4QJub[a] 1$_5$ ([אל]) 4QPentPar[b] 23.2$_4$, דבר אֶל־לֵב pi. *speak to (the) heart*, i.e. think, pray Gn 24$_{45}$, htp. *be spoken* to, with Ezk 2$_2$ 43$_6$.

ענה *respond* 4QJub[a] 2$_4$ ([אל]), נגד hi. *tell* 1 S 3$_{15}$ 4QpPs[a] 1.4$_5$ ([אל]יהם), ספר pi. *tell* Gn 37$_{10.10}$, צוה pi. *command, issue order* 50$_{16}$ Ex 16$_{34}$ Nm 15$_{23}$ 36$_{13}$ etc., 4QApocMos B 1.1$_1$, נבא ni. *prophesy* to (or, against, as §6) Jr 25$_{30}$ 26$_{11.12.12}$ 28$_8$ (|| עַל) etc. 4QpsEzek[a] 2$_8$ (הנבא א[ל]), משׁל *speak in figures* Ezk 17$_2$ 24$_3$, נסה pi. *attempt* (to speak) to Jb 4$_2$, שׁבע ni. *swear* to Jr 38$_{16}$, פלל htp. *entreat, pray* to Gn 20$_{17}$ Nm 11$_2$ 21$_7$ Dt 9$_{26}$ 1 S 1$_{26}$ etc. Si 38$_9$, עתר *entreat, pray* to Ex 8$_{4.25.26}$ 9$_{28}$ 10$_{18}$ etc. Si 37$_{15(B)}$, hi. Jb 22$_{27}$ Si 37$_{15(Bmg, D)}$ 38$_{14}$, חנן htp. *entreat, pray* to Gn 42$_{21}$ Dt 3$_{23}$ 1 K 8$_{33}$ (||2 C 6$_{24}$ לִפְנֵי *in the presence of*) 2 K 1$_{13}$ Ps 30$_9$ 142$_2$ Jb 8$_5$, רבה hi. *increase* (supplications) to 40$_{27}$, יעץ ni. *take counsel* with 2 K 6$_8$ 2 C 20$_{21}$ 4QapPs[b] 69$_3$ (ו[נ]ועץ), זבח *sacrifice* 4QMMT A 2$_9$ ([זובח]ים).

קרא *call* Gn 3$_9$ 19$_5$ 21$_{17}$ 22$_{11.15}$ etc. Si 46$_{5.16(Segal)}$ ([קרא א]ל) 47$_5$ 48$_{20}$ (וי[קר]או) 11QPs[a] 24$_3$ Dt 20$_{10}$=11QT 62$_6$ 4QJub[a] 1$_8$ ([ויקרא אל]) 4QPentPar[a] 3,2$_4$ ([אל]) 4Q372 1$_{16}$ 11QapPs[a] 1$_{10}$ (קר[א אל]) 3$_3$ (יקרא א[ל]) 4$_5$ ([קרא]), Siloam tunnel inscr.$_3$ (ק[ריא]), צעק *cry* Gn 4$_{10}$ 41$_{55}$ Ex 5$_{15}$ 8$_8$ 14$_{10}$ etc., זעק *cry* Jg 3$_{9.15}$ 6$_{6.7}$ 10$_{10}$ etc. 4Q462$_{11}$ 4QapPs[a] 2$_4$ ([ויזעקו אל]), שׁוע pi. *cry* Ps 18$_7$ 22$_{25}$ 28$_2$ 30$_3$ 31$_{23}$ 88$_{14}$ Jb 38$_{41}$, נהם *groan* to (one another) Ezk 24$_{23}$, צהל *neigh* at Jr 5$_8$, הלל pi. *speak well of* Gn 12$_{15}$, זמר pi. *sing* Ps 59$_{18}$, לשׁן hi. *slander* (one person) to (another) Pr 30$_{10}$, רגל pi. *slander* (one person) to (another) 2 S 19$_{28}$.

שׁמע *hear*, i.e. listen to Gn 16$_{11}$ (perh. אֶל = hear *about*) 21$_{17}$ 30$_{17}$ 49$_2$ Dt 4$_{1.1}$ etc. Si 16$_{24}$ 30$_{27}$ Dt 13$_4$ =11QT 54$_{11}$ CD 2$_2$, i.e. agree with, obey Gn 23$_{16}$ 28$_{7.7}$ 34$_{17.24.24}$ etc. Dt 17$_{12.12}$=11QT 56$_{9.9}$ Dt 21$_{18}$=11QT 64$_3$, hi. *make heard* by, *proclaim* to Is 62$_{11}$ Ezk 36$_{15}$, קשׁב hi. *listen* to Is 51$_4$ Jr 18$_{18.19}$ (|| לְ) Zc 1$_4$ Ps 142$_7$ Ne 9$_{34}$ (|| לְ) 11QPs[a] 24$_3$ 4QDibHam[a] 1.5$_{21}$ ([אל]) CD 20$_{19}$, אזן hi. *listen* to Dt 1$_{45}$ Is 51$_4$ Ps 143$_1$ Si 51$_{11}$, ראה *look* at Is 14$_{16}$ 17$_7$ Jr 4$_{23}$ (|| אֶת object-marker), ni. *appear* to, before (person) Gn 12$_{7.7}$ 17$_1$ 18$_1$ 26$_2$ etc., נבט hi. *look* at Ex 3$_6$ Nm 21$_9$ 2 K 3$_{14}$ Is 8$_{22}$ 51$_6$ Jon 2$_5$ Zc 12$_{10}$ Ps 34$_6$ etc. Si 16$_{19}$ 36$_{15}$ 2QapMoses 1$_5$ 1QH 4$_{11}$ 4QTanḥ 14$_4$, pay attention to 1 S 16$_{7.7}$ Is 22$_{8.11}$ 51$_{1.1.2.2}$ Si 9$_8$ 37$_{4(B)}$ 1QH 17$_{27}$, פקח *open (eyes)* to (poor) 4QBark[a] 2.1$_2$.

שׁמר *guard, look* after 1 S 26$_{15}$ 2 S 11$_{16}$, *wait* for (Y.) Ps 59$_{10}$ Lachish ost. 4$_{10}$, שׁעה *have regard* for, *pay attention* to Gn 4$_{4.4.5.5}$ Is 17$_8$ (17$_7$ עַל), *look diligently* for, towards (Y.) 2 S 22$_{42}$ (ms שׁוע pi. *cry*; ||Ps 18$_{42}$ שׁוע עַל pi.), שׁגח hi. *gaze* at Is 14$_{16}$ Ps 33$_{14}$, תמה *be astonished*, i.e. look in astonishment at Gn 43$_{33}$ Is 13$_8$, יפע hi. *reveal oneself* 1QpHab 11$_7$, גלה *reveal* Am 3$_7$, pi. Jr 11$_{20}$=20$_{12}$ Ezk 16$_{37}$, ni. *be revealed, reveal oneself* Gn 35$_7$ 1 S 2$_{27}$ 3$_{7.21}$ 14$_8$ etc., צפה pass. *be spied out*, i.e. destined for (sword) Jb 15$_{22}$, pi. *look out* for Lm 4$_{17}$ 4QShir[b] 42$_5$, קרה ni. *encounter, manifest oneself* to Nm 23$_{4.16}$.

בין *understand, have regard* for Ps 28$_{5.5}$, hi. 33$_{15}$ CD 1$_{10}$, htpol. *examine, look carefully* at (person) 1 K 3$_{21}$ Is 14$_{16}$ Si 41$_{20(M)}$, ידע ni. *be made known* to Ezk 20$_9$, ho. Lv 4$_{23.28}$, htp. *make oneself known* to Gn 45$_1$ Nm 12$_6$, זכר ni. *be remembered* by, in the presence of (God) Ps 109$_{14}$, hi. *recall, mention* to, in the presence of Gn 40$_{14}$ Is 19$_{17}$, שׂכל hi. *have consideration* for (person) Ps 41$_2$, *study, apply intelligence* to (words) Ne 8$_{13}$, דרשׁ *seek*, *look* to, in trust Dt 12$_5$ Jb 5$_8$, *ask* (of) (person) Dt 18$_{11}$ Is 8$_{19.19.19.19}$ etc. 11QT 60$_{19}$, הפך ni. *be changed* (in one's attitude) to Ex 14$_5$.

יחל pi. *wait*, in trust for (Y.) Is 51$_5$ Ps 130$_7$ 131$_3$, קוה pi. *wait*, in trust for (Y.) Is 51$_5$ Ho 12$_7$ Ps 27$_{14.14}$ 37$_{34}$, שׂבר pi. *hope* for (faithfulness) Is 38$_{18}$, *look*, in trust to (Y.) Ps 104$_{27}$ 145$_{15}$, בטח *trust* in Jg 20$_{36}$ 2 K 18$_{22}$||Is 36$_7$ Jr 7$_4$ Ps 4$_6$ 31$_7$ (31$_{15}$ עַל) 56$_4$ (56$_{5.12}$ בְּ trust *in*) Pr 3$_5$ Si 5$_5$, hi. *cause to trust* in 2 K 18$_{30}$||Is 36$_{15}$, שׁען ni. *rely* on (discernment) Pr 3$_5$, חלק hi. *flatter, be seductive* to Ps 36$_3$, חמל *have mercy* on Is 9$_{18}$ Jr 51$_3$, שׁלם hi. *make peace* with Jos 11$_{19}$, זנה *prostitute oneself* with Nm 25$_1$ Ezk 16$_{26.28}$, רבה hi. *increase* (prostitution) with 16$_{29}$.

כמר ni. *grow warm* (of emotions) Gn 43$_{30}$, ערג *long* for (Y.) Jl 1$_{20}$ Ps 42$_2$ (|| עַל), עגב *lust* for (person) Ezk 23$_5$ (|| עַל) 23$_{12}$, כמה *be faint* (with longing) for (water) Ps 63$_2$ (if em. בְּלִי *without* to אֵלַי), גרס *be crushed* (with longing) for (commandments) Ps 119$_{20}$, רנן pi. *exult* in (Y.) Ps 84$_3$, עשׂה חֶסֶד *show loyalty* to 2 S 3$_{8.8}$ (|| עִם), שׂחק *smile* at Jb 29$_{24}$, יטב hi. *be pleasing* 1 S 20$_{13}$, רעע *be displeasing* to Jon 4$_1$, רצה htp. *make oneself acceptable* 1 S 29$_4$, תמם *perfect* (heart) towards (Y) Si 49$_3$.

In nom. cl., of soul toward God Ps 62$_2$, of desire (for) Gn 3$_{16}$ 4$_7$ 1QM 13$_{12}$ (תשו[קתמה]) 15$_{10}$ (תשוק[תם]), וְלֹא פַחְדָּתִי אֵלַיִךְ *and fear of me is not to you*, i.e. you have no fear of me Jr 2$_{19}$ (or em. פָּחַדְתְּ אֵלַי *you were not frightened of me*), אֵינֶנּוּ אֵלַי *he is not disposed to me* as he was before Gn 31$_5$, אֵין־אֶתְכֶם אֵלַי *you were not to me*, i.e. you did not return to me Hg 2$_{17}$.

With adj., כָּלוֹת אֲלֵיהֶם eyes *yearning for them* Dt 28$_{32}$, לְבָבָם שָׁלֵם אֵלָיו *their heart is perfect towards*, i.e. completely disposed to, *him* 2 C 16$_9$, קַשֶּׁבֶת אֶל־ may your ear be *attentive to* the prayer of Ne 1$_{11.11}$, גְּדוֹלָה הִיא אֵלָי *this was important to me* Ec 9$_{13}$ (perh. אֶל = weigh heavily *upon*, as §3a).

<COLL> וכן עשיר אל איש נאצל *and thus is a wealthy man with respect to a deprived man* Si 13$_{17}$ (unless נאצל = *allied* to; perh. em. איש to רשׁ *poor man*), sim. 13$_{18.18}$, שׁוֹעַ אֶל־הָהָר *shouting to the mountain* Is 22$_5$ (or, *Shoa, on the mountain*, as §5a), מַחְשְׁבֹתֶיךָ אֵלֵינוּ *your thoughts towards us* Ps 40$_6$, פַּחַד אֵלַי *fear*, i.e. fearful, *to me* Jb 31$_{23}$ (unless nom. cl., *terror was*, i.e. came, *to me*, as §1a), דָּבָר טוֹב אֶל־י׳ *something good to*, i.e. in the opinion of, *Y.* 1 K 14$_{13}$.

3b. addressed to, intended for, + כתב *write* Jg 8$_{14}$ (perh. אֶל = *for [the benefit of]*, as §12) 2 S 11$_{14}$ 4QMMT B$_{10}$ ((וכתב[נו])) 4QMMT B$_{29}$ Lachish ost. 6$_9$ ((אלה[ם])) Arad ost. 40$_6$ ((וכתבת[י])), ni. *be written* Est 3$_{12.12.12}$ 8$_{9.9.9}$, נתן *give* letter Ne 2$_8$ (|| עַל 2$_7$), צוה pi. *command*, i.e. issue instruction for Jr 27$_4$ Est 4$_5$ (if em. עַל) 4$_{10}$, יעץ *advise*, i.e. give advice Si 37$_{7(B)}$ (Bmg, D עַל).

In nom. cl., of מִצְוָה *commandment* to priests Ml 2$_1$, בְּרָכָה *blessing* for Zion's enemies Ps 129$_8$.

<COLL> אֶל *to* addressee, at beginning of letters Lachish ost. 2$_1$ 6$_1$ Arad ost. 1$_1$ 2$_1$ 3$_1$ 4$_1$ 5$_1$ 6$_1$ 7$_1$ 8$_1$ ([א]ל) 9$_1$ 10$_1$ (both [אל]) 11$_1$ 12$_1$ 14$_1$ (both [אל]) 17$_1$ 18$_1$ 24$_1$, תְּפִלָּתוֹ אֶל־אֱלֹהָיו *his prayer to his God* 2 C 33$_{18}$, דְּבַר־י׳ אֶל־ *Y.'s message to* Jeremiah Dn 9$_2$, דָּבָר לִי אֶל (and vars.) *I have a message for* king, queen, prince Jg 3$_{19.20}$ 1 K 2$_{14}$ 2 K 9$_{5.5.5}$.

4. above, over, without contact, + נוף hi. *wave* hand 2 K 5$_{11}$, פרשׂ *stretch* wings 1 K 8$_7$ (||2 C 5$_8$ עַל), שׁקט *rest* over (lees) Jr 48$_{11}$.

5a. at, in, by, in the vicinity of, etc., with no clear sense of movement towards, + בנה *build* Jos 22$_{11.11}$ Ezk 16$_{25}$, זבח *sacrifice* Dt 16$_6$ (Sam בְּ), שׁחט *slaughter* (person) at (place) Jg 12$_6$ 2 K 10$_{14}$, (animals) on (table) Ezk 40$_{39.41}$, מול *circumcise* Jos 5$_3$, שׁפט *judge* Ezk 11$_{11}$, נכה hi. *strike* (Ahaziah) in (chariot) 2 K 9$_{27}$, ערך *marshal* troops Jg 20$_{20}$, קבר *bury* (1) at (place) Gn 23$_{19}$ 25$_{9.9}$ (unless אֶל = cave that was *in* the field) 49$_{29}$, (2) in (valley) Ezk 39$_{15}$, חנה *encamp* Jos 11$_5$, סחר *roam* through (land) Jr 14$_{18}$, מצא *find* 41$_{12}$.

מצה ni. *be drained out* at (base of altar) Lv 5$_9$, יצק *pour out* (blood) at (base of altar) 8$_{15}$ 9$_9$, שׁפך *pour out* (liquid) at (base of altar) Ex 29$_{12}$ Lv 4$_{7.18.25.30}$ etc., htp. *be poured out* (of life of child still) in (bosom) Lm 2$_{12}$, רצץ ni. *be broken* at (cistern) Ec 12$_6$ (|| עַל), רבע pass. *be squared off* at (edges) Ezk 43$_{16}$, ישׁב *sit* (1) at (meal) 1 S 20$_{24(Qr)}$ (Kt, 4QSam^b עַל; mss [Qr] אֶל), (2) on (seat, bed) 20$_{25}$ (|| עַל) 28$_{23}$, *live* (1) among (scorpions) Ezk 2$_6$, (2) at (place) 3$_{15}$, חבא ni. *be hidden* in, among (baggage) 1 S 10$_{22}$, חמם *tup* by, in front of (rods) Gn

30$_{39}$.

נשׂא *carry* on (shoulder) Ezk 12$_{12}$, שׁתל pass. *be planted* (1) in (field) 17$_{8}$, (2) by (water) 17$_{8}$, שׁכן *live* in (land) Dt 33$_{28}$ (Sam עַל), רבץ *lie down* in (dens) Ps 104$_{22}$, עמד *stand* (1) on (mountain, dry land) 1 S 17$_{3.3}$ Ezk 27$_{29}$, (2) at (roadside) Jr 48$_{19}$ Ezk 21$_{26}$, by, over (dead Goliath) 1 S 17$_{51}$ (2 S 1$_{10}$ עַל), נפל *fall* on (mountains) Ezk 31$_{12}$ (|| בְּ *in* valleys).

פוץ ni. *be scattered* on (mountains) 1 K 22$_{17}$ (||2 C 18$_{16}$ עַל), אכל *eat* on (mountains) Ezk 18$_{6.11}$ 22$_{9}$, רעה *graze* (intrans.) on (mountains) 34$_{14}$, trans. 34$_{13}$, עלה hi. *sacrifice* on (altar) Lv 2$_{12}$, טהר htp. *purify oneself* in (gardens) Is 66$_{17}$ (perh. אֶל = *[in order to go] into*), תאם *be joined* in (one ring) Ex 26$_{24}$||36$_{29}$ (if em. תַּמִּים *perfect*), at (the top) 36$_{29}$ (||26$_{24}$ עַל; if em. תַּמִּים).

שׁמע *hear* from, in (heaven) 1 K 8$_{30.30}$ (||2 C 6$_{21.21}$ מִן), ni. *be heard* on (mountains) Ezk 19$_{9}$, ראה *see* (someone) at (river) 43$_{3}$, בכה *weep* at (grave) 2 S 3$_{32}$, היה *be (situated)*, of border, at Jos 15$_{7}$ 18$_{14.19}$, of corpses, on Ezk 6$_{13}$ (|| בְּ; hill), of fugitives, on 7$_{16}$ (mountains), of birds, among 31$_{13}$ (branches), of dry area, on Jg 6$_{39.40}$ (|| עַל; fleece).

In nom. cl., of edge at side of ephod Ex 28$_{26}$||39$_{19}$, of teraphim in, on bed 1 S 19$_{16}$, of entrance at side of house 1 K 6$_{8}$, of supports at corners of stands 7$_{34}$, of camp at site 2 K 6$_{8}$, of fire in brazier Jr 36$_{23}$ (|| עַל), of shame on face Ezk 7$_{18}$ (|| בְּ), of stone in firmament 10$_{1}$, of gate by pillar 40$_{14}$, at border 48$_{32}$ (אֶל־פְּאַת; || פְּאַת, מִפְּאַת [without prep.]), of pavement, chambers at side of gate 40$_{18.44}$ (if em. לְשָׁכוֹת שָׁרִים בֶּחָצֵר הַפְּנִימִי אֲשֶׁר אֶל־ *chambers of [the] singers in the inner court which were next to* to לְשָׁכוֹת שְׁתַּיִם ... אַחַת אֶל־ *two chambers* in the inner court; *one was next to*) 40$_{44}$, of columns by pillars 40$_{49}$, of tables at side of vestibule 40$_{40.40}$, of palm-motifs on pillars 40$_{16.26.31.34.37}$, of carvings at side of vestibule 41$_{26}$, on wall 41$_{17}$, of flesh on tables 40$_{43}$, of trees on river bank 47$_{7}$, of Hazer-haticcon on border 47$_{16}$.

<COLL> אֶל־קְצוֹת *at the ends of* Ex 28$_{24}$ (||39$_{16}$ עַל), אֶל־הַכָּתֵף *at the side* 38$_{14}$ (||27$_{14}$ לְ), אֶל־הַמָּקוֹם *at the place* Jos 9$_{27}$, var. 1 K 10$_{19}$ (||2 C 9$_{18}$ עַל), אֶל־גְּבוּל *at the border of* Jos 17$_{8}$ Ezk 48$_{12}$, אֶל־פְּאַת נֶגֶב *at the southern edge* 48$_{28}$, יְרוּשָׁלַם אֶל־אַדְמַת יִשְׂרָאֵל *Jerusalem in the land of Israel* 12$_{19}$ (sim. 33$_{24}$ עַל; but perh. אמר אֶל *say concerning* [|| לְ], as §7), אֶל־נְהַר־פְּרָת in the territory *on the R. Euphrates* Jr 46$_{10}$, הָעַמִּים אֶל־אִיִּים *the peoples (living) on islands* Ezk 27$_{3}$, מְבֹא בֵית־י׳ אֶל־לִשְׁכַּת *the entrance of the temple of Y. at the chamber of* 2 K 23$_{11}$ (if em. מִבֹּא *from coming* to), בְּאַרְבַּע עֶשְׂרֵה רֹחַב אֶל אַרְבַּעַת רְבָעֶיהָ *with fourteen (cubits) of width*, i.e. 14 cubits wide, *at its four corners* Ezk 43$_{17}$.

5b. alongside, next to, + קבר *bury* with (ancestors) Gn 49$_{29}$ (or em. עִם *with*), עמד *stand* alongside (trees) Ezk 31$_{14}$ (if em. אֵלֵיהֶם *their terebinths* to אֲלֵיהֶם *alongside them*), יסף hi. *add* to 2 S 24$_{3}$ (mss אֵת object-marker; ||1 C 21$_{3}$ עַל) 1 K 10$_{7}$ (mss עַל; ||2 C 9$_{6}$ יסף עַל *add to*) Ezk 23$_{14}$ 1 C 17$_{18}$ (perh. אֶל = *for [the benefit of]*, as §12), pu. *be added* to 4QD$^{a}_{11}$ (+ מִן *(away) from* the living).

In nom. cl., of officers alongside king 2 K 11$_{14}$ (||2 C 23$_{13}$ עַל), window next to windows 1 K 7$_{4.5}$ (מוּל מֶחֱזָה אֶל־מֶחֱזָה *window was opposite window*), chambers next to pavement Ezk 40$_{17}$.

<COLL> אַחֲרָיו אֶל־הַמֵּתִים *afterwards—(they are)* counted *among the dead* Ec 9$_{3}$, אֶרֶז אֶל־הַבַּיִת *cedar around the house* 1 K 6$_{18}$, וְהַצְּלָעוֹת צֵלָע אֶל־צֵלָע שָׁלוֹשׁ וּשְׁלֹשִׁים פְּעָמִים *and the chambers (were arranged) chamber upon chamber, thirty-three times* Ezk 41$_{6}$, וּגְבוּלָהּ אֶל־שְׂפָתָהּ סָבִיב *with its border along its edge all the way round* 43$_{13}$.

5c. in the presence of, before, + חרשׁ hi. *be silent* Is 41$_{1}$, הסה *quieten* Nm 13$_{30}$, נכר htp. *behave as a stranger* to Gn 42$_{7}$, שׁחה htpal. *bow down* Is 45$_{14}$ GnzPs 3$_{22}$ (א[ליו י]שתחוו), כנע ni. *humble oneself* before (God) Si 4$_{25}$, דלף *shed* tears Jb 16$_{20}$, חלל pi. *profane* God Ezk 13$_{19}$, עמד *stand* before (master) 2 K 5$_{25}$, שׂים *place* (lawsuit) before (God) Jb 5$_{8}$, נשׂא *serve* (food) to Gn 43$_{34}$.

<COLL> אֶל־פָּנָיו do something (requite, argue, curse) *before his face*, i.e. in his (etc.) presence Dt 7$_{10.10}$ (Sam עַל in both) Jb 2$_{5}$ 13$_{15}$.

6. against, + לחם ni. *fight* Jr 1$_{19}$ 15$_{20}$ 34$_{7.7}$ (|| עַל), פשׁט *raid* Jg 20$_{37}$ 1 S 27$_{8.10(mss).10(mss)}$ (L עַל in both) 27$_{10}$ (mss עַל) 30$_{1.1}$, שׂרה *struggle* with Ho 12$_{5}$ (or em.

אֵל *[with] God* [and del. מַלְאָךְ *angel*] or אֵת *with*; || אֵת), רִיב *contend* with Jg $21_{22(Qr)}$ Jr 2_{29} 12_1 Jb 33_{13}, עטר *close in* on 1 S $23_{26.26}$, קום *rise up* Gn 4_8 1 S 22_{13} 24_8.

עבד hi. *put* army *to work* Ezk 29_{18}, ערך *marshal* troops, words Jb 32_{14} 1 C 19_{17}, צור *lay siege* to Dt 20_{19} (Sam עַל) 1 S $23_{8.8}$, פקד *inflict punishment* on Jr 46_{25} (|| עַל) $50_{18.18.18}$, עשׂה *do* evil 44_7, קוץ hi. *stir oneself* (into action) against Ezk 7_6, נתץ pass. *be pulled down* (of houses, in order to make defence) against (onslaught) Jr $33_{4.4}$, שׁפך *lay* (ramp) against (city) 2 S 20_{15}, חזק hi. *strengthen* (attack) against (city) 11_{25}.

רגז htp. *rage* 2 K $19_{27.28}$||Is $37_{28.29}$, כעס *be angry* with 2 C 16_{10}, קצף *be angry* with Jos 22_{18}, חרה אַף *be angry* with Nm 24_{10}, קשׁה hi. *harden* (oneself) against Jb 9_4, קשׁר htp. *conspire* 2 K 9_{14}, חשׁב *devise* plan Jr 49_{20} 50_{45}, pi. Ho 7_{15} Na 1_9, יעד *determine* action Jr $47_{7.7}$, יעץ *advise* against (nation) 49_{20}=50_{45}, יכח hi. *argue* with (God) Jb 13_3, שׁמע hi. *proclaim* Jr 49_2, *summon* (archers) 50_{29}, נטף hi. *preach* Ezk $21_{2.7}$, ענה *shout* Jr 25_{30}.

כלה *be determined* (of evil) 1 S 25_{17} (|| עַל) Est 7_7, בקשׁ pi. *seek* evil 1 S 25_{26}, גבר htp. *be heroic* against (God) Jb 15_{25}, זיד *act insolently* towards Jr $50_{29.29}$, מרר htpalp. *be embittered* Dn 8_7, כבד *go badly* (of battle) for 1 S 31_3 (||1 C 10_3 עַל), דבר *speak* (in some perh. אֶל = *about*) 1 K $16_{12.13}$ Jr 28_{16} $36_{7.31}$ etc., צוה pi. *order* (destruction) Is 23_{11}.

בוא *come*, in battle Jg 11_{12} 1 S $17_{43.45.45}$ 23_{10} etc. 11QT 2_5 (||Ex 34_{12} עַל), of evil, famine Jg 9_{57} 2 K 8_1 Jr 2_3 51_{60} Ezk 7_7, hi. *bring*, in battle 26_7, *bring* evil 2 S 17_{14} 1 K 14_{10} 21_{21} 2 K 22_{16} (|| עַל; ||2 C 34_{24} עַל both times; 2 K 22_{20} עַל for אֶל) etc., הלך *go*, in battle 1 S 23_3 2 S 5_6 1 K 22_{15}||2 C 18_{14} 2 K 3_7 2 C 18_5 (||1 K 22_6 עַל), יצא *go out*, in battle Jg 9_{33} 2 S 11_{23} Ezk 21_9 1QM 9_3, עלה *go up*, in battle Nm 13_{31} Jg 12_3 $20_{23.30}$ 1 S 7_7 etc., ירד *go down*, in battle 13_{12} 17_8 2 S 23_{21}||1 C 11_{23} 2 K 6_{18}.

קרב *approach, come near*, in battle Dt 20_{10}=11QT 62_6 Jg 20_{24}, שׁוב *go back*, in attack 20_{48} 11QPs^a 24_{12}, hi. *turn, direct* hand, anger Ezk 38_{12} (|| עַל) Jb 15_{13}, עבר *cross over*, in battle Jg 12_3, רוץ *run*, in attack Jb 15_{26} Dn 8_6, עור hi. *provoke* (wind) against Jr 51_1 (|| עַל), שׁלח *send* plague Ex 9_{14} (|| בְּ), *extend* hand, so as to harm Gn 22_{12} Ex 24_{11} 2 S 6_6 18_{12} Jb 1_{12}, pi. *send* plague Ezk $14_{19.21}$, נשׂא *raise* sword, etc. Is 2_4=Mc 4_3 Jr 51_{12} Zc 2_4, *raise* eyes, in scorn Is 37_{23} (|| עַל; ||2 K 19_{22} עַל both times), face, in approval (of rich in contest) against (poor) Si 32_{16}, פרשׂ *stretch* (wings) against (Moab) Jr 48_{40}.

אסף ni. *be assembled* against (hill) Jg 20_{11}, קבץ ni. *be assembled* against (Gibeonites) Jos 10_6, נטה *turn, direct* hand, weapon $8_{18.18}$ Ezk 30_{25} Jb 15_{25}, שׂים *lay* ambush Jg $20_{29.36}$, היה *be*, of battle 2 S 10_9||1 C 19_{10}, of Y.'s hand Ezk 13_9, of Y.'s word 1 K $16_{7.7}$, of outcry Ne 5_1.

In nom. cl., of deeds against Y. Is 3_8, anger against population Ezk $7_{12.14}$, הִנְנִי אֵלַיִךְ *behold, I am against you* (contrast Ezk 36_9 [§9]) Jr 50_{31} 51_{25} Ezk 29_{10} 35_3 38_3 39_1, var. Jr 21_{13} Ezk 13_8 21_8 Na 2_{14} 3_5, without sf. Ezk 13_{20} 29_{10} 30_{22} 34_{10}.

<COLL> חָרוֹן ... אֶל־ *anger ... against* Nm 32_{14}, לֹא־עָלֶיךָ ... כִּי אֶל־בֵּית *it is not against you (I come) ... but against the house of* 2 C 35_{21}, אֶל־הַגִּבְעָה סָבִיב *against Gibeah (and) around, against Gibeah on every side* Jg 20_{29}, חֶרֶב ... אֶל *(may there be) a sword ... against* Jr 50_{35} (|| עַל) $50_{35.35.36.36.37.37.37.37.37}$, sim. 50_{38}.

7. about, concerning, + חרשׁ hi. *be silent* about (tears) Ps 39_{13}, אמר *say* 2 K 19_{32}||Is 37_{33} Jr $22_{11.18}$ 27_{19} (|| עַל) 29_{16} etc., דבר *speak* 40_{16}, pi. in same sense (in some perh. אֶל = *against*, as §6) 2 S 7_{19} (||1 C 17_{17} עַל) Is 16_{13} 32_6 Jr 27_{13} 33_{14} (|| עַל) $50_{1.1}$ etc., צוה pi. *issue command* concerning (or, intended for, as §3b) Ex $6_{13.13}$ 25_{22} Lv 27_{34} Si 45_3 (ל[א]), נבא ni. *prophesy* Ezk 13_{16} (|| לְ), פלל htp. *pray* 1 S 1_{27} 2 K 19_{20}||Is 37_{21} (all three + אֶל pray *to*), ספר pi. *tell* Ps 2_7 69_{27}, צעק *cry* 2 K $8_{3.3}$ (+ אֶל cry *to*; $8_{5.5}$ עַל), קרא *proclaim* (liberty) in respect of (danger) Jr $34_{17.17.17}$.

ירה hi. *teach* about (behaviour) 2 C 6_{27} (||1 K 8_{36} אֶת object-marker), ידע hi. *make known* concerning, *tell* about Is 38_{19}, po. 1 S 21_3, יעץ ni. *take counsel* (with someone) about Si $37_{11(Bmg, D)}$ (B עַל) $37_{11(B, D).11(B)}$ (|| עַל; Bmg, D עַל in both), שׁאל *ask* 1QS 7_{21}, למד *learn* Jr 10_2 (or em. אֶת object-marker), שׁמע *hear* 1 S 31_{11} (אֵלָיו *about it*; mss, ||1 C 10_{11} כֹּל *all* the inhabitants) 2 K 19_9 (||Is 37_9 עַל), דרשׁ *ask* 1 K 14_5, כתב pass. *be written* Jr 51_{60}, ידד *cast* (lots) for (people) Jl 4_3, חמל *have mercy* in respect of, i.e. spare (arrows) Jr 50_{14}.

בכה *weep* for 2 S 1_{24} Ezk 27_{31}, אבל htp. *lament* for (Saul) 1 S 15_{35} 16_{1}, עצב ni. *grieve* for (David) 20_{34}, המה *moan*, in mourning for Jr 48_{36} (‖ לְ *for* Moab), הגה *moan*, in mourning for 48_{31} (‖ עַל *for* Moab), קון pilel *chant lament* over (Abner) 2 S 3_{33}, נשׂא *lift up*, i.e. sing (dirge) over Ezk 19_{1} 27_{32} (‖ עַל), קרח hi. *make oneself bald*, in mourning for (Tyre) 27_{31}.

נחם ni. *feel sorry* for (Benjaminites) Jg 21_{6}, *feel sorry* about, *repent* of (evil) 2 S 24_{16} (‖1 C 21_{15} עַל) Jr $26_{3.13.19}$ 42_{10}, pi. *console* (someone) about 2 S 10_{2} (‖1 C 19_{2} עַל), חרד *be anxious* about (Elisha) 2 K 4_{13}, שׂמח *rejoice* over Ezk 25_{6} Si 18_{32}, חנג htp. *take pleasure* in $37_{29(Bmg)}$ (D עַל), בושׁ *be ashamed* 4_{20} $41_{17(B).17(B)}$ (Bmg, M עַל in both) $42_{1(Bmg).2(Bmg)}$ (B, M עַל in both), זיד hi. *be excessive* with regard to $37_{29(D)}$, זרה *scatter*, perh. *be disparate* $37_{29(B, Bmg)}$.

אנה pu. *occur* to Ps 91_{10} (righteous), נגע hi. *occur* to (person) Ec $8_{14.14}$ Est 9_{26}, נפל *fall*, i.e. occur (of good fortune) to Si 37_{8} (perh. אֶל = *for [the benefit of]*, as §12), perh. בוא *come* true, i.e. occur to Dt 13_{3}=11QT 54_{9} (unless דבר אֶל pi. *speak to*, as §3a), קום hi. *cause to occur* to (Eli) 1 S 3_{12}, שׁנה ni. *occur twice* to (Pharaoh) Gn 41_{32}, כון pol. *establish* (behaviour) according to (commandments) GnzPs 1_{10}, היה *be*, of size, according to Ezk 45_{11} (measure).

In nom. cl., of vision of people Ezk 7_{13}.

With adj., טוֹב אֶל־ *good (news) concerning* 1 S 20_{12} 1 K 22_{13}‖2 C 18_{12}, הַחֲרֵדִים אֶל־דְּבָרוֹ *those who are anxious about his word* Is 66_{5}.

<COLL> דְּבַר־י׳ ... אֶל־ *Y.'s message ... concerning* Jr 47_{1} 49_{34} Zc 4_{6} Ml 1_{1}, sim. Jr 44_{1}, (הַשְּׁמֻעָה) אֶל־הִלָּקַח אֲרוֹן הָאֱלֹהִים *(the report) with reference to the taking of the ark of God* 1 S $4_{19.21}$ (+ וְאֶל־חָמִיהָ *and about her father-in-law*), (וְ)אֶל־ *(and) as for* at start of sentence, introducing new topic 1 K 8_{41}‖2 C 6_{32} 2 K 22_{18}‖2 C 34_{26} (unless אמר אֶל *say to*, as §3a) Ezk 11_{21} (or em. אֶל־לֵב appar. *as for a heart to* אֵלֶּה אַחֲרֵי *[as for] these, after* or אֵלֶּה בְּ *[as for] these, in*) Ne 11_{25}, יִהְיוּ אֶל־הַתְּרוּמָה הַזֹּאת לַנָּשִׂיא *they shall be—in respect of this offering—as the prince* Ezk 45_{16} (or em. יִהְיֶה אֵלָיו the people *shall be in addition to him*, as §13), לוֹא אֲלֵיכֶם *(may it) not (happen) to you* Lm 1_{12}; אֶל־נָכוֹן *in respect of (what is) certain, for certain* 1 S 23_{23} 26_{4}, נתן אֶל־פִּי *give* territory *in respect of*, i.e. according to, *the command of* Jos 15_{13} 17_{4} 21_{3}; הוֹי אֶל־ *woe to* Jr 48_{1}.

8. due to, because of, + אנח ni. *sigh* because of (news) Ezk 21_{12} (‖ עַל), קוט ni. *be loathsome* because of (sin) 6_{9}, כלה *be worn out* because of (vain help) Lm 4_{17}, בוא *come* because of (good news) 2 S 18_{27}, הלך *go* for, because of, i.e. in fear of (life) 1 K 19_{3}, נוס *flee* for, because of, i.e. in fear of (life) 2 K 7_{7}, נפל *fall* because of (beauty) Si $25_{21(C)}$, טול ho. *be cast down* at (sight) Jb 41_{1}.

נכה hi. *clap* Ezk 22_{13}, פרר hi. *breach* (covenant) by (action) 44_{7} (or em. עַל; perh. אֶל = *in addition to*, as §13), אמר *say* 6_{11} $25_{3.3.3}$, נתן *cause* (dynasty to be destroyed) because of (its anger) 1 K 21_{22}, ברר hi. perh. *clean* (hands) for (woman) Si 51_{20}=11QPs[a] 21_{17}.

In nom. cl., אֶל־שָׁאוּל וְאֶל־בֵּית הַדָּמִים *(it is) because of Saul and his house of blood* 2 S 21_{1} (mss עַל *against* in both).

<COLL> אֶל־חִנָּם *for nothing, in vain* Ezk 6_{10} $14_{23(mss)}$ (L lacks אֶל).

9. in aid of, in support of, + עור *rouse oneself* on behalf of Ps 7_{7}, גנן *defend, make defence* for (city) 2 K 19_{34} (‖Is 37_{35} עַל), שׁמר *guard* for (king) 11_{7}, פתח *open* (mouth) on behalf of (justice) Pr 31_{8}, קבץ *assemble* (people) behind, in support of (David) 2 S 3_{21}.

In nom. cl., of officers in support of king 2 K 6_{11}, הִנְנִי אֲלֵיכֶם *behold, I am for you* Ezk 36_{9} (contrast Jr 50_{31} [§6]).

10a. over, in charge of, + משׁל *rule* Jr 33_{26}, מלך hi. *make king* 2 S $2_{9.9.9}$ (‖ עַל), משׁח *anoint* (as king) 2 K $9_{3.6.6.12}$, חזק *compel, be dominant* over (Joab) 2 S 24_{4} (‖ עַל, as ‖1 C 21_{4}), פקד *appoint* Jr 49_{19}=50_{44}, שׂים *appoint* (1) to (task) Nm 4_{19} (‖ עַל), (2) over (bodyguard) 2 S 23_{23} (‖1 C 11_{25} עַל).

In nom. cl., of Joab in charge of army 2 S 20_{23} (‖8_{16} ‖1 C 18_{15} עַל).

With adj., פְּקֻדּוֹת אֶל־שַׁעֲרֵי הַבַּיִת *having charge of the temple gates* Ezk 44_{11}.

10b. under (the charge of), + עזב *leave* work Jb 39_{11}.

11. of, belonging to, + בחר pu. *be selected* as

belonging to living Ec $9_{4(Kt)}$, היה *be*, of shields belonging to servants 2 S 8_{7} (||1 C 18_{7} עַל *upon*, i.e. worn by), of territory belonging to temple Ezk 45_{2}.

In nom. cl., of goods belonging to Joseph Gn 47_{18}, באברו אליו *in the* (lit. *his*) *quarter (that is) to him* 4QToh A 1.1_{2}.

<COLL> הַלְּשָׁכוֹת ... אֶל־הַכֹּהֲנִים *the chambers ... belonging to the priests* Ezk 46_{19}, מַטּוֹת עֹז אֶל־שִׁבְטֵי מֹשְׁלִים *rods of strength belonging to (the category of) sceptres of rulers*, i.e. fit to be sceptres 19_{11} (unless אֶל = *for* sceptres, as §12).

12. for (the benefit of), + בקע *conquer* territory Is 7_{6} (hi.) 2 C 32_{1}, גרע *limit* wisdom to oneself Jb 15_{8}, תכן *regulate* truth, measure of righteousness 4Q416 5_{3}.

13. as well as, in addition to, + הרג *kill* Jos 13_{22}, בוא ho. *be brought* Ezk 23_{42}, לקח *take* wife Lv 18_{18}, רום hi. *offer* land Ezk 48_{20}. **<COLL>** אכל אֶל־הַדָּם *eat* meat *with the blood (in it)* 1 S 14_{34} (mss עַל *upon*, אֵת object-marker).

14. (in comparison) to, + קבל hi. *correspond* to Ex 26_{5}||36_{12}, דמה *be comparable* to Ezk $31_{2.8.8.18}$, pi. *compare* with Is $40_{18.25}$, משל ni. *be compared* with, i.e. become like Is 14_{10}, ערך *be comparable* to Ps 40_{6}, perh. קבל hi. *correspond* to Si 12_{5}.

15. perh. **to the tune,** in headings to psalms, אֶל־הַנְּחִילוֹת *to 'Nehiloth'* Ps 5_{1} (mss עַל; perh. *on flutes*), אֶל־שֹׁשַׁנִּים *to 'Shoshanim' (roses)* 80_{1} (both + לַמְנַצֵּחַ *for the director*).

16. to the point of, + שׂמח *rejoice* to the point of (joy), i.e. exceedingly Ho 9_{1} Jb 3_{22}.

17. perh. **with, by means of,** אֵלֶיךָ כִסִּתִי *I cover* (myself) *with you* Ps 143_{9}, אל לשונך אל תרגל *with your tongue, do not slander* Si 5_{14} (|| בְּ).

18. followed by other particles, etc. **a.** אֶל־אַחֲרֵי **behind, to the rear of** troops 2 S 5_{23} (+ סבב hi. *bring round* troops), chariot 2 K $9_{18.19}$ (+ סבב *go round*), horses Zc 6_{6} (+ יצא *go out*).

18b. אֶל־בֵּין **in between, among,** with ref. to boughs reaching to between clouds Ezk $31_{10.14}$ (+ נתן *place*), person or bulls entering wheels 10_{2} (בֵּינוֹת; + בוא *come*) 11QT 34_{4}, priests stepping between battle-lines 1QM $7_{9.14}$ (both + יצא *go out*).

18c. אֶל־מִבֵּית לְ **to within, behind** veil of tabernacle Lv 16_{15} (+ בוא hi. *bring*), lines of troops 2 K 11_{15} (||2 C 23_{14} lacks לְ; + יצא hi. *bring out*).

18d. אֶל־מוּל **in front of** mountain Ex 34_{3} (+ רעה *graze* intrans.) Jos $8_{33.33}$ (+ עמד *stand*, unless nom. cl. each time, חֶצְיוֹ אֶל־מוּל הַר־ *half of them were in front of Mt* Gerizim/Ebal), Canaan, i.e. on border of 22_{11} (+ בנה *build* altar), soldier 1 S 17_{30} (+ סבב *turn* intrans.; + מֵאֵצֶל *from beside*), הַיָּם ... אֶל־מוּל הַלְּבָנוֹן *the sea ... in front of Lebanon* Jos 9_{1}.

אֶל־מוּל פְּנֵי *in front of*, with ref. to front surfaces of smaller, cultic, objects, specif. tent Ex 26_{9} (+ כפל *fold over*), ephod 28_{25}||39_{18} (+ נתן *place*), turban 28_{37} (+ היה *be*) Lv 8_{9} (+ שׂים *place*), lampstand Nm 8_{2} (+ אור hi. *give light*) 8_{3} (+ עלה hi. *raise*, i.e. light candles), אֶל־מוּל פְּנֵי הַמִּלְחָמָה הַחֲזָקָה *at the front of the hardest fighting*, i.e. in the front line 2 S 11_{15} (+ יהב *place*).

18e. אֶל־מִחוּץ לְ **(to) outside** camp or city, in context of unclean activities or objects Lv $4_{12.21}$ 6_{4} (all three + יצא hi. *take out*) $10_{4.5}$ (both + נשׂא *carry*) 14_{3} (+ יצא *go out*) 14_{40} (+ שׁלך hi. *throw*) 14_{41} (+ שׁפך *pour*) 14_{45} (+ יצא hi.) 14_{53} (+ שׁלח pi. *dispatch*) 16_{27} $24_{14.23}$ (all three + יצא hi.) Nm $5_{3.4}$ (both + שׁלח pi.) 15_{36} 19_{3} (both + יצא hi.) 31_{13} Dt 23_{11} (both + יצא).

וְאֶל־מִצִּנִּים יִקָּחֵהוּ appar. *and from out of thorns he takes it* Jb 5_{5} (or em. וְאֹנָם צִנִּים *and as for their wealth, thorns* take it, or, וְאֵל מִשִּׁנָּיו *and God* takes it *from his teeth*, or, וַאֲלֻמִּים צְנֻמִים יִקַּח הוּא *and dried sheaves he takes*).

18f. אֶל־פְּנֵי **in front of, opposite** altar Lv 6_{7} (+ קרב hi. *present* offering), tent of meeting 9_{5} (+ לקח *take*) Nm 17_{8} (+ בוא *come*), mercy-seat Lv 16_{2} (+ בוא), temple Ezk 44_{4} (+ בוא hi. *bring*), rock Nm 20_{10} (+ קהל hi. *assemble* people), spring Ne 2_{13} (+ יצא *go out*; + אֶל of direction), Y. Ex 23_{17} (+ ראה ni. *appear*), king, to meet him 2 C 19_{2} (+ יצא), שׁלח ... אֶל־פְּנֵי הַשָּׂדֶה pi. *release ... into the open country* Lv 14_{53}, sim. Ezk 16_{5} (+ שׁלך ho. *be cast out*).

In nom. cl., with ref. to canopy opposite vestibule Ezk 41_{25}, entrance opposite area of certain length 42_{2}, wall opposite chambers 42_{7}, chambers opposite building 42_{10}, opposite yard $42_{10.13}$, building opposite yard 41_{12}.

<COLL> הַבִּנְיָן אֶל־פְּנֵי הַגִּזְרָה *the building in front of the yard* Ezk 41_{15}, עֶשְׂרִים אַמָּה אֶל־פְּנֵי הַהֵיכָל *twenty cubits in front of the nave* 41_4, אַתִּיק אֶל־פְּנֵי־אַתִּיק *ledge by ledge* 42_3, אֶל־פְּנֵי תְרוּמַת־הַקֹּדֶשׁ וְאֶל־פְּנֵי אֲחֻזַּת הָעִיר the territory *in front of the sacred reserve and in front of the property of the city* 45_7, אֶל־פְּנֵי ... תְּרוּמָה עַד־גְּבוּל קָדִימָה *(from) in front of ... (the) reserve up to the eastern border* 48_{21}.

18g. אֶל־תּוֹךְ **inside, into the middle of** sea Ex 14_{23} (+ בוא *come*), river Jos 4_5 (+ עבר *cross*) Jr 51_{63} (+ שׁלך hi. *cast*), fire Nm 19_6=4QToh B$^a_6$ ([תו]ך; + שׁלך hi.) Ezk 5_4 (+ שׁלך hi.), ground 11QT 32_{13} (+ פשׂה *spread out* intrans.), land 58_9 (+ בוא), camp Dt $23_{11.12}$ (Sam omits תּוֹךְ; both + בוא), congregation Nm 17_{12} (L תּוֹךְ; + רוץ *run*) 1QS 7_{13} (+ רקק *spit*) 1QSa $2_{10(Barthélemy)}$ ([העדה]; + בוא), population Ne 4_5 (+ בוא), gentiles 11QT 64_9 (+ ברח *flee*), battle victims 1QM 9_8 (+ בוא), city Jr 21_4 (+ אסף *gather* weapons) Jr 41_7 (+ בוא) Ezk 22_{19} (+ קבץ *gather* people) Si 48_{17} (+ נטה hi. *divert* water), town square Dt 13_{17}=11QT 55_8 (+ קבץ *gather* booty), house Dt 21_{12}=11QT 63_{12} (+ בוא hi. *bring* woman) Dt 22_2=11QT 64_{15} (+ אסף *bring* animal), temple Ne 6_{10} (+ יעד ni. *be assembled*) 11QT 46_{10} (+ בוא), courtyard 11QT 36_{14} (+ בוא), gate 2 S 3_{27} (+ נטה hi. *cause to turn*), cistern Jr 41_7 (+ שׁחט *slaughter* and throw bodies), cesspit 11QT 46_{15} (+ ירד), vessel Lv 11_{33} (+ נפל *fall*), ephah Zc 5_8 (+ שׁלך hi.), כַּנְפֵיהֶם אֶל־תּוֹךְ הַבַּיִת *their wings were inside the temple* 1 K 6_{27}, קְבֻצַת כֶּסֶף ... אֶל־תּוֹךְ כּוּר *the gathering of silver ... into a furnace* Ezk 22_{20}, אל תוך בני האדם *among human beings* 4QpsJub^c 2_3.

18h. אֶל־תַּחַת (1) **beneath** tree Jg 6_{19} (+ יצא hi. *bring out*) Jr 3_6 (+ הלך *go*) Zc $3_{10.10}$ (+ קרא *invite* to come), (wings of) cherubim 1 K 8_6||2 C 5_7 (+ בוא hi. *bring*) Ezk 10_2 (אֶל־תַּחַת לְ; + בוא *come*), room Jr 38_{11} (+ בוא), אֵין־לֶחֶם חֹל אֶל־תַּחַת יָדִי *there is no ordinary bread under my hand*, i.e. in my possession, 1 S 21_5 (21_9 lacks אֶל). (2) **instead of,** of new stones replacing old Lv 14_{42} (+ בוא hi.).

18i. other combinations, אֶל־נֹכַח פְּנֵי אֹהֶל־מוֹעֵד *toward the front of the tent of meeting* Nm 19_4 =4QToh B$^a_5$ ([א]ל נוכח א[והל]; + נזה hi. *sprinkle*), אֶל־מִנֶּגֶב the border went out *to the south of* Jos 15_3, אֶל־יַד *under the charge of* court official Est $2_{3.8.8.14}$, *alongside, next to* field 2 S 14_{30}, gate 18_4, Hamath Ezk 48_1, אֶל־יַד דֶּרֶךְ־ *along the way to* 48_1 (or em. אֶל־יַד to מִן־הַיָּם *from the sea*).

19. אֶל prob. corrupt for אַל **not,** הִשָּׁמֶר לְךָ אֶל־תֹּסֶף רְאוֹת פָּנַי *watch over yourself (not) to see my face again* Ex 10_{28} (mss אַל), וַיֹּאמֶר י׳ אֵלַי אֶל־תָּצַר *and Y. said to me (not) to harass* Dt 2_9 (mss אַל), אֹתָנוּ אֶל־תִּמְרֹדוּ perh. *against us do not rebel* Jos 22_{19} (mss אַל; or em. תַּמְרִדוּ *make* us *rebel*), אֶל־יִדְרֹךְ *let him not draw* bow Jr 51_3 (mss אַל; or em. יֶרֶף *let him* not *drop [hand]*), אֶל־יִתְעַל בְּסִרְיֹנוֹ *let him not put on his armour* 51_3 (mss אַל; perh. em. יִיגַע לְבֶשׁ סִרְיֹנוֹ *let him* not *weary of being clothed in armour;* unless שׁלח אֶל־ pi. *send against* him who draws, puts on armour).

Also 11QT $45_{5.18}$ + Sup 56_1 4Q487 20_2 23_3 1QSb 2_5 4QpIsa^d 2_2 4Q185 $1.3_{1.12}$ ([א]ל) 1QH 3_3 ([א]לי) 12_{27} 4QapLam$^b_8$ 4QFlor 2_4 1Q36 17_3 ([א]ל) 4QShir^b 18.3_{10} ([אל]יכה) 42_6 85_2 4QM$^{g(?)}$ 4_3 4QWiles 2_3 4Q251 3_{14} ([אל]) 4Q416 $8_{1.6}$ Mur 6 1_7 Mur 30 2_{19} ([אל]ך) 4QJub^a 1_4 ([אליו]) 4QapPs^b 15_9 28_2 31_2 50_6 4QPsJos^a 22.1_3 4QJub^d $1.2_{11.37}$ Lachish ost. 21_1 Arad ost. 3_9 (אלך) 8_8.

אֵלָא 1.0.0.2 pr.n.m. **Ela, 1.** father of Shimei, one of Solomon's officers, 1 K 4_{18}. **2.** father of Sallu (סלא), Seal 293 (Beirut). **3.** Samaria ost. 38_3.

→ אֵל *God.*

אלאמר 0.0.0.1 pr.n.m. **Eleamar,** Seal 136 (Megiddo, 7th cent.).

→ אֵל *God* + אמר *say.*

אלבא 0.0.0.1 pr.n.m. **Elba,** Samaria ost. 1_6.

→ perh. אֵל *God* + בוא *come.*

אֶלְגָּבִישׁ 3.0.1 n.[m.] **hail,** alw. אַבְנֵי אֶלְגָּבִישׁ *stones of hail* Ezk $13_{11.13}$ 38_{22} Si $46_{5(Segal)}$ (אבני [ברד וא]ל[גביש] lit. *stones of hail and hail*), <SUBJ> נפל *fall* Ezk $13_{11.13}$ (if em. לְכָלָה *for destruction;* both + גֶּשֶׁם שׁוֹטֵף/שֹׁטֵף *driving rain*), היה *be* 13_{13} (or em.). <OBJ> נתן *give* Ezk 13_{11}

13$_{11}$ (or del. וְאַתְּנָה *and I shall give*), מטר hi. *cause to rain down* 38$_{22}$ (+ גֶּשֶׁם שׁוֹטֵף, אֵשׁ *fire*, גָּפְרִית *brimstone*). <PREP> ענה בְּ *answer by, with* Si 46$_5$ (Segal); רוחות ה[עננים] *spirits of the clouds* ... לאלגביש *with hail* 4QJub^a 5$_7$ (|| עֲרָפֶל *deep darkness*, כְּפוֹר *hoar frost*, טַל *dew*, שֶׁלֶג *snow*, בָּרָד *hail*).

[אַלְגּוּם], see אַלְמֹג.

[אַלְגֻּם], see אַלְמֹג.

[אלדגן] pr.n.m. **Eldagan,** Seal 300 (אלדג[ן]; 8th cent.).
→ אֵל *God* + דָּגוֹן *Dagon*.

אֶלְדָּד 3 pr.n.m. **Eldad**—אֱלִידָד—**1.** recipient of gift of prophecy during exodus, Nm 11$_{26.27}$. **2.** perh. ident. with preceding, son of Chislon and leader of Benjamin, Nm 34$_{21}$ (אֱלִידָד *Elidad*; mss, Sam אלדד).
→ אֵל *God*.

[אלדלה] pr.n.m. **Eldalah,** Seal 140 (others אלרלה *Elralah*; 8th cent.).
→ אֵל *God* + perh. דלה *draw (water)*.

אֶלְדָּעָה 2 pr.n.m. **Eldaah**—אֶלְדָּעָה—son of Midian, Gn 25$_4$||1 C 1$_{33}$.
→ אֵל *God*.

אלה I 6 vb. **curse**—**Qal** Pf. אָלִית; inf. abs. אָלוֹת, אָלֹה—**1. curse,** perh. **swear oath** (Ho 10$_4$), <SUBJ> Micah's mother Jg 17$_2$, apostate Israelites Ho 10$_4$ (+ שָׁוְא swear *falsely*, or, curse *for no good reason*), אִישׁ *man* thought to have sinned 1 K 8$_{31}$||2 C 6$_{22}$ (if em. אָלָה *a curse* to וְאָלָה *and he curses*). **2.** inf. abs. as noun, **cursing,** אָלֹה וְכַחֵשׁ וְרָצֹחַ וְגָנֹב וְנָאֹף פָּרָצוּ *cursing and lying and murder and theft and adultery have broken out* Ho 4$_2$.

Hi. Impf. + waw וַיֹּאֶל; inf. cstr. הַאֲלֹתוֹ—**invoke a curse** on another, <SUBJ> רֵעַ *neighbour*, i.e. person sinned against 1 K 8$_{31}$||2 C 6$_{22}$, Saul 1 S 14$_{24}$. <OBJ> אִישׁ *man* thought to have sinned 1 K 8$_{31}$||2 C 6$_{22}$, עַם *people* of Israel 1 S 14$_{24}$.
→ אָלָה *curse*.

אלה II 1 vb. **mourn**—**Qal** Impv. אֱלִי—**mourn,** אֱלִי כִּבְתוּלָה חֲגֻרַת־שַׂק עַל־בַּעַל נְעוּרֶיהָ *mourn as a young woman girded in sackcloth for the husband of her youth* Jl 1$_8$.

אָלָה 37.1.8 n.f. **curse**—sf. אָלָתִי, אָלָתוֹ; pl. אָלוֹת (אָלֹת), cstr. אָלוֹת—**1. curse, imprecation,** Lv 5$_1$ Nm 5$_{23}$ Dt 30$_7$ 1 K 8$_{31.31}$||2 C 6$_{22.22}$ Is 24$_6$ Jr 23$_{10}$ Zc 5$_3$ Jb 31$_{30}$ Pr 29$_{24}$ Dn 9$_{11}$ 2 C 34$_{24}$ CD 9$_{12}$, sometimes against unknown evil-doer (e.g. Lv 5$_1$ Pr 29$_{24}$ CD 9$_{12}$). **2. covenant stipulation** expressed as curse (but distinction from §1 oft. unclear), sometimes perh. used collectively, **covenant,** Gn 24$_{41.41}$ 26$_{28}$ Dt 29$_{11.13.18.19.20}$ Ezk 16$_{59}$ 17$_{13.16.18.19}$ Ne 10$_{30}$ Si 41$_{19}$ 1QS 2$_{16}$ 5$_{12}$ CD 1$_{17}$ 15$_{2.3}$ 4QpsMos^e 2$_{6(Dimant)}$. **3. anathema,** i.e. object of curse, Nm 5$_{21.27}$ Jr 29$_{18}$ 42$_{18}$ 44$_{12}$.

<SUBJ> היה *be* between Isaac and Abimelech Gn 26$_{28}$ (+ בְּרִית *covenant*), רבץ *lie down* on one who breaks covenant Dt 29$_{19}$, כתב ptc. pass. *be written* 29$_{19.20(Sam)}$ Dn 9$_{11}$ (|| שְׁבוּעָה *oath*) 2 C 34$_{24}$ (הָאָלוֹת הַכְּתוּבוֹת עַל־ *the curses written in* the book; ||2 K 22$_{16}$ דִּבְרֵי *words of*), בוא *come*, i.e. be made, before altar 1 K 8$_{31}$||2 C 6$_{22}$ (or em. וְאָלָה *and he curses* or בְּאָלָה comes *with a curse*), דבק *cling* 1QS 2$_{16}$, אכל *eat* land Is 24$_6$, יצא *go out* over Israel Zc 5$_3$, נתך *be poured out* over Israel Dn 9$_{11}$.

<NOM CL> זֹאת הָאָלָה *this* (flying scroll) *is the curse* Zc 5$_3$.

<OBJ> שמע *hear* Pr 29$_{24}$, כתב *write* (of priest) Nm 5$_{23}$, ספר pi. *relate* Ps 59$_{13}$, נתן *give*, i.e. assign to Israel's enemies Dt 30$_7$, נשׂא *raise*, i.e. proclaim against sinner 1 K 8$_{31(mss)}$||2 C 6$_{22(mss)}$ (L נשׁא perh. *exact*), בוא hi. *bring* against Israel 2 C 34$_{24}$, כרת *cut*, i.e. impose, agree Dt 29$_{11.13}$ (both || בְּרִית *covenant*), בזה *despise* Ezk 16$_{59}$ 17$_{16.18.19}$ (all four + פרר בְּרִית hi. *breach covenant*), פרר hi. *breach* Si 41$_{19(M)}$ (|| בְּרִית) 4QpsMos^e 2$_{6(Dimant)}$ (ה[אלה וה]ברית), נתן *give*, i.e. requite Ezk 17$_{19}$ (perh. em. נְתַתִּיו *I shall requite it* [masc.] to נְתַתִּיהָ [fem.] or נְתַתִּין *I shall requite them*), דבק hi. *cause to cling* CD 1$_{17}$.

<CSTR> אָלוֹת הַבְּרִית *stipulations of the covenant* Dt 29$_{20}$ 1QS 2$_{16}$ 5$_{12}$ (ברית) CD 1$_{17}$ (בריתו) 15$_{2.3}$; קוֹל אָלָה *sound of a curse* Lv 5$_1$, שְׁבֻעַת אָלָה *oath of curse*, i.e. of

self-imprecation Nm 5$_{21}$ CD 9$_{12}$ (שבועת האלה), דִּבְרֵי הָאָלָה *words of the covenant stipulation* Dt 29$_{18}$, כָּל־הָאָלָה *every stipulation* Dt 29$_{19}$, כֹּל אָלוֹת *all (the) stipulations of* Dt 29$_{20}$ 1QS 2$_{16}$ (כול), כָּל־הָאָלוֹת *all the curses* Dt 30$_{7}$ 2 C 34$_{24}$ 4QPrFêtes[c] 5.2$_{5}$ (כו[ל]).

<APP> רָעָה ... אָלוֹת *misfortune ... curses* 2 C 34$_{24}$.

<ADJ> הָאָלָה הַזֹּאת *this curse* Dt 29$_{13.18}$, הָאָלוֹת הָאֵלֶּה *these curses* Nm 5$_{23}$ (הָאָלֹת) Dt 30$_{7}$.

<PREP> לְאָלָה *as anathema*, + היה *be* Nm 5$_{27}$ Jr 42$_{18}$ 44$_{12}$ (both || שַׁמָּה *horror*, קְלָלָה *cursing*, חֶרְפָּה *reproach*), נתן *give*, i.e. cause to be Nm 5$_{21}$ (|| שְׁבוּעָה *oath*) Jr 29$_{18}$ (|| שַׁמָּה, חֶרְפָּה, שְׁרֵקָה *whistling* [mss קְלָלָה]).

בְּ *into*, i.e. into acceptance of covenant stipulations, + עבר *pass* Dt 29$_{11}$ (Sam mss עבר hi. *cause to pass*), בוא *come* Ne 10$_{30}$ (|| שְׁבוּעָה *oath*), hi. *bring* Ezk 17$_{13}$, שׁבע בְּ ni. *swear by* CD 15$_{2}$ (ישׁ[בע]) 15$_{3}$ (נשׁ[בע]), נקם בְּ *take revenge by*, i.e. by fulfilling curse 1QS 5$_{12}$, בוא בְּ *come with curse* 1 K 8$_{31}$||2 C 6$_{22}$ (if em.; see Subj.), שׁאל בְּ *request* enemy's life *by means of* Jb 31$_{30}$.

בדל כְּ hi. *separate in accordance with* Dt 29$_{20}$.

נקה מִן ni. *be cleansed*, i.e. released, *from* Gn 24$_{41.41}$ (+ שְׁבוּעָה *oath* [24$_{8}$]); appar. לכד מִן ni. *be captured*, i.e. trapped, *by* Ps 59$_{13}$ (|| כַּחַשׁ *lying*, + גָּאוֹן *pride*).

מִפְּנֵי אָלָה אָבְלָה הָאָרֶץ *because of a curse the earth mourns* Jr 23$_{10}$ (mss אֵלֶּה *these [things]*).

<COLL> אָלָה פִּיהוּ מָלֵא *his mouth is full of perjury* Ps 10$_{7}$ (or em. אָלָה : אֲשֶׁר לֹא־בְרֶע *[which is] without trouble. Perjury* to אֲשֶׁר לֹא כֹרֵעַ אֵלֵךְ *each step unbowed I shall walk*; + מִרְמוֹת וָתֹךְ *deceits and oppression*).

Also 4QDibHam[a] 26$_{8}$.

<SYN> §§1–3 שְׁבוּעָה *oath*; §2 בְּרִית *covenant*; §3 שַׁמָּה *horror*, חֶרְפָּה *reproach*.

→ אלה *curse*.

אֵלָה I $_{17}$ n.f. **terebinth**—Pl. abs. אֵילִים (אֵלִים); cstr. אֵילֵי; sf. אֵלֵיהֶם—**terebinth** (one or more of three species of *pistacia*), associated with foreign worship (Ezk 6$_{13}$ Ho 4$_{13}$ Is 57$_{5}$), death of Absalom (2 S 18), used as landmark at named location (Gn 35$_{4}$ Jg 6$_{11}$ 1 C 10$_{12}$).

<SUBJ> עמד *stand* Ezk 31$_{14}$ (+ בְּגָבְהָם *in their height*; but perh. אֵלֵיהֶם = *their leaders* [אַיִל I]), נתן *give* Gn 49$_{21}$ (if em. אַיָּלָה *hind* to אֵילָה; obj. אִמְרֵי־שָׁפֶר *words of beauty*), שׁלח pass. *be sent* i.e. slender 49$_{21}$ (if em.). <NOM CL> נַפְתָּלִי אֵילָה *Naphtali is a terebinth* Gn 49$_{21}$ (if em.; see Subj.). <OBJ> חמד *desire* Is 1$_{29}$ (|| גַּנָּה *garden*), חול pol. *whirl* Ps 29$_{9}$ (if em. אַיָּלוֹת *hinds* to אֵילוֹת).

<CSTR> אֵילֵי הַצֶּדֶק *the terebinths of righteousness* Is 61$_{3}$ (|| מַטַּע י׳ *something planted of*, i.e. by, *Y.*, in figure of Israelites); שׂוֹבֶךְ הָאֵלָה *branches of the terebinth* 2 S 18$_{9}$, לֵב הָאֵלָה *heart of the terebinth* 18$_{14}$ (but perh. בְּלֵב = *in*), כָּל־אֵלָה *every terebinth* Ezk 6$_{13}$.

<APP> אֵלֵיהֶם ... כָּל־שֹׁתֵי מָיִם *their terebinths* (or, *leaders*; see Subj.) ..., *all drinkers of water* Ezk 31$_{14}$. <ADJ> הָאֵלָה הַגְּדוֹלָה *the large terebinth* 2 S 18$_{9}$, אֵלָה עֲבֻתָּה *leafy terebinth* Ezk 6$_{13}$ (+ עֵץ רַעֲנָן *green tree*).

<PREP> בְּ of place, *in*, + חזק *be caught* 2 S 18$_{9}$ (subj. ראשׁ *head*), תלה pass. *be hung* 2 S 18$_{10}$ (subj. Absalom), + חמם ni. *be inflamed* Is 57$_{5}$ (+ עֵץ רַעֲנָן *green tree*); כְּ *as*, + היה *be* Is 1$_{30}$ (+ נֹבֶלֶת עָלֶהָ *the leaves of which are withering*; || גַּנָּה *garden*) 6$_{13}$ (+ לְבָעֵר *for burning*; || אַלּוֹן *oak*); בושׁ מִן *be ashamed of* Is 1$_{29}$.

תַּחַת *under*, + היה *be* Ezk 6$_{13}$, טמן *conceal* cultic objects Gn 35$_{4}$, קום hi. *set up* stone Jos 24$_{26}$, ישׁב *sit* Jg 6$_{11.19}$ (אֶל־תַּחַת) 1 K 13$_{14}$, קטר pi. *burn incense* Ho 4$_{13}$ (+ כִּי טוֹב צִלָּהּ *because its shade is good*; || אַלּוֹן *oak*, לִבְנֶה *poplar*), קבר *bury* bones 1 C 10$_{12}$ (+ at Jabesh).

<SYN> אַלּוֹן *oak*, לִבְנֶה *poplar*, גַּנָּה *garden*.

→ אַלָּה *terebinth*, עֵמֶק הָאֵלָה *Valley of Elah*, בְּאֵר אֵילִים *Beer-elim*.

אֵלָה II $_{13}$ pr.n.m. **Elah, 1.** father of Hoshea, 2 K 15$_{30}$ 17$_{1}$ 18$_{1.9}$. **2.** son of Baasha and his successor as king of Israel, 1 K 16$_{6.8.13.14}$. **3.** Edomite chief, Gn 36$_{41}$||1 C 1$_{52}$. **4.** son of Caleb and father of Kenaz, 1 C 4$_{15.15}$. **5.** returning exile, son of Uzzi (mss אֵלֶּה בְּנֵי *these are the sons of* Uzzi), descendant of Benjamin, 1 C 9$_{8}$.

[אֶלָּה] $_{0.0.2}$ adv. **only**, [אין] צריך לו אחת אלה שלו *there is not one (matter) neccessary for him, only that there is (a necessity) for him (to)* MurEpJonathan$_{6}$, sim. Mur 48$_{5 (Milik)}$, [אין פליט] להן אלה אחי *there was to them no survivor, only my colleague* Mur45$_{8}$.

אַלָּה 1 n.[f.] **terebinth,** תַּחַת הָאַלָּה אֲשֶׁר בְּמִקְדַּשׁ י׳ *below the terebinth that is in the sanctuary of Y.* Jos 24$_{26}$ (or em. אֵלָה *terebinth*).

→ אֵלָה *terebinth*, perh. אַלַּמֶּלֶךְ *Allammelech.*

אֵלֶּה 755.17.139.1 demonstr. pronoun pl.m.&f. and adj. **these**—אֵל, Si אילו, Q, I אלו—**1.** as pronoun, **these, those, such,** in ref. to things, persons, etc., <SUBJ> (alw. with indicative verb) היה *be* Gn 36$_{13}$ Nm 3$_{17}$ 35$_{29}$ Jos 20$_9$ Is 66$_2$ 1 C 2$_{33.50}$ 3$_1$ 1QS 8$_{4.12}$ 9$_3$ 4QpsEzek^a 2$_2$, ברא ni. *be created* Si 39$_{29}$ (נב[ראו]) 39$_{30}$, כון ni. *be established* 1QS 8$_{10}$, כלה *be accomplished* Dn 12$_7$, pi. *complete* Ezr 9$_1$, קרא *occur* Jr 13$_{22}$ 4QapLam^a 1.1$_3$, בוא *come* Jg 18$_{18}$ Is 47$_9$ 49$_{12.12.12}$ Zc 2$_{4.4}$ 1 C 4$_{41}$ 1QSa 2$_4$ (see Coll.) 2$_8$ (יב[ואו]), הלך *go* 1QM 7$_5$, יצא *go out* Jos 8$_{22}$ 1 K 20$_{19}$, רדף *pursue* 1QM 9$_5$, מלט ni. *escape* Dn 11$_{41}$ CD 7$_{21(A)}$=19$_{10(B)}$, נטה hi. *turn* trans. Jr 5$_{25}$, טול hi. *throw* 1QM 6$_4$, עמד *stand* Dt 27$_{12.13}$, יצב htp. *stand* 1QM 2$_5$.

ישב *dwell* 1 C 8$_{28}$||9$_{34}$, *sit* 2 S 2$_{13.13}$, קיץ hi. *wake up* intrans. Dn 12$_{2.2}$, נשא *take* wife Ezr 10$_{44}$, *tell* proverb Hb 2$_6$, זכר hi. *call upon* Ps 20$_{8.8}$, עדר perh. *help* 1 C 12$_{39}$, חבר *join forces* Gn 14$_3$, חנה *encamp* 1 K 20$_{29}$, ילד ni. *be born* 1 C 3$_5$ 20$_8$ (אֵל; Seb, ||2 S 21$_{22}$ אֵלֶּה), pu. 2 S 3$_5$ 21$_{22}$, מות *die* Nm 16$_{29}$, בקשׁ pi. *seek* Ezr 2$_{62}$||Ne 7$_{64}$, שׁכח *forget* Is 49$_{15}$, בחר ni. *be chosen* Si 39$_{30(mg)}$, כבד ni. *be honoured* 44$_{7(B\ mg,\ M)}$.

<NOM CL> (1) אֵלֶּה הַ־ *these are the ones who* + pl. ptc. בוא *come* 1 C 4$_{38}$ 12$_1$, עלה *go up* Ezr 2$_{59}$||Ne 7$_{61}$, עמד *stand* 1 C 6$_{18}$, שׁרת pi. *minister* 2 C 17$_{19}$, קרא pass. *be called* Nm 1$_{16(Qr)}$, פקד pass. *be recorded* Ex 38$_{21}$ Nm 1$_{44}$ 2$_{32}$ 4$_{37.41.45}$ 26$_{51.57.63}$, כתב pass. *be recorded* 1 C 4$_{41}$, פלא ni. *be wonderful* 4Q181 2$_7$, שׁיר pol. *sing* 1 C 9$_{33}$, קשׁר htp. *conspire* 2 C 24$_{26}$; כָּל־אֵלֶּה שֹׁלְפֵי חֶרֶב *all of these could draw a sword* Jg 20$_{25}$, var. 20$_{35}$ (שֹׁלֵף).

(2) pl. noun as complement אִישׁ *man* Jg 20$_{44.46}$ Ezk 11$_2$ 1 C 4$_{12}$ 9$_9$ Si 44$_{10}$ 1QSa 1$_{27}$ 2$_1$ 4QM^a fr. 1$_{12}$, בֵּן *son* Gn 9$_{19}$ 10$_{20.29}$||1 C 1$_{23}$ Gn 10$_{31}$ 25$_4$||1 C 1$_{33}$ Gn 35$_{26}$ 36$_{5+14t}$ 46$_{15.18.22.25}$ Nm 26$_{30.35.36.37.41.42}$ Jos 17$_2$ Ezr 2$_1$ ||Ne 7$_6$ Ne 11$_7$ 1 C 2$_{1.18.23}$ 4$_{4.6.18}$ 5$_{14}$ 6$_{35}$ 7$_{8.11.17.33.40}$ 8$_{6.10.38}$||9$_{44}$ 9$_{8(mss)}$ (L אֵלָה בֶּן־ *Elah the son of* Uzzi) 23$_{10.24}$ 24$_{30}$ 25$_5$ 2 C 21$_2$, אַלּוּף *chief* Gn 36$_{15.16.17.18.19.21.29.30.43}$||1 C 1$_{54}$, רֹאשׁ *head* Ex 6$_{14.25}$ Ezr 8$_1$ Ne 11$_3$ 12$_7$ 1 C 5$_{24}$ 8$_{28}$||9$_{34}$ 11$_{10}$ 23$_9$ 4QShirShab^f 23.2$_{10}$, שַׂר *prince* 1 K 4$_2$ 9$_{23}$||2 C 8$_{10}$ 1 C 27$_{22.31}$, מֶלֶךְ *king* Gn 36$_{31}$||1 C 1$_{43}$ Jos 12$_{1.7}$, שֵׁד *demon* 11QapPs^a 1$_5$ ([השׁ]דים), כֹּהֵן *priest* Ne 10$_9$ 12$_1$, לֵוִי *Levite* 12$_1$, גִּבּוֹר *warrior* 2 C 14$_7$, אֱלֹהִים *god(s)* Ex 32$_{4.8}$, מִשְׁפָּחָה *family* Gn 10$_{32}$ Ex 6$_{14.15.19.24}$ Nm 26$_{7+11t}$ 1 C 4$_2$ 6$_4$, שֵׁבֶט *tribe* Gn 49$_{28}$, גּוֹי *nation* Jg 3$_1$.

חק *statute* Lv 26$_{46}$ Nm 30$_{17}$ Dt 4$_{45}$ 12$_1$ Ezk 43$_{18}$ 1QS 9$_{12}$ CD 12$_{20}$ 19$_{14}$, מִשְׁפָּט *judgment* Ex 21$_1$ Lv 26$_{46}$ Nm 36$_{13}$ Dt 4$_{45}$ 12$_1$ 1QS 8$_{20}$, תּוֹרָה *law* Lv 26$_{46}$, עֵדָה *testimony* Dt 4$_{45}$, מִצְוָה *commandment* Lv 27$_{34}$ Nm 36$_{13}$.

שֵׁם *name* Gn 25$_{13.16}$ 36$_{10.40}$ 46$_8$ Ex 1$_1$ 6$_{16}$ Nm 1$_5$ 3$_{2.3.18}$ 13$_{4.16}$ 27$_1$ 34$_{17.19}$ Jos 17$_3$ 2 S 5$_{14}$ 23$_8$ 1 K 4$_8$ Ezk 48$_1$ Ezr 8$_{13}$ 1 C 6$_2$ 8$_{38}$||9$_{44}$ 14$_4$, דָּבָר *word, thing* Ex 19$_6$ 35$_1$ Dt 1$_1$ 28$_{69}$ 2 S 23$_1$ Is 42$_{16}$ Jr 29$_1$ 30$_4$ Zc 8$_{16}$, מָשָׁל *proverb* Pr 25$_1$, מַעֲלָל *deed* Mc 2$_7$, מִדָּה *dimension* Ezk 43$_{13}$ 48$_{16}$, מִסְפָּר *number* 1 C 12$_{24}$, דֶּרֶךְ *way* 1QS 4$_2$, סוד *secret* 4$_6$.

קֶרֶן *horn* Zc 2$_{2.4}$, עַיִן *eye* 4$_{10}$, אֶבֶן *stone* 1 K 7$_9$, בֶּגֶד *garment* Ex 28$_4$ 4QM^a fr. 1$_{18}$, טְחוֹר *haemorrhoid* 1 S 6$_{17}$ (mss עֹפֶל *haemmorhoid*), בְּתוּלִים *(tokens of) virginity* Dt 22$_{17}$=11QT 65$_{12}$.

עִיר *city* Dt 3$_5$ 1 C 4$_{31}$, מִשְׁכָּן *home* Jb 18$_{21}$ (|| זֶה *this*), מוֹשָׁב *dwelling* 1 C 6$_{39}$, נַחֲלָה *possession* Jos 19$_{51}$, מַחֲלֹקֶת *division* Ezk 48$_{29}$ (|| זאת *this*) 1 C 26$_{19}$, קָצָה *end* Jb 26$_{14}$, תּוֹצָאָה *exit* Ezk 48$_{30}$, תּוֹלֵדָה *generation* Gn 2$_4$ 6$_9$ 10$_1$ 11$_{10.27}$ 25$_{12.19}$ 36$_{1.9}$ 37$_2$ Nm 3$_1$ Ru 4$_{18}$ 1 C 1$_{29}$, שָׁנָה *year* Gn 25$_{17}$, יוֹם *day* 25$_7$, מוֹעֵד *appointed feast* Lv 23$_{4.37}$, מַסָּע *order of march* Nm 10$_{28}$ 33$_{1.2}$; אֵלֶּה שְׁנֵי בְנֵי־הַיִּצְהָר *these are the two anointed* Zc 4$_{14}$, אֵלֶּה אַרְבַּע רֻחוֹת *these are the four winds of* 6$_5$, אלו ארונות הפנימית והחיצונית *these are (the) coffins, the inner and the outer* Beth Shearim inscr. 17.

(3) two or more pl. nouns conjoined by וְ *and* as complement Lv 26$_{46}$ Nm 36$_{13}$ Dt 4$_{45}$ 12$_1$ Ne 12$_1$.

(4) pl. adj. (used as noun) as complement טָמֵא *unclean* Lv 11$_{31}$, רָשָׁע *wicked* Ps 73$_{12}$.

(5) sg. noun as complement (אֵלֶּה = *these things comprise*) מַשָּׂא *task* Nm 4$_{15}$, עָשָׁן *smoke* Is 65$_5$, עַם *people* Ezk 36$_{20}$, בַּיִת *house* 46$_{24}$, מִסְפָּר *number* Ezr 1$_9$ 1 C 11$_{11}$, פְּקֻדָּה *enrollment* 2 C 17$_{14}$, תֹּכֶן *content* 1QS 5$_7$; אֵלֶּה אֲבִי עֵיטָם *these were (the sons of) the father of Etam* 1 C 4$_3$, אֵלֶּה הוּסַד שְׁלֹמֹה *these are the founding of Solomon,*

i.e. this is how Solomon founded 2 C 3$_{3}$.

(6) interrog. pronoun as complement, מִי־אֵלֶּה *who are these?* Gn 33$_{5}$ 48$_{8}$ Is 60$_{8}$, מָה־אֵלֶּה *what are these?* 2 S 16$_{2}$ Ezk 17$_{12}$ 24$_{19}$ 37$_{18}$ Zc 1$_{9}$ 2$_{2.4}$ (מָה אֵלֶּה) 4$_{4.13}$ 6$_{4}$.

(7) prep. as complement, לְ of possession, *to, of* Gn 32$_{18}$ 38$_{25}$ Pr 24$_{23}$, of benefit, *for* 2 C 29$_{32}$; בְּ of time, *in* Ne 12$_{26}$; מִן partitive, *(one) of* 1 C 8$_{40}$ 12$_{15}$ 26$_{8}$ 2 C 35$_{7}$ 4QMMT A 2$_{1}$, בַּתָּוֶךְ אֵלֶּה מִזֶּה וְאֵלֶּה מִזֶּה *in the middle — these (are) on this (side) and these (are) on this (side)* Jos 8$_{22}$; עַל־יַד *under the charge of* 1 C 25$_{6}$.

<OBJ> ע שׂ ה *do, make* Nm 15$_{13}$ 28$_{23}$ 29$_{39}$ Dt 18$_{12}$=11QT 60$_{20}$ Dt 22$_{5}$ 25$_{16}$ 2 S 23$_{17.22}$||1 C 11$_{19.24}$ Is 45$_{7}$ 66$_{2}$ Jr 3$_{7}$ 4$_{18}$ 5$_{19}$ 14$_{22}$ 30$_{15}$ Ezk 16$_{30}$ 17$_{15.18}$ 18$_{11}$ 23$_{30}$ Ps 15$_{5}$ 50$_{21}$ Si 35$_{23}$ GnzPs 2$_{14}$ 11QT 29$_{2(Yadin)}$ ([תעש]) 4QDibHam^{a} 1.6$_{4}$ 1QH 10$_{12}$ 18$_{21}$ fr. 2.1$_{5}$ 11$_{5}$ 4QShir^{b} 30$_{6}$ ([יעש]ה) 4QShirShab^{c} 4$_{11}$ 3Q9 2$_{1(Baillet)}$, פעל *do* Jb 33$_{29}$ GnzPs 3$_{6}$ 1QH 11$_{33}$, פלא hi. *do wondrously* fr. 2.1$_{16}$, ברא *create* Is 40$_{26}$, בוא hi. *bring* 4QpsMos^{e} 2.1$_{3}$, ילד *beget* Gn 22$_{23}$ 46$_{18.25}$ Is 49$_{21}$, גדל pi. *rear* 49$_{21}$.

כלה pi. *complete* Ezk 4$_{6}$, שׂים *place* Is 47$_{7}$, סרך *arrange* 1QM 2$_{6(mg)}$, כון hi. *prepare* 1QH 13$_{10}$ ([הכ]ינותה), עמד hi. *appoint* 1 C 6$_{16}$, נדב htp. *give freely* 29$_{17}$, קרב hi. *present* as sacrifice Lv 22$_{22}$, לקח *take* Gn 15$_{10}$ Lv 21$_{14}$, נחל *inherit* Jos 14$_{1}$, pi. *divide for inheritance* 13$_{32}$ 14$_{1}$, hi. *cause to inherit* Zc 8$_{12}$, פלג pi. *apportion* 1QH 13$_{16}$ (פל[גתה]), נכה hi. *strike* 2 K 10$_{9}$, אכל *eat* Lv 11$_{22}$ 11QT 48$_{3(Yadin)}$ ([אלה]) 48$_{4}$.

צוה pi. *command* Nm 34$_{29}$, דבר pi. *speak* 11QPs^{a} 27$_{11}$, 4QpsEzek^{a} 3$_{7}$, נגד hi. *tell* Is 48$_{14}$, מלל pi. *say* Jb 8$_{2}$, זכר *remember* Is 44$_{21}$ Ps 42$_{5}$, שׁמר *observe* 107$_{43}$, ראה hi. *show* Jg 13$_{23}$ (|| זֹאת *this*), שׁמע *hear* 1QH fr. 1$_{7(Licht)}$ (שמ[ענו]), ידע *know* 4QPrQuot 7$_{7(Baillet)}$ ([א]לה) 1QM 10$_{16}$ 4QDibHam^{a} 4$_{5}$=4QDibHam^{c} 31$_{10}$ 1QH 1$_{21}$ 5$_{3}$, בין hi. *understand* Si 16$_{23}$ (|| זֹאת) 1QH 1$_{38}$, צפן *hide* Jb 10$_{13}$ (+ זֹאת), שׂנא *hate* Zc 8$_{17}$, שׁקץ pi. *abominate* Lv 11$_{13}$.

<CSTR> אַחֲרִית אֵלֶּה *the outcome of these (things)* Dn 12$_{8}$, עֵינֵי־אֵלֶּה *the eyes of these (men)* 2 K 6$_{20}$, כָּל־אֵלֶּה *all these* Gn 10$_{29}$||1 C 1$_{23}$ Gn 14$_{3}$ 15$_{10}$ 25$_{4}$||1 C 1$_{33}$ Gn 49$_{28}$ Lv 18$_{24.24}$ 20$_{23}$ 22$_{25}$ Dt 3$_{5}$ Jg 13$_{23}$ 20$_{25.35.44.46}$ 1 K 7$_{9}$ 2 K 10$_{9}$ Is 45$_{7}$ 66$_{2.2}$ Jr 2$_{34}$ 3$_{7}$ 5$_{19}$ 14$_{22}$ Ezk 16$_{30.43}$ 17$_{18}$ 18$_{11}$ Hg 2$_{13}$ Zc 8$_{12.17}$ Jb 12$_{9}$ 33$_{29}$ Ec 7$_{8}$ 11$_{9}$ Dn 12$_{7}$ Ezr 10$_{44}$ 1 C 2$_{23}$ 7$_{8.11.40}$ 8$_{38.40}$ 9$_{9}$ 12$_{39}$ 25$_{5.6}$ 26$_{8}$ 27$_{31}$ 29$_{17}$ 2 C 14$_{7}$ 21$_{2}$ 29$_{32}$ Si 35$_{13}$ ([כ]ל [א]לה) 37$_{15}$ 44$_{7}$ GnzPs 2$_{14}$ 3$_{6}$ 4QPrQuot 7$_{7(Baillet)}$ ([כו]ל[א]לה) 1QM 2$_{6(mg)}$ 6$_{4}$ 7$_{5}$ 9$_{5}$ CD 8$_{12(A)}$=19$_{24(B)}$ 16$_{3}$ 1QDM 4$_{9}$ 4QapLam^{a} 1.1$_{3}$ 1QH 10$_{12}$ 13$_{16.17}$ 16$_{6}$ fr. 2.1$_{5}$ 11$_{5}$ 19$_{2}$ ([כו]ל) 11QPs^{a} 27$_{11}$ 4QShirShab^{c} 4$_{11}$ (כ[ו]ל) 4QMMT A 2$_{15}$ 4QMMT B$_{31}$ 4QJub^{a} 7$_{1.3}$ (both [כל אלה]) 4QapPs^{b} 1$_{7}$ 11QapPs^{a} 3$_{7}$.

<APP> אֵלֶּה followed by pl. (or collective) noun אִישׁ *man* 1 C 12$_{39}$, צֹאן *flock* 2 S 24$_{17}$||1 C 21$_{17}$, נֹאד *bottle* Jos 9$_{13}$, שַׂלְמָה *garment* 9$_{13}$, יוֹם *day* 11QT 43$_{4}$; אֵלֶּה כֻלָּם *these, all of them* Hb 2$_{6}$, אֵלֶּה הֵם *these, they (are)* Gn 25$_{16}$||1 C 1$_{31}$ Lv 23$_{2}$ Nm 3$_{20.21.27.33}$ (all four + מִשְׁפָּחָה *family*) 1 S 4$_{8}$ 1 C 8$_{6}$ 12$_{16}$ (introducing relative clause) 1QM 6$_{17}$ (המה) 4QpIsa^{b} 1.2$_{6}$, מָה־הֵמָּה אֵלֶּה *what are they, these things?* Zc 1$_{9}$ 4$_{5}$.

<PREP> (some referents of אֵלֶּה follow in brackets) לְ *to, by* Gn 31$_{43}$ (daughters) Lv 11$_{24}$ (animals) Nm 26$_{53}$ 1 K 22$_{17}$||2 C 18$_{16}$ (sheep) Ezk 9$_{5}$ 48$_{10}$ Mc 2$_{6}$ 1 C 26$_{12}$ 1QH fr. 7.2$_{10}$.

בְּ *in, through, among, by, with, because of* Lv 18$_{24.24}$ 25$_{54}$ 26$_{23}$ (punishments) Nm 26$_{64}$ 1 S 16$_{10}$ (sons) 17$_{39}$ (clothes) 1 K 22$_{11}$||2 C 18$_{10}$ (horns) Jr 9$_{23}$ Ezk 16$_{43}$ Hg 2$_{13}$ (foods) Jb 12$_{9}$ Ec 7$_{28}$ 1 C 7$_{29}$ (places) Si 16$_{5(B)}$ 50$_{28}$ 11QT 43$_{4}$ (days) 1QS 4$_{15}$ 6$_{1}$ 1QSa 2$_{4}$ (ב[א]לה; afflictions) CD 7$_{5}$ 8$_{2(A).12(A)}$=19$_{14(B).24(B)}$ 12$_{23}$ 13$_{3.4}$ 14$_{1}$ 1QH 13$_{17}$ 16$_{6}$ 18$_{11}$ 4QShirShab^{d} 1.1$_{41}$ 4QMMT B$_{5}$ 11QapPs^{a} 4$_{9}$ ([ב]אלה; gates), בין בְּ hi. *understand* 4QShirShab^{b} 16$_{4}$, אלה באלה mix *these with these* 11QT 35$_{12}$ 45$_{4}$, להריב אלה באלה *to dispute, these with these* 3QpsMos^{e} 2.1$_{6}$.

כְּ *as* Gn 27$_{46}$ Lv 10$_{19}$ Nm 28$_{24}$ 2 K 25$_{17}$||Jr 52$_{22}$ Is 66$_{8}$ (|| זֹאת *this*) Jr 10$_{16}$ 18$_{13}$ 51$_{19}$ Ezk 45$_{25}$ Jb 12$_{3}$ (כְּמוֹ־) 16$_{2}$ Si 16$_{5(A)}$ 40$_{8(M)}$ 1QH 10$_{4}$, רבות כאלה *many like these*, i.e. many such things Si 16$_{5}$, עוד כאלה *more like/than these* 43$_{27}$.

מִן *from, of, than* Gn 9$_{19}$ 10$_{5.32}$ (all three of ancestors) Lv 2$_{8}$ (ingredients) 22$_{25}$ (animals) Nm 22$_{15}$ Is 41$_{28}$ Jr 4$_{12}$ Ezk 8$_{15}$ (abominations) Ec 7$_{10}$ (times) 1 C 25$_{3}$ (ancestors) 23$_{4}$ (Levites) Si 43$_{32}$ ([מ]אלה; wonders) 1QS 8$_{12}$ 1QSa 2$_{9(Barthélemy)}$ ([מ]אלה]) CD 16$_{3}$, אַחַת מֵאֵלֶּה *one of these* Lv 5$_{4.5.13}$ Ezk 16$_{5}$ 18$_{10}$ (אַחַד), תחסרון מן אילו ואילו how long *will you lack from these things and these things?* Si 51$_{24}$ (or em. מאוכלה *from her* food), מאלו אבדו בחרב perh. *some of these perished by the sword* Mur 45$_7$.

עַל *above, on account of, against* Dt 25$_3$ Is 57$_6$ 64$_{11}$ Jr 2$_{34}$ 5$_{9.29}$ 9$_8$ Ec 11$_9$ Lm 1$_{16}$ 5$_{17}$ (|| זֶה *this*) Dn 10$_{21}$ Ne 13$_{26}$ Si 35$_{13}$ (וע]ל ... [א]לה]) 42$_1$ 4Q 397$_9$ ([אלה]) 11QapPs^a 3$_7$; על גב[ע] *on the basis of* 4QMMT B$_8$; עִם *with* Ps 126$_2$ 1 C 9$_{25}$ (gatekeepers) Si 37$_{15}$, אֵלֶּה עִם־אֵלֶּה *these with these* 1 C 24$_5$.

מִלְּבַד־אֵלֶּה *apart from these* claimants Dn 11$_4$; אֵלֶּה נֹכַח אֵלֶּה *these facing these* 1 K 20$_{29}$; עַד־אֵלֶּה *despite these* punishments Lv 26$_{18}$; מִפְּנֵי אֵלֶּה *because of these* adulterers Jr 23$_{10(mss)}$ (L אָלָה *curse*).

<COLL> גַּם־אֵלֶּה *these too* Is 28$_7$ 49$_{15}$ Pr 24$_{23}$ 25$_1$ Si 39$_{29.30(mg)}$, אֵלֶּה אֵיפֹה הֵם *as for these—where are they?* Is 49$_{21}$, אֵלֶּה פְקֻדָּתָם *as for these—their job* was 1 C 24$_{19}$, כול איש מנוגע ... אל יבוא בקהל אלה perh. *any man who is stricken ... these (men) are not to enter the congregation* 1QSa 2$_4$ (or perh. קהל אלה = קהל אל *assembly of God*), אשר לא יחזיקו באלה החקים *who do not adhere to 'These are are the statutes'* CD 19$_{14}$.

שְׁתֵּי־אֵלֶּה *these two* misfortunes Is 47$_9$, הַשָּׁלֹשׁ הָאֵלֶּה *these three* cities Dt 19$_9$, שְׁלֹשָׁה אֵלֶּה *these three* persons Gn 9$_{19}$, שְׁלָשׁ־אֵלֶּה *these three* conditions Ex 21$_{11}$, אַרְבַּעַת אֵלֶּה *these four* children 2 S 21$_{22}$, שִׁבְעָה־אֵלֶּה *these seven* lamps Zc 4$_{10}$, שְׁמֹנָה אֵלֶּה *these eight* sons Gn 22$_{23}$, שנים העשר האלה *these twelve* persons 4QOrd^a 2$_4$.

2. as demonstr. adj., **these,** (1) הָאֵלֶּה qualifying determined noun דָּבָר *word, event* Gn 15$_1$ (+ אַחַר *after*) 20$_8$ 22$_1$ (+ אַחַר) 22$_{20}$ (+ אַחֲרֵי *after*) 24$_{28}$ 29$_{13}$ 39$_7$ (+ אַחַר) 39$_{17.19}$ 40$_1$ (+ אַחַר) 43$_7$ 44$_{6.7}$ (|| זֶה *this*) 48$_1$ (+ אַחֲרֵי) Ex 19$_7$ 20$_1$ 24$_8$ 34$_{27.27}$ Nm 14$_{39}$ 16$_{31}$ Dt 4$_{30}$ 5$_{22}$ 6$_6$ 12$_{28}$ 30$_1$ 31$_{1.28}$ 32$_{45}$ Jos 24$_{26.29}$ (+ אַחֲרֵי) Jg 2$_4$ 9$_3$ 1 S 2$_{23}$ 11$_6$ 17$_{11.23}$ 18$_{23.24.26}$ 19$_7$ 21$_{13}$ 24$_{17}$ 25$_{9.12.37}$ 2 S 7$_{17}$||1 C 17$_{15}$ (|| זֶה *this*) 2 S 13$_{21}$ 14$_{19}$ 1 K 17$_{17}$ (+ אַחַר *after*) 18$_{36}$ 21$_1$ (+ אַחַר) 21$_{27}$ 2 K 1$_7$ 18$_{27}$||Is 36$_{12}$ 2 K 23$_{16.17}$ Jr 3$_{12}$ 7$_{27}$ 11$_6$ 16$_{10}$ (both || זֹאת *this*) 20$_1$ 22$_5$ 25$_{30}$ 26$_{7.10.15}$ 27$_{12}$ 34$_6$ 36$_{16.17.18.24}$ 38$_{4.24.27}$ 43$_1$ 45$_1$ 51$_{60.61}$ Zc 8$_9$ Jb 42$_7$ Est 2$_1$ 3$_1$ (both + אַחַר) 9$_{20.32}$ Dn 10$_{15}$ Ezr 7$_1$ (+ אַחַר) Ne 1$_4$ 5$_6$ 6$_{6.7.8}$ 2 C 15$_8$ 32$_1$ (+ אַחֲרֵי *after*) 4QRitPur 24$_4$ (אחר הדב[רי]ם ה[אלה]) 1QM 17$_{10}$ (+ אַחַר) 4QM^a fr. 13$_3$ ([הדב]רים]) 1QDM 2$_9$ 1Q29 5$_{1.4}$ 4QMMT A 2$_3$ ([האלה]) 4QMMT B$_{8.9}$ ([הדברים האלה]) 4QMMT B$_{13}$ (הדברי]ם ה[אלה) 4QJub^a 1$_{16}$ ([האלה]) 1$_{17}$ ([הדב]רים]).

מַעֲשֶׂה *deed* Nm 16$_{28}$ Jr 7$_{13}$, תּוֹעֵבָה *abomination* Lv 18$_{26.27}$ (הָאֵל; Sam הָאֵלֶּה) 18$_{29}$ Dt 18$_{12}$=11QT 60$_{20}$ 2 K 21$_{11}$ Jr 7$_{10}$ Ezk 18$_{13}$ Ezr 9$_{14}$, אוֹת *sign* Ex 4$_9$ Jos 24$_{17}$ 1 S 10$_{7.9}$, מוֹפֵת *wonder* Ex 11$_{10}$, מִצְוָה *commandment* Lv 26$_{14}$ Nm 15$_{22}$, מִשְׁפָּט *judgment* 35$_{24}$ Dt 7$_{12}$ 1QS 6$_{24(mg)}$ 4QM^a fr. 4$_3$ CD 12$_{19(A)}$ 20$_{27(B)}$ 5QRègle 9$_2$ ([המשפט]ים) 4QD^b 6, חֹק *statute* Dt 4$_6$ 6$_{24}$ 16$_{12}$ 17$_{19}$ (|| זֹאת *this*) 26$_{16}$ Jr 31$_{36}$ 1QS 5$_{7.20}$ 4QApocMos B 1.1$_2$ ([החו]קים]), רָעָה *misfortune* Dt 31$_{17}$ 4QPrFêtes^c 188$_4$, מַכָּה *wound* Zc 13$_6$, אִסָּר *curse* 2Q25 1$_2$ ([האל]ה]), אָלָה *curse* Nm 5$_{23}$ Dt 30$_7$, קְלָלָה *curse* 28$_{15.45}$, בְּרָכָה *blessing* 28$_2$.

אֱלֹהִים *god(s)* 1 S 4$_8$, כְּרוּב *cherub* 2 C 3$_{13}$, מִין *kind* 4QJub^a 6$_{4.10}$ (both [האלה]) 6$_{14}$ ([המינ]ים ... [האלה]) 7$_{4.9}$, אִישׁ *man* Gn 19$_8$ (הָאֵל; Seb, Sam הָאֵלֶּה) 34$_{21}$ Nm 1$_{17}$ 16$_{26.30}$ 22$_9$ Dt 13$_5$ (|| זֶה *this*) 2 S 3$_{39}$ 2 K 20$_{14}$||Is 39$_3$ Jr 38$_{9.16}$ Ezk 14$_{3.14.16.18}$ Jb 32$_1$ 1 C 11$_{19}$, יֶלֶד *youth* Dn 1$_{17}$, מֶלֶךְ *king* Dt 3$_{21}$ Jos 10$_{16.22.23.24.24.42}$ 11$_{5.12.18}$ 2 K 3$_{10.13}$, חַטָּא *sinner* Nm 17$_3$, עִבְרִי *Hebrew* 1 S 29$_3$ (|| זֶה), טָמֵא *unclean person* 4QToh A 1.1$_9$, עָרֵל *uncircumcised man* 14$_6$ 31$_4$||1 C 10$_4$, פְּלִשְׁתִּי *Philistine* 1 S 23$_2$.

אֶרֶץ *land* Gn 26$_{3.4}$ (both הָאֵל; Seb, Sam הָאֵלֶּה) Is 36$_{20}$ Jr 27$_6$, מַמְלָכָה *kingdom* Jos 11$_{10}$ Am 6$_2$, גּוֹי *nation* Dt 7$_{17.22}$ (הָאֵל; ms, Sam הָאֵלֶּה) 9$_{4.5}$ 11$_{23}$ 12$_{30}$ 18$_{14}$ =11QT 60$_{21}$ Dt 20$_{15}$=11QT 62$_{12}$ Dt 31$_3$ Jos 23$_{3.4.7.12.13}$ Jg 2$_{23}$ 2 K 17$_{41}$ Jr 25$_{9.11}$ (both || זֹאת *this*) 28$_{14}$ 2 C 32$_{14}$, עַם *people* Dt 20$_{16}$, שֵׁבֶט *tribe* Jos 21$_{16}$.

מַיִם *water(s)* Nm 5$_{19.22}$ 2 K 2$_{21}$ Ezk 47$_{8.9}$, רוּחַ *wind* Jr 49$_{36}$, מָקוֹם *place* 1 S 7$_{16}$, חָרְבָּה *ruin* Ezk 33$_{24}$, עִיר *city* Gn 19$_{25}$ (הָאֵל; or em. הָאֵלֶּ[ה]) Nm 21$_{25}$ 35$_{15}$ Dt 4$_{42}$ (הָאֵל; Seb, ms, Sam הָאֵלֶּה) 19$_{5.9.11}$ (הָאֵל; Seb, mss, Sam הָאֵלֶּה) Jos 11$_{14}$ 17$_{9.12}$ (|| זֹאת *this*) 19$_{8.16.31.48}$ 20$_4$ (+ הַהִיא *that*) 21$_{3.8.9}$||1 C 6$_{50}$ Jos 21$_{42.42}$ 1 K 9$_{13}$ 1 C 4$_{33}$ 2 C 14$_6$, שַׁעַר *gate* Jr 7$_2$ 17$_{20}$ 22$_2$ 11QT 36$_{13}$, בַּיִת *house* Jg 18$_{14}$, לִשְׁכָּה *room* Ezk 42$_9$, חַלּוֹן *window* 40$_{25}$, אֶבֶן *stone* Dt 27$_4$ Jos 4$_{6.7.20.21}$ Jr 43$_{10}$.

כְּלִי *object, vessel* Ex 25$_{39}$ 1 K 7$_{45(Qr)}$ (Kt perh. הָאֹהֶל the vessels [of] *the tent*) 2 K 4$_4$ 25$_{16}$||Jr 52$_{20}$ 2 C 4$_{18}$, סֵפֶר *document* Jr 32$_{14}$ (twice || זֶה *this*), גֶּזֶר *part* Gn 15$_{17}$, חֲרִיץ *portion* 1 S 17$_{18}$, כִּבְשָׂה *ewe-lamb* Gn 21$_{29}$, עֵץ *tree* 4QJub^d 1.2$_7$ ([העצים האלה]), תְּאֵנָה *fig* Jr 24$_5$, זַיִת *olive-tree* Zc 4$_{11}$, שְׂעֹרָה *(measure of) barley* Ru 3$_{17}$, זָנָב *tail* Is

7_4, עֶצֶם *bone* Ezk $37_{3.4.5.11}$, שָׁנָה *year* Gn 41_{35} 1 K 17_1 2 C 14_5 CD $4_{9.11.12}$, יוֹם *day* Zc $8_{9.15}$ Est 1_5 $9_{26.27.28.28.31}$ 11QT 17_{12} ([הא]לה) 4Q409 1_9, עֵת *time* 1QS 9_{21}, מִדָּה *dimension* Ezk $40_{24.28.29.32.33.35}$, תֹּכֶן *principle* 1QS 8_{13} (mg) 9_3.

ירא ni. ptc. *fearful* deed Dt 10_{21}, גָּדוֹל *mighty* deed 10_{21}, צרע pu. ptc. *leper* 2 K 7_8, הרג pass. ptc. *slain one* Ezk 37_9, נצב ni. ptc. *prefect* 1 K 5_7, עמד ptc. *person standing* Zc 3_7, שׁאר ni. ptc. *remaining* nation Jos $23_{7.12}$, טָמֵא *unclean person* 4QTohA 1.1_8.

(2) הָאֵלֶּה qualifying two or more sg. or pl. nouns conjoined by וְ *and* Dt 10_{21} Ezr 2_{65}||Ne 7_{67}; הַחֹתֶמֶת וְהַפְּתִילִים וְהַמַּטֶּה הָאֵלֶּה *this seal, cords, and staff* Gn 38_{25}, הַדְּבָרִים וְהָאֱמֶת הָאֵלֶּה *these deeds and truth*, i.e. these faithful deeds 2 C 32_1, האותות ואת המופ[תים] [האלה] *these signs and wonders* 11Qps^a 2_3.

(3) אֵלֶּה qualifying suffixed pl. noun עֶבֶד *servant* Ex 11_8 1 K 10_8||2 C 9_7 2 K 1_{13} Ezr 2_{65}||Ne 7_{67}, אָמָה *maidservant* Ezr 2_{65}||Ne 7_{67}, נָבִיא *prophet* 1 K 22_{23}||2 C 18_{22}, אוֹת *sign* Ex 10_1, דָּבָר *word* Dt 11_{18} 1 K 8_{59}, מַעֲשֶׂה *deed* Ne 6_{14}, עִיר *city* Jr 31_{21}.

<COLL> כול אלו אשמות *all these guilt offerings* 11QT 35_{14} (if em. אלי אשמות *rams for guilt offerings*), כָּל־הָעָם אֵלֶּה *all these people* 1 S 2_{23}, אֲנַחְנוּ אֵלֶּה *we ourselves* Dt 5_3.

Also 4QpIsa^b 1.3_5 1QDM $4_{3.10}$ 5QRègle 4_4 1QH fr. 18_9 4QCrypt 1.4_1 3Q9 3_3, Mur 24 3_{16} 5_{13}, 4Q521 3.1_4.

<SYN> זֶה *this* (masc.), זֹאת *this* (fem.).

אֱלַהּ, see אֱלוֹהַּ.

[אֱלֹהוּת] 0.0.3 n.[f.] **divinity**—Q אלוהות; sf. אלוהותו—שם כבוד אלוהות[כה] *name of glory of your divinity* 4QBer^b 1_8, רוממו ... אלוהות כבודו *exalt ... the divinity of his glory* 4QShirShab^d 1.1_{33}, באלהותו *in his divinity* 4QShirShab^a 1.1_2.

→ אֱלוֹהַּ *God*.

אֱלֹהִים +2603.29.213.3 n.m.pl. **God**—אֱלֹהִים (בֵּאלֹהִים, בָּאֱלֹהִים, לֵאלֹהִים, כֵּאלֹהִים, וֵאלֹהִים; sim. in cstr. & sf.; Q אלוהים); cstr. אֱלֹהֵי (אֱלוֹהֵי); sf. אֱלֹהַי (אֱלוֹהַי), אֱלֹהָ֑י (אֱלוֹהָ֑י), אֱלֹהֶיךָ (Q אלוהיכה), אֱלֹהַיִךְ (אֱלֹהָ֑יִךְ), אֱלֹהָיו, אֱלֹהֶיהָ, אֱלֹהֵינוּ, אֱלֹהֵיכֶם (Q אלוהיכמה), אֱלֹהֵיהֶם (Q אלוהיהמה), אֱלֹהֵיהֶן.

1. God, in ref. to Y., <SUBJ> עשׂה *do, make* Gn $1_{7.16.25}$ 2_{16} $41_{25.28.32}$ 42_{28} Ex 18_1 Jg 6_{40} 1 S 3_{17} 14_{44} 22_3 25_{22} 2 S $3_{9.35}$ 19_{14} 1 K 2_{23} 19_2 20_{10} 2 K 6_{31} Jon 3_{10} Ps 115_3 Ec $3_{11.14.14}$ $7_{14.29}$ 4Q185 1.3_{13} 11QapPs^a 1_{11} (אלוהי ... [עשה]), פעל *make* Ps 68_{29}, יסף hi. *do again* 1 K 19_2 20_{10} 2 K 6_{31}, אנה pi. *cause to happen* Ex 21_{13} Si 15_{13}, כלה pi. *complete* Gn 2_2 4QJub^a 5_2 ([כלה ... אלהים]), יכל *be able* 2 C 32_{14}, ברא *create* Gn $1_{1.21.27}$ 2_3 Dt 4_{32} Si 15_{14}, בנה *build* Ps 69_{36}.

נגע *touch* 1 S 10_{26}, בדל hi. *divide* Gn 1_4 Nm 16_9, בקע *split* Jg 15_{19}, נער pi. *shake* trans. Ne 5_{13}, פזר pi. *scatter* bones Ps 53_6, פרץ *break through* 1 C 14_{11} (||2 S 5_{20} י׳ Y.), טמטם pi. *block* Si 10_{16}, נכה hi. *strike* 1 S 4_8 2 S 6_7 (|| י׳) 1 C 14_{15} Si 10_{13}, נגף *strike* 2 C 13_{15}, מחץ *shatter* Ps 68_{22}, שׁחט *slaughter* 4QapPs^b 31_6, חבל pi. *destroy* Ec 5_5, שׁמד hi. *destroy* 1 C 5_{25}, קעקע *destroy* Si 10_{16}, כרת hi. *cut off* Dt 12_{29} 19_1, בלע *swallow* 4QapPs^b 17_3 ([א]להי).

שׁלט hi. *empower* Ec 5_{18} 6_2, אמץ pi. *strengthen* Si 42_{17} perh. $45_{2(B)}$ (Bmg י׳ Y.), חזק pi. *strengthen* 4QJub^d 1.2_{32} ([יחזק]), כבד pi. *honour* perh. $45_{2(B, Segal)}$ ([ויכבדהו]; Bmg י׳ Y.), ענה hi. *occupy someone* Ec 5_{19}, עור hi. *arouse* Ezr 1_5 1 C 5_{26}, שׂמח pi. *gladden* Ne 12_{43}, רצה *desire* Ec 9_7, חפץ *desire* Ps 115_3, חמד *desire* 68_{17}, שׂוש *rejoice* Is 62_5, עבר htp. *be angry* Ps 78_{59}, קצף *be angry* Ec 5_5, שׂנא *hate* Si $15_{13(B)}$ (A י׳ Y.), נחם ni. *regret* Jon $3_{9.10}$.

ראה *see* Gn 1_{4+6t} 6_{12} 22_8 31_{42} Ex 2_{25} Jon 3_{10} Ps 53_3 1 C 12_{18}, ni. *appear* Gn 35_9 2 C 1_7 (||1 K 3_5 י׳ Y.), hi. *show* Gn 48_{11} Ps 59_{11}, שׁקף hi. *look down* Ps 53_3 (+ מִשָּׁמַיִם *from heaven*), יפע hi. *send light* Ps 50_2, אור hi. *cause to shine* 4QShir^b 18.2_8 (ה[א]יר), גלה ni. *reveal oneself* Gn 35_9, שׁמע *hear* $21_{17.17}$ $30_{17.22}$ Ex 2_{24} Jg 9_7 13_9 Mc 7_7 Ps 66_{19} 78_{59} 4QapPs^b 31_4 ([אל]הי), עתר ni. *accept supplication* 2 S 21_{14}.

בוא *come* Gn 20_3 31_{24} Ex 20_{20} Nm $22_{9.20}$ 1 S 4_7 Ps 50_3, hi. *bring* Ec 11_9 12_{14} Ne 13_{18} 1 C 4_{10} Si 10_{13} ([ויבא]), הלך *go* 2 S 7_{23}||1 C 17_{21}, יצא *go out* Ps 60_{12} ||108_{12} (|| אֱלֹהִים) 1 C 14_{15} (||2 S 5_{24} י׳ Y.), hi. *let out* Ps 68_7, סור *turn* from 1 S 28_{15}, שׁוב *turn* from Jon $3_{9.9}$ 4QApocMos B 1.1_3, hi. *return* (trans.), *repay* Jg $9_{56.57}$ Ps 68_7, פקד *visit* Gn $50_{24.25}$ Ex 13_{19}, עלה *go up* Gn 17_{22}

35$_{13}$ Ps 47$_6$ (|| י׳ *Y.*), קרה ni. *meet* Ex 5$_3$ Nm 23$_4$, פלל pi. perh. *intervene* 1 S 2$_{25}$, מהר pi. *hurry* Gn 41$_{32}$, קדם pi. *precede* Ps 59$_{11}$, אסף pi. *act as rear guard* Is 52$_{12}$, נחה *lead* Ex 13$_{17}$, שׁלח *send* Gn 45$_{5.7}$ Ex 3$_{13}$ Jg 9$_{23}$ Ps 57$_4$ Ne 6$_{12}$ 1 C 21$_{15}$ 4QapPs^b 29$_4$ 33$_4$, עבר hi. *send across* Gn 8$_1$, תעה hi. *cause to wander* 20$_{13}$, סבב hi. *cause to wander* Ex 13$_{18}$, נצב ni. *stand* Ps 82$_1$ (+ בַּעֲדַת־אֵל *in the assembly of God*), ישׁב *sit, dwell* 1 K 8$_{27}$||2 C 6$_{18}$ (+ אֶת־הָאָדָם *with human beings*) Ps 47$_9$ (|| אֱלֹהִים), hi. *seat* Si 10$_{14}$, קום *arise* Ps 68$_2$ 74$_{22}$ 76$_{10}$ 4QapPs^b 24$_6$ ([א]להי) 50$_4$ ([אלהים]), hi. *establish, raise* 1 K 11$_{23}$, כון pol. *establish* Ps 48$_9$, hi. *establish* Jb 28$_{23(mss)}$ (L בין hi. *understand*) 2 C 29$_{36}$, פתה hi. *enlarge* Gn 9$_{27}$, רעה *shepherd* Gn 48$_{15}$, ירה hi. *shoot* Ps 64$_8$, *teach* Is 28$_{26}$.

נתן *give, place, allow* Gn 1$_{17}$ 27$_{28}$ 28$_4$ 30$_{18}$ 31$_7$ 43$_{23}$ 48$_9$ Jg 7$_{14}$ 8$_3$ 18$_{10}$ 1 S 1$_{17}$ 23$_{14}$ 1 K 5$_9$ 10$_{24}$||2 C 9$_{23}$ Ec 1$_{13}$ 3$_{10}$ 5$_{17.18}$ 6$_2$ 8$_{15}$ Dn 1$_{9.17}$ Ne 2$_{12}$ 7$_5$ (both + אֶל־לִבִּי *into my mind*) 13$_{26}$ 1 C 14$_{10}$ 25$_5$ 2 C 13$_{16}$ 18$_5$ (||1 K 22$_6$ אֲדֹנָי *my Lord*) 32$_{29}$ Si 15$_{14}$ 4Q525 1$_1$ (אלוה[ים]) 4QapPs^b 45$_6$, סגר pi. *hand over* 1 S 26$_8$, זבד perh. *give present to* Gn 30$_{20}$, לקח *take* 5$_{24}$ Ps 49$_{16}$, נצל hi. *take away, rescue* Gn 31$_{9.16}$ 2 C 32$_{14}$ (||2 K 18$_{35}$||Is 36$_{20}$ י׳ *Y.*, :: אֱלֹהִים *god*) 32$_{15}$ (:: אֱלוֹהַּ *god*) 32$_{17}$ (:: אֱלֹהִים *god*), אסף *take away* Gn 30$_{23}$, מצא *find* 44$_{16}$, שׂים *place* 45$_9$ 48$_{20}$ Nm 22$_{38}$, שׁית *place* Gn 4$_{25}$ Si 15$_{14}$, הפך *overturn* 1 S 10$_9$ Ne 13$_2$ Si 10$_{14}$, כשׁל hi. *cause to stumble* 2 C 25$_{8.8}$, שׁפל hi. *make low* Ps 75$_8$, נשׂא *raise* 2 S 14$_{14}$, ni. *be exalted* 4QapPs^b 33$_2$ ([תנשא]).

חשׁב *reckon* Gn 50$_{20}$, עשׁת htp. *consider* Jon 1$_6$, ידע *know* Gn 3$_5$ Ex 2$_{25}$ 2 C 32$_{31}$, ni. *be known* Ps 48$_4$ 76$_2$ Jb 28$_{23}$ 4QapPs^b 48$_7$, hi. *inform* Gn 41$_{39}$, בין *understand* Ps 94$_7$ (|| יָהּ *Y.*) Jb 28$_{23}$ (hi.; mss כון hi. *establish*), זכר *remember* Gn 8$_1$ 19$_{29}$ 30$_{22}$ Ex 2$_{24}$, נשׁה pi. *cause to forget* Gn 41$_{51}$.

חקר *search* Ps 44$_{22}$, בקשׁ pi. *seek* Ec 3$_{15}$, נסה pi. *test* Gn 22$_1$ Ex 20$_{20}$, שׁפט *judge* Gn 31$_{53}$ Ps 7$_{12}$ (|| אֵל *God*) 50$_6$ Ps 58$_{12}$ 75$_8$ 82$_1$ (+ בְּקֶרֶב אֱלֹהִים *among the gods*) Ec 3$_{17}$ 4QShir^b 18.2$_{10}$, דין *judge* Gn 30$_6$, לחם ni. *fight* Ne 4$_{14}$, ריב *contest* Ps 74$_{22}$, יכח hi. *reprove* 1 C 12$_{18}$, רשׁע hi. *condemn* Ex 22$_8$, פרר hi. *thwart* Ne 4$_9$, נכר pi. perh. *trick* 1 S 23$_7$ (or em. סִגַּר *delivered*), נשׁא hi. *deceive* 2 K 19$_{10}$||Is 37$_{10}$, המם *confuse* 2 C 15$_6$, שׁלם pi. *repay* Jg 1$_7$, מאס *reject* Ho 9$_{17}$ Ps 53$_6$ 78$_{59}$, זנח *reject* 60$_{12}$||108$_{12}$ (|| אֱלֹהִים), עזב *abandon* 71$_{11}$ Ezr 9$_9$ 2 C 32$_{31}$ 4QapPs^b 79$_6$ 4Q372 1$_{16}$ (|| אָב *father*), כנע hi. *subdue* Jg 4$_{23}$.

אמר *say* Gn 1$_{3+8t}$ 3$_{1.3}$ 6$_{13}$ 9$_{1.8.12.17}$ 17$_{9.15.19}$ 20$_6$ (+ בַּחֲלֹם *in the dream*) 21$_{12}$ 22$_{3.9}$ 31$_{16.24.29}$ 35$_{1.10.11}$ 43$_{29}$ 46$_{2.2}$ Ex 3$_{14.14.15}$ 13$_{17}$ 20$_1$ Nm 22$_{12}$ 2 S 23$_3$ 1 K 3$_{5.11}$||2 C 1$_{7.11}$ Is 40$_1$ 54$_6$ 57$_{21}$ 66$_9$ (|| י׳ *Y.*) Jon 4$_9$ Ps 50$_{16}$ 1 C 14$_{14}$ 28$_3$ 2 C 18$_{13}$ (||1 K 22$_{14}$ י׳ אֵלַי *Y.* says *to me* for אֱלֹהַי) 24$_{20}$ (+ כֹּה *thus*) 33$_7$ (||2 K 21$_7$ י׳) 35$_{21}$ 4QpGen^a 1$_1$ ([א]מר), דבר pi. *speak* Gn 8$_{15}$ 17$_{3.23}$ 21$_2$ 35$_{15}$ Ex 6$_2$ 20$_{1.19}$ Dt 5$_{24}$ Ps 60$_8$ 62$_{12}$ 108$_8$, קרא *call* Gn 1$_{5.5.8.10.10}$ Ex 3$_4$, ענה *answer* Gn 41$_{16}$ Ex 19$_{19}$ (+ בְּקוֹל *in thunder*) 1 S 28$_{15}$ 4QapPs^b 24$_8$, מנה pi. *appoint* Jon 4$_{7.8}$, יעד *appoint* 4QShir^b 2.2$_7$, משׁח *anoint* Ps 45$_8$, קדשׁ hi. *sanctify* 4QShir^b 35$_3$ (יקד[שׁ]), צוה pi. *command* Gn 7$_{9.16}$ 21$_4$ Ex 18$_{23}$ Ps 68$_{29}$ 1 C 14$_{16}$ (||2 S 5$_{25}$ י׳) 4Q385 1$_7$ 4QApoc Mos B 1.1$_1$, יעץ *advise* 2 C 25$_{16}$, חרשׁ *be silent* Ps 50$_3$.

ברך *bless* Ps 45$_3$, pass. be *blessed* 66$_{20}$ 68$_{36}$ 4QPsJos^b 22.2$_5$, pi. *bless* Gn 1$_{22.28}$ 2$_3$ 9$_1$ 25$_{11}$ Ps 67$_{2.7.8}$ 1 C 26$_5$, חנן *show favour* Gn 33$_{5.11}$ 43$_{29}$ Ps 67$_2$, רחם pi. *show mercy* 116$_5$ (|| י׳ *Y.*) GnzPs 2$_3$, בחר *choose* 1 C 29$_1$ 4QApoc Mos B 1.1$_8$, יטב hi. *be good to* Ex 1$_{20}$ 1 K 1$_{47}$, פרה hi. *make fruitful* Gn 41$_{52}$, צלח hi. *make prosper* 2 C 26$_5$, עזר *help* Ps 46$_6$ (|| אֱלֹהִים) 54$_6$ (|| אֲדֹנָי *my Lord*) 1 C 12$_{19}$ 2 C 25$_8$ 26$_7$ 4QapPs^b 15$_3$ ([א]להי), רפא *heal* Gn 20$_{17}$, פקח *open* someone's eyes 21$_{19}$, פדה *redeem* 2 S 7$_{23}$||1 C 17$_{21}$ Ps 49$_{16}$, ישׁע hi. *rescue* 69$_{36}$ 4QShir^b 1$_9$ (הושׁ[י]ע ה[אלוה]ים), נוח hi. *give peace to* 2 C 20$_{30}$.

היה *be* Gn 21$_{20}$ (+ אֵת *with*) 28$_{20}$ 31$_5$ (both + עִם *with*) 31$_{42}$ 48$_{21}$ Ex 18$_{19}$ (both + עִם) Is 49$_5$ (+ עֻזִּי *my strength*) 60$_{19}$ (+ לְתִפְאַרְתֵּךְ *as your beauty*, || י׳ *Y.*) Ps 94$_{22}$ (+ לְצוּר מַחְסִי *as the rock of my refuge*, || י׳) Ezr 1$_3$ (+ עִם *with*), גדל *be great* Ps 70$_5$, רום *be exalted* 2 S 22$_{47}$||Ps 18$_{47}$, hi. *raise* Ps 75$_8$, ירא ni. *be terrifying* 68$_{36}$, מלך *reign* Is 52$_7$ Ps 47$_9$ (|| אֱלֹהִים), משׁל *govern* 59$_{14}$.

<NOM CL> יֵשׁ(־)אֱלֹהִים *there is a God* 1 S 17$_{46}$ (+ לְיִשְׂרָאֵל *[belonging] to Israel* [mss בְּיִשְׂרָאֵל *in Israel*]) Ps 58$_{12}$, [אנכי אלהי ישראל] *I am the God of Israel* 4QJub^a 4$_9$, חַי הָאֱלֹהִים *(as) God is alive* 2 S 2$_{27}$, אֵין אֱלֹהִים *there is no God* Ps 14$_1$||53$_2$, אַיֵּה אֱלֹהֵיהֶם *where is their God?* Jl 2$_{17}$ Ps 79$_{10}$, sim. Ps 42$_{4.11}$ 115$_2$, אֱלֹהִים עִמְּךָ *God is with you* Gn 21$_{22}$, sim. 1 S 10$_7$ Zc 8$_{23}$ 1 C 17$_2$ (||2 S 7$_3$ י׳ *Y.*),

עִמָּנוּ בָרֹאשׁ הָאֱלֹהִים *with us, as our head, is God* 2 C 13$_{12}$ (+ כֹּהֵן *priest*), אֱלֹהִים בְּדוֹר צַדִּיק *God is with a righteous generation* Ps 14$_5$, י׳ אֱלֹהֶיךָ הוּא הָאֱלֹהִים *Y. your God—he is God* Dt 7$_9$, אֱלֹהִים עֵד *God is witness* Gn 31$_{50}$, מֶלֶךְ כָּל־הָאָרֶץ אֱלֹהִים *God is king of all the world* Ps 47$_8$, אֱלֹהֵי אָבִי בְּעֶזְרִי *the God of my father was as a help to me* Ex 18$_4$, אֱלֹהִים לִי *God is for me* Ps 56$_{10}$, עַמֵּךְ עַמִּי וֵאלֹהַיִךְ אֱלֹהָי *your people are my people and your God is my God* Ru 1$_{16}$, אֱלֹהִים בְּקִרְבָּהּ *God is among her* Ps 46$_6$, sim. Dt 31$_{17}$, מְעֹנָה אֱלֹהֵי קֶדֶם *the God of old is a refuge* 33$_{27}$, אֱלֹהִים לָנוּ מַחֲסֶה וָעֹז *God is for us a refuge and strength* Ps 46$_2$, sim. 62$_9$, מִשְׂגָּב־לָנוּ אֱלֹהֵי יַעֲקֹב *the God of Jacob is a refuge for us* 46$_{8.12}$ (both || י׳ צְבָאוֹת *Y. of Hosts*), אֱלֹהִים מִשְׂגַּבִּי *God is my refuge* 59$_{10.18}$, אֱלֹהִים צוּרָם *God is their rock* 78$_{35}$ (|| אֵל עֶלְיוֹן *God Most High*), חֶלְקִי אֱלֹהִים *my portion is God* 73$_{26}$, וֵאלֹהֵינוּ בַשָּׁמַיִם *and our God is in heaven* 115$_3$, הָאֱלֹהִים בַּשָּׁמַיִם וְאַתָּה עַל־הָאָרֶץ *God is in heaven and you are on the earth* Ec 5$_1$, הָעֲרָפֶל אֲשֶׁר־שָׁם אֱלֹהִים *the cloud where God is* Ex 20$_{21}$.

<OBJ> עבד *serve* Ex 3$_{12}$ Jos 24$_{15}$ (:: אֱלֹהִים *gods*) Ml 3$_{14}$, שׁרת pi. *minister to* Is 61$_6$ Jl 1$_{13}$ (both + כֹּהֵן *priest*), ירא *fear, revere* Gn 22$_{12}$ 42$_{18}$ Ex 1$_{17.21}$ 18$_{21}$=11QT 57$_8$ Dt 25$_{18}$ Ml 3$_{18}$ Ps 55$_{20}$ 66$_{16}$ Jb 1$_{1.8.9}$ 2$_3$ Ec 5$_6$ 7$_{18}$ 8$_{12}$ 12$_{13}$ Ne 7$_2$ 1 C 13$_{12}$ (||2 S 6$_9$ י׳ Y.) Si 10$_{20.24}$ (מ[י]רא), ערץ hi. *fear* Is 29$_{23}$, ידע *know* Ho 13$_4$ Dn 11$_{32}$ 1 C 28$_9$, זכר *remember* Ps 77$_4$ 4QJub[d] 1.1$_{14}$ ([זכרתי ... א]לוהינו), דרש *seek* Ex 18$_{15}$ 1 S 9$_9$ Ps 14$_2$ 53$_3$ 69$_{33}$ 1 C 21$_{30}$ 2 C 19$_3$ 26$_5$ 30$_{19}$, בקשׁ pi. *ask* 2 S 12$_{16}$, קרא *call* Ps 53$_5$ (||14$_5$ י׳ Y.), בחן *test* Ml 3$_{15}$, נסה pi. *test* Ps 78$_{56}$ 2 C 32$_{31}$, הלל pi. *praise* Ps 147$_{12}$ (|| י׳ Y.) Si 51$_1$ 4QShirShab[d] 1.1$_{30}$ 4Q372 1$_{26}$, זמר pi. *laud* Ps 47$_{7.7}$ (|| מַלְכֵּנוּ *our King*) 147$_1$ 4QShirShab[d] 1.1$_{42}$, ידה hi. *praise* Si 51$_1$ (א[ו]דיך), גדל hi. *magnify* 11QapPs[a] 1$_7$ (להגד[יל אל]והי), ברך pi. *bless* Jos 22$_{33}$ Ps 66$_8$ 68$_{27}$ (|| י׳ Y.) Si 50$_{22}$, *curse* 1 K 21$_{10.13}$ (both || מֶלֶךְ *king*) Jb 1$_5$ 2$_9$, חרף pi. *scorn* 1 S 17$_{45}$ 2 K 19$_{4.16}$||Is 37$_{4.17}$, נאץ pi. *scorn* Ps 10$_{13}$, קלל pi. *curse* Ex 22$_{27}$ Lv 24$_{15}$, לאה hi. *weary* Is 7$_{13}$ (:: אֲנָשִׁים *men*).

שׁכח *forget* Is 17$_{10}$ Ps 9$_{18}$, מאס *reject* 1 S 10$_{19}$, עזב *desert* Jg 10$_{10}$ (:: בְּעָלִים *Baals*), מרה *rebel against* Ps 78$_{56}$, ראה *see* Gn 32$_{31}$ Ex 24$_{10}$ Jg 13$_{22}$ Is 64$_3$ 2 C 26$_5$ (mss בְּיִרְאַת *in the fear of*), חזה *behold* Ex 24$_{11}$, שׂים *set* Ps 52$_9$ (+ מָעוּזּוֹ as *his refuge*) 54$_5$ (+ לְנֶגְדָּם *in front of them*), פקד *visit* Si 46$_{14}$.

<CSTR> אֱלֹהִים אֱלֹהֵי יִשְׂרָאֵל *God, God of Israel* Ps 68$_9$ (|| אֱלֹהִים זֶה סִינַי *God of Sinai*) 72$_{18}$ (+ י׳ Y.) Ezr 6$_{22}$, י׳ אֱלֹהֵי(־)יִשְׂרָאֵל *Y., God of Israel* Ex 5$_1$ 32$_{27}$ 34$_{23}$ Jos 7$_{13.19.20}$ 8$_{30}$ 9$_{18.19}$ 10$_{40.42}$ 13$_{14.33}$ 14$_{14}$ 22$_{24}$ 24$_{2.23}$ Jg 4$_6$ 5$_{3.5}$ 6$_8$ 11$_{21.23}$ 21$_3$ 1 S 2$_{30}$ 10$_{18}$ 14$_{41}$ 20$_{12}$ 23$_{10.11}$ 25$_{32.34}$ 2 S 12$_7$ 1 K 1$_{30.48}$ 8$_{15.17.20.23.25}$||2 C 6$_{4.7.10.14.16}$ 1 K 11$_{9.31}$ 14$_{7.13}$ 15$_{30}$ 16$_{13.26.33}$ 17$_{1.14}$ 22$_{54}$ 2 K 9$_6$ 10$_{31}$ 14$_{25}$ 18$_5$ 19$_{15}$||Is 37$_{16}$ (י׳ צְבָאוֹת) 2 K 19$_{20}$||Is 37$_{21}$ 2 K 21$_{12}$ 22$_{15.18}$||2 C 34$_{23.26}$ Is 17$_6$ 21$_{17}$ 24$_{15}$ Jr 11$_3$ 13$_{12}$ 21$_4$ 23$_2$ 24$_5$ 25$_{15}$ 30$_2$ 32$_{36}$ 33$_4$ 34$_{2.13}$ 37$_7$ 42$_9$ 45$_2$ Ezk 44$_2$ Ml 2$_{16}$ Ps 41$_{14}$ 106$_{48}$=1 C 16$_{36}$ Ru 2$_{12}$ Ezr 1$_3$ 4$_{1.3}$ 6$_{21}$ 7$_6$ 9$_{15}$ 1 C 15$_{12.14}$ 16$_4$ 22$_6$ 23$_{25}$ 24$_{19}$ 28$_4$ 29$_{10}$ 2 C 2$_{11}$ 6$_{17}$ 11$_{16}$ 13$_5$ 15$_{4.13}$ 20$_{19}$ 29$_{10}$ 30$_{1.5}$ 32$_{17}$ 33$_{16.18}$ 36$_{13}$ Si 50$_{22}$ 4Q522 24 (אלוהי) 4QpsJos[b] 22.2$_5$ (י[שראל]).

י׳ צְבָאוֹת אֱלֹהֵי יִשְׂרָאֵל *Y. of hosts, God of Israel* 2 S 7$_{27}$ Is 21$_{10}$ 37$_{16}$ Jr 7$_{3.21}$ 9$_{14}$ 16$_9$ 19$_{3.15}$ 25$_{27}$ 27$_{4.21}$ 28$_{2.14}$ 29$_{4.8.21.25}$ 31$_{23}$ 32$_{14.15}$ 35$_{13.18.19}$ 39$_{16}$ 42$_{15.18}$ 43$_{10}$ 44$_{2.11.25}$ 46$_{25}$ 48$_1$ 50$_{18}$ 51$_{33}$ Zp 2$_9$ 1 C 17$_{24}$.

אֱלֹהֵי(־)יִשְׂרָאֵל *God of Israel* (without י׳ צְבָאוֹת *Y. of hosts*) Gn 33$_{20}$ (+ אֵל *God*) Ex 24$_{10}$ Nm 16$_9$ Jos 22$_{16}$ 1 S 1$_{17}$ 5$_{7.8.10.11}$ 6$_{3.5}$ 2 S 23$_3$ 1 K 8$_{26}$ Is 29$_{23}$ (|| קְדוֹשׁ יַעֲקֹב *the Holy One of Jacob*) 41$_{17}$ 45$_{3.15}$ 48$_1$ (|| י׳ *Y.*) 48$_2$ 52$_{12}$ (|| י׳) Jr 35$_{17}$ 38$_{17}$ 44$_7$ Ezk 8$_4$ 9$_3$ 10$_{19.20}$ 11$_{22}$ 43$_2$ Ps 59$_6$ (+ י׳־אֱלֹהִים צְבָאוֹת *Y. the God, Sebaoth*) 69$_7$ (+ אֲדֹנָי י׳ צְבָאוֹת *my Lord Y. of hosts*) Ezr 3$_2$ 8$_{35}$ 9$_4$ 1 C 4$_{10}$ 5$_{26}$ 2 C 29$_7$ 4QJub[a] 4$_9$ ([אלהי ישראל]).

י׳ אֱלֹהֵי(־)צְבָאוֹת *Y., God of hosts* 2 S 5$_{10}$ 1 K 19$_{10.14}$ Jr 5$_{14}$ 15$_{16}$ 35$_{17}$ 38$_{17}$ 44$_7$ (all three + אֱלֹהֵי יִשְׂרָאֵל *God of Israel*) Ho 12$_6$ Am 3$_{13}$ (both הַצּ׳) 4$_{13}$ 5$_{14.15.16.27}$ 6$_{8.14}$ (הַצּ׳) Ps 89$_9$, י׳ צְבָאוֹת אֱלֹהֵי מַעַרְכוֹת יִשְׂרָאֵל *Y. of hosts, God of the battle-lines of Israel* 1 S 17$_{45}$, אֱלֹהֵי הָאֱלֹהִים *the God of gods* Dt 10$_{17}$ (|| אָדוֹן *lord*) Ps 136$_2$ 4QShir[b] 8$_{12}$ ([אל]והי ה[א]ל[והים]), אלוהי [אלוהי]ך *God of your gods* (unless app., *God, your God*) 1QDM 2$_{1(Milik)}$, sim. 2$_{6(Milik)}$, אלוהי אלים *God of gods* 4QShir[b] 16$_4$ ([אל]ים) 4QShirShab[a] 1.1$_{20}$ ([א]ל[וה]י) 4QShirShab[c] 4$_8$ 9$_2$ ([א]לוהי אלי[ם]) 4QShirShab[d] 1.1$_{26}$ ([א]ל[ו]ה[י]) MasShirShab 1$_9$ ([א]ל[וה]י) 11QShirShab 5$_5$ c$_1$ ([אל]והי) m$_5$ ([אל]ים) 11QapPs[a] 1$_{11}$ ([אלוהי אלים]), אֱלֹהֵי אָמֵן *God of reliability*, perh. the real God Is 65$_{16}$, אֱלֹהֵי אֱמֶת *God of truth*, i.e. the true God 2 C 15$_3$,

אלהי הכל *God of all* Si 33_{1} 45_{23} (אלוה[י] כל) 5QRègle 1 2 ([א]לוהי הכול), אלוהי דעות *God of knowledge* 4QShir^{a} 1_{2}, אלוהי פלא *God of wonder* 4QShir^{a} 1_{8}, אֱלֹהֵי עוֹלָם *God of eternity* Is 40_{28} 11QShirShab 5_{3} ([עול]מים), אֱלֹהֵי קֶדֶם *God of old* Dt 33_{27}, אֱלֹהֵי הַשָּׁמַיִם *God of heaven* Gn $24_{3.7}$ Jon 1_{9} Ezr 1_{2}||2 C 36_{23} Ne $1_{4.5}$ $2_{4.20}$, אֱלֹהֵי מָרוֹם *God of height*, the highest God Mc 6_{6} 4QShirShab^{d} 1.1_{30} (אלוהי מרומים), אֱלֹהֵי הָאָרֶץ *God of the earth/land* Gn 24_{3} 2 K $17_{26.26.27}$ (all three + מִשְׁפַּט *the law of*), אֱלֹהֵי כָל־הָאָרֶץ *God of all the earth* Is 54_{5} Kh. Beit Lei graf. $5_{1(Naveh)}$ (+ י׳ *Y.*), אֱלֹהֵי כָּל־בָּשָׂר *God of all flesh* Jr 32_{27}, אֱלֹהֵי הָרוּחֹת לְכָל־בָּשָׂר *God of the spirits of all flesh* Nm 16_{22} 27_{16}.

[אלו]הי קו[דש] *God of holiness* 4QShirShab^{d} 1.1_{6}, [א]לוהי כול קודש[ים] *God of all holinesses* 4QPrQuot 37_{3}, אלוהי [מ]לאכי רום *God of (the) angels of height* 4QShirShab^{d} 1.1_{1}, אלו[הי נ]ורא כוח *God of*, i.e. who is, *one that is terrible of might* 1.1_{41}, [א]לוהי ישע *God of salvation* 4QShir^{a} 2_{2}, אֱלֹהֵי יִשְׁעִי (and vars.) *God of my* (etc.) *salvation* Is 17_{10} Mc 7_{7} Hb 3_{18} Ps 24_{5} 25_{5} 27_{9} 65_{6} 79_{9} 85_{5} 1 C 16_{35} Si 51_{1}, אֱלֹהֵי יְשׁוּעָתִי *God of my salvation* Ps 88_{2}, אֱלֹהֵי תְּשׁוּעָתִי *God of my salvation* 51_{16}, אֱלֹהֵי צוּר יִשְׁעִי *God of the rock of my salvation* 2 S 22_{47}, אֱלֹהֵי צוּרִי *God of my rock*, i.e. my strong God 22_{3}, אלוהי צדק *God of righteousness* 4QShir^{b} 1_{5}, אלוהי דעת *God of knowledge* 4QShirShab^{a} 2_{8} 4QShirShab^{b} 11_{2} ([א]לוהי) 4QShirShab^{c} 4_{12} 4QShirShab^{f} 23.2_{12}, אֱלֹהֵי מָעוּזִּי *God of my refuge*, i.e. who is my refuge Ps 43_{2}, אֱלֹהֵי צִדְקִי *God of my justification* 4_{2}, אֱלֹהֵי חַסְדִּי *God of my loyalty*, i.e. who is loyal to me $59_{11(Qr).18}$, אֱלֹהֵי תְהִלָּתִי *God of my praise* 109_{1}, אֱלֹהֵי מִשְׁפָּט *God of justice* Is 30_{18} Ml 2_{17} (הַמִּשְׁפָּט) Si 32_{15}, אלהי הרחמן *the God of compassion* GnzPs 2_{3}, אלוהי עז *God of strength* 4QShirShab^{d} 1.1_{39}, אלוהי גבורות *God of strengths* 4Q Shir^{b} 2.2_{7} (אלוה[י] גבו[ר]ות) 4QShirShab^{d} 1.1_{2}.

י׳ אֱלֹהֵי(־)הָעִבְרִים *Y., God of the Hebrews* Ex 3_{18} (עִבְרִיִּים) 5_{3} (אֱלֹהֵי הָעִבְרִים) 7_{16} $9_{1.13}$ 10_{3}, אֱלֹהֵי יְרוּשָׁלִַם *the God of Jerusalem* 2 C 32_{19} Kh. Beit Lei graf. $5_{2(Naveh)}$ (ירשלם), אֱלֹהֵי אָבִי (and vars.) *God of my* (etc.) *ancestor* Gn $31_{5.29.42}$ $32_{10.10}$ 43_{23} $46_{1.3}$ 50_{17} Ex 3_{6} 15_{2} 18_{4} 1 C 28_{9} 2 C 17_{4} Si 51_{1}, י׳ אֱלֹהֵי אֲבֹתֵיכֶם (and vars.) *Y., God of your* (etc.) *ancestors* Ex 3_{13} (lacks י׳) $3_{15.16}$ 4_{5} Dt $1_{11.21}$ 4_{1} 6_{3} 12_{1} 26_{7} 27_{3} 29_{24} Jos 18_{3} Jg 2_{12} 2 K 21_{22} Ezr 7_{27} 8_{28} 10_{11} 1 C 5_{25} 12_{18} (both lack י׳) 29_{20} 2 C 7_{22} 11_{16} $13_{12.18}$ 14_{3} 15_{12} 19_{4} $20_{6.33}$ (lacks י׳) 21_{10} $24_{18.24}$ $28_{6.9.25}$ 29_{5} $30_{7.19.22}$ 33_{12} (lacks י׳) 34_{32} (lacks י׳) 34_{33} 36_{15} 11QT 54_{13} 4Q385 1_{8} (lacks י׳).

אֱלֹהֵי *God of* + pr.n.m., Shem Gn 9_{26}, Nahor Gn 31_{53}, Abraham Gn $24_{12.27.42.48}$ (all אֲדֹנִי אַבְרָהָם *of my lord Abraham*) 26_{24} 28_{13} $31_{42.53}$ Ex $3_{6.15}$ 4_{5} Ps 47_{10} (+ עַם *the people of*), Isaac Gn 28_{13} Ex $3_{6.15}$ 4_{5}, Jacob Ex $3_{6.15}$ 4_{5} 2 S 23_{1} Is 2_{3} Ps 20_{2} $46_{8.12}$ 75_{10} 76_{7} $81_{2.5}$ 84_{9} 94_{7} Si 46_{14}, David 2 K 20_{5}||Is 38_{5} 2 C 21_{12} 34_{3}, Hezekiah 2 C 32_{17}, Elijah 2 K 2_{14}; י׳ אֱלֹהֵי אַבְרָהָם יִצְחָק וְיִשְׂרָאֵל *Y. the God of Abraham, Isaac, and Israel* 1 K 18_{36} 1 C 29_{18} 2 C 30_{6}, אֱלֹהֵי אַבְרָהָם יִצְחָק וְיַעֲקֹב *the God of Abraham, Isaac, and Jacob* Ex 3_{16}, י׳ אֱלֹהֵי אֲדֹנִי הַמֶּלֶךְ *Y. the God of my lord the King* 1 K 1_{36}.

אֱלֹהֵי הָרִים *God of mountains* 1 K $20_{23.28}$, אֱלֹהֵי עֲמָקִים *God of valleys* 20_{28}, אֱלֹהֵי אוֹרִים *God of lights* 4QPrQuot 13_{1} 4QShirShab^{f} 46_{2} (אלוהי), אלוהי הנכבדים *God of the honoured ones* 4QShirShab^{a} 3.2_{8}.

עִיר אֱלֹהִים *city of God*, i.e. Jerusalem Ps 46_{5} (עִיר־) 48_{2} (אֱלֹהֵינוּ) 48_{9} (אֱלֹהֵינוּ; || י׳ *Y.*) 87_{3} (הָאֱלֹהִים), עָרֵי אֱלֹהֵינוּ *cities of our God* 2 S 10_{12}||1 C 19_{13}, מִקְדַּשׁ אֱלֹהָיו *sanctuary of his God* Lv 21_{12}=11QT 35_{7} ([מ]קדש אלוהיהמה), חַצְרוֹת אֱלֹהֵינוּ *courtyards of our God* Ps 92_{14} (mss חַצְרוֹת בֵּית *courtyards of the house of*; || י׳), בֵּית אֱלֹהִים *house*, i.e. temple, shrine, *of God* Gn 28_{17} (|| שַׁעַר הַשָּׁמָיִם *gate of heaven*) 28_{22} Ps 42_{5} 52_{10} 55_{15} 2 C 34_{9} (בֵּית־; ||2 K 22_{4} י׳ *Y.*) 4Q385 1_{4} (אלוהים), vars. (בֵּית הָאֱלֹהִים etc.) Jos 9_{23} Jg 17_{5} 18_{31} Is 2_{3} Ho 9_{8} Jl $1_{13.16}$ Am 2_{8} Mc 4_{2} (|| י׳ *Y.*) Ps 84_{11} $92_{14(mss)}$ 135_{2} (|| י׳ *Y.*) Ec 4_{17} Dn 1_{2} Ezr $1_{4.7}$ 2_{68} $3_{8.9}$ 6_{22} $8_{17.25.30.33.36}$ 9_{9} $10_{1.6.9}$ Ne 6_{10} 8_{16} 10_{33+6t} 11_{11}||1 C 9_{11} Ne $11_{16.22}$ 12_{40} $13_{4.7.9.11.14}$ 1 C 6_{33} $9_{13.26.27}$ 22_{2} 23_{28} (|| י׳ *Y.*) 25_{6} 26_{20} $28_{12.21}$ $29_{2.3.3.7}$ 2 C 3_{3} (||1 K 6_{1} בַּיִת לַי׳ *temple for Y.*) $4_{11.19}$ $5_{1.14}$ 7_{5} 15_{18} 22_{12} $23_{3.9}$ (||1 K $7_{40.48.51}$ $8_{11.63}$ 15_{15} 2 K $11_{3.4.10}$ י׳ *Y.*) $24_{5.7.13.27}$ 25_{24} (||2 K 14_{14} י׳) $28_{24.24}$ $31_{13.21}$ 33_{7} 35_{8} $36_{18.19}$.

[ממלכ]ות אלוהים *kingdoms of God* 4Q525 5_{3}, אֲרוֹן הָאֱלֹהִים *the ark of God* (and vars.) 1 S 3_{3} 4_{11+6t} 5_{1+5t} 6_{3} 14_{18} 2 S $6_{2.3}$|| 1 C $13_{6.7}$ 2 S $6_{4.6.7.12}$ 7_{2} $15_{24.25.29}$ 1 C $13_{3.5.12.14}$ (||2 S $6_{9.11}$ י׳ *Y.*) $15_{1.2.15.24}$ 16_{1} (||2 S 6_{17} י׳) 2 C

14, אֲרוֹן בְּרִית הָאֱלֹהִים *ark of the covenant of God* Jg 20$_{27}$ 1 S 4$_4$ 2 S 15$_{24}$ 1 C 16$_6$ (בְּרִית־), מִזְבַּח אֱלֹהִים *altar of God* Ps 43$_4$ Ezr 3$_2$ (מִזְבַּח אֱלֹהֵי), הֲדֹם רַגְלֵי אֱלֹהֵינוּ *footstool of our God* 1 C 28$_2$, מַטֵּה הָאֱלֹהִים *staff of God* Ex 4$_{20}$ 17$_9$, רֶכֶב אֱלֹהִים *chariot of God* Ps 68$_{18}$, נֵר אֱלֹהִים *lamp of God* in sanctuary 1 S 3$_3$, כְּלֵי קֹדֶשׁ הָאֱלֹהִים *vessels of the holiness of God*, i.e. cultic utensils 1 C 22$_{19}$, כְּלֵי שִׁיר הָאֱלֹהִים *vessels of the song of God*, i.e. instruments for sacred music 16$_{42}$, מִכְתַּב אֱלֹהִים *God's writing* Ex 32$_{16}$.

הַר הָאֱלֹהִים *the mountain of God* Ex 3$_1$ (+ חֹרֵב *Horeb*) 4$_{27}$ 18$_5$ 24$_{13}$ 1 K 19$_8$ (+ חֹרֵב) Ezk 28$_{16}$ (הַר־אֱלֹהִים) Ps 68$_{16}$ (הַר־אֱלֹהִים; + הַר־בָּשָׁן *Mt Bashan*; perh., as §3a, *mountain of gods* or *holy mountain*) 4Q372 1$_8$ (אלהי), הַר קֹדֶשׁ אֱלֹהִים *mountain of (the) holiness of God*, i.e. God's holy mountain Ezk 28$_{14}$ Dn 9$_{20}$ (הַר־קֹדֶשׁ אֱלֹהָי), גִּבְעַת הָאֱלֹהִים *the hill of God*, unless pl.n., *Gibeath-elohim* 1 S 10$_5$, גַּן־אֱלֹהִים *garden of God* Ezk 28$_{13}$ (+ עֵדֶן *Eden*) 31$_{8.8.9}$ (גַּן הָאֱלֹהִים), נְאוֹת אֱלֹהִים *pastures of God* Ps 83$_{13}$ (or em. נְוַת/נְוֵה *dwelling place of*), פֶּלֶג אֱלֹהִים *stream of God* 65$_{10}$, נַחֲלַת אֱלֹהִים *inheritance of*, i.e. from, *God* 2 S 14$_{16}$ 4QShir^b 2.1$_5$ (אל[והי]ם), גורל אלוהים *lot of God* 2.1$_8$.

עַם אֱלֹהִים *people of God* 2 S 14$_{13}$ Ps 47$_{10}$ (עַם אֱלֹהֵי; or em. עִם אָהֳלֵי *with the tents of*), קְהַל הָאֱלֹהִים *the assembly of God* Ne 13$_1$, מַחֲנֵה אֱלֹהִים *camp of God* Gn 32$_3$ 1 C 12$_{23}$ (+ כְּ גָּדוֹל *as large as*), מַעַרְכוֹת אֱלֹהִים *battle-lines of God* 1 S 17$_{26.36}$ (מַעַרְכֹת), זֶרַע אֱלֹהִים *seed of God*, i.e. godly offspring Ml 2$_{15}$, אִישׁ הָאֱלֹהִים *the man of God* (and vars.) with ref. to Moses Dt 33$_1$ Jos 14$_6$ Ps 90$_1$ Ezr 3$_2$ 1 C 23$_{14}$ 2 C 30$_{16}$, David Ne 12$_{24.36}$ 2 C 8$_{14}$, Elijah 1 K 17$_{18.24}$ 2 K 1$_{9.10.11.12.13}$, Elisha 2 K 4$_{7+8t}$ 5$_{8.14.15.20}$ 6$_{6.9.10.15}$ 7$_{2.17.18.19}$ 8$_{2.4.7.8.11}$ 13$_{19}$, Samuel 1 S 9$_{6.7.8.10}$, Shemaiah 1 K 12$_{22}$||2 C 11$_2$, Igdaliah Jr 35$_4$, like an angel Jg 13$_{6.8}$, others 1 S 2$_{27}$ 1 K 13$_{1+14t}$ 20$_{28}$ 2 K 23$_{16.17}$ 2 C 25$_{7.9}$ 4QapPs^b 24$_4$ (האל[הי]ם), נְזִיר אֱלֹהִים *Nazirite of God*, with ref. to Samson Jg 13$_{5.7}$ 16$_{17}$, נֵזֶר אֱלֹהָיו *consecration as Nazirite of his God* Nm 6$_7$, נְשִׂיא אֱלֹהִים *prince of God* Gn 23$_6$, מֹשֶׁה עֶבֶד־הָאֱלֹהִים *Moses, the servant of God* Dn 9$_{11}$ Ne 10$_{30}$ 1 C 6$_{34}$ (עֶבֶד הָאֱלֹהִים) 2 C 24$_9$, עַבְדֵי אֱלֹהֵי אָבִיךָ *servants of the God of your father* Gn 50$_{17}$, שָׂרֵי הָאֱלֹהִים *the officers of God* 1 C 24$_5$ (|| קֹדֶשׁ *holiness*), מַלְאַךְ הָאֱלֹהִים *the messenger of God* (supernatural except at 2 C 36$_{16}$) Gn 21$_{17}$ (אֱלֹהִים) 28$_{12}$ (מַלְאֲכֵי אֱלֹהִים) 31$_{11}$ 32$_2$ (מַלְאֲכֵי אֱלֹהִים) Ex 14$_{19}$ Jg 6$_{20}$ 13$_{6.9}$ 1 S 29$_9$ (אֱלֹהִים) 2 S 14$_{17.20}$ 19$_{28}$ 2 C 36$_{16}$ (מַלְאֲכֵי), נביא אלוהים *prophet of God* 11QPs^a 28$_{13}$, רוּחַ אֱלֹהִים *spirit of/from God* Gn 1$_2$ 41$_{38}$ Ex 31$_3$ 35$_{31}$ Nm 24$_2$ 1 S 10$_{10}$ 11$_6$ 16$_{15.16}$ (both + רָעָה *malign*) 16$_{23}$ (all four רוּחַ־) 18$_{10}$ (+ רָעָה) 19$_{20.23}$ Ezk 11$_{24}$ 2 C 15$_1$ 24$_{20}$, רוחות אל[והי] *spirits of the God of* 11QShirShab 3$_4$.

קָרְבַּן אֱלֹהֵיכֶם *offering of*, i.e. to, *your God* Lv 23$_{14}$, זִבְחֵי אֱלֹהִים *sacrifices of*, i.e. to, *God* Ps 51$_{19}$ (or em. זְבָחַי *my sacrifice, O God*), נִדְבוֹת הָאֱלֹהִים *the freewill offerings of*, i.e. to, *God* 2 C 31$_{14}$, לֶחֶם אֱלֹהָיו *bread of*, i.e sacrificial food for, *his God* Lv 21$_6$ (אֱלֹהֵיהֶם) 21$_8$ (אֱלֹהֶיךָ) 21$_{17.21.22}$ 22$_{25}$ (אֱלֹהֵיכֶם), מִשְׁמֶרֶת אֱלֹהֵיהֶם *service of*, i.e. due to, *their God* Ne 12$_{45}$, קִרְבַת אֱלֹהִים *approach of*, i.e. to, *God* Is 58$_2$ Ps 73$_{28}$ (קִרֲבַת; or del. אֱלֹהִים and em. קִרְבָתְךָ *your approach* to me), דרך אלוהים *way of God* 4QShir^b 2.1$_6$, יִרְאַת אֱלֹהִים *fear of*, i.e. reverence for, *God* Gn 20$_{11}$ 2 S 23$_3$ Ne 5$_9$ (אֱלֹהֵינוּ) 5$_{15}$ 2 C 26$_{5(mss)}$ (L בִּרְאֹת הָאֱלֹהִים *in the seeing of God*) Si 9$_{16}$ 10$_{22(A)}$ (י[רא]ת; B י״ *Y.*)) 40$_{26}$ (י[ר]את; || י״) 40$_{27}$, פַּחַד אֱלֹהִים *fear of God* Ps 36$_2$ 2 C 20$_{29}$, דַּעַת אֱלֹהִים *knowledge of*, i.e. about, *God* Ho 4$_1$ 6$_6$ Pr 2$_5$ (|| י״ *Y.*), שמחת אלוהים *joy of God* 4QShirShab^d 1.1$_{40}$, [רז]י אלוהים *secrets of*, i.e. about, *God* 4QShir^b 2.2$_6$ (Baillet), עלמי אלוהים *secrets of*, i.e. about, *God* 4Q525 5$_2$, חָכְמַת אֱלֹהִים *wisdom of*, i.e. from, *God* 1 K 3$_{28}$, מראה האלוהים *the vision of God* 4QVisSam 1$_5$, מַרְאוֹת אֱלֹהִים *visions of God* Ezk 1$_1$ 8$_3$ (mss מַרְאֵה *vision of*) 40$_2$.

בְּרִית אֱלֹהִים *covenant of*, i.e. with, *God* Lv 2$_{13}$ (אֱלֹהֶיךָ) Ps 78$_{10}$ Pr 2$_{17}$ (אֱלֹהֶיהָ) 2 C 34$_{32}$ 4Q385 1$_8$ (אלהי), תּוֹרַת אֱלֹהִים *law of God* Jos 24$_{26}$ (+ סֵפֶר *book of*) Is 1$_{10}$ (אֱלֹהֵינוּ) Ho 4$_6$ (אֱלֹהֶיךָ) Ps 37$_{31}$ (אֱלֹהָיו) Ne 8$_{18}$ (both + סֵפֶר) 10$_{29.30}$ (all four הָאֱלֹהִים), מִשְׁפַּט אֱלֹהֵיהֶם *judgment of their God* 2 K 17$_{26.27}$ (both אֱלֹהֵי) Is 58$_2$ (אֱלֹהָיו) Jr 5$_{4.5}$ (both || י״ *Y.*), מִצְוַת אֱלֹהֵינוּ *commandment of our God* Ps 119$_{115}$ (מִצְוֹת אֱלֹהָי) Ezr 10$_3$, חֻקֵּי הָאֱלֹהִים *the statutes of God* Ex 18$_{16}$, חֶסֶד אֱלֹהִים *loyalty of God* 2 S 9$_3$ Ps 52$_{10}$ (חֶסֶד־) 4QShirShab^a 1.2$_{20}$ (חסדי אלו[הים]), רחמי אלהים *mercies of God* Si 3$_{20}$, קִלְלַת אֱלֹהִים *curse of*, i.e. affront to, *God* Dt 21$_{23}$, שְׁבוּעַת אֱלֹהִים *vow of,* i.e. invoking, *God* Ec 8$_{2}$, אומר אלוהים *word of God* Si 42$_{15(B)}$ (M אֲדֹנָי *my Lord*), דְּבַר אֱלֹהִים *word of,* i.e. from, *God* Jg 3$_{20}$ (דְּבַר־) 1 S 9$_{27}$ 2 S 16$_{23}$ (הָאֱלֹהִים) 1 K 12$_{22}$ (הָאֱלֹהִים; + אֶל *to* prophet) Is 40$_{8}$ (דְּבַר־אֱלֹהֵינוּ) 1 C 17$_{3}$ (דְּבַר־; + אֶל *to* a prophet) 26$_{32}$ (הָאֱלֹהִים; מֶלֶךְ ∥ *king*), דִּבְרֵי אֱלֹהִים *words of God* Jr 23$_{36}$ Ezr 9$_{4}$ (אֱלֹהֵי־) 1 C 25$_{5}$ (הָאֱלֹהִים), מַעֲנֵה אֱלֹהִים *answer of,* i.e. from, *God* Mc 3$_{7}$, קוֹל אֱלֹהִים *voice of God* Dt 4$_{33}$ 5$_{26}$ (both + מִתּוֹךְ־הָאֵשׁ *from within the fire*), קֹלֹת אֱלֹהִים *thunderings of God* Ex 9$_{28}$, אֵשׁ אֱלֹהִים *fire of God* 2 K 1$_{12}$ (אֵשׁ־; mss lack אֱלֹהִים) Jb 1$_{16}$ (both + מִן־הַשָּׁמַיִם *from heaven*).

שֵׁם אֱלֹהִים *name of God* Lv 18$_{21}$ 19$_{12}$ (both אֱלֹהֶיךָ) 21$_{6}$ (אֱלֹהֵיהֶם) (all three + חלל pi. *profane*) Ps 20$_{2}$ (אֱלֹהֵי) 20$_{6}$ (שֵׁם־אֱלֹהֵינוּ) 44$_{21}$ (אֱלֹהֵינוּ) 69$_{31}$ (שֵׁם־) Pr 30$_{9}$ (אֱלֹהָי; ∥ ׳י *Y.*) 4QShirShab^{d} 1.1$_{10}$ (שם ... אלוהים), הֲדַר אֱלֹהֵינוּ *splendour of our God* Is 35$_{2}$ (∥ ׳י), כְּבֹד אֱלֹהִים *glory of God* Ezk 8$_{4}$ (mss כְּבוֹד ׳י אֱלֹהֵי יִשְׂרָאֵל *glory of Y., God of Israel*) 9$_{3}$ 10$_{19}$ 11$_{22}$ 43$_{2}$ (all five כְּבוֹד אֱלֹהֵי־יִשְׂרָאֵל *glory of the God of Israel*) Pr 25$_{2}$ (:: מֶלֶךְ *king*) MasShirShab 2$_{24}$ (כבוד אלוהים), כח אלה[יך] *strength of your God* 4QapPs^{a} 1.2$_{4}$, כוח אלוהי *strength of the God of* 11QShirShab 5$_{3}$, אומץ אלהים *strength of God* Si 42$_{17(Bmg)}$ (M אֲדֹנָי *my Lord*) [ג]בורת אלהינו *strength of our God* 4Q185 1.1$_{14}$, גבורות אלו[הי] *strong deeds of the God of* 11QShirShab 5$_{4}$, צֶלֶם אֱלֹהִים *image of God* Gn 1$_{27}$ 9$_{6}$, פְּנֵי אֱלֹהִים *face of God* 33$_{10}$ Ps 42$_{3}$ (both + ראה *see*) 4QShir^{b} 73$_{2}$ (אלוהים), פִּי אֱלֹהִים *mouth of God* 2 C 35$_{22}$ (mss מִפְּנֵי *in the presence of*), אֶצְבַּע אֱלֹהִים *finger of God* Ex 8$_{15}$ 31$_{18}$ Dt 9$_{10}$ (both + בְּ of instrument for writing law), יַד הָאֱלֹהִים *the hand of God* 1 S 4$_{8}$ 5$_{11}$ Ec 2$_{24}$ (+ מִן *from*) 9$_{1}$ (+ בְּ *in*) Ezr 7$_{9}$ (יַד־אֱלֹהָיו) 8$_{18}$ (both + טוֹבָה *good, benevolent* hand) 8$_{22.31}$ (all three יַד־אֱלֹהֵינוּ) Ne 2$_{8}$ (יַד־אֱלֹהַי) 2$_{18}$ (יַד אֱלֹהַי + טוֹבָה; all six + עַל *upon*) 2 C 30$_{12}$ Si 10$_{4.5}$ (both ביד אלהים), כַּף־אֱלֹהֶיךָ *hand of your God* Is 62$_{3}$ (∥ ׳י *Y.*).

מַעֲשֵׂה אֱלֹהִים *work of God* Ex 32$_{16}$ Ec 7$_{13}$ 8$_{17}$ 11$_{5}$ 12$_{14}$ (all four הָאֱלֹהִים), פֹּעַל אֱלֹהִים *act of God* Ps 64$_{10}$, מִפְעֲלוֹת אֱלֹהִים *acts of God* 66$_{5}$, נַפְתּוּלֵי אֱלֹהִים *wrestlings of,* perh. ordained by, *God* Gn 30$_{8}$, גְּמוּל אֱלֹהִים *recompense of God* Is 35$_{4}$, אַף אֱלֹהִים *anger of God* Nm 22$_{22}$ (ms, Sam ׳י *Y.*) Ps 78$_{31}$ Ezr 10$_{14}$ (אַף־אֱלֹהֵינוּ) 4QShir^{b} 35$_{2}$ (אפי אלוהים), גַּעֲרַת אֱלֹהָיִךְ *rebuke of your God* Is 51$_{20}$ (∥ ׳י), חֶרְדַּת אֱלֹהִים *terror of,* i.e. from, *God* 1 S 14$_{15}$, חִתַּת אֱלֹהִים *terror of,* i.e. from, *God* Gn 35$_{5}$, מַהְפֵּכַת אֱלֹהִים *God's overthow* of Sodom and Gomorrah Is 13$_{19}$ Jr 50$_{40}$ Am 4$_{11}$, יֵשַׁע אֱלֹהִים *deliverance of,* i.e. by, *God* Ps 50$_{23}$ (or em. יִשְׁעִי *my salvation*), יְשׁוּעַת אֱלֹהֵינוּ *victory of our God* Is 52$_{10}$ Ps 98$_{3}$, מַתַּת אֱלֹהִים *gift of God* Ec 3$_{13}$ 5$_{18}$, מֻכֵּה אֱלֹהִים *one struck of,* i.e. by, *God* Is 53$_{4}$, מקוללי אלוהים *ones cursed of,* i.e. by, *God* 11QT 64$_{12}$, קדושי אלוהים *holy ones of God* 4QShirShab^{d} 1.1$_{31}$.

<APP> אֱלֹהִים אֱלֹהָי *God, my God* Ps 43$_{4}$ 1 C 28$_{20}$, אֱלֹהִים אֱלֹהֵינוּ *God, our God* Ps 48$_{15}$ 67$_{7}$, אֱלֹהִים אֱלֹהֶיךָ *God, your God* 45$_{8}$ 50$_{7}$, אֱלֹהִים עֶלְיוֹן *God Most High* 57$_{3}$ (∥ אֵל *God*), [אל ע]ליון אלוהי ואלוהיכה *God most high, my God and your God* 4QJub^{d} 1.2$_{32}$, אֱלֹהִים מַלְכִּי *God, my King* Ps 74$_{12}$, אֵל אֱלֹהֵי *God, the God of* Gn 33$_{20}$ 46$_{3}$ Nm 16$_{22}$, אֵל אֱלֹהִים ׳י *God, God, Y.* Jos 22$_{22.22}$ Ps 50$_{1}$, ׳י הָאֱלֹהִים *God, Y.* 1 C 13$_{6}$ 2 C 30$_{19}$, אֱלֹהִים צְבָאוֹת *God, Sebaoth* Ps 59$_{6}$ 80$_{5.8.15.20}$ 84$_{9}$, ׳י אֱלֹהִים *Y. the God* Gn 2$_{4+10t}$ 3$_{1+8t}$ Ex 9$_{30}$ 2 S 7$_{25}$ 2 K 19$_{19}$ Jr 10$_{10}$ Jon 4$_{6}$ Ps 59$_{6}$ 72$_{18}$ 80$_{5.20}$ 84$_{9}$ (all three + צְבָאוֹת God of *Sebaoth*) 84$_{12}$ 1 C 17$_{16.17}$ 28$_{20}$ 29$_{1}$ 2 C 1$_{9}$ 6$_{41.41.42}$ 26$_{18}$ 11QPs^{a} 28$_{10}$ 4QJub^{a} 5$_{2}$ ([׳י אלהים]) perh. 4QapPs^{b} 24$_{4}$, [׳י אלוהי] *Y., God of* 11QapPs^{a} 1$_{11}$.

׳י אֱלֹהָי *Y. my God* Nm 22$_{18}$ Dt 4$_{5}$ 18$_{16}$ 26$_{14}$ Jos 14$_{8.9}$ 2 S 24$_{24}$ 1 K 3$_{7}$ 5$_{18.19}$∥2 C 2$_{3}$ 1 K 8$_{28}$∥2 C 6$_{19}$ 1 K 17$_{20.21}$ Jon 2$_{7}$ Hb 1$_{12}$ Zc 11$_{4}$ 14$_{5}$ Ps 7$_{2.4}$ 13$_{4}$ 18$_{29}$ (∥ 2 S 22$_{29}$ ׳י...׳י *Y. and Y.* [in two clauses]) 30$_{3.13}$ 35$_{24}$ 40$_{6}$ 86$_{12(mss)}$ (L אֲדֹנָי *my Lord*) 104$_{1}$ 109$_{26}$ Dn 9$_{4.20}$ Ezr 7$_{28}$ 9$_{5}$ 1 C 21$_{17}$ 22$_{7}$ 4Q372 1$_{26}$, ׳י אֱלֹהֵינוּ *Y. our God* Ex 3$_{18}$ 5$_{3}$ 8$_{6.22.23}$ 10$_{25.26}$ Dt 1$_{6.19.20.25.41}$ 2$_{29.33.36.37}$ 3$_{3}$ 4$_{7}$ 5$_{2.24.25.27}$ 6$_{4.20.24.25}$ 29$_{14.17.28}$ Jos 18$_{6}$ 22$_{19.29}$ 24$_{17.24}$ Jg 11$_{24}$ 1 S 7$_{8}$ 1 K 8$_{57.59.61.65}$ 2 K 18$_{22}$∥Is 36$_{7}$ 2 K 19$_{19}$∥Is 37$_{20}$ Is 26$_{13}$ Jr 3$_{22.23.25}$ 5$_{19.24}$ 8$_{14}$ 14$_{22}$ 16$_{10}$ 26$_{16}$ 31$_{6}$ 37$_{3}$ 42$_{6.20}$ 43$_{2}$ 50$_{28}$ 51$_{10}$ Mc 4$_{5}$ 7$_{17}$ Ps 20$_{8}$ 94$_{23}$ 99$_{5.8.9}$ 105$_{7}$∥1 C 16$_{14}$ Ps 106$_{47}$ 113$_{5}$ 122$_{9}$ 123$_{2}$ Dn 9$_{10.13.14}$ Ezr 9$_{8}$ Ne 10$_{35}$ 1 C 13$_{2}$ 15$_{13}$ 29$_{16}$ 2 C 2$_{3}$ 13$_{10.11}$ 14$_{6.10}$ 19$_{7}$ 29$_{6}$ 32$_{8.11}$ GnzPs 2$_{8}$ 2QapDavid 1.1$_{1}$ ([י]הוה אלהינ[ו]).

׳י אֱלֹהֶיךָ (and vars.) *Y. your* (masc. sg.) *God* Gn 27$_{20}$ Ex 15$_{26}$ 20$_{2.5.7.10.12}$ 23$_{19}$ 34$_{24.26}$ Dt 1$_{21.31}$ 2$_{7.30}$ 4$_{3}$ 12$_{27}$ 13$_{17.19}$=11QT 55$_{10.14}$ Dt 14$_{2}$=11QT 48$_{7.10}$ Dt 18$_{13}$=11QT

60_{21} (+ 219 times in Dt) Jos $1_{9.17}$ $9_{9.24}$ Jg 6_{26} 1 S 12_{19} 13_{13} $15_{15.21.30}$ 25_{29} 2 S $14_{11.17}$ 18_{28} $24_{3.23}$ 1 K 1_{17} 2_{3} 5_{19} 10_{9}||2 C 9_{8} 1 K $13_{6.21}$ 17_{12} 18_{10} 2 K 19_{4}||Is 37_{4} Is 7_{11} 41_{13} 43_{3} 48_{17} 51_{15} 55_{5} Jr 40_{2} $42_{2.3.5}$ Ho 12_{10} 13_{4} 14_{2} Am 9_{15} Ps 81_{11} 1 C 11_{2} $22_{11.12}$ 2 C 9_{8} 16_{7} 4QApocMos B 1.1_{2} (אלוהיכה) Arad ost. 6_{12} 11QT 53_{8} 54_{16} 63_{8} Kh. Beit Lei graf. $5_{1(\text{Cross})}$ (אלהיכה), י׳ אֱלֹהַיִךְ *Y. your* (fem. sg.) *God* Is 60_{9} Jr $2_{17.19}$ 3_{13} Mc 7_{10} Zp 3_{17}, י׳ אֱלֹהֵיכֶם *Y. your* (pl.) *God* Ex 6_{7} 8_{24} $10_{8.16.17}$ 16_{12} 23_{25} Lv 11_{44} $18_{2.4.30}$ 19_{2+7t} $20_{7.24}$ $23_{22.28.40.43}$ 24_{22} $25_{17.38.55}$ $26_{1.13}$ Nm $10_{9.10}$ 15_{41} Dt $1_{10.26.30.32}$ $3_{18.20.21.22}$ $4_{2.4.23.34}$ $5_{32.33}$ $6_{1.16.17}$ 8_{20} $9_{16.23}$ 10_{17} 11_{2+6t} $12_{4.5.7.10.11.12}$ $13_{4.5}$=11QT 54_{14} Dt 13_{6} 14_{1} =11QT 48_{8} Dt $20_{4.18}$ $29_{5.9}$ $31_{12.13.26}$ Jos $1_{11.13.15}$ 2_{11} $3_{3.9}$ $4_{5.23.23.24}$ (ms אֱלֹהֵינוּ) 8_{7} 10_{19} $22_{3.4.5}$ 23_{3+8t} Jg 6_{10} 1 S $12_{12.14}$ 2 K 17_{39} 23_{21} Jr 13_{16} 26_{13} $42_{4.13.20.21}$ Ezk $20_{5.7.19.20}$ Jl 1_{14} $2_{13.14.23.26.27}$ 4_{17} Zc 6_{15} Ps 76_{12} Ne 8_{9} 9_{5} 1 C $22_{18.19}$ 28_{8} 29_{20} 2 C 20_{20} 28_{10} $30_{8.9}$ 35_{3} 11QT fr. 1_{2} ([אלוה]יכם) 1Q29 $3_{2(\text{Milik})}$ ([י]הוה אלוהיכמה) 4QpPs Jos^{a} 1_{11} ([אלהיכ]מה).

י׳ אֱלֹהָיו *Y. his God* Ex 32_{11} Lv 4_{22} Nm 23_{21} Dt 17_{19} 18_{7} 1 S 30_{6} 1 K 5_{17} 11_{4} $15_{3.4}$ (ms lacks אֱלֹהָיו) 2 K 5_{11} 16_{2} Jr 7_{28} Jon 2_{2} Mc 5_{3} Ps 33_{12} 144_{15} 146_{5} Ezr 7_{6} 2 C 1_{1} $14_{1.10}$ 15_{9} 26_{16} 27_{6} 28_{5} 31_{20} 33_{12} 34_{8} $36_{5.12.23}$, י׳ אֱלֹהֵיהֶם *Y. their God* Ex 10_{7} $29_{46.46}$ Lv 26_{44} Jg 3_{7} 8_{34} 1 S 12_{9} 1 K 9_{9} 2 K $17_{7.9.14.16.19}$ 18_{12} Jr 3_{21} 22_{9} 30_{9} 43_{1} 50_{4} Ezk 28_{26} 34_{30} $39_{22.28}$ Ho 1_{7} 3_{5} 7_{10} Zp 2_{7} Hg 1_{12} Zc 9_{16} 10_{6} Neh $9_{3.3.4}$ 2 Chr 31_{6} 33_{17} 34_{33}.

<ADJ> אֱלֹהִים חַיִּים *living God* Dt $4_{44(\text{mss, Sam})}$ 5_{26} 1 S $17_{26.36}$ Jr 10_{10} (+ מֶלֶךְ עוֹלָם *eternal king*) 23_{36}, אֱלֹהִים חַי *living God* 2 K $19_{4.16}$||Is $37_{4.17}$, אֱלֹהִים קְדֹשִׁים *holy God* Jos 24_{19} (|| אֵל *God*), י׳ הָאֱלֹהִים הַקָּדוֹשׁ הַזֶּה *Y., this holy God* 1 S 6_{20}, י׳ הָאֱלֹהִים הַגָּדוֹל *Y. the great God* Ne 8_{6}, אֱלֹהִים צַדִּיק *righteous God* Ps 7_{10}, הָאֱלֹהִים הָאַדִּירִים הָאֵלֶּה *these mighty gods* (in ref. to Y.) 1 S 4_{8}, טוֹב לְיִשְׂרָאֵל אֱלֹהִים *God is good to Israel* Ps 73_{1}, גָּדוֹל אֱלֹהֵינוּ מִכָּל־הָאֱלֹהִים *our God is greater than all the gods* 2 C 2_{4}.

<PREP> לְ of possession, *of, (belonging) to* Gn 40_{8} Dt 1_{17} 32_{3} Ps 47_{10} 62_{12} 81_{5} 2 C 20_{15} Kh. Beit Lei graf. $5_{2(\text{Naveh})}$ (לאל[ה]י) 1QDM $2_{1(\text{Milik})}$ 4QShirShab^{c} 4_{8}, of direction, *to* Ne 12_{46} MasShirShab 2_{17}, + נתן *give* 1 S 6_{5} Ps 49_{8} 68_{35} Jb 1_{22}, לקח *take* Ex 18_{12}, קרב hi. *bring* Ezr 8_{35}, שׁחה htpal. *bow down* 2 S 15_{32}, כפף ni. *bow* Mc 6_{6}, רוץ *hasten* trans. Ps 68_{32}, אמר *say* Ps 66_{3} 2 C 1_{8}, קרא *call* Ps 57_{3} (|| אֵל *God*) 1 C 4_{10}, זעק *cry* 5_{20}, רוע hi. *shout* Ps 47_{2} 66_{1} 81_{2}, רנן hi. *shout* 81_{2}, שׁיר *sing* $68_{5.33}$, זמר pi. *sing praises* Ps 75_{10} 104_{33} 146_{2} 147_{7} (all three || י׳ Y.) 4QShirShab^{d} 1.1_{6} ([לאלו[הי]) 1.1_{39}, הלל pi. *give praise* 4QShirShab^{b} 1_{2} ([לאל[והי]) 4QShirShab^{f} 8_{2} 11QShir Shab 5_{5}, שׁבח *give praise* 4QShirShab^{d} 1.1_{2}, ידה hi. *give thanks* 136_{2}, כון hi. *direct* heart 2 C 20_{33}.

לְ of benefit, *to, for* Ps 40_{4} (+ תְּהִלָּה *psalm*), + זבח *sacrifice* Gn 46_{1} Ex 5_{8} 8_{21} Ps 50_{14} (|| עֶלְיוֹן *the Most High*), עלה hi. *offer* sacrifices 2 C 29_{7}, בנה *build* Ezr 4_{3} 4Q522 2_{4}, ישׁר pi. *straighten* Is 40_{3} (|| י׳ *Y.*), קרא *proclaim* Is 61_{2} (||י׳), שׁאר ni. *remain* Zc 9_{7}.

לְ *against*, + חטא *sin* Gn 39_{9}, נתן לְ *make as* 4Q ApocMos A 2.2_{6} קנא לְ pi. *be zealous for* Nm 25_{13}, צמא לְ *thirst for* Ps 42_{3} (|| אֵל חָי *the living God*), קָדוֹשׁ לְ *holy to* Lv $21_{6.7}$ Nm 15_{40}, יחל לְ hi. *wait for* Mc 7_{7} Ps $42_{6.12}$ 43_{5}, pi. 69_{4}, גיל לְ *rejoice in* 4QShir^{b} 1_{5}, דמם לְ *be silent before* Ps 62_{6}, עִיר גְּדוֹלָה לֵאלֹהִים *a city great before God* Jon 3_{3}, דרשׁ לְ *seek after* Ezr 4_{2} 2 C 17_{4} 31_{21} 34_{3}, רום לְ pol. *exalt* 4QShirShab^{a} 2_{8} 4QShirShab^{d} 1.1_{1}, ברך לְ pi. *bless* 4QShirShab^{f} 23.2_{12}, נִכְרָת־בְּרִית לֵאלֹהֵינוּ *let us make a covenant with our God* Ezr 10_{3}, אָהוּב לֵאלֹהָיו *loved by his God* Ne 13_{26}, היה לוֹ לֵאלֹהִים (and vars.) *be God to him* (etc.) Gn $17_{7.8}$ 28_{21} Ex 4_{16} 6_{7} 29_{45} Lv 11_{45} 22_{33} 25_{38} 26_{12}=11QT 59_{13} Lv 26_{45} Nm 15_{41} Dt 26_{17} 29_{12} 2 S 7_{24}||1 C 17_{22} Jr 7_{23} 11_{4} 24_{7} 30_{22} $31_{1.33}$ 32_{38} Ezk 11_{20} 14_{11} 34_{24} 36_{28} $37_{23.27}$ Zc 8_{8} 4QJub^{a} 7_{10} ([והייתי לאלהיהם]).

בְּ of instrument, *by, through* Ps 3_{3}, + עשׂה *do* 60_{14}||108_{14}, חזק pi. *strengthen* 1 S 23_{16}, דלג pi. *jump* 2 S 22_{30}||Ps 18_{30}, שׁוב *go back* Ho 12_{7}, *against*, + דבר pi. *speak* Nm 21_{5} (|| מֹשֶׁה *Moses*) Ps 78_{19}, מעל *act treacherously* Jos 22_{16} Ezr 10_{2} Ne 13_{27} 1 C 5_{25}, כחשׁ pi. *act deceitfully* Jos 24_{27}, מרה *rebel* Ho 14_{1}, שׁבע בְּ ni. *swear by* Gn 21_{23} 1 S 30_{15} Is 65_{16}, hi. *adjure by* Ne 13_{25} 2 C 36_{13}, ברך בְּ htp. *bless oneself by* Is 65_{16}, שׁאל בְּ *ask of* Jg 18_{5} 20_{18} 1 S 14_{37} $22_{13.15}$ 1 C $14_{10.14}$, זכר בְּ hi. *make mention of* Is 48_{1} (|| שֵׁם י׳ *the name of Y.*), שׁען בְּ ni. *lean upon* Is 50_{10} (|| שֵׁם י׳ *the name of Y.*), אמן בְּ hi. *trust in* Jon 3_{5} Ps 78_{22}, בטח בְּ *trust in* $56_{5.12}$, גיל בְּ *rejoice in* Is

61$_{10}$ Hb 3$_{18}$ (both || ׳י) 4QShir^{b} 8$_{2}$ 28$_{2}$ ([י]גילו]), רנן בְּ pi. *rejoice in* 4QShir^{a} 1$_{8}$, שׂמח בְּ *rejoice in* Ps 63$_{12}$, הלל בְּ pi. *praise* 44$_{9}$ 56$_{5.11}$ (|| ׳י), וְיָשִׂימוּ בֵאלֹהִים כִּסְלָם *so that they should set their hope in God* 78$_{7}$, מַחְסִי בֵּאלֹהִים *my refuge is in God* 62$_{8}$, יֶשׁ־כֹּחַ בֵּאלֹהִים *there is strength in God* 2 C 25$_{8}$.

מִי־אֵל גָּדוֹל כֵּאלֹהִים *who is a great god like God?* Ps 77$_{14}$.

מִן *arranged/ordained by* 1 C 5$_{22}$ 2 C 22$_{7}$ 25$_{20}$, perh. *in the presence of*, + רשׁע *be wicked* 2 S 22$_{22}$||Ps 18$_{22}$, צדק pi. *consider oneself justified* Jb 32$_{2}$, נשׂא מִן *receive from* Ps 24$_{5}$ (|| ׳י *Y.*), היה מִן ni. *be brought into being by* 4QShir Shab^{c} 4$_{12}$, עבר מִן *pass from* Is 40$_{27}$ (|| ׳י), חֲדַל־לְךָ מֵאֱלֹהִים *cease from God!*, i.e. leave God alone! 2 C 35$_{21}$, אַלְמָן מִן *widowed from* Jr 51$_{5}$ (|| ׳י), חֵלֶק מִן *portion from* Jb 20$_{29}$ (|| אֵל *God*), וְיָרֵאתָ מֵאֱלֹהֶיךָ *and you shall fear your God* Lv 19$_{14.32}$ 25$_{17.36.43}$; שׁוב מֵאַחֲרֵי hi. *turn* someone *from (following) after* 4QApocMos B 1.1$_{5}$ (להשׁ]יבכה])

אֶל of direction, *to*, Ps 62$_{2}$ (+ נֶפֶשׁ *soul*) 77$_{2.2}$ (both + קוֹל *voice*), + אמר *say* Gn 17$_{18}$ Ex 3$_{11.13}$ Nm 22$_{10}$ Jg 6$_{36.39}$ 1 C 21$_{8.17}$, פלל htp. *pray* Gn 20$_{17}$ Ne 2$_{4}$ 4$_{3}$, זעק *cry* Jg 10$_{14}$ Jr 11$_{12}$, שׁוע pi. *cry* Ps 18$_{7}$ (|| ׳י *Y.*), קרא *call* 2 S 22$_{7}$ (|| ׳י) Jon 1$_{6}$ 3$_{8}$ Ps 55$_{17}$, שׁוב *go back* Is 55$_{7}$ (|| ׳י) Ho 5$_{4}$ Ec 12$_{7}$, קרב *approach* 1 S 14$_{36}$ Zp 3$_{2}$ (|| ׳י), ni. Ex 22$_{7}$, עלה *go up* 2$_{23}$ 19$_{3}$ 1 S 10$_{3}$, בוא hi. *bring* Ex 18$_{19}$, נגשׁ hi. *bring* 21$_{6}$, אֶל־אֱלֹהִים אָשִׂים דִּבְרָתִי *I shall put my case to God* Jb 5$_{8}$ (|| אֵל *God*), נבט אֶל hi. *look at* Ex 3$_{6}$, דרשׁ אֶל *seek after* Is 8$_{19}$ Jb 5$_{8}$, קוה אֶל pi. *wait for* Ho 12$_{7}$, ראה אֶל ni. *show oneself to* Ps 84$_{8}$, דבר אֶל pi. *speak of* 2 C 32$_{19}$, כנע אֶל ni. *humble oneself before* Si 4$_{25}$.

סמך עַל *lean upon* Is 48$_{2}$, מָגִנִּי עַל־אֱלֹהִים *my shield* rests *upon Y.* Ps 7$_{11}$, עַל־אֱלֹהִים יִשְׁעִי *on God* rests *my deliverance* 62$_{8}$; מֵעַל *away from* Ho 9$_{1}$.

שׁוב עַד *return to* 4QApocMos B 1.1$_{2}$.

לִפְנֵי *in the presence of, before* Gn 6$_{11}$ Ex 18$_{12}$ Nm 10$_{10}$ Jos 24$_{1}$ Jg 21$_{2}$ Ps 56$_{14}$ 61$_{8}$ 68$_{4}$ Ec 2$_{26}$ 5$_{1}$ 7$_{26}$ 8$_{13}$ (מִלִּפְנֵי) Ne 1$_{4}$ 1 C 13$_{8.10}$ 16$_{1}$ Si 14$_{16(Amg)}$ 4QJub^{d} 1.1$_{34}$ ([לפני האלוהים]) 1$_{37}$ ([לפני האלוה]ים]), + ענה htp. *humble oneself* Dn 10$_{12}$ Ezr 8$_{21}$; כנע מִלִּפְנֵי ni. *humble oneself before* 2 C 33$_{12}$ 34$_{27}$.

מִפְּנֵי *from the presence of* Ps 68$_{3}$, *in the presence of* 2 C 35$_{22(mss)}$ (L מִפִּי *from the mouth of*), *because of* 68$_{9.9}$; בְּעֵינֵי *in the eyes of*, + מצא חֵן *find favour* Pr 3$_{4}$ (|| אָדָם *people*) Si 3$_{18(C)}$ (A אֵל *God*), רעע *be evil* 1 C 21$_{7}$.

הלך עִם *walk with* Mc 6$_{8}$, צפה עִם perh. *watch out for* Ho 9$_{8}$, רצה עִם *take pleasure in* Jb 34$_{9}$, עשׂה טוֹבָה עִם *do good to* 2 C 24$_{16}$, עשׂה עִם *do with the help of* 1 S 14$_{45}$; מֵעִם *from* Gn 41$_{32}$ 2 C 10$_{15}$.

<COLL> אֱלֹהִים וַאֲנָשִׁים *God and men* (see also §3a) Si 45$_{1}$ ([א]להים]) 11QT 64$_{12}$, אֱלֹהִים וְאָדָם *God and people* Pr 3$_{4}$, חָלִילָה לִּי אֱלֹהַי *my God forbid!* 1 C 11$_{19}$, אֵין־כָּמוֹךָ אֱלֹהִים *there is none like you, O God* 1 K 8$_{23}$ ||2 C 6$_{14}$, אלוהי *O, my God* 4QVisSam 3.2$_{2}$, אלוהים לכול מרנני דעת *God of all that sing (with) knowledge* 4QShirShab^{d} 1.1$_{37}$.

2a. other god(s), **<SUBJ>** היה *be* Jg 2$_{3}$ (+ לְמוֹקֵשׁ *as a trap*) Jr 2$_{28}$ 11$_{13}$ (both + מִסְפַּר עָרֶיךָ *the number of*, i.e. as numerous as, *your cities*), יכל *be able* 2 C 32$_{13.14}$, נתן *give* Jg 16$_{23.24}$, נסה pi. *attempt* Dt 4$_{34}$ (+ לָבוֹא *to come*), נצל hi. *rescue* 2 K 18$_{33.35}$||Is 36$_{18.20}$||2 C 32$_{13.14}$ 2 K 19$_{12}$||Is 37$_{12}$, שׁחה htp. *bow* to Y. Ps 97$_{7}$.

<NOM CL> אֵין אֱלֹהִים עִמָּדִי *there is no god with me* (Y.) Dt 32$_{39}$, אֵין אֱלֹהִים זוּלָתֶךָ *there is no deity apart from you* 2 S 7$_{22}$||1 C 17$_{20}$ Si 33$_{5}$, מִבַּלְעָדַי אֵין־אֱלֹהִים *apart from me there is no god* Is 44$_{6}$, sim 45$_{21}$, הַמִבְּלִי אֵין־אֱלֹהִים בְּיִשְׂרָאֵל *is it because there is no deity in Israel?* 2 K 1$_{3.6.16}$, אֵין אֱלֹהִים בְּכָל־הָאָרֶץ כִּי אִם־בְּיִשְׂרָאֵל *there is no god in all the world except in Israel* 5$_{15}$, כָּל־אֱלֹהֵי הָעַמִּים אֱלִילִים *all the gods of the peoples are idols* Ps 96$_{5}$||1 C 16$_{26}$, אֵי אֱלֹהֵימוֹ *where are their gods?* Dt 32$_{37}$, אַיֵּה אֱלֹהֶיךָ *where are your gods?* Jr 2$_{28}$, חֵי אֱלֹהֶיךָ *(as) your god is alive* Am 8$_{14}$ (+ אַשְׁמַת שֹׁמְרוֹן *wicked deed of Samaria*; or em. אֲשֵׁרַת *Asherah of* or אֲשִׁמַת *Ashima of*).

<OBJ> ירא *fear, revere* Jg 6$_{10}$ 2 K 17$_{7.35.37.38}$, עבד *serve* Ex 23$_{24}$ Dt 7$_{4.16}$ 11$_{16}$ 12$_{2.30}$ 13$_{3.7}$=11QT 54$_{10.21}$ Dt 13$_{14}$ 17$_{3}$=11QT 55$_{17}$ Dt 28$_{36}$=11QT 59$_{3}$ (+ עֵץ וָאֶבֶן made of *wood and stone*) Dt 28$_{64}$ 29$_{17.25}$ Jos 23$_{16}$ 24$_{2.15.15}$ (:: ׳י *Y.*) 24$_{16.20}$ Jg 3$_{6}$ 10$_{6+5t}$ 1 S 8$_{8}$ 26$_{19}$ 1 K 9$_{6}$||2 C 7$_{19}$ 2 K 17$_{33}$ 19$_{18}$ (+ עֵץ וָאֶבֶן) Jr 5$_{19}$ 16$_{13}$ 4Q386–9 4$_{15}$ 4QJub^{a} 2$_{6}$ ([א]להיהם]), ידע *know* Dt 13$_{14}$=11QT 55$_{4}$, הלל pi. *praise* Jg 16$_{24}$, בחר *choose* 5$_{8}$, מור hi. *exchange* Jr 2$_{11}$, דרשׁ *seek* 2 C 25$_{15.20}$, רזה perh. *shrivel* Zp 2$_{11}$.

2b. images of other gods (distinction from §2a not alw. clear).

<SUBJ> שׂרף ni. *be burned* 1 C 14$_{12}$. **<OBJ>** עשׂה *make* Ex 20$_{23.23}$ 32$_{1.23.31}$ 34$_{17}$ Lv 19$_{4}$ Jg 18$_{24}$ 1 K 14$_{9}$ 2 K 17$_{29}$ Jr 16$_{20}$, עמד hi. *set up* 2 C 25$_{14}$, גנב *steal* Gn 31$_{30}$ (31$_{19}$ תְּרָפִים *teraphim*), לקח *take* Jg 18$_{24}$ (|| כֹּהֵן *priest*), בוא hi. *bring* Dn 11$_{8}$ (|| נָסִיךְ *idol*, כְּלִי חֶמְדָּה *precious thing*) 2 C 25$_{14}$, מצא *find* Gn 31$_{32}$, סור hi. *remove* 35$_{2}$ Jos 24$_{14.23}$ Jg 10$_{16}$ 1 S 7$_{3}$ 2 C 33$_{15}$ (|| סֶמֶל *symbol*), עזב *abandon* 1 C 14$_{12}$ (|| 2 S 5$_{21}$ עָצָב *idol*), נתן *give* Gn 35$_{4}$ 2 K 19$_{18}$||Is 37$_{19}$, עבד *serve* Dt 4$_{28}$.

<CSTR> (§2a-b) אֱלֹהֵי נֵכָר *gods of foreignness*, i.e. foreign gods Gn 35$_{2.4}$ (both הַנֵּכָר) Dt 31$_{16}$ (נֵכַר־) Jos 24$_{20.23}$ Jg 10$_{16}$ 1 S 7$_{3}$ (all three הַנֵּכָר) Jr 5$_{19}$ 2 C 33$_{15}$ (הַנֵּכָר), אֱלֹהֵי הַגּוֹיִם *gods of the nations* Dt 29$_{17}$ 2 K 18$_{33}$||Is 36$_{18}$ 2 K 19$_{12}$||Is 37$_{12}$ 2 C 32$_{14}$, אֱלֹהֵי הָעַמִּים *gods of the peoples* Dt 6$_{14}$ 13$_{8}$ Jg 2$_{12}$ Ps 96$_{5}$||1 C 16$_{26}$, אֱלֹהֵי הָעָם *gods of the people* 2 C 25$_{15}$ (+ אֲשֶׁר לֹא־הִצִּילוּ אֶת־עַמָּם *who did not rescue their people*), אֱלֹהֵי גּוֹיֵ הָאֲרָצוֹת *gods of nations of the countries* 2 C 32$_{13.17}$, כָּל־אֱלֹהֵי הָאֲרָצוֹת *all the gods of the lands* 2 K 18$_{35}$||Is 36$_{20}$, אֱלֹהֵי עַמֵּי הָאָרֶץ *the gods of the peoples of the land* 1 C 5$_{25}$ (עַמֵּי־) 2 C 32$_{19}$, כָּל־אֱלֹהֵי הָאָרֶץ *all the gods of the earth* Zp 2$_{11}$, אֱלֹהֵי מַסֵּכָה *gods of metal* Ex 34$_{17}$ Lv 19$_{4}$ (+ אֱלִילִים *idols*), אֱלֹהֵי זָהָב *gods of gold* Ex 20$_{23}$ 32$_{31}$, אֱלֹהֵי כֶסֶף *gods of silver* 20$_{23}$.

אֱלֹהֵי הָאֱמֹרִי *god(s) of the Amorite(s)* Jos 24$_{15}$ Jg 6$_{10}$, אֱלֹהֵי בְנֵי־עַמּוֹן *god(s) of the Ammonites* 10$_{6}$ 1 K 11$_{33}$ (+ Milcom), אֱלֹהֵי אֲרָם *gods of Aram* Jg 10$_{6}$, אֱלֹהֵי מַלְכֵי־אֲרָם *gods of the kings of Aram* 2 C 28$_{23}$, אֱלֹהֵי מוֹאָב *gods of Moab* Jg 10$_{6}$ 1 K 11$_{33}$ (+ Chemosh), בַּעַל זְבוּב אֱלֹהֵי עֶקְרוֹן *Baal-zebub, god of Ekron* 2 K 1$_{2.3.6.16}$, אֱלֹהֵי דַרְמֶשֶׂק *gods of Damascus* 2 C 28$_{23}$, אֱלֹהֵי צִידוֹן *gods of Sidon* Jg 10$_{6}$, אֱלֹהֵי צִדֹנִים *god(s) of (the) Sidonians* 1 K 11$_{5}$ (|| שִׁקּוּץ *abomination*) 11$_{33}$ (צִדֹנִין [mss צִדֹנִים]; + Ashtoreth), אֱלֹהֵי פְלִשְׁתִּים *gods of (the) Philistines* Jg 10$_{6}$, אֱלֹהֵי מִצְרַיִם *gods of Egypt* Ex 12$_{12}$ Jr 43$_{12.13}$ (אֱלֹהֵי־), אֱלֹהֵי אֱדוֹם *gods of Edom* 2 C 25$_{20}$, אֱלֹהֵי בְּנֵי שֵׂעִיר *gods of the Seirites* 25$_{14}$, אֱלֹהֵי חֲמָת וְאַרְפָּד *gods of Hamath and Arpad* 2 K 18$_{34}$||Is 36$_{19}$, אֱלֹהֵי סְפַרְוַיִם *gods of Sepharvaim* 2 K 18$_{34}$||Is 36$_{19}$ (סְפַרְוָיִם), אֱלֹהֵי אֲבֹתָיו *gods of his ancestors* Dn 11$_{37}$.

בֵּית אֱלֹהִים *house*, i.e. temple, shrine, *of god(s)* Jg 9$_{27}$ (אֱלֹהֵיהֶם) Jr 43$_{12.13}$ (both בָּתֵּי אֱלֹהֵי) Na 1$_{14}$ (אֱלֹהֶיךָ) Ezr 1$_{7}$ (אֱלֹהָיו) 1 C 10$_{10}$ (אֱלֹהֵיהֶם; ||1 S 31$_{10}$ עַשְׁתָּרוֹת *of Ashtaroth*) 2 C 32$_{21}$ (אֱלֹהָיו; ||2 K 19$_{37}$||Is 37$_{38}$ בֵּית נִסְרֹךְ אֱלֹהָיו *house of Nisroch, his god*), זִבְחֵי אֱלֹהֵיהֶן *sacrifices of*, i.e. to, *their* (Moabites') *god(s)* Nm 25$_{2}$, שֵׁם אֱלֹהִים *god's name* Ex 23$_{13}$ Dt 18$_{20}$=11QT 61$_{1}$ (אלו[הים]) Jos 23$_{7}$ (אֱלֹהֵיהֶם) 1 K 18$_{24}$ (:: ׳י *Y.*) 18$_{25}$ (both אֱלֹהֵיכֶם) Mc 4$_{5}$ (אֱלֹהָיו; :: ׳י), פְּסִילֵי אֱלֹהֵיהֶם *images of their gods* Dt 7$_{25}$=11QT 2$_{7}$ (א[לוהיהמה]) Dt 12$_{3}$ Is 21$_{9}$ (אֱלֹהֶיהָ), כּוֹכַב אֱלֹהֵיכֶם *star of your gods* Am 5$_{26}$, כָּל־הָאֱלֹהִים *all (the) gods* (and vars.) usu. contrasted with Y. Gn 35$_{4}$ Ex 12$_{12}$ 18$_{11}$ 2 K 18$_{35}$||Is 36$_{20}$ Zp 2$_{11}$ Ps 95$_{3}$ 96$_{4.5}$ 97$_{7.9}$ 135$_{5}$ 1 C 16$_{25.26}$ 2 C 2$_{4}$ 32$_{14}$, מלך כו[ו]ל א[לוהי] *king of all the gods of* 11QShirShab h$_{6}$.

<APP> אֱלֹהִים מַעֲשֵׂה יְדֵי אָדָם עֵץ וָאֶבֶן *gods, the work of human hands—wood and stone* Dt 4$_{28}$ 11QT 59$_{3}$.

<ADJ> אֱלֹהִים אֲחֵרִים *other gods* Ex 20$_{3}$ 23$_{13}$ Dt 5$_{7}$ 6$_{14}$ 7$_{4}$ 8$_{19}$ 11$_{16.28}$ 13$_{3.7}$=11QT 54$_{10.21}$ Dt 13$_{14}$ 17$_{3}$=11QT 55$_{17}$ Dt 18$_{20}$=11QT 61$_{1}$ (אלו[הים אחר]ים) Dt 28$_{14.36.64}$ 29$_{25}$ 30$_{17}$ 31$_{18.20}$ Jos 23$_{16}$ 24$_{2.16}$ Jg 2$_{12.17.19}$ 10$_{13}$ 1 S 8$_{8}$ 26$_{19}$ 1 K 9$_{6.9}$||2 C 7$_{19.22}$ 1 K 11$_{4.10}$ 14$_{9}$ 2 K 5$_{17}$ 17$_{7.35.37.38}$ 22$_{17}$||2 C 34$_{25}$ Jr 1$_{16}$ 7$_{6.9.18}$ 11$_{10}$ 13$_{10}$ 16$_{11.13}$ 19$_{4.13}$ 22$_{9}$ 25$_{6}$ 32$_{29}$ 35$_{15}$ 44$_{3.5.8.15}$ Ho 3$_{1}$ 2 C 28$_{25}$ 4Q386–9 4$_{15}$ 4QJub^{a} 2$_{4}$ (אחר[ים]), אֱלֹהִים חֲדָשִׁים *new gods* Jg 5$_{8}$, אֱלֹהִים קְרֹבִים *a god who is near* Dt 4$_{7}$.

<PREP> לְ of direction, *to*, + שׁחה htp. *bow* Ex 23$_{24}$ Nm 25$_{2}$ Dt 30$_{17}$ Jr 22$_{9}$, of benefit, *to, for*, + עשׂה *do* Dt 12$_{31}$ 20$_{18}$=11QT 62$_{16}$ 2 K 5$_{17}$ 2 C 13$_{8}$, זבח *sacrifice* Ex 22$_{19}$ 34$_{15}$ Nm 25$_{2}$ 2 C 28$_{23}$, pi. *sacrifice* 1 K 11$_{8}$, קטר pi. *offer incense* 11$_{8}$ 2 K 22$_{17}$||2 C 34$_{25(Qr)}$ Jr 1$_{16}$ 19$_{4}$ 44$_{3.5.8.15}$ 48$_{35}$ 2 C 28$_{25}$, נסך hi. *offer libations* Jr 7$_{18}$ 19$_{13}$ 32$_{29}$, דרשׁ לְ *ask about* Dt 12$_{30}$, כרת בְּרִית לְ *make a covenant with* Ex 23$_{32}$, וַיָּשִׂימוּ לָהֶם בַּעַל בְּרִית לֵאלֹהִים *and they adopted Baal-berith as their god* Jg 8$_{33}$, וַיַּעֲמִידֵם לוֹ לֵאלֹהִים *and he established them as gods* 2 C 25$_{14}$.

אֵין־כָּמוֹךָ בָאֱלֹהִים אֲדֹנָי *there is none like you among the gods, my Lord* Ps 86$_{8}$, עשׂה שְׁפָטִים בְּ *make judgment against* Nm 33$_{4}$, קלל בְּ pi. *curse by* 1 S 17$_{43}$ Is 8$_{21}$ (perh. בְּ = *against*; || מֶלֶךְ *king*), חזק בְּ hi. *grasp* 1 K 9$_{9}$||2 C 7$_{22}$.

בְּקֶרֶב *among* Ps 82$_{1}$ (+ אֱלֹהִים *God*).

כְּ *as* 2 C 32$_{17}$.

מֵאֱלֹהֵי הָעַמִּים *from among the gods of the peoples* Dt 614 138 Jg 212.

אֶל of direction, *to*, + פנה *turn* Dt 3118.20 Ho 31, שׁוב *return* Ru 115 (|| עַם *people*), זעק *cry* Jon 15.

פקד עַל *bring punishment against* Jr 4625, בין עַל hi. *be concerned about* Dn 1137, דבר עַל pi. *speak about* 2 C 3219; מֵעַל *away from* 1 S 65.

אַחֲרֵי *after*, + הלך *go* Dt 614 819 1128 133 2814 Jg 212.19 1 K 1110 Jr 76.9 1110 1310 Jr 1611 256 3515, זנה *follow as prostitute* Ex 3415=11QT 213 ([אל]והיהמה) Ex 3416 Dt 3116 Jg 217 1 C 525, נטה hi. *incline* heart 1 K 112.4; פנה אחר *turn after* 4QJuba 24 ([פנו]); סוג מֵאַחַר ni. *turn away from* Is 5913; ישׁר בְּעֵינֵי *seem right to* Nm 2327.

3a. divine being, god, deity, in general וּבֵית דָּוִיד כֵּאלֹהִים כְּמַלְאַךְ י׳ *and the House of David will be as a divine being—as an angel of Y.* Zc 128, אלוהים נוראי כוח *divine beings, terrifying in strength* 11QShir Shab 53.

<SUBJ> ברך pi. *bless* 4QShirShabf 197 (אל[והי]ם), הלל pi. *praise* 23.16 (אלוה[י]ם), רוץ *run* 4QShirShabc 49 4QShirShabd 1.26 (א[לו]הים), מוט *be shaken* 4QShirShabf 23.14, רום pol. *exalt* 4QShirShabd 1.133.

<OBJ> כבד pi. *honour* Jg 99, שׂמח pi. *gladden* Jg 913, קבע *defraud* Ml 38 (:: אָדָם *human being*).

<CSTR> אלוהי כול קדושי קדושים *gods of all holy of holies* 4QShirShaba 1.12, אלוהי פלא *gods of wonder* 4QShirShabd 1.136, אלוהי כיליו *divine beings of his crown* or *of his whole offering* 4QShirShabf 23.15; לֵב אֱלֹהִים *mind of a god* Ezk 282.6, מוֹשַׁב אֱלֹהִים *seat of a god* Ezk 282, משא אלוהים *burden*, perh. utterance, *of divine beings* 11QShirShab 55, מלך *king of* 4QShirShaba 1.27 25 4QShirShabb 15 (אל[והי]) 4QShirc 3.212 (אלוהי) 4QShirShabf 23.113 243 (כול א[לוהים]), סוד *council of* 4QShirShabb 54 (א[לוהים]), משמע *hearing of* 4QShirShabd 1.212, מלחמת *battle of* 4QShirShabc 47, תבנית *structure of* 4QShirShabd 1.216, appar. ברך *blessing of* 4QShirShabf 20.213, קול דממת *sound of the silence of* 20.27.8, רוח דממת *spirit of the silence of gods* 4QShirShabf 183 (אלוהי[ם]), מחני *camps of* 4QShirShaba 22=4QShirShabb 14.18 4QShirShabf 20.213, רוחות *spirits of* 4QShirShabd 1.143 (רוחי [אלוה]ים) 1.28.9 4QShirShabe 55 4QShirShabf 67 20.211 ([א]לוהים) 23.110 (אֱלֹהִים = *God*), בדני *forms of* 146.7 (בדנ[י א]ל[והים]) 15.24 (אלו[הים]) 192, צורות *forms of* 194 ([צ]ורות; || רוּחַ *spirit*) 195, תושבחות כול אלוהים *praises of all divine beings* 4QShirShabd 1.132.33 (תשבחות).

<ADJ> אלוהים חיים *living gods* 4QShirShabd 1.144 =4QShirShabf 65 4QShirShabf 145.6 194.6 20.211 ([א]לוהים). **<PREP>** רנן בְּ *sing among* 4QShirShabd 1.136 4QShirShabe 43 ([רו]נן באל[והי]); וִהְיִיתֶם כֵּאלֹהִים *and you will be as gods* 35 (perh. *God*), [ויכבדהו כ]אלהים *and he honoured him like gods* Si 452(Segal); פ[לא] מאלוהים ואנשים *a wonder among gods and men* 4QShirShaba 2.23; שָׂרִיתָ עִם־אֱלֹהִים *you have struggled with gods*, or *God* Gn 3229, בוא עִם *come with* 4QShir Shabb 281 (אלוה[י]); ירא עַל ni. *be fearful over* 4QShir Shabf 23.113.

<COLL> אֱלֹהִים וַאֲנָשִׁים *gods and people* (see also §1) Gn 3229 Jg 99.13 4QShirShaba 2.23, לֹא אֱלֹהִים *non-gods* 2 K 1918||Is 3719 Jr 211 1620 2 C 139.

Esp. in בְּנֵי אֱלֹהִים **sons of gods** (and vars.), Gn 62.4 Jb 16 21 387, **<SUBJ>** בוא *come* Gn 64 (+ אֶל־בְּנוֹת הָאָדָם *to the daughters of humans*) Jb 16 21, יצב htp. *position oneself* 16 21, לקח *take* wives Gn 62, ראה *see* 62, רוע hi. *shout* Jb 387 (|| כּוֹכְבֵי בֹקֶר *morning stars*).

3b. ghost אֱלֹהִים רָאִיתִי עֹלִים מִן־הָאָרֶץ *a god* (Samuel) *I have seen rising from the ground* 1 S 2813.

Also 4QPrFêtesc 2142 4QMa fr. 11.120 4QShirb 2.110 (אל[והי]) 2.25 ([א]ל[ו]הים) 42 123 18.27 ([אלו]הים) 18.37 ([א]לוה[י]) 194 363 (אלוה[ים]) 1444 ([א]להים) 4QShir Shaba 1.15.6 3.13 4.13 (אל[ו]הים) 4QShirShabb 281 (אלוה[י]) 4QShirShabc 3.12.4 ([א]לוהי) 3.16 3.211 410 4QShirShabd 1.25 4QShirShabe 33 ([אלו]הים) 45 4QShir Shabf 3.114 (לאלוהי) 41 (אלוה[ים]) 198 (אלו[הי]ם) 244 292 ([אלו]הים) 302 353 443 4QShirShabg 12 MasShir Shab 210 11QShirShab 57 f6 k3 m2 ([א]לוהי) o4.6 ([א]לוהים) 4Q385 110 34 4Q525 28 (אלוה[ים]) 2.44 5.75 (וא[לוהים]) 4QapPsb 156.9 193 338 471 833 4QApocMos A 41 4Q409 210 4Q372 125 4QPsJosa 22.11 111.

→ אֱלוֹהַּ *God*, אֱלֹהוּת *divinity*.

[אֱלוֹ], see אֵלֶּה.

אִלּוּ 2 conj. **(even) if,** וְאִלּוּ חָיָה אֶלֶף שָׁנִים ... אֶחָד הַכֹּל הוֹלֵךְ אֶל־מָקוֹם *and even if he had lived a thousand years ... everyone goes to one place* Ec 6$_{6}$ (4QQoh[a] ואם לוא *and if* he had *not*), וְאִלּוּ ... נִמְכַּרְנוּ הֶחֱרַשְׁתִּי *and even if ... we had been sold, I should have kept silent* Est 7$_{4}$, וְאִילוּ הָאֶחָד שֶׁיִּפּוֹל וְאֵין שֵׁנִי לַהֲקִימוֹ *but if (it is) the (solitary) one that falls, there is no partner to help him up* Ec 4$_{10}$ (if em. אִי לוֹ *alas for him*).

→ אִלּוּלֵי *if not.*

[אַלְוָא] n.[m.] **aloe**—לאה—כלי דם לאה *vessels of blood of aloes* 3QTr 11$_{14}$ (Milik ד מן[ע] *resin*; Allegro דמ[ע] לאח *tithe of liquid*).

אֱלוֹהַּ 57.1.3 n.m. **God**—L אֱלוֹהַּ (L אֱלֹהַּ) cstr. אֱלוֹהַּ (L אֱלוֹהַּ); sf. לֵאלֹהוֹ—**1.** usu. **God,** in ref. to Y.. **2. other god,** Hb 1$_{11}$ Dn 11$_{37}$ (unless em. in both; see Prep.) 11$_{38.39}$ 2 C 32$_{15}$.

<SUBJ> רבה *be great* Jb 33$_{12}$ (L אֱלוֹהַּ; + מֵאֱנוֹשׁ *than a human being*), עשׂה *make,* i.e. create Dt 32$_{15}$ (L אֱלוֹהַּ; || צוּר *rock*) Jb 35$_{10}$, יכל *be able* to rescue 2 C 32$_{15}$ (L אֱלוֹהַּ; :: אֱלֹהִים *God* of Israel), בוא *come* from Teman Hb 3$_{3}$ (L אֱלוֹהַּ; || קָדוֹשׁ *holy [one]*), עזב *forsake* Israel Ne 9$_{17}$, שׁוב hi. *take back* Jb 9$_{13}$ (obj. אַף *anger*) 33$_{26}$ (obj. צְדָקָה *righteousness*), פתח *open* lips, i.e. speak 11$_{5}$, שׁלה *draw out* soul of godless one 27$_{8}$ (or em. יָשֶׁל *removes,* from שׁלל, or יִשְׁאַל *requires* or יִשָּׂא לֶאֱלוֹהַּ *lifts up* his soul *to God*).

צפן *store up* iniquity Jb 21$_{19}$ (or em. אַל let him *not*), יפע hi. *make shine* 37$_{15}$, קטל *kill* wicked Ps 139$_{19}$, דכא pi. *crush* Jb 6$_{9}$, בצע pi. *cut off* 6$_{9}$ 27$_{8}$ (obj. חָנֵף *godless one*), עות pi. *subvert* 19$_{6}$, נקף hi. *surround* 19$_{6}$, סוך *fence in* 3$_{23}$, נתן *give* 6$_{8}$ (obj. תִּקְוָה *[object of] hope*) 35$_{10}$ (obj. זְמִרוֹת בַּלָּיְלָה *songs in the night*), חלק *apportion* 39$_{17}$, שׁלם pi. *repay* wicked 21$_{19}$.

דרשׁ *seek* day of Job's birth 3$_{4}$, יאל hi. *be pleased* 6$_{9}$, רצה *be pleased* 33$_{26}$, שׁמר *keep* Jb 29$_{2}$, ראה *see* 11QPs[a] 28$_{7}$, שׁמע *hear* 28$_{7}$, אזן hi. *listen* 28$_{7}$, שׂים *place* Jb 37$_{15}$, *notice* unseemliness (mss תְּפִלָּה *prayer*) 24$_{12}$, נתר hi. *let loose* hand 6$_{9}$, סכך *cover* 29$_{4}$ (if em. סוֹד *council of*), דבר pi. *speak* 11$_{5}$, נגד hi. *tell* 11$_{6}$, ענה *answer* 12$_{4}$, ידע *know* Job's integrity 31$_{6}$, hi. *make known* 10$_{2}$, נשׁה hi. *cause to forget* 39$_{17}$, *cause to be forgotten* 11$_{6}$ (L אֱלוֹהַּ), יכח hi. *reprove* 5$_{17}$ (+ שַׁדַּי *Shaddai*), ריב *contend* 10$_{2}$, רשׁע hi. *condemn* 10$_{2}$.

<NOM CL> אַיֵּה אֱלוֹהַּ *where is God?* Jb 35$_{10}$, הֲיֵשׁ אֱלוֹהַּ מִבַּלְעָדַי *is there a God other than me?* Is 44$_{8}$ (|| צוּר *rock*), מִי אֱלוֹהַּ מִבַּלְעֲדֵי י׳ *who is God other than Y.?* Ps 18$_{32}$ (||2 S 22$_{32}$ אֵל *God*; || צוּר), הֲלֹא־אֱלוֹהַּ גֹּבַהּ שָׁמָיִם *is not God the height of,* i.e. as high as, *heaven?* Jb 22$_{12}$, אַתָּה אֱלוֹהַּ *you are a God of* Ne 9$_{17}$, הוא ... אלוה *he is ... a God of* Si 32$_{13}$.

<OBJ> בוא hi. *bring* Jb 12$_{6}$ (+ בְּיָדוֹ *in his hand,* i.e. under his control), קרא *call* 27$_{10}$ (mss add אֶל־ call *to*; + שַׁדַּי *Shaddai*), יכח hi. *reprove* 40$_{2}$ (+ שַׁדַּי *Shaddai*), חזה *see* (of Job) 19$_{26}$, ידע *know* 4QFlor 2$_{4(mg)}$ (=Dn 11$_{32}$ אֱלֹהָיו; subj. עַם *people*) Dn 11$_{38}$, שׁכח *forget* Ps 50$_{22}$, נטשׁ *forsake* (of Jeshurun) Dt 32$_{15}$.

<CSTR> אֱלוֹהַּ יַעֲקֹב *God of Jacob* Ps 114$_{7}$ (mss אֱלֹהֵי *God of*; || אָדוֹן *lord*), אֱלוֹהַּ סְלִיחוֹת *God of forgiveness(es)* Ne 9$_{17}$, אלוה תשלמות *God of rewards* Si 32$_{13}$, אֱלוֹהַּ מָעֻזִּים *God of strongholds* Dn 11$_{38}$, אֱלוֹהַּ נֵכָר *of foreignness,* i.e. foreign god Dn 11$_{39}$, אֱלוֹהַּ כָּל־גּוֹי וּמַמְלָכָה *god of any nation or kingdom* 2 C 32$_{15(L)}$.

אִמְרַת אֱלוֹהַּ *word of God* Pr 30$_{5}$, נִשְׁמַת *breath of* Jb 4$_{9}$ (L אֱלוֹהַּ), רוּחַ *breath of* 27$_{3}$, חֵלֶק *portion of,* i.e. from 31$_{2}$ (|| שַׁדַּי *Shaddai*), יַד *hand of* 19$_{21}$ (יַד־), שֵׁבֶט *rod of* 21$_{9}$, חֵקֶר אֱלוֹהַּ *searching,* i.e. profundity, *of* 11$_{7}$ (L אֱלוֹהַּ; || שַׁדַּי), סוֹד *council of* 15$_{8}$ (L אֱלוֹהַּ) 29$_{4}$ (or em. סוֹךְ *covering*), בִּעוּתֵי *terrors of* 6$_{4}$ (|| שַׁדַּי [ms שָׁמַיִם *heaven*]), יְמֵי *days of* 29$_{2}$, כָּל־אֱלוֹהַּ *any god* Dn 11$_{37}$ (or del.; see Prep.; + חֶמְדַּת נָשִׁים *desire of,* i.e. something desired by, *women,* אֱלֹהִים *gods*) 2 C 32$_{15}$ (L אֱלוֹהַּ).

<ADJ> אֱלוֹהַּ ... חַנּוּן וְרַחוּם אֶרֶךְ־אַפַּיִם וְרַב־חֶסֶד *a compassionate and merciful, long of,* i.e. slow to, *anger and abundant of,* i.e. abounding in, *loyalty* Ne 9$_{17(Qr)}$.

<PREP> קרא לְ *call to* Jb 12$_{4}$, נשׂא לְ *raise* soul *to* 27$_{8}$ (if em.; see Subj.), כבד לְ pi. *give honour to* Dn 11$_{38.38}$, זוּ כֹחוֹ לֵאלֹהוֹ *this, his strength, is as,* or *(ascribed) to* or *(belonging) to his god* Hb 1$_{11}$ (or em. לֵאלֹהָיו *to,* etc., *his gods*), עוֹד לֶאֱלוֹהַּ מִלִּים *there are still words for,* i.e. in support of, *God* Jb 36$_{2}$.

הַאֱנוֹשׁ מֵאֱלוֹהַּ יִצְדָּק *is a human being more righteous than God?* Jb 4$_{17(L)}$ (+ עֹשֵׂה ptc. *maker,* i.e. creator).

אֶל *to(wards)*, + אמר *say* Jb 10$_{2}$, קרא *call* 27$_{10(mss)}$, נשׂא *raise* face, i.e. look at 22$_{26}$, עתר *pray* 33$_{26}$, אֶל־אֱלוֹהַּ דָּלְפָה עֵינִי *my eye drips (with tears) before*, or is sleepless *(with waiting) for*, *God* 16$_{20(L)}$.

עַל בין *have regard for* Dn 11$_{37}$ (or del. עַל־כָּל־אֱלוֹהַּ), עַל־אֱלוֹהַּ נוֹרָא הוֹד *around God is fearful majesty* Jb 37$_{22}$.

עִם יכח hi. *argue* for a person *before* Jb 16$_{21}$, עשׂה עִם *do*, i.e. deal with, *with (the help of)* Dn 11$_{39}$ (or em. עַם make, i.e. settle, *people of* a foreign god).

תַּחַת שׁחח *bow down beneath* Jb 9$_{13}$; חול מִלִּפְנֵי *writhe before* Ps 114$_{7}$ (mss אֱלֹהֵי *God of* Jacob; or em. חוּלִי אָרֶץ *writhe, O earth* to כָּל־הָאָרֶץ lord of *all the earth*).

<COLL> יִזְבְּחוּ לַשֵּׁדִים לֹא אֱלֹהַּ *they sacrifice to the demons (who were) not God* Dt 32$_{17(L)}$, יודע אלה אמתך *knowing, O God, your trustworthiness* 1QIs[b] 38$_{19}$ (MT יוֹדִיעַ אֶל־אֲמִתֶּךָ *making known your trustworthiness*).

Also 4QapPs[a] 1.2$_{8}$

<SYN> §1 שַׁדַּי *Shaddai*, צוּר *rock*.

→ אֱלֹהִים *God*.

[אֱלוֹהִים], see אֱלֹהִים.

אֱלוּל I $_{1.0.2}$ pr.n.[m.] **Elul,** sixth month of post-exilic Jewish calendar, August/September, **<PREP>** עֶשְׂרִים וַחֲמִשָּׁה לֶאֱלוּל *(day) twenty-five of Elul* Ne 6$_{15}$, ארבעה עשר לאלול *(day) fourteen of Elul* Mur 29 1$_{9}$, sim. 1$_{1}$.

[אֱלוּל] II, see אֱלִיל.

[אִלּוּלֵי] $_{0.0.1}$ conj. **if not**—אללי—אללי שהגיים קרבים אלנו אזי עלתי *if the gentiles had not closed in on us, then I should have gone up* MurEpBeth-Mashiko$_{5}$.

→ אִלּוּ *(even) if*.

אֵלוֹן I $_{10.0.1}$ **terebinth**—cstr. אֵלוֹן; pl. cstr. אֵלוֹנֵי (אֵלֹנֵי) —oft. with pl.n. or pr.n. following, sometimes perh. as composite place name, **<SUBJ>** נצב ho. *be established* Jg 9$_{6}$ (unless אֵלוֹן מֻצָּב = *Elon-muzzab*, as pl.n.; or em. הַמַּצֵּבָה terebinth *of the pillar*). **<CSTR>** מִדֶּרֶךְ אֵלוֹן מְעוֹנְנִים *from the way of the terebinth of magicians*, or, as pl.n., *Elon-meonenim* Jg 9$_{37}$, אֵלוֹן תָּבוֹר *terebinth of Tabor* 1 S 10$_{3}$, אֵלוֹן מוֹרֶה *terebinth of Moreh* or *of (the) teacher* (in Shechem) Gn 12$_{6}$ Dt 11$_{30}$ (if em. אֵלוֹנֵי מֹרֶה *terebinths of Moreh*; Sam מורא), אֵלְנֵי מַמְרֵא *terebinths of Mamre* (in Hebron) Gn 13$_{18}$ 14$_{13}$ 18$_{1}$ (or, in all three, em. אֵלוֹן *terebinth of*) 4QAges 2.2$_{4}$ (אלוני ממרה). **<PREP>** בְּ *at, in* 4QAges 2.2$_{4}$ (Allegro מאלוני), + ישׁב *dwell* Gn 13$_{18}$, שׁכן *dwell* 14$_{13}$, ירא ni. *be seen* 18$_{1}$; מִן *from* Jos 19$_{33}$ (mss אַלּוֹן *oak*); עַד *unto*, + בוא *come* 1 S 10$_{3}$, עבר *pass* Gn 12$_{6}$, *by*, + נטה *extend* tent Jg 4$_{11}$; מִן *from* Jos 19$_{33}$; עִם מלך hi. *proclaim as king by* Jg 9$_{6}$; אֵצֶל *near* Dt 11$_{30}$. **<COLL>** אֵלוֹן בְּצַעֲנַנִּים *terebinth at Zaanannim* or *Elon-bezaanannim* (near Kedesh) Jos 19$_{33}$ (mss אַלּוֹן *oak* or *Allon-*) Jg 4$_{11(Qr)}$.

→ אֵילוֹן *Elon*, אֵילִם *Elim*.

אֵלוֹן II, see אֵילוֹן I.

אַלּוֹן I $_{9}$ n.m. **oak**—cstr. אַלּוֹן; pl. אַלּוֹנִים; cstr. אַלּוֹנֵי—**oak** or other large tree, **<SUBJ>** ילל hi. *howl* Zc 11$_{2}$ (+ אֶרֶז *cedar*, בְּרוֹשׁ *cypress*). **<OBJ>** עשׂה *make* into oars Ezk 27$_{6}$, לקח *take* for fashioning idol Is 44$_{14}$ (+ תִּרְזָה *oak*, אֶרֶז). **<CSTR>** אַלּוֹן בָּכוּת *Allon-bacuth*, lit. *oak of weeping*, as name of oak and place near Bethel Gn 35$_{8}$, אַלּוֹנֵי הַבָּשָׁן *oaks of Bashan* Zc 11$_{2}$, כָּל־אַלּוֹנֵי הַבָּשָׁן *all the oaks of Bashan* Is 2$_{13}$ (+ כָּל־אַרְזֵי הַלְּבָנוֹן *all the cedars of Lebanon*). **<PREP>** כְּ היה *be as* Is 6$_{13}$ (לְבָעֵר *for burning*; + אֵלָה), חָסֹן הוּא כָּאַלּוֹנִים *he* (Amorite) *was strong like the oaks* Am 2$_{9}$ (+ אֶרֶז *cedar*); גְּבוּלָם מֵחֵלֶף מֵאַלּוֹן בְּצַעֲנַנִּים *their boundary was from Heleph (and) from the oak tree in Zaanannim*, or *from Allon-bezaanannim* Jos 19$_{33(mss)}$ (L מֵאֵלוֹן *from the terebinth of* or *from Elon-*); עַל *against* Is 2$_{13}$; תַּחַת *beneath*, + קבר ni. *be buried* (of Rebekah's nurse) Gn 35$_{8}$, קטר pi. *burn (incense)* Ho 4$_{13}$ (כִּי טוֹב צִלָּהּ *because its shade is good*; + אֵלָה *terebinth*, לִבְנֶה *poplar*).

<COLL> אַלּוֹנִים מִבָּשָׁן *oaks from Bashan* Ezk 27$_{6}$.

אַלּוֹן II $_{1}$ pr.n.m. **Allon,** son of Jedaiah and father of Shiphi, descendant of Simeon, 1 C 4$_{37}$.

אַלּוּף I $_{60}$ n.m. **chief**—אַלֻּף; pl. abs. אַלֻּפִים; cstr. אַלּוּפֵי (אַלֻּפֵי); sf. אַלּוּפֵיהֶם (אַלֻּפֵיהֶם)—alw. in ref. to early

Edomite leaders except at Zc 9$_{7}$ 12$_{5.6}$ (Judaean leaders, unless em. in all three to אֶלֶף *clan*).

<SUBJ> היה *be* 1 C 1$_{51}$, אמר *say* Zc 12$_{5}$ (or em.), אכל *eat*, i.e. destroy Zc 12$_{6}$ (or em.), בהל ni. *be dismayed* Ex 15$_{15}$ (|| אַיִל *leader*). **<NOM CL>** אֵלֶּה אַלּוּפֵי *these are the chiefs of* Gn 36$_{15.16.17.18.21.29.30.43}$||1 C 1$_{54}$, אֵלֶּה אַלּוּפֵיהֶם *these are their chiefs* Gn 36$_{19}$, [אל]פי ישראל המה הרגלים *the chiefs of Israel are the feet* 4QpGen^{a} 5$_{3}$. **<OBJ>** אחז *hold* Ex 15$_{15}$, שׂים *place* Zc 12$_{6}$ (or em.).

<CSTR> אַלּוּפֵי אֱדוֹם *chiefs of Edom* Gn 36$_{43}$||1 C 1$_{54}$ Ex 15$_{15}$, אֱלִיפַז *of Eliphaz* Gn 36$_{16}$, רְעוּאֵל *of Reuel* 36$_{17}$, אָהֳלִיבָמָה *of Oholibamah* 36$_{18}$, הַחֹרִי *of the Horites* 36$_{21.29.30}$, אַלֻּפֵי יְהוּדָה *chiefs of Judah* Zc 12$_{5.6}$ (or em. in both to אַלְפֵי *clans of*), [אל]פי ישראל *chiefs of Israel* 4QpGen^{a} 5$_{3}$, אַלּוּפֵי בְנֵי־עֵשָׂו *chiefs of the sons of Esau* Gn 36$_{15}$, שְׁמוֹת אַלּוּפֵי עֵשָׂו *names of the chiefs of Esau* 36$_{40}$. **<APP>** אַלּוּף followed by name of person, 21 times in Gn 36$_{15-18.29.30}$, 11 times in Gn 36$_{40-43}$||1 C 1$_{51-54}$.

<PREP> אַלּוּפֵי הַחֹרִי לְאַלֻּפֵיהֶם *the chiefs of the Horites according to (the names of) their chiefs* Gn 36$_{30}$ (or em. אַלְפֵיהֶם according to *their clans*); וְהָיָה כְּאַלֻּף בִּיהוּדָה *and he will be as a chief in Judah* Zc 9$_{7}$ (or em. כְּאֶלֶף *as a clan*).

[אַלּוּף] II 1.1 **cow**—Si אלוף; pl. sf. אַלּוּפֵינוּ—אַלּוּפֵינוּ מְסֻבָּלִים *our cattle are burdened*, perh. pregnant Ps 144$_{14}$, באלוף ינהג *he guides the ox* Si 38$_{25}$ (|| שׁוֹר *ox* [mg בשיר *with a song*]).

→ אֶלֶף *cattle*.

אַלּוּף III 8 adj. **tame**—cstr. אַלּוּף; sf. אַלּוּפִי; pl. אַלֻּפִים—**1.** as noun, **companion, friend,** **<NOM CL>** אַלּוּף נְעֻרַי אָתָּה *you* (Y.) *are the companion of my youth* Jr 3$_{4}$ (+ אָב *father*), אַתָּה ... אַלּוּפִי *you* (enemy) *were ... my companion* Ps 55$_{14}$ (|| ידע pu. ptc. *intimate*). **<OBJ>** פקד *appoint* as head Jr 13$_{21}$, למד pi. *teach* 13$_{21}$, עזב *leave* Pr 2$_{17}$, פרד hi. *separate*, i.e. lose Pr 16$_{28}$ 17$_{9}$. **<CSTR>** אַלּוּף נְעוּרֶיהָ *companion of her youth* Pr 2$_{17}$ (or em. אִלּוּף *instruction of*; + בְּרִית *covenant*), אַלּוּף נְעֻרָי *companion of my youth* Jr 3$_{4}$. **<PREP>** אַל־תִּבְטְחוּ בְּאַלּוּף *do not trust in a companion* Mc 7$_{5}$ (|| רֵעַ *friend*).

2. as adj., **obedient,** כְּכֶבֶשׂ אַלּוּף יוּבַל לִטְבוֹחַ *as an obedient lamb led for slaughter* Jr 11$_{19}$.

→ אלף *learn*.

[אִלּוּף], see אַלּוּף III, §1, Cstr.

אָלוּשׁ 2 pl.n. **Alush,** station of exodus between Dophkah and Rephidim, Nm 33$_{13.14}$ (Sam אליש both times).

אֵלוֹת, see אֵילַת.

אֶלְזָבָד 2 pr.n.m. **Elzabad, 1.** Gadite warrior, 1 C 12$_{13}$. **2.** Korahite gatekeeper, son of Shemaiah, 1 C 26$_{7}$.

→ אֵל *God* + זבד *bestow*.

אלזכר 0.0.0.3 pr.n.m. **Elzachar, 1.** son of Jehohail (יהוחיל), Seal 42$_{1}$ (Palestine). **2.** father of Shebi (שבי), perh. ident. with preceding, Seal 43$_{2}$ (Palestine). **3.** father of Jathom (יתם), Seal 766$_{2}$ (7th cent.).

→ אֵל *God* + זכר *remember*.

אלח 3 vb. **be corrupt—Ni.** Pf. נֶאֱלָחוּ; ptc. נֶאֱלָח—יַחְדָּו נֶאֱלָחוּ אֵין עֹשֵׂה־טוֹב *together they have become corrupt, there is none who does good* Ps 14$_{3}$||53$_{4}$ (כֻּלּוֹ סָג), נִתְעָב וְנֶאֱלָח אִישׁ־שֹׁתֶה ... עַוְלָה *one abominable and corrupt, a man who drinks ... evil* Jb 15$_{16}$.

אֶלְחָנָן 4.0.0.2 pr.n.m. **Elhanan, 1.** one of David's warriors, son of Jaareoregim/Jair, 2 S 21$_{19}$||1 C 20$_{5(Qr)}$. **2.** one of David's warriors, son of Dodo, 2 S 23$_{24}$||1 C 11$_{26}$. **3.** father of Abigail (אבגיל), Seal 867$_{2}$ (8th/7th cent.). **4.** Seal 5 (8th cent.).

→ אֵל *God* + חנן *be gracious*.

אֱלִיאָב 21 pr.n.m. **Eliab, 1.** son of Helon (חֵלֹן) and leader of tribe of Zebulun, Nm 1$_{9}$ 2$_{7}$ 7$_{24.29}$ 10$_{16}$. **2.** father of Dathan and Abiram, descendant of Reuben, Nm 16$_{1.12}$ 26$_{8.9}$ Dt 11$_{6}$. **3.** eldest brother of David, 1 S 16$_{6}$ 17$_{13.28.28}$ 1 C 2$_{13}$ 27$_{18}$ (if em. אֱלִיהוּ *Elihu*) 2 C 11$_{18}$. **4.** Levite, son of Nahath (נַחַת; or em. תּוֹחַ *Toah* or תֹּחוּ *Tohu*) and father of Jeroham, appar. ident. with Eliel (אֱלִיאֵל) at 1 C 6$_{19}$ and Elihu (אֱלִיהוּא) at 1 S 1$_{1}$, 1 C

6₁₂. **5–6.** two of David's Gadite warriors, 1 C 12₁₀ 12(mss) (L אֱלִיאֵל *Eliel*). **7.** Levitical musician, 1 C 15₁₈.₂₀ 16₅.

→ אֵל *God* + אָב *father*.

אֱלִיאֵל 10 pr.n.m. **Eliel, 1.** Eliel the Mahavite (הַמַּחֲוִים; or em. הַמַּחֲנִי or הַמַּחֲנַיְמִי *the Mahan(aim)ite* or הַמְּעוֹנִי *the Maonite*), one of David's warriors, 1 C 11₄₆. **2.** one of David's Gadite warriors, 1 C 12₁₂ (mss אֱלִיאָב *Eliab*). **3.** another of David's warriors, 1 C 11₄₇. **4.** head of fathers' house in Manasseh, 1 C 5₂₄. **5.** son of Shimei (שִׁמְעִי; or em. שֶׁמַע *Shema*), descendant of Benjamin, 1 C 8₂₀. **6.** son of Shashak, descendant of Benjamin, 1 C 8₂₂. **7.** Levite, leader of sons of Hebron, 1 C 15₉.₁₁. **8.** Levite, son of Toah (תּוֹחַ; or em. תֹּחוּ *Tohu*) and father of Jeroham, appar. ident. with Eliab (אֱלִיאָב) at 1 C 6₁₂ and Elihu (אֱלִיהוּא) at 1 S 1₁, 1 C 6₁₉. **9.** Levite at time of Hezekiah, 2 C 31₁₃.

→ אֵל *God*.

אליאר 0.0.0.3 pr.n.m. **Eljair, 1.** father of Gedaliah (גדליהו [בן]), Arad ost. 21₂. **2.** son of Jeremiah, Seal 763₁ (c. 700). **3.** Seal 744₁ (c. 700).

→ אֵל *God* + אור *be light*.

אֱלִיאָתָה 2 pr.n.m. **Eliathah**—אֱלִיָּתָה—musician, son of Heman, 1 C 25₄.₂₇.

→ אֵל *God* + אתה *come*.

אליבר 0.0.0.1 **Elibar,** father of Elon (אלן), Seal 397₂ (7th cent.).

→ perh. אֵל *God* + ברר *purify*.

אֱלִידָד, see אֱלְדָד.

אֱלְיָדָע 4 pr.n.m. **Eliada, 1.** son of David, appar. ident. with Beeliada (בְּעֶלְיָדָע) at ||1 C 14₇, 2 S 5₁₆||1 C 3₈. **2.** father of Rezon, king of Damascus at time of Solomon, 1 K 11₂₃. **3.** descendant of Benjamin, military leader at time of Jehoshaphat, 2 C 17₁₇.

→ אֵל *God* + ידע *know*.

אַלְיָה 5.0.1 n.f. **fat tail** of sacrificial ram, alw. with article, **<OBJ>** לקח *take* Ex 29₂₂||Lv 8₂₅ (+ חֵלֶב *fat*, יֹתֶרֶת *appendage* of liver, כִּלְיָה *kidney*, שׁוֹק *thigh*), קרב hi. *present* in sacrifice Lv 3₉ 7₃ 11QT 15₈ + Sup ([האלי[ה; all three + חֵלֶב ,יֹתֶרֶת ,כִּלְיָה), מצא hi. *bring* Lv 9₁₉ (+ חֵלֶב ,יֹתֶרֶת ,כִּלְיָה), סור hi. *remove* 3₉ perh. 11QT 20₇ (+ חֵלֶב; both + לְעֻמַּת הֶעָצֶה *next to the backbone*), רום hi. *raise* 1 S 9₂₄ (if em. וְהֶעָלֶיהָ the thigh *and that which was on it* to וְהָאַלְיָה *and the fat tail*), שׂים *place* before Saul 9₂₄ (if em.). **<APP>** חֶלְבּוֹ הָאַלְיָה *its fat: (namely) the fat tail* Lv 3₉ (or em. וְהָאַלְיָה *and the fat tail*), sim. 7₃ (or em. וְאֵת הָאַלְיָה *and the fat tail*). **<ADJ>** הָאַלְיָה תְמִימָה *the entire fat tail* Lv 3₉ 11QT 15₈(Yadin) ([האלי[ה תמימה).

אֵלִיָּה, see אֵלִיָּהוּ.

אֵלִיָּהוּ 71.1.0.6 pr.n.m. **Elijah**—אֵלִיָּה—**1.** Elijah the Tishbite (הַתִּשְׁבִּי) from Gilead, prophet at time of Ahab, 1 K 17₁ (+ הַתִּשְׁבִּי) 17₁₃₊₇t 18₁₊₂₁t 19₁₊₇t 21₁₇.₂₀.₂₈ 2 K 1₃.₄.₈ (all three אֵלִיָּה) 1₁₀.₁₂ (אֵלִיָּה) 1₁₃.₁₅.₁₇ 2₁₊₁₁t 3₁₁ 9₃₆ (+ הַתִּשְׁבִּי) 10₁₀.₁₇ Ml 3₂₃ (אֵלִיָּה) 2 C 21₁₂ Si 48₄. **2.** priest, son of Harim and husband of foreign wife, Ezr 10₂₁ (אֵלִיָּה). **3.** son of Elam and husband of foreign wife, Ezr 10₂₆ (אֵלִיָּה). **4.** son of Jeroham (יְרֹחָם; or em. יְרֵמוֹת *Jeremoth*), descendant of Benjamin, 1 C 8₂₇ (אֵלִיָּה). **5.** son of Micah (מיכה [בן]), Seal 527₁ (T. Beit Mirsim?, 7th/6th cent.). **6.** Kenyon inscr. 213. **7.** Seal 344₁ (7th cent.). **8.** Seal 585₂ (T. Beit Mirsim?, 7th/6th cent.). **9.** Seal 747₂ (c. 700). **10.** Seal 762₁ (7th cent.).

→ אֵל *God* + י׳ *Y*.

אֱלִיהוּ, see אֱלִיהוּא.

אֱלִיהוּא 11 pr.n.m. **Elihu**—אֱלִיהוּ—**1.** friend of Job Jb 32₂.₄ (אֱלִיהוּ) 32₅.₆ 34₁ 35₁ (אֱלִיהוּ) 36₁. **2.** Korahite, gatekeeper, 1 C 26₇ (אֱלִיהוּ). **3.** brother of David, ident. with Eliab at 1 S 16₆ and 1 C 2₁₃, 1 C 27₁₈ (אֱלִיהוּ). **4.** Ephraimite, ancestor of Samuel, ident. with Eliab at 1 C 6₁₂ and Eliel at 6₁₉, 1 S 1₁. **5.** Manassite chief, supporter of David, 1 C 12₂₁.

→ אֵל *God* + הוּא *he*.

אֱלְיְהוֹעֵינַי, see אֶלְיוֹעֵינַי.

אֶלְיוֹעֵינַי 7 pr.n.m. **Elioenai**—אֱלְיְהוֹעֵינַי, אֶלְיוֹעֵנַי—**1.** leader of Simeon, 1 C 4₃₆. **2.** son of Becher and grandson of Benjamin, 1 C 7₈. **3.** son of Pashhur, member of priestly family at time of Ezra, one who divorced foreign wife, Ezr 10₂₂. **4.** priest assoc. with rededication of walls of Jerusalem, Ne 12₄₁. **5.** son of Zattu, husband of foreign wife at time of Ezra, Ezr 10₂₇ (אֶלְיוֹעֵנַי). **6.** returning exile, son of Zerahiah and descendant of Pahath-moab, Ezr 8₄ (אֶלְיְהוֹעֵינַי *Eliehoenai*). **7.** son of Neariah (נְעַרְיָה), descendant of David, 1 C 3₂₃.₂₄. **8.** gatekeeper, son of Meshelemiah, 1 C 26₃ (אֶלְיְהוֹעֵינַי). **9.** son of Shimei, descendant of Benjamin, 1 C 8₂₀ (if em. אֱלִיעֵנַי *Elienai*).
→ perh. אֶל *to* + ״ Y. + עַיִן *eye*.

אֶלְיוֹעֵנַי, see אֶלְיוֹעֵינַי.

אֶלְיַחְבָּא 2 pr.n.m. **Eliahba**, one of David's mighty warriors, 2 S 23₃₂‖1 C 11₃₃.
→ אֵל *God* + חבא *hide*.

אֱלִיחֹרֶף 1 pr.n.m. **Elihoreph**, one of Solomon's scribes 1 K 4₃.
→ אֵל *God* + חֹרֶף *autumn*.

אֱלִיל 20.1.3 n.m. **worthlessness**—אֱלִל, Kt אלול; pl. abs. אֱלִילִים; cstr. אֱלִילֵי, sf. אֱלִילֶיהָ—**1. worthlessness, worthless thing,** <NOM CL> אליל בעוף דבורה *a worthless thing among winged creatures is the bee* Si 11₃ (+ וראש תנובת פריה *but its fruit is the best of produce*).

<OBJ> נבא htp. *prophesy* Jr 14₁₄ (+ חֲזוֹן שֶׁקֶר *deceptive vision*, קֶסֶם *divination*, תַּרְמִית לֵב *deceit of heart*). <CSTR> רֹעִי הָאֱלִיל *the shepherd of worthlessness*, i.e. worthless shepherd Zc 11₁₇ or. em. הָאֱוִילִי [my] *foolish* [shepherd]; + עֹזְבִי הַצֹּאן *one who deserts the flock*), רֹפְאֵי אֱלִל *healers of worthlessness*, i.e. worthless physicians Jb 13₄ (‖ שֶׁקֶר *falsehood*).

2. worthless gods, idols, <SUBJ> חלף *vanish* Is 2₁₈ GnzPs 2₂₁, נוע *shake* Is 19₁. <NOM CL> כָּל־אֱלֹהֵי הָעַמִּים אֱלִילִים *all the gods of the peoples are idols* Ps 96₅ ‖1 C 16₂₆.

<OBJ> עשׂה *make* Lv 26₁ (‖ פֶּסֶל *carved image*, מַצֵּבָה *standing stone*; + אֶבֶן מַשְׂכִּית *figured stone*) Is 2₂₀.₂₀ 31₇.₇ Hb 2₁₈ (+ פֶּסֶל, מַסֵּכָה *molten image*, מוֹרֶה שֶּׁקֶר *teacher of deception*), עבד *serve* GnzPs 2₂₀ (+ מַעֲשֵׂה יָדַיִם *work of the hands*), מאס *reject* Is 31₇.₇, שׁלך hi. *throw away* 2₂₀.₂₀, שׁבת hi. *destroy* Ezk 30₁₃ (or em. אֵילִים *leaders*; ‖ גִּלּוּל *idol*, נָשִׂיא *prince*).

<CSTR> אֱלִילֵי כַסְפּוֹ *his idols of silver* Is 2₂₀ 31₇, אֱלִילֵי זְהָבוֹ *his idols of gold* 2₂₀ 31₇, אֱלִילֵי מִצְרַיִם *idols of Egypt* Is 19₁ 1QM 14₁; מַמְלְכֹת הָאֱלִיל *kingdoms of the idol(s)* Is 10₁₀ (+ פֶּסֶל *carved image*; perh. אֱלִיל = *worthlessness*). <ADJ> אֱלִילִים אִלְּמִים *dumb idols* Hb 2₁₈.

<PREP> עשׂה לְ *do for* Is 10₁₁ (+ עָצָב *idol*); בְּ *against* 1QM 14₁, הלל בְּ htp. *boast of* Ps 97₇ (+ פֶּסֶל *carved image*); פנה אֶל *turn to* Lv 19₄ (+ אֱלֹהֵי מַסֵּכָה *molten gods*), דרשׁ אֶל *inquire of* Is 19₃ (‖ יִדְּעֹנִי *familiar spirit*, אִטִּי *ghost*, אוֹב *ghost*).

<COLL> וַתִּמָּלֵא אַרְצוֹ אֱלִילִים ni. *and his land was filled with idols* Is 2₈ (+ מַעֲשֵׂה יָדַיִם *work of the hands*).

<SYN> פֶּסֶל *image*.

אֱלִימֶלֶךְ 6 pr.n.m. **Elimelech**, **1.** husband of Naomi, Ru 1₂.₃ 2₁.₃ 4₃.₉. **2.** Hazor inscr. 6₂ (אלמ[לך]; others אלמ[תן] *Elmattan*).
→ אֵל *God* + מֶלֶךְ *king*.

אליסמך, see אלסמך.

אֶלְיָסָף 6 pr.n.m. **Eliasaph**, **1.** son of Deuel (דְּעוּאֵל; Nm 2₁₄[L] רְעוּאֵל *Reuel* [mss, Sam [דְּעוּאֵל]) and leader of tribe of Gad, Nm 1₁₄ 2₁₄ 7₄₂.₄₇ 10₂₀. **2.** son of Lael (לָאֵל) and head of family of Gershon, Nm 3₂₄.
→ אֵל *God* + יסף *add*.

אליעז, see אלעז.

אֱלִיעֶזֶר 14.0.5 pr.n.m. **Eliezer**—**1.** Eliezer of Damascus, servant of Abraham, Gn 15₂. **2.** son of Moses and Zipporah, Ex 18₄ 1 C 23₁₅.₁₇.₁₇. **3.** son of Becher and grandson of Benjamin, 1 C 7₈. **4.** son of Dodavahu

(דֹּדָוָהוּ; or em. דֹּדָיָהוּ *Dodiah*) and prophet at time of Jehoshaphat, 2 C 20$_{37}$. **5.** priest at time of David, 1 C 15$_{24}$. **6.** Levite assoc. with temple treasury, 1 C 26$_{25}$. **7–9.** members of priestly or Levitical families at time of Ezra, who had married foreign wives, Ezr 10$_{18}$ (ms אֶלְעָזָר *Eleazar*) 10$_{23.31}$. **10.** appar. leading Levite summoned by Ezra, Ezr 8$_{16}$. **11.** son of Zichri and leader of Reuben at time of David, 1 C 27$_{16}$. **12.** son of Samuel and party to lease transaction, 5/6ḤevBA 44$_{3}$ fr. 1 fr. 2 5/6ḤevBA 45. **13.** MurEpJonathan$_{3}$.
→ אֵל *God* + עֶזֶר *help.*

אֱלִיעָם 2.0.0.1 pr.n.m. **Eliam, 1.** father of Bathsheba, perh. ident. with Ammiel at 1 C 3$_{5}$, 2 S 11$_{3}$. **2.** warrior among the thirty of David, appar. ident. with Ahijah at 1 C 11$_{36}$, 2 S 23$_{34}$. **3.** person known from Seal 6 (perh. Babylonia; or read אלנעם *Elnaam*).
→ אֵל *God* + עַם *people.*

אֱלִיעֵנַי 1 pr.n.m. **Elienai,** son of Shimei, descendant of Benjamin, 1 C 8$_{20}$ (or em. אֶלְיוֹעֵינַי *Elioenai*).
→ perh. אֶל *to* + ״ *Y.* + עַיִן *eye.*

אֱלִיפַז 15 pr.n.m. **Eliphaz**—אֱלִיפָז—**1.** son of Adah and Esau, Gn 36$_{4.10.11}$||1 C 1$_{35.36}$ Gn 36$_{12}$=4QpGen^{a} 4$_{1}$ Gn 36$_{12.15.16}$. **2.** Temanite, friend of Job, Jb 2$_{11}$ 4$_{1}$ 15$_{1}$ 22$_{1}$ 42$_{7.9}$.
→ אֵל *God* + פַּז *fine gold.*

אֱלִיפַל 1 pr.n.m. **Eliphal,** warrior of David and son of Ur, perh. ident. with Eliphelet (אֱלִיפֶלֶט) at ||2 S 23$_{34}$, 1 C 11$_{35}$.
→ אֵל *God* + פלל *intervene.*

[אֱלִיפָלָה], see אֱלִיפְלֵהוּ.

אֱלִיפְלֵהוּ 2 pr.n.m. **Elipheleh,** Levite, gatekeeper and musician, 1 C 15$_{18.21}$ (or em. in both אֱלִיפָלָה *Eliphalah*).
→ אֵל *God* + perh. פלה hi. *distinguish.*

אֱלִיפֶלֶט 9.0.0.1 pr.n.m. **Eliphelet**—אֶלְפֶּלֶט, אֱלִיפָלֶט—**1.** son of David, 2 S 5$_{16}$||1 C 3$_{8}$||14$_{7}$ 1 C 3$_{6}$||14$_{5}$ (אֶלְפָּלֶט; mss אֱלִיפֶלֶט). **2.** one of David's warriors, son of Ahasbai, perh. ident. with Eliphal at 1 C 11$_{35}$, 2 S 23$_{34}$. **3.** son of Eshek, descendant of Benjamin, 1 C 8$_{39}$. **4.** son of Adonikam, Ezr 8$_{13}$. **5.** son of Hashum, Ezr 10$_{33}$. **6.** T. el-'Oreme jug graf. (אלפלט).
→ אֵל *God* + פלט *escape.*

אֱלִיצוּר 5.0.0.1 pr.n.m. **Elizur**—I אליצר—**1.** son of Shedeur (שְׁדֵיאוּר) and leader of tribe of Reuben, Nm 1$_{5}$ 2$_{10}$ 7$_{30.35}$ 10$_{18}$. **2.** seal 498 (7th cent.).
→ אֵל *God* + צוּר *rock.*

אֱלִיצָפָן 6 pr.n.m. **Elizaphan**—אֶלְצָפָן (Sam אליצפן)—**1.** Levite, son of Uzziel, Ex 6$_{22}$ Lv 10$_{4}$ (both אֶלְצָפָן; Sam אליצפן) Nm 3$_{30}$ (BHS אֱלִיצָפָן) 1 C 15$_{8}$ 2 C 29$_{13}$. **2.** prince of Zebulun, son of Parnach, Nm 34$_{25}$.
→ אֵל *God* + צפן *hide.*

אֱלִיקָא 1 pr.n.m. **Elika,** one of David's warriors, אֱלִיקָא הַחֲרֹדִי *Elika the Harodite* 2 S 23$_{25}$ (mss הֲרֹרִי *Harorite* or אֲרֹדִי *Arodite*).
→ אֵל *God.*

אֶלְיָקִים 12.0.0.6 pr.n.m. **Eliakim**—I אליקם—**1.** son of Hilkiah and overseer of palace (עַל־הַבַּיִת *over the house*) at time of Hezekiah, 2 K 18$_{18.26.37}$||Is 36$_{3.11.22}$ 2 K 19$_{2}$||Is 37$_{2}$ Is 22$_{20}$. **2.** son of Josiah and his successor as king of Israel, name changed to Jehoiakim, 2 K 23$_{34}$||2 C 36$_{4}$. **3.** priest at time of Nehemiah, Ne 12$_{41}$. Seal 242$_{1}$ (אליקם; 6th cent.). **4.** Seal 108$_{1}$ (אליקם; Beth-Shemesh, 8th cent.). **5.** Seal 436$_{1}$ (אליקם; 7th cent.). **6.** Seal 486$_{1}$ (אליקם; T. Beit Mirsim, 8th cent.). **7.** Seal 277$_{1}$ (אליקם; Ramat Raḥel, 8th cent.). **8.** son of Johel (יוהל), Seal 829$_{1}$ (אליקם; City of David, 7th/6th cent.). **9.** son of Maaseiah (מעשיה).
→ אֵל *God* + קום *arise.*

אליקם, see אֶלְיָקִים.

אלירב 0.0.0.1 pr.n. **Elirab,** Lachish inscr. 32.
→ אֵל *God* + רבב *be many* or ריב *contend.*

אלירם, see אלרם.

אליש, see אָלוּשׁ.

אלישב, see אֶלְיָשִׁיב.

אֱלִישֶׁבַע 1 pr.n.f. **Elisheba,** wife of Aaron and daughter of Amminadab, Ex 6_{23}.

→ אֵל *God* + שׁבע *swear.*

אֱלִישָׁה 3 pr.n.m. **Elishah,** son of Javan and appar. eponymous ancestor of Cyprus, Gn 10_{4}||1 C 1_{7} Ezk 27_{7} (+ אִיֵּי *islands of*).

אֱלִישׁוּעַ 2 pr.n.m. **Elishua,** son of David, 2 S 5_{15}||1 C 14_{5} 1 C 3_{6} (if em. אֱלִישָׁמָע *Elishama*).

→ אֵל *God* + ישׁע hi. *save.*

אֶלְיָשִׁיב 17.0.1.21 pr.n.m. **Eliashib**—I אלשב, אלישב—**1.** priest at time of David, 1 C 24_{12}. **2.** high priest at time of Nehemiah, Ne $3_{1.20.21.21}$ $12_{10.10.22.23}$ $13_{4.7.28}$. **3.** father of Jehohanan (mss יְהוֹנָתָן *Jehonathan*), Ezr 10_{6}. **4.** singer at time of Ezra, Ezr 10_{24}. **5.** descendant of Zattu, Ezr 10_{27}. **6.** descendant of Bani, Ezr 10_{36}. **7.** son of Elioenai, descendant of Solomon, 1 C 3_{24}.

8. name of priestly course, 4QMish A 1.1_{8} (אלי[שיב]) 4QMish B[a] 1.1_{8} ([א]ל[ישיב]) 1.3_{4} 2.2_{1} (אלי[שיב]) 2.2_{5} 4QMish C[b] 1_{2} 4QMish C[c]$_{1}$ (all three [אלישיב]).

9. son of Shual (שעל), Seal 375_{1} (אלישב; 8th/7th cent.). **10.** father of Shelemiah ([ש]למיה[ו בן] אלישב), Seal 879_{2} (7th/6th cent.). **11.** Seal 872_{1} (אלישב; 7th/6th cent.). **12.** son of Ashiah (אשיהו), Arad ost. 17_{2} Seal 231_{1} (both אלישב) 232_{1} (אלשב [ב]ן אשיה) 282_{1} (אלישב; all three Arad, 7th cent.). **13.** administrator at Arad, Arad ost. 1_{1} 2_{1} 3_{1} 4_{1} 5_{1} 6_{1} 7_{1} 8_{1} (all eight אלישב) 9_{1} (אליש[ב]) 10_{1} (אלי[שב]) 11_{1} (אלישב) 12_{1} (אלי[שב]) 14_{1} ([אל]יש[ב]) 15_{1} (אלי[שב]) 16_{2} 18_{1} 24_{2} 38_{5} (all four אלישב) 47_{1} ([אל]ישב) 64_{2} (אליש[ב]). **14.** son of Ephroah (אפרח), Ḥorvat ʻUza ost. 2_{1} (אלישב). **15.** Lachish ost. 22_{8} (אליש[ב]).

→ אֵל *God* + שׁוב *return.*

אֱלִישָׁמָע 17.0.0.13 pr.n.m. **Elishama**—I אלשמע—**1.** son of Ammihud and chief of Ephraim, Nm 1_{10} 2_{18} $7_{48.53}$ 10_{22} 1 C 7_{26}. **2.** son of David, 2 S 5_{16}||1 C 3_{8}||14_{7} 3_{6} (mss אֱלִישָׁע *Elisha*; or em. אֱלִישׁוּעַ). **3.** member of royal family, father of Nethaniah, 2 K 25_{25}||Jr 41_{1}. **4.** scribe at time of Jehoiakim, Jr $36_{12.20.21}$. **5.** son of Jekamiah, descendant of Judah, 1 C 2_{41}. **6.** priest at time of Jehoshaphat, 2 C 17_{8}.

7. father of Elsagab (אלשגב), Seal 59_{2} (אלשמע; Palestine?, 7th cent.). **8.** son of the king (המלך), Seal 72_{1} (אלשמע; Palestine, 7th cent.). **9.** son of Gedaliah (גדליהו), Seal 100_{1} (אלשמע; Jerusalem?, 7th cent.). **10.** father of Jaush (יאש), Seal 566_{2} (אלשמע; T. Beit Mirsim?, 7th/6th cent.). **11.** father of Shallum (שלם), Seal 658_{2} (אלשמ[ע]) 659_{2} ([של]ם בן [אל]שמע) 660_{2} (של[ם בן] א[ל]ש[מע]; all three T. Beit Mirsim?, 7th/6th cent.). **12.** son of Semachiah (סמכיה), Seal 807_{1} (אלשמע; City of David, 7th/6th cent.). **13.** son of Joab (יהואב), Seal 810_{1} (אלשמע; City of David, 7th/6th cent.). **14.** father of Silla (סלא), Seal 835_{2} (אלשמע; City of David, 7th/6th cent.). **15.** Seal 224_{2} (אלשמע; Ramat Raḥel). **16.** Seal 244_{2} (אלשמע; 7th/6th cent.). **17.** Seal 423_{2} (אלשמע; 7th/6th cent.). **18.** Seal 504_{1} (אלשמע; T. Beit Mirsim?, 7th/6th cent.). **19.** Seal 729_{1} (אלשמע; 7th cent.). **20.** Seal 755_{1} (אלשמע; c. 700).

→ אֵל *God* + שׁמע *hear.*

אֱלִישָׁע 58.0.1.5 pr.n.m. **Elisha, 1.** Elijah's successor as prophet, 1 K $19_{16.17.19}$ 2 K $2_{1.2.2.3.4}$ (lacking in mss) 2_{5+7t} $3_{11.13.14}$ 4_{1+5t} 5_{8} (lacking in ms) $5_{9.10.20}$ (lacking in mss) 5_{25} 6_{1+10t} 7_{1} 8_{1+7t} 9_{1} 13_{14+6t} Si $48_{12(B)}$ ([א]ל[יש]ע) CD $8_{20(A)}$. **2.** son of Jeremiah (ירמיהו) and recipient of reinforcements at Ramath-negeb (רמתנג[ב]), Arad ost. $24_{15.19}$. **3.** son of Gargar (גרגר; others גרגד *Gargad*), Seal 317_{1} (6th cent.). **4.** Samaria ost. $1_{4.7}$ (אליש[ע]). **5.** Nimrud ivory inscr. 2.

→ אֵל *God* + ישׁע hi. *deliver.*

אֱלִישָׁפָט 1 pr.n.m. **Elishaphat,** son of Zichri and army officer at time of Athaliah, 2 C 23_{1}.

→ אֵל *God* + שׁפט *judge.*

אֱלִיָּתָה, see אֱלִיאָתָה.

[אֲלַכְסָא] 0.0.1 pr.n.[m.] **Alexander,** נקנר אלכסא *Nicanor Alexander* or *Nicanor (from) Alexandria* Frey 1256 (Jerusalem, 1st cent. CE).

אֱלִל, see אֱלִיל.

אַלְלַי 2 interj. **alas**—אַלְלַי־לִי—אַלְלַי לִי *alas for me* Mc 7$_{1}$ (+ כִּי *for* + pf.) Jb 10$_{15}$ (+ אִם *if* + pf.).

אִלְלֵי, see אִלּוּלֵי.

אלם I 8.0.6 vb. **be dumb—Ni.** Pf. נֶאֱלַמְתִּי, נֶאֱלָמָה (וְנֶאֱלַמְתִּי), Q נאלמו; impf. תֵּאָלַמְנָה, תֵּאָלֵם; + waw וַנֵּאָלַמְתָּ; ptc. Q נאלם, Q נאלמים—**be dumb, be silent.**
<SUBJ> psalmist Ps 39$_{3}$ (+ דּוּמִיָּה *[in] silence*; + חשׁה hi. *be silent*, עכר ni. *be aggravated*, of pain) 39$_{10}$ (+ פתח פֶּה not *open mouth*) 1QH 7$_{1}$ 12$_{32}$, Ezekiel Ezk 3$_{26}$ (+ יכח hi. be unable to *reprove*) 24$_{27}$ 33$_{22}$ (both + פתח ni. *be opened*, of previously dumb mouth), Daniel Dn 10$_{15}$, רָחֵל *ewe* Is 53$_{7}$ (+ פתח פֶּה), שָׂפָה *lip* Ps 31$_{19}$ 1QH 7$_{11}$ 8$_{36}$ (if em.), appar. דָּבָר *word* 8$_{36}$ (or em. נאלמו lips *were dumb*); subj. not specified 1QM 14$_{6}$ (לפתוח פה לנאלמים *to open [the] mouth of ones that are dumb*).
<PREP> לִפְנֵי *before* sheep shearers Is 53$_{7}$.
Also 1QH 8$_{39}$.
→ אֵלֶם *silence*, אִלֵּם *dumb.*

אלם II 1 vb. **bind—Pi.** Ptc. מְאַלְּמִים—**bind** sheaves, אֲנַחְנוּ מְאַלְּמִים אֲלֻמִּים בְּתוֹךְ הַשָּׂדֶה *we* (Joseph and his brothers) *were binding sheaves in the middle of the field* Gn 37$_{7}$.
→ אֲלֻמָּה *sheaf.*

אֵלֶם 2 n.[m.] **silence,** עַל־יוֹנַת אֵלֶם רְחֹקִים appar. *to (the tune of) A dove of silence, distant ones* Ps 56$_{1}$ (or em. אֵלִ[י]ם *of* distant *mighty ones* or *of* distant *terebinths*), הַאֻמְנָם אֵלֶם צֶדֶק תְּדַבֵּרוּן appar. *do you indeed (in) silence speak righteousness?* Ps 58$_{2}$ (or em. אֵלִ[י]ם *O leaders* or *O gods*).
→ אלם *be dumb.*

אִלֵּם 6.0.1 adj./n.m. **dumb**—pl. אִלְּמִים—**1.** as attributive adj. of כֶּלֶב *dog* Is 56$_{10}$, אֱלִיל *idol* Hb 2$_{18}$. **2.** as predicative adj. or noun, **dumb (one),** <SUBJ> בוא *come*, i.e. enter congregation 1QSa 2$_{6}$. <OBJ> שׂים *place*, i.e. make someone Ex 4$_{11}$ (+ חֵרֵשׁ *deaf*, עִוֵּר *blind*, פִּקֵּחַ *sighted*). <CSTR> לְשׁוֹן אִלֵּם *tongue of one that is dumb* Is 35$_{6}$ (+ פִּסֵּחַ *lame*), כול ... אלם *anyone (that is) ... dumb* 1QSa 2$_{6}$ (+ פִּסֵּחַ, עִוֵּר, חֵרֵשׁ). <PREP> פתח לְ *open* mouth *for* Pr 31$_{8}$; פתח כְּ not *open* mouth *as* Ps 38$_{14}$ (+ חֵרֵשׁ).
→ אלם *be dumb.*

אֻלָם, see אוּלָם II.

[אֵלָם], see אוּלָם II.

אלמא 0.0.3 pr.n.m. **Alma,** son of Judah and party to lease transaction, 5/6ḤevBA 44$_{4}$ fr. 1 fr. 2.

[אַלְמֹג] 6 n.[m]. **almug**—pl. אַלְמֻגִּים (mss אלמוגים), אַלְגּוּמִּים—type of tree, except at Ca 3$_{10}$ (if em.) alw. עֲצֵי אַלְמֻגִּים *timbers of almug* 1 K 10$_{11}$‖2 C 9$_{10}$ (2 C אַלְגּוּמִּים *algum* [mss אַלְמוּגִּים]) 1 K 10$_{12}$‖2 C 9$_{11}$ (1 K הָאַלְמֻגִּים; 2 C הָאַלְגּוּמִּים) 1 K 10$_{12}$ 2 C 2$_{7}$ (עֲצֵי אֲרָזִים בְּרוֹשִׁים וְאַלְגּוּמִּים *timbers of cedar, cypress, and algum*), as precious commodity from Ophir (and Lebanon 2 C 2$_{7}$), <SUBJ> בוא *come* 1 K 10$_{12}$, ראה ni. *be seen* 10$_{12}$. <OBJ> בוא hi. *bring* 1 K 10$_{11}$‖2 C 9$_{10}$ (+ אֶבֶן יְקָרָה *precious stone[s]*), שׁלח pi. *send* 2 C 2$_{7}$, עשׂה *make* 1 K 10$_{12}$‖2 C 9$_{11}$ (+ מְסִלָּה/מִסְעָד *[into] ramp*) Ca 3$_{10}$ (if em. אַרְגָּמָן *purple* to אַלְגֻּמִּן; as second obj.; + מֶרְכָּבָה *seat*).

[אֲלֻמָּה] 5 n.f. **sheaf**—sf. אֲלֻמָּתִי; pl. אֲלֻמִּים; sf. אֲלֻמֹּתָיו, אֲלֻמֹּתֵיכֶם—<SUBJ> קום *arise* Gn 37$_{7}$, נצב ni. *stand* 37$_{7}$, סבב *surround* 37$_{7}$, שׁחה htpal. *bow down* 37$_{7}$, צנם pass. *be dried* Jb 5$_{5}$ (if em.; see Obj.). <OBJ> אלם pi. *bind* Gn 37$_{7}$, נשׂא *carry* Ps 126$_{6}$, לקח *take* Jb 5$_{5}$ (if em. וְאֶל־מִצִּנִּים יִקָּחֵהוּ appar. *and from out of thorns he takes it* to וַאֲלֻמִּים צְנֻמִים יִקַּח הוּא *and dried sheaves he takes*). <PREP> שׁחה לְ htpal. *bow down to* Gn 37$_{7}$.
→ אלם *bind.*

[אַלְמוֹג], see אַלְמֹג.

אַלְמוֹדָד 2 pr.n.m. **Almodad,** son of Joktan, ancestor of a South Arabian people, Gn 10$_{26}$||1 C 1$_{20}$.

[אלמלך], see אֱלִימֶלֶךְ.

אַלַּמֶּלֶךְ 1 pl.n. **Allammelech,** in Asher, Jos 19$_{26}$.
→ perh. אֵלָה *terebinth* + מֶלֶךְ *king.*

אַלְמָן 1 adj. **widowed** (or perh. n.m. **widower**), לֹא־אַלְמָן יִשְׂרָאֵל וִיהוּדָה מֵאֱלֹהָיו *Israel and Judah are not widowed,* i.e. bereft, *of their God* Jr 51$_5$.
→ אַלְמָנָה *widow.*

אַלְמֹן 1 n.[m]. **widowhood,** שְׁכוֹל וְאַלְמֹן ... בָּאוּ עָלַיִךְ *complete bereavement and widowhood will come upon you* Is 47$_9$ (1QIsa[a] ואלמנה appar. *even [as] a widow*).
→ אַלְמָנָה *widow.*

אַלְמָנָה 56.2.2 n.f. **widow**—pl. אַלְמָנוֹת; sf. אַלְמְנֹתַיִךְ, אַלְמְנוֹתָיו (אַלְמְנֹתָיו, אַלְמְנֹתָו, L אַלְמְנוֹתָיו), אַלְמְנוֹתֶיהָ—1. **widow,** <SUBJ> היה *be* Ex 22$_{23}$ (+ אִשָּׁה *wife;* || יָתוֹם *orphan*) Lv 22$_{13}$ (+ בַּת־כֹּהֵן *daughter of priest;* || גְּרוּשָׁה *divorced woman*) 2 S 20$_3$ (if em.; see Adj.) Is 10$_2$=CD 16$_6$ (אלמ[נו]ת; + שָׁלָל *booty,* יָתוֹם *orphan*) Ezk 44$_{22}$ Jr 18$_{21}$ (+ אִשָּׁה, שַׁכּוּל *bereaved person*) Ps 109$_9$ (+ אִשָּׁה; || יָתוֹם), בוא *come* Dt 14$_{29}$ (+ לֵוִי *Levite*), אכל *eat* 14$_{29}$, שׂבע *be satisfied* 14$_{29}$, כול pilp. *feed* 1 K 17$_9$, שׂמח *rejoice* Dt 16$_{11}$ (+ לֵוִי) 16$_{14}$ (|| לֵוִי), קשׁשׁ pol. *collect* 1 K 17$_{10}$, לקח *take* 17$_{10}$, עצם *be numerous* Jr 15$_8$, רבה hi. *make great* complaint Si 32$_{17}$ (+ יָתוֹם), בטח *trust* Jr 49$_{11}$ (+ יָתוֹם), בכה *weep* Ps 78$_{64}$ Jb 27$_{15}$.

<NOM CL> אַלְמָנָה אָנִי *I am a widow* 2 S 14$_5$.

<OBJ> ענה pi. *afflict* Ex 22$_{21}$ (|| יָתוֹם *orphan*), עשׁק *oppress* Jr 7$_6$ Zc 7$_{10}$ (|| עָנִי *poor person*) Ml 3$_5$ (|| יָתוֹם; + שָׂכִיר *labourer,* גֵּר *sojourner*), ינה hi. *oppress* Jr 22$_3$ Ezk 22$_7$ (|| יָתוֹם; + אָב וָאֵם *father and mother,* גֵּר), ידע *know* carnally 19$_7$ (or em. אַרְמְנוֹתֵיהֶם *their strongholds;* || עִיר *city*), הרג *kill* Ps 94$_6$ (|| יָתוֹם, גֵּר), שׁלח pi. *send away* Jb 22$_9$ (+ יָתוֹם), נטשׁ *forsake* Si 32$_{17}$, צוה pi. *command* 1 K 17$_9$, ריב *plead for* Is 1$_{17}$ (|| יָתוֹם), רחם pi. *love* 9$_{16}$ (|| יָתוֹם; + בָּחוּר *youth*), עוד pol. *sustain* Ps 146$_9$ (|| יָתוֹם, גֵּר), רבה hi. *make many* Ezk 22$_{25}$, לקח *take (in marriage)* Lv 21$_{14}$ (|| חָלָל *defiled person,* זֹנָה *prostitute*) Ezk 44$_{22}$ (both || גְּרוּשָׁה *divorced woman,* :: בְּתוּלָה *virgin*) 44$_{22}$ (+ מִכֹּהֵן *of a priest*), יטב hi. *do good to* Jb 24$_{21}$ (+ עֲקָרָה *childless woman*).

<CSTR> נֶדֶר אַלְמָנָה *vow of a widow* Nm 30$_{10}$=11QT 54$_4$ (|| גְּרוּשָׁה *divorced woman*), בֶּגֶד *garment of* Dt 24$_{17}$ (+ גֵּר *sojourner,* יָתוֹם *orphan*), בֶּן־ *son of* 1 K 7$_{14}$, רִיב *dispute of* Is 1$_{23}$ (+ יָתוֹם), מִשְׁפַּט *justice of* Dt 10$_{18}$ (+ גֵּר) 27$_{19}$ (|| גֵּר; both || יָתוֹם), שׁוֹר *ox of* Jb 24$_3$ (|| יָתוֹם), לֵב *heart of* 29$_{13}$ (|| אבד ptc. *one about to perish*), עֵינֵי *eyes of* 31$_{16}$, גְּבוּל *boundary of* Pr 15$_{25}$ (:: גֵּאֶה *proud person*), דַּיַּן אַלְמָנוֹת *judge of widows* Ps 68$_6$ (|| יָתוֹם).

<APP> אִשָּׁה אַלְמָנָה *a woman, a widow* 2 S 14$_5$ (אִשָּׁה־) 1 K 7$_{14}$ 11$_{26}$ 17$_{9.10}$, צְרֻרוֹת ... אַלְמָנוֹת *women confined ... widows* 2 S 20$_3$ (if em.; see Adj.).

<ADJ> אַלְמָנוֹת חַיּוֹת *living widows* 2 S 20$_3$ (if em. אַלְמְנוּת חַיּוּת *widowhood of living*).

<PREP> לְ of benefit, *to, for,* + היה *be* Dt 24$_{19.20.21}$, נתן *give* 26$_{12.13}$ (both || לֵוִי *Levite*), היה ... תמור בעל לאלמנות *be ... instead of a husband to the widows* Si 4$_{10}$ (|| יָתוֹם *orphan*); עון בְּ *dwell among* (of jackals) Is 13$_{22}$ (or em. בְּאַלְמְנוֹתָיו [L] to בְּאַרְמְנוֹתֶיהָ *in her fortresses;* + הֵיכָל *palace*); כְּ *as* Lm 5$_3$, + היה *be* 1$_1$ (+ עִיר *city*); רעע עַל hi. *bring calamity upon* 1 K 17$_{20}$; גור עִם htpol. *sojourn with* 1 K 17$_{20}$.

<COLL> הַגֵּר הַיָּתוֹם וְהָאַלְמָנָה (and vars.) *the sojourner, the orphan and the widow* Dt 14$_{29}$ 16$_{11.14}$ 24$_{19.20.21}$ 26$_{12.13}$ 27$_{19}$ Jr 7$_6$ 22$_3$ Zc 7$_{10}$, ישׁב אַלְמָנָה *live as a widow* Gn 38$_{11}$ Is 47$_8$ (subj. Babylon; + שְׁכוֹל *bereavement*).

2. **widowhood,** of Babylon, שכול ואלמנה כתומם באו עליך *complete bereavement and widowhood will come upon you* 1QIsa[a] 47$_9$ (MT אַלְמֹן *widowhood*).

<SYN> גְּרוּשָׁה *divorced woman,* יָתוֹם *orphan,* גֵּר *sojourner,* לֵוִי *Levite.*
→ אַלְמָן *widowed.*

[אַלְמָנוּת] 4 n.f. **widowhood**—cstr. אַלְמְנוּת; sf. אַלְמְנוּתָהּ, אַלְמְנוּתֵךְ—<SUBJ> היה *be* 2 S 20$_3$. <CSTR> אַלְמְנוּת חַיּוּת *widowhood of living,* i.e. life of widowhood 2 S 20$_3$ (or em. אַלְמָנוֹת חַיּוֹת *living widows*); בִּגְדֵי אַלְמְנוּתָהּ *the*

garments of her widowhood Gn $38_{14.19}$, חֶרְפַּת אַלְמְנוּתַיִךְ *reproach of* Is 54_4 (|| עֲלוּמִים *youthfulness*). <APP> צְרֻרוֹת ... אַלְמְנוּת חַיּוּת *women confined ... a living widowhood* 2 S 20_3 (but see Cstr.).
→ אַלְמָן *widowed.*

אַלְמֹנִי 3 adj. **such and such, so and so**—אַלְמוֹנִי—only in פְּלֹנִי אַלְמֹנִי *such and such, so and so,* unnamed place or person, **1. such and such,** with ref. to a place, מְקוֹם פְּלֹנִי אַלְמֹנִי *such and such a place* 1 S 21_3 2 K 6_8. **2. so and so,** וַיֹּאמֶר סוּרָה שְׁבָה־פֹּה פְּלֹנִי אַלְמֹנִי *and he said, Turn, sit here, so and so* Ru 4_1 (or *sit here [in] such and such [a place]*).

אלמתן I 0.0.0.1 pl.n. **Elmattan,** perh. ident. with Immātīn, 12 km SSW of Samaria, Samaria ost. 28_3.

[אלמתן] II, see אֱלִימֶלֶךְ.

אלן, see אֵילוֹן I.

אֵלֹנִי 1 gent. **Elonite,** of the family of Elon son of Zebulun, Nm 26_{26}.
→ אֵילוֹן *Elon.*

[אֶלְנַעַם] 1 pr.n.m. **Elnaam**—אֶלְנָעַם—father of Jeribai and Joshaviah, two of David's warriors, 1 C 11_{46}.
→ אֵל *God* + נעם *be pleasant.*

אֶלְנָתָן 7.0.0.9 pr.n.m. **Elnathan, 1.** father of Nehushta, mother of Jehoiachin, 2 K 24_8. **2.** son of Achbor, perh. ident. with preceding, Jr 26_{22} $36_{12.25}$. **3–5.** leaders at time of Ezra, Ezr 8_{16} (mss יוֹנָתָן *Jonathan*) $8_{16.16}$. **6.** father of Jeconiah ([י]כניהו; others כניהו *Coniah*), Lachish ost. 3_{15}. **7.** son of Jaush (יאש), Seal 530_1 (אלנ[ת]ן; T. Beit Mirsim?, 7th/6th cent.). **8.** son of Bilgai (בלגי), Seal 820_1 (City of David, 7th/6th cent.). **9.** father of Gemariah (גמריהו), Seal 897_2 (7th cent.). **10.** Lachish ost. 11_3. **11.** Arad ost. 110_1 (אלנת[ן]). **12.** Seal 138 (8th/7th cent.). **13.** Seal 189_2 190_2 (אל[נתן]; both Gibeon, 8th cent.). **14.** Seal 430_2 (6th cent.). **15.** Stamp/Coin 17_1 18_2 (both 5th/4th cent.).
→ אֵל *God* + נתן *give.*

אלסמך 0.0.0.3 pr.n.m. **Elisamach**—אליסמך—**1.** father of Gaali (געלי), Seal 539_2 (אליסמך) 540_2 (both T. Beit Mirsim?, 7th/6th cent.). **2.** Seal 726_2 (7th/6th cent.).
→ אֵל *God* + סמך *lean.*

אלסמכי 0.0.0.1 pr.n.m. **Elsamchi,** Seal 129 (Transjordan, 7th cent.).
→ אֵל *God* + סמך *lean.*

אֶלָּסָר 2 pl.n. **Ellasar,** Mesopotamian kingdom, perh. ident. with Larsa (Senkere), אַרְיוֹךְ מֶלֶךְ אֶלָּסָר *Arioch, king of Ellasar* Gn $14_{1.9}$.

אֶלְעָד 1 pr.n.m. **Elead**—אֶלְעָד—descendant of Ephraim, 1 C 7_{21}.
→ אֵל *God* + עוד *testify.*

אֶלְעָדָה 1.0.0.1 pr.n.m. **Eleadah, 1.** descendant of Ephraim, 1 C 7_{20}. **2.** son of Karshon (כרשן), papMur 17_3.
→ אֵל *God* + עוד *testify.*

אֶלְעוּזַי 1 pr.n.m. **Eluzai,** one of David's warriors, 1 C 12_6.
→ אֵל *God* + עזז *be strong.*

אלעז 0.0.0.8 pr.n.m. **Eliaz**—אליעז—**1.** father of Joah (יחואח), Seal 571_2 (אליעז) 572_2 573_2 (all three T. Beit Mirsim?, 7th/6th cent.). **2.** son of Ahab (אחאב), Seal 517_1 518_1 (both T. Beit Mirsim?, 7th/6th cent.). **3.** son of Hoshea (הושע[יהו]), Seal 528_1 (אליעז; T. Beit Mirsim?, 7th/6th cent.). **4.** son of Azriel (עזראל), Seal 170_1 (c. 600). **5.** father of Micah (מכיהו), Seal 590_2 (T. Beit Mirsim?, 7th/6th cent.).
→ אֵל *God* + עזז *be strong.*

אֶלְעָזָר 72.3.27.2 pr.n.m. **Eleazar, 1.** priest, son of Aaron and Elisheba and father of Phinehas, Nm 20_{28} 1 C 5_{30} CD 5_3 1QDM 1_{11}, אֶלְעָזָר הַכֹּהֵן *Eleazar the priest* Nm 17_4 $19_{3.4}$ $26_{3.63}$ $27_{2.19.21.22}$ 31_{6+9t} $32_{2.28}$ 34_{17} Jos 14_1 17_4

19$_{51}$ 21$_{1}$ 22$_{13.31.32}$, אֶלְעָזָר בֶּן־אַהֲרֹן *Eleazar son of Aaron* Ex 6$_{25}$ Nm 3$_{32}$ 4$_{16}$ 17$_{2}$ 20$_{25}$ 25$_{7.11}$ 26$_{1}$ Jos 24$_{33}$ Jg 20$_{28}$ Ezr 7$_{5}$ 1QDM 1$_{3}$ (אלע[זר ב]ן אהר[ו]ן), אֶלְעָזָר בְּנוֹ *Eleazar his son* Nm 20$_{26.28}$ Dt 10$_{6}$ 1 C 6$_{35}$, פִּינְחָס בֶּן־אֶלְעָזָר *Phinehas son of Eleazar* Nm 25$_{7.11}$ 31$_{6}$ Jos 22$_{13.31.32}$ Jg 20$_{28}$ Ezr 7$_{5}$ 1 C 9$_{20}$ Si 45$_{23}$ ([ב]ן), אֶלְעָזָר וְאִיתָמָר *Eleazar and Ithamar* (and vars.) Ex 6$_{23}$ 28$_{1}$ Lv 10$_{6.12.16}$ Nm 3$_{2.4}$ 26$_{60}$ 1 C 5$_{29}$ 24$_{1+6t}$ 2QapMoses 1$_{1}$ (Baillet) (אלע[זר ואיתמר]) 4QPsJos[b] 17$_{5}$. **2.** son of Mahli and brother of Kish, 1 C 23$_{21.22}$ 24$_{28}$. **3.** son of Abinadab, custodian of ark at Kiriath-jearim, 1 S 7$_{1}$. **4.** son of Dodo, one of David's warriors, 2 S 23$_{9(Qr)}$||1 C 11$_{12}$. **5.** son of Phinehas, assistant to Meremoth, Ezr 8$_{33}$. **6.** son of Parosh, Ezr 10$_{25}$. **7.** priest at time of Nehemiah, Ne 12$_{42}$. **8.** son of Nahum (נחם), Seal 310$_{1}$ (6th/5th cent.). **9.** father of Jesus ben Sira, Si 50$_{27}$ 51$_{30}$. **10.** son of Hanniah, Bene Hezir inscr. **11.** perh. brother of Hanniah, Bene Hezir inscr. **12.** husband of Salome, Frey 1294. **13.** scribe, father of Judah, Frey 1308B. **14.** priest at time of Bar-Kochba, Bar-Kochba Revolt Year 1 coin 166 167 173 (all three + הכוהן *the priest*). **15.** perh. ident. with preceding, Mur 24 2$_{5}$ (אלעז[ר בן השלני] *Eleazar son of the Shilonite*). **16.** son of Zechariah, Mur 29 2$_{5}$ ([לאל]עזר) 2$_{12}$. **17-18.** Eleazar ben Eleazar ben Hitta, leaseholder at time of Bar-Kochba, 5/6ḤevBA 44$_{3}$ 5/6ḤevBA 44 fr. 1 fr. 2 5/6ḤevBA 45. **19.** father of vendor (דוסתוס *Dositheus*) in land sale, Mur 30 1$_{1}$ 2$_{10.32(Milik)}$ (אלעז[ר]). **20.** father of witness (Jonathan) to land sale, Mur 30 2$_{10}$ ([א]ל[עזר]). **21.** father of witness (Saul) to signature, MurEpBeth-Mashiko$_{11}$. **22.** administrator at time of Bar-Kochba, MurEpBeth-Mashiko$_{1}$. **23.** Seal 312 (6th/5th cent.). **24.** Frey 1247.

Also Frey 1534 (לעזר).

→ אֵל *God* + עזר *help*.

אֶלְעָלֵא, see אֶלְעָלֵה.

אֶלְעָלֵה 5 pl.n. **Elealeh**—אֶלְעָלֵא—Moabite town allotted to Reuben, perh. el-'Āl 3 km N of Heshbon, Nm 32$_{3.37}$ (אֶלְעָלֵא; mss, Sam אֶלְעָלֵה) Is 15$_{4}$||Jr 48$_{34}$ Is 16$_{9}$ (alw. + חֶשְׁבּוֹן *Heshbon*).

אלעש 0.0.0.1 pr.n.m. **Eleash,** Seal 340$_{2}$ (8th-6th cent.).

→ אֵל *God* + עוש *help*.

אֶלְעָשָׂה 6 pr.n.m. **El(e)asah, 1.** son of Helez and father of Sismai, descendant of Judah, 1 C 2$_{39.40}$. **2.** son of Raphah/Rephaiah (רְפָיָה/רָפָה) and father of Azel, descendant of Benjamin, 1 C 8$_{37}$ 9$_{43}$. **3.** son of Shaphan and messenger for Jeremiah, Jr 29$_{3}$. **4.** priest, descendant of Pashhur, Ezr 10$_{22}$.

→ אֵל *God* + עשׂה *do*.

אלף I 4 vb. **learn—Qal** Impf. תֶּאֱלַף—**learn, become acquainted with,** פֶּן־תֶּאֱלַף אֹרְחֹתָיו *in case you learn his* (angry man's) *ways* Pr 22$_{25(Qr)}$.

Pi. Impf. יְאַלֵּף; sf. + waw וַאֲאַלֶּפְךָ; ptc. + sf. מַלְּפֵנוּ—**teach.**

<SUBJ> עָוֹן *iniquity* Jb 15$_{5}$ (|| בחר *select*), Elihu 33$_{33}$, אֵל *God* 32$_{13}$ (if em. יִדְּפֶנּוּ *he drives*, i.e. defeats, *him to* יְאַלְּפֶנּוּ *he teaches him*; + מצא חָכְמָה *find wisdom*) 35$_{11}$ (|| חכם pi. *impart wisdom*), אִישׁ *man* 32$_{13}$ (if em.).

<OBJ> Job Jb 32$_{13}$ (if em.; see Subj.), Job's friends 33$_{33}$, humans 35$_{11}$, פֶּה *mouth* 15$_{5}$, חָכְמָה *wisdom* 33$_{33}$.

→ אַלּוּף *tame*.

אלף II 1 vb. **be a thousand—Hi.** Ptc. מַאֲלִיפוֹת—צֹאונֵנוּ מַאֲלִיפוֹת *our flocks number thousands* Ps 144$_{13}$ (|| רבב pu. *be numbered in the tens of thousands*).

→ אֶלֶף *thousand*.

[אָלֶף] 0.0.2 n.[m.] **aleph,** the Hebrew letter, [יש]בע וגם באלף ולמד וגם באלף ודלת *he should* not *swear either by Aleph and Lamedh,* i.e. אֵל *God, or by Aleph and Daleth,* i.e. אֲד(נָי) *Adonai* CD 15$_{1}$.

[אַלֻּף], see אַלּוּף I, III.

אֶלֶף I 496.6.45.4 n.m. **thousand**—אָלֶף; sf. אַלְפִּי; du. אַלְפַּיִם (אַלְפָּיִם) אלפים; pl. אֲלָפִים; cstr. אַלְפֵי; sf. אֲלָפָיו (Kt אלפו), אַלְפֵיכֶם, Q אלפיהם—**1.** as numeral or part of numeral, **a thousand. a.** of **money,** etc., אֶלֶף כֶּסֶף *a thousand (pieces) of silver* Gn 20$_{16}$ 2 S 18$_{12}$ Is 7$_{23}$ (+ בְּ of price) Ca 8$_{11}$, var. 8$_{12}$, אֶלֶף וּמֵאָה הַכֶּסֶף *the eleven* *hundred (pieces) of silver* Jg 17$_{2.3}$, var. 16$_5$, שֵׁשֶׁת אֲלָפִים זָהָב *six thousand (shekels) of gold* 2 K 5$_5$ (+ עֶשֶׂר כִּכְּרֵי־כֶסֶף *ten talents of silver*), אַלְפֵי זָהָב וָכָסֶף *thousands of (pieces of) gold and silver* Ps 119$_{72}$, specif. shekels (שֶׁקֶל) Ex 38$_{25.28}$ Nm 3$_{50}$ 7$_{85}$ 31$_{52}$ Jg 8$_{26}$ 1 S 17$_5$, talents (כִּכָּר) 2 K 15$_{19}$ Est 3$_9$ 1 C 19$_6$ 22$_{14.14}$ 29$_{4.4}$ 29$_{7.7.7.7}$ GnzPs 2$_{27}$, drachmas (דַּרְכְּמוֹן) Ezr 2$_{69}$ 8$_{27}$ (אֲדַרְכֹּן), minas (מָנֶה) Ezr 2$_{69}$||Ne 7$_{70.71}$.

1b. of units of **weight, measure,** למלך אל[ף] שמן *for the king, a thousand (units) of oil* T. Qasile ost. 1$_1$ (+ מֵאָה *hundred*), specif. kors (כֹּר) 1 K 5$_{25.25}$||2 C 2$_{9.9}$, baths (בַּת) 1 K 7$_{26}$||2 C 4$_5$ 2 C 2$_{9.9}$, cubits (אַמָּה) Nm 35$_{4.5.5.5.5}$ Jos 3$_4$ Ezk 45$_{1+7t}$ 48$_{8+27t}$ (Ezk lacks אַמָּה) Ne 3$_{13}$ 11QT 40$_8$ 46$_{16}$ 1QM 7$_7$ fr. 1$_7$ CD 10$_{21}$ 11$_6$ 4Q251 3$_5$ (אמ[ה]), וַיָּמָד אֶלֶף *and he measured out a thousand (cubits)* Ezk 47$_{4.4.5}$, sim. 47$_3$, וילכו המים ... במאתי[ם ו]אלף אמה *and the water flowed ... for 1200 cubits* Siloam tunnel inscr.$_5$.

1c. of **warriors,** mustered, killed, etc., Nm 31$_5$ Jos 4$_{13}$ 7$_{3.4}$ 8$_{3.12}$ Jg 3$_{29}$ 4$_{6.10.14}$ 7$_{3.3}$ 8$_{10.10}$ 12$_6$ 15$_{15.16}$ 20$_{2+9t}$ 21$_{10}$ 1 S 4$_{2.10}$ 11$_{8.8}$ 13$_{2.2.2.5}$ 15$_{4.4}$ 18$_8$ (|| רְבָבָה *ten thousand*) 24$_3$ 26$_2$ 2 S 6$_1$ 8$_{4.4.5.13}$||1 C 18$_{4.5.12}$ 2 S 10$_{6.6.6.18}$ ||1 C 19$_{18}$ 2 S 17$_1$ 18$_{3.4.7}$ 19$_{18}$ 24$_{9.9}$||1 C 21$_{5.5}$ 1 K 10$_{26}$ ||2 C 1$_{14}$ 1 K 12$_{21}$||2 C 11$_1$ 1 K 20$_{15.29.30}$ 2 K 13$_7$ 14$_7$||2 C 25$_{11}$ 2 K 19$_{35}$||Is 37$_{36}$ Is 30$_{17}$ Ps 60$_2$ 91$_7$ (|| רְבָבָה) 1 C 5$_{18}$ 12$_{15}$ (|| 100) 12$_{25+11t}$ 18$_{4.4}$ 2 C 12$_3$ 13$_{3.3.17}$ 14$_{7.7}$ 17$_{17.18}$, 25$_{5.12}$ Si 16$_{10}$ 46$_8$ 11QT 57$_{5.5.6}$ 1QM 5$_3$ 6$_{9.10.10.11}$ 9$_{4.5}$ 12$_4$ fr. 1$_{10}$ fr. 13$_2$ (11QapPs^a 2$_{12}$ (both א[לף]), specif. גִּבּוֹרֵי חַיִל *men of valour* 1 C 7$_{2+6t}$ 9$_{13}$ 2 C 17$_{14.16}$ 25$_6$, members of tribal armies Nm 2$_{4+22t}$.

הִכָּה שָׁאוּל בַּאֲלָפָיו וְדָוִד בְּרִבְבֹתָיו *Saul has killed in his thousands, and David in his tens of thousands* 1 S 18$_{7(Qr)}$ (Kt באלפו) 21$_{12(Qr)}$ (Kt באלפו, ברבבתו) 29$_{5(Qr)}$ (Kt ברבבתו), חַיִל אֶלֶף אֲלָפִים *an army of a million* 2 C 14$_8$.

1d. of **Israelites,** Ex 12$_{37}$ 20$_6$ Ex 38$_{26}$ Nm 11$_{21}$ Jg 5$_8$ 20$_{10}$ 1 S 6$_{19}$ 1 K 19$_{18}$ 2 C 25$_{13}$ 1QS 2$_{21}$ CD 13$_1$ (|| 100, 50, 10) 4QPsJos^a 22.1$_5$, specif. Levites Ex 32$_{28}$ Nm 3$_{22.28.34.39}$ 4$_{36.40.44.48}$ 26$_{62}$ 1 C 23$_{3.4.4.5.5}$ 26$_{30.32}$, Rebekah's descendants Gn 24$_{60}$, first-born sons Nm 3$_{43}$, returning exiles Ezr 2$_{3+10t}$||Ne 7$_{8+10t}$, members of tribes Nm 1$_{21+13t}$ 26$_{7+14t}$ Jg 15$_{11}$, of David's divisions 1 C 27$_{1+12t}$, of levy 1 K 5$_{27.28}$.

אֶלֶף לַמַּטֶּה *a thousand per tribe* Nm 31$_{4.4.5.6}$, רִבְבוֹת אֶפְרַיִם ... אַלְפֵי מְנַשֶּׁה *tens of thousands of Ephraim ... thousands of Manasseh* Dt 33$_{17}$, שש מאות האלף *the six hundred thousand* Israelites 4QOrd^a 1.2$_8$, הָעִיר הַיֹּצֵאת אֶלֶף תַּשְׁאִיר מֵאָה *the city that goes out as a thousand will be left with a hundred* Am 5$_3$.

1e. of **non-Israelites,** Nm 31$_{35.40.46}$ Jos 8$_{25}$ Jg 3$_{29}$ 8$_{10}$ 15$_{15.16}$ 16$_{27}$ 1 S 13$_5$ 29$_2$ 2 S 8$_{4.4.5.13}$||1 C 18$_{4.4.5.12}$ 2 S 10$_{6.6.6.18}$ 17$_1$ 1 K 20$_{29.30}$ 2 K 14$_7$||2 C 25$_{11}$ 2 K 19$_{35}$||Is 37$_{36}$ Ps 60$_2$ Est 9$_{16}$ 1 C 5$_{21}$ 2 C 2$_{16.16}$ 12$_3$ 25$_{12}$.

1f. of **other individuals,** dead Ex 32$_{28}$ Nm 17$_{14}$ 25$_9$ Jos 8$_{25}$ Jg 9$_{49}$ 2 S 24$_{15}$||1 C 21$_{14}$, captives Nm 31$_{35.40.46}$ 2 K 24$_{14.16.16}$ Jr 52$_{28.30}$ 1 C 5$_{21}$, servants Ezr 2$_{65}$||Ne 7$_{67}$, chiefs (שַׂר) 1 C 12$_{35}$, porters, 1 K 5$_{29}$||2 C 2$_{1.17}$, quarriers, 1 K 5$_{29}$||2 C 2$_{1.17}$, foremen 1 K 5$_{30}$||2 C 2$_{1.17}$.

1g. of **animals,** asses Ezr 2$_{67}$||Ne 7$_{68}$, horses 2 K 18$_{23}$||Is 36$_8$, for sacrifice 1 K 8$_{63.63}$||2 C 7$_{5.5}$ Mc 6$_7$ (|| רְבָבָה *ten thousand*) 1 C 29$_{21.21.21}$ 2 C 15$_{11}$, as booty Nm 31$_{32.+14t}$ 1 C 5$_{21.21.21}$, property 1 S 25$_{2.2}$ 2 K 3$_{4.4}$ Jb 1$_{3.3}$ 42$_{12.12.12.12}$, tribute 2 C 17$_{11.11}$, אחד מאלף אשר יצודו *one of each thousand (animals) that they trap* 11QT 60$_4$.

1h. of **other items,** burnt offerings 1 K 3$_4$||2 C 1$_6$, chariots 1 S 13$_5$ 1 K 10$_{26}$||2 C 1$_{14}$ Ps 68$_{18}$ (|| רְבָבָה *ten thousand*) 1 C 18$_4$ 19$_{7.18}$ 2 C 12$_3$, stalls 1 K 5$_6$||2 C 9$_{25}$, weapons אֶלֶף הַמָּגֵן תָּלוּי עָלָיו *a thousand are the shields hanging upon it* Ca 4$_4$; cultic utensils, Ezr 1$_{9.9.10.10.11}$, treasure chests Si 41$_{12}$, items of booty 11QT 58$_{13}$, vines Is 7$_{23}$, days, parts of days Ps 84$_{11}$ Dn 8$_{14}$ 12$_{11.12}$, years Ps 90$_4$ Si 41$_4$ (|| 100, 10), אֶלֶף שָׁנִים פַּעֲמַיִם *a thousand years twice* Ec 6$_6$, proverbs 1 K 5$_{12}$, psalms, songs 1 K 5$_{12}$ 11QPs^a 27$_{5.10}$.

<COLL> numbers compounded with אֶלֶף, 2000 = אַלְפַּיִם Nm 35$_{5.5.5.5}$ Jos 3$_4$ 7$_3$ (+ כְּ *about*) 1 K 7$_{26}$ 2 K 18$_{23}$||Is 36$_8$ Ne 7$_{71}$ 1 C 5$_{21}$ 1QM 7$_7$ (+ כְּ) fr. 1$_7$ CD 11$_6$ 4Q251 3$_5$, 3000 = שְׁלֹשֶׁת אֲלָפִים Ex 32$_{28}$ Jos 7$_{3.4}$ (+ כְּ) 1 K 5$_{12}$ 5$_{30}$||2 C 2$_{1.17}$ Jb 1$_3$ 1 C 12$_{30}$ 29$_4$ 2 C 4$_5$ 25$_{13}$ 11QT 46$_{16}$ (שלושת), 4000 = אַרְבַּעַת אֲלָפִים 1 C 23$_{5.5}$ 2 C 9$_{25}$ 1QM 6$_{10}$, 5000 = חֲמֵשֶׁת אֲלָפִים Jos 8$_{12}$ (+ כְּ) Ezk 45$_6$ 48$_{15}$ Ezr 2$_{69}$ 1 C 29$_7$, 6000 = שֵׁשֶׁת אֲלָפִים Nm 3$_{34}$ 2 K 5$_5$ Jb 42$_{12}$ 1 C 23$_4$ 1QM 6$_{11}$ 9$_5$, 7000 = שִׁבְעַת אֲלָפִים Nm 3$_{22}$ 1 K 19$_{18}$ 20$_{15}$ 2 K 24$_{16}$ Jb 1$_3$ 1 C 18$_4$ 29$_4$ 2 C 15$_{11}$,

8000 = שְׁמֹנַת אֲלָפִים Nm 3_{28} 1 C 29_{7}.

10,000 = עֲשֶׂרֶת אֲלָפִים Jg 3_{29} (+ כְּ *about*) $4_{6.10.14}$ 7_{3} 2 S 18_{3} (עֲשָׂרָה) 1 K 5_{28} 2 K 13_{7} 14_{7}||2 C 25_{11} 2 K $24_{14(Qr)}$ (Kt עשרה) Ezk $45_{1.3(Qr)}$ (Kt חמש) 45_{5} 48_{9+6t} Est 3_{9} 1 C 29_{7} 2 C 25_{12}, 20,000 = עֶשְׂרִים אֶלֶף 2 S 8_{4}||1 C 18_{4} 1 K $5_{25.25}$||2 C $2_{9.9}$ Ezk 45_{6} 2 C $2_{9.9}$, 25,000 =חֲמִשָּׁה וְעֶשְׂרִים אֶלֶף Ezk $45_{1.3.5.6}$ $48_{8.+10t}$, 26,000 = עֶשְׂרִים וְשִׁשָּׁה אֶלֶף 1 C 7_{40}, 27,000 = עֶשְׂרִים וְשִׁבְעָה אֶלֶף 1 K 20_{30}, 100,000 = מֵאָה(־)אֶלֶף 1 K 20_{29} 2 K $3_{4.4}$ 1 C 5_{21} 21_{5} 22_{14} 29_{7} 2 C 25_{6}, 1,000,000 = אֶלֶף אֲלָפִים 1 C 22_{14} 2 C 14_{8} GnzPs 2_{27}.

1005 = חֲמִשָּׁה וְאֶלֶף 1 K 5_{12}, 1200 = מאתי[ם ו]אלף Siloam tunnel inscr.$_{5}$, 2200 = אַלְפַּיִם וּמָאתָיִם Ne 7_{70}, 3600 = שלושת אלפים ושש מאות 11QPs[a] 27_{5}, 4050 = ארבעת אלפים וחמשים 27_{10}, 4500 =חֲמֵשׁ מֵאוֹת וְאַרְבַּעַת אֲלָפִים Ezk 48_{16+7t}, 61,000 = שֵׁשׁ־רִבֹּאוֹת וְאֶלֶף Ezr 2_{69}, 151,000 = מְאַת אֶלֶף וְאֶחָד וַחֲמִשִּׁים אֶלֶף Nm 2_{16}, 153,000 = מֵאָה וַחֲמִשִּׁים אֶלֶף וּשְׁלֹשֶׁת אֲלָפִים 2 C 2_{16}, 180,000 = מֵאָה וּשְׁמֹנִים אֶלֶף 1 K 12_{21}||2 C 11_{1}, 185,000 =מֵאָה (וּ)שְׁמֹנִים וַחֲמִשָּׁה אֶלֶף 2 K 19_{35}||Is 37_{36}, 186,000 = מְאַת אֶלֶף וּשְׁמֹנִים אֶלֶף וְשֵׁשֶׁת־אֲלָפִים Nm 2_{9}, 603,000 = שֵׁשׁ־מֵאוֹת אֶלֶף וּשְׁלֹשֶׁת אֲלָפִים Ex 38_{26} Nm 1_{46} 2_{32}, אַלְפֵי רְבָבָה *thousands of ten thousands* Gn 24_{60}.

אֶלֶף אֶחָד *a single thousand* Is 30_{17}, כְּאֶלֶף *about a thousand* Jg 9_{49} 11QT 40_{8}, עֲשָׂרָה ... לַמֵּאָה ... וּמֵאָה לָאֶלֶף וְאֶלֶף לָרְבָבָה *ten per hundred ..., and a hundred per thousand, and a thousand per ten thousand* Jg 20_{10}, לְמֵאוֹת וְלַאֲלָפִים *by hundreds and by thousands* 1 S 29_{2} 2 S 18_{4}, sim. 1QS 2_{21} 1QM fr. 1_{10} (לא[ל]פים) CD 13_{1} (both || 50, 10), לאלפיהם ולרבואותם *by their thousands and by their tens of thousands* 1QM 12_{4}.

אֶחָד מִנִּי־אֶלֶף *one out of a thousand* Jb 33_{23}, sim. 9_{3} Ec 7_{28} 11QT 58_{13} 60_{4}, בעל סודך אחד מאלף *your confidant* should be *one person in a thousand* Si 6_{6}, טוב אחד עושה רצון מאלף *one person who does what is pleasing is better than a thousand (others)* 16_{3}, אֵיכָה יִרְדֹּף אֶחָד אֶלֶף *how does one person pursue a thousand?* Dt 32_{30}, sim. Jos 23_{10}, [ה]קטן בכם ירדוף א[ל]ף *the smallest among you will pursue a thousand* 1QM fr. 13_{2}.

חֶסֶד לַאֲלָפִים show *loyalty to thousands* Ex 20_{6} 34_{7} Dt 5_{10} Jr 32_{18} CD 20_{21} ([לאלפים]), י׳ ... יֹסֵף עֲלֵיכֶם כָּכֶם אֶלֶף פְּעָמִים *may Y. ... increase you a thousand times* (lit. *increase you like you a thousand times*) Dt 1_{11}, אֶלֶף דּוֹר *a thousand generations* 7_{9} Ps 105_{8}||1 C 16_{15} CD $20_{22(B)}$ (all + לְ *for*) $7_{6(A)}$ 4QPs[a] 1.3_{1} $1.4_{3(Allegro)}$ ([דור]), לאלפי דורות *for thousands of generations* CD $19_{1(B)}$ ($7_{6[A]}$ אלף דור *[for] a thousand generations*), הַרְרֵי־אָלֶף perh. *hills of a thousand*, i.e. a thousand hills Ps 50_{10} (or em. הֲרָרַי the beasts on *my hills* are a thousand, or אֲלֶף = *of cattle*, or em. אֲלֶף to אֵל *of God*).

2. unit of a thousand men, usu. in military context, הַפְּקֻדִים אֲשֶׁר לְאַלְפֵי הַצָּבָא *commanders of the thousands of the army* Nm 31_{48}, שַׂר־הָאָלֶף *commander of the thousand* 1 S 17_{18} 18_{13} (שַׂר־אֲלֶף) 1QM 4_{2} (+ שרי מאיותיו *his centurions*), אות הא[ל]ף *standard of the thousand* 1QM 4_{1}.

שָׂרֵי (הָ)אֲלָפִים *(the) rulers of thousands* (alw. || מֵאָה *[unit of] a hundred* except 1 S 8_{12} [|| 50] 1 C 15_{25} 2 C 17_{14} 11QT 21_{3} + Sup [(ש)רי] 22_{2} [האלפ(ים)] 1QM 4_{1}) Ex $18_{21.25}$ Dt 1_{15} 11QT 57_{4} (all || 50, 10) Nm $31_{14.48.52.54}$ 1 S 22_{7} 1 C 13_{1} 27_{1} 29_{6} 11QT 42_{15} (all three + אָבוֹת *fathers' [households]*) 1 C 28_{1} 2 C 1_{2} 25_{5} (+ אָבוֹת) 11QT 58_{4} 1QS[a] 1_{29}.

Also 11QJub 4_{30} 1QSb 3_{7} ([א]ל[פי]כה *your thousands*) 4QRitMar 45_{2} Kadesh Barnea ost. $6_{3.6}$ (both אלפם).

<SYN> רְבָבָה *ten thousand*.

<ANT> אֶחָד *one*.

→ אלף *be a thousand*.

[אֶ֫לֶף] II $_{8}$ n.m. **cattle**—אֲלֶף; pl. אֲלָפִים; sf. אֲלָפֶ֫יךָ—**cattle** (collective), **head of cattle,** <SUBJ> עבד *work* land Is 30_{24} (|| עַיִר *ass*), אכל *eat* fodder 30_{24}. <NOM CL> בְּאֵין אֲלָפִים *where there are no cattle* Pr 14_{4} (|| שׁוֹר *ox*). <OBJ> שׁית *place* under control of humans Ps 8_{8} (+ צֹנֶה *flock*, בְּהֵמָה *animal*).

<CSTR> שְׁגַר(־)אֲלָפֶיךָ *offspring of your cattle* Dt 7_{13} $28_{4.18.51}$ (all four || צֹאן *flock*), בְּהֵמוֹת בְּהַרְרֵי־אֲלֶף *beasts on hills (full) of cattle* Ps 50_{10} (but perh. אֲלֶף = *thousand*, or em. אֵל *of God* or בַּהֲרָרַי אֲלֶף the beasts *on my hills are a thousand*).

<SYN> צֹאן *flock*.

אֶ֫לֶף III $_{13.0.2}$ n.m. **clan**—sf. אַלְפִּי; pl. אֲלָפִים; cstr.

אַלְפֵי; sf. אַלְפֵיכֶם—tribal unit smaller than שֵׁבֶט *tribe*, sometimes loosely equivalent to מִשְׁפָּחָה *family* (1 S 10_{19-21}) or מַטֶּה *tribe*; <SUBJ> אמר *say* Zc 12_5 (if em. אַלֻּפֵי *chiefs of*), אכל *eat*, i.e. destroy 12_6 (if em. אַלֻּפֵי). <NOM CL> אַלְפִּי הַדַּל בִּמְנַשֶּׁה *my clan is the poor(est) in Manasseh* Jg 6_{15}, הָאֲלָפִים אֲשֶׁר לִמְנַשֶּׁה *the clans that were*, i.e. belonged, *to Manasseh* 1 C 12_{21}. <OBJ> שׂים *place* Zc 12_6 (if em.). <CSTR> אַלְפֵי יְהוּדָה *clans of Judah* 1 S 23_{23} Mc 5_1 Zc $12_{5.6}$ (if em. in both), אַלְפֵי יִשְׂרָאֵל *clans of Israel* Jos 22_{14} Nm 31_5, רָאשֵׁי אַלְפֵי יִשְׂרָאֵל *heads of the clans of Israel* Nm 1_{16} (+ מַטֶּה *tribe*) 10_4 Jos 22_{14} (|| רֹאשׁ מַטֶּה *tribe*) $22_{21.30}$ 11QT 19_{16} 1QSa 1_{14}, רָאשֵׁי הָאֲלָפִים *heads of the clans* 1 C 12_{21}, כֹּל אַלְפֵי *all the clans of* 1 S 23_{23}. <PREP> לְ *belonging to* Jos 22_{14}, יצב לְ htp. *position oneself according to* 1 S 10_{19} (|| שֵׁבֶט *tribe*), אַלּוּפֵי הַחֹרִי לְאַלְפֵיהֶם *the chiefs of the Horites according to their clans* Gn 36_{30} (if em. אַלֻּפֵיהֶם *[the names of] their chiefs*); היה לְ *be as* Is 60_{22} (|| גּוֹי *nation*); בְּ *among*, + היה *be* Mc 5_1 (or em. הַצָּעִיר you are *the small[est]* among), חפשׂ pi. *seek* 1 S 23_{23}; היה כְּ *be as* Zc 9_7 (if em. כְּאַלֻּף *as a chief*); מסר מִן ni. *be handed over from* Nm 31_5.

<SYN> מַטֶּה *tribe*, שֵׁבֶט *tribe*, גּוֹי *nation*.

אֶלֶף IV, see צֵלַע הָאֶלֶף.

[אֱלְפֶּלֶט], see אֱלִיפֶלֶט.

[אֶלְפַּעַל] 3 pr.n.m. **Elpaal**—אֶלְפָּעַל—Benjaminite, a son of Shaharaim (or Ahiram, if em. שַׁחֲרַיִם at 1 C 8_8 to אֲחִירָם *Ahiram*) and Hushim (or Machsham, if em. אֹתָם חוּשִׁים sent *them—(namely) Hushim* at 1 C 8_8 to אֶת־מַחְשָׁם sent *Machsham* and מֵחֻשִׁים *by Hushim* at 8_{11} to מִמַּחְשָׁם *by Machsham*) and father of at least three sons, 1 C $8_{11.12.18}$.

→ אֵל *God* + פעל *do*.

אלץ 1 vb. **press**—**Pi.** Impf. + waw sf. וַתְּאַלְצֵהוּ—**press,** הֵצִיקָה לּוֹ בִדְבָרֶיהָ ... וַתְּאַלְצֵהוּ *she* (Delilah) *squeezed him* (Samson) *with her words ... and pressed him (to speak)* Jg 16_{16}.

[אלצדק] pr.n. **Elzedek,** Seal 584_2 ([א]לצד[ק]; T. Beit Mirsim?, 7th/6th cent.).

→ אֵל *God* + צדק *be righteous*.

אֶלְצָפָן, see אֱלִיצָפָן.

[אלצר] pr.n.m. **Elzar,** Beersheba ost. 2_1 (others הון[ ]ה).

אֶלְקוּם 1 perh. n.[m.] **God,** i.e. var. of אֱלֹהִים, וּמֶלֶךְ אַלְקוּם עִמּוֹ *and a king—God is with him* Pr 30_{31} (mss אַל־קוּם appar. against whom *no one stands*; or em. לְקוּם עַל עַמּוֹ *as he stands over his people* or אֵל קוֹס *the God Kos*; or אַלְקוּם = *the army*).

אֶלְקָנָה 19 pr.n.m. **Elkanah, 1.** father of Samuel, 1 S 1_{1+5t} $2_{11.20}$ 1 C $6_{12.19}$. **2.** son of Korah, Ex 6_{24} 1 C $6_{8.10}$. **3.** son of preceding, 1 C $6_{11.11}$ (lacking in mss). **4-5.** Levites, 1 C $6_{20.21}$. **6.** Levite, father of Asa, 1 C 9_{16}. **7.** one of David's warriors, 1 C 12_7. **8.** doorkeeper, 1 C 15_{23}. **9.** second in authority under Ahaz, 2 C 28_7.

→ אֵל *God* + קנה *acquire, create*.

אֶלְקֹשִׁי 1 gent. **Elkoshite,** appar. inhabitant or native of Elkosh, נַחוּם הָאֶלְקֹשִׁי *Nahum the Elkoshite* Na 1_1.

[אלרלה] pr.n.m. **Elralah,** Seal 140 (others אלדלה *Eldalah*; 8th cent.).

→ אֵל *God*.

אלרם 0.0.0.3 pr.n.m. **Eliram**—אלירם—**1.** Seal 529_1 (אלירם; T. Beit Mirsim?, 7th/6th cent.). **2.** son of Tomma (תמע), Seal 94_1 (5th cent.). **3.** Seal 220_1 (c. 700).

→ אֵל *God* + רום *be high*.

אלשב, see אֶלְיָשִׁיב.

אלשגב 0.0.0.1 pr.n.f. **Elsagab,** daughter of Elishama (בת אלשמע), Seal 59_1 (Palestine?, 7th cent.).

→ אֵל *God* + שׂגב *be high*.

אלשמע, see אֱלִישָׁמָע.

אֵלַת, see אֵילַת.

אֶלְתּוֹלַד 2 pl.n. **Eltolad**—mss אֶל(־)תּוֹלַד, אֶלְתּוֹלָד—town in Simeon, perh. ident. with Tolad (תּוֹלָד) at 1 C 4$_{29}$, Jos 15$_{30}$ 19$_{4}$.
→ ילד *give birth.*

אֶלְתְּקֵא 2 pl.n. **Eltekeh**—אֶלְתְּקֵה—Levitical city in Dan, perh. T. el-Melāt (T. Gibbetōn), Jos 19$_{44}$ (אֶלְתְּקֵה) 21$_{23}$.

אֶלְתְּקֵה, see אֶלְתְּקֵא.

אֶלְתְּקֹן 1 pl.n. **Eltekon,** town in hill country of Judah, Jos 15$_{59}$.

אִם +1071.68.125.6 conj. **if**—Q יאאם—**1.** as conditional particle, **if,** introducing protasis (which usu. precedes apodosis), generally expressing fulfilled or fulfillable conditions (exceptions Ho 9$_{12}$ Ps 7$_{4.4}$ 50$_{12}$ 73$_{15}$ 137$_{5}$ 139$_{8}$ Jb 31$_{5+10t}$), sometimes virtually equivalent to **when.**

1a. אִם with perfect in protasis, and apodosis with (1) perfect verb, or *waw*-consecutive with imperfect, אִם־בָּנֶיךָ חָטְאוּ־לוֹ וַיְשַׁלְּחֵם בְּיַד־פִּשְׁעָם *if your children sinned against him, he delivered them into the power of their transgression* Jb 8$_{4}$, אִם־חָכַמְתָּ חָכַמְתָּ לָּךְ *if you have become wise you have become wise for yourself* Pr 9$_{12}$, אם רע קראך נמצא שם *when misfortune came upon you, he was there* Si 12$_{17}$, אם עבר אשם הוא *if he then transgressed, he would become guilty* CD 15$_{3-4}$, אם לוא נגע בו כבס אותו *if he did not touch it, he shall wash it* 4QToh A 2.1$_{8}$, אם שמו בראישׁ[כ]ה למות הפקידהו *if he* (God) *has ordained it that you die in poverty, so has he appointed it* 4Q416 10.2$_{7}$.

(2) imperfect verb, or perfect with *waw*-consecutive, אִם־יָשַׁבְנוּ פֹה וָמָתְנוּ *if we sit here, we shall die* 2 K 7$_{4}$, אִם עָבַר וְרָמַס *when it passes, it tramples* Mc 5$_{7}$, אִם־שָׁכַבְתִּי וְאָמַרְתִּי *when I have lain down, I say* Jb 7$_{4}$, אִם־גֻּלַּחְתִּי וְסָר מִמֶּנִּי כֹחִי *if my hair was cut, my strength would go away from me* Jg 16$_{17}$, אִם־לֹא הֲבִיאֹתִיו ... וְחָטָאתִי *if I have not returned him ..., I shall be held guilty* Gn 43$_{9}$, אִם עָבַרְתָּ אִתִּי וְהָיִתָ עָלַי לְמַשָּׂא *if you crossed with me, you would be be a burden to me* 2 S 15$_{33}$, אִם־שַׁנּוֹתִי ... חַרְבִּי ... אָשִׁיב נָקָם *if I sharpened ... my sword ..., I could repay vengeance* Dt 32$_{41}$, אִם־שָׁכַחְנוּ שֵׁם אֱלֹהֵינוּ ... הֲלֹא אֱלֹהִים יַחֲקָר־זֹאת *if we forgot the name of our God ..., surely God would discover this* Ps 44$_{21}$, אִם־אַתָּה הֲכִינוֹתָ לִבֶּךָ ... כִּי־אָז תִּשָּׂא פָנֶיךָ מִמּוּם *if you had directed your heart* aright ..., *you would now hold up your head* free *from fault* Jb 11$_{13}$, אם קלל ... והבדילהו *if he has cursed ..., they are to set him apart* 1QS 7$_{1}$, אִם־עָשִׂיתִי זֹאת ... יִרַדֹּף אוֹיֵב נַפְשִׁי *had I done this ..., then the enemy would pursue my life* Ps 7$_{4}$, אִם־נִפְתָּה לִבִּי עַל־אִשָּׁה ... תִּטְחַן לְאַחֵר אִשְׁתִּי *if my mind has been misled because of a woman ..., may my wife grind for someone else* Jb 31$_{9}$, אם קרבת לא תאשם *when you have approached him, do nothing wrong* Si 9$_{13}$, אם מצא עת לא ישבע דם *if he could find an oppurtunity, he would never be sated with blood* 12$_{16}$ (conditional sentence here is also apodosis of main clause introduced by אִם), אם מתה ונשא לו אחרת *if she has died, then he is to marry another one* 11QT 57$_{18}$, אם קראתי אתה [ואח]ר אתננהו *when I have read it, afterwards I repeat it* Lachish ost. 3$_{11}$, אם על שלחן ... ישבתה אל תפתח ... גרנך *when you sit ... at table do not open wide ... your throat* Si 34$_{12}$, Gn 18$_{3}$ 33$_{10}$ 38$_{9}$ 47$_{6}$ Nm 5$_{27}$ 21$_{9}$ Jg 6$_{3}$ 2 K 7$_{4}$ Is 4$_{4}$ Si 13$_{23}$ 16$_{2.21}$ 30$_{34.40}$ 34$_{18}$ 11QT 58$_{6.7}$ (with ellipsis of verb) 58$_{11}$ 1QS 7$_{2}$ 4Q525 4$_{14}$ 4QToh A 1.1$_{5}$.

(3) imperative verb, הַגֵּד אִם־יָדַעְתָּ *tell, if you know* Jb 38$_{4.18}$, הָבוּ מִקְנֵיכֶם ... אִם־אָפֵס כָּסֶף *give your cattle ..., if your money has run out* Gn 47$_{16}$, אִם־נָא מָצָאתִי חֵן ... דַּבְּרוּ־נָא *please, if I have found favour ..., speak please* 50$_{4}$.

(4) noun clause, אם הלוית כמאבד *if you lend, you are as a loser* Si 8$_{12}$, אִם־יָצָאתִי הַשָּׂדֶה וְהִנֵּה חַלְלֵי־חֶרֶב *when I go out to the countryside, behold, those killed by the sword* Jr 14$_{18}$, אִם־מָצָאתָ וְיֵשׁ אַחֲרִית *if you found (it), then there is a future* Pr 24$_{14}$, Jr 14$_{18}$ Si 8$_{13}$.

(5) apodosis lacking or incomplete, 4QToh A 2.1$_{8}$ ([נגע]).

1b. אִם with imperfect in protasis, and apodosis with (1) perfect verb, or *waw*-consecutive with imperfect, אִם ... יְמֻתוּן ... לֹא י׳ שְׁלָחָנִי *if ... they die ..., Y. has not sent me* Nm 16_{29}, אִם־לֹא תַעֲשׂוּן כֵּן הִנֵּה חֲטָאתֶם *if you do not do this, behold you will have sinned* 32_{23}, אִם־שׁוֹב תָּשׁוּב בְּשָׁלוֹם לֹא־דִבֶּר י׳ בִּי *if you indeed return in safety, Y. has not spoken through me* 1 K 22_{28}, אִם־לֹא יִשְׂבְּעוּ וַיָּלִינוּ *if they are not satisfied, they stay all night* Ps 59_{16}, אם ינוח לא נחה לו *if he rests, it* (toil) *does not rest for him* Si 34_{4}, אם לוא יטהר ... טמא הוא *if he does not purify himself ..., then he has become defiled* 11QT 50_{7}, אם יוסף מן החי אל המת ... טמא הואה *if it has been increased from the living to the dead ..., he has become defiled* 4QD[a] $_{10}$, 1 S 6_{9} Jb 20_{12}.

(2) imperfect verb, or *waw*-consecutive with perfect, אם לא תרוץ לא תגיע ואם לא תבקש לא תמצא *if you do not run, you will not arrive; if you do not seek, you will not find* Si 11_{10}, אם לוא ימצא שם [עשרת צדיקים אשחית העיר] *if there are not found there ten righteous persons, I will destroy the city* 4QpGen[a] 3_{5}, יסור מלאך המשטמה מאחריו אם יקים את דבריו *the angel Mastema will leave him if he effects his words* CD 16_{5}, אִם־יְחַיֻּנוּ נִחְיֶה וְאִם־יְמִיתֻנוּ וָמָתְנוּ *if they let us live, we shall live; and if they kill us, we shall die* 2 K 7_{4}, אִם־יַחְתְּרוּ בִשְׁאוֹל מִשָּׁם יָדִי תִקָּחֵם *if they dig down to Sheol, my hand will take them from there* Am 9_{2}, אִם־יִכָּרֵת וְעוֹד יַחֲלִיף *if it is cut down, it renews itself once more* Jb 14_{7}, אִם־יִנּוֹעוּ וְנָפְלוּ *if they are shaken, they fall* Na 3_{12}, אִם־אֲדַבְּרָה לֹא־יֵחָשֵׂךְ כְּאֵבִי *were I to speak, my pain would not be relieved* Jb 16_{6}, אִם־יִשְׁכְּבוּ שְׁנַיִם וְחַם לָהֶם *if two lie down, they become warm* Ec 4_{11}, אִם־אַתָּה תְּשַׁחֵר אֶל־אֵל ... יָעִיר עָלֶיךָ *if you diligently seek God ..., he will rouse himself for you* Jb 8_{5}, אִם־אֶרְעַב לֹא־אֹמַר לָךְ *were I hungry, I should not tell you* Ps 50_{12}, אִם־אֶשְׁכָּחֵךְ יְרוּשָׁלָ͏ִם תִּשְׁכַּח יְמִינִי *were I to forget you, Jerusalem, my right hand would forget* 137_{5}, אִם־יִהְיֶה אֱלֹהִים עִמָּדִי ... וְהָיָה י׳ לִי לֵאלֹהִים *if God will be with me ..., then Y. will be my God* Gn 28_{20}, אִם־פָּקֹד יִפְקְדֵנִי אָבִיךָ וְאָמַרְתָּ *if your father does indeed notice me, you are to say* 1 S 20_{6}, אִם תֵּלֵךְ בִּדְרָכַי ... וְהַאֲרַכְתִּי אֶת־יָמֶיךָ *if you walk in my ways ..., I shall stretch out your days* 1 K 3_{14}, אִם־יוּכַל אִישׁ לִמְנוֹת אֶת־עֲפַר הָאָרֶץ גַּם־זַרְעֲךָ יִמָּנֶה *if a man were able to number the dust of the earth, so also shall your seed be numbered* Gn 13_{16}, לֹא אֶעֱשֶׂה אִם־אֶמְצָא שָׁם שְׁלֹשִׁים *I shall not do it, if I find thirty* people *there* 18_{30}, כִּי אִם־יְגַדְּלוּ אֶת־בְּנֵיהֶם וְשִׁכַּלְתִּים מֵאָדָם *were they to raise children, I should bereave them entirely* Ho 9_{12} (asseverative כִּי), אִם־מִזְבַּח אֲבָנִים תַּעֲשֶׂה־לִּי לֹא־תִבְנֶה אֶתְהֶן גָּזִית *if you make an altar of stones for me, you shall not make them of hewn stones* Ex 20_{25}, אִם־לֹא יֵעָלֶה הֶעָנָן וְלֹא יִסְעוּ *whenever the cloud was not taken up, they would not set out* 40_{37} (|| בְּ + inf. *when ...*), אם יסור מאחרי אשליכנו *if he turns from me, I shall cast him aside* Si 4_{19}, אם לתוך הבית יבוא עמה וטמא *if he comes into the house with her, he will be defiled* 11QT 50_{12}, אם נקבה תלד וטמאה [שבועים] *if she bears a female, she shall be unclean two weeks* 4Q251 3_{16}, כי אם תדור נדר לא תאחר לשלמו *if you make a vow, do not delay in fulfilling it* 11QT 53_{11} (asseverative or pleonastic כִּי; ||Dt 23_{22} lacks אִם), ... ונתתי לכה רחמים אם תשמע בקולי *and I shall give your mercy ... if you listen to my voice* 55_{13} (=Dt 13_{19} כִּי *if*), perh. יהו בו אצלך ... אם יחפצו לבו *they shall be there with you ..., if they desire to come* MurEpBarC[b] $_{6}$, אם לוא [יפחדו] ... ל[אסור אדם ... וישפוט] י׳ *if they are not afraid ... to imprison a man, ... Y. will judge* 11QapPs[a] 2_{9}, Gn $18_{26.28}$ $24_{8.41}$ 30_{31} 31_{8} 32_{9} 42_{37} Nm 16_{30} 30_{15} Dt $20_{11.12}$ 22_{25}=11QT $62_{6.8}$ 66_{4} Jg 4_{20} 1 S 1_{11} 6_{9} Am $9_{2.3.3.4}$ Jb 9_{3} Si 4_{19} $6_{12.32.32}$ $11_{10.10}$ 12_{15} $13_{4.4}$ $15_{15.15}$ 34_{4} 37_{12} 11QT 15_{15} 43_{13} $47_{15.16}$ 52_{9} 53_{12} (=Dt 15_{21} 23_{23} כִּי *if*) 53_{19} (=Nm 30_{6} with perfect in protasis [Sam imperfect]) $54_{8.19}$ $55_{2.15}$ (=Dt $13_{2.7.13}$ 17_{2} כִּי) 58_{10} (+ asseverative כִּי) $58_{15(mg)}$ 59_{16} 61_{7} (=Dt 19_{16} כִּי) 1QS $6_{13.14.18.21.24}$ CD 13_{4} 15_{3} 1QH 8_{24} 13_{19} 4Q251 4_{1} 4Q416 9.2_{2} ([אם י]קפוץ) perh. 4Q376 1.3_{1}.

(3) imperative verb, אִם־תּוּכַל הֲשִׁיבֵנִי *if you can, answer me* Jb 33_{5}, אִם־כֹּה אֹמַר ... לֵךְ *if I say this ..., leave* 1 S 20_{22}, אִם־אֹתָהּ תִּקַּח־לְךָ קָח *if you will take it, take it* 21_{10}, דבר נער אם צריך אתה *speak, lad, if you must* Si 35_{7} אם ישיבכה לכבודכה התהלך *if he restores you, conduct yourself honourably* 4Q416 10.2_{10}, Gn 31_{50} 1 S 20_{21} Si 12_{11} 34_{21} 35_{7} (with ellipsis of imperative).

(4) participle, אם אכזב ... מי יודע *if I lie ..., who knows?* Si 16_{21}.

(5) infinitive, אם ינוח לקבל תענוג *if he rests, it is to*

take pleasure Si 34$_{3}$.

(6) noun clause, אִם־אֶסַּק שָׁמַיִם שָׁם אָתָּה *were I to ascend to the skies, you would be there* Ps 139$_{8}$, תמה זה אם ינקה *it would be a marvel if he were held innocent* Si 16$_{11}$, אִם־תֵּיטִיב שְׂאֵת *if you do good, there is acceptance* Gn 4$_{7}$, אִם־אֶרְאֶה אוֹר ... גַּם־הוּא עָוֹן *were I to see light ..., that too would be a wickedness* Jb 31$_{26}$, היין חיים לאנוש אם ישתנו במתכנתו *wine is life for a man, if he drinks it in a proper amount* Si 34$_{27}$, אם תולידו לאנחה *if you have children, it is for*, i.e. leads to, *anguish* 41$_{9(M)}$, אם תפרו על יד אסון *if you are fruitful, it is for misfortune* 41$_{9(Bmg)}$, [א]ם תכשלו לשמחת עולם ואם תמותו לקללה *if you stumble, it is for*, i.e. leads to, *eternal rejoicing, and if you die, it is for*, i.e. leads to, *cursing* 41$_{9(B)}$, שמחה לכה אם תנקה ממנו *there will be joy for you, if you purify yourself of it* 4Q416 10.2$_{6}$.

(7) apodosis lacking or incomplete, 4QToh A 2.1$_{6}$ 3.2$_{7.8}$ 4Q416 5$_{13}$ 9.1$_{17.19.21.25}$ 9.2$_{2}$.

1c. אִם with infinitive in protasis, אִם־אָמְרִי אֶשְׁכְּחָה שִׂיחִי ... יָגֹרְתִּי כָל־עַצְּבֹתָי *were I to say, Let me forget my complaint ..., I should* still *fear all my pains* Jb 9$_{27}$, אם לש[מו]ע *were I to hear* 4QHymPr 7$_{3}$, אם לעבור ברית הוא יניאה *if it is to breach a covenant, he is to annul it* CD 16$_{12}$, אם לו ליוסף מן הח[יות] על המיתות והגיד *if it has begun to increase* (lit. *if it is to it to be increased*) *from the living to the dead, he is to tell* 4QD^{a}$_{11}$.

1d. אִם with participle in protasis, אִם־יֹסְפִים אֲנַחְנוּ לִשְׁמֹעַ ... וָמָתְנוּ *if we continue to hear ..., we shall die* Dt 5$_{25}$, אִם־לֹקֵחַ יַעֲקֹב אִשָּׁה ... לָמָּה לִּי חַיִּים *if Jacob takes a wife ..., why should I live?* Gn 27$_{46}$, אִם בֶּאֱמֶת אַתֶּם מֹשְׁחִים אֹתִי ... בֹּאוּ חֲסוּ *if you are anointing me in good faith ..., come, take shelter* Jg 9$_{15}$, אם אמנה היא העמידה *if it is well-trained, keep it* Si 7$_{22}$, אם נמוט לא יתכלכל *if sinking down, he will not provide for you* 12$_{15}$, אם עולה על לבך דבר ביראת אל ולא בחסר כל *if something comes into your mind, let it be because of reverence for God and not because of lack of anything else* 35$_{12}$, אם אין הוא בחון ... ויצא הג[ו]רל *if he is not experienced ..., the lot shall be drawn* CD 13$_{3}$, Jg 11$_{9}$ 4Q416 10.2$_{20}$.

1e. אִם with noun clause in protasis, וְאִם־מְעָט וְאֹסִפָה *and if it is* too *little, let me increase* 2 S 12$_{8}$, כי אם בתסבת הבקר ... וידע *for if (it is) in the morning tour, he will know* Lachish ost 4$_{9}$, אם לא לשר להש[ב את בגד] עב[דך ותת]ן אלו רח[מם] *if it is not (an obligation) to the official to return the garment of your servant, then have pity upon him* Meṣad Ḥashavyahu ost. 1$_{12}$ (others אמלא *I shall be satisfied*), אִם־גִּלְעָד אָוֶן אַךְ־שָׁוְא הָיוּ בַּגִּלְגָּל שְׁוָרִים זִבֵּחוּ *if Gilead is wickedness*, i.e. wicked, *then it was in vain that they were sacrificing bulls in Gilgal* Ho 12$_{12}$, אם עוד חמץ ונתת להם *if there is still some vinegar, you are to give it to them* Arad ost. 2$_{7}$, אם טוב תדיע למי תיטיב *if it is good* you plan to do, *you should know for whom you are doing good* Si 12$_{1}$, אם לא ממנו מי׳ *if it is not from him, then it is from Y.* 12$_{2}$, טוב העושר אם אין עון *wealth is good if there is not wickedness* 13$_{24}$, אם נפש אדם היא אשר תפול אל המי[ם] ... ישלח *if it is a human being who has fallen into the water ..., he will throw* 4Q251 2$_{6}$, ... אם שור נגח הוא [והמית ... יסקל] *if it is an ox accustomed to goring ... and it kills ..., it shall be stoned* 4Q251 4$_{4}$, אִם־לֹא קָרוֹב אָחִיךָ ... וַאֲסַפְתּוֹ *if your brother is not near ..., you are to collect it* Dt 22$_{2}$=11QT 64$_{14}$, אִם־הַשְּׂמֹאל וְאֵימִנָה וְאִם־הַיָּמִין וְאַשְׂמְאִילָה *if it is the left, then I shall go to the right, and if it is the right, then I shall go to the left* Gn 13$_{9}$, אִם־יֶשׁ־בִּי עָוֹן הֲמִיתֵנִי *if there is wickedness in me, kill me* 1 S 20$_{8}$, אִם־יֵשׁ נַפְשְׁכֶם אַל־יֵצֵא פָלִיט *if this is your desire, let no fugitive go out* 2 K 9$_{15}$, אִם־כֵּן לָמָּה זֶּה אָנֹכִי *if it be so, why am I such a person?* Gn 25$_{22}$, אִם־כֵּן אֵפוֹא זֹאת עֲשׂוּ *if it be so, then do this* 43$_{11}$, אִם־אַיִן מֵתָה אָנֹכִי *if there are none, I shall die* 30$_{1}$, אִם־אַיִן מְחֵנִי נָא *if not, destroy me, please* Ex 32$_{32}$, אל תבקש להיות מושל אם אין לך חיל להשבית זדון *do not seek to be a ruler, if you have not the strength to put down insolence* Si 7$_{6}$, אם יש אתך ענה ריעיך ואם אין שים ידך על פיך *if you can*, lit. *if there is to you, answer your friend, and if you cannot*, lit. *if there is not to you, put your hand on your mouth* 5$_{12(C)}$, Gn 23$_{8}$ Jg 9$_{15.20}$ 2 K 2$_{10}$ Si 13$_{5}$ 14$_{11.11}$ 16$_{2}$ 36$_{28}$ 37$_{12}$; esp. with יֵשׁ *there is* or אַיִן *there is not* followed by pronom. sf. & ptc. אִם־יֶשְׁךָ מוֹשִׁיעַ ... הִנֵּה אָנֹכִי מַצִּיג *if you are a saviour ..., behold, I present* Jg 6$_{36}$, אִם־יֶשְׁכֶם עֹשִׂים חֶסֶד ... הַגִּידוּ לִי *if you are going to behave loyally ..., tell me* Gn 24$_{49}$, ... אִם־יֶשְׁךָ מְשַׁלֵּחַ אֶת־אָחִינוּ נֵרְדָה ... וְאִם־אֵינְךָ מְשַׁלֵּחַ לֹא נֵרֵד *if you are going to send our brother ..., we shall go down ..., but if you are not* *going to send him, we shall not go down* 43_4, אִם־אֵינְךָ מֵשִׁיב דַּע כִּי *if you do not return* her ..., *know that* 20_7, 24_{42}.

<COLL> אִם followed by inf. absolute + impf. to emphasize condition, Ex 15_{26} 19_5 23_{22} (all with שׁמע *hear*) 21_5 $22_{3.11.12.16.22}$ Nm 21_2 30_{15} Jg 16_{11} 1 S 1_{11} 12_{25} $20_{6.21}$ 1 K 22_{28} 11QT 53_{19}, וְאִם־לֹא *but if not*, introducing alternative condition with ellipsis of verb, etc., from protasis of first condition, 1 S 2_{16} 6_9, אִם־נָא מָצָאתִי חֵן בְּעֵינֶיךָ *please, if I have found favour with you* Gn 18_3 30_{27} 33_{10} 47_{29} Ex 33_{13} 34_9 Jg 6_{17} 1 S 27_5, sim. Gn 50_4.

2a. in oaths, following imprecatory formula (here and in §2b אִם is used with negative oath, אִם־לֹא with positive; but see Gn $31_{52.52}$), כֹּה־יַעֲשֶׂה אֱלֹהִים ... אִם־אַשְׁאִיר ... מַשְׁתִּין בְּקִיר *thus may God do ..., if I let remain ... anyone who pisses on a wall*, i.e. any man 1 S 25_{22}, כֹּה־יַעֲשֶׂה־לְּךָ אֱלֹהִים ... אִם־תְּכַחֵד *thus may God do to you ..., if you conceal* 3_{17}, חָלִילָה לִּי אִם־אַצְדִּיק אֶתְכֶם *far be it from me, if I should declare you just* Jb 27_5, חָלִילָה חָלִילָה לִּי אִם־אֲבַלַּע וְאִם־אַשְׁחִית *far be it, far be it from me, if I should devour and I should destroy* 2 S 20_{20}, חַיֶּךָ וְחֵי נַפְשֶׁךָ אִם־אֶעֱשֶׂה אֶת־הַדָּבָר הַזֶּה *as you live, and as your soul lives, if I do*, i.e. I will not do, *this thing* 11_{11}, חַי־י׳ ... אִם־אֶקַּח *as Y. lives, if I take*, i.e. I will not take, *anything* 2 K 5_{16}, חיהוה אם נסה איש לקרא לי ספר לנצח *as Y. lives, if anyone has*, i.e. no one has, *ever tried to read me a letter* Lachish ost. 3_9, נִשְׁבַּעְתִּי בְאַפִּי אִם־יְבֹאוּן אֶל־מְנוּחָתִי *I adjured myself in my wrath, if they should*, i.e. that they should not, *enter my rest* Ps 95_{11}, הִשָּׁבְעָה ... בֵאלֹהִים ... אִם־תִּשְׁקֹר לִי *swear ... by God ..., if you*, i.e. that you will not, *lie to me* Gn 21_{23}, הִשְׁבַּעְתִּי אֶתְכֶם ... אִם־תָּעִירוּ וְאִם־תְּעוֹרְרוּ אֶת־הָאַהֲבָה *I have adjured you ..., if you*, i.e. that you do not, *wake up or rouse love* Ca 2_7= 3_5, נִכְרְתָה בְרִית עִמָּךְ׃ אִם־תַּעֲשֵׂה עִמָּנוּ רָעָה *let us make a covenant with you, if you*, i.e. that you will not, *cause us harm* Gn 26_{29}, 1 S 14_{45} 25_{34} 2 S 3_{35} (in both כִּי אִם emphatic or error for אִם or כִּי in same sense) Ezk 34_8.

2b. as asseverative particle, **surely, certainly (not)**, replacing imprecatory formula, oft. of vows made by Y., אִם־יִרְאֶה אִישׁ בָּאֲנָשִׁים הָאֵלֶּה *surely not one of these men will see* Dt 1_{35}, אִם־יְכֻפַּר הֶעָוֹן הַזֶּה *surely this sin will not be forgiven* Is 22_{14}, sim. 1 S 3_{14}, אִם־לֹא כַּאֲשֶׁר דִּמִּיתִי כֵּן הָיָתָה *surely, as I have planned, so it has happened* Is 14_{24}, אִם־לֹא בָּתִּים רַבִּים לְשַׁמָּה יִהְיוּ *surely many houses will become a ruin* 5_9, אִם־לֹא אֲשִׁיתְךָ מִדְבָּר *surely I shall make you a desert* Jr 22_6, אִם־לֹא אֲלֵיהֶם שְׁלַחְתִּיךָ *surely I shall send you to them* Ezk 3_6, אִם־לֹא דָם שָׂנֵאתָ *surely you have hated blood* 35_6; of oaths by others, מָגֵן אִם־יֵרָאֶה *surely a shield was not to be seen* Jg 5_8, עַל־פְּנֵיכֶם אִם־אֲכַזֵּב *surely I shall not lie to your face* Jb 6_{28}, אִם־לֹא נִכְחַד קִימָנוּ *surely our adversary was erased* 22_{20}, אִם־אֶקַּח מִכָּל־אֲשֶׁר־לָךְ *surely I shall not take anything belonging to you* Gn 14_{23}, אִם־לֹא אֶל־בֵּית־אָבִי תֵּלֵךְ *surely you shall go to my father's house* 24_{38}.

3. as interrogative particle, **is it the case that?**, oft. in rhetorical questions, **a.** introducing interrogative sentence, אִם מֵאֵת אֲדֹנִי הַמֶּלֶךְ נִהְיָה הַדָּבָר הַזֶּה *has this matter been brought about by my lord, the king?* 1 K 1_{27}, אִם־כַּחֹמֶר הַיֹּצֵר יֵחָשֵׁב *shall the potter be reckoned as the clay?* Is 29_{16}, אִם־כֹּחַ אֲבָנִים כֹּחִי אִם־בְּשָׂרִי נָחוּשׁ *is my strength the strength of rocks, is my flesh bronze?* Jb 6_{12}, כיוסף אם נולד גבר *has a man like Joseph been born?* Si 49_{15}, אם יש בכם כח להשיבני *do you have the strength to answer me?* 4QapPs[b] 76_9, Jb 39_{13}; also in indirect questions, דִּרְשׁוּ ... אִם־אֶחְיֶה *ask ... whether I shall live* 2 K 1_2, נִרְאֶה אִם פָּרְחָה הַגֶּפֶן *let us see whether the vine has flowered* Ca 7_{13}, בַקְשׁוּ ... אִם־תִּמְצְאוּ אִישׁ אִם־יֵשׁ עֹשֶׂה מִשְׁפָּט *seek ... whether you can find a man, whether there is one who does right* Jr 5_1, מִי־יוֹדֵעַ אִם *who knows whether?* Est 4_{14}; also הַאִם as emphatic interrogative, הַאִם תַּמְנוּ לִגְוֹעַ *shall we ever stop dying?* Nm 17_{28}, הַאִם אֵין עֶזְרָתִי בִי *is there really no help within me?* Jb 6_{13}.

3b. after clause beginning הֲ *is it the case that*, to introduce another question, הַלְּבֶן מֵאָה־שָׁנָה יִוָּלֵד וְאִם־שָׂרָה ... תֵּלֵד *can* a child *be born to a hundred-year old, or can Sarah give birth?* Gn 17_{17}, הֲנֵלֵךְ ... אִם־נֶחְדָּל *shall we go ... or shall we desist?* 1 K 22_{15}‖2 C 18_{14}, הֶהָיְתָה זֹּאת בִּימֵיכֶם וְאִם בִּימֵי אֲבֹתֵיכֶם *has this happened in your days, or in the days of your fathers?* Jl 1_2, Jb 21_4 (emphasizing מַדּוּעַ *why?*) 34_{17} 40_9; in indirect questions, לָדַעַת הַהִצְלִיחַ י׳ דַּרְכּוֹ אִם־לֹא *to know whether Y. would make* *his journey successful or not* Gn 24_{21}, וַאֲמֻשְׁךָ בְּנִי הַאַתָּה זֶה בְּנִי עֵשָׂו אִם־לֹא *that I might feel you, my son,* to see *whether you are indeed my son Esau or not* 27_{21}, הַכֶּר־נָא הַכְּתֹנֶת בִּנְךָ הִוא אִם־לֹא *look, please, whether this is your son's coat or not* 37_{32}, לְמַעַן אֲנַסֶּנּוּ הֲיֵלֵךְ בְּתוֹרָתִי אִם־לֹא *so that I can test it* (the people) *whether it walks in my law or not* Ex 16_{4}, וּרְאִיתֶם ... אֶת־הָעָם ... הַמְעַט הוּא אִם־רָב *and you are to see ... the people ... whether it is small or whether it is large* Nm 13_{18}, 13_{19}.

3c. introducing question similar to that of first clause, **or,** הֲמָלֹךְ תִּמְלֹךְ עָלֵינוּ אִם־מָשׁוֹל תִּמְשֹׁל בָּנוּ *will you indeed reign over us, or will you indeed govern us?* Gn 37_{8}, הַעַל־אֵלֶּה לֹא־אֶפְקֹד ... אִם ... לֹא תִתְנַקֵּם נַפְשִׁי *for these things, shall I not bring punishment ... or ... will not my soul take revenge?* Jr 5_{29}, הַאֱנוֹשׁ מֵאֱלוֹהַּ יִצְדָּק אִם מֵעֹשֵׂהוּ יִטְהַר־גָּבֶר *can a mortal be more just than God, or can a man be more pure than his maker?* Jb $4_{17(L)}$, הָאֵל יְעַוֵּת מִשְׁפָּט וְאִם־שַׁדַּי יְעַוֵּת־צֶדֶק *does God pervert justice, or does Shaddai pervert right?* 8_{3}, הֲכִימֵי אֱנוֹשׁ יָמֶיךָ אִם־שְׁנוֹתֶיךָ כִּימֵי גָבֶר *are your days as the days of a mortal, or are your years as the days of a man?* Jb 10_{5}, [הלוא יד]עתם אם לא שעתמה *do you not know, or have you not heard?* 4Q416 7_{8}, Is 10_{15} Jb $6_{5.6}$ 10_{4} $11_{2.7}$ 22_{3} 4QShir^b 30_{4} (ם[א]).

4. אִם as disjunctive particle, **either, or,** אִם ... אִם *either ... or,* אִם־בְּהֵמָה אִם־אִישׁ לֹא יִחְיֶה *be it an animal or a man, it shall not live* Ex 19_{13}, אִם־זָכָר אִם־נְקֵבָה *be it a male or a female* Lv 3_{1} 4QToh A 1.1_{7} (אם ... ואם), אִם־שׁוֹר אִם־שֶׂה *be it an ox or a sheep* Lv 27_{26} Dt 18_{3}, אִם־לְמָוֶת אִם־לְחַיִּים *be it for death or for life* 2 S 15_{21}, אם לטוב ואם לרע *be it for good or for evil* Si 13_{25}, שבועה אשר לא [י]דענה אם להקים היא ואם להניא *an oath that he does not know whether to fulfil or to annul* CD $16_{11(Rabin)}$, אִם־לְשֵׁבֶט אִם־לְאַרְצוֹ אִם־לְחֶסֶד *be it for a tribe or for his land or for the sake of loyalty* Jb 37_{13}, perh. אתה מבין אם בחכמת ידים המשילכה *you have understanding, whether because of the wisdom of (your) hands he has given you rule* 4Q416 1_{15}, להשכיל בכם אם תהיו לוא ואם [לא] *to consider among yourselves whether you will be his or not* 4QapPs^b 69_{7}; אִם ... וְעַד *either ... or,* אִם־מִחוּט וְעַד שְׂרוֹךְ־נַעַל *be it a thread or a shoe-lace* Gn 14_{23} (but perh. אִם is asseverative, §2b); אִם ... אוֹ *either ... or,* אִם־עֶבֶד יִגַּח הַשּׁוֹר אוֹ אָמָה *be it a male servant the bull gores or a woman servant* Ex 21_{32} (|| אוֹ ... אוֹ *either ... or*), אִם עַל־הַמִּשְׁכָּב הוּא אוֹ עַל־הַכְּלִי *whether it be on the bed or on the vessel* Lv 15_{23}, אם זוב [מבשרו או שכ]בת הזרע *whether (his touch) be a flux from his flesh or an emission of semen* 4QToh A 1.1_{8}, חטים חמש סאים אם יתיר או ח[סר] *five seahs of wheat, more or less* Mur 30_{14}, sim. Mur 30_{3} ([א]ן).

5. as concessive particle, **even though, even if,** אִם־צָדַקְתִּי לֹא אֶעֱנֶה *even if I had been in the right, I should not have answered* Jb 9_{15}, אִם־אֶצְדָּק פִּי יַרְשִׁיעֵנִי *even though I were in the right, my mouth would condemn me* 9_{20}, אם פתי הוא הוא יסגירנו *even if he is a dunce he is to lock him up* CD 13_{6}, אִם־יִהְיוּ חֲטָאֵיכֶם כַּשָּׁנִים כַּשֶּׁלֶג יַלְבִּינוּ *even though your sins were as scarlet, they would become white as snow* Is 1_{18}, אִם־יִהְיֶה עַמְּךָ יִשְׂרָאֵל כְּחוֹל הַיָּם שְׁאָר יָשׁוּב *even though your people Israel is as the sand of the sea* only *a remnant will return* 10_{22}, 1_{18} Jb 9_{30}; גַּם אִם *even if,* וגם אם יחסר מדעו עזוב לו *and even if his mind fails him, leave him alone* Si 3_{13}, Ec 8_{17} Si 12_{11} 16_{2}.

6. as desiderative particle, **if only, would that,** usu. followed by verb in second person, with impf. vb., שְׁמַע עַמִּי ... יִשְׂרָאֵל אִם־תִּשְׁמַע־לִי *listen, my people ..., Israel, if only you would listen to me* Ps 81_{9}, הַיּוֹם אִם־בְּקֹלוֹ תִשְׁמָעוּ *if only you would listen to his voice today* 95_{7}, אִם־תִּקְטֹל אֱלוֹהַּ רָשָׁע *O God, if only you would kill the wicked* 139_{19}, מָטִים לַהֶרֶג אִם־תַּחְשׂוֹךְ *if only you would restrain those who slip to slaughter* Pr 24_{11}, אִם־בָּרֵךְ תְּבָרְכֵנִי *if only you would really bless me* 1 C 4_{10}; with pf. vb. and כִּי for emphasis, כִּי אִם־זְכַרְתַּנִי ... כַּאֲשֶׁר יִיטַב לָךְ *if only you will remember me ... when things go well for you* Gn 40_{14}, חַי־י׳ כִּי־אִם־רַצְתִּי אַחֲרָיו *as Y. lives!, if only I had run after him* 2 K 5_{20} (but perh. אִם is asseverative).

7. אִם as relative particle, **that, which,** etc. in combination, עַד אִם **until,** אֶשְׁאָב עַד אִם־כִּלּוּ לִשְׁתֹּת *I shall draw water until they have finished drinking* Gn 24_{19}, תִּדְבָּקִין עַד אִם־כִּלּוּ אֵת כָּל־הַקָּצִיר *stay close until they have finished all the harvest* Ru 2_{21}, תָּנֻסוּ עַד אִם־נוֹתַרְתֶּם כַּתֹּרֶן *you shall flee until you are left like a flagstaff* Is 30_{17}, לֹא אֹכַל עַד אִם־דִּבַּרְתִּי דְּבָרָי *I shall not eat until I have spoken my words* Gn 24_{33}; עַד אֲשֶׁר אִם in same sense, לֹא אֶעֱזָבְךָ עַד אֲשֶׁר אִם־עָשִׂיתִי *I shall not leave you until I have done* Gn 28$_{15}$, נֵחָלֵץ ... עַד אֲשֶׁר אִם־הֲבִיאֹנֻם אֶל־מְקוֹמָם *we shall bear arms ... until we have brought them to their (proper) place* Nm 32$_{17}$, עַד־מָתַי ... עַד אֲשֶׁר אִם־שָׁאוּ עָרִים *how long? ... until cities lie waste* Is 6$_{11}$.

8a. אִם as adversative or exceptive particle, **but rather, except (for), unless,** לא ילך איש בשרירות לבו ... יאאם למול ... עורלת יצר *a man is not to walk in the stubbornness of his heart ..., rather he is to circumcise ... the foreskin of desire* 1QS 5$_{5}$, לֹא־יִתֵּן אֶתְכֶם ... לַהֲלֹךְ אִם לֹא בְּיָד חֲזָקָה *he would not allow you ... to go, except through a strong hand,* i.e. unless he was forced Ex 3$_{19}$ (if em. וְלֹא *and not*), אִישׁ יִגַּע בָּהֶם אִם לֹא בַבַּרְזֶל *a man touches them only if* (lit. *if not*) armed *with iron* 2 S 23$_{7}$ (if em. יִמָּלֵא בַרְזֶל *filled with iron*).

8b. in combination כִּי(־)אִם, **but rather, except, unless, but only,** לֹא יִירָשְׁךָ זֶה כִּי־אִם אֲשֶׁר יֵצֵא מִמֵּעֶיךָ הוּא יִירָשֶׁךָ *this one will not be your heir, rather it is one who will come out of your loins who will be your heir* Gn 15$_{4}$, לֹא יַעֲקֹב יֵאָמֵר עוֹד שִׁמְךָ כִּי אִם־יִשְׂרָאֵל *your name no longer will be called Jacob, but rather Israel* 32$_{29}$, לוא לכלת עולם [כי א]ם לקץ תעניות פשע *not for an everlasting destruction, but for a time for the humiliation of sin* 4QShir[a] 1$_{8(\text{Baillet})}$, אֵין זֶה כִּי אִם־בֵּית אֱלֹהִים *this is none other than the house of God* Gn 28$_{17}$, אֵין זֶה כִּי־אִם רֹעַ לֵב *this is none other than a bad mood* Ne 2$_{2}$, אין פה כסף וזהב [כי] אם [עצמתו] *there is not gold and silver here, only his bones* Silwan Royal Steward tomb inscr.2, לֹא אֲשַׁלֵּחֲךָ כִּי אִם־בֵּרַכְתָּנִי *I shall not release you unless you bless me* Gn 32$_{27}$, לוא יטהרו כי אם שבו מרעתם *they shall not be reckoned pure unless they turn from their wickedness* 1QS 5$_{14}$, אַל־תֹּאכְלוּ מִמֶּנּוּ ... מְבֻשָּׁל בַּמָּיִם כִּי אִם־צְלִי־אֵשׁ *do not eat any of it ... boiled, rather it is to be roasted on a fire* Ex 12$_{9}$, ... לֹא אֵלֵךְ כִּי אִם־אֶל־אַרְצִי אֵלֵךְ *I shall not go* with you, *rather, I shall go ... to my own land* Nm 10$_{30}$, לֹא־הָיוּ לוֹ בָּנִים כִּי אִם־בָּנוֹת *he had no sons, rather daughters* 26$_{33}$, לא קלל את חם כי אם בנו *he did not curse Ham but, on the contrary, his son* 4QpGen[a] 2$_{7}$, אֵין אֱלֹהִים בְּכָל־הָאָרֶץ כִּי אִם־בְּיִשְׂרָאֵל *there is no God in all the world except in Israel* 2 K 5$_{15}$, אַל־יִתְהַלֵּל עָשִׁיר בְּעָשְׁרוֹ כִּי אִם־בְּזֹאת יִתְהַלֵּל הַמִּתְהַלֵּל *let not the rich man glory in his wealth, rather let anyone who glories glory in this* Jr 9$_{23}$, מי בעל גמולות כי אם הוא *who is master of retribution except him?* Si 32$_{13(\text{mg})}$, עצת לבבך כך כי אם אמון ממנו *the advice of your own mind is such, unless there is something more trustworthy than it* 37$_{13(\text{D})}$, אין לו שמחת כל דבר כי אם דבריך *he has no joy in any word, except your words* GnzPs 2$_{24}$, דרך אנוש לא תכון כי אם ברוח יצר אל לו *the way of a human is not secured except by the spirit God fashions for him* 1QH 4$_{31}$, לא יצא מלפניך משפט שקר כי אם אמת ואמונה *deceitful justice does not go out from you, but rather truth and faith* GnzPs 4$_{20}$, לוא ישא מכול בנות הגויים כי אם מבית אביהו יקח *he is not to take* a wife *from any of the daughters of the Gentiles, rather he is to take* a wife *from his father's household* 11QT 57$_{16}$, אל ישלח את ידו ... כי אם בעצת חבור ישראל *let him not stretch out his hand ... unless* authorized *by the council of the society of Israel* CD 12$_{8}$, אל יאכלו כי אם נקרעו חיים *they are not to eat* (fish) *unless they have been torn apart when alive* 12$_{13}$, אל ישא ואל יתן ... כ[י] אם כף לכף *he is not to take and give,* i.e. trade, *... unless it is hand to hand,* i.e. in cash 13$_{15}$, אל יעש איש חבר ... כי אם הודיע למבקר *a man is not to enter a partnership unless he makes it known to the overseer* 13$_{15}$, מה אדבר כיא אם פתחתה פי ואיכה אבין כיא אם השכלתני *what can I say unless you have opened my mouth, and how can I understand unless you have made me perceive?* 1QH 12$_{33}$, [אל ילך כי אם רחוק מן המ]קדש שלושים רס *he should not walk* (on the sabbath) *unless he is thirty stadia distant from the temple* 4Q251 3$_{5}$, אל י]גע בזבה] או בדוה בנדתה כי אם טהרה [מנד]ת ה *he is not to touch the woman with a discharge or the menstruous woman in her impurity, but only when she is clean from her impurity* 4QToh A 1.1$_{7}$, [ה]ארץ לו תוכל ל[הטהר מדם האדם כי אם בדם שופכוה] *the earth cannot be purified from human blood except by the blood of the one who shed it* 4QJub[d] 1.2$_{19}$, Si 36$_{1}$ 11QT 3$_{6}$ 48$_{12}$ 52$_{14}$ CD 15$_{1}$ 1QH 12$_{34}$ 14$_{20}$ 1QMyst 1.2$_{4}$ 4QShir[b] 1$_{5}$ 4Q251 5$_{1}$ 4QToh A 3.2$_{6}$ 4QToh B[b]$_{10}$ (כ]יא אם]) 4QapPs[b] 76$_{11}$.

8c. in combination בִּלְתִּי אִם **except, unless,** לֹא נִשְׁאַר לִפְנֵי אֲדֹנִי בִּלְתִּי אִם־גְּוִיָּתֵנוּ *there is nothing left before my lord except for our bodies* Gn 47$_{18}$, אֵין זֹאת בִּלְתִּי אִם־חֶרֶב גִּדְעוֹן *this is none other than the sword of*

Gideon Jg 7_{14}, הֲיֵלְכוּ שְׁנַיִם יַחְדָּו בִּלְתִּי אִם־נוֹעָדוּ *do two walk together, unless they have arranged it?* Am 3_{3}, 3_{4}.

Also Si 34_{21} CD 15_{13} 4Q185 1.3_{14} 4QTanḥ 16_{4} 5QRègle 6_{3} 1QH 9_{20} 1QMyst $1.2_{4.7}$ 9_{2} 4QShir[b] 42_{10} Mur 22_{10} Arad ost. 16_{8} 28_{6} 4Q251 2_{8} 4QToh A $2.2_{2.8}$ 3.2_{5} 4Q416 9.2_{10} 4QD[a] 6.2_{9} 4Q464 2_{1}.

אֵם 220.9.23 n.f. **mother**—cstr. אֵם; sf. אִמִּי, אִמְּךָ (אִמֵּךְ, אִמָּם, אִמְּכֶן, אִמְּכֶם, אִמָּהּ, אִמּוֹ, אִמֵּךְ, (אמיכה, אמכה Q; pl. sf. אִמֹּתָם, אִמֹּתֵינוּ—**1a.** usu. human **mother** of children, but also of humanity (Eve as אֵם כָּל־חָי *ancestress of all living things* Gn 3_{20} Si $40_{1(B)}$), of a nation (דְּבוֹרָה שַׁקַּמְתִּי אֵם בְּיִשְׂרָאֵל *Deborah who rose up* as *a mother in Israel* Jg 5_{7}), or in ref. to a nation (Israel, Is 50_{1} Ezk $16_{3.44.45.45}$ $19_{2.10}$ 23_{2} Ho $2_{4.7}$ 4_{5}; Babylon, Jr 50_{12}).

2. animal **mother** שִׁבְעַת יָמִים יִהְיֶה עִם־אִמּוֹ *seven days it is to be with its mother* Ex 22_{29}, sim. Lv 22_{27} (תַּחַת *under* for עִם *with*), לֹא־תְבַשֵּׁל גְּדִי בַּחֲלֵב אִמּוֹ *you are not to boil a kid in its mother's milk* Ex 23_{19}=34_{26}=Dt 14_{21}, bird Dt $22_{6.6.7}$=11QT $65_{3.4.4}$, לֹא־תִקַּח הָאֵם עַל־הַבָּנִים *you shall not take the mother with the young* Dt 22_{6}=11QT 65_{4}, sim. 11QT 52_{6}, הָאֵם רֹבֶצֶת עַל־הָאֶפְרֹחִים אוֹ עַל־הַבֵּיצִים *the mother crouching over the young or the eggs* Dt 22_{6}=11QT 65_{3}, Dt 22_{7}=11QT 65_{4}.

3. junction, אֶל־אֵם הַדֶּרֶךְ בְּרֹאשׁ שְׁנֵי הַדְּרָכִים *at the junction of the road, at the head of two roads* Ezk 21_{26}, על אם הדרכים יעמוד *he stood at the junction of the roads* 4Q372 1_{9}.

<SUBJ> היה *be* Jr 20_{17} (+ קֶבֶר *grave* for unborn child) 2 C 22_{3} (+ יעץ ptc. *adviser* to king), עשׂה *make* Gn 27_{14} (obj. meal) 1 S 2_{19} (obj. coat) 1 K 15_{13}||2 C 15_{16} (obj. idol), קום *stand* 2 K 11_{1}||2 C 22_{10}, רבץ *crouch* Dt 22_{6}=11QT 65_{3}, בוא *come* Gn 37_{10} Jg 14_{5}, הלך *go* Ho 2_{7}, ירד *go down* Jg 14_{5}, עלה *go up* 1 S 2_{19}, hi. *take up* 2_{19}, שׁחה htpal. *prostrate oneself* Gn 37_{10} (|| אָח *brother*), אמר *say* Gn 24_{55} (|| אָח) 27_{13} Jg $17_{2.3}$ 2 K 4_{30} Ho 2_{7} Zc 13_{3} 1 C 4_{9}, דבר pi. *speak* 2 C $22_{10(L)}$ (mss, ||2 K 11_{1} אבד pi. *destroy*), קרא *name* a child 1 C 4_{9}, עטר pi. *crown* Ca 3_{11}, יסר pi. *teach* Pr 31_{1}, נחם pi. *comfort* Is 66_{13} 4QBark[c] $_{6}$, שׁאל *ask* 1 K 2_{20}, יבב pi. *shriek* Jg 5_{28}, ידע *know* 14_{4}, ראה *see* 2 K 11_{1}||2 C 22_{10}, שׁקף ni. *lean out of* window Jg 5_{28}, שׂמח *be happy* Ps 113_{9} Pr 23_{25} (|| ילד ptc. *one who gives birth*).

לקח *take* Gn 21_{21} (obj. wife for son) Dt 22_{15}=11QT 65_{9} (obj. proof of virginity) Jg 17_{4} (obj. son's money), נתן pass. *be given* 4QTNaph 2_{10} (נתון לו את *there was given to him* Bilhah my mother), יצא *go out* 1 S 22_{3} 2 K 24_{12}, hi. *bring out* Dt 21_{19}=11QT 64_{3} Dt 22_{15}=11QT 65_{9}, סור hi. *remove* adulterous behaviour Ho 2_{4}, שׁלח pu. *be sent away* Is 50_{1}, בושׁ *suffer shame* Jr 50_{12} (|| ילד ptc. *one who gives birth*), עזב *leave* child Ps 27_{10} 1QH 9_{35}, געל *reject* husband, child Ezk 16_{45}, זנה *be a whore* Ho 2_{7} (|| הרה ptc. *one who conceives*), תפשׂ *seize* refractory son Dt 21_{19}=11QT 64_{3}, יחם pi. *conceive* Ps 51_{7}, חבל pi. *have labour pains* Ca 8_{5}, ילד *give birth to* Jr 15_{10} 16_{3} 20_{14} 22_{26} Ca 8_{5} 1 C 4_{9} Zc $13_{3.3}$, שׁכל *suffer bereavement* 1 S 15_{33}, זקן *grow old* Pr 23_{22}, רטשׁ pu. *be smashed* Ho 10_{14}, מות *die* Est 2_{7}, אבד pi. *destroy* royal family 2 K 11_{1}||2 C $22_{10(mss)}$ (L דבר pi. *speak*), דקר *stab* son who is a prophet Zc 13_{3}.

<NOM CL> אִמְּךָ הִוא *she is your mother* Lv $18_{7(Qr)}$, הִיא אִמּוֹ *she is his mother* 1 K 3_{27}, הִיא אֵם *she was the mother of* 1 C 2_{26}, אֵין לָהּ אָב וָאֵם *she had no father nor mother* Est 2_{7}, אִמְּכֶם ... לֹא אִשְׁתִּי *your mother ... is not my wife* Ho 2_{4}, אִמֹּתֵינוּ כְּאַלְמָנוֹת *our mothers are as widows* Lm 5_{3}, אָבִיךְ הָאֱמֹרִי וְאִמֵּךְ חִתִּית *your father was an Amorite and your mother was a Hittite* Ezk 16_{3}, sim. 16_{45}, מָה אִמְּךָ לְבִיָּא *what a lioness your mother was!* 19_{2}, אִמְּךָ כַגֶּפֶן *your mother was as the vine* 19_{10}, כאדנים לגבר כן אמו *as legs to a man so is his mother* 4Q416 10.2_{17}.

<OBJ> קרא *call to* Ex 2_{8}, כבד pi. *show respect to* 20_{12} Dt 5_{16} Si 3_{6} 4Q416 10.2_{17} (אמיכה), ירא *revere* Lv 19_{3}, ברך pi. *bless* Pr 30_{11}, בכה *bewail* Dt 21_{13}=11QT 63_{13}, קלל pi. *insult* Ex 21_{17} Lv $20_{9.9}$ Pr 20_{20} Si $3_{11.16(A)}$, hi. *treat with contempt* Ezk 22_{7}, קלה hi. *insult* Dt 27_{16}, בזה *put to shame* Pr 15_{20}, בושׁ hi. *put to shame* 29_{15}, גזל *rob* 28_{24}, נכה hi. *strike* Ex 21_{15}, מות hi. *kill* 2 S 20_{19}, דמה *destroy* Ho 4_{5}, חיה hi. *let live* Jos 2_{13}, אסף *gather* 2_{18}, יצא hi. *bring out* 6_{23}, נוח hi. *place* 6_{23}, עזב *leave* Gn 2_{24} (:: אִשָּׁה *wife*, subj. man) Ru 2_{11} (subj. Ruth), ילד *bear* 4QTNaph 2_{4}, שׁלח pi. *release* Dt 22_{7}=11QT 65_{4}, *send away* Is 50_{1}, טול hi. *cast out* Jr 22_{26}, סור hi. *remove* 1 K

15$_{13}$||2 C 15$_{16}$, גלה hi. *exile* 2 K 24$_{15}$, ברח hi. *chase away* Pr 19$_{26}$, סחב *drag* Si 3$_{16(C)}$, לקח *take* Lv 20$_{14}$ Dt 22$_{6}$=11QT 65$_{4}$, נהג *take charge of* 4QTNaph 2$_{8}$.

<CSTR> אֵם *mother of* followed by personal name(s), Ahaziah 2 K 11$_{1}$||2 C 22$_{10}$, Asa 2 C 15$_{16}$, Jacob and Esau Gn 28$_{5}$, Joab 2 S 17$_{25}$, Onam 1 C 2$_{26}$, Sisera Jg 5$_{28}$, Solomon 1 K 1$_{11}$ 2$_{13}$, אֵם הַיֶּלֶד *mother of the boy* Ex 2$_{8}$, הַנַּעַר *of the boy* 2 K 4$_{30}$, בָּחוּר *of a young man* Jr 15$_{8}$ (or em.; see Prep.), הַבָּנִים *of sons* Ps 113$_{9}$ (־אֵם), הַמֶּלֶךְ *of the king* 1 K 2$_{19}$ 2 K 24$_{15}$; שֵׁם אִמּוֹ *his mother's name* was (followed by mother's name, esp. of king's mother) Lv 24$_{11}$ 1 K 11$_{26}$ 14$_{21}$||2 C 12$_{13}$ 1 K 14$_{31}$ 15$_{2}$ ||2 C 13$_{2}$ 1 K 15$_{10}$ 22$_{42}$||2 C 20$_{31}$ 2 K 8$_{26}$||2 C 22$_{2}$ 2 K 12$_{2}$ ||2 C 24$_{1}$ 2 K 14$_{2}$||2 C 25$_{1}$ 2 K 15$_{2}$||2 C 26$_{3}$ 2 K 15$_{33}$||2 C 27$_{1}$ 2 K 18$_{2}$||2 C 29$_{1}$ 2 K 21$_{1.19}$ 22$_{1}$ 23$_{31.36}$ 24$_{8.18}$||Jr 52$_{1}$.

אם אמי *mother of my mother* 4QTNaph 2$_{8}$, אבי ... אמי *father of ... my mother* 2$_{8}$, אֲבִי אִמֶּךָ *father of your mother* Gn 28$_{2}$, אֲחִי אִמֶּךָ *brother of your mother* Gn 28$_{2}$ (+ Laban), אִמּוֹ *of his mother* 29$_{10.10.10}$ (all three + Laban), אמה *of her mother* 4Q251 7$_{4}$, אֲחֵי אִמּוֹ *brothers of his mother* Jg 9$_{1.3}$ (־אֲחֵי), אֲחוֹת אִמְּךָ *sister of your mother* Lv 18$_{13}$ 20$_{19}$ (־אֲחוֹת), אמו *of his mother* 11QT 66$_{15}$ 4Q251 7$_{4}$ ([אחות אמו]), בַּת־אִמִּי *daughter of my mother* Gn 20$_{12}$ (|| אָחוֹת *sister*), אִמֶּךָ *of your mother* Lv 18$_{9}$, אִמֵּךְ *of your* (fem.) *mother* Ezk 16$_{45}$ (|| אָחוֹת), אִמּוֹ *of his mother* Lv 20$_{17}$ Dt 27$_{22}$ 11QT 66$_{14}$ (all || אָחוֹת) 4Q251 7$_{2}$ ([בת אמו]), בְּנוֹת אֵם *daughters of a mother* Ezk 23$_{2}$, בֶּן־אִמּוֹ *son of his mother* Gn 43$_{29}$ (|| אָח *brother*), אִמֶּךָ *of your mother* Dt 13$_{7}$=11QT 54$_{19}$ (אמכה) Ps 50$_{20}$ (אִמְּךָ) 11QT 66$_{13}$ (all || אָח), בְּנֵי אִמֶּךָ *sons of your mother* Gn 27$_{29}$ (|| אָח), אִמִּי *of my mother* Jg 8$_{19}$ (־בְּנֵי) Ps 69$_{9}$ (both || אָח) Ca 1$_{6}$, בֵּית אִמָּהּ *house(hold) of her mother* Gn 24$_{28}$ Ru 1$_{8}$, אִמִּי *of my mother* Ca 3$_{4}$ (|| הרה ptc. *one who conceives*) 8$_{2}$, בֵּית־אֲבִי אִמּוֹ *family of his mother* Jg 9$_{1}$.

רֶחֶם אִמּוֹ *womb of his mother* Nm 12$_{12}$ Si 40$_{1}$ (both + יצא מִן *come out from*), בֶּטֶן אִמִּי *womb of my mother* Jg 16$_{17}$ Jb 1$_{21}$ 31$_{18}$ Ps 22$_{11}$ (all + מִן *from*) 139$_{13}$ 1QH 9$_{30(Licht)}$ ([מבטן]), אִמּוֹ *of his mother* Ec 5$_{14}$ Si 46$_{13}$ (both + מִן), מְעֵי אִמִּי *womb of my mother* Is 49$_{1}$ Ps 71$_{6}$ (both + מִן), אמו *of his mother* 4QMMT A 2$_{46}$ ([מעי אמו]), שְׁדֵי אִמִּי *breasts of my mother* Ps 22$_{10}$ Ca 8$_{1}$, עֶרְוַת אִמְּךָ *nakedness of your mother* Lv 18$_{7}$ 1 S 20$_{30}$ (אִמֶּךָ), שְׁאֵר אִמְּךָ *flesh of your mother* Lv 18$_{13}$, קוֹל אִמּוֹ *voice of his mother* Dt 21$_{18}$, יִקְּהַת־אֵם *obedience of,* i.e. to, *a mother* Pr 30$_{17}$, תּוֹרַת אִמֶּךָ *instruction of your mother* 1$_{8}$ 6$_{20}$, תּוּגַת אִמּוֹ *grief of his mother* 10$_{1}$, סֵפֶר כְּרִיתוּת אִמְּכֶם *document of your* (pl.) *mother's divorce* Is 50$_{1}$, קֶבֶר ... אִמִּי *grave of ... my mother* 2 S 19$_{38}$, דֶּרֶךְ אֵם *mother's way* 1 K 22$_{53}$, חַטַּאת אִמּוֹ *sin of his mother* Ps 109$_{14}$, קללת אם *curse of a mother* Si 3$_{9}$, נְבִיאֵי אִמֶּךָ *prophets of your mother* 2 K 3$_{13}$, אֲבֶל־אֵם *mourner of,* i.e. for, *a mother* Ps 35$_{14}$, חֵיק אִמֹּתָם *bosom of their mothers* Lm 2$_{12}$.

<APP> אֵם *mother* + pronom. sf. with personal name (or personal name + אֵם *mother of*) Athaliah 2 K 11$_{1}$ ||2 C 22$_{10}$, Bathsheba 1 K 1$_{11}$ 2$_{13}$, Jezebel 2 K 9$_{22}$, Maacah 1 K 15$_{13}$||2 C 15$_{16}$, Sarah Gn 24$_{67}$, Zeruiah 2 S 17$_{25}$, Rebekah Gn 28$_{5}$, Leah Gn 30$_{14}$, Bilhah 4QTNaph 2$_{1}$ ([א]מי) 2$_{4.8.10}$, Hannah 2$_{8}$.

<ADJ> אֵם־אַחַת *one mother* Ezk 23$_{2}$.

<PREP> לְ of possession, *of, (belonging) to* Gn 44$_{20}$ Ca 6$_{9}$ (|| ילד ptc. *one who gives birth*), *except for* Lv 21$_{2}$, of direction, *to,* + נתן *give* Gn 24$_{53}$ (|| אָח *brother*) Jg 14$_{9}$ 1 K 17$_{23}$, בוא hi. *bring* 27$_{14}$, שׁוב hi. *bring back* Jg 17$_{3.4}$, אמר *say* Dt 33$_{9}$ Jg 17$_{2}$ 1 K 2$_{22}$ Lm 2$_{12}$, נגד hi. *tell* Jg 14$_{2.6.9.16}$, טמא לְ htp. *suffer impurity for* Lv 21$_{2.11}$ Nm 6$_{7}$ Ezk 44$_{25}$, שׂים לְ *place for (the use of)* 1 K 2$_{19}$, נשׁק לְ *kiss* 1 K 19$_{20}$.

בְּ *with, against,* + ריב *argue* Ho 2$_{4}$, קמה *stand up* Mc 7$_{6}$ (subj. daughter).

כְּ *as,* + עשׂה *do* evil 2 K 3$_{2}$, קדם pi. *meet* Si 15$_{2}$ (|| אִשָּׁה *wife* of one's youth), כְּאִמָּהּ בִּתָּהּ *the daughter is as her mother* Ezk 16$_{44}$.

אֶל of direction, *to,* + בוא *come* 1 K 2$_{13}$, hi. *bring* Gn 30$_{14}$ 2 K 4$_{20}$, הלך *go* Jg 14$_{9}$, נשׂא *carry* 2 K 4$_{19.20}$, אמר *say* Gn 27$_{11}$ 1 K 1$_{11}$, שׁמע *listen* Gn 28$_{7}$.

בושׁ מִן *be ashamed before* Si 41$_{17}$.

עַל *for the sake of* Jr 16$_{7}$, בוא עַל hi. *bring against* 15$_{8}$ (or em. עַל־אֵם בָּחוּר *against the mother of the young man* to לְאֹם מַחֲרִיב *a destroying nation*), אמר עַל *say concerning* 16$_{3}$, כְּגָמֻל עֲלֵי אִמּוֹ *as a suckling upon its mother* Ps 131$_{2}$.

נחם אַחֲרֵי ni. *be comforted after* (death of) Gn 24$_{67}$ (+ אִשָּׁה *wife*).

רַךְ וְיָחִיד לִפְנֵי אִמִּי *tender and the only child in my mother's presence* Pr 4$_{3}$.

<COLL> specif. mother of daughter (Gn 24$_{28.53.55}$ Lv 20$_{14}$ Dt 21$_{13}$=11QT 63$_{13}$ Dt 22$_{15}$=11QT 65$_{9}$ Jos 2$_{13.18}$ 6$_{23}$ Mc 7$_{6}$ Ru 1$_{8}$ 2$_{11}$ Ca 6$_{9}$ Est 2$_{7}$), אָב ... אֵם *father ... mother* (or reversed) Gn 2$_{24}$ 20$_{12}$ 27$_{14}$ 28$_{7}$ 37$_{10}$ 44$_{20}$ Ex 20$_{12}$ 21$_{15.17}$ Lv 18$_{7.9}$ 19$_{3}$ 20$_{9.9.17.19}$ 21$_{11}$ Dt 5$_{16}$ 13$_{7}$=11QT 54$_{19}$ Dt 21$_{13.18.19}$=11QT 64$_{3}$ Dt 22$_{15}$=11QT 65$_{9}$ Dt 27$_{16.22}$ Jg 14$_{2+6t}$ 1 S 22$_{3}$ 2 S 19$_{38}$ 1 K 19$_{20}$ 22$_{53}$ 2 K 3$_{2.13}$ 4$_{19}$ Jr 16$_{7}$ Ezk 22$_{7}$ Mc 7$_{6}$ Zc 13$_{3.3}$ Ps 27$_{10}$ 109$_{14}$ Pr 1$_{8}$ 4$_{3}$ 6$_{20}$ 10$_{1}$ 15$_{20}$ 19$_{26}$ 20$_{20}$ 23$_{22.25}$ 28$_{24}$ 30$_{11.17}$ Jb 17$_{14}$ Ru 2$_{11}$ Lm 5$_{3}$ Est 2$_{7.7}$ Si 3$_{9.11.16}$ 41$_{17}$ 1QH 9$_{35}$ 11QT 66$_{13.14.15}$, אֵם ... אָב ... בֵּן ... בַּת ... אָח *mother ... father ... son ... daughter ... brother* Lv 21$_{2}$, sim. Nm 6$_{7}$ Dt 33$_{9}$ Jos 2$_{13.18}$ 6$_{23}$ Ezk 44$_{25}$, בָּנִים ... בָּנוֹת ... אִמּוֹת ... אָבוֹת *sons ... daughters ... mothers ... fathers* Jr 16$_{3}$, אִשָּׁה וְאִמָּהּ *a woman and her mother* Lv 20$_{14}$, אֵם וְנָשִׁים *mother and wives* 2 K 24$_{15}$, יְהוֹיָכִין ... וְאִמּוֹ וַעֲבָדָיו וְשָׂרָיו וְסָרִיסָיו *Jehoiachin ... and his mother and his servants and his ministers and his eunuchs* 24$_{12}$, אֵם עַל־בָּנִים destroy *mother with children* Gn 32$_{12}$ Dt 22$_{6}$=11QT 65$_{4}$ Dt 22$_{7}$ Ho 10$_{14}$ 11QT 52$_{6}$, אֵם כָּל־חָי *ancestress of all living things* Gn 3$_{20}$ Si 40$_{1(B)}$ (Bmg אל *God*; + שׁוּב אֶל *return to*, i.e. die), עִיר וְאֵם בְּיִשְׂרָאֵל *a city and a mother in Israel* 2 S 20$_{19}$; in exclamations, אִמִּי וַאֲחֹתִי *my mother and my sister!* Jb 17$_{14}$, אָבִי וְאִמִּי *my father and my mother!* Is 8$_{4}$, אוֹי־לִי אִמִּי *woe is me, my mother* Jr 15$_{10}$.

Also Si 51$_{5}$ (לאמ[י]) 4QToh A 2.2$_{3}$.

<SYN> ילד ptc. *one who gives birth*, הרה ptc. *one who conceives*, אָח *brother*, אָחוֹת *sister*.

[אֹם] 0.0.3 n.m. **nation**—pl. אומים—<SUBJ> ספר pi. *recount* glory of Y. GnzPs 2$_{11}$, ראה *see* righteousness of Y. 2$_{11}$. <CSTR> כל האומים *all the (foreign) nations* GnzPs 1$_{18.23}$ (+ מֶלֶךְ *king of*) 2$_{11}$. <PREP> עלה מֵעַל *rise from above* GnzPs 1$_{18}$.

[אַמָּא], see אַמָּה III.

אָמָה 56.0.8.2 n.f. **maidservant**—cstr. I אמת; sf. אֲמָתִי, אֲמָתְךָ (אֲמָתֶךָ, Q אמתכה), אֲמָתוֹ (I אמתה), אֲמָתָהּ; pl. אֲמָהוֹת (אֲמָהֹת); cstr. אַמְהוֹת־; sf. אַמְהֹתַי, אַמְהֹתָיו, אַמְהֹתֵיהֶם, אַמְהֹתֵיכֶם, אַמְהֹתֶיהָ, (אמהותי[ו]ן Q).

1. maidservant, female slave, <SUBJ> עשׂה *do* Ex 20$_{10}$||Dt 5$_{14}$ (|| עֶבֶד *manservant*, בֵּן *son*, בַּת *daughter*, בְּהֵמָה *beast*, גֵּר *sojourner*), נוח *rest* Dt 5$_{14}$ (|| עֶבֶד), אכל *eat* offerings Dt 12$_{18}$ (|| עֶבֶד, בֵּן, בַּת, לֵוִי *Levite*), שׂמח *rejoice* at feast Dt 12$_{12}$ (|| עֶבֶד, בֵּן, בַּת, לֵוִי) 16$_{11.14}$ (both || עֶבֶד, בֵּן, בַּת, לֵוִי, גֵּר, יָתוֹם *orphan*, אַלְמָנָה *widow*), חשׁב *regard* Jb 19$_{15}$ (+ לְזָר *as a stranger*; || גור ptc. *alien*), נהג pi. *lament* (of maidservants of Nineveh) Na 2$_{8}$, תפף po. *beat* breast 2$_{8}$, היה *be* Lv 25$_{44}$ (+ לְ *[belonging] to* Israelite; || עֶבֶד).

<NOM CL> הִנֵּה אֲמָתִי *here is my maidservant* Gn 30$_{3}$.

<OBJ> שׁלח *send* Ex 2$_{5}$ (+ נַעֲרָה *maiden*), חמד *covet* 20$_{17}$ (|| עֶבֶד *manservant*, אִשָּׁה *wife*, שׁוֹר *ox*, חֲמוֹר *ass*, בַּיִת *house*), אוה htp. *desire* Dt 5$_{21}$ (|| עֶבֶד, שׁוֹר, חֲמוֹר, בַּיִת, שָׂדֶה *field*, אִשָּׁה), נכה hi. *strike* Ex 21$_{20}$ (|| עֶבֶד), נגח *gore* 21$_{32}$ (|| עֶבֶד), קנה *buy* Lv 25$_{44}$ (|| עֶבֶד), מכר *sell* CD 12$_{10}$ (|| עֶבֶד), מרא hi. *urge on* 11$_{12}$ (|| עֶבֶד, שׂכר ptc. *hired labourer*), רפא *heal* (so as to bear children) Gn 20$_{17}$ (|| אִשָּׁה), גרשׁ pi. *cast out* (so that son does not share inheritance) 21$_{10}$ (|| בֵּן *son*).

<CSTR> עֵין אֲמָתוֹ *eye of his maidservant* Ex 21$_{26}$ (|| עֶבֶד *manservant*), שֵׁן *tooth of* 21$_{27}$ (|| עֶבֶד), עצמ[ת] אמתה *bones of his maidservant* Silwan Royal Steward Inscr. 1$_{2}$, בֶּן־הָאָמָה *son of the maidservant* Gn 21$_{10.13}$ (Ishmael), בֶּן־אֲמָתוֹ *son of his maidservant* Jg 9$_{18}$ (Abimelech), בֶּן־אֲמָתְךָ *son of your bondmaid* Ex 23$_{12}$ (+ גֵּר *stranger*, שׁוֹר *ox*, חֲמוֹר *ass*), דְּבַר אֲמָתוֹ *the plea of his maidservant* 2 S 14$_{15}$ (+ שִׁפְחָה *bondmaid*), מִשְׁפַּט עַבְדִּי וַאֲמָתִי *just cause of my manservant or maidservant* Jb 31$_{13}$, אֹהֶל שְׁתֵּי הָאֲמָהֹת *tent of the two maidservants* Gn 31$_{33}$, עֵינֵי אַמְהוֹת עֲבָדָיו *eyes of his servants' maids* 2 S 6$_{20}$.

<APP> אֲמָתִי בִלְהָה *my maidservant Bilhah* Gn 30$_{3}$.

<PREP> מכר לְ *sell* daughter *as* a slave Ex 21$_{7}$ (+ עֶבֶד *slave*), עשׂה לְ *do to*, i.e. make a Hebrew maidservant a perpetual slave Dt 15$_{17}$ (+ עֶבֶד), היה לְאָכְלָה לְ *be food for* during sabbatical year Lv 25$_{6}$ (|| עֶבֶד, שָׂכִיר *hired labourer*, תּוֹשָׁב *sojourner*).

בוא אֶל *come to* for sex Gn 30$_{3}$; אַל־יֵרַע בְּעֵינֶיךָ עַל־הַנַּעַר וְעַל־אֲמָתֶךָ *do not be distressed over the boy or your maidservant* Gn 21$_{12}$.

ויתן לו את חנה אחת מאמהותי[ו]ן *and he* (Laban) *gave*

him (Rotheos) *Hannah, one of his maidservants* 4QT Naph 2_2.

כבד עִם ni. *be honoured with*, i.e. among 2 S 6_{22}; מִלְּבַד *apart from* Ezr 2_{65}||Ne 7_{67} (|| עֶבֶד *manservant*).

2. your maidservant, in self-deprecatory address (or on behalf of another, Jg 19_{19}), <SUBJ> דבר pi. *speak* (Abigail to David) 1 S 25_{24}, ראה *see* 25_{25}, ישׁן *sleep* (one of the mothers to Solomon) 1 K 3_{20}.

<NOM CL> הִנֵּה אֲמָתְךָ לְשִׁפְחָה *behold your handmaid is a servant* 1 S 25_{41} (+ לִרְחֹץ רַגְלֵי עַבְדֵי אֲדֹנִי *to wash the feet of the servants of my lord*), אָנֹכִי ... אֲמָתֶךָ *I am ... your maidservant* (Ruth to Boaz) Ru 3_9.

<OBJ> זכר *remember* 1 S 25_{31}, שׁכח *forget* (Hannah to God) 1_{11}, נתן לִפְנֵי *regard as* a base woman (Hannah to Eli) 1_{16}, נצל hi. *save* (woman of Tekoa to David) 2 S 14_{16} (+ שִׁפְחָה *bondmaid*).

<CSTR> בֶּן־אֲמָתֶךָ *son of your maidservant*, in address to God Ps 86_{16} 116_{16} (אֲמָתֶךָ) 1QS 11_{16} (בן אמתכה) 1QH 16_{18} (אמתך; all four + עֶבֶד *manservant*) 4QapPs[b] 15_2 33_5 (|| עֶבֶד), עֳנִי אֲמָתֶךָ *suffering of your* (God's) *maidservant* 1 S 1_{11}, פֶּשַׁע אֲמָתֶךָ *transgression of your maidservant* 25_{28}, דִּבְרֵי אֲמָתֶךָ *words of your maidservant* 1 S 25_{24} 2 S 20_{17} (אֲמָתֶךָ; wise woman of Abel Beth-maacah to Joab).

<APP> אֲנִי אֲמָתֶךָ *I your maidservant* 1 S 25_{25}, רוּת אֲמָתֶךָ *Ruth your maidservant* Ru 3_9.

<PREP> לְ *to, for* Jg 19_{19} (+ נַעַר *lad*, עֶבֶד *manservant*), + נתן *give* 1 S 1_{11}, שׁבע ni. *swear* (Bathsheba to Solomon) 1 K $1_{13.17}$; וּפָרַשְׂתָּ כְנָפֶךָ עַל־אֲמָתְךָ *and spread your skirt over your maidservant* Ru 3_9.

3. female official (corresponding to עֶבֶד *official*), לשלמית אמת אלנתן *to Shelomith the official of Elnathan* Stamp/Coin 18 (5th/4th cent.)$_2$, sim. Seal 157 (Amman c. 600)$_2$ (others אשת *wife of*).

Also perh. 5Q17 5_2

<SYN> עֶבֶד *manservant*, בֵּן *son*, בַּת *daughter*, לֵוִי *Levite*, גֵּר *sojourner*, אִשָּׁה *wife*.

אַמָּה I $_{246.0.124.3}$ n.f. **cubit**—Q אמה; cstr. אַמַּת; du. אַמָּתַיִם; pl. אַמּוֹת (I אמת)—**1. cubit, ell,** length of forearm, אַמַּת־אִישׁ *cubit of a man*, i.e. ordinary cubit Dt 3_{11}, אַמּוֹת בַּמִּדָּה הָרִאשׁוֹנָה *cubits by the former measure* 2 C 3_3, אַמָּה אַמָּה וָטֹפַח *a* (royal, long) *cubit was a cubit and a handbreadth* Ezk 43_{13}, sim. 40_5, measuring **a.** size of tabernacle and temple and their components and furnishings (most refs.), military banners, weapons, etc., 1QM $4_{15.15.16.16.17}$ $5_{6.6.7.7.12}$ $9_{12.12}$, bed, Dt $3_{11.11}$, flying scroll, Zc $5_{2.2}$, stone, 3QTr 10_9.

b. length of the ark, Gn $6_{15.15.15.16}$, tunnel, Siloam tunnel inscr.$_{2.5.6}$, breach in city wall, 2 K 14_{13} Ne 3_{13}.

c. dimensions of pasture land, Nm $35_{4.5.5.5.5}$.

d. distance between military camps, 1QM 7_7 4QM[a] fr. 1_7, battle formations, 1QM 5_{17}, ark and people, Jos 3_4, of permitted sabbath travel, CD 10_{21} 11_6 4Q251 3_5, of mourner from pure food 4QToh A 1.1_2, in instructions for locating treasure, 3QTr 1_{12} 2_8 4_4 5_{10} 7_6.

e. height of person 1 S 17_4 1 C 11_{23}, אמות וחצי רמו *cubits and a half was his height* 4QApocJos[c] 1_3, of gallows, Est 5_{14}, of quails' flight, Nm 11_{31}, at which treasure is to be located in building, 3QTr 1_{14}.

f. depth, of water, Gn 7_{20}, at which treasure is buried or hidden, 3QTr 1_2 (+ אריח perh. *cubits of laths*) 2_{14} $3_{2.12}$ $4_{7.14}$ $5_{3.10.14}$ $6_{4.10.12}$ $7_{9.12.15}$ $8_{5.9.12.15}$ $9_{2.5.8.12}$.

2. general measure, בָּא קִצֵּךְ אַמַּת בִּצְעֵךְ *your end has come, the measure* (lit. *cubit*) *of your extortion* Jr 51_{13}.

3. forearm of Y., אַמָּתוֹ הִיא סְמָכָתְהוּ *his forearm supported him* Is 59_{16} (if em. צִדְקָתוֹ *his righteousness* to אַמָּתוֹ), var. 63_5 (if em. חֲמָתִי *my wrath* to אַמָּתִי *my forearm*; both || זְרֹעַ *arm*), צִנָּה וְסֹחֵרָה אַמָּתוֹ *his forearm is a shield and buckler* Ps 91_4 (if em. אֲמִתּוֹ *his truth* to אַמָּתוֹ).

<COLL> מִדּוֹת הַמִּזְבֵּחַ בָּאַמּוֹת *the dimensions of the altar in cubits* Ezk 43_{13}.

אַמָּה = *(one) cubit* Gn 6_{16} (+ תְּכַלֶּנָּה *you shall finish it* to) Ex 25_{23}||37_{10} $26_{13.13}$ (both הָאַמָּה; + סרח pass. *be hung over*) $30_{2.2}$ $37_{25.25}$ Ezk 43_{13} (if em. חֵיק הָאַמָּה *bottom of the cubit* to חֵיקָהּ אַמָּה *its bottom was a cubit*, or הַחֵיק אַמָּה *the bottom was a cubit*) $43_{13.14}$ (if em. הָאַמָּה to אַמָּה) 43_{15} (if em. אַרְבַּע *four* to אַמָּה *a cubit*) 43_{17} 11QT 32_9, perh. 11QT 8_5 3QTr 4_{14} (אמת), חֲצִי הָאַמָּה *half a cubit* 1 K 7_{35} Ezk 43_{17} 1QM 5_7, אַמָּה וָחֵצִי *one and a half cubits* Ex $25_{10.10.17.23}$||$37_{1.1.6.10}$ $37_{1.1.6.10}$ 1QM $5_{6.12}$,

אַמָּה וַחֲצִי הָאַמָּה *a cubit and half a cubit* Ex 26_{16}||36_{21} 1 K $7_{31.32}$, אַמָּה וְטֹפַח *a cubit and a handbreadth* Ezk 40_{5} 43_{13}.

אַמָּתַיִם *two cubits* Ex 25_{23}||37_{10} 30_{2}||37_{25} Nm 11_{31}, אַמָּתַיִם וָחֵצִי *two and a half cubits* Ex $25_{10.17}$||$37_{1.6}$ 1QM 6_{5}.

אַמָּה, בָּאַמָּה with number, 1. אַמָּה(־)אַחַת *one cubit* Ezk $40_{12.42.42}$, אַמָּה אֶחָת $40_{12.42}$ 42_{4} 43_{14}, אַמָּה אַחַת וָחֵצִי *one and a half cubits* Ezk $40_{42.42}$. 2. Ezk 40_{9} $41_{3.22}$ 43_{14} 11QT $33_{12.12}$ 11QT 41_{17} + Sup 41_{17} + Sup 3QTr 10_{9}. 3. Ex 27_{1}||38_{1} 2 K 25_{17} Ezk $40_{48.48}$ 41_{22} 2 C 6_{13} 11QT 31_{11} 32_{1} ([אמו]ת) 11QT 38_{15} + Sup 42_{3} + Sup 11QT fr. 2_{2} 1QM 9_{12} 3QTr 1_{14} 3_{12} 4_{7} $5_{3(Allegro)}$ (אמ]ות שלו[ש) 5_{10} 6_{4} ([א]מות) 7_{15} 8_{9} Siloam tunnel inscr.$_{2}$, בָּאַמָּה 1 K 7_{27}. 4. Ex 36_{15} Dt 3_{11} 1 K 7_{19} Ezk 41_{5} $43_{14.15}$ 11QT $30_{8.10}$ ([אמות]) 31_{13} 32_{10} (אמ]ו[ת) 33_{12} 38_{14}, בָּאַמָּה Ex 26_{2}||36_{9} 26_{8} 1 K $7_{27.27.38}$. 5. Ex $27_{1.1.18}$||$38_{1.1.18}$ 1 K $6_{10.24.24}$||2 C $3_{11.11}$ 1 K 7_{16}||2 C 3_{15} 1 K 7_{16} Jr 52_{22} Ezk $40_{7.30.48.48}$ $41_{2.2.9.11.12}$ 2 C 3_{12} $6_{13.13}$ 11QT 7_{8} ([אמו]ת), בָּאַמָּה 1 K 6_{6} 7_{23}||2 C 4_{2} 1 C 11_{23}. 6. 1 S 17_{4} (+ וָזֶרֶת *and a span*) Ezk $40_{5.12.12}$ $41_{1.1.3.5.8}$ 3QTr 2_{12} 7_{9}, בָּאַמָּה 1 K 6_{6}. 7. Ezk 41_{3} 11QT 30_{7} 33_{9} 36_{5} 40_{9} 41_{12} fr. 2_{3} ([א]מות) 1QM 5_{7} 3QTr 5_{14} 7_{12} 9_{12}, בָּאַמָּה 1 K 6_{6}. 8. 1 K 7_{10} Ezk 40_{9} 1QM $4_{17(Yadin)}$ ([שמונ]ה) 1QM 9_{12} 3QTr 9_{5}. 9. Dt 3_{11} 11QT 42_{12} 1QM 4_{16} 3QTr 3_{2} 6_{10}.

10. Ex 26_{16}||36_{21} 1 K $6_{23.24}$ 7_{10} Ezk 40_{11} 41_{2} 42_{4} 2 C 4_{1} 11QT 6_{5} 42_{4}, בָּאַמָּה 1 K $6_{3.25.26}$ $7_{23.24}$||2 C $4_{2.3}$ Zc 5_{2} 11QT 4_{9} 41_{17} + Sup. 11. Ezk 40_{49} (or em.; see below) 3QTr 8_{15}. 12. 1 K 7_{15} Jr 52_{21} Ezk 40_{49} (if em. עַשְׁתֵּי עֶשְׂרֵה *eleven* to שְׁתֵּי עֶשְׂרֵה *twelve*) 1QM 4_{16} 3QTr 6_{12}, בָּאַמָּה 11QT 4_{11} ([ש]תים עשרה) 4QToh A 1.1_{2}. 13. Ezk 40_{11} 1QM 4_{15} ([שלוש ע]שרה) 3QTr $9_{2(Milik)}$ (שלוש עשרא]; + שתין *two*). 14. 1QM 4_{15}, בָּאַמָּה 11QT 36_{8} (ארבע [עשר]ה) 36_{10} 41_{14} 46_{6}. 15. Gn 7_{20} Ex $27_{14.15(Sam)}$ ||Ex $38_{14.15}$ 3QTr 3_{6}. 16. 3QTr 9_{8}. 17. 3QTr 8_{5}. 18. 1 K 7_{15} 2 K 25_{17} Jr 52_{21}. 19. 3QTr 2_{8}.

20. Ex 27_{16}||38_{18} 1 K $6_{2(mss)}$||2 C 3_{3} (1 K, L omit אַמָּה) 1 K $6_{3.20.20}$||2 C $3_{4.8.8}$ 1 K $6_{16.20}$ Ezk 40_{49} $41_{2.2.10}$ 2 C $3_{11.13}$ $4_{1.1}$ 11QT 31_{12} ([ע]שרים), בָּאַמָּה Zc 5_{2} 11QT 4_{13} 30_{6} 41_{17} + Sup 41_{17} + Sup. 21. 11QT 4_{12} 31_{11}, בָּאַמָּה 11QT $6_{7(Yadin)}$ + Sup ([אחת ועשרים]). 24. 3QTr 7_{6} (ערסרן [וארבע) 8_{12}. 25. Ezk $40_{13.25.29.30.33.36}$, בָּאַמָּה 40_{21}. 26. בָּאַמָּה 11QT 36_{7} ([ב]אמה). 28. בָּאַמָּה Ex 26_{2}||36_{9} 36_{9} 11QT 6_{3} ([ש]מונה ועשרי[ם באמ]ה) $39_{15.16}$, perh. 38_{15} (שמונ]ה ועשרים]) 41_{15}.

30. Gn 6_{15} 1 K 6_{2} $7_{2.6}$, בָּאַמָּה Ex 26_{8}||36_{15} 1 K 7_{23}||2 C 4_{2} 1QM 5_{17} ([ש]לושים). 35. 2 C 3_{15}. 36. בָּאַמָּה 11QT 41_{12}. 40. 1 K 6_{17} Ezk 41_{2} 3QTr 1_{2} 4_{4} ([ארבע]ין), בָּאַמָּה 11QT 6_{4} (אר[בעים] בא[מ]ה). 49. בָּאַמָּה 11QT 40_{10}.

50. Gn 6_{15} Ex $27_{12.13}$||$38_{12(mss, Sam).13}$ 1 K $7_{2.6}$ Ezk 40_{14} (if em. שִׁשִּׁים *sixty* to חֲמִשִּׁים *fifty*) $40_{15.21.25.29.33.36}$ $42_{2.7.8}$ 45_{2} Est 5_{14} 11QT 31_{11}, בָּאַמָּה Ex $27_{18(Sam)}$ (MT חֲמִשִּׁים בַּחֲמִשִּׁים) $38_{12(L)}$ 11QT 40_{12}. 60. 1 K 6_{2}||2 C 3_{3} Ezk 40_{14} (or em.; see above) 3QTr 5_{10}, בָּאַמָּה 11QT 4_{10} ([באמ]ה). 70. Ezk 41_{12}, בָּאַמָּה 40_{13}. 90. Ezk 41_{12}. 99. בָּאַמָּה 11QT $39_{14.16}$.

100. 1 K 7_{2} Ezk $40_{19.23.27.47.47}$ $41_{13.13.14.15}$ $42_{2.8}$ Siloam tunnel inscr.$_{6}$ ([א]מ), בָּאַמָּה Ex $27_{9.11(Sam)}$||$38_{9.11}$ (27_{11} MT אֹרֶךְ) 27_{18} 11QT 38_{12} 46_{9}. 120. בָּאַמָּה 11QT 36_{13}. 300. Gn 6_{15}. 360. בָּאַמָּה 11QT $40_{13.14}$ $41_{3(Yadin)}$ ([שלוש מאות וששים ב]אמה) $41_{4(Yadin)}$ ([ששים ושלוש]) $41_{6(Yadin)}$ + Sup (שש[י]ם [ו]שלוש) $41_{7.8.9.10.11}$. 400. 2 K 14_{13}||2 C 25_{23}. 480. בָּאַמָּה 11QT 38_{13} ([שמונים וארב[ע] מאות). 500. Ezk 42_{16} (if em. חֲמֵשׁ־אמות [Kt]/חֲמֵשׁ־מֵאוֹת [Qr] to חֲמֵשׁ־מֵאוֹת אַמּוֹת). 600. 11QT 40_{7} ([ש]ש מא[ות]), בָּאַמָּה $40_{8(Yadin)}$ (שש [מאות ב]אמה).

1000. Nm 35_{4} Ne 3_{13}, בָּאַמָּה Ezk 47_{3} CD 10_{21}. 1200. Siloam tunnel inscr.$_{5}$ (מאת[י]ם [ו]אלף). 2000. Jos 3_{4} 4QMª fr. 1_{7} 4Q251 3_{5}, בָּאַמָּה Nm $35_{5.5.5.5}$ 1QM 7_{7} CD 11_{6}. 3000. בָּאַמָּה 11QT 46_{16}.

Number missing. 3QTr 2_{14}, בָּאַמָּה 1 K 7_{31}.

Also 11QT 5_{2} 10_{17} $12_{9.16}$ 32_{9} ([א]מה).

[אַמָּה] II $_{1}$ n.[f.] **doorpost**—pl. cstr. אַמּוֹת—post, pivot, or perh. foundation, of door, וַיָּנֻעוּ אַמּוֹת הַסִּפִּים *and the doorposts of the thresholds shook* Is 6_{4}.

[אַמָּה] III $_{0.0.5}$ n.f. **conduit**—אמא; cstr. אמת—<CSTR> רוש אמת המים *head of the conduit of water* 3QTr 5_{1}, שולי האמא *margins* (perh. bottom) *of the conduit* 1_{1}.

<PREP> בְּ of place, *in* 3QTr 7_{3} (+ של conduit *of*) 8_{1} (בא[מא]; + שבדרך *which is on the way* to), + בוא *come* 4_{3} ([הבא]ה).

Also 11QT 32_{9} (לאמה).

אַמָּה IV 1 pl.n. **Ammah,** near Gibeon (or perh. אַמָּה III *conduit*), גִּבְעַת אַמָּה *hill of Ammah* 2 S 2$_{24.25}$ (if em.גִּבְעָה אַחַת *a certain hill*).

אַמָּה V, see מֶתֶג הָאַמָּה.

[אֻמָּה] 3.0.1 n.f. **people**—pl. אֻמִּים, אֻמּוֹת; appar. cstr. אֻמּוֹת; sf. אֻמֹּתָם—**people, tribe,** <SUBJ> שׁבח pi. *praise* Ps 117$_{1}$ (or em. הָאֻמִּים *the peoples* to הָעַמִּים *the peoples*, or, לְאֻמִּים *peoples*; ‖ גּוֹי *people*).

<CSTR> רָאשֵׁי אֻמּוֹת בֵּית־אָב appar. *head of tribes of an ancestral house* Nm 25$_{15}$ (but perh. בֵּית־אָב gloss on אֻמּוֹת); כָּל־הָאֻמִּים *all the peoples* Ps 117$_{1}$ (or em.; see above).

<PREP> שְׁנֵים־עָשָׂר נְשִׂיאִם לְאֻמֹּתָם *twelve princes according to their tribes* Gn 25$_{16}$, יסדתה [הע]מים למשפחותיהם ולשנות לאומותם *you established the peoples according to their families and the tongues of their tribes* 4QD^{b}10 (WA [ש]מים for [הע]מים), מְצַוֵּה לְאֻמִּים *a commander for peoples* Is 55$_{4}$ (if em. מְצַוֵּה לְאֻמִּים *a commander of peoples*, i.e. לְאֻמִּים from לְאֹם *people*).

[אָמוּל] II, see אמל I, Qal.

אָמוֹן I 1 n.m. **confidant,** וָאֶהְיֶה אֶצְלוֹ אָמוֹן *and I was with him (as) a confidant* Pr 8$_{30}$ (or em. אָמָּן *artisan* or אֱמוּן *reliable [one]*).

→ אמן *be trustworthy*.

אָמוֹן II 1 n.m. **multitude,** אֵת יֶתֶר הָאָמוֹן הֶגְלָה *the rest of the multitude he took into exile* Jr 52$_{15}$ (‖2 K 25$_{11}$ הֶמוֹן *multitude*; ‖Jr 39$_{9}$ עָם *people*; or em. אָמָּן *artisan[s]* or אֹמֶן *army*).

אָמוֹן III 17 pr.n.m. **Amon**—אָמֹן—**1.** governor of Samaria (שַׂר־הָעִיר) at time of Ahab, 1 K 22$_{26}$‖2 C 18$_{25}$ (1 K אָמֹן). **2.** king of Judah, son of Manasseh and Meshullemeth, 2 K 21$_{18.19}$‖2 C 33$_{20.21}$ 2 K 21$_{23.24}$‖2 C 33$_{25}$ 2 K 21$_{25}$ Jr 1$_{2}$ 25$_{3}$ Zp 1$_{1}$ 1 C 3$_{14}$ 2 C 33$_{22.23}$. **3.** servant of Solomon and father of returned exiles, Ne 7$_{59}$ (‖Ezr 2$_{57}$ אָמִי *Ami*).

→ אמן *be trustworthy*.

אָמוֹן IV 2 pr.n.m. **Amon,** Egyptian god, associated with No (Thebes), אָמוֹן מִנֹּא *Amon of No* Jr 46$_{25}$ (+ פַּרְעֹה *Pharaoh*, מִצְרַיִם *Egypt*), נֹא אָמוֹן *No-amon*, i.e. No, the city of Amon Na 3$_{8}$.

[אֵמוּן], see אֵמֻן I, II.

אֱמוּנָה 49.5.11 n.f. **faithfulness**—אֱמֻנָה (Q אימונה); cstr. אֱמוּנַת־; sf. אֱמוּנָתִי, אֱמוּנָתְךָ, אֱמוּנָתֶךָ (אֱמֻנָתְךָ), אֱמוּנָתוֹ (אֱמֻנָתוֹ), אֱמוּנָתָם (Q אמונתם); Q אמונתכה; pl. אֱמוּנוֹת—**1. faithfulness, trustworthiness, reliability. a.** of human beings, 1 S 26$_{33}$ 2 K 12$_{16}$ 22$_{7}$ Is 11$_{5}$ 59$_{4}$ Jr 5$_{1.3}$ 7$_{28}$ 9$_{2}$ Hb 2$_{4}$ Ps 37$_{3}$ 119$_{30}$ Pr 12$_{17.22}$ 28$_{20}$ 2 C 19$_{9}$ 31$_{12}$ 34$_{12}$ Si 6$_{14.15.16}$ 15$_{15}$ 45$_{4}$ GnzPs 2$_{16}$ 1QH 16$_{17}$ 17$_{14}$ 1QM 13$_{3}$ 1QS 8$_{3}$ 1QSb 5$_{26}$ 2QapMoses 1$_{2}$ 1QpHab 8$_{2}$ 11QPsa 19$_{14}$. **b.** of God, Dt 32$_{4}$ Ho 2$_{22}$ Ps 33$_{4}$ 36$_{6}$ 40$_{11}$ 88$_{12}$ 89$_{2.3.6.9.25.34.50}$ 92$_{3}$ 96$_{13}$ 98$_{3}$ 100$_{5}$ 119$_{75.90}$ 143$_{1}$ Lm 3$_{23}$ GnzPs 4$_{20}$ 4QShir^{b} 18.2$_{9}$ 4Q416 1$_{6}$ 5$_{10}$ 11QPs^{a} 19$_{9}$, perh. Is 33$_{6}$. **c.** of God's decrees, Is 25$_{1}$ Ps 119$_{86.138}$. **d.** of hands, **steadiness,** Ex 17$_{12}$.

<SUBJ> היה *be* Ex 17$_{12}$ (+ יָד *hand*) Is 11$_{5}$ (+ אֵזוֹר *girdle*; ‖ צֶדֶק *righteousness*) 33$_{6}$ 1QSb 5$_{26(Milik)}$ (אמונ[ה]); + אֵזוֹר; ‖ צֶדֶק), יצא *go out* GnzPs 4$_{20}$ (‖ אֱמֶת *reliability*; + שֶׁקֶר *falsehood*), אבד *perish* Jr 7$_{28}$, כרת ni. *be cut off* 7$_{28}$, ספר pu. *be declared* Ps 88$_{12}$ (‖ חֶסֶד *loyalty*, פֶּלֶא *wonder*, צְדָקָה *righteousness*).

<NOM CL> כָּל־מִצְוֹתֶיךָ אֱמוּנָה *all your commandments are reliability*, i.e. reliable Ps 119$_{86}$ (+ שֶׁקֶר *falsehood*), שופטי אמונה *my judge is faithfulness*, i.e. faithful 4QShir^{b} 18.2$_{9}$ (‖ צֶדֶק *righteousness*), רַבָּה אֱמוּנָתֶךָ *great is your faithfulness* Lm 3$_{23}$ (+ חֶסֶד *loyalty*, רַחֲמִים *mercy*), אֱמוּנָתְךָ עַד־שְׁחָקִים *your faithfulness is*, i.e. extends, *to the heavens* Ps 36$_{6}$ (‖ חֶסֶד), עַד־דֹּר וָדֹר אֱמוּנָתוֹ *his faithfulness is*, i.e. endures, *to all generations* 100$_{5}$ (‖ חֶסֶד), sim. 119$_{90}$, אֱמוּנָתְךָ סְבִיבוֹתֶיךָ *your faithfulness is around you* 89$_{9}$ (+ חֲסִין *mighty*), אֱמוּנָתִי ... עִמּוֹ *my faithfulness ... is with him* 89$_{25}$ (‖ חֶסֶד), אמונה לעשות רצון אל *faithfulness is the doing of God's will* Si 15$_{15(B)}$ (A, Bmg תבונה *understanding*).

<OBJ> עשׂה *do* Is 25$_{1}$ (‖ אֹמֶן *faithfulness*, פֶּלֶא *wonder*) Pr 12$_{22}$ (+ שֶׁקֶר *falsehood*), אמר *declare* Ps 40$_{11}$ (‖ תְּשׁוּעָה *deliverance*, צְדָקָה *righteousness*, חֶסֶד *loyalty*, אֱמֶת

reliability), ידע hi. *declare* 89$_2$ (|| חֶסֶד), ידה hi. *praise* 89$_6$ (|| פֶּלֶא *wonder*), נגד hi. *declare* 92$_3$ 11QPs^a 19$_9$ (|| שֵׁם *name*, both || חֶסֶד), פוח hi. *utter* Pr 12$_{17}$ (|| צֶדֶק *righteousness*, מִרְמָה *deceit*, but perh. em. יָפִיחַ *[one who] utters* to יָפֵחַ *witness of*), צוה pi. *command* Ps 119$_{138}$ (|| צֶדֶק).

כון hi. *establish* Ps 89$_3$ (subj. Y.; || חֶסֶד), שׁוב hi. *give back*, i.e. recompense 1 S 26$_{23}$ (|| צְדָקָה *righteousness*), רעה *associate (with)* (unless רעה = *feed [upon]*) Ps 37$_3$, שׁמר *keep* 1QS 8$_3$, זכר *remember* Ps 98$_3$ (subj. Y.; || חֶסֶד), בקשׁ pi. *seek* Jr 5$_1$ (|| מִשְׁפָּט *judgment*), אהב *love* Si 6$_{14.15.16}$.

<CSTR> אֱמוּנַת עִתֶּיךָ *faithfulness of*, i.e. that which can be relied upon during, *your times* Is 33$_6$ (if em. אֱמוּנַת עִתֵּי י׳ *the faithfulness of the times of Y.*); אֵל אֱמוּנָה *God of faithfulness*, i.e. faithful God Dt 32$_4$ (+ מִשְׁפָּט *judgment*, עָוֶל *iniquity*, צַדִּיק *just*, יָשָׁר *upright*), דֶּרֶךְ *way of* Ps 119$_{30}$ (+ מִשְׁפָּט, שֶׁקֶר *falsehood*), רוח *spirit of* 11QPs^a 19$_{14}$ (|| דַּעַת *knowledge*), יָפֵחַ *witness of* Pr 12$_{17}$ (if em.; see Obj.; :: שֶׁקֶר), אִישׁ אֱמוּנוֹת *man of faithfulness*, i.e. faithful man 28$_{20}$ (+ אָץ לְהַעֲשִׁיר *one who hastens to become rich*).

<PREP> גבר לְ *become strong because of* Jr 9$_2$ (+ שֶׁקֶר *falsehood*), עֵינֶיךָ הֲלוֹא לֶאֱמוּנָה *are not your eyes for faithfulness?* 5$_3$.

בְּ of accompaniment, *in, with*, Ps 33$_4$ (+ יָשָׁר *upright*), + עשׂה *do* 2 K 12$_{16}$ 22$_7$ 2 C 19$_9$ (+ יִרְאַת י׳ *fear of Y.*, לֵבָב שָׁלֵם with *a whole heart*) 34$_{12}$, הלך *walk* 4Q416 1$_2$, בוא hi. *bring* 31$_{12}$, שׁוב *go back* 1QH 16$_{17}$ (+ לב שלם with *a whole heart*), שׁוח *sink down* 4Q416 5$_{10}$, עבד *serve* GnzPs 2$_{16}$ 1QH 17$_{14}$, שׁפט *judge* Ps 96$_{13}$ (|| צֶדֶק *righteousness*), ni. *enter judgment* Is 59$_4$ (|| צֶדֶק), יכח hi. *reprove* 2QapMoses 1$_2$ (באמו[נ]ה; || אֱמֶת *reliability*), ידע *know* 1QM 13$_3$ (|| צֶדֶק), ענה *answer* Ps 143$_1$ (|| צְדָקָה *righteousness*), שׁבע ni. *swear* 89$_{50}$ (perh. בְּ = swear *by*; + חֶסֶד *loyalty*), חיה *live* Hb 2$_4$ (perh. בְּ = *by means of*; subj. צַדִּיק *righteous one*), ארשׂ pi. *betroth* Ho 2$_{22}$ (perh. בְּ = *for the price of*; || צֶדֶק, מִשְׁפָּט *judgment*, חֶסֶד *loyalty*, רַחֲמִים *mercy*), שׁקר בְּ pi. *be false to* Ps 89$_{34}$ (+ חֶסֶד), בחר בְּ *choose because of* Si 45$_4$.

בעבור ... אמונתם *on account of ... their fidelity* (|| עָמָל *toil*) 1QpHab 8$_2$.

<COLL> אמונתם במורה הצדק *their faithfulness to the teacher of righteousness* 1QpHab 8$_2$; אֱמוּנָה עִנִּיתָנִי *faithfully have you humbled me* Ps 119$_{75}$ (|| צֶדֶק).

2. office of trust given to Levites, <PREP> בֶּאֱמוּנָה *in an office of trust* (unless בֶּאֱמוּנָה = *because of trustworthiness*, or, *faithfully*) 1 C 9$_{26.31}$ (+ עַל *over*) 2 C 31$_{15}$, + יסד pi. *establish* 1 C 9$_{22}$, קדשׁ htp. *sanctify oneself* 2 C 31$_{18}$ (or em. בַּאֲבוֹתָם *because of their fathers*).

Also 4QShir^b 17$_1$ ([א]מונ[ת]) 4QPrFêtes^b 3$_{3 (Baillet)}$ ([ה]אמונתכ).

<SYN> §1 חֶסֶד *loyalty*, רַחֲמִים *mercy*, צֶדֶק *righteousness*, צְדָקָה *righteousness*, מִשְׁפָּט *judgment*, אֱמֶת *reliability*, פֶּלֶא *wonder*.

→ אמן *be trustworthy*.

אָמוֹץ 13.0.2.2 pr.n.m. **Amoz**—I אמץ—**1.** father of Isaiah, 2 K 19$_{2.20}$||Is 37$_{2.21}$ 2 K 20$_1$||Is 38$_1$ 1$_1$ 2$_1$ 13$_1$ 20$_2$ 37$_{21}$ 2 C 26$_{22}$ 32$_{20.32}$ CD 4$_{14}$ 7$_{10}$. **2.** scribe, Seal 74 (אמץ הספר; 7th cent.). **3.** T. Dan graf. (אמץ). **4.** Beersheba ost. 14 (אמץ; others אמם *Amam*).

→ אמץ *be strong*.

[אֵמוֹת], see מֵאָה.

אָמִי 1 pr.n.m. **Ami,** father of returning exiles, ident. with Amon (אָמוֹן) at ||Ne 7$_{59}$, Ezr 2$_{57}$.

[אֵמִי], see אֵמִים.

אמיה 0.0.0.1 pr.n.f. **Ammia,** from Beth-shean (הבשנית), Frey 1372.

אֵמִים 3 gent. **Emim**—אֵימִים—ancient inhabitants of Moab, Gn 14$_5$ (אֵימִים) Dt 2$_{10.11}$.

אֲמִינוֹן, see אַמְנוֹן.

אַמִּיץ 6.1 adj. **mighty**—אַמִּץ; cstr. אַמִּיץ—alw. as predicative adj. or noun, **mighty (one),** מֵרֹב אוֹנִים וְאַמִּיץ כֹּחַ *because of abundance of strength and (being) one that is mighty of strength* Is 40$_{26}$ (1QIsa^a אמץ *[because of] might of* strength, i.e. great strength),

חֲכַם לֵבָב וְאַמִּיץ כֹּחַ *(God is) one that is wise of heart and mighty of strength* Jb 9_{4}, אַמִּיץ הִנֵּה *behold, (God is) a mighty one* 9_{19}, אמיץ גבורות וחוזה כל *(Y. is) one that is mighty of strength(s) and one that sees all* Si $15_{18(B)}$,

חָזָק וְאַמִּץ לַאדֹנָי *my Lord has one that is strong and mighty* Is 28_{2} (or em. חֹזֶק וְאֹמֶץ *strength and might*), אַמִּיץ לִבּוֹ בַּגִּבּוֹרִים ... יָנוּס *one that is mighty of heart among the warriors ... will flee* Am 2_{16}, וַיְהִי הַקֶּשֶׁר אַמִּץ *and the conspiracy was mighty* 2 S 15_{12}, גֶּבֶר ... אִישׁ־דַּעַת מֵאַמִּיץ־כֹּחַ *stronger is ... a knowledgeable man than one that is mighty of strength* Pr 24_{5} (if em. גֶּבֶר ... מְאַמֶּץ־כֹּחַ *a man ... one that makes strength mighty*), כָּל־אַמִּיצַיִךְ אֻסְּרוּ *all your mighty ones were bound* Is 22_{3} (if em. נִמְצָאַיִךְ *your found ones*, i.e. those of you that are found).

→ אמץ *be strong*.

אָמִיר 2 n.m. **branch**, גַּרְגְּרִים בְּרֹאשׁ אָמִיר *berries in the head of*, i.e. topmost, *branch* Is 17_{6} (+ סָעִיף *bough*), כַּעֲזוּבַת הַחֹרֶשׁ וְהָאָמִיר *like the forsaken one of the woods and the branch* 17_{9} (or em. הַחִוִּי/הַחֹרִי וְהָאֱמֹרִי *of the Hivites/Horites and the Amorites*), הַנֹּתֵן אִמְרֵי־שָׁפֶר *that gives*, i.e. grows, *branches of* or *antlers of beauty* Gn 49_{21} (if em. אִמְרֵי־ *words of*).

אמל I 16 vb. **be feeble—Qal** Ptc. אֲמֻלָה—**be feeble**, מָה אֲמֻלָה לִבָּתֵךְ *how enfeebled is your heart* Ezk 16_{30} (or em. מַה־לִּי וְלִבְרִיתֵךְ *what is there to me and to*, i.e. what do I have to do with, *your covenant?* or אִמָּלֵא לִבָּתֵךְ *I am filled with your anger*, i.e. anger against you; or אמל II *be feverish* or אָמוּל *feverish*).

Pulal Pf. אֻמְלַל (אֻמְלָל) אֻמְלְלָה (אֻמְלָלָה), אֻמְלְלוּ (אֻמְלָלוּ)—**languish**, <**subj**> תֵּבֵל *world* Is 24_{4} (+ נבל *wither*, אבל *mourn*), מָרוֹם *exalted (place)*, i.e. heavens 24_{4} (if em. מְרוֹם עַם *exalted one of the people of* the earth to הַמָּרוֹם עִם *exalted [place] with* the earth), אֶרֶץ *earth* 24_{4} (if em.), *land* 33_{9} (+ אבל [or em. אֲבָל *alas*], חפר hi. *be ashamed*, קמל *wither*), בָּשָׁן *Bashan* Na 1_{4} (+ יבשׁ pi. *dry* sea, חרב hi. *dry* river), כַּרְמֶל *Carmel* 1_{4}, שְׁדֵמָה *field* of Heshbon Is 16_{8} (or em. כְּשַׁדְמוֹת *as the fields of*), פֶּרַח *bloom* of Lebanon Na 1_{4}, גֶּפֶן *vine* Is 16_{8} 24_{7} (+ אבל *mourn*, אנח ni. *groan*), תְּאֵנָה *fig* Jl 1_{12} (|| יבשׁ hi. *dry* vine or בושׁ hi. *be ashamed*), יִצְהָר *oil* 1_{10} (|| יבשׁ, אבל hi. or בושׁ hi., שׁדד pu. *be devastated*), שַׁעַר *gate* Jr 14_{2} (+ אבל, קדר *bow down*), חֵיל *rampart* Lm 2_{8} (+ טבע *sink*, אבל hi. *cause to mourn*), חוֹמָה *wall* Lm 2_{8}, רַב *(one that is) great*, i.e. that has many (children) 1 S 2_{5} (+ עָקָר *barren*), ילד ptc. *one that bears (children)* Jr 15_{9} (+ נפח *breathe out* life, בושׁ *be ashamed*, חפר *be ashamed*), פרשׂ ptc. *one that spreads* net Is 19_{8} (+ אבל *mourn*, אנה, בושׁ *mourn*), ישׁב ptc. *dweller* Ho 4_{3} (+ אבל, אסף ni. *be gathered*).

→ אֻמְלַל *languishing*, אֲמֵלָל *feeble*.

[אמל] II, see אמל I, Qal.

אמליוס 0.0.2 pr.n.m. **Aemilius**, appar. Aemilius Scaurus, Roman general, הרג אמליוס *Aemilius killed* 4QMish C^{d} 24.8.

אֻמְלַל 1 adj. **languishing**, חָנֵּנִי י׳ כִּי אֻמְלַל אָנִי *be gracious to me, O Y., for I am languishing* Ps 6_{3} (+ בהל ni. *be dismayed*), אֻמְלָלִים מִדֶּרֶךְ פִּשְׁעָם *languishing because of their sin* 107_{17} (if em. אֱוִלִים *fools*).

→ אמל *be feeble*.

[אֲמֵלָל] 1 adj. **feeble**— pl. אֲמֵלָלִים—מָה הַיְּהוּדִים הָאֲמֵלָלִים עֹשִׂים *what are the feeble Jews doing?* Ne 3_{34} (or ins. הָאֵלֶּה *these* feeble).

→ אמל *be feeble*.

[אמם], see אמן II, Ni.

אֲמָם 1.0.0.1 pl.n. **Amam**, **1.** in southern Judah, near Edomite border, Jos 15_{26}. **2. Beth-amam**, perh. ident. with preceding, Beersheba ost. 14 (בית אמם; others בזא אמץ *Baza, Amoz*).

אמן I 90.18.27 vb. **be trustworthy—Ni.** Pf. נֶאֱמַן, נֶאֶמְנָה, נֶאֶמְנוּ (נֶאֱמָנוּ); impf. יֵאָמֵן (יֵאָמֵן), יֵאָמְנוּ, תֵּאָמַנּוּ (Si יאמינו); ptc. נֶאֱמָן (Q נאמנך, נאמנו), נֶאֱמַן־, נֶאֱמָנָה, (נֶאֱמֶנֶת) נֶאֱמָנִים, נֶאֱמָנוֹת, נֶאֱמְנֵי.

1. be trustworthy, faithful, reliable, <**subj**> Y. Is 49_{7}, Israel Ho 12_{1} Ps 78_{37} (|| כון ni. *be established*),

David 1 S 22_{14}, Abraham Si 44_{20}, Samuel 46_{15}, treasurers Ne 13_{13}, witnesses CD 9_{21}, רוּחַ *spirit* Ps 78_{8} (+ כון hi. *establish*), לֵבָב *heart* Ne 9_{8}, פֶּצַע *wound* of friend Pr 27_{6} (:: עתר ni. *be profuse*).

<PREP> בְּ *to* Ps 78_{37} (+ בְּרִית *covenant*), *in* Si 46_{15} (+ דָּבָר *word*); כְּ *as* 1 S 22_{14} (+ David); עִם *with* Ho 12_{1} (+ קָדוֹשׁ *holy one*); אֵת *with* Ps 78_{8} (mss אֶל *to*; + אֵל *God*); לִפְנֵי *before* Y. Ne 9_{8}.

<COLL> נֶאֱמָן + verb, חשׁב ni. *be reckoned* trustworthy Ne 13_{13}, מצא *find* heart faithful Ne 9_{8}, ni. *be found* faithful Si 44_{20}; נאמן רועה *he was reliable as a seer* Si 46_{15} (רועה = רֹאֶה).

2. of witness, **be declared reliable,** אל יאמן איש על רעהו לעד *let no man be declared a reliable witness against his neighbour* CD 10_{2}.

3. be entrusted, attested, בְּכָל בֵּיתִי נֶאֱמָן הוּא *he* (Moses) *is entrusted with all my house* Nu 12_{7} (or understand as *he is faithful in*, §1), ויאמן בתורת[ו] *and he was entrusted with his law* 4QPsJos[b] 17_{3}, נֶאֱמָן שְׁמוּאֵל לְנָבִיא לַי׳ *Samuel was attested as a prophet of Y.* 1 S 3_{20}.

4. be firm, lasting, established, <SUBJ> Israel Is 7_{9} 2 C 20_{20} (|| צלח hi. *prosper*), מַמְלָכָה *kingdom*, 2 S 7_{16} (|| כון ni. *be established*), בַּיִת *house* 7_{16}, מַיִם *water* Is 33_{16} Jr 15_{18} (+ אַכְזָב *deceitful [brook]*), ברית *covenant* Ps 89_{29} (+ שׁמר לְעוֹלָם *keep* loyalty *forever*), חֶסֶד *loyalty* Si 50_{24} (+ קום hi. *establish* covenant), עֵדָה *testimony* Ps 93_{5}, עֵדוּת *testimony* 19_{8} (+ תָּמִים *perfect*) Si $34_{23.24(Bmg)}$ (B דַּעַת *knowledge*), פִּקּוּד *precept* Ps 111_{7}, שֵׁם *name* 1 C 17_{24} (|| גדל *be great*), עֵד *witness* Ps 89_{38} (or כִּסֵּא *throne*, if em. עֵד בַּשַּׁחַק *witness in the sky* to בְּעֹד הַשַּׁחַק *while the sky remains* or לְעַד כַּשַּׁחַק *for ever like the sky*; || כון ni.), טוּב *wealth* Si 44_{11}.

<PREP> לְ *to* Ps 89_{29}; עִם *with* Si $44_{11(B)}$ (M אם appar. *if*; + זֶרַע *descendant*) 50_{24}; עַד *until* 2 S 7_{16} 1 C 17_{24} (both + עוֹלָם *eternity*); ותאמנה באוו[זני] עבדכה עד עולם *and they are established in the ears of your servant for ever* 1QH $18_{5(Licht)}$ (or understand as pi. *you have established it*).

5. prove trustworthy, be fulfilled, <SUBJ> דָּבָר *word* Gn 42_{20} 1 K 8_{26}||2 C 6_{17} 1 C 17_{23} 2 C 1_{9}, נָבִיא *prophet* Si 36_{21}.

<PREP> עַד *until* 1 C 17_{23} (+ עוֹלָם *eternity*).

6. ptc. used as adj., **a. trustworthy, faithful, reliable,** of אֵל *God* Dt 7_{9} (+ שֹׁמֵר הַבְּרִית וְהַחֶסֶד *one who keeps the covenant and loyalty*), כֹּהֵן *priest* 2 S 2_{35}, נָבִיא *prophet* 4QApocMos B 1.1_{7} ([נ]אמן), עֵד *witness* Is 8_{2} Jr 42_{5} (עֵד אֱמֶת וְנֶאֱמָן *a true and faithful witness*) CD 9_{23} 4QapPs[b] 76_{9} (+ שפט אמת *judge of truth*), צִיר *messenger* Pr 25_{13}, רֵעַ *friend* Si 34_{2}, רעה ptc. *shepherd* 1QLitPr[b] 1.2_{8}, קִרְיָה *city* Is 1_{21} (+ מְלֵאֲתִי מִשְׁפָּט צֶדֶק יָלִין בָּהּ *full of justice, righteousness lodged in her*) 1_{26} (+ עִיר הַצֶּדֶק *city of righteousness*).

6b. firm, enduring, established, of, בַּיִת *house* 1 S 2_{35} 25_{28} 1 K 11_{38} CD 3_{19}, מָקוֹם *place* Is $22_{23.25}$, חֶסֶד *loyalty* Is 55_{3} (+ בְּרִית עוֹלָם *everlasting covenant*), מַכָּה *affliction*, Dt 28_{59} (|| גָּדוֹל *great*), חֳלִי *sicknesses* Dt 28_{59} (|| רַע *grievous*), כְּאֵב *pain* Si 30_{17} (|| עמד ptc. *lasting*; + נוחת עולם *eternal rest*), תֹּכֶן *decree* 1QH 12_{9}.

7. ptc. used as a noun, **a. trustworthy, reliable, faithful one, <SUBJ>** כסה pi. *cover*, i.e. keep secret (:: הוֹלֵךְ רָכִיל *one who goes about as a talebearer*) Pr 11_{13}, לין *spend night* Si 20_{4}. **<CSTR>** נֶאֶמְנֵי־אֶרֶץ *faithful ones of the land* Ps 101_{6} (+ הֹלֵךְ בְּדֶרֶךְ תָּמִים *he who walks in the way of the blameless*), נֶאֱמַן־רוּחַ *trustworthy one of spirit* Pr 11_{13}.

<PREP> בְּ *upon* Ps 101_{6}; מֵסִיר שָׂפָה לְנֶאֱמָנִים *he deprives trustworthy ones of speech* Jb 12_{20} (|| זָקֵן *elder*); יראו צדקתך על יד נאמנך *they will see your righteousness through your faithful one* GnzPs 2_{11}, הכביד ... מצות דברו על ידי נאמנו *he made heavy the command of his word through his faithful one* 4_{6} (|| עֶבֶד *servant*).

7b. trustworthiness, ובקרוה נאמנות *and they shall examine her concerning (her) trustworthiness* 4QOrd[a] 2_{9}.

7c. certainty, הוֹדַעְתִּי נֶאֱמָנָה *I proclaim a certainty* Ho 5_{9}.

8. fem. ptc. used as adv., **faithfully,** נאמנה שמעתי לסוד פלאכה *I have faithfully listened to your marvellous counsel* 1QH 12_{12}.

Also 1QM 16_{17} + Sup ([נ]אמן).

<SYN> כון ni. *be established*.

Pi. Pf. אמנתה; ptc. מאמנת—**a. establish,** בריתכה אמנתה לי *your covenant you established for me* 4QBark[a] 1_{4}. **b. trust,** רוח ... חכמת גבותה מאמנת בכול מעשי אל *a spirit of ... mighty wisdom which trusts in all* *the deeds of God* 1QS 4$_{3}$ (|| שׁען ni. *lean*). Perh. also ותאמנה 1QH 18$_{5}$ (see Ni., §3a).

Hi. Pf. הֶאֱמִין (הֶאֱמִן), הֶאֱמַנְתִּי (הֶאֱמַ֫נְתִּי), הֶאֱמִ֫ינוּ, הֶאֱמַנְתֶּם; impf. יַאֲמִין (יַאֲמֵן), 2ms תַּאֲמִין (תַּאֲמֵן, תַּאֲמֶן־), אַאֲמִין, יַאֲמִ֫ינוּ (Q יאמינוא), תַּאֲמִ֫ינוּ; + waw וַיַּאֲמֵן, וַיַּאֲמִ֫ינוּ; impv. הַאֲמִ֫ינוּ; ptc. מַאֲמִין, מַאֲמִינִים.

1a. believe, trust someone, <SUBJ> Israel Ex 4$_{1.8}$ 14$_{31}$ Dt 9$_{23}$ (all three || שׁמע *listen*) Is 43$_{10}$ 2 C 20$_{20}$ 32$_{15}$ (:: נשׁא hi. *deceive*, סות hi. *mislead*), עַם *people* Ex 14$_{31}$ 19$_{9}$, Jacob Gn 45$_{26}$, Sihon Jg 11$_{20}$, Achish 1 S 27$_{12}$, Jeremiah Jr 12$_{6}$, Gedaliah 40$_{14}$, Y. Jb 4$_{18}$ (:: שׂים *charge with error*) 15$_{15}$, subject not specified Is 53$_{1}$ Mc 7$_{5}$ (|| בטח *trust*) Pr 26$_{25}$ Si 7$_{26}$ 12$_{10}$ 36$_{31}$ 37$_{13}$ 4Q424 1$_{7}$ (תא[מין]) 1$_{8}$ (תאמ[ין]).

<OBJ> אִישׁ *man* 4Q424 1$_{7}$ (תא[מין]) 1$_{8}$ (תאמ[ין]).

<PREP> לְ of object, Gn 45$_{26}$ Ex 4$_{1.8}$ Dt 9$_{23}$ Is 43$_{10}$ 2 C 32$_{15}$ Jr 40$_{14}$ Si 37$_{13}$.

בְּ of object, Ex 14$_{31}$ 19$_{9}$ 1 S 27$_{12}$ Jr 12$_{6}$ Mc 7$_{5}$ (+ רֵעַ *friend*) Jb 4$_{18}$ (+ עֶבֶד *servant*) 15$_{15}$ (+ קָדוֹשׁ *holy one*) Pr 26$_{25}$ 2 C 20$_{20}$ (+ נָבִיא *prophet*) Si 7$_{26}$ 12$_{10}$ (+ שׂנא ptc. *enemy*) 36$_{31}$ (C + צָבָא *army*; D + גְּדוּד *troop*).

<COLL> מי יאמין *who will trust* Si 36$_{31}$ 37$_{13}$, var. Is 53$_{1}$, ושנואה אל תאמן בה *as for her that is hated, do not trust her* Si 7$_{26}$, לֹא־הֶאֱמִין סִיחוֹן אֶת־יִשְׂרָאֵל עֲבֹר בִּגְבֻלוֹ *Sihon did not trust Israel to pass through his territory* Jg 11$_{20}$ (or em. הֶאֱמִין סִיחוֹן to אָבָה וַיְמָאֵן סִיחוֹן תֵּת *Sihon* was not *willing and he refused to allow* Israel).

1b. believe, trust something, <SUBJ> Israel, Ex 4$_{8.9}$ (|| שׁמע *listen*) Ps 78$_{32}$ 106$_{12.24}$ 119$_{66}$, עבד ptc. *worshipper* GnzPs 1$_{8}$, Queen of Sheba 1 K 10$_{7}$||2 C 9$_{6}$, Job Jb 39$_{12}$, פֶּתִי *simple one* Pr 14$_{15}$ (:: בין *consider*), בגד ptc. *traitor* 1QpHab 2$_{4}$ (הבוג[דים]), appar. Kittim 2$_{14}$, רָשָׁע *wicked person* Jb 15$_{31}$, subj. not specified Si 13$_{11}$ (+ בטח *trust*) 16$_{3}$ (|| בטח) 1QH 8$_{14}$ 4Q424 2$_{1}$.

<PREP> לְ of object, Ex 4$_{8}$ (+ קוֹל *voice* of sign) 4$_{9}$ (+ אוֹת *sign*) 1 K 10$_{7}$||2 C 9$_{6}$ (+ דָּבָר *word*) Is 53$_{1}$ (+ שְׁמוּעָה *report*) Ps 106$_{24}$ (+ דָּבָר) Pr 14$_{15}$ (+ דָּבָר) Si 13$_{11}$ (+ רֹב *abundance* of speech) 1QH 8$_{14}$ (+ מָקוֹר *fountain* of life).

בְּ of object, Ps 78$_{32}$ (+ פלא ni. ptc. *wonder*) 106$_{12}$ (+ דָּבָר *word*) 119$_{66}$ (+ מִצְוָה *commandment*) Jb 15$_{31}$ (שָׁוְא *emptiness*) 39$_{12}$ Si 16$_{3}$ (+ חַיִּים *life*) GnzPs 1$_{8}$ (+ דָּבָר) 1QpHab 2$_{4}$ (+ בְּרִית *covenant*) 2$_{14}$ (+ חֹק *statute*).

1c. believe, trust, Y., <SUBJ> Israel Ex 14$_{31}$ Nm 14$_{11}$ (:: נאץ pi. *despise*) Dt 1$_{32}$ Ps 78$_{22}$ (|| בטח *trust*) 2 C 20$_{20}$, אָב *father* 2 K 17$_{14}$ (+ שׁמע *listen*, קשׁה עֹרֶף hi. *stiffen neck*), אִישׁ *man* of Nineveh Jon 3$_{5}$, Abraham Gn 15$_{6}$, Moses and Aaron Nm 20$_{12}$ (+ קדשׁ hi. *sanctify*), subj. not specified Si 15$_{15}$.

<PREP> בְּ of object, Gn 15$_{6}$ Ex 14$_{31}$ Nm 14$_{11}$ 20$_{12}$ Dt 1$_{32}$ 2 K 17$_{14}$ Jon 3$_{5}$ Ps 78$_{22}$ 2 C 20$_{20}$ Si 15$_{15}$.

1d. believe, trust that, (1) with כִּי, <SUBJ> Israel Ex 4$_{5}$, מֶלֶךְ *king* Lm 4$_{12}$, ישׁב ptc. *inhabitant* Lm 4$_{12}$, Job Jb 9$_{16}$, subj. not specified Hb 1$_{5}$.

<COLL> כִּי *that*, + verb (subj. in brackets) ראה ni. *appear* Ex 4$_{5}$ (Y.), אזן hi. *listen* Jb 9$_{16}$ (Y.), ספר pu. *be told* Hb 1$_{5}$ (deed), בוא *come* Lm 4$_{12}$ (emeny).

(2) with inf., הֶאֱמַנְתִּי לִרְאוֹת בְּטוּב־יי *I believe that I will see the goodness of Y.* Ps 27$_{13}$, לֹא־יַאֲמִין שׁוּב מִנִּי־חֹשֶׁךְ *he does not believe that he will return from the darkness* Jb 15$_{22}$.

1e. believe, have faith, used absolutely, <SUBJ> עַם *people* Ex 4$_{31}$, עָרִיץ *violent one* 1QpHab 2$_{6}$, Israel Is 7$_{9}$, psalmist Ps 116$_{10}$, subj. not specified Is 28$_{16}$ Jb 29$_{24}$.

<COLL> הַמַּאֲמִין לֹא יָחִישׁ *he who believes will not be in haste* Is 28$_{16}$.

2. have assurance of, confidence in, one's life continuing, וְלֹא תַאֲמִין בְּחַיֶּיךָ *and you will have no assurance of your life* Dt 28$_{66}$ (+ וְהָיוּ חַיֶּיךָ תְּלֻאִים *and your life shall be in suspense*), יָקוּם וְלֹא־יַאֲמִין בַּחַיִּין *he* (the wicked) *rises up, though he has no confidence in (his) life* Job 24$_{22}$ (mss בְּחַיָּיו *in his life*), [ל]וא נאמין בחיינו *we have no assurance of our lives* 4QPrFêtes[b] 39$_{2}$.

3. stand still, לֹא־יַאֲמִין כִּי־קוֹל שׁוֹפָר *he* (horse) *does not stand still at the sound of the trumpet* Jb 39$_{24}$.

Also Si 45$_{13}$ 4QDibHam[a] 3.2$_{12}$ fr. 7$_{16}$.

<SYN> בטח *trust*, שׁמע *listen*.

→ אֹמֶן *faithfulness*, אֱמוּנָה *faithfulness*, אֵמֻן *faithfulness*, אֵמֻן *faithful*, אֱמֶת *truth*, אָמֵן *Amen*, אָמְנָה *indeed*, אָמְנָם *indeed*, אֻמְנָם *indeed*, אֹמְנָה *doorpost*, אֲמָנָה *agreement*, אָמוֹן *confidant*, אָמוֹן *Amon*, אַמְנוֹן *Amnon*.

אמן II 9.1.6 vb. **foster—Qal** Ptc. אֹמֵן (Q אומן); f. אֹמֶנֶת (Q אומנתי, אֹמַנְתּוֹ); pl. אֹמְנִים (אֹמְנַיִךְ, Q אומניו); pass. Si אמנה; אֱמֻנִים (Q אמונים).

1a. active ptc. as noun, **guardian, foster parent, (wet-)nurse,** to young child (Ru 4$_{16}$ 1QH 7$_{22}$ 9$_{31.36}$), specif. sucklings (Nm 11$_{12}$ CD 11$_{11}$), and to older child (2 S 4$_4$), to royal children (2 S 4$_4$ 2 K 10$_{1.5}$).

<SUBJ> היה *be* Is 49$_{23}$ (+ מֶלֶךְ *king*; || ינק hi. ptc. fem. *nursing mother*), נשׂא *carry* child Nm 11$_{12}$ (+ בְּחֵיק *in bosom*; + הרה *conceive*, ילד *give birth*) 2 S 4$_4$ CD 11$_{11}$, נוס *flee* 2 S 4$_4$, שׁלח *send* reply 2 K 10$_5$ (|| זָקֵן *elder*, + אֲשֶׁר־עַל־הַבַּיִת *one who is over the palace*, אֲשֶׁר עַל־הָעִיר *one who is over the city*).

<CSTR> חיק אומניו *bosom of its foster parents* 1QH 7$_{22(mg)}$ (+ כשעשע עילול ב *as a child plays in*), בחיק אומנתי *in the bosom of my foster mother* 9$_{31}$ (+ אָב *father*, אֵם *mother*, הרה ptc. fem. *one who conceives*).

<PREP> לְ היה *be (as)* Ru 4$_{16}$ (+ שׁית בְּחֵיק hi. *place* child *in bosom*).

כְּ *as*, + שׂים *place*, i.e. appoint 1QH 7$_{21}$ (+ לאנשי מופת *to men of*, i.e. who cause, *marvel*; || אָב *father*), כול pilp. *provide*, i.e. nourish in bosom 9$_{36}$ (+ לכול מעש[י]כה *for all your works*; || רחם pi. ptc. fem. *one who gives birth*, + אֵם, אָב *mother*).

אֶל שׁלח *send* letters *to* 2 K 10$_1$ (|| זָקֵן *elder*, שַׂר *officer*).

<COLL> הָאֹמְנִים אַחְאָב appar. *the guardians (in respect of) Ahab* 2 K 10$_1$ (or del. אַחְאָב or em אֶת־בְּנֵי אַחְאָב those who were bringing up *the children of Ahab*, as §2).

1b. pass. ptc. as noun, **foster child,** <SUBJ> היה *be* Pr 8$_{30}$ (if em. אָמוּן *confidant*; + אֶצְלוֹ *beside him*).

2a. active ptc. as verb, **foster, bring up,** <SUBJ> Mordecai Est 2$_7$. <OBJ> Hadassah Est 2$_7$, בֵּן *child* 2 K 10$_1$ (if em.; see §1a, Coll.).

2b. pass. ptc. as verb, **be brought up, be trained,** הָאֱמֻנִים עֲלֵי תוֹלָע *those brought up on purple*, i.e. children of Jerusalem Lm 4$_5$=4QapLam^a 1.2$_{10}$ (תול[ע]), אם אמנה היא העמידה *if it* (animal) *is trained, maintain it* Si 7$_{22}$.

3. inf., **fostering, being fostered,** כַּאֲשֶׁר הָיְתָה בְאָמְנָה אִתּוֹ *as it was during her* (Esther's) *fostering with him* (Mordecai) Est 2$_{20}$ (if em. אָמְנָה *fosterage*).

<SYN> §1a אָב *father*, זָקֵן *elder*.

Ni. Impf. תֵּאָמַנָה—**be carried** (like an infant by its nurse), וּבְנֹתַיִךְ עַל־צַד תֵּאָמַנָה *and your daughters will be carried at the side* Is 60$_4$ (or em. תְּאַמֵּנָה *will lead the way*, from אמם; 1QIsa^b תנשינה *will be carried*).

→ אָמְנָה *fosterage*.

אָמָּן 1 n.m. **artisan,** <CSTR> כְּמוֹ חֲלָאִים מַעֲשֵׂה יְדֵי אָמָּן *like jewels, the work of an artisan's hands* Ca 7$_2$, וָאֶהְיֶה אֶצְלוֹ אָמָּן *and I was with him (as) an artisan* Pr 8$_{30}$ (if em. אָמוֹן *confidant*), אֵת יֶתֶר הָאָמָּן הֶגְלָה *the rest of the artisan(s) he took into exile* Jr 52$_{15}$ (if em. אָמוֹן *multitude*; ||2 K 25$_{11}$ הָמוֹן *multitude*; ||Jr 39$_9$ עָם *people*).

אָמֵן 30.0.35.1 adv. **amen, truly, 1.** solemn formula of confirmation, oft. אָמֵן אָמֵן *Amen, amen* (see Coll.), pronounced by individual, or, usu., group, **a.** in affirmation of oath or curse, וְאָמְרָה הָאִשָּׁה אָמֵן אָמֵן *and the woman shall say, Amen, Amen* Nm 5$_{22}$, וְעָנוּ כָל־הָעָם וְאָמְרוּ אָמֵן *and all the people shall answer and say, Amen* Dt 27$_{15}$, sim. 27$_{16+10t}$ Ne 5$_{13}$ 1QS 2$_{10.18}$ 4QBer^a 3.2$_{1.5.6}$ ([אמן אמן]) 3.2$_{10}$ 11QapPs^a 1$_1$ 4$_3$ 5$_3$ (both [אמן אמן]).

b. in affirmation of blessing or doxology, וַיְבָרֶךְ עֶזְרָא אֶת־י׳ ... וַיַּעֲנוּ כָל־הָעָם אָמֵן אָמֵן בְּמֹעַל יְדֵיהֶם *and Ezra blessed Y., ... and all the people responded, Amen, Amen, lifting up their hands* Ne 8$_6$, בָּרוּךְ י׳ לְעוֹלָם אָמֵן וְאָמֵן *blessed be Y. for ever! Amen and Amen* Ps 89$_{53}$, sim. 41$_{14}$ 72$_{19}$ 106$_{48}$=1 C 16$_{36}$ 1QS 1$_{20}$ 2$_{10}$ 4QPrFêtes^a 3$_2$ 4QPrFêtes^c 4$_5$ 4QDibHam^a 1.7$_2$ (אמ[ן]) 3.2$_3$ 4$_{15}$ 4QShir^b 63.4$_3$ 4QBer^a 2$_8$ 3.1$_7$ Alma inscr. ([א]מן).

c. in affirmation of other words, perh. regarded as in effect blessing or curse, 1 K 1$_{36}$ Jr 11$_5$ 28$_6$.

d. in support of someone's claim, אחי יענו לי אמן *my brothers will testify for me (saying), Amen* Meṣad Hashavyahu ost. 1$_{11}$.

<COLL> אָמֵן אָמֵן *Amen, Amen* Nm 5$_{22}$ Ne 8$_6$ 1QS 1$_{20}$ 2$_{10.18}$ 4QPrFêtes^a 3$_2$ 4QPrFêtes^b 20$_1$ 4QPrFêtes^c 4$_5$ 131.2$_3$ (אמן א[מן]) 4QDibHam^a 1.1$_{7(Baillet)}$ 1.7$_{2(Baillet)}$ (אמן [אמן]) 3.2$_{3(Baillet)}$ ([אמן] אמן) 4$_{15}$ 17.2$_{5(Baillet)}$ (אמן [אמן]) pap4QPrLit^b 1.3$_3$ (אמן א[מן]) 4QBer^a 2$_8$ 3.1$_7$ 3.2$_{1.5.6}$ ([אמן אמן]) 3.2$_{10}$ (אמן א[מן]) 4QShir^b 63.4$_3$ 111$_9$ (אמן א[מן]), אָמֵן וְאָמֵן Ps 41$_{14}$ 72$_{19}$ 89$_{53}$ 11QapPs^a 1$_1$ 4$_3$ 5$_3$ (both [אמן אמן]).

2. as noun, **Amen,** <CSTR> אֱלֹהֵי אָמֵן *the God of*

Amen Is 65_{16} (or em. אֱמוּן *of faithfulness* or אֹמֶן *of faithfulness*; + בְּ ברך htp. *bless oneself by*) 65_{16} (or em. אֱמוּן or אֹמֶן; + בְּ שׁבע ni. *swear by*).
→ אמן *be trustworthy.*

אָמֹן, see אָמוֹן III.

[אָמֹן], see אָמוֹן II.

אֹמֶן 1 n.m. **faithfulness,** עָשִׂיתָ פֶלֶא עֵצוֹת מֵרָחוֹק אֱמוּנָה אֹמֶן *you* (Y.) *have made wonder(s), counsels from afar, faithfulness (and more) faithfulness* Is 25_1 (or em. פֶּלֶא עֵצוֹת *wonders of counsel*; 1QIsa[a] perh. אָמֵן *amen*), בֵּאלֹהֵי אֹמֶן bless oneself/swear *by the God of faithfulness* $65_{16.16}$ (if, in both, em. אָמֵן).
→ אמן *be trustworthy.*

אֵמֻן I $5.0.2$ n.[m.] **faithfulness**—Q אמון; pl. אֱמוּנִים (אֱמֻנִים)—<NOM CL> בָּנִים לֹא־אֵמֻן בָּם *children in whom there is not faithfulness* Dt 32_{20} (Sam לא האמן *in whom he did not trust*; + דּוֹר תַּהְפֻּכֹת *generation of perversity*). <OBJ> שׁמר *keep* Is 26_2 (אֱמֻנִים; + צַדִּיק *righteous*) 1QS 10_{25} (+ מִשְׁפָּט *judgment*), בקשׁ pi. *seek* 4Q298 1_2.

<CSTR> אֱלֹהֵי אֵמֻן *God of faithfulness* Is $65_{16.16}$ (both if em. אָמֵן *Amen*), אִישׁ אֱמוּנִים *man of faithfulness* Pr 20_6 (+ חֶסֶד *loyalty*), עֵד *witness of* 14_5 (:: שֶׁקֶר *falsehood*), צִיר *messenger of* 13_{17} (+ רָשָׁע *wicked*).
→ אמן *be trustworthy.*

[אֵמֻן] II $3.1.2$ adj. **faithful**—(or [אָמוּן], qal ptc. pass. of אמן *be faithful*) Si אמן (אמון); pl. אֱמוּנִים; cstr. אֱמוּנֵי—**1. reliable, trustworthy,** מי יאמין לך אמן ממנו *whom can you trust (as) more reliable than it* (heart)? Si $37_{13(B)}$ (Bmg, D כי אם אמון *unless there is [something] more trustworthy*).

2. as noun, **faithful, trustworthy person,** <SUBJ> פסס *disappear* Ps 12_2 (unless em. פַּסּוּ to אָפְסוּ *they have ceased* or סָפוּ *they have come to an end*; ‖ חָסִיד *loyal person*). <OBJ> נצר *guard* Ps 31_{24} (+ חָסִיד *loyal person*, עֹשֵׂה גַאֲוָה *one who acts haughtily*), חלף hi. *cause to succeed* 4Q521 1.2_6.

<CSTR> שְׁלֻמֵי אֱמוּנֵי יִשְׂרָאֵל *the peacable ones of the faithful of Israel* 2 S 20_{19} (or em. וֶאֱמוּנֵי *and the faithful of*).

<COLL> וָאֶהְיֶה אֶצְלוֹ אָמוֹן *and I was with him (as) a reliable one* Pr 8_{30} (if em. אָמוֹן *confidant*).

Also 4QShir[b] 67_1.
→ אמן *be trustworthy.*

אֲמָנָה I $2.0.2$ n.f. **agreement**—sf. Q אמנתם—**agreement, covenant, pledge,** <NOM CL> אֲמָנָה עַל־הַמְשֹׁרְרִים *there was an agreement concerning the singers* Ne 11_{23} (+ מִצְוָה *commandment*). <OBJ> כרת *cut*, i.e. make Ne 10_1, קום pi. *establish* CD 20_{12} (‖ בְּרִית *covenant*). <PREP> מאס בְּ *despise* CD 20_{12}, בעבור עמלם ואמנתם במורה הצדק *on account of their toil and their covenant with the teacher of righteousness* 1QpHab 8_2 (but perh. אֱמֻנָתָם *their faithfulness*).
→ אמן *be trustworthy.*

אֲמָנָה II 2 pl.n. **Amana, 1.** appar. mountain in Lebanon or Syria, perh. Ǧebel Zebedāni, Ca 4_8 (+ רֹאשׁ *head*, perh. summit, *of*; + שְׂנִיר וְחֶרְמוֹן *Senir and Hermon*). **2.** river of Damascus, perh. Nahr Baradā which flows from Ǧebel Zebedāni, 2 K $5_{12(Qr)}$ (Kt אבנה *Abana*; +פַּרְפַּר *Parpar*).

אָמְנָה I 2 adv. **truly,** אָמְנָה אָנֹכִי חָטָאתִי *truly I have sinned* Jos 7_{20}, הִיא ... אָמְנָה אֲחֹתִי *truly she is ... my sister* Gn 20_{12} (Sam אָמְנָם *truly*).
→ אמן *be trustworthy.*

אָמְנָה II 1 n.f. **fosterage,** כַּאֲשֶׁר הָיְתָה בְאָמְנָה אִתּוֹ *as it was during her fosterage with him* Est 2_{20} (or em. אָמְנָהּ *her fostering*).
→ אמן *foster.*

[אֹמְנָה] 1 n.f. **doorpost**—pl. אֹמְנוֹת—<OBJ> קצץ pi. *cut down* 2 K 18_{16} (‖ דֶּלֶת *door*), צפה pi. *cover* 18_{16}, נתן *give* 18_{16}.
→ אמן *be trustworthy.*

אַמְנוֹן 28 pr.n.m. **Amnon**—אַמְנֹן, אֲמִינוֹן—**1.** son of David and Ahinoam, 2 S 3_2‖1 C 3_1 (אַמְנֹן) 2 S 13_{1+24t}

(13_{20} אֲמִינוֹן). **2.** son of Shimon, descendant of Judah, 1 C 4_{20}.

→ אמן *be trustworthy*.

אָמְנָם 9 adv. **truly, 1.** with verb, חרב hi. *destroy* 2 K 19_{17}||Is 37_{18}, ידע *know* Jb 9_2, שׁגה *stray* 19_4, גדל hi. *magnify* 19_5, רשׁע hi. *act wickedly* 34_{12}. **2.** in nom. cl., אָמְנָם אֲחֹתִי ... הִיא *truly she is ... my sister* Gn $20_{12(Sam)}$ (MT אָמְנָה *truly*), אָמְנָם כִּי אַתֶּם־עָם *truly you are (the) people* Jb 12_2, אָמְנָם לֹא־שֶׁקֶר מִלָּי *truly my words are not falsehood* 36_4, אָמְנָם כִּי גֹאֵל אָנֹכִי *truly, although I am a redeemer* Ru $3_{12(Qr)}$.

→ אמן *be trustworthy*.

אֻמְנָם 5 adv. **truly,** with verb, ילד *give birth* Gn 18_{13}, יכל *be able* Nm 22_{37}, ישׁב *dwell* 1 K 8_{27}||2 C 6_{18}, דבר pi. *speak* Ps 58_2. <COLL> הַאֻמְנָם *is it true that?* Nm 22_{37} 1 K 8_{27}||2 C 6_{18} Ps 58_2, הַאַף אֻמְנָם *is it indeed true (that)?* Gn 18_{13}.

→ אמן *be trustworthy*.

אַמְנֹן, see אַמְנוֹן.

אמץ 41.3.6.1 vb. **be strong—Qal** Pf. אָמְצוּ; impf. יֶאֱמַץ; + waw וַיֶּאֶמְצוּ; impv. אֱמַץ (אֱמָץ), אִמְצוּ.

1a. be strong, <SUBJ> לְאֹם *people* Gn 25_{23}, enemies 2 S 22_{18}||Ps 18_{18} (+ עַז *strong*), pursuers Ps 142_7, love and mercy 4Q372 1_{19}. <PREP> alw. with מִן of comparison, *than*.

1b. prevail, <SUBJ> Judah 2 C 13_{18} (:: כנע ni. *be defeated*).

2. be courageous, alw. impv. and || with חזק *be strong*, <SUBJ> Israel Dt 31_6 (:: ירא *fear*, ערץ *dread*), warriors Jos 10_{25} 2 C 32_7 1QM 15_7 (:: ערץ, חפז *tremble*, שׁוב *turn* back; all three :: ירא, חתת *be terrified*) 4QM[a] fr. 14_5, Joshua Dt $31_{7.23}$ Jos $1_{6.7}$ (+ מְאֹד *greatly*, לִשְׁמֹר לַעֲשׂוֹת *to observe faithfully*) 1_9 (:: ערץ, חתת) 1_{18} 4QPsJos[a] 3.2_{10} ([א]מץ), Solomon 1 C 22_{13} 28_{20} (|| עשׂה *do*; both :: ירא, חתת).

<SYN> חזק *be strong*.

<ANT> חתת *be terrified*, ירא *fear*, ערץ *dread*.

Pi. Pf. אִמֵּץ (אימץ Si), אִמַּצְתָּ (אִמַּצְתָּה), אִמַּצְתִּיךָ; impf. יְאַמֵּץ, 3fs תְּאַמְּצֶנּוּ, 2ms תְּאַמֵּץ, אֲאַמִּצְכֶם; + waw וַיְאַמֵּץ (וַיְאַמֶּץ־, Si ויאמצהו), 3fs וַתְּאַמֵּץ, וַיְאַמְּצוּ (וַיְאַמְּצֵהוּ); impv. אַמֵּץ (אַמְּצֵהוּ), אַמֵּצוּ; ptc. מְאַמֶּץ־, Q מאמצת; inf. אַמְּצוֹ.

1a. strengthen, make strong, physically, **make secure,** with limbs, buildings, etc. as object, <SUBJ> Y. Pr 8_{28} (+ עזז *be strong*) Si 33_7 (|| אדר hi. *make great*) 42_{17} (+ חזק htp. *stand firm*) 1QH 5_9 (+ יסד *establish*), Israel Is 35_3 2 C 11_{17} (both || חזק pi. *strengthen*), אִשָּׁה capable *wife* Pr 31_{17} (|| חגר *gird* with strength), Job Jb 4_4 (|| קום hi. *uphold*, חזק pi.), temple builders 2 C 24_{13} (|| עמד hi. *restore*).

<OBJ> Rehoboam 2 C 11_{17}, בֶּרֶךְ feeble *knee* Is 35_3 Jb 4_4, זְרוֹעַ *arm* Pr 31_{17} Si 33_7 Arad ost. 88_2, צָבָא *host* Si 42_{17}, temple 2 C 24_{13}, שַׁחַק *heaven* Pr 8_{28}, סוֹד *counsel* of truth 1QH 5_9.

<PREP> בְּ of place, *in* heart 1QH 5_9.

1b. strengthen, encourage, mentally or spiritually, with persons or heart as object, <SUBJ> Y. Is 41_{10} (|| עזר *help*, תמך *uphold*, :: ירא *fear*, שׁתע *fear*) Si 45_2 (|| חזק pi. *strengthen*), זְרוֹעַ *arm* of Y. Ps 89_{22} (+ כון ni. *be firm*), גְּבוּרָה *might* of Y. 1QM 1_{14} ([מאמ]צת; :: מסס hi. *melt*, כנע hi. *subdue*), Moses Dt 3_{28} (|| חזק pi.), Job Jb 16_5.

<OBJ> Israel Is 41_{10}, Joshua Dt 3_{28}, David Ps 89_{22}, Job's friends Jb 16_5, Moses Si 45_2, לֵבָב *heart* 1QM 1_{14} ([לבב]ל; אמץ לֵבָב pi. is usu. *harden the heart*, as in §2).

<PREP> בְּ of place, *in* Si $45_{2(B)}$ (+ מָרוֹם *height*), of instrument, *with* Jb 16_5 (+ פֶּה *mouth*) Si $45_{2(Bmg)}$ (+ מוֹרָא *fear*, i.e. fearful act).

1c. with obj. כֹּחַ, **retain strength,** <SUBJ> Israel Na 2_2 (+ מְאֹד *greatly*; || חזק pi. *strengthen*, i.e. gird, loins), חָזָק *strong person* Am 2_{14} (|| מלט pi. *save* one's life), אִישׁ *man* of knowledge Pr 24_5 (or em. מְאַמֶּץ־כֹּחַ *retains strength* to מֵאַמִּיץ־כֹּחַ *than one mighty of strength*); cf. מַאֲמַצֵּי־כֹחַ *efforts* Jb 36_{19}, אמוץ כוח *strength* 1QH 2_8.

2. with obj. לֵבָב, **harden heart,** <SUBJ> Y. Dt 2_{30} (|| קשׁה hi. *harden* spirit), Zedekiah 2 C 36_{13} (|| קשׁה hi. *stiffen* neck), Israel Dt 15_7 (|| קפץ *shut* hand).

<PREP> מִשּׁוּב *from turning*, i.e. so as not to turn, to Y. 2 C 36_{13}.

3. let grow strong, nurture, of trees, humans as trees, <SUBJ> Y. Ps 80_{16} (|| נטע *plant*) 80_{18}, חָרָשׁ *worker* in wood Is 44_{14} (|| נטע, גדל pi. *cause to grow*).

<OBJ> בֵּן *son* Ps $80_{16.18}$ (בֶּן־אָדָם *human being*), tree Is 44_{14}.

<PREP> alw. with לְ *for*, + sf.; בְּ *among* trees Is 44_{14}.

<SYN> §1, חזק pi. *strengthen*; §2, קשׁה hi. *harden*; §3, נטע *plant*.

Hi. Impf. יַאֲמֵץ (perh. Qal)—**exhibit strength, courage,** חֲזַק וְיַאֲמֵץ לִבֶּךָ *be strong and let your heart exhibit courage* Ps 27_{14}, var. 31_{25}.

Htp. Pf. הִתְאַמֵּץ; impf. + waw וַיִּתְאַמְּצוּ; impv. Q התאמצו; ptc. מִתְאַמֶּצֶת—**1. exert oneself, be determined,** <SUBJ> Rehoboam 1 K 12_{18}||2 C 10_{18}, Ruth Ru 1_{18}, בקשׁ pi. ptc. *one who seeks* Y. 4Q521 1.2_3 (+ בעבדתו *in his service*). <COLL> + inf. לַעֲלוֹת ... לָנוּס *to mount ... to flee* 1 K 12_{18}||2 C 10_{18}, לָלֶכֶת אִתָּהּ *to go with her* Ru 1_{18}.

2. press hard upon, וַיִּתְאַמְּצוּ עַל־רְחַבְעָם *they* (rebels) *pressed hard upon Rehoboam* 2 C 13_7 (:: חזק htp. *stand up to*).

→ אֹמֶץ *strength*, אַמְצָה *strength*, מַאֲמָץ *strength*, אַמִּיץ *mighty*, אַמְצִי *Amzi*, אֲמַצְיָהוּ *Amaziah*, אָמוֹץ *Amoz*.

[אָמֹץ] I 2 adj. **dappled**—pl. אֲמֻצִּים—סוּסִים בְּרֻדִּים אֲמֻצִּים *spotted, dappled horses* Zc 6_3 (or del. אֲמֻצִּים as gloss), הָאֲמֻצִּים יָצְאוּ *the dappled ones* (horses) *went out* 6_7 (or em. אֲדֻמִּים *red ones* or del.).

[אָמֹץ] II, see אָמוֹץ.

[אַמִּץ], see אַמִּיץ.

אֹמֶץ 1.1.6 n.[m]. **might**—Q, Si אומץ, Q אמוץ—<NOM CL> חֹזֶק וְאֹמֶץ לַאדֹנָי *strength and might are to my Lord* Is 28_2 (if em. חָזָק וְאַמִּץ *[one that is] strong and mighty*). <OBJ> יסף hi. *increase* Jb 17_9 4Q298 3_6, נתן *give* 1QM 14_7. <CSTR> אומץ אלהים *might of God* Si $42_{17(Bmg)}$ (B, M אמ[י]ץ God *has strengthened*), אמוץ מתנים *might of loins* 1QM 14_7 (+ חֹזֶק *strength*), אמוץ כוח *might of strength* 1QH 2_8 (+ חֹזֶק); כול [אומ]ץ *all might* 4Q298 1_3. <PREP> [מ]בלי אומ[ץ] *without might* 4QPrFêtes[c] 13_2, שׁ[מע]ו למלי בכול [אומ]ץ *hear my words with all (your) might* 4Q298 1_3.

→ אמץ *be strong*.

אַמְצָה 1 n.f. **might,** אַמְצָה לִי יֹשְׁבֵי יְרוּשָׁלַםִ appar. *there is might to me*, i.e. I am mighty, *O inhabitants of Jerusalem* Zc 12_5 (ms לְיֹשְׁבֵי *to the inhabitants of* for לִי יֹשְׁבֵי).

→ אמץ *be strong*.

אַמְצִי 2 pr.n.m. **Amzi, 1.** Levite, son of Bani and father of Hilkiah, descendant of Merari, 1 C 6_{31}. **2.** priest, son of Zechariah and father of Pelaliah, Ne 11_{12}.

→ אמץ *be strong*.

אֲמַצְיָה, see אֲמַצְיָהוּ.

אֲמַצְיָהוּ 40 pr.n.m. **Amaziah**—אֲמַצְיָה—**1.** king of Judah, 2 K 12_{22}||2 C 24_{27} (2 K אֲמַצְיָה) 2 K 13_{12} (אֲמַצְיָה) 14_1||2 C 25_1 2 K 14_8||2 C 25_{17} (2 K אֲמַצְיָה) 2 K $14_{9.11.11.13}$||2 C $25_{18.20.21.23}$ 2 K $14_{15.17.18}$||2 C $25_{25.26}$ 14_{21}||2 C 26_1 2 K 14_{23} 15_1 (אֲמַצְיָה) 15_3||2 C 26_4 1 C 3_{12} 2 C $25_{5.9.10.11.13.14.15.27}$. **2.** priest of Bethel at time of Amos, Am $7_{10.12.14}$ (all three אֲמַצְיָה). **3.** Levite, son of Hilkiah and father of Hashabiah, in line of Merari, 1 C 6_{30} (אֲמַצְיָה). **4.** father of Joshah and descendant of Simeon, 1 C 4_{34} (אֲמַצְיָה).

→ אמץ *be strong* + יי *Y*.

[אֶמְצַע] 0.0.2 n.m. **middle**—sf. אמצעו, אמצען—ועמוד בתוך באמצעו *and a column is in the middle—in the middle of it* 11QT 30_9, בין שני הבינין ... באמצען חפון *between the two tamarisks ... in their middle*, i.e. halfway between them, *(is) hollowed* 3QTr 4_7 (or em. חפור *is buried*; Allegro הבדין *the presses*).

אמר +5299.28.187.9 vb. **say**—**Qal** Pf. אָמַר (אָמָר), אָמְרָה, אֲמַרְתֶּם, אָמְרוּ, (אָמָרְתִּי) אָמַרְתִּי, אָמַרְתְּ, (אָמָרְתָּ) אָמַרְתָּ, אָמַרְנוּ; impf. יֹאמַר (Q יואמר), 3fs תֹּאמַר (תֹּאמָר), 2ms תֹּאמַר (תֹּאמָר), תֹּאמְרִי, אֹמַר (אוֹמְרָה), יֹאמְרוּ (יֹאמָרוּ), תֹּאמְרוּ (Q יומרו, יואמרו), 3fpl תֹּאמַרְנָה, יֹאמֶרְךָ, Q נֹאמַר (תֹּאמְרוּן, תֹּאמֵרוּ, תומרו, Q תֹּמְרוּ, [ת]ואמרו נואמרה); + waw וְאָמַרְתָּ (וְאָמָרְתָּ, Q ואמרתה), וְאָמַרְתִּי; וַיֹּאמֶר (וַיֹּאמַר, Q ויומר), 3fs וַתֹּאמֶר (וַתֹּאמַר, Q ותואמר), 2ms וַתֹּאמֶר (Q ותומר), וַתֹּאמְרִי, וָאֹמַר (וָאוֹמַר), וָאֹמְרָה,

וַתֹּאמְרוּ, (ותאמרו), וַתֹּאמַרְנָה (ותאמרן), 3fpl וַיֹּאמְרוּ, (ואומרה Q), וַנֹּאמֶר; impv. אֱמֹר (אֱמָר־), אִמְרִי, אִמְרוּ (Q אמורו); ptc. active אֹמֵר (אוֹמֵר), אֹמְרִים, אֹמְרָה (אֹמְרָה), אֹמֶרֶת, אֹמְרוֹת (אֹמְרֹת); pass. אָמוּר (Si אמורתכם); inf. abs. אָמֹר (אָמוֹר); cstr. אֱמֹר (אֱמָר־) לֵאמֹר (לֵאמוֹר), (לֵאמֹר), בֶּ/כֶּאֱמֹר, אָמְרִי, אָמְרָם, אֲמָרְךָ).

1. say, a. followed by or following direct speech (in DSS, following biblical quotation), e.g. וַיֹּאמֶר אֱלֹהִים יְהִי אוֹר *and God said, Let there be light* Gn 1$_{3}$, מי יאמר לך מה תעשה *who says to you, What are you doing?* Si 33$_{10}$, אמר אדני לא ידעתה קרא ספר *my lord said, Don't you know how to read a letter!* Lachish ost. 3$_{8}$; with כִּי introducing direct speech, e.g. Gn 21$_{30}$ Ex 17$_{16}$ 22$_{8}$ 1 K 1$_{13.30}$ etc. (perh. sometimes כִּי is asseverative); oft. preceded by כֹּה *thus*, e.g. כֹּה אָמַר בָּלָק *thus said Balak* Nm 22$_{16}$, esp. in expression כֹּה אָמַר (אֲדֹנָי) י׳ *thus said (my Lord) Y.* Ex 4$_{22}$ 5$_{1}$ 7$_{17.26}$ 8$_{16}$ etc.; in subordinate clause with אֲשֶׁר *concerning which, whom,* and introducing direct speech, וְהַמִּצְפָּה אֲשֶׁר אָמַר יִצֶף י׳ *and Mizpah concerning which he said, May Y. keep watch* Gn 31$_{49}$, כָּל־אֲבֵדָה אֲשֶׁר יֹאמַר כִּי הוּא זֶה *any missing thing concerning which one says, This is it* Ex 22$_{8}$, וַיַּעַבְדוּ הַגִּלֻּלִים אֲשֶׁר אָמַר י׳ לָהֶם לֹא תַעֲשׂוּ אֶת־הַדָּבָר הַזֶּה *and they worshipped filthy idols concerning which* action *Y. had said to them, You shall not do this thing* 2 K 17$_{12}$, ויהיו מסגירי הדלת אשר אמר אל מי בכם יסגור דלתו *and they will become door closers, concerning whom God said, Who among you will close his door?* CD 6$_{13}$, Is 8$_{12}$ Ho 13$_{10}$ CD 4$_{15.20}$ 6$_{8}$ 7$_{11}$ 8$_{9(A)}$=19$_{22(B)}$ 8$_{14.20}$ 9$_{2.7.9}$ 10$_{16}$ 16$_{6.10}$ ([אמ]ר) 16$_{15}$ 19$_{5}$ (כַּאֲשֶׁר) 19$_{11.26}$ 4QDa$_{9}$ 5QD$_{2}$ 4QpIsaa 8$_{21}$ 4QpIsab 1.1$_{3}$ 4QpIsac 4.2$_{7}$ 8$_{4}$ 22$_{4(Allegro)}$ ([אש]ר) 24$_{2(Allegro)}$ ([אמ]ר) 11QMelch 1$_{10.11}$ ([א]מר) 1$_{15.15}$ ([אמ]ר) 1$_{18.26}$ 11QMelch fr. 4Q183 1.2$_{9}$ 4QFlor 1$_{7}$ 4QCata 1$_{16}$ 12.1$_{2}$ 1QpHab 3$_{2.14}$ 5$_{6}$ 6$_{2}$ 7$_{3}$ 9$_{3}$ 10$_{2}$ 12$_{6}$ 4QMg 2$_{3}$ 4Q385 3$_{4}$ 4QpsEzeka 2$_{1}$ ([ואמרה]) 3.1$_{3.4}$ (both [ויאמר]) 2$_{5}$ ([ואמר[ת]) 2$_{6.8}$ (both [ויאמר]) 3$_{2.4}$ 4Q386–9 3.2$_{1.2.3}$ ([ויאמ]ר]) 3.2$_{7}$ 4QpGena 1$_{2}$ ([א]מר) 2$_{6}$ 3$_{8}$ (ויומר) 4$_{6}$ 4QTNaph 2$_{5}$ (ותואמר) perh. 4QToh A 1.1$_{3}$ 4QDb$_{9}$ (ויא[מר]; WA ואןמר]) 4QBera 3.2$_{2.7}$ ([ואמרו]) 4Q414 1.2$_{6}$ 4Q416 4$_{11.13}$ 4Q370 1$_{1.2}$ 4Q372 1$_{16}$ 4QApocMos B 1.1$_{6}$ 4QPsJosb 22.2$_{7}$; also with כַּאֲשֶׁר *as,* כַּאֲשֶׁר יֹאמַר מְשַׁל הַקַּדְמֹנִי מֵרְשָׁעִים יֵצֵא רֶשַׁע *as the ancient proverb says, From the wicked comes forth wickedness* 1 S 24$_{14}$, CD 7$_{8.14.16}$ 20$_{16}$ 4QpIsaa 2$_{2}$ ([כאש]ר) 4QpsEzeka 3$_{6}$ 4Q386–9 3.2$_{7}$ 4QDb$_{1}$ 4Q471a$_{3}$.

b. rarely, introducing indirect speech, e.g. אִמְרִי־נָא אֲחֹתִי אָתְּ *say, please, that you are my sister* Gn 12$_{13}$, [אנ]חנו אומרים שהם [זוח]ים *we say that they sacrifice* 4QMMT A 2$_{8}$, sim. 2$_{63.72}$ ([א]ומרים) 2$_{81}$; ... אם ויאמר *if* something has happened ..., then *he is to say* what has happened 4QOrda 2$_{8}$.

<SUBJ> E.g. God Gn 2$_{16.18}$ 3$_{1.9.13}$ Dt 17$_{16}$||11QT 56$_{17}$ 1QDM 1$_{2}$ CD 3$_{21}$ 4$_{13}$ 1QM 10$_{2.6}$ 11$_{6.11}$ 4QJub 7$_{9}$ ([ויאמר]) 4QapPsb 24$_{8}$ 4QApocMos A 9$_{3}$ 4Q370 1$_{1}$ (י[ה]וה) 1$_{2}$ 4Q464 3.2$_{3}$ etc., מַלְאָךְ *angel* Gn 16$_{9.10.11}$ 19$_{15}$ 21$_{17}$ 4QJub 5$_{1}$ ([ויאמר מלאך]) etc., שָׂרָף *seraph* Is 6$_{3.7}$, Satan Jb 1$_{7.9}$ 2$_{2.4}$, Joseph 4Q372 1$_{16}$, Moses Ex 3$_{3.4.11.13.14}$ 4$_{1}$ CD 5$_{8}$ etc., Joshua Ex 32$_{17}$ Nm 11$_{28}$ Jos 1$_{10.12.12.16}$ 4QTestim 1$_{22}$ 4QPsJosb 22.2$_{7}$ ([ויאמר]) etc., Ezekiel 4QpsEzeka 3$_{6}$ 4Q386–9 3.2$_{2}$ etc., Amariah Kuntillet ʿAjrud inscr. E2.2$_{1}$, מֶלֶךְ מִצְרַיִם *king of Egypt* Ex 1$_{15.18}$ 5$_{4}$ Ezk 29$_{3}$, א[שיו] ה[מל]ך *Joash the king* Kuntillet ʿAjrud inscr. E1, רָשָׁע *evildoer* 4Q185 1.2$_{9}$ (ל[א]מור), אהב ptc. *friend* Est 5$_{14}$ Si 37$_{1(D)}$, רֵעַ *friend* Dt 13$_{7}$=11QT 54$_{20}$ Jg 7$_{14}$ Si 37$_{3(B\ mg)}$, husband Dt 22$_{14.17}$ =11QT 65$_{8.12}$, יעץ ptc. *counsellor* Si 37$_{7(D)}$, covenanter 1QS 1$_{20.24}$ 2$_{10.18}$ 6$_{13}$, pious one 11QapPsa 2$_{1}$ 4$_{11}$, worshipper 1QH 2$_{25}$ 4$_{35}$, כֹּהֵן *priest* Nm 5$_{19.21}$ 31$_{21}$ Dt 20$_{3}$=11QT 61$_{15}$ Dt 27$_{9}$ Jg 18$_{6}$ 1QS 2$_{2.11}$ etc., נָבִיא *prophet* Jg 6$_{8}$ 1 S 22$_{5}$ 1 K 13$_{26}$ 18$_{36}$ 20$_{13}$ etc. perh. 6QAllegory 1$_{6}$ 4QApocMos B 1.1$_{6}$, שֹׁפֵט *judge* 11QT 62$_{3}$, אֹיֵב *enemy* Ex 15$_{9}$ Ezk 36$_{2}$ Ps 13$_{5}$ 41$_{6}$ 71$_{10}$ Lm 2$_{16}$ Si 33$_{12(mg)}$ 4QCata 7$_{12}$, מוֹאָב *Moab* Nm 22$_{4}$ Ezk 25$_{8}$ Si 33$_{12}$, מִצְרַיִם *Egypt* Gn 47$_{15}$ Ex 12$_{33}$ 14$_{25}$ 32$_{12}$ Jr 46$_{8}$ Ezk 29$_{9}$, יִשְׂרָאֵל *Israel* Nm 16$_{34}$ 21$_{2.21}$ Jg 7$_{2}$ 11$_{17}$ etc., עֵצָה *council* 4QBera 3.2$_{1}$, מִצְרַיִם *Egyptians* Gn 12$_{12}$, Israelites Ex 3$_{13}$ 16$_{15}$ 17$_{7}$ Nm 11$_{4}$ 17$_{27}$ Dt 17$_{14}$=11QT 56$_{13}$ CD 3$_{18}$, etc., בְּנֵי (־) בְלִיַּעַל *sons of Belial* Dt 13$_{14}$=11QT 55$_{4}$ Jg 19$_{22}$ 1 S 10$_{27}$ 1 K 21$_{10.13}$, Israel's religious leaders CD 5$_{12}$, בָּחִין *tested one* 4QapPsb 24$_{6}$ (|| הלל pi. *praise*), גּוֹיִם *nations* Nm 14$_{15}$ Dt 29$_{23}$ Mc 4$_{2.11}$ Ps 79$_{10}$ (mss בַּגּוֹיִם say *among the nations*) 115$_{2}$, כל העולמים *all the planets* GnzPs 3$_{18}$, נָחָשׁ *snake* Gn 3$_{1.4}$, סוּס *horse* Jb 39$_{25}$, אָתוֹן *she-ass* Nm 22$_{28.30}$, עֵץ *tree* Jg 9$_{8.10.12.14}$, זַיִת *olive-tree* 9$_{9}$,

תְּאֵנָה fig-tree 9_{11}, גֶּפֶן vine 9_{13}, אָטָד thornbush 9_{15}, חוֹחַ bramble 2 K 14_9, מַעֲשֶׂה creation Is 29_{16}, יֵצֶר creation 29_{16}, חֹמֶר clay 45_9, קוֹל voice 40_6, נֶפֶשׁ soul, חֶלְקִי י׳ אָמְרָה נַפְשִׁי *My soul said,* i.e. I thought, *Y. is my portion* Lm 3_{24}, מַה־תֹּאמַר נַפְשְׁךָ וְאֶעֱשֶׂה־לָּךְ *whatever your soul says,* i.e. whatever you think fit, *I shall do for you* 1 S 20_4, לֵב *heart* Ps 27_8, עֶצֶם *bone* 35_{10}, סֵפֶר *letter,* וספר טביהו ... לאמר השמר שלחה עב[ד]ך *and the letter of Tobiah ... saying, Beware, your servant has dispatched* Lachish ost. 3_{20}, 64 ([לאמ]ר), דָּבָר *word, message* Gn 15_1 1 K $12_{16.22}$ Ezk 3_{16} 29_{17} etc., מָשָׁל *proverb* 1 S 24_{14}, חָכְמוֹת *wisdom* Pr 1_{21} 9_4, כְּסִילוּת *folly* 9_{16}, רַע *wickedness* Si $37_{3(D)}$, לַיְלָה *night* Jb 3_3, בָּרָק *lightning* 38_{35}, אֵשׁ *fire* Pr 30_{16}, יָם *Sea* Is 23_4 Jb 28_{14}, תְּהוֹם *the deep* 28_{14}, אֲבַדּוֹן וָמָוֶת *Abaddon and Death* 28_{22}, impersonal הֲזֹאת הָעִיר שֶׁיֹּאמְרוּ כְּלִילַת יֹפִי *Is this the city about which they say, The perfection of beauty?* Lm 2_{15}, הֶאָמוּר בֵּית־יַעֲקֹב הֲקָצַר רוּחַ י׳ *Is it to be said, O house of Jacob, Is Y.'s patience limited?* Mc 2_7, דל דובר מי זה יאמרו *a pauper speaks—Who is this?, they say* Si 13_{23}, אין לאמר *there is no need* for anyone *to say* Si $39_{21.34(mg)}$, Ex 22_8 Dt 29_{24} 1 S 23_{22} Is 25_9 40_6 Jl 2_{17} etc.

<OBJ> e.g. דָּבָר *word* 1 S 10_{16} Jr 13_{12} 14_{17} 23_{38} (|| דבר pi. *speak* 5_{14}) 31_{23} Ne 2_{18} Si $34_{31(F)}$, אֹמֶר *word* Pr 1_{21}; also with objects the referents of which consist of words, e.g. כָּל־נָאָצוֹתֶיךָ אֲשֶׁר אָמַרְתָּ עַל־הָרֵי יִשְׂרָאֵל *all your taunts which you uttered against the mountains of Israel* Ezk 35_{12}, עַל־הַמִּשְׁפָּט אֲשֶׁר־יֹאמְרוּ לְךָ *according to the law that they recite to you* Dt 17_{11} (|| ירה hi. *teach*), אמר חוקיו *I shall recite his decrees* 1QS 10_{10}, 11QT $56_{4.6}$; with nominal expression elided, אָלִית וְגַם אָמַרְתְּ בְּאָזְנַי *you cursed and even said* the curse *in my hearing* Jg 17_2, הטה [ע]בדך [ל]בה על אשר אמ[רת] *your servant has inclined his heart concerning,* i.e., paid attention to, *what you said* Arad ost. 40_5.

<PREP> לְ introducing addressee, *to* Gn 1_{28} 3_9 4_{15} 9_1 15_5 etc., 1QS 10_{11} Mur24 2_5 (אמ[ר ל]) 3_5 [4_5] 5_4 5/6Ḥev/BA 45 1Q26 1_7 4Q464 3.2_3 Kuntillet ʿAjrud inscr. E1 $E2.2_1$ papMurPalimp$^b_1$ etc., *concerning,* אִמְרִי־לִי אָחִי הוּא *say of me, He is my brother* Gn 20_{13}, הָאֹמְרִים לָרַע טוֹב *those who say of evil, Good* Is 5_{20}, לֹא־תֹאמְרוּן קֶשֶׁר לְכֹל אֲשֶׁר־יֹאמַר הָעָם הַזֶּה קָשֶׁר *Do not say, Conspiracy, about everything of which this people says, Conspiracy* 8_{12}, כי אמרו לחזון דעת לא נכון *for they have said of the vision of knowledge, It is not correct* 1QH 4_{17}, Dt 33_9 Jg 9_{54} Jr 14_{10} 48_1 $49_{1.7.28}$ etc.; לִפְנֵי *in the presence of* Dt $26_{5.13}$ 1 S 20_1 Ezk 28_9 Ec 5_5 Ne 3_{34} 6_{19} (אמר = *mention* [§4]), לְעֵינֵי *in the sight of* Dt 31_7 Jos 10_{12} Jr $28_{1.5.11}$.

בְּ of time, place, *on, among* Dt 31_{17} Is $12_{1.4}$ 25_9 (all בַּיּוֹם הַהוּא *on that day*) Jl 2_{17} Jon 3_7 Si 39_{15}, בַּגּוֹיִם *among the nations* Ps 96_{10} 126_2 Lm 4_{15} 1 C 16_{31}, בְשַׁלְוִי *in my tranquillity* Ps 30_7, בְחָפְזִי *in my urgency* 31_{23} 116_{11}, בְּאָזְנֵי *in the hearing of* Jg 17_2 Is 49_{20} Ezk 9_5 Jb 33_8, ביד יחזקאל *through Ezekiel* CD 19_{11}, בְּלֶכְתּוֹ *as one goes along* 1 S 9_9 2 S 19_1.

אֶל introducing addressee, *to* Gn 3_1 12_{11} 13_{14} $24_{39.40.44.56}$ Dt 21_{20}=11QT 64_4 Dt 22_{16}=11QT 65_{10} 4QJub^a 1_{12} ([אליו]) 11QapPs^a 2_1 etc., *concerning* 2 K 19_{32}=Is 37_{33} Jr $22_{11.18}$ 27_{19} $29_{16.21.31}$ 32_{36}.

עַל *concerning* 11_{21} 12_{14} 14_{15} 16_3 22_6 etc., *against* Ezk 35_{12}.

<COLL> לֵאמֹר *to say, saying* (also finite forms of verb) following various verbs of hearing, saying—e.g. ענה *reply* Gn 18_{27} $23_{5.10.14}$ 41_{16} etc., קרא *call* Gn 5_{29} 30_{24} Ex 17_7 19_3 Jg 6_{32} etc., צוה pi. *order* Gn 2_{16} 3_{17} 26_{11} 28_6 32_5 11QT fr. 14 4QPentPar^b 23.24 4QJub^d 1.1_{12} etc., ברך pi. *bless* Gn 1_{22} 48_{20} 1 K 14_7 8_{55} Is 19_{25} 1QS 2_2 etc., htp. *bless oneself* Dt 29_{18}, אמר *say* Gn 9_8 21_{22} 27_6 31_{29} 34_4 4QJub^a 5_1 ([ויאמר ... לאמר]) etc., ni. *be said* Jos 2_2, דבר pi. *speak* Gn 8_{15} 17_3 $23_{3.8.13}$ Lv 24_1=11QT fr. 14 Dt 13_3=11QT 54_9 CD 4_{14} 1QM 10_6 4QJub^a 1_6 ([לאמר]) 4QPentPar^b 23.24 etc., שׁאל *ask* Gn 32_{18} 37_{15} 38_{21} 40_7 43_7 etc., נגד hi. *inform* 1 S 19_2 2 K 4_{31} 5_4 $9_{18.20}$ 1QM 11_6 etc., ho. *be informed* Gn 22_{20} $38_{13.24}$ Jos 10_{17} 1 S 15_{12} 19_{19} 2 S 6_{12} 1 K 15_1 22_9 2 K 6_{13} 8_7 Is 7_2 Lachish ost. 3_{14}, שׁבע ni. *vow* Gn 24_7 Ex 33_1 Nm 32_{10} Dt 13_4 34_4 4QJub^a 2_3 ([נשבעתי]) etc., hi. *adjure* Gn 24_{37} $50_{5.25}$ Ex 13_{19} Jos 6_{26} etc, שׁלח *send* message Gn 38_{25} Ex 7_{16} Nm 21_{21} Dt 9_{23} Jos 2_1 Lachish ost. 6_4 ([לאמ]ר) etc., כתב *write* Lachish ost. 6_9 ([לאמר]), אוץ hi. *hasten* Si 7_{17}, שׁמע *hear* Gn 24_{30} 31_1 41_{15} Dt 13_{13}=11QT 55_3 Jos 22_{11} etc.

וְעָנוּ וְאָמְרוּ לֵאמֹר (and vars.) *and they shall respond* (lit. *shall answer and say, saying*) Dt 21_7=11QT 63_5 Dt

25$_9$ 26$_5$ 27$_{14.15}$ 1QS 2$_5$ 4QRitMar 19$_{6(Baillet)}$ ([וענו] ואמרו) 4QPrQuot 1$_6$ ([וא]מ[רו]) 29$_{22}$ 34$_2$ ([ואמר]ו) 42$_4$ ([אמ]רו) 48$_7$ ([וא]רמו) 51$_{6(Baillet)}$ ([וענו וא]מרו) 51$_{12}$ (Baillet) ([ועג]ו) 65$_1$ ([ו]ענו) 84$_{3(Baillet)}$ ([ועג]ו) 221$_1$ ([ו]ענו) [וא]מרו) 4QRitPur 1$_1$ ([ואמ]ר) 29$_8$ ([וענ]ה) 33$_{6(Baillet)}$ ([וענה]) 40$_2$ 42.2$_{3(Baillet)}$ ([וענה]) 51.2$_8$ ([ואמ]ר) 1QM 13$_2$ 14$_4$ 15$_3$ + Sup ([וא]מר) 15$_7$ 16$_{15}$ 18$_6$ 4QM^a fr. 13$_8$ (ואמרו ... [וע]נו) 14$_5$ ([ו]ענה) 4QBer^a 3.2$_2$ 4Q414 1.2$_6$.

לֵאמֹר *that is to say, meaning, i.e.* 2 S 5$_6$, אַל־תֹּאמַר *do not say* Dt 9$_4$ (אמר = *think* [§7]) Jr 1$_7$ Pr 3$_{28}$ 20$_{22}$ 24$_{29}$ Ec 5$_5$ 7$_{10}$ Si 5$_{1.3.4.6}$ (+ ואמרת *nor are you to say*) 11$_{23.24}$ 15$_{11}$ 16$_{17}$ 34$_{12}$, מִי(־)יֹאמַר *who will say?* 2 S 16$_{10}$ Jb 9$_{12}$ 36$_{23}$ (אָמַר) Pr 20$_9$ Ec 8$_4$, מַה־נֹּאמַר (and vars.) *what shall we* (etc.) *say?* Gn 44$_{16}$ Ex 3$_{13}$ Jos 7$_8$ 1 S 10$_{15}$ 20$_4$ 2 K 8$_{14}$ 20$_{14}$=Is 39$_3$ Jr 13$_{21}$ Jb 23$_5$ 37$_{19}$ Ezr 9$_{10}$, איכה תאמרו *how can you say?* 4Q416 4$_{11}$, האמור יאמרו *would they* (the angels) *ever say?* 4$_{13}$, פֶּן־תֹּאמַר *lest you say* Is 48$_{5.7}$ Jb 32$_{13}$ (תֹּאמְרוּ) Si 15$_{12}$.

שָׁמַעְתִּי אֹמְרִים *I heard them saying* Gn 37$_{17}$, והתפללתי לפני י׳ ואמרתי *and I prayed to Y. and I said* GnzPs 2$_7$ 3$_{12}$ 4$_{17}$.

2. answer, e.g. וַיֹּאמֶר יִרְמְיָה הַנָּבִיא אֶל־חֲנַנְיָה הַנָּבִיא *and Jeremiah the prophet responded to Hananiah the prophet* Jr 28$_5$, וַיֹּאמֶר חֲזָאֵל מַדּוּעַ אֲדֹנִי בֹכֶה וַיֹּאמֶר כִּי־יָדַעְתִּי אֵת אֲשֶׁר־תַּעֲשֶׂה *and Hazael said, Why is my lord weeping? And he replied, Because I know what you will do* 2 K 8$_{12}$, וַיִּתְפַּלֵּל אֶל־י׳ וַיֹּאמֶר לוֹ וּמוֹפֵת נָתַן לוֹ *and he prayed to Y., and Y. responded and gave him a sign* 2 C 32$_{24}$, Gn 24$_{65}$ 27$_{20.32}$ 30$_{31}$ 32$_{28}$ 33$_5$ 47$_3$ Ex 4$_2$ etc.

3. with no words of speech following, **speak** (= דבר pi.) וַיֹּאמֶר קַיִן אֶל־הֶבֶל *and Cain spoke to Abel* Gn 4$_8$, אוֹיְבַי יֹאמְרוּ רַע לִי *my enemies speak evilly of me* Ps 41$_6$, כל אומר אמר אהבתי *every speaker has said, I am a friend* Si 37$_{1(B)}$, כל לאמר *finish speaking* Si 35$_8$, perh. באמר י׳ אליו *when Y. spoke to him* 4QApocMos A9$_3$.

4. speak of, mention, declare, e.g. טוֹבֹתָיו הָיוּ אֹמְרִים לְפָנַי *they used to speak of his merits in my presence* Ne 6$_{19}$, למען לא ישכח טובכם אמורתכם לדורות עולם *so that your goodness should not be forgotten, what is said concerning you* (forgotten) *by all future generations* Si 45$_{26}$ (Segal גבורתכם *your might*), אֲשֶׁר יֹאמְרֻךָ לִמְזִמָּה perh. *who mention you as a device* Ps 139$_{20}$, אֱמוּנָתְךָ וּתְשׁוּעָתְךָ אָמָרְתִּי לֹא־כִחַדְתִּי חַסְדְּךָ וַאֲמִתְּךָ *your fidelity and your salvation I have declared, I have not hidden your loyalty and your trustworthiness* 40$_{11}$, 145$_6$ (|| ספר pi. *recount*) 145$_{11}$ (|| דבר pi. *tell*), oft. with אֲשֶׁר in relative clause, e.g. הֲזֶה אֲחִיכֶם הַקָּטֹן אֲשֶׁר אֲמַרְתֶּם אֵלָי *is this your young brother whom you have mentioned to me?* Gn 43$_{29}$, אֲשֶׁר־יֹאמַר לָכֶם תַּעֲשׂוּ *whatever he says to you, do* Gn 41$_{55}$, כָּל־אֲשֶׁר תֹּאמַר יִנָּתֶן לָהּ *everything she named would be given to her* Est 2$_{13}$, אֶתֶּן לְךָ כְּכֹל אֲשֶׁר תֹּאמַר *I shall give to you in accordance with what you say* 1 K 5$_{20}$, Gn 34$_{12}$ (כַּאֲשֶׁר) 43$_{27}$ Nm 14$_{40}$ 2 S 6$_{22}$ Est 2$_{15}$, with אֶל introducing addressee אחד הֶהָרִים אֲשֶׁר אֹמַר אֵלֶיךָ *one of the mountains which I shall mention to you* Gn 22$_2$.

5. command, order, tell someone **to do** something, e.g. לְכָל־יִשְׂרָאֵל אָמַר הַמֶּלֶךְ הָעוֹלָה *the king commanded the sacrifice for all Israel* 2 C 29$_{24}$, וְלֶחֶם אָמַר לוֹ וְאֶרֶץ נָתַן לוֹ *he ordered food for him and gave him land* 1 K 11$_{18}$, לָהֶם הֵם אֹמְרִים זֹבְחֵי אָדָם *for these they commanded* people to be *sacrificers of humans* Ho 13$_2$, Jb 9$_7$.

With ellipsis of action ordered, לֹא־הִשְׁמִידוּ אֶת־הָעַמִּים אֲשֶׁר אָמַר י׳ לָהֶם *they did not destroy the peoples whom Y. had commanded them* to destroy Ps 106$_{34}$, וַיַּעַשׂ הָאִישׁ כַּאֲשֶׁר אָמַר יוֹסֵף *and the man did as Joseph had commanded* him to do Gn 43$_{17}$, אם יומרו לו ידבר *if they order him to do so, he is to speak* 1QS 6$_{13}$, יֹאמַר־נָא אֲדֹנֵנוּ עֲבָדֶיךָ ... יְבַקְשׁוּ *let our lord give the command. Then your servants ... will seek* 1 S 16$_{16}$, Nm 23$_{30}$ Jos 11$_9$ 2 S 16$_{11}$ 2 K 4$_{24}$ Ps 106$_{34}$.

Introducing subordinate clause with imperfect verb, אָמַר ... יָשׁוּב מַחֲשַׁבְתּוֹ ... עַל־רֹאשׁוֹ *he ordered ... that his idea return ... upon his own head* Est 9$_{25}$.

With *waw*-consecutive + verb, דַּבֵּר אֶל־בְּנֵי יִשְׂרָאֵל וְאָמַרְתָּ אֲלֵהֶם וְעָשׂוּ *speak to the Israelites and command them that they are to make* Nm 15$_{38}$, וָאֹמְרָה וַיְטַהֲרוּ *and I commanded that they cleanse* Ne 13$_9$, Ps 105$_{31.34}$ 107$_{25}$ Ne 13$_{19}$ 1 C 14$_{12}$ 2 C 24$_8$ etc.

With כִּי *that,* e.g. וַיִּגֶל אָזְנָם לַמּוּסָר וַיֹּאמֶר כִּי־יְשֻׁבוּן מֵאָוֶן *and he has opened their ear to instruction, and commanded that they return from wickedness* Jb 36$_{10}$.

With אֲשֶׁר *that,* e.g. וָאֹמְרָה אֲשֶׁר לֹא יִפְתָּחוּם *and I commanded that they should not open them* Ne 13$_{19}$,

וְאֹמְרָה לַלְוִיִּם אֲשֶׁר יִהְיוּ מִטַּהֲרִים *and I commanded the Levites that they should purify themselves* 13$_{22}$.

With לְ *to* + infinitive, וַיֹּאמֶר לְהַשְׁמִידָם לוּלֵי *and he would have given the command to destroy them unless* Ps 106$_{23}$, וַיֹּאמֶר הַמֶּלֶךְ לִקְרֹא לַחַרְטֻמִּים *and the king commanded* them *to call to the magicians* Dn 2$_{2}$, וֵאלֹהִים אָמַר לְבַהֲלֵנִי *and God gave orders to hasten me* 2 C 35$_{21}$, אמר לסור את דעתם perh. *he ordered their knowledge to depart* CD 10$_{9}$, Dt 9$_{25}$ 1 S 24$_{11}$ Est 1$_{17}$ 4$_{13.15}$ 6$_{1}$ 9$_{14}$ 1 C 21$_{17}$ 2 C 1$_{18}$ 29$_{27}$ 4QFlor 1$_{6}$ 4QJub^{a} 4$_{6}$ ([ויאמר]) 7$_{9}$ (אמ[ר]).

Oft. also with לְ introducing agent of action ordered, וַיֹּאמֶר לִיהוּדָה לִדְרוֹשׁ אֶת־י׳ *and he commanded Judah to seek Y.* 2 C 14$_{3}$, Ex 17$_{10}$ Est 1$_{10}$ Dn 1$_{3}$ Ne 9$_{15.23}$ 2 C 29$_{21.30}$ 31$_{4}$ Si 15$_{11(B)}$ (כל אשר שנא אמר לך *everything he hates he has commanded you*) 37$_{9(D)}$ CD 16$_{10}$ (אמ[ר ל]), with אֶל introducing agent, וּמַלְאַךְ י׳ אָמַר אֶל־גָּד לֵאמֹר לְדָוִיד *and an angel of Y. commanded Gad to say to David* 1 C 21$_{18}$, Ex 8$_{23}$.

<COLL> אמר עִם־הַסֵּפֶר *command by letter* (lit. *with the book*) Est 9$_{25}$.

6. promise, subj. Y. except Gn 41$_{54}$ (Joseph) Est 4$_{7}$ (Haman) Ps 119$_{57}$ (worshipper), e.g. וַי׳ פָּקַד אֶת־שָׂרָה כַּאֲשֶׁר אָמָר *and Y. visited Sarah as he had said* he would do Gn 21$_{1}$ (‖ דבר pi. *speak*), אָמַרְתִּי לִשְׁמֹר דְּבָרֶיךָ *I promised to keep your words* Ps 119$_{57}$, אָמַר י׳ לְהַרְבּוֹת אֶת־יִשְׂרָאֵל *Y. had promised to increase Israel* 1 C 27$_{23}$, Jr 48$_{8}$ (אֲשֶׁר) Jl 3$_{5}$; with לְ introducing recipient of promise אָמַר־לוֹ לָתֵת לוֹ נִיר *he promised him to give him a lamp* 2 K 8$_{19}$‖2 C 21$_{7}$, אמר לו לתת א[ת הארץ] *he promised to give him* (Abraham) *the land* 4Q464 7$_{3}$.

7. think, say to oneself, but oft. difficult to distinguish from §1a, וַיֹּאמַר אָכֵן נוֹדַע הַדָּבָר *and he thought, The matter is definitely known* Ex 2$_{14}$, אֲנִי־אָמַרְתִּי אֱלֹהִים אַתֶּם *I thought, You are gods* Ps 82$_{6}$, בֶּאֱמָרְכֶם שֻׁלְחַן י׳ נִבְזֶה הוּא *by your thinking, The table of Y. can be treated with scorn* Ml 1$_{7}$; with כִּי *that* introducing indirect speech, אָמֹר אָמַרְתִּי כִּי־שָׂנֹא שְׂנֵאתָהּ *I really thought that you despised her* Jg 15$_{2}$, or direct speech, וַיֹּאמֶר כִּי יִהְיֶה שָׁלוֹם וֶאֱמֶת בְּיָמָי *and he thought, There will be peace and stability in my days* Is 39$_{8}$ (but perh. כִּי asseverative; cf. ‖2 K 20$_{19}$). <SUBJ> God Jr 3$_{7.19}$ Zp 3$_{7}$, Abraham Gn 20$_{11}$, Isaac 26$_{9}$, Jacob 44$_{28}$, Moses Ex 2$_{14}$, Manoah Jg 15$_{2}$, Saul 1 S 20$_{26}$, David 2 S 12$_{22}$, Boaz Ru 4$_{4}$, Job Jb 29$_{18}$, Balak Nm 24$_{11}$, Naaman 2 K 5$_{11}$, Israelites Ml 1$_{7}$, mourner Lm 3$_{18}$. <COLL> שלא תהי אמור *so that you do not think* (lit. *are not being thought*) MurEp Beth-Mashiko$_{6}$.

8. in related expressions, **a.** אמר בְּלִבּוֹ **say in one's heart, think,** וַיִּצְחַק וַיֹּאמֶר בְּלִבּוֹ *and he laughed and said in his heart* Gn 17$_{17}$, <SUBJ> Abraham Gn 17$_{17}$ Esau Gn 27$_{41}$, Qohelet Ec 2$_{1.15}$ 3$_{17.18}$, Haman Est 6$_{6}$, Jeroboam 1 K 12$_{26}$, Babylon Is 47$_{10}$, Edom Ob$_{3}$, אַלֻּפֵי יְהוּדָה *chiefs of Judah* Zc 12$_{5}$, wicked Ps 10$_{6.11.13}$ 35$_{25}$, נָבָל *fool* 14$_{1}$ 53$_{2}$, destroyers of Jerusalem 74$_{8}$.

8b. אמר בִּלְבָבוֹ (and vars.) **say in one's heart, think,** or, without proposition following, **ponder** (Ps 4$_{5}$ 11QPs^{a} 28$_{5}$), <SUBJ> king of Babylon Is 14$_{13}$, Babylon 47$_{8}$, Nineveh Zp 2$_{15}$, Zion Is 49$_{21}$, Judah Jr 5$_{24}$ 13$_{22}$, Israelites Dt 7$_{17}$ 8$_{17}$ 9$_{4}$ 18$_{21}$=11QT 61$_{2}$, sybarites Zp 1$_{12}$; אִמְרוּ בִלְבַבְכֶם עַל־מִשְׁכַּבְכֶם *ponder on your beds* Ps 4$_{5}$, אמרתי אני בנפשי *I said in my soul, I thought* 11QPs^{a} 28$_{5}$.

8c. אמר אֶל־לִבּוֹ **say to one's heart, think,** <SUBJ> Y. Gn 8$_{21}$, David 1 S 27$_{1}$, Israelites 11QT 61$_{2(mg)}$; also אמר לִלְבָבוֹ introducing indirect speech, וּבַל־יֹאמְרוּ לִלְבָבָם כָּל־רָעָתָם זָכָרְתִּי *and they do not think* that *I have remembered all their wickedness* Ho 7$_{2}$.

8d. אמר לְ **think to, propose to,** sometimes perh. **threaten,** <SUBJ> Y. Dt 9$_{25}$ (sim. Ps 106$_{23}$, §5), Moses Ex 2$_{14}$, Solomon 1 K 5$_{19}$, Sennacherib 2 C 32$_{1}$, Ishbibenob 2 S 21$_{16}$, Israelites Jos 22$_{33}$ (perh. אמר לְ = *speak about*, cf. §3) 2 C 13$_{8}$ 28$_{10.13}$. <COLL> + verb, הרג *kill* Ex 2$_{14}$, נכה hi. *kill* 2 S 21$_{16}$, סקל *stone* 1 S 30$_{6}$, שׁמד hi. *destroy* Dt 9$_{25}$, כבשׁ *subjugate* 2 C 28$_{10}$, בקע *penetrate* 32$_{1}$, חזק htp. *withstand* 13$_{8}$, בנה *build* 1 K 5$_{19}$, עלה *go up* Jos 22$_{33}$, יסף hi. *add* 2 C 28$_{13}$, יטב hi. *do good* Jr 18$_{10}$.

Ni. Pf. נֶאֱמַר, Q נאמרה; impf. יֵאָמֵר (יֵאָמֵר, יֵאמֵר), 3fs Si תאמר; + waw וַיֵּאָמֵר—**1. be called, be named, a.** in explanations of place names, familiar statements, etc., לֹא יַעֲקֹב יֵאָמֵר עוֹד שִׁמְךָ כִּי אִם־יִשְׂרָאֵל *no longer will your name be called Jacob, but Israel* Gn 32$_{29}$, עַל־כֵּן יֵאָמַר כְּנִמְרֹד גִּבּוֹר צַיִד לִפְנֵי י׳ *therefore it is said, Like Nimrod—a mighty hunter before Y.* 10$_{9}$, 22$_{14}$ Nm 21$_{14}$.

b. in other contexts, עִיר הַהֶרֶס יֵאָמֵר לְאֶחָת *City of the Sun will be the name of* (lit. *will be called to*) *one* Is 19_{18}, לֹא־יֵאָמֵר עוֹד הַתֹּפֶת ... כִּי אִם־גֵּיא הַהֲרֵגָה *no longer will it be called Topheth ..., but Valley of Slaughter* Jr 7_{32}.

2. be said (of), with לְ *concerning* following יֵאָמֵר לְיַעֲקֹב ... מַה־פָּעַל אֵל *it will be said of Jacob ..., What has God done!* Nm 23_{23}, וְהַנּוֹתָר בִּירוּשָׁלַםִ קָדוֹשׁ יֵאָמֶר לוֹ *and whoever remains in Jerusalem, of him, 'Holy', will be said*, i.e. people will say, He is holy Is 4_3, 32_5 (of כִּילַי *knave*) 61_6 $62_{4.4}$ (all three of Israelites) (all || קרא ni. *be called*) Ps 87_5 (of Zion).

3. be said (to), be told (to), followed by direct speech, without addressee Jr 16_{14}, with addressee introduced by לְ, וַיֵּאָמַר לְמֶלֶךְ יְרִיחוֹ לֵאמֹר הִנֵּה אֲנָשִׁים בָּאוּ *and it was told to the king of Jericho, saying, Behold, men have come* Jos 2_2, Jr 4_{11} Zp 3_{16} (both with addressee Jerusalem) Ho $2_{1.1}$ (addressee Israel), by אֶל Ezk 13_{12} (addressee false prophets).

4. be recounted, וּמַרְאֵה הָעֶרֶב ... אֲשֶׁר נֶאֱמַר אֱמֶת הוּא *and the vision of the evening ... that was recounted was true* Dn 8_{26}, בפה חכם תאמר תהלה *by a wise mouth praise is declared* Si $15_{10(A)}$.

5. perh. **be mentioned, cited,** וַיִּקְרָא ... שֵׁם־הַמָּקוֹם הַהוּא י׳ יִרְאֶה אֲשֶׁר יֵאָמֵר הַיּוֹם בְּהַר י׳ יֵרָאֶה *and he called ... the name of that place, Y. sees, which is* still *mentioned today* in the saying, *On the mountain of Y. he is seen* Gn 22_{14}, of Wisdom, על אוכלםה בשבע נאמרה *When they eat to satisfaction, she is cited* 11QPsa 18_{11}.

<COLL> יֵאָמֵר בְּסֵפֶר *be said in a book* Nm 21_{14}; לֹא־יֵאָמֵר עוֹד (and var.) *no longer will it be called, said* Gn 32_{29} Jr 7_{32} 16_{14}.

Hi. Pf. הֶאֱמַרְתָּ, הֶאֱמִירְךָ—**proclaim, vow, bid,** a person to be (with לְ + infin.), or do, something, אֶת־י׳ הֶאֱמַרְתָּ הַיּוֹם לִהְיוֹת לְךָ לֵאלֹהִים וְלָלֶכֶת בִּדְרָכָיו *you have today proclaimed Y. to be your God and that you will walk* (lit. *to walk*) *in his ways* Dt 26_{17}, וַי׳ הֶאֱמִירְךָ הַיּוֹם לִהְיוֹת לוֹ לְעַם סְגֻלָּה ... וְלִשְׁמֹר כָּל־מִצְוֹתָיו *and Y. has today proclaimed you to be his treasured people ... and to keep all his commandments* 26_{18}.

Htp. Impf. יִתְאַמְּרוּ, Q אתימר, תִּתְיַמָּרוּ—**speak self-regardingly, boast,** יַבִּיעוּ יְדַבְּרוּ עָתָק יִתְאַמְּרוּ כָּל־פֹּעֲלֵי אָוֶן *all evil-doers spout forth, they speak arrogantly, all evil-doers boast* Ps 94_4, + בְּ *concerning, because of*, חֵיל גּוֹיִם תֹּאכֵלוּ וּבִכְבוֹדָם תִּתְיַמָּרוּ *you shall consume the wealth of nations and boast about their riches* Is 61_6, באהבתך אתימר *because of your love*, perh. love for you, *I boast* 4Q448 2_1.

Also 4QPrQuot 1_{18} ([ואמר]ו) 21_2 (ל[אמו]ר לנו) 4Q185 1.2_{11} 4QCata 1_1 (יואמ[ר]) 4QShira 7_2 ([ת]אומרו) 4QAges 2.1_7 Mur24 9_5 (אמ[ר]) 4QpIsab 1.3_7 11QMelch $1.1_{7(AHL)}$ (אמ[ר]) 4QCata 12.2_5 4QMish Cb 3_7 ([א]מרו) 4Q462 2 (ויא[מר]) 4Q462 3.9 4QapPsb 31_2 4Q464a 1_1 (ל[א]מר) Lachish ost. 21_7 ([א]מר).

→ אֹמֶר *word*, אִמְרָה *word*, אֲמַרְיָה *Amariah*, אִמְרִי *Imri*.

אֹמֶר 55.5.11 n.m. **word**—אֹ֫מֶר; cstr. Si אמר (אומר); sf. Si אמרי, אִמְרוֹ, Q אמרה, אמרם; pl. אֲמָרִים; cstr. אִמְרֵי; sf. אֲמָרַי (אֲמָרָי), אֲמָרָיו, אֲמָרֶיהָ, אֲמָרֵיכֶם, אִמְרֵיכֶם, Q אמריהמה (suffixed forms in sing. and all plurals vocalized as if abs. were אֵ֫מֶר)—**word,** sometimes perh. **command** or as collective, **speech.**

<SUBJ> היה *be* pleasing Ps 19_{15} (+ הִגָּיוֹן *thought*), קום *stand up*, i.e. be realized Jb 22_{28}, גמר *be finished* (of God's saving word) Ps 77_9, רחק *be distant* from wicked (of Wisdom's word) 11QPsa 18_{13}, נעם *be pleasant* Ps 141_6, מרץ ni. *be sick*, i.e. sickening Jb 6_{25} (or em. מלץ ni. *be sweet*).

<NOM CL> בְּצֶדֶק כָּל־אִמְרֵי־פִי *in righteousness*, i.e. correct, *are all my words* Pr 8_8, רוּחַ כַּבִּיר אִמְרֵי־פִיךָ *a great wind are the words of your mouth* Jb 8_2, יֹשֶׁר־לִבִּי אֲמָרָי *(leading to) uprightness of heart are my words* 33_3, טְהֹרִים אִמְרֵי־נֹעַם *words of pleasantness are pure* Pr 15_{26} (+ מַחֲשָׁבָה *thought*), צוּף־דְּבַשׁ אִמְרֵי־נֹעַם *words of pleasantness are a honeycomb* 16_{24}, אֵין־אֹמֶר *there is no word* Ps 19_4 (+ דָּבָר *word*), אמרהמה להודיע עוזו *their words are (uttered) to make known his strength* 11QPsa 18_{12}.

<OBJ> שׁמע *hear* Nm $24_{4.16}$ (+ דַּעַת *knowledge*) Dt 32_1 Jos 24_{27} Is 41_{26} Ps 138_4 141_6 4Q525 4_{23}, אזן hi. *listen* Ps 5_2 (+ הָגִיג *thought*), חשׁב *consider* as wind Jb 6_{26} (unless nom. cl., לְרוּחַ אִמְרֵי־נֹאָשׁ *the words of one who despairs are as wind*; + מִלָּה *word*), בין hi. *understand* Pr 1_2, לקח *take* 2_1 (|| מִצְוָה *commandment*) 4_{10}, שׁמר *observe* 7_1 (|| מִצְוָה) 4QapPsa 1.2_2 (אמ[ריו]), קרא *cry* (of wisdom) Pr

1$_{21}$ (if del. תֹּאמַר *she says*), אמר *say* 1$_{21}$ (or em.), דבר pi. *speak* 1$_{14}$, ידע hi. *make known* 22$_{21}$ (+ אֹמֶר), גזר *decree* (of Job) Jb 22$_{28}$, נתן *give* Gn 49$_{21}$ (but see Cstr.) Ps 68$_{12}$ (or em. to יִתֶּן־אֹמֶר הַמְבַשְּׂרוֹת *he gives a command; those that bear good news* to יִתֶּן־לַמְבַשְּׂרוֹת *he gives to those that bear good news*), נבע hi. *pour out* 19$_{3}$, פוק hi. *bring out* 4Q525 2.4$_{5}$ ([אמרי]), רבה hi. *increase* Jb 34$_{37}$, חשׂך *withhold* Pr 17$_{27}$ (+ דַּעַת *knowledge*, רוּחַ *spirit*), שׂים *place* in heart Jb 22$_{22}$ (+ תּוֹרָה *law*), צפן *store up* 23$_{12}$ (+ מִצְוָה), רדף pi. *pursue* Pr 19$_{7}$, חלק hi. *smooth*, i.e. flatter 2$_{16}$=7$_{5}$ 1QH 4$_{7}$ (אמ[רים]; || מְלִיצָה *word*), נשׂג hi. *understand* Si 12$_{12}$ (|| אֲנָחָה *sigh*) 34$_{22}$ (|| דָּבָר *word*), שׁוב hi. *take back*, i.e. reply Jg 5$_{29}$ Pr 22$_{21}$ (+ אֹמֶר), ענה *answer* Jb 32$_{12}$, כון hi. *establish* Si 36$_{4(F)}$, עשׂה *do*, i.e. effect 36$_{4(F)}$, מרה hi. *rebel (against)* Ps 107$_{11}$ (+ עֵצָה *counsel*), כחד pi. *falsify* Jb 6$_{10}$.

<CSTR> אומר אלהים *command of God* Si 42$_{15(B)}$ (M אמר אדני *command of the Lord*), [אמרי תבונה] *words of understanding* 4Q525 2.4$_{5}$, אמרי מלך *words of (the) king* 4QShirShab^{f} 23.1$_{11}$, אִמְרֵי ״ *words of Y.* Jos 24$_{27}$, קָדוֹשׁ *of (the) holy one* Jb 6$_{10}$, נוֹאָשׁ *of one who despairs* 6$_{26}$, אֱמֶת *of truth* Pr 22$_{21}$, כזב *of deceit* 4Q372 1$_{14}$, בִּינָה *of understanding* 1$_{2}$, אִמְרֵי־אֵל *words of God* Nm 24$_{4.16}$ Ps 107$_{11}$, פִּי *of my mouth* Dt 32$_{1}$ Ho 6$_{5}$ Ps 19$_{15}$ 54$_{4}$ 78$_{1}$ Pr 4$_{5}$ 5$_{7}$ 7$_{24}$ 8$_{8}$ 4Q525 2$_{12}$ ([מאמרי פי]), פִּיךָ *of your mouth* Ps 138$_{4}$ Pr 6$_{2}$ (or em. דִּבְרֵי שְׂפָתֶיךָ *word of your lips*) 6$_{2}$ Jb 8$_{2}$, פִּיו *of his mouth* 23$_{12}$ 1QS 9$_{25}$ 4QShirShab^{d} 1.1$_{35}$ (both פיהו), שֶׁקֶר *of falsehood* Is 32$_{7}$ 4QpPs^{a} 1.1$_{18}$, יֹשֶׁר *of uprightness* Jb 6$_{25}$, דַּעַת *of knowledge* Pr 19$_{27}$ (or em. מַאֲמָרִים רָעִים *evil words*) 23$_{12}$ (both + מוּסָר *discipline*), נֹעַם *of pleasantness* 15$_{26}$ 16$_{24}$, שֶׁפֶר *of beauty* Gn 49$_{21}$ (unless אֹמֶר *branch* or אִמֵּר *lamb*, or em. אֲמִרֵי *branches of* or *antlers of*); מַטּוֹת אֹמֶר *arrows (consisting) of speech* Hb 3$_{9}$ (or em. תֹּאמַר *you say*), נַחֲלַת אִמְרוֹ מֵאֵל *inheritance of his word from God* Jb 20$_{29}$, כָּל־אִמְרֵי *all the words of* Jos 24$_{27}$ Pr 8$_{8}$ (־אִמְרֵי) 1QS 9$_{25}$ (כו[ל]) 4Q372 1$_{14}$ ([כל]).

<APP> קֹשְׁטְ אִמְרֵי אֱמֶת *truth, words of truth* Pr 22$_{21}$, אֲמָרִים אֱמֶת *words, truth*, i.e. true words 22$_{21}$.

<PREP> לְ of direction, *to*, + נטה hi. *incline* ear Ps 78$_{1}$ (+ תּוֹרָה *law*) Pr 4$_{20}$ (|| דָּבָר *word*), בוא hi. *bring* ear 23$_{12}$, קשׁב hi. *attend* 7$_{24}$, אזן hi. *listen* Ps 54$_{4}$ (+ תְּפִלָּה *prayer*), היה לְ *be*, i.e. exist, *by* 4QShirShab^{d} 1.1$_{35}$.

בְּ of instrument, *by, with*, + חבל pi. *ruin* poor Is 32$_{7}$, הרג *kill* Ho 6$_{5}$ (or em. ידע hi. *make known*), שׁוב hi. *take back*, i.e. reply Jb 32$_{14}$ (|| מִלָּה *word*), יקשׁ ni. *be trapped* Pr 6$_{2}$ (or em. בִּדְבַר *by a word of*), לכד ni. *be captured* 6$_{2}$, ידע ni. *be known* (of wisdom) Si 4$_{24}$ (+ מַעֲנֶה *answer*), תעה hi. *lead astray* 4QpPs^{a} 1.1$_{18}$, באמר אדני מעשיו *by the command of the Lord are (effected) his works* Si 42$_{15(M)}$, sim. 42$_{15(Bmg)}$ (B רצונו *his pleasure*), כבוד אלוהי דעות באמריו *glory of the God of knowledge among his commandments* 4QShir^{b} 1$_{8}$.

מִן of direction, *from*, + נטה *turn* intrans. Pr 4$_{5}$, סור *turn* intrans. 5$_{7}$ 4Q525 2$_{12}$ ([מאמרי]), שׁגה *stray* Pr 19$_{27}$ (or em. לַהֲגוֹת מַאֲמָרִים רָעִים *to murmur evil words*), מאמרם הושיע ידו לו *at their* (judges) *command, his (own) hand has saved him* CD 9$_{10}$ (but perh. מַאֲמָרָם in the absence of *their word*).

עַל *against* 4QShirShab^{f} 23.1$_{11}$.

<SYN> מִצְוָה *commandment*, מִלָּה *word*, דָּבָר *word*.

→ אמר *say*.

[אֹמֶר], see אֹמֶר, esp. Cstr.

אִמֵּר I 2 pl.n. **Immer,** site in Babylonia from which exiles returned, Ezr 2$_{59}$||Ne 7$_{61}$.

אִמֵּר II 8.0.4 pr.n.m. **Immer, 1.** ancestor of priests at time of Ezra, Ezr 2$_{37}$||Ne 7$_{40}$ Ezr 10$_{20}$ Ne 3$_{29}$ 11$_{13}$||1 C 9$_{12}$. **2.** priest at time of David, perh. ident. with preceding, 1 C 24$_{14}$. **3.** priest, father of Passhur, perh. ident. with 1, Jr 20$_{1}$. **4.** name of priestly course, 4QMish A 1.2$_{1}$ 1.3$_{6}$ ([אמר]) 4QMish B^{a} 1.1$_{3}$ 1.2$_{1}$ ([אמר]) 2.1$_{6}$ ([אמר]) 2.3$_{6.7}$ ([אמר]) 2.3$_{9}$ 2.4$_{1}$ ([אמר]) 4QMish C$^{c}_{4}$ (אמ[ר]) 4QMish C$^{c}_{5}$ ([אמר]) 4QMish D 2$_{1}$ ([א]מר). **5.** Samaria ost. 29$_{3}$ (others קדר or גמר).

[אִמֵּר] III, see אֹמֶר, Cstr.

[אֶמְרָה], see אִמְרָה.

[אִמְרָה] 37.1.4 n.f. **word**—cstr. אִמְרַת; sf. אִמְרָתִי, אִמְרָתְךָ (Q אמרתכה), אִמְרָתֵךְ, אִמְרָתוֹ (אֶמְרָתוֹ), אִמְרָתֶךָ; pl.

אֲמָרוֹת; cstr. אִמְרוֹת—word of God except Gn 4_{23} (Lamech) Dt 32_{2} (Moses) Is $29_{4.4}$ (Jerusalem) Ps 17_{6} (worshipper).

<SUBJ> עמד *stand*, i.e. endure Ps 19_{10} (if em. יִרְאַת *fear of;* || מִשְׁפָּט *judgment*), אזל ni. *go out* Dt $32_{2(\text{Sam mss})}$ (MT נזל *flow*), חיה pi. *keep alive* Ps 119_{50}, חרף hi. *make cold* Si $43_{16(\text{M})}$ (Bmg אֵימָה *terror;* + כֹּחַ *strength*), צרף *test* Ps 105_{19}, pass. *be tested* 2 S 22_{31}||Ps 18_{31} (|| דֶּרֶךְ *way*) 119_{140} Pr 30_{5}, נזל *flow* like dew Dt 32_{2} (|| לֶקַח *instruction*), מלץ ni. *be smooth* to mouth, palate Ps 119_{103}, שׁחח ni. *be low* Is 29_{4}, עמק hi. *go deep down* Si $43_{23(\text{M Yadin})}$ (אמר]תו תע[מיק), צפף pilp. *chirp* from dust Is 29_{4} (|| קוֹל *voice*).

<NOM CL> אִמְרוֹת י׳ אֲמָרוֹת טְהֹרוֹת כֶּסֶף *the words of Y. are pure words, silver* Ps 12_{7}, אִמְרַת י׳ טְהוֹרָה *the word of Y. is pure* 19_{10} (if em.; see Subj.).

<OBJ> אזן hi. *listen to* Gn 4_{23} Is 32_{9} (both || קוֹל *voice*), שׁמע *hear* Is 28_{23} (|| קוֹל) Ps 17_{6}, קשׁב hi. *pay attention to* Is 28_{23}, ענה *sing* Ps 119_{172} (+ מִצְוָה *commandment*), צוה pi. *command* Lm 2_{17}, שׁמר *keep*, i.e. observe, fulfil Dt 33_{9} (|| בְּרִית *covenant*) Ps $119_{67.158}$, קום hi. *establish* 119_{38}, בצע pi. *accomplish* Lm 2_{17}, גדל hi. *magnify* Ps 138_{2}, שׁלח *send* to earth 147_{15} (+ דָּבָר *word*), צפן *store up* 119_{11}, אהב *love* 119_{140}, נאץ pi. *despise* Is 5_{24} (|| תּוֹרָה *law*), יצא hi. *bring out* 4Q525 4_{20} ([אמרו]תיכה), נבע hi. *pour out* 6.10_{1} ([אמרו]ת).

<CSTR> אִמְרַת י׳ *word of Y.* 2 S 22_{31}||Ps 18_{31} (אִמְרַת־) Ps 12_{7} (אִמְרוֹת *words of*) 19_{10} (if em.; see Subj.) 105_{19}, אֱלוֹהַּ *of God* Pr 30_{5}, קְדוֹשׁ־יִשְׂרָאֵל *of the Holy One of Israel* Is 5_{24}, צִדְקֶךָ *of your righteousness* Ps 119_{123}, אמרו]ת עולת] *words of folly* 4Q525 6.10_{1}; כָּל־אִמְרַת *every word of* Pr 30_{5}.

<APP> אֲמָרוֹת ... כֶּסֶף *words ... silver* Ps 12_{7}.

<ADJ> טָהוֹר *pure* Ps 12_{7} (if em. יִרְאַת *reverence of*).

<PREP> לְ חיה pi. *keep alive by* Ps 119_{154}, לְ כלה *be worn out (through looking) for* (of eyes) $119_{82.123}$ (|| יְשׁוּעָה *salvation*).

בְּ *by* or *in accordance with*, + כון hi. *establish* steps Ps 119_{133} (mss כְּ *according to*), סמך *support* $119_{116(\text{mss})}$ (L כְּ), נצל hi. *deliver* $119_{170(\text{mss})}$ (L כְּ), שׂיח בְּ *meditate on* 119_{148}.

כְּ *according to*, + בוא *come* (of loyalty, salvation) Ps 119_{41}, חנן *have mercy* 119_{58} 11QPsa 119_{107} (MT חיה כִּדְבָרֶךָ pi. *keep alive according to your word*) 119_{159} (MT חיה כְּחַסְדְּךָ pi. *keep alive according to your loyalty*), היה *be* (of loyalty) 119_{76}, סמך *support* Ps 119_{116} (mss בְּ *by*), כון hi. *establish* steps $119_{133(\text{mss})}$ (L בְּ), נצל hi. *deliver* 119_{170} (mss בְּ).

שׂישׂ עַל *rejoice at, because of* Ps 119_{162}.

<SYN> קוֹל *voice*.

→ אמר *say*.

אֱמֹרִי 86.0.3 gent. **Amorite**—Q אמורי—**1.** as collective noun, with article, הָאֱמֹרִי, **the Amorites,** race inhabiting Canaan, etc.; oft. in lists of Israel's enemies (and sometimes representative of all). **<SUBJ>** היה *be* Jg 1_{35} (+ לָמַס *subject to forced labour*), ישׁב *inhabit* Gn 14_{7} Nm 13_{29} Jos $24_{8.18}$ Jg 1_{35} 11_{21}, עזב *abandon* a place Is 17_{9} (if em. הָאָמִיר *the heath*), יצא *come out* to fight Dt 1_{44}, קרא *meet* in battle 1_{44}, לחם ni. *wage war* Jos $24_{8.11}$, רדף *pursue* Dt 1_{44}, לחץ *press hard* in battle Jg 1_{34}, כתת hi. *pulverize* Dt 1_{44}, עשׂה *do* 1 K 21_{26} 2 K 21_{11}, נתן *give, allow* Jg 1_{34}, יאל hi. *wish* 1_{35}, קרא *name* Dt 3_{9}.

<NOM CL> האמורי שם *the Amorite is there* 4Q522 2_{8}.

<OBJ> חרם hi. *exterminate* Dt 20_{17}=11QT 62_{14}, שׁמד hi. *destroy* Jos 24_{8} Am 2_{9}, נכה hi. *defeat* Gn 14_{7}, גרשׁ pi. *expel* Ex 33_{2} 34_{11} Jos 24_{18} 11QT $2_{2(\text{Yadin})}$ (... [גורש] [הא]מורי]), נשׁל *clear away* Dt 7_{1}, ירשׁ hi. *dispossess* Nm $21_{32(\text{Qr})}$ 32_{39} Jos 3_{10} Jg 11_{23} 1 K 21_{26} 4Q522 2_{3}, נתן *give* Jos 10_{12} perh. 12_{8} $24_{8.11}$, ילד *beget* (of Canaan) Gn 10_{16} ||1 C 1_{14}.

<CSTR> אֶרֶץ ... הָאֱמֹרִי *land of ... the Amorites* Ex 3_{17} 13_{5} Nm 21_{31} Jos 24_{8} Jg 10_{8} 11_{21} Ne 9_{8} Am 2_{10}, גְּבוּל *border of* Nm 21_{13} Jos 13_{4} Jg 1_{36} (or em. הָאֲדֹמִי *of the Edomites*) 11_{22}, עָרֵי *cities of* Nm 21_{25}, הַר *mountain(s) of* Dt $1_{7.19.20}$, מְקוֹם *place of* Ex 3_{8}, עֲזוּבַת *deserted site of* Is 17_{9} (if em.; see Subj.), סִיחוֹן מֶלֶךְ *Sihon, king of* Nm 21_{21} (מֶלֶךְ־) $21_{26.29(\text{Sam})}$ (MT אֱמֹרִי *Amorite* king, §2a) 21_{34} 32_{33} Dt 1_{4} 3_{2} 4_{46} Jos 12_{2} $13_{10.21}$ Jg 11_{19} (מֶלֶךְ־) 1 K 4_{19} Ps 135_{11} 136_{19}, מַלְכֵי *kings of* Dt 3_{8} 4_{47} Jos 2_{10} (+ שְׁנֵי *two*) 5_{1} 9_{10} (+ שְׁנֵי) 10_{5} (+ חֲמֵשֶׁת *five*) 10_{6} 24_{12} (+ שְׁנֵי) Dt 31_{4}, אֱלֹהֵי *gods of* Jos 24_{15} Jg 6_{10}, יֶתֶר *remnant of* 2 S 21_{2}, יַד *hand*, i.e. power, *of* Gn 48_{22} Dt 1_{27} Jos 7_{7}, עֲוֹן *wickedness of* Gn 15_{16}.

<APP> הָאָרֶץ הַזֹּאת ... הָאֱמֹרִי *this land ... (namely, of) the Amorites* Gn 15_{21}.

<PREP> אֶל of direction, *to* Ex 23_{23} Jos 11_3, אֶל־מוּל *towards* 9_1; לְ *belonging to* Ezr 9_1 (or em. אֲדֹמִי *Edomite;* + תּוֹעֵבָה *abomination*), עשׂה לְ *do to* Nm 22_2; בְּקֶרֶב *among* Jg 3_5; מִן *from* Jg 10_{11}, + יתר ni. *be left over* 1 K 9_{20}||2 C 8_7; בֵּין מוֹאָב וּבֵין הָאֱמֹרִי *between Moab and the Amorites* Nm 21_{13}, בֵּין יִשְׂרָאֵל וּבֵין הָאֱמֹרִי *between Israel and the Amorites* 1 S 7_{14}.

<COLL> הָאֱמֹרִי ... אֲשֶׁר כְּגֹבַהּ אֲרָזִים גָּבְהוֹ וְחָסֹן הוּא כָּאַלּוֹנִים *the Amorites ... whose height was as the height of cedars and who were as strong as the oaks* Am 2_9.

2a. as adj., **Amorite,** מֶלֶךְ אֱמֹרִי סִיחוֹן *an Amorite king, Sihon* Nm 21_{29} (Sam הָאֱמֹרִי king of *the Amorites,* §1).

2b. as sg. noun, **an Amorite,** <NOM CL> אֲבִיכֶן אֱמֹרִי *your father was an Amorite* Ezk 16_{45}, sim. 16_3 (both || חִתִּי *Hittite*).

<APP> מַמְרֵא הָאֱמֹרִי *Mamre the Amorite* Gn 14_{13} (+ אַבְרָם הָעִבְרִי *Abram the Hebrew*), סִיחֹן מֶלֶךְ־חֶשְׁבּוֹן הָאֱמֹרִי *Sihon, king of Heshbon, the Amorite* Dt 2_{24}.

אִמְרִי 2 pr.n.m. **Imri, 1.** ancestor of returning exile, son of Bani (Qr בָּנִי מִן *Bani from* the sons of Perez; Kt בנימן *Benjamin*) and father of Omri, descendant of Judah, perh. ident. with Amariah (אֲמַרְיָה) at ||Ne 11_4, 1 C $9_{4(Qr)}$. **2.** father of Zaccur, perh. ident. with preceding, Ne 3_2.

→ אמר *say.*

אֲמַרְיָה 16.0.0.9 pr.n.m. **Amariah**—אֲמַרְיָהוּ, I אמריו—**1.** son of Hezekiah and ancestor of Zephaniah (mss חִלְקִיָּה *Hilkiah*), Zp 1_1. **2.** son of Azariah and ancestor of Ezra, Ezr 7_3. **3.** descendant of Binnui, Ezr 10_{42}. **4.** son of Shephatiah and father of Zechariah, descendant of Judah, Ne 11_4. **5.** Levite, father of Ahitub and son of Meraioth, 1 C $5_{33.33}$ 6_{37}. **6.** Levite, father of Ahitub and son of Azariah, perh. ident. with preceding, 1 C $5_{37.37}$. **7.** chief priest at time of Jehoshaphat, 2 C 19_{11} (אֲמַרְיָהוּ). **8.** chief priest, Ne 10_4 $12_{2.13}$. **9.** Levite at time of Hezekiah, 2 C 31_{15} (אֲמַרְיָהוּ). **10.** Levite, 1 C 23_{19} 24_{23} (אֲמַרְיָהוּ). **11.** son of Joab, Seal 531_1 (T. Beit Mirsim?, 7th/6th cent.). **12.** Gibeon jar handle inscr. 14 15 16 17 18 ([א]מריהו) 19 ([אמריהו]) 61 (אמר[י]הו). **13.** Beersheba graf. 2_2 3 ([אמ]ריהו). **14.** Seal 211_2 (Kiriath-jearim, 7th/6th cent.). **15.** Kuntillet 'Ajrud inscr. E2.2_1 (אמריו).

→ אמר *say* + ׳י *Y.*

אֲמַרְיָהוּ, see אֲמַרְיָה.

אמריו, see אֲמַרְיָה.

אַמְרָפֶל 2 pr.n.m. **Amraphel,** king of Shinar, Gn $14_{1.9}$.

אֶמֶשׁ 5.0.0.1 n.[m.] **evening**—אָמֶשׁ—**1.** as adv., **last night** (Gn 19_{34} $31_{29.42}$), perh. less specif., **yesterday** (Lachish ost. 3_6), with verb, שׁכב *lie* with father Gn 19_{34}, אמר *say* in dream 31_{29}, יכח hi. *reprove* in dream 31_{42}, שׁלח *send* Lachish ost. 3_6. **2.** noun, **evening, twilight,** הָעֹרְקִים צִיָּה אֶמֶשׁ שׁוֹאָה וּמְשֹׁאָה *those that gnaw the wilderness—twilight, destruction, devastation* Jb 30_3 (ms אֱנוֹשׁ *human being of*; or em. אֵם *mother of* destruction).

אֱמֶת 127.7.204 n.f. **truth**—cstr. אֱמֶת; sf. אֲמִתְּךָ (אֲמִתֶּךָ, Q אמתכה, אמיתך), אֲמִתּוֹ, Si אמתה—senses oft. overlap.

1. reliability, dependability, trustworthiness, faithfulness, constancy, usu. as attribute of Y., also of Laban and Bethuel Gn 24_{49}, Joseph 47_{29}, צַדִּיק *righteous one* Ezk 18_9, secure king Pr 29_{14}, Joshua's scouts Jos 2_{14}; beneficiaries include Abraham Gn $24_{27.49}$, Jacob 32_{11} 47_{29} Mc 7_{20}, Ittai 2 S 15_{20}, Rahab's family Jos 2_{14}, people of Jabesh-gilead 2 S 2_6, חֹרְשֵׁי טוֹב *those who plan good* Pr 14_{22}.

<SUBJ> נצר *guard* Ps 40_{12} 61_8 Pr 20_{28} (all three || חֶסֶד *loyalty*), פגשׁ ni. *meet one another* Ps 85_{11} (+ חֶסֶד), צמח *sprout* 85_{12} (|| צֶדֶק *righteousness*), קדם pi. *proceed* 89_{15} (|| חֶסֶד), עזב *leave* Pr 3_3 (|| חֶסֶד), שׁעע pilp. *delight* trans. 1QH 10_{30} (|| בְּרִית *covenant*).

<NOM CL> אתה אמת *you are dependability,* i.e. dependable 1QH 4_{40} (+ צֶדֶק *righteousness*), אמת כול בחיריך *all your elect are trustworthiness,* i.e. trust

worthy 14_{15} (|| צַדִּיק *righteous*), אֵין־אֱמֶת וְאֵין־חֶסֶד וְאֵין־דַּעַת אֱלֹהִים בָּאָרֶץ *there is no trustworthiness or loyalty or knowledge of God in the land* Ho 4_1.

מִשְׁפְּטֵי־י׳ אֱמֶת *the judgments of Y. are trustworthy* Ps 19_{10}, צ[ד]ק ואמת משפטיך *righteous(ness) and trustworthy/trustworthiness are your judgments* CD 20_{30}, עַד־שְׁחָקִים אֲמִתֶּךָ *(reaching) up to the clouds is your dependability* Ps 57_{11}||108_5 (|| חֶסֶד *loyalty*), אֱמֶת־י׳ לְעוֹלָם *the dependability of Y. is forever* 117_2 (|| חֶסֶד), צִנָּה וְסֹחֵרָה אֲמִתּוֹ *his reliability is a shield and buckler* 91_4, אֲמִתְּךָ תְהִלָּתִי *your dependability is (the theme of) my praise* 22_{26} (if em. מֵאִתְּךָ *from you*).

מַעֲשֵׂי יָדָיו אֱמֶת וּמִשְׁפָּט *the works of his hands are trustworthiness and judgment* (or *trustworthy and just*) Ps 111_7, אמת אל היאה סלע פעמי *the reliability of God is the rock of my feet* 1QS 11_4 (|| גְּבוּרָה *strength*), אמת כול מעשיו *all his works are reliable* 10_{17}, חסד ואמת סביב פניו *loyalty and reliability are around his face* 11QPs^a 26_{10}, אמת ומשפט וצדק מכון כסאו *reliability and judgment and righteousness are the support of his throne* 26_{10}.

<OBJ> עשׂה *do*, i.e. behave reliably (towards) Gn 24_{49} 32_{11} (+ אֵת *with*, beneficiary of אֱמֶת) 47_{29} Jos 2_{14} 2 S 2_6 (all three + עִם *with*, beneficiary; all five || חֶסֶד *loyalty*) Ezk 18_9 Ne 9_{33} 2 C 31_{20} (|| טוֹב *goodness*, יָשָׁר *uprightness*) 1QS 1_5 5_3 (|| עֲנָוָה *humility*) 8_2 (both || אַהֲבַת חֶסֶד *love of loyalty*, all three || צְדָקָה *righteousness*, מִשְׁפָּט *judgment*), נתן *give* Mc 7_{20} (|| חֶסֶד *loyalty*).

יצא hi. *bring out* 1QH 4_{25} (|| מִשְׁפָּט *judgment*), שׁמר *keep*, i.e. remain trustworthy Ps 146_6, שׁלח *send* from heaven 57_4 (|| חֶסֶד *loyalty*), רבה hi. *increase* GnzPs 1_7 (|| מִשְׁפָּט), עזב *leave*, i.e. withhold Gn 24_{27}, מור hi. *exchange* 1QH 14_{20} (+ בהון *for wealth*, || מִשְׁפָּט), אהב *love* Zc 8_{19} (|| שָׁלוֹם *peace, integrity*), חפץ *desire* Ps 51_8 (+ בַּטֻּחוֹת *in the inner parts* of a person; || חָכְמָה *wisdom*; perh. אֱמֶת = *truth*, as §3), מנה pi. *appoint* 61_8, נגד hi. *declare* 30_{10}, כחד pi. *conceal* 40_{11} (|| חֶסֶד).

עבד *work*, i.e. work reliably Si 7_{20}, שׁפט *judge*, i.e. judge reliably Zc 8_{16} (+ מִשְׁפַּט שָׁלוֹם *judgment of peace*) Si 4_{15} (or em. אֻמּוֹת *nations*).

<CSTR> אֱמֶת־י׳ *dependability of Y.* Ps 117_2, perh. אֱמֶת יִשְׁעֶךָ *dependability of your salvation* 69_{14}, אמת אל *dependability of God* 1QS 11_4 1QM 4_6 (|| צֶדֶק *righteousness*, כָּבוֹד *glory*, מִשְׁפָּט *judgment*), אמת בריתך *trustworthiness of your covenant* 1QH 16_7 (+ רוח ק[ודשך] *your holy spirit*) 4Q414 1.2_3 ([א]מ[ת בריתכ[ה]).

מלך אמת וצדק *king of trustworthiness and righteousness* 4QShirShab^e 5_6, אִישׁ אֱמֶת *man of trustworthiness*, i.e. trustworthy man Ne 7_2 (+ יְרֵא אֱלֹהִים *fear God*), מִשְׁפַּט *judgment of* Ezk 18_8 Zc 7_9 (+ חֶסֶד וְרַחֲמִים *loyalty and compassion*) 1QM 11_{14} 1QH fr. 5_{10} (both אמתכה), *judgments of* 4QapPs^b 76_{13}, רַב־חֶסֶד וֶאֱמֶת *great of*, i.e. in, *loyalty and reliability* Ex 34_6 Ps 86_{15} 1QH 16_{16}.

נחלת אמת *inheritance of trustworthiness*, i.e. dependable inheritance 4QpPs^a 1.4_{12}, בת *daughter of* 4QRit Mar 2_3, יחד *community of* 1QS 2_{24} (+ עֲנָוָה *humility*, חֶסֶד *loyalty*, צֶדֶק *righteousness*) 2_{26} ([י]חד), עִיר־ *city of* Zc 8_3 (הָאֱמֶת), עתרות ... אמת *abundance of ... reliability* 4QBark^a 2.1_9 (|| שָׁלוֹם *peace*), שפט *judge of* 4QapPs^b 76_9 (+ עד נאמן *faithful witness*), דיין *judge of* GnzPs 4_{12} (|| צֶדֶק) 11QPs^a 24_6 (דין האמת), מוכיחי *ones who reprove (in respect) of* 1QH fr. 2.1_6, גמולי *benefits of*, i.e. due to 1Q36 15_3, אַנְשֵׁי אֱמֶת *men of trustworthiness*, i.e. trustworthy men Ex 18_{21}=11QT 57_8 (+ יִרְאֵי אֱלֹהִים *fear God*, שֹׂנְאֵי בָצַע *hate bribery*) 1QH 14_2 1QpHab 7_{10} (+ עושי התורה *those who do the law*) 4Q298 3_7.

רום אמת[ו] *height of his trustworthiness* 1.1_{20}, חוקי אמת *statutes of trustworthiness* 4QTNaph 4_5, אמתו *of his trustworthiness* 1QS 1_{15}, אמתכה *of your trustworthiness* 4QD^b $_{11}$ (|| קֹדֶשׁ *holiness*), פעלות אמת *deeds of trustworthiness* 4Q416 4_{13}, מעשי אמתיו *deeds of his trustworthiness* 1QS 1_{19} 1QM $13_{1.2}$ 11QShirShab 2_5 (אמת[ו]), רוב אמתכה *abundance of your reliability* 1QH 11_{29} (|| חֶסֶד *loyalty*), מ[קור] *source of* 18_{13}(Licht), מעשי *actions of* 1QM 13_9 14_{12} 1QH 1_{30}, ברכות אמת *blessings of trustworthiness*, i.e. trustworthy blessings 4QBer^a 3.1_4, כָּל־הָאֱמֶת *all the reliability* Gn 32_{11}, [כו]ל אמתו *all his reliability* 4QBer^a 3.1_8.

<PREP> לֶאֱמֶת *dependably*, + יצא hi. *issue* judgment Is 42_3, חבא *conceal* secret 1QS $4_{6(mg)}$.

בְּ of accompaniment, *with*, i.e. dependably, + שׁפט *judge* Pr 29_{14}, ישׁב *sit* Is 16_5 (|| חֶסֶד *loyalty*), נטע *plant* Jr 32_{41} (+ בְּכָל־לִבִּי וּבְכָל־נַפְשִׁי *with all my heart and with all my soul*), נתן *give* recompense Is 61_8 (+ וּבְרִית עוֹלָם אֶכְרוֹת לָהֶם *and an everlasting covenant shall*

I make with them), ענה *answer* Ps 69$_{14}$ (+ חֶסֶד), נגד hi. *declare* law 11QT 56$_4$.

בְּ of instrument, *by,* + צמת hi. *destroy* Ps 54$_7$, עשה *make, do* 2QapMoses 1$_{2(Baillet)}$ ([ע ש ה]; || אֱמוּנָה *reliability*), pass. *be done* Ps 111$_8$ (|| יָשָׁר *upright [one];* mss יוֹשֶׁר *uprightness*), כפר pu. *be atoned for* Pr 16$_6$ (|| חֶסֶד *loyalty*), *because of,* + עזר *help* 1QM 13$_{15}$ (לְ[עזו]ר, Yadin; :: אַשְׁמָה *culpability*), צדק hi. *justify* 4QShir^b 63.3$_4$ (:: אַשְׁמָה).

הלך בְּ htp. *walk in the presence of* Ps 26$_3$ (+ חֶסֶד *loyalty;* perh. אֱמֶת = *truth,* as §3) 4QapPs^b 47$_2$, שוה בְּ pi. *be equivalent to* (of wealth) 1QH 15$_{23}$, דבק בְּ *cleave to* 16$_7$, ידה בְּ *proclaim* 4QShirShab^d 1.1$_{38}$, כול מעשיהם באמתכה *all their works are in (accordance with) your dependability* 1QH 6$_9$ (+ חֶסֶד; perh. אֱמֶת = *truth,* as §3), באּ[מ]ת בריתכ[ה] *in the truth of your covenant* 4Q414 1.2$_3$.

שׂבר אֶל pi. *hope for* Is 38$_{18}$, ידע אֶל hi. *make known concerning* 38$_{19}$.

עַל *on account of* Ps 115$_1$ 138$_2$ (both || חֶסֶד *loyalty*).

אחר אמת לא ירצה *after truth he does not desire,* i.e. he is not zealous for truth 4Q424 1$_9$.

<COLL> חֶסֶד וֶאֱמֶת *loyalty and reliability* Gn 24$_{27}$ (חַסְדּוֹ וַאֲמִתּוֹ) 24$_{49}$ 32$_{11}$ (חֲסָדִים) 47$_{29}$ Ex 34$_6$ Jos 2$_{14}$ 2 S 2$_6$ 15$_{20}$ Ps 25$_{10}$ 40$_{11.12}$ (both חַסְדְּךָ וַאֲמִתְּךָ) 57$_4$ (חַסְדּוֹ וַאֲמִתּוֹ) 61$_8$ 85$_{11}$ (חֶסֶד־וֶאֱמֶת) 86$_{15}$ 89$_{15}$ Pr 3$_3$ 14$_{22}$ 16$_6$ 20$_{28}$ 1QH 16$_{16}$ 11QPs^a 26$_{10}$, חֶסֶד ... אֱמֶת *reliability ... loyalty* Ho 4$_1$ Mc 7$_{20}$, אֱמֶת וּמִשְׁפָּט *trustworthiness and judgment* Ps 111$_7$ GnzPs 1$_7$, הַדְּבָרִים וְהָאֱמֶת *the things and,* i.e. betokening, *(the) trustworthiness* 2 C 32$_1$.

2. stability of political conditions, <SUBJ> היה *be* 2 K 20$_{19}$||Is 39$_8$ (+ בְּיָמָי *in my days;* || שָׁלוֹם *peace*). <CSTR> שְׁלוֹם אֱמֶת *peace of stability,* i.e. lasting peace Jr 14$_{13}$ (mss שָׁלוֹם וֶאֱמֶת *peace and stability*), דִּבְרֵי שָׁלוֹם וֶאֱמֶת *words of,* i.e. concerning, *peace and stability* Est 9$_{30}$.

3. truth, correctness of words, statements, etc., <SUBJ> היה *be* Dt 22$_{20}$ 2 S 7$_{28}$ 1 K 10$_6$ (all three + דָּבָר *word*) Is 59$_{15}$ (+ עדר ni. *be lacking*), בוא hi. *bring* Ps 43$_3$, יצא *go out* GnzPs 4$_{20}$ (|| אֱמוּנָה *faithfulness*) 1QS 4$_{19}$, נחה hi. *lead* Ps 43$_3$, כשׁל *stumble* Is 59$_{14}$ (+ בָּרְחוֹב *in the street,* || נְכֹחָה *uprightness*).

<NOM CL> וְיִבָּחֲנוּ דִּבְרֵיכֶם הַאֱמֶת אִתְּכֶם *that your words might be examined (to see if there) is truth with you,* i.e. if you are telling the truth Gn 42$_{16}$, אֱמֶת הַדָּבָר *the word,* i.e. message, report, *was true* Dn 10$_1$ 2 C 9$_5$, דְּבַר־י׳ בְּפִיךָ אֱמֶת *the word of Y. in your mouth is true* 1 K 17$_{24}$ (or אֱמֶת = *really,* as §5), אמת פיכה *your mouth is,* i.e. utters, *truth* 1QH 11$_7$, תּוֹרָתְךָ אֱמֶת *your teaching is truth(ful)* Ps 119$_{142}$ (|| צֶדֶק *righteousness*), מִצְוֺתֶיךָ אֱמֶת *your commandments are truth(ful)* 119$_{151}$, רֹאשׁ־דְּבָרְךָ אֱמֶת *the head* (perh. sum, beginning) *of your message is correct* 119$_{160}$ (ms דבריך *your words*), perh. מאז אמתו *his truth is from of old* 4QM^a fr. 11.1$_{10}$.

<OBJ> ידע *know* 1QH 6$_{12}$ (|| כָּבוֹד *glory*), דרשׁ *seek* 4Q416 4$_7$, דבר *speak* Ps 15$_2$ (+ בִּלְבָבוֹ *in his heart*), pi. *speak* 1 K 22$_{16}$||2 C 18$_{15}$ (+ רַק *only*) Jr 9$_4$ Zc 8$_{16}$ 4QpPs^a 1.4$_4$, הגה *utter* Pr 8$_7$, נגד hi. *declare* Dn 11$_2$, ידה hi. *praise* Ps 71$_{22}$ 4QM^a fr. 5$_{1(Baillet)}$ ([להודות]), גדל hi. *magnify* Ps 138$_2$ (if em. אִמְרָתֶךָ *your word*), יפע hi. *cause to shine* 1QH 11$_{26}$ (or perh. subj., *shine*), חבא pi. *hide* 9$_{24}$, תעב pi. *abominate* 1QS 4$_{25}$, שׁלח *send* Ps 43$_3$ (|| אוֹר *light*), שׁלך hi. *throw* Dn 8$_{12}$ (perh. em. ho. *be thrown;* + אַרְצָה *to the ground*), קנה *buy* Pr 23$_{23}$ (+ חָכְמָה וּמוּסָר וּבִינָה *wisdom and discipline and insight*), מכר *sell* 23$_{23}$, נחל *inherit* 4Q416 7$_6$, ברר *choose* 4Q372 1$_{18}$.

<CSTR> אמת אל *truth of,* i.e. about, *God* 1QS 3$_6$, תבל *of (the) world* 4$_{19}$, עולם *of eternity* 9$_3$ 1QSb 2$_{28}$ (עול[ם]), כבודו *of his glory* 1QH 3$_{34}$, חוקי אל *of God's statutes* 1QS 1$_{12}$.

דֶּרֶךְ אֱמֶת *way of truth,* i.e. right way Gn 24$_{48}$ 1QS 4$_{17}$ (דרכי) CD 3$_{15}$ (דרכי אמתו; || צֶדֶק *righteousness,* רָצוֹן *pleasure,* כָּבוֹד *glory,* קֹדֶשׁ *holiness*) 4QBark^a 1$_6$ (דרכי [אמת]) 4Q416 10.2$_{15}$ (דרכ׳), עֵד *witness of* Jr 42$_5$ (+ נֶאֱמָן *trustworthy*) Pr 14$_{25}$ 1QS 8$_6$ (עדי) 4Q251 3$_8$ ([עדי אמת]), שְׂפַת־ *lip of,* i.e. that speaks Pr 12$_{19}$ (:: שֶׁקֶר *falsehood*), כְּתָב *book of* Dn 10$_{21}$, תּוֹרַת *law of,* i.e. correct teaching Ml 2$_6$ (+ עַוְלָה לֹא־נִמְצָא *perversion was not found*) Ne 9$_{13}$ (תּוֹרוֹת), דְּבַר־ *word of* Ps 45$_5$ (עַל־דְּבַר־ *for the cause of*) 119$_{43}$ Ec 12$_{10}$ (דִּבְרֵי).

אל אמת *God of truth* 1QH 15$_{25}$ 4Q416 3$_5$, רוח *spirit of* 1QS 3$_{19}$ (רוחות האמת; :: עָוֶל *injustice*) 4$_{21.23}$ (:: עָוֶל) 1QM 13$_{10}$ (both רוחי) 4QCat^a 12.1$_5$ 4QShirShab^f 17$_3$ (רוחי; || דַּעַת *knowledge,* בִּינָה *understanding*) 11QapPs^a

4_{13} ([רוח א]מת]), תועבת *abomination of* 1QS 4_{17}, סוד *counsel of* (sometimes perh. סוֹד = יְסוֹד *foundation* of) 1QH 1_{27} (האמת) 2_{10} (|| בִּינָה) $5_{9.26}$ 10_4 ([א]מתכה]) $11_{4.9}$ (|| פֶּלֶא *wonder;* both אמתכה) 11_{16} 4QBer^a 1_7 (|| קֹדֶשׁ *holiness*) 4Q416 8_6, מוסד *foundation of* 1QS 5_5, משקלת *level,* i.e. criterion, *of* 1QH 6_{26} ([א]מת]; others א]בן *stone;* || מִשְׁפָּט *judgment*), איפת אמת *ephah of* 4Q416 1_9, עבודת *service of* 1QpHab 7_{12} (האמת) 4QShir^b 63.2_4, עצת *council of* 1QS 3_6.

אִמְרֵי אֱמֶת *words of truth, true words* Pr 22_{21} (+ קֹשְׁטְ *truth*), בני אמת *children,* i.e. disciples, *of truth* 1QS $4_{5.6}$ 1QM 16_{17} + Sup ([בנ]י) 17_8 (אמתו) 1QH 6_{29} (א[מ]תו) 7_{30} 9_{35} ([בנ]י) 10_{27} $11_{11(mg)}$ (all four אמתכה) 4Q525 1_2 ([בני אמת]) 4QD$^{b}_{7}$ (אמתו), חסדי *pious ones of* 4QBer^a 1_8, בחירי *elect ones of* 4Q416 4_{10}, חוזי *seers of* CD 2_{13} 4QToh D$_7$ (ח[ו]זי אמ[תו]) 4QBer^a 3.2_{12} ([חוזי אמ]תו), רזי פלא ואמת *secrets of wonder and truth,* i.e. wonderful secrets of the truth 1QS 9_{18}.

מדת האמת *the measure,* i.e. criterion, *of truth* 1QS 8_4 (|| עֵת *time*), בית *house of* 5_6 8_9 (|| תמים ואמת *of perfection and truth*), לשון *tongue of* 4Q183 1.2_6, שמע *report of* 1QMyst 1.1_9, שם *name of,* i.e. the true name 1QpHab 8_9, תולדות *generations of* 1QS 3_{19} (:: עָוֶל *injustice*), ברכו[ת האמת] *blessings of truth* 4QJub^d 1.2_{33}.

ישור אמתכה *uprightness of your truth* 1QH 6_{10}, גורל *lot of* 1QM 13_{12}, מלאך אמתו *angel of his truth* 1QS 3_{24} 4QCat^a 12.1_7 ([מלא]ך), עדוות אמתו *testimonies of his truth* CD 20_{31} (+ צֶדֶק), נדבי א[מתו] *dedicated ones of,* i.e. those dedicated to, *his truth* 11QapPs^a 4_3.

<APP> אֲמָרִים אֱמֶת *words, truth,* i.e. true words Pr 22_{21}, שִׁמְךָ אֲמִתֶּךָ *your name, your truth,* i.e. your true name Ps 138_2 (if em. אִמְרָתֶךָ *your word*).

<PREP> לְ of direction, *to,* + שׁוּב *turn* intrans. 1QS 6_{15} (:: עָוֶל *wrong*), נפל hi. *cause to fall* 1QM 13_{10}, *with the goal of* 1QS 9_3, כול הנדבים לאמתו *all who devote themselves to his truth* 1_{11}, sim. 5_{10}.

בְּ of place, accompaniment, *in, with* 4Q416 5_2 4QJub^a 1_{17} ([באמת]), + דרך *tread* Si 51_{15}, hi. *lead* Ps 25_5, הלך pi. *walk* 86_{11} 4Q416 5_{11}, כון ni. *be established* 1QS 8_5 1QH 4_{14} fr. 2.1_{15} 4Q251 3_8 ([באמת]), hi. *establish* Si 37_{15} 1QH 7_{14} (|| לִמּוּד *teaching*), קום hi. *establish* 1QSb 3_{24}, הום *roar* 1QH 3_{34}, יחד *be united* 1QS 3_7, שׁעע pilp. *delight* 4Q416 4_{12}, נחלת איש באמת *share of a man in the truth* 1QS 4_{24} (|| צֶדֶק *righteousness*), פרשׂ *spread* 4Q416 5_4 ([פ]רשם).

בְּ of instrument, *by,* + ברר pi. *purify* 1QS 1_{12} 4_{20}, שׂכל hi. *make wise* Dn 9_{13} 1QH 7_{26} (|| רזי פל[אכה] *secrets of your wonder,* i.e. your wonderful secrets), סמך *support* 9_{32} (|| רוח קודשכה *your spirit of holiness,* i.e. your holy spirit), ידע *know* 9_{10} 10_{20} ([באמ]תכה, || כָּבוֹד *glory*), שׂמח pi. *gladden* 11_{30} (|| צְדָקָה *righteousness*).

תכן בְּ pi. *measure according to* 4Q181 2_8 4Q416 6_6, תמך בְּ *rely on* 1QH 7_{20} (|| בְּרִית *covenant*), שׁען בְּ ni. *rely on* 10_{17}, רדף בְּ *pursue* GnzPs 3_4 (ואדריף || צְדָקָה *righteousness*), לבגוד באמת *to betray the truth* 1QS 7_{18}.

כְּ *according to* 1QH 7_{28}.

נפל מִן hi. *cause* name *to fall from* 4QD^a 6.2_{10}.

עַל *upon* 4Q416 7_6.

תשכב עם האמת *you shall lie down with the truth* 4Q416 10.2_8.

<COLL> as adv., *truthfully* (but perh. sometimes *reliably,* §1), יְדַבֵּר דְּבָרִי אֱמֶת *may he speak my message truthfully* Jr 23_{28}, נִשְׁבַּע י׳ לְדָוִד אֱמֶת לֹא־יָשׁוּב מִמֶּנָּה *Y. swore to David truthfully; he will not turn back from it* Ps 132_{11}, לשפט אמת *to judge truthfully* 4QapPs^b 76_{12}; יֹאמְרוּ אֱמֶת *they say, It is true* Is 43_9.

4. sincerity, honesty; of motives, <CSTR> אוֹת אֱמֶת *sign of (a person's) sincerity* Jos 2_{12}.

<PREP> בְּ of accompaniment, *with,* i.e. sincerely, + משׁח *anoint* Jg 9_{15}, עשׂה *do,* i.e. behave $9_{16.19}$ (+ בְּתָמִים *with integrity*), הלך *go* 1 K 2_4 (+ בְּכָל־לְבָבָם וּבְכָל־נַפְשָׁם *with all their heart and with all their soul*) 3_6 (+ בִּצְדָקָה וּבְיִשְׁרַת לֵבָב *with righteousness and with uprightness of heart*) 2 K 20_3||Is 38_3 (htp.; + בְּלֵב שָׁלֵם *with a full heart*), עבד *worship* Jos 24_{14} (+ בְּתָמִים *with integrity*) 1 S 12_{24} (+ בְּכָל־לְבַבְכֶם *with all your heart*) 1QH 16_7 (+ לב שלם *full heart*), שׁען ni. *lean* on Y. Is 10_{20}, זכר hi. *invoke* Y. 48_1 (|| צְדָקָה *righteousness*), שׁבע ni. *swear* by Y. Jr 4_2 (|| מִשְׁפָּט *justice,* צְדָקָה), קרא *call upon* Y. Ps 145_{18}, יכח hi. *reprove* 1QS 5_{25} (א[מ]ת; || עֲנָוָה *humility,* אַהֲבַת חֶסֶד *love of loyalty*).

5. genuineness, reality of a thing, <NOM CL> וּמַרְאֵה הָעֶרֶב ... אֱמֶת הוּא *and the evening vision ... was* *genuine*, i.e. was a true representation of what would happen Dn 8$_{26}$, ואמת המשא *and the prophecy was genuine* 1QMyst 1.1$_{8}$ (|| כון ni. *be established*).

<CSTR> זֶרַע אֱמֶת *seed of genuineness*, i.e. genuine seed Jr 2$_{21}$, שֶׂכֶר *reward of* Pr 11$_{18}$, אֵל *God of* Ps 31$_{6}$, אֱלֹהֵי *God of* 2 C 15$_{3}$.

מטעת אמת *planting of genuineness*, i.e. genuine plant(ing) 1QH 8$_{10}$ 4QJub^{d} 1.2$_{30}$ (מטעת ה[אמת]), צדק *righteousness of* 1QS 4$_{2}$, צדקת *righteousness of* 11$_{14}$, דעת *knowledge of* 9$_{17}$ (|| צֶדֶק *righteousness*) 1QH 10$_{29}$ (but perh. דעת אמת = *knowledge of the truth*, as §3) 4QShirShab^{d} 1.1$_{18}$ ([אמ]תו) 4QShirShab^{f} 19$_{4}$ (|| צֶדֶק).

<APP> אֱלֹהִים אֱמֶת *genuine God* Jr 10$_{10}$ (+ אֱלֹהִים חַיִּים *living God*).

<PREP> בְּ of accompaniment, *with*, i.e. genuinely, really, + היה *be* Zc 8$_{8}$ (|| צְדָקָה *righteousness*), שׁלח *send* prophet (of Y.) Jr 26$_{15}$ 28$_{9}$, ידע *be familiar with* Si 7$_{20(A)}$, בושׁ *be ashamed* Si 42$_{1(B)}$, בייש באמת *truly ashamed* 42$_{1(M)}$, זהיר באמת *really careful* Si 42$_{8}$.

<COLL> as adv., *really*, וְהִנֵּה אֱמֶת נָכוֹן הַדָּבָר *and if the matter really is established* Dt 13$_{15}$=17$_{4}$=11QT 55$_{5=20}$, אֱמֶת שָׂם אָשָׁם נַפְשׁוֹ *he really offered his soul (as) a guilt offering* Is 53$_{10}$ (if em. אִם־תָּשִׂים *if you offer*), אמת נע[שתה] *it really happened* 1QDM 1$_{11(Milik)}$.

Also 4Q487 2$_{8}$ 1QS 1$_{26}$ 1QM 1$_{16}$ 4QpIsa^{a} 2$_{5}$ 11QMelch 1.1$_{21}$ 1QH 2$_{4}$ (mg צֶדֶק) 2$_{14}$ 6$_{25}$ 13$_{7}$ 16$_{4}$ 18$_{14}$ 1QH fr. 1$_{9}$ 26$_{2}$ 1QpPs 2$_{1}$ ([אמ]תו) 4QpPs^{a} 1.3$_{17}$ 6QHymn 6$_{4}$ 5Q17 5$_{2}$ 1Q36 15$_{2}$ 4QShir^{b} 1$_{10}$ 4QShirShab^{a} 3.2$_{3}$ 4QShirShab^{d} 1.1$_{12}$ 4QShirShab^{f} 3.1$_{12}$ 13$_{4}$ 20.2$_{5}$ (+ צֶדֶק *righteousness*) 23.1$_{13}$ (א[מ]תו) 4QBark^{c}3 ([א]מתם], Weinfeld [אש]מתם]) 4Q416 5$_{3}$ 7$_{7}$ ([בא]מת) 7$_{9}$ 4QapPs^{a} 1.2$_{8}$.

<SYN> §§1, 3, 4, 5 צְדָקָה *righteousness*; §§1, 3, 5 צֶדֶק *righteousness*; §§1, 3, 4 מִשְׁפָּט *judgment*; §§1, 2 שָׁלוֹם *peace*; §§1, 3 חָכְמָה *wisdom*; בְּרִית *covenant*; §§1, 4 אַהֲבַת חֶסֶד *love of loyalty*, עֲנָוָה *humility*; §§3, 4 תָּמִים *perfection*; §1 חֶסֶד *loyalty*.

<ANT> §3 עָוֶל *injustice*.

→ אמן *be trustworthy*; אֲמִתַּי *Amittai*.

[אַמְתַּחַת] 15 n.f. **sack**—cstr. אַמְתַּחַת; sf. אַמְתַּחְתִּי, אַמְתַּחְתּוֹ; pl. cstr. אַמְתְּחֹת; sf. אַמְתְּחֹתֵינוּ, אַמְתְּחֹתֵיכֶם—

<OBJ> פתח *open* Gn 43$_{21}$ 44$_{11}$, ירד hi. *take down* 44$_{11}$, מלא pi. fill 44$_{1}$. **<CSTR>** אַמְתַּחַת הַקָּטֹן *sack of the young(est one)* Gn 44$_{2}$, אַמְתַּחַת בִּנְיָמִן *Benjamin's sack* 44$_{12}$, אַמְתְּחֹת הָאֲנָשִׁים *sacks of the men* 44$_{1}$; פִּי אַמְתַּחְתּוֹ *mouth of his sack* 42$_{27}$ 43$_{12}$ (אַמְתְּחֹתֵיכֶם) 43$_{21}$ 44$_{1.2}$ (אַמְתַּחַת) 44$_{8}$ (אַמְתְּחֹתֵינוּ). **<PREP>** בְּ *in(to)* Gn 42$_{28}$, + מצא ni. *be found* 44$_{12}$, שׁוב *go back* 43$_{18}$ (Sam ho. *be returned*), שׂים *place* 43$_{22}$, נתן *give*, i.e. place 43$_{23}$.

אֲמִתַּי 2 pr.n.m. **Amittai**, father of Jonah the prophet, 2 K 14$_{25}$ Jon 1$_{1}$.

→ אֱמֶת *truth*..

אָן 42 interrog. adv. **where?**—+ ה- of direction אָנָה, אָנֶה—**1. where?, whither?**, usu. with ה- (except 1 S 10$_{14}$ 27$_{10[mss]}$), with verb, עשׂה *do*, i.e. work Ru 2$_{19}$ (+ אֵיפֹה *where?*), בוא *come* Gn 37$_{30}$, הלך *go* 16$_{8}$ (+ אֵי־מִזֶּה *whence?*) 32$_{18}$ (+ לְמִי *to whom?*) Jos 2$_{5}$ (+ ידע *know*) Jg 19$_{17}$ (both + מֵאַיִן *whence?*) 1 S 10$_{14}$ 1 K 2$_{42}$ 2 K 5$_{25}$ Zc 2$_{6}$ Ps 139$_{7}$ Ca 6$_{1}$ Ne 2$_{16}$ (+ ידע *know*; + מָה *what?*), hi. *bring* 2 S 13$_{13}$ Zc 5$_{10}$, יצא *go out* 1 K 2$_{36}$ Jr 15$_{2}$ (+ לְ of direction, *to*), פנה *turn* Ca 6$_{1}$, ברח *flee* Ps 139$_{7}$, עלה *go up* Dt 1$_{28}$ 2 S 2$_{1}$, נפל *fall* 2 K 6$_{6}$, פשׁט *raid* 1 S 27$_{10(mss)}$ (MT אַל *not*), יעד ho. *be intended* to turn Ezk 21$_{21}$ (+ שׂים hi. *direct* sword), עזב *leave* glory Is 10$_{3}$ (+ עַל־מִי *to whom?*).

<COLL> אָנֶה וָאָנָה *(to) anywhere at all* 1 K 2$_{36.42}$ 2 K 5$_{25}$.

2. מֵאָן **whence?**, מאן גֵּחֲזִי *whence*, i.e. where have you come from, *Gehazi?* 2 K 5$_{25(Kt)}$ (Qr, mss מֵאַיִן *whence?*).

3. עַד־אָנָה **how long?** (Jb 8$_{2}$ עַד־אָן), with verb, מאן pi. *refuse* Ex 16$_{28}$, שׁכח *forget* Ps 13$_{2}$, נאץ pi. *despise* Nm 14$_{11}$, יגה hi. *weary* Jb 19$_{2}$, דכא pi. *crush* 19$_{2}$, אמן hi. *believe* Nm 14$_{11}$, סתר hi. *hide* face Ps 13$_{2}$, שׁית *place*, i.e. take counsel 13$_{3}$, רום *be high* 13$_{3}$, רפה htp. *be relaxed* Jos 18$_{3}$, שׁקט *be quiet* Jr 47$_{6}$, שׁוע pi. *call out* Hb 1$_{2}$, זעק *call out* 1$_{2}$, הות pol. *shout* Ps 62$_{4}$, מלל pi. *speak* Jb 8$_{2}$.

4. עַד־אָנָה **how long until?**, with verb, תְּשִׂימוּן קִנְצֵי לְמִלִּין *how long until you put an end to words?* Jb 18$_{2}$.

אֵן, see בֵּן.

אֹן, see אוֹן III.

אָנָּא 13.0.2 interj. **oh!, please**—אָנָּה—addressee usu. Y. (Gn 50_{17} Joseph), **1. oh!,** expressing sorrow, etc., at past actions, with verb, חטא *sin* Ex 32_{31} (Sam הִנֵּה *behold*) Dn 9_4; introducing nom cl., Jon 4_2 Ps 116_{16} (mss lack אָנָּה). **2.** perh. **please,** with verb expressing action desired, usu. from person implored, also from another source (Jon 1_{14} Ne $1_{5.11}$ 4QDibHam[a] 1.6_{10}), עשׂה *do* 4QDibHam[a] 1.2_7 (+ נָא *please*), נשׂא *raise*, i.e. forgive Gn 50_{17} (+ נָא), ישׁע hi. *save* Ps 118_{25} (+ נָא), צלח hi. *forgive* 118_{25} (+ נָא), מלט pi. *rescue* 116_4, זכר *remember* 2 K 20_3||Is 38_3 (+ נָא), היה *be* attentive (of Y.'s ear) Ne $1_{5.11}$ (both + נָא), שׁוב *go back* (of Y.'s wrath) 4QDibHam[a] 1.6_{10} (+ נָא *please*), אבד not *die* (of intercessor and others) Jon 1_{14}.

<COLL> אָנָּא/אָנָּה י׳ *oh!, Y.* 2 K 20_3||Is 38_3 Jon 1_4 4_2 Ps $116_{4.16}$ $118_{25.25}$ Ne 1_5, אָנָּא אֲדֹנָי *oh!, my Lord* Dn 9_4 Ne 1_{11} 4QDibHam[a] 1.2_7 (אדו[ני]) 1.6_{10} (אדוני).

אנה I 2 vb. **mourn—Qal** Pf. + waw וְאָנוּ; ptc. אוֹנִים—<SUBJ> פֶּתַח *entrance* of Jerusalem Is 3_{26} (|| אבל *mourn*), דַּיָּג fisherman 19_8 (|| אבל).

→ אֳנָה *distress*, אֲנִיָּה *mourning*.

אנה II 4.1 vb. **happen—Pi.** Pf. אִנָּה; impf. Si יאננה—**allow to happen, allow to come,** <SUBJ> Y. Ex 21_{13} Ps 88_8 (if em. עִנִּיתָ *you have afflicted me* to אִנִּיתָ לִּי *you have allowed to come to me*), Si 15_{13}. <OBJ> אִישׁ *man* Ex 21_{13}, מִשְׁבָּר *breaker* Ps 88_8 (if em.), רָעָה *evil* Si 15_{13}. <PREP> לְ *to* person Ex 21_{13} Ps 88_8 (if em.) Si 15_{13}.

Pu. Impf. תְּאֻנֶּה, יְאֻנֶּה—**happen, come,** <SUBJ> רָעָה *evil* Ps 91_{10} (+ קרב *approach*), אָוֶן *iniquity* Pr 12_{21}. <PREP> לְ *to* person Pr 12_{21}; אֶל to *person* Ps 91_{10}.

Htp. Ptc. מִתְאַנֶּה—**seek occasion** to cause trouble, מִתְאַנֶּה הוּא לִי *he* (king of Aram) *is creating an occasion against me* (king of Israel) 2 K 5_7.

אָנֶה, see אָן.

אָנָה, see אָנָּא.

אָנֶה, see אָן.

[אֹנֶה] 3.0.2 n.m. **distress**—perh. אוֹן IV or אוֹנִי/אֹנִי; sf. אֹנִי (אוֹנִי), Q אונה, אונמה; pl. אוֹנִים—**distress, mourning, weariness,** <OBJ> זכר *remember* Ps 89_{48} (if em. זְכָר־אֲנִי מֶה־חָלֶד perh. *remember, what duration I am* to זְכָר־אֹנִי יְמֵי־הַחֶלֶד *remember my distress, the days of my duration*). <CSTR> בֶּן־אוֹנִי *son of my distress* (Benjamin) Gn 35_{18}, לֶחֶם אוֹנִים *bread of mourning* Ezk $24_{17.22}$ (both if em. אֲנָשִׁים *men*) Ho 9_4.

<PREP> לֹא־אָכַלְתִּי בְאֹנִי *I did not eat* of tithe *in my distress*, i.e. while mourning Dt 26_{14}; ... לוא יואכלו לאונמה *they will not eat* of tithe ... *in their weariness*, i.e. during working days 11QT 43_{16}.

Also 4QPrFêtes[c] 3_1 (אונה, appar. אוֹנָה).

→ אנה *mourn*.

[אֲנוּ] 1.0.17 pronoun **we**, with ref. to Johanan Jr $42_{6(Kt)}$, Jezaniah $42_{6(Kt)}$ (or em. עֲזַרְיָה *Azariah*), עַם *people* $42_{6(Kt)}$, שַׂר *officer* $42_{6(Kt)}$, עבר ptc. *one who passes (into)* covenant 1QS 1_{25}, כֹּהֵן *priest* 1QM $13_{7.12}$ $14_{8.12}$, לֵוִי *Levite* $13_{7.12}$ $14_{8.12}$, זָקֵן *elder* $13_{7.12}$ $14_{8.12}$, community 4QD[b]$_{13.14}$; elsewhere uncertain.

<SUBJ> חיה *live* 4QPrFêtes[b] 39_1, שׁלח *send* Jr $42_{6(Kt)}$ (Qr אֲנַחְנוּ *we*), עמד *stand* 4QM[a] fr. 14_3 (עו[מ]דים), קום hi. *establish* 4QD[b]$_{14}$ (:: אַתָּה *you*), פשׁע *sin* 1QS 1_{25}, חטא *sin* 1_{25}, רשׁע hi. *do evil* 1_{25}, שׂמח *rejoice* 1QM 13_{12}, שׂישׂ *rejoice* 13_{12}, גיל *rejoice* 13_{12}, הלל *praise* 14_{12}, ברך pi. *bless* 1QM $14_{8(Yadin)}$ (נ[ברכה]), רום pol. *exalt* 14_{12} 4QPrQuot 11_3, ידה hi. *praise* 1QLitPr[b] 1.1_6.

<NOM CL> אנו בעולה מרחם *we are in iniquity from the womb* 4QPrFêtes[a] $1_{2(Baillet)}$ (AHL אֲנִי *I*), אנו עם [עו]לם *we are the people of eternity* $13_{7(Yadin)}$, אנו עם פדותכה וצון מרעיתך *we are your redeemed people and the sheep of your pasture* 4QD[b]$_{13}$.

<APP> אנו גורל אמתכה *we, the lot of your truth* 1QM 13_{12}, אנו שא[ר עמכה] *we, the remnant of your people* $14_{8(Yadin)}$, אנו עם קודשכה *we, the people of your holiness* 14_{12}, sim. 4QPrQuot 1_{20} 11_3 (both קודשו *his holiness*).

<COLL> אנו [וא]בותינו *we and our fathers* 1QS 1_{25},

אנו הננו *we, behold we* are standing 4QM^{a} fr. 14$_{3}$, וגם אנו *and we too* 4QPrFêtes^{c} 53$_{1}$.

Also 4QPrQuot 28$_{5}$ 29$_{20}$ 4QPrFêtes^{c} 16$_{8}$ 4QDibHam^{c} 31$_{2}$.

→ אֲנַחְנוּ *we*.

אֱנוֹשׁ I $_{42.19.25}$ n.m. **person**—Q אינוש; cstr. אֱנוֹשׁ—**1.** individual **man, human being,** <SUBJ> עשׂה *do* Is 56$_{2}$ (+ בֶּן־אָדָם *human being*), שׁמר *watch* Jr 20$_{10}$, 1QH 9$_{15}$ (|| גֶּבֶר *man*), ראה *see* Jb 10$_{4}$, ידע *know* 28$_{13}$, הגה *meditate* Si 14$_{20}$, הום *murmer* 4Q416 7$_{11}$ (+ [בן אדם]), בין ni. *have understanding* Si 34$_{19.19}$, כון hi. *establish* 1QS 11$_{10}$ 1QH 15$_{13}$ (both + אָדָם *human being*), ספר pi. *recount* 1QH 12$_{5}$, יכל *be able* 1QH 15$_{13}$, עצל ni. *be lazy* 4Q416 7$_{11}$, חטא *sin* Si 15$_{20}$.

<OBJ> עצב *grieve* Si 14$_{1}$, צוה pi. *command* 15$_{20}$ (+ אִישׁ *man*), יכח hi. *reprove* Jb 5$_{17}$, שׁגה hi. *lead astray* 4QWiles 1$_{17}$ (+ בני איש *human beings*).

<CSTR> אֱנוֹשׁ שְׁלוֹמִי *man of my peace*, i.e. my friend Jr 20$_{10}$, מפעל אנוש *deed of a person* Si 15$_{19(B)}$ (A איש *of a person*), רוח *spirit of* 1QH 13$_{2}$, לב *heart of* Si 13$_{25}$ 37$_{14}$, לְבַב־ *heart of* Is 13$_{7}$ (לְבָב) Ps 104$_{15.15}$ (or em. לְבַב־אֱנוֹשׁ to לְבָבוֹ *his heart*), די *sufficiency of* Si 34$_{19.19}$, בני *children of* 1QH 13$_{4}$, כֹּל *all of* Jr 20$_{10}$.

<APP> אַתָּה אֱנוֹשׁ כְּעֶרְכִּי אַלּוּפִי וּמְיֻדָּעִי *you, a man of my own rank,* lit. according to my valuation, *my companion and my familiar friend* Ps 55$_{14}$.

<PREP> לְ *to, for,* Si 34$_{27}$, + שׁוב hi. *restore* Jb 33$_{26}$ Si 32$_{24}$ (|| אָדָם *human being*), בזה *have contempt* Si 7$_{11}$, נאוה לְ *seemly for* Si 10$_{18}$.

רוּחַ־הִיא בֶאֱנוֹשׁ *it is the spirit in a person* Jb 32$_{8}$, תלל בְּ hi. *trifle with* 13$_{9}$.

מִן of comparison, *than,* + רבה *be greater* Jb 33$_{12}$, צדק *be righteous* 1QH 9$_{15}$.

<COLL> אֱנוֹשׁ כְּעֶרְכִּי *a man of my own rank* Ps 55$_{14}$, אַשְׁרֵי אֱנוֹשׁ *blessed is the man* Is 56$_{2}$ Jb 5$_{17}$ Si 14$_{1.20}$.

2. frail **mortal,** <SUBJ> עשׂה *do* 4QapPs^{b} 31$_{6}$, צדק *be righteous* Jb 4$_{17}$ (|| גֶּבֶר *human being*) 9$_{2}$ 25$_{4}$ (|| ילד pass. *one born*), זכה *be pure* 15$_{14}$ (|| ילד pass.), יסף hi. *do again* Ps 10$_{18}$, ערץ *terrorize* 10$_{18}$, צוץ *flourish* 103$_{15}$.

<NOM CL> מָה־אֱנוֹשׁ *what is a mortal?* Ps 8$_{5}$ (+ בֶּן־אָדָם *human being*) Jb 7$_{17}$ 15$_{14}$, אֱנוֹשׁ רִמָּה *a mortal (who is) a maggot* 25$_{6}$ (+ בֶּן־אָדָם).

<OBJ> בושׁ pi. *insult* Si 8$_{6}$ ([אנו[ש), זכר *remember* Ps 8$_{5}$, גדל pi. *magnify* Jb 7$_{17}$.

<CSTR> בֶּן־אֱנוֹשׁ *son of a mortal* Ps 144$_{3}$ (|| אָדָם *human being*), תִּקְוַת *hope of* Jb 14$_{19}$ Si 7$_{17}$, חיי *life of* 37$_{25(D)}$ (B איש *of a man*), יְמֵי *days of* Jb 10$_{5}$ (|| גֶּבֶר *man*).

<ADJ> יָשִׁישׁ *old* Si 8$_{6}$ (אנו[ש י]שיש).

<PREP> הֲלֹא־צָבָא לֶאֱנוֹשׁ *does a mortal not have a term of service?* Jb 7$_{1}$; שׁית אֶל *set* mind *upon* Jb 7$_{17}$.

<COLL> אֱנוֹשׁ מִן־הָאָרֶץ *a mortal from the earth* Ps 10$_{18}$, אֱנוֹשׁ כֶּחָצִיר יָמָיו *as for a mortal, his days are as grass* 103$_{15}$.

3. collective **people, humankind,** <SUBJ> שׁאר ni. *be left* Is 24$_{6}$, עזז *be strong* Ps 9$_{20}$ (+ גּוֹיִם *nations*) 4QapPs^{b} 46$_{5}$, עצר *prevail* against Y. 2 C 14$_{10}$, שׁאף *trample upon* Ps 56$_{2}$ (|| לחם ptc. *one who fights*), נבט hi. *see* Jb 36$_{25}$ (|| אָדָם *human being*), הלך htp. *walk* 1QS 3$_{17}$, מות *die* Is 51$_{12}$, שׁחה htpal *bow down* 4QTNaph 4$_{7}$.

<NOM CL> אֱנוֹשׁ הֵמָּה *they are human* Ps 9$_{21}$ (+ גּוֹיִם *nations*).

<OBJ> יקר hi. *make precious* Is 13$_{12}$ (|| אָדָם *humankind*), חשׁב *consider* 33$_{8}$, רכב hi. *cause to ride* Ps 66$_{12}$, שׁוב hi. *cause to return* 90$_{3}$ (+ בְּנֵי־אָדָם *human beings*), ידע hi. *make known* Si 38$_{5}$, ברא *create* 1QS 3$_{17}$, טהר pi. *to purify* 1QH 4$_{37}$ (לט]הר אנו[ש) 11$_{10}$, בין hi. *give discernment* fr. 15 1$_{5}$, שׂכל hi *instruct* 4QTNaph 4$_{5}$ ([אנש]).

<CSTR> חֶרְפַּת אֱנוֹשׁ *reproach of people* Is 51$_{7}$, חֶרֶט *stylus of* 8$_{1}$, עָמָל *trouble of* Ps 73$_{5}$ (+ אָדָם *humankind*), נדת *impurity of* 1QS 11$_{15}$ (+ בני אדם *human beings*), פשׁע *transgression of* CD 3$_{17}$, דרך *way of* 1QH 4$_{31}$, תשׁובת *return of* 1QH 11$_{20}$, קטני *least of* GnzPs 3$_{19}$ (אינוש; || אָדָם), [ראשי אנוש] *heads of humanity* 4QJub^{a} 7$_{14}$, כול אנש *all humanity* 4QTNaph 4$_{5}$ ([כול אנש]) 4$_{7}$.

<APP> אֱנוֹשׁ מִזְעָר *people, a few* Is 24$_{6}$.

<PREP> זרע לאנוש *seed of humanity* Si 10$_{19.19}$, לא לאנוש צדקה *righteousness does not belong to humankind* 1QH 4$_{30}$ (+ בן אדם *human being*), נתן ל *give to* 38$_{6}$, שׂים לְ *designate for* 1QS 3$_{17}$.

מִן *from,* + שׁבת hi. *make* memory *cease* Dt 32$_{26}$, עלם ni. *be hidden* Si 11$_{4(B)}$, סתר ni. *be hidden* 1QS 11$_{6}$ (מאנ[ו]ש), דלל *hang* Jb 28$_{4}$, ירא מִן *be afraid of* Is 51$_{12}$ (+ בֶּן־אָדָם *human being*).

Also 1QSb 4$_{1}$ 1QH 14$_{11}$ 4QMish Cf 1.2$_{1}$.

<SYN> גֶּבֶר *man*, אָדָם *human being*, ילד pass. *one born*.

→ אֱנוֹשׁ *Enosh*.

אֱנוֹשׁ II 7.1 pr.n.m. **Enosh,** son of Seth, Gn 4$_{26}$ 5$_{6.7.9.10.11}$ 1 C 1$_{1}$ Si 49$_{16}$.

→ אֱנוֹשׁ *person*.

אנח 12.3.2 vb. **sigh—Ni.** Pf. נֶאֶנְחוּ, נֶאֶנְחָה; impf. יֵאָנַח, תֵּאָנַח, Q יאנחו; + waw וַיֵּאָנְחוּ; impv. הֵאָנַח; ptc. נֶאֱנָח, נֶאֱנָחִים, נֶאֱנָחָה—**sigh, groan,** <SUBJ> Israelites Ex 2$_{23}$, שָׂמֵחַ ptc. *one who is merry* of heart Is 24$_{7}$ (|| אבל *mourn*, אמל pu'lal *languish*), אִישׁ *man* Ezk 9$_{4}$ (אנק ni. *groan*), בֶּן־אָדָם *human being* 21$_{11.11}$, Ezekiel 21$_{12}$, בְּהֵמָה *beast* Jl 1$_{18}$, עַם *people* Pr 29$_{2}$ (:: שׂמח *rejoice*) Lm 1$_{11}$, כֹּהֵן *priest* 1$_{4}$ (|| יגה ni. *grieve*; + מרר *be bitter*), Jerusalem 1$_{8.21}$, מות ptc. *dead person* 4Q416 4$_{5}$.

<PREP> בְּ of accompaniment, *with* Ezk 21$_{11}$ (+ שִׁבָּרוֹן *breaking* of loins) 21$_{11}$ (+ מְרִירוּת *bitterness*), בִּמְשֹׁל רָשָׁע *when the wicked rule* Pr 29$_{2}$; לְעֵינֵיהֶם *before their eyes* Ezk 21$_{11}$; מִן־הָעֲבֹדָה *because of the servitude* Ex 2$_{23}$; עַל *on account of* 4Q416 4$_{5}$ Ezk 9$_{4}$ (+ כָּל־הַתּוֹעֵבוֹת *all the abominations*).

<COLL> מצחות נאנחים *the foreheads of those who sigh* CD 19$_{12}$ (|| אנק ni. *groan*).

Htp. Impf. Si יתאנח, 2ms Si תתאנח; ptc. Si מתאנח, Q מתאנחים—**sigh, groan,** <SUBJ> בַּעַל *husband* Si 25$_{18}$, סָרִיס *eunuch* 30$_{20}$ (if em. סירים; || חבק pi. *embrace* girl), Israelites 11QT 59$_{5}$ (|| זעק *cry*); subj. not specified, Si 12$_{12}$ (but see Prep.).

<PREP> לאנחתי perh. *because of my sighing* Si 12$_{12}$ (or em. לתוכחתי *regarding my reproof*, or, לאמרותי *regarding my words*, or, לאחותי *regarding my declaration*; also, perh. em. תתאנח *you will sigh* to תתמה *you will be amazed* at my words); בלא טעמו *without his discernment* Si 25$_{18}$; מפני עול כבד *because of a heavy yoke* 11QT 59$_{5}$.

→ אֲנָחָה *sigh*.

אֲנָחָה 11.4.8 n.f. **sigh, sighing**—sf. אַנְחָתִי, אַנְחָתָה, אַנְחֹתַי—<SUBJ> נוס *flee* Is 35$_{10}$=51$_{11}$ (|| יָגוֹן *grief*; + בֹּשֶׁת *shame*), סתר ni. *be hidden* Ps 38$_{10}$ (|| תַּאֲוָה *desire*), בוא *come* Jb 3$_{24}$ (שְׁאָגָה *groaning*), סבב pol. *surround* 1QH 5$_{34}$ (יָגוֹן || [א]נחה).

<NOM CL> רַבּוֹת אַנְחֹתַי *my sighs are many* Lm 1$_{22}$, אנחה על מרודיה *there is sighing for her homeless ones* Si 32$_{19}$ (or em. מורידה *the one who causes it* [a tear] *to fall*), אנחה על משכבך *there is sighing upon your bed* 47$_{20}$ (+ אַף *anger*), אין ... אנחה *there is not ... sighing* 1QH 11$_{26}$ (|| יָגוֹן *grief*; + עַוְלָה *iniquity*).

<OBJ> שבת hi. *bring to an end* Is 21$_{2}$, הגה *murmur* 1QH 11$_{22}$ (|| יָגוֹן *grief*). <CSTR> קול אנחה *voice of sighing* Ps 102$_{6}$ (אַנְחָתִי) 1QH 9$_{4}$, לחם *bread of* 5$_{33}$, מושב *seat of* 4QToh A 1.1$_{1}$.

<PREP> אנח לְ htp. *sigh because of* Si 12$_{12}$ (or em. לאנחתי *because of my sighing* to לתוכחתי *regarding my reproof*, or לאמרותי *regarding my words*, or לאחותי *regarding my declaration*; also, perh. em. תתאנח *you will sigh* to תתמה *you will be amazed* at my words), המה לְ *roar at* 1QH 6$_{24}$; אם תולידו לאנחה *if you beget (children), it will be for sighing* Si 41$_{9}$; בְּ of cause, *by reason of, with*, + יגע *be weary* Jr 45$_{3}$ Ps 6$_{7}$, כלה *be ended* 31$_{11}$ (|| יָגוֹן *grief*; + עָוֹן *iniquity*), נכר בְּ hi. *recognize* 1QH 5$_{13}$ (but perh. הכרתה = *you have cut off*, from כרת hi.); כבד עַל *be heavy* (of hand, i.e. be weary) *by reason of* Jb 23$_{2}$ (+ שִׂיחַ *complaint*).

<SYN> יָגוֹן *grief*.

→ אנח *sigh*.

אֲנַחְנוּ 104.0.11 pronoun **we**—אֲנָחְנוּ—<SUBJ> **a. with a finite verb,** היה *be* Gn 44$_{9}$ (+ לַאדֹנִי לַעֲבָדִים *as slaves for my lord*) 46$_{34}$ (+ אַנְשֵׁי מִקְנֶה *keepers of cattle*) 47$_{19}$ (+ עֲבָדִים לְפַרְעֹה *slaves to Pharaoh*) 1 S 8$_{20}$ (+ כְּכָל־הַגּוֹיִם *as all the nations*), הלך *go* Mc 4$_{5}$, עלה *go up* Dt 1$_{41}$, נתן *give* Jg 16$_{5}$, ni. *be given* Ezr 9$_{7}$, עשׂה *do* Jr 44$_{17}$ Ps 100$_{3(Kt)}$, עבד *serve* Jos 24$_{18}$ Jg 9$_{28}$, שׁמע *hear* Jr 35$_{8}$, ידע *know* Ex 10$_{26}$ 2 C 20$_{12}$, יכל *be able* Jg 21$_{18}$ (+ לָתֵת *to give*) Ne 4$_{4}$ (+ לִבְנוֹת *to build*), עמד *stand* 2 K 10$_{4}$, קום *rise* Ps 20$_{9}$ (:: הֵמָּה *they*) Ne 2$_{20}$, בנה *build* Ezr 4$_{3}$, סבל *bear* iniquity Lm 5$_{7}$.

חטא *sin* Jr 3$_{25}$, רשׁע *act wickedly* CD 20$_{29}$ (+ אנו *we*), hi. Ne 9$_{33}$, מעל *be unfaithful* Ezr 10$_{2}$, מות *die* Gn 43$_{8}$ 47$_{19}$ Nm 20$_{4}$, פשׁט *raid* 1 S 30$_{14}$, חלץ ni. *be armed* Nm

32$_{17}$, מלט ni. *escape* Is 20$_{6}$ Ps 124$_{7}$, ישׁע ni. *be saved* Jr 8$_{20}$, שׁבע ni. *swear* Jos 9$_{19}$ Jg 21$_{7}$, 1 S 20$_{42}$, זכר hi. *mention* Ps 20$_{8}$ (or em. נַזְכִּיר *we will mention* to נַגְבִּיר *we will prevail*; :: אֵלֶּה *these*), ידה hi. *give thanks* 79$_{13}$, ברך pi. *bless* 115$_{18}$, יעד ni. *be gathered* 1QH fr. 10$_{6}$, קנה *buy* Ne 5$_{8}$, חשׁב *reckon* Is 53$_{4}$, כרת *cut* 2 C 2$_{15}$, כתב *write* 4QMMT B$_{29}$.

b. with a participle, בוא *come* Jos 2$_{18}$, ho. *be brought* Gn 43$_{18}$, הלך *go* Jg 18$_{5}$, נסע *journey* Nm 10$_{29}$, עלה *go up* Dt 1$_{28}$, עבר *pass* Jg 19$_{18}$ 1 S 14$_{8}$, שׁלח *send* Jr 42$_{6(Qr)}$ (Kt אנו *we*), ישׁב *dwell* 2 K 6$_{1}$, *sit* 7$_{3}$ Jr 8$_{14}$, בנה *build* Ne 3$_{33}$, שׁחת hi. *destroy* Gn 19$_{13}$, אלם pi. *bind* sheaves 37$_{7}$, כרת *cut*, i.e. make, covenant Ne 10$_{1}$, חשׁב *reckon* 4QMMT A 2$_{2}$ ([אנח]נ[ו]) 2$_{10}$ ([אנ]חנו חושבים]) 2$_{34.44}$ ([אנחנו חושבים]) 2$_{45}$ ([אנח]נו]) 2$_{50}$, עשׂה *do* Dt 12$_{8}$ 2 K 7$_{9}$ Jr 26$_{19}$ Ne 4$_{15}$, יסף *do again* Dt 5$_{25}$ (+ לִשְׁמֹעַ *to hear*), שׁמע *hear* 2 K 18$_{26}$‖Is 36$_{11}$, אמר *say* 4QMMT A 2$_{8}$ ([אנחנו אומרים]) 2$_{63.72}$ ([א]ומרים]) 2$_{81}$, נכר hi. *recognize* 4QMMT B$_{23}$, נפל hi. *make fall*, i.e. present, supplications Dn 9$_{18}$, ידה hi. *give thanks* 1 C 29$_{13}$, ירא *be afraid* 1 S 23$_{3}$, קטר pi. *burn incense* Jr 44$_{19}$, זבח *sacrifice* Ezr 4$_{2}$, מקק ni. *pine away* 33$_{10}$, חשׁה hi. *be silent* 1 K 22$_{3}$ 2 K 7$_{9}$, אשׁר pi. *pronounce blessed* Ml 3$_{15}$, פשׁט *strip* clothing Ne 4$_{17}$, ערב *give as security* 5$_{2}$ (if em.; see Nom. Cl.) 5$_{3}$, כבשׁ *bring into bondage* 5$_{5}$, שׁמר *keep* charge 2 C 13$_{11}$ (:: אַתֶּם *you*), פרד ni. *be separated* Ne 4$_{13}$.

<NOM CL> אַחִים אֲנָחְנוּ *we are brothers* Gn 13$_{8}$ (אֲנָחְנוּ; + אֲנָשִׁים *men*) 42$_{13}$ (+ שְׁנֵים עָשָׂר *twelve*, בְּנֵי אִישׁ־אֶחָד *sons of one man*), var. 42$_{32}$ (+ שְׁנֵים עָשָׂר), אֲחֵי אֲחַזְיָהוּ אֲנַחְנוּ *we are brothers of Ahaziah* 2 K 10$_{13}$, הִנְנוּ עַצְמְךָ וּבְשָׂרְךָ אֲנָחְנוּ *behold, we are your bone and flesh* 2 S 5$_{1}$‖1 C 11$_{1}$ (הִנֵּה), אֲנַחְנוּ הַבָּשָׂר *we are the flesh* Ezk 11$_{3}$, אֲנַחְנוּ הַחֹמֶר *we are the clay* Is 64$_{7}$, עָפָר אֲנָחְנוּ *we are dust* Ps 103$_{14}$.

חֲכָמִים אֲנַחְנוּ *we are wise* Jr 8$_{8}$, כֵּנִים אֲנַחְנוּ *we are honest* Gn 42$_{11.31}$ (אֲנָחְנוּ), נְקִיִּם אֲנַחְנוּ *we are innocent* Jos 2$_{17}$, sim. 2$_{19}$, אֲשֵׁמִים אֲנַחְנוּ *we are guilty* Gn 42$_{21}$, אֲנַחְנוּ טְמֵאִים *we are unclean* Nm 9$_{7}$, אֲנַחְנוּ רְעֵבִים *we are hungry* 2 K 7$_{12}$, רְחֹקִים אֲנַחְנוּ *we are far* Jos 9$_{22}$, אֲנַחְנוּ רַבִּים *we are many* Ne 5$_{2}$ (or em. רַבִּים to עֹרְבִים we *give as security* our sons and daughters) Ezk 33$_{24}$.

עֲבָדִים אֲנַחְנוּ *we are slaves* Ezr 9$_{9}$, vars. Jos 9$_{8.11}$ (אֲנָחְנוּ) 2 K 10$_{5}$ Ne 9$_{36.36}$, הִנֶּנּוּ עֲבָדִים לַאדֹנִי ... אֲנַחְנוּ *behold, we ... are slaves of my lord* Gn 44$_{16}$, לוֹ אֲנַחְנוּ *we are his* Ps 100$_{3(Qr)}$, רֹעֵי צֹאן ... אֲנַחְנוּ *we ... are shepherds* Gn 47$_{3}$ (if em. רֹעֵה *a shepherd*), אֲנַחְנוּ עַם מַרְעִיתוֹ וְצֹאן יָדוֹ *we are the people of his pasture and the sheep of his hand* Ps 95$_{7}$, גִּבּוֹרִים אֲנָחְנוּ וְאַנְשֵׁי חַיִל *we are warriors and men of valour* Jr 48$_{14}$, גֵרִים אֲנַחְנוּ *we are sojourners* 1 C 29$_{15}$.

אֲנַחְנוּ בְקָדֵשׁ *we are from Haran* Gn 29$_{4}$, מֵחָרָן אֲנָחְנוּ *we are in Kadesh* Nm 20$_{16}$, אֵין ... זוּלָתִי שְׁתַּיִם אֲנַחְנוּ בַּבָּיִת *there was no one ... except the two of us in the house* 1 K 3$_{18}$, אֲנַחְנוּ בְּאַשְׁמָה *we are in guilt* Ezr 9$_{7}$, אֲנַחְנוּ בָהּ *we are in it* (trouble) Ne 2$_{17}$, אֲנַחְנוּ ... בְּצָרָה *we are ... in distress* 9$_{37}$, אֲנַחְנוּ עִמָּךְ *we are with you* Ezr 10$_{4}$, תְמוֹל אֲנַחְנוּ *we are (of) yesterday* Jb 8$_{9}$, אֲנַחְנוּ יַחְדָּו *we were together* 1 K 3$_{18}$.

<APP> עֲבָדֶיךָ ... אֲנַחְנוּ *your servants ... we* Gn 42$_{13}$ 46$_{34}$ 47$_{3}$, var. Ne 2$_{20}$, אֲנַחְנוּ עַמְּךָ וְצֹאן מַרְעִיתֶךָ *we, your people and the flock of your pasture* Ps 79$_{13}$, אִתָּנוּ אֲנַחְנוּ אֵלֶּה פֹה הַיּוֹם כֻּלָּנוּ חַיִּים *with us, all these of us alive here today* Dt 5$_{13}$, שְׁנֵינוּ אֲנַחְנוּ *we, both of us* 1 S 20$_{42}$, [אנחנו] כל מלאכי הפנים וכל מלאכי קודש שני[המינים האלה *we, all the angels of the presence and all the angels of holiness, these two kinds* 4QJub[a] 7$_{8}$.

<COLL> וַאֲנַחְנוּ י׳ אֱלֹהֵינוּ *but as for us, Y. is our God* 2 C 13$_{10}$, אֲנַחְנוּ and other subjects, **a.** גַּם־אֲנַחְנוּ גַּם־ *both we and* Gn 43$_{8}$ 44$_{16}$ 46$_{34}$ 47$_{3.19}$ CD 20$_{29}$; **b.** without גַּם, Gn 47$_{19}$ Nm 20$_{4}$ Jr 3$_{25}$ 35$_{8}$ 44$_{17}$ Ezr 9$_{7}$ Ne 5$_{2}$ (unless em.; see Nom. Cl.).

Also 2Q27 1$_{5}$ 4QpsMos[e] 2.2$_{6}$.

→ אֲנוּ *we*, נַחְנוּ *we*.

אֲנָחֲרַת 1 pl.n. **Anaharath**—אֲנָחֲרַת—town in Issachar, perh. Naʿūra, 14 km SE of Nazareth, Jos 19$_{19}$.

אני 0.0.0.1 pr.n.m. **Ani**, Seal 80 (8th cent.).

אֳנִי, see אֳנִיָּה.

אֲנִי 871.4.103.1 pronoun **I**—אֲנִי (BHS אָנִי), Q אניא—rarely with ref. to female speaker, Gn 18$_{13}$ 1 S 1$_{26}$ 25$_{24.25}$ 2 S 13$_{13}$ 14$_{5}$ 1 K 1$_{21.26}$ 3$_{17}$ Is 49$_{21}$ Ru 1$_{21}$ Ca 1$_{5.6}$ 2$_{1.5.16}$ 5$_{2.5.6.8}$ 6$_{3}$ 7$_{11}$ 8$_{10}$ Est 4$_{11.16}$ 7$_{4}$ 8$_{5}$.

<SUBJ> a. of **non-participial** forms, היה *be* Jg 12$_{2}$ (+ אִישׁ *man*) 2 S 15$_{34}$ (+ עֶבֶד *servant*) 1 K 1$_{21}$ (+ adj.) Ps 109$_{25}$ (+ חֶרְפָּה *reproach*) Ec 1$_{12}$ (+ מֶלֶךְ *king*) Dn 8$_{2}$ (+ עַל *by* river) 8$_{5}$ 10$_{2}$ (both + ptc.) 10$_{4}$ (+ עַל) 10$_{9}$ (+ ptc.) Ne 1$_{1}$ (+ בְּ *in*) 1$_{11}$ (+ מַשְׁקֶה *wine-steward*) Si 51$_{13(B)}$ (+ נַעַר *lad*) 1QH 2$_{11}$ (+ נְגִינָה subject of *song*) 5$_{22}$ (+ עַל) Mur 24 3$_{14}$ ([אנ]י; + ptc.); + לְ of possession, *(belonging) to*, etc. 1 S 14$_{40}$ (:: אַתֶּם *you* pl.) 2 S 7$_{14}$||1 C 17$_{13}$ (:: הוּא *he*) Ezk 34$_{24}$ Zc 2$_{9}$ 1 C 28$_{6}$ 1QH 8$_{14}$, וְהָיוּ(־)לִי לְעָם וַאֲנִי אֶהְיֶה לָהֶם לֵאלֹהִים *and they will be to me as a people and I shall be to them as God* Jr 32$_{38}$ Ezk 11$_{20}$ 14$_{11}$ 37$_{23}$ Zc 8$_{8}$, sim. 1 C 22$_{10(mss)}$ (L אֲנִי־לוֹ *I am for him*; :: הוּא).

היה ni. *be exhausted* Dn 8$_{27}$, קדם pi. *be first* Si 30$_{25}$, כלה *be finished* Ps 39$_{11}$, pi. *complete* Gn 24$_{45}$, יתר ni. *remain* 1 K 18$_{22}$ 19$_{10.14}$ Dn 10$_{13}$, שׁאר ni. *remain* Is 49$_{21}$ Dn 10$_{8}$, שׁנה *suffer change* Ml 3$_{6}$ (unless Nom. Cl.; see App.; :: אַתֶּם), פלה ni. *be separate* Ex 33$_{16}$.

בוא *come* Gn 37$_{10}$ Jg 20$_{4}$ 2 S 11$_{11}$ 1 K 1$_{14}$ Ps 5$_{8}$ Dn 9$_{23}$ 10$_{12}$ Ne 6$_{10}$, hi. *bring* Lv 26$_{41}$ Is 48$_{15}$, הלך *go* Gn 22$_{5}$ Lv 26$_{24.41}$ Jg 1$_{3}$ 1 K 18$_{12}$ 2 K 6$_{3}$ Is 45$_{2}$ Ho 5$_{14}$ Zc 8$_{21}$ Ps 26$_{1.11}$ Ru 1$_{21}$, hi. *lead* 2 S 13$_{13}$, htp. *go* 1 S 12$_{2}$, יצא *go out* 19$_{3}$ 2 S 18$_{2}$, hi. *take out* Ex 29$_{46}$ Lv 25$_{55}$ Nm 15$_{41}$ (unless nom. cl. in all three; see App.) Ezk 21$_{10}$, ירד *go down* 1 S 26$_{6}$, עלה *go up* 2 K 19$_{23}$||Is 37$_{24}$, קרב *approach* Jos 8$_{5}$.

שׁוב *go back* Gn 22$_{5}$ Ec 4$_{1.7}$, hi. *bring back* Gn 42$_{37}$, *answer* Jb 35$_{4}$, סבב *turn* intrans. Ec 2$_{20}$ 7$_{25}$, פנה *turn* intrans. 2$_{11.12}$, עוד htpol. *be restored* 1QH 4$_{22}$ (וא[נ]י), עבר *pass* Gn 31$_{52}$ (:: אַתָּה) Ho 10$_{11}$ (or em. hi.), hi. *cause to pass* Ex 33$_{19}$ Ho 10$_{11}$ (if em.), עזב *desert* Ps 119$_{87}$ 2 C 12$_{5}$ (:: אַתֶּם), נוס *flee* 1 S 4$_{16}$ (|| אָנֹכִי *I*), מלט ni. *escape* Jb 1$_{15.16.17.19}$, pi. *rescue* Is 46$_{4}$, רוץ *run* 2 S 18$_{22}$, דלג pi. *leap* 4QapPs^{b} 48$_{6}$, נהל htp. *journey* Gn 33$_{14}$.

עמד *stand* 1 S 19$_{3}$ Ne 12$_{40}$, קום *arise* Ca 5$_{5}$ Ne 2$_{12}$ 1QH 4$_{22}$ (וא[נ]י), hi. *establish* Ezk 16$_{62}$, שׁכב *lie down* Ps 3$_{6}$, ישׁן *sleep* 3$_{6}$, שׁחה htpal. *bow down* Gn 22$_{5}$ Ps 5$_{8}$, כחשׁ pi. *cringe* 4QapPs^{b} 33$_{9}$, שׁפל hi. *bring low* Ezk 17$_{24}$, גבה hi. *make high* 17$_{24}$, שׂים *place* Lv 20$_{5}$, אסף *gather* trans. Is 10$_{14}$, קבץ pi. *gather* trans. Jr 23$_{3}$, פוץ hi. *disperse* trans. Ne 1$_{8}$, שׁלח *send* Jr 14$_{15}$ 29$_{31}$, pi. *send* 1 K 20$_{34}$, נשׂא *raise* Is 46$_{4}$ Ezk 20$_{15.23}$ 36$_{7}$ Ho 5$_{14}$, סמך ni. *support oneself* 11QPs^{a} 19$_{13}$, תמך *support oneself* 1QH fr. 1$_{10}$, שׁען ni. *support oneself* 1QH 7$_{18}$, מוט *totter* 1QS 11$_{11}$, כשׁל *stumble* 1QH fr. 15$_{(Licht)}$ ([כשלתי]).

ראה *see* 1 S 25$_{25}$ Jr 23$_{24}$ Ps 118$_{7}$ Jb 5$_{3}$ Ec 2$_{13.24}$ 4$_{4}$ 5$_{17}$ Dn 8$_{15}$ 10$_{7}$ 12$_{5}$, hi. *show* Zc 1$_{9}$ appar. 4QpsEzek^{a} 2$_{3}$ ([אני אראה]), חזה *see* Ps 17$_{15}$ Jb 19$_{27}$ (|| עֵינַי *my eyes*), שׁור *see* Ho 14$_{9}$, צפה pi. *look out* Mc 7$_{7}$, שׁקד *keep watch* Si 36$_{16}$, שׁמע *hear* Gn 41$_{15}$ Ex 6$_{5}$ Is 65$_{24}$ (:: הֵם *they*) Ezk 35$_{12.13}$ Dn 12$_{8}$ 2 C 7$_{14}$ 34$_{27}$ (||2 K 22$_{19}$ אָנֹכִי), hi. *inform* Is 45$_{21}$, חלם *dream* Gn 41$_{11}$.

ידע *know* Ex 3$_{19}$ 1 S 17$_{28}$ 2 K 2$_{3.5}$ Jr 48$_{30}$ Ezk 11$_{5}$ Ho 5$_{3}$ 13$_{5}$ Ps 51$_{5}$ 135$_{5}$ Jb 13$_{2}$ (+ אָנֹכִי) 19$_{25}$ Ec 2$_{14}$ 2 C 2$_{7}$ 1QH 4$_{30}$ 11$_{7}$ 12$_{11}$ (unless Nom. Cl.; see App.) 13$_{21}$ 14$_{12.17}$ ([ואנ]י) 15$_{12.22.25}$ ([ידעת]י) 4Q372 1$_{31}$, חרשׁ hi. *be silent* Jb 6$_{24}$, אלם ni. *be silent* 1QH 7$_{1}$ 12$_{32}$, שׂיח *muse* Ps 119$_{78}$, חשׁב ni. *be reckoned* 4QM^{a} fr. 11.1$_{18(Baillet)}$ ([אחש]ב), htp. 11.1$_{14}$, קדשׁ ni. *be hallowed* Lv 22$_{32.33}$ (unless nom. cl. in both; see App.), חכם *be wise* Ec 2$_{15}$, בין *understand* Dn 9$_{2}$ 12$_{8}$, hi. 1QH 17$_{21}$, htpol. 4QapPs^{b} 15$_{7}$, זכר *remember* Ex 6$_{5}$ Lv 26$_{45}$ (unless nom. cl.; see App.) Ezk 16$_{60}$ 4QapPs^{b} 33$_{11}$, שׁכח *forget* Ho 4$_{6}$, בטח *trust* Ps 13$_{6}$ (|| לִבִּי *my heart*) 31$_{7.15}$ 55$_{24}$ 56$_{4}$ 4QapPs^{b} 45$_{3}$, שׁמר *observe* Ps 17$_{4}$ perh. Ec 8$_{2}$ (see Coll.), נצר *keep* commandments Ps 119$_{69}$, יחל pi. *wait* 71$_{14}$, צדק *be vindicated* Jb 13$_{18}$, אהב *love* Is 43$_{4}$ Pr 8$_{17}$ 11QPs^{a} 19$_{11}$ 22$_{2}$ Kh. Beit Lei graf. 5$_{1(Cross)}$ ([אנ]י); (unless nom. cl.; see App.), בחר *choose* Is 66$_{4}$ Jb 34$_{33}$ (:: אַתָּה) 1QH 16$_{10}$, חמל *have pity* Ezk 5$_{11}$, חוס *have pity* Jon 4$_{11}$, סלח *forgive* 2 C 7$_{14}$, עלז *rejoice* Hb 3$_{18}$, שׁעע pilp. *delight in* Ps 119$_{70}$, שׂחק *laugh* Pr 1$_{26}$.

לעג *mock* Pr 1$_{26}$, קנא hi. *cause jealousy* Dt 32$_{21}$ (:: הֵם), קשׁר *conspire* 2 K 10$_{9}$ (+ אַתֶּם), פתה pi. *seduce* 1 K 22$_{21}$||2 C 18$_{20}$ Ezk 14$_{9}$, שׂנא *hate* 1K 22$_{8}$||2 C 18$_{7}$ Ec 2$_{18}$, מאס *reject* 1 S 16$_{1}$ Jr 31$_{37}$, קצף *be angry* Zc 1$_{15}$, חרף pi. *reproach* 1 S 17$_{10}$, כאב hi. *cause pain* Ezk 13$_{22}$, חלה ni. *be made ill* Dn 8$_{27}$, hi. *make ill* Mc 6$_{13}$, בושׁ *be ashamed* Jr 17$_{18}$, חתת *fear* 17$_{18}$ (:: הֵמָּה), פחד *fear* 1QH fr. 4$_{9}$, חטא *sin* 2 S 19$_{21}$ Ne 1$_{6}$, ענה II *be afflicted* Ps 116$_{10}$, pi. *afflict* 35$_{13}$, שׁמד ni. *be destroyed* Gn 34$_{30}$.

אמר *say* Is 38$_{10}$ 49$_{4}$ Jr 5$_{4}$ 10$_{19}$ Jon 2$_{5}$ Ps 30$_{7}$ 31$_{23}$ 41$_{5}$ 82$_{6}$ 116$_{11}$ Ru 4$_{4}$ Ec 2$_{1.15}$ 3$_{17.18}$ 9$_{16}$ 1 C 21$_{17}$ 11QPs^{a} 28$_{5}$ 1QH 2$_{25}$ 4$_{35}$, דבר pi. *speak* Nm 14$_{35}$ 1 S 19$_{3}$ 20$_{23}$ Is 48$_{15}$ Jr 4$_{12}$ 34$_{5}$ Ezk 5$_{13.15.17}$ 6$_{10}$ (unless nom. cl.; see App.)

12$_{25}$ 13$_{7}$ 17$_{21.24}$ 21$_{22.37}$ 22$_{14}$ 23$_{34}$ 24$_{14}$ 26$_{5.14}$ 28$_{10}$ 30$_{12}$ 34$_{24}$ 36$_{36}$ 37$_{14}$ 39$_{5}$ Jb 13$_{3.13}$ Ec 1$_{16}$, נגד hi. *tell* Is 45$_{21}$ 57$_{12}$ Ps 75$_{10}$, חוה pi. *declare* Jb 32$_{10.17}$, ענה I *answer* Is 41$_{17}$ 65$_{24}$ Ho 14$_{9}$ Zc 13$_{9}$ (:: הוּא) Jb 32$_{17}$, ni. Ezk 14$_{4}$, שׁאל *ask* GnzPs 3$_{1}$, דרשׁ *seek* Jb 5$_{8}$ 4Q416 10.2$_{13}$, ni. *be asked* Ezk 20$_{31}$.

צוה pi. *command* 2 S 14$_{8}$ Is 13$_{3}$, קרא *call* 1 K 18$_{24}$ Is 42$_{6}$ (unless nom. cl.; see App.) 48$_{15}$ Ps 17$_{6}$ 55$_{17}$ 1QH 16$_{19}$ (קר[א]ת[י]), ni. *be called* Est 4$_{11}$, שׁוע pi. *call* Ps 88$_{14}$, שׁיר *sing* 59$_{17}$, זמר pi. *sing* 71$_{22}$ 75$_{10}$, רנן pi. *praise* 59$_{17}$, ידה hi. *praise* 71$_{22}$ Jb 40$_{14}$, הלל pi. *praise* 4QRit Pur 39.2$_{1}$ (אה[ל]לה) 1QH 10$_{20\text{(Licht)}}$ ([אהללה]), שׁבח pi. *commend* Ec 4$_{2}$ 8$_{15}$, ברך pi. *bless* Nm 6$_{27}$, יעץ *advise* 2 S 17$_{15}$, עזר *help* Is 41$_{13.14}$, צלח hi. *cause to prosper* 48$_{15}$, עשׁר hi. *enrich* Gn 14$_{23}$.

עשׂה *do, make* Ex 12$_{12}$ (unless nom. cl.; see App.) Lv 26$_{16}$ Dt 12$_{30}$ 2 S 12$_{12}$ (:: אַתָּה *you*) 19$_{39}$ 1 K 5$_{22}$ 18$_{23}$ Is 41$_{4}$ 46$_{4}$ 57$_{16}$ Ezk 8$_{18}$ 17$_{24}$ 22$_{14}$ 29$_{3.9}$ 36$_{36}$ 37$_{14}$ Ne 5$_{15}$ 2 C 32$_{13}$, פעל *make* Is 41$_{4}$, רבץ hi. *make lie down* Ezk 34$_{15}$, יסף hi. *do again, add* Jg 2$_{21}$ 1 K 12$_{11.14}$||2 C 10$_{11.14}$ (both :: אָבִי *my father*) Ps 71$_{14}$ Ec 1$_{16}$, חושׁ hi. *hasten* Is 60$_{22}$ (unless nom. cl.; see App.), יכל *be able* 1 S 17$_{9}$ Jr 36$_{5}$, רבה hi. *multiply* Ex 7$_{3}$ 4QapPs^{b} 33$_{9}$, גדל hi. *make great* Ezk 24$_{9}$ Ec 1$_{16}$, פרה hi. *make fruitful* Ezk 17$_{24}$, חזק pi. *strengthen* Ex 4$_{21}$ Ho 7$_{15}$, htp. *be encouraged* Ezr 7$_{28}$, קשׁה hi. *harden* heart Ex 7$_{3}$, כבד hi. *make heavy* 10$_{1}$, נוח hi. *appease* Ezk 21$_{22}$, ברא *create* Is 45$_{8}$ 11QT 29$_{9}$.

מצא *find* Ex 33$_{16}$, נתן *give* Gn 48$_{22}$ Ex 2$_{9}$ 6$_{8}$ (unless nom. cl.; see App.) 31$_{6}$ Lv 17$_{11}$ Nm 18$_{8}$ 2 S 21$_{6}$ 1 K 21$_{7}$ Jr 1$_{18}$ Ezk 4$_{5}$ 20$_{25}$ Am 4$_{6}$ Ml 2$_{9}$ Ps 89$_{28}$, *place* Lv 20$_{3}$ Ezk 16$_{43}$ 17$_{22}$, גמל *repay* 1 S 24$_{18}$ (:: אַתָּה *you*), חכר *rent* from Mur 24 2$_{6}$ ([חכרתי]) 3$_{5}$ (אנ[י]) 5$_{5}$ ([א]ני ... [ח]כרת[י]; all three + מרצוני *of my free will*) 5/6Ḥev BA 45 fr. 2, hi. *let* to 5/6ḤevBA 45 fr. 1, לקח *take* Nm 3$_{12}$ 18$_{6}$ Jg 17$_{2}$ 2 S 7$_{8}$||1 C 17$_{7}$ Ezk 17$_{22}$, pu. *be taken* 1QH 12$_{24}$ (לחק[תי]), לכד *capture* 2 S 12$_{28}$, מכר ni. *be sold* Est 7$_{4}$.

כרת *make (covenant)* Gn 31$_{44}$ 2 S 3$_{13}$ (+ אָנֹכִי), עבד *serve* 16$_{19}$, נסך *enthrone* Ps 2$_{6}$, זבח *sacrifice* Jon 2$_{10}$, נדב htp. *offer freely* 1 C 29$_{17}$, סבל *carry* Is 46$_{4.4}$, חשׂף *strip* trans. Jr 13$_{26}$ 49$_{10}$, אוץ *press* 17$_{16}$, שׁפך *pour* Ezk 22$_{22}$, פתח *open* Ca 5$_{6}$, בנה *build* Ezk 36$_{36}$ 2 C 6$_{2}$, קור *dig* 2 K 19$_{24}$||Is 37$_{25}$, שׁתל *plant* Ezk 17$_{22}$, נטע *plant* 36$_{36}$, רעה *tend* 34$_{15}$, בער pi. *kindle* 21$_{4}$, טרף *tear* Ho 5$_{14}$, הרס *tear down* Ml 1$_{4}$ (:: הֵמָּה), קרץ pu. *be cut* Jb 33$_{6}$.

ישׁב *dwell* 4QM^{a} fr. 11.1$_{13}$, hi. *cause to dwell* Lv 23$_{43}$ (unless nom. cl.; see App.), שׁכן *dwell* Pr 8$_{12}$, אכל *eat* Ne 5$_{14}$, שׁתה *drink* Nm 20$_{19}$ 2 K 19$_{24}$||Is 37$_{25}$, צום *fast* Est 4$_{16}$, שׁבר hi. *conceive* Is 66$_{9}$, ילד *beget* Ps 2$_{7}$ (:: אַתָּה *you* sg.), hi. *beget* Is 66$_{9}$, חיה pi. *give life* Dt 32$_{39}$ Jr 49$_{11}$, רפא *heal* Dt 32$_{39}$ 2 C 7$_{14}$, זקן *be old* Gn 18$_{13}$ Jos 23$_{2}$ 1 S 12$_{2}$ 4QJub^{d} 1.1$_{12}$ (זק[נתי]), שׂיב *be grey* 1 S 12$_{2}$, יבשׁ *become dry* Ps 102$_{12}$ (|| יָמַי *my days*), hi. *make dry* Ezk 17$_{24}$.

משׁל *rule* Jg 8$_{23}$, מלך *rule* 1 K 1$_{5}$ Arad ost. 88$_{1}$, שׁפט *judge* Ps 75$_{3}$, רשׁע hi. *condemn* Jb 15$_{6}$ (:: פִּיךָ *your mouth*), חשׂך *restrain* 7$_{11}$, עצר *restrain* Is 66$_{9}$, יסר pi. *chastise* Lv 26$_{28}$ 1 K 12$_{11.14}$||2 C 10$_{11.14}$ (both :: אָבִי *my father*) Ho 7$_{15}$, נכה hi. *strike* Lv 26$_{24}$ 1 S 17$_{9}$ Ezk 21$_{22}$, ירה hi. *shoot* 1 S 20$_{20}$, לחם ni. *fight* Jr 21$_{5}$, שׁמם hi. *devastate* Lv 26$_{32}$, גרע *diminish* Ezk 5$_{11}$, מות hi. *kill* Dt 32$_{39}$.

b. of participles, בוא *come* Gn 37$_{30}$ Ex 18$_{6}$, hi. *bring* Gn 6$_{17}$ Lv 18$_{3}$ 20$_{22}$ Nm 15$_{18}$ 2 K 10$_{24}$ 22$_{20}$||2 C 34$_{28}$ Jr 42$_{17}$ Ezk 6$_{3}$ 37$_{5}$, הלך *go* Jg 19$_{18}$ (+ אָנֹכִי *I*) 2 S 12$_{23}$ (:: הוּא *he*) 15$_{20.20}$, יצא *go out* Ex 11$_{4}$ Dn 10$_{20}$, שׁוב hi. *bring back* Jr 28$_{3.4}$, נשׂא *raise* 2 K 3$_{14}$, קום hi. *establish* Gn 9$_{9}$, נפל hi. *set down* Jr 38$_{26}$, אסף ni. *be gathered* Gn 49$_{29}$, כון ni. *be ready* Ps 38$_{18}$, שׁלח *send* Ex 9$_{14}$ Ezk 2$_{3.4}$, pi. Lv 18$_{24}$ 20$_{23}$, רעשׁ hi. *shake* Hg 2$_{6.21}$, הרס *pull down* Jr 45$_{4}$, נתץ *pull down* 45$_{4}$, נטה *extend to, offer* 1 C 21$_{10}$ (||2 S 24$_{12}$ אָנֹכִי), רכב *ride* 2 K 9$_{25}$ Ne 2$_{12}$, מלא *fill* Jr 23$_{24}$, perh. כלא *be shut in* Ps 88$_{9}$ (lacking in MT).

ראה *see* 2 S 18$_{27}$ 2 K 9$_{17}$ 23$_{17}$ Jr 1$_{11.13}$ Zc 5$_{2}$ (all three :: אַתָּה *you* sg.) Est 5$_{13}$, hi. *show* Ex 25$_{9}$ Ezk 40$_{4}$, שׁקד *watch* Jr 1$_{12}$, חקר *search* 17$_{10}$, בחן *test* 17$_{10}$, אמר *say* Ps 45$_{2}$, דבר *speak* Is 45$_{19}$ Jr 38$_{20}$, pi. Ezk 2$_{8}$ 44$_{5}$ Dn 9$_{20.21}$, נגד hi. *tell* Is 42$_{9}$ 45$_{19}$ 11QT 51$_{7}$, צוה pi. *command* Gn 27$_{8}$, קרא *call* Is 41$_{4}$ 48$_{13}$ Jr 25$_{29}$ (+ אָנֹכִי), pass. *be called* Est 5$_{12}$, ענה ni. *answer* Ezk 14$_{7}$, שׁאל *ask* Jr 38$_{14}$, עוד hi. *call to witness* MurEpBarC$^{a}_{3}$, שׁבע hi. *cause to vow* 1 K 22$_{16}$||2 C 18$_{15}$, ברך pi. *bless* 4QRitMar 10$_{2\text{(Baillet)}}$ ([מברך]).

ידע *know* Jon 1$_{12}$ Ec 8$_{12}$, שׁמע hi. *make known* 4Q

Shir^{a} 1$_{4}$ (unless nom. cl.; see App.), זכר hi. *recall* Gn 41$_{9}$, בטח *trust* Ps 27$_{3}$, חשׁה hi. *be silent* Is 57$_{11}$, כתב *write* Jr 36$_{18}$, ידה hi. *acknowledge* 5/6Ḥev BA 45 fr. 1 (מודא אני), ירא *fear* Gn 42$_{18}$ Jon 1$_{9}$ (|| אָנֹכִי) Dn 1$_{10}$, pi. *cause to fear* 4QShir^{b} 35$_{6}$ 8QHymn 1$_{1}$, דאג *be concerned* Jr 38$_{19}$, אהב *love* 2 S 13$_{4}$ Is 61$_{8}$, שׂנא *hate* Is 61$_{8}$, קצף *be angry* Zc 1$_{15}$, שׁגג *err* Ps 119$_{67}$, שׂחק pi. *joke* Pr 26$_{19}$.

עשׂה *do, make* Gn 18$_{17}$ Ex 34$_{10}$ (+ אָנֹכִי) Jg 15$_{3}$ Is 5$_{5}$ 45$_{7}$ (unless nom. cl.; see App.) 66$_{22}$ Jr 9$_{23}$ (unless nom. cl.; see App.) 29$_{32}$ Ezk 22$_{14}$ 36$_{22.32}$ Ml 3$_{17.21}$ Ne 2$_{16}$ 6$_{3}$, ברא *create* Is 65$_{18}$, עצר pass. *be prohibited* Jr 36$_{5}$, נתן *give* Gn 9$_{12}$ Lv 14$_{34}$ 23$_{10}$ 25$_{2}$ Nm 13$_{2}$ 15$_{2}$ Dt 32$_{49.52}$ 1 S 23$_{4}$ Ezk 2$_{8}$ 3$_{3}$, *place* MurEpBarC$^{a}_{5}$, נשׁה *lend* Ne 5$_{10}$, לקח *take* Ezk 37$_{19.21}$, מצא *find* Ec 7$_{26}$, כסה pi. *conceal* Gn 18$_{17}$, פתח *open* Ezk 37$_{12}$, פשׁט *strip* trans. Ne 4$_{17}$, בדל hi. *divide* 4QJub^{a} 7$_{9}$ ([אני מבדיל]).

ישׁב *dwell, sit* 1 K 3$_{17}$ Jr 40$_{10}$ (:: אַתֶּם *you* pl.) Ezk 8$_{1}$ Ezr 9$_{4}$, גור htpol. *dwell* 1 K 17$_{20}$, שׁכן *dwell* Nm 5$_{3}$ 35$_{34}$ =11QT 51$_{7}$ Jl 4$_{17}$ (unless nom. cl.; see App.) 11QT 45$_{13.14}$ 46$_{4}$ + Sup, שׁאר ni. *remain* Ezk 9$_{8}$ (וְנֵאשֲׁאַר), חלה *be ill* Ca 2$_{5}$ 5$_{8}$, כאב *be in pain* Ps 69$_{30}$, גוע *expire* 88$_{16}$, צום *fast* 2 S 12$_{23}$, אנח ni. *groan* Lm 1$_{21}$, רושׁ *be poor* 4Q416 10.2$_{13}$ (+ אַתָּה *you* sg.), פלל htp. *pray* Dn 9$_{20}$, זבח *sacrifice* Ex 13$_{15}$ Ezk 39$_{17}$, קדשׁ pi. *sanctify* Ex 31$_{13}$ Lv 20$_{8}$ 21$_{15.23}$ 22$_{9.16}$ (unless nom. cl. in all five; see App.) Ezk 20$_{12}$ 37$_{28}$, בנה *build* 2 C 2$_{3.4.8}$, שׁפט *judge* 1 S 3$_{13}$, חסר pi. *deprive* Ec 4$_{8}$, פקד *punish* Jr 44$_{29}$, נכה hi. *strike* Ezk 7$_{9}$, ישׁע hi. *rescue* Is 49$_{26}$ (unless nom. cl.; see App.) 60$_{16}$, רפא *heal* Ex 15$_{26}$ (unless nom. cl.; see App.), חזק pi. *strengthen* 14$_{17}$, נצר *guard* Is 27$_{3}$, שׂבע *be satisfied* 4QJub^{d} 1.1$_{12}$ ([אני שבע]).

<NOM CL> with singular noun, יֵצֶר *creature* 1QH 1$_{21}$ 3$_{23}$ 18$_{25.31}$ fr. 1$_{8}$ 3$_{11(mg)}$ 52$_{3}$ ([יצ]ר), אִישׁ *man* Jg 13$_{11}$ 1 K 13$_{14}$ (both with ellipsis of predicate; || אַתָּה *you* sg.) 2 K 1$_{10.12}$ 1QH fr. 1$_{4}$, אִשָּׁה *woman* 1 S 1$_{26}$ 2 S 14$_{5}$, גֶּבֶר *man* Lm 3$_{1}$, אָב *father* Ml 1$_{6}$, בֵּן *son* Gn 27$_{32}$ 2 K 16$_{7}$ Is 19$_{11}$ Ps 116$_{16}$ 4QJub^{d} 1.1$_{13}$, נַעַר *lad* Si 51$_{13}$ (=11QPs^{a} 21$_{11}$), מֶלֶךְ *king* 2 S 19$_{23}$ Ml 1$_{14}$, שַׂר *prince* Jos 5$_{14}$, גִּבּוֹר *warrior* Jl 4$_{10}$, נָבִיא *prophet* 1 K 13$_{18}$, נָזִיר *Nazirite* Jg 16$_{17}$, חָבֵר *companion* Ps 119$_{63}$, קַבְּלָן *recipient* Mur 22 1$_{4}$ Mur 30 1$_{5}$ 2$_{22}$, עֶבֶד *servant* 2 S 15$_{34.34}$ 1 K 18$_{36}$ (:: אַתָּה) 2 K 16$_{7}$ Ps 116$_{16.16}$ 119$_{125}$ 143$_{12}$ 1QH 14$_{25}$ (but perh. app., ואני עבדך *and as for me, your servant*).

חֵלֶק your *portion* Nm 18$_{20}$ 1Q26 1$_{7(Milik)}$ ([חל]קכה), אֲחֻזָּה their *portion* Ezk 44$_{28}$, נַחֲלָה their *portion* 44$_{28}$, עַם *people* Jos 17$_{14}$, יָם *sea* Jb 7$_{12}$, חוֹמָה *wall* Ca 8$_{10}$ (|| שָׁדַי *my breasts*), עֵץ *tree* Is 56$_{3}$, חֲבַצֶּלֶת *crocus* Ca 2$_{1}$, מוֹפֵת their *sign* Ezk 12$_{11}$, הֶדֶר *ornament* 4QM^{a} fr. 12$_{4}$ (but perh. app.), מַנְגִּינָה *(theme of) song* Lm 3$_{63}$, יְשׁוּעָה your *salvation* Ps 35$_{3}$, מוּסָר *chastisement* Ho 5$_{2}$, בַּעַר *brutishness*, i.e. brutish Ps 73$_{22}$, שָׁלוֹם *peace*, i.e. peaceable 120$_{7}$ (:: הֵמָּה *they*), תְּפִלָּה *prayer*, i.e. prayerful 109$_{4}$ (or em. תְּפִלָּתִי לָהֶם as for me, *my prayer was for them* or אֵין תִּפְלָה *there was no unsavouriness*, i.e. unseemly behaviour), בִּינָה *understanding* Pr 8$_{14}$, עַצְמְכֶם וּבְשַׂרְכֶם אָנִי *I am your bones and your flesh* Jg 9$_{2(L)}$, אני עפר ואפר *I am dust and ashes* 1QH 10$_{5}$.

Pharaoh Gn 41$_{44}$, Joseph 45$_{3.4}$, Joab 2 S 20$_{17}$ (with ellipsis of predicate; || אַתָּה *you* sg., + אָנֹכִי *I*), El Shaddai Gn 17$_{1}$ 35$_{11}$, אֵל *God* Is 43$_{12}$ 45$_{22}$ Ezk 28$_{2}$ (:: אַתָּה), אֱלֹהִים *God* 2 K 5$_{7}$ Is 41$_{10}$ Jr 23$_{23}$ Ezk 28$_{9}$ (:: אַתָּה) 34$_{31}$, אֲדֹנָי י׳ *my Lord Y.* 13$_{9}$ 23$_{49}$ 24$_{24}$ 28$_{24}$ 29$_{16}$.

י׳ *Y.* Gn 15$_{7}$ 28$_{13}$ Ex 6$_{2.6.29}$ 7$_{5.17}$ (+ אָנֹכִי) 10$_{2}$ 14$_{4.18}$ Lv 18$_{5.6.21}$ 19$_{12.14.16.18.28.30.32.37}$ 22$_{3.8.30.31}$ 1 K 20$_{13.28}$ Is 42$_{8}$ 43$_{15}$ 45$_{5.6.18}$ 49$_{23}$ Jr 24$_{7}$ 32$_{27}$ Ezk 6$_{7.13.14}$ 7$_{4.27}$ 11$_{10.12}$ 12$_{15.16.20}$ 13$_{14.21.23}$ 14$_{8}$ 15$_{7}$ 16$_{62}$ 20$_{26.38.42.44}$ 22$_{16}$ 24$_{27}$ 25$_{5.7.11.17}$ 26$_{6}$ 28$_{22.23}$ 29$_{6.9.21}$ 30$_{8.19.25.26}$ 32$_{15}$ 33$_{29}$ 34$_{27}$ 35$_{4.9.15}$ 36$_{11.23.38}$ 37$_{6.13}$ 38$_{23}$ 39$_{6}$ 4QpsEzek^{a} 2$_{4}$ ([אני י׳]) 4Q386–9 3.2$_{1}$, אֲנִי י׳ אֱלֹהֵיכֶם *I, Y., am your God* Ex 6$_{7}$ 16$_{12}$ Lv 11$_{44}$ 18$_{2.4.30}$ 19$_{3.4.10.25.31.34.36}$ 20$_{7.24}$ 23$_{22}$ 24$_{22}$ 25$_{17.38}$ 26$_{1.13}$ Nm 10$_{10}$ 15$_{41}$ Dt 29$_{5}$ Jg 6$_{10}$ Ezk 20$_{5.7.19.20}$ Jl 2$_{27}$ 11QT fr. 1$_{2}$ ([אלוה]יכם), sim. Ex 29$_{46}$ Lv 26$_{44}$ Is 41$_{13}$ 43$_{3}$ 48$_{17}$ Ezk 28$_{26}$ 39$_{22.28}$ Zc 10$_{6}$ 11QT 53$_{8}$.

With plural noun, רֶגֶל *foot* Jb 29$_{15}$ (unless אֲנִי subj. of היה *be*), אָדוֹן *lord* Ml 1$_{6}$, אֲנִי מְתֵי מִסְפָּר *I am people (few) of number* Gn 34$_{30}$.

With pronoun, הוּא *he, the one* Dt 32$_{39}$ Is 41$_{4}$ 43$_{10.13}$ 46$_{4}$ 48$_{12}$ 52$_{6}$ (אֲנִי־הוּא הַמְדַבֵּר *I am he that speaks*) 1 C 21$_{17}$ (אֲנִי־הוּא אֲשֶׁר־חָטָאתִי *I am he that has sinned*), זֶה *this* Gn 27$_{24}$ 1 K 18$_{8}$ (both || אַתָּה) Is 63$_{1}$ (|| מִי *who?*; all three with ellipsis of predicate), מִי *who?* 1 C 17$_{16}$ (||2 S 7$_{18}$ אָנֹכִי; || בֵּיתִי *my household*) 29$_{14}$ (|| עַמִּי *my people*) 2 C 2$_{5}$, מָה *what?* 1QH 3$_{24}$ 11$_{3}$ fr. 2.1$_{4}$, זְכָר־אֲנִי מֶה־חָלֶד perh. *remember, what duration I am* Ps 89$_{48}$ (or em. אֲדֹנָי

O, my Lord or מֶה־חָדֵל אָנִי *how lacking I am* or אֲנִי יְמֵי־הַחֶלֶד *my sorrow, the days of my duration*), אֲנִי הַמּוֹלִיד *I am the one that makes fertile* Is 66$_{9}$, אֲנִי י׳ הַקּוֹרֵא *I, Y., am the one that calls* 45$_{3}$, אֲנִי י׳ הַמַּעֲלֶה *I, Y., am the one that brought* you *up* Lv 11$_{45}$ (unless in both אֲנִי י׳ *I am Y.*).

With adjective, צָעִיר *small* Jb 32$_{6}$ (:: אַתֶּם), יָשֵׁן *sleeping* Ca 5$_{2}$ (:: לִבִּי *my heart*), קָדוֹשׁ *holy* Lv 11$_{44.45}$ 19$_{2}$ 20$_{26}$ 21$_{8}$ Ezk 39$_{7}$ (unless אֲנִי י׳ *I am Y.*), חַנּוּן *merciful* Ex 22$_{26}$, חָסִיד *loyal* Jr 3$_{12}$ Ps 86$_{2}$, כְּלִיל *perfect* Ezk 27$_{3}$ (or em. אָמַרְתְּ אֲנִי *you said, I* to אֳנִיָּה *ship*), טוֹב *good* Est 8$_{5}$, תָּם *sound* Jb 9$_{20.21}$, זַךְ *pure* 33$_{9}$ (|| אָנֹכִי), נָאוֶה *lovely* Ca 1$_{5}$, שְׁחוֹר *black* 1$_{5}$, שְׁחַרְחֹר *black* 1$_{6}$, עָמֵל *working* Ec 2$_{18}$ 4$_{8}$, שְׁכוּל *bereaved* Is 49$_{21}$, גַּלְמוּד *barren* Is 49$_{21}$, עָנִי *poor, afflicted* Ps 25$_{16}$ 40$_{18}$ 69$_{30}$ 70$_{6}$ 86$_{1}$ 88$_{16}$, אֶבְיוֹן *poor* 40$_{18}$ 70$_{6}$ 86$_{1}$, אֻמְלַל *feeble* 6$_{3}$ (+ עֲצָמַי *my bones*), יָחִיד *alone* 25$_{16}$, אַחֲרוֹן *last* Is 44$_{6}$ 48$_{12}$, רִאשׁוֹן *first* 44$_{6}$ 48$_{12}$, חָדֵל *lacking* Ps 39$_{5}$, חָסֵר *lacking* 1 S 21$_{16}$, עָרֵל *uncircumcised* Ex 6$_{12.30}$, רָשָׁע *wicked* 9$_{27}$.

With preposition, לְ of possession, *(belonging) to* 1 K 20$_{4}$ Is 44$_{5}$ Ps 119$_{94}$ Jb 33$_{6}$ Ca 2$_{16}$ 6$_{3}$ 7$_{11}$ (all three :: דּוֹדִי *my love*) 1QS 11$_{9.9}$, of benefit, *for, (disposed) to* Zc 8$_{11}$ 1 C 22$_{10}$ (mss אֲנִי אֶהְיֶה לוֹ *I shall be for him*; :: הוּא); בְּ of place, *in*, Ex 8$_{18}$ (unless אֲנִי י׳ *I am Y.*) Jr 26$_{14}$ Ezk 1$_{1}$ Jl 2$_{27}$ Dn 8$_{2}$; partitive, *(some) of* 4QPrFêtes^{a} 1$_{2}$ (Baillet אנו *we*); כְּ *as* Jr 11$_{19}$ Ho 5$_{12}$ 14$_{9}$ Ps 38$_{14}$ 52$_{10}$; מִן comparative, *(greater) than* 2 S 19$_{44}$; אֶל *(disposed) to* you Ho 3$_{3}$; עַל *against* Ezk 5$_{8}$; אֵת *with* Is 43$_{2.5}$ Jr 1$_{8.19}$ 15$_{20}$ 30$_{11}$ 42$_{11}$ 46$_{28}$ Ezk 34$_{30}$ Hg 1$_{13}$ 2$_{4}$; עִם *with* you Is 41$_{10}$ Ps 73$_{23}$; תַּחַת *in place of* God Gn 50$_{19}$; אַחֲרֵי *behind* Ne 12$_{38}$.

With adverb, שָׁם *there* 2 S 14$_{32}$ Is 48$_{16}$ Pr 8$_{27}$.

<APP> + אָמָה your *handmaid* 1 S 25$_{25}$, עֶבֶד your *servant* 1 K 1$_{26}$ 1QH 13$_{21}$, חֹתֵן your *father-in-law* Ex 18$_{6}$, שׂכל hi. ptc. *sage* 1QH 12$_{11}$ (Licht משכלי *by my intelligence*) 4QShir^{a} 1$_{4}$ (but perh. in both nom. cl.).

י׳ *Y.* (see also אֲנִי י׳ אֱלֹהֵיכֶם *I, Y., am your God* at nom. cl.) Ex 6$_{8}$ 8$_{18}$ 12$_{12}$ 15$_{26}$ 29$_{46}$ 31$_{13}$ Lv 11$_{45}$ 19$_{2}$ 20$_{8.26}$ 21$_{8.12.15.23}$ 22$_{2.9.16.32.33}$ 23$_{43}$ 25$_{55}$ 26$_{2.45}$ Nm 3$_{13.41.45}$ 14$_{35}$ 15$_{41}$ 35$_{34}$=11QT 51$_{7}$ Is 27$_{3}$ 41$_{4.13.17}$ 42$_{6}$ 45$_{3.7.8.19.21}$ 49$_{26}$ 60$_{16.22}$ 61$_{8}$ Jr 9$_{23}$ 17$_{10}$ Ezk 5$_{13.15.17}$ 6$_{10}$ 7$_{9}$ 12$_{25}$ 14$_{4.7.9}$ 17$_{21.24.24}$ 20$_{12}$ 21$_{4.10.22.37}$ 22$_{14.22}$ 24$_{14}$ 26$_{14}$ 30$_{12}$ 34$_{24.24.30}$ 35$_{12}$ 36$_{36.36}$ 37$_{14.28}$ 39$_{7}$ Jl 4$_{17}$ Ml 3$_{6}$ 11QT 45$_{14}$ Kh. Beit Lei graf. 5$_{1(Cross)}$ ([אנ]י) (but perh. nom. cl. here and at Ex 6$_{8}$ 8$_{18}$ 12$_{12}$ 15$_{26}$ 29$_{46}$ Lv 11$_{45}$ 20$_{8}$ 21$_{15.23}$ 22$_{9.16.32.33}$ 23$_{43}$ 26$_{45}$ Nm 3$_{45}$ 15$_{41}$ Is 42$_{6}$ 45$_{3.7}$ 49$_{26}$ 60$_{22}$ Jr 9$_{23}$ Ezk 6$_{10}$ 7$_{9}$ 39$_{7}$ Jl 4$_{17}$ Ml 3$_{6}$).

Wisdom Pr 8$_{12}$, Koheleth Ec 1$_{12}$, Daniel Dn 8$_{1.15.27}$ 9$_{2}$ 10$_{2.7}$ 12$_{5}$, Bar-Hizka Mur 22 1$_{4}$, Joseph 1$_{5}$ (יה[וסף]), Halipha Mur 24 3$_{14}$ ([א]ני חליפא), Salome Mur 30 1$_{6}$ 2$_{25}$.

<COLL> אֲנִי וְ *I and* + singular noun, אֵם *mother* Gn 37$_{10}$, בֵּן *son* 1 K 1$_{21}$, נַעַר *lad* Gn 22$_{5}$, פִּלֶגֶשׁ *concubine* Jg 20$_{4}$, אִשָּׁה *woman* 1 K 3$_{17}$, Jonathan 1 S 14$_{40}$, לֵב my *heart* Ec 7$_{25}$, אֲנִי וְאַתָּה *I and you* Gn 31$_{44}$ 1 S 20$_{23}$ 2 K 9$_{25}$ 5/6Ḥev BA 45 fr. 2, אֲנִי וָהוּא *I and he* Gn 41$_{11}$, בַּיִת *household* Gn 34$_{30}$ Ne 1$_{6}$, עַם *people* Ex 9$_{27}$ 33$_{16.16}$ Jos 8$_{5}$ Jg 12$_{2}$ Est 7$_{4}$, מִקְנֶה *cattle* Nm 20$_{19}$, אֲנִי וַחֲצִי הַסְּגָנִים *I and half the prefects* Ne 12$_{40}$, אֲנִי וְכָל־אֲשֶׁר־לִי *I and all that is mine* 1 K 20$_{4}$.

+ plural noun, אָב *ancestor* 2 C 32$_{13}$, אִישׁ *man* Ne 2$_{12}$ 4$_{17}$, אָח *relative* Gn 37$_{10}$ Ne 4$_{17}$ 5$_{10.14}$, נַעַר *lad* Ne 4$_{17}$ 5$_{10}$, נַעֲרָה *lass* Est 4$_{16}$.

אֲנִי וְאַפְסִי עוֹד *I am, and there is none other than me* Is 47$_{8.10}$ Zp 2$_{15}$, הִנְנִי־אָנִי *here I am* Ezk 34$_{11.20}$, אֲנִי ... לְבַדִּי *I ... alone* 1 K 19$_{10.14}$ Is 49$_{21}$ Jb 1$_{15.16.17.19}$ (all four + רַק *only*) Dn 10$_{8}$, אַתָּה ... וְלֹא־אָנִי *you... and not I* Jb 34$_{33}$, sim. 15$_{6}$, בִּי־אֲנִי ... הֶעָוֹן *on me alone ... be the guilt* 1 S 25$_{24}$, חַי־אָנִי *as I live* Nm 14$_{21.28}$ Is 49$_{18}$ Jr 22$_{24}$ 46$_{18}$ Ezk 5$_{11}$ 14$_{16.18.20}$ 16$_{48}$ 17$_{16}$ (all six + נְאֻם אֲדֹנָי י׳ *oracle of my lord Y.*) 17$_{19}$ 18$_{3}$ 20$_{3.31.33}$ 33$_{11}$ (all five + נְאֻם אֲדֹנָי י׳) 33$_{27}$ 34$_{8}$ 35$_{6.11}$ (all three + נְאֻם אֲדֹנָי י׳) Zp 2$_{9}$.

אֲנִי פִּי־הַמֶּלֶךְ שְׁמוֹר *let me observe the command of the king* Ec 8$_{2}$ (or em. אֶת־ object-marker or אַנְפֵּי *face of*).

גַּם־אָנִי *I too*, etc. Ex 6$_{5}$ (גַּם אֲנִי) Lv 26$_{24}$ Dt 12$_{30}$ Jg 1$_{3}$ 2$_{21}$ 2 S 18$_{2.22}$ 1 K 13$_{18}$ 2 K 2$_{3.5}$ Jr 4$_{12}$ 31$_{37}$ Ezk 5$_{8.11}$ 8$_{18}$ 9$_{10}$ 16$_{43}$ 20$_{15.23.25}$ 21$_{22}$ 24$_{9}$ Ho 3$_{3}$ 4$_{6}$ Am 4$_{6}$ Mc 6$_{13}$ Zc 8$_{21}$ Ml 2$_{9}$ Ps 71$_{22}$ Jb 7$_{11}$ 13$_{2}$ 33$_{6}$ 40$_{14}$ Pr 1$_{26}$ 23$_{15}$ Ec 2$_{14.15}$ Ne 5$_{10}$ 2 C 34$_{27}$ Si 30$_{25}$ 36$_{16}$ 4Q414 3$_{4}$, בָּרְכֵנִי גַם־אָנִי *bless me too* Gn 27$_{34.38}$, אַף־אָנִי *even I*, etc. 40$_{16}$ Lv 26$_{16.24.28.41}$ Is 48$_{12}$ (אַף אֲנִי) Ps 89$_{28}$ Jb 32$_{10.17.17}$ 2 C 12$_{5}$ 4Q385 3$_{3}$, אֲנִי ... אֲנִי *I ... I* for emphasis, etc. Gn 37$_{30}$ Dt 32$_{39}$ 2 S 15$_{34}$ Is 48$_{15}$ Ho 5$_{14}$.

אֲנִי *as for me*, etc., when not functioning as subject, Gn 17$_{4}$ 43$_{14}$ 48$_{7}$ 1 K 1$_{26}$ Is 45$_{12}$ (+ אָנֹכִי) 59$_{21}$ Ezk 9$_{10}$ Ps

41$_{13}$ 69$_{14}$ 73$_{2.28}$ 109$_{4}$ (if em.; see Nom. Cl.), Ec 2$_{15}$ Lm 1$_{16}$ Dn 10$_{17}$ 11$_{1}$ 1QS 11$_{2.11}$ 4QRitMar 19$_{4 (Baillet)}$ 1QH 2$_{28}$ 4$_{33}$ 9$_{6}$ 11$_{19}$ 14$_{25}$ (unless Nom. Cl.) 4QShir[b] 28$_{3}$ 63.3$_{1}$ Mur 30 1$_{6}$ 2$_{25}$, esp. emphasizing possession, וְלֹא יְחַלְּלוּ אֶת־שֵׁם קָדְשִׁי ... אֲנִי י׳ *so that they do not profane my holy name ..., mine, Y.'s* Lv 22$_{2}$, sim. 21$_{12}$ 26$_{2}$ Nm 3$_{13.41.45}$ (but perh. in all six nom. cl.) 2 S 19$_{1}$ Pr 23$_{15}$ Dn 8$_{1}$, אֲנִי (הָיָה) עִם־לְבָבִי *it was in my heart* 1 C 22$_{7}$ 28$_{2}$, הֲצוֹם צַמְתֻּנִי אָנִי *did you really fast for me?* Zc 7$_{5}$.

Also 4QRitMar 182$_{1}$ 512 33$_{8}$ ([ואנ]י) 42.2$_{5}$ 1QH 7$_{35}$ 9$_{18}$ 4QShir[b] 36$_{4}$ ([ואנ]י) Mur 48$_{3}$ ([שאנ]י) 4QapPs[b] 24$_{9}$.

אֳנִי 7 n.m. and f. **fleet**—cstr. אֳנִי—<SUBJ> בוא *come* 1 K 10$_{22}$, hi. *bring* wood, stone 10$_{11}$, נשׂא *carry* gold, silver 10$_{11.22}$, הלך *go* Is 33$_{21}$ (+ צִי *ship*), מוט htpol. *be tossed about* Si 36$_{2 (E, F)}$ (if em. אזנו appar. *his ear* to אוני). <OBJ> עשׂה *make* 1 K 9$_{26}$. <CSTR> אֳנִי חִירָם *fleet of Hiram* 1 K 10$_{11.22}$, אֳנִי תַרְשִׁישׁ *fleet of Tarshish* 10$_{22.22}$, אֳנִי־שַׁיִט *fleet of*, i.e. driven by, *oar(s)* Is 33$_{21}$. <PREP> שׁלח בְּ *send in* or *with* 1 K 9$_{27}$; עִם *with* 1 K 10$_{22}$.

→ אֳנִיָּה *ship.*

אֳנִיָּה 20.0.4 n.f. **ship**—Q אוניה; pl. אֳנִיּוֹת (אֳנִיֹּת, Kt אוניות); cstr. אֳנִיּוֹת; sf. אֳנִיּוֹתֵיהֶם—<SUBJ> היה *be* Ezk 27$_{9}$ (+ בָּךְ *in you*; ‖ מַלָּח *sailor*), עצר *be able* to go 2 C 20$_{37}$, בוא *come* Jon 1$_{3}$ 2 C 9$_{21}$, hi. *bring* Is 60$_{9}$, הלך *go* 1 K 22$_{49}$ ‖2 C 20$_{36}$ 2 C 9$_{21}$ (+ לַמֶּלֶךְ *belonging to the king*; ‖1 K 10$_{22}$ אֳנִי *fleet*) 20$_{37}$, pi. *go about* Ps 104$_{26}$ (‖ לִוְיָתָן *Leviathan*), שׁוּר *travel* Ezk 27$_{25}$ (if em. שָׁרוֹתַיִךְ מַעֲרָבֵךְ *your travellers, your merchandise* to שָׁרוֹת לָךְ בְּמַעֲרָבֵךְ *travelling for you with merchandise*), נשׂא *carry* 2 C 9$_{21}$, חשׁב pi. *be minded*, i.e. be about (to break) Jon 1$_{4}$, שׁבר ni. *be broken, break* intrans. 1$_{4}$ 2 C 20$_{37}$, ילל hi. *wail* Is 23$_{1.14}$, קוה pi. *await* 60$_{9}$ (if וָאֳנִיּוֹת תַּרְשִׁישׁ בָּרִאשֹׁנָה = *with ships of Tarshish at the front*; but perh. nom. cl.; see Nom. Cl.)

<NOM CL> וָאֳנִיּוֹת תַּרְשִׁישׁ בָּרִאשֹׁנָה *and ships of Tarshish are at the front* Is 60$_{9}$ (but see Subj.), אֳנִיּוֹת תַּרְשִׁישׁ שָׁרוֹתַיִךְ מַעֲרָבֵךְ *ships of Tarshish were your travellers, your merchandise* Ezk 27$_{25}$ (but see Subj.).

<OBJ> עשׂה *make* 1 K 22$_{49 (Qr)}$‖2 C 20$_{36}$, מצא *find* Jon 1$_{3}$, שׁבר pi. *shatter* Ps 48$_{8}$, שׁלח *send* 2 C 8$_{18}$ (Kt אוניות; or em. וַיָּשֶׂם *and he placed*, i.e. made; ‖ עֶבֶד *servant* [unless em.; see Prep]).

<CSTR> אֳנִיּוֹת סוֹחֵר *ships of a merchant* Pr 31$_{14}$, אֵבֶה *of papyrus* Jb 9$_{26}$, תַּרְשִׁישׁ *of Tarshish* 1 K 22$_{49}$ Is 2$_{16}$ (‖ שְׂכִיָּה perh. *ship*) 23$_{1.14}$ 60$_{9}$ Ezk 27$_{25}$ Ps 48$_{8}$ 2 C 9$_{21}$, רִנָּתָם *of their exulting* Is 43$_{14}$, הַיָּם *of the sea* Ezk 27$_{9}$; דֶּרֶךְ אֳנִיָּה *way of a ship* Pr 30$_{19}$ (‖ נֶשֶׁר *eagle*, נָחָשׁ *serpent*, גֶּבֶר *man*), חוֹף אֳנִיּוֹת *shore of ships* Gn 49$_{13}$, אַנְשֵׁי *men of*, i.e. sailors 1 K 9$_{27}$, כָּל־ *all* Is 2$_{16}$ Ezk 27$_{9}$.

<PREP> וַיִּשְׁלַח לוֹ לָאֳנִיּוֹת עֲבָדִים *and he sent him servants by ships* 2 C 8$_{18}$ (if em. וַעֲבָדִים *and servants*; perh. also em. וַיִּשְׁלַח, see Obj.); בְּ of place, *in*, Jon 1$_{5}$ 1QH 6$_{22}$, + שׁוב hi. *send back* Dt 28$_{68}$, הלך *go* 1 K 22$_{50}$, ירד *go down* Ps 107$_{23}$, hi. *bring down* Is 43$_{14}$, שׂער בְּ htp. *storm against* Dn 11$_{40}$ (‖ רֶכֶב *chariot*, פָּרָשׁ *cavalry*); עַל *against* Is 2$_{16}$; ירד מִן *go down from* Ezk 27$_{29}$; חלף עִם *pass by with* Jb 9$_{26}$; כְּ *as* + היה *be* Pr 31$_{14}$, שׂים *make* 1QH 3$_{6}$ (‖ עִיר *city*), רעע ni. *be broken, break* intrans. 3$_{13}$, עלה *go up* 7$_{4}$.

<ADJ> אֳנִיּוֹת רַבּוֹת *many ships* Dn 11$_{40}$. <COLL> כאוניה על פני מים *as a ship upon the waters* 1QH 3$_{13}$, וְדָן לָמָּה יָגוּר אֳנִיּוֹת *and Dan, why did he linger (by) the ships?* Jg 5$_{17}$, יְהוֹשָׁפָט עשׂר אֳנִיּוֹת perh. *Jehoshaphat was rich in ships* 1 K 22$_{49 (Kt)}$.

→ אֳנִי *fleet.*

אֲנִיָּה 2 n.f. **mourning**, <SUBJ> היה *be* Is 29$_{2}$ (‖ תַּאֲנִיָּה *mourning*). <OBJ> רבה hi. *increase* Lm 2$_{5}$ (‖ תַּאֲנִיָּה).

<SYN> תַּאֲנִיָּה *mourning.*

→ אנה *mourn.*

אניהו 0.0.0.3 pr.n.m. **Oniah, 1.** son of Hariah (הריהו), Seal 273$_{1}$ (Gibeon). **2.** son of Merab (מירב), Seal 730$_{1}$ (8th/7th cent.). **3.** Kh. el-Qom tomb inscr. 3$_{4}$. **4.** Ketef Hinnom inscr. 2$_{2}$ (others וניהו).

[אָנִין] 0.0.1 n.[m.] **sighing**—sf. Q אנינם—perh. רבה אנינם *great is their sighing* 1QH fr. 5$_{8}$.

→ אנן *sigh.*

אֲנִיעָם 1 pr.n.m. **Aniam,** son of Shemida, descendant of Manasseh, 1 C 7$_{19}$.

אֲנָךְ 4 **lead,** <SUBJ> נצב ni. *be positioned* by wall Am 7$_7$ (if em. אֲדֹנָי נִצָּב עַל־חוֹמַת אֲנָךְ וּבְיָדוֹ אֲנָךְ *my lord was standing by a wall of lead and in his hand was lead* to אֲנָךְ נִצָּב עַל־חוֹמָה *lead*, i.e. plumbline, *was positioned by a wall*). <NOM CL> בְּיָדוֹ אֲנָךְ *in his hand was lead*, i.e. plumbline Am 7$_7$ (unless em.). <OBJ> ראה *see* Am 7$_8$, שׂים *place* 7$_8$. <CSTR> חוֹמַת אֲנָךְ *wall of lead*, perh. built with a plumbline Am 7$_7$ (unless em.).

אָנֹכִי 359.0.32 pronoun **I**—אָנֹכִי (אָנֹ֫כִי), Q אנוכי—rarely of female speaker, Gn 16$_{5.8}$ 24$_{24}$ 25$_{22}$ 29$_{33}$ 30$_{1.3}$ 38$_{25}$ Jg 11$_{37}$ 1 S 1$_{15.28}$ 2 S 11$_5$ 1 K 2$_{18.20}$ 2 K 4$_{13}$ Ru 2$_{10.13}$ 3$_9$, freq. of Y. (esp. in 11QT).

<SUBJ> **a. with verbs,** היה *be* Ex 4$_{12.15}$ Dt 31$_{23}$ (:: אַתָּה *you* sg.; all + עִם *with*) Ru 2$_{13}$ (+ כְּ *as*), + לְ of possession Ho 1$_9$ (:: אַתֶּם *you* pl.), *as, in the capacity of* Jg 11$_9$ 1 S 23$_{17}$ (:: אַתָּה), וִהְיִיתֶם לִי לְעָם וְאָנֹכִי אֶהְיֶה לָכֶם לֵאלֹהִים *and you will be to me as a people and I shall be to you as God* Jr 11$_4$ 30$_{22}$ Ezk 36$_{28}$, sim. Jr 24$_7$ (+ אֲנִי *I*) 11QT 29$_7$, בעל *be master* Jr 3$_{14}$ 31$_{32}$.

יצא *go out* Nm 22$_{32}$, hi. *bring out* Jg 6$_8$, ירד *go down* Gn 46$_4$, עבר *pass* Ps 141$_{10}$, עלה hi. *bring up* Gn 46$_4$ Jg 6$_8$ 1 S 10$_{18}$ Am 2$_{10}$, עמד *stand* Dt 10$_{10}$, ישׁב *sit, stay* Jg 6$_{18}$ 1 S 20$_5$, קרה ni. *meet* trans. Nm 23$_{15}$, פצה *open* mouth Jg 11$_{35}$, שׁלח *send* Ex 3$_{12}$ Jr 23$_{32}$, pi. Gn 38$_{17}$ Ex 8$_{24}$, הלך hi. *lead* Am 2$_{10}$, סבב perh. *bring about* 1 S 22$_{22}$, שׂים *place* Ex 4$_{11.11}$.

ראה *see* Jr 7$_{11}$, חזה *see* Pr 24$_{32}$, ידע *know* Gn 20$_6$ 28$_{16}$ Dt 31$_{27}$ Jr 29$_{11}$, hi. *inform* 1 S 16$_3$, זכר *remember* GnzPs 4$_9$, שׁכח *forget* Is 49$_{15}$ (:: אֵלֶּה *these*), אמר *say* Jr 3$_{19}$ 11QT 56$_{17}$, דבר pi. *speak* 1 K 2$_{18}$ Jr 35$_{14}$ Jb 16$_4$ 21$_3$ 33$_{31}$ 42$_4$, נגד hi. *tell* Is 43$_{12}$, דמה pi. *speak in figures* Ho 12$_{11}$, צוה pi. *command* 2 S 13$_{28}$ Jr 1$_{17}$, שׁבע ni. *swear* Gn 21$_{24}$, ענה *answer* Jb 9$_{14}$ 13$_{22}$ 14$_{15}$, שׁמע *hear* Gn 21$_{26}$ (+ אַתָּה) 2 K 22$_{19}$ (‖2 C 34$_{27}$ אֲנִי), hi. *tell* Is 43$_{12}$, רגל tiphel *teach to walk* Ho 11$_3$, דרשׁ *seek* Dt 18$_{19}$, שׁיר *sing* Jg 5$_3$, תקע *sound* trumpet Jg 7$_{18}$ (:: אַתֶּם), בכה *weep* Jg 11$_{37}$, נחם pi. *comfort* Is 66$_{13}$, שׂמח *rejoice* Ps 104$_{34}$.

עשׂה *do, make* Gn 30$_{30}$ 47$_{30}$ 2 S 2$_6$ (:: י׳ Y.) Is 45$_{12}$ Jr 27$_5$, יכל *be able* Gn 19$_{19}$ Nm 11$_{14}$ Jg 11$_{35}$, מלא *be full* Mc 3$_8$, pi. *be wholehearted* Jos 14$_8$, ברא *create* Is 54$_{16.16}$, נטע *plant* Jr 2$_{21}$, רבה hi. *multiply* visions Ho 12$_{11}$, נתן *give* Gn 16$_5$ Jg 17$_{10}$ Jr 27$_6$ Ho 2$_{10}$ (+ הִיא *she*), שׁית *place* Pr 24$_{32}$, שׁאל hi. *lend* 1 S 1$_{28}$, תכן pi. *regulate* Ps 75$_4$, חשׂך *withhold* Gn 20$_6$, מנע *withhold* Am 4$_7$, סתר hi. *conceal* Dt 31$_{18}$, ירשׁ hi. *dispossess* Jos 13$_6$, עור hi. *rouse* trans. Is 45$_{13}$, ריב *contend* 49$_{25}$, פנה pi. *prepare* house Gn 24$_{31}$, כול pilp. *provide for* 50$_{21}$, הרה *become pregnant* Nm 11$_{12}$, ילד *give birth* 11$_{12}$, בנה ni. *be built up* Gn 30$_3$.

נצל hi. *rescue* 1 S 10$_{18}$ 2 S 12$_7$, ישׁע hi. *rescue* Is 43$_{12}$ 49$_{25}$, גאל *redeem* Ru 3$_{13}$ 4$_4$, פדה *redeem* Ho 7$_{13}$ (:: הֵמָּה *they*), סלח *forgive* 11QT 53$_{21}$ 54$_3$, ערב *guarantee* Gn 43$_9$, עבד *serve* Jos 24$_{15}$, כרת *make (covenant)* Jr 34$_{13}$, משׁח *anoint* 2 S 12$_7$, חטא *sin* Jos 7$_{20}$ Jg 11$_{27}$ (:: אַתָּה) 2 S 24$_{17}$ (‖1 C 21$_{17}$ אֲנִי), pi. *suffer loss* Gn 31$_{39}$, עוה hi. *sin* 2 S 24$_{17}$, רשׁע *be condemned* Jb 9$_{29}$, מרה *rebel* Is 50$_5$, מות pol. *kill* 2 S 1$_{16}$, שׁמד hi. *destroy* Am 2$_9$, שׁחת hi. *destroy* 4QpGen^a 3$_4$ ([אנוכ]י לא [אשחית]).

b. with participles, בוא *come* Ex 3$_{13}$ 19$_9$ Jg 7$_{17}$ 1 S 4$_{16}$ (הַבָּא I am *[the] one that is coming*; ‖ אֲנִי *I*) 17$_{45}$ (:: אַתָּה *you* sg.) Is 66$_{18}$, hi. *bring* Jr 4$_6$ 6$_{19}$ 32$_{42}$ 51$_{64}$, הלך *go* Gn 15$_2$ 24$_{42}$ 25$_{32}$ 28$_{20}$ Jos 23$_{14}$ Jg 17$_9$ 1 K 2$_2$, יצא *go out* Ex 8$_{25}$, ירד *go down* 1 S 10$_8$, רדף *pursue* Jg 8$_5$, ברח *flee* Gn 16$_8$, שׁלח *send* Ex 23$_{20}$ 1 S 21$_3$ Jr 25$_{15.16.27}$ 26$_5$ Ml 3$_{23}$, pass. *be sent* 1 K 14$_6$, עמד *stand* Dt 5$_5$ Is 21$_8$, נצב ni. *stand* Gn 24$_{13.43}$ Ex 17$_9$ Is 21$_8$, נפל *fall* Jb 12$_3$ 13$_2$ (+ אֲנִי), קום hi. *raise* Zc 11$_{16}$, עלה hi. *raise* Jr 50$_9$, נשׂא *raise* Am 5$_1$, נטל *raise* 2 S 24$_{12}$ (‖1 C 21$_{10}$ אֲנִי), שׂים *place* Zc 12$_2$, יצג hi. *lay* Jg 6$_{37}$, רבץ hi. *lay* Is 54$_{11}$, עוק hi. *press* Am 2$_{13}$, מהה htpalp. *delay* intrans. 2 S 15$_{28}$.

ראה *see* Gn 31$_5$, שׁמע *hear* Ex 32$_{18}$ 1 S 2$_{23.24}$ 15$_{14}$ 2 S 20$_{17}$, ידע *know* Jr 29$_{23}$(Qr) (הַיּוֹדֵעַ I am *the one that knows*; Kt הו[א] יֹדֵעַ I am *he who knows*), חשׁב *devise* 18$_{11}$ 26$_3$ 29$_{11}$ 36$_3$, דבר *speak* Dt 5$_1$ Jr 28$_7$ 32$_{42}$ Jon 3$_2$ Dn 10$_{11}$, pi. 11QT 31$_9$, נגד hi. *tell* 1QDM 1$_7$ ([א]נו[כי]) 4QJub^a 1$_{12}$, צוה pi. *command* Ex 34$_{11}$ Dt 4$_{2.2.40}$ 6$_{2.6}$ 7$_{11}$ 8$_{1.11}$ 10$_{13}$ 11$_{8.13.22.27.28}$ 12$_{11.14.28}$ 13$_1$=11QT 54$_6$ Dt 13$_{19}$=11QT 55$_{13}$ Dt 15$_{5.11.15}$ 19$_{7.9}$ 24$_{18.22}$ 27$_{1.4.10}$ 28$_{1.13.14.15}$ 30$_{2.8.11.16}$ Am 9$_9$ 1QDM 1$_9$ (אנו[כי מ]צו[ך]) 2$_4$(Milik) ([מצו]ך) 4QpsMos^e 1$_3$ ([מצ]ו[ך]), עוד hi. *bear witness* Dt 32$_{46}$, למד pi. *teach* 4$_1$, שׁאל *ask* 2 S 3$_{13}$ (‖ אֲנִי) 14$_{18}$ 1 K 2$_{16.20}$, בקשׁ pi. *seek* Gn 37$_{16}$, פלל htp. *pray* Ne 1$_6$ (+ אֲנִי), שׂישׂ *rejoice* Ps 119$_{162}$, ירא *fear* Gn 32$_{12}$, תעב pi. *detest* Am 6$_8$, שׂנא pass. *be hated* Gn 29$_{33}$, בזה ni. *be despised* Ps 119$_{141}$.

עשה *do* 1 S 3$_{11}$ Is 44$_{24}$ (unless nom. cl.; see App.) Jr 33$_{9.9}$, חלל hi. *begin* 25$_{29}$ (:: אַתֶּם *you* pl., + אֲנִי), ישב *dwell* Gn 24$_{3.37}$ 2 S 7$_{2}$||1 C 17$_{1}$ (אֲרוֹן *ark*) 2 K 4$_{13}$ Is 6$_{5}$, שׁכן *dwell* 11QT 46$_{12}$ 47$_{18}$, pi. *cause to dwell* 47$_{11}$, מצא hi. *bring* Zc 11$_{6}$, נתן *give* Dt 4$_{8}$ 5$_{31}$ 11$_{26.32}$ Jos 1$_{2}$ 11$_{6}$ 1 S 24$_{5}$ 11QT 51$_{16}$ 55$_{2}$ ([א]נוכי) 55$_{16}$ 56$_{12}$ 60$_{16}$ 62$_{11.13}$ 64$_{12}$ fr. 1$_{5}$ (אנ[וכי]) 4QPentPar^{b} 23.2$_{4}$ ([א]נוכי), ירשׁ hi. *dispossess* 60$_{20}$, שׁקל *weigh* silver 2 S 18$_{12}$, יצר *form* Jr 18$_{11}$.

גאל *redeem* Ru 3$_{12}$, נסה pi. *test* 11QT 54$_{12}$ (מנשה), דין *judge* Gn 15$_{14}$, פתה pi. *seduce* Ho 2$_{16}$, מטר hi. *send rain* Gn 7$_{4}$, ישׁע hi. *rescue* Is 43$_{11}$ (unless nom. cl.; see App.), עור hi. *rouse* trans. Jr 50$_{9}$, רגע *disturb* Is 51$_{15}$ (unless nom. cl.; see App.), ירה hi. *shoot* 1 S 20$_{36}$, נכה hi. *strike* Ex 7$_{17}$ (+ אֲנִי), נגף *strike* 7$_{27}$, הרג *kill* 4$_{23}$, כלה pi. *destroy* Jr 14$_{12}$, כרת *make* covenant Ex 34$_{10}$ Dt 29$_{13}$ 4QJub^{a} 1$_{14}$ ([א]נכי), קדשׁ pi. *sanctify* 11QT 52$_{19}$, משׁח pass. *be anointed* 2 S 3$_{39}$, הרה *be pregnant* Gn 38$_{25}$ 2 S 11$_{5}$, מות *die* Gn 30$_{1}$ 48$_{21}$ 50$_{5.24}$ Dt 4$_{22}$ (:: אַתֶּם *you* pl.).

<NOM CL> with singular noun, אָב *father* Jb 29$_{16}$, בֵּן *son* 2 S 1$_{13}$ (:: אַתָּה *you* sg.; + אִישׁ גֵּר of a *man [who is] a sojourner*) Am 7$_{14}$ (+ נָבִיא of a *prophet*), בֶּן־ ... שָׁנָה *son of ... year(s) (of age)* Dt 31$_{2}$ Jos 14$_{7.10}$ 2 S 19$_{36}$, בַּת *daughter* Gn 24$_{24}$ (+ בְּתוּאֵל of *Bethuel*), אִישׁ *man* 27$_{11}$ (:: אָח my *brother*; + חָלָק *smooth*) Ex 4$_{10}$ (+ דְּבָרִים of *words*) 1 S 18$_{23}$ (+ רושׁ ptc. *[who is] poor*) Is 6$_{5}$ (+ טְמֵא־שְׂפָתַיִם *[who is] unclean of lips*) Ps 22$_{7}$, *husband* Ho 2$_{4}$ (:: הִיא *she*) Zc 13$_{5}$ (+ עֹבֵד אֲדָמָה *[who] works the land*).

אִשָּׁה *woman* 1 S 1$_{15}$ (+ קְשַׁת־רוּחַ *[who is] hard of spirit*), נַעַר *lad* 30$_{13}$ (+ מִצְרִי *Egyptian*) 1 K 3$_{7}$ (+ קָטֹן *young*; both :: אַתָּה) Jr 1$_{6.7}$, נָבִיא *prophet* Am 7$_{14}$ Zc 13$_{5}$, עֵד *witness* Jr 29$_{23}$, ראה ptc. *seer* 1 S 9$_{19}$, שׁמר ptc. *guardian* Gn 4$_{9}$, בּוֹקֵר *herdsman* Am 7$_{14}$, בּוֹלֵס *tender of figs* 7$_{14}$, עֶבֶד *servant* Gn 24$_{34}$, גֵּר *sojourner* 23$_{4}$ Ps 39$_{13}$ 119$_{19}$, תּוֹשָׁב *inhabitant* Gn 23$_{4}$ Ps 39$_{13}$.

אֵל *God* Gn 31$_{13}$ (+ בֵּית־אֵל of *Bethel*) 46$_{3}$ (+ אֱלֹהֵי אָבִיךָ *[who was] the God of your father*) Ex 20$_{5}$ Dt 5$_{9}$ (unless in both אָנֹכִי י׳ *I am Y.*; both + קַנָּא *jealous*) Is 46$_{9}$ Ho 11$_{9}$, [אנכי אלהי ישראל ואב] *I am the God of Israel and father* to the sons of Jacob 4QJub^{a} 4$_{9}$, אֱלֹהִים *God* Gn 26$_{24}$ Ex 3$_{6}$ (both + אָבִיךָ of *your father*) Is 46$_{9}$ Ps 46$_{11}$ 50$_{7}$, אָנֹכִי י׳ אֱלֹהֶיךָ *I am Y. your God* Ex 20$_{2}$ Dt 5$_{6}$ Ho 12$_{10}$ 13$_{4}$ Ps 81$_{11}$, Esau Gn 27$_{19}$, Ruth Ru 3$_{9}$.

אָתוֹן your *she-ass* Nm 22$_{30}$, כֶּלֶב *dog* 1 S 17$_{43}$ (:: אַתָּה *you* sg.), sim. 2 S 3$_{8}$, תּוֹלַעַת *worm* Ps 22$_{7}$, מָגֵן *shield* Gn 15$_{1}$, בַּעַר *brutishness*, i.e. brutish Pr 30$_{2}$, אָנֹכִי עָפָר וָאֵפֶר *I am dust and ashes* Gn 18$_{27}$.

With plural participle, אָנֹכִי שְׁלֻמֵי *I am (of) the peacable ones of* the faithful of Israel 2 S 20$_{19}$.

With pronoun, הוּא *he (who)* Is 43$_{25}$ (+ מחה *efface*) 51$_{12}$ (+ נחם pi. *comfort*) Jr 29$_{23(Kt)}$ (Qr הַיּוֹדֵעַ *the one that knows*), מִי *who?* Ex 3$_{11}$ 1 S 18$_{18}$ (|| חַיַּי *my life*) 2 S 7$_{18}$ (|| בֵּיתִי *my house*; ||1 C 17$_{16}$ אֲנִי *I*); לָמָּה זֶּה אָנֹכִי *why am I (in) this (state)?* Gn 25$_{22}$, הַאַתָּה זֶה ... וַיֹּאמֶר אָנֹכִי *is it you ...? And he said, (It is) I* 2 S 2$_{20}$.

With gentilic, פְּלִשְׁתִּי *Philistine* 1 S 17$_{8}$ (:: אַתֶּם *you* pl.), עֲמָלֵקִי *Amalekite* 2 S 1$_{8}$ (:: אַתָּה *you* sg.), עִבְרִי *Hebrew* Jon 1$_{9}$ (+ אֲנִי), לֵוִי *Levite* Jg 17$_{9}$, בֶּן־יְמִינִי *Benjaminite* 1 S 9$_{21}$.

With adjective, עֵירֹם *naked* Gn 3$_{10}$, עָיֵף *weary* 25$_{30}$, עָנִי *poor* Ps 109$_{22}$ (|| לֵב my *heart*; + אֶבְיוֹן *poor*), צָעִיר *small* Jg 6$_{15}$ (|| אֶלֶף my *clan*) Ps 119$_{141}$, טוֹב *good* 1 S 1$_{8}$, נָקִי *innocent* 2 S 3$_{28}$, חַף *innocent* Jb 33$_{9}$ (אָנֹכִי; || אֲנִי *I*), רַךְ *tender* 2 S 3$_{39}$, נָכְרִי *foreign* Ru 2$_{10}$, חַי *alive* (in oath) Dt 32$_{40}$.

With preposition, מִן of place, *from* Jg 19$_{18}$ (+ אֲנִי *I*); כְּ *as* Ho 5$_{14.14}$ (+ אֲנִי), לְאֹתוֹת I and the children are *as signs* Is 8$_{18}$; עִם *with* Gn 28$_{15}$ 31$_{38}$ Ps 91$_{15}$ 11QT 61$_{14}$; אֵת *with* Gn 26$_{24}$, תַּחַת *in place of* God Gn 30$_{2}$; אַחֲרֵי *after*, i.e. subordinate, to you Ru 4$_{4}$; בְּקֶרֶב *among* Nm 11$_{21}$.

With adverb, כֵּן *thus* Jb 9$_{35}$ (+ עִמָּדִי *with*, i.e. in, *myself*).

<APP> אָנֹכִי י׳ *I, Y.* Ex 4$_{11}$ (Ex 20$_{2.5}$ Dt 5$_{6.9}$ Is 43$_{11}$ 44$_{24}$ 51$_{15}$ Ho 12$_{10}$ 13$_{4}$ Ps 81$_{11}$ are prob. Nom. Cl.).

<COLL> אָנֹכִי וְ *I and* with collective singular noun, בַּיִת my *household* Jos 24$_{15}$, מַמְלָכָה my *kingdom* 2 S 3$_{28}$; with plural noun, רֵעַ my *friend* Jg 11$_{37(Qr)}$, יֶלֶד *child* Is 8$_{18}$; אָנֹכִי וְכָל־אֲשֶׁר אִתִּי *I and all who are with me* Jg 7$_{18}$.

אָנֹכִי אָנֹכִי *I, I* for emphasis Is 43$_{11.25}$ 51$_{12}$, sim. Jg 5$_{3}$, אָנֹכִי לְבַדִּי *I alone* Nm 11$_{14}$, יַחַד אָנֹכִי perh. *I alone* Ps 141$_{10}$ (or move יַחַד to preceding colon), גַּם אָנֹכִי *I too*, etc. Gn 206.6 (גַּם־) 2126 303.30 (both גַּם־) 1 S 128 1223 2 S 26 2 K 2219 Jr 711 Am 47 Jb 164 GnzPs 49, אָנֹכִי *as for me*, etc. Gn 2427 1 S 1223 Ps 1418 (if em. כִּי *for*) Jb 214 (הֶאָנֹכִי).

Also 11QPsa 2814 Lachish ost. 68 ([י]אנכ).

אנן 2.1 vb. **sigh—Htpo.** Impf. יִתְאוֹנֵן (Si יתונן); ptc. מִתְאוֹנְנִים—**complain,** <SUBJ> אָדָם *human being* Lm 339, עֶבֶד *slave* Si 1025(A); subj. unspecified, Nm 111 (וַיְהִי הָעָם כְּמִתְאֹנְנִים *and the people were as ones that complain*).

→ אָנִין *sighing*.

אנס 1.1.1 vb. **force—Qal** Ptc. אֹנֵס, Q אונס—הַשְּׁתִיָּה כַדָּת אֵין אֹנֵס *the drinking was in accordance with the law—there was no one forcing* to drink or not to drink Est 18, אל ידור ... מאום אנוס *he is not to (offer in fulfilment of) vow ... something forced*, i.e. taken by force CD 1613.

Ni. Pf Si נאנסתה—אם נאנסתה במטעמים *if you are forced with*, i.e. to eat, *delicacies* Si 3421(B).

→ אֹנֶס *force*.

[אָנֵס], see אֹנֵס.

אנף 14.1.1 vb. **be angry—Qal** Pf. אָנַפְתָּ; impf. יֶאֱנַף, 2ms תֶּאֱנַף; + waw וְאָנַפְתָּ—<SUBJ> Y. 1 K 846||2 C 636 Is 121 Ps 603 (+ זנח *reject*, פרץ *break out* against) 795 (+ לָנֶצַח *forever*, בער *burn*, of jealousy) 856 (+ משך *prolong* anger) Ezr 914 (+ עַד־כַּלֵּה *unto destruction*), בַּר *son* Ps 212 (+ בער *burn*, of anger). <PREP> בְּ *against, with* 1 K 846||2 C 636 Is 121 Ps 856 Ezr 914.

Htp. Pf. הִתְאַנַּף; + waw וַיִּתְאַנַּף, 2ms Q תתאנף—as Qal, **be angry,** <SUBJ> Y. Dt 137 421 98 (+ קצף hi. *enrage*) 920 1 K 119 2 K 1718 Si 4519 4QDibHama 28. <PREP> בְּ *against, with* Dt 137 421 98.20 1 K 119 2 K 1718 4QDibHama 28; בִּגְלַלְכֶם *because of you* Dt 137; עַל־דִּבְרֵיכֶם *because of you* (lit. *because of your things*) Dt 421.

→ אַף *nose*, אַפַּיִם *Appaim*.

אֲנָפָה 2 n.f. **heron** or other unclean bird, perh. cormorant, flamingo, ostrich, or vulture, <OBJ> שׁקץ pi. *abominate* Lv 1119, אכל not *eat* 1119(Sam)||Dt 1418. <COLL> הָאֲנָפָה לְמִינָהּ *the heron according to its kind* Lv 1119||Dt 1418.

אנק 4 vb. **groan—Qal** Impf. יֶאֱנֹק; inf. אֱנֹק—**groan,** <SUBJ> חָלָל *one who is wounded* Jr 5152 Ezk 2615 (|| הרג ni. *be killed*).

Ni. Impv. הֵאָנֵק, ptc. נֶאֱנָקִים—as Qal, **groan,** in mourning, <SUBJ> אִישׁ *man*, i.e. inhabitant, of Jerusalem Ezk 94 (|| אנח ni. *sigh*), Ezekiel 2417 (+ עשׂה אֵבֶל *make mourning*; see also Coll.).

<PREP> עַל *concerning* Ezk 94 (+ תּוֹעֵבָה *abomination*). <COLL> הֵאָנֵק דֹּם *groan, be silent*, i.e. groan quietly Ezk 2417.

→ אֲנָקָה *groan(ing)*.

אֲנָקָה I 4.1 n.f. **groan(ing)**—cstr. אֶנְקַת—<SUBJ> בוא *come* Ps 7911 (+ לִפְנֵי *before* Y.). <OBJ> שׁמע *hear* Ps 10221, נטשׁ *disregard* Si 3217(Bmg); כַּסּוֹת ... אֶת־מִזְבַּח י׳ ... אֲנָקָה *to cover ... the altar of Y. ... with groaning* Ml 213 (|| בְּכִי *weeping*, דִּמְעָה *tear[s]*, or nom. cl., *there is weeping and groaning*).

<CSTR> אֶנְקַת אָסִיר *groaning of (the) prisoner* Ps 7911 10221, יתום *of (the) orphan* Si 3217(Bmg) (B צעקת *cry of*), אֶבְיוֹנִים *of the poor* Ps 126 (|| שֹׁד *despoiling*). <PREP> קום מן *arise because of* Ps 126.

→ אנק *groan*.

אֲנָקָה II 1 n.f. perh. **gecko** (*hemidactylus turcicus*), in list of reptiles, as unclean, Lv 1130.

אנשׁ 9.0.4 vb. **be weak—Qal** Ptc. אָנוּשׁ (אָנֻשׁ), אֲנוּשָׁה—usu. **be incurable,** also **be unerasable** (Is 81 [if em.]), <SUBJ> כְּאֵב *pain* Is 1711 1QH 528 828, מַכָּה *blow* Jr 1518 Mc 19, לֵב *heart* Jr 179 (or em. אֱנֹשׁ *human being* or נוֹאָשׁ *despairing*), יוֹם *day* 1716 (or em. אֱנוֹשׁ), שֶׁבֶר *breach* 3012 (if em. אָנוּשׁ לְשִׁבְרֵךְ appar. *it is incurable for your breach* to אָנוּשׁ שִׁבְרֵךְ לָךְ *incurable is your breach for you*), מַכְאֹב *pain* 3015, חֵץ *arrow*, i.e. effects of arrow Jb 346 (or em. מַחַץ *wound*), חֶרֶט *stylus* Is 81 (if em. אֱנוֹשׁ *of a human being*). <COLL> אשר יהלך לפני רעהו ערום ולוא היה

אנושׁ *one that parades before his fellow naked, though he be not incurable*, i.e. very ill 1QS 7_{12} (or em. אָנוּס [or אָנוּשׁ] *compelled*).

Ni. Impf. + waw וַיֵּאָנַשׁ—as Qal, **be incurable,** **<SUBJ>** יֶלֶד Bathsheba's *child* 2 S 12_{15} (ms, 4QSam[a] omit).

Also 1QH 8_{40} 4QapLam[a] 1.1_{14} (Allegro איש *man*).

אֱנֹשׁ, see אֱנוֹשׁ.

אנתיכוס 0.0.1 pr.n.m. **Antiochus,** perh. Antiochus IV Epiphanes, מלכי יון מאנתיכוס *the kings of Greece from (the time of) Antiochus* 4QpNah 3.1_{3}.

אָסָא 58 pr.n.m. **Asa, 1.** king of Judah, 1 K 15_{8}||2 C 13_{23} 1 K $15_{9.11}$||2 C 14_{1} 1 K $15_{13.14}$||2 C $15_{16.17}$ 1 K $15_{16.17.18}$ ||2 C $16_{1.2}$ 1 K $15_{18.20.22}$||2 C $16_{4.6}$ 1 K $15_{22.23.24}$||2 C $16_{11.13}$ 1 K $15_{25.28.32.33}$ $16_{8.10.15.23.29}$ $22_{41.43}$||2 C 20_{32} 1 K 22_{47} Jr 41_{9} 1 C 3_{10} 2 C $14_{7.9.10.11.12}$ $15_{2.2.8.10.16.19}$ $16_{1.7.10.10.12}$ 17_{2} 21_{12}. **2.** Levite, son of Elkanah and father of Berechiah, 1 C 9_{16} (mss אָסָף *Asaph*).

אָסוּךְ 1 n.m. **jar** or other vessel, אֵין לְשִׁפְחָתְךָ ... כִּי אִם־ אָסוּךְ שָׁמֶן *there is nothing to your maidservant ... except a jar (of) oil* 2 K 4_{2}.

→ סוך *anoint.*

אָסוֹן 5.3 n.m. **harm,** **<SUBJ>** היה *be* Ex $21_{22.23}$, קרא *meet*, i.e. befall Benjamin Gn $42_{4.38}$ 44_{29} (קרה), נגע *strike* Si 34_{22}. **<OBJ>** יצא hi. *take out*, i.e. produce (of contention) Si 38_{18}. **<CSTR>** על יד אסון *by the hand*, i.e. by means, *of harm* Si $41_{9(Bmg)}$, כל אוסן *all harm* Si 34_{22}.

אֵסוּר 3 n.m. **bond**—pl. אֲסוּרִים; sf. אֱסוּרָיו—**<SUBJ>** **bond, fetter,** perh. **girdle** (Is 11_{5}), היה *be* Is 11_{5} (if em. אֵזוֹר *girdle*; + צֶדֶק *righteousness*; || אֵזוֹר), מסס ni. *be melted* Jg 15_{14} (+ מֵעַל יָדָיו *from off his hands*; + עֲבֹת *rope*).

<NOM CL> אֲסוּרִים יָדֶיהָ *her hands are fetters* Ec 7_{26} (+ חֵרֶם *net*, מָצוֹד *net*).

<CSTR> אֵסוּר מָתְנָיו *girdle of his loins* Is 11_{5} (if em.; see above); בֵּית הָאֵסוּר *house of (the) fetter*, i.e. prison Jr 37_{15}.

<PREP> ויסרתיהו באסורים perh. *and I shall punish him in fetters* Si 4_{17} (but prob. אִסּוּרִים *chastisements*).

→ אסר *bind.*

אסטאן 0.0.1 n.[m.] **portico,** מתחת פנת האסטאן הדרומית *below the southern corner of the portico* 3QTr 11_{2}.

אָסִיף 2.0.0.1 n.[m.] **harvest**—אָסִף—**harvest, ingathering,** תִּשְׁמֹר ... חַג הָאָסִף בְּצֵאת הַשָּׁנָה בְּאָסְפְּךָ אֶת־מַעֲשֶׂיךָ *you are to observe ... the festival of ingathering at the end of the year when you gather your produce* Ex 23_{16} (+ חַג הַמַּצּוֹת *the festival of unleavened bread*, חַג הַקָּצִיר *the festival of harvest*), תַּעֲשֶׂה ... חַג הָאָסִיף תְּקוּפַת הַשָּׁנָה *you are to hold ... the festival of ingathering at the turn of the year* 34_{22} (+ חַג שָׁבֻעֹת, חַג הַמַּצּוֹת *festival of weeks*), ירחו אסף *months of harvest*, or, *its two months are the harvest* Gezer Calendar$_{1}$.

→ אסף *gather.*

אָסִיר 13.0.1 n.m. **prisoner**—pl. אֲסִירִים (אֲסִרִם); cstr. אֲסִירֵי; sf. L אֲסִירָיךְ, אֲסִירָיו—**<SUBJ>** שׁוב *go back* Zc 9_{12}, שׁאן palel *be at ease* Jb 3_{18}, שׁמע *hear* 3_{18}. **<NOM CL>** הָאֲסִירִם אֲשֶׁר בְּבֵית הַסֹּהַר *the prisoners who were in the prison* Gn 39_{22}.

<OBJ> נתן *give* Gn 39_{22}, פתח *release* Is 14_{17} (+ בַּיְתָה *homeward*), שׁלח pi. *send away*, i.e. release Zc 9_{11} (+ מִבּוֹר *from a pit*), יצא hi. *take out* Ps 68_{7}, בזה *despise* 69_{34}, דכא pi. *crush* Lm 3_{34}, רעה htp. *make friends with* 4QPrFêtes[c] 13_{6} ([אסירי]ם).

<CSTR> אֲסִירֵי הַתִּקְוָה *prisoners of hope*, i.e. waiting in hope, Zc 9_{12}, עֳנִי וּבַרְזֶל *of affliction and iron* Ps 107_{10}, אֶרֶץ *of (the) land* Lm 3_{34}; אֶנְקַת אָסִיר *groaning of (the) prisoner* Ps 79_{11} 102_{21}, בֵּית האסירים *house of the prisoners* Jg $16_{21(Kt).25(Kt)}$, כָּל־הָאֲסִירִם *all the prisoners* Gn 39_{22}, כֹּל אֲסִירֵי *all prisoners of* Lm 3_{34}.

<COLL> אסיר עד קץ רצונכה *a prisoner until the end of your desire*, i.e. until you desire it otherwise 1QH fr. $9_{8(Licht)}$ (unless אסיר = *I shall turn away*; AHL אסור).

→ אסר *bind.*

[אָסִיר], see אַסִּיר I, §1, Prep.

אָסִיר I 4 n.m. **prisoner**—אַסִר—**1.** collective, **prisoners, <SUBJ>** אסף pu. *be gathered* Is 24_{22} (+ עַל־ בּוֹר *in a dungeon*). **<OBJ>** יצא hi. *bring out* Is 42_{7} (+ מִמַּסְגֵּר *from prison;* || ישׁב ptc. *one who dwells* in darkness). **<APP>** אֲסֵפָה אַסִּיר *a gathering, prisoners* Is 24_{22} (or em. אֹסֶף הָאַסִּיר *gathering of the prisoners*). **<PREP>** בִּלְתִּי כָּרַע תַּחַת אַסִּיר *unless he crouches beneath the prisoners* Is 10_{4} (or em. בִּלְתִּי כֹּרַעַת חַת אֹסִיר *Beltis crouches, Osiris is shattered*).

2. as sing. noun, **prisoner,** בְּנֵי יְכָנְיָה אַסִּר *the sons of Jeconiah, a prisoner* 1 C 3_{17} (or em. הָאַסִּר *the prisoner;* perh. אַסִּר = אַסִּיר II *Assir*).

→ אסר *bind.*

אַסִּיר II 4 pr.n.m. **Assir, 1.** son of Korah, Ex 6_{24} 1 C 6_{7}. **2.** son of Ebiasaph and father of Tahath, 1 C $6_{8.22}$. **3.** perh. son of Jeconiah, if בְּנֵי יְכָנְיָה אַסִּר = *the sons of Jeconiah, Assir,* 1 C 3_{17} (but prob. אָסִיר I *prisoner*).

→ אסר *bind.*

אסם 0.0.0.2 vb. **store—Qal** Pf. אסם—**store** harvest, **<SUBJ>** עבד *servant* Meṣad Ḥashavyahu ost. 1_{5} (+ קצר *harvest,* כלה pi. *finish* or כול *measure*) 1_{6} (+ כלה pi. or כול).

→ אָסָם *storehouse,* חצראסם *Hazar-asam.*

[אָסָם] 2.0.1 n.m. **storehouse**—sf. Sam אסימך; pl. sf. אֲסָמֶיךָ (Q אסמיכה)—**<SUBJ>** מלא ni. *be filled* Pr 3_{10}. **<OBJ>** רוה hi. *drench,* i.e. fill with well-watered crops Ps 104_{13} (if em. מִפְּרִי מַעֲשֶׂיךָ *from the fuit of your deeds* to מְרִי אֲסָמֶיךָ *drenching your storehouses*). **<PREP>** יְצַו י׳ אִתְּךָ אֶת־הַבְּרָכָה בַּאֲסָמֶיךָ *may Y. command for you blessing in your storehouses* (Sam יצוה ... באסימך), הבא בטנאיכה ובאסמיכה *bring in(to) your baskets and your storehouses* 4Q416 2_{2}.

→ אסם *store.*

אַסְנָה 1 pr.n.m. **Asnah,** head of a family of temple servants (נְתִינִים), Ezr 2_{50} (||Ne 7_{52} omits).

אָסְנַת 3 pr.n.f. **Asenath,** wife of Joseph, Gn $41_{45.50}$ 46_{20}.

אסף 200.7.23 vb. **gather—Qal** Pf. אָסַף, אָסַפְתָּ, אָסַפְתִּי (אָסַפְתִּי), אָסְפוּ; impf. יֶאֱסֹף (Q [י]אסוף), יַאַסְפֵנִי, יַאַסְפְךָ (אֹסְפָה, אֹסִפְךָ), אֶאֱסֹף, תַּאַסְפִי (תֹּסֵף) תֶּאֱסֹף, (וַיַּאַסְפֵהוּ), וַיֹּסֶף; + waw וְאָסַפְתִּי, (וַאֲסַפְתִּי, וְאָסַפְתּוֹ, וְאָסַפְתָּה) וְאָסַפְתָּ, נֶאֱסֹף, וַיֶּאֶסְפוּ, ותוסף Q), (וַיַּאַסְפֵם, וַיַּאַסְפָה, וַיַּאַסְפֵהוּ) (Q ויוספוה); impv. אֱסֹף (Si אסוף, אָסְפָה־), אִסְפִי, אִסְפוּ; ptc. אֹסֵף (אֹסִפְךָ, אֹסְפָם), אֲסֵפִי; inf. אָסֹף, אֱסֹף (אָסְפְּךָ, אָסְפְּכֶם).

1a. gather (people) **together,** specif. for war Nm 21_{23} Jg 3_{13} 11_{20} 1 S 14_{52} 17_{1} 2 S 6_{1} 10_{17}||1 C 19_{17} 2 S $12_{28.29}$ Zc 14_{2} Dn 11_{10}, to make decision or hear proclamation 1 S $5_{8.11}$ 2 K 23_{1}||2 C 34_{29} 2 C 29_{4}, for communal intercession Jl 1_{14} $2_{16.16}$, for imprisonment Gn 42_{17}, for punishment, death Jr 8_{13} Zp 1_{2} 3_{8} Ezk 34_{29} 1QM 3_{10} 14_{5}, from exile Ezk 11_{17} 4QPrFêtes[c] $3_{3(\text{Baillet})}$.

<SUBJ> Y. Is 11_{12} (|| קבץ pi. *collect*) Jr 8_{13} 21_{4} Ezk 11_{17} Mc 2_{12} (both || קבץ pi.) Zp 1_{2} 3_{8} (|| קבץ *collect*) 3_{18} Zc 14_{2} 4QPrFêtes[c] 3_{3} 1QM 3_{10} 14_{5} (+ לכלה *to destroy*) Si 33_{13}, Laban Gn 29_{22}, Joseph 42_{17}, Moses Ex 3_{16} 4_{29} (both || הלך *go*) Nm $11_{16.24}$ 21_{16}, Sihon 21_{23} Jg 11_{20}, Joshua Jos 24_{1}, Rahab 2_{18}, Eglon Jg 3_{13}, Saul 1 S 14_{52}, David 2 S 6_{1} 10_{17}||1 C 19_{17} 2 S $12_{28.29}$ 1 C 15_{4} 23_{2}, Solomon 1 K 10_{26}||2 C 1_{14}, king of Assyria Is 10_{14}, Josiah 2 C 34_{29} (|| שׁלח *send*), Josiah's servants 2 K 23_{1} (|| שׁלח), Hezekiah 2 C 29_{4} (|| בוא hi. *bring*) 29_{20}, king of the north's sons Dn 11_{10}, Philistines 1 S 17_{1}, Ashdodites 5_{8} (|| שׁלח), Ekronites 5_{11} (|| שׁלח), Chaldaeans Hb $1_{9.15}$ 2_{5} (|| קבץ *collect*), mourner Si 38_{16}, priests Jl 1_{14} $2_{16.16}$ (|| קבץ) 2 C 29_{15}, heaven and earth Ps 50_{5}.

<OBJ> אִישׁ *man* Gn 29_{22} Nm $11_{16.24}$, שַׂר *officer* 1 C 23_{2} 2 C 29_{20}, סֶרֶן Philistine *officer* 1 S $5_{8.11}$, פָּרָשׁ *horseman* 1 K 10_{26}||2 C 1_{14}, בָּחוּר *warrior* 2 S 6_{1}, גִּבּוֹר *warrior* 1 S 14_{52}, זָקֵן *elder* Ex 3_{16} 4_{29} Jl 1_{14} 2 K 23_{1}||2 C 34_{29}, priests (and Levites) 1 C 15_{4} 23_{2} 2 C $29_{4.15}$, חָסִיד *pious person* Ps 50_{5}, נדח ni. ptc. *one who is banished* Is 11_{12}, יגן ni. ptc. *one who is weary* Zp 3_{18} (or em. נוּגֵי מִמּוֹעֵד *those weary of a festival* to כְּיוֹם מוֹעֵד *as [on] a feast day* and מִמֵּךְ *from you* to מֻכִּם *ones stricken* or הָיוּ *they were* to הֹוָה *ruin* Zp 3_{18}), exiles Ezk 11_{17}, corrupt officials Jr 8_{13}.

עוֹלָל *child* Jl 2_{16}, ינק ptc. *suckling* 2_{16}, Joseph's brothers Gn 42_{17}, Ammonites and Amalekites Jg 3_{13},

Chaldaeans Jr 21$_{4}$, Israelites Jl 1$_{14}$, עַם *people* Nm 21$_{16.23}$ Jg 11$_{20}$ 2 S 12$_{28.29}$ Jl 2$_{16}$, גּוֹי *nation* Hb 2$_{5}$ Zp 3$_{8}$ Zc 14$_{2}$ 1QM 14$_{5}$, שֵׁבֶט *tribe* Jos 24$_{1}$ Si 33$_{13}$, בַּיִת *household* Jos 2$_{18}$ (+ בַּיְתָה *into the house*), מַחֲנֶה *camp* 1 S 17$_{1}$, רֶכֶב *chariotry* 1 K 10$_{26}$||2 C 1$_{14}$, הָמוֹן *multitude* of forces Dn 11$_{10}$, שְׁבִי *captives* Hb 1$_{9}$ (+ כַּחוֹל *as sand*), Israel 2 S 10$_{17}$||1 C 19$_{17}$ Mc 2$_{12}$, אָדָם *humanity* (as fish) Hb 1$_{15}$, שְׁאֵר *next of kin* Si 38$_{16}$ (or אסף שארו = *take his body*; as §2), אֶרֶץ *world* Is 10$_{14}$, כֹּל *everything* Zp 1$_{2}$, חַיָּה *beast* Jr 12$_{9}$ (|| הלך *go*); with ellipsis of object, 1QM 3$_{10}$ (enemies of Y.).

1b. gather in, bring back an individual to a larger group, **<SUBJ>** Y. 2 K 22$_{20}$||2 C 34$_{28}$ Mc 4$_{6}$ (|| קבץ pi. *collect*), David 2 S 11$_{27}$ (|| שלח *send*), זָקֵן *elder* Jos 20$_{4}$. **<OBJ>** Bathsheba 2 S 11$_{27}$, Josiah 2 K 22$_{20}$||2 C 34$_{28}$, רצח ptc. *one who kills* unintentionally Jos 20$_{4}$ (+ הָעִירָה *into the town*), צלע ptc. *one that limps*, i.e. lame animal Mc 4$_{6}$.

1c. collect, gather up, oft. specif. **harvest** produce, etc., **<SUBJ>** Noah Gn 6$_{21}$, Ezekiel Ezk 24$_{4}$, Ruth Ru 2$_{7}$ (|| לקט pi. *collect*, i.e. glean), Ahaz 2 C 28$_{24}$, Israelites Ex 23$_{10.16}$ Lv 23$_{39}$ 25$_{3.20}$ Nm 11$_{32.32}$ Dt 11$_{14}$ 16$_{13}$ 28$_{38}$, Judaeans Jr 40$_{10.12}$, Levites 2 K 22$_{4}$||2 C 34$_{9}$ 2 C 24$_{11}$, קצר ptc. *reaper* Is 17$_{5}$ (if em. קָצִיר *harvest*; || לקט pi. *collect*), אִישׁ *man* Nm 19$_{9.10}$ Ps 39$_{7}$ (:: צבר *pile up* goods) 1QDM 3$_{3(\text{Baillet})}$ (איש [אסוף]), חטא ptc. *sinner* Ec 2$_{26}$ (|| כנס *collect*), ישׁב ptc. *one who dwells* under siege Jr 10$_{17(\text{Qr})}$, רְאֵם *wild ox* Jb 39$_{12(\text{Qr})}$ (|| שׁוב hi. *take back*).

<OBJ> (1) noun in singular, קָצִיר *harvest* Is 17$_{5}$, תְּבוּאָה *produce* Ex 23$_{10}$ Lv 23$_{39}$ 25$_{3.20}$, מַאֲכָל *food* Gn 6$_{21}$, מְעַט *a little* produce Dt 28$_{38}$, מְאוּמָה *anything*, i.e. any produce 1QDM 3$_{3(\text{Baillet})}$ ([מאומה],), שְׂלָו *quail* Nm 11$_{32}$, דָּגָן *grain* Dt 11$_{14}$, גֹּרֶן *threshing floor*, i.e. its contents Jb 39$_{12}$, קַיִץ *summer fruit* Jr 40$_{10.12}$, יַיִן *wine* 40$_{10.12}$, תִּירוֹשׁ *wine* Dt 11$_{14}$, שֶׁמֶן *oil* Jr 40$_{10}$, יִצְהָר *oil* Dt 11$_{14}$, אֵפֶר *ash* Nm 19$_{9.10}$ 4QToh B^{a} 7 (והאוס[ף]) 4QMMT A 2$_{14}$, כֶּסֶף *money* 2 K 22$_{4}$||2 C 34$_{9}$ 2 C 24$_{11}$, כִּנְעָה *bundle* Jr 10$_{17}$, רוּחַ *wind* Pr 30$_{4}$ (|| צרר *wrap up* water).

(2) noun in plural, מַעֲשֶׂה fruit of *labour* Ex 23$_{16}$, בֵּיצָה *egg* Is 10$_{14}$, חֹמֶר *homer* Nm 11$_{32}$, עֶצֶם *bone* 2 S 21$_{13}$, נֵתַח *piece* of meat Ezk 24$_{4}$, כְּלִי *vessel* 2 C 28$_{24}$.

(3) with ellipsis of obj., Dt 16$_{13}$ (produce) Ps 39$_{7}$ Ec 2$_{26}$ (possessions) Ru 2$_{7}$ (grain).

2. take away, remove single item, person, etc., **<SUBJ>** Y. Gn 30$_{23}$ Jr 16$_{5}$ Ps 2$_{7}$ (if em. אֲסַפְּרָה *let me relate*) 26$_{9}$ 27$_{10}$ (:: עזב *abandon*) 85$_{4}$ (+ שׁוב hi. *take back*) 104$_{29}$ Jb 34$_{14}$ 1QH 5$_{14}$, Jacob Gn 49$_{33}$, Micah Jg 18$_{25}$, Ahijah 1 S 14$_{19}$, מֶלֶךְ *king* of Israel 2 K 5$_{6.7}$, Elisha 5$_{3.11}$, Israelite Dt 22$_{2}$=11QT 64$_{15}$, אִישׁ *man* Is 4$_{1}$, enemies 1QH 5$_{33}$, כּוֹכָב *star* Jl 2$_{10}$=4$_{15}$.

<OBJ> Naaman 2 K 5$_{3.6.7}$, מֶלֶךְ *king* Ps 2$_{7}$ (if em.; see Subj.), psalmist (as abandoned child) Ps 27$_{10}$, stray beast Dt 22$_{2}$=11QT 64$_{15}$, יָד *hand* 1 S 14$_{19}$, רֶגֶל *leg* Gn 49$_{33}$, לָשׁוֹן *tongue* 1QH 5$_{14}$, צרע pu. ptc. *leprous area* 2 K 5$_{11}$, רוּחַ *breath* Ps 104$_{29}$ (+ יִגְוָעוּן and then *they die*) Jb 34$_{14}$, נְשָׁמָה *breath* 34$_{14}$, חַיִּים *life* Ps 26$_{9}$, נֶפֶשׁ *life* Jg 18$_{25.25}$ Ps 26$_{9}$ 1QH 5$_{33}$, שָׁלוֹם *peace* Jr 16$_{5}$, חֶסֶד *loyalty* Jr 16$_{5}$, רַחֲמִים *mercy* Jr 16$_{5}$, עֶבְרָה *wrath* Ps 85$_{4}$, חֶרְפָּה *reproach* Gn 30$_{23}$ Is 4$_{1}$, נֹגַהּ *brightness* Jl 2$_{10}$=4$_{15}$.

<PREP> (§§1–2) בְּ of place, *in, among* Hb 1$_{15}$ (+ מִכְמֶרֶת *net*) Hb 1$_{15}$ Pr 30$_{4}$ (+ חֹפֶן *palm*) Ru 2$_{7}$ (+ עֹמֶר *sheaf*), בָעֳמָרִים אַחֲרֵי הַקּוֹצְרִים *among the sheaves behind the reapers* Ru 2$_{7}$.

אֶל gather people/things *around* oneself, keep them *with* one Gn 6$_{21}$ Jos 2$_{18}$ 20$_{4}$ 1 S 14$_{52}$ 2 K 23$_{1}$; לְ in same sense Ps 50$_{5}$.

אֶל gather people/things *in* a place, specif. בַּיִת *house* Dt 22$_{2}$=11QT 64$_{15}$ 2 S 11$_{27}$, מִשְׁמָר *prison* Gn 42$_{17}$, עִיר *city* Jr 21$_{4}$ (אֶל־תּוֹךְ), מִטָּה *bed* Gn 49$_{33}$ (וַיֶּאֱסֹף רַגְלָיו אֶל־הַמִּטָּה וַיִּגְוַע *and he drew up his legs into the bed and died*), סִיר *cauldron* Ezk 24$_{4}$.

לְ gather people *in* a place, specif. רְחוֹב *street* 2 C 29$_{4}$, צוּקָה *narrow place* 1QH 5$_{33}$.

אֹסִפְךָ אֶל־/עַל־אֲבֹתֶיךָ *I shall gather you to your ancestors*, i.e. cause you to die, be buried 2 K 22$_{20}$||2 C 34$_{28}$, אֹסִפְךָ אֶל־חֵיקִי *I shall take you to my chest*, perh. as ritual of adoption Ps 2$_{7}$ (if em. אֲסַפְּרָה אֶל־חֹק י׳ *let me relate the statute of Y*).

ותוסף לשונם כחרב אל תערה *and you will remove their tongue like a sword into its scabbard* 1QH 5$_{14}$.

מִן of place, *from* Ex 23$_{16}$ Dt 16$_{13}$ Jr 10$_{17}$ Ezk 11$_{17}$ Zp 1$_{2}$ 2 C 34$_{9.9.9}$ (מִיַּד), אסף מִצָּרַעַת *remove from*, i.e.

relieve of, *leprosy* 2 K 5$_{3.6.7}$; מֵאֵת *away from* people 2 K 22$_{4}$ Jr 16$_{5}$; אַחֲרֵי *behind* reapers Ru 2$_{7}$; עִם *with* sinners Ps 26$_{9.9}$.

<COLL> אָסֹף אָסֵף/אֲסִיפֵם *I shall indeed put an end (to them)* Jr 8$_{13}$ Zp 1$_{2}$ (סוף hi. *put an end to* with אסף inf. absol. for paranomasia, esp. at Jr 8$_{13}$, unless אָסֹף = הָסֵף, hi. inf. absol. of סוף), אָסֹף אֶאֱסֹף *I shall indeed gather* Mc 2$_{12}$.

אֹסֶף רָעָב אֹסְפֵי *ones gathered in*, i.e. killed, *by famine* Ezk 34$_{29}$, כֶּאֱסֹף בֵּיצִים עֲזֻבוֹת כָּל־הָאָרֶץ אֲנִי אָסָפְתִּי *as one might collect abandoned eggs, I have gathered the whole earth* Is 10$_{14}$.

3. bring up the rear, act as rearguard, as Pi., §3a, כְּבוֹד י׳ יַאַסְפֶךָ *the glory of Y. brings up your rear* Is 58$_{8}$ (or em. יְאַסְּפֶךָ pi.; + הלך לִפְנֵי *go in front of*).

<SYN> §1 קבץ pi. *collect*, לקט pi. *collect*, הלך *go*, שׁלח *send*, שׁוב hi. *take back*.

Ni. Pf. נֶאֱסַף; Si, Q נאספה ,נאספו נֶאֶסְפוּ (נֶאֱסָפוּ); impf. יֵאָסֵף, 3fs תֵּאָסֵף, 2ms תֵּאָסֵף ,תֵּאָסְפוּ יֵאָסְפוּ (יֵאָסֵפוּ ,יֵאָסְפוּן); + waw וַיֵּאָסֵף (וַיֵּאָסְפוּ), וַיֵּאָסֵף ;וְנֶאֱסַפְתֶּם ,וְנֶאֱסַפְתָּ ,וְנֶאֶסְפָה; impv. הֵאָסֵף ,הֵאָסְפִי ,הֵאָסְפוּ; ptc. נֶאֱסָף ,נֶאֱסָפִים; inf. הֵאָסֵף ,הֵאָסֵף, Q האספו, Q האספם (Q הספם)—**1a. be gathered** to ancestors, etc., **in death,** וַיֵּאָסֶף אֶל־עַמָּיו *and he was gathered to his ancestors* (and vars.), perh. with ref. to family grave, of Abraham Gn 25$_{8}$, Ishmael 25$_{17}$, Isaac 35$_{29}$ (all three ‖ גוע *expire*, מות *die*), Jacob Gn 49$_{29}$ (עַמִּי *my people*) 49$_{33}$ (‖ גוע), Moses Nm 27$_{13}$ 31$_{2}$ Dt 32$_{50}$, Aaron Nm 20$_{24}$ Dt 32$_{50}$, וְנֶאֱסַפְתָּ אֶל־קִבְרֹתֶיךָ *and you* (Josiah) *will be gathered to your graves* 2 K 22$_{20}$‖2 C 34$_{28}$, כָּל־הַדּוֹר הַהוּא נֶאֶסְפוּ אֶל־אֲבוֹתָיו *all that generation were gathered to its ancestors* Jg 2$_{10}$; without prep. phrase, טוב נאסף ממסתולל perh. *better dead than grovelling* Si 40$_{28(B)}$ (M מפני חצף *than an impudent face*), כלנו נאספים *all of us are about to die* 8$_{7}$, of Aaron Nm 20$_{26}$ (‖ מות *die*) 27$_{13}$, ירה hi. ptc. *teacher* CD 19$_{35}$=20$_{14}$ (יורה), גְּוִיָּה *body* Si 44$_{14(M)}$ (ג[וית]ם; + שלום *in peace*), רַגְלִי *infantry* 16$_{10}$.

2a. be gathered, be brought together by someone else, **<SUBJ>** מִקְנֶה *livestock* Gn 29$_{7}$, עֵדֶר *flock* 29$_{3.8}$ (Sam in both רעה ptc. *shepherd*), Israel Is 49$_{5}$ (‖ שׁוב pol. *restore* to someone), מַיִם *water* 2 S 14$_{14}$.

2b. be taken away, removed, <SUBJ> Pharaoh (as sea monster) Ezk 29$_{5}$ (‖ קבץ ni. *be collected*), חָלָל *one that is slain* Jr 25$_{33}$ (‖ קבר ni. *be buried*, ספד ni. *be mourned*), אִישׁ loyal *man* Is 57$_{1}$ (‖ אבד *perish*), צַדִּיק *righteous (one)* 57$_{1}$, שִׂמְחָה *joy* 16$_{10}$ Jr 48$_{33}$, גִּיל *joy* Is 16$_{10}$ Jr 48$_{33}$, רוּחַ *spirit* 4Q416 9.2$_{2}$ ([רו]ח), עֶצֶם *bone* 8$_{2}$ (‖ קבר ni. *be buried*), לָשׁוֹן *tongue* 1QH 8$_{35}$, דָּג *fish* Nm 11$_{22}$ Ho 4$_{3}$, עֵשֶׂב *grass* Pr 27$_{25}$, wealth Jb 27$_{19}$; subj. not specified, Si 42$_{21(M)}$ (לא נאסף *nothing* of God *is taken away*).

2c. be brought into, return to a place, **<SUBJ>** Moses Nm 11$_{30}$, Miriam 12$_{14.15}$ (both :: סגר ni. *be shut out*), Absalom 2 S 17$_{13}$, אָדָם *person* Ex 9$_{19}$ (+ בַּיְתָה *into the house* for security), כְּפִיר *lion-cub* Ps 104$_{22}$, בְּהֵמָה *beast* Ex 9$_{19}$ (+ בַּיְתָה), חֶרֶב *sword* Jr 47$_{6}$, לַיְלָה *night* 1QH 12$_{7}$, אַשְׁמוּרָה night *watch* 1QS 10$_{2}$, אוֹר *light* 10$_{1}$, מָאוֹר *light* 10$_{3}$, יָרֵחַ *moon* Is 60$_{20}$ (‖ בוא *come*, i.e. set).

3. gather (intrans.), **come together,** specif. for war Gn 34$_{30}$ Jos 10$_{5}$ Jg 6$_{33}$ 10$_{17}$ 20$_{11}$ 1 S 13$_{5.11}$ 17$_{1}$ 2 S 10$_{15}$ 17$_{11}$ 23$_{9}$‖1 C 11$_{13}$ 2 S 23$_{11}$ Is 13$_{4}$ Mc 4$_{11}$ Zc 12$_{3}$ 1 C 19$_{7}$ 1QM 18$_{4}$ 19$_{9}$ + Sup, for protection Jr 4$_{5}$ 8$_{14}$, for judgment Is 43$_{9}$, to celebrate festival Jg 16$_{23}$ 2 C 30$_{3.13}$, to hear proclamation Gn 49$_{1}$ Ne 8$_{1}$.

<SUBJ> Israelites Lv 26$_{25}$ Jg 10$_{17}$ (‖ חנה *encamp*) Jg 20$_{11}$ 1 S 17$_{2}$ (‖ חנה) 2 S 17$_{11}$ Jr 4$_{5}$ 8$_{14}$ (both ‖ בוא *come*) Ne 9$_{1}$, sons of light 1QM 19$_{9}$ + Sup (+ המחנה *into the camp*) 4QCat^{a} 12.1$_{11}$, Levites Ex 32$_{26}$ Ne 8$_{13}$, Shechemites Jg 9$_{6}$, Benjaminites 20$_{14}$, עֵדָה *congregation* of Israel 1QSa 1$_{1}$, Aram 2 S 10$_{15}$ (+ יַחַד *together*), Midian and Amalek Jg 6$_{33}$ (+ יַחַד), Canaanites and Perizzites Gn 34$_{30}$, Ashdodites and Egyptians Am 3$_{9}$ (unless em. בְּאַשְׁדּוֹד *in Ashdod* to בְּאַשּׁוּר *in Assyria*), Philistines 1 S 13$_{5.11}$ 17$_{1}$ (‖ חנה) 2 S 23$_{9}$‖1 C 11$_{13}$ 2 S 23$_{11}$, Ammonites 1 C 19$_{7}$.

עַם *people* Ezr 3$_{1}$‖Ne 8$_{1}$ (+ כְּאִישׁ אֶחָד *as a single man*) 2 C 30$_{3.13}$, גּוֹי *nation* Is 13$_{4}$ Mc 4$_{11}$ Zc 12$_{3}$, לְאֹם *nation* Is 43$_{9}$ (‖ קבץ ni. *be collected*), מַמְלָכָה *kingdom* 1QH 6$_{7}$ (מ[מל]כות), אִישׁ *man*, i.e. member, of community 1QS 5$_{7}$, בֵּן *son* Gn 49$_{1}$, רֹאשׁ *head* of fathers' house Ne 8$_{13}$ 1QM 3$_{4}$, singers Ne 12$_{28}$, חָרֵד *(one who is) fearful* of Y. Ezr 9$_{4}$, נָדִיב *noble (one)* Ps 47$_{10}$, שַׂר *officer* 2 C 12$_{5}$, סֶרֶן Philistine *officer* Jg 16$_{23}$, מֶלֶךְ Amorite *king* Jos 10$_{5}$ (‖ חנה *encamp*), נָכֶה *stricken (one)*, i.e. wretch Ps 35$_{15.15}$,

מַעֲרָכָה *battle line* 1QM 18_4, birds and beasts Ezk 39_{17} (‖ קבץ ni. *be collected*, בוא *come*).

<PREP> (§§2–3) ... בְּיוֹם עֶשְׂרִים וְאַרְבָּעָה ... נֶאֶסְפוּ בְּצוֹם וּבְשַׂקִּים *on the twenty-fourth day ... they gathered ... in a fast and with sackcloth* Ne 9_1, ויאספו המחנה בלילה *and they will gather into camp at night* 1QM 19_9 + Sup.

אֶל *against* Jg 20_{11}; אֶל *around* a person Ex 32_{26} Ezr 9_4 Ne 8_{13} 1QM 18_4.

אֶל of direction, *(in)to* a place, specif. עִיר *city* Lv 26_{25} 2 S 17_{13}, Jerusalem Ezr 3_1 2 C 12_5, רְחוֹב *street* Ne 8_1, מְעוֹנָה *dwelling place* 1QH 12_7, מַחֲנֶה *camp* Nm 11_{30}, תַּעַר *scabbard* Jr $47_{6(mss)}$ (L אַל *not*).

עַל *against* Mc 4_{11} Zc 12_3 Ps 35_{15}, *upon* Am 3_9; עַל *around* 2 S 17_{11}; עַל *in(to)*, with + מָעוֹן *dwelling place* 1QS 10_1.

לְ of benefit, *for* Nm 11_{22}, בהאספם ליחד *when they join the community* 1QS 5_7 1QSa $1_{1(Barthélemy)}$ ([ליחד]); לְ *around* Is $49_{5(Qr)}$; לְ *in(to)*, with בַּיִת *house* 1QM 3_4, מָעוֹן *dwelling place* 1QS 10_3, Jerusalem 2 C 30_3.

מִן of direction, *from* Jg 20_{14} Is 16_{10}=Jr 48_{33} Ne 12_{28} 1 C 19_7; מִסָּבִיב *from all around* Ezk 39_{17}.

<COLL> הֵאָסֹף יֵאָסֵף ... כָל־יִשְׂרָאֵל *all Israel ... must indeed gather* 2 S 17_{11}.

<SYN> §1a גוע *die*; §2b קבר ni. *be buried*; §3 חנה *encamp*, בוא *come*, קבץ ni. *be collected*.

Pi. Ptc. מְאַסֵּף (מְאַסִּפְכֶם), מְאַסְפָיו—**1. gather, remove,** מְאַסְפָיו יֹאכְלֻהוּ *those who harvest it* (דָּגָן *grain*) *will eat it* Is 62_9 (‖ קבץ pi. *collect*), ... וְנָפְלָה נִבְלַת הָאָדָם כְּעָמִיר מֵאַחֲרֵי הַקֹּצֵר וְאֵין מְאַסֵּף *the corpses of humans shall fall ... as sheaves behind the reaper, with no one gathering them* Jr 9_{21}.

2. take in guest, וְאֵין אִישׁ מְאַסֵּף אוֹתִי/אוֹתָם הַבָּיְתָה *and no man would take me/them home* Jg $19_{15.18}$.

3a. bring up the rear, act as rearguard, דֶּגֶל מַחֲנֵה בְנֵי־דָן מְאַסֵּף לְכָל־הַמַּחֲנֹת *the standard of the camp of the Danites bringing up the rear of all the camps* Nm 10_{25}, מְאַסִּפְכֶם אֱלֹהֵי יִשְׂרָאֵל *the God of Israel is bringing up your rear* Is 52_{12} (+ הלך לִפְנֵי *go in front of*).

b. ptc. as noun, **rearguard,** וְהַמְאַסֵּף הֹלֵךְ אַחֲרֵי הָאָרוֹן *with the rear guard going behind the ark* Jos $6_{9.13}$ (אֲרוֹן יי) (both + הלך לִפְנֵי *go in front of*).

Pu. + waw וְאֻסַּף, וְאֻסְּפוּ; ptc. מְאֻסָּף—**be gathered together,** <SUBJ> מֶלֶךְ *king* (as prisoner) Is 24_{22}, עַם *people* Ezk 38_{12} Ho 10_{10}, שָׁלָל *booty* (as swarm of locusts) Is 33_4, חַיִל *wealth* Zc 14_{14}. <PREP> מִן of direction, *from* Ezk 38_{12}; עַל *against* Ho 10_{10}.

Htp. Inf. הִתְאַסֵּף—**assemble** (intrans.), <SUBJ> רֹאשׁ *head* of people Dt 33_5 (+ יַחַד *together*) 33_{21} (if em. סָפוּן וַיֵּתֵא *reserved; and he came* to וְהִתְאַסְּפוּן *and they assembled*).

→ אסף *harvest*, אָסֹף *storehouse*, אָסִיף *ingathering*, אֲסֵפָה *collecting*, אֲסֻפָּה *collection*, אֲסַפְסֻף *rabble*, אָסָף *Asaph*, אספי *Aspi*.

אָסָף 46.0.0.1 pr.n.m. **Asaph, 1.** Levite, singer and chief musician of David (1 C 15_{19} $16_{5.5.7.37}$ 25_9), ancestor of temple choristers (בְּנֵי אָסָף *sons of Asaph*), son of Berechiah (1 C 6_{24}; 15_{17}) and father of Zabdi (זַבְדִּי Ne 11_{17}‖1 C $9_{15(mss)}$; L זִכְרִי *Zichri*), and/or Zaccur (זַכּוּר Ne 12_{35}), oft. assoc. with Heman and Jeduthun (e.g. 1 C 6_{24} 25_6 2 C 5_{12}).

<CSTR> בְּנֵי אָסָף *sons of Asaph* Ezr 2_{41} 3_{10} (בְּנֵי־) Ne 7_{44} 11_{22} 1 C $25_{1.2}$ 2 C 20_{14} 29_{13}. <APP> אָסָף הַחֹזֶה *Asaph the seer* 2 C 29_{30}. <PREP> מִזְמוֹר לְאָסָף *psalm of/for/by Asaph* Ps 50_1 73_1 75_1 76_1 79_1 82_1 83_1, לְאָסָף מִזְמוֹר *of/for/by Asaph, a psalm* 77_1 80_1 $81_{1(mss)}$ (L lacks מִזְמוֹר), מַשְׂכִּיל לְאָסָף *maskil of/for/by Asaph* 74_1 78_1. <COLL> דָּוִיד וְאָסָף *David and Asaph* Ne 12_{46} 2 C 29_{30} 35_{15}.

2. father of Joah (יוֹאָח), Hezekiah's recorder, 2 K $18_{18.37}$‖Is $36_{3.22}$. **3.** keeper of Artaxerxes' royal forest, Ne 2_8. **4.** Levite at time of Nehemiah, son of Elkanah and father of Berechiah, 1 C $9_{16(mss)}$ (L אָסָא *Asa*). **5.** ancestor of family of gatekeepers, 1 C 26_1 (or em. אֲבִיאָסָף *Abiasaph*, or אֶבְיָסָף *Ebiasaph*). **6.** Seal 7 (Megiddo, 8th cent.).

→ אסף *gather*.

אָסִף, see אָסִיף.

[אָסֹף] 3.0.1 n.[m.] **storehouse**—sf. אספיו; pl. אֲסֻפִּים; cstr. אֲסֻפֵּי—**storehouse,** or perh. **threshold,** <NOM CL> לְעֹבֵד אֱדֹם ... בֵּית הָאֲסֻפִּים *to Obed-edom ... was (assigned) the house of the storehouses* 1 C 26_{15} (or em.

הַסִּפִּים *of the thresholds*). <OBJ> כבס pi. *wash* to purify house in which death has occurred 11QT 49_{13} (+ מַשְׁקוֹף *lintel,* מְזוּזָה *doorpost,* מַנְעוּל *lock*). <CSTR> אֲסֻפֵּי הַשְּׁעָרִים *hallways of the gates*, i.e. their interiors Ne 12_{25}; בֵּית הָאֲסֻפִּים *house of the storehouses* 1 C 26_{15} (or em.). <PREP> לְ *assigned to* 1 C 26_{17}; בְּ stand guard *at* Ne 12_{25}.

→ אסף *gather*.

אֹסֶף 3 n.m. **harvest, group**—cstr. אֹסֶף; pl. cstr. אָסְפֵּי—**1. harvest, picking,** <SUBJ> בוא *come* Is 32_{10} (+ בָּצִיר *grape-harvest*). <CSTR> אָסְפֵּי־קַיִץ *pickings of harvest* Mc 7_1 (or em. אֹסְפֵי *one that gathers*; + עֹלְלֹת בָּצִיר *gleanings of grape-harvest*). <PREP> כְּ היה *be as* Mc 7_1 (or em.). **2. group, swarm,** <SUBJ> אסף pu. *be gathered* Is 24_{22} (if em. אֲסֵפָה *collecting*) 33_4 (or em. שְׁלַלְכֶם אֹסֶף *your booty, a swarm of* to שָׁלָל כְּמוֹ אֹסֶף *booty as a swarm of*). <CSTR> אֹסֶף הָאַסִּיר *group of prisoners* Is 24_{22} (if em. אֲסֵפָה אַסִּיר *gathering [of] prisoners*), אֹסֶף הֶחָסִיל *swarm of (the) locusts* Is 33_4. <APP> שְׁלַלְכֶם אֹסֶף *your booty, a swarm of* Is 33_4 (unless em.).

→ אסף *gather*.

אֲסֵפָה 1 n.f. **gathering,** וְאֻסְּפוּ אֲסֵפָה אַסִּיר *and they will be gathered (into) a gathering (of) prisoners* Is 24_{22} (or em. אֹסֶף הָאַסִּיר *group of prisoners*).

[אֲסֻפָּה] 1 n.f. **collection**—pl. אֲסֻפּוֹת—בַּעֲלֵי אֲסֻפּוֹת נִתְּנוּ מֵרֹעֶה אֶחָד *masters of*, i.e. those that understand, *collections (of proverbs) given from a single shepherd* Ec 12_{11}.

→ אסף *gather*.

אספי 0.0.0.1 pr.n.m. **Aspi,** Seal 757_2 (8th–6th cent.).

→ אסף *gather*.

[אֲסַפְסוּף], see אֲסַפְסֻף.

[אֲסַפְסֻף] 1.0.1 n.[m.] **rabble**—Q אספסוף; with article הָאסַפְסֻף—וְהָאסַפְסֻף אֲשֶׁר בְּקִרְבּוֹ הִתְאַוּוּ תַּאֲוָה *and the rabble that was among it was filled with longing* Nm 11_4, אנשי בליעל וכול האספסוף *men of Belial and all the rabble* 4QCatª 7_5.

Also 4QCatª 30_2 (אס[פסוף]).

→ אסף *gather*.

אַסְפָּתָא 1 pr.n.m. **Aspatha**—אַסְפָּתָא—son of Haman, Est 9_7.

אסר 72.0.15 **bind—Qal** Pf. אֲסָרָם, אָסְרָה, אֲסַרְנֻהוּ, אֲסַרְתֶּם, אֲסָרוּךָ; impf. יֶאְסֹר, יֶאְסָרְךָ, נֶאֱסָרְךָ, יַאַסְרוּנִי (יַאַסְרֻנִי), + waw וַיֶּאְסֹר (וַיֶּאֱסֹר, וַיַּאַסְרֵהוּ), וַתַּאַסְרֵהוּ, וַיַּאַסְרוּהוּ (וַיַּאַסְרוּם, וַיַּאַסְרֻהוּ); impv. אֱסֹר, אִסְרוּ; ptc. אֹסְרִי, Q אוסרים, אָסוּר, אֲסוּרִים (הָסוּרִים [for הָאֲסוּרִים]), Kt אסורי, אֲסֻרוֹת; inf. אָסֹר (אָסוֹר), אֱסוֹר (אֱסֹר, אֱסָרְךָ, לֶאְסֹר, אָסְרָם).

1a. bind, tie up a person for imprisonment, <SUBJ> (1) with active verb, God Jb 36_{13} Ho 7_{12} (if em. אַיְסִרֵם *I shall chastise them* to אֶאֱסָרֵם *I shall bind them*) 11QapPsª 4_8 ([יאסר]ך), Joseph Gn 42_{24} Ps 105_{22} (|| חכם pi. *make wise*), Nebuchadnezzar 2 C 36_6, Delilah Jg $16_{8.12}$, פְּלִשְׁתִּי *Philistine* 15_{10} 16_{21} (|| נקר pi. *gouge out* eyes), סֶרֶן *lord* of Philistines $16_{5.7.11}$, אִישׁ *man* of Judah $15_{12.13.13}$, חַיִל *army* of Chaldaeans 2 K 25_7||Jr 39_7||52_{11} (|| עור pi. *blind*), שַׂר *officer* of Assyrian army 2 C 33_{11} (|| לכד *capture*), חָסִיד *devotee* Ps 149_8.

(2) with passive verb, Jeremiah Jr 40_1, צַדִּיק *righteous person* Jb 36_8 (|| לכד ni. *be captured*), מֶלֶךְ *king* Ca 7_6.

<OBJ> Simeon Gn 42_{24}, Samson Jg $15_{10.12.13.13}$ 16_5 (+ לְעַנּוֹת *in order to subdue*) $16_{7.8.11.12.21}$, Zedekiah 2 K 25_7||Jr 39_7||52_{11}, Manasseh 2 C 33_{11}, Jehoiakim 36_6, Belial 11QapPsª 4_8 ([יאסר]ך), אָדָם *human being* 11QapPsª 2_9 ([ל]אסור אדם), שַׂר *officer* Ps 105_{22}, כבד ni. ptc. *honoured person* 49_8, מֶלֶךְ *king* 149_8, חנף ptc. *impious person* Jb 36_{13}, Israel Ho 7_{12} (if em.; see Subj.).

<PREP> בְּ of instrument, *with, by,* Jg $16_{7.8}$ (both + יֶתֶר *cord*) $16_{11.12}$ (both + עֲבֹת *rope*) 16_{21} (+ נְחֻשְׁתַּ *fetter*) 2 K 25_7||Jr 39_7||52_{11} (+ נְחֻשְׁתַּ) Jr 40_1 (+ זִק *fetter*) Ezk 3_{25} (+ עֲבֹת) Ps 149_8 (+ כֶּבֶל *chain*) Jb 36_8 (both + זִק) Ca 7_6 (+ רַהַט *tress*) 2 C 33_{11} 36_6 (both + נְחֻשְׁתַּ), of place, *in,* 11QapPsª 4_8 ([יאסר]ך [בשאו]ל); בְּאָסְרָם לִשְׁתֵּי עוֹנֹתָם *in their binding*, i.e. when they are bound, *for their two sins* Ho 10_{10}(Qr) (or em. בְּהִוָּסְרָם/בְּיִסְּרָם *in their being*

disciplined or לְיַסְּרָם *to discipline them*).

1b. tie up, to prevent escape, <SUBJ> with passive verb, יָד *hand* of prisoner 2 S 3_{34} (|| נגשׁ ho. *be brought* into fetters). <OBJ> קֶרֶן *horn* of bull 11QT $34_{6(AHL)}$, ראשׁ *head* of bull 11QT $34_{6(Yadin)}$.

<PREP> בְּ of instrument, *with, by,* א]סורות ידיך [לוא בזקים *your hands were bound not by fetters* 4QSam^a 2 S 3_{34}; אֶל *to* a thing, 11QT 34_6 (+ טַבַּעַת *ring*).

2a. imprison, <SUBJ> (1) with active verb, Shalmaneser 2 K 17_4, Neco 23_{33}; (2) with passive verb, אָסִיר *prisoner* Gn $39_{20(Qr)}$ (Kt אסורי), אפה ptc. *baker* 40_5, מַשְׁקֶה *cupbearer* 40_5, Joseph 40_3. <OBJ> Hoshea 2 K 17_4 (+ בֵּית כֶּלֶא in *prison*), Jehoahaz 23_{33}.

<PREP> בְּ of place, *in,* Gen 40_5 (+ בֵּית הַסֹּהַר *prison*) 2 K 23_{33} (+ רִבְלָה *Riblah*).

2b. pass. ptc. as noun, **prisoner,** <SUBJ> אסר pass. *be bound* Gn $39_{20(Kt)}$, יצא *go out* Is 49_9 (+ אֲשֶׁר בַּחֹשֶׁךְ *those who are in darkness*). <NOM CL> אֲנִי ... גֹּלָה וַאֲסוּרָה *I was ... an exile and a prisoner* Is 49_{21} (if em. וְסוּרָה *and thrust out*). <OBJ> נתר hi. *release* Ps 146_7 4Q521 1.2_8 (|| עִוֵּר *blind person*).

<CSTR> אֲסוּרֵי הַמֶּלֶךְ *prisoners of the king* Gn $39_{20(Kt)}$; בֵּית הָאֲסוּרִים *the house of prisoners, prison* Jg $16_{21(Qr).25(Qr)}$, Ec 4_{14} (הָסוּרִים). <PREP> לְ of direction, *to,* + אמר *say* Is 49_9, קרא *proclaim* liberty 61_1 (|| שׁבה pass. ptc. *captive*); באילך מאסור *by your arbitration from a prisoner* 4Q416 9.2_3.

3. tether animal, <SUBJ> (1) with active verb, Judah Gn 49_{11}; (2) with passive verb, סוּס *horse* 2 K 7_{10}, חֲמוֹר *donkey* 7_{10}. <OBJ> סוּס *horse* Jr 46_4, עַיִר *young donkey* Gn 49_{11}, בֶּן־אָתוֹן *son of a she-donkey* 49_{11}, חַג perh. sacrificial beast for *festival* Ps 118_{27}.

<PREP> לְ *to* a thing, Gn 49_{11} (+ גֶּפֶן *vine*, שֹׂרֵקָה *vine*); עַד *to* a thing, Ps 118_{27} (+ קֶרֶן *horn* of altar); בְּ of instrument, *with* Ps 118_{27} (+ עֲבֹת *rope*).

4a. harness an animal, **prepare** a chariot, etc., <SUBJ> אִישׁ *man* 1 S 6_{10}, פְּלִשְׁתִּי *Philistine* 6_7. <OBJ> פָּרָה milch *cow* 1 S $6_{7.10}$. <PREP> בָּעֲגָלָה *to the cart* 1 S $6_{7.10}$.

4b. prepare a vehicle pulled by an animal, <SUBJ> Joseph Gn 46_{29}, Pharaoh Ex 14_6, Ahab 1 K 18_{44}. <OBJ> מֶרְכָּבָה *chariot* Gn 46_{29}, רֶכֶב *chariot* Ex 14_6 2 K 9_{21}; obj. not expressed, 1 K 18_{44} 2 K 9_{21}.

5. join battle, <SUBJ> Ahab 1 K 20_{14}, Abijah 2 C 13_3. <OBJ> מִלְחָמָה *battle* 1 K 20_{14} 2 C 13_3.

6. tie clothing, equipment onto someone, <SUBJ> (1) with active verb, God Jb 12_{18}; (2) with passive verb, חֶרֶב *sword* Ne 4_{12}. <OBJ> אֵזוֹר *girdle* Jb 12_{18}. <PREP> בְּמָתְנֵיִם *around the thighs* Jb 12_{18}; עַל־מָתְנַיִם *against the thighs* Ne 4_{12}.

7. vow, i.e. bind oneself by oath, <SUBJ> אִישׁ *man* Nm 30_3=11QT 53_{15}, אִשָּׁה *woman* Nm $30_{4.5.5.6}$=11QT $53_{16.18.19.21}$ Nm $30_{7.8.9.10}$=11QT 54_4 Nm $30_{11.12}$. <OBJ> אִסָּר *oath* Nm $30_{3.4.5.5.6}$=11QT $53_{15.16.18.19.21}$ Nm $30_{8.11.12}$, נֶדֶר *vow* 30_6 11QT 53_{21} 54_4, מִבְטָא *utterance* Nm 30_9. <PREP> אסר עַל־נֶפֶשׁ *vow by one's life* Nm $30_{3.5.5.6.10}$=11QT $53_{15.16.18.19.21}$ 54_4 Nm $30_{7.8.9.11.12}$. <COLL> אסור עד קץ רצונכה *bound* (by vow) *until the end of your desire,* i.e. until you desire it otherwise 1QH fr. $9_{8(AHL)}$ (Sukenik אסיר).

Ni. Pf. Q נאסרתי; impf. יֵאָסֵר, תֵּאָסֵר; impv. הֵאָסְרוּ—**1. be bound, tied up,** <SUBJ> Samson Jg $16_{6.10.13}$, worshipper 1QH 5_{36}, Belial 11QapPs^a 3_{10} ([ותאסר]). <PREP> בְּ of instrument, *with* Jg $16_{6.10.13}$ 1QH 5_{36} (עֲבֹת *rope*), עד עולם *for ever* 11QapPs^a 3_{10} ([ותאסר]). <COLL> + לְעַנּוֹת *in order to subdue* Jg 16_6.

2. stay in prison, <SUBJ> Joseph's brothers Gn $42_{16.19}$.

3. consist of, be constituted, על אלף איש תסאר המערכה *the battle (line) consists of a thousand men* 1QM 5_3.

4. be forbidden, אסר [כול עבודה ת] *all work is forbidden* 1QDM $3_{11(Milik)}$.

Pu. Pf. אֻסְּרוּ (אֻסָּרוּ)—**be captured,** <SUBJ> קָצִין *officer* Is 22_3 (+ מִקֶּשֶׁת *without a bow*), מצא ni. ptc. *one present* 22_3 (+ יַחְדָּו *together*).

Also 11QMelch 1.$1_{4(AHL)}$ (Milik [י]אמור) 4QMish C^a 1_7.

→ אָסִיר *prisoner*, אַסִּיר *prisoner*, אִסָּר *vow*, אֵסוּר *bond*, מוֹסֵר *bond*, מָסֹרֶת *bond*, אַסִּיר *Assir*, מוֹסֵרָה *Moserah*, מֹסֵרוֹת *Moseroth*.

אֵסֶר, see אַסִּיר I.

אִסָּר $_{11.0.8}$ n.m. **vow**—sf. forms are vocalized as if from אֱסָר; cstr. אִסַּר; sf. אֱסָרָהּ; pl. Q אסרים; sf. אֱסָרֶיהָ (אֱסָרֶהָ)—a promise that binds one, <SUBJ> קום *stand*, i.e. need to be fulfilled Nm 30$_{5.6}$=11QT 53$_{19.20}$ Nm 30$_{8.12.13}$ (|| נֶדֶר *vow*).

<OBJ> אסר *vow* Nm 30$_3$=11QT 53$_{15}$ (with subj. אִישׁ *man*; + נֶדֶר *vow*) Nm 30$_{4.5.5.6}$=11QT 53$_{16.18.19.20}$ Nm 30$_8$ (all five || נֶדֶר) 30$_{11.12}$ (|| נֶדֶר; all seven with subj. אִשָּׁה *woman*), קום hi. *fulfil* Nm 30$_{14}$ (+ נֶדֶר) 30$_{15}$ (|| נֶדֶר; both with subj. אִישׁ), פרר hi. *annul* 30$_{13.14.16}$ (all with subj. אִישׁ), שׁמע *hear* Nm 30$_5$=11QT 53$_{18}$.

<CSTR> אִסַּר נַפְשָׁהּ *vow of her soul*, i.e. made of her free will Nm 30$_{13}$, שְׁבֻעַת אִסָּר *swearing of vow*, i.e. a sworn vow 30$_{14}$ 1QS 5$_8$ CD 16$_7$, כָּל־אִסָּר *every vow* Nm 30$_5$=11QT 53$_{19}$ Nm 30$_{12}$. <ADJ> האסרים האל[ה] *these vows* 2Q25 1$_2$.

<PREP> כָּל־מוֹצָא שְׂפָתֶיהָ לִנְדָרֶיהָ וּלְאִסַּר נַפְשָׁהּ *every issue of her lips, whether it be her vows* (under duress) *or a vow made of her own free will* Nm 30$_{13}$.

<SYN> נֶדֶר *vow*.

→ אסר *bind*.

אֵסַר־חַדֹּן $_3$ pr.n.m. **Esarhaddon**—אֱסַר חַדֹּן, Q אסרחודן—Sennacherib's son, king of Assyria, 2 K 19$_{37}$||Is 37$_{38}$ Ezr 4$_2$.

אֶסְתֵּר $_{55}$ pr.n.f. **Esther**, also called הֲדַסָּה *Hadassah*, cousin and protégée of Mordecai; queen of Persia, wife of Xerxes, and deliverer of the Jews from Haman's plot, Est 2$_{7+11t}$ 4$_{5+8t}$ 5$_{1+7t}$ 6$_{14}$ 7$_{2.6.8}$ 8$_{1.2.3.4.4.7}$ 9$_{13.32}$, אֶסְתֵּר הַמַּלְכָּה *Queen Esther* 2$_{22}$ 5$_{2.3.12}$ 7$_{1.2.3.5.7}$ 8$_{1.7}$ 9$_{12.29.31}$.

[אִסְתִּרָא] $_{0.0.1}$ n.[f.] **stater**—pl. אסתרין—coin of high value, אסתרין ארבע *four staters* 3QTr 9$_3$.

אַף I $_{134.4.24}$ conj. **also**—+ הוּא, Q אפהוא (אפהו)—**1. also, and, moreover. a.** usu. introducing second or third clause or noun (1) beginning sentence, Lv 26$_{39.40}$ Nm 16$_{14}$ Dt 15$_{17}$ Is 26$_{9.11}$ 35$_2$ 40$_{24.24.24}$ 41$_{23.26.26.26}$ 44$_{15.15.16.19}$ 45$_{21}$ 48$_{12.13}$ Hb 2$_{15}$ Ps 16$_{6.7.9}$ 18$_{49}$ (|| 2 S 22$_{49}$ וְ *and*) 68$_{9.17}$ 74$_{16}$ 77$_{17.18}$ 89$_{12.22.44}$ 96$_{12}$ (if em. אָז *then*) 119$_3$ 135$_{17}$ Jb 6$_{27}$ 14$_3$ 36$_{16}$ 37$_{1.11}$ Pr 9$_2$ 23$_{28}$ Ca 1$_{16}$ Ec 1$_5$ (if em. שׁוֹאֵף *gasping* to שָׁב אַף *and [then] returning*) 2$_9$ Si 16$_{19}$ 38$_{27}$ 4QpNah 3.2$_6$ 4QMMT A 2$_9$ ([אף]) 2$_{13.21.22}$ ([אף]) 2$_{45}$ ([אף]) 2$_{50.57}$ ([אף]) 2$_{60.63.64.70.72.74.79}$ ([אף]) 2$_{88}$ ([אף]) 4QMMT B$_6$ ([אף]) 4QMMT B$_{12.15}$ ([אף]) 4QMMT B$_{21.28}$ MurEpBeth-Mashiko$_5$; אַף כִּי *moreover*, Ezk 23$_{40}$ Hb 2$_5$ Ne 9$_{18}$; (2) before verb, subj. Y., רום pol. *raise* 1 S 2$_7$, שׂגב pi. *exalt* 11QapPs^a 5$_{13}$ ([ישגבך]; MT Ps 91$_{14}$ lacks אַף), תמך pi. *uphold* Is 41$_{10}$, עזר *help* 41$_{10}$, צרח hi. *roar* 42$_{13}$, עשׂה *do, make* 43$_7$ 46$_{11}$, שׁחה htpal. *bow down* 46$_6$, דבר *speak* 46$_{11}$, בוא hi. *bring* 46$_{11}$, קרא *call* 48$_{15}$; subj. עֲמָקִים *valleys*, שׁיר *sing* Ps 65$_{14}$; (3) before object-noun, בְּרִית *covenant* Lv 26$_{42.42}$, אֱמוּנָה *faithfulness* Ps 89$_6$, דָּבָר *word* Ne 2$_{18}$, קָדְקֹד *pate* Dt 33$_{20}$, יַיִן *wine* Ne 13$_{15}$; (4) before subject-noun, יְשׁוּעָה *salvation* Is 33$_2$.

1b. before pronoun, *even I*, etc. אֲנִי *I* Gn 40$_{16}$ Lv 26$_{16.24.28.41}$ Jb 32$_{10.17}$, אַתָּה *you* Pr 22$_{19}$, הוּא *he* 2 K 2$_{14}$ (perh. §1a), הִיא *she, it* Dt 2$_{20(Qr)}$ Jg 5$_{29}$, הֵם *they* Dt 2$_{11}$ 1 C 9$_{38}$||8$_{32}$ (הֵמָּה), אֲנַחְנוּ *we* 4QMMT B$_{29}$.

2. emphatic particle, **really, indeed,** modifying (1) sentence, Gn 3$_1$ 1 S 14$_{30}$ (both + כִּי *that*) Am 2$_{11}$ Jb 34$_{12}$ (+ אָמְנָם *truly*) 34$_{17}$ 36$_{29}$ 40$_8$; (2) verb, ילד *give birth* Gn 18$_{13}$ (+ אֻמְנָם *truly*), חבב *love* Dt 33$_3$, קוה pi. *wait* Is 26$_8$, צעק *call* 46$_7$, כון ni. *be established* 1 C 16$_{30}$, בוא hi. *bring* Est 5$_{12}$, שׁגה *err* Jb 19$_4$ (+ אָמְנָם *truly*), ספה *sweep away* Gn 18$_{23.24}$; (3) preposition, אַף־אַחֲרָיו *right behind him* 2 S 20$_{14}$; (4) adjective, אַף נָעִים *truly lovely* Ca 1$_{16}$. <COLL> preceded by הֲ interrogative, Gn 18$_{13.23.24}$ Am 2$_{11}$ Jb 34$_{17}$ 40$_8$, מה אף הוא (and vars.) *what indeed is he?* 1QS 11$_{20}$ 1QH 10$_{3.12}$ 12$_{31}$ 15$_{21}$ fr. 4$_{10}$.

3. even, specifying, אָדָם וְאַף סוֹרְרִים *human beings, even rebellious ones* Ps 68$_{19}$, וַאֲזַמְּרָה אַף־כְּבוֹדִי *and I shall praise him, even my dignity (will praise him)* 108$_2$.

4. so, therefore, of consequence, Is 43$_{19}$ Ps 89$_{28}$ 93$_1$ 96$_{10}$ 2 C 12$_5$.

5. nonetheless, even so, Lv 26$_{44}$ (וְאַף־גַּם־זֹאת *and even in spite of this*) Ps 44$_{10}$ 58$_3$ (+ אָמְנָם *truly*; perh. §2) Jb 15$_4$ Ne 9$_{34}$ (if em. אֶת־ appar. introducing subject of transitive verb).

6. אַף כִּי, **a. how much more** true, appropriate, etc., following הֵן *behold* Dt 31$_{27}$ Pr 11$_{31}$; הִנֵּה *behold* 1 S 23$_3$

2 S 16$_{11}$; כִּי *when* 2 S 4$_{11}$; כִּי אִם *surely* 1 S 21$_{6}$; no particle 2 K 5$_{13}$ Ezk 14$_{21}$ Pr 15$_{11}$ 19$_{7}$ 21$_{27}$. **b. how much less,** true, appropriate, etc., following הֵן *behold* Jb 4$_{19}$ 15$_{16}$ 25$_{16}$; הִנֵּה *behold* 1 K 8$_{27}$‖2 C 6$_{18}$ Ezk 15$_{5}$; אַף *surely* Jb 35$_{14}$; כִּי *surely* 2 C 32$_{15}$; no particle Pr 17$_{7}$ 19$_{10}$ Si 16$_{11}$.

6c. how then?, Jb 9$_{14}$.

Also Si 40$_{8(mg)}$ 4Q385 3$_{3}$ 4QMMT A 2$_{24}$ ([א]ף) 4Q416 9.2$_{10}$.

אַף II $_{277.12.71}$ n.m. **anger, nose**—אַף; cstr. אַף; sf. אַפִּי (Q אפיא), אַפְּךָ (אַפֶּךָ, Q אפכה), אַפּוֹ, אַפֵּךְ, אַפָּהּ, אַפְּכֶם, אַפָּם; du. אַפַּיִם (אַפָּיִם); cstr. אַפֵּי; sf. אַפֶּיךָ, אַפָּיו, אַפֶּיהָ, אַפֵּינוּ.

1. anger—**<SUBJ>** חרה *be inflamed*, with אַף *anger of* person, Y. Ex 4$_{14}$ 22$_{23}$ 32$_{10.11}$ Nm 11$_{1.10}$ (+ מְאֹד *greatly*) 11$_{33}$ 12$_{9}$ 22$_{22}$ 25$_{3}$ 32$_{10.13}$ Dt 6$_{15}$ 7$_{4}$ 11$_{17}$ 29$_{19(Sam).26}$ 31$_{17}$ Jos 7$_{1}$ 23$_{16}$ Jg 2$_{14.20}$ 3$_{8}$ 6$_{39}$ 10$_{7}$ 2 S 6$_{7}$‖1 C 13$_{10}$ 2 S 24$_{1}$ 2 K 13$_{3}$ 23$_{26}$ Is 5$_{25}$ Ho 8$_{5}$ Zc 10$_{3}$ (+ עַל *against*) Ps 106$_{40}$ Jb 19$_{11}$ (if em. וַיִּחַר *and he inflamed* his anger) 42$_{7}$ 2 C 25$_{15}$ CD 1$_{21}$ 2$_{21}$ 3$_{8}$ 5$_{16}$ 8$_{13(A).18(A)}$=19$_{26(B).31(B)}$ 10$_{9}$ 20$_{16}$ 1QDM 2$_{9}$, Jacob Gn 30$_{2}$, Joseph Gn 44$_{18}$, Moses Ex 32$_{19.22}$, Samson Jg 14$_{19}$, Saul 1 S 11$_{6}$ (+ מְאֹד) 20$_{30}$, David 2 S 12$_{5}$ (+ מְאֹד), Eliab 1 S 17$_{28}$, Potiphar Gn 39$_{19}$, Balaam Nm 22$_{27}$, Balak 24$_{10}$ (+ אֶל *against*), Zebul Jg 9$_{30}$, Elihu Jb 32$_{2.2.3.5}$, Ephraimites 2 C 25$_{10}$ (+ מְאֹד), foreign nations Ps 124$_{3}$; + בְּ be inflamed *against* Gn 30$_{2}$ 44$_{18}$ Ex 4$_{14}$ 32$_{10.11}$ Nm 11$_{33}$ 12$_{9}$ 25$_{3}$ 32$_{13}$ Dt 6$_{15}$ 7$_{4}$ 11$_{17}$ 29$_{19(Sam).26}$ 31$_{17}$ Jos 7$_{1}$ 23$_{16}$ Jg 2$_{14.20}$ 3$_{8}$ 6$_{39}$ 10$_{7}$ 1 S 17$_{28}$ 20$_{30}$ 2 S 6$_{7}$‖1 C 13$_{10}$ 2 S 12$_{5}$ 24$_{1}$ 2 K 13$_{3}$ 23$_{26}$ Is 5$_{25}$ Ho 8$_{5}$ Ps 106$_{40}$ 124$_{3}$ Jb 32$_{2.3}$ 42$_{7}$ 2 C 25$_{10.15}$ CD 1$_{21}$ 2$_{21}$ 3$_{8}$ 5$_{16}$ 8$_{13(A)}$=19$_{26(B).31}$ 10$_{9}$ (all seven + עֵדָה *congregation*) 20$_{16}$ 1QDM 2$_{9(Milik)}$.

בער *burn* intrans. Is 30$_{27}$ Ho 7$_{6}$ (if em. אֹפֵהֶם *their baker*) Ps 2$_{12}$ (+ אנף *be angry*) 1QS 2$_{15}$ (+ קנאת משפטיו *jealousy of his judgments*), עשׁן *smoke* Dt 29$_{19}$ (Sam חרה *be inflamed*; + בְּ *against*, ‖ קִנְאָה *jealousy*) Ho 7$_{6}$ (if em. יָשֵׁן אֹפֵהֶם *their baker is sleeping* to יֶעְשַׁן אַפְּהֶם *their anger smokes*) Ps 74$_{1}$, ישׁן *sleep*, i.e. subside Ho 7$_{6}$ (see above), יסף hi. *do again* 2 S 24$_{1}$.

שׁוב *go back*, i.e. abate Gn 27$_{45}$ Is 12$_{1}$ (+ אנף *be angry*) Jr 2$_{35}$ 23$_{20}$ Is 5$_{25}$=9$_{11=16=20}$=10$_{4}$ (‖ יָד *hand*) Ho 14$_{5}$ Jb 14$_{13}$ Dn 9$_{16}$ (‖ חֵמָה *wrath*) 2 C 12$_{12}$ 1QM 3$_{9}$ 4QDibHam^{a} 1.2$_{11}$ 1.6$_{11}$ (both ‖ חֵמָה) 4Q416 9.1$_{15}$, פקד *visit*, i.e. punish Jb 35$_{15}$, ארר pass. *be cursed* Gn 49$_{7}$ (+ כִּי עָז *for it is strong*; ‖ עֶבְרָה *wrath*), כלה *be completed* Is 10$_{25}$ (‖ זַעַם *wrath*) Ezk 5$_{13}$, נתך ni. *be poured out* Jr 7$_{20}$ 42$_{18}$ 44$_{6}$ (all three ‖ חֵמָה), עלה *arise* Ps 78$_{21}$ (‖ אֵשׁ *fire*) 78$_{31}$ (both + בְּ *against*) 4QapLam^{a} 1.2$_{1}$, טרף *tear* Am 1$_{11}$ (‖ עֶבְרָה *wrath*) Jb 16$_{9}$, קצר pi. *shorten* days Si 30$_{24}$ (קִנְאָה ‖ ואו[ף]; *jealousy*).

<NOM CL> אִם בַּנְּהָרִים אַפֶּךָ *was your anger against the rivers?* Hb 3$_{8}$ (‖ עֶבְרָה *wrath*), עֻזּוֹ וְאַפּוֹ עַל כָּל־עֹזְבָיו *his strength and his anger is against all who forsake him* Ezr 8$_{22}$, אף אל ... על בליעל ובכול אנשי גורלו *the anger of God ... is against Belial and against all the men of his lot* 1QM 4$_{1}$, רחמים ואף עמו *mercy and anger are with him* Si 5$_{6}$ (עִ[מ]וֹ) 16$_{11}$, גָּדוֹל הָאַף *great is the anger* Jr 36$_{7}$ (‖ חֵמָה *wrath*), אפו להשמיד ולהכרית *his anger is for destroying and for cutting off* 1QM 1$_{4}$.

<OBJ> חרה hi. *inflame*, i.e. provoke Jb 19$_{11}$ (or em. וַיִּחַר to וַיִּחַר *and* his anger *was inflamed*; + עַל *against*), עשׂה *do*, i.e. show Ezk 35$_{11}$, חזק hi. *strengthen* Mc 7$_{18}$, שׂים *place*, i.e. store up Jb 36$_{13}$, משׁך *prolong* Ps 85$_{6}$ (+ אנף *be angry*), שׁפך *pour out* Is 42$_{25}$, בוא hi. *bring* Si 47$_{20(Segal)}$ ([להביא]; + עַל *against* descendants; ‖ אֲנָחָה *sighing*), שׁוב hi. *turn*, i.e. let loose 66$_{15}$ (+ בְּחֵמָה *in wrath*), restrain Ps 78$_{38}$ Jb 9$_{13}$ Pr 24$_{18}$ 29$_{8}$ 1QS 10$_{19}$ 4Q416 1$_{10}$, שׁלח pi. *dispatch* Ezk 7$_{3}$ (+ בְּ *against*).

עור hi. *rouse* Si 33$_{8}$ (‖ חֵמָה *wrath*), כלה pi. *fulfil* Ezk 5$_{13}$ 7$_{8}$ 20$_{8.21}$ (all + בְּ *against*, ‖ חֵמָה), ארך hi. *constrain* Is 48$_{9}$ Pr 19$_{11}$ Si 30$_{22}$ 1QH 13$_{7}$, כפה *subdue* Pr 21$_{14}$ (‖ חֵמָה), שׁבת hi. *destroy* Si 48$_{10}$, עלה hi. *bring up*, i.e. provoke Pr 15$_{1}$ (‖ חֵמָה) 1QS 5$_{12}$, נגד hi. *tell* Jb 36$_{33}$ (unless em. מִקְנֶה *cattle* to מְקַנֵּא *provoking* anger), ספח pi. *join together* wrath and anger Hb 2$_{15}$ (or em. מְסַפֵּחַ *joining together* to מִסַּף *from the cup of*; but prob. אַף I *also*).

<CSTR> אַף(־)י׳ *anger of Y.* Ex 4$_{14}$ Nm 11$_{10.33}$ 12$_{9}$ 22$_{22(ms, Sam)}$ 25$_{3.4}$ 32$_{10.13.14}$ Dt 6$_{15}$ 7$_{4}$ 11$_{17}$ 29$_{19}$ 29$_{26}$ Jos 7$_{1}$ 23$_{16}$ Jg 2$_{14.20}$ 3$_{8}$ 10$_{7}$ 2 S 6$_{7}$‖1 C 13$_{10}$ 2 S 24$_{1}$ 2 K 13$_{3}$ 24$_{20}$‖Jr 52$_{3}$ Is 5$_{25}$ Jr 4$_{8}$ 12$_{13}$ 23$_{20}$ 25$_{37}$ 30$_{24}$ 51$_{45}$ Zp 2$_{2.3}$ (both + יוֹם *day* of Y.'s anger) Ps 106$_{40}$ Lm 2$_{22}$ (+ יוֹם) 2 C 12$_{12}$ 25$_{15}$ 28$_{11}$ 11QapPs^{b} 3$_{11}$ (י[הוה]), אַף(־)אֱלֹהִים

anger of God Nm 22$_{22}$ (ms, Sam 'י *Y.*) Ezr 10$_{14}$ 1QDM 2$_{9(Milik)}$ ([אלוהיכם]), אפי אלוהים *anger of God* 4QShir^{b} 35$_{2}$, אף אל *anger of God* 1QM 4$_{1}$ 6$_{3}$ CD 1$_{21}$ 3$_{8}$ 8$_{13(A)}$ =19$_{26(B)}$ 10$_{9}$ 20$_{16}$ 4QapLam^{a} 1.2$_{1}$, אַף אֲדֹנִי *anger of my lord* Ex 32$_{22}$, אַף *anger of* Moses Ex 32$_{19}$, Saul 1 S 20$_{30}$, David 2 S 12$_{5}$, Eliab 1 S 17$_{28}$, Balaam Nm 22$_{27}$, Balak 24$_{10}$, Rezin Is 7$_{4}$, Elihu Jb 32$_{2}$, אַף־אָחִיךָ *your brother's anger* Gn 27$_{45}$, אַף אֹיְבַי *anger of my enemies* Ps 138$_{7}$, אף עברה *anger of wrath,* i.e. fierce wrath 1QS 4$_{12}$ 4QBer^{a} 3.2$_{10}$ ([עברו[ת).

חֲרוֹן אַף *inflammation of anger* of Y. Ex 32$_{12}$ Nm 25$_{4}$ 32$_{14}$ (both + 'י Y.) Dt 13$_{18}$=11QT 55$_{11}$ Jos 7$_{26}$ 1 S 28$_{18}$ 2 K 23$_{26}$ Is 13$_{9.13}$ Jr 4$_{8}$ (+ 'י) 4$_{26}$ 12$_{13}$ 25$_{37}$ (both + 'י) 25$_{38}$ 30$_{24}$ (+ 'י) 49$_{37}$ 51$_{45}$ (+ 'י) Ho 11$_{9}$ Jon 3$_{9}$ Na 1$_{6}$ Zp 2$_{2}$ (+ 'י) 3$_{8}$ Ps 69$_{25}$ 78$_{49}$ 85$_{4}$ Jb 20$_{23}$ Lm 1$_{12}$ 4$_{11}$ Ezr 10$_{14}$ 2 C 28$_{11}$ (+ 'י) 28$_{13}$ 29$_{10}$ 30$_{8}$ Si 45$_{19}$ (+ אנף htp. *become enraged*) 4QDibHam^{a} 1.3$_{11}$ CD 9$_{4.6}$ 10$_{9}$ 1QpHab 3$_{12}$ (ח[רו]ן) 1Q36 18$_{3}$ 11QapPs^{b} 3$_{11}$ 4QAocMos B 1.1$_{13}$, חרוני אפכה 4QDibHam^{a} 1.5$_{5}$.

חֳרִי־אַף *inflammation of anger* Ex 11$_{8}$ Dt 29$_{23}$ (חֳרִי) 1 S 20$_{34}$ Is 7$_{4}$ Lm 2$_{3}$ 2 C 25$_{10}$ 4QDibHam^{a} 1.5$_{5(erased)}$, זַעַם־אַפּוֹ *wrath of his anger* Lm 2$_{6}$, עֹז אַפֶּךָ *strength of your anger* Ps 76$_{8}$ (if em. מֵאָז *from the time of*) 90$_{11}$, עזוז אף *strength of anger* Si 45$_{18}$, זַעַף אַף *raging of anger* Is 30$_{30}$ 4QWiles 2$_{6}$ (Allegro ואף אף perh. *and anger of anger*), זעף אפים *raging of anger* 1QpHab 3$_{13}$ 4QShir^{b} 35$_{2}$ (זע[ף] אפי), עֶבְרוֹת אַפֶּךָ *ragings of your anger* Jb 40$_{11}$.

שֵׁבֶט אַפִּי *rod of my anger* Is 10$_{5}$ (+ זַעַם *wrath*), מִיץ אַפַּיִם *squeeezing of anger* Pr 30$_{33}$, פני אפו *face of his anger,* i.e. his angry face 1QS 2$_{9}$,

אֶרֶךְ אַפַּיִם *(one) long of,* i.e. slow to, *anger* Ex 34$_{6}$ Nm 14$_{18}$ Jl 2$_{13}$ Jon 4$_{2}$ Na 1$_{3}$ Ps 86$_{15}$ 103$_{8}$ 145$_{8}$ Pr 14$_{29}$ 15$_{18}$ 16$_{32}$ Ne 9$_{17}$ Si 5$_{4}$, אֹרֶךְ אַפַּיִם *length,* i.e. restraining, *of anger* Jr 15$_{15}$ (if em. אֶרֶךְ *long of*) Pr 25$_{15}$ 1QS 4$_{3}$ CD 2$_{4}$ 4QShir^{b} 108$_{1(Baillet)}$ ([אור]ך) 4QM^{g} 4$_{3}$ (אורך א[פים]) 4Q525 4$_{25}$ ([ארך]) 5$_{8}$ ([אפים]; ‖ חָרוֹן *wrath*).

קְצַר־אַפַּיִם *short of anger,* i.e. impatient Pr 14$_{17}$ 4Q424 1$_{12}$ (אפי[ם]) 4Q477 2$_{4}$, קוצר אפים *shortness of anger,* i.e. impatience 1QS 4$_{10}$ (קצור) 6$_{26}$, שֶׁטֶף אַף *flood of anger* Pr 27$_{4}$ (‖ חֵמָה *wrath,* + קִנְאָה *jealousy*), יוֹם אַף *day of anger* Zp 2$_{2.3}$ Ps 110$_{5}$ Jb 20$_{28}$ Lm 2$_{1.21.22}$, עֵת אַפְּךָ *time of your anger* Jr 18$_{23}$, גורל אף *lot of anger* 1QH 3$_{27}$, [מש]פט אף *judgment of anger* 1Q36 16$_{3(Milik)}$, גֹּבַהּ אַפּוֹ *arrogance of his anger* Ps 10$_{4}$ (but perh. אַף = *nose/face,* as §2/3), נקמת אפו *vengeance of his anger* 1QM 3$_{6}$, עזות אף *insolence of anger* Si 10$_{18}$, בַּעַל אַף *possessor of,* i.e. one prone to, *anger* Pr 22$_{24}$ (‖ חֵמָה) Si 8$_{16}$, אִישׁ־אַף *man of,* i.e. prone to, *anger* Pr 29$_{22}$ (‖ חֵמה), מֵאָז אַפֶּךָ *from the time of your anger,* i.e. when your anger is roused Ps 76$_{8}$ (or em. מֵעֹז *from the strength of*), מושבי אף כבודו *dwelling places of the anger of his glory* 4QShirShab^{f} 23.1$_{12}$.

<APP> חֵמָה אַפּוֹ *wrath (and) his anger,* i.e. his furious anger Is 42$_{25}$, מִקְנֶה אַף *cattle, anger* Jb 36$_{33}$ (or em. מַקְנִיא *provoking* anger).

<ADJ> גָּדוֹל *great* Dt 29$_{23}$ 4QApocMos B 1.1$_{3}$.

<PREP> קָרָאתִי גִּבּוֹרַי לְאַפִּי *I have called my warriors to my anger* Is 13$_{3}$, יְפַלֵּס נָתִיב לְאַפּוֹ *he makes straight a path for his anger* Ps 78$_{50}$.

בְּ of accompaniment, *with, in* 4QBer^{a} 3.2$_{10}$ perh. 4QapPs^{b} 17$_{3}$ (‖ חֵמָה *wrath*), + הפך *overturn* Dt 29$_{22}$ (‖ חֵמָה *wrath*) Am 4$_{10}$ (if em.; see §2, Prep.) Jb 9$_{5}$, ירד hi. *cast down* Ps 56$_{8}$, נטה hi. *turn someone away* 27$_{9}$, נתשׁ *uproot* Dt 29$_{27}$ (‖ חֵמָה, קֶצֶף *wrath*), רדף *pursue* Lm 3$_{66}$, נדח hi. *banish* Jr 32$_{37}$, קום *rise* Ps 7$_{7}$, רום pol. *be lifted up* 4QApocMos A 2.2$_{3}$, יסר pi. *chastise* Jr 10$_{24}$ (:: בְּמִשְׁפָּט *with justice, fairly*), יכח hi. *reprove* Ps 6$_{2}$ (‖ חֵמָה), לחם ni. *fight* Jr 21$_{5}$, נכה hi. *strike* 33$_{5}$ (‖ חֵמָה), טרף *tear* Jb 18$_{4}$, רדה *subjugate* Is 14$_{6}$, דרך *tread down* 63$_{3}$ (‖ חֵמָה), בוס *tread down* 63$_{6}$ (‖ חֵמָה), דושׁ *tread down* Hb 3$_{12}$ (‖ זַעַם *wrath*), הרג *slaughter* Gn 49$_{6}$ (‖ רָצוֹן *desire*), אכל *consume* Ezk 43$_{8}$, בלע pi. *swallow* Ps 21$_{10}$, שׂטם *bear a grudge* 55$_{4}$, עוב hi. *darken* Lm 2$_{1}$, עשׂה *do, execute* Ezk 5$_{15}$ (obj. שְׁפָטִים *judgments,* ‖ חֵמָה) Mc 5$_{14}$ (obj. נָקָם *vengeance,* ‖ חֵמָה), עור pol. *stir up* 1QH 9$_{3}$ (obj. קִנְאָה *jealousy*), קבץ *gather* Ezk 22$_{20}$ (‖ חֵמָה), נתן מֶלֶךְ *give* someone *a king* Ho 13$_{11}$ (‖ עֶבְרָה *wrath*), דבר pi. *speak* Ps 2$_{5}$ (‖ חָרוֹן *wrath*) 1QS 5$_{25}$ (‖ תְּלֻנָּה *grumbling*), שׁבע ni. *swear* Ps 95$_{11}$, קפץ רַחֲמִים *shut up compassion* Ps 77$_{10}$, חלק חֲבָלִים pi. *apportion pains* Jb 21$_{17}$.

תַּעֲלֶה חֲמָתִי בְּאַפִּי *my wrath rises in my anger* Ezk 38$_{18}$, רֶגַע בְּאַפּוֹ *(he is but) a moment in his anger* Ps 30$_{6}$ (or em. רֹגֶז *shaking* with anger; :: רָצוֹן *desire*),

סַכֹּתָה בְאַף *you have clothed yourself with anger* Lm 3:43, אטור באף *I shall stay in anger* 1QS 10:20.

בְּ of cause, instrument, *because of, by* perh. 4QBer[a] 3.2:10, + היה *be* (of deluge) Ezk 13:13 (perh. בְּ of accompaniment; || חֵמָה *wrath*), בלע *swallow* 4QapPs[b] 17:3, שבר ni. *be broken* Dn 11:20 (|| מִלְחָמָה *war*), כלה *be finished* Ps 90:7 (|| חֵמָה), שחת עולמים באף עברת אל *the pit of ages*, i.e. eternal damnation, *because of the wrathful anger of God* 1QS 4:12, חללים באף אל *victims of the wrath of God* 1QM 6:3, באפכה כול משפטי נגע *all judgments of suffering are due to your anger* 1QH 11:8, אֵשׁ קָדְחָה בְאַפִּי *a fire blazed because of my anger* Dt 32:22 Jr 15:14, var. 17:4.

כְּ עשׂה *do according to* Ezk 25:14 (|| חֵמָה *wrath*) 35:11 (|| קִנְאָה *jealousy*).

רפה מִן hi. *refrain from* Ps 37:8 (|| חֵמָה *wrath*).

עַל *because of* 2 K 24:20||Jr 52:3, חיה עַל pi. *keep alive against* Ps 138:7, עַל־אַפִּי ... הָיְתָה לִּי הָעִיר *the city has been ... a cause of my anger* Jr 32:31 (|| חֵמָה *wrath*).

מִפְּנֵי *on account of* Dt 9:19 (|| חֵמָה *wrath*); לִפְנֵי *in the presence of* 1QH 12:18 ([אפכ[ה) 12:30.

<COLL> הייתי ... קנאה ואף *I have become ... (an object of) jealousy and wrath* 1QH 5:23, וגם אף במקדוש perh. *and anger even against the sanctuary* 4QTanḥ 16:1 (but perh. אַף I *also*).

2. nose, nostril, of humans and animals (Jb 40:24.26 Pr 11:22 perh. Am 4:2 [if em.; see Subj.]), **<SUBJ>** נשׂא ni. *be lifted up* with hooks Am 4:2 (if em. וְנִשָּׂא אֶתְכֶם appar. *and you will be lifted up*). **<NOM CL>** אַפֵּךְ כְּמִגְדַּל הַלְּבָנוֹן *your nose is as the tower of Lebanon* Ca 7:5 (|| צַוָּאר *neck*, עַיִן *eye*), אַף לָהֶם וְלֹא יְרִיחוּן *they have a nose, but they cannot smell* Ps 115:6 (|| אֹזֶן *ear*). **<OBJ>** סור hi. *remove* Ezk 23:25 (|| אֹזֶן *ear*), נקב *pierce* Jb 40:24.

<CSTR> אַף חֲזִיר *pig's nose* Pr 11:22; רוּחַ אַף *breath of (Y.'s) nose* 2 S 22:16||Ps 18:16 Jb 4:9, רוּחַ אַפַּיִם *breath of nostrils* Ex 15:8 Lm 4:20, אפך *of your nose* 4QapPs[b] 29:3, רֵיחַ אַפֵּךְ *scent of*, i.e. from, *your nose* Ca 7:9, מִיץ־אַף *squeeezing of nose* Pr 30:33, נֶזֶם אַף *ring of nose*, i.e. nose ring Is 3:21.

<PREP> בְּ of place, *on, in(to)*, Gn 7:22 Is 2:22 (both + נְשָׁמָה *breath*) 65:5 (+ עָשָׁן *smoke*) Jb 27:3 (+ רוּחַ *breath*) Pr 11:22 (+ נֶזֶם *ring*), + נפח *blow* Gn 2:7 4QDibHam[a] 8:5 (נפח[תה]), שׂים *place* Dt 33:10 (+ קְטוֹרָה *incense*) 2 K 19:28||Is 37:29 (+ חַח *ring*, || שָׂפָה *lip*) Jb 40:26 (+ אַגְמוֹן *cord*), עלה *go up* 4QapPs[b] 24:11, hi. *cause* stench *to go up* Am 4:10 (or em. בְּאֵשׁ *stench of* your camps to בָּאֵשׁ I shall cause your camps to rise, i.e. be destroyed, *with fire*, and em. וּבְאַפְּכֶם *even into your nostril* to וּבְאַפִּי *and in my anger* I shall overturn).

ערב בְּאַף *be sweet in the nose*, i.e. smell sweet 11QPs[a] 22:11, עָלָה עָשָׁן בְּאַפּוֹ *smoke went up from his nose* 2 S 22:9||Ps 18:9 (|| פֶּה *mouth*).

עַל *on, through*, + שׂים *place* ring Gn 24:47 (|| יָד *hand*), נתן *place* ring Ezk 16:12 (|| אֹזֶן *ear*, ראשׁ *head*).

יצא מִן *come out from* Nm 11:20.

הִנָּם שֹׁלְחִים אֶת־הַזְּמוֹרָה אֶל־אַפָּם *behold, they extend the branch to their nose* Ezk 8:17 (Tiq soph אַפִּי/אַפַּי *my nose*, i.e. *they provoke me to anger*).

3. in dual, **face, <OBJ>** שׁוב hi. *turn* in rebuff Si 41:21(B) (M פני *face of*; Bmg מי השע פי *who would cause the mouth of* your neighbour *to cry out?*).

<CSTR> אפי רעך *face of your neighbour* Si 41:21(B); זֵעַת אַפַּיִם *sweat of face* Gn 3:19.

<PREP> לְאַפַּיִם *onto one's face, face-downward*, + שחה htpal. *bow down* Gn 48:12 Nm 22:31 2 S 18:28, נפל *fall* 1 S 20:41, לְאַפֵּי = לִפְנֵי *in front of* 1 S 25:23; עַל אַפַּיִם *face downward*, + שחה htpal. *bow down* 2 S 14:33 1 K 1:23, נפל *fall* 2 S 14:4.

<COLL> אַרְצָה אַפַּיִם, אַפַּיִם אַרְצָה *the face toward the ground* in gesture of obeisance, + שחה htpal. *bow down* Gn 19:1 42:6 48:12 1 S 25:41 2 S 14:33 18:28 24:20||1 C 21:21 Is 49:23 (אֶרֶץ) Ne 8:6, קדד *bow down* 1 S 24:9 28:14 1 K 1:31 (אֶרֶץ; mss, Seb אַרְצָה) 2 C 20:18, כרע *bow down* 2 C 7:3, נפל *fall* 1 S 20:41 2 S 14:4.

4. perh. **side,** מָנָה אַחַת אַפָּיִם *a portion (consisting of) one of two sides*, i.e. only half a portion 1 S 1:5.

Also 1QSb 16:2 1QH 18:5 1QpZeph 1:5 ([א]ף).

<SYN> §1 חֵמָה *wrath*, עֶבְרָה *wrath*, זַעַם *wrath*, קִנְאָה *jealousy*; §3 אֹזֶן *ear*.

→ אנף *be angry*.

אפד 2 vb. **dress in ephod—Qal** + waw וְאָפַדְתָּ, וַיֶּאְפֹּד— וְאָפַדְתָּ לוֹ בְּחֵשֶׁב הָאֵפֹד *and you are to dress him with the decorated band of the ephod* Ex 29:5 (|| Lv 8:7 וַיֶּאְפֹּד לוֹ בּוֹ

and he dressed him with it).
→ אֵפֹד I *ephod,* אֵפֹד II *Ephod.*

אֵפֹד I 52.1.2 n.m. **ephod**—אֵפוֹד; cstr. אֲפֻדַּת, sf. אֲפֻדָּתוֹ; pl. Q אפודות; sf. Q אפודיהם (cstr., sf., and pl. as if from [אֲפֻדָּה])—**1. ephod,** priestly garment, **a.** costly decorative tunic for Aaron, alw. assoc. with חֹשֶׁן *breastplate,* **<NOM CL>** אפוד ... בגדי קדש *the holy clothes (included) ... an ephod* Si 45$_{10}$. **<OBJ>** עשׂה *make* Ex 28$_{6}$‖39$_{2}$, לבשׁ hi. *dress (with)* 29$_{5}$, נתן *place* 29$_{5(Sam)}$‖Lv 8$_{7}$.

<CSTR> כִּתְפוֹת הָאֵפֹד *shoulder-pieces of the ephod* Ex 28$_{12}$‖39$_{7}$ (כְּתֵפֹת) 28$_{25}$‖39$_{18}$ (39$_{18}$ כִּתְפֹת) 28$_{27}$‖39$_{20}$ (28$_{27}$ הָאֵפוֹד; 39$_{20}$ כִּתְפֹת), חֵשֶׁב הָאֵפֹד *decorated band of,* i.e. around, *the ephod* 28$_{8}$‖39$_{5}$ (אֲפֻדָּתוֹ) 28$_{27.28}$‖39$_{20.21}$ (28$_{27.28}$ הָאֵפוֹד) 29$_{5}$‖Lv 8$_{7}$, טַבְּעֹת הָאֵפֹד *rings of the ephod* Ex 28$_{28}$‖39$_{21}$, מְעִיל הָאֵפוֹד *robe of the ephod* 28$_{31}$‖39$_{22}$ (39$_{22}$ הָאֵפֹד; Sam הַמְּעִיל) 29$_{5}$ (הָאֵפֹד; ‖Lv 8$_{7}$, Sam הַמְּעִיל), מַעֲשֵׂה אֵפֹד *work,* i.e. style, *of (the) ephod* Ex 28$_{15}$‖39$_{8}$ (Sam הָאֵפוֹד), עֵבֶר הָאֵפֹד *side of the ephod* 28$_{26}$‖39$_{19}$.

<PREP> לְ of benefit, *for,* + לקח *take* precious stones Ex 25$_{7}$‖35$_{9}$, בוא hi. *bring* precious stones 35$_{27}$; זחח מֵעַל ni. *be moved from (being) on* (of breastplate) Ex 28$_{28}$‖39$_{21}$.

1b. simpler religious vestment, **<NOM CL>** עַל־דָּוִיד אֵפוֹד *around David there was an ephod* 1 C 15$_{27}$. **<OBJ>** נשׂא *carry,* i.e. wear 1 S 2$_{28}$ (+ לְפָנַי *before me* [Y.]) 14$_{3}$ 22$_{18}$, חגר pass. *be girded (with)* 1 S 2$_{18}$ (4QSam[a] חוגר *wearing*) 2 S 6$_{14}$. **<ADJ>** אֵפוֹד בָּד *ephod of linen* 1 S 2$_{18}$ 22$_{18}$ 2 S 6$_{14}$ 1 C 15$_{27}$.

2. perh. **oracle,** precious object, kept in local shrine and used for divination (1 S 23$_{6.9}$ 30$_{7.7}$), **<SUBJ>** ירד *go down* 1 S 23$_{6}$ (אֵפוֹד יָרַד בְּיָדוֹ *an ephod went down in his hand,* appar. *he went down with an ephod in his hand*). **<NOM CL>** יֵשׁ ... אֵפוֹד *there is ... an ephod* Jg 18$_{14}$.

<OBJ> עשׂה *make* (of Micah) Jg 17$_{5}$, לקח 18$_{17.18}$ (if em.; see Cstr.; in both subj. Danites) 18$_{20}$ (subj. priest), נגשׁ hi. *bring forward* 1 S 14$_{18}$ (if em. אֲרוֹן הָאֱלֹהִים *ark of God,* subj. Ahijah) 23$_{9}$ 30$_{7.7}$ (all three with subj. Abiathar), נשׂא *carry* 14$_{18}$ (if em. הָיָה אֲרוֹן הָאֱלֹהִים *the ark of Y. was* to הוּא הָיָה נֹשֵׂא הָאֵפוֹד *he used to carry the ephod*) 1 K 2$_{26}$ (if em. אֲרוֹן אֲדֹנָי י׳ *ark of my Lord Y.;* subj. Abiathar), טמא pi. *defile* (of Israelites) Is 30$_{22}$.

<CSTR> אֲפֻדַּת מַסֵּכַת זְהָבֶךָ *ephod of your idol(s) of gold* Is 30$_{22}$ (‖ צִפּוּי *covering*), פֶּסֶל הָאֵפוֹד *image of the ephod* Jg 18$_{18}$ (or em. אֶת־הַפֶּסֶל וְאֶת־הָאֵפוֹד take *the image and the ephod*).

<PREP> עשׂה לְ *make* booty *into* (of Gideon) Jg 8$_{27}$; לוּטָה בַשִּׂמְלָה אַחֲרֵי הָאֵפוֹד sword *wrapped in the cloth, behind the ephod* 1 S 21$_{10}$ (4QSam[a] אחר אפד).

<COLL> אֵפוֹד ... תְּרָפִים *ephod ... teraphim* Jg 17$_{5}$ 18$_{14.17.18}$ (all three + פֶּסֶל *image,* מַסֵּכָה *idol*) 18$_{20}$ (+ פֶּסֶל) Ho 3$_{4}$ (+ מַצֵּבָה *pillar,* זֶבַח *sacrifice,* שַׂר *prince,* מֶלֶךְ *king*), in inventory of buried treasure 3QTr 1$_{9}$ (אפודת; Allegro אפורין *amphorae*), ישׁב ... אֵין אֵפוֹד *dwell ... without ephod* Ho 3$_{4}$.

Also 4QShirShab[f] 23.2$_{5}$ 11QShirShab 7$_{6}$.
→ אפד *dress in ephod.*

אֵפֹד II 1 pr.n.m. **Ephod,** father of Hanniel, chief of Manasseh, Nm 34$_{23}$.
→ אפד *dress in ephod.*

[אֲפֻדָּה], see אֵפֹד I.

[אַפֶּדֶן] 1 n.[m.] **palace**—sf. אַפַּדְנוֹ—וְיִטַּע אָהֳלֵי אַפַּדְנוֹ *and he will plant the tents of his palace,* i.e. his royal pavilion Dn 11$_{45(L)}$ (mss אָהֳלֵי; or em. וְיִטֶּה אָהֳלוֹ אַפַּדְנוֹ *and he will stretch out his tent—his palace*), אַפֶּדֶן עָשָׂה לוֹ Solomon *made himself a palace* Ca 3$_{9}$ (if em. אַפִּרְיוֹן *palanquin*).

אפה 25 vb. **bake—Qal** Pf. אָפָה, אָפִיתִי, אָפוּ; impf. יֹאפוּ, תֹּאפוּ; + waw וַתֹּפֵהוּ, וַיֹּאפוּ, וְאָפִיתָ; impv. אֵפוּ; ptc. אֹפֶה (אֹפֵהֶם), אֹפִים (אוֹפִים), אֹפוֹת—**1. bake, <SUBJ>** Lot Gn 19$_{3}$ (‖ עשׂה *make* feast), בֶּן־יִשְׂרָאֵל *Israelite* Ex 12$_{39}$ 16$_{23.23}$ (‖ בשׁל pi. *boil*) Lv 24$_{5}$, אָדָם *human being* Is 44$_{15}$ (‖ שׂלק hi. *make fire*) 44$_{19}$ (‖ צלה *roast*), אִשָּׁה *woman* Lv 26$_{26}$ 1 S 28$_{24}$ (‖ לושׁ *knead*), כֹּהֵן *priest* Ezk 46$_{20}$ (‖ בשׁל pi.).

<OBJ> בָּצֵק *dough* Ex 12$_{39}$, עֻגָה *cake* of unleavened bread 12$_{39}$, מַצָּה *unleavened bread* 1 S 28$_{24}$, חַלָּה *loaf* Lv 24$_{5}$, לֶחֶם *bread* 26$_{26}$ Is 44$_{15.19}$. **<PREP>** בְּתַנּוּר *in an oven* Lv 26$_{26}$, עַל־גֶּחָלָיו *on its coals* Is 44$_{19}$.

2. ptc. as noun, **baker,** <SUBJ> חטא *sin* Gn 40$_{1}$ (|| שׁקה hi. ptc. *butler*), אסר pass. *be bound* (|| שׁקה hi. ptc.) 40$_{5}$, ישׁן *sleep* Ho 7$_{6}$, חלם *dream* Gn 40$_{5}$, שׁבת *cease* Hos 7$_{4}$. <CSTR> מַעֲשֵׂה אֹפֶה *produce of a baker* Gn 40$_{17}$, שַׂר הָאֹפִים *chief of the bakers* 40$_{2}$ (הָאוֹפִים; || שׁקה hi. ptc. *butler*) 40$_{16.20.22}$ (both || שׁקה hi. ptc.) 41$_{10}$ Jerusalem pithos inscr. (האו[פים]; others [האפ[ם]), חוץ *street of* Jr 37$_{21}$. <PREP> אֶת־בְּנוֹתֵיכֶם יִקָּח ... לְאֹפוֹת *your daughters he will take ... as bakers* 1 S 8$_{13}$ (|| רַקָּח *perfumer*, טַבָּח *cook*).

Ni. Impf. תֵּאָפֶה, תֵּאָפֶינָה—**be baked,** <SUBJ> מִנְחָה *meal offering* Lv 6$_{10}$ (+ חָמֵץ with *yeast*) 7$_{9}$, לֶחֶם *bread* 23$_{17}$ (+ חָמֵץ). <PREP> בַּתַּנּוּר *in the oven* Lv 7$_{9}$. <COLL> חָמֵץ *with yeast* Lv 6$_{10}$ 23$_{17}$.

→ מַאֲפֶה *something baked.*

אֵפָה, see אֵיפָה.

אֵפוֹ, see אֵפוֹא.

אֵפוֹא 15 part. **then**—אֵפוֹ—**then, therefore, 1.** with interrog., מָה *what?* Gn 27$_{37}$ Ex 33$_{16}$ Is 22$_{1}$, מִי *who?* Gn 27$_{33}$, אַיֵּה *where?* Jg 9$_{38}$ 2 K 2$_{14}$ (if em. אַף־הוּא *indeed he*) Ho 13$_{10}$ (if em. אֱהִי *I shall be*) Jb 17$_{15}$, אֵי *where?* Is 19$_{12}$. **2.** in commands, wishes, דְּעוּ אֵפוֹא כִּי *know, then, that* 2 K 10$_{10}$ Jb 19$_{6}$ (דְּעוּ־אֵפוֹ), עֲשֵׂה זֹאת אֵפוֹא *do this, then* Pr 6$_{3}$, מִי־יִתֵּן אֵפוֹ וְיִכָּתְבוּן מִלַּי *would, then, that my words were written* Jb 19$_{23}$. **3.** in conditional sentence with אִם *if,* אִם־כֵּן אֵפוֹא זֹאת עֲשׂוּ *if so, then do this* Gn 43$_{11}$, אִם־לֹא אֵפוֹא מִי־הוּא *if it is not he, then who is it?* Jb 9$_{24}$, וְאִם־לֹא אֵפוֹ מִי יַכְזִיבֵנִי *if not, then who will prove me a liar?* 24$_{25}$.

אֵפוֹד, see אֵפֹד I.

[אפודה], see אֵפֹד I.

אֲפִיחַ 1 pr.n.m. **Aphiah,** father of Becorath and ancestor of Saul, 1 S 9$_{1}$.

[אָפִיל] 1 adj. **late**—pl. f. אֲפִילֹת—with ref. to crops, הַחִטָּה וְהַכֻּסֶּמֶת לֹא נֻכּוּ כִּי אֲפִילֹת הֵנָּה *the wheat and the spelt were not damaged for they are late (crops)* Ex 9$_{32}$.

אַפַּיִם I, see אַף II, §4.

אַפַּיִם II 2 pr.n.m. **Appaim**—אַפָּיִם—son of Nadab and father of Ishi, descendant of Judah, 1 C 2$_{30.31}$.

→ אַף *nose.*

[אָפִיק] I 18.1.2 n.m. **channel**—cstr. אֲפִיק; pl. אֲפִיקִים; cstr. אֲפִיקֵי (אֲפִקֵי); sf. אֲפִיקָיו, אֲפִיקֶיךָ—**1. channel** for water, in valley, etc.

<SUBJ> היה *be* Ezk 36$_{4}$ (+ לְבַז וּלְלַעַג *as booty and mockery;* || חָרְבָּה *ruin,* עִיר *city*), ראה ni. *appear* 2 S 22$_{16}$||Ps 18$_{16}$ (|| מוֹסָד *foundation*), נשׂא *bear* reproach Ezk 36$_{6}$, מלא ni. *be filled* with 32$_{6}$ (+ הַר *mountain*), יבשׁ *be dry* Jl 1$_{20}$ (+ נָוֶה *pasture*), הלך *flow* with water 4$_{18}$ (|| הַר, גִּבְעָה *hill,* + מַעְיָן *spring*). <OBJ> עשׂה ... [כל צבאם] ואפיקים *he* (Y.) *made* heaven and earth and *all their host and watercourses* 4QapPs^{b} 1$_{4}$.

<CSTR> אֲפִיק נְחָלִים *channel(s) of streams* Jb 6$_{15}$ (+ נַחַל *stream*), אֲפִיקֵי יְהוּדָה *channels of Judah* Jl 4$_{18}$, הָאָרֶץ *of the land* Ezk 31$_{12}$ (+ הַר *mountain,* גַּיְא *valley*), מַיִם *of water* 2 S 22$_{16}$ (if em.; see below) Jl 1$_{20}$ Ps 18$_{16}$ (or em. יָם *of [the] sea*) 42$_{2}$ (אֲפִיקֵי־) Ca 5$_{12}$ (מָיִם), אֲפִקֵי יָם *channels of the sea* 2 S 22$_{16}$ (or em. מַיִם *of water*) Ps 18$_{16}$ (if em.; see above), כול אפיקים *all channels* 4QBer^{a} 2$_{2}$, כָּל־אֲפִיקֵי *all the channels of* Ezk 31$_{12}$ (כֹּל) Jl 4$_{18}$, כָּל־אֲפִיקָיו *all his channels* Is 8$_{7}$ (|| גָּדָה *bank*) Ezk 35$_{8}$ (if em. אֲפִיקֶיךָ *your channels*).

<ADJ> אפיק אדיר *mighty channel* Si 40$_{13(B)}$ (|| נַחַל *stream*).

<PREP> אמר לְ *say to* Ezk 6$_{3}$ 36$_{4}$ 36$_{6}$ (all three || הַר *mountain,* גִּבְעָה *hill,* גַּיְא *valley*); בְּ of place, *in,* + רעה *tend* flock Ezk 34$_{13}$ (|| מוֹשָׁב *settlement,* + הַר), נפל *fall* 35$_{8}$ (unless em. בָּהֶם *in them* to בָּךְ *in you;* || גִּבְעָה, גַּיְא), שׁבר ni. *be broken* 31$_{12}$; כְּ *as* Ps 126$_{4}$ (+ בַּנֶּגֶב *in the Negeb*) Jb 6$_{15}$ (+ אָח *brother*) Si 40$_{13(Bmg)}$ (+ חַיִל *wealth*); מאפיק perh. *more than a channel* Si 40$_{13(B)}$; עַל *by* Ca 5$_{12}$ (+ יוֹנָה *dove*), עלה עַל *rise over* Is 8$_{7}$, בוא עַל hi. *bring* sword *upon* Ezk 6$_{3}$, ערג עַל *long for* Ps 42$_{2}$.

2. tube, furrow, in descr. of Behemoth and Leviathan, עֲצָמָיו אֲפִיקֵי נְחוּשָׁה *his bones are tubes of bronze*

Jb 40$_{18}$, גַּאֲוָה אֲפִיקֵי מָגִנִּים *(his) pride is furrows of shields* 41$_{7}$ (or em. גֵּוֹה *his back*).
<SYN> הַר *mountain*, גִּבְעָה *hill*, גַּיְא *valley*.
→ אפק *be strong*.

[אָפִיק] II 1 adj. **mighty**—pl. אֲפִיקִים—מְזִיחַ אֲפִיקִים *belt of the mighty* Jb 12$_{21}$ (+ נָדִיב *noble*).
→ אפק *be strong*.

אֲפִיק, see אֲפֵק.

אֹפִיר, see אוֹפִיר I.

אֹפֶל 9.0.1 n.m. **darkness**, <SUBJ> לקח *take* Jb 3$_{6}$, בוא *come* 30$_{26}$ (|| רַע *evil*, :: אוֹר *light*). <OBJ> כסה pi. *cover*, i.e. conceal Jb 23$_{17}$ (+ מִפָּנַי *from my face*, חֹשֶׁךְ *darkness*).
<PREP> בְּ of place, *in, through*, + הלך *walk* Ps 91$_{6}$ (+ צָהֳר pl. *noon*), ירה *shoot* arrows 11$_{2}$ (בְּמוֹ); ראה מִן *see out of* Is 29$_{18}$ (|| חֹשֶׁךְ *darkness*; 1QIsaa אפלה *darkness*); יפע כְּמוֹ hi. *shine as* Jb 10$_{22}$, עֵיפָתָה כְּמוֹ אֹפֶל *gloom as darkness* 10$_{22}$.
<COLL> חוֹקֵר אֶבֶן אֹפֶל וְצַלְמָוֶת *seeking a (precious) stone (in) darkness and utter gloom* Jb 28$_{3}$.
Also 4Q525 5$_{1}$.
→ אֲפֵלָה *darkness*, מַאֲפֵל *darkness*, מַאְפֵּלְיָה *deep darkness*, אָפֵל *dark*.

אָפֵל 1 adj. **dark**, perh. as noun, **darkness**, הֲלֹא־חֹשֶׁךְ יוֹם י׳ וְלֹא־אוֹר וְאָפֵל וְלֹא־נֹגַהּ לוֹ *is not the day of Y. darkness and not light, dark(ness) and has no brightness?* Am 5$_{20}$.
→ אֹפֶל *darkness*.

אֲפֵלָה 10.0.5 n.f. **darkness**—cstr. Q אפלת; sf. אֲפֵלָתְךָ; pl. אֲפֵלוֹת; cstr. Q אפלות—**darkness**, <NOM CL> אֲפֵלָתְךָ כַּצָּהֳרָיִם *your darkness will be as the noon* Is 58$_{10}$ (+ וְזָרַח בַּחֹשֶׁךְ אוֹרֶךָ *and your light will shine in darkness*), מכסיה אפלות נשף *her garments are shades of twilight* 4QWiles 1$_{5}$.
<CSTR> אפלת אש עולמים *darkness of eternal fire* 1QS 2$_{8}$; חֹשֶׁךְ־אֲפֵלָה *darkness of*, i.e. deepest, *darkness* Ex 10$_{22}$, יוֹם חֹשֶׁךְ וַאֲפֵלָה *day of darkness and gloom* Jl 2$_{2}$ Zp 1$_{15}$ (+ עֶבְרָה *wrath*, צָרָה *distress*, מְצוּקָה *distress*, שֹׁאָה *ruin*, מְשׁוֹאָה *ruin*, שׁוֹפָר *[sound of] trumpet*, תְּרוּעָה *alarm*; both + עָנָן *cloud*, עֲרָפֶל *dense cloud*).
<PREP> ויחשך מאור פני לאפלה *the light of my countenance was darkened into darkness* 1QH 5$_{32}$; בְּ of place, *in, through*, + הלך pi. *walk* Is 59$_{9}$ (+ חֹשֶׁךְ *darkness*), צעד *step* Pr 7$_{9}$ (בְּאִישׁוֹן לַיְלָה וַאֲפֵלָה *in the middle of the night, [in] darkness*), משׁשׁ pi. *grope in* Dt 28$_{29}$ (:: צָהֳר pl. *noon*), דחח ni. *be pushed* Jr 23$_{12}$, נפל *fall* 23$_{12}$, זעם pass. *be cursed* 1QS 2$_{8}$; מִן of direction/place, *(away) from*, + ראה *see* 1QIsaa 29$_{18}$ (|| חֹשֶׁךְ *darkness*; MT אֹפֶל *darkness*), בדל hi. *separate* 11QPsa 26$_{11}$ (obj. אוֹר *light*) 4QapPsa 7.2$_{3}$; דֶּרֶךְ רְשָׁעִים כָּאֲפֵלָה *the way of the wicked is as darkness* Pr 4$_{19}$ (+ אוֹר נֹגַהּ *shining light*).
<COLL> אֲפֵלָה מְנֻדָּח *driven (into) darkness* Is 8$_{22}$ (or em. מִנֹּגַהּ *without brightness*; + צָרָה *distress*, חֲשֵׁכָה *darkness*, מְעוּף צוּקָה *darkness of distress*).
Also 6QHymn 2$_{3}$ (חושך ואפ[לה] *darkness and darkness*).
<SYN> חֹשֶׁךְ *darkness*.
→ אֹפֶל *darkness*.

אפלי 0.0.0.1 pr.n.m. perh. **Aphulai**, son of Shema (שמע), Seal 245$_{1}$ (7th/6th cent.).

אֶפְלָל 2 pr.n.m. **Ephlal**, son of Zabad and father of Obed, descendant of Judah, 1 C 2$_{37.37}$.

[אֹפֶן] 1.1 n.[m.] **occasion**—du./pl. אופנים; sf. אָפְנָיו—דָּבָר דָּבֻר עַל־אָפְנָיו *word spoken at its (appropriate) occasion* Pr 25$_{11}$, מוסר שכל ומושל אופנים *discipline of intelligence and being master of (appropriate) occasions* Si 50$_{27}$ (or em. משלי *proverbs of*, i.e. suited to occasions).

אפס 5.1 vb. **cease**—**Qal** Pf. אָפֵס; ptc. Si אפס—<SUBJ> כֶּסֶף *silver* Gn 47$_{15}$ (+ תמם *be complete*) 47$_{16}$, אמן ptc. pass. *faithful one* Ps 12$_{2}$ (if em. פַּסּוּ *they have ceased* to אָפְסוּ *they have ceased*), מֵץ *oppressor* Is 16$_{4}$ (|| כלה *be complete*, תמם), עָרִיץ *tyrant* 29$_{20}$ (|| כלה, כרת ni. *be cut off*), חֶסֶד *loyalty* Ps 77$_{9}$ (|| גמר *cease*, + לָנֶצַח *forever*), מַרְאֶה *sight* (unless המראה = *rebelliousness*) Si 41$_{2(Bmg)}$, מָרָה appar. *sustenance* 41$_{2(M)}$ (|| אבד *be lost*).

<PREP> מִבְּנֵי אָדָם ... אָפְסוּ the faithful ones *have ceased from (living among) human beings* Ps 12_{2} (if em.; see Subj.).

<SYN> כלה *be complete*, תמם *be complete*.

→ אֶפֶס *end*, אֹפֶס *extremity*.

אֶפֶס 43.4.10 n.m. **end**—אַפְסִי; pl. cstr. אַפְסֵי; sf. Q אפסיו—**1. end, limit,** of time or space, <SUBJ> פנה *turn* Is 45_{22}, ישׁע ni. *be delivered* 45_{22}, שׁוב *return* Ps 22_{28} (+ מִשְׁפָּחָה *family*), ירא *fear* 67_{8}, ראה *see* Is 52_{10} (+ גּוֹי *nation*) Ps 98_{3} Si $36_{22(Bmg)}$, ידע *know* Si 36_{22}, זכר *remember* Ps 22_{28}.

<OBJ> נגח pi. *gore* Dt 33_{17} (|| עַם *people*), דין *judge* 1 S 2_{10}, נתן *give* Ps 2_{8} (|| גּוֹי *nation*), קום hi. *establish* Pr 30_{4}. <NOM CL> אין אפס *there is no end* 1QH 6_{17} 12_{10}.

<CSTR> אַפְסֵי־אָרֶץ *ends of the earth* Dt 33_{17} 1 S 2_{10} Is 45_{22} 52_{10} (both + כָּל־ *all*) Jr 16_{19} Mc 5_{3} Zc 9_{10} (|| יָם *sea*; + נָהָר *river*) Ps 2_{8} 22_{28} (+ כָּל־) 59_{14} (אַפְסֵי הָאָרֶץ) 67_{8} (+ כָּל־) 72_{8} (|| יָם; + נָהָר) 98_{3} Pr 30_{4} Si 36_{22} (all three + כָּל־) 44_{21} (|| יָם; + נָהָר) GnzPs 1_{16}.

<PREP> לְ משׁל *rule unto* Ps 59_{14}; אַשּׁוּר בְּאֶפֶס עֲשָׁקוֹ *at the end, Assyria oppressed him* Is 52_{4} (+ בָּרִאשֹׁנָה *in the beginning*; but perh. אֶפֶס = for *nothing* in return; cf. §2a), בוא מִן *come from* Jr 16_{19}; עַד *unto*, Zc 9_{10} (+ מָשְׁלוֹ *his dominion* is), + גדל Mi 5_{3} *be great*, רדה *rule* Ps 72_{8}, נחל hi. *cause to inherit* Si 44_{21}, כון hi. *establish* GnzPs 1_{16}.

2a. as noun, **nothing(ness), worthlessness,** <SUBJ> היה *be* Is 34_{12} (+ שַׂר *prince*). <NOM CL> אֶפֶס מַעֲשֵׂיהֶם *their deeds are nothing* Is 41_{29} (|| אָוֶן *nothing*), פָּעָלְכֶם אָפֶס *your deed is nothing* 41_{24} (if em. מֵאָפַע; + אַיִן *nothing*). <PREP> חשׁב מִן ni. *be reckoned as* Is 40_{17} (|| תֹּהוּ *nothing*); כל מאפס אל אפס ישוב *everything from nothing returns to nothing* Si $41_{10(B, M)}$ (Bmg כל מאונים אל אונים; + תֹּהוּ); כְּ *as*, + היה *be* Is 41_{12} (|| אַיִן *nothing*), חשׁב ni. *be reckoned* 4QDibHam[a] $1.3_{3(mg)}$ (ו[כ]אפס נחש[בו]; || אַיִן, תֹּהוּ).

2b. בְּאֶפֶס **without** (lit. *in there not being*, or *with nothingness of*), + noun, תִּקְוָה *hope* Jb 7_{6}, לְאֹם *people* Pr 14_{28} (+ בְּרָב־ *in a multitude of*), עֵץ *wood* 26_{20} (+ בְּאֵין *without*), יָד *hand* Dn 8_{25}.

3. as negative particle, **there is not, there is no one,** אֶפֶס בָּר *there is no corn* Pr 14_{4} (if em. אֵבוּס *stall*), וְאָמַר ... הַעוֹד עִמָּךְ וְאָמַר אָפֶס *and he will say, Is there anyone else with you? And he will say, There is not* Am 6_{10}, אֶפֶס אֱלֹהִים *there is no (other) god* Is 45_{14} (|| אַיִן *there is not*), עַד אֶפֶס מָקוֹם *until there is no place* 5_{8}, אֶפֶס עָצוּר וְעָזוּב *there is no bound or free* Dt 32_{36}, sim. 2 K 14_{26}, אפס כול שותיהם *all those who drink of them are not*, i.e. are no more 1QH 3_{30}.

ואפס יצר עולה *the creature of iniquity is not*, i.e. is no more 1QH fr. 3_{10}, אֲנִי וְאַפְסִי עוֹד *I am and there is no one else* Is 47_{10} Zp 2_{15}, הַאֶפֶס עוֹד אִישׁ *is there no one else?* 2 S 9_{3}.

אֶפֶס בִּלְעָדָי *there is no one apart from me* Is 45_{6} (|| אַיִן), אֶפֶס כָּמוֹנִי *there is no one like me* 46_{9} (|| אַיִן), אפס כמוה *there is no one like it* 1QH 3_{36}, אֶפֶס מֵאוֹתִי *it is not from me* Is 54_{15}.

4. in restrictive uses, **a.** as adv., **only,** אֶפֶס אֶת־הַדָּבָר אֲשֶׁר־אֲדַבֵּר ... תְדַבֵּר *you will only speak ... the word that I speak* Nm 22_{35}, אֶפֶס קָצֵהוּ תִרְאֶה *you will only see its extremity* 23_{13}.

4b. in conj., אֶפֶס כִּי **except that,** qualifying a preceding statement, + verbal clause, usu. with לֹא *not*, Dt 15_{4} Jg 4_{9} 2 S 12_{14} (without לֹא) Am 9_{8} 1QH 2_{33} (לא יד[עו]); + nom. cl., Nm 13_{28}.

Also 4QShirShab[f] 6_{8} 5Q16 1_{4} (ובאפסיו).

<SYN> §1 יָם *sea*, נָהָר *river*; §2a אַיִן *nothing*, תֹּהוּ *nothing*; §3 אַיִן *there is not*.

→ אפס *cease*.

אֶפֶס דַּמִּים 1 pl.n. **Ephes-dammim,** Philistine camp between Socoh and Azekah, perh. ident. with Pas-dammim (פַּס דַּמִּים) at 1 C 11_{13}, 1 S 17_{1}.

→ אֶפֶס *end* + דָּם *blood*.

[אֹפֶס] 1 n.m. **extremity**—du. אָפְסַיִם—**extremity of body, ankle,** מֵי אָפְסָיִם *waters of ankles*, i.e. ankle-deep water Ezk 47_{3} (+ בֶּרֶךְ *knee*, מֹתֶן *hip*).

→ אפס *cease*.

[אֶפַע], see אֶפְעֶה I, II.

אֶפְעֶה I 3 n.[m.] **viper**—Q אפעא—venomous snake,

perh. Echis colorata, <SUBJ> בקע ni. *break out*, i.e. be hatched (cf. אֶפְעֶה II, Subj.) Is 59$_5$ (1QIsa^a אפע; + צִפְעוֹנִי *adder*, עַכָּבִישׁ *spider*). <CSTR> perh. אֶרֶץ ... אֶפְעֶה *land of ... viper(s)* Is 30$_6$ (+ לָבִיא *lion[ess]*, לַיִשׁ *lion*, שָׂרָף *serpent*), לְשׁוֹן אֶפְעֶה *tongue of viper* Jb 20$_{16}$ (+ פֶּתֶן *asp*).

[אֶפְעֶה] II 1.0.4 n.[m.] **nothing**—אֶפַע—<SUBJ> **nothing, worthlessness,** or, perh., **groaning,** בקע ni. *break out* (cf. אֶפְעֶה I, Subj.) 1QH 2$_{28}$ (|| שָׁוְא *emptiness*). <CSTR> הרית אפעה *one pregnant of,* i.e. with/by, *nothing* 1QH 3$_{12}$, מעשי *acts of* 3$_{17}$, רוחי *spirits of* 3$_{18}$. <PREP> פָּעָלְכֶם מֵאָפַע *your work is of nothing,* i.e. worthless, futile Is 41$_{24}$ (if em. אֶפֶס *nothing;* || אַיִן *nothing;* lacking in 1QIsa^a).

אפף 5.0.2 vb. **surround**—**Qal** Pf. אָפְפוּ (אֲפָפֻנִי, אֲפָפוּנִי)—<SUBJ> (alw. pl.) מַיִם *waters* Jon 2$_6$ (|| סבב *surround*), חֶבֶל *cord* of death Ps 18$_5$ (||2 S 22$_5$ מִשְׁבָּר *breaker;* || בעת pi. *overwhelm*) 116$_3$ (|| מצא *find*) 1QH 3$_{28}$, רָעָה *evil* Ps 40$_{13}$, נַחַל *stream* of Belial 1QH 5$_{39(Licht)}$ (ונחלי [ב]ליעל). <OBJ> נֶפֶשׁ *soul* 1QH 5$_{39}$. <PREP> אפף עַל *surround* Ps 40$_{13}$.

אפצח 0.0.0.2 pr.n. **Ephezach,** Samaria ost. 31$_2$ 90$_2$ (אפצ[ח]).

→ perh. פצח *break out*.

אפק 7.1.3 vb. **be strong**—**Htp.** Pf. הִתְאַפָּקוּ; impf. יִתְאַפַּק, 2ms תִּתְאַפַּק, אֶתְאַפָּק; + waw וָאֶתְאַפַּק; inf. הִתְאַפֵּק; ptc. Q [מ]תאפקים—**1. force oneself,** וָאֶתְאַפַּק וָאַעֲלֶה *and I* (Saul) *forced myself and I offered* 1 S 13$_{12}$.

2. restrain oneself from tears, anger, etc., <SUBJ> Y. Is 42$_{14}$ (|| חרש hi. *be silent*) 64$_{11}$ (+ ענה pi. *afflict;* both || חשה hi. *be silent*) 63$_{15}$ (if em. to אַל־נָא תִּתְאַפָּק *do not, pray, restrain yourself [with regard to]* your yearnings) Si 32$_{22(B)}$ (|| מהה htpalp. *delay* intrans.), Joseph Gn 43$_{31}$ 45$_1$, Haman Est 5$_{10}$, גִּבּוֹר *warrior* Si 32$_{22(Bmg)}$, הֲמוֹן *yearning* Is 63$_{15}$ (or em.; see above), רַחֲמִים *compassion* 63$_{15}$ (or em.; see above), subj. not specified 4Q525 2$_4$.

<PREP> לְ *in front of* attendants Gn 45$_1$; בְּ of instrument, *with* disciplines 5Q525 2$_1$; כְּ *as* warrior Si 32$_{22(B)}$; להתאפק על עליל[ות] רשע *to restrain oneself against acts of wickedness* 1QH 14$_9$; יתאפק עד ימחץ *he restrains himself until he destroys* Si 32$_{22}$, [מ]תאפקים עד [יום] משפטיכה *those who restrain themselves until the day of your judgments* 1QH 14$_{4(Licht)}$.

<SYN> חשה hi. *be silent*.

→ אָפִיק *channel*, אָפִיק *mighty*, אֲפֵק *Aphek*, אֲפֵקָה *Aphekah*.

אֲפֵק 9 pl.n. **Aphek**—אֲפִיק (mss אֲפֵק); + ה- of direction אֲפֵקָה—**1.** city, appar. in the Sharon (לַשָּׁרוֹן *[belonging] to the Sharon* Jos 12$_{18}$), assoc. with Philistines, perh. T. Rās el-ʿĒn, Jos 12$_{18}$ 1 S 4$_1$ 29$_1$. **2.** city in Asher, perh. mod. T. el-Kerdāne (T. Afēk), near Acre, Jos 19$_{30}$ Jg 1$_{31}$ (L אֲפִיק; mss אֲפֵק or אֲפֵק). **3.** city on Canaanite–Amorite border (or Gebalite border, if em. גְּבוּל הָאֱמֹרִי : וְהָאָרֶץ הַגִּבְלִי *the Amorite border; and the Gebalite territory* to גְּבוּל הַגִּבְלִי *border of the Gebalites*), perh. mod. Kh. Afqā, N of Beirut at the source of the Nahr Ibrāhīm, or ident. with one of the preceding, Jos 13$_4$. **4.** city in the Golan, assoc. with Aramaeans, perh. mod. Fīq, 6 km E of Sea of Galilee, 1 K 20$_{26.30}$ 2 K 13$_{17}$.

→ אפק *be strong*.

אֲפֵקָה 1 pl.n. **Aphekah**—אֲפֵקָה—town in hill country of Judah, perh. mod. Kh. Kanʿān, Jos 15$_{53}$.

→ אפק *be strong*.

אֵפֶר 22.3.6 n.[m.] **dust**—cstr. אֵפֶר—**dust, ash(es),** <SUBJ> היה *be* Ml 3$_{21}$ (+ רָשָׁע *wicked person*, תַּחַת *under* soles of feet), יצע ho. *be spread out* Est 4$_3$ (|| שַׂק *sackcloth;* + אֵבֶל *mourning*, צוֹם *fast*, בְּכִי *weeping*, מִסְפֵּד *mourning*), גאה *be proud* Si 10$_9$ (|| עָפָר *dust*).

<NOM CL> אָנֹכִי עָפָר וָאֵפֶר *I am dust and ashes* Gn 18$_{27}$, var. 1QH 10$_5$ (ואני).

<OBJ> אסף *gather* Nm 19$_{9.10}$ 4QToh B$^a{}_7$ ([והאוס]ף), לקח *take*, i.e. place 2 S 13$_{19}$ (+ עַל *upon* head), יצע hi. *spread out* Is 58$_5$ (|| שַׂק *sackcloth*), אכל *eat* Ps 102$_{10}$ (+ כַּלֶּחֶם *as bread*), רעה *graze (on)* Is 44$_{20}$, לבשׁ *be dressed (in)* Est 4$_1$ (|| שַׂק) Si 40$_{3(mg)}$ (|| עָפָר *dust*), עטה *wrap oneself (in)* Si 11$_{4(A)}$ (א[פ]ר; B אזור *girdle*).

<CSTR> אפר קודש *ashes of holiness* 4QRitPur 1_{3}, אֵפֶר הַפָּרָה *ashes of the heifer* Nm $19_{9.10}$ 4QToh B$^{a}_{7}$; שח עפר ואפר *humble one of dust and ashes* Si 40_{3} (if em. שוב *returning* to שח), מע[שה] אפר *work of ashes* 1QH fr.2.1_{7} (+ עָפָר *dust*), מִשְׁלֵי־אֵפֶר *proverbs of ashes* Jb 13_{12}, מקוי אפר *heaps of ashes* 1QH fr. 3_{6}.

<PREP> נתן לְ *give as*, i.e. make into Ezk 28_{18} (+ עַל־הָאָרֶץ *upon the earth*); בְּ of place, *in*, + פלשׁ htp. *roll oneself* Jr 6_{26} (+ שַׂק *sackcloth*, אֵבֶל *mourning*, מִסְפֵּד *mourning*) Ezk 27_{30} (+ עָפָר *dust*), כבשׁ hi. *trample* Lm 3_{16} (+ חָצָץ *gravel*), ירד hi. *bring down* kings Is 10_{13} (if em. כְּאַבִּיר *as a bull*), בקשׁ בְּ pi. *seek* prayer *with* Dn 9_{3} (|| צוֹם, שַׂק *fast*).

עַל *upon*, + נחם pi. *repent* Jb 42_{6} (|| עָפָר *dust*; but perh. עַל = *[covered] in*, or, *concerning*), ישׁב *sit* Jon 3_{6} (+ שַׂק *sackcloth*); כְּ *as* Ps 147_{16} (+ כְּפוֹר *frost*, || צֶמֶר *wool*), + משׁל htp. *be comparable* to Jb 30_{19} (|| עָפָר *dust*, + חֹמֶר *mud*); ישׁב בְּתוֹךְ *sit among* Jb 2_{8}; לָתֵת ... פְּאֵר תַּחַת אֵפֶר *to give ... a garland instead of ashes* Is 61_{3} (|| אֵבֶל *mourning*, + רוּחַ כֵּהָה *faint spirit*).

<COLL> עָפָר וָאֵפֶר *dust and ashes* Gn 18_{27} Jb 30_{19} 42_{6} Si 40_{3} (+ עד לשוב *until returning [as* or *to]* [or em. שוב to שח unto *the humble one of*]) 1QH 10_{5} 4QShir^{b} $126_{2(\text{Baillet})}$ (ואני עפר וא[פר]).

<SYN> עָפָר *dust*, שַׂק *sackcloth*.

אֲפֵר 2 n.[m.] **covering**, וַיִּתְחַפֵּשׂ בָּאֲפֵר עַל־עֵינָיו *and he disguised himself with a covering over his eyes* 1 K 20_{38}, וַיָּסַר אֶת־הָאֲפֵר מֵעֲלֵי עֵינָיו *and he removed the covering from over his eyes* $20_{41(\text{Qr})}$.

[אֹפֶר], see אוֹפִיר I.

[אֶפְרֹחַ] I 4.0.2 n.m. **nestling**—pl. אֶפְרֹחִים (Q אפרוחים); sf. Qr אֶפְרֹחָיו (Kt אפרחו), אֶפְרֹחֶיהָ—<SUBJ> עלע pi. *suck* Jb 39_{30}. <OBJ> שִׁית *place* Ps 84_{4}. <PREP> רבץ עַל *crouch over* Dt 22_{6}=11QT 65_{3} (|| בֵּיצָה *egg*). <COLL> קַן־צִפּוֹר ... אֶפְרֹחִים אוֹ בֵיצִים *a bird's nest ... (with) nestlings or eggs* Dt 22_{6}=11QT 65_{3}.

<SYN> בֵּיצָה *egg*.

→ פרח I *sprout*.

[אֶפְרֹחַ] II 0.0.0.8 pr.n.m. **Ephroah, 1.** father of Eliashib (אלישב), Ḥorvat 'Uza ost. 2_{1}. **2.** son of Semachiah ([בן] סמכיהו), Seal 239_{1} (8th/7th cent.). **3.** father of Ahab, Seal 519_{2} (T. Beit Mirsim?, 7th/6th cent.). **4.** son of Joshua (יהושע), Seal 520_{1} ([א]פרח) 521_{1} (both T. Beit Mirsim?, 7th/6th cent.). **5.** son of Shahar (שחר), Seal 522_{1} ([ב]ן [א]פרח) 523_{1} ([בן שח]ר; both T. Beit Mirsim?, 7th/6th cent.). **6.** father of Rephaiah (רפאיהו), Seal 817_{2} (City of David, 7th/6th cent.). **7.** Seal 415 (7th/6th cent.). **8.** Seal 809_{1} (City of David, 7th/6th cent.).

→ פרח *sprout*.

אַפִּרְיוֹן 1 n.[m.] **palanquin,** אַפִּרְיוֹן עָשָׂה לוֹ הַמֶּלֶךְ שְׁלֹמֹה *King Solomon made himself a palanquin* Ca 3_{9} (Gnz אִפְּרְיוֹן; or em. אַפֶּדֶן *throne*; + מִטָּה *couch*).

אֶפְרַיִם I 180.2.11 pr.n.m. **Ephraim**—אֶפְרָיִם—**1.** second son of Joseph, Gn 41_{52} 46_{20} 48_{1+7t} 50_{23} Nm 1_{10} 26_{28} 1 C $7_{20.22}$.

2a. tribe of Ephraim, sometimes with ref. to territory of tribe (e.g. Dt 34_{2} Jg 12_{15} 2 C 30_{10}), Nm 1_{33} $2_{18.24}$ 13_{8} Dt 33_{17} Jos 16_{10} $17_{9.10}$ $21_{5.20}$ Jg 1_{29} 5_{14} 7_{24} $8_{1.2}$ 10_{9} 12_{1+8t} 2 S 2_{9} Ezk $48_{5.6}$ Ps 60_{9}=108_{9} 78_{67} (or understand both as §4) 80_{3} 1 C 6_{51} 2 C 28_{7}, אֶפְרַיִם וּמְנַשֶּׁה *Ephraim and Manasseh* Dt 34_{2} 2 C 15_{9} $30_{1.10.18}$ 31_{1} 4QpPs^{a} 1.2_{17}, sim. Jos 17_{17} Is 9_{20}, מְנַשֶּׁה וְאֶפְרַיִם *Manasseh and Ephraim* 2 C $34_{6.9}$ Jos 14_{4} 16_{4}, sim. Is 9_{20}. **2b.** בְּנֵי אֶפְרַיִם *people of Ephraim*, Nm 1_{32} 2_{18} 7_{48} 10_{22} $26_{35.37}$ 34_{24} Jos $16_{5.8.9}$ 17_{8} Ps 78_{9} (or em. בָּנִים פְּרֻצִים *unruly children*) 1 C 9_{3} 12_{30} $27_{10.14\ 20}$ 2 C 28_{12}, cf. also 25_{7} (§4), וּמְנַשֶּׁה *and Manasseh* 11QT 24_{13}, sim. 11QT 44_{13}.

3. הַר אֶפְרַיִם *hill country of Ephraim*, a range of hills in central Palestine, extending into territory of Manasseh and Benjamin, Jos 17_{15} 19_{50} 20_{7} 21_{21} $24_{30.33}$ Jg 2_{9} 3_{27} 4_{5} 7_{24} 10_{1} $17_{1.8}$ $18_{2.13}$ $19_{1.16.18}$ 1 S 1_{1} 9_{4} 14_{22} 2 S 20_{21} 1 K 4_{8} 12_{25} 2 K 5_{22} Jr 4_{15} 31_{5} 50_{19} 1 C 6_{52} 2 C 13_{4} 15_{8} 19_{4}.

4. northern kingdom of Israel, Is $7_{2.5.8.9.17}$ 9_{8} $11_{13.13.13}$ 17_{3} $28_{1.3}$ Jr 7_{15} $31_{9.18.20}$ Ezk $37_{16.19}$ Hos 4_{17} 5_{3+8t} $6_{4.10}$ $7_{1.8.8.11}$ $8_{9.11}$ 9_{3+5t} $10_{6.11.11}$ $11_{3.8.9}$ $12_{1.2.9.15}$

13$_{1.12}$ 14$_9$ Ob$_{19}$ Zc 9$_{10.13}$ 10$_7$ 2 C 17$_2$ 25$_{7.10}$ Si 47$_{21.23}$ 4QTestim 1$_{27}$ CD 7$_{13}$ 4QpHos^b 2$_3$ 4QpNah 3.2$_{2.8}$ 3.3$_5$ 3.4$_{5(\text{Horgan})}$ ([א]פרים) 4QapPs^b 24$_5$ 4QPsJos^b 22.2$_{13a}$ (|| יִשְׂרָאֵל *Israel,* יְהוּדָה *Judah*).

5. יַעַר אֶפְרַיִם *forest of Ephraim*, perh. a wooded area E. of the Jordan, 2 S 18$_6$.

6. שַׁעַר אֶפְרַיִם *gate of Ephraim*, major gate of Jerusalem, 2 K 14$_{13}$||2 C 25$_{23}$ Ne 8$_{16}$ 12$_{39}$.

אֶפְרַיִם II $_1$ pl.n. **Ephraim,** N of Jerusalem and S of Baal-Hazor, perh. ident. with Ophrah (עָפְרָה) at 1 S 13$_{17}$ and Ephron at 2 C 13$_{19(\text{Kt, mss})}$ (Qr עֶפְרַיִן *Ephrain*), perh. ident. with Eṭ-Ṭaiyibe, 2 S 13$_{23}$.

אֶפְרָת, see אֶפְרָתָה I–II.

אֶפְרָתָה I $_3$ pr.n.f. **Ephrathah**—אֶפְרָת—second wife of Caleb and mother of Hur, also wife of Hezron, father of Caleb, and mother of Ashhur (if em.), 1 C 2$_{19}$ (אֶפְרָת) 2$_{24}$ (if em. בְּכָלֵב אֶפְרָתָה וְאֵשֶׁת *in Caleb, Ephrathah; and the wife of* to בָּא כָלֵב אֶפְרָתָה אֵשֶׁת *Caleb came to Ephrathah wife of*) 2$_{50}$ 4$_4$.

אֶפְרָתָה II $_8$ pl.n. **Ephrathah**—אֶפְרָת—appar. ident. with or near to Bethlehem, Gn 35$_{16.19}$ (mss אֶפְרָת) 48$_{7.7}$ (אֶפְרָת; Sam אֶפְרָתָה) Mc 5$_1$ (perh. em. אֶפְרָתָה צָעִיר לִהְיוֹת *Ephrathah [which] is [too] small to be* to אֶפְרָת הַצָּעִיר *Ephrath is the smallest*) Ps 132$_6$ Ru 4$_{11}$ 1 C 2$_{24}$ (or em. בְּכָלֵב אֶפְרָתָה וְאֵשֶׁת *in Caleb, Ephrathah; and the wife of* to בָּא כָלֵב אֶפְרָתָה אֵשֶׁת *Caleb came to Ephrathah wife of*).

אֶפְרָתִי $_5$ gent. **Ephrathite**—אֶפְרָתִי, pl. אֶפְרָתִים—**1.** as noun, appar. member of tribe of Ephraim, Jg 12$_5$ 1 S 1$_1$ 1 K 11$_{26}$. **2.** as adj. and noun, (person) from Ephrathah, 1 S 17$_{12}$ Ru 1$_2$.

אֶצְבֹּן $_2$ pr.n.m. **Ezbon**—אֶצְבֹּן, Sam אצבעון—**1.** son of Gad (appar. ident. with Ozni at Nm 26$_{16}$), Gn 46$_{16}$ (אֶצְבֹּן; Sam אצבעון). **2.** grandson of Benjamin 1 C 7$_7$.

אֶצְבַּע $_{31.0.10}$ n.f. **finger, toe**—cstr. אֶצְבַּע; sf. אֶצְבָּעוֹ, אֶצְבָּעֲךָ; pl. אֶצְבָּעוֹת (אֶצְבָּעוֹת); cstr. אֶצְבְּעוֹת (אֶצְבְּעֹת); sf. אֶצְבְּעוֹתַי (אֶצְבְּעֹתַי), אֶצְבְּעֹתֶיךָ, אֶצְבְּעֹתָיו, אֶצְבְּעוֹתֵיכֶם—**1. finger,** esp. forefinger (e.g. Ex 29$_{12}$ Lv 4$_{6.17}$), sometimes used in measurement (Jr 52$_{21}$ 1QM 5$_{13}$), also of finger of God (Ex 8$_{15}$ 31$_{18}$ Dt 9$_{10}$ Ps 8$_4$).

<SUBJ> עשׂה *make* Is 2$_8$ 17$_8$ (both + יָד *hand*) 11QPs^a 28$_4$, גאל ni. *be defiled* Is 59$_3$ (|| כַּף *hand*), נטף *drip* Ca 5$_5$ (|| יָד). <NOM CL> אֶצְבַּע אֱלֹהִים הִיא *it is the finger of God* Ex 8$_{15(\text{Qr})}$, אֶצְבְּעֹת יָדָיו ... שֵׁשׁ *the fingers of his hands ... were six* 2 S 21$_{20}$, אצבעות ידיו [ע]בות *the fingers of his hands are thick* 4QCrypt 1.3$_3$, [א]צבעות ידיו דקות [וארוכ]ות *the fingers of his hands are thin and long* 2.1$_4$, עָבְיוֹ אַרְבַּע אֶצְבָּעוֹת *its thickness was four fingers* Jr 52$_{21}$, רוחבו ארבע אצבעות *its width shall be four fingers* 1QM 5$_{13}$, אצב[עך] גדולה וחזקה *your finger is great and mighty* 4Q372 1$_{18}$.

<OBJ> טבל *dip* Lv 4$_{6.17}$ 9$_9$ 14$_{16}$, שׁלח *send*, i.e. point Is 58$_9$ 1QS 11$_2$ (both || אָוֶן *wickedness*), למד pi. *train* Ps 144$_1$ (|| יָד *hand*). <CSTR> אֶצְבַּע אֱלֹהִים *the finger of God* Ex 8$_{15}$ 31$_{18}$ Dt 9$_{10}$, אֶצְבְּעֹת יָדָיו *the fingers of his hands* 2 S 21$_{20}$; מַעֲשֵׂי אֶצְבְּעֹתֶיךָ *the works of your fingers* Ps 8$_4$. <ADJ> אֶצְבָּעוֹ הַיְמָנִית *his right finger* Lv 14$_{16.27}$.

<PREP> בְּ of instrument, *with*, + נתן *place* Ex 29$_{12}$ Lv 8$_{15}$ 11QT 16$_{16}$ 23$_{12}$, לקח *take* Lv 4$_{25.30.34}$ Nm 19$_4$, נזה hi. *sprinkle* Lv 14$_{16.27}$ 16$_{14.14.19}$ 4QToh B$^a_4$ 4QApocMos B 1.2$_4$ (באצבע[ו]), ירה hi. *point* Pr 6$_{13}$ (|| עַיִן *eye*, רֶגֶל *foot*), כתב pass. *be written* Ex 31$_{18}$ Dt 9$_{10}$; קשׁר עַל *bind upon* Pr 7$_3$ (+ לוּחַ לִבֶּךָ *the tablet of your heart*). <COLL> אַרְבַּע אֶצְבָּעוֹת *four fingers* Jr 52$_{21}$ 1QM 5$_{13}$.

2. toe, also of fingers and toes (1 C 20$_6$), <NOM CL> אֶצְבְּעוֹת רַגְלָיו שֵׁשׁ *the toes of his feet were six* 2 S 21$_{20}$, אֶצְבְּעֹתָיו שֵׁשׁ *his fingers and toes were six* 1 C 20$_6$, אצבעות רגליו דקות וארוכות *the toes of his feet are thin and long* 4QCrypt 1.2$_5$, אצבעות רגליו עבות וקצרות *the toes of his feet are thick and short* 1.3$_5$.

<CSTR> אֶצְבְּעוֹת רַגְלָיו *the toes of his feet* 2 S 21$_{20}$ 4QCrypt 1.2$_5$ 1.3$_5$. <SYN> יָד *hand*, אָוֶן *wickedness*.

[אָצִיל] I $_1$ n.[m.] **side**—pl. sf. אֲצִילֶיהָ (Q אציליהא)—**side, edge** of earth, מֵאֲצִילֶיהָ קְרָאתִיךָ *I called you from its edges* Is 41$_9$ (+ קְצוֹת הָאָרֶץ *ends of the earth*).

→ אצל *withhold.*

[אָצִיל] II $_{1}$ n.[m.] **leader**—pl. cstr. אֲצִילֵי—with ref. to Moses, Aaron, Nadab, Abihu and the seventy elders, וְאֶל־אֲצִילֵי בְּנֵי יִשְׂרָאֵל לֹא שָׁלַח יָדוֹ וַיֶּחֱזוּ ... וַיֹּאכְלוּ וַיִּשְׁתּוּ *he did not extend his hand against the leaders of the sons of Israel, and they saw* God *and ate, and drank* Ex 24_{11} (Sam mss וַיֹּאחֲזוּ *and they held*).

→ perh. אצל *withhold.*

[אַצִּיל] $_{3.1}$ n.[f.] **joint**—Si אציל; appar. + ה- of direction אַצִּילָה; pl. cstr. אַצִּילֵי, אַצִּלוֹת—**1. joint** of hand, arm (יָד), with ref. to armpit (Jr 38_{12}) and perh. to wrist (Ezk 13_{18}) or elbow (Si 41_{19}).

<OBJ> נטה hi. *stretch out* Si 41_{19} (+ על/אל לחם *at a meal*). **<CSTR>** אַצִּלוֹת יָדֶיךָ *joints of your arms* Jr 38_{12}, כָּל־אַצִּילֵי יָדַי *all the joints of my hands* Ezk 13_{18} (or em. יָדַיִם or יָד *of [your/their] hand[s]*). **<PREP>** על תפר pi. *sew* magic bands *on* Ezk 13_{18} (+ ראשׁ *head*), שִׂים תַּחַת *place* clothes *under* Jr 38_{12}.

2. appar. **joint, edge**of foundations of temple side chambers, מוֹסְדוֹת צְלָעוֹת מְלוֹ הַקָּנֶה שֵׁשׁ אַמּוֹת אַצִּילָה *the foundations of the side chambers were a full rod—six cubits to the joint* Ezk $41_{8(Qr)}$ (or em. אֶצְלָהּ *beside it*, i.e. flush with platform [גִּבְהָ]).

→ perh. אצל *withhold.*

אצל I $_{5.3}$ vb. **withhold**—Pf. אָצַלְתָּ, אָצַלְתִּי; + waw וַיָּאצֶל, וְאָצַלְתִּי (perh. hi.)—**withhold, set aside, <SUBJ>** Y. Nm $11_{17.25}$ (Sam נצל hi. *seize* in both), Isaac Gn 27_{36} (+ לקח *take*), Koheleth Ec 2_{10} (+ מנע *withhold*). **<OBJ>** בְּרָכָה *blessing* Gn 27_{36}. **<PREP>** לְ of benefit, *for* Esau Gn 27_{36}; מִן privative, *(away) from* enjoyment Ec 2_{10}, partitive, *(some) of* spirit Nm $11_{17.25}$.

Ni. Pf. נֶאֱצַל, Si נאצלו; ptc. Si נאצל—**1. be set aside, be taken away,** [לא נוסף] ולא נאצל *nothing is added and nothing is taken away* Si $42_{21(B[Segal])}$ (M נאסף *gathered [away]*), הם בשנים נאצלו משש מאות אלף appar. *they* (Joshua and Caleb), *as two, were set aside from six hundred thousand* 46_{8}, perh. Ezk 42_{6} (see below, §3).

2. ptc. appar. used as adj., **poor** (i.e. from whom wealth is withheld), כן עשיר אל איש נאצל *so is a rich man with regard to a poor man* Si 13_{17} (unless נאצל = *makes alliance* with, i.e. אצל II; perh. em. איש to רש *poor*).

3. perh. **be recessed,** נֶאֱצַל מֵהַתַּחְתֹּנוֹת וּמֵהַתִּיכֹנוֹת מֵהָאָרֶץ appar. the upper chambers (הַלְּשָׁכוֹת) *were recessed (further) from the ground than the lower and middle (chambers)* Ezk 42_{6} (but perh. נֶאֱצַל = *it* (space) *was taken away* [as §1] from other chambers, or em. נֶאֶצְלוּ *were recessed* or נֶאֱצַר *it* (space) *was stored up* compared to other chambers).

→ אֵצֶל *beside,* אָצִיל I *side,* אֲצַלְיָהוּ *Azaliah,* perh. אַצִּיל *joint,* אָצִיל II *leader,* אָצַל *Azal,* אָצֵל *Azel.*

אצל II, see אצל I, §2.

אֵצֶל $_{61.2.24}$ prep. **beside**—sf. אֶצְלִי, Q אצלך, אֶצְלוֹ, אֶצְלָהּ, Q הצלכם (Q אצלכן), אֶצְלָם (Q אצלן).

1. prep. **beside, with, near,** followed by noun or pronoun, Sarah 2QJub[a] $23_{7(Baillet)}$ ([אצל שרה]), Potiphar's wife Gn $39_{10.15.16.18}$, Ezekiel Ezk 43_{6}, Nehemiah Ne 4_{12}, Ezra 8_{4}, Sanballat 3_{35}, Jeshua MurEpBethMashiko$_{7}$ MurEpBarC[a]$_{4}$ MurEpBarC[b]$_{4.5}$, Jonathan MurEpJonathan$_{4}$, people of En-Gedi 5/6ḤevEp 12 fr; Gibeah Jg 19_{14}, En-rogel 1 K 1_{9}, Zarethan 4_{12}, Bethlehem Jr 41_{17}.

פַּר *bull* 11QT 26_{9} $34_{12.13}$, פָּרָה *cow* Gn 41_{3}, אַיִל *ram* Dn 8_{7}, חַיָּה *living creature* Ezk $1_{15.19}$, כְּרוּב *cherub* $10_{9.9.16}$, נְבֵלָה *corpse* 1 K $13_{24.24.25.28}$, עֶצֶם *bone* 13_{31} Ezk 39_{15}, אֵלוֹן *terebinth* Dt 11_{30}, מִין *kind* Si 13_{16}, Y. Pr 8_{30}, Dagon 1 S 5_{2}, מֶלֶךְ *king* Dn 10_{13} Ne 2_{6}, צַר *enemy* 4_{6}, אָח *brother* 2 C 28_{15}, בני יהודה *descendants of Judah* 11QT 44_{11}, reader Si 12_{12}.

מִזְבֵּחַ *altar* Lv 1_{16} 6_{3} 10_{12} Dt 16_{21} 1 K 2_{29} 2 K 12_{10} Ezk 9_{2} Am 2_{8}, כְּלִי *vessel* 3QTr 5_{7} $11_{1.4.11.15}$ (or in all five אצלם = *figured coins* from צלם *image*), אֶבֶן *stone* 1 S 20_{19} (or em. אֶבֶן to אַרְגָּב *mound*), בַּיִת *house* 1 K 21_{2} Ne 3_{23} 11QT $32_{12(Yadin)}$, הֵיכָל *palace* 1 K 21_{1}, לִשְׁכָּה *room* Jr 35_{4}, מְקֵרָה *cool room* 3QTr 7_{8}, קִיר *wall* Ezk 33_{30} 11QT 37_{9}, מְזוּזָה *doorpost* Ezk 43_{8}, פִּנָּה *corner* Pr $7_{8.12}$, perh. גִּבְהָ *platform* Ezk 41_{8} (if em.; see below), שַׁעַר *gate* 11QT 38_{6} 42_{7}, יָד *hand*, i.e. armrest, of throne 1 K 10_{19}‖2 C 9_{18}, גְּבוּל *border* Is 19_{19}, עֹמֶד *place of standing* Dn 8_{17}, אוֹפָן *wheel* Ezk 10_{6}.

With verb, היה *be* 1 K 21_{1} Is 19_{19} Pr 8_{30} MurEpBar

Cb$_5$, שׁכב *to lie* Gn 39$_{10}$, עזב *leave* 39$_{15.18}$, נוח hi. *place* 39$_{16}$ 1 K 13$_{31}$, קבר *bury* 2QJub^a 23$_{7(Baillet)}$ (... [ויקבוהו] [א]צל), עמד *stand* Gn 41$_3$ 1 K 10$_{19}$||2 C 9$_{18}$ 1 K 13$_{24.24.25.28}$ Ezk 9$_2$ 10$_6$ 43$_6$ Ne 8$_4$, hi. *cause to stand* Si 12$_{12}$, שׁלך hi. *cast* Lv 1$_{16}$, שׂים *set* 6$_3$, נטע *plant* Dt 16$_{21}$, אכל *eat* Lv 10$_{12}$ 11QT 38$_6$ ([אוכ]ל[ים]), ישׁב *dwell, sit* Dt 11$_{30}$ 1 S 20$_{19}$ Ne 4$_6$ 2$_6$, נצג hi. *set* 1 S 5$_2$, נתן *place* 2 K 12$_{10}$ Ezk 43$_8$, הלך *go* 1$_{19}$ 10$_{16}$, דבר ni. *speak with one another* Ezk 33$_{30}$, בנה *build* 39$_{15}$, נטה hi. *stretch out* intrans. Am 2$_8$, עבר *pass by* Pr 7$_8$, ארב *wait in ambush* Pr 7$_{12}$, בוא *enter* Jg 19$_{14}$ Dn 8$_{17}$, hi. *bring* 2 C 28$_{15}$, ho. *be brought* 4Q251 3$_{13}$ ([אצ]ל), נגע hi. *approach* Dn 8$_7$, יתר ni. *remain* 10$_{13}$, חזק hi. *repair* Ne 3$_{23}$, שׂרף *burn* 11QT 26$_9$, עשׂה *make* 32$_{12}$ 37$_9$ (וע[ש]יתמה) 42$_7$, חלק *allot* 44$_{11}$, עלה *go up* MurEpBeth-Mashiko$_7$.

Without verb, אֲשֶׁר אֵצֶל *which is near* 1 K 1$_9$ 4$_{12}$ Jr 35$_4$ 41$_{17}$, שאצל *which is next to* 3QTr 7$_{8.8}$, הִנֵּה אֵצֶל *behold, he is beside* the altar 1 K 2$_{29}$, הוּא קָרוֹב אֵצֶל *it,* vineyard, *is near* my house 21$_2$, אוֹפַן אֶחָד ... אֵצֶל *a wheel ... beside* creatures/cherubim Ezk 1$_{15}$ 10$_9$, טוֹבִיָּה הָעַמֹּנִי אֶצְלוֹ *Tobiah the Ammonite was beside him* Ne 3$_{35}$, הַתּוֹקֵעַ בַּשּׁוֹפָר אֶצְלִי *the one who sounded the trumpet was beside me* 4$_{12}$, מוֹסְדוֹת צְלָעוֹת מְלוֹ הַקָּנֶה שֵׁשׁ אַמּוֹת אֶצְלָה *the foundations of the side chambers were a full rod-six cubits beside it* Ezk 41$_{8(Qr)}$ (if em. אַצִּילָה *to the joint*), מין כל בשר אצלו *the kind of all flesh is beside it,* i.e. all flesh is with its own kind Si 13$_{16}$, ופר פר ונתחיו אצלו *each bull and its pieces beside it* 11QT 34$_{12}$, יין נסכו אצלו *the wine of its drink offering beside it* 34$_{13}$, בחכן אצלם *in measure next to them,* i.e. right next to them 3QTr 5$_7$ 11$_{1.4}$ (ותכן) 11$_{11}$ (אצלן) 11$_{15}$, הגללאים שהצלכם *the Galilaeans who are with you* MurEpBarC$^a_4$, אצלך בדעת those who are *beside you in knowledge,* i.e. known to you MurEpBarC$^b_4$, הוא כן אצלי בעין גד[י] *he is here with me in En-Gedi* MurEpJonathan$_4$, ... משפינא שאצלכן *from the ship ... that is with you* 5/6ḤevEp 12 fr.

2. מֵאֵצֶל **from beside, from near, beside,** with noun or pronoun, Eliab 1 S 17$_{30}$, זנה ptc. *prostitute* 1 K 3$_{20}$, prophet 20$_{36}$, כְּרוּב *cherub* Ezk 10$_{16}$, אוּלָם *porch* Ezk 40$_7$, נֶגֶב *south* 1 S 20$_{41}$ (or em. נֶגֶב to אַרְגָּב *mound*).

With verb, סבב *turn* intrans. 1 S 17$_{30}$ (+ אֶל־מוּל אַחֵר *towards another*), ni. Ezk 10$_{16}$, קום *arise* 1 S 20$_{41}$, לקח *take* 1 K 3$_{20}$, הלך *go* 20$_{36}$.

Without verb, סַף הַשַּׁעַר מֵאֵצֶל *the threshold of the gate beside* the porch of the gate Ezk 40$_7$.

3. אֶל־אֵצֶל **to beside, to the side of,** יַגִּיעַ גֵּי־הָרִים אֶל־אֶצְלוֹ *the valley of the mountains will reach to beside it* Zc 14$_5$ (if em. אָצַל will reach to *Azal*).

Also 11QT 37$_7$ 4QMish C^d 3$_1$.

→ אצל *withhold.*

אָצֵל 6 pr.n.m. **Azel**—אָצֵל—son of Eleasah, descendant of Saul, 1 C 8$_{37.38.38}$=9$_{43.44.44}$.

→ perh. אצל *withhold.*

אָצַל 1 pl.n. **Azal**—אָצַל—appar. river near Mt of Olives, Zc 14$_5$ (or em. אֶצְלוֹ reach to *beside it*).

→ perh. אצל *withhold.*

אֲצַלְיָהוּ 2.0.0.2 pr.n.m. **Azaliah, 1.** son of Meshullam and father of Shaphan, 2 K 22$_3$||2 C 34$_8$. **2.** son of Meshullam (בן משלם), perh. ident. with foregoing, Seal 853$_1$ (7th cent.). **3.** son of Ido (בן ידו), Seal 752$_1$ (7th cent.).

→ אצל *withhold* + י' Y.

אֹצֶם 2 pr.n.m. **Ozem, 1.** sixth son of Jesse, 1 C 2$_{15}$. **2.** son of Jerahmeel, 1 C 2$_{25}$.

אֶצְעָדָה 2 n.f. **bracelet,** <**OBJ**> מצא *find* Nm 31$_{50}$ (|| צָמִיד *bracelet,* טַבַּעַת *ring,* עָגִיל *anklet,* כּוּמָז *bead*), לקח *take* 2 S 1$_{10}$ (|| נֵזֶר *diadem*), בוא hi. *bring* 1$_{10}$, קרב hi. *present* Nm 31$_{50}$. <**NOM CL**> אֶצְעָדָה אֲשֶׁר עַל־זְרֹעוֹ *a bracelet that was upon his arm* 2 S 1$_{10}$ (or em. הַצְּעָדָה *the bracelet*). <**COLL**> כְּלִי־זָהָב אֶצְעָדָה *article(s) of gold: armlet(s)* Nm 31$_{50}$ (mss Seb כְּלֵי *articles*).

[אצן], see און.

אצר 5 vb. **store up**—Pf. אָצְרוּ; ptc. אוֹצְרִים—<**SUBJ**> אָב *ancestor* 2 K 20$_{17}$||Is 39$_6$, בַּיִת *house* Mc 6$_{10}$ (if em.; see אוֹצָר *treasure,* App.). <**OBJ**> חָמָס *violence* Am 3$_{10}$, שֹׁד *robbery* 3$_{10}$, אוֹצָר *treasure* Mc 6$_{10}$ (if em.; see אוֹצָר).

<PREP> עַד־הַיּוֹם הַזֶּה *until this day* 2 K 20$_{17}$||Is 39$_{6}$, בְּאַרְמְנוֹתֵיהֶם *in their strongholds* Am 3$_{10}$ (or em. בְּאַשּׁוּר *in Assyria*).

Ni. Impf. יֵאָצֵר—**be stored up, <SUBJ>** סַחַר *profit* Is 23$_{18}$ (|| חסן ni. *be hoarded*), אֶתְנַן *fee* 23$_{18}$, perh. לִשְׁכָּה *chamber* Ezk 46$_{6}$ (if em.; see אצל *withhold*, §3).

Hi. + waw וָאוֹצְרָה—**appoint as treasurer,** וָאוֹצְרָה עַל־אוֹצָרוֹת שֶׁלֶמְיָה *and I* (Nehemiah) *appointed Shelemiah as treasurer in charge of treasuries* Ne 13$_{13}$ (or em. וָאֲצַוֶּה *and I commanded* Shelemiah to be in charge).

→ אוֹצָר *treasure,* אוֹצָרָה *treasure,* perh. אֵצֶר *Ezer.*

אֵ֫צֶר 5 pr.n.m. **Ezer,** a son of Seir the Horite, Gn 36$_{21.27}$ ||1 C 1$_{38.42}$ Gn 36$_{30}$.

→ perh. אצר *store up.*

[אֹצָרָה], see אוֹצָרָה.

אֶקְדָּח 1 n.[m.] **beryl**—Q אוקדח—**beryl, red granite,** or sim., וְשַׂמְתִּי ... שְׁעָרַיִךְ לְאַבְנֵי אֶקְדָּח *and I shall place ... your gates as stones of beryl* Is 54$_{12}$ (+ כַּדְכֹּד *agate*).

אַקּוֹ 1 n.m. **wild goat** (perh. *capra aegagrus*), fit for consumption, **<OBJ>** אכל *eat* Dt 14$_{5}$.

אֹר, see יְאֹר.

[אֲרָא] 1.0.0.1 pr.n.m. **Ara**—L וַאֲרָא (mss וַאֲרָא)—**1.** Asherite chief, son of Jether, 1 C 7$_{38}$. **2.** Seal 328$_{2}$ (6th cent.).

אַרְאָ, see אֲרָא.

אראיל, see אֲרִיאֵל III.

[אַרְאֵל] n.m. **hero,** הִכָּה אֵת שְׁנֵי אַרְאֵלֵי מוֹאָב *he struck the two heroes of Moab* 2 S 23$_{20}$||1 C 11$_{22}$ (if em. אֲרִ[י]אֵל *Ariel*), אַרְאֶלָּם צָעֲקוּ *heroes will cry out* Is 33$_{7}$ (if em. אֵרָאֶה לָם perh. *I shall appear to them*).

אַרְאֵל, see אֲרִיאֵל I.

אַרְאֵלִי I 2 pr.n.m. **Areli,** son of Gad, Gn 46$_{16}$ Nm 26$_{17}$ (Sam ארולי appar. *Arvalli* in both).

→ אַרְאֵלִי *Arelite;* cf. אֲרִיאֵל *Ariel.*

אַרְאֵלִי II 1 gent. **Arelite,** of the family of Areli, Nm 26$_{17}$ (Sam ארולי appar. *Arvallite*).

→ אַרְאֵלִי *Areli.*

אֶרְאֶלָּם, see אֲרִיאֵל, אַרְאֵלִי I, II, ראה.

ארב I 26.4.6 vb. **wait in ambush—Qal** Pf. אָרְבוּ, אָרַבְתִּי; impf. יֶאֱרֹב, 3fs תֶּאֱרֹב (Q תארוב), יֶאֶרְבוּ (Q יורבו), וַיֶּאֶרְבוּ; + waw (וַיָּרֶב) וַיֶּאֱרֹב, וַאֲרַבְתֶּם, וְאָרַב, נֶאֶרְבָה; impv. אֱרֹב; ptc. אֹרֵב (אוֹרֵב), אֹרְבִים (Q אורבים); inf. אֱרָב־.

1. ambush, lie in wait, <SUBJ> גִּבּוֹר *warrior* Jos 8$_{4}$, עַז *strong person* Ps 59$_{4}$ (|| גור *cause conflict,* unless em. יָגוּרוּ *they cause conflict* to יָגוֹדּוּ *they attack,* from גדד *cut*), עַם *people* with Abimelech Jg 9$_{34}$, Gazites 16$_{2}$ (+ סבב *surround*), Benjaminites 21$_{20}$, Job Jb 31$_{9}$ (+ פתה ni. *be deceived,* of heart), Abimelech Jg 9$_{32.34.43}$.

רָשָׁע *wicked person* Ps 10$_{9.9}$ (+ לַחֲטוֹף *to seize*) Pr 24$_{15}$ (unless subj. is בֵּן my *son,* and רָשָׁע = *[as] a wicked person;* + שׁדד pi. *act violently*), חַטָּא *sinner* 1$_{11.18}$ (both || צפן *hide,* intrans.), wicked person(s) Mc 7$_{2}$ (+ צוד *hunt*), רדף ptc. *pursuer* (|| דלק *pursue*) Lm 4$_{19}$, רכל ptc. *pedlar* Si 11$_{30}$.

אִישׁ worthless *man* Si 11$_{32}$, זנה ptc. fem. *prostitute* Pr 23$_{28}$, אִשָּׁה *woman* dressed as prostitute 7$_{12}$ 4QWiles 1$_{11(Allegro)}$ (ה[זונ]ה), דָּבָר *word* of the wicked Pr 12$_{6}$, זְאֵב *wolf* Si 11$_{30}$, דֹּב *bear* Lm 3$_{10}$, כְּפִיר *(young) lion* 1QH 5$_{10(AHL)}$ (יורבו; others וירבו *and they ambushed,* unless וירבו = *and they were many;* + פצה *open* mouth).

<OBJ> דָּם *blood* Pr 12$_{6}$. **<PREP>** לְ *against, for* Dt 19$_{11}$ (+ רֵעַ *neighbour,* קום *rise,* נכה hi. *smite,* || שׂנא *hate*) Jos 8$_{4}$ (+ עִיר *city*) Jg 16$_{2}$ (+ שִׁמְשׁוֹן *Samson*) Mc 7$_{2}$ (+ דָּם *blood*) Ps 59$_{4}$ (+ נֶפֶשׁ *soul*) Pr 1$_{11.18}$ (both + דָּם) 24$_{15}$ (+ נָוֶה *dwelling-place*) Lm 4$_{19}$ Si 11$_{30}$ (+ טֶרֶף *prey*) 11$_{30}$ (+ בַּיִת *house*) 11$_{32}$ (+ דָּם); בְּ of place, *in* Jg 9$_{32.43}$ (both + שָׂדֶה *field*) 21$_{20}$ (+ כֶּרֶם *vineyard*) Ps 10$_{9}$ (+ מִסְתָּר *secret place*) Lm 4$_{19}$ (+ מִדְבָּר *desert*) 4QWiles 1$_{11}$ (+ מִסְתָּר), בְּחֶתֶף *in robbery* Pr 23$_{28}$ (if em.; see below); כְּ *as* Ps 10$_{9}$

(+ אַרְיֵה בְסֻכֹּה *a lion in his lair*) Pr 23$_{28}$ (+ חֶתֶף *robber*, or, *as if for robbery*; perh. em. בְּ *in* robbery) Si 11$_{30}$ (+ זְאֵב *wolf*); עַל־פֶּתַח רֵעִי *at my neighbour's entrance* Jb 31$_{9}$; מֵאַחֲרֵי הָעִיר *from behind the city* Jos 8$_{4}$; אֵצֶל כָּל־פִּנָּה *beside every corner* Pr 7$_{12}$.

2. ptc. as noun, **one lying in wait** (Jg 20$_{29}$ 1 S 22$_{8.13}$ Ezr 8$_{31}$), **ambush,** usu. sg. coll. <SUBJ> ישׁב *sit* Jg 16$_{9.12}$ (both + בַּחֶדֶר *in the room*), קום *rise* Jos 8$_{19}$ (+ מִמְּקוֹמוֹ *from its place*) 4QMª fr. 1$_{13}$ (ה]אור[ב]; + מִמְּקוֹמוֹ), גיח hi. *rush out* Jg 20$_{33}$ (+ מִמְּקוֹמוֹ), חושׁ *hurry* 20$_{37}$, פשׁט *make a dash* 20$_{37}$, משׁך *spread out* 20$_{37}$, לָכַד *capture* Jos 8$_{21}$, נכה hi. *smite* Jg 20$_{37}$.

<NOM CL> אֹרֵב לוֹ *there was an ambush against him behind the city* Jos 8$_{14}$ (+ מֵאַחֲרֵי הָעִיר *from behind the city*). <OBJ> שׂים *place* Jos 8$_{2}$ (+ לָעִיר *against the city*) 8$_{12}$ Jg 20$_{29.36}$ (both + אֶל־הַגִּבְעָה *against Gibeah*) 1QM 9$_{17}$ 4QMª fr. 1$_{12}$ (both + למערכת *for a formation*), כון hi. *prepare* Jr 51$_{12}$ (‖ שׁמר ptc. *lookout*).

<CSTR> מערכות אורבים *formations of ambush(es)* 4QMª fr. 1$_{12}$, כַּף אוֹיֵב וְאוֹרֵב *hand of (the) enemy and ambusher* Ezr 8$_{31}$ (+ נצל מִן hi. *deliver from*).

<PREP> לְ *as* + קום *rise up* against 1 S 22$_{13}$, hi. *raise* someone *up* against 22$_{8}$; כְּ *as* Si 8$_{11}$; מִן *from* + קום Jos 8$_{7}$; בטח אֶל־ *trust in* Jg 20$_{36}$; היה עִם־ *be with* Jg 20$_{38}$.

Pi. ptc. as noun, **one lying in wait, ambush**—ptc. מְאָרְבִים—<OBJ> שׂים *place* Jg 9$_{25}$, נתן *place* 2 C 20$_{22}$.

Hi. lie in wait—+ waw וַיָּרֶב—וַיָּרֶב בַּנָּחַל *and he* (Saul) *lay in wait in the valley* 1 S 15$_{5}$.

<SYN> צפן *hide*.

→ אֶרֶב *ambush*, אֹרֶב *lying in wait*; מַאֲרָב *ambush*, perh. אֲרֻבָּה *window*, אָרְבָּה *skill*, אֲרַב *Arab*, אַרְבִּי *Arbite*, אֲרֻבּוֹת *Arubboth*.

[ארב] II, see אָבַר, §2.

אֲרַב 1 pl.n. **Arab,** city in Judaean hill country, perh. Kh. er-Rābiye SW of Hebron or Kh. Arrūb N of Hebron, Jos 15$_{52}$.

→ perh. ארב *wait in ambush*.

[אֹרֶב] 2 n.[m.] **lying in wait**—אֹרֶב—**1. place of lying in wait, lair,** וַתָּבוֹא חַיָּה בְמוֹ־אָרֶב *and an animal comes into a lair* Jb 37$_{8}$ (‖ מְעוֹנָה *den*). **2.** perh. act of **lying in wait,** יֵשְׁבוּ בַסֻּכָּה לְמוֹ־אָרֶב *they remain in a thicket, for lying in wait* Jb 38$_{40}$ (or, אֹרֶב = *lair*, as §1; subj. lions; + מְעוֹנָה).

<SYN> מְעוֹנָה *den*.

→ ארב *wait in ambush*.

אֶרֶב 18 n.m. **ambush**—אוֹרֵב; cstr. אֹרֶב; pl. אֹרְבִים—**ambush, ambush party,** <SUBJ> בוא *come* Jos 8$_{19}$, קום *arise* 8$_{19}$, לכד *capture* 8$_{19.21}$, ישׁב *sit* Jg 16$_{9.12}$, גיח hi. *burst out* 20$_{33}$, רוץ *run* Jos 8$_{19}$, חושׁ hi. *hasten* Jg 20$_{37}$, מהר pi. *hasten* Jos 8$_{19}$, פשׁט *raid* Jg 20$_{37}$, משׁך *drag (oneself)*, i.e. move stealthily 20$_{37}$, נכה hi. *strike* 20$_{37}$, יצת hi. *set alight* Jos 8$_{19}$.

<NOM CL> אֹרֵב לוֹ מֵאַחֲרֵי הָעִיר *there was an ambush for him behind the city* Jos 8$_{14}$. <OBJ> שׂים *place* Jos 8$_{2.12}$ Jg 20$_{29.36}$, כון hi. *prepare* Jr 51$_{12}$ (‖ שׁמר ptc. *guard*).

<CSTR> אֹרֵב יִשְׂרָאֵל *ambush (on the part) of Israel* Jg 20$_{33}$; כַּף אוֹיֵב וְאוֹרֵב from *the hand of enemy and ambush* Ezr 8$_{31}$ (+ עַל־הַדָּרֶךְ *along the way*).

<PREP> לְ *as, in,* + קום *stand* 1 S 22$_{13}$, hi. *raise* 22$_{8}$.

קום מִן *arise from* Jos 8$_{7}$.

בטח אֶל *trust in* Jg 20$_{36}$.

אִישׁ יִשְׂרָאֵל עִם־הָאֹרֵב appointed signal of *Israelite(s) with the ambush*, i.e. between them Jg 20$_{38}$.

→ ארב *wait in ambush*.

אַרְבֵאל, see בֵּית אַרְבֵאל.

אַרְבֶּה 24.1.1 n.m. **locust,** perh. *schistocerca gregaria*, an edible species (Lv 11$_{22}$=11QT 48$_{3}$), usu. collective, <SUBJ> היה *be* 1 K 8$_{37}$‖2 C 6$_{28}$ (‖ שִׁדָּפוֹן *blight*, יֵרָקוֹן *mildew*, חָסִיל *locust*) Ex 10$_{14}$, כבד *be heavy* in number 10$_{14}$, בוא *come* Ps 105$_{34}$ (‖ יֶלֶק *locust*), עלה *go up* Ex 10$_{14}$, נוח *settle* 10$_{14}$, שׁאר ni. *remain* 10$_{19}$, חסל *consume* Dt 28$_{38}$, אכל *eat* Jl 1$_{4}$ (‖ יֶלֶק, חָסִיל, + גָּזָם *locust*) 2$_{25}$ (‖ יֶלֶק, חָסִיל, גָּזָם) Ps 105$_{34}$ (‖ יֶלֶק).

<OBJ> בוא hi. *bring* Ex 10$_{4}$, נשׂא *raise* Ex 10$_{13.19}$, תקע *thrust* 10$_{19}$, אכל *eat* Lv 11$_{22}$=11QT 48$_{3}$ (+ לְמִינוֹ *according to its kind*, ‖ סָלְעָם *locust*, חַרְגֹּל *locust*, חָגָב *locust*). <CSTR> יֶתֶר הָאַרְבֶּה *the remainder of*, i.e. what is left by, *the locust* Jl 1$_{4}$, דֵּי־אַרְבֶּה *sufficiency of locusts* Jg

65 (+ לָרֹב *for multitude*). **<ADJ>** אַרְבֶּה אֶחָד *one locust* Ex 10$_{19}$.

<PREP> נתן לְ *give to* Ps 78$_{46}$ (‖ חָסִיל *locust*), מֶלֶךְ אֵין לָאַרְבֶּה *the locust has no king* Pr 30$_{27}$; נטה בְּ *stretch out* hand *for* Ex 10$_{12}$; כְּ *as*, + נפל *fall* Jg 7$_{12}$ (+ לָרֹב *for multitude*), כבד htp. *multiply* Na 3$_{15}$ (‖ יֶלֶק *locust*), נער ni. *be shaken off* Ps 109$_{23}$, רעשׁ hi. *cause to leap* Jb 39$_{20}$, שׁכן *settle* Si 43$_{17}$, מִנְּזָרַיִךְ כָּאַרְבֶּה *your princes are as locusts* Na 3$_{17}$ (‖ גּוֹב *locust*); רבב מִן *be more numerous than* Jr 46$_{23}$.

<SYN> חָסִיל *locust*, יֶלֶק *locust*, גָּזָם *locust*.

→ רבה *be many*.

[אָרְבָּה] 1 n.f. perh. **skill**—pl. cstr. אָרְבּוֹת—וְהִשְׁפִּיל גַּאֲוָתוֹ עִם אָרְבּוֹת יָדָיו *and he will lay low his pride together with* (or, *despite*) *the skill of his hands* Is 25$_{11}$.

→ perh. ארב *wait in ambush*.

אֲרֻבָּה 9.0.2 n.f. **window**—pl. אֲרֻבּוֹת; cstr. אֲרֻבּוֹת (אֲרֻבֹּת); sf. אֲרֻבֹּתֵיהֶם—**window**, **<SUBJ>** פתח ni. *be opened* Gn 7$_{11}$ Is 24$_{18}$ 4QpGen[a] 1$_{5}$ 4Q370 1$_{4}$, סכר ni. *be stopped up* Gn 8$_{2}$ (:: מַעְיָן *fountain* of deep). **<OBJ>** פתח *open* Ml 3$_{10}$, עשׂה *make* 2 K 7$_{2.19}$. **<CSTR>** אֲרֻבֹּת הַשָּׁמַיִם *windows of the sky* Gn 7$_{11}$ 8$_{2}$ Ml 3$_{10}$ 4QpGen[a] 1$_{5}$ 4Q370 1$_{4}$; כל ארבות *all windows of* 4Q370 1$_{4}$.

<PREP> ראה בְּ *look through* Ec 12$_{3}$; עָשָׁן מֵאֲרֻבָּה *smoke from a window* Hos 13$_{3}$. **<COLL>** אֲרֻבּוֹת בַּשָּׁמַיִם *windows in the sky* 2 K 7$_{2.19}$, אֲרֻבּוֹת מִמָּרוֹם *windows of the sky* (lit. *from on high*) Is 24$_{18}$.

→ perh. ארב *wait in ambush*.

אֲרֻבּוֹת 1 pl.n. **Arubboth,** one of Solomon's administrative centres, perh. T. el-Asāwir (T. Ēsūr) 12 km E of Caesarea, 1 K 4$_{10}$.

→ perh. ארב *wait in ambush*.

אַרְבִּי 1 gent. **Arbite,** perh. inhabitant of Arab (אֲרָב), 2 S 23$_{35}$ (mss אַרְכִּי *Archite*).

→ perh. ארב *wait in ambush*.

אַרְבַּע I 454.1.117.2 n.m. and f. **four**—m. אַרְבָּעָה; cstr. אַרְבַּעַת; sf. אַרְבַּעְתָּם; f. אַרְבַּע; cstr. אַרְבַּע; sf. אַרְבַּעְתָּן; du. אַרְבַּעְתָּיִם; pl. אַרְבָּעִים (Q ארבעין ,רבעים).

אַרְבָּעָה/אַרְבַּע **four,** אַרְבָּעִים **forty.** See Coll. for listing of numbers compounded with אַרְבַּע, not alw. specified in §§1-7.

1. of periods of time, **a.** days (יוֹם), usu. אַרְבָּעִים except Jg 11$_{40}$ (4) 1 K 8$_{65}$ (14) 4QMMT A 1$_{172}$ (שלוש מאת ו[ששים וארבעה]) 4QpGen[a] 2$_{3}$ (both 364) Arad ost. 2$_{3}$ (לארבעת הימם *for the four days*), Gn 7$_{17}$ 8$_{6}$ 50$_{3}$ (‖ 70) Nm 13$_{25}$ 14$_{34}$ 1 S 17$_{16}$ Ezk 4$_{6}$ Jon 3$_{4}$ 11QT 21$_{13}$ 2QJub[a] 23$_{7}$ 4QpGen[a] 1$_{12}$, 40 days and 40 nights (לַיְלָה) Gn 7$_{4.12}$ Ex 24$_{18}$ 34$_{28}$ Dt 9$_{9.11.18.25}$ (אֶת־אַרְבָּעִים הַיּוֹם וְאֶת־אַרְבָּעִים הַלָּיְלָה) 10$_{10}$ 1 K 19$_{8}$ 4QpGen[a] 1$_{6}$ 4QJub[a] 1$_{120}$ ([ארבעים יום וארבעים לילה]). **b.** weeks (שָׁבוּעַ), 2QJub[a] 23$_{8(Baillet)}$ (ארֹ[בעה שבועי]; ‖ 3). **c.** feast days (מוֹעֵד), 4QRitPur 33$_{2}$. **d.** months (חֹדֶשׁ), Jg 19$_{2}$ 20$_{47}$ 1 S 27$_{7}$.

1e. years (שָׁנָה), alw. אַרְבָּעִים unless specified after ref., Gn 31$_{41}$ (14) 47$_{28}$ (147) Jos 14$_{10}$ (45) 2 S 15$_{7}$ (4) 1 K 6$_{1}$ (480) Ezk 40$_{1}$ (14) 4QpGen[a] 1$_{1}$ (ש]נת]; 480) 4QPsJos[b] 12$_{4}$ (41) 4Q464 3.2$_{4}$ ([ארבע מאות שנה]; 400); with ref. to time spent in wilderness Ex 16$_{35}$ Nm 14$_{33.34}$ 33$_{38}$ (בִּשְׁנַת הָאַרְבָּעִים *in the fortieth year*) Dt 1$_{3}$ (בְּאַרְבָּעִים שָׁנָה *in the fortieth year*) 2$_{7}$ 8$_{2.4}$ 29$_{4}$ Jos 5$_{6}$ Am 2$_{10}$ 5$_{25}$ Ps 95$_{10}$ Ne 9$_{21}$ 1QDM 2$_{5}$, to king's reign (e.g. age of accession, duration, point where an incident occurs) Gn 14$_{5}$ (14) 1 S 4$_{18}$ (Eli) 2 S 2$_{10}$ 5$_{4}$ 1 K 2$_{11}$‖1 C 29$_{27}$ 1 K 11$_{42}$‖2 C 9$_{30}$ 1 K 14$_{21}$‖2 C 12$_{13}$ 1 K 15$_{10}$ (both 41) 15$_{33}$ (24) 22$_{41}$ (4) 2 K 12$_{2}$‖2 C 24$_{1}$ 2 K 14$_{23}$ (41) 18$_{13}$‖Is 36$_{1}$ (14) Zc 7$_{1}$ (4) 1 C 26$_{31}$ 2 C 3$_{2}$ (4) 16$_{13}$ (41) 22$_{2}$ (42); שנת ארבע ... לגאלת ציון *the fourth year ... of Israel's redemption* Jewish War Year 4 Coin 161 162 163, sim. Mur 30 2$_{8}$.

With ref. to person's age Gn 5$_{13}$ (840) 11$_{13.15}$ (both 403) 11$_{16}$ (34) 11$_{17}$ (430) 25$_{20}$ 26$_{34}$ Jos 14$_{7}$ Jb 42$_{16}$ 4QpGen[a] 2$_{8}$ (מאה וארֹ[ב]עים; 140) 1QM 6$_{14}$ (45) 6$_{14}$ 7$_{1.1(erased).2}$, to time of peace Jg 3$_{11}$ 5$_{31}$ 8$_{28}$, to time of national bondage, humiliation Gn 15$_{13}$ (400) Ex 12$_{40.41}$ (both 430) Jg 13$_{1}$ Ezk 29$_{11.12.13}$, to jubilee Lv 25$_{8}$ (49) 4QJub[d] 1.2$_{35}$ (שלושה וארֹ[בעים היובל]), to end-time CD 20$_{15}$ 1QpPs[a] 1.2$_{7}$.

1f. in dates, with יוֹם *day*, in ref. to fourteenth day Ex 12$_{6.18}$ Nm 9$_{3.5.11}$ 28$_{16}$ Jos 5$_{10}$ Ezk 45$_{21}$ Est 9$_{15.17.18}$.

$_{19.21}$ 4QPrQuot 1$_{9}$ ([היו]ם ארבעה ע[שר]) 4QpGen^{a} 1$_{8}$, twenty-fourth day Hg 1$_{15}$ 2$_{18}$ Zc 1$_{7}$ Dn 10$_{4}$ Ne 9$_{1}$ 4QpGen^{a} 1$_{17}$ (ארבעה [עשרים]); without יום, in ref. to fourth day Zc 7$_{1}$ GnzPs 4$_{17}$ 11QJub 4$_{7}$ 4QShirShab^{a} 1.1$_{1}$ 4QMish B^{a} 1.1$_{2}$ ([ארבעה]) 1.1$_{7}$ 1.2$_{2.2}$ ([ארבעה]) 1.2$_{3.3}$ (ארב[ע ה]) 1.2$_{6}$ (ארבע[ה]) 1.3$_{4.5.5.7.7}$ 2.1$_{2.4}$ ([אר]בעה) 2.1$_{4.7}$ 4QMMT A 1$_{2.49.98.143}$ (all four [ארבעה]) 4QMish C^{a} 2$_{2}$ ([אר]ב ע ה) 4QMish C^{c}$_{5}$ (אר[ב]עה) 4QMish C^{d} 1.2$_{8}$ (א]רבע[ה) 2$_{6}$ ([ארבעה]) 4QOtot 1$_{10.11}$, fourteenth day Lv 23$_{5}$ Ezr 6$_{19}$ 2 C 30$_{15}$ 35$_{1}$ 11QT 17$_{6}$ ([ארב]עה) Mur 29 2$_{9}$ 4QMish B^{a} 1.2$_{5}$ 4QMMT A 1$_{6.21.33.76.131.170}$ (all six [ארבעה עשר]) 4QMish C^{a} 1$_{2}$ 4QMish C^{c}$_{3}$ ([ארבעה] עשר) 4QMish D 2$_{5}$ ([ארב]עה עשר), twenty-fourth day Hg 2$_{10.20}$ 4QMish B^{a} 1.1$_{2}$ (ארו]בעה ועשרים]) 1.3$_{3}$ (ארבעה] עשר]ים) 2.1$_{1}$ (אר]בעה עשר[ים).

2. of units of measurement, currency, etc., cubits (אַמָּה) Ex 26$_{2.8}$||36$_{9.15}$ Dt 3$_{11}$ 1 K 6$_{17}$ 7$_{19.27.27.38}$ 2 K 14$_{13}$||2 C 25$_{23}$ Ezk 41$_{2.5}$ 43$_{14.15.17.17}$ 48$_{16+7t}$ 11QT 6$_{4}$ (אר]בעים]) 30$_{7.9}$ ([אמות]) 31$_{13}$ 32$_{10}$ 33$_{12}$ 36$_{4.8.10}$ 38$_{13.14}$ 40$_{10}$ (רבעים) 41$_{14.17}$ + Sup (ארב[ע]) 46$_{6}$ 1QM 4$_{15}$ 3QTr 1$_{3}$ 7$_{6}$ 8$_{13}$, fingers (אֶצְבַּע) as units of length Jr 52$_{21}$ 1QM 5$_{13}$, thumbs (גּוּדָל) 5$_{13}$, hand-breadths (טֶפַח) 5$_{13}$, baths (בַּת) 1 K 7$_{38}$, hins (הִין) 11QT 19$_{14}$, kors (כֹּר) Mur 24 2$_{17}$ ([כ]ורין), shekels (שֶׁקֶל) Gn 23$_{15.16}$ Ex 38$_{29}$ Nm 7$_{85}$ Ne 5$_{15}$ Meṣad Ḥashavyahu ost. 6$_{2}$, talents (כִּכָּר) 1 K 9$_{28}$||2 C 8$_{18}$ 3QTr 1$_{14}$ 4$_{4}$ 7$_{7}$, stater (אִסְתְּרָא) 3QTr 9$_{3}$, sela (סֶלַע) דינרין ששה עשר שהם סלעים ארבע *sixteen dinars, which are (equivalent to) four selas* 5/6ḤevBA 44$_{8.8}$, sim. 46$_{1}$.

3. of people, warriors (who are mustered, killed, etc.) Gn 32$_{7}$ 33$_{1}$ Jos 4$_{13}$ Jg 5$_{8}$ 12$_{6}$ 20$_{2.17}$ 1 S 4$_{2}$ 22$_{2}$ 25$_{13}$ 30$_{10.17}$ 2 S 10$_{18}$||1 C 19$_{18}$ 2 S 21$_{22}$ 1 C 5$_{18}$ 7$_{7}$ 12$_{27.37}$ 21$_{5}$ 2 C 13$_{3}$ 1QM 6$_{10}$, members of tribes Nm 1$_{21+9t}$, members of tribal armies Nm 2$_{4+11t}$ Ne 11$_{6}$, returning exiles Ezr 2$_{7+8t}$||Ne 7$_{12+8t}$ Ezr 2$_{15.15.64}$||Ne 7$_{66}$ Ne 7$_{23.44.62.67}$ 11$_{6.13.18}$, Levites 1 C 9$_{26}$ 23$_{4.5.5}$ 26$_{17.17.18}$ CD 10$_{5}$, Sodomites Gn 18$_{28.29.29}$, kings (מֶלֶךְ) Gn 14$_{9}$ (|| 5) Dn 8$_{22}$, administrators 1 C 27$_{1+12t}$, smiths (חָרָשׁ) Zc 2$_{3}$, relatives (אָח) 2 K 10$_{14}$, children Gn 46$_{22}$ Jg 12$_{14}$ 2 K 2$_{24}$ Dn 1$_{17}$ 1 C 3$_{5}$ 7$_{1}$ 21$_{20}$ 23$_{10.12}$ 25$_{5}$, wives 2 C 13$_{21}$, captives Jg 21$_{12}$ Jr 52$_{30.30}$, lepers 2 K 7$_{3}$, dead people Nm 17$_{14}$ 25$_{9}$, false prophets, idolaters 1 K 18$_{19.19.22}$ 22$_{6}$||2 C 18$_{5}$.

4. Of animals, camels (גָּמָל) 2 K 8$_{9}$ Ezr 2$_{67}$||Ne 7$_{68}$, mules (פֶּרֶד) Ezr 2$_{66}$, bulls (פַּר) Nm 7$_{88}$, cows Gn 32$_{16}$ (פָּרָה) Nm 7$_{7}$ (בָּקָר), sheep (צֹאן) Ex 21$_{37}$ (|| 5) Jb 42$_{12}$, lambs (כֶּבֶשׂ) Nm 29$_{13+7t}$ 11QT 20$_{2(Yadin)}$ + Sup ([בני]) 22$_{3(Yadin)}$ + Sup ([כבשי]ם ב[ני שנה]) 28$_{3(Yadin)}$ (כבשים] [ארבעה) 28$_{7.10}$ (14 in all 5).

5. of items of cultic furniture, pillars (עַמּוּד) Ex 26$_{32}$ ||36$_{36}$ 27$_{16}$||38$_{19}$ 1 K 7$_{3}$ perh. 11QT 12$_{15}$ (עמוד[י]ם), bases (אֶדֶן) Ex 26$_{19.21.32}$||36$_{24.26.36}$ 27$_{16}$||38$_{19}$, tables (שֻׁלְחָן) Ezk 40$_{41.41.42}$, rings (טַבַּעַת) Ex 27$_{4}$||38$_{5}$ 25$_{12.26}$||37$_{3.13}$, ornamental cups (גָּבִיעַ) 25$_{34}$||37$_{20}$, ornamental pomegranates (רִמּוֹן) 1 K 7$_{42}$||2 C 4$_{13}$; cultic vessels (כְּלִי) Ezr 1$_{10.11}$, rows (טוּר) of jewels, pillars Ex 28$_{17}$||39$_{10}$ 1 K 7$_{2}$, feet (פַּעַם) Ex 25$_{12}$||37$_{3}$ 1 K 7$_{30}$.

6. of end-points of objects, corners Ex 25$_{26}$||37$_{13}$ (פֵּאָה) 27$_{2}$||38$_{2}$ 1 K 7$_{34}$ Ezk 43$_{20}$ 45$_{19}$ (all five פִּנָּה) 46$_{21.22.23}$ (all three מִקְצוֹעַ) Jb 1$_{19}$ 11QT 15$_{18}$ + Sup 16$_{17}$ (both [אר]בע) 23$_{13}$ 30$_{6}$ (all five פִּנָּה) QT 37$_{13}$ 3QTr 10$_{17}$ (both מִקְצוֹעַ), end (קָצָה) Ex 27$_{4}$||38$_{5}$ (קָצָה) Dt 22$_{12}$ Is 11$_{12}$ (both כָּנָף) Jr 49$_{36}$ (קָצָה) Ezk 7$_{2}$ (כָּנָף).

7. of other things, specif. cities Nm 35$_{6.7}$ Jos 15$_{36}$ 18$_{28}$ 19$_{7}$ 21$_{18+8t}$ 11QT 48$_{13}$, gates (שַׁעַר) 11QT 5$_{8}$ 4QPrQuot 1$_{3(Baillet)}$ ([ארבע]ה שערי), foundations (מוּסָד) 11QShirShab 5$_{4}$, chambers (נִשְׁכָּה) 11QT 44$_{8}$, carts (עֲגָלָה) Nm 7$_{8}$, chariots (רֶכֶב) 1 K 10$_{26}$||2 C 1$_{14}$ 1QM 6$_{10}$, (מֶרְכָּבָה) Zc 6$_{1}$, stalls (אֻרְיָה) 1 K 5$_{6}$||2 C 9$_{25}$, wheels (אוֹפַן) 1 K 7$_{30.32}$, wheels as heavenly beings Ezk 1$_{16.18}$ 10$_{9.10.12}$, heavenly beings (חַיָּה) 1$_{5.8.10.10.10}$ 4QpsEzek^{a} 4$_{6}$, winds, directions (רוּחַ) Jr 49$_{36}$ Ezk 37$_{9}$ 42$_{20}$ Zc 2$_{10}$ 6$_{5}$ Dn 8$_{8}$ 11$_{4}$ 1 C 9$_{24}$ 11QT 6$_{6(Yadin)}$ ([רוחותיה]) 3QTr 7$_{5}$ (רוח[ות]; Allegro דודי[ן] *pots*) 4QM^{a} fr. 1$_{14}$ ([אר]בעת הרוח[ות]) 4QpsEzek^{a} 2$_{8}$ 4Q386–9 3.2$_{9}$ ([אר]בע) 4QToh D 1$_{5}$ 4QapPs^{b} 14$_{3}$, supports (כָּתֵף) 1 K 7$_{34}$, legs (רֶגֶל) of table Ex 25$_{26}$ ||37$_{13}$, of animal Lv 11$_{23}$, הלך עַל־אַרְבַּע *go on all fours* 11$_{20.21}$=11QT 48$_{4}$ Lv 11$_{27.42}$, wings (כָּנָף) Ezk 1$_{6}$ 10$_{21}$, faces (פָּנִים) 1$_{6.15}$ 10$_{14.21.21}$, horns (קֶרֶן) 43$_{15.20}$ (horns of altar) Zc 2$_{1}$ Dn 8$_{8.22}$ 11QT 23$_{12}$ (horns of altar), fingers and toes (אֶצְבַּע) 2 S 21$_{20}$||1 C 20$_{6}$, jars (כַּד) 1 K 18$_{34}$, rods (שַׁרְבִיט) Si 37$_{18(D)}$, berries (גַּרְגַּר) Is 17$_{6}$ (|| 5), carobs (חָרוּב) Mur 22 2$_{13}$, sources (רֹאשׁ) of river Gn 2$_{10}$, of army Jg 9$_{34}$, fractional parts (יָד) Gn 47$_{24}$ (|| חֲמִישִׁית *a fifth*), quarters (רֶבַע) Ezk 1$_{8.17}$ 10$_{11}$ 43$_{16.17}$, columns (דֶּלֶת) of scroll Jr 36$_{23}$ (|| 3), types (מִשְׁפָּחָה) of destroyer 15$_{3}$, kinds (מִין) 4QJub[a] 6$_{4}$ ([ארבעת המינים]) 7$_{3}$ ([ארבעה]), times (פַּעַם) Ne 6$_{4}$, lot 1 C 24$_{13.18}$ (אָחַז) 25$_{21.31}$ (גּוֹרָל), judgments (שֶׁפֶט) Ezk 14$_{21}$, sins (פֶּשַׁע) Am 1$_{3.6.9.11.13}$ 2$_{1.4.6}$ (all || 3), blows (מַכָּה) Dt 25$_{3}$, generations (דּוֹר) Jb 42$_{16}$, songs 11QPs[a] 27$_{6.9.9.10.10}$, things that are insatiable Pr 30$_{15}$, incomprehensible 30$_{18}$, unbearable 30$_{21}$, small 30$_{24}$ (all || 3), of good bearing 30$_{29}$.

<COLL> numbers compounded with אַרְבַּע, 14 = אַרְבַּע(־)עֶשְׂרֵה, אַרְבָּעָה עָשָׂר Gn 14$_{5}$ 31$_{41}$ 46$_{22}$ Ex 12$_{6.18}$ Lv 23$_{5}$ Nm 9$_{3.5.11}$ 28$_{16}$ 29$_{13+7t}$ Jos 5$_{10}$ 15$_{36}$ 18$_{28}$ 1 K 8$_{65}$ 2 K 18$_{13}$||Is 36$_{1}$ Ezk 40$_{1}$ 43$_{17.17}$ 45$_{21}$ Est 9$_{15.17.18}$ (all three || 13) 9$_{19.21}$ (|| 15) Ezr 6$_{19}$ 1 C 24$_{13}$ (|| 13) 25$_{5}$ (|| 3) 25$_{21}$ 2 C 13$_{21}$ 30$_{15}$ 35$_{1}$ 11QT 17$_{6}$ 20$_{2}$ (both ארב[עה]) 22$_{3}$ (עש[ר]) 28$_{3(Yadin)}$ ([ארבעה]) 28$_{7.10}$ 36$_{8}$ (עשר[ה]) 36$_{10}$ 41$_{14.17}$ + Sup (ארב[ע עשרה]) 46$_{6}$ 1QM 4$_{15}$ 4QPrQuot 1$_{9}$ (ע[שר]) Mur 29 2$_{9}$, 24 = עֶשְׂרִים וְאַרְבַּע, עֶשְׂרִים וְאַרְבָּעָה, אַרְבָּעָה וְעֶשְׂרִים Nm 7$_{88}$ 2 S 21$_{20}$||1 C 20$_{6}$ Hg 1$_{15}$ 2$_{10.18.20}$ Zc 1$_{7}$ Dn 10$_{4}$ Ne 9$_{1}$ 1 C 24$_{18}$ 25$_{31}$ 3QTr 7$_{6}$ (עסרן [ואר]בע]) 8$_{13}$ 4QMish B[a] 1.1$_{2}$ (אר[בעה ועשרים]), 34 = אַרְבַּע וּשְׁלֹשִׁים Gn 11$_{16}$, 54 = אַרְבַּע וַחֲמִשִּׁים 11QT 44$_{8}$, 74 = שִׁבְעִים וְאַרְבָּעָה Ezr 2$_{40}$||Ne 7$_{43}$.

40 = אַרְבָּעִים Gn 5$_{13}$ (840) 7$_{4.4.12.12.17}$ 8$_{6}$ 18$_{29.29}$ 25$_{20}$ 26$_{34}$ 32$_{16}$ 50$_{3}$ Ex 16$_{35}$ 24$_{18.18}$ 34$_{28.28}$ Nm 13$_{25}$ 14$_{33.34.34}$ 32$_{13}$ 33$_{38}$ Dt 1$_{3}$ 2$_{7}$ 8$_{2.4}$ 9$_{9+7t}$ 10$_{10.10}$ 29$_{4}$ Jos 5$_{6}$ 14$_{7}$ Jg 3$_{11}$ 5$_{31}$ 8$_{28}$ 12$_{14}$ (|| 30) 13$_{1}$ 1 S 4$_{18}$ 17$_{16}$ 2 S 2$_{10}$ 5$_{4}$ 1 K 2$_{11}$||1 C 29$_{27}$ 1 K 6$_{17}$ 7$_{38}$ 11$_{42}$||2 C 9$_{30}$ 1 K 19$_{8.8}$ 2 K 8$_{9}$ 12$_{2}$||2 C 24$_{1}$ Ezk 4$_{6}$ 29$_{11.12.13}$ 41$_{2}$ (|| 20) Am 2$_{10}$ 5$_{25}$ Jon 3$_{4}$ Ps 95$_{10}$ Ne 5$_{15}$ 9$_{21}$ 1 C 26$_{31}$ 11QT 6$_{4}$ (אר[בעים]) 36$_{4}$ 2QJub[a] 23$_{7}$ 1QM 6$_{14}$ 7$_{1.1(erased).2}$ (all 4 || 50) CD 20$_{15}$ 1QpPs[a] 1.2$_{7}$ 3QTr 1$_{3.14}$ 4$_{4}$ (ארבע[ין]) 5/6ḤevBA 46$_{1}$.

41 = אַרְבָּעִים וְאַחַת 1 K 14$_{21}$||2 C 12$_{13}$ 1 K 15$_{10}$ 2 K 14$_{23}$ 2 C 16$_{13}$ 3QTr 4$_{4(Milik)}$ (ארבע[ין ואח]ת) 4QPsJos[b] 1 2$_{4}$ (א[חד ו]ארבעים), 42 = אַרְבָּעִים וּשְׁתַּיִם, אַרְבָּעִים וּשְׁנַיִם Nm 35$_{6}$ 2 K 2$_{24}$ 10$_{14}$ Ezr 2$_{24}$||Ne 7$_{28}$ 2 C 22$_{2}$, 43 = שלושה וארן[בעים] 4QJub[d] 1.2$_{35}$, 45 = אַרְבָּעִים וַחֲמִשָּׁה, חָמֵשׁ וְאַרְבָּעִים, וְחָמֵשׁ אַרְבָּעִים Gn 18$_{28}$ Jos 14$_{10}$ 1 K 7$_{3}$ 1QM 6$_{14}$ (|| 30), 48 = אַרְבָּעִים וּשְׁמֹנֶה Nm 35$_{7}$ Jos 21$_{41}$, 49 = תֵּשַׁע וְאַרְבָּעִים Lv 25$_{8}$ 11QT 21$_{13}$ (תשעה) 40$_{10}$ (ורבעים).

400 = אַרְבַּע(־)מֵאוֹת Gn 15$_{13}$ 23$_{15.16}$ 32$_{7}$ 33$_{1}$ Jg 21$_{12}$ 1 S 22$_{2}$ 25$_{13}$ (+ כְּ *about*) 30$_{10}$ (|| 200) 30$_{17}$ 1 K 7$_{42}$||2 C 4$_{13}$ 1 K 18$_{19}$ 22$_{6}$||2 C 18$_{5}$ (1 K + כְּ) 2 K 14$_{13}$||2 C 25$_{23}$ 11QT 38$_{13}$ 3QTr 7$_{7}$ 4Q464 3.2$_{4}$ ([ארבע מאות]), 4,000 = אַרְבַּעַת אֲלָפִים 1 S 4$_{2}$ (+ כְּ) 1 C 23$_{5.5}$ 2 C 9$_{25}$, 40,000 = אַרְבָּעִים אֶלֶף Jos 4$_{13}$ (+ כְּ) Jg 5$_{8}$ 2 S 10$_{18}$ 1 K 5$_{6}$ 1 C 12$_{37}$ 19$_{18}$, 400,000 = אַרְבַּע(־)מֵאוֹת אֶלֶף Jg 20$_{2.17}$ 2 C 13$_{3}$ (|| 800,000).

אַרְבַּעְתָּן/ם *the four of them* Ezk 1$_{8.10.10.10.16.18}$ 10$_{10.12}$, אַרְבַּעַת אֵלֶּה *these four* 2 S 21$_{22}$, אַרְבַּעְתַּיִם repay *fourfold* 12$_{6}$, קִרְיַת (הָ)אַרְבַּע *Kiriath-arba*, perh. *city of (the) four* (quarters, founders?) (but see אַרְבַּע II *Arba*), i.e. Hebron Gn 23$_{2}$ 35$_{27}$ Jos 14$_{15}$ 15$_{13.54}$ 20$_{7}$ 21$_{11}$ Jg 1$_{10}$ Ne 11$_{25}$.

Also 11QT 12$_{7}$ 30$_{10}$ 37$_{3}$ 1Q30 1$_{5}$ 3QTr 2$_{14}$ 4QShir Shab[f] 93$_{1}$ ([א]רבעה).

→ רבע I *make square*.

אַרְבַּע II $_{3}$ pr.n.m. **Arba,** ancestor or chief of Anakim, in pl.n. קִרְיַת אַרְבַּע *Kiriath-arba* (Hebron), Jos 14$_{15}$ 15$_{13}$ 21$_{11}$.

ארג $_{14.1.2}$ vb. **weave**—Impf. יֶאֱרֹ֫גוּ, תַּאַרְגִי (Q יירגו); ptc. אֹרֵג (Si, Q אורג), אֹרְגִים (Q אורגים), אֹרְגוֹת—**1. weave** cloth, etc., <SUBJ> Delilah Jg 16$_{13}$, אִשָּׁה *woman* 2 K 23$_{7}$. <OBJ> מַחְלָפָה *plait* of hair Jg 16$_{13}$, בַּיִת *house* or *hanging* 2 K 23$_{7}$ (or em. בַּתִּים *vestments*; + לָאֲשֵׁרָה *for Asherah*), קוּר *web* of spider Is 59$_{5}$ (1QIsa[a] יירגו; or em. קוּרֵי to קוּי *threads of*; || בקע pi. *hatch* eggs), קַו *line*, i.e. thread 59$_{5}$ (if em. קוּרֵי).

2. ptc. used as noun, **weaver,** <SUBJ> בוש *be ashamed* Is 19$_{9}$ (1QIsa[a] אורגים חורו *weavers have grown pale* for אֹרְגִים חוֹרָי *weavers [in] white material*; perh. em. חוֹרָי to חָוְרוּ or יֶחֱוָרוּ *will be pale*; || עבד ptc. *worker* in combed flax), חור *be pale* 19$_{9}$ (if em. חוֹרָי).

<CSTR> מַעֲשֵׂה אֹרֵג *work of a weaver* Ex 28$_{32}$||39$_{22}$ 39$_{27}$ Si 45$_{11}$ (אורג) 4QShirShab fr. 2 23.2$_{7}$ (+ רוקמה *variegated material*) 23.2$_{10}$ (both מעשי אורג) 11QShir Shab 8$_{5}$ (מ[עשי אורג]; + רוקמה), אֹרֵג ... כָּל־מְלֶאכֶת *all the work of ... a weaver* Ex 35$_{35}$, מְנוֹר אֹרְגִים *beam of*

weavers 1 S 17_{7} 2 S 21_{19}||1 C 20_{5} 1 C 11_{23}. **<APP>** חָרָשׁ וְחֹשֵׁב וְרֹקֵם ... וְאֹרֵג עֹשֵׂי כָּל־מְלָאכָה וְחֹשְׁבֵי מַחֲשָׁבֹת *a craftsman or a designer or an embroiderer ... or a weaver, ones doing any (kind of) work and skilful designers* Ex 35_{35}.

<PREP> כְּ *as*, + קפד pi. *roll up* life Is 38_{12} (if em. קִפַּדְתִּי כָאֹרֵג *I have rolled up as a weaver* to קִפַּדְתָּ כְּאָרְ[י]ג *you have rolled up* my life *as cloth*), ספר *cut* life 1QIsa[a] 38_{12} (כאורג).

3. in pr.n.m., **Jaareoregim** (lit. *forests of weavers*), וַיַּךְ אֶלְחָנָן בֶּן־יַעְרֵי אֹרְגִים בֵּית הַלַּחְמִי אֵת גָּלְיָת *and Elhanan son of Jaareoregim, the Bethlehemite, struck Goliath* 2 S 21_{19} (||1 C $20_{5[Qr]}$ בֶּן־יָעִיר אֶת־לַחְמִי אֲחִי גָּלְיָת and Elhanan *son of Jair* struck *Lahmi, brother of Goliath*).

→ אֶרֶג *loom*, אָרִיג *cloth*.

[אָרְג], see ארג, §2, Prep.

אֶרֶג 2 n.[m.] **shuttle** of loom—אֶרֶג—יָמַי קַלּוּ מִנִּי־אָרֶג *my days are swifter than a shuttle* Jb 7_{6}, וַיִּסַּע אֶת־הַיְתַד הָאֶרֶג אֶת־הַמַּסָּכֶת *he pulled away the peg, the shuttle, (and) the web* Jg 16_{14} (or הַיְתַד = *the pin of*, and, by synecdoche, אֶרֶג = *loom*).

→ ארג *weave*.

[אַרְגָּב], see אֵצֶל §1, §2.

אַרְגֹּב I 1 pr.n.m. **Argob**, appar. officer of Pekahiah, 2 K 15_{25} (or del. אֶת־אַרְגֹּב וְאֶת־הָאַרְיֵה *Argob and Arieh* and ins. at 15_{29}, as pl.n., after גִּלְעָד *Gilead*).

אַרְגֹּב II 4 pl.n. **Argob**, territory of Og in Bashan around upper Yarmuk, חֶבֶל אַרְגֹּב *area of Argob* Dt $3_{4.13}$ (הָאַרְגֹּב) 3_{14} 1 K 4_{13} 2 K 15_{29} (if del. אֶת־אַרְגֹּב וְאֶת־הָאַרְיֵה *Argob and Arieh*, as pr.n., at 15_{25} and ins. after גִּלְעָד *Gilead*).

אַרְגְּוָן, see אַרְגָּמָן.

אַרְגַּז 3 **box**, or other kind of receptacle, perh. **saddlebag**, **<NOM CL>** הָאַרְגַּז אֲשֶׁר־אִתּוֹ *the box that was with it* (ark). **<OBJ>** שׂים *place* 1 S $6_{11.15}$, ירד hi. *take down* from cart 6_{15}. **<PREP>** שׂים בְּ *place* golden figures *in* 1 S 6_{8}.

אַרְגָּמָן 39.1.5 n.m. **purple**—Q ארגמון, אַרְגְּוָן—thread, cloth, etc. dyed purple, esp. in תְּכֵלֶת וְאַרְגָּמָן וְתוֹלַעַת שָׁנִי (and vars.) *blue and purple and scarlet (material)*, used in tabernacle/temple hangings and sacred vestments, Ex 25_{4}||35_{6} $26_{1.31.36}$||$36_{8.35.37}$ 27_{16}||38_{18} $28_{5.33}$ ||$39_{1.24}$ $35_{23.25.35}$ 38_{23} $39_{3.29}$ 1QM 7_{11} perh. 11QT 3_{2} (תכלת וארגמן) 10_{14} ([א]רגמן ותול[ע]), תְּכֵלֶת וְאַרְגָּמָן וְכַרְמִיל וּבוּץ *purple and blue and crimson and fine linen* 2 C 3_{14}.

<SUBJ> היה *be* Ex 28_{8} (+ חֵשֶׁב *decoration* of ephod, || זָהָב *gold*, שֵׁשׁ *fine linen*) Ezk 27_{7} (+ מְכַסֶּה *covering*, מֵאִיֵּי אֱלִישָׁה *from the islands of Elishah*, || תְּכֵלֶת *blue [material]*), מצא ni. *be found* Ex 35_{23} (|| שֵׁשׁ, עִז *[hair of] goat*, עוֹר *skin*).

<NOM CL> חֵשֶׁב ... הוּא ... אַרְגָּמָן *the decoration* of the ephod ... *is ... purple* Ex 39_{5} (|| זָהָב *gold*, שֵׁשׁ *fine linen*), אַרְגָּמָן לְבוּשָׁם *their clothing is purple* Jr 10_{9} (|| תְּכֵלֶת *blue [material]*), אַרְגָּמָן לְבוּשָׁהּ *her clothing is purple* Pr 31_{22} (|| שֵׁשׁ *fine linen*).

<OBJ> בוא hi. *bring* Ex 35_{6} (for parallels, see ||Ex 25_{4} in Coll.) 35_{25} (|| שֵׁשׁ *fine linen*), לקח *take* 28_{5} (|| שֵׁשׁ, זָהָב *gold*), נתן *give* Ezk 27_{16} (|| נֹפֶךְ *emerald*, רִקְמָה *embroidery*, בּוּץ *fine linen*, רָאמֹת *coral*, כַּדְכֹּד *agate*; + בְּעִזְבוֹנָיִךְ *in exchange for your wares*).

עשׂה *make* something of purple Ex 26_{1}||36_{8} (+ יְרִיעָה *curtain*) 26_{31}||36_{35} (+ פָּרֹכֶת *veil*) 26_{36}||36_{37} 27_{16}||38_{18} (both + מָסָךְ *screen*) 28_{6}||39_{2} (+ אֵפוֹד *ephod*) 28_{15}||39_{8} (+ חֹשֶׁן *breastpiece*; both || זָהָב *gold*) 39_{29} (+ אַבְנֵט *sash*; all seven + שֵׁשׁ מָשְׁזָר *fine twined linen*) Ca 3_{10} (+ מֶרְכָּב *seat*, or understand מֶרְכָּבוֹ אַרְגָּמָן as nom. cl., *its seat was of purple*; or em. אַלְגֻּמִּן *algum*; || זָהָב, כֶּסֶף *silver*) 2 C 3_{14} (+ פָּרֹכֶת).

<CSTR> תַּכְרִיךְ ... אַרְגָּמָן *mantle of ... purple* Est 8_{15} (|| בּוּץ *fine linen*; + תְּכֵלֶת *blue [material]*, חוּר *white [material]*, זָהָב *gold*), ... אבנט *girdle of* ... 1QM 7_{11} (+ שֵׁשׁ מָשְׁזָר *fine twined linen*), בֶּגֶד *garment of* Nm 4_{13}, ... בִּגְדֵי *garments of* ... Jg 8_{26} Si 45_{10} (|| תְּכֵלֶת, זָהָב), ... חַבְלֵי־ *cords of* ... Est 1_{6} (|| בּוּץ), ... רִמֹּנֵי *pomegranates of* ... Ex 28_{33}||39_{24} (39_{24} + מָשְׁזָר *twined*; perh. add וְשֵׁשׁ

and fine twined linen), נצני ארגמון flowers of 4QMish D 35.

<APP> מַטְוֶה ... אַרְגָּמָן yarn ... (of) purple Ex 3525, בגדי קודש ... ארגמן clothes of holiness ... of purple Si 4510, perh. ארגמן אדום purple, red, of Temple furnishings 11QT 1012.

<PREP> בְּ of instrument, i.e. material, in, with, + רקם embroider Ex 3535 3823 (both || שֵׁשׁ fine linen), + עשה work 2 C 26 (אַרְגְּוָן) 213 (|| אֶבֶן stone, עֵץ wood, תְּכֵלֶת blue [material], בּוּץ linen; both || זָהָב gold, כֶּסֶף silver, נְחֹשֶׁת bronze, בַּרְזֶל iron, כַּרְמִיל crimson); דַּלַּת רֹאשֵׁךְ כָּאַרְגָּמָן the loose hair of your head is as purple Ca 76 (|| כַּרְמֶל Carmel; or em. כַּרְמִיל crimson); עשה מִן make garments from Ex 391; עשה בְּתוֹךְ work thread into Ex 393 (|| שֵׁשׁ fine linen).

<COLL> זֹאת הַתְּרוּמָה ... אַרְגָּמָן this is the offering ... purple Ex 254 (|| זָהָב gold, כֶּסֶף silver, נְחֹשֶׁת copper, שֵׁשׁ fine linen, עֵז [hair of] goat, עוֹר skin, עֵץ wood, שֶׁמֶן oil, בֹּשֶׂם spice, אֶבֶן stone).

<SYN> זָהָב gold, כֶּסֶף silver, תְּכֵלֶת blue (material), שֵׁשׁ fine linen, בּוּץ fine linen, כַּרְמִיל crimson (material), תּוֹלֵעָה scarlet (material) (תּוֹלַעַת שָׁנִי).

אַרְדְּ 2 pr.n.m. **Ard**—אֶרֶד—**1.** son of Bela, Nm 2640.40 (if ins. לְאַרְדְּ to Ard before מִשְׁפַּחַת הָאַרְדִּי the Ardite family). **2.** son of Benjamin and brother of Bela (or ident. with preceding if ins. וַיִּהְיוּ בְנֵי בֶלַע and the sons of Bela were before גֵּרָא Gera at Gn 4621), appar. ident. with Addar (אַדָּר) at 1 C 83 (mss אַרְדְּ), Gn 4621.
→ אַרְדִּי Ardite.

אַרְדּוֹן 1 pr.n.m. **Ardon,** son of Caleb, 1 C 218.

אַרְדִּי 1 gent. **Ardite,** of the family of Ard, Nm 2640.
→ אַרְדְּ Ard.

אֲרִדַי 1 pr.n.m. **Aridai,** son of Haman, Est 99.

אֲרֹדִי, see אֲרוֹדִי II.

ארה 2 vb. **pluck—Qal** Pf. אָרִיתִי מוֹרִי—אָרִיתִי, אָרוּהָ I have plucked my myrrh with my spice Ca 51 (|| עִם־בְּשָׂמִי אכל eat, שׁתה drink), אָרוּהָ כָּל־עֹבְרֵי דָרֶךְ all passers by plucked it (vine) Ps 8013.

[אֹרָה] 1 n.[f.] **mallow**—pl. אֹרֹת—vegetable, perh. mallow (malva rotundifolia), <OBJ> לקט pi. gather 2 K 439.

אֲרוֹד 1 pr.n.m. **Arod,** son of Gad, appar. ident. with Arodi at Gn 4616, Nm 2617 (Sam אֲרוֹדִי Arodi).
→ אֲרוֹדִי Arodi(te).

אַרְוַד 2 pl.n. **Arvad,** Phoenician port, perh. mod. T. Ru'ād, Ezk 278 (|| צִידוֹן Sidon) 2711 (|| חֵילֵךְ Helech).
→ אַרְוָדִי Arvadite.

אֲרוֹדִי I 1 pr.n.m. **Arodi,** son of Gad, appar. ident. with Arod, Gn 4616 Nm 2617(Sam) (MT אֲרוֹד Arod).
→ אֲרוֹד Arod, אֲרוֹדִי Arodite.

אֲרוֹדִי II 1 gent. **Arodite,** of the family of Arod/Arodi, Nm 2617 2 S 2325(mss) (MT חֲרֹדִי Harodite; mss הֲרֹרִי Harorite).
→ אֲרוֹד Arod, אֲרוֹדִי Arodi.

אַרְוָדִי 2 gent. **Arvadite,** Canaanite people from Arvad, Gn 1018||1 C 116.
→ אַרְוַד Arvad.

[אֻרְוָה] 4 n.f. **stall**—pl. אֻרָוֹת (אֻוָרוֹת); cstr. אֻרְוֹת (אֻרְיוֹת) —**stall** for horses, etc., <SUBJ> היה be 1 K 56||2 C 925 (+ לִשְׁלֹמֹה to Solomon, || פָּרָשׁ horseman).

<OBJ> עשה make 2 C 3228 (+ לְכָל־בְּהֵמָה וּבְהֵמָה for every beast, || אוֹצָר treasury, מִסְכְּנוֹת storehouses) 3228 (if em.; see Prep.).

<CSTR> אֻרְוֹת סוּסִים stalls of horses 1 K 56||2 C 925 (2 C אֻרְיוֹת; + מֶרְכָּב chariot[ry]).

<PREP> עֲדָרִים לָאֲוֵרוֹת flocks for the stalls 2 C 3228 (if em. אֻרָוֹת לָעֲדָרִים stalls for the flocks).

<COLL> אַרְבָּעִים אֶלֶף אֻרְוֹת forty thousand stalls of horses 1 K 56, אַרְבַּעַת אֲלָפִים אֻרְיוֹת four thousand stalls of horses 2 C 925.

[אָרוּז] 1 adj. **secure**—pl. אֲרֻזִים—בַּחֲבָלִים חֲבֻשִׁים וַאֲרֻזִים fabrics *bound with cords and (made) secure* Ezk 27$_{24}$.

אֲרוּכָה 6 n.f. **restoration**—אֲרֻכָה; cstr. אֲרֻכַת; sf. אֲרֻכָתְךָ—**a.** of person, **healing,** Is 58$_8$ Jr 8$_{22}$ 30$_{17}$ 33$_6$; **b.** of building, **repair,** Ne 4$_1$ 2 C 24$_{13}$.

<SUBJ> צמח *spring up* Is 58$_8$ (|| אוֹר *light*), עלה *arise* Jr 8$_{22}$ Ne 4$_1$ 2 C 24$_{13}$. <OBJ> עלה hi. *raise,* i.e. bring Jr 30$_{17}$ (+ רפא *heal* someone of wounds) 33$_6$ (|| מַרְפֵּא *healing*). <CSTR> אֲרֻכַת בַּת־עַמִּי *healing of the daughter of my people* Jr 8$_{22}$.

→ ארך *be long.*

ארולי, see אַרְאֵלִי I, II.

[אֲרוּמָה] 1 pl.n. **Arumah**—בָּארוּמָה–dwelling place of Abimelech, perh. Kh. el-'Orēme 8 km S of Shechem, perh. ident. with Tormah (תָּרְמָה) at Jg 9$_{31}$ and Rumah (רוּמָה) at 2 K 23$_{36}$, Jg 9$_{31}$ (if em. בְּתָרְמָה *at Tormah*) 9$_{41}$.

אֲרוֹן 201.0.3.2 n.m. (sometimes f.) **ark**—הָאָרוֹן (הָאָרֹן); cstr. אֲרוֹן (אֲרֹן); sf. 3mpl Q ארונן; pl. Q ארונות—**1.** usu. **ark** of covenant. **2. coffer,** chest for money, 2 K 12$_{10.11}$||2 C 24$_{8.11}$ 2 C 24$_{10}$. **3. coffin,** Beth Shearim inscr. 17 22.

<SUBJ> היה *be* 1 S 14$_{18}$ (or em. הָיָה אֲרוֹן הָאֱלֹהִים *the ark of God was* to הוּא הָיָה נֹשֵׂא הָאֵפוֹד *he used to carry the ephod;* + וּבְנֵי יִשְׂרָאֵל *and the Israelites* [or em. עִם בְּנֵי יִשְׂרָאֵל *with the Israelites* or לִפְנֵי יִשְׂרָאֵל *before Israel*]) 6$_1$ (+ בְּ *in* field) 2 S 6$_{16}$||1 C 15$_{29}$ (+ בָּא [עַד] עִיר *coming to the city of;* or em. בְּבֵית *in the house of*), ישב *dwell,* i.e. remain 1 S 5$_7$ 7$_2$ 2 S 6$_{11}$||1 C 13$_{14}$ 2 S 7$_2$ 11$_{11}$ (|| יִשְׂרָאֵל *Israel,* יְהוּדָה *Judah*), בוא *come* 1 S 4$_{5.6}$ 5$_{10}$ 2 S 6$_9$ 2 C 8$_{11}$, הלך *go* Jos 6$_8$, נסע *set out* Nm 10$_{33.35}$, מושׁ *depart* 14$_{44}$, עבר *pass* Jos 3$_{11}$ 4$_{11}$, שׁוב *go back* 1 S 5$_{11}$, סבב *be brought round* 5$_8$, קום *arise* Ps 132$_8$||2 C 6$_{41}$ (|| י׳ *Y.*), לקח ni. *be taken* 1 S 4$_{11.17.19.21.22}$, מות hi. *kill* Philistines 5$_{11}$.

<NOM CL> מִשְׁמַרְתָּם הָאָרֹן *their charge was the ark* Nm 3$_{31}$ (|| שֻׁלְחָן *table,* מְנֹרָה *lampstand,* מִזְבֵּחַ *altar,* כְּלִי sacred *vessel,* מָסָךְ *screen*), שָׁם אֲרוֹן אֱלֹהִים *the ark of God was there* 1 S 3$_3$, sim. Jg 20$_{27}$, אֲרוֹן בְּרִית־י׳ תַּחַת יְרִיעוֹת *the ark of the covenant of Y. is under curtains,* i.e. in a tent 1 C 17$_1$, אלו ארונות *these are (the) coffins* Beth Shearim inscr. 17, זוא ארונן שלשלושת בניו *this is the coffin of* (lit. *which is to*) *his three sons* Beth Shearim inscr. 22.

<OBJ> בוא hi. *bring* Ex 26$_{33}$||40$_{21}$ 39$_{35}$ 1 S 7$_1$ 2 S 6$_{17}$||1 C 16$_1$ 1 K 8$_6$||2 C 5$_7$ 1 C 13$_{5.12}$ 22$_{19}$ 2 C 24$_{11}$, נגשׁ hi. *bring* 1 S 14$_{18}$ (unless em.; see Cstr.), ירד hi. *bring down* 6$_{15}$, שׁוב hi. *bring back* 6$_{21}$ 2 S 15$_{25.29}$ 1 C 13$_5$ 2 C 24$_{11}$, עלה hi. *bring up* 1 S 7$_1$ 2 S 6$_2$||1 C 13$_6$ 2 S 6$_{12.15}$||1 C 15$_{25.28}$ 1 K 8$_{1.4}$||2 C 5$_{2.5}$ 1 C 15$_{3.12.14}$ 2 C 1$_4$, שׁלח pi. *send away* 1 S 5$_{10.11}$ 6$_3$, סבב hi. *take round* 5$_{8.10}$ Jos 6$_{11}$ 1 C 13$_3$, סור hi. *remove* 2 S 6$_{10}$||1 C 13$_{13}$, נוח hi. *cause to rest* 1 S 6$_{18}$.

נשׂא *carry* Ex 25$_{14}$||37$_5$ Dt 10$_8$ 31$_{9.25}$ Jos 3$_{6+7t}$ 4$_{9.10.16.18}$ 6$_{6.12}$ 8$_{33}$ 1 S 4$_4$ 2 S 6$_{3.4.13}$ 15$_{24}$ 1 K 2$_{26}$ (unless em.; see Cstr.) 8$_3$||2 C 5$_4$ 1 C 15$_{2.2.15.26.27}$ 2 C 24$_{11}$, רכב hi. *carry* 2 S 6$_3$||1 C 13$_7$, שׂים *place* Ex 40$_3$ 1 S 6$_{11}$ 2 C 6$_{11}$, יצק hi. *place* 2 S 15$_{24}$, נתן *place* 1 K 6$_{19}$ 2 C 35$_3$, לקח *take* 1 S 4$_{3.11}$ 5$_{1.2}$ 6$_8$ 2 K 12$_{10}$, אחז *seize* 1 C 13$_9$, עשׂה *make* Ex 25$_{10}$||37$_1$ 31$_7$||35$_{12}$ (31$_7$ + לָעֵדֻת *for the testimony*) Dt 10$_{1.3}$ 2 C 24$_8$, ערה pi. *empty* 24$_{11}$, כסה pi. *cover* Nm 4$_5$, משׁח *anoint* Ex 30$_{26}$, ראה *see* Jos 3$_3$ 1 S 6$_{13}$, זכר hi. *cause to remember* 4$_{18}$, שׁמר *keep* 7$_1$.

<CSTR> אֲרוֹן הָאֱלֹהִים *ark of God* 1 S 3$_3$ (אֱלֹהִים) 4$_{3.4.4}$ (if em. in all three; see below) 4$_{11}$ (אֱלֹהִים) 4$_{13+5t}$ 5$_{1.2.10}$ 14$_{18.18}$ (or em. in both אֲרוֹן הָאֱלֹהִים to הָאֵפוֹד *the ephod*) 2 S 6$_{2+6t}$ 7$_2$ 15$_{24.25.29}$ 1 C 13$_{5.6.7.12.14}$ 15$_{1.2.15.24}$ 16$_1$ 2 C 1$_4$, אֱלֹהֵינוּ *of our God* 1 C 13$_3$, אֱלֹהֵי יִשְׂרָאֵל *of the God of Israel* 1 S 5$_{7+5t}$ 6$_3$, י׳ *of Y.* Jos 3$_{13}$ 4$_{5.11}$ (אֲרוֹן־) 6$_{6.7.11}$ (אֲרוֹן־) 6$_{12.13.13}$ 7$_6$ 1 S 4$_4$ (mss; see below) 4$_6$ 5$_{3.4}$ 6$_1$ (אֲרוֹן־) 6$_{2+5t}$ 7$_{1.1}$ 2 S 6$_{9.10.11.13}$ (אֲרוֹן־) 6$_{15.16.17}$ 1 K 2$_{26}$ (if em.; see below) 8$_4$ 1 C 15$_{2.3.12.14}$ 16$_4$ 2 C 8$_{11}$, אֲדֹנָי *of my Lord* 1 K 2$_{26}$ (or em. אֲרוֹן אֲדֹנָי to אֲרוֹן [בְּרִית] י׳ *the ark of [the covenant of] Y.* or הָאֵפוֹד *the ephod*).

אֲרוֹן הַבְּרִית *ark of the covenant* Jos 3$_{6.6.8}$ (אֲרוֹן־) 3$_{11.14}$ (if em.; see App.) 4$_9$ 6$_6$, בְּרִית י׳ *of the covenant of Y.* Nm 10$_{33}$ 14$_{44}$ Dt 10$_8$ 31$_9$ (בְּרִית־י׳) 31$_{25.26}$ Jos 3$_{3.17}$ (if em.; see App.) 4$_{7.18}$ 6$_8$ (בְּרִית־י׳) 8$_{33}$ Jg 20$_{27}$ (mss; see below) 1 S 4$_3$ (בְּרִית־י׳; or em. [בְּרִית] הָאֱלֹהִים *of [the covenant of] God*) 4$_4$ (בְּרִית־י׳ צְבָאוֹת *of the covenant of Y. of hosts;* or em. אֲרוֹן הָאֱלֹהִים *ark of God*) 4$_5$ 1 K 2$_{26}$ (if em.; see above) 6_{19} (בְּרִית־י׳) $8_{1.6}$‖2 C $5_{2.7}$ (at 1 K 8_6 perh. em. אֲרוֹן בְּרִית י׳ to הָאָרוֹן *the ark*) Jr 3_{16} 1 C $15_{25.26.28.29}$ (בְּרִית־י׳) 16_{37} 17_1 22_{19} $28_{2.18}$, בְּרִית הָאֱלֹהִים *of the covenant of God* Jg 20_{27} (mss [אֱלֹהִים]״ *of Y. [God]* for הָאֱלֹהִים) 1 S 4_3 (if em.; see above) 4_4 (or em. אֲרוֹן הָאֱלֹהִים *ark of God*; mss [האל]״ *of Y. [God]*) 2 S 15_{24} 1 C 16_6, בְּרִית־אֲדֹנָי *of the covenant of my Lord* 1 K 3_{15}.

אֲרוֹן הָעֵדוּת *ark of the testimony* Ex 25_{22} (אֲרֹן הָעֵדֻת) $26_{33.34}$ (הָעֵדֻת) 30_6 (אֲרֹן הָעֵדֻת) 30_{26} (הָעֵדֻת) 39_{35} (אֲרֹן הָעֵדֻת) $40_{3.5}$ (הָעֵדֻת) 40_{21} Nm 4_5 7_{89} (both אֲרֹן הָעֵדֻת) Jos 4_{16} 4QApocMos B 1.2_7, אֲרוֹן־הַקֹּדֶשׁ *ark of holiness* 2 C 35_3, אֲרוֹן עֵץ *ark of wood* Dt 10_1, עֲצֵי שִׁטִּים *of acacia wood* Ex 25_{10} Dt 10_3, עֻזֶּךָ *of your strength* Ps 132_8‖1 C6_{41}.

מְקוֹם הָאָרוֹן *place of the ark* 1 K 8_7‖2 C 5_8, מָנוֹחַ *resting place of* 1 C 6_{16}, צַד אֲרוֹן *side of the ark of* Ex 31_{26} (see Prep.), צַלְעֹת הָאָרֹן *sides of the ark* Ex 25_{14}‖37_5, טַבְּעֹת *rings of* 25_{15}.

<APP> הָאָרוֹן הַבְּרִית *the ark, the covenant* Jos $3_{14.17}$ (בְּרִית־י׳ *the covenant of Y.*; in both perh. em. אֲרוֹן *the ark of*), אֲרוֹן הַבְּרִית אֲדוֹן כָּל־הָאָרֶץ *ark of the covenant, the lord of all the earth* 3_{11}, ארונות הפנימית והחיצונית *coffins, the inner and the outer* Beth Shearim inscr. 17.

<ADJ> אֲרוֹן אֶחָד *one coffer* 2 K 12_{10}‖2 C 24_8.

<PREP> לְ of benefit, *to, for* 1 C $15_{23.24}$ (both + שֹׁעֵר *gatekeeper*), + עשׂה *do* 1 S 5_8 6_2, כון hi. *prepare* place 1 C 15_1, בנה *build* house 28_2, שׂים *set* place 1 K 8_{21}, שׁלך לְ hi. *cast* tax *into* 2 C 24_{10}, עמד מִזֶּה וּמִזֶּה לְ *stand on each side of* Jos 8_{33}, [ונגש ע]ד לארון *and he shall draw near to the ark of* 4QApocMos B 1.2_7.

בְּ of place, direction, *in(to)* 1 K 8_9‖2 C 5_{10} (+ לוּחַ *tablet*) 2 K 12_{11} (+ כֶּסֶף *money*), + היה *be* CD 5_3 (subj. סֵפֶר *book* of law), שׂים *place* tablet Dt $10_{2.5}$, ho. *be placed* Gn 50_{26} (if em.; see below), ישׂם *place* Joseph 50_{26} (or em. וַיִּשֶׂם to וַיּוּשַׂם *and he was placed*), ראה בְּ *look at* 1 S 6_{19}.

ראה מִן ni. *be seen from*, i.e. project beyond 2 C 5_9 (or em. הַקֹּדֶשׁ *the sanctuary*), מלמעלה מן הארון *(from) above the ark* 11QT 7_{12}; שׂים מִצַּד *place* book of law *beside* Dt 31_{26}.

אֶל *(in)to*, + נתן *place* testimony Ex $25_{16.21}$ 40_{20}, שׁלח *stretch out* 2 S 6_6 (obj. יָד *hand*, if em. וַיִּשְׁלַח עֻזָּא *and Uzzah stretched out* to וַיִּשְׁלַח עֻזָּא אֶת־יָדוֹ *and Uzzah stretched out his hand*).

עַל *upon, over* Ex 25_{22} (+ כַּפֹּרֶת *mercy seat*) 30_6 (+ פָּרֹכֶת *veil*) Lv 16_2 Nm 7_{89} (both + כַּפֹּרֶת), + נתן *place* mercy seat Ex 25_{21} 26_{34} 40_{20}, שׂים *place* pole 40_{20}, סכך *cover* 40_3 (+ אֶת־הַפָּרֹכֶת *with the veil*) 40_{21} (hi.) 1 K 8_7 1 C 28_{18}, שׁלח עַל *stretch out* hand *to* 1 C 13_{10}, חָרֵד עַל *trembling about* 1 S 4_{13}, כסה עַל pi. *cover* 2 C 5_8 (subj. cherubim; ‖ בַּד *pole*).

לִפְנֵי *before* 1 C 16_6 (+ בַּחֲצֹצְרוֹת *with trumpets*), + חצר hi. *blow* trumpet 15_{24}, נשׂא *carry* trumpet Jos $6_{4.6.13}$, שׁרת pi. *minister* 1 C 16_{37}, הלך *go* 2 S 6_4, עבר *pass* Jos 4_5 6_7, עמד *stand* 1 K 3_{15}, נפל *fall* to ground Jos 7_6 1 S $5_{3.4}$, נתן *place* Ex 40_5 (obj. מִזְבֵּחַ *altar*) 1 C 16_4 (+ מִן־הַלְוִיִּם *some of the Levites*), יעד ni. *gather* intrans. 1 K 8_5‖2 C 5_6, עזב *leave* 1 C 16_{37}; כרת מִפְּנֵי ni. *be cut off before* Jos 4_7.

עִם *with* 1 S 4_4 2 S 6_4 (appar. + עֲגָלָה *cart*), + מות *die* 6_7; הלך אַחֲרֵי *follow* Jos $6_{9.13}$; ברך בַּעֲבוּר pi. *bless* house *because of* 1 S 6_{12}.

אֲרַוְנָה 21 pr.n.m. **Araunah**—הָאֲרַוְנָה (Kt האורנה), אָרְנָן, Kt ארניה—Jebusite whose threshing floor in Jerusalem David bought as site for temple, 2 S 24_{16}‖1 C 21_{15} (2 S Kt האורנה, Qr הָאֲרַוְנָה) 2 S 24_{18}‖1 C 21_{18} (2 S Kt ארניה) 2 S 24_{20}‖1 C 21_{20} 2 S $24_{20.21.22}$‖1 C 21_{23} 2 S $24_{23.23.24}$‖1 C 21_{24} 1 C $21_{20.21.21.22.25.28}$ (in 1 C all eleven אָרְנָן) 2 C 3_1 (אָרְנָן).

אֶרֶז $73_{.1.11}$ n.m. **cedar,** usu. cedar of Lebanon, but sometimes a species of juniper (*oxycedrus* or *phoenicia*)—אֶרֶז; cstr. אֶרֶז; pl. אֲרָזִים; cstr. אַרְזֵי; sf. אֲרָזֶיךָ, אֲרָזָיו—**cedar,** usu. cedar tree, oft. in ref. to height (e.g. Am 2_9 CD 2_{19}), also cut cedar (e.g. 2 S 5_{11}‖1 C 14_1 1 K $5_{22.24}$ 9_{11} Ezr 3_7 2 C 2_7) or cedar wood (e.g. 1 K $6_{18.18.20}$ $7_{3.7.11}$ Jr 22_{14} Ca 8_9 11QT 36_{11}), **<SUBJ>** שׂמח *rejoice* Is 14_8 (‖ בְּרוֹשׁ *cypress*), עמם *overshadow* Ezk 31_8 (‖ בְּרוֹשׁ, עַרְמוֹן *plane-tree*), נפל *fall* Zc 11_2 (+ בְּרוֹשׁ), כסה pu. *be covered with* Ps 80_{11}, שׂבע *be satisfied* 104_{16} (‖ עֵץ *tree*), הלל pi. *praise* 148_9 (‖ עֵץ פְּרִי *fruit tree*, הַר *mountain*, גִּבְעָה *hill*).

<NOM CL> אַשּׁוּר אֶרֶז בַּלְּבָנוֹן *Assyria was a cedar in Lebanon* Ezk 31$_3$ (+ יְפֵה עָנָף ... וּגְבַהּ קוֹמָה *fair of branch ... and tall of height*), אֶרֶז ... מִקְלַעַת פְּקָעִים *(the) cedar ... was a carving of gourds* 1 K 6$_{18}$, הַכֹּל אֶרֶז *the whole was cedar* 6$_{18}$ (+ אֵין אֶבֶן נִרְאָה *no stone was seen*), וּמִלְמַעְלָה אֲבָנִים ... וָאֶרֶז *above were stones ... and cedar* 7$_{11}$, קֹרוֹת בָּתֵּינוּ אֲרָזִים *the beams of our house are cedars* Ca 1$_{17}$.

<OBJ> אכל *consume* Jg 9$_{15}$, נתן *place* Is 41$_{19}$ (|| שִׁטָּה *acacia*, הֲדַס *myrtle*, עֵץ שֶׁמֶן *olive-tree*, + בְּרוֹשׁ *cypress*, תִּדְהָר *elm*, תְּאַשּׁוּר *box-tree*), *make* 1 K 10$_{27}$||2 C 1$_{15}$||9$_{27}$ (+ כַּשִּׁקְמִים *as sycamores*), בוא hi. *bring* 4Q522 2$_5$ (|| בְּרוֹשׁ; [יבן]יא) חלף hi. *replace with* Is 9$_9$ (+ שִׁקְמָה *sycamore*), כרת *cut* 1 K 5$_{20}$ Is 44$_{14}$ (+ תִּרְזָה *holm-oak*, אַלּוֹן *oak*, אֹרֶן *cedar* [mss אֶרֶז *cedar*], עֲצֵי יַעַר *trees of the forest*), שׁלך hi. *cast* 4QToh B^a 5 (+ תולע *crimson stuff*), לקח *take* Ezk 27$_5$ (+ בְּרוֹשׁ), שׁבר *break* Ps 29$_5$, pi. *shatter* 29$_5$, שׁלח *send* 2 C 2$_2$.

<CSTR> אַרְזֵי הַלְּבָנוֹן *cedars of Lebanon* Jg 9$_{15}$ (+ אָטָד *thorn*) Is 2$_{13}$ (+ אַלּוֹנֵי הַבָּשָׁן *oaks of Bashan*) 14$_8$ (לְבָנוֹן; || בְּרוֹשׁ *cypress*) Ps 29$_5$ (+ אֲרָזִים *cedars*) 104$_{16}$ (לְבָנוֹן; + עֲצֵי י׳ *trees of Y.*) 4QpIsa^c 8$_3$(Allegro) ([ואר]זי לבנון; || בְּרוֹשׁ) 4QBer^a 2$_5$ ([ארזי לבנו]ן), אַרְזֵי־אֵל *cedars of God* Ps 80$_{11}$.

מִזְבַּח אֶרֶז *altar of cedar* 1 K 6$_{20}$, לוּחַ *panel of* Ca 8$_9$, כִּיּוּר *panelling of* 11QT 36$_{11}$, עֵץ הָאֶרֶז *wood (consisting) of cedar* Lv 14$_4$ (אֶרֶז) 14$_{6.49}$ (אֶרֶז) 14$_{51}$ (עֵץ־) 14$_{52}$ (all five + צִפֹּר *bird*) Nm 19$_6$ (all six + שְׁנִי תוֹלַעַת *crimson stuff*, אֵזוֹב *hyssop*) 11QT 41$_{16.17}$ + Sup 49$_3$ (+ אֵזוֹב; all four אֶרֶז), עצי ארז *trees of cedar* 42$_6$ + Sup, עֲצֵי אֲרָזִים *trees of cedar* 2 S 5$_{11}$||1 C 14$_1$ 1 K 5$_{22.24}$ (both + בְּרוֹשׁ *cypress*) 6$_{10}$ 9$_{11}$ (+ בְּרוֹשׁ, זָהָב *gold*) Ezr 3$_7$ 2 C 2$_7$ (+ בְּרוֹשׁ, אַלְגּוּם *algum*).

דמע א[ר]ז *resin of cedar* 3QTr 11$_{10}$(Milik; Allegro או *or*) (|| סוּחַ *fir-tree*), צַמֶּרֶת הָאֶרֶז *top of the cedar* Ezk 17$_3$ (הָאֶרֶז) 17$_{22}$, גֹּבַהּ אֲרָזִים *height of cedars* Am 2$_9$ (+ אַלּוֹן *oak*), רוּם *height of* CD 2$_{19}$ (+ הַר *mountain*), קוֹמַת *height*, i.e. tallest, *of* 2 K 19$_{23}$||Is 37$_{24}$ (אֲרָזָיו; || בְּרוֹשׁ *cypress*), מִבְחַר *choicest of* Jr 22$_7$ (אֲרָזֶיךָ), שתילי *cuttings of* Si 50$_{12}$ (+ ערבי נחל *willows of the brook*), בַּיִת *house of* 2 S 7$_2$||1 C 17$_1$ (1 C הָאֲרָזִים) 2 S 7$_7$||1 C$_6$, צַלְעוֹת *planks of* 1 K 6$_{15}$, כְּרֻתֹת *beams of* 6$_{36}$ 7$_{2.12}$, עַמּוּדֵי *columns of* 7$_2$, כָּל־ *all* Is 2$_{13}$ (אַרְזֵי) Ps 148$_9$ 4QBer^a 2$_5$ (כול ארזי).

<ADJ> אֶרֶז אַדִּיר *majestic cedar* Ezk 17$_{23}$, אַרְזֵי הַלְּבָנוֹן הָרָמִים וְהַנִּשָּׂאִים *the high and exalted cedars of Lebanon* Is 2$_{13}$.

<PREP> היה לְ *come to be* Ezk 17$_{23}$.

בְּ *in, with*, + ספן *roof* 1 K 6$_9$ 7$_{3.7}$ Jr 22$_{14}$, חרה tiphel *compete* 22$_{15}$, קנן pu. *be nested* 22$_{23}$ (|| לְבָנוֹן *Lebanon*), אכל בְּ *consume some of* Zc 11$_1$.

כְּ *as* Nm 24$_6$ (|| נַחַל *valley*, גַּן *garden*, אֲהָל *aloe*), + שׂגה *grow* Ps 92$_{13}$ (|| תָּמָר *palm-tree*), רמח כארז *a spear like a cedar* 4QApocJos^c 1$_3$, מַרְאֵהוּ ... בָּחוּר כָּאֲרָזִים *his appearance is ... choice as the cedars* Ca 5$_{15}$ (|| לְבָנוֹן *Lebanon*), יַחְפֹּץ זְנָבוֹ כְמוֹ־אָרֶז *he bends his tail like a cedar* Jb 40$_{17}$.

עֵצִים מִן־הָאֶרֶז *trees from*, i.e. including, *the cedar* (:: אֵזוֹב *hyssop*) 1 K 5$_{13}$.

שׁלח אֶל *send* message *to* 2 K 14$_9$||2 C 25$_{18}$.

יוֹם לַי׳ ... עַל כָּל־אַרְזֵי לְבָנוֹן *Y. has a day ... against all the cedars of Lebanon* Is 2$_{13}$.

<COLL> + אֶרֶז, בַּלְּבָנוֹן *in Lebanon* 1 K 5$_{13}$ 2 K 14$_9$||2 C 25$_{18}$ Ezk 31$_3$ Ps 92$_{13}$ Si 50$_{12}$, מִן־הַלְּבָנוֹן *from Lebanon* 1 K 5$_{20}$ Ezr 3$_7$ 2 C 2$_7$ (מֵהַלְּבָנוֹן), עֲלֵי־מָיִם *by the waters* Nm 24$_6$, לְאֵין מִסְפָּר *without number* 1 C 22$_4$, אֶל־הַבַּיִת פְּנִימָה *inside the house* 1 K 6$_{18}$.

<SYN> בְּרוֹשׁ *cypress*, אַלּוֹן *oak*, עֵץ *tree*, אֵזוֹב *hyssop*, הַר *mountain*, לְבָנוֹן *Lebanon*.

→ אַרְזָה *cedar work*.

אַרְזָה 1 n.f. **cedarwork** (unless rd אַרְזָהּ *her cedar*), כִּי אַרְזָה עֵרָה *for he has stripped the cedarwork* Zp 2$_{14}$.

→ אֶרֶז *cedar*.

ארח 6.2.2 vb. **journey—Qal** + waw וְאָרַח; ptc. אֹרֵחַ, אֹרְחִים (Q אורחינו); inf. Q ארוח (אָרְחִי).

1. journey, go, <SUBJ> גֶּבֶר *man* Jb 34$_8$. <PREP> לְחֶבְרָה *for company* Jb 34$_8$, עִם *with* wicked Jb 34$_8$. <COLL> אָרְחִי וְרִבְעִי *my travelling and my lying down* Ps 139$_3$ (unless אֹרַח *way*).

2. ptc. as noun, **wanderer, traveller,** <SUBJ> נטה *turn aside* to pass night Jr 14$_8$ (|| גֵּר *sojourner*), בוא *come* 2 S 12$_4$, שׁמר *keep* discipline Pr 10$_{17}$ (if em. אֹרַח *path*). <OBJ> ראה *see* Jg 19$_{17}$. <CSTR> מְלוֹן אֹרְחִים *lodging* *place of travellers* Jr 9₁, חשבון ארח *account of traveller* Si 42₃(Bmg) (unless אֹרַח *way*; B אֲדוֹן *lord*, i.e. employer). **<APP>** הָאִישׁ הָאֹרֵחַ *the man, the traveller* Jg 19₁₇, לָאֹרֵחַ הַבָּא *for the traveller, the one that comes* 2 S 12₄. **<PREP>** עשׂה לְ *do for* 2 S 12₄, פתח לְ *open* door *to* Jb 31₃₂ (if em. אֹרַח *way*); היה כְּ *be as* Jr 14₈. **<COLL>** אֹרֵחַ לְחַיִּים *one that travels to life* Pr 10₁₇ (if em. אֹרַח *way of*), ובנ]ז[וינו ואורחינו ואביונינו *and our despised, and our wayfarers, and our poor* 4QPrFêtes^b 21₂.

Hi. Impf. Si יאריח—**set on journey,** ירח יאריח]י[עתות *(the) moon sets (the) seasons on their journey* Si 43₆(M) (B ירח ירח appar. *the moon, as for the moon*).

Also 4QDibHam^a 18₅.

→ אֹרַח *way,* אֹרְחָה *caravan,* אֲרֻחָה *provisions.*

אָרַח 4 pr.n.m. **Arah, 1.** head of family of returning exiles, Ezr 2₅||Ne 7₁₀. **2.** perh. ident with preceding, father of Shecaniah, the father-in-law of Tobiah, Ne 6₁₈. **3.** son of Ulla (עֻלָּא), descendant of Asher, 1 C 7₃₉.

→ ארח *journey.*

אֹרַח 59.4.4 n.m. **way**—mss אוֹרַח; cstr. אֹרַח; sf. אָרְחִי, אָרְחוֹ, אָרְחֵךְ; pl. אֳרָחוֹת; cstr. אָרְחוֹת (Q אורחות); sf. אָרְחֹתָיו, (אֹרְחֹתֶיךָ) אֹרְחוֹתֶיךָ, אָרְחֹתַי (Kt ארחתו, Si ארחתיה (Q אורחותיה), Si אורחותיו), אָרְחוֹתָם (אָרְחֹתֵיהֶם).

1. path, way, a. marked out by previous travellers, Gn 49₁₇ Jg 5₆.₆ Is 33₈ 41₃ (or em.; see Obj.) Ps 8₉ Jb 16₂₂ Si 49₆ 4QapLam^a 2₇. **b.** a course of movement, a route dictated by the traveller, Jl 2₇ Ps 19₆ Pr 9₁₅ (or §3) Si 42₃.

2. way, an action or course of action viewed ethically, sometimes simply 'the' way, as prescribed by God or justice Is 26₈ 40₁₄ Ps 44₁₉ 119₁₅ Pr 2₁₃.₂₀ 4₁₈ 8₂₀ 12₂₈ 17₂₃, God's own ways as taught to humans Ps 25₄.₁₀ Is 2₃||Mc 4₂, 'the' way as the right action(s) Is 30₁₁ Pr 15₁₀, way watched to assess moral quality Ps 17₄ Jb 13₂₇=33₁₁ Jr 12₄ (if em.; see Obj.), way as task entrusted to someone else 4Q424 1₇, care needed in one's ways Si 35₂₂, ways destroyed by leaders Is 3₁₂, bad ways Ps 49₁₄ (if em.; see Nom. Cl.) 119₁₀₁.₁₀₄.₁₂₈ Jb 8₁₃ (or em.; see Nom. Cl.) 22₁₅ Pr 1₁₉ (or em.; see Nom. Cl.) 2₁₅ 4₁₄ 22₂₅ 4QWiles 1₉.

3. way, in ref. to life viewed as a path Ps 142₄, smooth or straight for the righteous Is 26₇ Ps 27₁₁ 143₁₀(mss) (see Cstr.) Pr 3₆ 15₁₉ (perh. 9₁₅, §1) Si 39₂₄, leading to 'life' Ps 16₁₁ Pr 2₁₉ 5₆ 10₁₇ (or em.; see Nom. Cl.) 15₂₄ 22₁₉ (if em.; see Cstr.), preserved 2₈, purified Ps 119₉, glorious 73₂₄ (if em.; see Cstr.) Zc 2₁₂ (if em.; see Cstr.), blocked Jb 19₈, not reached by the wicked 4Q525 5₈, made evil Ps 16₄ (if em.; see Obj.), requited Jb 34₁₁, wisdom for one's ways Pr 19₂₀ (if em.; see Prep.).

4. way, manner, חָדַל לִהְיוֹת לְשָׂרָה אֹרַח כַּנָּשִׁים *the manner of women had ceased to be to Sarah* Gn 18₁₁ (or em. כְּאֹרַח נָשִׁים *according to the manner of women*).

5. embankment, earthwork, for siege, וַיָּסֹלּוּ עָלַי אָרְחוֹת אֵידָם *and they cast up against me their ramparts of destruction* Jb 30₁₂.

6. traveller, דְּלָתַי לָאֹרַח אֶפְתָּח *I have opened my doors to the traveller* Jb 31₃₂ (or em. אֹרֵחַ *traveller*).

7. caravan, חָדְלוּ אֲרָחוֹת *caravans ceased* Jg 5₆ (or em. אֹרְחוֹת *caravans*), יִלָּפְתוּ אָרְחוֹת דַּרְכָּם יַעֲלוּ בַתֹּהוּ וְיֹאבֵדוּ *the caravans wind about their way, they go up into the waste and perish* Jb 6₁₈ (or em. אֹרְחוֹת), הִבִּיטוּ אָרְחוֹת תֵּמָא *the caravans of Tema look* 6₁₉ (or em. אֹרְחוֹת; || הֲלִיכָה *caravan*).

§§ 1-3 **<SUBJ>** סלל pass. *be raised as a highway* Pr 15₁₉ (|| דֶּרֶךְ *way*), ישׁר *be level* Si 39₂₄(Segal) (ארחו]ת[).

<NOM CL> אֹרַח צַדִּיקִים כְּאוֹר *the way of the righteous is as the light of* dawn Pr 4₁₈, וכמסככה כול אורחו]ת[י]ה[*and all her paths are like a woman who is shut away* 4QapLam^a 2₇(Allegro), אָרְחוֹת י׳ חֶסֶד וֶאֱמֶת *the ways of Y. are steadfastness and truth* Ps 25₁₀, אֹרַח לַצַּדִּיק מֵישָׁרִים *the path of the righteous is level* Is 26₇ (+ מַעְגָּל *path*), אֹרַח לְחַיִּים שׁוֹמֵר מוּסָר *the one who keeps discipline is a path to life* Pr 10₁₇ (or em. אֹרֵחַ *traveller*), אֹרַח רַע לְעֹזֵב מוּסָר *there is an evil path to one who abandons discipline* Pr 15₁₀ (if em. מוּסָר רָע לְעֹזֵב אֹרַח *there is severe discipline for one who abandons the path*), אורחותיה שבילי חטאת *her ways are paths of sin* 4QWiles 1₉ (|| דֶּרֶךְ *way*, מַעְגָּל *path*), אֹרַח חַיִּים לְמַעְלָה לְמַשְׂכִּיל *the path of life is upward for the wise* Pr 15₂₄, אָרְחֹתֵיהֶם עִקְּשִׁים *their ways are crooked* 2₁₅ (or em.

מְעַקְּשִׁים they *make crooked* or מְעֻקָּשִׁים are *made crooked*), ... כֵּן אָרְחוֹת *such are the paths of* ... Jb 8$_{13}$ (or em. אַחֲרִית *end of*) Pr 1$_{19}$ (or em. אַחֲרִית), זֶה ... אָרְחוֹתָם *this is ... their paths* Ps 49$_{14}$ (if em. אַחֲרֵיהֶם *after them*; || דֶּרֶךְ *way*).

<OBJ> ישׁר pi. *make straight* Pr 3$_{6}$ 9$_{15}$ (|| דֶּרֶךְ *way*), פלס pi. *make level*, i.e. have regard for 5$_{6}$ (+ מַעְגָּל *path*) 4Q424 1$_{7}$, נטה hi. *pervert* Pr 17$_{23}$, עקשׁ pi. *make crooked* 2$_{15}$ (if em.; see Nom. Cl.), pu. *be made crooked* 2$_{15}$ (if em.; see Nom. Cl.), שׁמם hi. *make desolate* Si 49$_{6}$, עבט pi. *change* Jl 2$_{7}$ (or em. יְעַבְּטוּן to יְעַוְּתוּן *make crooked*; + דֶּרֶךְ), קוה pi. *wait for* Is 26$_{8}$ (if em. קִוִּינוּךָ *we have waited for you* to קִוִּינוּ *we have waited for* the path), עזב *abandon* Pr 2$_{13}$ (|| דֶּרֶךְ) 15$_{10}$ (unless em.; see Nom. Cl.), שׁמר *keep* Ps 17$_{4}$ Jb 13$_{27}$ 22$_{15}$ 33$_{11}$ Pr 2$_{20}$ (|| דֶּרֶךְ), נצר *keep* 2$_{8}$, אלף *learn* 22$_{25}$ (Kt ארחתו), למד pi. *teach* Ps 25$_{4}$ (|| דֶּרֶךְ), ידע hi. *make known* 16$_{11}$ 22$_{19}$ (if em.; see Cstr.), ראה *see* Jr 12$_{4}$ (if em. אֶת־אַחֲרִיתֵנוּ *our end* to אָרְחוֹתֵנוּ *our ways*), נבט hi. *behold* Ps 119$_{15}$ (|| פִּקּוּד *precept*), זכה pi. *make pure* 119$_{9}$, נשׂג hi. *attain to* Pr 2$_{19}$, גדר *wall up* Jb 19$_{8}$ (|| נְתִיבָה *path*), בלע pi. *swallow up*, i.e. destroy Is 3$_{12}$, רעע hi. *make evil* Ps 16$_{4}$ (if em. אַחֵר מָהָרוּ *they have acquired another* to אָרְחָם הֵרֵעוּ *they have made their path wicked*), מור hi. *change* 16$_{4}$ (if em. אַחֵר מָהָרוּ to אָרְחָם הֵמִירוּ *they change their way*), שׂנא *hate* 119$_{104.128}$.

Obj. of place, *in, by a way*, + הלך *go* Jg 5$_{6}$ (+ נְתִיבָה *path*) Jb 16$_{22}$ (אֹרַח לֹא־אָשׁוּב *a way by which I shall not return*), pi. Ps 142$_{4}$ (+ נְתִיבָה), עבר *pass* Is 33$_{8}$ 41$_{3}$ (אֹרַח בְּרַגְלָיו לֹא יָבוֹא *a path his foot has not entered*; or em. אֹרֵחַ *traveller*) Ps 8$_{9}$, רוץ *run* 19$_{6}$, קוה pi. *wait for* Is 26$_{8}$ (unless em.; see above), לקח *take* Ps 73$_{24}$ (if em.; see Cstr.), שׁלח *send* Zc 2$_{12}$ (if em.; see Cstr.).

<CSTR> אֹרַח מִשְׁפָּט *path of justice* Is 40$_{14}$ (|| דֶּרֶךְ *way*), צְדָקָה *of righteousness* Pr 8$_{20}$ (אֹרַח־ || נְתִיבָה *path*) 12$_{28}$ (אֹרַח־ || דֶּרֶךְ + נְתִיבָה), מִישׁוֹר *of uprightness* Ps 27$_{11}$ (+ דֶּרֶךְ) 143$_{10(mss)}$ (L אֶרֶץ *land of*), שֶׁקֶר *of falsehood* 119$_{104}$ (שָׁקֶר) 119$_{128}$, כָּבוֹד *of glory* 73$_{24}$ (if em. אַחַר *after*) Zc 2$_{12}$ (if em. אַחַר), עוֹלָם *of antiquity* Jb 22$_{15}$, אִישׁ *of a man* 34$_{11}$, חַיִּים *of life* Ps 16$_{11}$ Pr 5$_{6}$ 15$_{24}$, רְשָׁעִים *of the wicked* 4$_{14}$ (|| דֶּרֶךְ), יְשָׁרִים *of the upright* 15$_{19}$ (or em. חֲרוּצִים *of the diligent*), מִשְׁפָּטֶיךָ *of your judgments* Is 26$_{8}$.

אָרְחוֹת יֹשֶׁר *paths of uprightness* Pr 2$_{13}$, מִשְׁפָּט *of justice* Pr 2$_{8}$ 17$_{23}$, תמים *of virtuous one* Si 39$_{24(Segal)}$ (ארחו[ת]), פָּרִיץ *of violent one* Ps 17$_{4}$ (mss פֶּרֶץ *of violence*), חַיִּים *of life* Pr 2$_{19}$ 22$_{19}$ (if em. הַיּוֹם אַף־אָתָּה *today, even you*) 4Q525 5$_{8}$ (אורחות), צַדִּיקִים *of righteous ones* 2$_{20}$ 4$_{18}$, יַמִּים *of the seas* Ps 8$_{9}$, כָּל־שֹׁכְחֵי אֵל *of all who forget God* Jb 8$_{13}$ (or em.; see Nom Cl.), כָּל־בֹּצֵעַ בָּצַע *of everyone who makes gain by violence* Pr 1$_{19}$ (or em.; see Nom Cl.).

דֶּרֶךְ אֹרְחֹתֶיךָ *path of your ways* Is 3$_{12}$.

כָּל־אֹרַח *every path* Ps 119$_{101.104.128}$, כָּל־אָרְחוֹת י׳ *all the paths of Y.* 25$_{10}$, כָּל־אָרְחֹתָי *all my paths* Jb 13$_{27}$ 33$_{11}$, כל ארחותיך *all your paths* 4Q424 1$_{7}$.

<ADJ> אֹרַח רָע *evil path* Ps 119$_{101}$ Pr 15$_{10}$ (if em.; see Nom. Cl.), אֳרָחוֹת עֲקַלְקַלּוֹת *winding paths* Jg 5$_{6}$ (or del. אֳרָחוֹת).

<PREP> בְּ *in, by* Pr 12$_{28}$, + הלך *walk* Is 2$_{3}$||Mc 4$_{2}$ (+ דֶּרֶךְ *way*), pi. Pr 8$_{20}$, בוא *enter* 4$_{14}$, נחה *lead* Ps 27$_{11}$ 143$_{10(mss)}$, טמן *hide* trans. 142$_{4}$, חכם *be wise* Pr 19$_{20}$ (if em. בְּאַחֲרִיתֶךָ *in your end* to בְּאֹרְחֹתֶיךָ *in your paths*), זהר ni. *take heed* Si 35$_{22(B)}$, למד בְּ pi. *teach concerning* Is 40$_{14}$.

כְּאֹרַח אִישׁ יַמְצִאֶנּוּ *according to a man's way he will make (it) find him* Jb 34$_{11}$.

מִן of direction, *from*, + כלא *restrain* Ps 119$_{101}$, נטה *turn* 44$_{19}$ (מִנִּי), hi. Is 30$_{11}$ (מִנִּי; || דֶּרֶךְ *way*).

יְהִי־דָן ... שְׁפִיפֹן עֲלֵי־אֹרַח *may Dan be a viper upon the path* Gn 49$_{17}$, בושׁ עַל *be ashamed of* Si 42$_{3(Bmg)}$ (B אדון *Lord*; M דרך *way*).

<SYN> דֶּרֶךְ *way*, נְתִיבָה *path*, מַעְגָּל *path*.

→ ארח *journey*.

[אֹרְחָה] 2 n.f. **caravan**—cstr. אֹרְחַת; pl. cstr. אֹרְחוֹת— **<SUBJ>** בוא *come* from Gilead Gn 37$_{25}$, לין *pass the night* in forest, desert Is 21$_{13}$, חדל *cease* Jg 5$_{6}$ (if em. אֳרָחוֹת *ways*), לפת pi. *twist* way Jb 6$_{18}$ (if em. יִלָּפְתוּ אָרְחוֹת *the ways of* their way *are twisted*), עלה *go up* 6$_{18}$ (if em.), אבד *disappear* 6$_{18}$ (if em.), נבט hi. *look* 6$_{19}$ (if em. אָרְחוֹת *ways of*; || הֲלִיכָה *caravan*). **<CSTR>** אֹרְחַת יִשְׁמְעֵאלִים *caravan of Ishmaelites* Gn 37$_{25}$, אֹרְחוֹת דְּדָנִים *caravans of Dedanites* Is 21$_{13}$, אֹרְחוֹת תֵּמָא *caravans of Tema* Jb 6$_{19}$ (if em.). → ארח *journey*.

אֲרֻחָה 6 n.f. **ration of food**—cstr. אֲרֻחַת; sf. אֲרֻחָתוֹ—אֲרֻחָתוֹ אֲרֻחַת תָּמִיד נִתְּנָה־לּוֹ מֵאֵת הַמֶּלֶךְ *his ration was a ration of continuity,* i.e. regular allowance, *given him from the king* 2 K 25$_{30}$‖Jr 52$_{34}$ (מֶלֶךְ־בָּבֶל *the king of Babylon*), וַיִּתֶּן־לוֹ ... אֲרֻחָה וּמַשְׂאֵת וַיְשַׁלְּחֵהוּ *and he gave him ... rations and a present and he dispatched him* Jr 40$_{5}$, טוֹב אֲרֻחַת יָרָק וְאַהֲבָה־שָׁם *a ration of vegetable(s) where there is love is better* than a fatted ox Pr 15$_{17}$.

→ ארח *journey.*

אֲרִי 35.1.3 n.m. **lion**—pl. אֲרָיוֹת (אֲרָיִים)—**1. lion,** **<SUBJ>** היה *be* 2 K 17$_{25}$ (+ הרג ptc. *killing*), בוא *come* 1 S 17$_{34}$ (‖ דֹּב *bear*), נשׂא *carry off* 17$_{34}$, שׁבר *break* bones 1QH 5$_{7}$ (‖ לָבִיא *lion[ess]*), טרף *tear* prey Ezk 22$_{25}$, שׁנן *sharpen* tongue 1QH 5$_{13}$, מות hi. *kill* 2 K 17$_{26}$, שׁכב *lie down* Nm 23$_{24}$ (‖ לָבִיא), אכל *eat* 23$_{24}$, שׁתה *drink* 23$_{24}$ 1QH 5$_{7}$, נדח hi. *scatter* Jr 50$_{17}$, שׁאג *roar* Ezk 22$_{25}$ Zp 3$_{3}$ (‖ זְאֵב *wolf*), נהם *growl* Pr 28$_{15}$ (‖ דֹּב).

<NOM CL> אֲרִי בַחוּץ *a lion is outside* Pr 22$_{13}$, אֲרִי בֵּין הָרְחֹבוֹת *a lion is in the streets* 26$_{13}$ (‖ שַׁחַל *lion*), שָׂרֶיהָ ... אֲרָיוֹת *her princes ... are lions* Zp 3$_{3}$, ... אֲרִי מֹשֵׁל *a ruler ... is a lion* Pr 28$_{15}$, הוּא ... אֲרִי *he is a lion* Lm 3$_{10(Qr)}$ (Kt אריה) (+ בְּמִסְתָּרִים *in hiding,* ‖ דֹּב *bear*).

<OBJ> נכה hi. *smite* 1 S 17$_{36}$ (‖ דֹּב *bear*) 2 S 23$_{20(Qr)}$ (Kt אריה) ‖1 C 11$_{22}$, שׁלח pi. *let loose* 2 K 17$_{25.26}$. **<CSTR>** כְּפִיר *young of* Jg 14$_{5}$, גּוּר *cub of* Na 2$_{12}$, גּוֹרֵי *cubs of* Jr 51$_{38}$, יַד *hand of* 1 S 17$_{37}$ (+ נצל מִן hi. *deliver from,* ‖ דֹּב *bear*), פִּי *mouth of* Am 3$_{12}$ (+ נצל מִן hi.) perh. 1QH 5$_{19}$ (or כֹּחַ *strength of*), מְעוֹן *den of* Na 2$_{12}$ (+ כְּפִיר *[young] lion*) Ca 4$_{8}$ (מְעֹנוֹת; ‖ נָמֵר *leopard*) 1QH 5$_{13}$, מַאֲכַל *food of* Si 13$_{19}$.

<PREP> כְּ *as* Ps 22$_{17}$ (of trussed quarry; or em. כָּרוּ *they pierced*), + נשׂא htp. *raise oneself* Nm 23$_{24}$ (‖ לָבִיא *lion[ess]*), שׁכב *lie* 24$_{9}$ (+ לָבִיא), שׁבר pi. *break* bones Is 38$_{13}$, קֶשֶׁר ... כַּאֲרִי the *conspiracy ... (is) as a lion* Ezk 22$_{25}$.

מִן of comparison, *than,* Jg 14$_{18}$ (+ עַז *strong,* דְּבַשׁ *honey*), + גבר *be strong* 2 S 1$_{23}$ (‖ נֶשֶׁר *eagle*); מִיַּד, see Cstr.; בֵּין אֲרָיוֹת רָבָצָה *among lions she crouched* Ezk 19$_{2}$ (‖ כְּפִיר *[young] lion*), הלך בְּתוֹךְ htp. *roam among* 19$_{6}$ (+ כְּפִיר), נוס מִפְּנֵי *flee from before* Am 5$_{19}$ (+ דֹּב *bear*).

2. in representations, **lion-relief,** etc., **<SUBJ>** עמד *stand* 1 K 10$_{19.20}$ ‖2 C 9$_{18.19}$. **<NOM CL>** עַל־הַמִּסְגְּרוֹת ... אֲרָיוֹת ... *on the panels ... were lions* 1 K 7$_{29}$ (‖ בָּקָר *ox,* כְּרוּב *cherub*). **<OBJ>** פתח pi. *engrave* 1 K 7$_{36}$ (‖ כְּרוּב *cherub,* תִּמֹּרָה *palm-tree*).

<PREP> מִתַּחַת לַאֲרָיוֹת *below the lions* 1 K 7$_{29}$ (‖ בָּקָר *ox*). **<COLL>** שְׁנַיִם אֲרָיוֹת *two lions* 1 K 10$_{19}$ ‖2 C 9$_{18}$, שְׁנַיִם עָשָׂר אֲרָיִים *twelve lions* 1 K 10$_{20}$ ‖2 C 9$_{19}$ (אֲרָיוֹת).

<SYN> §1 כְּפִיר *(young) lion,* לָבִיא *lion(ess),* דֹּב *bear;* §2 בָּקָר *ox,* כְּרוּב *cherub.*

→ אַרְיֵה *lion,* אֲרִיאֵל *Ariel,* אַרְאֵלִי *Areli, Arelite,* אֲרִיאֵלִי *Arielite.*

אֲרִי, see אוּרִי.

אֲרִיאֵל I 3 pr.n.m. **Ariel**—אֲרִאֵל—**1.** Moabite, 2 S 23$_{20}$‖1 C 11$_{22}$ (שְׁנֵי אֲרִ[י]אֵל מוֹאָב) appar. he struck *the two [sons] of Ariel of Moab;* perh. em. אַרְאֵלֵי *heroes of* or אֲרִ[י]אֵלֵי *priests of,* or אֲרִיאֵל IV *lion[s] of God.* **2.** a leader of returning exiles, Ezr 8$_{16}$.

→ אֵל *God* + אֲרִי *lion.*

אֲרִיאֵל II 5 pl.n. **Ariel,** i.e. Jerusalem, Is 29$_{1.1.2.2.7}$.

→ אֵל *God* + אֲרִי *lion.*

אֲרִיאֵל III 3 n.[m.] **altar hearth**—הַרְאֵל, Kt אראיל—וְהַהַרְאֵל אַרְבַּע אַמּוֹת *and the altar hearth will be four cubits (high)* Ezk 43$_{15}$ (or em. וְהָאֲרִיאֵל), וְהָאֲרִיאֵל שְׁתֵּים עֶשְׂרֵה אֹרֶךְ *and the altar hearth will be twelve cubits in length* 43$_{16(Qr)}$, וּמֵהָאֲרִיאֵל וּלְמַעְלָה הַקְּרָנוֹת אַרְבַּע *and from the altar hearth and above, the horns are four* 43$_{15(Qr)}$.

[אֲרִיאֵל] IV, see אֲרִיאֵל I.

[אֲרִיאֵלִי] I gent. **Arielite,** i.e. Jerusalemite, inhabitant of Ariel (אֲרִיאֵל II), Is 33$_{7}$ (if em. אֶרְאֶלָּם perh. *I shall appear to them* to אֲרִאֵלִים).

[אֲרִיאֵלִי] II n.m. **priest,** i.e. person connected with altar hearth (אֲרִיאֵל III), הִכָּה אֵת שְׁנֵי אֲרִ(י)אֵלֵי מוֹאָב *he struck the two priests of Moab* 2 S 23$_{20}$‖1 C 11$_{22}$ (if em. אֲרִ[י]אֵל *Ariel*), אֶרְאֶלִּים צָעֲקוּ *priests will cry out* Is 33$_{7}$

(if em. אֵרָאֶלָם perh. *I shall appear to them*).

[אָרִיג], see ארג, §2, Prep.

[אֲרִידַי], see אֲרִדַי.

אֲרִידָתָא 1 pr.n.m. **Aridatha**—אֲרִידָתָא—son of Haman, Est 9_{8}.

[אריה], see אוּרִיָּה.

אֲרִיֵה I $_{45.1}$ n.m. **lion**, <SUBJ> היה *be* Is 35_{9} (+ שָׁם *there*, פָּרִיץ *ferocious one*), מצא *find* 1 K 13_{24} 20_{36}, עמד *stand* 13_{24} (|| חֲמוֹר *donkey*) $13_{25.28}$ (|| חֲמוֹר), הלך *go* Na 2_{12} (+ גּוּר *cub*), עלה *go up* Jr 4_{7} (+ מִסֻּבְּכוֹ *from its lair*, || שחת hi. ptc. *destroyer*).

מות *die* Ec 9_{4}, hi. *kill* 1 K $13_{24.26}$, נכה hi. *strike* $20_{36.36}$ Jr 5_{6} (+ מִיַּעַר *from the forest*, || זְאֵב *wolf*, נָמֵר *leopard*), שחת hi. *destroy* Jr 2_{30}, חנק pi. *strangle* Na 2_{13} (+ לְלִבְאֹתָיו *for his lionesses*), שבר *maul* 1 K $13_{26.28}$, טרף *tear* Na 2_{13} Ps 17_{12} (|| כְּפִיר *[young] lion*) 22_{14}, מלא *fill* lair with prey Na 2_{13}.

כסף *desire* Ps 17_{12}, שאג *roar* Am 3_{4} (+ בַּיַּעַר *in the forest*, || כְּפִיר *[young] lion*) 3_{8} Ps 22_{14}, הגה *growl* Is 31_{4} (+ עַל־טַרְפּוֹ *over its prey*, || כְּפִיר), קרא *call* 21_{8} (perh. אַרְיֵה of warrior, or *[as] a lion*, or em. with 1QIsa[a] הָרֹאֶה *the lookout*), פצה *open* mouth Ps 22_{14}, אכל *eat* 1 K 13_{28} Is 11_{7} (+ דֹּב *bear*) 65_{25} (+ זְאֵב *wolf*; both + כַּבָּקָר *as the ox*).

<OBJ> שית *set* Is 15_{9} (|| יסף ptc. fem. *additional* troubles; or em. אֶרְאֶה *I shall see*), נכה hi. *strike* 2 S $23_{20(Kt)}$ (Qr אֲרִי), ראה *see* 1 K 13_{25}.

<CSTR> גּוּר *cub of* Gn 49_{9} Dt 33_{22} Na 2_{12}, לֵב *heart of* 2 S 17_{10}, פְּנֵי *face of* Ezk 1_{10} (|| שׁוֹר *ox*) 10_{14} (|| כְּרוּב *cherub*, נֶשֶׁר *eagle*; both || אָדָם *human being*) 1 C 12_{9}, שִׁנֵּי *teeth of* Jl 1_{6} (|| לָבִיא *lion[ess]*), פִּי *mouth of* Ps 22_{22} (|| רְאֵם *wild ox*), מַפֶּלֶת *carcass of* Jg 14_{8}, גְּוִיַּת *carcass of* $14_{8.9}$, שַׁאֲגַת *roar of* Jb 4_{10} (|| שַׁחַל *lion*, + כְּפִיר *[young] lion*).

<NOM CL> הוא ... אריה *he ... is a lion* Lm $3_{10(Kt)}$ (Qr אֲרִי; + בְּמִסְתָּרִים *in hiding*, || דֹּב *bear*). <APP> אַרְיֵה לָבִיא *lion (and) lion(ess)* Na 2_{12}.

<PREP> כְּ *as* Ps 17_{12} (+ דִּמְיֹן *appearance*), + היה *be* Jr 12_{8} (or em. אֲרִיָה *enclosure*; + בַּיַּעַר *in the forest*) Mi 5_{7} (+ בְּבַהֲמוֹת יַעַר *among the beasts of the forest*, || כְּפִיר *[young] lion*) Si 4_{30} (+ בביתך *in your house*), רבץ *crouch* Gn 49_{9} (+ לָבִיא *lion[ess]*), שאג *roar* Hos 11_{10}, ארב *lie in wait* Ps 10_{9}, רוץ hi. *chase* Jr 49_{19}=$50_{44(Qr)}$, טרף *tear* Ps 7_{3}, אכל *eat* Jr 2_{30}; נתן לְ *give to* 1 K 13_{26}.

<SYN> כְּפִיר *(young) lion*, לָבִיא *lion(ess)*, דֹּב *bear*, זְאֵב *wolf*, חֲמוֹר *donkey*, אָדָם *human being*.

→ אֲרִי *lion*, אַרְיֵה *Arieh*.

אַרְיֵה II 1 pr.n.m. **Arieh**, appar. officer of Pekahiah, 2 K 15_{25} (הָאַרְיֵה; or em. חַוֹּת יָעִיר *Havvot-jair*, as gloss to גִּלְעָד *Gilead* at 15_{29}).

[אֲרִיָה], see אֻרְוָה.

אריהו, see אוּרִיָּה.

אריו, see אוּרִיָּה.

אַרְיוֹךְ 2 pr.n.m. **Arioch**, king of Ellasar, ally of Chedarlaomer, Gn $14_{1.9}$.

אֲרִים, see אור I, §2b.

[אריסטבולוס] pr.n.m. **Aristobulos**, brother and opponent of Hyrcanus II, 4QMish C[a] 2_{6} ([אריסטבולוס]) 4QMish C[b] 3_{6} ([אר]יסטבולוס).

אֲרִיסַי 1 pr.n.m. **Arisai**, son of Haman, Est 9_{9}.

ארך $_{34.2.4}$ vb. **be long**—**Qal** Pf. אָרְכוּ־; impf. Q יארוך, יַאֲרִכוּ; + waw וַתֶּאֱרַכְנָה—**last long, grow long**, <SUBJ> יוֹם *day* (alw. pl.) Gn 26_{8} Ezk 12_{22}, קֵץ *end* time 1QpHab 7_{7} (others יאריך, i.e. Hi., §2, in same sense, or §1, *he will prolong*), פֹּארָה *branch* Ezk 31_{5} (|| רבה *be many*). <PREP> לוֹ *for him* Gn 26_{8}.

Hi. Pf. הֶאֱרִיךְ, הֶאֱרִיכוּ, הַאֲרַכְתֶּם; impf. יַאֲרִיךְ, יַאֲרִיכוּן, יַאֲרִכוּ (Q ויארך), תַּאֲרִיךְ, אַאֲרִיךְ, יַאֲרִיכוּ (תַּאֲרִיכֻן) תַּאֲרִיכוּ (יַאֲרִכֻן, יַאֲרִיכֻן; + waw וְהַאֲרַכְתָּ (Q והארכתה), L וְהַאֲרַכְתִּי (mss וְהַאֲרַכְתִּי), וַיַּאֲרִכוּ;

impv. Si האריך, הַאֲרִיכִי, Q האריכו; ptc. מַאֲרִיךְ; inf. abs. Si האריך, cstr. הַאֲרִיךְ.

1. prolong one's days (obj. alw. יוֹם pl., also חֹדֶשׁ *month* Nm 9$_{22}$), days of another (1 K 3$_{14}$), <SUBJ> Y. 1 K 3$_{14}$ (L וְהַאֲרַכְתִּי), Israelites Dt 4$_{26.40}$ 5$_{33}$ 11$_{9}$ (8QPhyl ירבו ימיכם *your days shall be many*) 22$_{7}$=11QT 65$_{5}$ (+ יטב *be good* for you) Dt 30$_{18}$ 32$_{47}$, מֶלֶךְ *king* of Israel 17$_{20}$=11QT 59$_{21}$, עֶבֶד *servant* of Y. Is 53$_{10}$ (+ ראה זֶרַע *see seed*, i.e. descendants), זָקֵן *elder* Jos 24$_{31}$ Jg 2$_{7}$, שׂנא ptc. *one who hates* unjust gain Pr 28$_{16}$, רָשָׁע *wicked person* Ec 8$_{13}$, חטא ptc. *sinner* 8$_{12}$ (if em. מְאַת וּמַאֲרִיךְ *a hundred times, and he endures*, as §2, to וְאֶת־יָמָיו מַאֲרִיךְ *and he prolongs his days*), עָנָן *cloud* Nm 9$_{19.22}$.

<PREP> לוֹ *for himself* Ec 8$_{12}$ (if em.; see Subj.); בָּאָרֶץ *in the land* Dt 5$_{33}$; כַּצֵּל *as the shadow* Ec 8$_{13}$ (unless כַּצֵּל = days *that are as a shadow*); עַל־הָאֲדָמָה *upon the land* Dt 4$_{26}$ (עָלֶיהָ) 4$_{40}$ 11$_{9}$ 30$_{18}$ 32$_{47}$, עַל־הַמִּשְׁכָּן *over the tabernacle* Nm 9$_{19.22}$, עַל־מַמְלַכְתּוֹ *over his kingdom* Dt 17$_{20}$ (=11QT 59$_{21}$ מלכותו; Sam על כסא ממלכתו *on the throne of his kingdom*); אַחֲרֵי יְהוֹשֻׁעַ *after (death of) Joshua* Jos 24$_{31}$ Jg 2$_{7}$ (יְהוֹשׁוּעַ).

2. be long, last long, endure, <SUBJ> יוֹם *day* (alw. pl.) Ex 20$_{12}$ Dt 5$_{16}$ (+ יטב *be good* for you) 6$_{2}$ 25$_{15}$, appar. אֶרֶץ *land* Pr 28$_{2}$ (but see Prep.), מֶלֶךְ *king* Ps 72$_{5}$ (if em. יִירָאוּךָ *may they fear you* to וְיַאֲרִיךְ; + דּוֹר דּוֹרִים *generation upon generations*), Esau Gn 27$_{40}$ (if em. תָּרִיר *you will be restless*), רָשָׁע *wicked person* Ec 7$_{15}$ (:: אבד *perish*), חטא ptc. *sinner* 8$_{12}$ (unless em.; see §1, Subj.), בַּד *pole* 1 K 8$_{8}$||2 C 5$_{9}$ (+ וַיֵּרָאוּ רָאשֵׁי הַבַּדִּים *so that the ends of the staves were seen*).

<PREP> לוֹ *for himself* Ec 8$_{12}$ (unless em.; see §1, Subj.).

בְּרָעָתוֹ *with*, or *despite, his wickedness* Ec 7$_{15}$, בְּאָדָם מֵבִין יֹדֵעַ כֵּן יַאֲרִיךְ *by means of an intelligent and knowledgeable person, thus will it* (land) *last long* Pr 28$_{2}$ (or em. יִדְעָכוּן *they* [enemies] *will be extinguished*).

עַל הָאֲדָמָה *upon the land* Ex 20$_{12}$ Dt 5$_{16}$ 25$_{15}$.

3. hold back, postpone, <SUBJ> Y. Is 48$_{9}$, אָדָם *person* Si 30$_{22}$, שֶׂכֶל *intelligence* Pr 19$_{11}$, דכא ni. ptc. *one crushed* by poverty 1QH 13$_{6(Licht)}$ (נדכ[א]), Job Jb 6$_{11}$.

<OBJ> אַף *anger* Is 48$_{9}$ (|| חטם *restrain*) Pr 19$_{11}$ (+ עבר *pass* over, i.e. ignore) Si 30$_{22}$ 1QH 13$_{6}$, נֶפֶשׁ *soul* Jb 6$_{11}$ (+ יחל pi. *wait*).

4. extend, stretch out (trans.), <SUBJ> God Si 33$_{7(Bmg)}$ (B האדר *make glorious*), Jerusalem Is 54$_{2}$, wicked Israelites 57$_{4}$, חרשׁ ptc. *one who ploughs* Ps 129$_{3}$.

<OBJ> יָד *hand* Si 33$_{7(Bmg)}$, לָשׁוֹן *tongue*, i.e. speak Is 57$_{4}$ (|| רחב hi. *widen* mouth), מֵיתָר *rope* 54$_{2}$ (|| רחב hi. *widen* area of tent, חזק pi. *make* pegs *firm*).

<PREP> הֶאֱרִיכוּ לְמַעֲנִיתָם *they stretched out (in respect of) their furrow* Ps 129$_{3(Qr)}$; עַל *against* Is 57$_{4}$.

<SYN> §4 רחב hi. *widen*.

→ אָרֵךְ *long*, אֹרֶךְ *length*, אֲרוּכָה *restoration*.

[אָרֵךְ], see אָרֹךְ.

[אָרֹךְ] 18.1.11 adj. **long**—abs. Q ארוך, f. אֲרֻכָּה, pl. Q ארוכים, f. Q ארוכות; cstr. אֶרֶךְ (L אֲרֶךְ), pl. Q ארוכי—

1. in absolute, **a.** as predicative adj., of person 4QCrypt 2.1$_{3}$ (:: קָצֵר *short*), אֶצְבַּע *finger* 2.1$_{5}$ (|| וארוכ[ות]; || דַּק *thin*), *toe* 1.2$_{5}$ (|| דַּק), שׁוֹק *thigh* 1.2$_{6}$ (|| דַּק), מִגְדָּל *tower* 1QM 9$_{12}$ (+ היה *be*, שלוש אמות *three cubits*), מִלְחָמָה *war* 2 S 3$_{1}$ (+ היה), מִדָּה *dimension* Jb 11$_{9}$ (+ מֵאֶרֶץ *than the earth*, || רָחָב *wide*, עָמֹק *deep*), exile Jr 29$_{28}$. **b.** as attributive adj., of רֹמַח *spear* 1QM 6$_{15}$ (+ שמונה *eight* cubits).

c. ארוך אפים **long (in respect) of anger, patient,** of Y., 4QShirb 52$_{1}$ 1QH 1$_{6}$ 16$_{16}$ (א[רו]ך א[פי]ם) 17$_{17}$.

2. in construct, **a.** as adj., **long of,** אֶרֶךְ אַפַּיִם *long of*, i.e. slow to, *anger* (of Y.) Ex 34$_{6}$ Nm 14$_{18}$ Jl 2$_{13}$ Jon 4$_{2}$ (all four + רַב־חֶסֶד *abundant of*, i.e. abounding in, *loyalty*) Na 1$_{3(Qr)}$ (+ גְּדָל־כֹּחַ *great of strength*) Ps 86$_{15}$ 103$_{8}$ (both + רַב־חֶסֶד) 145$_{8}$ (+ גְּדָל־חָסֶד *great of loyalty*) Ne 9$_{17}$ (+ רַב־חֶסֶד) Si 5$_{4}$, ארוכי רוח *long of*, i.e. able to sustain, *breath* (of warhorses) 1QM 6$_{12}$ (|| קַל *swift*, רַךְ *soft*), אֶרֶךְ הָאֵבֶר *long of the wings* (of eagle) Ezk 17$_{3}$.

b. as noun, **one long of,** אֶרֶךְ אַפַּיִם *one long of*, i.e. slow to, *anger* Jr 15$_{15}$ (or em. אֹרֶךְ *length of*) Pr 14$_{29}$ 15$_{18}$ 16$_{32}$, אֶרֶךְ־רוּחַ *one long of spirit*, i.e. patient Ec 7$_{8}$, <SUBJ> שׁקט hi. *silence* strife Pr 15$_{18}$ (L אֲרֶךְ; + אִישׁ חֵמָה *wrathful man*). <NOM CL> + רַב *abundant* in understanding Pr 14$_{29}$ (+ קְצַר־רוּחַ *one short of spirit*, i.e. irascible), טוֹב *good*, i.e. better than warrior, proud person 16$_{32}$ (+ מֹשֵׁל בְּרוּחוֹ *one who rules his spirit*, i.e. controls his temper) Ec 7$_{8}$. **<PREP>** לְ *as, being* Jr 15$_{15}$ (or em. לְאֹרֶךְ *because of length of*).

→ ארך *be long*.

אֹרֶךְ 95.1.20 n.[m.] **length**—Q אורך; cstr. אֹרֶךְ (Q אורך, Q ארוך); sf. אָרְכּוֹ (Q אורכו), אָרְכָּהּ, אָרְכָּם, אָרְכָּן— **<NOM CL>** ארך אפים עמו *length*, i.e. restraining, *of anger is with him* CD 2$_{4}$, הוּא חַיֶּיךָ וְאֹרֶךְ יָמֶיךָ *that is your life and your length of days* Dt 30$_{20}$=1QDM 2$_{5}$, אֹרֶךְ יָמִים בִּימִינָהּ *length of days is in her hand* Pr 3$_{16}$, אֹרֶךְ ... אַמָּה *length is ... cubit(s)* Ezk 40$_{11.30.33.36.47.49}$ 41$_{12}$ 42$_{2}$ (if del. אֶל־פְּנֵי־ *to the face of* the length of, i.e. to the long side of) 2 C 3$_{3.8}$ (all ten ‖ רֹחַב *width*) Ex 36$_{15}$ Ezk 40$_{42}$ (‖ רֹחַב, גֹּבַהּ *height*) 41$_{13.13.22}$ (‖ גָּבֹהַּ *high*) 42$_{7.8}$ 2 C 3$_{4}$ (if em. עַל־פְּנֵי *in front of* the length to עַל־פָּנָיו *in front of it*) 3$_{11}$ 1QM 4$_{15}$ 5$_{6.7.12}$ 9$_{12}$, אֹרֶךְ ... בָּאַמָּה *length is ... in cubit(s)* Ex 26$_{2}$‖36$_{9}$ 26$_{8}$ 27$_{18}$ Zc 5$_{2}$ (‖ רֹחַב) 11QT 38$_{13}$ 41$_{17}$ + Sup (‖ גֹּבַהּ *height*), אַמָּה ... אֹרֶךְ *cubit(s) is ... length* Gn 6$_{15}$ Ex 25$_{10.23}$‖37$_{1.10}$ 27$_{1}$‖38$_{1}$ 30$_{2}$‖37$_{25}$ 38$_{18}$ 1 K 6$_{2.20}$ 7$_{2}$ 2 C 4$_{1}$ 6$_{13}$ (all ‖ רֹחַב, קוֹמָה *height*) Ex 25$_{17}$‖37$_{6}$ Dt 3$_{11}$ 1 K 6$_{3}$ 7$_{6}$ Ezk 40$_{21.25.29}$ (all ‖ רֹחַב) Ex 26$_{16}$‖36$_{21}$ 2 C 3$_{15}$.

בָּאַמָּה ... אֹרֶךְ *in cubit(s) is ... length* Ex 27$_{9}$ 1 K 7$_{27}$, אֹרֶךְ *length is* + number of cubits Ezk 42$_{20}$ 45$_{1.6}$ 48$_{9.10.13}$ (all ‖ רֹחַב *width*), number of cubits is אֹרֶךְ *is length* Ex 27$_{11}$ Ezk 43$_{16.17}$ 45$_{5}$ 46$_{22}$ 48$_{13}$ (all ‖ רֹחַב *width*) 45$_{1}$, קָנֶה אֶחָד אֹרֶךְ *(its) length* (of תָּא *recess*) *is one reed* 40$_{7}$ (‖ רֹחַב), גֹּמֶד אָרְכָּהּ *its length* (of sword) *is a gomed* Jg 3$_{16}$, זֶרֶת אָרְכּוֹ וְזֶרֶת רָחְבּוֹ *its length* (of breast-plate) *is a span and its width is a span* Ex 28$_{16}$‖39$_{9}$, כַּמָּה־רָחְבָּהּ וְכַמָּה אָרְכָּהּ *how much is its* (Jerusalem's) *width and how much is its length?* Zc 2$_{6}$, אֹרֶךְ כְּאַחַד הַחֲלָקִים *(its) length* (of תְּרוּמָה *sacred area*) *is (the same) as one of the portions* Ezk 48$_{8}$ (‖ רֹחַב), וְאָרְכּוֹ וְקִירֹתָיו עֵץ *and its length* (of הֵיכָל *hall*) *and its walls were wood* 41$_{22}$ (or em. וְאַדְנוֹ/וַאֲדָנָיו *and its base[s]*).

<OBJ> מדד *measure* Ezk 40$_{20}$ 41$_{2.4}$ (both ‖ רֹחַב *width*) 41$_{15}$ 45$_{3}$ (‖ רֹחַב), ספר pi. *recount* 1QH 17$_{17}$, נתן *give* Ps 21$_{5}$, יסף hi. *add* Pr 3$_{2}$, נשׂג hi. *attain* 4Q298 1$_{3}$ ([השיג]ו אורך]).

<CSTR> אֹרֶךְ אַפַּיִם *length*, i.e. restraining, *of anger* Jr 15$_{15}$ (if em. אֶרֶךְ *long of*) Pr 25$_{15}$ (+ לָשׁוֹן רַכָּה *gentle tongue*) 1QS 4$_{3}$ (mg אורך) CD 2$_{4}$ 4QShir[b] 108$_{1 (Baillet)}$ ([אור]ך) 4QM[g] 4$_{3}$ (א[פים]) 4Q525 4$_{24}$ ([ארך]) 5$_{8}$ ([ארך]), ארך רוח *length of spirit*, i.e. patience Si 5$_{11 (A)}$ (C ארך, with ellipsis of רוח), אֹרֶךְ יָמִים *length of days*, i.e. long life Ps 21$_{5}$ 23$_{6}$ 91$_{16}$ (+ אַשְׂבִּיעֵהוּ *I shall satisfy him with*) 93$_{5}$ Jb 12$_{12}$ (+ יָשִׁישׁ *old*) Pr 3$_{2.16}$ Lm 5$_{20}$ (‖ לָנֶצַח *forever*) 1QS 4$_{7}$ (אורכ) 1QM 1$_{9}$ (אורך) 1QDM 2$_{5}$ ([אורך ימ]יכה) 1QH 13$_{21}$ (אורך) 4Q416 10.2$_{20}$ (אורך ימיכיה) Kuntillet ʿAjrud inscr. D2 (ארך ימם; others ברך), [ארוך] חיים *length of life* 4Q298 1$_{3}$, אֹרֶךְ דָּלִיּוֹתָיו *length of its branches* Ezk 31$_{7}$ (or em. רֹב *abundance of*; ‖ גֹּדֶל *greatness*).

אורך המגן *length of the shield* 1QM 5$_{6}$ (‖ רֹחַב *width*), הכידון *of the dagger* 5$_{12}$ (‖ רֹחַב *width*), הרמח *of the spear* 5$_{7}$.

אֹרֶךְ־הַבִּנְיָן *length of the building* Ezk 41$_{15}$, הֶחָצֵר *of the court* Ex 27$_{18}$ (‖ רֹחַב *width*, קוֹמָה *height*), הָאֻלָם *of the porch* Ezk 40$_{49}$, הַלְּשָׁכוֹת *of the chambers* 42$_{8}$, הַשַּׁעַר *of the gate* 40$_{11.18}$ (הַשְּׁעָרִים), הַתֵּבָה *of the ark* Gn 6$_{15}$, הַמְּכוֹנָה *of the stand* 1 K 7$_{27}$ (‖ רֹחַב, קוֹמָה), הַיְרִיעָה *of the curtain* Ex 26$_{2.8}$‖36$_{9.15}$ (both ‖ רֹחַב *width*) 26$_{13}$ (יְרִיעֹת), הַקָּרֶשׁ *of the plank* 26$_{16}$‖36$_{21}$ (‖ רֹחַב).

פְּנֵי־אֹרֶךְ אַמּוֹת הַמֵּאָה to *the face of the length*, i.e. the long side, *of a hundred cubits* Ezk 42$_{2}$ (or del. אֶל־פְּנֵי־; see Nom. Cl.), כָּל־אֹרֶךְ *the whole length* 48$_{13}$ (or em. הַכֹּל *the whole [area] was [of] length*).

<APP> אֹרֶךְ חֲמִשָּׁה וְעֶשְׂרִים אֶלֶף *length, twenty-five thousand (cubits)* Ezk 45$_{3 (Qr)}$.

<PREP> לְאֹרֶךְ יָמִים *during length of*, i.e. many, *days*, + ישׁב *dwell* Ps 23$_{6}$, נאה pilel *befit* 93$_{5}$, עזב *abandon* Lm 5$_{20}$, אַל־לְאֹרֶךְ אַפְּךָ תִּקָּחֵנִי *do not, because of your patience, take me* Jr 15$_{15}$ (if em. אֶרֶךְ *long of*), הִתְהַלֵּךְ בָּאָרֶץ לְאָרְכָּהּ *go around in the land across its length* Gn 13$_{17}$ (‖ רֹחַב *width*).

בְּ of accompaniment, *with* Jb 12$_{12}$ (with ellipsis of בְּ) 4QM[g] 4$_{3}$ 4Q525 5$_{8}$, + ענה *answer* Si 5$_{11 (C)}$, שׁוב hi. *return*, i.e. reply 5$_{11 (A)}$, יצא hi. *send forth* words 4Q525 4$_{24}$ ([בארך]), of cause, *because of*, + יפה *be fair* Ezk 31$_{7}$ (or em. בְּרֹב *because of the abundance of*) 1QS 4$_{7}$, of instrument, *by means of*, + פתה pu. *be persuaded* Pr 25$_{15}$, ש[ש] מא[ות] אמה באורך *six hundred cubits in length* 11QT 40$_8$, לִפְאַת צָפוֹן בָּאֹרֶךְ *for the north side along its (whole) length* Ex 27$_{11}$, באורך ימים *during length of days* 1QS 4$_7$, עֹדֵף בְּאֹרֶךְ *excess in length of* Ex 26$_{13}$, הַנּוֹתָר בָּאֹרֶךְ *the remainder in*, i.e. of, *the length* Ezk 48$_{18}$.

כְּאָרְכָּן כֵּן רָחְבָּן *their width was as their length* Ezk 42$_{11}$ (or em. וּכְרָחְבָּן as their length *and as their width*); לְעֻמַּת *corresponding to* Ezk 40$_{18}$; עַל־פְּנֵי *in front of* 2 C 3$_4$ (or em. עַל־פָּנָיו *in front of it*; see Nom. Cl.).

<COLL> אֹרֶךְ לְ *length to*, i.e. of Ex 27$_9$ 11QT 38$_{13.13}$, אֹרֶךְ לְעֻמּוֹת *a length corresponding to* Ezk 45$_7$.

Also 11QT 8$_5$ ([או]רכו).

<SYN> רֹחַב *width*, קוֹמָה *height*.

→ ארך *be long*.

אֶרֶךְ 1 pl.n. **Erech**, part of Nimrod's kingdom, mod. Warka on left bank of lower Euphrates, Gn 10$_{10}$.

אַרְכִּי 6 gent. **Archite, 1.** a particular **Archite,** חוּשַׁי הָאַרְכִּי *Hushai the Archite* 2 S 15$_{32}$ 16$_{16}$ 17$_{5.14}$ 1 C 27$_{33}$, פַּעֲרַי הָאַרְכִּי *Paarai the Archite* 2 S 23$_{35}$ (mss for הָאַרְבִּי *the Arbite*). **2.** as collective, **Archites,** גְּבוּל הָאַרְכִּי *border of the Archites* Jos 16$_2$.

אֲרָם 143.0.3 pr.n.m. **Aram**—cstr. אֲרַם—**1. Aram,** territory belonging to various Aramaean states and peoples, esp. to NE of Israel, <SUBJ> נוח *rest* i.e. ally oneself Is 7$_2$ (+ עַל־אֶפְרָיִם *upon Ephraim*), לקח *take* territory 1 C 2$_{23}$.

<CSTR> שְׂדֵה אֲרָם *field of Aram* Ho 12$_{13}$ (see §2f), עָרֵי *cities of* Zc 9$_1$ (if em. עֵין אָדָם *eye of human beings*), עַם־ *people of* Am 1$_5$, בני *sons of* 1QM 2$_{11}$ (+ שאר *remnant of*), בְּנוֹת־ *daughters of* Ezk 16$_{57}$ (mss אדם *Edom*), מֶלֶךְ(־)אֲרָם *king of Aram* Jg 3$_{10}$ (+ Cushan-rishathaim) 1 K 15$_{18}$‖2 C 16$_2$ 1 K 20$_{1.20}$ 2 K 6$_{24}$ 8$_{7.9}$ (all + Ben-hadad) 8$_{28.29}$‖2 C 22$_{5.6}$ 2 K 9$_{14.15}$ 12$_{18.19}$ 13$_{3.22.24}$ (all + Hazael) 2 K 15$_{37}$ 16$_5$‖Is 7$_1$ 2 K 16$_6$ (or em. אֱדוֹם; all + Rezin) 1 K 20$_{22.23}$ 22$_{3.31}$‖2 C 18$_{30}$ 2 K 5$_{1.5}$ 6$_{8.11}$ 13$_{4.7}$ 16$_7$ 2 C 16$_{7.7}$ (or em. יִשְׂרָאֵל *of Israel*) 28$_5$, מַלְכֵי *kings of* 1 K 10$_{29}$‖2 C 1$_{17}$ 2 C 28$_{23}$ (ms מֶלֶךְ *king of*), אֱלֹהֵי *gods of* Jg 10$_6$, חֵיל *army of* Jr 35$_{11}$ 2 C 24$_{23.24}$, רֶכֶב *chariotry of* Is 22$_6$ (if em. אָדָם *of human beings*), יַד־ *hand*, i.e. control, *of* 2 K 13$_5$, ... אַף *anger of* ... Is 7$_4$, ראשׁ *head of*, i.e. Damascus 7$_8$, עֵין *eye of* Zc 9$_1$ (if em. אָדָם).

<PREP> מִן of direction, *from*, + נחה *lead* Nm 23$_7$ (or em. אֱדֹם *Edom*), בוא *come* 2 C 20$_2$ (ms אֱדֹם), קדשׁ hi. *consecrate* 2 S 8$_{12}$ (mss אֱדֹם, as ‖1 C 18$_{11}$); ישׁב בְּ *dwell in* 2 S 15$_8$; שׁוב לְ hi. *recover* Elath *for* 2 K 16$_6$ (or em. אֱדוֹם); מלך עַל *reign over* 1 K 11$_{25}$ (mss אֱדֹם), מֶלֶךְ עַל *king over* 19$_{15}$ 2 K 8$_{13}$; וְדָבָר אֵין־לָהֶם עִם־אֲרָם *and there was nothing to them*, i.e. they had no dealings, *with Aram* Jg 18$_{7.28}$ (if, in both, em. אָדָם *human beings*); בֵּין אֲרָם וּבֵין יִשְׂרָאֵל *between Aram and Israel* 1 K 22$_1$.

<COLL> אֲרָם וְכָל־סְבִיבוֹתֶיהָ *Aram and all her neighbours* Ezk 16$_{57}$, גְּשׁוּר־וַאֲרָם *Geshur and Aram* 1 C 2$_{23}$.

2. in compound names orig. signifying *the Aramaeans of* a particular region (Zobah, etc.), and sometimes still best interpreted thus (e.g. אֲרַם צוֹבָא וּרְחוֹב *the Aramaeans of Zobah and of Rehob* 2 S 10$_8$). **a. Aram-naharaim, Aram of Mesopotamia,** also אֲרָם אֲשֶׁר מֵעֵבֶר הַנָּהָר *the Aramaeans who are on the other side of the River* Habur or Euphrates 2 S 10$_{16}$‖1 C 19$_{16}$; in this way distinguished from (Syrian) Aramaeans living immediately adjacent to Israel, <SUBJ> בוא *come* 2 S 10$_{16}$. <OBJ> יצא *bring out* 2 S 10$_{16}$‖1 C 19$_{16}$. <CSTR> מֶלֶךְ אֲרַם נַהֲרָיִם Jg 3$_8$ (= Aram at 3$_{10}$; + Cushan-rishathaim). <APP> פְּתוֹר אֲרַם נַהֲרַיִם *Pethor* (in) *Aram-naharaim*, home of Balaam, Dt 23$_5$. <PREP> הלך אֶל *go to* Gn 24$_{10}$; שׂכר מִן *hire* soldiers *from* 1 C 19$_6$ (+ Aram-maacah, Zobah); לחם בְּ ni. *fight against* 1QM 2$_{10}$; נצה אֶת hi. *struggle with* Ps 60$_2$ (+ Aram-zobah, Edom).

b. Aram-zobah—צוֹבָא, צוֹבָה—state in southern Syria north of Aram Beth-rehob, led by Hadadezer, defeated by David (2 S 10‖1 C 19) (see also צוֹבָה *Zobah*), <NOM CL> אֲרַם צוֹבָא ... לְבַדָּם בַּשָּׂדֶה (*the warriors of*) *Aram-zobah ... were on their own in the field* 2 S 10$_8$ (+ Aram Beth-rehob, Maacah). <OBJ> שׂכר *hire* (warriors of) 2 S 10$_6$ (+ Aram Beth-rehob, Maacah). <PREP> נצה אֶת hi. *struggle with* Ps 60$_2$ (+ Aram-naharaim, Edom).

c. Aram-Damascus, Aram of Damascus—דַּמֶּשֶׂק,

דַּרְמֶשֶׂק—successor to Aram-zobah as Aramaean state under Ben-Hadad II, Hazael, Ben-Hadad III and Rezin, <SUBJ> בוא *come* 2 S 8$_{5}$||1 C 18$_{5}$, עזר *help* 2 S 8$_{5}$||1 C 18$_{5}$ (obj. Hadadezer, king of Zobah). <PREP> שׂים בְּ *place* garrisons *in* 2 S 8$_{6}$||1 C 18$_{6}$ (+ אֱרָם, §3).

d. Aram-maacah, region in Golan (see also מַעֲכָה *Maacah*), <PREP> שׂכר מִן *hire from* 1 C 19$_{6}$ (+ Aram-naharaim, Zobah).

e. Aram Beth-rehob, home-territory of Hadadezer, who united it with neighbouring Aram Zobah (see also רְחוֹב *Rehob*), <OBJ> שׂכר *hire* people of 2 S 10$_{6}$ (+ Aram-zobah, Maacah).

f. Paddan-aram, Paddan of Aram, prob. ident. with Aram-naharaim, as Aram. equivalent of שְׂדֵה אֲרָם *field of Aram* (Ho 12$_{13}$), Laban's home in Mesopotamia, also פַּדָּן *Paddan* Gn 48$_{7}$, <PREP> בְּ of place, *in*, + רכשׁ *gain possession* Gn 31$_{18}$, ילד *give birth* 46$_{15}$, pu. *be born* 35$_{26}$; מִן of direction, *from* Gn 25$_{20}$, + בוא *come* 33$_{18}$ 35$_{9}$; with ה- of direction, פַּדֶּנָה אֲרָם *towards Paddan-aram* Gn 28$_{2.5.6.7}$; without prep or ה-, 4QPentPara 3.2$_{7}$ (פ[דן ארם).

3. Aramaeans, inhabitants of Mesopotamia and Syria, antagonists of Israel (and Judah), <SUBJ> (oft. with pl. verb) היה *be* 2 S 8$_{6}$ (+ לְדָוִד לַעֲבָדִים *to David as servants*; ||1 C 18$_{6}$ 4QSama לְדָוִד עֲבָדִים), עשׂה *do* 2 K 7$_{12}$, ראה *see* 2 S 10$_{15}$||1 C 19$_{16}$, ידע *know* 2 K 7$_{12}$, ירא *fear* 2 S 10$_{19}$, אבה *be willing* 1 C 19$_{19}$, אמר *say* 1 K 20$_{28}$, יעץ *counsel* Is 7$_{5}$, נתן *give* Ezk 27$_{16}$ (mss אֱדֹם *Edom*), שׁלך hi. *throw away* 2 K 7$_{15}$, בוא *come* 2 K 7$_{12}$, נחת *descend* 6$_{9}$ (if em.; see Nom. Cl.), חבא ni. *hide oneself* 26$_{9}$ (if em.; see Nom. Cl.), מלא pi. *fill* 1 K 20$_{27}$, סחר *trade with* Ezk 27$_{16}$, ישׁע hi. *rescue* 2 S 10$_{19}$||1 C 19$_{19}$, שׁלח *send* for help 1 C 19$_{16}$, יצא *come out* 2 K 5$_{2}$ 7$_{12}$, hi. *bring out* military assistance 1 C 19$_{16}$, אסף ni. *be grouped* 2 S 10$_{15}$, ערך *group for battle* 10$_{17}$, קרא *encounter* in battle 10$_{17}$, לחם ni. *fight* 10$_{17}$||1 C 19$_{17}$, תפשׂ *capture* 2 K 7$_{12}$, שׁבה *capture* 5$_{2}$, חזק *be strong* 2 S 10$_{11}$||1 C 19$_{12}$, עוה *act wickedly* against Y. Zc 9$_{1}$ (if em. עֵין אָדָם *eye of human beings* to עָווּ אֲרָם *the Aramaeans acted wickedly*), אכל *devour* Is 9$_{11}$, נוס *flee* from battle 2 S 10$_{13.14.18}$||1 C 19$_{14.15.18}$, נגף ni. *suffer defeat* 2 S 10$_{15}$||1 C 19$_{16}$.

<NOM CL> שָׁם אֲרָם נְחִתִּים *there the Aramaeans are descending* 2 K 6$_{9}$ (or em. נְחִתִּים to נֹחֲתִים *descending*, or נֶחְבָּאִים *hiding themselves*).

<OBJ> עלה hi. *lift* Am 9$_{7}$ (subj. Y.), פקד *muster* 1 K 20$_{26}$, קרא *encounter* in battle 2 S 10$_{9}$||1 C 19$_{10}$ 1 C 19$_{17}$, נכה hi. *defeat* 2 S 8$_{13}$ (mss אֱדוֹם *Edom*, as in 2 C 18$_{12}$) 1 K 20$_{29}$ 2 K 13$_{17.19.19}$, כלה pi. *destroy* 1 K 22$_{11}$||2 C 18$_{10}$, נגח pi. *gore* 1 K 22$_{11}$||2 C 18$_{10}$, I סוך pilp. *incite* Is 9$_{11}$. <CSTR> מַחֲנֵה אֲרָם *battle-camp of Aramaeans* 2 K 7$_{4.5.5.6.10.14}$ (מַחֲנֵה־) 7$_{16}$, שְׁאָר *remnant of* Is 17$_{3}$, גְּדוּדֵי *troops of* 2 K 6$_{23}$ 24$_{2}$ (or em. אֱדֹם *Edom*).

<APP> אֹיְבָיו ... אֲרָם מִקֶּדֶם וּפְלִשְׁתִּים מֵאָחוֹר *his enemies ... the Aramaeans from the east and the Philistines from the west* Is 9$_{11}$.

<PREP> בְּ *against* 2 S 10$_{13}$, + נכה hi. *inflict defeat* upon 1 K 20$_{21}$; הרג מִן *slay of* 2 S 10$_{18}$||1 C 19$_{18}$; נגשׁ לִפְנֵי *draw near before* 1 C 19$_{14}$; נֹכַח *facing* 1 K 22$_{35}$||2 C 18$_{34}$.

4. ancestor of Aramaeans, son of Shem, Gn 10$_{22.23}$ 1 C 1$_{17}$. **5.** great-nephew of Abraham, Gn 22$_{21}$. **6.** son of Shemer, descendant of Asher, 1 C 7$_{34}$.

→ אֲרַמִּי *Aramaean*, אֲרָמִית *in Aramaic*.

אַרְמוֹן 32.0.1 n.m. **fortress**—cstr. אַרְמוֹן; pl. אַרְמְנוֹת; cstr. אַרְמְנוֹת; sf. אַרְמְנוֹתַיִךְ, אַרְמְנֹתָיו, אַרְמְנוֹתֶיהָ, אַרְמְנֹתֶיהָ (Q ארמונתיה), אַרְמְנוֹתֵיהֶם, אַרְמְנֹתֵינוּ—**fortress, fortification,** oft. of defences of Jerusalem, <SUBJ> ישׁב *dwell* Jr 30$_{18}$ (+ עַל־מִשְׁפָּטוֹ *in its proper place*, עִיר *city*), בזז ni. *be plundered* Am 3$_{11}$ (|| עֹז *strength*), נטשׁ pu. *be abandoned* Is 32$_{14}$ (+ הֲמוֹן עִיר *multitude of a city*).

<NOM CL> כל ארמונתיה ... כעקרה *all her fortresses ... are as an infertile woman* 4QapLama 2$_{6}$(Allegro).

<OBJ> שׂים *place*, i.e. cause (city) to be Is 25$_{2}$, שׂנא *hate* Am 6$_{8}$, ערר po. *lay bare* Is 23$_{13}$ (|| בַּחוּן *siege tower*), שׁחת hi. *destroy* Jr 6$_{5}$, שׂרף *burn* 2 C 36$_{19}$ (|| חוֹמָה *wall*, בַּיִת *house* of God), אכל *devour* Jr 17$_{27}$ 49$_{27}$ (+ חוֹמָה) Ho 8$_{14}$ (+ עִיר *city*) Am 1$_{4.7.10}$ (both + חוֹמָה) 1$_{12.14}$ (+ חוֹמָה) 2$_{2.5}$, בלע pi. *swallow up* Lm 2$_{5}$ (|| מִבְצָר *fortification*), פסג pi. *pass (through)* Ps 48$_{14}$ (or em. פִּקְדוּ *visit*; + חֵיל *rampart*).

<CSTR> אַרְמוֹן בֵּית־הַמֶּלֶךְ *fortress of the house of the king*, i.e. palace citadel 1 K 16$_{18}$ 2 K 15$_{25}$(Qr), זָרִים *of strangers* Is 25$_{2}$ (mss זֵדִים *of insolent ones*), אַרְמְנוֹת

יְרוּשָׁלַםִ *fortresses of Jerusalem* Jr 17$_{27}$ Am 2$_5$, בָּצְרָה *of Bozrah* 1$_{12}$, הַקְּרִיּוֹת *of Kirioth* 2$_2$ (or em. אַרְמְנֹתֶיהָ *her fortresses*), בֶּן־הֲדַד *of Ben-hadad* Jr 49$_{27}$ Am 1$_4$.

בְּרִיחַ אַרְמוֹן *bar of fortress* Pr 18$_{19}$, חוֹמֹת אַרְמְנוֹתֶיהָ *walls of her fortresses* Lm 2$_7$ (or em. חֶמְדַּת אֹצְרוֹתֶיהָ *delight of her treasures*), כָּל־אַרְמְנוֹתֶיהָ *all her fortresses* 2$_5$ (or em. אַרְמְנוֹתָו *his fortresses*) 2 C 36$_{19}$ 4QapLam^a 2$_6$ (ארמונתיה).

<PREP> בְּ of place, *in, into, among*, + היה *be* (of peace) Ps 122$_7$ (|| חֵיל *rampart*), ידע ni. *be known* (of Y.) 48$_4$, אצר *store up* violence and robbery Am 3$_{10}$, בוא *come* (of death) Jr 9$_{20}$ (|| חַלּוֹן *window*), דרך *tread* (of Assyria) Mc 5$_4$ (|| אֶרֶץ *land*), נכה hi. *strike* Pekahiah *in* 2 K 15$_{25}$, ענה *dwell* (of jackals) Is 13$_{22}$ (if em. בְּאַלְמְנוֹתָיו [L] *among your widows* to בְּאַרְמְנוֹתֶיהָ; + הֵיכָל *palace*).

בוא אֶל *come to* 1 K 16$_{18}$.

שׁמע עַל hi. *proclaim to* Am 3$_9$ (+ בְּאַשְׁדּוֹד *in Ashdod*; or em. בְּאַשּׁוּר *in Assyria*) 3$_9$ (+ בְּאֶרֶץ מִצְרָיִם *in the land of Egypt*).

<COLL> וְעָלְתָה אַרְמְנֹתֶיהָ סִירִים *and thorns will grow up (in) her fortresses* Is 34$_{13}$ (+ מִבְצָר *fortification*).

<SYN> חֵיל *rampart*, מִבְצָר *fortification*, חוֹמָה *wall*.

→ אַרְמֹנִי *Armoni*.

אֲרַמִּי 13 gent. **Aramaean**—f. אֲרַמִּיָּה; pl. אֲרַמִּים (הָרַמִּים [= הָאֲרַמִּים])—**1.** as plur. noun, **Aramaeans,** <SUBJ> בוא *come* 2 K 16$_6$(Kt, mss) (Qr אֲדֹמִים *Edomites*), ישׁב *dwell* 16$_6$(Kt, mss), נכה hi. *strike* 8$_{28}$||2 C 22$_5$ (2 C הָרַמִּים) 2 K 8$_{29}$ (||2 C 22$_6$ lacks אֲרַמִּים) 9$_{15}$.

2. as sing. noun, a particular **Aramaean,** אֲרַמִּי אֹבֵד אָבִי *an Aramaean on the point of death was my father* Dt 26$_5$, לָבָן הָאֲרַמִּי *Laban the Aramaean* Gn 25$_{20}$ 31$_{20.24}$, בְּתוּאֵל הָאֲרַמִּי *Bethuel the Aramaean* 25$_{20}$ 28$_5$, נַעֲמָן הָאֲרַמִּי הַזֶּה *Naaman this Aramaean* 2 K 5$_{20}$.

3. as attributive adj., **Aramaean,** פִּילַגְשׁוֹ הָאֲרַמִּיָּה *his Aramaean concubine* 1 C 7$_{14}$.

→ אֲרָם *Aram*, אֲרָמִית *in Aramaic*.

אֲרָמִית 5 adv. **in Aramaic,** with verb, דבר pi. *speak* 2 K 18$_{26}$||Is 36$_{11}$ (:: יְהוּדִית *in Judaean*, i.e. Hebrew) Dn 2$_4$ (or em. וַיֹּאמְרוּ *and they said*), כתב pass. *be written* Ezr 4$_7$, תרגם pass. *be translated* appar. from Aramaic 4$_7$. <COLL> introduces text in Aramaic, Dn 2$_4$ (unless em.) Ezr 4$_7$.

→ אֲרָם *Aram*.

אַרְמֹנִי 1 pr.n.m. **Armoni,** son of Saul and Rizpah, 2 S 21$_8$.

→ אַרְמוֹן *fortress*.

אֲרָן 2 pr.n.m. **Aran,** Edomite, son of Dishan and brother of Uz, Gn 36$_{28}$||1 C 1$_{42}$.

אֹרֶן I 1 n.[m.] **laurel,** נָטַע אֹרֶן וְגֶשֶׁם יְגַדֵּל *he plants a laurel and the rain makes it grow* Is 44$_{14}$ (with shortened ן-; mss Kt אֶרֶז *cedar* ; + אֶרֶז, תִּרְזָה *holm*, אַלּוֹן *oak*).

אֹרֶן II 1 pr.n.m. **Oren,** son of Jerahmeel, 1 C 2$_{25}$.

אַרְנֶבֶת 2 n.f. **hare,** unclean animal, <SUBJ> עלה hi. *raise*, i.e. chew cud Lv 11$_6$||Dt 14$_7$ (+ שָׁפָן *rock badger*, גָּמָל *camel*), פרס hi. *split*, i.e. have bipartite foot Lv 11$_6$||Dt 14$_7$. <OBJ> אכל *chew* Lv 11$_6$||Dt 14$_7$.

אַרְנוֹן 25 pl.n. **Arnon**—אַרְנֹן—river forming boundary between Moab and Amorites (Nm 21$_{13}$ Jg 11$_{18}$), prob. Sēl el-Mōǧib that enters Dead Sea opposite En-gedi, esp. assoc. with Moab (Is 16$_2$ Jr 48$_{20}$), oft. in descr. of territorial borders.

<NOM CL> אַרְנוֹן גְּבוּל מוֹאָב *Arnon is the border of Moab* Nm 21$_{13}$=Jg 11$_{18}$. <CSTR> נַחַל אַרְנוֹן *river (of) Arnon* Dt 2$_{24.36}$ 3$_{8.12.16}$ 4$_{48}$ (all six אַרְנֹן) Jos 12$_{1.2}$ 13$_{9.16}$ 2 K 10$_{33}$ (אַרְנֹן), בָּמוֹת אַרְנֹן *high places of Arnon* Nm 21$_{28}$, גְּבוּל אַרְנֹן *border (consisting) of the Arnon* 22$_{36}$ (or del. גְּבוּל), עֵבֶר אַרְנוֹן *side of Arnon* 21$_{13}$ Jg 11$_{18}$, יְדֵי אַרְנוֹן *hands*, i.e. sides, *of Arnon* 11$_{26}$. <APP> הַנְּחָלִים אַרְנוֹן *the rivers* (that form) *Arnon* Nm 21$_{14}$ (or em. הַנְּחָלִים אַרְנוֹן *the rivers. Arnon*). <PREP> נגד בְּ hi. *tell in* Jr 48$_{20}$; מִן *from*, + ירשׁ *possess* land Nm 21$_{24}$ Jg 11$_{22}$, לקח *take* land; לקח עַד *take* land *unto Arnon* Nm 21$_{26}$. <COLL> מַעְבְּרֹת לְאַרְנוֹן *fords of Arnon* Is 16$_2$.

ארניה, see אֲרַוְנָה.

אַרְנָן 1 pr.n. **Arnan,** descendant of Zerubbabel, 1 C 321.

אַרְנֹן, see אַרְנוֹן.

אָרְנָן, see אֲרַוְנָה.

ארס, see ארשׁ.

[אַרְעִיבוֹת] n.f.pl. **juniper cedar,** ועץ זית והדס ודפנה [וא]רעיבו[ת בושם] *olive wood and myrtle, and laurel wood and juniper cedar and balsam* 4QJub[d] 1.27.

אַרְפַּד 6 pl.n. **Arpad**—אַרְפָּד—Aramaean city, perh. T. Erfād/T. Rif'at, 30 km N of Aleppo, alw. assoc. with Hamath, 2 K 1834||Is 3619 (+ אֱלֹהֵי) 2 K 1913||Is 3713 (+ מֶלֶךְ) Is 109 Jr 4923.

אַרְפַּכְשַׁד 9.0.1 pr.n.m. **Arpachshad**—אַרְפַּכְשָׁד—son of Shem and father of Shelah and others, Gn 1022.24||1 C 117.18 Gn 1110.11.12.13 1 C 124 1QM 211 (+ בני *sons of*).

[ארץ], see אֶרֶץ, §3b, Prep.

אֶרֶץ +2504.24.224.3 n.f. (sometimes m.) **land**—אֶרֶץ (כָּ/לָ/וָ/הָ/בָּאָרֶץ); + ה- of direction אַרְצָה (אָרְצָה); cstr. אֶרֶץ (אֶרֶץ); sf. אַרְצִי, אַרְצְךָ (אַרְצֶךָ, Q ארצכה), אַרְצֵךְ, אַרְצוֹ, אַרְצָהּ, אַרְצֵנוּ, אַרְצְכֶם (Q ארצכמה), אַרְצָם (Q ארצמה); pl. אֲרָצוֹת (אֲרָצֹת); cstr. אַרְצוֹת (אַרְצֹת); sf. אַרְצֹתָם, Q ארצותיכה.

1. land, territory, usu. as possessed by people, nation, or representative individual (e.g. 1 K 1013||2 C 912); also plots and estates of land (e.g. Gn 2315 Lv 199 Jos 81 1 K 1118), regions within country (e.g. Gn 4711 1 S 94.5 1 K 911) or world (e.g. Gn 1010 Zc 66.8); types of terrain (without emphasis on ownership, e.g. אֶרֶץ צִיָּה *land of dryness, parched land*; see also §3); inhabitants of land (e.g. 1 S 1425 279 2 S 1523 Is 3718 Ezk 1413 Ho 12).

הָאָרֶץ *the land* sometimes refers to Judah or the land of Israel (e.g. 1 K 419 918 2 K 327 1320 Is 6516; see also Gn 341), אֶרֶץ י׳ *Y.'s land* Ho 93, ארצכה *your* (Y.'s) *land* 1QM 1212 194, defined as כָּל־הָאָרֶץ ... הַגִּלְעָד עַד־דָּן *all the land ..., Gilead to Dan* Dt 341, כָּל־הָאָרֶץ הָהָר וְהַנֶּגֶב וְהַשְּׁפֵלָה וְהָאֲשֵׁדוֹת *all the land—the hill country, the Negeb, the Shephelah, and the slopes* Jos 1040.

<SUBJ> היה *be* Gn 4720 (+ לְ *to*) Ex 2329 Lv 2633 (both + שְׁמָמָה *desolation*) Nm 3412 Jos 149 (both + לְ) Jr 2538 (+ שַׁמָּה *desolation*) 4422 (+ חָרְבָּה *desolation*) Ezk 1220 1416 158 (all three + שְׁמָמָה) 3510 (+ לְ, || גּוֹי *nation*) Mc 713 (+ שְׁמָמָה) 4QapPs[b] 692 ([היתה]; + נִדָּה *defilement*), קרא ni. *be named* Dt 313, יכל *be able* Gn 367 Am 710.

מלא *be full* Lv 1929 Is 119 (perh. אֶרֶץ = *world*) Jr 2310 515 Ezk 723, ni. *be filled* Ex 17 2 K 320 Is 27.7.8 Ezk 99 (|| עִיר *city*), כול hi. *contain* Am 710, שׁקט *be peaceful* Jos 1415 Jg 311.30 531 828 1 C 440 2 C 1323 145 (+ וְאֵין־עִמּוֹ מִלְחָמָה *and he* [Asa] *had no war*).

שׁכן *dwell* quietly 4Q386–9 3.27 ([תש]כון), להה *faint* from famine Gn 4713.13 (Sam לאה *be weary*), באשׁ *stink* Ex 810, קיא *vomit* inhabitants Lv 1825.28 2022, אכל *devour* inhabitants Lv 2638 Nm 1332, ni. *be consumed* Zp 118, אבל *mourn* Is 339 Jr 124.11 2310, ספד *mourn* Zc 1212, אמל pulal *languish* Is 339, אבד *perish* Jr 911, שׁכל pi. *be unfruitful* 2 K 219.

ישׁב *be inhabited* Jr 176, ni. Ex 1635 Jr 68, נשׂא *sustain* Gn 367 Na 15, עשׂה *produce* Gn 4147, נתן *yield* Lv 2519 264.20, נוב pol. *yield* 11QBer 1.29, זוב *flow* Ex 38 (|| מָקוֹם *place*) 317 135 333 Lv 2024 (|| אֲדָמָה *land*) Nm 148 1613.14 Dt 63 119 (|| אֲדָמָה) 269 (|| מָקוֹם) 2615 (|| אֲדָמָה) 273 Jos 56 Jr 115 3222 Si 468 4QJub[a] 23 4QPsJos[a] 116 ([ארץ זבת]; all + חָלָב וּדְבָשׁ with *milk and honey*), רוה *be drenched* Is 347 4QapPs[b] 786 ([הא]רץ).

נתן ni. *be given* Ezk 1115 3324 (both + לְמוֹרָשָׁה *as a possession*) Jb 1519, pu. *be given* Nm 325 (+ לַאֲחֻזָּה *as a possession*), מכר ni. *be sold* Lv 2523, חלק ni. *be divided* Nm 2653 (or em. pi., *divide* land) 2655, עזב ni. *be abandoned* Lv 2643, נפל *fall* as lot Ezk 4714.

כבשׁ ni. *be conquered* Nm 3222.29 Jos 181, שׁדד pu. *be despoiled* Jr 420, עתם ni. perh. *be burned* Is 918 (1QIsa[a] נתעם; or em. נִתְּעָה *was led astray*), שׁמם *be devastated* CD 310, ni. Jr 1211 Ezk 307 3215 3634.35 Zc 714, ישׁם *be desolate* Ezk 197 CD 521, חטא *sin* Ezk 1413, זנה *be a prostitute* Lv 1929 Ho 12, חנף *be defiled* Jr 31 Ps 10638, טמא *be defiled* Lv 1825, בושׁ *feel shame* Jr 5147, שׁאר ni. *be left over* Jos $13_{1.2}$.

בוא *come* 1 S 14_{25} (ms עַם *people*), סבב *be transformed* Zc 14_{10}, שׁוב pulal *be restored* Ezk 38_8, טהר pu. *be cleansed* 22_{24} (or em. מטר ho. *be rained [upon]*) 4QapPs^{b} 69_6, שׁמע *hear* Jr 22_{29}, ברך pu. *be blessed* Dt 33_{13}, בכה *weep* 2 S 15_{23}; perh. אֶרֶץ = *soil*, רצה *enjoy, make up for* missed sabbaths, sin Lv $26_{34.43}$ 2 C 36_{21}, hi. *be compensated for* missed sabbaths Lv 26_{34}, שׁבת *observe sabbath* Lv 25_2 26_{34}.

<NOM CL> מָה הָאָרֶץ *what is the land* like? Nm $13_{19.20}$, מָה אַרְצֶךָ *what is your country?* Jon 1_8, זֹאת הָאָרֶץ *this is the land* Jos 13_2 Ezk 48_{29}, אַרְצְכֶם שְׁמָמָה *your land is a desolation* Is 1_7 (+ עִיר *city*), sim. 4QDibHam^{a} 1.5_3; with predicative adj., טוֹבָה/טוֹב *good* Nm 13_{19} 14_7 Jg 18_9, נְעֵמָה *pleasant* Gn 49_{15}, רַחֲבַת יָדַיִם *broad (of hands)* Jg 18_{10} 1C 4_{40}, שְׁלֵוָה *peaceful* 4_{40}, שְׁמֵנָה *fat, fertile* Nm 13_{20}, רָעָה *bad* 13_{19}, טְמֵאָה *unclean* Jos 22_{19}, רָזָה *lean*, i.e. unproductive Nm 13_{20}, חָרֵב *desolate* 4Q386–9 3.3_5 ([א]רצם), סְבִיב הָאָרֶץ *surrounding the land* Am 3_{11}, הָאֲרָצוֹת אֲשֶׁר סְבִיבוֹתֶיהָ *the lands that are around it* Ezk 5_6 (|| גּוֹי *nation*), sim. 5_5 2 C 17_{10}.

אֶרֶץ לֹא לָהֶם *a land that is not theirs* Gn 15_{13}, אַרְצִי לְפָנֶיךָ *my land is before you* 20_{15}, לִי הָאָרֶץ *the land is mine* Lv 25_{23}, לְמִי־אָרֶץ *whose land is it?* 2 S 3_{12}, כְּגַן־עֵדֶן הָאָרֶץ לְפָנָיו *as the Garden of Eden is the land before him* Jl 2_3, עוֹדֶנּוּ הָאָרֶץ לְפָנֵינוּ *while the land is still before us* 2 C 14_6.

<OBJ> נתן *give* Gn 12_7 $13_{15.17}$ $15_{7.18}$ 17_8 24_7 26_3 $28_{4.13}$ 35_{12} 48_4 (+ אֲחֻזָּה *as a possession*) Ex $6_{4.8}$ 12_{25} $13_{5.11}$ 32_{13} 33_1 23_{10} $25_{2.38}$ Lv 14_{34} (+ אֲחֻזָּה) Nm 13_2 14_8 15_2 $20_{12.24}$ 21_{34} (|| עַם *people*) 27_{12} $32_{7.9.29}$ (+ אֲחֻזָּה) 32_{33} 33_{53} 36_2 Dt $1_{25.35.36}$ $2_{12.19.24.29}$ 3_2 (|| עַם) $3_{18.20}$ $4_{1.21}$ (|| נַחֲלָה *inheritance*) 4_{38} 5_{31} $6_{10.23}$ 8_{10} $9_{6.23}$ 10_{11} $11_{17.31}$ 12_1 15_4 (+ נַחֲלָה) 15_7 16_{20} 17_{14}=11QT 56_{12} Dt 18_9=11QT 60_{16} Dt $19_{1.2.8.8.10.14}$ 24_4 (+ נַחֲלָה) $25_{15.19}$ 26_1 (+ נַחֲלָה) $26_{2.3.9}$ $27_{2.3}$ $28_{8.52}$ 29_7 31_7 $32_{49.52}$ 34_4 Jos $1_{6.11.13.14.15}$ $2_{9.14.24}$ 5_6 8_1 (|| עִיר, עַם *city*) 9_{24} 11_{23} (+ נַחֲלָה) 15_{19}=Jg 1_{15} Jos 18_3 21_{43} 22_4 23_{16} $24_{3.8.13}$ Jg 1_2 6_9 18_{10} (|| מָקוֹם *place*) 1 K $8_{36.48}$||2 C $6_{27.38}$ 1 K 11_{18} (|| לֶחֶם *food*) Jr 3_{19} 7_7 (|| מָקוֹם) 11_5 27_6 30_3 $32_{22.22}$ Ezk $20_{15.28.42}$ (|| אֲדָמָה *land*) $29_{19.20}$ 36_5 (+ לְמוֹרָשָׁה *as a possession*) 36_{28} 37_{25} 47_{14} Ps 105_{11}||1 C 16_{18} Ps 105_{32} 135_{12} 136_{21} (both + נַחֲלָה) Ne $9_{8.15.36}$ 2 C 20_7 11QT 51_{16} 11QT fr. 1_4 (+ נַחֲלָה) 4QpGen^{a} 2_8 4QJub^{a} 2_3 ([אתנה ארץ]) 4QPentPar^{b} 23.2_4 4Q464 7_3 ([הארץ]), *place*, i.e. cause to be $1_{8.21}$ 2_{31} (all three + לִפְנֵי *before*) Ezk 6_{14} 33_{28} (both + שְׁמָמָה *desolation*) Ne 9_{35} (+ לִפְנֵי).

שׁית *place*, i.e. cause to be Jr 2_{15} 50_3 (both + שַׁמָּה *devastation*), שׂים *place*, i.e. cause to be 4_7 18_{16} Zc 7_{14} (all + שַׁמָּה).

ירשׁ *take possesion (of)* Gn 15_7 28_4 Lv 20_{24} (|| אֲדָמָה *land*) Nm $21_{24.35}$ Dt 2_{31} $3_{12.18.20}$ $4_{1.5.14.22.26.47}$ 5_{31} $6_{1.18}$ =11QT 51_{16} Dt 7_1 8_1 $9_{4.5.6}$ 10_{11} 11_{8+6t} 12_1 15_4 16_{20} 17_{14} =11QT 56_{12} Dt $19_{2.14}$ 23_{21} 25_{19} 26_1 $30_{5.5.16}$ Jos $1_{11.11.15}$ 12_1 13_1 18_3 21_{43} 23_5 24_8 Jg 2_6 11_{21} 18_9 Is 14_{21} (+ תֵּבֵל *world*, perh. אֶרֶץ = *world*) 60_{21} Jr 30_3 Ezk 35_{10} Am 2_{10} Ps 25_{13} $37_{9.11.22.29.34}$ (perh. in all five אֶרֶץ = *world*) 44_4 Ezr 9_{11} Ne $9_{15.22.22.22.23.24}$ 1 C 28_8 CD 1_8 4Q386–9 2_3 ([את ארצם]), hi. *give possession (of)* Nm 33_{53}.

שׁבע ni. *vow* to give Gn 50_{24} Ex 13_5 Nm $14_{16.23}$ Dt 6_{18} 8_1 $31_{21.23}$ Jg 2_1 Jr 32_{22}, חלק *apportion* Jos 14_5, pi. *apportion* Nm 26_{53} (if em. תֵּחָלֵק *shall be divided*) 13_7 18_{10} 19_{51} 1 K 18_6 Ezk 47_{21} Jl 4_2, לקח *take* Dt 3_8 29_7 Jos $11_{16.23}$ Jg $11_{13.15.15}$, אחז ni. *take possession (of)* Jos 22_9.

נחל *inherit* Ex 23_{30} 32_{13} Nm $34_{17.18}$ Is 57_{13} 4Q416 1_{14}, hi. *give someone as a possession* Dt 3_{28} 19_3 Jos 1_6 1 C 28_8, htp. *share with one another* Nm 33_{54} 34_{13} Ezk 47_{13}, פלה hi. *set apart* Ex 8_{18}, נפל hi. *allot* Ezk 45_1 48_{29}, כתב *make inventory (of)* Jos $18_{4.6.8.8.9}$, משׁל *rule* Is 16_1, חנה *encamp (in)* 2 S 17_{26}, חמשׁ pi. *take a fifth part (of produce of)* Gn 41_{34}, מכר *sell* Ezk 30_{12}.

ידע *recognize* Nm 14_{31} (or em. וְיִרְעוּ *and they will tend flocks [in]*) Jr 15_{14} 16_{13} 17_4 Ezk 32_9, זכר *remember* Lv 26_{42}, חמד *desire* Ex 34_{24}, מאס *despise* Nm 14_{31}, ראה *see* Gn 13_{15} 49_{15} (|| מְנֻחָה *resting place*) Ex 10_5 Nm 13_{18} $14_{23.23}$ 27_{12} $32_{1.8.9}$ Dt 1_{35} 3_{25} (|| הַר *mountain*) 3_{28} 32_{52} Jos 2_1 Jg 18_9 Is 33_{17} Jr $22_{10.12}$ Ezk $12_{6.12.13}$, hi. *show* Gn 12_1 Jos 5_6.

רגל pi. *spy out* Gn 42_{30} Jos 6_{22} 7_2 14_7 Jg $18_{2.14.17}$ 1 C 19_3, תור *spy out* Nm $13_{16.21.25.32.32}$ $14_{6.7.34.38}$ Ezk 20_6, חפר *search* Dt 1_{22} Jos $2_{2.3}$, חקר *search* Jg 18_2 1C 19_3, דרשׁ *seek* Dt 11_{12}, סחר *ply* for trade Gn 34_{10} 43_{24}, ענשׁ *tax* 2 C 36_3, ערך hi. *tax* 2 K 23_{35}, סבב *go around* Gn 2_{11}

Nm 214, עבר *cross* Is 2310, בזא perh. *divide* 182.7.

מלא *fill* 1 K 2027 Ezk 817 3011, pi. *fill* Ps 8010 (mss ni. *be filled*) 1QM 1212 194 (both || נַחֲלָה), עזב *leave* 2 K 86 Jr 918 Ezk 812 (subj. Y.) Ru 211 4Q386–9 46.12 (in both, subj. Y.) 414, קום hi. *re-establish* Is 498, עמד hi. *maintain* Hb 36 (if em. וַיְמֹדֶד *and he measured* to וַיַּעֲמֵד) Pr 294, שׁקה hi. *drench* Ezk 326, רצה *favour* Ps 852, נצל hi. *save* 2 K 1833||Is 3618||2 C 3213 2 K 1835||Is 3620 (||2 C 3214 עַם *people*), טהר pi. *cleanse* Ezk 3912.16 2 C 348 (|| בַּיִת *temple*) 1QM 72, רפא *heal* 2 C 714.

נכה hi. *strike, conquer* Nm 324 1 S 279 Jos 1040 Is 114 (perh. אֶרֶץ = *world*) Ml 324, לכד *capture* Jos 1042, חרב hi. *devastate* Jg 1624 2 K 1917||Is 3718 1QSb 524 (perh. אֶרֶץ = *world*) 1QpHab 68, חרם hi. *exterminate* 2 K 1911||Is 3711, שׁחת pi. *destroy* Jos 2233 Jg 65 Is 1420 (|| עַם) Ezk 3011, hi. *destroy* 2 K 1825||Is 3610 Is 3610 Jr 3629 1QpHab 413 ([הא]רץ), שׁמד hi. *destroy* 4Q464 5.24, בקק po. *empty* Jr 512, שׁמם hi. *devastate* Lv 2632 Ezk 3012, אכל *devour* 2 C 713, כלה pi. *destroy* (of famine) Gn 4130.

הפך *overthrow* 1 C 193 (||2 S 103 עִיר *city*), הרס *overthrow* Pr 294, שׁטף *overwhelm* Jr 472 (|| עִיר), דושׁ *crush* 1QpHab 310 (perh. אֶרֶץ = *ground*), עכר *trouble* 1 S 1429, חנף hi. *defile* Jr 32.9, חלל *defile* Jr 1618, טמא pi. *defile* Nm 3534=11QT 4811 Jr 27, חטא hi. *cause to sin* Dt 244.

<CSTR> אֶרֶץ *the land of*, or אַרְצָה *to the land of* + pl.n. or pr.n., Ararat 2 K 1937||Is 3738, Assyria Is 718 2713 Ho 1111 Mc 55, Babylon Jr 5028 5129, Bashan 1 C 511, Benjamin Jg 2121 1 S 94.16 2 S 2114 Jr 11 1726 328.44 3313 3712, Cabul 1 K 913, Canaan Gn 1131 125.5 (all אַרְצָה) Gn 1312 163 178 232.19 3118 (אַרְצָה) 3318 356 365.6 371 425.7.13.29 (אַרְצָה) 4232 448 4517 (אַרְצָה) 4525 466.12.31 471.4.13.14.15 483.7 4930 505.13 (אַרְצָה) Ex 64 1635 Lv 1434 183 2538 Nm 132.17 2619 3230.32 (Seb אַרְצָה) 3340.51 342 (הָאָרֶץ כְּנַעַן) 342 (+ לִגְבֻלֹתֶיהָ *to* the full extent of *its boundaries*) 3429 3510 (אַרְצָה) 3514 Dt 3249 Jos 512 141 212 229.10.11.32 243 Jg 2112 Ezk 1629 174 Ps 10511||1 C 1618 4QpGen^a 210.13 ([א]רץ) 4QPsJos^b 125, Cush Gn 213, Damascus CD 65.19 821(A)=1934(B) 2012, Edom Gn 3616.17.21.31||1 C 143 Nm 2023 214 3337 Jg 1118 1 K 926 ||2 C 817 Is 346.

Egypt Gn 1310 2121 4119+15t 458 (|| בַּיִת *house*) 4518.19.20.26 4620 476+6t 485 507 Ex 420 (אַרְצָה) 512 613.26.28 73.4.19.21 81.2.3.12.13.20 99+6t 1012+6t 113.5.6.9 121+8t 1315.18 161.3.6.32 191 202 (|| בֵּית עֲבָדִים *house of slaves*) 2220 239 2946 321.4.7.8.11.23 331 Lv 1145 183 1934.36 2233 2343 2538.42.55 2613.45 Nm 11 313 817 91 142 1541 264 331.38 Dt 127 56 (|| בֵּית עֲבָדִים) 515 612 814 (both || בֵּית עֲבָדִים) 97 1019 1110 136=11QT 5416 Dt 1311 (both || בֵּית עֲבָדִים) 1515 163.3 201=11QT 6114 Dt 2422 291.15.24 3411, Jos 2417 (|| בֵּית עֲבָדִים) Jg 212 1930 1 S 126 278 1 K 61 89.21 99||2 C 722 1 K 1228 2 K 177.36 Is 1116 1918.19.20 2713 Jr 26 722.25 114.7 1614 237 248 3132 3220.21 3413 (|| בֵּית עֲבָדִים) 4214.16 437.11.12.13 441+11t 4613 Ezk 194 205.6.8.9.10.36 2319.27 299.10.12.19.20 3013.13.25 3215 Ho 217 716 115 1210 134 Am 210 31.9 97 Mc 64 (|| בֵּית עֲבָדִים) 715 Zc 1010 Ps 7812 816.11 Dn 915 1142 2 C 65 (||1 K 816 מִצְרַיִם *Egypt*) 2010 11QT fr. 12 ([מצר]ים) 1QDM 26(Milik) ([מצרים]) 4QPsJos^b 124 ([א]רץ).

Ephraim Dt 342 Jg 1215 (|| הַר *mountain*) 2 C 3010, Gad 1 S 137, Galilee 1 K 911, Gilead Nm 321.29 Jos 175.6 229.13.15.32 Jg 104 201 2 S 1726 2 K 1033 1 C 222 59, Goshen Gn 4510 4628 (אַרְצָה) 4634 471.4.6.27 508 Ex 818 926 Jos 1041 1116, Hadrach Zc 91, Ham Ps 10523.27 10622, Hamath 2 K 2333 2521||Jr 5227 Jr 395||529, Havilah Gn 211, Hepher 1 K 410.

Israel 1 S 1319 2 K 52.4 623 Ezk 2717 402 4718 (+ בֵּין *between*) 1 C 222 2 C 216 3025 (|| יִשְׂרָאֵל *Israel*) 347 11QT 586 4QMMT A 271, Jazer Nm 321, Jerusalem 4Q385 12, Jordan Ps 427, Judah Dt 342 1 S 225 3016 2 K 2324 2522 Is 261 Jr 3123 371 3910 4012 434.5 449.14.28 Am 712 Zc 24 Ru 17 Ne 514 1 C 640 2 C 911 158 172 CD 43 65 1QpZeph 15 ([א]רץ).

Magog Ezk 382, Merathaim Jr 5021, Midian Ex 215 Hb 37 (+ יְרִיעוֹת *pavilions of*), Mizpah Jos 113, Moab Dt 15 2869 3249 345.6 Jg 1115.18 Jr 4824.33, Moriah Gn 222, Naphtali Is 823 (אַרְצָה) 1 K 1520 2 K 1529, Pathros Jr 441 Ezk 2914, the Negeb Gn 201 (אַרְצָה) 2462 Nm 1329 Jos 1519||Jg 115, Nimrod Mc 55, Nod Gn 416, Og Dt 447 Ne 922.

Rameses Gn 4711, Rephaim Dt 220 313, Seir Gn 324 (|| שָׂדֶה *land*; אַרְצָה) 3630, Shaalim 1 S 94, Shalishah 94, Shinar Gn 1010 112 Zc 511 Dn 12, Shual 1 S 1317, Sihon

Dt 4_{46} 1 K 4_{19} Ne 9_{22}, Tob Jg $11_{3.5}$, Tahtim-hodshi 2 S 24_{6}, Tappuah Jos 17_{8}, Tema Is 21_{14}, Uz Jr 25_{20} Jb 1_{1} Lm 4_{21}, Zebulun Jg 12_{12} Is 8_{23} (אַרְצָה), Zuph 1 S 9_{5}.

+ gentilic, Amorites Ex 3_{17} 13_{5} Nm 21_{31} Jos 24_{8} Jg 10_{8} 11_{21} Ne 9_{8} Am 2_{10}, Canaanites Ex 3_{17} $13_{5.11}$ Dt 1_{7} 11_{30} Jos 13_{4} Ezk 16_{3} Ne 9_{8}, Chaldaeans Is 23_{13} Jr 24_{5} 25_{12} $50_{1.8.25.45}$ $51_{4.54}$ Ezk 1_{3} 12_{13}, Gadites 2 K 10_{33}, Gebalites Jos 13_{5}, Hebrews Gn 40_{15}, Hittites Jos 1_{4} Jg 1_{26}, Kittim Is 23_{1}, Perizzites Jos 17_{15}, Philistines Gn $21_{32.34}$ Ex 13_{17} 1 S 27_{1} 29_{11} 30_{16} 31_{9}‖1 C 10_{9} 1 K 5_{1}‖2 C 9_{26} 2 K $8_{2.3}$ Jr 25_{20} Zp 2_{5}, Sinim Is 49_{12}, Temanites Gn 36_{34}‖1 C 1_{45}.

אַרְצָה בְּנֵי־קֶדֶם *to the land of the people of the east* Gn 29_{1}, אֶרֶץ בְּנֵי עַמּוֹן *land of the Ammonites* Nm 22_{5} (if em. בְּנֵי־עַמּוֹ *his relatives*) Dt $2_{19.37}$ (בְּנֵי־) Jos 13_{25} Jg 11_{15} 2 S 10_{2}‖1 C 19_{2} (1 C בְּנֵי־) 1 C 20_{1} (בְּנֵי־), בְּנֵי יִשְׂרָאֵל *of (the) Israelites* Jos 11_{22}, מֶלֶךְ חֶשְׁבּוֹן *of (the) king of Heshbon* Ne 9_{22}, ארצות הגוים *lands of the gentiles* 1QM 2_{7}.

אֶרֶץ הַבְּרִית *land of,* i.e. that has entered, *the covenant* Ezk 30_{5}, הַכִּכָּר *of the Plain* Gn 19_{28}, הַמִּישֹׁר *of the Plateau* Dt 4_{43} Jr 48_{21}, הָעֵמֶק *of the Valley* Jos 17_{16} (אֶרֶץ־; in all four *of = that forms*), הַכַּרְמֶל *(full) of (the) farmland* Jr 2_{7}, הַצְּבִי *of (the) beauty*, i.e. beautiful Dn 11_{16} (אֶרֶץ־) 11_{41}.

אֶרֶץ עָנְיִי *land of my,* i.e. where I suffer, *affliction* Gn 41_{52}, הֲרִסֻתֵךְ *of your overthrow*, i.e. your devastated land Is 49_{19} (or em. הֲרַסְתִּיךְ *I overthrew you*).

אֶרֶץ פְּרִי *land (full) of fruit* Ps 107_{34}, מִקְנֶה *of,* i.e. fit for, *cattle* Nm 32_{4}, מִדְבָּר *(full) of desert* Dt 32_{10} (Sam הַמִּדְבָּר) Pr 21_{19} (אֶרֶץ־), מִישׁוֹר *of level place*, i.e. flat Ps 143_{10} (mss אֹרַח *way*, דֶּרֶךְ *way*), עֲרָבָה *(full) of desert* Jr 2_{6} (+ וְשׁוּחָה *and of pit*) 1QM 10_{13}, חֶמְדָּה *of desire* Jr 3_{19} Zc 7_{14} Ps 106_{24} GnzPs 1_{21} (א]רץ חמ[דה) 4QApocMos A 2.1_{4} (חמדות), חֵפֶץ *of delight* Ml 3_{12}, כָּבוֹד *of glory* 4QDibHam^{a} 8_{7}, מֶרְחָק *of distance*, i.e. distant Is 13_{5} 46_{11} Jr 4_{16} (הַמֶּרְחָק) 6_{20} 8_{19} (מַרְחַקִּים) Pr 25_{25}, צָפוֹן *of (the) north* Jr 3_{18} 6_{22} 10_{22} 23_{8} (צָפוֹנָה) 31_{8} 46_{10} 50_{9} Zc 2_{10} $6_{6.8.8}$ CD 7_{14}, מִזְרָח *of (the) east* Zc 8_{7}, מְבוֹא הַשֶּׁמֶשׁ *of the setting of the sun*, i.e. west 8_{7}, הַתֵּימָן *of the south* 6_{6}.

אֶרֶץ צַלְמָוֶת *land of gloom* Is 9_{1} Jr 2_{6} Jb 10_{21}, חֹשֶׁךְ *of darkness* Is 45_{19} Jb 10_{21}, עֵיפָתָה *of darkness* 10_{22}, מַאְפֵּלְיָה *of darkness* Jr 2_{31}, רְפָאִים *of shades* Is 26_{19}, נִדָּה *of impurity* Ezr 9_{11}, [ארץ ר]שעה *land of wickedness* 4QPsJos^{b} 2.2_{13}, פְּסִלִים *(full) of idols* Jr 50_{38}, צִיָּה *of dryness, drought* Is 41_{18} (‖ מִדְבָּר *desert*) 53_{2} Jr 2_{6} 51_{43} Ezk 19_{13} Ho 2_{5} (both ‖ מִדְבָּר) Jl 2_{20} Ps 63_{2} (אֶרֶץ־) 107_{35} 1QH 8_{4} 4QCat^{a} 12.1_{8} (+ שְׁמָמָה *of desolation*) 4QBer^{a} 2_{2} ([ציי[ה perh. *of beauty*), תַּלְאֻבוֹת *of droughts* Ho 13_{5}, מְלֵחָה *of saltiness* Jr 17_{6}, מוֹלֶדֶת *of (one's) birth* Gn 11_{28} (מוֹלַדְתּוֹ) 24_{7} 31_{13} (מוֹלַדְתֶּךָ) Jr 22_{10} (מוֹלַדְתּוֹ) 46_{16} (מוֹלַדְתֵּנוּ) Ezk 23_{15} (מוֹלַדְתָּם), מְכֻרָה *of origin* 21_{35} (‖ מָקוֹם *place*) 29_{14} (מְכוּרָה), אוֹיֵב *of an enemy* 1 K 8_{46} (הָאוֹיֵב) Jr 31_{16}, גְּזֵרָה *of separation*, i.e. inaccessible Lv 16_{22}, נְשִׁיָּה *of oblivion* Ps 88_{13}.

אֶרֶץ שִׁבְיִ *land of captivity* Jr 30_{10}=46_{27} 2 C 6_{37} (‖1 K 8_{47} שֹׁבֶה ptc. *captive*) 2 C 6_{38} 4QpsMos^{e} 1_{5} (שבים) 4Q385 1_{6} ([שבי[אם) 1_{8} ([ארן]ץ שבים) 4_{3} (ארצות שבים), שִׁבְיָה *of captivity* Ne 3_{36}, מֶמְשֶׁלֶת *of,* i.e. under the, *rule of* 1 K 9_{19}‖2 C 8_{6} Jr 34_{1} (perh. אֶרֶץ = *world*, as §2) 51_{28}, אֲחֻזָּה *of (one's) possession*, i.e. that one possesses Gn 36_{43} Lv 14_{34} (אֲחֻזַּתְכֶם) 25_{24} Nm 35_{28} (אֲחֻזָּתוֹ) Jos 22_{4} (אֲחֻזַּתְכֶם) 22_{9} (אֲחֻזָּתָם) 22_{19} (אֲחֻזַּתְכֶם).

אֶרֶץ צִלְצַל כְּנָפַיִם *land of the clashing of armies* Is 18_{1}, רַחֲבַת יָדַיִם *of breadth of hands*, i.e. broad 22_{18}, אַרְבַּע מֵאֹת שֶׁקֶל *of (value) 400 shekels* Gn 23_{15}, זֵית יִצְהָר וּדְבַשׁ *of olive oil and honey* 2 K 18_{32}, זֵית שֶׁמֶן וּדְבָשׁ *of olive oil and honey* Dt 8_{8} (אֶרֶץ־) 4QPsJos^{a} 11_{6} ([ארץ זית שמן ו]דבש), חִטָּה וּשְׂעֹרָה וְגֶפֶן וּתְאֵנָה וְרִמּוֹן *(full) of wheat and barley and vines and figs and pomegranates* 8_{8} 4QPsJos^{a} 11_{5} (חטה ושער]ה וגפן [ותאנה ורמון), צָרָה וְצוּקָה *of distress and hardship* Is 30_{6}, דָּגָן וְתִירוֹשׁ *of grain and wine* Dt 33_{28} 2 K 18_{32}‖Is 36_{17}, לֶחֶם וּכְרָמִים *of bread and vineyards* 2 K 18_{32}‖Is 36_{17}.

אֶרֶץ אָבוֹת *land of parents* Gn 31_{3} 48_{21} 11QT 59_{12}, מְגוּרִים *of sojournings* Gn 17_{8} 28_{4} (both מְגֻרֶיךָ) 37_{1} Ex 6_{4} (מְגֻרֵיהֶם) Ezk 20_{38}, נְכֹחוֹת *of uprightness* Is 26_{10}, חַיִּים *of (the) living*, or *of life* 38_{11} (הַחַיִּים) 53_{8} Jr 11_{19} Ezk 26_{20} 32_{23+6t} Ps 27_{13} 52_{7} 116_{9} (אַרְצוֹת הַחַיִּים *lands of*) 142_{6} Jb 28_{13} (both הַחַיִּים), תַּחְתִּיּוֹת *of lowest places*, i.e. Sheol Ezk 26_{20} $32_{18.24}$, נַחֲלֵי מַיִם *of watery streams* Dt 8_{7} (מָיִם) 10_{7} (מָיִם) 6QDeut(?) $1_{2(\text{Baillet})}$ ([נחל[י מים), הָרִים וּבְקָעֹת *(full) of mountains and valleys* Dt 11_{11}.

אֶרֶץ פְּרָזוֹת *land (full) of villages* Ezk 38_{11}, אֶרֶץ מוֹשְׁבֹתֵיכֶם *land of your dwelling-places* Nm 15_{2}, שְׁעָרָיו *of* its gates, perh. *any city in its land* 1 K 8$_{37}$||2 C 6$_{28}$, אֹיְבֵיהֶם *of their enemies* Lv 26$_{36.39(mss, Sam)}$ (both אַרְצֹת) 26$_{41.44}$ (Sam ארצות) 1 K 8$_{48}$ Ezk 39$_{27}$ (אַרְצוֹת) 11QT 59$_{5}$ (ארצות אויביהמה) 4QBark^{a} 2.1$_{12}$ ([באר]ץ), אֹיְבֵיכֶם *of your enemies* Lv 26$_{34.38}$.

בֵּית אֶרֶץ *house of the land of* Lv 14$_{34}$, חֲמַס־אֶרֶץ *violence of*, i.e. against, *(the) land* Hb 2$_{8=17}$ (|| אָדָם *human being[s]*), חֲצִי אֶרֶץ *half of (the) land of* Jos 13$_{25}$, פֶּשַׁע אֶרֶץ *sin of*, i.e. in, *a land* Pr 28$_{2}$ (or em. עָרִיץ *tyrant*), יִתְרוֹן אֶרֶץ *profit of a land* Ec 5$_{8}$, צְבִי אֶרֶץ *glory of (the) land* Ezk 25$_{9}$, קְצֵה אֶרֶץ *edge, border, of land (of)* Ex 16$_{35}$ Nm 33$_{37}$ Is 26$_{15}$ (קַצְוֵי־אָרֶץ) Jr 12$_{12}$ (קְצֵה־) 12$_{12}$ (הָאָרֶץ), נחלת ארצות *allocation of lands* 1QM 10$_{15}$.

עַם הָאָרֶץ *(common) people of the land* Gn 23$_{7}$ (עַם־) 23$_{12.13}$ 42$_{6}$ Ex 5$_{5}$ Lv 4$_{27}$ 20$_{2.4}$ Nm 14$_{9}$ 2 K 11$_{14}$||2 C 23$_{13}$ 2 K 11$_{18.19.20}$||2 C 23$_{20.21}$ (עַם־) 2 K 15$_{5}$||2 C 26$_{21}$ 2 K 16$_{15}$ 21$_{24}$||2 C 33$_{25}$ (עַם־) 2 K 23$_{30}$||2 C 36$_{1}$ (עַם־) 2 K 23$_{35}$ 24$_{14}$ (עַם־) 25$_{3.19.19}$||Jr 52$_{6.25.25}$ Jr 1$_{18}$ 34$_{19}$ 37$_{2}$ 44$_{21}$ Ezk 7$_{27}$ (עַם־) 12$_{19}$ 22$_{29}$ 33$_{2}$ (עַם־) 39$_{13}$ 45$_{16.22}$ 46$_{3.9}$ (עַם־) Hg 2$_{4}$ Zc 7$_{5}$ Jb 12$_{24}$ (עַם־; perh. אֶרֶץ = *world*) Dn 9$_{6}$ Ezr 4$_{4}$ (עַם־) Ne 9$_{10}$ (עַם אַרְצוֹ) Si 50$_{19}$.

יֹשֵׁב הָאָרֶץ *dweller(s) of*, i.e. in, *the land* Gn 34$_{30}$ 50$_{11}$ Nm 14$_{14}$ (both יוֹשֵׁב) Jos 24$_{18}$ Jg 11$_{21}$ (יוֹשֵׁב), נְשִׂיא *prince of* Gn 34$_{2}$, אֶזְרַח *native of* Ex 12$_{19.48}$ Nm 9$_{14}$, דַּלַּת *poor(est) of the land* 2 K 25$_{12}$||Jr 52$_{16}$ (דַּלּוֹת) Jr 40$_{7}$, אֲחֻזַּת *portion of the land* Lv 27$_{24}$, תְּרוּמַת *reserved portion of* Ezk 48$_{12}$, שְׂדֵה *field(s) of* Lv 25$_{31}$, זְהַב *gold of* Gn 2$_{12}$, פְּרִי *produce of* Nm 13$_{26}$ Dt 1$_{25}$ Is 4$_{2}$, יְבוּל *produce of* Jg 6$_{4}$, תְּבוּאַת *produce of* Lv 23$_{39}$ 4QPrFêtes^{b} 22$_{3}$ (ארצנו [תב]ואת) 4QPrFêtes^{c} 8$_{4(Baillet)}$ ([תבואת אר]צנו), לֶחֶם *bread of*, i.e. food grown in Nm 15$_{19}$, עֲבוּר *produce of* Jos 5$_{11.12}$, מַעְשַׂר *tithe of* Lv 27$_{30}$, טוּב *bounty of* Is 1$_{19}$ Ezr 9$_{12}$ (both טוּב־), זִמְרַת *choice produce of* Gn 43$_{11}$, רֵאשִׁית *first fruits of* Ezk 48$_{14}$, זֶרַע *seed of*, i.e. from 17$_{5}$, שַׁבַּת *sabbath of* Lv 25$_{6}$ 4QBer^{a} 1$_{11}$ (שבתות), קִיטֹר *smoke of*, i.e. rising from Gn 19$_{28}$, דִּבַּת *rumour of*, i.e. about Nm 13$_{32}$ 14$_{37}$ (דִּבַּת־).

עֵין הָאָרֶץ *eye*, i.e. surface, *of* Ex 10$_{5.15}$ (כָּל־הָאָרֶץ) Nm 22$_{5.11}$, פְּנֵי *face*, i.e. surface area, *of* Gn 19$_{28}$ (אֶרֶץ) Dt 11$_{25}$ 1 S 30$_{16}$ 2 S 18$_{8}$ Zc 5$_{3}$ (all four כָּל־הָאָרֶץ), גְּלוֹת *captivity of* Jg 18$_{30}$, שְׁבוּת *restoration of* Jr 33$_{11}$ (שְׁבוּת־), עֲוֹן *guilt of* Zc 3$_{9}$, עֶרְוַת *nakedness of* Gn 42$_{9.12}$, טַבּוּר *middle of* Jg 9$_{37}$, כִּבְרַת *distance of* Gn 35$_{16}$ (כִּבְרַת־) 2 K 5$_{19}$ (כִּבְרַת־אָרֶץ), חרבן הארץ *destruction of the land* CD 5$_{20}$ 4QpsMos^{e} 1$_{8}$, חובת הארץ *condemnation of the land* 4QpIsa^{c} 1.2$_{1}$, [יצ]הר הארץ *oil of the land* 11QT 22$_{16}$.

חמדת ארצם *desire*, i.e. thing desired, *of their land* 4QDibHam^{a} 1.4$_{11}$, דֶּרֶךְ אַרְצָם *way of*, i.e. to, *their land* Ex 13$_{17}$ (אֶרֶץ) 1 K 8$_{48}$||2 C 6$_{38}$, מְטַר־אַרְצְכֶם *rain of your land* Dt 11$_{14}$ (Sam, ms אַרְצְךָ) 28$_{12}$ (אַרְצְךָ) 28$_{24}$, קְצִיר אַרְצְכֶם *harvest of your land* Lv 19$_{9}$ 23$_{22}$, רֹחַב־אַרְצְךָ *breadth of your land* Is 8$_{8}$, גְּבוּל אַרְצְךָ *border of your land* Nm 20$_{23}$ (אֶרֶץ) Dt 19$_{3}$ Ezk 47$_{15}$ (הָאָרֶץ), עֵת אַרְצוֹ *appointed time of his country* Jr 27$_{7}$.

רִגְעֵי־אֶרֶץ *peaceful ones of a land* Ps 35$_{20}$, נֶאֶמְנֵי־אֶרֶץ *faithful ones of a land* 101$_{6}$, מַחֲשַׁכֵּי־אֶרֶץ *dark places of (the) land* 74$_{20}$.

אֱלֹהֵי הָאָרֶץ *god(s) of the land* Dt 31$_{16(ms)}$ 2 K 17$_{26.26.27}$ 18$_{35}$||Is 36$_{20}$ (הָאֲרָצוֹת; ||2 C 32$_{14}$ גּוֹיִם *nations*), אֱלֹהֵי נֵכַר־הָאָרֶץ *gods of foreignness*, i.e. foreign gods, *of the land* Dt 31$_{16}$.

מַלְכֵי הָאָרֶץ *kings of the land* Jos 12$_{1.7}$ 1 S 21$_{12}$ (מֶלֶךְ) Jr 25$_{20.20}$ (both אֶרֶץ) Ezr 9$_{7}$ (מַלְכֵי הָאֲרָצוֹת), פַּחוֹת *governors of* 1 K 10$_{15}$||2 C 9$_{14}$, אֵילֵי *chiefs of* 2 K 24$_{15(Qr)}$ Ezk 17$_{13}$, זִקְנֵי *elders of* 1 K 20$_{7}$ Jr 26$_{17}$ Pr 31$_{23}$ (זִקְנֵי־), אֲדֹנֵי *lord of* Gn 42$_{30.33}$, עַנְוֵי *poor of* Is 11$_{4}$ (עַנְוֵי־) Am 8$_{4}$ Zp 2$_{3}$ Jb 24$_{4}$ (עֲנִיֵּי־) 1QSb 5$_{22}$ ([ע]נוי [א]רץ), אַנְשֵׁי *men of* Lv 18$_{27}$ (אַנְשֵׁי־), בְּנוֹת *daughters of* Gn 27$_{46}$, מוֹשְׁבֵי *settlements of*, i.e. in Ezk 34$_{13}$, עָרֵי *cities of* Nm 32$_{33}$ Mc 5$_{10}$ (אַרְצֶךָ) 1QpHab 3$_{1}$, מַכּוֹת *afflictions of* Dt 29$_{21}$, כַּנְפוֹת four *corners of* Ezk 7$_{2}$, ידי הא[רץ ו]ה[ע]יר *the hands (of the people) of the land and the city* Lachish ost. 6$_{7(Torczyner)}$.

עַמֵּי הָאָרֶץ *(non-Israelite) peoples of the land* Est 8$_{17}$ Ezr 10$_{2.11}$ Ne 9$_{24}$ (עַמְמֵי) 10$_{31.32}$ 1 C 5$_{25}$ (עַמֵּי־) 4QapPs^{b} 69$_{1}$ ([הא]רץ), יֹשְׁבֵי *dwellers of*, i.e. in Gn 36$_{20}$ Ex 23$_{31}$ Nm 32$_{17}$ 33$_{52.55}$ Jos 2$_{9.24}$ 7$_{9}$ 9$_{11}$ (אַרְצֵנוּ) 9$_{24}$ 13$_{21}$ Jg 1$_{32.33}$ 2$_{2}$ (יוֹשְׁבֵי) Is 21$_{14}$ (אֶרֶץ) Jr 1$_{14}$ 6$_{12}$ 10$_{18}$ (יוֹשְׁבֵי) 13$_{13}$ Ho 4$_{1}$ Jl 1$_{2}$ (both יוֹשְׁבֵי) Jl 1$_{14}$ 2$_{1}$ Zp 1$_{18}$ Zc 11$_{6}$ Ne 9$_{24}$ 1 C 11$_{4}$ 22$_{18}$ 2 C 20$_{7}$ 1QpZeph 1$_{5(Milik)}$ ([יושבי] ארץ), גּוֹיֵ־ *(non-Israelite) nations of* Ezr 6$_{21}$, שַׁעֲרֵי אַרְצֵךְ *gates (of the cities) of your land* Na 3$_{13}$, מָעוּזֵּי אַרְצוֹ *fortresses of his land* Dn 11$_{19}$.

יוֹשְׁבֵי הָאֲרָצוֹת *dwellers of the lands* 2 C 15$_{5}$, גּוֹיֵי *nations of the (other) lands* 32$_{13.17}$, מַמְלְכוֹת *kingdoms of* 1 C 29$_{30}$ 2 C 12$_8$ 17$_{10}$ 20$_{29}$, מִשְׁפְּחוֹת *families of* Ezk 20$_{32}$, עַמֵּי *peoples of* Ezr 3$_3$ 9$_{1.2.11}$ Ne 9$_{30}$ 10$_{29}$ 2 C 13$_9$ 32$_{13}$ 1QM 10$_9$ 4QVisSam 3.2$_5$ (ארצותיכה) 1QH 4$_{26}$.

כָּל־הָאָרֶץ *all the land* Gn 13$_{9.15}$ Ex 10$_{15}$ 32$_{13}$ Dt 11$_{25}$ 19$_8$ 34$_1$ Jos 2$_{3.24}$ 6$_{27}$ 9$_{24}$ 10$_{40}$ 11$_{16.23}$ 21$_{43}$ 1 S 13$_3$ 14$_{25}$ 30$_{16}$ 2 S 15$_{23}$ 18$_8$ 24$_8$ 2 K 17$_5$ Is 7$_{24}$ 10$_{23}$ 28$_{22}$ Jr 1$_{18}$ 4$_{20.27}$ 8$_{16}$ 12$_{11}$ 15$_{10}$ 23$_{15}$ 25$_{11}$ 40$_4$ 45$_4$ Zp 1$_{18}$ Zc 5$_{3.6}$ 13$_8$ Zech 14$_{10}$ Jb 42$_{15}$ 4QapPs^b 69$_2$.

כָּל־אֶרֶץ *all the land of* Gn 2$_{11.13}$ 17$_8$ 41$_{19+7t}$ 45$_{8.20.26}$ Ex 5$_{12}$ 7$_{19.21}$ 8$_{12.13.20}$ 9$_{9.9.22.24.25}$ 10$_{14.15.22}$ 11$_6$ Lv 25$_{24}$ (כֹּל) Dt 34$_2$ Jos 1$_4$ (כֹּל) 10$_{41}$ 11$_{16}$ 13$_4$ 24$_3$ Jg 11$_{21}$ 1 S 13$_{19}$ (כֹּל) 1 K 4$_{10}$ (כֹּל) 9$_{19}$||2 C 8$_6$ (כֹּל) 1 K 15$_{20}$ 2 K 10$_{33}$ 15$_{29}$ (כֹּל) Jr 44$_{26}$ 51$_{28}$ 2 C 15$_8$ 34$_7$.

כָּל־הָאֲרָצוֹת *all the lands* Gn 26$_{3.4}$ (both הָאֲרָצֹת) 41$_{54}$ 2 K 19$_{11}$||Is 37$_{11}$ Is 37$_{18}$ Jr 16$_{15}$ 23$_{3.8}$ (all three כֹּל) 27$_6$ 32$_{37}$ 40$_{11}$ Ezk 20$_{6.15}$ 22$_4$ 36$_{24}$ Dn 9$_7$ 1 C 14$_{17}$ 22$_5$ 2 C 9$_{28}$ 11$_{23}$ (כָּל־אַרְצוֹת) 34$_{33}$ 1QM 11$_{13}$ (+ [או]יבי *enemies from*) 4QDibHam^a 1.5$_{12}$ 1.6$_{13(\text{Baillet})}$ ([כול]) 4QApoc MosA 2.1$_4$ (הרצות) 2.2$_5$ 4Q372 1$_5$.

כָּל־אַרְצוֹת *all the lands of* 1 C 13$_2$ 2 C 11$_{23}$ 1QM 2$_7$, כָּל־אַרְצְךָ *all your* (sg.) *land* Dt 28$_{52.52}$ 11QT 52$_3$, כָּל־אַרְצְכֶם *all your* (pl.) *land* Lv 25$_9$, כָּל־אַרְצוֹ *all his land* Nm 21$_{26}$ Dt 11$_3$ 29$_1$ 34$_{11}$, כָּל־אַרְצָהּ *all its land* Jr 51$_{47.52}$.

<ADJ> הָאָרֶץ הַזֹּאת *this land* Gn 12$_7$ 15$_{7.18}$ 24$_{5.7}$ 26$_3$ 31$_{13}$ 48$_4$ 50$_{24}$ Ex 32$_{13}$ Nm 14$_{3.8.14}$ 32$_{5.22}$ Dt 3$_{12.18}$ 4$_{22.22}$ 9$_{4.6}$ 26$_9$ Jos 11$_{16}$ 13$_7$ 17$_{12}$ Jg 1$_{27}$ 2$_2$ 1 K 9$_8$||2 C 7$_{21}$ (|| בַּיִת *house*) 2 K 18$_{25}$||Is 36$_{10}$ Is 36$_{10}$ (||2 K 18$_{25}$ מָקוֹם *place*) Jr 13$_{13}$ 14$_{15}$ 16$_{3.6.13}$ 22$_{12}$ 24$_6$ $_8$ 25$_{9.11}$ 26$_{20}$ (|| עִיר *city*) 32$_{15.22.41.43}$ 36$_{29}$ 37$_{19}$ 42$_{10.13}$ Ezk 47$_{14.21}$ 2 C 20$_7$ 30$_9$, הָאָרֶץ הַלֵּזוּ *this land* Ezk 36$_{35}$.

הָאָרֶץ הַהִיא *that land* Gn 2$_{12(Qr)}$ 10$_{11(Qr)}$ 26$_{12(Qr)}$ 35$_{22(Qr)}$ Ex 3$_{8(Qr)}$ Dt 29$_{21(Qr).26(Qr)}$ Jg 11$_{21}$ Jr 3$_1$ 25$_{13}$ Ezk 14$_{17.19}$ Zc 3$_9$, הָאֲרָצֹת הָאֵלֶּה *these lands* Is 36$_{20}$ Jr 27$_6$, var. Gn 26$_{3.4}$.

אֶרֶץ טוֹבָה *good land* Ex 3$_8$ Dt 1$_{35}$ 3$_{25}$ 4$_{21.22}$ 6$_{18}$ 8$_{7.10}$ 9$_6$ 11$_{17}$ Jos 23$_{16}$ 1 C 28$_8$ 4QPsJos^a 11$_4$, אֶרֶץ רְחָבָה *spacious land* Ex 3$_8$ Ne 9$_{35}$ 4QPsJos^a 11$_4$, אֶרֶץ שְׁמֵנָה *fat, rich land* 9$_{35}$ (perh. אֶרֶץ = *soil*), אֶרֶץ נוֹרָאָה *frightening land* Is 21$_1$, אֶרֶץ עֲיֵפָה *weary land* 32$_2$ (+ כְּצֵל סֶלַע־כָּבֵד בְּ *as the shadow of a large rock in/on*, perh. אֶרֶץ = *ground*) Ps 63$_2$ (עָיֵף) 143$_6$, אֶרֶץ רְחוֹקָה *distant land* Dt 29$_{21}$ Jos 9$_{6.9}$ 1 K 8$_{46}$||2 C 6$_{36}$ 2 K 20$_{14}$||Is 39$_3$ 2 C 6$_{36}$ 4QDibHam^a 1.6$_{13}$, אֶרֶץ קְרוֹבָה *nearby land* 1 K 8$_{46}$||2 C 6$_{36}$ 4QDibHam^a 1.6$_{13}$, אֶרֶץ תַּחְתִּית *lowest land*, i.e. Sheol Ezk 31$_{14.16.18}$, אֶרֶץ נָכְרִיָּה *foreign country* Ex 2$_{22}$ 18$_3$, אֶרֶץ אַחֶרֶת *another land* Dt 29$_{27}$ Jr 22$_{26}$, אֲרָצוֹת רַבּוֹת *many lands* Jr 28$_8$ 11QT 59$_2$ 1QpHab 6$_8$.

<PREP> לְ of benefit, *to, for* Gn 41$_{36}$ Jb 37$_{13}$ 1QS 9$_4$ (+ רָצוֹן *favour*), + עשׂה *do* Dt 2$_{12}$ 29$_{23}$ 31$_4$ 2 S 7$_{23}$ 1 K 9$_8$||2 C 7$_{21}$ (|| בַּיִת *temple*), קנא pi. *be jealous* Jl 2$_{18}$ (|| עַם *people*), עתר pi. *accept supplication* 2 S 21$_{14}$ 24$_{25}$, כפר pu. *be atoned* Nm 35$_{33}$ (perh. אֶרֶץ = *soil*), יתר hi. *leave* remnant CD 2$_{11}$, כְּטוֹב לְאַרְצוֹ *the better for his land* Ho 10$_1$.

לְ of possession, *(belonging) to*, Lv 25$_4$ (+ שַׁבָּת *sabbath*) 25$_5$ (+ שָׁנָה *year*), גְּבוּל קָדִימָה : לָאָרֶץ perh. *the eastern boundary of the land* Ezk 45$_8$, of direction, *(in)to*, + בוא *come* Jr 44$_{28}$ 4QPsJos^b 12$_5$, hi. *bring* 11QT 59$_{12}$, הלך *go* Gn 30$_{25}$ (|| מָקוֹם *place*) 1 K 10$_{13}$||2 C 9$_{12}$ Jr 51$_9$, שׁוב *go back* Gn 32$_{10}$ (|| מוֹלֶדֶת *place of birth*) Jos 1$_{15}$ 2 K 3$_{27}$ 19$_7$ Jr 37$_7$ Dn 11$_{28}$ 2 C 30$_9$ 32$_{21}$, hi. *return* trans. Jr 12$_{15}$ (|| נַחֲלָה *inheritance*), נוס *flee* 50$_{16}$, מלט ni. *escape* CD 7$_{14}$, נתן *give* Lv 25$_{24}$, קרא לְ ni. *be called* Is 62$_4$, מִזְרַח־שֶׁמֶשׁ לְאֶרֶץ *east of the land of* Jg 11$_{18}$.

בְּ of place, *in(to)* Gn 10$_{10}$ 12$_6$ 23$_{2.19}$ 33$_{18}$ 35$_6$ 36$_{16.17.21.30.31.43}$ 41$_{30.31.48.53}$ 42$_{13.32}$ 46$_{31}$ 47$_{1.11.11.14.14.28}$ 48$_3$ 49$_{30}$ 50$_5$ Ex 6$_{28}$ 7$_3$ 8$_{21}$ 9$_{5.22.22.26}$ 10$_{13}$ 11$_{3.9}$ 12$_{1.12.13.29}$ 13$_{15}$ 23$_{26}$ Lv 22$_{24}$ 25$_{7.10}$ 26$_{1.6.34.36.39.44}$ Nm 3$_{13}$ 8$_{17}$ 10$_9$ 18$_{13.20}$ 32$_{30}$ 34$_{29}$ 35$_{14}$ Dt 1$_5$ 4$_{14.17.43.46}$ 5$_{15.31.33}$ 6$_1$ 11$_{30}$ 12$_1$ 15$_{4.7}$ (+ שְׁעָרִים *gates*) 15$_{11.15}$ 19$_{14}$ 24$_{22}$ 25$_{19}$ 28$_{8.69}$ 29$_1$ 30$_{16}$ 32$_{10.49}$ 34$_{11}$ Jos 1$_{13.22}$ 14$_1$ 17$_{15}$ 21$_2$ 22$_{9.10}$ Jg 10$_{4.8}$ 18$_7$ 21$_{12}$ 1 S 23$_{23}$ 2 S 14$_{20}$ 21$_{14}$ 24$_{13}$||1 C 21$_{12}$ 1 K 4$_{19.19}$ 8$_{37.47.47.48}$||2 C 6$_{28.37.37.38}$ 1 K 9$_{11.18.26}$||2 C 8$_{17}$ 1 K 10$_6$||2 C 9$_5$ 1 K 14$_{24}$ 17$_7$ 2 K 15$_{20}$ 19$_7$||Is 37$_7$ 2 K 23$_{24.33}$ 25$_{21}$ Is 7$_{18}$ 14$_{25}$ (|| הָרִים *mountains*) 19$_{18.20}$ 26$_{1.10}$ 30$_6$ 34$_6$ 38$_{11}$ 42$_4$ 60$_{18}$ (|| גְּבוּלִים *borders*) 61$_7$ 65$_{16.16}$ Jr 1$_1$ 4$_5$ 5$_{19.19.30}$ 17$_4$ 23$_5$ 31$_{22.23}$ 32$_{8.15.20.43.44}$ 33$_{13.15}$ 39$_5$||52$_9$ 42$_{16}$ 43$_{13}$ 44$_{8.9.24.26.27}$ 46$_{10}$ 50$_{22.25}$ 51$_{4.46}$ Ezk 1$_3$ 20$_{5.40}$ 21$_{35}$ (|| מָקוֹם *place*) 23$_{19}$ 30$_{13}$ 31$_{16}$ 32$_{23.24.25.26.27.32}$ 37$_{22}$ Ho 4$_1$ 7$_{16}$ 13$_5$ Am 3$_9$ Zc 5$_{11}$ 6$_8$ 11$_{16}$ Ps 16$_3$ (+ קְדוֹשִׁים *holy ones*) 27$_{13}$ 41$_3$ 58$_3$ (perh. אֶרֶץ = *world*) 72$_{16}$ 74$_8$ 78$_{12}$ (|| שָׂדֶה *field*) 88$_{13}$ 105$_{27.32.35.36}$ 106$_{22}$ 112$_2$ 119$_{87}$ (perh.

אֶרֶץ = *world*) Jb 1$_{1}$ Dn 11$_{16}$ Ne 3$_{36}$ 5$_{14}$ 1 C 2$_{22}$ 6$_{40}$ 2 C 2$_{16}$ 9$_{11}$ 17$_{2}$ 32$_{31}$ GnzPs 1$_{21}$ ([באר]ץ) 11QT 51$_{19}$ 52$_{3}$ 59$_{5}$ 11QT fr. 1$_{6}$ ([בארצ]כמה) 11QJub 4$_{9}$ ([בא]רץ) 1QS 1$_{6}$ (perh. אֶרֶץ = *world*) 8$_{3}$ 4QTestim 1$_{28}$ 4QDibHam^{a} 1.5$_{3.12}$ 4QVisSam 3.2$_{5}$ (|| יָם *sea*) CD 6$_{19}$ 8$_{21(A)}$=19$_{34(B)}$ 20$_{12}$ 1QH 8$_{4}$ 4QAcademyFr. 1$_{4}$ 11QBer 1.2$_{10.13}$ 4Q386–9 4$_{3}$ 4QMMT A 2$_{71}$ 4Q372 1$_{5}$ 4QPsJos^{b} 2.22$_{13}$ ([בארץ]).

+ היה *be* 4Q464 3.2$_{3}$ ([יהיה ... בארץ]; + גֵּר *resident alien*), ישׁב *dwell* Gn 4$_{16}$ 13$_{7.12}$ 16$_{3}$ 24$_{37.62}$ 34$_{21}$ 37$_{1.1}$ 45$_{10}$ 46$_{34}$ 47$_{4.6.27.27}$ Ex 2$_{15}$ 23$_{33}$ Lv 26$_{5}$ Nm 13$_{28.29}$ 21$_{31}$ 33$_{40}$ 35$_{32}$ Dt 12$_{10.29}$ 29$_{15}$ Jos 1$_{14}$ 17$_{12.16}$ 24$_{15}$ Jg 1$_{27}$ 6$_{10}$ 11$_{3}$ 2 K 25$_{24}$||Jr 40$_{9}$ Is 9$_{1}$ Jr 24$_{8}$ 42$_{10.13}$ 43$_{4}$ 44$_{1.1.13.15.26}$ Ezk 36$_{28}$ Ho 9$_{3}$ Lm 4$_{21}$ 1 C 5$_{11.23}$ CD 13$_{21}$, hi. *settle* trans. Ezk 26$_{20}$, שׁכן *take up residence* Gn 26$_{2}$ 35$_{22}$ Ps 85$_{10}$, pi. *settle* trans. Jr 7$_{7}$ (|| מָקוֹם), גור *be resident alien* Gn 15$_{13}$ 21$_{23}$ 26$_{3}$ 47$_{4}$ Ex 2$_{22}$ 18$_{3}$ 22$_{20}$ 23$_{9}$ Lv 19$_{33.34}$ Dt 10$_{19}$ 23$_{8}$ 24$_{14}$ (+ שְׁעָרִים) Jr 14$_{8}$ 43$_{5}$ 44$_{12.14}$ Ps 105$_{23}$ 1 C 22$_{2}$ CD 6$_{5}$.

בוא *come* Jos 2$_{18}$ Jg 6$_{5}$ 1 S 9$_{5}$ 2 K 6$_{23}$ 13$_{20}$ Mc 5$_{4}$ (|| אַרְמְנוֹת *citadels*) 5$_{5}$ (|| גְּבוּל *border*) Dn 11$_{40.41}$, hi. *bring* Lv 26$_{41}$ 4QJub^{a} 2$_{2}$ ([אביאם באר]ץ), הלך *go* through 1 K 18$_{5}$, hi. *lead* through Jr 2$_{6.6.6}$, htp. *walk about* Gn 13$_{17}$ Jos 18$_{4.8}$ Ps 116$_{9}$ 4QDibHam^{a} 8$_{7}$, עבר *pass* through Ex 12$_{12}$ Lv 26$_{6}$ Nm 20$_{17}$ Dt 2$_{27}$ Jos 18$_{9}$ Jg 11$_{17.19}$ 1 S 9$_{4.4.4}$ Ezk 14$_{17}$ 39$_{14.15}$ 2 C 30$_{10}$, hi. *cause to pass* through Jr 15$_{14}$ (mss עבד hi. *cause to serve*) Ezk 14$_{15}$, שׁלח pi. *send* (messengers) through 1 S 31$_{9}$||1 C 10$_{9}$.

יתר ni. *be left* Jos 11$_{22}$ 1 K 9$_{21}$||2 C 8$_{8}$, שׁאר ni. *be left* 2 K 25$_{22}$ Jr 24$_{8}$ 40$_{6}$, hi. *leave* 39$_{10}$, עזב *leave* Gn 50$_{8}$, אבד *be lost* Is 27$_{13}$, שׁוט *wander* 2 S 24$_{8}$, בוך ni. *become confused, lost* Ex 14$_{3}$, נדח ni. *be banished* to Is 27$_{13}$, פרץ *spread out* intrans. Jb 1$_{10}$, זרה ni. *be scattered* throughout Ezk 6$_{8}$ 36$_{19}$ (both || גּוֹי *nation*), pi. *scatter* (trans.) throughout 12$_{15}$ 20$_{23}$ 22$_{15}$ 29$_{12}$ 30$_{23.26}$ Ps 106$_{27}$ (all || גּוֹי), פוץ hi. *scatter* (trans.) throughout Ezk 11$_{16}$ (|| גּוֹי), בזר pi. *scatter* (trans.) throughout 11QT 59$_{2}$, פזר pi. *scatter* (trans.) throughout 4QCat^{a} 12.1$_{8}$, טול ho. *be cast* 4Q372 1$_{10}$.

עשׂה *do* 4Q385 1$_{6}$ 4QPsJos^{b} 22.2$_{14}$ ([עשו]), רבה *multiply* Jr 3$_{16}$ 1 C 5$_{9}$, פרה *be fruitful* Gn 26$_{22}$ Jr 3$_{16}$, hi. *make fruitful* Gn 41$_{52}$, זרע *sow* 26$_{12}$ Ho 2$_{25}$ (in both perh. אֶרֶץ = *ground*), נטע *plant* people Jr 32$_{41}$ 4QApocMos A 2.1$_{4}$, רכשׁ *acquire property* Gn 36$_{6}$ 46$_{6}$, בנה *build* 4QPentPar^{b} 23.2$_{6}$, שׁמר *keep* covenant 4Q385 1$_{8}$ ([בארץ]), כון ni. *be established* Ps 140$_{12}$, ילד ni. *be born* Gn 46$_{20}$ 48$_{5}$ 1 C 7$_{21}$, pu. *be born* Gn 36$_{5}$, hi. *beget* Lv 25$_{45}$ Jr 16$_{3}$, גבר *grow old* 9$_{2}$, ישׁן *grow old* Dt 4$_{25}$, מות *die* Gn 11$_{28}$ 46$_{12}$ 48$_{7}$ Ex 11$_{5}$ 16$_{3}$ Nm 14$_{2}$ 26$_{19}$ Dt 4$_{22}$ 34$_{5}$ Jr 16$_{6}$, hi. *kill* 2 K 25$_{21}$||Jr 52$_{27}$, שׁחת hi. *destroy* 4QBark^{a} 2.1$_{12}$ ([בארץ]), קבר *bury* Dt 34$_{6}$, ni. *be buried* Jg 12$_{12.15}$.

רָעָב בָּאָרֶץ *famine in the land* Gn 12$_{10}$ 26$_{1}$ 41$_{36.56}$ 42$_{5}$ 43$_{1}$ 47$_{4}$ 2 S 24$_{13}$ 1 K 8$_{37}$||2 C 6$_{28}$ 2 K 4$_{38}$ Jr 14$_{15}$ Ezk 34$_{29}$ Am 8$_{11}$ Ru 1$_{1}$, חֵלֶק בָּאָרֶץ *share in the land, portion of territory* Jos 14$_{4}$ Ps 142$_{6}$ Jb 24$_{18}$ (חֶלְקָה).

בְּ of authority, *over*, + מלך *reign* Gn 36$_{31}$||1 C 1$_{43}$, hi. *appoint as king* Jr 37$_{1}$, פקד *appoint* governor 40$_{7}$ 41$_{2.18}$, עמד hi. *appoint* judge 2 C 19$_{5}$, שׂים *appoint* judge 2 S 15$_{4}$, *against* Zc 9$_{1}$ (+ דָּבָר *word*), + חרה אַף *become angry* Dt 29$_{26}$, לחם ni. *fight* Jg 11$_{12}$, שׁלח יָד *extend one's hand* Dn 11$_{42}$, עלה *go up* 2 K 17$_{5}$.

בטח בְּ *have confidence in* Jr 12$_{5}$, מאס בְּ *despise* Ps 106$_{24}$, עֵינֵיהֶם יָשִׁיתוּ לִנְטוֹת בָּאָרֶץ *they set their eyes to survey the land* 17$_{11}$, בְּאַרְצֹתָם perh. *according to their lands* in genealogical lists Gn 10$_{5.20.31}$ (all + גּוֹי *people*); בְּקֶרֶב *in* Gn 45$_{6}$ Ex 8$_{18}$ Dt 4$_{5}$ 19$_{10}$ Is 5$_{8}$ 6$_{12}$ 7$_{22}$ 1QDM 1$_{9}$ 4QpsMos^{e} 2.2$_{9}$; בְּתוֹךְ *in* Dt 19$_{2}$ Is 19$_{19}$ Ezk 20$_{8}$ 21$_{37}$ 2 C 32$_{4}$ 11QT 47$_{14}$ 48$_{13}$ 4QJub^{a} 2$_{10}$ ([בתוך]).

מִן partitive, *(some, any) of* Dt 2$_{5.9.19}$ (both + יְרֻשָּׁה as *an inheritance*) Ezk 45$_{1.4}$ (both + קֹדֶשׁ *sacred area*), of direction, *from*, 2 K 5$_{4}$ Is 46$_{11}$ Jr 8$_{19}$ 10$_{22}$ 30$_{10}$ 46$_{27}$ 51$_{54}$ Ezk 16$_{3}$ 30$_{13}$ Ho 11$_{11}$ 12$_{10}$ 13$_{4}$ Ps 42$_{7}$ Pr 25$_{25}$, + בוא *come* Gn 42$_{7}$ Dt 29$_{21}$ Jos 9$_{6.9}$ 1 K 8$_{41}$||2 C 6$_{32}$ 2 K 20$_{14}$||Is 39$_{3}$ Is 13$_{5}$ 21$_{1}$ 49$_{12}$ Jr 3$_{18}$ 4$_{16}$ 6$_{20.22}$ 17$_{26}$ 2 C 20$_{10}$ 30$_{25}$, hi. *bring* Dt 26$_{2}$ Jr 23$_{8}$ 31$_{8}$.

יצא *go out* Gn 10$_{11}$ 31$_{13}$ Ex 12$_{41}$ 16$_{1}$ 19$_{1}$ Nm 1$_{1}$ 9$_{1}$ 26$_{4}$ 33$_{1.38}$ Dt 9$_{7}$ 16$_{3}$ 1 K 6$_{1}$ 8$_{9.21}$ 2 K 24$_{7}$ Jr 7$_{25}$ 50$_{8}$ Ezk 21$_{24}$ 36$_{20}$ Mc 7$_{15}$ 4QPsJos^{b} 12$_{4}$ ([מאר]ץ), hi. *bring out* Ex 6$_{13.26}$ 7$_{4}$ 12$_{17.42.51}$ 16$_{6.32}$ 20$_{2}$ 29$_{46}$ 32$_{11}$ Lv 19$_{36}$ 22$_{33}$ 23$_{43}$ 25$_{38.42.55}$ 26$_{13.45}$ Nm 15$_{41}$ Dt 1$_{27}$ 5$_{6}$ 6$_{12}$ 8$_{14}$ 13$_{6}$=11QT 54$_{16}$ Dt 13$_{11}$ 29$_{24}$ Jg 2$_{12}$ 1 K 9$_{9}$||2 C 7$_{22}$ Jr 7$_{22}$ 11$_{4}$ 31$_{32}$ 32$_{21}$ 34$_{13}$ Ezk 20$_{6.9.10.38}$ (|| אֲדָמָה *land*) Dn 9$_{15}$ 2 C 6$_{5}$ 11QT fr. 1$_{2}$ CD 4$_{3}$ 6$_{5}$ 1QDM 2$_{6}$ ([צ]את[נו]).

שׁוּב *go back* Jos 22$_{32}$ 2 K 8$_3$ Jr 31$_{16}$ 44$_{28}$, hi. *take back* trans. Gn 44$_8$ Zc 10$_{10}$, עלה *go up* Ex 1$_{10}$ 13$_{18}$ Is 11$_{16}$ Ho 2$_{2.17}$ 4QpsMos^e 1$_5$, hi. *take up* Gn 50$_{24}$ Ex 3$_8$ 32$_{1.4.7.8.23}$ Lv 11$_{45}$ Nm 16$_{13}$ Dt 20$_1$=11QT 61$_{14}$ Jos 24$_{17}$ Jg 19$_{30}$ 1 S 12$_6$ 1 K 12$_{28}$ 2 K 17$_{7.36}$ Jr 2$_6$ 16$_{14.15}$ 23$_{7.8}$ 50$_9$ Am 2$_{10}$ 3$_1$ 9$_7$ Mc 6$_4$ Ps 81$_{11}$, ברח *flee* 2 S 19$_{10}$, נוס *flee* Jr 50$_{28}$ Zc 2$_{10}$, גרשׁ pi. *expel* Ex 6$_1$ Nm 22$_6$, נדח hi. *expel* 1QH 4$_8$, שׁלח *send* 1 S 9$_{16}$, pi. *expel* Ex 6$_1$ 7$_2$ 11$_{10}$ 12$_{33}$.

לקח *take* Gn 21$_{21}$ 22$_2$ 24$_7$ 45$_{19}$ Jg 11$_5$ 1 S 30$_{16.16}$, קבץ *collect* Ezk 20$_{34.41}$ 34$_{13}$ 39$_{27}$ (עַמִּים ‖ אֲרָצוֹת *peoples* in all four) Ps 107$_3$, אסף *gather* Ezk 11$_{17}$ (‖ עַם *people*), ni. *be gathered, removed* Jr 48$_{33}$, שׁבה *take captive* 2 K 5$_2$, ni. *be taken captive* 4Q385 1$_2$, גנב pu. *be stolen* Gn 40$_{15}$, ישׁע hi. *rescue* Zc 8$_{7.7}$, גלה ni. *be revealed* Is 23$_1$.

תמם *be exhausted* Gn 47$_{15.15}$, אפס *cease* Is 16$_4$, אבד *perish* Mc 7$_2$ Ps 10$_{16}$ Jb 18$_{17}$ (מִנִּי; + חוּץ *street*), pi. *destroy* Ps 21$_{11}$, hi. *destroy* Ezk 25$_7$, שׁמד hi. *destroy* 4Q372 1$_6$, שׁבת hi. *remove* Lv 26$_6$ Ezk 23$_{27.48}$ 34$_{25}$, עבר hi. *remove* 1 K 15$_{12}$ Zc 13$_2$, גזר ni. *be cut off* Is 53$_8$, כרת *cut off* Jr 11$_{19}$, ni. *be cut off* Pr 2$_{22}$, hi. *cut off* Jos 7$_9$ 1 S 28$_9$ Zc 13$_2$, בער pi. *destroy* 2 S 4$_{11}$ (perh. אֶרֶץ = *world*) 1 K 22$_{47}$ 2 C 19$_3$, שׁבר *break* Ho 2$_{20}$, נכא ni. *be whipped out* Jb 30$_8$, שׁרשׁ pi. *uproot* Ps 52$_7$, נסח *tear away* Pr 2$_{22}$ (or em. ni.), ni. *be torn away* Si 48$_{15}$, סתר pi. *hide* face CD 2$_8$, חֻשָׁם מֵאֶרֶץ הַתֵּימָנִי *Husham from, or, belonging to, the land of the Temanite(s)* Gn 36$_{34}$‖1 C 1$_{45}$ (חוּשָׁם), מרה מִן hi. *rebel more than* Ezk 5$_6$, לְבַד מִן *apart from, in addition to* Jos 17$_5$; מִקֶּרֶב הָאָרֶץ *from within the land* Dt 15$_{11}$; מִתּוֹךְ *from* ([מתוך הארץ]) 4QJub^a 2$_{15}$.

אֶל *against* Jr 28$_8$ (‖ מַמְלָכָה *kingdom*) Ezk 30$_{25}$ 38$_8$ Zc 2$_4$ 1 C 19$_2$, of direction, *(in)to* Ex 33$_3$ 1 K 22$_{36}$ Is 22$_{18}$, + בוא *come* Ex 12$_{25}$ 16$_{35}$ Lv 14$_{34}$ 19$_{23}$ 23$_{10}$ 25$_2$ Nm 13$_{27}$ 14$_{30}$ 20$_{24}$ 32$_9$ 34$_2$ Dt 4$_{21}$ 17$_{14}$=11QT 56$_{12}$ Dt 18$_9$=11QT 60$_{16}$ Dt 26$_{1.3}$ 27$_3$ 31$_7$ 32$_{52}$ 2 K 8$_1$ (subj. famine) Ne 9$_{23}$ Jos 22$_{15}$ 2 S 24$_6$ Jr 48$_{21}$ (subj. מִשְׁפָּט *judgment*) 11QT fr. 1$_4$ 4QPentPar^b 23.2$_4$, hi. *bring* Ex 6$_8$ 13$_{5.11}$ Nm 14$_{3.8.16.24}$ 16$_{14}$ (‖ נַחֲלָה *inheritance*) 20$_{12}$ Dt 6$_{10}$ 7$_1$ 8$_7$ 9$_{28}$ 11$_{29}$ 30$_5$ 31$_{21}$ (Sam אדמה *ground*) 31$_{23}$ Jos 24$_8$ Jg 2$_1$ Jr 2$_7$ Ezk 17$_4$ 19$_4$ 20$_{15.28.42}$ 40$_2$ Zc 10$_{10}$ Ne 9$_{23}$.

הלך *go* Gn 12$_1$ 22$_2$ 24$_4$ (‖ מוֹלֶדֶת *place of birth*) 24$_5$ 36$_6$ Ex 18$_{27}$ Nm 10$_{30}$ (‖ מוֹלֶדֶת) Jos 22$_{4.9.9}$ 1 K 11$_{21.22}$, שׁוּב *go back* Gn 21$_{32}$ 31$_{3.13}$ Nm 35$_{28}$ Jos 22$_{32}$ 1 S 29$_{11}$ Is 37$_7$ Jr 46$_{16}$ Ho 11$_5$ Jb 10$_{21}$ Ru 1$_7$, hi. *return* trans. Gn 24$_5$ 48$_{21}$ Jr 30$_3$, עלה *go up* Is 36$_{10}$, hi. *raise* Gn 50$_{24}$ Ex 3$_{8.17.17}$ 33$_1$, יצא *go out* Zc 6$_{6.6.8}$ 4QpGen^a 2$_{10}$ ([אל]) 2$_{13}$ ([אל ארץ]), hi. *bring out* Ezk 20$_6$, עבר *cross* Nm 32$_7$ 33$_{51}$ Dt 2$_{29}$ 27$_2$ Jos 1$_2$ 22$_{19}$, קרב *approach* Dt 23$_7$, ירד *go down* Ezk 32$_{24}$, hi. *bring down* 32$_{18}$, ho. *be brought down* 31$_{18}$, פנה *turn* intrans. 1 S 13$_{17}$.

נדח hi. *expel* Jl 2$_{20}$, מלט ni. *escape* 1 S 27$_1$, ברח *flee* Am 7$_{12}$, נוס *flee* Is 13$_{14}$, לקח *take* 2 K 18$_{32}$‖Is 36$_{17}$, שׁבה *take captive* 1 K 8$_{46}$‖2 C 6$_{36}$, רבה *multiply, extend* Ezk 16$_{29}$, נתן ni. *be handed over* 31$_{14}$, נשׂא *carry* Lv 16$_{22}$, שׁלח *send* Nm 13$_{27}$ Jos 22$_{13}$, pi. *send* Gn 25$_6$ Ezk 14$_{19}$, שׁלך hi. *cast* Dt 29$_{27}$, דבר אֶל pi. *speak about* Jr 50$_1$, פקד אֶל *punish* 50$_{18}$ (‖ מֶלֶךְ *king*), שׁכן אֶל *take up residence in* Dt 33$_{28}$, סחר אֶל *ply trade throughout* Jr 14$_{18}$ (or em. נִסְחֲבוּ *they were dragged*), חשׁב אֶל *calculate concerning* 50$_{45}$; בוא אֶל תּוֹךְ *come into the middle of* 11QT 58$_9$.

עַל of place/direction, *to* (sometimes perh. *against*) Ex 10$_{21}$, + בוא *come* 2 K 15$_{19}$ Jr 3$_{18}$ 37$_{19}$ Ezk 33$_3$ (obj. חֶרֶב *sword*), hi. *bring* Jr 25$_{9.13}$ Ezk 14$_{17}$ (obj. חֶרֶב) 33$_2$ (obj. חֶרֶב) 38$_{16}$, יצא *go out* across Gn 41$_{45}$ Ps 81$_6$, שׁוב *go back* Jr 22$_{27}$ 4QapPs^b 69$_6$, hi. *return* trans. 24$_6$ Ezk 29$_{14}$, שׁלך ho. *be cast* Jr 22$_{28}$, טול hi. *hurl* 22$_{26}$, *upon*, + עלה hi. *raise* Ex 8$_{1.3}$ 10$_{12}$, נתן *give* rain, etc. 1 K 8$_{36}$‖2 C 6$_{27}$ Ezk 32$_8$, *place*, i.e. impose tax 2 K 23$_{33}$ Est 10$_1$ (+ אִיֵּי הַיָּם *islands of the sea*), ירד hi. *send down* rain 11QBer 1.2$_7$, מטר *send rain, hail* Ex 9$_{23}$ Jb 38$_{26}$, נטה *stretch* (trans.) over Ex 10$_{12.13}$, *in* Dt 23$_{21}$, + ישׁב *live* Lv 25$_{18}$ Ezk 37$_{25}$, *against* Is 28$_{22}$ Jr 1$_{18}$, + עלה *go up* 2 K 18$_{25}$‖Is 36$_{10}$ Is 36$_{10}$ (‖2 K 18$_{25}$ מָקוֹם *place*) Jr 50$_{21}$ Ezk 38$_{11}$ Jl 1$_6$, פשׁט *raid* 1 S 23$_{27}$, צרר *be hostile* Nm 33$_{55}$, נבא ni. *prophesy* Jr 26$_{20}$ (‖ עִיר *city*), קרא *summon* Ps 105$_{16}$, פקד *take retribution* Jr 25$_{12}$, יצא hi. *send out* rumour Nm 14$_{36}$.

עַל of authority, *over* Gn 42$_6$ (+ שַׁלִּיט *ruler*), + מלך *reign* 2 K 11$_3$‖2 C 22$_{12}$, שׁית *place* governor Gn 41$_{33}$, פקד hi. *appoint* 41$_{34}$, ברך עַל pi. *bless* Y. *for* Dt 8$_{10}$, כפר עַל pi. *atone for* 4Q251 3$_9$ (ה[א]רץ); מֵעַל *away from, from off*, + עבד *perish* Dt 4$_{26}$ 11$_{17}$ Jos 23$_{16}$, טול hi. *cast* Jr 16$_{13}$, קלל hi. *lighten* hand 1 S 6$_5$ (‖ אֱלֹהִים *gods*).

כְּ *as* Ho 2$_5$, כְּאֶרֶץ מִצְרַיִם *as the land of Egypt* Gn 13$_{10}$ Dt 11$_{10}$ (both ‖ גַּן *garden*), אֶרֶץ כְּאַרְצְכֶם *a land like your land* 2 K 18_{32}||Is 36_{17}; עשׂה חֶסֶד עִם *show loyalty to* Gn 21_{23}; בְּעַד הָאָרֶץ *for, on behalf of the land* Ezk 22_{30} 1QDM 4_{1} ([א]ר[ץ]), + כפר pi. *atone* 1QS $8_{6.10}$.

<COLL> אֶרֶץ לֹא־אִישׁ *a land of no one, uninhabited land* Jb 38_{26}, יָרַדְתִּי הָאָרֶץ perh. *I went down to the* (underworld) *land* Jon 2_{7} (|| שַׁחַת *pit*), שְׁתֵּי הָאֲרָצוֹת *the two lands* Ezk 35_{10}, אֶרֶץ אֲשֶׁר אֲבָנֶיהָ בַרְזֶל *a land whose stones are iron* Dt 8_{9}, אֶרֶץ שֶׁמַּלְכֵּךְ *O land whose king (is)* Ec $10_{16.17}$, אִי־לָךְ אֶרֶץ *woe to you, O land* 10_{16}, אַשְׁרֵיךְ אֶרֶץ *happy are you, O land* 10_{17}, אֶרֶץ אֶרֶץ אָרֶץ *O land, land, land!* Jr 22_{29}.

2. earth, world, oft. + הַשָּׁמַיִם *heaven, the sky* (see Coll.); also with ref. to earth's inhabitants (e.g. Gn 9_{19} $11_{1.9}$ 41_{57} 1 S 17_{46} 1 K 10_{24} Ps 66_{4}).

<SUBJ> היה *be* Gn 1_{1} (+ תֹהוּ וָבֹהוּ *chaos*) Dt 28_{23} (+ אֲשֶׁר תַּחְתֶּיךָ *that is below you*) Jr 7_{34} (+ חָרְבָּה *desolation*), כלה pu. *be completed* Gn 2_{1}, ברא ni. *be created* 2_{4}, יבשׁ *be dry* after flood 8_{14}, פלג ni. *be divided* 10_{25}, נפץ *disperse* 9_{19}, מלא *be full* 6_{13} Jr 46_{12} Hb 3_{3} Ps 33_{5} 104_{24} 119_{64} 4QTNaph 4_{4}, ni. *be filled* Gn 6_{11} Nm 14_{21} Hb 2_{14}.

נוח *rest* Is 14_{7}, שׁקט *be quiet* 14_{7} Zc 1_{11} Ps 76_{9} 4QAcademyFr. 1_{4}, hi. *be quiet* Jb 37_{17}, בוא *come* Gn 41_{57}, ישׁב *sit, stay* Zc 1_{11}, עמד *stand, endure* Is 66_{22} Ec 1_{4}, יכל *be able* Pr 30_{21} (+ שְׂאֵת *to sustain itself*) 4QJub^{d} 1.2_{19} (+ ל[הטהר] *to be purified*), אור hi. *shine* Ezk 43_{2}, מור hi. *be changed* Ps 46_{3} (or em. מוג ni. *be melted* or מור II ni. *be shaken*), קום htpol. *arise* Jb 20_{27}.

בלע *swallow* Ex 15_{12} Nm $16_{32.34}$ 26_{10} Dt 11_{6} Ps 106_{17}, פתח *open up* Nm 16_{32} 26_{10} Is 45_{8} Ps 106_{17}, פצה *open* mouth Dt 11_{6}, כסה pi. *cover* Nm 16_{33} Ps 106_{17} Jb 16_{18}, רעשׁ *quake* Jg 5_{4} 2 S 22_{8}||Ps 18_{8} Is 13_{13} Jr 8_{16} (perh. אֶרֶץ = *land*) 10_{10} 49_{21} 51_{29} Jl 4_{16} Ps 68_{9} 77_{19} (|| תֵּבֵל *world*) 4QapPs^{b} 24_{10}, ni. *be shaken* Jr 50_{46}, געשׁ *quake* 2 S 22_{8}||Ps 18_{8}, רגז *quake* 1 S 14_{15} Jl 2_{10} Ps 77_{19} Pr 30_{21}, נוט *quake* Ps 99_{1} (|| עַמִּים *peoples*), נוע *move* intrans. Is 24_{20}.

בקע ni. *be split* 1 K 1_{40} Hb 3_{9} (if em. תְּבַקַּע *you split*), רעע htpo. *fall apart* Is 24_{19} 4QShir^{b} 3_{7}, פרר htpo. *be split asunder* Is 24_{19}, מוט ni. *be moved* Ps 104_{5}, htpol. *be shaken apart* Is 24_{19}, מוג *melt* Am 9_{5} Ps 46_{7}, ni. *melt* 75_{4}, רעד *quake* 104_{32}, הום ni. *reverberate* 1 S 4_{5}, חול *writhe, dance* Jr 51_{29} Ps 96_{9}||1 C 16_{30} Ps 97_{4} 114_{7} Si $43_{17(B)}$ 4QShir^{b} 37_{3} (ו[תח]ול ה[ארץ]), ho. *be born* Is 66_{8}.

ראה *see* Ps 97_{4}, שׁמע *hear* Dt 32_{21} Is 34_{1} (|| תֵּבֵל *world*) Jr 6_{19} 4Q521 1.2_{1}, אזן hi. *hear* Is 1_{2}, קשׁב hi. *listen* Mc 1_{2}, ענה *answer* Ho 2_{24}, ידע *know* 1 S 17_{46}, ירה hi. *teach* Jb 12_{8}, גלה pi. *reveal* Is 26_{21}, בקשׁ pi. *seek* 1 K 10_{24}, רוע hi. *shout* Ps 66_{1} 98_{4} 100_{1}, רנן pi. *shout* Jr 51_{48} Ps 98_{4}, זמר pi. *laud* 98_{4}, צרח *cry out* 1QH 3_{32}, הלל pi. *praise* Ps 69_{35} (|| יָם *sea*), פצח *burst out* in song Is 14_{7} Ps 98_{4}, שׁיר *sing* 96_{1}||1 C 16_{23}, שׂמח *rejoice* Ezk 35_{14}, גיל *rejoice* Is 49_{13} Ps 97_{1} (|| אִיִּים *islands*) 96_{11}||1 C 16_{31} (|| הָרִים *mountains*) perh. 4Q521 1.3_{4} (ה[אר]ץ).

ירא *fear* Ps 33_{8} 76_{9}, אבל *mourn* Is 24_{4} (|| תֵּבֵל) Jr 4_{28} Ho 4_{3} (perh. אֶרֶץ = *land*), שׁחה htp. *prostrate oneself* Ps 66_{4}, שׁחת ni. *corrupt oneself* Gn 6_{11}, חנף *be defiled* Is 24_{5}, אכל ni. *be consumed* Zp 3_{8}, נבל *wither* Is 24_{4}, בקק ni. *be emptied* 24_{3}, עזב ni. *be abandoned* Jb 18_{4}.

יצא hi. *yield* produce Gn $1_{12.24}$, דשׁא hi. *make sprout* 1_{11}, נתן *yield* produce Ezk 34_{27} Zc 8_{12} Ps 67_{7} 85_{13}, ni. *be given* Jb 9_{24}, כלא *withhold* produce Hg 1_{10}, שׂבע *be satisfied* Ps 104_{13} Pr 30_{16}, שׁרץ *swarm* with Ps 105_{30} (in all perh. אֶרֶץ = *ground, soil*).

<NOM CL> הָאָרֶץ הֲדֹם רַגְלָי *the earth is my footstool* Is 66_{1}, לִי כָּל־הָאָרֶץ *the whole world is mine* Ex 19_{5}, sim. Ps 89_{12} GnzPs 4_{3} (both || תֵּבֵל *world*), לַי׳ הָאָרֶץ *the world is Y.'s* Ex 9_{29} Dt 10_{14} Ps 24_{1}, שָׁמַיִם לָרוּם וָאָרֶץ לָעֹמֶק *heaven is for height and earth is for depth* Pr 25_{3}.

<OBJ> עשׂה *make* Gn 2_{4} Ex 20_{11} (|| יָם *sea*) 31_{17} 2 K 19_{15}||Is 37_{16} Is 45_{12} (|| אָדָם *humanity*) 66_{22} Jr 10_{12} (|| תֵּבֵל *world*) 27_{5} (|| אָדָם, בְּהֵמָה *animals*) 32_{17} 51_{15} Ps 115_{15} 121_{2} 124_{8} 134_{3} 146_{6} (|| יָם *sea*) Pr 8_{26} (|| חוּץ *open country*; perh. אֶרֶץ = *soil*) 2 C 2_{11} 11QPs^{a} 26_{14} (|| תֵּבֵל) 4QapPs^{b} 1_{3} 11QapPs^{a} 1_{11} ([עשה ... הארץ]) 2_{3}, ברא *create* Gn 1_{1} Is 65_{17} 1QM 10_{12} 1QH 1_{13} (|| יַמִּים *seas*, תְּהוֹמוֹת *abysses*) 4QpNah $1_{2(Allegro)}$ (ב[ראם]) 4QTanḥ 16_{2} (ה[ארץ] בר[א]) 4QJub^{a} 5_{4} ([ברא ... הארץ]), קנה *create* Gn $14_{19.22}$ Jerusalem ost. 1_{3} (קן ארץ), חול hi. *cause to writhe* Si $43_{17(Bmg, M)}$, pol. *give birth to* Ps 90_{2}, יצר *fashion* Is 45_{18}, רקע *spread out* 42_{5} 44_{24} Ps 136_{6}, מדד po. *measure* Hb 3_{6} (or em. עמד hi. *maintain*), תלה *hang* Jb 26_{7}.

יסד *establish* Is 48_{13} $51_{13.16}$ Zc 12_{1} Ps 78_{69} 102_{26} 104_{5} Jb 38_{4} Pr 3_{19}, כון pol. *establish* Ps 119_{90}, שׁוק pol. *richly endow* 65_{10}, רוה hi. *drench* Is 55_{10} (perh. אֶרֶץ = *soil*) Jr

46$_{8}$ (‖ עָרִים *cities*), נתן *give* Ps 115$_{16}$ (+ לִבְנֵי־אָדָם *to humans*), *place*, i.e. cause to be Lv 26$_{19}$ (+ כַּנְּחֻשָׁה *as copper*), שׂים *place*, i.e. cause to be Is 13$_{9}$ (+ שַׁמָּה *desolation*), רגע hi. *give rest to* Jr 50$_{34}$.

מלא *fill* Gn 9$_{1}$ Jr 23$_{24}$ 4QDibHam^{a} 8$_{14(mg, Baillet)}$ 4Q525 5.7$_{2}$ ([ארץ]) 4Q462$_{7}$ ([הארץ]; ‖ מַיִם *water*), כסה pi. *cover* Is 60$_{2}$ (subj. חֹשֶׁךְ *darkness*, ‖ לְאֻמִּים *nations*) Ezk 38$_{9}$ (subj. עָנָן *cloud*) Ps 104$_{9}$ (subj. מַיִם *water*) Si 47$_{15}$ (subj. Solomon and his repute) 1QM 12$_{9}$ (subj. עָב *cloud*) 19$_{2}$ (ל[כ]סות), בקק *empty* Is 24$_{1}$, ישׁב *inhabit* 24$_{6}$ 26$_{21}$ Jr 25$_{29.30}$ Ps 33$_{14}$ CD 10$_{9}$, שׁכן *inhabit* Is 18$_{3}$ (‖ תֵּבֵל) Pr 2$_{21}$ 10$_{30}$, דור *inhabit* Si 36$_{11}$ ([הא]רץ) 44$_{3}$, רדה *rule* 44$_{3(mg)}$, צעד *tread* Hb 3$_{12}$.

ראה *see* Jr 4$_{23}$, פקד *visit* Ps 65$_{10}$ CD 7$_{9}$=19$_{6}$ 4pIsa^{c} 1.2$_{2}$ (perh. אֶרֶץ = *land*), קרא *summon* Ps 50$_{1}$ (+ מִמִּזְרַח־שֶׁמֶשׁ עַד־מְבֹאוֹ *from the rising of the sun to its setting*), עוד hi. *call as witness* Dt 30$_{19}$, ענה *answer* Ho 2$_{23}$, שׁפט *judge* Gn 18$_{25}$ Is 40$_{23}$ Ps 2$_{10}$ 82$_{8}$ 94$_{2}$ 96$_{13}$‖1 C 16$_{33}$ Ps 98$_{9}$ (both ‖ תֵּבֵל) 148$_{11}$, דין *judge* 11QapPs^{a} 2$_{7}$ ([ידין]).

ערץ *terrify* Is 2$_{19.21}$, אסף *gather up* 10$_{14}$, אכל *consume* Dt 32$_{22}$ Is 24$_{6}$, חבל pi. *destroy* 13$_{5}$, שׁחת hi. *destroy* Gn 6$_{13}$ Jr 51$_{25}$, pi. *destroy* Gn 9$_{11}$, שׁכר hi. *inebriate* Jr 51$_{7}$, הפך *overthrow* Jb 12$_{15}$, רעשׁ hi. *shake* Hg 2$_{6.21}$ Ps 60$_{4}$, רגז hi. *shake* Is 14$_{16}$ (‖ מַמְלָכוֹת *kingdoms*) Jb 9$_{6}$, בקע pi. *split* Hb 3$_{9}$ (or em. תִּבָּקַע *be split*), כתת pi. *crush* Zc 11$_{6}$, חנף hi. *defile* 4QJub^{d} 1.2$_{19}$ ([מחניף ... הארץ]).

<CSTR> מֶגֶד אֶרֶץ *choice things of (the) earth* Dt 33$_{16}$, מְצֻקֵי *pillars of* 1 S 2$_{8}$ (+ וַיָּשֶׁת עֲלֵיהֶם תֵּבֵל *and he put the world on them*), מֶרְחֲבֵי *broad places of* Hb 1$_{6}$, עַנְוֵי־ *poor ones of* Ps 76$_{10}$, מָגִנֵּי־ *shields of* 47$_{10}$ (or em. סִגְנֵי *rulers of*), דִּשְׁנֵי־ *fat ones of* 22$_{30}$ (or em. יְשֵׁנֵי *sleeping ones of*), תנובת ארץ *produce of (the) earth* 1QLitPr^{b} 1.1$_{4}$.

אַפְסֵי־אָרֶץ *ends of (the) earth* Dt 33$_{17}$ (Sam הָאָרֶץ) 1 S 2$_{10}$ Is 45$_{22}$ 52$_{10}$ Jr 16$_{19}$ (both אָרֶץ) Mc 5$_{3}$ Zc 9$_{10}$ Ps 2$_{8}$ (all three אָרֶץ) 22$_{28}$ 59$_{14}$ (אַפְסֵי הָאָרֶץ) 67$_{8}$ 72$_{8}$ (both אָרֶץ) 98$_{3}$ Pr 30$_{4}$ Si 36$_{22}$ 44$_{21}$ GnzPs 1$_{16}$.

גְּבוּלוֹת אָרֶץ *boundaries of (the) earth* Ps 74$_{17}$, בָּמֳתֵי *high places of* Dt 32$_{13(Qr)}$ (אָרֶץ) Is 58$_{14(Qr)}$ Am 4$_{13}$ Mc 1$_{3(Qr)}$ (אָרֶץ) Si 46$_{9}$ 4Q386–9 4$_{12}$ ([ב]מתי א[רץ]; perh. אֶרֶץ = *land*), יֹעֲצֵי *counsellors (of the affairs) of* Jb 3$_{14}$, מֶרְחַקֵּי־ *distant places of* Is 8$_{9}$ Ps 95$_{4(ms)}$ (L מֶחְקְרֵי־ *depths of*; + הָרִים *mountains*), רַחֲבֵי־ *expanses of* Jb 38$_{18}$, קְטַנֵּי־ *small ones of* Pr 30$_{24}$.

מוֹסְדֵי אָרֶץ *foundations of (the) earth* Is 24$_{18}$ 40$_{21}$ (מוֹסְדוֹת הָאָרֶץ) Jr 31$_{37}$ (מוֹסְדֵי־אָרֶץ) Mc 6$_{2}$ (מֹסְדֵי אָרֶץ) Ps 82$_{5}$ Pr 8$_{29}$ 4QShir^{b} 1$_{12}$ 42$_{6}$ (הארץ) 4Q370 1$_{4}$ ([אר]ץ), תַּחְתִּיּוֹת *depths of* Is 44$_{23}$ (אָרֶץ) Ps 63$_{10(mss)}$ (L הָאָרֶץ) 139$_{15}$, עַתּוּדֵי *chiefs of* Is 14$_{9}$, אֲסִירֵי *prisoners of* Lm 3$_{34}$, נִכְבַּדֵּי־ *ones honoured of*, i.e. by Is 23$_{8.9}$, יַרְכְּתֵי־ *ends of* Jr 25$_{32}$ 50$_{41}$, קַדְמֵי־ *origins of* Pr 8$_{23}$.

חוּג הָאָרֶץ *vault of the earth* Is 40$_{22}$, טַבּוּר *centre of* Ezk 38$_{12}$, קְצֵה *end*, or *edge, of* Dt 13$_{8.8}$ 28$_{49.64.64}$ Is 5$_{26}$ 40$_{28}$ 41$_{5.9}$ (all three קְצוֹת) 42$_{10}$ 43$_{6}$ 48$_{20}$ 49$_{6}$ 62$_{11}$ Jr 10$_{13(Qr)}$ 25$_{31.33.33}$ 51$_{16}$ (קְצֵה־אָרֶץ) Ps 46$_{10}$ 48$_{11}$ (קַצְוֵי־אֶרֶץ) 61$_{3}$ 65$_{6}$ (קַצְוֵי־אֶרֶץ) 135$_{7}$ Jb 28$_{24}$ (קְצוֹת־) Pr 17$_{24}$ (קְצֵה־אָרֶץ), מְשׂוֹשׂ *joy of* Is 24$_{11}$ Ps 48$_{3}$ (כָּל־הָאָרֶץ), חַיַּת הָאָרֶץ *beasts of the world* Gn 1$_{24}$ (חַיְתוֹ־אֶרֶץ) 1$_{25}$ (‖ אֲדָמָה *earth*) 9$_{2.10.10}$ 1 S 17$_{46}$ Ezk 29$_{5}$ 32$_{4}$ (חַיַּת כָּל־; mss כָּל־חַיַּת) Ps 79$_{2}$ (חַיְתוֹ־אָרֶץ; all four + עוֹף הַשָּׁמַיִם *birds of the heavens*) Jb 5$_{22}$ 12$_{8}$ (if em. שִׂיחַ לָאָרֶץ *speak to the earth*) 4QJub^{a} 7$_{1}$ ([חי]ת הארץ), בֶּהֱמַת *beasts of* Dt 28$_{26}$ Is 18$_{6.6}$ Jr 7$_{33}$ 15$_{3}$ 16$_{4}$ 19$_{7}$ 34$_{20}$ Jb 35$_{11}$ (בַּהֲמוֹת אָרֶץ).

סרך הארץ *rule of the earth* CD 7$_{6(A)}$=1 9$_{3(B)}$, שרץ הארץ *swarming creatures of the earth* 11QT 50$_{20}$, ט]ל הארץ] *dew of the earth* 4QJub^{a} 6$_{2}$, מלוא ה[שמ]ים והארץ *fulness of the heaven and the earth* 1QH 16$_{3}$, תֵּבֵל אַרְצוֹ *world of his earth*, appar. *the entire world* Jb 37$_{12}$ (if em.; see Coll.) Pr 8$_{31}$.

פְּנֵי הָאָרֶץ *surface of the earth* (alw. + עַל *upon*, except at Si 38$_{8}$) Gn 1$_{29}$ 7$_{3}$ 8$_{9}$ 11$_{4.8}$ (all five פְּנֵי כָל־הָאָרֶץ) 11$_{9}$ (פְּנֵי כָּל־הָאָרֶץ) Nm 11$_{31}$ (mss פְּנֵי כָל־הָאָרֶץ) Jr 27$_{5}$ Ezk 39$_{14}$ Am 5$_{8}$=9$_{6}$ Jb 5$_{10}$ (‖ פְּנֵי־אָרֶץ, + חוּץ *outside*, i.e. open country; perh. אֶרֶץ = *soil*, as §3) Dn 8$_{5}$ (פְּנֵי כָל־הָאָרֶץ) Si 38$_{8(Bmg)}$ (פני ארצו or בני ארצו *sons of his world*; B בני אדם *human beings*) 4QJub^{a} 5$_{14}$ ([פני כל] הארץ) 4QapPs^{b} 46$_{4}$ ([פ]ני הארץ), כַּנְפוֹת *corners of* Is 11$_{12}$ 24$_{16}$ (כְּנַף) Jb 37$_{3}$ 38$_{13}$, יְמֵי *days of* Gn 8$_{22}$, תְּהֹמוֹת *depths of* Ps 71$_{20}$, אֲפִקֵי *channels of* Ezk 31$_{12}$, שְׁמַנֵּי *fat*, i.e. fertile *places, of* Gn 27$_{28.39}$.

אֱלֹהֵי הָאָרֶץ *God/gods of the earth* Gn 24$_{3}$ (וֵאלֹהֵי) Zp 2$_{11}$, מַלְכֵי *kings of* 1 K 5$_{14}$ 10$_{23}$‖2 C 9$_{22}$ Ezk 27$_{33}$ (מַלְכֵי־אָרֶץ) Ps 2$_{2}$ (מַלְכֵי־אֶרֶץ) 76$_{13}$ 89$_{28}$ (both מַלְכֵי־

(אֶרֶץ) 102$_{16}$ 138$_{4}$ (מַלְכֵי־אָֽרֶץ) 148$_{11}$ Lm 4$_{12}$ (both מַלְכֵי־אֶרֶץ; מַלְכֵי || תֵּבֵל world) 2 C 9$_{23}$ (||1 K 10$_{24}$ lacks מַלְכֵי) GnzPs 2$_{12}$ (מלכי ארץ; || תֵּבֵל), נְשִׂיאֵי, princes of Ezk 39$_{18}$, רִשְׁעֵי wicked ones of 7$_{21}$ Ps 75$_{9}$ (רִשְׁעֵי־אָֽרֶץ) 101$_{8}$ (רִשְׁעֵי־אָֽרֶץ; perh. אֶרֶץ = land, as §1).

מַמְלְכוֹת הָאָרֶץ kingdoms of the earth (except at Ps 68$_{33}$, alw. preceded by כָּל־/כֹּל all) Dt 28$_{25}$ 2 K 19$_{15.19}$ ||Is 37$_{16.20}$ Is 23$_{17}$ Jr 15$_{4}$ 24$_{9}$ 25$_{26}$ (הַמַּמְלְכוֹת הָאָרֶץ; or em. הַמַּמְלָכוֹת and del. הָאָרֶץ) 29$_{18}$ 34$_{1}$ (אֶרֶץ; perh. אֶרֶץ = land, as §1) 34$_{17}$ Ps 68$_{33}$ Ezr 1$_{2}$||2 C 36$_{23}$, גּוֹיֵי nations of (alw. preceded by כָּל־/כֹּל) Gn 18$_{18}$ 22$_{18}$ 26$_{4}$ Dt 28$_{1}$ (mss and Sam גּוֹי) Jr 26$_{6}$ 33$_{9}$ 44$_{8}$ Zc 12$_{3}$ 4QapPs^{b} 76$_{16}$ (גוי), עַמֵּי peoples of (except at 2 C 32$_{19}$, alw. preceded by כָּל־/כֹּל) Dt 28$_{10}$ Jos 4$_{24}$ 1 K 8$_{43}$||2 C 6$_{33}$ 1 K 8$_{53.60}$ Ezk 31$_{12}$ Zp 3$_{20}$ 2 C 32$_{19}$, מִשְׁפְּחוֹת families of Zc 14$_{17}$, שַׁעֲרֵי gates, i.e. cities, of Jr 15$_{7}$.

תקומי הארץ perh. powers of the earth GnzPs 3$_{17}$, דורות הארץ generations of the earth 4QJub^{f} 21$_{24}$ (דור[ות] [הארץ]) 4QJub^{d} 1.2$_{34}$, תּוֹלְדוֹת הַשָּׁמַיִם וְהָאָרֶץ generations of the heavens and the earth Gn 2$_{4}$, מעשי שמים וארץ works of heaven and earth 4QBark^{c} 3.

כָּל־הָאָרֶץ all the earth Gn 1$_{26.29}$ 7$_{3}$ 8$_{9}$ 9$_{19}$ 11$_{1.4.8.9}$ 18$_{25}$ 41$_{57}$ 47$_{13}$ Ex 9$_{14.16}$ 19$_{5}$ 34$_{10}$ (+ גּוֹיִם nations) Nm 14$_{21}$ 1 K 10$_{24}$ 2 K 5$_{15}$ Is 6$_{3}$ 10$_{14}$ 12$_{5}$ 13$_{5}$ 14$_{7.26}$ 25$_{8}$ Jr 51$_{7.25}$ Ezk 32$_{4}$ 35$_{14}$ Hb 2$_{20}$ Zp 3$_{8.19}$ Zc 1$_{11}$ 4$_{10}$ 14$_{9}$ Ps 8$_{2.10}$ 19$_{5}$ 33$_{8}$ (+ תֵּבֵל world) 45$_{17}$ 47$_{3}$ 48$_{3}$ 57$_{6.12}$ 66$_{1.4}$ 72$_{19}$ 83$_{19}$ 96$_{1.9}$||1 C 16$_{23.30}$ Ps 97$_{9}$ 98$_{4}$ 100$_{1}$ 105$_{7}$||1 C 16$_{14}$ Ps 108$_{6}$ Lm 2$_{15}$ Dn 8$_{5}$ 2 C 16$_{9}$ Si 48$_{15}$ GnzPs 1$_{9}$ 4QJub^{f} 21$_{22}$ 4QDibHam^{a} 1.3$_{10(Baillet)}$ ([כו]ל) 4$_{3}$ 4Q525 5.7$_{2}$ (כול [הארץ]) 4QJub^{a} 5$_{14}$ ([כ]ל) 7$_{3}$ ([כל הארץ]) 11QapPs^{a} 2$_{7}$ ([כו]ל) 2$_{8}$ ([כול האר]ץ) 3$_{3}$ 4QJub^{d} 1.2$_{34}$ ([כול הא]רץ).

דֶּרֶךְ כָּל־הָאָרֶץ way of, i.e. what occurs naturally in, all the world Gn 19$_{31}$ Jos 23$_{14}$ 1 K 2$_{2}$, אֲדוֹן כָּל־ lord of all Jos 3$_{11.13}$ (perh. אֶרֶץ = promised land, as §1) Mc 4$_{13}$ Zc 4$_{14}$ 6$_{5}$ Ps 97$_{5}$, תְּהִלַּת כָּל־ praise of all Jr 51$_{41}$, מֶלֶךְ כָּל־ king of all Ps 47$_{8}$ (mss מֶלֶךְ עַל king over, as Ps 47$_{3}$ Zc 14$_{9}$), פַּטִּישׁ כָּל־ hammer, i.e. conqueror, of all Jr 50$_{23}$, אֱלֹהֵי כָל־ God of all Is 54$_{5}$ Kh. Beit Lei graf. 5$_{1(Naveh)}$, חַלְלֵי כָל־ wounded of all Jr 51$_{49}$.

<ADJ> + אֶרֶץ חֲדָשָׁה new earth Is 65$_{17}$, sim. 66$_{22}$, אֶרֶץ רַבָּה wide world Ps 110$_{6}$.

<PREP> לְ of possession, (belonging) to, of Is 26$_{9}$ (+ מִשְׁפָּט judgment, || תֵּבֵל world), חשׁך לְ darken Am 8$_{9}$, נבט לְ pi. look at Is 5$_{30}$ (perh. אֶרֶץ = dry ground), hi. look at Ps 104$_{32}$, כון לְ hi. prepare rain for 147$_{8}$, שׂיח לְ speak to Jb 12$_{8}$ (or em. חַיַּת הָאָרֶץ beasts of the world), מַיִם מִתַּחַת לָאָרֶץ waters under the earth Ex 20$_{4}$||Dt 5$_{8}$ Dt 4$_{18}$; שׁוב אֶל go back to Si 40$_{11}$, נבט אֶל hi. look at Is 8$_{22}$ 51$_{6}$ (+ מִתַּחַת the earth below) Ps 102$_{20}$, קרא אֶל summon 50$_{4}$.

בְּ of place, in(to) Gn 2$_{5}$ 4$_{14}$ 6$_{4.5.6.17}$ Ex 20$_{4}$||Dt 5$_{8}$ Dt 4$_{17}$ Jr 9$_{23}$ Ps 46$_{9}$ 73$_{25}$ 113$_{6}$ 135$_{6}$ (|| יָם sea, תְּהוֹם depth) Ec 7$_{20}$ 1 C 29$_{11}$ Si 50$_{22}$ 11QJub 4$_{7}$ ([בא]רץ) 4QJub^{f} 21$_{24}$ (ב[אר]ץ) 4QDibHam^{a} 5.1$_{6}$ ([באר]ץ) 1QH fr. 2.1$_{3}$ fr. 13$_{3}$ ([באר]ץ) 4QpPs^{a} 1.2$_{7}$ 4QJub^{a} 6$_{9.13}$ (both [בא]רץ) 7$_{5}$, + שׁרץ swarm Gn 8$_{17}$ 9$_{7}$, הלך go Ps 73$_{9}$, htp. go about Zc 1$_{11}$ 6$_{7.7.7}$ Jb 1$_{7}$ 2$_{2}$, שׁוט roam 1$_{7}$ 2$_{2}$, pol. roam Zc 4$_{10}$ 2 C 16$_{9}$.

ילד ni. be born 4Q525 5$_{1}$ ([בארץ]), גור sojourn Ps 119$_{19}$, גבר become strong upon 1QNoah 1$_{2}$, רבה multiply Gn 1$_{22}$ 9$_{7}$, פרד ni. spread out 10$_{32}$, פוץ be scattered Si 48$_{15}$, קום hi. raise up 4QJub^{d} 1.2$_{30}$ ([הקים]), שׁפט judge Ps 58$_{12}$, ידע know 67$_{3}$ (|| גּוֹיִם nations), שׂים establish Jb 38$_{33}$, עשׂה make 4QJub^{a} 5$_{9}$ ([עשה באר]ץ) 11QapPs^{a} 2$_{4}$ (ע[שה ... ב]ארץ), נטע plant righteousness GnzPs 1$_{7}$ (טעתה; || עוֹלָם world), קבר ni. be buried 11QJub 4$_{29}$ ([יק]בר ב[ארץ]), שׁלם pu. be recompensed Pr 11$_{31}$, שׁבת keep sabbath 4QJub^{a} 7$_{9}$ ([לשבות ... בארץ]), שׁלט בְּ rule over 11QapPs^{a} 3$_{10}$ ([תשלט]), נגע בְּ touch Am 9$_{5}$ Dn 8$_{5}$ (perh. אֶרֶץ = ground).

נָע וָנָד בָּאָרֶץ a ceaseless wanderer in the world Gn 4$_{14}$, שְׂאוּ־נֵס בָּאָרֶץ raise a standard in the world! Jr 51$_{27}$ (|| גּוֹיִם nations), לְאֻמִּים בָּאָרֶץ nations in, i.e. of, the world Ps 67$_{5}$, הוּא הֵחֵל לִהְיוֹת גִּבֹּר בָּאָרֶץ he was the first person in the world to be a hero Gn 10$_{8}$||1 C 1$_{10}$, הַגְּדֹלִים אֲשֶׁר בָּאָרֶץ the heroes that are in the world 2 S 7$_{9}$||1 C 17$_{8}$, אִישׁ אֵין בָּאָרֶץ there is no one in the world Gn 19$_{31}$, שִׂים שְׁאֵרִית בָּאָרֶץ establish offspring in the world 45$_{7}$, אֵין־שָׁם מַחְסוֹר כָּל־דָּבָר אֲשֶׁר בָּאָרֶץ the place lacked nothing in the world Jg 18$_{10}$.

גּוֹי אֶחָד בָּאָרֶץ a unique nation in the world 2 S 7$_{23}$||1 C 17$_{21}$, תְּהִלָּה בָּאָרֶץ (object of) praise in the world Is 62$_{7}$, אֵין כָּמֹנִי בְּכָל־הָאָרֶץ there is none like me in all the world Ex 9$_{14}$, sim. Jb 2$_{3}$ 2 C 6$_{14}$, מִי־אֵל בַּשָּׁמַיִם וּבָאָרֶץ what

God is there in heaven or earth? Dt 3$_{24}$, sim. 1QM 10$_{8}$, אֵין אֱלֹהִים בְּכָל־הָאָרֶץ כִּי אִם־בְּיִשְׂרָאֵל *there is no God in all the world except in Israel* 2 K 5$_{15}$, אָרוּם בָּאָרֶץ *I shall be exalted in the world* Ps 46$_{11}$ (|| גּוֹיִם *nations*); בְּקֶרֶב *in* Gn 48$_{16}$ Is 19$_{24}$ 24$_{13}$ Ps 74$_{12}$, [להיותכה] לברכה [בכול הא]רץ *that you may be a blessing in all the earth* 4QJub^{d} 1.2$_{34}$.

מִן of place, *from*, + שׁבת *cease* (or hi., *make* seed *cease*) *from* Si 10$_{17}$, מחה ni. *be wiped out* Gn 7$_{23}$, כחד ni. *be wiped out* Ex 9$_{15}$, תמם *be destroyed* Ps 104$_{35}$, כרת hi. *cut off* Na 2$_{14}$ Ps 34$_{17}$ 109$_{15}$ 4QJub^{d} 1.2$_{6}$ (מהארץ), ni. *be cut off* Ps 109$_{15}$ (if em. יַכְרֵת *he will cut off* to יִכָּרֵת) Pr 2$_{22}$, אבד *perish* 4QJub^{f} 21$_{22}$, pi. *destroy* Ps 21$_{11}$ (|| בְּנֵי אָדָם *human beings*), כלה pi. *destroy* 1QpHab 13$_{4}$, אכל *consume* Pr 30$_{14}$ (|| אָדָם *humanity*), הלל pi. *(send) praise* Ps 148$_{7}$, יצא *come forth* Jb 28$_{5}$ (מִנִּי), צמח *grow* 4QJub^{a} 6$_{14}$ ([הצמח מהארץ]).

כל מארץ *everything (that proceeds) from the earth* Si 40$_{11}$, כִּי־גָבְהוּ שָׁמַיִם מֵאָרֶץ *for the heavens are higher than the earth* Is 55$_{9}$ (or em. כְּגֹבַהּ *as* the heavens *are higher*), אֲרֻכָּה מֵאֶרֶץ מִדָּהּ *its measure is longer than the world* Jb 11$_{9}$ (|| יָם *sea*), אֱנוֹשׁ מִן־הָאָרֶץ *person from the earth*, i.e. ungodly Ps 10$_{18}$, דשׁן מֵאֶרֶץ htp. *cause to grow fat by means of the earth* 1QH 10$_{26}$.

עַל *concerning* Is 14$_{26}$ (|| גּוֹיִם *nations*), of place/ direction *over, (up)on, to* Gn 7$_{6.10.12}$ 9$_{14.16.17}$ Lv 11$_{2}$ Dt 4$_{36.39}$ Jos 2$_{11}$ 1 K 8$_{23}$ (all three + מִתַּחַת the earth *below*; :: שָׁמַיִם *heaven/sky*) Ps 148$_{13}$ Ec 5$_{1}$ 8$_{14.16}$ 11$_{2}$ Ps 110$_{6}$ (עַל = *throughout*) Jb 7$_{1(Qr)}$ (+ אֱנוֹשׁ *human being*) 8$_{9}$ (both עֲלֵי) 1 C 29$_{15}$ 4Q483 1$_{2}$ ([ע]ל) 5Q185 1.1$_{13}$ (הא[רץ]; all three + יָמִים *days* on earth) 4QJub^{a} 6$_{7}$ 7$_{2}$ (both [על הארץ]) 11QapPs^{a} 2$_{3}$ ([על ה]ארץ), + היה *be* (of flood waters, rain) 4QpGen^{a} 1$_{3.6}$, בוא hi. *bring* flood Gn 6$_{17}$, שׁוב *go back* Ec 12$_{7}$, יצא *come out* (of sun) Gn 19$_{23}$ 4QPrQuot 35$_{1}$ (בצ[א]ת ... ה[ארץ]) 35$_{10(Baillet)}$ ([בצאת] ... ה[ארץ]), עבר *pass* over Is 54$_{9}$, hi. *cause to pass* Gn 8$_{1}$, שׂים *place* Jb 20$_{4}$ (עֲלֵי; + אָדָם *humanity*).

יצר ni. *be created* Si 49$_{14}$, דשׁא hi. *sprout vegetation* Gn 1$_{11}$, אור hi. *shine* on 1$_{15.17}$ 4QPrQuot 1$_{12}$ 10$_{1}$ 24$_{3}$ (Baillet) ([להאיר]) 29$_{7}$ ([להאיר ע]ל[הא] ר ץ) 48$_{7}$ ([להא]יר על [הא]רץ) 64$_{7(Baillet)}$ ([להאיר]) 4QJub^{a} 6$_{6}$ ([להאיר על הארץ]), עוף pol. *fly* Gn 1$_{20}$, גבה *be high* Ps 103$_{11}$, רמשׂ *creep* Gn 1$_{26.28.30}$ 7$_{14.21}$ 8$_{17.19}$ Lv 11$_{44}$ 4QJub^{a} 7$_{1}$ ([הרמש על הארץ]) 7$_{3}$ (ה[רומש על הארץ]), שׁרץ *swarm* Gn 7$_{21}$ Lv 11$_{29.41.42.46}$, מטר *send rain* Gn 2$_{5}$ 7$_{4}$, ריק hi. *pour out* (of clouds) Ec 11$_{3}$, פוץ *be scattered* (of winds) Jb 38$_{24}$ (עֲלֵי), שׁלח *send* sin 11QapPs^{a} 2$_{8}$ (ישׁ[ל]ח[ו] על [כול האר]ץ).

שׁחת hi. *behave destructively* Gn 6$_{12}$ 1QNoah 1$_{3(Milik)}$ ([השחית] ... על הארץ), נכה hi. *smite* 11QapPs^{a} 3$_{3}$ ([על הארץ]), ברא *create* humanity Dt 4$_{32}$, יסד *establish* God's home Am 9$_{6}$, ישׁב *dwell* (of Y.) 1 K 8$_{27}$||2 C 6$_{18}$, רבה *multiply* Gn 7$_{18}$ 8$_{17}$, גבר *become strong* 7$_{18.19.24}$, כִּימֵי הַשָּׁמַיִם עַל־הָאָרֶץ *as long as the heavens are above the earth* Dt 11$_{21}$, עֶלְיוֹן עַל־כָּל־הָאָרֶץ *the Most High over all the world* Ps 83$_{19}$ 97$_{9}$ (|| אֱלֹהִים *gods*), קרא עַל *summon* drought *against* Hg 1$_{11}$, גבר עַל *be strong against* 4QpGen^{a} 1$_{7}$ (ה[א]רץ).

מֵעַל *(from) above, on top of*, + רום *rise up* Gn 7$_{17}$ Ezk 10$_{16}$, נשׂא ni. *be raised up* (of heavenly creatures) 1$_{19.21}$, שׁוב *go back* (of flood) Gn 8$_{3}$, יבשׁ *dry up* (of flood) 8$_{7}$, חרב *dry up* (of flood) 8$_{13}$=4QpGen^{a} 1$_{21}$ ([מעל הארץ]), קלל *abate* (of flood) 8$_{11}$=4QpGen^{a} 1$_{18}$ ([קלו]), רדף *pursue* 11QapPs^{a} 3$_{3}$ (ר[דף ... מעל]).

בֵּינִי וּבֵין הָאָרֶץ *between me and the world* Gn 9$_{13}$, בֵּין הָאָרֶץ וּבֵין הַשָּׁמַיִם *between earth and heaven/the sky* Ezk 8$_{3}$ Zc 5$_{9}$ 1 C 21$_{16}$, sim. 2 S 18$_{9}$; עִם *with* 1QH 13$_{12}$ (|| יַמִּים *seas*, תְּהוֹמוֹת *abysses*); כְּ *as* Ps 78$_{69}$; כְּנֶגֶד *in front of* GnzPs 1$_{9}$.

<COLL> appar. with ה- of direction, מִי־פָקַד עָלָיו אָרְצָה *who gave him authority* extending even *to the earth?* Jb 34$_{13}$ (but perh. ה accusative, or em. אַרְצֹה [ms אַרְצוֹ] who assigned [to] him *his earth/the earth?*; || תֵּבֵל *world*), יְצַוֵּם עַל־פְּנֵי תֵבֵל אָרְצָה *he commands them on the face of (the world of) the earth* 37$_{12}$ (or em. אַרְצֹה *his earth*).

וַיִּקְרָא אֱלֹהִים לַיַּבָּשָׁה אֶרֶץ *and God called the dry (ground) earth* Gn 1$_{10}$, הָאָרֶץ מִתַּחַת *the earth/world below* Ex 20$_{4}$||Dt 5$_{8}$, יְשׁוּעֹת בַּל־נַעֲשֶׂה אֶרֶץ *we win no victory in the world* Is 26$_{18}$, אֶרֶץ וְתֵבֵל *earth and world*, perh. *the whole universe* Ps 90$_{2}$, תהום וארץ *abyss and earth* Si 16$_{18}$, הַס ... כָּל־הָאָרֶץ *Hush ..., all the world!* Hb 2$_{20}$.

שָׁמַיִם וָאָרֶץ *heaven and earth* Gn 2$_{1.4}$ (both הַשָּׁמַיִם וְהָאָרֶץ) 14$_{19.22}$ Jr 33$_{25}$ 51$_{48}$ Jl 4$_{16}$ Ps 69$_{35}$ 115$_{15}$ 121$_{2}$ 124$_{8}$

134$_{3}$ 146$_{6}$ 1QH 16$_{3}$ (השמים והארץ) 4QpNah 1$_{2}$ (שמיו וארצו *his heaven and his earth*) 4Q181 1$_{2(Allegro)}$ (ש[מים] וארץ) 4Q521 1.2$_{1}$ (הש[מים והארץ]) 4QBark^{c}$_{3}$ 4QapPs^{b} 1$_{3}$ 76$_{16}$ (שמ[ים וארץ]) 4Q372 1$_{30}$ ([השמים] והארץ), אֶרֶץ וְשָׁמַיִם *earth and heaven* Gn 2$_{4}$ Ps 148$_{13}$ 4QShir^{b} 37$_{(Baillet)}$ (שמי[ם וארץ]), אֶת־הַשָּׁמַיִם וְאֵת־הָאָרֶץ *the heaven and the earth* (as obj. of verbs) Gn 1$_{1}$ (אֵת) Ex 20$_{11}$ 31$_{17}$ Dt 4$_{26}$ 30$_{19}$ 31$_{28}$ 2 K 19$_{15}$||Is 37$_{16}$ Jr 23$_{24}$ 32$_{17}$ Hg 2$_{6.21}$ 2 C 2$_{11}$ 11QapPs^{a} 1$_{11}$ ([ואת הארץ]).

3. ground, soil, oft. difficult to distinguish §3a–b from §2 ('earth, world'; see, e.g., Dt 28$_{23}$ Ps 85$_{12}$ 104$_{14}$) and §1 ('land, territory'; see, e.g., Ps 52$_{7}$ Pr 2$_{22}$).

3a. ground, <OBJ> גמא pi. *swallow*, i.e. bound across (of horse) Jb 39$_{24}$.

<CSTR> אֶרֶץ מִישׁוֹר *ground of evenness*, i.e. level Ps 143$_{10}$ (mss אוֹרַח *path of*); עֲפַר הָאָרֶץ *dust of*, i.e. on, *the ground* (perh. *dust of the earth*, as §2) Gn 13$_{16.16}$ 28$_{14}$ Ex 8$_{12.13}$ 2 S 22$_{43}$ (עֲפַר־אֶרֶץ; + חוּצָה *outside*) Is 40$_{12}$ Am 2$_{7}$ (עֲפַר־אֶרֶץ) Jb 14$_{19}$ (עפר־אָרֶץ) 2 C 1$_{9}$ 4QShir^{b} 30$_{5}$ (הא[ר]ץ), חֵיק *bosom of*, i.e. trench in, Ezk 43$_{14}$, פַּח *trap of*, i.e. on, in, Am 3$_{5}$, זֹחֲלֵי אֶרֶץ *crawlers of*, i.e. beings that crawl on, *(the) ground* Mc 7$_{17}$, כושלי ארץ perh. *stumblers of*, i.e. on, *(the) ground* 1QH fr. 7.2$_{4(mg)}$.

<PREP> לְ of direction, *(right down) (in)to*, + ירד *go down* Ezk 26$_{11}$ Ec 3$_{21}$ (perh. אֶרֶץ = *world*), hi. *cast down* Is 63$_{6}$ Lm 2$_{10}$, נפל *fall* Ezk 38$_{20}$ Am 3$_{14}$, נטה *stretch* intrans. Jb 15$_{29}$, מגר pi. *hurl* Ps 89$_{45}$, שׁלך ho. *be cast down* Ezk 19$_{12}$, גדע ni. *be hewn down* Is 14$_{12}$, נגע hi. *cast down* Is 25$_{12}$ (|| עָפָר *dust*) Lm 2$_{2}$, נוח hi. *cast down* Is 28$_{2}$ Am 5$_{7}$, שׁפך *pour* Jb 16$_{13}$, ni. *be poured* Lm 2$_{11}$, רמס *trample* Ps 7$_{6}$ (|| עָפָר *dust*), שׁבר pi. *shatter* Is 21$_{9}$, דכא pi. *crush* Ps 143$_{3}$, צרף *refine* 12$_{7}$, חלל pi. *defile* 74$_{7}$ 89$_{40}$, קדר *mourn* Jr 14$_{2}$, דבק לְ *stick to* Ps 44$_{26}$ (|| עָפָר *dust*), ישׁב לְ *sit on* Is 3$_{26}$ 47$_{1}$ Jb 2$_{13}$ Lm 2$_{10}$, שׁכב לְ *lie on* 2$_{21}$, עזב לְ *leave on* Jb 39$_{14}$ (|| עָפָר).

בְּ of place, *in(to)* 1QH 8$_{23}$, + טמן pass. *be hidden* Jos 7$_{21}$ Jb 18$_{10}$, צנח *go down* (of tent-peg) Jg 4$_{21}$, טבע *sink* (of gates) Lm 2$_{9}$, מעך pass. *be pressed* 1 S 26$_{7}$, אַכֶּנּוּ נָא בַחֲנִית וּבָאָרֶץ *please let me strike him with the spear right into the ground* 1 S 26$_{8}$, שׁרשׁ po. *take root* Is 40$_{24}$, *on(to)*, + נטשׁ *leave* Ezk 32$_{4}$ (|| שָׂדֶה *field*), נחה hi. *lead* Ps 143$_{10}$ (mss אֹרַח *way*, דֶּרֶךְ *way*), בקע *split* 141$_{7}$, שׁפך *pour* Jl 4$_{19}$ 1QDM 4$_{2}$, אוֹפַן אֶחָד בָּאָרֶץ *one wheel on the ground* Ezk 1$_{15}$, נגע בְּ *touch* Dn 8$_{5}$; אבד בְּתוֹךְ *disappear into* 11QT 32$_{14}$.

מִן of place, *from*, + עלה *go up* Gn 2$_{6}$ (subj. water) 1 S 28$_{13}$ (subj. ghosts; in both perh. אֶרֶץ = *world*), נשׂא *raise* voice, i.e. speak (from grave) Si 46$_{20}$, רום hi. *raise* voice, i.e. speak (from grave) Si 51$_{9}$, יצא hi. *bring forth* Ps 104$_{14}$ Si 38$_{4}$ (in both perh. אֶרֶץ = *world*), קום hi. *raise* 2 S 12$_{17}$, נתר *leap* (of insect) 11QT 48$_{5}$, אסף *pick up* bundle Jr 10$_{17}$, סחה pi. *scrape away* Si 10$_{17}$, צמח *grow* Ps 85$_{12}$ (|| שָׁמַיִם, perh. אֶרֶץ = *world*) 4Q185 1.1$_{10}$; גובהמה מן ארץ *their height from the ground* 11QT 32$_{10}$.

עמד אֶל *stand on* dry land (perh. אֶרֶץ = *world*) 27$_{29}$, נגע אֶל *bring down to* Ezk 13$_{14}$; ירד אֶל תּוֹךְ *go down into* (of conduit) 11QT 32$_{13}$; עַל of place/direction, *on(to)* Ex 16$_{14}$ (+ כְּפוֹר *frost*) Dt 22$_{6}$ (|| עֵץ *tree*) Jg 6$_{37.39.40}$ (both + טַל *dew*) Ezk 28$_{18}$ (+ אֵפֶר *ash*), + שׁפך *pour* Dt 12$_{16}$=11QT 53$_{5}$ Dt 12$_{24}$ 15$_{23}$=11QT 52$_{12}$ Ezk 24$_{7}$ (+ עָפָר *dust*) 36$_{18}$ (perh. אֶרֶץ = *land*), נתר pi. *leap* (of insect) Lv 11$_{21}$, יצג hi. *set foot* Dt 28$_{56}$, הלך *walk* Ec 10$_{7}$, ישׁב *sit* Ezk 26$_{16}$, שׁלך hi. *cast* 28$_{17}$, שׁפל hi. *cast down* Is 26$_{5}$ (|| עָפָר) Ps 147$_{6}$ (עֲדֵי).

שרשם עד ארץ קעקע *he tears away their root, right down to the ground* Si 10$_{16}$; כְּאוֹב מֵאֶרֶץ *as a ghost from the ground* Is 29$_{4}$; וַתָּשִׂימִי כָאָרֶץ גֵּוֵךְ *and you have made your back like the ground* 51$_{23}$ (|| חוּץ *street*).

אַרְצָה *to/on the ground* (perh. *to the earth* at Gn 28$_{12}$ Ex 9$_{23.33}$ 1 S 3$_{19}$ 2 K 10$_{10}$ Ho 6$_{3}$ Ps 147$_{15}$ Lm 2$_{1}$ [all three אֶרֶץ] Dn 8$_{10}$), + שׁחה htpal. *bow down* Gn 18$_{2}$ 19$_{1}$ (+ אַף *[on one's] face*) 24$_{52}$ 33$_{3}$ 37$_{10}$ 38$_{9}$ 42$_{6}$ (+ אַף) 43$_{26}$ 48$_{12}$ (+ אַף) 1 S 25$_{23}$ (אֶרֶץ) 25$_{41}$ 2 S 14$_{33}$ 18$_{28}$ 24$_{20}$||1 C 21$_{21}$ 1 K 1$_{23}$ (all six + אַף) 2 K 2$_{15}$ 4$_{37}$ Is 49$_{23}$ (אֶרֶץ; + אַף) Ru 2$_{10}$ Ne 8$_{6}$ (+ אַף), קדד *bow down* Ex 34$_{8}$ 1 S 24$_{9}$ 28$_{14}$ 1 K 1$_{31}$ (אֶרֶץ) 2 C 20$_{18}$ (all four + אַף), כרע *bow* 7$_{3}$ (+ אַף), גהר *crouch* 1 K 18$_{42}$.

נפל *fall* Gn 44$_{14}$ (+ פָּנִים on one's *face*) Jos 5$_{14}$ 7$_{6}$ (both + פָּנִים) Jg 3$_{25}$ (of dead person) 13$_{20}$ (+ פָּנִים) 1 S 5$_{3.4}$ (of idol; both + פָּנִים) 14$_{45}$ (of hair) 17$_{49}$ (+ פָּנִים) 20$_{41}$ (+ אַף) 26$_{20}$ (of blood) 28$_{20}$ (+ מְלֹא־קוֹמָתוֹ *full-length*) 2 S 1$_{2}$ 14$_{4}$ (+ אַף) 14$_{11}$ (of hair) 14$_{22}$ (+ פָּנִים) 1 K 1$_{52}$ (of hair) 2 K 10$_{10}$ (of Y.'s word) Jb 1$_{20}$ Am 9$_{9}$ (of pebble; אֶרֶץ) 2 C 20$_{24}$ (of corpse) Si 50$_{17}$ (+ פָּנִים), hi.

cast down 1 S 3$_{19}$ (of Y.'s word) Dn 8$_{10}$ (of stars) Si 47$_{22}$ (of Y.'s word), הוא *fall* Jb 37$_{6}$ (of snow; אֶרֶץ).

שׁלח *send* Ps 147$_{15}$ (of Y.'s word; אֶרֶץ), שׁלך hi. *throw* Ex 4$_{3.3}$ (of rod) Lm 2$_{1}$ (of Zion; אֶרֶץ) Dn 8$_{7}$ (of ram) 8$_{12}$ (of truth), ירה *throw* Ho 6$_{3}$ (of rain; אֶרֶץ; or em. יַרְוֶה *he will drench*, as §3b), ירד hi. *put down* Gn 44$_{11}$ (of sack) Ob$_{3}$ (אֶרֶץ), הלך *go* Ex 9$_{23}$, נתן *turn* face Dn 10$_{15}$, נצב ho. *be set up* Gn 28$_{12}$ (of ladder), שׁכב *lie* 2 S 12$_{16}$ 13$_{31}$, hi. *lay* captive 2 S 8$_{2}$, רדם ni. *fall asleep* Dn 8$_{18}$ 10$_{9}$ (both + פָּנִים), שׁפך *pour out* blood, viscera 2 S 20$_{10}$ 1 C 22$_{8}$, נגר ni. *be poured* (of water) 2 S 14$_{14}$, נתך ni. *be poured* (of rain, hail) Ex 9$_{33}$, נכה *strike* 2 S 2$_{22}$ 18$_{11}$ 2 K 13$_{18}$ (of arrow), שׁחת hi. *destroy* Jg 20$_{21.25}$, pi. *waste* semen Gn 38$_{9}$, שׁחט *slaughter* animal 1 S 14$_{32}$.

<COLL> הָאָרֶץ עַד־הַחַלֹּנוֹת *(from) the ground up to the windows* Ezk 41$_{16}$ (or em. וּמֵהָאָרֶץ *and from the ground*).

3b. soil, with more emphasis on composition and productivity of ground, <SUBJ> זרע pass. *be sown* Jr 2$_{2}$, ni. *be sown* Dt 29$_{22}$ (Sam hi. *sow* soil), עבד ni. *be worked* Ezk 36$_{34}$, צמח hi. *yield growth* Dt 29$_{22}$, היה *be* Is 34$_{9}$ (+ זֶפֶת *pitch*, || עָפָר *topsoil*), יצא hi. *yield* growth 61$_{11}$ (|| גַּן *garden*, perh. אֶרֶץ = *world*). <NOM CL> שְׂרֵפָה כָל־אַרְצָהּ *all its soil is burning*, i.e. burnt Dt 29$_{22}$. <OBJ> זרע *sow* Ex 23$_{10}$, hi. *sow* Dt 29$_{22(Sam)}$, רוה hi. *drench* Ho 6$_{3}$ (if em. יוֹרֶה *throwing*, as §3a).

<CSTR> פְּרִי הָאָרֶץ *produce of the soil* Nm 13$_{20}$, זֶרַע הָאָרֶץ what has been grown from *seed of the soil* Lv 27$_{30}$ (|| עֵץ *tree*), עֵשֶׂב הָאָרֶץ *foliage of*, i.e. growing from, *the soil* Ex 10$_{12.15}$ Am 7$_{2}$ Ps 72$_{16}$ Jb 5$_{25}$, זַרְזִיף אָרֶץ *dripping*, i.e. irrigation, *of the soil* Ps 72$_{6}$ (+ גֵּז *lawn*).

<PREP> בְּ of place, *in, on* Jr 14$_{4}$ (+ גֶּשֶׁם *rain*, || אֲדָמָה *soil*), + כתב ni. *be inscribed* Jr 17$_{13}$ (or em. יִכָּרֵתוּ *will be cut off* or יֵכָּלֵמוּ *will be put to shame* in the land), זקן hi. *grow old* Jb 14$_{8}$ (|| עָפָר *dust*), מִמָּטָר דֶּשֶׁא מֵאָרֶץ appar. *after*, or, *because of, rain, grass is*, i.e. sprouts, *from the soil* 2 S 23$_{4}$ (or em. מַאֲרִץ rain *makes fruitful*, i.e. ארץ hi.).

Also 4QPrQuot 15$_{9}$ ([אר]ץ) 72$_{5}$ 4QPrFêtes^{b} ([אר]ץ) 4QPrFêtes^{c} 131.2$_{8}$ (עלי ארץ) 189$_{2}$ 4QOrd^{b} 15$_{2}$ (לארצ) 1QM 12$_{5}$ 4QDibHam^{a} 1.7$_{13}$ 3.2$_{11}$ 4$_{3}$ 22$_{4}$ 26$_{6}$ 4QDibHam^{b} 24$_{2}$ ([הא]רץ]) 4QDibHam^{c} 31$_{8}$ ([הא]רץ]) 4QPrayers 1.3$_{8}$ (עלי ארץ) 4QpIsa^{a} 2$_{5}$ 1Q25 5$_{2}$ 4QapLam^{a} 1.1$_{12}$ 4QpPs^{a} 1.2$_{10}$ 4QFlor 8$_{2}$ 4QAges 2.2$_{3}$ 5$_{2}$ (על [הארן]ץ) 1Q26 2$_{3}$ 1QLitPr^{b} 1.1$_{6}$ 1Q41 3$_{1}$ 4Q178 1$_{3}$ 4QShir^{b} 30$_{1}$ ([א]רץ]) 1$_{2}$ ([א]רץ) 6QDeut(?) 1$_{2}$ ([הא]רץ]) 5Q23$_{1}$ 4Q285 3$_{3.6}$ 4Q385 3$_{6}$ (both מן הארץ) 4QpsJub^{c} 2$_{3}$ ([א]רץ]) 4QToh A 3.2$_{7}$ 4QBer^{a} 2$_{1}$ 3.1$_{1}$ 4QapPs^{b} 44$_{2}$ 50$_{4}$ 4QApocMos A 1$_{2}$ 6$_{1}$ 11QapPs^{a} fr. A$_{5}$.

<SYN> §1 מָקוֹם *place*, נַחֲלָה *inheritance*, מוֹלֶדֶת *place of birth*, בַּיִת *house, temple*, מִדְבָּר *desert*; §2 תֵּבֵל *world*, שָׁמַיִם *heaven*, תְּהוֹם *abyss*, אָדָם *humanity*; §3 עָפָר *dust*, עֵץ *tree*; §§1, 2 גּוֹי *nation*, עִיר *city*, עַם *people*, מַמְלָכָה *kingdom*, יָם *sea*, הַר *mountain*; §§1, 3 שָׂדֶה *field*; §§1, 2, 3 אֲדָמָה *land, earth, soil*, חוּצָה/חוּץ *street, open land*.

אַרְצָא 1 pr.n.m. **Arza**, overseer (עַל־הַבַּיִת) of Baasha's palace at Tirzah, 1 K 16$_{9}$.

ארצטון 0.0.1 pr.n.m. **Ariston**, father of Joseph, MurEpBeth-Mashiko$_{3}$.

ארר 63.0.22.6 vb. **curse—Qal** Pf. אָרוֹתִיהָ; impf. תָּאֹר, אָאֹר; + waw וְאָרוֹתִי; impv. אָרָה־, אֹרוּ, (אוֹרוּ) אֹרוּ; ptc. active אֹרְרֵי (אֹרְרֶיךָ), pass. אָרוּר (I ארר), אֲרוּרָה, אֲרוּרִים, Q אוררי; inf. אָרוֹר—**1. curse,** <SUBJ> Y. Gn 12$_{3}$ (:: ברך pi. *bless*) 4QD^{b} 13.14, Israelites Ex 22$_{27}$ (|| קלל pi. *curse*), Balaam Nm 22$_{6.6}$ (:: ברך pi.) 22$_{12}$ 23$_{7}$ (|| זעם *be indignant*), Levites and inhabitants of camps 4QD^{b} 17; subj. not specified, Gn 27$_{29}$ Nm 24$_{9}$ (both :: ברך pi.) Jg 5$_{23.23}$.

<OBJ> קלל pi. ptc. *one who curses* Gn 12$_{3}$, Jacob 27$_{29}$, נָשִׂיא *prince* Ex 22$_{27}$, Israel Nm 22$_{6.12}$ 23$_{7}$, Meroz Jg 5$_{23}$, יוֹם *day* Jb 3$_{8}$, ישׁב ptc. *inhabitant* Jg 5$_{23}$, בְּרָכָה *blessing* Ml 2$_{2.2}$, עבר ptc. *one who crosses, transgresses* 4QD^{b} 13.14, נטה ptc. *one who turns aside* from law 4QD^{b} 17.

<COLL> אוֹרוּ אָרוֹר *bitterly curse* Jg 5$_{23}$.

2a. pass. ptc., **accursed,** used as predicative adj., **cursed, cursed be,** <SUBJ> רָשָׁע *wicked one* 4QBer^{a} 3.2$_{5}$ (הרש[ע]; || זעם *be indignant*), מֶלֶךְ wicked *king* 4QToh D$_{2}$ ([אר]ור), מַלְאָךְ *angel* 4QBer^{a} 3.2$_{7}$ (... [ארור מלא]ך), Gibeonites Jos 9$_{23}$, Cain Gn 4$_{11}$, Canaan 9$_{25}$ 4QpGen^{a} 2$_{6}$, Belial 1QM 13$_{4}$ (א[רור] בליעל)=4QBer^{a} 3.2$_{2}$ (ארור [ב]ליעל; || זעם) 11QapPs^{a} 4$_{6}$ ([ארור]), רוּחַ

spirit of Belial 1QM 13$_4$=4QBer^a 3.2$_3$ (רו]חי גו[רלו).

אִישׁ *man* of Belial 1QS 2$_{5.7}$ (‖ זעם *be indignant*) 4QPsJos^b 22.2$_9$ ([אר]ור [איש בליעל]), who makes idol Dt 27$_{15}$, who rebuilds Jericho Jos 6$_{26}$ 4QPsJos^b 22.2$_8$ ([א]רור א[יש), who eats in violation of oath 1 S 14$_{24.28}$, who announced Jeremiah's birth Jr 20$_{15}$, who does not heed covenant 11$_3$, גֶּבֶר *man* who relies on humans 17$_5$, בֶּן־אָדָם *man* who incites Saul 1 S 26$_{19}$.

עשׂה ptc. *one who does* evil 4QToh D$_5$ ([עוש]'; ‖ זעם *be indignant*) 4QBer 3.2$_{11}$ ([ארורים]... עוש]'), treachery Jr 48$_{10}$, קלל hi. ptc. *one who dishonours* parents Dt 27$_{16}$ (or em. to pi., *one who curses* parents), ארר ptc. *one who curses* Gn 27$_{29}$ Nm 24$_9$ (both :: ברך *bless*), נכה hi. ptc. *one who strikes* neighbour Dt 27$_{24}$, בוא ptc. *one who comes* into covenant 1QS 2$_{11}$, סוג hi. ptc. *one who removes* landmark Dt 27$_{17}$, שׁגה hi. ptc. *one who misleads* blind 27$_{18}$, נטה hi. ptc. *one who turns aside* justice 27$_{19}$, לקח ptc. *one who takes* bribe 27$_{25}$, נכל ptc. *cheat* Ml 1$_{14}$, שׁכב ptc. *one who lies* with relative, beast, neighbour's wife Dt 27$_{20.21.22.23}$, מנע ptc. *one who withholds* sword Jr 48$_{10}$, נתן ptc. *one who gives* daughter to Benjaminite Jg 21$_{18}$, one who breaches covenant Dt 27$_{26}$ 28$_{16.16.19.19}$, one who opens or defiles grave Silwan royal steward tomb inscr. 1$_2$ Kh. Beit Lei graf. 1$_1$ 2 (others אר for ארר) 3 (others ארדח for ארר) 4 (ארר; others אורר appar. *one who curses*) En-Gedi cave inscr., one who trusts in saints Ps 16$_3$ (if em. וְאַדִּירֵי כָּל־חֶפְצִי־בָם *and noble ones of all [whom] my delight is in them* to וַאֲרוּרִים כָּל־חֶפְצֵי־בָם *and cursed are all who delight in them*).

נָחָשׁ *snake* Gn 3$_{14}$, אֲדָמָה *earth* 3$_{17}$, פְּרִי *fruit* Dt 28$_{18.18}$, שֶׁגֶר *offspring* 28$_{18}$, עַשְׁתְּרוֹת *ewes* 28$_{18}$, טֶנֶא *basket* 28$_{17}$, מִשְׁאֶרֶת *kneading-trough* 28$_{17}$, יוֹם *day* of birth Jr 20$_{14}$, אַף *anger* Gn 49$_7$, עֶבְרָה *wrath* 49$_7$; subj. not specified, 4Q525 5$_4$ ([ארר]ים).

<PREP> בְּ *in respect of* 4QBer^a 3.2$_{2.3}$ (both + מַחֲשָׁבָה *plan*) 3.2$_5$ ([בכול]; + מֶמְשָׁלָה *dominion*).

<COLL> אָרוּר אַתָּה *cursed are you* (sg.) Gn 3$_{14}$ 4$_{11}$ Dt 28$_{16.16.19.19}$ 1QS 2$_{5.7}$ 4QToh D$_2$, אֲרוּרִים אַתֶּם *cursed are you* (pl.) Jos 9$_{23}$, אֲרוּרִים הֵם *cursed are they* 1 S 26$_{19}$.

<PREP> במחשבת משטמתו *in respect of his* (Belial's) *plan of enmity* 4QBer^a 3.2$_2$; [מ]אדם *from among humanity* 11QapPs^a 4$_6$ ([ארור]).

2b. as noun, **accursed one,** <SUBJ> שׁגה *stray* from commandments Ps 119$_{21}$ (but perh. אֲרוּרִים הַשֹּׁגִים = *cursed are those who stray*, as §2a). <OBJ> גער *rebuke* Ps 119$_{21}$, פקד *make arrangements (for)* 2 K 9$_{34}$.

<CSTR> ארורי עולמים *cursed ones of eternity* 1QS 2$_{17}$.

<APP> זֵדִים אֲרוּרִים *accursed insolent ones* Ps 119$_{21}$ (mss זָרִים *strangers*, ms גּוֹיִם *nations*, but see Subj.).

<ADJ> ארור אחד בליעל *a cursed one of Belial* 4QTestim 1$_{23}$ (mg איש ארור אחד *a certain cursed man*).

<PREP> בְּתוֹךְ *among* 1QS 2$_{17}$.

3. bewitch, cast spell (upon), וַיָּאֶר אֶת־הַלָּיְלָה *and he* (perh. angel of Y.) *cast a spell upon the night* Ex 14$_{20}$ (if em. וַיָּאֶר *and he lit up*).

<SYN> §2a זעם *be indignant*.

<ANT> §§1, 2a ברך (pi.) *bless*.

Ni. Pf. Q נארותה; ptc. נֵאָרִים—**suffer curse,** <SUBJ> perh. worshipper 1Q26 1$_6$, Israel Ml 3$_9$. <PREP> בכול תבואתכה *in respect of all your produce* 1Q26 1$_6$, בַּמְּאֵרָה *with the curse* Ml 3$_9$.

Pi. Pf. אֵרְרָהּ, Q ארורהו; ptc. מְאָרֲרִים—**1. curse,** <SUBJ> Y. Gn 5$_{29}$, קָדוֹשׁ *holy one* CD 20$_8$. <OBJ> בוא ptc. *one who comes* into congregation CD 20$_8$, אֲדָמָה *earth* Gn 5$_{29}$. **2.** as technical term in ordeal, **effect curse,** of bitter waters, Nm 5$_{18.19.22.24.24.27}$ (or em. in all הַמְּאוֹרֲרִים *that bring clarification* or הָאוּרִים *the Urim* or הַמּוֹרִים *that instruct*; Sam המארים *that give light*).

Ho. Impf. יוּאַר, Q יוארו—**suffer curse,** <SUBJ> זֶרַע *seed* of Israel CD 12$_{22}$, one cursed by Balaam Nm 22$_6$ (:: ברך pu. *be blessed*).

→ מְאֵרָה *curse*, אֲרָרָה *curse*, perh. אוּרִים *Urim*.

[אֲרָרָה] 0.0.1 n.[f.] **curse**—pl. cstr. ארורות—ארורות [נ]צח *curses of eternity* 5Q16 1$_3$.

→ ארר *curse*.

[ארדח], see ארר, Qal, §2a.

אֲרָרַט 4 pl.n. **Ararat**—אֲרָרָט (Q הוררט)—Armenia or part thereof, <CSTR> אֶרֶץ אֲרָרָט *land of Ararat* 2 K 19$_{37}$‖Is 37$_{38}$ (1QIsa^a הוררט), הָרֵי אֲרָרָט Gn 8$_4$, מַמְלְכוֹת אֲרָרַט *kingdoms of Ararat*, Minni, and Ashkenaz Jr 51$_{27}$

(or em. מַמְלְכוֹת *kingdoms:* Ararat).

[אֲרָרִי], see הֲרָרִי.

ארשׂ $_{11.0.2}$ **desire—Pi.** Pf. אֵרַשְׂתִּי, אֵרַשׂ (mss אֵרַסְתִּי); impf. תְּאָרֵשׂ; + waw וְאֵרַשְׂתִּיךְ—**betroth oneself** to woman, **<SUBJ>** אִישׁ *man* Dt 20$_{7}$ (ǁ לקח *take [in marriage]*), Y. Ho 2$_{21.21.22}$, David 2 S 3$_{14}$, Israelite Dt 28$_{30}$. **<OBJ>** אִשָּׁה *woman* Dt 20$_{7}$ 28$_{30}$ (:: שׁגל *violate* [Kt]) 2 S 3$_{14}$ (mss ארס), Israel Ho 2$_{21.21.22}$, Michal 2 S 3$_{14}$. **<PREP>** וְאֵרַשְׂתִּיךְ לִי *and I shall betroth to me,* i.e. take as my betrothed Ho 2$_{21}$ (+ לְעוֹלָם *for ever*) 2$_{21.22}$, var. 2 S 3$_{14}$ (all three + בְּ *for the price of* or *by means of*).

Pu. Pf. אֹרָשָׂה (Q אורשה); ptc. מְאֹרָשָׂה (Q מאורשה)—**1. be betrothed** to man, **<SUBJ>** בְּתוּלָה *virgin* Ex 22$_{15}$ Dt 22$_{23.28}$=11QT 66$_{9}$ נַעֲרָה *girl* Dt 22$_{23(Qr).25(Qr).27(Qr).28(Qr)}$=11QT 66$_{8.9}$. **<PREP>** לְאִישׁ *to a man* Dt 22$_{23}$.

→ אֲרֶשֶׁת *desire.*

[אֲרֶשֶׁת] $_{1}$ n.f. **desire**—cstr. אֲרֶשֶׁת—**<OBJ>** (subj. Y.) מנע *withhold* Ps 21$_{3}$, נתן 61$_{6}$ (if em. יְרֻשַּׁת *inheritance of*). **<CSTR>** אֲרֶשֶׁת שְׂפָתָיו *desire of,* i.e. expressed through, *his lips* Ps 21$_{3}$ (+ תַּאֲוַת לִבּוֹ *desire of his heart*), אֲרֶשֶׁת יִרְאֵי שְׁמֶךָ *the desire of those who fear your name* 61$_{6}$ (if em.).

→ ארשׂ *desire.*

אֹרַת, see אֹרָה.

אַרְתַּחְשַׁסְתְּ $_{9}$ pr.n.m. **Artaxerxes**—אַרְתַּחְשַׁסְתְּ (Kt ארתחשסתא), אַרְתַּחְשַׁשְׂתְּא (Kt ארתחששתא), אַרְתַּחְשַׁשְׂתְּ —prob. Artaxerxes I, ruler of Persian empire at time of Ezra's return, **<CSTR>** בִּימֵי אַרְתַּחְשַׁשְׂתָּא *in the days of Artaxerxes* Ezr 4$_{7}$. **<APP>** אַרְתַּחְשַׁסְתְּ הַמֶּלֶךְ *Artaxerxes, the king* Ezr 7$_{7(Qr)}$ 8$_{1(Qr)}$ Ne 2$_{1(Qr)}$ 5$_{14(Qr)}$, הַמֶּלֶךְ אַרְתַּחְשַׁסְתְּא *the king, Artaxerxes* Ezr 7$_{11(Qr)}$, אַרְתַּחְשַׁשְׂתְּ מֶלֶךְ פָּרָס *Artaxerxes, king of Persia* 4$_{7(Qr)}$ 7$_{1(Qr)}$ (אַרְתַּחְשַׁסְתְּ מֶלֶךְ־), אַרְתַּחְשַׁסְתְּ מֶלֶךְ־בָּבֶל *Artaxerxes, king of Babylon* Ne 13$_{6(Qr)}$.

אֲשַׂרְאֵל $_{1}$ pr.n.m. **Asarel, 1.** son of Jehallelel, descendant of Judah, 1 C 4$_{16}$. **2.** musician, son of Asaph, 1 C 25$_{2}$ (if em. אֲשַׂרְאֵלָה *Asarelah*) 25$_{14}$ (if em. יְשַׂרְאֵלָה *Jesarelah*).

אֲשַׂרְאֵלָה $_{1}$ pr.n.m. **Asarelah,** musician, son of Asaph, perh. ident. with יְשַׂרְאֵלָה *Jesarelah* at 1 C 25$_{14}$ (or em. אֲשַׂרְאֵל *Asarel*), 1 C 25$_{2}$ (mss אֲשַׁרְאֵלָה *Asharelah*; or em. אֲשַׂרְאֵל *Asarel*).

אַשְׂרִיאֵל $_{3}$ pr.n.m. **Asriel,** descendant of Manasseh, Nm 26$_{31}$ (Sam אשרואל) Jos 17$_{2}$ 1 C 7$_{14}$ (or del.).

→ אַשְׂרִיאֵלִי *Asrielite.*

אַשְׂרִיאֵלִי $_{1}$ gent. **Asrielite,** belonging to the family of Asriel, Nm 26$_{31}$.

→ אַשְׂרִיאֵל *Asriel.*

אֵשׁ I $_{379.17.49}$ n.f. and m. **fire**—cstr. אֵשׁ; sf. אִשּׁוֹ, אֶשְׁכֶם, אִשָּׁם (Kt אשתם); pl. Si אשות—**1. supernatural fire. a.** assoc. with **theophany**, etc. of Y. (many refs. also belong to §2), Gn 15$_{17}$ (ǁ עָשָׁן *smoke*) Ex 3$_{2.2}$ 13$_{21.22}$ 14$_{24}$ (all three ǁ עָנָן *cloud*) 19$_{18}$ 24$_{17}$ 40$_{38}$ (+ עָנָן) Lv 9$_{24}$ 10$_{2}$ Nm 9$_{15.16}$ (both + עָנָן) 11$_{1.2.3}$ 14$_{14}$ (ǁ עָנָן) 16$_{35}$ 21$_{28}$=Jr 48$_{45}$ Dt 1$_{33}$ (ǁ עָנָן) Dt 4$_{11}$ (+ חֹשֶׁךְ עָנָן וַעֲרָפֶל *darkness, cloud, and gloom*) 4$_{12.15.24.33.36.36}$ (ǁ שָׁמַיִם *heaven*) 5$_{4.5.22}$ (ǁ עָנָן, עֲרָפֶל *gloom*) 5$_{23.24.25.26}$ 9$_{3.10.15}$ 10$_{4}$ 18$_{16}$ 33$_{2(Qr)}$ 2 S 22$_{9}$ǁPs 18$_{9}$ (ǁ עָשָׁן, גֶּחָלֶת *coal*) 2 S 22$_{13}$ǁPs 18$_{13.14}$ (both ǁ בָּרָד *hail*) 1 K 18$_{24.38}$ 19$_{12.12.12}$ 2 K 1$_{10.10.12.12.14}$ (all five + מִן־הַשָּׁמַיִם *from heaven*) Is 4$_{5}$ (ǁ עָשָׁן, עָנָן *cloud*) 10$_{16.17}$ (ǁ לֶהָבָה *flame*) 26$_{11}$ (ǁ קִנְאָה *zeal*) 30$_{30}$ 33$_{14}$ 65$_{1}$ (ǁ עָשָׁן) 66$_{15.15.16}$ (ǁ חֶרֶב *sword*) Ezk 1$_{4}$ (ǁ עָנָן) 1$_{4+5t}$ Jl 3$_{3}$ (+ דָּם *blood,* עָשָׁן) Am 5$_{6}$ Zc 2$_{9}$ Ps 29$_{7}$ 50$_{3}$ 78$_{14}$ 97$_{3}$ 105$_{39}$ (ǁ עָנָן) Jb 1$_{16}$ Ne 9$_{12.19}$ (both ǁ עָנָן) 1 C 21$_{26}$ 2 C 7$_{1.3}$ (both + כְּבוֹד י׳ *glory of Y.*) Si 45$_{19}$ (ǁ אַף *anger*) 48$_{3}$ 4QDib Ham^{a} 6$_{10}$ (ǁ עָנָן) 1QH 8$_{12}$ (ǁ Gn 3$_{24}$ חֶרֶב) 4QpsEzek^{a} 4$_{12}$ 4Q386–9 3.2$_{10}$ 4QBer^{a} 1$_{3}$ 4QJub^{a} 1$_{9}$.

Oft. assoc. with storms, etc., e.g. Gn 19$_{24}$ Ezk 38$_{22}$ (both ǁ גָּפְרִית *sulphur*) Ex 9$_{23.24}$ Ps 148$_{8}$ (all three + בָּרָד *hail*) Nm 26$_{10}$ Is 29$_{6}$.

1b. miraculous fire, assoc. with other sources, specif. bush Ex 3$_{2.2}$ Jg 9$_{15}$, Leviathan, i.e. crocodile Jb 41$_{11}$, humans Jg 9$_{20.20}$, heavenly beings 2 K 2$_{11.11}$ 6$_{17}$ Ezk 8$_{2.2}$ 10$_{2.6.7}$ 28$_{14.16}$ Ps 104$_{4}$ Dn 10$_{6}$ Si 48$_{9}$ 4Q185 1.1$_{8}$

4QShirShab^{d} 1.2$_{9}$ 4QShirShab^{f} 15.2$_{3}$ 20.2$_{10.10}$ 4QBer^{b} 1$_{4}$ 4QJub^{a} 5$_{6}$.

2. fire of sacrifice, Ex 29$_{14}$ Lv 1$_{7.7.8.12.17}$ 3$_{5}$ 6$_{2.3.5.6}$ 10$_{1}$ 16$_{12.13}$ Nm 3$_{4}$ 6$_{18}$ 18$_{9}$ 26$_{61}$ Jg 6$_{21}$ 1 K 18$_{23.23.25}$ Is 30$_{33}$ Jr 7$_{31}$ 19$_{5}$ Si 50$_{9}$ 11QT 34$_{12}$ perh. 1Q29 1$_{3}$ 2$_{3}$, fire in censer Lv 10$_{1.1}$ Nm 16$_{7.18}$ 17$_{2.11}$ 11QT 3$_{13}$, fire of child sacrifice Gn 22$_{6}$ (|| מַאֲכֶלֶת *knife*) 22$_{7}$ (+ עֵץ *wood*) Dt 12$_{31}$ 18$_{10}$=11QT 60$_{18}$ 2 K 16$_{3}$||2 C 28$_{3}$ 2 K 17$_{17.31}$ 21$_{6}$||2 C 33$_{6}$ 2 K 23$_{10}$ Jr 7$_{18}$ (|| עֵץ *wood*) 7$_{31}$ Ezk 20$_{31}$ Si 45$_{25}$ (unless אִשׁ *man*) 4QJub^{d} 1.1$_{34}$.

3a. fire of destruction, Is 50$_{11.11}$ Jr 23$_{29}$ (|| פַּטִּישׁ *hammer*) Ezk 15$_{7.7}$ 21$_{37}$ (+ לְאָכְלָה *as fuel*) 23$_{25}$ Jl 2$_{3}$ (|| לֶהָבָה) Am 7$_{4}$ Ob$_{18}$ (|| לֶהָבָה *flame*) Na 3$_{15}$ Ps 78$_{63}$ (both || חֶרֶב *sword*) Jb 28$_{5}$ (fire as component of the earth) Lm 1$_{13}$ 2$_{3}$ Si 15$_{16}$ (:: מַיִם *water*, || מָוֶת *death*) 16$_{6}$ (|| חֵמָה *wrath*) 39$_{29}$ (in list of items created למשפט *for judgment* with hail, wickedness, and pestilence) 51$_{4}$ CD 5$_{13}$ (|| זִק *spark*) 4QCat^{a} 1$_{7}$.

b. Specif. destructive of left-overs or unclean parts of sacrifice Ex 12$_{10}$ 29$_{34}$ Lv 4$_{12}$ 6$_{23}$ 7$_{17.19}$ 8$_{17.32}$ 9$_{11}$ 16$_{27}$ 19$_{6}$ 11QT 43$_{11}$, clothing Lv 13$_{52.55.57}$ Is 9$_{4}$, idols Ex 32$_{20}$ Dt 7$_{5.25}$ 9$_{21}$ 12$_{3}$ 2 K 19$_{18}$||Is 37$_{19}$ 1 C 14$_{12}$ 1QM 14$_{1}$, אֶתְנַן gifts given as *fee* Mc 1$_{7}$.

c. burning אוּד *brand* Zc 3$_{2}$, מְגִלָּה *scroll* Jr 36$_{23.23.32}$, פִּשְׁתִּים *flax* Jg 15$_{14}$, פָּתִיל *thread* 16$_{9}$, hair Ezk 5$_{4.4.4}$, קַשׁ *chaff* Is 5$_{24}$ 47$_{14}$ (|| לֶהָבָה *flame*, אוּר *flame*) Jl 2$_{5}$, דּוֹנַג *wax* Mc 1$_{4}$ Ps 68$_{3}$ 1QH 4$_{33}$, wood Jr 5$_{14}$ Ezk 15$_{4.6}$ (both + לְאָכְלָה *as fuel*) 15$_{4.5}$ Zc 12$_{6}$ Pr 26$_{20}$ (|| מָדוֹן *contention*) 26$_{21}$ (|| גַּחֶלֶת *coal*) Si 8$_{3}$, הֲמָס *brushwood* Is 64$_{1}$, thorns 2 S 23$_{7}$ Is 9$_{17}$ 33$_{12}$ Ps 118$_{12}$ (+ דְּבֹרָה *bee*), בְּרִיחַ *bar* Na 3$_{13}$, weapons Ezk 39$_{9.10}$, chariots Jos 11$_{6.9}$ 2 K 23$_{11}$ Ps 46$_{10}$, booty 11QT 55$_{9}$.

d. land, farmland Ex 22$_{5}$ Jg 15$_{5}$ 2 S 14$_{30.30.31}$ Ezk 30$_{8}$ Jl 1$_{19}$ (|| לֶהָבָה *flame*) 1$_{20}$ Zc 12$_{6}$ Ps 105$_{32}$ 1QM 11$_{10}$, tree(s) Jr 11$_{16}$ 21$_{14}$ 22$_{7}$ Ezk 19$_{12.14}$ 21$_{3}$ Zc 11$_{1}$ Ps 80$_{17}$ (humans as vine) 83$_{15}$ (|| לֶהָבָה) 1QH 2$_{26}$ 3$_{29}$ 8$_{20}$, marshland (אֲגַם) Jr 51$_{32}$.

e. buildings, esp. fortifications Jg 9$_{49.52}$ 12$_{1}$ 14$_{15}$ 18$_{27}$ 1 K 16$_{18}$ 2 K 8$_{12}$ (|| חֶרֶב *sword*) 25$_{9}$||Jr 52$_{13}$ Is 64$_{10}$ Jr 38$_{18}$ 39$_{8}$ 43$_{13}$ 49$_{27}$ 51$_{58}$ Ezk 16$_{41}$ 23$_{47}$ Am 1$_{4.7.10.12.14}$ 2$_{2.5}$ Ps 74$_{7}$ Ne 1$_{3}$ 2$_{3.13.17}$ 2 C 35$_{13}$ 4QapLam^{a} 1.1$_{5}$.

f. city Nm 21$_{28}$=Jr 48$_{45}$ (|| לֶהָבָה *flame*) Nm 31$_{10}$ Dt 13$_{17}$ Jos 6$_{24}$ 8$_{8.19}$ 11$_{11}$ Jg 1$_{8}$ 18$_{27}$ 20$_{48}$ 1 S 30$_{1.3.14}$ 1 K 9$_{16}$ Is 1$_{7}$ Jr 21$_{10}$ 32$_{29}$ 34$_{2.22}$ 37$_{8.10}$ 38$_{17.23}$ 43$_{12}$ 49$_{2}$ 50$_{32}$ Ezk 24$_{10}$ (|| עֵץ *wood*) 28$_{18}$ 30$_{14.16}$ Ho 8$_{14}$ Zc 9$_{4}$ Lm 4$_{11}$ 11QT 55$_{9}$.

g. in punishment, specif. capital punishment Lv 20$_{14}$ 21$_{9}$ Jos 7$_{15.25}$ (|| אֶבֶן *stone*), punishment of wicked Is 66$_{24}$ Ps 11$_{6}$ (|| גָּפְרִית *sulphur*) 21$_{10.10}$ 106$_{18}$ (|| לֶהָבָה *flame*) 140$_{11}$ Jb 15$_{34}$ 20$_{26}$ 22$_{20}$ 31$_{12}$ 1QS 2$_{8}$ 4$_{13}$ 1QH 6$_{18}$ 17$_{13}$ 1QpHab 10$_{5.13}$ 4QShir^{a} 2$_{4}$ 4Q416 10.2$_{5}$.

h. as cause of injury, Lv 13$_{24}$ Is 43$_{2}$ (|| לֶהָבָה *flame*, :: מַיִם *water*), in murder Jg 14$_{15}$ 15$_{16}$.

4. cleansing fire, for metal booty Nm 31$_{23.23}$ (:: מַיִם *water*), for use in the preparation of objects in metal, clay, etc. Ex 32$_{24}$ Is 54$_{16}$ Jr 6$_{29}$ Ezk 22$_{20}$ 24$_{12}$ Zc 13$_{9}$ Ml 3$_{2}$ (|| בֹּרִית *soap*) Ps 66$_{12}$ (|| מַיִם *water*) 1QH 5$_{16}$.

5. domestic fire, Ex 12$_{8.9}$ 35$_{3}$ Is 30$_{14}$ (|| מַיִם *water*) Jr 36$_{23.23}$ Ps 21$_{10}$ 2 C 35$_{13}$ Si 39$_{26}$ (with water, iron, salt as essentials for life), for boiling water Is 64$_{1}$, for preparing food Lv 2$_{14}$ Is 44$_{16.19}$ Jr 29$_{22}$ (wicked humans as roast meat) CD 12$_{14}$ (|| מַיִם).

6. fire **in symbolic assoc.** with **a.** anger (usu. of Y.) Dt 32$_{22}$ Is 30$_{27}$ 65$_{5}$ Jr 4$_{4}$ 15$_{14}$ 17$_{4}$ 21$_{12}$ Ezk 21$_{36}$ 22$_{21.31}$ 38$_{19}$ Ho 7$_{6}$ Na 1$_{6}$ Ps 39$_{4}$ (anger of worshipper) 78$_{21}$ (|| אַף *anger*) 89$_{47}$ Lm 2$_{4}$ 1QM 14$_{1}$. **b.** jealousy Ezk 36$_{5}$ Zp 1$_{18}$ 3$_{8}$ Ps 79$_{5}$ 4QDibHam^{a} 1.5$_{5}$ 4QBark^{c} 2.1$_{6}$. **c.** erotic love Ca 8$_{6}$ Si 9$_{8}$, adultery Pr 6$_{27}$ (+ גַּחֶלֶת *coal*), incest Si 23$_{16}$.

d. other matters, e.g. pain 1QH 8$_{30}$, insatiability Pr 30$_{16}$ (|| אֶרֶץ *earth*), human endeavour Jb 18$_{5}$, prophetic inspiration Jr 20$_{9}$ Si 48$_{1}$ (|| תַּנּוּר *oven*), sin Si 3$_{30}$ (:: מַיִם *water*, || חַטָּאת *sin*) 8$_{10}$ 40$_{30}$, evil words Pr 16$_{27}$, perh. insubstantiality יגע ... בְּדֵי־אֵשׁ *toil ... for the sake of fire* Jr 51$_{58}$ Hb 2$_{13}$ (both || רִיק *nothing*; perh. אֵשׁ II *triviality*), perh. speed of chariot Na 2$_{4}$, instability 4Q424 1$_{5}$.

<SUBJ> היה *be* Ex 40$_{38}$ (+ in the cloud) Ob$_{18}$ (+ house of Jacob), ברא ni. *be created* Si 39$_{29}$ (נב[ראו]), עשׂה *do* Y.'s command Ps 148$_{8}$, זור *be strange* to Y. Lv 10$_{1}$ Nm 3$_{4}$ 26$_{61}$, אמר *say*, Enough! Pr 30$_{16}$.

אכל *consume* Ex 24$_{17}$ Lv 6$_{3}$ Nm 16$_{35}$ 21$_{28}$ 26$_{10}$ Dt 4$_{24}$ 5$_{25}$ 9$_{3}$ 32$_{22}$ Jg 6$_{21}$ 2 S 22$_{9}$||Ps 18$_{9}$ 1 K 18$_{38}$ Is 26$_{11}$ 29$_{6}$ 30$_{27.30}$ 33$_{11.14}$ Jr 17$_{27}$ 21$_{14}$ 48$_{45}$ 49$_{27}$ 50$_{32}$ Ezk 15$_{4.5.7}$

19$_{12.14}$ 21$_{3}$ 28$_{18}$ Ho 8$_{14}$ Jl 1$_{19.20}$ 2$_{3.5}$ Am 1$_{4.7.10.12.14}$ 2$_{2.5}$ 5$_{6}$ 7$_{4.4}$ Na 3$_{13.15}$ Zc 11$_{1}$ Ps 21$_{10}$ 50$_{3}$ 78$_{63}$ Jb 1$_{16}$ 15$_{34}$ 20$_{26}$ 22$_{20}$ Lm 2$_{3}$ 2 C 7$_{1}$ 1QM 11$_{10}$ 1QH 2$_{26}$ 3$_{29}$.

בער *burn* intrans. Nm 11$_{1.3}$ Jr 20$_{9}$ Ps 39$_{4}$ Jb 1$_{16}$ Si 23$_{16}$ 40$_{30(Bmg)}$ 1QH 6$_{18}$ 8$_{30}$ 4QShir[a] 2$_{4}$ 4Q386–9 3.2$_{10}$ (ש[א]) 4QJub[a] 1$_{9}$ ([כאש בוערת]) 4QapPs[b] 46$_{9}$, trans. Ps 83$_{15}$, pu. intrans. Jr 36$_{22}$ (if em. אֶת־), שׂרף *burn* trans. Is 47$_{14}$, להט *burn* intrans. Ps 104$_{4}$, pi. trans. Dt 32$_{22}$, intrans. Ps 97$_{3}$, יקד *burn* intrans. Dt 32$_{22}$ Is 10$_{16}$ 65$_{5}$ Si 16$_{6}$, ho. intrans. Lv 6$_{2.5.6}$ Jr 15$_{14}$ 17$_{4}$, שׂלק ni. *be lighted* Ps 78$_{21}$, קדח *be lighted* Dt 32$_{22}$ Jr 15$_{14}$, *set ablaze* Is 64$_{1}$, יצת *set ablaze* 9$_{17}$, תמם *be consumed* Jr 6$_{29}$ (if em.; see Prep.).

כבה *be extinguished* Lv 6$_{5.6}$ Is 66$_{24}$ Jr 17$_{27}$ Pr 26$_{20}$, נפח pu. *be blown*, i.e. cooled Jb 20$_{26}$, שׁקע *die out* Nm 11$_{2}$, לחך pi. *lick* water 1 K 18$_{38}$, נתך hi. *melt* trans. Ezk 22$_{20}$ (or em. ni. *be melted*).

אור hi. *illuminate* Ps 105$_{39}$, נגה *shine* Jb 18$_{5}$, לקח htp. perh. *flash* Ex 9$_{24}$ Ezk 1$_{4}$.

יצא *go out, break out* Lv 9$_{24}$ 10$_{2}$ Nm 16$_{35}$ 21$_{28}$=Jr 48$_{45}$ Jg 9$_{15.20.20}$ Ezk 5$_{4}$ 19$_{14}$, הלך *go*, i.e. spread Ex 9$_{23}$ (+ אַרְצָה *to the land*) Ps 97$_{3}$, עלה *come up* Jg 6$_{21}$, נפל *fall* 1 K 18$_{38}$ Jb 1$_{16}$, ירד *come down* 2 K 1$_{10.10.12.12.14}$ 2 C 7$_{1.3}$, בעה *boil* trans. Is 64$_{1}$, עצר pass. *be constrained* 1QH 8$_{30}$, יצק ho. *be poured out* Si 15$_{16}$.

<NOM CL> אֵשׁ הִיא *it is a fire* Jb 31$_{12}$, אֵשׁ ... ״י *Y. ... is a fire* Dt 4$_{24}$, אַחַר הָרַעַשׁ אֵשׁ *after the earthquake there was fire* 1 K 19$_{12}$, מְדֻרָתָהּ אֵשׁ וְעֵצִים הַרְבֵּה *its pyre is fire and plenty of wood* Is 30$_{33}$, רוּחֲכֶם אֵשׁ *your breath is fire* 33$_{11}$, מִמַּרְאֵה מָתְנָיו וּלְמַטָּה אֵשׁ *from the appearance of his loins downwards there was fire* Ezk 8$_{2}$.

הָאֵשׁ אֲשֶׁר עַל־הַמִּזְבֵּחַ *the fire that is on the altar* Lv 1$_{8.12}$ 3$_{5(Sam)}$ 11QT 34$_{12}$ 4QJub[d] 1.1$_{34}$ (האש אשר על] [המזבח), הָאֵשׁ אֲשֶׁר־תַּחַת זֶבַח הַשְּׁלָמִים *the fire that is beneath the sacrifice of the peace offering* Nm 6$_{18}$, הָאֵשׁ אֲשֶׁר עַל־/אֶל־הָאָח *the fire on the brazier* Jr 36$_{23.23}$, מִימִינוֹ אֵשׁ דָּת לָמוֹ appar. *at his right hand fire was law for them* Dt 33$_{2(Qr)}$ (Kt אשדת).

<OBJ> עשׂה *make (into)* minister Ps 104$_{4}$, נתן *place* Lv 1$_{7}$ 10$_{1}$ Nm 16$_{7.18}$ 17$_{11}$ Ezk 30$_{8.14.16}$ Jl 3$_{3}$, שׂים *place* 1 K 18$_{23.23.25}$, שׁלח *send* Lm 1$_{13}$, pi. *dispatch* Ezk 39$_{6}$ Ho 8$_{14}$ Am 1$_{4.7.10.12}$ 2$_{2.5}$, לקח *take* Gn 22$_{6}$ Ezk 10$_{6}$, חתה *snatch* Is 30$_{14}$ Pr 6$_{27}$, בוא hi. *bring* 11QT 3$_{13(Yadin)}$ ([לה]ביא), קרב hi. *bring forward* Lv 10$_{1}$ Nm 3$_{4}$ 26$_{61}$, יצא hi. *take out* Ezk 28$_{18}$, בער pi. *light* Ex 35$_{3}$ (Sam hi.; + בְּיוֹם הַשַּׁבָּת *on the sabbath*) Jr 7$_{18}$ Ezk 39$_{9.10}$, hi. *light* Jg 15$_{5}$ (+ בַּלַּפִּידִים *in the torches*), קדח *light* Is 50$_{11}$ Jr 17$_{4}$ CD 5$_{13}$, דלק hi. *light* Ezk 24$_{10}$, יצת hi. *light* Jr 11$_{16}$ 17$_{27}$ 21$_{14}$ 43$_{12}$ 49$_{27}$ 50$_{32}$ Ezk 21$_{3}$ Am 1$_{14}$ Lm 4$_{11}$.

כבה pi. *extinguish* Am 5$_{6}$ Si 3$_{30}$ 51$_{4}$, מטר hi. *rain down* Gn 19$_{24}$ Ezk 38$_{22}$ Ps 11$_{6}$, נפח *blow* Ezk 22$_{20}$, זרה *scatter* Nm 17$_{2}$, פרשׂ *stretch out* Ps 105$_{39}$, ראה *see* Dt 18$_{16}$, רוח hi. *smell* Jg 16$_{9}$.

<CSTR> אֵשׁ לֶהָבָה *fire of flame*, i.e. flaming fire Is 4$_{5}$ Ho 7$_{6}$ Ps 105$_{32}$ Lm 2$_{3}$ 4Q185 1.1$_{8}$, גופרית *of sulphur* 1QpHab 10$_{5}$, פֶּחָם *of coal* Is 54$_{16}$, תָּמִיד *of continuity*, i.e. perpetual Lv 6$_{6}$, עולמים *of ages*, i.e. eternal 1QS 2$_{8}$ 4QShir[a] 2$_{4}$ (ש[א]), לבונה *of incense* Si 50$_{9}$, מְצָרֵף *of smelter* Ml 3$_{2}$, ״י *of Y.* Nm 11$_{1.3}$ 1 K 18$_{38}$ (אֵשׁ־), אֱלֹהִים *of God* 2 K 1$_{12}$ Jb 1$_{16}$, הָאָח *of the brazier* Jr 36$_{22}$ (if em. אֶת־), הַמִּזְבֵּחַ *of the altar* Lv 6$_{2}$, עֶבְרָתִי *of my wrath* Ezk 21$_{36}$ 22$_{21.31}$ 38$_{19}$ (אֵשׁ־) 1QM 14$_{1}$ (עברתו), קִנְאָתִי *of my jealousy* Ezk 36$_{5}$ Zp 1$_{18}$ (קִנְאָתוֹ) 3$_{8}$ 4QDibHam[a] 1.5$_{5}$ (קנאתכה) 4QBark[a] 2.1$_{6}$ (קנאת), לַפִּדוֹת *of torches* Na 2$_{4}$ (if em. אֵשׁ־פְּלָדוֹת perh. *fire of steel*), קוֹצִים *of thorns* Ps 118$_{12}$ (or em. בְּקוֹצִים *in thorns*), מחשכים *of dark places* 1QS 4$_{13}$.

מִכְוַת־אֵשׁ *burn of*, i.e. from, *fire* Lv 13$_{24}$, תַּנּוּר *oven of* Ps 21$_{10}$, חוֹמַת *wall of* Zc 2$_{9}$, כִּיּוֹר *pot of*, i.e. brazier 12$_{6}$, מַאֲכֹלֶת *fuel of* Is 9$_{4.18}$, עַמּוּד *pillar of* Ex 13$_{21.22}$ (הָאֵשׁ) 14$_{24}$ Nm 14$_{14}$ Ne 9$_{12.19}$ (הָאֵשׁ) 4QDibHam[a] 6$_{10}$, רֶכֶב *chariot(s) of* 2 K 2$_{11}$ (רֶכֶב־) 6$_{17}$, נַחֲלַת *inheritance of* Si 45$_{25}$ (unless אִשׁ *of a* single *man*), לַפִּיד *torch of* Gn 15$_{17}$ Zc 12$_{6}$ Dn 10$_{6}$ (לַפִּידֵי) 1QM 11$_{10}$, שְׂרֵפַת *(result of) burning of*, i.e. by Is 64$_{10}$ 4QapLam[a] 1.1$_{5}$, צְלִי־ *roasted of*, i.e. by Ex 12$_{8.9}$ (+ נָא ... מְבֻשָּׁל בַּמָּיִם *raw* or *boiled in water*).

אוֹר *light of* Ps 78$_{14}$, נֹגַהּ *brightness of* Is 4$_{5}$, מַרְאֵה־ *appearance of* Nm 9$_{15.16}$ Ezk 1$_{27.27}$ 8$_{2}$ 4QShirShab[f] 20.2$_{10}$ (מראי), אפלת *shadow of* 1QS 2$_{8}$, לַבַּת־ *flame of* Ex 3$_{2}$ (Sam להבת *flame of*), להט *flame of* 1QH 8$_{12}$, שְׁבִיב *flame of* Jb 18$_{5}$ Si 8$_{10}$ (אשו), אוּר *flame of* Is 50$_{11}$, לְשׁוֹן *tongue*, i.e. flame, *of* 5$_{24}$ 1Q29 1$_{3}$ 2$_{3}$ (both לשונות), לַהַב *flame of* Is 29$_{6}$ 30$_{30}$ 66$_{15}$ (לַהֲבֵי־) Jl 2$_{5}$ Am 7$_{4}$ (if em.

לָרִב בָּאֵשׁ *to contend with fire*) Ps 29$_7$ (לְהָבוֹת) 4QShirShab^d 1.2$_9$ (להבת) 4QShirShab^f 15.2$_3$ 4Q487 1.2$_4$ CD 2$_5$ (all three להבי), כִּידוֹדֵי *flames of* Jb 41$_{11}$.

רִשְׁפֵּי *sparks of* Ca 8$_6$, שבולי *streams of* 4QShirShab^f 20.2$_{10}$ 4QpsEzek^a 4$_{11}$ ([שבלי אש]), גַּחֲלֵי־ *coals of* Lv 16$_{12}$ 2 S 22$_{13}$||Ps 18$_{13.14}$ Ezk 1$_{13}$ 10$_2$ 4QpsEzek^a 4$_{12}$ 4QapPs^b 28$_1$, אַבְנֵי־ *stones of*, i.e. coals Ezk 28$_{14.16}$, מוסדי *foundations of* 4QBer^a 1$_3$, משפטי *judgments of* 1QpHab 10$_{13}$, מעשי *workings of* 1QH 5$_{16}$, גדודי *troops of* Si 48$_9$, מלאכי *angels of* 4QBer^b 1$_4$ (|| עָנָן *cloud*), [מ]לאכי רוחות האש *the angels of the spirits of fire* 4QJub^a 5$_6$, סוּסֵי *horses of* 2 K 2$_{11}$.

<ADJ> + גָּדוֹל *great* Dt 4$_{36}$ 5$_{25}$ 18$_{16}$ (both + זֹאת *this*), אֵשׁ צָרֶבֶת *burning fire* Pr 16$_{27}$.

<PREP> לְ of direction, *to*, + נתן *give* Ezk 15$_6$, ni. *be given* Ezk 15$_4$, of benefit, *for* (burning in), + היה *be* Ezk 21$_{37}$, עֵצִים לָאֵשׁ *wood is for fire* Pr 26$_{21}$, וְהָיָה אוֹר־יִשְׂרָאֵל לְאֵשׁ *and the light of Israel will be as a fire* Is 10$_{17}$, [והיה] לאש *and it will be as a fire* 1QH 6$_{18(Licht)}$, הִנְנִי נֹתֵן דְּבָרַי בְּפִיךָ לְאֵשׁ *behold I am placing my words in your mouth as a fire* Jr 5$_{14}$, נֹגַהּ לָאֵשׁ *the fire was bright* Ezk 1$_{13}$.

בְּ of place, accompaniment, *in(to), through, with*, + הלך *go* Dt 1$_{33}$ Is 43$_2$, בוא *come* Nm 31$_{23}$ Is 66$_{15}$ (mss כְּ *as*) Ps 66$_{12}$ CD 12$_{14}$ 4QM^g 2$_4$, hi. *bring* Zc 13$_9$, ירד *go down* Ex 19$_{18}$, נתן *place* 2 K 19$_{18}$||Is 37$_{19}$, שׁלך hi. *throw* Ex 32$_{24}$, נפל hi. *drop* Ps 140$_{11}$, *through*, + עבר hi. *make* children *pass* Dt 18$_{10}$=11QT 60$_{18}$ 2 K 16$_3$||2 C 28$_3$ 2 K 17$_{17}$ 21$_6$||2 C 33$_6$ 2 K 23$_{10}$ Ezk 20$_{31}$, *make* metal *pass* Nm 31$_{23}$, שׁפך ni. *be poured out* 4QDibHam^a 1.5$_5$ ([נשפ]כה), פרה *let loose* weapons 1QH 2$_{26}$, לֹא בָאֵשׁ י׳ *Y. was not in the fire* 1 K 19$_{12}$, בְּאֵשׁ חֶלְאָתָהּ *into a fire its rust (is to go)* Ezk 24$_{12}$ (mss בָּאֵשׁ), כלמת כלה באש מחשכים *disgrace of destruction in fire of dark places* 1QS 4$_{13}$.

בְּ of instrument, *by (means of), with*, + שׂרף *burn* trans. Ex 12$_{10}$ 29$_{14.34}$ 32$_{20}$ Lv 4$_{12}$ 8$_{17.32}$ 9$_{11}$ 13$_{55.57}$ 16$_{27}$ 20$_{14}$ Nm 31$_{10}$ Dt 7$_{5.25}$ 9$_{21}$ 12$_{3.31}$ 13$_{17}$ Jos 6$_{24}$ 7$_{25}$ 11$_{6.9.11}$ Jg 9$_{52}$ 12$_1$ 14$_{15}$ 15$_6$ 18$_{27}$ 1 S 30$_{1.14}$ 1 K 9$_{16}$ 16$_{18}$ 2 K 17$_{17}$ 23$_{11}$ 25$_9$||Jr 52$_{13}$ Is 44$_{16.19}$ Jr 7$_{31}$ 19$_5$ (all four perh. בְּ of place) 21$_{10}$ 34$_{22}$ 36$_{32}$ (perh. בְּ of place) 37$_{8.10}$ 38$_{18.23}$ 39$_8$ 43$_{13}$ 51$_{32}$ Ezk 5$_4$ (perh. בְּ of place) 16$_{41}$ 23$_{47}$ Ps 46$_{10}$ 2 C 36$_{19}$ 11QT 55$_9$, pass. *be burned* 1 S 30$_3$ Ps 80$_{17}$ (or em. שְׂרָפֻהָ *they have burnt her*), ni. *be burned* Lv 6$_{23}$ 7$_{17.19}$ 13$_{52}$ 19$_6$ 21$_9$ Jos 7$_{15}$ 2 S 23$_7$ Jr 38$_{17}$ Mc 1$_7$ 1 C 14$_{12}$ 11QT 43$_{11}$.

בער *burn* intrans. Ex 3$_2$ (perh. בְּ of place) Dt 4$_{11}$ 5$_{23}$ 9$_{15}$ Jg 15$_{14}$ (perh. בְּ of place), hi. trans. Ezk 5$_2$ (if em. אוּר *fire*), יצת *be set alight* Is 33$_{12}$, ni. *be burned* Ne 1$_3$ 2$_{17}$ 4Q416 10.2$_5$, hi. *set alight* Jos 8$_{8.19}$ Jg 9$_{49}$ 2 S 14$_{30.30.31}$ Jr 32$_{29}$ 49$_2$ 51$_{58}$, להט pi. *set alight* Si 9$_8$, שׁלח pi. *dispose of* Jg 1$_8$ 20$_{48}$ 2 K 8$_{12}$ Ps 74$_7$, כלה pi. *destroy* Ezk 22$_{31}$, אכל ni. *be consumed* Ezk 23$_{25}$ Zp 1$_{18}$ 3$_8$ Zc 9$_4$, pu. *be consumed* Ne 2$_{3.13}$.

קלה *roast* Lv 2$_{14}$ Jr 29$_{22}$, בשׁל pi. *boil* 2 C 35$_{13}$, פוח hi. *blow* Ezk 21$_{36}$, נפח *blow* 22$_{21}$, דבר pi. *speak* 36$_5$ 38$_{19}$, ענה *answer* 1 K 18$_{24}$ 1 C 21$_{26}$, שׁפט *judge* 1QpHab 10$_5$ 4QBark^a 2.1$_6$, ni. *be judged* 4Q185 1.1$_8$ (Allegro כאש ... ישפט[ו] *as a fire ... they will judge*), ריב *contend* Am 7$_4$ (or em. לַהֶבֶת אֵשׁ *flame of fire*), שׁפט ni. *contend* Is 66$_{16}$, בְּאֵשׁ־פְּלָדוֹת הָרֶכֶב *by fire of steel is (made) the chariotry* Na 2$_4$ (or em. כְּאֵשׁ לַפִּדוֹת *as fire of torches*).

מִן of direction, *from*, + יצא *go out* Ezk 1$_{13}$ 15$_7$, נצל ho. *be saved* Zc 3$_2$, of instrument, *by*, + תמם *be complete*, i.e. used up (of lead) Jr 6$_{29(Qr, mss)}$ (Kt מֵאִשְׁתָּם עֹפָרֶת *lead is from their fire*; or em. מֵאֵשׁ תַּם *by fire* lead *will be consumed* or תֵּחַם אֵשׁ *fire is warm* with lead), partitive, *of, from* Nm 18$_9$ (or em. אִשֶּׁה *fire offering*).

מִתּוֹךְ *from within*, + דבר pi. *speak* Dt 4$_{12.15.33}$ 5$_{4.22.26}$ 9$_{10}$ 10$_4$, שׁמע *hear* 4$_{36}$ 5$_{24}$, כְּעֵין הַחַשְׁמַל מִתּוֹךְ הָאֵשׁ *as the gleam of amber from within the fire* Ezk 1$_4$.

מִפְּנֵי *in the presence of, because of*, + מסס ni. *melt* (of wax) Mc 1$_4$ Ps 68$_3$ 1QH 4$_{33}$ (erased מלפני), + ירא *fear* Dt 5$_5$.

עמד לִפְנֵי *stand before* 4Q424 1$_5$.

כְּ *as* Ex 24$_{17}$ (+ כָּבוֹד *glory* of Y.) Is 30$_{27}$ (+ לָשׁוֹן *tongue* of Y.) Jr 23$_{29}$ (+ דָּבָר *word* of Y.) Na 2$_4$ (if em. בְּ *by*) Jb 28$_5$ (כְּמוֹ) Pr 16$_{27(Qr)}$ (+ עַל־שְׂפָתוֹ *[what is] on his lip*) 1QM 14$_1$ 4Q386–9 3.2$_{10}$ ([כא]ש) 4QJub^a 1$_9$ (כאש), + היה *be* Jr 20$_9$ 4QCat^a 1$_{7(Allegro)}$ ([ו]היו), בוא *come* Ml 3$_2$ (if em. הוא *he is* as fire), יצא *go out*, i.e. spread Jr 4$_4$=21$_{12}$, רדף *pursue* Ps 83$_{15}$, צלח *rush* Am 5$_6$, קום *arise* Si 48$_1$, בער *burn* intrans. Is 9$_{17}$ Ho 7$_6$ Ps 79$_5$ 89$_{47}$ (both כְּמוֹ) Lm 2$_3$ Si 40$_{30}$ (B כְּמוֹ), דעך pu. *be extin-*

guished Ps 118$_{12}$ (or em. בער *burn*), פרח *sprout*, i.e. spread 1QH 8$_{30}$, נתך ni. *be poured out* Na 1$_{6}$, הדר ni. *be glorious* Si 50$_{9}$, שָׁפַךְ כָּאֵשׁ חֲמָתוֹ *he has poured out his wrath like fire* Lm 2$_{4}$, נֶהְפַּךְ כְּמוֹ־אֵשׁ *it is turned over, as if by,* or *into, fire* Jb 28$_{5}$.

עַל *on, in* Lv 1$_{8.12.17}$ 3$_{5}$ Jr 36$_{23}$ 4QJub^{d} 1.1$_{34}$ ([על האש]), ערך *arrange* wood Lv 1$_{7}$, נתן *place* 16$_{13}$ Nm 6$_{18}$ Si 8$_{3}$, נפל hi. *drop* cedars Jr 22$_{7}$, קטר hi. *burn* flesh 11QT 34$_{12}$; אֶל *(on)to,* + שׁלח *send*, i.e. extend, hand Ezk 10$_{7}$, שׁלך hi. *throw* pieces of scroll Jr 36$_{23}$; אֶל־תּוֹךְ *into the middle of,* + שׁלךְ hi. *throw* hair Ezk 5$_{4}$; אַחַר הָאֵשׁ קוֹל *after the fire was a sound* 1 K 19$_{12}$.

Also 4Q487 15$_{2}$ 6QD 2$_{1}$ 4QShir^{b} 44$_{3}$ 4QpGen^{a} 2$_{12}$.

<SYN> לֶהָבָה *flame,* עָשָׁן *smoke,* עָנָן *cloud,* בָּרָד *hail,* גָּפְרִית *sulphur,* גַּחֶלֶת *coal,* עֵץ *wood,* מַיִם *water,* חֶרֶב *sword,* אַף *anger,* רִיק *nothing.*

<ANT> מַיִם *water.*

→ אִשֶּׁה *fire offering.*

[אֵשׁ] II, see אֵשׁ I, §6d.

אִשׁ 3 part. **there is**—אִשׁ—אִם־אִשׁ לְהֵמִין וּלְהַשְׂמִיל *if there is*, i.e. if it is possible, *to turn right or to turn left* 2 S 14$_{19}$ (Gnz Qr אִישׁ if *a man* [is able] to turn), הַאִשׁ ... אֹצְרוֹת רֶשַׁע *are there ... treasuries of wickedness?* Mi 6$_{10}$ (or em. הַאֶשֶּׁה *shall I forget?* or הַאֶשָּׂא *shall I bear?*), אִישׁ רֵעִים לְהִתְרֹעֵעַ *there are friends for shattering,* who destroy, *one another* Pr 18$_{24}$ (or em. לְהִתְרָעוֹת *for being companions to one another;* but perh. אִישׁ *man* of, i.e. with, friends; Seb יֵשׁ *there is;* ||יֵשׁ).

[אֹשׁ] 0.0.10 n.m. **foundation**—pl. cstr. אושי—<SUBJ> רעע ni. *be broken* 1QH 3$_{13}$ 7$_{4}$, רעד *be shaken* 3$_{35}$, מוג htpol. *be melted* 3$_{35}$. <OBJ> כון hi. *establish* 1QSb 3$_{20}$ 1QH 7$_{9}$. <CSTR> אושי קיר *foundations of wall* 1QH 3$_{13}$, חמר *of clay* 3$_{30}$, עולם *of eternity* 3$_{35}$ 7$_{9}$, מבניתי *of my structure* 7$_{4}$, מעשיהם *of their works* fr. 18$_{7}$ (א[ו]ש׳); כול אושי *all the foundations of* 1QSb 3$_{20}$ 1QH 7$_{4}$, כול אושיהם *all their foundations* 11QShirShab 5$_{7}$.

Also 1Q36 17$_{2}$ 4QBer^{a} 2$_{4}$.

→ אשׁשׁ *be firm.*

אשא 0.0.0.8 pr.n.m. **Isha, 1.** Samaria ost. 22$_{2}$ 23$_{2}$ 24$_{1}$ ([א]אש) 26$_{1}$ 27$_{1}$ 28$_{1}$ 29$_{1}$ 37$_{3}$ 39$_{3}$ (א[אש]) perh. 102 ([א]ש[א]). **2.** Kenyon inscr. 175 (אש[א]) **3.** seal 316 (Hebron? 8th/7th cent.).

אשבאל, see אַשְׁבֵּל.

אַשְׁבֵּל 3 pr.n.m. **Ashbel,** head of Benjaminite family, Gn 46$_{21}$ Nm 26$_{38}$ (Sam mss אשבאל) 1 C 8$_{1}$.

→ אַשְׁבֵּלִי *Ashbelite.*

אַשְׁבֵּלִי 1 gent. **Ashbelite,** belonging to family of Ashbel, Nm 26$_{38}$.

→ אַשְׁבֵּל *Ashbel.*

אֶשְׁבָּן 2 pr.n.m. **Eshban,** son of Dishon (Gn 36$_{26}$ דִּישָׁן *Dishan;* Sam דִּישׁוֹן), Gn 36$_{26}$||1 C 1$_{41}$.

אַשְׁבֵּעַ, see בֵּית אַשְׁבֵּעַ.

[אֶשְׁבַּעַל] 2 pr.n.m. **Eshbaal**—אֶשְׁבָּעַל—son of Saul, ident. with Ishbosheth (אִישׁ־בֹּשֶׁת) at 2 S 2$_{8}$ etc., 1 C 8$_{33}$ 9$_{39}$.

→ בַּעַל *Baal.*

[אֶשֶׁד] 7 n.f. **slope of mountains, hills**—cstr. אֶשֶׁד; pl. אֲשֵׁדוֹת; cstr. אַשְׁדּוֹת (אַשְׁדֹּת).

<SUBJ> היה *be* Jos 13$_{20}$, נטה *extend* intrans. Nm 21$_{15}$.

<OBJ> נכה hi. *strike* Jos 10$_{40}$ (+ הַר *mountain,* שְׁפֵלָה *lowland,* נֶגֶב *Negeb*).

<CSTR> אֶשֶׁד הַנְּחָלִים *slope of the valleys* Nm 21$_{15}$ (Sam אֲשֶׁר הִנְחִלָם *which he apportioned*), אַשְׁדֹּת הַפִּסְגָּה *the slopes of Pisgah* Dt 3$_{17}$ 4$_{49}$ Jos 12$_{3}$ 13$_{20}$ (both אַשְׁדּוֹת).

<PREP> נתן בְּ *give* land *in* or *consisting of* Jos 12$_{8}$ (+ הַר, שְׁפֵלָה, עֲרָבָה, נֶגֶב *Arabah,* מִדְבָּר *desert*); תַּחַת *beneath* Dt 3$_{17}$ 4$_{49}$ Jos 12$_{3}$.

אַשְׁדּוֹד 17 pl.n. **Ashdod**—+ ־ה of direction אַשְׁדּוֹדָה—**1.** Philistine coastal city, Esdūd (T. Ašdōd), Jos 11$_{22}$ 15$_{46.47}$ 1 S 5$_{1.5.6.7}$ (+ אַנְשֵׁי *men of*) 6$_{17}$ Is 20$_{1.1}$ Jr 25$_{20}$ (+ שְׁאֵרִית *remnant of*) Am 1$_{8}$ 3$_{9}$ (or em. אַשּׁוּר *Assyria*) Zp

2$_{4}$ Zc 9$_{6}$ 2 C 26$_{6}$ (חוֹמַת *wall of*).

→ אַשְׁדּוֹדִי *Ashdodite.*

אַשְׁדּוֹדִי $_{6}$ gent.n. **Ashdodite**—אַשְׁדּוֹדִית; pl. אַשְׁדּוֹדִים, אַשְׁדֳּדִיּוֹת (Kt אשדודיות). **1.** as (collective) noun, **a.** with ref. to inhabitant(s) of Ashdod, Jos 13$_{3}$ 1 S 5$_{3.6}$ Ne 4$_{1}$. **b.** with ref. to language/dialect of Ashdod, חֲצִי מְדַבֵּר אַשְׁדּוֹדִית *half were speaking Ashdodite* Ne 13$_{24}$ (ms חֶצְיָם *half of them*). **2.** as adj., from Ashdod, נָשִׁים אַשְׁדֳּדִיּוֹת *Ashdodite women* Ne 13$_{23(Qr)}$ (Kt אשדודיות).

→ אַשְׁדּוֹד *Ashdod.*

אשדת, see אֵשׁ I, Nom. Cl.

אִשָּׁה $_{782.42.57.7}$ n.f. **woman**—אִשָּׁה (אֵשֶׁת); cstr. אֵשֶׁת; sf. אִשְׁתִּי, אִשְׁתְּךָ, (אִשְׁתֶּךָ, אֶשְׁתְּךָ), אִשְׁתּוֹ, pl. נָשִׁים; cstr. נְשֵׁי (אִשֹּׁת); sf. נָשַׁי, נָשֶׁיךָ, נָשָׁיו, נָשֵׁינוּ, נְשֵׁיכֶם, נְשֵׁיהֶם.

1. usu. **wife,** legitimate sexual partner of a man, and mother of his children (see esp. Gn 16$_{3}$ 20$_{17}$ 30$_{4.9}$ 37$_{2}$ Jg 11$_{2}$ 19$_{1}$ 2 S 5$_{13}$ 15$_{16}$).

2a. woman, without ref. to marital status, e.g. Gn 12$_{11.14}$ 31$_{35}$ Ex 19$_{15}$ 21$_{28}$ Lv 26$_{26}$ Jos 2$_{1}$ Zc 5$_{9}$.

2b. used distributively, **each woman,** אִשָּׁה ... רְעוּתָהּ *each woman ... her neighbour* Ex 3$_{22(Sam)}$ (MT אִשָּׁה ... שְׁכֶנְתָּהּ *each woman ... her neighbour*) 11$_{2}$ (both ‖ אִישׁ *man*) Jr 9$_{19}$, תֵּצֶאנָה אִשָּׁה *you will come out, each one* of you Am 4$_{3}$ (with ref. to פָּרוֹת הַבָּשָׁן *cows of Bashan*), שֹׁבְנָה אִשָּׁה *return, each one* of you Ru 1$_{8}$, וּמְצֶאןָ מְנוּחָה אִשָּׁה *and may you find rest, each one* of you 1$_{9}$ (both with ref. to Orpah and Ruth).

3a. female animal, in ark, תִּקַּח־לְךָ ... אִישׁ וְאִשְׁתּוֹ *take ... a male and its mate* Gn 7$_{2.2}$ (Sam in both זָכָר וּנְקֵבָה *male and female*).

3b. used distributively, **each animal,** דַּיּוֹת אִשָּׁה רְעוּתָהּ *(female) buzzards—each one with her neighbour* Is 34$_{15}$, אִשָּׁה רְעוּתָהּ לֹא פָקָדוּ *not one lacked her companion* 34$_{16}$, תֹּאכַלְנָה אִשָּׁה אֶת־בְּשַׂר רְעוּתָהּ *each one* (sheep) *will eat the flesh of its companion* Zc 11$_{9}$.

4. with ref. to inanimate objects, used distributively, **each thing,** אִשָּׁה אֶל־אֲחֹתָהּ *each one to its partner* (lit. *sister*) Ex 26$_{3.3.5.6.17}$ (Sam and ‖36$_{10.10.12.13.22}$ אַחַת אֶל־אַחַת lit. *one to one*) Ezk 1$_{9.23}$ 3$_{13}$, with ref. to יְרִיעָה *curtain* (Ex 26$_{3.3.6}$), לוּלָי *loop* (Ex 26$_{5}$), יָד *handle* (Ex 26$_{17}$), כָּנָף *wing* (Ezk 1$_{9.23}$ 3$_{13}$).

<SUBJ> היה *be* Gn 2$_{25}$ (+ עָרוֹם *naked*) 3$_{20}$ (+ אֵם *mother*) 19$_{26}$ (+ נְצִיב מֶלַח *pillar of salt*) 24$_{51}$ (+ לְ married *to*) Ex 21$_{4}$ 22$_{23}$ (+ אַלְמָנָה *widow*) Lv 15$_{19.19.25}$ (+ טְמֵאָה *impure*) Nm 5$_{27}$ (+ לְאָלָה *as an object of curse*) 14$_{3}$ (+ לָבַז *as booty*) 32$_{26}$ Dt 21$_{15}$ 25$_{5}$ Jg 8$_{30}$ 14$_{20}$ (all four + לְ married *to*) 2 S 14$_{2}$ 1 K 11$_{3}$ Jr 3$_{1}$ (both + לְ married *to*) 18$_{21}$ (+ שַׁכּוּל *childless,* אַלְמָנָה) Ezk 23$_{2}$ Ps 109$_{9}$ (+ אַלְמָנָה, ‖ בֵּן *child*) Pr 31$_{14}$ Ru 1$_{2}$ 1 C 2$_{26}$ 4$_{5}$ (both + לְ married *to*) 2 C 21$_{6}$ 22$_{11}$ (+ אֲחוֹת *sister of*) 11QT 50$_{10}$ (+ מְלֵאָה *full,* i.e. pregnant) 57$_{16}$ (+ לְבַדָּהּ *only her*) 4QRitPur 40$_{2}$ (וה[י]ה]).

שׁבה ni. *be captured* 1 S 30$_{3.5}$, לכד ni. *be captured* Jr 6$_{11}$, חפשׁ pu. *be freed* Lv 19$_{20}$, סבב ni. *be handed over* Jr 6$_{12}$ (‖ שָׂדֶה *field,* בַּיִת *house*), שׁגל ni. *be violated* Is 13$_{16(Kt)}$ Zc 14$_{2(Kt)}$, מות *die* Gn 3$_{4}$ 38$_{12}$ Dt 22$_{22}$ Ezk 24$_{18}$ 11QT 57$_{18}$, ho. *be killed* Lv 19$_{20}$ 20$_{11.16.27}$, נכה ho. *be killed* Nm 25$_{15}$, כרת ni. *be cut off* Lv 20$_{18}$, שׁמד ni. *be destroyed* Jg 21$_{16}$, רצח ni. *be murdered* 20$_{4}$, קבר pu. *be buried* Gn 25$_{10}$.

ראה *see* Gn 3$_{6}$ Ex 2$_{2}$ (both + כִּי[־]טוֹב *that [it was] good*) Jg 13$_{19.20}$ 1 S 28$_{12.13.13.21}$, נבט hi. *look* Gn 19$_{26}$, צפה *watch* Pr 31$_{27}$, שׁמע *hear* Dt 31$_{12}$ 1 S 4$_{19}$ 2 S 11$_{26}$ Is 32$_{9}$ (‖ בַּת *daughter*) Jr 9$_{19}$, אזן hi. *listen* Gn 4$_{23}$, למד *learn* Dt 31$_{12}$ Si 9$_{1}$, pi. *teach* daughter Jr 9$_{19}$, שׂכל hi. *be intelligent* Pr 19$_{14}$ Si 7$_{19}$ 25$_{8}$ 40$_{23}$, שׁכח *forget* child Is 49$_{15.15}$, זמם *plan* Pr 31$_{16}$, אמר *say* Gn 3$_{2.13}$ 39$_{7}$ Nm 5$_{22}$ Jos 2$_{4}$ Jg 13$_{6}$ (mss נגד hi. *tell*) 13$_{10.23}$ 14$_{16}$ 1 S 18$_{7}$ 27$_{11}$ 28$_{9.11.12.13.21}$ 2 S 14$_{4}$ (mss בוא *come*) 14$_{4+6t}$ 17$_{20}$ 20$_{17.17.21}$ 1 K 3$_{17.22.22.26.26.26}$ 17$_{24}$ 21$_{7}$ 2 K 4$_{1}$ 6$_{26.28.28}$ Is 4$_{1}$ Jr 38$_{22}$ Jb 2$_{9}$ Pr 30$_{20}$ Ru 4$_{14}$ Est 1$_{17}$ 5$_{14}$ (‖ אהב ptc. *friend*) 6$_{13}$ (‖ חָכָם *adviser*), דבר pi. *speak* Gn 39$_{19}$ 2 S 20$_{16}$ 1 K 3$_{22}$ 21$_{5}$ Jr 44$_{25}$, ענה *answer* 2 S 14$_{19}$, נגד hi. *tell* Jg 13$_{6(mss)}$ (L אמר *say*) 13$_{10}$ 1 S 19$_{11}$ 25$_{37}$ 27$_{11}$ 2 S 11$_{5}$, ספר pi. *recount* 2 K 8$_{6}$, קרא *call, name* Gn 4$_{25}$ Jg 13$_{24}$ 2 S 20$_{16}$ 1 C 7$_{16}$, ni. *be called* Gn 2$_{23}$ Est 4$_{11}$.

שׁאל *ask* Ex 3$_{22}$ 11$_{2}$, דרשׁ *seek* 1 K 14$_{5}$ Pr 31$_{13}$, מצא *find* favour Dt 24$_{1}$, ni. *be found* Dt 17$_{2}$=11QT 55$_{16}$ Jb 42$_{15}$, צפן *conceal* Ex 2$_{2}$ Jos 2$_{4}$, סתר hi. *conceal* 2 C 22$_{11}$, כחד pi. *conceal* 2 S 14$_{18}$, שׁנה htp. *disguise oneself* 1 K

14$_{2}$, נכר htp. *disguise oneself* 14$_{5.6}$, שׁוה nithpael *be similar (to)* Pr 27$_{15}$ (or em. ni., נִשְׁוָתָה, in same sense), חבא htp. *hide oneself* Gn 3$_{8}$.

זעק *cry out* 1 S 28$_{12}$, צעק *cry out* 2 K 4$_{1}$ 6$_{26}$ 8$_{3.5}$, שׁיר *sing* 1 S 18$_{6(Qr)}$, ענה *sing* 18$_{7}$, חול pol. *dance* 1 S 18$_{6}$, שׂחק *laugh* 18$_{7}$ Pr 31$_{25}$, נצר pass. *be kept* of heart, i.e. secretive Pr 7$_{10}$ (or em. נְצֻרַת לוֹט *one enclosed by a veil*).

פלל htp. *pray* 1 S 1$_{26}$, קסם *divine* 28$_{8}$, נדר *vow* Nm 6$_{2}$ 30$_{4}$=11QT 53$_{16}$, אסר *bind oneself* Nm 30$_{4}$=11QT 53$_{16}$, נזר hi. *become a Nazirite* Nm 6$_{2}$, מלא pi. *fulfil* Jr 44$_{25}$, צבא *minister* 1 S 2$_{22}$, קטר pi. *offer incense* Jr 44$_{15}$.

שׂטה *stray* from husband Nm 5$_{12.19.29}$, גלה pi. *uncover* pudendum Lv 20$_{18}$, זנה *be a prostitute* (see also App.) Am 7$_{17}$, נאף pi. *commit adultery* Ezk 16$_{32}$ Ho 3$_{1}$ Pr 30$_{20}$, מעל *act treacherously* Nm 5$_{6.12.27}$, בגד *betray* Jr 3$_{20}$, עבר *transgress* Dt 17$_{2}$=11QT 55$_{16}$, הרג *kill* Jg 9$_{54}$, נקה ni. *be found innocent* Nm 5$_{19.28}$, טמא *be impure* Lv 12$_{2.2}$ 15$_{18}$ 11QT 50$_{10}$, ni. *defile oneself* Nm 5$_{14.14.27.28.29}$, עצר pass. *be prohibited* 1 S 21$_{6}$, בושׁ htpol. *feel shame* Gn 2$_{25}$, חטא hi. *lead into sin* Ne 13$_{26}$, פרץ *break through*, i.e. persuade 1 S 28$_{23}$ (mss פצר *press*), נטה hi. *lead astray* 1 K 11$_{3.4}$, סות hi. *incite* Dt 13$_{7}$=11QT 54$_{20}$ 1 K 21$_{25}$, פתה pi. *deceive* Jg 14$_{15}$.

נתן *give* Gn 3$_{6.12}$ 16$_{3}$ Pr 31$_{15.24}$ Est 1$_{20}$, ni. *be given (in marriage)* 4Q251 7$_{4}$ ([ואל תנתן אישה]), מכר *sell* Pr 31$_{24}$, גמל *repay* 31$_{12}$, לקח *take* Gn 16$_{3}$ Ex 2$_{9}$ Jos 2$_{4}$ 1 S 28$_{24}$ 2 S 17$_{19}$ 1 K 17$_{10}$ Ezk 16$_{32}$ Pr 31$_{16}$, ho. *be taken* Gn 12$_{15}$, נשׂא *raise, carry* 39$_{7}$ (obj. eyes) Nm 5$_{31}$ (obj. sin), קבל pi. *take (in marriage)* Si 36$_{26}$ (א[שה], obj. [ז]כר *man*), שׁוב hi. *bring back* Lv 26$_{26}$, *go back* 2 K 8$_{3}$.

בעל pass. *be married* Gn 20$_{3}$ Dt 22$_{22}$, צרר *be a rival wife* Lv 18$_{18}$, גרשׁ pass. *be driven out, divorced* Lv 21$_{7}$, עזב pass. *be deserted* Is 54$_{6}$.

יפה *be beautiful* Si 26$_{16}$ (א[שה]) 36$_{26(mg)}$, ישׁר *be pleasing* Jg 14$_{7}$, אהב pass. *be loved* Dt 21$_{15}$ Ho 3$_{1}$, חשׁק ni. *be beloved* Si 40$_{19}$, הלל htp. *be praised* Pr 31$_{30}$, אבה *consent* Gn 24$_{5.8}$, שׂמח *rejoice* Ne 12$_{43}$, יטב hi. *do good (to)* husband Si 26$_{13}$, אשׁר pi. *make* husband *happy* 25$_{23}$, דשׁן pi. *make* husband *fat* 26$_{2}$.

שׂנא pass. *be hated* Dt 21$_{15}$, מאס ni. *be despised* Is 54$_{6}$, עצב pass. *be hurt* 54$_{6}$, ירא *fear* Dt 31$_{12}$ 1 S 28$_{13}$ Pr 31$_{21}$, יסר ni. *be chastened* Ezk 23$_{48}$, בכה *weep* Dt 21$_{13}$=11QT 63$_{14}$ Jg 14$_{16}$, pi. *mourn* Ezk 8$_{14}$, ספד *mourn* 2 S 11$_{26}$ Zc 12$_{12.12.13.13.14}$, אבל htp. *mourn* 2 S 14$_{2.2}$.

ידע *know* Pr 9$_{13}$ (or em. אֵשֶׁת כְּסִילוּת *woman of folly* to כְּסִילוּת), know sexually Nm 31$_{17.35}$ Jg 21$_{11}$, הרה *conceive* Gn 4$_{1.17}$ Ex 2$_{2}$ 1 S 4$_{19}$ 2 S 11$_{5.5}$ 2 K 4$_{17}$ 1 C 7$_{23}$, זרע ni. *become pregnant* Lv 12$_{2(Sam)}$ (MT hi.) Nm 5$_{28}$, hi. appar. in same sense Lv 12$_{2}$=4Q251 3$_{14}$ ([אשה כי תזריע]; Sam ni.), קנה *acquire* Gn 4$_{1}$, חול *writhe* Is 45$_{10}$ (|| אָב *father*), צרר hi. *suffer birth pains* Jr 48$_{41}$ 49$_{22}$, ילד *give birth* Gn 3$_{16}$ 4$_{1.17.25}$ 16$_{1}$ 17$_{19}$ 20$_{17}$ 24$_{36}$ 36$_{14}$ 44$_{27}$ Ex 2$_{2}$ 6$_{20.23.25}$ 21$_{4}$ Lv 12$_{2}$=4Q251 3$_{14}$ ([אשה כי תזריע וילדה]) Nm 26$_{59.59}$ Jg 13$_{2.24}$ 1 S 4$_{19.19}$ 2 S 11$_{27}$ 12$_{15.24}$ 1 K 3$_{17.18.18}$ 2 K 4$_{17}$ Jr 29$_{6}$ Ru 4$_{13}$ 1 C 2$_{24.29.35}$ 4$_{18}$ 7$_{16.23}$, ינק hi. *suckle* Ex 2$_{7.7.9}$ 1 S 1$_{23}$, גמל *wean* 1$_{23}$.

בוא *come* Gn 6$_{18.18}$ 7$_{7.7.13.13}$ 11$_{31}$ 12$_{5}$ Ex 18$_{5.6}$ 35$_{22}$ (Sam hi. *bring*) Jg 13$_{6}$ 19$_{26}$ 1 S 28$_{21}$ 2 S 14$_{4(mss)}$ (L אמר *say*) 20$_{22}$ 1 K 3$_{16}$ 14$_{4.5.5.6.17.17}$ 21$_{5}$ Is 27$_{11}$ Ru 1$_{2}$ 3$_{14}$ 4$_{11}$ Est 4$_{11}$ 11QT 39$_{7}$ 50$_{10}$ 1QM 7$_{3}$, hi. *bring* Ex 35$_{22(Sam).22.25.29}$ 1 S 27$_{11}$ Pr 31$_{14}$, קרב *approach* Lv 20$_{16}$ Dt 25$_{11}$, נגשׁ ni. *approach* 4QRitPur 40$_{2}$, קרא *meet* Pr 7$_{10}$, הלך *go* Gn 11$_{31}$ 12$_{5}$ 24$_{5.8.39}$ 1 S 1$_{18}$ 2 S 14$_{8}$ 1 K 14$_{2.4.17}$ 2 K 8$_{1.2}$ Jr 3$_{1}$ 4QpNah 3.4$_{4}$, יצא *go out* Gn 8$_{16.16.18.18}$ 11$_{31}$ 12$_{5}$ Ex 15$_{20}$ 21$_{3}$ Nm 16$_{27}$ 1 S 18$_{6}$ 2 K 8$_{3}$ Zc 5$_{9}$, ho. *be led out* Jr 38$_{22}$.

מהר pi. *hasten* intrans. Jg 13$_{10}$ 1 S 28$_{24}$, רוץ *run* Jg 13$_{10}$, נוס *flee* 9$_{51}$, סור *turn* from common sense Pr 11$_{22}$, hi. *turn* king's heart 11QT 56$_{18}$, עלה *go up* Gn 13$_{1}$ Jg 9$_{51}$ 2 S 2$_{2}$, hi. *raise* dead 1 S 28$_{8.11.11}$, שׁכב *lie down* 1 K 3$_{19}$ Ru 3$_{8}$, ni. *be laid* Is 13$_{16(Qr)}$ (|| עוֹלֵל *suckling*) Zc 14$_{2(Qr)}$ (|| בַּיִת *house*), נפל *fall* Jg 13$_{20}$ 19$_{26.27}$ 2 S 14$_{4}$, שׁחה htp. *prostrate oneself* 14$_{4}$, קום *stand* 1 K 14$_{2.4.17}$ 2 K 8$_{1.2}$ Is 32$_{9}$ Pr 31$_{15}$, עמד *stand* Lv 18$_{23}$ 1 K 3$_{16}$ Jr 44$_{15}$ 2 C 20$_{13}$, נצב ni. *stand* 1 S 1$_{26}$.

שׁלח *send* Dt 25$_{11}$ (obj. hand) 2 S 11$_{5}$, תמך *obtain* Pr 11$_{16}$, חזק hi. *grasp, urge* Dt 25$_{11}$ 2 K 4$_{8}$ Is 4$_{1}$, אמץ pi. *strengthen* Pr 31$_{17}$, שׁלך hi. *throw* Jg 9$_{53}$ 2 S 11$_{21}$, סגר *close* Jg 9$_{51}$, דרך hi. *trample* Si 9$_{2}$, נבע hi. *cause to flow*, i.e. produce household, daughter 42$_{14(B)}$.

ישׁב *dwell* Gn 11$_{31}$ Dt 3$_{19}$ 21$_{13}$=11QT 63$_{13}$ Jos 1$_{14}$ 1 S 1$_{23}$ 1 K 3$_{17}$ 2 K 22$_{14}$||2 C 34$_{22}$ 2 C 8$_{11}$, *sit* Jg 13$_{9}$ Ezk 8$_{14}$ Zc 5$_{7}$, שׁאר ni. *remain* Jr 38$_{22}$ Ru 1$_{5}$, גור *sojourn* 2 K 8$_{1.2}$

Ru 1$_{1}$, אכל *eat* Gn 3$_{1.2.3.6}$ 1 S 1$_{18}$ 2 K 6$_{28}$ Is 4$_{1}$ Pr 30$_{20}$ 31$_{27}$ Lm 2$_{20}$ (obj. children), שׁתה *drink* Jr 35$_{8}$, טעם *taste* Pr 31$_{18}$ (+ כִּי־טוֹב *that* it is *good*), זוב *have a discharge* Lv 15$_{19.25}$, רחץ *wash* 15$_{18}$ 2 S 11$_{2}$, לבשׁ *get dressed* 2 S 14$_{2}$ Is 4$_{1}$, חגר *put on belt* Pr 31$_{17}$, סוך *anoint* 2 S 14$_{2}$, מחה *wipe* mouth Pr 30$_{20}$.

טוה *spin* Ex 35$_{25.26}$, ארג *weave* 2 K 23$_{7}$, פרשׂ *spread something out* 2 S 17$_{19}$, שׁטח *scatter* grain 17$_{19}$, טחן *grind*, i.e. have sex with Jb 31$_{10}$, קשׁשׁ po. *gather* wood 1 K 17$_{10}$, צוד *hunt* adulterer's life Pr 6$_{26}$, אור hi. *light a fire* Is 27$_{11}$, כול pilp. *provide for* 1 K 17$_{9}$ Si 25$_{22}$, שׁמר *look after* house 2 S 15$_{16}$ 20$_{3}$, אפה *bake* Lv 26$_{26}$ 1 S 28$_{24}$, לושׁ *knead* 28$_{24}$ Jr 7$_{18}$.

עשׂה *do, make* Gn 3$_{13}$ Ex 36$_{6}$ Nm 5$_{6}$ Dt 17$_{2}$=11QT 55$_{16}$ Dt 17$_{5}$ 31$_{12}$ 1 K 14$_{4}$ 2 K 8$_{2}$ Jr 44$_{9}$ Ezk 23$_{48}$ Pr 31$_{13.22.24}$, פעל *do* 30$_{20}$, פלא hi. *do something extraordinary* Nm 6$_{2}$, משׁל *rule* Is 3$_{12}$, שׁפט *judge* Jg 4$_{4}$, נצל hi. *rescue* Dt 25$_{11}$, המה *be noisy* Pr 9$_{13}$ (or em.; see above).

<NOM CL> אִשְׁתּוֹ זֹאת *this is his wife* Gn 12$_{12}$, sim. 2 K 8$_{5}$ perh. Zc 5$_{7}$, אִשְׁתְּךָ הִיא *she is your wife* Gn 12$_{18(Qr)}$ 26$_{9(Qr)}$ (both || אֲחוֹת *sister*), הִיא לֹא אִשְׁתִּי *she is not my wife* Ho 2$_{4}$ (|| אִישׁ *husband*), אַתְּ־אִשְׁתּוֹ *you are his wife* Gn 39$_{9}$, אַתְּ אֵשֶׁת *you are the wife of* 1 K 14$_{2(Qr)}$, sim. Ru 3$_{11}$, אִשָּׁה ... אָתְּ *you are a ... woman* Gn 12$_{11}$, אִשָּׁה ... אֲנִי/אָנֹכִי *I am ... a woman* 1 S 1$_{15}$ 2 S 14$_{5}$, var. 1 S 1$_{26}$.

דְּבוֹרָה אִשָּׁה *Deborah was a woman* Jg 4$_{4}$, אֵשֶׁת חֶצְרוֹן אֲבִיָּה *the wife of Hezron was Abijah* 1 C 2$_{24}$ (or em. אֶפְרָתָה אֵשֶׁת חֶצְרוֹן אֲבִיהוּ to *Ephrathah, wife of Hezron his father*), עַמֵּךְ נָשִׁים *your people are women* Na 3$_{13}$, אֶשְׁתְּךָ כְּגֶפֶן פֹּרִיָּה *your wife is like a fruitful vine* Ps 128$_{3}$ (|| בֵּן *child*), אֵשֶׁת־חַיִל עֲטֶרֶת בַּעְלָהּ *a competent wife is the crown of her husband* Pr 12$_{4}$, אֵשֶׁת כְּסִילוּת ... פְּתַיּוּת *a woman of folly ... is simplicity*, i.e. simple 9$_{13}$ (or em. כְּסִילוּת ... וּמְפַתָּה *folly* is noisy *and deceives*), אשה ... מנה *a wife is ... a portion* Si 26$_{3}$ (Segal מתנה *gift*), אשה לך *(if) you have a wife* 7$_{26}$.

אַיֵּה ... אִשְׁתֶּךָ *where is ... your wife?* Gn 18$_{9}$, שָׁם אִשָּׁה *a woman was there* 1 K 17$_{10}$ 2 K 4$_{8}$, שָׁם הַנָּשִׁים *the women were there* Ezk 8$_{14}$, הַאֵין ... אִשָּׁה *is there not ... a woman?* Jg 14$_{3}$, הִנֵּה אִשְׁתְּךָ *here is your wife* Gn 12$_{19}$, יֵשׁ אִשָּׁה *there is a woman* Si 36$_{26(mg)}$, יֵשׁ מֵהֶם נָשִׁים *there were among them women* Ezr 10$_{44}$ (or em. וַיְשַׁלְּחוּם *and they dispatched* or וַיָּשִׂימוּ *and they appointed*), וכהם הנשים *and the women are like them* CD 5$_{10}$, נָשֵׁינוּ בַּשְּׁבִי *our wives are in captivity* 2 C 29$_{9}$.

אִשְׁתּוֹ ... עֲקָרָה *his wife ... was infertile* Gn 25$_{21}$ Jg 13$_{2}$, הָאִשָּׁה טוֹבַת־שֶׂכֶל וִיפַת תֹּאַר *the woman was good of wit and fair of form* 1 S 25$_{3}$, הָאִשָּׁה טוֹבַת מַרְאֶה *the woman was good of appearance* 2 S 11$_{2}$.

<OBJ> לקח *take* Gn 11$_{31}$ 12$_{5.19}$ 19$_{15}$ 32$_{23}$ 36$_{6}$ Ex 4$_{20}$ (|| בֵּן *child*) 18$_{2}$ Jg 15$_{6}$ 21$_{22}$ 2 S 12$_{11}$ 14$_{2}$ Jr 43$_{6}$ (|| גֶּבֶר *man*), in marriage Gn 4$_{19}$ 6$_{2}$ 11$_{29}$ 20$_{3}$ 21$_{21}$ 24$_{3.4.7.37.38.40}$ (all six + לִבְנִי *for my son*) 25$_{1}$ 26$_{34}$ 27$_{46}$ 28$_{1.2.6.6}$ 31$_{50}$ 36$_{2}$ 38$_{6}$ Lv 18$_{18}$ 20$_{14.21}$ 21$_{7.7.13.14}$ Nm 12$_{1.1}$ Dt 20$_{7.7}$ 22$_{13.14}$ =11QT 65$_{7.8}$ Dt 23$_{1}$=11QT 66$_{12}$ Dt 24$_{1.4.5.5}$ Jg 14$_{3}$ 19$_{1}$ 2 S 5$_{13}$ 12$_{9.10}$ 1 K 16$_{31}$ Jr 16$_{2}$ 29$_{6.6}$ Ho 1$_{2}$ Ezr 2$_{61}$||Ne 7$_{63}$ 1 C 7$_{15}$ 14$_{3}$ 2 C 11$_{18}$ 11QT 57$_{16.17}$ 66$_{12}$ CD 4$_{21}$ 7$_{7}$ 19$_{3}$ appar. 4Q416 10.2$_{21.21}$ 4QPentPar^{a} 3.2$_{7}$ ([אשה]).

רבה hi. *multiply* Dt 17$_{17}$=11QT 56$_{18}$ 1 C 7$_{4}$, בקשׁ pi. *seek* 1 S 28$_{7}$, מצא *find* Pr 18$_{22}$ (|| טוֹב *good*) 31$_{10}$ Ec 7$_{26.28}$ (perh. :: אָדָם *man*) 11QT 66$_{4}$ (||Dt 22$_{25}$ נַעֲרָה *girl*), בחר *choose* Gn 6$_{2}$, יכח hi. *decree* 24$_{44}$, קנה *acquire* Ru 4$_{5}$ Si 36$_{29}$ (+ ראשית קנין as *a foremost possession*), ארשׂ pi. *become engaged (to)* Dt 20$_{7}$ 28$_{30}$ 2 S 3$_{14}$, נתן *give* Gn 3$_{12}$ 30$_{26}$ Nm 5$_{21}$ (+ לְאָלָה *as an object of curse*) 2 S 20$_{3}$ 1 K 20$_{5}$ Jr 8$_{10}$ (|| שָׂדֶה *field*) Ru 4$_{11}$, *give (in marriage)* Ex 21$_{4}$ Jg 15$_{6}$ 21$_{14.18.18.22}$ 1 S 25$_{44}$ 2 S 3$_{14}$ 12$_{8.11}$ 1 K 11$_{19}$, יהב *give* Gn 29$_{21}$, פקד hi. *entrust* Jr 40$_{7}$, שׂים *place*, i.e. appoint Ezr 10$_{44}$ (if em. יֵשׁ *there were*).

בוא hi. *bring* Gn 2$_{22}$ Nm 5$_{15}$ Est 5$_{10}$ (|| אהב ptc. *friend*), הלך hi. *lead* into exile 2 K 24$_{15}$, יצא hi. *bring out* Dt 17$_{5}$=11QT 55$_{21}$ Jos 6$_{22}$ Jr 38$_{23}$, *expel, divorce* Ezr 10$_{3.19}$, נהג *lead* 1 S 30$_{22}$, אסף *incorporate* in household 2 S 11$_{27}$, שׁלח pi. *send away, divorce* Gn 12$_{20}$ Dt 22$_{19.29}$=11QT 66$_{11}$ Dt 24$_{1.3.4}$ Jr 3$_{1}$ Ezr 10$_{44}$ (if em. יֵשׁ *there were*) 1 C 8$_{8}$, גרשׁ *drive out* Mc 2$_{9}$, שׁוב hi. *return* Gn 14$_{16}$ (|| עַם *people*) 20$_{7.14}$ Jr 41$_{16}$ (|| גֶּבֶר *man*), ישׁב ho. *marry* Ezr 10$_{2.10.14.17.18}$ Ne 13$_{23.27}$, עזב *leave behind* 2 S 15$_{16}$, נוח hi. *leave behind* 2 S 20$_{3}$, שׁאר hi. *allow to remain* Dt 23$_{4}$, קהל hi. *congregate* Dt 31$_{12}$, נשׂא *raise* Gn 31$_{17}$ 46$_{5}$, *marry* Jg 21$_{23}$ Ru 1$_{4}$ Ezr 10$_{44}$ 2 C 11$_{21}$ 13$_{21}$ 24$_{3}$ 11QT 57$_{15}$, *cause to marry* Si 7$_{23(A)}$, עמד hi. *cause to stand* Nm 5$_{18.30}$, רכב hi. *cause to ride* Ex 4$_{20}$.

ראה *see* Gn 12$_{14}$ 33$_{5}$ Dt 21$_{11}$=11QT 63$_{11}$ Jg 14$_{1.2}$ 16$_{1}$ 2 S 11$_{2}$, חמד *desire* Ex 20$_{17}$ Dt 5$_{21}$, אהב *love* Ex 21$_{5}$ Jg 16$_{4}$ 1 K 11$_{1}$ Ho 3$_{1}$ Ec 9$_{9}$, שׂמח pi. *delight* Dt 24$_{5}$ (Sam שׂמח אֶת *be happy with*), שׂנא *hate* Dt 22$_{13.16}$=11QT 65$_{7.11}$ Dt 24$_{3}$, מאס *despise* Si 7$_{19}$, תעב pi. *abominate* 7$_{26}$, בזה hi. *cause to despise* husband Est 1$_{17}$ (or em. לְהִבָּזוֹת *so that* their husbands *would be despised*), נשׁא hi. *deceive* Gn 3$_{13}$, רמה pi. *deceive* 1 S 28$_{12}$, קנא pi. *be jealous*, i.e. suspicious (of) Nm 5$_{14.14.30}$ Si 9$_{1}$.

בעל *marry* Dt 24$_{1}$ 11QT 65$_{7}$, פקד *visit* Jg 15$_{1}$, ידע *know, be intimate with* Gn 4$_{1.17.25}$ 1 S 1$_{19}$ 1QSa 1$_{10}$, נחם pi. *comfort* 2 S 12$_{24}$, שׁכב *lie with* Gn 26$_{10}$ Lv 15$_{18}$ 19$_{20}$ 20$_{11.18}$ Nm 5$_{19}$ Dt 28$_{30(Qr)}$ 1 S 2$_{22}$, (|| בַּיִת *house*), רבע *lie with* Lv 18$_{23}$ 20$_{16}$, נאף *commit adultery with* Lv 20$_{10}$ Pr 6$_{32}$, pi. *commit adultery with* Jr 29$_{23}$, יבם pi. *consummate levirate marriage with* Gn 38$_{8}$ Dt 25$_{5}$.

שׁקה hi. *cause to drink* Nm 5$_{24.26.27}$, לבשׁ hi. *clothe* Gn 3$_{21}$, שׁמר *keep* Est 2$_{3.8.15}$ (all שֹׁמֵר הַנָּשִׁים *guardian of the women*), כול pilp. *provide for* 2 S 20$_{3}$, רפא *heal* Gn 20$_{17}$, נצל hi. *rescue* 1 S 30$_{18}$, חיה hi. *allow to live* Nm 31$_{18}$, pi. Jg 21$_{14}$ 1 S 27$_{9}$, משׁל hi. *give authority to* Si 30$_{28}$ 47$_{19}$, קבר *bury* Gn 23$_{19}$ 49$_{31.31}$.

קרא *call* Ex 2$_{7}$, שׁאל *ask* 2 S 14$_{18}$, צוה pi. *command* 2 S 14$_{19}$ 1 K 17$_{9}$, שׁבע hi. *adjure* Nm 5$_{19.21}$, ברך pi. *bless* 1 S 2$_{20}$, אשׁר pi. *declare blessed* Pr 31$_{28}$, הלל pi. *praise* 31$_{28.31}$.

שׁבה *capture* Gn 34$_{29}$ Nm 31$_{9}$ 1 S 30$_{2}$ 2 C 21$_{17}$ 28$_{8}$, חטף *seize* Jg 21$_{21}$, בזז *plunder* Gn 34$_{29}$ Dt 20$_{14}$=11QT 62$_{10}$, ענה pi. *violate* Dt 22$_{24.29}$=11QT 66$_{3.11}$ (both || נַעֲרָה *girl*) Lm 5$_{11}$ (|| בְּתוּלָה *virgin*), שׁגל *violate* Dt 28$_{30(Kt)}$, טמא pi. *defile* Ezk 18$_{6.11.15}$ 33$_{26}$, נכה hi. *strike* Ex 21$_{28(Sam)}$ (MT נגח *gore*) Jg 21$_{10}$, נגף *strike* Ex 21$_{22}$, נגח *gore* 21$_{28}$=4Q251 4$_{3}$ (א]שה ... יגח]; Sam נכה *strike*), דקר *stab* Nm 25$_{8}$ (|| אִישׁ *man*), שׂרף *burn* Lv 20$_{14}$ Jg 15$_{6}$ (|| אָב *father*), רגם *stone* Lv 20$_{27}$, סקל *stone* Dt 17$_{5}$=11QT 55$_{21}$, מות hi. *kill* Ex 21$_{29}$=4Q251 4$_{5}$ ([והמית]), הרג *kill* Lv 20$_{16}$ Nm 31$_{17}$ Ezk 9$_{6}$ Est 3$_{13}$, כרת hi. *cut off* Jr 44$_{7}$, נפץ pi. *shatter* Jr 51$_{22}$, חרם hi. *put to ban* Dt 3$_{6}$ Jg 21$_{11}$ (|| זָכָר *male*), שׁכל pi. *make childless* 1 S 15$_{33}$.

<CSTR> אֵשֶׁת *wife of* + pr.n.m., Noah Gn 7$_{13}$, Abra(ha)m Gn 11$_{29}$ 11$_{31}$ 12$_{17}$ 16$_{1.3}$ 20$_{18}$, Nahor Gn 11$_{29}$ 24$_{15}$, Esau 36$_{10+7t}$, Judah 38$_{12}$ Frey 1295, Jacob Gn 46$_{19}$, Hezron 1 C 2$_{24}$, Abishur 2$_{29}$, Hodiah 4$_{19}$, Machir 7$_{16}$, Moses Ex 18$_{2}$, Amram Nm 26$_{59}$, Lappidoth Jg 4$_{4}$, Heber 4$_{17.21}$ 5$_{24}$, Gilead 11$_{2}$, Samson 14$_{15.16.20}$, Mahlon Ru 4$_{10}$, Phinehas 1 S 4$_{19}$, Saul 14$_{50}$, David 25$_{44}$ 2 S 3$_{5}$, Nabal 1 S 25$_{14}$ 27$_{3}$ 30$_{5}$ 2 S 2$_{2}$ 3$_{3}$, Uriah 2 S 11$_{3.26}$ 12$_{10.15}$, Solomon 1 K 9$_{16}$, Jeroboam 14$_{2.4.5.6.17}$, Naaman 2 K 5$_{2}$, Jehoiada 2 C 22$_{11}$ (|| בַּת *daughter*), Shallum 2 K 22$_{14}$ ||2 C 34$_{22}$, Asaiah Seal 62$_{2}$, Joshua Seal 63$_{2}$, Pashhur 152$_{1}$, Hananel 157$_{2}$, Eleazar Frey 1294, Dositheus Mur 30 1$_{6}$ 2$_{25}$ (אשתו של דוסתס), נְשֵׁי לֶמֶךְ *wives of Lamech* Gn 4$_{23}$, נְשֵׁי־דָוִד *wives of David* 1 S 30$_{5}$, נְשֵׁי מִדְיָן *women of Midian* Nm 31$_{9}$, נְשֵׁי יָבֵשׁ גִּלְעָד *women of Jabesh-gilead* Jg 21$_{14}$.

אֵשֶׁת־הָאִישׁ *wife of the man* Gn 20$_{7}$ Lv 20$_{10}$ Pr 6$_{26}$ (both אֵשֶׁת אִישׁ), אֵשֶׁת הָאֶחָד *the wife of one (of them)* Dt 25$_{11}$, אֵשֶׁת־הַמֵּת *wife of the deceased* Dt 25$_{5}$ Ru 4$_{5}$, נְשֵׁי הַמֶּלֶךְ *wives of the king* 2 K 24$_{15}$, אֵשֶׁת אֲדֹנָיו *wife of his lord* Gn 24$_{36}$ (אֲדֹנִי) 39$_{7}$ (אֵשֶׁת־) 39$_{8}$ 2 S 12$_{8}$ (נְשֵׁי אֲדֹנֶיךָ + בְּחֵיקֶךָ *in your bosom*; || בֵּית *house*), נְשֵׁי עַמִּי *wives of my people* Mc 2$_{9}$, אֵשֶׁת אָבִיו *his father's wife* Gn 37$_{2}$ (נְשֵׁי) Lv 18$_{8}$ (אֵשֶׁת־אָבִיךָ) 20$_{11}$ Dt 23$_{1}$=11QT 66$_{12}$ (אביהו) Dt 27$_{20}$, אֵשֶׁת אָחִיו *his brother's wife* Gn 38$_{8}$ (אָחִיךָ) 38$_{9}$ Lv 18$_{16}$ (אֵשֶׁת־אָחִיךָ) 20$_{21}$ 11QT 66$_{12}$ (אחיהו), אֵשֶׁת בִּנְךָ *your son's wife* Lv 18$_{15}$, נְשֵׁי־בָנָיו *his sons' wives* Gn 6$_{18}$ (בָנֶיךָ) 7$_{7.13}$ 8$_{16}$ (בָנֶיךָ) 8$_{18}$ 46$_{26}$ (נְשֵׁי בְנֵי־), אֵשֶׁת רֵעֵהוּ *his neighbour's wife* Ex 20$_{17}$ (רֵעֶךָ) Lv 20$_{10}$ Dt 5$_{21}$ (רֵעֶךָ) 22$_{24}$=11QT 66$_{3}$ Jr 5$_{8}$ Ezk 18$_{6.11.15}$ 22$_{11}$ 33$_{26}$ Pr 6$_{29}$, נְשֵׁי רֵעֵיהֶם *their neighbours' wives* Jr 29$_{23}$, אֵשֶׁת עֲמִיתְךָ *your neighbour's wife* Lv 18$_{20}$.

אֵשֶׁת חֵיקֶךָ *wife of your bosom*, i.e. your cherished wife Dt 13$_{7}$=11QT 54$_{20}$ (חיקכה) Dt 28$_{54}$ (חֵיקוֹ) Si 9$_{1}$, אֵשֶׁת נְעוּרִים *wife of (one's) youth* Is 54$_{6}$ Ml 2$_{14.15}$ (both נְעוּרֶיךָ) Pr 5$_{18}$ (נְעוּרֶךָ) Si 15$_{2}$, אֵשֶׁת בְּרִיתֶךָ *wife of your covenant*, i.e. to whom you have vowed Ml 2$_{14}$, אֵשֶׁת לֵדָה *wife (of) giving birth* Jr 13$_{21}$ 1QH 3$_{7}$, אֵשֶׁת בַּעֲלַת־אוֹב *woman of*, i.e. who is, *a possessor of a familiar spirit* 1 S 28$_{7.7}$, אֵשֶׁת יְפַת־תֹּאַר *woman of*, i.e. who is, *fair of form* Dt 21$_{11}$=11QT 63$_{11}$ (11QT, Sam אִשָּׁה יְפַת תֹּאַר *a woman, fair of form*), אֵשֶׁת־חֵן *woman of grace*, i.e. graceful woman Pr 11$_{16}$ Si 9$_{8}$ (+ יפי לא לך *fairness that is not yours*), אֵשֶׁת חַיִל *wife of valour*, i.e. doughty wife Pr 12$_{4}$ (:: מְבִישָׁה *one that brings shame*)

31_{10} (both אֵשֶׁת־) Ru 3_{11} Si 26_{2}.

אֵשֶׁת מְרוֹרִים *woman of bitterness(es)* 4QapLam^{a} 2_{7}, אֵשֶׁת רָע *woman of evil,* i.e. bad woman Pr 6_{24} (or em. אִשָּׁה זָרָה *strange woman* or אֵשֶׁת רֵעַ *wife of a neighbour*), אִשֹּׁת הַזִּמָּה *the women of wickedness* Ezk 23_{44} (or em. לַעֲשׂוֹת זִמָּה *to do wickedness*), אשת זדון *woman of impudence* Si 12_{14}, אֵשֶׁת זְנוּנִים *woman of,* i.e. that practices, *fornication* Ho 1_{2}, אֵשֶׁת כְּסִילוּת *woman of folly* Pr 9_{13} (or em. אֵשֶׁת כְּסִילוּת to כְּסִילוּת), אשת לשון *wife of tongue,* i.e. garrulous Si 25_{20} (+ אִישׁ *husband*), אֵשֶׁת מִדְיָנִים *wife of arguments,* i.e. argumentative Pr 21_{9}=$25_{24(Qr)}$ (+ בַּיִת *house*) $21_{19(Qr)}$ $27_{15(Qr)}$.

בַּעַל אִשָּׁה *husband of a woman* Ex $21_{3.22}$ (הָאִשָּׁה) Si 25_{8}, אִישׁ הָאִשָּׁה *husband of the woman* Jg 20_{4}, יְלוּד אִשָּׁה *(one) born of woman* Jb 14_{1} (+ אָדָם *human being*) 15_{14} 25_{4} Si 10_{18} (all three + אֱנוֹשׁ *human being*) 1QS 11_{21} (+ בֶּן־אָדָם *human being*) 1QH 13_{17} $18_{13.16}$ (א[שה]) pap4QJub $13_{29(Baillet)}$ (אש[ה]) 4QapLam^{b}$_{5}$, בֶּן־אִשָּׁה *son of a woman* Lv $24_{10.11}$ (הָאִשָּׁה) Jg $11_{1.2}$ (בְּנֵי־הָאִשָּׁה) 11_{2} 1 K 3_{19} (הָאִשָּׁה) 7_{14}||2 C 2_{13} 1 K 17_{17} (הָאִשָּׁה) 1 C 4_{19} (בְּנֵי אֵשֶׁת; or em. בְּנֵי אִשְׁתּוֹ), בַּת־אֵשֶׁת *daughter of the wife of* Lv 18_{11}, בַּת הַנָּשִׁים *daughter of the women* Dn 11_{17} (or em. אֲנָשִׁים *of men*), אֲחוֹת אִשְׁתּוֹ *sister of his wife* 1 K 11_{19}, חַכְמוֹת נָשִׁים *wise(st) ones of women* Pr 14_{1} (or em. חָכְמוֹת תָּשִׁים *wisdom places*), נֵפֶל אֵשֶׁת appar. *miscarriage of a woman* Ps 58_{9} (or em. אֵשֶׁת to אִשָּׁה, or נֵפֶל אֵשֶׁת בַּל־חָזוּ שָׁמֶשׁ *[as] the miscarriage of a woman, they have not seen [the] sun* to וְאֵשֶׁת בַּל־חָזָה שָׁמֶשׁ *and [as] a mole [that] has not seen [the] sun*; + שַׁבְּלוּל *snail*).

חֶמְדַּת נָשִׁים *one beloved of women* Dn 11_{37}, אַהֲבַת נָשִׁים *love of women* 2 S 1_{26}, נֶפֶשׁ נָשֶׁיךָ *soul of your wives* 19_{6}, קוֹל אִשְׁתֶּךָ *voice of your wife* Gn 3_{17}, דִּבְרֵי הָאִשָּׁה *words of the woman* 39_{19} (אִשְׁתּוֹ) 2 K 6_{30}, שבועת האשה *vow of the woman* CD 16_{10}, מִדְיְנֵי אִשָּׁה *arguments of,* i.e. from, *a wife* Pr 19_{13} (Gnz מִדִינֵי), צַעֲקַת הָעָם וּנְשֵׁיהֶם *outcry of,* i.e. from, *the people and their wives* Ne 5_{1}, מַעֲשֵׂה אִשָּׁה *action of a woman* Ezk 16_{30}, שֵׁם הָאִשָּׁה *the woman's name* Gn 3_{20} (אִשְׁתּוֹ) $11_{29.29}$ (both אֵשֶׁת־) 36_{39}||1 C 1_{50} (אִשְׁתּוֹ) Nm 25_{15} 26_{59} 1 S 14_{50} (both אֵשֶׁת) 25_{3} Ru 1_{2} (both אִשְׁתּוֹ) 1 C 2_{29} (אֵשֶׁת) 8_{29}||9_{35} (אִשְׁתּוֹ; 9_{35} mss אֲחֹתוֹ *of his sister*), תואר אשה *woman's figure* Si 36_{27}, יופי אשה *woman's fairness* 25_{21}, עֶרְוַת אִשָּׁה *woman's nakedness* Lv $18_{8.16}$ (both אֵשֶׁת־) 18_{17}, יַד הָאִשָּׁה *the woman's hand* Gn 19_{16} (יַד־אִשְׁתּוֹ) 38_{20} Nm 5_{25} (both לקח מִן *take from*) Jg 4_{9} (יַד־אִשָּׁה; + מכר בְּ *sell into*), יְדֵי נָשִׁים *women's hands* Lm 4_{10}, רֹאשׁ הָאִשָּׁה *the woman's head* Nm 5_{18}, מֵצַח אִשָּׁה *woman's forehead* Jr 3_{3} (or em. אִשָּׁה זוֹנָה *of a woman* that *is a prostitute* to נְחֻשָׁה *of bronze*), אָזְנֵי נְשֵׁיכֶם *your women's ears* Ex 32_{2}, לֵב אִשָּׁה *woman's heart* Jr 48_{41} 49_{22}.

שִׂמְלַת אִשָּׁה *woman's garment* Dt 22_{5} 4QOrd^{a} 2_{7} (שלמות, both || גֶּבֶר *man*), כתונ[ת] אשה *woman's tunic* 2_{7}, תַּמְרוּקֵי הַנָּשִׁים *ointments of,* i.e. for, *the women* Est 2_{12}, מִשְׁכְּבֵי אִשָּׁה *sexual actions of a woman* Lv 18_{22} 20_{13}, דֶּרֶךְ נָשִׁים *way of women,* i.e. menstruation Gn 31_{35}, דָּת הַנָּשִׁים *law of,* i.e. for, *women* Est 2_{12}.

עֲוֹן הָאִשָּׁה *sin (in respect) of the woman* 2 S 3_{8}, רע אשה *woman's wickedness* Si 25_{17}, רעת אשה *woman's wickedness* 25_{19} 42_{13}, רָעֹת נְשֵׁיכֶם *your wives' sins* Jr 44_{9} (רָעוֹת נָשָׁיו; or em. רָעוֹת נְשֵׁיהֶם) 44_{9}, טיב אשה *woman's nature* Si $42_{14(B, M)}$ (Bmg טוב *goodness*; || אִישׁ *man*).

בֵּית־אִשָּׁה *woman's house* Jos 2_{1} 6_{22} (הָאִשָּׁה), בֵּית הַנָּשִׁים *house of the women,* i.e. harem Est $2_{3.9.11}$ (חֲצַר בֵּית־) $2_{13.14}$ Si $42_{12(B)}$ (ובית נשים *and [in] a house of women,* unless בית = *between*; or em. בין *between*), מִשְׁתֵּה נָשִׁים *banquet of,* i.e. for, *women* Est 1_{9}, הֲמוֹן נָשִׁים *abundance of wives* 2 C 11_{23}, כָּל־אִשָּׁה *each woman* Ex 35_{25} Jg 21_{11}, כָּל־הַנָּשִׁים *all the women* Ex 15_{20} 35_{26} 1 K 11_{8} (נָשָׁיו) Ezk 23_{48} Est $1_{17.20}$ 2_{17} Ezr 10_{3} (נָשִׁים; ms הַנָּשִׁים; or em. נָשֵׁינוּ).

<APP> אִשָּׁה in cstr. or with sf. *wife of, his wife,* etc., preceded by pr.n.f., Eve Gn 4_{1}, Sarah 11_{31} $12_{5.11.17}$ $16_{1.3}$ $17_{15.19}$ $18_{9.10}$ $20_{2.14.18}$ 23_{19} 24_{36} 25_{10} 49_{31}, Milcah 24_{15}, Rebekah 25_{21} 26_{8} 49_{31} 4QPentPar^{a} 3.2_{4} (רבקה] [אשתו), Adah Gn $36_{10.12}$, Basemath $36_{10.13.17}$, Oholibamah $36_{14.18.18}$, the daughter of Shua 38_{12}, Ephrathah 1 C 2_{24} (if em.; see Nom. Cl.), Rachel Gn 46_{19}, Azubah 1 C 2_{18}, Maacah 7_{16}, Hodesh 8_{9}, Zipporah Ex 18_{2}, Jael Jg $4_{17.21}$ 5_{24}, Ruth Ru 4_{10}, Hannah 1 S 1_{19}, Peninnah 1_{4}, Michal 19_{11} 25_{44}, Abigail 25_{14} 27_{3} 30_{5} 2 S 2_{2} 3_{3} Seal 62_{2}, Eglah 2 S 3_{5}||1 C 3_{3}, Bathsheba 2 S 11_{3} 12_{24}, Jezebel 1 K $21_{5.7.25}$, Jehoshabeath 2 C 22_{11}, Huldah 2 K 22_{14}||2 C 34_{22}, Zeresh Est $5_{10.14}$ $6_{13.13}$, Ahathmelech Seal 63_{1}, Adatha 152_{1}, Alijah 157_{1}, Salome Frey 1294 1295 Mur 30 1_{6} 2_{25} (both || בַּת

daughter).

אִשָּׁה ... יְהוּדִית *a wife ... Judith* Gn 26$_{34}$, אִשָּׁה ... אִיזֶבֶל *a wife ... Jezebel* 1 K 16$_{31}$, אִשָּׁה ... מָחֲלַת *a wife ... Mahalath* 2 C 11$_{18}$, נָשָׁיו ... עָדָה ... אָהֳלִיבָמָה *his wives ... Adah ... Oholibamah* Gn 36$_{2}$, שְׁתֵּי נָשִׁים חֶלְאָה וְנַעֲרָה *two wives, Helah and Naarah* 1 C 4$_{5}$, חוּשִׁים ... בַּעֲרָא נָשָׁיו *Hushim ... Baara, his wives* 8$_{8}$, אִשְׁתּוֹ הַיְהֻדִיָּה *his wife, the Judaean* 1 C 4$_{18}$, כַּלָּתוֹ אֵשֶׁת־ *his daughter-in-law, the wife of* 1 S 4$_{19}$, בִּתּוֹ אֵשֶׁת־ *his daughter, the wife of* 1 S 25$_{44}$ 1 K 9$_{16}$, שְׁתַּיִם נָשִׁים בְּנוֹת אֵם־אַחַת *two women, daughters of the same mother* Ezk 23$_{2}$.

אִשָּׁה(־)אַלְמָנָה *woman* who is *a widow* 2 S 14$_{5}$ 1 K 7$_{14}$ 11$_{26}$ 17$_{9.10}$, אִשָּׁה נְבִיאָה *woman* who is *a prophetess* Jg 4$_{4}$, אִשָּׁה פִילֶגֶשׁ *woman* who is *a concubine* 19$_{1.27}$, var. 2 S 15$_{16}$ 20$_{3}$, אִשָּׁה נִדָּה *woman* who is *an impurity*, i.e. impure Ezk 18$_{6}$, אִשָּׁה יִרְאַת־י׳ *a woman* who possesses *reverence for Y.* Pr 31$_{30}$, הָאִשָּׁה בַּעֲלַת הַבָּיִת *the woman* who was *the mistress of the household* 1 K 17$_{17}$, אִשָּׁה ... בְתוּלָה *virgin* ... he shall take as *a wife* Lv 21$_{14}$, אִשָּׁה זוֹנָה *woman* who is *a prostitute* Lv 21$_{7}$ (זֹנָה) Jos 2$_{1}$ 6$_{22}$ (הָאִשָּׁה הַזּוֹנָה) Jg 11$_{1}$ 16$_{1}$ 1 K 3$_{16}$ (נָשִׁים זֹנוֹת) Jr 3$_{3}$ (or em. נְחֻשָׁה forehead *of bronze*) Ezk 16$_{30}$ (אִשָּׁה־) 23$_{44}$ Pr 6$_{26}$ (or em.; see Prep.), אִשָּׁה ... שִׁית זוֹנָה נְצֻרַת לוֹט *woman ... (one dressed in) a garment of a prostitute, one that is enclosed by a veil* 7$_{10}$ (if em. נְצֻרַת לֵב *kept of heart*), נָשִׁים שָׂרוֹת *women* who are *princesses* 1 K 11$_{3}$.

<ADJ> אִשָּׁה אַחַת *a certain woman* Jg 9$_{53}$ 2 K 4$_{1}$ Zc 5$_{7}$, הָאִשָּׁה הָאַחַת *the first woman* 1 K 3$_{17}$, הָאִשָּׁה הַזֹּאת *this woman* 1 S 2$_{20}$ 1 K 3$_{17.18.19}$ 2 K 6$_{28}$, הָאִשָּׁה הַהִיא *that woman* Nm 5$_{31(Qr)}$, נָשִׁים רַבּוֹת *many women* Jg 8$_{30}$ 1 K 11$_{1}$ Ezk 16$_{41}$.

אִשָּׁה הָרָה *pregnant woman* Ex 21$_{22}$, אִשָּׁה דָּוָה *sick woman* Lv 20$_{18}$, אִשָּׁה חֲדָשָׁה *new wife* Dt 24$_{5}$, אִשָּׁה ... חֲלָלָה *defiled ... woman* Lv 21$_{7}$, אִשָּׁה גְדוֹלָה *great, important woman* 2 K 4$_{8}$, אִשָּׁה טוֹבָה *good wife* Si 26$_{1.3}$ ([ט]ובה), אִשָּׁה רָעָה *bad wife* 42$_{6}$, אִשָּׁה יָפָה *beautiful woman* Pr 11$_{22}$, var. Gn 12$_{14}$ Jb 42$_{15}$, אִשָּׁה חֲכָמָה *wise woman* 2 S 14$_{2}$ 20$_{16}$, אִשָּׁה בַּיֶּשֶׁת *decorous wife* Si 26$_{15}$, נָשִׁים שַׁאֲנַנּוֹת *carefree women* Is 32$_{9}$, נָשִׁים רַחֲמָנִיּוֹת *compassionate women* Lm 4$_{10}$.

אִשָּׁה יִשְׂרְאֵלִית *Israelite woman* Lv 24$_{10.11}$, אִשָּׁה כֻשִׁית *Cushite wife* Nm 12$_{1.1}$, הָאִשָּׁה הַתְּקֹעִית *the Tekoan woman* 2 S 14$_{4.9}$, אִשָּׁה זָרָה *strange*, or *foreign*, *woman* Pr 2$_{16}$ 6$_{24}$ (if em. אֵשֶׁת רָע *woman of evil*) 7$_{5}$ Si 9$_{3}$ (|| זוֹנָה *prostitute*), אִשָּׁה אַחֶרֶת *another woman* Jg 11$_{2}$ 1 K 3$_{22}$ 1 C 2$_{26}$ 11QT 57$_{17}$, נָשִׁים מִצְרִיֹּת *Egyptian women* Ex 1$_{19}$, נָשִׁים ... מֹאֲבִיּוֹת *Moabite ... wives* Ru 1$_{4}$ Ne 13$_{23}$ (+ עַמֳּנִיּוֹת *Ammonite*, אַשְׁדֳּדִיּוֹת *Ashdodite*), נָשִׁים נָכְרִיּוֹת *foreign wives* 1 K 11$_{1.8}$ Ezr 10$_{2.3(ms)+6t}$ Ne 13$_{26.27}$.

אִשָּׁה חַכְמַת־לֵב *woman* that is *wise of mind* Ex 35$_{25}$, אִשָּׁה יְפַת־מַרְאֶה *woman* that is *beautiful in appearance* Gn 12$_{11}$ 2 S 14$_{27}$, אִשָּׁה קְשַׁת־רוּחַ *woman* who is *hard of spirit* 1 S 1$_{15}$.

<PREP> לְ of direction, *to*, + אמר *say* Gn 3$_{13}$ 4$_{23}$ Nm 5$_{21}$ Jg 14$_{15}$ 2 S 14$_{5}$ 1 K 14$_{2}$ Is 45$_{10}$, דבר pi. *speak* Jg 14$_{7}$, נגד hi. *tell* 1 S 25$_{14}$, ספר pi. *recount* Est 6$_{13}$ (|| אהב ptc. *friend*), שׁאל *ask* 2 K 8$_{6}$, נתן *give* 1 S 1$_{4}$ 1 K 3$_{26}$ 9$_{16}$ 2 K 8$_{6}$ Jb 42$_{15}$ Pr 31$_{3.31}$ Ru 4$_{13}$ Si 47$_{19}$, of possession, *of, (belonging) to* 1 S 28$_{24}$ 2 S 3$_{5}$||1 C 3$_{3}$, of benefit, *for*, + עשׂה *do, make* Gn 3$_{21}$ Nm 5$_{30}$ 1 K 11$_{8}$ 11QT 48$_{16}$, לקח *take* wagons Gn 45$_{19}$.

לקח לוֹ לְאִשָּׁה *take for him(self) as a wife* (and vars.) Gn 12$_{19}$ 25$_{20}$ 28$_{9}$ 34$_{4.21}$ Ex 6$_{20.23.25}$ Dt 21$_{11}$=11QT 63$_{11}$ Dt 24$_{3}$ 25$_{5}$ Jg 3$_{6}$ 14$_{2}$ 1 S 25$_{39.40}$ 2S 12$_{9}$ 1 K 4$_{15}$ Ezk 44$_{22}$ 4Q251 7$_{3}$ ([אל יקח ... לאישתו]), קָנִיתִי לִי לְאִשָּׁה *I have acquired for myself as a wife* Ru 4$_{10}$, נתן לוֹ לְאִשָּׁה *give to him as a wife* (and vars.) Gn 16$_{3}$ 29$_{28}$ 30$_{4.9}$ 34$_{8.12}$ 38$_{14}$ (ni. *be given*) 41$_{45}$ Dt 22$_{16}$=11QT 65$_{11(mg)}$ Jos 15$_{16.17}$=Jg 1$_{12.13}$ Jg 21$_{1.7}$ 1 S 18$_{17.19}$ (ni.) 18$_{27}$ 1 K 2$_{17.21}$ (ho. *be given*) 2 K 14$_{9}$||2 C 25$_{18}$ 1 C 2$_{35}$ 4Q251 7$_{4}$ (ואל תנתן] [אישה ... לאישתו).

היה לוֹ לְאִשָּׁה *become to him as a wife, become his wife* (and vars.) Gn 20$_{12}$ 24$_{67}$ Nm 36$_{3.6.6.8.11.12}$ Dt 21$_{13}$=11QT 63$_{14}$ 22$_{19.29}$=11QT 66$_{11}$ Dt 24$_{4}$ 1 S 25$_{42.43}$ 2 S 11$_{27}$ 12$_{10}$ 1 K 4$_{11}$ 2 K 8$_{18}$||2 C 21$_{6(mss)}$ (L אִשָּׁה) Ru 4$_{13}$, מָהֹר יִמְהָרֶנָּה לּוֹ לְאִשָּׁה *he must pay her bride-price for her to be to him as a wife* Ex 22$_{15}$.

דרשׁ לְ *ask about* 2 S 11$_{3}$, שׁאל לְ *ask about* Gn 26$_{7}$, שׁלח לְ *send for* 1 K 20$_{7}$, היה לְ *become as* Jr 50$_{37}$ 51$_{30}$, זור לְ *be loathsome to* Jb 19$_{17}$ (|| בֵּן *child*), קנא לְ pi. *be suspicious of* Si 9$_{2}$, מַה־נַּעֲשֶׂה ... לְנָשִׁים *what shall we do ... for wives?* Jg 21$_{7.16}$, וַיִּבֶן י׳ אֱלֹהִים אֶת־הַצֵּלָע ... מִן־הָאָדָם לְאִשָּׁה *and Y. God built the rib ... from the man as a woman* Gn 2$_{22}$, שֵׁם לְנָשִׁים *a byword among women*

Ezk 23$_{10}$.

בְּ *for the sake of (acquiring)*, + עבד *serve* Ho 12$_{13}$, + שׁמר *keep* sheep 12$_{13}$, יחשׂ בְּ htp. *be registered in addition to* 2 C 31$_{18}$, דבק בְּ *cleave to* Gn 2$_{24}$, נגף בְּ *strike against* with plague 2 C 21$_{14}$, משׁל בְּ *rule over* Gn 3$_{16}$, נגע בְּ *touch* 26$_{11}$ (|| אִישׁ *man*), חזק בְּ hi. *seize* 11QT 66$_{4}$, חשׁק בְּ *desire* Dt 21$_{11}$=11QT 63$_{11}$, טמא בְּ *defile onself by* Lv 18$_{20}$, בגד בְּ *betray* Ml 2$_{14.15}$, רעע עַיִן בְּ hi. *look wickedly at* Dt 28$_{54}$, וְכֹל הַטַּף בַּנָּשִׁים *each infant among the women*, i.e. every young woman Nm 31$_{18}$, הַיָּפָה בַּנָּשִׁים *the fair(est) of the women* Ca 1$_{8}$ 5$_{9}$ 6$_{1}$.

מִן of direction, *from*, + יצא *go out* Si 42$_{13}$, שׁמר *keep away* 1 S 21$_{5}$ Pr 6$_{24}$ 7$_{5}$, בדל ni. *separate oneself* Ezr 10$_{11}$, עלם hi. *avert* eye Si 9$_{8}$, נצל hi. *save* Pr 2$_{16}$, of cause, *by means of*, + שׂים *establish* offspring 1 S 2$_{20}$, מאשה תחלת עון *by means of a woman was the beginning of sin* Si 25$_{24}$, partitive, *some of*, *(any)one of* Nm 31$_{35}$ (specifying נֶפֶשׁ אָדָם *human beings*) 2 K 4$_{1}$, comparative, *than* Jg 21$_{14}$ Pr 21$_{9.19}$ 25$_{24}$, + אהב *love* Est 2$_{17}$ 2 C 11$_{21}$ (both + כָּל־ *all*), ברך pu. *be blessed* Jg 5$_{24.24}$, שׁכל *be made childless* 1 S 15$_{33}$, וַיְהִי־בָךְ הֵפֶךְ מִן־הַנָּשִׁים *and there was in you a difference from the women* Ezk 16$_{34}$, שׂמח מִן *rejoice in* Pr 5$_{18}$, ילד מִן hi. *have children by* 1 C 8$_{9}$.

כְּ *as* Ex 1$_{19}$ 2 S 14$_{2}$ Is 19$_{16}$ 54$_{6}$ Jr 13$_{21}$ (כְּמוֹ) Si 15$_{2}$ 4QapLam^{a} 2$_{7(mg)}$ 1QH 3$_{7}$ (כְּמוֹ), אֹרַח כַּנָּשִׁים *the normal way of women* Gn 18$_{11}$.

אֶל of direction, *to*, + אמר *say* Gn 3$_{1.4.16}$ 12$_{11}$ Nm 5$_{19}$ Jg 13$_{13.22}$ 1 S 28$_{8}$ 2 S 14$_{2.8.18}$ Jr 44$_{24}$ (+ כָּל־ *all*), *say concerning* Gn 20$_{2}$, דבר pi. *speak* Jg 13$_{11}$ 1 K 14$_{5}$ 2 K 4$_{17}$ 8$_{1}$ 22$_{14}$||2 C 34$_{22}$, קרא *call* 1 K 17$_{10}$ ([אשתו]), צהל *neigh* lustfully Jr 5$_{8}$, נגשׁ *approach* Ex 19$_{15}$, הלך *go* 2 K 22$_{14}$||2 C 34$_{22}$, ירד *go down* Jg 14$_{10}$, שׁוב *go back* Jr 3$_{1}$, בוא *come* Jg 13$_{9.10}$ 1 S 28$_{8}$ 2 S 17$_{20}$, for sex Gn 29$_{21}$ 38$_{8.9}$ Dt 21$_{13}$=11QT 63$_{14}$ Dt 22$_{13}$ (=11QT 65$_{7}$ וּבְעָלָהּ *and he married her*) Jg 15$_{1}$ 16$_{1}$ 2 S 12$_{24}$ 20$_{3}$ Ezk 23$_{44}$ Pr 6$_{29}$ Ru 4$_{13}$ 1 C 7$_{23}$, for marriage Dt 25$_{5(Sam)}$ (MT עַל), קרב *approach* 2 S 20$_{17}$, for sex Lv 18$_{14.19}$ Dt 22$_{14}$=11QT 65$_{8}$ Ezk 18$_{6}$ Si 9$_{3}$ 1QSa 1$_{10(Milik)}$ ([י]קרב), נתן שְׁכֹבֶת אֶל *give sex to*, i.e. have sex with Lv 18$_{20}$, ראה אֶל ni. *appear to* Jg 13$_{3.21}$, חבר אֶל *associate with* Si 12$_{14}$.

עַל *on* the body of (of clothes) Dt 22$_{5}$ 4QOrd^{a} 2$_{6}$, *on account of* Gn 20$_{3}$, *in addition to* 28$_{9}$ Ex 35$_{22}$ (+ אֲנָשִׁים *men*) 11QT 57$_{16}$, *concerning* 2 S 14$_{8}$ Jb 31$_{9}$, בוא עַל *come to* for marriage Dt 25$_{5}$ (Sam אֶל), יצא עַל *go out to* Est 1$_{17}$, עַל־דְּבַר *on account of* Gn 20$_{11.18}$, לחם עַל ni. *fight for* Ne 4$_{8}$, עַל־אֹדוֹת *concerning* Nm 12$_{1}$, אמר עַל *say to* Jr 44$_{20}$ (|| גֶּבֶר *man*).

אֵת *with*, + עשׂה *do* abomination Ezk 22$_{11}$, צחק pi. *play* Gn 26$_{8}$, ילד אֵת hi. *have children by* 1 C 2$_{18}$.

עִם *with*, + שׁכב *lie (sexually)* Dt 22$_{22.22}$ 27$_{20}$ 2 S 11$_{11}$ 12$_{11.24}$ 11QT 45$_{11}$ 66$_{4(mg).4(mg)}$ (||Dt 22$_{25[Qr]}$ נַעֲרָה *girl*) CD 12$_{1}$, ראה חַיִּים *enjoy life* Ec 9$_{9}$, יעץ עִם ni. *take advice from* Si 37$_{11}$ (+ אל צרתה *concerning her rival*), גַּם־אִישׁ עִם־אִשָּׁה *both man with*, i.e. and, *woman* Jr 6$_{11}$.

מֵאִישׁ (וְ)עַד־אִשָּׁה *including both man and woman* Jos 6$_{21}$ 8$_{25}$ 1 S 15$_{3}$ 22$_{19}$ 2 S 6$_{19}$||1 C 16$_{3}$ Ne 8$_{2}$ 2 C 15$_{13}$, מטף עד נשים *including both infants and wives* 1QSa 1$_{4}$.

שׁחת בְּעַד ho. *be destroyed because of* Si 9$_{8}$, בְּעַד אִשָּׁה זוֹנָה appar. *on account of a woman (who is) a prostitute* Pr 6$_{26}$ (or em. בְּעַד אִשָּׁה to בְּעַד or בִּקְשָׁה a prostitute *has sought*); הלך אַחֲרֵי *go after* Jg 13$_{11}$; לְעֵינֵי *in the sight of* Ezk 16$_{41}$; לִפְנֵי *before* 2 K 5$_{2}$, נֶגֶד *before* Ne 8$_{3}$; לְנֹכַח *on behalf of* Gn 25$_{21}$; מִלְּבַד *excepting* Gn 46$_{26}$.

בֵּינְךָ וּבֵין הָאִשָּׁה *between you and the woman* Gn 3$_{15}$, בֵּין אִישׁ לְאִשְׁתּוֹ *between a man and his wife* Nm 30$_{17}$ (|| בַּת *daughter*).

<COLL> אִישׁ ... אוֹ ... אִשָּׁה *a man ... or ... a woman* Ex 21$_{28}$=4Q251 4$_{3}$ ([את איש או את א]שה) Ex 21$_{29}$=4Q251 4$_{5}$ ([אי]ש) Lv 13$_{29.38}$ 20$_{27}$ Nm 5$_{6}$ (|| נֶפֶשׁ *person*) 6$_{2}$ Dt 17$_{2.5}$=11QT 55$_{16.21}$ Dt 17$_{5}$ 29$_{17}$ 4QRitPur 40$_{2(Baillet)}$ ([אי]ש), אִישׁ וְאִשָּׁה *man and/or woman* Ex 35$_{29}$ (+ כָּל־ *any*) 36$_{6}$ Jg 9$_{49}$ (+ כְּאֶלֶף *about a thousand*) 16$_{27}$ (+ כִּשְׁלֹשֶׁת אֲלָפִים *about three thousand*) 1 S 27$_{9.11}$ Jr 44$_{7}$ (אִישׁ־) 51$_{22}$ Est 4$_{11}$, אִישׁ אִשְׁתּוֹ *each man* is to seize *his wife* Jg 21$_{21.22}$, אֲנָשִׁים וְנָשִׁים *men and women* Dt 31$_{12}$ Jg 9$_{51}$ (+ כָּל־ *all*) 16$_{27}$ Jr 40$_{7}$ Ezr 10$_{1}$ (+ יְלָדִים *children*) Ne 8$_{3}$, אשישים ונשים *men and women* 4QRitMar 34$_{3}$, נער זעטוט ואשה *young lad and/or woman* 1QM 7$_{3}$ (+ כל *every*), var. 4QM^{a} fr. 1$_{6}$ (א[ש]ה).

שְׁתֵּי נָשִׁים *two wives* Gn 4$_{19}$ Dt 21$_{15}$ 1 S 1$_{2}$ 27$_{3}$ 30$_{5.18}$ 2 S 2$_{2}$ 1 C 4$_{5}$ CD 4$_{21}$, שְׁתַּיִם נָשִׁים *two women* 1 K 3$_{16}$ Ezk 23$_{2}$ Zc 5$_{9}$, var. 2 C 24$_{3}$, שְׁלֹשֶׁת נָשִׁים *three wives* Gn 7$_{13}$, שֶׁבַע נָשִׁים *seven women* Is 4$_{1}$ (:: אִישׁ אֶחָד *one man*), עֶשֶׂר נָשִׁים *ten women* Lv 26$_{26}$ 2 S 15$_{16}$ 20$_{3}$, אַרְבַּע עֶשְׂרֵה נָשִׁים

fourteen wives 2 C 13$_{21}$, נָשִׁים שְׁמוֹנֶה־עֶשְׂרֵה *eighteen wives* 11$_{21}$, נָשִׁים שְׁבַע מֵאוֹת *seven hundred wives* 1 K 11$_{3}$.

וְאִשְׁתּוֹ *and his wife* preceded by pr.n.m., Noah Gn 7$_{7}$ 8$_{18}$ Abimelech 20$_{17}$, Abraham 25$_{10}$, Manoah Jg 13$_{19.20}$, Elkanah 1 S 2$_{20}$, Eleazar Frey 1247, הָאָדָם וְאִשְׁתּוֹ *the man and his wife* Gn 2$_{25}$ 3$_{8.21}$, הוּא וְאִשְׁתּוֹ *he and his wife* 13$_{1}$ Ru 1$_{1}$, אַתָּה ... וְאִשְׁתְּךָ *you* (sg.) *and your wife* Gn 6$_{18}$ 8$_{16}$, אַתֶּם וּנְשֵׁיכֶם *you* (pl.) *and your wives* Jr 44$_{25}$.

הָאִשָּׁה וִילָדֶיהָ *the wife and her children* Ex 21$_{4}$, sim. Ho 1$_{2}$ Ne 8$_{3}$ 11QT 39$_{7}$, הָאִשָּׁה ... בְּנָהּ *the woman ... her son* 2 K 8$_{5}$, בֵּן וְאִשָּׁה your *son and wife* Si 30$_{28}$, אִשָּׁה וּבִתָּהּ *a woman and her daughter* Lv 18$_{17}$, אִשָּׁה ... בָּנִים *wife ... children/sons* Ex 4$_{20}$ 18$_{2.6}$ 21$_{5}$ (+ אָדוֹן *master*) Dt 28$_{54}$ (+ אָח *brother*) 1 S 30$_{22}$ Jb 19$_{17}$ (בֵּן), var. Gn 6$_{18}$ 7$_{7.13}$ 8$_{16.18}$ Ex 18$_{5}$, אִשָּׁה ... בָּנוֹת *wife ... daughters* Gn 19$_{15.16}$.

נָשִׁים ... יְלָדִים *wives ... children* Gn 30$_{26}$ 32$_{23}$ (+ שְׁפָחוֹת *maidservants*) 33$_{5}$ Ne 12$_{43}$, נָשִׁים ... בָּנִים *wives ... children/sons* Ex 22$_{23}$ Nm 16$_{27}$ 1 K 20$_{3.5.7}$ (all three + כֶּסֶף *silver*, זָהָב *gold*) Jr 38$_{23}$ 1 C 7$_{4}$, var. Gn 31$_{17}$ 2 C 20$_{13}$ 21$_{14.17}$, אִשָּׁה ... בָּנִים ... בָּנוֹת *wife ... sons ... daughters* 1 S 1$_{4}$ Jr 16$_{2}$ Am 7$_{17}$, var. Dt 13$_{7}$=11QT 54$_{20}$ (+ אָח *brother*), נָשִׁים ... בָּנִים ... בָּנוֹת *wives ... sons ... daughters* Gn 36$_{6}$ Ex 32$_{2}$ 1 S 30$_{3}$ Jr 14$_{16}$ 29$_{6}$ 35$_{8}$ Ne 10$_{29}$ 2 C 28$_{8}$ 31$_{18}$, var. 2 S 19$_{6}$ Ne 4$_{8}$ (+ אָח, בַּיִת *house*) 2 C 29$_{9}$.

טַף ... נָשִׁים *infants ... wives* Gn 34$_{29}$ 45$_{19}$ 46$_{5}$ Nm 32$_{26}$ (+ מִקְנֶה *livestock*) Dt 20$_{14}$=11QT 62$_{10}$ (both + בְּהֵמָה *beasts*) Dt 29$_{10}$ (+ גֵּר *foreigner*) Ezk 9$_{6}$ (+ בְּתוּלָה *young woman*, בָּחוּר *young man*, זָקֵן *old person*) Est 3$_{13}$ 8$_{11}$ 2 C 20$_{13}$ 31$_{18}$ (+ כֹּל־ *all*), var. Nm 14$_{3}$ 16$_{27}$ 31$_{9}$ Dt 2$_{34}$ 3$_{6}$ (+ מַת *man*) 3$_{19}$ (+ מִקְנֶה) 31$_{12}$ (+ גֵּר) Jos 1$_{14}$ (+ מִקְנֶה) 8$_{35}$ (+ גֵּר) Jg 21$_{10}$ Jr 40$_{7}$ 41$_{16}$ (+ סָרִיס *eunuch*) 43$_{6}$ (both + גֶּבֶר *man*) 1QpHab 6$_{11}$ (‖ אִישׁ, זָקֵן *man*, נַעַר *lad*) 4QpNah 3.4$_{4}$ (‖ עוֹלֵל *suckling*), נָשִׁים וְהַנּוֹלָד מֵהֶם *women and whoever was born of them* Ezr 10$_{3}$.

נָשִׁים ... אֲנָשִׁים ... בַּחוּרִים *wives ... men ... young men* Jr 18$_{21}$, בָּנִים ... אָבוֹת ... נָשִׁים *children ... fathers ... wives* Jr 7$_{18}$, הָעָם וּנְשֵׁיהֶם *the people and their wives* Ne 5$_{1}$, אִשָּׁה ... אִמָּהּ *woman ... her mother* Lv 20$_{14}$, אֵם ... נָשִׁים *mother ... wives* 2 K 24$_{15}$, אִשְׁתּוֹ וְאַמְהֹתָיו *his wife and his maidservants* Gn 20$_{17}$, נָשִׁים ... פִּלַגְשִׁים *wives ... concubines* 2 S 19$_{6}$ 1 K 11$_{3}$ 2 C 11$_{21.21}$, var. 2 S 5$_{13}$.

יין ונשים *wine and women* Si 19$_{2}$, באין אשה *without a wife* Si 36$_{30}$, וְגַם־הָאִשָּׁה *and also the woman* 1 S 28$_{23}$, אִשָּׁה לִי *a wife of mine* 2 C 8$_{11}$, יָרֵא לֵאמֹר אִשְׁתִּי *he was frightened of saying, My wife* Gn 26$_{7}$ (‖ אָחוֹת *sister*), וּנְשֵׁיהֶם לְבָד *and their wives on their own* Zc 12$_{12.12.13.}$ 13.14, אִשָּׁה זוֹנָה ... וְאֵשֶׁת אִישׁ perh. *a woman (who is) a prostitute ... and (who is) a wife of a man*, i.e. an adulteress Pr 6$_{26}$ (or em.; see Prep.).

Also Si 41$_{21(Bmg)}$ 11QT fr. 5 11QJub 4$_{14}$ 4QRitMar 1$_{3}$ 4QDibHam[c] 31$_{3}$ 4QOrd[c] 1.1$_{1}$. 4QapPs[b] 1$_{7}$ (א[שתו])

<SYN> (§§ 1–2) אִישׁ *man*, גֶּבֶר *man*, אֱנוֹשׁ *man*, אַלְמָנָה *widow*, בֵּן *son/child*, בַּת *daughter*, נַעַר *lad*, נַעֲרָה *girl*, יֶלֶד *child*, טַף *infant(s)*, עוֹלֵל *suckling*, אָב *father*, אֵם *mother*, אָח *brother*, אָחוֹת *sister*, שִׁפְחָה *maidservant*, פִּילֶגֶשׁ *concubine*, אהב ptc. *friend*, זָקֵן *old man*, גֵּר *sojourner*, בַּיִת *house*, שָׂדֶה *field*, מִקְנֶה *livestock*, בְּהֵמָה *beast*.

אִשֶּׁה 65.3.8 n.m. **fire offering**—cstr. אִשֵּׁה; pl. cstr. אִשֵּׁי; sf. אִשַּׁי (אִשָּׁי)—**fire offering,** i.e. offering made by fire.

<SUBJ> היה *be* Lv 23$_{18}$ 24$_{7}$ (+ לְבֹנָה *frankincense*).

<NOM CL> אִשֶּׁה הוּא לַי׳ *it is a fire offering to Y.* Ex 29$_{25}$ Lv 8$_{21}$ (‖ עֹלָה *burnt offering*) 8$_{28}$ (‖ מִלֻּאִים *consecration offering*), vars. Ex 29$_{18}$ (‖ עֹלָה) Lv 1$_{13.17}$, זֶה הָאִשֶּׁה *this is the fire offering* Nm 28$_{3}$, אִשֵּׁי י׳ ... הוּא נַחֲלָתוֹ *the fire offerings of Y. ... are his* (Levi's) *inheritance* Jos 13$_{14}$ (if em. אִשֵּׁי ׳י to ׳י *Y.* is his inheritance), sim. Si 45$_{22(Segal)}$, אשי י׳ בידם *the fire offerings of Y. were in their hand* Si 50$_{13}$, עולה היא אשה *it is a burnt offering, a fire offering* 11QT 15$_{13}$, vars. 16$_{10}$ ([עו]לה הוא) 22$_{4}$ + Sup (עולה הואה), [הוא] ... אשי *it is fire offerings of* 28$_{2(Yadin)}$, מִנְחָתוֹ ... אִשֶּׁה *its grain offering is ... a fire offering* Lv 23$_{13}$.

<OBJ> קטר hi. *burn* Ex 30$_{20}$ Lv 1$_{9}$ 2$_{2.9.11.16}$ 3$_{5}$ (+ עֹלָה *burnt offering*) 7$_{5}$ (+ אָשָׁם *guilt offering*) Nm 18$_{17}$ (+ רֵיחַ נִיחֹחַ לַי׳ *a pleasing odour to Y.*) 11QT 20$_{8(Yadin)}$ 23$_{17}$ 34$_{14}$ 4QJub[d] 1.13$_{4}$ ([ויק]טירו) ([תקטיר ... אשה]), קרב hi. *offer* Lv 3$_{3.9}$ (both + מִזֶּבַח הַשְּׁלָמִים *from the sacrifice of the peace offerings*) 3$_{14}$ 7$_{25}$ 21$_{6.21}$ (‖ לֶחֶם *bread*) 23$_{8.25.27.36.36.37}$ Nm 15$_{13}$ 28$_{3.13.19}$ 29$_{13.36}$ 11QT 28$_{1(Yadin)}$ + Sup ([והקרבתמה]), בוא hi. *bring* Lv 7$_{30}$ (+ חֵלֶב *fat*) Nm 15$_{25}$ (‖ חַטָּאת *sin offering*), נתן *give* Lv 22$_{22}$ (+ לַי׳ *to Y.*) 1 S 2$_{28}$ (+ לְ *to* Eli's house), עשׂה *make*, i.e. offer Ex 29$_{41}$ Nm 15$_{3}$ (+ לַעֲשׂוֹת רֵיחַ נִיחֹחַ *to make a pleasing*

odour) 15$_{10.14}$ 28$_{8}$ 29$_{6}$ (+ לְרֵיחַ נִיחֹחַ for a pleasing odour), אכל eat Dt 18$_{1}$ (|| נַחֲלָה inheritance) Si 45$_{21}$.

<CSTR> אִשֵּׁה רֵיחַ(־)נִיחֹחַ fire offering of pleasing odour Lv 1$_{9}$ (נִיחֹחַ) 1$_{13.17}$ 2$_{2.9}$ 3$_{5}$ 23$_{18}$ Nm 15$_{10.13.14}$ 28$_{8.24}$ 29$_{13.36}$ (all fourteen + לַי׳ to Y.) 11QT 15$_{13}$ 16$_{10(Yadin)}$ (both ניחוח) 20$_{8(Yadin)}$ (ני[ח]ו[ח]) 22$_{4(Yadin)}$ + Sup ([ניחוח]) 34$_{14}$ (ניחוח) 4QJub^{d} 1.1$_{34}$ (אשה ריח ניחוח), אִשֵּׁה י׳ fire offering of Y. Dt 18$_{1(mss)}$ (L אִשֵּׁי fire offerings of), אשי ריח ניחוח fire offering(s) of pleasing odour 11QT 23$_{17}$ 28$_{2(Yadin)}$ (ר[יח ניחוח]), אִשֵּׁי י׳ fire offerings of Y. Lv 2$_{3.10}$ 4$_{35}$ 5$_{12}$ 6$_{10}$ (if em. אִשַּׁי my fire offerings) 6$_{11}$ 7$_{30.35}$ 10$_{12.13}$ 21$_{6.21}$ 24$_{9}$ Dt 18$_{1}$ (mss אִשֵּׁה) Jos 13$_{14}$ Si 45$_{21.22}$ (אשי י[יי]) 50$_{13}$, הַחֲלָבִים of fat Lv 10$_{15}$, בְּנֵי יִשְׂרָאֵל of the Israelites 1 S 2$_{28}$; קָרְבַּן אִשֶּׁה oblation of fire offering Lv 22$_{27}$, לֶחֶם אִשֶּׁה appar. food of fire offering (unless app.) 3$_{11.16}$ (+ רֵיחַ נִיחֹחַ) Nm 28$_{24}$ (אִשֵּׁה), לַחְמִי אִשַּׁי bread of my fire offerings 28$_{2}$ (if em.; see App.), כָּל־אִשֵּׁי all the fire offerings of 1 S 2$_{28}$.

<APP> אִשֶּׁה preceded by עֹלָה burnt offering Lv 1$_{9.13.17}$ 23$_{18}$ Nm 28$_{6}$ 29$_{6.13.36}$ 11QT 15$_{13}$ 16$_{10}$ (עו[לה]) perh. 20$_{8(Yadin)}$ (העול[ה]) 22$_{4(Yadin)}$ + Sup (+ ריח odour); עֹלָה, רֵיחַ נִיחֹחַ pleasing odour Nm 28$_{13}$; עֹלָה אוֹ־זֶבַח burnt offering or sacrifice 15$_{10}$; כֶּבֶשׂ lamb 28$_{8}$; פַּר bull, אַיִל ram, כֶּבֶשׂ 29$_{6}$; רֵיחַ נִיחֹחַ Ex 29$_{18.41}$; אַזְכָּרָה memorial offering Lv 2$_{2.9.16}$ 24$_{7}$; קָרְבָּן offering 3$_{14}$ Nm 15$_{25}$; חֵלֶב fat 18$_{17}$; חֵלֶב, כְּלָיוֹת kidneys, יֹתֶרֶת appendage Lv 3$_{5}$ 7$_{5}$; שְׁנֵי עֶשְׂרֹנִים סֹלֶת two tenths (of an ephah of) flour 23$_{13}$; כָּל־שְׂאֹר וְכָל־דְּבַשׁ any leaven or honey 2$_{11}$; הכול ... אשה everything ... a fire offering 11QT 34$_{14}$ 4QJub^{d} 1.1$_{34}$ ([הכול ... אשה]), sim. 11QT 23$_{17}$ (אשי).

אִשֶּׁה followed by עֹלָה Nm 28$_{3}$; עֹלָה, מִנְחָה grain offering, זֶבַח sacrifice, נֶסֶךְ drink offering Lv 23$_{37}$; עֹלָה אוֹ־זֶבַח Nm 15$_{3}$; פַּר, אַיִל, כֶּבֶשׂ 28$_{19}$; כֶּבֶשׂ 29$_{13.36}$; רֵיחַ נִיחֹחַ Lv 23$_{13}$ Nm 28$_{2}$ (if em. לַחְמִי לְאִשַּׁי רֵיחַ נִיחֹחִי my bread for my fire offerings, my pleasing odour to לַחְמִי אִשַּׁי לְרֵיחַ נִיחֹחִי the bread of my fire offerings for my pleasing odour); חֵלֶב Lv 3$_{3.9}$; חֵלֶב, כְּלָיוֹת, יֹתֶרֶת 3$_{14}$; לֶחֶם bread 21$_{6}$.

<PREP> עשה לְ offer as Ex 29$_{41}$ Nm 28$_{6}$ (pass.), לַחְמִי לְאִשַּׁי my bread for my fire offerings 28$_{2}$ (if em.; see App); מִן partitive, of, from Lv 2$_{3.10}$ (both + קֹדֶשׁ holiness) 6$_{11}$ (+ חֹק statute) 7$_{35}$ (+ מִשְׁחָה consecrated portion) 10$_{13}$ (+ חֹק) 24$_{9}$ Nm 18$_{9}$ (if em. אֵשׁ fire; both + קֹדֶשׁ), + יתר ni. remain 10$_{12}$ (+ מִנְחָה grain offering), נתן give portion 6$_{10}$ (if em. מֵאִשַּׁי from my fire offerings to מֵאִשֵּׁי י׳ from the fire offerings of Y.); קטר עַל hi. burn upon Lv 4$_{35}$ 5$_{12}$ (+ חַטָּאת sin offering), בוא עַל hi. bring sacrificial portions with 10$_{15}$.

<COLL> אִשֶּׁה ... לַי׳ fire offering ... to Y. Ex 29$_{18.25.41}$ 30$_{20}$ Lv 1$_{9.13.17}$ 2$_{2.9.11.16}$ 3$_{3.5.9.11.14}$ 7$_{5.25}$ 8$_{21.28}$ 22$_{22.27}$ 23$_{8.13.18.25.27.36.36.37}$ 24$_{7}$ Nm 15$_{3.10.14.25}$ 18$_{17}$ 28$_{3.6.8.13.19.24}$ 29$_{6.13.36}$ 11QT 23$_{17}$ (אשי) 22$_{4(Yadin)}$ + Sup 28$_{(Yadin)}$ + Sup 28$_{2(Yadin)}$ (all three [לי׳]); אשה ... לפני י׳ fire offering ... before Y. 11QT 15$_{13}$ (לפיני) 16$_{10(Yadin)}$ (ל[פני י׳]) 20$_{8(Yadin)}$ ([לפני]) 34$_{14}$.

<SYN> עֹלָה burnt offering, חַטָּאת sin offering.

→ אֵשׁ fire.

[אָשׁוּחַ], see אָשִׁיחַ.

[אשויה], see אָשְׁיָה.

[אֱשׁוֹן] 1 n.[m.] **beginning**—cstr. אֱשׁוֹן—בֶּאֱשׁוֹן חֹשֶׁךְ at the beginning of darkness Pr 20$_{20(Qr)}$ (Kt בְּאִישׁוֹן at the pupil, i.e. middle, of), בֶּאֱשׁוֹן לַיְלָה at the beginning of night Pr 7$_{9}$ (if em. בְּאִישׁוֹן).

אַשּׁוּר 150.1.5 pl.n. **Assyria**—אַשֻּׁר—**1. Assyria,** capital city, land, and empire centred on the river Tigris at Qal'at Šerqāṭ, Gn 2$_{14}$ 10$_{11}$ 2 K 15$_{29}$ 17$_{6.23}$ 18$_{11}$ Is 27$_{13}$ Jr 2$_{18}$ Hos 5$_{13}$ 7$_{11}$ 8$_{9}$ 9$_{3.6}$ (if em. מִשֹּׁד from destruction) 10$_{6}$ 11$_{11}$ Am 3$_{10}$ (if em. אַרְמְנוֹתֵיהֶם their palaces) Zp 2$_{13}$; assoc. with Egypt Is 11$_{11.16}$ 19$_{23.23}$ Mc 7$_{12}$ Zc 10$_{10.11}$; מֶלֶךְ(־)אַשּׁוּר king of Assyria 2 K 15$_{19.20.20.29}$ 16$_{7.8.9.9.10.18}$ 17$_{3+8t}$ 18$_{7.9.11}$ 18$_{13}$||Is 36$_{1}$ 2 K 18$_{14.14.16.17}$||Is 36$_{2}$ 2 K 18$_{19}$||Is 36$_{4}$||2 C 32$_{10}$ 2 K 18$_{23.28.30.31.33}$||Is 36$_{8.13.15.16.18}$ 2 K 19$_{4.6.8.10.20.32.36}$||Is 37$_{4.6.8.10.21.33.37}$ 2 K 20$_{6}$||Is 38$_{6}$ 2 K 23$_{29}$ Is 7$_{17.20}$ 8$_{4.7}$ 10$_{12}$ 20$_{1.4.6}$ Jr 50$_{17.18}$ Na 3$_{18}$ Ezr 4$_{2}$ 6$_{22}$ 1 C 5$_{6}$ (אַשֻּׁר) 5$_{26.26}$ 2 C 28$_{16.20.21}$ 32$_{1+6t}$ 33$_{11}$; מַלְכֵי אַשּׁוּר kings of Assyria 2 K 19$_{11.17}$||Is 37$_{11.18}$ Ne 9$_{32}$ 2 C 30$_{6}$ 32$_{4}$, אֶרֶץ אַשּׁוּר land of Assyria Is 7$_{18}$ Mc 5$_{5}$, רֹכְלֵי ... אַשּׁוּר merchants of ... Assyria Ezk 27$_{23}$.

2. appar. ident. with Shur (שׁוּר), Gn 25$_{18}$ (or em.

שׁוּרָה *to Shur*).

3. as gent., **Assyrian,** people, army of Assyria, Nm 24$_{22.24}$ Is 10$_{5.24}$ 14$_{25}$ 23$_{13}$ 30$_{31}$ 31$_{8}$ 52$_{4}$ Jr 2$_{36}$ Ezk 23$_{5}$ 31$_{3}$ (or em. תְּאַשּׁוּר *box-tree*) 32$_{22}$ Hos 11$_{5}$ 12$_{2}$ 14$_{4}$ Mc 5$_{4.5}$ Ps 83$_{9}$ 1QM 1$_{6}$ 18$_{2}$; assoc. with Egypt Is 19$_{23.23}$ Lm 5$_{6}$, with Egypt and Israel Is 19$_{24.25}$; מַחֲנֵה אַשּׁוּר *camp of Assyria* 2 K 19$_{35}$||Is 37$_{36}$ Si 48$_{21}$ ([מ]חנה), בְּנֵי(־)אַשּׁוּר *Assyrians* Ezk 16$_{28}$ 23$_{7.9.12.23}$ 1QM 2$_{12}$, גדודי כתיי אשור *troops of the Kittim of Assyria* 1$_{2}$; הומן אשור *multitude of Assyria* 19$_{10}$.

4. as pr.n.m., **Asshur,** son of Shem, Gn 10$_{22}$||1 C 1$_{17}$.

אֲשׁוּרִי 1 gent. **Ashurite,** or perh. **Assyrian,** וַיַּמְלִכֵהוּ אֶל־הַגִּלְעָד וְאֶל־הָאֲשׁוּרִי *and he made him king over Gilead and the Ashurites* 2 S 2$_{9}$ (or em. אָשֵׁרִי *Asherites*).

אַשּׁוּרִם 1 pr.n.m. **Asshurim,** son of Dedan and appar. ancestor of north Arabian people, Gn 25$_{3}$ (or em. אַשּׁוּר *Assyria*).

אַשְׁחוּר 2.0.0.2 pr.n.m. **Ashhur**—I אשחר—**1.** son of Hezron and Abijah (or Caleb and Ephrathah, if em. בָּא כָלֵב אֶפְרָתָה אֵשֶׁת חֶצְרוֹן אָבִיהוּ *Caleb went in to Ephrathah, the wife of Hezron his father*), 1 C 2$_{24}$ 4$_{5}$. **2.** son of Asaiah ([בן] עשיהו), Seal 532$_{1}$ (אשחר; T. Beit Mirsim?, 7th/6th cent.). **3.** Samaria ost. 13$_{3}$ (אשחר).

אשחר, see אַשְׁחוּר.

אשיה, see אשיהו.

[אָשְׁיָה] 1 n.f. **tower**—pl. sf. אָשְׁיוֹתֶיהָ (Kt אשויתיה)—<SUBJ> נפל *fall* Jr 50$_{15}$ (|| חוֹמָה *wall*).

אשיהו 0.0.0.9 pr.n.m. **Ashiah**—אשיה—**1.** son of Ezer and father of Eliashib, Arad ost. 17$_{3}$ 35$_{2}$ ([אש]יהו) 40$_{7}$ ([ואשיהו]) 40$_{11}$ (ו[א]ש[יה]ו) 51$_{1}$ Seal 231$_{2}$ 232$_{2}$ (אשיה) 282$_{2}$ (all three Arad, 7th cent.) 370$_{1}$ (8th/7th cent.). **2.** son of Shemaiah, Seal 533$_{1}$ 605$_{2}$ 610$_{2}$ (all three T. Beit Mirsim?, 7th/6th cent.). **3.** Lachish ost. 22$_{6}$ ([לאש]יהו). **4.** Jerusalem decanter inscr. ([לאש]יהו).

→ י׳ *Y*.

אשיו, see יְהוֹאָשׁ *Joash*.

[אָשִׁיחַ] 0.1.4 n.m. **reservoir**—Si, Q אשיח (Allegro אשוח); cstr. Q אשיח (Allegro אשוח); pl./du. Allegro אשוחין—**reservoir, cistern,** <SUBJ> כרה ni. *be dug* Si 50$_{3}$ (+ מִקְוֶה *pool*). <NOM CL> אשיח שיבית הכרם *reservoir that is (at) Beth-haccherem* 3QTr 10$_{5}$. <CSTR> מז[רח] אשיח שלומו *east of the reservoir of Solomon* 3QTr 5$_{6}$ (Allegro [ב]בזר *in the lining of*), בית אשוחין *house of the (two) reservoirs* 11$_{12}$(Allegro) (AHL בית אשדתין or אשרחין *Beth-eshdatin* or *Beth-eshrahin*). <PREP> בְּ *in* 3QTr 10$_{5}$ 11$_{12}$. <ADJ> האשיח הצפו[ני הגד]ול *the large northern reservoir* 3QTr 7$_{4}$.

→ שׁוח *sink down*.

אֲשִׁימָא 1 pr.n.f. **Ashima,** Hamathite god, אַנְשֵׁי חֲמָת עָשׂוּ אֶת־אֲשִׁימָא *the men of Hamath made Ashima* 2 K 17$_{30}$, הַנִּשְׁבָּעִים בְּאַשְׁמַת שֹׁמְרוֹן *those who swear by Ashima of Samaria* Am 8$_{14}$ (if em. בְּאַשְׁמַת *by the wicked deed of*).

אֲשֵׁירָה, see אֲשֵׁרָה.

[אָשִׁישׁ] 1.0.5 n.m. **adult**—pl. Q אשישים; cstr. אֲשִׁישֵׁי; sf. Q אשישיהם—<OBJ> אבד pi. *destroy* 1QpHab 6$_{11}$. <CSTR> אשישי צדק *adults of righteousness*, i.e. righteous adults 4QRitMar 9$_{9}$, appar. אֲשִׁישֵׁי קִיר־חֲרֶשֶׂת *adults of Kir-hareseth* Is 16$_{7}$ (but perh. אֲשִׁישָׁה *raisin-cake*; ||Jr 46$_{31}$ אַנְשֵׁי *men of*). <APP> רבים ... נערים אשישים וזקנים נשים וטף *many ... youths, adults and old people, women and children* 1QpHab 6$_{11}$.

Also 4QRitMar 9$_{4}$ (+ נַעַר *lad*) 9$_{11}$ 10$_{3}$ ([א]שישי) 34$_{3}$ (+ אִשָּׁה *woman*).

אֲשִׁישָׁה 4 n.f. **raisin cake**—pl. אֲשִׁישׁוֹת, cstr. אֲשִׁישֵׁי—<OBJ> אהב *love* Ho 3$_{1}$, חלק pi. *apportion* 2 S 6$_{19}$||1 C 16$_{3}$ (+ לֶחֶם *bread*, אֶשְׁפָּר *date cake*). <CSTR> אֲשִׁישֵׁי עֲנָבִים *raisin cakes (made) of (dried) grapes* Ho 3$_{1}$, perh. אֲשִׁישֵׁי קִיר־חֲרֶשֶׂת *raisin cakes of Kir-hareseth* Is 16$_{7}$ (but prob. אָשִׁישׁ *adult*; ||Jr 46$_{31}$ אַנְשֵׁי *men of*). <PREP> סמך בְּ pi. *sustain with* Ca 2$_{5}$ (|| תַּפּוּחַ *apple*).

[אֶשֶׁךְ] 1 n.[m.] **testicle**—אָשֶׁךְ—מְרוֹחַ אָשֶׁךְ *one that is* *crushed of testicle* (and may therefore not serve at altar) Lv 21$_{20}$.

[אַשְׁכּוּז], see אַשְׁכְּנַז.

אֶשְׁכּוֹל I 9 n.m. **cluster**—cstr. אֶשְׁכּוֹל (אֶשְׁכֹּל); pl. אַשְׁכְּלֹת (אַשְׁכֹּלֹת); cstr. אַשְׁכְּלוֹת; sf. אַשְׁכְּלֹתֶיהָ—usu. on grapevine, also on henna shrub (Ca 1$_{14}$). **<SUBJ>** בשל hi. *ripen* into grapes Gn 40$_{10}$. **<NOM CL>** אַשְׁכְּלֹת מְרֹרֹת לָמוֹ *(their) clusters are bitter for them* Dt 32$_{32}$ (+ עֵנָב *grape*), אֵין־אֶשְׁכּוֹל *there is no cluster* Mc 7$_1$ (+ בִּכּוּרָה *early fig*), אֶשְׁכֹּל הַכֹּפֶר דּוֹדִי לִי *my beloved is a cluster of henna (blossom) to me* Ca 1$_{14}$. **<OBJ>** אכל *eat* Mc 7$_1$, כרת *cut* Nm 13$_{23}$ (+ זְמוֹרָה *branch*) 13$_{24}$. **<CSTR>** אֶשְׁכּוֹל עֲנָבִים *cluster of grapes* Nm 13$_{23}$, אֶשְׁכֹּל הַכֹּפֶר *cluster of henna (blossom)* Ca 1$_{14}$, אַשְׁכְּלוֹת הַגֶּפֶן *clusters of the vine* 7$_9$ (+ תַּפּוּחַ *apple*). **<ADJ>** אֶחָד *one* Nm 13$_{23}$. **<PREP>** שָׁדַיִךְ לְאַשְׁכֹּלוֹת *your breasts are as clusters* Ca 7$_8$; מצא בְּ *be found in* (of new wine) Is 65$_8$; היה כְּ *be as* (of breasts) Ca 7$_9$; עַל אֹדוֹת *on account of* Nm 13$_{24}$.
→ אֶשְׁכּוֹל II–III *Eshcol*.

[אֶשְׁכּוֹל] II 2 pr.n.m. **Eshcol**—אֶשְׁכֹּל—Amorite ally of Abram and brother of Mamre and Aner, Gn 14$_{13.24}$.
→ אֶשְׁכּוֹל I *cluster*.

אֶשְׁכּוֹל III 4 pl.n. **Eshcol,** near Hebron, visited by Israelite spies, אֶשְׁכּוֹל *valley of Eshcol* Nm 13$_{23}$ (אֶשְׁכֹּל) 13$_{24}$ 32$_9$ Dt 1$_{24}$ (אֶשְׁכֹּל).
→ אֶשְׁכּוֹל I *cluster*.

אַשְׁכְּנַז 3 pr.n.m. **Ashkenaz**—אַשְׁכְּנַז, L אַשְׁכֲּנַז **1.** descendant of Japheth, Gn 10$_3$||1 C 1$_6$ (אַשְׁכֲּנַז; mss אַשְׁכְּנַז). **2.** people descended from preceding, appar. ident. with Scythians, Jr 51$_{27}$ (אַשְׁכְּנָז).

אֶשְׁכָּר 2.0.0.1 n.[m.] **payment**—sf. אֶשְׁכָּרֵךְ—**payment, tribute,** **<OBJ>** קרב hi. *present* (of kings) Ps 72$_{10}$ (|| מִנְחָה *tribute*), שׁוב hi. *bring back*, i.e. bring precious goods as payment Ezk 27$_{15}$. **<ADJ>** perh. אשכר טב *good payment* Kadesh Barnea add. ost.

אֵשֶׁל 3 n.[m.] **tamarisk**—mss אֶשֶׁל—**<OBJ>** נטע *plant* Gn 21$_{33}$ (בִּבְאֵר שָׁבַע *at Beer-sheba*). **<PREP>** תַּחַת *under*, + ישׁב *sit* 1 S 22$_6$ (+ בָּרָמָה *on the height*), קבר *bury* bones 31$_{13}$ (+ בְּיָבֵשָׁה *at Jabesh*, ||1 C 10$_{12}$ אֵלָה *terebinth*).

אשׁם 36.1.9 vb. **be guilty**—**Qal** Pf אָשֵׁם (אָשַׁם), אָשְׁמָה, אָשַׁמְתְּ (Q אשמתה), אָשַׁמְתְּ, אָשְׁמוּ; impf. יֶאְשַׁם, תֶּאְשַׁם, נֶאְשָׁם, תֶּאְשְׁמוּ, (יֶאְשָׁמוּ) יֶאְשְׁמוּ; + waw וַיֶּאְשַׁם, וַיֶּאְשְׁמוּ; inf. אָשׁוֹם (אָשֹׁם), לְאַשְׁמָה—**1a.** usu. **be guilty, incur guilt, trespass,** esp. in respect of infringements of holiness. **b.** trans., **be guilty of,** 11QT 59$_9$ 4QJub^d 1.2$_{25}$.

2. be accounted guilty, Ezk 6$_6$ Hos 10$_2$ Is 24$_6$ Zc 11$_5$ Pr 30$_{10}$ perh. Jg 21$_{22}$ Ho 4$_{15}$ etc.

3. acknowledge guilt or **be free of guilt, expiate guilt,** עַד אֲשֶׁר־יֶאְשְׁמוּ וּבִקְשׁוּ פָנָי *until they acknowledge,* or *are free of, (their) guilt and seek my presence* Ho 5$_{15}$, יאשמו כול רשעי עמו אשר שמרו את מצוותו *all the wicked ones of his people who have (nonetheless) kept his commandments will acknowledge,* or *will be free of, (their) guilt* 1QpHab 5$_5$ (unless יאשמו ... אשר = *those who* have kept commandments ... *will declare* the wicked *guilty*).

<SUBJ> יִשְׂרָאֵל *Israel* Ho 10$_2$, Israelites 11QT 59$_9$, עֵדָה *congregation* of Israel Lv 4$_{13}$ (|| שׁגה *err*, עשׂה *do*), יְהוּדָה *Judah* Ho 4$_{15}$ 5$_{15}$, אֶפְרַיִם *Ephraim* 5$_{15}$ 13$_1$ (+ מות *die*), שֹׁמְרוֹן *Samaria* 14$_1$ (+ נפל *fall*), אֱדוֹם *Edom* Ezk 25$_{12}$ (|| נקם ni. *avenge oneself*), עִיר *city*, i.e. Jerusalem 22$_4$ (|| טמא *be unclean*), כַּשְׂדִּי *Chaldaean* Hb 1$_{11}$ (if em. וְיָשֶׂם [1QpHab וישם] *and he will place*, i.e. impute; perh. also em. כַּשְׂדִּי to גִּבּוֹר *warrior*; + עבר *transgress*). Isaac 4QJub^f 21$_{22}$ (ו[א]שמתה), רָשָׁע *wicked (one)* 1QpHab 5$_5$, אכל ptc. *one who devours* Israel Jr 2$_3$, צַר *adversary* of Israel 50$_7$, one who kills sheep, i.e. enemy of Israel Zc 11$_5$, שׂנא ptc. *one who hates* righteous Ps 34$_{22}$, קָרוֹב *(one who is) near* to heretics CD 5$_{15}$ (+ נקה ni. not *be accounted innocent*), מִזְבֵּחַ pagan *altar* Ezk 6$_6$ (or understand as וְיֵשַׁמּוּ *and they will be made desolate*; || חרב *be desolate*, שׁבר ni. *be broken*, שׁבת ni. *be made to cease*).

ישׁב ptc. *one who dwells* in land Is 24$_6$, נָשִׂיא *prince* Lv 4$_{22}$ (|| חטא *sin*, עשׂה *do*), priest, etc. 2 C 19$_{10}$, אָב *father*

Jg 21$_{22}$, אָח *brother* 21$_{22}$ 2 C 19$_{10}$, נֶפֶשׁ *soul*, i.e. individual Lv 4$_{27}$ (|| עשׂה, חטא) 5$_{2}$ (|| טמא *be unclean* [Gnz יָדַע *if he knows, then*]) 5$_{3.4.17}$ (+ נשׂא *bear* iniquity) 5$_{19.23}$ (|| חטא) Nm 5$_{6}$ (+ ידה htp. *confess*), שׁמע ptc. *one who hears* oath CD 9$_{12}$, one who breaks vow 15$_{4}$, one cursed by servant Pr 30$_{10}$, one who approaches powerful person Si 9$_{13}$.

<OBJ> אַשְׁמָה *wickedness* 11QT 59$_{9}$ 4QJubd 1.2$_{25}$.

<PREP> לְ *in respect of* an offence Lv 5$_{5}$, *against* Y. 5$_{19}$ 2 C 19$_{10}$, a person Nm 5$_{7}$; בְּ *with, because of* Ezk 22$_{4}$ Ho 13$_{1}$.

<COLL> אָשֹׁם אָשַׁם *he is indeed guilty* Lv 5$_{19}$, וַיֶּאְשְׁמוּ אָשׁוֹם *and they are most seriously guilty* Ezk 25$_{12}$, כהרביתו יאשם *according to his multiplication, he is guilty*, i.e. the more he does it, the more guilty he becomes CD 5$_{15}$; after conditional clause with עבר *transgress* CD 15$_{4}$, עשׂה *do* evil Nm 5$_{6}$, ידע *know* about an offence 5$_{2(Gnz).3.4.17}$ (+ לֹא *not*) CD 9$_{12}$.

<SYN> §1 חטא *sin*, טמא *be unclean*.

Ni. Pf. נֶאְשָׁמוּ—**be accounted guilty,** as Qal, §2, of עֶדְרֵי צֹאן *flocks of sheep* suffering because of Israel's guilt Jl 1$_{18}$ (or understand as נָשַׁמּוּ *they are made desolate*).

Hi. Impv. הַאֲשִׁימֵם; inf. Q האשים—**1. punish,** of God punishing wicked Ps 5$_{11}$ (+ נפל *fall*).

2. make guilty, wicked, of Belial leading humanity astray 1QM 13$_{11}$ (|| רשׁע hi. *make wicked*).

→ אָשָׁם *guilt*, אַשְׁמָה *guilt*, אָשֵׁם *guilty*.

אָשָׁם 46.0.5 n.m. **guilt**—sf. אֲשָׁמוֹ, אֲשָׁמָם; sf. אֲשָׁמָיו, Q אשמותמה—**1.** usu. **guilt offering, trespass offering,** typically of animal (but also golden haemorrhoids and golden mice 1 S 6$_{4.17}$, soul of servant of Y., Is 53$_{10}$), as reparation, esp. for violation of vow or contact with uncleanness.

<NOM CL> אָשָׁם הוּא *it* (sacrifice) *is a guilt offering* Lv 5$_{19}$ 7$_{5}$, כַּחַטָּאת הָאָשָׁם הוּא לַכֹּהֵן קֹדֶשׁ קָדָשִׁים הוּא *the guilt offering is as the sin offering—it is for the priest; it is most holy* 14$_{13}$ (Sam, ms כְּאָשָׁם; see Prep.), מָה הָאָשָׁם *what is the guilt offering?* 1 S 6$_{4}$, אָשָׁם ... רָצוֹן *a guilt offering ... is a pleasure* Pr 14$_{9}$ (+ בֵּין יְשָׁרִים *among upright individuals*; or em.; see §2, Subj., Nom. Cl.), וַאֲשָׁמָם אֵיל־צֹאן *and their guilt offering was a ram of the flock* Ezr 10$_{19}$ (if em. וְאֲשֵׁמִים *and as for [the] guilty ones*; + עַל־אַשְׁמָתָם *[in atonement] for their wickedness*).

<OBJ> בוא hi. *bring* Lv 5$_{6.7.15.25}$ 19$_{21}$ (all five + לי׳ *to Y.*) 4Q 266$_{3}$ (|| חַטָּאת *sin offering*), לקח *take* Lv 14$_{21}$ (+ לִתְנוּפָה *as a wave offering*), שׁוב hi. *give back* in recompense Nm 18$_{9}$ (|| מִנְחָה, חַטָּאת *meal offering*, קָרְבָּן *offering*) 1 S 6$_{3.4.8.17}$ (in both as second object), נוח hi. *place* Ezk 42$_{13}$ (|| מִנְחָה, חַטָּאת), שׂים *place*, i.e. cause (soul) to be Is 53$_{10}$ (or em. תֻּשַׂם if his soul *were to be placed* as a guilt offering), שׁחט *slaughter* Lv 7$_{2}$ Ezk 40$_{39}$ (|| עוֹלָה, חַטָּאת *burnt offering*), בשׁל pi. *boil* 46$_{20}$ (|| חַטָּאת), אכל *eat* 44$_{29}$ (|| מִנְחָה, חַטָּאת), חטא *sin (in respect of* or *so as to incur*) Lv 5$_{7}$, אשׁם *be guilty (in respect of* or *so as to incur*) Nm 18$_{9(Sam)}$ (MT שׁוב hi. *give back*), ליץ *scorn* Pr 14$_{9}$ (or em. יָלִין *pass the night*; see §2, Subj.).

<CSTR> אֵיל הָאָשָׁם *ram of the guilt offering* Lv 5$_{16}$ 19$_{21}$ (אֵיל אָשָׁם) 19$_{22}$ CD 9$_{14}$, כול אלי אשמות *all (the) rams of guilt offerings* 11QT 35$_{14}$ (others אלו אשמות *all these guilt offerings*; + חַטָּאת *sin offering*), כֶּבֶשׂ הָאָשָׁם *lamb of the guilt offering* Lv 14$_{24}$ (+ לֹג הַשָּׁמֶן *log of oil*) 14$_{25}$, דַּם הָאָשָׁם *blood of the guilt offering* 14$_{14.17.25.28}$, לחם אשמים *flesh of guilt offerings* Si 7$_{31}$ (if em. אברים *bulls* or *limbs*), כֶּסֶף אָשָׁם *money of*, i.e. to purchase, *guilt offering* 2 K 12$_{17}$ (|| חַטָּאת *sin offering*), תּוֹרַת הָאָשָׁם *law of the guilt offering* Lv 7$_{1}$, כָּל־אֲשָׁמָם *every guilt offering of theirs* Nm 18$_{9}$.

<APP> אֲשָׁמוֹ ... אַיִל תָּמִים *his guilt offering ... an unblemished ram* Lv 5$_{15}$, sim. 5$_{25}$ 19$_{21}$, אֲשָׁמוֹ ... נְקֵבָה ... כִּשְׂבָּה אוֹ־שְׂעִירַת עִזִּים *his guilt offering ... a female ..., a lamb or a kid of goats* 5$_{6}$, אֲשָׁמוֹ ... שְׁתֵּי תֹרִים אוֹ־שְׁנֵי בְנֵי־יוֹנָה *his guilt offering ... two turtledoves or two young pigeons* 5$_{7}$, כֶּבֶשׂ אֶחָד אָשָׁם *one lamb, a guilt offering* 14$_{21}$.

<PREP> עשׂה לְ *make* place *for* 11QT 35$_{11.12}$ (both || חַטָּאת *sin offering*), בוא לְ hi. *bring as* Lv 5$_{15.18.25}$ Nm 6$_{12}$, law *concerning* Lv 7$_{7}$ (|| חַטָּאת) 7$_{37}$ (|| עוֹלָה, חַטָּאת *burnt offering*, מִנְחָה *meal offering*, + זֶבַח שְׁלָמִים *peace offering*, מִלּוּאִים *consecration offerings*).

כַּחַטָּאת כָּאָשָׁם *as the sin offering is (as) the guilt offering* Lv 7$_{7}$ 14$_{13(Sam, ms)}$, קֹדֶשׁ קָדָשִׁים הִיא כַּחַטָּאת וְכָאָשָׁם *it is most holy as the sin offering and as the guilt offering* 6$_{10(Qr)}$.

2. guilt, wickedness, wicked deed, **<SUBJ>** שׁוב ho. *be returned,* i.e. be recompensed Nm 5$_{8}$, לין *pass the night* Pr 14$_{9}$ (if em. אֱוִלִים יָלִיץ *fools scorn* to בְּבָתֵּי אֱוִילִים יָלִין *in the houses of fools* wickedness *passes the night;* :: רָצוֹן *pleasure,* i.e. what is pleasing). **<NOM CL>** אָהֳלֵי לֵצִים אָשָׁם *the tents of scoffers are (full of) wickedness* Pr 14$_{9}$ (if em. אֱוִלִים יָלִיץ *fools scorn*). **<OBJ>** שׁוב hi. *give back,* i.e. recompense Nm 5$_{7.8}$, בוא hi. *bring* Gn 26$_{10}$ (+ עַל *upon*).

<CSTR> תערובת [א]שם *mixture of guilt,* i.e. sinful mingling 4QMMT A 2$_{59}$.

<PREP> מִתְהַלֵּךְ בַּאֲשָׁמָיו *wandering about in his wicked deeds* Ps 68$_{22}$; אמן נקתי מא[שם] *truly I am innocent of wickedness* Meṣad Ḥashavyahu ost. 1$_{11}$.

<COLL> אַרְצָם מָלְאָה אָשָׁם *their land is full of wickedness* Jr 51$_{5}$ (+ מִן *against*).

3. stolen item, the possession of which incurs guilt, כל אשם מושב אשר אין בעלים *every stolen item that is returned (for) which there are no owners* CD 9$_{13}$.

Also 11QT 32$_{6}$ (אשמם; Yadin אשמתם *their wicked deeds*) 4QPsJos^{a} 6.1$_{7}$ ([א]שמכה).

<SYN> §1 חַטָּאת *sin offering,* מִנְחָה *meal offering,* עוֹלָה *burnt offering.*

→ אשׁם *be guilty.*

אָשֵׁם 3.0.1 adj. **guilty**—pl. אֲשֵׁמִים (Q אשימים)—as predicative adj. or noun, **guilty (one),** אֲבָל אֲשֵׁמִים אֲנַחְנוּ עַל־אָחִינוּ *we are indeed guilty concerning our brother* Gn 42$_{21}$, וידעו כי אשימים הם *and they knew that they were guilty* CD 1$_{9}$ (erased אנשים *men*), וַאֲשֵׁמִים אֵיל־צֹאן עַל־אַשְׁמָתָם *and as for the guilty ones, there was a ram of the flock (in atonement) for their wickedness* Ezr 10$_{19}$ (or em. וַאֲשָׁמָם *and their guilt offering* was a ram), וּמִדַּבֵּר הַמֶּלֶךְ הַדָּבָר הַזֶּה כְּאָשֵׁם *and because the king has said this thing (he is) as a guilty one* 2 S 14$_{13}$.

→ אשׁם *be guilty.*

אַשְׁמָה 19.0.78 n.f. **guilt**—cstr. אַשְׁמַת; sf. Q אשמתי, Q אשמתכה, אַשְׁמָתוֹ, Q אשמתה, אַשְׁמָתֵנוּ (אַשְׁמָתֵינוּ), אַשְׁמָתָם; pl. אֲשָׁמוֹת; cstr. Q אשמות; sf. אַשְׁמוֹתַי—**1. guilt,** **<NOM CL>** רַבָּה אַשְׁמָה לָנוּ *great is our guilt* 2 C 28$_{13}$. **<OBJ>** רבה hi. *increase* 2 C 33$_{23}$, נחל hi. *cause to inherit* 4Q181 2$_{4}$ (‖ עַוְלָה *iniquity*).

<CSTR> אַשְׁמַת הָעָם *guilt of the people* Lv 4$_{3}$, יִשְׂרָאֵל *of Israel* Ezr 10$_{10}$, ׳י *(in the eyes) of Y.* 2 C 28$_{13}$, אשמת קצי נגוע[י] עוונות *guilt of the periods of those stricken by iniquities* 4QShir^{a} 1$_{7(mg)}$, אשמת גורלו *guilt of his lot* 4QM^{g} 4$_{6}$.

עֲוֹן אַשְׁמָה *iniquity of,* i.e. resulting in, *guilt* Lv 22$_{16}$ (+ נשׂא hi. *cause to bear [responsibility for]*) 11QT 35$_{8}$ (+ נשׂא *bear [responsibility for]*) 1QS 5$_{15}$ (+ נשׂא hi.) 4QRitPur 16$_{1}$ 1QpHab 8$_{12(erased)}$ (all four עוון), חטא אשמה *sin of,* i.e. resulting in, *guilt* 11QT 35$_{15}$ (+ נשׂא), משגת *error of* 4QFlor 1$_{9}$ (א[ש]מה), יגון *weariness of* 1QH 11$_{21}$ (+ חַטָּאָה *sin*), בני *sons of* 5$_{7}$ 6$_{30}$ (+ בני א[מ]תו *sons of his truth*) 7$_{11}$ ([ב]ני), אנשי *men of* 6$_{19}$, זדון אשמתם *insolence of their guilt* 4QpNah 3.3$_{4}$, פשעי אשמתם *sins of their guilt* 1QS 1$_{23}$ (+ עָוֹן *iniquity,* חַטָּאת *sin*), רשע אשמתכה *wickedness of your guilt* 2$_{5}$, פשעי אשמתי *sins of my guilt* 4QShir^{b} 18.2$_{10}$, כול עוון ואשמה *all iniquity and guilt* 11QT 58$_{17}$.

<ADJ> גְּדֹלָה *great* Ezr 9$_{7}$ (+ עֲוֹנֹתֵינוּ *our iniquities*) 9$_{13}$ (+ מַעֲשֵׂינוּ הָרָעִים *our evil deeds*).

<PREP> לְאַשְׁמָה *incurring guilt* Lv 4$_{3}$ 5$_{26}$ 1 C 21$_{3}$ 1QS 5$_{12}$, *in addition to guilt* 2 C 28$_{13}$; בְּאַשְׁמָה *(burdened) with guilt* Ezr 9$_{7.15}$, *because of guilt,* perh. 4QM^{g} 4$_{6}$, + בוא *come* against Israel Ezr 9$_{13}$, רשׁע hi. *condemn* wicked 4QShir^{b} 63.3$_{4}$ (:: אֱמֶת *truth*), perh. *during (time of) guilt* 4QShir^{a} 1$_{7}$; כְּ *according to* 1QS 1$_{10}$ 1QH 5$_{5}$; מִן *(free) of,* + טהר pi. *cleanse* 1QH 4$_{37}$, htp. *be cleansed* 6$_{8}$, שׁמר מִן ni. *keep oneself from* 11QT 58$_{17}$; יסף עַל hi. *add to* Ezr 10$_{10}$.

2. wickedness, wicked deed, oft. difficult to distinguish from §1, **<SUBJ>** היה *be* 4QAcademyFr. 1$_{4}$ (+ בארץ *in the land*), גדל *be great* Ezr 9$_{6}$ (+ עַד לַשָּׁמָיִם *unto heaven,* ‖ עָוֹן *iniquity*), כחד ni. *be hidden* from God Ps 69$_{6}$ (+ אִוֶּלֶת *folly*).

<NOM CL> עִמָּכֶם אֲשָׁמוֹת לַי׳ *with you are,* i.e. you have committed, *wicked deeds against Y.* 2 C 28$_{10}$ (or em. עֲלֵיכֶם עֹמְסִם you *are burdening on yourselves* wicked deeds), אשמתם ... בממשלתו *their wicked deeds ... are under his rule* 1QS 3$_{22}$ (+ עָוֹן *iniquity,* חַטָּאָה *sin,* פֶּשַׁע *sin*), נתיבו[תיה] אשמות פשע *her paths are wicked deeds of sin* 4QWiles 1$_{10}$.

<OBJ> עשה *do* 11QT 51$_{14}$, אָשֵׁם *be guilty (of)* 59$_{9}$ 4QJub^{d} 1.2$_{25}$, כלה pi. *destroy* 1QM 11$_{11}$, כפר pi. *atone for* 1QH fr. 2.1$_{13}$, זכר *remember* 1QH 4$_{34}$ (+ מַעַל *unfaithfulness*), עמס *burden* 2 C 28$_{10}$ (if em.; see Nom. Cl.).

<CSTR> אַשְׁמַת שֹׁמְרוֹן *wicked deed of Samaria* Am 8$_{14}$ (or em. אֲשֵׁרַת *Asherah of* or אֲשִׁמַת *Ashimah of*), אשמת פשע *wicked deed of sin* 1QS 9$_{4}$ (|| מַעַל *unfaithfulness*) 3Q9 3$_{2}$ (אש[מת]), רשעה *of wickedness* 1QH fr. 1$_{5}$, מעל *of unfaithfulness* 1QH 4$_{30}$ (+ עָוֺן *iniquity*) 11$_{11}$ (+ תועבות נדה *abominations of impurity*), מות *of death*, i.e. a mortal sin 4QJub^{d} 1.2$_{25}$, אשמות פשע *wicked deeds of sin* 4QWiles 1$_{3(\text{Allegro})}$ ([פשע]) 1$_{10}$ (+ מָוֶת *death*), מע[ל] *of unfaithfulness* 4QWiles 4$_{5(\text{Allegro})}$, אשמות ילוד אשה *transgressions of one born of woman* 1QH 18$_{12}$ (+ דֶּרֶךְ *way*, i.e. behaviour).

לב אשמה *heart of wickedness* 1QS 1$_{6}$ (+ עיני זנות *eyes of lust*) 4Q487 2$_{7}$, פי *mouth of* 15$_{3}$ (אשמת), יד *hand of* 4QShir^{b} 20.1$_{3}$, בשר *flesh of* 1QM 12$_{12}$, קרן *horn of* 4QM^{a} fr. 4$_{4}$ ([אש]מ[ה]), יצר *inclination of*, i.e. towards CD 2$_{16}$ (+ עני זנות *eyes of lust*) 1QH 6$_{32}$ 4QBer^{a} 3.2$_{8}$ ([א]שמתכה), גורל אשמתו *lot of his wickedness* 3.2$_{2}$, עצת אשמתם *counsel of their wickedness* 4QpNah 3.2$_{6}$, משרת אשמתו *service of* 4QBer^{a} 3.2$_{3.9}$ (משרת] ... [אשמתכ]ה), בית אשמ[תם] *house of their wickedness* 1QpHab 4$_{11}$.

חללי האשמה *those slain (because) of wickedness* 1QM 6$_{17}$ (אשמתם) 17$_{14}$ + Sup ([האש]מה) 4QM^{a} fr. 1$_{13}$, מעשי אשמה *deeds of wickedness* 4QShir^{b} 48$_{6}$, פגרי *corpses of* 1QM 14$_{3}$ (האשמה) 4QpNah 3.2$_{6}$, נסתר[ו]ת אשמ[ה] *hidden deeds of wickedness* 4QRitPur 34$_{3}$, [ד]ורות אשמתי *generations of my wickedness* 4QShir^{b} 42$_{5}$.

כול אשמה *every wickedness* 11QT 59$_{9}$, כול ... אשמתם *all ... their wicked deeds* 18$_{7}$ ([אשמת]ם) 26$_{12}$ (אשמתמה; || עָוֺן *iniquity*, חַטָּאת *sin*) 1QS 3$_{22}$.

<ADJ> אַשְׁמָתָם זֹאת *this transgression of theirs* 2 C 24$_{18}$, אשמה גדולה *great wickedness* 11QT 51$_{14}$.

<PREP> בְּ of cause, instrument, *by*, *because of* 2 C 24$_{18}$, + שׁנה pi. *change* works of God 1QH 5$_{36}$, כחד hi. *destroy* 4QPsJos^{a} 22.1$_{1}$, of accompaniment, *with*, *in (a state of)* 1QH 4$_{30}$ 4QWiles 4$_{5}$, + גלל htpo. *roll about* 1QH 6$_{22}$, הלך *walk* 4QWiles 1$_{3}$ (ב[א]שמות), שׁמד בְּ hi. *destroy* 1QM 13$_{15}$, שׁבע בְּ ni. *swear by* Am 8$_{14}$ (or em. בַּאֲשֵׁרַת/בַּאֲשִׁמַת *by Asherah/Ashima of*).

מִן perh. cleanse *from* 11QT 18$_{7}$; עַל *(in atonement) for* Ezr 10$_{19}$, + כפר pi. *make atonement* 1QS 9$_{4}$, יסף עַל hi. *add to* 2 C 28$_{13}$ (|| חַטָּאת *sin*); עם *with* 11QT 26$_{12}$; למען אשמתם *because of their guilt* 1QH 5$_{26}$.

3. perh. **guilt offering**, בְּיוֹם אַשְׁמָתוֹ *on the day of (the sacrifice of) his guilt offering* Lv 5$_{24}$ (but perh. *when he realizes his guilt*, as §1).

Also 11QT 32$_{6(\text{Yadin})}$ (AHL אשמם *their guilt [offering]*) 1QH 6$_{5}$ fr. 6$_{12}$ 4Q181 1$_{1}$ (לאשמה) 4QShir^{b} 99$_{1}$ (כאשמ[ת]) 4QRitPur 1$_{12}$ 4QOrd^{b} 2.2$_{6}$.

<SYN> §2 עָוֺן *iniquity*, חַטָּאת *sin*.

→ אשׁם *be guilty*.

[אַשְׁמוֹן], see אַשְׁמָן.

[אַשְׁמוּר], see אַשְׁמוּרָה.

אַשְׁמוּרָה 7.1.1 n.f. **watch**—אַשְׁמֹרֶת; cstr. אַשְׁמֹרֶת; sf. Si אשמורתם; pl. אַשְׁמֻרוֹת; cstr. Q אשמורי; sf. Si אשמרותם—period of night, esp. as observed by soldiers (Ex 14$_{24}$ Jg 7$_{19}$ 1 S 11$_{11}$), <NOM CL> אֶלֶף שָׁנִים ... אַשְׁמוּרָה בַלָּיְלָה *a thousand years ... are (as) a watch in the night* Ps 90$_{4}$ (or em. כְּאַשְׁמוּרָה *as a watch*). <OBJ> קדם pi. *precede* (of worshipper's eyes) Ps 119$_{148}$. <CSTR> אַשְׁמֹרֶת הַבֹּקֶר *watch of the morning* Ex 14$_{24}$ 1 S 11$_{11}$, רשית אשמורי חושך *beginning of the watches of darkness* 1QS 10$_{2}$, רֹאשׁ הָאַשְׁמֹרֶת *(at) the head*, i.e. beginning, *of the watch* Jg 7$_{19}$ Lm 2$_{19}$ (אַשְׁמֻרוֹת *of watches*). <ADJ> הָאַשְׁמֹרֶת הַתִּיכוֹנָה *the middle watch* Jg 7$_{19}$. <PREP> בְּ *during*, + היה *be* Ex 14$_{24}$, בוא *come* 1 S 11$_{11}$, הגה *moan*, i.e. meditate Ps 63$_{7}$, שׁחח ni. *be bowed down*, i.e. relax guard Si 43$_{10(B, M)}$, ישׁן *sleep* or שׁנה *be changed* 43$_{10(Bmg)}$. → שׁמר *keep*.

[אַשְׁמָן] 1 adj. **healthy**—pl. אַשְׁמַנִּים (ms, Q אשמונים)—כָּשַׁלְנוּ בַצָּהֳרַיִם כַּנֶּשֶׁף בָּאַשְׁמַנִּים כַּמֵּתִים *we have stumbled in the middle of the day as (though it were) twilight, among the healthy ones as (though we were) the dead ones* Is 59$_{10}$ (or em. בְּמַחֲשַׁכִּים *in darkness*).

→ שׁמן *be fat*.

[אַשְׁמֹרֶת], see אַשְׁמוּרָה.

אשנא 0.0.0.2 pr.n.m. **Ashna, 1.** servant of Ahaz (עבד אחז), Seal 141$_1$ (8th cent.). **2.** Seal 413 (8th/7th cent.). **3.** Seal 488 (לא[שנא]; 8th cent.).

אֶשְׁנָב 2.1 n.m. **window**—sf. אֶשְׁנַבִּי—<SUBJ> היה *be* Si 42$_{11(B)}$. <PREP> בְּעַד *through,* + יבב pi. *cry out* Jg 5$_{28}$ (or em. נבט hi. *look*), שקף ni. *lean* 5$_{28}$ Pr 7$_6$ (both || חַלּוֹן *window*).

אַשְׁנָה 2 pl.n. **Ashnah, 1.** town in the lowland of Judah, perh. mod. ʿAslīn, Jos 15$_{33}$. **2.** appar. a different town in same area, perh. mod. Idna, Jos 15$_{43}$.

אֶשְׁעָן 1 pl.n. **Eshan,** town in hill country of Judah, perh. mod. Kh. Ḫallat Samʿa, 16 km SW of Hebron, Jos 15$_{52}$.
→ perh. שׁען *lean.*

[אַשָּׁף] 2 n.m. **conjuror**—pl. אַשָּׁפִים—perh. specif. exorcist, עֶשֶׂר יָדוֹת עַל ... הָאַשָּׁפִים *ten times better than ... the conjurors* Dn 1$_{20}$ (+ חַרְטֹם *magician*), ... לִקְרֹא לָאַשָּׁפִים ... לְהַגִּיד לַמֶּלֶךְ חֲלֹמֹתָיו *to call ... the conjurors ... to explain to the king his dreams* 2$_2$ (|| חַרְטֹם, כשׁף pi. ptc. *sorcerer,* כַּשְׂדִּי *Chaldaean*).
<SYN> חַרְטֹם *magician.*

אַשְׁפָּה 6.0.0.1 n.f. **quiver**—Q אשפא; sf. אַשְׁפָּתוֹ; pl. perh. I אשפת—<SUBJ> רנה *rattle,* perh. of arrows by metonymy, Jb 39$_{23}$. <NOM CL> אַשְׁפָּתוֹ כְּקֶבֶר פָּתוּחַ *his quiver is as an open grave* Jr 5$_{16}$ (or em. אֲשֶׁר פִּיהוּ *whose mouth*). <OBJ> נשׂא *carry* Is 22$_6$ (|| מָגֵן *shield,* + רֶכֶב *chariot,* פָּרָשׁ *horse rider*), מלא pi. *fill* Ps 127$_5$ (+ מִן *with* sons).
<CSTR> בְּנֵי אַשְׁפָּתוֹ *sons of his quiver,* i.e. arrows Lm 3$_{13}$ (+ קֶשֶׁת *bow,* חֵץ *arrow*), מַטּוֹת אַשְׁפָּתֶךָ *the rods,* i.e. arrows, *of your quiver* Hb 3$_9$ (if em. מַטּוֹת אֹמֶר *rods of word;* + קֶשֶׁת *bow*). <PREP> בְּ סתר hi. *conceal* servant of Y. *in* Is 49$_2$ (+ חֵץ *arrow*).
Also Lachish ost. 13$_3$ (4 את אשפת).

אַשְׁפְּנַז 1 pr.n.m. **Ashpenaz,** Nebuchadnezzar's chief eunuch, Dn 1$_3$.

אֶשְׁפָּר 2 n.[m.] **date cake,** וַיְחַלֵּק ... אֶשְׁפָּר אֶחָד *and he distributed* to all the Israelites ... *a date cake* 2 S 6$_{19}$||1 C 16$_3$ (lacks אֶחָד; + לֶחֶם *bread,* אֲשִׁישָׁה *raisin cake*).

אַשְׁפֹּת 6.0.2 n.[m.] **refuse heap**—אַשְׁפּוֹת; pl. אַשְׁפַּתּוֹת (Q אשפותות)—**1. midden, ash heap,** <OBJ> חבק pi. *embrace* Lm 4$_5$. <PREP> מִן רום hi. *raise* poor *from* 1 S 2$_8$=Ps 113$_7$=GnzPs 3$_{13}$ (|| עָפָר *dust*). **2.** in name of gate of Jerusalem, שַׁעַר הָאַשְׁפֹּת *gate of ashes, Dung Gate,* Ne 2$_{13}$ 3$_{13}$ (הַשְּׁפוֹת) 3$_{14}$ (אַשְׁפּוֹת) 12$_{31}$.
Also 4QapLam^a 1.2$_7$ (אשפותות).
→ שׁפת *set on fire.*

אַשְׁקְלוֹן 12 pl.n. **Ashkelon,** Philistine coastal city between Gaza and Ashdod, ʿAsqalān (T. Ašqelōn), Jg 1$_{18}$ 14$_{19}$ 1 S 6$_{17}$ 2 S 1$_{20}$ (+ חוּצֹת *streets of*) Jr 25$_{20}$ 47$_{5.7}$ Am 1$_8$ Zp 2$_{4.7}$ (+ בָּתֵּי *houses of*) Zc 9$_{5.5}$.
→ אֶשְׁקְלוֹנִי *Ashkelonite.*

אֶשְׁקְלוֹנִי 1 gent. **Ashkelonite,** ... סַרְנֵי פְלִשְׁתִּים הָעַזָּתִי ... הָאֶשְׁקְלוֹנִי *Philistine generals—the Gazan ..., the Ashkelonite* Jos 13$_3$.
→ אַשְׁקְלוֹן *Ashkelon.*

אשׁר I 7.1 vb. **go forward**—**Qal** Impv. אִשְׁרוּ—**go forward,** <SUBJ> perh. פֶּתִי *simple one* Pr 9$_6$. <PREP> בְּ of place, *in,* Pr 9$_6$ (+ דֶּרֶךְ *way* of evil ones).
Pi. Pf. אִשְּׁרוּ; impf. Si ואאשרנו, תְּאַשֵּׁר; impv. אַשֵּׁר, אַשְּׁרוּ; ptc. מְאַשְּׁרֵי, מְאַשְּׁרֶיךָ—**1.** as Qal, **go forward,** <SUBJ> אֵל *God* Dt 33$_2$ (if em. אֵשְׁדָּת לָמוֹ *fire was a law for them* to אִשְּׁרוּ אֵלִים *the gods advanced*), בֵּן *son* Pr 4$_{14}$ (|| בוא *enter*).
<PREP> בְּ of place, *in,* Pr 4$_{14}$ (+ דֶּרֶךְ *way* of evil ones); מִן of place, *at,* Dt 33$_2$ (if em.; see Subj.; + יָמִין *right hand*).
2a. lead, direct, <SUBJ> בֵּן *son* Pr 23$_{19}$ (+ שׁמע *hear*), חָכְמָה *wisdom* Si 4$_{18}$. <OBJ> לֵב *heart* Pr 23$_{19}$, one who has wisdom Si 4$_{18}$. <PREP> בְּ of place, *in,* Pr 23$_{19}$ (+ דֶּרֶךְ *way*).

2b. ptc. used as noun, **leader,** <SUBJ> היה *be* Is 9_{15} (+ תעה hi. *mislead*), תעה hi. 3_{12} (|| נגשׂ ptc. *oppressor*), בלע pi. *swallow up* 3_{12}. <CSTR> מְאַשְּׁרֵי הָעָם *leaders of the people* Is 9_{15}.

3. correct, דִּרְשׁוּ מִשְׁפָּט אַשְּׁרוּ חָמוֹץ *seek judgment, put right (the) oppressor* Is 1_{17} (or em. חָמוּץ *oppressed person*).

4. verify, עָרוּם יָבִין לְאַשְּׁרוֹ *an astute person understands (how) to verify it* (דָּבָר *word*) Pr 14_{15} (if em. לַאֲשֻׁרוֹ *for his step*).

Pu. Ptc. מְאֻשָּׁרָיו—ptc. used as noun, **one who is led,** מְאֻשָּׁרָיו מְבֻלָּעִים *those led by them are swallowed up* Is 9_{15}.

→ אֲשֻׁר *step,* אֲתָרִים *Atharim,* perh. תְּאַשּׁוּר *box-tree.*

אשׁר II 9.5 vb. **be happy—Pi.** Pf. אִשְּׁרוּ, (sf. אִשְּׁרוּנִי); impf. 3fs Si תאשר 2ms Si תאשר (תאשרנו), Si נאשרנו, יְאַשְּׁרוּהוּ (Si יְאַשְּׁרוּהָ, יאשריהו); + waw וַתְּאַשְּׁרֵנִי; ptc. מְאַשְּׁרִים—**1. pronounce happy, blessed, deem successful,** <SUBJ> בֵּן *child* Pr 31_{28} (|| הלל pi. *praise,* + קום *rise*), בַּת *daughter* Gn 30_{13} (+ אָשֵׁר *Asher*) Ca 6_9 (|| ראה *see,* הלל pi.), ראה ptc. *one who sees* Si 37_{24}, Y. Dt 33_{29} (if em. וַאֲשֶׁר *and who [is]* to וְאִשֵּׁר *and he will pronounce blessed*), גּוֹי *nation* Ml 3_{12} Ps 72_{17} (+ ברך htp. *bless oneself*), Israel Ml 3_{15}, אֹזֶן *ear* Jb 29_{11} (|| עוד hi. *witness,* + שׁמע *hear*); subj. not specified, Si 11_{27} (תאשׁ[רה]ו) 11_{28} 34_9.

<OBJ> Leah Gn 30_{13}, Job Jb 29_{11}, Israel Ml 3_{12}, זיד ptc. *one who is presumptuous* 3_{15}, מֶלֶךְ *king* Ps 72_{17}, אָדָם *person* Si 11_{27} (תאשׁ[רה]ו), אִישׁ *man* 34_9, גֶּבֶר *man* 11_{28}, בַּעַל *husband* 25_{23}, אִשָּׁה *wife* Pr 31_{28}, יוֹנָה *dove,* i.e. lover Ca 6_9, חָכָם *wise person* Si 37_{24}, חֶרֶב *sword* Dt 33_{29} (if em.; see Subj.).

2. make happy, אשה לא תאשר את בעלה *a woman (who) does not make her husband happy* Si 25_{23}.

Pu. Impf. Kt יאשר (Si יאושר); + waw Qr וְאֻשַּׁר; ptc. מְאֻשָּׁר—**be pronounced happy, blessed,** <SUBJ> שׂכל hi. ptc. *one who pays attention* to poor Ps 41_3, תמך ptc. *one who holds onto* wisdom Pr 3_{18}, אָדָם *person* Si 11_{27}. <PREP> בָּאָרֶץ *in the land* Ps 41_3, באחריתו *at his* (life's) *end* Si 11_{27}.

<SYN> הלל pi. *praise.*

→ אֶשֶׁר *happiness,* אֹשֶׁר *happiness,* אַשְׁרֵי *happy,* perh. אָשֵׁר *Asher,* אָשֵׁרִי *Asherite,* אשריחת *Asheriahath.*

אָשֵׁר $43.0.5$ pr.n.m. **Asher, 1.** son of Jacob and Zilpah, Gn 30_{13} 35_{26} 46_{17} Ex 1_4 Nm 26_{46} 1 C 2_2.

2. tribe descended from preceding, and its territory, Gn 49_{20} Nm $1_{13.40.41}$ $2_{27.27}$ 7_{72} 10_{26} 13_{13} $26_{44.47}$ 34_{27} Dt 27_{13} 33_{24} Jos $17_{10.11}$ $19_{24.31.34}$ $21_{6.30}$ Jg 1_{31} 5_{17} 6_{35} 7_{23} 1 K 4_{16} Ezk $48_{2.3}$ 1 C $6_{47.59}$ $7_{30.40}$ 12_{37} 2 C 30_{11} 11QT 23_2 (unless אֲשֶׁר *which*) 24_{16} 39_{13}.

<CSTR> (§§1-2) בַּת־ *daughter of* Nm 26_{46}, בְּנֵי *sons of* Gn 46_{17} Nm 1_{40} 2_{27} 7_{72} 10_{26} $26_{44.47}$ 34_{27} Jos $19_{24.31}$ (all four בְּנֵי־) 1 C $7_{30.40}$ (בְּנֵי־), מַטֵּה *tribe of* Nm 1_{41} 2_{27} 13_{13} Jos 21_6 (מַטֵּה־) 21_{30} 1 C $6_{47.59}$, גְּבוּל *border of* Ezk 48_3, עולת *burnt offering of* 11QT 24_{16}.

3. name of city gate, Ezk 48_{34} 11QT $41_{10.11}$.

4. town or tribal territory on border of Manasseh, Jos 17_7.

→ אָשֵׁרִי *Asherite;* perh. אשׁר II *be happy.*

אֲשֶׁר $†5495.57.†944.29$ part. of relation, **which, that, who** (invariable as to number, gender, and case).

1. as **pronoun** introducing relative clause, **which, that, who(m).**

a. אֲשֶׁר is **subject** of relative clause, (1) with **finite verb,** הָאֲדָמָה אֲשֶׁר פָּצְתָה אֶת־פִּיהָ *the earth that opened its mouth* Gn 4_{11}, כָּל־מַאֲכָל אֲשֶׁר יֵאָכֵל *all food that is eaten* 6_{21}, מחזיקים ... אשר נותרו *those holding fast ... who remained* CD 3_{13}, sim. Gn 14_{24} 15_{17} $19_{5.8}$ 24_{27} etc. Si 30_{19} 34_{16} 44_{20} 46_1 $47_{13.23}$ 49_{10} $50_{27.27}$ 11QPs^a^ 27_{11} GnzPs $1_{8.9.27}$ Lv 23_{29}=11QT 25_{11} 11QT $27_{7.7}$ 35_5 $37_{11.14}$ 4QJub^a^ 2_4 $7_{2.13}$ (all three [אשר]) etc. Lachish ost. 3_{11} Silwan royal steward tomb inscr. 1_2 Nimrud ivory inscr. 1_2 (איש אשר יב[א]), with resumptive pronoun, חֲמַת יְ׳ אֲשֶׁר־הִיא נִצְּתָה *Y.'s anger which has been kindled* 2 K 22_{13}.

בְּתוּלָה אֲשֶׁר לֹא־אֹרָשָׂה *a girl that is not engaged* Ex 22_{15} Dt 22_{28}=11QT 66_9, מִשְׁפָּטוֹ אֲשֶׁר הָרְאֵיתָ *its design which you were shown* Ex 26_{30}, כָּל־עַמְּךָ יִשְׂרָאֵל אֲשֶׁר יֵדְעוּ(ן) אִישׁ *all your people, Israel, who know, each one* 1 K 8_{38}||2 C 6_{29}, כול הרשעה ... אשר יתמו *all the wicked ... who will cease* 4QpPs^a^ 1.2_7, perh. בֵּית יֹאשִׁיָּה ... אֲשֶׁר־

בָּאוּ מִבָּבֶל *the household of Josiah ... that came from Babylon* Zc 6$_{10}$.

אֲשֶׁר היה *which is*, with prep., Gn 26$_{1}$ 30$_{30}$ 41$_{36.53}$ Ex 13$_{12}$ etc. 11QT 49$_{16}$ Dt 19$_{17}$=11QT 61$_{9}$ Dt 20$_{14}$=11QT 62$_{10}$ 1QS 6$_{9}$ 7$_{22}$ CD 2$_{20}$ 5$_{2}$ 12$_{18}$ 14$_{11}$ perh. 19$_{3}$; with adj., Nm 9$_{6}$ Ezk 26$_{17}$ 2 C 7$_{21}$ 1QM 7$_{6}$ 4QM^{a} fr. 1$_{10(Baillet)}$ ([טהור]) perh. 4QCrypt 1.1$_{4}$ (יהיה ק[]); with ptc., 1 K 12$_{6}$||2 C 10$_{6}$ Ezk 34$_{2}$ 11QT 42$_{15}$ 46$_{9}$ 57$_{13}$ 4QCat^{a} 1$_{8.8}$, רוחי גורלו אש[ר המה ה]יו [ה]ממרים *the spirits of his lot who were those that rebelled* 11QMelch 1$_{12(Milik)}$; with noun, Jr 52$_{25}$ Ezk 44$_{22}$ 4QpPs^{a} 1.3$_{5}$ 4QpPs^{b} 3$_{2(Allegro)}$ (ק[הל]).

כָּבוֹד ... אֲשֶׁר לֹא־הָיָה כֵן *glory ... the like of which there has not been* (lit. *which there has not been thus*) 2 C 1$_{12}$, כול אשר יהיה *whatever might be* 1QS 9$_{26}$.

Verb in אֲשֶׁר clause agrees with subject of preceding noun clause, e.g. אֲנִי י׳ אֲשֶׁר הוֹצֵאתִיךָ *I am Y. who brought you out* Gn 15$_{7}$ (sim. Ex 20$_{2}$ 29$_{46}$ Lv 19$_{36}$ 25$_{38}$ 26$_{13}$ Nm 15$_{41}$ Dt 5$_{6}$), אֲנִי י׳ ... אֲשֶׁר־הִבְדַּלְתִּי אֶתְכֶם *I am Y. ... who has separated you* Lv 20$_{24}$, אֲנִי־הוּא אֲשֶׁר־חָטָאתִי *I am the one who sinned* 1 C 21$_{17}$, הַאַתָּה הָאִישׁ אֲשֶׁר־דִּבַּרְתָּ *are you the man who spoke?* Jg 13$_{11}$ (sim. 1 K 13$_{14}$), אם נפש אדם היא אשר תפול *if it is a human being that falls* 4Q251 2$_{6}$, אַתָּה־הוּא י׳ ... אֲשֶׁר בָּחַרְתָּ *you are Y. ... who chose* Ne 9$_{7}$, וְעַתָּה אֲדֹנָי אֱלֹהֵינוּ אֲשֶׁר הוֹצֵאתָ *and now, my Lord, our God, who brought out* Dn 9$_{15}$, אל או[רי]ם אשר חדשתה *God of lights who has renewed* 4QPrQuot 29$_{9}$.

מִי כָמוֹנִי אֲשֶׁר־יָבוֹא *who is like me that would come?*, i.e. would such as I come? Ne 6$_{11}$, בְּרוּכָה אָתְּ אֲשֶׁר כְּלִתִנִי *blessed are you who restrained me* 1 S 25$_{33}$ (sim. 2 S 2$_{5}$ 4QPrQuot 34$_{4}$ [(ברו)ך] 1QH 11$_{27}$ (...את(ה]), אֵלֶּה הֵם אֲשֶׁר עָבְרוּ ,([(א)שר] *these are the ones that crossed* 1 C 12$_{16}$, אַתְּ ... אֲשֶׁר פִּלַּלְתְּ *you ... who have interceded* Ezk 16$_{52}$, sim. Est 7$_{5}$ 4QpIsa^{b} 1.2$_{7}$.

Verb in אֲשֶׁר clause agrees with person in preceding clause, e.g. כָּל־מִסְפַּרְכֶם ... אֲשֶׁר הֲלִינֹתֶם *all your number ... who complained* Nm 14$_{29}$, קוּמִי יְרוּשָׁלַםִ אֲשֶׁר שָׁתִית *arise, O Jerusalem, (you) who have drunk* Is 51$_{17}$, הַאוֹתִי לֹא־תִירָאוּ ... אֲשֶׁר־שַׂמְתִּי *do you not fear me ... who placed* Jr 5$_{22}$, כַּאֲשֶׁר עָשִׂית אֲשֶׁר־בָּזִית *as you, who despised ..., have done* Ezk 16$_{59}$, ... בְּרֹאשְׁכֶם : אֲשֶׁר־כַּסְפִּי לְקַחְתֶּם *on the head of you who have taken ... my silver* Jl 4$_{4}$, כבודכה אשר נקדשתה *the glory of you who are sanctified* 4QDibHam^{a} 1.4$_{9}$ (sim. 1.5$_{10}$), במועלם אשר עזבוהו *because of the transgression of those who forsook him* CD 1$_{3}$, מי כמוהו אשר לא שכח *who is like him who has not forgotten?* GnzPs 4$_{8}$ (sim. 1QM 10$_{8}$).

(2) with **participle**, סִיחֹן ... אֲשֶׁר יוֹשֵׁב בְּחֶשְׁבּוֹן *Sihon ... who lives at Heshbon* Nm 21$_{34}$, [הכו]הן הרשע אשר צ[ופ]ה *the wicked priest who keeps watch* 4QpPs^{a} 1.4$_{8(Allegro)}$, י׳ ... אֲשֶׁר ... נִרְאָה *Y. ... who ... is seen* Nm 14$_{14}$, י׳ אֲשֶׁר נֶאֱמָן *Y. who is faithful* Is 49$_{7}$, הַמַּשְׁקֶה וְהָאֹפֶה ... אֲשֶׁר אֲסוּרִים *the cupbearer and the baker ... who were confined* Gn 40$_{5}$, כול אשר נותר *all that is left* 11QT 43$_{10}$, כְּתָב אֲשֶׁר־נִכְתָּב *a document that is written* Est 8$_{8}$, הדבר אשר כתוב *the word that was written* CD 19$_{7}$, תַּבְנִיתָם אֲשֶׁר־אַתָּה מָרְאֶה *their design that you are being shown* Ex 25$_{40}$, sim. 2 S 14$_{7}$ Is 11$_{10}$ 2 C 34$_{10}$ perh. 34$_{21}$ (נִמְצָא, ||2 K 22$_{13}$ הַנִּמְצָא).

With resumptive subject pronoun, כָּל־הַבְּהֵמָה אֲשֶׁר הִיא מַפְרֶסֶת פַּרְסָה *every animal that has a cloven hoof* Lv 11$_{26(Qr)}$, אֶרֶץ אֲשֶׁר־הִיא זָבַת חָלָב *a land that is flowing with milk* Nm 14$_{8(Qr)}$, מורי הצדק אשר הואה [יורה] *the teacher of righteousness who teaches* 1QpMic 8$_{6(Milik)}$, אֱלֹהֵיכֶם אֲשֶׁר־הוּא מוֹשִׁיעַ *your God, who saves* 1 S 10$_{19}$, הנפש אשר ה[ואה] *the soul that is* 1QDM 4$_{7(Milik)}$, כֹּל אֲשֶׁר־אֵינֶנּוּ ... טָלוּא *everything that is not ... spotted* Gn 30$_{33}$, אוזן אשר איננה שומעת *an ear that does not hear* 4Q424 2$_{5}$, כַּשָּׁפֵיכֶם אֲשֶׁר־הֵם אֹמְרִים *your sorcerers who say* Jr 27$_{9}$, חוֹמֹת יְרוּשָׁלַםִ אֲשֶׁר־הֵם פְּרוּצִים *the walls of Jerusalem that were breached* Ne 2$_{13(Qr)}$.

(3) with **verbless predicate, a. noun**, with resumptive pronoun, סָרִיס אֶחָד אֲשֶׁר־הוּא פָקִיד *a certain eunuch who was an overseer* 2 K 25$_{19}$ (||Jr 52$_{25}$ הָיָה *was* for הוּא), אִישׁ נָכְרִי אֲשֶׁר לֹא־אָחִיךָ הוּא *a foreign man who is not your kin* Dt 17$_{15}$=11QT 56$_{15}$; without resumptive pronoun, בְּנֵי יִשְׂרָאֵל אֲשֶׁר־כְּנַעֲנִים appar. *the Israelites that are Canaanites*, i.e. who live in Canaan Ob 20 (+ אֲשֶׁר בִּסְפָרַד *that are in Sepharad*).

b. adjective, מַעַלְלֵיכֶם אֲשֶׁר לֹא־טוֹבִים *your deeds which were not good* Ezk 36$_{31}$, with resumptive pronoun, כַּלָּתֵךְ ... אֲשֶׁר־הִיא טוֹבָה *your daughter-in-law ... who is good* Ru 4$_{15}$, sim. Ne 2$_{18}$, הָאִישׁ אֲשֶׁר־הוּא טָהוֹר

the man who is clean Nm 9$_{13}$, בֵּיתִי אֲשֶׁר־הוּא חָרֵב *my house that is ruined* Hg 1$_9$, הַחַיִּים אֲשֶׁר הֵמָּה חַיִּים עֲדֶנָה *the living who are still alive* Ec 4$_2$, הכתיאים א[שר המ]ה קלים *the Kittim who are swift* 1QpHab 2$_{12}$, sim. Gn 9$_3$ Nm 35$_{31}$, הַבְּהֵמָה אֲשֶׁר לֹא טְהֹרָה הִיא *the animal that is not clean* Gn 7$_{2(Qr)}$ 7$_8$ (אֵינֶנָּה טְהוֹרָה), sim. Gn 30$_{33}$.

c. preposition, כבודו אשר מאחד *his glory which is from (the) one* 4Q462$_7$, כל קהל עמך ישראל אשר בארבע רוחות שמים *all the congregation of your people, Israel, who are throughout the four winds of heaven* 4Q448 1$_5$, הַמַּיִם אֲשֶׁר מִתַּחַת לָרָקִיעַ *the waters that were below the expanse* Gn 1$_7$, הָעֵץ אֲשֶׁר בְּתוֹךְ־הַגָּן *the tree that was in the middle of the garden* 3$_3$, sim. 1$_{7.29}$ 6$_4$ 7$_{19.22}$ etc. Si 51$_8$ 11QT 3$_{9.15}$ ([א]שר) 7$_9$ 15$_7$ + Sup 16$_7$ etc. perh. Arad ost. 29$_7$ (אשר בכבן), esp. with לְ of possession, etc. Gn 12$_{20}$ 13$_1$ 14$_{23}$ 19$_{12}$ 20$_7$ etc. 11QT 13$_{14}$ (העו[לה] אשר לו) 15$_{11}$ + Sup 16$_{14}$ 26$_7$ 36$_{13}$ etc. perh. Arad ost. 8$_9$ 7$_{12}$, כָּל־אֲשֶׁר יֶשׁ־לוֹ *everything he has* Gn 39$_{5.5}$ 4QToh A 3.2$_3$ (כול; var. Gn 39$_8$, sim. 11QT 58$_3$).

הַכֶּלֶב הַמֵּת אֲשֶׁר כָּמוֹנִי *a dead dog like me* (lit. *the dead dog that is like me*) 2 S 9$_8$, גּוֹי אֲשֶׁר־כָּזֶה *a nation that is like this* Jr 5$_{9.29}$ 9$_8$, וְהַקְטִיר אִתּוֹ אֲשֶׁר לִפְנֵי י׳ *and he would burn incense with it* (altar) *which was before Y.* 1 K 9$_{25}$; with resumptive subject pronoun, כָּל בֶּן־נֵכָר אֲשֶׁר לֹא מִזַּרְעֲךָ הוּא *every foreigner who is not of your seed* Gn 17$_{12}$ (sim. Nm 17$_5$ 1 K 8$_{41}$||2 C 6$_{32}$ 1 K 9$_{20}$||2 C 8$_7$ Ezk 43$_{19}$), האיש הזה אשר הוא מבני *this man who is of the children of* 8QHymn 1$_2$, הַבְּהֵמָה אֲשֶׁר־הִיא לָכֶם *the animal which is yours* Lv 11$_{39}$.

לִקְדוֹשִׁים אֲשֶׁר־בָּאָרֶץ הֵמָּה *as for saints that are in the land* Ps 16$_3$, כָּל־בֵּית יִשְׂרָאֵל אֲשֶׁר־הֵמָּה בְּתוֹכָם *all of the house of Israel that are among them* Ezk 12$_{10}$; with שָׁם *there*, הָאֱמֹרִי אֲשֶׁר־שָׁם *the Amorites who were there* Nm 21$_{32}$, sim. 2 K 23$_{16.20}$.

אֲשֶׁר לֹא בְּ *without* (lit. *which is not with*), usu. used adverbially, אשר לוא במשפט *without law*, i.e. unjustifiably, incorrectly, etc. 1QS 7$_{8.18}$, 5$_{17}$ 6$_{1.12}$ 7$_{11}$ CD 9$_3$, בַּל־אֶמּוֹט לְדֹר וָדֹר אֲשֶׁר לֹא־בְרָע perh. *I shall not be moved—generation to generation without trouble* Ps 10$_6$ (or em. אֹשֶׁר *happiness* or אַשֻּׁר לֹא כֹרֵעַ *each step unbowed* I shall walk).

With omission of preposition of place, אֲשֶׁר־פֶּתַח אֹהֶל מוֹעֵד *that was (at) the entrance to the tent of meeting* Lv 1$_5$ 4$_{7.18}$ (sim. Gn 19$_{11}$ 2 K 23$_8$ Jr 19$_2$), הַחֲנִית אֲשֶׁר מְרַאֲשֹׁתָיו *the spear that was (at) his head* 1 S 26$_{11(Qr)}$ (sim. 26$_{16}$), קֶבֶר אָבִיו אֲשֶׁר בֵּית לָחֶם *his father's grave which was (at) Bethlehem* 2 S 2$_{32}$, sim. 2 K 2$_3$ 10$_{29}$ (|| אֲשֶׁר בְּ *which was in*), כָּל־הַכֵּלִים אֲשֶׁר בֵּית *all the vessels that were (in) the temple* of Y. 1 K 7$_{48}$||2 C 4$_{19}$, sim. 2 K 25$_{13}$ (|| אֲשֶׁר בְּ; ||Jr 52$_{17}$ לְ that *belonged to*) Jr 32$_2$ 2 C 23$_9$ (||2 K 11$_{10}$ אֲשֶׁר בְּ), הַלְּשָׁכוֹת אֲשֶׁר דֶּרֶךְ *the chambers that were (in) the direction of*, i.e. that faced Ezk 42$_{11.12}$.

לַמּוֹעֵד אֲשֶׁר שְׁמוּאֵל *for the time that was (set by) Samuel* 1 S 13$_8$ (or ins. שָׂם that Samuel *had set*), וְאֶת־הָרָעָה אֲשֶׁר הֲדָד *and (was) along with the evil that was Hadad* 1 K 11$_{25}$ (or ins. עָשָׂה that Hadad *did*), כָּל־חֵיל כַּשְׂדִּים אֲשֶׁר רַב־טַבָּחִים *all the army of Chaldaeans that were (with) the chief of the guard* 2 K 25$_{10}$ (or ins. with ||Jr 52$_{14}$ אֶת־ *with*).

1b. אֲשֶׁר is **object** of relative clause, (1) with **finite verb,** כָּל־אֲשֶׁר עָשָׂה *everything that he had done* Gn 1$_{31}$, הָאָדָם אֲשֶׁר יָצָר *the human being whom he had formed* 2$_8$, הַצֵּלָע אֲשֶׁר־לָקַח *the rib that he had taken* 2$_{22}$, sim. Gn 1$_{21}$ 2$_{2.2.3}$ 3$_1$ etc. Si 8$_9$ 15$_{11(B)}$ 34$_{15(Bmg)}$ (B ש) 11QPs^a 27$_9$ GnzPs 1$_{18}$ 11QT 29$_{5.6.10}$ 30$_4$ 47$_4$ 4QJub^a 1$_{7.14}$ 2$_1$ (all three [אשר]) 2$_{9.9}$ 5$_{2.9.9.10}$ (all five [אשר]) 4QPentPar^b 23.2$_6$ etc. Lachish ost. 2$_6$ 3$_5$ 4$_{2.4.11}$ 18$_2$ Arad ost. 40$_6$ ([אשר ר]צה) 40$_{15}$ (אש[ר] אד[ם עשתה]) Kuntillet ʻAjrud add. inscr. 2 papMurPalimp^b$_2$.

מֵאַחֶרֶת אֲשֶׁר־עָשִׂיתָ *than (the) other (evil) that you did* 2 S 13$_{16}$, וַיָּמֶת אֹתוֹ אֲשֶׁר־הִפְקִיד מֶלֶךְ־בָּבֶל *and he killed him whom the king of Babylon had appointed* Jr 41$_2$, להאבידמה ... אשר לוא יותיר *to destroy them ... whom he will not leave over* 4QCat^a 12.14 (sim. Lv 25$_{42.55}$ Jos 1$_{15}$ Ne 9$_{29}$ 2 C 35$_{20}$), אַתָּה ... אֲשֶׁר הֶחֱזַקְתִּיךָ : *you ... whom I took* Is 41$_8$, השב ... דבר ... אשר נעשה מחר *return*, i.e. reply with, *... (the) matter ... that we are to undertake tomorrow* Lachish ost. 9$_7$, מעשינו אשר הרעונו *our deeds that we did badly*, i.e. our bad deeds 1QM 11$_4$.

As obj. of infinitive, כֹּל אֲשֶׁר יָזְמוּ לַעֲשׂוֹת *everything that they propose to do* Gn 11$_6$, הָאֲתֹנוֹת אֲשֶׁר הָלַכְתָּ לְבַקֵּשׁ *the asses that you went to seek* 1 S 10$_2$, כָּל־כֶּסֶף אֲשֶׁר יַעֲלֶה עַל לֶב־אִישׁ לְהָבִיא *all money that it comes into a* man's heart to bring 2 K 12$_{5}$, sim. 1 S 14$_{4}$ 2 S 7$_{23}$||1 C 17$_{21}$ 1 K 9$_{21}$ Jr 13$_{6}$ 26$_{3}$ Ne 9$_{23}$ 11QT 43$_{13}$.

הָאָרֶץ ... אֲשֶׁר נִשְׁבַּעְתִּי לָתֵת לַאֲבֹתֵיכֶם *the land ... that I vowed to give to your ancestors* Dt 13$_{5}$ (sim. Ex 13$_{5}$ Dt 1$_{8}$ 6$_{10}$ 7$_{13}$ 10$_{11}$ 11$_{9}$ Jos 1$_{6}$ etc.), הָאָרֶץ אֲשֶׁר נָשָׂאתִי אֶת־יָדִי לָתֵת אֹתָהּ לְאַבְרָהָם *the land that I raised my hand*, i.e. vowed, *to give to Abraham* Ex 6$_{8}$ (sim. Ezk 20$_{28.42}$ 47$_{14}$ Ne 9$_{15}$).

With resumptive pronoun, (a) suffixed, רֵיחַ שָׂדֶה אֲשֶׁר בֵּרֲכוֹ י׳ *the smell of a field that Y. has blessed* Gn 27$_{27}$, הַדָּבָר אֲשֶׁר לֹא־דִבְּרוֹ י׳ *the word that Y. has not spoken* Dt 18$_{21}$=11QT 61$_{3}$ Dt 18$_{22}$, sim. Ex 18$_{9}$ 28$_{3}$ Dt 13$_{3}$=11QT 54$_{10}$ Dt 28$_{48}$ 33$_{8}$ 34$_{10}$ Jos 7$_{14.14.14}$ 1 S 25$_{26}$ 1 K 9$_{21}$||2 C 8$_{8}$ 2 K 19$_{4}$||Is 37$_{4}$ 2 K 19$_{16}$ (lacking in ||Is 37$_{17}$) Is 19$_{25}$ 50$_{1}$ Jr 8$_{2.2}$ 13$_{6}$ 27$_{20}$ 28$_{9}$ 29$_{22}$ Ezk 36$_{21}$ (without pronoun in 36$_{22}$) Ps 94$_{12}$ 2 C 21$_{6}$ 8$_{8}$ 22$_{7}$ 4QOrd^{a} 1.2$_{6}$ CD 16$_{11}$ 1QH 17$_{9}$ ([א]שר) 1QMyst 1.1$_{10}$ 1QpHab 8$_{1}$ 9$_{9}$ 12$_{13}$ 4QpNah 1$_{2(Allegro)}$ (ב[רא]ם) 3.1$_{11(Allegro)}$ (י[']תנוהו) 4QMMT A 23$_{7}$ ([בחר בו]), מורה הצדק אשר הודיעו אל *the teacher of righteousness whom God informed* 1QpHab 7$_{4}$.

(b) independent, מִשְׁפָּטַי ... אֲשֶׁר יַעֲשֶׂה אֹתָם הָאָדָם *my judgments ... that a person fulfils* Lv 18$_{5}$ 16$_{32}$ Ezk 20$_{11.13.21}$ (without pronoun at Ne 9$_{29}$ CD 3$_{15}$ 4QD^{b}$_{12}$), sim. Ex 6$_{5}$ Lv 23$_{2.4.37}$ 25$_{42.55}$ etc., לַמְּלָאכָה אֲשֶׁר־צִוָּה י׳ לַעֲשֹׂת אֹתָהּ *for the work that Y. commanded us to do* Ex 36$_{5}$.

With antecedent repeated, שְׂדֵה הַמַּכְפֵּלָה ... אֲשֶׁר קָנָה אַבְרָהָם אֶת־הַשָּׂדֶה *the field of Machpelah ... that Abraham had bought* Gn 49$_{30}$, כַּבְּרִית אֲשֶׁר כָּרַתִּי ... אֲשֶׁר־הֵמָּה הֵפֵרוּ אֶת־בְּרִיתִי *like the covenant that I made ... which covenant of mine they broke* Jr 31$_{32}$, מֵי נֹחַ זֹאת לִי אֲשֶׁר נִשְׁבַּעְתִּי מֵעֲבֹר מֵי־נֹחַ עוֹד *this is (like) the waters of Noah to me which I vowed would not pass again* Is 54$_{9}$ (or em. כַּאֲשֶׁר *as*).

With (part of) antecedent following אֲשֶׁר, כֹּל אֲשֶׁר־דִּבֶּר אֶת־הַטּוֹבָה *all the good that he mentioned* 1 S 25$_{30}$, אֵת אֲשֶׁר־תַּעֲשֶׂה ... רָעָה *the evil ... that you will do* 2 K 8$_{12}$, (אֵת) אֲשֶׁר אֲדַבֵּר דָּבָר *the word that I speak* Ezk 12$_{25.28}$, sim. Ex 25$_{9}$ Nm 33$_{4}$ 1 K 22$_{31}$ perh. Ezk 47$_{13}$ (from §2b, 6).

With verbs of saying, etc. (which do not usually have direct obj.), נדבות רצונכה אשר צויתה *gifts of your pleasing that you commanded* 4QPrFêtes^{c} 131.2$_{6}$ pap4QPrLit^{b} 1.3$_{6}$, הַתּוֹרָה אֲשֶׁר(־)צִוָּה י׳ *the law that Y. commanded* Nm 19$_{2}$ 31$_{21}$ Ne 8$_{14}$ (sim. Jos 1$_{7}$ 22$_{5}$ 2 K 14$_{6}$ 17$_{13}$ 21$_{8}$ Mal 3$_{22}$ Ne 8$_{1}$ 1 C 16$_{40}$ 4QDibHam^{a} 4$_{8}$ [צ(וית)]) 1QDM 1$_{4}$ ([ה(תור)ה אשר צוי(תי)]), [כל אשר א]צוך *everything that I have commanded you* 4QJub^{a} 2$_{5}$, (כְּ)כֹל/כָּל־אֲשֶׁר(־)צִוָּה י׳ *(according to) everything that Y. commanded* Ex 35$_{10}$ 36$_{1}$ 38$_{22}$ 39$_{32.42}$ etc. (sim. Gn 6$_{22}$ 7$_{5}$ Ex 29$_{35}$ 31$_{6.11}$ etc. 1QS 9$_{25}$ 4QDibHam^{a} 1.5$_{14}$ 1QH 15$_{11.18}$ 4QFlor 11$_{2}$), [בדר]כי ... אשר תעיד בהם *in my ways ... (concerning) which you will bear witness among them* 4QpsMos^{e} 1$_{3}$, כל מצותי אשר אצוה *all my commandments (about) which I command you* 2.1$_{5}$, פָּעֳלוֹ אֲשֶׁר שֹׁרְרוּ אֲנָשִׁים *his work (of) which men sing* Jb 36$_{24}$.

הָאָרֶץ אֲשֶׁר נִשְׁבַּע לָהֶם *the land that he had vowed to them* Nm 14$_{16}$ (sim. Gn 50$_{24}$ Ex 33$_{1}$ Nm 11$_{12}$ 14$_{23}$ 32$_{11}$ etc.), בָּאָרֶץ אֲשֶׁר אֹמַר אֵלֶיךָ *in the land that I shall say to you* Gn 26$_{2}$ (sim. 22$_{2.3.9}$ 43$_{27.29}$ etc.), הָעִיר אֲשֶׁר דִּבַּרְתָּ *the city that you mentioned* 19$_{21}$ (sim. 23$_{16}$ Dt 9$_{28}$ 13$_{3}$=11QT 54$_{9}$ Jos 14$_{12}$ 20$_{2}$), הָרָעָה אֲשֶׁר(־)דִּבֶּר *the evil that he pronounced* Jr 26$_{13.19}$, כָּעֵת ... אֲשֶׁר־דִּבֶּר אֵלֶיהָ אֱלִישָׁע *(at) about the time that Elisha had told her* 2 K 4$_{17}$, with resumptive pronoun, לַמּוֹעֵד אֲשֶׁר־דִּבֶּר אֹתוֹ אֱלֹהִים *at the time that God had said* Gn 21$_{2}$.

כָּל־צְבָא הַשָּׁמַיִם אֲשֶׁר לֹא־צִוִּיתִי *the whole host of heaven (concerning) which I did not command you* Dt 17$_{3}$, לֹא־הִשְׁמִידוּ אֶת־הָעַמִּים אֲשֶׁר אָמַר י׳ לָהֶם *they did not destroy the peoples whom Y. commanded them (to destroy)* Ps 106$_{34}$, כָּל־הָאָרֶץ ... אֲשֶׁר אָמַרְתִּי אֶתֵּן *all the land ... that I said I should give* Ex 32$_{13}$, טַפְּכֶם אֲשֶׁר אֲמַרְתֶּם לָבַז יִהְיֶה *your infants whom you said would be as plunder* Nm 14$_{31}$ Dt 1$_{39}$.

כָּל־אֲבֵדָה אֲשֶׁר יֹאמַר כִּי־הוּא זֶה *every lost item (of) which one says, This is it* Ex 22$_{8}$, הַמִּצְפָּה אֲשֶׁר אָמַר יִצֶף י׳ *Mizpah (concerning) which he said, May Y. watch* Gn 31$_{49}$, sim. Dt 28$_{68}$ 1 S 9$_{17.23}$ 24$_{5}$ 1 K 8$_{29}$ etc. CD 4$_{20}$ 6$_{7}$ 11QMelch 1$_{4[Milik]}$ ([אשר (אמר)]) 4QCat^{a} 12.1$_{2}$ ([א]שר), בַּמָּקוֹם אֲשֶׁר דִּבֶּר אֵלֶיךָ אַל־תֹּאכַל *in the place of which he said to you, You are not to eat* 1 K 13$_{22}$.

לדבר אשר צותני *as for the matter (about) which you*

commanded me Arad ost. 18_7, הָעֵץ אֲשֶׁר צִוִּיתִיךָ לֵאמֹר לֹא תֹאכַל מִמֶּנּוּ *the tree (about) which I commanded you, saying, You are not to eat from it* Gn 3_{17}, הָעֵץ אֲשֶׁר צִוִּיתִיךָ לְבִלְתִּי אֲכָל־מִמֶּנּוּ *the tree (about) which I commanded you in order that you would not eat from it* 3_{11}, עַם תֹּעֵי לֵבָב הֵם ... : אֲשֶׁר־נִשְׁבַּעְתִּי בְאַפִּי אִם־יְבֹאוּן *they are a wayward people ... (concerning) whom I vowed, They will not come* Ps 95_{11}.

With other verbs that do not usually have direct obj., כל דבר אשר ימעל איש *every matter (concerning) which one sins* CD 9_{16}, בַּדָּבָר אֲשֶׁר זָדוּ *in the matter (concerning) which they were insolent* Ex 18_{11}, הַדֶּשֶׁן אֲשֶׁר תֹּאכַל הָאֵשׁ אֶת־הָעֹלָה *the ash (to) which the fire consumes the sacrifice* Lv 6_3, אֲשָׁמוֹ אֲשֶׁר חָטָא *his guilt offering which he has incurred by sinning* 5_7 (sim. 5_{11}).

(2) with **participle** (or adjective, Ec 9_9), אוֹת־הַבְּרִית אֲשֶׁר־אֲנִי נֹתֵן *the sign of the covenant that I give* Gn 9_{12}, כָּל־הָאָרֶץ אֲשֶׁר־אַתָּה רֹאֶה *all the land that you see* 13_{15}, הַלֶּחֶם אֲשֶׁר־הוּא אוֹכֵל *the bread that he eats* 39_6, [הדב]רים אשר אנכי מגיד לך *the words that I am telling you* 4QJub^a 1_{12}, sim. Gn 21_{22} 31_{43} 39_3 47_{14} Ex 5_8 etc. 11QT 31_9 51_{16} 52_{19} 54_5 Dt 13_{19}=11QT 55_{13} 4QJub^a 1_{14} ([אשר]) 4QPentPar^b 23.2_4 etc., תְּלֻנּוֹת בְּנֵי יִשְׂרָאֵל אֲשֶׁר הֵמָּה מַלִּינִים *the complaints of the Israelites which they murmur* Nm 14_{27} 17_{20} (הֵם), נוֹרָא הוּא אֲשֶׁר אֲנִי עֹשֶׂה עִמָּךְ *that which I am doing with you is wonderful* Ex 34_{10}, הַלַּחַץ אֲשֶׁר מִצְרַיִם לֹחֲצִים אֹתָם *the hardship that Egypt inflicts on them* 3_9, עֲמָלְךָ אֲשֶׁר־אַתָּה עָמֵל *your work that you do* Ec 9_9, כָּל־אֲשֶׁר עֹשִׂים *all that (they) do* Gn 39_{22}, הָאֲבָנִים ... אֲשֶׁר אָנֹכִי מְצַוֶּה אֶתְכֶם *the stones (about) which I am commanding you* Dt 27_4 (sim. 4QpsMos^e 1_3 ([מצ(ו)ך]), המה אשר אני מגיד *those things that I declare* 11QT 51_6, זבחי שלמיהמה אשר יהיו זובחים *their peace offerings that they will be sacrificing* 37_{11}.

2. אֲשֶׁר is not subject or object of relative clause; connection with antecedent is made by a suffixed preposition, a construct case, or an adverb like שָׁם *there.*

2a. אֲשֶׁר introduces **nominal clause,** with (1) suffixed preposition, הָאֲדָמָה אֲשֶׁר־הֵם עָלֶיהָ *the ground that they are upon* (lit. *upon it*) Ex 8_{17}, אִישׁ אֲשֶׁר רוּחַ אֱלֹהִים בּוֹ *a man who possesses God's spirit* (lit. *that God's spirit is in him*) Gn 41_{38}, כָּל־בָּשָׂר אֲשֶׁר־בּוֹ רוּחַ חַיִּים *all flesh in which there is a living spirit* 6_{17} 7_{15}, הָרָעָה אֲשֶׁר אֲנַחְנוּ בָהּ *the trouble that we are in* Ne 2_{17}, sim. Gn $1_{29.30}$ 30_{35} Lv 13_{45} 14_{40} etc. 11QT 48_{17} Dt 19_{17}=11QT $61_{8(mg)}$ CD 10_{12} 4QJub^a 5_{13} ([אשר בתוך]) 6_{13} 7_5.

אִישׁ אֲשֶׁר־לוֹ עָרְלָה *a man who has a foreskin* Gn 34_{14}, אִישׁ אֲשֶׁר־אֵלֶּה לּוֹ *the man to whom these belong* Gn 38_{25}, לַשְּׂעִירִם אֲשֶׁר הֵם זֹנִים אַחֲרֵיהֶם *to the satyrs after whom they played the whore* Lv 17_7, הבא ... אשר אין לו *the one who comes ... who has nothing* 4QOrd^a 1.2_4, כֹּל אֲשֶׁר אֵין־לוֹ סְנַפִּיר *everything that does not have fins* Lv 11_{10} ||Dt 14_{10} Lv 11_{12}, כַּצֹּאן אֲשֶׁר אֵין־לָהֶם רֹעֶה *as sheep that have no shepherd* Nm 27_{17} 1 K 22_{17}||2 C 18_{16} (sim. Lv 25_{31} Jr 8_{17} 39_{10} Pr 6_7 Si $36_{31[Bmg, C, D]}$ CD 14_{15} [(אי)ן] 14_{16} [(א)שר]), גַּנָּה אֲשֶׁר־מַיִם אֵין לָהּ *a garden that has no water* Is 1_{30}.

פְּרִי ... אֲשֶׁר זַרְעוֹ־בוֹ *fruit ... that has its seed in it* (lit. *fruit that its seed is in it*) Gn $1_{11.12}$, כֹּל אֲשֶׁר נִשְׁמַת־רוּחַ חַיִּים בְּאַפָּיו *everything in whose nostrils is the breath of a living spirit* Gn 7_{22}, אָחִיו אֲשֶׁר עַל־יָדוֹ הַשָּׁנִי *his brother on whose hand was the crimson (thread)* 38_{30}, שמץ תענוג אשר פי שנים רישו *a little enjoyment the distress of,* i.e. associated with, *which is double* Si 18_{32}, אשר ברכת אדני ברצונו *for whom the blessing of my Lord is at his pleasure* 4Q521 1.3_3 (unless אשר = *I shall sing*).

אֶרֶץ אֲשֶׁר אֲבָנֶיהָ בַרְזֶל *a land the stones of which are iron* Dt 8_9, הַשַּׁעַר אֲשֶׁר פָּנָיו דֶּרֶךְ *the gate the face of which was,* i.e. faced, *towards* Ezk 40_6 (שַׁעַר) $40_{20.22}$ 42_{15} 43_4 (שַׁעַר; sim. $40_{45.46}$), צֹר ... אֲשֶׁר סֹחֲרֶיהָ שָׂרִים *Tyre ... whose traders are princes* Is $23_{8(L)}$, פִּלַגְשֵׁיהֶם אֲשֶׁר בְּשַׂר־חֲמוֹרִים בְּשָׂרָם *their lovers whose flesh was the flesh of donkeys* Ezk 23_{20}, בניהם אשר כרום ארזים גבהם *their children whose size was as the height of cedars* CD 2_{19} (sim. 1QH 5_9), כָּל־הָעָם אֲשֶׁר־אַתָּה בְקִרְבּוֹ *all the people among whom you are* Ex 34_{10} (sim. Nm 11_{21} Ezk 20_9).

הכתיאים אשר פחדם ... על כול הגואים *the Kittim, whose dread was ... on all the nations* 1QpHab $3_{4(mg)}$, נֹא אָמוֹן ... אֲשֶׁר־חֵיל ... חוֹמָתָהּ *No-amon ... whose wall was ... a rampart* Na 3_8, הָאִשָּׁה אֲשֶׁר־בְּנָהּ הַחַי *the woman whose son was the live one* 1 K 3_{26},

איש ... אשר בלבבו כלבבך *a man ... who in his heart is like your heart* Si $37_{12(\text{Bmg, D})}$, אשר אין גורלו בתוך *whose lot is not among* CD $20_{5(\text{erased})}$, אתה ... אשר מעשיך הכול *you ... whose works are everything* 1QH 16_8, כֹּל שֶׁרֶץ הָעוֹף ... אֲשֶׁר־לֹא כְרָעַיִם מִמַּעַל לְרַגְלָיו *all flying swarming creatures ... that do not have joints above their legs* Lv $11_{21(\text{Kt})}$ (Qr, 11_{23} אֲשֶׁר־לוֹ *that has*).

כול כלים אשר יש להמה טהרה *all vessels that can be cleaned* (lit. *vessels that there is to them cleaning*) 11QT 49_{15}, העוף ... אשר יש לו כרעים *the fowl ... that has legs* 48_4, כול איש אשר יש אתו דבר לדבר *everyone who has something to say* 1QS 6_{12} (sim. Jon 4_{11} 11QT 52_{17}), כעשב הוא אשר [י]ש הרחש תחתו *he is as a plant below which there is a worm* 4QD$^{a}_{8(\text{Milik})}$, אֲדוֹן כָּל־הָאָרֶץ׃ אֲשֶׁר־בָּהּ הַסּוּסִים הַשְּׁחֹרִים יֹצְאִים *the lord of all the earth, where the black horses go out* Zc 6_5 (or em. הָאֲדֻמִּים יֹצְאִים אֶל־אֶרֶץ to אֲשֶׁר־בָּהּ הַסּוּסִים הַשְּׁחֹרִים הַקֶּדֶם וְהַשְּׁחֹרִים *the red ones go out to the land of the east and the black ones*), [כל אשר על הארץ] *all that is upon the earth* 4QJub^{a} 7_2.

(2) preposition prefixed to אֲשֶׁר, סרי מדרך [חטאים על] אשר כתוב *those that turn from the way of the wicked concerning whom it is written* 4QFlor $1_{14(\text{Brooke})}$, הַמִּדְבָּר אֲשֶׁר־הוּא חֹנֶה שָׁם *the desert where he encamped* Ex 18_5.

(3) שָׁם *there*, אֶרֶץ הַחֲוִילָה אֲשֶׁר־שָׁם הַזָּהָב *the land of Havilah where there is gold* (lit. *which there is gold*) Gn 2_{11}, הַמָּקוֹם אֲשֶׁר־אַתָּה שָׁם *the place where you are* 13_{14}, הַבָּתִּים אֲשֶׁר אַתֶּם שָׁם *the houses where you are* Ex 12_{13}, בַּיִת אֲשֶׁר אֵין־שָׁם מֵת *a house where there was not a dead person* 12_{30} (sim. Jg 18_{10}), sim. Ex 9_{26} 20_{21} Jg 19_{26} 1 S 3_3 9_{10} etc., הַבָּמָה אֲשֶׁר־אַתֶּם הַבָּאִים שָׁם *the high place where you go* Ezk 20_{29}.

(4) no preposition or שָׁם *there*, מָקוֹם צָר אֲשֶׁר אֵין־דֶּרֶךְ *a narrow place (in) which there was no room* Nm 22_{26}, צִמָּאוֹן אֲשֶׁר אֵין־מָיִם *a parched land (in) which there is not water* Dt 8_{15}, חָמֵשׁ שָׁנִים אֲשֶׁר אֵין־חָרִישׁ *five years (during) which there is no ploughing* Gn 45_6, עת אשר בידו מצלחת *an occasion (at) which success is in his hand* Si 38_{13}, כָּל־יְמֵי אֲשֶׁר הַנֶּגַע בּוֹ *all the days (during) which the affliction is with him* Lv 13_{46}, כָּל־הַיָּמִים אֲשֶׁר־הֵם חַיִּים עַל־פְּנֵי הָאֲדָמָה *all the days (during) which they are alive on the earth* 1 K 8_{40}‖2 C 6_{31} (sim. Dt 4_{10} 12_1 31_{13} 1 S 20_{31} 1QDM $1_{6[\text{Milik}]}$ [(כול) ... (חיים על האד)מה]), לַמְיַלְּדֹת הָעִבְרִיֹּת אֲשֶׁר שֵׁם הָאַחַת שִׁפְרָה וְשֵׁם הַשֵּׁנִית פּוּעָה *to the Hebrew midwives (of) whom the name of the one was Shiphrah and the name of the second was Puah* Ex 1_{15} (sim. 18_3 Jg 20_{31}), איש אשר לא קן *one (for) whom there is no nest* Si $36_{31(\text{B})}$ (Bmg, C, D אשר אין לו קן[י]ן in same sense), כל אשם מושב אשר אין בעלים *every restored misappropriated object (for) which there are no owners* CD 9_{13}.

(5) noun with pronoun suffix referring to antecedent, הַגּוֹיִם אֲשֶׁר י׳ ... נֹתֵן לְךָ אֶת־אַרְצָם *the nations ... whose land Y. is giving you* Dt 19_1, הָאֲדָמָה אֲשֶׁר אַתָּה קָץ מִפְּנֵי שְׁנֵי מְלָכֶיהָ *the land before whose two kings you are in dread* Is 7_{16}, מַחֲנֵיהֶם אֲשֶׁר אֲנִי שֹׁכֵן בְּתוֹכָם *their camps among which I dwell* Nm 5_3 (sim. 35_{34} 11QT 45_{13} 47_{18}), בְּנוֹת הַכְּנַעֲנִי אֲשֶׁר אָנֹכִי יֹשֵׁב בְּאַרְצוֹ *the daughters of the Canaanite in whose land I live* Gn 24_{37} (sim. 24_3 Jos 24_{15} Jg 6_{10}), [מלאכי] שמים אשר חיים עולם נחלתם *angels of heaven, whose inheritance is life (and) eternity* 4Q416 4_{13}, perh. מקור מים חיים אשר הכול *source of living water all of which* 4Q416 2_5 (context fragmentary), אַתָּה ... אֲשֶׁר־עֵינֶיךָ פְּקֻחוֹת *you ... whose eyes are opened* Jr 32_{19}.

2b. אֲשֶׁר introduces **verbal clause**, with (1) suffixed preposition, הָאָרֶץ אֲשֶׁר־גַּרְתָּה בָּהּ *the land in which you stayed* Gn 21_{23}, הַדֶּרֶךְ אֲשֶׁר תֵּלְכוּ־בָהּ *the road on which you walk* 42_{38} Dt 1_{33} Jos 3_4 (sim. Gn 24_{42} Dt 1_{22} Jos 24_{17} Jg $18_{5.6}$ etc.), הבגד אשר תהיה עליו *the garment in which it is (found)* 4QToh A 2.1_5 (sim. 2.1_7), הַיָּמִים אֲשֶׁר־הָיָה לָהֶם הַמִּשְׁתֶּה *the days that they had of their feast* Jg 14_{17}, האנשים אשר יהיה להמה מקרה *the men that have an accident* 11QT 46_{18}, שׁוֹר וָשֶׂה אֲשֶׁר יִהְיֶה בוֹ מוּם *an ox or a sheep in which there is a defect* Dt 17_1=11QT 52_4 (sim. Lv 13_{52} $21_{17.19}$), לְעֵינֵי הַגּוֹיִם אֲשֶׁר הוֹצֵאתִים לְעֵינֵיהֶם *in view of the nations before whose eyes I had brought them out* Ezk 20_{14} (var. 20_{22}).

כְּלֵי הַקֹּדֶשׁ אֲשֶׁר יְשָׁרְתוּ בָהֶם *the holy vessels with which they ministered* Nm 3_{31} (sim. $4_{9.12.14}$ 2 K 25_{14}‖Jr 52_{18} Ezk 42_{14}), כָּל־אִישׁ אֲשֶׁר־נִמְצָא אִתּוֹ *every man with whom was found* Ex 35_{23} (sim. 35_{24}), אַהֲרֹן וּמֹשֶׁה אֲשֶׁר אָמַר י׳ לָהֶם *Aaron and Moses to whom Y. said* 6_{26},

הַנַּעֲרָה אֲשֶׁר אֹמַר אֵלֶיהָ *the girl to whom I say* Gn $24_{14(Qr)}$, המחנה אשר גנב בו *the camp in which it was stolen* CD 9_{11}.

הַחַטָּאת אֲשֶׁר חָטְאוּ עָלֶיהָ *the sin through which they became sinful* Lv 4_{14}, כלי [א]שר יגע בו הזב או אשר ישב *a vessel (against) which one with a discharge will touch or upon which he will sit* 4QToh A 1.1_{4}, [אש]ר כפר בם clothes *in which they made atonement* 4QToh B^{b}_{4} (sim. 4QToh B^{a}_{1}), הַבְּהֵמָה אֲשֶׁר יַקְרִיב מִמֶּנָּה אִשֶּׁה *the animal from which one presents an offering by fire* Lv 7_{25}, בָּרָד ... אֲשֶׁר לֹא־הָיָה כָמֹהוּ *hail ... the like of which there has not been* Ex $9_{18.24}$ (sim. CD 3_{19}), נָשַׁי ... אֲשֶׁר עָבַדְתִּי אֹתְךָ בָּהֵן *my wives ... on whose account I have served you* Gn 30_{26}, י׳ אֲשֶׁר־הִתְהַלַּכְתִּי לְפָנָיו *Y. before whom I have walked* 24_{40} (sim. 48_{15}), מָרְדֳּכַי אֲשֶׁר הַחִלּוֹתָ לִנְפֹּל לְפָנָיו *Mordecai before whom you have started to fall* Est 6_{13}, סיר אשר הוא נוקש בו והוא נשבר *a cauldron that it knocks against and is broken* Si 13_{2}.

הַדֶּרֶךְ אֲשֶׁר צִוְּךָ י׳ ... לָלֶכֶת בָּהּ *the way along which Y. ... commanded you to go* Dt 13_{6}=11QT 54_{17}, דרך ... אשר יהיו באים בו *a way ... by which they will come* 11QT 31_{6} (sim. $32_{11[Yadin]}$ [יהי(ו באי)ם (בה)ם] 32_{13} 33_{14} 46_{7} 48_{13}), השבת אשר שבת ב[ו] *the sabbath day on which he ceased* $4QJub^{a}$ 7_{5}, העת אשר היה כתוב עליה *the time about which it was written* CD 1_{13}, בורות ... אשר תהיה הצואה יורדת אל תוכמה *pits ... into the middle of which the excrement will descend* 11QT 46_{15} (sim. Lv 11_{33}), sim. Gn 19_{29} 28_{13} Ex 3_{5} 4_{17} 8_{18} etc. 11QT $20_{9.10}$ ([א]שר) $26_{5(Yadin)}$ (אשר על[ה עליו]) 29_{3} (Yadin) (בית אשר א[שכין] שמי עליו) 29_{8} etc.

הֶחֳדַלְתִּי אֶת־דִּשְׁנִי אֲשֶׁר־בִּי יְכַבְּדוּ אֱלֹהִים *should I, by whom they honour gods, be made to leave my fatness* Jg 9_{9} (or em. בּוֹ *by which*), נַחַל ... אֲשֶׁר לֹא־יֵעָבֵד בּוֹ *a stream that has not been worked* Dt 21_{4} (=11QT 63_{2} omits בּוֹ), י׳ ... אֲשֶׁר הִתְפַּלַּלְתָּ אֵלַי *Y. ... to whom you have prayed* Is 37_{21} (‖2 K 19_{20} אֲשֶׁר = *that which*, as §3), עַבְדִּי־אָתָּה יִשְׂרָאֵל אֲשֶׁר־בְּךָ אֶתְפָּאָר *you are my servant, Israel, by whom I am glorified* 49_{3}, קֹדֶשׁ הֵמָּה אֲשֶׁר־בָּאָה אֲלֵיהֶם אֲרוֹן י׳ *holy are they to whom Y.'s ark has come* 2 C 8_{11}.

(2) preposition prefixed to אֲשֶׁר, בַּאֲשֶׁר ... חֲבָרַיִךְ יָגַעַתְּ *your enchantments ... at which you laboured* Is 47_{12}, דְּבָר ... עַל אֲשֶׁר יִחַלְתָּנִי your *word about which you made me hope* Ps 119_{49}, אֲנָשִׁים ... לַאֲשֶׁר רָחַצְתְּ כָּחַלְתְּ עֵינַיִךְ *men ... for whom you washed, made up your eyes* Ezk 23_{40}, אֶל כָּל־אֲשֶׁר יָבוֹא שָׁם נַחֲלַיִם *every (place) to which the currents come* Ezk 47_{9}.

(3) שָׁם *there*, הַמָּקוֹם אֲשֶׁר דִּבֶּר אִתּוֹ שָׁם אֱלֹהִים *the place where God spoke with him* Gn 35_{15}, חֶבְרוֹן אֲשֶׁר־גָּר־שָׁם אַבְרָהָם *Hebron where Abraham had stayed* 35_{27} (sim. Dt 18_{6} Ezr 1_{4}), כָּל־הַגּוֹיִם ... אֲשֶׁר הִדַּחְתִּי אֶתְכֶם שָׁם *all the nations ... where I expelled you* Jr 29_{14} (var. 29_{18}, sim. 30_{11} 43_{5} Ezk 4_{13} 6_{9}), הַגּוֹיִם אֲשֶׁר־בָּאוּ שָׁם *the nations where they came* Ezk 12_{16} 36_{20} (sim. Jr 49_{36} Ezk 36_{22} 37_{21}), Gn 13_{3} 19_{27} $31_{13.13}$ (see Coll.) 33_{19} etc. 1QS $6_{3.6}$ 1QM 5_{17} 14_{3} 19_{9} + Sup, הַמָּקוֹם אֲשֶׁר אָמַרְתָּ לָשׂוּם שִׁמְךָ שָׁם *the place where you promised to put your name* 2 C 6_{20}, אַרְזֵי לְבָנוֹן ... : אֲשֶׁר־שָׁם צִפֳּרִים יְקַנֵּנוּ *cedars of Lebanon ... where birds make nests* Ps 104_{17}, מְקוֹם הַמִּזְבֵּחַ אֲשֶׁר־עָשָׂה שָׁם *the place where he had made the altar* (lit. *the place of the altar that he had made there*) Gn 13_{4}, כִּסְּתוֹתֵיכֶנָה אֲשֶׁר אַתֵּנָה מְצֹדְדוֹת שָׁם appar. *your armbands by which you hunt* Ezk 13_{20}, אשר יהיו מניחים [ש]ם עליהמה *upon which (there) they will place* 11QT 32_{10} (Yadin).

(4) שָׁמָּה *thither, there*, מָקוֹם אֲשֶׁר יָנוּס שָׁמָּה *a place to which he might flee* Ex 21_{13}, אֹהֶל מוֹעֵד אֲשֶׁר אִוָּעֵד לְךָ שָׁמָּה *the tent of meeting where I shall come to meet you* 30_{36} (sim. 29_{42} 30_{6} Nm 17_{19}), הָאָרֶץ אֲשֶׁר אֲנִי מֵבִיא אֶתְכֶם שָׁמָּה *the land to which I am bringing you* Lv 20_{22} Nm 15_{18} (sim. Lv 18_{3}), הָאָרֶץ אֲשֶׁר אַתֶּם עֹבְרִים שָׁמָּה לְרִשְׁתָּהּ *the land to which you are crossing to possess* Dt 4_{14} 6_{1} (both בָּאָרֶץ) $11_{8.11}$ (sim. 4_{26} 30_{18} 31_{13} 32_{47}), בַּגּוֹיִם אֲשֶׁר יְנַהֶג י׳ אֶתְכֶם שָׁמָּה *among the nations to which Y. will lead you* Dt 4_{27} (sim. 12_{29} 30_{1} Jr 46_{28} Ezk 36_{21}), Gn 20_{13} Nm 14_{24} $35_{25.26}$ Dt 3_{21} etc. $4QDibHam^{a}$ 1.5_{12} 4QFlor 1_{3}.

מקום ... אשר יהיו יוצאים שמה *a place ... to which they will go out* 11QT 46_{13}, מק[ו]ם ... אשר יהיו מבשלים שמה *a place ... where you will boil* 37_{14}, אחד שעריכה ... אשר הוא גר שמה *one of your gates ... where he lives* 60_{12}, הַמָּקוֹם אֲשֶׁר הָיְתָה־שָׁמָּה *the place where she was* Ru 1_{7}.

(5) מִשָּׁם *thence*, כַּסְלֻחִים אֲשֶׁר יָצְאוּ מִשָּׁם פְּלִשְׁתִּים *Casluhim from where (the) Philistines went out* Gn 10_{14} ‖1 C 1_{12}, הָאֲדָמָה אֲשֶׁר לֻקַּח מִשָּׁם *the earth from whence he*

was taken Gn 3$_{23}$ (sim. 1QH 12$_{27}$ at §3f), הָאָרֶץ אֲשֶׁר־יָצָאתָ מִשָּׁם *the land from which you went out* 24$_{5}$, Nm 23$_{13}$ Dt 9$_{28}$ 11$_{10}$ Jos 20$_{6}$.

(6) אֲשֶׁר meaning **where, when,** etc., like בַּאֲשֶׁר, כַּאֲשֶׁר, בַּמִּדְבָּר ... אֲשֶׁר נְשָׂאֲךָ י׳ *in the desert ... (in) which Y. lifted you* Dt 1$_{31}$ (sim. 4QDibHam^a 7$_{14}$ [במד(בר)]), הַבְּאֵר אֲשֶׁר אָמַר י׳ *the well where Y. said* Nm 21$_{16}$, חֹרֵב אֲשֶׁר כָּרַת י׳ *Horeb where Y. made (a covenant)* 1 K 8$_{9}$||2 C 5$_{10}$, מִצְרַיִם אֲשֶׁר בָּרַח *Egypt whither he had fled* 1 K 12$_{2}$||2 C 10$_{2}$, דרכיו אשר יצא *his ways (by) which he goes out* 11QT 58$_{21}$, בְּסֵפֶר ... מֹשֶׁה אֲשֶׁר־צִוָּה י׳ *in the book ... of Moses where Y. commanded* 2 K 14$_{6}$||2 C 25$_{4}$, קֵן ... אֲשֶׁר־שָׁתָה *a nest ... where she has placed* Ps 84$_{4}$, הָאָרֶץ אֲשֶׁר שְׁלַחְתָּנוּ *the land (to) which you sent us* Nm 13$_{27}$, בָעִיר אֲשֶׁר כֵּן־עָשׂוּ *in the city where they had acted thus* Ec 8$_{10}$, שִׁקֲתוֹת הַמַּיִם אֲשֶׁר תָּבֹאןָ הַצֹּאן *water troughs (to) which the flock would come* Gn 30$_{38(Qr)}$.

With antecedent מָקוֹם *place,* מְקוֹם אֲשֶׁר *(the) place (in) which, the place where* Gn 39$_{20}$ 1 K 21$_{19}$ Ezk 21$_{35}$ Est 4$_{3}$ 8$_{17}$ Ne 4$_{14}$; with resumptive שָׁם *there* Gn 40$_{3}$ Nm 9$_{17}$ 2 S 15$_{21}$ Jr 22$_{12}$ Ezk 6$_{13}$; בִּמְקוֹם אֲשֶׁר(־)יִשְׁחַט *in the place where one slaughters* Lv 4$_{24.33}$ 6$_{18}$ (תִּשָּׁחֵט) 7$_{2}$ (יִשְׁחֲטוּ) 14$_{13}$, בִּמְקוֹם אֲשֶׁר־יֵאָמֵר ... יֵאָמֵר *in the place where it is said* (or, *instead of it being said*) *... it will be said* Ho 2$_{1}$; בַּמָּקוֹם אֲשֶׁר־דִּבֶּר אִתּוֹ *at the place (at) which he spoke with him* Gn 35$_{13.14}$, מְקוֹמוֹ אֲשֶׁר תִּהְיֶה רַגְלוֹ *his place where his foot is* 1 S 23$_{22}$, הַמָּקוֹם ... אֲשֶׁר יֹאפוּ *the place ... where they bake* Ezk 46$_{20}$, כָּל־הַמָּקוֹם אֲשֶׁר אַזְכִּיר אֶת־שְׁמִי *every place where I cause my name to be remembered* Ex 20$_{24}$, הַמָּקוֹם אֲשֶׁר־יִפְנֶה הָרֹאשׁ *the place (to) which the head turned* Ezk 10$_{11}$, perh. הַמָּקוֹם אֲשֶׁר־תִּשְׁלָחֵנִי *the place (to) which you send* me 1 K 5$_{23}$, מקומות ... אשר יהיו באים המצורעים *places ... (to) which the lepers will come* 11QT 46$_{17}$.

הַגּוֹיִם אֲשֶׁר עֲבַרְתֶּם *the nations (through) whom you passed* Dt 29$_{15}$, בַּדֶּרֶךְ הַזֶּה אֲשֶׁר אָנֹכִי הוֹלֵךְ *on this road (upon) which I walk* Gn 28$_{20}$ (sim. 35$_{3}$ Dt 1$_{31}$ 8$_{2}$ Jg 2$_{17}$ 4$_{9}$ etc.), כֹּל אֲשֶׁר(־)תֵּלֵךְ *wherever you go (to)* Gn 28$_{15}$ Jos 1$_{7.9}$ (sim. 2 S 7$_{7.9}$||1 C 17$_{6.8}$ 2 S 8$_{6.14}$||1 C 18$_{6.13}$), כָּל־אֲשֶׁר תִּשְׁלָחֵנוּ *wherever you send us (to)* Jos 1$_{16}$ (sim. 1 S 18$_{5}$ Jr 1$_{7}$), כַּמִּשְׁפָּט הָרִאשׁוֹן אֲשֶׁר הָיִיתָ מַשְׁקֵהוּ *like the former situation (during) which you were his cupbearer* 40$_{13}$, עֶשְׂרִים שָׁנָה אֲשֶׁר(־)בָּנָה שְׁלֹמֹה *twenty years (during) which Solomon built* 1 K 9$_{10}$||2 C 8$_{1}$.

With antecedent עֵת *time,* בעת אש[ר] *at the time when* 11QT 33$_{2}$, בָּעֵת הַהִיא אֲשֶׁר אָשִׁיב *at that time when I shall restore* Jl 4$_{1(Qr)}$ (sim. CD 10$_{15}$ 4QFlor 4$_{3}$ 4QCat^a 1$_{5}$), עֵת אֲשֶׁר שָׁלַט הָאָדָם בְּאָדָם *a time when one person dominates another* Ec 8$_{9}$ (sim. 2 C 25$_{27}$ 4QTestim 1$_{21}$), כָּל־עֵת אֲשֶׁר אֲנִי רֹאֶה *all the time that I see* Est 5$_{13}$; with antecedent יוֹם *day,* אַרְבָּעִים הַיּוֹם ... אֲשֶׁר הִתְנַפָּלְתִּי *the forty days (during) which I prostrated myself* Dt 9$_{25}$, הַיּוֹם הַזֶּה אֲשֶׁר יְצָאתֶם מִמִּצְרַיִם *this day (on) which you went out from Egypt* Ex 13$_{3}$, וְהַיָּמִים אֲשֶׁר מָלַךְ *and the days (during) which he reigned* 1 K 2$_{11}$||1 C 29$_{27}$ 1 K 11$_{42}$ 14$_{20}$ 2 K 10$_{36}$, יום הברכה אשר אברא אני את מקדשי *the day of blessing (on) which I shall create my sanctuary* 11QT 29$_{9}$, כול הימים אשר הוא בתוכה מת *all the days he is inside her, dead* 50$_{10}$, Gn 5$_{5}$ 25$_{7}$ Nm 6$_{5}$ 9$_{18}$ 14$_{34}$ etc. 11QT 39$_{8}$ 46$_{4(Yadin)}$ (כול הימים אשר א[ני שוכ]ן בתוכם) 49$_{11.13}$ 57$_{2}$ 4QDibHam^a 1.6$_{5}$ CD 8$_{3(A)}$=19$_{15(B)}$ 16$_{4}$ 4Q Cat^a 7$_{15}$.

כָּל־אֲשֶׁר שְׁלָחוֹ יוֹאָב *everything (about) which Joab had sent him* 2 S 11$_{22}$ (sim. 1 S 21$_{3}$ 1 K 20$_{9}$ Jr 42$_{5.21}$ 43$_{1}$), sim. Dt 11$_{10}$ 1 K 8$_{44}$||2 C 6$_{34}$ Is 64$_{10}$ Jr 42$_{5}$ 43$_{1}$ 11QT 60$_{13}$ CD 6$_{6}$ 1QpHab 10$_{3}$ 12$_{9}$, הַזְּרֹעַ ... אֲשֶׁר הוֹצִאֲךָ י׳ *the arm ... (with) which Y. brought you out* Dt 7$_{19}$, מִשְׁלַח יֶדְכֶם ... אֲשֶׁר בֵּרַכְךָ י׳ *your activity ... (in) which Y. has blessed you* 12$_{7}$, רֹעַ מַעֲלָלֶיךָ אֲשֶׁר עֲזַבְתָּנִי *the evil of your deeds (through) which you deserted me* 28$_{20}$, ויבינו בכל אשר עזבו *and they will understand everything (through) which they deserted* 4QpsMos^e 1$_{4}$ (sim. 2.1$_{8}$ [אשר עז]בוני])).

לְכֹל אֲשֶׁר־יֵעָשֶׂה הָעוֹר לִמְלָאכָה *concerning every (activity) for which the skin is used* (lit. *for everything which the skin is used for work*) Lv 13$_{51}$, גְּבוּל אֲשֶׁר תִּתְנַחֲלוּ אֶת־הָאָרֶץ *(the) boundary (by) which you are to apportion the land* Ezk 47$_{13}$, שֹׁפְטֶיךָ אֲשֶׁר אָמַרְתָּ *your judges (to) whom you said* Ho 13$_{10}$, כול רשי ... העדה אשר יצא הגורל להתי[צב] *all the heads of ... the congregation (for) whom the lot goes out to be positioned* 1QSa 1$_{16(mg)}$.

(7) noun with pronoun suffix referring to antecedent, רָשָׁע ... אֲשֶׁר־בָּא יוֹמוֹ *wicked one ..., whose day has*

come Ezk 21$_{30}$ (sim. 21$_{34}$), גּוֹי ... אֲשֶׁר בָּזְאוּ נְהָרִים אַרְצוֹ *a nation ... whose land the rivers have divided* 18$_{2.7}$, כְּרָחֵל וּכְלֵאָה אֲשֶׁר בָּנוּ שְׁתֵּיהֶם *like Rachel and like Leah, the two of whom built* Ru 4$_{11}$, איש אשר לוא השיגה ידו *a person who hand has not reached* 4QToh A 2.1$_{6}$, בְּנֵי יְהוּדָה אֲשֶׁר־שָׁפְכוּ דָם־נָקִיא בְּאַרְצָם *the people of Judah in whose land they spilt innocent blood* Jl 4$_{19}$, כִּזְבֵיהֶם אֲשֶׁר־הָלְכוּ אֲבוֹתָם אַחֲרֵיהֶם *their delusions after which their ancestors went* Am 2$_{4}$, הָאִשָּׁה אֲשֶׁר־הֶחֱיָה אֶת־בְּנָהּ *the woman whose son he had revived* 2 K 8$_{1}$, אִישׁ אֲשֶׁר אִמּוֹ תְּנַחֲמֶנּוּ *a man whose mother comforts him* Is 66$_{13}$=4QBarkc$_{6}$, כָּל־אִישׁ אֲשֶׁר יִדְּבֶנּוּ לִבּוֹ *each man whose heart moves him* Ex 25$_{2}$ (sim. 35$_{21.21.26.29}$ 36$_{2}$ etc. Si 45$_{23}$), הָאִישׁ אֲשֶׁר נִמְצָא הַגָּבִיעַ בְּיָדוֹ *the man in whose hand is found the cup* Gn 44$_{17}$, לָעִיר ... : ... אֲשֶׁר עֲשִׁירֶיהָ מָלְאוּ חָמָס *to the city ... whose wealthy are full of violence* Mc 6$_{12}$.

הכוהן אשר גבר קלונו מכבודו *the priest whose shame was greater than his honour* 1QpHab 11$_{12}$, ספרי הנביאים אשר בזה ישראל את דבריהם *the books of the prophets whose words Israel despised* CD 7$_{18}$, לָאִישׁ ... אֲשֶׁר תֵּדַע אֶת־לְבָבוֹ *to the man ... whose heart you know* 1 K 8$_{39}$||2 C 6$_{30}$, גּוֹי אֲשֶׁר לֹא־תִשְׁמַע לְשֹׁנוֹ *a nation whose language you will not understand* Dt 28$_{49}$, עפר ואפר אשר בחייו יורם גויו *(creature of) dust and ash whose body rots in his own lifetime* Si 10$_{9}$, גבולות ... אשר את עובריהם ארותה *boundaries ... the crossers of which you have cursed* 4QD^{b}$_{13}$, sim. Ex 36$_{2}$ Lv 16$_{27.32}$ (unless כֹּהֵן *priest* is subj. of מלא pi. *fill* hand) 21$_{10}$ Nm 3$_{3}$ etc. Si 46$_{11}$ 50$_{1.2.3}$ 11QT 59$_{13}$ (unless מֶלֶךְ *king* is subj. of זנה *prostitute* eyes) 1QS 7$_{18}$ 1QM 17$_{2}$ CD 10$_{1}$ 1QH 2$_{32}$ 1QpHab 7$_{11}$ 4QpNah 1$_{5(mg)}$ 3.2$_{1}$ 3.3$_{3.7}$ 3.4$_{3.6}$, הֲלוֹא־הוּא אֲשֶׁר הֵסִיר חִזְקִיָּהוּ אֶת־בָּמֹתָיו *is it not he whose high places Hezekiah removed* 2 K 18$_{22}$||Is 36$_{7}$, וַאֲשֶׁר הִסְתַּרְתִּי פָנַי ... עַל כָּל־רָעָתָם *and on account of whose wickedness ... I have hidden my face* Jr 33$_{5}$, צֹאן הַהֲרֵגָה : אֲשֶׁר קֹנֵיהֶן יַהַרְגֻן *sheep for slaughter, whose buyers will slay them* Zc 11$_{5}$.

מֹסְרוֹת עָרוֹד ... : אֲשֶׁר־שַׂמְתִּי עֲרָבָה בֵיתוֹ *the bonds of the donkey ... whose home I have made the steppe* Jb 39$_{5}$, להם אשר חרה אף אל בכל עדתו *to them against all of whose congregation God's anger has been kindled* CD 8$_{13}$, אֲנִי י׳ אֲשֶׁר לֹא־יֵבֹשׁוּ קֹוָי *I am Y., of whom those that wait for me will not be shamed* Is 49$_{23}$, אֲנִי י׳ אֲשֶׁר בְּחֻקַּי לֹא הֲלַכְתֶּם *I am Y. in whose statutes you did not walk* Ezk 11$_{12}$, י׳ ... אֲשֶׁר תְּנָה הוֹדְךָ *Y. ... whose majesty is recounted* Ps 8$_{2}$ (if em. אֲשֶׁר תְּנָה appar. *who gives*), הָאִשָּׁה אֲשֶׁר־הִיא מְצוֹדִים וַחֲרָמִים לִבָּהּ *the woman, who is a trap and whose heart is snares* Ec 7$_{26}$.

<COLL> a. אֲשֶׁר ... אֲשֶׁר, two relatives with one antecedent, הַחֵלֶב אֲשֶׁר עֲלֵ(י)הֶן אֲשֶׁר עַל־הַכְּסָלִים *the fat that is on them, that is at the loins* 3$_{4.10.15}$ 4$_{9}$ 7$_{4}$, בָּנֶיךָ אֲשֶׁר יֵצְאוּ מִמְּךָ אֲשֶׁר תּוֹלִיד *your sons who will come out of you, whom you will father* 2 K 20$_{18}$||Is 39$_{7}$, שמעון ... אשר בדורו ... אשר בימיו ... אשר בדורו *Simeon ... in whose generation ... in whose days ... in whose generation* Si 50$_{1}$, האיש אשר יוכל ... [ו]אשר ידרוש ... ואשר [י]ואת *the man that eats ... and that seeks ... and that enjoys* 4QD^{b}$_{15}$, כָּל־הָעֵץ אֲשֶׁר בַּשָּׂדֶה אֲשֶׁר בְּכָל־גְּבֻלוֹ *every tree that was in the field, (i.e.) that was in all its boundary* Gn 23$_{17}$, י׳ ... אֲשֶׁר לְקָחַנִי ... וַאֲשֶׁר דִּבֶּר־לִי וַאֲשֶׁר נִשְׁבַּע־לִי *Y. ... who took me ... and who spoke to me and who swore to me* 24$_{7}$, אֱלֹהִים ... : אֲשֶׁר־עָשִׂיתָ גְדֹלוֹת ... : אֲשֶׁר הִרְאִיתַנִי צָרוֹת *O God ..., you who have done great things ..., who have shown me troubles* Ps 71$_{19(Qr)}$, בֵּית־אֵל אֲשֶׁר מָשַׁחְתָּ שָּׁם מַצֵּבָה אֲשֶׁר נָדַרְתָּ לִּי שָׁם נֶדֶר *Bethel where you anointed a pillar (and) where you took a vow to me* Gn 31$_{13}$, יושב אשר החטיים אשר לוא דרשתי *a dweller, who is the Hittites, whom I did not seek* 4Q522 2$_{9}$, האיש אשר יעשה בו מלאכה או אשר לוא יתענו בו *the man who does work on it or who does not afflict himself on it* 11QT 27$_{7}$, sim. Gn 23$_{9}$ 40$_{5}$ Lv 4$_{18}$ Si 37$_{12}$ 50$_{27}$ CD 9$_{3.9}$ etc, הַמְּקֹמוֹת אֲשֶׁר עָבְדוּ־שָׁם הַגּוֹיִם אֲשֶׁר אַתֶּם יֹרְשִׁים אֹתָם *the places at which the nations whom you dispossessed worshipped* Dt 12$_{2}$, כֹּל אֲשֶׁר־עָשׂוּ הָאֱמֹרִי אֲשֶׁר לְפָנָיו *all that the Amorites who were before him did* 2 K 21$_{11}$, בְּרִיתוֹ דָּבָר צִוָּה ... : אֲשֶׁר כָּרַת *his covenant, a promise he established, ... that he made* 1 C 16$_{16}$.

b. אֲשֶׁר ... אֲשֶׁר, the antecedent of the second in the first relative clause, הָעֵצִים אֲשֶׁר עַל־הָאֵשׁ אֲשֶׁר עַל־הַמִּזְבֵּחַ *the sticks that are on the fire that is on the altar* Lv 1$_{8.12}$, sim. 3$_{5}$, שְׂדֵה עֶפְרוֹן אֲשֶׁר בַּמַּכְפֵּלָה אֲשֶׁר לִפְנֵי מַמְרֵא *Ephron's field which was at Machpelah which was opposite Mamre* Gn 23$_{17}$, sim. CD 7$_{10}$ etc.

c. אֲשֶׁר separated from antecedent by main clause verb, etc., e.g. רִבְקָה יֹצֵאת אֲשֶׁר יֻלְּדָה לִבְתוּאֵל *Rebekah, who had been born to Bethuel, comes out* Gn 24$_{15}$, הַגֹּאֵל עֹבֵר אֲשֶׁר דִּבֶּר־בֹּעַז *the redeemer, whom Boaz mentioned, passes* Ru 4$_{1}$, הֲיוֹנָתָן יָמוּת אֲשֶׁר עָשָׂה הַיְשׁוּעָה *should Jonathan, who has wrought the victory, die?* 1 S 14$_{45}$ (sim. Jos 5$_{6}$ 1 S 14$_{21}$ Lm 1$_{10}$ 2 C 36$_{13}$ 1QMyst 1.1$_{10}$), נְבִיאֶיךָ הָרָגוּ אֲשֶׁר־הֵעִידוּ *they killed your prophets who had borne witness* Ne 9$_{26}$ (sim. Dt 19$_{9}$ Is 56$_{5}$ 2 C 1$_{12}$ 1QDM 1$_{5}$ 4QpHos^{a} 1.2$_{4}$), אֶת־הַמַּטֶּה הַזֶּה תִּקַּח בְּיָדֶךָ אֲשֶׁר תַּעֲשֶׂה־בּוֹ אֶת־הָאֹתֹת *take in your hand this rod with which you will perform the signs* Ex 4$_{17}$, שלמה מלך ... ואל הניח לו מסביב אשר הכין בית *Solomon reigned ... and God gave him rest all round, who founded a temple* Si 47$_{13}$ (sim. Lv 22$_{2}$ Hb 2$_{5}$ Si 44$_{20}$ 45$_{23}$ 49$_{10}$), לֹא־תַסְגִּיר עֶבֶד אֶל־אֲדֹנָיו אֲשֶׁר־יִנָּצֵל אֵלֶיךָ *you are not to deliver a servant, who has escaped to you, to his master* Dt 23$_{16}$ (sim. Jg 18$_{16}$ 1 S 24$_{20}$ 1 K 8$_{39}$||2 C 6$_{30}$ 1 K 10$_{3}$||2 C 9$_{2}$ 2 K 10$_{10}$ Is 29$_{22}$ Jr 18$_{8}$ 32$_{9}$ Mc 7$_{20}$ Ps 84$_{4}$ Jb 6$_{4}$ 1 C 17$_{11}$ 11QT 47$_{18}$ 1QM 10$_{8}$ CD 10$_{1}$ 12$_{18}$ 4QpGen^{a} 5$_{4}$), אַרְיֵה ... אֲשֶׁר אִם עָבַר וְרָמַס *a lion ... which, if it passes, tramples* Mc 5$_{7}$, אֲשֶׁר בְּשַׁלֶּכֶת מַצֶּבֶת בָּם as a terebinth or an oak *of which, after felling, there is a stump* Is 6$_{13}$, כפיר החרון ... אשר יתלה *the lion of wrath ... who hangs* people 4QpNah 3.1$_{7}$, הֲתַחַת אֱלֹהִים אָנֹכִי אֲשֶׁר־מָנַע מִמֵּךְ *am I in place of God who has withheld from you?* Gn 30$_{2}$, שור ... בתוך עירי אשר אנוכי מקדש ... אשר לוא יבוא *an ox ..., within my city that I consecrate ..., which is not to come* 11QT 52$_{20}$ (sim. Nm 14$_{14}$ Dt 32$_{38}$ 2 S 3$_{8}$ Ezk 16$_{45}$ 2 C 22$_{9}$).

d. אֲשֶׁר–clause precedes antecedent, וַיִּוָּלֵד לְיוֹסֵף בְּאֶרֶץ מִצְרַיִם אֲשֶׁר יָלְדָה־לּוֹ אָסְנַת ... אֶת־מְנַשֶּׁה וְאֶת־אֶפְרָיִם *and to Joseph was born in the land of Egypt, whom Asenath bore to him ..., Manasseh and Ephraim* Gn 46$_{20}$

e. verb in relative clause is cognate with antecedent, רְכוּשָׁם אֲשֶׁר רָכָשׁוּ *their property which they had acquired* Gn 12$_{5}$ 46$_{6}$ (sim. 31$_{18}$), מַעֲשִׂים אֲשֶׁר לֹא־יֵעָשׂוּ *deeds that are not done* 20$_{9}$, הַשְּׁבֻעָה אֲשֶׁר נִשְׁבַּעְתִּי *the vow that I vowed* 26$_{3}$ Jr 11$_{5}$ (sim. Dt 7$_{8}$ Jos 9$_{20}$ 4QDibHam^{a} 6$_{18}$ [(השבו]עה אשר נשב(עתה)]), הַמְּלָכִים אֲשֶׁר מָלְכוּ *the kings that reigned* Gn 36$_{31}$||1 C 1$_{43}$, ההריגה אשר הרגוה *the slaughter that they committed* GnzPs 2$_{8(mg)}$, הַדָּבָר אֲשֶׁר דִּבַּרְתִּי *the word I spoke* Gn 41$_{28}$ (sim. 39$_{19}$ 44$_{2}$ 45$_{27}$ Ex 4$_{30}$ 14$_{12}$ etc. papMurPalimp^{b}$_{2}$), הַחֲלֹמוֹת אֲשֶׁר חָלָם *the dreams that he dreamt* 42$_{9}$ (sim. 37$_{6.10}$ Jr 29$_{8}$), sim. Gn 6$_{21}$ 27$_{41}$ 30$_{26}$ 44$_{15}$ Ex 3$_{9}$ etc., חֲרוֹן אַפּוֹ ... אֲשֶׁר־חָרָה אַפּוֹ *the burning of his wrath ... (with) which his anger burned* 2 K 23$_{26}$.

f. antecedent is governed noun (*nomen rectum*), e.g. שֶׁם־בְּנוֹ אֲשֶׁר־יָלְדָה הָגָר *the name of his son, whom Hagar had borne* Gn 16$_{15}$, וַתִּכְלֶינָה שֶׁבַע שְׁנֵי הַשָּׂבָע אֲשֶׁר הָיָה בְּאֶרֶץ מִצְרָיִם *and the seven years of the plenty that had been in Egypt came to an end* 41$_{53}$, בְּכוֹר הַשִּׁפְחָה אֲשֶׁר אַחַר הָרֵחָיִם *the first-born of the maidservant who is behind the mill* Ex 11$_{5}$, נַאֲקַת בְּנֵי יִשְׂרָאֵל אֲשֶׁר מִצְרַיִם מַעֲבִדִים אֹתָם *the groaning of the Israelites whom the Egyptians are oppressing* 6$_{5}$, פִּתְגָם הַמֶּלֶךְ אֲשֶׁר־יַעֲשֶׂה *the decree of the king that he makes* Est 1$_{20}$, שירי דויד אשר אמר *the songs of David who said* 11QMelch 1$_{10}$ (sim. 1$_{15}$ [(אמ(ר]), sim. Jos 12$_{9}$ 15$_{8}$ Jg 6$_{21}$ 16$_{3}$ 19$_{12}$ etc.

g. antecedent is governing noun (*nomen regens*) alone, not the combination of governing and governed nouns, e.g. בֶּן־מִלְכָּה אֲשֶׁר יָלְדָה לְנָחוֹר *the son of Milcah whom she bore to Nahor* Gn 24$_{24}$ (sim. 21$_{9}$ 34$_{1}$ 46$_{15}$ 2 S 21$_{8.8}$), בְּנֵי חֶצְרוֹן אֲשֶׁר נוֹלַד־לוֹ *the sons of Hezron that were born to him* 1 C 2$_{9}$ (sim. 3$_{1}$); also [איש] מבני אהרון אשר ישבה *a man from the sons of Aaron who is in captivity* 4QD^{a} 6.2$_{5}$.

h. מִי אֲשֶׁר *whoever, the one who* (alw. as subj.) Ex 32$_{33}$ Jg 21$_{5}$ 2 S 20$_{11.11}$ Ec 9$_{4}$.

i. מָה אֲשֶׁר *whatever, what* ולוא ידעו מה אשר יבוא *and they did not know what would come* 1QMyst 1.1$_{4}$.

j. clause introduced by אֲשֶׁר is parallel to a participle, e.g. הָאֲנָשִׁים הַבָּאִים אֵלַיִךְ אֲשֶׁר־בָּאוּ לְבֵיתֵךְ *the people that come to you, that come to your house* Jos 2$_{3}$, sim. 24$_{17}$ Jg 16$_{24}$ Ezk 3$_{15}$ 16$_{45}$ Jb 9$_{5}$ Ezr 10$_{14}$ 11QT 49$_{6}$ 4QToh A 2.1$_{5}$.

k. אֲשֶׁר is parallel to שֶׁ־ *which, that,* Jon 4$_{10}$ Ec 3$_{15}$ 4$_{2}$ 5$_{4}$ 5$_{14}$ 8$_{7}$ (both כַּאֲשֶׁר *as*) 8$_{14}$ 10$_{14}$.

3. as **noun**, meaning **that which, what, the one who(m), whatever,** etc., without explicit antecedent.

a. אֲשֶׁר is subject of the verb in its clause, אֶהְיֶה אֲשֶׁר אֶהְיֶה *I am what I am* Ex 3$_{14}$, וְאַגִּידָה לָכֶם אֵת אֲשֶׁר־יִקְרָא

אֶתְכֶם *and I shall tell you what will befall you* Gn 49_{1}, אֲשֶׁר הָיָה נַעֲשֶׂה *what was done* Ne 5_{18}, אל תשפל נפשכה [ל]אשר לא ישוה בכה *do not make low your soul for one that is not equal to you* 4Q416 9.2_{15}, תן אשר לו *give what is his* 4Q416 10.2_{6}.

וַאֲשֶׁר לֹא צָדָה *and whoever has not lain in wait* Ex 21_{13}, וַאֲשֶׁר יָבֹא אֶת־רֵעֵהוּ *and whoever comes with his fellow* Dt 19_{5}, ארר אשר ימחה *cursed be whoever erases* En-Gedi cave inscr.$_{1}$ Kh. Beit Lei graf. 1_{2} ([א]שר [י]מחה; others ישר מחר), אשר חוטא *whoever sins* Si 38_{15}, אשר ראך ומת *whoever sees you (and) dies* 48_{11} (or em. אַשְׁרֵי *happy is* the one that sees), [ואשר יו]תר *and what remains* 1QDM $3_{2(Milik)}$ etc., Si $15_{11.16.17(A)}$ (B כל ש *everything which*) 40_{11} (with ellipsis of verb; ‖ כֹּל *everything*) 11QPs^{a} 26_{12} 11QT 15_{17} + Sup $23_{15.16}$ 1QS $6_{25.27}$ (ו[א]שר]) 4QJub^{a} 1_{11} ([אשר]) etc. Arad ost. 40_{5} (אל אשר אמ[רת]).

רַק אֲשֶׁר־לְפָנִים לֹא יְדָעוּם *only those that formerly had not known them* Jg 3_{2}, יָדַעְתָּ ... אֵת אֲשֶׁר־הָיָה מִקְנְךָ אִתִּי *you know what has been*, i.e. the state of, *your cattle with me* Gn 30_{29}, אֲשֶׁר הָיָה דְבַר־י׳ אֶל־יִרְמְיָהוּ *that which was the word of Y. to Jeremiah* Jr 14_{1} 46_{1} 47_{1} 49_{34}, וְאַתָּה אֱנוֹשׁ כְּעֶרְכִּי ... אֲשֶׁר יַחְדָּו נַמְתִּיק סוֹד *and you, a man like myself ... we who had sweet counsel together* Ps 55_{15}, וַיֵּלֶךְ חִלְקִיָּהוּ וַאֲשֶׁר הַמֶּלֶךְ *and Hilkiah and those that were (belonging to) the king went* 2 C 34_{22} (or em. אֲשֶׁר־אָמַר *those whom* the king *had ordered*), כַּאֲשֶׁר אֲבֵלִים יְנַחֵם *as one that comforts mourners* Jb 29_{25}, כַּאֲשֶׁר יִהְיֶה מִי יַגִּיד לוֹ *how* (lit. *as what*) *it will be, who can tell him?* 8_{7}, אַחֲרָיו לֹא־הָיָה כָמֹהוּ בְּכֹל מַלְכֵי יְהוּדָה וַאֲשֶׁר הָיוּ לְפָנָיו *after him there was none like him among all the kings of Judah, nor (among) those who had been before him* 2 K 18_{5}, מה נורא אתה אליהו ואשר כ[מו]ך יתפאר perh. *how wonderful you are, Elijah, and the one that, like you, receives glory* Si 48_{4}, יד לאשר *the hand of whoever* Kh. el-Qom tomb inscr. $3_{3(Dever)}$.

אֲשֶׁר עַל־הַבַּיִת *(the one) who is over the household* Gn $43_{16.19}$ (אִישׁ *man*) $44_{1.4}$ 1 K 16_{9} (Arza) 18_{3} (Obadiah) 2 K 10_{5} (‖ אֲשֶׁר עַל־הָעִיר *the one who is over the city*) $18_{18.37}$‖Is $36_{3.22}$ (both ‖ מַזְכִּיר *recorder*) 2 K 19_{2}‖Is 37_{2} (Eliakim in all three; all three ‖ סֹפֵר *scribe*) Is 22_{15} (Shebna) Silwan royal steward tomb inscr.$_{1}$ (perh. Shebna, Hilkiah) Seal 149 ([א]שר; Gedaliah) 501 502 (Adonijah in both) 503 ([ע]ל; Nathan) 860 ([ע]ל; Iddo), אֲשֶׁר עַל־הַמֶּלְתָּחָה *the one who is over the wardrobe* 2 K 10_{22}, אֲשֶׁר עַל־הַמַּס *the one who was over the forced labour* 1 K 12_{18}‖2 C 10_{18} (Adoram/Hadoram) Seal 782_{4} (Pelaiah).

אֲשֶׁר הַמִּתְבָּרֵךְ בָּאָרֶץ יִתְבָּרֵךְ *whoever blesses himself in the land will bless himself* Is 65_{16} with additional subject pronoun, אֲשֶׁר יֵצֵא מִמֵּעֶיךָ הוּא יִירָשֶׁךָ *the one that will go out from your body, that one will inherit from you* Gn 15_{4}, sim. Ex 12_{16}.

3b. אֲשֶׁר is object of the verb in its clause, אֲשֶׁר יִרְאֶה יַגִּיד *what he sees he will announce* Is 21_{6}, אֲשֶׁר לֹא־יָדַעְתִּי יִשְׁאָלוּנִי *they ask me what I do not know* Ps 35_{11}, אִיעָצְךָ אֲשֶׁר יַעֲשֶׂה הָעָם *I shall tell you what the people will do* Nm 24_{14} (Sam אֵת אֲשֶׁר), עַל אֲשֶׁר־עָשָׂה *because of what he did* Jr 15_{4} (mss כָּל־אֲשֶׁר *all that*), אֲשֶׁר יִרְאֶה הָאָדָם *that which a human being sees* 1 S 16_{7}, ב[כל מאשר ריאתי] *among all those that I have seen* 4QJub^{a} 7_{11}, מִשְׁנֶה עַל אֲשֶׁר־יִלְקְטוּ יוֹם יוֹם *a second (portion) above what they would gather daily* Ex 16_{5}, הַמְכַסֶּה אֲנִי ... אֲשֶׁר אֲנִי עֹשֶׂה *do I hide ... what I do?* Gn 18_{17}, מִלְּבַד אֲשֶׁר נָתַן *apart from what he gave* 1 K 10_{13}‖2 C 9_{12}, sim. Gn 9_{24}=4QpGen^{a} 2_{5} Gn 18_{19} $27_{8.45}$ GnzPs 3_{21}, אֲשֶׁר(־)תַּשִּׂיג יָדוֹ *what his hand can reach*, i.e. what he can afford Lv $14_{22.30.31}$ Nm 6_{21} Ezk 46_{7} (כַּאֲשֶׁר) (var. Lv 27_{8}), אַנְשֵׁי יָבֵישׁ גִּלְעָד אֲשֶׁר קָבְרוּ אֶת־שָׁאוּל *the men of Jabesh-gilead were the ones who buried Saul* 2 S 2_{4}.

אֲשֶׁר(־)אֹמַר אֵלֶיךָ *the one (of) which I say to you* Jg 7_{4}, לֹא יְחַלְּלוּ אֶת־קָדְשֵׁי בְּנֵי יִשְׂרָאֵל אֵת אֲשֶׁר־יָרִימוּ לַי׳ *they will not profane the holy things of the Israelites, whatever they offer to Y.* Lv 22_{15}, חַג הַקָּצִיר בִּכּוּרֵי מַעֲשֶׂיךָ אֲשֶׁר תִּזְרַע *the festival of harvest, (of) the first-fruits of your labour, (of) what you sow* Ex 23_{16}, וַיֵּרַע בְּעֵינֵי י׳ אֲשֶׁר עָשָׂה *and what he had done was evil in Y.'s eyes* Gn 38_{10}, הֲרֵעֹתֶם אֲשֶׁר עֲשִׂיתֶם *what you have done you have done wrongly* 44_{5} (sim. Dt 18_{17} 2 S 24_{10} Jr 38_{9}), אֲשֶׁר רְאִיתֶם אֶת־מִצְרַיִם הַיּוֹם *what you have seen today, Egypt* Ex 14_{13} (or, *Egypt that you have seen today*, or em. כַּאֲשֶׁר *when*), אַתָּה אֲשֶׁר־הִכִּיתָ רָדָפוּ *the one whom you* (lit. *you, the one whom you*) *struck they pursued* Ps 69_{27} (or em. אֵת אֲשֶׁר

the one whom or אתה *him whom*), אשר כנפשכה *those that are like you* 1QH 4$_{21}$, מָה הַמַּכּוֹת הָאֵלֶּה ... אֲשֶׁר הֻכֵּיתִי בֵּית מְאַהֲבָי *what are these wounds? ... Those I received at my friends' house* Zc 13$_{6}$, אחד מאלף אשר יצודו *one in a thousand of what they hunt* 11QT 60$_{5}$, אֲשֶׁר נָתְנוּ ... זָהָב *what they gave ... was gold* Ne 7$_{71}$.

With resumptive object pronoun, אֲשֶׁר שָׁמַעְנוּ וַנֵּדָעֵם *things that we have learnt and known* Ps 78$_{3}$, אֵת אֲשֶׁר־כְּבָר עָשׂוּהוּ *what they have already done* Ec 2$_{12}$, לְתַקֵּן אֵת אֲשֶׁר עִוְּתוֹ *to straighten what he has bent* 7$_{13}$, אֶת־אֲשֶׁר־יֹאמַר י׳ אֵלַי אֹתוֹ אֲדַבֵּר *what Y. says to me I speak* 1 K 22$_{14}$||2 C 18$_{13}$ (אֱלֹהַי), ... את אשר אנו[כי] מצוך לע[שו]ת אותם *what I am commanding you ... to do* 1QDM 1$_{8(Milik)}$.

3c. אֲשֶׁר is subject of a nominal clause, לַאֲשֶׁר בְּבָתֵּיכֶם *for whoever is in your houses* Gn 47$_{24}$, מֵאֲשֶׁר לְאַהֲרֹן *from what is Aaron's* Ex 29$_{27}$, אֶת אֲשֶׁר־בָּעִיר ... לָקָחוּ *whatever was in the city ... they took* Gn 34$_{28}$, אֲשֶׁר אֵינֶנּוּ יֹצֵא *whoever does not go out* 1 S 11$_{7}$, אֲשֶׁר לִהְיוֹת כְּבָר הָיָה *what is to be has already been* Ec 3$_{15}$, נוֹדָע אֲשֶׁר־הוּא אָדָם *it is known what a human being is* 6$_{10}$ (or em. אֲשֶׁר־הוּא to אַשְׁרֵהוּ *happy is he*), אֶל־אֲשֶׁר לָעָם *to the (area) that pertains to the people* Ezk 42$_{14}$, בְּתוֹךְ אֲשֶׁר לַנָּשִׂיא *in the middle of the (area) that pertains to the prince* 48$_{22}$, וַיִּשָּׁאֶר אַךְ־נֹחַ וַאֲשֶׁר אִתּוֹ *and there remained only Noah and whoever was in the ark with him* Gn 7$_{23}$; with resumptive subject pronoun, אֲשֶׁר אֵינֶנּוּ זֹבֵחַ *one that does not sacrifice* Ec 9$_{2}$, אשר איננו נקשר *one that is not tied* CD 13$_{18}$, אֶת־אֲשֶׁר יֶשְׁנוֹ פֹּה ... וְאֵת אֲשֶׁר אֵינֶנּוּ פֹּה *with whoever is here ... and with whoever is not here* Dt 29$_{14}$, כָּל־תְּמוּנָה אֲשֶׁר בַּשָּׁמַיִם מִמַּעַל וַאֲשֶׁר בָּאָרֶץ מִתָּחַת *any image—(of) what is in the heavens above and (of) what is in the earth below* Ex 20$_{4}$=Dt 5$_{8}$, אִישׁ אֲשֶׁר כְּבִרְכָתוֹ בֵּרַךְ אֹתָם *he blessed each one (with) that which was according to his blessing*, i.e. he gave each one an appropriate blessing Gn 49$_{28}$ (or em. אִישׁ אֲשֶׁר to אִישׁ אִישׁ *each one*), הַנִּשְׁבָּע כַּאֲשֶׁר שְׁבוּעָה יָרֵא *the vower is as one that fears a vow* Ec 9$_{2}$, נְצִיב אֶחָד אֲשֶׁר בָּאָרֶץ *a single garrison was (what was) in the land* 1 K 4$_{19}$, וְיֵשׁ אֲשֶׁר אֹמְרִים *and there are those that say* Ne 5$_{2.3.4}$, Gn 44$_{1}$ 2 C 17$_{19}$.

3d. אֲשֶׁר is object of a participle in a nominal clause, אֲשֶׁר־הֵם בּוֹנִים *what they are building* Ne 3$_{35}$, בַּאֲשֶׁר הוּא עָמֵל *from what he does* Ec 3$_{9}$, אֵת אֲשֶׁר הָאֱלֹהִים עֹשֶׂה הִגִּיד לְפַרְעֹה *what God is doing he has told Pharaoh* Gn 41$_{25}$, גִּילוּ ... אֲשֶׁר אֲנִי בוֹרֵא *rejoice ... (in) what I am creating* Is 65$_{18}$, בַּשְּׂרִידִים אֲשֶׁר י׳ קֹרֵא *among the survivors will be those whom Y. calls* Jl 3$_{5}$, אֲשֶׁר אָנֹכִי מְצַוְּךָ הַיּוֹם לְאַהֲבָה *what I am commanding you today is to love* Dt 30$_{16}$.

3e. אֲשֶׁר refers to a pronoun or pronominal suffix in its clause, עֲבָדִים ... גַּם־אֲנַחְנוּ גַּם אֲשֶׁר־נִמְצָא הַגָּבִיעַ בְּיָדוֹ *both we and he in whose hand the goblet is found ... are slaves* Gn 44$_{16}$, אֲשֶׁר יִמָּצֵא אִתּוֹ יִהְיֶה־לִּי עָבֶד *the one with whom it is found will be my slave* 44$_{10}$ (sim. 44$_{9}$), בְּיַד אֲשֶׁר־אַתָּה יָגוֹר מִפְּנֵיהֶם *into the hand of those before whom you are in dread* Jr 22$_{25}$ (sim. Ezk 23$_{28}$), תּוֹרַת אֲשֶׁר־בּוֹ נֶגַע *the law of*, i.e. for, *one in whom there is illness* Lv 14$_{32}$, אֲשֶׁר אֵין־לוֹ כָּסֶף *one that has no money* Is 55$_{1}$ (sim. 8$_{20.23}$ Si 44$_{9[B]}$ [M שֶׁ *which*]), אֲשֶׁר־אֵין מִשְׁפָּטָם לִשְׁתּוֹת *those whose sentence is not to drink* Jr 49$_{12}$, לאשר להמה טמא *to those that have an unclean (thing)* 4QCat^{a} 7$_{17(Allegro)}$, אֲשֶׁר חִצָּיו שְׁנוּנִים *one whose arrows are sharpened* Is 5$_{28}$, אֲשֶׁר־בְּגָדֶיךָ חַמִּים *you whose clothes are hot* Jb 37$_{17}$, אֲשֶׁר יִזֶּה עָלֶיהָ תְּכַבֵּס *that which it spurts upon, you are to launder* Lv 6$_{20}$, אֲשֶׁר תֵּצֵא מִמֶּנּוּ *one from whom there issues* 15$_{32}$, אֵת אֲשֶׁר־לֹא־אֶעֱשֶׂה כָּמֹהוּ עוֹד *the like of which I shall not do again* Ezk 5$_{9}$, sim. Lv 5$_{5}$ 13$_{54.57}$ 27$_{24.24}$ Nm 5$_{7}$ etc.

3f. אֲשֶׁר is prefixed by a preposition, עִם אֲשֶׁר תִּמְצָא אֶת־אֱלֹהֶיךָ לֹא יִחְיֶה *whoever you find your gods with will not live* Gn 31$_{32}$, בַּאֲשֶׁר לֹא־חָפַצְתִּי בָּחָרוּ *they have chosen what I did not desire* Is 66$_{4}$=4QpsMos^{e} 2.1$_{8}$ (sim. Is 65$_{12}$), באשר הורשיתה התבונן *concentrate on what you are empowered (to do)* Si 3$_{22(C)}$ (A מָה *what?*, i.e. that which), לאשר אין כוחכה perh. *one to whom there is not your strength* 4Q416 9.2$_{16}$.

3g. אֲשֶׁר is **complement** of nom. cl., הוא אשר הכ[ה] שאול *he is the one whom Saul struck* 4QpGen^{a} 4$_{1}$, הוא אשר אמר *this is what he has said* 4QToh A 1.1$_{3}$, מִי ... אֲשֶׁר יָכוֹל *who ... was the one that was able?* 2 C 32$_{14}$ (sim. ||2 K 18$_{35}$||Is 36$_{20}$), זֶה אֲשֶׁר תַּעֲשֶׂה אֹתָהּ *this is what*, i.e. the shape, *you are to make it* (the ark) Gn 6$_{15}$ (sim. Ex 29$_{38}$), זֶה אֲשֶׁר לֹא־תֹאכְלוּ *this is what you are* *not to eat* Dt 14_{12}, זֶה אֲשֶׁר־יִקְרָא־לָהּ *this is what she will be called* Jr 33_{16}, זֹאת אֲשֶׁר־דִּבֶּר *this is what he said* Gn 49_{28}, זֹאת אֲשֶׁר לַלְוִיִּם *this is what is for the Levites* Nm 8_{24}, הוּא אֲשֶׁר(־)דִּבֶּר י׳ *this is what Y. said* Ex 16_{23} Lv 10_3 (sim. Gn 42_{14}), הוא אשר אמר *this is what he said* CD 10_{16} 16_{15} 1QpHab $3_{2.13}$ 5_6, הוּא אֲשֶׁר כִּהֵן *he was the one that ministered* 1 C 5_{36}, הוא אשר שכן *he is the one that dwelt* 4QAges 2.2_1, הוּא אֲשֶׁר עָשָׂה הַמֶּלֶךְ *it was the one that the king had made* Jr 41_9, אֵלֶּה אֲשֶׁר *these are the ones whom, the things which*, with pf., Nm 34_{29} Jos 13_{32} 14_1 Zc 1_{10} 1 C 6_{16} 1QH 13_{10}, אֶת־כָּל־אֵלֶּה אֲשֶׁר שָׂנֵאתִי *all these are things that I hate* Zc 8_{17}; with resumptive pronoun, זֶה אֲשֶׁר יִשְׁתֶּה אֲדֹנִי בּוֹ *this is what my lord drinks from* Gn 44_5. המה אשר כתוב עליהם *they are the ones of whom it is written* 4QFlor 1_{16} (עליה[מ]ה) 4QCat^{a} 1_7 (sim. 5_{11}).

3h. the place which, where, wherever, בַּאֲשֶׁר בַּאֲשֶׁר חֲלָלִים *where there are wounded* Jb 39_{30}, בַּאֲשֶׁר כָּרַע שָׁם נָפַל *in the place where he sank down, there he fell* Jg 5_{27}, לָגוּר בַּאֲשֶׁר יִמְצָא *to stay wherever he might find* 17_8 (sim. Ex 5_{11} Jg 17_9), המרגיע באשר יערב *who looks for lodgings wherever evening falls* Si $36_{31(B, D)}$, עַל אֲשֶׁר לֹא־אֵדָע *to where I do not know* 1 K 18_{12}, אֶל אֲשֶׁר־דִּבַּרְתִּי *to the place that I mentioned* Ex 32_{34}.

With resumptive שָׁם *there*, בַּאֲשֶׁר הוּא־שָׁם *in the place where he is* Gn 21_{17}, אֶל אֲשֶׁר־יֵצֵא לוֹ שָׁמָּה הַגּוֹרָל *wherever the lot goes out to him* Nm 33_{54}, אל אשר לקח משם *to where he was taken from* 1QH 12_{27}, אֶל אֲשֶׁר יִהְיֶה־שָׁמָּה הָרוּחַ לָלֶכֶת יֵלֵכוּ *to wherever the wind would go, they would go* Ezk 1_{12} (sim. 1_{20}), with omission of prep. or שָׁם, וַאֲשֶׁר שָׁכַב לֹא־יוֹסִיף לָקוּם *and (from) where he has lain down he will not again rise up* Ps 41_9, with cognate verbs, וַיִּתְהַלְּכוּ בַּאֲשֶׁר יִתְהַלָּכוּ *and they wandered wherever they might wander* 1 S 23_{13}, sim. 2 S 15_{20} 2 K 8_1 Ru $1_{16.16.17}$.

3i. the manner in which, how, יֶתֶר דִּבְרֵי יָרָבְעָם אֲשֶׁר נִלְחַם וַאֲשֶׁר מָלָךְ *the rest of the words about Jeroboam—how he fought and how he reigned* 1 K 14_{19}, sim. 22_{46} 2 K 13_{12}||$14_{15.28}$ 20_{20}, אֵת כָּל־אֲשֶׁר גִּדְּלוֹ הַמֶּלֶךְ וְאֵת אֲשֶׁר נִשְּׂאוֹ *the whole manner in which the king had magnified him and how he had promoted him* Est 5_{11} (sim. 10_2), וּמָלְאוּ בָתֶּיךָ ... אֲשֶׁר לֹא־רָאוּ אֲבֹתֶיךָ *and they will fill your houses ... in a way that your ancestors did not see* Ex 10_6, [כתוב כל דב]רי הבריה כאשר בים הששי כלה י׳ *write all the words of the creation—how on the sixth day Y. completed* his works 4QJub^{a} 5_1.

3j. with regard to that which, ואשר אמר *and as for that which he said* followed by text (usu. biblical) CD $8_{14(A)}$=$19_{26(B)}$ 9_2 $16_{6.10}$ 4QD$^{a}_{8}$ 4QpIsa^{a} 8_{21} 4QpIsa^{b} $1.1_{3.4(Allegro)}$ ([אמר]) 4QpIsa^{c} 4.2_7 8_4 11QMelch fr. (ו[א]שר) 11QMelch 1_{11} ([א]מר) 1_{26} 4Q183 1.2_9 1QpHab 6_2 7_3 9_2 10_1 12_6 4QpUnid $1_{2(Allegro)}$ ([אמר]) 4QFlor 1_7 4QCat^{a} 1_{16}, sim. CD 9_8, ואשר ד[ברת]ה ביד מושה *and as for that which you said through Moses* 1QM 10_6.

3k. perh. **the reason that, why,** [זה א]שר נשיב לכה appar. *this is the reason that we shall reply to you* 4QPr Fêtes^{b} $1_{3(Baillet)}$.

4. as **conjunction, a.** אֲשֶׁר introduces **object**-clause, **(the extent) that, how (much),** after verbs of saying, knowing, seeing, etc.

(1) אֲשֶׁר, with pf., רָאִיתָ אֲשֶׁר נְשָׂאֲךָ י׳ אֱלֹהֶיךָ כַּאֲשֶׁר יִשָּׂא־אִישׁ אֶת־בְּנוֹ *you have seen how Y. your God has carried you, as a man carries his son* Dt 1_{31} $11_{4.6}$ 25_{18} Jos 4_7 2 K 20_{20} Ezk 6_9 (or em. אֲשֶׁר נִשְׁבַּרְתִּי remember *how I was broken* to וְשָׁבַרְתִּי *and I shall break*) Ps 78_{43} 132_2 Ec $7_{22.29}$ Est 6_2 8_{11} (אֲשֶׁר appar. *[saying] that*) Ne 2_{10}, זֶה הַדָּבָר אֲשֶׁר *this is the reason that* (with pf.) Jos 5_4 1 K 11_{27}, עַתָּה אֲשֶׁר־בָּאתִי *now (it is) that I have come* 2 S 14_{15}.

With impf., Gn 24_3 Ex 11_7 1 K 22_{16}||2 C 18_{15} Jr 32_{40} Ec 8_{12} Est 1_{19} 2_{10} Dn $1_{8.8}$ Ezr 2_{63}||Ne 7_{65} Ne 2_5 $8_{14.15}$ 10_{31} $13_{1.19.22}$ Si 37_{15} 38_{14} 1QJub^{b} $35_{9(Milik)}$ ([יד]עתי אשר) 1QH $6_{7(Licht)}$ (אשר לו[א תענה]) 4QFlor $1_{16(Allegro)}$ (אשר לו[א יטמאו]), מגיד [א]נו[כי] א ש ר יעזב[וני] *I declare that they will abandon me* 1QDM 1_7, דְּעוּ חַטַּאתְכֶם אֲשֶׁר תִּמְצָא אֶתְכֶם *know that your sin will find you* Nm 32_{23}, וְיֵשׁ אֲשֶׁר יִהְיֶה הֶעָנָן *and (if) it happened that the cloud were* $9_{20.21}$, טוֹב אֲשֶׁר לֹא־תִדֹּר *it is better that you do not vow* Ec 5_4 (sim. 7_{18}), אֵין טוֹב מֵאֲשֶׁר יִשְׂמַח הָאָדָם *there is nothing better than that a person should be happy* 3_{22}, המשפט אשר לוא ישפוט איש *the law (saying) that a man is not to judge* 1QS 8_{24}, ואשר אמר לדויד ... אשר יניח *and as for what he said to*

David ... (namely) that he would give him rest 4QFlor 1_{7}, עַד אֲשֶׁר יָבֹאוּ עַמִּים *again (it will be) that nations come* Zc 8_{20}, בַּיָּמִים הָהֵמָּה אֲשֶׁר יַחֲזִיקוּ *in those days (it will be) that* ten people *grasp* 8_{23}, וְהָיָה ... אֲשֶׁר יְגַלֵּחַ *and it would be ... that he would cut* his hair 2 S 14_{26}, וּבְמַעֲלוֹת אֲשֶׁר יַעֲלוּ אֵלָיו *and it was by the steps that they would go up to it* Ezk 40_{49} (or em. וּבְמַעֲלוֹת עֶשֶׂר *and by ten steps* they would go up, as 40_{22}), לְבַד מֵאֲשֶׁר יוֹשִׁיט־לוֹ הַמֶּלֶךְ *except that,* i.e. unless, *the king would extend to him* Est 4_{11} (unless לְבַד מֵאֲשֶׁר = *apart from the one [to] whom*).

With ptc., וַיַּרְא שָׁאוּל אֲשֶׁר־הוּא מַשְׂכִּיל *and Saul saw that he was successful* 1 S 18_{15}, 2 C 2_{7}.

With nom. cl., etc., יֶשׁ־הֶבֶל ... אֲשֶׁר יֵשׁ צַדִּיקִים *there is a vanity ... that there are upright people* Ec 8_{14}, אֲשֶׁר־רָאִיתִי אָנִי טוֹב אֲשֶׁר־יָפֶה לֶאֱכוֹל *that which I have seen is good is that (it is) pleasant to eat* 5_{17}, יֹדְעִים אֲשֶׁר כָּל־אִישׁ וְאִשָּׁה אֲשֶׁר יָבוֹא ... לְהָמִית *knowing that any man or woman that would come ... (was) to kill,* i.e. to be killed Est 4_{11}, הִגִּיד לָהֶם אֲשֶׁר־הוּא יְהוּדִי *he had told them that he was a Jew* 3_{4}, sim. Ezk 20_{26} Ec 9_{1} Ne 2_{17} 1QJub[b] $35_{9(Milik)}$ ([אשר הו]ארע).

פשרו אשר *its interpretation is that* 4QpIsa[a] 8_{22} 4Qp Isa[c] 28_{2} ([פ[ש]רו]) 4QpIsa[d] $1_{2(Allegro)}$ ([פשרו אש]ר) 1Qp Hab 4_{1} 5_{7} $6_{3.6}$ $7_{7.15}$ 4QpHos[a] $1.2_{3(Allegro)}$ ([פשר]ן) $1.2_{12.15}$ 4QpHos[b] 16_{1} ([פ]שרו), פשרו ... אשר *its interpretation ... is that* 4QpNah 3.2_{5}, פשר הדבר אשר *the interpretation of the passage is that* 4QpIsa[b] 1.1_{2} 1QpHab 5_{3} 4Q Cat[a] 1_{6}.

(2) introducing **direct speech,** 1 S 15_{20} 2 S 1_{4} CD 4_{16} 4QD[b] $_{2}$ perh. Ne 4_{6} (or em. כָּל־הַמְּזִמּוֹת אֲשֶׁר־חָשְׁבוּ *all the intrigues that they devised*).

(3) appar. introducing **command**, usu. negative, with impf., אשר לוא ילך איש *(it is the case that) a man is not to go* 1QS 5_{4}, sim. $5_{14.15.16}$, ואשר לוא להוכיח *and (it is the case that one is) not to argue* 9_{16}, ואשר יקים בברית *and (it is the case that) he is to establish by a covenant* 5_{10} (5_{8} ויקם *and he is to establish*).

(4) אֵת אֲשֶׁר, with pf., יְדַעְתֶּם אֵת אֲשֶׁר־יָשַׁבְנוּ ... וְאֵת אֲשֶׁר־עָבַרְנוּ *you know that we dwelt ... and that we passed* Dt 29_{15}, יָדַעְתָּ אֵת אֲשֶׁר עֲבַדְתִּיךָ *you know how I served you* Gn 30_{29}, לְמַעַן תְּסַפֵּר ... אֵת אֲשֶׁר הִתְעַלַּלְתִּי בְּמִצְרַיִם *so that you might tell ... how I diverted myself with Egypt* Ex 10_{2}, Dt 9_{7} Jos 2_{10} 5_{1} 1 S 12_{24} $24_{11.19.19}$ 28_{9} 2 S 19_{20} 1 K 19_{1} (אֵת כָּל־אֲשֶׁר) 2 K 8_{5} 20_{3}||Is 38_{3}; with impf. 2 S 11_{20} perh. 2 K 8_{12}.

4b. introducing **final** clause, **so that, in order that,** (1) אֲשֶׁר, with pf., נָתַתִּי לְךָ לֵב ... אֲשֶׁר כָּמוֹךָ לֹא־הָיָה *I have given you (such) a mind that there will not have been (a king) like you* 1 K 3_{12} (sim. 3_{13}).

With impf., Gn 11_{7} Ex 20_{26} Dt $4_{10.40}$ $6_{3.3}$ $28_{27.35}$ 32_{46} Jos 3_{7} 2 K 9_{37} Jr 19_{11} Ml 3_{19} Ps 58_{6} Ru 3_{1} Ec 7_{21} Est 9_{1} Ne 2_{7} 2 C 1_{11} Si 16_{15} 45_{24} 50_{24} 11QT $48_{15.16}$ 57_{10} (unless אֲשֶׁר = *the ones who*) 57_{11} 58_{9} 1QDM $2_{2(Milik)}$ ([אשר [תעשה]), מִי י׳ אֲשֶׁר אֶשְׁמַע בְּקֹלוֹ *who is Y., that I should listen to his voice?* Ex 5_{2} (sim. 2 C 2_{5}), רָעָה ... אֲשֶׁר כָּל־שֹׁמְעָהּ תְּצִלֶּנָה אָזְנָיו *evil ... so that—everyone who hears of it—his ears will tingle* Jr 19_{3} (sim. 1 S 3_{11} 2 K 21_{12}), הָרָעוֹת רָעוֹת מְאֹד אֲשֶׁר לֹא־תֵאָכַלְנָה *the bad ones were very bad so that they could not be eaten* Jr 24_{3}, מִבְּלִי אֲשֶׁר לֹא־יִמְצָא הָאָדָם *so that a human being will not find* Ec 3_{11}, אֲשֶׁר לָמָּה יִרְאֶה *lest* (lit. *so that why*) *he see* Dn 1_{10}.

With conditional sentence, אֲשֶׁר אִם־יוּכַל אִישׁ לִמְנוֹת אֶת־עֲפַר הָאָרֶץ גַּם־זַרְעֲךָ יִמָּנֶה *so that if a man were able to count the dust of the earth, your seed also could be counted* Gn 13_{16}, אֲשֶׁר בְּהַעֲוֺתוֹ וְהֹכַחְתִּיו *so that when he sins, I shall reprove him* 2 S 7_{14}, sim. Gn 13_{16}.

(2) אֵת אֲשֶׁר, with impf., וְעָשִׂיתִי אֵת אֲשֶׁר־בְּחֻקַּי תֵּלֵכוּ *and I shall act so that you will walk in my statutes* Ezk 36_{27}.

(3) לְמַעַן אֲשֶׁר, with impf. Gn 18_{19} Lv 17_{5} Nm 17_{5} Dt 20_{18}=11QT 62_{15} Dt 27_{3} Jos 3_{4} 2 S 13_{5} Jr 42_{6} Ezk 20_{26} (+ לְמַעַן) 31_{14} 36_{30} 46_{18} 4QD[a] $_{9}$ 4QpsMos[e] 1_{10} ([למען] אשר לא י[כ]ל[ו]).

4c. introducing **causal** clause, **on account of the fact that, because, for,** (1) אֲשֶׁר, with pf., Gn 30_{18} $34_{13.27}$ 42_{21} Ex 5_{21} Nm 20_{13} (unless אֲשֶׁר = *the place where*) Dt 23_{5} Jos 4_{23} 5_{6} Jg 9_{17} 1 S 2_{23} 15_{15} 20_{42} $26_{16.23}$ 2 S 2_{6} 14_{22} 1 K 2_{32} 3_{19} $15_{5.13}$||2 C 15_{16} 2 K 12_{3} 17_{4} Is 65_{7} Jr 1_{16} 13_{25} 32_{3} 44_{23} Ezk 29_{20} 39_{29} Zc 1_{15} 11_{2} (or del.) Ps 31_{8} 119_{158} Ec 10_{15} Dn 9_{8} 1 C 21_{8} Si 16_{7} GnzPs 3_{25} 4_{5} (both + כִּי *for*) 11QT 59_{8} (|| מִפְּנֵי *because of*) 4QOrd[a] 2_{6} 4QDibHam[a] 1.6_{6} CD 2_{18} 6_{13} 12_{11} 1QpHab 10_{13} 4Qp Gen[a] 4_{5}.

With impf., לֹא־נֹאמַר עוֹד אֱלֹהֵינוּ לְמַעֲשֵׂה יָדֵינוּ אֲשֶׁר־בְּךָ יְרֻחַם יָתוֹם *we shall no more say, Our God, to the work of our hands, for it is by you that the orphan is spared* Ho 14_{4} (unless אֲשֶׁר־בְּךָ = *thou by whom*), sim. 1 K 8_{33} (‖2 C 6_{24} כִּי *because*) Jr 16_{13} Jb 9_{17} Ec 8_{12}.

With ptc., אשר אנוכי שוכן בתוכמה *because I dwell among them* 11QT 46_{12}, אֲשֶׁר אֵינֶנּוּ יָרֵא *because he does not fear* Ec 8_{13}, אשר אין הם מבדיל *because they do not distinguish* CD 5_{6}, אֲשֶׁר אֵין־נַעֲשָׂה פִתְגָם *because a decree is not executed* Ec 8_{11} (+ עַל־כֵּן *therefore*).

With nom. cl., etc., אֲשֶׁר הָעִיר ... חֲרֵבָה *seeing that the city ... is desolate* Ne 2_{3}, טוֹבִים הַשְּׁנַיִם ... אֲשֶׁר יֵשׁ־לָהֶם שָׂכָר *two are better ... for to them there is recompense* Ec 4_{9}, אֲשֶׁר אֵין־טוֹב *for there is nothing better* 8_{15}, אֲשֶׁר מִי־יַגִּיד *for who will tell?* 6_{12}, sim. Dt 3_{24}.

(2) אֲשֶׁר עַל־כֵּן, with pf., אֲשֶׁר עַל־כֵּן סָרוּ מֵאַחֲרָיו *because they turned away from him* Jb 34_{27}.

(3) עַל אֲשֶׁר, with pf., עַל אֲשֶׁר עָזְבוּ *because they deserted Y.* Dt 29_{24} 1 K 9_{9}‖2 C 7_{22} Jr 16_{11} 22_{9}, sim. Ex 32_{35} Nm 20_{24} Dt $32_{51.51}$ 1 S 24_{6} 2 S 3_{30} 6_{8} 8_{10}‖1 C 18_{10} 2 S 12_{6} 21_{1} 1 K 16_{7} 2 K 18_{12} 22_{13}‖2 C 34_{21} Ezk 23_{30} 35_{15} 39_{23} Jb 32_{3} Est 1_{15} 8_{7} 1 C 13_{10}.

(4) יַעַן אֲשֶׁר, with pf., יען אשר לא הקים *because he did not establish* CD 9_{7}, Gn 22_{16} Dt 1_{36} Jos 14_{14} Jg 2_{20} 1 S 30_{22} 1 K 3_{11} 8_{18}‖2 C 6_{8} 1 K $11_{11.33}$ $14_{7.15}$ 16_{2} $20_{28.36}$ 2 K 1_{16} 10_{30} $21_{11.15}$ Jr 19_{4} 25_{8} $29_{23.25.31}$ 35_{18} Ezk 16_{43} 21_{9} 26_{2} 31_{10} Ps 109_{16} 2 C 1_{11}; with impf., Ezk 12_{12} 44_{12} (or em. to pf. verb).

(5) בַּאֲשֶׁר, with pf., ידענו באשר חנואת[נו] *we knew because you favoured us (with)* 4QDibHam[a] 4_{5} 4QDib Ham[c] $31_{11 (Baillet)}$ ([בא]שר [חנו]את[נו]); with nom. cl., בַּאֲשֶׁר לְמִי־הָרָעָה הַזֹּאת *on account of whom is this great misfortune?* Jon 1_{8}, sim. Gn $39_{9.23}$ Ec 7_{2} 8_{4}.

(6) עַל־דְּבַר אֲשֶׁר, with pf., Dt $22_{24.24}$=11QT $66_{2.3}$ Dt 23_{5} 2 S 13_{22}.

(7) עֵקֶב אֲשֶׁר, with pf. Gn 22_{18} 26_{5} 2 S 12_{6}.

(8) מִפְּנֵי אֲשֶׁר, with pf. Ex 19_{18} Jr 44_{23}.

(9) מֵאֲשֶׁר, with pf., מאשר לא סרו *since they did not turn* CD 8_{4}, sim. Is 43_{4} 4QTNaph 2_{7} ([מ]ת), perh. Nm 6_{11} (but prob. מֵאֲשֶׁר = atone him *from that which* he has sinned); with nom. cl., מאשר אין בהם בינה *since there is no understanding in them* CD 5_{17}.

(10) עַל־אוֹדוֹת אֲשֶׁר, with pf. עַל־כָּל־אֹדוֹת אֲשֶׁר נִאֲפָה *because she had fornicated so often* Jr 3_{8}.

(11) כְּפִי אֲשֶׁר, with ptc., נָתַתִּי אֶתְכֶם נִבְזִים ... כְּפִי אֲשֶׁר אֵינְכֶם שֹׁמְרִים אֶת־דְּרָכַי *I made you despised ... for not observing my ways* Ml 2_{9}.

(12) perh. בְּשֶׁל אֲשֶׁר, with impf., בְּשֶׁל אֲשֶׁר יַעֲמֹל הָאָדָם *seeing that a person works* Ec 8_{17} (unless אֲשֶׁר = *although*).

4d. introducing **temporal** clause, **when,** (1) אֲשֶׁר, with pf., Jos 14_{10} Ps 139_{15} (unless אֲשֶׁר = *how* or *although*); with impf., אֲשֶׁר יִשְׁאָלוּן בְּנֵיכֶם *when your sons ask* Jos 4_{21}, והיה [א]שר יבואו ... הקלל[ות] *and it will happen, when the curses ... come* 1QDM 1_{10}, אֲשֶׁר יִקָּרֵא עָלָיו מְלֹא רֹעִים *when a group of shepherds is called against him* Is 31_{4} (unless אֲשֶׁר ... עָלָיו = *against whom*), הַנְּפִלִים הָיוּ בָאָרֶץ ... אֲשֶׁר יָבֹאוּ בְּנֵי הָאֱלֹהִים *the Nephilim were on the earth ... when the divine beings would come* Gn 6_{4}, תַּחְתַּי אֶרְגָּז אֲשֶׁר אָנוּחַ לְיוֹם צָרָה perh. *in my place I tremble while I wait quietly for the day of distress* Hb 3_{16} (or em. יִרְגְּזוּ אֲשֻׁרָי *my footsteps tremble*), מקץ שלוש[י]ם [ואחד יום משלח]ה אשר לא י[ספה] שוב *at the end of thirty-one days from sending her, when it did not return* 4QpGen[a] 1_{20}.

(2) עַד אֲשֶׁר *until*, with pf., Ex 32_{20} Dt 2_{14} 9_{21} Jos 3_{17} 8_{26} Jg 4_{24} 1 K 10_{7}‖2 C 9_{6} 1 K 17_{17} 2 K $17_{20.23}$ 21_{16} Ezk 34_{21} CD 2_{21} Si 47_{23} $48_{1.15}$.

With impf., Gn 27_{44} 29_{8} 33_{14} Ex 23_{30} 24_{14} Lv 22_{4} Nm 11_{20} 20_{17} 21_{22} Dt 2_{29} 3_{20} Jos 1_{15} 1 S 22_{3} Ho 5_{15} Jon 4_{5} Mc 7_{9} Ps 112_{8} Ru 1_{13} 3_{18} Ec 2_{3} Ne 2_{7} 4_{5} 1 C 19_{5} Si 13_{7} 11QT 45_{8} ([יש]לים) $45_{17.18}$ 50_{3} 58_{20} 1QS 6_{17} 8_{18} 4Qps Ezek[a] 3_{2} 4Q386–9 4_{5} ([עד]) 4QToh A 2.1_{3} 4QJub[a] 4_{5} ([עד אשר ארד]) 4_{7} ([עד אש]ר), עַד אֲשֶׁר לֹא־יָבֹאוּ *until they do not come*, i.e. before they come Ec 12_{1}, sim. $12_{2.6}$.

With ptc., 2 S 17_{13}, עַד אֲשֶׁר אֵין־בָּהֶם כֹּחַ *until there was no strength in them* 1 S 30_{4}.

עַד אֲשֶׁר־עַד־כֹּה *until now* Jos 17_{14}.

עַד אֲשֶׁר אִם *until*, with pf., Gn 28_{15} Nm 32_{17} Is 6_{11}.

4e. appar. introducing **conditional** clause, **if,** (1) אֲשֶׁר, with impf., אֲשֶׁר תִּשְׂטֶה אִשָּׁה *if a woman strays* Nm 5_{29}, Lv 4_{22} (‖ אִם *if* $4_{3.27}$) 6_{20} 25_{33} Dt 11_{27} (‖ אִם 11_{28}) 18_{22}=11QT 61_{3}; with pf., אֲשֶׁר לֹא־גָזַלְתִּי אָז אָשִׁיב perh.

if I have not stolen, then do I repay? Ps 69$_5$ (unless אֲשֶׁר = *that which*).

(2) אֶת אֲשֶׁר, with impf., 1 K 8$_{31}$ (||2 C 6$_{22}$ אִם *if*).

4f. appar. introducing **comparative** clause, **(just) as,** אֲשֶׁר לֹא־יִסָּפֵר צְבָא הַשָּׁמַיִם ... כֵּן אַרְבֶּה אֶת־זֶרַע דָּוִד *as the host of heaven cannot be counted ... so shall I increase David's offspring* Jr 33$_{22}$, וְנִשְׁמַד הַמִּישֹׁר אֲשֶׁר אָמַר י׳ *and the plain will be destroyed, as Y. has said* 48$_8$, אשר כתוב *as (it is) written* 4QpIsa^e 1$_2$ 6$_{2(\text{Allegro})}$ ([כ]תוב) 8$_{2(\text{Allegro})}$ ([ו]א[שר כ]תוב]) 4QCat^a 5$_{5(\text{Allegro})}$ ([אשר כתוב]).

4g. perh. introducing **concessive** clause, **although,** (1) אֲשֶׁר, אֲשֶׁר הָלַךְ חֲשֵׁכִים ... יִבְטַח בְּשֵׁם י׳ *although he walked in darkness ... he trusts in Y.'s name* Is 50$_{10}$, אָבוֹא אֶל־הַמֶּלֶךְ אֲשֶׁר לֹא־כַדָּת *I shall go to the king, although (it is) against the law* Est 4$_{16}$, כָּרוּ־לִי זֵדִים שִׁיחוֹת אֲשֶׁר לֹא כְתוֹרָתֶךָ *the insolent have dug pits for me, although (it is) against your law* Ps 119$_{85}$, אֲשֶׁר חֹטֵא עֹשֶׂה רָע ... כִּי גַּם־יוֹדֵעַ אָנִי *although a sinner does evil ... I also know* Ec 8$_{12}$, לִשְׂרֹף אֶת־בְּנֵיהֶם ... בָּאֵשׁ ... אֲשֶׁר לֹא(־)צִוִּיתִי *in order to burn their sons ... in the fire ... although I did not command (it)* Jr 7$_{31}$ 19$_5$, sim. 32$_{35}$.

(2) אֲשֶׁר אִם, אֲשֶׁר אִם־צָדַקְתִּי לֹא אֶעֱנֶה *although I am right I do not respond* Jb 9$_{15}$.

4h. perh. as **desiderative** particle, **may (it be),** אֲשֶׁר בָּנֵינוּ כִּנְטִעִים *may our sons be as plants* Ps 144$_{12}$ (unless אֲשֶׁר = *because*, or *we whose*; or em. אַשְׁרֵי *happy are* or אַשֵּׁר *bless!*).

4i. perh. **lest,** [ל]וא תחמדו כסף ... אש[ר תוקש] *do not desire silver ... lest you be ensnared* 11QT 2$_{8(\text{Yadin})}$ (=Dt 7$_{25}$ פֶּן *lest*).

5. כַּאֲשֶׁר. **a.** usu. introduces **comparative** clause, **in the way that, (just) as** (perh. lit. *as that which*; as §3), less oft., **as though,** etc. (e.g. Ex 21$_{22}$ Dt 28$_{49}$ 1K 14$_{15}$ Is 65$_8$ Ezk 1$_{16}$ 10$_{10}$ Am 5$_{19}$ Zc 10$_6$ Dn 1$_{13}$ Si 44$_9$), introduces verb as כְּ *as* introduces noun, e.g. כְּשִׂמְחַת בַּקָּצִיר כַּאֲשֶׁר יָגִילוּ בְּחַלְּקָם שָׁלָל *as joy at harvest, as they rejoice when they divide spoil* Is 9$_2$; with cognate verbs, וּמָשַׁחְתָּ אֹתָם כַּאֲשֶׁר מָשַׁחְתָּ אֶת־אֲבִיהֶם *and you are to anoint them as you anointed their father* Ex 40$_{15}$, sim. Lv 4$_{10.20.21.31.35}$ etc.

Oft. כַּאֲשֶׁר ... כֵּן *as ... so,* כַּאֲשֶׁר יְעַנּוּ אֹתוֹ כֵּן יִרְבֶּה *as they would oppress him, so he would increase* Ex 1$_{12}$, sim. Gn 41$_{13}$ Ex 7$_6$ 12$_{28.50}$ 27$_8$ etc. Si 33$_4$ 11QT 24$_{10}$ 4QpIsa^a 8$_{23}$ 4Q416 10.2$_{18}$; also כֵּן ... כַּאֲשֶׁר Gn 18$_5$ 50$_{12}$ Ex 7$_{10.20}$ 10$_{10}$ etc., כַּאֲשֶׁר ... כָּכָה Ec 11$_5$, כָּכָה ... כַּאֲשֶׁר Jr 19$_{11}$, הִנֵּה ... כַּאֲשֶׁר Am 2$_{13}$ 9$_9$, perh. כַּאֲשֶׁר ... הִנֵּה 2 C 2$_2$ (see 2$_3$), כַּאֲשֶׁר צִוָּה י׳ ... וַיַּנִּיחֵהוּ אַהֲרֹן *as Y. commanded ... Aaron placed* Ex 16$_{34}$, כאשר יאמרו ... ואמרו *as they will say ... so they will say* 4Q386–9 3.2$_7$, כאשר גלה אוזנכה ... כבדם *as he opened your ear ..., honour them* 4Q416 10.2$_{18}$, כַּאֲשֶׁר תִּרְאֶה עֲשֵׂה *as you see, do* Dn 1$_{13}$.

כַּאֲשֶׁר with pf., Gn 7$_{9.16}$ 8$_{21}$ 17$_{23}$ 18$_5$ etc. Si 7$_{31}$ 33$_{4.5}$ 11QT 16$_{15}$ 24$_{10}$ 53$_{10.14}$ 55$_{12}$ Dt 19$_{19}$=11QT 61$_{10}$ 1QS 8$_{16(\text{mg})}$ 11$_{16}$ 1QSb 3$_{24}$ ([כאש]ר) 4QPrFêtes^c 5.2$_6$ 1QM 11$_5$ ([כא]שר) CD 3$_{20}$ 7$_4$ 19$_{11}$ 1QpHab 7$_{13}$ 12$_6$ (unless כַּאֲשֶׁר = *because*) 4QFlor 1$_5$ perh. 4QRitPur 48$_6$ ([כ]אשר [לקח]תנו) 5QRègle 1$_5$ (כאשר עש) 4QFlor 1$_8$ (Allegro) (כאשר באו perh. *when they came*) 1Q26 1$_4$ (כאשר גלה) 4Q386–9 3.2$_8$ 4Q416 10.2$_{18.18}$ 4Q462$_{17}$ 4QJub^a 7$_{12}$ ([כאשר ברכם]) 4Q464 3.2$_3$.

כַּאֲשֶׁר דִּבֶּר ... י׳ *as Y. ... had said* Gn 12$_4$ 24$_{51}$ Ex 7$_{13.22}$ 8$_{11.15}$ 9$_{12.35}$ Nm 5$_4$ 17$_5$ 27$_{23}$ Dt 1$_{21}$ 2$_1$ 6$_{3.19}$ 9$_3$ 10$_9$ 27$_3$ 31$_3$ Jos 4$_8$ 14$_{12}$ 23$_5$ Jg 2$_{15}$ 1 K 5$_{19}$ 8$_{20}$||2 C 6$_{10}$ 2 K 24$_{13}$ Jr 27$_{13}$ 2 C 23$_3$ (sim. 4QpGen^a 4$_2$), כַּאֲשֶׁר צִוָּה ... י׳ *as Y. ... had commanded* Ex 7$_{6.10.20}$ 12$_{28.50}$ 16$_{34}$ 34$_4$ 39$_{1.5.7.21.26.29.31.43}$ 40$_{19.21.23.25.27.29.32}$ Lv 8$_{4.9.13.17.21.29}$ 9$_{7.10}$ 10$_{15}$ 16$_{34}$ 24$_{23}$ Nm 1$_{19}$ 2$_{33}$ 3$_{42.51}$ 8$_{3.22}$ 15$_{36}$ 17$_{26}$ 20$_{27}$ 26$_4$ 27$_{11.22}$ 31$_{7.31.41.47}$ 36$_{10}$ Dt 1$_{19}$ 4$_5$ (צִוַּנִי) 5$_{12.16}$ (both צִוְּךָ) 5$_{32}$ 10$_5$ (צִוַּנִי) 20$_{17}$=11QT 62$_{15}$ (צִוְּךָ) Dt 34$_9$ Jos 10$_{40}$ 11$_{15.20}$ 14$_{2.5}$ 21$_8$ 2 S 5$_{25}$ (צִוָּהוּ) 24$_{19}$ Jr 13$_5$ 1 C 24$_{19}$ (צִוָּהוּ), כאשר צוה *as he* (Y.) *commanded* 1QS 1$_2$ 3$_{10}$ 8$_{21}$ 9$_{15.24}$ 1QSb 3$_{24}$.

כַּאֲשֶׁר צִוָּה מֹשֶׁה *as Moses commanded* Ex 16$_{24}$ Lv 9$_{21}$ Jos 8$_{31.33}$ 11$_{12}$ 1 C 15$_{15}$, כאשר אמר *as he* (Y.) *said* followed by biblical text CD 7$_{8(A)}$=19$_{5(B)}$ 7$_{14.16}$ 20$_{16}$ 4QpIsa^a 2$_2$ ([כאש]ר), sim. CD 4$_{13}$ 19$_{15}$ 4QpsEzek^a 3$_6$, כאשר לא היו היו *they have become as though they had never existed* Si 44$_9$.

With impf., Gn 34$_{12}$ Ex 8$_{23}$ 21$_{22}$ 33$_{11}$ Lv 4$_{10.35}$ 24$_{20}$ 27$_{14}$ Nm 2$_{17}$ 11$_{12}$ 15$_{14}$ 22$_8$ Dt 1$_{31.44}$ 8$_5$ 12$_{22}$ 16$_{10}$ 28$_{29.49}$ Jg 7$_{17}$ 9$_{33}$ 16$_9$ 1 S 2$_{16}$ 24$_{5.14}$ 26$_{20}$ 2 S 17$_{12}$ 19$_4$ 1 K 14$_{10.15}$ 2 K 21$_{13}$ Is 9$_2$ 25$_{11}$ 29$_{8.8}$ 31$_4$ 55$_{10}$ 65$_8$ 66$_{20}$ Jr 13$_{11}$ 19$_{11}$

39_{12} 43_{12} Ezk 1_{16} 10_{10} 46_{12} Am 2_{13} 3_{12} 5_{19} 9_{9} Ml 3_{17} Dn 1_{13} Si $36_{31(C)}$ (unless כַּאֲשֶׁר = *when*) GnzPs 3_{3} 1QS 6_{16} 4QpIsa^{a} 8_{23} 4Q386–9 3.2_{7}, כאשר סריס יחבק נערה *as a eunuch embraces a girl* Si 30_{20} (if em. סירים appar. *pots*).

כִּי כַּאֲשֶׁר יָקוּם אִישׁ ... כֵּן הַדָּבָר הַזֶּה *for as a man (who) rises ... is this matter* Dt 22_{26}=11QT 66_{6}, כַּאֲשֶׁר יוּכְלוּן שְׂאֵת *as (much as) they can carry* Gn 44_{1}, יְהִי כֵן י׳ עִמָּכֶם כַּאֲשֶׁר אֲשַׁלַּח אֶתְכֶם *may Y. be with you just as I (intend to) send you* Ex 10_{10} (unless כַּאֲשֶׁר = *when*), כַּאֲשֶׁר יִשְׁאַל־אִישׁ בִּדְבַר הָאֱלֹהִים כֵּן כָּל־עֲצַת אֲחִיתֹפֶל *as one asks for a divine word, so was all Ahithophel's advice* 2 S $16_{23(Qr)}$.

With active ptc., לוא תעשו ... כאשר הגויים עושים *you are not to behave ... as the nations do* 11QT 48_{11} 51_{19}, Gn 34_{22} Nm $32_{25.27}$ 2 K 2_{19} Is 66_{22} Jr 42_{2} Ne 5_{12} 2 C 29_{8} 30_{7}, כַּאֲשֶׁר אֵינְךָ יוֹדֵעַ *just as you do not know* Ec 11_{5}; with pass. ptc., כַּאֲשֶׁר כָּתוּב *as (it is) written* 1 K 21_{11} Dn 9_{13} 1QS 5_{17} 8_{14} CD 7_{19} 4QpIsa^{c} $1_{3(Allegro)}$ ([כאשר כ]תוב) 4.2_{18} 11QMelch $1_{9.24}$ 4QFlor $1_{2.12}$ 4QCat^{a} 7_{1} 4Q178 3_{2} 4QpGen^{a} 3_{1}, וַעֲשׂוּיָה אֲלֵיהֶן ... כְּרוּבִים ... כַּאֲשֶׁר עֲשׂוּיִם לַקִּירוֹת *and done on them ... were cherubs just as had been done on the walls* Ezk 41_{25}.

With nom. cl., etc., כַּאֲשֶׁר בִּהְיוֹת הַתֶּבֶן *just as when there was straw* Ex 5_{13}, כַּאֲשֶׁר בַּתְּחִלָּה *as (it was) in the beginning* Gn 41_{21}, כַּאֲשֶׁר בָּרִאשֹׁנָה *as (it was) in the beginning* Jos $8_{5.6}$ 2 S 7_{10}||1 C 17_{9} (בָּרִאשׁוֹנָה), כַּאֲשֶׁר עִם־לְבָבִי *as (it was) with my heart*, i.e. as I felt Jos 14_{7}, כאשר בנפשך *as (it is) in your soul* 4QDibHam^{a} $5.2_{7(Baillet)}$ ([בנפש]כה) 1QH fr. 11_{9}, עוֹדֶנִּי ... כַּאֲשֶׁר בְּיוֹם *I am still today ... as (I was) on the day of* Jos 14_{11}, הַמַּחֲנֶה כַּאֲשֶׁר־הִיא *the camp was just as it had been* 2 K 7_{7} (sim. 7_{10}), הֲיֵשׁ אֶת־לְבָבְךָ יָשָׁר כַּאֲשֶׁר לְבָבִי עִם־לְבָבֶךָ *is your heart upright as my heart (is upright) with (regard to) your heart?* 10_{15}.

5b. introducing **temporal** clause, **when, after,** with pf., Gn 12_{11} 20_{13} 24_{52} 29_{10} 30_{25} etc. 1QNoah 3_{4} 1QpHab 8_{9} 4QCat^{a} $5_{6(Allegro)}$ ([אמר]) 4QTNaph $2_{5.7.9}$ 4QD$^{b}_{1}$ 4Q416 1_{4}, כַּאֲשֶׁר כִּלָּה *when he had finished* Gn 18_{33} 24_{22} (כִּלּוּ) 27_{30} 43_{2} (כִּלּוּ) Jg 3_{18} Meṣad Ḥashavyahu ost. 1_{6} (כל) 1_{8} (כלת), וישבתו כאשר שבתו *and they ceased (completely) when they ceased* Si 44_{9}; with impf., Gn 27_{40} 40_{14} Ex $17_{11.11}$ Ezk 35_{11} 37_{18} Ho 7_{12} Ec 4_{17} 5_{3} Ne 6_{3} Si 12_{15} (|| אִם *if*; perh. כַּאֲשֶׁר = *if* in these three) 11QT 39_{10} 45_{18} CD 15_{12} perh. 11QT 45_{3} (כאשר י) 1Q39 1_{5} (כאשר יסו) 4Q521 1.2_{11} (+ אָז *then*) 4QToh A 1.1_{9}.

With ptc., כ[אשר הוא] מקטיר ושחטו *when he is burning (it), they will slaughter* 11QT $23_{10(Yadin)}$, [כא]שר א[תה] עובר *when you cross* 1QDM $2_{2(Milik)}$; כַּאֲשֶׁר מִשְׁפָּטֶיךָ לָאָרֶץ *when your judgments are*, i.e. have come, *to the earth* Is 26_{9}, כַּאֲשֶׁר־שֵׁמַע לְמִצְרָיִם perh. *when a report is*, i.e. comes, *to Egypt* 23_{5}, כאשר כרצונו תשפט עמו appar. *when it is according to his will*, i.e. when he wants, *you will judge with him* Si 8_{14} (or em. כאשר ירצה *as he wishes*).

5c. introducing **conditional** clause, **if,** כַּאֲשֶׁר שָׁכֹלְתִּי שָׁכָלְתִּי *if I am bereaved, I am bereaved* Gn 43_{14}, כַּאֲשֶׁר אָבַדְתִּי אָבָדְתִּי *if I perish, I perish* Est 4_{16}.

5d. introducing **causal** clause, **because,** כַּאֲשֶׁר מְרִיתֶם *because you rebelled* Nm 27_{14}, with pf., Jg 6_{27} 1 S 28_{18} (unless כַּאֲשֶׁר = *after*) 1 K 3_{6} 2 K 8_{19}||2 C 21_{7} (unless כַּאֲשֶׁר = *as*) Is 51_{13} (unless כַּאֲשֶׁר = *when*) Jr 5_{19} Mc 3_{4} (unless כַּאֲשֶׁר = *as*) Hg 1_{12} (unless כַּאֲשֶׁר = *when*) 11QT 53_{13} (unless כַּאֲשֶׁר = *as*) 1QH 11_{31}; with ptc., כַּאֲשֶׁר אֵינָם יֹדְעִים *because they do not know* 2 K 17_{26}; with nom. cl., כַּאֲשֶׁר לַכֹּל מִקְרֶה אֶחָד *because there is one fate for everybody* Ec 9_{2} (or em. בַּאֲשֶׁר *because*).

5e. perh. **that which,** like אֲשֶׁר in same sense (§3), הבחרה באשר יורני וארצה כאשר ישופטני *I shall choose what you teach me, and I shall delight in what you judge for me* (perh. *in how you judge me*) 1QS 10_{12}, לבחור את אשר רצה ולמאוס כאשר שנא *to choose what he wanted and to reject what he hated* CD 2_{15}.

5f. introducing noun, not clause, כַּאֲשֶׁר = כְּ, כַּאֲשֶׁר עֵץ־הַגֶּפֶן *as the wood of the vine* Ezk 15_{6}, עבדך יספר בנפלאותך כאשר כוחו ורוח דבריו *your servant will relate your wonders according to*, i.e. to the extent of, *his strength and the power of his words* GnzPs 2_{23}.

6. אַחֲרֵי אֲשֶׁר. **a.** introducing **temporal** clause, **after,** with pf., Dt 24_{4} Jos 2_{7} (כַּאֲשֶׁר) 7_{8} 9_{16} 23_{1} 24_{20}, אַחַר אֲשֶׁר הֻכְּתָה הָעִיר *after the city had been defeated* Ezk 40_{1}, אחר אשר למדנונו *after we had instructed him* 4QpsJub^{c} 2_{1}.

6b. introducing causal clause, **because, seeing that,** with pf., Jg 11_{36} 19_{23} 2 S 19_{31}.

7. תַּחַת אֲשֶׁר. **a.** introducing **causal** clause, **because of,** with pf., Nm 25_{13} Dt 21_{14} 22_{29}=11QT 66_{11} Dt 28_{47} 1 S 26_{21} 2 K 22_{17}‖2 C 34_{25} Is 53_{12} Jr 29_{19} 50_{7} 2 C 21_{12}. **b.** + היה pf., **instead of being,** הָאָרֶץ ... תֵּעָבֵד תַּחַת אֲשֶׁר הָיְתָה שְׁמָמָה *the land ... will be worked instead of being a desolation* Ezk 36_{34}, Dt 28_{62}.

8. בַּעֲבוּר אֲשֶׁר. **a.** introducing **final** clause, **so that,** with impf., וְהֵבֵאתָ לְאָבִיךָ ... בַּעֲבֻר אֲשֶׁר יְבָרֶכְךָ *and take (it) to your father ... that he might bless you* Gn 27_{10}, בעבור אשר לא יגדפו *so that they do not* (or, *lest they*) *blaspheme* CD 12_{7} (sim. 12_{9}), בעבור אשר ל[ו]א תגאל *so that she does not defile* 4QToh A 1.1_{6}.

8b. introducing **causal** clause, **because,** with pf., בעבור אשר דרשו *because they sought* CD 1_{18}, 1QpHab 9_{11} ([א]שר).

Also 11QT 3_{1} $30_{4(\text{AHL})}$ $38_{9(\text{AHL})}$ $58_{3(\text{erased})}$ fr. 6_{2} 2QJub^{b} fr. $1_{2.3}$ 4Q485 1_{6} 4Q487 1.2_{6} 4QRitMar 1_{7} (אש[ר]) 95_{1} 126_{2} ([א]שר]) 4QPrQuot 1_{19} (לילה אשר הו[אה]) 33_{6} 42_{6} (אש[ר]) 48_{8} 56.1_{5} (לילה אשר) 4QPrFêtes^{c} 2_{5} (אשר על) 9_{3} 11_{9} 17_{5} 4QRitPur 29_{20} (all three אש[ר]) 4QOrd^{a} 2_{10} ([א]שר) 5_{3} 4QOrd^{b} 9.1_{2} 1QM 2_{15} + Sup 4QM^{f} fr. 32_{4} (ה[רש]ענו אשר) 4QDibHam^{a} 3.2_{16} 4_{9} CD 15_{17} (Rabin א[מ]ר) 4QpIsa^{c} 21_{4} 1QDM 4_{6} 45_{2} 6QapSam/Kings 30_{2} (הנופלים אשר) 1QH fr. 4_{2} 1QMyst 3_{3} 1Q29 1_{2} (כאשר) 4QpHos^{b} 4_{5} 19_{4} 4QpUnid 2_{1} 4QFlor 5_{1} (כאשר) 8_{1} 4QCat^{a} 1_{1} $7_{3.13}$ 21_{6} 4QAges $2.2_{2.8}$ (Allegro אש) 4QShir^{b} 95_{3} (both אש[ר]) 4Q521 3.2_{6} 4Q385 3_{5} (עד אש[ר]) 4Q522 1_{7} 4QpsMos^{e} 2.1_{9} 4QpsJub^{c} 2_{6} ([א]שר לוא ישגו) 4QToh A 2.1_{1} ([א]שר יזו עליו) 2.2_{9} 3.1_{7} (אש[ר ימעכו]) 3.2_{11} (אשר בתוכו) 4Q298 2_{10} 4Q414 2_{3} (ישראל אשר) 3_{5} (היום אשר) 4Q416 3_{2} (כול אשר) 10.2_{19} (וכ[אשר]) 4Q477 $2_{2.5}$ (חוכיחו אשר) 2_{7} (הוא[ה]) 2_{7} (חוכ[יחו א]שר) 2_{7} (אשר איננו) Arad ost. 5_{4} ([א]שר) 5_{10} 21_{7} (אש[ר]) Samaria stele inscr. Silwan tomb inscr.$_{2}$.

[אֶשֶׁר], see אַשְׁרֵי.

[אֹשֶׁר] $_{1.1}$ n.[m.] **happiness**—Si אשר; sf. אָשְׁרִי—בְּאָשְׁרִי *in my happiness,* i.e. how happy I am Gn 30_{13} (or em. בָּא אָשְׁרִי *my happiness has come*), בְּאֹשֶׁר לֹא־בְרָע *in happiness, not in misfortune* Ps 10_{6} (if em. אֲשֶׁר *which is*), אשר ראך ומת *happiness,* i.e. happy, *is the one that sees you and dies* Si 48_{11}.

→ אשר *be happy.*

[אָשֻׁר] $_{10}$ n.f. **step**—sf. אַשֻּׁרִי (as if from אַשֻּׁר), אֲשֻׁרוֹ, mss אֲשֻׁרֵנוּ; pl. אֲשֻׁרִים; sf. אֲשֻׁרַי אֲשֻׁרָי (אֲשֻׁרַי), אֲשֻׁרָיו, אֲשֻׁרֵינוּ (אֲשֻׁרֵינוּ [as if from אַשֻּׁר])—also **track** left by footstep of Y. (Jb 23_{11}), <SUBJ> תמך *hold* to path Ps 17_{5} (+ פַּעַם *step*), מעד *shake* 37_{31}, שׁפך pu. *be poured out,* i.e. slip 73_{2} (+ רֶגֶל *leg*), רגז *tremble* Hb 3_{16} (if em. אֶרְגַּז אֲשֶׁר *I tremble because* to יִרְגְּזוּ־אֲשֻׁרָי *my footsteps tremble*), נטה *turn aside* from way Ps 44_{19} (or em. to וַתֵּט *and you turned our steps aside*) Jb 31_{7}, סבב *surround* Ps 17_{11} (or em. אַשֻּׁרֵינוּ appar. *our steps* to יְשֻׁרוּנִי *they look at me*). <OBJ> כון pol. *establish* Ps 40_{3} (+ רֶגֶל *leg*), נטה *turn aside* 44_{19} (if em.). <CSTR> בַּת־אֲשֻׁרִים appar. *daughter,* i.e. made of, *steps* Ezk 27_{6} (or em. בִּתְאַשֻּׁרִים *of cypresses*). <PREP> בין לְ hi. *discern* Pr 14_{15} (or em. לְאַשְּׁרוֹ *to pronounce him happy* or לִתְשׁוּבָה *return*); אחז בְּ *hold to* Jb 23_{11} (+ דֶּרֶךְ *way*).

→ אשר *advance.*

אֲשַׁרְאֵלָה, see אֲשַׂרְאֵלָה.

אֲשֵׁרָה $_{40.0.1.6}$ [pr.] n.f. **Asherah**—אֲשֵׁירָה; sf. 3ms I אשרתה; pl. אֲשֵׁרִים (אֲשֵׁרוֹת); sf. אֲשֵׁרֶיךָ (אֲשֵׁירֶיךָ), אֲשֵׁרָיו, אֲשֵׁרֵיהֶם (אֲשֵׁירֵיהֶם)—Canaanite goddess and wooden pole or tree representing her, <SUBJ> כרת pu. *be cut down* Jg 6_{28} (+ מִזְבֵּחַ *altar*), עמד *stand,* i.e. remain 2 K 13_{6}, קום *rise,* i.e. remain Is 27_{9} (‖ חַמָּן *incense altar*).

<NOM CL> אֲנִי עֲנָתוֹ וַאֲשֵׁרָתוֹ *I am his Anat and his Asherah* Ho 14_{9} (if em. אֲנִי עָנִיתִי וַאֲשׁוּרֶנּוּ *I have answered and watched him*).

<OBJ> נטע *plant* Dt 16_{21} 11QT 51_{20} (‖ מַצֵּבָה *pillar,* + אֶבֶן figured *stone*), יצא hi. *bring forth* 2 K 23_{6}, עשׂה *make* 1 K 14_{15} 16_{33} 2 K 17_{16} (+ מַסֵּכָה שְׁנֵים עֲגָלִים *a molten image, two calves*) 21_{3} (+ בָּמָה *high place,* מִזְבֵּחַ *altar*) 2 C 33_{3} (+ מִזְבֵּחַ, בָּמָה) 4QJub^{a} 2_{10} ([אשרות]), בנה *build* 1 K 14_{23} (‖ מַצֵּבָה, בָּמָה), נצב hi. *set up* 2 K 17_{10} (‖ מַצֵּבָה), עמד hi. *set up* 2 C 33_{19} (‖ פָּסִיל *graven image,* +

בָּמָה), כרת *cut down* Ex 34$_{13}$ (|| מִזְבֵּחַ, מַצֵּבָה) Jg 6$_{25.30}$ (both + מִזְבֵּחַ) 2 K 18$_4$ (|| בָּמָה, מַצֵּבָה, נְחָשׁ bronze *serpent*) 23$_{14}$ (|| מַצֵּבָה), גדע pi. *cut down* Dt 7$_5$ (|| מִזְבֵּחַ, מַצֵּבָה, פָּסִיל) 2 C 14$_2$ (|| מִזְבֵּחַ, בָּמָה, מַצֵּבָה) 17$_6$ (|| בָּמָה, מַצֵּבָה, בָּמָה) 31$_1$ (|| מַצֵּבָה, בָּמָה, מִזְבֵּחַ), בער pi. *root out* 19$_3$, שׁבר pi. *break* 34$_4$ (|| פָּסִיל, מַסֵּכָה *molten image*, + מִזְבֵּחַ, חַמָּן *incense altar*), נתשׁ *pluck up* Mc 5$_{13}$, נתץ pi. *tear down* 2 C 34$_7$ (|| מִזְבֵּחַ, + פָּסִיל, חַמָּן), שׂרף *burn* Dt 12$_3$ (|| מִזְבֵּחַ, מַצֵּבָה, פָּסִיל) 2 K 23$_{15}$ (+ מִזְבֵּחַ, בָּמָה), ראה *see* Is 17$_8$ (|| מִזְבֵּחַ, + חַמָּן), זכר *remember* Jr 17$_2$ (|| מִזְבֵּחַ), עבד *serve* Jg 3$_7$ (|| בַּעַל *Baal*) 6$_{25}$ (+ מִזְבֵּחַ) 2 C 24$_{18}$ (|| עָצָב *idol*).

<CSTR> אֲשֵׁרַת שֹׁמְרוֹן *Asherah of Samaria* Am 8$_{13}$ (if em. אַשְׁמַת *wicked deed of*); פֶּסֶל הָאֲשֵׁרָה *graven image of Asherah* 2 K 21$_7$, אַלּוֹן אֲשֵׁרָה *oak of Asherah* Is 6$_{13}$ (if em. אֲשֶׁר *which*), עֲצֵי הָאֲשֵׁרָה *wood of the Asherah* Jg 6$_{26}$, נְבִיאֵי הָאֲשֵׁרָה *prophets of Asherah* 1 K 18$_{19}$ (|| בַּעַל *Baal*).

<PREP> לְ of benefit, *to, for,* + עשׂה *make* 1 K 15$_{13}$ ||2 C 15$_{16}$ (obj. מִפְלֶצֶת *abominable thing*), pass. *be made* 2 K 23$_4$ (subj. כְּלִי *vessel*; || בַּעַל *Baal*, + כֹּל צְבָא הַשָּׁמַיִם *all the host of heaven*), ארג *weave* 2 K 23$_7$ (obj. appar. בַּיִת *hanging*), ברך לְ pi. *bless by* Kuntillet ʿAjrud inscr. E1 Kuntillet ʿAjrud inscr. E2.2$_2$ Kh. el-Qom tomb inscr. 3$_3$ (perh. ברך pass. *be blessed*; all three || יי *Y.*), ולאשרתה *and by his Asherah* Kuntillet ʿAjrud add. inscr. 1 (|| יי) Kh. el-Qom tomb inscr. 3$_5$.

שׁבע בְּ ni. *swear by* Am 8$_{13}$ (if em. בְּאַשְׁמַת *by the wicked deed of*).

טהר מִן pi. *purify* Judah and Jerusalem *of* 2 C 34$_3$ (|| בָּמָה *high place*, פָּסִיל *graven image*, מַסֵּכָה *molten image*).

<COLL> אֲשֵׁרָה כָּל־עֵץ אֵצֶל מִזְבַּח יי *an Asherah, any tree beside the altar of Y.* Dt 16$_{21}$.

Also Kuntillet ʿAjrud inscr. D2$_2$ (אשרת; + יי *Y.*) Kh. el-Qom tomb inscr. 3$_6$ (א[ש]רתה).

<SYN> בַּעַל *Baal*, בָּמָה *high place*, מַצֵּבָה *pillar*, מִזְבֵּחַ *altar*, חַמָּן *incense altar*, פָּסִיל *graven image*, מַסֵּכָה *molten image*.

אשרחי 0.0.0.1 pr.n.m. **Asherahi,** Seal 534$_1$ (א[שׁ]רח׳) 626$_2$ (both T. Beit Mirsim?, 7th/6th cent.).

אָשֵׁרִי 1 gent. **Asherite,** collective, members of tribe of Asher, Jg 1$_{32}$ 2 S 2$_9$ (if em. הָאֲשׁוּרִי *the Ashurites*).
→ אָשֵׁר *Asher*.

אַשְׁרֵי 45.8.11 interj. **happy**—sf. אַשְׁרֶיךָ, אַשְׁרַיִךְ, אַשְׁרָיו, אַשְׁרֵהוּ, אַשְׁרֵיכֶם (Q אשריכמה)—**happy, blessed is/are** (lit. happiness, blessedness of, pl. cstr. of אֶשֶׁר), **a.** followed by noun, אִישׁ *man* 1 K 10$_8$||2 C 9$_7$ (or em. אֲנָשֶׁיךָ *your men* to נָשֶׁיךָ *your wives*) Ps 1$_1$ 112$_1$ Si 14$_2$ 34$_8$ 50$_{28}$, אֱנוֹשׁ *person* Is 56$_2$ Jb 5$_{17}$ Si 14$_{1.20}$, אָדָם *person* Is 56$_2$ (בֶּן־אָדָם) Ps 32$_2$ 84$_{6.13}$ Pr 3$_{13}$ 8$_{34}$ 28$_{14}$ 4Q185 1.2$_{8.13}$ 5Q525 2$_3$, גֶּבֶר *man* Ps 34$_9$ 40$_5$ 94$_{12}$ 127$_5$ GnzPs 1$_{27}$, בַּעַל *husband* Si 25$_8$ 26$_1$, בֵּן *son* Pr 20$_7$ Ps 144$_{12}$ (if em. אֲשֶׁר perh. *may* our sons be as plants), עֶבֶד *servant* 1 K 10$_8$||2 C 9$_7$, עַם *people* Ps 89$_{16}$ 144$_{15.15}$, גּוֹי *nation* 33$_{12}$, צַדִּיק *righteous person* Is 3$_{10}$ (if em. אִמְרוּ *say!*), תְּמִים *one perfect* of way Ps 119$_1$.

b. followed by pron. sf., with ref. to Israel Dt 33$_{29}$, אֶרֶץ *land* Ec 10$_{17}$, אָדָם *man* 6$_{10}$ (if em. אֲשֶׁר הוּא *what is* to אַשְׁרֵהוּ *happy is he*), king GnzPs 3$_{17}$, one who fears Y. Ps 128$_2$ (+ וְטוֹב לָךְ *and it shall be well for you*), בטח ptc. *one who trusts* in Y. Pr 16$_{20}$ (+ יִמְצָא־טוֹב *he shall find wellbeing*), שׁמר ptc. *one who keeps* law 29$_{18}$ (or em. אִשְּׁרֵהוּ *it*, i.e. the law, *disciplines him*), חנן po. ptc. *one who shows favour* to poor 14$_{21}$, זרע ptc. *one who sows* Is 32$_{20}$.

c. followed by ptc. of חכה *wait* Is 30$_{18}$, pi. in same sense Dn 12$_{12}$, חסה *seek refuge* Ps 2$_{12}$, דרשׁ *seek* wisdom 4Q525 2$_2$, נשׂא pass. *be forgiven* Ps 32$_1$, כסה pass. *be covered* 32$_1$, שׂכל hi. *pay attention* to poor 41$_2$, ישׁב *dwell* 84$_5$, שׁמר *keep* justice, etc. 106$_3$ GnzPs 4$_{27}$, עשׂה *do* righteousness Ps 106$_3$, נצר *keep* testimonies 119$_2$, תמך *uphold* statutes 4Q525 2$_1$, ירא *fear* Y. Ps 128$_1$, הלך *walk* in ways of Y. 128$_1$, גיל *rejoice* in wisdom 4Q525 2$_2$.

d. followed by (1) שֶׁ־ *who*, + שׁלם pi. *requite* Ps 137$_8$, אחז *seize* 137$_9$, נפל *fall* Si 25$_8$, מצא *find* GnzPs 3$_1$; אַשְׁרֵי שֶׁאֵל יַעֲקֹב בְּעֶזְרוֹ *happy is the one whose help is the God of Jacob* Ps 146$_5$.

(2) verb, without relative, אַשְׁרֵי תִּבְחַר וּתְקָרֵב *blessed is the one whom you choose and bring near* Ps 65$_5$, אַשְׁרֵי דְּרָכַי יִשְׁמֹרוּ *happy are those who keep my ways* Pr 8$_{32}$, אשרי יזכה בקדושתך *blessed is the one who is worthy*

of your sanctity, or *who is pure* GnzPs 4_{25}.
⇒ אשׁר *be happy*.

[אשריחת] pr.n.m. **Asheriahath,** Seal 627_{2} ([א]שריחת; T. Beit Mirsim?, 7th/6th cent.).
⇒ perh. אשׁר *be happy* + חתת *be shattered*.

אשׁשׁ 1 vb. **be firm—Htpo.** Impv. הִתְאֹשָׁשׁוּ—**make firm** in mind, or perh. **experience grief,** זִכְרוּ־זֹאת וְהִתְאֹשָׁשׁוּ *remember this and make (it) firm*, or *and be grieved* Is 46_{8}.
⇒ אֹשׁ *foundation*.

אֶשֶׁת, see אִשָּׁה.

[אֵשֶׁת], see אִשָּׁה, Cstr.

אֶשְׁתָּאוֹל, see אֶשְׁתָּאֹל.

אֶשְׁתָּאֹל 7 pl.n. **Eshtaol**—אֶשְׁתָּאוֹל—town in Dan, once (Jos 15_{33}) in lowland of Judah, alw. assoc. with Zorah (צָרְעָה), Jos 15_{33} 19_{41} (both אֶשְׁתָּאוֹל) Jg 13_{25} 16_{31} $18_{2.8.11}$.
⇒ אֶשְׁתָּאֻלִי *Eshtaolite*.

אֶשְׁתָּאֻלִי 1 gent. **Eshtaolite,** מֵאֵלֶּה יָצְאוּ הַצָּרְעָתִי וְהָאֶשְׁתָּאֻלִי *from these went out the Zorathites and the Eshtaolites* 1 C 2_{53}.
⇒ אֶשְׁתָּאֹל *Eshtaol*.

אֶשְׁתּוֹן 2 pr.n.m. **Eshton,** son of Mehir, descendant of Judah, 1 C $4_{11.12}$.

אשתם, see אֵשׁ I, Prep.

אֶשְׁתְּמֹה, see אֶשְׁתְּמֹעַ I.

אֶשְׁתְּמֹעַ I 4 pl.n. **Eshtemoa**—אֶשְׁתְּמֹה—**1.** Levitical city in hill country of Judah, perh. mod. Es-Semū'a, 15 km SSW of Hebron, Jos 15_{50} (אֶשְׁתְּמֹה) 21_{14} 1 S 30_{28} 1 C 6_{42}.
⇒ שׁמע *hear*.

אֶשְׁתְּמֹעַ II 2 pr.n.m. **Eshtemoa,** Maacathite, son of Ishbah, 1 C $4_{17.19}$.
⇒ שׁמע *hear*.

[אַתְּ], see אַתְּ, אַתָּה.

אַתְּ 60.0.2 pronoun **you** (fem. sg.)—אָתְּ (L אָתְּ), mss, Sam, Kt אתי—of Sarai Gn $12_{11.13}$, Rebekah $24_{23.47.60}$, Bathsheba 1 K $2_{15.22}$, Abigail 1 S 25_{33}, Ruth Ru $3_{9.10.11.16}$, Esther Est 4_{14}, Shunammite woman 2 K $4_{16.23}$ 8_{1}, Jeroboam's wife 1 K $14_{2.6.12}$, Manoah's wife Jg 13_{3}, Potiphar's wife Gn 39_{9}, Jephthah's daughter Jg 11_{35}, Micah's mother 17_{2}, wife of disciple of Elisha 2 K 4_{7}, lover Ca 6_{4}, אֵשֶׁת־חַיִל *doughty woman* Pr 31_{29}, suspected adulteress Nm 5_{20}, Israel Jr 2_{20} 3_{1} Ezk 22_{24} 36_{13}, Jerusalem Is 51_{12} Jr 4_{30} 13_{21} 15_{6} Ezk $16_{7.33.45.45.48.52.52.55.58}$ 23_{35} Zc 9_{11}, Nineveh Na $3_{11.11}$, Tyre Ezk 27_{3} perh. 28_{14} (or em. אֶת־ *with* cherub), Moab Jr 48_{7}, Babylon 50_{24}, Y. 4QDb$_{9(mg).9}$, זְרוֹעַ *arm* of Y. Is $51_{9.10}$, תְּאֵנָה *fig tree* Jg 9_{10}, גֶּפֶן *vine* 9_{12}, אֶבֶן *stone*, as divine image Jr 2_{27}; at Nm 11_{15} Dt 5_{27} (mss, Sam, אַתָּ[ה] *you* (masc. sg.).

<**SUBJ**> היה *be* Gn 24_{60} (+ לְ *as*) Jg 11_{35} (+ בְּ *as*) Ezk 36_{13} (+ שׁכל pi. ptc. *one who bereaves*) Na 3_{11} (+ עלם ni. ptc. *concealed*, i.e. dazed; or em. נֶעֱלָפָה *powerless* or נִלְעָמָה *subjugated*), ברך pass. *be blessed* Ru 3_{10} 1 S 25_{33} 4QDb$_{9(mg)}$, עשׂה *do* Nm 11_{15} (or em., see above) Jr 4_{30} Ezk 16_{48}, חיה *live* 2 K 4_{7}, אבד *perish* Est 4_{14}, הלך *go* Jg $9_{10.12}$ 1 K 14_{12} 2 K 4_{23} 8_{1} Jr 15_{6}, קום *arise* 1 K 14_{12} 2 K 8_{1}, עלה *go up* Pr 31_{29}, שׁוב *go back* Ezk 16_{55}, נטשׁ *desert* Jr 15_{6}, שׂטה *stray* in adultery Nm 5_{20}.

צעה *recline* Jr 2_{20} (+ זנה ptc. *[as] prostitute*), שׁכר *become drunk* Na 3_{11}, זנה *be a prostitute* Jr 3_{1}, טמא ni. *be unclean* Nm 5_{20}, חבק *embrace* 2 K 4_{16}, ילד *give birth (to)* Jr 2_{27} (:: אַתָּה *you* [masc. sg.]), נתן *give* Ezk 16_{33}, נשׂא *carry* $16_{52.52.58}$ 23_{35}, כלה *restrain* 1 S 25_{33}, מלך *reign* Jg $9_{10.12}$, לכד ni. *be captured* Jr 48_{7}, שׁדד pass. *be devastated* 4_{30}.

אמר *say* Jg 17_{2} Ezk 27_{3} (or em.; see Nom. Cl.), דבר pi. *speak* Dt 5_{27}, שׁאל *ask* 1 K 2_{22}, בקשׁ pi. *seek* Na 3_{11}, אלה *curse* Jg 17_{2}, ידע *know* 1 K 2_{15} Jr 50_{24}, ירא *fear* Is 51_{12} (or em. מִי־אַתְּ וַתִּירָא *who are you* [masc.] *that you fear?*), למד pi. *teach* Jr 13_{21}, בושׁ *be ashamed* Ezk 16_{52},

לבשׁ *be dressed (in)* Jr 430, עדה *be decorated (with)* 430, נכר htp. *disguise oneself* 1 K 146, אכל *eat*, i.e. devour, people Ezk 3613.

<NOM CL> מִי־אַתְּ *who are you?* Ru 39 (L אַתְּ; :: אָנֹכִי *I*) 316 Is 5112 (or em. אַתָּה *you* [masc.]), בַּת־מִי אַתְּ *whose daughter are you?* Gn 2423 (:: אָנֹכִי *I*) 2447, אֲחֹתִי אַתְּ *you are my sister* 1213, בַּת־אִמֵּךְ אַתְּ ... וַאֲחוֹת אֲחוֹתֵךְ אַתְּ *you are your mother's daughter ... and your sister's sister*, i.e. just like them Ezk 1645 (or em. אֲחָיוֹתַיִךְ), הֲלוֹא אַתְּ־הִיא *are you not the one?* Is 519.10, אַתְּ־אִשְׁתּוֹ *you are his wife* Gn 399, אֵשֶׁת חַיִל אָתְּ *you are a woman of valour* Ru 311, אַתְּ אֵשֶׁת יָרָבְעָם *you are Jeroboam's wife* 1 K 142(Qr), אַתְּ ... אִשָּׁה ... אָתְּ *you are ... a woman* Gn 1211 (Sam אתי), אַתְּ עֵרֹם וְעֶרְיָה *you are naked and bare* Ezk 167, אַתְּ־עֲקָרָה *you are infertile* Jg 133, יָפָה אַתְּ *you are beautiful* Ca 64, אַתְּ אֶרֶץ *you are a land* Ezk 2224, אַתְּ־כְּרוּב *you are a cherub* 2814 (or em. אֶת־ *with*), אַתְּ אֳנִיָּה *you are a ship* 273 (if em. אַתְּ אָמַרְתְּ אֲנִי *you said, I*), את הו הכול *you* (Y.) *are everything* 4QDb9.

<APP> אַתְּ רַעְיָתִי *you, my companion* Ca 64 (Gnz רַעְיָתִי), אַתְּ בִּתִּי *you, my daughter* Ru 316.

<COLL> אַתְּ with impv. Gn 2460 Jg 910.12 1 K 1412 2 K 81 Ezk 1652.52, גַּם־אַתְּ *and as for you* Zc 911, *you too* Jr 487 Ezk 1652.52 2335 Na 311.11, אַתְּ וּבֵיתֵךְ *you and your household* 2 K 81(Qr), אַתְּ וּבֵית־אָבִיךְ *you and your father's household* Est 414 (Gnz lacks אַתְּ), אַתְּ וּבְנוֹתַיִךְ *you and your daughters* Ezk 1648 (וּבְנוֹתָיִךְ) 1655, אַתְּ וּבָנַיִךְ *you and your sons* 2 K 47(Qr).

→ אַתָּה *you* masc. sg.

אֵת I +10898.55.+866.33 **object-marker**—אֵת, אֶת־ (אֵת) [Ps 475 602 Pr 312] אֶת־ [Jb 4126 Est 931(L)]; in Bar-Kochba letters, etc. normal form is ת, for both את and –ת־ה־, usu. prefixed to object); with sf. אוֹתִי (אֹתִי), אוֹתְךָ (אֹתְךָ, אֹתָךְ, אוֹתָךְ [Nm 2233] אֹתְכָה [Ex 2935]), אוֹתָנוּ (אֹתָהּ) אוֹתָהּ (אֹתָה I), (אֹתוֹ) אוֹתוֹ, (אֹתְךָ) אוֹתְךָ אוֹתְכֶם (אֹתָנוּ), אֶתְכֶם (fem. Am 42 Zc 119 Ca 27 35 58 84, [Jos 2315], Q אתכמה), אוֹתָם (oft. fem., אֹתָם, אוֹתְהֶם [fem. Ezk 2345], אֶתְהֶם [fem. Ezk 3412 1 C 650], Q אותמה), אֹתָן (Ezk 1654), אוֹתָנָה (Ezk 3421), אֹתָנָה (Ex 3526), אוֹתְהֶן (Ezk 2347), אֶתְהֶן (Lv 2014).

1. with **determined direct object. a.** with **definite article,** בָּרָא אֱלֹהִים אֵת הַשָּׁמַיִם וְאֵת הָאָרֶץ *God created the heavens and the earth* Gn 11, ביום עזבו את הארץ *on the day of his leaving the land* 4Q386–9 412, sim. Gn 14.7.16.16.16 etc. Si 4333(Segal) 4822(Segal) (עשה *do* restored in both) 11QT 22.2.3.3(all four Yadin) (all three [את ה–]) 23(Yadin) (גורש *driving out* restored in all five) 4QJuba 110.10 212 54 (all four [את ה–]) 54.4 ([את ה–]) 59.12 62.3.5 (all four [את ה–]) 65.5.11 ([את ה–]) 72.12 4QPentParb 23.29 4Q464 73 ([א]ת ה–]) etc. Lachish ost. 48 (את הע[ד]; others אתה עוד *him again*) 55 (את [ה]ס[פר]ם) 614 Arad ost. 511 (י[שלח] לך את) 132 (תש[לח את הש]מן) 164 2416 Siloam tunnel inscr.1 ([מנפים את]) Nimrud ivory inscr. 13 ([א]ת הספר).

כל הבשר יאהב מינו וכל אדם את הדומה לו *all flesh loves its (own) sort and each person the one who is like him* Si 1315, אֶת־הַכֹּל *everything* Lv 19.13 827 Dt 236 Jos 1119 2 S 1931 1 K 1426‖2 C 129 Ec 311 715 1019 1115 Si 4333 1QDM 14 Mur 24 212 (quoted at §3b) 4QJuba 213.

1b. with **suffixed pronoun,** וַיִּתֵּן אֹתָם אֱלֹהִים *and God placed them* Gn 117, גֵּרַשְׁתָּ אֹתִי *you have expelled me* 414, אֹתְךָ רָאִיתִי *I saw you* 71, sim. 122.27.27.28 23 etc. Si 313 723 3611 381 3931 4525 5126 11QT 178 2016 279 347.8 4QJuba 113 214 (both [אותם]) 215 ([אתם]) 53.3 (both [אתו]) 66 ([אותם]) 72.10 (both [אתם]) 711.11 (both [אתו]) 4QPent Para 3.27 ([אותו]) 4QPentParb 23.26 etc. Lachish ost. 312 124 (א[תה]) Arad ost. 122 ([א]תם) 176 2413 Kuntillet ʿAjrud inscr. E1.

Pronoun suffix is used when אֵת (1) precedes the verb, אֹתְךָ רָאִיתִי *I saw you* Gn 71; (2) follows a suffixed indirect object, וְהִרְאַנִי אֹתוֹ *and he will show me it* 2 S 1525; (3) follows an infinitive absolute, וְנָתוֹן אֹתוֹ *and placed him* Gn 4143. (4) follows a noun with possessive suffix, מִיִּרְאָתוֹ אֹתוֹ *because of his fearing him* 2 S 311, באהבתכה אותם *in your loving them* 4QDibHama 1.29.

Pronoun suffix to אֵת may indicate (1) emphasis, e.g. הַאֹתִי הֵם מַכְעִסִים *is it me they are enraging?* Jr 719, הַאוֹתִי לֹא־תִירָאוּ *is it not me you should fear?* 522, הָאֹתִי תִּשְׁאָלוּנִי *is it me you ask?* Is 4511 (if em. הָאֹתִיּוֹת שְׁאֵלוּנִי *they have asked me the things to come*). (2) reflexivity of verb (or some such word) הֲלוֹא אֹתָם *is it not they themselves* they are enraging? Jr 719, הוֹי רֹעֵי־יִשְׂרָאֵל אֲשֶׁר הָיוּ רֹעִים אוֹתָם *woe to the shepherds* of Israel who have been tending themselves Ezk 34_{2} (sim. $34_{8.10}$), וַיִּרְאוּ שֹׁטְרֵי בְנֵי־יִשְׂרָאֵל אֹתָם בְּרָע *and the Israelite foremen found* (lit. *saw*) *themselves in trouble* Ex 5_{19}, בְּיוֹם ... נִזְרוֹ יָבִיא אֹתוֹ אֶל־פֶּתַח אֹהֶל מוֹעֵד perh. *on the day ... of his Nazirite vow he is to bring himself to the entrance of the tent of meeting* Nm 6_{13} (or em. יָבִיאוּ *they are to bring* him, or, יָבוֹא *he is to come* and del. אֹתוֹ), הַפָּנִים אֲשֶׁר רָאִיתִי ... מַרְאֵיהֶם וְאוֹתָם *the faces which I had seen ... —their appearances and they themselves* Ezk 10_{22} (or move athnach and em. וְאַוָּתָם *and their desire [was]* or וְהֵמָּה *and they [were]* or וּבְלֶכְתָּם/וּבְצֵאתָם *and when they went [out]*), וְנָסַב אֹתוֹ הַגְּבוּל *and the boundary turned (itself)* Jos 19_{14}.

[הנוש]א אותה נבלתה perh. *the one that carries it—the carcase*, i.e. carries that same carcase 4QMMT A 2_{23} (unless נבלתה = *her carcase*).

1c. with **suffixed noun,** אֶת־קֹלְךָ שָׁמַעְתִּי *I heard your voice* Gn 3_{10}, sim. $4_{2.11.17.25.25}$ etc. Si 4_{23} $7_{29.30}$ 8_{15} 9_{13} (ת[א]) 13_{23} 20_{22} 25_{23} 33_{3} $36_{11(mg).19}$ $44_{1(mg)}$ $45_{5.15.15}$ 47_{20} $49_{13.13}$ 11QPs^{a} $19_{8(mg).11}$ $24_{4.8.9}$ $28_{6.6}$ GnzPs $1_{11.11.17.19}$ 2_{14} $3_{4.27}$ 4_{10} 11QT $16_{9.9}$ (ואת נס[כו]) $16_{11.17}$ (ואת [מנ]חתו) 16_{18} (ואת נ[סכ]ו) 4QJub^{a} 2_{1} ([את מרים]) את [מצותי ... ואת שבתותי) 2_{8} ([את]) 2_{8} (את א[להיהם]) 2_{5} (א]ת שמי]) 2_{10} ([את משכני ואת] מקדש[י]) 2_{9} (ואת קדשי] 7_{13} ([את מצוותיו]) etc. Lachish ost. 2_{4} (את [ע]בדה) 6_{1} Meṣad Ḥashavyahu ost. 1_{6} (if em. קצרו/ה *his harvest*) $1_{9.12}$ ([השב ... את]).

1d. with **name** of person, place, or people, etc., וְהָאָדָם יָדַע אֶת־חַוָּה *and the man knew Eve* Gn 4_{1}, וַתֵּלֶד אֶת־קַיִן *and she gave birth to Cain* 4_{1} (sim. $4_{2.17.18.18.18}$ etc. 4QpGen^{a} 4_{1} 4QTNaph 2_{10}), sim. $14_{4.23}$ 16_{3} $19_{10.29.29}$ etc. Si 45_{6} 48_{18} $49_{9.10}$ 1QJub^{b} 35_{9} 1QM 11_{1},

אֶת־יי *Y.* Gn 24_{48} 25_{22} 29_{35} Ex 5_{2} 10_{7} etc. Si 45_{25} 50_{22} GnzPs 3_{19} perh. 4Q385 3_{3} (unless אֵת = *with*; + צבאות *of hosts*), אֶת אֲדֹנָי *Adonai* Is 6_{1} Am 9_{1} Ne 4_{8} 4QBark^{a} 2_{1} (אדוני) 4Q521 1.2_{4} perh. 4_{11} (unless אֵת = *with*), אֶת־אֱלֹהִים *God* Ps 14_{2}||53_{3} 78_{56}, את אל *God* CD 10_{2} 4QpHos^{a} 1.2_{3} 4QpHos^{b} 7_{2} perh. 4QBer^{a} 3.1_{8}, את אל ישועות *the God of victories* 1QS 1_{19}, את מיכאל *Michael* 4Q285 2_{3} (or, *with Michael*), את בליעל *Belial* 1QM 13_{2} (בלי[על]) 4QBer^{a} 3.2_{1}.

אֶת־יִשְׂרָאֵל *Israel* Gn 50_{2} (in ref. to Jacob) Ex $5_{2.2}$ $14_{5.30}$ etc. Si 46_{1} 47_{23} 4QDibHam^{a} 1.4_{5} ([ישראל]) 1.5_{7} CD 5_{20}=6QD 3_{3} CD 6_{1} 4QpHos^{b} $7_{2(Horgan)}$ (יש[רא]ל) 4QCat^{a} 5_{7} (ישרא[ל]) 4Q181 2_{3} ([א]ת) 4Q386–9 4_{10} (verb missing in all four) 4_{11}, [את יעקוב] 4QPentPar^{a} 3.2_{7}, את לוי *Levi* 5QRègle 2_{7} (verb missing), אֶת־מְנַשֶּׁה *Manasseh* Gn $48_{1.13}$ Jg 11_{29} land of Manasseh) Is 9_{20} 2 C 33_{11} (King Manasseh) 4QpNah $3.3_{9(Horgan)}$ ([המחזק]ים את מ[נשה]), אֶת־חָם *Ham* Gn 5_{32} 6_{10} 4QpGen^{a} 2_{7} perh. 4Q462$_{1}$ ([א]ת; unless אֵת = *with*), אֶת־יֶפֶת *Japheth* Gn 5_{32} 6_{10} perh. 4Q462$_{1}$ (unless אֵת = *with*), אֶת־רִבְקָה *Rebekah* Gn 22_{23} $24_{59.60.67}$ 25_{20} 49_{31} 4QTNaph 2_{1} (רבק[ה]), אֶת־זִלְפָּה *Zilpah* Gn 29_{24} 30_{9} 4QTNaph 2_{3}, את בלהה *Bilhah* $2_{4.10}$, אֶת־חַנָּה *Hannah* 1 S $1_{5.19}$ 2_{21} 4QTNaph $2_{2.8}$, אֶת־עוֹג *Og* Dt 1_{4} (אֵת) 3_{3} perh. 4QApocJos^{c} 1_{2} (unless אֵת = *with*), אֶת־שְׁמוּאֵל *Samuel* 1 S 3_{16} 9_{18} $12_{11.18}$ $28_{11.12}$ 11QPs^{a} 28_{8}, אֶת־דָּוִ(י)ד *David* 1 S 16_{19} $17_{38.42.43.55}$ etc. 4QMMT B$_{28}$, אֶת־יוֹחָנָן *Johanan* Jr 41_{13} 1 C 5_{35} perh. 4Q477 2_{3} (unless אֵת = *with*), אֶת־חֲנַנְיָה *Hananiah* Ne 7_{2} 4Q477 $2_{5.9}$ ([ואת חנניה ... הוכיחו] *and Hananiah ... they reproved*), את הודויהו *Hodaviah* Lachish ost. 3_{16}, את נחם *Nahum* Arad ost. 16_{10}, אֶת־מִצְרַיִם *Egypt* Ex $3_{20.22}$ (מִצְרָיִם) $12_{23.27.36}$ (מִצְרָיִם) etc. 4Q386–9 4_{11}, אֶת־יְרוּשָׁלַםִ *Jerusalem* 1 K 15_{4} (יְרוּשָׁלָםִ) 2 K 18_{35}||Is 36_{20} 2 K $21_{13.16}$ 23_{27} etc. 4Q462$_{18}$ (erased [ישרא[ל *Israel*), אֶת־צִיּוֹן *Zion* Zc 1_{17} Ps 51_{20} 137_{1} 4QDibHam^{a} 1.4_{11}, את עזקה *Azekah* Lachish ost. 4_{12}, perh. sim. 5QToponyms 1_{2} 2_{1} 5_{1} (both [א]ת) 5_{2} $6_{1.2}$ 4Q522 1.1_{1+16t} (1_{8} א[ת], $1_{9.10}$ [א]ת; verb missing in all twenty-one).

את כול בני אור *all (the) sons of light* 1QS 3_{13}, מִצְרַיִם יָלַד אֶת־לוּדִים *Egypt engendered (the) Ludim* 1 C $1_{11(Qr)}$ (sim. $1_{11.11.11.12.12.12}$), נכה אֶת־פְּלִשְׁתִּים hi. *defeat (the) Philistines* Jg 3_{31} 2 S 5_{25} 8_{1}||1 C 18_{1} 2 S 23_{12}||1 C 11_{14} 2 K 18_{8}, את פלשתיים הכנ[יע] *he humiliated (the) Philistines* 1QM 11_{2} (sim. 1 S 7_{11} 23_{4} Jr 47_{4} Ob$_{19}$), אֶת־אֹהֶל מוֹעֵד *(the) tent of meeting* Ex 29_{44} 30_{26} 31_{7} (אֵת) 40_{34} Lv $16_{20.33}$ Nm 4_{25} 8_{15} Jos 18_{1} 1 K 8_{4}||2 C 5_{5}, וַיִּשְׂרֹף ... אֶת־בֵּית־מֶלֶךְ *and he burned ... (the) palace* 1 K 16_{18}, ויק[ח א]ת כלי בית אלוהים *and he took the vessels of (the) house of God* 4Q385 1_{4}.

1e. with (determined) **construct chain,** וַיִּשְׁמְעוּ

אֶת־קוֹל י׳ *and they heard the sound of Y.* Gn 3$_{8}$, לִשְׁמֹר אֶת־דֶּרֶךְ עֵץ הַחַיִּים *to guard the way to the tree of life* 3$_{24}$, וַיִּרְאוּ ... אֶת־בְּנוֹת הָאָדָם *and they saw ... the daughters of humans* 6$_{2}$, sim. 1$_{16}$ 3$_{18}$ 4$_{11}$ 8$_{6.13}$ etc. Si 6$_{9}$ 9$_{1}$ 16$_{15}$ 36$_{21}$ 39$_{35(mg)}$ 41$_{21(M)}$ 47$_{5.10}$ ([א]ת) 51$_{8.12}$ 11QPs^a 28$_{7}$ GnzPs 1$_{13.15}$ 2$_{9.13.13}$ 3$_{25}$ 4$_{13}$ 11QT 2$_{7(Yadin)}$ (ואת פסילי ... [תשרפון]; ||Dt 7$_{25}$ lacks אֵת) 15$_{9}$ + Sup 15$_{12(Yadin).12(Yadin)}$ 16$_{6(Yadin)}$ ([א]ת חלב הפר]) 4QJub^a 1$_{11}$ ([את מ]חלקות [הע]תים) 2$_{8}$ ([את מועד]י בריתי) 6$_{3}$ 7$_{5}$ ([את יום] השבת) 2$_{13}$ 4QPentPar^b 23.2$_{4}$ etc. Lachish ost. 6$_{3}$ ([א]ת ספ[ר]) 6$_{4}$ ([ואת]) Meṣad Ḥashavyahu ost. 1$_{2.8.9.13}$ ([להש]ב את בגד] עב[דך]) 1$_{14}$ ([והש]בת את[בגד] [ע]בדך) papMurPalimp^b$_{1}$.

אֶת־יוֹם הַשְּׁבִיעִי *the seventh day* Gn 2$_{3}$, לפנות שם את דרך הואהא *to clear there the way of him* 1QS 8$_{13}$.

אֵת/אֶת־כָּל־ *all* followed by determined expression (see also Ps 72$_{19}$ at §4c), Gn 1$_{25.29}$ 2$_{6.11.13}$ etc. GnzPs 1$_{13}$ 11QT 3$_{8}$ 15$_{4(Yadin)}$ (כ[ו]ל) 16$_{7(Yadin)}$ ([ואת כול]) 20$_{5}$ 26$_{11}$ 4QJub^a 1$_{17}$ 2$_{5}$ ([את כל]) ([כ]ל) 5$_{2.4}$ ([את כל]) 6$_{2.3.12}$ ([את כל]) 6$_{12}$ ([את]) 6$_{12}$ (כ[ל]) 6$_{12}$ ([את כל]) 7$_{1.1.1}$ (both [את כל]) 4QPentPar^a 3.2$_{5}$ etc.

1f. with **demonstrative pronoun,** etc., עִבְדוּ אֶת־י׳ כִּי אֹתָהּ אַתֶּם מְבַקְשִׁים *serve Y., for that is what you seek (to do)* Ex 10$_{11}$.

(1) אֶת־זֶה *this one* (masc.), אֶת־זֶה לֹא תֹאכְלוּ *this one you are not to eat* Lv 11$_{4}$||Dt 14$_{7}$, sim. Gn 29$_{33}$ 44$_{29}$ Lv 11$_{9}$||Dt 14$_{9}$ Lv 11$_{21}$ 1 S 21$_{16}$ 1 K 22$_{27}$ Ec 7$_{14}$ 8$_{9}$ 9$_{1.1}$ (all three אֶת־כָּל־זֶה *all this*).

(2) אֶת־זֹאת *this one* (fem.), ארור האדם אשר יפתח את זאת *cursed be whoever opens this* Siloam royal steward tomb inscr. 1$_{3}$, sim. Gn 29$_{27}$ 41$_{39}$ (אֶת־כָּל־זֹאת) Jos 22$_{24}$ 2 S 13$_{17}$ Jr 9$_{11}$ Ps 92$_{7}$.

(3) אֶת־אֵלֶּה *these ones* Gn 46$_{18.25}$ Lv 11$_{13.22}$ 21$_{14}$ Nm 15$_{13}$ 28$_{23}$ Is 48$_{14}$ 49$_{21}$ Ezk 4$_{6}$ 4QShir^b 30$_{6}$ Mur 24 3$_{16}$ 5$_{13}$ (in both תאלה and missing verb), אֶת־כָּל־אֵלֶּה *all these* Gn 15$_{10}$ Lv 20$_{23}$ (+ עשׂה *do*) Jg 13$_{23}$ 2 K 10$_{9}$ Is 66$_{2}$ Jr 3$_{7}$ 5$_{19}$ 14$_{22}$ Ezk 16$_{30}$ 18$_{11}$ (all six + עשׂה) Zc 8$_{12}$ GnzPs 3$_{6}$ 1QM 2$_{6(mg)}$ 4QDibHam^a 1.6$_{4}$ (+ עשׂה) 1QDM 4$_{9}$ (verb missing) 1QH 16$_{9(Licht)}$ ([את כו]ל אלה]; + עשׂה).

(4) אֶת־מִי *(to) whom?*, בַּחֲרוּ ... אֶת־מִי תַעֲבֹדוּן *choose ... whom you will serve* Jos 24$_{15}$, sim. 1 S 12$_{3.3}$ 28$_{11}$ 2 K 19$_{22}$||Is 37$_{23}$ Is 6$_{8}$ 28$_{9.9}$ 57$_{11}$, ופקדתי ת מי שיתן *and I have ordered whoever will give* MurEpBarC^b$_{8}$.

1g. אֵת אֲשֶׁר **the one who, that which** (see also אֲשֶׁר *which*, §3), Gn 9$_{24}$=4QpGen^a 2$_{5}$ Gn 18$_{19}$ 27$_{45}$ 28$_{15}$ 30$_{29}$ etc. Si 15$_{11}$ 11QPs^a 26$_{12}$ 11QT 15$_{17}$ + Sup 23$_{15.16}$ CD 1$_{12}$ 2$_{13.15}$ 13$_{18}$ (verb missing) 1QDM 1$_{8}$ 1QH 13$_{14}$ 17$_{21}$ 4Q385 1$_{6}$ 4QD^b$_{19}$ ([את אשר]) 4Q416 9.1$_{20}$ 4QJub^a 1$_{10}$ ([את אשר]) 2$_{5}$ ([את כל אשר]) 4$_{4}$ ([את אשר]), אֵת אֲשֶׁר יֶחֱטָא אִישׁ *if a man sins* 1 K 8$_{31}$ (||2 C 6$_{22}$ אִם־ *if* for אֵת אֲשֶׁר).

1h. with verbs that more usually take **preposition** rather than direct object (some of the following are perh. accusatives of respect, as §3b).

(1) with verbs of motion, וַיִּגַּשׁ דָּוִד אֶת־הָעָם *and David approached the people* 1 S 30$_{21}$ (mss אֶל *to*; sim. Nm 4$_{19}$ [mss, Sam אֶל] 1 S 9$_{18}$ [mss אֶל־]), וַנֵּלֶךְ אֵת כָּל־הַמִּדְבָּר *we walked (through) all the desert* Dt 1$_{19}$ (sim. 2$_{7}$), עֹבְרִים עַל־פְּנֵי־דֶרֶךְ אֶת־הַמִּדְבָּר appar. *crossing along the road to the desert* 2 S 15$_{23}$ (mss lack אֶת; mss אֶל), אֶת־בֵּית י׳ אֲנִי הֹלֵךְ *I am going (to) the house of Y.* Jg 19$_{18}$ (or em. אֶל־בֵּיתִי *to my house*), ובאתה את האולם *and you will come (along) the vestibule*, i.e. the vestibule's length will be 11QT 4$_{8}$, לָבוֹא חֶרֶב אֵת רַבַּת בְּנֵי־עַמּוֹן וְאֶת־יְהוּדָה *for the sword to come (to) Rabbah of the Annonites and (to) Judah* Ezk 21$_{25}$ (or em. אֶל־ *against*).

(2) with other verbs, e.g. ענה *reply* (also ענה בְּ), וַיַּעַן עֶפְרוֹן ... אֶת־אַבְרָהָם *and Ephron answered ... Abraham* Gn 23$_{10.14}$, sim. 23$_{5}$ 34$_{13}$ 35$_{3}$ 41$_{16.16}$ 42$_{22}$ etc. 11QT 59$_{7}$, זכר *remember* (also זכר לְ), וַיִּזְכֹּר אֱלֹהִים אֶת־נֹחַ *and God remembered Noah* Gn 8$_{1}$, זכר אדני את [ע]בדה *my lord has remembered his servant* Lachish ost. 2$_{4}$, sim. Gn 9$_{15}$ 19$_{29}$ 30$_{22}$ 40$_{23}$ 42$_{9}$ etc., עבד *serve* (also עבד לְ) Gn 14$_{4}$ 15$_{14}$ 27$_{40}$ 30$_{26}$ 31$_{6}$ etc. GnzPs 1$_{11}$ 2$_{20}$ 3$_{27}$ 11QT 54$_{14}$ 1QSa 1$_{13}$ CD 5$_{4}$ (||Jg 2$_{13}$ לְ) 1QpHab 13$_{2.2}$.

צוה pi. *command* (also צוה לְ pi.), כֹּל אֲשֶׁר צִוָּה אֹתוֹ *all that he commanded him* Gn 6$_{22}$, sim. 7$_{9.16}$ 21$_{4}$ 27$_{8}$ 32$_{5}$ etc. 1QDM 1$_{3}$ (וצויתו[ה א]ת), בכה *weep* (also בכה עַל), וּבָכְתָה אֶת־אָבִיהָ וְאֶת־אִמָּהּ *and she is to bewail her father and her mother* Dt 21$_{13}$=11QT 63$_{13}$, sim. Gn 50$_{3}$ Lv 10$_{6}$ Nm 20$_{29}$ Dt 34$_{8}$ 1 S 20$_{41}$ (perh. אֵת = *with*) Jr 8$_{23}$, קוה

pi. *wait* (cf. קוה לְ pi.), אוֹתְךָ קִוִּיתִי *I awaited you* Ps 25$_{5}$, רצה *take pleasure*, כְּאָב אֶת־בֵּן יִרְצֶה *as a father takes pleasure in (his) son* Pr 3$_{12}$, sim. Ezk 43$_{27}$ Ml 1$_{13}$ Ps 102$_{15}$ 147$_{11}$ Ec 9$_{7}$ (רצה אֵת appar. *compensate for* missed sabbaths, iniquity Lv 26$_{34.41.43.43}$ 2 C 36$_{21}$).

ערב *become surety* for (also ערב לְ Pr 6$_{1}$), עַבְדְּךָ עָרַב אֶת־הַנַּעַר *your servant has become surety for the lad* Gn 44$_{32}$, sim. Jr 30$_{21}$, מרה *rebel* against (also מרה בְּ), אֹתִי מָרָתָה *against me you rebelled* Jr 4$_{17}$, sim. Nm 20$_{24}$ 1 S 12$_{15}$ 1 K 13$_{26}$ (all three + פֶּה *mouth*, i.e. command) Ps 105$_{28}$, hi. Dt 1$_{26}$ 9$_{23}$ Jos 1$_{18}$ 1 S 12$_{14}$ (all four + פֶּה) Ezk 5$_{6}$ Ps 78$_{56}$ 106$_{33}$ 1QS 6$_{26}$ (+ פֶּה), גזל *rob* (also גזל מִן), לגזול את עניי עמו *to rob the poor of his people* CD 6$_{16}$, sim. Jg 9$_{25}$, סבב ni. *surround* (also סבב עַל ni. Gn 19$_{4}$ Jos 7$_{9}$), נָסַבּוּ אֶת־הַבַּיִת *they surrounded the house* Jg 19$_{22}$, ידה htp. *confess* (also ידה עַל htp. Ne 1$_{6}$ 9$_{2}$), וְהִתְוַדּוּ אֶת־עֲוֺנָם *and they will confess their iniquity* Lv 26$_{40}$, sim. 16$_{21}$=11QT 26$_{11}$ Lv 16$_{21}$ 26$_{40}$ Nm 5$_{7}$.

(3) שׁכב אֵת *lie with*, in sexual contexts (Gn 19$_{33.34}$ 26$_{10}$ 34$_{7}$ 35$_{22}$ Lv 18$_{22}$ [+ מִשְׁכָּב pl. *(having) intercourse*] 19$_{20}$ [+ שִׁכְבַת־זֶרַע *[with] semen*] 20$_{11.12.13}$ [+ מִשְׁכָּב pl.] 20$_{18.20}$ 1 S 2$_{22}$ and the refs. below), may be transitive ('lay'); note שׁכב with אֹתָהּ *her* (שׁכב אִתָּהּ *lie with her* is unattested) at Gn 34$_{2}$ (|| ענה pi. *rape*) Lv 15$_{18}$ (+ שִׁכְבַת־זֶרַע) 15$_{24}$ Nm 5$_{13}$ (+ שִׁכְבַת־זֶרַע) 5$_{19}$ 2 S 13$_{14}$ (|| ענה pi.) Ezk 23$_{8}$, also יִשְׁכָּבֶנָּה *he will lay her down* Dt 28$_{30(Qr)}$ (Kt ישגלנה *he will rape her* (Kt שׁגל, Qr שׁכב also at Is 13$_{16}$ Jr 3$_{2}$ Zc 14$_{2}$); but שׁכב עִם *lie with* is also common, sometimes near שׁכב אֵת (thus Gn 19$_{32-35}$).

(4) אֵת with cognate accusative, e.g. וְהוּא שֹׁכֵב אֵת מִשְׁכַּב הַצָּהֳרָיִם *and while he was having a midday nap* (lit. *lying the bed of noon*) 2 S 4$_{5}$ (sim. Lv 18$_{22}$ 19$_{20}$ 20$_{13}$ Nm 5$_{13}$, §1h [3]), לעבוד את עבודת העד[ה] *to do the work of the congregation* 1QSa 1$_{13}$, הַזָּב אֶת־זוֹבוֹ *the one that has a flow* (lit. *that flows his flow*) Lv 15$_{33}$ 4QD$^{a}_{14}$.

<COLL> (1) אֵת follows noun, etc., that has verbal force, כְּמַהְפֵּכַת אֱלֹהִים אֶת־סְדֹם וְאֶת־עֲמֹרָה *as God's overturning of Sodom and Gomorrah* Is 13$_{19}$ Jr 50$_{40}$ Am 4$_{11}$, לְיֵשַׁע אֶת־מְשִׁיחֶךָ *for the salvation of your anointed* Hb 3$_{13}$ (or em. ־אֶת to לְיֵשַׁע עַם *for the salvation of the people of* or לְהוֹשִׁיעַ אֶת־עַם *to save the people of*), לְכָבוֹד אֶת־עַבְדֶּךָ *for the honouring of your servant* 1 C 17$_{18}$ (or em. לְכַבֵּד *to honour*), לְמַסַּע אֶת־הַמַּחֲנוֹת *for the travelling of the camps* Nm 10$_{2}$, לְמַשְׂאוֹת אוֹתָהּ *for carrying it* Ezk 17$_{9}$ (or em. לְהַשְׂאוֹת in same sense or לְיוֹם צֵאת *on the day of going out*), מֹצַאֲכֶם אֹתוֹ *your finding him* Gn 32$_{20}$, מְשָׁרְתֵי אֹתִי *those who minister to me* Jr 33$_{22}$ (or em. מְשָׁרְתַי אִתּוֹ *my ministers with him*), הַגְּבוּל סָבִיב אוֹתָהּ *the rim around*, or, *surrounding, it* Ezk 43$_{17}$ (or em. סְבִיבוֹתָיו *around it*), יָצִיעַ סָבִיב אֶת־קִירוֹת הַבַּיִת סָבִיב לַהֵיכָל וְלַדְּבִיר *a structure around the walls of the temple, around the hall and the shrine* 1 K 6$_{5(Qr)}$, וּמְשׂוֹשׂ אֶת־רְצִין perh. *and exaltation of*, i.e. exalting in, *Rezin* Is 8$_{6}$ (or del. אֶת־רְצִין and em. וּמְסוֹס *and melting away*), מִי מָנָה עֲפַר יַעֲקֹב וּמִסְפָּר אֶת־רֹבַע יִשְׂרָאֵל *who has counted the dust of Jacob or 'number-ed' the quarter of Israel?* Nm 23$_{10}$ (Sam וּמִי סָפַר אֶת־ *and who has numbered?*), גולת אל את אישון עינו appar. *God's revelation of*, or *exiling of*, *the apple of his eye* 4QToh A 3.1$_{1}$.

(2) אֵת more closely defines determined object, e.g. וַתִּרְאֵהוּ אֶת־הַיֶּלֶד *and she saw him—the boy* Ex 2$_{6}$, אֹתוֹ כְהַיּוֹם תִּמְצְאוּן אֹתוֹ *him you will find immediately* 1 S 9$_{13}$ (cf. גַּם־אֹתוֹ הַכֻּהוּ *him too, kill* 2 K 9$_{27}$), שלח נביאו למושחני את שמואל *he sent his prophet to anoint me—Samuel* 11QPs^{a} 28$_{8}$, ושלחו לו מחצית העם את אנשי הצבא *and they will send him half the people—the men of war* 11QT 58$_{10}$, וּסְקַלְתֶּם אֹתָם בָּאֲבָנִים וָמֵתוּ אֶת־הַנַּעֲרָה ... וְאֶת־הָאִישׁ *and you will stone them with stones and they will die—the girl ... and the man* Dt 22$_{24(Qr)}$=11QT 66$_{2}$ (וסקלום), כָּל נְדִיב לִבּוֹ יְבִיאֶהָ אֵת תְּרוּמַת י׳ *all the generosity of his heart he is to bring—the contribution for Y.* Ex 35$_{5}$, ויצוהו הַמֶּלֶךְ־אָחָז אֶת־אוּרִיָּה *and King Ahaz commanded him—Uriah* 2 K 16$_{15(Kt)}$, עֲוֺנוֹתָיו יִלְכְּדֻנוֹ אֶת־הָרָשָׁע *his transgressions capture him—the wicked (person)* Pr 5$_{22(L)}$, וּנְטַשְׁתִּיךָ הַמִּדְבָּרָה אוֹתְךָ *and I shall cast you—yes, you—into the desert* Ezk 29$_{5}$, לִהְיוֹת בְּמִקְדָּשִׁי לְחַלְּלוֹ אֶת־בֵּיתִי *to be in my sanctuary to profane it—my temple* 44$_{7}$, יֹאכְלֵם חֹדֶשׁ אֶת־חֶלְקֵיהֶם *a new moon will consume them—their fields* Ho 5$_{7}$ (perh. אֵת = *with*), וַיַּכֵּם חֲזָאֵל ... : ... אֵת כָּל־אֶרֶץ הַגִּלְעָד הַגָּדִי וְהָרְאוּבֵנִי *and Hazael struck them ...—all the land of Gilead, the Gadites, and the Reubenites* 2 K 10$_{33(L)}$, וְשָׁפַט אֶת־יִשְׂרָאֵל אֵת כָּל־הַמְּקוֹמוֹת הָאֵלֶּה *and he judged*

Israel—all these places 1 S 7_{16} (unless אֵת = *with*, specif. near to).

(3) אֵת more closely defines undetermined object, e.g. וַיַּעַשׂ הַמֶּלֶךְ מִשְׁתֶּה ... אֵת מִשְׁתֵּה אֶסְתֵּר *and the king held a feast—the feast of Esther* Est 2_{18}, עָזְבוּ מְקוֹר מַיִם־חַיִּים אֶת־י׳ *they forsook the source of fresh water—Y.* Jr 17_{13}, [ותלד בת] ראישונה את זלפה *and she gave birth to a first daughter—Zilpah* 4QTNaph 2_3, וְחַקּוֹתָ עָלֶיהָ עִיר אֶת־יְרוּשָׁלָםִ *and you are to engrave upon it a city—Jerusalem* Ezk 4_1, אהללה נא אנשי חסד את אבותינו *let me now praise loyal men—our ancestors* Si $44_{1(\mathrm{Bmg})}$, לְעֹשֵׂה אוֹרִים גְּדֹלִים ... : אֶת־הַשֶּׁמֶשׁ ... : אֶת־הַיָּרֵחַ *to the maker of great lights ... the sun ..., the moon* Ps 136_7, וַהֲקִמֹתִי ... רֹעֶה אֶחָד ... אֵת עַבְדִּי דָוִיד *and I shall appoint ... a single shepherd ... —my servant David* Ezk 34_{23}, יָבִיא י׳ עָלֶיךָ ... יָמִים אֲשֶׁר לֹא־בָאוּ ... אֵת מֶלֶךְ אַשּׁוּר *Y. will bring against you ... days (the like of) which have never occurred ... —the king of Assyria* Is 7_{17}, קַדְּשׁוּ עָלֶיהָ גוֹיִם אֶת־מַלְכֵי מָדַי *prepare against her nations—the kings of the Medes* Jr 51_{28}.

(4) (וְ)אֵת follows object without אֵת, e.g. עֹשֶׂה שָׁמַיִם וָאָרֶץ אֶת־הַיָּם וְאֶת־כָּל־אֲשֶׁר־בָּם *maker of heaven and earth, the sea and everything in them* Ps 146_6, וְהָרָאָה וְאֶת־הָאַיָּה וְהַדַּיָּה *and the kite and the falcon and the buzzard* Dt 14_{13} (‖Lv 11_{14} וְאֶת־הַדָּאָה וְאֶת־הָאַיָּה).

וַהֲבֵאתֶם גָּזוּל וְאֶת־הַפִּסֵּחַ וְאֶת־הַחוֹלֶה *and you bring a stolen one or the lame or the sick* Ml 1_{13}, וְיָרְשׁוּ הַנֶּגֶב אֶת־הַר עֵשָׂו וְהַשְּׁפֵלָה אֶת־פְּלִשְׁתִּים *and they will possess the Negeb, Mount Esau, and the Shephelah, (the land of the) Philistines* Ob_{19}, וְיָרְשׁוּ אֶת־שְׂדֵה אֶפְרַיִם ... וּבִנְיָמִן אֶת־הַגִּלְעָד *and they will possess the country of Ephraim ... and Benjamin, Gilead* Ob_{19} (but perh. אֵת defines preceding location more closely, as Coll., §2), יכתובו עם אל ואת שם ישראל ואהרון ושמות *they will write, People of God, and the name of Israel and Aaron and the names of* 1QM 3_{13}.

(5) (וְ)אֵת follows verb with subject suffix, וַיְשַׁנֶּהָ וְאֶת־נַעֲרוֹתֶיהָ *and he changed her and her girls* Est 2_9, אַצִּילְךָ וְאֵת הָעִיר *I shall deliver you and the city* 2 K 20_6‖Is 38_6

2. אֵת before syntactically **undetermined direct object. a.** with כֹּל *all*, נָתַתִּי לָכֶם אֶת־כֹּל *I have given you everything* Gn 9_3.

אֶת־כָּל־ before undetermined object, וַיִּבְרָא אֱלֹהִים ... אֵת כָּל־עוֹף כָּנָף *and God created ... all winged fowl* Gn 1_{21}, נָתַתִּי לָכֶם אֶת־כָּל־עֵשֶׂב זֹרֵעַ זֶרַע *I have given you all seed-producing grass* 1_{29}, sim. 1_{30} 8_{21} 39_{23} 41_{48} Lv $4_{35(\mathrm{L})}$ 11_{15} Nm 34_2 Dt 2_{34} Jos 10_{39} 2 S 6_1 2 K 25_9 Jr 25_{23} 47_4 Ezk 27_5 Jb 41_{26} Ec 4_4 12_{14} Est 2_3 8_{11} 9_{29} (perh. אֵת = *with*).

אֶת־כָּל־אֲשֶׁר (and vars.) *everything that* Gn 1_{31} 12_{20} 24_{36} 25_5 $31_{1.12}$ etc. Dt 13_{16}=11QT 55_7 1QS 1_4 5_{18} 1QH 14_{10} Arad ost. 40_6 ([את כל אשר]).

2b. with אִישׁ *(any) man*, אִשָּׁה *(any) woman*, אִם־נָשַׁךְ הַנָּחָשׁ אֶת־אִישׁ *if a serpent had bitten a man* Nm 21_9 (Sam אֶת־הָאִישׁ *the man*), כִּי־יִגַּח שׁוֹר אֶת־אִישׁ אוֹ אֶת־אִשָּׁה *if an ox gores anyone—male or female* Ex 21_{28}=4Q251 4_4, הַכֹּהֵן הַמַּקְרִיב אֶת־עֹלַת אִישׁ *the priest who presents anyone's sacrifice* Lv 7_8, וַיָּשֶׂם י׳ אֵת חֶרֶב אִישׁ *and Y. set the sword of each man* Jg 7_{22}, הָרְגוּ אֶת־אִישׁ־צַדִּיק *they have killed a righteous person* 2 S 4_{11}, הִכָּה אֶת־אִישׁ מִצְרִי אִישׁ מַרְאֶה *he killed (the) Egyptian man, a man of (striking) appearance* 23_{21} (‖1 C 11_{23} אֶת־הָאִישׁ הַמִּצְרִי *the Egyptian man*), להדף את איש יודע מלחמות *to drive out whoever knows war* (Goliath) Si 47_5, אִישׁ אֲשֶׁר יִקַּח אֶת־אִשָּׁה *a man who takes a woman* Lv 20_{14}, אִישׁ אֲשֶׁר יִנְאַף אֶת־אֵשֶׁת אִישׁ *a man who commits adultery with the wife of a(nother) man* 20_{10}.

2c. with numeral, לֹא הֲרֵעֹתִי אֶת־אַחַד מֵהֶם *I did not harm one of them* Nm 16_{15}, קַח ... אֶת־אַחַד מֵהַנְּעָרִים *take ... one of the lads* 1 S 9_3, וַיָּמָד אֶת־סַף הַשַּׁעַר ... וְאֵת סַף אֶחָד *and he measured the threshold of the gate ... and one threshold* Ezk 40_6, וְלָקַחְתָּ אֶת־שְׁתֵּי אַבְנֵי־שֹׁהַם *and you are to take (the) two stones of onyx* Ex 28_9 ($35_{27.27}$ 39_6 (אֶת־אַבְנֵי הַשֹּׁהַם), אתן לך את שני [לוחות] האבן *I will give you the two tablets of stone* 4QJub[a] 1_6, [את ארבעת מינים] הגדולים האלה] עשה *these four great kinds he made* 6_4, sim. 6_{10} ([את שלשה]) 6_{14} ([את] של[ושה]) 7_3 ([את] ארבעה), אֶת־שֶׁבַע כְּבָשֹׂת תִּקַּח *you will take (the) seven ewes* Gn 21_{30} (Sam הַכְּבָשׂוֹת), וַיִּקַּח ... אֵת עֶשֶׂר־נָשִׁים פִּלַגְשִׁים *and he took ... (the) ten women (who were) concubines* 2 S 20_3 (sim. 15_{16}), בַּאֲכֹל הָאֵשׁ אֵת חֲמִשִּׁים וּמָאתַיִם אִישׁ *when the fire consumed (the) two hundred and fifty men* Nm 26_{10}, וַיִּבֶן אֶת־עֶשְׂרִים אַמָּה *and he built* (the) twenty cubits 1 K 6$_{16}$.

2d. with other objects, וְהִשִּׂיג לָכֶם דַּיִשׁ אֶת־בָּצִיר וּבָצִיר יַשִּׂיג אֶת־זָרַע *and for you, threshing will overtake vintage and vintage will overtake sowing* Lv 26$_{5}$, וִיאַבֵּד אֶת־לֵב מַתָּנָה *and a gift destroys reason* Ec 7$_{7}$, וּמָדְדוּ אֶת־תָּכְנִית *and they will measure (the) plan* Ezk 43$_{10}$, כְּאָב אֶת־בֵּן יִרְצֶה *as a father* reproves *a son he loves* Pr 3$_{12}$.

לָעוּת אֶת־יָעֵף דָּבָר perh. *to help (the) weary somewhat* Is 50$_{4}$, הָאֱלֹהִים יְבַקֵּשׁ אֶת־נִרְדָּף *God seeks (the) pursued* Ec 3$_{15}$, וַיְחַזֵּק חָרָשׁ אֶת־צֹרֵף *and (the) carpenter encourages (the) smith* Is 41$_{7}$, פָּגַעְתָּ אֶת־שָׂשׂ *you encounter (the) one who rejoices* 64$_{4}$, וָאֶשְׁמַע אֵת מִדַּבֵּר אֵלָי *and I hear one speaking to me* Ezk 2$_{2}$ (sim. 43$_{6}$ lacks אֵת).

וַיַּצֶּב ... אֶת־מַצֶּבֶת אֲשֶׁר בְּעֵמֶק־הַמֶּלֶךְ *and he erected ... (the) pillar that is in the valley of the king* 2 S 18$_{18}$, כָּרַת אֶת־כְּנַף אֲשֶׁר לְשָׁאוּל *he cut (the) hem belonging to Saul* 1 S 24$_{6}$ (mss ins. הַמְּעִיל hem *of the robe*), את מקו[ם ש]ל *(the) land that belongs to* Mur 22 1$_{2}$.

עבד אֶת־אֱלֹהִים *serve (foreign) gods* Jos 24$_{14.15}$ Jr 16$_{13}$ (sim. GnzPs 2$_{20}$), י׳ שֹׁמֵר אֶת־גֵּרִים *Y. guards (the) strangers* Ps 146$_{9}$, תִּקַּח אֶת־זָרִים *she receives strangers* Ezk 16$_{32}$ (or em. אֶתְנַנִּים *fees*), וְאֶת־צַדִּיקִים יְשַׁלֶּם־טוֹב *and he will reward righteous ones well* Pr 13$_{21}$, יכבד את חסידים *he will honour loyal ones* 4Q521 1.2$_{7}$, אֶת־יְתוֹמִים יָבֹזּוּ *they plundered (the) orphans* Is 10$_{2}$, וּפָגְשׁוּ צִיִּים אֶת־אִיִּים *and wild animals will meet hyenas* 34$_{14}$, וַיַּעַשׂ אֶת־אֵילִים *and he made (the) pillars* Ezk 40$_{14}$.

לְבַקֵּשׁ אֶת־פַּרְעֹשׁ אֶחָד *to seek a single flea* 1 S 26$_{20}$, תבער את דם נקי *you will purge (the) innocent blood* 11QT 63$_{7}$ (||Dt 21$_{9}$ תְּבַעֵר הַדָּם הַנָּקִי), אֶת־קַשׁ יָבֵשׁ תִּרְדֹּף *will you pursue dry chaff?* Jb 13$_{25}$, וְאֶת־כָּל־בֵּית גָּדוֹל שָׂרַף *and every large house he burned* 2 K 25$_{9}$||Jr 52$_{13}$ (הַגָּדוֹל), וְאֶת־עַם עָנִי תּוֹשִׁיעַ *and a poor people you save* 2 S 22$_{28}$ (or em. וְאַתָּ *and you*; ||Ps 18$_{28}$ כִּי־אַתָּה *for you*), אֶת־עַם נוֹעָז לֹא תִרְאֶה *a savage people you will not see* Is 33$_{19}$ (or em. אַתָּ), השליך ... [את שני] תולע *throw ... (the) scarlet material* 4QToh B^{a}$_{6}$ (Lv 14$_{6.51}$ אֵת/אֶת־שְׁנִי הַתּוֹלַעַת).

וַיִּתֶּן־לָהּ ... אֵת גֻּלֹּת עִלִּיּוֹת וְאֵת גֻּלֹּת תַּחְתִּיּוֹת *and he gave her ... (the) upper pools and (the) lower pools* Jos 15$_{19}$=Jg 1$_{15}$ (perh. pl.n. 'Upper and Lower Gulloth'; sim. 4Q522 1$_{15}$), ברכו את שם הקדוש *bless the holy name* Si 39$_{35}$ (unless הקדוש = *of the holy one*; sim. GnzPs 1$_{22}$).

חובש את עצם דכים *binding the bone of (the) crushed* GnzPs 4$_{1}$, וַיִּשְׂרֹף אֶת־עַצְמוֹת אָדָם *and he burned bones of people* 2 K 23$_{20}$ (sim. 1 K 13$_{2}$), לָמָּה תִשְׁמַע אֶת־דִּבְרֵי אָדָם *why do you hear (the) words of human beings?* 1 S 24$_{10}$, הִצִּיל אֶת־נֶפֶשׁ אֶבְיוֹן *he rescued (the) soul of (the) poor* Jr 20$_{13}$, אֶת־דַּכְּאֵי־רוּחַ יוֹשִׁיעַ *(the) crushed of spirit he saves* Ps 34$_{19}$, וַיַּעַשׂ אֶת־בֵּית בָּמוֹת *and he made the house of*, or perh. *for, (the) high places* 1 K 12$_{31}$, כְּשָׁמְעֲךָ אֶת־קוֹל צְעָדָה *when you hear a sound of marching* 2 S 5$_{24(Qr)}$ (||1 C 14$_{15}$ הַצְּעָדָה).

אַל־תִּלְחַם אֶת־לֶחֶם רַע עָיִן *do not eat a miser's food* Pr 23$_{6}$ (ms lacks לֶחֶם, with אֵת = *with* a miser), וידע את שני מעמד *and he knows (the) years of (their) existence* CD 2$_{9}$, המציל את חוסי בו *who rescues those wo take refuge in him* Si 51$_{8}$, [ועשי]תה את מסבה צפון להיכל *and you are to make (the) staircase north of the temple* 11QT 30$_{5}$, וּמַדֹּתֶם ... אֶת־פְּאַת־קֵדְמָה ... וְאֶת־פְּאַת־נֶגֶב ... וְאֶת־פְּאַת־יָם ... וְאֵת פְּאַת צָפוֹן *and you are to measure ... (the) east side ... and (the) south side ... (and) the west side ... and (the) north side* Nm 35$_{5}$, כל [ע]בדך את קצר ואסם *your servant finished harvest(ing) and stored* Meṣad Ḥashavyahu ost. 1$_{6}$ (or em. קצרו/ה; others קצרו אסם *his harvest, [then] he stored*), perh. את אדם *humanity* or *a person* 4Q521 4$_{6}$, את זבול *loftiness* 4Q298 3$_{3}$ (verb missing in both).

3a. אֵת before **indirect object,** e.g. וְהִנְחַלְתִּי אֶת־שְׁאֵרִית הָעָם הַזֶּה אֶת־כָּל־אֵלֶּה *and I shall bequeath the remnant of this people all these things* Zc 8$_{12}$, הַיְלָדִים אֲשֶׁר־חָנַן אֱלֹהִים אֶת־עַבְדֶּךָ *the children whom God spared (for) your servant* Gn 33$_{5}$, וְלֹא־עָנוּ ... אֹתוֹ דָּבָר *but they did not reply ... anything to him* 1 K 18$_{21}$ 2 K 18$_{36}$||Is 36$_{21}$, יבכר י׳ את א[דנ]י דבר *may Y. quickly cause my lord to know a matter* Lachish ost. 2$_{5}$, וימלא אותי כול משאלות לבי *and he has fulfilled for me all the desires of my heart* GnzPs 3$_{7}$.

הַגֵּד אֶת־בֵּית־יִשְׂרָאֵל אֶת־הַבַּיִת *describe the temple (to) the Israelites* Ezk 43$_{10}$, אֶת־מִי הִגַּדְתָּ מִלִּין *(to) whom have you told things?* Jb 26$_{4}$, הֶרְאָה אֹתִי אֱלֹהִים גַּם אֶת־זַרְעֶךָ *God has also shown me your offspring* Gn 48$_{11}$ (sim. Lachish ost. 6$_{1}$; contrast, e.g., הֶרְאָנוּ אֶת־כָּל־אֵלֶּה *he showed us all these things* Jg 13$_{23}$), [אני אראה א]ת

בני ישראל וידעו appar. *I shall show the sons of Israel* (with ellipsis of direct object), *that they might know* 4QpsEzek^{a} 2_{3}, הִשְׁמִיעַ אֶת־מַחֲנֵה אֲרָם קוֹל רֶכֶב *he caused the camp of Aram to hear the sound of chariotry* 2 K 7_{6}, יַשְׁמִעוּ דְּבָרַי אֶת־עַמִּי *let them proclaim my words to my people* Jr 23_{22}, ישמע י׳ את אדני ש[מ]עת שלם *may Y. cause my lord to hear a report of peace* Lachish ost. 2_{2} 3_{3} ([את]), sim. 4_{1} 5_{1} (both [את]) 8_{1} 9_{1}.

וְלִמַּדְתֶּם אֹתָם אֶת־בְּנֵיכֶם *and you are to teach your children them* Dt 11_{19}, גַּם אֶת־הָרָעוֹת לִמַּדְתְּ אֶת־דְּרָכָיִךְ *you have even taught the wicked women your ways* Jr $2_{33(Qr)}$, לִמַּדְתִּי אֶתְכֶם חֻקִּים *I have taught you statutes* Dt 4_{5} (sim. $4_{1.14}$ 6_{1} $31_{19.22}$ Ec 12_{9} Si $45_{17.17}$), יִרְאוּ אֶת־הַלֶּחֶם אֲשֶׁר הֶאֱכַלְתִּי אֶתְכֶם *they will see the bread which I fed (to) them* Ex 16_{32}, וְהַאֲכַלְתִּי אֶת־מוֹנַיִךְ אֶת־בְּשָׂרָם *and I shall feed (to) your oppressors their own flesh* Is 49_{26}, וְהִשְׁקָה אֶת־הָאִשָּׁה אֶת־מֵי הַמָּרִים *and he will make the woman drink the bitter water* Nm 5_{24} (sim. 5_{26}), וְהִשְׁקִיתָה אוֹתוֹ אֶת־כָּל־הַגּוֹיִם *and you are to make all the nations drink it* Jr 25_{15}, משיאים את העם עוון *making the people bear iniquity* 4QMMT A 2_{32} (sim. 2_{13} Lv 22_{16}).

3b. אֵת before **accusative of respect,** חָלָה אֶת־רַגְלָיו *he was ill with his feet* 1 K 15_{23} (|| 2 C 16_{12} בְּ in same sense), וּנְמַלְתֶּם אֵת בְּשַׂר עָרְלַתְכֶם *and you are to be circumcised in your foreskin* Gn 17_{11} (sim. 17_{14}), אַחַר הִתְגַּלְּחוֹ אֶת־נִזְרוֹ *after he has shaved himself of his Nazirite (hair)* Nm 6_{19}, נִשְׁבַּרְתִּי אֶת־לִבָּם ... וְאֵת עֵינֵיהֶם *I was broken with respect to their heart ... and their eyes* Ezk 6_{9} (or em. וְשָׁבַרְתִּי *and I shall break*), ונענשו את רביעית לחמו *and he will be fined a quarter of his food* 1QS 6_{25} (אֵת with passive verb, as §4c; sim. 4Q251$_{4.9}$ [both ונענש]), וַיִּתְנַכְּלוּ אֹתוֹ *and they conspired against him* Gn 37_{18}, נָגַשׂ אֶת־הַכֶּסֶף וְאֶת־הַזָּהָב אֶת־עַם הָאָרֶץ *he oppressed the people of the land in respect of silver and gold,* i.e. he exacted money from them 2 K 23_{35}, וְאֵת פְּדוּיֵי ... הָעֹדְפִים ... : וְלָקַחְתָּ חֲמֵשֶׁת חֲמֵשֶׁת שְׁקָלִים *and as the redemption price of ... the additional persons ... you are to take five shekels apiece* Nm 3_{46}.

וכסה את בגדיו *and he will cover in respect of,* i.e. put on, *his clothes* 4QRitPur 1_{14}, אם נצחו את אויביהמה *if they are victorious in respect of,* i.e. defeat, *their enemies* 11QT 58_{11}, ו[נפסד את] הכול appar. *and he will be lost in respect of,* i.e. will lose, *everything* Mur 24 2_{12} (unless *and everything will be lost,* as §4c).

3c. with **objects of time,** וּזְרַעְתֶּם אֵת הַשָּׁנָה הַשְּׁמִינִת *and you are to sow the eighth year* Lv 25_{22}, וָאֶתְנַפַּל ... אֵת אַרְבָּעִים הַיּוֹם וְאֶת־אַרְבָּעִים הַלַּיְלָה *and I prostrated myself ... (the) forty days and (the) forty nights* Dt 9_{25}, יזו את השנ[ית] *they will sprinkle the second (time)* 11QT $50_{3(Yadin)}$ (sim. 4QToh A 2.1_{1}), ישקודו ... את שלישית כול לילות השנה *they will keep watch ... a third of all the nights of the year* 1QS 6_{7}, [חכרתי מן ש]מעון ... את [ח]מ[ש שנים] *I have leased from Simeon ... (for) five years* Mur 24 2_{10}, בהושע ישראל את הראשונה *when Israel was saved the first time* CD 5_{19}, מַצּוֹת יֵאָכֵל אֵת שִׁבְעַת הַיָּמִים *unleavened bread will be eaten seven days* Ex 13_{7} (in both אֵת with passive verb, as §4c), יהו בו אצלך תשבת *may they be there with you (on the) Sabbath* MurEpBarC$^{b}_{6}$ (אֵת with היה, as §4a, 2).

3d. מלא אֵת **be full of,** שׂבע אֵת **be satisfied with,** אֶת חֲמַת י׳ מָלֵאתִי *I am full of Y.'s anger* Jr 6_{11}, מָלֵאתִי כֹחַ אֶת־רוּחַ י׳ *I am full of strength, of the spirit of Y.* Mc 3_{8}, הֶחָצֵר מָלְאָה אֶת־נֹגַהּ כְּבוֹד י׳ *the court was full of the shining of Y.'s glory* Ezk 10_{4}, וּמָלְאוּ בָּתֵּי מִצְרַיִם אֶת־הֶעָרֹב *and the houses of Egypt will be full of swarms (of insects)* Ex 8_{17} (also without אֵת, e.g. Jg 16_{27} Hb 3_{3} Ps 33_{5} 104_{24} 119_{64}.

מלא אֵת ni. *be filled with,* וַיִּמָּלֵא הַבַּיִת אֶת־הֶעָנָן *and the temple was filled with the cloud* Ezk 10_{4}, וַתִּמָּלֵא הָאָרֶץ אֹתָם *and the land was filled with them* Ex 1_{7}, sim. 1 K $7_{14.14.14}$ 2 K 3_{20} (see also Nm 14_{21} Ps 72_{19} at §4c).

מלא אֵת pi. *fill with,* מלא ציון את הודך *fill Zion with your glory* Si $36_{19(B)}$ (|| מִן *with;* Bmg מִן both times), לְמַלְאָם אֶת־פִּגְרֵי הָאָדָם *to fill them with human corpses* Jr 33_{5}.

וְעַמִּי אֶת־טוּבִי יִשְׂבָּעוּ *and my people will be satisfied with my goodness* Jr 31_{14}, וּשְׂבַעְתֶּם אֹתוֹ *and you will be satisfied with it* Jl 2_{19}.

4a. אֵת before **subject of active verb.**

(1) with intransitive verb, פן תסוב את נחלתך *lest your inheritance go away* Si 9_{6} (or em. תָּסֵב *you cause your inheritance to go away*), אֶת־עַמּוּד הֶעָנָן לֹא־סָר ... וְאֶת־עַמּוּד הָאֵשׁ ... לְהָאִיר לָהֶם וְאֶת־הַדֶּרֶךְ *and the pillar of cloud did not depart ..., nor the pillar of fire ...*

to light for them, nor the way Ne 9$_{19}$ (mss אֶת־הַדֶּרֶךְ to show them *the way*), אֶת־נַהֲרֹתֶיהָ הֹלֵךְ *her rivers (were) going* Ezk 31$_{4}$ (perh. אֵת = *with*; or em. הֹלִיכָה *she caused* her rivers *to go*), אֵת כָּל־הָרָעָה הַזֹּאת בָּאָה *all this trouble has come* Dn 9$_{13}$, וְאֶת־הַבַּרְזֶל נָפַל אֶל־הַמָּיִם *and the iron (blade) fell into the water* 2 K 6$_{5}$, אֵת כָּל־מִבְרָחָיו ... יִפֹּלוּ *all his fugitives ... will fall* Ezk 17$_{21(Qr)}$, אֶת־הַנָּשִׂיא נָשִׂיא הוּא יֵשֶׁב־בּוֹ *the prince will sit there* 44$_{3}$ (or em. אַךְ *only* the prince), לֹא יִמַּס אֶת־לְבַב אֶחָיו *the heart of his comrades will not melt* Dt 20$_{8}$=11QT 62$_{4}$ (Sam יָמֵיס he will not *cause* his comrades' heart *to melt*), אֵת כָּל־דְּגַת יְאֹרֶיךָ בְּקַשְׂקְשֹׂתֶיךָ תִּדְבָּק *all the fish of your Nile will stick in your scales* Ezk 29$_{4}$, כִּי־יֵיטַב אֶל־אָבִי אֶת־הָרָעָה עָלֶיךָ *if your misfortune is pleasing to my father* 1 S 20$_{13}$, אַל־יֵרַע בְּעֵינֶיךָ אֶת־הַדָּבָר *let not the matter be bad in your eyes* 2 S 11$_{25}$ (mss lack אֶת־), אַל־יִמְעַט לְפָנֶיךָ אֵת כָּל־הַתְּלָאָה *let not all the weariness be too little for you* Ne 9$_{32}$ (sim. Jos 22$_{17}$ at §4b), וַתֶּחֱנַף אֶת־הָאָרֶץ *and the land was polluted* Jr 3$_{9}$ (or em. וַתַּחֲנִף *and she polluted*), אמר לסור את דעתם *he commanded that their knowledge depart* CD 10$_{9}$.

(2) with היה *be*, אִישׁ אֶת־קֳדָשָׁיו לוֹ יִהְיוּ *(for) each man —his holy things are his own* Nm 5$_{10}$, אֶת־שְׁנֵי הַגּוֹיִם וְאֶת־שְׁתֵּי הָאֲרָצוֹת לִי תִהְיֶינָה *the two nations and the two lands will be mine* Ezk 35$_{10}$, אֵת אֲשֶׁר־עֲדֶן לֹא הָיָה *the one who has still not been* Ec 4$_{3}$, וַיְהִי לִמְנַשֶּׁה ... בֵּית־שְׁאָן וּבְנוֹתֶיהָ ... וְאֶת־יֹשְׁבֵי דֹאר וּבְנֹתֶיהָ *and to Manasseh belonged Beth-shean and its villages ... and the inhabitants of Dor and its villages* Jos 17$_{11}$, [וא]ת הלחיים ואת הקבה לכהנים יהיה ... וללויים את השכם *and the cheeks and the stomach will be for the priests ... and the shoulder for the Levites* 11QT 22$_{9}$.

(3) with transitive verb, אֶת־מַלְכֵינוּ ... לֹא עָשׂוּ תּוֹרָתֶךָ *our kings ... did not carry out your law* Ne 9$_{34}$ (or em. אַף *but*), חַי־י׳ אֵת אֲשֶׁר עָשָׂה־לָנוּ אֶת־הַנֶּפֶשׁ *by the life of Y. who made for us the soul* Jr 38$_{16(Kt)}$, וְאֵת אֲשֶׁר לֹא־יִתֵּן אֶת־צַוָּארוֹ *and whoever does not place his neck* 27$_{8}$.

4b. אֵת before **subject or predicate of nom. cl.**, אֶת־כָּל־אֵלֶּה אֲשֶׁר שָׂנֵאתִי *all these are things that I hate* Zc 8$_{17}$, אֶת־כָּל־אֵלֶּה אַנְשֵׁי־חָיִל *all these were warriors* Jg 20$_{44.46}$, הַנּוֹתָר אֶת־הֶהָמוֹן הַזֶּה *what remains is this pile* 2 C 31$_{10}$, הַמְעַט־לָנוּ אֶת־עֲוֹן פְּעוֹר *was the sin of Peor too little for us?* Jos 22$_{17}$, אֵי־חֲנִית הַמֶּלֶךְ וְאֶת־צַפַּחַת הַמַּיִם *where is the king's spear and the jar of water?* 1 S 26$_{16}$ (or em. וְאֵי־ *and where is?*), וְאֶת־הָאָח לְפָנָיו מְבֹעָרֶת *the brazier was in front of him, burning* Jr 36$_{22}$ (or em. וְאֵשׁ־ *and the fire of* the brazier), וְאֶת־כָּל־הָאָרֶץ הִיא *and that is the whole land* 45$_{4}$ (mss, KtOr לִי *[belong] to me* for הִיא; or em. חִיא to אַכֶּה *I shall strike*), אֵת הֶעָרִים אֲשֶׁר תִּתְּנוּ לַלְוִיִּם אֵת שֵׁשׁ־עָרֵי הַמִּקְלָט *the cities you are to give the Levites are the six cities of refuge* Nm 35$_{6}$, כָּל־הֶעָרִים ... אַרְבָּעִים וּשְׁמֹנֶה עִיר אֶתְהֶן וְאֶת־מִגְרְשֵׁיהֶן *all the cities ... are forty-eight—these and their pastures* 35$_{7}$, וְלִבְנֵי גֵרְשׁוֹן ... אֶת־עִיר מִקְלַט הָרֹצֵחַ *and to the Gershonites ... was the city of refuge for a killer* Jos 21$_{27}$ (sim. 21$_{28-39}$; but perh. אֵת marks objects of נתן *give* [21$_{21}$] throughout), וּבְנֵי חֶצְרוֹן ... אֶת־יְרַחְמְאֵל וְאֶת־רָם וְאֶת־כְּלוּבָי *and the sons of Hezron ... were Jerahmeel, Ram, and Chelubai* 1 C 2$_{9}$, וְאֵת הִתְיַחֵשׂ הַכֹּהֲנִים לְבֵית אֲבוֹתֵיהֶם *and the enrolment of the priests was by ancestral household* 2 C 31$_{17}$ (or em. זֹאת *this was*), מֶה הָאָדָם שֶׁיָּבוֹא אַחֲרֵי הַמֶּלֶךְ אֵת אֲשֶׁר־כְּבָר עָשׂוּהוּ *what is the person who comes after the king? What they have already done* Ec 2$_{12}$ (or em. מַה־יַּעֲשֶׂה הָאָדָם *what will the person do?* and עָשָׂה הוּא *he has done* for עָשׂוּהוּ [mss עָשָׂהוּ *he has done (it)*]), אֵת אֲשֶׁר־נָתַן י׳ *(it is) what Y. has given* 1 S 30$_{23}$ (perh. אֵת = *with*; or em. אַחֲרֵי *seeing* what Y. has given), אֶת־הַדָּבָר אֲשֶׁר *(it) is the word that* Hg 2$_{5}$ (perh. אֵת = *with*; or em. זֹאת הַבְּרִית *this is the covenant* or del. אֵת), הֲלוֹא אֶת־הַדְּבָרִים אֲשֶׁר *surely (they) are the words that* Zc 7$_{7}$ (or em. אֶת־ to אֵלֶּה *these are*), וְאֵת פְּאַת *and (this is) the boundary of* Ezk 47$_{17.18.19}$ (mss זֹאת *this is* in all three), אֵין־אֶתְכֶם אֵלַי *you were not to me*, i.e. you did not return to me Hg 2$_{17}$, [ו]ל[ו] את הממשלה appar. *and to him is the government* 4Q462$_{8}$.

4c. אֵת before **subject of passive verb** (some perh. accusatives of respect, as §3b), אֶת־אַרְבַּעַת אֵלֶּה יֻלְּדוּ לְהָרָפָה *these four were born to the giants* 2 S 21$_{22}$ (‖1 C 20$_{8}$ אֵל נוּלְּדוּ *these were born*), הֻלֶּדֶת אֶת־פַּרְעֹה *Pharoah's being born* Gn 40$_{20}$ (sim. Ezk 16$_{4.5}$; all three + יוֹם *the day of*), וַיִּוָּלֵד לַחֲנוֹךְ אֶת־עִירָד *and to Enoch was born Irad* Gn 4$_{18}$ (sim. 21$_{5}$ 46$_{20.20}$ Nm 26$_{60.60.60.60}$), הִגָּמֵל אֶת־יִצְחָק *Isaac's being weaned* Gn 21$_{8}$ (+ יוֹם), לֹא־יִקָּרֵא עוֹד אֶת־שִׁמְךָ אַבְרָם *no more will your name be called Abram*

17_5 (mss, Sam omit אֵת), הִמָּשַׁח אֹתוֹ *his being anointed* Lv 6_{13} Nm $7_{10.84}$ (all three + יוֹם) 7_{88}, וַיֻּגַּד לְדָוִד אֵת אֲשֶׁר־עָשְׂתָה רִצְפָּה *and it was told David what Rizpah had done* 2 S 21_{11} (sim. Gn 27_{42} Jos 9_{24} 1 K 18_{13}), הוּקַם אֶת־דִּבְרֵי יְהוֹנָדָב *the words of Jonadab have been fulfilled* Jr 35_{14}, יְבֻקַּשׁ אֶת־עֲוֹן יִשְׂרָאֵל ... וְאֶת־חַטֹּאת יְהוּדָה *the iniquity of Israel ... and the sins of Judah will be sought* 50_{20}, ואת חק יתרדף appar. *and (the) statute will be pursued* 4Q521 1.3_1 (אֵת with undetermined noun, as §2d), וְיִמָּלֵא כְבוֹדוֹ אֶת־כֹּל הָאָרֶץ *and all the earth was full of his glory* Ps 72_{19} (sim. Nm 14_{21}), ואחר [יוזה עליו] את מימי ח[ז]יה ... ואת כול *and afterwards there will be sprinkled on him the waters of sprinkling ... and all* 4QRitPur 1_6 (mg Baillet) (sim. 1_7), אַחֲרֵי הֻכַּבֵּס אֹתוֹ *after it has been washed* Lv 13_{56} (Sam הכבסו *they washed*; sim. 13_{55}), אַחֲרֵי הִטּוֹחַ אֶת־הַבָּיִת *after the house has been replastered* 14_{48}, אִם אֶת־כָּל־דְּגֵי הַיָּם יֵאָסֵף לָהֶם *or were all the fish of the sea gathered for them* Nm 11_{22}, בְּגוֹרָל יֵחָלֵק אֶת־הָאָרֶץ *by lot will the land be divided* 26_{55}, יוּמַת נָא אֶת־הָאִישׁ *let, pray, the man be killed* Jr 38_4, הַנִּלְכָּד בַּחֵרֶם יִשָּׂרֵף בָּאֵשׁ אֹתוֹ וְאֶת־כָּל־אֲשֶׁר־לוֹ *anyone captured in the ban will be burnt in the fire—he and all that he has* Jos 7_{15}, וְאֵת הַפָּר הַשֵּׁנִי הֹעֲלָה *and the second bull had been sacrificed* Jg 6_{28}, גַּם־אוֹתוֹ לְאַשּׁוּר יוּבָל *it too will be carried to Assyria* Ho 10_6 (or em. יוֹבִלוּ *they will carry*), וַיּוּשַׁב אֶת־מֹשֶׁה וְאֶת־אַהֲרֹן אֶל־פַּרְעֹה *and Moses and Aaron were taken back to Pharaoh* Ex 10_8, וְנִשָּׂא־בָם אֶת־הַשֻּׁלְחָן *and by them the table will be carried* 25_{28} (Sam וְנָשְׂאוּ *and they will carry*; ||37_{15} לָשֵׂאת אֶת־הַשֻּׁלְחָן *to carry the table*), וְנִשָּׂא אֶתְכֶם בְּצִנּוֹת perh. *and you will be lifted up with hooks* Am 4_2 (or em. אַפְּכֶן *your nose* will), בַּחֵיק יוּטַל אֶת־הַגּוֹרָל *the lot is cast into the lap* Pr 16_{33}, וְהוּבָא אֶת־בַּדָּיו בַּטַּבָּעֹת *and its poles will be brought through the rings* Ex 27_7 (Sam וְהֵבֵאתָ *and you will bring*; ||38_7 וַיָּבֵא *and he brought*), לֹא־הוּבָא אֶת־דָּמָהּ *its blood was not brought* Lv 10_{18} (sim. 16_{27}), לֹא תִנָּתֵן אֶת־הָעִיר *let not the city be given* 2 K 18_{30} (||Is 36_{15} lacks אֶת־), יֻתַּן אֶת־הָאָרֶץ *let the land be given* Nm 32_5, יֻתַּן אֶת־אֲבִישַׁג *let Abishag be given* 1 K 2_{21}, אֵת כָּל־אֲשֶׁר תֹּאמַר יִנָּתֵן לָהּ *let everything she mentions be given her* Est 2_{13}, perh. ונתון לו את בלהה *and Bilhah was given to him* 4QTNaph 2_{10} (unless נָתוֹן *one gave*, as §1d), את רוחו לא תבלע *his spirit will not be swallowed* 4Q416 9.1_3 (unless תִּבְלַע *you will swallow*, as §1c), הפקח נא את אזן עבדך *let, pray, your servant's ear be opened* Lachish ost. 3_5 (unless הַפְּקַח *open*, pray).

5. as resumptive or **emphatic particle,** בְּמִשְׁפָּטַי מָאָסוּ וְאֶת־חֻקּוֹתַי לֹא־הָלְכוּ בָהֶם *they rejected my judgments and did not walk in my statutes* Ezk 20_{16}, עַל־הָרָעָה אֲשֶׁר הֵבֵאתִי עַל־יְרוּשָׁלַםִ אֵת כָּל־אֲשֶׁר הֵבֵאתִי עָלֶיהָ *concerning the misfortune I have brought against Jerusalem—everything that I have brought against it* 14_{22} (or em. אֶל־ *concerning*), אל יגע בו את לחמו *let him not touch it—his bread* 4QToh A 2.1_7, וְנָתַתִּי אוֹתָם עָלָיו אֶת־עֵץ יְהוּדָה *and I shall place them upon it—the stick of Judah* Ezk 37_{19} (or del. עָלָיו and em. אוֹתָם to אִתּוֹ *with it* or אֶת־ to עַל *upon*), אֵלֶּה בְּנֵי לֵאָה ... וְאֵת דִּינָה *these are the sons of Leah ... and Dinah* Gn 46_{15}, מֵאֵל אָבִיךָ ... וְאֵת שַׁדַּי *from your father's God ... and Shaddai* 49_{25} (mss, Sam אֵל *El*-Shaddai), הברית אשר כרת משה ... את הבר[י]ת לש[וב] *the covenant which Moses made ... the covenant to return* CD 15_9, וְהִבִּיטוּ אֵלַי אֵת אֲשֶׁר־דָּקָרוּ *and they will look at me—the one that they have stabbed* Zc 12_{10}, בַּעֲבֹדָה קָשָׁה ... אֵת כָּל־עֲבֹדָתָם *with hard work ... —all their work* Ex 1_{14}, אֶת־מְקוֹם כִּסְאִי וְאֶת־מְקוֹם כַּפּוֹת רַגְלַי *(this is) the place of my throne and the place of the soles of my feet* Ezk 43_7 (or ins. הֲרָאִיתָ *have you seen?*, or em. אֵת to זֶה *this is*, מַה־מַּשָּׂא י׳ ... אֶת־מַה־מַּשָּׂא וְנָטַשְׁתִּי אֶתְכֶם *what is the burden of Y.? ... What is (the) burden? (That) I shall cast you off* Jr 23_{33} (or em. אַתֶּם הַמַּשָּׂא *you are the burden*), עַל־כֵּן יֵאָמַר ... אֶת־וָהֵב ... וְאֶת־הַנְּחָלִים *therefore it is said ..., Waheb ... and the streams* Nm 21_{14}.

Also 11QPs^{a} 28_{14} 11QT 3_{10} 19_2 20_1 + Sup (ת[א]) 20_1 + Sup 21_4 + Sup 23_{17} $24_{1.2}$ 45_{18} $49_{2.4}$ fr. $2_{1.3}$ 4QRitMar 94_5 4QPrQuot 40.2_1 4QPrFêtes^{c} 12.2_4 (אותכ[ה]) 58_4 143_3 $183_{10(mg)}$ (Baillet אתן) 188_2 4QRitPur 16_6 23_3 (ת[א]) 4QOrd^{a} 1.2_2 5_4 4QOrd^{b} $10.2_{4.5}$ $20_{3(mg)}$ 4QM^{a} fr. 16_5 4QDibHam^{a} 1.3_7 1.8_5 7_1 12_2 (אותנ[ו]) 26_6 4QVisSam 2_1 4QpIsa^{e} 6_7 1QDM 3_7 1QNoah $3_{5.6}$ 6QapSam/Kings $58_{2(mg)}$ 4QapLam^{a} 1.1_4 4QHymSap 15_1 4QpPs^{a} 1.3_{20} 1.4_{14} 4QpHos^{b} 19_2 4QpUnid 1_4 4QFlor 4_1 6_1 11_2 4QCat^{a} $1_{5.12.12}$ 7_4 4QAges 1_5 1Q30 1_3 1Q36 7_3 4QTanḥ 16_2 2Q27 1_3 6QfrProph 1_2 5QToponyms 1_2 2_2 4_1 (ת[א])

51.2 (both [וא[ת]) 4QpsMose 2.110.11 4QpsJubc 13 24 4Qp Gena 63 4QToh A 2.21 4QBerb 21 4Q285 42 4QMish Ce 12 4Q416 110 512 4Q525 51.4 ([א]ת) 4QJuba 43.3 4QAcademyFr 13.7 Mur 22 12 Mur 24 411 5/6ḤevBA 447 Bar-Kochba Deed of Sale 5/6ḤevBA 46 (twice) MurEpJonathan3.5 Arad ost. 57 125 ([א]ת) 166.8 4014 1119.

אֵת II 931.7.41.9 prep. **with**—אֶת־; with sf. אִתִּי (אִתִּי, אוֹתִי), אִתְּךָ (Q אתכה, אוֹתְךָ, אִתָּךְ, אוֹתָךְ, אִתֵּךְ, אִתָּךְ, אִתְּךָ) אִתָּךְ (Q אתוה, I אתה, אוֹתוֹ, אִתּוֹ) אִתּוֹ (מֵאִתֵּךְ, אוֹתָךְ, אִתָּךְ), אִתָּם (אֶתְכֶם) אִתְּכֶם (אוֹתָנוּ, אִתָּנוּ) אִתָּנוּ, אִתָּהּ, אִתָּם, Q אתמה, אוֹתָם).

1. together with, along with, and, joining two nouns (or noun and pronoun, two pronouns, noun-phrase and noun, etc.), **a.** each having similar semantic role in relation to verb, היה *be* Gn 2120 345 (+ מִקְנֶה *livestock*) 392.21 Nm 14 Jos 219 627 Jg 119 1411 1 S 293 1 K 1125 (or em. זֹאת *this* was the evil) 2 K 113‖2 C 2212 2 K 118‖2 C 237 2 K 1519 (subj. יָד *hand*) 2525 Jr 2624 (subj. יָד) 412.3.3 Ezk 2117 Am 514 Pr 241 Ru 32, מצא ni. *be found* Gn 449.10 Ex 3523.24 1 C 298 2 C 2929, הלך *go* Gn 124 135 1424 Nm 1029 2220 2313(Qr) Jos 1024 Jg 13.3.17 74.4 (‖ עִם *with*) 1 S 2323 2 S 316 1326 (‖ עִם) 1511.19 1617 1927 1 K 1315 224 (‖2 C 183 עִם) 2 K 37 63.4 828‖2 C 225 2 K 1016 Jr 1910 5159 Ml 26 Pr 111.15 1320 Ru 118 1QS 820 919 1QM 75, htp. *walk together* 1QS 62, בוא *come* Ex 11 Dt 195 317 1 S 165 1734 (וְאֶת־הַ־; mss וְהַ־) 296.10 1 K 137.16 Jr 404.4 Pr 2224 Ca 48.8 4QMa fr. 110 ([א]יבו), יצא *go out* Gn 1131 1 S 223 281 296 2 S 2117 Jr 2916.

ירד *go down* Gn 4423 1 S 266 2 K 115.15 Ezk 3117 3230 1QM 76, hi. *send down* Ezk 2620 3116 3218 (or em. אַתָּה *you*), ho. *be sent down* 3118, נפל *fall* 305 4722 (or em. hi. *cause to fall*), שכב *lie down* 2 S 712 119 Ezk 3118 3227.28.29.29.30, ho. *be laid* 3219.32, שׁוּב *go back* 1 K 1316.19 Ru 110 1QS 625 (others יָשִׁיב *he will answer*, with אֵת object-marker), עבר *cross* Nm 3229.30 2 S 1533 1934.37.39, עלה *go up* Gn 507.14 Ex 1238 Jg 13.16 1 S 219 2 S 1935, hi. *raise* Is 6311 (perh. אֵת object marker), עמד *stand* Gn 451 Nm 15, רום *be high* Ezk 1017, נשׂא *carry* Ex 1822 Nm 1117 Ezk 3224.25.30, נתן *place* Is 539 Ezk 3229, חיה *live* Zc 109, גדל *grow up* 1 K 128.10‖2 C 108.10, pi. *magnify* Ps 344, מול ni. *be circumcised* Gn 1727, ישׁב *dwell* 2455 3410.16.22.23 Ex 221 Jos 1563 Jg 116.21 1711 194 1 S 2223 2 S 1618 1 K 218 Jr 168 405.6 5039 Pr 329 Ru 223 2 C 618, *sit* 2 K 632 Jb 213, hi. *accommodate* Ezk 2620, לין *pass the night* Lv 1913 (subj. פְּעֻלָּה *wage*) 2 S 178 (unless hi. with object marker, *cause* people *to pass night*) 198 Jb 194 (subj. מְשׁוּגָה *error*), אכל *eat* Gn 4316.32.32 1 K 1316, ברה *eat* 2 S 1217, לחם *eat* Pr 231, שׁתה *drink* 1 K 1316, קצר *harvest* Meṣad Ḥashavyahu ost. 110, צחק pi. *play* Gn 268, שׂמח *rejoice* Is 6610 (‖ בְּ *with*, + Jerusalem), שׂושׂ *rejoice* 6610, המה *murmur* 4QpsEzeka 32 (ולבי[ן] הומה את נפשי *and my heart murmurs, with my soul*), יעץ ni. *take counsel* 1 K 126.8‖2 C 106.8 Is 4014, עלל htpo. *behave* wickedly Ps 1414, נכה hi. *strike* 2 K 1525.25 (or move אֶת־הָאַרְגֹּב וְאֶת־הָאַרְיֵה *with Argob and with Arieh* to 1529, with אֵת object marker), ho. *be struck* Nm 2514, סוף hi. *destroy* Zp 13, ספה *destroy* Dt 2918, שׁחת hi. *destroy* Gn 613 (+ אֶרֶץ *earth*), רעה *shepherd* Gn 372.

1b. in nom. cl., מִי אִתִּי *who is with me?* 2 K 932, י׳ אוֹתִי *Y. is with me* Jos 1412 Jr 2011, י׳ אִתּוֹ *Y. is with him* Gn 393.23, י׳ אִתָּנוּ *Y. is with us* Nm 149, אִתְּךָ אֲנִי *I am with you* (sg.) Is 432.5 (־אֲנִי in both) Jr 18.19 1520 3011 4628, אִתְּךָ אָנֹכִי *I am with you* Gn 2624, אֲנִי אִתְּכֶם *I am with you* (pl.) Hg 113 24, var. Jr 4211, אִתָּם ... אֲנִי *I ... am with them* Ezk 3430, מלך הכבוד אתנו *the king of glory is with us* 1QM 128 191, אֲחִיתֹפֶל אִתּוֹ *Ahithophel was with him* 2 S 1615, אֶת־אָבִינוּ ... הַקָּטֹן *the little one ... is with our father* Gn 4213.32, אֲחִיכֶם אִתְּכֶם *your brother is with you* 433.5, שָׁם אִתָּנוּ נַעַר *a lad was with us there* 4112, בָּנַי הִנָּם אִתְּכֶם *my sons, behold, are with you* 1 S 122, אִתְּכֶם בְּנֵי אֲדֹנֵיכֶם *with you are your master's sons* 2 K 102, בְּנֵי הַמֶּלֶךְ ... אֶת־גְּדֹלֵי הָעִיר *the king's sons ... were with the elders of the city* 106, שְׁלֹשִׁים וּשְׁנַיִם מֶלֶךְ אִתּוֹ *thirty-two kings were with him* 1 K 201, עֲשֶׂרֶת אֲלָפִים אֶת־אִישׁ יְהוּדָה *ten thousand were with*, i.e. from, *the men of Judah* 1 S 154.

פָּרַס ... אִתָּם *Persia ... is with them* Ezk 385, צֶאֱצָאֵיהֶם אִתָּם *their offspring are with them* Is 6523, עַמִּים רַבִּים אִתָּךְ *many peoples are with you* Ezk 386.15 (unless with verb בוא *come*), כָּל־בְּנֵי אַשּׁוּר אוֹתָם *all the Assyrians are with them* Ezk 23$_{23}$ (mss אִתָּם; unless with verb בוא hi. *bring*).

אֶת־מִי־אֵין כְּמוֹ־אֵלֶּה *with whom are there not such things?* Jb 12$_{3}$, את אל משפט כול חי *with God is the judgment of each living being* 1QS 10$_{18}$, שַׁעֲשֻׁעַי אֶת־בְּנֵי אָדָם *my delight was (to be) with human beings* Pr 8$_{31}$, אֶת־יְשָׁרִים סוֹדוֹ *his counsel is with the upright* 3$_{32}$, אֶת־צְנוּעִים חָכְמָה *wisdom is with the modest* 11$_{2}$, אֶת־נוֹעָצִים חָכְמָה *wisdom is with those who take advice* 13$_{10}$, כָּבוֹד אִתִּי *glory is with me* 8$_{18}$, כול כבוד אתכה הוא *all glory is with you* 1QH 11$_{8}$, אתכה אור *with you is light* 18$_{3}$, רוב הדר אתם *abundance of splendour is with them* 4Q416 4$_{14}$, דבר המלך אתכם *the king's word is with*, i.e. binding on, *you* Arad ost. 24$_{17}$, [מס]פר שמות כול צבאם אתכה *the number of the names of all their army is with you* 1QM 12$_{2(\text{Yadin})}$, תּוֹרַת י׳ אִתָּנוּ *the law of Y. is with us* Jr 8$_{8}$, הַאֱמֶת אִתְּכֶם *is truth with you?*, i.e. are you speaking the truth? Gn 42$_{16}$.

הֲיַד יוֹאָב אִתָּךְ *is the hand of Joab with you?* 2 S 14$_{19}$, שְׂפָתֵינוּ אִתָּנוּ *our lip is with us* Ps 12$_{5}$, נפשו אתו *his soul is with him*, i.e. he feels well Si 34$_{20}$, מָה אִתָּנוּ *what is with us?*, i.e. what do we have? 1 S 9$_{7}$, הַכֶּסֶף אִתִּי *the money is with me* Jg 17$_{2}$, כַּסְפָּם וּזְהָבָם אִתָּם *their silver and their gold is with them* Is 60$_{9}$ (unless with verb בוא hi. *bring*), אִתָּנוּ אֲחֻזַּת נַחֲלָתֵנוּ *with us is the possession of our inheritance* Nm 32$_{32}$ (or em. אַתָּ[ה] תְּנָה *you, give!* or אָתָנוּ *has come to us*), אִתְּכֶם הָרֶכֶב *with you is the chariotry* 2 K 10$_{2}$, שְׂכָרוֹ אִתּוֹ וּפְעֻלָּתוֹ לְפָנָיו *his payment is with him and his reward is before him* Is 40$_{10}$ 62$_{11}$.

כָּל־הָעָם אֲשֶׁר אֶת־ *all the people who were with* + pr.n.m. 1 S 13$_{22}$ 2 S 20$_{15}$ Jr 41$_{13}$, הָעָם אֲשֶׁר(־)אִתּוֹ *the people who are with him* Gn 32$_{8}$ Jos 8$_{11}$ (הָעָם הַמִּלְחָמָה) Jg 4$_{13}$ 7$_{1}$ 9$_{33.35.48}$ 1 S 14$_{17}$ (לָעָם) 14$_{20}$ 30$_{4.21}$ 2 S 3$_{31}$ 6$_{2}$ 15$_{30}$ 16$_{14}$ 17$_{2.16.22.29}$ (לָעָם) 18$_{1}$, הָעָם אֲשֶׁר(־)אִתָּךְ *the people who are with you* Jg 7$_{2}$ 9$_{32}$, הָעָם אֲשֶׁר אִתִּי *the people who are with me* Gn 33$_{15}$ Jos 8$_{5}$, עַמִּים אֲשֶׁר אִתָּךְ *peoples that are with you* Ezk 39$_{4}$, sim. 38$_{22}$, רַבִּים אֲשֶׁר אִתָּנוּ מֵאֲשֶׁר אוֹתָם *those who are with us are greater than those who are with them* 2 K 6$_{16}$.

חֵיל כַּשְׂדִּים אֲשֶׁר אֶת־רַב־טַבָּחִים *the army of Chaldaeans that was with the captain of the guards* Jr 52$_{14}$, הַצָּבָא אֲשֶׁר־אִתּוֹ *the army that was with him* 2 S 3$_{23}$, הַחַיִל אֲשֶׁר־אִתּוֹ *the army that was with him* 24$_{2}$, בְּנֵי־חַיִל אֲשֶׁר אִתּוֹ *the warriors that were with him* 17$_{10}$, רָאשֵׁי אַלְפֵי יִשְׂרָאֵל אֲשֶׁר אִתּוֹ *the heads of the clans of Israel that were with him* Jos 22$_{30}$, כול בני ישראל אשר אתו *all the Israelites that are with him* 11QT 58$_{20}$, עֲבָדָיו אֲשֶׁר־אִתּוֹ *his servants who were with him* 2 S 15$_{14}$, סְרִיסֵי פַרְעֹה אֲשֶׁר אִתּוֹ *Pharaoh's eunuchs who were with him* Gn 40$_{7}$, הָאֲנָשִׁים אֲשֶׁר(־)אִתּוֹ *the men that were with him* 24$_{32}$ 1 S 22$_{6}$ (אֲנָשִׁים) 2 S 1$_{11}$ 17$_{12}$ Jr 41$_{7}$, מֵאָה־אִישׁ אֲשֶׁר־אִתּוֹ *a hundred men that were with him* Jg 7$_{19}$, שְׁלֹשׁ־מֵאוֹת הָאִישׁ אֲשֶׁר אִתּוֹ *the three hundred men that were with him* 8$_{4}$, sim. 1 S 30$_{9}$.

הַמְּלָכִים אֲשֶׁר אִתּוֹ *the kings that were with him* Gn 14$_{5.17}$ 2 K 25$_{28}$‖Jr 52$_{32(\text{Qr})}$, הַשָּׂרִים אֲשֶׁר אִתּוֹ *the princes that were with him* Nm 22$_{40}$ (לַשָּׂרִים) Est 3$_{1}$, sim. Jr 41$_{11.13.16}$ 42$_{8}$, ה[לויי]ם אשר אתו *the Levites who are with him* 1QM 18$_{6(\text{Yadin})}$, הַטַּף אֲשֶׁר אִתּוֹ *the infants that are with him* 2 S 15$_{22}$, הַקְּרֻאִים אֲשֶׁר אִתּוֹ *the guests that were with him* 1 K 1$_{41}$.

כָּל־אֲשֶׁר אִתִּי *everyone who is with me* Jg 7$_{18}$, sim. Gn 7$_{23}$ 20$_{16}$ 2 S 16$_{21}$, הַנָּבִיא אֲשֶׁר־אִתּוֹ חֲלוֹם ... וַאֲשֶׁר דְּבָרִי אִתּוֹ *the prophet with whom there is a dream ... and whoever my word is with* Jr 23$_{28}$, כָּל־נֶפֶשׁ (הַ)חַיָּה אֲשֶׁר אִתְּכֶם *every living creature that is with you* Gn 9$_{10.12}$, sim. 8$_{1.17}$ 9$_{10}$, הָאַרְגַּז אֲשֶׁר־אִתּוֹ *the chest that was with it* 1 S 6$_{15}$, בִּגְדֵי עֵשָׂו ... אֲשֶׁר אִתָּהּ בַּבָּיִת *the clothes of Esau ... which were with her in the house* Gn 27$_{15}$, כָּל־אֲשֶׁר אִתָּהּ בַּבַּיִת *everyone who is with her in the house* Jos 6$_{17}$, אֲשֶׁר יִמָּצֵא אִתּוֹ *whoever it is found with* Gn 44$_{9.10}$, sim. Ex 35$_{23.24}$.

יֵשׁ אִתָּךְ *there is with you*, i.e. you have, you can Pr 3$_{28}$ Si 5$_{12}$, יֵשׁ אוֹתוֹ דְּבַר־י׳ *the word of Y. is with him* 2 K 3$_{12}$, sim. Jr 27$_{18}$, איש אשר יש אתו דבר *a man that has a message* 1QS 6$_{12}$, יש אתי דבר *I have a message* 6$_{13}$, אִם־יֵשׁ אֶת־נַפְשְׁכֶם *if there is with your soul*, i.e. if you wish Gn 23$_{8}$, הֲיֵשׁ אֶת־לְבָבְךָ יָשָׁר *is there with your heart straightforwardness?* 2 K 10$_{15}$ (or del. אֶת־, *is your heart straightforward[ness]?*), יֵשׁ־אֶת־עֲבָדֶיךָ חֲמִשִּׁים אֲנָשִׁים *there are with your servants fifty men* 2$_{16}$, יֵשׁ אָחִינוּ הַקָּטֹן אִתָּנוּ *our youngest brother is with us* Gn 44$_{26}$.

לִבְּךָ אֵין אִתִּי *your heart is not with me* Jg 16$_{15}$, אין אתם

יראת י' *they have no reverence for Y.* Si 16$_{2}$, אֵינֶנּוּ אִתָּנוּ *he is not with us* Gn 44$_{26.30}$, sim. 44$_{34}$, אִישׁ אֵין אִתָּךְ *there is no one with you* 1 S 21$_{2}$, sim. Is 63$_{3}$, אֵין־זָר אִתָּנוּ בַּבַּיִת *there was no stranger with us in the house* 1 K 3$_{18}$, לֹא־אִתָּנוּ יֹדֵעַ *there is no one with us that knows* Ps 74$_{9}$, אוֹר־עֵינַי ... אֵין אִתִּי *the light of my eyes ... is not with me* 38$_{11}$, הֵיטִיב אֵין אוֹתָם *to do good is not with,* i.e. impossible for, *them* Jr 10$_{5}$, טוֹב שְׁפַל־רוּחַ אֶת־עֲנָוִים *it is better (to be) lowly of spirit with the poor* Pr 16$_{19(Qr)}$.

<COLL> הוּא נַעַר אֶת־בְּנֵי בִלְהָה וְאֶת־בְּנֵי זִלְפָּה *he was a lad with the sons of Bilhah and with the sons of Zilpah* Gn 37$_{2}$, מַה־לַתֶּבֶן אֶת־הַבָּר *what is there to straw with wheat,* i.e. what have they in common? Jr 23$_{28}$.

הַמִּשְׁכָּן ... וְאֶת־מָסַךְ פֶּתַח הֶחָצֵר ... וְאֵת מֵיתָרָיו perh. the duty of the sons of Gershon was *the Tabernacle ... with both the screen for the entrance to the court ... and its cords* Nm 3$_{26}$.

הָרָוָה אֶת־הַצְּמֵאָה *the quenched with the thirsty* Dt 29$_{18}$, הָאֲרִי וְאֶת־הַדּוֹב *the lion with the bear* 1 S 17$_{34}$ (mss וְהַדּוֹב), צִיִּים אֶת־אִיִּים *jackals with wild beasts* Jr 50$_{39}$, איש את רעהו *a man with his fellow, with one another* 1QS 6$_{2}$ 8$_{20}$ 9$_{19}$, המשיח אתם *the Messiah with them* 1QSa 2$_{12}$, אֵשֶׁת נֹחַ ... אִתָּם *Noah's wife ... with them* Gn 7$_{13}$, הָעֹבְרִים אֶת־הַנּוֹתָרִים *the travellers with those who remain* Ezk 39$_{14}$, הַמַּכְשֵׁלוֹת אֶת־הָרְשָׁעִים *the stumbling blocks with the wicked* Zp 1$_{3}$, שְׁאוֹל אֶת־עֹזְרָיו *Sheol with its helpers* Ezk 32$_{21}$ (unless with verb דבר pi. *speak*), [עצמתו] ועצמ[ת] אמתה א[ת]ה *his bones and the bones of his maidservant with him* Siloam royal steward tomb inscr. 1$_{2}$.

י' ... אֶת־אַחֲרֹנִים *Y ..., with (the) last (ones)* Is 41$_{4}$, אַתָּה וּבָנֶיךָ אִתָּךְ *you and your sons with you* Lv 10$_{9}$ Nm 18$_{1.2.7}$ (אִתָּךְ), sim. Gn 9$_{8}$ 46$_{7}$ Ex 28$_{1.41}$ 29$_{21.21}$||Lv 8$_{30.30}$ Lv 8$_{2}$ 10$_{14.15}$ Nm 18$_{1}$, שְׁנֵי בְנֵיכֶם אִתְּכֶם *your two sons with you* 2 S 15$_{27}$, כָּל־אַחֶיךָ ... אִתָּךְ *all your brothers ... with you* Nm 16$_{10}$, אַתָּה וּבָנֶיךָ וְאִשְׁתְּךָ וּנְשֵׁי־בָנֶיךָ אִתָּךְ *you and your sons and your wife and your sons' wives with you* Gn 6$_{18}$, var. 8$_{16}$, sim. 7$_{7}$ 8$_{18}$, לְבָנֶיךָ וְלִבְנֹתֶיךָ אִתָּךְ *to your sons and your daughters with you* Nm 18$_{11.19}$, לְךָ וּלְזַרְעֲךָ אִתָּךְ *to you and your descendants with you* Gn 28$_{4}$ Nm 18$_{19}$.

כָּל־יֹשְׁבֵי יְרוּשָׁלַםִ אִתּוֹ *all the inhabitants of Jerusalem with him* 2 K 23$_{2}$, הוּא וְעַמּוֹ אִתּוֹ *he and his people with him* Ezk 30$_{11}$, הוּא וְכָל־בְּנֵי־יִשְׂרָאֵל אִתּוֹ *he and and all the Israelites with him* Nm 27$_{21}$, יַעֲקֹב וְכָל־זַרְעוֹ אִתּוֹ *Jacob and all his descendants with him* Gn 46$_{6}$, חֲשַׁבְיָה וְאִתּוֹ יְשַׁעְיָה *Hashabiah and with him Jeshaiah* Ezr 8$_{19}$, שָׂרֵי מוֹאָב אִתּוֹ *the princes of Moab with him* Nm 23$_{17}$, צָדוֹק וְכָל־הַלְוִיִּם אִתּוֹ *Zadok and all the Levites with him* 2 S 15$_{24}$, הָעָם ... אֶת־אַבְשָׁלוֹם *the people ... with Absalom* 15$_{12}$, האנשם את אלישע perh. *the men with Elisha* Arad ost. 24$_{19}$, וַאֲנָשִׁים ... אִתּוֹ *and men ... with him* 1 K 11$_{17}$ Jr 26$_{22}$, עֲשָׂרָה אֲנָשִׁים אִתּוֹ *ten men with him* 2 K 25$_{25}$||Jr 41$_{1}$, sim. 2 S 3$_{20}$, אִתּוֹ שְׁלֹשֶׁת־אֲלָפִים אִישׁ *thirty men with him* 1 S 26$_{2}$, עֶשְׂרִים עֲבָדָיו אִתּוֹ *his twenty servants with him* 2 S 19$_{18}$, עֲדַת יִשְׂרָאֵל ... אִתּוֹ *the congregation of Israel ... with him* 1 K 8$_{5}$.

וַיַּרְא ... אִתָּם אֶת־בִּנְיָמִין *when he saw ... Benjamin with them* Gn 43$_{16}$ (Sam אִתָּם וְאֶת־ *them and Benjamin*), לֹא תַעֲשׂוּן אִתִּי אֱלֹהֵי כֶסֶף *you are not to make gods of silver (to be) with me* Ex 20$_{23}$, אֵין לְזָרִים אִתָּךְ *not for strangers (who are) with you* Pr 5$_{17}$, זְכַרְתַּנִי אִתְּךָ *remember me (when I was) with you* Gn 40$_{14}$, זְכֹר אֲנִי וָאַתָּה אֵת רֹכְבִים צְמָדִים אַחֲרֵי אַחְאָב *remember me and you with riders close behind Ahab* 2 K 9$_{25}$, לְהַחֲיוֹת אִתָּךְ *to keep (them) alive with you* Gn 6$_{19}$, אם צריך אתך *if needing is with you,* perh. if you must Si 35$_{7(Bmg)}$ (B אם צריך אתה *if you must;* F אם צורך אותך appar. *if there is a need with you,* i.e. if you need), בני את כל מלאכתיך בענוה הלוך *my son, with all your possessions, go humbly* Si 3$_{17(C)}$ (A בְּ *despite,* or *with*).

2. with, to, linking verb (+ object noun) to additional noun; in transitive constructions, some confusion with אֵת I (object marker) is possible, + דבר pi. *speak* Gn 17$_{3.22.23}$ 21$_{2}$ 23$_{8}$ 34$_{6.8}$ 35$_{13.14.15}$ 41$_{9}$ 42$_{7.30}$ 45$_{15}$ Ex 25$_{22}$ 31$_{18}$ 34$_{29.32.33.34.35}$ Nm 3$_{1}$ 7$_{89}$ (|| אֶל speak *to*) 26$_{3}$ Dt 5$_{24}$ Jos 17$_{14}$ 22$_{15.21}$ 2 S 3$_{27}$ 7$_{7}$||1 C 17$_{6}$ 1 K 8$_{15}$||2 C 6$_{4}$ 1 K 22$_{24}$||2 C 18$_{23}$ 2 K 25$_{6}$||Jr 39$_{5}$||52$_{9}$ 2 K 25$_{28}$||Jr 52$_{32}$ Jr 1$_{16}$ 4$_{12}$ 5$_{5}$ 7$_{22}$ 9$_{7}$ 12$_{1}$ 34$_{3}$ 35$_{2}$ 38$_{25}$ Ezk 2$_{1}$ 3$_{22.24.27}$ 14$_{4}$ (|| אֶל) 20$_{3}$ 33$_{30.30}$ 44$_{5}$ Zc 8$_{16}$ Ps 12$_{3}$ 109$_{2}$ 127$_{5}$ Dn 1$_{19}$ 2 C 10$_{10}$ (||1 K 12$_{10}$ אֶל) 22$_{10}$ (perh. אֵת = *against,* i.e. condemn) 1QS 7$_{5}$, חוה pi. *speak* Jb 32$_{6}$, אור hi. *make* face *shine* upon Ps 67$_{2}$.

כרת *cut* covenant (except Hg 2$_{5}$ דָּבָר *word*) Gn 15$_{18}$

Ex 34$_{27.27}$ Dt 5$_{3.3}$ 28$_{69.69}$ 29$_{13.14.14}$ 31$_{16}$ 2 S 3$_{12.13.21}$ 2 K 17$_{15.35.38}$ Is 28$_{15}$ (|| עִם *with;* + מָוֶת *death*) Jr 11$_{10}$ 31$_{31.31.32.33}$ 34$_{8.13}$ Ezk 17$_{13}$ Hg 2$_5$ Zc 11$_{10}$ Ps 105$_9$||1 C 16$_{16}$ (11QPs^a עם) 4QDibHam^a 3.2$_{13}$, קום *be established* (of agreement with Sheol) Is 28$_{18}$, hi. *establish* covenant (except 1 K 6$_{12}$ דָּבָר) Gn 6$_{18}$ 9$_{9.9}$ (+ זֶרַע *seed*) 9$_{10}$ (+ נֶפֶשׁ *life*) 9$_{11}$ 17$_{21}$ Ex 6$_4$ Lv 26$_9$ 1 K 6$_{12}$ Ezk 16$_6$, פרר hi. *break* covenant Lv 26$_{44}$ Jg 2$_1$ 1 K 15$_{19}$||2 C 16$_3$ Jer 14$_{21}$ Ezk 17$_{16}$ 4QDibHam^a 1.5$_8$, ho. *be cancelled* (of covenant) Jr 33$_{21.21}$, כפר pu. *be cancelled* (of covenant with death) Is 28$_{18}$.

היה *be* (of covenant) Ezk 37$_{26}$ Ml 2$_{4.5}$, שׁאר ni. *remain* Jos 23$_{7.12}$, חלק pi. *share* booty Is 53$_{12}$ Pr 16$_{19}$, נחל *have a portion* with Nm 32$_{19}$, מנה ni. *be counted* Is 53$_{12}$, יחד *be united* 14$_{20}$, שׂיח pol. *consider* Is 53$_8$, חתן htp. *become related* (through marriage) to one another Gn 34$_9$ 1 K 3$_1$, אמן ni. *be constant* to Ps 78$_8$, באשׁ ni. *be odious* to 2 S 16$_{21}$, תעב ni. *be repugnant* to 1 C 21$_6$ (subj. דָּבָר *matter*), עזב *abandon* loyalty Ru 2$_{20.20}$.

עשׂה *do, perform* to, for Gn 24$_{49}$ (obj. חֶסֶד *loyalty*, אֱמֶת *reliability*) 32$_{11}$ (obj. אֱמֶת) Dt 1$_{30}$ 10$_{21}$ Jg 11$_{27}$ (obj. רָעָה *evil*) 1 S 12$_{7.7}$ (obj. צְדָקָה *righteousness*) 24$_{19}$ 2 S 2$_6$ (both with obj. טוֹבָה *goodness*) 2 K 18$_{31}$||Is 36$_{16}$ (obj. בְּרָכָה *blessing*) Jr 33$_9$ (obj. טוֹבָה) Ezk 17$_{17}$ 22$_{11}$ (obj. תּוֹעֵבָה *abomination*) Mc 5$_{14}$ Zc 7$_9$ (obj. חֶסֶד) Ru 2$_{11}$, *deal* with Jr 21$_2$ Ezk 7$_{27}$ 16$_{59}$ 20$_{44}$ 22$_{14}$ 23$_{25.29}$ 39$_{24}$ Zp 3$_{19}$ Zc 1$_6$ Ps 109$_{21}$.

כון hi. *appoint* for 2 C 35$_{20}$, פקד hi. *assign* to Gn 40$_4$ Jr 40$_7$ 41$_{10}$, ho. *be assigned* to Lv 5$_{23}$, צוה pi. *command* (blessing) for Dt 28$_8$, חשׁב pi. *reckon*, i.e. keep a check on 2 K 12$_{16}$ 22$_7$, משׁך *extend* hand Ho 7$_5$, ערב htp. *come to terms* with 2 K 18$_{23}$||Is 36$_8$ 2 K 18$_{23}$ (אֶת־מֶלֶךְ *with the king of;* mss, ||Is 36$_8$ הַמֶּלֶךְ *the king*), שׁלם hi. *make peace* with Jos 10$_{1.4.4}$ 2 S 10$_{19}$ Pr 16$_7$, רעה htp. *associate* with Pr 22$_{24}$, שׁכן *make one's abode* Lv 16$_{16}$ Is 57$_{15}$ 11QT 29$_8$, גור *take up residence* Ex 12$_{48}$ Lv 19$_{33.34}$ Nm 9$_{14}$ 15$_{14.16}$ Ezk 47$_{23}$ (|| בְּתוֹךְ *among* 47$_{22}$).

בוא *come* Ezk 16$_8$ (+ בִּבְרִית *into a covenant*), hi. *bring* with Gn 46$_7$, קרב hi. *bring near* with Nm 18$_2$, שׁוב hi. *bring* with 1 K 13$_{18}$, עלה hi. *raise, take* with Ex 13$_{19}$, לקח *take* with Gn 22$_3$ Ex 17$_5$ 1 S 9$_3$ 2 K 3$_{26}$, צפן *store* Pr 2$_1$ 7$_1$, יצא hi. *bring out* with Gn 8$_{17(Kt)}$, שׁלח *send* with 24$_{40}$ 42$_4$ 2 S 13$_{27}$ 1 K 1$_{44}$, pi. Gn 43$_4$.

In nom. cl., מִשְׁפָּטִי אֶת־י׳ וּפְעֻלָּתִי אֶת־אֱלֹהָי *my judgment is with Y. and my recompense with my God* Is 49$_4$.

<COLL> זֶה חַסְדְּךָ אֶת־רֵעֶךָ *is this your loyalty to your friend?* 2 S 16$_{17}$, זֹאת בְּרִיתִי אוֹתָם *this is my covenant with them* Is 59$_{21}$, מִשְׁפַּט הַכֹּהֲנִים אֶת־הָעָם *the judgment of the priests (in connection) with the people* 1 S 2$_{13}$, אֵין לוֹ חֵלֶק ... אִתְּכֶם *he has no share ... with you* Dt 12$_{12}$. חַסְדּוֹ אֶת־הַחַיִּים וְאֶת־הַמֵּתִים *his loyalty to the living and to the dead* Ru 2$_{20}$, בְּרִיתוֹ אֶת־אַבְרָהָם אֶת־יִצְחָק וְאֶת־יַעֲקֹב *his covenant with Abraham, with Isaac, and with Jacob* Ex 2$_{24}$, sim. 2 K 13$_{23}$, בְּרִיתִי אוֹתָךְ *my covenant with you* Ezk 16$_{60}$, var. Gn 17$_4$, לֹא אֶת־בְּנֵיכֶם *it was not with your children* Dt 11$_2$ (perh. ellipsis of כרת בְּרִית *make a covenant*), יִפָּתַח פִּיךָ אֶת־הַפָּלִיט *your mouth will be opened to the fugitive* Ezk 24$_{27}$, שְׁלֵמִים הֵם אִתָּנוּ *they are at peace with us* Gn 34$_{21}$, וּבָחַנְתָּ לִבִּי אִתָּךְ *and you have tested my heart,* i.e. attitude, *towards you* Jr 12$_3$.

3. under the control of, in the care of, e.g. צְרוּרָה בִּצְרוֹר הַחַיִּים אֵת י׳ *bound up in the bundle of life, or in the document of the living, in the care of Y.* 1 S 25$_{29}$, אֲשֶׁר יִהְיֶה לְךָ אֶת־אָחִיךָ *whatever you possess (that is) under the control of,* i.e. lent to, *your brother* Dt 15$_3$, אֲשֶׁר־הָיָה מִקְנְךָ אִתִּי *what has been (the condition of) your livestock in my care* Gn 30$_{29}$, מִסְפַּר־חֳדָשָׁיו אִתָּךְ *the number of his months is under your control* Jb 14$_5$, נָתַתִּי אִתּוֹ אֵת אָהֳלִיאָב *I have put Oholiab at his disposal* Ex 31$_6$, אִתּוֹ אָהֳלִיאָב *Oholiab was at his disposal* 38$_{23}$, כָּל־הַנֶּפֶשׁ אֲשֶׁר הִנִּיחַ ... אֶת־גְּדַלְיָהוּ *all the people whom he had left ... in the care of Gedaliah* Jr 43$_6$, שִׁלְחָה הַנַּעַר אִתִּי *send the lad in my care* Gn 43$_8$, גָּנוּב הוּא אִתִּי perh. *it is stolen (if it is) in my care* 30$_{33}$, בְּאָמְנָה אִתּוֹ *during (her) fosterage with him* Est 2$_{20}$.

4a. in the presence of, near to, e.g. וַיִּתְהַלֵּךְ חֲנוֹךְ אֶת־הָאֱלֹהִים *and Enoch walked in the presence of God* Gn 5$_{22.24}$, אֶת־הָאֱלֹהִים הִתְהַלֶּךְ־נֹחַ *Noah walked in the presence of God* 6$_9$, הִתְהַלַּכְנוּ אִתָּם בִּהְיוֹתֵנוּ בַּשָּׂדֶה *we lived in their presence when we were in the field* 1 S 25$_{15}$, וְאֵת כֹּל וְנֹכַחַת perh. *and before all you will be justified* Gn 20$_{16}$, שָׁתָה אֶפְרֹחֶיהָ אֶת־מִזְבְּחוֹתֶיךָ *she placed her chicks before your altars* Ps 84$_4$, כָּתְבָהּ עַל־לוּחַ אִתָּם *write it on a* *tablet in their presence* Is 30_{8} (or del. אִתָּם), פְּשָׁעֵינוּ אִתָּנוּ *our sins are before us* 59_{12}, וְנוֹדְעָה יַד־י׳ אֶת־עֲבָדָיו *and the hand of Y. is revealed in the presence of his servants* 66_{14}, בַּעֲוֹנֹת אֲבֹתָם אִתָּם יִמָּקּוּ *because of the iniquities of their ancestors they will pine away in their presence*, i.e. because of them, *(as well)* Lv 26_{39}, בְּתִתָּם סִפָּם אֶת־סִפִּי *when they put their threshold by my threshold* Ezk 43_{8} (‖ אֵצֶל *alongside*), מָקוֹם אִתִּי *there is a place next to me* Ex 33_{21}, in geographical descriptions, הַפְּסִילִים ... אֶת־הַגִּלְגָּל *Pesilim ... near Gilgal* Jg 3_{19}, אֵלוֹן בְּצַעֲנַנִּים ... אֶת־קֶדֶשׁ *Elon-bezaanannim ... near Kedesh* 4_{11}, עֶצְיוֹן־גֶּבֶר ... אֶת־אֵלוֹת *Ezion-geber ... near Eloth* 1 K 9_{26}, גּוּר ... אֶת־יִבְלְעָם *Gur ... near Ibleam* 2 K 9_{27} (all with אֲשֶׁר *which is* after first name).

4b. usu. אֶת־פְּנֵי **in the presence of, in front of,** like לִפְנֵי, followed by י׳ *Y.* (including pronom. ref. to Y.) unless stated, + גדל *be great* Gn 19_{13}, היה *be* great 1 S 2_{17}, ישׁב *dwell* Ps 140_{14}, חנה *encamp* Gn 33_{18} (+ עִיר *city*), עמד *stand* 19_{27} 1 K 12_{6} (+ Solomon; ‖2 C 10_{6} לִפְנֵי), ראה ni. *show oneself* Ex $34_{23.24}$ Dt $16_{16.16}$ 31_{11} 1 S 1_{22}, נחה hi. *lead* 22_{4} (+ מֶלֶךְ מוֹאָב *king of Moab*), נזה hi. *sprinkle* Lv $4_{6.17}$ (both + פָּרֹכֶת *curtain*, ‖ לִפְנֵי), חדה pi. *gladden* Ps 21_{7}, שׁרת pi. *minister* 1 S 2_{11} (+ Eli) 2_{18} Est 1_{10} (+ Ahasuerus); in nom. cl., אֶת־פְּנֵי מֵבִין חָכְמָה *before the understanding person is wisdom* Pr 17_{24}, שֹׂבַע שְׂמָחוֹת אֶת־פָּנֶיךָ *there is fulness of joy in your presence* Ps 16_{11}.

5. in contention with, against, + היה *be* (of battle) 2 S 21_{15} 1 C 20_{5} (‖2 S 21_{19} עִם *against*), עשׂה *do, make* Gn $14_{2.2}$ Jos 11_{18} (all three with obj. מִלְחָמָה *war*) Jr 5_{18} 30_{11} 46_{28} (both ‖ בְּ *against*) Ezk 11_{13} 20_{17} Zp 1_{18} (all six with obj. כָּלָה *destruction*) 2 C 24_{24} (obj. שֶׁפֶט *judgment*), יכל *prevail* Jr 38_{5}, ערך *be arrayed* for war Gn $14_{8.9.9}$ Jg 20_{20}, לחם *make war* Ps 35_{1}, ni. Jos 10_{25} 24_{8} Jg 12_{4} 1 S 17_{9} 2 S 11_{17} 21_{15} 1 K 20_{23} $22_{31.31.31}$‖2 C $18_{30.30.30}$ 2 K 8_{29}‖2 C 22_{6} 2 K 9_{15} 19_{9}‖Is 37_{9} Jr $21_{4.4.5}$ 32_{5} 33_{5} 37_{10}, קרא *wage (war)* Jos 11_{20}.

שׂרה *struggle* Ho 12_{4}, ריב *contend* Nm 20_{13} Jg 8_{1} Is $45_{9.9}$ 49_{25} 50_{8} Jr $2_{9.9}$ Mc 6_{1} Ps 35_{1} Pr 23_{11} 25_{9} Ne $5_{7.7}$ $13_{11.17}$, גור *contend* Is 54_{15}, שׁפט ni. *enter judgment* 1 S 12_{7} Is 66_{16} Jr 2_{35} Ezk 17_{20} $20_{35.36.36}$ 38_{22} Pr 29_{9} 4Q285 7_{3}, בּוֹא בְמִשְׁפָּט *come into judgment* Ps 143_{2}, קוּם לַמִּשְׁפָּט *stand in judgment* Is 54_{17}, רוץ *run* race Jr 12_{5}, חרה htp. *contend* 12_{5} (+ סוּס *horse*).

In nom. cl., סָרָבִים וְסַלּוֹנִים אוֹתָךְ *thistles and thorns are against you* Ezk 2_{6}.

6a. instrumental, **by (means of), with,** e.g. קָנִיתִי אִישׁ אֶת־י׳ *I have acquired a person by means of Y.* Gn 4_{1}, וְדַשְׁתִּי אֶת־בְּשַׂרְכֶם אֶת־קוֹצֵי הַמִּדְבָּר וְאֶת־הַבַּרְקֳנִים *I shall thresh their flesh by means of desert thorns and by means of briars* Jg 8_{7} (‖ בְּ of instrument 8_{16}), וצררת אתם בצק *and you are to wrap up (the) dough with them* Arad ost. 3_{6}, וְהַקְטִיר אִתּוֹ *and he would burn incense by means of it* 1 K 9_{25} (or del. אִתּוֹ אֲשֶׁר *by means of it which was* before).

6b. without, apart from, לֹא־יָדַע אִתּוֹ מְאוּמָה *he did not know anything without him* Gn 39_{6}, אֲדֹנִי לֹא־יָדַע אִתִּי מַה־בַּבָּיִת *without me, my master does not know what is in the house* 39_{8}.

7a. מֵאֵת (also מֵאִתּוֹ, מֵאתוֹ, etc.) **from being with, away from, from,** + לקח *take* Gn 42_{24} Ex $25_{2.3}$ 30_{16} 35_{5} Lv 7_{34} 16_{5} 25_{36} Nm $3_{49.50}$ 7_{5} $17_{17.17}$ $18_{26.28}$ $31_{51.54}$ Dt 3_{4} 1 S 7_{14} 2 S 21_{12} 1 K 20_{34} 2 K $5_{15.20}$ $12_{6.8.9}$ Zc $6_{10.10.10}$ 1 C 2_{23} CD 16_{14}, pu. *be taken* 2 K 2_{10}, קבל pi. *receive* Jb 2_{10}, אסף *collect* 2 K 22_{4} Jr 16_{5}, גנב pi. *steal* 23_{30}, קנה *buy* Gn 25_{10} 49_{30} 50_{13} Lv $25_{15.44}$ (‖ מִן *from* 25_{45}) 27_{24} Jos 24_{32} 2 S 24_{24} (מֵאוֹתְךָ) 1 K 16_{24} Jr 32_{9} Ru 4_{5} (‖ מִיַּד *from the hand of*), כרה *buy* Dt 2_{6}, שׁבר *buy* 2_{6}, רבה hi. *take much* Nm 35_{8} (+ רַב *large quantity*) מעט hi. *take little* 35_{8} (+ מְעַט *small quantity*), נתן *give* 18_{26} Jos $21_{16.34}$, pass. *be given* Nm 3_{9} (מֵאֵת = *from among*), ni. *be given* 2 K 25_{30}‖Jr 52_{34}.

בוא *come* 1 K 5_{14} Jr 51_{53} Lachish ost. 3_{20} (subj. סֵפֶר *letter*) Arad ost. 40_{8} (ב[א]), הלך *go* Gn 26_{31} Jos 22_{9} Jg 19_{2} 1 K 18_{12} 20_{36} 2 K 4_{5} 5_{19} 8_{14} Jr 3_{1} 9_{1}, יצא *go out* Gn 44_{28} Ex 5_{20} Nm 16_{35} Is 51_{4} Jr 2_{37} 23_{15} Ezk 33_{30} Jb 2_{7} 4QJub[d] 1.2_{34} (מאתוה), ירד *go down* Gn 38_{1} Mc 1_{12}, נפל *fall* 1 K 20_{25} (מֵאוֹתָךְ), מושׁ *move away* Is 54_{10} 1QS 6_{3}, נסע *set out* Nm 11_{31}, עבר *pass* Dt 2_{8} 1 K 22_{24}‖2 C 18_{23}, קום *go up*, i.e. be transferred (of property) Gn 23_{20}, עלה *go up* Is 57_{8} Zc 14_{17}, ברח *flee* 1 K 11_{23}, שׁוב *go back* Jos $22_{32.32}$, hi. *take back* Jr 41_{16}, סור hi. *turn* trans. Ps 66_{20}, נשׂא *carry* 24_{5} Si 38_{2} (obj. מַשְׂאֵת *portion* of food), רום hi. *raise* tax Nm $31_{28.52.52}$, שׁלח pi. *dispatch* Gn 8_{8}

26$_{27}$ 1QS 7$_{16}$ Arad ost. 5$_2$ 6$_2$ 9$_2$ ([שלח] מאת[ך]).

עשׂה *do, make* 1 K 6$_{33}$ (מֵאֵת רְבִעִית *from a fourth*; or em. מְזֻזוֹת רְבֻעוֹת *squared doorposts*), ni. *be accomplished* by Ne 6$_{16}$, שׁאל *ask* Ex 11$_{2.2}$ Jos 15$_{18}$=Jg 1$_{14}$ 1 S 8$_{10}$ 2 S 3$_{13}$ 1 K 2$_{16.20}$ 2 K 4$_3$ (|| מִן *from*) 4$_{28}$ Ps 27$_4$ Pr 30$_7$, דרשׁ *inquire* 1 K 22$_{7.8}$||2 C 18$_{6.7}$ (מֵאוֹתוֹ 1 K 22$_7$) 2 K 3$_{11}$ 8$_8$ (both מֵאוֹתוֹ), שׁמע *hear* 1 S 2$_{23}$ Is 21$_{10}$ 28$_{22}$ Jr 49$_{14}$ Ob$_1$ (all four מֵאֵת י׳ *from Y.*), חכם pi. *become wise, receive wisdom* Si 38$_2$.

נקם *take revenge* on Nm 31$_2$, חלץ ni. *be equipped* 31$_3$ (מֵאֵת = *from among*), נוף hi. *designate as a wave-offering* 8$_{11}$ (מֵאֵת = *from among*), גלה pi. *reveal (oneself)* Is 57$_8$ (מֵאֵת = *when away from* me, i.e. in my absence; or em. גָּלִיתָ *you have departed*), כלה *be determined* by Est 7$_7$, מטר hi. *cause to rain* Gn 19$_{24}$ (מֵאֵת י׳ מִן־הַשָּׁמָיִם *from Y., from heaven*).

היה *be* Ex 29$_{28}$ Dt 18$_{3.3}$ Jos 11$_{20}$ Zc 7$_{12}$ Ps 118$_{23}$ Ezr 9$_8$ (all five מֵאֵת י׳), ni. *be caused* by 1 K 12$_7$ 12$_{24}$||2 C 11$_4$, הַדָּבָר אֲשֶׁר(־)הָיָה אֶל־יִרְמְיָהוּ מֵאֵת י׳ *the word that was to Jeremiah from Y.* Jr 7$_1$ 11$_1$ 18$_1$ 21$_1$ 30$_1$ 32$_1$ 34$_{1.8.12}$ 35$_1$ 40$_1$, sim. 26$_1$ 27$_1$ 36$_1$.

In nom. cl., מאת אל יד מלחמה *from God is the power of battle* 1QM 4$_2$ (unless מְאַת אֵל *hundred of God*), מֵאִתְּךָ תְהִלָּתִי *my praise is from you* Ps 22$_{26}$, מאתכה משפט *judgment is from you* 4QShir^b 52$_4$, מאתכה [ס]וד *from you is counsel* 52$_5$, מאתכה הגבורה ולוא לנו *strength is from you, and not (belonging) to us* 1QM 11$_4$, מאתכה מעמדי *my position is from you* 1QH 2$_{22}$, מאתכה מצעדי *my step is from you* 2$_{23.33}$ (מאתך), מאתך דרך כול חי *from you is the way of every living being* 15$_{22}$, מִקְנֵה הַשָּׂדֶה ... מֵאֵת בְּנֵי־חֵת *the purchase of the field ... was from the Hittites* Gn 49$_{32}$, אֶפֶס מֵאוֹתִי *nothing is from me* Is 54$_{15}$ (or del. אֶפֶס, they stir up strife *[apart] from me*, i.e. without my consent), זֹאת הָרָעָה מֵאֵת י׳ *this evil is from Y.* 2 K 6$_{33}$.

<**COLL**> חֹק ... מֵאֵת פַּרְעֹה *a statute ... from Pharoah* Gn 47$_{22}$, חֻקַּת עוֹלָם ... מֵאֵת בְּנֵי יִשְׂרָאֵל *an eternal statute ... from*, i.e. binding on, *the Israelites* Ex 27$_{21}$ (sim. 29$_{28}$ Lv 7$_{34.36}$), מֵאֵת בְּנֵי־יִשְׂרָאֵל בְּרִית עוֹלָם *an eternal covenant from*, i.e. binding on, *the Israelites* 24$_8$.

זֹאת חֲנֻכַּת הַמִּזְבֵּחַ ... מֵאֵת נְשִׂיאֵי יִשְׂרָאֵל *this was the altar-dedication (offering) ... from the princes of Israel* Nm 7$_{84}$, ללויים ... השכם מאת זובחי הזבח *to the Levites is*, i.e. belongs, ... *the shoulder from those making sacrifice* 11QT 60$_7$, זֹאת פְּעֻלַּת שֹׂטְנַי מֵאֵת י׳ *may this be my accusers' reward from Y.* Ps 109$_{20}$, זֹאת ... צִדְקָתָם מֵאִתִּי *this is ... their justification from me* Is 54$_{17}$, זֶה־לְּךָ הָאוֹת מֵאֵת י׳ *this is the sign for you from Y.* 2 K 20$_9$||Is 38$_7$, זֶה גוֹרָלֵךְ ... מֵאִתִּי *this is your lot ... from me* Jr 13$_{25}$.

הֲיֵשׁ דָּבָר מֵאֵת י׳ *is there a word from Y.?* Jr 37$_{17}$, הִנֵּה מֵאֵת י׳ *behold! (it is) from Y.* Hb 2$_{13}$, רוּחַ ... מֵאֵת י׳ *a spirit from Y.* 1 S 16$_{14}$, כְּטַל מֵאֵת י׳ *as dew from Y.* Mc 5$_6$, מִקְנַת־כֶּסֶף מֵאֵת בֶּן־נֵכָר *a purchase from a foreigner* Gn 17$_{27}$, עולת [יום] ... מאת בני ישראל *a daily sacrifice ... from the Israelites* 11QT 29$_5$, והמה מאתכה גרו *and on account of you they have attacked*, or, *and they, (sent) from you, have attacked* 1QH 2$_{23(mg)}$, רֹקַע הָאָרֶץ מֵאִתִּי *fashioning the earth from myself*, perh. according to my own plan Is 44$_{24(Qr)}$ (|| לְבַדִּי *on my own*; Kt מי אתי *who was with me?*), אֵין־לְךָ מֵאֵת הַמֶּלֶךְ *there is no one (belonging) to you from the king* 2 S 15$_3$.

7b. מֵאֵת פְּנֵי **(away) from the presence of, from,** + גרשׁ pi. *expel* Ex 10$_{11}$, יצא *go out* Gn 27$_{30}$, נשׂא *carry* 43$_{34}$ Lv 10$_4$ (+ קֹדֶשׁ *sanctuary*), קרב hi. *bring* 2 K 16$_{14}$ (+ בַּיִת *temple*).

Also 4Q522 2$_{10}$ Mur 24 1$_{10}$ Lachish ost. 13$_2$ ([א]ת עבדה) 13$_3$ (4 את אשפת) Arad ost. 16$_7$ (אתך).

[אֵת] III 5 n.[m.] **blade**—sf. אִתּוֹ; pl. אִתִּים (אֵתִים); sf. אִתֵּיכֶם—in list of agricultural cutting instruments (1 S 13$_{20.21}$). <**SUBJ**> נפל *fall* 2 K 6$_5$ (unless אֵת object-marker introducing subject). <**OBJ**> לטשׁ *sharpen* 1 S 13$_{20}$, חדד hi. *sharpen* Zc 2$_4$ (if em. לְהַחֲרִיד אֹתָם *to terrify them* to לְהָחֵד אִתִּים), כתת *beat* into swords Jl 4$_{10}$. <**CSTR**> אֶת־הַבַּרְזֶל perh. *blade of iron* 2 K 6$_5$ (unless אֵת object-marker introducing subject). <**PREP**> לְ charge *for (sharpening)* 1 S 13$_{21}$, כתת לְ *beat* swords *into* Is 2$_4$=Mc 4$_3$.

אֹת, see אוֹת.

אֶתְבַּעַל 1 pr.n.m. **Ethbaal,** king of Sidon, father of Jezebel, 1 K 16$_{31}$.

→ בַּעַל *Baal.*

אתה 21.1 vb. **come—Qal** Pf. אָתָה, אָתָנוּ; impf. יֶאֱתֶה, תֶּאֱתֶה, יֶאֱתָיוּ; + waw וַיֵּתֵא (וַיֵּאת) וַיֶּאֱתָיֶנִי, (וַיֶּאֱתָיוּן); impv. אֵתָיוּ, ptc. אֹתִיּוֹת (Q אותות)—**1. come,** **<SUBJ>** Y. Dt 33_{2} (‖ בוא *come*), Cyrus Is 41_{25}, foreign nations 41_{5} (‖ קרב *approach*) 1QIsa[a] 45_{20} (ואתיו; MT יַחְדָּו *together*; ‖ בוא), Israelites Jr 3_{22} (‖ שׁוב *go back*, + אַתָּה *you*), Job's adversaries Jb 30_{14} (+ גלל htpalp. *roll about*), חַיָּה *beast* Is 56_{9} (+ לֶאֱכֹל *to eat*), זָהָב *gold* Jb 37_{22}, חַשְׁמַן *noble* Ps 68_{32} (or em. יַאֲתִיוּ *they will bring* noble gifts).

בֹּקֶר *morning* Is 21_{12}, לַיְלָה *night* 21_{12}, שָׁנָה *year* Jb 16_{22}, אֲחֻזָּה *possession* Nm 32_{32} (if em. אִתָּנוּ *with us* to אָתָנוּ *has come to us*), מֶמְשָׁלָה *government* Mc 4_{8} (‖ בוא *come*), אֵיד *disaster* Pr 1_{27} (‖ בוא), פַּחַד *fear* Jb 3_{25} (‖ בוא); subj. unspecified, Gn 20_{16} (if em. אִתָּךְ all who are *with you* to אָתָךְ all that *has come*, i.e. occurred, *[to] you*) Dt 33_{21} (or em. סָפוּן וַיֵּתֵא *reserved; and he came* to וְהִתְאַסְּפוּן *and they were gathered*) Is 21_{12} (‖ שׁוב *go back*) 56_{12}.

<PREP> כְּפֶרֶץ רָחָב *as a wide breach* Jb 30_{14}, כְּסוּפָה *as a whirlwind* Pr 1_{27} (Gnz כַּסּוּפָה).

מִן of direction, *from* Nm 32_{32} (if em. אִתָּנוּ *with us*) Dt 33_{2} (if em. מֵרִבְבֹת קֹדֶשׁ perh. *consisting of ten thousands of holy beings* to מִמְּרִבַת קָדֵשׁ *from Meribah of Kadesh*) Ps 68_{32} (+ מִצְרַיִם *Egypt*) Jb 37_{22} (+ צָפוֹן *north*).

עָדֶיךָ *unto you* Mc 4_{8}.

2. fem. ptc. as noun, **that which is to come,** alw. pl. except Jr 33_{2} (if em.; see Obj.), **<OBJ>** נגד hi. *tell* Is 41_{23} (+ לְאָחוֹר *hereafter*) 44_{7} (or em. מִשּׂוּמִי עַם־עוֹלָם וְאֹתִיּוֹת *since my appointing a people of eternity; and things to come* to מִי הִשְׁמִיעַ מֵעוֹלָם אוֹתִיּוֹת *who proclaimed from eternity things to come?*; + אֲשֶׁר תָּבֹאנָה *that which is to come*) 44_{8}, שׁמע hi. *proclaim* 44_{7} (if em.; see above) 44_{8}, שׁאל *ask* 45_{11} (or em. הָאֹתִיּוֹת שְׁאָלוּנִי *ask me the things to come!* to הַאֹתִי תִּשְׁאָלוּנִי *do you ask me?*; 1QIsa[a] אותות; + עַל־בָּנַי *concerning my children*), נבט hi. *look (at)* Si $42_{18(M)}$ (+ כֹּל *everything*), יצר *fashion* Jr 33_{2} (if em. אוֹתָהּ *her* to אֹתִיָּה). **<CSTR>** אתיות עולם *future events of eternity* Si $42_{18(M)}$.

<SYN> §1 בוא *come*, שׁוב *go back*.

Hi. Impv. הֵתָיוּ (Q האתיו)—**bring,** **<SUBJ>** Temanites Is 21_{14} (+ קדם pi. *go before*), prophet Jr 12_{9} (or em. אֵתָיוּ *come!*, of beasts). **<OBJ>** מַיִם *water* Is 21_{14}, חַיָּה *beast* Jr 12_{9} (+ לְאָכְלָה *to*, or *for, food*), חַשְׁמַן *noble (gift)* Ps 68_{32} (if em. יֶאֱתָיוּ *let* nobles *come*).

אַתָּה 744.7.163.1 pronoun **you** (masc. sg.)—אַתָּה (אָתָּה), I, Q, Kt את (for Qr אַתְּ at Nm 11_{15} Dt 5_{27} Ezk 28_{14}, see אַתְּ *you* fem.)—**<SUBJ>** **a.** of **verbs,** היה *be* Gn 41_{40} (+ עַל *in charge of*) 45_{10} (+ קָרוֹב *near*) Nm 16_{16} (+ לִפְנֵי *before*) 2 S $5_{2(Qr)}$ (+ הַמּוֹצִיא *the one who brings out*) 13_{13} (+ כְּ *as*, :: אֲנִי *I*) Ezk 2_{8} (+ מְרִי *rebellious[ness]*) 35_{4} (+ שְׁמָמָה *devastation*) 38_{9} (+ כְּ) Ps 10_{14} (+ ptc.) 90_{1} (+ מָעוֹן *refuge*) 1 C 11_{2} (+ נָגִיד *leader*) 1QSb $1_{6(Milik)}$ ([תה]יה), + לְ of possession, etc. Ex 4_{16} (:: הוּא *he*) 18_{19} Dt 28_{44} (:: הוּא) 2 S 5_{2} 7_{24}‖1 C 17_{22} 4QVisSam 6_{1} 1QH 13_{15}, שׁוה *be as* Pr 26_{4} perh. 4Q416 9.2_{4}.

בוא *come* Gn 6_{18} 7_{1} 15_{15} Ex 3_{18} Dt 1_{37} 31_{7} Jos 13_{1} 1 S 13_{11} Jr 20_{6} 36_{6} Ezk 38_{15} Zc 6_{10} 2 C 25_{8}, hi. *bring* Dt 31_{23} 2 S 9_{10}, הלך *go* Ex 19_{24} 33_{1} Jg 9_{14} 2 S 15_{19} 1 K 9_{4}‖2 C 7_{17} (mss עַתָּה *now*) Jr 20_{6} Dn 12_{13}, htp. *go about* 4Q416 5_{11}, יצא *go out* Gn 8_{16} Ex 11_{8} 1 S 28_{1} Is 7_{3} Ezk 12_{4}, hi. *bring out* 12_{3}, עלה *go up* Ex 19_{24} 24_{1} 33_{1}, hi. *bring up* 2 C 2_{15} (:: אֲנַחְנוּ *we*), ירד *go down* Ex 19_{24} Dt 28_{43} (:: גֵּר *sojourner*), hi. *send down* Ps 55_{24}.

שׁוב *go back* Dt 30_{8} 2 S 19_{15} Jr 15_{19} (:: הֵמָּה *they*) Ho 12_{7} Ps 85_{7}, hi. *bring back* 1 K 8_{34}‖2 C 6_{25} 1QH 5_{18}, קרב *approach* Dt 5_{27}, hi. *bring forward* Nm 16_{17}, *assemble* trans. Ex 28_{1}, רחק *be distant* Ps 22_{20}, עבר *cross over* Gn 31_{52} (:: אֲנִי) Jos 1_{2} 2 S 19_{34}.

קום *arise* Jos 1_{2} Jg 8_{21} 9_{32} Jr 1_{17} Ps 102_{14} 132_{8}‖2 C 6_{41}, hi. *raise* 1QM 14_{10}, עמד *stand, persist* Dt 5_{31} 1 S 9_{27} 2 S 20_{4} Ps 102_{27} (:: הֵמָּה) 1QDM 1_{2}, יצב htp. *position oneself* 2 S 18_{13}, קוץ hi. *rouse oneself* Ps 59_{6} (unless Nom. Cl., אַתָּה ... אֱלֹהֵי יִשְׂרָאֵל *you ... are the God of Israel*), ישׁב *be enthroned* 102_{13} Lm 5_{19}, hi. *accommodate* Ps 4_{9}, שׁכב *lie down* Ezk 4_{4} 32_{28}, נפל *fall* 2 K 14_{10}‖2 C 25_{19} Ezk 39_{4}.

רום hi. *raise* Ex 14_{16}, שׂים *place* 18_{21} Ezk 4_{4} 13_{17} 21_{24} Ps 56_{9} 91_{9} 1QH 6_{25} 8_{16}, שׁית *place* 4QapPs[b] 33_{2}, אסף ni. *be gathered* in death Nm 27_{13}, שׁלח *send* Jr 29_{25} 4QapPs[b] 33_{4}, עזב *abandon* Ne 9_{19}, שׁלך hi. *throw* Ps 50_{17}, ho. *be thrown* Is 14_{19}, סבב *turn* intrans. 1 S 22_{18}, hi. trans. 1 K 18_{37}, נטה *stretch* trans. Ex 14_{16} 1QH 1_{9}, פרשׂ *stretch* hands Jb 11_{13}, פתח *open* 1QH 5_{32}, סגר *close* $5_{14(mg)}$.

רדף *pursue* 2 S 20_{6}, אסר *commence (battle)* 1 K 20_{14}, צור *besiege* Ezk 4_{3}, ארב *lay ambush* Jg 9_{32}, נכה hi. *strike* Ezk 21_{19} Ps 69_{27} (or em. אֶת object-marker) Pr 23_{14}, שׂרף *burn* Jr 36_{29}, שׁלל *plunder* Hb 2_{8}, בער pi. *destroy* Dt 21_{9}=11QT 63_{7}, רצץ pi. *shatter* Ps 74_{14}, שׁבר ni. *be broken* Ezk 32_{28}, שׁוף *bruise* Gn 3_{15} (:: הוא), דכא pi. *crush* Ps 89_{11} 4QapPs^{b} 15_{5} ([ד]כאת), תפשׂ ni. *be captured* Jr 34_{3}, נצל ni. *be saved* 2 K 19_{11}||Is 37_{11}, hi. *save* Jg 10_{15} Ezk $3_{19.21}$ 33_{9} Ne 9_{28}, מלט ni. *escape* Jr 34_{3} $38_{18.23}$, נקה ni. *be held innocent* 49_{12}.

גלה *uncover* 2 S 7_{27}||1 C 17_{25} 1QH fr. 4_{7}, *be exiled* Ezk 12_{3}, pi. *reveal* secret 1QH 13_{6}, אור hi. *illuminate* Ps 18_{29}, חלק *divide* 2 S 19_{30}, בדל hi. *separate* 1 K 8_{53} 4Q416 1_{2}, בקע *split* trans. Ex 14_{16} Ps 74_{15}, פרד I hi. *frustrate* Jb 15_{4}, פרד II po. *split* Ps 74_{13}, סתם *block* Dn 8_{26} 12_{4}, חתם *seal* 12_{4} 4QShir^{b} 30_{3} ([חתמ]תה), חשׂך *withhold* Ezr 9_{13}, גרע *restrain* Jb 15_{4}, כלא *withhold* Ps 40_{12}, סתר ni. *hide oneself* Jr 36_{19}, pi. *conceal* 1QH 5_{11}.

ראה *see* Is 33_{19} (if em. אֶת־ object-marker) Jr 12_{3} Ob$_{13}$, ho. *be shown* Dt 4_{35}, נבט hi. *look* Ps 10_{14}, שׁמע *hear* Gn 23_{13} Dt 4_{33} 5_{27} (|| אַתְּ *you* masc.) 9_{2} $30_{2.8}$ Jos 14_{12} 1 S 28_{22} 1 K $8_{30.32.34.36.39.43}$||2 C $6_{21.23.25.27.30.33}$ Jr 22_{2} Ezk 2_{8} Zc 3_{8} Ps 61_{6} Jb 33_{33} Pr 23_{19} Ne $9_{27.28}$.

אמר *say* Gn 32_{13} Ex 3_{18} Nm 11_{21} 1 K 1_{24} Is 14_{13} Jr 25_{30} 32_{25} Ezk 21_{33} 28_{2} $33_{10.12}$ 36_{1} $39_{1.17}$, דבר pi. *speak* Ex 7_{2} 20_{19} 28_{3} 31_{13} Nm 20_{8} Dt $5_{27(Sam)}$ (אתה for MT אַתְּ) 1 S 20_{23} 2 S 7_{29} 17_{6} Jr 1_{17} 51_{62}, נגד hi. *tell* Gn 21_{26} (|| אָנֹכִי *I*) 1 S $24_{19(Qr)}$ Ezk 43_{10}, ספר pi. *tell* Is 43_{26}, ענה *answer* Ps 38_{16} 99_{8} 1QH 4_{18}, קרא *call* 1 S 26_{14}, *read* Jr 36_{6}, קהל *summon (assembly)* Nm 20_{8}.

צוה pi. *command* Ex 27_{20} Jos 3_{8} Ps 119_{4} 1QH 6_{20}, pu. *be commanded* Gn 45_{19}, עוד hi. *command* Ex 19_{23}, שׁבע ni. *vow* 1 K $1_{13.17}$, נבא ni. *prophesy* Jr 25_{30} Ezk 13_{17} $21_{19.33}$ 36_{1} 39_{1}, ירה hi. *teach* Ps 119_{102} Jb 34_{32} 1QS 11_{17}, קדשׁ pi. *sanctify* 4QRitPur 51.2_{10}, ברך pi. *bless* Ps 5_{13} 109_{28} (:: הֵמָּה, || עֶבֶד your *servant*) 1 C 17_{27}, ארר *curse* 4QD$^{b}{}_{14}$, קלל pi. *curse* Ec $7_{22(Qr)}$, pu. *be cursed* 11QapPs^{a} 3_{10} ([א]תה תקלל), hi. *lighten* 1 K $12_{4.10}$||2 C 10_{10} (both :: אָב your *father*).

זהר hi. *warn* Ezk $3_{19.21}$ 33_{9}, שׁבח pi. *silence* Ps 89_{10} 4QapPs^{b} 15_{4}, שׁאל *ask* 1 S 17_{56}, בקשׁ pi. *seek* Jr 45_{5}, דרשׁ *seek* 4Q416 1_{7}, פלל htp. *pray* Jb 7_{16} 11_{14}, פגע *intercede* 7_{16}, *attack* Jg 8_{21} 1 S 22_{18}, כפר pi. *atone* Ps 65_{4}, כרת *make (covenant)* Gn 31_{44}.

חוס *pity* Jon 4_{10}, חנן *have mercy* Ps 41_{11} Kh. Beit Lei graf. 6 (others אל *God*), htp. *pray* Jb 8_{5}, רחם pi. *have mercy* Zc 1_{12} Ps 102_{14}, נחם pi. *console* Ps 86_{17}, סלח *forgive* 1 K $8_{34.36.39}$||2 C $6_{25.37.30}$ Lm 3_{42}, עזר *help* Ps 86_{17} 1QH 2_{34} 4QapPs^{b} 15_{3} ([אתה]), בטח *trust* 4Q416 9.2_{14} (א[תה]), hi. *cause to trust* Jr 28_{15}, ישׁע hi. *save* 2 S 22_{28}||Ps 18_{28} (at 2 S if em. אֶת־ object-marker) Ps 86_{2} (unless Nom. Cl., אַתָּה אֱלֹהַי *you, my God*; + אֲנִי *I*), סלח *forgive* 4QDibHam^{a} 4_{7}.

חכם *be wise* Pr 23_{19}, בחן *test* Jr 12_{3}, חרץ *decide* 1 K 20_{40}, בחר *choose* Jb 34_{33} (:: אֲנִי) 1QH fr. $2.1_{7(Licht)}$ ([בחרתה]), זנח *reject* Ps 60_{12} 89_{39}, מאס *reject* Ho 4_{6} Ps 89_{39}, ירא *fear* Ex 9_{30} Dt 6_{2} Is 41_{8} Jr 30_{10} $46_{27.28}$ Ezk 2_{6}, חתת *fear* Jr 30_{10} 46_{27}, שׂנא *hate* Ps 50_{17}, נאץ *despise* 1QH 4_{12}, קצף *be angry* Is 64_{4}, קשׁר *conspire* 1 S 22_{13}, עכר *cause trouble* 1 K 18_{18}, בגד *betray* Ml 2_{14}, חשׁק *love* Is 38_{17}, שׂמח *rejoice* Dt 14_{26} $16_{11.14}$ 26_{11}, גיל *rejoice* Is 41_{16}, הלל pi. *praise* 4Q416 1_{1}, htp. *glory* Is 41_{16}, שׂחק *laugh* Ps 59_{9}.

ידע *know* Gn $30_{26.29}$ Ex 32_{22} Nm 20_{14} Dt 9_{2} 13_{7} =11QT 54_{21} Dt $28_{36.64}$ Jos 14_{6} 1 S 28_{2} (ms עַתָּה *now*) 28_{9} 2 S 7_{20}||1 C 17_{18} 2 S 17_{8} 1 K $2_{5.44}$ $5_{17.20}$ 8_{39}||2 C 6_{30} 2 K 4_{1} Jr 12_{3} 15_{15} 17_{16} 18_{23} Ezk 35_{4} 37_{3} Ps 40_{10} $69_{6.20}$ 139_{2} 142_{4} Jb 5_{27} 1 C 28_{9} 4QPrFêtes^{b} 2_{4} 1QM 18_{10} 4QDibHam^{a} 8_{10} 1QH $7_{13.16}$ $9_{12.29}$ 4QapPs^{b} 31_{6}, hi. *inform* Ex 33_{12} 1QS $11_{17(erased)}$ (הודיתה perh. *you praised*) 1QH $9_{23(Licht)}$ ([הודעתני]), זכר *remember* Ps 25_{7}, שׁכח *forget* Jb 11_{16} (or em. עַתָּה *now*).

מצא *find* Gn 38_{23}, נתן *give* Ex 10_{25} Nm 32_{32} (if em. אִתָּנוּ *with us* to אַתָּ[ה] תְּנָה *you, give!*) Jg 15_{18} 1 K $8_{36.39}$||2 C $6_{27.30}$ Ezr 9_{13} 2 C 20_{7} 11QPs^{a} 19_{4} 1QH 7_{10}, *place* Ezk $41_{3.9}$, ni. *be given* Jr 34_{3}, לקח *take* Gn 6_{21} Ex 30_{23} Nm 20_{8} 2 S 20_{6} Ezk $41_{3.9}$ 5_{1} 37_{16}, אחז *take* Ex 18_{21}, נחל *possess* Ps 82_{8}, hi. *cause to possess* Dt 31_{7} Jos 1_{6} Ps $82_{8(ms)}$ 4QPsJos^{a} 3.2_{10} ([את]ה), עבט *borrow* Dt 15_{6}, לוה *borrow* 28_{12}, hi. *lend* 28_{44} (:: הוא), חכר *rent* 5/6ḤevBA 45 fr. 2, גמל *repay* 1 S 24_{18} (:: אֲנִי), שׁלם pi. *repay* Ps 62_{13}, גאל *redeem* Ru 4_{6}, פדה *redeem* 1QM $13_{9(Yadin)}$ ([פ]דיתנו) 4QDibHam^{a} 4_{7}.

חיה *live* Gn 43_{8} (|| אֲנַחְנוּ) Dt 30_{19} Jr 38_{17} Si 15_{15}, ערל

ni. *be uncircumcised* Hb 2$_{16}$, זקן *be old* Jos 13$_{1}$ 1 S 8$_{5}$, חלה pu. *be made ill* Is 14$_{10}$, אנח ni. *groan* Ezk 21$_{11}$, נבל *languish* Ex 18$_{18}$, ירשׁ *take possession* Jg 11$_{23}$, ni. *be impoverished* Gn 45$_{11}$, hi. *dispossess* Ps 44$_{3}$ 2 C 20$_{7}$, מות *die* Gn 20$_{7}$ 43$_{8}$ 1 S 22$_{16}$ Jr 20$_{6}$ 27$_{13}$ Am 7$_{17}$, hi. *kill* 1 S 20$_{8}$, שׁחט *kill* 4QapPs^{b} 31$_{6}$, קבר ni. *be buried* Jr 20$_{6}$.

עשׂה *do, make* Ex 20$_{10}$ Dt 5$_{14}$ 30$_{8}$ Jg 10$_{15}$ 1 S 15$_{6}$ 2 S 12$_{12}$ (:: אֲנִי) 1 K 3$_{6}$ 5$_{23}$ 8$_{32.43}$||2 C 6$_{23.33}$ 1 K 8$_{39}$ 21$_{7}$ 2 K 19$_{15}$||Is 37$_{16}$ Jr 14$_{22}$ 32$_{17}$ Ezk 4$_{9}$ 12$_{3}$ Jon 1$_{14}$ Ps 39$_{10}$ 40$_{6}$ (or em. אִתָּנוּ *with us*) 99$_{4}$ 109$_{21.27}$ Lm 1$_{21}$ Ne 9$_{6(Qr)}$ 2 C 1$_{8}$ 1QM 13$_{10}$ 18$_{8}$ 4QDibHam^{a} 1.2$_{18}$ 1.6$_{4}$ 1QH 16$_{9}$ 4Q414 4$_{1}$ 4Q372 1$_{17}$, פעל *do* 1QH 11$_{33}$, ברא *create* Ps 89$_{13}$ GnzPs 2$_{18}$ 4QVisSam 3.2$_{6}$ 1QH 1$_{13.27}$ 4$_{38}$ 15$_{14}$ (Licht) ([ברא]תה) 4QBer^{b} 2$_{4}$, קנה *create* Ps 139$_{13}$, יצר *form* 1QH 1$_{8}$ 10$_{22}$ 15$_{22}$.

נצב hi. *establish* Ps 74$_{17}$, יסד *establish* Ps 89$_{12}$ 1QH 9$_{12}$ 4QapPs^{b} 15$_{5}$ ([י]סדתם), חזק pi. *strengthen* 4QDibHam^{a} 1.6$_{8}$ 1QH 1$_{31}$, סמך *support* 9$_{21(Licht)}$ ([סמכתני]), כול pilp. *sustain* 9$_{34}$, חלל hi. *begin* Dt 3$_{24}$, שׁמר *observe* Gn 17$_{9}$ Nm 18$_{7}$ Ho 12$_{7}$ 4Q376 1.2$_{3}$, *guard* Zc 3$_{7}$ Ps 12$_{8}$, אחר pi. *be slow* 40$_{18}$||70$_{6}$, שׁחר pi. *make haste* Jb 8$_{5}$, קוה pi. *wait* Ho 12$_{7}$, חסר *lack* 4Q416 9.1$_{17}$.

מלך *be king* Jg 9$_{14}$ 1 S 23$_{17}$ (+ אָנֹכִי), hi. *make king* 1 K 3$_{7}$ 2 C 1$_{9}$, משׁל *rule* Gn 4$_{7}$ Jg 8$_{22}$, שׁפט *judge* 1 K 8$_{32}$||2 C 6$_{23}$ Ezk 22$_{2}$, דין *judge* Zc 3$_{7}$, שׂוך *protect* Jb 1$_{10(Qr)}$ 1QH 8$_{11}$ ([את]ה), נצר *guard* Ps 12$_{8}$, מנה *appoint* 1 K 20$_{25}$, יעד *appoint* 1QM 13$_{18}$.

אכל *eat* Lv 10$_{14}$ Dt 12$_{18}$ 14$_{26}$ 15$_{20}$ 2 S 9$_{7}$ Ezk 2$_{8}$ Mc 6$_{14}$, שׁתה *drink* Gn 24$_{44}$ Lv 10$_{9}$ Mc 6$_{15}$ Hb 2$_{16}$, שׂבע *be satisfied* Mc 6$_{14}$, סוך *anoint* 6$_{15}$, לבשׁ *be clothed* 1 K 22$_{30}$||2 C 18$_{29}$, אזר *gird (loins)* Jr 1$_{17}$, זרע *sow* Mc 6$_{15}$, נטע *plant* Ps 44$_{3}$, קצר *reap* Mc 6$_{15}$, עבד *work (land)* 2 S 9$_{10}$, *serve* Nm 18$_{7}$ 1 C 28$_{9}$, רעה *shepherd* 2 S 5$_{2}$||1 C 11$_{2}$, בנה *build* 2 S 7$_{5}$||1 C 17$_{4}$ 1 K 8$_{19}$||2 C 6$_{9}$ (:: הוא, בֵּן your *son*).

כתב *write* Ezk 37$_{16}$ 4QJub^{a} 1$_{17}$ ([אתה כתוב]), חקק *inscribe* 4$_{1}$, רשׁם *record* 1QH 16$_{10}$, פקד *register* Nm 1$_{3}$, hi. *appoint* 1$_{50}$, נשׂא *carry* 11$_{17}$ 18$_{1.1}$, *list* 31$_{26}$, *receive* 1 K 5$_{23}$, *forgive* Ps 32$_{5}$, *utter* prayer, lament Jr 7$_{16}$ 11$_{14}$ Ezk 19$_{1}$ 27$_{2}$, כון ni. *be established* 1 S 20$_{31}$, *be ready* Ezk 38$_{7}$, hi. *prepare* 38$_{7}$ 1QH 13$_{13}$ 15$_{22}$ ([הכינו]תה), *place* Ezk 4$_{3}$ Ps 74$_{16}$ Jb 11$_{13}$, pol. *sustain* Ps 68$_{10}$ 99$_{4}$, יבשׁ hi. *dry* trans. 74$_{15}$, דרך *tread* Dt 33$_{29}$ Mc 6$_{15}$.

b. of participles, ראה *see* Gn 13$_{15}$ 31$_{43}$ Jg 9$_{36}$ 2 S 15$_{27}$ Jr 1$_{11.13}$ (both :: אֲנִי *I*) 24$_{3}$ Ezk 8$_{6}$ 40$_{4}$ Am 7$_{8}$ 8$_{2}$ Zc 4$_{2}$ 5$_{2}$ (:: אֲנִי), ni. *be seen* Nm 14$_{14}$, ho. *be shown* Ex 25$_{40}$, ירא *fear* Gn 22$_{12}$ Dt 7$_{19}$ Jg 7$_{10}$, ni. *be terrifying* Ps 76$_{8}$ Si 48$_{4}$ 1QM 12$_{7}$ ([נ]ורא) 4QapPs^{b} 50$_{3}$, קוץ *dread* Is 7$_{16}$, קנא pi. *be jealous* Nm 11$_{29}$.

ברך pass. *be blessed* Gn 26$_{29}$ Dt 28$_{3.3.6.6}$ 1 S 15$_{13}$ 26$_{25}$ Ps 119$_{12}$ 1 C 29$_{10}$ GnzPs 2$_{2}$ 4$_{13}$ 1QS 11$_{15}$ 4QPrQuot 34$_{4}$ ([ברו]ך) 35$_{7(Baillet)}$ ([ברוך] א[תה]) 4QRitPur 29$_{8.21}$ (Baillet) ([ברוך]) 33$_{6}$ 40$_{3(mg)}$ ([בר]וך) 1QH 5$_{20}$ 10$_{14}$ 11$_{27}$ ([את]ה) 11$_{29(mg).32}$ ([א]תה) 16$_{8}$ fr. 4$_{15}$ 15.1$_{6(Holm-Nielsen)}$ ([ברוך]) 4QShir^{b} 16$_{4}$ ([בר]וך) 4Q414 1.2$_{6}$ ([א]תה), ארר pass. *be cursed* Gn 3$_{14}$ 4$_{11}$ Dt 28$_{16.16.19.19}$ 1QS 2$_{5.7}$ 4QToh D$_{2}$ ([אר]ור), זעם pass. *be denounced* 1QS 2$_{7}$ 4QToh D$_{5}$ 4QBer^{a} 3.2$_{8}$ ([ז]עום), בזה pass. *be despised* Ob$_{2}$.

אמר *say* Ex 2$_{14}$ 33$_{12}$ 1 K 18$_{11.14}$ Am 7$_{16}$ Ne 5$_{12}$ 6$_{8}$, דבר *speak* Jr 40$_{16}$, pi. in same sense Jg 6$_{17}$ Jr 43$_{2}$, נבא ni. *prophesy* 32$_{3}$, ידע *know* 4QJub 35$_{9}$ ([יו]דע), חשׁב *plan* Ne 6$_{6}$, בדא *devise* 6$_{8}$, בטח *trust* Dt 28$_{52}$ 2 K 19$_{10}$||Is 37$_{10}$ Jr 5$_{17}$ 12$_{5}$, hi. *keep secure* Ps 22$_{10}$ (mss מִבְטַחִי *my security*), בקשׁ pi. *seek* Jg 4$_{22}$ 2 S 17$_{3}$ 20$_{19}$ Ne 2$_{4}$, בחן *test* 1 C 29$_{17}$, בחר *choose* 1 S 20$_{30}$, ברר *choose* 4Q372 1$_{18}$, אבל htp. *lament* 1 S 16$_{1}$ (:: אֲנִי), נחם pi. *console* 1QH fr. 21$_{3}$.

בוא *come* Ex 34$_{12}$ Dt 7$_{1}$ 9$_{5}$ 11$_{10.29}$ 12$_{29}$ 18$_{9}$ 23$_{21}$ 28$_{21.63}$ 30$_{16}$ 1 S 17$_{43.45}$ (both :: אָנֹכִי *I*) 2 S 11$_{10}$ Ezk 38$_{13}$, הלך *go* Nm 14$_{14}$ Jg 4$_{9}$ 14$_{3}$ Zc 2$_{6}$ Ec 9$_{10}$, עלה *go up* Dt 32$_{50}$.

עבר *cross over* Dt 2$_{18}$ 3$_{21}$ 9$_{1}$ 30$_{18}$, *transgress* Est 3$_{3}$, רוץ *run* 2 S 18$_{22}$, עמד *stand* Ex 3$_{5}$ Jos 5$_{15}$, נצב ni. *stand* Nm 22$_{34}$, ישׁב *sit, dwell* Ex 18$_{14}$ (:: עָם the *people*) Jos 9$_{7}$ Ezk 2$_{6}$ 12$_{2}$, שׁכב *lie down* Gn 28$_{13}$ Ezk 4$_{9}$, נפל *fall* Jos 7$_{10}$, *desert* Jr 37$_{13}$, יעד ni. *be assembled* Nm 16$_{11}$, שׁלח *send* 2 K 1$_{6}$, pass. *be sent* Ezk 3$_{5}$.

נתן *give* 1 K 18$_{9}$ Ps 145$_{15}$, ירשׁ *take possession* Dt 18$_{14}$, נשׁה *lend* 24$_{11}$, חסר *lack* 1 K 11$_{22}$, רושׁ *be poor* 4Q416 9.2$_{20}$ 10.2$_{3}$ 10.2$_{20}$.

גאל *redeem* Ru 3$_{9}$ (+ אָנֹכִי), תמך *hold* Ps 16$_{5}$, חתם *seal* Ezk 28$_{12}$, גזה *sever* Ps 71$_{6}$, חתה *pile* coals Pr 25$_{22}$, בנה *build* 1 K 6$_{12}$ Ne 6$_{6}$, גיח *bring out* from womb Ps 22$_{10}$.

רדף *pursue* 1 S 24$_{15}$, צדה *lie in wait* 24$_{12}$, נקשׁ htp.

entrap 28$_{9}$, נכה hi. *strike* 2 K 6$_{22}$, שׁחת hi. *destroy* Ezk 9$_{8}$, שׁדד pass. *be pillaged* Is 33$_{1}$, גלה *be exiled* 2 S 15$_{19}$, אנח ni. *groan* Ezk 21$_{12}$, חלה *be ill* Ne 2$_{2}$ (+ אֵינְךָ *you are not*), מות *die* 2 K 20$_{1}$||Is 38$_{1}$ Jr 28$_{16}$, ho. *be killed* 1 S 19$_{11}$.

עשׂה *do* Gn 21$_{22}$ Ex 18$_{14.17}$ Nm 11$_{15(Sam)}$ (אתה for MT אַתְּ) Jg 11$_{27}$ 18$_{3}$ 2 S 3$_{25}$ Ezk 11$_{13}$ 12$_{9}$ 24$_{19}$, יצר *form* Is 64$_{7}$ (:: אֲנַחְנוּ *we*), חרה htp. *contend* Jr 22$_{15}$, זנה *prostitute oneself* Ho 4$_{15}$, אור ni. *be resplendent* Ps 76$_{5}$, משׁל *rule* Ps 89$_{10}$ 1 C 29$_{12}$ 2 C 20$_{6}$ 4QapPs^{b} 15$_{4}$ ([אתה משל]), הוה *be* Ne 6$_{6}$, חיה pi. *give life* 9$_{6}$.

<NOM CL> (predicate oft. with 1st person sg. sf.) with singular noun, אָב *father* Is 63$_{16.16}$ 64$_{7}$ Jr 2$_{27}$ (|| אַתְּ *you* fem.) Ps 89$_{27}$ Jb 17$_{14}$ Si 51$_{10}$ 1QH 9$_{35}$, בֵּן *son* Jg 11$_{2}$ 1 S 17$_{58}$ Ps 2$_{7}$ (+ אֲנִי *I*), בְּכוֹר *first-born* Gn 49$_{3}$ =4QpGen^{a} 4$_{3}$, נַעַר *lad* 1 S 17$_{33}$ (:: הוּא *he*), חָתָן *bridegroom* Ex 4$_{25}$, אָח *kinsman* Gn 29$_{15}$.

אָדָם *human* Ezk 28$_{2.9}$, אִישׁ *man* Jg 13$_{11}$ (|| אֲנִי) 1 S 26$_{15}$ 2 S 12$_{7}$ 16$_{8}$ 18$_{20}$ 1 K 1$_{42}$ 2$_{9.26}$ 13$_{14}$ 17$_{24}$ 1 C 28$_{3}$, מֶלֶךְ *king* 1QH 10$_{8}$, אָדוֹן *lord* 10$_{8}$, שַׂר *prince* 10$_{8}$, נָשִׂיא *prince* Gn 23$_{6}$, ראשׁ *head* 1 S 15$_{17}$ Jr 22$_{6}$, כֹּהֵן *priest* Ps 110$_{4}$, עֶבֶד *servant* Is 41$_{9}$ 44$_{21.21}$ 49$_{3}$, אַלּוּף *companion* Jr 3$_{4}$, בַּעַל *possessor* Pr 23$_{2}$.

מַחְסֶה *refuge* Jr 17$_{17}$ Ps 71$_{7}$ 142$_{6}$, מְצוּדָה *refuge* 31$_{4}$ 71$_{3}$, מָעוֹז *refuge* 31$_{5}$, סֵתֶר *hiding-place* 32$_{7}$ 119$_{114}$, מִשְׁמֶרֶת *safekeeping*, i.e. safe 1 S 22$_{23}$, מָגֵן *shield* Ps 3$_{4}$ 119$_{114}$, מַפֵּץ *war-club* Jr 51$_{20}$, סֶלַע *rock* Ps 31$_{4}$ 71$_{3}$, עָפָר *dust* Gn 3$_{19}$, נֵר *lamp* 2 S 22$_{29}$, שֶׁבַח *praise* 11QPs^{a} 19$_{16}$, כָּבוֹד *glory* 24$_{13}$, חושך אתה ולוא אור *you* (Belial) *are darkness and not light* 11QapPs^{a} 4$_{7}$, עַצְמִי וּבְשָׂרִי אָתָּה *you are my bone and flesh* Gn 29$_{14}$ 2 S 19$_{14}$.

עַם *people* Ex 33$_{3}$ Dt 7$_{6}$ 14$_{2.21}$ Jos 17$_{15.17}$ Is 51$_{16}$ Ho 2$_{25}$ 11QT 48$_{7.10}$, מָרוֹם *height*, i.e. exalted Ps 92$_{9}$, תִּפְאֶרֶת *glory* 89$_{18}$ 4QapPs^{b} 15$_{7}$ ([אתה]), תְּהִלָּה *praise* Jr 17$_{14}$, תִּקְוָה *hope* Ps 71$_{5}$, יֵשַׁע *salvation* Si 51$_{10}$ (unless predicate is גִּבּוֹר *mighty one*), אֱמֶת *truthfulness* 1QH 4$_{40}$, עֶזְרָתִי וּמְפַלְטִי אַתָּה *you are my help and my rescuer* Ps 40$_{18}$||70$_{6(ms)}$ (L עֶזְרִי), הֲשָׁלוֹם אַתָּה *are you (at) peace?* 2 S 20$_{9}$ Kuntillet ‘Ajrud inscr. E2.2$_{1}$ (השלם את), var. 1 S 25$_{6}$ (|| בַּיִת your *household*).

אֵל *God* Gn 16$_{13}$ Is 45$_{15}$ Ezk 28$_{2.9}$ Jon 4$_{2}$ Ps 5$_{5}$ 77$_{15}$ 86$_{15}$ 90$_{2}$ Ne 9$_{31}$ Si 36$_{22}$ 4QDibHam^{a} 1.5$_{8}$ 4$_{4}$ 1QH 7$_{31}$ 15$_{25}$ fr. 3$_{12}$ 4QShir^{b} 52$_{1(Baillet)}$ ([אל]), אֵלִי *my God* Is 44$_{17}$ Ps 22$_{11}$ 63$_{2}$ 118$_{28}$ 140$_{7}$, אֱלוֹהַּ *God* Ne 9$_{17}$, אֱלֹהִים *God* 1 K 18$_{36}$ (:: אֲנִי) 18$_{37}$ Ps 25$_{5}$ 43$_{2}$ 86$_{10}$ 4QShir^{b} 8$_{12}$ ([אל]והי]) Kh. Beit Lei graf. 5$_{2}$ (י׳ את אלהי ירשלם *Y., you are the God of Jerusalem;* others יהד לולאלהי the mountains *of Judah belong to him, to the God of* Jerusalem), אֱלֹהַי *my God* Is 25$_{1}$ Jr 31$_{18}$ (unless י׳ *Y.* is predicate) Ps 31$_{15}$ 143$_{10}$, אֱלֹהֵינוּ *our God* Jr 3$_{22}$ (unless י׳ Y. is predicate), Y. Is 37$_{20}$ 2 C 14$_{10}$ (unless אֱלֹהֵינוּ *our God* is predicate), אֲדֹנָי *my Lord* Ps 16$_{2}$, Saul 1 S 28$_{12}$, Ziba 2 S 9$_{2}$, Joab 20$_{17}$ (:: אֲנִי *I*).

With plural noun, חֲמוּדוֹת *preciousness*, i.e. precious Dn 9$_{23}$.

With pronoun, מִי *who?* Gn 27$_{18.32}$ (:: אֲנִי) 1 S 26$_{14}$ 2 S 1$_{8}$ (:: אָנֹכִי) Zc 4$_{7}$ 11QapPs^{a} 2$_{2}$ ([א]תה) 4$_{6}$, (הַ)אַתָּה זֶה *this is you(?)* Gn 27$_{21.24}$ 2 S 2$_{20}$ (:: אָנֹכִי) 1 K 18$_{17}$, אַתָּה־הוּא *you are the one* Jr 14$_{22}$ 49$_{12}$ (אַתָּה הוּא) Ezk 38$_{17}$ GnzPs 4$_{19}$ 1QH 13$_{4}$, *you are the same* Ps 102$_{28}$, אַתָּה־הוּא (הָ)אֱלֹהִים *you are God* 2 S 7$_{28}$||1 C 17$_{26}$ 2 K 19$_{15}$||Is 37$_{16}$ 2 C 20$_{6}$, אַתָּה־הוּא י׳ *you are Y.* Ne 9$_{6.7}$, אַתָּה־הוּא מַלְכִּי *you are my king* Ps 44$_{5}$, אַתָּה הַמּוֹצִיא וְהַמֵּבִיא *you were the one who took out and brought (back)* 1 C 11$_{2}$.

With preposition, לְ of possession, *(belonging) to* Gn 32$_{18}$ 1 S 30$_{13}$ Is 43$_{1}$ 1QH 7$_{25}$ 1Q26 3$_{2}$, הֲלָנוּ אַתָּה *are you for us?* Jos 5$_{13}$; בְּ *with* illness 2 C 21$_{15}$, בְּקֶרֶב *among* Ex 34$_{10}$ Nm 14$_{14}$ Jr 14$_{9}$ 1QM 10$_{1}$ 4QDibHam^{a} 6$_{10}$; כְּ *as* Ezk 32$_{2}$ Ob$_{11}$ 1QSb 4$_{24}$; עַל *upon* Ec 5$_{1}$ (+ אֶרֶץ the *earth*, || אֱלֹהִים *God*); עִם *with* 1 S 28$_{19}$ Ps 23$_{4}$; מִן of place 1 S 30$_{13}$ 2 S 1$_{13}$ 15$_{2}$ Jon 1$_{8}$, מֵעוֹלָם *from eternity* Ps 93$_{2}$ (|| כִּסֵּא your *throne*), מִקֶּדֶם *from eternity* Hb 1$_{12}$; לִפְנֵי *in front of* Nm 18$_{2}$.

With adjective, אֶפְרָתִי *Ephrathite* Jg 12$_{5}$, נָכְרִי *foreign* 2 S 15$_{19}$, חַי *alive* 4QDibHam^{a} 8$_{2}$, עֵירֹם *naked* Gn 3$_{11}$, עָמֵל *toiling* Ec 9$_{9}$, עָיֵף *weary* Dt 25$_{18}$, יָגֵעַ *weary* Dt 25$_{18}$, דַּל *poor* 2 S 13$_{4}$, אֶבְיוֹן *poor* 4Q416 10.2$_{9.13}$ (+ אֲנִי *I*), יָגוֹר *fearful* Jr 22$_{25}$ 39$_{17}$, חָפֵץ *desiring* 1 K 21$_{6}$, קָטֹן *small* 1 S 15$_{17}$, קָשֶׁה *hard* Is 48$_{4}$, קָרוֹב *near* Jr 12$_{2}$ Ps 119$_{151}$, רָחוֹק *far* Jr 12$_{2}$.

קָדוֹשׁ *holy* Ps 22$_{4}$, תָּמִים *perfect* Ezk 28$_{15}$, גָּדוֹל *great* Jr 10$_{6}$ (|| שֵׁם your *name*) Si 3$_{18(C)}$ 4QPentPar^{b} 6.2$_{3}$, עֶלְיוֹן *exalted* Ps 97$_{9}$, צַדִּיק *righteous* 1 S 24$_{18}$ Jr 12$_{1}$ Ps 119$_{137}$ (|| מִשְׁפָּט your *commandments*) Pr 24$_{24}$ Ezr 9$_{15}$ Ne 9$_{8.33}$ 1QH 14$_{15}$ (|| בָּחִיר *elect*), טוֹב *good* Jg 11$_{25}$ 1 S 29$_{6.9}$ Ps

86$_{5}$ 119$_{68}$, יָשָׁר upright 1 S 29$_{6}$ Jb 8$_{6}$, זַךְ pure 8$_{6}$, חָכָם *wise* Ezk 28$_{3}$, סַלָּח *forgiving* Ps 86$_{5}$, מָאֵן *refusing* Ex 7$_{27}$ (+ אָנֹכִי) 9$_{2}$ 10$_{4}$ Jr 38$_{21}$, רחמון וחנון אתה *you are merciful and compassionate* 4QapPsb 47$_{1}$, אם צריך אתה *if you must* Si 35$_{7}$ (mg אתך *you* accusative), אין אתה צריך *you do not need* any help 4Q372 1$_{17}$.

With adverb, שָׁם *there* Gn 13$_{14}$ 1 S 19$_{3}$ (+ אֲנִי) Ps 139$_{8}$, לְבַדְּךָ *on you own* 1 S 21$_{2}$ Ps 83$_{19}$.

<APP> אַתָּה followed by noun, sometimes vocative, Elijah Si 48$_{4}$, Daniel Dn 12$_{4}$, Solomon 1 C 28$_{9}$, Pashhur Jr 20$_{6}$, Melchiresha 4QToh D$_{2}$, Israel Is 41$_{8}$, Migdal-eder, or *tower of the flock* Mc 4$_{8}$, Bethlehem 5$_{1}$, בֶּן־אָדָם *human being,* in addressing Ezekiel Ezk 2$_{6.8}$ 3$_{25}$ 4$_{1}$ 5$_{1}$ 7$_{2}$ 12$_{3}$ 13$_{17}$ 21$_{11.19.24.33}$ 22$_{2}$ 24$_{25}$ 27$_{2}$ 33$_{7.10.12.30}$ 36$_{1}$ 37$_{16}$ 39$_{1.17}$ 43$_{10}$, נַעַר *lad* 1 S 17$_{58}$, אָח *brother* 2 S 20$_{9}$, גִּבּוֹר *mighty (one)* Si 51$_{10}$ (but perh. nom. cl.).

י׳ ... אַתָּה *you ..., (O) Y.* Nm 14$_{14.14}$ 2 S 7$_{24}$||1 C 17$_{22}$ 2 S 7$_{27.29}$||1 C 17$_{27}$ 2 S 22$_{29}$ 1 K 18$_{37}$ 2 K 19$_{19}$ Is 63$_{16}$ Jr 3$_{22}$ (but perh. nom. cl.) 12$_{1.3}$ 14$_{9.22}$ 15$_{15}$ 18$_{23}$ 31$_{18}$ (but perh. nom. cl.) 32$_{17.25}$ Jon 1$_{14}$ Hb 1$_{12}$ Ps 3$_{4}$ 4$_{9}$ 6$_{4(Qr)}$ 12$_{8}$ 22$_{20}$ 40$_{6.12}$ 41$_{11}$ 59$_{6.9}$ 70$_{6(L)}$ (mss, ||40$_{18}$ אֱלֹהַי *my God*) 86$_{17}$ 92$_{9}$ 97$_{9}$ 102$_{13}$ 109$_{21.27}$ 119$_{12.137.151}$ Lm 5$_{19}$ 11QPsa 19$_{16}$ 24$_{13}$ GnzPs 2$_{2.18}$ 4$_{13}$, אַתָּה ... י׳ *O Y., ... you* Ps 40$_{10}$ 99$_{8}$ 132$_{8}$||2 C 6$_{41}$ 2 C 14$_{10}$ (unless Nom. Cl.) Kh. Beit Lei graf. 5$_{2}$ (את; but see Nom. Cl.).

אַתָּה אֵל *you, (O) God* 4QPrQuot 34$_{4}$ ([א]ל) 35$_{7}$ ([את]ה א[ל]) 4QRitPur 29$_{8(Baillet)}$ ([אל]) 29$_{21}$ ([את]ה) 33$_{6(Baillet)}$ ([אל]) 40$_{3(mg)}$ 64$_{5}$ 1QM 12$_{7}$ 13$_{7}$ ([ו]אתה) 13$_{9(Yadin)}$ ([אל]) 18$_{8}$ 1QH 1$_{26}$ 4$_{12.18}$ 6$_{20}$ 8$_{11}$ (את]ה א[ל) 11$_{29(mg)}$ fr. 4$_{15}$, var. 1QM 10$_{1}$, אַתָּה אֱלֹהִים *you, God* Ps 55$_{24}$ 60$_{12}$ 61$_{6}$ 4QShirb 16$_{4}$, var. Ps 69$_{6}$, אַתָּה אֱלֹהַי *you, my God* 40$_{18}$||70$_{6(mss)}$ (L י׳ Y.) 86$_{2}$ (but perh. Nom. Cl.) 1 C 17$_{25}$, אַתָּה אֵלִי *you, my God* 1QS 11$_{15}$ 1QH 2$_{34}$ 5$_{11.14.18.32}$ 7$_{10}$ 8$_{16}$ 9$_{23}$ 4QShirb 30$_{3}$ ([אל]י) 52$_{1}$, אַתָּה אֱלֹהֵינוּ *you, our God* Ezr 9$_{13}$ 2 C 20$_{7}$.

אַתָּה ... אֲדֹנָי *you ..., my Lord* Ps 38$_{16}$ 86$_{5.15}$ 4QDibHama 1.6$_{3(mg)}$ 1QH 5$_{20(mg)}$ 10$_{14}$ 11$_{27(Licht)}$ ([את]ה אדוני) 11$_{32}$ ([את]ה) 16$_{8}$ fr. 15.1$_{6}$, אַתָּה אֲדֹנִי הַמֶּלֶךְ *you, my lord king* 1 K 1$_{13.20}$, sim. 1$_{17}$, אתה מושיע *you, a saviour* 4QPentParb 6.2$_{3}$, אַתָּה אֱנוֹשׁ כְּעֶרְכִּי *you, a person like me* Ps 55$_{14}$, אַתָּה חָלָל רָשָׁע *you, profaned wicked one* Ezk 21$_{30}$ (or em. חֲלַל רֶשַׁע *profaned,* or *slain, of,* i.e. by, *wickedness*), [ארור] אתה *you, cursed one* 11QapPsa 4$_{6}$, אַתָּה הַר־הַגָּדוֹל *you, great mountain* Zc 4$_{7}$, אתה מבין perh. *you, understanding one* 4Q416 1$_{15}$.

<COLL> אַתָּה וְ *you and* + noun (oft. with 2nd person sg. sf.) in singular בֵּן *son* Ex 20$_{10}$ Dt 5$_{14}$ 6$_{2}$ 12$_{18}$ 16$_{11.14}$ 1 S 22$_{13}$, אִשָּׁה *wife* Gn 8$_{16}$, לֵוִי *Levite* Dt 26$_{11}$, Aaron Ex 19$_{24}$ 24$_{1}$ Nm 1$_{3}$ 16$_{17}$ 20$_{8}$, Eleazar 31$_{26}$ 1QDM 1$_{2}$ ([אלע]זר), Purah Jg 7$_{10}$, Ziba 2 S 19$_{30}$, Shear-jashub Is 7$_{3}$, Jeremiah Jr 36$_{19}$, אֲרוֹן *ark* Ps 132$_{8}$||2C 6$_{41}$, אֲנִי וָאַתָּה *I and you* Gn 31$_{44}$ 1 S 20$_{23}$ 2 K 9$_{25}$ 5/6HevBA 45.

בַּיִת *household* Gn 7$_{1}$ 45$_{11}$ Dt 14$_{26}$ 15$_{20}$ 1 S 22$_{16}$ 1 K 18$_{18}$ Jr 38$_{17}$, עֵדָה *congregation* Nm 16$_{11.16}$, קָהָל *assembly* Ezk 38$_{7}$, מַלְכוּת *kingdom* 1 S 20$_{31}$, זֶרַע *seed* Gn 17$_{9}$ Dt 30$_{19}$, עַם *people* Ex 11$_{8}$ 33$_{1}$ Jos 1$_{2}$ Jg 9$_{32}$ Jr 27$_{13}$, Judah 2 K 14$_{10}$||2 C 25$_{19}$, אַתָּה וְכָל־אֲשֶׁר־לָךְ *you and all that belongs to you* Gn 20$_{7}$.

With plural noun אָב *ancestor* Dt 13$_{7}$=11QT 54$_{21(Yadin)}$ ([ואבותיכה]) Dt 28$_{36.64}$ Jr 20$_{6}$, בֵּן *son* Gn 6$_{18}$ 45$_{10}$ Lv 10$_{9.14}$ (+ בַּת *daughter*) Nm 18$_{1.1.2.7}$ Dt 30$_{2}$ 1 S 28$_{19}$ 2 S 9$_{10}$, זָקֵן *elder* Ex 3$_{18}$, עֶבֶד *servant* 9$_{30}$ 2 S 19$_{15}$ Jr 22$_{2}$, רֵעַ *companion* Zc 3$_{8}$, אִישׁ *man* 1 S 28$_{1}$, יְהוּדִי *Jew* Ne 6$_{6}$, עַם *people* Ezk 38$_{15}$, אֲגַף *troop* 38$_{9}$ 39$_{4}$, אַתָּה וָהֵם *you and they* Nm 16$_{16}$.

לְבַדְּךָ ... אַתָּה *you ... alone* Nm 11$_{17}$ 1 K 8$_{39}$||2 C 6$_{30}$ 2 K 19$_{15.19}$||Is 37$_{16.20}$ Ps 86$_{10}$ Ne 9$_{6}$ 4QDibHama 1.5$_{8}$, לְבָדָד ... אַתָּה *you ... alone* Ps 4$_{9}$, רק אתה *only you* 1QH 15$_{14}$, גַּם־אַתָּה *you too,* etc. Gn 24$_{44}$ 43$_{8}$ Ex 10$_{25}$ Nm 27$_{13}$ Dt 1$_{37}$ 1 S 28$_{22}$ 2 S 15$_{19}$ 1 K 2$_{5}$ (גַּם אַתָּה) Is 14$_{10}$ Ob$_{11.13}$ Hb 2$_{16}$ Zc 3$_{7}$ Pr 26$_{4}$ Ec 7$_{22(Qr)}$ Si 15$_{15}$ 4Q416 6$_{4}$, גַּם־אַתָּה גַּם־הָעָם *both you and the people* Ex 18$_{18}$, גַּם־אַתָּה גַּם־בִּנְךָ *both you and your son* Jg 8$_{22}$.

אַתָּה *as for you,* etc. when not functioning as subject Gn 49$_{8}$ Dt 18$_{14}$ 1 K 1$_{20}$ Ezk 3$_{25}$ 7$_{2}$ 21$_{30}$ 24$_{25}$ 33$_{7.30}$ Mc 4$_{8}$ 5$_{1}$ Ps 6$_{4(Qr)}$ 55$_{14}$ 76$_{8}$ 1QM 13$_{7}$ ([ו]אתה; but perh. nom. cl.) 4Q416 1$_{3}$, אֶת־דָּמְךָ גַּם־אָתָּה *your own blood* 1 K 21$_{19}$, אַתָּה יָדְךָ *you (with) your hand* Ps 44$_{3}$, הוֹדַעְתִּיךָ הַיּוֹם אַף־אָתָּה *I have told you today—yes, you* Pr 22$_{19}$ (or em. אֹרְחֹתֶיךָ *your ways,* אֹרְחֹתָיו *his ways* or אָרְחוֹת חַיִּים *the ways of life*), לך אתה ... הצדקה *righteousness ... pertains to you—yes, you* 4QDibHama 1.6$_{3}$ (לכה) 1QH 16$_{9}$ 17$_{20}$, sim. 1$_{26}$ 4Q416 1$_{6.9}$, לֹא־עָלֶיךָ אַתָּה *it is not against you personally* 2 C 35$_{21}$; אַתָּה דַּע־לָךְ *know it yourself* Jb 5$_{27}$,

כִּי אִם־בֹּא אַתָּה *but come on your own* 2 C 25$_{8}$.

זָכֹר אֲנִי וָאַתָּה אֵת רֹכְבִים *remember me and you with riders* 2 K 9$_{25}$.

Also 4QPrQuot 48$_{5}$ 4QPrFêtes[b] 5$_{1}$ 4QPrFêtes[c] 147$_{2}$ 4QRitPur 73$_{5}$ ([א]תה) 1QM 18$_{12}$ 4QDibHam[a] 6$_{13}$ 4QVisSam 6$_{2}$ 1QH 11$_{36}$ fr. 9$_{7}$ 4QShir[b] 28$_{6}$ 4Q416 4$_{15}$ 9.2$_{14}$ 4QapPs[b] 13$_{3}$ 94$_{2}$ 4QApocMos A 3$_{1}$ 10$_{3}$.

אָתוֹן 34 n.f. **she-ass**—sf. אֲתֹנוֹ, אֲתֹנְךָ; pl. אֲתֹנוֹת (אֲתוֹנוֹת, אֲתֹנֹת)—belonging to Balaam (Nm 22$_{21+13t}$), Kish (1 S 9$_{3.5.20}$ 10$_{2.14.16}$), Job (Jb 1$_{3.14}$ 42$_{12}$) Shunammite woman (2 K 4$_{22.24}$), Abraham (Gn 12$_{16}$), Jacob (Gn 32$_{16}$), Joseph (Gn 45$_{23}$), Judah (Gn 49$_{11}$), David (1 C 27$_{30}$), messiah (Zc 9$_{9}$); in inventory of herd animals, etc. (Gn 12$_{16}$ 32$_{16}$ Jb 1$_{3}$ 42$_{12}$ 1 C 27$_{30}$).

<SUBJ> נשׂא *carry* food Gn 45$_{23}$ (‖ חֲמוֹר *ass*), הלך *go* Nm 22$_{23}$, נטה *turn aside* intrans. 22$_{23.33}$, אבד *go astray* 1 S 9$_{3.20}$ (both + לְ perh. *[belonging] to* Kish), מצא ni. *be found* 9$_{20}$ 10$_{2.16}$, רעה *graze* Jb 1$_{14}$, לחץ *squeeze* Balaam's foot Nm 22$_{25}$, ni. *squeeze oneself* into confined area 22$_{25}$, רבץ *crouch* 22$_{27}$, ראה *see* angel 22$_{23.25.27.33}$, אמר *say* to Balaam 22$_{28.30}$, עלל htp. *make sport (of)* Balaam 22$_{29}$ (Sam הִתְעַלַּלְתִּי *I* [Balaam] *have made a fool of myself*).

<NOM CL> הֲלוֹא אָנֹכִי אֲתֹנְךָ *am I not your she-ass?* Nm 22$_{30}$.

<OBJ> רכב *ride* Jg 5$_{10}$, חבשׁ *bind*, i.e. prepare for riding Nm 22$_{21}$ 2 K 4$_{24}$, נכה hi. *strike* Nm 22$_{23.25.27.32}$, הרג *kill* 22$_{29}$, נטה hi. *turn* 22$_{23}$, בקשׁ pi. *seek* 1 S 9$_{3}$ (+ נַעַר *lad*) 10$_{2.14}$, שׁלח *send* Gn 45$_{23}$ 2 K 4$_{22}$ (‖ נַעַר), חיה hi. *keep alive* Nm 22$_{33}$.

<CSTR> פִּי הָאָתוֹן *mouth of the she-ass* Nm 22$_{28}$, בְּנִי אֲתֹנוֹ *son of his she-ass* Gn 49$_{11}$ (+ עַיִר *ass*), בֶּן־אֲתֹנוֹת *son of she-asses* Zc 9$_{9}$ (+ עַיִר, חֲמוֹר *ass*), אַחַת הָאֲתֹנוֹת *one of the she-asses* 2 K 4$_{22}$, דִּבְרֵי הָאֲתֹנוֹת *matters of*, i.e. concerning, *the she-asses* 1 S 10$_{2}$ (mss דְּבַר *matter of*).

<APP> עַל־חֲמוֹר וְעַל־עַיִר בֶּן־אֲתֹנוֹת *on an ass, (and) on a (male) ass, a son of she-asses* Zc 9$_{9}$.

<ADJ> אֲתֹנוֹת צְחֹרוֹת *tawny she-asses* Jg 5$_{10}$.

<PREP> אמר לְ *say to* Nm 22$_{29}$, שׂים לְ *place* heart *towards*, i.e. be concerned about 1 S 9$_{20}$.

חדל מִן *cease from (being concerned about)* 1 S 9$_{5}$.

רכב עַל *ride upon* Nm 22$_{22.30}$ Zc 9$_{9}$ (+ עָנִי *humble* [of rider]), עַל־הָאֲתֹנוֹת יֶחְדְּיָהוּ *over*, i.e. in charge of, *the she-asses was Jehdeiah* 1 C 27$_{30}$.

<COLL> עֶשֶׂר אֲתֹנֹת *ten she-asses* Gn 45$_{23}$, אֲתֹנֹת עֶשְׂרִים *twenty she-asses* 32$_{16}$, חֲמֵשׁ מֵאוֹת אֲתוֹנוֹת *five hundred she-asses* Jb 1$_{3}$ אֶלֶף אֲתוֹנוֹת *a thousand she-asses* 42$_{12}$.

[אַתּוּק], see אַתִּיק.

[אַתִּי], see אַתְּ.

אִתַּי 9 pr.n.m. **Ittai**—אִיתַי—**1.** Gittite (i.e. from Gath), one of David's officers at time of Absalom's revolt, 2 S 15$_{19.21.22.22}$ 18$_{2.5.12}$. **2.** son of Ribai from Gibeah, one of David's warriors, 2 S 23$_{29}$ (‖1 C 11$_{31}$ אִיתַי).

[אַתָּיָה], see אתה.

אַתִּיק 5 n.m. **ledge, gallery**—pl. אַתִּיקִים; sf. אַתִּיקֶיהָא (K אתוקיהא)—**<SUBJ>** אכל *eat*, i.e. take up space Ezk 42$_{5}$ (mss יכל *be able*). **<NOM CL>** הָאַתִּיקִים סָבִיב לִשְׁלָשְׁתָּם *the ledges were around the three of them* (three sections of temple) Ezk 41$_{16}$ (+ סַף *threshold*, חַלּוֹן *window*), נֶגֶד רִצְפָה ... אַתִּיק *opposite a pavement ... was a ledge* 42$_{3}$ (or em. אַתִּיקִים *ledges*). **<OBJ>** מדד *measure* Ezk 41$_{15}$. **<PREP>** אֶל־פְּנֵי־אַתִּיק *next to ledge* Ezk 42$_{3}$.

אַתֶּם 279.0.12 pronoun **you** (masc. pl.)—Q אתמה, אתן—(appar. fem. in אַתֶּם מְצֹדְדוֹת *you hunt* Ezk 13$_{20}$).

<SUBJ> **a.** of **verbs**, היה *be* Gn 44$_{10}$ (+ נָקִי *innocent*) 1 S 12$_{14}$ (+ אַחַר *behind*) 2 S 19$_{13}$ (+ אַחֲרוֹן *last*) Ml 3$_{12}$ (+ אֶרֶץ חֵפֶץ *land of delight*), + לְ of possession, *(belonging) to*, etc. Ex 19$_{6}$ Lv 26$_{12}$ 1 S 8$_{17}$ 14$_{40}$ (:: אֲנִי *I*) Jr 7$_{23}$ Ezk 11$_{11}$.

בוא *come* Nm 14$_{30}$, hi. *bring* Gn 42$_{19}$ Jos 18$_{6}$, הלך *go* Gn 42$_{19}$ Ex 5$_{11}$ 12$_{31}$ Jos 3$_{3}$ 1 K 9$_{6}$‖2 C 7$_{19}$ Jr 7$_{23}$ Ezk 20$_{39}$ (or em. לְכוּ *go!* to הַשְׁלִיכוּ *throw!*), עלה *go up* Gn 44$_{17}$, hi. *raise* 1 C 15$_{12}$, יצא *go out* Ex 12$_{22.31}$, עבר *pass* Jos 1$_{14}$ Ezk 20$_{39(mss)}$ (L עבד *worship*), פנה *turn* intrans. Dt 1$_{40}$, סור *turn* intrans. Ml 2$_{8}$, שׁוב *go back* Jos 22$_{18}$ 1 K 9$_{6}$‖2 C 7$_{19}$ Jr 34$_{15}$, קרב *approach* Is 57$_{3}$, נסע *travel* Dt 1$_{40}$ Jos 3$_{3}$.

קום *arise* Ex 12$_{31}$ Jos 8$_{7}$ Jg 9$_{18}$, עמד *stand (still)* Jos

10_{19}, ישׁב *stay (seated)* Nm 22_{19} 32_6 Jr 40_{10}, *dwell* Hg 1_4 (see Coll.), hi. *become married to* Ezr 10_{10}, שׁחה htpal. *bow down* 1 K 9_6||2 C 7_{19}, רדף *pursue* Jos 10_{19}, שׁלח *send (away)* Gn 45_8 Jr 42_{20}, pi.Gn 26_{27}, שׁלך *throw* Ezk 20_{39} (if em. לְכוּ *go!*), עזב *desert* Jg 10_{13} 2 C 7_{19} 12_5 (:: אֲנִי *I*) 13_{11} (:: אֲנַחְנוּ *we*), גרשׁ pi. *expel* Jg 11_7, כשׁל hi. *cause to stumble* Ml 2_8, שׂים *place* Jr 40_{10} 42_{15}.

ראה *see* Ex 19_4 20_{22} Dt 29_1 Jos 23_3 Jr 23_1 44_2, חזה *see* Jb 27_{12}, חרשׁ hi. *be quiet* Ex 14_{14}, שׁמע *hear* Jos 22_2 Jr 27_9 29_{20} 34_{17}, חשׁב *think* Gn 50_{20}, ni. *be accounted* 4Q471a$_5$, ידע *know* 44_{27} Ex 23_9 Dt 29_{15} 2 K 9_{11} Jr 16_{13} 44_3, זכר *remember* 1QM 17_2, בחר *choose* Jos 24_{22}, מאס *reject* 1 S 10_{19}, אמר *say* 10_{19} Ml 1_5 (|| עֵינֵיכֶם *your eyes*), דבר pi. *speak* Jr 44_{25} (or em.; see Coll.), נגד hi. *tell* Is 48_6, קרא ni. *be called* 61_6, צעק *cry* 65_{14} (:: עֲבָדַי *my servants*), ילל hi. *howl* 65_{14}, שׂנא *hate* Gn 26_{27} Jg 11_7, ירא *fear* Nm 14_9 2 C 20_{15} 1QM 17_4, חתת *fear* 2 C 20_{15}, בושׁ *feel shame* Is 65_{13} (:: עֲבָדַי), שׂמח *rejoice* Dt $12_{7.12}$, חנן *have mercy* Jb 19_{21}, חמל *have mercy* 1 S 23_{21}.

עשׂה *do* Jos 2_{12} 1 S 12_{20} 2 S 2_5 Jr 34_{15}, יכל *be able* 13_{23}, מהר pi. *hurry* intrans. 2 C 24_5, שׁמר *keep* Lv 18_{26} Jos 6_{18} 22_2 1 K 9_6, מלא pi. *fulfil* Jr 44_{25} (or em.; see Coll.), נתן *give* Nm 18_{28} Jos 2_{12} Jg 14_{13} 21_{22} Ezk 36_8, *allow* Jos 10_{19}, נשׂא *yield* produce Ezk 36_8, לקח *take* Ex 5_{11}, אסף *gather* trans. Jr 40_{10}, לקט pu. *be garnered* Is 27_{12}, אסר ni. *be bound* Gn 42_{16}, ירשׁ *possess* Lv 20_{24} Dt 4_{22}, hi. Jos 8_7, מכר *sell* Ne 5_8.

אכל *eat* Nm 18_{31} Dt 12_7, שׁתה *drink* 2 K 3_{17} Jr 35_6, רעב *be hungry* Is 65_{13} (:: עֲבָדַי *my servants*), צמא *be thirsty* 65_{13} (:: עֲבָדַי), כתב *write* Jos 18_6 Est 8_8, חתם *seal* 8_8, תקע *sound* trumpet Jg 7_{18} (+ אָנֹכִי *I*), קבר *bury* 2 S 2_5, חנה *encamp* Nm 31_{19}, מלך hi. *make king* Jg 9_{18}, ריב *contend* 6_{31}, ישׁע hi. *deliver* 6_{31}.

חטא *sin* Ex 32_{30}, htp. *clear oneself of sin* Nm 31_{19}, מעל *sin* Ezr 10_{10} Ne 1_8 (:: אֲנִי *I*), רעע hi. *do evil* Jr 16_{12}, שׁחת pi. *corrupt* Ml 2_8, נקה ni. *be held innocent* Jr 25_{29} (+ אָנֹכִי, אֲנִי), קדשׁ htp. *sanctify oneself* 1 C 15_{12}, רום hi. *offer* sacrifice Nm 18_{28}, קטר pi. *burn* incense Jr 44_{21}, כרת *make (covenant)* Jg 2_2 Jr 34_{15}, עבד *worship* Ex 12_{31} Jg 10_{13} 1 K 9_6||2 C 7_{19} Ezk 20_{39} (mss עבר *pass*).

מרד *rebel* Jos 22_{18}, פגע *attack* Jg 15_{12}, הרג *kill* 9_{18}, בער pi. *destroy* Is 3_{14}, זנב pi. *utterly destroy* Jos 10_{19}, נתץ *tear down* Jg 2_2, כלה *be consumed* Ml 3_6 (:: אֲנִי *I*), ספה ni. *be destroyed* 1 S 12_{25}, מות *die* Nm 18_3, hi. *kill* 17_6, חזק *be strong* 2 C 15_7, htp. *take courage* 1QM $17_{4.8}$, פרה *be fruitful* Gn 9_7, רבה *be many* 9_7, אבד *die* Jr 27_{15} (+ הֵם *they*).

b. of participles, בוא *come* Nm 34_2 Dt 4_5 Jr 44_8 Ezk $20_{3.29}$ (if em. הַבָּאִים you are *those who come* to בָּאִים you *are coming*) Ezr 9_{11}, הלך *go* 2 K 1_3, יצא *go out* Ex 13_4, עבר *cross over* Nm 33_{51} 35_{10} Dt 2_4 $4_{14.22.26}$ 6_1 $11_{8.11.31}$ 31_{13} 32_{47} Jos 1_{11}, *transgress* Nm 14_{41} 2 C 24_{20}, שׁוב *go back* 1 S 7_3, hi. *bring back* Jg 11_9, ישׁב *dwell* Nm 33_{54} 35_{34} Jos 9_{22} 24_{15} Jg 6_{10} 2 C 32_{10}, *sit* 5/6ḤevEp 12_3 (ואתן יושבן[י]ן), גור *sojourn* Jr 35_7, לין *pass night* Ne 13_{21}, נצב ni. *stand* Dt 29_9, פסח *limp* 1 K 18_{21}, רוץ *run* Hg 1_9, נשׂא *bear* Ne 5_7 (if em. נֹשִׁים [Qr] *exacting*), עמס *burden* 2 C 28_{10} (if em. עִמָּכֶם *with you*; see Coll.)

ראה *see* Hg 2_3 Ne 2_{17} (+ אֲנַחְנוּ *we*) 2 C 29_8 30_7, ידע *know* 4QMMT A $24_{6.54}$ (both [ואתם יודעים]) $27_{6.87}$ (וא[תם]) 4QMMT B_7 ([ואתם יודעים]) 4QMMT B_8 ([י]ודעים), חלם hi. *dream* Jr 29_8, חרשׁ hi. *be silent* 2 S 19_{11}, חשׁה hi. *be silent* Jg 18_9, שׁמע *hear* Dt 4_{12} 2 K 10_6, אמר *say* Ex 5_{17} 2 S 21_4 Jr $32_{36.43}$ 33_{10} Ezk 20_{32} 2 C 13_8 $28_{10.13}$, יעץ ni. *counsel* 1 K $12_{6.9}$||2 C $10_{6.9}$, משׁל *speak figuratively* Ezk 18_2, לון hi. *complain* Ex 16_8, בטח *trust* Jr $7_{8.14}$ 2 C 32_{10}, בקשׁ pi. *seek* Ex 10_{11} Ml 3_1, ירא *fear* Jr $42_{11.16}$, דאג *be concerned* 42_{16} 5/6ḤevEp 12_3.

עשׂה *do* Jg 18_{18} Jr 44_7 Ne 2_{19} 5_9 13_{17} 2 C 19_6, רפה ni. *be idle* Ex 5_{17}, htp. *dally* Jos 18_3, נתן *give* Jr 26_{15}, שׁלם pi. *repay* Jl 4_4, גמל *repay* 4_4, ירשׁ *dispossess* Dt 12_2, יסף hi. *add* Ne 13_{18}, אכל *eat* Jos 24_{13} Zc 7_6 5/6ḤevEp 12_3, שׁתה *drink* Zc 7_6 (הֲלוֹא אַתֶּם הָאֹכְלִים וְאַתֶּם הַשֹּׁתִים *is it not you who are those that eat and you who are those that drink?*) 5/6ḤevEp 12_3, משׁח *anoint* Jg 9_{15}, טפל *smear* Jb 13_4 (|| כֻּלְּכֶם *all of you*).

טמא ni. *defile oneself* Ezk $20_{30.31}$ (+ אֲנִי *I*), חלל pi. *profane* Ml 1_{12} Ne 13_{17}, זנה *prostitute oneself* Nm 15_{39} Ezk 20_{30}, רגל pi. *spy* Gn $42_{9.14.16.34}$, מרד *rebel* Ne 2_{19}, לחם ni. *fight* Jos 10_{25} Jr 21_4, צוד pilel *hunt* Ezk 13_{20} (|| אַתֵּנָה *you* fem. pl.), ארב *lay ambush* Jos 8_4, קבע *rob* Ml $3_{8.9}$, נשׁה *exact (interest)* Ne $5_{7(Qr)}$ (or em. נֹשְׂאִים *bearing*) 5_{11}, מות hi. *kill* Jr 26_{15}, ארר pass. *be cursed* Jos 9_{23}, ni. Ml 3_9, ברך pass. *be blessed* 1 S 23_{21} 2 S 2_5 Ps 115_{15}.

<NOM CL> with collective singular noun, עַם *people* Ex 33$_5$ Ho 1$_9$ (:: אָנֹכִי *I*) 2$_1$ Jb 12$_2$, צֹאן *flock* Ezk 34$_{31(mss)}$ (L אַתֵּן *you* fem. pl.) 34$_{31}$ (:: אֲנִי *I*), הָמוֹן *crowd* 2 C 13$_8$, עַצְמִי וּבְשָׂרִי אַתֶּם *you are my bone and my flesh* 2 S 19$_{13}$, אַתֶּם הַמְעַט מִכָּל־הָעַמִּים *you are the least numerous of all the peoples* Dt 7$_7$, אַתֶּם קֹדֶשׁ *you are holiness*, i.e. holy Ezr 8$_{28}$.

With plural noun, יֶלֶד *child* Is 57$_4$ (+ פֶּשַׁע *of sin*), בֵּן *child* Dt 14$_1$=11QT 48$_7$ (+ לַי׳ *of Y.*) 1 S 26$_{16}$ (+ מָוֶת *of*, i.e. destined for, *death*), אָח *brother* 2 S 19$_{13}$, תּוֹשָׁב *inhabitant* Lv 25$_{23}$, גֵּר *sojourner* 25$_{23}$, פָּלִיט *fugitive* Jg 12$_4$, רֹאשׁ *chief* 1 C 15$_{12}$, עֶבֶד *servant* 1 S 17$_8$ (:: אָנֹכִי *I*), עֵד *witness* Jos 24$_{22}$ Is 43$_{10.12}$ (+ אֲנִי) 44$_8$ Ru 4$_{9.10}$; אֱלֹהִים אַתֶּם *you are gods* Is 41$_{23}$ Ps 82$_6$ (‖ כֻּלְּכֶם *all of you*), sim. Is 42$_{17}$.

With interrog. pronoun, מִי *who?* Jos 9$_8$ 2 K 10$_{13}$, מָה *what?* Jg 18$_8$ (מָה אַתֶּם appar. *how are you?* or *what is your news?*) Jl 4$_4$ (+ לִי *to me*).

With preposition, לְ *in support of* 2 K 10$_6$, כִּי לְמַבָּרִאשׁוֹנָה לֹא אַתֶּם *because you were not there at the beginning* 1 C 15$_{13}$; בְּ of place, *in*, *among* Lv 26$_{34}$ Nm 35$_{33}$; מִן partitive, *(some) of*, אַתֶּם מֵאַיִן *you are of nothing* Is 41$_{24}$; כְּ *as* Am 9$_7$.

With adverb, שָׁם *there* Ex 12$_{13}$, אֵיפֹה *where?* Jr 36$_{19}$, מֵאַיִן *whence?* Gn 29$_4$; כֵּן־אַתֶּם *thus you are* Jr 18$_6$.

With adjective (in plural), חַי *alive* Dt 4$_4$ 12$_1$ 31$_{13}$, יָשִׁישׁ *elderly* Jb 32$_6$ (:: אֲנִי *I*), צַדִּיק *righteous* 2 K 10$_9$, כֵּן *upright* Gn 42$_{19.33.34}$, קָרֵב *approaching* Dt 20$_3$=11QT 61$_{15}$, חָפֵץ *delighting in* Ml 3$_1$; אַתֶּם הָרַבִּים *you are the many*, i.e. more numerous 1 K 18$_{25}$.

<APP> (oft. as vocative) דּוֹר *generation* Jr 2$_{31}$, כָּל־הַגּוֹלָה *all the diaspora* 29$_{20}$, הַגּוֹי כֻּלּוֹ *the whole nation* Ml 3$_9$, בֵּית(־)יִשְׂרָאֵל *house of Israel* Jr 18$_6$ Ezk 20$_{39}$, בְּנֵי יִשְׂרָאֵל *children of Israel* Am 9$_7$, בְּנֵי־יַעֲקֹב *children of Jacob* Ml 3$_6$, בני בריתו *children of his covenant* 1QM 17$_8$, בני אדם *children of humans* 4Q185 1.1$_9$, בְּנֵי עֹנְנָה *children of a sorceress* Is 57$_3$, כֹּל גִּבּוֹרֵי הַחַיִל *all the warriors* Jos 1$_{14}$, כּוּשִׁים *Cushites* Zp 2$_{12}$, צֹר וְצִידוֹן *Tyre and Sidon* Jl 4$_4$, הָרֵי יִשְׂרָאֵל *mountains of Israel* Ezk 36$_8$, רֵעָי *my friends* Jb 19$_{21}$, אַתֶּם ... אִישׁ *you ..., each one (of you)* Ezk 20$_{39}$ Hg 1$_9$, sim. Ne 5$_7$, אַתֶּם ... כֻּלְּכֶם *you ..., all of you* Dt 29$_9$ Jb 27$_{12}$, וְאַתֶּם עֹזְבֵי י׳ הַשְּׁכֵחִים ... הָעֹרְכִים ... וְהַמְמַלְאִים *as for you, who desert Y., who forget ..., who set* a table ... *and who fill* a cup Is 65$_{11}$, אַתֶּם הַדְּבֵקִים *you who held firm* Dt 4$_4$.

<COLL> אַתֶּם וְ *you and* with collective singular noun, בַּיִת *household* Nm 18$_{31}$, שְׁבִי *captive(s)* 31$_{19}$, בְּהֵמָה *beast(s)* 2 K 3$_{17}$; with plural noun, בַּיִת *household* Dt 12$_7$, אָב *ancestor* Jr 16$_{13}$ 44$_{3.21}$, אִשָּׁה *wife* 44$_{25}$ (or em. אַתֵּנָה הַנָּשִׁים *you are the wives*), אָח *brother* 1 C 15$_{12}$, בֵּן *child, son* Dt 12$_{12}$ (+ בַּת *daughter*) 1 K 9$_6$ Jr 35$_6$, נָבִיא *prophet* 27$_{15}$, מִקְנֶה *herd* 2 K 3$_{17}$ (or em. מַחֲנֶה *camp*); הֵמָּה אַתֶּם וְ *they, you, and* Jr 44$_3$.

גַּם־אַתֶּם *you too*, etc. Nm 18$_{28}$ 22$_{19}$ Jos 2$_{12}$ Jg 7$_{18}$ Jr 13$_{23}$ Zp 2$_{12}$ Ne 5$_8$, גַּם־אַתֶּם גַּם־ *both you and* Ex 12$_{31}$ 1 S 12$_{14}$ (וְגַם־) 12$_{25}$, גַּם־הֵם גַּם־אַתֶּם *neither they nor you* Nm 18$_3$.

אַתֶּם *as for you*, when not functioning as subject Nm 14$_{32}$ (unless פִּגְרֵיכֶם אַתֶּם is nom cl., *your corpses are you*, i.e. you will become corpses, or app., *your corpses, you*, i.e. your very corpses, or sim.) Jos 23$_9$ Is 65$_{11}$ Zp 2$_{12}$ 2 C 28$_{10}$ (or em. אַתֶּם עִמָּכֶם *as for you, with you are wicked deeds* to אַתֶּם עֲלֵיכֶם עֹמְסִם *you are burdening on yourselves* wicked deeds), הַעֵת לָכֶם אַתֶּם לָשֶׁבֶת ... וְהַבַּיִת הַזֶּה חָרֵב *is it a time for yourselves to dwell* in your panelled houses *while this house is ruined?* Hg 1$_4$.

Also 4Q185 1.2$_7$ (אתמה) 4Q416 4$_6$.

אֵתָם 4 pl.n. **Etham**, second station of exodus, Ex 13$_{20}$ Nm 33$_{6.7.8}$ (+ מִדְבַּר *desert of*).

אֶתְמוֹל 31.2 n.[m.] **previous time**—אִתְמוֹל, אֶתְמוּל, תְּמוֹל, תְּמֹל—usu. with שִׁלְשׁוֹם *a third (day)*, i.e. the day before yesterday (except Ex 5$_{14}$ 1 S 2$_{27}$ 2 S 15$_{20}$ Is 30$_{33}$ Mc 2$_8$ Ps 90$_4$ Jb 8$_9$), appar. in same sense as אֶתְמוֹל alone.

1. past, previous time, perh. specif. **yesterday,** <NOM CL> לו אתמול ולך היום *he has the past, you have today* Si 38$_{22}$, תְמוֹל אֲנַחְנוּ *we are (as) yesterday*, i.e. without long experience Jb 8$_9$. <CSTR> יוֹם אֶתְמוֹל *a day of previous time, as yesterday* Ps 90$_4$.

<PREP> מֵאֶתְמוֹל *from a previous time*, i.e. already, + ערך pass. *be prepared* (of Topheth), Is 30$_{33}$ (perh. em.

(מֵאֶתְמוֹל) מִתְּמוֹל שִׁלְשׁוֹם *from a previous time* Ex 4_{10} (לֹא אִישׁ דְּבָרִים אָנֹכִי גַּם מִתְּמוֹל גַּם מִשִּׁלְשֹׁם *I am not a man [in command] of words, not from a previous time nor from before,* i.e. I have never been a good speaker) 21_{29} =4Q251 4_4 ([מאתמול [שלשום]) Ex 21_{36} (all three שׁוֹר נַגָּח הוּא מִתְּמוֹל שִׁלְשֹׁם [and var.] *he is a goring ox from a previous time,* i.e. he has already gored), + שׂנא *hate* (of unpremeditated murderer) Dt 4_{42} 19_4 (שִׁלְשֹׁם) 19_6 Jos 20_5, עבר *pass* 3_4, ידע *know* 1 S 10_{11} (מֵאֶתְמוֹל), עצר *be restrained* $21_{6(mss)}$ (שִׁלְשֹׁם; L כִּתְמוֹל, as §2).

2. (כְּ)אֶתְמוֹל as adv., **(as) previously,** perh. specif. **(as) yesterday,** + היה *be* 1 S 4_7 14_{21} 19_7 2 S 3_{17} 5_2, הלך *go* Jos 4_{18}, בוא *come* 1 S 20_{27} 2 S 15_{20} (תְּמוֹל בּוֹאֶךָ; + הַיּוֹם *today, now*), hi. *bring* 1 C 11_2, יצא hi. *take out* 11_2, קום pol. *establish* oneself Mc 2_8 (or em. אֶתְמוֹל עַמִּי *previously my people* to אַתֶּם לְעַמִּי *you* rise up as an enemy *to my people*), ישׁב *dwell* 2 K 13_5, עשׂה *do* Ex 5_8, כלה pi. *finish,* i.e. fulfil instruction $5_{14.14}$, נתן *give* straw 5_7, ידע *know* people Ru 2_{11}, עצר pass. *be restrained,* i.e. be kept away (of women) 1 S 21_6 (mss מִתְּמוֹל *from a previous time,* as §1, Prep.).

<COLL> כִּתְמוֹל שִׁלְשֹׁם *as previously* Ex $5_{7.14}$ Jos 4_{18} (שִׁלְשׁוֹם) 1 S 14_{21} 19_7 (both כְּאֶתְמוֹל שִׁלְשׁוֹם) 21_6 2 K 13_5 (שִׁלְשׁוֹם), אֵינֶנּוּ עִמּוֹ כִּתְמוֹל שִׁלְשׁוֹם *it was not with him as previously* Gn 31_2 (Sam אֵינָם), sim. 31_5.

גַּם־אֶתְמוֹל גַּם־שִׁלְשׁוֹם *both previously and before* 2 S 3_{17} 5_2‖1 C 11_2 (גַּם־תְּמוֹל, (גַּם־תְּמוֹל גַּם־שִׁלְשֹׁם) גַּם־תְּמוֹל גַּם־הַיּוֹם *both previously and today* Ex 5_{14} 1 S 20_{27}, גַּם מִתְּמוֹל גַּם מִשִּׁלְשֹׁם גַּם מֵאָז *from a previous time, from before (then), and from now,* i.e. as §1, Ex 4_{10}.

אֶתָן, see אֵיתָן I.

אַתֵּן, see אַתֵּנָה ,אַתֶּם.

[אַתֵּן], see אַתֵּנָה.

אַתֵּנָה 5 pronoun **you** (fem. pl.)—אַתֵּן—of Rachel and Leah Gn 31_6, false prophets Ezk 13_{20}, Israel $34_{17.31}$, hailstones 13_{11}.

<SUBJ> ידע *know* Gn 31_6, נפל *fall* Ezk 13_{11}, צוד pol. *hunt* 13_{20} (‖ אַתֶּם *you* [masc. pl.]). **<NOM CL>** אַתֵּן צֹאנִי *you are my flock* Ezk 34_{31} (mss אַתֶּם *you* [masc. pl.]; ‖ אַתֶּם), אַתֵּנָה הַנָּשִׁים *you are the wives* Jr 44_{25} (if em. אַתֶּם וּנְשֵׁיכֶם *you and your wives*).

<APP> וְאַתֵּנָה צֹאנִי *as for you, my flock* Ezk 34_{17}, וְאַתֵּנָה אַבְנֵי אֶלְגָּבִישׁ *and you, stones of hail* 13_{11} (but perh. del. אַתֵּנָה אַבְנֵי).

אֶתְנָה, see אֶתְנַן I, Nom. Cl.

אֶתְנִי 1 pr.n.m. **Ethni,** ancestor of Asaph, perh. ident. with Jeatherai (יְאָתְרַי) at 1 C 6_6, 1 C 6_{26}.

אֵתָנִים, see אֵיתָן I.

אֶתְנַן I 12 n.m. **fee**—אֶתְנָה (אֶתְנָן); cstr. אֶתְנַן; sf. אֶתְנַנָּהּ (אֶתְנַנָּה); pl. sf. אֶתְנַנֶּיהָ—payment, sometimes not monetary (Mc 1_7 Ho 2_{14}), to prostitute, or given by prostitute (Ezk $16_{34.41}$) to attract clients, **<SUBJ>** היה *be* Is 23_{18} (+ קֹדֶשׁ לי״ *holiness,* i.e. something holy, *to Y.,* ‖ סַחַר *gain*), נתן ni. *be given* Ezk 16_{34}, שׂרף ni. *be burned* Mc 1_7 (‖ פְּסִיל *idol*). **<NOM CL>** אֶתְנָה הֵמָּה לִי *they* (vine and fig-tree) *are my fee* Ho 2_{14} (or em. אֶתְנַן). **<OBJ>** בוא hi. *bring* Dt 23_{19} (+ בֵּית י״ into *Y.'s house,* ‖ מְחִיר *price*), נתן *give* Ezk $16_{34.41}$ Ho 2_{14}, לקח *take* Ezk 16_{32} (if em. אֶת־זָרִים *strangers* to אֶתְנַנִּים *fees*), אהב *love* Ho 9_1 (+ עַל כָּל־גָּרְנוֹת דָּגָן *on every threshing floor*), קלס pi. *despise* Ezk 16_{31} (or em. לקט pi. *glean*). **<CSTR>** אֶתְנַן זוֹנָה *fee of prostitute* Dt 23_{19} Mc $1_{7.7}$; כָּל־אֶתְנַנֶּיהָ *all her fees* Mc 1_7. **<PREP>** שׁוּב לְ *go back to* Is 23_{17}; שׁוּב עַד *go back to* Mc 1_7; קבץ מִן pi. *collect* idols *from (the proceeds of)* Mc 1_7 (or em. pu. *be collected*).

→ נתן *give*.

[אֶתְנַן] II 1 pr.n.m. **Ethnan**—אֶתְנָן—son of Helah and Asshur, descendant of Judah, 1 C 4_7.

אֲתָרִים 1 pl.n. **Atharim,** on route of exodus, appar. near Arad, Nm 21_1 (or em. הָאֲתָרִים *Atharim* to תָּרִים *spies*).

ENGLISH–HEBREW INDEX